THE
STUDENT'S
MILTON

THE STUDENT'S MILTON

Being the complete poems of
JOHN MILTON
with the greater part of his prose works,
now printed in one volume, together
with new translations into English of
his Italian, Latin, and Greek poems

Edited by
FRANK ALLEN PATTERSON

Revised Edition

APPLETON-CENTURY-CROFTS, INC.
New York

PREFACE

This edition has been prepared because of the need which the editor has keenly felt for several years of laying before students and the happily ever-increasing number of Milton readers throughout the country a one-volume text of all Milton's poetry and of his most important prose.

Living almost three centuries after Milton, we are beginning to realize, better than our fathers did, the real significance of the man. Professor Grierson and Professor Whitehead have agreed essentially in calling the seventeenth century the most important of eras, for in that age our modern ideas began to take form and grow into living thought. And in that beginning and young growth of far-reaching ideas Milton stood foremost. His brilliant and profound mind illuminated every subject it touched, shedding a clear light far forward upon many a question that to-day challenges the intellect of lovers of human and individual liberty. Milton thought so deeply and so truly that we, with the advantage of three centuries, often find difficulty in reaching him. In his day Milton led the van, and he is still there. But this is not all. Milton advanced on many fronts. While one fighter led almost a forlorn hope in the struggle for the separation of church and state and another fought in the cause of toleration, Milton was fighting and leading, always present and never surrendering, even in apparent defeat. That is why in the twentieth century he is still our leader, still "our sacred Milton," "a bold inquirer into morals and religion," and even more.

Until we have attained complete liberty in these and many other fields of thought, Milton will furnish us both the material and the inspiration for waging the fight. Saurat remarks that in his major contentions Milton is always right. Three hundred years have proved him so. The statement is no exaggeration. His words and his ideals will not become obsolete until our swords rest in our hands after we have built Jerusalem. And that time, you and I shall never see.

But there is still more. Milton added to deep thought consummate art. Even in his prose we to-day recognize an art surpassing that of most writers. Masson's apologetic excuses for his hero are no longer needed or acceptable; the critic is obsolete, the author remains. In his poetry Milton expressed his profound thought with such exquisite and appropriate art that he stands to-day the greatest of our poets, dramatic art alone excepted. Not in one poem but in many did he reach the high-water mark. The most captious critic has difficulty in suggesting improvements even in the minor verse. In his great poems he has been the teacher of many generations of poets, the despair of imitators.

Unlike most other poets Milton is not good in spots alone; he is consistently good. It is true, he has his heights, but to mention purple patches is to imply a drabness between that does not exist. He was a gifted but also a trained poet, disciplined by life and by severe study to know the best thought in the best form. The result of conscientious, truthful, and faithful application of such a mind is art—constant, not varying, sustained, not failing. Milton had faith in himself and a deep belief in the value of art. That faith brought forth realization.

In the belief that Milton's words are more valuable than anything that can be written about him, the editor has omitted in the interests of a more complete text both introduction and notes. The omission of an introduction will be readily excused, since the serious reader will always have on his desk Hanford's *Milton Handbook*, where he will find the results of the latest scholarly researches and illuminating criticism on both the poetry and the prose, together with an adequate bibliography.

The glossary contains the proper names, except those too obvious to mention, the geographical names, the classical and scriptural references, and obsolete words. As no such dictionary has existed for the prose, the editor ventures to hope that his assistance will prove helpful. In its preparation he has found especially useful Professor Allan H. Gilbert's *Geographical Dictionary*. After all, the best commentary on Milton's poetry is his own prose.

The text has been prepared with care. In the poetry the spelling and punctuation of the first editions have been faithfully preserved, or at least as faithfully as painstaking composition and proof-reading could make them. The reading is that of the original editions except in places where evidently Milton himself revised the reading in the second editions. Such emendations are recorded in the textual notes in the back of the volume. The editor is especially proud to announce that the translation of the Latin and Greek poems has been made by Nelson G. McCrea, Anthon Professor of Latin in Columbia University, and that the Italian poems have been translated afresh by Dino Bigongiari, Da Ponte Professor of Italian in Columbia University.

The text of the prose has been modernized from the original editions. Few scholars realize how corrupt is the standard edition of the prose commonly found in our libraries. The good editor of many generations ago thought often to improve a Milton gone astray, and where he did not knowingly alter, he often carelessly copied; but this last may be easily forgiven to an age ignorant of type-writers and untrained in careful proof-reading. To him the present editor owes too much in labor saving to be crabbed. But in this age when, as a recent British critic has said, every comma in Milton is sacred, the wilful altering of a word is treasonous; needless to say no such changes have intentionally been introduced into the text.

The text of the translation of the *De Doctrina* has been derived from that published in the Bohn Library. It has been condensed by the omission of all scriptural references, except those embedded in Milton's own language. Not only has the text been thus reduced about half, but, it is believed, a real service has been rendered in making Milton's ideas more easily available. The reader should remember that for nearly every statement Milton uses Biblical authority; if curious, he should consult the translation in the Bohn Library.

The gratifying pleasure yet remains of cordially and sincerely thanking those who have aided most in the somewhat arduous work of preparing this book. To the publishers, Mr. F. S. Crofts and his associates, the editor is indebted for intelligent and enthusiastic coöperation in making the volume approach the ideal which he had set. They have allowed no obstacle, financial or other, to stand in the way of possible success. Professors Marjorie Nicolson, James Holly Hanford, J. William Hebel, and David H. Stevens have been constant and faithful in aid and counsel, never-failing helps in times of need. It is always a keen pleasure to an instructor to acknowledge unusual assistance from his own students. To four of those in my graduate class in Milton I am indebted far beyond any acknowledgment that I can make here or elsewhere. Miss A. Marion Osborn, Miss Muriel J. Hughes, and Mr. Charles B. Anderson have faithfully read proof hour upon hour and day by day, declaring that Milton's ideas were a sufficient reward. Mr. Anderson, who has in preparation a biographical study of persons mentioned by Milton, has also assisted with the glossary. Miss Ruth Mowry Chapman, Secretary of the Facsimile Text Society, has worked untiringly upon the glossary and proofs, and in other numerous ways has helped efficiently to smooth out difficulties. My greatest indebtedness is due to one whose name by merit should appear on the title-page, but who would not consent even to this veiled allusion, did she know that it exists. Many hours has she stolen from a life already too busily crowded to read aloud, or to listen to, Milton's prose. Very few discrepancies, I am sure, have escaped her keen ear and trained mind. To all these are due my thanks, but upon my own head rest the imperfections.

F. A. P.

Columbia University
June 2, 1930

PREFACE TO THE SECOND EDITION

The cordial reception given to the first edition of the *Student's Milton* by scholars and students throughout America has led the editor to listen, with reluctance, to the repeated demand for interpretative notes. He has hesitated because it has seemed to him that Milton is his own best interpreter and that no one, least of all a confessed admirer of Milton, should rush in to place himself between the man and his audience. But *fata obstant,* or, at least, the editor was brought to feel that he too, like Cromwell's antagonist, might possibly be mistaken.

This second edition has brought one much wished for opportunity, the possibility of revising the text. In the first edition there were some obvious misprints. Some of these have been pointed out in reviews and in personal correspondence. The editor especially desires to thank Professor Harris Fletcher for his able and helpful review in the *Journal of English and Germanic Philology.* He has now collated afresh both the poetry and the prose and hopes that no serious errors remain.

As a further reward for writing these notes, the editor is grateful for the permission, which the publishers graciously granted, of adding about one hundred pages of text. These new selections include the *Prolusions* and the *Familiar Letters,* complete in translation, the *Letter to a Friend,* from the Cambridge Manuscript, the subjects for poems and plays, from the same source, the four early lives of Milton, and selections from the three *Defences* and the *History of Britain;* there are also selections from the lives by Toland and Richardson of data not given in the preceding biographies, and also selections of typical early opinions concerning Milton and his work. These additions, together with the notes and introduction, will make the *Student's Milton* a more adequate text for a study of the great poet and prose writer in the seventeenth century.

In writing the notes, the editor has endeavored to meet the needs of three classes of students. First, he has tried to make his notes alive and interesting to the average sophomore, who does not know whether he is interested in Milton or not, or even whether he is interested in poetry. It has seemed to the editor that an essential attitude of all students, and especially of those who are making their first real acquaintance with a great poet, is that, after all, life is greater than art can ever be, and that the first question to be settled must always be "What relation does this poetry have to the life that we are living in this age of international ties, of domestic problems, and of lively discussions on the nature of religious thought and feeling and the bounds of true liberty?" If poetry is alive, it must be a factor in present thought. The editor at all times has tried to show that it is because Milton fulfills this condition, that he is still among the giants of literature,—that he was great in life before he was great in art, and that Milton's life indeed was his greatest poem, a deep well and living source for such poetry as *Paradise Lost.*

Second, he has tried to meet the needs of the advanced student of junior or senior standing who has taken a study of Milton as a serious piece of specialization. For him he has included more textual notes and notes involving a deeper consideration of some of the problems raised by a study of Milton's thought.

Finally, he has had in mind the graduate student who is making a special study of Milton and of the seventeenth century. For him he has added a complete list of all the departures from the original editions, including the typographical errors on the part of the seventeenth century printers; he has also added the original errata pages, and occasionally he has suggested subjects for further study.

In writing the notes to *Comus,* the editor felt that the situation is different from that in most of the other poems, for with the content of this poem the student is already familiar from intensive study in the secondary school. He has preferred, therefore, to use his short space for printing the important departures of the printed text from the Cambridge and Bridgewater Manuscripts and thereby has given the average student a better idea of Milton's care in his extensive revisions, and has shown the advanced student the nature of many problems still awaiting solution. If the student is ingenious at solving puzzles, he will find in these two manuscripts and in their connections with possible earlier drafts, now lost, and in the relations of the manuscripts to the printed editions, ample material of a fascinating nature upon which profitably to exercise his "riddling" mind. He may learn that scholarship is not all of one kind and that he too may become a scholar. In the notes on *Paradise Lost* the editor took occasion to incorporate Bishop Sumner's pertinent notes to the *Christian Doctrine*.

It is hardly an exaggeration to say that the preparation of this revised and augmented second edition has entailed more labor than did that of the first. Without the cordial help and criticism of many friends this last edition in its present form would not have been possible. The editor and publishers are indebted to the Columbia University Press for their permission to use the translation of the *Prolusions* made especially for the *Columbia Milton* by Mr. Bromley Smith of the Johns Hopkins University. As this translation will not be published in the *Columbia Milton* until the autumn of 1935, this kindness is indeed unusual, and cordial thanks are here expressed to Mr. Frederick Coykendall, Director of the Columbia University Press. Thanks also are due to The Macmillan Company for their permission to use the translation of the *Familiar Letters* made by Masson and printed in his *Life of Milton*. The editor owes much also to Dr. David H. Stevens of the General Education Board and to Mr. Donald Roberts of the College of the City of New York for reading many of the notes and for the suggestions they have made. Fortunately for the edition, this year Professor H. J. C. Grierson of the University of Edinburgh was the visiting professor of English at Columbia University. He obligingly read the more important notes, such as the headnote to *Paradise Lost* and made valuable criticisms in his inimitable way.

The editor's own graduate students in Milton have rendered active and important services. To name them all would make too long a list. He must not fail, however, to mention those who have been consistently the hard and faithful workers. Mr. Theodore G. Ehrsam, of Lehigh University, voluntarily offered to make a third collation of the text of the entire poetry with the original editions. Mr. Frederick C. Shipley helped in collating the prose. Mr. Ernest Mossner gave similar assistance and made also the selections from the *Second Defence* and from the *Defensio pro se*. Mr. Maximilian G. Walten helped in the collation of the prose and is responsible for the selections from the *History of Britain*. Mr. Ray L. Armstrong under the editor's direction culled the early opinions of Milton and his work. Mr. Joseph W. Martin assisted in the collation of the prose and prepared the early lives for publication,—no inconsiderable task. Lastly, she, whose inspiration and faith over many years have reached far beyond the confines of Miltonic study, has exerted beneficent influence. Without the assistance of these enthusiastic coadjutors, this edition could not have been printed for many months to come, and then would not have been such as the editor hopes it now is.

F. A. P.

Columbia University
June 23, 1933

CONTENTS

CONTENTS

CONTENTS

INTRODUCTION

John Milton was born in Bread Street in the heart of London on December 9, 1608. His father, John Milton, was born near Oxford. While attending the University he changed his religious adherence from the Catholic faith of his father to the popular Protestant state church. He evidently made this change after due consideration; but, as he stubbornly refused to recant, his irate parent repudiated him and all his works. Left without support, he abandoned his university career and migrated to the metropolis, where he proposed to shift for himself. Ultimately he became a scrivener, engaged in writing deeds and contracts and attending to minor details in connection with the law. In time he married, prospered, bought his own home, reared three children, and enjoyed the best that middle class life in London could afford him. At night and after business hours he amused himself composing and playing music, entertaining friends, conversing about notions more or less liberal and perhaps radical, and superintending the education of his two sons, who, he had determined, should have something of what had been denied him. As his fortune grew, his wife interested herself more and more in works of charity toward the poor of the city. His chief pride lay in his oldest child, John, who, as a mere boy, had shown himself a son after his father's own heart; in him, the elder Milton saw what, under happier circumstances, he himself might have been. His hopes for the boy grew with the passing years. And well they might.

When young John was only ten, the father had his portrait done in oil by a contemporary artist—a picture that is now one of the most prized possessions of the Pierpont Morgan Library. At about this time he encouraged the lad to study late at night by ordering a servant to sit with him till he was ready to retire at twelve or one, little dreaming what tragedy he was laying up for later years. As time passed and the boy entered his teens, Thomas Young, a Scotchman of the Reformed faith, and a liberal, was employed to assist in fitting the talented boy for school and the university. At home young Milton entered with enthusiasm into the cultural recreations of his father, translated Psalms into English verse for his father to set to music, and doubtless listened to the liberal views expressed when his father met friends for an evening's enjoyment of that best of pleasures, amateur art.

In due time he entered St. Paul's, an excellent training school of the city, in preparation for one of the universities. About this time his Scottish instructor departed the shores of England to act as a shepherd for the English Puritan merchants settled in Hamburg. While at St. Paul's, Milton continued his efficient and careful study of Latin, Greek, and Hebrew, growing daily in favor with his father and with his own friends. Here also he had his enthusiasm for his native language quickened under the inspiration of young Alexander Gill, a teacher, the son of the active headmaster. Meanwhile his custom of writing in English verse and of reading all the contemporary English poetry that he could lay hands on grew upon him. His style in writing verse soon became more and more his own; moreover it had certain vital signs that told his friends that it would live. His self-esteem and just confidence in his own worth and powers also increased, for his idealism held him rigidly to what reason and his study told him was best in life. He emerged, trained in the languages as few pupils were then trained, and as perhaps few are now, ready for his university career, but with many rather dangerous traits, such as an idealism that might easily lead to an opposite extreme of loose living, or else to a fanatic's excess, and an independence of thought that boded no good to accepted conservative ideas of life, such as his unknown grandfather up near the university town of Oxford cherished and even defended with his money and happiness. It was written in the stars that John Milton, the younger, should be a radical like John Milton, the elder, that he should be so thorough-going that three hundred years later conservatives would hold their breaths while they read his searching invectives against cherished beliefs held from father to son for generations.

At Cambridge Milton continued his independent way, studying till midnight and later, writing English poetry whenever he felt moved so to do, sending letters in careful, elegant Latin to his former tutor, writing to his best friend, the talented son of an Italian, now an English citizen, and thinking to himself, "What a mess my church is in, and what a mess for a young fellow to project himself into! I don't know that I am going to do it. I wonder what my dear old father will say." The college men at Cambridge, too, were a little gay. Milton liked to be a good fellow, when the fun was innocent. He could joke with the best of them in Latin, and in rather coarse fashion too, if he so pleased. He enjoyed the Cam; he enjoyed the rides on old Hobson's famous horses, and he loved the eccentric old man, seeing the real beneath the shrewd exterior of the successful man of business. And all the while he heard time's winged chariot drawing near and thought how good it might be to grow up.

As one year crept on to the next, the spirit of the whole place changed toward the undergraduate who combined genius with scholarship. His tutors, from a sad experience of one of them who had probably tried to correct him on a Latin word, had learned to respect the attainments of this young man; and his acquaintances among the students had changed the scornful, "Lady of Christ's" into an affectionate tribute to his idealism and a fair exterior. Milton went his way. His degree came on schedule; after seven years he should have been a candidate for a fellowship, but he allowed the honor to pass uncontested to a younger friend, Edward King; and the reason only he knew—the church had become impossible for John Milton, and a fellowship meant studying for the church. Let King have it and welcome; King was an idealist too. Milton prepared to leave the University after seven years of study, while his friends, of whom he had many, made it known how much better it would have pleased them had he planned to return for the next term.

His father, meanwhile, feeling the cares of life and the infirmities of age growing upon him, wished to secure a little quiet leisure by retiring into the country at Horton, about twenty miles away from London; from here he could ride in occasionally, look over his property, see how the writing of contracts was prospering, and have an hour of music and talk with old cronies. To Horton Milton betook himself, with a welcome such as we can easily imagine. It was not long before he was settled into a program of study and recreation, all directed toward the ideal of a sound mind in a sound body. Reading Latin, Greek, and Hebrew, brushing up his Italian and French, dipping more deeply into advanced mathematics, reading history, all in Latin, and writing English poetry of the most elegant kind he could master—these were the chief items in the five-year plan of this idealistic youth, fresh from seven years at Cambridge, and ambitious to grow up. How much of this he accomplished we can judge by the results. At Horton we know that he wrote *Comus, Lycidas,* and probably other poems. Statements in his letters show that he worked consistently and hard at his schedule. But in all this work, his dominating thought concerned the future and the best use he could make of the great talent that God had bestowed upon him. He must not be a faithless steward and return without interest or investment. He desired ardently and prayerfully to grow up but found that man does not add to his mental or physical stature at will.

When his mother died in 1637, the time seemed propitious for some things to be settled. Friends, too, whom he doubtless respected, mildly at least, began to carp and curiously to wonder what this young fellow thought he was about. It was time to decide things. And the first thing should come first: would his father give his consent to a life of writing and of study? Father and son talked it out in many a conversation and thought it out by themselves much more deeply. One of the final states of these talks the son expressed in a Latin poem addressed to his father. At length that matter was settled, and settled as the younger man wished it. Then came the question of further study, and the Milton fortune, or at least as much of it as was necessary, was placed at the son's command. With this aid he left for a prolonged trip to the Continent, accompanied by a man servant.

On this Continental tour Milton had one chief desire—he wished to become a cultured and living poet in the best tradition of the greatest masters the world had known. He was interested above all in life, and he sought out and made friends with those who best represented contemporary letters in the Italian centers of culture. At Naples he cultivated an intimacy with that generous old man, Manso, the erstwhile friend of Tasso. With deliberate care he made every turn count toward his great ambition—to write that which the world would not willingly let die, and to make his own life such a poem.

On his return to England life called to him in stronger accents, for the time, than art; liberty was at stake. That battle had to be fought and won. Like most battles this turned out to be a continuous struggle, long drawn out. For eighteen years Milton fought the good fight as he saw the truth—only occasionally and never for long devoting his attention to art. His life in England from 1640 to 1658 was but a logical continuation of what the thirty-two years preceding had been—a preparation by intense study and deep thinking for writing great poetry. In his prose writings during these years he fought for tolerance in religion, for the complete separation of church and state, for the liberty of the subject under a tyrannous government, for the liberty of printing, writing, and thinking, for a reasonable liberty in domestic relations, and for a sound foundation for national greatness and virtue.

Exactly when he actually began to write his great epic is not known. We used to think that he probably began as late as 1658, but scholars are now inclined to put the date much earlier, some even believing that he may have been working on it, or at least actively preparing for it, as early as 1644, or at any rate by 1646.

With the return of Charles II and his court Milton's life became more obscure. He was blind when he was only forty-three and had gradually dropped from the public eye. We know that for a while following the Restoration he was on the list of those who might well suffer punishment; we know that he spent a few months in prison and that he was finally released. His life thenceforth was that of a retired man of letters, interested still in life, genial with his many friends, working on his poetry, which now at last had become what he had always wanted it to be, the real passion of his life. In 1667 the first edition of *Paradise Lost* was published. In 1671 *Paradise Regain'd* and *Samson Agonistes* were published in one volume. In 1673 he re-issued the 1645 edition of his short poems, adding to that edition whatever he had written of a similar nature during the years between 1645 and 1673, including also some other minor verse which he thought might be worth preserving. With characteristic tact and a view to practical results he wisely omitted four sonnets which he knew were not suitable reading for the times. In 1673 the old warrior again joined battle, as he watched with growing apprehensions the king's tolerant attitude toward the Catholic church; he knew that this could not mean peace to England; he could not foresee that this attitude allowed to grow would ultimately contribute its share to cause the revolution of 1688, when many of the ideas for which he had fought throughout his life would become so thoroughly established that they could never be dislodged from English national life. One cannot but regret that the old man could not have lived until 1688; but, if he had, he doubtless would not have realized the full significance of that "glorious revolution." Only we can see that then were those principles finally established that have made England the foremost of the nations of the world in her love for political liberty.

In 1674 Milton issued a revised and augmented edition of his great epic. The hand of the old poet, suffering from blindness and "gout struck in," had not weakened. The lines he added are not inferior. That revision was the last work that he did. The four early lives will give us further facts about this fighter of our battles; they will also leave us with the impression of a friendly, genial man of culture and refinement. Let us not delay longer to acquaint ourselves with these old biographies.

BIOGRAPHIES OF MILTON

I. THE LIFE OF MR. JOHN MILTON

[Anonymous]

To WRITE the lives of single persons is then a commendable undertaking, when by it some moral benefit is designed to mankind. He who has that in aim, will not employ his time or pen to record the history of bad men, how successful or great soever they may have been; unless by relating their tragical ends (which, through the just judgment of the Almighty, most commonly overtakes them) or by discriminating, with a due note of infamy, whatever is criminal in their actions, he warn the reader to flee their example.

But to celebrate, whether the gifts or graces, the natural endowments, or acquired laudable habits of persons eminent in their generations, while it gives glory to God, the bestower of all good things, and (by furnishing a model) tends to the edification of our brethren, is little less than the duty of every Christian; which seems acknowledged by the late supervisors of our Common Prayer when they added to the Collect for the church militant, a clause commemorating the *Saints and Servants of God departed this life in his Fear*.

That he who is the subject of this discourse, made it his endeavor to be thought worthy of that high character, will, I make no doubt, appear to the impartial reader from the particulars, which I shall with all sincerity relate of his life and works.

The learned Mr. John Milton, born about the year sixteen hundred and eight, is said to be descended from an ancient knightly family in Buckinghamshire, that gave name to the chief place of their abode. However that be, his father was entitled to a true nobility in the Apostle Paul's Heraldry; having been disinherited about the beginning of Queen Elizabeth's reign by his father a Romanist, who had an estate of five hundred pound a year at Stainton St. John in Oxfordshire, for reading the Bible. Upon this occasion he came young to London, and being taken care of by a relation of his, a scrivener. he became free of that profession; and was so prosperous in it, and the consortship of a prudent, virtuous wife, as to be able to breed up in a liberal manner, and provide a competency for two sons and a daughter. After which, out of a moderation not usual with such as have tasted the sweets of gain, and perhaps naturally inclined rather to a retired life by his addiction to music (for his skill in which he stands registered among the composers of his time), he gave over his trade, and went to live in the country.

This his eldest son had his institution to learning both under public and private masters; under whom, through the pregnancy of his parts and his indefatigable industry (sitting up constantly at his study till midnight), he profited exceedingly; and early in that time wrote several grave and religious poems, and paraphrased some of David's Psalms.

At about eighteen years of age he went to Christ's College in Cambridge; where for his diligent study, his performance of public exercises, and for choice verses, written on the occasions usually solemnized by the universities, as well for his virtuous and sober life, he was in high esteem with the best of his time.

After taking his degree of Master of Arts he left the university, and, having no design to take upon him any of the particular learned professions, applied himself for five years, at his father's house in the country, to the diligent reading of the best classic authors, both divine and human; sometimes repairing to London, from which he was not far distant, for learning music and the mathematics.

Being now become master of what useful knowledge was to be had in books, and competently skilled amongst others, in the Italian language, he made choice of that country to travel into, in order to polish his conversation, and learn to know men. And having received instructions how to demean himself with that wise, observing nation, as well as how to shape his journey, from Sir Henry Wotton, whose esteem of him appears in an elegant letter to him upon that subject, he took his way through France. In this kingdom, the manners and genius of which he had in no admiration, he made small stay, nor contracted any acquaintance; save that, with the recommendation of the Lord Scudamore, our King's Ambassador at Paris, he waited on Hugo Grotius, who was there under that character from the Crown of Sweden.

Hasting to Italy by the way of Nice, and passing through Genoa, Leghorn, and Pisa he arrived at Florence. Here he lived two months in familiar and elegant conversation with the choice wits of that city, and was admitted by them to their private academies; an economy much practised among the virtuosi of those parts, for the communication of polite literature, as well as for the cementing of friendships. The reputation he had with them they expressed in several commendatory verses, which are extant in his book of poems. From Florence he went to Rome, where, as in all places, he spent his time in the choicest company; and amongst others there, in that of Lucas Holstein.

At Naples, which was his next remove, he became acquainted with Marquis Manso, a learned person, and so aged as to have been contemporary and intimate with Torquato Tasso, the famous Italian heroic. This nobleman obliged him by very particular civilities, accompanying him to see the rarities of the place, and paying him visits at his lodging; also sent him the testimony of a great esteem in this distich:

> Ut Mens, Forma, Decor Facies, Mos, si Pietas sic,
> Non Anglus, verum herclè Angelus ipse fores.

Yet excused himself at parting for not having been able to do him more honor by reason of his resolute owning his religion. This he did whensoever by any one's enquiry occasion was offered; not otherwise forward to enter upon discourses of that nature. Nor did he decline its defense in the like circumstances even in Rome itself on his return thither; though he had been advised by letters from some friends to Naples, that the English Jesuits designed to do him mischief on that account. Before his leaving Naples he returned the Marquis an acknowledgment of his great favors in an elegant copy of verses entitled *Mansus*, which is extant amongst his other Latin poems.

From Rome he revisited Florence for the sake of his charming friends there; and then proceeded to Venice, where he shipped what books he had bought, and through the delicious country of Lombardy, and over the Alps to Geneva, where he lived in familiar conversation with the famous Diodati. Thence through France he returned home, having, with no ill management of his time, spent about fifteen months abroad.

He had by this time laid in a large stock of knowledge, which as he designed not for the purchase of wealth, so neither intended he it, as a miser's hoard, to lie useless. Having therefore taken a house, to be at full ease and quiet, and gotten his books about him, he set himself upon compositions, tending either to the public benefit of mankind, and especially his countrymen, or to the advancement of the Commonwealth of Learning. And his first labors were very happily dedicated to what had the chiefest place in his affections, and had been no small part of his study, the service of religion.

It was now the year 1640, and the nation was much divided upon the controversies about church government, between the Prelatical party, and the Dissenters, or, as they were commonly then called, Puritans. He had studied religion in the Bible and the best authors, had strictly lived up to its rules, and had no temporal concern depending upon any hierarchy to render him suspected, either to himself or others, as one that writ for interest; and, therefore, with great boldness and zeal offered his judgment, first in two *Books of Reformation* by way of address to a friend, and then, in answer to a bishop, he writ of *Prelatical Episcopacy* and *The Reason of Church Government*. After that, *Animadversions upon the Remonstrants defence* (the work of Bishop Hall) *against Smectymnuus* and *Apology for those Animadversions.*

In this while, his manner of settlement fitting him for the reception of a wife, he in a month's time (according to his practice of not wasting that precious talent) courted, married, and brought home from Forresthall, near Oxford, a daughter of Mr. Powell. But she, that was very young, and had been bred in a family of plenty and freedom, being not well pleased with his reserved manner of life, within a few days left him, and went back into the country with her mother. Nor though he sent several pressing invitations could he prevail with her to return, till about four years after, when Oxford was surrendered (the nighness of her father's house to that garrison having for the most part of the meantime hindered any communication between them), she of her own accord came, and submitted to him, pleading that her mother had been the inciter of her to that frowardness. He, in the interval, who had entered into that state for the end designed by God and nature, and was then in the full vigor of his manhood, could ill bear the disappointment he met with by her obstinate absenting; and, therefore, thought upon a divorce, that he might be free to marry another; concerning which he also was in treaty. The lawfulness and expedience of this, duly regulate in order to all those purposes for which marriage was at first instituted, had upon full consideration and reading good authors been formerly his opinion; and the necessity of justifying himself now concurring with the opportunity, acceptable to him, of instructing others in a point of so great concern to the peace and preservation of families, and so likely to prevent temptations as well as mischiefs, he first writ *The Doctrine and Discipline of Divorce,* then *Colasterion,* and after *Tetrachordon.* In these he taught the right use and design of marriage; then the original and practice of divorces amongst the Jews, and showed that our Saviour, in those four places of the Evangelists, meant not the abrogating but rectifying the abuses of it; rendering to that purpose another sense of the word fornication (and which is also the opinion amongst others of Mr. Selden in his *Uxor Hebræa*) than what is commonly received. Martin Bucer's *Judgment* in this matter he likewise translated into English. The Assembly of Divines then sitting at Westminster, though formerly obliged by his learned pen in the defense of Smectymnuus, and other their controversies with the bishops, now impatient of having the clergies' jurisdiction, as they reckoned it, invaded, instead of answering, or disproving what those books had asserted, caused him to be summoned for them before the Lords. But that house, whether approving the doctrine, or not favoring his accusers, soon dismissed him.

This was the mending of a decay in the superstructure, and had for object only the well-being of private persons, or at most of families. His small treatise *of Education*, addressed to Mr. Hartlib, was the laying a foundation also of public weal. In it he prescribed an easy and delightful method for training up gentry in such a manner to all sorts of literature, as that they might at the same time by like degrees advance in virtue and abilities to serve their country, subjoining directions for their attaining other necessary or ornamental accomplishments; and it seemed he designed in some measure to put this in practise. He had, from his first settling, taken care of instructing his two nephews by his sister Phillips, and, as it happened, the son of some friend. Now he took a large house, where the Earle of Barrimore, sent by his aunt the Lady Ranalagh, Sir Thomas Gardiner of Essex, and others were under his tuition. But whether it were that the tempers of our gentry would not bear the strictness of his discipline, or for what other reason, he continued that course but a while.

His next public work, and which seemed to be his particular province, who was so jealous in promoting knowledge, was *Areopagitica,* written in manner of an oration, to vindicate the freedom of the press from the tyranny of licensers; who either enslaved to the dictates of those that put them into office, or prejudiced by their own ignorance, are wont to hinder the coming out of any thing which is not consonant to the common received opinions, and by that means deprive the public of the benefit of many useful labors.

Hitherto all his writings had for subject the propagation of religion or learning, or the bettering some more private concerns of mankind. In political matters he had published nothing. And it was now the time of the King's coming upon his trial, when some of the Presbyterian ministers, out of malignity to the Independent party, who had supplanted them, more than from any principles of loyalty, asserted clamorously in their sermons and writings the privilege of kings from all accountableness. Or (to speak in the language of this time) non-resistance and passive obedience to be the doctrine of all the Reformed Churches. This general thesis, which encouraged all manner of tyranny, he opposed by good arguments, and the authorities of several eminently learned protestants in a book titled *The Tenure of Kings,* but without any particular application to the dispute then on foot in this nation.

Upon the change of government which succeeded the King's death he was, without any seeking of his, by the means of a private acquaintance, who was then a member of the new Council of State, chosen Latin Secretary. In this public station his abilities and the acuteness of his parts, which had lain hid in his privacy, were soon taken notice of, and he was pitched upon to elude the artifice of Εἰκὼν Βασιλική. This he had no sooner performed answerably to the expectation from his wit and pen, in Εἰκονοκλάστης, but another adventure expected him.

Salmasius, a professor in Holland, who had in a large treatise, not long before, maintained the parity of church governors against Episcopacy, put out *Defensio Caroli Regis,* and in it, amongst other absurdities, justified (as indeed it was unavoidable in the defense of that cause, which was styled *Bellum Episcopale*) to the contradiction of his former book, the pretensions of the bishops. Him Mr. Milton, by the order of his masters, answered in *Defensio pro populo Anglicano,* both in more correct Latin, to the shame of the other's grammarship, and by much better reasoning. For Salmasius being a foreigner, and grossly ignorant of our laws and constitution (which in all nations are the respective distinguishing principles of government), either brought no arguments from thence, or such only (and by him not seldom mistaken or misapplied) as were partially suggested to him by those whose cause he had undertaken; and which, having during the many years of our divisions been often ventilated, received an easy solution. Nor had he given proof of deeper learning in that which is properly called politics, while he made use of trite instances, as that of the government of bees, and such like to prove the preeminency of monarchy; and all along so confounded it with tyranny (as also he did the Episcopal with the Papal government), that he might better have passed for a defender of the grand Signor, and the Council of Trent, than of a lawful king and a reformed church. For this and reneging his former principles he was by Mr. Milton facetiously exposed; nor did he ever reply, though he lived three years after.

But what he wisely declined, the further provoking such an adversary, or persisting to defend a cause he so ill understood, was attempted in *Clamor Regii Sanguinis,* etc., in which Salmasius was hugely extolled, and Mr. Milton as falsely defamed. The anonymous author, Mr. Milton, who had by his last book gained great esteem and many friends among the learned abroad, by whom, and by public ministers coming hither he was often visited, soon discovered to be Morus, formerly a professor and minister at Geneva, then living in Holland. Him, in *Secunda Defensio pro populo Anglicano,* he rendered ridiculous for his trivial and weak treatise under so tragical a title, containing little of argument, which had not before suffered with Salmasius. And because it consisted most of railing and false reproaches, he, in no unpleasant manner, from very good testimonies retorted upon him the true history of his notorious impurities, both at Geneva and Leyden. Himself he also, by giving a particular ingenuous account of his whole life, vindicated from those scurrilous aspersions, with which that book had endeavored to blemish him; adding perhaps thereby also reputation to the cause he defended, at least with impartial readers, when they should reflect upon the different qualifications of the respective champions. And when Morus afterwards strove to clear himself of being the author, and to represent Mr. Milton as an injurious defamer in that particular, he in *Defensio pro se* by very good testimonies, and other circumstantial proofs justified his having fixed it there, and made good sport of the other's shallow evasions.

While he was thus employed his eyesight totally failed him; not through any immediate or sudden judgment, as his adversaries insultingly affirmed, but from a weakness which his hard, nightly study in his youth had first occasioned, and which by degrees had for some time before deprived him of the use of one eye. And the issues and seatons, made use of to save or retrieve that, were thought by drawing away the spirits, which should have supplied the optic vessels, to have hastened the loss of the other. He was, indeed, advised by his physicians of the danger, in his condition, attending so great intentness as that work required. But he, who was resolute in going through with what upon good consideration he at any time designed, and to whom the love of truth and his country was dearer than all things, would not for any danger decline their defense.

Nor did his darkness discourage or disable him from prosecuting, with the help of amanuenses, the former design of his calmer studies. And he had now more leisure, being dispensed with by having a substitute allowed him, and sometimes instructions sent home to him, from attending in his office of secretary.

It was now that he began that laborious work of amassing out of all the classic authors, both in prose and verse, a *Latin Thesaurus* to the emendation of that done by Stephanus; also the composing *Paradise Lost,* and the framing a body of divinity out of the Bible. All which, notwithstanding the several calamities befalling him in his fortunes, he finished after the Restoration: as also the *British History* down to the Conquest, *Paradise Regained, Samson Agonistes,* a tragedy, *Logica and Accedence, commenced Grammar* and had begun a *Greek Thesaurus;* having scarce left any part of learning unimproved by him, as in *Paradise Lost* and *Regained* he more especially taught all virtue.

In these works, and the instruction of some youth or other at the intreaty of his friends, he in great serenity spent his time and expired no less calmly in the year 1674.

He had naturally a sharp wit, and steady judgment; which helps toward attaining learning he improved by an indefatigable attention to his study; and was supported in that by a temperance, always observed by him, but in his youth even with great nicety. Yet did he not reckon this talent but as entrusted with him; and therefore dedicated all his labors to the glory of God and some public good; neither binding himself to any of the gainful professions, nor having any worldly interest for aim in what he taught. He made no address or court for the employment of Latin secretary, though his eminent fitness for it appear by his printed letters of that time. And he was so far from being concerned in the corrupt designs of his masters, that whilst in his first and second *Defensio pro populo Anglicano* he was an advocate for liberty against tyranny and oppression (which to him seemed the case, as well by the public declarations on the one side [and he was a stranger to their private counsels], as by the arguments on the other side, which run mainly upon the justifying of exorbitant and lawless power), he took care all along strictly to define and persuade to true liberty, and especially in very solemn perorations at the close of those books; where he also, little less than prophetically, denounced the punishments due to the abusers of that specious name. And as he was not linked to one party by self interest, so neither was he divided from the other by animosity; but was forward to do any of them good offices, when their particular cases afforded him ground to appear on their behalf. And especially, if on the score of wit or learning, they could lay claim to his peculiar patronage. Of which were instances, among others the grand-child of the famous Spencer, a papist suffering in his concerns in Ireland, and Sir William Davenant, when taken prisoner, for both of whom he procured relief.

This his sincerity, and disentanglement of any private ends with his sentiments relating to the public, proceeded no doubt from a higher principle, but was in great part supported, and temptations to the contrary avoided by his constant frugality; which enabled him at first to live within compass of the moderate patrimony his father left him, and afterwards to bear with patience, and no discomposure of his way of living, the great losses which befell him in his fortunes. Yet he was not sparing to buy good books, of which he left a fair collection; and was generous in relieving the wants of his friends. Of his gentleness and humanity he likewise gave signal proof in receiving home, and living in good accord till her death with his first wife, after she had so obstinately absented from him. During which time, as neither in any other scene of his life, was he blemished with the least unchastity.

From so Christian a life, so great learning, and so unbiassed a search after truth it is not probable any errors in doctrine should spring. And, therefore, his judgment in his body of divinity concerning some speculative points, differing perhaps from that commonly received (and which is thought to be the reason that never was printed) neither ought rashly to be condemned, and however himself not to be uncharitably censured; who, by being a constant champion for the liberty of opining, expressed much candor towards others. But that this age is insensible of the great obligations it has to him, is too apparent in that he has no better a pen to celebrate his memory.

He was of a moderate stature, and well proportioned, of a ruddy complexion, light brown hair, and handsome features; save that his eyes were none of the quickest. But his blindness, which proceeded from a gutta serena, added no further blemish to them. His deportment was sweet and affable; and his gate erect and manly, bespeaking courage and undauntedness (or a *nil conscire*), on which account he wore a sword while he had his sight, and was skilled in using it. He had an excellent ear, and could bear a part both in vocal and instrumental music. His moderate estate left him by his father was, through his good economy, sufficient to maintain him. Out of his secretary's salary he had saved two thousand pounds, which, being lodged in the excise, and that bank failing upon the Restoration, he utterly lost. Besides which, and the ceasing of his employment, he had no damage by that change of affairs. For he early sued out his pardon; and by means of that, when the Sergeant of the house of Commons had officiously seized him, was quickly set at liberty. He had, too, at the first return of the Court in good manners left his house in Petty France, which had a door into the park; and in all other things demeaning himself peaceably, was so far from being reckoned disaffected, that he was visited at his house on Bunhill by a chief officer of state, and desired to employ his pen on their behalf. And when the subject of divorce was under consideration with the Lords, upon the account of the Lord Ross, he was consulted by an eminent member of that house. By the great fire in 1666 he had a house in Bread Street burnt, which was all the real estate he had.

He rendered his studies and various works more easy and pleasant by alloting them their several portions of the day. Of these the time friendly to the Muses fell to his poetry; and he, waking early, (as is the use of temperate men) had commonly a good stock of verses ready against his amanuensis came; which if it happened to be later then ordinary, he would complain, saying *he wanted to be milked*. The evenings he likewise spent in reading some choice poets, by way of refreshment after the days toil, and to store his fancy against morning. Besides his ordinary lectures out of the Bible and the best commentators on the week day, that was his sole subject on Sundays. And David's Psalms were in esteem with him above all poetry. The youths that he instructed from time to time served him often as amanuenses, and some elderly persons were glad for the benefit of his learned conversation, to perform that office. His first wife died a while after his blindness seized him, leaving him three daughters, that lived to be women. He married two more, whereof one survived him. He died in a fit of the gout, but with so little pain or emotion, that the time of his expiring was not perceived by those in the room. And though he had been long troubled with that disease, insomuch that his knuckles were all callous, yet was he not ever observed to be very impatient. He had this elegy in common with the patriarchs and kings of Israel, that he was gathered to his people; for he happened to be buried in Cripplegate, where about thirty years before he had by chance also interred his father.

II. MINUTES OF THE LIFE OF MR. JOHN MILTON

BY JOHN AUBREY

[His parentage]

MR. JOHN MILTON was of an Oxfordshire family. His mother was a Bradshaw.

His grandfather, . . . , (a Roman Catholic), of Holton, in Oxfordshire, near Shotover.

His father was brought up in the University of Oxon, at Christ Church, and his grandfather disinherited him because he kept not to the Catholic religion. He found a Bible in English in his chamber. So thereupon he came to London, and became a scrivener (brought up by a friend of his; was not an apprentice), and got a plentiful estate by it, and left it off many years before he died. He was an ingenious man; delighted in music; composed many songs now in print, especially that of *Oriana*.

I have been told that the father composed a song of fourscore parts for the Landgrave of Hesse, for which [his] highness sent a medal of gold, or a noble present. He died about 1647; buried in Cripplegate church, from his house in the Barbican.

[His birth]

His son John was born in Bread Street, in London, at the Spread Eagle, which was his house (he had also in that street another house, the Rose; and other houses in other places).

He was born Anno Domini . . . the . . . day of . . . , about . . . o'clock, in the . . .

(John Milton was born the 9th of December, 1608, die Veneris, half an hour after 6 in the morning.)

[His precocity]

Anno Domini 1619, he was ten years old, as by his picture; and was then a poet.

[School, college and travel]

His school-master then was a Puritan, in Essex, who cut his hair short.

He went to school to old Mr. Gill, at Paul's school. Went, at his own charge only, to Christ's College in Cambridge at fifteen, where he stayed eight years at least. Then he travelled into France and Italy (had Sir H. Wotton's commendatory letters). At Geneva he contracted a great friendship with the learned Dr. Diodati of Geneva (vide his poems). He was acquainted with Sir Henry Wotton, Ambassador at Venice, who delighted in his company. He was several years < Quaere, how many? Resp., two years. > beyond sea, and returned to England just upon the breaking out of the civil wars.

From his brother, Christopher Milton: When he went to school, when he was very young, he studied very hard, and sat up very late, commonly till twelve or one o'clock at night, and his father ordered the maid to sit up for him; and in those years (10) composed many copies of verses which might well become a riper age. And was a very hard student in the University, and performed all his exercises there with very good applause. His first tutor there was Mr. Chapell; from whom receiving some unkindness <whipped him>, he was afterwards (though it seemed contrary to the rules of the college) transferred to the tuition of one Mr. Tovell, who died parson of Lutterworth.

He went to travel about the year 1638 and was abroad about a year's space, chiefly in Italy.

[Return to England]

Immediately after his return he took a lodging at Mr. Russell's, a tailor, in St. Bride's churchyard, and took into his tuition his sister's two sons, Edward and John Phillips, the first 10, the other 9 years of age; and in a year's time made them capable of interpreting a Latin author at sight, etc., and within three years they went through the best of Latin and Greek poets.—Lucretius and Manilius <and with him the use of the globes and some rudiments of arithmetic and geometry> of the Latins, Hesiod, Aratus, Dionysius Afer, Oppian, Apollonii *Argonautica,* and Quintus Calaber. Cato, Varro, and Columella *De re rustica* were the very first authors they learned. As he was severe on one hand, so he was most familiar and free in his conversation to those to whom most severe in his way of education. N. B. He made his nephews songsters, and sing, from the time they were with him.

[First wife and children]

He married his first wife, . . . Powell, of . . . Fosthill, in Oxfordshire, Anno Domini . . . , by whom he had 4 children. Hath two daughters living: Deborah was his amanuensis; he taught her Latin, and to read Greek to him when he had lost his eyesight, which was Anno Domini . . .

[Separation from his first wife]

(She went from him to her mother at . . . the King's quarters, near Oxford), Anno Domini . . . and [he] wrote the *Triplechord,* about divorce.

Two opinions do not well on the same bolster. She was a . . . Royalist and went to her mother, near Oxford (the King's quarters). I have so much charity for her that she might not wrong his bed: but what man, especially contemplative, would like to have a young wife environed and stormed by the sons of Mars, and those of the enemy party?

His first wife (Mrs. Powell, a Royalist) was brought up and lived where there was a great deal of company and merriment (dancing etc.). And when she came to live with her husband, at Mr. Russell's in St. Bride's churchyard, she found it very solitary: no company came to her; oftentimes heard his nephews beaten and cry. This life was irksome to her, and so she went to her parents at Fosthill. He sent for her, after some time; and I think his servant was evilly entreated: but as for the matter of wronging his bed, I never heard the least suspicions; nor had he, of that, any jealousy.

[Second wife]

He had a middle wife, whose name was (he thinks Katherine) Woodcock. No child living by her.

[Third wife]

He married his second wife, Mrs. Elizabeth Minshull, Anno . . . (the year before the sickness): a gentle person, a peaceful and agreeable humour.

[His public employment]

He was Latin secretary to the Parliament.

[*His blindness*]

His sight began to fail him at first upon his writing against Salmasius, and before it was fully completed one eye absolutely failed. Upon the writing of other books, after that, his other eye decayed.

His eyesight was decaying about 20 years before his death. His father read without spectacles at 84. His mother had very weak eyes, and used spectacles presently after she was thirty years old.

[*Writings after his blindness*]

After he was blind he wrote these following books, viz.: *Paradise Lost, Paradise Regained, Grammar, Dictionary* (imperfect).

I heard that after he was blind that he was writing a Latin dictionary. <In the hands of Moses Pitt. > Vidua affirmat she gave all his papers (among which this dictionary, imperfect) to his nephew that he brought up, a sister's son, . . . Phillips, who lives near the Maypole in the Strand. She has a great many letters by her from learned men, his acquaintance, both of England and beyond the sea.

[*His later residences*]

He lived in several places, e. g. Holburn near Kingsgate. He died in Bunhill, opposite to the Artillery-garden wall.

[*His death and burial*]

He died of the gout struck in, the 9th or 10th of November, 1674, as appears by his apothecary's book.

He lies buried in St. Gile's Cripplegate, upper end of chancel at the right hand (vide his gravestone). Memorandum: his stone is now removed; for, about two years since (now 1681), the two steps to the communion table were raised. I guess John Speed and he lie together.

[*Personal characteristics*]

His harmonical and ingenious soul did lodge in a beautiful and well-proportioned body.
In toto nusquam corpore menda fuit.
Ovid.

He was a spare man. He was scarce so tall as I am. <Quaere, quot feet I am high. Resp., of middle stature.>

He had auburn hair. His complexion exceeding fair—he was so fair that they called him *the lady of Christ's College.* Oval face. His eye a dark gray.

He had a delicate tuneable voice, and had good skill. His father instructed him. He had an organ in his house: he played on that most.

Of a very cheerful humour: he would be cheerful even in his gout fits, and sing.

He was very healthy and free from all diseases (seldom took any physic, only sometimes he took manna); only towards his latter end he was visited with the gout, spring and fall.

He had a very good memory; but I believe that his excellent method of thinking and disposing did much to help his memory.

He pronounced the letter R (littera canina) very hard. ("A certain sign of a satirical wit"—from John Dryden.)

[*Portraits of him*]

His widow has his picture, drawn very well and like, when a Cambridge scholar.

She has his picture when a Cambridge scholar, which ought to be engraven; for the pictures before his books are not *at all* like him.

Write his name in red letters on his picture, with his widow, to preserve.

[*His habits*]

His exercise was chiefly walking.

He was an early riser (scil. at 4 o'clock manè); yea, after he lost his sight. He had a man read to him. The first thing he read was the Hebrew Bible, and that was at 4 h. manè, ½ h. +. Then he contemplated.

At 7 his man came to him again, and then read to him again, and wrote till dinner: the writing was as much as the reading. His (2nd) daughter, Deborah (married in Dublin to one Mr. Clarke (sells silk, etc.); very like her father), could read to him Latin, Italian and French, and Greek. The other (1st) sister is Mary, more like her mother.

After dinner he used to walk 3 or 4 hours at a time (he always had a garden where he lived); went to bed about 9.

Temperate, rarely drank between meals.

Extreme pleasant in his conversation, and at dinner, supper, etc; but satirical.

[*Notes about some of his works*]

From Mr. E. Phillips:—All the time of writing his *Paradise Lost*, his vein began at the autumnal equinoctial and ceased at the vernal or thereabouts (I believe about May); and this was 4 or 5 years of his doing it. He began about 2 years before the King came in, and finished about 3 years after the King's Restoration.

In the 4th book of *Paradise Lost* there are about 6 verses of Satan's exclamation to the sun, which Mr. E. Phillips remembers about 15 or 16 years before ever his poem was thought of. Which verses were intended for the beginning of a tragedy which he had designed; but was diverted from it by other business.

Whatever he wrote against monarchy was out of no animosity to the King's person, or out of any faction or interest, but out of a pure zeal to the liberty [of] mankind, which he thought would be greater under a free state than under a monarchial government. His being so conversant in Livy and the Roman authors, and the greatness he saw done by the Roman Commonwealth and the virtue of their great commanders induced him to.

From Mr. Abraham Hill:—Memorandum: his sharp writing against Alexander More, of Holland, upon a mistake, notwithstanding he had given him by the Ambassador < Quaere the Ambassador's name of Mr. Hill. Resp., Newport, the Dutch Ambassador. > all satisfaction to the contrary: viz., that the book called "Clamor" was writ by Peter du Moulin. Well, that was all one; he having writ it, it should go into the world; one of them was as bad as the other.

Memorandum:—Mr. Theodore Haak, Regiae Societatis Socius, hath translated half his *Paradise Lost* into High Dutch in such blank verse, which is very well liked of by Germanus Fabricius, Professor at Heidelberg, who sent Mr. Haak a letter upon this translation: "Incredible est quantum nos omnes affecerit gravitas styli, et copia lectissimorum verborum," etc,—vide the letter.

Mr. John Milton made two admirable panegyrics as to sublimity of wit: one on Oliver Cromwell and the other on Thomas, Lord Fairfax, both which his nephew Mr. Phillips hath. But he hath hung back these two years as to imparting copies to me for the collection of mine with you. Wherefore I desire you in your next to intimate your desire of having these two copies of verses aforesaid. Were they made in commendation of the devil, 'twere all one to me: 'tis the ὕψος that I look after. I have been told 'tis beyond Waller's or anything in that kind.

[*His acquaintance*]

He was visited much by learned [men], more than he did desire.

He was mightily importuned to go into France and Italy. Foreigners came much to see him and much admired him, and offered to him great preferments to come over to them: and the only inducement of several foreigners that came over into England was chiefly to see Oliver Protector and Mr. John Milton; and would see the house and chamber where he was born. He was much more admired abroad than at home.

His familiar learned acquaintance were:

Mr. Andrew Marvell, Mr. Skinner, Dr. Paget, M. D.

Mr. . . . Skinner, who was his disciple.

John Dryden, Esq., Poet Laureate, who very much admires him, and went to him to have leave to put his *Paradise Lost* into a drama in rhyme. Mr. Milton received him civilly and told him he would give him leave to tag his verses.

His widow assures me that Mr. Hobbes was not one of his acquaintance, that her husband did not like him at all; but he would acknowledge him to be a man of great parts and a learned man. Their interests and tenets did run counter to each other—vide Mr. Hobbes' *Behemoth*.

III. A SELECTION FROM FASTI OXONIENSIS

BY ANTHONY WOOD, 1691

1635. This year was incorporated Master of Arts John Milton, not that it appears so in the register, for the reason I have told you in the incorporations, 1629, but from his own mouth to my friend, who was well acquainted with, and had from him, and from his relations after his death, most of this account of his life and writings following.

(1) That he was born in Breadstreet within the City of London, between six and seven o'clock in the morning of the ninth of Decemb. an. 1608. (2) That his father, John Milton, who was a scrivener living at the Spread Eagle in the said street, was a native of Halton in Oxfordshire, and his mother, named Sarah, was of the ancient family of the Bradshaws. (3) That his grandfather Milton, whose Christian name was John, as he thinks, was an under-ranger or keeper of the forest of Shotover, near to the said town of Halton, but descended from those of his name who had lived beyond all record at Milton near Halton and Thame in Oxfordshire. Which grandfather being a zealous papist, did put away, or, as some say, disinherit, his son, because he was a protestant, which made him retire to London, to seek, in a manner, his fortune. (4) That he, the said John Milton, the author, was educated mostly in Paul's School under Alex. Gill, senior, and thence at fifteen years of age was sent to Christ's Coll. in Cambridge, where he was put under the tuition of Will. Chappell, afterwards Bishop of Ross in Ireland; and there, as at school for three years before, 'twas usual with him to sit up till midnight at his book, which was the first thing that brought his eyes into the danger of blindness. By this his indefatigable study he profited exceedingly, wrote then several poems, paraphrased some of David's *Psalms*, performed the collegiate and academical exercise to the admiration of all, and was esteemed to be a virtuous and sober person, yet not to be ignorant of his own parts. (5) That after he had taken the degrees in Arts, he left the university of his own accord, and was not expelled for misdemeanors, as his adversaries have said. Whereupon, retiring to his father's house in the country, he spent some time in turning over Latin and Greek authors, and now and then made excursions into the great city to buy books, to the end that he might be instructed in mathematics and music; in which last he became excellent, and by the help of his mathematics could compose a song or lesson. (6) That after five years being thus spent, and his mother (who was very charitable to the poor) dead, he did design to travel, so that obtaining the rudiments of the Ital. tongue, and instructions how to demean himself from Sir Hen. Wotton, who delighted in his company, and gave him letters of commendation to certain persons living at

Venice, he travelled into Italy, an. 1638. (7) That in his way thither, he touched at Paris, where Joh. Scudamore, Viscount Slego, Ambassador from K. Ch. I. to the French King, received him kindly, and by his means became known to Hugo Grotius, then and there Ambassador from the Qu. of Sweden; but the manners and genius of that place being not agreeable to his mind, he soon left it. (8) That thence by Geneva and other places of note, he went into Italy, and through Leghorn, Pisa, &c. he went to Florence, where continuing two months, he became acquainted with several learned men, and familiar with the choicest wits of that great city, who introduced and admitted him into their private academies, whereby he saw and learned their fashions of literature. (9) That from thence he went to Siena and Rome, in both which places he spent his time among the most learned there, Lucas Holsteinius being one; and from thence he journeyed to Naples, where he was introduced into the acquaintance of Joh. Bapt. Mansus, an Italian Marquis (to whom Torquatus Tassus, an Italian poet, wrote his book *De Amicitia*) who showed great civilities to him, accompanied him to see the rarities of that place, visited him at his lodgings, and sent to, the testimony of his great esteem for, him, in this distich,

> *Ut mens, forma, decor, facies, mos, si pietas sic,*
> *Non Anglus, verum herculè Angelus ipse fores.*

And excused himself at parting for not having been able to do him more honor, by reason of his resolute owning his (protestant) religion; which resoluteness he using at Rome, many there were that dared not to express their civilities towards him, which otherwise they would have done. And I have heard it confidently related, that for his said resolutions, which out of policy and for his own safety, might have been then spared, the English priests at Rome were highly disgusted, and it was questioned, whether the Jesuits, his countrymen there, did not design to do him mischief. Before he left Naples he returned the Marquis an acknowledgment of his great favors in an elegant copy of verses entitled *Mansus,* which is among the Latin poems. (10) That from thence (Naples) he thought to have gone into Sicily and Greece, but upon second thoughts he continued in Italy, and went to Lucca, Bononia, Ferrara, and at length to Venice; where continuing a month, he went and visited Verona and Milan. (11) That after he had shipped the books and other goods which he had bought in his travels, he returned through Lombardy, and over the Alps to Geneva, where spending some time, he became familiar with the famous Joh. Deodati, D.D. Thence, going through France, he returned home, well fraught with knowledge and manners, after he had been absent one year and three months. (12) That soon after he settled in an house in St. Bride's Churchyard near Fleet Street in London, where he instructed in the Lat. tongue two youths named John and Edw. Philips, the sons of his sister Anne by her husband Edward Philips: both which were afterwards writers, and the eldest principled as his uncle. But the time soon after changing, and the rebellion thereupon breaking forth, Milton sided with the faction, and being a man of parts, was therefore more capable than another of doing mischief, especially by his pen, as by those books which I shall anon mention, will appear. (13) That at first we find him a Presbyterian and a most sharp and violent opposer of prelacy, the established ecclesiastical discipline and the orthodox clergy. (14) That shortly after he did set on foot and maintained very odd and novel positions concerning divorce, and then taking part with the Independents, he became a great anti-monarchist, a bitter enemy to K. Ch. I., and at length arrived to that monstrous and unparalleled height of profligate impudence, as in print to justify the most execrable murder of him the best of kings, as I shall anon tell you. Afterwards, being made Latin secretary to the Parliament, we find him a Commonwealth's man, a hater of all things that looked towards a single person, a great reproacher of the universities, scholastical degrees, decency and uniformity in the church. (15) That when Oliver ascended the throne, he became the Latin secretary, and proved to him very serviceable when employed in business of weight and moment, and did great matters to obtain a name and wealth. To conclude, he was a person of wonderful parts, of a very sharp, biting, and satirical wit. He was a good philosopher and historian, an excellent poet, Latinist, Grecian and Hebritian, a good mathematician and musician, and so rarely endowed by nature, that had he been but honestly principled, he might have been highly useful to that party, against which he all along appeared with much malice and bitterness. As for the things which he hath published, are these: (1) *Of Reformation, touching Church Discipline in England, and the causes that hitherto have hindered it,* &c. Lond. 1641. qu. At which time, as before, the nation was much divided upon the controversies about church government between the prelatical party and Puritans, and therefore Milton did with great boldness and zeal offer his judgment as to those matters in his said book of Reformation. (2) *Animadversions upon the Remonstrant's defence against Smectymnuus.* Lond. 1641. qu. Which *Rem. Defence* was written (as 'tis said) by Dr. Jos. Hall, Bishop of Exeter. (3) *Apology against the humble Remonstrant.* This was written in vindication of his *Animadversions.* (4) *Against Prelatical Episcopacy.* This I have not yet seen. (5) *The Reason of Church Government;* nor this. (6) *The Doctrine and Discipline of Divorce,* &c. in two books. Lond. 1644-45, qu. To which is added in some copies a translation of *The Judgment of Mart. Bucer concerning Divorce,* &c. It must be now known, that after his settlement, upon his return from his travels, he in a month's time courted, married, and brought home to his house in London, a wife from Forsthill, lying between Halton and Oxford, named Mary, the daughter of Mr. . . . Powell of that place, Gent. But she, who was very young, and had been bred in a family of plenty and freedom, being not well pleased with her husband's retired manner of life, did shortly after leave him and went back in the country with her mother. Whereupon, though he sent divers pressing invitations, yet he could not prevail with her to come back till about 4 years after, when the garrison of Oxen was surrendered (the nighness of her father's house to which having for the most part of the meantime hindered any communication between them), she of her own accord returned and submitted to him, pleading that her mother had been the chief promoter of her frowardness. But he, being not able to bear this abuse, did therefore upon consideration, after he had consulted many eminent authors, write the said book of divorce, with intentions to be separated from her, but by the compromising of her relations the matter did not take effect: so that she continuing with him ever after till her death, he had several children by her, of whom Deborah was the third daughter, trained up by the father in Lat. and Greek, and made by him his amanuensis. (7) *Tetrachordon: Expositions upon the four chief places in Scripture which treat on marriage,* On Gen. 1. 27, 28, &c. Lond. 1646. qu. (8) *Colasterion: A reply to a nameless answer against the doctrine and discipline of divorce,* &c. printed 1645. qu. Upon his publication of the said three books of marriage and divorce, the assembly of divines then sitting at Westminster took special notice of them, and thereupon, though the author had obliged them by his pen in his defence of Smectymnuus and other their controversies had with the bishops, they, impatient of having the clergy's jurisdiction (as they reckoned it) invaded, did, instead of answering, or disproving what those books had asserted, cause him to be summoned before the House of Lords; but that House, whether approving the doctrine, or not favoring his accusers, did soon dismiss him.

To these things I must add, that after his Majesty's restoration, when the subject of divorce was under consideration with the Lords upon the account of John, Lord Ros, or Roos, his separation from his wife, Anne Pierpont, eldest daughter to Henry, Marquis of Dorchester, he was consulted by an eminent member of that house, as he was about that time by a chief officer of state, as being the prime person that was knowing in that affair. (9) *Of Education,* written or addressed to Mr. Sam. Hartlib. In this treatise he prescribed an easy and delightful method for the training up of gentry to all sorts of literature, that they might at the same time by like degrees advance in virtue and abilities to serve their country, subjoining directions for their obtaining other necessary or ornamental accomplishments. And to this end that he might put it in practice, he took a larger house, where the Earl of Barrimore sent by his aunt, the Lady Ranalagh, Sir Thomas Gardner of Essex, to be there with others (besides his two nephews) under his tuition. But whether it were that the tempers of our gentry would not bear the strictness of his discipline, or for what other reasons I cannot tell, he continued that course but a while. (10) *Areopagitica: A speech for the liberty of unlicensed printing, to the Parliament of England.* Lond. 1644. qu.; written to vindicate the freedom of the press from the tyranny of licensers, who for several reasons deprive the public of the benefit of many useful authors. (11) *Poemata: quorum pleraque intra annum œtatis vigesimum conscripsit author,* &c. Lond. 1645. oct. (12) *A Mask.*—printed 1645. oct. (13) *Poems,* &c.—printed the same year. Hitherto we find him only to have published political things, but when he saw, upon the coming of K. Charles I. to his trial, the Presbyterian ministers clamorously to assert in their sermons and writings the privileges of kings from all accountableness, or (to speak in the language of that time) non-resistance and passive obedience to be the doctrine of all the reformed churches (which he took to be only their malignity against the Independents who had supplanted them more than for any principles of loyalty) he therefore to oppose that thesis (which as he conceived did encourage all manner of tryanny) did write and publish from divers arguments and authorities. (13) *The Tenure of Kings and Magistrates: proving that it is lawful, &c. to call to account a Tyrant or King, and after due conviction to depose and put him to death,* &c. Lond. 1649–50. qu. Soon after the king being beheaded to the great astonishment of all the world, and the government thereupon changed, he was, without any seeking of his, by the endeavors of a private acquaintance who was a member of the new Council of State, chosen Latin secretary, as I have before told you. In this public station his abilities and acuteness of parts, which had been in a manner kept private, were soon taken notice of, and he was pitched upon to elude the artifice (so it was then by the faction called) of *Eikon Basilicé.* Whereupon he soon after published (14) *Iconoclastes: in Answer to a book entitled Eikon Basilicé, the Portraiture of his Sacred Majesty in his Solitudes and Sufferings.* Lond. 1649–50. qu. *ib.* 1690, oct.; which being published to the horror of all sober men, nay even to the Presbyterians themselves, yet by the then dominant party it was esteemed an excellent piece, and performed answerably to the expectation of his wit and pen. After the return of King Charles II, this book was called in by proclamation, dated 13 Aug. 1660, at which time the author (who a little before had left his house in Petty France, which had a door going into St. James's Park) absconded, for fear of being brought to a legal trial, and so consequently of receiving condign punishment. At the same time also, was called in a book of John Goodwin, then lately a minister in Coleman Street in Lond. entitled *The Obstructors of Justice,* written in defence of the sentence against his Majesty Charles I. At which time also the said Goodwin absconded to prevent justice. Soon after the publication of *Iconoclastes,* Salmasius, a professor in Holland, who had in a large treatise not long before, maintained, as 'tis said, the parity of Church Governors against Episcopacy, did publish *Defensio Regia, pro Carolo I. Rege Angliæ,* wherein he justified several matters, as Milton conceived, to the contradiction of his former book. Whereupon he wrote and published (15) *Pro Populo Anglicano defensio contra Claudii Anonymi alias Salmasii defensionem regiam.* Lond. 1651. fol.; said to be written in more correct Latin than that of Salmasius. While Milton was writing the said book, his sight began to fail him, and before it was fully completed, one of his eyes did absolutely perish. In the month of June the same year (1651) the said book was burnt at Toulouse by an arrest from the Parliament, under the government of the Duke of Orleans. And in Sept. following it was the usual practice of Marchm. Needham a great crony of Milton, to abuse Salmasius in his public Mercury called *Politicus,* (as Milton had done before in his *Defensio*) by saying among other things that Christina, Qu. of Sweden had cashiered him her favor, by under-standing that he was a pernicious parasite, and a promoter of tyranny. After his Majesty's restoration, this book also was called in by the same proclamation before mentioned. But so it was, that in 1652, a certain book entitled *Regii sanguinis clamor,* &c. being published Salmasius was highly extolled in it, and Milton had his just character given therein. The nameless author of which being for a considerable time sought out, but in vain, by Milton, he at length learned by certain ministers of state sent to the Republic of England, (who would sometimes visit him as a learned man) that it was written by one Alex. More, formerly a professor and minister at Geneva, then living in Holland. Whereupon he published (16) *Pro populo Anglicano, defensio secunda, contra infamem libellum Anonymum, cui titulus, Regii sanguinis clamor ad cœlum adversus patricidas Anglicanos.* Lond. 1654, and at Hag. Com. the same year, in oct. Upon the writing of this book, the author, Milton, lost the other eye; and though to his charge he used many means, yet he could never recover either of his eyes. This book entitled *Regii sanguinis clamor* &c. though written by Dr. Peter du Moulin, Prebendary of Canterbury, as it afterwards well appeared, yet Milton upon the reports before mentioned, could not be convinced to the contrary, but that it was written by the said More, and therefore not only abused him in his answers, but by his friend Needham in his *Politicus,* whereby the reputation of that learned person was severely touched. (17) *Pro se defensio contra Alex. Morum Ecclesiaste libelli famosi, cui titulus, Regii sanguinis clamor,* &c. Lond. 1655, oct. In this book he is exceeding bitter against Morus, and pretends to give a true history of his notorious impurities both at Geneva and Leyden, and an account of his own particular life to vindicate himself from what, as he thought, was scurrilously said of him by Morus. At the end of the said book, the author, Milton, added *Ad Alex. Mori supplementum responsio.* About the time that he had finished these things, he had more leisure and time at command, and being dispensed with by having a substitute allowed him, and sometimes instructions sent home to him from attending his office of secretary, he began that laborious work of amassing out of all the classic authors both in prose and verse a Latin *Thesaurus,* to the emendation of that done by Stephanus, also the composing of *Paradise Lost,* and of the framing of a *Body of Divinity* out of the Bible. All which, notwithstanding the several troubles that befell him in his fortunes, he finished after his Majesty's restoration. But to go on with the catalogue of his books according to time, take these as they follow, (18) *Treatise of civil power in ecclesiastical causes,* &c. Lond. 1659. in tw. (19) *Considerations touching the likeliest means to remove Hirelings out of the Church,* Lond. 1659. in tw. (20) *Ready and easy way to establish a free Commonwealth, and the excellencies thereof compared with,* &c. Lond. 1659, in two sheets and an half in qu. This being published in Feb. the same year, was answered by G. S. in his *Dignity of Kingship.* (21) *Brief notes upon a late sermon titled, The fear of God and the King,* &c. Lond. 1660. qu. See more in Matthew Griffith *Among the Writers,* an. 1665. (22) *Accedence commenced Grammar,* &c. pr. 1661. in oct. (23) *Paradise Lost:* a Poem in 10 books, Lond. 1669. qu.; pr. in fol. with cuts, an. 1688. (24) *Paradise Regained:* a Poem in four books, Lond. 1670, qu.; pr. in fol. with cuts, an. 1688. (25) *History of Britany from the first traditional beginning, continued to the Norman Conquest.* Lond. 1670, qu. This history when it first came abroad, had only the reputation of the putting of our old authors neatly together in a connected story, not abstaining from some lashes at the ignorance, or I know not what, of those times. (26) *Artis logicæ plenior institutio ad Petri Rami methodum concinnata.* Lond. 1672. in tw. (27) *Of True Religion, Heresy, Schism, Toleration, and what best means may be used against the growth and increase of Popery.* Lond. 1673, qu. (28) *Poems,* &c. *on several occasions, both English and Latin,* &c. *composed at several times.* Lond. 1673-4. oct. Among these are mixed some of his poems before mentioned, made in his youthful years. (29) *Epistolarum familiarium lib.* 1 Lond. 1674. oct. (30) *Prolusiones quædam Oratoriæ in Coll. Christi habitæ,* printed with the *familiar Epistles.* (31) *Literæ Pseudosenatus Anglicani Cromwellii, reliquorum perduellium nomine ac jussu conscripte,* printed in 1676, in tw. (32) *Character of the Long Parliament and of the Assembly of Divines.* Lond. 1681, in 2 sheets in qu. In which book is a notable account of their ignorance, treachery, and hypocrisy. (33) *Brief History of Muscovia and of other less known countries, lying eastward of Russia as far as Cathay,* &c. Lond. 1682, oct. (34) *The Rights of the People over Tyrants,* printed lately in qu. These, I think, are all the things that he hath yet extant: those that are not, are *The Body of Divinity,* which my friend calls *Idea Theologiæ,* now, or at least lately, in the hands of the author's acquaintance called Cyr. Skinner, living in Mark Lane, London, and the Latin *Thesaurus* in those of Edw. Philips, his nephew. At length this great scholar and frequent writer dying in his house at Bunhill, near London, in a fit of the gout, but with so little pain, that the time of his expiring was not perceived by those in the room, on the ninth or tenth day of Novemb. 1674, was buried in the grave of his father (who died very aged about 1647), in the chancel of the Church of St. Giles near Cripplegate, London. See more of him in Sir Walter Raleigh *Among the Writers,* number 458. He was of a moderate stature, and well proportioned, of a ruddy complexion, light brown hair, and had handsome features, yet his eyes were none of the quickest. When he was a student in Cambridge he was so fair and clear, that many called him the Lady of Christ's College. His deportment was affable, and his gait erect and manly, bespeaking courage and un-dauntedness. On which account he wore a sword while he had his sight, and was skilled in using it. He had a delicate, tuneable voice, an excellent ear, could play on the organ, and bear a part in vocal and instrumental music. The estate which his father left him was but indifferent, yet by his frugality he made it serve him and his. Out of his secretary's salary he saved 2000 £ which being lodged in the excise, and that bank failing upon his Majesty's restoration, he utterly lost that sum. By the great fire which happened in London in the beginning of Sept. 1666, he had a house in Bread Street burned, which was all the real estate that he had then left. To conclude, he was more admired abroad and by for-eigners, than at home; and was much visited by them when he lived in Petty France, some of whom have out of pure devotion gone to Bread Street to see the house and chamber where he was born, &c.

IV. THE LIFE OF MR. JOHN MILTON

BY EDWARD PHILIPS, 1694

OF all the several parts of history, that which sets forth the lives, and commemorates the most remarkable actions, sayings, or writings of famous and illustrious persons, whether in war or peace, whether many together, or any one in particular, as it is not the least useful in itself, so it is in highest vogue and esteem among the studious and reading part of mankind.

The most eminent in this way of history were, among the ancients, Plutarch and Diogenes Laertius; of the Greeks, the first wrote the lives, for the most part, of the most renowned heroes and warriors of the Greeks and Romans; the other, the lives of the ancient Greek Philosophers. And Cornelius Nepos (or as some will have it Æmilius Probus) of the Latins, who wrote the lives of the most illustrious Greek and Roman generals.

Among the moderns, Machiavelli, a noble Florentine, who elegantly wrote the life of Castruccio Castracani, Lord of Lucca. And of our nation, Sir Fulke Greville, who wrote the life of his most intimate friend, Sir Philip Sidney; Mr. Thomas Stanley of Cumberlo-Green, who made a most elaborate improvement to the aforesaid Laertius, by adding to what he found in him, what by diligent search and enquiry he collected from other au-thors of best authority; [and] Isaac Walton, who wrote the lives of Sir Henry Wotton, Dr. Donne, and for his divine poems, the admired Mr. George Herbert. Lastly, not to mention several other biographers of considerable note, the great Gassendus of France, the worthy celebrator of two no less worthy subjects of his impartial pen; *viz.* the noble philosopher Epicurus, and the most politely learned virtuoso of his age, his countryman, Monsieur Peiresk.

And pity it is the person whose memory we have here undertaken to perpetuate by recounting the most memorable transactions of his life (though his works sufficiently recommend him to the world), finds not a well-informed pen able to set him forth, equal with the best of those here mentioned; for doubtless, had his fame been as much spread through Europe in Thuanus's time, as now it is, and hath been for several years, he had justly merited from that great historian, an eulogy not inferior to the highest by him given to all the learned and ingenious that lived within the compass of his history. For we may safely and justly affirm, that take him in all respects, for acumen of wit, quickness of apprehension, sagacity of judgment, depth of argument, and elegancy of style, as well in Latin as English, as well in verse as prose, he is scarce to be paralleled by any the best of writers our nation hath in any age brought forth.

He was born in London, in a house in Breadstreet, the lease whereof, as I take it, but for certain it was a house in Breadstreet, became in time part of his estate, in the year of our Lord 1606. His father John Milton, an honest, worthy, and substantial citizen of London, by profession a scrivener; to which he voluntarily betook himself, by the advice and assistance of an intimate friend of his, eminent in that calling, upon his being cast out by his father, a bigoted Roman Catholic, for embracing, when young, the protestant faith, and abjuring the popish tenets. For he is said to have been descended of an ancient family of the Miltons, of Milton near Abingdon in Oxfordshire; where they had been a long time seated, as appears by the monuments still to be seen in Milton church; till one of the family having taken the wrong side, in the contest between the Houses of York and Lancaster, was sequestered of all his estate, but what he held by his wife. However, certain it is, that this vocation he followed for many years, at his said house in Breadstreet, with success suitable to his industry and prudent conduct of his affairs. Yet did he not so far quit his own generous and ingenious inclinations, as to make himself wholly a slave to the world; for he sometimes found vacant hours to the study (which he made his recreation) of the noble science of music, in which he advanced to that perfection, that as I have been told, and as I take it by our author himself, he composed an *In Nomine* of forty parts; for which he was rewarded with a gold medal and chain by a Polish prince, to whom he presented it. However, this is a truth not to be denied, that for several songs of his composition, after the way of these times, (three or four of which are still to be seen in Old Wilby's set of Airs, besides some compositions of his in Ravenscroft's Psalms), he gained the reputation of a considerable master in this most charming of all the liberal sciences. Yet all this while, he managed his grand affair of this world with such prudence and diligence, that by the assistance of divine Providence favoring his honest endeavors, he gained a competent estate, whereby he was enabled to make a handsome provision both for the education and maintenance of his children; for three he had, and no more, all by one wife, Sarah, of the family of the Castons, derived originally from Wales, a woman of incomparable virtue and goodness: John the eldest, the subject of our present work; Christopher; and an only daughter Ann.

Christopher being principally designed for the study of the common law of England, was entered young a student of the Inner Temple, of which house he lived to be an ancient bencher, and keeping close to that study and profession all his life time, except in the time of the civil wars of England; when being a great favorer and asserter of the King's cause, and obnoxious to the Parliament's side, by acting to his utmost power against them, so long as he kept his station at Reading; and after that town was taken by the Parliament forces, being forced to quit his house there, he steered his course according to the motion of the King's army. But when the war was ended with victory and success to the Parliament party, by the valor of General Fairfax, and the craft and conduct of Cromwell, and his composition made by the help of his brother's interest with the then prevailing power, he betook himself again to his former study and profession, following chamber-practice every term; yet came to no advancement in the world in a long time, except some small employ in the town of Ipswich, where (and near it) he lived all the latter time of his life; for he was a person of a modest, quiet temper, preferring justice and virtue before all worldly pleasure or grandeur. But in the beginning of the reign of

King James the II., for his known integrity and ability in the law, he was by some persons of quality recommended to the King, and at a call of sergeants received the coif, and the same day was sworn one of the barons of the Exchequer, and soon after made one of the judges of the Common Pleas. But his years and indisposition not well brooking the fatigue of public employment, he continued not long in either of these stations; but having his *quietus est,* retired to a country life, his study and devotion.

Ann, the only daughter of the said John Milton, the elder, had a considerable dowry given her by her father in marriage with Edward Philips, (the son of Edward Philips of Shrewsbury,) who, coming up young to town, was bred up in the crown-office in Chancery, and at length came to be secondary of the office under old Mr. Bembo. By him she had, besides other children that died infants, two sons yet surviving, of whom more hereafter; and by a second husband, Mr. Thomas Agar (who, upon the death of his intimate friend Mr. Philips, worthily succeeded in the place, which, except some time of exclusion before and during the Interregnum, he held for many years, and left it to Mr Thomas Milton, the son of the aforementioned Sir Christopher, who at this day executes it with great reputation and ability), two daughters, Mary who died very young, and Ann yet surviving.

But to hasten back to our matter in hand. John, our author, who was destined to be the ornament and glory of his country, was sent, together with his brother, to Paul's school, whereof Dr. Gill the elder was then chief master; where he was entered into the first rudiments of learning, and advanced therein with that admirable success, not more by the discipline of the school and good instructions of his masters (for that he had another master, possibly at his father's house, appears by the *Fourth Elegy* of his Latin poems written in his 18th year, to Thomas Young, pastor of the English Company of Merchants at Hamburg, wherein he owns and styles him his master), than by his own happy genius, prompt wit and apprehension, and insuperable industry: for he generally sat up half the night, as well in voluntary improvements of his own choice, as the exact perfecting of his school exercises.

So that at the age of 15 he was full ripe for academic learning, and accordingly was sent to the University of Cambridge; where in Christ's College under the tuition of a very eminent learned man, whose name I cannot call to mind, he studied seven years, and took his degree of Master of Arts; and for the extraordinary wit and reading he had shown in his performances to attain his degree (some whereof, spoken at a *Vacation Exercise* in his 19th year of age, are to be yet seen in his *Miscellaneous Poems*), he was loved and admired by the whole university, particularly by the fellows and most ingenious persons of his house. Among the rest there was a young gentleman, one Mr. King, with whom, for his great learning and parts, he had contracted a particular friendship and intimacy; whose death (for he was drowned on the Irish seas in his passage from Chester to Ireland) he bewails in that most excellent monody in his forementioned poems, intituled *Lycidas.* Never was the loss of friend so elegantly lamented; and among the rest of his *Juvenile Poems,* some he wrote at the age of 15, which contain a poetical genius scarce to be paralleled by any English writer.

Soon after he had taken his Master's degree, he thought fit to leave the university: not upon any disgust or discontent for want of preferment, as some ill-willers have reported; nor upon any cause whatsoever forced to fly, as his detractors maliciously feign; but from which aspersion he sufficiently clears himself in his *Second Answer to Alexander Morus,* the author of a book called, *Clamor Regii Sanguinis ad Cœlum,* the chief of his calumniators; in which he plainly makes it out, that after his leaving the university, to the no small trouble of his fellow-collegiates, who in general regretted his absence, he for the space of five years lived for the most part with his father and mother at their house at Horton near Colebrook in Berkshire; whither his father, having got an estate to his content, and left off all business, was retired from the cares and fatigues of the world.

After the said term of five years, his mother then dying, he was willing to add to his acquired learning the observation of foreign customs, manners, and institutions; and thereupon took a resolution to travel, more especially designing for Italy: and accordingly, with his father's consent and assistance, he put himself into an equipage suitable to such a design; and so, intending to go by the way of France, he set out for Paris, accompanied only with one man, who attended him through all his travels; for his prudence was his guide, and his learning his introduction and presentation to persons of most eminent quality. However, he had also a most civil and obliging letter of direction and advice from Sir Henry Wotton, then Provost of Eton, and formerly resident Ambassador from King James the First to the state of Venice; which letter is to be seen in the first edition of his *Miscellaneous Poems.*

At Paris, being recommended by the said Sir Henry and other persons of quality, he went first to wait upon my Lord Scudamore, then Ambassador in France from King Charles the First. My Lord received him with wonderful civility; and understanding he had a desire to make a visit to the great Hugo Grotius, he sent several of his attendants to wait upon him, and to present him in his name to that renowned doctor and statesman, who was at that time Ambassador from Christina, Queen of Sweden, to the French king. Grotius took the visit kindly, and gave him entertainment suitable to his worth, and the high commendations he had heard of him. After a few days, not intending to make the usual tour of France, he took his leave of my Lord, who at his departure from Paris, gave him letters to the English merchants residing in any part through which he was to travel, in which they were requested to show him all the kindness, and do him all the good offices that lay in their power.

From Paris he hastened on his journey to Nice, where he took shipping, and in a short space arrived at Genoa; from whence he went to Leghorn, thence to Pisa, and so to Florence. In this city he met with many charming objects, which invited him to stay a longer time than he intended; the pleasant situation of the place, the nobleness of the structures, the exact humanity and civility of the inhabitants, the more polite and refined sort of language there, than elsewhere. During the time of his stay here, which was about two months, he visited all the private academies of the city, which are places established for the improvement of wit and learning, and maintained a correspondence and perpetual friendship among gentlemen fitly qualified for such an institution; and such sort of academies there are in all or most of the noted cities in Italy. Visiting these places, he was soon taken notice of by the most learned and ingenious of the nobility, and the grand wits of Florence, who caressed him with all the honors and civilities imaginable; particularly Jacobo Gaddi, Carolo Dati, Antonio Francini, Frescobaldo, Cultellino, Bonmatthei and Clementillo: whereof Gaddi hath a large, elegant Italian canzonet in his praise, [and] Dati, a Latin epistle, both printed before his Latin poems, together with a Latin distich of the Marquis of Villa, and another of Selvaggi, and a Latin tetrastich of Giovanni Salsilli, a Roman.

From Florence he took his journey to Siena, from thence to Rome; where he was detained much about the same time he had been in Florence; as well by his desire of seeing all the rarities and antiquities of that most glorious and renowned city, as by the conversation of Lucas Holstenius, and other learned and ingenious men, who highly valued his acquaintance, and treated him with all possible respect.

From Rome he travelled to Naples, where he was introduced by a certain hermit, who accompanied him in his journey from Rome thither, into the knowledge of Giovanni Baptista Manso, Marquis of Villa, a Neapolitan by birth, a person of high nobility, virtue, and honor, to whom the famous Italian poet, Torquato Tasso, wrote his treatise *De Amicitia;* and moreover mentions him with honor in that illustrious poem of his, entitled, *Gierusalemme Liberata.* This noble marquis received him with extraordinary respect and civility, and went with him himself to give him a sight of all that was of note and remark in the city, particularly the viceroy's palace, and was often in person to visit him at his lodging. Moreover, this noble marquis honored him so far, as to make a Latin distich in his praise, as hath been already mentioned; which being no less pithy then short, though already in print, it will not be unworth the while here to repeat.

> *Ut mens, forma, decor, facies, mos, si pietas* [1] *sic*
> *Non Anglus, verum herculè Angelus ipse fores.*

In return of this honor, and in gratitude for the many favors and civilities received of him, he presented him at his departure with a large Latin eclogue, intitled *Mansus,* afterwards published among his *Latin Poems.* The marquis at his taking leave of him, gave him this compliment: that he would have done him many more offices of kindness and civility, but was therefore rendered incapable, in regard he had been over-liberal in his speech against the religion of the country.

He had entertained some thoughts of passing over into Sicily and Greece, but was diverted by the news he received from England, that affairs there were tending toward a civil war; thinking it a thing unworthy in him to be taking his pleasure in foreign parts, while his countrymen at home were fighting for their liberty: but first resolved to see Rome once more; and though the merchants gave him a caution that the Jesuits were hatching designs against him in case he should return thither, by reason of the freedom he took in all his discourses of religion; nevertheless he ventured to prosecute his resolution, and to Rome the second time he went; determining with himself not industriously to begin to fall into any discourse about religion, but, being asked, not to deny or endeavor to conceal his own sentiments.

Two months he stayed at Rome; and in all that time never flinched, but was ready to defend the orthodox faith against all opposers; and so well he succeeded therein, that, good Providence guarding him, he went safe from Rome back to Florence, where his return to his friends of that city was welcomed with as much joy and affection, as, had it been to his friends and relations in his own country, he could not have come a more joyful and welcome guest.

Here, having stayed as long as at his first coming, excepting an excursion of a few days to Lucca, crossing the Apennine, and passing through Bononia and Ferrara, he arrived at Venice; where when he had spent a month's time in viewing of that stately city, and shipped up a parcel of curious and rare books which he had picked up in his travels (particularly a chest or two of choice music-books of the best masters flourishing about that time in Italy, namely, Luca Marenzo, Monte Verde, Horatio Vecchi, Cifa, the Prince of Venosa, and several others), he took his course through Verona, Milan, and the Pœnine Alps, and so by the lake Leman to Geneva; where he stayed for some time, and had daily converse with the most learned Giovanni Deodati, theology professor in that city; and so returning through France, by the same way he had passed in going to Italy, he, after a peregrination of one complete year and about three months, arrived safe in England, about the time of the King's making his second expedition against the Scots.

Soon after his return, and visits paid to his father and other friends, he took him a lodging in St. Bride's Churchyard, at the house of one Russel, a tailor, where he first undertook the education and instruction of his sister's two sons, the younger whereof had been wholly committed to his charge and care.

And here by the way, I judge it not impertinent to mention the many authors both of the Latin and Greek, which through his excellent judgment and way of teaching, far above the pedantry of common public schools (where such authors are scarce ever heard of), were run over within no greater compass of time, than from ten to fifteen or sixteen years of age. Of the Latin, the four grand authors *De Re Rustica,* Cato, Varro, Columella and Palladius; Cornelius Celsus, an ancient physician of the Romans; a great part of Pliny's *Natural History;* Vitruvius his *Architecture;* Frontinus his *Stratagems;* with the two egregious poets, Lucretius and Manilius. Of the Greek, Hesiod, a poet equal with Homer;

---

[1] This word relates to his being a Protestant not a Roman Catholic.

Aratus his *Phænomena,* and *Diosemeia;* Dionysius Afer *De Situ Orbis;* Oppian's *Cyne-
getics* and *Halieutics;* Quintus Calaber his *Poem of the Trojan War* continued from
Homer; Apollonius Rhodius his *Argonautics:* and in prose, Plutarch's *Placita Philoso-
phorum,* and Περι Παιδων Ἀγογιας [*sic*]; Geminus's *Astronomy;* Xenophon's *Cyri Institutio,* and *Anabasis;* Ælian's *Tactics;* and Polyænus his *Warlike Stratagems.* Thus by
teaching, he in some measure increased his own knowledge, having the reading of all
these authors as it were by proxy; and all this might possibly have conduced to the preserving of his eyesight, had he not moreover been perpetually busied in his own laborious
undertakings of the book and pen.

Nor did the time thus studiously employed in conquering the Greek and Latin tongues,
hinder the attaining to the chief oriental languages, *viz.,* the Hebrew, Chaldee, and Syriac,
so far as to go through the *Pentateuch,* or Five Books of Moses in Hebrew, to make a
good entrance into the *Targum,* or Chaldee Paraphrase, and to understand several chapters
of St. Matthew in the Syriac Testament: besides an introduction into several arts and sciences, by reading Urstisius his *Arithmetic,* Riff's *Geometry,* Petiscus his *Trigonometry,*
Joannes de Sacro Bosco *De Sphæra;* and into the Italian and French tongues, by reading in
Italian Giovan Villani's *History of the Transactions between several petty States of Italy;*
and in French a great part of Pierre Davity, the famous geographer of France in his time.

The Sunday's work was, for the most part, the reading each day a chapter of the Greek
Testament, and hearing his learned exposition upon the same (and how this savored of
atheism in him, I leave to the courteous backbiter to judge). The next work after this,
was the writing from his own dictation, some part, from time to time, of a tractate which
he thought fit to collect from the ablest of divines who had written of that subject:
Amesius, Wollebius, &c., *viz. A Perfect System of Divinity,* of which more hereafter.

Now persons so far manuducted into the highest paths of literature both divine and human, had they received his documents with the same acuteness of wit and apprehension,
the same industry, alacrity, and thirst after knowledge, as the instructor was indued with,
what prodigies of wit and learning might they have proved! The scholars might in some
degree have come near to the equalling of the master, or at least have in some sort made
good what he seems to predict in the close of an elegy he made in the seventeenth year of
his age, upon the death of one of his sister's children (a daughter), who died in her infancy:

> "Then thou, the mother of so sweet a child,
>   Her false, imagin'd loss cease to lament,
>   And wisely learn to curb thy sorrows wild:
>   This if thou do, he will an offspring give,
> That till the world's last end shall make thy name to live."

But to return to the thread of our discourse. He made no long stay in his lodgings in
St. Bride's Church-yard; necessity of having a place to dispose his books in, and other
goods fit for the furnishing of a good, handsome house, hastening him to take one; and,
accordingly, a pretty garden-house he took in Aldersgate-street, at the end of an entry, and
therefore the fitter for his turn, by the reason of the privacy; besides that there are few
streets in London more free from noise than that. Here first it was that his academic erudition was put in practice, and vigorously proceeded, he himself giving an example to those
under him (for it was not long after his taking this house, ere his elder nephew was put
to board with him also) of hard study and spare diet; only this advantage he had, that
once in three weeks or a month, he would drop into the society of some young sparks of
his acquaintance, the chief whereof were Mr. Alphry, and Mr. Miller, two gentlemen of
Gray's Inn, the beaux of those times, but nothing near so bad as those now-a-days; with
these gentlemen he would so far make bold with his body, as now and then to keep a
gawdy-day.

In this house he continued several years, in the one or two first whereof, he set out several treatises, *viz.*, that *Of Reformation;* that *Against Prelatical Episcopacy; The Reason of Church-Government; The defence of Smectymnuus,* at least the greatest part of them, but as I take it, all; and some time after, one sheet *Of Education* which he dedicated to Mr. Samuel Hartlib, he that wrote so much of husbandry (this sheet is printed at the end of the second edition of his *Poems*), and lastly *Areopagitica.*

During the time also of his continuance in this house, there fell out several occasions of the increasing of his family. His father, who till the taking of Reading by the Earl of Essex his forces, had lived with his other son at his house there, was upon that son's dis-settlement necessitated to betake himself to this his eldest son, with whom he lived for some years, even to his dying day. In the next place he had an addition of some scholars; to which may be added, his entering into matrimony; but he had his wife's company so small a time, that he may well be said to have become a single man again soon after.

About Whitsuntide it was, or a little after, that he took a journey into the country; no body about him certainly knowing the reason, or that it was any more than a journey of recreation; after a month's stay, home he returns a married man, that went out a bachelor; his wife being Mary, the eldest daughter of Mr. Richard Powell, then a justice of peace, of Forresthill, near Shotover in Oxfordshire; some few of her nearest relations accompanying the bride to her new habitation; which by reason the father nor any body else were yet come, was able to receive them; where the feasting held for some days in celebration of the nuptials, and for entertainment of the bride's friends. At length they took their leave, and returning to Foresthill, left the sister behind; probably not much to her satisfaction, as appeared by the sequel. By that time she had for a month or thereabout led a philosophical life (after having been used to a great house, and much company and joviality), her friends, possibly incited by her own desire, made earnest suit by letter, to have her company the remaining part of the summer, which was granted, on condition of her return at the time appointed, Michaelmas, or thereabout. In the meantime came his father, and some of the forementioned disciples.

And now the studies went on with so much the more vigor, as there were more hands and heads employed; the old gentleman living wholly retired to his rest and devotion, without the least trouble imaginable. Our author, now as it were a single man again, made it his chief diversion now and then in an evening, to visit the lady Margaret Lee, daughter to the —— Lee, Earl of Marlborough, Lord High Treasurer of England, and President of the Privy Council, to King James the First. This lady being a woman of great wit and ingenuity had a particular honor for him, and took much delight in his company, as likewise her husband Captain Hobson, a very accomplished gentleman; and what esteem he at the same time had for her, appears by a sonnet he made in praise of her, to be seen among his other *Sonnets* in his extant *Poems.*

Michaelmas being come, and no news of his wife's return, he sent for her by letter; and receiving no answer, sent several other letters, which were also unanswered; so that at last he dispatched down a foot messenger with a letter, desiring her return. But the messenger came back not only without an answer, at least a satisfactory one, but to the best of my remembrance, reported that he was dismissed with some sort of contempt. This proceeding, in all probability, was grounded upon no other cause but this, namely, that the family being generally addicted to the cavalier party, as they called it, and some of them possibly engaged in the King's service, who by this time had his headquarters at Oxford, and was in some prospect of success, they began to repent them of having matched the eldest daughter of the family to a person so contrary to them in opinion; and thought it would be a blot in their escutcheon, whenever that court should come to flourish again.

However, it so incensed our author, that he thought it would be dishonorable ever to receive her again, after such a repulse; so that he forthwith prepared to fortify himself with arguments for such a resolution, and accordingly wrote two treatises, by which he undertook to maintain, that it was against reason, and the enjoinment of it not provable by Scripture, for any married couple disagreeable in humor and temper, or having an aversion to each [other], to be forced to live yoked together all their days. The first was, his *Doctrine and Discipline of Divorce;* of which there was printed a second edition, with some additions. The other in prosecution of the first, was styled *Tetrachordon.* Then the better to confirm his own opinion by the attestation of others, he set out a piece called *The Judgment of Martin Bucer,* a protestant minister, being a translation, out of that reverend divine, of some part of his works, exactly agreeing with him in sentiment. Lastly, he wrote in answer to a pragmatical clerk, who would needs give himself the honor of writing against so great a man, his *Colasterion, or Rod of Correction for a Saucy Impertinent.*

Not very long after the setting forth of these treatises, having application made to him by several gentlemen of his acquaintance for the education of their sons, as understanding haply the progress he had infixed by his first undertakings of that nature, he laid out for a larger house, and soon found it out.

But in the interim before he removed, there fell out a passage, which though it altered not the whole course he was going to steer, yet it put a stop or rather an end to a grand affair, which was more than probably thought to be then in agitation; it was indeed a design of marrying one of Dr. Davis's daughters, a very handsome and witty gentlewoman, but averse, as it is said, to this motion. However, the intelligence hereof, and the then declining state of the King's cause, and consequently of the circumstances of Justice Powell's family, caused them to set all engines on work, to restore the late married woman to the station wherein they a little before had planted her. At last this device was pitched upon. There dwelt in the lane of St. Martin's-le-Grand, which was hard by, a relation of our author's, one Blackborough, whom it was known he often visited, and upon this occasion the visits were the more narrowly observed, and possibly there might be a combination between both parties; the friends on both sides concentring in the same action, though on different behalfs. One time above the rest, he making his usual visit, the wife was ready in another room, and on a sudden he was surprised to see one whom he thought to have never seen more, making submission and begging pardon on her knees before him. He might probably at first make some show of aversion and rejection; but partly his own generous nature, more inclinable to reconciliation than to perseverance in anger and revenge, and partly the strong intercession of friends on both sides, soon brought him to an act of oblivion, and a firm league of peace for the future; and it was at length concluded, that she should remain at a friend's house, till such time as he was settled in his new house at Barbican, and all things for her reception in order; the place agreed on for her present abode, was the widow Webber's house in St. Clement's Church-yard, whose second daughter had been married to the other brother many years before. The first fruits of her return to her husband was a brave girl, born within a year after; though, whether by ill constitution or want of care, she grew more and more decrepit.

But it was not only by children that she increased the number of the family; for in no very long time after her coming, she had a great resort of her kindred with her in the house, *viz.* her father and mother, and several of her brothers and sisters, which were in all pretty numerous; who upon his father's sickening and dying soon after, went away.

And now the house looked again like a house of the Muses only, though the accession of scholars was not great. Possibly his proceeding thus far in the education of youth may have been the occasion of some of his adversaries calling him pedagogue and schoolmaster; whereas it is well known he never set up for a public school to teach all the young fry of the parish, but only was willing to impart his learning and knowledge to relations, and the sons of some gentlemen that were his intimate friends; besides, that neither his converse, nor his writings, nor his manner of teaching ever savored in the least anything of pedantry; and probably he might have some prospect of putting in practice his academical institution, according to the model laid down in his sheet *Of Education.* The progress of which design was afterwards diverted by a series of alteration in the affairs of state; for I am much mistaken, if there were not about this time a design in agitation of making him adjutant-general in Sir William Waller's army. But the new modeling of the army soon following, proved an obstruction to that design; and Sir William, his commission being laid down, began, as the common saying is, to turn *cat in pan*.

It was not long after the march of Fairfax and Cromwell through the city of London with the whole army, to quell the insurrections Brown and Massey, now malcontents also, were endeavoring to raise in the city against the army's proceedings, ere he left his great house in Barbican, and betook himself to a smaller in High Holburn, among those that open backward into Lincoln's Inn Fields. Here he lived a private and quiet life, still prosecuting his studies and curious search into knowledge, the grand affair perpetually of his life; till such time as, the war being now at an end, with complete victory to the Parliament's side, as the Parliament then stood purged of all its dissenting members, and the King after some treaties with the army *re infecta,* brought to his trial; the form of government being now changed into a free state, he was hereupon obliged to write a treatise, called *The Tenure of Kings and Magistrates.*

After which his thoughts were bent upon retiring again to his own private studies, and falling upon such subjects as his proper genius prompted him to write of, among which was the history of our own nation from the beginning till the Norman Conquest, wherein he had made some progress. When (for this his last treatise, reviving the fame of other things he had formerly published) being more and more taken notice of for his excellency of style, and depth of judgment, he was courted into the service of this new common-wealth, and at last prevailed with (for he never hunted after preferment, nor affected the tintamar and hurry of public business) to take upon him the office of Latin secretary to the Council of State, for all their letters to foreign princes and states; for they stuck to this noble and generous resolution, not to write to any, or receive answers from them, but in a language most proper to maintain a correspondence among the learned of all nations in this part of the world; scorning to carry on their affairs in the wheedling, lisping jargon of the cringing French, especially having a minister of state able to cope with the ablest any prince or state could employ, for the Latin tongue. And so well he acquitted himself in this station, that he gained from abroad both reputation to himself, and credit to the state that employed him.

And it was well the business of his office came not very fast upon him; for he was scarce well warm in his secretaryship before other work flowed in upon him, which took him up for some considerable time. In the first place there came out a book said to have been written by the king, and finished a little before his death, intituled εἰκὼν βασιλική, that is, *The Royal Image;* a book highly cried up for its smooth style, and pathetical composure; wherefore to obviate the impression it was like to make among the many, he was obliged to write an answer, which he intituled εἰκονοκλάστης or *Image-Breaker.*

And upon the heels of that, out comes in public the great kill-cow of Christendom, with his *Defensio Regis contra Populum Anglicanum;* a man so famous and cried up for his Plinian Exercitations, and other pieces of reputed learning, that there could no where have been found a champion that durst lift up the pen against so formidable an adversary, had not our little English David had the courage to undertake this great French Goliath. To whom he gave such a hit in the forehead, that he presently staggered, and soon after fell. For immediately upon the coming out of the answer, intituled, *Defensio Populi Anglicani contra Claudium Anonymum,* &c. he that till then had been chief minister and superin-tendent in the court of the learned Christina, Queen of Sweden, dwindled in esteem to that degree, that he at last vouchsafed to speak to the meanest servant. In short, he was dismissed with so cold and slighting an adieu, that after a faint dying reply, he was glad to have recourse to death, the remedy of evils, and ender of controversies.

And now I presume our author had some breathing space, but it was not long. For though Salmasius was departed, he left some stings behind; new enemies started up, barkers, though no great biters. Who the first asserter of Salmasius his cause was, is not certainly known, but variously conjectured at. some supposing it to be one Janus, a lawyer of Gray's

Inn, some Dr. Bramhal, made by King Charles the Second, after his restoration, Arch-bishop of Armagh in Ireland; but whoever the author was, the book was thought fit to be taken into correction; and our author not thinking it worth his own undertaking, to the disturbing the progress of whatever more chosen work he had then in hands, committed this task to the youngest of his nephews; but with such exact emendations before it went to the press, that it might have very well passed for his, but that he was willing the person that took the pains to prepare it for his examination and polishment, should have the name and credit of being the author; so that it came forth under this title, *Joannis Philippi Angli Defensio pro Populo Anglicano contra,* &c.

During the writing and publishing of this book, he lodged at one Thomson's next door to the Bull-head tavern at Charing-Cross, opening into the Spring-Garden; which seems to have been only a lodging taken till his designed apartment in Scotland-Yard was pre-pared for him. For hither he soon removed from the foresaid place; and here his third child, a son, was born, which through the ill usage, or bad constitution, of an ill-chosen nurse, died an infant.

From this apartment, whether he thought it not healthy, or otherwise convenient for his use, or whatever else was the reason, he soon after took a pretty garden-house in Petty-France in Westminster, next door to the Lord Scudamore's, and opening into St. James's Park. Here he remained no less than eight years, namely, from the year 1652, till within a few weeks of King Charles the Second's restoration.

In this house his first wife dying in childbed, he married a second, who after a year's time died in childbed also. This his second marriage was about two or three years after his being wholly deprived of sight, which was just going about the time of his answering Salmasius; whereupon his adversaries gladly take occasion of imputing his blindness as a judgment upon him for his answering the King's book, &c. whereas it is most certainly known, that his sight, what with his continual study, his being subject to the headache, and his per-petual tampering with physic to preserve it, had been decaying for above a dozen years before, and the sight of one for a long time clearly lost. Here he wrote, by his amanuensis, his two *Answers to Alexander More,* who upon the last answer quitted the field.

So that being now quiet from state adversaries and public contests, he had leisure again for his own studies and private designs; which were his foresaid *History of England;* and a new *Thesaurus Linguæ Latinæ,* according to the manner of Stephanus, a work he had been long since collecting from his own reading, and still went on with it at times, even very near to his dying day; but the papers after his death were so discomposed and de-ficient that it could not be made fit for the press; however, what there was of it, was made use of for another dictionary.

But the height of his noble fancy and invention began now to be seriously and mainly employed in a subject worthy of such a Muse, *viz.* a heroic poem, entitled, *Paradise Lost;* the noblest in the general esteem of learned and judicious persons, of any yet written by any either ancient or modern. This subject was first designed a tragedy, and in the fourth book of the poem there are ten verses, which several years before the poem was begun, were shown to me and some others, as designed for the very beginning of the said tragedy. The verses are these:—

> "O thou that with surpassing glory crown'd!
> Look'st from thy sole dominion, like the god
> Of this new world; at whose sight all the stars
> Hide their diminish'd heads; to thee I call,
> But with no friendly voice; and add thy name,
> O Sun! to tell thee how I hate thy beams
> That bring to my remembrance, from what state
> I fell, how glorious once above thy sphere;
> Till pride and worse ambition threw me down,
> Warring in Heaven, against Heaven's glorious King."

There is another very remarkable passage in the composure of this poem, which I have a particular occasion to remember; for whereas I had the perusal of it from the very beginning, for some years, as I went from time to time to visit him, in a parcel of ten, twenty, or thirty verses at a time, which being written by whatever hand came next, might possibly want correction as to the orthography and pointing; having as the summer came on, not been showed any for a considerable while, and, desiring the reason thereof was answered: that his vein never happily flowed but from the autumnal equinoctial to the vernal, and that whatever he attempted was never to his satisfaction, though he courted his fancy never so much, so that in all the years he was about this poem, he may be said to have spent but half his time therein.

It was but a little before the King's restoration that he wrote and published his book *In Defence of a Commonwealth;* so undaunted he was in declaring his true sentiments to the world; and not long before, his *Power of the Civil Magistrate in Ecclesiastical Affairs,* and his *Treatise against Hirelings,* just upon the King's coming over; having a little before been sequestered from his office of Latin secretary, and the salary thereunto belonging.

He was forced to leave his house also in Petty-France, where all the time of his abode there, which was eight years, as above-mentioned, he was frequently visited by persons of quality, particularly my Lady Ranalagh, whose son for some time he instructed; all learned foreigners of note, who could not part out of the city, without giving a visit to a person so eminent; and lastly, by particular friends that had a high esteem for him, *viz.* Mr. Andrew Marvel, young Lawrence (the son of him that was president of Oliver's council), to whom there is a sonnet among the rest, in his printed *Poems;* Mr. Marchamont Needham, the writer of *Politicus;* but above all, Mr. Cyriac Skinner whom he honored with two sonnets, one long since public among his *Poems,* the other but newly printed.

His next removal was, by the advice of those that wished him well, and had a concern for his preservation, into a place of retirement and abscondence, till such time as the current of affairs for the future should instruct him what farther course to take. It was a friend's house in Bartholomew Close, where he lived till the act of oblivion came forth; which it pleased God, proved as favorable to him as could be hoped or expected, through the intercession of some that stood his friends both in Council and Parliament; particularly in the House of Commons, Mr. Andrew Marvel, a member for Hull, acted vigorously in his behalf, and made a considerable party for him; so that, together with John Goodwin of Coleman Street, he was only so far excepted as not to bear any office in the Commonwealth.

Soon after appearing again in public, he took a house in Holborn near Red Lyon Fields; where he stayed not long, before his pardon having passed the seal, he removed to Jewin Street. There he lived when he married his 3d wife, recommended to him by his old friend Dr. Paget in Coleman Street.

But he stayed not long after his new marriage, ere he removed to a house in the Artillery-walk leading to Bunhill Fields. And this was his last stage in this world, but it was of many years continuance, more perhaps than he had had in any other place besides.

Here he finished his noble poem, and published it in the year 1666. The first edition was printed in quarto by one Simons, a printer in Aldersgate Street; the other in a large octavo, by Starky near Temple-Bar, amended, enlarged, and differently disposed as to the number of books by his own hand, that is by his own appointment; the last set forth, many years since his death, in a large folio, with cuts added, by Jacob Tonson.

Here it was also that he finished and published his history of our nation till the Conquest, all complete so far as he went, some passages only excepted; which, being thought too sharp against the clergy, could not pass the hand of the licenser, were in the hands of the late Earl of Anglesey while he lived; where at present is uncertain.

It cannot be certainly concluded when he wrote his excellent tragedy entitled *Samson Agonistes,* but sure enough it is that it came forth after his publication of *Paradise Lost,* together with his other poem called *Paradise Regain'd.* which doubtless was begun and finished and printed after the other was published, and that in a wonderful short space considering the sublimeness of it; however, it is generally censured to be much inferior to the other, though he could not hear with patience any such thing when related to him. Possibly the subject may not afford such variety of invention; but it is thought by the most judicious to be little or nothing inferior to the other for style and decorum.

The said Earl of Anglesey, whom he presented with a copy of the unlicensed papers of his history, came often here to visit him, as very much coveting his society and converse; as likewise others of the nobility, and many persons of eminent quality; nor were the visits of foreigners ever more frequent than in this place, almost to his dying day.

His treatise *Of True Religion, Heresy, Schism and Toleration,* &c. was doubtless the last thing of his writing that was published before his death. He had, as I remember, prepared for the press an answer to some little scribing quack in London, who had written a scurrilous libel against him; but whether by the dissuasion of friends, as thinking him a fellow not worth his notice, or for what other cause I know not, this answer was never published.

He died in the year 1673, towards the latter end of the summer, and had a very decent interment according to his quality, in the church of St. Giles, Cripplegate, being attended from his house to the church by several gentlemen then in town, his principal well-wishers and admirers.

He had three daughters who survived him many years (and a son) all by his first wife (of whom sufficient mention hath been made): Anne his eldest as above said, and Mary his second, who were both born at his house in Barbican; and Deborah the youngest, who is yet living, born at his house in Petty-France, between whom and his second daughter, the son, named John, was born as above-mentioned, at his apartment in Scotland Yard. By his second wife, Catharine, the daughter of captain Woodcock of Hackney, he had only one daughter, of which the mother, the first year after her marriage, died in child-bed, and the child also within a month after. By his third wife Elizabeth, the daughter of one Mr. Minshal of Cheshire, (and kinswoman to Dr. Paget), who survived him, and is said to be yet living, he never had any child.

And those he had by the first he made serviceable to him in that very particular in which he most wanted their service, and supplied his want of eyesight by their eyes and tongue. For though he had daily about him one or other to read to him; some persons of man's estate, who of their own accord greedily catched at the opportunity of being his readers, that they might as well reap the benefit of what they read to him, as oblige him by the benefit of their reading; others of younger years sent by their parents to the same end; yet, excusing only the eldest daughter by reason of her bodily infirmity and difficult utterance of speech (which to say the truth I doubt was the principal cause of excusing her), the other two were condemned to the performance of reading, and exactly pronouncing of all the languages of whatever book he should at one time or other think fit to peruse; *viz.* the Hebrew (and I think the Syriac), the Greek, the Latin, the Italian, Spanish, and French. All which sorts of books to be confined to read, without understanding one word, must needs be a trial of patience almost beyond endurance; yet it was endured by both for a long time. Yet the irksomeness of this employment could not be always concealed, but broke out more and more into expressions of uneasiness; so that at length they were all (even the eldest also) sent out to learn some curious and ingenious sorts of manufacture, that are proper for women to learn, particularly embroideries in gold or silver. It had been happy indeed, if the daughters of such a person had been made in some measure inheritrixes of their father's learning; but since fate otherwise decreed, the greatest honor that can be ascribed to this now living (and so would have been to the others, had they lived) is to be daughter to a man of his extraordinary character.

He is said to have died worth 1500 £ in money (a considerable estate, all things considered) besides household goods; for he sustained such losses as might well have broke any person less frugal and temperate than himself; no less than 2000 £ which he had put for security and improvement into the excise office, but neglecting to recall it in time, could never after get it out, with all the power and interest he had in the great ones of those times; besides another great sum, by mismanagement and for want of good advice.

Thus I have reduced into form and order whatever I have been able to rally up, either from the recollection of my own memory of things transacted while I was with him, or the information of others, equally conversant afterwards, or from his own mouth by frequent visits to the last.

I shall conclude with two material passages, which though they relate not immediately to our author, or his own particular concerns, yet in regard they happened during his public employ, and consequently fell most especially under his cognizance, it will not be amiss here to subjoin them. The first was this:

Before the war broke forth between the States of England and the Dutch, the Hollanders sent over three ambassadors in order to an accommodation; but they returning *re infecta,* the Dutch sent away a plenipotentiary, to offer peace upon much milder terms, or at least to gain more time. But this plenipotentiary could not make such haste, but that the Parliament had procured a copy of their instructions in Holland, which were delivered by our author to his kinsman that was then with him, to translate for the Council to view, before the said plenipotentiary had taken shipping for England; an answer to all he had in charge lay ready for him, before he made his public entry into London.

In the next place there came a person with a very sumptuous train, pretending himself an agent from the prince of Condé, then in arms against Cardinal Mazarin: the Parliament mistrusting him, set their instrument so busily at work, that in four or five days they had procured intelligence from Paris, that he was a spy from King Charles; whereupon the very next morning our author's kinsman was sent to him, with an order of Council commanding him to depart the kingdom within three days, or expect the punishment of a spy.

By these two remarkable passages, we may clearly discover the industry and good intelligence of those times.

V. JOHN TOLAND

[These excerpts from the biographies of Toland (1698) and Richardson (1734) contain data not mentioned in the preceding lives. The page references are to Miss Helen Darbishire's convenient edition, *The Early Lives of Milton,* London, 1932.]

p. 95—". . . I forgot all this while to mention that he paid a visit to Galileo, then an old man, and a prisoner to the Inquisition for thinking otherwise in astronomy than pleased the Franciscan friars."

p. 160—(concerning the European reception of the *First Defence of the English People*): " . . . and, as if the old Grecian republics had revived to decree the accustomed honors to the assertors of liberty, Leonardus Philaras, an Athenian born and ambassador from the Duke of Parma to the French King, wrote a fine commendation of his Defence, and sent him his picture, together with a personal elogium."

p. 176—". . . His admirer Leonardus Philaras coming upon some occasions to London, went to see Milton, who, though he could not see him again, was extremely pleased with his conversation. He afterwards acquainted Milton by a letter that there was a physician who performed wonders on blind people at Paris, and requests him to send in writing the state and progress of his distemper; which to gratify his friend our author performed, yet without expressing any hopes of a cure."

p. 179—". . . Homer, whose two poems he could almost repeat without book: . . ."

p. 180—(concerning the first publication of *Paradise Lost*): ". . . I must not forget that we had like to be eternally deprived of this treasure by the ignorance or malice of the Licenser; who, among other frivolous exceptions, would needs suppress the whole poem for imaginary treason in the following lines.

> —As, when the Sun new risen
> Looks thro the Horizontal misty Air
> Shorn of his Beams, or from behind the Moon
> In dim Eclipse disasterous Twilight sheds
> On half the Nations, and with fear of change
> Perplexes Monarchs."

p. 186—". . . He [Sir Robert Howard] was a great admirer of Milton to his dying day; and, being his particular acquaintance, would tell many pleasant stories of him, as that he himself having demanded of him once what made him side with the Republicans? Milton answered, among other reasons, because theirs was the most frugal government; for that the trappings of a monarchy might set up an ordinary commonwealth."

p. 192–93—". . . Towards the latter part of his time he contracted his library, both because the heirs he left could not make a right use of it, and that he thought he might sell it more to their advantage than they could be able to do themselves. His enemies reported that poverty constrained him thus to part with his books; . . ."

p. 193—"All his learned and great friends in London, not without a friendly concourse of the vulgar, accompanied his body to the Church of St. Giles near Cripplegate, where he lies buried in the chancel, and where the piety of his admirers will shortly erect a monument becoming his worth, and the encouragement of letters in King William's reign."

p. 194—". . . when blindness and age confined him, he played much upon an organ he kept in the house; and had a Pully to swing and keep him in motion."

p. 194—". . . when he was not disposed to rise at his usual hours, he always had one to read to him by his bedside."

p. 194—". . . he used frequently to tell those about him the entire satisfaction of his mind that he had constantly employed his strength and faculties in the defence of liberty and in a direct opposition to slavery."

p. 195—". . . in the latter part of his life he was not a professed member of any particular sect among Christians, he frequented none of their assemblies, nor made use of their peculiar rites in his family."

VI. JONATHAN RICHARDSON

p. 202—(concerning Milton's appearance: ". . . in his habit plain, clean and neat . . . his hair was a light brown, which he wore parted a-top and somewhat flat, long and waving, a little curled."

p. 203—"One that had often seen him told me he used to come to a house where he lived, and he has also met him in the street, led by Millington, the same who was so famous an auctioneer of books about the time of the Revolution and since. This man was then a seller of old books in Little Britain and Milton lodged at his house. This was three or four years before he died. He then wore no sword that my informer remembers, though probably he did; at least it was his custom not long before to wear one with a small silver hilt, and in cold weather a grey camblet coat. His band was usually not of the sort as that in the print I have given (that is, as my original is) but like what are in the common prints of him, the band usually worn at that time: to have a more exact idea of his figure, let it be remembered that the fashion of the coat then was not much unlike what the Quakers wear now.

"I have heard many years since that he used to sit in a grey coarse cloth coat at the door of his house, near Bunhill Fields without Moorgate, in warm sunny weather to enjoy the fresh air and so, as well as in his room, received the visits of people of distinguished parts as well as quality. And very lately I had the good fortune to have another picture of him from an ancient clergyman in Dorsetshire, Dr. Wright. He found him in a small house, he thinks but one room on a floor; in that, up one pair of stairs, which was hung with a rusty green, he found John Milton, sitting in an elbow chair, black clothes and neat enough, pale but not cadaverous, his hands and fingers gouty and with chalk stones. Among other discourse he expressed himself to this purpose: that was he free from the pain this gave him, his blindness would be tolerable."

p. 204—"Music he loved extremely and understood well. It is said he composed, though nothing of that has been brought down to us. He diverted himself with performing, which they say he did well on the organ and bass viol. And this was a great relief to him after he had lost his sight.

"In relation to his love of music and the effect it had upon his mind, I remember a story I had from a friend I was happy in for many years and who loved to talk of Milton, as he often did. Milton, hearing a lady sing finely, 'Now will I swear' (says he) 'this lady is handsome.' His ears now were eyes to him."

p. 205—"When he was a youth he sometimes read romances; . . . In this spring of life he also sometimes saw a play, and visited public walks and such kind of diversions. He was a cheerful companion, but no joker: his conversation was lively, but with dignity."

p. 223—"I don't remember to have ever heard he was sour, ill natured or morose in general, and in common life; but the contrary: . . ."

p. 229—(concerning Milton's alleged unkindness to his daughters):

"As we are at a loss as to the particulars of the affair, what I have suggested will, I hope, be sufficient; only let me add that that daughter, who was certainly one (if there was really more than one) that was thus serviceable to her excellent father in his distress, expressed no uneasiness that I ever heard of when she gave accounts of Milton's affairs to the many inquirers lately; but, on the contrary, spoke of him with great tenderness: particularly I have been told she said he was delightful company, the life of the conversation, and that on account of a flow of subject and an unaffected cheerfulness and civility. One instance of her tender remembrance of him I cannot forbear relating. The picture in crayons I have of him was shown her after several others (or which were pretended to be his). When those were shown and she was asked if she could recollect if she had ever seen such a face: 'No, No.' But when this was produced, in a transport: ' 'Tis my father, 'tis my dear father! I see him! 'Tis him!' And then she put her hands to several parts of her face: ' 'Tis the very man! Here, here—' "

p. 238—(concerning Milton's aversions, late in life, to the crabbed Puritan divines): ". . . Milton had a servant who was a very honest silly fellow, and a zealous and constant follower of these teachers. When he came from the Meeting, his master would frequently ask him what he had heard, and divert himself with ridiculing their fooleries or (it may be) the poor fellow's understanding; both one and the other probably. However, this was so grievous to the good creature that he left his service upon it."

p. 272—(how Milton escaped punishment at the Restoration): ". . . 'Twas Sir William Davenant obtained his remission in return for his own life procured by Milton's interest when himself was under condemnation, anno 1650. . . . It will now be expected I should declare what authority I have for this story. My first answer is

Mr. Pope told it to me. Whence had he it? From Mr. Betterton. Sir William was his patron. . . ."

p. 276—(concerning Milton's state of mind after the Restoration): ". . . he was in perpetual terror of being assassinated; though he had escaped the talons of the law, he knew he had made himself enemies in abundance. He was so dejected he would lie awake whole nights. He then kept himself as private as he could. This Dr. Tancred Robinson had from a relation of Milton's, Mr. Walker of the Temple. . . ."

p. 277–8—(concerning Milton's burial in St. Giles Cripplegate): ". . . The circumstances of his family excused a monument, nor was any such necessary.

"I have heard however that one was a few years ago intended to have been set up for him in Westminster Abbey; by whom I know not; but it was not permitted upon account of his political principles. . . ."

p. 280—(concerning the alleged offer of the Latin Secretaryship to Milton by Charles II): "My authority is Henry Bendish, Esq., a descendant by his mother's side from the Protector Oliver Cromwell; their family and Milton's were in great intimacy before and after his death, and the thing was known among them. Mr. Bendish has heard the widow or daughter or both say it: that soon after the Restoration the King offered to employ this pardoned man as his Latin Secretary, the post in which he served Cromwell with so much integrity and ability. (That a like offer was made to Thurlow is not disputed as ever I heard.) Milton withstood the offer; the wife pressed his compliance. 'Thou art in the right,' says he 'You, as other women, would ride in your coach; for me, my aim is to live and die an honest man.' "

p. 291—". . . Other stories I have heard concerning the posture he was usually in when he dictated; that he sat leaning backward obliquely in an easy chair, with his leg flung over the elbow of it. That he frequently composed lying in bed in a morning ('twas winter sure then) I have been well informed; that when he could not sleep, but lay awake whole nights, he tried; not one verse could he make: at other times flowed easy his unpremeditated verse with a certain *Impetus* and *Æstro,* as himself seemed to believe. Then, at what hour soever, he rung for his daughter to secure what came. I have been also told he would dictate many, perhaps 40 lines, as it were in a breath, and then reduce them to half the number. . . ."

p. 292—". . . The price this great man condescended to take for such a work—such a work!—was ten pounds, and if a certain number went off, then it was to be made up to fifteen. The contract was in being a few years since; I need not tell you I have tried to get a sight of it; they say 'tis lost."

p. 295–6—(concerning the early reception of *Paradise Lost*): ". . . Sir George Hungerford, an ancient member of Parliament, told me, many years ago, that Sir John Denham came into the house one morning with a sheet, wet from the press, in his hand. 'What have you there, Sir John?' 'Part of the noblest poem that ever was wrote in any language or in any age.' This was *Paradise Lost.* However, 'tis certain the book was unknown till about two years after, when the Earl of Dorset produced it. Dr. Tancred Robinson has given permission to use his name, and what I am going to relate he had from Fleet Shephard, at the Grecian Coffee House and who often told the story. My Lord was in Little Britain, beating about for books to his taste; there was *Paradise Lost;* he was surprised with some passages he struck upon, dipping here and there, and bought it; the bookseller begged him to speak in its favour if he liked it, for that they lay on his hands as waste paper. Jesus!— Shephard was present. My Lord took it home, read it, and sent it to Dryden, who in a short time returned it. 'This man' (says Dryden) 'cuts us all out, and the ancients too.' Much the same character he gave of it to a North-country gentleman to whom I mentioned the book, he being a great reader, but not in a right train, coming to town seldom and keeping little company. Dryden amazed him with speaking so loftily of it. 'Why, Mr. Dryden,' says he (Sir W. L. told me the thing himself), ''tis not in rhyme.' 'No. Nor would I have done my Virgil in rhyme if I was to begin it again.' It was when that work was in hand. . . .''

VII. FROM THE HISTORY OF THE LIFE OF THOMAS ELLWOOD

WRITTEN BY HIS OWN HAND . . . 1714

I committed the care of the house to a tenant of my father's, who lived in the town, and taking my leave of Crowell, went up to my sure friend Isaac Penington again. Where understanding that the mediation used for my admittance to John Milton, had succeeded so well, that I might come when I would, I hastened to London, and in the first place went to wait upon him.

He received me courteously, as well for the sake of Dr. Paget, who introduced me, as of Isaac Penington, who recommended me; to both whom he bore a good respect. And having inquired divers things of me, with respect to my former progression in learning, he dismissed me, to provide myself of such accommodations as might be most suitable to my future studies.

I went therefore and took myself a lodging as near to his house (which was then in Jewyn-street) as conveniently as I could, and from thenceforward went every day in the afternoon, except on the first-days of the week, and sitting by him in his dining room, read to him in such books in the Latin tongue as he pleased to hear me read.

At my first sitting to read to him, observing that I used the English pronunciation, he told me, if I would have the benefit of the Latin tongue, not only to read and understand Latin authors, but to converse with foreigners, either abroad or at home, I must learn the foreign pronunciation. To this I consenting, he instructed me how to sound the vowels; so different from the common pronunciation used by the English, who speak Anglice their Latin, that (with some few other variations in sounding some consonants, in particular cases; as C before E or I, like Ch. Sc before I, like Sh, &c.) the Latin thus spoken, seemed as different from that which was delivered, as the English generally speak it, as if it were another language.

I had before, during my retired life at my father's, by unwearied diligence and industry, so far recovered the rules of grammar (in which I had once been very ready) that I could both read a Latin author, and after a sort hammer out his meaning. But this change of pronunciation proved a new difficulty to me. It was now harder to me to read, than it was before to understand when read. But

> *Labor omnia vincit*
> *Improbus.*

> Incessant pains,
> The end obtains.

And so did I. Which made my reading the more acceptable to my master. He, on the other hand, perceiving with what earnest desire I pursued learning, gave me not only all the encouragement, but all the help he could. For, having a curious ear, he understood by my tone, when I understood what I read, and when I did not; and accordingly would stop me, examine me, and open the most difficult passages to me.

Thus went I on for about six weeks time, reading to him in the afternoons; and exercising myself with my own books, in my chamber in the forenoons, I was sensible of an improvement.

But, alas! I had fixed my studies in a wrong place. London and I could never agree for health; my lungs, as I suppose, were too tender to bear the sulphurous air of that city, so that I soon began to droop; and in less than two months time, I was fain to leave both my studies and the city, and return into the country to preserve life; and much ado I had to get thither. . . . I was very kindly received by my master, who had conceived so good an opinion of me, that my conversation, I found, was acceptable to him, and he seemed heartily glad of my recovery and return; and into our old method of study we fell again, I reading to him, and he explaining to me, as occasion required.

But, as if learning had been a forbidden fruit to me, scarce was I well settled in my work, before I met with another diversion, which turned me quite out of my work . . .

Being now at liberty, I visited more generally my friends that were still in prison, and more particularly my friend and benefactor William Penington, at his house, and then went to wait upon my master Milton: with whom yet I could not propose to enter upon my inter- mitted studies, until I had been in Buckinghamshire, to visit my worthy friends Isaac Penington, and his virtuous wife, with other friends in that country. . . .

Some little time before I went to Aylesbury prison, I was desired by my quondam master, Milton, to take an house for him in the neighbourhood where I dwelt, that he might go out of the city, for the safety of himself and his family, the pestilence then growing hot in London. I took a pretty box for him in Giles Chalfont, a mile from me, of which I gave him notice, and intended to have waited on him, and seen him well settled in it, but was pre- vented by that imprisonment.

But now being released, and returned home, I soon made a visit to him, to welcome him into the country.

After some common discourses had passed between us, he called for a manuscript of his; which being brought he delivered to me, bidding me take it home with me, and read it at my leisure, and when I had so done, return it to him with my judgment thereupon.

When I came home, and sat myself to read it, I found it was that excellent Poem, which he intitled PARADISE LOST. After I had, with the best attention, read it through, I made him another visit, and returned him his book, with due acknowledgment of the favour he had done me in communicating it to me. He asked me how I liked it, and what I thought of it; which I modestly but freely told him; and after some further discourse about it, I pleasantly said to him, 'Thou hast said much here of Paradise Lost, but what hast thou to say of Paradise Found?' He made me no answer, but sat some time in a muse; then brake off that discourse, and fell upon another subject.

After the sickness was over, and the city well cleansed, and become safely habitable again, he returned thither. And when afterwards I went to wait on him there (which I seldom failed of doing, whenever my occasions drew me to London), he shewed me his second Poem, called PARADISE REGAINED, and in a pleasant tone said to me, 'This is owing to you, for you put it into my head by the question you put to me at Chalfont, which before I had not thought of.' But from this digression I return to the family I then lived in.

VIII. A FEW SEVENTEENTH AND EIGHTEENTH CENTURY OPINIONS OF MILTON AND HIS WORKS

Roger Williams to Mrs. Sadleir, Winter of 1652–3
. . . I also humbly wish that you may please to read over impartially Mr. Milton's answer to the king's book.

Mrs. Sadleir to Roger Williams:
For Milton's book, that you desire I should read, if I be not mistaken, that is he that has wrote a book of the lawfulness of divorce; and, if report says true, he had, at that time, two or three wives living. This, perhaps, were good doctrine in New England; but it is most abominable in Old England. For his book that he wrote against the late king that you would have me read, you should have taken notice of God's judgment upon him,

who stroke him with blindness, and, as I have heard, he was fain to have the help of one Andrew Marvell, or else he could not have finished that most accursed libel. God has began his judgment upon him here—his punishment will be hereafter in hell. But have you seen the answer to it? If you can get it, I assure you it is worth your reading.

Letter, July 12, 1654

It pleased the Lord to call me for some time, and with some persons, to practice the Hebrew, the Greek, Latin, French and Dutch. The Secretary of the Council (Mr. Milton) for my Dutch I read him, read me many more languages.

Evelyn's Diary, 24 Oct. 1663

Mr. Edward Phillips came to be my sonns preceptor: this gentleman was nephew to Milton, who wrote against Salmasius's 'Defensio,' but was not at all infected with his principles, tho' he was brought up by him.

James Heath, *A Brief Chronicle*, 1663

To better also his condition as to his Kingdoms, came forth several defences of his Authority in several Treatises, especially that of *Salmasius*, called *The Royal Defence* (which one *Milton*, since stricken with blindness cavilled at, who wrote also against that incomparable Book and Remains of King *Charles* the Martyr, about this time produced to light, though endeavoured by all means to be supprest, called *Eikon Basilike*, in an impudent and blasphemous Libel, called *Iconoclastes*, since deservedly burnt by the Common Executioner) doth justly challenge to be here registred.

Charles Blount, *Liberty of the Press*, 1695

Books being therefore in the main so useful to Human Society, I cannot but herein agree with Mr. *Milton*, and say, that (unless it be effected with great Caution) you had almost as good kill a Man, as a good Book; for he that kills a Man, kills but a Reasonable Creature, God's Image: whereas he that destroys a good Book, kills Reason it self, which is as it were the very Eye of God.

Wood, *Athenæ Oxonienses*

This Edw. Phillips hath a brother called Joh. Phillips, who having early imbib'd in a most plentiful manner the rankest antimonarchical principles, from that villanous leading incendiary Joh. Milton his uncle, but not in any university, proved in a short time so notable a proficient in his bloody school of king-killing, that he judged himself sufficiently qualified publicly to engage in and espouse his master's quarrel: and this he did in his *Miltoni Defensio*, &c.

Preface to the Second Part of Waller's *Poems*, 1690. Supposed to be by Francis Atterbury.

In other kinds of writing it [rhyme] continues still, and will do so till some excellent spirit arises, that has leisure enough, and resolution, to break the charm, and free us from the troublesome bondage of rhyming, as Mr. Milton very well calls it, and has proved it as well by what he has wrote in another way. But this is a thought for times at some distance; the present age is a little too warlike; it may perhaps furnish out matter for a good poem in the next, but it will hardly encourage one now.

Langbaine, *Lives and Characters* &c., 1699

An Author of that Excellence of Genius and Learning, that none of any Age or Nation, I think, has excel'd him: during the Civil Wars, and after the Death of King *Charles* the First, he was advanced to considerable Posts in the Government, as Under Secretary of State, &c. and he was a strenuous Defender of the Power and Liberty of the People, upon which that Government immediately stood.

William Winstanley, *Lives of the most Famous English Poets*, 1687

John Milton was one, whose natural parts might deservedly give him a place amongst the principal of our English Poets, having written two Heroick Poems and a Tragedy; namely, *Paradice Lost, Paradice Regain'd* and *Sampson Agonista;* But his Fame is gone out like a Candle in a Snuff, and his Memory will always stink, which might have ever lived in honourable Repute, had not he been a notorious Traytor, and most impiously and villanously bely'd that blessed Martyr King *Charles* the First.

Adam Martindale, *Diary*

He [a new preacher in the parish] was a young man of very pregnant parts for preaching, prayer, writing, and disputation, and so zealous and painfull in his worke that he killed himselfe with it in the best of his time; but he spent his booke in proving the rulers then over us to be no usurpers (I meane so well as he could, for to me he might as well have offered to prove the moon to be made of greene cheese). He went much upon the principles of Knox, Buchanan, Lex, Rex, and Grotius, *de jure belli et pacis;* trod much in Milton's steps, and being overwhelmed with melancholly, which by times made him peevish and morose, he managed the controversie with so much bitterness and severe reflections &c.

William Prynne, *The Re-Publicans and others spurious Good Old Cause,* 1659

But our new *Salt-peter-men,* have with an high strong hand fully executed, accomplished whatever they designed; and because they miscarried not in it, like them, but by God's justice upon them, us, our King, Lords, Parliament for all our crying sins, have prospered in this *Fœlix Scelus,* and brought their *wicked devices to pass;* they glory in it, as the (g) *Highest Act of Justice,* the *Best of Causes; the Greatest Mercy and Deliverance that ever befell* the English Nation; etc.

The marginal reference:

(g) See their Declaration of 17 March, 1648. & May 6, 1659. John Godwins Obstructors of Justice, Cooks & Bradshawes Speeches, John Miltons Answer to Salmatius, and sundry other printed Pamphlets.

Robert Baillie, *Letters and Journals*

. . . but it was the justice of God that brought Peters, Harrison, and others to a shamefull death; . . . to disgrace the two Goodwins, blind Milton, . . . and others of that maleficent crew.

Thomas Hobbes, *Behemoth,* 1679

. . . About this time came out two Books; one written by *Salmasius,* a *Presbyterian,* against the Murder of the King; another written by *Milton,* an *Independent* in *England,* in Answer to it. . . . I have seen them both; they are very good Latine both, and hardly to be judged which is better; and both very ill reasoning, and hardly to be judged which is worst: like two Declamations *Pro* and *Con,* for exercise only in a Rhetorick School, by one and the same man: so like is a Presbyterian to an Independent.

Joseph Jane, *Eikon Aklastos, The Image Vnbroaken,* 1651

His Majest: booke hath passed the censure of the greatest part of the learned world, being translated into the most spred Languages, and strangers honour his Memory, and abhorre his murtherers, but such, as regarde not the al seeing eye of God beholding their wickedness, despise the judgment of the whole world, and there is a man found out, that will breake downe the united reason of mankinde, & he tells men, they must take his word above their owne, and all mens reason, this he vndertakes, that lookes on kings, as Ants, and the kings booke, as wanting all moment of Soliditie, and if, as he chose the Title of Iconoclastes he had written his booke in a Forraigne, or learned language, his vnfaithfullness and impudence would be as open, and odius as his vanitie is ridiculous.

Daniel Elsevier to Sir Joseph Williamson, Sec'y of State, 20, Nov. 1676

Il m'a dit que vous avez esté informé, Monsieur, que je debvois imprimer tous les ouvrages de Milton ensemble. Je vous puis protester de n'y avoir jamais pensé, et que j'aurois horreur d'imprimer les traités qu'il a fait pour la defense d'une si meschante et abominable cause. Outre qu'il ne seroit pas bienseant au fils de celuy qui a imprimé le premier "Salmasii Defensionem Regiam," et qui auroit donné sa vie s'il eust pu sauver le feu roy de glorieuse memoire, d'imprimer un livre si detesté de tous les honnestes geans.

Roger L'Estrange: *No Blinde Guides, &c.* 1660
Mr. Milton,

Although in your *Life,* and *Doctrine,* you have *Resolved one* great *Question;* by *evidencing* that *Devils may indue Humane shapes;* and proving your *self,* even to your own *Wife,* an *Incubus: you have yet Started Another;* and that is, whether *you* are not of *That* Regiment, *which carried the Herd of Swine headlong into the Sea: and moved the People to beseech Jesus to depart out of their coasts. (This* may be very well imagined, from your suitable practises *Here*) Is it possible to read your *Proposals of the benefits of a Free-State,* without Reflecting upon your Tutours—*All this will I give thee, if thou wilt fall down, and worship me?* Come, come Sir, lay the Devil aside; do not proceed with so much *malice,* and against *Knowledge:*—Act like a *Man;*—that a good Christian may not be affraid to pray for you.

Was it not *You,* that scribled a Justification of the *Murther* of the *King,* against *Salmasius:* and made it *good* too, Thus? *That murther was an Action meritorious, compared with your superiour wickedness,* 'Tis *There,* (as I remember) that you *Common place* your self into *Set forms* of *Rayling,* two Pages thick: and lest, your Infamy should not extend it self enough, within the Course and Usage of your *Mother-tongue,* the *Thing* is Dress'd up in a *Travailing Garb,* and *Language:* to blast the English Nation to the Universe; and to give every man a Horrour for *Mankind,* when he Considers, *You are of the Race.* In This, you are above all *Others;* but in your *Iconoclastes,* you exceed your self.

There, not content to see that Sacred Head divided from the *Body;* your piercing Malice enters into the private Agonies of his struggling *Soul;* with a Blasphemous Insolence, invading the prerogative of God himself: (Omniscience) and by Deductions most *Unchristian,* and *Illogical,* aspersing his *Last Pieties,* (the almost certain *Inspirations* of the *Holy Spirit*) with *Juggle,* and *Prevarication.* Nor are the *Words* ill fitted to the *Matter.* The Bold *Design* being suited with a conform *Irreverence of Language.* (but I do not love to Rake long in a Puddle.)

James Howell, *Familiar Letters.* ed. J. Jacobs
(To Dr. D. Featly, 1 Aug. 1644)
Sir,

I receiv'd your Answer to that futilous Pamphlet, with your desire of my opinion touching it. Truly, Sir, I must tell you, that never poor Cur was toss'd in a Blanket as you have toss'd that poor Coxcomb in the Sheet you pleas'd to send me: For whereas a fillip might have fell'd him, you have knock'd him down with a kind of *Herculean* Club, *sans resource.* . . . But I hope the Times will mend, and your *Man* also, if he hath any grace, you have so well corrected him.
(To Sir Edw. Spencer, Kt., London, 24 Jan. ?)

But that opinion of a poor shallow-brain'd Puppy, who upon any cause of disaffection would have men to have a privilege to change their Wives, or to repudiate them, deserves to be hiss'd at rather than confuted; for nothing can tend more to usher in all confusion and beggary thro'out the World: Therefore that Wiseacre deserves of all other to wear a toting horn.

John Toland *Amyntor, or a Defence of Milton's Life.* 1699

AY but, say these Gentlemen, you have made an Inroad on our Persuasion, and directly attack'd the sacred Majesty of Kings, the venerable Order of Bishops, the best constituted Church in the World, our holy Liturgy, and decent Ceremonies, the Authority of Councils, the Testimony of the Fathers, and a hundred other things which we profoundly respect and admire: nor are we the only Sufferers; for almost all other Sects and Parties have equal Reasons of Complaint against you. Well, be it so then; but, good Sirs, betake your selves for Reparation to JOHN MILTON; or, if he is not to be brought to easie Terms, defend your Castles and Territories against him with all the Vigor you can. For, I assure you I am no further concern'd in the Quarrel than to shew you the Enemy, and to give a true Account of his Forces.

Dryden, *The Author's Apology for Heroic Poetry, &c.*

After this, I cannot, without injury to the deceased author of *Paradise Lost,* but acknowledge, that this poem has received its entire foundation, part of the design, and many of the ornaments, from him. What I have borrowed will be so easily discerned from my mean productions, that I shall not need to point the reader to the places: and truly I should be sorry, for my own sake, that any one should take the pains to compare them together; the original being undoubtedly one of the greatest, most noble, and most sublime poems which either this age or nation has produced. And though I could not refuse the partiality of my friend, . . .

Preface to *Sylvæ*

Milton's *Paradise Lost* is admirable; but am I therefore bound to maintain, that there are no flats amongst his elevations, when 'tis evident he creeps along sometimes for above an hundred lines together? Cannot I admire the height of his invention, and the strength of his expression, without defending his antiquated words, and the perpetual harshness of their sound? It is as much commendation as a man can bear, to own him excellent; all beyond it is idolatry.

Original and Progress of Satire

The English have only to boast of Spenser and Milton, who neither of them wanted either genius or learning to have been perfect poets, and yet both of them are liable to many censures. . . . As for Mr. Milton, whom we all admire with so much justice, his subject is not that of an Heroic Poem, properly so called. His design is the losing of our happiness; his event is not prosperous, like that of all other epic works; his heavenly machines are many, and his human persons are but two . . . his thoughts are elevated, his words sounding, and that no man has so happily copied the manner of Homer, or so copiously translated his Grecisms, and the Latin elegancies of Virgil. 'Tis true, he runs into a flat of thought, sometimes for a hundred lines together, but it is when he is got into a track of Scripture. His antiquated words were his choice, not his necessity; for therein he imitated Spenser, as Spenser did Chaucer. . . . Neither will I justify Milton for his blank verse, though I may excuse him, by the example of Hannibal Caro, and other Italians, who have used it; for whatever causes he alleges for the abolishing of rhyme, (which I have not now the leisure to examine,) his own particular reason is plainly this, that rhyme was not his talent; he had neither the ease of doing it, nor the graces of it; which is manifest in his *Juvenilia,* or verses written in his youth, where his rhyme is always constrained and forced, and comes hardly from him, at an age when the soul is most pliant, and the passion of love makes almost every man a rhymer, though not a poet.

Ibid.

Then I consulted a greater genius, (without offence to the *Manes* of that noble author,) I mean Milton. But as he endeavours everywhere to express Homer, whose age had not arrived to that fineness, I found in him a true sublimity, lofty thoughts, which were clothed with admirable Grecisms, and ancient words, which he had been digging from the mines of Chaucer and Spenser, and which, with all their rusticity, had somewhat of venerable in them; but I found not there neither that for which I looked.

Epitaph on Milton

[First engraved, without the author's name, beneath the portrait in Tonson's edition of *Paradise Lost,* 1688.]

Three poets, in three distant ages born,
Greece, Italy, and England did adorn.
The first in loftiness of thought surpass'd,
The next in majesty, in both the last:
The force of Nature could no farther go;
To make a third, she join'd the former two.

Dr. Francis Atterbury, Bishop of Rochester, to Alexander Pope, June 15, 1722

I long to see the original MS. of Milton; but do not know how to come at it without your repeated assistance.

I hope you will not utterly forget what passed in the coach about Samson Agonistes. I shall not press you as to time, but some time or other, I wish you would review, and polish that piece. If upon a new perusal of it (which I desire you to make) you think as I do, that it is written in the very spirit of the ancients, it deserves your care, and is capable of being improved, with little trouble, into a perfect model and standard of tragic poetry—always alluring for its being a story taken out of the Bible; which is an objection that at this time of day I know is not to be got over.

(Note by Bowles: "What are we to think of a poem of Milton, *polished* even by Pope? Pope, however, did not presume to touch it; but the request of Atterbury must ever remain a monument, I will not say of his *want* of *taste* (for no one seems more pleased with Milton,) but of the *submission* of his *taste,* and almost faculties, where poetry was concerned, to Pope.")

Pope's Works (Elwin and Courthope), Vol. IX, p. 49 and note.

Dr. Francis Atterbury to Pope (written from his prison in the Tower, April 10, 1723)

You and I have spent many hours together upon much pleasanter subjects; and, that I may preserve the old custom, I shall not part with you now till I have closed this letter, with three lines of Milton, which you will, I know, readily and not without some degree of concern apply to your ever affectionate, etc.

"Some natural tears he dropped, but wiped them soon;
The world was all before him, where to choose
His place of rest, and Providence his guide."

(Note by Warton: "He repeated these lines to some of the upper scholars of Westminster school, who went to visit him in the Tower.")

The Poetical Works of William Somerville (Cooke's Edition)

"Epistle to Mr. Thomson
On the First Edition of His Seasons"

Read Philips much, consider Milton more;
But from their dross extract the purer ore."
(p. 41)

Hudibras and Milton Reconciled
(a burlesque imitation of Milton's "grand style," p. 284).

The Poetical Works of Dr. Armstrong (*Works of the British Poets,* edited by Thomas Park, 1808, Vol. 34, p. 103)

"Taste: An Epistle to a Young Critic"
(first printed in the year 1753)

[Shakespeare referred to as]
The great stupendous genius of our stage,
Boast of our island, pride of human-kind,

Had faults to which the boxes are not blind.
His frailties are to every gossip known:
Yet Milton's pedantries not shock the town.

The lords who starv'd old Ben were learn'dly fond
Of Chaucer, whom with bungling toil they conn'd:
Their sons, whose ears bold Milton could not seize,
Would laugh o'er Ben like mad, and snuff and sneeze,
And swear, and seem as tickled as you please:
Their spawn, the pride of this sublimer age,
Feel to the toes and horns grave Milton's rage:
Though liv'd he now, he might appeal with scorn
To lords, knights, 'squires, and doctors, yet unborn:
Or, justly mad, to Moloch's burning fane
Devote the choicest children of his brain.

MILTON'S
Complete
POEMS

POEMS

OF

Mr. *John Milton,*

BOTH

ENGLISH and LATIN

Compos'd at several times.

[The text of the Shorter English Poems, usually called The Minor Poems, is from the edition of 1645, unless otherwise stated.]

THE STATIONER

TO THE READER.

It is not any private respect of gain, Gentle Reader, *for the slightest Pamphlet is now adayes more vendible then the Works of learnedest men; but it is the love I have to our own Language that hath made me diligent to collect, and set forth such* Peeces *both in Prose and Vers, as may renew the wonted honour and esteem of our English tongue: and it's the worth of these both English and Latin* Poems, *not the flourish of any prefixed* encomions *that can invite thee to buy them, though these are not without the highest Commendations and Applause of the learnedst* Academicks, *both domestick and forrein: And amongst those of our own Countrey, the unparallel'd attestation of that renowned Provost of* Eaton, *Sir* Henry Wootton: *I know not thy palat how it relishes such dainties, nor how harmonious thy soul is; perhaps more trivial Airs may please thee better. But howsoever thy opinion is spent upon these, that incouragement I have already received from the most ingenious men in their clear and courteous entertainment of Mr.* Wallers *late choice Peeces, hath once more made me adventure into the World, presenting it with these ever-green, and not to be blasted Laurels. The Authors more peculiar excellency in these studies, was too well known to conceal his Papers, or to keep me from attempting to sollicit them from him. Let the event guide it self which way it will, I shall deserve of the age, by bringing into the Light as true a Birth, as the Muses have brought forth since our famous* Spencer *wrote; whose Poems in these English ones are as rarely imitated, as sweetly excell'd. Reader, if thou art Eagle-eied to censure their worth, I am not tearful to expose them to thy exactest perusal.*

Thine to command.

HUMPH. MOSELEY.

3

On the Morning of Christs Nativity.

Compos'd 1629

I

This is the Month, and this the happy morn
Wherin the Son of Heav'ns eternal King,
Of wedded Maid, and Virgin Mother born,
Our great redemption from above did bring;
For so the holy sages once did sing,
   That he our deadly forfeit should release,
And with his Father work us a perpetual peace.

II

That glorious Form, that Light unsufferable,
And that far-beaming blaze of Majesty,
Wherwith he wont at Heav'ns high Councel-Table,
To sit the midst of Trinal Unity,
He laid aside; and here with us to be,
   Forsook the Courts of everlasting Day,
And chose with us a darksom House of mortal Clay.

III

Say Heav'nly Muse, shall not thy sacred vein
Afford a present to the Infant God?
Hast thou no vers, no hymn, or solemn strein,
To welcom him to this his new abode,
Now while the Heav'n by the Suns team untrod,
   Hath took no print of the approching light,
And all the spangled host keep watch in squadrons bright?

IV

See how from far upon the Eastern rode
The Star-led Wisards haste with odours sweet:
O run, prevent them with thy humble ode,
And lay it lowly at his blessed feet;
Have thou the honour first, thy Lord to greet,
   And joyn thy voice unto the Angel Quire,
From out his secret Altar toucht with hallow'd fire.

The Hymn.

I

It was the Winter wilde,
While the Heav'n-born-childe,
   All meanly wrapt in the rude manger lies;
Nature in aw to him
Had dofft her gawdy trim,
   With her great Master so to sympathize:
It was no season then for her
To wanton with the Sun her lusty Paramour.

II

Onely with speeches fair
She woo's the gentle Air
   To hide her guilty front with innocent Snow;
And on her naked shame,
Pollute with sinfull blame,
   The Saintly Vail of Maiden white to throw,
Confounded, that her Makers eyes
Should look so neer upon her foul deformities.

III

But he her fears to cease,
Sent down the meek-eyd Peace,
   She crown'd with Olive green, came softly sliding
Down through the turning sphear
His ready Harbinger,
   With Turtle wing the amorous clouds dividing,
And waving wide her mirtle wand,
She strikes a universall Peace through Sea and Land.

IV

No War, or Battails sound
Was heard the World around:
   The idle spear and shield were high up hung;
The hooked Chariot stood
Unstain'd with hostile blood,
   The Trumpet spake not to the armed throng,
And Kings sate still with awfull eye,
As if they surely knew their sovran Lord was by.

V

But peacefull was the night
Wherin the Prince of light
   His raign of peace upon the earth began:
The Windes with wonder whist,
Smoothly the waters kist,
   Whispering new joyes to the milde Ocean,
Who now hath quite forgot to rave,
While Birds of Calm sit brooding on the charmed wave.

30

40

50

60

VI

The Stars with deep amaze
Stand fixt in stedfast gaze,   70
   Bending one way their pretious influence,
And will not take their flight,
For all the morning light,
   Or *Lucifer* that often warn'd them thence;
But in their glimmering Orbs did glow,
Untill their Lord himself bespake, and bid them go.

VII

And though the shady gloom
Had given day her room,
  , The Sun himself with-held his wonted speed,
And hid his head for shame,   80
As his inferiour flame,
   The new-enlightn'd world no more should **need**;
He saw a greater Sun appear
Then his bright Throne, or burning Axletree could bear.

VIII

The Shepherds on the Lawn,
Or ere the point of dawn,
   Sate simply chatting in a rustick row;
Full little thought they than,
That the mighty *Pan*
   Was kindly com to live with them below;   90
Perhaps their loves, or els their sheep,
Was all that did their silly thoughts so busie keep.

IX

When such musick sweet
Their hearts and ears did greet,
   As never was by mortall finger strook,
Divinely-warbled voice
Answering the stringed noise,
   As all their souls in blisfull rapture took:
The Air such pleasure loth to lose,
With thousand echo's still prolongs each heav'nly close.   100

X

Nature that heard such sound
Beneath the hollow round
   Of *Cynthia's* seat, the Airy region thrilling.
Now was almost won
To think her part was don,
   And that her raign had here its last fulfilling;
She knew such harmony alone
Could hold all Heav'n and Earth in happier union.

XI

At last surrounds their sight
A Globe of circular light,
   That with long beams the shame-fac't night array'd,   110
The helmed Cherubim
And sworded Seraphim,
   Are seen in glittering ranks with wings displaid,
Harping in loud and solemn quire,
With unexpressive notes to Heav'ns new-born Heir.

XII

Such Musick (as 'tis said)
Before was never made,
   But when of old the sons of morning sung,
While the Creator Great   120
His constellations set,
   And the well-ballanc't world on hinges hung,
And cast the dark foundations deep,
And bid the weltring waves their oozy channel keep.

XIII

Ring out ye Crystall sphears,
Once bless our human ears,
   (If ye have power to touch our senses so)
And let your silver chime
Move in melodious time;
   And let the Base of Heav'ns deep Organ blow,   130
And with your ninefold harmony
Make up full consort to th'Angelike symphony.

XIV

For if such holy Song
Enwrap our fancy long,
   Time will run back, and fetch the age of gold,
And speckl'd vanity
Will sicken soon and die,
   And leprous sin will melt from earthly mould,
And Hell it self will pass away,
And leave her dolorous mansions to the peering day.   140

XV

Yea Truth, and Justice then
Will down return to men,
   Orb'd in a Rain-bow; and like glories wearing
Mercy will sit between,
Thron'd in Celestiall sheen, '
   With radiant feet the tissued clouds down stearing.
And Heav'n as at som festivall,
Will open wide the Gates of her high Palace Hall.

XVI

But wisest Fate sayes no,
This must not yet be so,   150
   The Babe lies yet in smiling Infancy,
That on the bitter cross
Must redeem our loss;
   So both himself and us to glorifie:
Yet first to those ychain'd in sleep,
The wakefull trump of doom must thunder through the deep,

XVII

With such a horrid clang
As on mount *Sinai* rang
   While the red fire, and smouldring clouds out brake:
The aged Earth agast   160
With terrour of that blast,
   Shall from the surface to the center shake;
When at the worlds last session,
The dreadfull Judge in middle Air shall spread his throne.

XVIII

And then at last our bliss
Full and perfect is,
   But now begins; for from this happy day
Th'old Dragon under ground
In straiter limits bound,
   Not half so far casts his usurped sway,   170
And wrath to see his Kingdom fail,
Swindges the scaly Horrour of his foulded tail.

XIX

The Oracles are dumm,
No voice or hideous humm
   Runs through the arched roof in words deceiving.
Apollo from his shrine
Can no more divine,
   With hollow shreik the steep of *Delphos* leaving.
No nightly trance, or breathed spell,
Inspire's the pale-ey'd Priest from the prophetic cell.   180

XX

The lonely mountains o're,
And the resounding shore,
   A voice of weeping heard, and loud lament;
From haunted spring, and dale
Edg'd with poplar pale.
   The parting Genius is with sighing sent,
With flowre-inwov'n tresses torn
The Nimphs in twilight shade of tangled thickets mourn.

XXI

In consecrated Earth,
And on the holy Hearth,
  The *Lars,* and *Lemures* moan with midnight plaint,
In Urns, and Altars round,
A drear, and dying sound
  Affrights the *Flamins* at their service quaint;
And the chill Marble seems to sweat,
While each peculiar power forgoes his wonted seat.

190

XXII

Peor, and *Baalim,*
Forsake their Temples dim,
  With that twise batter'd god of *Palestine,*
And mooned *Ashtaroth,*
Heav'ns Queen and Mother both,
  Now sits not girt with Tapers holy shine,
The Libyc *Hammon* shrinks his horn,
In vain the *Tyrian* Maids their wounded *Thamuz* mourn.

200

XXIII

And sullen *Moloch* fled,
Hath left in shadows dred,
  His burning Idol all of blackest hue,
In vain with Cymbals ring,
They call the grisly king,
  In dismall dance about the furnace blue,
The brutish gods of *Nile* as fast,
Isis and *Orus,* and the Dog *Anubis* hast.

210

XXIV

Nor is *Osiris* seen
In *Memphian* Grove, or Green,
  Trampling the unshowr'd Grasse with lowings loud:
Nor can he be at rest
Within his sacred chest,
  Naught but profoundest Hell can be his shroud,
In vain with Timbrel'd Anthems dark
The sable-stoled Sorcerers bear his worshipt Ark.

220

XXV

He feels from *Juda's* Land
The dredded Infants hand,
  The rayes of *Bethlehem* blind his dusky eyn;
Nor all the gods beside,
Longer dare abide,
  Not *Typhon* huge ending in snaky twine:
Our Babe to shew his Godhead true,
Can in his swadling bands controul the damned crew.

XXVI

So when the Sun in bed,
Curtain'd with cloudy red,
　　Pillows his chin upon an Orient wave.
The flocking shadows pale,
Troop to th'infernall jail,
　　Each fetter'd Ghost slips to his severall grave,
And the yellow-skirted *Fayes,*
Fly after the Night-steeds, leaving their Moon-lov'd maze.

230

XXVII

But see the Virgin blest,
Hath laid her Babe to rest.
　　Time is our tedious Song should here have ending,
Heav'ns youngest teemed Star,
Hath fixt her polisht Car.
　　Her sleeping Lord with Handmaid Lamp attending.
And all about the Courtly Stable,
Bright-harnest Angels sit in order serviceable.

240

A Paraphrase on *Psalm* 114.

This and the following *Psalm* were don by the Author at fifteen yeers old.

WHEN the blest seed of *Terah's* faithfull Son,
After long toil their liberty had won,
And past from *Pharian* fields to *Canaan* Land,
Led by the strength of the Almighties hand,
Jehovah's wonders were in *Israel* shown,
His praise and glory was in *Israel* known.
That saw the troubl'd Sea, and shivering fled,
And sought to hide his froth-becurled head
Low in the earth, *Jordans* clear streams recoil,
As a faint host that hath receiv'd the foil.
The high, huge-bellied Mountains skip like Rams
Amongst their Ews, the little Hills like Lambs.
Why fled the Ocean? And why skipt the Mountains?
Why turned *Jordan* toward his Crystall Fountains?
Shake earth, and at the presence be agast
Of him that ever was, and ay shall last,
That glassy flouds from rugged rocks can crush,
And make soft rills from fiery flint-stones gush.

10

Psalm 136.

LET us with a gladsom mind
Praise the Lord, for he is kind,
　　For his mercies ay endure,
　　Ever faithfull, ever sure.

Let us blaze his Name abroad,
For of gods he is the God;
　　For. *&c.*

O let us his praises tell,
Who doth the wrathfull tyrants quell.
   For, &c.   10

Who with his miracles doth make
Amazed Heav'n and Earth to shake.
   For, &c.

Who by his wisdom did create
The painted Heav'ns so full of state.
   For his, &c.   20

Who did the solid Earth ordain
To rise above the watry plain.
   For his, &c.

Who by his all-commanding might,
Did fill the new-made world with light.
   For his, &c.

And caus'd the Golden-tressed Sun,
All the day long his cours to run.
   For his, &c.   30

The horned Moon to shine by night,
Amongst her spangled sisters bright.
   For his, &c.

He with his thunder-clasping hand,
Smote the first-born of *Egypt* Land.
   For his, &c.   40

And in despight of *Pharao* fell,
He brought from thence his *Israel*.
   For, &c.

The ruddy waves he cleft in twain,
Of the *Erythræan* main.
   For, &c.

The floods stood still like Walls of Glass,
While the Hebrew Bands did pass.
   For, &c.   50

But full soon they did devour
The Tawny King with all his power.
   For, &c.

His chosen people he did bless
In the wastfull Wildernes.
   For, &c.   60

In bloody battail he brought down
Kings of prowess and renown.
   For, &c.

He foild bold *Seon* and his host,
That rul'd the *Amorrean* coast.
   For, &c.

And large-lim'd *Og* he did subdue,
With all his over hardy crew.
   For, &c.

And to his servant *Israel,*
He gave their Land therin to dwell.
   For, &c.

He hath with a piteous eye
Beheld us in our misery.
   For, &c.

And freed us from the slavery
Of the invading enimy.
   For, &c.

All living creatures he doth feed,
And with full hand supplies their need.
   For, &c.

Let us therfore warble forth
His mighty Majesty and worth.
   For, &c.

That his mansion hath on high
Above the reach of mortall ey.
   For his mercies ay endure,
   Ever faithfull, ever sure.

70

80

90

Anno aetatis 17.

On the Death of a fair Infant dying of a Cough.

[Not in 1645; from 1673.]

I

O FAIREST flower no sooner blown but blasted,
Soft silken Primrose fading timelesslie,
Summers chief honour if thou hadst out-lasted
Bleak winters force that made thy blossome drie;
For he being amorous on that lovely die
   That did thy cheek envermeil, thought to kiss
But kill'd alas, and then bewayl'd his fatal bliss.

II

For since grim Aquilo his charioter
By boistrous rape th' Athenian damsel got,
He thought it toucht his Deitie full neer,
If likewise he some fair one wedded not,
Thereby to wipe away th' infamous blot,
    Of long-uncoupled bed, and childless eld,
Which 'mongst the wanton gods a foul reproach was held.

III

So mounting up in ycie-pearled carr,
Through middle empire of the freezing aire
He wanderd long, till thee he spy'd from farr,
There ended was his quest, there ceast his care.
Down he descended from his Snow-soft chaire,
    But all unwares with his cold-kind embrace
Unhous'd thy Virgin Soul from her fair biding place.

IV

Yet art thou not inglorious in thy fate;
For so *Apollo,* with unweeting hand
Whilome did slay his dearly-loved mate
Young *Hyacinth* born on *Eurotas'* strand,
Young *Hyacinth* the pride of *Spartan* land;
    But then transform'd him to a purple flower
Alack that so to change thee winter had no power.

V

Yet can I not perswade me thou art dead
Or that thy coarse corrupts in earths dark wombe,
Or that thy beauties lie in wormie bed,
Hid from the world in a low delved tombe;
Could Heav'n for pittie thee so strictly doom?
    Oh no! for something in thy face did shine
Above mortalitie that shew'd thou wast divine.

VI

Resolve me then oh Soul most surely blest
(If so it be that thou these plaints dost hear)
Tell me bright Spirit where e're thou hoverest
Whether above that high first-moving Spheare
Or in the Elisian fields (if such here were.)
    Oh say me true if thou wert mortal wight
And why from us so quickly thou didst take thy flight.

VII

Wert thou some Starr which from the ruin'd roofe
Of shak't Olympus by mischance didst fall;
Which carefull *Jove* in natures true behoofe
Took up, and in fit place did reinstall?
Or did of late earths Sonnes besiege the wall
    Of sheenie Heav'n, and thou some goddess fled
Amongst us here below to hide thy nectar'd head.

VIII

Or wert thou that just Maid who once before   50
Forsook the hated earth, O tell me sooth
And cam'st again to visit us once more?
Or wert thou that sweet smiling Youth!
Or that c[r]own'd Matron sage white-robed Truth?
  Or any other of that heav'nly brood
Let down in clowdie throne to do the world some good.

IX

Or wert thou of the golden-winged hoast,
Who having clad thy self in humane weed,
To earth from thy præfixed seat didst poast,
And after short abode flie back with speed,   60
As if to shew what creatures Heav'n doth breed,
  Thereby to set the hearts of men on fire
To scorn the sordid world, and unto Heav'n aspire.

X

But oh why didst thou not stay here below
To bless us with thy heav'n-lov'd innocence,
To slake his wrath whom sin hath made our foe
To turn Swift-rushing black perdition hence,
Or drive away the slaughtering pestilence,
  To stand 'twixt us and our deserved smart
But thou canst best perform that office where thou art.   70

XI

Then thou the mother of so sweet a child
Her false imagin'd loss cease to lament,
And wisely learn to curb thy sorrows wild;
Think what a present thou to God hast sent,
And render him with patience what he lent;
  This if thou do he will an off-spring give,
That till the worlds last-end shall make thy name to live.

Anno Aetatis 19. *At a Vacation Exercise in the Colledge, part* Latin, *part* English. *The* Latin *speeches ended, the* English *thus began.*

[Not in 1645; from 1673.]

Hail native Language, that by sinews weak
Didst move my first endeavouring tongue to speak,
And mad'st imperfect words with childish tripps,
Half unpronounc't, slide through my infant-lipps,
Driving dum silence from the portal dore,
Where he had mutely sate two years before:
Here I salute thee and thy pardon ask,
That now I use thee in my latter task:
Small loss it is that thence can come unto thee,
I know my tongue but little Grace can do thee: 10

Thou needst not be ambitious to be first,
Believe me I have thither packt the worst:
And, if it happen as I did forecast,
The daintest dishes shall be serv'd up last.
I pray thee then deny me not thy aide
For this same small neglect that I have made:
But haste thee strait to do me once a Pleasure,
And from thy wardrope bring thy chiefest treasure;
Not those new fangled toys, and triming slight
Which takes our late fantasticks with delight,   20
But cull those richest Robes, and gay'st attire
Which deepest Spirits, and choicest Wits desire:
I have some naked thoughts that rove about
And loudly knock to have their passage out;
And wearie of their place do only stay
Till thou hast deck't them in thy best aray;
That so they may without suspect or fears
Fly swiftly to this fair Assembly's ears;
Yet I had rather if I were to chuse,
Thy service in some graver subject use,   30
Such as may make thee search thy coffers round,
Before thou cloath my fancy in fit sound:
Such where the deep transported mind may soare
Above the wheeling poles, and at Heav'ns dore
Look in, and see each blissful Deitie
How he before the thunderous throne doth lie,
Listening to what unshorn *Apollo* sings
To th' touch of golden wires, while *Hebe* brings
Immortal Nectar to her Kingly Sire:
Then passing through the Spherse of watchful fire,   40
And mistie Regions of wide air next under,
And hills of Snow and lofts of piled Thunder,
May tell at length how green-ey'd *Neptune* raves,
In Heav'ns defiance mustering all his waves,
Then sing of secret things that came to pass
When Beldam Nature in her cradle was;
And last of Kings and Queens and *Hero's* old,
Such as the wise *Demodocus* once told
In solemn Songs at King *Alcinous* feast,
While sad *Ulisses* soul and all the rest   50
Are held with his melodious harmonie
In willing chains and sweet captivitie.
But fie my wandring Muse how thou dost stray!
Expectance calls thee now another way,
Thou know'st it must be now thy only bent
To keep in compass of thy Predicament:
Then quick about thy purpos'd business come,
That to the next I may resign my Roome.

Then Ens *is represented as Father of the* Prædicaments *his ten Sons, whereof the Eldest stood for* Substance *with his Canons, which* Ens *thus speaking, explains.*

Good luck befriend thee Son; for at thy birth
The Faiery Ladies daunc't upon the hearth;   60

Thy drowsie Nurse hath sworn she did them spie
Come tripping to the Room where thou didst lie;
And sweetly singing round about thy Bed
Strew all their blessings on thy sleeping Head.
She heard them give thee this, that thou should'st still
From eyes of mortals walk invisible,
Yet there is something that doth force my fear,
For once it was my dismal hap to hear
A *Sybil* old, bow-bent with crooked age,
That far events full wisely could presage,   70
And in Times long and dark Prospective Glass
Fore-saw what future dayes should bring to pass,
Your Son, said she, (nor can you it prevent)
Shall subject be to many an Accident.
O're all his Brethren he shall Reign as King,
Yet every one shall make him underling,
And those that cannot live from him asunder
Ungratefully shall strive to keep him under,
In worth and excellence he shall out-go them,
Yet being above them, he shall be below them;   80
From others he shall stand in need of nothing,
Yet on his Brothers shall depend for Cloathing.
To find a Foe it shall not be his hap,
And peace shall lull him in her flowry lap;
Yet shall he live in strife, and at his dore
Devouring war shall never cease to roare:
Yea it shall be his natural property
To harbour those that are at enmity.
What power, what force, what mighty spell, if not
Your learned hands, can loose this Gordian knot?   90

The next Quantity *and* Quality, *spake in Prose, then* Relation *was call'd by his Name.*

Rivers arise; whether thou be the Son,
Of utmost *Tweed,* or *Oose,* or gulphie *Dun,*
Or *Trent,* who like some earth-born Giant spreads
His thirty Armes along the indented Meads,
Or sullen *Mole* that runneth underneath,
Or *Severn* swift, guilty of Maidens death,
Or Rockie *Avon,* or of Sedgie *Lee,*
Or Coaly *Tine,* or antient hallowed *Dee,*
Or *Humber* loud that keeps the *Scythians* Name,
Or *Medway* smooth, or Royal Towred *Thame.*   100

The rest was Prose.

The Passion.

I

Ere-while of Musick, and Ethereal mirth,
Wherwith the stage of Ayr and Earth did ring,
And joyous news of heav'nly Infants birth,
My muse with Angels did divide to sing;
But headlong joy is ever on the wing,
  In Wintry solstice like the shortn'd light
Soon swallow'd up in dark and long out-living night.

II

For now to sorrow must I tune my song,
And set my Harpe to notes of saddest wo,
Which on our dearest Lord did sease er'e long,   10
Dangers, and snares, and wrongs, and worse then so,
Which he for us did freely undergo.
   Most perfect *Heroe,* try'd in heaviest plight
Of labours huge and hard, too hard for human wight.

III

He sov'ran Priest stooping his regall head
That dropt with odorous oil down his fair eyes,
Poor fleshly Tabernacle entered,
His starry front low-rooft beneath the skies;
O what a Mask was there, what a disguise!
   Yet more; the stroke of death he must abide,   20
Then lies him meekly down fast by his Brethrens side.

IV

These latter scenes confine my roving vers,
To this Horizon is my *Phœbus* bound,
His Godlike acts, and his temptations fierce,
And former sufferings other where are found;
Loud o're the rest *Cremona's* Trump doth sound;
   Me softer airs befit, and softer strings
Of Lute, or Viol still, more apt for mournful things.

V

Befriend me night best Patroness of grief,
Over the Pole thy thickest mantle throw,   30
And work my flatter'd fancy to belief,
That Heav'n and Earth are colour'd with my wo;
My sorrows are too dark for day to know:
   The leaves should all be black wheron I write,
And letters where my tears have washt a wannish white.

VI

See see the Chariot, and those rushing wheels,
That whirl'd the Prophet up at *Chebar* flood,
My spirit som transporting *Cherub* feels,
To bear me where the Towers of *Salem* stood,
Once glorious Towers, now sunk in guiltles blood;   40
   There doth my soul in holy vision sit
In pensive trance, and anguish, and ecstatick fit.

VII

Mine eye hath found that sad Sepulchral rock
That was the Casket of Heav'ns richest store,
And here though grief my feeble hands up-lock,
Yet on the softned Quarry would I score
My plaining vers as lively as before;
   For sure so well instructed are my tears,
That they would fitly fall in order'd Characters.

VIII

Or should I thence hurried on viewles wing,   50
Take up a weeping on the Mountains wilde,
The gentle neighbourhood of grove and spring
Would soon unboosom all thir Echoes milde,
And I (for grief is easily beguild)
  Might think th'infection of my sorrows loud,
Had got a race of mourners on som pregnant cloud.

This Subject the Author finding to be above the yeers he had, when he wrote it, and nothing satisfi'a with what was begun, left it unfinisht.

On Time.

FLY envious *Time,* till thou run out thy race,
Call on the lazy leaden-stepping hours,
Whose speed is but the heavy Plummets pace;
And glut thy self with what thy womb devours,
Which is no more then what is false and vain,
And meerly mortal dross;
So little is our loss,
So little is thy gain.
For when as each thing bad thou hast entomb'd,
And last of all, thy greedy self consum'd,   10
Then long Eternity shall greet our bliss
With an individual kiss;
And Joy shall overtake us as a flood,
When every thing that is sincerely good
And perfectly divine,
With Truth, and Peace, and Love shall ever shine
About the supreme Throne
Of him, t'whose happy-making sight alone,
When once our heav'nly-guided soul shall clime,
Then all this Earthy grosnes quit,   20
Attir'd with Stars, we shall for ever sit,
  Triumphing over Death, and Chance, and thee O Time.

Upon the Circumcision.

YE flaming Powers, and winged Warriours bright,
That erst with Musick, and triumphant song
First heard by happy watchful Shepherds ear,
So sweetly sung your Joy the Clouds along
Through the soft silence of the list'ning night;
Now mourn, and if sad share with us to bear
Your fiery essence can distill no tear,
Burn in your sighs, and borrow
Seas wept from our deep sorrow,
He who with all Heav'ns heraldry whileare   10
Enter'd the world, now bleeds to give us ease;
Alas, how soon our sin
  Sore doth begin
    His Infancy to sease!

O more exceeding love or law more just?
Just law indeed, but more exceeding love!
For we by rightfull doom remediles
Were lost in death, till he that dwelt above
High thron'd in secret bliss, for us frail dust
Emptied his glory, ev'n to nakednes;
And that great Cov'nant which we still transgress
Intirely satisfi'd,
And the full wrath beside
Of vengeful Justice bore for our excess,
And seals obedience first with wounding smart
This day, but O ere long
Huge pangs and strong
    Will pierce more neer his heart.

At a Solemn Musick.

BLEST pair of *Sirens,* pledges of Heav'ns joy,
Sphear-born harmonious Sisters, Voice, and Vers,
Wed your divine sounds, and mixt power employ
Dead things with inbreath'd sense able to pierce,
And to our high-rais'd phantasie present,
That undisturbed Song of pure concent,
Ay sung before the saphire-colour'd throne
To him that sits theron
With Saintly shout, and solemn Jubily,
Where the bright Seraphim in burning row
Their loud up-lifted Angel trumpets blow,
And the Cherubick host in thousand quires
Touch their immortal Harps of golden wires,
With those just Spirits that wear victorious Palms,
Hymns devout and holy Psalms
Singing everlastingly;
That we on Earth with undiscording voice
May rightly answer that melodious noise;
As once we did, till disproportion'd sin
Jarr'd against natures chime, and with harsh din
Broke the fair musick that all creatures made
To their great Lord, whose love their motion sway'd
In perfect Diapason, whilst they stood
In first obedience, and their state of good.
O may we soon again renew that Song,
And keep in tune with Heav'n, till God ere long
To his celestial consort us unite,
To live with him, and sing in endles morn of light.

An Epitaph on the Marchioness of *Winchester*.

THIS rich Marble doth enterr
The honour'd Wife of *Winchester,*
A Vicounts daughter, an Earls heir,
Besides what her vertues fair

Added to her noble birth,
More then she could own from Earth.
Summers three times eight save one
She had told, alas too soon,
After so short time of breath,
To house with darknes, and with death.   10
Yet had the number of her days
Bin as compleat as was her praise,
Nature and fate had had no strife
In giving limit to her life.
Her high birth, and her graces sweet,
Quickly found a lover meet;
The Virgin quire for her request
The God that sits at marriage feast;
He at their invoking came
But with a scarce-wel-lighted flame;   20
And in his Garland as he stood,
Ye might discern a Cipress bud.
Once had the early Matrons run
To greet her of a lovely son,
And now with second hope she goes,
And calls *Lucina* to her throws;
But whether by mischance or blame
Atropos for *Lucina* came;
And with remorsles cruelty,
Spoil'd at once both fruit and tree: 30
The haples Babe before his birth
Had burial, yet not laid in earth,
And the languisht Mothers Womb
Was not long a living Tomb.
So have I seen som tender slip
Sav'd with care from Winters nip,
The pride of her carnation train,
Pluck't up by som unheedy swain,
Who onely thought to crop the flowr
New shot up from vernall showr;   40
But the fair blossom hangs the head
Side-ways as on a dying bed,
And those Pearls of dew she wears,
Prove to be presaging tears
Which the sad morn had let fall
On her hast'ning funerall.
Gentle Lady may thy grave
Peace and quiet ever have;
After this thy travail sore
Sweet rest sease thee evermore,   50
That to give the world encrease,
Shortned hast thy own lives lease,
Here besides the sorrowing
That thy noble House doth bring,
Here be tears of perfect moan
Weept for thee in *Helicon,*
And som Flowers, and som Bays,

For thy Hears to strew the ways,
Sent thee from the banks of *Came,*
Devoted to thy vertuous name;   60
Whilst thou bright Saint high sit'st in glory,
Next her much like to thee in story,
That fair *Syrian* Shepherdess,
Who after yeers of barrennes,
The highly favour'd *Joseph* bore
To him that serv'd for her before,
And at her next birth much like thee,
Through pangs fled to felicity,
Far within the boosom bright
Of blazing Majesty and Light,   70
There with thee, new welcom Saint,
Like fortunes may her soul acquaint,
With thee there clad in radiant sheen,
No Marchioness, but now a Queen.

SONG

On *May* morning.

Now the bright morning Star, Dayes harbinger,
Comes dancing from the East, and leads with her
The Flowry *May,* who from her green lap throws
The yellow Cowslip, and the pale Primrose.
  Hail bounteous *May* that dost inspire
  Mirth and youth, and warm desire,
  Woods and Groves, are of thy dressing,
  Hill and Dale, doth boast thy blessing.
Thus we salute thee with our early Song,
And welcom thee, and wish thee long.   10

On *Shakespear.* 1630.

WHAT needs my *Shakespear* for his honour'd Bones,
The labour of an age in piled Stones,
Or that his hallow'd reliques should be hid
Under a Star-ypointing *Pyramid?*
Dear son of memory, great heir of Fame,
What need'st thou such weak witnes of thy name?
Thou in our wonder and astonishment
Hast built thy self a live-long Monument.
For whilst to th' shame of slow-endeavouring art,
Thy easie numbers flow, and that each heart   10
Hath from the leaves of thy unvalu'd Book,
Those Delphick lines with deep impression took,
Then thou our fancy of it self bereaving,
Dost make us Marble with too much conceaving;
And so Sepulcher'd in such pomp dost lie,
That Kings for such a Tomb would wish to die.

On the University Carrier who

sickn'd in the time of his vacancy, being
forbid to go to *London,* by reason of
the Plague.

HERE lies old *Hobson,* Death hath broke his girt,
And here alas, hath laid him in the dirt,
Or els the ways being foul, twenty to one,
He's here stuck in a slough, and overthrown.
'Twas such a shifter, that if truth were known,
Death was half glad when he had got him down;
For he had any time this ten yeers full,
Dodg'd with him, betwixt *Cambridge* and the Bull.
And surely, Death could never have prevail'd,
Had not his weekly cours of carriage fail'd;   10
But lately finding him so long at home,
And thinking now his journeys end was come,
And that he had tane up his latest Inne,
In the kind office of a Chamberlin
Shew'd him his room where he must lodge that night,
Pull'd off his Boots, and took away the light:
If any ask for him, it shall be sed,
Hobson has supt, and's newly gon to bed.

Another on the same.

HERE lieth one who did most truly prove,
That he could never die while he could move,
So hung his destiny never to rot
While he might still jogg on, and keep his trot,
Made of sphear-metal, never to decay
Untill his revolution was at stay.
Time numbers motion, yet (without a crime
'Gainst old truth) motion number'd out his time;
And like an Engin mov'd with wheel and waight,
His principles being ceast, he ended strait,   10
Rest that gives all men life, gave him his death,
And too much breathing put him out of breath;
Nor were it contradiction to affirm
Too long vacation hastned on his term.
Meerly to drive the time away he sickn'd,
Fainted, and died, nor would with Ale be quickn'd;
Nay, quoth he, on his swooning bed outstretch'd,
If I may not carry, sure Ile ne're be fetch'd,
But vow though the cross Doctors all stood hearers,
For one Carrier put down to make six bearers.   20
Ease was his chief disease, and to judge right,
He di'd for heavines that his Cart went light,
His leasure told him that his time was com,
And lack of load, made his life burdensom,
That even to his last breath (ther be that say't)
As he were prest to death, he cry'd more waight;
But had his doings lasted as they were,

He had bin an immortall Carrier.
Obedient to the Moon he spent his date
In cours reciprocal, and had his fate   30
Linkt to the mutual flowing of the Seas,
Yet (strange to think) his wain was his increase:
His Letters are deliver'd all and gon,
Onely remains this superscription.

L'Allegro.

HENCE loathed Melancholy
    Of *Cerberus,* and blackest midnight born,
In *Stygian* Cave forlorn
    'Mongst horrid shapes, and shreiks, and sights unholy,
Find out som uncouth cell,
    Wher brooding darknes spreads his jealous wings,
And the night-Raven sings;
    There under *Ebon* shades, and low-brow'd Rocks,
As ragged as thy Locks,
    In dark *Cimmerian* desert ever dwell.   10

But com thou Goddes fair and free,
In Heav'n ycleap'd *Euphrosyne,*
And by men, heart-easing Mirth,
Whom lovely *Venus* at a birth
With two sister Graces more
To Ivy-crowned *Bacchus* bore;
Or whether (as som Sager sing)
The frolick Wind that breathes the Spring,
Zephir with *Aurora* playing,
As he met her once a Maying,   20
There on Beds of Violets blew,
And fresh-blown Roses washt in dew,
Fill'd her with thee a daughter fair,
So bucksom, blith, and debonair.
Haste thee nymph, and bring with thee
Jest and youthful Jollity,
Quips and Cranks, and wanton Wiles,
Nods, and Becks, and Wreathed Smiles,
Such as hang on *Hebe's* cheek,
And love to live in dimple sleek;   30
Sport that wrincled Care derides,
And Laughter holding both his sides.
Com, and trip it as ye go
On the light fantastick toe,
And in thy right hand lead with thee,
The Mountain Nymph, sweet Liberty;
And if I give thee honour due,
Mirth, admit me of thy crue
To live with her, and live with thee,
In unreproved pleasures free;   40
To hear the Lark begin his flight,
And singing startle the dull night,

From his watch-towre in the skies,
Till the dappled dawn doth rise;
Then to com in spight of sorrow,
And at my window bid good morrow,
Through the Sweet-Briar, or the Vine,
Or the twisted Eglantine.
While the Cock with lively din,
Scatters the rear of darknes thin,   50
And to the stack, or the Barn dore,
Stoutly struts his Dames before,
Oft list'ning how the Hounds and horn,
Chearly rouse the slumbring morn,
From the side of som Hoar Hill,
Through the high wood echoing shrill.
Som time walking not unseen
By Hedge-row Elms, on Hillocks green,
Right against the Eastern gate,
Wher the great Sun begins his state,   60
Rob'd in flames, and Amber light,
The clouds in thousand Liveries dight.
While the Plowman neer at hand,
Whistles ore the Furrow'd Land,
And the Milkmaid singeth blithe,
And the Mower whets his sithe,
And every Shepherd tells his tale
Under the Hawthorn in the dale.
Streit mine eye hath caught new pleasures
Whilst the Lantskip round it measures,   70
Russet Lawns, and Fallows Gray,
Where the nibling flocks do stray,
Mountains on whose barren brest
The labouring clouds do often rest:
Meadows trim with Daisies pide,
Shallow Brooks, and Rivers wide.
Towers, and Battlements it sees
Boosom'd high in tufted Trees,
Wher perhaps som beauty lies,
The Cynosure of neighbouring eyes.   80
Hard by, a Cottage chimney smokes,
From betwixt two aged Okes,
Where *Corydon* and *Thyrsis* met,
Are at their savory dinner set
Of Hearbs, and other Country Messes,
Which the neat-handed *Phillis* dresses;
And then in haste her Bowre she leaves,
With *Thestylis* to bind the Sheaves;
Or if the earlier season lead
To the tann'd Haycock in the Mead,   90
Som times with secure delight
The up-land Hamlets will invite,
When the merry Bells ring round,
And the jocond rebecks sound
To many a youth, and many a maid,

Dancing in the Chequer'd shade;
And young and old com forth to play
On a Sunshine Holyday,
Till the live-long day-light fail,
Then to the Spicy Nut-brown Ale,   100
With stories told of many a feat,
How *Faery Mab* the junkets eat,
She was pincht, and pull'd she sed,
And by the Friars Lanthorn led
Tells how the drudging *Goblin* swet,
To ern his Cream-bowle duly set,
When in one night, ere glimps of morn,
His shadowy Flale hath thresh'd the Corn
That ten day-labourers could not end,
Then lies him down the Lubbar Fend.   110
And stretch'd out all the Chimney's length,
Basks at the fire his hairy strength;
And Crop-full out of dores he flings,
Ere the first Cock his Mattin rings.
Thus don the Tales, to bed they creep,
By whispering Windes soon lull'd asleep.
Towred Cities please us then,
And the busie humm of men,
Where throngs of Knights and Barons bold,
In weeds of Peace high triumphs hold,   120
With store of Ladies, whose bright eies
Rain influence, and judge the prise
Of Wit, or Arms, while both contend
To win her Grace, whom all commend.
There let *Hymen* oft appear
In Saffron robe, with Taper clear,
And pomp, and feast, and revelry,
With mask, and antique Pageantry,
Such sights as youthfull Poets dream
On Summer eeves by haunted stream.   130
Then to the well-trod stage anon,
If *Jonsons* learned Sock be on,
Or sweetest *Shakespear* fancies childe,
Warble his native Wood-notes wilde,
And ever against eating Cares,
Lap me in soft *Lydian* Aires,
Married to immortal verse
Such as the meeting soul may pierce
In notes, with many a winding bout
Of lincked sweetnes long drawn out,   140
With wanton heed, and giddy cunning,
The melting voice through mazes running;
Untwisting all the chains that ty
The hidden soul of harmony.
That *Orpheus* self may heave his head
From golden slumber on a bed
Of heapt *Elysian* flowres, and hear
Such streins as would have won the ear

Of *Pluto,* to have quite set free
His half regain'd *Eurydice.*
These delights, if thou canst give,
Mirth with thee, I mean to live.

150

Il Penseroso.

HENCE vain deluding joyes,
  The brood of folly without father bred,
How little you bested,
  Or fill the fixed mind with all your toyes;
Dwell in som idle brain,
  And fancies fond with gaudy shapes possess,
As thick and numberless
  As the gay motes that people the Sun Beams,
Or likest hovering dreams
  The fickle Pensioners of *Morpheus* train.

10

But hail thou Goddes, sage and holy,
Hail divinest Melancholy,
Whose Saintly visage is too bright
To hit the Sense of human sight;
And therfore to our weaker view,
Ore laid with black staid Wisdoms hue.
Black, but such as in esteem,
Prince *Memnons* sister might beseem,
Or that Starr'd *Ethiope* Queen that strove
To set her beauties praise above
The Sea Nymphs, and their powers offended.
Yet thou art higher far descended,
Thee bright-hair'd *Vesta* long of yore,
To solitary *Saturn* bore;
His daughter she (in *Saturns* raign,
Such mixture was not held a stain)
Oft in glimmering Bowres, and glades
He met her, and in secret shades
Of woody *Ida's* inmost grove,
While yet there was no fear of *Jove.*
Com pensive Nun, devout and pure,
Sober, stedfast, and demure,
All in a robe of darkest grain,
Flowing with majestick train,
And sable stole of *Cipres* Lawn,
Over thy decent shoulders drawn.
Com, but keep thy wonted state,
With eev'n step, and musing gate,
And looks commercing with the skies,
Thy rapt soul sitting in thine eyes:
There held in holy passion still,
Forget thy self to Marble, till
With a sad Leaden downward cast,
Thou fix them on the earth as fast.
And joyn with thee calm Peace, and Quiet,

20

30

40

Spare Fast, that oft with gods doth diet,
And hears the Muses in a ring,
Ay round about *Joves* Altar sing.
And adde to these retired leasure,
That in trim Gardens takes his pleasure;   50
But first, and chiefest, with thee bring,
Him that yon soars on golden wing,
Guiding the fiery-wheeled throne,
The Cherub Contemplation,
And the mute Silence hist along,
'Less *Philomel* will daign a Song,
In her sweetest, saddest plight,
Smoothing the rugged brow of night,
While *Cynthia* checks her Dragon yoke,
Gently o're th'accustom'd Oke;   60
Sweet Bird that shunn'st the noise of folly,
Most musicall, most melancholy!
Thee Chauntress oft the Woods among,
I woo to hear thy eeven-Song;
And missing thee, I walk unseen
On the dry smooth-shaven Green,
To behold the wandring Moon,
Riding neer her highest noon,
Like one that had bin led astray
Through the Heav'ns wide pathles way;   70
And oft, as if her head she bow'd,
Stooping through a fleecy cloud.
Oft on a Plat of rising ground,
I hear the far-off *Curfeu* sound,
Over som wide-water'd shoar,
Swinging slow with sullen roar;
Or if the Ayr will not permit,
Som still removed place will fit,
Where glowing Embers through the room
Teach light to counterfeit a gloom,   80
Far from all resort of mirth,
Save the Cricket on the hearth,
Or the Belmans drousie charm,
To bless the dores from nightly harm:
Or let my Lamp at midnight hour,
Be seen in som high lonely Towr,
Where I may oft out-watch the *Bear,*
With thrice great *Hermes,* or unsphear
The spirit of *Plato* to unfold
What Worlds, or what vast Regions hold   90
The immortal mind that hath forsook
Her mansion in this fleshly nook:
And of those *Dæmons* that are found
In fire, air, flood, or under ground,
Whose power hath a true consent
With Planet, or with Element.
Som time let Gorgeous Tragedy
In Scepter'd Pall com sweeping by,

Presenting *Thebs,* or *Pelops* line,
Or the tale of *Troy* divine.   100
Or what (though rare) of later age,
Ennobled hath the Buskind stage.
But, O sad Virgin, that thy power
Might raise *Musæus* from his bower,
Or bid the soul of *Orpheus* sing
Such notes as warbled to the string,
Drew Iron tears down *Pluto*'s cheek,
And made Hell grant what Love did seek.
Or call up him that left half told
The story of *Cambuscan* bold,   110
Of *Camball,* and of *Algarsife,*
And who had *Canace* to wife,
That own'd the vertuous Ring and Glass,
And of the wondrous Hors of Brass,
On which the *Tartar* King did ride;
And if ought els, great *Bards* beside,
In sage and solemn tunes have sung,
Of Turneys and of Trophies hung;
Of Forests, and inchantments drear,
Where more is meant then meets the ear.   120
Thus night oft see me in thy pale career,
Till civil-suited Morn appeer,
Not trickt and frounc't as she was wont,
With the Attick Boy to hunt,
But Cherchef't in a comly Cloud,
While rocking Winds are Piping loud,
Or usher'd with a shower still,
When the gust hath blown his fill,
Ending on the russling Leaves,
With minute drops from off the Eaves.   130
And when the Sun begins to fling
His flaring beams, me Goddes bring
To arched walks of twilight groves,
And shadows brown that *Sylvan* loves
Of Pine, or monumental Oake,
Where the rude Ax with heaved stroke,
Was never heard the Nymphs to daunt,
Or fright them from their hallow'd haunt.
There in close covert by som Brook,
Where no profaner eye may look,   140
Hide me from Day's garish eie,
While the Bee with Honied thie,
That at her flowry work doth sing,
And the Waters murmuring
With such consort as they keep,
Entice the dewy-feather'd Sleep;
And let som strange mysterious dream,
Wave at his Wings in Airy stream,
Of lively portrature display'd,
Softly on my eye-lids laid.   150
And as I wake, sweet musick breath

Above, about, or underneath,
Sent by som spirit to mortals good,
Or th'unseen Genius of the Wood.
But let my due feet never fail,
To walk the studious Cloysters pale,
And love the high embowed Roof,
With antick Pillars massy proof,
And storied Windows richly dight,
Casting a dimm religious light.   160
There let the pealing Organ blow,
To the full voic'd Quire below,
In Service high, and Anthems cleer,
As may with sweetnes, through mine ear,
Dissolve me into extasies,
And bring all Heav'n before mine eyes.
And may at last my weary age
Find out the peacefull hermitage,
The Hairy Gown and Mossy Cell,
Where I may sit and rightly spell,   170
Of every Star that Heav'n doth shew,
And every Herb that sips the dew;
Till old experience do attain
To somthing like Prophetic strain.
These pleasures *Melancholy* give,
And I with thee will choose to live.

Sonnets.

I

O Nightingale, that on yon bloomy Spray
  Warbl'st at eeve, when all the Woods are still,
  Thou with fresh hope the Lovers heart dost fill,
  While the jolly hours lead on propitious *May,*
Thy liquid notes that close the eye of Day,
  First heard before the shallow Cuccoo's bill
  Portend success in love; O if *Jove's* will
  Have linkt that amorous power to thy soft lay,
Now timely sing, ere the rude Bird of Hate
  Foretell my hopeles doom in som Grove ny: 10
  As thou from yeer to yeer hast sung too late
For my relief; yet hadst no reason why,
  Whether the Muse, or Love call thee his mate,
  Both them I serve, and of their train am I.

[The translation of the Italian poems is at page 110.]

II

Donna leggiadra il cui bel nome honora
  L'herbosa val di Rheno, e il nobil varco,
  Ben è colui d'ogni valore scarco
  Qual tuo spirto gentil non innamora,
Che dolcemente mostra si di fuora
  De suoi atti soavi giamai parco,
  E i don', che son d'amor saette ed arco,

Lu onde l' alta tua virtù s'infiora.
Quando tu vaga parli, o lieta canti
   Che mover possa duro alpestre legno,
   Guardi ciascun a gli occhi, ed a gli orecchi
L'entrata, chi di te si truova indegno;
   Gratia sola di sù gli vaglia, inanti   10
   Che'l disio amoroso al cuor s'invecchi.

III

Qual in colle aspro, al imbrunir di sera
   L'avezza giovinetta pastorella
   Va bagnando l'herbetta strana e bella
   Che mal si spande a disusata spera
Fuor di sua natia alma primavera,
   Cosi Amor meco insù la lingua snella
   Desta il fior novo di strania favella,
   Mentre io di te, vezzosamente altera,
Canto, dal mio buon popol non inteso
   E'l bel Tamigi cangio col bel Arno.   10
Amor lo volse, ed io a l'altrui peso
Seppi ch' Amor cosa mai volse indarno.
   Deh! foss' il mio cuor lento e'l duro seno
   A chi pianta dal ciel si buon terreno.

Canzone.

Ridonsi donne e giovani amorosi
M' accostandosi attorno, e perche scrivi,
Perche tu scrivi in lingua ignota e strana
Verseggiando d'amor, e come t'osi?
Dinne, se la tua speme sia mai vana,
E de pensieri lo miglior t' arrivi;
Cosi mi van burlando, altri rivi
Altri lidi t' aspettan, & altre onde
Nelle cui verdi sponde
Spuntati ad hor, ad hor a la tua chioma   10
L'immortal guiderdon d'eterne frondi
Perche alle spalle tue soverchia soma?
   Canzon dirotti, e tu per me rispondi
Dice mia Donna, e'l suo dir, è il mio cuore
Questa è lingua di cui si vanta Amore.

IV

Diodati, e te'l dirò con maraviglia,
   Quel ritroso io ch'amor spreggiar soléa
   E de suoi lacci spesso mi ridéa
   Gia caddi, ov'huom dabben talhor s'impiglia.
Ne treccie d'oro, ne guancia vermiglia
   M' abbaglian sì, ma sotto nova idea
   Pellegrina bellezza che'l cuor bea,
   Portamenti alti honesti, e nelle ciglia
Quel sereno fulgor d' amabil nero,
   Parole adorne di lingua piu d'una,   10

E'l cantar che di mezzo l'hemispero
Traviar ben può la faticosa Luna,
  E degli occhi suoi auventa si gran fuoco
  Che l'incerar gli orecchi mi fia poco.

V

Per certo i bei vostr'occhi Donna mia
  Esser non puo che non fian lo mio sole
  Si mi percuoton forte, come ei suole
  Per l'arene di Libia chi s'invia,
Mentre un caldo vapor (ne sentì pria)
  Da quel lato si spinge ove mi duole,
  Che forse amanti nelle lor parole
  Chiaman sospir; io non so che si sia:
Parte rinchiusa, e turbida si cela
  Scosso mi il petto, e poi n'uscendo poco   10
  Quivi d' attorno o s'agghiaccia, o s'ingiela;
Ma quanto a gli occhi giunge a trovar loco
  Tutte le notti a me suol far piovose
  Finche mia Alba rivien colma di rose.

VI

Giovane piano, e semplicetto amante
  Poi che fuggir me stesso in dubbio sono,
  Madonna a voi del mio cuor l'humil dono
  Farò divoto; io certo a prove tante
L'hebbi fedele, intrepido, costante,
  De pensieri leggiadro, accorto, e buono;
  Quando rugge il gran mondo, e scocca il tuono,
  S'arma di se, e d' intero diamante,
Tanto del forse, e d' invidia sicuro,
  Di timori, e speranze al popol use   10
  Quanto d'ingegno, e d' alto valor vago,
E di cetra sonora, e delle muse:
  Sol troverete in tal parte men duro
  Ove Amor mise l'insanabil ago.

VII

How soon hath Time the suttle theef of youth,
  Stoln on his wing my three and twentith yeer!
  My hasting dayes flie on with full career,
  But my late spring no bud or blossom shew'th.
Perhaps my semblance might deceive the truth,
  That I to manhood am arriv'd so near,
  And inward ripenes doth much less appear,
  That som more timely-happy spirits indu'th.
Yet be it less or more, or soon or slow,
  It shall be still in strictest measure eev'n,   10
  To that same lot, however mean, or high,
Toward which Time leads me, and the will of Heav'n;
  All is, if I have grace to use it so,
  As ever in my great task Masters eye.

VIII

Captain or Colonel, or Knight in Arms,
  Whose chance on these defenceless dores may sease,
  If deed of honour did thee ever please,
  Guard them, and him within protect from harms,
He can requite thee, for he knows the charms
  That call Fame on such gentle acts as these,
  And he can spred thy Name o're Lands and Seas,
  What ever clime the Suns bright circle warms.
Lift not thy spear against the Muses Bowre,
  The great *Emathian* Conqueror bid spare
  The house of *Pindarus,* when Temple and Towre
Went to the ground: And the repeated air
  Of sad *Electra*'s Poet had the power
  To save th' *Athenian* Walls from ruine bare.

IX

Lady that in the prime of earliest youth,
  Wisely hast shun'd the broad way and the green,
  And with those few art eminently seen,
  That labour up the Hill of heav'nly Truth,
The better part with *Mary,* and with *Ruth,*
  Chosen thou hast, and they that overween,
  And at thy growing vertues fret their spleen,
  No anger find in thee, but pity and ruth.
Thy care is fixt and zealously attends
  To fill thy odorous Lamp with deeds of light,
  And Hope that reaps not shame. Therefore be sure
Thou, when the Bridegroom with his feastfull friends
  Passes to bliss at the mid hour of night,
  Hast gain'd thy entrance, Virgin wise and pure.

X

Daughter to that good Earl, once President
  Of *Englands* Counsel, and her Treasury,
  Who liv'd in both, unstain'd with gold or fee,
  And left them both, more in himself content,
Till the sad breaking of that Parlament
  Broke him, as that dishonest victory
  At *Chæronéa,* fatal to liberty
  Kil'd with report that Old man eloquent,
Though later born, then to have known the dayes
  Wherin your Father flourisht, yet by you
  Madam, me thinks I see him living yet;
So well your words his noble vertues praise,
  That all both judge you to relate them true,
  And to possess them, Honour'd *Margaret.*

[The remaining sonnets are not in 1645; from 1673, unless otherwise stated.]

XI

A Book was writ of late call'd *Tetrachordon;*
    And wov'n close, both matter, form and stile;
    The Subject new: it walk'd the Town a while,
    Numbring good intellects; now seldom por'd on.
Cries the stall-reader, bless us! what a word on
    A title page is this! and some in file
    Stand spelling fals, while one might walk to Mile-
End Green. Why is it harder Sirs then Gordon,
Colkitto, or Macdonnel, or Galasp?
    Those rugged names to our like mouths grow sleek
    That would have made *Quintilian* stare and gasp.
Thy age, like ours, O Soul of Sir *John Cheek,*
    Hated not Learning wors then Toad or Asp;
    When thou taught'st *Cambridge,* and King *Edward* Greek.

XII. *On the same.*

I did but prompt the age to quit their cloggs
    By the known rules of antient libertie,
    When strait a barbarous noise environs me
    Of Owles and Cuckoes, Asses, Apes and Doggs.
As when those Hinds that were transform'd to Froggs
    Raild at *Latona's* twin-born progenie
    Which after held the Sun and Moon in fee.
    But this is got by casting Pearl to Hoggs;
That bawle for freedom in their senceless mood,
    And still revolt when truth would set them free.
    Licence they mean when they cry libertie;
For who loves that, must first be wise and good;
    But from that mark how far they roave we see
    For all this wast of wealth, and loss of blood.

To Mr. H. Lawes, *on his Aires.*

XIII

Harry whose tuneful and well measur'd Song
    First taught our English Musick how to span
    Words with just note and accent, not to scan
    With *Midas* Ears, committing short and long;
Thy worth and skill exempts thee from the throng,
    With praise enough for Envy to look wan;
    To after age thou shalt be writ the man,
    That with smooth aire couldst humor best our tongue.
Thou honour'st Verse, and Verse must lend her wing
    To honour thee, the Priest of *Phœbus* Quire
    That tun'st their happiest lines in Hymn, or Story.
Dante shall give Fame leave to set thee higher
    Then his *Casella,* whom he woo'd to sing
    Met in the milder shades of Purgatory.

XIV

When Faith and Love which parted from thee never,
  Had ripen'd thy just soul to dwell with God,
  Meekly thou didst resign this earthy load
  Of Death, call'd Life; which us from Life doth sever.
Thy Works and Alms and all thy good Endeavour
  Staid not behind, nor in the grave were trod;
  But as Faith pointed with her golden rod,
  Follow'd thee up to joy and bliss for ever.
Love led them on, and Faith who knew them best
  Thy hand-maids, clad them o're with purple beams   10
  And azure wings, that up they flew so drest,
And speak the truth of thee on glorious Theams
  Before the Judge, who thenceforth bid thee rest
  And drink thy fill of pure immortal streams.

[Sonnets XV, XVI, XVII and XXII are not in 1673; from the Cambridge MS.]

On the Lord Gen. Fairfax *at the seige of* Colchester.

XV

Fairfax, whose name in armes through Europe rings
  Filling each mouth with envy, or with praise,
  And all her jealous monarchs with amaze,
  And rumors loud, that daunt remotest kings,
Thy firm unshak'n vertue ever brings
  Victory home, though new rebellions raise
  Thir Hydra heads, & the fals North displaies
  Her brok'n league, to impe their serpent wings,
O yet a nobler task awaites thy hand;
  For what can Warr, but endless warr still breed,   10
  Till Truth, & Right from Violence be freed,
And Public Faith cleard from the shamefull brand
  Of Public Fraud. In vain doth Valour bleed
  While Avarice, & Rapine share the land.

To the Lord Generall Cromwell *May* 1652.

On the proposalls of certaine ministers at the Committee for Propagation of the Gospell.

XVI

Cromwell, our cheif of men, who through a cloud
  Not of warr onely, but detractions rude,
  Guided by faith & matchless Fortitude
  To peace & truth thy glorious way hast plough'd,
And on the neck of crowned Fortune proud
  Hast reard Gods Trophies, & his work pursu'd,
  While Darwen stream with blood of Scotts imbru'd,
  And *Dunbarr feild* resounds thy praises loud,

And Worsters laureat wreath; yet much remaines
   To conquer still; peace hath her victories   10
   No less renownd then warr, new foes aries
Threatning to bind our soules with secular chaines:
   Helpe us to save free Conscience from the paw
   Of hireling wolves whose Gospell is their maw.

To Sr *Henry Vane the younger.*

XVII

Vane, young in yeares, but in sage counsell old,
   Then whome a better Senatour nere held
   The helme of Rome, when gownes not armes repelld
   The feirce Epeirot & the African bold,
Whether to settle peace, or to unfold
   The drift of hollow states, hard to be spelld,
   Then to advise how warr may best, upheld,
   Move by her two maine nerves, Iron & Gold
In all her equipage; besides to know
   Both spirituall powre & civill, what each meanes   10
   What severs each thou 'hast learnt, which few have don.
The bounds of either sword to thee wee ow.
   Therfore on thy firme hand religion leanes
   In peace, & reck'ns thee her eldest son.

On the late Massacher in Piemont.

XVIII

Avenge O Lord thy slaughter'd Saints, whose bones
   Lie scatter'd on the Alpine mountains cold,
   Ev'n them who kept thy truth so pure of old
   When all our Fathers worship't Stocks and Stones,
Forget not: in thy book record their groanes
   Who were thy Sheep and in their antient Fold
   Slayn by the bloody *Piemontese* that roll'd
   Mother with Infant down the Rocks. Their moans
The Vales redoubl'd to the Hills, and they
   To Heav'n. Their martyr'd blood and ashes sow   10
   O're all th'*Italian* fields where still doth sway
The triple Tyrant: that from these may grow
   A hunder'd-fold, who having learnt thy way
   Early may fly the *Babylonian* wo.

XIX

When I consider how my light is spent,
   E're half my days, in this dark world and wide,
   And that one Talent which is death to hide,
   Lodg'd with me useless, though my Soul more bent
To serve therewith my Maker, and present
   My true account, least he returning chide,
   Doth God exact day-labour, light deny'd,

I fondly ask; But patience to prevent
That murmur, soon replies, God doth not need
   Either man's work or his own gifts, who best
   Bear his milde yoak, they serve him best, his State
Is Kingly. Thousands at his bidding speed
   And post o're Land and Ocean without rest:
   They also serve who only stand and waite.

XX

Lawrence of vertuous Father vertuous Son,
   Now that the Fields are dank, and ways are mire,
   Where shall we sometimes meet, and by the fire
   Help wast a sullen day; what may be won
From the hard Season gaining: time will run
   On smoother, till *Favonius* re-inspire
   The frozen earth; and cloth in fresh attire
   The Lillie and Rose, that neither sow'd nor spun.
What neat repast shall feast us, light and choice,
   Of Attick tast, with Wine, whence we may rise
   To hear the Lute well toucht, or artfull voice
Warble immortal Notes and *Tuskan* Ayre?
   He who of those delights can judge, And spare
   To interpose them oft, is not unwise.

XXI

Cyriack, whose Grandsire on the Royal Bench
   Of Brittish *Themis,* with no mean applause
   Pronounc't and in his volumes taught our Lawes,
   Which others at their Barr so often wrench;
To day deep thoughts resolve with me to drench
   In mirth, that after no repenting drawes;
   Let *Euclid* rest and *Archimedes* pause,
   And what the *Swede* intend, and what the *French.*
To measure life, learn thou betimes, and know
   Toward solid good what leads the nearest way;
   For other things mild Heav'n a time ordains,
And disapproves that care, though wise in show,
   That with superfluous burden loads the day,
   And when God sends a cheerful hour, refrains.

To Mr. Cyriack Skinner *upon his Blindness.*

XXII

Cyriack, this three years day these eys, though clear
   To outward view, of blemish or of spot;
   Bereft of light thir seeing have forgot,
   Nor to thir idle orbs doth sight appear
Of Sun or Moon or Starre throughout the year,
   Or man or woman. Yet I argue not
   Against heavns hand or will, nor bate a jot

Of heart or hope; but still bear vp and steer
Right onward. What supports me, dost thou ask?
    The conscience, Friend, to have lost them overply'd   10
    In libertyes defence, my noble task,
Of which all Europe talks from side to side.
    This thought might lead me through the world's vain mask
    Content though blind, had I no better guide.

XXIII

Methought I saw my late espoused Saint
    Brought to me like *Alcestis* from the grave,
    Whom *Joves* great Son to her glad Husband gave,
    Rescu'd from death by force though pale and faint.
Mine as whom washt from spot of child-bed taint,
    Purification in the old Law did save,
    And such, as yet once more I trust to have
    Full sight of her in Heaven without restraint,
Came vested all in white, pure as her mind:
    Her face was vail'd, yet to my fancied sight,   10
    Love, sweetness, goodness, in her person shin'd
So clear, as in no face with more delight.
    But O as to embrace me she enclin'd
    I wak'd, she fled, and day brought back my night.

Finis.

The Fifth Ode of Horace. Lib. I.

[Not in 1645; from 1673.]

Quis multa gracilis te puer in Rosa, *Rendred almost word for word without Rhyme according to the Latin Measure, as near as the Language will permit.*

    What slender Youth bedew'd with liquid odours
    Courts thee on Roses in some pleasant Cave,
        Pyrrha for whom bindst thou
        In wreaths thy golden Hair,
    Plain in thy neatness; O how oft shall he
    On Faith and changed Gods complain: and Seas
        Rough with black winds and storms
        Unwonted shall admire:
    Who now enjoyes thee credulous, all Gold,
    Who always vacant always amiable   10
        Hopes thee; of flattering gales
        Unmindfull. Hapless they
    To whom thou untry'd seem'st fair. Me in my vow'd
    Picture the sacred wall declares t' have hung
        My dank and dropping weeds
        To the stern God of Sea.

On the new forcers of Conscience under the Long PARLIAMENT.

[Not in 1645; from 1673.]

Because you have thrown of your Prelate Lord,
    And with stiff Vowes renounc'd his Liturgie
    To seise the widdow'd whore Pluralitie
    From them whose sin ye envi'd, not abhor'd,
Dare ye for this adjure the Civill Sword
    To force our Consciences that Christ set free,
    And ride us with a classic Hierarchy
    Taught ye by meer *A. S.* and *Rotherford?*
Men whose Life, Learning, Faith and pure intent
    Would have been held in high esteem with *Paul*   10
    Must now be nam'd and printed Hereticks
By shallow *Edwards* and Scotch what d'ye call:
    But we do hope to find out all your tricks,
    Your plots and packing wors then those of *Trent,*
              That so the Parliament
May with their wholsom and preventive Shears
Clip your Phylacteries, though bauk your Ears,
             And succour our just Fears
When they shall read this clearly in your charge
New Presbyter is but *Old Priest* writ Large.   20

Arcades.

Part of an entertainment presented to the Countess Dowager of *Darby* at *Harefield,* by som Noble persons of her Family, who appear on the Scene in pastoral habit, moving toward the seat of State, with this Song.

1. SONG

Look Nymphs, and Shepherds look,
What sudden blaze of majesty
Is that which we from hence descry
Too divine to be mistook:
    This this is she
To whom our vows and wishes bend,
Heer our solemn search hath end.

Fame that her high worth to raise,
Seem'd erst so lavish and profuse,
We may justly now accuse
Of detraction from her praise,   10
    Less then half we find exprest,
    Envy bid conceal the rest.

Mark what radiant state she spreds,
In circle round her shining throne,
Shooting her beams like silver threds,
This this is she alone,
    Sitting like a Goddes bright,
    In the center of her light.

Might she the wise *Latona* be,
Or the towred *Cybele*,
Mother of a hunderd gods;
Juno dare's not give her odds;
    Who had thought this clime had held
    A deity so unparalel'd?

As they com forward, the Genius of the Wood appears, and turning toward them, speaks.

Gen. Stay gentle Swains, for though in this disguise,
I see bright honour sparkle through your eyes,
Of famous *Arcady* ye are, and sprung
Of that renowned flood, so often sung,
Divine *Alpheus,* who by secret sluse,   30
Stole under Seas to meet his *Arethuse;*
And ye the breathing Roses of the Wood,
Fair silver-buskind Nymphs as great and good,
I know this quest of yours, and free intent
Was all in honour and devotion ment
To the great Mistres of yon princely shrine,
Whom with low reverence I adore as mine,
And with all helpful service will comply
To further this nights glad solemnity;
And lead ye where ye may more neer behold   40
What shallow-searching *Fame* hath left untold;
Which I full oft amidst these shades alone
Have sate to wonder at, and gaze upon:
For know by lot from *Jove* I am the powr
Of this fair Wood, and live in Oak'n bowr,
To nurse the Saplings tall, and curl the grove
With Ringlets quaint, and wanton windings wove.
And all my Plants I save from nightly ill,
Of noisom winds, and blasting vapours chill.
And from the Boughs brush off the evil dew,   50
And heal the harms of thwarting thunder blew,
Or what the cross dire-looking Planet smites,
Or hurtfull Worm with canker'd venom bites.
When Eev'ning gray doth rise, I fetch my round
Over the mount, and all this hallow'd ground,
And early ere the odorous breath of morn
Awakes the slumbring leaves, or tasseld horn
Shakes the high thicket, haste I all about,
Number my ranks, and visit every sprout
With puissant words, and murmurs made to bless,   60
But els in deep of night when drowsines
Hath lockt up mortal sense, then listen I
To the celestial *Sirens* harmony,
That sit upon the nine enfolded Sphears,
And sing to those that hold the vital shears,
And turn the Adamantine spindle round,
On which the fate of gods and men is wound.
Such sweet compulsion doth in musick ly,
To lull the daughters of *Necessity,*
And keep unsteddy Nature to her law,   70

And the low world in measur'd motion draw
After the heavenly tune, which none can hear
Of human mould with grosse unpurged ear;
And yet such musick worthiest were to blaze
The peerles height of her immortal praise,
Whose lustre leads us, and for her most fit,
If my inferior hand or voice could hit
Inimitable sounds, yet as we go,
What ere the skill of lesser gods can show,
I will assay, her worth to celebrate,   80
And so attend ye toward her glittering state;
Where ye may all that are of noble stemm
Approach, and kiss her sacred vestures hemm.

2. SONG

O're the smooth enameld green
Where no print of step hath been,
  Follow me as I sing,
  And touch the warbled string.
Under the shady roof
Of branching Elm Star-proof,
  Follow me,   90
I will bring you where she sits,
Clad in splendor as befits
  Her deity.
Such a rural Queen
All *Arcadia* hath not seen.

3. SONG

Nymphs and Shepherds dance no more
By sandy *Ladons* Lillied banks.
On old *Lycæus* or *Cyllene* hoar,
  Trip no more in twilight ranks,
Though *Erymanth* your loss deplore,   100
  A better soyl shall give ye thanks.
From the stony *Mænalus,*
Bring your Flocks, and live with us,
Here ye shall have greater grace,
To serve the Lady of this place.
  Though *Syrinx* your *Pans* Mistres were,
  Yet *Syrinx* well might wait on her.
  Such a rural Queen
All *Arcadia* hath not seen.

Lycidas.

In this Monody the Author bewails a learned Friend, unfortunatly drown'd in his Passage from *Chester* on the *Irish* Seas, 1637. And by occasion foretels the ruine of our corrupted Clergy then in their height.

Yet once more, O ye Laurels, and once more
Ye Myrtles brown, with Ivy never-sear,
I com to pluck your Berries harsh and crude,
And with forc'd fingers rude,
Shatter your leaves before the mellowing year.

Bitter constraint, and sad occasion dear,
Compels me to disturb your season due:
For *Lycidas* is dead, dead ere his prime
Young *Lycidas,* and hath not left his peer:
Who would not sing for *Lycidas?* he knew
Himself to sing, and build the lofty rhyme.
He must not flote upon his watry bear
Unwept, and welter to the parching wind,
Without the meed of som melodious tear.
  Begin then, Sisters of the sacred well,
That from beneath the seat of *Jove* doth spring,
Begin, and somwhat loudly sweep the string.
Hence with denial vain, and coy excuse,
So may som gentle Muse
With lucky words favour my destin'd Urn,
And as he passes turn,
And bid fair peace be to my sable shrowd.
For we were nurst upon the self-same hill,
Fed the same flock; by fountain, shade, and rill.
  Together both, ere the high Lawns appear'd
Under the opening eye-lids of the morn,
We drove a field, and both together heard
What time the Gray-fly winds her sultry horn,
Batt'ning our flocks with the fresh dews of night,
Oft till the Star that rose, at Ev'ning, bright
Toward Heav'ns descent had slop'd his westering wheel.
Mean while the Rural ditties were not mute,
Temper'd to th'Oaten Flute,
Rough *Satyrs* danc'd, and *Fauns* with clov'n heel,
From the glad sound would not be absent long,
And old *Damœtas* lov'd to hear our song.
  But O the heavy change, now thou art gon,
Now thou art gon, and never must return!
Thee Shepherd, thee the Woods, and desert Caves,
With wilde Thyme and the gadding Vine o'regrown,
And all their echoes mourn.
The Willows, and the Hazle Copses green,
Shall now no more be seen,
Fanning their joyous Leaves to thy soft layes.
As killing as the Canker to the Rose,
Or Taint-worm to the weanling Herds that graze,
Or Frost to Flowers, that their gay wardrop wear,
When first the White thorn blows;
Such, *Lycidas,* thy loss to Shepherds ear.
  Where were ye Nymphs when the remorseless deep
Clos'd o're the head of your lov'd *Lycidas?*
For neither were ye playing on the steep,
Where your old *Bards,* the famous *Druids* ly,
Nor on the shaggy top of *Mona* high,
Nor yet where *Deva* spreads her wisard stream:
Ay me, I fondly dream!
Had ye bin there—for what could that have don?
What could the Muse her self that *Orpheus* bore,

The Muse her self, for her inchanting son
Whom Universal nature did lament, 60
When by the rout that made the hideous roar,
His goary visage down the stream was sent,
Down the swift *Hebrus* to the *Lesbian* shore.
     Alas! What boots it with uncessant care
To tend the homely slighted Shepherds trade,
And strictly meditate the thankles Muse,
Were it not better don as others use,
To sport with *Amaryllis* in the shade,
Or with the tangles of *Neæra*'s hair?
Fame is the spur that the clear spirit doth raise 70
(That last infirmity of Noble mind)
To scorn delights, and live laborious dayes;
But the fair Guerdon when we hope to find,
And think to burst out into sudden blaze,
Comes the blind *Fury* with th'abhorred shears,
And slits the thin-spun life. But not the praise,
Phœbus repli'd, and touch'd my trembling ears;
Fame is no plant that grows on mortal soil,
Nor in the glistering foil
Set off to th'world, nor in broad rumour lies, 80
But lives and spreds aloft by those pure eyes,
And perfet witnes of all judging *Jove;*
As he pronounces lastly on each deed,
Of so much fame in Heav'n expect thy meed.
     O Fountain *Arethuse,* and thou honour'd floud,
Smooth-sliding *Mincius,* crown'd with vocall reeds,
That strain I heard was of a higher mood:
But now my Oate proceeds,
And listens to the Herald of the Sea
That came in *Neptune*'s plea, 90
He ask'd the Waves, and ask'd the Fellon winds,
What hard mishap hath doom'd this gentle swain?
And question'd every gust of rugged wings
That blows from off each beaked Promontory,
They knew not of his story,
And sage *Hippotades* their answer brings,
That not a blast was from his dungeon stray'd,
The Ayr was calm, and on the level brine,
Sleek *Panope* with all her sisters play'd.
It was that fatall and perfidious Bark 100
Built in th'eclipse, and rigg'd with curses dark,
That sunk so low that sacred head of thine.
     Next *Camus,* reverend Sire, went footing slow,
His Mantle hairy, and his Bonnet sedge,
Inwrought with figures dim, and on the edge
Like to that sanguine flower inscrib'd with woe.
Ah! Who hath reft (quoth he) my dearest pledge?
Last came, and last did go,
The Pilot of the *Galilean* lake,
Two massy Keyes he bore of metals twain, 110
(The Golden opes, the Iron shuts amain)

He shook his Miter'd locks, and stern bespake,
How well could I have spar'd for thee young swain,
Anow of such as for their bellies sake,
Creep and intrude, and climb into the fold?
Of other care they little reck'ning make,
Then how to scramble at the shearers feast,
And shove away the worthy bidden guest.
Blind mouthes! that scarce themselves know how to hold
A Sheep-hook, or have learn'd ought els the least   120
That to the faithfull Herdmans art belongs!
What recks it them? What need they? They are sped;
And when they list, their lean and flashy songs
Grate on their scrannel Pipes of wretched straw,
The hungry Sheep look up, and are not fed,
But swoln with wind, and the rank mist they draw,
Rot inwardly, and foul contagion spread:
Besides what the grim Woolf with privy paw
Daily devours apace, and nothing sed,
But that two-handed engine at the door,   130
Stands ready to smite once, and smite no more.
    Return *Alpheus,* the dread voice is past,
That shrunk thy streams; Return *Sicilian* Muse,
And call the Vales, and bid them hither cast
Their Bels, and Flourets of a thousand hues.
Ye valleys low where the milde whispers use,
Of shades and wanton winds, and gushing brooks,
On whose fresh lap the swart Star sparely looks,
Throw hither all your quaint enameld eyes,
That on the green terf suck the honied showres,   140
And purple all the ground with vernal flowres.
Bring the rathe Primrose that forsaken dies.
The tufted Crow-toe, and pale Gessamine,
The white Pink, and the Pansie freakt with jeat,
The glowing Violet.
The Musk-rose, and the well attir'd Woodbine,
With Cowslips wan that hang the pensive hed,
And every flower that sad embroidery wears:
Bid *Amaranthus* all his beauty shed,
And Daffadillies fill their cups with tears,   150
To strew the Laureat Herse where *Lycid* lies.
For so to interpose a little ease,
Let our frail thoughts dally with false surmise.
Ay me! Whilst thee the shores, and sounding Seas
Wash far away, where ere thy bones are hurld,
Whether beyond the stormy *Hebrides,*
Where thou perhaps under the whelming tide
Visit'st the bottom of the monstrous world;
Or whether thou to our moist vows deny'd,
Sleep'st by the fable of *Bellerus* old,   160
Where the great vision of the guarded Mount
Looks toward *Namancos* and *Bayona's* hold;
Look homeward Angel now, and melt with ruth.
And, O ye *Dolphins,* waft the haples youth.

Weep no more, woful Shepherds weep no more,
For *Lycidas* your sorrow is not dead,
Sunk though he be beneath the watry floar,
So sinks the day-star in the Ocean bed,
And yet anon repairs his drooping head,
And tricks his beams, and with new spangled Ore,   170
Flames in the forehead of the morning sky:
So *Lycidas* sunk low, but mounted high,
Through the dear might of him that walk'd the waves
Where other groves, and other streams along,
With *Nectar* pure his oozy Lock's he laves,
And hears the unexpressive nuptiall Song,
In the blest Kingdoms meek of joy and love.
There entertain him all the Saints above,
In solemn troops, and sweet Societies
That sing, and singing in their glory move,   180
And wipe the tears for ever from his eyes.
Now *Lycidas* the Shepherds weep no more;
Hence forth thou art the Genius of the shore,
In thy large recompense, and shalt be good
To all that wander in that perilous flood.
    Thus sang the uncouth Swain to th'Okes and rills,
While the still morn went out with Sandals gray,
He touch'd the tender stops of various Quills,
With eager thought warbling his *Dorick* lay:
And now the Sun had stretch'd out all the hills,   190
And now was dropt into the Western bay;
At last he rose, and twitch'd his Mantle blew:
To morrow to fresh Woods, and Pastures new.

A

MASK

of the same Author

PRESENTED

At LUDLOW-Castle,
1634.

To the Right Honourable, John Lord Vicount
Bracly, Son and Heir apparent to the
Earl of *Bridgewater*, &c.

My Lord,
    *This Poem, which receiv'd its first occasion of Birth from your Self, and others of
your Noble Family, and much honour from your own Person in the performance, now
returns again to make a finall Dedication of it self to you. Although not openly acknowledg'd by the Author, yet it is a legitimate off-spring, so lovely, and so much desired, that
the often Copying of it hath tir'd my Pen to give my severall friends satisfaction, and
brought me to a necessity of producing it to the publike view; and now to offer it up*

in all rightfull devotion to those fair Hopes, and rare Endowments of your much-promising Youth, which give a full assurance, to all that know you, of a future excellence. Live sweet Lord to be the honour of your Name, and receive this as your own, from the hands of him, who hath by many favours been long oblig'd to your most honour'd Parents, and as in this representation your attendant Thyrsis, *so now in all reall expression*

> Your faithfull, and most
> humble Servant
> H. Lawes.

The Copy of a Letter writt'n by Sir Henry Wootton, to the Author, upon the following Poem.

From the Colledge, this 13. *of April,* 1638.

SIR,

It was a special favour, when you lately bestowed upon me here, the first taste of your acquaintance, though no longer then to make me know that I wanted more time to value it, and to enjoy it rightly; and in truth, if I could then have imagined your farther stay in these parts, which I understood afterwards by Mr. *H.*, I would have been bold in our vulgar phrase to mend my draught (for you left me with an extreme thirst) and to have begged your conversation again, joyntly with your said learned Friend, at a poor meal or two, that we might have banded together som good Authors of the antient time: Among which, I observed you to have been familiar.

Since your going, you have charg'd me with new Obligations, both for a very kinde Letter from you dated the sixth of this Month, and for a dainty peece of entertainment which came therwith. Wherin I should much commend the Tragical part, if the Lyrical did not ravish me with a certain Dorique delicacy in your Songs and Odes, wherunto I must plainly confess to have seen yet nothing parallel in our Language: *Ipsa mollities.* But I must not omit to tell you, that I now onely owe you thanks for intimating unto me (how modestly soever) the true Artificer. For the work it self I had view'd som good while before, with singular delight, having receiv'd it from our common Friend Mr. *R.* in the very close of the late *R's* Poems, Printed at *Oxford,* wherunto it was added (as I now suppose) that the Accessory might help out the Principal, according to the Art of *Stationers,* and to leave the Reader *Con la bocca dolce.*

Now Sir, concerning your travels, wherin I may chalenge a little more priviledge of Discours with you; I suppose you will not blanch *Paris* in your way; therfore I have been bold to trouble you with a few lines to Mr. *M. B.* whom you shall easily find attending the young Lord *S.* as his Governour, and you may surely receive from him good directions for the shaping of your farther journey into *Italy,* where he did reside by my choice som time for the King, after mine own recess from *Venice.*

I should think that your best Line will be thorow the whole length of *France* to *Marseilles,* and thence by Sea to *Genoa,* whence the passage into *Tuscany* is as Diurnal as a *Gravesend* Barge: I hasten as you do to *Florence,* or *Siena,* the rather to tell you a short story from the interest you have given me in your safety.

At *Siena* I was tabled in the House of one *Alberto Scipioni* an old *Roman* Courtier in dangerous times, having bin Steward to the *Duca di Pagliano,* who with all his Family were strangled, save this onely man that escap'd by foresight of the Tempest: With him I had often much chat of those affairs; Into which he took pleasure to look back from his Native Harbour; and at my departure toward *Rome* (which had been the center of his experience) I had wonn confidence enough to beg his advice, how I might carry my self securely there, without offence of others, or of mine own conscience. *Signor Arrigo mio* (sayes he) *I pensieri stretti, & il viso sciolto* will go safely over the whole World:

Of which *Delphian* Oracle (for so I have found it) your judgement doth need no commentary; and therfore (Sir) I will commit you with it to the best of all securities, Gods dear love, remaining

Your Friend as much at command
as any of longer date
Henry Wootton.

Postscript.

SIR, *I have expresly sent this my Foot-boy to prevent your departure without som acknowledgement from me of the receipt of your obliging Letter, having my self through som busines, I know not how, neglected the ordinary conveyance. In any part where I shall understand you fixed, I shall be glad, and diligent to entertain you with Home-Novelties; even for som fomentation of our friendship, too soon interrupted in the Cradle.*

The Persons

The attendant Spirit afterwards in the habit of *Thyrsis.*
Comus with his crew.
The Lady.
1. Brother.
2. Brother.
Sabrina the Nymph.

The cheif persons which presented, were

The Lord *Bracly,*
Mr. *Thomas Egerton* his Brother,
The Lady *Alice Egerton.*

A
MASK

PRESENTED

At LUDLOW-Castle,
1634. &c.

The first Scene discovers a wilde Wood.

The attendant Spirit descends or enters.

BEFORE the starry threshold of *Joves* Court
My mansion is, where those immortal shapes
Of bright aëreal Spirits live insphear'd
In Regions milde of calm and serene Ayr,
Above the smoak and stirr of this dim spot,
Which men call Earth, and with low-thoughted care
Confin'd, and pester'd in this pin-fold here,
Strive to keep up a frail, and Feaverish being
Unmindfull of the crown that Vertue gives
After this mortal change, to her true Servants   10
Amongst the enthron'd gods on Sainted seats.
Yet som there be that by due steps aspire
To lay their just hands on that Golden Key
That ope's the Palace of Eternity:
To such my errand is, and but for such,
I would not soil these pure Ambrosial weeds,

With the rank vapours of this Sin-worn mould.
　　But to my task. *Neptune* besides the sway
Of every salt Flood, and each ebbing Stream,
Took in by lot 'twixt high, and neather *Jove,*　　　　20
Imperial rule of all the Sea-girt Iles
That like to rich, and various gemms inlay
The unadorned boosom of the Deep,
Which he to grace his tributary gods
By course commits to severall goverment.
And gives them leave to wear their Saphire crowns,
And weild their little tridents, but this Ile
The greatest, and the best of all the main
He quarters to his blu-hair'd deities,
And all this tract that fronts the falling Sun　　　　30
A noble Peer of mickle trust, and power
Has in his charge, with temper'd awe to guide
An old, and haughty Nation proud in Arms:
Where his fair off-spring nurs't in Princely lore,
Are coming to attend their Fathers state,
And new-entrusted Scepter, but their way
Lies through the perplex't paths of this drear Wood,
The nodding horror of whose shady brows
Threats the forlorn and wandring Passinger.
And here their tender age might suffer perill,　　　　40
But that by quick command from Soveran *Jove*
I was dispatcht for their defence, and guard;
And listen why, for I will tell ye now
What never yet was heard in Tale or Song
From old, or modern Bard in Hall, or Bowr.
　　Bacchus that first from out the purple Grape,
Crush't the sweet poyson of mis-used Wine
After the *Tuscan* Mariners transform'd
Coasting the *Tyrrhene* shore, as the winds listed,
On *Circes* Iland fell (who knows not *Circe*　　　　50
The daughter of the Sun? Whose charmed Cup
Whoever tasted, lost his upright shape,
And downward fell into a groveling Swine)
This Nymph that gaz'd upon his clustring locks,
With Ivy berries wreath'd, and his blithe youth,
Had by him, ere he parted thence, a Son
Much like his Father, but his Mother more,
Whom therfore she brought up and *Comus* nam'd,
Who ripe, and frolick of his full grown age,
Roaving the *Celtick,* and *Iberian* fields,　　　　60
At last betakes him to this ominous Wood,
And in thick shelter of black shades imbowr'd,
Excells his Mother at her mighty Art,
Offring to every weary Travailer,
His orient liquor in a Crystal Glasse,
To quench the drouth of *Phœbus,* which as they taste
(For most do taste through fond intemperate thirst)
Soon as the Potion works, their human count'nance,
Th' express resemblance of the gods, is chang'd

Into som brutish form of Woolf, or Bear,
Or Ounce, or Tiger, Hog, or bearded Goat,
All other parts remaining as they were,
And they, so perfect is their misery,
Not once perceive their foul disfigurement,
But boast themselves more comely then before
And all their friends, and native home forget
To roule with pleasure in a sensual stie.
Therfore when any favour'd of high *Jove*,
Chances to passe through this adventrous glade,
Swift as the Sparkle of a glancing Star,   80
I shoot from Heav'n to give him safe convoy,
As now I do: But first I must put off
These my skie robes spun out of *Iris* Wooff,
And take the Weeds and likenes of a Swain,
That to the service of this house belongs,
Who with his soft Pipe, and smooth-dittied Song,
Well knows to still the wilde winds when they roar,
And hush the waving Woods, nor of lesse faith,
And in this office of his Mountain watch,
Likeliest, and neerest to the present ayd   90
Of this occasion. But I hear the tread
Of hatefull steps, I must be viewles now.

Comus *enters with a Charming Rod in one hand, his Glass in the other, with him a rout of Monsters headed like sundry sorts of wilde Beasts, but otherwise like Men and Women, their Apparel glistring, they com in making a riotous and unruly noise, with Torches in their hands.*

Comus. The Star that bids the Shepherd fold,
Now the top of Heav'n doth hold,
And the gilded Car of Day,
His glowing Axle doth allay
In the steep *Atlantick* stream,
And the slope Sun his upward beam
Shoots against the dusky Pole,
Pacing toward the other gole   100
Of his Chamber in the East.
Mean while welcom Joy, and Feast,
Midnight shout, and revelry,
Tipsie dance, and Jollity.
Braid your Locks with rosie Twine
Dropping odours, dropping Wine.
Rigor now is gon to bed,
And Advice with scrupulous head,
Strict Age, and sowre Severity,
With their grave Saws in slumber ly.   110
We that are of purer fire
Imitate the Starry Quire,
Who in their nightly watchfull Sphears,
Lead in swift round the Months and Years.
The Sounds, and Seas with all their finny drove
Now to the Moon in wavering Morrice move,
And on the Tawny Sands and Shelves,
Trip the pert Fairies and the dapper Elves;

By dimpled Brook, and Fountain brim,
The Wood-Nymphs deckt with Daisies trim,   120
Their merry wakes and pastimes keep:
What hath night to do with sleep?
Night hath better sweets to prove,
Venus now wakes, and wak'ns Love.
Com let us our rights begin,
Tis onely day-light that makes Sin
Which these dun shades will ne're report.
Hail Goddesse of Nocturnal sport
Dark vaild *Cotytto,* t' whom the secret flame
Of mid-night Torches burns; mysterious Dame   130
That ne're art call'd, but when the Dragon woom
Of Stygian darknes spets her thickest gloom,
And makes one blot of all the ayr,
Stay thy cloudy Ebon chair,
Wherin thou rid'st with *Hecat',* and befriend
Us thy vow'd Priests, till utmost end
Of all thy dues be done, and none left out,
Ere the blabbing Eastern scout,
The nice Morn on th' *Indian* steep
From her cabin'd loop hole, peep,   140
And to the tel-tale Sun discry
Our conceal'd Solemnity.
Com, knit hands, and beat the ground,
In a light fantastick round.

The Measure.

Break off, break off, I feel the different pace,
Of som chast footing neer about this ground.
Run to your shrouds, within these Brakes and Trees,
Our number may affright: Som Virgin sure
(For so I can distinguish by mine Art)
Benighted in these Woods. Now to my charms,   150
And to my wily trains, I shall e're long
Be well stock't with as fair a herd as graz'd
About my Mother *Circe.* Thus I hurl
My dazling Spells into the spungy ayr,
Of power to cheat the eye with blear illusion,
And give it false presentments, lest the place
And my quaint habits breed astonishment,
And put the Damsel to suspicious flight,
Which must not be, for that's against my course;
I under fair pretence of friendly ends,   160
And well plac't words of glozing courtesie
Baited with reasons not unplausible
Wind me into the easie-hearted man,
And hugg him into snares. When once her eye
Hath met the vertue of this Magick dust,
I shall appear som harmles Villager
And hearken, if I may her busines hear.
But here she comes, I fairly step aside.

The Lady enters.

This way the noise was, if mine ear be true,
My best guide now, me thought it was the sound   170
Of Riot, and ill manag'd Merriment,
Such as the jocond Flute, or gamesom Pipe
Stirs up among the loose unleter'd Hinds,
When for their teeming Flocks, and granges full
In wanton dance they praise the bounteous *Pan,*
And thank the gods amiss. I should be loath
To meet the rudenesse, and swill'd insolence
Of such late Wassailers; yet O where els
Shall I inform my unacquainted feet
In the blind mazes of this tangl'd Wood?   180
My Brothers when they saw me wearied out
With this long way, resolving here to lodge
Under the spreading favour of these Pines,
Stept as they se'd to the next Thicket side
To bring me Berries, or such cooling fruit
As the kind hospitable Woods provide.
They left me then, when the gray-hooded Eev'n
Like a sad Votarist in Palmers weed
Rose from the hindmost wheels of *Phœbus* wain.
But where they are, and why they came not back,   190
Is now the labour of my thoughts, 'tis likeliest
They had ingag'd their wandring steps too far,
And envious darknes, e're they could return,
Had stole them from me, els O theevish Night
Why shouldst thou, but for som fellonious end,
In thy dark lantern thus close up the Stars,
That nature hung in Heav'n, and fill'd their Lamps
With everlasting oil, to give due light
To the misled and lonely Travailer?
This is the place, as well as I may guess,   200
Whence eev'n now the tumult of loud Mirth
Was rife, and perfet in my list'ning ear,
Yet nought but single darknes do I find.
What might this be? A thousand fantasies
Begin to throng into my memory
Of calling shapes, and beckning shadows dire,
And airy tongues, that syllable mens names
On Sands, and Shoars, and desert Wildernesses.
These thoughts may startle well, but not astound
The vertuous mind, that ever walks attended   210
By a strong siding champion Conscience.——
O welcom pure-ey'd Faith, white-handed Hope,
Thou hovering Angel girt with golden wings,
And thou unblemish't form of Chastity,
I see ye visibly, and now beleeve
That he, the Supreme good, t' whom all things ill
Are but as slavish officers of vengeance,
Would send a glistring Guardian if need were
To keep my life and honour unassail'd.

Was I deceiv'd, or did a sable cloud   220
Turn forth her silver lining on the night?
I did not err, there does a sable cloud
Turn forth her silver lining on the night,
And casts a gleam over this tufted Grove.
I cannot hallow to my Brothers, but
Such noise as I can make to be heard farthest
Ile venter, for my new enliv'nd spirits
Prompt me; and they perhaps are not far off.

SONG.

> Sweet Echo, sweetest Nymph that liv'st unseen
> Within thy airy shell   230
> By slow Meander's margent green,
> And in the violet imbroider'd vale
> Where the love-lorn Nightingale
> Nightly to thee her sad Song mourneth well.
> Canst thou not tell me of a gentle Pair
> That likest thy Narcissus are?
> O if thou have
> Hid them in som flowry Cave,
> Tell me but where
> Sweet Queen of Parly, Daughter of the Sphear,   240
> So maist thou be translated to the skies,
> And give resounding grace to all Heav'ns Harmonies.

Com. Can any mortal mixture of Earths mould
Breath such Divine inchanting ravishment?
Sure somthing holy lodges in that brest,
And with these raptures moves the vocal air
To testifie his hidd'n residence;
How sweetly did they float upon the wings
Of silence, through the empty-vaulted night
At every fall smoothing the Raven doune   250
Of darknes till it smil'd: I have oft heard
My mother *Circe* with the Sirens three,
Amidst the flowry-kirtl'd *Naiades*
Culling their Potent hearbs, and balefull drugs,
Who as they sung, would take the prison'd soul,
And lap it in *Elysium, Scylla* wept,
And chid her barking waves into attention,
And fell *Charybdis* murmur'd soft applause:
Yet they in pleasing slumber lull'd the sense,
And in sweet madnes rob'd it of it self,   260
But such a sacred, and home-felt delight,
Such sober certainty of waking bliss
I never heard till now. Ile speak to her
And she shall be my Queen. Hail forren wonder
Whom certain these rough shades did never breed
Unlesse the Goddes that in rurall shrine
Dwell'st here with *Pan,* or *Silvan,* by blest Song
Forbidding every bleak unkindly Fog

To touch the prosperous growth of this tall Wood.

La. Nay gentle Shepherd ill is lost that praise 270
That is addrest to unattending Ears,
Not any boast of skill, but extreme shift
How to regain my sever'd company
Compell'd me to awake the courteous Echo
To give me answer from her mossie Couch.

Co. What chance good Lady hath bereft you thus?

La. Dim darknes, and this leavy Labyrinth.

Co. Could that divide you from neer-ushering guides?

La. They left me weary on a grassie terf.

Co. By falshood, or discourtesie, or why? 280

La. To seek i'th vally som cool friendly Spring.

Co. And left your fair side all unguarded Lady?

La. They were but twain, and purpos'd quick return.

Co. Perhaps fore-stalling night prevented them.

La. How easie my misfortune is to hit!

Co. Imports their loss, beside the present need?

La. No less then if I should my brothers loose.

Co. Were they of manly prime, or youthful bloom?

La. As smooth as *Hebe*'s their unrazor'd lips.

Co. Two such I saw, what time the labour'd Oxe 290
In his loose traces from the furrow came,
And the swink't hedger at his Supper sate;
I saw them under a green mantling vine
That crawls along the side of yon small hill,
Plucking ripe clusters from the tender shoots,
Their port was more then human, as they stood;
I took it for a faëry vision
Of som gay creatures of the element
That in the colours of the Rainbow live
And play i'th plighted clouds. I was aw-strook, 300
And as I past, I worshipt; if those you seek
It were a journey like the path to Heav'n,
To help you find them. *La.* Gentle villager
What readiest way would bring me to that place?

Co. Due west it rises from this shrubby point.

La. To find out that, good Shepherd, I suppose,
In such a scant allowance of Star-light,
Would overtask the best Land-Pilots art,
Without the sure guess of well-practiz'd feet.

Co. I know each lane, and every alley green 310
Dingle, or bushy dell of this wilde Wood,
And every bosky bourn from side to side
My daily walks and ancient neighbourhood,
And if your stray attendance be yet lodg'd,
Or shroud within these limits, I shall know
Ere morrow wake, or the low-roosted lark
From her thatch't pallat rowse, if otherwise
I can conduct you Lady to a low
But loyal cottage, where you may be safe
Till further quest'. *La.* Shepherd I take thy word, 320
And trust thy honest offer'd courtesie,

Which oft is sooner found in lowly sheds
With smoaky rafters, then in tapstry Halls
And Courts of Princes, where it first was nam'd,
And yet is most pretended: In a place
Less warranted then this, or less secure
I cannot be, that I should fear to change it.
Eie me blest Providence, and square my triall
To my proportiond'd strength. Shepherd lead on.——

The two Brothers.

Eld. Bro. Unmuffle ye faint stars, and thou fair Moon   330
That wontst to love the travailers benizon,
Stoop thy pale visage through an amber cloud,
And disinherit *Chaos,* that raigns here
In double night of darknes, and of shades;
Or if your influence be quite damm'd up
With black usurping mists, som gentle taper
Though a rush Candle from the wicker hole
Of som clay habitation visit us
With thy long levell'd rule of streaming light,
And thou shalt be our star of *Arcady,*   340
Or *Tyrian* Cynosure. *2. Bro.* Or if our eyes
Be barr'd that happines, might we but hear
The folded flocks pen'd in their watled cotes,
Or sound of pastoral reed with oaten stops,
Or whistle from the Lodge, or village cock
Count the night watches to his feathery Dames,
'Twould be som solace yet, som little chearing
In this close dungeon of innumerous bowes.
But O that haples virgin our lost sister
Where may she wander now, whether betake her   350
From the chill dew, amongst rude burrs and thistles?
Perhaps som cold bank is her boulster now
Or 'gainst the rugged bark of som broad Elm
Leans her unpillow'd head fraught with sad fears.
What if in wild amazement, and affright,
Or while we speak within the direfull grasp
Of Savage hunger, or of Savage heat?
Eld. Bro. Peace brother, be not over-exquisite
To cast the fashion of uncertain evils;
For grant they be so, while they rest unknown,   360
What need a man forestall his date of grief,
And run to meet what he would most avoid?
Or if they be but false alarms of Fear,
How bitter is such self-delusion?
I do not think my sister so to seek,
Or so unprincipl'd in vertues book,
And the sweet peace that goodnes boosoms ever,
As that the single want of light and noise
(Not being in danger, as I trust she is not)
Could stir the constant mood of her calm thoughts,   370
And put them into mis-becoming plight.

Vertue could see to do what vertue would
By her own radiant light, though Sun and Moon
Were in the flat Sea sunk. And Wisdoms self
Oft seeks to sweet retired Solitude,
Where with her best nurse Contemplation
She plumes her feathers, and lets grow her wings
That in the various bussle of resort
Were all to ruffl'd, and somtimes impair'd.
He that has light within his own cleer brest
May sit i'th center, and enjoy bright day,   380
But he that hides a dark soul, and foul thoughts
Benighted walks under the mid-day Sun;
Himself is his own dungeon.
   2. *Bro.* Tis most true
That musing meditation most affects
The Pensive secrecy of desert cell,
Far from the cheerfull haunt of men, and herds,
And sits as safe as in a Senat house,
For who would rob a Hermit of his Weeds,
His few Books, or his Beads, or Maple Dish,   390
Or do his gray hairs any violence?
But beauty like the fair Hesperian Tree
Laden with blooming gold, had need the guard
Of dragon watch with uninchanted eye,
To save her blossoms, and defend her fruit
From the rash hand of bold Incontinence.
You may as well spred out the unsun'd heaps
Of Misers treasure by an out-laws den,
And tell me it is safe, as bid me hope
Danger will wink on Opportunity,   400
And let a single helpless maiden pass
Uninjur'd in this wilde surrounding wast.
Of night, or lonelines it recks me not,
I fear the dred events that dog them both,
Lest som ill greeting touch attempt the person
Of our unowned sister.
   Eld. Bro. I do not, brother,
Inferr, as if I thought my sisters state
Secure without all doubt, or controversie:
Yet where an equall poise of hope and fear
Does arbitrate th'event, my nature is   410
That I encline to hope, rather then fear,
And gladly banish squint suspicion.
My sister is not so defenceless left
As you imagine, she has a hidden strength
Which you remember not.
   2. *Bro.* What hidden strength,
Unless the strength of Heav'n, if you mean that?
   Eld. Bro. I mean that too, but yet a hidden strength
Which if Heav'n gave it, may be term'd her own:
'Tis chastity, my brother, chastity:
She that has that, is clad in compleat steel,
And like a quiver'd Nymph with Arrows keen   420

May trace huge Forests, and unharbour'd Heaths,
Infamous Hills, and sandy perilous wildes,
Where through the sacred rayes of Chastity,
No savage fierce, Bandite, or mountaneer
Will dare to soyl her Virgin purity,
Yea there, where very desolation dwels
By grots, and caverns shag'd with horrid shades,
She may pass on with unblench't majesty,
Be it not don in pride, or in presumption.   430
Som say no evil thing that walks by night
In fog, or fire, by lake, or moorish fen,
Blew meager Hag, or stubborn unlaid ghost,
That breaks his magick chains at *curfeu* time,
No goblin, or swart Faëry of the mine,
Hath hurtfull power o're true virginity.
Do ye beleeve me yet, or shall I call
Antiquity from the old Schools of Greece
To testifie the arms of Chastity?
Hence had the huntress *Dian* her dred bow   440
Fair silver-shafted Queen for ever chaste,
Wherwith she tam'd the brinded lioness
And spotted mountain pard, but set at nought
The frivolous bolt of *Cupid,* gods and men
Fear'd her stern frown, and she was queen oth' Woods.
What was that snaky-headed *Gorgon* sheild
That wise *Minerva* wore, unconquer'd Virgin,
Wherwith she freez'd her foes to congeal'd stone?
But rigid looks of Chast austerity,
And noble grace that dash't brute violence   45.
With sudden adoration, and blank aw.
So dear to Heav'n is Saintly chastity,
That when a soul is found sincerely so,
A thousand liveried Angels lacky her,
Driving far off each thing of sin and guilt,
And in cleer dream, and solemn vision
Tell her of things that no gross ear can hear,
Till oft convers with heav'nly habitants
Begin to cast a beam on th'outward shape,
The unpolluted temple of the mind,   460
And turns it by degrees to the souls essence,
Till all be made immortal: but when lust
By unchaste looks, loose gestures, and foul talk,
But most by leud and lavish act of sin,
Lets in defilement to the inward parts,
The soul grows clotted by contagion,
Imbodies, and imbrutes, till she quite loose
The divine property of her first being.
Such are those thick and gloomy shadows damp
Oft seen in Charnell vaults, and Sepulchers   470
Lingering, and sitting by a new made grave.
As loath to leave the body that it lov'd,
And link't it self by carnal sensualty
To a degenerate and degraded state.

2. *Bro.* How charming is divine Philosophy!
Not harsh, and crabbed as dull fools suppose,
But musical as is *Apollo's* lute,
And a perpetual feast of nectar'd sweets,
Where no crude surfet raigns. *Eld. Bro.* List, list, I hear
Som far off hallow break the silent Air.   480
 2. *Bro.* Me thought so too; what should it be?
Eld. Bro. For certain
Either som one like us night-founder'd here,
Or els som neighbour Wood-man, or at worst,
Som roaving Robber calling to his fellows.
 2. *Bro.* Heav'n keep my sister, agen agen and neer,
Best draw, and stand upon our guard.
 Eld. Bro. Ile hallow,
If he be friendly he comes well, if not,
Defence is a good cause, and Heav'n be for us.

The attendant Spirit habited like a Shepherd.

That hallow I should know, what are you? speak;
Com not too neer, you fall on iron stakes else.   490
 Spir. What voice is that, my young Lord? speak agen.
 2. *Bro.* O brother, 'tis my father Shepherd sure.
 Eld. Bro. Thyrsis? Whose artful strains have oft delaid
The huddling brook to hear his madrigal,
And sweeten'd every muskrose of the dale,
How cam'st thou here good Swain? hath any ram
Slip't from the fold, or young Kid lost his dam,
Or straggling weather the pen't flock forsook?
How couldst thou find this dark sequester'd nook?
 Spir. O my lov'd masters heir, and his next joy,   500
I came not here on such a trivial toy
As a stray'd Ewe, or to pursue the stealth
Of pilfering Woolf, not all the fleecy wealth
That doth enrich these Downs, is worth a thought
To this my errand, and the care it brought.
But O my Virgin Lady, where is she?
How chance she is not in your company?
 Eld. Bro. To tell thee sadly Shepherd, without blame,
Or our neglect, we lost her as we came.
 Spir. Ay me unhappy then my fears are true.   510
 Eld. Bro. What fears good *Thyrsis?* Prethee briefly shew.
 Spir. Ile tell ye, 'tis not vain, or fabulous,
(Though so esteem'd by shallow ignorance)
What the sage Poëts taught by th' heav'nly Muse,
Storied of old in high immortal vers
Of dire *Chimera's* and inchanted Iles,
And rifted Rocks whose entrance leads to hell,
For such there be, but unbelief is blind.
 Within the navil of this hideous Wood,
Immur'd in cypress shades a Sorcerer dwels   520
Of *Bacchus,* and of *Circe* born, great *Comus,*
Deep skill'd in all his mothers witcheries,

And here to every thirsty wanderer,
By sly enticement gives his banefull cup,
With many murmurs mixt, whose pleasing poison
The visage quite transforms of him that drinks,
And the inglorious likenes of a beast
Fixes instead, unmoulding reasons mintage
Character'd in the face; this have I learn't
Tending my flocks hard by i'th hilly crofts,   530
That brow this bottom glade, whence night by night
He and his monstrous rout are heard to howl
Like stabl'd wolves, or tigers at their prey,
Doing abhorred rites to *Hecate*
In their obscured haunts of inmost bowres.
Yet have they many baits, and guilefull spells
To inveigle and invite th'unwary sense
Of them that pass unweeting by the way.
This evening late by then the chewing flocks
Had ta'n their supper on the savoury Herb   540
Of Knot-grass dew-besprent, and were in fold,
I sate me down to watch upon a bank
With Ivy canopied, and interwove
With flaunting Hony-suckle, and began
Wrapt in a pleasing fit of melancholy
To meditate my rural minstrelsie,
Till fancy had her fill, but ere a close
The wonted roar was up amidst the Woods,
And fill'd the Air with barbarous dissonance,
At which I ceas't, and listen'd them a while,   550
Till an unusuall stop of sudden silence
Gave respit to the drowsie frighted steeds
That draw the litter of close-curtain'd sleep.
At last a soft and solemn breathing sound
Rose like a steam of rich distill'd Perfumes,
And stole upon the Air, that even Silence
Was took e're she was ware, and wish't she might
Deny her nature, and be never more
Still to be so displac't. I was all eare,
And took in strains that might create a soul   560
Under the ribs of Death, but O ere long
Too well I did perceive it was the voice
Of my most honour'd Lady, your dear sister.
Amaz'd I stood, harrow'd with grief and fear,
And O poor hapless Nightingale thought I,
How sweet thou sing'st, how neer the deadly snare!
Then down the Lawns I ran with headlong hast
Through paths, and turnings oft'n trod by day,
Till guided by mine ear I found the place
Where that damn'd wisard hid in sly disguise   570
(For so by certain signes I knew) had met
Already, ere my best speed could prævent,
The aidless innocent Lady his wish't prey,
Who gently ask't if he had seen such two,
Supposing him som neighbour villager;

Longer I durst not stay, but soon I guess't
Ye were the two she mean't, with that I sprung
Into swift flight, till I had found you here,
But furder know I not. 2. *Bro.* O night and shades,
How are ye joyn'd with hell in triple knot   580
Against th'unarmed weakness of one Virgin
Alone, and helpless! Is this the confidence
You gave me Brother? *Eld. Bro.* Yes, and keep it still,
Lean on it safely, not a period
Shall be unsaid for me: against the threats
Of malice or of sorcery, or that power
Which erring men call Chance, this I hold firm,
Vertue may be assail'd, but never hurt,
Surpriz'd by unjust force, but not enthrall'd,
Yea even that which mischief meant most harm,   590
Shall in the happy trial prove most glory.
But evil on it self shall back recoyl,
And mix no more with goodness, when at last
Gather'd like scum, and setl'd to it self
It shall be in eternal restless change
Self-fed, and self-consum'd, if this fail,
The pillar'd firmament is rott'nness,
And earths base built on stubble. But com let's on.
Against th' opposing will and arm of Heav'n
May never this just sword be lifted up,   600
But for that damn'd magician, let him be girt
With all the greisly legions that troop
Under the sooty flag of *Acheron,*
Harpyies and *Hydra's,* or all the monstrous forms
'Twixt *Africa* and *Inde,* Ile find him out,
And force him to restore his purchase back,
Or drag him by the curls, to a foul death,
Curs'd as his life.
   Spir. Alas good ventrous youth,
I love thy courage yet, and bold Emprise,
But here thy sword can do thee little stead,   610
Farr other arms, and other weapons must
Be those that quell the might of hellish charms,
He with his bare wand can unthred thy joynts,
And crumble all thy sinews.
   Eld. Bro. Why prethee Shepherd
How durst thou then thy self approach so neer
As to make this relation?
   Spir. Care and utmost shifts
How to secure the Lady from surprisal,
Brought to my mind a certain Shepherd Lad
Of small regard to see to, yet well skill'd
In every vertuous plant and healing herb   620
That spreds her verdant leaf to th'morning ray,
He lov'd me well, and oft would beg me sing,
Which when I did, he on the tender grass
Would sit, and hearken even to extasie,
And in requitall ope his leather'n scrip,

And shew me simples of a thousand names
Telling their strange and vigorous faculties;
Amongst the rest a small unsightly root,
But of divine effect, he cull'd me out;
The leaf was darkish, and had prickles on it,   630
But in another Countrey, as he said,
Bore a bright golden flowre, but not in this soyl:
Unknown, and like esteem'd, and the dull swayn
Treads on it daily with his clouted shoon,
And yet more med'cinal is it then that *Moly*
That *Hermes* once to wise *Ulysses* gave;
He call'd it *Hæmony,* and gave it me,
And bad me keep it as of sovran use
'Gainst all inchantments, mildew blast, or damp
Or gastly furies apparition;   640
I purs't it up, but little reck'ning made,
Till now that this extremity compell'd,
But now I find it true; for by this means
I knew the foul inchanter though disguis'd,
Enter'd the very lime-twigs of his spells,
And yet came off: if you have this about you
(As I will give you when we go) you may
Boldly assault the necromancers hall;
Where if he be, with dauntless hardihood,
And brandish't blade rush on him, break his glass   650
And shed the lushious liquor on the ground,
But sease his wand, though he and his curst crew
Feirce signe of battail make, and menace high,
Or like the sons of *Vulcan* vomit smoak,
Yet will they soon retire, if he but shrink.
    Eld. Bro. Thyrsis lead on apace, Ile follow thee,
And som good angel bear a sheild before us.

The Scene changes to a stately Palace, set out with all manner of deliciousness: soft Musick, Tables spred with all dainties. Comus *appears with his rabble, and the Lady set in an inchanted Chair, to whom he offers his Glass, which she puts by, and goes about to rise.*

    Comus. Nay Lady sit; if I but wave this wand,
Your nervs are all chain'd up in Alablaster,
And you a statue; or as *Daphne* was   660
Root-bound, that fled *Apollo.*
    La. Fool do not boast,
Thou canst not touch the freedom of my minde
With all thy charms, although this corporal rinde
Thou haste immanacl'd, while Heav'n sees good.
    Co. Why are you vext Lady? why do you frown?
Here dwel no frowns, nor anger, from these gates
Sorrow flies farr: See here be all the pleasures
That fancy can beget on youthfull thoughts,
When the fresh blood grows lively, and returns
Brisk as the *April* buds in Primrose-season.   670
And first behold this cordial Julep here
That flames, and dances in his crystal bounds
With spirits of balm, and fragrant Syrops mixt.

Not that *Nepenthes* which the wife of *Thone,*
In *Egypt* gave to *Jove*-born *Helena*
Is of such power to stir up joy as this,
To life so friendly, or so cool to thirst.
Why should you be so cruel to your self,
And to those dainty limms which nature lent
For gentle usage, and soft delicacy?   680
But you invert the cov'nants of her trust,
And harshly deal like an ill borrower
With that which you receiv'd on other terms,
Scorning the unexempt condition
By which all mortal frailty must subsist,
Refreshment after toil, ease after pain,
That have been tir'd all day without repast,
And timely rest have wanted, but fair Virgin
This will restore all soon.
　　La. 'Twill not false traitor,
'Twill not restore the truth and honesty   690
That thou hast banish't from thy tongue with lies,
Was this the cottage, and the safe abode
Thou told'st me of? What grim aspects are these,
These oughly-headed Monsters? Mercy guard me!
Hence with thy brew'd inchantments, foul deceiver,
Hast thou betrai'd my credulous innocence
With visor'd falshood, and base forgery,
And wouldst thou seek again to trap me here
With lickerish baits fit to ensnare a brute?
Were it a draft for *Juno* when she banquets,   700
I would not taste thy treasonous offer; none
But such as are good men can give good things,
And that which is not good, is not delicious
To a wel-govern'd and wise appetite.
　　Co. O foolishnes of men! that lend their ears
To those budge doctors of the *Stoick* Furr,
And fetch their precepts from the *Cynick* Tub,
Praising the lean and sallow Abstinence.
Wherefore did Nature powre her bounties forth,
With such a full and unwithdrawing hand,   710
Covering the earth with odours, fruits, and flocks,
Thronging the Seas with spawn innumerable,
But all to please, and sate the curious taste?
And set to work millions of spinning Worms,
That in their green shops weave the smooth-hair'd silk
To deck her Sons, and that no corner might
Be vacant of her plenty, in her own loyns
She hutch't th'all-worshipt ore, and precious gems
To store her children with; if all the world
Should in a pet of temperance feed on Pulse,   720
Drink the clear stream, and nothing wear but Freize,
Th'all-giver would be unthank't, would be unprais'd,
Not half his riches known, and yet despis'd,
And we should serve him as a grudging master,
As a penurious niggard of his wealth,

And live like Natures bastards, not her sons,
Who would be quite surcharg'd with her own weight,
And strangl'd with her waste fertility;
Th'earth cumber'd, and the wing'd air dark't with plumes,
The herds would over-multitude their Lords,   730
The Sea o'refraught would swell, & th'unsought diamonds
Would so emblaze the forhead of the Deep,
And so bestudd with Stars, that they below
Would grow inur'd to light, and com at last
To gaze upon the Sun with shameless brows.
List Lady be not coy, and be not cosen'd
With that same vaunted name Virginity,
Beauty is natures coyn, must not be hoorded,
But must be currant, and the good thereof
Consists in mutual and partak'n bliss,   740
Unsavoury in th'injoyment of it self
If you let slip time, like a neglected rose
It withers on the stalk with languish't head.
Beauty is natures brag, and must be shown
In courts, at feasts, and high solemnities
Where most may wonder at the workmanship;
It is for homely features to keep home,
They had their name thence; course complexions
And cheeks of sorry grain will serve to ply
The sampler, and to teize the huswifes wooll.   750
What need a vermeil-tinctur'd lip for that
Love-darting eyes, or tresses like the Morn?
There was another meaning in these gifts,
Think what, and be adviz'd, you are but young yet.
    _La._ I had not thought to have unlockt my lips
In this unhallow'd air, but that this Jugler
Would think to charm my judgement, as mine eyes
Obtruding false rules pranckt in reasons garb.
I hate when vice can bolt her arguments,
And vertue has no tongue to check her pride: 760
Impostor do not charge most innocent nature,
As if she would her children should be riotous
With her abundance, she good cateress
Means her provision onely to the good
That live according to her sober laws,
And holy dictate of spare Temperance:
If every just man that now pines with want
Had but a moderate and beseeming share
Of that which lewdly-pamper'd Luxury
Now heaps upon som few with vast excess,   770
Natures full blessings would be well dispenc't
In unsuperfluous eeven proportion,
And she no whit encomber'd with her store,
And then the giver would be better thank't,
His praise due paid, for swinish gluttony
Ne're looks to Heav'n amidst his gorgeous feast,
But with besotted base ingratitude
Cramms, and blasphemes his feeder. Shall I go on?

Or have I said anough? To him that dares
Arm his profane tongue with contemptuous words   780
Against the Sun-clad power of Chastity,
Fain would I somthing say, yet to what end?
Thou hast nor Eare, nor Soul to apprehend
The sublime notion, and high mystery
That must be utter'd to unfold the sage
And serious doctrine of Virginity,
And thou art worthy that thou shouldst not know
More happines then this thy present lot.
Enjoy your deer Wit, and gay Rhetorick
That hath so well been taught her dazling fence,   790
Thou art not fit to hear thy self convinc't;
Yet should I try, the uncontrouled worth
Of this pure cause would kindle my rap't spirits
To such a flame of sacred vehemence,
That dumb things would be mov'd to sympathize,
And the brute Earth would lend her nerves, and shake,
Till all thy magick structures rear'd so high,
Were shatter'd into heaps o're thy false head.
  Co. She fables not, I feel that I do fear
Her words set off by som superior power;   800
And though not mortal, yet a cold shuddring dew
Dips me all o're, as when the wrath of *Jove*
Speaks thunder, and the chains of *Erebus*
To som of *Saturns* crew. I must dissemble,
And try her yet more strongly. Com, no more,
This is meer moral babble, and direct
Against the canon laws of our foundation;
I must not suffer this, yet 'tis but the lees
And setlings of a melancholy blood;
But this will cure all streight, one sip of this   810
Will bathe the drooping spirits in delight
Beyond the bliss of dreams. Be wise, and taste.—

The Brothers rush in with Swords drawn, wrest his Glass out of his hand, and break it against the
ground; his rout make signe of resistance, but are all driven in; The attendant Spirit comes in.

  Spir. What, have you let the false enchanter scape?
O ye mistook, ye should have snatcht his wand
And bound him fast; without his rod revers't,
And backward mutters of dissevering power,
We cannot free the Lady that sits here
In stony fetters fixt, and motionless;
Yet stay, be not disturb'd, now I bethink me,
Som other means I have which may be us'd,   820
Which once of *Meliboeus* old I learnt
The soothest Shepherd that ere pip't on plains.
  There is a gentle Nymph not farr from hence,
That with moist curb sways the smooth Severn stream,
Sabrina is her name, a Virgin pure,
Whilom she was the daughter of *Locrine,*
That had the Scepter from his father *Brute.*
She guiltless damsell flying the mad pursuit

Of her enraged stepdam *Guendolen,*
Commended her fair innocence to the flood   830
That stay'd her flight with his cross-flowing course,
The water Nymphs that in the bottom plaid,
Held up their pearled wrists and took her in,
Bearing her straight to aged *Nereus* Hall,
Who piteous of her woes, rear'd her lank head,
And gave her to his daughters to imbathe
In nectar'd lavers strew'd with Asphodil,
And through the porch and inlet of each sense
Dropt in Ambrosial Oils till she reviv'd,
And underwent a quick immortal change   840
Made Goddess of the River; still she retains
Her maid'n gentlenes, and oft at Eeve
Visits the herds along the twilight meadows,
Helping all urchin blasts, and ill luck signes
That the shrewd medling Elfe delights to make,
Which she with pretious viold liquors heals.
For which the Shepherds at their festivals
Carrol her goodnes lowd in rustick layes,
And throw sweet garland wreaths into her stream
Of pancies, pinks, and gaudy Daffadils.   850
And, as the old Swain said, she can unlock
The clasping charm, and thaw the numming spell,
If she be right invok't in warbled Song,
For maid'nhood she loves, and will be swift
To aid a Virgin, such as was her self
In hard besetting need, this will I try
And adde the power of som adjuring verse.

                          SONG

      Sabrina fair
          Listen where thou art sitting
      Under the glassie, cool, translucent wave,   860
          In twisted braids of Lillies knitting
      The loose train of thy amber-dropping hair,
          Listen for dear honours sake,
          Goddess of the silver lake,
                      Listen and save.

Listen and appear to us
In name of great *Oceanus,*
By the earth-shaking *Neptune*'s mace,
And *Tethys* grave majestick pace,
By hoary *Nereus* wrincled look,   870
And the *Carpathian* wisards hook,
By scaly *Tritons* winding shell,
And old sooth-saying *Glaucus* spell,
By *Leucothea*'s lovely hands,
And her son that rules the strands,
By *Thetis* tinsel-slipper'd feet,
And the Songs of *Sirens* sweet,

By dead *Parthenope*'s dear tomb,
And fair *Ligea*'s golden comb,
Wherwith she sits on diamond rocks   880
Sleeking her soft alluring locks,
By all the *Nymphs* that nightly dance
Upon thy streams with wily glance,
Rise, rise, and heave thy rosie head
From thy coral-pav'n bed,
And bridle in thy headlong wave,
Till thou our summons answer'd have.

                              Listen and save.

Sabrina rises, attended by water-Nymphes, and sings.

  By the rushy-fringed bank,
Where grows the Willow and the Osier dank,   890
  My sliding Chariot stayes,
Thick set with Agat, and the azurn sheen
Of Turkis blew, and Emrauld green
  That in the channell strayes,
Whilst from off the waters fleet
Thus I set my printless feet
O're the Cowslips Velvet head,
  That bends not as I tread,
Gentle swain at thy request
  I am here.   900

  Spir. Goddess dear
We implore thy powerful hand
To undoe the charmed band
Of true Virgin here distrest,
Through the force, and through the wile
Of unblest inchanter vile.
  Sab. Shepherd 'tis my office best
To help insnared chastity;
Brightest Lady look on me,
Thus I sprinkle on thy brest   910
Drops that from my fountain pure,
I have kept of pretious cure,
Thrice upon thy fingers tip,
Thrice upon thy rubied lip,
Next this marble venom'd seat
Smear'd with gumms of glutenous heat
I touch with chaste palms moist and cold,
Now the spell hath lost his hold;
And I must haste ere morning hour
To wait in *Amphitrite*'s bowr.   920

Sabrina descends, and the Lady rises out of her seat.

  Spir. Virgin, daughter of *Locrine*
Sprung of old *Anchises* line,
May thy brimmed waves for this
Their full tribute never miss

From a thousand petty rills,
That tumble down the snowy hills:
Summer drouth, or singed air
Never scorch thy tresses fair,
Nor wet *Octobers* torrent flood
Thy molten crystal fill with mudd,   930
May thy billows rowl ashoar
The beryl, and the golden ore,
May thy lofty head be crown'd
With many a tower and terrass round,
And here and there thy banks upon
With Groves of myrrhe, and cinnamon.

Com Lady while Heaven lends us grace,
Let us fly this cursed place,
Lest the Sorcerer us intice
With som other new device.   940
Not a waste, or needless sound
Till we com to nolier ground,
I shall be your faithfull guide
Through this gloomy covert wide,
And not many furlongs thence
Is your Fathers residence,
Where this night are met in state
Many a friend to gratulate
His wish't presence, and beside
All the Swains that there abide,   950
With Jiggs, and rural dance resort,
We shall catch them at their sport,
And our sudden coming there
Will double all their mirth and chere;
Com let us haste, the Stars grow high,
But night sits monarch yet in the mid sky.

The Scene changes, presenting Ludlow *Town and the Presidents Castle, then com in Countrey-Dancers, after them the attendant Spirit, with the two Brothers and the Lady.*

SONG

    Spir. *Back Shepherds, back, anough your play,*
Till next Sun-shine holiday,
Here be without duck or nod
Other trippings to be trod   960
Of lighter toes, and such Court guise
As Mercury *did first devise*
With the mincing Dryades
On the Lawns, and on the Leas.

This second Song presents them to their father and mother.

Noble Lord, and Lady bright,
I have brought ye new delight,
Here behold so goodly grown
Three fair branches of your own,
Heav'n hath timely tri'd their youth,

Their faith, their patience, and their truth.   970
And sent them here through hard assays
With a crown of deathless Praise,
*   To triumph in victorious dance*
O're sensual Folly, and Intemperance.

                The dances ended, the Spirit Epiloguizes.

    Spir. To the Ocean now I fly,
And those happy climes that ly
Where day never shuts his eye,
Up in the broad fields of the sky:
There I suck the liquid ayr
All amidst the Gardens fair   980
Of *Hesperus,* and his daughters three
That sing about the golden tree:
Along the crisped shades and bowres
Revels the spruce and jocond Spring,
The Graces, and the rosie-boosom'd Howres,
Thither all their bounties bring,
That there eternal Summer dwels,
And West winds, with musky wing
About the cedar'n alleys fling
Nard, and *Cassia's* balmy smels.   990
Iris there with humid bow,
Waters the odorous banks that blow
Flowers of more mingled hew
Then her purfl'd scarf can shew,
And drenches with *Elysian* dew
(List mortals, if your ears be true)
Beds of *Hyacinth,* and roses
Where young *Adonis* oft reposes,
Waxing well of his deep wound
In slumber soft, and on the ground   1000
Sadly sits th' *Assyrian* Queen;
But farr above in spangled sheen
Celestial *Cupid* her fam'd Son advanc't,
Holds his dear *Psyche* sweet intranc't
After her wandring labours long,
Till free consent the gods among
Make her his eternal Bride,
And from her fair unspotted side
Two blissful twins are to be born,
Youth and Joy; so *Jove* hath sworn.   1010
    But now my task is smoothly don,
I can fly, or I can run
Quickly to the green earths end,
Where the bow'd welkin slow doth bend,
And from thence can soar as soon
To the corners of the Moon.
    Mortals that would follow me,
Love vertue, she alone is free,
She can teach ye how to clime

Higher then the Spheary chime;
Or if Vertue feeble were,
Heav'n it self would stoop to her.

The End.

[The following translations are not in 1645; from 1673.]

PSAL. I. Done into Verse, 1653

BLESS'D is the man who hath not walk'd astray
In counsel of the wicked, and ith'way
Of sinners hath not stood, and in the seat
Of scorners hath not sate. But in the great
Jehovahs Law is ever his delight,
And in his Law he studies day and night.
He shall be as a tree which planted grows
By watry streams, and in his season knows
To yield his fruit, and his leaf shall not fall,
And what he takes in hand shall prosper all.   10
Not so the wicked, but as chaff which fann'd
The wind drives, so the wicked shall not stand
In judgment, or abide their tryal then,
Nor sinners in th'assembly of just men.
For the Lord knows th'upright way of the just,
And the way of bad men to ruine must.

PSAL. II. Done Aug. 8. 1653. *Terzetti*

WHY do the Gentiles tumult, and the Nations
    Muse a vain thing, the Kings of th'earth upstand
    With power, and Princes in their Congregations
Lay deep their plots together through each Land,
    Against the Lord and his Messiah dear.
    Let us break off, say they, by strength of hand
Their bonds, and cast from us, no more to wear,
    Their twisted cords: he who in Heaven doth dwell
    Shall laugh, the Lord shall scoff them, then severe
Speak to them in his wrath, and in his fell   10
    And fierce ire trouble them; but I saith hee
    Anointed have my King (though ye rebell)
On Sion my holi' hill. A firm decree
    I will declare; the Lord to me hath say'd
    Thou art my Son I have begotten thee
This day; ask of me, and the grant is made;
    As thy possession I on thee bestow
    Th'Heathen, and as thy conquest to be sway'd
Earths utmost bounds: them shalt thou bring full low
    With Iron Scepter bruis'd, and them disperse   20
    Like to a potters vessel shiver'd so.
And now be wise at length ye Kings averse
    Be taught ye Judges of the Earth; with fear

Jehovah serve, and let your joy converse
With trembling; kiss the Son least he appear
   In anger and ye perish in the way
   If once his wrath take fire like fuel sere.
Happy all those who have in him their stay.

PSAL. 3. Aug. 9. 1653

When he fled from Absalom

LORD how many are my foes
   How many those
That in arms against me rise
   Many are they
   That of my life distrustfully thus say,
No help for him in God there lies.
But thou Lord art my shield my glory,
      Thee through my story
      Th' exalter of my head I count
         Aloud I cry'd   10
Unto Jehovah, he full soon reply'd
And heard me from his holy mount.
I lay and slept, I wak'd again,
         For my sustain
      Was the Lord. Of many millions
      The populous rout
   I fear not though incamping round about
They pitch against me their Pavillions.
Rise Lord, save me my God for thou
      Hast smote ere now   20
      On the cheek-bone all my foes,
         Of men abhor'd
   Hast broke the teeth. This help was from the Lord
Thy blessing on thy people flows.

PSAL. IV. Aug. 10. 1653

ANSWER me when I call
God of my righteousness
In straights and in distress
Thou didst me disinthrall
And set at large; now spare,
   Now pity me, and hear my earnest prai'r.
Great ones how long will ye
My glory have in scorn
How long be thus forborn
Still to love vanity,   10
   To love, to seek, to prize
   Things false and vain and nothing else but lies?
Yet know the Lord hath chose
Chose to himself a part
The good and meek of heart
(For whom to chuse he knows)

Jehovah from on high
   Will hear my voyce what time to him I crie.
Be aw'd, and do not sin,
Speak to your hearts alone,
Upon your beds, each one,
And be at peace within.
Offer the offerings just
   Of righteousness and in Jehovah trust.
Many there be that say
Who yet will shew us good?
Talking like this worlds brood;
But Lord, thus let me pray,
On us lift up the light
   Lift up the favour of thy count'nance bright.
Into my heart more joy
And gladness thou hast put
Then when a year of glut
Their stores doth over-cloy
And from their plenteous grounds
   With vast increase their corn and wine abounds.
In peace at once will I
Both lay me down and sleep
For thou alone dost keep
Me safe where ere I lie
As in a rocky Cell
   Thou Lord alone in safety mak'st me dwell.

PSAL. V. Aug. 12. 1653

Jehovah to my words give ear
    My meditation waigh
The voyce of my complaining hear
My King and God for unto thee I pray.
   Jehovah thou my early voyce
    Shalt in the morning hear
   Ith'morning I to thee with choyce
Will rank my Prayers, and watch till thou appear.
   For thou art not a God that takes
    In wickedness delight
   Evil with thee no biding makes
Fools or mad men stand not within thy sight.
   All workers of iniquity
    Thou hat'st; and them unblest
   Thou wilt destroy that speak a ly
The bloodi' and guileful man God doth detest.
   But I will in thy mercies dear
    Thy numerous mercies go
   Into thy house; I in thy fear
Will towards thy holy temple worship low.
   Lord lead me in thy righteousness
    Lead me because of those
   That do observe if I transgress,
Set thy wayes right before, where my step goes.

For in his faltring mouth unstable
    No word is firm or sooth
Their inside, troubles miserable;
An open grave their throat, their tongue they smooth.
    God, find them guilty, let them fall
        By their own counsels quell'd; ·
    Push them in their rebellions all   30
Still on; for against thee they have rebell'd;
    Then all who trust in thee shall bring
        Their joy, while thou from blame
Defend'st them, they shall ever sing
And shall triumph in thee, who love thy name.
    For thou Jehovah wilt be found
        To bless the just man still,
    As with a shield thou wilt surround
Him with thy lasting favour and good will.   40

PSAL. VI. Aug. 13. 1653

LORD in thine anger do not reprehend me
    Nor in thy hot displeasure me correct;
Pity me Lord for I am much deject
    Am very weak and faint; heal and amend me,
For all my bones, that even with anguish ake,
    Are troubled, yea my soul is troubled sore
And thou O Lord how long? turn Lord, restore
    My soul, O save me for thy goodness sake
For in death no remembrance is of thee;
    Who in the grave can celebrate thy praise?   10
Wearied I am with sighing out my dayes,
    Nightly my Couch I make a kind of Sea;
My Bed I water with my tears; mine Eie
    Through grief consumes, is waxen cld and dark
Ith' mid'st of all mine enemies that mark.
    Depart all ye that work iniquitie.
Depart from me, for the voice of my weeping
    The Lord hath heard, the Lord hath heard my prai'r
My supplication with acceptance fair
    The Lord will own, and have me in his keeping.   20
Mine enemies shall all be blank and dash't
    With much confusion; then grow red with shame,
They shall return in hast the way they came
    And in a moment shall be quite abash't.

PSAL. VII. Aug. 14. 1653

Upon the words of Chush *the* Benjamite *against him.*

    LORD my God to thee I flie
    Save me and secure me under
    Thy protection while I crie,
    Least as a Lion (and no wonder)
    He hast to tear my Soul asunder
    Tearing and no rescue nigh.

Lord my God if I have thought
Or done this, if wickedness
Be in my hands, if I have wrought
Ill to him that meant me peace,
Or to him have render'd less,
And not fre'd my foe for naught;

Let th'enemy pursue my soul
And overtake it, let him tread
My life down to the earth and roul
In the dust my glory dead,
In the dust and there out spread
Lodge it with dishonour foul.

Rise Jehovah in thine ire
Rouze thy self amidst the rage
Of my foes that urge like fire;
And wake for me, their furi' asswage;
Judgment here thou didst ingage
And command which I desire.

So th' assemblies of each Nation
Will surround thee, seeking right,
Thence to thy glorious habitation
Return on high and in their sight.
Jehovah judgeth most upright
All people from the worlds foundation.

Judge me Lord, be judge in this
According to my righteousness
And the innocence which is
Upon me: cause at length to cease
Of evil men the wickedness
And their power that do amiss.

But the just establish fast,
Since thou art the just God that tries
Hearts and reins. On God is cast
My defence, and in him lies
In him who both just and wise
Saves th' upright of Heart at last.

God is a just Judge and severe,
And God is every day offended;
If th' unjust will not forbear,
His Sword he whets, his Bow hath bended
Already, and for him intended
The tools of death, that waits him near.

(His arrows purposely made he
For them that persecute.) Behold
He travels big with vanitie,
Trouble he hath conceav'd of old
As in a womb, and from that mould
Hath at length brought forth a Lie.

10

20

30

40

50

He dig'd a pit, and delv'd it deep,
And fell into the pit he made,
His mischief that due course doth keep,
Turns on his head, and his ill trade
Of violence will undelay'd
Fall on his crown with ruine steep.   60

Then will I Jehovah's praise
According to his justice raise
And sing the Name and Deitie
Of Jehovah the most high.

PSAL. VIII. Aug. 14. 1653

O Jehovah our Lord how wondrous great
    And glorious is thy name through all the earth?
So as above the Heavens thy praise to set
    Out of the tender mouths of latest bearth,

Out of the mouths of babes and sucklings thou
    Hast founded strength because of all thy foes
To stint th'enemy, and slack th'avengers brow
    That bends his rage thy providence to oppose.

When I behold thy Heavens, thy Fingers art,
    The Moon and Starrs which thou so bright hast set,   10
In the pure firmament, then saith my heart,
    O what is man that thou remembrest yet,

And think'st upon him; or of man begot
    That him thou visit'st and of him art found;
Scarce to be less then Gods, thou mad'st his lot,
    With honour and with state thou hast him crown'd.

O're the works of thy hand thou mad'st him Lord,
    Thou hast put all under his lordly feet,
All Flocks, and Herds, by thy commanding word,
    All beasts that in the field or forrest meet.   20

Fowl of the Heavens, and Fish that through the wet
    Sea-paths in shoals do slide. And know no dearth.
O Jehovah our Lord how wondrous great
    And glorious is thy name through all the earth.

April, 1648. J. M.

Nine of the Psalms done into Metre, wherein all but what is in a different Character, are the very words of the Text, translated from the Original.

PSAL. LXXX

1 THOU Shepherd that dost Israel *keep*
　　Give ear *in time of need,*
Who leadest like a flock of sheep
　　Thy loved Josephs seed,
That sitt'st between the Cherubs *bright*
　　Between their wings out-spread
Shine forth, *and from thy cloud give light,*
　　And on our foes thy dread.

2 In Ephraims view and Benjamins,
　　And in Manasse's sight
Awake * thy strength, come, and *be seen*
　　To save us *by thy might.*

3 Turn us again, *thy grace divine*
　　To us O God *vouchsafe;*
Cause thou thy face on us to shine
　　And then we shall be safe.

4 Lord God of Hosts, how long wilt thou,
　　How long wilt thou declare
Thy * smoking wrath, *and angry brow*
　　Against thy peoples praire.

5 Thou feed'st them with the bread of tears,
　　Their bread with tears they eat,
And mak'st them * largely drink the tears
　　Wherwith their cheeks are wet.

6 A strife thou mak'st us *and a prey*
　　To every neighbour foe,
Among themselves they * laugh, they * play,
　　And * flouts at us they throw.

7 Return us, *and thy grace divine,*
　　O God of Hosts *vouchsafe*
Cause thou thy face on us to shine,
　　And then we shall be safe.

8 A Vine from Ægypt thou hast brought,
　　Thy free love made it thine,
And drov'st out Nations *proud and haut*
　　To plant this *lovely* Vine.

9 Thou did'st prepare for it a place
　　And root it deep and fast
That it *began to grow apace,*
　　And fill'd the land *at last.*

10 With her *green* shade *that* cover'd *all,*
　　The Hills were *over-spread*
Her Bows as *high as* Cedars tall
　　Advanc'd their lofty head.

11 Her branches *on the western side*

* *Gnorera.*

* *Gnashanta.*

* *Shalish.*

* *Jilgnagu.*

10

20

30

40

Down to the Sea she sent,
And *upward* to that river *wide*
Her other branches *went.*

12 Why hast thou laid her Hedges low
And brok'n down her Fence,   50
That all may pluck her, as they go,
With rudest violence?

13 The *tusked* Boar out of the wood
Up turns it by the roots,
Wild Beasts there brouze, and make their food
Her Grapes and tender Shoots.

14 Return now, God of Hosts, look down
From Heav'n, thy Seat divine,
Behold *us, but without a frown,*
And visit this *thy* Vine.   60

15 Visit this Vine, which thy right hand
Hath set, and planted *long,*
And the young branch, that for thy self
Thou hast made firm and strong.

16 But now it is consum'd with fire,
And cut *with Axes* down,
They perish at thy dreadfull ire,
At thy rebuke and frown.

17 Upon the man of thy right hand
Let thy *good* hand be *laid,*   70
Upon the Son of Man, whom thou
Strong for thy self hast made.

18 So shall we not go back from thee
To wayes of sin and shame,
Quick'n us thou, then *gladly* wee
Shall call upon thy Name.
Return us, *and thy grace divine*
Lord God of Hosts *voutsafe,*
Cause thou thy face on us to shine,
And then we shall be safe.   80

PSAL. LXXXI

1 To God our strength sing loud, *and clear,*
Sing loud to God *our King,*
To Jacobs God, *that all may hear*
Loud acclamations ring.

2 Prepare a Hymn, prepare a Song
The Timbrel hither bring
The *cheerfull Psaltry* bring along
And Harp *with* pleasant *string.*

3 Blow, *as is wont,* in the new Moon
With Trumpets *lofty sound,*   10
Th' appointed time, the day wheron
Our solemn Feast *comes round.*

4 This was a Statute *giv'n of old*
For Israel *to observe*
A Law of Jacobs God, *to hold*

From whence they might not swerve.
5 This he a Testimony ordain'd
   In Joseph, *not to change,*
 When as he pass'd through Ægypt land;
   The Tongue I heard, was strange.   20
6 From burden, *and from slavish toyle*
   I set his shoulder free;
   His hands from pots, *and mirie soyle*
   Deliver'd were *by me.*
7 When trouble did thee sore assaile,
   On me then didst thou call,
   And I to free thee *did not faile,*
   And led thee out of thrall.
   I answer'd thee in * thunder deep   * Be Sether rag-
   With clouds encompass'd round;   nam.
   I tri'd thee at the water *steep*   30
   Of Meriba *renown'd.*
8 Hear O my people, *heark'n well,*
   I testifie to thee
   Thou antient flock of Israel,
   If thou wilt list to mee,
9 Through out the land of thy abode
   No alien God shall be
 Nor shalt thou to a forein God
   In honour bend thy knee.   40
10 I am the Lord thy God which brought
   Thee out of Ægypt land
 Ask large enough, and I, *besought,*
   Will grant thy full demand.
11 And yet my people would not *hear,*
   Nor hearken to my voice;
   And Israel *whom I lov'd so dear*
   Mislik'd me for his choice.
12 Then did I leave them to their will
   And to their wandring mind;   56
   Their own conceits they follow'd still
   Their own devises blind.
13 O that my people would *be wise*
   To serve me *all their daies,*
   And O that Israel would *advise*
   To walk my *righteous* waies.
14 Then would I soon bring down their foes
   That now so proudly rise,
   And turn my hand against *all those*
   That are their enemies.   60
15 Who hate the Lord should *then be fain*
   To bow to him and bend,
 But *they, his people, should remain,*
   Their time should have no end.
16 And he would feed them *from the shock*
   With flowr of finest wheat,
 And satisfie them from the rock
   With Honey *for their Meat.*

PSAL. LXXXII

1 God in the * great * assembly stands   * *Bagnadath-el.*
   Of Kings and lordly States,
Among the gods † on both his hands   † *Bekerev.*
   He judges and debates.
2 How long will ye * pervert the right   * *Tishphetu*
   With * judgment false and wrong   *gnavel.*
Favouring the wicked *by your might,*
   Who thence grow bold and strong?
3 * Regard the * weak and fatherless   * *Shiphtu-dal.*
   * Dispatch the * poor mans cause,   1c
And † raise the man in deep distress
   By † just and equal Lawes.   † *Hatzdiku.*
4 Defend the poor and desolate,
   And rescue from the hands
Of wicked men the low estate
   Of him *that help demands.*
5 They know not nor will understand,
   In darkness they walk on,
The Earths foundations all are * mov'd   * *Jimmotu.*
   And * out of order gon.   2c
6 I said that ye were Gods, yea all
   The Sons of God most high
7 But ye shall die like men, and fall
   As other Princes *die.*
8 Rise God, * judge thou the earth *in might,*
This *wicked* earth * redress,   * *Shiphta.*
For thou art he who shalt by right
   The Nations all possess.

PSAL. LXXXIII

1 Be not thou silent *now at length*
   O God hold not thy peace,
Sit not thou still O God of *strength*
   We cry and do not cease.
2 For lo thy *furious* foes *now* * swell
   And * storm outrageously,   * *Jehemajun.*
And they that hate thee *proud and fell*
   Exalt their heads full hie.
3 Against thy people they † contrive   † *Jagnarimu.*
   † Their Plots and Counsels deep,   † *Sod.*
* Them to ensnare they chiefly strive   10
   * Whom thou dost hide and keep.   * *Jithjagnatsu*
                                           gnal.
                                           * *Tsephuneca.*
4 Come let us cut them off say they,
   Till they no Nation be
That Israels name for ever may
   Be lost in memory.
5 For they consult † with all their might,   † *Lev jachdau.*
   And all as one in mind
Themselves against thee they unite
   And in firm union bind.   20

6 The tents of Edom, and the brood
    Of *scornful* Ishmael,
  Moab, with them of Hagars blood
    That in the Desart dwell,
7 Gebal and Ammon *there conspire,*
    And *hateful* Amalec,
  The Philistims, and they of Tyre
    Whose bounds the Sea doth check.
8 With them *great* Asshur also bands
    And doth confirm the knot,   30
  All these have lent their armed hands
    To aid the Sons of Lot.
9 Do to them as to Midian *bold*
    That wasted all the Coast.
  To Sisera, and as *is told*
    Thou didst to Jabins *hoast,*
  When at the brook of Kishon *old*
    They were repulst and slain,
10 At Endor quite cut off, and rowl'd   40
    As dung upon the plain.
11 As Zeb and Oreb evil sped
    So let their Princes *speed.*
  As Zeba, and Zalmunna *bled*
    So let their Princes *bleed.*
12 *For they amidst their pride* have said
    By right now shall we seize
  Gods houses, and *will now invade*
    † Their stately Palaces.
13 My God, oh make them as a wheel
    No quiet let them find,
  Giddy and *restless* let *them reel*
    Like stubble from the wind.
14 As *when* an *aged* wood takes fire
    Which on a sudden straies,   50
  The *greedy* flame runs hier and hier
    Till all the mountains blaze,
15 So with thy whirlwind them pursue,
    And with thy tempest chase;
16 * And till they * yield thee honour due,
    Lord fill with shame their face.   60
17 Asham'd and troubl'd let them be,
    Troubl'd and sham'd for ever,
  Ever confounded, and so die
    With shame, *and scape it never.*
18 Then shall they know that thou whose name
    Jehova is alone,
  Art the most high, *and thou the same*
    O're all the earth *art one.*

PSAL. LXXXIV

1 How lovely are thy dwellings fair!
    O Lord of Hoasts, how dear
  The *pleasant* Tabernacles are!

Where thou do'st dwell so near.

2 My Soul doth long and almost die
    Thy Courts O Lord to see,
My heart and flesh aloud do crie,
    O living God, for thee.

3 There ev'n the Sparrow *freed from wrong*
    Hath found a house of *rest,*   10
The Swallow there, to lay her young
    Hath built her *brooding* nest,
Ev'n *by* thy Altars Lord of Hoasts
    They find their safe abode,
And home they fly from round the Coasts
    Toward thee, My King, my God.

4 Happy, who in thy house reside
    Where thee they ever praise,

5 Happy, whose strength in thee doth bide,
    And in their hearts thy waies.   20

6 They pass through Baca's *thirstie* Vale,
    That dry and barren ground
As through a fruitfull watry Dale
    Where Springs and Showrs abound.

7 They journey on from strength to strength
    With joy and gladsom cheer
Till all before *our* God *at length*
    In Sion do appear.

8 Lord God of Hoasts hear *now* my praier
    O Jacobs God give ear,   30

9 Thou God our shield look on the face
    Of thy anointed *dear.*

10 For one day in thy Courts *to be*
    Is better, *and more blest*
Then *in the joyes of Vanity,*
    A thousand daies *at best.*
I in the temple of my God
    Had rather keep a dore,
Then dwell in Tents, *and rich abode*
    With Sin *for evermore.*   40

11 For God the Lord both Sun and Shield
    Gives grace and glory *bright,*
No good from them shall be with-held
    Whose waies are just and right.

12 Lord *God* of Hoasts *that raign'st on high,*
    That man is *truly* blest,
Who *only* on thee doth relie,
    And in thee only rest.

PSAL. LXXXV

1 THY Land to favour graciously
    Thou hast not Lord been slack,
Thou hast from *hard* Captivity
    Returned Jacob back.

2 Th' iniquity thou didst forgive
 That wrought thy people woe,
 'And all their Sin, *that did thee grieve*
 Hast hid *where none shall know*.
3 Thine anger all thou hadst remov'd,
 And *calmly* didst return
From thy † fierce wrath which we had prov'd
 Far worse then fire to burn.
4 God of our saving health and peace,
 Turn us, and us restore,
Thine indignation cause to cease
 Toward us, *and chide no more*.
5 Wilt thou be angry without end,
 For ever angry thus
Wilt thou thy frowning ire extend
 From age to age on us?
6 Wilt thou not * turn, and *hear our voice*
 And us again * revive,
That so thy people may rejoyce
 By thee preserv'd alive.
7 Cause us to see thy goodness Lord,
 To us thy mercy shew
Thy saving health to us afford
 And life in us renew.
8 *And now* what God the Lord will speak
 I will *go strait and* hear,
For to his people he speaks peace
 And to his Saints *full dear,*
To his dear Saints he will speak peace
 But let them never more
Return to folly, *but surcease*
 To trespass as before.
9 Surely to such as do him fear
 Salvation is at hand
And glory shall *ere long appear*
 To dwell within our Land.
10 Mercy and Truth *that long were miss'd*
 Now *joyfully* are met
Sweet Peace and Righteousness have kiss'd
 And hand in hand are set.
11 Truth from the earth *like to a flowr*
 Shall bud and blossom *then,*
And Justice from her heavenly bowr
 Look down *on mortal men.*
12 The Lord will also then bestow
 Whatever thing is good
Our Land shall forth in plenty throw
 Her fruits *to be our food.*
13 Before him Righteousness shall go
 His Royal Harbinger,
Then * will he come, and not be slow
 His footsteps cannot err.

† Heb. *The burning heat of thy wrath.*

* Heb. *Turn to quicken us.*

* Heb. *He will set his steps to the way.*

10

20

30

40

50

PSAL. LXXXVI

1 THY *gracious* ear, O Lord, encline,
   O hear me I *thee pray,*
For I am poor, and almost pine
   With need, *and sad decay.*

2 Preserve my soul, for † I have trod
   Thy waies, and love the just,
Save thou thy servant O my God
   Who *still* in thee doth trust.

3 Pitty me Lord for daily thee
   I call; 4 O make rejoyce
Thy Servants Soul; for Lord to thee
   I lift my soul *and voice,*

5 For thou art good, thou Lord art prone
   To pardon, thou to all
Art full of mercy, thou *alone*
   To them that on thee call.

6 Unto my supplication Lord
   Give ear, and to the crie
Of my *incessant* praiers afford
   Thy hearing graciously.

7 I in the day of my distress
   Will call on thee *for aid;*
For thou wilt *grant* me *free access*
   And answer, *what I pray'd.*

8 Like thee among the gods is none
   O Lord, nor any works
Of all that other gods have done
   Like to thy *glorious* works.

9 The Nations all whom thou hast made
   Shall come, *and all shall frame*
To bow them low before thee Lord,
   And glorifie thy name.

10 For great thou art, and wonders great
   By thy strong hand are done,
Thou *in thy everlasting Seat*
   Remainest God alone.

11 Teach me O Lord thy way *most right,*
   I in thy truth will bide,
To fear thy name my heart unite
   So shall it never slide.

12 Thee will I praise O Lord my God
   Thee honour, and adore
With my whole heart, and blaze abroad
   Thy name for ever more.

13 For great thy mercy is toward me,
   And thou hast free'd my Soul
Eev'n from the lowest Hell set free
   From deepest darkness foul.

14 O God the proud against me rise
   And violent men are met
To seek my life, and in their eyes

† Heb. *I am good,
loving, a doer
of good and
holy things.*

10

20

30

40

50

No fear of thee have set.
15 But thou Lord art the God most mild
    Readiest thy grace to shew,
  Slow to be angry, and *art stil'd*
    Most mercifull, most true.
16 O turn to me *thy face at length,*
    And me have mercy on,
  Unto thy servant give thy strength,
    And save thy hand-maids Son.   60
17 Some sign of good to me afford,
    And let my foes *then* see
  And be asham'd, because thou Lord
    Do'st help and comfort me.

PSAL. LXXXVII

1 AMONG the holy Mountains *high*
    Is his foundation fast,
  There Seated in his Sanctuary,
    His Temple there is plac't.
2 Sions *fair* Gates the Lord loves more
    Then all the dwellings *faire*
  Of Jacobs *Land, though there be store,*
    And all within his care.
3 City of God, most glorious things
    Of thee *abroad* are spoke;   10
4 I mention Egypt, *where proud Kings*
    Did our forefathers yoke,
  I mention Babel to my friends,
    Philistia *full of scorn,*
  And Tyre with Ethiops *utmost ends,*
    Lo this man there was born:
5 But *twise that praise shall in our ear*
    Be said of Sion *last*
  This and this man was born in her,
    High God shall fix her fast.   20
6 The Lord shall write it in a Scrowle
    That ne're shall be out-worn
  When he the Nations doth enrowle
    That this man there was born.
7 Both they who sing, and they who dance
    With sacred Songs are there,
  In thee *fresh brooks, and soft streams glance*
    And all my fountains *clear.*

PSAL. LXXXVIII

1 LORD God that dost me save and keep,
    All day to thee I cry;
  And all night long, before thee *weep*
    Before thee *prostrate lie.*
2 Into thy presence let my praier
    With sighs devout ascend

And to my cries, that *ceaseless are,*
   Thine ear with favour bend.
3 For cloy'd with woes and trouble store
   Surcharg'd my Soul doth lie,
My life *at deaths uncherful dore*   10
   Unto the grave draws nigh.
4 Reck'n'd I am with them that pass
   Down to the *dismal* pit
I am a * man, but weak alas   * Heb. *A man*
   And for that name unfit.   *without manly*
                                    strength.
5 From life discharg'd and parted quite
   Among the dead *to sleep,*
And like the slain *in bloody fight*
   That in the grave lie *deep.*   20
Whom thou rememberest no more,
   Dost never more regard,
Them from thy hand deliver'd o're
   Deaths hideous house hath barr'd.
6 Thou in the lowest pit *profound*
   Hast set me *all forlorn,*
Where thickest darkness *hovers round,*
   In horrid deeps *to mourn.*
7 Thy wrath *from which no shelter saves*
   Full sore doth press on me;   30
* Thou break'st upon me all thy waves,   * The Heb.
  * And all thy waves break me.   *bears both.*
8 Thou dost my friends from me estrange,
   And mak'st me odious,
Me to them odious, *for they change,*
   And I here pent up thus.
9 Through sorrow, and affliction great
   Mine eye grows dim and dead,
Lord all the day I thee entreat,
   My hands to thee I spread.   40
10 Wilt thou do wonders on the dead,
   Shall the deceas'd arise
And praise thee *from their loathsom bed*
   With pale and hollow eyes?
11 Shall they thy loving kindness tell
   On whom the grave *hath hold,*
Or they *who* in perdition *dwell*
   Thy faithfulness *unfold?*
12 In darkness can thy mighty *hand*
   Or wondrous acts be known,
Thy justice in the *gloomy* land   50
   Of *dark* oblivion?
13 But I to thee O Lord do cry
   E're yet my life be spent,
And *up to thee* my praier *doth hie*
   Each morn, and thee prevent.
14 Why wilt thou Lord my soul forsake,
   And hide thy face from me,
15 That am already bruis'd, and † shake   † Heb. *Præ Con-*
                                  cussione.

With terror sent from thee;   60
Bruz'd and afflicted and *so low*
As ready to expire,
While I thy terrors undergo
Astonish'd with thine ire.
16 Thy fierce wrath over me doth flow
Thy threatnings cut me through.
17 All day they round about me go,
Like waves they me persue.
18 Lover and friend thou hast remov'd
And sever'd from me far.   70
They *fly me now* whom I have lov'd,
And as in darkness are.

[The text of the Latin and Greek poems is at page 111.]

TRANSLATIONS OF LATIN AND GREEK POEMS

The author is well aware that in the tributes which follow he is not so much appreciated as over-appreciated, because men of distinguished ability who are also friends are apt, in their eagerness to praise, to express everything in terms that accord rather with their own fine qualities than with the actual facts. Nevertheless, he is unwilling that the high regard which these gentlemen have for him should not be known, especially since others have been urgent with him to bring this about. For while he is doing his utmost to avert from himself the odium of extravagant praise, and prefers that nothing should be ascribed to him which exceeds the bounds of fairness, still he cannot deny that he regards this estimate of men who are famous for their genius as a mark of the highest honor to himself.

Giovanni Battista Manso, Marquis of Villa, of Naples, to John Milton, Englishman.

If your piety were such as is your mind, your form, charm, face, and manners, then you would be not an Angle but indeed a veritable Angel.

To John Milton, Englishman, who deserves to be crowned with the triple laurel of poetry, Greek, Latin, and Tuscan, an epigram of Giovanni Salsilli, of Rome.

Yield, Meles; let Minicus yield with lowered urn; let Sebetus cease to speak always of Tasso; but let the Thames victoriously exalt its waters above them all; for through thee, Milton, it alone will be the peer of all three.

To John Milton

Let Greece boast of Maeonides and Rome of Maro; England boasts of Milton, the peer of both.

Selvaggi.

To John Milton, English Nobleman.

ODE

Raise me, Clio, to the celestial sphere, that I may entwine a wreath of stars and not of the eternal branches of the fair god in Pindus and Helicon. Greater merit deserves greater ornaments. celestial praise is meet for heavenly virtue.

A lofty eternal salve cannot be a prey to destructive Time. Consuming oblivion cannot steal exalted honor from our memories. May virtue affix a strong arrow upon the bow of my lyre and I shall strike down Death itself. England girt by the broad expanses of the deep ocean stands off separated from the world. Therefore its worth excels that of other human beings. This fertile land brings forth heroes who rightly may be called super-human.

Their breasts afford a trusted shelter to banished virtue, which alone is dear to them because they know how to find in it joy and pleasure. Do thou repeat it, John, and do thou show by thy true virtue that my song is truthful.

Zeuxis was driven away from his native land by his eager desire; for he had heard the world wide renown of Helen's fame and in order to be able to reproduce her adequately he culled the rarest of all the fairest beauties.

Thus the industrious bee extracts laboriously its valued juice from lilies and roses and all the other flowers that adorn the lawns. Different chords make one pleasing sound, and various voices make a concordant melody.

Milton, lover of fair Renown, thou didst depart from thy native land to set thy wandering foot in various countries in quest of sciences and arts. Thou sawest the kingdoms of the swaying Gaul, and the worthiest heroes of Italy.

Thy almost divinely creating thought, in search of virtue only, saw in every land all those who tread the path of noble value. It discerned the best from the good and used it to forge therewith the image of all virtues.

All those who were born in Florence, or who learned there the art of speaking the Tuscan language, those whose memory, perpetuated in learned books, is honored by the world, all were sought out and cherished by you; and you conversed with them through their works.

Jehovah in vain, as far as thou art concerned, confused the languages in lofty Babel, —the tower which crashed to earth, a self-made trophy of various speeches. For thou hast mastered the languages of Spain, France, Tuscany, Greece and Rome.

Thou hast clearly penetrated the most profound mysteries which nature conceals on earth and in the heavens and which sometimes it hides in its avarice even from super-human intellects. And thou dost reach in the end the great threshold of moral virtue.

Let Time halt its wings. Let it stop; and so may the years pause which consume the memories of immortal virtue. For if there ever were deeds worthy of poetry or of history, thou hast them present in thy mind.

Give me thy sweet lyre if I am to speak of thy sweet song which reaps its reward in making thee a heavenly man in raising thee to the skies. The Thames will boast that because of thee, its Swan, it now can rival the river Permessus.

I, who on the banks of the Arno strive to proclaim your lofty merit, I know that I toil in vain and that I learn how to admire it, but not how to praise it. Therefore I curb my tongue and I listen to my heart which undertakes to praise thee with wonder.

Antonio Francini, noble man of Florence.

To John Milton of London.

To a young man distinguished alike for his nationality and for his excellences;

to a man who in his travels has examined many places upon the earth's surface, who in his studies has examined them all, in order that, like a modern Ulysses, he might everywhere learn everything from every one;

to a polyglot on whose lips languages now quite dead so live again that in his praise all forms of speech are inadequate; and who in these forms is so nicely expert that he understands the expressions of popular admiration and applause called forth by the wisdom that is his, and his alone;

to him whose endowments of mind and of person stir the senses to admiration and through that very admiration deprive everyone of power to act; whose works summon to applause, but by their charm render his admirers speechless;

to one in whose memory lives the whole world; in whose understanding wisdom; in whose will the passion for fame; on whose lips eloquence; who with Astronomy to guide him hears the harmonies of the heavenly spheres; who with Philosophy to teach him deciphers the meanings of the marvels of nature through which the greatness of God is portrayed; who with constant reading of authors as his companion, in the places in which the facts of ancient history lie hidden, in the ruins of bygone time, in the mazes of scholarship, interrogates, restores, traverses (but why do I strain up the steeps?);

to him in the publishing of whose excellences the tongues of Rumor would not suffice, nor in their praise the amazement of his fellow-beings, in token of reverence and love this tribute of admiration due to his desert is offered by Charles Dato, a Patrician of Florence, devoted servant of so great a man, devoted lover of excellence so great.

ELEGIES AND EPIGRAMS.

Liber Primus.

Elegy I to *Charles Diodati.*

At last, dear friend, a letter from you has come to me and the note-paper, your messenger, has brought me your words, brought them, in fact, from the western bank of the Dee, near Chester, where the descending current seeks the Vergivian Sea. Great, believe me, is my delight that a region so far away has cherished a heart that loves me and a soul so loyal, and that that distant country owes me my engaging comrade and is willing to give him back to me presently at my bidding.

I am housed in the city which the Thames washes with its refluent waves and am well content to be in my dear native town. No longer am I interested in returning to the Cam and its reeds, nor am I tormented with longing for my room there from which I have long been debarred. Those bare fields that grant no pleasant shade do not attract me (How ill does that place beseem the votaries of Phoebus!), nor am I disposed to continue to endure the threats of the stern Master and the other incidents to which my nature cannot submit. If this be exile, to be again in my father's home and, without a care, to follow the pleasant suggestions of leisure, then I reject neither the name nor the lot of a rusticated man, but rather am happy in the terms of my exile. (Oh, that the poet, that sad exile in the region of Tomis, had suffered nothing worse; then he would not have yielded in aught to Ionian Homer, and thou, Maro, wouldst have been surpassed and so deprived of thy primacy of praise.) For here I may give my hours without restriction to the gentle Muses and am wholly absorbed in my books, which, indeed, constitute my life. When I am weary, I am rapt away by the pageantry of the rounded theatre and the voices on the stage call me to their due applause. Now I listen to the shrewdness of age, now to the prodigal heir; now the suitor appears, now the soldier without his helmet, or the lawyer with his inexhaustible ten-year case thunders out barbarous words to an uneducated court. Often the cunning slave comes to the help of his young master in a love affair, and at every point deceives the very nose of the unbending father; often the maiden, wondering at the new warmth of her feelings, knows not what love is, and even while she knows not, loves. Now frenzied Tragedy shakes her bloodstained sceptre; her hair streams wildly as she rolls her eyes. I am distressed but continue to watch, and find pleasure in watching though distressed. From time to time there is in my tears a sweet bitterness, as when an unfortunate lad has left his joys untasted and falls pitifully because of thwarted love; or some fierce avenger of crime comes back across the Styx from the darkness, startling guilty hearts with Death's own torch; or the house of Pelops, or, it may be, the house of noble Ilus mourns, or the palace of Creon pays the penalties of his incestuous line.

But I do not always seclude myself in the house, nor even in the city, and the spring days do not pass without yielding me some proper enjoyment. I, too, may be found in the groves where the elms stand close together or under the noble shade of some spot near the city. Here often one may see groups of maidens go by, stars breathing soft flames. Ah, how many times have I been entranced by the miracle of some wondrous beauty such as might make even aged Jove a youth again. Ah, how many times have I seen eyes that surpassed gems and all the stars that either pole keeps in revolution, necks that outshone the arms of Pelops twice alive and the Way that flows moist with pure nectar; how many times exquisite beauty of brow and waving tresses, golden snares that deceiving Love spreads, and alluring cheeks in comparison with which the crimson of the hyacinth and even the blush of thy flower, Adonis, lack lustre. Yield, ye Heroides, so often praised in days of old, and every leman that captivated inconstant Jove; yield, ye Achaemenian maids with towering head-dress, and all that dwell in Susa and in Memnonian Nineveh; do ye also, maidens of Danaus, lower the *fasces,* and ye, brides of Ilium and of Romulus. Let not the Tarpeian Muse boast of Pompey's colonnade and of the theatre full of Ausonian stoles. It is to the maids of England that the foremost glory is due; let it be enough for thee, foreign woman, to be able to follow after. And thou, oh city of London, built by Dardanian settlers, conspicuous far and wide for thy turreted head, thou, fortunate to excess, dost enclose within thy walls all the beauty that the pendent earth possesses. Not so many are the stars that sparkle in thy clear air, hosts that attend upon Endymion's goddess, as are the maidens that, conspicuous for golden beauty, move through thy streets, a radiant throng to see. Men believe that to this spot came life-giving Venus herself, drawn by her twin doves, with her quivered soldier close to her side, ready to rank this city above Cnidos and the valleys that are watered by the stream of Simois, above Paphos too and rosy Cyprus.

But I, while the indulgent mood of the blind boy permits, am preparing to leave these happy precincts with all convenient speed, and to keep far away from the ill-famed halls of treacherous Circe, using the help of the divine plant of moly. I am resolved also to go back to the rush-grown marshes of the Cam, and to hear again the hoarse murmur of the school-room. Meantime, take this slight gift of a faithful friend, these few words brought into elegiac measures.

Elegy II.

On the Death of the Beadle of the University of Cambridge.

It was your custom as you drew all eyes with your glittering mace, to call together again and again the company of Pallas; now grim Death, the last beadle of all, carries you, too, off, beadle though you are, and shows no indulgence even to her own office. Though the hair on your forehead was whiter than the plumage beneath which, as tradition tells us, Jove hid for safety, nevertheless,—Oh, you should have grown young again through an Haemonian elixir; should have been able to reach the years of Aeson; should have been called back from the Stygian waters by the son of Coronis through his healing art in answer to the repeated entreaties of the goddess. If you had been ordered to summon the robed lines and to go, a swift messenger, from your Phoebus, you used to stand as stood wing-footed Cyllenius in the Trojan hall, sent from the ethereal citadel of his father; you used to speak as spoke Eurybates when he delivered the stern command of the leader Atrides before the face of furious Achilles. Oh, mighty queen of the tombs, attendant upon Avernus, too cruel to the Muses, to Pallas too cruel, why should you not seize those who are a mere useless weight of earth? It is such a crowd that deserves to be attacked by your shafts. For this man, therefore, Academe, in sable vestments mourn, and let his black bier be wet with your tears. Let complaining Elegy in person pour forth sad strains, and let a dirge fill all the schools with mournful sound.

Elegy III.

On the Death of the Bishop of Winchester.

I was sad, and with none to bear me company, sat in silence, and many sorrows had found a home in my soul. And lo, all suddenly, there rose before me the vision of the deadly havoc which Libitina had wrought on English soil, when dire Death, formidable with her sepulchral torch, entered the lustrous marble palaces of princes, struck walls that were heavy with gold and jasper, and did not fear to lay prostrate with her scythe the hosts of rulers. Then I recalled that distinguished duke and his revered brother (their bones were consumed on pyres before their time), and I recalled also those heroes whom all Belgia saw snatched away to the skies and wept the while for the leaders she had lost. But for you, especially, I mourned, right worthy Bishop, once the great glory of your Winchester. I burst into tears and thus in accents sad made my plaint: "O ruthless Death, Goddess second to Tartarean Jove, is it not enough that the forest feels thy anger, that authority is given thee over the green fields, that at the taint of thy breath the lilies droop, the crocus too and the rose sacred to lovely Cypris? Thou dost not permit the oak on the brink of the stream to marvel forever at the soft motion of the passing water; to thee succumb the birds, prescient though they are, that in flocks are borne on their pinions in the clear sky; all the thousands of animals that wander in the dark forests, and the mute herd that the caves of Proteus sustain. Envious Goddess, seeing that power so great has been granted thee, what pleasure dost thou gain from staining thy hands in human blood, from sharpening thy unerring arrows against a noble breast, and driving from its abode a soul half divine?

While with tears I revolved these thoughts deep in my heart, dewy Hesperus came up from the western waters, and Phoebus had submerged his chariot in the sea of Tartessus, completing his journey from the shores of the Orient. I delayed not, but stretched my limbs in hope of refreshment on my yielding couch; night and sleep had sealed my eyes, when suddenly I seemed to be walking in a broad demesne. Alas, my powers are inadequate to describe the scene. There all things shone with roseate light, as when the mountain ridges redden with the morning sun; and the ground was bright with a garment of many colors as when Thaumas's daughter displays her riches. Not with such varied blossoms did the goddess Chloris, beloved by light Zephyr, adorn the gardens of Alcinous. Silver streams lapped the green fields, the sands showed a deeper yellow than Hesperian Tagus; through those fragrant riches stole the light breath of Favonius, a breath born all dewy beneath countless roses. Such at the farthest bounds of the land of the Ganges is the home of royal Lucifer imagined to be. While I myself was marveling at the dense shade cast by the clustering vines, and the luminous spaces all about me, lo, all suddenly, the Bishop of Winchester stood before me! A starry radiance shone on his bright face; his lustrous vestment flowed down to his golden sandals, a white fillet encircled his sainted head. And while thus clad the venerable old man moved onward, the blossoming earth shook with joyous sounds. The heavenly hosts joyfully moved their jeweled wings; the pure air resounded with a triumphal clarion. Each angel greeted with embrace and song his new companion, and One uttered from his peaceful lips these words: "Come, my son, and joyously receive the happiness of thy Father's kingdom; henceforth forever, my son, rest from thy hard labors." He spoke, and the winged hosts touched their harps. But for me, golden rest was driven away together with the darkness; and I wept that my slumbers were disturbed by the beloved of Cephalus. May such dreams often be my happy lot!

Elegy IV.

To Thomas Young, his tutor, performing the duties of Chaplain to the English merchants resident in Hamburg.

Make haste, my letter, make haste to cross the illimitable sea; go; over the smooth waters seek the borders of Germany; break the bonds of sluggish delay; let nothing, I pray, impede you as you go, let nothing stay your journey as you hasten on. I myself will importune Aeolus, who curbs the winds in his Sicanian cavern, and the sea-green gods, and azure Doris with her attendant nymphs, to grant you a quiet pathway through their realms. But do you, if you can, gain for yourself the swift team that bore the Colchian as she fled from the face of her husband, or the team that brought Triptolemus into the borders of Scythia, a welcome lad sent from the city of Eleusis. And when you shall see the yellow sands of Germany, turn your steps to the walls of wealthy Hamburg, which is said to derive its name from Hama, to whom a Cimbrian club gave the death-blow. In that city there lives a minister, famous for his noble practice of old-time piety and skilled in feeding the sheep that love Christ. That man is indeed more than the other half of my soul; I am now forced to live with only half of my life. Ah me, how many seas, how many mountains intervene to deprive me of the other part of myself! Dearer is he to me than were you, most learned of the Greeks, to Clinias's son, who traced his lineage to Telamon; than the great Stagirite to his royal pupil whom the loving daughter of Chaonia bore to Libyan Jove. As was the son of Amyntor, as was the heroic son of Philyra to the King of the Myrmidons, such is this man to me. With him to lead the way, I first traversed the Aonian glens and the sacred boskage of the twice-cloven peak, drank of the Pierian spring, and by Clio's grace thrice wet my happy lips with Castalia's wine. But flaming Aethon had thrice beheld the Sign of the Ram and covered its fleecy back with new gold, and twice, Chloris, thou hadst scattered fresh grass over the aged earth, and twice had Auster carried off thy riches; but not yet had it been my privilege to feed my eyes on his face or with my ears to drink in the sweet sounds of his voice.

Go, then, and outstrip sonorous Eurus in thy course. What need there is of admonition the facts declare and you yourself see. You will find him, perhaps, sitting by the side of his sweet wife, caressing on his lap the dear pledges of their love; or, it may be, turning the pages of the huge tomes of the ancient Fathers or the Holy Books of the true God, or refreshing with celestial dew tender souls, the great and saving task of religion. Let it be your care to give him, in customary fashion, hearty greeting, such as it would befit your master to express if only he were there. Remember, too, to say these words deferentially as you fix for a while your modest eyes upon the ground: These lines, if indeed in the midst of fighting there is leisure for the peaceful Muses, a faithful hand sends to you from the shores of England. Accept his sincere greeting, late though it be, and for this very reason may it be more welcome to you. Late, it is true, but from the heart came that greeting which chaste Penelope, Icarus's daughter, received from her laggard husband. But why do I wish to blot out an obvious fault which my master himself is quite unable to extenuate? He is proven to be a laggard, as indeed he really is; he confesses his misdoing and is ashamed to have failed in his duty. Pray grant pardon to one who has confessed and who asks for pardon; faults which are acknowledged become less grave. Not against those who tremble does the wild beast open wide his jaws, nor does the lion seize with lacerating claw the prostrate. Often the cruel hearts of pike-bearing Thracians have softened at the pitiful entreaties of a suppliant; hands outstretched turn aside the lightning stroke, and a simple victim propitiates angry gods.

For a long time he was fain to write to you, and now love has not suffered him to prolong delay any further. For wandering Rumor (alas, true messenger of calamity!) declares that in the regions about you the tide of war is rising, that you and your city are surrounded by overbearing soldiers and that the Saxon chieftains have already taken up arms. Round about you, far and wide, Enyo is making the fields desolate, and now blood waters ground where the flesh of men has been sown. To the Germans Thrace has yielded its own Mars, to that country Father Mars has driven his Odrysian coursers. Now the ever-burgeoning olive is losing its foliage and the goddess that hates the brazen sound of the trumpet has fled, see, she has fled from earth, and now the Maid of Justice, unwilling to be the last, is believed to have flown to mansions in the skies. Meantime, around you resounds the horrid din of war; you live alone and penniless in a strange land, you in your poverty seek in an alien country the sustenance which your own country did not provide. Fatherland, stern parent, more cruel than the white cliffs upon which break in foam the waves of your coast, does it become you thus to expose your innocent children, do you thus with heart of iron force them to a foreign shore, and permit those to seek their livelihood in distant regions whom God himself in his foresight had sent to you, who bring you glad tidings from Heaven and show the way that after death leads to the stars? Thou dost indeed deserve to live imprisoned in Stygian darkness and to perish by the unending hunger of the soul! Just so did the prophet of the land of the Tishbites once tread with unaccustomed step the trackless wilds and the desert wastes of Arabia, as he fled from the hands of King Ahab and from thy hands too, ruthless woman of Sidon. In such wise, his limbs torn by the strident scourge, was Cilician Paul driven from the Emathian city, and Jesus Himself was ordered to depart from the borders of fishy Gergessa by its ungrateful citizens.

But take courage; let not hope fail because of carking care, let not pallid fear make your very bones tremble. For though you are beset by gleaming weapons and a thousand javelins threaten you with death, by no weapons shall your side, though defenceless, be injured, and of your blood shall no spear-point drink. For you yourself shall be safe under the gleaming aegis of God. He shall be your guardian, He your defender, He who beneath the walls of the citadel of Zion routed in the silence of the night the warriors of Assyria and put to flight those whom immemorial Damascus had sent from her ancient fields into the borders of Samaria, who terrified the serried cohorts with their trembling king, when in the empty air rang out the clear trumpet, when the horny hoofs beat the plain into dust, when the chariot, forward driven, shook the sandy ground, and there was heard the neighing of chargers rushing into battle, and the clash of steel and the deep roar of men's voices. Remember to hope (for this is left for the wretched), overcome thy misfortunes with courageous soul, and do not doubt that some day you will enjoy better times and once again will be able to see your home in your native land.

Elegy V.

On the Coming of Spring.

Time, revolving in an unbroken circle, now as the spring gains in warmth calls back new zephyrs; Earth, its losses made good, puts on for a brief space the garment of youth and, now released from the chains of cold, the ground becomes magically green. Am I deceived? Or do not my poetic powers also return? Is not inspiration mine, through bounty of the spring? Through bounty of the spring it is mine, and once again (who would believe it?) gains strength therefrom and now demands for itself some enterprise. Castaly and the twin peaks hover before my eyes and at night dreams bring to me Pirene; my breast is afire with mysterious emotions, and madness and divine sounds excite me within. The Delian god himself comes (I see his locks entwined with the laurel of Peneis), the Delian god in person. Now my mind is swept away into the heights of the clear sky and through the wandering clouds I move released from the body; through the shadows I am borne on and through caverns, those sanctuaries of poets, and the inner shrines of the gods lie open to me. My mind beholds all that is done on Olympus and dark Tartarus does not elude my vision.

To what lofty strain does my spirit give utterance with parted lips? To what does this madness, this divine frenzy, give birth? The spring, which has brought me inspiration, shall by that inspiration be sung. In this way she shall gain through the return of her own gift.

Now, Philomel, hidden in the young leaves, thou dost begin thy sweet cadences, while silence reigns throughout the woods. Let us begin together, I, in the city, thou amidst the trees, and let us both together sing the coming of spring. Joy! the change to spring has come again. Let us celebrate the glories of the spring, and let the Muse each year take up this enterprise. Now the sun, fleeing from the Ethiopians and the fields of Tithonus, turns to the regions of the North his golden reins. Short is the journey of night, short the stay of darksome night, abhorred night is bound for exile with her darkness. And now Lycaonian Boötes, no longer, as before, follows wearily the heavenly Wain on a long journey; now even the stars only here and there, through the sky, keep their wonted watches around the courts of Jove; for with the night are gone guile and slaughter and violence, and the gods are free from fear of the wickedness of the Giants. It may be that some shepherd, reclining on the summit of a cliff, exclaims as the dewy earth flushes with the first rays of the sun: "This night, Phoebus, thou certainly hadst no sweet dalliance to detain thy swift courses." Cynthia, as she sees from on high those light-bringing wheels, joyously goes back to her forests, assumes her quiver, and laying aside her faint rays, seems to rejoice that by her brother's help her own duties are so greatly lessened. "Aurora," Phoebus exclaims, "leave the chamber of thy aged lover; what pleasure does that ineffectual couch give thee? For thee on the green grass the hunter, Aeolus's son, is waiting. Up; towering Hymettus is keeping thy flame for thee." The golden-haired goddess by her blushes admits her fault, and more swiftly speeds the horses of the dawn.

Earth, re-born, puts off hated old age and longs, Phoebus, to submit to thy embraces. She longs for them and is worthy of them. For what is more beautiful than she as she voluptuously displays her fecund breasts, her breath redolent of Arabian harvests, her lovely lips sweet with balsam and Paphian roses. See, her lofty brow is crowned with sacred groves, as the towering pines encircle the goddess Ops on Mount Ida; and she entwines with many-colored flowers her dewy tresses, the flowers themselves adding to the pleasure she gives, even as the Sicanian goddess pleased the god of Taenarum when she had bound her flowing locks with blossoms. Look, Phoebus, yielding love calls to thee, and the spring breezes carry honeyed prayers; perfume-laden Zephyrus lightly moves his cinnamon-scented wings, and the very birds seem to bring blandishments. And not without dower does earth rashly seek thy affection, for it is not in poverty that she asks for the coveted nuptials. The life-giving goddess offers thee wholesome herbs for healing, and thus herself enhances thy fame. And if riches, if dazzling gifts move thee (for it is by gifts that love is often purchased), she proudly displays to thee all the wealth that she hides under the great sea and beneath the mountain heights. Ah! how often, when in weariness thou dost plunge down from the slopes of Olympus into the waters of the West, does she say: "Why, Phoebus, is it the cerulean mother who receives thee in the Hesperian waters when thou art faint with thy day's journey? What have you to do with Tethys? What with the waters of Tartessus? Why do you bathe your divine face in impure brine? Thou wilt do better, Phoebus, to seek coolness in my shade. Come hither: moisten thy heated locks in my dew. Softer slumber will come to thee on the cool grass. Come hither and lay thy brightness on my breast. Where thou liest, a softly whispering breeze will soothe us both as we rest on dewy roses. Believe me, the fate of Semele does not terrify me, nor the axle-trees that smoked for the horses of Phaethon. When thou shalt more wisely use thy fires, come hither and lay thy brightness on my breast."

Thus the wanton earth sighs forth her love, and all her children tumultuously follow the example of their mother. For now roving Cupid speeds o'er the whole wide earth and re-kindles his failing torch from the fire of the sun. The deadly horns of his bow ring with new strings; his flashing arrows sparkle dangerously with new steel. And now he essays to conquer even unconquerable Diana, even chaste Vesta, as she sits by her hallowed hearth. Venus herself, at this season of the year, renews her youth and is believed to have risen again from the warm waters of the sea. Through cities built of marble, the young men cry "Hymenaeus"; the shores and hollow rocks resound with the cry "Io Hymen." Hymen himself appears in festal array, comely in fitting tunic, his fragrant robe redolent of the crimson crocus. In crowds the maidens with gold-cinctured breasts go forth to gain the joys of the lovely spring. Each has her own prayer; still the prayer of all is one and the same, that Cytherea may give her the man that she desires.

Now, too, the shepherd modulates his theme on his pipe of seven reeds, and Phyllis has her songs to add thereto. The sailor propitiates his stars with song by night, and calls the light dolphins to the surface of the waters. Jupiter himself makes holiday with his consort on high Olympus and summons to his feast even the gods that serve him. Now, also, the satyrs, as the late twilight gathers, flit in swift bands over the blossoming fields, and with them Sylvanus, crowned with the leaves of his own cypress, at once a god half goat, a goat half god. And the Dryads that have been hidden deep within the old trees, now roam over the ridges, over the lonely fields. Maenalian Pan storms over sown fields and woodland copses; scarce is mother Cybele safe, scarce Ceres. Faunus, love-possessed, would fain ravish some Oread, while the trembling nymph takes to her heels for safety; now she hides, and though she does so, desires, since she is poorly concealed, to be seen, and flees, and though she flees, is anxious to be caught. The very gods do not hesitate to give the woods preference over the skies and every grove has its own divinity.

And long may every grove have its own divinity! Go not, I pray, ye gods, from your homes in the forest. May the ages of gold bring you back, O Jupiter, to the wretched earth! Why return to the clouds, thy direful armories? At least, Phoebus, drive on thy rapid coursers as slowly as thou mayest, and let the hours of spring pass insensibly. Let rough winter bring to us tardily its long, long nights, and let the shadows attack our pole later than is their wont.

Elegy VI.

To Charles Diodati, now staying in the country.

Who, having written on the 13th of December asking for indulgence for his verses (in case they should not seem as good as usual) on the ground that in the midst of the festivities with which his friends had welcomed him, he had not been able to give fruitful service to the Muses, received this reply.

I, who have eaten but little, send you a wish for good health which you, who have eaten too much, perhaps lack. But why does your Muse challenge mine and refuse to allow it to seek the seclusion that it desires? You would fain know through verse how much I love and cherish you; believe me, you will scarcely be able to discover this through verse, for my love cannot be imprisoned in contracted measures, and does not come whole and complete to a metre that limps.

How well you describe the stately feasts and the joys of December, the ceremonies that commemorate the Deity who came down from heaven, the delights of the country in winter and the Gallic must quaffed by the merry fireside. But why do you complain that poetry absents itself from wine and feasting? Song loves Bacchus and Bacchus loves song, and Phoebus was not ashamed to wear the green ivy clusters and to prefer that ivy to his own laurel. Right often on the Aonian hills have the ninefold throng, mingling with the rout of Thyoneus, cried "Euoe." Naso sent poor poetry from the Corallaean fields; for in that country there were no feasts nor planted vines. Of what but wine and roses and Lyaeus with his grapes did the Teian Muse sing in her short measures? Teumesian Euan inspires the poetry of Pindar and every page is redolent of the wine that had been quaffed, as it pictures the crash of the heavy chariot, overturning because the axle is broken, or the speed of the rider, dark with Elean dust. Only when his lips were moist with four-year-old wine did the Roman lyrist sing sweetly of Glycera, and of Chloe with her yellow hair. Your laden table with its noble provision strengthens your mind and kindles your inspiration. Your Massic cups foam with a fertile vein of song and from the jar itself you pour the verses stored therein. To these helps we add the devices of art, and Apollo, who enters the inner chambers of the heart; Bacchus, Apollo and Ceres, all give their favor to one person. No wonder, then, that such sweet verses should have been composed by three deities through you, when to this end they were agreed.

Now also the Thracian lute, all repoussé of gold, sounds for you, touched softly by skilled fingers, and against the background of hanging draperies is heard the music of the lyre, guiding with its vibrant art the dancing feet of the maidens. Let such scenes at least hold the attention of your Muses and call back all the creative power that your deadening indulgence drives away. Believe me, when the ivory sounds, and in time with the plectrum the gay throng fills the perfume-ladened rooms, you will feel Phoebus stealing silently into your heart, even as sudden warmth courses through your veins. And as the maiden plays, through her eyes and through her fingers, Thalia will slip swiftly into every nook and corner of your being.

For light Elegy is the concern of many gods, and calls to her measures whatever god she will. Bacchus comes to aid elegies, and Erato and Ceres and Venus, and tender Love with his rosy mother. To such poets, then, bountiful feasts are permitted, and frequent draughts of old wine. But the poet who sings of wars and of heaven subject now to mature Jove, and of pious heroes and leaders half divine, who sings now of the sacred conferences of the high gods, now of the abysmal realms where barks a savage dog, that poet should live sparingly as did the Samian teacher and should find in herbs his simple food. Let the crystal water stand beside him in a beechen cup, and let him drink only sober draughts from a pure spring. Let him have, in addition, a youth chaste and free from evil, uncompromising standards, and stainless hands. Such is your character, augur, when, bright with sacred vestments and lustral waters, you rise to approach the angry gods. In this fashion, we learn that wise Tiresias lived after he lost his eyesight and Ogygian Linus and Calchas, fugitive from his doomed home, and aged Orpheus, taming wild creatures amid those lonely caves. So Homer, eating but little and drinking but water, carried the Dulichian hero over the long stretches of sea and through the monster-making hall of Persa's daughter, child of Phoebus, and the waters made treacherous by the songs of women, and through thy realms, O King of the Lower World, where it is said that he held with black blood the hosts of the shades. For the poet is sacred to the gods and is their priest. His inmost soul and lips breathe Jove.

But if you shall desire to know what I am doing (if only at least you think it worth while to learn what I am doing), I am hymning the king of heavenly lineage, prince of peace, and the happy days promised by the sacred books; the wailing of the Christ child and the stabling under a poor roof of Him who rules, together with his Father, the realms on high; and the starry heavens and the hosts that sang in the upper air and the gods suddenly shattered in their own shrines. This is my gift to the birthday of Christ, the first rays of its dawn brought the theme to me. For you are waiting themes also studied on my native reeds, you shall be the judge to whom I shall recite them.

Elegy VII.

Not yet, sweet Amathusia, did I know thy laws, and my heart was yet void of Paphian fire. Often did I disdain the arrows of Cupid (mere childish weapons), and especially thy divinity, O Love. "Boy," I said, "pierce gentle doves, easy battles become so tender a general; or else, little one, celebrate a vainglorious triumph over sparrows; for thy warfare these are the fitting trophies. Why dost thou direct thy silly weapons against mankind? Against strong men that quiver of thine has no power." The Cyprian could not endure these taunts (for no god is quicker to anger) and so in fury blazed with double fire.

It was spring and, shining o'er the roofs of the houses, the light had brought to thee, O May, thy first day; but my eyes still sought receding night and could not endure the brightness of dawn. Beside my couch stood Love, tireless Love with iridescent wings. The motion of his quiver betrayed the presence of the god, his face, too, betrayed him, as did his sweetly threatening eyes, and all that beseemed a boy and Love. In such a guise did the lad of Sigeum mix full cups for amorous Jove on eternal Olympus; such the guise of him who drew to his kisses the beautiful nymphs, Hylas, Thiodamas's son, drawn down by the Naiad. He was angry (but you would have thought this anger becoming) and he uttered savage threats of exceeding bitterness. "Wretched man," he said, "you would with greater safety have gained wisdom from the example of others; now, you shall yourself bear witness to the might of my right hand. You shall be numbered among those who have experienced my power, in fact I shall increase belief in me through your sufferings. It was I myself (if you are unaware of the fact), that conquered Phoebus, proud as he was of his victory over the Python, and even that god bowed to me; and as often as he recalls the daughter of Peneus, he himself admits that my darts inflict a surer and severer injury. Compared with me the Parthian horseman who conquers a foe that is behind him cannot with greater skill bend his tense bow, the Cydonian hunter yields to me, and he also who all unwitting caused his wife's death. Giant Orion also was conquered by me, and strong-handed Hercules, and Hercules's friend, as well. Jove himself may hurl his thunderbolts at me, but my darts will first pierce the side of Jove. Your other doubts my arrows will better instruct, and your heart which I shall attack in no light fashion; stupid man, your Muses will not be able to defend you, and Phoebus's serpent will give you no help." Thus he spoke, and shaking his golden-pointed arrow he flew away to the warm breast of Cypris. But I was disposed to laugh as he thus savagely thundered his threats and had no fear at all of the boy.

Sometimes, in the city where our citizens promenade, sometimes where the fields near the town give pleasure, groups of maidens with goddess-like faces move radiantly to and fro along the walks; and with this accession of brightness the day shines with double splendor. Am I deceived? Or does Phoebus draw his rays from this source also? These pleasing sights I did not shun through any austerity; and I followed instinctively the suggestion of my youthful impulses; and taking no thought of the future I sent my glances to meet theirs; I could not control my eyes. As it chanced, I noted one maiden who outshone all the rest; that radiance was the beginning of my trouble. So Venus herself might wish to appear to mortals; so the queen of the gods should be the cynosure of all eyes. This maiden that villain Cupid had put in my path and quite alone had already laid this snare for me. The cunning god was in hiding near by, with a bunch of arrows and his heavy torch hanging on his back. There was no waiting; now he clung to her eyelids, now to her virgin face, he sprang thence to her lips, then nestled in her cheeks, and whenever the agile archer wanders, ah me, in a thousand places he smites my unarmed breast. Straightway, unwonted ardors filled my heart. I was consumed within with love and was all flame. Meantime, to my misery she who now alone pleased me, vanished, never again to meet my eyes; in mournful silence, I went on quite distraught, and in doubtful mood I wished again and again to turn back. I am torn in twain, part of me stands still, the other part follows my prayers, and I find pleasure in weeping for the joys so suddenly snatched from me. So did Juno's offspring mourn for his lost heaven when he was flung down upon the hearths of Lemnos; in such wise did Amphiaraus, as he was swept down to Orcus by his panicstricken horses, look back at the sunlight of which he was bereft. What am I to do, unhappy man that I am, o'ercome with sorrow? I may neither put away the love that has begun nor follow it up. Oh, that I may have the privilege of seeing once again that beloved face, and of telling her my sad tale. Perhaps she is not made of unimpressionable adamant, perhaps she would not be deaf to my prayers! Believe me, no one has ever burned with love so unhappily; I shall be put down as the first and only example. Be merciful, I pray, since thou art the winged deity of tender love; and let not thy deeds be at variance with thy office. Now, oh certainly now, thy bow fills me with terror, goddess-born, thou that art powerful by thy darts no less than by thy fire. Thy altars shall smoke with my gifts, and thou alone shall be the most exalted for me among the high gods. Take away my madness, I pray, or rather, do not take it away. I know not why, every one who loves is sweetly wretched. Do thou only graciously grant that if hereafter any maiden is to be mine, a single arrow shall pierce both the hearts whose destiny is love.

In these verses I once with froward mind and ill-directed zeal set up idle trophies of my folly. For baneful error caught and drove me thus astray, and my heedless youth was an unsound teacher; until the shade-embowered Academy offered me its Socratic rills and taught me to reject the yoke that I had accepted. Straightway all flame was quenched, and from that time my breast is rigid, encased in thick ice; whence it comes that the Boy himself fears cold for his arrows and even Venus dreads a Diomedean strength.

On the Gunpowder Plot.

When recently, traitorous Fawkes, you dared your unspeakable crime alike against the King and the nobles of Britain,—am I mistaken? or did you wish to seem in some degree kind and to offset your guilt with specious piety? You meant, of course, to send them to the courts of high heaven in a chariot of sulphurous flames with wheels of flying fire; just as he whose head the savage Parcae found inviolable left Jordan's fields, by whirlwind snatched away.

On the Same.

Was it thus, Beast that lurks upon the Seven Hills, that you tried to bestow heaven upon King James? Unless your divinity is able to offer better guerdons, be sparing, I pray, treacherous creature, of your gifts. The king, 'tis true, has late in time gone without you to his companionate stars, making no use of the aid of your hellish powder. Hurl rather, then, into heaven your shameful cowls and all the senseless gods of profane Rome; for unless in this or in some other way you aid each one, believe me, he will with scant comfort climb the road to Heaven.

On the Same.

King James made mock of the purgatorial fires without which the mansions of the skies may not be attained. Thereat, the triple-crowned Latin monster gnashed its teeth, and shook its ten horns with menace dire. "Not without punishment," it cried, "shall you, Briton, make light of my rites; you shall pay the penalty for your scorn of religion. For if you shall ever enter the starry citadel, only a painful way through flames will be open to you." Oh, how close to fatal reality were the words of your prophecy, words that barely lacked complete fulfilment! For it almost happened that swept up on high by Tartarean fire he went, a burned shade, to the precincts of Heaven.

On the Same.

Him whom just now impious Rome had by her curses devoted to the nether world, and had condemned to the Styx and the Taenarian abyss, him by a complete change she now longs to raise to the stars, and is eager to lift up to the high gods.

On the Inventor of Gunpowder.

Antiquity in its blindness praised Iapetus's son, who brought from the chariot of the Sun the heavenly torch; but, to my mind, he will be found to be the greater who, as we believe, stole from Jupiter his lurid arms and three-forked thunderbolt.

To Leonora singing in Rome.

To each person (believe it, ye peoples) has been assigned his own angel from heaven's ranks. What wonder, Leonora, if a greater glory is yours? For your voice itself expresses in sound Deity present among us. Either God or certainly the Third Mind of Heaven come down to earth, steals mysteriously through your throat, steals and graciously teaches mortal hearts the power to accustom themselves insensibly to eternal sounds. For if all things be God, and He pervade them all, in you alone He speaks, in all the rest He is present but silent.

To the Same.

Another Leonora captivated the poet Torquato, and in his mad love for her he lost his reason. Ah, unfortunate man, how much more happily would he have been destroyed in your time, Leonora, and for your sake! For he would have heard you sing with Pierian voice as you touched the golden strings of your mother's lyre. Although he rolled his eyes more wildly than Dircaean Pentheus, or even completely lost all intelligence, you, nevertheless, could likewise have been able to compose by your voice his blindly whirling senses, and, breathing peace deep into his love-sick heart, you could by your soul-stirring singing have restored him to himself.

To the Same.

Why, credulous Naples, boast of your liquid-voiced Siren and the famous shrine of Achelous's daughter, Parthenope? Why boast that the Naiad of the shore, when she died on your coast, had her holy body placed upon a Chalcidian pyre? Let me assure you, she still lives, and has exchanged the deep murmurs of Posilipo for the fair waters of the Tiber. There, crowned with the enthusiastic favor of the sons of Romulus, she holds rapt by her singing both mortals and gods.

A Fable about a Peasant and his Master.

A peasant gathered every year from an apple tree fruit of the finest flavor and brought it to his master in the city. The latter, taken by the incredible sweetness of the fruit, transferred the tree itself to his own garden. Up to that time the tree had been notably productive, but now, exhausted by length of years and moved from its accustomed soil, it straightway ceased to bear altogether. When this, at length, became clear to the master, finding himself mocked by his vain hope, he cursed the hands that had been so swift to their own harm, and cried, "How much better it had been to receive with gratitude those gifts of my tenant, small though they were; I could have curbed my desire for more and my greedy appetite; as it is, I have lost both the fruit and the tree as well.

Against the Hundred of Salmasius.

Who made Salmasius's "Hundred" easy for him? And taught this magpie to attempt our language? 'Twas his stomach that taught him this skill, and the hundred Jacobuses, the very life-blood of the purse of the exiled prince. For, if there dawns a hope for unrighteous money, then the very man who has just threatened to dissipate by a single puff the Primacy of the Pope, the Anti-Christ, will of his own accord join in the chant of the Cardinals.

Against Salmasius.

Rejoice, ye mackerel, and all the fish that are in the sea, ye that in the freezing winter shiver in your homes in the water! In pity for you, that distinguished knight Salmasius is graciously planning to clothe your nudity; and, being generous with scrivener's material, he is preparing for you paper wrappings, giving preference to the insignia, name and glory of Claudius Salmasius, in order that through the whole fish market you may carry the clients of this Knight who are most welcome to the libraries and bookshelves of gentlemen who wipe their noses on their elbows.

POEMS IN VARIOUS METRES.

On the Death of the Vice-Chancellor, a Physician.

Ye descendants of Iapetus who inhabit the pendulous rounded earth, learn to obey the laws of Fate and in token thereof stretch out suppliant hands to the Parcae. If once roving Death, issuing from Taenarum, summons you in accents melancholy, alas, delays and tricks are tried in vain. You must needs pass through the darkness of the Styx. If one's strong right arm availed to keep away the fated hour of Death, fierce Hercules would not have lain dead on Emathian Oeta, poisoned by Nessus's blood; and Ilion would not have seen Hector slain by the base deceit of envious Pallas, nor him whom as Jove wept the wraith of the son of Peleus destroyed with Locrian sword. If the spells of Hecate could keep grim Fate at bay, the mother of Telegonus would still live and still be notorious, and likewise through the use of her potent wand the sister of Aegialus. If the arts of physicians and unknown simples could deceive the threefold divinity, Machaon, deep-versed in herbs, would not have fallen by the spear of Eurypylus; and the blood-stained arrow of Echidna would not have slain you, son of Philyra, nor you, boy cut from your mother's womb, the shafts and bolt of thy grandfather.

And you, who are greater than your protégé Apollo, you to whom authority over our robed circle was granted, whom now leafy Cirrha mourns, and spring-encircled Helicon, would still be happily alive, would still be presiding over the company of Pallas, and not, indeed, without distinction; you would not in Charon's skiff have traversed the dismal recesses of the abyss. But Persephone broke the thread of your life, angry when she saw that by your arts and potent elixirs you had rescued so many from the black jaws of Death. Cherished Master, I pray that your body may rest beneath soft turf and that from your grave may grow roses and marigolds and the hyacinth with its purple bloom. Gentle be the judgment that Aeacus passes on you, and may Aetnaean Proserpine smile upon thee, and may you walk forever among the blessed in the Elysian fields.

On the Fifth of November.

Now, good King James, coming from the far-distant North, ruled Troy-sprung peoples and the far-stretching realms of Albion's sons, and now an inviolable treaty had united the sceptres of England and the Caledonian Scots. Peace-bringer, successful and rich, he sat on his new throne, without thought of hidden conspiracy or open enemy; when the fierce tyrant who reigns over Acheron's river of fire, father of the Eumenides, a wandering exile from ethereal Olympus, had, as it chanced, gone up and down the wide, wide world, counting the associates of his guilt, his faithful slaves destined to be sharers in his kingdom after the pangs of death.

Here he stirs furious tempests in mid-air; there he contrives hatred between inseparable friends. He arms invincible nations against each other's very lives and ruins realms that bloom with olive-bearing peace. Whomsoever he sees enamoured of stainless virtue he longs to bring under his sway and, himself an adept in guile, tries to seduce hearts that are closed against crime; he makes secret plots, stretches concealed snares to catch the unwary, even as the Caspian tigress follows her trembling prey through trackless wastes at night when no moon shines and the stars wink half-asleep. With such disasters does Summanus, wrapped in a smoking whirlwind of blue flame, assail peoples and cities.

And now there comes in sight a land white with cliffs against which the breakers dash, a land beloved by the god of the sea, to which long ago the son of Neptune had given his name, not hesitating to cross the ocean and challenge fierce Amphitryoniades to mortal combat before the cruel years of captured Troy. As soon as he beheld this land blessed with wealth and festal peace, its fields rich with the bounty of Ceres, and (what distressed him more) a people worshiping the holy will of the true God, he finally burst into sighs that reeked with Tartarean fires and lurid sulphur; such sighs as the savage monster Typhoeus, imprisoned by Jove in Trinacrian Aetna, breathes from his corruption-laden mouth. Fire flashes from his eyes, and he grinds together his rows of adamantine teeth with a sound like the din of arms and the stroke of spear upon spear. And then he cried: "I have traveled the whole world o'er and found only this sight food for tears; this people alone rebels against me, despises my yoke, and exceeds in power my arts. Still, if my efforts can accomplish anything, they shall not long do this with impunity, they shall not go unpunished." This and no more; then with his pitch-black wings he swims in the liquid air. Wherever he flies, warring winds in battalions race before him, the clouds thicken, and the thunder and lightning are incessant.

And now he had swiftly passed over the ice-mantled Alps and was within the borders of Ausonia. On his left was cloud-capped Apennine, and the old Sabine country; on his right Etruria, notorious for its many poisonings; he also saw thee, Tiber, stealing kisses from Thetis. And now he alighted upon the citadel of Mavors's son, Quirinus. By this time the late twilight had rendered vision uncertain, when through the whole city the Wearer of the Triple Crown, carrying the gods made of bread was borne on the shoulders of men; kings came before him on bended knee, and a long line of mendicant friars holding wax tapers in their hands—for they are blind, born in Cimmerian darkness and dragging out their lives therein. Then they enter the temples bright with many a torch (it was the Eve sacred to Peter) and the noise of the choristers at intervals fills the empty domes and wide spaces; in such wise do Bromius and his rout howl as they celebrate their orgies on Echionian Aracynthus, while Asopus, overcome, quivers in his crystal waves, and even Cithaeron, far away, replies from his hollow cliff.

When, therefore, these ceremonies were concluded according to the prescribed ritual, Night silently left the embraces of ancient Erebus, and, with whip to urge them on, drives her coursers at head-long speed, blind Typhlon, fierce Melanchaetes, wilful Siope, born of an Acherontean sire, and Phrix, rough with shaggy hair.

Meantime the tamer of Kings, the heir of Phlegethon, enters his bridal chamber (for the secret adulterer prolongs no barren nights without a yielding leman); but scarce had sleep closed his eyes when the black lord of shades, the ruler of the silent folk, who preys upon men, stood beside him, disguised under a false appearance. His forehead shone with the white locks he had assumed, a long beard covered his breast; his ash-colored robe swept the ground in a long train, from his shaven head hung a cowl; and, that nothing might be lacking to the perfection of his device, he had bound his lustful loins with a hempen rope, and stepped slowly in latticed sandals. In such a guise (so the story goes) Francis used to wander all alone through the grewsome haunts of wild beasts in the wastes of the desert; and, himself impious, brought to the woodland people the pious words of salvation, and tamed wolves and Libyan lions.

Thus attired, the crafty Serpent deceitfully opened his accursed lips with these words: "Sleepest thou, my son? Does slumber still engulf thy limbs? O unmindful of the Faith and forgetful of thy sheep, while a barbarous people born under the Hyperborean sky mocks at thy throne, venerable priest, and at thy triple diadem, while the quiver-bearing Britons disdain thy authority! Rise, sluggard, whom the Latin Caesar reverences, to whom the unbarred portal of the vaulted sky is wide open. Break their haughty spirit and their shameless pride, and let this sacrilegious people know the potency of thy curse, and the power that lies in you as the custodian of the apostolic key. Mindful of the past, avenge Hesperia's scattered fleet and the standards of the Iberians sunk in the wide deep, and the many bodies of thy saints nailed to the shameful cross in the recent reign of the Thermodoontean Maiden. If, however, thou dost prefer to lie lazily on thy soft bed, and art unwilling to bruise the growing strength of the foe, he will fill the Tyrrhenian Sea with thousands of soldiers and will plant his gleaming standards on the Aventine hill; he will destroy all that is left of ancient treasures, and will burn them with flames; he will trample with his profane feet on thy holy neck, on thine whose sandal kings used to be glad to kiss. Still, thou shouldst not assail him with open warfare; fruitless would be such an effort; do thou rather be crafty and use deceit; it is right to spread any sort of net for heretics. Even now the great king is summoning to council patricians from the uttermost ends of his kingdom, men born of noble ancestry, and agéd fathers, venerable with robe and snowy hair. These thou shalt be able to scatter limb from limb into the air, to reduce them to ashes by placing the fire of nitrous powder in the depths of the building where they have assembled. Straightway, therefore, do thou thyself inform all the faithful that England has of the plan and its execution; will any one of thy people dare not to perform the bidding of the Supreme Pope? And when they are stricken with sudden fear and overwhelmed by disaster, then let either the fierce Gaul invade them or the savage Iberian. Thus at length the days of Mary will return to that land, and thou shalt again be sovereign over the warlike English. And, to free you from all fear, know that the gods and goddesses and all the deities that are celebrated in your calendar are propitious." He spoke, and laying aside the garments he had donned, the perfidious one fled to dreadful Lethe, the realm that knows no joy.

Now rosy Tithonia, opening the portals of the Orient, clothed the earth with the gold of the returning light, and still lamenting the sad death of her swarthy son, she bedews the mountain heights with ambrosial drops, while the doorkeeper of the starry courts drove away slumber, dispelling the pleasant visions and dreams of the night.

There is a place enclosed in the eternal darkness of night, formerly the vast foundations of a long ruined building, now the cavern of fierce Murder and of two-tongued Treachery, whom brutal Discord bore at one birth. Here amid rubble and broken rock lie unburied bones of men and corpses pierced with steel. Here ever sits black Guile with twisted eyes, and Altercations, and Calumny, her jaws armed with stings; here may be seen Frenzy, and a thousand ways of dying, and Terror also; about the place flits bloodless Horror, and through the deep silences the unsubstantial Manes howl without ceasing; the earth, full conscious, is a swamp of blood. Murder and Treachery themselves lurk affrighted in the inner recesses of the cavern, and though none pursues them, the guilty pair with many a backward glance flee through the cavern, a cavern dismal with jagged rocks and black with deadly shadows.

These defenders of Rome, faithful through long ages, the Babylonish priest summons forth, and thus he speaks: "By the sea that sweeps round the borders of the West dwells a people whom I abhor; Nature in her wisdom declined to unite this unworthy race with our world. Hasten thither (this is my command) with swift steps. Let them be blown by Tartarean powder into thin air, King and nobles alike, an accursed stock; and all that are afire with love for the true faith take as associates in the scheme and helpers in its execution." He finished; the ruthless twins obeyed him with delight.

Meanwhile the Lord, who makes the heavens revolve in a wide sweep, who sends down lightning from the ethereal heights, looks down and smiles at the idle efforts of the perverse cabal, for he will gladly himself defend the cause of his own people.

The story goes that there is a place where fertile Europe is separated from the land of Asia, a place that looks towards the waters of the Mareotic lake. Here stands the lofty tower of Titanian Rumor, brazen, broad, resounding, nearer the glittering stars than Athos or Pelion superimposed on Ossa. A thousand doors and entrances stand wide open, a thousand windows too, and through the thin walls gleam the spacious courts. Here a dense crowd of people start varied whisperings; even as swarms of flies buzz around the milk pails, or in the sheepfold of woven rushes, while in summer time the Dog-Star seeks on high the zenith. Rumor herself, avenger of her mother, is seated at the summit of her citadel. On every side of her head are countless ears with which she draws to herself the slightest sound, and strives to catch the faintest murmurs from the outermost borders of the wide, wide world. And even thou, Arestor's son, unkind watcher of the heifer of Isis, didst not turn so many eyes in thy ruthless face, eyes that never blink in silent sleep, eyes that survey far and wide the lands that lie beneath them. With these eyes of hers she is wont to scrutinize places quite devoid of light, and even impervious to the radiant sun; babbling with a thousand tongues she heedlessly pours forth to any random gossip all that she has heard or seen, now subtracting from the truth through lies, now exaggerating it through manufactured tales.

None the less, Rumor, thou hast earned commendation from my song for a kindly report than which none has been truer; worthy art thou to be sung by me, and I shall not regret having praised thee at such length; for we English, saved by thy good offices, roving Goddess, give thee fair return. God, who regulates the motion of the eternal stars, launched his thunderbolts, and, as the earth trembled, spoke to thee: "Art silent, Rumor? Or dost thou fail to see the impious band of Papists that has conspired against me and my Britons, and the strange form of murder plotted against sceptered James?" This and no more; she understood at once the mandate of the Thunderer, and swift as she was before, she now put on whirring wings, clothed her slim body in many-colored feathers, and took in her right hand a sounding trumpet of Temesaean brass. Straightway with the oarage of her wings she clove the yielding air; and, not content to outstrip in her flight the swift clouds, she leaves behind now the winds, now the horses of the sun. At first, in her usual fashion, she scattered through the cities of England ambiguous phrases, indefinite hints; presently she spread abroad the plots, the detestable scheme of treachery, and the facts in all their dreadful significance. She adds the names of the conspirators, and in her garrulity she does not omit to mention the place chosen for this nefarious attempt. At these reports all are confounded; young men, young women, and feeble old men tremble alike. The consciousness of impending utter ruin suddenly takes possession of every age.

Meantime, the heavenly Father from on high takes pity upon the people and blocks the cruel machinations of the worshipers of the Pope. They are arrested and haled to condign punishment. And to God holy incense and grateful honors are offered; all the crossroads smoke joyfully with festal bonfires; crowds of young people engage in the dance; and there is no day in the whole calendar more celebrated than the Fifth of November.

On the death of the Bishop of Ely.

My cheeks were still wet and unsightly with tears, and my eyes, not yet dry, still swollen from the salty rain which I had recently from pure affection shed while I was paying my sad tribute at the bier of our beloved Bishop of Winchester, when hundred-tongued Rumor (Ah! always true messenger of evil and calamity!) spread through the cities of wealthy Britain and the peoples that are sons of Neptune the news that you, an ornament of Mankind, who were the head of the church in that island which bears the name of Ely, had yielded to Death and the iron-hearted Sisters. Then my anguished breast straightway seethed with hot anger, again and again cursing the sovereign goddess of the graves. Naso did not utter from the depths of his soul worse imprecations against Ibis, and the Greek poet less bitterly execrated the shameful treachery of Lycambes and his own betrothed Neobule. But lo, while I was pouring forth furious curses and invoking death upon Death, I seemed to my astonishment to hear these words breathed softly on the air: "Away with your blind fury, away with your gleaming bile and your fruitless threats. Why do you rashly wrong the deities which cannot be harmed but which can be suddenly roused to anger? It is not true, as you, poor deluded creature, think, that Death is the sable daughter of Night. Nor is she born of Erebus or of Erinys, nor was her birthplace in illimitable Chaos. Rather is it true that, sent from the starry heavens, she gathers everywhere the harvest of God, and calls into the light of the upper air souls that are buried under the weight of the flesh (even as the flying Hours, daughters of Themis and of Jove, call forth the day) and brings them face to face with the eternal Father; and in her righteousness she seizes and carries off the impious to the sad realms of dusky Tartarus and to abodes in the nether world. When to my joy I heard this voice calling, with all speed I left behind me my loathsome dungeon and, with winged soldiers all about me, I was borne upward in an ecstasy toward the stars, as long ago that aged prophet, driving a chariot of fire, was caught up to the skies. No terror came upon me from the Wain of bright Boötes, slow-moving from the cold, or from the arms of the formidable Scorpion, or from thy sword, Orion. I flew past the globe of the gleaming sun and far beneath my feet I saw the tri-form goddess as with her golden reins she sought to curb her dragon team. Up through the ranks of the planets and through the Milky Way I swept, again and again marveling at this unaccustomed speed, until I came to the bright portals of Olympus and the crystalline palace and the emerald-paved courts. But at this point I will say no more, for who that is born of mortal father would be able to tell of the loveliness of that place? For me, it is enough to enjoy it forever."

That Nature is not subject to Old Age.

Ah, how unbroken are the misconceptions by which the wandering mind of man is driven and made weary, so that, plunged in utter darkness, his thoughts revolve in a veritable night of Oedipus. His unbalanced mind dares to measure the actions of the gods by his own, dares to conceive the laws graven on everlasting adamant as resembling his own, and connects with his own transitory hours the designs of fate that no lapse of time can change.

Is it then true that the face of nature shall waste away and be covered with deep wrinkles? Shall the Mother of all things, contracting her all-generating womb, grow barren with age? Shall she move, confessing that age, with uncertain footsteps, her starry head ever trembling? Shall repellent old age and the eternal hunger of the years and filth and decay vex the stars? Shall insatiable Time devour Heaven and take into its maw its own father? Alas, could not improvident Jupiter have defended his own strongholds against this disaster, freed them from this evil work of time, and given them ceaseless rounds of motion? 'Twill happen, then, that some day, collapsing with tremendous uproar, the framework of Heaven will fall in ruin, and each pole, as it meets the stroke, shall sound stridently, as the Olympian falls from his mansion in the skies and Pallas, too, causing dismay by her uncovered Gorgon's head. So Juno's offspring, cast down from the sacred threshold of the skies, fell upon Aegean Lemnos. Thou, too, O Phoebus, shalt imitate in thy swift-descending chariot the downfall of thy son, and shalt be swept down in sudden ruin; and, as thy torch is extinguished, Nereus shall smoke and give forth baleful hisses from his astounded waters. Then, too, as the foundations of aerial Haemus are shattered, the summit will be rent in twain and the Ceraunian heights, dashed into the depths of the abyss, shall terrify Stygian Dis, heights that had once been used against the high gods and in fratricidal strife.

Ah! No! The Omnipotent Father has taken counsel for the universe by establishing the stars on a firmer basis, has adjusted the scales of Fate by unchanging weights, and given command that every individual element in the great order should ceaselessly keep the even tenor of its way. Hence it comes that the First Wheel of the Universe rolls on in its diurnal course, and with like whirling speed sweeps along the spheres that it encloses. Saturn is not slower than was his wont, and fierce Mars, as in days of yore, flashes from his crested helmet ruddy lightnings. Blooming Phoebus, bright with eternal youth, does not, as his team descends the slopes, warm regions no longer fruitful; but, always strong with friendly light, speeds on through the same signs of the Zodiac. In equal beauty rises from the fragrant Indies the star that gathers its ethereal flock on white Olympus, calling them in the morning and driving them in the evening to the pastures of the sky, dividing the realms of time with aspect dual. Still shines the Delian goddess, and passes through her phases with alternating horns, clasping with changeless arms the cerulean light. Nor do the elements break faith; with wonted crash the lurid lightning strikes and blasts the cliffs. Corus rages through the void with roar no less deep, and with like chill savage Aquilo attacks the armed Scythians with breath of storm and eddying clouds. The King of the sea in wonted fashion lashes the foundations of Sicilian Pelorus and the waters round about ring with the hoarse conch of Ocean's trumpeter; and the Balearic whales bear on their backs an Aegaeon no less vast in bulk. Nor, Earth, does thy ancient vigor fail thee. The narcissus still keeps its fragrance, and thy boy, O Phoebus, and thine too, Cypris, keep their beauty. Earth, still rich as of yore, conceals with guilty conscience in its mountains the gold destined to cause crime, or under its waters, pearls.

Thus, in brief, the perfect succession of all things shall go on forever until the final conflagration, wrapping far and wide the poles and the summits of the mighty sky, shall ravage the whole world and on that stupendous pyre shall blaze the structure of the universe.

On the Platonic Idea as Understood by Aristotle.

Tell me, ye goddesses that preside over the sacred groves, and thou, O Memory, blessèd mother of the nine-fold divinity, and thou, Eternity, that dost at ease recline far away in thy spacious cavern, guarding the records and the established laws of Jove, the calendar of Heaven and the daybooks of the gods,—tell me, who was that primal man in whose image cunning Nature fashioned the human race, a man eternal, incorruptible, of equal age with the sky, at once single and universal, the model of the Deity. Certainly he does not exist, concealed within the mind of Jove, a twin to virgin Pallas; but, although his nature is quite general, nevertheless he exists apart in the manner of an individual, and, wonders of wonders, he is limited by a definite spatial area; whether, as the sempiternal comrade of the constellations, he wanders through the ten-fold ranks of heaven, or dwells on the orb of the Moon, nearest to earth; or, sitting among the souls that are destined to enter human bodies, he lives bemused beside the Lethean waters of oblivion; or perchance in some far-distant part of the world he moves, a giant huge, this Archetype of Man, and lifts his lofty head, affrighting the gods, taller than Atlas who bears the burden of the stars. No such being did the Dircaean augur, to whom blindness gave special clarity of vision, see in the depths of his heart; no such being did the wingèd grandson of Pleïone show in the silence of the night to the acute company of seers; no such being did the Assyrian priest know, though he could recall the long line of ancestors of ancient Ninus, and Belus of old and famous Osiris; no such being did Hermes Trismegistus, that wondrous creature with the triple name (though he was an adept in mysteries), bequeath to the worshipers of Isis.

But you, everlasting glory of the umbrageous Academy (if indeed you were the first to bring these portentous imaginings into the Schools) must forthwith, being yourself the greatest of myth-makers, call back the poets whom you banished from your city, or else go forth yourself from the city which you founded.

To my Father.

Now I would fain have the Pierian springs turn their refreshing courses through my heart and pour over my lips the whole stream that is released from the twin summits, in order that, forgetting all trivial melodies, my Muse may rise on adventurous wings to do honor to my revered father. This song, a modest effort, she meditates for you, honored father, though uncertain of its acceptability. Yet I do not myself know what gifts of mine can more fitly match yours to me, although not even my greatest gifts could equal yours, much less could your gifts be balanced by a gratitude that finds but dry expression in empty words. But still this page displays my rating; I have enumerated on this sheet the wealth that I have, which is, in fact, nothing except what golden Clio has given me and what dreams have created for me in some secluded cavern, dreams and the laurel copses of the sacred grove, the shadows of Parnassus.

Do not look down upon divine song, the poet's function, than which there is nothing that more commends his ethereal birth and heavenly ancestry, that more commends the mind of man because of its origin. For song retains the sacred traces of the Promethean fire. The gods on high love song; and song has power to stir the trembling depths of Tartarus and to fetter the gods of the lower world; it grips the unsympathetic Manes with triple adamant. It is with song that the priestesses of Phoebus and the pallid lips of trembling Sibyls reveal the secrets of the far-distant future. It is a song that the sacrificing priest makes at the hallowed altar, whether he strikes down the bull that is shaking its gilded horns, or when he expertly consults the will of fate hidden in the smoking flesh, and seeks to discover destiny in the warm entrails. We, too, when we shall return again to our native Olympus and the periods of unchanging time shall be fixed forever, shall move through the spaces of the sky wearing wreaths of gold and blending sweet songs with the soft-sounding plectrum, songs with which the stars and the vaults of the twin poles shall resound. Even now the fiery Spirit that circles the swiftly moving orbs is singing, himself, among the starry bands an imperishable strain, a hymn that cannot be told, while the glowing Serpent curbs his burning hisses and fierce Orion with lowered sword becomes gentle, and Mauretanian Atlas feels no longer the burden of the stars.

Poetry used to add beauty to royal banquets, when luxury and the measureless depths of insatiable appetites were not yet known, but the feast sparkled with wine temperately enjoyed. Then as he sat at the festal board, as tradition enjoined, the minstrel, with his unshorn locks encircled with oak leaves, would sing of the prowess of heroes and of deeds that deserve imitation, and of Chaos and the broad-based foundations of the universe, and the creeping gods and the acorns that nourished those deities, and of the thunderbolt not yet sought from the cavern of Aetna. In fine, what avails the empty modulations of the voice, when devoid of words and their meaning and of rhythmical language? Such a melody befits the choruses of the woods, not Orpheus, who checked the course of streams and added ears to the oaks by his poetry, not by his lyre, and by his singing reduced to tears the ghosts of the dead. It is from song that he has this glory. Do not, I beg, continue to think lightly of the holy Muses, nor regard as useless and poor those through whose boon you yourself skilfully adjust a thousand sounds to fitting rhythms and, expert in varying your melodious voice by a thousand tuneful changes, may justly be heir to Arion's name. If it has been your fate to beget in me a poet, why do you think it strange if, being so closely united by the precious tie of blood, we pursue kindred art and related interests? Phoebus himself, in his desire to divide himself between two persons, gave one-half to me and the other half to my sire, and thus we, father and son, possess the divided deity.

Nevertheless, though you pretend to dislike the tender Muses, I think that you do not really dislike them, for you did not, father, bid me go where a broad way lies open, where the opportunities for gain are easier, and the golden hope of amassing riches shines steadily. Nor do you force me to the civil code, and the ill-guarded principles of national justice, and thus condemn my ears to senseless clamor. But in your desire to enrich still further my cultivated mind you took me far away from the din of the city to those high retreats of delightful leisure along the Aonian stream and permitted me to walk a happy comrade by Phoebus's side.

I pass over in silence the normal attachment to a dear parent; in my case something greater is demanded. When at your expense, my noble father, there were revealed to me the eloquence of the language of Romulus and the graces of Latin, and also the sonorous vocabulary developed by the oratorical Greeks, a vocabulary that befitted the mouth of Jove, you urged me to add the beauties of which the French language is so proud, and the speech that with degenerate lips testifying by his words to the wars of the barbarians the Italian of today pours forth, and the mysteries uttered by the prophets of Palestine. In fine, whatever heaven holds, and mother earth below the sky, and the air that moves between earth and sky, whatever also the waters cover, and the tossing shimmering surface of the sea, all this I may now and in the future come to know because of you; and, as the clouds divide, Science comes into view, and naked bends her lovely face to my kisses, unless I should wish to flee, unless it should be irksome to me to sip those sweets.

Go now, amass riches, all ye who with perverted desires prefer the ancient riches of Austria and the kingdoms of Peru! What greater gift could my father, or even Jove himself, have given me, though he gave me everything, the heavens alone excepted? Not more desirable was the gift, however safe it might have been, of him who entrusted to his son the universal light and the chariot of Hyperion and the reins of day and the tiara with its luminous waves. Therefore, since now I am one of the company of scholars, though the humblest of them all, I shall take my seat in the midst of the ivy and laurel wreaths of the victor. No longer shall

I be lost in the obscurity of the stupid crowd, and my footsteps shall shun the eyes of the uninitiated. Hence, wakeful Cares, hence Complaints, and the glance of Envy with its twisted look askance; savage Calumny, open not your snaky jaws; over me, loathsome crew, you have no power for ill; I come not under your jurisdiction, and safely with breast free from care I shall walk high above your viperous strokes.

But for you, dear father, now that I cannot adequately requite your kindnesses nor repay your gifts by deeds, let it be enough that I have enumerated them all and have recounted with grateful soul the long list of them and placed them in the keeping of a faithful mind.

And you, my youthful verses, with which I once toyed, if only you shall be bold enough to hope for unending years, and outliving the obsequies of your master, still to see the light, if you shall not be snatched away by dark forgetfulness to the depths of crowded Orcus, perhaps you will preserve as an example for the ages yet to come these praises and the name of my father which I have sung.

Psalm CXIV.

When the children of Israel, when the famous tribes of Jacob left the land of Egypt, a land abhorred, of barbarous speech, then, certainly, the only holy race was that of the sons of Judah; and among those peoples the Lord God was a mighty King. The sea saw this, and deferentially heartened the fugitives by piling itself up in roaring waves, and the sacred Jordan was driven back towards its silver springs; the towering mountains leaped and bounded like vigorous rams in a luxuriant enclosure, and all the lower crags skipped like lambs around their dear mother when the shepherd pipes. Why, pray, dread and monstrous sea, didst thou hearten the fugitives by piling thyself up in roaring waves, and why wast thou, O sacred Jordan, driven back towards thy silver springs? Why, pray, ye towering mountains, did ye leap and bound like vigorous rams in a luxuriant enclosure? And why, ye lower crags, did ye skip like lambs around their dear mother when the shepherd pipes? Quake, O Earth, in fear of the Lord, who shapeth great works, in fear, O Earth, of the Lord, highest and holiest God of the sons of Isaac, who from crags made roaring rivers pour, from dripping rock an ever-running spring.

It chanced that together with some criminals a philosopher was arrested, a man unknown and quite innocent. The King, ignorant of the facts, condemned him. As he went along the road to death, he suddenly sent to the King these lines.

O King, if you destroy me, a man who observes the laws and has done absolutely no wrong to any one, you will easily (be assured of this) take from earth a head supremely wise; later, however, you will understand, and will then bitterly complain (but in vain) that you have taken from your city such a renowned means of defence.

Against a sculptor who made a likeness of him.

If you were looking at the original itself, you would perhaps say that this likeness had been made by an inexpert hand; but since, my friends, you cannot tell whose presentment this is, you laugh at the poor reproduction of a worthless artist.

Scazons to Salsilli, a Roman poet, in his illness.

Oh, Muse, that art willing to move along with limping gait, and takest pleasure in walking slowly like Vulcan, and dost not think that such movement is less pleasing than is fairhaired Deïope when she dances with comely ankles before the golden couch of Juno, come, pray, and carry these few words to Salsilli, who is so fond of my Muse that he gives it quite undeservedly the preference over really great poets. Well, then, that Milton, London's son, who lately, leaving his own nest and stretch of sky (where the worst of winds, utterly without control over its furious lungs, keeps in swift action beneath the sky its panting blasts) came to the fertile soil of Italy to see her cities known through their proud fame, her men, her trained and gifted youth, wishes you now abundant prosperity, Salsilli, and good health for thy weary body; for now accumulation of bile attacks your veins, deep in your vitals spreads its infection, and in its impiety has not spared you because with such polish you pour forth Lesbian melody from your Roman lips.

O sweet boon of the Gods, O Health, own sister of Hebe! and thou, Apollo, terror of diseases, since thou didst slay the Python (or Paean, if thou dost more gladly hear that name), this man is thy priest. Ye oak forests of Faunus and ye hills beneficent with the dew of the grape, home of kindly Evander, if any health-giving plant grow in your valleys, do ye vie with one another in carrying it to help your sick poet. So he, restored again to the dear Muses, will charm the neighboring fields with his sweet song. Numa himself, under the dark trees where he enjoys happy ease forever, always, as he reclines, gazing at his Egeria, will marvel; and the swelling Tiber god himself, propitiated by the music, will show favor to the husbandman's hope of the year; he will not proceed to attack the kings in their tombs by rushing on with left rein too loosely held, but will more effectively curb his waves all the way down to the salt realms of curving Portumnus.

To Manso.

Giovanni Battista Manso, Marquis of Villa, is a man of the highest distinction among the Italians for the fame of his genius, his enthusiasm for letters, and his prowess in war. There is still extant a Dialogue on Friendship dedicated to him by Torquato Tasso, for he was a most intimate friend of Tasso and was by him celebrated among the nobles of Campania in the poem entitled Gerusalemme Conquistata, Book XX:

> Among the cavaliers high-minded and courteous
> Shone Manso.

When the author was sojourning in Naples, this gentleman displayed the greatest good will and showed him many acts of kindness. His guest, therefore, before leaving the city, sent him the following poem that he might not seem unappreciative.

These verses, too, Manso, the Pierides meditate in praise of you, of you, Manso, so well known to the choir of Phoebus, for he has deemed no other worthy of equal honor since Gallus died and Etruscan Maecenas. You, too, if the breath of my Muse has so much power, shall sit in the midst of the ivy and the laurel wreaths of the victor.

Long ago a happy friendship united you to great Tasso and wrote your names on immortal records. Presently the all-knowing Muse brought to you sweet-tongued Marini; he rejoiced to be called your protégé as he sang in fluent numbers the Assyrian loves of the gods and with his soft strains held the Ausonian nymphs spellbound.

At his death the poet, conscious of his debt to you, left to you alone the disposition of his body and the execution of his final wishes. Your dear affection did not fail the Manes of your friend; for we have seen the poet smiling at us from the sculptured bronze. But even this did not seem enough for both friends, and your loyal services did not cease at the tomb; it was your wish to rescue both completely from Orcus in so far as you could and to cheat the greedy laws of the Parcae. You therefore portrayed the lineage of both, the varied phases of their lives, their characters, and the gifts bestowed by Minerva; emulous of him who, born near lofty Mycale, eloquently told the story of Aeolian Homer's life. I therefore, father Manso, in the name of Clio and mighty Phoebus, wish for you health and strength for many years to come, I, a youthful traveler from the Hyperborean realms. And you in your kindness will not disdain so distant a Muse, who, reared under hard conditions in the frozen North, recently dared in her rashness to fly through the cities of Italy. I, too, believe that on my river I have heard in the shadows of the night the swans singing where the silver Thames with its spreading crystal waters laves its grey locks in ocean's tide. Why, even Tityrus once came to these shores of yours.

But we who live where the region of the sky that is furrowed by the seven-fold Wain endures wintry Boötes and interminable night, we are neither an uncultivated race nor useless to Phoebus. We also worship him; we have, in fact, sent gifts to Phoebus (unless the old tradition is baseless), ears of golden grain and yellow apples in baskets and fragrant crocuses; sent, too, chosen bands from the Druids. (The Druids, an ancient folk occupied with the rites of the gods, used to sing the praises of heroes and their deeds so worthy of emulation.) Therefore, as often as on grassy Delos the Greek maidens move round the altar with festal song in the old, old fashion, they recall to memory in their joyous strains Loxo, daughter of Corineus, and prophetic Upis, and Hecaërge, with her golden hair, maidens whose nude breasts were dyed with Caledonian woad.

Fortunate old man! Therefore, wherever throughout the world the great glory and name of Torquato shall be celebrated and the bright fame of immortal Marini shall increase, your name also shall come again and again upon the lips of men for their applause; you in like flight with them will pursue the road to immortality. It shall be said that Cynthius of his own prompting dwelt in your home, and that the Muses came to your threshold to serve you. Yet, it was not of his own prompting that that same Apollo, when a fugitive from the skies, came to the fields of King Pheretiades, though the latter had been host to mighty Alcides. Only, when he wished to escape from the noisy ploughmen he would retire to the famous cavern of gentle Chiron, among the moist glades and leafy shelters beside the river Peneus; there often under a dark ilex, yielding to the persuasive entreaty of his friend, he would, to the accompaniment of the lyre, assuage the grievous troubles of his exile by singing. Then neither the banks of the stream nor the rocks at the bottom of the abyss stayed in their usual place; the Trachinian cliff began to move in unison and ceased to be aware of the huge weight of the familiar woods; the ash trees made haste to leave their hillsides and the spotted lynxes were enthralled by this strange music.

Old man, beloved of the gods! It must be that kindly Jupiter and Phoebus and the grandson of Atlas shed a gentle light upon you at your birth, for no one, unless from his infancy he is dear to the high gods, will be able to be the patron of a great poet. Therefore it is that your lengthening years are still green with lingering blossoms, and in vitality gain the spindles of Aeson, keeping for you still the unfading glories of your brow, your active mind and the ripe keenness of your judgment. Oh, if only my lot would grant me such a friend, who would know so well how to honor the votaries of Phoebus, if ever I shall call back into the realms of song our native kings and Arthur, who wars even beneath the earth; or if I shall sing of the high-souled heroes of the Table invincible through their comradeship, and (Oh, that the inspiration may be mine!) if I shall break the Saxon phalanxes under the war god of the Britons! At length, when, after finishing the years of a life by no means silent, when, full of years, I shall yield to Death her rights, that friend will stand by my bedside with tearful eyes; it will suffice for me to say to him as he stands there, "May I be the object of thy care." He will have my limbs, relaxed in ashen death, laid to rest softly in a small urn; perhaps he will sculpture my features in marble, wreathing my locks with Paphian myrtle or Parnassian laurel, and I shall find rest in perfect peace. Then, too, if there is any loyalty, if there are definite rewards for the righteous, I myself, removed to the ethereal regions of the gods on high, whither toil and a pure mind and an aspiring virtue carry men, shall (in so far as destiny permits) from some part of that distant universe behold these things, and with a soul filled with smiling serenity, my face shall be suffused with rosy light and with joy I shall applaud myself on high Olympus.

Damon's Epitaph.

Theme

Thyrsis and Damon, shepherds of the same countryside, and interested in the same pursuits, were from boyhood inseparable friends. Thyrsis, going abroad for purposes of study, received the news of Damon's death. When later he returned home, and found that it was really so, he bemoans himself and his loneliness in the following elegy. Damon here stands for Charles Diodati, Italian in so far as his father's family came from the Tuscan city of Lucca, but in all other respects English; a young man distinguished, during his brief life, for his talents, learning, and all other notable virtues.

Ye nymphs of Himera (for 'tis you who keep in mind Daphnis and Hylas and the long lamented fate of Bion), sing through the cities on the Thames a Sicilian strain: the words, the sighs, which wretched Thyrsis uttered, the constant plaints with which he wearied the caverns, the streams, the bubbling springs, and the depths of the forest while he mourned the fact that Damon had been wrested from him prematurely; even the midnight heard his lamentations, as he wandered in lonely places. And now twice had the stalk with its green grain grown up, and twice had the barns counted the golden harvests since his last day had taken Damon into the shadows, and Thyrsis was not yet returned; for love of the sweet Muse kept that shepherd in a Tuscan city. But when the completion of his studies and concern for the flock that he had left behind called him back home, and he sat once more beneath the familiar elm, then, then at last he felt the loss of his friend and essayed thus to disburden himself of immeasurable sorrow:—

Go home, my lambs, unfed; your master has now no time for you. Ah me, what deities shall I say are on the earth, what deities in the sky, now that they have snatched thee, Damon, away in ruthless death? Is it thus that thou dost leave us? Shall thy worth go thus nameless and too soon be lost among the obscure shades? But that deity who separates the souls with his golden wand would not wish this; he would lead thee into a company worthy of thyself, and keep far away all the ignoble herd of the silent dead.

Go home, my lambs, unfed; your master has now no time for you. Whatever shall come to pass, certainly, unless the wolf shall see me first, thou shalt not waste away in a tomb unmourned. Thy honor shall stand fast and shall long live among the shepherds. To thee, next after Daphnis, they shall rejoice to pay their vows, of thee, next after Daphnis, to sing the praises, so long as Pales, so long as Faunus shall love the fields; if this signifies aught, to have cherished old-time faith and piety, and the arts of Pallas, and to have had a comrade skilled in song.

Go home, my lambs, unfed; your master has now no time for you. These rewards, Damon, are surely thine, these rewards shall always be thine. But what, pray, is to become of me? What faithful comrade will be ever at my side, as was thy wont when the cold was intense and the ground covered with hoarfrost, or under the scorching sun when all green things were dying of thirst, whether it was needful to go afield against the great lions, or to frighten away the ravening wolves from the high defences of the folds? Who will always while away the day with conversation and song?

Go home, my lambs, unfed; your master has now no time for you. To whom shall I now entrust my heart? Who will teach me to soothe eating cares? Who to cheat the long, long night with sweet converse, when before the cheerful blaze the ripe pears simmer and the nuts snap on the hearth while boisterous Auster outside brings confusion in its train, and comes roaring down upon the elms.

Go home, my lambs, unfed; your master has now no time for you. Or, in the summer time, when the day is turning in mid-career, when Pan is fast asleep, hidden under the shade of the oak, and the Nymphs seek again their familiar haunts beneath the water, and the shepherds are no longer visible, and the peasant snores under the hedge, who will bring back to me your charm, your laughter, your Cecropian wit, and your fine cultivation?

Go home, my lambs, unfed; your master has now no time for you. But now, all alone, I wander through the fields, now through the meadows all alone; where the branching shadows are thick in the valley, there I await the evening; over my head the rain and Eurus make a mournful sound in the unquiet twilight of the disturbed forest.

Go home, my lambs, unfed; your master has now no time for you. Alas, how completely my fields, once well cultivated, are now covered with unmannerly weeds, and the grain itself, though high, is now bursting open with decay! The grapes, too, unwedded, are wasting with neglected clusters, and the myrtle copses please me not. I am weary of my sheep as well, while they mourn and turn their eyes upon their master.

Go home, my lambs, unfed; your master has now no time for you. Tityrus is calling me to the hazels, Alphesiboeus to the ash trees, Aegon to the willows, handsome Amyntas to the streams: "Here are cool springs, here intermingled grass and moss, here the sound of the zephyrs in the arbutus blends with that of the tranquil waters." They sing to a deaf ear. I find a thicket and am gone.

Go home, my lambs, unfed; your master has now no time for you. Mopsus observed this, for he chanced to note my return (Mopsus is an expert in the language of the birds and the lore of the stars), and said, "Thyrsis, what means this? What unreasoning melancholy torments you? Either love is destroying you, or some star casts an evil spell upon you; the star of Saturn has often been baleful to shepherds and has pierced their very hearts with leaden dart aslant."

Go home, my lambs, unfed; your master has now no time for you. The nymphs are filled with wonder. "What is to become of thee, Thyrsis?" they say. "What is your purpose? This lowering brow, these eyes distraught, and features set, belong not to youth; youth's natural quest is the dance and light merriment and always love. Twice wretched is he who loves too late."

Go home, my lambs, unfed; your master has now no time for you. Hyas comes, and Dryope, and Aegle, the daughter of Baucis, skilled in music, and mistress of the lyre, but spoiled by pride; Chloris comes, who dwells beside the Idumanian stream. Their blandishments, their words of solace, affect me not; nothing, in fact, that is present moves me and I have no hope for the future.

Go home, my lambs, unfed; your master has now no time for you. Ah me, how similar are the cattle as they sport in the meadows, all of them companions thinking alike by the law of their being! No one selects from the herd one comrade rather than another. Thus in great numbers the wolves come to feed, and the shaggy wild asses find in turn their mates. The law of the sea is the same; Proteus on the deserted shore counts the ranks of his seals, and the common sparrow has always some one with whom to associate, some one with whom he cheerfully flits from one heap of spelt to another, returning late to his own shelter. But if Fate has condemned to death this comrade, whether killed by a kite with hookéd beak or pierced by a peasant's arrow, straightway he seeks another to bear him company in his flights. But we men are a hard race, driven by ruthless fate, diverse in feeling and at variance in sentiment. Scarcely out of a thousand does a man find one comrade for himself, or, if Fate, at last kind to our prayers, has granted that single one, on some unthought-of day, at an hour quite unexpected, he is snatched away, leaving a vacant place forever.

Go home, my lambs, unfed; your master has now no time for you. Alas, what vagrant impulse drew me to unknown shores, to travel among the towering crags and snow-capped Alps? Was it worth so much to see buried Rome (even though she were such as when long, long ago Tityrus himself left his sheep and farm to see her) that I could bring myself to be separated from thee, so dear a friend, that I could have the heart to put so many deep seas between us, so many mountains, forests, cliffs, and roaring streams? Ah, certainly I might have touched at the end thy hand and lovingly closed thy eyes in peaceful death, and said "Farewell, be mindful of me in thy journey to the stars."

Go home, my lambs, unfed; thy master has now no time for you. And yet I shall never weary of remembering you, ye Tuscan shepherds, youths devoted to the Muses, for there are Grace and Charm and thou, too, Damon, wert a Tuscan, tracing thy lineage from the ancient city of Lucumo. Oh, how puissant was I when, stretched beside cool murmuring

Arno and its poplar groves where the grass is softest, I was able to pluck now violets, now the tips of the myrtles, and to listen to the contest of Menalcas and Lycidas! I even dared to contend myself, and I think that I did not wholly displease; for I have still in my possession your gifts, baskets of rush and interwoven osiers, and waxen fastenings for my reed-pipe. Why, Dati and Francini taught my name to their own beech trees; both men were famous for their poetry and their learning, and both were of Lydian blood.

Go home, my lambs, unfed; thy master has now no time for you. These thoughts the dewy moon was wont to suggest to me in my happiness while all alone I was shutting my tender kids in their safe enclosure. Ah, how often did I say, at the very time when you were lying dead, "Now Damon is singing; now he is setting traps for a hare; now he is weaving osiers for his various needs." And all that then with tranquil mind I hoped might come to pass, I lightheartedly took for granted in my wishes, and conceived it as already realized. "Say, my good friend, you are not busy, are you? Unless, perhaps, something holds thee back, shall we go and for a while lie in the shade of the rustling trees, either by the waters of Colne, or in the countryside of Cassibelaunus? Thou shalt, to please me, describe thy healing medicaments, hellebore, the low-growing crocus, the leaf of the hyacinth, and all the herbs that this or that marsh supplies and the arts of the healers." Ah, perish the herbs, and perish the arts of the healers, now that they have been unable to help the master himself. I myself also—for my pipe was trying to utter some lofty strain (it is now eleven nights and a day)—had chanced to put my lips to new reeds; but they snapped asunder as their fastenings broke, and could not further endure that mighty volume of sound. I fear, too, that I may be conceited; still I will tell the story. Do you, ye woods, withdraw.

Go home, my lambs, unfed; your master has now no time for you. I shall sing, yes, I myself, of the Dardanian ships moving on Rutupian waters, and the ancient kingdom of Imogene, daughter of Pandrasus, and of the chieftains Brennus and Arviragus and of ancient Belinus, and of the Armorican settlers who came at length under the laws of the Britons. And then I shall sing of Igraine pregnant with Arthur through a fateful trick, and those false lineaments, and the wearing of the arms of Gorlois,—all this the guile of Merlin. Oh, if then life shall still be mine, you, my reed-pipe, will hang on an aged pine far away, quite forgotten by me, or else, all changed, you shall stridently emit a British note for my native Muses. For consider. One man may not do all things, one man may not hope all things; for me there will be a sufficiently ample reward, a sufficiently great glory (though I then be unknown to fame forever and altogether without repute in the outside world), if only fairhaired Ouse shall read me and he who drinks of Alan and eddying Humber and all the woods of Trent; and if above all the rest my own Thames and dark-metaled Tamar, and the Orkneys, whose waves are at the end of the world, shall commit my verse to memory.

Go home, my lambs, unfed; your master has now no time for you. These were the plans I was keeping for you under the soft-barked laurel, these, and even more. I was saving for you, also, the two cups which Manso had given me, Manso, not the least glory of the Chalcidian shore, cups of marvelous artistry, as Manso himself is a marvel. Around them he had a double theme engraved. In the center are the waters of the Red Sea, and fragrant spring, the long coast of Arabia, and the woods exuding balsam; among the trees the Phoenix, divine bird, like none other on earth, all brilliant blue with iridescent wings, watches Aurora as she rises over the shimmering waves. On the other side are a wide expanse of sky and towering Olympus; and (who would believe it?) here is Love also with his quiver limned against the clouds, his flashing weapons, his torches, his darts tinged with burning bronze. And from this point he does not attack trivial souls and the ignoble hearts of the crowd; but, turning hither and thither his shining eyes, he ever shoots his arrows upward towards the stars, and never tires nor looks aside to make a downward stroke. In this way the minds of the elect are inflamed and the shapes of the gods.

Thou, too, Damon, art with the gods—for no vain hope deceives me—thou too art certainly with them. For where else could thy sweet and blessed innocence go? Where else thy shining virtues? It would certainly not be right to seek thee in the depths of Lethaean Orcus. Tears befit thee not, and we shall weep no more. Begone, tears, pure Damon now dwells in the pure ether, and barely walks even on the rainbow. And among the souls of heroes and the ever-living gods he quaffs ethereal draughts and drinks joys with his holy lips.

And now that thou hast gained the privileges of Heaven, be propitious to me and graciously favor me by what name soever thou art called, whether thou shalt be our own Damon, or the name Diodati is sweeter to thy ears, by which divine name all the dwellers in heaven shall know thee while in the woods thou shalt be called Damon. Because the flush of innocence and stainless youth were dear to thee, because thou didst not know the joy of marriage, lo, for thee, virginal honors are reserved. Thou, with thy bright head haloed in glory, and carrying in thy hand a leafy canopy of joyous palms, shalt to all eternity take part in immortal nuptial songs, where music abounds, and the ecstatic melodies of the lyre blend with the choruses of the blessed and the joyous revelry grows ever wilder under the touch of the thyrsus of Zion.

To *John Rouse*, Librarian of Oxford University.

An ode on the loss of a book of poems, a second copy of which he wished sent to him, that he might place it in the Public Library with the rest of my works.

Strophe 1.

Book in twin parts that rejoices in a single cover, albeit doubly wreathed, and bright with graces unlaborious, which once a youthful hand brought to you, conscientious, but not yet the hand of a master poet; while in his travels now in umbrageous Italy, now in verdant England, he composed light verse, unaffected by the people; and forsaking the common paths, he indulged his native lute, and presently in like fashion with Daunian quill called forth for his neighbors a melody from far away, his feet scarce touching the ground;

Antistrophe.

Who stole you, little book, who craftily stole you from your brothers, when, sent from the city at the insistent entreaty of a learned friend, you pursued your glorious journey to the cradle of the Thames, blue Father Thames, where are the clear springs of the Muses and the hallowed Bacchic dance, already known to the world as the Heavens revolve through the immeasurable lapse of the ages, and destined to be famous forever?

Strophe 2.

Only may some God or some scion of a god, commiserating the pristine nobility of our race (if we have sufficiently atoned for our former misdeeds and for the degenerate ease that comes from soft luxury) take away our hideous civil strife, and through his purity call back the studies that give life, and with them the homeless Muses now banished from almost the whole domain of England's sons; and the unclean birds whose claws are almost upon us may he pierce with arrows from Apollo's quiver, and drive the curse of Phineus far from the Pegasean stream!

Antistrophe.

But as for you, little book, though once through the bad faith or the drowsiness of the messenger you strayed from the band of your brothers, whether you are now lodged in some den or some hiding place where perhaps you are being thumbed by the disgusting calloused hands of an unintelligent dealer, rejoice in your happiness; for, lo, upon you shines a new hope of being able to escape the abyss of Lethe and to mount up into the high courts of Jove by the oarage of your wings.

Strophe 3.

For Rouse wishes you to belong to his own special treasures, and complains that, though you were promised to him, you are still lacking to the full number; that you come is the prayer of him to whose care have been entrusted the famous monuments of men; he wishes you also to be placed in the hallowed shrines over which he himself presides, the faithful guardian of immortal masterpieces and curator of riches nobler than those committed to the charge of Ion, the famous scion of Erechtheus, in the wealthy temple of the god his father, with its golden tripods and Delphic offerings, Ion, son of Actaean Creusa.

Antistrophe.

So, then, you shall go to see the lovely groves of the Muses; you shall enter again the divine home of Phoebus, in which he dwells in Oxford's vale, holding it dearer than Delos and the twice-cleft summit of Parnassus. You shall go in full honor, now that you also have gained a glorious destiny, and leave me, solicited by the entreaties of an appreciative friend. There you shall be read among the lofty names of authors, the ancient luminaries and true glory of the Greek and Latin races.

Epode.

As for you, my labors, in the end not without significance, whatever this barren mind of mine has poured forth, now, albeit late, I bid you hope for peaceful repose, knowing no more of envy, and for the blessed abodes that gracious Hermes and Rouse's expert guardianship will grant you, abodes into which the unmannerly tongues of the vulgar shall not penetrate, and from which the crowd of undiscriminating readers will keep far away. But our distant descendants and a more understanding age will perhaps with sound judgment make a fairer estimate of things. Then, when jealousy has been completely buried, our deserts will be known by a sane posterity—all thanks to Rouse.

The ode consists of three strophes, an equal number of antistrophes, and an epode at its close These divisions, though they do not precisely correspond either in the number of verses or in sections that are everywhere unchangeable, we have made in the way mentioned above, having in view the convenience of the reader rather than an arrangement by which they might be sung according to the ancient measures.
In other respects this poetic form should perhaps have been more correctly called monostrophic. The metres in part follow a definite scheme, in part are used freely. The Phalaecean verses twice admit a spondee in the third foot, a substitution that Catullus makes at will in the second foot.

TRANSLATION OF ITALIAN POEMS

II

My beautiful lady whose fair name brings honor to the grassy vale of the Reno River and to the noble pass; truly is he bereft of all worth, who is not conquered by your noble spirit, as it gently reveals itself, ever lavishly in its suave aspects, nor by whose attractions—arrows and bow of love—wherewith your lofty virtue clothes itself.

As charmingly you speak and joyously sing (in such a wise that you could stir to motion the rooted alpine timber), let each one guard the entrance to his eyes and ears, whoso is unworthy of thee. Grace alone from heaven avail him before the loving desire ages in his heart.

III

As in a barren cliff at dusk the young, experienced shepherdess waters the strange and beautiful grass which with difficulty spreads over the unwonted plot, away from its fostering native springlike clime, so love draws from my agile tongue the new blossom of a strange speech while of thee, beautiful in thy pride, I sing not understood by my good people, having exchanged the language of the Thames for that of the Arno. It is love that would have it thus and I to one's woe have found that Love never willed aught in vain. Would that my insensible heart and stony breast were fruitful soil for him who sows from Heaven.

Canzone

Ladies and loving swains drawing near to me laugh and ask how I dare write my love poetry in an unknown and strange tongue. "Tell us"—they say jokingly—"if your hope is ever in vain and if the fairest of your thoughts ever comes true." "Other shores await you and other streams on whose green banks now grows the undying guerdon of eternal boughs to wreathe your locks. Why do you place this excessive burden on your shoulder?"

My song! to thee I'll answer and do thou reply in my behalf: my lady, in whose words my heart is to be found, says! "This is the language whereof Love is proud."

IV

Diodati, I'll tell thee a wondrous tale: that restive one who was wont to despise love, the snares of which he often mocked, has fallen where good people oft are caught.

Not golden locks, nor ruddy cheeks have charmed me, but an exotic beauty incarnate of a new idea, which brings bliss to my heart; in her a behaviour of lofty dignity, in her eyes the unclouded radiance of lovely brown; hers a speech adorned of many tongues, and a power to sing such that it could divert from its orbit in the midst of heaven the laboring Moon. Her eyes dart forth such flames that useless it were to wax one's ears.

V

Surely your eyes, my lady, cannot but be my Sun, since indeed their rays fall upon me as the Sun does upon the traveler in the Libyan wastes. While a burning vapor—nor did I ever feel it before—presses against my suffering—it is what lovers in their speech call sigh. I know not what it is: while it stirs enclosed within it shakes my bosom, then but little issuing forth, what remains freezes and congeals therein; but when it succeeds in finding its way to the eyes, then it makes all my nights rainy [with tears] until rosy dawn appears again.

VI

I, a simple and unexperienced lover, uncertain whether to forsake my own self, devotedly, my lady, bestow upon you the humble gift of my heart. I have tested it repeatedly, and found it faithful, fearless and constant, adorned with pleasing thoughts, keen and good: when the world outside roars, and the thunder claps, it dons the armor of its own strength, of perfect adamant; feeling as secure from the attacks of Fortune and of Envy, of vulgar fears and hopes as he is fond of glory, of valor, of the tuneful lyre and of the Muse: only in one spot you will find this heart less resistent, and that is where love stuck its fatal point.

JOANNIS MILTONI

Londinensis

Poemata.

Quorum pleraque intra **Annum** ætatis Vigesimum Conscripsit.

Hæc quæ sequuntur de Authore testimonia, tametsi ipse intelligebat non tam de se quam supra se esse dicta, eo quod præclaro ingenio viri, nec non amici ita fere solent laudare, ut omnia suis potius virtutibus, quam veritati congruentia nimis cupide affingant, noluit tamen horum egregiam in se voluntatem non esse notam; Cum alii præsertim ut id faceret magnopere suaderent. Dum enim nimiæ laudis invidiam totis ab se viribus amovitur, sibique quod plus æquo est non attributum esse mavult, judicium interim hominum cordatorum atque illustrium quin summo sibi honori ducat, negare non potest.

*Joannes Baptista Mansus, Marchio Villensis Neapolitanus ad Joannem Mil-
tonium Anglum.*

Ut mens, forma, decor, facies, mos, si pietas sic,
    Non Anglus, verùm herclè Angelus ipse fores.

Ad Joannem Miltonem Anglum triplici poeseos laureâ coronandum Græcâ
nimirum, Latinâ, *atque* Hetruscâ, *Epigramma Joannis Salsilli Romani.*

Cede Meles, cedat depressa Mincius urna;
    Sebetus Tassum desinat usque loqui;
At Thamesis victor cunctis ferat altior undas
    Nam per te Milto par tribus unus erit.

Ad Joannem Miltonum.

Græcia Mæonidem, jactet sibi Roma Maronem,
    Anglia Miltonum jactat utrique parem.
                   Selvaggi.

Al Signor Gio. Miltoni Nobile Inglese.

ODE

Ergimi all' Etra ò Clio
Perche di stelle intreccierò corona
Non più del Biondo Dio
La Fronde eterna in Pindo, e in Elicona,
Diensi a merto maggior, maggiori i fregi,
A' celeste virtù celesti pregi.

Non puo del tempo edace
Rimaner preda, eterno alto valore
Non puo l' oblio raepace
Furar dalle memorie eccelso onore,
Su l' arco di mia cetra un dardo forte
Virtù m' adatti, e ferirò la morte.

Del Ocean profondo
Cinta dagli ampi gorghi Anglia resiede
Separata dal mondo,
Però che il suo valor l' umano eccede:
Questa feconda sà produrre Eroi,
Ch' hanno a ragion del sovruman tra noi.

Alla virtù sbandita
Danno ne i petti lor fido ricetto,
Quella gli è sol gradita,
Perche in lei san trovar gioia, e diletto;
Ridillo tu Giovanni e mostra in tanto
Con tua vera virtù, vero il mio Canto.

Lungi dal Patrio lido
Spinse Zeusi l' industre ardente brama;
Ch' udio d' Helena il grido
Con aurea tromba rimbombar la fama,
E per poterla effigiare al paro
Dalle più belle Idee trasse il priù raro.   30

Cosi l' Ape Ingegnosa
Trae con industria il suo liquor pregiato
Dal giglio e dalla rosa,
E quanti vaghi fiori ornano il prato;
Formano un dolce suon diverse Chorde,
Fan varie voci melodia concorde.

Di bella gloria amante
Milton dal Ciel natio per varie parti
Le peregrine piante
Volgesti a ricercar scienze, ed arti;   40
Del Gallo regnator vedesti i Regni,
E dell' Italia ancor gl' Eroi piu degni.

Fabro quasi divino
Sol virtù rintracciando il tuo pensıero
Vide in ogni confino
Chi di nobil valor calca il sentiero;
L' ottimo dal miglior dopo scegliea
Per fabbricar d' ogni virtu l' Idea.

Quanti nacquero in Flora
O in lei del parlar Tosco appreser l' arte,   50
La cui memoria onora
Il mondo fatta eterna in dotte carte,
Volesti ricercar per tuo tesoro,
E parlasti con lor nell' opre loro.

Nell' altera Babelle
Per te il parlar confuse Giove in vano,
Che per varie favelle
Di se stessa trofeo cadde su'l piano:
Ch' Ode oltr' all Anglia il suo piu degno Idioma
Spagna, Francia, Toscana, e Grecia e Roma.   60

I piu profondi arcani
Ch' occulta la natura e in cielo e in terra
Ch' a Ingegni sovrumani
Troppo avara tal' hor gli chiude, e serra,
Chiaramente conosci, e giungi al fine
Della moral virtude al gran confine.

Non batta il Tempo l' ale,
Fermisi immoto, e in un ferminsi gl' anni,
Che di virtù immortale
Scorron di troppo ingiuriosi a i danni;   70
Che s' opre degne di Poema o storia
Furon gia, l' hai presenti alla memoria.

Dammi tua dolce Cetra
Se vuoi ch' io dica del tuo dolce canto,
Ch' inalzandoti all' Etra
Di farti huomo celeste ottiene il vanto,
Il Tamigi il dirà che gl' è concesso
Per te suo cigno pareggiar Permesso.

Io che in riva del Arno
Tento spiegar tuo merto alto, e preclaro   80
So che fatico indarno,
E ad ammirar, non a lodarlo imparo;
Freno dunque la lingua, e ascolto il core
Che ti prende a lodar con lo stupore.

Del sig. Antonio Francini gentilhuomo Fiorentino.

JOANNI MILTONI

LONDINIENSI

Juveni Patria, virtutibus eximio,

Viro *qui multa peregrinatione, studio cuncta orbis terrarum loca perspexit, ut novus Ulysses omnia ubique ab omnibus apprehenderet;*

Polyglotto, in cujus ore linguæ jam deperditæ sic reviviscunt, ut idiomata omnia sint in ejus laudibus infacunda; Et jure ea percallet ut admirationes & plausus populorum ab propria sapientia excitatos, intelligat;

Illi, cujus animi dotes corporisque sensus ad admirationem commovent, & per ipsam motum cuique auferunt; cujus opera ad plausus hortantur, sed venustate vocem laudatoribus adimunt;

Cui in Memoria totus Orbis: In intellectu Sapientia: in voluntate ardor gloriæ: in ore Eloquentia: Harmonicos celestium Sphærarum sonitus Astronomia Duce audienti; Characteres mirabilium naturæ per quos Dei magnitudo describitur magistra Philosophia legenti; Antiquitatum latebras, vetustatis excidia, eruditionis ambages comite assidua autorum Lectione,

Exquirenti, restauranti, percurrenti
(At cur nitor in arduum?);

Illi in cujus virtutibus evulgandis ora Famæ non sufficiant, nec hominum stupor in laudandis satis est, Reverentiæ & amoris ergo hoc ejus meritis debitum admirationis tributum offert Carolus Datus Patricius Florentinus,

Tanto homini servus, tantæ virtutis amator.

ELEGIARUM

Liber Primus.

Elegia prima *ad Carolum Diodatum.*

Tandem, chare, tuæ mihi pervenere tabellæ,
    Pertulit & voces nuntia charta tuas,
Pertulit occiduâ Devæ Cestrensis ab orâ
    Vergivium prono quà petit amne salum.
Multùm crede juvat terras aluisse remotas
    Pectus amans nostri, tamque fidele caput,
Quòdque mihi lepidum tellus longinqua sodalem

Debet, at unde brevi reddere jussa velit.
Me tenet urbs refluâ quam Thamesis alluit undâ,
   Meque nec invitum patria dulcis habet.   10
Jam nec arundiferum mihi cura revisere Camum,
   Nec dudum vetiti me laris angit amor.
Nuda nec arva placent, umbrasque negantia molles,
   Quàm male Phœbicolis convenit ille locus!
Nec duri libet usque minas perferre magistri
   Cæteraque ingenio non subeunda meo.
Si sit hoc exilium patrios adiisse penates,
   Et vacuum curis otia grata sequi,
Non ego vel profugi nomen, sortemve recuso,
   Lætus & exilii conditione fruor.   20
O utinam vates nunquam graviora tulisset
   Ille Tomitano flebilis exul agro;
Non tunc Jonio quicquam cessisset Homero
   Neve foret victo laus tibi prima Maro.
Tempora nam licet hîc placidis dare libera Musis,
   Et totum rapiunt me mea vita libri.
Excipit hinc fessum sinuosi pompa theatri,
   Et vocat ad plausus garrula scena suos.
Seu catus auditur senior, seu prodigus hæres,
   Seu procus, aut positâ casside miles adest,   30
Sive decennali fœcundus lite patronus
   Detonat inculto barbara verba foro,
Sæpe vafer gnato succurrit servus amanti,
   Et nasum rigidi fallit ubique Patris;
Sæpe novos illic virgo mirata calores
   Quid sit amor nescit, dum quoque nescit, amat.
Sive cruentatum furiosa Tragœdia sceptrum
   Quassat, & effusis crinibus ora rotat,
Et dolet, & specto, juvat & spectasse dolendo,
   Interdum & lacrymis dulcis amaror inest: 40
Seu puer infelix indelibata reliquit
   Gaudia, & abrupto flendus amore cadit,
Seu ferus è tenebris iterat Styga criminis ultor
   Conscia funereo pectora torre movens,
Seu mæret Pelopeia domus, seu nobilis Ili,
   Aut luit incestos aula Creontis avos.
Sed neque sub tecto semper nec in urbe latemus,
   Irrita nec nobis tempora veris eunt.
Nos quoque lucus habet vicinâ consitus ulmo
   Atque suburbani nobilis umbra loci.   50
Sæpius hic blandas spirantia sydera flammas
   Virgineos videas præteriisse choros.
Ah quoties dignæ stupui miracula formæ
   Quæ posset senium vel reparare Iovis:
Ah quoties vidi superantia lumina gemmas,
   Atque faces quotquot volvit uterque polus;
Collaque bis vivi Pelopis quæ brachia vincant,
   Quæque fluit puro nectare tincta via,
Et decus eximium frontis, tremulosque capillos,
   Aurea quæ fallax retia tendit Amor.   6c

Pellacesque genas, ad quas hyacinthina sordet
  Purpura, & ipse tui floris, Adoni, rubor.
Cedite laudatæ toties Heroides olim,
  Et quæcunque vagum cepit amica Jovem.
Cedite Achæmeniæ turritâ fronte puellæ,
  Et quot Susa colunt, Memnoniamque Ninon.
Vos etiam Danaæ fasces submittite Nymphæ,
  Et vos Iliacæ, Romuleæque nurus.
Nec Pompeianas Tarpëia Musa columnas
  Jactet, & Ausoniis plena theatra stolis.   70
Gloria Virginibus debetur prima Britannis,
  Extera sat tibi sit fœmina posse sequi.
Tuque urbs Dardaniis Londinum structa colonis
  Turrigerum latè conspicienda caput,
Tu nimium felix intra tua mœnia claudis
  Quicquid formosi pendulus orbis habet.
Non tibi tot cælo scintillant astra sereno
  Endymioneæ turba ministra deæ,
Quot tibi conspicuæ formáque auróque puellæ
  Per medias radiant turba videnda vias.   80
Creditur huc geminis venisse invecta columbis
  Alma pharetrigero milite cincta Venus,
Huic Cnidon, & riguas Simoentis flumine valles,
  Huic Paphon, & roseam posthabitura Cypron.
Ast ego, dum pueri sinit indulgentia cæci,
  Mœnia quàm subitò linquere fausta paro;
Et vitare procul malefidæ infamia Circes
  Atria, divini Molyos usus ope.
Stat quoque juncosas Cami remeare paludes,
  Atque iterum raucæ murmur adire Scholæ.   90
Interea fidi parvum cape munus amici,
  Paucaque in alternos verba coacta modos.

Elegia secunda, Anno ætatis 17.

In obitum Præconis Academici Cantabrigiensis.

TE, qui conspicuus baculo fulgente solebas
  Palladium toties ore ciere gregem,
Ultima præconum præconem te quoque sæva
  Mors rapit, officio nec favet ipsa suo.
Candidiora licet fuerint tibi tempora plumis
  Sub quibus accipimus delituisse Jovem,
O dignus tamen Hæmonio juvenescere succo,
  Dignus in Æsonios vivere posse dies,
Dignus quem Stygiis medicâ revocaret ab undis
  Arte Coronides, sæpe rogante dea.   10
Tu si jussus eras acies accire togatas,
  Et celer à Phoebo nuntius ire tuo,
Talis in Iliacâ stabat Cyllenius aula
  Alipes, æthereâ missus ab arce Patris.
Talis & Eurybates ante ora furentis Achillei
  Rettulit Atridæ jussa severa ducis.
Magna sepulchrorum regina, satelles Averni

Sæva nimis Musis, Palladi sæva nimis,
   Quin illos rapias qui pondus inutile terræ,
     Turba quidem est telis ista petenda tuis.
Vestibus hunc igitur pullis Academia luge,
   Et madeant lachrymis nigra feretra tuis.
Fundat & ipsa modos querebunda Elegëia tristes,
   Personet & totis nænia mœsta scholis.

Elegia tertia, Anno ætatis 17.

In obitum Præsulis Wintoniensis.

MŒSTUS eram, & tacitus nullo comitante sedebam,
   Hærebantque animo tristia plura meo,
Protinus en subiit funestæ cladis Imago
   Fecit in Angliaco quam Libitina solo;
Dum procerum ingressa est splendentes marmore turres
   Dira sepulchrali mors metuenda face;
Pulsavitque auro gravidos & jaspide muros,
   Nec metuit satrapum sternere falce greges.
Tunc memini clarique ducis, fratrisque verendi
   Intempestivis ossa cremata rogis.
Et memini Heroum quos vidit ad æthera raptos,
   Flevit & amissos Belgia tota duces.
At te præcipuè luxi dignissime præsul,
   Wintoniæque olim gloria magna tuæ;
Delicui fletu, & tristi sic ore querebar,
   Mors fera Tartareo diva secunda Jovi,
Nonne satis quod sylva tuas persentiat iras,
   Et quod in herbosos jus tibi detur agros,
Quodque afflata tuo marcescant lilia tabo,
   Et crocus, & pulchræ Cypridi sacra rosa,
Nec sinis ut semper fluvio contermina quercus
   Miretur lapsus prætereuntis aquæ?
Et tibi succumbit liquido quæ plurima cœlo
   Evehitur pennis quamlibet augur avis,
Et quæ mille nigris errant animalia sylvis,
   Et quod alunt mutum Proteos antra pecus.
Invida, tanta tibi cum sit concessa potestas,
   Quid juvat humanâ tingere cæde manus?
Nobileque in pectus certas acuisse sagittas,
   Semideamque animam sede fugâsse suâ?
Talia dum lacrymans alto sub pectore volvo,
   Roscidus occiduis Hesperus exit aquis,
Et Tartessiaco submerserat æquore currum
   Phœbus, ab eöo littore mensus iter.
Nec mora, membra cavo posui refovenda cubili,
   Condiderant oculos noxque soporque meos.
Cum mihi visus eram lato spatiarier agro,
   Heu nequit ingenium visa referre meum.
Illic puniceâ radiabant omnia luce,
   Ut matutino cum juga sole rubent.
Ac veluti cum pandit opes Thaumantia proles,
   Vestitu nituit multicolore solum.

Non dea tam variis ornavit floribus hortos
    Alcinoi, Zephyro Chloris amata levi.
Flumina vernantes lambunt argentea campos,
    Ditior Hesperio flavet arena Tago.
Serpit odoriferas per opes levis aura Favoni,
    Aura sub innumeris humida nata rosis.
Talis in extremis terræ Gangetidis oris
    Luciferi regis fingitur esse domus.   50
Ipse racemiferis dum densas vitibus umbras
    Et pellucentes miror ubique locos,
Ecce mihi subito præsul Wintonius astat,
    Sydereum nitido fulsit in ore jubar;
Vestis ad auratos defluxit candida talos,
    Infula divinum cinxerat alba caput.
Dumque senex tali incedit venerandus amictu,
    Intremuit læto florea terra sono.
Agmina gemmatis plaudunt cælestia pennis,
    Pura triumphali personat æthra tubâ.   60
Quisque novum amplexu comitem cantuque salutat,
    Hosque aliquis placido misit ab ore sonos;
Nate veni, & patrii felix cape gaudia regni,
    Semper ab hinc duro, nate, labore vaca.
Dixit, & aligeræ tetigerunt nablia turmæ,
    At mihi cum tenebris aurea pulsa quies.
Flebam turbatos Cephaleiâ pellice somnos,
    Talia contingant somnia sæpe mihi.

Elegia quarta. Anno ætatis 18.

Ad Thomam Junium præceptorem suum apud mercatores Anglicos Ham-
burgæ agentes Pastoris munere fungentem.

CURRE per immensum subitò mea littera pontum,
    I, pete Teutonicos læve per æquor agros,
Segnes rumpe moras, & nil, precor, obstet eunti,
    Et festinantis nil remoretur iter.
Ipse ego Sicanio frænantem carcere ventos
    Æolon, & virides sollicitabo Deos;
Cæruleamque suis comitatam Dorida Nymphis,
    Ut tibi dent placidam per sua regna viam.
At tu, si poteris, celeres tibi sume jugales,
    Vecta quibus Colchis fugit ab ore viri.   10
Aut queis Triptolemus Scythicas devenit in oras
    Gratus Eleusinâ missus ab urbe puer.
Atque ubi Germanas flavere videbis arenas
    Ditis ad Hamburgæ mœnia flecte gradum,
Dicitur occiso quæ ducere nomen ab Hamâ,
    Cimbrica quem fertur clava dedisse neci.
Vivit ibi antiquæ clarus pietatis honore
    Præsul Christicolas pascere doctus oves;
Ille quidem est animæ plusquam pars altera nostræ,
    Dimidio vitæ vivere cogor ego.   20
Hei mihi quot pelagi, quot montes interjecti

Me faciunt aliâ parte carere mei!
Charior ille mihi quam tu doctissime Graium
    Cliniadi, pronepos qui Telamonis erat.
Quámque Stagirites generoso magnus alumno,
    Quem peperit Libyco Chaonis alma Jovi.
Qualis Amyntorides, qualis Philyrëius Heros
    Myrmidonum regi, talis & ille mihi.
Primus ego Aonios illo præeunte recessus
    Lustrabam, & bifidi sacra vireta jugi,   30
Pieriosque hausi latices, Clioque favente,
    Castalio sparsi læta ter ora mero.
Flammeus at signum ter viderat arietis Æthon,
    Jnduxitque auro lanea terga novo,
Bisque novo terram sparsisti Chlori senilem
    Gramine, bisque tuas abstulit Auster opes:
Necdum ejus licuit mihi lumina pascere vultu,
    Aut linguæ dulces aure bibisse sonos.
Vade igitur, cursuque Eurum præverte sonorum,
    Quàm sit opus monitis res docet, ipsa vides.   40
Invenies dulci cum conjuge forte sedentem,
    Mulcentem gremio pignora chara suo,
Forsitan aut veterum prælarga volumina patrum
    Versantem, aut veri biblia sacra Dei.
Cælestive animas saturantem rore tenellas,
    Grande salutiferæ religionis opus.
Utque solet, multam sit dicere cura salutem,
    Dicere quam decuit, si modo adesset, herum.
Hæc quoque paulum oculos in humum defixa modestos,
    Verba verecundo sis memor ore loqui: 50
Hæc tibi, si teneris vacat inter prælia Musis
    Mittit ab Angliaco littore fida manus.
Accipe sinceram, quamvis sit sera, salutem;
    Fiat & hoc ipso gratior illa tibi.
Sera quidem, sed vera fuit, quam casta recepit
    Icaris a lento Penelopeia viro.
Ast ego quid volui manifestum tollere crimen,
    Ipse quod ex omni parte levare nequit.
Arguitur tardus meritò, noxamque fatetur,
    Et pudet officium deseruisse suum.   60
Tu modò da veniam fasso, veniamque roganti,
    Crimina diminui, quæ patuere, solent.
Non ferus in pavidos rictus diducit hiantes,
    Vulnifico pronos nec rapit ungue leo.
Sæpe sarissiferi crudelia pectora Thracis
    Supplicis ad mœstas deliquere preces.
Extensæque manus avertunt fulminis ictus,
    Placat & iratos hostia parva Deos.
Jamque diu scripsisse tibi fuit impetus illi,
    Neve moras ultra ducere passus Amor.   70
Nam vaga Fama refert, heu nuntia vera malorum!
    In tibi finitimis bella tumere locis,
Teque tuàmque urbem truculento milite cingi,
    Et iam Saxonicos arma parasse duces.

Te circum latè campos populatur Enyo,
  Et sata carne virûm jam cruor arva rigat.
Germanisque suum concessit Thracia Martem,
  Illuc Odrysios Mars pater egit equos.
Perpetuóque comans jam deflorescit oliva,
  Fugit & ærisonam Diva perosa tubam,   80
Fugit io terris, & jam non ultima virgo
  Creditur ad superas justa volasse domos.
Te tamen intereà belli circumsonat horror,
  Vivis & ignoto solus inópsque solo;
Et, tibi quam patrii non exhibuere penates
  Sede peregrinâ quæris egenus opem.
Patria dura parens, & saxis sævior albis
  Spumea quæ pulsat littoris unda tui,
Siccine te decet innocuos exponere fætus;
  Siccine in externam ferrea cogis humum,   90
Et sinis ut terris quærant alimenta remotis
  Quos tibi prospiciens miserat ipse Deus,
Et qui læta ferunt de cælo nuntia, quique
  Quæ via post cineres ducat ad astra, docent?
Digna quidem Stygiis quæ vivas clausa tenebris,
  Æternâque animæ digna perire fame!
Haud aliter vates terræ Thesbitidis olim
  Pressit inassueto devia tesqua pede,
Desertasque Arabum salebras, dum regis Achabi
  Effugit atque tuas, Sidoni dira, manus.   100
Talis & horrisono laceratus membra flagello,
  Paulus ab Æmathiâ pellitur urbe Cilix.
Piscosæque ipsum Gergessæ civis Jesum
  Finibus ingratus jussit abire suis.
At tu sume animos, nec spes cadat anxia curis
  Nec tua concutiat decolor ossa metus.
Sis etenim quamvis fulgentibus obsitus armis,
  Intententque tibi millia tela necem,
At nullis vel inerme latus violabitur armis,
  Deque tuo cuspis nulla cruore bibet.   110
Namque eris ipse Dei radiante sub ægide tutus,
  Ille tibi custos, & pugil ille tibi;
Ille Sionææ qui tot sub mœnibus arcis
  Assyrios fudit nocte silente viros; .
Inque fugam vertit quos in Samaritidas oras
  Misit ab antiquis prisca Damascus agris,
Terruit & densas pavido cum rege cohortes,
  Aere dum vacuo buccina clara sonat,
Cornea pulvereum dum verberat ungula campum,
  Currus arenosam dum quatit actus humum,   120
Auditurque hinnitus equorum ad bella ruentûm,
  Et strepitus ferri, murmuraque alta virûm.
Et tu (quod superest miseris) sperare memento,
  Et tua magnanimo pectore vince mala.
Nec dubites quandoque frui melioribus annis,
  Atque iterum patrios posse videre lares.

Elegia quinta, Anno ætatis 20.

In adventum veris.

IN se perpetuo Tempus revolubile gyro
   Jam revocat Zephyros vere tepente novos.
Induiturque brevem Tellus reparata juventam,
   Jamque soluta gelu dulce virescit humus.
Fallor? an & nobis redeunt in carmina vires,
   Ingeniumque mihi munere veris adest?
Munere veris adest, iterumque vigescit ab illo
   (Quis putet) atque aliquod jam sibi poscit opus.
Castalis ante oculos, bifidumque cacumen oberrat,
   Et mihi Pyrenen somnia nocte ferunt.   10
Concitaque arcano fervent mihi pectora motu,
   Et furor, & sonitus me sacer intùs agit.
Delius ipse venit, video Penëide lauro
   Implicitos crines, Delius ipse venit.
Jam mihi mens liquidi raptatur in ardua cœli,
   Perque vagas nubes corpore liber eo.
Perque umbras, perque antra feror penetralia vatum,
   Et mihi fana patent interiora Deûm.
Intuiturque animus toto quid agatur Olympo,
   Nec fugiunt oculos Tartara cæca meos.   20
Quid tam grande sonat distento spiritus ore?
   Quid parit hæc rabies, quid sacer iste furor?
Ver mihi, quod dedit ingenium, cantabitur illo;
   Profuerint isto reddita dona modo.
Jam Philomela tuos foliis adoperta novellis
   Instituis modulos, dum silet omne nemus.
Urbe ego, tu sylvâ simul incipiamus utrique,
   Et simul adventum veris uterque canat.
Veris io rediere vices, celebremus honores
   Veris, & hoc subeat Musa quotannis opus.   30
Jam sol Æthiopas fugiens Tithoniaque arva,
   Flectit ad Arctöas aurea lora plagas.
Est breve noctis iter, brevis est mora noctis opacæ,
   Horrida cum tenebris exulat illa suis.
Jamque Lycaonius plaustrum cæleste Boötes
   Non longâ sequitur fessus ut ante viâ,
Nunc etiam solitas circum Jovis atria toto
   Excubias agitant sydera rara polo.
Nam dolus & cædes, & vis cum nocte recessit,
   Neve Giganteum Dii timuere scelus.   40
Forte aliquis scopuli recubans in vertice pastor,
   Roscida cum primo sole rubescit humus,
Hac, ait, hac certè caruisti nocte puellâ
   Phœbe tuâ, celeres quæ retineret equos.
Læta suas repetit sylvas, pharetramque resumit
   Cynthia, Luciferas ut videt alta rotas,
Et tenues ponens radios gaudere videtur
   Officium fieri tam breve fratris ope.

20 quotannis] perennis *1673*

Desere, Phœbus ait, thalamos Aurora seniles,
  Quid juvat effœto procubuisse toro?   5o
Te manet Æolides viridi venator in herba,
  Surge, tuos ignes altus Hymettus habet.
Flava verecundo dea crimen in ore fatetur,
  Et matutinos ocyus urget equos.
Exuit invisam Tellus rediviva senectam,
  Et cupit amplexus Phœbe subire tuos;
Et cupit, & digna est, quid enim formosius illâ,
  Pandit ut omniferos luxuriosa sinus,
Atque Arabum spirat messes, & ab ore venusto
  Mitia cum Paphiis fundit amoma rosis.   6o
Ecce coronatur sacro frons ardua luco,
  Cingit ut Idæam pinea turris Opim;
Et vario madidos intexit flore capillos,
  Floribus & visa est posse placere suis.
Floribus effusos ut erat redimita capillos
  Tænario placuit diva Sicana Deo.
Aspice Phœbe tibi faciles hortantur amores,
  Mellitasque movent flamina verna preces.
Cinnameâ Zephyrus leve plaudit odorifer alâ,
  Blanditiasque tibi ferre videntur aves.   70
Nec sine dote tuos temeraria quærit amores
  Terra, nec optatos poscit egena toros,
Alma salutiferum medicos tibi gramen in usus
  Præbet, & hinc titulos adjuvat ipsa tuos.
Quòd si te pretium, si te fulgentia tangunt
  Munera, (muneribus sæpe coemptus Amor)
Illa tibi ostentat quascunque sub æquore vasto,
  Et superinjectis montibus abdit opes.
Ah quoties cum tu clivoso fessus Olympo
  In vespertinas præcipitaris aquas,   8o
Cur te, inquit, cursu languentem Phœbe diurno
  Hesperiis recipit Cærula mater aquis?
Quid tibi cum Tethy? Quid cum Tartesside lymphâ,
  Dia quid immundo perluis ora salo?
Frigora Phœbe meâ melius captabis in umbrâ,
  Huc ades, ardentes imbue rore comas.
Mollior egelidâ veniet tibi somnus in herbâ,
  Huc ades, & gremio lumina pone meo.
Quáque jaces circum mulcebit lene susurrans
  Aura per humentes corpora fusa rosas.   9o
Nec me (crede mihi) terrent Semelëia fata,
  Nec Phäetontéo fumidus axis equo;
Cum tu Phœbe tuo sapientius uteris igni,
  Huc ades & gremio lumina pone meo.
Sic Tellus lasciva suos suspirat amores;
  Matris in exemplum cætera turba ruunt.
Nunc etenim toto currit vagus orbe Cupido,
  Languentesque fovet solis ab igne faces.
Insonuere novis lethalia cornua nervis,
  Triste micant ferro tela corusca novo.   100
Jamque vel invictam tentat superasse Dianam,

Quæque sedet sacro Vesta pudica foco.
Ipsa senescentem reparat Venus annua formam,
    Atque iterum tepido creditur orta mari.
Marmoreas juvenes clamant Hymenæe per urbes,
    Litus io Hymen, & cava saxa sonant.
Cultior ille venit tunicâque decentior aptâ,
    Puniceum redolet vestis odora crocum.
Egrediturque frequens ad amœni gaudia veris
    Virgineos auro cincta puella sinus.   110
Votum est cuique suum, votum est tamen omnibus unum,
    Ut sibi quem cupiat, det Cytherea virum.
Nunc quoque septenâ modulatur arundine pastor,
    Et sua quæ jungat carmina Phyllis habet.
Navita nocturno placat sua sydera cantu,
    Delphinasque leves ad vada summa vocat.
Jupiter ipse alto cum conjuge ludit Olympo,
    Convocat & famulos ad sua festa Deos.
Nunc etiam Satyri cum sera crepuscula surgunt,
    Pervolitant celeri florea rura choro,   120
Sylvanusque suâ Cyparissi fronde revinctus,
    Semicaperque Deus, semideusque caper.
Quæque sub arboribus Dryades latuere vetustis
    Per juga, per solos expatiantur agros.
Per sata luxuriat fruticetaque Mænalius Pan,
    Vix Cybele mater, vix sibi tuta Ceres,
Atque aliquam cupidus prædatur Oreada Faunus,
    Consulit in trepidos dum sibi Nympha pedes,
Jamque latet, latitansque cupit male tecta videri,
    Et fugit, & fugiens pervelit ipsa capi.   130
Dii quoque non dubitant cælo præponere sylvas,
    Et sua quisque sibi numina lucus habet.
Et sua quisque diu sibi numina lucus habeto,
    Nec vos arboreâ dii precor ite domo.
Te referant miseris te Jupiter aurea terris
    Sæcla, quid ad nimbos aspera tela redis?
Tu saltem lentè rapidos age Phœbe jugales
    Quà potes, & sensim tempora veris eant.
Brumaque productas tardè ferat hispida noctes,
    Ingruat & nostro serior umbra polo.   140

Elegia sexta.

Ad Carolum Diodatum ruri commorantem.

Qui cum idibus Decemb. scripsisset, & sua carmina excusari postulasset si solito minus essent bona, quòd inter lautitias quibus erat ab amicis exceptus, haud satis felicem operam Musis dare se posse affirmabat, hunc habuit responsum.

Mitto tibi sanam non pleno ventre salutem,
    Quâ tu distento forte carere potes.
At tua quid nostram prolectat Musa camœnam,
    Nec sinit optatas posse sequi tenebras?
Carmine scire velis quàm te redamémque colámque,

Crede mihi vix hoc carmine scire queas.
Nam neque noster amor modulis includitur arctis,
    Nec venit ad claudos integer ipse pedes.
Quàm bene solennes epulas, hilaremque Decembrim
    Festaque cœlifugam quæ coluere Deum,   10
Deliciasque refers, hyberni gaudia ruris,
    Haustaque per lepidos Gallica musta focos.
Quid quereris refugam vino dapibusque poesin?
    Carmen amat Bacchum, Carmina Bacchus amat.
Nec puduit Phœbum virides gestasse corymbos,
    Atque hederam lauro præposuisse suæ.
Sæpius Aoniis clamavit collibus Euœ
    Mista Thyonêo turba novena choro.
Naso Corallæis mala carmina misit ab agris:
    Non illic epulæ non sata vitis erat.   20
Quid nisi vina, rosasque racemiferumque Lyæum
    Cantavit brevibus Tëia Musa modis?
Pindaricosque inflat numeros Teumesius Euan,
    Et redolet sumptum pagina quæque merum,
Dum gravis everso currus crepat axe supinus,
    Et volat Eléo pulvere fuscus eques.
Quadrimoque madens Lyricen Romanus Jaccho
    Dulce canit Glyceran, flavicomamque Chloen.
Jam quoque lauta tibi generoso mensa paratu,
    Mentis alit vires, ingeniumque fovet.   30
Massica fœcundam despumant pocula venam,
    Fundis & ex ipso condita metra cado.
Addimus his artes, fusumque per intima Phœbum
    Corda, favent uni Bacchus, Apollo, Ceres.
Scilicet haud mirum tam dulcia carmina per te
    Numine composito tres peperisse Deos.
Nunc quoque Thressa tibi cælato barbitos auro
    Insonat argutâ molliter icta manu;
Auditurque chelys suspensa tapetia circum,
    Virgineos tremulâ quæ regat arte pedes.   40
Illa tuas saltem teneant spectacula Musas,
    Et revocent, quantum crapula pellit iners.
Crede mihi dum psallit ebur, comitataque plectrum
    Implet odoratos festa chorea tholos,
Percipies tacitum per pectora serpere Phœbum,
    Quale repentinus permeat ossa calor,
Perque puellares oculos digitumque sonantem
    Irruet in totos lapsa Thalia sinus.
Namque Elegía levis multorum cura deorum est,
    Et vocat ad numeros quemlibet illa suos;   50
Liber adest elegis, Eratoque, Ceresque, Venusque,
    Et cum purpureâ matre tenellus Amor.
Talibus inde licent convivia larga poetis,
    Sæpius & veteri commaduisse mero.
At qui bella refert, & adulto sub Jove cælum,
    Heroasque pios, semideosque duces,
Et nunc sancta canit superum consulta deorum,
    Nunc latrata fero regna profunda cane,

Ille quidem parcè Samii pro more magistri
    Vivat, & innocuos præbeat herba cibos; 60
Stet prope fagineo pellucida lympha catillo,
    Sobriaque è puro pocula fonte bibat.
Additur huic scelerisque vacans, & casta juventus,
    Et rigidi mores, & sine labe manus.
Qualis veste nitens sacrâ, & lustralibus undis
    Surgis ad infensos augur iture Deos.
Hoc ritu vixisse ferunt post rapta sagacem
    Lumina Tiresian, Ogygiumque Linon,
Et lare devoto profugum Calchanta, senemque
    Orpheon edomitis sola per antra feris; 70
Sic dapis exiguus, sic rivi potor Homerus
    Dulichium vexit per freta longa virum,
Et per monstrificam Perseiæ Phœbados aulam,
    Et vada fœmineis insidiosa sonis,
Perque tuas rex ime domos, ubi sanguine nigro
    Dicitur umbrarum detinuisse greges.
Diis etenim sacer est vates, divûmque sacerdos,
    Spirat & occultum pectus, & ora Jovem.
At tu si quid agam, scitabere (si modò saltem
    Esse putas tanti noscere siquid agam) 80
Paciferum canimus cælesti semine regem,
    Faustaque sacratis sæcula pacta libris,
Vagitumque Dei, & stabulantem paupere tecto
    Qui suprema suo cum patre regna colit,
Stelliparumque polum, modulantesque æthere turmas,
    Et subitò elisos ad sua fana Deos.
Dona quidem dedimus Christi natalibus illa
    Illa sub auroram lux mihi prima tulit.
Te quoque pressa manent patriis meditata cicutis,
    Tu mihi, cui recitem, judicis instar eris. 90

Elegia septima, Anno ætatis undevigesimo.

NONDUM blanda tuas leges Amathusia nôram,
    Et Paphio vacuum pectus ab igne fuit.
Sæpe cupidineas, puerilia tela, sagittas,
    Atque tuum sprevi maxime, numen, Amor.
Tu puer imbelles dixi transfige columbas,
    Conveniunt tenero mollia bella duci.
Aut de passeribus tumidos age, parve, triumphos,
    Hæc sunt militiæ digna trophæa tuæ.
In genus humanum quid inania dirigis arma?
    Non valet in fortes ista pharetra viros. 10
Non tulit hoc Cyprius, (neque enim Deus ullus ad iras
    Promptior) & duplici jam ferus igne calet.
Ver erat, & summæ radians per culmina villæ
    Attulerat primam lux tibi Maie diem:
At mihi adhuc refugam quærebant lumina noctem
    Nec matutinum sustinuere jubar.
Astat Amor lecto, pictis Amor impiger alis,

Prodidit astantem mota pharetra Deum:
Prodidit & facies, & dulce minantis ocelli,
    Et quicquid puero, dignum & Amore fuit.   20
Talis in æterno juvenis Sigeius Olympo
    Miscet amatori pocula plena Jovi;
Aut qui formosas pellexit ad oscula nymphas
    Thiodamantæus Naiade raptus Hylas;
Addideratque iras, sed & has decuisse putares,
    Addideratque truces, nec sine felle minas.
Et miser exemplo sapuisses tutiùs, inquit,
    Nunc mea quid possit dextera testis eris.
Inter & expertos vires numerabere nostras,
    Et faciam vero per tua damna fidem.   30
Ipse ego si nescis strato Pythone superbum
    Edomui Phœbum, cessit & ille mihi;
Et quoties meminit Peneidos, ipse fatetur
    Certiùs & graviùs tela nocere mea.
Me nequit adductum curvare peritiùs arcum,
    Qui post terga solet vincere Parthus eques.
Cydoniusque mihi cedit venator, & ille
    Inscius uxori qui necis author erat.
Est etiam nobis ingens quoque victus Orion,
    Herculeæque manus, Herculeusque comes.   40
Jupiter ipse licet sua fulmina torqueat in me,
    Hærebunt lateri spicula nostra Jovis.
Cætera quæ dubitas meliùs mea tela docebunt,
    Et tua non leviter corda petenda mihi.
Nec te stulte tuæ poterunt defendere Musæ,
    Nec tibi Phœbæus porriget anguis opem.
Dixit, & aurato quatiens mucrone sagittam,
    Evolat in tepidos Cypridos ille sinus.
At mihi risuro tonuit ferus ore minaci,
    Et mihi de puero non metus ullus erat.   50
Et modò quà nostri spatiantur in urbe Quirites
    Et modò villarum proxima rura placent,
Turba frequens, faciéque simillima turba dearum
    Splendida per medias itque reditque vias.
Auctaque luce dies gemino fulgore coruscat,
    Fallor? an & radios hinc quoque Phœbus habet.
Hæc ego non fugi spectacula grata severus,
    Impetus & quò me fert juvenilis, agor.
Lumina luminibus malè providus obvia misi,
    Neve oculos potui continuisse meos.   60
Unam forte aliis supereminuisse notabam,
    Principium nostri lux erat illa mali.
Sic Venus optaret mortalibus ipsa videri,
    Sic regina Deûm conspicienda fuit.
Hanc memor objecit nobis malus ille Cupido,
    Solus & hos nobis texuit antè dolos.
Nec procul ipse vafer latuit, multæque sagittæ,
    Et facis a tergo grande pependit onus.
Nec mora, nunc ciliis hæsit, nunc virginis ori,
    Insilit hinc labiis, insidet inde genis: 70

Et quascunque agilis partes jaculator oberrat,
  Hei mihi, mille locis pectus inerme ferit.
Protinus insoliti subierunt corda furores,
  Uror amans intùs, flammaque totus eram.
Interea misero quæ jam mihi sola placebat,
  Ablata est oculis non reditura meis.
Ast ego progredior tacitè querebundus, & excors,
  Et dubius volui sæpe referre pedem.
Findor, & hæc remanet, sequitur pars altera votum,
  Raptaque tàm subitò gaudia flere juvat.   80
Sic dolet amissum proles Junonia cœlum,
  Inter Lemniacos præcipitata focos.
Talis & abreptum solem respexit, ad Orcum
  Vectus ab attonitis Amphiaraus equis.
Quid faciam infelix, & luctu victus, amores
  Nec licet inceptos ponere, neve sequi.
O utinam spectare semel mihi detur amatos
  Vultus, & coràm tristia verba loqui;
Forsitan & duro non est adamante creata,
  Forte nec ad nostras surdeat illa preces.   90
Crede mihi nullus sic infeliciter arsit,
  Ponar in exemplo primus & unus ego.
Parce precor teneri cum sis Deus ales amoris,
  Pugnent officio nec tua facta tuo.
Jam tuus O certè est mihi formidabilis arcus,
  Nate deâ, jaculis nec minus igne potens:
Et tua fumabunt nostris altaria donis,
  Solus & in superis tu mihi summus eris.
Deme meos tandem, verùm nec deme furores,
  Nescio cur, miser est suaviter omnis amans: 100
Tu modo da facilis, posthæc mea siqua futura est,
  Cuspis amaturos figat ut una duos.

      Hæc ego mente olim lævâ, studioque supino
        Nequitiæ posui vana trophæa meæ.
      Scilicet abreptum sic me malus impulit error,
        Indocilisque ætas prava magistra fuit,
      Donec Socraticos umbrosa Academia rivos
        Præbuit, admissum dedocuitque jugum.
      Protinus extinctis ex illo tempore flammis,
        Cincta rigent multo pectora nostra gelu.   110
      Unde suis frigus metuit puer ipse Sagittis,
        Et Diomedéam vim timet ipse Venus.

In Proditionem Bombardicam.

Cum simul in regem nuper satrapasque Britannos
  Ausus es infandum perfide Fauxe nefas,
Fallor? an & mitis voluisti ex parte videri,
  Et pensare malâ cum pietate scelus;
Scilicet hos alti missurus ad atria cæli,
  Sulphureo curru flammivolisque rotis.
Qualiter ille feris caput inviolabile Parcis
  Liquit Jördanios turbine raptus agros.

In eandem.

SICCINE tentasti cælo donâsse Jäcobum
    Quae septemgemino Bellua monte lates?
Ni meliora tuum poterit dare munera numen,
    Parce precor donis insidiosa tuis.
Ille quidem sine te consortia serus adivit
    Astra, nec inferni pulveris usus ope.
Sic potiùs fœdos in cælum pelle cucullos,
    Et quot habet brutos Roma profana Deos.
Namque hac aut aliâ nisi quemque adjuveris arte,
    Crede mihi cæli vix bene scandet iter.   10

In eandem.

PURGATOREM animæ derisit Jäcobus ignem,
    Et sine quo superûm non adeunda domus.
Frenduit hoc trinâ monstrum Latiale coronâ
    Movit & horrificùm cornua dena minax.
Et nec inultus ait temnes mea sacra Britanne,
    Supplicium spretâ relligione dabis.
Et si stelligeras unquam penetraveris arces,
    Non nisi per flammas triste patebit iter.
O quàm funesto cecinisti proxima vero,
    Verbaque ponderibus vix caritura suis!   10
Nam prope Tartareo sublime rotatus ab igni
Ibat ad æthereas umbra perusta plagas.

In eandem.

QUEM modò Roma suis devoverat impia diris,
    Et Styge damnarât Tænarioque sinu,
Hunc vice mutatâ jam tollere gestit ad astra,
    Et cupit ad superos evehere usque Deos.

In inventorem Bombardæ.

JAPETIONIDEM laudavit cæca vetustas,
    Qui tulit æthaeream solis ab axe facem;
At mihi major erit, qui lurida creditur arma,
    Et trifidum fulmen surripuisse Jovi.

Ad Leonoram Romæ canentem.

ANGELUS unicuique suus (sic credite gentes)
    Obtigit æthereis ales ab ordinibus.
Quid mirum? Leonora tibi si gloria major,
    Nam tua præsentem vox sonat ipsa Deum.
Aut Deus, aut vacui certè mens tertia cœli
    Per tua secretò guttura serpit agens;
Serpit agens, facilisque docet mortalia corda
    Sensim immortali assuescere posse sono.
Quòd si cuncta quidem Deus est, per cunctaque fusus,
    In te unâ loquitur, cætera mutus habet.

Ad eandem.

ALTERA Torquatum cepit Leonora Poëtam,
    Cujus ab insano cessit amore furens.
Ah miser ille tuo quantò feliciùs ævo
    Perditus, & propter te Leonora foret!
Et te Pieriâ sensisset voce canentem
    Aurea maternæ fila movere lyræ;
Quamvis Dircæo torsisset lumina Pentheo
    Sævior, aut totus desipuisset iners,
Tu tamen errantes cæcâ vertigine sensus
    Voce eadem poteras composuisse tuâ;   10
Et poteras ægro spirans sub corde quietem
    Flexanimo cantu restituisse sibi.

Ad eandem.

CREDULA quid liquidam Sirena Neapoli jactas,
    Claraque Parthenopes fana Achelöiados,
Littoreamque tuâ defunctam Naiada ripâ
    Corpora Chalcidico sacra dedisse rogo?
Illa quidem vivitque, & amœnâ Tibridis undâ
    Mutavit rauci murmura Pausilipi.
Illic Romulidûm studiis ornata secundis,
    Atque homines cantu detinet atque Deos.

Elegiarum Finis.

[Added in Second Edition, 1673.]

Apologus de Rustico & Hero.

RUSTICUS ex Malo sapidissima poma quotannis
    Legit, & urbano lecta dedit Domino:
Hic incredibili fructûs dulcedine Captus
    Malum ipsam in proprias transtulit areolas.
Hactenus illa ferax, sed longo debilis ævo,
    Mota solo assueto, protinùs aret iners.
Quod tandem ut patuit Domino, spe lusus inani,
    Damnavit celeres in sua damna manus.
Atque ait, Heu quantò satius fuit illa Coloni
    (Parva licet) grato dona tulisse animo!   10
Possem Ego avaritiam frœnare, gulamque voracem:
    Nunc periere mihi & fœtus & ipsa parens.

[From *Defensio pro populo anglicano,* 1651.]

In Salmasii Hundredam.

QUIS expedivit Salmasio suam Hundredam,
Picámque docuit nostra verba conari?
Magister artis venter, et Jacobaei
Centum, exulantis viscera marsupii regis.

Quod si dolosi spes refulserit nummi,
Ipse Antichristi qui modò primatum Papæ
Minatus uno est dissipare sufflatu,
Cantabit ultrò Cardinalitium melos.

[From *Defensio secunda*, 1654.]

In Sàlmasium.

GAUDETE scombri, et quicquid est piscium salo,
Qui frigida hyeme incolitis algentes freta!
Vestrum misertus ille Salmasius Eques
Bonus, amicire nuditatem cogitat;
Chartæque largus, apparat papyrinos
Vobis cucullos, præterentes Claudii
Insignia, nomenque et decus, Salmasii:
Gestetis ut per omne cetarium forum
Equitis clientes, scriniis mungentium
Cubito virorum, et capsulis, gratissimos.

10

SYLVARUM LIBER.

Anno ætatis 16. In obitum Procancellarii medici.

PARÉRE fati discite legibus,
Manusque Parcæ jam date supplices,
    Qui pendulum telluris orbem
      Jäpeti colitis nepotes.
Vos si relicto mors vaga Tænaro
Semel vocârit flebilis, heu moræ
    Tentantur incassùm dolique;
      Per tenebras Stygis ire certum est.
Si destinatam pellere dextera
Mortem valeret, non ferus Hercules
    Nessi venenatus cruore
      Æmathiâ jacuisset Oetâ.

10

Nec fraude turpi Palladis invidæ
Vidisset occisum Ilion Hectora, aut
    Quem larva Pelidis peremit
      Ense Locro, Jove lacrymante.
Si triste fatum verba Hecatëia
Fugare possint, Telegoni parens
    Vixisset infamis, potentique
      Ægiali soror usa virgâ.

20

Numenque trinum fallere si queant
Artes medentûm, ignotaque gramina,
    Non gnarus herbarum Machaon
      Eurypyli cecidisset hastâ.
Læsisset & nec te Philyreie
Sagitta echidnæ perlita sanguine,
    Nec tela te fulmenque avitum
      Cæse puer genitricis alvo.
Tuque O alumno major Apolline,
Gentis togatæ cui regimen datum,

30

Frondosa quem nunc Cirrha luget,
  Et mediis Helicon in undis,
Jam præfuisses Palladio gregi
Lætus, superstes, nec sine gloria,
  Nec puppe lustrasses Charontis
    Horribiles barathri recessus.
At fila rupit Persephone tua
Irata, cum te viderit artibus
    Succoque pollenti tot atris
      Faucibus eripuisse mortis.   40
Colende præses, membra precor tua
Molli quiescant cespite, & ex tuo
    Crescant rosæ, calthæque busto,
      Purpureoque hyacinthus ore.
Sit mite de te judicium Æaci,
Subrideatque Ætnæa Proserpina,
    Interque felices perennis
      Elysio spatiere campo.

In quintum Novembris, Anno ætatis 17.

Jam pius extremâ veniens Jäcobus ab arcto
Teucrigenas populos, latéque patentia regna
Albionum tenuit, jamque inviolabile fœdus
Sceptra Caledoniis conjunxerat Anglica Scotis:
Pacificusque novo felix divesque sedebat
In solio, occultique doli securus & hostis:
Cum ferus ignifluo regnans Acheronte tyrannus,
Eumenidum pater, æthereo vagus exul Olympo,
Forte per immensum terrarum erraverat orbem,
Dinumerans sceleris socios, vernasque fideles,   10
Participes regni post funera mœsta futuros;
Hic tempestates medio ciet aëre diras,
Illic unanimes odium struit inter amicos,
Armat & invictas in mutua viscera gentes;
Regnaque olivifera vertit florentia pace,
Et quoscunque videt puræ virtutis amantes,
Hos cupit adjicere imperio, fraudumque magister
Tentat inaccessum sceleri corrumpere pectus,
Insidiasque locat tacitas, cassesque latentes
Tendit, ut incautos rapiat, seu Caspia Tigris   20
Insequitur trepidam deserta per avia prædam
Nocte sub illuni, & somno nictantibus astris.
Talibus infestat populos Summanus & urbes
Cinctus cæruleæ fumanti turbine flammæ.
Jamque fluentisonis albentia rupibus arva
Apparent, & terra Deo dilecta marino,
Cui nomen dederat quondam Neptunia proles
Amphitryoniaden qui non dubitavit atrocem
Æquore tranato furiali poscere bello,
Ante expugnatæ crudelia sæcula Troiæ.   30

At simul hanc opibusque & festâ pace beatam
Aspicit, & pingues donis Cerealibus agros,
Quodque magis doluit, venerantem numina veri
Sancta Dei populum, tandem suspiria rupit
Tartareos ignes & luridum olentia sulphur.
Qualia Trinacriâ trux ab Jove clausus in Ætna
Efflat tabifico monstrosus ab ore Tiphœus.
Ignescunt oculi, stridetque adamantinus ordo
Dentis, ut armorum fragor, ictaque cuspide cuspis.
Atque pererrato solum hoc lacrymabile mundo   40
Inveni, dixit, gens hæc mihi sola rebellis,
Contemtrixque jugi, nostrâque potentior arte.
Illa tamen, mea si quicquam tentamina possunt,
Non feret hoc impune diu, non ibit inulta,
Hactenus; & piceis liquido natat aëre pennis;
Quà volat, adversi præcursant agmine venti,
Densantur nubes, & crebra tonitrua fulgent.

   Jamque pruinosas velox superaverat alpes,
Et tenet Ausoniæ fines, à parte sinistrâ
Nimbifer Appenninus erat, priscique Sabini,   50
Dextra veneficiis infamis Hetruria, nec non
Te furtiva Tibris Thetidi videt oscula dantem;
Hinc Mavortigenæ consistit in arce Quirini.
Reddiderant dubiam jam sera crepuscula lucem,
Cum circumgreditur totam Tricoronifer urbem,
Panificosque Deos portat, scapulisque virorum
Evehitur, præeunt summisso poplite reges,
Et mendicantum series longissima fratrum;
Cereaque in manibus gestant funalia cæci,
Cimmeriis nati in tenebris, vitamque trahentes.   60
Templa dein multis subeunt lucentia tædis
(Vesper erat sacer iste Petro) fremitúsque canentum
Sæpe tholos implet vacuos, & inane locorum.
Qualiter exululat Bromius, Bromiique caterva,
Orgia cantantes in Echionio Aracyntho,
Dum tremit attonitus vitreis Asopus in undis,
Et procul ipse cavâ responsat rupe Cithæron.

   His igitur tandem solenni more peractis,
Nox senis amplexus Erebi taciturna reliquit,
Præcipitesque impellit equos stimulante flagello,   70
Captum oculis Typhlonta, Melanchætemque ferocem,
Atque Acherontæo prognatam patre Siopen
Torpidam, & hirsutis horrentem Phrica capillis.
Interea regum domitor, Phlegetontius hæres,
Ingreditur thalamos (neque enim secretus adulter
Producit steriles molli sine pellice noctes)
At vix compositos somnus claudebat ocellos,
Cum niger umbrarum dominus, rectorque silentum,
Prædatorque hominum falsâ sub imagine tectus
Astitit, assumptis micuerunt tempora canis,   80
Barba sinus promissa tegit, cineracea longo
Syrmate verrit humum vestis, pendetque cucullus
Vertice de raso, & ne quicquam desit ad artes,

Cannabeo lumbos constrinxit fune salaces,
Tarda fenestratis figens vestigia calceis.
Talis, uti fama est, vastâ Franciscus eremo
Tetra vagabatur solus per lustra ferarum,
Sylvestrique tulit genti pia verba salutis
Impius, atque lupos domuit, Lybicosque leones.
  Subdolus at tali Serpens velatus amictu   90
Solvit in has fallax ora execrantia voces;
Dormis nate? Etiamne tuos sopor opprimit artus
Immemor O fidei, pecorumque oblite tuorum,
Dum cathedram venerande tuam, diademaque triplex
Ridet Hyperboreo gens barbara nata sub axe,
Dumque pharetrati spernunt tua jura Britanni;
Surge, age, surge piger, Latius quem Cæsar adorat,
Cui reserata patet convexi janua cæli,
Turgentes animos, & fastus frange procaces,
Sacrilegique sciant, tua quid maledictio possit,   100
Et quid Apostolicæ possit custodia clavis;
Et memor Hesperiæ disjectam ulciscere classem,
Mersaque Iberorum lato vexilla profundo,
Sanctorumque cruci tot corpora fixa probrosæ,
Thermodoontéa nuper regnante puella.
At tu si tenero mavis torpescere lecto
Crescentesque negas hosti contundere vires,
Tyrrhenum implebit numeroso milite Pontum,
Signaque Aventino ponet fulgentia colle:
Relliquias veterum franget, flammisque cremabit,   110
Sacraque calcabit pedibus tua colla profanis,
Cujus gaudebant soleis dare basia reges.
Nec tamen hunc bellïs & aperto Marte lacesses,
Irritus ille labor, tu callidus utere fraude,
Quælibet hæreticis disponere retia fas est;
Jamque ad consilium extremis rex magnus ab oris
Patricios vocat, & procerum de stirpe creatos,
Grandævosque patres trabeâ canisque verendos;
Hos tu membratim poteris conspergere in auras,
Atque dare in cineres, nitrati pulveris igne   120
Ædibus injecto, quà convenere, sub imis.
Protinus ipse igitur quoscumque habet Anglia fidos
Propositi, factique mone, quisquámne tuorum
Audebit summi non jussa facessere Papæ.
Perculsosque metu subito, casúque stupentes
Invadat vel Gallus atrox, vel sævus Iberus.
Sæcula sic illic tandem Mariana redibunt,
Tuque in belligeros iterum dominaberis Anglos.
Et nequid timeas, divos divasque secundas
Accipe, quotque tuis celebrantur numina fastis.   130
Dixit & adscitos ponens malefidus amictus
Fugit ad infandam, regnum illætabile, Lethen.
  Jam rosea Eoas pandens Tithonia portas
Vestit inauratas redeunti lumine terras;
Mæstaque adhuc nigri deplorans funera nati
Irrigat ambrosiis montana cacumina guttis;

Cum somnos pepulit stellatæ janitor aulæ
Nocturnos visus, & somnia grata revolvens.
  Est locus æternâ septus caligine noctis
Vasta ruinosi quondam fundamina tecti,   140
Nunc torvi spelunca Phoni, Prodotæque bilinguis
Effera quos uno peperit Discordia partu.
Hic inter cæmenta jacent semifractaque saxa,
Ossa inhumata virûm, & trajecta cadavera ferro;
Hic Dolus intortis semper sedet ater ocellis,
Jurgiaque, & stimulis armata Calumnia fauces,
Et Furor, atque viæ moriendi mille videntur,
Et Timor, exanguisque locum circumvolat Horror,
Perpetuoque leves per muta silentia Manes
Exululant, tellus & sanguine conscia stagnat.   150
Ipsi etiam pavidi latitant penetralibus antri
Et Phonos, & Prodotes, nulloque sequente per antrum
Antrum horrens, scopulosum, atrum feralibus umbris
Diffugiunt sontes, & retrò lumina vortunt,
Hos pugiles Romæ per sæcula longa fideles
Evocat antistes Babylonius, atque ita fatur.
Finibus occiduis circumfusum incolit æquor
Gens exosa mihi, prudens natura negavit
Indignam penitùs nostro conjungere mundo;
Illuc, sic jubeo, celeri contendite gressu,   160
Tartareoque leves difflentur pulvere in auras
Et rex & pariter satrapæ, scelerata propago
Et quotquot fidei caluere cupidine veræ
Consilii socios adhibete, operisque ministros.
Finierat, rigidi cupidè paruere gemelli.
  Interea longo flectens curvamine cælos
Despicit ætherea dominus qui fulgurat arce,
Vanaque perversæ ridet conamina turbæ,
Atque sui causam populi volet ipse tueri.
  Esse ferunt spatium, quà distat ab Aside terra   170
Fertilis Europe, & spectat Mareotidas undas;
Hic turris posita est Titanidos ardua Famæ
Ærea, lata, sonans, rutilis vicinior astris
Quàm superimpositum vel Athos vel Pelion Ossæ
Mille fores aditusque patent, totidemque fenestræ,
Amplaque per tenues translucent atria muros;
Excitat hic varios plebs agglomerata susurros;
Qualiter instrepitant circum mulctralia bombis
Agmina muscarum, aut texto per ovilia junco,
Dum Canis æstivum cœli petit ardua culmen   180
Ipsa quidem summâ sedet ultrix matris in arce,
Auribus innumeris cinctum caput eminet olli,
Queis sonitum exiguum trahit, atque levissima captat
Murmura, ab extremis patuli confinibus orbis.
Nec tot Aristoride servator inique juvencæ
Isidos, immiti volvebas lumina vultu,
Lumina non unquam tacito nutantia somno,
Lumina subjectas late spectantia terras.

Istis illa solet loca luce carentia sæpe
Perlustrare, etiam radianti impervia soli.   190
Millenisque loquax auditaque visaque linguis
Cuilibet effundit temeraria, veráque merdax
Nunc minuit, modò confictis sermonibus auget.
Sed tamen a nostro meruisti carmine laudes
Fama, bonum quo non aliud veracius ullum,
Nobis digna cani, nec te memorasse pigebit
Carmine tam longo, servati scilicet Angli
Officiis vaga diva tuis, tibi reddimus æqua.
Te Deus æternos motu qui temperat ignes,
Fulmine præmisso alloquitur, terrâque tremente: 200
Fama siles? an te latet impia Papistarum
Conjurata cohors in meque meosque Britannos,
Et nova sceptrigero cædes meditata Jäcobo:
Nec plura, illa statim sensit mandata Tonantis,
Et satis antè fugax stridentes induit alas,
Induit & variis exilia corpora plumis;
Dextra tubam gestat Temesæo ex ære sonoram.
Nec mora jam pennis cedentes remigat auras,
Atque parum est cursu celeres prævertere nubes,
Jam ventos, jam solis equos post terga reliquit: 210
Et primò Angliacas solito de more per urbes
Ambiguas voces, incertaque murmura spargit,
Mox arguta dolos, & detestabile vulgat
Proditionis opus, nec non facta horrida dictu,
Authoresque addit sceleris, nec garrula cæcis
Insidiis loca structa silet; stupuere relatis,
Et pariter juvenes, pariter tremuere puellæ,
Effætique senes pariter, tantæque ruinæ
Sensus ad ætatem subitò penetraverat omnem.
Attamen interea populi miserescit ab alto   220
Æthereus pater, & crudelibus obstitit ausis
Papicolûm; capti pœnas raptantur ad acres;
At pia thura Deo, & grati solvuntur honores;
Compita læta focis genialibus omnia fumant;
Turba choros juvenilis agit: Quintoque Novembris
Nulla Dies toto occurrit celebratior anno.

Anno ætatis 17. In obitum Præsulis Eliensis.

ADHUC madentes rore squalebant genæ,
    Et sicca nondum lumina
Adhuc liquentis imbre turgebant salis,
    Quem nuper effudi pius,
Dum mœsta charo justa persolvi rogo
    Wintoniensis præsulis.
Cum centilinguis Fama (proh semper mali
    Cladisque vera nuntia)
Spargit per urbes divitis Britanniæ,
    Populosque Neptuno satos,   10
Cessisse morti, & ferreis sororibus

Te generis humani decus,
Qui rex sacrorum illâ fuisti in insulâ
   Quæ nomen Anguillæ tenet.
Tunc inquietum pectus irâ protinus
   Ebulliebat fervidâ,
Tumulis potentem sæpe devovens deam:
   Nec vota Naso in Ibida
Concepit alto diriora pectore,
   Graiusque vates parciùs   20
Turpem Lycambis execratus est dolum,
   Sponsamque Neobolen suam.
At ecce diras ipse dum fundo graves,
   Et imprecor neci necem,
Audisse tales videor attonitus sonos
   Leni, sub aurâ, flamine:
Cæcos furores pone, pone vitream
   Bilemque & irritas minas,
Quid temerè violas non nocenda numina,
   Subitoque ad iras percita.   30
Non est, ut arbitraris elusus miser,
   Mors atra Noctis filia,
Erebóve patre creta, sive Erinnye,
   Vastóve nata sub Chao:
Ast illa cælo missa stellato, Dei
   Messes ubique colligit;
Animasque mole carneâ reconditas
   In lucem & auras evocat:
Ut cum fugaces excitant Horæ diem
   Themidos Jovisque filiæ;   40
Et sempiterni ducit ad vultus patris;
   At justa raptat impios
Sub regna furvi luctuosa Tartari,
   Sedesque subterraneas.
Hanc ut vocantem lætus audivi, citò
   Fœdum reliqui carcerem,
Volatilesque faustus inter milites
   Ad astra sublimis feror:
Vates ut olim raptus ad cœlum senex
   Auriga currus ignei,   50
Non me Boötis terruere lucidi
   Sarraca tarda frigore, aut
Formidolosi Scorpionis brachia,
   Non ensis Orion tuus.
Prætervolavi fulgidi solis globum,
   Longéque sub pedibus deam
Vidi triformem, dum coercebat suos
   Frænis dracones aureis.
Erraticorum syderum per ordines,
   Per lacteas vehor plagas,   60
Velocitatem sæpe miratus novam,
   Donec nitentes ad fores
Ventum est Olympi, & regiam Crystallinam, &
   Stratum smaragdis Atrium.

Sed hic tacebo, nam quis effari queat
   Oriundus humano patre
Amœnitates illius loci, mihi
   Sat est in æternum frui.

Naturam non pati senium.

Heu quàm perpetuis erroribus acta fatiscit
Avia mens hominum, tenebrisque immersa profundis
Œdipodioniam volvit sub pectore noctem!
Quæ vesana suis metiri facta deorum
Audet, & incisas leges adamante perenni
Assimilare suis, nulloque solubile sæclo
Consilium fati perituris alligat horis.
  Ergóne marcescet sulcantibus obsita rugis
Naturæ facies, & rerum publica mater
Omniparum contracta uterum sterilescet ab ævo?   10
Et se fassa senem malè certis passibus ibit
Sidereum tremebunda caput? num tetra vetustas
Annorumque æterna fames, squalorque situsque
Sidera vexabunt? an & insatiabile Tempus
Esuriet Cælum, rapietque in viscera patrem?
Heu, potuitne suas imprudens Jupiter arces
Hoc contra munisse nefas, & Temporis isto
Exemisse malo, gyrosque dedisse perennes?
Ergo erit ut quandoque sono dilapsa tremendo
Convexi tabulata ruant, atque obvius ictu   20
Stridat uterque polus, superâque ut Olympius aulâ
Decidat, horribilisque retectâ Gorgone Pallas.
Qualis in Ægæam proles Junonia Lemnon
Deturbata sacro cecidit de limine cæli.
Tu quoque Phœbe tui casus imitabere nati
Præcipiti curru, subitáque ferere ruinâ
Pronus, & extinctâ fumabit lampade Nereus,
Et dabit attonito feralia sibila ponto.
Tunc etiam aërei divulsis sedibus Hæmi
Dissultabit apex, imoque allisa barathro   30
Terrebunt Stygium dejecta Ceraunia Ditem
In superos quibus usus erat, fraternaque bella.
  At Pater omnipotens fundatis fortius astris
Consuluit rerum summæ, certoque peregit
Pondere fatorum lances, atque ordine summo
Singula perpetuum jussit servare tenorem.
Volvitur hinc lapsu mundi rota prima diurno;
Raptat & ambitos sociâ vertigine cælos.
Tardior haud solito Saturnus, & acer ut olim
Fulmineùm rutilat cristatâ casside Mavors.   40
Floridus æternùm Phœbus juvenile coruscat,
Nec fovet effœtas loca per declivia terras
Devexo temone Deus; sed semper amicâ
Luce potens eadem currit per signa rotarum,
Surgit odoratis pariter formosus ab Indis
Æthereum pecus albenti qui cogit Olympo

Mane vocans, & serus agens in pascua cæli,
Temporis & gemino dispertit regna colore.
Fulget, obitque vices alterno Delia cornu,
Cæruleumque ignem paribus complectitur ulnis.   50
Nec variant elementa fidem, solitóque fragore
Lurida perculsas jaculantur fulmina rupes.
Nec per inane furit leviori murmure Corus,
Stringit & armiferos æquali horrore Gelonos
Trux Aquilo, spiratque hyemem, nimbosque volutat.
Utque solet, Siculi diverberat ima Pelori
Rex maris, & raucâ circumstrepit æquora conchâ
Oceani Tubicen, nec vastâ mole minorem
Ægæona ferunt dorso Balearica cete.
Sed neque Terra tibi sæcli vigor ille vetusti   60
Priscus abest, servatque suúm Narcissus odorem,
Et puer ille suum tenet & puer ille decorem
Phœbe tuusque & Cypri tuus, nec ditior olim
Terra datum sceleri celavit montibus aurum
Conscia, vel sub aquis gemmas. Sic denique in ævum
Ibit cunctarum series justissima rerum,
Donec flamma orbem populabitur ultima, latè
Circumplexa polos, & vasti culmina cæli;
Ingentique rogo flagrabit machina mundi.

De Idea Platonica quemadmodum Aristoteles intellexit.

DICITE sacrorum præsides nemorum deæ,
Tuque O noveni perbeata numinis
Memoria mater, quæque in immenso procul
Antro recumbis otiosa Æternitas,
Monumenta servans, & ratas leges Jovis,
Cælique fastos atque ephemeridas Deûm,
Quis ille primus cujus ex imagine
Natura sollers finxit humanum genus,
Æternus, incorruptus, æquævus polo,
Unusque & universus, exemplar Dei?   10
Haud ille Palladis gemellus innubæ
Interna proles insidet menti Jovis;
Sed quamlibet natura sit communior,
Tamen seorsùs extat ad morem unius,
Et, mira, certo stringitur spatio loci;
Seu sempiternus ille syderum comes
Cæli pererrat ordines decemplicis,
Citimúmve terris incolit Lunæ globum:
Sive inter animas corpus adituras sedens
Obliviosas torpet ad Lethes aquas: 20
Sive in remotâ forte terrarum plagâ
Incedit ingens hominis archetypus gigas,
Et diis tremendus erigit celsum caput
Atlante major portitore syderum.
Non cui profundum cæcitas lumen dedit
Dircæus augur vidit hunc alto sinu;
Non hunc silenti nocte Plëiones nepos

Vatum sagaci præpes ostendit choro;
Non hunc sacerdos novit Assyrius, licet
Longos vetusti commemoret atavos Nini,
Priscumque Belon, inclytumque Osiridem.
Non ille trino gloriosus nomine
Ter magnus Hermes (ut sit arcani sciens)
Talem reliquit Isidis cultoribus.
At tu perenne ruris Academi decus
(Hæc monstra si tu primus induxti scholis)
Jam jam pöetas urbis exules tuæ
Revocabis, ipse fabulator maximus,
Aut institutor ipse migrabis foras.

Ad Patrem.

Nunc mea Pierios cupiam per pectora fontes
Irriguas torquere vias, totumque per ora
Volvere laxatum gemino de vertice rivum;
Ut tenues oblita sonos audacibus alis
Surgat in officium venerandi Musa parentis.
Hoc utcunque tibi gratum pater optime carmen
Exiguum meditatur opus, nec novimus ipsi
Aptiùs à nobis quæ possint munera donis
Respondere tuis, quamvis nec maxima possint
Respondere tuis, nedum ut par gratia donis
Esse queat, vacuis quæ redditur arida verbis.
Sed tamen hæc nostros ostendit pagina census,
Et quod habemus opum chartâ numeravimus istâ,
Quæ mihi sunt nullæ, nisi quas dedit aurea Clio
Quas mihi semoto somni peperere sub antro,
Et nemoris laureta sacri Parnassides umbræ.
  Nec tu vatis opus divinum despice carmen,
Quo nihil æthereos ortus, & semina cæli,
Nil magis humanam commendat origine mentem,
Sancta Prometheæ retinens vestigia flammæ.
Carmen amant superi, tremebundaque Tartara carmen
Ima ciere valet, divosque ligare profundos,
Et triplici duros Manes adamante coercet.
Carmine sepositi retegunt arcana futuri
Phœbades, & tremulæ pallentes ora Sibyllæ;
Carmina sacrificus solennes pangit ad aras
Aurea seu sternit motantem cornua taurum;
Seu cùm fata sagax fumantibus abdita fibris
Consulit, & tepidis Parcam scrutatur in extis.
Nos etiam patrium tunc cum repetemus Olympum,
Æternæque moræ stabunt immobilis ævi,
Ibimus auratis per cæli templa coronis,
Dulcia suaviloquo sociantes carmina plectro,
Astra quibus, geminique poli convexa sonabunt.
Spiritus & rapidos qui circinat igneus orbes.
Nunc quoque sydereis intercinit ipse choreis
Immortale melos, & inenarrabile carmen;
Torrida dum rutilus compescit sibila serpens,
Demissoque ferox gladio mansuescit Orion;

Stellarum nec sentit onus Maurusius Atlas.
Carmina regales epulas ornare solebant,
Cum nondum luxus, vastæque immensa vorago
Nota gulæ, & modico spumabat cœna Lyæo.
Tum de more sedens festa ad convivia vates
Æsculeâ intonsos redimitus ab arbore crines,
Heroumque actus, imitandaque gesta canebat,
Et chaos, & positi latè fundamina mundi,
Reptantesque Deos, & alentes numina glandes,
Et nondum Ætneo quæsitum fulmen ab antro.
Denique quid vocis modulamen inane juvabit,
Verborum sensusque vacans, numerique loquacis?
Silvestres decet iste choros, non Orphea cantus,
Qui tenuit fluvios & quercubus addidit aures
Carmine, non cithará, simulachraque functa canendo
Compulit in lacrymas; habet has à carmine laudes.
  Nec tu perge precor sacras contemnere Musas,
Nec vanas inopesque puta, quarum ipse peritus
Munere, mille sonos numeros componis ad aptos,
Millibus & vocem modulis variare canoram
Doctus, Arionii meritò sis nominis hæres.
Nunc tibi quid mirum, si me genuisse poëtam
Contigerit, charo si tam propè sanguine juncti
Cognatas artes, studiumque affine sequamur:
Ipse volens Phœbus se dispertire duobus,
Altera dona mihi, dedit altera dona parenti,
Dividuumque Deum genitorque puerque tenemus.
  Tu tamen ut simules teneras odisse camœnas,
Non odisse reor, neque enim, pater, ire jubebas
Quà via lata patet, quà pronior area lucri,
Certaque condendi fulget spes aurea nummi:
Nec rapis ad leges, malè custoditaque gentis
Jura, nec insulsis damnas clamoribus aures.
Sed magis excultam cupiens ditescere mentem,
Me procul urbano strepitu, secessibus altis
Abductum Aoniæ jucunda per otia ripæ
Phœbæo lateri comitem sinis ire beatum.
Officium chari taceo commune parentis,
Me poscunt majora, tuo pater optime sumptu
Cùm mihi Romuleæ patuit facundia linguæ,
Et Latii veneres, & quæ Jovis ora decebant
Grandia magniloquis elata vocabula Graiis,
Addere suasisti quos jactat Gallia flores,
Et quam degeneri novus Italus ore loquelam
Fundit, Barbaricos testatus voce tumultus,
Quæque Palæstinus loquitur mysteria vates.
Denique quicquid habet cælum, subjectaque cœlo
Terra parens, terræque & cœlo interfluus aer,
Quicquid & unda tegit, pontique agitabile marmor,
Per te nosse licet, per te, si nosse libebit.
Dimotáque venit spectanda scientia nube,
Nudaque conspicuos inclinat ad oscula vultus,
Ni fugisse velim, ni sit libâsse molestum.

I nunc, confer opes quisquis malesanus avitas
Austriaci gazas, Perüanaque regna præoptas.
Quæ potuit majora pater tribuisse, vel ipse
Jupiter, excepto, donâsset ut omnia, cœlo?
Non potiora dedit, quamvis & tuta fuissent,
Publica qui juveni commisit lumina nato
Atque Hyperionios currus, & fræna diei,
Et circùm undantem radiatâ luce tiaram.　100
Ergo ego jam doctæ pars quamlibet ima catervæ
Victrices hederas inter, laurosque sedebo,
Jamque nec obscurus populo miscebor inerti,
Vitabuntque oculos vestigia nostra profanos.
Este procul vigiles curæ, procul este querelæ,
Invidiæque acies transverso tortilis hirquo,
Sæva nec anguiferos extende Calumnia rictus;
In me triste nihil fædissima turba potestis,
Nec vestri sum juris ego; securaque tutus
Pectora, vipereo gradiar sublimis ab ictu.　110

At tibi, chare pater, postquam non æqua merenti
Posse referre datur, nec dona rependere factis,
Sit memorâsse satis, repetitaque munera grato
Percensere animo, fidæque reponere menti.

Et vos, O nostri, juvenilia carmina, lusus,
Si modo perpetuos sperare audebitis annos,
Et domini superesse rogo, lucemque tueri,
Nec spisso rapient oblivia nigra sub Orco,
Forsitan has laudes, decantatumque parentis
Nomen, ad exemplum, sero servabitis ævo.　120

[The text of the Greek poems has been modernized.]

Psalm 114.

Ἰσραὴλ ὅτε παῖδες, ὅτ' ἀγλαὰ φῦλ' Ἰακώβου
Αἰγύπτιον λίπε δῆμον, ἀπεχθέα, βαρβαρόφωνον,
Δὴ τότε μοῦνον ἔην ὅσιον γένος υἷες Ἰούδα.
Ἐν δὲ θεὸς λαοῖσι μέγα κρείων βασίλευεν.
Εἶδε, καὶ ἐντροπάδην φυγάδ' ἐρρώησε θάλασσα
Κύματι εἰλυμένη ῥοθίῳ, ὁδ' ἄρ' ἐστυφελίχθη
Ἱρὸς Ἰορδάνης ποτὶ ἀργυροειδέα πηγήν.
Ἐκ δ' ὄρεα σκαρθμοῖσιν ἀπειρέσια κλονέοντο,
Ὡς κριοὶ σφριγόωντες ἐΰτραφερῷ ἐν ἀλωῇ.
Βαιότεραι δ' ἅμα πᾶσαι ἀνασκίρτησαν ἐρίπναι,　10
Οἷα παραὶ σύριγγι φίλῃ ὑπὸ μητέρι ἄρνες.
Τίπτε σύγ' αἰνὰ θάλασσα πέλωρ φυγάδ' ἐρρώησας;
Κύματι εἰλυμένη ῥοθίῳ; τί δ' ἄρ' ἐστυφελίχθης
Ἱρὸς Ἰορδάνη ποτὶ ἀργυροειδέα πηγήν;
Τίπτ' ὄρεα σκαρθμοῖσιν ἀπειρέσια κλονέεσθε
Ὡς κριοὶ σφριγόωντες ἐΰτραφερῷ ἐν ἀλωῇ;
Βαιότεραι τί δ' ἄρ' ὕμμες ἀνασκιρτησατ' ἐρίπναι,
Οἷα παραὶ σύριγγι φίλῃ ὑπὸ μητέρι ἄρνες,
Σείεο γαῖα τρέουσα θεὸν μεγάλ' ἐκτυπέοντα
Γαῖα, θεὸν τρείουσ' ὕπατον σέβας Ἰσσακίδαο
Ὅς τε καὶ ἐκ σπιλάδων ποταμοὺς χέε μορμύροντας
Κρήνην τ' ἀέναον πέτρης ἀπὸ δακρυοέσσης.

*Philosophus ad regem quendam qui eum ignotum & insontem inter reos forte
captum inscius damnaverat* τὴν ἐπὶ θανάτῳ πορευόμενος, *hæc subito misit.*

'Ω ἄνα εἰ ὀλέσῃς με τὸν ἔννομον, οὐδέ τιν' ἀνδρῶν
Δεινὸν ὅλως δράσαντα, σοφώτατον ἴσθι κάρηνον
Ῥηϊδίως ἀφέλοιο, τόδ' ὕστερον αὖθι νοήσεις,
Μαψ αὖτως δ' ἄρ' ἔπειτα χρόνῳ μάλα πολλὸν ὀδύρῃ,
Τοιόνδ' ἐκ πόλεως περιώνυμον ἄλκαρ ὀλέσσας.

In Effigiei ejus Sculptorem.

'Αμαθεῖ γεγράφθαι χειρὶ τήνδε μὲν εἰκόνα
Φαίης τάχ' ἄν, πρὸς εἶδος αὐτοφυὲς βλέπων·
Τὸν δ' ἐκτυπωτὸν οὐκ ἐπιγνόντες, φίλοι,
Γελᾶτε φαύλου δυσμίμημα ζωγράφου.

Ad Salsillum poetam Romanum ægrotantem.

SCAZONTES.

O MUSA gressum quæ volens trahis claudum,
Vulcanioque tarda gaudes incessu,
Nec sentis illud in loco minus gratum,
Quàm cùm decentes flava Dëiope suras
Alternat aureum ante Junonis lectum,
Adesdum & hæc s'is verba pauca Salsillo
Refer, camœna nostra cui tantum est cordi,
Quamque ille magnis prætulit immeritò divis.
Hæc ergo alumnus ille Londini Milto,
Diebus hisce qui suum linquens nidum   10
Polique tractum, (pessimus ubi ventorum,
Insanientis impotensque pulmonis
Pernix anhela sub Jove exercet flabra)
Venit feraces Itali soli ad glebas,
Visum superbâ cognitas urbes famâ
Virosque doctæque indolem juventutis,
Tibi optat idem hic fausta multa Salsille,
Habitumque fesso corpori penitùs sanum;
Cui nunc profunda bilis infestat renes,
Præcordiisque fixa damnosùm spirat.   20
Nec id pepercit impia quòd tu Romano
Tam cultus ore Lesbium condis melos.
O dulce divûm munus, O salus Hebes
Germana! Tuque Phœbe morborum terror
Pythone cæso, sive tu magis Pæan
Libenter audis, hic tuus sacerdos est.
Querceta Fauni, vosque rore vinoso
Colles benigni, mitis Euandri sedes,
Siquid salubre vallibus frondet vestris,
Levamen ægro ferte certatim vati.   30
Sic ille charis redditus rursùm Musis
Vicina dulci prata mulcebit cantu.

4 Μαψιδίως δ' ἄρ' ἔπειτα τεὸν πρὸς θυμὸν ὀδύρῃ *1673*

Ipse inter atros emirabitur lucos
Numa, ubi beatum degit otium æternum,
Suam reclivis semper Ægeriam spectans.
Tumidusque & ipse Tibris hinc delinitus
Spei favebit annuæ colonorum:
Nec in sepulchris ibit obsessum reges
Nimiùm sinistro laxus irruens loro:
Sed fræna melius temperabit undarum,   40
Adusque curvi salsa regna Portumni.

Mansus.

Joannes Baptista Mansus Marchio Villensis vir ingenii laude, tum literarum studio, nec non & bellicâ virtute apud Italos clarus in primis est. Ad quem Torquati Tassi dialogus extat de Amicitiâ scriptus; erat enim Tassi amicissimus; ab quo etiam inter Campaniæ principes celebratur, in illo poemate cui titulus Gerusalemme conquistata, *lib. 20.*

Fra cavalier magnanimi, è cortesi
Risplende il Manso———

Is authorem Neapoli commorantem summâ benevolentiâ prosecutus est, multaque ei detulit humanitatis officia. Ad hunc itaque hospes ille antequam ab eâ urbe discederet, ut ne ingratum se ostenderet, hoc carmen misit.

Hæc quoque Manse tuæ meditantur carmina laudi
Pierides, tibi Manse choro notissime Phœbi,
Quandoquidem ille alium haud æquo est dignatus honore,
Post Galli cineres, & Mecænatis Hetrusci.
Tu quoque si nostræ tantùm valet aura Camœnæ,
Victrices hederas inter, laurosque sedebis.
Te pridem magno felix concordia Tasso
Junxit, & æternis inscripsit nomina chartis.
Mox tibi dulciloquum non inscia Musa Marinum
Tradidit, ille tuum dici se gaudet alumnum,   10
Dum canit Assyrios divûm prolixus amores;
Mollis & Ausonias stupefecit carmine nymphas.
Ille itidem moriens tibi soli debita vates
Ossa tibi soli, supremaque vota reliquit.
Nec manes pietas tua chara fefellit amici,
Vidimus arridentem operoso ex ære poetam.
Nec satis hoc visum est in utrumque, & nec pia cessant
Officia in tumulo, cupis integros rapere Orco,
Quà potes, atque avidas Parcarum eludere leges:
Amborum genus, & variâ sub sorte peractam   20
Describis vitam, moresque, & dona Minervæ;
Æmulus illius Mycalen qui natus ad altam
Rettulit Æolii vitam facundus Homeri.
Ergo ego te Cliûs & magni nomine Phœbi
Manse pater, jubeo longum salvere per ævum
Missus Hyperboreo juvenis peregrinus ab axe.
Nec tu longinquam bonus aspernabere Musam,
Quæ nuper gelidâ vix enutrita sub Arcto
Imprudens Italas ausa est volitare per urbes.
Nos etiam in nostro modulantes flumine cygnos   30
Credimus obscuras noctis sensisse per umbras,
Quà Thamesis latè puris argenteus urnis
Oceani glaucos perfundit gurgite crines.

Quin & in has quondam pervenit Tityrus oras.
Sed neque nos genus incultum, nec inutile Phœbo,
Quà plaga septeno mundi sulcata Trione
Brumalem patitur longâ sub nocte Boöten.
Nos etiam colimus Phœbum, nos munera Phœbo
Flaventes spicas, & lutea mala canistris,
Halantemque crocum (perhibet nisi vana vetustas)   40
Misimus, & lectas Druidum de gente choreas.
(Gens Druides antiqua sacris operata deorum
Heroum laudes imitandaque gesta canebant)
Hinc quoties festo cingunt altaria cantu
Delo in herbosâ Graiæ de more puellæ
Carminibus lætis memorant Corineïda Loxo,
Fatidicamque Upin, cum flavicomâ Hecaërge
Nuda Caledonio variatas pectora fuco.
Fortunate senex, ergo quacunque per orbem
Torquati decus, & nomen celebrabitur ingens,   50
Claraque perpetui succrescet fama Marini,
Tu quoque in ora frequens venies plausumque virorum,
Et parili carpes iter immortale volatu.
Dicetur tum sponte tuos habitasse penates
Cynthius, & famulas venisse ad limina Musas:
At non sponte domum tamen idem, & regis adivit
Rura Pheretiadæ cælo fugitivus Apollo;
Ille licet magnum Alciden susceperat hospes;
Tantùm ubi clamosos placuit vitare bubulcos,
Nobile mansueti cessit Chironis in antrum,   60
Irriguos inter saltus frondosaque tecta
Peneium prope rivum: ibi sæpe sub ilice nigrâ
Ad citharæ strepitum blandâ prece victus amici
Exilii duros lenibat voce labores.
Tum neque ripa suo, barathro nec fixa sub imo,
Saxa stetere loco, nutat Trachinia rupes,
Nec sentit solitas, immania pondera, silvas,
Emotæque suis properant de collibus orni,
Mulcenturque novo maculosi carmine lynces.
Diis dilecte senex, te Jupiter æquus oportet   70
Nascentem, & miti lustrarit lumine Phœbus,
Atlantisque nepos; neque enim nisi charus ab ortu
Diis superis poterit magno favisse poetae.
Hinc longæva tibi lento sub flore senectus
Vernat, & Æsonios lucratur vivida fusos,
Nondum deciduos servans tibi frontis honores,
Ingeniumque vigens, & adultum mentis acumen.
O mihi si mea sors talem concedat amicum
Phœbæos decorâsse viros qui tam bene norit,
Si quando indigenas revocabo in carmina reges,   80
Arturumque etiam sub terris bella moventem;
Aut dicam invictæ sociali fœdere mensæ,
Magnanimos Heroas, & (O modo spiritus adsit)
Frangam Saxonicas Britonum sub Marte phalanges.
Tandem ubi non tacitæ permensus tempora vitæ,
Annorumque satur cineri sua jura relinquam,

Ille mihi lecto madidis astaret ocellis,
Astanti sat erit si dicam sim tibi curæ;
Ille meos artus liventi morte solutos
Curaret parvâ componi molliter urnâ.   90
Forsitan & nostros ducat de marmore vultus,
Nectens aut Paphiâ myrti aut Parnasside lauri
Fronde comas, at ego securâ pace quiescam.
Tum quoque, si qua fides, si præmia certa bonorum,
Ipse ego cælicolûm semotus in æthera divûm,
Quò labor & mens pura vehunt, atque ignea virtus
Secreti hæc aliquâ mundi de parte videbo
(Quantum fata sinunt) & totâ mente serenùm
Ridens purpureo suffundar lumine vultus
Et simul æthereo plaudam mihi lætus Olympo.   100

Epitaphium

DAMONIS.

Argumentum

Thyrsis & Damon ejusdem viciniæ Pastores, eadem studia sequuti a pueritiâ amici erant, ut qui pluri-
mùm. Thyrsis animi causâ profectus peregrè de obitu Damonis nuncium accepit. Domum postea reversus,
& rem ita esse comperto, se, suamque solitudinem hoc carmine deplorat. Damonis autem sub personâ
hìc intelligitur Carolus Deodatus ex urbe Hetruriæ Luca paterno genere oriundus, cætera Anglus; ingenio,
doctrina, clarissimisque cæteris virtutibus, dum viveret, juvenis egregius.

HIMERIDES nymphæ (nam vos & Daphnin & Hylan,
Et plorata diu meministis fata Bionis)
Dicite Sicelicum Thamesina per oppida carmen:
Quas miser effudit voces, quæ murmura Thyrsis,
Et quibus assiduis exercuit antra querelis,
Fluminaque, fontesque vagos, nemorumque recessus,
Dum sibi præreptum queritur Damona, neque altam
Luctibus exemit noctem loca sola pererrans.
Et jam bis viridi surgebat culmus arista,
Et totidem flavas numerabant horrea messes,   10
Ex quo summa dies tulerat Damona sub umbras,
Nec dum aderat Thyrsis; pastorem scilicet illum
Dulcis amor Musæ Thusca retinebat in urbe.
Ast ubi mens expleta domum, pecorisque relicti
Cura vocat, simul assuetâ sedítque sub ulmo,
Tum vero amissum tum denique sentit amicum,
Cœpit & immensum sic exonerare dolorem.
   Ite domum impasti, domino jam non vacat, agni.
Hei mihi! quæ terris, quæ dicam numina cœlo,
Postquam te immiti rapuerunt funere Damon;   20
Siccine nos linquis, tua sic sine nomine virtus
Ibit, & obscuris numero sociabitur umbris?
At non ille, animas virgâ qui dividit aureâ,
Ista velit, dignumque tui te ducat in agmen,
Ignavumque procul pecus arceat omne silentum.
   Ite domum impasti, domino jam non vacat, agni.
Quicquid erit, certè nisi me lupus antè videbit,
Indeplorato non comminuere sepulchro,

Constabitque tuus tibi honos, longúmque vigebit
Inter pastores: Illi tibi vota secundo   30
Solvere post Daphnin, post Daphnin dicere laudes
Gaudebunt, dum rura Pales, dum Faunus amabit:
Si quid id est, priscamque fidem coluisse, piúmque,
Palladiásque artes, sociúmque habuisse canorum.
　Ite domum impasti, domino jam non vacat, agni.
Hæc tibi certa manent, tibi erunt hæc præmia Damon,
At mihi quid tandem fiet modò? quis mihi fidus
Hærebit lateri comes, ut tu sæpe solebas
Frigoribus duris, & per loca fœta pruinis,
Aut rapido sub sole, siti morientibus herbis?   40
Sive opus in magnos fuit eminùs ire leones
Aut avidos terrere lupos præsepibus altis;
Quis fando sopire diem, cantuque solebit?
　Ite domum impasti, domino jam non vacat, agni.
Pectora cui credam? quis me lenire docebit
Mordaces curas, quis longam fallere noctem
Dulcibus alloquiis, grato cùm sibilat igni
Molle pyrum, & nucibus strepitat focus, at malus auster
Miscet cuncta foris, & desuper intonat ulmo.
　Ite domum impasti, domino jam non vacat, agni.   50
Aut æstate, dies medio dum vertitur axe,
Cum Pan æsculeâ somnum capit abditus umbrâ,
Et repetunt sub aquis sibi nota sedilia nymphæ.
Pastoresque latent, stertit sub sepe colonus,
Quis mihi blanditiásque tuas, quis tum mihi risus,
Cecropiosque sales referet, cultosque lepores?
　Ite domum impasti, domino jam non vacat, agni.
At jam solus agros, jam pascua solus oberro,
Sicubi ramosæ densantur vallibus umbræ,
Hic serum expecto, supra caput imber & Eurus   60
Triste sonant, fractæque agitata crepuscula silvæ.
　Ite domum impasti, domino jam non vacat, agni.
Heu quàm culta mihi priùs arva procacibus herbis
Involvuntur, & ipsa situ seges alta fatiscit!
Innuba neglecto marcescit & uva racemo,
Nec myrteta juvant; ovium quoque tædet, at illæ
Moerent, inque suum convertunt ora magistrum.
　Ite domum impasti, domino jam non vacat, agni.
Tityrus ad corylos vocat, Alphesibœus ad ornos,
Ad salices Ægon, ad flumina pulcher Amyntas,   70
Hîc gelidi fontes, hîc illita gramina musco,
Hîc Zephyri, hîc placidas interstrepit arbutus undas;
Ista canunt surdo, frutices ego nactus abibam.
　Ite domum impasti, domino jam non vacat, agni.
Mopsus ad hæc, nam me redeuntem forte notârat
(Et callebat avium linguas, & sydera Mopsus)
Thyrsi quid hoc? dixit, quæ te coquit improba bilis?
Aut te perdit amor, aut te malè fascinat astrum,
Saturni grave sæpe fuit pastoribus astrum,
Intimaque obliquo figit præcordia plumbo.   80
　Ite domum impasti, domino jam non vacat, agni.

Mirantur nymphæ, & quid te Thyrsi futurum est?
Quid tibi vis? ajunt, non hæc solet esse juventæ
Nubila frons, oculique truces, vultusque severi,
Illa choros, lususque leves, & semper amorem
Jure petit, bis ille miser qui serus amavit.
    Ite domum impasti, domino jam non vacat, agni.
Venit Hyas, Dryopéque, & filia Baucidis Ægle
Docta modos, citharæque sciens, sed perdita fastu,
Venit Idumanii Chloris vicina fluenti;   90
Nil me blanditiæ, nil me solantia verba,
Nil me, si quid adest, movet, aut spes ulla futuri.
    Ite domum impasti, domino jam non vacat, agni.
Hei mihi quam similes ludunt per prata juvenci,
Omnes unanimi secum sibi lege sodales,
Nec magis hunc alio quisquam secernit amicum
De grege, sic densi veniunt ad pabula thoes,
Inque vicem hirsuti paribus junguntur onagri;
Lex eadem pelagi, deserto in littore Proteus
Agmina Phocarum numerat, vilisque volucrum   100
Passer habet semper quicum sit, & omnia circum
Farra libens volitet, serò sua tecta revisens,
Quem si fors letho objecit, seu milvus adunco
Fata tulit rostro, seu stravit arundine fossor,
Protinus ille alium socio petit inde volatu.
Nos durum genus, & diris exercita fatis
Gens homines aliena animis, & pectore discors,
Vix sibi quisque parem de millibus invenit unum,
Aut si sors dederit tandem non aspera votis,
Illum inopina dies quâ non speraveris horâ   110
Surripit, æternum linquens in sæcula damnum.
    Ite domum impasti, domino jam non vacat, agni.
Heu quis me ignotas traxit vagus error in oras
Ite per aëreas rupes, Alpemque nivosam!
Ecquid erat tanti Romam vidisse sepultam?
Quamvis illa foret, qualem dum viseret olim,
Tityrus ipse suas & oves & rura reliquit;
Ut te tam dulci possem caruisse sodale,
Possem tot maria alta, tot interponere montes,
Tot sylvas, tot saxa tibi, fluviosque sonantes.   120
Ah certè extremùm licuisset tangere dextram,
Et bene compositos placidè morientis ocellos,
Et dixisse vale, nostri memor ibis ad astra.
    Ite domum impasti, domino jam non vacat, agni.
Quamquam etiam vestri nunquam meminisse pigebit
Pastores Thusci, Musis operata juventus,
Hic Charis, atque Lepos; & Thuscus tu quoque Damon,
Antiquâ genus unde petis Lucumonis ab urbe.
O ego quantus eram, gelidi cum stratus ad Arni
Murmura, populeumque nemus, quà mollior herba,   130
Carpere nunc violas, nunc summas carpere myrtos,
Et potui Lycidæ certantem audire Menalcam.
Ipse etiam tentare ausus sum, nec puto multùm
Displicui, nam sunt & apud me munera vestra

Fiscellæ, calathique & cerea vincla cicutæ,
Quin & nostra suas docuerunt nomina fagos
Et Datis, & Francinus, erant & vocibus ambo
Et studiis noti, Lydorum sanguinis ambo.
   Ite domum impasti, domino jam non vacat, agni.
Hæc mihi tum læto dictabat roscida luna,   140
Dum solus teneros claudebam cratibus hœdos.
Ah quoties dixi, cùm te cinis ater habebat,
Nunc canit, aut lepori nunc tendit retia Damon,
Vimina nunc texit, varios sibi quod sit in usus;
Et quæ tum facili sperabam mente futura
Arripui voto levis, & præsentia finxi,
Heus bone numquid agis? nisi te quid forte retardat,
Imus? & argutâ paulùm recubamus in umbra,
Aut ad aquas Colni, aut ubi jugera Cassibelauni?
Tu mihi percurres medicos, tua gramina, succos,   150
Helleborúmque, humilésque crocos, foliúmque hyacinthi,
Quasque habet ista palus herbas, artesque medentûm,
Ah pereant herbæ, pereant artesque medentûm
Gramina, postquam ipsi nil profecere magistro.
Ipse etiam, nam nescio quid mihi grande sonabat
Fistula, ab undecimâ jam lux est altera nocte,
Et tum forte novis admôram labra cicutis,
Dissiluere tamen rupta compage, nec ultra
Ferre graves potuere sonos, dubito quoque ne sim
Turgidulus, tamen & referam, vos cedite silvæ.   160
   Ite domum impasti, domino jam non vacat, agni.
Ipse ego Dardanias Rutupina per æquora puppes
Dicam, & Pandrasidos regnum vetus Inogeniæ,
Brennúmque Arviragúmque duces, priscúmque Belinum,
Et tandem Armoricos Britonum sub lege colonos;
Tum gravidam Arturo fatali fraude Jögernen
Mendaces vultus, assumptáque Gorlöis arma,
Merlini dolus. O mihi tum si vita supersit,
Tu procul annosa pendebis fistula pinu
Multùm oblita mihi, aut patriis mutata camœnis   170
Brittonicum strides, quid enim? omnia non licet uni
Non sperâsse uni licet omnia, mi satis ampla
Merces, & mihi grande decus (sim ignotus in ævum
Tum licet, externo penitúsque inglorius orbi)
Si me flava comas legat Usa, & potor Alauni,
Vorticibúsque frequens Abra, & nemus omne Treantæ,
Et Thamesis meus ante omnes, & fusca metallis
Tamara, & extremis me discant Orcades undis.
   Ite domum impasti, domino jam non vacat, agni.
Hæc tibi servabam lentâ sub cortice lauri,   180
Hæc, & plura simul, tum quæ mihi pocula Mansus,
Mansus Chalcidicæ non ultima gloria ripæ
Bina dedit, mirum artis opus, mirandus & ipse,
Et circùm gemino cælaverat argumento:
In medio rubri maris unda, & odoriferum ver
Littora longa Arabum, & sudantes balsama silvæ,
Has inter Phœnix divina avis, unica terris

Cæruleùm fulgens diversicoloribus alis
Auroram vitreis surgentem respicit undis.
Parte alia polus omnipatens, & magnus Olympus,   190
Quis putet? hic quoque Amor, pictæque in nube pharetræ,
Arma corusca faces, & spicula tincta pyropo;
Nec tenues animas, pectúsque ignobile vulgi
Hinc ferit, at circùm flammantia lumina torquens
Semper in erectum spargit sua tela per orbes
Impiger, & pronos nunquam collimat ad ictus,
Hinc mentes ardere sacræ, formæque deorum.
    Tu quoque in his, nec me fallit spes lubrica Damon,
Tu quoque in his certè es, nam quò tua dulcis abiret
Sanctáque simplicitas, nam quò tua candida virtus?   200
Nec te Lethæo fas quæsivisse sub orco,
Nec tibi conveniunt lacrymæ, nec flebimus ultrà,
Ite procul lacrymæ, purum colit æthera Damon,
Æthera purus habet, pluvium pede reppulit arcum;
Heroúmque animas inter, divósque perennes,
Æthereos haurit latices & gaudia potat
Ore Sacro. Quin tu cœli post jura recepta
Dexter ades, placidúsque fave quicúnque vocaris,
Seu tu noster eris Damon, sive æquior audis
Diodotus, quo te divino nomine cuncti   210
Cœlicolæ nôrint, sylvísque vocabere Damon.
Quòd tibi purpureus pudor, & sine labe juventus
Grata fuit, quòd nulla tori libata voluptas,
En etiam tibi virginei servantur honores;
Ipse caput nitidum cinctus rutilante corona,
Letáque frondentis gestans umbracula palmæ
Æternùm perages immortales hymenæos;
Cantus ubi, choreisque furit lyra mista beatis,
Festa Sionæo bacchantur & Orgia Thyrso.

Finis.

[Added in Second Edition, 1673.]

Jan. 23. 1646.

Ad *Joannem Rousium* Oxoniensis Academiæ Bibliothecarium.

De libro Poematum amisso, quem ille sibi denuo mitti postulabat, ut cum aliis nostris in Bibliothecâ
publica reponeret, Ode.

Strophe I.

GEMELLE cultu simplici gaudens liber,
  Fronde licet geminâ,
  Munditiéque nitens non operosâ,
    Quam manus attulit
    Juvenilis olim,
  Sedula tamen haud nimii Poetæ;
  Dum vagus Ausonias nunc per umbras,
  Nunc Britannica per vireta lusit

Insons populi, barbitóque devius
Indulsit patrio, mox itidem pectine Daunio 10
Longinquum intonuit melos
Vicinis, & humum vix tetigit pede;

Antistrophe.

Quis te, parve liber, quis te fratribus
Subduxit reliquis dolo?
Cum tu missus ab urbe,
Docto jugiter obsecrante amico,
Illustre tenebas iter
Thamesis ad incunabula
Cærulei patris,
Fontes ubi limpidi 20
Aonidum, thyasusque sacer
Orbi notus per immensos
Temporum lapsus redeunte cœlo,
Celeberque futurus in ævum;

Strophe 2.

Modò quis deus, aut editus deo
Pristinam gentis miseratus indolem
(Si satis noxas luimus priores
Mollique luxu degener otium)
Tollat nefandos civium tumultus,
Almaque revocet studia sanctus 30
Et relegatas sine sede Musas
Jam penè totis finibus Angligenûm;
Immundasque volucres
Unguibus imminentes
Figat Apollineâ pharetrâ,
Phinéamque abigat pestem procul amne Pegaséo.

Antistrophe.

Quin tu, libelle, nuntii licet malâ
Fide, vel oscitantiâ
Semel erraveris agmine fratrum,
Seu quis te teneat specus,
Seu qua te latebra, forsan unde vili 40
Callo teréris institoris insulsi,
Lætare felix, en iterum tibi
Spes nova fulget posse profundam
Fugere Lethen, vehique Superam
In Jovis aulam remige pennâ;

Strophe 3.

Nam te Roüsius sui
Optat peculî, numeróque justo
Sibi pollicitum queritur abesse,
Rogatque venias ille cujus inclyta 50
Sunt data virûm monumenta curæ:

Téque adytis etiam sacris
Voluit reponi quibus & ipse præsidet
Æternorum operum custos fidelis,
Quæstorque gazæ nobilioris,
Quàm cui præfuit Iön
Clarus Erechtheides
Opulenta dei per templa parentis
Fulvosque tripodas, donaque Delphica
Iön Actæâ genitus Creusâ.   60

Antistrophe.

Ergo tu visere lucos
Musarum ibis amœnos,
Diamque Phœbi rursus ibis in domum
Oxoniâ quam valle colit
Delo posthabitâ,
Bifidóque Parnassi jugo:
Ibis honestus,
Postquam egregiam tu quoque sortem
Nactus abis, dextri prece sollicitatus amici.
Illic legéris inter alta nomina   7c
Authorum, Graiæ simul & Latinæ
Antiqua gentis lumina, & verum decus.

Epoaos.

Vos tandem haud vacui mei labores,
Quicquid hoc sterile fudit ingenium,
Jam serò placidam sperare jubeo
Perfunctam invidiâ requiem, sedesque beatas
Quas bonus Hermes
Et tutela dabit solers Roüsi,
Quò neque lingua procax vulgi penetrabit, atque longè
Turba legentum prava facesset;   80
At ultimi nepotes,
Et cordatior ætas
Judicia rebus æquiora forsitan
Adhibebit integro sinu.
Tum livore sepulto,
Si quid meremur sana posteritas sciet
Roüsio favente.

Ode tribus constat Strophis, totidémque Antistrophis unâ demum epodo clausis, quas, tametsi omnes nec versuum numero, nec certis ubique colis exactè respondeant, ita tamen secuimus, commodè legendi potius, quam ad antiquos concinendi modos rationem spectantes. Alioquin hoc genus rectiùs fortasse dici monostrophicum debuerat. Metra partim sunt κατὰ σχέσιν, partim ἀπολελυμένα. Phaleucia quæ sunt, spondæum tertio loco bis admittunt, quod idem in secundo loco Catullus ad libitum fecit.

[The text is that of the first edition, 1645, unless otherwise stated.]

PARADISE LOST.

Paradise Lost

A

POEM

IN

TWELVE BOOKS

The Author
JOHN MILTON

IN

Paradisum Amissam

Summi Poetæ

JOHANNIS MILTONI.

Qui legis Amissam Paradisum, grandia magni
  Carmina Miltoni, *quid nisi cuncta legis?*
Res cunctas, & cunctarum primordia rerum,
  Et fata, & fines continet iste liber.
Intima panduntur magni penetralia mundi,
  Scribitur & toto quicquid in Orbe latet.
Terræque, tractusque maris, cœlumque profundum
  Sulphureumque Erebi flammivomumque specus.
Quæque colunt terras, Portumque & Tartara cæca,
  Quæque colunt summi lucida regna Poli.
Et quodcunque ullis conclusum est finibus usquam.
  Et sine fine Chaos, & sine fine Deus;
Et sine fine magis, si quid magis est sine fine,
  In Christo erga homines conciliatus amor.
Hæc qui speraret quis crederet esse futurum?
  Et tamen hæc hodie terra Britanna *legit.*
O quantos in bella Duces! quæ protulit arma!
  Quæ canit, et quanta prælia dira tuba.
Cœlestes acies! atque in certamine Cœlum!
  Et quæ Cœlestes pugna deceret agros!
Quantus in ætheriis tollit se Lucifer *armis!*
  Atque ipso graditur vix Michaele *minor!*
Quantis, & quam funestis concurritur iris
  Dum ferus hic stellas protegit, ille rapit!
Dum vulsos Montes ceu Tela reciproca torquent,
  Et non mortali desuper igne pluunt:
Stat dubius cui se parti concedat Olympus,
  Et metuit pugnæ non superesse suæ.
At simul in cœlis Messiæ insignia fulgent,
  Et currus animes, armaque digna Deo,
Horrendumque rotæ strident, & sæva rotarum
  Erumpunt torvis fulgura luminibus,
Et flammæ vibrant, & vera tonitrua rauco
Admistis flammis insonuere Polo:
Excidit attonitis mens omnis, & impetus omnis
  Et cassis dextris irrita Tela cadunt.
Ad pœnas fugiunt, & ceu foret Orcus asylum
  Infernis certant condere se tenebris.
Cedite Romani *scriptores, cedite* Graii
  Et quos fama recens vel celebravit anus.
Hæc quicunque leget tantum cecinisse putabit
  Mæonidem ranas, Virgilium *culices.*

S. B., M. D.

ON

Paradise Lost.

WHEN I beheld the Poet blind, yet bold,
In slender Book his vast Design unfold,
Messiah Crown'd, Gods Reconcil'd Decree,
Rebelling Angels, the Forbidden Tree,
Heav'n, Hell, Earth, Chaos, All; the Argument
Held me a while misdoubting his Intent,
That he would ruine (for I saw him strong)
The sacred Truths to Fable and old Song
(So *Sampson* groap'd the Temples Posts in spight)
The World o'rewhelming to revenge his sight.
  Yet as I read, soon growing less severe,
I lik'd his Project, the success did fear;
Through that wide Field how he his way should find
O're which lame Faith leads Understanding blind;
Lest he perplex'd the things he would explain,
And what was easie he should render vain.
  Or if a Work so infinite he spann'd,
Jealous I was that some less skilful hand
(Such as disquiet always what is well,
And by ill imitating would excell)
Might hence presume the whole Creations day
To change in Scenes, and show it in a Play.
  Pardon me, Mighty Poet, nor despise
My causeless, yet not impious, surmise.
But I am now convinc'd, and none will dare
Within thy Labours, to pretend a share.
Thou hast not miss'd one thought that could be fit,
And all that was improper dost omit:
So that no room is here for Writers left,
But to detect their Ignorance or Theft.
  That Majesty which through thy Work doth Reign
Draws the Devout, deterring the Profane.
And things divine thou treatst of in such state
As them preserves, and thee, inviolate.
At once delight and horrour on us seise,
Thou singst with so much gravity and ease;
And above humane flight dost soar aloft
With Plume so strong, so equal, and so soft,
The Bird nam'd from that Paradise you sing
So never flaggs, but always keeps on Wing.
  Where couldst thou words of such a compass find?
Whence furnish such a vast expence of mind?
Just Heav'n thee like *Tiresias* to requite
Rewards with Prophesie thy loss of sight.
  Well mightst thou scorn thy Readers to allure
With tinkling Rhime, of thy own sense secure;
While the *Town-Bayes* writes all the while and spells,
And like a Pack-horse tires without his Bells:
Their Fancies like our Bushy-points appear,

The Poets tag them, we for fashion wear.
I too transported by the Mode offend,
And while I meant to Praise thee must Commend.
Thy Verse created like thy Theme sublime,
In Number, Weight, and Measure, needs not Rhime.

                                        A. M.

The Printer to the Reader

Courteous Reader, there was no Argument at first intended to the Book, but for the satisfaction of many that have desired it, I have procur'd it, and withall a reason of that which stumbled many others, why the Poem Rimes not.

                                        S. Simmons.

THE VERSE.

THE Measure is *English* Heroic Verse without Rime, as that of *Homer* in *Greek,* and of *Virgil* in *Latin;* Rime being no necessary Adjunct or true Ornament of Poem or good Verse, in longer Works especially, but the Invention of a barbarous Age, to set off wretched matter and lame Meeter; grac't indeed since by the use of some famous modern Poets, carried away by Custom, but much to their own vexation, hindrance, and constraint to express many things otherwise, and for the most part worse than else they would have exprest them. Not without cause therefore some both *Italian* and *Spanish* Poets of prime note have rejected Rime both in longer and shorter Works, as have also long since our best *English* Tragedies, as a thing of it self, to all judicious eares, triveal and of no true musical delight; which consists only in apt Numbers, fit quantity of Syllables, and the sense variously drawn out from one Verse into another, not in the jingling sound of like endings, a fault avoyded by the learned Ancients both in Poetry and all good Oratory. This neglect then of Rime so little is to be taken for a defect, though it may seem so perhaps to vulgar Readers, that it rather is to be esteem'd an example set, the first in *English,* of ancient liberty recover'd to Heroic Poem from the troublesom and modern bondage of Rimeing.

PARADISE LOST

BOOK I.

The Argument

THE first Book proposes first in brief the whole Subject, *Mans disobedience, and the loss thereupon of Paradise wherein he was plac't:* Then touches *the prime cause of his fall, the Serpent, or rather* Satan *in the Serpent; who revolting from God, and drawing to his side many Legions of Angels, was by the command of God driven out of Heaven with all his Crew into the great Deep.* Which action past over, the Poem hasts into the midst of things, presenting *Satan with his Angels now fallen into Hell,* describ'd here, *not in the Center* (for Heaven and Earth may be suppos'd as yet not made, certainly not yet accurst) *but in a place of utter darknesse, fitliest call'd* Chaos: *Here* Satan *with his Angels lying on the burning Lake, thunder struck and astonisht, after a certain space recovers, as from confusion, calls up him who next in Order and Dignity lay by him; they confer of thir miserable fall.* Satan *awakens all his Legions, who lay till then in the same manner confounded; They rise, thir Numbers, array of Battel, thir chief Leaders nam'd, according to the Idols known afterwards in* Canaan *and the Countries adjoyning. To these* Satan *directs his Speech, comforts them with hope yet of regaining Heaven, but tells them lastly of a new World and new kind of Creature to be created, according to an ancient Prophesie or report in Heaven; for that Angels were long before this visible Creation, was the opinion of many ancient Fathers. To find out the truth of this Prophesie, and what to determin thereon he refers to a full Councell. What his Associates thence attempt.* Pandemonium *the Palace of* Satan *rises, suddenly built out of the Deep: The infernal Peers there sit in Counsel.*

OF Mans First Disobedience, and the Fruit
Of that Forbidden Tree, whose mortal tast
Brought Death into the World, and all our woe,
With loss of *Eden,* till one greater Man
Restore us, and regain the blissful Seat,
Sing Heav'nly Muse, that on the secret top
Of *Oreb,* or of *Sinai,* didst inspire
That Shepherd, who first taught the chosen Seed,
In the Beginning how the Heav'ns and Earth
Rose out of *Chaos:* or if *Sion* Hill   10
Delight thee more, and *Siloa's* Brook that flow'd
Fast by the Oracle of God; I thence
Invoke thy aid to my adventrous Song,
That with no middle flight intends to soar
Above th' *Aonian* Mount, while it pursues
Things unattempted yet in Prose or Rhime.
And chiefly Thou O Spirit, that dost prefer
Before all Temples th' upright heart and pure,
Instruct me, for Thou know'st; Thou from the first
Wast present, and with mighty wings outspread   20
Dove-like satst brooding on the vast Abyss
And mad'st it pregnant: What in me is dark
Illumine, what is low raise and support;
That to the highth of this great Argument
I may assert Eternal Providence,
And justifie the wayes of God to men.
   Say first, for Heav'n hides nothing from thy view
Nor the deep Tract of Hell, say first what cause
Mov'd our Grand Parents in that happy State,
Favour'd of Heav'n so highly, to fall off   30
From their Creator, and transgress his Will
For one restraint, Lords of the World besides?
Who first seduc'd them to that fowl revolt?
Th' infernal Serpent; he it was, whose guile
Stird up with Envy and Revenge, deceiv'd
The Mother of Mankinde, what time his Pride
Had cast him out from Heav'n, with all his Host
Of Rebel Angels, by whose aid aspiring
To set himself in Glory above his Peers,
He trusted to have equal'd the most High,   40
If he oppos'd; and with ambitious aim
Against the Throne and Monarchy of God
Rais'd impious War in Heav'n and Battel proud
With vain attempt. Him the Almighty Power
Hurld headlong flaming from th' Ethereal Skie
With hideous ruine and combustion down
To bottomless perdition, there to dwell
In Adamantine Chains and penal Fire,
Who durst defie th' Omnipotent to Arms.
Nine times the Space that measures Day and Night   50
To mortal men, he with his horrid crew
Lay vanquisht, rowling in the fiery Gulfe
Confounded though immortal: But his doom

Reserv'd him to more wrath; for now the thought
Both of lost happiness and lasting pain
Torments him; round he throws his baleful eyes
That witness'd huge affliction and dismay
Mixt with obdurate pride and stedfast hate:
At once as far as Angels kenn he views
The dismal Situation waste and wilde,   60
A Dungeon horrible, on all sides round
As one great Furnace flam'd, yet from those flames
No light, but rather darkness visible
Serv'd only to discover sights of woe,
Regions of sorrow, doleful shades, where peace
And rest can never dwell, hope never comes
That comes to all; but torture without end
Still urges, and a fiery Deluge, fed
With ever-burning Sulphur unconsum'd:
Such place Eternal Justice had prepar'd   70
For those rebellious, here their Prison ordain'd
In utter darkness, and their portion set
As far remov'd from God and light of Heav'n
As from the Center thrice to th' utmost Pole.
O how unlike the place from whence they fell!
There the companions of his fall, o'rewhelm'd
With Floods and Whirlwinds of tempestuous fire,
He soon discerns, and weltring by his side
One next himself in power, and next in crime,
Long after known in *Palestine,* and nam'd   80
Bëelzebub. To whom th' Arch-Enemy,
And thence in Heav'n call'd Satan, with bold words
Breaking the horrid silence thus began.
   If thou beest he; But O how fall'n! how chang'd
From him, who in the happy Realms of Light
Cloth'd with transcendent brightnes didst outshine
Myriads though bright: If he whom mutual league,
United thoughts and counsels, equal hope,
And hazard in the Glorious Enterprize,
Joynd with me once, now misery hath joynd   90
In equal ruin: into what Pit thou seest
From what highth fal'n, so much the stronger provd
He with his Thunder: and till then who knew
The force of those dire Arms? yet not for those
Nor what the Potent Victor in his rage
Can else inflict do I repent or change,
Though chang'd in outward lustre; that fixt mind
And high disdain, from sence of injur'd merit,
That with the mightiest rais'd me to contend,
And to the fierce contention brought along   100
Innumerable force of Spirits arm'd
That durst dislike his reign, and me preferring,
His utmost power with adverse power oppos'd
In dubious Battel on the Plains of Heav'n,
And shook his throne. What though the field be lost?
All is not lost; the unconquerable Will,

And study of revenge, immortal hate,
And courage never to submit or yield:
And what is else not to be overcome?
That Glory never shall his wrath or might   110
Extort from me. To bow and sue for grace
With suppliant knee, and deifie his power
Who from the terrour of this Arm so late
Doubted his Empire, that were low indeed,
That were an ignominy and shame beneath
This downfall; since by Fate the strength of Gods
And this Empyreal substance cannot fail,
Since through experience of this great event
In Arms not worse, in foresight much advanc't,
We may with more successful hope resolve   120
To wage by force or guile eternal Warr
Irreconcileable, to our grand Foe,
Who now triumphs, and in th' excess of joy
Sole reigning holds the Tyranny of Heav'n.
   So spake th' Apostate Angel, though in pain,
Vaunting aloud, but rackt with deep despare:
And him thus answer'd soon his bold Compeer.
   O Prince, O Chief of many Throned Powers,
That led th' imbattelld Seraphim to Warr
Under thy conduct, and in dreadful deeds   130
Fearless, endanger'd Heav'ns perpetual King;
And put to proof his high Supremacy,
Whether upheld by strength, or Chance, or Fate,
Too well I see and rue the dire event,
That with sad overthrow and foul defeat
Hath lost us Heav'n, and all this mighty Host
In horrible destruction laid thus low,
As far as Gods and Heav'nly Essences
Can Perish: for the mind and spirit remains
Invincible, and vigour soon returns,   140
Though all our Glory extinct, and happy state
Here swallow'd up in endless misery.
But what if he our Conquerour, (whom I now
Of force believe Almighty, since no less
Then such could hav orepow'rd such force as ours)
Have left us this our spirit and strength intire
Strongly to suffer and support our pains,
That we may so suffice his vengeful ire,
Or do him mightier service as his thralls
By right of Warr, what e're his business be   150
Here in the heart of Hell to work in Fire,
Or do his Errands in the gloomy Deep;
What can it then avail though yet we feel
Strength undiminisht, or eternal being
To undergo eternal punishment?
Whereto with speedy words th' Arch-fiend reply'd.
   Fall'n Cherube, to be weak is miserable
Doing or Suffering: but of this be sure,
To do ought good never will be our task,

But ever to do ill our sole delight,   160
As being the contrary to his high will
Whom we resist. If then his Providence
Out of our evil seek to bring forth good,
Our labour must be to pervert that end,
And out of good still to find means of evil;
Which oft times may succeed, so as perhaps
Shall grieve him, if I fail not, and disturb
His inmost counsels from their destind aim.
But see the angry Victor hath recall'd
His Ministers of vengeance and pursuit   170
Back to the Gates of Heav'n: The Sulphurous Hail
Shot after us in storm, oreblown hath laid
The fiery Surge, that from the Precipice
Of Heav'n receiv'd us falling, and the Thunder,
Wing'd with red Lightning and impetuous rage,
Perhaps hath spent his shafts, and ceases now
To bellow through the vast and boundless Deep.
Let us not slip th' occasion, whether scorn,
Or satiate fury yield it from our Foe.
Seest thou yon dreary Plain, forlorn and wilde,   180
The seat of desolation, voyd of light,
Save what the glimmering of these livid flames
Casts pale and dreadful? Thither let us tend
From off the tossing of these fiery waves,
There rest, if any rest can harbour there,
And reassembling our afflicted Powers,
Consult how we may henceforth most offend
Our Enemy, our own loss how repair,
How overcome this dire Calamity,
What reinforcement we may gain from Hope,   190
If not what resolution from despare.
    Thus Satan talking to his neerest Mate
With Head up-lift above the wave, and Eyes
That sparkling blaz'd, his other Parts besides
Prone on the Flood, extended long and large
Lay floating many a rood, in bulk as huge
As whom the Fables name of monstrous size,
Titanian, or Earth-born, that warr'd on Jove,
Briarios or Typhon, whom the Den
By ancient Tarsus held, or that Sea-beast   200
Leviathan, which God of all his works
Created hugest that swim th' Ocean stream:
Him haply slumbring on the Norway foam
The Pilot of some small night-founder'd Skiff,
Deeming some Island, oft, as Sea-men tell,
With fixed Anchor in his skaly rind
Moors by his side under the Lee, while Night
Invests the Sea, and wished Morn delayes:
So stretcht out huge in length the Arch-fiend lay
Chain'd on the burning Lake, nor ever thence   210
Had ris'n or heav'd his head, but that the will
And high permission of all-ruling Heaven

Left him at large to his own dark designs,
That with reiterated crimes he might
Heap on himself damnation, while he sought
Evil to others, and enrag'd might see
How all his malice serv'd but to bring forth
Infinite goodness, grace and mercy shewn
On Man by him seduc't, but on himself
Treble confusion, wrath and vengeance pour'd.   220
Forthwith upright he rears from off the Pool
His mighty Stature; on each hand the flames
Drivn backward slope their pointing spires, & rowld
In billows, leave i' th' midst a horrid Vale.
Then with expanded wings he stears his flight
Aloft, incumbent on the dusky Air
That felt unusual weight, till on dry Land
He lights, if it were Land that ever burn'd
With solid, as the Lake with liquid fire;
And such appear'd in hue, as when the force   230
Of subterranean wind transports a Hill
Torn from *Pelorus,* or the shatter'd side
Of thundring *Ætna,* whose combustible
And fewel'd entrals thence conceiving Fire,
Sublim'd with Mineral fury, aid the Winds,
And leave a singed bottom all involv'd
With stench and smoak: Such resting found the sole
Of unblest feet. Him followed his next Mate,
Both glorying to have scap't the *Stygian* flood
As Gods, and by their own recover'd strength,   240
Not by the sufferance of supernal Power.
   Is this the Region, this the Soil, the Clime,
Said then the lost Arch Angel, this the seat
That we must change for Heav'n, this mournful gloom
For that celestial light? Be it so, since hee
Who now is Sovran can dispose and bid
What shall be right: fardest from him is best
Whom reason hath equald, force hath made supream
Above his equals. Farewel happy Fields
Where Joy for ever dwells: Hail horrours, hail   250
Infernal world, and thou profoundest Hell
Receive thy new Possessor: One who brings
A mind not to be chang'd by Place or Time.
The mind is its own place, and in it self
Can make a Heav'n of Hell, a Hell of Heav'n.
What matter where, if I be still the same,
And what I should be, all but less then hee
Whom Thunder hath made greater? Here at least
We shall be free; th' Almighty hath not built
Here for his envy, will not drive us hence: 260
Here we may reign secure, and in my choyce
To reign is worth ambition though in Hell:
Better to reign in Hell, then serve in Heav'n.
But wherefore let we then our faithful friends,
Th' associates and copartners of our loss

Lye thus astonisht on th' oblivious Pool,
And call them not to share with us their part
In this unhappy Mansion, or once more
With rallied Arms to try what may be yet
Regaind in Heav'n, or what more lost in Hell?　　　　　270
　　So *Satan* spake, and him *Bëëlzebub*
Thus answer'd. Leader of those Armies bright,
Which but th' Omnipotent none could have foyld,
If once they hear that voyce, their liveliest pledge
Of hope in fears and dangers, heard so oft
In worst extreams, and on the perilous edge
Of battel when it rag'd, in all assaults
Their surest signal, they will soon resume
New courage and revive, though now they lye
Groveling and prostrate on yon Lake of Fire,　　　　　280
As we erewhile, astounded and amaz'd,
No wonder, fall'n such a pernicious highth.
　　He scarce had ceas't when the superiour Fiend
Was moving toward the shore; his ponderous shield
Ethereal temper, massy, large and round,
Behind him cast; the broad circumference
Hung on his shoulders like the Moon, whose Orb
Through Optic Glass the *Tuscan* Artist views
At Ev'ning from the top of *Fesole,*
Or in *Valdarno,* to descry new Lands,　　　　　290
Rivers or Mountains in her spotty Globe.
His Spear, to equal which the tallest Pine
Hewn on *Norwegian* hills, to be the Mast
Of some great Ammiral, were but a wand,
He walkt with to support uneasie steps
Over the burning Marle, not like those steps
On Heavens Azure, and the torrid Clime
Smote on him sore besides, vaulted with Fire;
Nathless he so endur'd, till on the Beach
Of that inflamed Sea, he stood and call'd　　　　　300
His Legions, Angel Forms, who lay intrans't
Thick as Autumnal Leaves that strow the Brooks
In *Vallombrosa,* where th' *Etrurian* shades
High overarch't imbowr; or scatterd sedge
Afloat, when with fierce Winds *Orion* arm'd
Hath vext the Red-Sea Coast, whose waves orethrew
Busiris and his *Memphian* Chivalrie,
While with perfidious hatred they pursu'd
The Sojourners of *Goshen,* who beheld
From the safe shore their floating Carkases　　　　　310
And broken Chariot Wheels, so thick bestrown
Abject and lost lay these, covering the Flood,
Under amazement of their hideous change.
He call'd so loud, that all the hollow Deep
Of Hell resounded. Princes, Potentates,
Warriers, the Flowr of Heav'n, once yours, now lost,
If such astonishment as this can sieze
Eternal spirits; or have ye chos'n this place

After the toyl of Battel to repose
Your wearied vertue, for the ease you find   320
To slumber here, as in the Vales of Heav'n?
Or in this abject posture have ye sworn
To adore the Conquerour? who now beholds
Cherube and Seraph rowling in the Flood
With scatter'd Arms and Ensigns, till anon
His swift pursuers from Heav'n Gates discern
Th' advantage, and descending tread us down
Thus drooping, or with linked Thunderbolts
Transfix us to the bottom of this Gulfe.
Awake, arise, or be for ever fall'n.   330
    They heard, and were abasht, and up they sprung
Upon the wing, as when men wont to watch
On duty, sleeping found by whom they dread,
Rouse and bestir themselves ere well awake.
Nor did they not perceave the evil plight
In which they were, or the fierce pains not feel;
Yet to their Generals Voyce they soon obeyd
Innumerable. As when the potent Rod
Of *Amrams* Son in *Egypts* evill day
Wav'd round the Coast, up call'd a pitchy cloud   340
Of *Locusts,* warping on the Eastern Wind,
That ore the Realm of impious *Pharaoh* hung
Like Night, and darken'd all the Land of *Nile*:
So numberless were those bad Angels seen
Hovering on wing under the Cope of Hell
'Twixt upper, nether, and surrounding Fires;
Till, as a signal giv'n, th' uplifted Spear
Of their great Sultan waving to direct
Thir course, in even ballance down they light
On the firm brimstone, and fill all the Plain;   350
A multitude, like which the populous North
Pour'd never from her frozen loyns, to pass
Rhene or the *Danaw,* when her barbarous Sons
Came like a Deluge on the South, and spread
Beneath *Gibraltar* to the *Lybian* sands.
Forthwith from every Squadron and each Band
The Heads and Leaders thither hast where stood
Their great Commander; Godlike shapes and forms
Excelling human, Princely Dignities,
And Powers that earst in Heaven sat on Thrones;   360
Though of their Names in heav'nly Records now
Be no memorial, blotted out and ras'd
By thir Rebellion, from the Books of Life.
Nor had they yet among the Sons of *Eve*
Got them new Names, till wandring ore the Earth,
Through Gods high sufferance for the tryal of man,
By falsities and lyes the greatest part
Of Mankind they corrupted to forsake
God their Creator, and th' invisible
Glory of him, that made them, to transform   370
Oft to the Image of a Brute, adorn'd

With gay Religions full of Pomp and Gold,
And Devils to adore for Deities:
Then were they known to men by various Names,
And various Idols through the Heathen World.
Say, Muse, their Names then known, who first, who last,
Rous'd from the slumber, on that fiery Couch,
At thir great Emperors call, as next in worth
Came singly where he stood on the bare strand,
While the promiscuous croud stood yet aloof?   380
The chief were those who from the Pit of Hell
Roaming to seek their prey on earth, durst fix
Their Seats long after next the Seat of God,
Their Altars by his Altar, Gods ador'd
Among the Nations round, and durst abide
Jehovah thundring out of *Sion,* thron'd
Between the Cherubim; yea, often plac'd
Within his Sanctuary it self their Shrines,
Abominations; and with cursed things
His holy Rites, and solemn Feasts profan'd,   390
And with their darkness durst affront his light.
First *Moloch,* horrid King besmear'd with blood
Of human sacrifice, and parents tears,
Though for the noyse of Drums and Timbrels loud
Their childrens cries unheard, that past through fire
To his grim Idol. Him the *Ammonite*
Worshipt in *Rabba* and her watry Plain,
In *Argob* and in *Basan,* to the stream
Of utmost *Arnon.* Nor content with such
Audacious neighbourhood, the wisest heart   400
Of *Solomon* he led by fraud to build
His Temple right against the Temple of God
On that opprobrious Hill, and made his Grove
The pleasant Vally of *Hinnom, Tophet* thence
And black *Gehenna* call'd, the Type of Hell.
Next *Chemos,* th' obscene dread of *Moabs* Sons,
From *Aroer* to *Nebo,* and the wild
Of Southmost *Abarim;* in *Hesebon*
And *Horonaim, Seons* Realm, beyond
The flowry Dale of *Sibma* clad with Vines,   410
And *Eleale* to th' *Asphaltick* Pool.
Peor his other Name, when he entic'd
Israel in *Sittim* on their march from *Nile*
To do him wanton rites, which cost them woe.
Yet thence his lustful Orgies he enlarg'd
Even to that Hill of scandal, by the Grove
Of *Moloch* homicide, lust hard by hate;
Till good *Josiah* drove them thence to Hell.
With these came they, who from the bordring flood
Of old *Euphrates* to the Brook that parts   420
Egypt from *Syrian* ground, had general Names
Of *Baalim* and *Ashtaroth,* those male,
These Feminine. For Spirits when they please
Can either Sex assume, or both; so soft

And uncompounded is their Essence pure,
Not ti'd or manacl'd with joynt or limb,
Nor founded on the brittle strength of bones,
Like cumbrous flesh; but in what shape they choose
Dilated or condens't, bright or obscure,
Can execute their aerie purposes,   430
And works of love or enmity fulfill.
For those the Race of *Israel* oft forsook
Their living strength, and unfrequented left
His righteous Altar, bowing lowly down
To bestial Gods; for which their heads as low
Bow'd down in Battel, sunk before the Spear
Of despicable foes. With these in troop
Came *Astoreth,* whom the *Phœnicians* call'd
Astarte, Queen of Heav'n, with crescent Horns;
To whose bright Image nightly by the Moon   440
Sidonian Virgins paid their Vows and Songs,
In *Sion* also not unsung, where stood
Her Temple on th' offensive Mountain, built
By that uxorious King, whose heart though large,
Beguil'd by fair Idolatresses, fell
To Idols foul. *Thammuz* came next behind,
Whose annual wound in *Lebanon* allur'd
The *Syrian* Damsels to lament his fate
In amorous dittyes all a Summers day,
While smooth *Adonis* from his native Rock   450
Ran purple to the Sea, suppos'd with blood
Of *Thammuz* yearly wounded: the Love-tale
Infected *Sions* daughters with like heat,
Whose wanton passions in the sacred Porch
Ezekiel saw, when by the Vision led
His eye survay'd the dark Idolatries
Of alienated *Judah.* Next came one
Who mourn'd in earnest, when the Captive Ark
Maim'd his brute Image, head and hands lopt off
In his own Temple, on the grunsel edge,   460
Where he fell flat, and sham'd his Worshipers:
Dagon his Name, Sea Monster, upward Man
And downward Fish: yet had his Temple high
Rear'd in *Azotus,* dreaded through the Coast
Of *Palestine,* in *Gath* and *Ascalon,*
And *Accaron* and *Gaza's* frontier bounds.
Him follow'd *Rimmon,* whose delightful Seat
Was fair *Damascus,* on the fertil Banks
Of *Abbana* and *Pharphar,* lucid streams.
He also against the house of God was bold: 470
A Leper once he lost and gain'd a King,
Ahaz his sottish Conquerour, whom he drew
Gods Altar to disparage and displace
For one of *Syrian* mode, whereon to burn
His odious offrings, and adore the Gods
Whom he had vanquisht. After these appear'd
A crew who under Names of old Renown,

Osiris, Isis, Orus and their Train
With monstrous shapes and sorceries abus'd
Fanatic *Egypt* and her Priests, to seek   480
Thir wandring Gods disguis'd in brutish forms
Rather then human. Nor did *Israel* scape
Th' infection when their borrow'd Gold compos'd
The Calf in *Oreb*: and the Rebel King
Doubl'd that sin in *Bethel* and in *Dan*,
Lik'ning his Maker to the Grazed Ox,
Jehovah, who in one Night when he pass'd
From *Egypt* marching, equal'd with one stroke
Both her first born and all her bleating Gods.
Belial came last, then whom a Spirit more lewd   490
Fell not from Heaven, or more gross to love
Vice for it self: To him no Temple stood
Or Altar smoak'd; yet who more oft then hee
In Temples and at Altars, when the Priest
Turns Atheist, as did *Ely*'s Sons, who fill'd
With lust and violence the house of God.
In Courts and Palaces he also Reigns
And in luxurious Cities, where the noyse
Of riot ascends above thir loftiest Towrs,
And injury and outrage: And when Night   500
Darkens the Streets, then wander forth the Sons
Of *Belial*, flown with insolence and wine.
Witness the Streets of *Sodom*, and that night
In *Gibeah*, when the hospitable door
Expos'd a Matron to avoid worse rape.
These were the prime in order and in might;
The rest were long to tell, though far renown'd,
Th' *Ionian* Gods, of *Javans* Issue held
Gods, yet confest later then Heav'n and Earth
Thir boasted Parents; *Titan* Heav'ns first born   510
With his enormous brood, and birthright seis'd
By younger *Saturn*, he from mightier *Jove*
His own and *Rhea*'s Son like measure found;
So *Jove* usurping reign'd: these first in *Creet*
And *Ida* known, thence on the Snowy top
Of cold *Olympus* rul'd the middle Air,
Thir highest Heav'n; or on the *Delphian* Cliff,
Or in *Dodona*, and through all the bounds
Of *Doric* Land; or who with *Saturn* old
Fled over *Adria* to th' *Hesperian* Fields,   520
And ore the *Celtic* roam'd the utmost Isles.
All these and more came flocking; but with looks
Down cast and damp, yet such wherein appear'd
Obscure som glimps of joy, to have found thir chief
Not in despair, to have found themselves not lost
In loss it self; which on his count'nance cast
Like doubtful hue: but he his wonted pride
Soon recollecting, with high words, that bore
Semblance of worth not substance, gently rais'd
Their fainted courage, and dispel'd their fears.   530

Then strait commands that at the warlike sound
Of Trumpets loud and Clarions be upreard
His mighty Standard; that proud honour claim'd
Azazel as his right, a Cherube tall:
Who forthwith from the glittering Staff unfurld
Th' Imperial Ensign, which full high advanc't
Shon like a Meteor streaming to the Wind
With Gemms and Golden lustre rich imblaz'd,
Seraphic arms and Trophies: all the while
Sonorous mettal blowing Martial sounds: 540
At which the universal Host upsent
A shout that tore Hells Concave, and beyond
Frighted the Reign of *Chaos* and old Night.
All in a moment through the gloom were seen
Ten thousand Banners rise into the Air
With Orient Colours waving: with them rose
A Forrest huge of Spears: and thronging Helms
Appear'd, and serried Shields in thick array
Of depth immeasurable: Anon they move
In perfect *Phalanx* to the *Dorian* mood   550
Of Flutes and soft Recorders; such as rais'd
To highth of noblest temper Hero's old
Arming to Battel, and in stead of rage
Deliberate valour breath'd, firm and unmov'd
With dread of death to flight or foul retreat,
Nor wanting power to mitigate and swage
With solemn touches, troubl'd thoughts, and chase
Anguish and doubt and fear and sorrow and pain
From mortal or immortal minds. Thus they
Breathing united force with fixed thought   560
Mov'd on in silence to soft Pipes that charm'd
Thir painful steps o're the burnt soyle; and now
Advanc't in view they stand, a horrid Front
Of dreadful length and dazling Arms, in guise
Of Warriers old with order'd Spear and Shield,
Awaiting what command thir mighty Chief
Had to impose: He through the armed Files
Darts his experienc't eye, and soon traverse
The whole Battalion views, thir order due,
Thir visages and stature as of Gods,   570
Thir number last he summs. And now his heart
Distends with pride, and hardning in his strength
Glories: For never since created man,
Met such imbodied force, as nam'd with these
Could merit more then that small infantry
Warr'd on by Cranes: though all the Giant brood
Of *Phlegra* with th' Heroic Race were joyn'd
That fought at *Theb's* and *Ilium,* on each side
Mixt with auxiliar Gods; and what resounds
In Fable or *Romance* of *Uthers* Son   580
Begirt with *British* and *Armoric* Knights;
And all who since, Baptiz'd or Infidel
Jousted in *Aspramont* or *Montalban,*

Damasco, or *Marocco,* or *Trebisond,*
Or whom *Biserta* sent from *Afric* shore
When *Charlemain* with all his Peerage fell
By *Fontarabbia.* Thus far these beyond
Compare of mortal prowess, yet observ'd
Thir dread Commander: he above the rest
In shape and gesture proudly eminent   590
Stood like a Towr; his form had yet not lost
All her Original brightness, nor appear'd
Less then Arch Angel ruind, and th' excess
Of Glory obscur'd: As when the Sun new ris'n
Looks through the Horizontal misty Air
Shorn of his Beams, or from behind the Moon
In dim Eclips disastrous twilight sheds
On half the Nations, and with fear of change
Perplexes Monarchs. Dark'n'd so, yet shon
Above them all th' Arch Angel: but his face 600
Deep scars of Thunder had intrencht, and care
Sat on his faded cheek, but under Browes
Of dauntless courage, and considerate Pride
Waiting revenge: cruel his eye, but cast
Signs of remorse and passion to behold
The fellows of his crime, the followers rather
(Far other once beheld in bliss) condemn'd
For ever now to have their lot in pain,
Millions of Spirits for his fault amerc't
Of Heav'n, and from Eternal Splendors flung 610
For his revolt, yet faithfull how they stood,
Thir Glory witherd. As when Heavens Fire
Hath scath'd the Forrest Oaks, or Mountain Pines,
With singed top their stately growth though bare
Stands on the blasted Heath. He now prepar'd
To speak; whereat their doubl'd Ranks they bend
From Wing to Wing, and half enclose him round
With all his Peers: attention held them mute.
Thrice he assayd, and thrice in spite of scorn,
Tears such as Angels weep, burst forth: at last 620
Words interwove with sighs found out their way.
 O Myriads of immortal Spirits, O Powers
Matchless, but with th' Almighty, and that strife
Was not inglorious, though th' event was dire,
As this place testifies, and this dire change
Hateful to utter: but what power of mind
Foreseeing or presaging, from the Depth
Of knowledge past or present, could have fear'd,
How such united force of Gods, how such
As stood like these, could ever know repulse? 630
For who can yet beleeve, though after loss,
That all these puissant Legions, whose exile
Hath emptied Heav'n, shall faile to re-ascend
Self-rais'd, and repossess their native seat.
For me, be witness all the Host of Heav'n,
If counsels different, or danger shun'd

By me, have lost our hopes. But he who reigns
Monarch in Heav'n, till then as one secure
Sat on his Throne, upheld by old repute,
Consent or custome, and his Regal State   640
Put forth at full, but still his strength conceal'd,
Which tempted our attempt, and wrought our fall.
Henceforth his might we know, and know our own
So as not either to provoke, or dread
New warr, provok't; our better part remains
To work in close design, by fraud or guile
What force effected not: that he no less
At length from us may find, who overcomes
By force, hath overcome but half his foe.
Space may produce new Worlds; whereof so rife   650
There went a fame in Heav'n that he ere long
Intended to create, and therein plant
A generation, whom his choice regard
Should favour equal to the Sons of Heaven:
Thither, if but to prie, shall be perhaps
Our first eruption, thither or elsewhere:
For this Infernal Pit shall never hold
Cælestial Spirits in Bondage, nor th' Abysse
Long under darkness cover. But these thoughts
Full Counsel must mature: Peace is despaird,   660
For who can think Submission? Warr then, Warr
Open or understood must be resolv'd.
    He spake: and to confirm his words, out-flew
Millions of flaming swords, drawn from the thighs
Of mighty Cherubim; the sudden blaze
Far round illumin'd hell: highly they rag'd
Against the Highest, and fierce with grasped arm's
Clash'd on their sounding shields the din of war,
Hurling defiance toward the vault of Heav'n.
    There stood a Hill not far whose griesly top   670
Belch'd fire and rowling smoak; the rest entire
Shon with a glossie scurff, undoubted sign
That in his womb was hid metallic Ore,
The work of Sulphur. Thither wing'd with speed
A numerous Brigad hasten'd. As when bands
Of Pioners with Spade and Pickaxe arm'd
Forerun the Royal Camp, to trench a Field,
Or cast a Rampart. *Mammon* led them on,
Mammon, the least erected Spirit that fell
From heav'n, for ev'n in heav'n his looks & thoughts   680
Were always downward bent, admiring more
The riches of Heav'ns pavement, trod'n Gold,
Then aught divine or holy else enjoy'd
In vision beatific: by him first
Men also, and by his suggestion taught,
Ransack'd the Center, and with impious hands
Rifl'd the bowels of thir mother Earth
For Treasures better hid. Soon had his crew

Op'nd into the Hill a spacious wound
And dig'd out ribs of Gold. Let none admire　　　690
That riches grow in Hell; that soyle may best
Deserve the pretious bane. And here let those
Who boast in mortal things, and wondring tell
Of *Babel,* and the works of *Memphian* Kings,
Learn how thir greatest Monuments of Fame,
And Strength and Art are easily outdone
By Spirits reprobate, and in an hour
What in an age they with incessant toyle
And hands innumerable scarce perform.
Nigh on the Plain in many cells prepar'd,　　　700
That underneath had veins of liquid fire
Sluc'd from the Lake, a second multitude
With wondrous Art found out the massie Ore,
Severing each kinde, and scum'd the Bullion dross:
A third as soon had form'd within the ground
A various mould, and from the boyling cells
By strange conveyance fill'd each hollow nook,
As in an Organ from one blast of wind
To many a row of Pipes the sound-board breaths.
Anon out of the earth a Fabrick huge　　　710
Rose like an Exhalation, with the sound
Of Dulcet Symphonies and voices sweet,
Built like a Temple, where *Pilasters* round
Were set, and Doric pillars overlaid
With Golden Architrave; nor did there want
Cornice or Freeze, with bossy Sculptures grav'n,
The Roof was fretted Gold. Not *Babilon,*
Nor great *Alcairo* such magnificence
Equal'd in all thir glories, to inshrine
Belus or *Serapis* thir Gods, or seat　　　720
Thir Kings, when *Ægypt* with *Assyria* strove
In wealth and luxurie. Th' ascending pile
Stood fixt her stately highth, and strait the dores
Op'ning thir brazen foulds discover wide
Within, her ample spaces, o're the smooth
And level pavement: from the arched roof
Pendant by suttle Magic many a row
Of Starry Lamps and blazing Cressets fed
With *Naphtha* and *Asphaltus* yeilded light
As from a sky. The hasty multitude　　　730
Admiring enter'd, and the work some praise
And some the Architect: his hand was known
In Heav'n by many a Towred structure high,
Where Scepter'd Angels held thir residence,
And sat as Princes, whom the supreme King
Exalted to such power, and gave to rule,
Each in his Herarchie, the Orders bright.
Nor was his name unheard or unador'd
In ancient *Greece;* and in *Ausonian* land
Men call'd him *Mulciber;* and how he fell　　　740

From Heav'n, they fabl'd, thrown by angry *Jove*
Sheer o're the Chrystal Battlements: from Morn
To Noon he fell, from Noon to dewy Eve,
A Summers day; and with the setting Sun
Dropt from the Zenith like a falling Star,
On *Lemnos* th' *Ægæan* Ile: thus they relate,
Erring; for he with this rebellious rout
Fell long before; nor aught avail'd him now
To have built in Heav'n high Towrs; nor did he scape
By all his Engins, but was headlong sent   750
With his industrious crew to build in hell.
Mean while the winged Haralds by command
Of Sovran power, with awful Ceremony
And Trumpets sound throughout the Host proclaim
A solemn Councel forthwith to be held
At *Pandæmonium,* the high Capital
Of Satan and his Peers: thir summons call'd
From every Band and squared Regiment
By place or choice the worthiest; they anon
With hunderds and with thousands trooping came   760
Attended: all access was throng'd, the Gates
And Porches wide, but chief the spacious Hall
(Though like a cover'd field, where Champions bold
Wont ride in arm'd, and at the Soldans chair
Defi'd the best of *Panim* chivalry
To mortal combat or carreer with Lance)
Thick swarm'd, both on the ground and in the air,
Brusht with the hiss of russling wings. As Bees
In spring time, when the Sun with Taurus rides,
Poure forth thir populous youth about the Hive   770
In clusters; they among fresh dews and flowers
Flie to and fro, or on the smoothed Plank,
The suburb of thir Straw-built Cittadel,
New rub'd with Baume, expatiate and confer
Thir State affairs. So thick the aerie crowd
Swarm'd and were straitn'd; till the Signal giv'n,
Behold a wonder! they but now who seemd
In bigness to surpass Earths Giant Sons
Now less then smallest Dwarfs, in narrow room
Throng numberless, like that Pigmean Race   780
Beyond the *Indian* Mount, or Faerie Elves,
Whose midnight Revels, by a Forrest side
Or Fountain some belated Peasant sees,
Or dreams he sees, while over head the Moon
Sits Arbitress, and neerer to the Earth
Wheels her pale course, they on thir mirth & dance
Intent, with jocond Music charm his ear;
At once with joy and fear his heart rebounds.
Thus incorporeal Spirits to smallest forms
Reduc'd thir shapes immense, and were at large,   790
Though without number still amidst the Hall
Of that infernal Court. But far within
And in thir own dimensions like themselves

The great Seraphic Lords and Cherubim
In close recess and secret conclave sat
And thousand Demy-Gods on golden seat's,
Frequent and full. After short silence then
And summons read, the great consult began.

The End of the First Book.

PARADISE LOST.

BOOK II.

The Argument.

The Consultation begun, Satan debates whether another Battel be to be hazarded for the recovery of Heaven: some advise it, others dissuade: A third proposal is prefer'd, mention'd before by Satan, to search the truth of that Prophesie or Tradition in Heaven concerning another world and another kind of creature equal or not much inferiour to themselves, about this time to be created: Thir doubt who shall be sent on this difficult search: Satan thir chief undertakes alone the voyage, is honourd and applauded. The Council thus ended, the rest betake them several wayes & to several imployments, as thir inclinations lead them, to entertain the time till Satan return. He passes on his Journey to Hell Gates, finds them shut, and who sat there to guard them, by whom at length they are op'nd, and discover to him the great Gulf between Hell and Heaven; with what difficulty he passes through, directed by Chaos, the Power of that place, to the sight of this new World which he sought.

HIGH on a Throne of Royal State, which far
Outshon the wealth of *Ormus* and of *Ind,*
Or where the gorgeous East with richest hand
Showrs on her Kings *Barbaric* Pearl & Gold,
Satan exalted sat, by merit rais'd
To that bad eminence; and from despair
Thus high uplifted beyond hope, aspires
Beyond thus high, insatiate to pursue
Vain Warr with Heav'n, and by success untaught
His proud imaginations thus displaid.   10
   Powers and Dominions, Deities of Heav'n,
For since no deep within her gulf can hold
Immortal vigor, though opprest and fall'n,
I give not Heav'n for lost. From this descent
Celestial vertues rising, will appear
More glorious and more dread then from no fall,
And trust themselves to fear no second fate:
Mee though just right, and the fixt Laws of Heav'n
Did first create your Leader, next, free choice,
With what besides, in Counsel or in Fight,   20
Hath bin achievd of merit, yet this loss
Thus farr at least recover'd, hath much more
Establisht in a safe unenvied Throne
Yeilded with full consent. The happier state
In Heav'n, which follows dignity, might draw
Envy from each inferior; but who here
Will envy whom the highest place exposes
Formost to stand against the Thunderers aime
Your bulwark, and condemns to greatest share
Of endless pain? where there is then no good   30

For which to strive, no strife can grow up there
From Faction; for none sure will claim in hell
Precedence, none, whose portion is so small
Of present pain, that with ambitious mind
Will covet more. With this advantage then
To union, and firm Faith, and firm accord,
More then can be in Heav'n, we now return
To claim our just inheritance of old,
Surer to prosper then prosperity
Could have assur'd us; and by what best way,   40
Whether of open Warr or covert guile,
We now debate; who can advise, may speak.
   He ceas'd, and next him *Moloc,* Scepter'd King
Stood up, the strongest and the fiercest Spirit
That fought in Heav'n; now fiercer by despair:
His trust was with th' Eternal to be deem'd
Equal in strength, and rather then be less
Car'd not to be at all; with that care lost
Went all his fear: of God, or Hell, or worse
He reckd not, and these words thereafter spake.   50
   My sentence is for open Warr: Of Wiles,
More unexpert, I boast not: them let those
Contrive who need, or when they need, not now.
For while they sit contriving, shall the rest,
Millions that stand in Arms, and longing wait
The Signal to ascend, sit lingring here
Heav'ns fugitives, and for thir dwelling place
Accept this dark opprobrious Den of shame,
The Prison of his Tyranny who Reigns
By our delay? no, let us rather choose   60
Arm'd with Hell flames and fury all at once
O're Heav'ns high Towrs to force resistless way,
Turning our Tortures into horrid Arms
Against the Torturer; when to meet the noise
Of his Almighty Engin he shall hear
Infernal Thunder, and for Lightning see
Black fire and horror shot with equal rage
Among his Angels; and his Throne it self
Mixt with *Tartarean* Sulphur, and strange fire,
His own invented Torments. But perhaps   70
The way seems difficult and steep to scale
With upright wing against a higher foe.
Let such bethink them, if the sleepy drench
Of that forgetful Lake benumme not still,
That in our proper motion we ascend
Up to our native seat: descent and fall
To us is adverse. Who but felt of late
When the fierce Foe hung on our brok'n Rear
Insulting, and pursu'd us through the Deep,
With what compulsion and laborious flight   80
We sunk thus low? Th' ascent is easie then;
Th' event is fear'd; should we again provoke
Our stronger, some worse way his wrath may find

To our destruction: if there be in Hell
Fear to be worse destroy'd: what can be worse
Then to dwell here, driv'n out from bliss, condemn'd
In this abhorred deep to utter woe;
Where pain of unextinguishable fire
Must exercise us without hope of end
The Vassals of his anger, when the Scourge   90
Inexorably, and the torturing houre
Calls us to Penance? More destroy'd then thus
We should be quite abolisht and expire.
What fear we then? what doubt we to incense
His utmost ire? which to the highth enrag'd,
Will either quite consume us, and reduce
To nothing this essential, happier farr
Then miserable to have eternal being:
Or if our substance be indeed Divine,
And cannot cease to be, we are at worst   100
On this side nothing; and by proof we feel
Our power sufficient to disturb his Heav'n,
And with perpetual inrodes to Allarme,
Though inaccessible, his fatal Throne:
Which if not Victory is yet Revenge.
    He ended frowning, and his look denounc'd
Desperate revenge, and Battel dangerous
To less then Gods. On th' other side up rose
Belial, in act more graceful and humane;
A fairer person lost not Heav'n; he seemd   110
For dignity compos'd and high exploit:
But all was false and hollow; though his Tongue
Dropt Manna, and could make the worse appear
The better reason, to perplex and dash
Maturest Counsels: for his thoughts were low;
To vice industrious, but to Nobler deeds
Timorous and slothful: yet he pleas'd the eare,
And with perswasive accent thus began.
    I should be much for open Warr, O Peers,
As not behind in hate; if what was urg'd   120
Main reason to perswade immediate Warr,
Did not disswade me most, and seem to cast
Ominous conjecture on the whole success:
When he who most excels in fact of Arms,
In what he counsels and in what excels
Mistrustful, grounds his courage on despair
And utter dissolution, as the scope
Of all his aim, after some dire revenge.
First, what Revenge? the Towrs of Heav'n are fill'd
With Armed watch, that render all access   130
Impregnable; oft on the bordering Deep
Encamp thir Legions, or with obscure wing
Scout farr and wide into the Realm of night,
Scorning surprize. Or could we break our way
By force, and at our heels all Hell should rise
With blackest Insurrection, to confound

Heav'ns purest Light, yet our great Enemie
All incorruptible would on his Throne
Sit unpolluted, and th' Ethereal mould
Incapable of stain would soon expel   140
Her mischief, and purge off the baser fire
Victorious. Thus repuls'd, our final hope
Is flat despair: we must exasperate
Th' Almighty Victor to spend all his rage,
And that must end us, that must be our cure,
To be no more; sad cure; for who would loose,
Though full of pain, this intellectual being,
Those thoughts that wander through Eternity,
To perish rather, swallowd up and lost
In the wide womb of uncreated night,   150
Devoid of sense and motion? and who knows,
Let this be good, whether our angry Foe
Can give it, or will ever? how he can
Is doubtful; that he never will is sure.
Will he, so wise, let loose at once his ire,
Belike through impotence, or unaware,
To give his Enemies thir wish, and end
Them in his anger, whom his anger saves
To punish endless? wherefore cease we then?
Say they who counsel Warr, we are decreed,   160
Reserv'd and destin'd to Eternal woe;
Whatever doing, what can we suffer more,
What can we suffer worse? is this then worst,
Thus sitting, thus consulting, thus in Arms?
What when we fled amain, pursu'd and strook
With Heav'ns afflicting Thunder, and besought
The Deep to shelter us? this Hell then seem'd
A refuge from those wounds: or when we lay
Chain'd on the burning Lake? that sure was worse.
What if the breath that kindl'd those grim fires   170
Awak'd should blow them into sevenfold rage
And plunge us in the Flames? or from above
Should intermitted vengeance Arme again
His red right hand to plague us? what if all
Her stores were op'n'd, and this Firmament
Of Hell should spout her Cataracts of Fire,
Impendent horrors, threatning hideous fall
One day upon our heads; while we perhaps
Designing or exhorting glorious Warr,
Caught in a fierie Tempest shall be hurl'd   180
Each on his rock transfixt, the sport and prey
Of racking whirlwinds, or for ever sunk
Under yon boyling Ocean, wrapt in Chains;
There to converse with everlasting groans,
Unrespited, unpitied, unrepreev'd,
Ages of hopeless end; this would be worse.
Warr therefore, open or conceal'd, alike ·
My voice disswades; for what can force or guile
With him, or who deceive his mind, whose eye

Views all things at one view? he from heav'ns highth   190
All these our motions vain, sees and derides;
Not more Almighty to resist our might
Then wise to frustrate all our plots and wiles.
Shall we then live thus vile, the race of Heav'n
Thus trampl'd, thus expell'd to suffer here
Chains & these Torments? better these then worse
By my advice; since fate inevitable
Subdues us, and Omnipotent Decree,
The Victors will. To suffer, as to doe,
Our strength is equal, nor the Law unjust   200
That so ordains: this was at first resolv'd,
If we were wise, against so great a foe
Contending, and so doubtful what might fall.
I laugh, when those who at the Spear are bold
And vent'rous, if that fail them, shrink and fear
What yet they know must follow, to endure
Exile, or ignominy, or bonds, or pain,
The sentence of thir Conquerour: This is now
Our doom; which if we can sustain and bear,
Our Supream Foe in time may much remit   210
His anger, and perhaps thus farr remov'd
Not mind us not offending, satisfi'd
With what is punish't; whence these raging fires
Will slack'n, if his breath stir not thir flames.
Our purer essence then will overcome
Thir noxious vapour, or enur'd not feel,
Or chang'd at length, and to the place conformd
In temper and in nature, will receive
Familiar the fierce heat, and void of pain;
This horror will grow milde, this darkness light,   220
Besides what hope the never-ending flight
Of future days may bring, what chance, what change
Worth waiting, since our present lot appeers
For happy though but ill, for ill not worst,
If we procure not to our selves more woe.
     Thus *Belial* with words cloath'd in reasons garb
Counsel'd ignoble ease, and peaceful sloath,
Not peace: and after him thus *Mammon* spake.
     Either to disinthrone the King of Heav'n
We warr, if warr be best, or to regain   230
Our own right lost: him to unthrone we then
May hope, when everlasting Fate shall yeild
To fickle Chance, and *Chaos* judge the strife:
The former vain to hope argues as vain
The latter: for what place can be for us
Within Heav'ns bound, unless Heav'ns Lord supream
We overpower? Suppose he should relent
And publish Grace to all, on promise made
Of new Subjection; with what eyes could we
Stand in his presence humble, and receive   240
Strict Laws impos'd, to celebrate his Throne
With warbl'd Hymns, and to his Godhead sing

Forc't Halleluiah's; while he Lordly sits
Our envied Sovran, and his Altar breathes
Ambrosial Odours and Ambrosial Flowers,
Our servile offerings. This must be our task
In Heav'n, this our delight; how wearisom
Eternity so spent in worship paid
To whom we hate. Let us not then pursue
By force impossible, by leave obtain'd   250
Unacceptable, though in Heav'n, our state
Of splendid vassalage, but rather seek
Our own good from our selves, and from our own
Live to our selves, though in this vast recess,
Free, and to none accountable, preferring
Hard liberty before the easie yoke
Of servile Pomp. Our greatness will appear
Then most conspicuous, when great things of small,
Useful of hurtful, prosperous of adverse
We can create, and in what place so e're   260
Thrive under evil, and work ease out of pain
Through labour and endurance. This deep world
Of darkness do we dread? How oft amidst
Thick clouds and dark doth Heav'ns all-ruling Sire
Choose to reside, his Glory unobscur'd,
And with the Majesty of darkness round
Covers his Throne; from whence deep thunders roar
Must'ring thir rage, and Heav'n resembles Hell?
As he our Darkness, cannot we his Light
Imitate when we please? This Desart soile   270
Wants not her hidden lustre, Gemms and Gold;
Nor want we skill or art, from whence to raise
Magnificence; and what can Heav'n shew more?
Our torments also may in length of time
Become our Elements, these piercing Fires
As soft as now severe, our temper chang'd
Into their temper; which must needs remove
The sensible of pain. All things invite
To peaceful Counsels, and the settl'd State
Of order, how in safety best we may   280
Compose our present evils, with regard
Of what we are and where, dismissing quite
All thoughts of Warr: ye have what I advise.
   He scarce had finisht, when such murmur filld
Th' Assembly, as when hollow Rocks retain
The sound of blustring winds, which all night long
Had rous'd the Sea, now with hoarse cadence lull
Sea-faring men orewatcht, whose Bark by chance
Or Pinnace anchors in a craggy Bay
After the Tempest: Such applause was heard   290
As *Mammon* ended, and his Sentence pleas'd,
Advising peace: for such another Field
They dreaded worse then Hell: so much the fear
Of Thunder and the Sword of *Michael*
Wrought still within them: and no less desire

To found this nether Empire, which might rise
By pollicy, and long process of time,
In emulation opposite to Heav'n.
Which when *Bëëlzebub* perceiv'd, then whom,   300
Satan except, none higher sat, with grave
Aspect he rose, and in his rising seem'd
A Pillar of State; deep on his Front engraven
Deliberation sat and publick care;
And Princely counsel in his face yet shon,
Majestick though in ruin: sage he stood
With *Atlantean* shoulders fit to bear
The weight of mightiest Monarchies; his look
Drew audience and attention still as Night
Or Summers Noon-tide air, while thus he spake.

   Thrones and imperial Powers, off-spring of heav'n,   310
Ethereal Vertues; or these Titles now
Must we renounce, and changing stile be call'd
Princes of Hell? for so the popular vote
Inclines, here to continue, and build up here
A growing Empire; doubtless; while we dream,
And know not that the King of Heav'n hath doom'd
This place our dungeon, not our safe retreat
Beyond his Potent arm, to live exempt
From Heav'ns high jurisdiction, in new League
Banded against his Throne, but to remaine   320
In strictest bondage, though thus far remov'd,
Under th' inevitable curb, reserv'd
His captive multitude: For he, be sure,
In highth or depth, still first and last will Reign
Sole King, and of his Kingdom loose no part
By our revolt, but over Hell extend
His Empire, and with Iron Scepter rule
Us here, as with his Golden those in Heav'n.
What sit we then projecting Peace and Warr?
Warr hath determin'd us, and foild with loss   330
Irreparable; tearms of peace yet none
Voutsaf't or sought; for what peace will be giv'n
To us enslav'd, but custody severe,
And stripes, and arbitrary punishment
Inflicted? and what peace can we return,
But to our power hostility and hate,
Untam'd reluctance, and revenge though slow,
Yet ever plotting how the Conquerour least
May reap his conquest, and may least rejoyce
In doing what we most in suffering feel?   340
Nor will occasion want, nor shall we need
With dangerous expedition to invade
Heav'n, whose high walls fear no assault or Siege,
Or ambush from the Deep. What if we find
Some easier enterprize? There is a place
(If ancient and prophetic fame in Heav'n
Err not) another World, the happy seat
Of som new Race call'd *Man,* about this time

To be created like to us, though less
In power and excellence, but favour'd more   350
Of him who rules above; so was his will
Pronounc'd among the Gods, and by an Oath,
That shook Heav'ns whol circumference, confirm'd.
Thither let us bend all our thoughts, to learn
What creatures there inhabit, of what mould,
Or substance, how endu'd, and what thir Power,
And where thir weakness, how attempted best,
By force or suttlety: Though Heav'n be shut,
And Heav'ns high Arbitrator sit secure
In his own strength, this place may lye expos'd   360
The utmost border of his Kingdom, left
To their defence who hold it: here perhaps
Som advantagious act may be achiev'd
By sudden onset, either with Hell fire
To waste his whole Creation, or possess
All as our own, and drive as we were driven,
The punie habitants, or if not drive,
Seduce them to our Party, that thir God
May prove thir foe, and with repenting hand
Abolish his own works. This would surpass   370
Common revenge, and interrupt his joy
In our Confusion, and our Joy upraise
In his disturbance; when his darling Sons
Hurl'd headlong to partake with us, shall curse
Thir frail Original, and faded bliss,
Faded so soon. Advise if this be worth
Attempting, or to sit in darkness here
Hatching vain Empires. Thus *Bëëlzebub*
Pleaded his devilish Counsel, first devis'd
By *Satan,* and in part propos'd: for whence,   380
But from the Author of all ill could Spring
So deep a malice, to confound the race
Of mankind in one root, and Earth with Hell
To mingle and involve, done all to spite
The great Creatour? But thir spite still serves
His glory to augment. The bold design
Pleas'd highly those infernal States, and joy
Sparkl'd in all thir eyes; with full assent
They vote: whereat his speech he thus renews.
  Well have ye judg'd, well ended long debate,   390
Synod of Gods, and like to what ye are,
Great things resolv'd; which from the lowest deep
Will once more lift us up, in spight of Fate,
Neerer our ancient Seat; perhaps in view
Of those bright confines, whence with neighbouring Arms
And opportune excursion we may chance
Re-enter Heav'n; or else in some milde Zone
Dwell not unvisited of Heav'ns fair Light
Secure, and at the brightning Orient beam
Purge off this gloom; the soft delicious Air,   400
To heal the scarr of these corrosive Fires

Shall breath her balme. But first whom shall we send
In search of this new world, whom shall we find
Sufficient? who shall tempt with wandring feet
The dark unbottom'd infinite Abyss
And through the palpable obscure find out
His uncouth way, or spread his aerie flight
Upborn with indefatigable wings
Over the vast abrupt, ere he arrive
The happy Ile; what strength, what art can then   410
Suffice, or what evasion bear him safe
Through the strict Senteries and Stations thick
Of Angels watching round? Here he had need
All circumspection, and wee now no less
Choice in our suffrage; for on whom we send,
The weight of all and our last hope relies.
    This said, he sat; and expectation held
His look suspence, awaiting who appeer'd
To second, or oppose, or undertake
The perilous attempt: but all sat mute,   420
Pondering the danger with deep thoughts; & each
In others count'nance red his own dismay
Astonisht: none among the choice and prime
Of those Heav'n-warring Champions could be found
So hardie as to proffer or accept
Alone the dreadful voyage; till at last
Satan, whom now transcendent glory rais'd
Above his fellows, with Monarchal pride
Conscious of highest worth, unmov'd thus spake.
    O Progeny of Heav'n, Empyreal Thrones,   430
With reason hath deep silence and demurr
Seis'd us, though undismaid: long is the way
And hard, that out of Hell leads up to Light;
Our prison strong, this huge convex of Fire,
Outrageous to devour, immures us round
Ninefold, and gates of burning Adamant
Barr'd over us prohibit all egress.
These past, if any pass, the void profound
Of unessential Night receives him next
Wide gaping, and with utter loss of being   440
Threatens him, plung'd in that abortive gulf.
If thence he scape into what ever world,
Or unknown Region, what remains him less
Then unknown dangers and as hard escape.
But I should ill become this Throne, O Peers,
And this Imperial Sov'ranty, adorn'd
With splendor, arm'd with power, if aught propos'd
And judg'd of public moment, in the shape
Of difficulty or danger could deterre
Me from attempting. Wherefore do I assume   450
These Royalties, and not refuse to Reign,
Refusing to accept as great a share
Of hazard as of honour, due alike
To him who Reigns, and so much to him due

Of hazard more, as he above the rest
High honourd sits? Go therfore mighty powers,
Terror of Heav'n, though fall'n; intend at home,
While here shall be our home, what best may ease
The present misery, and render Hell
More tollerable; if there be cure or charm   460
To respite or deceive, or slack the pain
Of this ill Mansion: intermit no watch
Against a wakeful Foe, while I abroad
Through all the coasts of dark destruction seek
Deliverance for us all: this enterprize
None shall partake with me. Thus saying rose
The Monarch, and prevented all reply,
Prudent, least from his resolution rais'd
Others among the chief might offer now
(Certain to be refus'd) what erst they feard;   470
And so refus'd might in opinion stand
His rivals, winning cheap the high repute
Which he through hazard huge must earn. But they
Dreaded not more th' adventure then his voice
Forbidding; and at once with him they rose;
Thir rising all at once was as the sound
Of Thunder heard remote. Towards him they bend
With awful reverence prone; and as a God
Extoll him equal to the highest in Heav'n:
Nor fail'd they to express how much they prais'd,   480
That for the general safety he despis'd
His own: for neither do the Spirits damn'd
Loose all thir vertue; least bad men should boast
Thir specious deeds on earth, which glory excites,
Or close ambition varnisht o're with zeal.
Thus they thir doubtful consultations dark
Ended rejoycing in thir matchless Chief:
As when from mountain tops the dusky clouds
Ascending, while the North wind sleeps, o'respread
Heavn's chearful face, the lowring Element   490
Scowls ore the dark'nd lantskip Snow, or showre;
If chance the radiant Sun with farewell sweet
Extend his ev'ning beam, the fields revive,
The birds thir notes renew, and bleating herds
Attest thir joy, that hill and valley rings.
O shame to men! Devil with Devil damn'd
Firm concord holds, men onely disagree
Of Creatures rational, though under hope
Of heavenly Grace: and God proclaiming peace,
Yet live in hatred, enmitie, and strife   500
Among themselves, and levie cruel warres,
Wasting the Earth, each other to destroy:
As if (which might induce us to accord)
Man had not hellish foes anow besides,
That day and night for his destruction waite.
   The *Stygian* Councel thus dissolv'd; and forth
In order came the grand infernal Peers,

Midst came thir mighty Paramount, and seemd
Alone th' Antagonist of Heav'n, nor less
Then Hells dread Emperour with pomp Supream, 510
And God-like imitated State; him round
A Globe of fierie Seraphim inclos'd
With bright imblazonrie, and horrent Arms.
Then of thir Session ended they bid cry
With Trumpets regal sound the great result:
Toward the four winds four speedy Cherubim
Put to thir mouths the sounding Alchymie
By Haralds voice explain'd: the hollow Abyss
Heard farr and wide, and all the host of Hell
With deafning shout, return'd them loud acclaim. 520
Thence more at ease thir minds and somwhat rais'd
By false presumptuous hope, the ranged powers
Disband, and wandring, each his several way
Pursues, as inclination or sad choice
Leads him perplext, where he may likeliest find
Truce to his restless thoughts, and entertain
The irksome hours, till his great Chief return.
Part on the Plain, or in the Air sublime
Upon the wing, or in swift race contend,
As at th' Olympian Games or *Pythian* fields; 530
Part curb thir fierie Steeds, or shun the Goal
With rapid wheels, or fronted Brigads form.
As when to warn proud Cities warr appears
Wag'd in the troubl'd Skie, and Armies rush
To Battel in the Clouds, before each Van
Pric forth the Aerie Knights, and couch thir spears
Till thickest Legions close; with feats of Arms
From either end of Heav'n the welkin burns.
Others with vast *Typhœan* rage more fell
Rend up both Rocks and Hills, and ride the Air 540
In whirlwind; Hell scarce holds the wilde uproar.
As when *Alcides* from *Oechalia* Crown'd
With conquest, felt th' envenom'd robe, and tore
Through pain up by the roots *Thessalian* Pines,
And *Lichas* from the top of *Oeta* threw
Into th' *Euboic* Sea. Others more milde,
Retreated in a silent valley, sing
With notes Angelical to many a Harp
Thir own Heroic deeds and hapless fall
By doom of Battel; and complain that Fate 550
Free Vertue should enthrall to Force or Chance.
Thir song was partial, but the harmony
(What could it less when Spirits immortal sing?)
Suspended Hell, and took with ravishment
The thronging audience. In discourse more sweet
(For Eloquence the Soul, Song charms the Sense,)
Others apart sat on a Hill retir'd,
In thoughts more elevate, and reason'd high
Of Providence, Foreknowledge, Will, and Fate,
Fixt Fate, free will, foreknowledge absolute, 560

And found no end, in wandring mazes lost.
Of good and evil much they argu'd then,
Of happiness and final misery,
Passion and Apathie, and glory and shame,
Vain wisdom all, and false Philosophie:
Yet with a pleasing sorcerie could charm
Pain for a while or anguish, and excite
Fallacious hope, or arm th' obdured brest
With stubborn patience as with triple steel.
Another part in Squadrons and gross Bands,   570
On bold adventure to discover wide
That dismal World, if any Clime perhaps
Might yeild them easier habitation, bend
Four ways thir flying March, along the Banks
Of four infernal Rivers that disgorge
Into the burning Lake thir baleful streams;
Abhorred *Styx* the flood of deadly hate,
Sad *Acheron* of sorrow, black and deep;
Cocytus, nam'd of lamentation loud
Heard on the ruful stream; fierce *Phlegeton*   580
Whose waves of torrent fire inflame with rage.
Farr off from these a slow and silent stream,
Lethe the River of Oblivion roules
Her watrie Labyrinth, whereof who drinks,
Forthwith his former state and being forgets,
Forgets both joy and grief, pleasure and pain.
Beyond this flood a frozen Continent
Lies dark and wilde, beat with perpetual storms
Of Whirlwind and dire Hail, which on firm land
Thaws not, but gathers heap, and ruin seems   590
Of ancient pile; all else deep snow and ice,
A gulf profound as that *Serbonian* Bog
Betwixt *Damiata* and mount *Casius* old,
Where Armies whole have sunk: the parching Air
Burns frore, and cold performs th' effect of Fire.
Thither by harpy-footed Furies hail'd,
At certain revolutions all the damn'd
Are brought: and feel by turns the bitter change
Of fierce extreams, extreams by change more fierce,
From Beds of raging Fire to starve in Ice   600
Thir soft Ethereal warmth, and there to pine
Immovable, infixt, and frozen round,
Periods of time, thence hurried back to fire.
They ferry over this *Lethean* Sound
Both to and fro, thir sorrow to augment,
And wish and struggle, as they pass, to reach
The tempting stream, with one small drop to loose
In sweet forgetfulness all pain and woe,
All in one moment, and so neer the brink;
But fate withstands, and to oppose th' attempt   610
Medusa with *Gorgonian* terror guards
The Ford, and of it self the water flies
All taste of living wight, as once it fled

The lip of *Tantalus*. Thus roving on
In confus'd march forlorn, th' adventrous Bands
With shuddring horror pale, and eyes agast
View'd first thir lamentable lot, and found
No rest: through many a dark and drearie Vaile
They pass'd, and many a Region dolorous,
O're many a Frozen, many a Fierie Alpe,   620
Rocks, Caves, Lakes, Fens, Bogs, Dens, and shades of death,
A Universe of death, which God by curse
Created evil, for evil only good,
Where all life dies, death lives, and nature breeds,
Perverse, all monstrous, all prodigious things,
Abominable, inutterable, and worse
Then Fables yet have feign'd, or fear conceiv'd,
Gorgons and *Hydra's,* and *Chimera's* dire.
   Mean while the Adversary of God and Man,
Satan with thoughts inflam'd of highest design,   630
Puts on swift wings, and toward the Gates of Hell
Explores his solitary flight; som times
He scours the right hand coast, som times the left,
Now shaves with level wing the Deep, then soares
Up to the fiery concave touring high.
As when farr off at Sea a Fleet descri'd
Hangs in the Clouds, by *Æquinoctial* Winds
Close sailing from *Bengala,* or the Iles
Of *Ternate* and *Tidore,* whence Merchants bring
Thir spicie Drugs: they on the trading Flood   640
Through the wide *Ethiopian* to the Cape
Ply stemming nightly toward the Pole. So seem'd
Farr off the flying Fiend: at last appeer
Hell bounds high reaching to the horrid Roof,
And thrice threefold the Gates; three folds were Brass,
Three Iron, three of Adamantine Rock,
Impenitrable, impal'd with circling fire,
Yet unconsum'd. Before the Gates there sat
On either side a formidable shape;
The one seem'd Woman to the waste, and fair,   650
But ended foul in many a scaly fould
Voluminous and vast, a Serpent arm'd
With mortal sting: about her middle round
A cry of Hell Hounds never ceasing bark'd
With wide *Cerberean* mouths full loud, and rung
A hideous Peal: yet, when they list, would creep,
If aught disturb'd thir noyse, into her woomb,
And kennel there, yet there still bark'd and howl'd
Within unseen. Farr less abhorrd then these
Vex'd *Scylla* bathing in the Sea that parts   660
Calabria from the hoarce *Trinacrian* shore:
Nor uglier follow the Night-Hag, when call'd
In secret, riding through the Air she comes
Lur'd with the smell of infant blood, to dance
With *Lapland* Witches, while the labouring Moon
Eclipses at thir charms. The other shape,

If shape it might be call'd that shape had none
Distinguishable in member, joynt, or limb,
Or substance might be call'd that shadow seem'd,
For each seem'd either; black it stood as Night, 670
Fierce as ten Furies, terrible as Hell,
And shook a dreadful Dart; what seem'd his head
The likeness of a Kingly Crown had on.
Satan was now at hand, and from his seat
The Monster moving onward came as fast,
With horrid strides, Hell trembled as he strode.
Th' undaunted Fiend what this might be admir'd,
Admir'd, not fear'd; God and his Son except,
Created thing naught vallu'd he nor shun'd;
And with disdainful look thus first began. 680
  Whence and what art thou, execrable shape,
That dar'st, though grim and terrible, advance
Thy miscreated Front athwart my way
To yonder Gates? through them I mean to pass,
That be assur'd, without leave askt of thee:
Retire, or taste thy folly, and learn by proof,
Hell-born, not to contend with Spirits of Heav'n.
  To whom the Goblin full of wrauth reply'd,
Art thou that Traitor Angel, art thou hee,
Who first broke peace in Heav'n, and Faith, till then 690
Unbrok'n, and in proud rebellious Arms
Drew after him the third part of Heav'ns Sons
Conjur'd against the highest, for which both Thou
And they outcast from God, are here condemn'd
To waste Eternal daies in woe and pain?
And reck'n'st thou thy self with Spirits of Heav'n,
Hell-doomd, and breath'st defiance here and scorn,
Where I reign King, and to enrage thee more,
Thy King and Lord? Back to thy punishment,
False fugitive, and to thy speed add wings, 700
Least with a whip of Scorpions I pursue
Thy lingring, or with one stroke of this Dart
Strange horror seise thee, and pangs unfelt before.
  So spake the grieslie terrour, and in shape,
So speaking and so threatning, grew ten fold
More dreadful and deform: on th' other side
Incenc't with indignation *Satan* stood
Unterrifi'd, and like a Comet burn'd,
That fires the length of *Ophiucus* huge
In th' Artick Sky, and from his horrid hair 710
Shakes Pestilence and Warr. Each at the Head
Level'd his deadly aime; thir fatall hands
No second stroke intend, and such a frown
Each cast at th' other, as when two black Clouds
With Heav'ns Artillery fraught, come rattling on
Over the *Caspian*, then stand front to front
Hov'ring a space, till Winds the signal blow
To joyn thir dark Encounter in mid air:
So frownd the mighty Combatants, that Hell

Grew darker at thir frown, so matcht they stood;   720
For never but once more was either like
To meet so great a foe: and now great deeds
Had been achiev'd, whereof all Hell had rung,
Had not the Snakie Sorceress that sat
Fast by Hell Gate, and kept the fatal Key,
Ris'n, and with hideous outcry rush'd between.
   O Father, what intends thy hand, she cry'd,
Against thy only Son? What fury O Son,
Possesses thee to bend that mortal Dart
Against thy Fathers head? and know'st for whom;   730
For him who sits above and laughs the while   .
At thee ordain'd his drudge, to execute
What e're his wrath, which he calls Justice, bids,
His wrath which one day will destroy ye both.
   She spake, and at her words the hellish Pest
Forbore, then these to her *Satan* return'd:
   So strange thy outcry, and thy words so strange
Thou interposest, that my sudden hand
Prevented spares to tell thee yet by deeds
What it intends; till first I know of thee,   740
What thing thou art, thus double-form'd, and why
In this infernal Vaile first met thou call'st
Me Father, and that Fantasm call'st my Son?
I know thee not, nor ever saw till now
Sight more detestable then him and thee.
   T' whom thus the Portress of Hell Gate reply'd;
Hast thou forgot me then, and do I seem
Now in thine eye so foul, once deemd so fair
In Heav'n, when at th' Assembly, and in sight
Of all the Seraphim with thee combin'd   750
In bold conspiracy against Heav'ns King,
All on a sudden miserable pain
Surpris'd thee, dim thine eyes, and dizzie swumm
In darkness, while thy head flames thick and fast
Threw forth, till on the left side op'ning wide,
Likest to thee in shape and count'nance bright,
Then shining heav'nly fair, a Goddess arm'd
Out of thy head I sprung: amazement seis'd
All th' Host of Heav'n; back they recoild affraid
At first, and call'd me *Sin,* and for a Sign   760
Portentous held me; but familiar grown,
I pleas'd, and with attractive graces won
The most averse, thee chiefly, who full oft
Thy self in me thy perfect image viewing
Becam'st enamour'd, and such joy thou took'st
With me in secret, that my womb conceiv'd
A growing burden. Mean while Warr arose,
And fields were fought in Heav'n; wherein remain
(For what could else) to our Almighty Foe
Cleer Victory, to our part loss and rout   770
Through all the Empyrean: down they fell
Driv'n headlong from the Pitch of Heaven, down

Into this Deep, and in the general fall
I also; at which time this powerful Key
Into my hand was giv'n, with charge to keep
These Gates for ever shut, which none can pass
Without my op'ning. Pensive here I sat
Alone, but long I sat not, till my womb
Pregnant by thee, and now excessive grown
Prodigious motion felt and rueful throes.   780
At last this odious offspring whom thou seest
Thine own begotten, breaking violent way
Tore through my entrails, that with fear and pain
Distorted, all my nether shape thus grew
Transform'd: but he my inbred enemie
Forth issu'd, brandishing his fatal Dart
Made to destroy: I fled, and cry'd out *Death;*
Hell trembl'd at the hideous Name, and sigh'd
From all her Caves, and back resounded *Death.*
I fled, but he pursu'd (though more, it seems,   790
Inflam'd with lust then rage) and swifter far,
Me overtook his mother all dismaid,
And in embraces forcible and foule
Ingendring with me, of that rape begot
These yelling Monsters that with ceasless cry
Surround me, as thou sawst, hourly conceiv'd
And hourly born, with sorrow infinite .
To me, for when they list into the womb
That bred them they return, and howle and gnaw
My Bowels, their repast; then bursting forth   800
Afresh with conscious terrours vex me round,
That rest or intermission none I find.
Before mine eyes in opposition sits
Grim *Death* my Son and foe, who sets them on,
And me his Parent would full soon devour
For want of other prey, but that he knows
His end with mine involvd; and knows that I
Should prove a bitter Morsel, and his bane,
When ever that shall be; so Fate pronounc'd.
But thou O Father, I forewarn thee, shun   810
His deadly arrow; neither vainly hope
To be invulnerable in those bright Arms,
Though temper'd heav'nly, for that mortal dint,
Save he who reigns above, none can resist.
    She finish'd, and the suttle Fiend his lore
Soon learnd, now milder, and thus answerd smooth.
Dear Daughter, since thou claim'st me for thy Sire,
And my fair Son here showst me, the dear pledge
Of dalliance had with thee in Heav'n, and joys
Then sweet, now sad to mention, through dire change   820
Befalln us unforeseen, unthought of, know
I come no enemie, but to set free
From out this dark and dismal house of pain,
Both him and thee, and all the heav'nly Host
Of Spirits that in our just pretenses arm'd

Fell with us from on high: from them I go
This uncouth errand sole, and one for all
My self expose, with lonely steps to tread
Th' unfounded deep, & through the void immense
To search with wandring quest a place foretold   830
Should be, and, by concurring signs, ere now
Created vast and round, a place of bliss
In the Pourlieues of Heav'n, and therein plac't
A race of upstart Creatures, to supply
Perhaps our vacant room, though more remov'd,
Least Heav'n surcharg'd with potent multitude
Might hap to move new broiles: Be this or aught
Then this more secret now design'd, I haste
To know, and this once known, shall soon return,
And bring ye to the place where Thou and Death   840
Shall dwell at ease, and up and down unseen
Wing silently the buxom Air, imbalm'd
With odours; there ye shall be fed and fill'd
Immeasurably, all things shall be your prey.
He ceas'd, for both seemd highly pleasd, and Death
Grinnd horrible a gastly smile, to hear
His famine should be fill'd, and blest his mawe
Destin'd to that good hour: no less rejoyc'd
His mother bad, and thus bespake her Sire.
    The key of this infernal Pit by due,   850
And by command of Heav'ns all-powerful King
I keep, by him forbidden to unlock
These Adamantine Gates; against all force
Death ready stands to interpose his dart,
Fearless to be o'rematcht by living might.
But what ow I to his commands above
Who hates me, and hath hither thrust me down
Into this gloom of *Tartarus* profound,
To sit in hateful Office here confin'd,
Inhabitant of Heav'n, and heav'nlie-born,   860
Here in perpetual agonie and pain,
With terrors and with clamors compasst round
Of mine own brood, that on my bowels feed:
Thou art my Father, thou my Author, thou
My being gav'st me; whom should I obey
But thee, whom follow? thou wilt bring me soon
To that new world of light and bliss, among
The Gods who live at ease, where I shall Reign
At thy right hand voluptuous, as beseems
Thy daughter and thy darling, without end.   870
    Thus saying, from her side the fatal Key,
Sad instrument of all our woe, she took;
And towards the Gate rouling her bestial train,
Forthwith the huge Porcullis high up drew,
Which but her self not all the *Stygian* powers
Could once have mov'd; then in the key-hole turns
Th' intricate wards, and every Bolt and Bar
Of massie Iron or sollid Rock with ease

Unfast'ns: on a sudden op'n flie
With impetuous recoile and jarring sound   880
Th' infernal dores, and on thir hinges grate
Harsh Thunder, that the lowest bottom shook
Of *Erebus*. She op'nd, but to shut
Excel'd her power; the Gates wide op'n stood,
That with extended wings a Bannerd Host
Under spread Ensigns marching might pass through
With Horse and Chariots rankt in loose array;
So wide they stood, and like a Furnace mouth
Cast forth redounding smoak and ruddy flame.
Before thir eyes in sudden view appear   890
The secrets of the hoarie deep, a dark
Illimitable Ocean without bound,
Without dimension, where length, breadth, and highth,
And time and place are lost; where eldest Night
And *Chaos,* Ancestors of Nature, hold
Eternal *Anarchie,* amidst the noise
Of endless warrs, and by confusion stand.
For hot, cold, moist, and dry, four Champions fierce
Strive here for Maistrie, and to Battel bring
Thir embryon Atoms; they around the flag   900
Of each his faction, in thir several Clanns,
Light-arm'd or heavy, sharp, smooth, swift or slow,
Swarm populous, unnumber'd as the Sands
Of *Barca* or *Cyrene's* torrid soil,
Levied to side with warring Winds, and poise
Thir lighter wings. To whom these most adhere,
Hee rules a moment; *Chaos* Umpire sits,
And by decision more imbroiles the fray
By which he Reigns: next him high Arbiter
Chance governs all. Into this wilde Abyss,   910
The Womb of nature and perhaps her Grave,
Of neither Sea, nor Shore, nor Air, nor Fire,
But all these in thir pregnant causes mixt
Confus'dly, and which thus must ever fight,
Unless th' Almighty Maker them ordain
His dark materials to create more Worlds,
Into this wilde Abyss the warie fiend
Stood on the brink of Hell and look'd a while,
Pondering his Voyage; for no narrow frith
He had to cross. Nor was his eare less peal'd   920
With noises loud and ruinous (to compare
Great things with small) then when *Bellona* storms,
With all her battering Engines bent to rase
Som Capital City, or less then if this frame
Of Heav'n were falling, and these Elements
In mutinie had from her Axle torn
The stedfast Earth. At last his Sail-broad Vannes
He spreads for flight, and in the surging smoak
Uplifted spurns the ground, thence many a League
As in a cloudy Chair ascending rides   930
Audacious, but that seat soon failing, meets

A vast vacuitie: all unawares
Fluttring his pennons vain plumb down he drops
Ten thousand fadom deep, and to this hour
Down had been falling, had not by ill chance
The strong rebuff of som tumultuous cloud
Instinct with Fire and Nitre hurried him
As many miles aloft: that furie stay'd,
Quencht in a Boggie *Syrtis,* neither Sea,
Nor good dry Land: nigh founderd on he fares,   940
Treading the crude consistence, half on foot,
Half flying; behoves him now both Oare and Saile.
As when a Gryfon through the Wilderness
With winged course ore Hill or moarie Dale,
Pursues the *Arimaspian,* who by stelth
Had from his wakeful custody purloind
The guarded Gold: So eagerly the fiend
Ore bog or steep, through strait, rough, dense, or rare,
With head, hands, wings, or feet pursues his way,
And swims or sinks, or wades, or creeps, or flyes: 950
At length a universal hubbub wilde
Of stunning sounds and voices all confus'd
Born through the hollow dark assaults his eare
With loudest vehemence: thither he plyes,
Undaunted to meet there what ever power
Or Spirit of the nethermost Abyss
Might in that noise reside, of whom to ask
Which way the neerest coast of darkness lyes
Bordering on light; when strait behold the Throne
Of *Chaos,* and his dark Pavilion spread   960
Wide on the wasteful Deep; with him Enthron'd
Sat Sable-vested Night, eldest of things,
The consort of his Reign; and by them stood
Orcus and *Ades,* and the dreaded name
Of *Demogorgon;* Rumor next and Chance,
And Tumult and Confusion all imbroild,
And Discord with a thousand various mouths.
    T' whom *Satan* turning boldly, thus. Ye Powers
And Spirits of this nethermost Abyss,
Chaos and *ancient Night,* I come no Spie,   970
With purpose to explore or to disturb
The secrets of your Realm, but by constraint
Wandring this darksome desart, as my way
Lies through your spacious Empire up to light,
Alone, and without guide, half lost, I seek
What readiest path leads where your gloomie bounds
Confine with Heav'n; or if som other place
From your Dominion won, th' Ethereal King
Possesses lately, thither to arrive
I travel this profound, direct my course;   980
Directed, no mean recompence it brings
To your behoof, if I that Region lost,
All usurpation thence expell'd, reduce
To her original darkness and your sway

(Which is my present journey) and once more
Erect the Standerd there of *ancient Night;*
Yours be th' advantage all, mine the revenge.
    Thus *Satan;* and him thus the Anarch old
With faultring speech and visage incompos'd
Answer'd. I know thee, stranger, who thou art,   990
That mighty leading Angel, who of late
Made head against Heav'ns King, though overthrown.
I saw and heard, for such a numerous host
Fled not in silence through the frighted deep
With ruin upon ruin, rout on rout,
Confusion worse confounded; and Heav'n Gates
Pourd out by millions her victorious Bands
Pursuing. I upon my Frontieres here
Keep residence; if all I can will serve,
That little which is left so to defend   1000
Encroacht on still through our intestine broiles
Weakning the Scepter of old Night: first Hell
Your dungeon stretching far and wide beneath;
Now lately Heaven and Earth, another World
Hung ore my Realm, link'd in a golden Chain
To that side Heav'n from whence your Legions fell:
If that way be your walk, you have not farr;
So much the neerer danger; goe and speed;
Havock and spoil and ruin are my gain.
    He ceas'd; and *Satan* staid not to reply,   1010
But glad that now his Sea should find a shore,
With fresh alacritie and force renew'd
Springs upward like a Pyramid of fire
Into the wilde expanse, and through the shock
Of fighting Elements, on all sides round
Environ'd wins his way; harder beset
And more endanger'd, then when *Argo* pass'd
Through *Bosporus* betwixt the justling Rocks:
Or when *Ulysses* on the Larbord shunnd
Charybdis, and by th' other whirlpool steard.   1020
So he with difficulty and labour hard
Mov'd on, with difficulty and labour hee;
But hee once past, soon after when man fell,
Strange alteration! Sin and Death amain
Following his track, such was the will of Heav'n,
Pav'd after him a broad and beat'n way
Over the dark Abyss, whose boiling Gulf
Tamely endur'd a Bridge of wondrous length
From Hell continu'd reaching th' utmost Orbe
Of this frail World; by which the Spirits perverse   1030
With easie intercourse pass to and fro
To tempt or punish mortals, except whom
God and good Angels guard by special grace.
But now at last the sacred influence
Of light appears, and from the walls of Heav'n
Shoots farr into the bosom of dim Night
A glimmering dawn; here Nature first begins

Her fardest verge, and *Chaos* to retire
As from her outmost works a brok'n foe
With tumult less and with less hostile din,   1040
That *Satan* with less toil, and now with ease
Wafts on the calmer wave by dubious light
And like a weather-beaten Vessel holds
Gladly the Port, though Shrouds and Tackle torn;
Or in the emptier waste, resembling Air,
Weighs his spread wings, at leasure to behold
Farr off th' Empyreal Heav'n, extended wide
In circuit, undetermind square or round,
With Opal Towrs and Battlements adorn'd
Of living Saphire, once his native Seat;   1050
And fast by hanging in a golden Chain
This pendant world, in bigness as a Starr
Of smallest Magnitude close by the Moon.
Thither full fraught with mischievous revenge,
Accurst, and in a cursed hour he hies.

The End of the Second Book.

PARADISE LOST.

BOOK III.

The Argument.

God *sitting on his Throne sees* Satan *flying towards this world, then newly created; shews him to the Son who sat at his right hand; foretells the success of* Satan *in perverting mankind; clears his own Justice and Wisdom from all imputation, having created Man free and able enough to have with-stood his Tempter; yet declares his purpose of grace towards him, in regard he fell not of his own malice, as did* Satan, *but by him seduc't. The Son of God renders praises to his Father for the manifestation of his gracious purpose towards Man; but God again declares, that Grace cannot be extended towards Man without the satisfaction of divine Justice; Man hath offended the majesty of God by aspiring to Godhead, and therefore with all his Progeny devoted to death must dye, unless some one can be found sufficient to answer for his offence, and undergoe his Punishment. The Son of God freely offers himself a Ransome for Man: the Father accepts him, ordains his incarnation, pronounces his exaltation above all Names in Heaven and Earth; commands all the Angels to adore him; they obey, and hymning to their Harps in full Quire, celebrate the Father and the Son. Mean while* Satan *alights upon the bare convex of this Worlds outermost Orb; where wandring he first finds a place since call'd The Lymbo of Vanity; what persons and things fly up thither; thence comes to the Gate of Heaven, describ'd ascending by stairs, and the waters above the Firmament that flow about it: His passage thence to the Orb of the Sun; he finds there* Uriel *the Regent of that Orb, but first changes himself into the shape of a meaner Angel; and pretending a zealous desire to behold the new Creation and Man whom God had plac't here, inquires of him the place of his habitation, and is directed; alights first on Mount* Niphates.

Hail holy light, ofspring of Heav'n first-born,
Or of th' Eternal Coeternal beam
May I express thee unblam'd? since God is light,
And never but in unapproached light
Dwelt from Eternitie, dwelt then in thee,
Bright effluence of bright essence increate.
Or hear'st thou rather pure Ethereal stream,
Whose Fountain who shall tell? before the Sun,
Before the Heavens thou wert, and at the voice
Of God, as with a Mantle didst invest   10

The rising world of waters dark and deep,
Won from the void and formless infinite.
Thee I re-visit now with bolder wing,
Escap't the *Stygian* Pool, though long detain'd
In that obscure sojourn, while in my flight
Through utter and through middle darkness borne
With other notes then to th' *Orphean* Lyre
I sung of *Chaos* and *Eternal Night,*
Taught by the heav'nly Muse to venture down
The dark descent, and up to reascend,   20
Though hard and rare: thee I revisit safe,
And feel thy sovran vital Lamp; but thou
Revisit'st not these eyes, that rowle in vain
To find thy piercing ray, and find no dawn;
So thick a drop serene hath quencht thir Orbs,
Or dim suffusion veild. Yet not the more
Cease I to wander where the Muses haunt
Cleer Spring, or shadie Grove, or Sunnie Hill,
Smit with the love of sacred song; but chief
Thee *Sion* and the flowrie Brooks beneath   30
That wash thy hallowd feet, and warbling flow,
Nightly I visit: nor somtimes forget
Those other two equal'd with me in Fate,
So were I equal'd with them in renown,
Blind *Thamyris* and blind *Mæonides,*
And *Tiresias* and *Phineus* Prophets old.
Then feed on thoughts, that voluntarie move
Harmonious numbers; as the wakeful Bird
Sings darkling, and in shadiest Covert hid
Tunes her nocturnal Note. Thus with the Year   40
Seasons return, but not to me returns
Day, or the sweet approach of Ev'n or Morn,
Or sight of vernal bloom, or Summers Rose,
Or flocks, or herds, or human face divine;
But cloud in stead, and ever-during dark
Surrounds me, from the chearful waies of men
Cut off, and for the Book of knowledg fair
Presented with a Universal blanc
Of Natures works to mee expung'd and ras'd,
And wisdome at one entrance quite shut out.   50
So much the rather thou Celestial light
Shine inward, and the mind through all her powers
Irradiate, there plant eyes, all mist from thence
Purge and disperse, that I may see and tell
Of things invisible to mortal sight.
  Now had the Almighty Father from above,
From the pure Empyrean where he sits
High Thron'd above all highth, bent down his eye,
His own works and their works at once to view:
About him all the Sanctities of Heaven   60
Stood thick as Starrs, and from his sight receiv'd
Beatitude past utterance; on his right
The radiant image of his Glory sat,

His onely Son; On Earth he first beheld
Our two first Parents, yet the onely two
Of mankind, in the happie Garden plac't,
Reaping immortal fruits of joy and love,
Uninterrupted joy, unrivald love
In blissful solitude; he then survey'd
Hell and the Gulf between, and *Satan* there   70
Coasting the wall of Heav'n on this side Night
In the dun Air sublime, and ready now
To stoop with wearied wings, and willing feet
On the bare outside of this World, that seem'd
Firm land imbosom'd without Firmament,
Uncertain which, in Ocean or in Air.
Him God beholding from his prospect high,
Wherein past, present, future he beholds,
Thus to his onely Son foreseeing spake.

    Onely begotten Son, seest thou what rage   80
Transports our adversarie, whom no bounds
Prescrib'd, no barrs of Hell, nor all the chains
Heapt on him there, nor yet the main Abyss
Wide interrupt can hold; so bent he seems
On desperat revenge, that shall redound
Upon his own rebellious head. And now
Through all restraint broke loose he wings his way
Not farr off Heav'n, in the Precincts of light,
Directly towards the new created World,
And Man there plac't, with purpose to assay   90
If him by force he can destroy, or worse,
By som false guile pervert; and shall pervert;
For man will heark'n to his glozing lyes,
And easily transgress the sole Command,
Sole pledge of his obedience: So will fall
Hee and his faithless Progenie: whose fault?
Whose but his own? ingrate, he had of mee
All he could have; I made him just and right,
Sufficient to have stood, though free to fall.
Such I created all th' Ethereal Powers   100
And Spirits, both them who stood & them who faild;
Freely they stood who stood, and fell who fell.
Not free, what proof could they have givn sincere
Of true allegiance, constant Faith or Love,
Where onely what they needs must do, appeard,
Not what they would? what praise could they receive?
What pleasure I from such obedience paid,
When Will and Reason (Reason also is choice)
Useless and vain, of freedom both despoild,
Made passive both, had servd necessitie,   110
Not mee. They therefore as to right belongd,
So were created, nor can justly accuse
Thir maker, or thir making, or thir Fate;
As if Predestination over-rul'd
Thir will, dispos'd by absolute Decree
Or high foreknowledge; they themselves decreed

Thir own revolt, not I: if I foreknew,
Foreknowledge had no influence on their fault,
Which had no less prov'd certain unforeknown.
So without least impulse or shadow of Fate, 　　　　　　120
Or aught by me immutablie foreseen,
They trespass, Authors to themselves in all
Both what they judge and what they choose; for so
I formd them free, and free they must remain,
Till they enthrall themselves: I else must change
Thir nature, and revoke the high Decree
Unchangeable, Eternal, which ordain'd
Thir freedom, they themselves ordain'd thir fall.
The first sort by thir own suggestion fell,
Self-tempted, self-deprav'd: Man falls deceiv'd 　　　130
By the other first: Man therefore shall find grace,
The other none: in Mercy and Justice both,
Through Heav'n and Earth, so shall my glorie excel,
But Mercy first and last shall brightest shine.
　　Thus while God spake, ambrosial fragrance fill'd
All Heav'n, and in the blessed Spirits elect
Sense of new joy ineffable diffus'd:
Beyond compare the Son of God was seen
Most glorious, in him all his Father shon
Substantially express'd, and in his face 　　　　　　140
Divine compassion visibly appeerd,
Love without end, and without measure Grace,
Which uttering thus he to his Father spake.
　　O Father, gracious was that word which clos'd
Thy sovran sentence, that Man should find grace;
For which both Heav'n and Earth shall high extoll
Thy praises, with th' innumerable sound
Of Hymns and sacred Songs, wherewith thy Throne
Encompass'd shall resound thee ever blest.
For should Man finally be lost, should Man 　　　　150
Thy creature late so lov'd, thy youngest Son
Fall circumvented thus by fraud, though joynd
With his own folly? that be from thee farr,
That farr be from thee, Father, who art Judge
Of all things made, and judgest onely right.
Or shall the Adversarie thus obtain
His end, and frustrate thine, shall he fulfill
His malice, and thy goodness bring to naught,
Or proud return though to his heavier doom,
Yet with revenge accomplish't and to Hell 　　　　160
Draw after him the whole Race of mankind,
By him corrupted? or wilt thou thy self
Abolish thy Creation, and unmake,
For him, what for thy glorie thou hast made?
So should thy goodness and thy greatness both
Be questiond and blaspheam'd without defence.
　　To whom the great Creatour thus reply'd.
O Son, in whom my Soul hath chief delight,
Son of my bosom, Son who art alone

My word, my wisdom, and effectual might,   170
All hast thou spok'n as my thoughts are, all
As my Eternal purpose hath decreed:
Man shall not quite be lost, but sav'd who will,
Yet not of will in him, but grace in me
Freely voutsaft; once more I will renew
His lapsed powers, though forfeit and enthrall'd
By sin to foul exorbitant desires;
Upheld by me, yet once more he shall stand
On even ground against his mortal foe,
By me upheld, that he may know how frail   180
His fall'n condition is, and to me ow
All his deliv'rance, and to none but me.
Some I have chosen of peculiar grace
Elect above the rest; so is my will:
The rest shall hear me call, and oft be warnd
Thir sinful state, and to appease betimes
Th' incensed Deitie, while offerd grace
Invites; for I will cleer thir senses dark,
What may suffice, and soft'n stonie hearts
To pray, repent, and bring obedience due.   190
To prayer, repentance, and obedience due,
Though but endevord with sincere intent,
Mine eare shall not be slow, mine eye not shut.
And I will place within them as a guide
My Umpire *Conscience,* whom if they will hear,
Light after light well us'd they shall attain,
And to the end persisting, safe arrive.
This my long sufferance and my day of grace
They who neglect and scorn, shall never taste;
But hard be hard'nd, blind be blinded more,   200
That they may stumble on, and deeper fall;
And none but such from mercy I exclude.
But yet all is not don; Man disobeying,
Disloyal breaks his fealtie, and sinns
Against the high Supremacie of Heav'n,
Affecting God-head, and so loosing all,
To expiate his Treason hath naught left,
But to destruction sacred and devote,
He with his whole posteritie must die,
Die hee or Justice must; unless for him   210
Som other able, and as willing, pay
The rigid satisfaction, death for death.
Say Heav'nly Powers, where shall we find such love,
Which of ye will be mortal to redeem
Mans mortal crime, and just th' unjust to save,
Dwels in all Heaven charitie so deare?
  He ask'd, but all the Heav'nly Quire stood mute,
And silence was in Heav'n: on mans behalf
Patron or Intercessor none appeerd,
Much less that durst upon his own head draw   220
The deadly forfeiture, and ransom set.
And now without redemption all mankind

Must have bin lost, adjudg'd to Death and Hell
By doom severe, had not the Son of God,
In whom the fulness dwels of love divine,
His dearest mediation thus renewd.
    Father, thy word is past, man shall find grace;
And shall grace not find means, that finds her way,
The speediest of thy winged messengers,
To visit all thy creatures, and to all   230
Comes unprevented, unimplor'd, unsought,
Happie for man, so coming; he her aide
Can never seek, once dead in sins and lost;
Attonement for himself or offering meet,
Indebted and undon, hath none to bring:
Behold mee then, mee for him, life for life
I offer, on mee let thine anger fall;
Account mee man; I for his sake will leave
Thy bosom, and this glorie next to thee
Freely put off, and for him lastly die   240
Well pleas'd, on me let Death wreck all his rage;
Under his gloomie power I shall not long
Lie vanquisht; thou hast givn me to possess
Life in my self for ever, by thee I live,
Though now to Death I yeild, and am his due
All that of me can die, yet that debt paid,
Thou wilt not leave me in the loathsom grave
His prey, nor suffer my unspotted Soule
For ever with corruption there to dwell;
But I shall rise Victorious, and subdue   250
My Vanquisher, spoild of his vanted spoile;
Death his deaths wound shall then receive, & stoop
Inglorious, of his mortall sting disarm'd.
I through the ample Air in Triumph high
Shall lead Hell Captive maugre Hell, and show
The powers of darkness bound. Thou at the sight
Pleas'd, out of Heaven shalt look down and smile,
While by thee rais'd I ruin all my Foes,
Death last, and with his Carcass glut the Grave:
Then with the multitude of my redeemd   260
Shall enter Heaven long absent, and returne,
Father, to see thy face, wherein no cloud
Of anger shall remain, but peace assur'd,
And reconcilement; wrauth shall be no more
Thenceforth, but in thy presence Joy entire.
    His words here ended, but his meek aspect
Silent yet spake, and breath'd immortal love
To mortal men, above which only shon
Filial obedience: as a sacrifice
Glad to be offer'd, he attends the will   270
Of his great Father. Admiration seis'd
All Heav'n, what this might mean, & whither tend
Wondring; but soon th' Almighty thus reply'd:
    O thou in Heav'n and Earth the only peace
Found out for mankind under wrauth, O thou

My sole complacence! well thou know'st how dear,
To me are all my works, nor Man the least
Though last created, that for him I spare
Thee from my bosom and right hand, to save,
By loosing thee a while, the whole Race lost.　　　　　280
Thou therefore whom thou only canst redeeme,
Thir Nature also to thy Nature joyne;
And be thy self Man among men on Earth,
Made flesh, when time shall be, of Virgin seed,
By wondrous birth: Be thou in *Adams* room
The Head of all mankind, though *Adams* Son.
As in him perish all men, so in thee
As from a second root shall be restor'd,
As many as are restor'd, without thee none.
His crime makes guiltie all his Sons, thy merit　　　　290
Imputed shall absolve them who renounce
Thir own both righteous and unrighteous deeds,
And live in thee transplanted, and from thee
Receive new life. So Man, as is most just,
Shall satisfie for Man, be judg'd and die,
And dying rise, and rising with him raise
His Brethren, ransomd with his own dear life.
So Heav'nly love shal outdo Hellish hate,
Giving to death, and dying to redeeme,
So dearly to redeem what Hellish hate　　　　　300
So easily destroy'd, and still destroyes
In those who, when they may, accept not grace.
Nor shalt thou by descending to assume
Mans Nature, less'n or degrade thine owne.
Because thou hast, though Thron'd in highest bliss
Equal to God, and equally enjoying
God-like fruition, quitted all to save
A World from utter loss, and hast been found
By Merit more then Birthright Son of God,
Found worthiest to be so by being Good,　　　　　310
Farr more then Great or High; because in thee
Love hath abounded more then Glory abounds,
Therefore thy Humiliation shall exalt
With thee thy Manhood also to this Throne;
Here shalt thou sit incarnate, here shalt Reigne
Both God and Man, Son both of God and Man,
Anointed universal King; all Power
I give thee, reign for ever, and assume
Thy Merits; under thee as Head Supream
Thrones, Princedoms, Powers, Dominions I reduce:　　　　320
All knees to thee shall bow, of them that bide
In Heaven, or Earth, or under Earth in Hell;
When thou attended gloriously from Heav'n
Shalt in the Skie appeer, and from thee send
The summoning Arch-Angels to proclaime
Thy dread Tribunal: forthwith from all Windes
The living, and forthwith the cited dead
Of all past Ages to the general Doom

Shall hast'n, such a peal shall rouse thir sleep.
Then all thy Saints assembl'd, thou shalt judge 330
Bad men and Angels, they arraignd shall sink
Beneath thy Sentence; Hell, her numbers full,
Thenceforth shall be for ever shut. Mean while
The World shall burn, and from her ashes spring
New Heav'n and Earth, wherein the just shall dwell
And after all thir tribulations long
See golden days, fruitful of golden deeds,
With Joy and Love triumphing, and fair Truth.
Then thou thy regal Scepter shalt lay by,
For regal Scepter then no more shall need, 340
God shall be All in All. But all ye Gods,
Adore him, who to compass all this dies,
Adore the Son, and honour him as mee.
　No sooner had th' Almighty ceas't, but all
The multitude of Angels with a shout
Loud as from numbers without number, sweet
As from blest voices, uttering joy, Heav'n rung
With Jubilee, and loud Hosanna's fill'd
Th' eternal Regions: lowly reverent
Towards either Throne they bow, & to the ground 350
With solemn adoration down they cast
Thir Crowns inwove with Amarant and Gold,
Immortal Amarant, a Flour which once
In Paradise, fast by the Tree of Life
Began to bloom, but soon for mans offence
To Heav'n remov'd where first it grew, there grows,
And flours aloft shading the Fount of Life,
And where the river of Bliss through midst of Heavn
Rowls o're *Elisian* Flours her Amber stream;
With these that never fade the Spirits Elect 360
Bind thir resplendent locks inwreath'd with beams,
Now in loose Garlands thick thrown off, the bright
Pavement that like a Sea of Jasper shon
Impurpl'd with Celestial Roses smil'd.
Then Crown'd again thir gold'n Harps they took,
Harps ever tun'd, that glittering by their side
Like Quivers hung, and with Præamble sweet
Of charming symphonie they introduce
Thir sacred Song, and waken raptures high;
No voice exempt, no voice but well could joine 370
Melodious part, such concord is in Heav'n.
　Thee Father first they sung Omnipotent,
Immutable, Immortal, Infinite,
Eternal King; thee Author of all being,
Fountain of Light, thy self invisible
Amidst the glorious brightness where thou sit'st
Thron'd inaccessible, but when thou shad'st
The full blaze of thy beams, and through a cloud
Drawn round about thee like a radiant Shrine,
Dark with excessive bright thy skirts appeer, 380
Yet dazle Heav'n, that brightest Seraphim

Approach not, but with both wings veil thir eyes.
Thee next they sang of all Creation first,
Begotten Son, Divine Similitude,
In whose conspicuous count'nance, without cloud
Made visible, th' Almighty Father shines,
Whom else no Creature can behold; on thee
Impresst the effulgence of his Glorie abides,
Transfus'd on thee his ample Spirit rests.
Hee Heav'n of Heavens and all the Powers therein   390
By thee created, and by thee threw down
Th' aspiring Dominations: thou that day
Thy Fathers dreadful Thunder didst not spare,
Nor stop thy flaming Chariot wheels, that shook
Heav'ns everlasting Frame, while o're the necks
Thou drov'st of warring Angels disarraid.
Back from pursuit thy Powers with loud acclaime
Thee only extold, Son of thy Fathers might,
To execute fierce vengeance on his foes,
Not so on Man; him through their malice fall'n,   400
Father of Mercie and Grace, thou didst not doome
So strictly, but much more to pitie encline:
No sooner did thy dear and onely Son
Perceive thee purpos'd not to doom frail Man
So strictly, but much more to pitie enclin'd,
He to appease thy wrauth, and end the strife
Of Mercy and Justice in thy face discern'd,
Regardless of the Bliss wherein hee sat
Second to thee, offerd himself to die
For mans offence. O unexampl'd love,   410
Love no where to be found less then Divine!
Hail Son of God, Saviour of Men, thy Name
Shall be the copious matter of my Song
Henceforth, and never shall my Harp thy praise
Forget, nor from thy Fathers praise disjoine.
    Thus they in Heav'n, above the starry Sphear,
Thir happie hours in joy and hymning spent.
Mean while upon the firm opacous Globe
Of this round World, whose first convex divides
The luminous inferior Orbs, enclos'd   420
From *Chaos* and th' inroad of Darkness old,
Satan alighted walks: a Globe farr off
It seem'd, now seems a boundless Continent
Dark, waste, and wild, under the frown of Night
Starless expos'd, and ever-threatning storms
Of *Chaos* blustring round, inclement skie;
Save on that side which from the wall of Heav'n
Though distant farr som small reflection gaines
Of glimmering air less vext with tempest loud:
Here walk'd the Fiend at large in spacious field.   430
As when a Vultur on *Imaus* bred,
Whose snowie ridge the roving *Tartar* bounds,
Dislodging from a Region scarce of prey
To gorge the flesh of Lambs or yeanling Kids

On Hills where Flocks are fed, flies toward the Springs
Of *Ganges* or *Hydaspes, Indian* streams;
But in his way lights on the barren plaines
Of *Sericana,* where *Chineses* drive
With Sails and Wind thir canie Waggons light:
So on this windie Sea of Land, the Fiend   440
Walk'd up and down alone bent on his prey,
Alone, for other Creature in this place
Living or liveless to be found was none,
None yet, but store hereafter from the earth
Up hither like Aereal vapours flew
Of all things transitorie and vain, when Sin
With vanity had filld the works of men:
Both all things vain, and all who in vain things
Built thir fond hopes of Glorie or lasting fame,
Or happiness in this or th' other life;   450
All who have thir reward on Earth, the fruits
Of painful Superstition and blind Zeal,
Naught seeking but the praise of men, here find
Fit retribution, emptie as thir deeds;
All th' unaccomplisht works of Natures hand,
Abortive, monstrous, or unkindly mixt,
Dissolvd on earth, fleet hither, and in vain,
Till final dissolution, wander here,
Not in the neighbouring Moon, as some have dreamd;
Those argent Fields more likely habitants,   460
Translated Saints, or middle Spirits hold
Betwixt th' Angelical and Human kinde:
Hither of ill-joynd Sons and Daughters born
First from the ancient World those Giants came
With many a vain exploit, though then renownd:
The builders next of *Babel* on the Plain
Of *Sennaar,* and still with vain designe
New *Babels,* had they wherewithall, would build:
Others came single; hee who to be deemd
A God, leap'd fondly into *Ætna* flames,   470
Empedocles, and hee who to enjoy
Plato's Elysium, leap'd into the Sea,
Cleombrotus, and many more too long,
Embryo's and Idiots, Eremits and Friers
White, Black and Grey, with all thir trumperie.
Here Pilgrims roam, that stray'd so farr to seek
In *Golgotha* him dead, who lives in Heav'n;
And they who to be sure of Paradise
Dying put on the weeds of *Dominic,*
Or in *Franciscan* think to pass disguis'd;   480
They pass the Planets seven, and pass the fixt,
And that Crystalline Sphear whose ballance weighs
The Trepidation talkt, and that first mov'd;
And now Saint *Peter* at Heav'ns Wicket seems
To wait them with his Keys, and now at foot
Of Heav'ns ascent they lift thir Feet, when loe
A violent cross wind from either Coast

Blows them transverse ten thousand Leagues awry
Into the devious Air; then might ye see
Cowles, Hoods and Habits with thir wearers tost   490
And flutterd into Raggs, then Reliques, Beads,
Indulgences, Dispenses, Pardons, Bulls,
The sport of Winds: all these upwhirld aloft
Fly o're the backside of the World farr off
Into a *Limbo* large and broad, since calld
The Paradise of Fools, to few unknown
Long after, now unpeopl'd, and untrod;
All this dark Globe the Fiend found as he pass'd,
And long he wanderd, till at last a gleame
Of dawning light turnd thither-ward in haste   500
His travell'd steps; farr distant hee descries
Ascending by degrees magnificent
Up to the wall of Heaven a Structure high,
At top whereof, but farr more rich appeerd
The work as of a Kingly Palace Gate
With Frontispice of Diamond and Gold
Imbellisht, thick with sparkling orient Gemmes
The Portal shon, inimitable on Earth
By Model, or by shading Pencil drawn.
The Stairs were such as whereon *Jacob* saw   510
Angels ascending and descending, bands
Of Guardians bright, when he from *Esau* fled
To *Padan-Aram* in the field of *Luz,*
Dreaming by night under the open Skie,
And waking cri'd, This is the Gate of Heav'n.
Each Stair mysteriously was meant, nor stood
There alwaies, but drawn up to Heav'n somtimes
Viewless, and underneath a bright Sea flow'd
Of Jasper, or of liquid Pearle, whereon
Who after came from Earth, sayling arriv'd,   520
Wafted by Angels, or flew o're the Lake
Rapt in a Chariot drawn by fiery Steeds.
The Stairs were then let down, whether to dare
The Fiend by easie ascent, or aggravate
His sad exclusion from the dores of Bliss.
Direct against which op'nd from beneath,
Just o're the blissful seat of Paradise,
A passage down to th' Earth, a passage wide,
Wider by farr then that of after-times
Over Mount *Sion,* and, though that were large,   530
Over the *Promis'd Land* to God so dear,
By which, to visit oft those happy Tribes,
On high behests his Angels to and fro
Pass'd frequent, and his eye with choice regard
From *Paneas* the fount of *Jordans* flood
To *Bëersaba,* where the *Holy Land*
Borders on *Ægypt* and the *Arabian* shoare;
So wide the op'ning seemd, where bounds were set
To darkness, such as bound the Ocean wave.
Satan from hence now on the lower stair   540

That scal'd by steps of Gold to Heav'n Gate
Looks down with wonder at the sudden view
Of all this World at once. As when a Scout
Through dark and desart wayes with peril gone
All night; at last by break of chearful dawne
Obtains the brow of some high-climbing Hill,
Which to his eye discovers unaware
The goodly prospect of some forein land
First seen, or some renownd Metropolis
With glistering Spires and Pinnacles adornd,   550
Which now the Rising Sun guilds with his beams.
Such wonder seis'd, though after Heaven seen,
The Spirit maligne, but much more envy seis'd
At sight of all this World beheld so faire.
Round he surveys, and well might, where he stood
So high above the circling Canopie
Of Nights extended shade; from Eastern Point
Of *Libra* to the fleecie Starr that bears
Andromeda farr off *Atlantick* Seas
Beyond th' *Horizon;* then from Pole to Pole   560
He views in bredth, and without longer pause
Down right into the Worlds first Region throws
His flight precipitant, and windes with ease
Through the pure marble Air his oblique way
Amongst innumerable Starrs, that shon
Stars distant, but nigh hand seemd other Worlds,
Or other Worlds they seemd, or happy Iles,
Like those *Hesperian* Gardens fam'd of old,
Fortunate Fields, and Groves and flourie Vales,
Thrice happy Iles, but who dwelt happy there   570
He stayd not to enquire: above them all
The golden Sun in splendor likest Heaven
Allur'd his eye: Thither his course he bends
Through the calm Firmament; but up or downe
By center, or eccentric, hard to tell,
Or Longitude, where the great Luminarie
Alooff the vulgar Constellations thick,
That from his Lordly eye keep distance due,
Dispenses Light from farr; they as they move
Thir Starry dance in numbers that compute   580
Days, months, and years, towards his all-chearing Lamp
Turn swift their various motions, or are turnd
By his Magnetic beam, that gently warms
The Univers, and to each inward part
With gentle penetration, though unseen,
Shoots invisible vertue even to the deep:
So wondrously was set his Station bright.
There lands the Fiend, a spot like which perhaps
Astronomer in the Sun's lucent Orbe
Through his glaz'd Optic Tube yet never saw.   590
The place he found beyond expression bright,
Compar'd with aught on Earth, Medal or Stone;

Not all parts like, but all alike informd
With radiant light, as glowing Iron with fire;
If mettal, part seemd Gold, part Silver cleer;
If stone, Carbuncle most or Chrysolite,
Rubie or Topaz, to the Twelve that shon
In *Aarons* Brest-plate, and a stone besides
Imagind rather oft then elsewhere seen,
That stone, or like to that which here below   600
Philosophers in vain so long have sought,
In vain, though by thir powerful Art they binde
Volatil *Hermes,* and call up unbound
In various shapes old *Proteus* from the Sea,
Draind through a Limbec to his Native forme.
What wonder then if fields and regions here
Breathe forth *Elixir* pure, and Rivers run
Potable Gold, when with one vertuous touch
Th' Arch-chimic Sun so farr from us remote
Produces with Terrestrial Humor mixt   610
Here in the dark so many precious things
Of colour glorious and effect so rare?
Here matter new to gaze the Devil met
Undazl'd, farr and wide his eye commands,
For sight no obstacle found here, nor shade,
But all Sun-shine, as when his Beams at Noon
Culminate from th' *Æquator,* as they now
Shot upward still direct, whence no way round
Shadow from body opaque can fall, and the Aire,
No where so cleer, sharp'nd his visual ray   620
To objects distant farr, whereby he soon
Saw within kenn a glorious Angel stand,
The same whom *John* saw also in the Sun:
His back was turnd, but not his brightness hid;
Of beaming sunnie Raies, a golden tiar
Circl'd his Head, nor less his Locks behind
Illustrious on his Shoulders fledge with wings
Lay waving round; on som great charge imploy'd
Hee seemd, or fixt in cogitation deep.
Glad was the Spirit impure; as now in hope   630
To find who might direct his wandring flight
To Paradise the happie seat of Man,
His journies end and our beginning woe.
But first he casts to change his proper shape,
Which else might work him danger or delay:
And now a stripling Cherube he appeers,
Not of the prime, yet such as in his face
Youth smil'd Celestial, and to every Limb
Sutable grace diffus'd, so well he feignd;
Under a Coronet his flowing haire   640
In curles on either cheek plaid, wings he wore
Of many a colourd plume sprinkl'd with Gold,
His habit fit for speed succinct, and held
Before his decent steps a Silver wand.

He drew not nigh unheard, the Angel bright,
Ere he drew nigh, his radiant visage turnd,
Admonisht by his eare, and strait was known
Th' Arch-Angel *Uriel,* one of the seav'n
Who in Gods presence, nearest to his Throne
Stand ready at command, and are his Eyes   650
That run through all the Heav'ns, or down to th' Earth
Bear his swift errands over moist and dry,
O're Sea and Land: him *Satan* thus accostes.
  Uriel, for thou of those seav'n Spirits that stand
In sight of Gods high Throne, gloriously bright,
The first are wont his great authentic will
Interpreter through highest Heav'n to bring,
Where all his Sons thy Embassie attend;
And here art likeliest by supream decree
Like honour to obtain, and as his Eye   660
To visit oft this new Creation round;
Unspeakable desire to see, and know
All these his wondrous works, but chiefly Man,
His chief delight and favour, him for whom
All these his works so wondrous he ordaind,
Hath brought me from the Quires of Cherubim
Alone thus wandring. Brightest Seraph tell
In which of all these shining Orbes hath Man
His fixed seat, or fixed seat hath none,
But all these shining Orbes his choice to dwell;   670
That I may find him, and with secret gaze,
Or open admiration him behold
On whom the great Creator hath bestowd
Worlds, and on whom hath all these graces powrd;
That both in him and all things, as is meet,
The Universal Maker we may praise;
Who justly hath drivn out his Rebell Foes
To deepest Hell, and to repair that loss
Created this new happie Race of men
To serve him better: wise are all his wayes.   680
  So spake the false dissembler unperceivd;
For neither Man nor Angel can discern
Hypocrisie, the only evil that walks
Invisible, except to God alone,
By his permissive will, through Heav'n and Earth:
And oft though wisdom wake, suspicion sleeps
At wisdoms Gate, and to simplicitie
Resigns her charge, while goodness thinks no ill
Where no ill seems: Which now for once beguil'd
Uriel, though Regent of the Sun, and held   690
The sharpest sighted Spirit of all in Heav'n;
Who to the fraudulent Impostor foule
In his uprightness answer thus returnd.
Faire Angel, thy desire which tends to know
The works of God, thereby to glorifie
The great Work-Maister, leads to no excess

That reaches blame, but rather merits praise
The more it seems excess, that led thee hither
From thy Empyreal Mansion thus alone,
To witness with thine eyes what some perhaps   700
Contented with report heare onely in heav'n:
For wonderful indeed are all his works,
Pleasant to know, and worthiest to be all
Had in remembrance always with delight;
But what created mind can comprehend
Thir number, or the wisdom infinite
That brought them forth, but hid thir causes deep.
I saw when at his Word the formless Mass,
This worlds material mould, came to a heap:
Confusion heard his voice, and wilde uproar   710
Stood rul'd, stood vast infinitude confin'd;
Till at his second bidding darkness fled,
Light shon, and order from disorder sprung:
Swift to thir several Quarters hasted then
The cumbrous Elements, Earth, Flood, Aire, Fire,
And this Ethereal quintessence of Heav'n
Flew upward, spirited with various forms,
That rowld orbicular, and turnd to Starrs
Numberless, as thou seest, and how they move;
Each had his place appointed, each his course,   720
The rest in circuit walles this Universe.
Look downward on that Globe whose hither side
With light from hence, though but reflected, shines;
That place is Earth the seat of Man, that light
His day, which else as th' other Hemisphere
Night would invade, but there the neighbouring Moon
(So call that opposite fair Starr) her aide
Timely interposes, and her monthly round
Still ending, still renewing through mid Heav'n,
With borrowd light her countenance triform   730
Hence fills and empties to enlighten the Earth,
And in her pale dominion checks the night.
That spot to which I point is *Paradise*,
Adams abode, those loftie shades his Bowre.
Thy way thou canst not miss, me mine requires.
    Thus said, he turnd, and *Satan* bowing low,
As to superior Spirits is wont in Heav'n,
Where honour due and reverence none neglects,
Took leave, and toward the coast of Earth beneath,
Down from th' Ecliptic, sped with hop'd success,   740
Throws his steep flight in many an Aerie wheele,
Nor staid, till on *Niphates* top he lights.

The End of the Third Book.

PARADISE LOST.

BOOK IV.

The Argument.

Satan *now in prospect of* Eden, *and nigh the place where he must now attempt the bold enterprize which he undertook alone against God and Man, falls into many doubts with himself, and many passions, fear, envy, and despare; but at length confirms himself in evil, journeys on to Paradise, whose outward prospect and scituation is described, overleaps the bounds, sits in the shape of a Cormorant on the Tree of life, as highest in the Garden to look about him. The Garden describ'd; Satans first sight of Adam and Eve; his wonder at thir excellent form and happy state, but with resolution to work thir fall; over- hears thir discourse, thence gathers that the Tree of knowledge was forbidden them to eat of, under penalty of death; and thereon intends to found his temptation, by seducing them to transgress: then leaves them a while, to know further of thir state by some other means. Mean while* Uriel *descending on a Sun-beam warns* Gabriel, *who had in charge the Gate of Paradise, that some evil spirit had escap'd the Deep, and past at Noon by his Sphere in the shape of a good Angel down to Paradise, discovered after by his furious gestures in the Mount.* Gabriel *promises to find him out ere morning. Night coming on,* Adam *and* Eve *discourse of going to thir rest: thir Bower describ'd; thir Evening worship.* Gabriel *draw- ing forth his Bands of Night-watch to walk the round of Paradise, appoints two strong Angels to* Adams *Bower, least the evill spirit should be there doing some harm to* Adam *or* Eve *sleeping; there they find him at the ear of* Eve, *tempting her in a dream, and bring him, though unwilling, to* Gabriel; *by whom ques- tion'd, he scornfully answers, prepares resistance, but hinder'd by a Sign from Heaven, flies out of Para- dise.*

    O for that warning voice, which he who saw
Th' *Apocalyps,* heard cry in Heaven aloud,
Then when the Dragon, put to second rout,
Came furious down to be reveng'd on men,
Wo to the inhabitants on Earth! that now,
While time was, our first Parents had bin warnd
The coming of thir secret foe, and scap'd
Haply so scap'd his mortal snare; for now
Satan, now first inflam'd with rage, came down,
The Tempter ere th' Accuser of man-kind,   10
To wreck on innocent frail man his loss
Of that first Battel, and his flight to Hell:
Yet not rejoycing in his speed, though bold,
Far off and fearless, nor with cause to boast,
Begins his dire attempt, which nigh the birth
Now rowling, boiles in his tumultuous brest,
And like a devellish Engine back recoiles
Upon himself; horror and doubt distract
His troubl'd thoughts, and from the bottom stirr
The Hell within him, for within him Hell   20
He brings, and round about him, nor from Hell
One step no more then from himself can fly
By change of place: Now conscience wakes despair
That slumberd, wakes the bitter memorie
Of what he was, what is, and what must be
Worse; of worse deeds worse sufferings must ensue.
Sometimes towards *Eden* which now in his view
Lay pleasant, his grievd look he fixes sad,
Sometimes towards Heav'n and the full-blazing Sun,
Which now sat high in his Meridian Towre: 30
Then much revolving, thus in sighs began.

O thou that with surpassing Glory crownd,
Look'st from thy sole Dominion like the God
Of this new World; at whose sight all the Starrs
Hide thir diminisht heads; to thee I call,
But with no friendly voice, and add thy name
O Sun, to tell thee how I hate thy beams
That bring to my remembrance from what state
I fell, how glorious once above thy Spheare;
Till Pride and worse Ambition threw me down   40
Warring in Heav'n against Heav'ns matchless King:
Ah wherefore! he deservd no such return
From me, whom he created what I was
In that bright eminence, and with his good
Upbraided none; nor was his service hard.
What could be less then to afford him praise,
The easiest recompence, and pay him thanks,
How due! yet all his good prov'd ill in me,
And wrought but malice; lifted up so high
I sdeind subjection, and thought one step higher   50
Would set me highest, and in a moment quit
The debt immense of endless gratitude,
So burthensome, still paying, still to ow;
Forgetful what from him I still receivd,
And understood not that a grateful mind
By owing owes not, but still pays, at once
Indebted and dischargd; what burden then?
O had his powerful Destiny ordaind
Me some inferiour Angel, I had stood
Then happie; no unbounded hope had rais'd   60
Ambition. Yet why not? som other Power
As great might have aspir'd, and me though mean
Drawn to his part; but other Powers as great
Fell not, but stand unshak'n, from within
Or from without, to all temptations arm'd.
Hadst thou the same free Will and Power to stand?
Thou hadst: whom hast thou then or what to accuse,
But Heav'ns free Love dealt equally to all?
Be then his Love accurst, since love or hate,
To me alike, it deals eternal woe.   70
Nay curs'd be thou; since against his thy will
Chose freely what it now so justly rues.
Me miserable! which way shall I flie
Infinite wrauth, and infinite despaire?
Which way I flie is Hell; my self am Hell;
And in the lowest deep a lower deep
Still threatning to devour me opens wide,
To which the Hell I suffer seems a Heav'n.
O then at last relent: is there no place
Left for Repentance, none for Pardon left?   80
None left but by submission; and that word
Disdain forbids me, and my dread of shame
Among the Spirits beneath, whom I seduc'd
With other promises and other vaunts

Then to submit, boasting I could subdue
Th' Omnipotent. Ay me, they little know
How dearly I abide that boast so vaine,
Under what torments inwardly I groane:
While they adore me on the Throne of Hell,
With Diadem and Scepter high advanc't   90
The lower still I fall, onely supream
In miserie; such joy Ambition findes.
But say I could repent and could obtaine
By Act of Grace my former state; how soon
Would highth recal high thoughts, how soon unsay
What feign'd submission swore: ease would recant
Vows made in pain, as violent and void.
For never can true reconcilement grow
Where wounds of deadly hate have peirc'd so deep:
Which would but lead me to a worse relapse,   100
And heavier fall: so should I purchase deare
Short intermission bought with double smart.
This knows my punisher; therefore as farr
From granting hee, as I from begging peace:
All hope excluded thus, behold in stead
Of us out-cast, exil'd, his new delight,
Mankind created, and for him this World.
So farwel Hope, and with Hope farwel Fear,
Farwel Remorse: all Good to me is lost;
Evil be thou my Good; by thee at least   110
Divided Empire with Heav'ns King I hold
By thee, and more then half perhaps will reigne;
As Man ere long, and this new World shall know.
      Thus while he spake, each passion dimm'd his face
Thrice chang'd with pale, ire, envie and despair,
Which marrd his borrow'd visage, and betraid
Him counterfet, if any eye beheld.
For heav'nly mindes from such distempers foule
Are ever cleer. Whereof hee soon aware,
Each perturbation smooth'd with outward calme,   120
Artificer of fraud; and was the first
That practisd falshood under saintly shew,
Deep malice to conceale, couch't with revenge:
Yet not anough had practisd to deceive
Uriel once warnd; whose eye pursu'd him down
The way he went, and on th' Assyrian mount
Saw him disfigur'd, more then could befall
Spirit of happie sort: his gestures fierce
He markd and mad demeanour, then alone,
As he suppos'd, all unobserv'd, unseen.   130
So on he fares, and to the border comes
Of Eden, where delicious Paradise,
Now nearer, Crowns with her enclosure green,
As with a rural mound the champain head
Of a steep wilderness, whose hairie sides
With thicket overgrown, grottesque and wilde,
Access deni'd; and over head up grew

Insuperable highth of loftiest shade,
Cedar, and Pine, and Firr, and branching Palm,
A Silvan Scene, and as the ranks ascend   140
Shade above shade, a woodie Theatre
Of stateliest view. Yet higher then thir tops
The verdurous wall of Paradise up sprung:
Which to our general Sire gave prospect large
Into his neather Empire neighbouring round.
And higher then that Wall a circling row
Of goodliest Trees loaden with fairest Fruit,
Blossoms and Fruits at once of golden hue
Appeerd, with gay enameld colours mixt:
On which the Sun more glad impress'd his beams   150
Then in fair Evening Cloud, or humid Bow,
When God hath showrd the earth; so lovely seemd
That Lantskip: And of pure now purer aire
Meets his approach, and to the heart inspires
Vernal delight and joy, able to drive
All sadness but despair: now gentle gales
Fanning thir odoriferous wings dispense
Native perfumes, and whisper whence they stole
Those balmie spoiles. As when to them who saile
Beyond the *Cape of Hope,* and now are past   160
Mozambic, off at Sea North-East windes blow
Sabean Odours from the spicie shoare
Of *Arabie* the blest, with such delay
Well pleas'd they slack thir course, and many a League
Cheard with the grateful smell old Ocean smiles.
So entertaird those odorous sweets the Fiend
Who came thir bane, though with them better pleas'd
Then *Asmodeus* with the fishie fume,
That drove him, though enamourd, from the Spouse
Of *Tobits* Son, and with a vengeance sent   170
From *Media* post to *Ægypt,* there fast bound.
    Now to th' ascent of that steep savage Hill
Satan had journied on, pensive and slow;
But further way found none, so thick entwin'd,
As one continu'd brake, the undergrowth
Of shrubs and tangling bushes had perplext
All path of Man or Beast that past that way:
One Gate there onely was, and that look'd East
On th' other side: which when th' arch-fellon saw
Due entrance he disdaind, and in contempt,   180
At one slight bound high overleap'd all bound
Of Hill or highest Wall, and sheer within
Lights on his feet. As when a prowling Wolfe,
Whom hunger drives to seek new haunt for prey,
Watching where Shepherds pen thir Flocks at eeve
In hurdl'd Cotes amid the field secure,
Leaps o're the fence with ease into the Fould:
Or as a Thief bent to unhoord the cash
Of some rich Burgher, whose substantial dores,
Cross-barrd and bolted fast, fear no assault,   190

In at the window climbes, or o're the tiles;
So clomb this first grand Thief into Gods Fould:
So since into his Church lewd Hirelings climbe.
Thence up he flew, and on the Tree of Life,
The middle Tree and highest there that grew,
Sat like a Cormorant; yet not true Life
Thereby regaind, but sat devising Death
To them who liv'd; nor on the vertue thought
Of that life-giving Plant, but only us'd
For prospect, what well us'd had bin the pledge   200
Of immortalitie. So little knows
Any, but God alone, to value right
The good before him, but perverts best things
To worst abuse, or to thir meanest use.
Beneath him with new wonder now he views
To all delight of human sense expos'd
In narrow room Natures whole wealth, yea more,
A Heaven on Earth: for blissful Paradise
Of God the Garden was, by him in the East
Of *Eden* planted; *Eden* stretchd her Line   210
From *Auran* Eastward to the Royal Towrs
Of Great *Seleucia,* built by *Grecian* Kings,
Or where the Sons of *Eden* long before
Dwelt in *Telassar:* in this pleasant soile
His farr more pleasant Garden God ordaind;
Out of the fertil ground he caus'd to grow
All Trees of noblest kind for sight, smell, taste;
And all amid them stood the Tree of Life,
High eminent, blooming Ambrosial Fruit
Of vegetable Gold; and next to Life   220
Our Death the Tree of Knowledge grew fast by,
Knowledge of Good bought dear by knowing ill.
Southward through *Eden* went a River large,
Nor chang'd his course, but through the shaggie hill
Pass'd underneath ingulft, for God had thrown
That Mountain as his Garden mould high rais'd
Upon the rapid current, which through veins
Of porous Earth with kindly thirst up drawn,
Rose a fresh Fountain, and with many a rill
Waterd the Garden; thence united fell   230
Down the steep glade, and met the neather Flood,
Which from his darksom passage now appeers,
And now divided into four main Streams,
Runs divers, wandring many a famous Realme
And Country whereof here needs no account,
But rather to tell how, if Art could tell,
How from that Saphire Fount the crisped Brooks,
Rowling on Orient Pearl and sands of Gold,
With mazie error under pendant shades
Ran Nectar, visiting each plant, and fed   240
Flours worthy of Paradise which not nice Art
In Beds and curious Knots, but Nature boon
Powrd forth profuse on Hill and Dale and Plaine,

Both where the morning Sun first warmly smote
The open field, and where the unpierc't shade
Imbround the noontide Bowrs: Thus was this place,
A happy rural seat of various view;
Groves whose rich Trees wept odorous Gumms and Balme,
Others whose fruit burnisht with Golden Rinde
Hung amiable, *Hesperian* Fables true,　　　　　　　　　250
If true, here onely, and of delicious taste:
Betwixt them Lawns, or level Downs, and Flocks
Grasing the tender herb, were interpos'd,
Or palmie hilloc, or the flourie lap
Of som irriguous Valley spread her store,
Flours of all hue, and without Thorn the Rose:
Another side, umbrageous Grots and Caves
Of coole recess, o're which the mantling Vine
Layes forth her purple Grape, and gently creeps
Luxuriant; mean while murmuring waters fall　　　　　260
Down the slope hills, disperst, or in a Lake,
That to the fringed Bank with Myrtle crownd,
Her chrystall mirror holds, unite thir streams.
The Birds thir quire apply; aires, vernal aires,
Breathing the smell of field and grove, attune
The trembling leaves, while Universal *Pan*
Knit with the *Graces* and the *Hours* in dance
Led on th' Eternal Spring. Not that faire field
Of *Enna,* where *Proserpin* gathring flours
Her self a fairer Floure by gloomie *Dis*　　　　　　　270
Was gatherd, which cost *Ceres* all that pain
To seek her through the world; nor that sweet Grove
Of *Daphne* by *Orontes,* and th' inspir'd
Castalian Spring might with this Paradise
Of *Eden* strive; nor that *Nyseian* Ile
Girt with the River *Triton,* where old *Cham,*
Whom Gentiles *Ammon* call and *Libyan Jove,*
Hid *Amalthea* and her Florid Son
Young *Bacchus* from his Stepdame *Rhea's* eye;
Nor where *Abassin* Kings thir issue Guard,　　　　　280
Mount *Amara,* though this by som suppos'd
True Paradise under the *Ethiop* Line
By *Nilus* head, enclos'd with shining Rock,
A whole dayes journey high, but wide remote
From this *Assyrian* Garden, where the Fiend
Saw undelighted all delight, all kind
Of living Creatures new to sight and strange:
Two of far nobler shape erect and tall,
Godlike erect, with native Honour clad
In naked Majestie seemd Lords of all,　　　　　　　290
And worthie seemd, for in thir looks Divine
The image of thir glorious Maker shon,
Truth, Wisdome, Sanctitude severe and pure,
Severe, but in true filial freedom plac't;
Whence true autoritie in men; though both
Not equal, as thir sex not equal seemd;

For contemplation hee and valour formd,
For softness shee and sweet attractive Grace,
Hee for God only, shee for God in him:
His fair large Front and Eye sublime declar'd   300
Absolute rule; and Hyacinthin Locks
Round from his parted forelock manly hung
Clustring, but not beneath his shoulders broad:
Shee as a vail down to the slender waste
Her unadorned golden tresses wore
Dissheveld, but in wanton ringlets wav'd
As the Vine curles her tendrils, which impli'd
Subjection, but requir'd with gentle sway,
And by her yeilded, by him best receivd,
Yeilded with coy submission, modest pride,   310
And sweet reluctant amorous delay.
Nor those mysterious parts were then conceald,
Then was not guiltie shame, dishonest shame
Of natures works, honor dishonorable,
Sin-bred, how have ye troubl'd all mankind
With shews instead, meer shews of seeming pure,
And banisht from mans life his happiest life,
Simplicitie and spotless innocence.
So passd they naked on, nor shund the sight
Of God or Angel, for they thought no ill: 320
So hand in hand they passd, the lovliest pair
That ever since in loves imbraces met,
Adam the goodliest man of men since borne
His Sons, the fairest of her Daughters *Eve*.
Under a tuft of shade that on a green
Stood whispering soft, by a fresh Fountain side
They sat them down, and after no more toil
Of thir sweet Gardning labour then suffic'd
To recommend coole *Zephyr,* and made ease
More easie, wholsom thirst and appetite   330
More grateful, to thir Supper Fruits they fell,
Nectarine Fruits which the compliant boughes
Yeilded them, side-long as they sat recline
On the soft downie Bank damaskt with flours:
The savourie pulp they chew, and in the rinde
Still as they thirsted scoop the brimming stream;
Nor gentle purpose, nor endearing smiles
Wanted, nor youthful dalliance as beseems
Fair couple, linkt in happie nuptial League,
Alone as they. About them frisking playd   340
All Beasts of th' Earth, since wilde, and of all chase
In Wood or Wilderness, Forrest or Den;
Sporting the Lion rampd, and in his paw
Dandl'd the Kid; Bears, Tygers, Ounces, Pards
Gambold before them, th' unwieldy Elephant
To make them mirth us'd all his might, & wreathd
His Lithe Proboscis; close the Serpent sly
Insinuating, wove with Gordian twine
His breaded train, and of his fatal guile

Gave proof unheeded; others on the grass　　　　　350
Coucht, and now fild with pasture gazing sat,
Or Bedward ruminating: for the Sun
Declin'd was hasting now with prone carreer
To th' Ocean Iles, and in th' ascending Scale
Of Heav'n the Starrs that usher Evening rose:
When *Satan* still in gaze, as first he stood,
Scarce thus at length faild speech recoverd sad.
　O Hell! what doe mine eyes with grief behold,
Into our room of bliss thus high advanc't
Creatures of other mould, earth-born perhaps,　　　360
Not Spirits, yet to heav'nly Spirits bright
Little inferior; whom my thoughts pursue
With wonder, and could love, so lively shines
In them Divine resemblance, and such grace
The hand that formd them on thir shape hath pourd.
Ah gentle pair, yee little think how nigh
Your change approaches, when all these delights
Will vanish and deliver ye to woe,
More woe, the more your taste is now of joy;
Happie, but for so happie ill secur'd　　　　　370
Long to continue, and this high seat your Heav'n
Ill fenc't for Heav'n to keep out such a foe
As now is enterd; yet no purpos'd foe
To you whom I could pittie thus forlorne
Though I unpittied: League with you I seek,
And mutual amitie so streight, so close,
That I with you must dwell, or you with me
Henceforth; my dwelling haply may not please
Like this fair Paradise, your sense, yet such
Accept your Makers work; he gave it me,　　　380
Which I as freely give; Hell shall unfould,
To entertain you two, her widest Gates,
And send forth all her Kings; there will be room,
Not like these narrow limits, to receive
Your numerous ofspring; if no better place,
Thank him who puts me loath to this revenge
On you who wrong me not for him who wrongd.
And should I at your harmless innocence
Melt, as I doe, yet public reason just,
Honour and Empire with revenge enlarg'd,　　　390
By conquering this new World, compels me now
To do what else though damnd I should abhorre.
　So spake the Fiend, and with necessitie,
The Tyrants plea, excus'd his devilish deeds.
Then from his loftie stand on that high Tree
Down he alights among the sportful Herd
Of those fourfooted kindes, himself now one,
Now other, as thir shape servd best his end
Neerer to view his prey, and unespi'd
To mark what of thir state he more might learn　　　400
By word or action markt: about them round
A Lion now he stalkes with fierie glare,

Then as a Tiger, who by chance hath spi'd
In some Purlieu two gentle Fawnes at play,
Strait couches close, then rising changes oft
His couchant watch, as one who chose his ground
Whence rushing he might surest seise them both
Grip't in each paw: when *Adam* first of men
To first of women *Eve* thus moving speech,
Turnd him all eare to heare new utterance flow.   410
   Sole partner and sole part of all these joyes,
Dearer thy self then all; needs must the Power
That made us, and for us this ample World
Be infinitly good, and of his good
As liberal and free as infinite,
That rais'd us from the dust and plac't us here
In all this happiness, who at his hand
Have nothing merited, nor can performe
Aught whereof hee hath need, hee who requires
From us no other service then to keep   420
This one, this easie charge, of all the Trees
In Paradise that beare delicious fruit
So various, not to taste that onely Tree
Of knowledge, planted by the Tree of Life,
So neer grows Death to Life, what ere Death is,
Som dreadful thing no doubt; for well thou knowst
God hath pronounc't it death to taste that Tree,
The only sign of our obedience left
Among so many signes of power and rule
Conferrd upon us, and Dominion giv'n   430
Over all other Creatures that possesse
Earth, Aire, and Sea. Then let us not think hard
One easie prohibition, who enjoy
Free leave so large to all things else, and choice
Unlimited of manifold delights:
But let us ever praise him, and extoll
His bountie, following our delightful task
To prune these growing Plants, & tend these Flours,
Which were it toilsom, yet with thee were sweet.
   To whom thus *Eve* repli'd. O thou for whom   440
And from whom I was formd flesh of thy flesh,
And without whom am to no end, my Guide
And Head, what thou hast said is just and right.
For wee to him indeed all praises owe,
And daily thanks, I chiefly who enjoy
So farr the happier Lot, enjoying thee
Preeminent by so much odds, while thou
Like consort to thy self canst no where find.
That day I oft remember, when from sleep
I first awak't, and found my self repos'd   450
Under a shade on flours, much wondring where
And what I was, whence thither brought, and how.
Not distant far from thence a murmuring sound
Of waters issu'd from a Cave and spread
Into a liquid Plain, then stood unmov'd

Pure as th' expanse of Heav'n; I thither went
With unexperienc't thought, and laid me downe
On the green bank, to look into the cleer
Smooth Lake, that to me seemd another Skie.
As I bent down to look, just opposite,   460
A Shape within the watry gleam appeerd
Bending to look on me, I started back,
It started back, but pleasd I soon returnd,
Pleas'd it returnd as soon with answering looks
Of sympathie and love, there I had fixt
Mine eyes till now, and pin'd with vain desire,
Had not a voice thus warnd me, What thou seest,
What there thou seest fair Creature is thy self,
With thee it came and goes: but follow me,
And I will bring thee where no shadow staies   470
Thy coming, and thy soft imbraces, hee
Whose image thou art, him thou shall enjoy
Inseparablie thine, to him shalt beare
Multitudes like thy self, and thence be call'd
Mother of human Race: what could I doe,
But follow strait, invisibly thus led?
Till I espi'd thee, fair indeed and tall,
Under a Platan, yet methought less faire,
Less winning soft, less amiablie milde,
Then that smooth watry image; back I turnd,   480
Thou following cryd'st aloud, Return fair *Eve,*
Whom fli'st thou? whom thou fli'st, of him thou art,
His flesh, his bone; to give thee being I lent
Out of my side to thee, neerest my heart
Substantial Life, to have thee by my side
Henceforth an individual solace dear;
Part of my Soul I seek thee, and thee claim
My other half: with that thy gentle hand
Seisd mine, I yeilded, and from that time see
How beauty is excelld by manly grace   490
And wisdom, which alone is truly fair.
    So spake our general Mother, and with eyes
Of conjugal attraction unreprov'd,
And meek surrender, half imbracing leand
On our first Father, half her swelling Breast
Naked met his under the flowing Gold
Of her loose tresses hid: he in delight
Both of her Beauty and submissive Charms
Smil'd with superior Love, as *Jupiter*
On *Juno* smiles, when he impregns the Clouds   500
That shed *May* Flowers; and press'd her Matron lip
With kisses pure: aside the Devil turnd
For envie, yet with jealous leer maligne
Ey'd them askance, and to himself thus plaind.
    Sight hateful, sight tormenting! thus these two
Imparadis't in one anothers arms
The happier *Eden,* shall enjoy thir fill
Of bliss on bliss. while I to Hell am thrust,

Where neither joy nor love, but fierce desire,
Among our other torments not the least,   510
Still unfulfill'd with pain of longing pines;
Yet let me not forget what I have gain'd
From thir own mouths; all is not theirs it seems:
One fatal Tree there stands of Knowledge call'd,
Forbidden them to taste: Knowledge forbidd'n?
Suspicious, reasonless. Why should thir Lord
Envie them that? can it be sin to know,
Can it be death? and do they onely stand
By Ignorance, is that thir happie state,
The proof of thir obedience and thir faith?   520
O fair foundation laid whereon to build
Thir ruine! Hence I will excite thir minds
With more desire to know, and to reject
Envious commands, invented with designe
To keep them low whom knowledge might exalt
Equal with Gods; aspiring to be such,
They taste and die: what likelier can ensue?
But first with narrow search I must walk round
This Garden, and no corner leave unspi'd;
A chance but chance may lead where I may meet   530
Some wandring Spirit of Heav'n, by Fountain side,
Or in thick shade retir'd, from him to draw
What further would be learnt. Live while ye may,
Yet happie pair; enjoy, till I return,
Short pleasures, for long woes are to succeed.
    So saying, his proud step he scornful turn'd,
But with sly circumspection, and began
Through wood, through waste, o're hil, o're dale his roam.
Mean while in utmost Longitude, where Heav'n
With Earth and Ocean meets, the setting Sun   540
Slowly descended, and with right aspect
Against the eastern Gate of Paradise
Leveld his eevning Rayes: it was a Rock
Of Alablaster, pil'd up to the Clouds,
Conspicuous farr, winding with one ascent
Accessible from Earth, one entrance high;
The rest was craggie cliff, that overhung
Still as it rose, impossible to climbe.
Betwixt these rockie Pillars *Gabriel* sat
Chief of th' Angelic Guards, awaiting night;   550
About him exercis'd Heroic Games
Th' unarmed Youth of Heav'n, but nigh at hand
Celestial Armourie, Shields, Helmes, and Speares
Hung high with Diamond flaming, and with Gold.
Thither came *Uriel*, gliding through the Eeven
On a Sun beam, swift as a shooting Starr
In *Autumn* thwarts the night, when vapors fir'd
Impress the Air, and shews the Mariner
From what point of his Compass to beware
Impetuous winds: he thus began in haste.   560
    Gabriel, to thee thy cours by Lot hath giv'n

Charge and strict watch that to this happie place
No evil thing approach or enter in;
This day at highth of Noon came to my Spheare
A Spirit, zealous, as he seem'd, to know
More of th' Almighties works, and chiefly Man
Gods latest Image: I describ'd his way
Bent all on speed, and markt his Aerie Gate;
But in the Mount that lies from *Eden* North,
Where he first lighted, soon discernd his looks   570
Alien from Heav'n, with passions foul obscur'd:
Mine eye pursu'd him still, but under shade
Lost sight of him; one of the banisht crew
I fear, hath ventur'd from the deep, to raise
New troubles; him thy care must be to find.
    To whom the winged Warriour thus returnd:
Uriel, no wonder if thy perfet sight,
Amid the Suns bright circle where thou sitst,
See farr and wide: in at this Gate none pass
The vigilance here plac't, but such as come   580
Well known from Heav'n; and since Meridian hour
No Creature thence: if Spirit of other sort,
So minded, have oreleapt these earthie bounds
On purpose, hard thou knowst it to exclude
Spiritual substance with corporeal barr.
But if within the circuit of these walks
In whatsoever shape he lurk, of whom
Thou telst, by morrow dawning I shall know.
    So promis'd hee, and *Uriel* to his charge
Returnd on that bright beam, whose point now raisd   590
Bore him slope downward to the Sun now fall'n
Beneath th' *Azores;* whither the prime Orb,
Incredible how swift, had thither rowl'd
Diurnal, or this less volubil Earth
By shorter flight to th' East, had left him there
Arraying with reflected Purple and Gold
The Clouds that on his Western Throne attend:
Now came still Eevning on, and Twilight gray
Had in her sober Liverie all things clad;
Silence accompanied, for Beast and Bird,   600
They to thir grassie Couch, these to thir Nests
Were slunk, all but the wakeful Nightingale;
She all night long her amorous descant sung;
Silence was pleas'd: now glow'd the Firmament
With living Saphirs: *Hesperus* that led
The starrie Host, rode brightest, till the Moon
Rising in clouded Majestie, at length
Apparent Queen unvaild her peerless light,
And o're the dark her Silver Mantle threw.
    When *Adam* thus to *Eve:* Fair Consort, th' hour   6
Of night, and all things now retir'd to rest
Mind us of like repose, since God hath set
Labour and rest, as day and night to men
Successive, and the timely dew of sleep

Now falling with soft slumbrous weight inclines
Our eye-lids; other Creatures all day long
Rove idle unimploid, and less need rest;
Man hath his daily work of body or mind
Appointed, which declares his Dignitie,
And the regard of Heav'n on all his waies;   620
While other Animals unactive range,
And of thir doings God takes no account.
To morrow ere fresh Morning streak the East
With first approach of light, we must be ris'n,
And at our pleasant labour, to reform
Yon flourie Arbors, yonder Allies green,
Our walks at noon, with branches overgrown,
That mock our scant manuring, and require
More hands then ours to lop thir wanton growth:
Those Blossoms also, and those dropping Gumms,   630
That lie bestrowne unsightly and unsmooth,
Ask riddance, if we mean to tread with ease;
Mean while, as Nature wills, Night bids us rest.
  To whom thus *Eve* with perfet beauty adornd.
My Author and Disposer, what thou bidst
Unargu'd I obey; so God ordains,
God is thy Law, thou mine: to know no more
Is womans happiest knowledge and her praise.
With thee conversing I forget all time,
All seasons and thir change, all please alike.   640
Sweet is the breath of morn, her rising sweet,
With charm of earliest Birds; pleasant the Sun
When first on this delightful Land he spreads
His orient Beams, on herb, tree, fruit, and flour,
Glistring with dew; fragrant the fertil earth
After soft showers; and sweet the coming on
Of grateful Eevning milde, then silent Night
With this her solemn Bird and this fair Moon,
And these the Gemms of Heav'n, her starrie train:
But neither breath of Morn when she ascends   650
With charm of earliest Birds, nor rising Sun
On this delightful land, nor herb, fruit, floure,
Glistring with dew, nor fragrance after showers,
Nor grateful Evening mild, nor silent Night
With this her solemn Bird, nor walk by Moon,
Or glittering Starr-light without thee is sweet.
But wherfore all night long shine these, for whom
This glorious sight, when sleep hath shut all eyes?
  To whom our general Ancestor repli'd.
Daughter of God and Man, accomplisht *Eve,*   660
Those have thir course to finish, round the Earth,
By morrow Eevning, and from Land to Land
In order, though to Nations yet unborn,
Ministring light prepar'd, they set and rise;
Least total darkness should by Night regaine
Her old possession, and extinguish life
In Nature and all things, which these soft fires

Not only enlighten, but with kindly heate
Of various influence foment and warme,
Temper or nourish, or in part shed down   670
Thir stellar vertue on all kinds that grow
On Earth, made hereby apter to receive
Perfection from the Suns more potent Ray.
These then, though unbeheld in deep of night,
Shine not in vain, nor think, though men were none,
That heav'n would want spectators, God want praise;
Millions of spiritual Creatures walk the Earth
Unseen, both when we wake, and when we sleep:
All these with ceaseless praise his works behold
Both day and night: how often from the steep   680
Of echoing Hill or Thicket have we heard
Celestial voices to the midnight air,
Sole, or responsive each to others note
Singing thir great Creator: oft in bands
While they keep watch, or nightly rounding walk
With Heav'nly touch of instrumental sounds
In full harmonic number joind, thir songs
Divide the night, and lift our thoughts to Heaven.
    Thus talking hand in hand alone they pass'd
On to thir blissful Bower; it was a place   690
Chos'n by the sovran Planter, when he fram'd
All things to mans delightful use; the roofe
Of thickest covert was inwoven shade
Laurel and Mirtle, and what higher grew
Of firm and fragrant leaf; on either side
Acanthus, and each odorous bushie shrub
Fenc'd up the verdant wall; each beauteous flour,
Iris all hues, Roses, and Gessamin
Rear'd high thir flourisht heads between, and wrought
Mosaic; underfoot the Violet,   700
Crocus, and Hyacinth with rich inlay
Broiderd the ground, more colour'd then with stone
Of costliest Emblem: other Creature here
Beast, Bird, Insect, or Worm durst enter none;
Such was thir awe of man. In shadier Bower
More sacred and sequesterd, though but feignd,
Pan or *Silvanus* never slept, nor Nymph,
Nor *Faunus* haunted. Here in close recess
With Flowers, Garlands, and sweet-smelling Herbs
Espoused *Eve* deckt first her Nuptial Bed,   710
And heav'nly Quires the Hymenæan sung,
What day the genial Angel to our Sire
Brought her in naked beauty more adorn'd,
More lovely then *Pandora,* whom the Gods
Endowd with all thir gifts, and O too like
In sad event, when to the unwiser Son
Of *Japhet* brought by *Hermes,* she ensnar'd
Mankind with her faire looks, to be aveng'd
On him who had stole *Joves* authentic fire.
    Thus at thir shadie Lodge arriv'd, both stood,   720

Both turnd, and under op'n Skie ador'd
The God that made both Skie, Air, Earth & Heav'n
Which they beheld, the Moons resplendent Globe
And starrie Pole: Thou also mad'st the Night,
Maker Omnipotent, and thou the Day,
Which we in our appointed work imployd
Have finisht happie in our mutual help
And mutual love, the Crown of all our bliss
Ordain'd by thee, and this delicious place
For us too large, where thy abundance wants   730
Partakers, and uncropt falls to the ground.
But thou hast promis'd from us two a Race
To fill the Earth, who shall with us extoll
Thy goodness infinite, both when we wake,
And when we seek, as now, thy gift of sleep.
     This said unanimous, and other Rites
Observing none, but adoration pure
Which God likes best, into thir inmost bower
Handed they went; and eas'd the putting off
These troublesom disguises which wee wear,   740
Strait side by side were laid, nor turnd I weene
Adam from his fair Spouse, nor *Eve* the Rites
Mysterious of connubial Love refus'd:
Whatever Hypocrites austerely talk
Of puritie and place and innocence,
Defaming as impure what God declares
Pure, and commands to som, leaves free to all.
Our Maker bids increase, who bids abstain
But our Destroyer, foe to God and Man?
Haile wedded Love, mysterious Law, true sourse   750
Of human ofspring, sole proprietie,
In Paradise of all things common else.
By thee adulterous lust was driv'n from men
Among the bestial herds to raunge, by thee
Founded in Reason, Loyal, Just, and Pure,
Relations dear, and all the Charities
Of Father, Son, and Brother first were known.
Farr be it, that I should write thee sin or blame,
Or think thee unbefitting holiest place,
Perpetual Fountain of Domestic sweets,   760
Whose Bed is undefil'd and chast pronounc't,
Present, or past, as Saints and Patriarchs us'd.
Here Love his golden shafts imploies, here lights
His constant Lamp, and waves his purple wings,
Reigns here and revels; not in the bought smile
Of Harlots, loveless, joyless, unindeard,
Casual fruition, nor in Court Amours
Mixt Dance, or wanton Mask, or Midnight Bal,
Or Serenate, which the starv'd Lover sings
To his proud fair, best quitted with disdain.   770
These lulld by Nightingales imbraceing slept,
And on thir naked limbs the flourie roof
Showrd Roses, which the Morn repair'd. Sleep on,

Blest pair; and O yet happiest if ye seek
No happier state, and know to know no more.
  Now had night measur'd with her shaddowie Cone
Half way up Hill this vast Sublunar Vault,
And from thir Ivorie Port the Cherubim
Forth issuing at th' accustomd hour stood armd
To thir night watches in warlike Parade,   780
When *Gabriel* to his next in power thus spake.
  Uzziel, half these draw off, and coast the South
With strictest watch; these other wheel the North,
Our circuit meets full West. As flame they part
Half wheeling to the Shield, half to the Spear.
From these, two strong and suttle Spirits he calld
That neer him stood, and gave them thus in charge.
  Ithuriel and *Zephon,* with wingd speed
Search through this Garden, leav unsearcht no nook,
But chiefly where those two fair Creatures Lodge,   790
Now laid perhaps asleep secure of harme.
This Eevning from the Sun's decline arriv'd
Who tells of som infernal Spirit seen
Hitherward bent (who could have thought?) escap'd
The barrs of Hell, on errand bad no doubt:
Such where ye find, seise fast, and hither bring.
  So saying, on he led his radiant Files,
Daz'ling the Moon; these to the Bower direct
In search of whom they sought: him there they found
Squat like a Toad, close at the eare of *Eve;*   800
Assaying by his Devilish art to reach
The Organs of her Fancie, and with them forge
Illusions as he list, Phantasms and Dreams,
Or if, inspiring venom, he might taint
Th' animal Spirits that from pure blood arise
Like gentle breaths from Rivers pure, thence raise
At least distemperd, discontented thoughts,
Vain hopes, vain aimes, inordinate desires
Blown up with high conceits ingendring pride.
Him thus intent *Ithuriel* with his Spear   810
Touch'd lightly; for no falshood can endure
Touch of Celestial temper, but returns
Of force to its own likeness: up he starts
Discoverd and surpriz'd. As when a spark
Lights on a heap of nitrous Powder, laid
Fit for the Tun som Magazin to store
Against a rumord Warr, the Smuttie graine
With sudden blaze diffus'd, inflames the Aire:
So started up in his own shape the Fiend.
Back stept those two fair Angels half amaz'd   820
So sudden to behold the grieslie King;
Yet thus, unmovd with fear, accost him soon.
  Which of those rebell Spirits adjudg'd to Hell
Com'st thou, escap'd thy prison, and transform'd,
Why satst thou like an enemie in waite
Here watching at the head of these that sleep?

Know ye not then said *Satan,* filld with scorn,
Know ye not me? ye knew me once no mate
For you, there sitting where ye durst not soare;
Not to know mee argues your selves unknown,   830
The lowest of your throng; or if ye know,
Why ask ye, and superfluous begin
Your message, like to end as much in vain?
To whom thus *Zephon,* answering scorn with scorn.
Think not, revolted Spirit, thy shape the same,
Or undiminisht brightness, to be known
As when thou stoodst in Heav'n upright and pure;
That Glorie then, when thou no more wast good,
Departed from thee, and thou resembl'st now
Thy sin and place of doom obscure and foule.   840
But come, for thou, be sure, shalt give account
To him who sent us, whose charge is to keep
This place inviolable, and these from harm.
    So spake the Cherube, and his grave rebuke
Severe in youthful beautie, added grace
Invincible: abasht the Devil stood,
And felt how awful goodness is, and saw
Vertue in her shape how lovly, saw, and pin'd
His loss; but chiefly to find here observd
His lustre visibly impar'd; yet seemd   850
Undaunted. If I must contend, said he,
Best with the best, the Sender not the sent,
Or all at once; more glorie will be wonn,
Or less be lost. Thy fear, said *Zephon* bold,
Will save us trial what the least can doe
Single against thee wicked, and thence weak.
    The Fiend repli'd not, overcome with rage;
But like a proud Steed reind, went hautie on,
Chaumping his iron curb: to strive or flie
He held it vain; awe from above had quelld   860
His heart, not else dismai'd. Now drew they nigh
The western point, where those half-rounding guards
Just met, & closing stood in squadron joind
Awaiting next command. To whom thir Chief
Gabriel from the Front thus calld aloud.
    O friends, I hear the tread of nimble feet
Hasting this way, and now by glimps discerne
Ithuriel and *Zephon* through the shade,
And with them comes a third of Regal port,
But faded splendor wan; who by his gate   870
And fierce demeanour seems the Prince of Hell,
Not likely to part hence without contest;
Stand firm, for in his look defiance lours.
    He scarce had ended, when those two approachd
And brief related whom they brought, wher found,
How busied, in what form and posture coucht.
    To whom with stern regard thus *Gabriel* spake.
Why hast thou, *Satan,* broke the bounds prescrib'd
To thy transgressions, and disturbd the charge

Of others, who approve not to transgress　　　　　　　　880
By thy example, but have power and right
To question thy bold entrance on this place;
Imploi'd it seems to violate sleep, and those
Whose dwelling God hath planted here in bliss?
　　To whom thus *Satan* with contemptuous brow.
Gabriel, thou hadst in Heav'n th' esteem of wise,
And such I held thee; but this question askt
Puts me in doubt. Lives ther who loves his pain?
Who would not, finding way, break loose from Hell,
Though thither doomd? Thou wouldst thy self, no doubt,　　890
And boldly venture to whatever place
Farthest from pain, where thou mightst hope to change
Torment with ease, & soonest recompence
Dole with delight, which in this place I sought;
To thee no reason; who knowst only good,
But evil hast not tri'd: and wilt object
His will who bound us? let him surer barr
His Iron Gates, if he intends our stay
In that dark durance: thus much what was askt.
The rest is true, they found me where they say;　　900
But that implies not violence or harme.
　　Thus hee in scorn. The warlike Angel mov'd,
Disdainfully half smiling thus repli'd.
O loss of one in Heav'n to judge of wise,
Since *Satan* fell, whom follie overthrew,
And now returns him from his prison scap't,
Gravely in doubt whether to hold them wise
Or not, who ask what boldness brought him hither
Unlicenc't from his bounds in Hell prescrib'd;
So wise he judges it to fly from pain　　910
However, and to scape his punishment.
So judge thou still, presumptuous, till the wrauth,
Which thou incurr'st by flying, meet thy flight
Seavenfold, and scourge that wisdom back to Hell,
Which taught thee yet no better, that no pain
Can equal anger infinite provok't.
But wherefore thou alone? wherefore with thee
Came not all Hell broke loose? is pain to them
Less pain, less to be fled, or thou then they
Less hardie to endure? courageous Chief,　　920
The first in flight from pain, had'st thou alleg'd
To thy deserted host this cause of flight,
Thou surely hadst not come sole fugitive.
　　To which the Fiend thus answerd frowning stern.
Not that I less endure, or shrink from pain,
Insulting Angel, well thou knowst I stood
Thy fiercest, when in Battel to thy aide
The blasting volied Thunder made all speed
And seconded thy else not dreaded Spear.
But still thy words at random, as before,　　930
Argue thy inexperience what behooves
From hard assaies and ill successes past

A faithful Leader, not to hazard all
Through wayes of danger by himself untri'd.
I therefore, I alone first undertook
To wing the desolate Abyss, and spie
This new created World, whereof in Hell
Fame is not silent, here in hope to find
Better abode, and my afflicted Powers
To settle here on Earth, or in mid Aire;   940
Though for possession put to try once more
What thou and thy gay Legions dare against;
Whose easier business were to serve thir Lord
High up in Heav'n, with songs to hymne his **Throne,**
And practis'd distances to cringe, not fight.
    To whom the warriour Angel soon repli'd.
To say and strait unsay, pretending first
Wise to flie pain, professing next the Spie,
Argues no Leader, but a lyar trac't,
Satan, and couldst thou faithful add? O name,   950
O sacred name of faithfulness profan'd!
Faithful to whom? to thy rebellious crew?
Armie of Fiends, fit body to fit head;
Was this your discipline and faith ingag'd,
Your military obedience, to dissolve
Allegeance to th' acknowledg'd Power supream?
And thou sly hypocrite, who now wouldst seem
Patron of liberty, who more then thou
Once fawn'd, and cring'd, and servilly ador'd
Heav'ns awful Monarch? wherefore but in hope   96·
To dispossess him, and thy self to reigne?
But mark what I arreede thee now, avant;
Flie thither whence thou fledst: if from this houre
Within these hallowd limits thou appeer,
Back to th' infernal pit I drag thee chaind,
And Seale thee so, as henceforth not to scorne
The facil gates of hell too slightly barrd.
    So threatn'd hee, but *Satan* to no threats
Gave heed, but waxing more in rage repli'd.
    Then when I am thy captive talk of chaines,   970
Proud limitarie Cherube, but ere then
Farr heavier load thy self expect to feel
From my prevailing arme, though Heavens King
Ride on thy wings, and thou with thy Compeers,
Us'd to the yoak, draw'st his triumphant wheels
In progress through the rode of Heav'n Star-pav'd.
    While thus he spake, th' Angelic Squadron bright
Turnd fierie red, sharpning in mooned hornes
Thir Phalanx, and began to hemm him round
With ported Spears, as thick as when a field   980
Of *Ceres* ripe for harvest waving bends
Her bearded Grove of ears, which way the wind
Swayes them; the careful Plowman doubting stands
Least on the threshing floore his hopeful sheaves
Prove chaff. On th' other side *Satan* allarm'd

Collecting all his might dilated stood,
Like *Teneriff* or *Atlas* unremov'd:
His stature reacht the Skie, and on his Crest
Sat horror Plum'd; nor wanted in his graspe
What seemd both Spear and Shield: now dreadful deeds
Might have ensu'd, nor onely Paradise
In this commotion, but the Starrie Cope
Of Heav'n perhaps, or all the Elements
At least had gon to rack, disturbd and torne
With violence of this conflict, had not soon
Th' Eternal to prevent such horrid fray
Hung forth in Heav'n his golden Scales, yet seen
Betwixt *Astrea* and the *Scorpion* signe,
Wherein all things created first he weighd,
The pendulous round Earth with ballanc't Aire
In counterpoise, now ponders all events,
Battels and Realms: in these he put two weights
The sequel each of parting and of fight;
The latter quick up flew, and kickt the beam;
Which *Gabriel* spying, thus bespake the Fiend.
    Satan, I know thy strength, and thou knowst mine,
Neither our own but giv'n; what follie then
To boast what Arms can doe, since thine no more
Then Heav'n permits, nor mine, though doubld now
To trample thee as mire: for proof look up,
And read thy Lot in yon celestial Sign
Where thou art weigh'd, & shown how light, how weak,
If thou resist. The Fiend lookt up and knew
His mounted scale aloft: nor more; but fled
Murmuring, and with him fled the shades of night.

The End of the Fourth Book.

PARADISE LOST.

BOOK V.

The Argument.

Morning approach't, Eve *relates to* Adam *her troublesome dream; he likes it not, yet comforts her: They come forth to thir day labours: Thir Morning Hymn at the Door of thir Bower. God to render Man inexcusable sends* Raphael *to admonish him of his obedience, of his free estate, of his enemy near at hand; who he is, and why his enemy, and whatever else may avail* Adam *to know.* Raphael *comes down to Paradise, his appearance describ'd, his coming discern'd by* Adam *afar off sitting at the door of his Bower; he goes out to meet him, brings him to his lodge, entertains him with the choycest fruits of Paradise got together by* Eve; *thir discourse at Table:* Raphael *performs his message, minds* Adam *of his state and of his enemy; relates at* Adams *request who that enemy is, and how he came to be so, beginning from his first revolt in Heaven, and the occasion thereof; how he drew his Legions after him to the parts of the North, and there incited them to rebel with him, perswading all but only* Abdiel *a Seraph, who in Argument dissuades and opposes him, then forsakes him.*

Now Morn her rosie steps in th' Eastern Clime
Advancing, sow'd the Earth with Orient Pearle,
When *Adam* wak't, so customd, for his sleep
Was Aerie light, from pure digestion bred,

990

1000

1010

And temperat vapors bland, which th' only sound
Of leaves and fuming rills, *Aurora's* fan,
Lightly dispers'd, and the shrill Matin Song
Of Birds on every bough; so much the more
His wonder was to find unwak'nd *Eve*
With Tresses discompos'd, and glowing Cheek,   10
As through unquiet rest: he on his side
Leaning half-rais'd, with looks of cordial Love
Hung over her enamour'd, and beheld
Beautie, which whether waking or asleep,
Shot forth peculiar Graces; then with voice
Milde, as when *Zephyrus* on *Flora* breathes,
Her hand soft touching, whisperd thus. Awake
My fairest, my espous'd, my latest found,
Heav'ns last best gift, my ever new delight,
Awake, the morning shines, and the fresh field   20
Calls us, we lose the prime, to mark how spring
Our tended Plants, how blows the Citron Grove,
What drops the Myrrhe, & what the balmie Reed,
How Nature paints her colours, how the Bee
Sits on the Bloom extracting liquid sweet.
     Such whispering wak'd her, but with startl'd eye
On *Adam,* whom imbracing, thus she spake.
     O Sole in whom my thoughts find all repose,
My Glorie, my Perfection, glad I see
Thy face, and Morn return'd, for I this Night,   30
Such night till this I never pass'd, have dream'd,
If dream'd, not as I oft am wont, of thee,
Works of day pass't, or morrows next designe,
But of offence and trouble, which my mind
Knew never till this irksom night; methought
Close at mine ear one call'd me forth to walk
With gentle voice, I thought it thine; it said,
Why sleepst thou *Eve?* now is the pleasant time,
The cool, the silent, save where silence yields
To the night-warbling Bird, that now awake   40
Tunes sweetest his love-labor'd song; now reignes
Full Orb'd the Moon, and with more pleasing light
Shadowie sets off the face of things; in vain,
If none regard; Heav'n wakes with all his eyes,
Whom to behold but thee, Natures desire,
In whose sight all things joy, with ravishment
Attracted by thy beauty still to gaze.
I rose as at thy call, but found thee not;
To find thee I directed then my walk;
And on, methought, alone I pass'd through ways   50
That brought me on a sudden to the Tree
Of interdicted Knowledge: fair it seem'd,
Much fairer to my Fancie then by day:
And as I wondring lookt, beside it stood
One shap'd & wing'd like one of those from Heav'n
By us oft seen; his dewie locks distill'd
Ambrosia; on that Tree he also gaz'd;

And O fair Plant, said he, with fruit surcharg'd,
Deigns none to ease thy load and taste thy sweet,
Nor God, nor Man; is Knowledge so despis'd?   60
Or envie, or what reserve forbids to taste?
Forbid who will, none shall from me withhold
Longer thy offerd good, why else set here?
This said he paus'd not, but with ventrous Arme
He pluckt, he tasted; mee damp horror chil'd
At such bold words voucht with a deed so bold:
But he thus overjoy'd, O Fruit Divine,
Sweet of thy self, but much more sweet thus cropt,
Forbidd'n here, it seems, as onely fit
For Gods, yet able to make Gods of Men: 70
And why not Gods of Men, since good, the more
Communicated, more abundant growes,
The Author not impair'd, but honourd more?
Here, happie Creature, fair Angelic *Eve,*
Partake thou also; happie though thou art,
Happier thou mayst be, worthier canst not be:
Taste this, and be henceforth among the Gods
Thy self a Goddess, not to Earth confind,
But somtimes in the Air, as wee, somtimes
Ascend to Heav'n, by merit thine, and see   80
What life the Gods live there, and such live thou.
So saying, he drew nigh, and to me held,
Even to my mouth of that same fruit held part
Which he had pluckt; the pleasant savourie smell
So quick'nd appetite, that I, methought,
Could not but taste. Forthwith up to the Clouds
With him I flew, and underneath beheld
The Earth outstretcht immense, a prospect wide
And various: wondring at my flight and change
To this high exaltation; suddenly   90
My Guide was gon, and I, me thought, sunk down,
And fell asleep; but O how glad I wak'd
To find this but a dream! Thus *Eve* her Night
Related, and thus *Adam* answerd sad.
  Best Image of my self and dearer half,
The trouble of thy thoughts this night in sleep
Affects me equally; nor can I like
This uncouth dream, of evil sprung I fear;
Yet evil whence? in thee can harbour none,
Created pure. But know that in the Soule   100
Are many lesser Faculties that serve
Reason as chief; among these Fansie next
Her office holds; of all external things,
Which the five watchful Senses represent,
She forms Imaginations, Aerie shapes,
Which Reason joyning or disjoyning, frames
All what we affirm or what deny, and call
Our knowledge or opinion; then retires
Into her private Cell when Nature rests.
Oft in her absence mimic Fansie wakes   110

To imitate her; but misjoyning shapes,
Wilde work produces oft, and most in dreams,
Ill matching words and deeds long past or late.
Som such resemblances methinks I find
Of our last Eevnings talk, in this thy dream,
But with addition strange; yet be not sad.
Evil into the mind of God or Man
May come and go, so unapprov'd, and leave
No spot or blame behind: Which gives me hope
That what in sleep thou didst abhorr to dream,   120
Waking thou never wilt consent to do.
Be not disheart'nd then, nor cloud those looks
That wont to be more chearful and serene
Then when fair Morning first smiles on the World,
And let us to our fresh imployments rise
Among the Groves, the Fountains, and the Flours
That open now thir choicest bosom'd smells
Reservd from night, and kept for thee in store.
  So cheard he his fair Spouse, and she was cheard,
But silently a gentle tear let fall   130
From either eye, and wip'd them with her haire;
Two other precious drops that ready stood,
Each in thir chrystal sluce, hee ere they fell
Kiss'd as the gracious signs of sweet remorse
And pious awe, that feard to have offended.
  So all was cleard, and to the Field they haste.
But first from under shadie arborous roof,
Soon as they forth were come to open sight
Of day-spring, and the Sun, who scarce up risen
With wheels yet hov'ring o're the Ocean brim,   140
Shot paralel to the earth his dewie ray,
Discovering in wide Lantskip all the East
Of Paradise and *Edens* happie Plains,
Lowly they bow'd adoring, and began
Thir Orisons, each Morning duly paid
In various style, for neither various style
Nor holy rapture wanted they to praise
Thir Maker, in fit strains pronounc't or sung
Unmeditated, such prompt eloquence
Flowd from thir lips, in Prose or numerous Verse,   150
More tuneable then needed Lute or Harp
To add more sweetness, and they thus began.
  These are thy glorious works, Parent of good,
Almightie, thine this universal Frame,
Thus wondrous fair; thy self how wondrous then!
Unspeakable, who sitst above these Heavens
To us invisible or dimly seen
In these thy lowest works, yet these declare
Thy goodness beyond thought, and Power Divine:
Speak yee who best can tell, ye Sons of light,   160
Angels, for yee behold him, and with songs
And choral symphonies, Day without Night,
Circle his Throne rejoycing, yee in Heav'n,

On Earth joyn all yee Creatures to extoll
Him first, him last, him midst, and without end.
Fairest of Starrs, last in the train of Night,
If better thou belong not to the dawn,
Sure pledge of day, that crownst the smiling Morn
With thy bright Circlet, praise him in thy Spheare
While day arises, that sweet hour of Prime.
Thou Sun, of this great World both Eye and Soule,   170
Acknowledge him thy Greater, sound his praise
In thy eternal course, both when thou climb'st,
And when high Noon hast gaind, & when thou fallst.
Moon, that now meetst the orient Sun, now fli'st
With the fixt Starrs, fixt in thir Orb that flies,
And yee five other wandring Fires that move
In mystic Dance not without Song, resound
His praise, who out of Darkness call'd up Light.
Aire, and ye Elements the eldest birth   180
Of Natures Womb, that in quaternion run
Perpetual Circle, multiform; and mix
And nourish all things, let your ceaseless change
Varie to our great Maker still new praise.
Ye Mists and Exhalations that now rise
From Hill or steaming Lake, duskie or grey,
Till the Sun paint your fleecie skirts with Gold,
In honour to the Worlds great Author rise,
Whether to deck with Clouds the uncolourd skie,
Or wet the thirstie Earth with falling showers,   190
Rising or falling still advance his praise.
His praise ye Winds, that from four Quarters blow,
Breathe soft or loud; and wave your tops, ye Pines,
With every Plant, in sign of Worship wave.
Fountains and yee, that warble, as ye flow,
Melodious murmurs, warbling tune his praise.
Joyn voices all ye living Souls, ye Birds,
That singing up to Heaven Gate ascend,
Bear on your wings and in your notes his praise;
Yee that in Waters glide, and yee that walk   200
The Earth, and stately tread, or lowly creep;
Witness if I be silent, Morn or Eeven,
To Hill, or Valley, Fountain, or fresh shade
Made vocal by my Song, and taught his praise.
Hail universal Lord, be bounteous still
To give us onely good; and if the night
Have gathered aught of evil or conceald,
Disperse it, as now light dispels the dark.
  So pray'd they innocent, and to thir thoughts
Firm peace recovered soon and wonted calm.   210
On to thir mornings rural work they haste
Among sweet dewes and flours; where any row
Of Fruit-trees overwoodie reachd too farr
Thir pamperd boughes, and needed hands to check
Fruitless imbraces: or they led the Vine
To wed her Elm; she spous'd about him twines

Her mariageable arms, and with her brings
Her dowr th' adopted Clusters, to adorn
His barren leaves. Them thus imploid beheld
With pittie Heav'ns high King, and to him call'd   220
Raphael, the sociable Spirit, that deign'd
To travel with *Tobias,* and secur'd
His marriage with the seaventimes-wedded Maid.
   Raphael, said hee, thou hear'st what stir on Earth
Satan from Hell scap't through the darksom Gulf
Hath raisd in Paradise, and how disturbd
This night the human pair, how he designes
In them at once to ruin all mankind.
Go therefore, half this day as friend with friend
Converse with *Adam,* in what Bowre or shade   230
Thou find'st him from the heat of Noon retir'd,
To respit his day-labour with repast,
Or with repose; and such discourse bring on,
As may advise him of his happie state,
Happiness in his power left free to will,
Left to his own free Will, his Will though free,
Yet mutable; whence warne him to beware
He swerve not too secure: tell him withall
His danger, and from whom, what enemie
Late falln himself from Heav'n, is plotting now   240
The fall of others from like state of bliss;
By violence, no, for that shall be withstood,
But by deceit and lies; this let him know,
Least wilfully transgressing he pretend
Surprisal, unadmonisht, unforewarnd.
   So spake th' Eternal Father, and fulfilld
All Justice: nor delaid the winged Saint
After his charge receivd; but from among
Thousand Celestial Ardors, where he stood
Vaild with his gorgeous wings, up springing light   250
Flew through the midst of Heav'n; th' angelic Quires
On each hand parting, to his speed gave way
Through all th' Empyreal road; till at the Gate
Of Heav'n arriv'd, the gate self-opend wide
On golden Hinges turning, as by work
Divine the sov'ran Architect had fram'd.
From hence, no cloud, or, to obstruct his sight,
Starr interpos'd, however small he sees,
Not unconform to other shining Globes,
Earth and the Gard'n of God, with Cedars crownd   260
Above all Hills. As when by night the Glass
Of *Galileo,* less assur'd, observes
Imagind Lands and Regions in the Moon:
Or Pilot from amidst the *Cyclades*
Delos or *Samos* first appeering kenns
A cloudy spot. Down thither prone in flight
He speeds, and through the vast Ethereal Skie
Sailes between worlds & worlds, with steddie wing
Now on the polar windes, then with quick Fann

Winnows the buxom Air; till within soare
Of Towring Eagles, to all the Fowles he seems
A *Phœnix,* gaz'd by all, as that sole Bird   270
When to enshrine his reliques in the Sun's
Bright Temple, to *Ægyptian Theb's* he flies.
At once on th' Eastern cliff of Paradise
He lights, and to his proper shape returns
A Seraph wingd; six wings he wore, to shade
His lineaments Divine; the pair that clad
Each shoulder broad, came mantling o're his brest
With regal Ornament; the middle pair   280
Girt like a Starrie Zone his waste, and round
Skirted his loines and thighes with downie Gold
And colours dipt in Heav'n; the third his feet
Shaddowd from either heele with featherd maile
Skie-tinctur'd grain. Like *Maia's* son he stood,
And shook his Plumes, that Heav'nly fragrance filld
The circuit wide. Strait knew him all the Bands
Of Angels under watch; and to his state,
And to his message high in honour rise;
For on som message high they guessd him bound.   290
Thir glittering Tents he passd, and now is come
Into the blissful field, through Groves of Myrrhe,
And flouring Odours, Cassia, Nard, and Balme;
A Wilderness of sweets; for Nature here
Wantond as in her prime, and plaid at will
Her Virgin Fancies, pouring forth more sweet,
Wilde above rule or Art; enormous bliss.
Him through the spicie Forrest onward com
Adam discernd, as in the dore he sat
Of his coole Bowre, while now the mounted Sun   300
Shot down direct his fervid Raies to warme
Earths inmost womb, more warmth then *Adam* needs;
And *Eve* within, due at her hour prepar'd
For dinner savourie fruits, of taste to please
True appetite, and not disrelish thirst
Of nectarous draughts between, from milkie stream,
Berrie or Grape: to whom thus *Adam* call'd.
     Haste hither *Eve,* and worth thy sight behold
Eastward among those Trees, what glorious shape
Comes this way moving; seems another Morn   310
Ris'n on mid-noon; som great behest from Heav'n
To us perhaps he brings, and will voutsafe
This day to be our Guest. But goe with speed,
And what thy stores contain, bring forth and poure
Abundance, fit to honour and receive
Our Heav'nly stranger; well we may afford
Our givers thir own gifts, and large bestow
From large bestowd, where Nature multiplies
Her fertil growth, and by disburd'ning grows
More fruitful, which instructs us not to spare.   320
     To whom thus *Eve. Adam,* earths hallowd mould,
Of God inspir'd, small store will serve. where store,

All seasons, ripe for use hangs on the stalk;
Save what by frugal storing firmness gains
To nourish, and superfluous moist consumes:
But I will haste and from each bough and break,
Each Plant & juciest Gourd will pluck such choice
To entertain our Angel guest, as hee
Beholding shall confess that here on Earth
God hath dispenst his bounties as in Heav'n.   330
   So saying, with dispatchful looks in haste
She turns, on hospitable thoughts intent
What choice to chuse for delicacie best,
What order, so contriv'd as not to mix
Tastes, not well joynd, inelegant, but bring
Taste after taste upheld with kindliest change,
Bestirs her then, and from each tender stalk
Whatever Earth all-bearing Mother yeilds
In *India* East or West, or middle shoare
In *Pontus* or the *Punic* Coast, or where   340
Alcinous reign'd, fruit of all kindes, in coate,
Rough, or smooth rin'd, or bearded husk, or shell
She gathers, Tribute large, and on the board
Heaps with unsparing hand; for drink the Grape
She crushes, inoffensive moust, and meathes
From many a berrie, and from sweet kernels prest
She tempers dulcet creams, nor these to hold
Wants her fit vessels pure, then strews the ground
With Rose and Odours from the shrub unfum'd.
Mean while our Primitive great Sire, to meet   350
His god-like Guest, walks forth, without more train
Accompani'd then with his own compleat
Perfections, in himself was all his state,
More solemn then the tedious pomp that waits
On Princes, when thir rich Retinue long
Of Horses led, and Grooms besmeard with Gold
Dazles the croud, and sets them all agape.
Neerer his presence *Adam* though not awd,
Yet with submiss approach and reverence meek,
As to a superior Nature, bowing low,   360
   Thus said. Native of Heav'n, for other place
None can then Heav'n such glorious shape contain;
Since by descending from the Thrones above,
Those happie places thou hast deignd a while
To want, and honour these, voutsafe with us
Two onely, who yet by sov'ran gift possess
This spacious ground, in yonder shadie Bowre
To rest, and what the Garden choicest bears
To sit and taste, till this meridian heat
Be over, and the Sun more coole decline.   370
   Whom thus the Angelic Vertue answerd milde.
Adam, I therefore came, nor art thou such
Created, or such place hast here to dwell,
As may not oft invite, though Spirits of Heav'n
To visit thee; lead on then where thy Bowre

Oreshades; for these mid-hours, till Eevning rise
I have at will. So to the Silvan Lodge
They came, that like *Pomona's* Arbour smil'd
With flourets deck't and fragrant smells; but *Eve*
Undeckt, save with her self more lovely fair   380
Then Wood-Nymph, or the fairest Goddess feign'd
Of three that in Mount *Ida* naked strove,
Stood to entertain her guest from Heav'n; no vaile
Shee needed, Vertue-proof, no thought infirme
Alterd her cheek. On whom the Angel *Haile*
Bestowd, the holy salutation us'd
Long after to blest *Marie,* second *Eve.*
    Haile Mother of Mankind, whose fruitful Womb
Shall fill the World more numerous with thy Sons
Then with these various fruits the Trees of God   390
Have heap'd this Table. Rais'd of grassie terf
Thir Table was, and mossie seats had round,
And on her ample Square from side to side
All *Autumn* pil'd, though *Spring* and *Autumn* here
Danc'd hand in hand. A while discourse they hold;
No fear lest Dinner coole; when thus began
Our Authour. Heav'nly stranger, please to taste
These bounties which our Nourisher, from whom
All perfet good unmeasur'd out, descends,
To us for food and for delight hath caus'd   400
The Earth to yeild; unsavourie food perhaps
To spiritual Natures; only this I know,
That one Celestial Father gives to all.
    To whom the Angel. Therefore what he gives
(Whose praise be ever sung) to man in part
Spiritual, may of purest Spirits be found
No ingrateful food: and food alike those pure
Intelligential substances require
As doth your Rational; and both contain
Within them every lower facultie   410
Of sense, whereby they hear, see, smell, touch, taste,
Tasting concoct, digest, assimilate,
And corporeal to incorporeal turn.
For know, whatever was created, needs
To be sustaind and fed; of Elements
The grosser feeds the purer, earth the sea,
Earth and the Sea feed Air, the Air those Fires
Ethereal, and as lowest first the Moon;
Whence in her visage round those spots, unpurg'd
Vapours not yet into her substance turnd.   420
Nor doth the Moon no nourishment exhale
From her moist Continent to higher Orbes.
The Sun that light imparts to all, receives
From all his alimental recompence
In humid exhalations, and at Even
Sups with the Ocean: though in Heav'n the Trees
Of life ambrosial frutage bear, and vines
Yeild Nectar, though from off the boughs each Morn

We brush mellifluous Dewes, and find the ground
Cover'd with pearly grain: yet God hath here   430
Varied his bounty so with new delights,
As may compare with Heaven; and to taste
Think not I shall be nice. So down they sat,
And to thir viands fell, nor seemingly
The Angel, nor in mist, the common gloss
Of Theologians, but with keen dispatch
Of real hunger, and concoctive heate
To transubstantiate; what redounds, transpires
Through Spirits with ease; nor wonder; if by fire
Of sooty coal the Empiric Alchimist   440
Can turn, or holds it possible to turn
Metals of drossiest Ore to perfet Gold
As from the Mine. Mean while at Table *Eve*
Ministerd naked, and thir flowing cups
With pleasant liquors crown'd: O innocence
Deserving Paradise! if ever, then,
Then had the Sons of God excuse to have bin
Enamour'd at that sight; but in those hearts
Love unlibidinous reign'd, nor jealousie
Was understood, the injur'd Lovers Hell.   450
    Thus when with meats & drinks they had suffic'd,
Not burd'nd Nature, sudden mind arose
In *Adam,* not to let th' occasion pass
Given him by this great Conference to know
Of things above his World, and of thir being
Who dwell in Heav'n, whose excellence he saw
Transcend his own so farr, whose radiant forms
Divine effulgence, whose high Power so far
Exceeded human, and his wary speech
Thus to th' Empyreal Minister he fram'd.   460
    Inhabitant with God, now know I well
Thy favour, in this honour done to man,
Under whose lowly roof thou hast voutsaf't
To enter, and these earthly fruits to taste,
Food not of Angels, yet accepted so,
As that more willingly thou couldst not seem
At Heav'ns high feasts to have fed: yet what compare?
    To whom the winged Hierarch repli'd.
O *Adam,* one Almightie is, from whom
All things proceed, and up to him return,   470
If not deprav'd from good, created all
Such to perfection, one first matter all,
Indu'd with various forms, various degrees
Of substance, and in things that live, of life;
But more refin'd, more spiritous, and pure,
As neerer to him plac't or neerer tending
Each in thir several active Sphears assignd,
Till body up to spirit work, in bounds
Proportiond to each kind. So from the root
Springs lighter the green stalk, from thence the leaves   480
More aerie, last the bright consummate floure

Spirits odorous breathes: flours and thir fruit
Mans nourishment, by gradual scale sublim'd
To vital Spirits aspire, to animal,
To intellectual, give both life and sense,
Fansie and understanding, whence the soule
Reason receives, and reason is her being,
Discursive, or Intuitive; discourse
Is oftest yours, the latter most is ours,
Differing but in degree, of kind the same.   490
Wonder not then, what God for you saw good
If I refuse not, but convert, as you,
To proper substance; time may come when men
With Angels may participate, and find
No inconvenient Diet, nor too light Fare:
And from these corporal nutriments perhaps
Your bodies may at last turn all to Spirit,
Improv'd by tract of time, and wingd ascend
Ethereal, as wee, or may at choice
Here or in Heav'nly Paradises dwell;   500
If ye be found obedient, and retain
Unalterably firm his love entire
Whose progenie you are. Mean while enjoy
Your fill what happiness this happie state
Can comprehend, incapable of more.
   To whom the Patriarch of mankind repli'd.
O favourable spirit, propitious guest,
Well hast thou taught the way that might direct
Our knowledge, and the scale of Nature set
From center to circumference, whereon   510
In contemplation of created things
By steps we may ascend to God. But say,
What meant that caution joind, *if ye be found
Obedient?* can wee want obedience then
To him, or possibly his love desert
Who formd us from the dust, and plac'd us here
Full to the utmost measure of what bliss
Human desires can seek or apprehend?
   To whom the Angel. Son of Heav'n and Earth,
Attend: That thou art happie, owe to God;   520
That thou continu'st such, owe to thy self,
That is, to thy obedience; therein stand.
This was that caution giv'n thee; be advis'd.
God made thee perfet, not immutable;
And good he made thee, but to persevere
He left it in thy power, ordaind thy will
By nature free, not over-rul'd by Fate
Inextricable, or strict necessity;
Our voluntarie service he requires,
Not our necessitated, such with him   530
Findes no acceptance, nor can find, for how
Can hearts, not free, be tri'd whether they serve
Willing or no, who will but what they must
By Destinie, and can no other choose?

My self and all th' Angelic Host that stand
In sight of God enthron'd, our happie state
Hold, as you yours, while our obedience holds;
On other surety none; freely we serve,
Because wee freely love, as in our will
To love or not; in this we stand or fall: 540
And som are fall'n, to disobedience fall'n,
And so from Heav'n to deepest Hell; O fall
From what high state of bliss into what woe!
 To whom our great Progenitor. Thy words
Attentive, and with more delighted eare
Divine instructer, I have heard, then when
Cherubic Songs by night from neighbouring Hills
Aereal Music send: nor knew I not
To be both will and deed created free;
Yet that we never shall forget to love   550
Our maker, and obey him whose command
Single, is yet so just, my constant thoughts
Assur'd me and still assure: though what thou tellst
Hath past in Heav'n, som doubt within me move,
But more desire to hear, if thou consent,
The full relation, which must needs be strange,
Worthy of Sacred silence to be heard;
And we have yet large day, for scarce the Sun
Hath finisht half his journey, and scarce begins
His other half in the great Zone of Heav'n.   560
 Thus *Adam* made request, and *Raphael*
After short pause assenting, thus began.
 High matter thou injoinst me, O prime of men,
Sad task and hard, for how shall I relate
To human sense th' invisible exploits
Of warring Spirits; how without remorse
The ruin of so many glorious once
And perfet while they stood; how last unfould
The secrets of another world, perhaps
Not lawful to reveal? yet for thy good   570
This is dispenc't, and what surmounts the reach
Of human sense, I shall delineate so,
By lik'ning spiritual to corporal forms,
As may express them best, though what if Earth
Be but the shaddow of Heav'n, and things therein
Each to other like, more then on earth is thought?
 As yet this world was not, and *Chaos* wilde
Reignd where these Heav'ns now rowl, where Earth now rests
Upon her Center pois'd, when on a day
(For Time, though in Eternitie, appli'd   580
To motion, measures all things durable
By present, past, and future) on such day
As Heav'ns great Year brings forth, th' Empyreal Host
Of Angels by Imperial summons call'd,
Innumerable before th' Almighties Throne
Forthwith from all the ends of Heav'n appeerd
Under thir Hierarchs in orders bright

Ten thousand thousand Ensignes high advanc'd,
Standards, and Gonfalons twixt Van and Reare
Streame in the Aire, and for distinction serve   590
Of Hierarchies, of Orders, and Degrees;
Or in thir glittering Tissues bear imblaz'd
Holy Memorials, acts of Zeale and Love
Recorded eminent. Thus when in Orbes
Of circuit inexpressible they stood,
Orb within Orb, the Father infinite,
By whom in bliss imbosom'd sat the Son,
A midst as from a flaming Mount, whose top
Brightness had made invisible, thus spake.
   Hear all ye Angels, Progenie of Light,   600
Thrones, Dominations, Princedoms, Vertues, Powers,
Hear my Decree, which unrevok't shall stand.
This day I have begot whom I declare
My onely Son, and on this holy Hill
Him have anointed, whom ye now behold
At my right hand; your Head I him appoint;
And by my Self have sworn to him shall bow
All knees in Heav'n, and shall confess him Lord:
Under his great Vice-gerent Reign abide
United as one individual Soule   610
For ever happie: him who disobeyes
Mee disobeyes, breaks union, and that day
Cast out from God and blessed vision, falls
Into utter darkness, deep ingulft, his place
Ordaind without redemption, without end.
  So spake th' Omnipotent, and with his words
All seemd well pleas'd, all seem'd, but were not all.
That day, as other solem dayes, they spent
In song and dance about the sacred Hill,
Mystical dance, which yonder starrie Spheare   620
Of Planets and of fixt in all her Wheeles
Resembles nearest, mazes intricate,
Eccentric, intervolv'd, yet regular
Then most, when most irregular they seem:
And in thir motions harmonie Divine
So smooths her charming tones, that Gods own ear
Listens delighted. Eevning now approachd
(For we have also our Eevning and our Morn,
We ours for change delectable, not need)
Forthwith from dance to sweet repast they turn   630
Desirous, all in Circles as they stood,
Tables are set, and on a sudden pil'd
With Angels Food, and rubied Nectar flows:
In Pearl, in Diamond, and massie Gold,
Fruit of delicious Vines, the growth of Heav'n.
On flours repos'd, and with fresh flourets crownd,
They eate, they drink, and in communion sweet
Quaff immortalitie and joy, secure
Of surfet where full measure onely bounds
Excess, before th' all bounteous King, who showrd   640

With copious hand, rejoycing in thir joy.
Now when ambrosial Night with Clouds exhal'd
From that high mount of God, whence light & shade
Spring both, the face of brightest Heav'n had changd
To grateful Twilight (for Night comes not there
In darker veile) and roseat Dews dispos'd
All but the unsleeping eyes of God to rest,
Wide over all the Plain; and wider farr
Then all this globous Earth in Plain outspread,
(Such are the Courts of God) Th' Angelic throng   650
Disperst in Bands and Files thir Camp extend
By living Streams among the Trees of Life,
Pavilions numberless, and sudden reard,
Celestial Tabernacles, where they slept
Fannd with coole Winds, save those who in thir course
Melodious Hymns about the sovran Throne
Alternate all night long: but not so wak'd
Satan, so call him now, his former name
Is heard no more in Heav'n; he of the first,
If not the first Arch-Angel, great in Power,   660
In favour and præeminence, yet fraught
With envie against the Son of God, that day
Honourd by his great Father, and proclaimd
Messiah King anointed, could not beare
Through pride that sight, and thought himself impaird.
Deep malice thence conceiving & disdain,
Soon as midnight brought on the duskie houre
Friendliest to sleep and silence, he resolv'd
With all his Legions to dislodge, and leave
Unworshipt, unobey'd the Throne supream   670
Contemptuous, and his next subordinate
Awak'ning, thus to him in secret spake.
    Sleepst thou Companion dear, what sleep can close
Thy eye-lids? and remembrest what Decree
Of yesterday, so late hath past the lips
Of Heav'ns Almightie. Thou to me thy thoughts
Wast wont, I mine to thee was wont to impart;
Both waking we were one; how then can now
Thy sleep dissent? new Laws thou seest impos'd;
New Laws from him who reigns, new minds may raise   680
In us who serve, new Counsels, to debate
What doubtful may ensue, more in this place
To utter is not safe. Assemble thou
Of all those Myriads which we lead the chief;
Tell them that by command, ere yet dim Night
Her shadowie Cloud withdraws, I am to haste,
And all who under me thir Banners wave,
Homeward with flying march where we possess
The Quarters of the North, there to prepare
Fit entertainment to receive our King   690
The great *Messiah,* and his new commands,
Who speedily through all the Hierarchies
Intends to pass triumphant, and give Laws.

So spake the false Arch-Angel, and infus'd
Bad influence into th' unwarie brest
Of his Associate; hee together calls,
Or several one by one, the Regent Powers,
Under him Regent, tells, as he was taught,
That the most High commanding, now ere Night,
Now ere dim Night had disincumberd Heav'n,   700
The great Hierarchal Standard was to move;
Tells the suggested cause, and casts between
Ambiguous words and jealousies, to sound
Or taint integritie; but all obey'd
The wonted signal, and superior voice
Of thir great Potentate; for great indeed
His name, and high was his degree in Heav'n;
His count'nance, as the Morning Starr that guides
The starrie flock, allur'd them, and with lyes
Drew after him the third part of Heav'ns Host: 710
Mean while th' Eternal eye, whose sight discernes
Abstrusest thoughts, from forth his holy Mount
And from within the golden Lamps that burne
Nightly before him, saw without thir light
Rebellion rising, saw in whom, how spred
Among the sons of Morn, what multitudes
Were banded to oppose his high Decree;
And smiling to his onely Son thus said.
    Son, thou in whom my glory I behold
In full resplendence, Heir of all my might,   720
Neerly it now concernes us to be sure
Of our Omnipotence, and with what Arms
We mean to hold what anciently we claim
Of Deitie or Empire, such a foe
Is rising, who intends to erect his Throne
Equal to ours, throughout the spacious North;
Nor so content, hath in his thought to trie
In battel, what our Power is, or our right.
Let us advise, and to this hazard draw
With speed what force is left, and all imploy   730
In our defence, lest unawares we lose
This our high place, our Sanctuarie, our Hill.
    To whom the Son with calm aspect and cleer
Light'ning Divine, ineffable, serene,
Made answer. Mightie Father, thou thy foes
Justly hast in derision, and secure
Laugh'st at thir vain designes and tumults vain,
Matter to mee of Glory, whom thir hate
Illustrates, when they see all Regal Power
Giv'n me to quell thir pride, and in event   740
Know whether I be dextrous to subdue
Thy Rebels, or be found the worst in Heav'n.
    So spake the Son, but *Satan* with his Powers
Farr was advanc't on winged speed, an Host
Innumerable as the Starrs of Night,
Or Starrs of Morning, Dew-drops, which the Sun

Impearls on every leaf and every flouer.
Regions they pass'd, the mightie Regencies
Of Seraphim and Potentates and Thrones
In thir triple Degrees, Regions to which   750
All thy Dominion, *Adam,* is no more
Then what this Garden is to all the Earth,
And all the Sea, from one entire globose
Stretcht into Longitude; which having pass'd
At length into the limits of the North
They came, and *Satan* to his Royal seat
High on a Hill, far blazing, as a Mount
Rais'd on a Mount, with Pyramids and Towrs
From Diamond Quarries hew'n, & Rocks of Gold,
The Palace of great *Lucifer,* (so call   760
That Structure in the Dialect of men
Interpreted) which not long after, hee
Affecting all equality with God,
In imitation of that Mount whereon
Messiah was declar'd in sight of Heav'n,
The Mountain of the Congregation call'd;
For thither he assembl'd all his Train,
Pretending so commanded to consult
About the great reception of thir King,
Thither to come, and with calumnious Art   770
Of counterfeted truth thus held thir ears.
   Thrones, Dominations, Princedomes, Vertues, Powers,
If these magnific Titles yet remain
Not meerly titular, since by Decree
Another now hath to himself ingross't
All Power, and us eclipst under the name
Of King anointed, for whom all this haste
Of midnight march, and hurried meeting here,
This onely to consult how we may best
With what may be devis'd of honours new   780
Receive him coming to receive from us
Knee-tribute yet unpaid, prostration vile,
Too much to one, but double how endur'd,
To one and to his image now proclaim'd?
But what if better counsels might erect
Our minds and teach us to cast off this Yoke?
Will ye submit your necks, and chuse to bend
The supple knee? ye will not, if I trust
To know ye right, or if ye know your selves
Natives and Sons of Heav'n possest before   790
By none, and if not equal all, yet free,
Equally free; for Orders and Degrees
Jarr not with liberty, but well consist.
Who can in reason then or right assume
Monarchie over such as live by right
His equals, if in power and splendor less,
In freedome equal? or can introduce
Law and Edict on us, who without law

Erre not, much less for this to be our Lord,
And look for adoration to th' abuse   800
Of those Imperial Titles which assert
Our being ordain'd to govern, not to serve?
    Thus farr his bold discourse without controule
Had audience, when among the Seraphim
Abdiel, then whom none with more zeale ador'd
The Deitie, and divine commands obei'd,
Stood up, and in a flame of zeale severe
The current of his fury thus oppos'd.
    O argument blasphemous, false and proud!
Words which no eare ever to hear in Heav'n   810
Expected, least of all from thee, ingrate
In place thy self so high above thy Peeres.
Canst thou with impious obloquie condemne
The just Decree of God, pronounc't and sworn,
That to his only Son by right endu'd
With Regal Scepter, every Soule in Heav'n
Shall bend the knee, and in that honour due
Confess him rightful King? unjust thou saist
Flatly unjust, to binde with Laws the free,
And equal over equals to let Reigne,   820
One over all with unsucceeded power.
Shalt thou give Law to God, shalt thou dispute
With him the points of libertie, who made
Thee what thou art, & formd the Pow'rs of Heav'n
Such as he pleasd, and circumscrib'd thir being?
Yet by experience taught we know how good,
And of our good, and of our dignitie
How provident he is, how farr from thought
To make us less, bent rather to exalt
Our happie state under one Head more neer   830
United. But to grant it thee unjust,
That equal over equals Monarch Reigne:
Thy self though great & glorious dost thou count,
Or all Angelic Nature joind in one,
Equal to him begotten Son, by whom
As by his Word the mighty Father made
All things, ev'n thee, and all the Spirits of Heav'n
By him created in thir bright degrees,
Crownd them with Glory, & to thir Glory nam'd
Thrones, Dominations, Princedoms, Vertues, Powers   840
Essential Powers, nor by his Reign obscur'd,
But more illustrious made, since he the Head
One of our number thus reduc't becomes,
His Laws our Laws, all honour to him done
Returns our own. Cease then this impious rage,
And tempt not these; but hast'n to appease
Th' incensed Father, and th' incensed Son,
While Pardon may be found in time besought.
    So spake the fervent Angel, but his zeale
None seconded, as out of season judg'd,   85

Or singular and rash, whereat rejoic'd
Th' Apostat, and more haughty thus repli'd.
That we were formd then saist thou? & the work
Of secondarie hands, by task transferd
From Father to his Son? strange point and new!
Doctrin which we would know whence learnt: who saw
When this creation was? rememberst thou
Thy making, while the Maker gave thee being?
We know no time when we were not as now;
Know none before us, self-begot, self-rais'd   860
By our own quick'ning power, when fatal course
Had circl'd his full Orbe, the birth mature
Of this our native Heav'n, Ethereal Sons.
Our puissance is our own, our own right hand
Shall teach us highest deeds, by proof to try
Who is our equal: then thou shalt behold
Whether by supplication we intend
Address, and to begirt th' Almighty Throne
Beseeching or besieging. This report,
These tidings carrie to th' anointed King;   870
And fly, ere evil intercept thy flight.
     He said, and as the sound of waters deep
Hoarce murmur echo'd to his words applause
Through the infinite Host, nor less for that
The flaming Seraph fearless, though alone
Encompass'd round with foes, thus answerd bold.
     O alienate from God, O spirit accurst,
Forsak'n of all good; I see thy fall
Determind, and thy hapless crew involv'd
In this perfidious fraud, contagion spred   880
Both of thy crime and punishment: henceforth
No more be troubl'd how to quit the yoke
Of Gods *Messiah;* those indulgent Laws
Will not be now voutsaf't, other Decrees
Against thee are gon forth without recall;
That Golden Scepter which thou didst reject
Is now an Iron Rod to bruise and breake
Thy disobedience. Well thou didst advise,
Yet not for thy advise or threats I fly
These wicked Tents devoted, least the wrauth   890
Impendent, raging into sudden flame
Distinguish not: for soon expect to feel
His Thunder on thy head, devouring fire.
Then who created thee lamenting learne,
When who can uncreate thee thou shalt know.
     So spake the Seraph *Abdiel* faithful found,
Among the faithless, faithful only hee;
Among innumerable false, unmov'd,
Unshak'n, unseduc'd, unterrifi'd
His Loyaltie he kept, his Love, his Zeale;   900
Nor number, nor example with him wrought
To swerve from truth, or change his constant mind
Though single. From amidst them forth he passd,

Long way through hostile scorn, which he susteind
Superior, nor of violence fear'd aught;
And with retorted scorn his back he turn'd
On those proud Towrs to swift destruction doom'd.

The End of the Fifth Book.

PARADISE LOST.

BOOK VI.

The Argument.

Raphael *continues to relate how* Michael *and* Gabriel *were sent forth to Battel against* Satan *and his Angels. The first Fight describ'd:* Satan *and his Powers retire under Night: He calls a Councel, invents devilish Engines, which in the second dayes Fight put* Michael *and his Angels to some disorder; But they at length pulling up Mountains overwhelm'd both the force and Machins of* Satan: *Yet the Tumult not so ending, God on the third day sends* Messiah *his Son, for whom he had reserv'd the glory of that Victory: Hee in the Power of his Father coming to the place, and causing all his Legions to stand still on either side, with his Chariot and Thunder driving into the midst of his Enemies, pursues them unable to resist towards the wall of Heaven; which opening, they leap down with horrour and confusion into the place of punishment prepar'd for them in the Deep:* Messiah *returns with triumph to his Father.*

ALL night the dreadless Angel unpursu'd
Through Heav'ns wide Champain held his way, till Morn,
Wak't by the circling Hours, with rosie hand
Unbarr'd the gates of Light. There is a Cave
Within the Mount of God, fast by his Throne,
Where light and darkness in perpetual round
Lodge and dislodge by turns, which makes through Heav'n
Grateful vicissitude, like Day and Night;
Light issues forth, and at the other dore
Obsequious darkness enters, till her houre   10
To veile the Heav'n, though darkness there might well
Seem twilight here; and now went forth the Morn
Such as in highest Heav'n, arrayd in Gold
Empyreal, from before her vanisht Night,
Shot through with orient Beams: when all the Plain
Coverd with thick embatteld Squadrons bright,
Chariots and flaming Armes, and fierie Steeds
Reflecting blaze on blaze, first met his view:
Warr he perceav'd, warr in procinct, and found
Already known what he for news had thought   20
To have reported: gladly then he mixt
Among those friendly Powers who him receav'd
With joy and acclamations loud, that one
That of so many Myriads fall'n, yet one
Returnd not lost: On to the sacred hill
They led him high applauded, and present
Before the seat supream; from whence a voice
From midst a Golden Cloud thus milde was heard.
   Servant of God, well done, well hast thou fought
The better fight, who single hast maintaind   30
Against revolted multitudes the Cause

Of Truth, in word mightier then they in Armes;
And for the testimonie of Truth hast born
Universal reproach, far worse to beare
Then violence: for this was all thy care
To stand approv'd in sight of God, though Worlds
Judg'd thee perverse: the easier conquest now
Remains thee, aided by this host of friends,
Back on thy foes more glorious to return
Then scornd thou didst depart, and to subdue   40
By force, who reason for thir Law refuse,
Right reason for thir Law, and for thir King
Messiah, who by right of merit Reigns.
Goe *Michael* of Celestial Armies Prince,
And thou in Military prowess next
Gabriel, lead forth to Battel these my Sons
Invincible, lead forth my armed Saints
By Thousands and by Millions rang'd for fight;
Equal in number to that Godless crew
Rebellious, them with Fire and hostile Arms   50
Fearless assault, and to the brow of Heav'n
Pursuing drive them out from God and bliss,
Into thir place of punishment, the Gulf
Of *Tartarus,* which ready opens wide
His fiery *Chaos* to receave thir fall.
   So spake the Sovran voice, and Clouds began
To darken all the Hill, and smoak to rowl
In duskie wreathes, reluctant flames, the signe
Of wrauth awak't: nor with less dread the loud
Ethereal Trumpet from on high gan blow: 60
At which command the Powers Militant,
That stood for Heav'n, in mighty Quadrate joyn'd
Of Union irresistible, mov'd on
In silence thir bright Legions, to the sound
Of instrumental Harmonie that breath'd
Heroic Ardor to advent'rous deeds
Under thir God-like Leaders, in the Cause
Of God and his *Messiah.* On they move
Indissolubly firm; nor obvious Hill,
Nor streit'ning Vale, nor Wood, nor Stream divides   70
Thir perfet ranks; for high above the ground
Thir march was, and the passive Air upbore
Thir nimble tread; as when the total kind
Of Birds in orderly array on wing
Came summond over *Eden* to receive
Thir names of thee; so over many a tract
Of Heav'n they march'd, and many a Province wide
Tenfold the length of this terrene: at last
Farr in th' Horizon to the North appeer'd
From skirt to skirt a fierie Region, stretcht   80
In battailous aspect, and neerer view
Bristl'd with upright beams innumerable
Of rigid Spears, and Helmets throng'd, and Shields
Various, with boastful Argument portraid,

The banded Powers of *Satan* hasting on
With furious expedition; for they weend
That self same day by fight, or by surprize
To win the Mount of God, and on his Throne
To set the envier of his State, the proud
Aspirer, but thir thoughts prov'd fond and vain
In the mid way: though strange to us it seemd
At first, that Angel should with Angel warr,
And in fierce hosting meet, who wont to meet
So oft in Festivals of joy and love
Unanimous, as sons of one great Sire
Hymning th' Eternal Father: but the shout
Of Battel now began, and rushing sound
Of onset ended soon each milder thought.
High in the midst exalted as a God
Th' Apostat in his Sun-bright Chariot sate
Idol of Majestie Divine, enclos'd
With Flaming Cherubim, and golden Shields;
Then lighted from his gorgeous Throne, for now
'Twixt Host and Host but narrow space was left,
A dreadful interval, and Front to Front
Presented stood in terrible array
Of hideous length: before the cloudie Van,
On the rough edge of battel ere it joyn'd,
Satan with vast and haughtie strides advanc't,
Came towring, armd in Adamant and Gold;
Abdiel that sight endur'd not, where he stood
Among the mightiest, bent on highest deeds,
And thus his own undaunted heart explores.
　O Heav'n! that such resemblance of the Highest
Should yet remain, where faith and realtie
Remain not; wherfore should not strength & might
There fail where Vertue fails, or weakest prove
Where boldest; though to sight unconquerable?
His puissance, trusting in th' Almightie's aide,
I mean to try, whose Reason I have tri'd
Unsound and false; nor is it aught but just,
That he who in debate of Truth hath won,
Should win in Arms, in both disputes alike
Victor; though brutish that contest and foule,
When Reason hath to deal with force, yet so
Most reason is that Reason overcome.
　So pondering, and from his armed Peers
Forth stepping opposite, half way he met
His daring foe, at this prevention more
Incens't, and thus securely him defi'd.
　Proud, art thou met? thy hope was to have reacht
The highth of thy aspiring unoppos'd,
The Throne of God unguarded, and his side
Abandond at the terror of thy Power
Or potent tongue; fool, not to think how vain
Against th' Omnipotent to rise in Arms;
Who out of smallest things could without end

90

100

110

120

130

Have rais'd incessant Armies to defeat
Thy folly; or with solitarie hand
Reaching beyond all limit, at one blow   140
Unaided could have finisht thee, and whelmd
Thy Legions under darkness; but thou seest
All are not of thy Train; there be who Faith
Prefer, and Pietie to God, though then
To thee not visible, when I alone
Seemd in thy World erroneous to dissent
From all: my Sect thou seest, now learn too late
How few somtimes may know, when thousands err.
    Whom the grand foe with scornful eye askance
Thus answerd. Ill for thee, but in wisht houre   150
Of my revenge, first sought for thou returnst
From flight, seditious Angel, to receave
Thy merited reward, the first assay
Of this right hand provok't, since first that tongue
Inspir'd with contradiction durst oppose
A third part of the Gods, in Synod met
Thir Deities to assert, who while they feel
Vigour Divine within them, can allow
Omnipotence to none. But well thou comst
Before thy fellows, ambitious to win   160
From me som Plume, that thy success may show
Destruction to the rest: this pause between
(Unanswerd least thou boast) to let thee know;
At first I thought that Libertie and Heav'n
To heav'nly Soules had bin all one; but now
I see that most through sloth had rather serve,
Ministring Spirits, trained up in Feast and Song;
Such hast thou arm'd, the Minstrelsie of Heav'n,
Servilitie with freedom to contend,
As both thir deeds compar'd this day shall prove.   170
    To whom in brief thus *Abdiel* stern repli'd.
Apostat, still thou errst, nor end wilt find
Of erring, from the path of truth remote:
Unjustly thou deprav'st it with the name
Of *Servitude* to serve whom God ordains,
Or Nature; God and Nature bid the same,
When he who rules is worthiest, and excells
Them whom he governs. This is servitude,
To serve th' unwise, or him who hath rebelld
Against his worthier, as thine now serve thee,   180
Thy self not free, but to thy self enthrall'd;
Yet leudly dar'st our ministring upbraid.
Reign thou in Hell thy Kingdom, let mee serve
In Heav'n God ever blesst, and his Divine
Behests obey, worthiest to be obey'd,
Yet Chains in Hell, not Realms expect: mean while
From mee returnd, as erst thou saidst, from flight,
This greeting on thy impious Crest receive.
    So saying, a noble stroke he lifted high,
Which hung not, but so swift with tempest fell   190

On the proud Crest of *Satan,* that no sight,
Nor motion of swift thought, less could his Shield
Such ruin intercept: ten paces huge
He back recoild; the tenth on bended knee
His massie Spear upstaid; as if on Earth
Winds under ground or waters forcing way
Sidelong, had push't a Mountain from his seat
Half sunk with all his Pines. Amazement seis'd
The Rebel Thrones, but greater rage to see
Thus foil'd thir mightiest, ours joy filld, and shout,   200
Presage of Victorie and fierce desire
Of Battel: whereat *Michael* bid sound
Th' Arch-angel trumpet; through the vast of Heav'n
It sounded, and the faithful Armies rung
Hosanna to the Highest: nor stood at gaze
The adverse Legions, nor less hideous joyn'd
The horrid shock: now storming furie rose,
And clamour such as heard in Heav'n till now
Was never, Arms on Armour clashing bray'd
Horrible discord, and the madding Wheeles   210
Of brazen Chariots rag'd; dire was the noise
Of conflict; over head the dismal hiss
Of fiery Darts in flaming volies flew,
And flying vaulted either Host with fire.
So under fierie Cope together rush'd
Both Battels maine, with ruinous assault
And inextinguishable rage; all Heav'n
Resounded, and had Earth bin then, all Earth
Had to her Center shook. What wonder? when
Millions of fierce encountring Angels fought   220
On either side, the least of whom could weild
These Elements, and arm him with the force
Of all thir Regions: how much more of Power
Armie against Armie numberless to raise
Dreadful combustion warring, and disturb,
Though not destroy, thir happie Native seat;
Had not th' Eternal King Omnipotent
From his strong hold of Heav'n high over-rul'd
And limited thir might; though numberd such
As each divided Legion might have seemd   230
A numerous Host, in strength each armed hand
A Legion; led in fight, yet Leader seemd
Each Warriour single as in Chief, expert
When to advance, or stand, or turn the sway
Of Battel, open when, and when to close
The ridges of grim Warr; no thought of flight,
None of retreat, no unbecoming deed
That argu'd fear; each on himself reli'd,
As onely in his arm the moment lay
Of victorie; deeds of eternal fame   240
Were don, but infinite: for wide was spred
That Warr and various; somtimes on firm ground
A standing fight, then soaring on main wing

Tormented all the Air; all Air seemd then
Conflicting Fire: long time in eeven scale
The Battel hung; till *Satan,* who that day
Prodigious power had shewn, and met in Armes
No equal, raunging through the dire attack
Of fighting Seraphim confus'd, at length
Saw where the Sword of *Michael* smote, and fell'd   250
Squadrons at once, with huge two-handed sway
Brandisht aloft the horrid edge came down
Wide wasting; such destruction to withstand
He hasted, and oppos'd the rockie Orb
Of tenfold Adamant, his ample Shield
A vast circumference: At his approach
The great Arch-Angel from his warlike toile
Surceas'd, and glad as hoping here to end
Intestine War in Heav'n, the arch foe subdu'd
Or Captive drag'd in Chains, with hostile frown   260
And visage all enflam'd first thus began.
    Author of evil, unknown till thy revolt,
Unnam'd in Heav'n, now plenteous, as thou seest
These Acts of hateful strife, hateful to all,
Though heaviest by just measure on thy self
And thy adherents: how hast thou disturb'd
Heav'ns blessed peace, and into Nature brought
Miserie, uncreated till the crime
Of thy Rebellion? how hast thou instill'd
Thy malice into thousands, once upright   270
And faithful, now prov'd false. But think not here
To trouble Holy Rest; Heav'n casts thee out
From all her Confines. Heav'n the seat of bliss
Brooks not the works of violence and Warr.
Hence then, and evil go with thee along
Thy ofspring, to the place of evil, Hell,
Thou and thy wicked crew; there mingle broiles,
Ere this avenging Sword begin thy doome,
Or som more sudden vengeance wing'd from God
Precipitate thee with augmented paine.   280
    So spake the Prince of Angels; to whom thus
The Adversarie. Nor think thou with wind
Of airie threats to aw whom yet with deeds
Thou canst not. Hast thou turnd the least of these
To flight, or if to fall, but that they rise
Unvanquisht, easier to transact with mee
That thou shouldst hope, imperious, & with threats
To chase me hence? erre not that so shall end
The strife which thou call'st evil, but wee style
The strife of Glorie: which we mean to win,   290
Or turn this Heav'n it self into the Hell
Thou fablest, here however to dwell free,
If not to reign: mean while thy utmost force,
And join him nam'd *Almightie* to thy aid,
I flie not, but have sought thee farr and nigh.
    They ended parle, and both addrest for fight

Unspeakable; for who, though with the tongue
Of Angels, can relate, or to what things
Liken on Earth conspicuous, that may lift
Human imagination to such highth   300
Of Godlike Power: for likest Gods they seemd,
Stood they or mov'd, in stature, motion, arms
Fit to decide the Empire of great Heav'n.
Now wav'd thir fierie Swords, and in the Aire
Made horrid Circles; two broad Suns thir Shields
Blaz'd opposite, while expectation stood
In horror; from each hand with speed retir'd
Where erst was thickest fight, th' Angelic throng,
And left large field, unsafe within the wind
Of such commotion, such as to set forth   310
Great things by small, If Natures concord broke,
Among the Constellations warr were sprung,
Two Planets rushing from aspect maligne
Of fiercest opposition in mid Skie,
Should combat, and thir jarring Sphears confound.
Together both with next to Almightie Arme,
Uplifted imminent one stroke they aim'd
That might determine, and not need repeate,
As not of power, at once; nor odds appeerd
In might or swift prevention; but the sword   320
Of *Michael* from the Armorie of God
Was giv'n him temperd so, that neither keen
Nor solid might resist that edge: it met
The sword of *Satan* with steep force to smite
Descending, and in half cut sheere, nor staid,
But with swift wheele reverse, deep entring shar'd
All his right side; then *Satan* first knew pain,
And writh'd him to and fro convolv'd; so sore
The griding sword with discontinuous wound
Pass'd through him, but th' Ethereal substance clos'd   330
Not long divisible, and from the gash
A stream of Nectarous humor issuing flow'd
Sanguin, such as Celestial Spirits may bleed,
And all his Armour staind ere while so bright.
Forthwith on all sides to his aide was run
By Angels many and strong, who interpos'd
Defence, while others bore him on thir Shields
Back to his Chariot; where it stood retir'd
From off the files of warr; there they him laid
Gnashing for anguish and despite and shame   340
To find himself not matchless, and his pride
Humbl'd by such rebuke, so farr beneath
His confidence to equal God in power.
Yet soon he heal'd; for Spirits that live throughout
Vital in every part, not as frail man
In Entrailes, Heart or Head, Liver or Reines,
Cannot but by annihilating die;
Nor in thir liquid texture mortal wound
Receive, no more then can the fluid Aire:

All Heart they live, all Head, all Eye, all Eare,   350
All Intellect, all Sense, and as they please,
They Limb themselves, and colour, shape or size
Assume, as likes them best, condense or rare.
   Mean while in other parts like deeds deservd
Memorial, where the might of *Gabriel* fought,
And with fierce Ensignes pierc'd the deep array
Of *Moloc* furious King, who him defi'd,
And at his Chariot wheeles to drag him bound
Threatn'd, nor from the Holie One of Heav'n
Refrein'd his tongue blasphemous; but anon   360
Down clov'n to the waste, with shatterd Armes
And uncouth paine fled bellowing. On each wing
Uriel and *Raphael* his vaunting foe,
Though huge, and in a Rock of Diamond Armd,
Vanquish'd *Adramelec,* and *Asmadai,*
Two potent Thrones, that to be less then Gods
Disdain'd, but meaner thoughts learnd in thir flight,
Mangl'd with gastly wounds through Plate and Maile.
Nor stood unmindful *Abdiel* to annoy
The Atheist crew, but with redoubl'd blow   370
Ariel and *Arioc,* and the violence
Of *Ramiel* scorcht and blasted overthrew.
I might relate of thousands, and thir names
Eternize here on Earth; but those elect
Angels contented with thir fame in Heav'n
Seek not the praise of men: the other sort
In might though wondrous and in Acts of Warr,
Nor of Renown less eager, yet by doome
Canceld from Heav'n and sacred memorie,
Nameless in dark oblivion let them dwell.   380
For strength from Truth divided and from Just,
Illaudable, naught merits but dispraise
And ignominie, yet to glorie aspires
Vain glorious, and through infamie seeks fame:
Therfore Eternal silence be thir doome.
   And now thir mightiest quelld, the battel swerv'd,
With many an inrode gor'd; deformed rout
Enter'd, and foul disorder; all the ground
With shiverd armour strow'n, and on a heap
Chariot and Charioter lay overturnd   390
And fierie foaming Steeds; what stood, recoyld
Orewearied, through the faint Satanic Host
Defensive scarce, or with pale fear surpris'd,
Then first with fear surpris'd and sense of paine
Fled ignominious, to such evil brought
By sinne of disobedience, till that hour
Not liable to fear or flight or paine.
Far otherwise th' inviolable Saints
In Cubic Phalanx firm advanc't entire,
Invulnerable, impenitrably arm'd: 400
Such high advantages thir innocence
Gave them above thir foes, not to have sinnd.

Not to have disobei'd; in fight they stood
Unwearied, unobnoxious to be pain'd
By wound, though from thir place by violence mov'd.
　　Now Night her course began, and over Heav'n
Inducing darkness, grateful truce impos'd,
And silence on the odious dinn of Warr:
Under her Cloudie covert both retir'd,
Victor and Vanquisht: on the foughten field　　　　410
Michael and his Angels prevalent
Encamping, plac'd in Guard thir Watches round,
Cherubic waving fires: on th' other part
Satan with his rebellious disappeerd,
Far in the dark dislodg'd, and void of rest,
His Potentates to Councel call'd by night;
And in the midst thus undismai'd began.
　　O now in danger tri'd, now known in Armes
Not to be overpowerd, Companions deare,
Found worthy not of Libertie alone,　　　　420
Too mean pretense, but what we more affect,
Honour, Dominion, Glorie, and renowne,
Who have sustaind one day in doubtful fight,
(And if one day, why not Eternal dayes?)
What Heavens Lord had powerfullest to send
Against us from about his Throne, and judg'd
Sufficient to subdue us to his will,
But proves not so: then fallible, it seems,
Of future we may deem him, though till now
Omniscient thought. True is, less firmly arm'd,　　　　430
Some disadvantage we endur'd and paine,
Till now not known, but known as soon contemnd,
Since now we find this our Empyreal forme
Incapable of mortal injurie
Imperishable, and though peirc'd with wound,
Soon closing, and by native vigour heal'd.
Of evil then so small as easie think
The remedie; perhaps more valid Armes,
Weapons more violent, when next we meet,
May serve to better us, and worse our foes,　　　　440
Or equal what between us made the odds,
In Nature none: if other hidden cause
Left them Superiour, while we can preserve
Unhurt our mindes, and understanding sound,
Due search and consultation will disclose.
　　He sat; and in th' assembly next upstood
Nisroc, of Principalities the prime;
As one he stood escap't from cruel fight,
Sore toild, his riv'n Armes to havoc hewn,
And cloudie in aspect thus answering spake.　　　　450
Deliverer from new Lords, leader to free
Enjoyment of our right as Gods; yet hard
For Gods, and too unequal work we find
Against unequal armes to fight in paine,
Against unpaind, impassive; from which evil

Ruin must needs ensue; for what availes
Valour or strength, though matchless, quelld with pain
Which all subdues, and makes remiss the hands
Of Mightiest. Sense of pleasure we may well
Spare out of life perhaps, and not repine,   460
But live content, which is the calmest life:
But pain is perfet miserie, the worst
Of evils, and excessive, overturnes
All patience. He who therefore can invent
With what more forcible we may offend
Our yet unwounded Enemies, or arme
Our selves with like defence, to mee deserves
No less then for deliverance what we owe.
    Whereto with look compos'd *Satan* repli'd.
Not uninvented that, which thou aright   470
Beleivst so main to our success, I bring;
Which of us who beholds the bright surface
Of this Ethereous mould whereon we stand,
This continent of spacious Heav'n, adornd
With Plant, Fruit, Flour Ambrosial, Gemms & Gold,
Whose Eye so superficially surveyes
These things, as not to mind from whence they grow
Deep under ground, materials dark and crude,
Of spiritous and fierie spume, till toucht
With Heav'ns ray, and temperd they shoot forth   480
So beauteous, op'ning to the ambient light.
These in thir dark Nativitie the Deep
Shall yeild us, pregnant with infernal flame,
Which into hallow Engins long and round
Thick-rammd, at th' other bore with touch of fire
Dilated and infuriate shall send forth
From far with thundring noise among our foes
Such implements of mischief as shall dash
To pieces, and orewhelm whatever stands
Adverse, that they shall fear we have disarmd   490
The Thunderer of his only dreaded bolt.
Nor long shall be our labour, yet ere dawne,
Effect shall end our wish. Mean while revive;
Abandon fear; to strength and counsel joind
Think nothing hard, much less to be despaird.
He ended, and his words thir drooping chere
Enlightn'd, and thir languisht hope reviv'd.
Th' invention all admir'd, and each, how hee
To be th' inventer miss'd, so easie it seemd
Once found, which yet unfound most would have thought   500
Impossible: yet haply of thy Race
In future dayes, if Malice should abound,
Some one intent on mischief, or inspir'd
With dev'lish machination might devise
Like instrument to plague the Sons of men
For sin, on warr and mutual slaughter bent.
Forthwith from Councel to the work they flew,
None arguing stood, innumerable hands

Were ready, in a moment up they turnd
Wide the Celestial soile, and saw beneath　　　　510
Th' originals of Nature in thir crude
Conception; Sulphurous and Nitrous Foame
They found, they mingl'd, and with suttle Art,
Concocted and adusted they reduc'd
To blackest grain, and into store conveyd:
Part hidd'n veins diggd up (nor hath this Earth
Entrails unlike) of Mineral and Stone,
Whereof to found thir Engins and thir Balls
Of missive ruin; part incentive reed
Provide, pernicious with one touch to fire.　　　　520
So all ere day spring, under conscious Night
Secret they finish'd, and in order set,
With silent circumspection unespi'd.
Now when fair Morn Orient in Heav'n appeerd
Up rose the Victor Angels, and to Arms
The matin Trumpet Sung: in Arms they stood
Of Golden Panoplie, refulgent Host,
Soon banded; others from the dawning Hills
Lookd round, and Scouts each Coast light-armed scoure,
Each quarter, to descrie the distant foe,　　　　530
Where lodg'd, or whither fled, or if for fight,
In motion or in alt: him soon they met
Under spred Ensignes moving nigh, in slow
But firm Battalion; back with speediest Sail
Zophiel, of Cherubim the swiftest wing,
Came flying, and in mid Aire aloud thus cri'd.
　　Arme, Warriours, Arme for fight, the foe at hand,
Whom fled we thought, will save us long pursuit
This day, fear not his flight; so thick a Cloud
He comes, and settl'd in his face I see　　　　540
Sad resolution and secure: let each
His Adamantine coat gird well, and each
Fit well his Helme, gripe fast his orbed Shield,
Born eevn or high, for this day will pour down,
If I conjecture aught, no drizling showr,
But ratling storm of Arrows barbd with fire.
So warnd he them aware themselves, and soon
In order, quit of all impediment;
Instant without disturb they took Allarm,
And onward move Embattelld; when behold　　　　550
Not distant far with heavie pace the Foe
Approaching gross and huge; in hollow Cube
Training his devilish Enginrie, impal'd
On every side with shaddowing Squadrons Deep,
To hide the fraud. At interview both stood
A while, but suddenly at head appeerd
Satan: And thus was heard Commanding loud.
　　Vangard, to Right and Left the Front unfould;
That all may see who hate us, how we seek
Peace and composure, and with open brest　　　　560
Stand readie to receive them, if they like

Our overture, and turn not back perverse;
But that I doubt, however witness Heaven,
Heav'n witness thou anon, while we discharge
Freely our part: yee who appointed stand
Do as you have in charge, and briefly touch
What we propound, and loud that all may hear.
　　So scoffing in ambiguous words, he scarce
Had ended; when to Right and Left the Front
Divided, and to either Flank retir'd.　　　　　　　　　570
Which to our eyes discoverd new and strange,
A triple-mounted row of Pillars laid
On Wheels (for like to Pillars most they seem'd
Or hollow'd bodies made of Oak or Firr
With branches lopt, in Wood or Mountain fell'd)
Brass, Iron, Stonie mould, had not thir mouthes
With hideous orifice gap't on us wide,
Portending hollow truce; at each behind
A Seraph stood, and in his hand a Reed
Stood waving tipt with fire; while we suspense,　　　580
Collected stood within our thoughts amus'd,
Not long, for sudden all at once thir Reeds
Put forth, and to a narrow vent appli'd
With nicest touch. Immediate in a flame,
But soon obscurd with smoak, all Heav'n appeerd,
From those deep-throated Engins belcht, whose roar
Emboweld with outragious noise the Air,
And all her entrails tore, disgorging foule
Thir devillish glut, chaind Thunderbolts and Hail
Of Iron Globes, which on the Victor Host　　　　　590
Level'd, with such impetuous furie smote,
That whom they hit, none on thir feet might stand,
Though standing else as Rocks, but down they fell
By thousands, Angel on Arch-Angel rowl'd;
The sooner for thir Arms, unarm'd they might
Have easily as Spirits evaded swift
By quick contraction or remove; but now
Foule dissipation follow'd and forc't rout;
Nor serv'd it to relax thir serried files.
What should they do? if on they rusht, repulse　　　600
Repeated, and indecent overthrow
Doubl'd, would render them yet more despis'd,
And to thir foes a laughter; for in view
Stood rankt of Seraphim another row
In posture to displode thir second tire
Of Thunder: back defeated to return
They worse abhorr'd. *Satan* beheld thir plight,
And to his Mates thus in derision call'd.
　　O Friends, why come not on these Victors proud?
Ere while they fierce were coming, and when wee,　　610
To entertain them fair with open Front
And Brest, (what could we more?) propounded terms
Of composition, strait they chang'd thir minds,
Flew off, and into strange vagaries fell,

As they would dance, yet for a dance they seemd
Somwhat extravagant and wilde, perhaps
For joy of offerd peace: but I suppose
If our proposals once again were heard
We should compel them to a quick result.
   To whom thus *Belial* in like gamesom mood.   620
Leader, the terms we sent were terms of weight,
Of hard contents, and full of force urg'd home,
Such as we might perceive amus'd them all,
And stumbl'd many, who receives them right,
Had need from head to foot well understand;
Not understood, this gift they have besides,
They shew us when our foes walk not upright.
   So they among themselves in pleasant veine
Stood scoffing, highthn'd in thir thoughts beyond
All doubt of Victorie, eternal might   630
To match with thir inventions they presum'd
So easie, and of his Thunder made a scorn,
And all his Host derided, while they stood
A while in trouble; but they stood not long,
Rage prompted them at length, & found them arms
Against such hellish mischief fit to oppose.
Forthwith (behold the excellence, the power
Which God hath in his mighty Angels plac'd)
Thir Arms away they threw, and to the Hills
(For Earth hath this variety from Heav'n   640
Of pleasure situate in Hill and Dale)
Light as the Lightning glimps they ran, they flew,
From thir foundations loosning to and fro
They pluckt the seated Hills with all thir load,
Rocks, Waters, Woods, and by the shaggie tops
Up lifting bore them in thir hands: Amaze,
Be sure, and terrour seis'd the rebel Host,
When coming towards them so dread they saw
The bottom of the Mountains upward turn'd,
Till on those cursed Engins triple-row   650
They saw them whelmd, and all thir confidence
Under the weight of Mountains buried deep,
Themselves invaded next, and on thir heads
Main Promontories flung, which in the Air
Came shadowing, and opprest whole Legions arm'd,
Thir armor help'd their harm, crush't in and brus'd
Into thir substance pent, which wrought them pain
Implacable, and many a dolorous groan,
Long strugling underneath, ere they could wind
Out of such prison, though Spirits of purest light,   660
Purest at first, now gross by sinning grown.
The rest in imitation to like Armes
Betook them, and the neighbouring Hills uptore;
So Hills amid the Air encounterd Hills
Hurl'd to and fro with jaculation dire,
That under ground they fought in dismal shade;
Infernal noise; Warr seem'd a civil Game

To this uproar; horrid confusion heapt
Upon confusion rose: and now all Heav'n
Had gone to wrack, with ruin overspred,   670
Had not th' Almightie Father where he sits
Shrin'd in his Sanctuarie of Heav'n secure,
Consulting on the sum of things, foreseen
This tumult, and permitted all, advis'd:
That his great purpose he might so fulfill,
To honour his Anointed Son aveng'd
Upon his enemies, and to declare
All power on him transferr'd: whence to his Son
Th' Assessor of his Throne he thus began.
    Effulgence of my Glorie, Son belov'd,   680
Son in whose face invisible is beheld
Visibly, what by Deitie I am,
And in whose hand what by Decree I doe,
Second Omnipotence, two dayes are past,
Two dayes, as we compute the dayes of Heav'n,
Since *Michael* and his Powers went forth to tame
These disobedient; sore hath been thir fight,
As likeliest was, when two such Foes met arm'd;
For to themselves I left them, and thou knowst,
Equal in their Creation they were form'd,   690
Save what sin hath impaird, which yet hath wrought
Insensibly, for I suspend thir doom;
Whence in perpetual fight they needs must last
Endless, and no solution will be found:
Warr wearied hath perform'd what Warr can do,
And to disorder'd rage let loose the reines,
With Mountains as with Weapons arm'd, which makes
Wild work in Heav'n, and dangerous to the maine.
Two dayes are therefore past, the third is thine;
For thee I have ordain'd it, and thus farr   700
Have sufferd, that the Glorie may be thine
Of ending this great Warr, since none but Thou
Can end it. Into thee such Vertue and Grace
Immense I have transfus'd, that all may know
In Heav'n and Hell thy Power above compare,
And this perverse Commotion governd thus,
To manifest thee worthiest to be Heir
Of all things, to be Heir and to be King
By Sacred Unction, thy deserved right.
Go then thou Mightiest in thy Fathers might,   710
Ascend my Chariot, guide the rapid Wheeles
That shake Heav'ns basis, bring forth all my Warr,
My Bow and Thunder, my Almightie Arms
Gird on, and Sword upon thy puissant Thigh;
Pursue these sons of Darkness, drive them out
From all Heav'ns bounds into the utter Deep:
There let them learn, as likes them, to despise
God and *Messiah* his anointed King.
    He said, and on his Son with Rayes direct
Shon full, he all his Father full exprest   720

Ineffably into his face receiv'd,
And thus the filial Godhead answering spake.
    O Father, O Supream of heav'nly Thrones,
First, Highest, Holiest, Best, thou alwayes seekst
To glorifie thy Son, I alwayes thee,
As is most just; this I my Glorie account,
My exaltation, and my whole delight,
That thou in me well pleas'd, declarst thy will
Fulfill'd, which to fulfil is all my bliss.
Scepter and Power, thy giving, I assume,   730
And gladlier shall resign, when in the end
Thou shalt be All in All, and I in thee
For ever, and in mee all whom thou lov'st:
But whom thou hat'st, I hate, and can put on
Thy terrors, as I put thy mildness on,
Image of thee in all things; and shall soon,
Armd with thy might, rid heav'n of these rebell'd,
To thir prepar'd ill Mansion driven down
To chains of Darkness, and th' undying Worm,
That from thy just obedience could revolt,   740
Whom to obey is happiness entire.
Then shall thy Saints unmixt, and from th' impure
Farr separate, circling thy holy Mount
Unfained *Halleluiahs* to thee sing,
Hymns of high praise, and I among them chief.
So said, he o're his Scepter bowing, rose
From the right hand of Glorie where he sate,
And the third sacred Morn began to shine
Dawning through Heav'n: forth rush'd with whirlwind sound
The Chariot of Paternal Deitie,   750
Flashing thick flames, Wheele within Wheele undrawn,
It self instinct with Spirit, but convoyd
By four Cherubic shapes, four Faces each
Had wondrous, as with Starrs thir bodies all
And Wings were set with Eyes, with Eyes the Wheels
Of Beril, and careering Fires between;
Over thir heads a chrystal Firmament,
Whereon a Saphir Throne, inlaid with pure
Amber, and colours of the showrie Arch.
Hee in Celestial Panoplie all armd   760
Of radiant *Urim,* work divinely wrought,
Ascended, at his right hand Victorie
Sate Eagle-wing'd, beside him hung his Bow
And Quiver with three-bolted Thunder stor'd,
And from about him fierce Effusion rowld
Of smoak and bickering flame, and sparkles dire;
Attended with ten thousand thousand Saints,
He onward came, farr off his coming shon,
And twentie thousand (I thir number heard)
Chariots of God, half on each hand were seen: 770
Hee on the wings of Cherub rode sublime
On the Crystallin Skie, in Saphir Thron'd.
Illustrious farr and wide, but by his own

First seen, them unexpected joy surpriz'd,
When the great Ensign of *Messiah* blaz'd
Aloft by Angels born, his Sign in Heav'n:
Under whose Conduct *Michael* soon reduc'd
His Armie, circumfus'd on either Wing,
Under thir Head imbodied all in one.
Before him Power Divine his way prepar'd;   780
At his command the uprooted Hills retir'd
Each to his place, they heard his voice and went
Obsequious, Heav'n his wonted face renewd,
And with fresh Flourets Hill and Valley smil'd.
This saw his hapless Foes, but stood obdur'd,
And to rebellious fight rallied thir Powers
Insensate, hope conceiving from despair.
In heav'nly Spirits could such perverseness dwell?
But to convince the proud what Signs availe,
Or Wonders move th' obdurate to relent?   790
They hard'nd more by what might most reclame,
Grieving to see his Glorie, at the sight
Took envie, and aspiring to his highth,
Stood reimbattell'd fierce, by force or fraud
Weening to prosper, and at length prevaile
Against God and *Messiah,* or to fall
In universal ruin last, and now
To final Battel drew, disdaining flight,
Or faint retreat; when the great Son of God
To all his Host on either hand thus spake.   800
    Stand still in bright array ye Saints, here stand
Ye Angels arm'd, this day from Battel rest;
Faithful hath been your Warfare, and of God
Accepted, fearless in his righteous Cause,
And as ye have receivd, so have ye don
Invincibly; but of this cursed crew
The punishment to other hand belongs,
Vengeance is his, or whose he sole appoints;
Number to this dayes work is not ordain'd
Nor multitude, stand onely and behold   810
Gods indignation on these Godless pourd
By mee; not you but mee they have despis'd,
Yet envied; against mee is all thir rage,
Because the Father, t'whom in Heav'n supream
Kingdom and Power and Glorie appertains,
Hath honourd me according to his will.
Therefore to mee thir doom he hath assig'n'd;
That they may have thir wish, to trie with mee
In Battel which the stronger proves, they all,
Or I alone against them, since by strength   820
They measure all, of other excellence
Not emulous, nor care who them excells;
Nor other strife with them do I voutsafe.
    So spake the Son, and into terrour chang'd
His count'nance too severe to be beheld
And full of wrauth bent on his Enemies

At once the Four spred out thir Starrie wings
With dreadful shade contiguous, and the Orbes
Of his fierce Chariot rowld, as with the sound
Of torrent Floods, or of a numerous Host.　　　　　　　　830
Hee on his impious Foes right onward drove,
Gloomie as Night; under his burning Wheeles
The stedfast Empyrean shook throughout,
All but the Throne it self of God. Full soon
Among them he arriv'd; in his right hand
Grasping ten thousand Thunders, which he sent
Before him, such as in thir Soules infix'd
Plagues; they astonisht all resistance lost,
All courage; down thir idle weapons drop'd;
O're Shields and Helmes, and helmed heads he rode　　840
Of Thrones and mighty Seraphim prostrate,
That wish'd the Mountains now might be again
Thrown on them as a shelter from his ire.
Nor less on either side tempestuous fell
His arrows, from the fourfold-visag'd Foure,
Distinct with eyes, and from the living Wheels,
Distinct alike with multitude of eyes,
One Spirit in them rul'd, and every eye
Glar'd lightning, and shot forth pernicious fire
Among th' accurst, that witherd all thir strength,　　850
And of thir wonted vigour left them draind,
Exhausted, spiritless, afflicted, fall'n.
Yet half his strength he put not forth, but check'd
His Thunder in mid Volie, for he meant
Not to destroy, but root them out of Heav'n:
The overthrown he rais'd, and as a Heard
Of Goats or timerous flock together throngd
Drove them before him Thunder-struck, pursu'd
With terrors and with furies to the bounds
And Chrystall wall of Heav'n, which op'ning wide,　　860
Rowld inward, and a spacious Gap disclos'd
Into the wastful Deep; the monstrous sight
Strook them with horror backward, but far worse
Urg'd them behind; headlong themselvs they threw
Down from the verge of Heav'n, Eternal wrauth
Burnt after them to the bottomless pit.
　　Hell heard th' unsufferable noise, Hell saw
Heav'n ruining from Heav'n and would have fled
Affrighted; but strict Fate had cast too deep
Her dark foundations, and too fast had bound.　　　870
Nine dayes they fell; confounded *Chaos* roard,
And felt tenfold confusion in thir fall
Through his wilde Anarchie, so huge a rout
Incumberd him with ruin: Hell at last
Yawning receavd them whole, and on them clos'd,
Hell thir fit habitation fraught with fire
Unquenchable, the house of woe and paine.
Disburd'nd Heav'n rejoic'd, and soon repaird
Her mural breach, returning whence it rowld.

Sole Victor from th' expulsion of his Foes   880
Messiah his triumphal Chariot turnd:
To meet him all his Saints, who silent stood
Eye witnesses of his Almightie Acts,
With Jubilie advanc'd; and as they went,
Shaded with branching Palme, each order bright,
Sung Triumph, and him sung Victorious King,
Son, Heire, and Lord, to him Dominion giv'n,
Worthiest to Reign: he celebrated rode
Triumphant through mid Heav'n, into the Courts
And Temple of his mightie Father Thron'd   890
On high; who into Glorie him receav'd,
Where now he sits at the right hand of bliss.
    Thus measuring things in Heav'n by things on Earth
At thy request, and that thou maist beware
By what is past, to thee I have reveal'd
What might have else to human Race bin hid;
The discord which befel, and Warr in Heav'n
Among th' Angelic Powers, and the deep fall
Of those too high aspiring, who rebelld
With *Satan,* hee who envies now thy state,   900
Who now is plotting how he may seduce
Thee also from obedience, that with him
Bereavd of happiness thou maist partake
His punishment, Eternal miserie;
Which would be all his solace and revenge,
As a despite don against the most High,
Thee once to gaine Companion of his woe.
But list'n not to his Temptations, warne
Thy weaker; let it profit thee to have heard
By terrible Example the reward   910
Of disobedience; firm they might have stood,
Yet fell; remember, and fear to transgress.

The End of the Sixth Book.

PARADISE LOST.

BOOK VII.

The Argument.

Raphael *at the request of* Adam *relates how and wherefore this World was first created; that God,
after the expelling of* Satan *and his Angels out of Heaven, declar'd his pleasure to create another World
and other Creatures to dwell therein; sends his Son with Glory and attendance of Angels to perform the
work of Creation in six dayes: the Angels celebrate with Hymns the performance thereof, and his reas-
cention into Heaven.*

DESCEND from Heav'n *Urania,* by that name
If rightly thou art call'd, whose Voice divine
Following, above th' *Olympian* Hill I soare,
Above the flight of *Pegasean* wing.
The meaning, not the Name I call: for thou

Nor of the Muses nine, nor on the top
Of old *Olympus* dwell'st, but Heav'nlie borne,
Before the Hills appeerd, or Fountain flow'd,
Thou with Eternal wisdom didst converse,
Wisdom thy Sister, and with her didst play   10
In presence of th' Almightie Father, pleas'd
With thy Celestial Song. Up led by thee
Into the Heav'n of Heav'ns I have presum'd,
An Earthlie Guest, and drawn Empyreal Aire,
Thy tempring; with like safetie guided down
Return me to my Native Element:
Least from this flying Steed unrein'd, (as once
Bellerophon, though from a lower Clime)
Dismounted, on th' *Aleian* Field I fall
Erroneous, there to wander and forlorne.   20
Half yet remaines unsung, but narrower bound
Within the visible Diurnal Spheare;
Standing on Earth, not rapt above the Pole,
More safe I Sing with mortal voice, unchang'd
To hoarce or mute, though fall'n on evil dayes,
On evil dayes though fall'n, and evil tongues;
In darkness, and with dangers compast round,
And solitude; yet not alone, while thou
Visit'st my slumbers Nightly, or when Morn
Purples the East: still govern thou my Song,   30
Urania, and fit audience find, though few.
But drive farr off the barbarous dissonance
Of *Bacchus* and his Revellers, the Race
Of that wilde Rout that tore the *Thracian* Bard
In *Rhodope,* where Woods and Rocks had Eares
To rapture, till the savage clamor dround
Both Harp and Voice; nor could the Muse defend
Her Son. So fail not thou, who thee implores:
For thou art Heav'nlie, shee an empty dreame.
  Say Goddess, what ensu'd when *Raphael,*   40
The affable Arch-angel, had forewarn'd
Adam by dire example to beware
Apostasie, by what befell in Heaven
To those Apostates, least the like befall
In Paradise to *Adam* or his Race,
Charg'd not to touch the interdicted Tree,
If they transgress, and slight that sole command,
So easily obeyd amid the choice
Of all tasts else to please thir appetite,
Though wandring. He with his consorted *Eve*   50
The storie heard attentive, and was fill'd
With admiration, and deep Muse to heare
Of things so high and strange, things to thir thought
So unimaginable as hate in Heav'n,
And Warr so neer the Peace of God in bliss
With such confusion: but the evil soon
Driv'n back redounded as a flood on those
From whom it sprung, impossible to mix

With Blessedness. Whence *Adam* soon repeal'd
The doubts that in his heart arose: and now   60
Led on, yet sinless, with desire to know
What neerer might concern him, how this World
Of Heav'n and Earth conspicuous first began,
When, and whereof created, for what cause,
What within *Eden* or without was done
Before his memorie, as one whose drouth
Yet scarce allay'd still eyes the current streame,
Whose liquid murmur heard new thirst excites,
Proceeded thus to ask his Heav'nly Guest.

   Great things, and full of wonder in our eares,   70
Farr differing from this World, thou hast reveal'd
Divine Interpreter, by favour sent
Down from the Empyrean to forewarne
Us timely of what might else have bin our loss,
Unknown, which human knowledg could not reach:
For which to the infinitly Good we owe
Immortal thanks, and his admonishment
Receave with solemne purpose to observe
Immutably his sovran will, the end
Of what we are. But since thou hast voutsaf't   80
Gently for our instruction to impart
Things above Earthly thought, which yet concernd
Our knowing, as to highest wisdom seemd,
Deign to descend now lower, and relate
What may no less perhaps availe us known,
How first began this Heav'n which we behold
Distant so high, with moving Fires adornd
Innumerable, and this which yeelds or fills
All space, the ambient Aire wide interfus'd
Imbracing round this florid Earth, what cause   90
Mov'd the Creator in his holy Rest
Through all Eternitie so late to build
In *Chaos,* and the work begun, how soon
Absolv'd, if unforbid thou maist unfould
What wee, not to explore the secrets aske
Of his Eternal Empire, but the more
To magnifie his works, the more we know.
And the great Light of Day yet wants to run
Much of his Race though steep, suspens in Heav'n
Held by thy voice, thy potent voice he heares,   100
And longer will delay to heare thee tell
His Generation, and the rising Birth
Of Nature from the unapparent Deep:
Or if the Starr of Eevning and the Moon
Haste to thy audience, Night with her will bring
Silence, and Sleep listning to thee will watch,
Or we can bid his absence, till thy Song
End, and dismiss thee ere the Morning shine.

   Thus *Adam* his illustrous Guest besought:
And thus the Godlike Angel answerd milde.   110
This also thy request with caution askt

Obtaine: though to recount Almightie works
What words or tongue of Seraph can suffice,
Or heart of man suffice to comprehend?
Yet what thou canst attain, which best may serve
To glorifie the Maker, and inferr
Thee also happier, shall not be withheld
Thy hearing, such Commission from above
I have receav'd, to answer thy desire
Of knowledge within bounds; beyond abstain   120
To ask, nor let thine own inventions hope
Things not reveal'd, which th' invisible King,
Onely Omniscient, hath supprest in Night,
To none communicable in Earth or Heaven:
Anough is left besides to search and know.
But Knowledge is as food, and needs no less
Her Temperance over Appetite, to know
In measure what the mind may well contain,
Oppresses else with Surfet, and soon turns
Wisdom to Folly, as Nourishment to Winde.   130
    Know then, that after *Lucifer* from Heav'n
(So call him, brighter once amidst the Host
Of Angels, then that Starr the Starrs among)
Fell with his flaming Legions through the Deep
Into his place, and the great Son returnd
Victorious with his Saints, th' Omnipotent
Eternal Father from his Throne beheld
Thir multitude, and to his Son thus spake.
    At least our envious Foe hath fail'd, who thought
All like himself rebellious, by whose aid   140
This inaccessible high strength, the seat
Of Deitie supream, us dispossest,
He trusted to have seis'd, and into fraud
Drew many, whom thir place knows here no more;
Yet farr the greater part have kept, I see,
Thir station, Heav'n yet populous retaines
Number sufficient to possess her Realmes
Though wide, and this high Temple to frequent
With Ministeries due and solemn Rites:
But least his heart exalt him in the harme   150
Already done, to have dispeopl'd Heav'n,
My damage fondly deem'd, I can repaire
That detriment, if such it be to lose
Self-lost, and in a moment will create
Another World, out of one man a Race
Of men innumerable, there to dwell,
Not here, till by degrees of merit rais'd
They open to themselves at length the way
Up hither, under long obedience tri'd,
And Earth be chang'd to Heavn, & Heav'n to Earth,   160
One Kingdom, Joy and Union without end.
Mean while inhabit laxe, ye Powers of Heav'n,
And thou my Word, begotten Son, by thee
This I perform, speak thou, and be it don:

My overshadowing Spirit and might with thee
I send along, ride forth, and bid the Deep
Within appointed bounds be Heav'n and Earth,
Boundless the Deep, because I am who fill
Infinitude, nor vacuous the space.
Though I uncircumscrib'd my self retire,   170
And put not forth my goodness, which is free
To act or not, Necessitie and Chance
Approach not mee, and what I will is Fate.
    So spake th' Almightie, and to what he spake
His Word, the Filial Godhead, gave effect.
Immediate are the Acts of God, more swift
Then time or motion, but to human ears
Cannot without process of speech be told,
So told as earthly notion can receave.
Great triumph and rejoycing was in Heav'n   180
When such was heard declar'd the Almightie's will;
Glorie they sung to the most High, good will
To future men, and in thir dwellings peace:
Glorie to him whose just avenging ire
Had driven out th' ungodly from his sight
And th' habitations of the just; to him
Glorie and praise, whose wisdom had ordain'd
Good out of evil to create, in stead
Of Spirits maligne a better Race to bring
Into thir vacant room, and thence diffuse   190
His good to Worlds and Ages infinite.
So sang the Hierarchies: Mean while the Son
On his great Expedition now appeer'd,
Girt with Omnipotence, with Radiance crown'd
Of Majestie Divine, Sapience and Love
Immense, and all his Father in him shon.
About his Chariot numberless were pour'd
Cherub and Seraph, Potentates and Thrones,
And Vertues, winged Spirits, and Chariots wing'd,
From the Armoury of God, where stand of old   200
Myriads between two brazen Mountains lodg'd
Against a solemn day, harnest at hand,
Celestial Equipage; and now came forth
Spontaneous, for within them Spirit livd,
Attendant on thir Lord: Heav'n op'nd wide
Her ever during Gates, Harmonious sound
On golden Hinges moving, to let forth
The King of Glorie in his powerful Word
And Spirit coming to create new Worlds.
On heav'nly ground they stood, and from the shore   210
They view'd the vast immeasurable Abyss
Outrageous as a Sea, dark, wasteful, wilde,
Up from the bottom turn'd by furious windes
And surging waves, as Mountains to assault
Heav'ns highth, and with the Center mix the Pole.
    Silence, ye troubl'd waves, and thou Deep, peace,
Said then th' Omnific Word, your discord end:

    Nor staid, but on the Wings of Cherubim
Uplifted, in Paternal Glorie rode
Farr into *Chaos,* and the World unborn;   220
For *Chaos* heard his voice: him all his Traine
Follow'd in bright procession to behold
Creation, and the wonders of his might.
Then staid the fervid Wheeles, and in his hand
He took the golden Compasses, prepar'd
In Gods Eternal store, to circumscribe
This Universe, and all created things:
One foot he center'd, and the other turn'd
Round through the vast profunditie obscure,
And said, thus farr extend, thus farr thy bounds,   230
This be thy just Circumference, O World.
Thus God the Heav'n created, thus the Earth,
Matter unform'd and void: Darkness profound
Cover'd th' Abyss: but on the watrie calme
His brooding wings the Spirit of God outspred,
And vital vertue infus'd, and vital warmth
Throughout the fluid Mass, but downward purg'd
The black tartareous cold infernal dregs
Adverse to life: then founded, then conglob'd
Like things to like, the rest to several place   240
Disparted, and between spun out the Air,
And Earth self-ballanc't on her Center hung.
    Let ther be Light, said God, and forthwith Light
Ethereal, first of things, quintessence pure
Sprung from the Deep, and from her Native East
To journie through the airie gloom began,
Sphear'd in a radiant Cloud, for yet the Sun
Was not; shee in a cloudie Tabernacle
Sojourn'd the while. God saw the Light was good;
And light from darkness by the Hemisphere   250
Divided: Light the Day, and Darkness Night
He nam'd. Thus was the first Day Eev'n and Morn:
Nor past uncelebrated, nor unsung
By the Celestial Quires, when Orient Light
Exhaling first from Darkness they beheld;
Birth-day of Heav'n and Earth; with joy and shout
The hollow Universal Orb they fill'd,
And touch't thir Golden Harps, & hymning prais'd
God and his works, Creatour him they sung,
Both when first Eevning was, and when first Morn.   260
    Again, God said, let ther be Firmament
Amid the Waters, and let it divide
The Waters from the Waters: and God made
The Firmament, expanse of liquid, pure,
Transparent, Elemental Air, diffus'd
In circuit to the uttermost convex
Of this great Round: partition firm and sure,
The Waters underneath from those above
Dividing: for as Earth, so hee the World
Built on circumfluous Waters calme, in wide   270

Crystallin Ocean, and the loud misrule
Of *Chaos* farr remov'd, least fierce extreames
Contiguous might distemper the whole frame:
And Heav'n he nam'd the Firmament: So Eev'n
And Morning *Chorus* sung the second Day.
   The Earth was form'd, but in the Womb as yet
Of Waters, Embryon immature involv'd,
Appeer'd not: over all the face of Earth
Main Ocean flow'd, not idle, but with warme
Prolific humour soft'ning all her Globe,   280
Fermented the great Mother to conceave,
Satiate with genial moisture, when God said
Be gather'd now ye Waters under Heav'n
Into one place, and let dry Land appeer.
Immediately the Mountains huge appeer
Emergent, and thir broad bare backs upheave
Into the Clouds, thir tops ascend the Skie:
So high as heav'd the tumid Hills, so low
Down sunk a hollow bottom broad and deep,
Capacious bed of Waters: thither they   290
Hasted with glad precipitance, uprowld
As drops on dust conglobing from the drie;
Part rise in crystal Wall, or ridge direct,
For haste; such flight the great command impress'd
On the swift flouds: as Armies at the call
Of Trumpet (for of Armies thou hast heard)
Troop to thir Standard, so the watrie throng,
Wave rowling after Wave, where way they found,
If steep, with torrent rapture, if through Plaine,
Soft-ebbing; nor withstood them Rock or Hill,   300
But they, or under ground, or circuit wide
With Serpent errour wandring, found thir way,
And on the washie Oose deep Channels wore;
Easie, e're God had bid the ground be drie,
All but within those banks, where Rivers now
Stream, and perpetual draw thir humid traine.
The dry Land, Earth, and the great receptacle
Of congregated Waters he call'd Seas:
And saw that it was good, and said, Let th' Earth
Put forth the verdant Grass, Herb yeilding Seed,   310
And Fruit Tree yeilding Fruit after her kind;
Whose Seed is in her self upon the Earth.
He scarce had said, when the bare Earth, till then
Desert and bare, unsightly, unadorn'd,
Brought forth the tender Grass, whose verdure clad
Her Universal Face with pleasant green,
Then Herbs of every leaf, that sudden flour'd
Op'ning thir various colours, and made gay
Her bosom smelling sweet: and these scarce blown,
Forth flourish't thick the clustring Vine, forth crept 320
The swelling Gourd, up stood the cornie Reed
Embattell'd in her field: add the humble Shrub,
And Bush with frizl'd hair implicit: last

Rose as in Dance the stately Trees, and spred
Thir branches hung with copious Fruit; or gemm'd
Thir Blossoms: with high Woods the Hills were crownd,
With tufts the vallies & each fountain side,
With borders long the Rivers. That Earth now
Seemd like to Heav'n, a seat where Gods might dwell,
Or wander with delight, and love to haunt   330
Her sacred shades: though God had yet not rain'd
Upon the Earth, and man to till the ground
None was, but from the Earth a dewie Mist
Went up and waterd all the ground, and each
Plant of the field, which e're it was in the Earth
God made, and every Herb, before it grew
On the green stemm; God saw that it was good:
So Eev'n and Morn recorded the Third Day.
    Again th' Almightie spake: Let there be Lights
High in th' expanse of Heaven to divide   340
The Day from Night; and let them be for Signes,
For Seasons, and for Dayes, and circling Years,
And let them be for Lights as I ordaine
Thir Office in the Firmament of Heav'n
To give Light on the Earth; and it was so.
And God made two great Lights, great for thir use
To Man, the greater to have rule by Day,
The less by Night alterne: and made the Starrs,
And set them in the Firmament of Heav'n
To illuminate the Earth, and rule the Day   350
In thir vicissitude, and rule the Night,
And Light from Darkness to divide. God saw,
Surveying his great Work, that it was good:
For of Celestial Bodies first the Sun
A mightie Spheare he fram'd, unlightsom first,
Though of Ethereal Mould: then form'd the Moon
Globose, and everie magnitude of Starrs,
And sowd with Starrs the Heav'n thick as a field:
Of Light by farr the greater part he took,
Transplanted from her cloudie Shrine, and plac'd   360
In the Suns Orb, made porous to receive
And drink the liquid Light, firm to retaine
Her gather'd beams, great Palace now of Light.
Hither as to thir Fountain other Starrs
Repairing, in thir gold'n Urns draw Light,
And hence the Morning Planet guilds his horns;
By tincture or reflection they augment
Thir small peculiar, though from human sight
So farr remote, with diminution seen.
First in his East the glorious Lamp was seen,   370
Regent of Day, and all th' Horizon round
Invested with bright Rayes, jocond to run
His Longitude through Heav'ns high rode: the gray
Dawn, and the *Pleiades* before him danc'd
Shedding sweet influence: less bright the Moon,
But opposite in leveld West was set

His mirror, with full face borrowing her Light
From him, for other light she needed none
In that aspect, and still that distance keepes
Till night, then in the East her turn she shines,   380
Revolvd on Heav'ns great Axle, and her Reign
With thousand lesser Lights dividual holds,
With thousand thousand Starres, that then appeer'd
Spangling the Hemisphere: then first adornd
With thir bright Luminaries that Set and Rose,
Glad Eevning & glad Morn crownd the fourth day.
   And God said, let the Waters generate
Reptil with Spawn abundant, living Soule:
And let Fowle flie above the Earth, with wings
Displayd on the op'n Firmament of Heav'n.   390
And God created the great Whales, and each
Soul living, each that crept, which plenteously
The waters generated by thir kindes,
And every Bird of wing after his kinde;
And saw that it was good, and bless'd them, saying,
Be fruitful, multiply, and in the Seas
And Lakes and running Streams the waters fill;
And let the Fowle be multiply'd on the Earth.
Forthwith the Sounds and Seas, each Creek & Bay
With Frie innumerable swarme, and Shoales   400
Of Fish that with thir Finns & shining Scales
Glide under the green Wave, in Sculles that oft
Bank the mid Sea: part single or with mate
Graze the Sea weed thir pasture, & through Groves
Of Coral stray, or sporting with quick glance
Show to the Sun thir wav'd coats dropt with Gold,
Or in thir Pearlie shells at ease, attend
Moist nutriment, or under Rocks thir food
In jointed Armour watch: on smooth the Seale,
And bended Dolphins play: part huge of bulk   410
Wallowing unweildie, enormous in thir Gate
Tempest the Ocean: there Leviathan
Hugest of living Creatures, on the Deep
Stretcht like a Promontorie sleeps or swimmes,
And seems a moving Land, and at his Gilles
Draws in, and at his Trunck spouts out a Sea.
Mean while the tepid Caves, and Fens and shoares
Thir Brood as numerous hatch, from the Egg that soon
Bursting with kindly rupture forth disclos'd
Thir callow young, but featherd soon and fledge   420
They summ'd thir Penns, and soaring th' air sublime
With clang despis'd the ground, under a cloud
In prospect; there the Eagle and the Stork
On Cliffs and Cedar tops thir Eyries build:
Part loosly wing the Region, part more wise
In common, rang'd in figure wedge thir way,
Intelligent of seasons, and set forth
Thir Aierie Caravan high over Sea's
Flying, and over Lands with mutual wing

Easing thir flight; so stears the prudent Crane　　　　430
Her annual Voiage, born on Windes; the Aire
Floats, as they pass, fann'd with unnumber'd plumes:
From Branch to Branch the smaller Birds with song
Solac'd the Woods, and spred thir painted wings
Till Ev'n, nor then the solemn Nightingal
Ceas'd warbling, but all night tun'd her soft layes:
Others on Silver Lakes and Rivers Bath'd
Thir downie Brest; the Swan with Arched neck
Between her white wings mantling proudly, Rowes
Her state with Oarie feet: yet oft they quit　　　　440
The Dank, and rising on stiff Pennons, towre
The mid Aereal Skie: Others on ground
Walk'd firm; the crested Cock whose clarion sounds
The silent hours, and th' other whose gay Traine
Adorns him, colour'd with the Florid hue
Of Rainbows and Starrie Eyes. The Waters thus
With Fish replenisht, and the Aire with Fowle,
Ev'ning and Morn solemniz'd the Fift day.
　　The Sixt, and of Creation last arose
With Eevning Harps and Mattin, when God said,　　　　450
Let th' Earth bring forth Fowle living in her kinde,
Cattel and Creeping things, and Beast of the Earth,
Each in their kinde. The Earth obey'd, and strait
Op'ning her fertil Woomb teem'd at a Birth
Innumerous living Creatures, perfet formes,
Limb'd and full grown: out of the ground up rose
As from his Laire the wilde Beast where he wonns
In Forrest wilde, in Thicket, Brake, or Den;
Among the Trees in Pairs they rose, they walk'd:
The Cattel in the Fields and Meddowes green:　　　　460
Those rare and solitarie, these in flocks
Pasturing at once, and in broad Herds upsprung.
The grassie Clods now Calv'd, now half appeer'd
The Tawnie Lion, pawing to get free
His hinder parts, then springs as broke from Bonds,
And Rampant shakes his Brinded main; the Ounce,
The Libbard, and the Tyger, as the Moale
Rising, the crumbl'd Earth above them threw
In Hillocks; the swift Stag from under ground
Bore up his branching head: scarse from his mould　　　　470
Behemoth biggest born of Earth upheav'd
His vastness: Fleec't the Flocks and bleating rose,
As Plants: ambiguous between Sea and Land
The River Horse and scalie Crocodile.
At once came forth whatever creeps the ground,
Insect or Worme; those wav'd thir limber fans
For wings, and smallest Lineaments exact
In all the Liveries dect of Summers pride
With spots of Gold and Purple, azure and green:
These as a line thir long dimension drew,　　　　480
Streaking the ground with sinuous trace; not all
Minims of Nature; some of Serpent kinde

Wondrous in length and corpulence involv'd
Thir Snakie foulds, and added wings. First crept
The Parsimonious Emmet, provident
Of future, in small room large heart enclos'd,
Pattern of just equalitie perhaps
Hereafter, join'd in her popular Tribes
Of Commonaltie: swarming next appeer'd
The Femal Bee that feeds her Husband Drone   490
Deliciously, and builds her waxen Cells
With Honey stor'd: the rest are numberless,
And thou thir Natures know'st, and gav'st them Names,
Needless to thee repeated; nor unknown
The Serpent suttl'st Beast of all the field,
Of huge extent somtimes, with brazen Eyes
And hairie Main terrific, though to thee
Not noxious, but obedient at thy call.
Now Heav'n in all her Glorie shon, and rowld
Her motions, as the great first-Movers hand   500
First wheeld thir course; Earth in her rich attire
Consummate lovly smil'd; Aire, Water, Earth,
By Fowl, Fish, Beast, was flown, was swum, was walkt
Frequent; and of the Sixt day yet remain'd;
There wanted yet the Master work, the end
Of all yet don; a Creature who not prone
And Brute as other Creatures, but endu'd
With Sanctitie of Reason, might erect
His Stature, and upright with Front serene
Govern the rest, self-knowing, and from thence   510
Magnanimous to correspond with Heav'n,
But grateful to acknowledge whence his good
Descends, thither with heart and voice and eyes
Directed in Devotion, to adore
And worship God Supream, who made him chief
Of all his works: therefore the Omnipotent
Eternal Father (For where is not hee
Present) thus to his Son audibly spake.
    Let us make now Man in our image, Man
In our similitude, and let them rule   520
Over the Fish and Fowle of Sea and Aire,
Beast of the Field, and over all the Earth,
And every creeping thing that creeps the ground.
This said, he formd thee, *Adam*, thee O Man
Dust of the ground, and in thy nostrils breath'd
The breath of Life; in his own Image hee
Created thee, in the Image of God
Express, and thou becam'st a living Soul.
Male he created thee, but thy consort
Femal for Race; then bless'd Mankinde, and said,   530
Be fruitful, multiplie, and fill the Earth,
Subdue it, and throughout Dominion hold
Over Fish of the Sea, and Fowle of the Aire,
And every living thing that moves on the Earth.
Wherever thus created, for no place

Is yet distinct by name, thence, as thou know'st
He brought thee into this delicious Grove,
This Garden, planted with the Trees of God,
Delectable both to behold and taste;
And freely all thir pleasant fruit for food   540
Gave thee, all sorts are here that all th' Earth yeelds,
Varietie without end; but of the Tree
Which tasted works knowledge of Good and Evil,
Thou mai'st not; in the day thou eat'st, thou di'st;
Death is the penaltie impos'd, beware,
And govern well thy appetite, least sin
Surprise thee, and her black attendant Death.
Here finish'd hee, and all that he had made
View'd, and behold all was entirely good;
So Ev'n and Morn accomplish't the Sixt day: 550
Yet not till the Creator from his work
Desisting, though unwearied, up returnd
Up to the Heav'n of Heav'ns his high abode,
Thence to behold this new created World
Th' addition of his Empire, how it shew'd
In prospect from his Throne, how good, how faire,
Answering his great Idea. Up he rode
Followd with acclamation and the sound
Symphonious of ten thousand Harpes that tun'd
Angelic harmonies: the Earth, the Aire   560
Resounded, (thou remember'st, for thou heardst)
The Heav'ns and all the Constellations rung,
The Planets in thir stations list'ning stood,
While the bright Pomp ascended jubilant.
Open, ye everlasting Gates, they sung,
Open, ye Heav'ns, your living dores; let in
The great Creator from his work returnd
Magnificent, his Six days work, a World;
Open, and henceforth oft; for God will deigne
To visit oft the dwellings of just Men   570
Delighted, and with frequent intercourse
Thither will send his winged Messengers
On errands of supernal Grace. So sung
The glorious Train ascending: He through Heav'n,
That open'd wide her blazing Portals, led
To Gods Eternal house direct the way,
A broad and ample rode, whose dust is Gold
And pavement Starrs, as Starrs to thee appeer,
Seen in the Galaxie, that Milkie way
Which nightly as a circling Zone thou seest   580
Pouderd with Starrs. And now on Earth the Seaventh
Eev'ning arose in *Eden,* for the Sun
Was set, and twilight from the East came on,
Forerunning Night; when at the holy mount
Of Heav'ns high-seated top, th' Impereal Throne
Of Godhead, fixt for ever firm and sure,
The Filial Power arriv'd, and sate him down
With his great Father. for he also went

Invisible, yet staid (such priviledge
Hath Omnipresence) and the work ordain'd,   590
Author and end of all things, and from work
Now resting, bless'd and hallowd the Seav'nth day,
As resting on that day from all his work,
But not in silence holy kept; the Harp
Had work and rested not, the solemn Pipe,
And Dulcimer, all Organs of sweet stop,
All sounds on Fret by String or Golden Wire
Temper'd soft Tunings, intermixt with Voice
Choral or Unison: of incense Clouds
Fuming from Golden Censers hid the Mount.   600
Creation and the Six dayes acts they sung,
Great are thy works, *Jehovah,* infinite
Thy power; what thought can measure thee or tongue
Relate thee; greater now in thy return
Then from the Giant Angels; thee that day
Thy Thunders magnifi'd; but to create
Is greater then created to destroy.
Who can impair thee, mighty King, or bound
Thy Empire? easily the proud attempt
Of Spirits apostat and thir Counsels vaine   610
Thou hast repeld, while impiously they thought
Thee to diminish, and from thee withdraw
The number of thy worshippers. Who seekes
To lessen thee, against his purpose serves
To manifest the more thy might: his evil
Thou usest, and from thence creat'st more good.
Witness this new-made World, another Heav'n
From Heaven Gate not farr, founded in view
On the cleer *Hyaline,* the Glassie Sea;
Of amplitude almost immense, with Starr's   620
Numerous, and every Starr perhaps a World
Of destind habitation; but thou know'st
Thir seasons: among these the seat of men,
Earth with her nether Ocean circumfus'd,
Thir pleasant dwelling place. Thrice happie men,
And sons of men, whom God hath thus advanc't,
Created in his Image, there to dwell
And worship him, and in reward to rule
Over his Works, on Earth, in Sea, or Air,
And multiply a Race of Worshippers   630
Holy and just: thrice happie if they know
Thir happiness, and persevere upright.
   So sung they, and the Empyrean rung,
With *Halleluiahs:* Thus was Sabbath kept.
And thy request think now fulfill'd, that ask'd
How first this World and face of things began,
And what before thy memorie was don
From the beginning, that posteritie
Informd by thee might know; if else thou seekst
Aught, not surpassing human measure, say.   640

The End of the Seventh Book.

PARADISE LOST.

BOOK VIII.

The Argument.

Adam *inquires concerning celestial Motions, is doubtfully answer'd, and exhorted to search rather things more worthy of knowledg:* Adam *assents, and still desirous to detain* Raphael, *relates to him what he remember'd since his own Creation, his placing in Paradise, his talk with God concerning solitude and fit society, his first meeting and Nuptials with* Eve, *his discourse with the Angel thereupon; who after admonitions repeated departs.*

THE Angel ended, and in *Adams* Eare
So Charming left his voice, that he a while
Thought him still speaking, still stood fixt to hear;
Then as new wak't thus gratefully repli'd.
What thanks sufficient, or what recompence
Equal have I to render thee, Divine
Hystorian, who thus largely hast allayd
The thirst I had of knowledge, and voutsaf't
This friendly condescention to relate
Things else by me unsearchable, now heard   10
With wonder, but delight, and, as is due,
With glorie attributed to the high
Creator; some thing yet of doubt remaines,
Which onely thy solution can resolve.
When I behold this goodly Frame, this World
Of Heav'n and Earth consisting, and compute,
Thir magnitudes, this Earth a spot, a graine,
An Atom, with the Firmament compar'd
And all her numberd Starrs, that seem to rowle
Spaces incomprehensible (for such   20
Thir distance argues and thir swift return
Diurnal) meerly to officiate light
Round this opacous Earth, this punctual spot,
One day and night; in all thir vast survey
Useless besides, reasoning I oft admire,
How Nature wise and frugal could commit
Such disproportions, with superfluous hand
So many nobler Bodies to create,
Greater so manifold to this one use,
For aught appeers, and on thir Orbs impose   30
Such restless revolution day by day
Repeated, while the sedentarie Earth,
That better might with farr less compass move,
Serv'd by more noble then her self, attaines
Her end without least motion, and receaves,
As Tribute such a sumless journey brought
Of incorporeal speed, her warmth and light;
Speed, to describe whose swiftness Number failes.
    So spake our Sire, and by his count'nance seemd
Entring on studious thoughts abstruse, which *Eve* 40
Perceaving where she sat retir'd in sight,
With lowliness Majestic from her seat,

And Grace that won who saw to wish her stay,
Rose, and went forth among her Fruits and Flours.
To visit how they prosper'd, bud and bloom,
Her Nurserie; they at her coming sprung
And toucht by her fair tendance gladlier grew.
Yet went she not, as not with such discourse
Delighted, or not capable her eare
Of what was high: such pleasure she reserv'd,   50
Adam relating, she sole Auditress;
Her Husband the Relater she preferr'd
Before the Angel, and of him to ask
Chose rather; hee, she knew would intermix
Grateful digressions, and solve high dispute
With conjugal Caresses, from his Lip
Not Words alone pleas'd her. O when meet now
Such pairs, in Love and mutual Honour joyn'd?
With Goddess-like demeanour forth she went;
Not unattended, for on her as Queen   60
A pomp of winning Graces waited still,
And from about her shot Darts of desire
Into all Eyes to wish her still in sight.
And *Raphael* now to *Adam's* doubt propos'd
Benevolent and facil thus repli'd.
   To ask or search I blame thee not, for Heav'n
Is as the Book of God before thee set,
Wherein to read his wondrous Works, and learne
His Seasons, Hours, or Days, or Months, or Yeares:
This to attain, whether Heav'n move or Earth,   70
Imports not, if thou reck'n right, the rest
From Man or Angel the great Architect
Did wisely to conceal, and not divulge
His secrets to be scann'd by them who ought
Rather admire; or if they list to try
Conjecture, he his Fabric of the Heav'ns
Hath left to thir disputes, perhaps to move
His laughter at thir quaint Opinions wide
Hereafter, when they come to model Heav'n
And calculate the Starrs, how they will weild   80
The mightie frame, how build, unbuild, contrive
To save appeerances, how gird the Sphear
With Centric and Eccentric scribl'd o're,
Cycle and Epicycle, Orb in Orb:
Alreadie by thy reasoning this I guess,
Who art to lead thy ofspring, and supposest
That Bodies bright and greater should not serve
The less not bright, nor Heav'n such journies run,
Earth sitting still, when she alone receaves
The benefit: consider first, that Great   90
Or Bright inferrs not Excellence: the Earth
Though, in comparison of Heav'n, so small,
Nor glistering, may of solid good containe
More plenty then the Sun that barren shines,
Whose vertue on it self workes no effect,

But in the fruitful Earth; there first receavd
His beams, unactive else, thir vigor find.
Yet not to Earth are those bright Luminaries
Officious, but to thee Earths habitant.
And for the Heav'ns wide Circuit, let it speak   100
The Makers high magnificence, who built
So spacious, and his Line stretcht out so farr;
That Man may know he dwells not in his own;
An Edifice too large for him to fill,
Lodg'd in a small partition, and the rest
Ordain'd for uses to his Lord best known.
The swiftness of those Circles attribute,
Though numberless, to his Omnipotence,
That to corporeal substances could adde
Speed almost Spiritual; mee thou thinkst not slow,   110
Who since the Morning hour set out from Heav'n
Where God resides, and ere mid-day arriv'd
In *Eden,* distance inexpressible
By Numbers that have name. But this I urge,
Admitting Motion in the Heav'ns, to shew
Invalid that which thee to doubt it mov'd;
Not that I so affirm, though so it seem
To thee who hast thy dwelling here on Earth.
God to remove his wayes from human sense,
Plac'd Heav'n from Earth so farr, that earthly sight,   120
If it presume, might erre in things too high,
And no advantage gaine. What if the Sun
Be Center to the World, and other Starrs
By his attractive vertue and thir own
Incited, dance about him various rounds?
Thir wandring course now high, now low, then hid,
Progressive, retrograde, or standing still,
In six thou seest, and what if sev'nth to these
The Planet Earth, so stedfast though she seem,
Insensibly three different Motions move?   130
Which else to several Sphears thou must ascribe,
Mov'd contrarie with thwart obliquities,
Or save the Sun his labour, and that swift
Nocturnal and Diurnal rhomb suppos'd,
Invisible else above all Starrs, the Wheele
Of Day and Night; which needs not thy beleefe,
If Earth industrious of her self fetch Day
Travelling East, and with her part averse
From the Suns beam meet Night, her other part
Still luminous by his ray. What if that light   140
Sent from her through the wide transpicuous aire,
To the terrestrial Moon be as a Starr
Enlightning her by Day, as she by Night
This Earth? reciprocal, if Land be there,
Feilds and Inhabitants: Her spots thou seest
As Clouds, and Clouds may rain, and Rain produce
Fruits in her soft'nd Soile, for some to eate
Allotted there; and other Suns perhaps

With thir attendant Moons thou wilt descrie
Communicating Male and Femal Light,   150
Which two great Sexes animate the World,
Stor'd in each Orb perhaps with some that live.
For such vast room in Nature unpossest
By living Soule, desert and desolate,
Onely to shine, yet scarce to contribute
Each Orb a glimps of Light, conveyd so farr
Down to this habitable, which returnes
Light back to them, is obvious to dispute.
But whether thus these things, or whether not,
Whether the Sun predominant in Heav'n   160
Rise on the Earth, or Earth rise on the Sun,
Hee from the East his flaming rode begin,
Or Shee from West her silent course advance
With inoffensive pace that spinning sleeps
On her soft Axle, while she paces Eev'n,
And bears thee soft with the smooth Air along,
Sollicit not thy thoughts with matters hid,
Leave them to God above, him serve and feare;
Of other Creatures, as him pleases best,
Wherever plac't, let him dispose: joy thou   170
In what he gives to thee, this Paradise
And thy fair *Eve;* Heav'n is for thee too high
To know what passes there; be lowlie wise:
Think onely what concernes thee and thy being;
Dream not of other Worlds, what Creatures there
Live, in what state, condition or degree,
Contented that thus farr hath been reveal'd
Not of Earth onely but of highest Heav'n.
     To whom thus *Adam* cleerd of doubt, repli'd.
How fully hast thou satisfi'd mee, pure   180
Intelligence of Heav'n, Angel serene,
And freed from intricacies, taught to live,
The easiest way, nor with perplexing thoughts
To interrupt the sweet of Life, from which
God hath bid dwell farr off all anxious cares,
And not molest us, unless we our selves
Seek them with wandring thoughts, and notions vaine.
But apt the Mind or Fancie is to roave
Uncheckt, and of her roaving is no end;
Till warn'd, or by experience taught, she learne,   190
That not to know at large of things remote
From use, obscure and suttle, but to know
That which before us lies in daily life,
Is the prime Wisdom, what is more, is fume,
Or emptiness, or fond impertinence,
And renders us in things that most concerne
Unpractis'd, unprepar'd, and still to seek.
Therefore from this high pitch let us descend
A lower flight, and speak of things at hand
Useful, whence haply mention may arise   200
Of somthing not unseasonable to ask

By sufferance, and thy wonted favour deign'd.
Thee I have heard relating what was don
Ere my remembrance: now hear mee relate
My Storie, which perhaps thou hast not heard;
And Day is yet not spent; till then thou seest
How suttly to detaine thee I devise,
Inviting thee to hear while I relate,
Fond, were it not in hope of thy reply:
For while I sit with thee, I seem in Heav'n,   210
And sweeter thy discourse is to my eare
Then Fruits of Palm-tree pleasantest to thirst
And hunger both, from labour, at the houre
Of sweet repast; they satiate, and soon fill,
Though pleasant, but thy words with Grace Divine
Imbu'd, bring to thir sweetness no satietie.
    To whom thus *Raphael* answer'd heav'nly meek.
Nor are thy lips ungraceful, Sire of men,
Nor tongue ineloquent; for God on thee
Abundantly his gifts hath also pour'd   220
Inward and outward both, his image faire:
Speaking or mute all comliness and grace
Attends thee, and each word, each motion formes.
Nor less think wee in Heav'n of thee on Earth
Then of our fellow servant, and inquire
Gladly into the wayes of God with Man:
For God we see hath honour'd thee, and set
On Man his equal Love: say therefore on;
For I that Day was absent, as befell,
Bound on a voyage uncouth and obscure,   230
Farr on excursion toward the Gates of Hell;
Squar'd in full Legion (such command we had)
To see that none thence issu'd forth a spie,
Or enemie, while God was in his work,
Least hee incenst at such eruption bold,
Destruction with Creation might have mixt.
Not that they durst without his leave attempt,
But us he sends upon his high behests
For state, as Sovran King, and to enure
Our prompt obedience. Fast we found, fast shut   240
The dismal Gates, and barricado'd strong;
But long ere our approaching heard within
Noise, other then the sound of Dance or Song,
Torment, and lowd lament, and furious rage.
Glad we return'd up to the coasts of Light
Ere Sabbath Eev'ning: so we had in charge.
But thy relation now; for I attend,
Pleas'd with thy words no less then thou with mine.
    So spake the Godlike Power, and thus our Sire.
For Man to tell how human Life began   250
Is hard; for who himself beginning knew?
Desire with thee still longer to converse
Induc'd me. As new wak't from soundest sleep
Soft on the flourie herb I found me laid

In Balmie Sweat, which with his Beames the Sun
Soon dri'd, and on the reaking moisture fed.
Strait toward Heav'n my wondring Eyes I turnd,
And gaz'd a while the ample Skie, till rais'd
By quick instinctive motion up I sprung,
As thitherward endevoring, and·upright   260
Stood on my feet; about me round I saw
Hill, Dale, and shadie Woods, and sunnie Plaines,
And liquid Lapse of murmuring Streams; by these,
Creatures that livd, and movd, and walk'd, or flew,
Birds on the branches warbling; all things smil'd,
With fragrance and with joy my heart oreflow'd.
My self I then perus'd, and Limb by Limb
Survey'd, and sometimes went, and sometimes ran
With supple joints, as lively vigour led:
But who I was, or where, or from what cause,   270
Knew not; to speak I tri'd, and forthwith spake,
My Tongue obey'd and readily could name
What e're I saw. Thou Sun, said I, faire Light,
And thou enlight'nd Earth, so fresh and gay,
Ye Hills and Dales, ye Rivers, Woods, and Plaines.
And ye that live and move, fair Creatures, tell,
Tell, if ye saw, how came I thus, how here?
Not of my self; by some great Maker then,
In goodness and in power præeminent;
Tell me, how may I know him, how adore,   280
From whom I have that thus I move and live,
And feel that I am happier then I know.
While thus I call'd, and stray'd I knew not whither,
From where I first drew Aire, and first beheld
This happie Light, when answer none return'd,
On a green shadie Bank profuse of Flours
Pensive I sate me down; there gentle sleep
First found me, and with soft oppression seis'd
My droused sense, untroubl'd, though I thought
I then was passing to my former state   290
Insensible, and forthwith to dissolve:
When suddenly stood at my Head a dream,
Whose inward apparition gently mov'd
My Fancy to believe I yet had being,
And livd: One came, methought, of shape Divine,
And said, thy Mansion wants thee, *Adam,* rise,
First Man, of Men innumerable ordain'd
First Father, call'd by thee I come thy Guide
To the Garden of bliss, thy seat prepar'd.
So saying, by the hand he took me rais'd,   300
And over Fields and Waters, as in Aire
Smooth sliding without step, last led me up
A woodie Mountain; whose high top was plaine,
A Circuit wide, enclos'd, with goodliest Trees
Planted, with Walks, and Bowers, that what I saw
Of Earth before scarce pleasant seemd. Each Tree
Load'n with fairest Fruit, that hung to the Eye

Tempting, stirr'd in me sudden appetite
To pluck and eate; whereat I wak'd, and found
Before mine Eyes all real, as the dream   310
Had lively shadowd: Here had new begun
My wandring, had not hee who was my Guide
Up hither, from among the Trees appeer'd,
Presence Divine. Rejoycing, but with aw
In adoration at his feet I fell
Submiss: he rear'd me, & Whom thou soughtst I am,
Said mildely, Author of all this thou seest
Above, or round about thee or beneath.
This Paradise I give thee, count it thine
To Till and keep, and of the Fruit to eate: 320
Of every Tree that in the Garden growes
Eate freely with glad heart; fear here no dearth:
But of the Tree whose operation brings
Knowledg of good and ill, which I have set
The Pledge of thy Obedience and thy Faith,
Amid the Garden by the Tree of Life,
Remember what I warne thee, shun to taste,
And shun the bitter consequence: for know,
The day thou eat'st thereof, my sole command
Transgrest, inevitably thou shalt dye;   330
From that day mortal, and this happie State
Shalt loose, expell'd from hence into a World
Of woe and sorrow. Sternly he pronounc'd
The rigid interdiction, which resounds
Yet dreadful in mine eare, though in my choice
Not to incur; but soon his cleer aspect
Return'd and gratious purpose thus renew'd.
Not onely these fair bounds, but all the Earth
To thee and to thy Race I give; as Lords
Possess it, and all things that therein live,   340
Or live in Sea, or Aire, Beast, Fish, and Fowle.
In signe whereof each Bird and Beast behold
After thir kindes; I bring them to receave
From thee thir Names, and pay thee fealtie
With low subjection; understand the same
Of Fish within thir watry residence,
Not hither summond, since they cannot change
Thir Element to draw the thinner Aire.
As thus he spake, each Bird and Beast behold
Approaching two and two, These cowring low   350
With blandishment, each Bird stoop'd on his wing.
I nam'd them, as they pass'd, and understood
Thir Nature, with such knowledg God endu'd
My sudden apprehension: but in these
I found not what me thought I wanted still;
And to the Heav'nly vision thus presum'd.
    O by what Name, for thou above all these,
Above mankinde, or aught then mankinde higher,
Surpassest farr my naming, how may I
Adore thee, Author of this Universe,   360

And all this good to man, for whose well being
So amply, and with hands so liberal
Thou hast provided all things: but with mee
I see not who partakes. In solitude
What happiness, who can enjoy alone,
Or all enjoying, what contentment find?
Thus I presumptuous; and the vision bright,
As with a smile more bright'nd, thus repli'd.

   What call'st thou solitude, is not the Earth
With various living creatures, and the Aire   370
Replenisht, and all these at thy command
To come and play before thee, know'st thou not
Thir language and thir wayes, they also know,
And reason not contemptibly; with these
Find pastime, and beare rule; thy Realm is large.
So spake the Universal Lord, and seem'd
So ordering. I with leave of speech implor'd,
And humble deprecation thus repli'd.

   Let not my words offend thee, Heav'nly Power,
My Maker, be propitious while I speak.   380
Hast thou not made me here thy substitute,
And these inferiour farr beneath me set?
Among unequals what societie
Can sort, what harmonie or true delight?
Which must be mutual, in proportion due
Giv'n and receiv'd; but in disparitie
The one intense, the other still remiss
Cannot well suite with either, but soon prove
Tedious alike: Of fellowship I speak
Such as I seek, fit to participate   390
All rational delight, wherein the brute
Cannot be human consort; they rejoyce
Each with thir kinde, Lion with Lioness;
So fitly them in pairs thou hast combin'd;
Much less can Bird with Beast, or Fish with Fowle
So well converse, nor with the Ox the Ape;
Wors then can Man with Beast, and least of all.

   Whereto th' Almighty answer'd, not displeas'd.
A nice and suttle happiness I see
Thou to thy self proposest, in the choice   400
Of thy Associates, *Adam,* and wilt taste
No pleasure, though in pleasure, solitarie.
What thinkst thou then of mee, and this my State,
Seem I to thee sufficiently possest
Of happiness, or not? who am alone
From all Eternitie, for none I know
Second to mee or like, equal much less.
How have I then with whom to hold converse
Save with the Creatures which I made, and those
To me inferiour, infinite descents   410
Beneath what other Creatures are to thee?

   He ceas'd, I lowly answer'd. To attaine
The highth and depth of thy Eternal wayes

All human thoughts come short, Supream of things;
Thou in thy self art perfet, and in thee
Is no deficience found; not so is Man,
But in degree, the cause of his desire
By conversation with his like to help,
Or solace his defects. No need that thou
Shouldst propagat, already infinite;   420
And through all numbers absolute, though One;
But Man by number is to manifest
His single imperfection, and beget
Like of his like, his Image multipli'd,
In unitie defective, which requires
Collateral love, and deerest amitie.
Thou in thy secresie although alone,
Best with thy self accompanied, seek'st not
Social communication, yet so pleas'd,
Canst raise thy Creature to what highth thou wilt   430
Of Union or Communion, deifi'd;
I by conversing cannot these erect
From prone, nor in thir wayes complacence find.
Thus I embold'nd spake, and freedom us'd
Permissive, and acceptance found, which gain'd
This answer from the gratious voice Divine.

   Thus farr to try thee, *Adam,* I was pleas'd,
And finde thee knowing not of Beasts alone,
Which thou hast rightly nam'd, but of thy self,
Expressing well the spirit within thee free,   440
My Image, not imparted to the Brute,
Whose fellowship therefore unmeet for thee
Good reason was thou freely shouldst dislike,
And be so minded still; I, ere thou spak'st,
Knew it not good for Man to be alone,
And no such companie as then thou saw'st
Intended thee, for trial onely brought,
To see how thou could'st judge of fit and meet:
What next I bring shall please thee, be assur'd,
Thy likeness, thy fit help, thy other self,   450
Thy wish, exactly to thy hearts desire.

   Hee ended, or I heard no more, for now
My earthly by his Heav'nly overpowerd,
Which it had long stood under, streind to the highth
In that celestial Colloquie sublime,
As with an object that excels the sense,
Dazl'd and spent, sunk down, and sought repair
Of sleep, which instantly fell on me, call'd
By Nature as in aide, and clos'd mine eyes.
Mine eyes he clos'd, but op'n left the Cell   460
Of Fancie my internal sight, by which
Abstract as in a transe methought I saw,
Though sleeping, where I lay, and saw the shape
Still glorious before whom awake I stood;
Who stooping op'nd my left side, and took
From thence a Rib, with cordial spirits warme,

And Life-blood streaming fresh; wide was the wound,
But suddenly with flesh fill'd up & heal'd:
The Rib he formd and fashond with his hands;
Under his forming hands a Creature grew,   470
Manlike, but different sex, so lovly faire,
That what seemd fair in all the World, seemd now
Mean, or in her summd up, in her containd
And in her looks, which from that time infus'd
Sweetness into my heart, unfelt before,
And into all things from her Aire inspir'd
The spirit of love and amorous delight.
She disappeerd, and left me dark, I wak'd
To find her, or for ever to deplore
Her loss, and other pleasures all abjure: 480
When out of hope, behold her, not farr off,
Such as I saw her in my dream, adornd
With what all Earth or Heaven could bestow
To make her amiable: On she came,
Led by her Heav'nly Maker, though unseen,
And guided by his voice, nor uninformd
Of nuptial Sanctitie and marriage Rites:
Grace was in all her steps, Heav'n in her Eye,
In every gesture dignitie and love.
I overjoyd could not forbear aloud,   490
    This turn hath made amends; thou hast fulfill'd
Thy words, Creator bounteous and benigne,
Giver of all things faire, but fairest this
Of all thy gifts, nor enviest. I now see
Bone of my Bone, Flesh of my Flesh, my Self
Before me; Woman is her Name, of Man
Extracted; for this cause he shall forgoe
Father and Mother, and to his Wife adhere;
And they shall be one Flesh, one Heart, one Soule.
    She heard me thus, and though divinely brought,   500
Yet Innocence and Virgin Modestie,
Her vertue and the conscience of her worth,
That would be woo'd, and not unsought be won,
Not obvious, not obtrusive, but retir'd,
The more desirable, or to say all,
Nature her self, though pure of sinful thought,
Wrought in her so, that seeing me, she turn'd;
I follow'd her, she what was Honour knew,
And with obsequious Majestie approv'd
My pleaded reason. To the Nuptial Bowre   510
I led her blushing like the Morn: all Heav'n,
And happie Constellations on that houre
Shed thir selectest influence; the Earth
Gave sign of gratulation, and each Hill;
Joyous the Birds; fresh Gales and gentle Aires
Whisper'd it to the Woods, and from thir wings
Flung Rose, flung Odours from the spicie Shrub,
Disporting, till the amorous Bird of Night
Sung Spousal, and bid haste the Eevning Starr

On his Hill top, to light the bridal Lamp.   520
Thus I have told thee all my State, and brought
My Storie to the sum of earthly bliss
Which I enjoy, and must confess to find
In all things else delight indeed, but such
As us'd or not, works in the mind no change,
Nor vehement desire, these delicacies
I mean of Taste, Sight, Smell, Herbs, Fruits, & Flours,
Walks, and the melodie of Birds; but here
Farr otherwise, transported I behold,
Transported touch; here passion first I felt,   530
Commotion strange, in all enjoyments else
Superiour and unmov'd, here onely weake
Against the charm of Beauties powerful glance.
Or Nature faild in mee, and left some part
Not proof enough such Object to sustain,
Or from my side subducting, took perhaps
More then enough; at least on her bestow'd
Too much of Ornament, in outward shew
Elaborate, of inward less exact.
For well I understand in the prime end   540
Of Nature her th' inferiour, in the mind
And inward Faculties, which most excell,
In outward also her resembling less
His Image who made both, and less expressing
The character of that Dominion giv'n
O're other Creatures; yet when I approach
Her loveliness, so absolute she seems
And in her self compleat, so well to know
Her own, that what she wills to do or say,
Seems wisest, vertuousest, discreetest, best;   550
All higher knowledge in her presence falls
Degraded, Wisdom in discourse with her
Looses discount'nanc't, and like folly shewes;
Authoritie and Reason on her waite,
As one intended first, not after made
Occasionally; and to consummate all,
Greatness of mind and nobleness thir seat
Build in her loveliest, and create an awe
About her, as a guard Angelic plac't.
To whom the Angel with contracted brow.   560
  Accuse not Nature, she hath don her part;
Do thou but thine, and be not diffident
Of Wisdom, she deserts thee not, if thou
Dismiss not her, when most thou needst her nigh,
By attributing overmuch to things
Less excellent, as thou thy self perceav'st.
For what admir'st thou, what transports thee so,
An outside? fair no doubt, and worthy well
Thy cherishing, thy honouring, and thy love,
Not thy subjection: weigh with her thy self;   570
Then value: Oft times nothing profits more
Then self-esteem, grounded on just and right

Well manag'd; of that skill the more thou know'st,
The more she will acknowledge thee her Head,
And to realities yeild all her shows;
Made so adorn for thy delight the more,
So awful, that with honour thou maist love
Thy mate, who sees when thou art seen least wise.
But if the sense of touch whereby mankind
Is propagated seem such dear delight   580
Beyond all other, think the same voutsaf't
To Cattel and each Beast; which would not be
To them made common & divulg'd, if aught
Therein enjoy'd were worthy to subdue
The Soule of Man, or passion in him move.
What higher in her societie thou findst
Attractive, human, rational, love still;
In loving thou dost well, in passion not,
Wherein true Love consists not; love refines
The thoughts, and heart enlarges, hath his seat   590
In Reason, and is judicious, is the scale
By which to heav'nly Love thou maist ascend,
Not sunk in carnal pleasure, for which cause
Among the Beasts no Mate for thee was found.
    To whom thus half abash't *Adam* repli'd.
Neither her out-side formd so fair, nor aught
In procreation common to all kindes
(Though higher of the genial Bed by far,
And with mysterious reverence I deem)
So much delights me, as those graceful acts,   600
Those thousand decencies that daily flow
From all her words and actions, mixt with Love
And sweet compliance, which declare unfeign'd
Union of Mind, or in us both one Soule;
Harmonie to behold in wedded pair
More grateful then harmonious sound to the eare.
Yet these subject not; I to thee disclose
What inward thence I feel, not therefore foild,
Who meet with various objects, from the sense
Variously representing; yet still free   610
Approve the best, and follow what I approve.
To love thou blam'st me not, for love thou saist
Leads up to Heav'n, is both the way and guide;
Bear with me then, if lawful what I ask;
Love not the heav'nly Spirits, and how thir Love
Express they, by looks onely, or do they mix
Irradiance, virtual or immediate touch?
    To whom the Angel with a smile that glow'd
Celestial rosie red, Loves proper hue,
Answer'd. Let it suffice thee that thou know'st   620
Us happie, and without Love no happiness.
Whatever pure thou in the body enjoy'st
(And pure thou wert created) we enjoy
In eminence, and obstacle find none
Of membrane, joynt, or limb, exclusive barrs:

Easier then Air with Air, if Spirits embrace,
Total they mix, Union of Pure with Pure
Desiring; nor restrain'd conveyance need
As Flesh to mix with Flesh, or Soul with Soul.
But I can now no more; the parting Sun   630
Beyond the Earths green Cape and verdant Isles
Hesperean sets, my Signal to depart.
Be strong, live happie, and love, but first of all
Him whom to love is to obey, and keep
His great command; take heed least Passion sway
Thy Judgement to do aught, which else free Will
Would not admit; thine and of all thy Sons
The weal or woe in thee is plac't; beware.
I in thy persevering shall rejoyce,
And all the Blest: stand fast; to stand or fall   640
Free in thine own Arbitrement it lies.
Perfet within, no outward aid require;
And all temptation to transgress repel.
　So saying, he arose; whom *Adam* thus
Follow'd with benediction. Since to part,
Go heavenly Guest, Ethereal Messenger,
Sent from whose sovran goodness I adore.
Gentle to me and affable hath been
Thy condescension, and shall be honour'd ever
With grateful Memorie: thou to mankind   650
Be good and friendly still, and oft return.
　So parted they, the Angel up to Heav'n
From the thick shade, and *Adam* to his Bowre.

The End of the Eighth Book.

PARADISE LOST.

BOOK IX.

The Argument.

Satan *having compast the Earth, with meditated guile returns as a mist by Night into Paradise, enters into the Serpent sleeping.* Adam *and* Eve *in the Morning go forth to thir labours, which* Eve *proposes to divide in several places, each labouring apart:* Adam *consents not, alledging the danger, lest that Enemy, of whom they were forewarn'd, should attempt her found alone:* Eve *loath to be thought not circumspect or firm enough, urges her going apart, the rather desirous to make tryal of her strength;* Adam *at last yields: The Serpent finds her alone; his subtle approach, first gazing, then speaking, with much flattery extolling* Eve *above all other Creatures.* Eve *wondring to hear the Serpent speak, asks how he attain'd to human speech and such understanding not till now; the Serpent answers, that by tasting of a certain Tree in the Garden he attain'd both to Speech and Reason, till then void of both:* Eve *requires him to bring her to that Tree, and finds it to be the Tree of Knowledge forbidden: The Serpent now grown bolder, with many wiles and arguments induces her at length to eat; she pleas'd with the taste deliberates awhile whether to impart thereof to* Adam *or not, at last brings him of the Fruit, relates what perswaded her to eat thereof:* Adam *at first amaz'd, but perceiving her lost, resolves through vehemence of love to perish with her; and extenuating the trespass, eats also of the Fruit: The Effects thereof in them both; they seek to cover thir nakedness; then fall to variance and accusation of one another.*

No more of talk where God or Angel Guest
With Man, as with his Friend, familiar us'd
To sit indulgent, and with him partake
Rural repast, permitting him the while
Venial discourse unblam'd: I now must change
Those Notes to Tragic; foul distrust, and breach
Disloyal on the part of Man, revolt,
And disobedience: On the part of Heav'n
Now alienated, distance and distaste,
Anger and just rebuke, and judgement giv'n,   10
That brought into this World a world of woe,
Sinne and her shadow Death, and Miserie
Deaths Harbinger: Sad task, yet argument
Not less but more Heroic then the wrauth
Of stern *Achilles* on his Foe pursu'd
Thrice Fugitive about *Troy* Wall; or rage
Of *Turnus* for *Lavinia* disespous'd,
Or *Neptun*'s ire or *Juno*'s, that so long
Perplex'd the *Greek* and *Cytherea*'s Son;
If answerable style I can obtaine   20
Of my Celestial Patroness, who deignes
Her nightly visitation unimplor'd,
And dictates to me slumbring, or inspires
Easie my unpremeditated Verse:
Since first this Subject for Heroic Song
Pleas'd me long choosing, and beginning late;
Not sedulous by Nature to indite
Warrs, hitherto the onely Argument
Heroic deem'd, chief maistrie to dissect
With long and tedious havoc fabl'd Knights   30
In Battels feign'd; the better fortitude
Of Patience and Heroic Martyrdom
Unsung; or to describe Races and Games,
Or tilting Furniture, emblazon'd Shields,
Impreses quaint, Caparisons and Steeds;
Bases and tinsel Trappings, gorgious Knights
At Joust and Torneament; then marshal'd Feast
Serv'd up in Hall with Sewers, and Seneshals;
The skill of Artifice or Office mean,
Not that which justly gives Heroic name   40
To Person or to Poem. Mee of these
Nor skilld nor studious, higher Argument
Remaines, sufficient of it self to raise
That name, unless an age too late, or cold
Climat, or Years damp my intended wing
Deprest, and much they may, if all be mine,
Not Hers who brings it nightly to my Ear.
    The Sun was sunk, and after him the Starr
Of *Hesperus,* whose Office is to bring
Twilight upon the Earth, short Arbiter   50
Twixt Day and Night, and now from end to end
Nights Hemisphere had veild the Horizon round:
When *Satan* who late fled before the threats

Of *Gabriel* out of *Eden,* now improv'd
In meditated fraud and malice, bent
On mans destruction, maugre what might hap
Of heavier on himself, fearless return'd.
By Night he fled, and at Midnight return'd
From compassing the Earth, cautious of day,
Since *Uriel* Regent of the Sun descri'd   60
His entrance, and forewarnd the Cherubim
That kept thir watch; thence full of anguish driv'n,
The space of seven continu'd Nights he rode
With darkness, thrice the Equinoctial Line
He circl'd, four times cross'd the Carr of Night
From Pole to Pole, traversing each Colure;
On the eighth return'd, and on the Coast averse
From entrance or Cherubic Watch, by stealth
Found unsuspected way. There was a place,
Now not, though Sin, not Time, first wraught the change,   70
Where *Tigris* at the foot of Paradise
Into a Gulf shot under ground, till part
Rose up a Fountain by the Tree of Life;
In with the River sunk, and with it rose
Satan involv'd in rising Mist, then sought
Where to lie hid; Sea he had searcht and Land
From *Eden* over *Pontus,* and the Poole
Mæotis, up beyond the River *Ob;*
Downward as farr Antartic; and in length
West from *Orontes* to the Ocean barr'd   80
At *Darien,* thence to the Land where flowes
Ganges and *Indus:* thus the Orb he roam'd
With narrow search; and with inspection deep
Consider'd every Creature, which of all
Most opportune might serve his Wiles, and found
The Serpent suttlest Beast of all the Field.
Him after long debate, irresolute
Of thoughts revolv'd, his final sentence chose
Fit Vessel, fittest Imp of fraud, in whom
To enter, and his dark suggestions hide   90
From sharpest sight: for in the wilie Snake,
Whatever sleights none would suspicious mark,
As from his wit and native suttletie
Proceeding, which in other Beasts observ'd
Doubt might beget of Diabolic pow'r
Active within beyond the sense of brute.
Thus he resolv'd, but first from inward griefe
His bursting passion into plaints thus pour'd:
     O Earth, how like to Heav'n, if not preferr'd
More justly, Seat worthier of Gods, as built   100
With second thoughts, reforming what was old!
For what God after better worse would build?
Terrestrial Heav'n, danc't round by other Heav'ns
That shine, yet bear thir bright officious Lamps,
Light above Light, for thee alone, as seems,
In thee concentring all thir precious beams

Of sacred influence: As God in Heav'n
Is Center, yet extends to all, so thou
Centring receav'st from all those Orbs; in thee,
Not in themselves, all thir known vertue appeers   110
Productive in Herb, Plant, and nobler birth
Of Creatures animate with gradual life
Of Growth, Sense, Reason, all summ'd up in Man.
With what delight could I have walk't thee round
If I could joy in aught, sweet interchange
Of Hill and Vallie, Rivers, Woods and Plaines,
Now Land, now Sea, & Shores with Forrest crownd,
Rocks, Dens, and Caves; but I in none of these
Find place or refuge; and the more I see
Pleasures about me, so much more I feel   120
Torment within me, as from the hateful siege
Of contraries; all good to me becomes
Bane, and in Heav'n much worse would be my state.
But neither here seek I, no nor in Heav'n
To dwell, unless by maistring Heav'ns Supreame;
Nor hope to be my self less miserable
By what I seek, but others to make such
As I, though thereby worse to me redound:
For onely in destroying I finde ease
To my relentless thoughts; and him destroyd,   130
Or won to what may work his utter loss,
For whom all this was made, all this will soon
Follow, as to him linkt in weal or woe,
In wo then; that destruction wide may range:
To mee shall be the glorie sole among
The infernal Powers, in one day to have marr'd
What he *Almightie* styl'd, six Nights and Days
Continu'd making, and who knows how long
Before had bin contriving, though perhaps
Not longer then since I in one Night freed   140
From servitude inglorious welnigh half
Th' Angelic Name, and thinner left the throng
Of his adorers: hee to be aveng'd,
And to repair his numbers thus impair'd,
Whether such vertue spent of old now faild
More Angels to Create, if they at least
Are his Created or to spite us more,
Determin'd to advance into our room
A Creature form'd of Earth, and him endow,
Exalted from so base original,   150
With Heav'nly spoils, our spoils: What he decreed
He effected; Man he made, and for him built
Magnificent this World, and Earth his seat,
Him Lord pronounc'd, and, O indignitie!
Subjected to his service Angel wings,
And flaming Ministers to watch and tend
Thir earthie Charge: Of these the vigilance
I dread, and to elude, thus wrapt in mist
Of midnight vapor glide obscure, and prie

In every Bush and Brake, where hap may finde   160
The Serpent sleeping, in whose mazie foulds
To hide me, and the dark intent I bring.
O foul descent! that I who erst contended
With Gods to sit the highest, am now constraind
Into a Beast, and mixt with bestial slime,
This essence to incarnate and imbrute,
That to the hight of Deitie aspir'd;
But what will not Ambition and Revenge
Descend to? who aspires must down as low
As high he soard, obnoxious first or last   170
To basest things. Revenge, at first though sweet,
Bitter ere long back on it self recoiles;
Let it; I reck not, so it light well aim'd,
Since higher I fall short, on him who next
Provokes my envie, this new Favorite
Of Heav'n, this Man of Clay, Son of despite,
Whom us the more to spite his Maker rais'd
From dust: spite then with spite is best repaid.
    So saying, through each Thicket Danck or Drie,
Like a black mist low creeping, he held on   180
His midnight search, where soonest he might finde
The Serpent: him fast sleeping soon he found
In Labyrinth of many a round self-rowld,
His head the midst, well stor'd with suttle wiles:
Not yet in horrid Shade or dismal Den,
Nor nocent yet, but on the grassie Herbe
Fearless unfeard he slept: in at his Mouth
The Devil enterd, and his brutal sense,
In heart or head, possessing soon inspir'd
With act intelligential; but his sleep   190
Disturbd not, waiting close th' approach of Morn.
Now whenas sacred Light began to dawne
In *Eden* on the humid Flours, that breathd
Thir morning Incense, when all things that breath,
From th' Earths great Altar send up silent praise
To the Creator, and his Nostrils fill
With gratefull Smell, forth came the human pair
And joynd thir vocal Worship to the Quire
Of Creatures wanting voice, that done, partake
The season, prime for sweetest Sents and Aires: 200
Then commune how that day they best may ply
Thir growing work: for much thir work outgrew
The hands dispatch of two Gardning so wide.
And *Eve* first to her Husband thus began.
    Adam, well may we labour still to dress
This Garden, still to tend Plant, Herb and Flour.
Our pleasant task enjoyn'd, but till more hands
Aid us, the work under our labour grows,
Luxurious by restraint; what we by day
Lop overgrown, or prune, or prop, or bind,   210
One night or two with wanton growth derides
Tending to wilde. Thou therefore now advise

Or hear what to my mind first thoughts present,
Let us divide our labours, thou where choice
Leads thee, or where most needs, whether to wind
The Woodbine round this Arbour, or direct
The clasping Ivie where to climb, while I
In yonder Spring of Roses intermixt
With Myrtle, find what to redress till Noon:
For while so near each other thus all day   220
Our task we choose, what wonder if so near
Looks intervene and smiles, or object new
Casual discourse draw on, which intermits
Our dayes work brought to little, though begun
Early, and th' hour of Supper comes unearn'd.
  To whom mild answer *Adam* thus return'd.
Sole *Eve,* Associate sole, to me beyond
Compare above all living Creatures deare,
Well hast thou motion'd, wel thy thoughts imployd
How we might best fulfill the work which here   230
God hath assign'd us, nor of me shalt pass
Unprais'd: for nothing lovelier can be found
In woman, then to studie houshold good,
And good workes in her Husband to promote.
Yet not so strictly hath our Lord impos'd
Labour, as to debarr us when we need
Refreshment, whether food, or talk between,
Food of the mind, or this sweet intercourse
Of looks and smiles, for smiles from Reason flow,
To brute deni'd, and are of Love the food,   240
Love not the lowest end of human life.
For not to irksom toile, but to delight
He made us, and delight to Reason joyn'd.
These paths and Bowers doubt not but our joynt hands
Will keep from Wilderness with ease, as wide
As we need walk, till younger hands ere long
Assist us: But if much converse perhaps
Thee satiate, to short absence I could yeild.
For solitude somtimes is best societie,
And short retirement urges sweet returne.   25c
But other doubt possesses me, least harm
Befall thee sever'd from me; for thou knowst
What hath bin warn'd us, what malicious Foe
Envying our happiness, and of his own
Despairing, seeks to work us woe and shame
By sly assault; and somwhere nigh at hand
Watches, no doubt, with greedy hope to find
His wish and best advantage, us asunder,
Hopeless to circumvent us joynd, where each
To other speedie aide might lend at need;   26o
Whether his first design be to withdraw
Our fealtie from God, or to disturb
Conjugal Love, then which perhaps no bliss
Enjoy'd by us excites his envie more;
Or this, or worse, leave not the faithful side

That gave thee being, stil shades thee and protects.
The Wife, where danger or dishonour lurks,
Safest and seemliest by her Husband staies,
Who guards her, or with her the worst endures.
   To whom the Virgin Majestie of *Eve,*   270
As one who loves, and some unkindness meets,
With sweet austeer composure thus reply'd.
   Ofspring of Heav'n and Earth, and all Earths Lord,
That such an Enemie we have, who seeks
Our ruin, both by thee informd I learne,
And from the parting Angel over-heard
As in a shadie nook I stood behind,
Just then returnd at shut of Evening Flours.
But that thou shouldst my firmness therfore doubt
To God or thee, because we have a foe   280
May tempt it, I expected not to hear.
His violence thou fearst not, being such,
As wee, not capable of death or paine,
Can either not receave, or can repell.
His fraud is then thy fear, which plain inferrs
Thy equal fear that my firm Faith and Love
Can by his fraud be shak'n or seduc't;
Thoughts, which how found they harbour in thy brest,
Adam, missthought of her to thee so dear?
   To whom with healing words *Adam* reply'd.   290
Daughter of God and Man, immortal *Eve,*
For such thou art, from sin and blame entire:
Not diffident of thee do I dissuade
Thy absence from my sight, but to avoid
Th' attempt it self, intended by our Foe.
For hee who tempts, though in vain, at least asperses
The tempted with dishonour foul, suppos'd
Not incorruptible of Faith, not prooff
Against temptation: thou thy self with scorne
And anger wouldst resent the offer'd wrong,   300
Though ineffectual found: misdeem not then,
If such affront I labour to avert
From thee alone, which on us both at once
The Enemie, though bold, will hardly dare,
Or daring, first on mee th' assault shall light.
Nor thou his malice and false guile contemn;
Suttle he needs must be, who could seduce
Angels, nor think superfluous others aid.
I from the influence of thy looks receave
Access in every Vertue, in thy sight   310
More wise, more watchful, stronger, if need were
Of outward strength; while shame, thou looking on,
Shame to be overcome or over-reacht
Would utmost vigor raise, and rais'd unite.
Why shouldst not thou like sense within thee feel
When I am present, and thy trial choose
With me, best witness of thy Vertue tri'd.
   So spake domestick *Adam* in his care

And Matrimonial Love, but *Eve,* who thought
Less attributed to her Faith sincere,   320
Thus her reply with accent sweet renewd.
   If this be our condition, thus to dwell
In narrow circuit strait'nd by a Foe,
Suttle or violent, we not endu'd
Single with like defence, wherever met,
How are we happie, still in fear of harm?
But harm precedes not sin: onely our Foe
Tempting affronts us with his foul esteem
Of our integritie: his foul esteeme
Sticks no dishonor on our Front, but turns   330
Foul on himself; then wherfore shund or feard
By us? who rather double honour gaine
From his surmise prov'd false, finde peace within,
Favour from Heav'n, our witness from th' event.
And what is Faith, Love, Vertue unassaid
Alone, without exterior help sustaind?
Let us not then suspect our happie State
Left so imperfet by the Maker wise,
As not secure to single or combin'd.
Fraile is our happiness, if this be so,   340
And *Eden* were no *Eden* thus expos'd.
   To whom thus *Adam* fervently repli'd.
O Woman, best are all things as the will
Of God ordaind them, his creating hand
Nothing imperfet or deficient left
Of all that he Created, much less Man,
Or ought that might his happie State secure,
Secure from outward force; within himself
The danger lies, yet lies within his power:
Against his will he can receave no harme.   350
But God left free the Will, for what obeyes
Reason, is free, and Reason he made right,
But bid her well beware, and still erect,
Least by some faire appeering good surpris'd
She dictate false, and missinforme the Will
To do what God expresly hath forbid.
Not then mistrust, but tender love enjoynes,
That I should mind thee oft, and mind thou me.
Firm we subsist, yet possible to swerve,
Since Reason not impossibly may meet   360
Some specious object by the Foe subornd,
And fall into deception unaware,
Not keeping strictest watch, as she was warnd.
Seek not temptation then, which to avoide
Were better, and most likelie if from mee
Thou sever not: Trial will come unsought.
Wouldst thou approve thy constancie, approve
First thy obedience; th' other who can know,
Not seeing thee attempted, who attest?
But if thou think, trial unsought may finde   370
Us both securer then thus warnd thou seemst,

Go; for thy stay, not free, absents thee more;
Go in thy native innocence, relie
On what thou hast of vertue, summon all,
For God towards thee hath done his part, do thine.
   So spake the Patriarch of Mankinde, but *Eve*
Persisted, yet submiss, though last, repli'd.
   With thy permission then, and thus forewarnd
Chiefly by what thy own last reasoning words
Touchd onely, that our trial, when least sought,   380
May finde us both perhaps farr less prepar'd,
The willinger I goe, nor much expect
A Foe so proud will first the weaker seek;
So bent, the more shall shame him his repulse.
Thus saying, from her Husbands hand her hand
Soft she withdrew, and like a Wood-Nymph light
Oread or *Dryad,* or of *Delia's* Traine,
Betook her to the Groves, but *Delia's* self
In gate surpass'd and Goddess-like deport,
Though not as shee with Bow and Quiver armd,   390
But with such Gardning Tools as Art yet rude,
Guiltless of fire had formd, or Angels brought.
To *Pales,* or *Pomona,* thus adornd,
Likeliest she seemd, *Pomona* when she fled
Vertumnus, or to *Ceres* in her Prime,
Yet Virgin of *Proserpina* from *Jove.*
Her long with ardent look his Eye pursu'd
Delighted, but desiring more her stay.
Oft he to her his charge of quick returne
Repeated, shee to him as oft engag'd   400
To be returnd by Noon amid the Bowre,
And all things in best order to invite
Noontide repast, or Afternoons repose.
O much deceav'd, much failing, hapless *Eve,*
Of thy presum'd return! event perverse!
Thou never from that houre in Paradise
Foundst either sweet repast, or sound repose;
Such ambush hid among sweet Flours and Shades
Waited with hellish rancor imminent
To intercept thy way, or send thee back   410
Despoild of Innocence, of Faith, of Bliss.
For now, and since first break of dawne the Fiend,
Meer Serpent in appearance, forth was come,
And on his Quest, where likeliest he might finde
The onely two of Mankinde, but in them
The whole included Race, his purposd prey.
In Bowre and Field he sought, where any tuft
Of Grove or Garden-Plot more pleasant lay,
Thir tendance or Plantation for delight,
By Fountain or by shadie Rivulet   420
He sought them both, but wish'd his hap might find
Eve separate, he wish'd, but not with hope
Of what so seldom chanc'd, when to his wish,
Beyond his hope, *Eve* separate he spies,

Veild in a Cloud of Fragrance, where she stood,
Half spi'd, so thick the Roses bushing round
About her glowd, oft stooping to support
Each Flour of slender stalk, whose head though gay
Carnation, Purple, Azure, or spect with Gold,
Hung drooping unsustaind, them she upstaies   430
Gently with Mirtle band, mindless the while,
Her self, though fairest unsupported Flour,
From her best prop so farr, and storm so nigh.
Neerer he drew, and many a walk travers'd
Of stateliest Covert, Cedar, Pine, or Palme,
Then voluble and bold, now hid, now seen
Among thick-wov'n Arborets and Flours
Imborderd on each Bank, the hand of *Eve:*
Spot more delicious then those Gardens feign'd
Or of reviv'd *Adonis,* or renownd   440
Alcinous, host of old *Laertes* Son,
Or that, not Mystic, where the Sapient King
Held dalliance with his faire *Egyptian* Spouse.
Much hee the Place admir'd, the Person more.
As one who long in populous City pent,
Where Houses thick and Sewers annoy the Aire,
Forth issuing on a Summers Morn to breathe
Among the pleasant Villages and Farmes
Adjoynd, from each thing met conceaves delight,
The smell of Grain, or tedded Grass, or Kine,   450
Or Dairie, each rural sight, each rural sound;
If chance with Nymphlike step fair Virgin pass,
What pleasing seemd, for her now pleases more,
She most, and in her look summs all Delight.
Such Pleasure took the Serpent to behold
This Flourie Plat, the sweet recess of *Eve*
Thus earlie, thus alone; her Heav'nly forme
Angelic, but more soft, and Feminine,
Her graceful Innocence, her every Aire
Of gesture or lest action overawd   460
His Malice, and with rapine sweet bereav'd
His fierceness of the fierce intent it brought:
That space the Evil one abstracted stood
From his own evil, and for the time remaind
Stupidly good, of enmitie disarm'd,
Of guile, of hate, of envie, of revenge;
But the hot Hell that always in him burnes,
Though in mid Heav'n, soon ended his delight,
And tortures him now more, the more he sees
Of pleasure not for him ordain'd: then soon   470
Fierce hate he recollects, and all his thoughts
Of mischief, gratulating, thus excites.
    Thoughts, whither have ye led me, with what sweet
Compulsion thus transported to forget
What hither brought us, hate, not love, nor hope
Of Paradise for Hell, hope here to taste
Of pleasure, but all pleasure to destroy,

Save what is in destroying, other joy
To me is lost. Then let me not let pass
Occasion which now smiles, behold alone　　　　　　480
The Woman, opportune to all attempts,
Her Husband, for I view far round, not nigh,
Whose higher intellectual more I shun,
And strength, of courage hautie, and of limb
Heroic built, though of terrestrial mould,
Foe not informidable, exempt from wound,
I not; so much hath Hell debas'd, and paine
Infeebl'd me, to what I was in Heav'n.
Shee fair, divinely fair, fit Love for Gods,
Not terrible, though terrour be in Love　　　　　　490
And beautie, not approacht by stronger hate,
Hate stronger, under shew of Love well feign'd,
The way which to her ruin now I tend.
　　So spake the Enemie of Mankind, enclos'd
In Serpent, Inmate bad, and toward *Eve*
Address'd his way, not with indented wave,
Prone on the ground, as since, but on his reare,
Circular base of rising foulds, that tour'd
Fould above fould a surging Maze, his Head
Crested aloft, and Carbuncle his Eyes;　　　　　　500
With burnisht Neck of verdant Gold, erect
Amidst his circling Spires, that on the grass
Floted redundant: pleasing was his shape,
And lovely, never since of Serpent kind
Lovelier, not those that in *Illyria* chang'd
Hermione and *Cadmus,* or the God
In *Epidaurus;* nor to which transformd
Ammonian Jove, or *Capitoline* was seen,
Hee with *Olympias,* this with her who bore
Scipio the highth of *Rome.* With tract oblique　　　510
At first, as one who sought access, but feard
To interrupt, side-long he works his way.
As when a Ship by skilful Stearsman wrought
Nigh Rivers mouth or Foreland, where the Wind
Veres oft, as oft so steers, and shifts her Saile;
So varied hee, and of his tortuous Traine
Curld many a wanton wreath in sight of *Eve,*
To lure her Eye; shee busied heard the sound
Of rusling Leaves, but minded not, as us'd
To such disport before her through the Field,　　　520
From every Beast, more duteous at her call,
Then at *Circean* call the Herd disguis'd.
Hee boulder now, uncall'd before her stood;
But as in gaze admiring: Oft he bowd
His turret Crest, and sleek enamel'd Neck,
Fawning, and lick'd the ground whereon she trod.
His gentle dumb expression turnd at length
The Eye of *Eve* to mark his play; he glad
Of her attention gaind, with Serpent Tongue
Organic, or impulse of vocal Air,　　　　　　　530

His fraudulent temptation thus began.
    Wonder not, sovran Mistress, if perhaps
Thou canst, who art sole Wonder, much less arm
Thy looks, the Heav'n of mildness, with disdain,
Displeas'd that I approach thee thus, and gaze
Insatiate, I thus single, nor have feard
Thy awful brow, more awful thus retir'd.
Fairest resemblance of thy Maker faire,
Thee all things living gaze on, all things thine
By gift, and thy Celestial Beautie adore   540
With ravishment beheld, there best beheld
Where universally admir'd; but here
In this enclosure wild, these Beasts among,
Beholders rude, and shallow to discerne
Half what in thee is fair, one man except,
Who sees thee? (and what is one?) who shouldst be seen
A Goddess among Gods, ador'd and serv'd
By Angels numberless, thy daily Train.
    So gloz'd the Tempter, and his Proem tun'd;
Into the Heart of *Eve* his words made way,   550
Though at the voice much marveling; at length
Not unamaz'd she thus in answer spake.
What may this mean? Language of Man pronounc't
By Tongue of Brute, and human sense exprest?
The first at lest of these I thought deni'd
To Beasts, whom God on thir Creation-Day
Created mute to all articulat sound;
The latter I demurre, for in thir looks
Much reason, and in thir actions oft appeers.
Thee, Serpent, suttlest beast of all the field   560
I knew, but not with human voice endu'd;
Redouble then this miracle, and say,
How cam'st thou speakable of mute, and how
To me so friendly grown above the rest .
Of brutal kind, that daily are in sight?
Say, for such wonder claims attention due.
    To whom the guileful Tempter thus reply'd.
Empress of this fair World, resplendent *Eve,*
Easie to mee it is to tell thee all
What thou commandst, and right thou shouldst be obeyd: 570
I was at first as other Beasts that graze
The trodden Herb, of abject thoughts and low,
As was my food, nor aught but food discern'd
Or Sex, and apprehended nothing high:
Till on a day roaving the field, I chanc'd
A goodly Tree farr distant to behold
Loaden with fruit of fairest colours mixt,
Ruddie and Gold: I nearer drew to gaze;
When from the boughes a savorie odour blow'n,
Grateful to appetite, more pleas'd my sense   580
Then smell of sweetest Fenel, or the Teats
Of Ewe or Goat dropping with Milk at Eevn,
Unsuckt of Lamb or Kid, that tend thir play.

To satisfie the sharp desire I had
Of tasting those fair Apples, I resolv'd
Not to deferr; hunger and thirst at once,
Powerful perswaders, quick'nd at the scent
Of that alluring fruit, urg'd me so keene.
About the Mossie Trunk I wound me soon,
For high from ground the branches would require　　　590
Thy utmost reach or *Adams:* Round the Tree
All other Beasts that saw, with like desire
Longing and envying stood, but could not reach.
Amid the Tree now got, where plentie hung
Tempting so nigh, to pluck and eat my fill
I spar'd not, for such pleasure till that hour
At Feed or Fountain never had I found.
Sated at length, ere long I might perceave
Strange alteration in me, to degree
Of Reason in my inward Powers, and Speech　　　600
Wanted not long, though to this shape retaind.
Thenceforth to Speculations high or deep
I turnd my thoughts, and with capacious mind
Considerd all things visible in Heav'n,
Or Earth, or Middle, all things fair and good;
But all that fair and good in thy Divine
Semblance, and in thy Beauties heav'nly Ray
United I beheld; no Fair to thine
Equivalent or second, which compel'd
Mee thus, though importune perhaps, to come　　　610
And gaze, and worship thee of right declar'd
Sovran of Creatures, universal Dame.
　　So talk'd the spirited sly Snake; and *Eve*
Yet more amaz'd unwarie thus reply'd.
　　Serpent, thy overpraising leaves in doubt
The vertue of that Fruit, in thee first prov'd:
But say, where grows the Tree, from hence how far?
For many are the Trees of God that grow
In Paradise, and various, yet unknown
To us, in such abundance lies our choice,　　　620
As leaves a greater store of Fruit untoucht,
Still hanging incorruptible, till men
Grow up to thir provision, and more hands
Help to disburden Nature of her Bearth.
　　To whom the wilie Adder, blithe and glad.
Empress, the way is readie, and not long,
Beyond a row of Myrtles, on a Flat,
Fast by a Fountain, one small Thicket past
Of blowing Myrrh and Balme; if thou accept
My conduct, I can bring thee thither soon.　　　630
　　Lead then, said *Eve.* Hee leading swiftly rowld
In tangles, and made intricate seem strait,
To mischief swift. Hope elevates, and joy
Bright'ns his Crest, as when a wandring Fire
Compact of unctuous vapor, which the Night
Condenses, and the cold invirons round,

Kindl'd through agitation to a Flame,
Which oft, they say, some evil Spirit attends,
Hovering and blazing with delusive Light,
Misleads th' amaz'd Night-wanderer from his way　　　640
To Boggs and Mires, & oft through Pond or Poole,
There swallow'd up and lost, from succour farr.
So glister'd the dire Snake, and into fraud
Led *Eve* our credulous Mother, to the Tree
Of prohibition, root of all our woe;
Which when she saw, thus to her guide she spake.
　　Serpent, we might have spar'd our coming hither,
Fruitless to me, though Fruit be here to excess,
The credit of whose vertue rest with thee,
Wondrous indeed, if cause of such effects.　　　650
But of this Tree we may not taste nor touch;
God so commanded, and left that Command
Sole Daughter of his voice; the rest, we live
Law to our selves, our Reason is our Law.
　　To whom the Tempter guilefully repli'd.
Indeed? hath God then said that of the Fruit
Of all these Garden Trees ye shall not eate,
Yet Lords declar'd of all in Earth or Aire?
　　To whom thus *Eve* yet sinless. Of the Fruit
Of each Tree in the Garden we may eate,　　　660
But of the Fruit of this fair Tree amidst
The Garden, God hath said, Ye shall not eate
Thereof, nor shall ye touch it, least ye die.
　　She scarse had said, though brief, when now more bold
The Tempter, but with shew of Zeale and Love
To Man, and indignation at his wrong,
New part puts on, and as to passion mov'd,
Fluctuats disturbd, yet comely, and in act
Rais'd, as of som great matter to begin.
As when of old som Orator renound　　　670
In *Athens* or free *Rome,* where Eloquence
Flourishd, since mute, to som great cause addrest,
Stood in himself collected, while each part,
Motion, each act won audience ere the tongue,
Somtimes in highth began, as no delay
Of Preface brooking through his Zeal of Right.
So standing, moving, or to highth upgrown
The Tempter all impassiond thus began.
　　O Sacred, Wise, and Wisdom-giving Plant,
Mother of Science, Now I feel thy Power　　　680
Within me cleere, not onely to discerne
Things in thir Causes, but to trace the wayes
Of highest Agents, deemd however wise.
Queen of this Universe, doe not believe
Those rigid threats of Death; ye shall not Die:
How should ye? by the Fruit? it gives you Life
To Knowledge? By the Threatner, look on mee,
Mee who have touch'd and tasted, yet both live,
And life more perfet have attaind then Fate

Meant mee, by ventring higher then my Lot.   690
Shall that be shut to Man, which to the Beast
Is open? or will God incense his ire
For such a petty Trespass, and not praise
Rather your dauntless vertue, whom the pain
Of Death denounc't, whatever thing Death be,
Deterrd not from atchieving what might leade
To happier life, knowledge of Good and Evil;
Of good, how just? of evil, if what is evil
Be real, why not known, since easier shunnd?
God therefore cannot hurt ye, and be just;   700
Not just, not God; not feard then, nor obeid:
Your feare it self of Death removes the feare.
Why then was this forbid? Why but to awe,
Why but to keep ye low and ignorant,
His worshippers; he knows that in the day
Ye Eate thereof, your Eyes that seem so cleere,
Yet are but dim, shall perfetly be then
Op'nd and cleerd, and ye shall be as Gods,
Knowing both Good and Evil as they know.
That ye should be as Gods, since I as Man,   710
Internal Man, is but proportion meet,
I of brute human, yee of human Gods.
So ye shall die perhaps, by putting off
Human, to put on Gods, death to be wisht,
Though threat'nd, which no worse then this can bring.
And what are Gods that Man may not become
As they, participating God-like food?
The Gods are first, and that advantage use
On our belief, that all from them proceeds;
I question it, for this fair Earth I see,   720
Warm'd by the Sun, producing every kind,
Them nothing: If they all things, who enclos'd
Knowledge of Good and Evil in this Tree,
That whoso eats thereof, forthwith attains
Wisdom without their leave? and wherein lies
Th' offence, that Man should thus attain to know?
What can your knowledge hurt him, or this Tree
Impart against his will if all be his?
Or is it envie, and can envie dwell
In heav'nly brests? these, these and many more   730
Causes import your need of this fair Fruit.
Goddess humane, reach then, and freely taste.
    He ended, and his words replete with guile
Into her heart too easie entrance won:
Fixt on the Fruit she gaz'd, which to behold
Might tempt alone, and in her ears the sound
Yet rung of his perswasive words, impregn'd
With Reason, to her seeming, and with Truth;
Meanwhile the hour of Noon drew on, and wak'd
An eager appetite, rais'd by the smell   740
So savorie of that Fruit, which with desire,
Inclinable now grown to touch or taste,

Sollicited her longing eye; yet first
Pausing a while, thus to her self she mus'd.
　　Great are thy Vertues, doubtless, best of Fruits,
Though kept from Man, & worthy to be admir'd,
Whose taste, too long forborn, at first assay
Gave elocution to the mute, and taught
The Tongue not made for Speech to speak thy praise: 750
Thy praise hee also who forbids thy use,
Conceales not from us, naming thee the Tree
Of Knowledge, knowledge both of good and evil;
Forbids us then to taste, but his forbidding
Commends thee more, while it inferrs the good
By thee communicated, and our want:
For good unknown, sure is not had, or had
And yet unknown, is as not had at all.
In plain then, what forbids he but to know,
Forbids us good, forbids us to be wise?
Such prohibitions binde not. But if Death   760
Bind us with after-bands, what profits then
Our inward freedom? In the day we eate
Of this fair Fruit, our doom is, we shall die.
How dies the Serpent? hee hath eat'n and lives,
And knows, and speaks, and reasons, and discernes,
Irrational till then. For us alone
Was death invented? or to us deni'd
This intellectual food, for beasts reserv'd?
For Beasts it seems: yet that one Beast which first
Hath tasted, envies not, but brings with joy   770
The good befall'n him, Author unsuspect,
Friendly to man, farr from deceit or guile.
What fear I then, rather what know to feare
Under this ignorance of Good and Evil,
Of God or Death, of Law or Penaltie?
Here grows the Cure of all, this Fruit Divine,
Fair to the Eye, inviting to the Taste,
Of vertue to make wise: what hinders then
To reach, and feed at once both Bodie and Mind?
　　So saying, her rash hand in evil hour   780
Forth reaching to the Fruit, she pluck'd, she eat:
Earth felt the wound, and Nature from her seat
Sighing through all her Works gave signs of woe,
That all was lost. Back to the Thicket slunk
The guiltie Serpent, and well might, for *Eve*
Intent now wholly on her taste, naught else
Regarded, such delight till then, as seemd,
In Fruit she never tasted, whether true
Or fansied so, through expectation high
Of knowledg, nor was God-head from her thought.   790
Greedily she ingorg'd without restraint,
And knew not eating Death: Satiate at length,
And hight'nd as with Wine, jocond and boon,
Thus to her self she pleasingly began.
　　O Sovran, vertuous, precious of all Tree

In Paradise, of operation blest
To Sapience, hitherto obscur'd, infam'd,
And thy fair Fruit let hang, as to no end
Created; but henceforth my early care,
Not without Song, each Morning, and due praise   800
Shall tend thee, and the fertil burden ease
Of thy full branches offer'd free to all;
Till dieted by thee I grow mature
In knowledge, as the Gods who all things know;
Though others envie what they cannot give;
For had the gift bin theirs, it had not here
Thus grown. Experience, next to thee I owe,
Best guide; not following thee, I had remaind
In ignorance, thou op'nst Wisdoms way,
And giv'st access, though secret she retire.   810
And I perhaps am secret; Heav'n is high,
High and remote to see from thence distinct
Each thing on Earth; and other care perhaps
May have diverted from continual watch
Our great Forbidder, safe with all his Spies
About him. But to *Adam* in what sort
Shall I appeer? shall I to him make known
As yet my change, and give him to partake
Full happiness with mee, or rather not,
But keep the odds of Knowledge in my power   820
Without Copartner? so to add what wants
In Femal Sex, the more to draw his Love,
And render me more equal, and perhaps,
A thing not undesireable, sometime
Superior; for inferior who is free?
This may be well: but what if God have seen,
And Death ensue? then I shall be no more,
And *Adam* wedded to another *Eve,*
Shall live with her enjoying, I extinct;
A death to think. Confirm'd then I resolve,   830
Adam shall share with me in bliss or woe:
So dear I love him, that with him all deaths
I could endure, without him live no life.
  So saying, from the Tree her step she turnd,
But first low Reverence don, as to the power
That dwelt within, whose presence had infus'd
Into the plant sciential sap, deriv'd
From Nectar, drink of Gods. *Adam* the while
Waiting desirous her return, had wove
Of choicest Flours a Garland to adorne   840
Her Tresses, and her rural labours crown
As Reapers oft are wont thir Harvest Queen.
Great joy he promis'd to his thoughts, and new
Solace in her return, so long delay'd;
Yet oft his heart, divine of somthing ill,
Misgave him; hee the faultring measure felt;
And forth to meet her went, the way she took
That Morn when first they parted; by the Tree

Of Knowledge he must pass, there he her met,
Scarse from the Tree returning; in her hand   850
A bough of fairest fruit that downie smil'd,
New gatherd, and ambrosial smell diffus'd.
To him she hasted, in her face excuse
Came Prologue, and Apologie to prompt,
Which with bland words at will she thus addrest.
  Hast thou not wonderd, *Adam,* at my stay?
Thee I have misst, and thought it long, depriv'd
Thy presence, agonie of love till now
Not felt, nor shall be twice, for never more
Mean I to trie, what rash untri'd I sought,   860
The paine of absence from thy sight. But strange
Hath bin the cause, and wonderful to heare:
This Tree is not as we are told, a Tree
Of danger tasted, nor to evil unknown
Op'ning the way, but of Divine effect
To open Eyes, and make them Gods who taste;
And hath bin tasted such: the Serpent wise,
Or not restraind as wee, or not obeying,
Hath eat'n of the fruit, and is become,
Not dead, as we are threatn'd, but thenceforth   870
Endu'd with human voice and human sense,
Reasoning to admiration, and with mee
Perswasively hath so prevaild, that I
Have also tasted, and have also found
Th' effects to correspond, opener mine Eyes
Dimm erst, dilated Spirits, ampler Heart,
And growing up to Godhead; which for thee
Chiefly I sought, without thee can despise.
For bliss, as thou hast part, to me is bliss,
Tedious, unshar'd with thee, and odious soon.   880
Thou therfore also taste, that equal Lot
May joyne us, equal Joy, as equal Love;
Least thou not tasting, different degree
Disjoyne us, and I then too late renounce
Deitie for thee, when Fate will not permit.
  Thus *Eve* with Countnance blithe her storie told;
But in her Cheek distemper flushing glowd.
On th' other side, *Adam,* soon as he heard
The fatal Trespass don by *Eve,* amaz'd,
Astonied stood and Blank, while horror chill   890
Ran through his veins, and all his joynts relax'd;
From his slack hand the Garland wreath'd for *Eve*
Down drop'd, and all the faded Roses shed:
Speechless he stood and pale, till thus at length
First to himself he inward silence broke.
  O fairest of Creation, last and best
Of all Gods Works, Creature in whom excell'd
Whatever can to sight or thought be formd,
Holy, divine, good, amiable, or sweet!
How art thou lost, how on a sudden lost,   900
Defac't, deflourd, and now to Death devote?

Rather how hast thou yeelded to transgress
The strict forbiddance, how to violate
The sacred Fruit forbidd'n! som cursed fraud
Of Enemie hath beguil'd thee, yet unknown,
And mee with thee hath ruind, for with thee
Certain my resolution is to Die;
How can I live without thee, how forgoe
Thy sweet Converse and Love so dearly joyn'd,
To live again in these wilde Woods forlorn?   910
Should God create another *Eve,* and I
Another Rib afford, yet loss of thee
Would never from my heart; no no, I feel
The Link of Nature draw me: Flesh of Flesh,
Bone of my Bone thou art, and from thy State
Mine never shall be parted, bliss or woe.
    So having said, as one from sad dismay
Recomforted, and after thoughts disturbd
Submitting to what seemd remediless,
Thus in calme mood his Words to *Eve* he turnd.   920
    Bold deed thou hast presum'd, adventrous *Eve,*
And peril great provok't, who thus hast dar'd
Had it bin onely coveting to Eye
That sacred Fruit, sacred to abstinence,
Much more to taste it under banne to touch.
But past who can recall, or don undoe?
Not God Omnipotent, nor Fate, yet so
Perhaps thou shalt not Die, perhaps the Fact
Is not so hainous now, foretasted Fruit,
Profan'd first by the Serpent, by him first   930
Made common and unhallowd ere our taste;
Nor yet on him found deadly, he yet lives,
Lives, as thou saidst, and gaines to live as Man
Higher degree of Life, inducement strong
To us, as likely tasting to attaine
Proportional ascent, which cannot be
But to be Gods, or Angels Demi-gods.
Nor can I think that God, Creator wise,
Though threatning, will in earnest so destroy
Us his prime Creatures, dignifi'd so high,   940
Set over all his Works, which in our Fall,
For us created, needs with us must faile,
Dependent made; so God shall uncreate,
Be frustrate, do, undo, and labour loose,
Not well conceav'd of God, who though his Power
Creation could repeate, yet would be loath
Us to abolish, least the Adversary
Triumph and say; Fickle their State whom God
Most Favors, who can please him long? Mee first
He ruind, now Mankind; whom will he next?   950
Matter of scorne, not to be given the Foe.
However I with thee have fixt my Lot,
Certain to undergoe like doom, if Death
Consort with thee, Death is to mee as Life;

So forcible within my heart I feel
The Bond of Nature draw me to my owne,
My own in thee, for what thou art is mine;
Our State cannot be severd, we are one,
One Flesh; to loose thee were to loose my self.
    So *Adam,* and thus *Eve* to him repli'd.   960
O glorious trial of exceeding Love,
Illustrious evidence, example high!
Ingaging me to emulate, but short
Of thy perfection, how shall I attaine,
Adam, from whose deare side I boast me sprung,
And gladly of our Union heare thee speak,
One Heart, one Soul in both; whereof good prooff
This day affords, declaring thee resolvd,
Rather then Death or aught then Death more dread
Shall separate us, linkt in Love so deare,   970
To undergoe with mee one Guilt, one Crime,
If any be, of tasting this fair Fruit,
Whose vertue, for of good still good proceeds,
Direct, or by occasion hath presented
This happie trial of thy Love, which else
So eminently never had bin known.
Were it I thought Death menac't would ensue
This my attempt, I would sustain alone
The worst, and not perswade thee, rather die
Deserted, then oblige thee with a fact   980
Pernicious to thy Peace, chiefly assur'd
Remarkably so late of thy so true,
So faithful Love unequald; but I feel
Farr otherwise th' event, not Death, but Life
Augmented, op'nd Eyes, new Hopes, new Joyes,
Taste so Divine, that what of sweet before
Hath toucht my sense, flat seems to this, and harsh.
On my experience, *Adam,* freely taste,
And fear of Death deliver to the Windes.
    So saying, she embrac'd him, and for joy   990
Tenderly wept, much won that he his Love
Had so enobl'd, as of choice to incurr
Divine displeasure for her sake, or Death.
In recompence (for such compliance bad
Such recompence best merits) from the bough
She gave him of that fair enticing Fruit
With liberal hand: he scrupl'd not to eat
Against his better knowledge, not deceav'd,
But fondly overcome with Femal charm.
Earth trembl'd from her entrails, as again   1000
in pangs, and Nature gave a second groan,
Skie lowr'd, and muttering Thunder, som sad drops
Wept at compleating of the mortal Sin
Original; while *Adam* took no thought,
Eating his fill, nor *Eve* to iterate
Her former trespass fear'd, the more to soothe
Him with her lov'd societie, that now

As with new Wine intoxicated both
They swim in mirth, and fansie that they feel
Divinitie within them breeding wings   1010
Wherewith to scorn the Earth: but that false Fruit
Farr other operation first displaid,
Carnal desire enflaming, hee on *Eve*
Began to cast lascivious Eyes, she him
As wantonly repaid; in Lust they burne:
Till *Adam* thus 'gan *Eve* to dalliance move.
  Eve, now I see thou art exact of taste,
And elegant, of Sapience no small part,
Since to each meaning savour we apply,
And Palate call judicious; I the praise   1020
Yeild thee, so well this day thou hast purvey'd.
Much pleasure we have lost, while we abstain'd
From this delightful Fruit, nor known till now
True relish, tasting; if such pleasure be
In things to us forbidden, it might be wish'd,
For this one Tree had bin forbidden ten.
But come, so well refresh't, now let us play,
As meet is, after such delicious Fare;
For never did thy Beautie since the day
I saw thee first and wedded thee, adorn'd   1030
With all perfections, so enflame my sense
With ardor to enjoy thee, fairer now
Then ever, bountie of this vertuous Tree.
  So said he, and forbore not glance or toy
Of amorous intent, well understood
Of *Eve,* whose Eye darted contagious Fire.
Her hand he seis'd, and to a shadie bank,
Thick overhead with verdant roof imbowr'd
He led her nothing loath; Flours were the Couch,
Pansies, and Violets, and Asphodel,   1040
And Hyacinth, Earths freshest softest lap.
There they thir fill of Love and Loves disport
Took largely, of thir mutual guilt the Seale,
The solace of thir sin, till dewie sleep
Oppress'd them, wearied with thir amorous play.
Soon as the force of that fallacious Fruit,
That with exhilerating vapour bland
About thir spirits had plaid, and inmost powers
Made erre, was now exhal'd, and grosser sleep
Bred of unkindly fumes, with conscious dreams   1050
Encumberd, now had left them, up they rose
As from unrest, and each the other viewing,
Soon found thir Eyes how op'nd, and thir minds
How dark'nd; innocence, that as a veile
Had shadow'd them from knowing ill, was gon,
Just confidence, and native righteousness,
And honour from about them, naked left
To guiltie shame hee cover'd, but his Robe
Uncover'd more. So rose the *Danite* strong
Herculean Samson from the Harlot-lap   1060

Of *Philistean Dalilah,* and wak'd
Shorn of his strength, They destitute and bare
Of all thir vertue: silent, and in face
Confounded long they sate, as struck'n mute,
Till *Adam,* though not less then *Eve* abasht,
At length gave utterance to these words constraind.

O *Eve,* in evil hour thou didst give eare
To that false Worm, of whomsoever taught
To counterfet Mans voice, true in our Fall,
False in our promis'd Rising; since our Eyes   1070
Op'nd we find indeed, and find we know
Both Good and Evil, Good lost, and Evil got,
Bad Fruit of Knowledge, if this be to know,
Which leaves us naked thus, of Honour void,
Of Innocence, of Faith, of Puritie,
Our wonted Ornaments now soild and staind,
And in our Faces evident the signes
Of foul concupiscence; whence evil store;
Even shame, the last of evils; of the first
Be sure then. How shall I behold the face   1080
Henceforth of God or Angel, earst with joy
And rapture so oft beheld? those heav'nly shapes
Will dazle now this earthly, with thir blaze
Insufferably bright. O might I here
In solitude live savage, in some glade
Obscur'd, where highest Woods impenetrable
To Starr or Sun-light, spread thir umbrage broad,
And brown as Evening: Cover me ye Pines,
Ye Cedars, with innumerable boughs
Hide me, where I may never see them more.   1090
But let us now, as in bad plight, devise
What best may for the present serve to hide
The Parts of each from other, that seem most
To shame obnoxious, and unseemliest seen,
Some Tree whose broad smooth Leaves together sowd,
And girded on our loyns, may cover round
Those middle parts, that this new commer, Shame,
There sit not, and reproach us as unclean.

So counsel'd hee, and both together went
Into the thickest Wood, there soon they chose   1100
The Figtree, not that kind for Fruit renown'd,
But such as at this day to *Indians* known
In *Malabar* or *Decan* spreds her Armes
Braunching so broad and long, that in the ground
The bended Twigs take root, and Daughters grow
About the Mother Tree, a Pillard shade
High overarch't, and echoing Walks between;
There oft the *Indian* Herdsman shunning heate
Shelters in coole, and tends his pasturing Herds
At Loopholes cut through thickest shade: Those Leaves   1110
They gatherd, broad as *Amazonian* Targe,
And with what skill they had, together sowd,
To gird thir waste, vain Covering if to hide

Thir guilt and dreaded shame; O how unlike
To that first naked Glorie. Such of late
Columbus found th' *American* so girt
With featherd Cincture, naked else and wilde
Among the Trees on Iles and woodie Shores.
Thus fenc't, and as they thought, thir shame in part
Coverd, but not at rest or ease of Mind,   1120
They sate them down to weep, nor onely Teares
Raind at thir Eyes, but high Winds worse within
Began to rise, high Passions, Anger, Hate,
Mistrust, Suspicion, Discord, and shook sore
Thir inward State of Mind, calme Region once
And full of Peace, now tost and turbulent:
For Understanding rul'd not, and the Will
Heard not her lore, both in subjection now
To sensual Appetite, who from beneathe
Usurping over sovran Reason claimd   1130
Superior sway: From thus distemperd brest,
Adam, estrang'd in look and alterd stile,
Speech intermitted thus to *Eve* renewd.

   Would thou hadst heark'nd to my words, & stai'd
With me, as I besought thee, when that strange
Desire of wandring this unhappie Morn,
I know not whence possessd thee; we had then
Remaind still happie, not as now, despoild
Of all our good, sham'd, naked, miserable.
Let none henceforth seek needless cause to approve   1140
The Faith they owe; when earnestly they seek
Such proof, conclude, they then begin to faile.

   To whom soon mov'd with touch of blame thus *Eve.*
What words have past thy Lips, *Adam* severe,
Imput'st thou that to my default, or will
Of wandering, as thou call'st it, which who knows
But might as ill have happ'nd thou being by,
Or to thy self perhaps: hadst thou bin there,
Or here th' attempt, thou couldst not have discernd
Fraud in the Serpent, speaking as he spake;   1150
No ground of enmitie between us known,
Why hee should mean me ill, or seek to harme.
Was I to have never parted from thy side?
As good have grown there still a liveless Rib.
Being as I am, why didst not thou the Head
Command me absolutely not to go,
Going into such danger as thou saidst?
Too facil then thou didst not much gainsay,
Nay, didst permit, approve, and fair dismiss.
Hadst thou bin firm and fixt in thy dissent,   1160
Neither had I transgress'd, nor thou with mee.

   To whom then first incenst *Adam* repli'd.
Is this the Love, is this the recompence
Of mine to thee, ingrateful *Eve,* exprest
Immutable when thou wert lost, not I,
Who might have liv'd and joyd immortal bliss,

Yet willingly chose rather Death with thee:
And am I now upbraided, as the cause
Of thy transgressing? not enough severe,
It seems, in thy restraint: what could I more?   1170
I warn'd thee, I admonish'd thee, foretold
The danger, and the lurking Enemie
That lay in wait; beyond this had bin force,
And force upon free Will hath here no place.
But confidence then bore thee on, secure
Either to meet no danger, or to finde
Matter of glorious trial; and perhaps
I also err'd in overmuch admiring
What seemd in thee so perfet, that I thought
No evil durst attempt thee, but I rue   1180
That errour now, which is become my crime,
And thou th' accuser. Thus it shall befall
Him who to worth in Women overtrusting
Lets her Will rule; restraint she will not brook,
And left to her self, if evil thence ensue,
Shee first his weak indulgence will accuse.
          Thus they in mutual accusation spent
The fruitless hours, but neither self-condemning:
And of thir vain contest appeer'd no end.

The End of the Ninth Book.

PARADISE LOST.

BOOK X.

The Argument.

Mans transgression known, the Guardian Angels forsake Paradise, and return up to Heaven to approve thir vigilance, and are approv'd, God declaring that the entrance of Satan could not be by them prevented. He sends his Son to judge the Transgressors, who descends and gives Sentence accordingly; then in pity cloaths them both, and reascends. Sin and Death sitting till then at the Gates of Hell, by wondrous sympathie feeling the success of Satan in this new World, and the sin by Man there committed, resolve to sit no longer confin'd in Hell, but to follow Satan thir Sire up to the place of Man: To make the way easier from Hell to this World to and fro, they pave a broad Highway or Bridge over Chaos, according to the Track that Satan first made; then preparing for Earth, they meet him proud of his success returning to Hell; thir mutual gratulation. Satan arrives at Pandemonium, in full assembly relates with boasting his success against Man; instead of applause is entertained with a general hiss by all his audience, transform'd with himself also suddenly into Serpents, according to his doom giv'n in Paradise; then deluded with a shew of the forbidden Tree springing up before them, they greedily reaching to take of the Fruit, chew dust and bitter ashes. The proceedings of Sin and Death; God foretels the final Victory of his Son over them, and the renewing of all things; but for the present commands his Angels to make several alterations in the Heavens and Elements. Adam more and more perceiving his fall'n condition heavily bewailes, rejects the condolement of Eve; she persists and at length appeases him: then to evade the Curse likely to fall on thir Ofspring, proposes to Adam violent wayes, which he approves not, but conceiving better hope, puts her in mind of the late Promise made them, that her Seed should be reveng'd on the Serpent, and exhorts her with him to seek Peace of the offended Deity, by repentance and supplication.

MEANWHILE the hainous and despightfull act
Of *Satan* done in Paradise, and how
Hee in the Serpent had perverted *Eve*,
Her Husband shee, to taste the fatall fruit,

Was known in Heav'n; for what can scape the Eye
Of God All-seeing, or deceave his Heart
Omniscient, who in all things wise and just,
Hinder'd not *Satan* to attempt the minde
Of Man, with strength entire, and free Will arm'd,
Complete to have discover'd and repulst
Whatever wiles of Foe or seeming Friend.
For still they knew, and ought to have still remember'd
The high Injunction not to taste that Fruit,
Whoever tempted; which they not obeying,
Incurr'd, what could they less, the penaltie,
And manifold in sin, deserv'd to fall.
Up into Heav'n from Paradise in hast
Th' Angelic Guards ascended, mute and sad
For Man, for of his state by this they knew,
Much wondring how the suttle Fiend had stoln
Entrance unseen. Soon as th' unwelcome news
From Earth arriv'd at Heaven Gate, displeas'd
All were who heard, dim sadness did not spare
That time Celestial visages, yet mixt
With pitie, violated not thir bliss.
About the new-arriv'd, in multitudes
Th' ethereal People ran, to hear and know
How all befell: they towards the Throne Supream
Accountable made haste to make appear
With righteous plea, thir utmost vigilance,
And easily approv'd; when the most High
Eternal Father from his secret Cloud,
Amidst in Thunder utter'd thus his voice.
    Assembl'd Angels, and ye Powers return'd
From unsuccessful charge, be not dismaid,
Nor troubl'd at these tidings from the Earth,
Which your sincerest care could not prevent,
Foretold so lately what would come to pass,
When first this Tempter cross'd the Gulf from Hell.
I told ye then he should prevail and speed
On his bad Errand, Man should be seduc't
And flatter'd out of all, believing lies
Against his Maker; no Decree of mine
Concurring to necessitate his Fall,
Or touch with lightest moment of impulse
His free Will, to her own inclining left
In eevn scale. But fall'n he is, and now
What rests, but that the mortal Sentence pass
On his transgression, Death denounc't that day,
Which he presumes already vain and void,
Because not yet inflicted, as he fear'd,
By some immediate stroak; but soon shall find
Forbearance no acquittance ere day end.
Justice shall not return as bountie scorn'd.
But whom send I to judge them? whom but thee
Vicegerent Son, to thee I have transferr'd
All Judgement, whether in Heav'n, or Earth, or Hell.

10

20

30

40

50

Easie it may be seen that I intend
Mercie collegue with Justice, sending thee
Mans Friend, his Mediator, his design'd   60
Both Ransom and Redeemer voluntarie,
And destin'd Man himself to judge Man fall'n.
　So spake the Father, and unfoulding bright
Toward the right hand his Glorie, on the Son
Blaz'd forth unclouded Deitie; he full
Resplendent all his Father manifest
Express'd, and thus divinely answer'd milde.
　Father Eternal, thine is to decree,
Mine both in Heav'n and Earth to do thy will
Supream, that thou in mee thy Son belov'd   70
Mayst ever rest well pleas'd. I go to judge
On Earth these thy transgressors, but thou knowst,
Whoever judg'd, the worst on mee must light,
When time shall be, for so I undertook
Before thee; and not repenting, this obtaine
Of right, that I may mitigate thir doom
On me deriv'd, yet I shall temper so
Justice with Mercie, as may illustrate most
Them fully satisfied, and thee appease.
Attendance none shall need, nor Train, where none   80
Are to behold the Judgement, but the judg'd,
Those two; the third best absent is condemn'd,
Convict by flight, and Rebel to all Law
Conviction to the Serpent none belongs.
　Thus saying, from his radiant Seat he rose
Of high collateral glorie: him Thrones and Powers,
Princedoms, and Dominations ministrant
Accompanied to Heaven Gate, from whence
Eden and all the Coast in prospect lay.
Down he descended strait; the speed of Gods   90
Time counts not, though with swiftest minutes wing'd.
Now was the Sun in Western cadence low
From Noon, and gentle Aires due at thir hour
To fan the Earth now wak'd, and usher in
The Eevning coole when he from wrauth more coole
Came the mild Judge and Intercessor both
To sentence Man: the voice of God they heard
Now walking in the Garden, by soft windes
Brought to thir Ears, while day declin'd, they heard,
And from his presence hid themselves among   100
The thickest Trees, both Man and Wife, till God
Approaching, thus to *Adam* call'd aloud.
　Where art thou *Adam,* wont with joy to meet
My coming seen far off? I miss thee here,
Not pleas'd, thus entertaind with solitude,
Where obvious dutie erewhile appear'd unsaught:
Or come I less conspicuous, or what change
Absents thee, or what chance detains? Come forth.
He came, and with him *Eve,* more loth, though first
To offend, discount'nanc't both, and discompos'd;   110

Love was not in thir looks, either to God
Or to each other, but apparent guilt,
And shame, and perturbation, and despaire,
Anger, and obstinacie, and hate, and guile.
Whence *Adam* faultring long, thus answer'd brief.
　I heard thee in the Garden, and of thy voice
Affraid, being naked, hid my self. To whom
The gracious Judge without revile repli'd.
　My voice thou oft hast heard, and hast not fear'd,
But still rejoyc't, how is it now become　　　　　　120
So dreadful to thee? that thou art naked, who
Hath told thee? hast thou eaten of the Tree
Whereof I gave thee charge thou shouldst not eat?
　To whom thus *Adam* sore beset repli'd.
O Heav'n! in evil strait this day I stand
Before my Judge, either to undergoe
My self the total Crime, or to accuse
My other self, the partner of my life;
Whose failing, while her Faith to me remaines,
I should conceal, and not expose to blame　　　　130
By my complaint; but strict necessitie
Subdues me, and calamitous constraint,
Least on my head both sin and punishment,
However insupportable, be all
Devolv'd; though should I hold my peace, yet thou
Wouldst easily detect what I conceale.
This Woman whom thou mad'st to be my help,
And gav'st me as thy perfet gift, so good,
So fit, so acceptable, so Divine,
That from her hand I could suspect no ill,　　　　140
And what she did, whatever in it self,
Her doing seem'd to justifie the deed;
Shee gave me of the Tree, and I did eate.
　To whom the sovran Presence thus repli'd.
Was shee thy God, that her thou didst obey
Before his voice, or was shee made thy guide,
Superior, or but equal, that to her
Thou did'st resigne thy Manhood, and the Place
Wherein God set thee above her made of thee,
And for thee, whose perfection farr excell'd　　　150
Hers in all real dignitie: Adornd
She was indeed, and lovely to attract
Thy Love, not thy Subjection, and her Gifts
Were such as under Government well seem'd,
Unseemly to beare rule, which was thy part
And person, had'st thou known thy self aright.
　So having said, he thus to *Eve* in few:
Say Woman, what is this which thou hast done?
　To whom sad *Eve* with shame nigh overwhelm'd,
Confessing soon, yet not before her Judge　　　　160
Bold or loquacious, thus abasht repli'd.
　The Serpent me beguil'd and I did eate.
　Which when the Lord God heard, without delay

To Judgement he proceeded on th' accus'd
Serpent though brute, unable to transferre
The Guilt on him who made him instrument
Of mischief, and polluted from the end
Of his Creation; justly then accurst,
As vitiated in Nature: more to know
Concern'd not Man (since he no further knew)   170
Nor alter'd his offence; yet God at last
To Satan first in sin his doom apply'd,
Though in mysterious terms, judg'd as then best:
And on the Serpent thus his curse let fall.
  Because thou hast done this, thou art accurst
Above all Cattel, each Beast of the Field;
Upon thy Belly groveling thou shalt goe,
And dust shalt eat all the days of thy Life.
Between Thee and the Woman I will put
Enmitie, and between thine and her Seed;   180
Her Seed shall bruise thy head, thou bruise his heel.
  So spake this Oracle, then verifi'd
When *Jesus* son of *Mary* second *Eve,*
Saw Satan fall like Lightning down from Heav'n,
Prince of the Aire; then rising from his Grave
Spoild Principalities and Powers, triumpht
In open shew, and with ascension bright
Captivity led captive through the Aire,
The Realme it self of Satan long usurpt,
Whom he shall tread at last under our feet;   190
Eevn hee who now foretold his fatal bruise,
And to the Woman thus his Sentence turn'd.
  Thy sorrow I will greatly multiplie
By thy Conception; Childern thou shalt bring
In sorrow forth, and to thy Husbands will
Thine shall submit, hee over thee shall rule.
  On *Adam* last thus judgement he pronounc'd.
Because thou hast heark'nd to the voice of thy Wife,
And eaten of the Tree concerning which
I charg'd thee, saying: Thou shalt not eate thereof,   200
Curs'd is the ground for thy sake, thou in sorrow
Shalt eate thereof all the days of thy Life;
Thornes also and Thistles it shall bring thee forth
Unbid, and thou shalt eate th' Herb of th' Field,
In the sweat of thy Face shalt thou eate Bread,
Till thou return unto the ground, for thou
Out of the ground wast taken, know thy Birth,
For dust thou art, and shalt to dust returne.
  So judg'd he Man, both Judge and Saviour sent,
And th' instant stroke of Death denounc't that day   210
Remov'd farr off; then pittying how they stood
Before him naked to the aire, that now
Must suffer change, disdain'd not to begin
Thenceforth the forme of servant to assume,
As when he wash'd his servants feet, so now
As Father of his Familie he clad

Thir nakedness with Skins of Beasts, or slain,
Or as the Snake with youthful Coate repaid;
And thought not much to cloath his Enemies:
Nor hee thir outward onely with the Skins   220
Of Beasts, but inward nakedness, much more
Opprobrious, with his Robe of righteousness,
Araying cover'd from his Fathers sight.
To him with swift ascent he up returnd.
Into his blissful bosom reassum'd
In glory as of old, to him appeas'd
All, though all-knowing, what had past with Man
Recounted, mixing intercession sweet.
Meanwhile ere thus was sin'd and judg'd on Earth,
Within the Gates of Hell sate Sin and Death,   230
In counterview within the Gates, that now
Stood open wide, belching outrageous flame
Farr into *Chaos,* since the Fiend pass'd through,
Sin opening, who thus now to Death began.
    O Son, why sit we here each other viewing
Idlely, while Satan our great Author thrives
In other Worlds, and happier Seat provides
For us his ofspring deare? It cannot be
But that success attends him; if mishap,
Ere this he had return'd, with fury driv'n   240
By his Avenger, since no place like this
Can fit his punishment, or their revenge.
Methinks I feel new strength within me rise,
Wings growing, and Dominion giv'n me large
Beyond this Deep; whatever drawes me on,
Or sympathie, or som connatural force
Powerful at greatest distance to unite
With secret amity things of like kinde
By secretest conveyance. Thou my Shade
Inseparable must with mee along: 250
For Death from Sin no power can separate.
But least the difficultie of passing back
Stay his returne perhaps over this Gulfe
Impassable, impervious, let us try
Adventrous work, yet to thy power and mine
Not unagreeable, to found a path
Over this Maine from Hell to that new World
Where Satan now prevailes, a Monument
Of merit high to all th' infernal Host,
Easing thir passage hence, for intercourse,   260
Or transmigration, as thir lot shall lead.
Nor can I miss the way, so strongly drawn
By this new felt attraction and instinct.
    Whom thus the meager Shadow answerd soon.
Goe whither Fate and inclination strong
Leads thee, I shall not lag behinde, nor erre
The way, thou leading, such a sent I draw
Of carnage, prey innumerable, and taste
The savour of Death from all things there that live:

Nor shall I to the work thou enterprisest   270
Be wanting, but afford thee equal aid.
   So saying, with delight he snuff'd the smell
Of mortal change on Earth. As when a flock
Of ravenous Fowl, though many a League remote,
Against the day of Battel, to a Field,
Where Armies lie encampt, come flying, lur'd
With sent of living Carcasses design'd
For death, the following day, in bloodie fight.
So sented the grim Feature, and upturn'd
His Nostril wide into the murkie Air,   280
Sagacious of his Quarrey from so farr.
Then Both from out Hell Gates into the waste
Wide Anarchie of *Chaos* damp and dark
Flew divers, & with Power (thir Power was great)
Hovering upon the Waters; what they met
Solid or slimie, as in raging Sea
Tost up and down, together crowded drove
From each side shoaling towards the mouth of Hell.
As when two Polar Winds blowing adverse
Upon the *Cronian* Sea, together drive   290
Mountains of Ice, that stop th' imagin'd way
Beyond *Petsora* Eastward, to the rich
Cathaian Coast. The aggregated Soyle
Death with his Mace petrific, cold and dry,
As with a Trident smote, and fix't as firm
As *Delos* floating once; the rest his look
Bound with *Gorgonian* rigor not to move,
And with *Asphaltic* slime; broad as the Gate,
Deep to the Roots of Hell the gather'd beach
They fasten'd, and the Mole immense wraught on   300
Over the foaming deep high Archt, a Bridge
Of length prodigious joyning to the Wall
Immoveable of this now fenceless world
Forfeit to Death; from hence a passage broad,
Smooth, easie, inoffensive down to Hell.
So, if great things to small may be compar'd,
Xerxes, the Libertie of *Greece* to yoke,
From *Susa* his *Memnonian* Palace high
Came to the Sea, and over *Hellespont*
Bridging his way, *Europe* with *Asia* joyn'd,   310
And scourg'd with many a stroak th' indignant waves.
Now had they brought the work by wondrous Art
Pontifical, a ridge of pendent Rock
Over the vext Abyss, following the track
Of *Satan,* to the self same place where hee
First lighted from his Wing, and landed safe
From out of *Chaos* to the outside bare
Of this round World: with Pinns of Adamant
And Chains they made all fast, too fast they made
And durable; and now in little space   320
The Confines met of Empyrean Heav'n
And of this World, and on the left hand Hell

With long reach interpos'd; three sev'ral wayes
In sight, to each of these three places led.
And now thir way to Earth they had descri'd,
To Paradise first tending, when behold
Satan in likeness of an Angel bright
Betwixt the *Centaure* and the *Scorpion* stearing
His *Zenith,* while the Sun in *Aries* rose:
Disguis'd he came, but those his Childern dear   330
Thir Parent soon discern'd, though in disguise.
Hee, after *Eve* seduc't, unminded slunk
Into the Wood fast by, and changing shape
To observe the sequel, saw his guileful act
By *Eve,* though all unweeting, seconded
Upon her Husband, saw thir shame that sought
Vain covertures; but when he saw descend
The Son of God to judge them, terrifi'd
Hee fled, not hoping to escape, but shun
The present, fearing guiltie what his wrauth   340
Might suddenly inflict; that past, return'd
By Night, and listning where the hapless Paire
Sate in thir sad discourse, and various plaint,
Thence gatherd his own doom, which understood
Not instant, but of future time. With joy
And tidings fraught, to Hell he now return'd,
And at the brink of *Chaos,* neer the foot
Of this new wondrous Pontifice, unhop't
Met who to meet him came, his Ofspring dear.
Great joy was at thir meeting, and at sight   350
Of that stupendious Bridge his joy encreas'd.
Long hee admiring stood, till Sin, his faire
Inchanting Daughter, thus the silence broke.
  O Parent, these are thy magnific deeds,
Thy Trophies, which thou view'st as not thine own,
Thou art thir Author and prime Architect:
For I no sooner in my Heart divin'd,
My Heart, which by a secret harmonie
Still moves with thine, joyn'd in connexion sweet,
That thou on Earth hadst prosper'd, which thy looks   360
Now also evidence, but straight I felt
Though distant from thee Worlds between, yet felt
That I must after thee with this thy Son;
Such fatal consequence unites us three:
Hell could no longer hold us in her bounds,
Nor this unvoyageable Gulf obscure
Detain from following thy illustrious track.
Thou hast atchiev'd our libertie, confin'd
Within Hell Gates till now, thou us impow'rd
To fortifie thus farr, and overlay   370
With this portentous Bridge the dark Abyss.
Thine now is all this World, thy vertue hath won
What thy hands builded not, thy Wisdom gain'd
With odds what Warr hath lost, and fully aveng'd
Our foile in Heav'n; here thou shalt Monarch reign,

There didst not; there let him still Victor sway,
As Battel hath adjudg'd, from this new World
Retiring, by his own doom alienated,
And henceforth Monarchie with thee divide
Of all things, parted by th' Empyreal bounds,   380
His Quadrature, from thy Orbicular World,
Or trie thee now more dang'rous to his Throne.
   Whom thus the Prince of Darkness answerd glad.
Fair Daughter, and thou Son and Grandchild both,
High proof ye now have giv'n to be the Race
Of *Satan* (for I glorie in the name,
Antagonist of Heav'ns Almightie King)
Amply have merited of me, of all
Th' Infernal Empire, that so neer Heav'ns dore
Triumphal with triumphal act have met,   390
Mine with this glorious Work, & made one Realm
Hell and this World, one Realm, one Continent
Of easie thorough-fare. Therefore while I
Descend through Darkness, on your Rode with ease
To my associate Powers, them to acquaint
With these successes, and with them rejoyce,
You two this way, among those numerous Orbs
All yours, right down to Paradise descend;
There dwell & Reign in bliss, thence on the Earth
Dominion exercise and in the Aire,   400
Chiefly on Man, sole Lord of all declar'd,
Him first make sure your thrall, and lastly kill.
My Substitutes I send ye, and Create
Plenipotent on Earth, of matchless might
Issuing from mee: on your joynt vigor now
My hold of this new Kingdom all depends,
Through Sin to Death expos'd by my exploit.
If your joynt power prevaile, th' affaires of Hell
No detriment need feare, goe and be strong.
   So saying he dismiss'd them, they with speed   410
Thir course through thickest Constellations held
Spreading thir bane; the blasted Starrs lookt wan,
And Planets, Planet-strook, real Eclips
Then sufferd. Th' other way *Satan* went down
The Causey to Hell Gate; on either side
Disparted *Chaos* over built exclaimd,
And with rebounding surge the barrs assaild,
That scorn'd his indignation: through the Gate,
Wide open and unguarded, *Satan* pass'd,
And all about found desolate; for those   420
Appointed to sit there, had left thir charge,
Flown to the upper World; the rest were all
Farr to the inland retir'd, about the walls
Of *Pandæmonium,* Citie and proud seate
Of *Lucifer,* so by allusion calld,
Of that bright Starr to *Satan* paragond.
There kept thir Watch the Legions, while the Grand
In Council sate, sollicitous what chance

Might intercept thir Emperour sent, so hee
Departing gave command, and they observ'd.   430
As when the *Tartar* from his *Russian* Foe
By *Astracan* over the Snowie Plaines
Retires, or *Bactrian* Sophi from the hornes
Of *Turkish* Crescent, leaves all waste beyond
The Realme of *Aladule,* in his retreate
To *Tauris* or *Casbeen.* So these the late
Heav'n-banisht Host, left desert utmost Hell
Many a dark League, reduc't in careful Watch
Round thir Metropolis, and now expecting
Each hour their great adventurer from the search   440
Of Forrein Worlds: he through the midst unmarkt,
In shew plebeian Angel militant
Of lowest order, past; and from the dore
Of that *Plutonian* Hall, invisible
Ascended his high Throne, which under state
Of richest texture spred, at th' upper end
Was plac't in regal lustre. Down a while
He sate, and round about him saw unseen:
At last as from a Cloud his fulgent head
And shape Starr bright appeer'd, or brighter, clad   450
With what permissive glory since his fall
Was left him, or false glitter: All amaz'd
At that so sudden blaze the *Stygian* throng
Bent thir aspect, and whom they wish'd beheld,
Thir mighty Chief returnd: loud was th' acclaime:
Forth rush'd in haste the great consulting Peers,
Rais'd from thir dark *Divan,* and with like joy
Congratulant approach'd him, who with hand
Silence, and with these words attention won.
    Thrones, Dominations, Princedoms, Vertues, Powers,   460
For in possession such, not onely of right,
I call ye and declare ye now, returnd
Successful beyond hope, to lead ye forth
Triumphant out of this infernal Pit
Abominable, accurst, the house of woe,
And Dungeon of our Tyrant: Now possess,
As Lords, a spacious World, to our native Heaven
Little inferiour, by my adventure hard
With peril great atchiev'd. Long were to tell
What I have don, what sufferd, with what paine   470
Voyag'd th' unreal, vast, unbounded deep
Of horrible confusion, over which
By Sin and Death a broad way now is pav'd
To expedite your glorious march; but I
Toild out my uncouth passage, forc't to ride
Th' untractable Abysse, plung'd in the womb
Of unoriginal *Night* and *Chaos* wilde,
That jealous of thir secrets fiercely oppos'd
My journey strange, with clamorous uproare
Protesting Fate supreame; thence how I found   480
The new created World, **which fame** in Heav'n

Long had foretold, a Fabrick wonderful
Of absolute perfection, therein Man
Plac't in a Paradise, by our exile
Made happie: Him by fraud I have seduc'd
From his Creator, and the more to increase
Your wonder, with an Apple; he thereat
Offended, worth your laughter, hath giv'n up
Both his beloved Man and all his World,
To Sin and Death a prey, and so to us,   490
Without our hazard, labour, or allarme,
To range in, and to dwell, and over Man
To rule, as over all he should have rul'd.
True is, mee also he hath judg'd, or rather
Mee not, but the brute Serpent in whose shape
Man I deceav'd: that which to mee belongs,
Is enmity, which he will put between
Mee and Mankinde; I am to bruise his heel;
His Seed, when is not set, shall bruise my head:
A World who would not purchase with a bruise,   500
Or much more grievous pain? Ye have th' account
Of my performance: What remaines, ye Gods,
But up and enter now into full bliss.
    So having said, a while he stood, expecting
Thir universal shout and high applause
To fill his eare, when contrary he hears
On all sides, from innumerable tongues
A dismal universal hiss, the sound
Of public scorn; he wonderd, but not long
Had leasure, wondring at himself now more;   510
His Visage drawn he felt to sharp and spare,
His Armes clung to his Ribs, his Leggs entwining
Each other, till supplanted down he fell
A monstrous Serpent on his Belly prone,
Reluctant, but in vaine, a greater power
Now rul'd him, punisht in the shape he sin'd,
According to his doom: he would have spoke,
But hiss for hiss returnd with forked tongue
To forked tongue, for now were all transform'd
Alike, to Serpents all as accessories   520
To his bold Riot: dreadful was the din
Of hissing through the Hall, thick swarming now
With complicated monsters, head and taile,
Scorpion and Asp, and *Amphisbæna* dire,
Cerastes hornd, *Hydrus,* and *Ellops* drear,
And *Dipsas* (Not so thick swarm'd once the Soil
Bedropt with blood of *Gorgon,* or the Isle
Ophiusa) but still greatest hee the midst,
Now Dragon grown, larger then whom the Sun
Ingenderd in the *Pythian* Vale on slime,   530
Huge *Python,* and his Power no less he seem'd
Above the rest still to retain; they all
Him follow'd issuing forth to th' open Field,
Where all ye. left of that revolted Rout

Heav'n-fall'n, in station stood or just array,
Sublime with expectation when to see
In Triumph issuing forth thir glorious Chief;
They saw, but other sight instead, a crowd
Of ugly Serpents; horror on them fell,
And horrid sympathie; for what they saw,   540
They felt themselvs now changing; down thir arms,
Down fell both Spear and Shield, down they as fast,
And the dire hiss renew'd, and the dire form
Catcht by Contagion, like in punishment,
As in thir crime. Thus was th' applause they meant,
Turnd to exploding hiss, triumph to shame
Cast on themselves from thir own mouths. There stood
A Grove hard by; sprung up with this thir change,
His will who reigns above, to aggravate
Thir penance, laden with fair Fruit, like that   550
Which grew in Paradise, the bait of *Eve*
Us'd by the Tempter: on that prospect strange
Thir earnest eyes they fix'd, imagining
For one forbidden Tree a multitude
Now ris'n, to work them furder woe or shame;
Yet parcht with scalding thurst and hunger fierce,
Though to delude them sent, could not abstain,
But on they rould in heaps, and up the Trees
Climbing, sat thicker then the snakie locks
That curld *Megæra*: greedily they pluck'd   560
The Frutage fair to sight, like that which grew
Neer that bituminous Lake where *Sodom* flam'd;
This more delusive, not the touch, but taste
Deceav'd; they fondly thinking to allay
Thir appetite with gust, instead of Fruit
Chewd bitter Ashes, which th' offended taste
With spattering noise rejected: oft they assayd,
Hunger and thirst constraining, drugd as oft,
With hatefullest disrelish writh'd thir jaws
With soot and cinders fill'd; so oft they fell   570
Into the same illusion, not as Man
Whom they triumph'd once lapst. Thus were they plagu'd
And worn with Famin, long and ceasless hiss,
Till thir lost shape, permitted, they resum'd,
Yearly enjoynd, some say, to undergo
This annual humbling certain number'd days,
To dash thir pride, and joy for Man seduc't.
However some tradition they dispers'd
Among the Heathen of thir purchase got,
And Fabl'd how the Serpent, whom they calld   580
Ophion with *Eurynome,* the wide-
Encroaching *Eve* perhaps, had first the rule
Of high *Olympus,* thence by *Saturn* driv'n
And *Ops,* ere yet *Dictæan Jove* was born.
Mean while in Paradise the hellish pair
Too soon arriv'd, *Sin* there in power before,
Once actual, now in body, and to dwell

Habitual habitant; behind her *Death*
Close following pace for pace, not mounted yet
On his pale Horse: to whom *Sin* thus began.   550
    Second of *Satan* sprung, all conquering *Death*,
What thinkst thou of our Empire now, though earnd
With travail difficult, not better farr
Then stil at Hels dark threshold to have sate watch,
Unnam'd, undreaded, and thy self half starv'd?
    Whom thus the Sin-born Monster answerd soon.
To mee, who with eternal Famin pine,
Alike is Hell, or Paradise, or Heaven,
There best, where most with ravin I may meet;
Which here, though plenteous, all too little seems   600
To stuff this Maw, this vast unhide-bound Corps.
    To whom th' incestuous Mother thus repli'd.
Thou therefore on these Herbs, and Fruits, & Flours
Feed first, on each Beast next, and Fish, and Fowle,
No homely morsels, and whatever thing
The Sithe of Time mowes down, devour unspar'd,
Till I in Man residing through the Race,
His thoughts, his looks, words, actions all infect,
And season him thy last and sweetest prey.
    This said, they both betook them several wayes,   610
Both to destroy, or unimmortal make
All kinds, and for destruction to mature
Sooner or later; which th' Almightie seeing
From his transcendent Seat the Saints among,
To those bright Orders utterd thus his voice.
    See with what heat these Dogs of Hell advance
To waste and havoc yonder World, which I
So fair and good created, and had still
Kept in that state, had not the folly of Man
Let in these wastful Furies, who impute   620
Folly to mee, so doth the Prince of Hell
And his Adherents, that with so much ease
I suffer them to enter and possess
A place so heav'nly, and conniving seem
To gratifie my scornful Enemies,
That laugh, as if transported with some fit
Of Passion, I to them had quitted all,
At random yeilded up to their misrule;
And know not that I call'd and drew them thither
My Hell-hounds, to lick up the draff and filth   630
Which mans polluting Sin with taint hath shed
On what was pure, till cramm'd and gorg'd, nigh burst
With suckt and glutted offal, at one sling
Of thy victorious Arm, well-pleasing Son,
Both *Sin*, and *Death*, and yawning *Grave* at last
Through *Chaos* hurld, obstruct the mouth of Hell
For ever, and seal up his ravenous Jawes.
Then Heav'n and Earth renewd shall be made pure
To sanctitie that shall receive no staine:
Till then the Curse pronounc't on both precedes.   640

Hee ended, and the heav'nly Audience loud
Sung *Halleluia,* as the sound of Seas,
Through multitude that sung: Just are thy ways,
Righteous are thy Decrees on all thy Works;
Who can extenuate thee? Next, to the Son,
Destin'd restorer of Mankind, by whom
New Heav'n and Earth shall to the Ages rise,
Or down from Heav'n descend. Such was thir song,
While the Creator calling forth by name
His mightie Angels gave them several charge,   650
As sorted best with present things. The Sun
Had first his precept so to move, so shine,
As might affect the Earth with cold and heat
Scarce tollerable, and from the North to call
Decrepit Winter, from the South to bring
Solstitial summers heat. To the blanc Moone
Her office they prescrib'd, to th' other five
Thir planetarie motions and aspects
In *Sextile, Square,* and *Trine,* and *Opposite,*
Of noxious efficacie, and when to joyne   660
In Synod unbenigne, and taught the fixt
Thir influence malignant when to showre,
Which of them rising with the Sun, or falling,
Should prove tempestuous: To the Winds they set
Thir corners, when with bluster to confound
Sea, Aire, and Shoar, the Thunder when to rowle
With terror through the dark Aereal Hall.
Some say he bid his Angels turne ascanse
The Poles of Earth twice ten degrees and more
From the Suns Axle; they with labour push'd   670
Oblique the Centric Globe: Som say the Sun
Was bid turn Reines from th' Equinoctial Rode
Like distant breadth to *Taurus* with the Seav'n
Atlantick Sisters, and the *Spartan* Twins
Up to the *Tropic* Crab; thence down amaine
By *Leo* and the *Virgin* and the *Scales,*
As deep as *Capricorne,* to bring in change
Of Seasons to each Clime; else had the Spring
Perpetual smil'd on Earth with vernant Flours,
Equal in Days and Nights, except to those   680
Beyond the Polar Circles; to them Day
Had unbenighted shon, while the low Sun
To recompence his distance, in thir sight
Had rounded still th' *Horizon,* and not known
Or East or West, which had forbid the Snow
From cold *Estotiland,* and South as farr
Beneath *Magellan.* At that tasted Fruit
The Sun, as from *Thyestean* Banquet, turn'd
His course intended; else how had the World
Inhabited, though sinless, more then now,   690
Avoided pinching cold and scorching heate?
These changes in the Heav'ns, though slow, produc'd
Like change on Sea and Land, sideral blast.

Vapour, and Mist, and Exhalation hot,
Corrupt and Pestilent: Now from the North
Of *Norumbega,* and the *Samoed* shoar
Bursting thir brazen Dungeon, armd with ice
And snow and haile and stormie gust and flaw,
Boreas and *Cæcias* and *Argestes* loud
And *Thrascias* rend the Woods and Seas upturn;   700
With adverse blast up-turns them from the South
Notus and *Afer* black with thundrous Clouds
From *Serraliona;* thwart of these as fierce
Forth rush the *Levant* and the *Ponent* Windes
Eurus and *Zephir* with thir lateral noise,
Sirocco, and *Libecchio.* Thus began
Outrage from liveless things; but Discord first
Daughter of Sin, among th' irrational,
Death introduc'd through fierce antipathie:
Beast now with Beast gan war, & Fowle with Fowle,   710
And Fish with Fish; to graze the Herb all leaving,
Devourd each other; nor stood much in awe
Of Man, but fled him, or with count'nance grim
Glar'd on him passing: these were from without
The growing miseries, which *Adam* saw
Alreadie in part, though hid in gloomiest shade,
To sorrow abandond, but worse felt within,
And in a troubl'd Sea of passion tost,
Thus to disburd'n sought with sad complaint.
   O miserable of happie! is this the end   720
Of this new glorious World, and mee so late
The Glory of that Glory, who now becom
Accurst of blessed, hide me from the face
Of God, whom to behold was then my highth
Of happiness: yet well, if here would end
The miserie, I deserv'd it, and would beare
My own deservings; but this will not serve;
All that I eate or drink, or shall beget,
Is propagated curse. O voice once heard
Delightfully, *Encrease and multiply,*   730
Now death to heare! for what can I encrease
Or multiplie, but curses on my head?
Who of all Ages to succeed, but feeling
The evil on him brought by me, will curse
My Head, Ill fare our Ancestor impure,
For this we may thank *Adam;* but his thanks
Shall be the execration; so besides
Mine own that bide upon me, all from mee
Shall with a fierce reflux on mee redound,
On mee as on thir natural center light   740
Heavie, though in thir place. O fleeting joyes
Of Paradise, deare bought with lasting woes!
Did I request thee, Maker, from my Clay
To mould me Man, did I sollicite thee
From darkness to promote me, or here place
In this delicious Garden? as my Will

Concurd not to my being, it were but right
And equal to reduce me to my dust,
Desirous to resigne, and render back
All I receav'd, unable to performe   750
Thy terms too hard, by which I was to hold
The good I sought not. To the loss of that,
Sufficient penaltie, why hast thou added
The sense of endless woes? inexplicable
Thy Justice seems; yet to say truth, too late,
I thus contest; then should have been refusd
Those terms whatever, when they were propos'd:
Thou didst accept them; wilt thou enjoy the good,
Then cavil the conditions? and though God
Made thee without thy leave, what if thy Son   760
Prove disobedient, and reprov'd, retort,
Wherefore didst thou beget me? I sought it not:
Wouldst thou admit for his contempt of thee
That proud excuse? yet him not thy election,
But Natural necessity begot.
God made thee of choice his own, and of his own
To serve him, thy reward was of his grace,
Thy punishment then justly is at his Will.
Be it so, for I submit, his doom is fair,
That dust I am, and shall to dust returne: 770
O welcom hour whenever! why delayes
His hand to execute what his Decree
Fixd on this day? why do I overlive,
Why am I mockt with death, and length'nd out
To deathless pain? how gladly would I meet
Mortalitie my sentence, and be Earth
Insensible, how glad would lay me down
As in my Mothers lap? there I should rest
And sleep secure; his dreadful voice no more
Would Thunder in my ears, no fear of worse   780
To mee and to my ofspring would torment me
With cruel expectation. Yet one doubt
Pursues me still, least all I cannot die,
Least that pure breath of Life, the Spirit of Man
Which God inspir'd, cannot together perish
With this corporeal Clod; then in the Grave,
Or in some other dismal place, who knows
But I shall die a living Death? O thought
Horrid, if true! yet why? it was but breath
Of Life that sinn'd; what dies but what had life   790
And sin? the Bodie properly hath neither.
All of me then shall die: let this appease
The doubt, since humane reach no further knows.
For though the Lord of all be infinite,
Is his wrauth also? be it, man is not so,
But mortal doom'd. How can he exercise
Wrath without end on Man whom Death must end?
Can he make deathless Death? that were to make
Strange contradiction, which to God himself

Impossible is held, as Argument   800
Of weakness, not of Power. Will he, draw out,
For angers sake, finite to infinite
In punisht man, to satisfie his rigour
Satisfi'd never; that were to extend
His Sentence beyond dust and Natures Law,
By which all Causes else according still
To the reception of thir matter act,
Not to th' extent of thir own Spheare. But say
That Death be not one stroak, as I suppos'd,
Bereaving sense, but endless miserie   810
From this day onward, which I feel begun
Both in me, and without me, and so last
To perpetuitie; Ay me, that fear
Comes thundring back with dreadful revolution
On my defensless head; both Death and I
Am found Eternal, and incorporate both,
Nor I on my part single, in mee all
Posteritie stands curst: Fair Patrimonie
That I must leave ye, Sons; O were I able
To waste it all my self, and leave ye none!   820
So disinherited how would ye bless
Me now your Curse! Ah, why should all mankind
For one mans fault thus guiltless be condemn'd,
If guiltless? But from mee what can proceed,
But all corrupt, both Mind and Will deprav'd,
Not to do onely, but to will the same
With me? how can they then acquitted stand
In sight of God? Him after all Disputes
Forc't I absolve: all my evasions vain
And reasonings, though through Mazes, lead me still   830
But to my own conviction: first and last
On mee, mee onely, as the sourse and spring
Of all corruption, all the blame lights due;
So might the wrauth. Fond wish! couldst thou support
That burden heavier then the Earth to bear,
Then all the World much heavier, though divided
With that bad Woman? Thus what thou desir'st,
And what thou fearst, alike destroyes all hope
Of refuge, and concludes thee miserable
Beyond all past example and future,   840
To *Satan* onely like both crime and doom.
O Conscience, into what Abyss of fears
And horrors hast thou driv'n me; out of which
I find no way, from deep to deeper plung'd!
    Thus *Adam* to himself lamented loud
Through the still Night, not now, as ere man fell,
Wholsom and cool, and mild, but with black Air
Accompanied, with damps and dreadful gloom,
Which to his evil Conscience represented
All things with double terror: On the ground   850
Outstretcht he lay, on the cold ground, and oft
Curs'd his Creation, Death as oft accus'd

Of tardie execution, since denounc't
The day of his offence. Why comes not Death,
Said hee, with one thrice acceptable stroke
To end me? Shall Truth fail to keep her word,
Justice Divine not hast'n to be just?
But Death comes not at call, Justice Divine
Mends not her slowest pace for prayers or cries.
O Woods, O Fountains, Hillocks, Dales and Bowrs,   860
With other echo late I taught your Shades
To answer, and resound farr other Song.
Whom thus afflicted when sad *Eve* beheld,
Desolate where she sate, approaching nigh,
Soft words to his fierce passion she assay'd:
But her with stern regard he thus repell'd.
   Out of my sight, thou Serpent, that name best
Befits thee with him leagu'd, thy self as false
And hateful; nothing wants, but that thy shape,
Like his, and colour Serpentine may shew   870
Thy inward fraud, to warn all Creatures from thee
Henceforth; least that too heav'nly form, pretended
To hellish falshood, snare them. But for thee
I had persisted happie, had not thy pride
And wandring vanitie, when lest was safe,
Rejected my forewarning, and disdain'd
Not to be trusted, longing to be seen
Though by the Devil himself, him overweening
To over-reach, but with the Serpent meeting
Fool'd and beguil'd, by him thou, I by thee,   880
To trust thee from my side, imagin'd wise,
Constant, mature, proof against all assaults,
And understood not all was but a shew
Rather then solid vertu, all but a Rib
Crooked by nature, bent, as now appears,
More to the part sinister from me drawn,
Well if thrown out, as supernumerarie
To my just number found. O why did God,
Creator wise, that peopl'd highest Heav'n
With Spirits Masculine, create at last   890
This noveltie on Earth, this fair defect
Of Nature, and not fill the World at once
With Men as Angels without Feminine,
Or find some other way to generate
Mankind? this mischief had not then befall'n,
And more that shall befall, innumerable
Disturbances on Earth through Femal snares,
And straight conjunction with this Sex: for either
He never shall find out fit Mate, but such
As some misfortune brings him, or mistake,   900
Or whom he wishes most shall seldom gain
Through her perverseness, but shall see her gaind
By a farr worse, or if she love, withheld
By Parents, or his happiest choice too late
Shall meet, alreadie linkt and Wedlock-bound

To a fell Adversarie, his hate or shame:
Which infinite calamitie shall cause
To Humane life, and houshold peace confound.
    He added not, and from her turn'd, but *Eve*
Not so repulst, with Tears that ceas'd not flowing,   910
And tresses all disorderd, at his feet
Fell humble, and imbracing them, besaught
His peace, and thus proceeded in her plaint.
    Forsake me not thus, *Adam,* witness Heav'n
What love sincere, and reverence in my heart
I beare thee, and unweeting have offended,
Unhappilie deceav'd; thy suppliant
I beg, and clasp thy knees; bereave me not,
Whereon I live, thy gentle looks, thy aid,
Thy counsel in this uttermost distress,   920
My onely strength and stay: forlorn of thee,
Whither shall I betake me, where subsist?
While yet we live, scarse one short hour perhaps,
Between us two let there be peace, both joyning,
As joyn'd in injuries, one enmitie
Against a Foe by doom express assign'd us,
That cruel Serpent: On me exercise not
Thy hatred for this miserie befall'n,
On me already lost, mee then thy self
More miserable; both have sin'd, but thou   930
Against God onely, I against God and thee,
And to the place of judgement will return,
There with my cries importune Heaven, that all
The sentence from thy head remov'd may light
On me, sole cause to thee of all this woe,
Mee mee onely just object of his ire.
    She ended weeping, and her lowlie plight,
Immoveable till peace obtain'd from fault
Acknowledg'd and deplor'd, in *Adam* wraught
Commiseration; soon his heart relented   940
Towards her, his life so late and sole delight,
Now at his feet submissive in distress,
Creature so faire his reconcilement seeking,
His counsel whom she had displeas'd, his aide;
As one disarm'd, his anger all he lost,
And thus with peaceful words uprais'd her soon.
    Unwarie, and too desirous, as before,
So now of what thou knowst not, who desir'st
The punishment all on thy self; alas,
Beare thine own first, ill able to sustaine   950
His full wrauth whose thou feelst as yet lest part,
And my displeasure bearst so ill. If Prayers
Could alter high Decrees, I to that place
Would speed before thee, and be louder heard,
That on my head all might be visited,
Thy frailtie and infirmer Sex forgiv'n,
To me committed and by me expos'd.
But rise, let us no more contend, nor blame

Each other, blam'd enough elsewhere, but strive
In offices of Love, how we may light'n   960
Each others burden in our share of woe;
Since this days Death denounc't, if ought I see,
Will prove no sudden, but a slow-pac't evill,
A long days dying to augment our paine,
And to our Seed (O hapless Seed!) deriv'd.
    To whom thus *Eve,* recovering heart, repli'd.
Adam, by sad experiment I know
How little weight my Words with thee can finde,
Found so erroneous, thence by just event
Found so unfortunate; nevertheless,   970
Restor'd by thee, vile as I am, to place
Of new acceptance, hopeful to regaine
Thy Love, the sole contentment of my heart,
Living or dying from thee I will not hide
What thoughts in my unquiet brest are ris'n,
Tending to som relief of our extremes,
Or end, though sharp and sad, yet tolerable,
As in our evils, and of easier choice.
If care of our descent perplex us most,
Which must be born to certain woe, devourd   98.,
By Death at last, and miserable it is
To be to others cause of misery,
Our own begotten, and of our Loines to bring
Into this cursed World a woful Race,
That after wretched Life must be at last
Food for so foule a Monster, in thy power
It lies, yet ere Conception to prevent
The Race unblest, to being yet unbegot.
Childless thou art, Childless remaine:
So Death shall be deceav'd his glut, and with us two   990
Be forc'd to satisfie his Rav'nous Maw.
But if thou judge it hard and difficult,
Conversing, looking, loving, to abstain
From Loves due Rites, Nuptial embraces sweet,
And with desire to languish without hope,
Before the present object languishing
With like desire, which would be miserie
And torment less then none of what we dread,
Then both our selves and Seed at once to free
From what we fear for both, let us make short,   1000
Let us seek Death, or hee not found, supply
With our own hands his Office on our selves;
Why stand we longer shivering under feares,
That shew no end but Death, and have the power,
Of many wayes to die the shortest choosing,
Destruction with destruction to destroy.
    She ended heer, or vehement despaire
Broke off the rest; so much of Death her thoughts
Had entertaind, as di'd her Cheeks with pale.
But *Adam* with such counsel nothing sway'd,   1010
To better hopes his more attentive minde

Labouring had rais'd, and thus to *Eve* repli'd.
    Eve, thy contempt of life and pleasure seems
To argue in thee somthing more sublime
And excellent then what thy minde contemnes;
But self-destruction therefore saught, refutes
That excellence thought in thee, and implies,
Not thy contempt, but anguish and regret
For loss of life and pleasure overlov'd.
Or if thou covet death, as utmost end   1020
Of miserie, so thinking to evade
The penaltie pronounc't, doubt not but God
Hath wiselier arm'd his vengeful ire then so
To be forestall'd; much more I fear least Death
So snatcht will not exempt us from the paine
We are by doom to pay; rather such acts
Of contumacie will provoke the highest
To make death in us live: Then let us seek
Som safer resolution, which methinks
I have in view, calling to minde with heed   1030
Part of our Sentence, that thy Seed shall bruise
The Serpents head; piteous amends, unless
Be meant, whom I conjecture, our grand Foe
Satan, who in the Serpent hath contriv'd
Against us this deceit: to crush his head
Would be revenge indeed; which will be lost
By death brought on our selves, or childless days
Resolv'd, as thou proposest; so our Foe
Shall scape his punishment ordain'd, and wee
Instead shall double ours upon our heads.   1040
No more be mention'd then of violence
Against our selves, and wilful barrenness,
That cuts us off from hope, and savours onely
Rancor and pride, impatience and despite,
Reluctance against God and his just yoke
Laid on our Necks. Remember with what mild
And gracious temper he both heard and judg'd
Without wrauth or reviling; wee expected
Immediate dissolution, which we thought
Was meant by Death that day, when lo, to thee   1050
Pains onely in Child-bearing were foretold,
And bringing forth, soon recompenc't with joy,
Fruit of thy Womb: On mee the Curse aslope
Glanc'd on the ground, with labour I must earne
My bread; what harm? Idleness had bin worse;
My labour will sustain me; and least Cold
Or Heat should injure us, his timely care
Hath unbesaught provided, and his hands
Cloath'd us unworthie, pitying while he judg'd;
How much more, if we pray him, will his ear   1060
Be open, and his heart to pitie incline,
And teach us further by what means to shun
Th' inclement Seasons, Rain, Ice, Hail and Snow,
Which now the Skie with various Face begins

To shew us in this Mountain, while the Winds
Blow moist and keen, shattering the graceful locks
Of these fair spreading Trees; which bids us seek
Som better shroud, som better warmth to cherish
Our Limbs benumm'd, ere this diurnal Starr
Leave cold the Night, how we his gather'd beams   1070
Reflected, may with matter sere foment,
Or by collision of two bodies grinde
The Air attrite to Fire, as late the Clouds
Justling or pusht with Winds rude in thir shock
Tine the slant Lightning, whose thwart flame driv'n down
Kindles the gummie bark of Firr or Pine,
And sends a comfortable heat from farr,
Which might supplie the Sun: such Fire to use,
And what may else be remedie or cure
To evils which our own misdeeds have wrought,   1080
Hee will instruct us praying, and of Grace
Beseeching him, so as we need not fear
To pass commodiously this life, sustain'd
By him with many comforts, till we end
In dust, our final rest and native home.
What better can we do, then to the place
Repairing where he judg'd us, prostrate fall
Before him reverent, and there confess
Humbly our faults, and pardon beg, with tears
Watering the ground, and with our sighs the Air   1090
Frequenting, sent from hearts contrite, in sign
Of sorrow unfeign'd, and humiliation meek.
Undoubtedly he will relent and turn
From his displeasure; in whose look serene,
When angry most he seem'd and most severe,
What else but favor, grace, and mercie shon?
  So spake our Father penitent, nor *Eve*
Felt less remorse: they forthwith to the place
Repairing where he judg'd them prostrate fell
Before him reverent, and both confess'd   1100
Humbly thir faults, and pardon beg'd, with tears
Watering the ground, and with thir sighs the Air
Frequenting, sent from hearts contrite, in sign
Of sorrow unfeign'd, and humiliation meek.

The End of the Tenth Book.

PARADISE LOST.

BOOK XI.

The Argument.

The Son of God presents to his Father the Prayers of our first Parents now repenting, and intercedes for them: God accepts them, but declares that they must no longer abide in Paradise; sends Michael *with a Band of Cherubim to dispossess them; but first to reveal to Adam future things:* Michaels *coming down. Adam shews to Eve certain ominous signs; he discerns Michaels approach, goes out to meet him: the Angel denounces thir departure. Eve's Lamentation. Adam pleads, but submits: The Angel leads him up to a high Hill, sets before him in vision what shall happ'n till the Flood.*

THUS they in lowliest plight repentant stood
Praying, for from the Mercie-seat above
Prevenient Grace descending had remov'd
The stonie from thir hearts, and made new flesh
Regenerat grow instead, that sighs now breath'd
Unutterable, which the Spirit of prayer
Inspir'd, and wing'd for Heav'n with speedier flight.
Then loudest Oratorie: yet thir port
Not of mean suiters, nor important less
Seem'd thir Petition, then when th' ancient Pair   10
In Fables old, less ancient yet then these,
Deucalion and chaste *Pyrrha* to restore
The Race of Mankind drownd, before the Shrine
Of *Themis* stood devout. To Heav'n thir prayers
Flew up, nor missd the way, by envious windes
Blow'n vagabond or frustrate: in they passd
Dimentionless through Heav'nly dores; then clad
With incense, where the Golden Altar fum'd,
By thir great Intercessor, came in sight
Before the Fathers Throne: Them the glad Son   20
Presenting, thus to intercede began.
    See Father, what first fruits on Earth are sprung
From thy implanted Grace in Man, these Sighs
And Prayers, which in this Golden Censer, mixt
With Incense, I thy Priest before thee bring,
Fruits of more pleasing savour from thy seed
Sow'n with contrition in his heart, then those
Which his own hand manuring all the Trees
Of Paradise could have produc't, ere fall'n
From innocence. Now therefore bend thine eare   30
To supplication, heare his sighs though mute;
Unskilful with what words to pray, let mee
Interpret for him, mee his Advocate
And propitiation, all his works on mee
Good or not good ingraft, my Merit those
Shall perfet, and for these my Death shall pay.
Accept me, and in mee from these receave
The smell of peace toward Mankinde, let him live
Before thee reconcil'd, at least his days
Numberd, though sad, till Death, his doom (which I   40
To mitigate thus plead, not to reverse)
To better life shall yeeld him, where with mee
All my redeemd may dwell in joy and bliss,
Made one with me as I with thee am one.
    To whom the Father, without Cloud, serene.
All thy request for Man, accepted Son,
Obtain, all thy request was my Decree:
But longer in that Paradise to dwell,
The Law I gave to Nature him forbids:
Those pure immortal Elements that know   50
No gross, no unharmoneous mixture foule,
Eject him tainted now, and purge him off
As a distemper, gross to aire as gross,

And mortal food, as may dispose him best
For dissolution wrought by Sin, that first
Distemperd all things, and of incorrupt
Corrupted. I at first with two fair gifts
Created him endowd, with Happiness
And Immortalitie: that fondly lost,
This other serv'd but to eternize woe;   60
Till I provided Death; so Death becomes
His final remedie, and after Life
Tri'd in sharp tribulation, and refin'd
By Faith and faithful works, to second Life,
Wak't in the renovation of the just,
Resignes him up with Heav'n and Earth renewd.
But let us call to Synod all the Blest
Through Heavn's wide bounds; from them I will not hide
My judgments, how with Mankind I proceed,
As how with peccant Angels late they saw;   70
And in thir state, though firm, stood more confirmd.
   He ended, and the Son gave signal high
To the bright Minister that watchd, hee blew
His Trumpet, heard in *Oreb* since perhaps
When God descended, and perhaps once more
To sound at general Doom. Th' Angelic blast
Filld all the Regions: from thir blissful Bowrs
Of *Amarantin* Shade, Fountain or Spring,
By the waters of Life, where ere they sate
In fellowships of joy: the Sons of Light   80
Hasted, resorting to the Summons high,
And took thir Seats; till from his Throne supream
Th' Almighty thus pronouncd his sovran Will.
   O Sons, like one of us Man is become
To know both Good and Evil, since his taste
Of that defended Fruit; but let him boast
His knowledge of Good lost, and Evil got,
Happier, had it suffic'd him to have known
Good by it self, and Evil not at all.
He sorrows now, repents, and prayes contrite,   90
My motions in him, longer then they move,
His heart I know, how variable and vain
Self-left. Least therefore his now bolder hand
Reach also of the Tree of Life, and eat,
And live for ever, dream at least to live
For ever, to remove him I decree,
And send him from the Garden forth to Till
The Ground whence he was taken, fitter soile.
   Michael, this my behest have thou in charge,
Take to thee from among the Cherubim   100
Thy choice of flaming Warriours, least the Fiend
Or in behalf of Man, or to invade
Vacant possession som new trouble raise:
Hast thee, and from the Paradise of God
Without remorse drive out the sinful Pair,
From hallowd ground th' unholie, and denounce

To them and to thir Progenie from thence
Perpetual banishment. Yet least they faint
At the sad Sentence rigorously urg'd,
For I behold them soft'nd and with tears   110
Bewailing thir excess, all terror hide.
If patiently thy bidding they obey,
Dismiss them not disconsolate; reveale
To *Adam* what shall come in future dayes,
As I shall thee enlighten, intermix
My Cov'nant in the Womans seed renewd;
So send them forth, though sorrowing, yet in peace:
And on the East side of the Garden place,
Where entrance up from *Eden* easiest climbes,
Cherubic watch, and of a Sword the flame   120
Wide waving, all approach farr off to fright,
And guard all passage to the Tree of Life:
Least Paradise a receptacle prove
To Spirits foule, and all my Trees thir prey,
With whose stol'n Fruit Man once more to delude.
    He ceas'd; and th' Archangelic Power prepar'd
For swift descent, with him the Cohort bright
Of watchful Cherubim; four faces each
Had, like a double *Janus,* all thir shape
Spangl'd with eyes more numerous then those   130
Of *Argus,* and more wakeful then to drouze,
Charm'd with *Arcadian* Pipe, the Pastoral Reed
Of *Hermes,* or his opiate Rod. Mean while
To resalute the World with sacred Light
Leucothea wak'd, and with fresh dews imbalmd
The Earth, when *Adam* and first Matron *Eve*
Had ended now thir Orisons, and found,
Strength added from above, new hope to spring
Out of despaire, joy, but with fear yet linkt;
Which thus to *Eve* his welcome words renewd.   140
    Eve, easily may Faith admit, that all
The good which we enjoy, from Heav'n descends
But that from us ought should ascend to Heav'n
So prevalent as to concerne the mind
Of God high-blest, or to incline his will,
Hard to belief may seem; yet this will Prayer,
Or one short sigh of humane breath, up-borne
Ev'n to the Seat of God. For since I saught
By Prayer th' offended Deitie to appease,
Kneel'd and before him humbl'd all my heart,   150
Methought I saw him placable and mild,
Bending his eare; perswasion in me grew
That I was heard with favour; peace returnd
Home to my brest, and to my memorie
His promise, that thy Seed shall bruise our Foe;
Which then not minded in dismay, yet now
Assures me that the bitterness of death
Is past, and we shall live. Whence Haile to thee
Eve rightly call'd, Mother of all Mankind,

Mother of all things living, since by thee   160
Man is to live, and all things live for Man.
    To whom thus *Eve* with sad demeanour meek.
Ill worthie I such title should belong
To me transgressour, who for thee ordaind
A help, became thy snare; to mee reproach
Rather belongs, distrust and all dispraise:
But infinite in pardon was my Judge,
That I who first brought Death on all, am grac't
The sourse of life; next favourable thou,
Who highly thus to entitle me voutsaf'st,   170
Farr other name deserving. But the Field
To labour calls us now with sweat impos'd,
Though after sleepless Night; for see the Morn,
All unconcern'd with our unrest, begins
Her rosie progress smiling; let us forth,
I never from thy side henceforth to stray,
Wherere our days work lies, though now enjoind
Laborious, till day droop; while here we dwell,
What can be toilsom in these pleasant Walkes?
Here let us live, though in fall'n state, content.   180
    So spake, so wish'd much-humbl'd *Eve,* but Fate
Subscrib'd not; Nature first gave Signs, imprest
On Bird, Beast, Aire, Aire suddenly eclips'd
After short blush of Morn; nigh in her sight
The Bird of *Jove,* stoopt from his aerie tour,
Two Birds of gayest plume before him drove:
Down from a Hill the Beast that reigns in Woods,
First Hunter then, pursu'd a gentle brace,
Goodliest of all the Forrest, Hart and Hinde;
Direct to th' Eastern Gate was bent thir flight.   190
Adam observ'd, and with his Eye the chase
Pursuing, not unmov'd to *Eve* thus spake.
    O *Eve,* some furder change awaits us nigh,
Which Heav'n by these mute signs in Nature shews
Forerunners of his purpose, or to warn
Us haply too secure of our discharge
From penaltie, because from death releast
Some days; how long, and what till then our life,
Who knows, or more then this, that we are dust,
And thither must return and be no more.   200
Why else this double object in our sight
Of flight pursu'd in th' Air and ore the ground
One way the self-same hour? why in the East
Darkness ere Dayes mid-course, and Morning light
More orient in yon Western Cloud that draws
O're the blew Firmament a radiant white,
And slow descends, with somthing heav'nly fraught.
    He err'd not, for by this the heav'nly Bands
Down from a Skie of Jasper lighted now
In Paradise, and on a Hill made alt,   210
A glorious Apparition, had not doubt
And carnal fear that day dimm'd *Adams* eye.

Not that more glorious, when the Angels met
Jacob in *Mahanaim,* where he saw
The field Pavilion'd with his Guardians bright;
Nor that which on the flaming Mount appeerd
In *Dothan,* cover'd with a Camp of Fire,
Against the *Syrian* King, who to surprize
One man, Assassin-like had levied Warr,
Warr unproclam'd. The Princely Hierarch   220
In thir bright stand, there left his Powers to seise
Possession of the Garden; hee alone,
To finde where *Adam* shelterd, took his way,
Not unperceav'd of *Adam,* who to *Eve,*
While the great Visitant approachd, thus spake.
   Eve, now expect great tidings, which perhaps
Of us will soon determin, or impose
New Laws to be observ'd; for I descrie
From yonder blazing Cloud that veils the Hill
One of the heav'nly Host, and by his Gate   230
None of the meanest, some great Potentate
Or of the Thrones above, such Majestie
Invests him coming; yet not terrible,
That I should fear, nor sociably mild,
As *Raphael,* that I should much confide,
But solemn and sublime, whom not to offend,
With reverence I must meet, and thou retire.
He ended; and th' Arch-Angel soon drew nigh,
Not in his shape Celestial, but as Man
Clad to meet Man; over his lucid Armes   240
A militarie Vest of purple flowd
Livelier then *Melibœan,* or the graine
Of *Sarra,* worn by Kings and Hero's old
In time of Truce; *Iris* had dipt the wooff;
His starrie Helme unbuckl'd shew'd him prime
In Manhood where Youth ended; by his side
As in a glistering *Zodiac* hung the Sword,
Satans dire dread, and in his hand the Spear.
Adam bowd low, hee Kingly from his State
Inclin'd not, but his coming thus declar'd.   250
   Adam, Heav'ns high behest no Preface needs:
Sufficient that thy Prayers are heard, and Death,
Then due by sentence when thou didst transgress,
Defeated of his seisure many dayes
Giv'n thee of Grace, wherein thou may'st repent,
And one bad act with many deeds well done
Mayst cover: well may then thy Lord appeas'd
Redeem thee quite from Deaths rapacious claime;
But longer in this Paradise to dwell
Permits not; to remove thee I am come,   260
And send thee from the Garden forth to till
The ground whence thou wast tak'n, fitter Soile.
   He added not, for *Adam* at the newes
Heart-strook with chilling gripe of sorrow stood,
That all his senses bound; *Eve,* who unseen

Yet all had heard, with audible lament
Discover'd soon the place of her retire.
    O unexpected stroke, worse then of Death!
Must I thus leave thee Paradise? thus leave
Thee Native Soile, these happie Walks and Shades,   270
Fit haunt of Gods? where I had hope to spend,
Quiet though sad, the respit of that day
That must be mortal to us both. O flours,
That never will in other Climate grow,
My early visitation, and my last
At Eev'n, which I bred up with tender hand
From the first op'ning bud, and gave ye Names,
Who now shall reare ye to the Sun, or ranke
Your Tribes, and water from th' ambrosial Fount?
Thee lastly nuptial Bowre, by mee adornd   280
With what to sight or smell was sweet; from thee
How shall I part, and whither wander down
Into a lower World, to this obscure
And wilde, how shall we breath in other Aire
Less pure, accustomed to immortal Fruits?
    Whom thus the Angel interrupted milde.
Lament not *Eve*, but patiently resigne
What justly thou hast lost; nor set thy heart,
Thus over fond, on that which is not thine;
Thy going is not lonely, with thee goes   290
Thy Husband, him to follow thou art bound;
Where he abides, think there thy native soile.
    Adam by this from the cold sudden damp
Recovering, and his scatterd spirits returnd,
To *Michael* thus his humble words addressd.
    Celestial, whether among the Thrones, or nam'd
Of them the Highest, for such of shape may seem
Prince above Princes, gently hast thou tould
Thy message, which might else in telling wound,
And in performing end us; what besides   300
Of sorrow and dejection and despair
Our frailtie can sustain, thy tidings bring,
Departure from this happy place, our sweet
Recess, and onely consolation left
Familiar to our eyes, all places else
Inhospitable appeer and desolate,
Nor knowing us nor known: and if by prayer
Incessant I would hope to change the will
Of him who all things can, I could not cease
To wearie him with my assiduous cries: 310
But prayer against his absolute Decree
No more availes then breath against the winde,
Blown stifling back on him that breaths it forth:
Therefore to his great bidding I submit.
This most afflicts me, that departing hence,
As from his face I shall be hid, deprivd
His blessed count'nance; here I could frequent,
With worship, place by place where he voutsaf'd

Presence Divine, and to my Sons relate;
On this Mount he appeerd, under this Tree   320
Stood visible, among these Pines his voice
I heard, here with him at this Fountain talk'd:
So many grateful Altars I would reare
Of grassie Terfe, and pile up every Stone
Of lustre from the brook, in memorie,
Or monument to Ages, and thereon
Offer sweet smelling Gumms & Fruits and Flours:
In yonder nether World where shall I seek
His bright appearances, or footstep trace?
For though I fled him angrie, yet recall'd   330
To life prolongd and promisd Race, I now
Gladly behold though but his utmost skirts
Of glory, and farr off his steps adore.
       To whom thus *Michael* with regard benigne.
Adam, thou know'st Heav'n his, and all the Earth:
Not this Rock onely; his Omnipresence fills
Land, Sea, and Aire, and every kinde that lives,
Fomented by his virtual power and warmd:
All th' Earth he gave thee to possess and rule,
No despicable gift; surmise not then   340
His presence to these narrow bounds confin'd
Of Paradise or *Eden*: this had been
Perhaps thy Capital Seate, from whence had spred
All generations, and had hither come
From all the ends of th' Earth, to celebrate
And reverence thee thir great Progenitor.
But this præeminence thou hast lost, brought down
To dwell on eeven ground now with thy Sons:
Yet doubt not but in Vallie and in Plaine
God is as here, and will be found alike   350
Present, and of his presence many a signe
Still following thee, still compassing thee round
With goodness and paternal Love, his Face
Express, and of his steps the track Divine.
Which that thou mayst beleeve, and be confirmd,
Ere thou from hence depart, know I am sent
To shew thee what shall come in future dayes
To thee and to thy Ofspring; good with bad
Expect to hear, supernal Grace contending
With sinfulness of Men; thereby to learn   360
True patience, and to temper joy with fear
And pious sorrow, equally enur'd
By moderation either state to beare,
Prosperous or adverse: so shalt thou lead
Safest thy life, and best prepar'd endure
Thy mortal passage when it comes. Ascend
This Hill; let *Eve* (for I have drencht her eyes)
Here sleep below while thou to foresight wak'st,
As once thou slepst, while Shee to life was formd.
       To whom thus *Adam* gratefully repli'd.   370
Ascend, I follow thee, safe Guide, the path

Thou lead'st me, and to the hand of Heav'n submit,
However chast'ning, to the evil turne
My obvious breast, arming to overcom
By suffering, and earne rest from labour won,
If so I may attain. So both ascend
In the Visions of God: It was a Hill
Of Paradise the highest, from whose top
The Hemisphere of Earth in cleerest Ken
Stretcht out to amplest reach of prospect lay.   380
Not higher that Hill nor wider looking round,
Whereon for different cause the Tempter set
Our second *Adam* in the Wilderness,
To shew him all Earths Kingdomes and thir Glory.
His Eye might there command wherever stood
City of old or modern Fame, the Seat
Of mightiest Empire, from the destind Walls
Of *Cambalu*, seat of *Cathaian Can*
And *Samarchand* by *Oxus, Temirs* Throne,
To *Paquin* of *Sinæan* Kings, and thence   390
To *Agra* and *Lahor* of great *Mogul*
Down to the golden *Chersonese,* or where
The *Persian* in *Ecbatan* sate, or since
In *Hispahan,* or where the *Russian Ksar*
In *Mosco,* or the Sultan in *Bizance,*
Turchestan-born; nor could his eye not ken
Th' Empire of *Negus* to his utmost Port
Ercoco and the less Maritine Kings
Mombaza, and *Quiloa,* and *Melind,*
And *Sofala* thought *Ophir,* to the Realme   400
Of *Congo,* and *Angola* fardest South;
Or thence from *Niger* Flood to *Atlas* Mount
The Kingdoms of *Almansor, Fez* and *Sus,*
Marocco and *Algiers,* and *Tremisen;*
On *Europe* thence, and where *Rome* was to sway
The World: in Spirit perhaps he also saw
Rich *Mexico* the seat of *Motezume,*
And *Cusco* in *Peru,* the richer seat
Of *Atabalipa,* and yet unspoil'd
Guiana, whose great Citie *Geryons* Sons   410
Call *El Dorado*: but to nobler sights
Michael from *Adams* eyes the Filme remov'd
Which that false Fruit that promis'd clearer sight
Had bred; then purg'd with Euphrasie and Rue
The visual Nerve, for he had much to see;
And from the Well of Life three drops instill'd.
So deep the power of these Ingredients pierc'd,
Eevn to the inmost seat of mental sight,
That *Adam* now enforc't to close his eyes,
Sunk down and all his Spirits became intranst: 420
But him the gentle Angel by the hand
Soon rais'd, and his attention thus recall'd.
    Adam, now ope thine eyes, and first behold
Th' effects which thy original crime hath wrought

In some to spring from thee, who never touch'd
Th' excepted Tree, nor with the Snake conspir'd,
Nor sinn'd thy sin, yet from that sin derive
Corruption to bring forth more violent deeds.
    His eyes he op'nd, and beheld a field,
Part arable and tilth, whereon were Sheaves   430
New reapt, the other part sheep-walks and foulds;
Ith' midst an Altar as the Land-mark stood
Rustic, of grassie sord; thither anon
A sweatie Reaper from his Tillage brought
First Fruits, the green Eare, and the yellow Sheaf,
Uncull'd, as came to hand; a Shepherd next
More meek came with the Firstlings of his Flock
Choicest and best; then sacrificing, laid
The Inwards and thir Fat, with Incense strew'd,
On the cleft Wood, and all due Rites perform'd.   440
His Offring soon propitious Fire from Heav'n
Consum'd with nimble glance, and grateful steame;
The others not, for his was not sincere;
Whereat hee inlie rag'd, and as they talk'd,
Smote him into the Midriff with a stone
That beat out life; he fell, and deadly pale
Groand out his Soul with gushing bloud effus'd.
Much at that sight was *Adam* in his heart
Dismai'd, and thus in haste to th' Angel cri'd.
    O Teacher, some great mischief hath befall'n   450
To that meek man, who well had sacrific'd;
Is Pietie thus and pure Devotion paid?
    T' whom *Michael* thus, hee also mov'd, repli'd.
These two are Brethren, *Adam,* and to come
Out of thy loyns; th' unjust the just hath slain,
For envie that his Brothers Offering found
From Heav'n acceptance; but the bloodie Fact
Will be aveng'd, and th' others Faith approv'd
Loose no reward, though here thou see him die,
Rowling in dust and gore. To which our Sire.   460
    Alas, both for the deed and for the cause!
But have I now seen Death? Is this the way
I must return to native dust? O sight
Of terrour, foul and ugly to behold,
Horrid to think, how horrible to feel!
    To whom thus *Michael*. Death thou hast seen
In his first shape on man; but many shapes
Of Death, and many are the wayes that lead
To his grim Cave, all dismal; yet to sense
More terrible at th' entrance then within.   470
Some, as thou saw'st, by violent stroke shall die,
By Fire, Flood, Famin, by Intemperance more
In Meats and Drinks, which on the Earth shal bring
Diseases dire, of which a monstrous crew
Before thee shall appear; that thou mayst know
What miserie th' inabstinence of *Eve*
Shall bring on men. Immediately a place

Before his eyes appeard, sad, noysom, dark,
A Lazar-house it seemd, wherein were laid
Numbers of all diseas'd, all maladies   480
Of gastly Spasm, or racking torture, qualmes
Of heart-sick Agonie, all feavorous kinds,
Convulsions, Epilepsies, fierce Catarrhs,
Intestin Stone and Ulcer, Colic pangs,
Dæmoniac Phrenzie, moaping Melancholie
And Moon-struck madness, pining Atrophie,
Marasmus, and wide-wasting Pestilence,
Dropsies, and Asthma's, and Joint-racking Rheums.
Dire was the tossing, deep the groans, despair
Tended the sick busiest from Couch to Couch;   490
And over them triumphant Death his Dart
Shook, but delaid to strike, though oft invok't
With vows, as thir chief good, and final hope.
Sight so deform what heart of Rock could long
Drie-ey'd behold? *Adam* could not, but wept,
Though not of Woman born; compassion quell'd
His best of Man, and gave him up to tears
A space, till firmer thoughts restraind excess,
And scarce recovering words his plaint renew'd.
    O miserable Mankind, to what fall   500
Degraded, to what wretched state reserv'd!
Better end heer unborn. Why is life giv'n
To be thus wrested from us? rather why
Obtruded on us thus? who if we knew
What we receive, would either not accept
Life offer'd, or soon beg to lay it down,
Glad to be so dismist in peace. Can thus
Th' Image of God in man created once
So goodly and erect, though faultie since,
To such unsightly sufferings be debas't   510
Under inhuman pains? Why should not Man,
Retaining still Divine similitude
In part, from such deformities be free,
And for his Makers Image sake exempt?
    Thir Makers Image, answerd *Michael,* then
Forsook them, when themselves they villifi'd
To serve ungovern'd appetite, and took
His Image whom they serv'd, a brutish vice,
Inductive mainly to the sin of *Eve.*
Therefore so abject is thir punishment,   520
Disfiguring not Gods likeness, but thir own,
Or if his likeness, by themselves defac't
While they pervert pure Natures healthful rules
To loathsom sickness, worthily, since they
Gods Image did not reverence in themselves.
    I yeild it just, said *Adam,* and submit.
But is there yet no other way, besides
These painful passages, how we may come
To Death, and mix with our connatural dust?
    There is, said Michael, if thou well observe   530

The rule of not too much, by temperance taught
In what thou eatst and drinkst, seeking from thence
Due nourishment, not gluttonous delight,
Till many years over thy head return:
So maist thou live, till like ripe Fruit thou drop
Into thy Mothers lap, or be with ease
Gatherd, not harshly pluckt, for death mature:
This is old age; but then thou must outlive
Thy youth, thy strength, thy beauty, which will change
To withered weak & gray; thy Senses then   540
Obtuse, all taste of pleasure must forgoe,
To what thou hast, and for the Aire of youth
Hopeful and cheerful, in thy blood will reigne
A melancholly damp of cold and dry
To waigh thy spirits down, and last consume
The Balme of Life. To whom our Ancestor.
  Henceforth I flie not Death, nor would prolong
Life much, bent rather how I may be quit
Fairest and easiest of this combrous charge,
Which I must keep till my appointed day   550
Of rendring up, and patiently attend
My dissolution. *Michael* repli'd,
  Nor love thy Life, nor hate; but what thou livst
Live well, how long or short permit to Heav'n:
And now prepare thee for another sight.
  He lookd and saw a spacious Plaine, whereon
Were Tents of various hue; by some were herds
Of Cattel grazing: others, whence the sound
Of Instruments that made melodious chime
Was heard, of Harp and Organ; and who moovd   560
Thir stops and chords was seen: his volant touch
Instinct through all proportions low and high
Fled and pursu'd transverse the resonant fugue.
In other part stood one who at the Forge
Labouring, two massie clods of Iron and Brass
Had melted (whether found where casual fire
Had wasted woods on Mountain or in Vale,
Down to the veins of Earth, thence gliding hot
To som Caves mouth, or whether washt by stream
From underground) the liquid Ore he dreind   570
Into fit moulds prepar'd; from which he formd
First his own Tooles; then, what might else be wrought
Fusil or grav'n in mettle. After these,
But on the hether side a different sort
From the high neighbouring Hills, which was thir Seat,
Down to the Plain descended: by thir guise
Just men they seemd, and all thir study bent
To worship God aright, and know his works
Not hid, nor those things lost which might preserve
Freedom and Peace to men: they on the Plain   580
Long had not walkt, when from the Tents behold
A Beavie of fair Women, richly gay
In Gems and wanton dress; to the Harp they sung

Soft amorous Ditties, and in dance came on:
The Men though grave, ey'd them, and let thir eyes
Rove without rein, till in the amorous Net
Fast caught, they lik'd, and each his liking chose;
And now of love they treat till th' Eevning Star
Loves Harbinger appeerd; then all in heat
They light the Nuptial Torch, and bid invoke   590
Hymen, then first to marriage Rites invok't;
With Feast and Musick all the Tents resound.
Such happy interview and fair event
Of love & youth not lost, Songs, Garlands, Flours,
And charming Symphonies attach'd the heart
Of *Adam,* soon enclin'd to admit delight,
The bent of Nature; which he thus express'd.
     True opener of mine eyes, prime Angel blest,
Much better seems this Vision, and more hope
Of peaceful dayes portends, then those two past;   600
Those were of hate and death, or pain much worse,
Here Nature seems fulfilld in all her ends.
     To whom thus *Michael.* Judg not what is best
By pleasure, though to Nature seeming meet,
Created, as thou art, to nobler end
Holie and pure, conformitie divine.
Those Tents thou sawst so pleasant, were the Tents
Of wickedness, wherein shall dwell his Race
Who slew his Brother; studious they appere
Of Arts that polish Life, Inventers rare,   610
Unmindful of thir Maker, though his Spirit
Taught them, but they his gifts acknowledg'd none.
Yet they a beauteous ofspring shall beget;
For that fair femal Troop thou sawst, that seemd
Of Goddesses, so blithe, so smooth, so gay,
Yet empty of all good wherein consists
Womans domestic honour and chief praise;
Bred onely and completed to the taste
Of lustful appetence, to sing, to dance,
To dress, and troule the Tongue, and roule the Eye.   620
To these that sober Race of Men, whose lives
Religious titl'd them the Sons of God,
Shall yeild up all thir vertue, all thir fame
Ignobly, to the traines and to the smiles
Of these fair Atheists, and now swim in joy,
(Erelong to swim at larg) and laugh; for which
The world erelong a world of tears must weepe.
     To whom thus *Adam* of short joy bereft.
O pittie and shame, that they who to live well
Enterd so faire, should turn aside to tread   630
Paths indirect, or in the mid way faint!
But still I see the tenor of Mans woe
Holds on the same, from Woman to begin.
     From Mans effeminate slackness it begins,
Said th' Angel, who should better hold his place
By wisdome, and superiour gifts receavd.

But now prepare thee for another Scene.
  He lookd and saw wide Territorie spred
Before him, Towns, and rural works between,
Cities of Men with lofty Gates and Towrs,   640
Concours in Arms, fierce Faces threatning Warr,
Giants of mightie Bone, and bould emprise;
Part wield thir Arms, part courb the foaming Steed,
Single or in Array of Battel rang'd
Both Horse and Foot, nor idely mustring stood;
One way a Band select from forage drives
A herd of Beeves, faire Oxen and faire Kine
From a fat Meddow ground; or fleecy Flock,
Ewes and thir bleating Lambs over the Plaine,
Thir Bootie; scarce with Life the Shepherds flye,   650
But call in aide, which tacks a bloody Fray;
With cruel Tournament the Squadrons joine;
Where Cattel pastur'd late, now scatterd lies
With Carcasses and Arms th' ensanguind Field
Deserted: Others to a Citie strong
Lay Siege, encampt; by Batterie, Scale, and Mine,
Assaulting; others from the Wall defend
With Dart and Jav'lin, Stones and sulfurous Fire;
On each hand slaughter and gigantic deeds.
In other part the scepter'd Haralds call   660
To Council in the Citie Gates: anon
Grey-headed men and grave, with Warriours mixt,
Assemble, and Harangues are heard, but soon
In factious opposition, till at last
Of middle Age one rising, eminent
In wise deport, spake much of Right and Wrong,
Of Justice, of Religion, Truth and Peace,
And Judgement from above: him old and young
Exploded, and had seiz'd with violent hands,
Had not a Cloud descending snatch'd him thence   670
Unseen amid the throng: so violence
Proceeded, and Oppression, and Sword-Law
Through all the Plain, and refuge none was found.
Adam was all in tears, and to his guide
Lamenting turnd full sad; O what are these,
Deaths Ministers, not Men, who thus deal Death
Inhumanly to men, and multiply
Ten thousand fould the sin of him who slew
His Brother; for of whom such massacher
Make they but of thir Brethren, men of men?   680
But who was that Just Man, whom had not Heav'n
Rescu'd, had in his Righteousness bin lost?
  To whom thus *Michael;* These are the product
Of those ill-mated Marriages thou saw'st;
Where good with bad were matcht, who of themselves
Abhor to joyn; and by imprudence mixt,
Produce prodigious Births of bodie or mind.
Such were these Giants, men of high renown;
For in those dayes Might onely shall be admir'd,

Book XI | PARADISE LOST   347

690

700

710

720

730

740

And Valour and Heroic Vertu call'd;
To overcome in Battel, and subdue
Nations, and bring home spoils with infinite
Man-slaughter, shall be held the highest pitch
Of human Glorie, and for Glorie done
Of triumph, to be styl'd great Conquerours,
Patrons of Mankind, Gods, and Sons of Gods,
Destroyers rightlier call'd and Plagues of men.
Thus Fame shall be achiev'd, renown on Earth,
And what most merits fame in silence hid.
But hee the seventh from thee, whom thou beheldst
The onely righteous in a World perverse,
And therefore hated, therefore so beset
With Foes for daring single to be just,
And utter odious Truth, that God would come
To judge them with his Saints: Him the most High
Rapt in a balmie Cloud with winged Steeds
Did, as thou sawst, receave, to walk with God
High in Salvation and the Climes of bliss,
Exempt from Death; to shew thee what reward
Awaits the good, the rest what punishment;
Which now direct thine eyes and soon behold.
    He look'd, & saw the face of things quite chang'd;
The brazen Throat of Warr had ceast to roar,
All now was turn'd to jollitie and game,
To luxurie and riot, feast and dance,
Marrying or prostituting, as befell,
Rape or Adulterie, where passing faire
Allurd them; thence from Cups to civil Broiles.
At length a Reverend Sire among them came,
And of thir doings great dislike declar'd,
And testifi'd against thir wayes; hee oft
Frequented thir Assemblies, wheresc met,
Triumphs or Festivals, and to them preacha
Conversion and Repentance, as to Souls
In prison under Judgements imminent:
But all in vain: which when he saw, he ceas'd
Contending, and remov'd his Tents farr off;
Then from the Mountain hewing Timber tall,
Began to build a Vessel of huge bulk,
Measur'd by Cubit, length, & breadth, and highth,
Smeard round with Pitch, and in the side a dore
Contriv'd, and of provisions laid in large
For Man and Beast: when loe a wonder strange!
Of everie Beast, and Bird, and Insect small
Came seavens, and pairs, and enterd in, as taught
Thir order; last the Sire, and his three Sons
With thir four Wives; and God made fast the dore.
Meanwhile the Southwind rose, & with black wings
Wide hovering, all the Clouds together drove
From under Heav'n; the Hills to their supplie
Vapour, and Exhalation dusk and moist,
Sent up amain; and now the thick'nd Skie

Like a dark Ceeling stood; down rush'd the Rain
Impetuous, and continu'd till the Earth
No more was seen; the floating Vessel swum
Uplifted; and secure with beaked prow
Rode tilting o're the Waves, all dwellings else
Flood overwhelmd, and them with all thir pomp
Deep under water rould; Sea cover'd Sea,
Sea without shoar; and in thir Palaces   750
Where luxurie late reign'd, Sea-monsters whelp'd
And stabl'd; of Mankind, so numerous late,
All left, in one small bottom swum imbark't.
How didst thou grieve then, *Adam,* to behold
The end of all thy Ofspring, end so sad,
Depopulation; thee another Floud,
Of tears and sorrow a Floud thee also drown'd,
And sunk thee as thy Sons; till gently reard
By th' Angel, on thy feet thou stoodst at last,
Though comfortless, as when a Father mourns   760
His Childern, all in view destroyd at once;
And scarce to th' Angel utterdst thus thy plaint.
    O Visions ill foreseen! better had I
Liv'd ignorant of future, so had borne
My part of evil onely, each dayes lot
Anough to bear; those now, that were dispenst
The burd'n of many Ages, on me light
At once, by my foreknowledge gaining Birth
Abortive, to torment me ere thir being,
With thought that they must be. Let no man seek   •   770
Henceforth to be foretold what shall befall
Him or his Children, evil he may be sure,
Which neither his foreknowing can prevent,
And hee the future evil shall no less
In apprehension then in substance feel
Grievous to bear: but that care now is past,
Man is not whom to warne: those few escap't
Famin and anguish will at last consume
Wandring that watrie Desert: I had hope
When violence was ceas't, and Warr on Earth,   780
All would have then gon well, peace would have crownd
With length of happy days the race of man;
But I was farr deceav'd; for now I see
Peace to corrupt no less then Warr to waste.
How comes it thus? unfould, Celestial Guide,
And whether here the Race of man will end.
To whom thus *Michael.* Those whom last thou sawst
In triumph and luxurious wealth, are they
First seen in acts of prowess eminent
And great exploits, but of true vertu void;   790
Who having spilt much blood, and don much waste
Subduing Nations, and achievd thereby
Fame in the World, high titles, and rich prey,
Shall change thir course to pleasure, ease, and sloth,

Surfet, and lust, till wantonness and pride
Raise out of friendship hostil deeds in Peace.
The conquerd also, and enslav'd by Warr
Shall with thir freedom lost all vertu loose
And feare of God, from whom thir pietie feign'd
In sharp contest of Battel found no aide   800
Against invaders; therefore coold in zeale
Thenceforth shall practice how to live secure,
Worldlie or dissolute, on what thir Lords
Shall leave them to enjoy; for th' Earth shall bear
More then anough, that temperance may be tri'd:
So all shall turn degenerate, all deprav'd,
Justice and Temperance, Truth and Faith forgot;
One Man except, the onely Son of light
In a dark Age, against example good,
Against allurement, custom, and a World   810
Offended; fearless of reproach and scorn,
Or violence, hee of thir wicked wayes
Shall them admonish, and before them set
The paths of righteousness, how much more safe,
And full of peace, denouncing wrauth to come
On thir impenitence; and shall returne
Of them derided, but of God observd
The one just Man alive; by his command
Shall build a wondrous Ark, as thou beheldst,
To save himself and houshold from amidst   820
A World devote to universal rack.
No sooner hee with them of Man and Beast
Select for life shall in the Ark be lodg'd,
And shelterd round, but all the Cataracts
Of Heav'n set open on the Earth shall powre
Raine day and night, all fountaines of the Deep
Broke up, shall heave the Ocean to usurp
Beyond all bounds, till inundation rise
Above the highest Hills: then shall this Mount
Of Paradise by might of Waves be moovd   830
Out of his place, pushd by the horned floud,
With all his verdure spoil'd, and Trees adrift
Down the great River to the op'ning Gulf,
And there take root an Iland salt and bare,
The haunt of Seales and Orcs, and Sea-mews clang.
To teach thee that God attributes to place
No sanctitie, if none be thither brought
By Men who there frequent, or therein dwell.
And now what further shall ensue, behold.
      He lookd, and saw the Ark hull on the floud,   840
Which now abated, for the Clouds were fled,
Drivn by a keen North-winde, that blowing drie
Wrinkl'd the face of Deluge, as decai'd;
And the cleer Sun on his wide watrie Glass
Gaz'd hot, and of the fresh Wave largely drew,
As after thirst, which made thir flowing shrink

From standing lake to tripping ebbe, that stole
With soft foot towards the deep, who now had stopt
His Sluces, as the Heav'n his windows shut.
The Ark no more now flotes, but seems on ground   850
Fast on the top of som high mountain fixt.
And now the tops of Hills as Rocks appeer;
With clamor thence the rapid Currents drive
Towards the retreating Sea thir furious tyde.
Forthwith from out the Arke a Raven flies,
And after him, the surer messenger,
A Dove sent forth once and agen to spie
Green Tree or ground whereon his foot may light;
The second time returning, in his Bill
An Olive leafe he brings, pacific signe: 860
Anon drie ground appeers, and from his Arke
The ancient Sire descends with all his Train;
Then with uplifted hands, and eyes devout,
Grateful to Heav'n, over his head beholds
A dewie Cloud, and in the Cloud a Bow
Conspicuous with three listed colours gay,
Betok'ning peace from God, and Cov'nant new.
Whereat the heart of *Adam* erst so sad
Greatly rejoyc'd, and thus his joy broke forth.
    O thou who future things canst represent   870
As present, Heav'nly instructer, I revive
At this last sight, assur'd that Man shall live
With all the Creatures, and thir seed preserve.
Farr less I now lament for one whole World
Of wicked Sons destroyd, then I rejoyce
For one Man found so perfet and so just,
That God voutsafes to raise another World
From him, and all his anger to forget.
But say, what mean those colourd streaks in Heavn,
Distended as the Brow of God appeas'd,   880
Or serve they as a flourie verge to binde
The fluid skirts of that same watrie Cloud,
Least it again dissolve and showr the Earth?
    To whom th' Archangel. Dextrously thou aim'st;
So willingly doth God remit his Ire,
Though late repenting him of Man deprav'd,
Griev'd at his heart, when looking down he saw
The whole Earth fill'd with violence, and all flesh
Corrupting each thir way; yet those remoov'd,
Such grace shall one just Man find in his sight,   890
That he relents, not to blot out mankind,
And makes a Covenant never to destroy
The Earth again by flood, nor let the Sea
Surpass his bounds, nor Rain to drown the World
With Man therein or Beast; but when he brings
Over the Earth a Cloud, will therein set
His triple-colour'd Bow, whereon to look
And call to mind his Cov'nant: Day and Night,

Seed time and Harvest, Heat and hoary Frost
Shall hold thir course, till fire purge all things new,　　　900
Both Heav'n and Earth, wherein the just shall dwell.

The End of the Eleventh Book.

PARADISE LOST.

BOOK XII.

The Argument.

The Angel Michael *continues from the Flood to relate what shall succeed; then, in the mention of* Abraham, *comes by degrees to explain, who that Seed of the Woman shall be which was promised* Adam *and* Eve *in the Fall; his Incarnation, Death, Resurrection, and Ascension; the state of the Church till his second Coming.* Adam *greatly satisfied and recomforted by these Relations and Promises descends the Hill with* Michael; *wakens* Eve, *who all this while had slept, but with gentle dreams compos'd to quietness of mind and submission.* Michael *in either hand leads them out of Paradise, the fiery Sword waving behind them, and the Cherubim taking thir Stations to guard the Place.*

As one who in his journey bates at Noone,
Though bent on speed, so heer the Archangel paus'd
Betwixt the world destroy'd and world restor'd,
If *Adam* aught perhaps might interpose;
Then with transition sweet new Speech resumes.
　Thus thou hast seen one World begin and end;
And Man as from a second stock proceed.
Much thou hast yet to see, but I perceave
Thy mortal sight to faile; objects divine
Must needs impaire and wearie human sense:　　　10
Henceforth what is to com I will relate,
Thou therefore give due audience, and attend.
This second sours of Men, while yet but few,
And while the dread of judgement past remains
Fresh in thir mindes, fearing the Deitie,
With some regard to what is just and right
Shall lead thir lives, and multiplie apace,
Labouring the soile, and reaping plenteous crop,
Corn wine and oyle; and from the herd or flock,
Oft sacrificing Bullock, Lamb, or Kid,　　　20
With large Wine-offerings pour'd, and sacred Feast
Shal spend thir dayes in joy unblam'd, and dwell
Long time in peace by Families and Tribes
Under paternal rule; till one shall rise
Of proud ambitious heart, who not content
With fair equalitie, fraternal state,
Will arrogate Dominion undeserv'd
Over his brethren, and quite dispossess
Concord and law of Nature from the Earth;
Hunting (and Men not Beasts shall be his game)　　　30
With Warr and hostile snare such as refuse
Subjection to his Empire tyrannous:
A mightie Hunter thence he shall be styl'd

Before the Lord, as in despite of Heav'n,
Or from Heav'n claming second Sovrantie;
And from Rebellion shall derive his name,
Though of Rebellion others he accuse.
Hee with a crew, whom like Ambition joyns
With him or under him to tyrannize,
Marching from *Eden* towards the West, shall finde   40
The Plain, wherein a black bituminous gurge
Boiles out from under ground, the mouth of Hell;
Of Brick, and of that stuff they cast to build
A Citie & Towre, whose top may reach to Heav'n;
And get themselves a name, least far disperst
In foraign Lands thir memorie be lost,
Regardless whether good or evil fame.
But God who oft descends to visit men
Unseen, and through-thir habitations walks
To mark thir doings, them beholding soon,   50
Comes down to see thir Citie, ere the Tower
Obstruct Heav'n Towrs, and in derision sets
Upon thir Tongues a various Spirit to rase
Quite out thir Native Language, and instead
To sow a jangling noise of words unknown:
Forthwith a hideous gabble rises loud
Among the Builders; each to other calls
Not understood, till hoarse, and all in rage,
As mockt they storm; great laughter was in Heav'n
And looking down, to see the hubbub strange   60
And hear the din; thus was the building left
Ridiculous, and the work Confusion nam'd.
    Whereto thus *Adam* fatherly displeas'd.
O execrable Son so to aspire
Above his Brethren, to himself assuming
Authoritie usurpt, from God not giv'n:
He gave us onely over Beast, Fish, Fowl
Dominion absolute; that right we hold
By his donation; but Man over men
He made not Lord; such title to himself   70
Reserving, human left from human free.
But this Usurper his encroachment proud
Stayes not on Man; to God his Tower intends
Siege and defiance: Wretched man! what food
Will he convey up thither to sustain
Himself and his rash Armie, where thin Aire
Above the Clouds will pine his entrails gross,
And famish him of Breath, if not of Bread?
    To whom thus *Michael.* Justly thou abhorr'st
That Son, who on the quiet state of men   80
Such trouble brought, affecting to subdue
Rational Libertie; yet know withall,
Since thy original lapse, true Libertie
Is lost, which alwayes with right Reason dwells
Twinn'd, and from her hath no dividual being:

Reason in man obscur'd, or not obeyd,
Immediately inordinate desires
And upstart Passions catch the Government
From Reason, and to servitude reduce
Man till then free. Therefore since hee permits   90
Within himself unworthie Powers to reign
Over free Reason, God in Judgement just
Subjects him from without to violent Lords;
Who oft as undeservedly enthrall
His outward freedom: Tyrannie must be,
Though to the Tyrant thereby no excuse.
Yet somtimes Nations will decline so low
From vertue, which is reason, that no wrong,
But Justice, and some fatal curse annext
Deprives them of thir outward libertie,   100
Thir inward lost: Witness th' irreverent Son
Of him who built the Ark, who for the shame
Don to his Father, heard this heavie curse,
Servant of Servants, on his vitious Race.
Thus will this latter, as the former World,
Still tend from bad to worse, till God at last
Wearied with their iniquities, withdraw
His presence from among them, and avert
His holy Eyes; resolving from thenceforth
To leave them to thir own polluted wayes;   110
And one peculiar Nation to select
From all the rest, of whom to be invok'd,
A Nation from one faithful man to spring:
Him on this side *Euphrates* yet residing,
Bred up in Idol-worship; O that men
(Canst thou believe?) should be so stupid grown,
While yet the Patriark liv'd, who scap'd the Flood,
As to forsake the living God, and fall
To worship thir own work in Wood and Stone
For Gods! yet him God the most High voutsafes   120
To call by Vision from his Fathers house,
His kindred and false Gods, into a Land
Which he will shew him, and from him will raise
A mightie Nation, and upon him showre
His benediction so, that in his Seed
All Nations shall be blest; hee straight obeys,
Not knowing to what Land, yet firm believes:
I see him, but thou canst not, with what Faith
He leaves his Gods, his Friends, and native Soile
Ur of *Chaldæa,* passing now the Ford   130
To *Haran,* after him a cumbrous Train
Of Herds and Flocks, and numerous servitude;
Not wandring poor, but trusting all his wealth
With God, who call'd him, in a land unknown.
Canaan he now attains, I see his Tents
Pitcht about *Sechem,* and the neighbouring Plaine
Of *Moreh;* there by promise he receaves

Gift to his Progenie of all that Land;
From *Hamath* Northward to the Desert South
(Things by thir names I call, though yet unnam'd)　　　140
From *Hermon* East to the great Western Sea,
Mount *Hermon,* yonder Sea, each place behold
In prospect, as I point them; on the shoare
Mount *Carmel;* here the double-founted stream
Jordan, true limit Eastward; but his Sons
Shall dwell to *Senir,* that long ridge of Hills.
This ponder, that all Nations of the Earth
Shall in his Seed be blessed; by that Seed
Is meant thy great deliverer, who shall bruise
The Serpents head; whereof to thee anon　　　150
Plainlier shall be reveald. This Patriarch blest,
Whom *faithful Abraham* due time shall call,
A Son, and of his Son a Grand-childe leaves,
Like him in faith, in wisdom, and renown;
The Grandchilde with twelve Sons increast, departs
From *Canaan,* to a land hereafter call'd
Egypt, divided by the River *Nile;*
See where it flows, disgorging at seaven mouthes
Into the Sea: to sojourn in that Land
He comes invited by a yonger Son　　　160
In time of dearth, a Son whose worthy deeds
Raise him to be the second in that Realme
Of *Pharao:* there he dies, and leaves his Race
Growing into a Nation, and now grown
Suspected to a sequent King, who seeks
To stop thir overgrowth, as inmate guests
Too numerous; whence of guests he makes them slaves
Inhospitably, and kills thir infant Males:
Till by two brethren (those two brethren call
Moses and *Aaron*) sent from God to claime　　　170
His people from enthralment, they return
With glory and spoile back to thir promis'd Land.
But first the lawless Tyrant, who denies
To know thir God, or message to regard,
Must be compelld by Signes and Judgements dire;
To blood unshed the Rivers must be turnd,
Frogs, Lice and Flies must all his Palace fill
With loath'd intrusion, and fill all the land;
His Cattel must of Rot and Murren die,
Botches and blaines must all his flesh imboss,　　　180
And all his people; Thunder mixt with Haile,
Haile mixt with fire must rend th' *Egyptian* Skie
And wheel on th' Earth, devouring where it rouls;
What it devours not, Herb, or Fruit, or Graine,
A darksom Cloud of Locusts swarming down
Must eat, and on the ground leave nothing green:
Darkness must overshadow all his bounds,
Palpable darkness, and blot out three dayes;
Last with one midnight stroke all the first-born
Of *Egypt* must lie dead. Thus with ten wounds　　　190

This River-dragon tam'd at length submits
To let his sojourners depart, and oft
Humbles his stubborn heart, but still as Ice
More hard'nd after thaw, till in his rage
Pursuing whom he late dismissd, the Sea
Swallows him with his Host, but them lets pass
As on drie land between two christal walls,
Aw'd by the rod of *Moses* so to stand
Divided, till his rescu'd gain thir shoar:
Such wondrous power God to his Saint will lend,　　　　200
Though present in his Angel, who shall goe
Before them in a Cloud, and Pillar of Fire,
By day a Cloud, by night a Pillar of Fire,
To guide them in thir journey, and remove
Behinde them, while th' obdurat King pursues:
All night he will pursue, but his approach
Darkness defends between till morning Watch;
Then through the Firey Pillar and the Cloud
God looking forth will trouble all his Host
And craze thir Chariot wheels: when by command　　　210
Moses once more his potent Rod extends
Over the Sea; the Sea his Rod obeys;
On thir imbattelld ranks the Waves return,
And overwhelm thir Warr: the Race elect
Safe towards *Canaan* from the shoar advance
Through the wilde Desert, not the readiest way,
Least entring on the *Canaanite* allarmd
Warr terrifie them inexpert, and feare
Return them back to *Egypt,* choosing rather
Inglorious life with servitude; for life　　　　220
To noble and ignoble is more sweet
Untraind in Armes, where rashness leads not on.
This also shall they gain by thir delay
In the wide Wilderness, there they shall found
Thir government, and thir great Senate choose
Through the twelve Tribes, to rule by Laws ordaind:
God from the Mount of *Sinai,* whose gray top
Shall tremble, he descending, will himself
In Thunder Lightning and loud Trumpets sound
Ordaine them Lawes; part such as appertaine　　　　230
To civil Justice, part religious Rites
Of sacrifice, informing them, by types
And shadowes, of that destind Seed to bruise
The Serpent, by what meanes he shall achieve
Mankinds deliverance. But the voice of God
To mortal eare is dreadful; they beseech
That *Moses* might report to them his will,
And terror cease; he grants what they besaught,
Instructed that to God is no access
Without Mediator, whose high Office now　　　　240
Moses in figure beares, to introduce
One greater, of whose day he shall foretell,
And all the Prophets in thir Age the times

Of great *Messiah* shall sing. Thus Laws and Rites
Establisht, such delight hath God in Men
Obedient to his will, that he voutsafes
Among them to set up his Tabernacle,
The holy One with mortal Men to dwell:
By his prescript a Sanctuary is fram'd
Of Cedar, overlaid with Gold, therein   250
An Ark, and in the Ark his Testimony,
The Records of his Cov'nant, over these
A Mercie-seat of Gold between the wings
Of two bright Cherubim, before him burn
Seaven Lamps as in a Zodiac representing
The Heav'nly fires; over the Tent a Cloud
Shall rest by Day, a fierie gleame by Night,
Save when they journie, and at length they come,
Conducted by his Angel to the Land
Promisd to *Abraham* and his Seed: the rest   260
Were long to tell, how many Battels fought,
How many Kings destroyd, and Kingdoms won,
Or how the Sun shall in mid Heav'n stand still
A day entire, and Nights due course adjourne,
Mans voice commanding, Sun in *Gibeon* stand,
And thou Moon in the vale of *Aialon,*
Till *Israel* overcome; so call the third
From *Abraham,* Son of *Isaac,* and from him
His whole descent, who thus shall *Canaan* win.

  Here *Adam* interpos'd. O sent from Heav'n,   270
Enlightner of my darkness, gracious things
Thou hast reveald, those chiefly which concerne
Just *Abraham* and his Seed: now first I finde
Mine eyes true op'ning, and my heart much eas'd,
Erwhile perplext with thoughts what would becom
Of mee and all Mankind; but now I see
His day, in whom all Nations shall be blest,
Favour unmerited by me, who sought
Forbidd'n knowledge by forbidd'n means.
This yet I apprehend not, why to those   280
Among whom God will deigne to dwell on Earth
So many and so various Laws are giv'n;
So many Laws argue so many sins
Among them; how can God with such reside?
  To whom thus *Michael.* Doubt not but that sin
Will reign among them, as of thee begot;
And therefore was Law given them to evince
Thir natural pravitie, by stirring up
Sin against Law to fight; that when they see
Law can discover sin, but not remove,   290
Save by those shadowie expiations weak,
The bloud of Bulls and Goats, they may conclude
Some bloud more precious must be paid for Man,
Just for unjust, that in such righteousness
To them by Faith imputed, they may finde
Justification towards God, and peace

Of Conscience, which the Law by Ceremonies
Cannot appease, nor Man the moral part
Perform, and not performing cannot live.
So Law appears imperfet, and but giv'n   300
With purpose to resign them in full time
Up to a better Cov'nant, disciplin'd
From shadowie Types to Truth, from Flesh to Spirit,
From imposition of strict Laws, to free
Acceptance of large Grace, from servil fear
To filial, works of Law to works of Faith.
And therefore shall not *Moses,* though of God
Highly belov'd, being but the Minister
Of Law, his people into *Canaan* lead;
But *Joshua* whom the Gentiles *Jesus* call,   310
His Name and Office bearing, who shall quell
The adversarie Serpent, and bring back
Through the worlds wilderness long wanderd man
Safe to eternal Paradise of rest.
Meanwhile they in thir earthly *Canaan* plac't
Long time shall dwell and prosper, but when sins
National interrupt thir public peace,
Provoking God to raise them enemies:
From whom as oft he saves them penitent
By Judges first, then under Kings; of whom   320
The second, both for pietie renownd
And puissant deeds, a promise shall receive
Irrevocable, that his Regal Throne
For ever shall endure; the like shall sing
All Prophecie, That of the Royal Stock
Of *David* (so I name this King) shall rise
A Son, the Womans Seed to thee foretold,
Foretold to *Abraham,* as in whom shall trust
All Nations, and to Kings foretold, of Kings
The last, for of his Reign shall be no end.   330
But first a long succession must ensue,
And his next Son for Wealth and Wisdom fam'd,
The clouded Ark of God till then in Tents
Wandring, shall in a glorious Temple enshrine.
Such follow him, as shall be registerd
Part good, part bad, of bad the longer scrowle,
Whose foul Idolatries, and other faults
Heapt to the popular summe, will so incense
God, as to leave them, and expose thir Land,
Thir Citie, his Temple, and his holy Ark   340
With all his sacred things, a scorn and prey
To that proud Citie, whose high Walls thou saw'st
Left in confusion, *Babylon* thence call'd.
There in captivitie he lets them dwell
The space of seventie years, then brings them back,
Remembring mercie, and his Cov'nant sworn
To *David,* stablisht as the dayes of Heav'n.
Returnd from *Babylon* by leave of Kings
Thir Lords, whom God dispos'd, the house of God

They first re-edifie, and for a while   350
In mean estate live moderate, till grown
In wealth and multitude, factious they grow;
But first among the Priests dissension springs,
Men who attend the Altar, and should most
Endeavour Peace: thir strife pollution brings
Upon the Temple it self: at last they seise
The Scepter, and regard not *Davids* Sons,
Then loose it to a stranger, that the true
Anointed King *Messiah* might be born
Barr'd of his right; yet at his Birth a Starr   360
Unseen before in Heav'n proclaims him com,
And guides the Eastern Sages, who enquire
His place, to offer Incense, Myrrh, and Gold;
His place of birth a solemn Angel tells
To simple Shepherds, keeping watch by night;
They gladly thither haste, and by a Quire
Of squadrond Angels hear his Carol sung.
A Virgin is his Mother, but his Sire
The Power of the most High; he shall ascend
The Throne hereditarie, and bound his Reign   370
With earths wide bounds, his glory with the Heav'ns.
    He ceas'd, discerning *Adam* with such joy
Surcharg'd, as had like grief bin dew'd in tears,
Without the vent of words, which these he breathd.
    O Prophet of glad tidings, finisher
Of utmost hope! now clear I understand
What oft my steddiest thoughts have searcht in vain,
Why our great expectation should be call'd
The seed of Woman: Virgin Mother, Haile,
High in the love of Heav'n, yet from my Loynes   380
Thou shalt proceed, and from thy Womb the Son
Of God most High; So God with man unites.
Needs must the Serpent now his capital bruise
Expect with mortal paine: say where and when
Thir fight, what stroke shall bruise the Victors heel.
    To whom thus *Michael*. Dream not of thir fight,
As of a Duel, or the local wounds
Of head or heel: not therefore joynes the Son
Manhood to God-head, with more strength to foil
Thy enemie; nor so is overcome   390
Satan, whose fall from Heav'n, a deadlier bruise,
Disabl'd not to give thee thy deaths wound:
Which hee, who comes thy Saviour, shall recure,
Not by destroying *Satan,* but his works
In thee and in thy Seed: nor can this be,
But by fulfilling that which thou didst want,
Obedience to the Law of God, impos'd
On penaltie of death, and suffering death,
The penaltie to thy transgression due,
And due to theirs which out of thine will grow: 400
So onely can high Justice rest appaid.
The Law of God exact he shall fulfill

Both by obedience and by love, though love
Alone fulfill the Law; thy punishment
He shall endure by coming in the Flesh
To a reproachful life and cursed death,
Proclaming Life to all who shall believe
In his redemption, and that his obedience
Imputed becomes theirs by Faith, his merits
To save them, not thir own, though legal works.   410
For this he shall live hated, be blasphem'd,
Seis'd on by force, judg'd, and to death condemnd
A shameful and accurst, naild to the Cross
By his own Nation, slaine for bringing Life;
But to the Cross he nailes thy Enemies,
The Law that is against thee, and the sins
Of all mankinde, with him there crucifi'd,
Never to hurt them more who rightly trust
In this his satisfaction; so he dies,
But soon revives, Death over him no power   420
Shall long usurp; ere the third dawning light
Returne, the Starres of Morn shall see him rise
Out of his grave, fresh as the dawning light,
Thy ransom paid, which Man from death redeems,
His death for Man, as many as offerd Life
Neglect not, and the benefit imbrace
By Faith not void of workes: this God-like act
Annuls thy doom, the death thou shouldst have dy'd,
In sin for ever lost from life; this act
Shall bruise the head of *Satan,* crush his strength   430
Defeating Sin and Death, his two maine armes,
And fix farr deeper in his head thir stings
Then temporal death shall bruise the Victors heel,
Or theirs whom he redeems, a death like sleep,
A gentle wafting to immortal Life.
Nor after resurrection shall he stay
Longer on Earth then certaine times to appeer
To his Disciples, Men who in his Life
Still follow'd him; to them shall leave in charge
To teach all nations what of him they learn'd   440
And his Salvation, them who shall beleeve
Baptizing in the profluent streame, the signe
Of washing them from guilt of sin to Life
Pure, and in mind prepar'd, if so befall,
For death, like that which the redeemer dy'd.
All Nations they shall teach; for from that day
Not onely to the Sons of *Abrahams* Loines
Salvation shall be Preacht, but to the Sons
Of *Abrahams* Faith wherever through the world;
So in his seed all Nations shall be blest.   450
Then to the Heav'n of Heav'ns he shall ascend
With victory, triumphing through the aire
Over his foes and thine; there shall surprise
The Serpent, Prince of aire, and drag in Chaines
Through all his realme, & there confounded leave;

Then enter into glory, and resume
His Seat at Gods right hand, exalted high
Above all names in Heav'n; and thence shall come,
When this worlds dissolution shall be ripe,
With glory and power to judge both quick & dead,   460
To judge th' unfaithful dead, but to reward
His faithful, and receave them into bliss,
Whether in Heav'n or Earth, for then the Earth
Shall all be Paradise, far happier place
Then this of *Eden,* and far happier daies.
   So spake th' Archangel *Michael,* then paus'd,
As at the Worlds great period; and our Sire
Replete with joy and wonder thus repli'd.
   O goodness infinite, goodness immense!
That all this good of evil shall produce,   470
And evil turn to good; more wonderful
Then that which by creation first brought forth
Light out of darkness! full of doubt I stand,
Whether I should repent me now of sin
By mee done and occasiond, or rejoyce
Much more, that much more good thereof shall spring,
To God more glory, more good will to Men
From God, and over wrauth grace shall abound.
But say, if our deliverer up to Heav'n
Must reascend, what will betide the few   480
His faithful, left among th' unfaithful herd,
The enemies of truth; who then shall guide
His people, who defend? will they not deale
Wors' with his followers then with him they dealt?
   Be sure they will, said th' Angel; but from Heav'n
Hee to his own a Comforter will send,
The promise of the Father, who shall dwell
His Spirit within them, and the Law of Faith
Working through love, upon thir hearts shall write,
To guide them in all truth, and also arme   490
With spiritual Armour, able to resist
Satans assaults, and quench his fierie darts,
What Man can do against them, not affraid,
Though to the death, against such cruelties
With inward consolations recompenc't,
And oft supported so as shall amaze
Thir proudest persecuters: for the Spirit
Powrd first on his Apostles, whom he sends
To evangelize the Nations, then on all
Baptiz'd, shall them with wondrous gifts endue   500
To speak all Tongues, and do all Miracles,
As did thir Lord before them. Thus they win
Great numbers of each Nation to receave
With joy the tidings brought from Heav'n: at length
Thir Ministry perform'd, and race well run,
Thir doctrine and thir story written left,
They die; but in thir room, as they forewarne,
Wolves shall succeed for teachers, grievous Wolves.

Who all the sacred mysteries of Heav'n
To thir own vile advantages shall turne　　　510
Of lucre and ambition, and the truth
With superstitions and traditions taint,
Left onely in those written Records pure,
Though not but by the Spirit understood.
Then shall they seek to avail themselves of names,
Places and titles, and with these to joine
Secular power, though feigning still to act
By spiritual, to themselves appropriating
The Spirit of God, promisd alike and giv'n
To all Beleevers; and from that pretense,　　　520
Spiritual Lawes by carnal power shall force
On every conscience; Laws which none shall finde
Left them inrould, or what the Spirit within
Shall on the heart engrave. What will they then
But force the Spirit of Grace it self, and binde
His consort Libertie; what, but unbuild
His living Temples, built by Faith to stand,
Thir own Faith not anothers: for on Earth
Who against Faith and Conscience can be heard
Infallible? yet many will presume:　　　530
Whence heavie persecution shall arise
On all who in the worship persevere
Of Spirit and Truth; the rest, farr greater part,
Will deem in outward Rites and specious formes
Religion satisfi'd; Truth shall retire
Bestuck with slandrous darts, and works of Faith
Rarely be found: so shall the World goe on,
To good malignant, to bad men benigne,
Under her own waight groaning, till the day
Appeer of respiration to the just,　　　540
And vengeance to the wicked, at return
Of him so lately promis'd to thy aid,
The Womans seed, obscurely then foretold,
Now amplier known thy Saviour and thy Lord,
Last in the Clouds from Heav'n to be reveald
In glory of the Father, to dissolve
Satan with his perverted World, then raise
From the conflagrant mass, purg'd and refin'd,
New Heav'ns, new Earth, Ages of endless date
Founded in righteousness and peace and love,　　　550
To bring forth fruits Joy and eternal Bliss.
　　He ended; and thus *Adam* last reply'd.
How soon hath thy prediction, Seer blest,
Measur'd this transient World, the Race of time,
Till time stand fixt: beyond is all abyss,
Eternitie, whose end no eye can reach.
Greatly instructed I shall hence depart,
Greatly in peace of thought, and have my fill
Of knowledge, what this vessel can containe;
Beyond which was my folly to aspire.
Henceforth I learne, that to obey is best,　　　560

And love with feare the onely God, to walk
As in his presence, ever to observe
His providence, and on him sole depend,
Merciful over all his works, with good
Still overcoming evil, and by small
Accomplishing great things, by things deemd weak
Subverting worldly strong, and worldly wise
By simply meek; that suffering for Truths sake
Is fortitude to highest victorie,   570
And to the faithful Death the Gate of Life;
Taught this by his example whom I now
Acknowledge my Redeemer ever blest.
       To whom thus also th' Angel last repli'd:
This having learnt, thou hast attained the summe
Of wisdom; hope no higher, though all the Starrs
Thou knewst by name, and all th' ethereal Powers,
All secrets of the deep, all Natures works,
Or works of God in Heav'n, Air, Earth, or Sea,
And all the riches of this World enjoydst,   580
And all the rule, one Empire; onely add
Deeds to thy knowledge answerable, add Faith,
Add Vertue, Patience, Temperance, add Love,
By name to come call'd Charitie, the soul
Of all the rest: then wilt thou not be loath
To leave this Paradise, but shalt possess
A Paradise within thee, happier farr.
Let us descend now therefore from this top
Of Speculation; for the hour precise
Exacts our parting hence; and see the Guards,   590
By mee encampt on yonder Hill, expect
Thir motion, at whose Front a flaming Sword,
In signal of remove, waves fiercely round;
We may no longer stay: go, waken *Eve;*
Her also I with gentle Dreams have calm'd
Portending good, and all her spirits compos'd
To meek submission: thou at season fit
Let her with thee partake what thou hast heard,
Chiefly what may concern her Faith to know,
The great deliverance by her Seed to come   600
(For by the Womans Seed) on all Mankind.
That ye may live, which will be many dayes,
Both in one Faith unanimous though sad,
With cause for evils past, yet much more cheer'd
With meditation on the happie end.
       He ended, and they both descend the Hill;
Descended, *Adam* to the Bowre where *Eve*
Lay sleeping ran before, but found her wak't;
And thus with words not sad she him receav'd.
       Whence thou returnst, & whither wentst, I know;   610
For God is also in sleep, and Dreams advise,
Which he hath sent propitious, some great good
Presaging, since with sorrow and hearts distress
Wearied I fell asleep: but now lead on;

In mee is no delay; with thee to goe,
Is to stay here; without thee here to stay,
Is to go hence unwilling; thou to mee
Art all things under Heav'n, all places thou,
Who for my wilful crime art banisht hence.
This further consolation yet secure   620
I carry hence; though all by mee is lost,
Such favour I unworthie am voutsaft,
By mee the Promis'd Seed shall all restore.
    So spake our Mother *Eve,* and *Adam* heard
Well pleas'd, but answer'd not; for now too nigh
Th' Archangel stood, and from the other Hill
To thir fixt Station, all in bright array
The Cherubim descended; on the ground
Gliding meteorous, as Ev'ning Mist
Ris'n from a River o're the marish glides,   630
And gathers ground fast at the Labourers heel
Homeward returning. High in Front advanc't,
The brandisht Sword of God before them blaz'd
Fierce as a Comet; which with torrid heat,
And vapour as the *Libyan* Air adust,
Began to parch that temperate Clime; whereat
In either hand the hastning Angel caught
Our lingring Parents, and to th' Eastern Gate
Led them direct, and down the Cliff as fast
To the subjected Plaine; then disappeer'd.   640
They looking back, all th' Eastern side beheld
Of Paradise, so late thir happie seat,
Wav'd over by that flaming Brand, the Gate
With dreadful Faces throng'd and fierie Armes:
Som natural tears they drop'd, but wip'd them soon;
The World was all before them, where to choose
Thir place of rest, and Providence thir guide:
They hand in hand with wandring steps and slow,
Through *Eden* took thir solitarie way.

The End.

PARADISE
REGAIN'D.
A
POEM.

In IV *BOOKS*
To which is added
SAMSON AGONISTES
The Author
JOHN MILTON

PARADISE REGAIN'D.

[The text is that of the first edition, 1671.]

The First Book.

I who e're while the happy Garden sung,
By one mans disobedience lost, now sing
Recover'd Paradise to all mankind,
By one mans firm obedience fully tri'd
Through all temptation, and the Tempter foil'd
In all his wiles, defeated and repuls't,
And *Eden* rais'd in the wast Wilderness.
  Thou Spirit who ledst this glorious Eremite
Into the Desert, his Victorious Field
Against the Spiritual Foe, and broughtst him thence
By proof the undoubted Son of God, inspire,
As thou art wont, my prompted Song else mute,
And bear through highth or depth of natures bounds
With prosperous wing full summ'd to tell of deeds
Above Heroic, though in secret done,
And unrecorded left through many an Age,

364

Worthy t' have not remain'd so long unsung.
   Now had the great Proclaimer with a voice
More awful then the sound of Trumpet, cri'd
Repentance, and Heavens Kingdom nigh at hand   20
To all Baptiz'd: to his great Baptism flock'd
With aw the Regions round, and with them came
From *Nazareth* the Son of *Joseph* deem'd
To the flood *Jordan*, came as then obscure,
Unmarkt, unknown; but him the Baptist soon
Descri'd, divinely warn'd, and witness bore
As to his worthier, and would have resign'd
To him his Heavenly Office, nor was long
His witness unconfirm'd: on him baptiz'd
Heaven open'd, and in likeness of a Dove   30
The Spirit descended, while the Fathers voice
From Heav'n pronounc'd him his beloved Son.
That heard the Adversary, who roving still
About the world, at that assembly fam'd
Would not be last, and with the voice divine
Nigh Thunder-struck, th' exalted man, to whom
Such high attest was giv'n, a while survey'd
With wonder, then with envy fraught and rage
Flies to his place, nor rests, but in mid air
To Councel summons all his mighty Peers,   40
Within thick Clouds and dark ten-fold involv'd,
A gloomy Consistory; and them amidst
With looks agast and sad he thus bespake.
   O ancient Powers of Air and this wide world,
For much more willingly I mention Air,
This our old Conquest, then remember Hell
Our hated habitation; well ye know
How many Ages, as the years of men,
This Universe we have possest, and rul'd
In manner at our will th' affairs of Earth,   50
Since *Adam* and his facil consort *Eve*
Lost Paradise deceiv'd by me, though since
With dread attending when that fatal wound
Shall be inflicted by the Seed of *Eve*
Upon my head, long the decrees of Heav'n
Delay, for longest time to him is short;
And now too soon for us the circling hours
This dreaded time have compast, wherein we
Must bide the stroak of that long threatn'd wound,
At least if so we can, and by the head   60
Broken be not intended all our power
To be infring'd, our freedom and our being
In this fair Empire won of Earth and Air;
For this ill news I bring, the Womans seed
Destin'd to this, is late of woman born,
His birth to our just fear gave no small cause,
But his growth now to youths full flowr, displaying
All vertue, grace and wisdom to atchieve
Things highest, greatest, multiplies my fear.

Before him a great Prophet, to proclaim   70
His coming, is sent Harbinger, who all
Invites, and in the Consecrated stream
Pretends to wash off sin, and fit them so
Purified to receive him pure, or rather
To do him honour as their King; all come,
And he himself among them was baptiz'd,
Not thence to be more pure, but to receive
The testimony of Heaven, that who he is
Thenceforth the Nations may not doubt; I saw
The Prophet do him reverence, on him rising   80
Out of the water, Heav'n above the Clouds
Unfold her Crystal Dores, thence on his head
A perfect Dove descend, what e're it meant,
And out of Heav'n the Sov'raign voice I heard,
This is my Son belov'd, in him am pleas'd.
His Mother then is mortal, but his Sire,
He who obtains the Monarchy of Heav'n,
And what will he not do to advance his Son?
His first-begot we know, and sore have felt,
When his fierce thunder drove us to the deep;   90
Who this is we must learn, for man he seems
In all his lineaments, though in his face
The glimpses of his Fathers glory shine.
Ye see our danger on the utmost edge
Of hazard, which admits no long debate,
But must with something sudden be oppos'd,
Not force, but well couch't fraud, well woven snares,
E're in the head of Nations he appear
Their King, their Leader, and Supream on Earth.
I, when no other durst, sole undertook   100
The dismal expedition to find out
And ruine *Adam*, and the exploit perform'd
Successfully; a calmer voyage now
Will waft me; and the way found prosperous once
Induces best to hope of like success.
    He ended, and his words impression left
Of much amazement to th' infernal Crew,
Distracted and surpriz'd with deep dismay
At these sad tidings; but no time was then
For long indulgence to their fears or grief: 110
Unanimous they all commit the care
And management of this main enterprize
To him their great Dictator, whose attempt
At first against mankind so well had thriv'd
In *Adam*'s overthrow, and led thir march
From Hell's deep-vaulted Den to dwell in light,
Regents and Potentates, and Kings, yea gods
Of many a pleasant Realm and Province wide.
So to the Coast of *Jordan* he directs
His easie steps; girded with snaky wiles,   120
Where he might likeliest find this new-declar'd,
This man of men, attested Son of God,

Temptation and all guile on him to try;
So to subvert whom he suspected rais'd
To end his Raign on Earth so long enjoy'd:
But contrary unweeting he fulfill'd
The purpos'd Counsel pre-ordain'd and fixt
Of the most High, who in full frequence bright
Of Angels, thus to *Gabriel* smiling spake.
    Gabriel this day by proof thou shalt behold,   130
Thou and all Angels conversant on Earth
With man or mens affairs, how I begin
To verifie that solemn message late,
On which I sent thee to the Virgin pure
In *Galilee,* that she should bear a Son
Great in Renown, and call'd the Son of God;
Then toldst her doubting how these things could be
To her a Virgin, that on her should come
The Holy Ghost, and the power of the highest
O're-shadow her: this man born and now up-grown,   140
To shew him worthy of his birth divine
And high prediction, henceforth I expose
To Satan; let him tempt and now assay
His utmost subtilty, because he boasts
And vaunts of his great cunning to the throng
Of his Apostasie; he might have learnt
Less over-weening, since he fail'd in *Job,*
Whose constant perseverance overcame
Whate're his cruel malice could invent.
He now shall know I can produce a man   150
Of female Seed, far abler to resist
All his sollicitations, and at length
All his vast force, and drive him back to Hell,
Winning by Conquest what the first man lost
By fallacy surpriz'd. But first I mean
To exercise him in the Wilderness,
There he shall first lay down the rudiments
Of his great warfare, e're I send him forth
To conquer Sin and Death the two grand foes,
By Humiliation and strong Sufferance: 160
His weakness shall o'recome Satanic strength
And all the world, and mass of sinful flesh;
That all the Angels and Ætherial Powers,
They now, and men hereafter may discern,
From what consummate vertue I have chose
This perfect Man, by merit call'd my Son,
To earn Salvation for the Sons of men.
    So spake the Eternal Father, and all Heaven
Admiring stood a space, then into Hymns
Burst forth, and in Celestial measures mov'd,   170
Circling the Throne and Singing, while the hand
Sung with the voice, and this the argument.
    Victory and Triumph to the Son of God
Now entring his great duel, not of arms,
But to vanquish by wisdom hellish wiles.

The Father knows the Son; therefore secure
Ventures his filial Vertue, though untri'd,
Against whate're may tempt, whate're seduce,
Allure, or terrifie, or undermine.
Be frustrate all ye stratagems of Hell,   180
And devilish machinations come to nought.
    So they in Heav'n their Odes and Vigils tun'd:
Mean while the Son of God, who yet some days
Lodg'd in *Bethabara* where *John* baptiz'd,
Musing and much revolving in his brest,
How best the mighty work he might begin
Of Saviour to mankind, and which way first
Publish his God-like office now mature,
One day forth walk'd alone, the Spirit leading;
And his deep thoughts, the better to converse   190
With solitude, till far from track of men,
Thought following thought, and step by step led on,
He entred now the bordering Desert wild,
And with dark shades and rocks environ'd round,
His holy Meditations thus persu'd.
    O what a multitude of thoughts at once
Awakn'd in me swarm, while I consider
What from within I feel my self, and hear
What from without comes often to my ears,
Ill sorting with my present state compar'd.   200
When I was yet a child, no childish play
To me was pleasing, all my mind was set
Serious to learn and know, and thence to do
What might be publick good; my self I thought
Born to that end, born to promote all truth,
All righteous things: therefore above my years,
The Law of God I read, and found it sweet,
Made it my whole delight, and in it grew
To such perfection, that e're yet my age
Had measur'd twice six years, at our great Feast   210
I went into the Temple, there to hear
The Teachers of our Law, and to propose
What might improve my knowledge or their own;
And was admir'd by all, yet this not all
To which my Spirit aspir'd, victorious deeds
Flam'd in my heart, heroic acts, one while
To rescue *Israel* from the *Roman* yoke,
Then to subdue and quell o're all the earth
Brute violence and proud Tyrannick pow'r,
Till truth were freed, and equity restor'd: 220
Yet held it more humane, more heavenly first
By winning words to conquer willing hearts,
And make perswasion do the work of fear;
At least to try, and teach the erring Soul
Not wilfully mis-doing, but unware
Misled; the stubborn only to subdue.
These growing thoughts my Mother soon perceiving
By words at times cast forth inly rejoyc'd,

And said to me apart, high are thy thoughts
O Son, but nourish them and let them soar   230
To what highth sacred vertue and true worth
Can raise them, though above example high;
By matchless Deeds express thy matchless Sire.
For know, thou art no Son of mortal man,
Though men esteem thee low of Parentage,
Thy Father is the Eternal King, who rules
All Heaven and Earth, Angels and Sons of men,
A messenger from God fore-told thy birth
Conceiv'd in me a Virgin, he fore-told
Thou shouldst be great and sit on *David*'s Throne,   240
And of thy Kingdom there should be no end.
At thy Nativity a glorious Quire
Of Angels in the fields of *Bethlehem* sung
To Shepherds watching at their folds by night,
And told them the Messiah now was born,
Where they might see him, and to thee they came;
Directed to the Manger where thou lais't,
For in the Inn was left no better room:
A Star, not seen before in Heaven appearing
Guided the Wise Men thither from the East,   250
To honour thee with Incense, Myrrh, and Gold,
By whose bright course led on they found the place,
Affirming it thy Star new grav'n in Heaven,
By which they knew thee King of *Israel* born.
Just *Simeon* and Prophetic *Anna,* warn'd
By Vision, found thee in the Temple, and spake
Before the Altar and the vested Priest,
Like things of thee to all that present stood.
This having heard, strait I again revolv'd
The Law and Prophets, searching what was writ   260
Concerning the Messiah, to our Scribes
Known partly, and soon found of whom they spake
I am; this chiefly, that my way must lie
Through many a hard assay even to the death,
E're I the promis'd Kingdom can attain,
Or work Redemption for mankind, whose sins
Full weight must be transferr'd upon my head.
Yet neither thus disheartn'd or dismay'd,
The time prefixt I waited, when behold
The Baptist, (of whose birth I oft had heard,   270
Not knew by sight) now come, who was to come
Before Messiah and his way prepare.
I as all others to his Baptism came,
Which I believ'd was from above; but he
Strait knew me, and with loudest voice proclaim'd
Me him (for it was shew'n him so from Heaven)
Me him whose Harbinger he was; and first
Refus'd on me his Baptism to confer,
As much his greater, and was hardly won;
But as I rose out of the laving stream,   280
Heaven open'd her eternal doors, from whence

The Spirit descended on me like a Dove,
And last the sum of all, my Father's voice,
Audibly heard from Heav'n, pronounc'd me his,
Me his beloved Son, in whom alone
He was well pleas'd; by which I knew the time
Now full, that I no more should live obscure,
But openly begin, as best becomes
The Authority which I deriv'd from Heaven.
And now by some strong motion I am led   290
Into this wilderness, to what intent
I learn not yet, perhaps I need not know;
For what concerns my knowledge God reveals.
    So spake our Morning Star then in his rise,
And looking round on every side beheld
A pathless Desert, dusk with horrid shades;
The way he came not having mark'd, return
Was difficult, by humane steps untrod;
And he still on was led, but with such thoughts
Accompanied of things past and to come   300
Lodg'd in his brest, as well might recommend
Such Solitude before choicest Society.
Full forty days he pass'd, whether on hill
Sometimes, anon in shady vale, each night
Under the covert of some ancient Oak,
Or Cedar, to defend him from the dew,
Or harbour'd in one Cave, is not reveal'd;
Nor tasted humane food, nor hunger felt
Till those days ended, hunger'd then at last
Among wild Beasts: they at his sight grew mild,   310
Nor sleeping him nor waking harm'd, his walk
The fiery Serpent fled, and noxious Worm,
The Lion and fierce Tiger glar'd aloof.
But now an aged man in Rural weeds,
Following, as seem'd, the quest of some stray Ewe,
Or wither'd sticks to gather; which might serve
Against a Winters day when winds blow keen,
To warm him wet return'd from field at Eve,
He saw approach, who first with curious eye
Perus'd him, then with words thus utt'red spake.   320
    Sir, what ill chance hath brought thee to this place
So far from path or road of men, who pass
In Troop or Caravan, for single none
Durst ever, who return'd, and dropt not here
His Carcass, pin'd with hunger and with droughth?
I ask the rather, and the more admire,
For that to me thou seem'st the man, whom late
Our new baptizing Prophet at the Ford
Of *Jordan* honour'd so, and call'd thee Son
Of God; I saw and heard, for we sometimes   330
Who dwell this wild, constrain'd by want, come forth
To Town or Village nigh (nighest is far)
Where ought we hear, and curious are to hear,
What happ'ns new; Fame also finds us out.

To whom the Son of God. Who brought me hither
Will bring me hence, no other Guide I seek.
    By Miracle he may, reply'd the Swain,
What other way I see not, for we here
Live on tough roots and stubs, to thirst inur'd   340
More then the Camel, and to drink go far,
Men to much misery and hardship born;
But if thou be the Son of God, Command
That out of these hard stones be made thee bread;
So shalt thou save thy self and us relieve
With Food, whereof we wretched seldom taste.
    He ended, and the Son of God reply'd.
Think'st thou such force in Bread? is it not written
(For I discern thee other then thou seem'st)
Man lives not by Bread only, but each Word   350
Proceeding from the mouth of God; who fed
Our Fathers here with Manna; in the Mount
Moses was forty days, nor eat nor drank,
And forty days *Eliah* without food
Wandred this barren waste, the same I now:
Why dost thou then suggest to me distrust,
Knowing who I am, as I know who thou art?
    Whom thus answer'd th' Arch Fiend now undisguis'd.
'Tis true, I am that Spirit unfortunate,
Who leagu'd with millions more in rash revolt   360
Kept not my happy Station, but was driv'n
With them from bliss to the bottomless deep,
Yet to that hideous place not so confin'd
By rigour unconniving, but that oft
Leaving my dolorous Prison I enjoy
Large liberty to round this Globe of Earth,
Or range in th' Air, nor from the Heav'n of Heav'ns
Hath he excluded my resort sometimes.
I came among the Sons of God, when he
Gave up into my hands *Uzzean Job*   370
To prove him, and illustrate his high worth;
And when to all his Angels he propos'd
To draw the proud King *Ahab* into fraud
That he might fall in *Ramoth,* they demurring,
I undertook that office, and the tongues
Of all his flattering Prophets glibb'd with lyes
To his destruction, as I had in charge.
For what he bids I do; though I have lost
Much lustre of my native brightness, lost
To be belov'd of God, I have not lost   380
To love, at least contemplate and admire
What I see excellent in good, or fair,
Or vertuous, I should so have lost all sense.
What can be then less in me then desire
To see thee and approach thee, whom I know
Declar'd the Son of God, to hear attent
Thy wisdom, and behold thy God-like deeds?
Men generally think me much a foe

To all mankind: why should I? they to me
Never did wrong or violence, by them
I lost not what I lost, rather by them   390
I gain'd what I have gain'd, and with them dwell
Copartner in these Regions of the World,
If not disposer; lend them oft my aid,
Oft my advice by presages and signs,
And answers, oracles, portents and dreams,
Whereby they may direct their future life.
Envy they say excites me, thus to gain
Companions of my misery and wo.
At first it may be; but long since with wo
Nearer acquainted, now I feel by proof,   400
That fellowship in pain divides not smart,
Nor lightens aught each mans peculiar load.
Small consolation then, were Man adioyn'd:
This wounds me most (what can it less) that Man,
Man fall'n shall be restor'd, I never more.
   To whom our Saviour sternly thus reply'd.
Deservedly thou griev'st, compos'd of lyes
From the beginning, and in lies wilt end;
Who boast'st release from Hell, and leave to come
Into the Heav'n of Heavens; thou com'st indeed,   410
As a poor miserable captive thrall,
Comes to the place where he before had sat
Among the Prime in Splendour, now depos'd,
Ejected, emptyed, gaz'd, unpityed, shun'd,
A spectacle of ruin or of scorn
To all the Host of Heaven; the happy place
Imparts to thee no happiness, no joy,
Rather inflames thy torment, representing
Lost bliss, to thee no more communicable,
So never more in Hell then when in Heaven.   420
But thou art serviceable to Heaven's King.
Wilt thou impute to obedience what thy fear
Extorts, or pleasure to do ill excites?
What but thy malice mov'd thee to misdeem
Of righteous *Job,* then cruelly to afflict him
With all inflictions, but his patience won?
The other service was thy chosen task,
To be a lyer in four hundred mouths;
For lying is thy sustenance, thy food.
Yet thou pretend'st to truth; all Oracles   430
By thee are giv'n, and what confest more true
Among the Nations? that hath been thy craft,
By mixing somewhat true to vent more lyes.
But what have been thy answers, what but dark
Ambiguous and with double sense deluding,
Which they who ask'd have seldom understood,
And not well understood as good not known?
Who ever by consulting at thy shrine
Return'd the wiser, or the more instruct
To flye or follow what concern'd him most,   440

And run not sooner to his fatal snare?
For God hath justly giv'n the Nations up
To thy Delusions; justly, since they fell
Idolatrous, but when his purpose is
Among them to declare his Providence
To thee not known, whence hast thou then thy truth,
But from him or his Angels President
In every Province, who themselves disdaining
To approach thy Temples, give thee in command
What to the smallest tittle thou shalt say   450
To thy Adorers; thou with trembling fear,
Or like a Fawning Parasite obey'st;
Then to thy self ascrib'st the truth fore-told.
But this thy glory shall be soon retrench'd;
No more shalt thou by oracling abuse
The Gentiles; henceforth Oracles are ceast,
And thou no more with Pomp and Sacrifice
Shalt be enquir'd at *Delphos* or elsewhere,
At least in vain, for they shall find thee mute.
God hath now sent his living Oracle   460
Into the World, to teach his final will,
And sends his Spirit of Truth henceforth to dwell
In pious Hearts, an inward Oracle
To all truth requisite for men to know.
    So spake our Saviour; but the subtle Fiend,
Though inly stung with anger and disdain,
Dissembl'd, and this Answer smooth return'd.
    Sharply thou hast insisted on rebuke,
And urg'd me hard with doings, which not will
But misery hath rested from me; where   470
Easily canst thou find one miserable,
And not inforc'd oft-times to part from truth;
If it may stand him more in stead to lye,
Say and unsay, feign, flatter, or abjure?
But thou art plac't above me, thou art Lord;
From thee I can and must submiss endure
Check or reproof, and glad to scape so quit.
Hard are the ways of truth, and rough to walk,
Smooth on the tongue discourst, pleasing to th' ear,
And tuneable as Silvan Pipe or Song;   480
What wonder then if I delight to hear
Her dictates from thy mouth? most men admire
Vertue, who follow not her lore: permit me
To hear thee when I come (since no man comes)
And talk at least, though I despair to attain.
Thy Father, who is holy, wise and pure,
Suffers the Hypocrite or Atheous Priest
To tread his Sacred Courts, and minister
About his Altar, handling holy things,
Praying or vowing, and vouchsaf'd his voice   490
To *Balaam* Reprobate, a Prophet yet
Inspir'd; disdain not such access to me.
    To whom our Saviour with unalter'd brow.

Thy coming hither, though I know thy scope,
I bid not or forbid; do as thou find'st
Permission from above; thou canst not more.
   He added not; and Satan bowing low
His gray dissimulation, disappear'd
Into thin Air diffus'd: for now began
Night with her sullen wing to double-shade   500
The Desert, Fowls in thir clay nests were couch't;
And now wild Beasts came forth the woods to roam.

The End of the First Book.

PARADISE REGAIN'D.

The Second Book.

MEAN while the new-baptiz'd, who yet remain'd
At *Jordan* with the Baptist, and had seen
Him whom they heard so late expresly call'd
Jesus Messiah Son of God declar'd,
And on that high Authority had believ'd,
And with him talkt, and with him lodg'd, I mean
Andrew and *Simon,* famous after known
With others though in Holy Writ not nam'd,
Now missing him thir joy so lately found,
So lately found, and so abruptly gone,   10
Began to doubt, and doubted many days,
And as the days increas'd, increas'd thir doubt:
Sometimes they thought he might be only shewn,
And for a time caught up to God, as once
Moses was in the Mount, and missing long;
And the great *Thisbite* who on fiery wheels
Rode up to Heaven, yet once again to come.
Therefore as those young Prophets then with care
Sought lost *Eliah,* so in each place these
Nigh to *Bethabara;* in *Jerico*   20
The City of Palms, *Ænon,* and *Salem* Old,
Machærus and each Town or City wall'd
On this side the broad lake *Genezaret,*
Or in *Perea,* but return'd in vain.
Then on the bank of *Jordan,* by a Creek:
Where winds with Reeds, and Osiers whisp'ring play
Plain Fishermen, no greater men them call,
Close in a Cottage low together got
Thir unexpected loss and plaints out breath'd.
Alas, from what high hope to what relapse   30
Unlook'd for are we fall'n, our eyes beheld
Messiah certainly now come, so long
Expected of our Fathers; we have heard
His words, his wisdom full of grace and truth,
Now, now, for sure, deliverance is at hand,
The Kingdom shall to *Israel* be restor'd:

Thus we rejoyc'd, but soon our joy is turn'd
Into perplexity and new amaze:
For whither is he gone, what accident
Hath rapt him from us? will he now retire   40
After appearance, and again prolong
Our expectation? God of *Israel,*
Send thy Messiah forth, the time is come;
Behold the Kings of the Earth how they oppress
Thy chosen, to what highth thir pow'r unjust
They have exalted, and behind them cast
All fear of thee, arise and vindicate
Thy Glory, free thy people from thir yoke,
But let us wait; thus far he hath perform'd,
Sent his Anointed, and to us reveal'd him,   50
By his great Prophet, pointed at and shown,
In publick, and with him we have convers'd;
Let us be glad of this, and all our fears
Lay on his Providence; he will not fail
Nor will withdraw him now, nor will recall,
Mock us with his blest sight, then snatch him hence,
Soon we shall see our hope, our joy return.
   Thus they out of their plaints new hope resume
To find whom at the first they found unsought:
But to his Mother *Mary,* when she saw   60
Others return'd from Baptism, not her Son,
Nor left at *Jordan,* tydings of him none;
Within her brest, though calm; her brest though pure,
Motherly cares and fears got head, and rais'd
Some troubl'd thoughts, which she in sighs thus clad.
   O what avails me now that honour high
To have conceiv'd of God, or that salute
Hale highly favour'd, among women blest;
While I to sorrows am no less advanc't,
And fears as eminent, above the lot   70
Of other women, by the birth I bore,
In such a season born when scarce a Shed
Could be obtain'd to shelter him or me
From the bleak air; a Stable was our warmth,
A Manger his, yet soon enforc't to flye
Thence into *Egypt,* till the Murd'rous King
Were dead, who sought his life, and missing fill'd
With Infant blood the streets of *Bethlehem;*
From *Egypt* home return'd, in *Nazareth*
Hath been our dwelling many years, his life   80
Private, unactive, calm, contemplative,
Little suspicious to any King; but now
Full grown to Man, acknowledg'd, as I hear,
By *John* the Baptist, and in publick shown,
Son own'd from Heaven by his Father's voice;
I look't for some great change; to Honour? no,
But trouble, as old *Simeon* plain fore-told,
That to the fall and rising he should be
Of many in *Israel,* and to a sign

Spoken against, that through my very Soul
A sword shall pierce, this is my favour'd lot,
My Exaltation to Afflictions high;
Afflicted I may be, it seems, and blest;
I will not argue that, nor will repine.
But where delays he now? some great intent
Conceals him: when twelve years he scarce had seen,
I lost him, but so found, as well I saw
He could not lose himself; but went about
His Father's business; what he meant I mus'd,
Since understand; much more his absence now   100
Thus long to some great purpose he obscures.
But I to wait with patience am inur'd;
My heart hath been a store-house long of things
And sayings laid up, portending strange events.
   Thus *Mary* pondering oft, and oft to mind
Recalling what remarkably had pass'd
Since first her Salutation heard, with thoughts
Meekly compos'd awaited the fulfilling:
The while her Son tracing the Desert wild,
Sole but with holiest Meditations fed,   110
Into himself descended, and at once
All his great work to come before him set;
How to begin, how to accomplish best
His end of being on Earth, and mission high:
For Satan with slye preface to return
Had left him vacant, and with speed was gon
Up to the middle Region of thick Air,
Where all his Potentates in Council sate;
There without sign of boast, or sign of joy,
Sollicitous and blank he thus began.   120
    Princes, Heavens antient Sons, Æthereal Thrones,
Demonian Spirits now, from the Element
Each of his reign allotted, rightlier call'd,
Powers of Fire, Air, Water, and Earth beneath,
So may we hold our place and these mild seats
Without new trouble; such an Enemy
Is ris'n to invade us, who no less
Threat'ns then our expulsion down to Hell;
I, as I undertook, and with the vote
Consenting in full frequence was impowr'd,   130
Have found him, view'd him, tasted him, but find
Far other labour to be undergon
Then when I dealt with *Adam* first of Men,
Though *Adam* by his Wives allurement fell,
However to this Man inferior far,
If he be Man by Mothers side at least,
With more then humane gifts from Heaven adorn'd,
Perfections absolute, Graces divine,
And amplitude of mind to greatest Deeds.
Therefore I am return'd, lest confidence   140
Of my success with *Eve* in Paradise
Deceive ye to perswasion over-sure

Of like succeeding here; I summon all
Rather to be in readiness, with hand
Or counsel to assist; lest I who erst
Thought none my equal, now be over-match'd.
　So spake the old Serpent doubting, and from all
With clamour was assur'd thir utmost aid
At his command; when from amidst them rose
Belial the dissolutest Spirit that fell,　　　　　　　　　　150
The sensuallest, and after *Asmodai*
The fleshliest Incubus, and thus advis'd.
　Set women in his eye and in his walk,
Among daughters of men the fairest found;
Many are in each Region passing fair
As the noon Skie; more like to Goddesses
Then Mortal Creatures, graceful and discreet,
Expert in amorous Arts, enchanting tongues
Perswasive, Virgin majesty with mild
And sweet allay'd, yet terrible to approach,　　　　　　　　160
Skill'd to retire, and in retiring draw
Hearts after them tangl'd in Amorous Nets.
Such object hath the power to soft'n and tame
Severest temper, smooth the rugged'st brow,
Enerve, and with voluptuous hope dissolve,
Draw out with credulous desire, and lead
At will the manliest, resolutest brest,
As the Magnetic hardest Iron draws.
Women, when nothing else, beguil'd the heart
Of wisest *Solomon,* and made him build,　　　　　　　　170
And made him bow to the Gods of his Wives.
　To whom quick answer Satan thus return'd.
Belial, in much uneven scale thou weigh'st
All others by thy self; because of old
Thou thy self doat'st on womankind, admiring
Thir shape, thir colour, and attractive grace,
None are, thou think'st, but taken with such toys.
Before the Flood thou with thy lusty Crew,
False titl'd Sons of God, roaming the Earth
Cast wanton eyes on the daughters of men,　　　　　　　　180
And coupl'd with them, and begot a race.
Have we not seen, or by relation heard,
In Courts and Regal Chambers how thou lurk'st,
In Wood or Grove by mossie Fountain side,
In Valley or Green Meadow to way-lay
Some beauty rare, *Calisto, Clymene,*
Daphne, or *Semele, Antiopa,*
Or *Amymone, Syrinx,* many more
Too long, then lay'st thy scapes on names ador'd,
Apollo, Neptune, Jupiter, or *Pan,*　　　　　　　　190
Satyr, or Fawn, or Silvan? But these haunts
Delight not all; among the Sons of Men,
How many have with a smile made small account
Of beauty and her lures, easily scorn'd
All her assaults, on worthier things intent?

Remember that *Pellean* Conquerour,
A youth, how all the Beauties of the East
He slightly view'd, and slightly over-pass'd;
How hee sirnam'd of *Africa* dismiss'd
In his prime youth the fair *Iberian* maid.   200
For *Solomon* he liv'd at ease, and full
Of honour, wealth, high fare, aim'd not beyond
Higher design then to enjoy his State;
Thence to the bait of Women lay expos'd;
But he whom we attempt is wiser far
Then *Solomon,* of more exalted mind,
Made and set wholly on the accomplishment
Of greatest things; what woman will you find,
Though of this Age the wonder and the fame,
On whom his leisure will vouchsafe an eye   210
Of fond desire? or should she confident,
As sitting Queen ador'd on Beauties Throne,
Descend with all her winning charms begirt
To enamour, as the Zone of *Venus* once
Wrought that effect on *Jove,* so Fables tell;
How would one look from his Majestick brow
Seated as on the top of Vertues hill,
Discount'nance her despis'd, and put to rout
All her array; her female pride deject,
Or turn to reverent awe? for Beauty stands   220
In the admiration only of weak minds
Led captive; cease to admire, and all her Plumes
Fall flat and shrink into a trivial toy,
At every sudden slighting quite abasht:
Therefore with manlier objects we must try
His constancy, with such as have more shew
Of worth, of honour, glory, and popular praise;
Rocks whereon greatest men have oftest wreck'd;
Or that which only seems to satisfie
Lawful desires of Nature, not beyond;   230
And now I know he hungers where no food
Is to be found, in the wide Wilderness;
The rest commit to me, I shall let pass
No advantage, and his strength as oft assay.
  He ceas'd, and heard thir grant in loud acclaim;
Then forthwith to him takes a chosen band
Of Spirits likest to himself in guile
To be at hand, and at his beck appear,
If cause were to unfold some active Scene
Of various persons each to know his part;   240
Then to the Desert takes with these his flight;
Where still from shade to shade the Son of God
After forty days fasting had remain'd,
Now hungring first, and to himself thus said.
  Where will this end? four times ten days I have pass'd
Wandring this woody maze, and humane food
Nor tasted, nor had appetite; that Fast
To Vertue I impute not, or count part

Of what I suffer here; if Nature need not,
Or God support Nature without repast   250
Though needing, what praise is it to endure?
But now I feel I hunger, which declares,
Nature hath need of what she asks; yet God
Can satisfie that need some other way,
Though hunger still remain: so it remain
Without this bodies wasting, I content me,
And from the sting of Famine fear no harm,
Nor mind it, fed with better thoughts that feed
Mee hungring more to do my Fathers will.
   It was the hour of night, when thus the Son   260
Commun'd in silent walk, then laid him down
Under the hospitable covert nigh
Of Trees thick interwoven; there he slept,
And dream'd, as appetite is wont to dream,
Of meats and drinks, Natures refreshment sweet;
Him thought, he by the Brook of *Cherith* stood
And saw the Ravens with their horny beaks
Food to *Elijah* bringing Even and Morn,
Though ravenous, taught to abstain from what they brought:
He saw the Prophet also how he fled   270
Into the Desert, and how there he slept
Under a Juniper; then how awakt,
He found his Supper on the coals prepar'd,
And by the Angel was bid rise and eat,
And eat the second time after repose,
The strength whereof suffic'd him forty days;
Sometimes that with *Elijah* he partook,
Or as a guest with *Daniel* at his pulse.
Thus wore out night, and now the Herald Lark
Left his ground-nest, high towring to descry   280
The morns approach, and greet her with his Song:
As lightly from his grassy Couch up rose
Our Saviour, and found all was but a dream,
Fasting he went to sleep, and fasting wak'd.
Up to a hill anon his steps he rear'd,
From whose high top to ken the prospect round,
If Cottage were in view, Sheep-cote or Herd;
But Cottage, Herd or Sheep-cote none he saw,
Only in a bottom saw a pleasant Grove,
With chaunt of tuneful Birds resounding loud;   290
Thither he bent his way, determin'd there
To rest at noon, and entr'd soon the shade
High rooft and walks beneath, and alleys brown
That open'd in the midst a woody Scene,
Natures own work it seem'd (Nature taught Art)
And to a Superstitious eye the haunt
Of Wood-Gods and Wood-Nymphs; he view'd it round,
When suddenly a man before him stood,
Not rustic as before, but seemlier clad,
As one in City, or Court, or Palace bred,   300
And with fair speech these words to him address'd.

With granted leave officious I return,
But much more wonder that the Son of God
In this wild solitude so long should bide
Of all things destitute, and well I know,
Not without hunger. Others of some note,
As story tells, have trod this Wilderness;
The Fugitive Bond-woman with her Son
Out cast *Nebaioth,* yet found he relief
By a providing Angel; all the race   310
Of *Israel* here had famish'd, had not God
Rain'd from Heaven Manna, and that Prophet bold
Native of *Thebez* wandring here was fed
Twice by a voice inviting him to eat.
Of thee these forty days none hath regard,
Forty and more deserted here indeed.
    To whom thus Jesus; what conclud'st thou hence?
They all had need, I as thou seest have none.
    How hast thou hunger then? Satan reply'd,
Tell me if Food were now before thee set,   320
Would'st thou not eat? Thereafter as I like
The giver, answer'd Jesus. Why should that
Cause thy refusal, said the subtle Fiend,
Hast thou not right to all Created things,
Owe not all Creatures by just right to thee
Duty and Service, nor to stay till bid,
But tender all their power? nor mention I
Meats by the Law unclean, or offer'd first
To Idols, those young *Daniel* could refuse;
Nor proffer'd by an Enemy, though who   330
Would scruple that, with want opprest? behold
Nature asham'd, or better to express,
Troubl'd that thou shouldst hunger, hath purvey'd
From all the Elements her choicest store
To treat thee as beseems, and as her Lord
With honour, only deign to sit and eat.
    He spake no dream, for as his words had end,
Our Saviour lifting up his eyes beheld
In ample space under the broadest shade
A Table richly spred, in regal mode,   340
With dishes pil'd, and meats of noblest sort
And savour, Beasts of chase, or Fowl of game,
In pastry built, or from the spit, or boyl'd,
Gris-amber-steam'd; all Fish from Sea or Shore,
Freshet, or purling Brook, of shell or fin,
And exquisitest name, for which was drain'd
Pontus and *Lucrine* Bay, and *Afric* Coast.
Alas how simple, to these Cates compar'd,
Was that crude Apple that diverted *Eve!*
And at a stately side-board by the wine   350
That fragrant smell diffus'd, in order stood
Tall stripling youths rich clad, of fairer hew
Then *Ganymed* or *Hylas,* distant more
Under the Trees now trip'd, now solemn stood

Nymphs of *Diana*'s train, and *Naiades*
With fruits and flowers from *Amalthea*'s horn,
And Ladies of th' *Hesperides,* that seem'd
Fairer then feign'd of old, or fabl'd since
Of Fairy Damsels met in Forest wide
By Knights of *Logres,* or of *Lyones,*   360
Lancelot or *Pelleas,* or *Pellenore,*
And all the while Harmonious Airs were heard
Of chiming strings, or charming pipes and winds
Of gentlest gale *Arabian* odors fann'd
From their soft wings, and *Flora*'s earliest smells.
Such was the Splendour, and the Tempter now
His invitation earnestly renew'd.
    What doubts the Son of God to sit and eat?
These are not Fruits forbidden, no interdict
Defends the touching of these viands pure,   370
Thir taste no knowledge works, at least of evil,
But life preserves, destroys life's enemy,
Hunger, with sweet restorative delight.
All these are Spirits of Air, and Woods, and Springs,
Thy gentle Ministers, who come to pay
Thee homage, and acknowledge thee thir Lord:
What doubt'st thou Son of God? sit down and eat.
    To whom thus Jesus temperately reply'd:
Said'st thou not that to all things I had right?
And who withholds my pow'r that right to use?   380
Shall I receive by gift what of my own,
When and where likes me best, I can command?
I can at will, doubt not, as soon as thou,
Command a Table in this Wilderness,
And call swift flights of Angels ministrant
Array'd in Glory on my cup to attend:
Why shouldst thou then obtrude this diligence,
In vain, where no acceptance it can find,
And with my hunger what hast thou to do?
Thy pompous Delicacies I contemn,   390
And count thy specious gifts no gifts but guiles.
    To whom thus answer'd Satan malecontent:
That I have also power to give thou seest,
If of that pow'r I bring thee voluntary
What I might have bestow'd on whom I pleas'd,
And rather opportunely in this place
Chose to impart to thy apparent need,
Why shouldst thou not accept it? but I see
What I can do or offer is suspect;
Of these things others quickly will dispose   400
Whose pains have earn'd the far fet spoil. With that
Both Table and Provision vanish'd quite
With sound of Harpies wings, and Talons heard;
Only the importune Tempter still remain'd,
And with these words his temptation pursu'd.
    By hunger, that each other Creature tames,
Thou art not to be harm'd, therefore not mov'd:

Thy temperance invincible besides,
For no allurement yields to appetite,
And all thy heart is set on high designs,   410
High actions; but wherewith to be atchiev'd?
Great acts require great means of enterprise,
Thou art unknown, unfriended, low of birth,
A Carpenter thy Father known, thy self
Bred up in poverty and streights at home;
Lost in a Desert here and hunger-bit:
Which way or from what hope dost thou aspire
To greatness? whence Authority deriv'st,
What Followers, what Retinue canst thou gain,
Or at thy heels the dizzy Multitude,   420
Longer then thou canst feed them on thy cost?
Money brings Honour, Friends, Conquest, and Realms;
What rais'd *Antipater* the *Edomite,*
And his Son *Herod* plac'd on *Juda's* Throne;
(Thy throne) but gold that got him puissant friends?
Therefore, if at great things thou wouldst arrive,
Get Riches first, get Wealth, and Treasure heap,
Not difficult, if thou hearken to me,
Riches are mine, Fortune is in my hand;
They whom I favour thrive in wealth amain,   430
While Virtue, Valour, Wisdom sit in want.
     To whom thus Jesus patiently reply'd;
Yet Wealth without these three is impotent,
To gain dominion or to keep it gain'd.
Witness those antient Empires of the Earth,
In highth of all thir flowing wealth dissolv'd:
But men endu'd with these have oft attain'd
In lowest poverty to highest deeds;
Gideon and *Jephtha,* and the Shepherd lad,
Whose off-spring on the Throne of *Juda* sat   440
So many Ages, and shall yet regain
That seat, and reign in *Israel* without end.
Among the Heathen, (for throughout the World
To me is not unknown what hath been done
Worthy of Memorial) canst thou not remember
Quintius, Fabricius, Curius, Regulus?
For I esteem those names of men so poor
Who could do mighty things, and could contemn
Riches though offer'd from the hand of Kings.
And what in me seems wanting, but that I   450
May also in this poverty as soon
Accomplish what they did, perhaps and more?
Extol not Riches then, the toyl of Fools,
The wise mans cumbrance if not snare, more apt
To slacken Virtue, and abate her edge,
Then prompt her to do aught may merit praise.
What if with like aversion I reject
Riches and Realms; yet not for that a Crown,
Golden in shew, is but a wreath of thorns,
Brings dangers, troubles, cares, and sleepless nights   400

To him who wears the Regal Diadem,
When on his shoulders each mans burden lies;
For therein stands the office of a King,
His Honour, Vertue, Merit and chief Praise,
That for the Publick all this weight he bears.
Yet he who reigns within himself, and rules
Passions, Desires, and Fears, is more a King;
Which every wise and vertuous man attains:
And who attains not, ill aspires to rule
Cities of men, or head-strong Multitudes,   470
Subject himself to Anarchy within,
Or lawless passions in him which he serves.
But to guide Nations in the way of truth
By saving Doctrine, and from errour lead
To know, and knowing worship God aright,
Is yet more Kingly, this attracts the Soul,
Governs the inner man, the nobler part,
That other o're the body only reigns,
And oft by force, which to a generous mind
So reigning can be no sincere delight.   480
Besides to give a Kingdom hath been thought
Greater and nobler done, and to lay down
Far more magnanimous, then to assume.
Riches are needless then, both for themselves,
And for thy reason why they should be sought,
To gain a Scepter, oftest better miss't.

The End of the Second Book.

PARADISE REGAIN'D.

The Third Book.

So spake the Son of God, and Satan stood
A while as mute confounded what to say,
What to reply, confuted and convinc't
Of his weak arguing, and fallacious drift;
At length collecting all his Serpent wiles,
With soothing words renew'd, him thus accosts.
   I see thou know'st what is of use to know,
What best to say canst say, to do canst do;
Thy actions to thy words accord, thy words
To thy large heart give utterance due, thy heart   10
Conteins of good, wise, just, the perfect shape.
Should Kings and Nations from thy mouth consult,
Thy Counsel would be as the Oracle
Urim and *Thummim,* those oraculous gems
On *Aaron's* breast: or tongue of Seers old
Infallible; or wert thou sought to deeds
That might require th' array of war, thy skill
Of conduct would be such, that all the world
Could not sustain thy Prowess, or subsist

In battel, though against thy few in arms.   20
These God-like Vertues wherefore dost thou hide?
Affecting private life, or more obscure
In savage Wilderness, wherefore deprive
All Earth her wonder at thy acts, thy self
The fame and glory, glory the reward
That sole excites to high attempts the flame
Of most erected Spirits, most temper'd pure
Ætherial, who all pleasures else despise,
All treasures and all gain esteem as dross,
And dignities and powers all but the highest?   30
Thy years are ripe, and over-ripe, the Son
Of *Macedonian Philip* had e're these
Won *Asia* and the Throne of *Cyrus* held
At his dispose, young *Scipio* had brought down
The *Carthaginian* pride, young *Pompey* quell'd
The *Pontic* King and in triumph had rode.
Yet years, and to ripe years judgment mature,
Quench not the thirst of glory, but augment.
Great *Julius,* whom now all the world admires
The more he grew in years, the more inflam'd   40
With glory, wept that he had liv'd so long
Inglorious: but thou yet art not too late.
    To whom our Saviour calmly thus reply'd.
Thou neither dost perswade me to seek wealth
For Empires sake, nor Empire to affect
For glories sake by all thy argument.
For what is glory but the blaze of fame,
The peoples praise, if always praise unmixt?
And what the people but a herd confus'd,
A miscellaneous rabble, who extol   50
Things vulgar, & well weigh'd, scarce worth the praise.
They praise and they admire they know not what;
And know not whom, but as one leads the other;
And what delight to be by such extoll'd,
To live upon thir tongues and be thir talk,
Of whom to be disprais'd were no small praise?
His lot who dares be singularly good.
Th' intelligent among them and the wise
Are few, and glory scarce of few is rais'd.
This is true glory and renown, when God   60
Looking on the Earth, with approbation marks
The just man, and divulges him through Heaven
To all his Angels, who with true applause
Recount his praises; thus he did to *Job,*
When to extend his fame through Heaven & Earth,
As thou to thy reproach mayst well remember,
He ask'd thee, hast thou seen my servant *Job?*
Famous he was in Heaven, on Earth less known;
Where glory is false glory, attributed
To things not glorious, men not worthy of fame.   70
They err who count it glorious to subdue
By Conquest far and wide, to over-run

Large Countries, and in field great Battels win,
Great Cities by assault: what do these Worthies,
But rob and spoil, burn, slaughter, and enslave
Peaceable Nations, neighbouring, or remote,
Made Captive, yet deserving freedom more
Then those thir Conquerours, who leave behind
Nothing but ruin wheresoe're they rove,
And all the flourishing works of peace destroy,   80
Then swell with pride, and must be titl'd Gods,
Great Benefactors of mankind, Deliverers,
Worship't with Temple, Priest and Sacrifice;
One is the Son of *Jove,* of *Mars* the other,
Till Conquerour Death discover them scarce men,
Rowling in brutish vices, and deform'd,
Violent or shameful death thir due reward.
But if there be in glory aught of good,
It may by means far different be attain'd
Without ambition, war, or violence;   90
By deeds of peace, by wisdom eminent,
By patience, temperance; I mention still
Him whom thy wrongs with Saintly patience born,
Made famous in a Land and times obscure;
Who names not now with honour patient *Job?*
Poor *Socrates* (who next more memorable?)
By what he taught and suffer'd for so doing,
For truths sake suffering death unjust, lives now
Equal in fame to proudest Conquerours.
Yet if for fame and glory aught be done,   100
Aught suffer'd; if young *African* for fame
His wasted Country freed from *Punic* rage,
The deed becomes unprais'd, the man at least,
And loses, though but verbal, his reward.
Shall I seek glory then, as vain men seek
Oft not deserv'd? I seek not mine, but his
Who sent me, and thereby witness whence I am.
   To whom the Tempter murmuring thus reply'd.
Think not so slight of glory; therein least
Resembling thy great Father: he seeks glory,   110
And for his glory all things made, all things
Orders and governs, nor content in Heaven
By all his Angels glorifi'd, requires
Glory from men, from all men good or bad,
Wise or unwise, no difference, no exemption;
Above all Sacrifice, or hallow'd gift
Glory he requires, and glory he receives
Promiscuous from all Nations, Jew, or Greek,
Or Barbarous, nor exception hath declar'd;
From us his foes pronounc't glory he exacts.   120
   To whom our Saviour fervently reply'd.
And reason; since his word all things produc'd,
Though chiefly not for glory as prime end,
But to shew forth his goodness, and impart
His good communicable to every soul

Freely; of whom what could he less expect
Then glory and benediction, that is thanks,
The slightest, easiest, readiest recompence
From them who could return him nothing else,
And not returning that would likeliest render   130
Contempt instead, dishonour, obloquy?
Hard recompence, unsutable return
For so much good, so much beneficence.
But why should man seek glory? who of his own
Hath nothing, and to whom nothing belongs
But condemnation, ignominy, and shame?
Who for so many benefits receiv'd
Turn'd recreant to God, ingrate and false,
And so of all true good himself despoil'd,
Yet, sacrilegious, to himself would take   140
That which to God alone of right belongs;
Yet so much bounty is in God, such grace,
That who advance his glory, not thir own,
Them he himself to glory will advance.
    So spake the Son of God; and here again
Satan had not to answer, but stood struck
With guilt of his own sin, for he himself
Insatiable of glory had lost all.
Yet of another Plea bethought him soon.
    Of glory as thou wilt, said he, so deem,   150
Worth or not worth the seeking, let it pass:
But to a Kingdom thou art born, ordain'd
To sit upon thy Father *David*'s Throne;
By Mother's side thy Father, though thy right
Be now in powerful hands, that will not part
Easily from possession won with arms;
Judæa now and all the promis'd land
Reduc't a Province under Roman yoke,
Obeys *Tiberius;* nor is always rul'd
With temperate sway; oft have they violated   160
The Temple, oft the Law with foul affronts,
Abominations rather, as did once
Antiochus: and think'st thou to regain
Thy right by sitting still or thus retiring?
So did not *Machabeus:* he indeed
Retir'd unto the Desert, but with arms;
And o're a mighty King so oft prevail'd,
That by strong hand his Family obtain'd,
Though Priests, the Crown, and *David*'s Throne usurp'd,
With *Modin* and her Suburbs once content.   170
If Kingdom move thee not, let move thee Zeal,
And Duty; Zeal and Duty are not slow;
But on Occasions forelock watchful wait.
They themselves rather are occasion best,
Zeal of thy Fathers house, Duty to free
Thy Country from her Heathen servitude;
So shalt thou best fullfil, best verifie
The Prophets old, who sung thy endless raign,

The happier raign the sooner it begins,
Raign then; what canst thou better do the while?   180
    To whom our Saviour answer thus return'd.
All things are best fullfil'd in their due time,
And time there is for all things, Truth hath said:
If of my raign Prophetic Writ hath told
That it shall never end, so when begin
The Father in his purpose hath decreed,
He in whose hand all times and seasons roul.
What if he hath decreed that I shall first
Be try'd in humble state, and things adverse,
By tribulations, injuries, insults,   190
Contempts, and scorns, and snares, and violence,
Suffering, abstaining, quietly expecting
Without distrust or doubt, that he may know
What I can suffer, how obey? who best
Can suffer, best can do; best reign, who first
Well hath obey'd; just tryal e're I merit
My exaltation without change or end.
But what concerns it thee when I begin
My everlasting Kingdom, why art thou
Sollicitous, what moves thy inquisition?   200
Know'st thou not that my rising is thy fall,
And my promotion will be thy destruction?
    To whom the Tempter inly rackt reply'd.
Let that come when it comes; all hope is lost
Of my reception into grace; what worse?
For where no hope is left, is left no fear;
If there be worse, the expectation more
Of worse torments me then the feeling can.
I would be at the worst; worst is my Port,
My harbour and my ultimate repose,   210
The end I would attain, my final good.
My error was my error, and my crime
My crime; whatever for it self condemn'd,
And will alike be punish'd; whether thou
Raign or raign not; though to that gentle brow
Willingly I could flye, and hope thy raign,
From that placid aspect and meek regard,
Rather then aggravate my evil state,
Would stand between me and thy Fathers ire,
(Whose ire I dread more then the fire of Hell)   220
A shelter and a kind of shading cool
Interposition, as a summers cloud.
If I then to the worst that can be hast,
Why move thy feet so slow to what is best,
Happiest both to thy self and all the world,
That thou who worthiest art should'st be thir King?
Perhaps thou linger'st in deep thoughts detain'd
Of the enterprize so hazardous and high;
No wonder, for though in thee be united
What of perfection can in man be found,   230
Or human nature can receive, consider

Thy life hath yet been private, most part spent
At home, scarce view'd the *Gallilean* Towns,
And once a year *Jerusalem,* few days
Short sojourn; and what thence could'st thou observe?
The world thou hast not seen, much less her glory,
Empires, and Monarchs, and thir radiant Courts,
Best school of best experience, quickest in sight
In all things that to greatest actions lead.
The wisest, unexperienc't, will be ever   240
Timorous and loath, with novice modesty,
(As he who seeking Asses found a Kingdom)
Irresolute, unhardy, unadventrous:
But I will bring thee where thou soon shalt quit
Those rudiments, and see before thine eyes
The Monarchies of the Earth, thir pomp and state,
Sufficient introduction to inform
Thee, of thy self so apt, in regal Arts,
And regal Mysteries; that thou may'st know
How best their opposition to withstand.   250
    With that (such power was giv'n him then) he took
The Son of God up to a Mountain high.
It was a Mountain at whose verdant feet
A spatious plain out stretch't in circuit wide
Lay pleasant; from his side two rivers flow'd,
Th' one winding, the other strait and left between
Fair Champain with less rivers interveind,
Then meeting joyn'd thir tribute to the Sea:
Fertil of corn the glebe, of oyl and wine,
With herds the pastures throng'd, with flocks the hills,   260
Huge Cities and high towr'd, that well might seem
The seats of mightiest Monarchs, and so large
The Prospect was, that here and there was room
For barren desert fountainless and dry.
To this high mountain top the Tempter brought
Our Saviour, and new train of words began.
    Well have we speeded, and o're hill and dale,
Forest and field, and flood, Temples and Towers
Cut shorter many a league; here thou behold'st
Assyria and her Empires antient bounds,   270
Araxes and the *Caspian* lake, thence on
As far as *Indus* East, *Euphrates* West,
And oft beyond; to South the *Persian* Bay,
And inaccessible the *Arabian* drouth:
Here *Ninevee,* of length within her wall
Several days journey, built by *Ninus* old,
Of that first golden Monarchy the seat,
And seat of *Salmanassar,* whose success
Israel in long captivity still mourns;
There *Babylon* the wonder of all tongues,   280
As antient, but rebuilt by him who twice
Judah and all thy Father *David*'s house
Led captive, and *Jerusalem* laid waste,
Till *Cyrus* set them free; *Persepolis*

His City there thou seest, and *Bactra* there;
Ecbatana her structure vast there shews,
And *Hecatompylos* her hunderd gates,
There *Susa* by *Choaspes,* amber stream,
The drink of none but Kings; of later fame
Built by *Emathian,* or by *Parthian* hands,   290
The great *Seleucia, Nisibis,* and there
Artaxata, Teredon, Tesiphon,
Turning with easie eye thou may'st behold.
All these the *Parthian,* now some Ages past,
By great *Arsaces* led, who founded first
That Empire, under his dominion holds
From the luxurious Kings of *Antioch* won.
And just in time thou com'st to have a view
Of his great power; for now the *Parthian* King
In *Ctesiphon* hath gather'd all his Host   300
Against the *Scythian,* whose incursions wild
Have wasted *Sogdiana;* to her aid
He marches now in hast; see, though from far,
His thousands, in what martial equipage
They issue forth, Steel Bows, and Shafts their arms
Of equal dread in flight, or in pursuit;
All Horsemen, in which fight they most excel;
See how in warlike muster they appear,
In Rhombs and wedges, and half moons, and wings.
    He look't and saw what numbers numberless   310
The City gates out powr'd, light armed Troops
In coats of Mail and military pride;
In Mail thir horses clad, yet fleet and strong,
Prauncing their riders bore, the flower and choice
Of many Provinces from bound to bound;
From *Arachosia,* from *Candaor* East,
And *Margiana* to the *Hyrcanian* cliffs
Of *Caucasus,* and dark *Iberian* dales,
From *Atropatia* and the neighbouring plains
Of *Adiabene, Media,* and the South   320
Of *Susiana* to *Balsara's* hav'n.
He saw them in thir forms of battell rang'd,
How quick they wheel'd, and flying behind them shot
Sharp sleet of arrowie showers against the face
Of thir pursuers, and overcame by flight;
The field all iron cast a gleaming brown,
Nor wanted clouds of foot, nor on each horn,
Cuirassiers all in steel for standing fight;
Chariots or Elephants endorst with Towers
Of Archers, nor of labouring Pioners   330
A multitude with Spades and Axes arm'd
To lay hills plain, fell woods, or valleys fill,
Or where plain was raise hill, or over-lay
With bridges rivers proud, as with a yoke;
Mules after these, Camels and Dromedaries,
And Waggons fraught with Utensils of war.
Such forces met not, nor so wide a camp,

When *Agrican* with all his Northern powers
Besieg'd *Albracca,* as Romances tell;
The City of *Gallaphrone,* from thence to win   340
The fairest of her Sex *Angelica*
His daughter, sought by many Prowest Knights,
Both *Paynim,* and the Peers of *Charlemane.*
Such and so numerous was thir Chivalrie;
At sight whereof the Fiend yet more presum'd,
And to our Saviour thus his words renew'd.
    That thou may'st know I seek not to engage
Thy Vertue, and not every way secure
On no slight grounds thy safety; hear, and mark
To what end I have brought thee hither and shewn   350
All this fair sight; thy Kingdom though foretold
By Prophet or by Angel, unless thou
Endeavour, as thy Father *David* did,
Thou never shalt obtain; prediction still
In all things, and all men, supposes means,
Without means us'd, what it predicts revokes.
But say thou wer't possess'd of *David's* Throne
By free consent of all, none opposite,
Samaritan or *Jew;* how could'st thou hope
Long to enjoy it quiet and secure,   360
Between two such enclosing enemies
Roman and *Parthian?* therefore one of these
Thou must make sure thy own, the *Parthian* first
By my advice, as nearer and of late
Found able by invasion to annoy
Thy country, and captive lead away her Kings
Antigonus, and old *Hyrcanus* bound,
Maugre the *Roman:* it shall be my task
To render thee the *Parthian* at dispose;
Chuse which thou wilt by conquest or by league.   370
By him thou shalt regain, without him not,
That which alone can truly reinstall thee
In *David's* royal seat, his true Successour,
Deliverance of thy brethren, those ten Tribes
Whose off-spring in his Territory yet serve
In *Habor,* and among the *Medes* dispers't,
Ten Sons of *Jacob,* two of *Joseph* lost
Thus long from *Israel;* serving as of old
Thir Fathers in the land of *Egypt* serv'd,
This offer sets before thee to deliver.   380
These if from servitude thou shalt restore
To thir inheritance, then, nor till then,
Thou on the Throne of *David* in full glory,
From *Egypt* to *Euphrates* and beyond
Shalt raign, and *Rome* or *Cæsar* not need fear.
    To whom our Saviour answer'd thus unmov'd.
Much ostentation vain of fleshly arm,
And fragile arms, much instrument of war
Long in preparing, soon to nothing brought,

Before mine eyes thou hast set; and in my ear   390
Vented much policy, and projects deep
Of enemies, of aids, battels and leagues,
Plausible to the world, to me worth naught.
Means I must use thou say'st, prediction else
Will unpredict and fail me of the Throne:
My time I told thee, (and that time for thee
Were better farthest off) is not yet come;
When that comes think not thou to find me slack
On my part aught endeavouring, or to need
Thy politic maxims, or that cumbersome   400
Luggage of war there shewn me, argument
Of human weakness rather then of strength.
My brethren, as thou call'st them; those Ten Tribes
I must deliver, if I mean to raign
David's true heir, and his full Scepter sway
To just extent over all Israel's Sons;
But whence to thee this zeal, where was it then
For Israel, or for David, or his Throne,
When thou stood'st up his Tempter to the pride
Of numbring Israel, which cost the lives   410
Of threescore and ten thousand Israelites
By three days Pestilence? such was thy zeal
To Israel then, the same that now to me.
As for those captive Tribes, themselves were they
Who wrought their own captivity, fell off
From God to worship Calves, the Deities
Of Egypt, Baal next and Ashtaroth,
And all the Idolatries of Heathen round,
Besides thir other worse then heathenish crimes;
Nor in the land of their captivity   420
Humbled themselves, or penitent besought
The God of their fore-fathers; but so dy'd
Impenitent, and left a race behind
Like to themselves, distinguishable scarce
From Gentils, but by Circumcision vain,
And God with Idols in their worship joyn'd.
Should I of these the liberty regard,
Who freed, as to their antient Patrimony,
Unhumbl'd, unrepentant, unreform'd,
Headlong would follow; and to thir Gods perhaps   430
Of Bethel and of Dan? no, let them serve
Thir enemies, who serve Idols with God.
Yet he at length, time to himself best known,
Remembring Abraham by some wond'rous call
May bring them back repentant and sincere,
And at their passing cleave the Assyrian flood,
While to their native land with joy they hast,
As the Red Sea and Jordan once he cleft,
When to the promis'd land thir Fathers pass'd;
To his due time and providence I leave them.   440
  So spake Israel's true King, and to the Fiend

Made answer meet, that made void all his wiles.
So fares it when with truth falshood contends.

The End of the Third Book.

PARADISE REGAIN'D.

The Fourth Book.

PERPLEX'D and troubl'd at his bad success
The Tempter stood, nor had what to reply,
Discover'd in his fraud, thrown from his hope,
So oft, and the perswasive Rhetoric
That sleek't his tongue, and won so much on *Eve,*
So little here, nay lost; but *Eve* was *Eve,*
This far his over-match, who self deceiv'd
And rash, before-hand had no better weigh'd
The strength he was to cope with, or his own:
But as a man who had been matchless held   10
In cunning, over-reach't where least he thought,
To salve his credit, and for very spight
Still will be tempting him who foyls him still,
And never cease, though to his shame the more;
Or as a swarm of flies in vintage time,
About the wine-press where sweet moust is powr'd,
Beat off, returns as oft with humming sound;
Or surging waves against a solid rock,
Though all to shivers dash't, the assault renew,
Vain battry, and in froth or bubbles end: 20
So Satan, whom repulse upon repulse
Met ever; and to shameful silence brought,
Yet gives not o're though desperate of success,
And his vain importunity pursues.
He brought our Saviour to the western side
Of that high mountain, whence he might behold
Another plain, long but in bredth not wide;
Wash'd by the Southern Sea, and on the North
To equal length back'd with a ridge of hills
That screen'd the fruits of the earth and seats of men   30
From cold *Septentrion* blasts, thence in the midst
Divided by a river, of whose banks
On each side an Imperial City stood,
With Towers and Temples proudly elevate
On seven small Hills, with Palaces adorn'd,
Porches and Theatres, Baths, Aqueducts,
Statues and Trophees, and Triumphal Arcs,
Gardens and Groves presented to his eyes,
Above the highth of Mountains interpos'd.
By what strange Parallax or Optic skill   40
Of vision multiplyed through air, or glass
Of Telescope, were curious to enquire:
And now the Tempter thus his silence broke.
The City which thou seest no other deem

Then great and glorious *Rome,* Queen of the Earth
So far renown'd, and with the spoils enricht
Of Nations; there the Capitol thou seest
Above the rest lifting his stately head
On the *Tarpeian* rock, her Cittadel
Impregnable, and there Mount *Palatine*   50
The Imperial Palace, compass huge, and high
The Structure, skill of noblest Architects,
With gilded battlements, conspicuous far,
Turrets and Terrases, and glittering Spires.
Many a fair Edifice besides, more like
Houses of Gods (so well I have dispos'd.
My Aerie Microscope) thou may'st behold
Outside and inside both, pillars and roofs
Carv'd work, the hand of fam'd Artificers
In Cedar, Marble, Ivory or Gold.   60
Thence to the gates cast round thine eye, and see
What conflux issuing forth, or entring in,
Pretors, Proconsuls to thir Provinces
Hasting or on return, in robes of State;
Lictors and rods the ensigns of thir power,
Legions and Cohorts, turmes of horse and wings:
Or Embassies from Regions far remote
In various habits on the *Appian* road,
Or on the *Æmilian,* some from farthest South,
Syene, and where the shadow both way falls,   70
Meroe Nilotic Isle, and more to West,
The Realm of *Bocchus* to the Black-moor Sea;
From the *Asian* Kings and *Parthian* among these,
From *India* and the golden *Chersoness,*
And utmost *Indian* Isle *Taprobane,*
Dusk faces with white silken Turbants wreath'd:
From *Gallia, Gades,* and the *Brittish* West,
Germans and *Scythians,* and *Sarmatians* North
Beyond *Danubius* to the *Tauric* Pool.
All Nations now to *Rome* obedience pay,   80
To *Rome's* great Emperour, whose wide domain
In ample Territory, wealth and power,
Civility of Manners, Arts, and Arms,
And long Renown thou justly may'st prefer
Before the *Parthian;* these two Thrones except,
The rest are barbarous, and scarce worth the sight,
Shar'd among petty Kings too far remov'd;
These having shewn thee, I have shewn thee all
The Kingdoms of the world, and all thir glory.
This Emperour hath no Son, and now is old,   90
Old, and lascivious, and from *Rome* retir'd
To *Capreæ* an Island small but strong
On the *Campanian* shore, with purpose there
His horrid lusts in private to enjoy,
Committing to a wicked Favourite
All publick cares, and yet of him suspicious,
Hated of all, and hating; with what ease

Indu'd with Regal Vertues as thou art,
Appearing, and beginning noble deeds,
Might'st thou expel this monster from his Throne　　　　　100
Now made a stye, and in his place ascending
A victor people free from servile yoke?
And with my help thou may'st; to me the power
Is given, and by that right I give it thee.
Aim therefore at no less then all the world,
Aim at the highest, without the highest attain'd
Will be for thee no sitting, or not long
On *David's* Throne, be propheci'd what will.
　　To whom the Son of God unmov'd reply'd.　　　　　110
Nor doth this grandeur and majestic show
Of luxury, though call'd magnificence,
More then of arms before, allure mine eye,
Much less my mind; though thou should'st add to tell
Thir sumptuous gluttonies, and gorgeous feasts
On *Cittron* tables or *Atlantic* stone;
(For I have also heard, perhaps have read)
Their wines of *Setia, Cales,* and *Falerne,*
Chios and *Creet,* and how they quaff in Gold,
Crystal and Myrrhine cups imboss'd with Gems
And studs of Pearl, to me should'st tell who thirst　　　　　120
And hunger still: then Embassies thou shew'st
From Nations far and nigh; what honour that,
But tedious wast of time to sit and hear
So many hollow complements and lies,
Outlandish flatteries? then proceed'st to talk
Of the Emperour, how easily subdu'd,
How gloriously; I shall, thou say'st, expel
A brutish monster: what if I withal
Expel a Devil who first made him such?
Let his tormenter Conscience find him out,　　　　　130
For him I was not sent, nor yet to free
That people victor once, now vile and base,
Deservedly made vassal, who once just,
Frugal, and mild, and temperate, conquer'd well,
But govern ill the Nations under yoke,
Peeling thir Provinces, exhausted all
By lust and rapine; first ambitious grown
Of triumph that insulting vanity;
Then cruel, by thir sports to blood enur'd
Of fighting beasts, and men to beasts expos'd,　　　　　140
Luxurious by thir wealth, and greedier still,
And from the daily Scene effeminate.
What wise and valiant man would seek to free
These thus degenerate, by themselves enslav'd,
Or could of inward slaves make outward free?
Know therefore when my season comes to sit
On *David's* Throne, it shall be like a tree
Spreading and over-shadowing all the Earth,
Or as a stone that shall to pieces dash
All Monarchies besides throughout the world,　　　　　150

And of my Kingdom there shall be no end:
Means there shall be to this, but what the means,
Is not for thee to know, nor me to tell.
   To whom the Tempter impudent repli'd.
I see all offers made by me how slight
Thou valu'st, because offer'd, and reject'st:
Nothing will please the difficult and nice,
Or nothing more then still to contradict:
On the other side know also thou, that I
On what I offer set as high esteem,   160
Nor what I part with mean to give for naught;
All these which in a moment thou behold'st,
The Kingdoms of the world to thee I give;
For giv'n to me, I give to whom I please,
No trifle; yet with this reserve, not else,
On this condition, if thou wilt fall down,
And worship me as thy superior Lord,
Easily done, and hold them all of me;
For what can less so great a gift deserve?
   Whom thus our Saviour answer'd with disdain.   170
I never lik'd thy talk, thy offers less,
Now both abhor, since thou hast dar'd to utter
The abominable terms, impious condition;
But I endure the time, till which expir'd,
Thou hast permission on me. It is written
The first of all Commandments, Thou shalt worship
The Lord thy God, and only him shalt serve;
And dar'st thou to the Son of God propound
To worship thee accurst, now more accurst
For this attempt bolder then that on *Eve,*   180
And more blasphemous? which expect to rue.
The Kingdoms of the world to thee were giv'n,
Permitted rather, and by thee usurp't,
Other donation none thou canst produce:
If given, by whom but by the King of Kings,
God over all supreme? if giv'n to thee,
By thee how fairly is the Giver now
Repaid? But gratitude in thee is lost
Long since. Wert thou so void of fear or shame,
As offer them to me the Son of God,   190
To me my own, on such abhorred pact,
That I fall down and worship thee as God?
Get thee behind me; plain thou now appear'st
That Evil one, Satan for ever damn'd.
   To whom the Fiend with fear abasht reply'd.
Be not so sore offended, Son of God;
Though Sons of God both Angels are and Men,
If I to try whether in higher sort
Then these thou bear'st that title, have propos'd
What both from Men and Angels I receive,   200
Tetrarchs of fire, air, flood, and on the earth
Nations besides from all the quarter'd winds,
God of this world invok't and world beneath;

Who then thou art, whose coming is foretold
To me so fatal, me it most concerns.
The tryal hath indamag'd thee no way,
Rather more honour left and more esteem;
Me naught advantag'd, missing what I aim'd.
Therefore let pass, as they are transitory,
The Kingdoms of this world; I shall no more   210
Advise thee, gain them as thou canst, or not.
And thou thy self seem'st otherwise inclin'd
Then to a worldly Crown, addicted more
To contemplation and profound dispute,
As by that early action may be judg'd,
When slipping from thy Mothers eye thou went'st
Alone into the Temple; there was found
Among the gravest Rabbies disputant
On points and questions fitting *Moses* Chair,
Teaching not taught; the childhood shews the man,   220
As morning shews the day. Be famous then
By wisdom; as thy Empire must extend,
So let extend thy mind o're all the world,
In knowledge, all things in it comprehend,
All knowledge is not couch't in *Moses* Law,
The *Pentateuch* or what the Prophets wrote,
The *Gentiles* also know, and write, and teach
To admiration, led by Natures light;
And with the *Gentiles* much thou must converse,
Ruling them by perswasion as thou mean'st,   230
Without thir learning how wilt thou with them,
Or they with thee hold conversation meet?
How wilt thou reason with them, how refute
Thir Idolisms, Traditions, Paradoxes?
Error by his own arms is best evinc't.
Look once more e're we leave this specular Mount
Westward, much nearer by Southwest, behold
Where on the *Ægean* shore a City stands
Built nobly, pure the air, and light the soil,
Athens the eye of *Greece*, Mother of Arts   240
And Eloquence, native to famous wits
Or hospitable, in her sweet recess,
City or Suburban, studious walks and shades;
See there the Olive Grove of *Academe,*
Plato's retirement, where the *Attic* Bird
Trills her thick-warbl'd notes the summer long,
There flowrie hill *Hymettus* with the sound
Of Bees industrious murmur oft invites
To studious musing; there *Ilissus* rouls
His whispering stream; within the walls then view   50
The schools of antient Sages; his who bred
Great *Alexander* to subdue the world,
Lyceum there, and painted *Stoa* next:
There thou shalt hear and learn the secret power
Of harmony in tones and numbers hit
By voice or hand, and various measur'd verse,

Æolian charms and *Dorian Lyric* Odes,
And his who gave them breath, but higher sung,
Blind *Melesigenes* thence *Homer* call'd,
Whose Poem *Phœbus* challeng'd for his own.   260
Thence what the lofty grave Tragœdians taught
In *Chorus* or *Iambic,* teachers best
Of moral prudence, with delight receiv'd
In brief sententious precepts, while they treat
Of fate, and chance, and change in human life;
High actions, and high passions best describing:
Thence to the famous Orators repair,
Those antient, whose resistless eloquence
Wielded at will that fierce Democratie,
Shook the Arsenal and fulmin'd over *Greece,*   270
To *Macedon,* and *Artaxerxes* Throne;
To sage Philosophy next lend thine ear,
From Heaven descended to the low-rooft house
Of *Socrates,* see there his Tenement,
Whom well inspir'd the Oracle pronounc'd
Wisest of men; from whose mouth issu'd forth
Mellifluous streams that water'd all the schools
Of Academics old and new, with those
Sirnam'd *Peripatetics,* and the Sect
Epicurean, and the *Stoic* severe;   280
These here revolve, or, as thou lik'st, at home,
Till time mature thee to a Kingdom's waight;
These rules will render thee a King compleat
Within thy self, much more with Empire joyn'd.
    To whom our Saviour sagely thus repli'd.
Think not but that I know these things, or think
I know them not; not therefore am I short
Of knowing what I aught: he who receives
Light from above, from the fountain of light,
No other doctrine needs, though granted true;   290
But these are false, or little else but dreams,
Conjectures, fancies, built on nothing firm.
The first and wisest of them all profess'd
To know this only, that he nothing knew;
The next to fabling fell and smooth conceits,
A third sort doubted all things, though plain sence;
Others in vertue plac'd felicity,
But vertue joyn'd with riches and long life,
In corporal pleasure he, and careless ease,
The Stoic last in Philosophic pride,   300
By him call'd vertue; and his vertuous man,
Wise, perfect in himself, and all possessing
Equal to God, oft shames not to prefer,
As fearing God nor man, contemning all
Wealth, pleasure, pain or torment, death and life,
Which when he lists, he leaves, or boasts he can,
For all his tedious talk is but vain boast,
Or subtle shifts conviction to evade.
Alas what can they teach, and not mislead;

Ignorant of themselves, of God much more,   310
And how the world began, and how man fell
Degraded by himself, on grace depending?
Much of the Soul they talk, but all awrie,
And in themselves seek vertue, and to themselves
All glory arrogate, to God give none,
Rather accuse him under usual names,
Fortune and Fate, as one regardless quite
Of mortal things. Who therefore seeks in these
True wisdom, finds her not, or by delusion
Far worse, her false resemblance only meets,   320
An empty cloud. However many books
Wise men have said are wearisom; who reads
Incessantly, and to his reading brings not
A spirit and judgment equal or superior,
(And what he brings, what needs he elsewhere seek)
Uncertain and unsettl'd still remains,
Deep verst in books and shallow in himself,
Crude or intoxicate, collecting toys,
And trifles for choice matters, worth a spunge;
As Children gathering pibles on the shore.   330
Or if I would delight my private hours
With Music or with Poem, where so soon
As in our native Language can I find
That solace? All our Law and Story strew'd
With Hymns, our Psalms with artful terms inscrib'd,
Our Hebrew Songs and Harps in *Babylon,*
That pleas'd so well our Victors ear, declare
That rather *Greece* from us these Arts deriv'd;
Ill imitated, while they loudest sing
The vices of thir Deities, and thir own   340
In Fable, Hymn, or Song, so personating
Thir Gods ridiculous, and themselves past shame.
Remove their swelling Epithetes thick laid
As varnish on a Harlots cheek, the rest,
Thin sown with aught of profit or delight,
Will far be found unworthy to compare
With *Sion's* songs, to all true tasts excelling,
Where God is prais'd aright, and Godlike men,
The Holiest of Holies, and his Saints;
Such are from God inspir'd, not such from thee;   350
Unless where moral vertue is express't
By light of Nature not in all quite lost.
Thir Orators thou then extoll'st, as those
The top of Eloquence, Statists indeed,
And lovers of thir Country, as may seem;
But herein to our Prophets far beneath,
As men divinely taught, and better teaching
The solid rules of Civil Government
In thir majestic unaffected stile
Then all the Oratory of *Greece* and *Rome.*   360
In them is plainest taught, and easiest learnt,
What makes a Nation happy, and keeps it so,

What ruins Kingdoms, and lays Cities flat;
These only with our Law best form a King.
  So spake the Son of God; but Satan now
Quite at a loss, for all his darts were spent,
Thus to our Saviour with stern brow reply'd.
  Since neither wealth, nor honour, arms nor arts,
Kingdom nor Empire pleases thee, nor aught
By me propos'd in life contemplative, 370
Or active, tended on by glory, or fame,
What dost thou in this World? the Wilderness
For thee is fittest place, I found thee there,
And thither will return thee, yet remember
What I foretell thee, soon thou shalt have cause
To wish thou never hadst rejected thus
Nicely or cautiously my offer'd aid,
Which would have set thee in short time with ease
On *David*'s Throne; or Throne of all the world,
Now at full age, fulness of time, thy season, 380
When Prophesies of thee are best fullfill'd.
Now contrary, if I read aught in Heaven,
Or Heav'n write aught of Fate, by what the Stars
Voluminous, or single characters,
In their conjunction met, give me to spell,
Sorrows, and labours, opposition, hate,
Attends thee, scorns, reproaches, injuries,
Violence and stripes, and lastly cruel death,
A Kingdom they portend thee, but what Kingdom,
Real or Allegoric I discern not, 390
Nor when, eternal sure, as without end,
Without beginning; for no date prefixt
Directs me in the Starry Rubric set.
  So saying he took (for still he knew his power
Not yet expir'd) and to the Wilderness
Brought back the Son of God, and left him there,
Feigning to disappear. Darkness now rose,
As day-light sunk, and brought in lowring night
Her shadowy off-spring unsubstantial both,
Privation meer of light and absent day. 400
Our Saviour meek and with untroubl'd mind
After his aerie jaunt, though hurried sore,
Hungry and cold betook him to his rest,
Wherever, under some concourse of shades
Whose branching arms thick intertwind might shield
From dews and damps of night his shelter'd head,
But shelter'd slept in vain, for at his head
The Tempter watch'd, and soon with ugly dreams
Disturb'd his sleep; and either Tropic now
'Gan thunder, and both ends of Heav'n, the Clouds 410
From many a horrid rift abortive pour'd
Fierce rain with lightning mixt, water with fire
In ruine reconcil'd: nor slept the winds
Within thir stony caves, but rush'd abroad
From the four hinges of the world, and fell

On the vext Wilderness, whose tallest Pines,
Though rooted deep as high, and sturdiest Oaks.
Bow'd their Stiff necks, loaden with stormy blasts,
Or torn up sheer: ill wast thou shrouded then,
O patient Son of God, yet only stoodst   420
Unshaken; nor yet staid the terror there,
Infernal Ghosts, and Hellish Furies, round
Environ'd thee, some howl'd, some yell'd, some shriek'd,
Some bent at thee thir fiery darts, while thou
Sat'st unappall'd in calm and sinless peace.
Thus pass'd the night so foul till morning fair
Came forth with Pilgrim steps in amice gray;
Who with her radiant finger still'd the roar
Of thunder, chas'd the clouds, and laid the winds,
And grisly Spectres, which the Fiend had rais'd   430
To tempt the Son of God with terrors dire.
And now the Sun with more effectual beams
Had chear'd the face of Earth, and dry'd the wet
From drooping plant, or dropping tree; the birds
Who all things now behold more fresh and green,
After a night of storm so ruinous,
Clear'd up their choicest notes in bush and spray
To gratulate the sweet return of morn;
Nor yet amidst this joy and brightest morn
Was absent, after all his mischief done,   440
The Prince of darkness, glad would also seem
Of this fair change, and to our Saviour came,
Yet with no new device, they all were spent,
Rather by this his last affront resolv'd,
Desperate of better course, to vent his rage,
And mad despight to be so oft repell'd.
Him walking on a Sunny hill he found,
Back'd on the North and West by a thick wood,
Out of the wood he starts in wonted shape;
And in a careless mood thus to him said.   450
   Fair morning yet betides thee Son of God,
After a dismal night; I heard the rack
As Earth and Skie would mingle; but my self
Was distant; and these flaws, though mortals fear them
As dangerous to the pillard frame of Heaven,
Or to the Earths dark basis underneath,
Are to the main as inconsiderable,
And harmless, if not wholsom, as a sneeze
To mans less universe, and soon are gone;
Yet as being oft times noxious where they light   460
On man, beast, plant, wastful and turbulent,
Like turbulencies in the affairs of men,
Over whose heads they rore, and seem to point,
They oft fore-signifie and threaten ill:
This Tempest at this Desert most was bent;
Of men at thee, for only thou here dwell'st.
Did I not tell thee, if thou didst reject
The perfect season offer'd with my aid

To win thy destin'd seat, but wilt prolong
All to the push of Fate, persue thy way   470
Of gaining *David*'s Throne no man knows when,
For both the when and how is no where told,
Thou shalt be what thou art ordain'd, no doubt;
For Angels have proclaim'd it, but concealing
The time and means: each act is rightliest done,
Not when it must, but when it may be best.
If thou observe not this, be sure to find,
What I foretold thee, many a hard assay
Of dangers, and adversities and pains,
E're thou of *Israel*'s Scepter get fast hold;   480
Whereof this ominous night that clos'd thee round,
So many terrors, voices, prodigies
May warn thee, as a sure fore-going sign.
　　So talk'd he, while the Son of God went on
And staid not, but in brief him answer'd thus.
　　Mee worse then wet thou find'st not; other harm
Those terrors which thou speak'st of, did me none;
I never fear'd they could, though noising loud
And threatning nigh; what they can do as signs
Betok'ning, or ill boding, I contemn   490
As false portents, not sent from God, but thee;
Who knowing I shall raign past thy preventing,
Obtrud'st thy offer'd aid, that I accepting
At least might seem to hold all power of thee,
Ambitious spirit, and wouldst be thought my God,
And storm'st refus'd, thinking to terrifie
Mee to thy will; desist, thou art discern'd
And toil'st in vain, nor me in vain molest.
　　To whom the Fiend now swoln with rage reply'd:
Then hear, O Son of *David*, Virgin-born;   500
For Son of God to me is yet in doubt,
Of the Messiah I have heard foretold
By all the Prophets; of thy birth at length
Announc't by *Gabriel* with the first I knew,
And of the Angelic Song in *Bethlehem* field,
On thy birth-night, that sung thee Saviour born.
From that time seldom have I ceas'd to eye
Thy infancy, thy childhood, and thy youth,
Thy manhood last, though yet in private bred;
Till at the Ford of *Jordan* whither all   510
Flock'd to the Baptist, I among the rest,
Though not to be Baptiz'd, by voice from Heav'n
Heard thee pronounc'd the Son of God belov'd.
Thenceforth I thought thee worth my nearer view
And narrower Scrutiny, that I might learn
In what degree or meaning thou art call'd
The Son of God, which bears no single sence;
The Son of God I also am, or was,
And if I was, I am; relation stands;
All men are Sons of God; yet thee I thought   520
In some respect far higher so declar'd.

Therefore I watch'd thy footsteps from that hour,
And follow'd thee still on to this wast wild;
Where by all best conjectures I collect
Thou art to be my fatal enemy.
Good reason then, if I before-hand seek
To understand my Adversary, who
And what he is; his wisdom, power, intent,
By parl, or composition, truce, or league
To win him, or win from him what I can.   530
And opportunity I here have had
To try thee, sift thee, and confess have found thee
Proof against all temptation as a rock
Of Adamant, and as a Center, firm
To the utmost of meer man both wise and good,
Not more; for Honours, Riches, Kingdoms, Glory
Have been before contemn'd, and may agen:
Therefore to know what more thou art then man,
Worth naming Son of God by voice from Heav'n,
Another method I must now begin.   540
    So saying he caught him up, and without wing
Of *Hippogrif* bore through the Air sublime
Over the Wilderness and o're the Plain;
Till underneath them fair *Jerusalem*,
The holy City lifted high her Towers,
And higher yet the glorious Temple rear'd
Her pile, far off appearing like a Mount
Of Alabaster, top't with golden Spires:
There on the highest Pinacle he set
The Son of God; and added thus in scorn: 550
    There stand, if thou wilt stand; to stand upright,
Will ask thee skill; I to thy Fathers house
Have brought thee, and highest plac't, highest is best,
Now shew thy Progeny; if not to stand,
Cast thy self down; safely if Son of God:
For it is written, He will give command
Concerning thee to his Angels, in thir hands
They shall up lift thee, lest at any time
Thou chance to dash thy foot against a stone.
    To whom thus Jesus: also it is written,   560
Tempt not the Lord thy God, he said and stood.
But Satan smitten with amazement fell
As when Earths Son *Antæus* (to compare
Small things with greatest) in *Irassa* strove
With *Joves Alcides*, and oft foil'd still rose,
Receiving from his mother Earth new strength,
Fresh from his fall, and fiercer grapple joyn'd,
Throttl'd at length in the Air, expir'd and fell;
So after many a foil the Tempter proud,
Renewing fresh assaults, amidst his pride   570
Fell whence he stood to see his Victor fall.
And as that *Theban* Monster that propos'd
Her riddle, and him, who solv'd it not, devour'd;
That once found out and solv'd, for grief and spight

Cast her self headlong from th' *Ismenian* steep,
So strook with dread and anguish fell the Fiend,
And to his crew, that sat consulting, brought
Joyless triumphals of his hop't success,
Ruin, and desperation, and dismay,
Who durst so proudly tempt the Son of God.   580
So Satan fell and strait a fiery Globe
Of Angels on full sail of wing flew nigh,
Who on their plumy Vans receiv'd him soft
From his uneasie station, and upbore
As on a floating couch through the blithe Air,
Then in a flowry valley set him down
On a green bank, and set before him spred
A table of Celestial Food, Divine,
Ambrosial, Fruits fetcht from the tree of life,
And from the fount of life Ambrosial drink,   590
That soon refresh'd him wearied, and repair'd
What hunger, if aught hunger had impair'd,
Or thirst, and as he fed, Angelic Quires
Sung Heavenly Anthems of his victory
Over temptation, and the Tempter proud.
   True Image of the Father whether thron'd
In the bosom of bliss, and light of light
Conceiving, or remote from Heaven, enshrin'd
In fleshly Tabernacle, and human form,
Wandring the Wilderness, whatever place,   600
Habit, or state, or motion, still expressing
The Son of God, with Godlike force indu'd
Against th' Attempter of thy Fathers Throne,
And Thief of Paradise; him long of old
Thou didst debel, and down from Heav'n cast
With all his Army, now thou hast aveng'd
Supplanted *Adam,* and by vanquishing
Temptation, hast regain'd lost Paradise,
And frustrated the conquest fraudulent:
He never more henceforth will dare set foot   610
In Paradise to tempt; his snares are broke:
For though that seat of earthly bliss be fail'd,
A fairer Paradise is founded now
For *Adam* and his chosen Sons, whom thou
A Saviour art come down to re-install.
Where they shall dwell secure, when time shall be
Of Tempter and Temptation without fear.
But thou, Infernal Serpent, shalt not long
Rule in the Clouds; like an Autumnal Star
Or Lightning thou shalt fall from Heav'n trod down   620
Under his feet: for proof, e're this thou feel'st
Thy wound, yet not thy last and deadliest wound
By this repulse receiv'd, and hold'st in Hell
No triumph; in all her gates *Abaddon* rues
Thy bold attempt; hereafter learn with awe
To dread the Son of God: he all unarm'd
Shall chase thee with the terror of his voice

From thy Demoniac holds, possession foul,
Thee and thy Legions, yelling they shall flye,
And beg to hide them in a herd of Swine,   630
Lest he command them down into the deep
Bound, and to torment sent before thir time.
Hail Son of the most High, heir of both worlds,
Queller of Satan, on thy glorious work
Now enter, and begin to save mankind.
      Thus they the Son of God our Saviour meek
Sung Victor, and from Heavenly Feast refresht
Brought on his way with joy; hee unobserv'd
Home to his Mothers house private return'd.

The End.

SAMSON

AGONISTES,

A

DRAMATIC POEM.

The Author

JOHN MILTON.

[The text is that of the first edition, 1671.]

Of that sort of Dramatic Poem which is call'd Tragedy.

TRAGEDY, as it was antiently compos'd, hath been ever held the gravest, moralest, and most profitable of all other Poems: therefore said by *Aristotle* to be of power by raising pity and fear, or terror, to purge the mind of those and such like passions, that is to temper and reduce them to just measure with a kind of delight, stirr'd up by reading or seeing those passions well imitated. Nor is Nature wanting in her own effects to make good his assertion: for so in Physic things of melancholic hue and quality are us'd against melancholy, sowr against sowr, salt to remove salt humours. Hence Philosophers and other gravest Writers, as *Cicero, Plutarch* and others, frequently cite out of Tragic Poets, both to adorn and illustrate thir discourse. The Apostle *Paul* himself thought it not unworthy to insert a verse of *Euripides* into the Text of Holy Scripture, 1 Cor. 15. 33. and *Paraeus* commenting on the *Revelation,* divides the whole Book as a Tragedy, into Acts distinguisht each by a Chorus of Heavenly Harpings and Song between. Heretofore Men in highest dignity have labour'd not a little to be thought able to compose a Tragedy. Of that honour *Dionysius* the elder was no less ambitious, then before of his attaining to the Tyranny. *Augustus Cæsar* also had begun his *Ajax,* but unable to please his own judgment with what he had begun, left it unfinisht. *Seneca* the Philosopher is by some thought the Author of those Tragedies (at lest the best of them) that go under that name. *Gregory Nazianzen* a Father of the Church, thought it not unbeseeming the sanctity of his person to write a Tragedy, which he entitl'd, *Christ Suffering.* This is mention'd to vindicate Tragedy from the small esteem, or rather infamy, which in the account of many it undergoes at this day with other common Interludes; hap'ning through the Poets error of intermixing Comic stuff with Tragic sadness and gravity; or introducing trivial and vulgar persons, which by all judicious hath bin counted absurd; and brought in without discretion, corruptly to gratifie the people. And though antient Tragedy use no Prologue, yet using sometimes, in case of self defence, or explanation, that which *Martial* calls an Epistle; in behalf of this Tragedy coming forth after the antient manner, much different from what among us passes for best, thus much before-hand may be Epistl'd; that *Chorus* is here introduc'd after the Greek manner, not antient only but modern, and still in use among the *Italians.* In the modelling therefore of this Poem, with good reason, the Antients and *Italians* are rather follow'd, as of much more authority and fame. The measure of Verse us'd in the Chorus is of all sorts, call'd by the Greeks *Monostrophic,* or rather *Apolelymenon,* without regard had to *Strophe, Antistrophe* or *Epod,* which were a kind of Stanza's fram'd only for the Music, then us'd with the Chorus that sung; not essential to the Poem, and therefore not material; or being divided into Stanza's or Pauses, they may be call'd *Allæostropha.* Division into Act and Scene referring chiefly to the Stage (to which this work never was intended) is here omitted.

It suffices if the whole Drama be found not produc't beyond the fift Act, of the style and uniformitie, and that commonly call'd the Plot, whether intricate or explicit, which is nothing indeed but such œconomy, or disposition of the fable as may stand best with verisimilitude and decorum; they only will best judge who are not unacquainted with *Æschulus, Sophocles,* and *Euripides,* the three Tragic Poets unequall'd yet by any, and the best rule to all who endeavour to write Tragedy. The circumscription of time wherein the whole Drama begins and ends, is according to antient rule, and best example, within the space of 24 hours.

The Argument.

Samson *made Captive, Blind, and now in the Prison at Gaza, there to labour as in a common workhouse, on a Festival day, in the general cessation from labour, comes forth into the open Air, to a place nigh, somewhat retir'd there to sit a while and bemoan his condition. Where he happens at length to be visited by certain friends and equals of his tribe, which make the Chorus, who seek to comfort him what they can; then by his old Father* Manoa, *who endeavours the like, and withal tells him his purpose to procure his liberty by ransom; lastly, that this Feast was proclaim'd by the* Philistins *as a day of Thanksgiving for thir deliverance from the hands of* Samson, *which yet more troubles him.* Manoa *then departs to prosecute his endeavour with the* Philistian *Lords for* Samson's *redemption; who in the mean while is visited by other persons; and lastly by a publick Officer to require his coming to the Feast before the Lords and People, to play or shew his strength in thir presence; he at first refuses, dismissing the publick Officer with absolute denyal to come; at length perswaded inwardly that this was from God, he yields to go along with him, who came now the second time with great threatnings to fetch him; the Chorus yet remaining on the place,* Manoa *returns full of joyful hope, to procure e're long his Sons deliverance: in the midst of which discourse an Ebrew comes in haste confusedly at first; and afterward more distinctly relating the Catastrophe, what* Samson *had done to the* Philistins, *and by accident to himself; wherewith the Tragedy ends.*

The Persons.

Samson.
Manoa *the Father of* Samson.
Dalila *his Wife.*
Harapha *of Gath.*
Publick Officer.
Messenger.
Chorus *of Danites.*

The Scene before the Prison in Gaza.

SAMSON

AGONISTES.

Sams. A LITTLE onward lend thy guiding hand
To these dark steps, a little further on;
For yonder bank hath choice of Sun or shade,
There I am wont to sit, when any chance
Relieves me from my task of servile toyl,
Daily in the common Prison else enjoyn'd me,
Where I a Prisoner chain'd, scarce freely draw
The air imprison'd also, close and damp,
Unwholsom draught: but here I feel amends,
The breath of Heav'n fresh-blowing, pure and sweet,   10
With day-spring born; here leave me to respire.
This day a solemn Feast the people hold
To *Dagon* thir Sea-Idol, and forbid
Laborious works, unwillingly this rest
Thir Superstition yields me; hence with leave
Retiring from the popular noise, I seek
This unfrequented place to find some ease,
Ease to the body some, none to the mind
From restless thoughts, that like a deadly swarm
Of Hornets arm'd, no sooner found alone,   20
But rush upon me thronging, and present
Times past, what once I was, and what am now.
O wherefore was my birth from Heaven foretold
Twice by an Angel, who at last in sight
Of both my Parents all in flames ascended
From off the Altar, where an Off'ring burn'd,
As in a fiery column charioting
His Godlike presence, and from some great act
Or benefit reveal'd to *Abraham*'s race?
Why was my breeding order'd and prescrib'd   30
As of a person separate to God,
Design'd for great exploits; if I must dye
Betray'd, Captiv'd, and both my Eyes put out,
Made of my Enemies the scorn and gaze;
To grind in Brazen Fetters under task
With this Heav'n-gifted strength? O glorious strength
Put to the labour of a Beast, debas't
Lower then bondslave! Promise was that I
Should *Israel* from *Philistian* yoke deliver;
Ask for this great Deliverer now, and find him   40
Eyeless in *Gaza* at the Mill with slaves,
Himself in bonds under *Philistian* yoke;
Yet stay, let me not rashly call in doubt
Divine Prediction; what if all foretold
Had been fulfilld but through mine own default,
Whom have I to complain of but my self?
Who this high gift of strength committed to me,
In what part lodg'd, how easily bereft me,
Under the Seal of silence could not keep,

But weakly to a woman must reveal **it**,   50
O'recome with importunity and tears.
O impotence of mind, in body strong!
But what is strength without a double share
Of wisdom, vast, unwieldy, burdensom,
Proudly secure, yet liable to fall
By weakest suttleties, not made to rule,
But to subserve where wisdom bears command.
God, when he gave me strength, to shew withal
How slight the gift was, hung it in my Hair.
But peace, I must not quarrel with the will   60
Of highest dispensation, which herein
Happ'ly had ends above my reach to know:
Suffices that to me strength is my bane,
And proves the sourse of all my miseries;
So many, and so huge, that each apart
Would ask a life to wail, but chief of all,
O loss of sight, of thee I most complain!
Blind among enemies, O worse then chains,
Dungeon, or beggery, or decrepit age!
Light the prime work of God to me is extinct,   70
And all her various objects of delight
Annull'd, which might in part my grief have eas'd,
Inferiour to the vilest now become
Of man or worm; the vilest here excel me,
They creep, yet see, I dark in light expos'd
To daily fraud, contempt, abuse and wrong,
Within doors, or without, still as a fool,
In power of others, never in my own;
Scarce half I seem to live, dead more then half.
O dark, dark, dark, amid the blaze of noon,   80
Irrecoverably dark, total Eclipse
Without all hope of day!
O first created Beam, and thou great Word,
Let there be light, and light was over all;
Why am I thus bereav'd thy prime decree?
The Sun to me is dark
And silent as the Moon,
When she deserts the night
Hid in her vacant interlunar cave.
Since light so necessary is to life,   90
And almost life it self, if it be true
That light is in the Soul,
She all in every part; why was the sight
To such a tender ball as th' eye confin'd?
So obvious and so easie to be quench't,
And not as feeling through all parts diffus'd,
That she might look at will through every pore?
Then had I not been thus exil'd from light;
As in the land of darkness yet in light,
To live a life half dead, a living death,   100
And buried; but O yet more miserable!
My self, my Sepulcher, a moving Grave,

Buried, yet not exempt
By priviledge of death and burial
From worst of other evils, pains and wrongs,
But made hereby obnoxious more
To all the miseries of life,
Life in captivity
Among inhuman foes.
But who are these? for with joint pace I hear   110
The tread of many feet stearing this way;
Perhaps my enemies who come to stare
At my affliction, and perhaps to insult,
Thir daily practice to afflict me more.
  Chor. This, this is he; softly a while,
Let us not break in upon him;
O change beyond report, thought, or belief!
See how he lies at random, carelessly diffus'd,
With languish't head unpropt,
As one past hope, abandon'd,   120
And by himself given over;
In slavish habit, ill-fitted weeds
O're worn and soild;
Or do my eyes misrepresent? Can this be hee,
That Heroic, that Renown'd,
Irresistible *Samson?* whom unarm'd
No strength of man, or fiercest wild beast could withstand;
Who tore the Lion, as the Lion tears the Kid,
Ran on embattelld Armies clad in Iron,
And weaponless himself,   130
Made Arms ridiculous, useless the forgery
Of brazen shield and spear, the hammer'd Cuirass,
Chalybean temper'd steel, and frock of mail
Adamantean Proof;
But safest he who stood aloof,
When insupportably his foot advanc't,
In scorn of thir proud arms and warlike tools,
Spurn'd them to death by Troops. The bold *Ascalonite*
Fled from his Lion ramp, old Warriors turn'd
Thir plated backs under his heel;   14
Or grovling soild thir crested helmets in the dust.
Then with what trivial weapon came to hand,
The Jaw of a dead Ass, his sword of bone,
A thousand fore-skins fell, the flower of *Palestin*
In *Ramath-lechi* famous to this day:
Then by main force pull'd up, and on his shoulders bore
The Gates of *Azza,* Post, and massie Bar
Up to the Hill by *Hebron,* seat of Giants old,
No journey of a Sabbath day, and loaded so;
Like whom the Gentiles feign to bear up Heav'n.   15(
Which shall I first bewail,
Thy Bondage or lost Sight,
Prison within Prison
Inseparably dark?
Thou art become (O worst imprisonment!)

The Dungeon of thy self; thy Soul
(Which Men enjoying sight oft without cause complain)
Imprison'd now indeed,
In real darkness of the body dwells,
Shut up from outward light   160
To incorporate with gloomy night;
For inward light alas
Puts forth no visual beam.
O mirror of our fickle state,
Since man on earth unparallel'd?
The rarer thy example stands,
By how much from the top of wondrous glory,
Strongest of mortal men,
To lowest pitch of abject fortune thou art fall'n.
For him I reckon not in high estate   170
Whom long descent of birth
Or the sphear of fortune raises;
But thee whose strength, while vertue was her mate,
Might have subdu'd the Earth,
Universally crown'd with highest praises.
    Sam. I hear the sound of words, thir sense the air
Dissolves unjointed e're it reach my ear.
    Chor. Hee speaks, let us draw nigh. Matchless in might,
The glory late of *Israel,* now the grief;
We come thy friends and neighbours not unknown   180
From *Eshtaol* and *Zora's* fruitful Vale
To visit or bewail thee, or if better,
Counsel or Consolation we may bring,
Salve to thy Sores, apt words have power to swage
The tumors of a troubl'd mind,
And are as Balm to fester'd wounds.
    Sam. Your coming, Friends, revives me, for I learn
Now of my own experience, not by talk,
How counterfeit a coin they are who friends
Bear in their Superscription (of the most   190
I would be understood) in prosperous days
They swarm, but in adverse withdraw their head
Not to be found, though sought. Yee see, O friends,
How many evils have enclos'd me round;
Yet that which was the worst now least afflicts me,
Blindness, for had I sight, confus'd with shame,
How could I once look up, or heave the head,
Who like a foolish Pilot have shipwrack't,
My Vessel trusted to me from above,
Gloriously rigg'd; and for a word, a tear,   200
Fool, have divulg'd the secret gift of God
To a deceitful Woman: tell me Friends,
Am I not sung and proverbd for a Fool
In every street, do they not say, how well
Are come upon him his deserts? yet why?
Immeasurable strength they might behold
In me, of wisdom nothing more then mean;
This with the other should, at least, have paird,

These two proportiond ill drove me transverse.

 Chor. Tax not divine disposal, wisest Men   210
Have err'd, and by bad Women been deceiv'd;
And shall again, pretend they ne're so wise.
Deject not then so overmuch thy self,
Who hast of sorrow thy full load besides;
Yet truth to say, I oft have heard men wonder
Why thou shouldst wed *Philistian* women rather
Then of thine own Tribe fairer, or as fair,
At least of thy own Nation, and as noble.

 Sam. The first I saw at *Timna,* and she pleas'd
Mee, not my Parents, that I sought to wed,   220
The daughter of an Infidel: they knew not
That what I motion'd was of God; I knew
From intimate impulse, and therefore urg'd
The Marriage on; that by occasion hence
I might begin *Israel*'s Deliverance,
The work to which I was divinely call'd;
She proving false, the next I took to Wife
(O that I never had! fond wish too late)
Was in the Vale of *Sorec, Dalila,*
That specious Monster, my accomplisht snare.   230
I thought it lawful from my former act,
And the same end; still watching to oppress
Israel's oppressours: of what now I suffer
She was not the prime cause, but I my self,
Who vanquisht with a peal of words (O weakness!)
Gave up my fort of silence to a Woman.

 Chor. In seeking just occasion to provoke
The *Philistine,* thy Countries Enemy,
Thou never wast remiss, I bear thee witness:
Yet *Israel* still serves with all his Sons.   240

 Sam. That fault I take not on me, but transfer
On *Israel*'s Governours, and Heads of Tribes,
Who seeing those great acts which God had done
Singly by me against their Conquerours
Acknowledg'd not, or not at all consider'd
Deliverance offerd: I on th' other side
Us'd no ambition to commend my deeds,
The deeds themselves, though mute, spoke loud the dooer;
But they persisted deaf, and would not seem
To count them things worth notice, till at length   250
Thir Lords the *Philistines* with gather'd powers
Enterd *Judea* seeking mee, who then
Safe to the rock of *Etham* was retir'd,
Not flying, but fore-casting in what place
To set upon them, what advantag'd best;
Mean while the men of *Judah* to prevent
The harass of thir Land, beset me round;
I willingly on some conditions came
Into thir hands, and they as gladly yield me
To the uncircumcis'd a welcom prey,   260
Bound with two cords; but cords to me were threds

Toucht with the flame: on thir whole Host I flew
Unarm'd, and with a trivial weapon fell'd
Their choicest youth; they only liv'd who fled.
Had *Judah* that day join'd, or one whole Tribe,
They had by this possess'd the Towers of *Gath,*
And lorded over them whom now they serve;
But what more oft in Nations grown corrupt,
And by thir vices brought to servitude,
Then to love Bondage more then Liberty,   270
Bondage with ease then strenuous liberty;
And to despise, or envy, or suspect
Whom God hath of his special favour rais'd
As thir Deliverer; if he aught begin,
How frequent to desert him, and at last
To heap ingratitude on worthiest deeds?
    Chor. Thy words to my remembrance bring
How *Succoth* and the Fort of *Penuel*
Thir great Deliverer contemn'd,
The matchless *Gideon* in pursuit   280
Of *Madian* and her vanquisht Kings:
And how ingrateful *Ephraim*
Had dealt with *Jephtha,* who by argument,
Not worse then by his shield and spear
Defended *Israel* from the *Ammonite,*
Had not his prowess quell'd thir pride
In that sore battel when so many dy'd
Without Reprieve adjudg'd to death,
For want of well pronouncing *Shibboleth.*
    Sam. Of such examples adde mee to the roul,   290
Mee easily indeed mine may neglect,
But Gods propos'd deliverance not so.
    Chor. Just are the ways of God,
And justifiable to Men;
Unless there be who think not God at all,
If any be, they walk obscure;
For of such Doctrine never was there School,
But the heart of the Fool,
And no man therein Doctor but himself.
    Yet more there be who doubt his ways not just,   300
As to his own edicts, found contradicting,
Then give the rains to wandring thought,
Regardless of his glories diminution;
Till by thir own perplexities involv'd
They ravel more, still less resolv'd,
But never find self-satisfying solution.
    As if they would confine th' interminable,
And tie him to his own prescript,
Who made our Laws to bind us, not himself,
And hath full right to exempt   310
Whom so it pleases him by choice
From National obstriction, without taint
Of sin, or legal debt;
For with his own Laws he can best dispence.

He would not else who never wanted means,
Nor in respect of the enemy just cause
To set his people free,
Have prompted this Heroic *Nazarite*,
Against his vow of strictest purity,
To seek in marriage that fallacious Bride,   320
Unclean, unchaste.
　　Down Reason then, at least vain reasonings down,
Though Reason here aver
That moral verdit quits her of unclean:
Unchaste was subsequent, her stain not his.
　　But see here comes thy reverend Sire
With careful step, Locks white as doune,
Old *Manoah:* advise
Forthwith how thou oughtst to receive him.
　　Sam. Ay me, another inward grief awak't,   330
With mention of that name renews th' assault.
　　Man. Brethren and men of *Dan,* for such ye seem,
Though in this uncouth place; if old respect,
As I suppose, towards your once gloried friend,
My Son now Captive, hither hath inform'd
Your younger feet, while mine cast back with age
Came lagging after; say if he be here.
　　Chor. As signal now in low dejected state,
As earst in highest, behold him where he lies.
　　Man. O miserable change! is this the man,   340
That invincible *Samson,* far renown'd,
The dread of *Israel's* foes, who with a strength
Equivalent to Angels walk'd thir streets,
None offering fight; who single combatant
Duell'd thir Armies rank't in proud array,
Himself an Army, now unequal match
To save himself against a coward arm'd
At one spears length. O ever failing trust
In mortal strength! and oh what not in man
Deceivable and vain! Nay what thing good   350
Pray'd for, but often proves our woe, our bane?
I pray'd for Children, and thought barrenness
In wedlock a reproach; I gain'd a Son,
And such a Son as all Men hail'd me happy;
Who would be now a Father in my stead?
O wherefore did God grant me my request,
And as a blessing with such pomp adorn'd?
Why are his gifts desirable, to tempt
Our earnest Prayers, then giv'n with solemn hand
As Graces, draw a Scorpions tail behind?   360
For this did the Angel twice descend? for this
Ordain'd thy nurture holy, as of a Plant;
Select, and Sacred, Glorious for a while,
The miracle of men: then in an hour
Ensnar'd, assaulted, overcome, led bound,
Thy Foes derision, Captive, Poor, and Blind
Into a Dungeon thrust, to work with Slaves?

Alas methinks whom God hath chosen once
To worthiest deeds, if he through frailty err,
He should not so o'rewhelm, and as a thrall   370
Subject him to so foul indignities,
Be it but for honours sake of former deeds.
    Sam. Appoint not heavenly disposition, Father,
Nothing of all these evils hath befall'n me
But justly; I my self have brought them on,
Sole Author I, sole cause: if aught seem vile,
As vile hath been my folly, who have profan'd
The mystery of God giv'n me under pledge
Of vow, and have betray'd it to a woman,
A *Canaanite,* my faithless enemy.   380
This well I knew, nor was at all surpris'd,
But warn'd by oft experience: did not she
Of *Timna* first betray me, and reveal
The secret wrested from me in her highth
Of Nuptial Love profest, carrying it strait
To them who had corrupted her, my Spies,
And Rivals? In this other was there found
More Faith? who also in her prime of love,
Spousal embraces, vitiated with Gold,
Though offer'd only, by the sent conceiv'd   390
Her spurious first-born; Treason against me?
Thrice she assay'd with flattering prayers and sighs,
And amorous reproaches to win from me
My capital secret, in what part my strength
Lay stor'd, in what part summ'd, that she might know;
Thrice I deluded her, and turn'd to sport
Her importunity, each time perceiving
How openly, and with what impudence
She purpos'd to betray me, and (which was worse
Then undissembl'd hate) with what contempt   400
She sought to make me Traytor to my self;
Yet the fourth time, when mustring all her wiles,
With blandisht parlies, feminine assaults,
Tongue-batteries, she surceas'd not day nor night
To storm me over-watch't, and wearied out.
At times when men seek most repose and rest,
I yielded, and unlock'd her all my heart,
Who with a grain of manhood well resolv'd
Might easily have shook off all her snares:
But foul effeminacy held me yok't   410
Her Bond-slave; O indignity, O blot
To Honour and Religion! servil mind
Rewarded well with servil punishment!
The base degree to which I now am fall'n,
These rags, this grinding, is not yet so base
As was my former servitude, ignoble,
Unmanly, ignominious, infamous,
True slavery, and that blindness worse then this,
That saw not how degenerately I serv'd.
    Man. I cannot praise thy Marriage choises, Son,   420

Rather approv'd them not; but thou didst plead
Divine impulsion prompting how thou might'st
Find some occasion to infest our Foes.
I state not that; this I am sure; our Foes
Found soon occasion thereby to make thee
Thir Captive, and thir triumph; thou the sooner
Temptation found'st, or over-potent charms
To violate the sacred trust of silence
Deposited within thee; which to have kept
Tacit, was in thy power; true; and thou bear'st   430
Enough, and more the burden of that fault;
Bitterly hast thou paid, and still art paying
That rigid score. A worse thing yet remains,
This day the *Philistines* a popular Feast
Here celebrate in *Gaza;* and proclaim
Great Pomp, and Sacrifice, and Praises loud
To *Dagon,* as their God who hath deliver'd
Thee *Samson* bound and blind into thir hands,
Them out of thine, who slew'st them many a slain.
So *Dagon* shall be magnifi'd, and God,   440
Besides whom is no God, compar'd with Idols,
Disglorifi'd, blasphem'd, and had in scorn
By th' Idolatrous rout amidst thir wine;
Which to have come to pass by means of thee,
Samson, of all thy sufferings think the heaviest,
Of all reproach the most with shame that ever
Could have befall'n thee and thy Fathers house.
    Sam. Father, I do acknowledge and confess
That I this honour, I this pomp have brought
To *Dagon,* and advanc'd his praises high   450
Among the Heathen round; to God have brought
Dishonour, obloquie, and op't the mouths
Of Idolists, and Atheists; have brought scandal
To *Israel,* diffidence of God, and doubt
In feeble hearts, propense anough before
To waver, or fall off and joyn with **Idols;**
Which is my chief affliction, shame and sorrow,
The anguish of my Soul, that suffers not
Mine eie to harbour sleep, or thoughts to rest.
This only hope relieves me, that the strife   460
With me hath end; all the contest is now
'Twixt God and *Dagon; Dagon* hath presum'd,
Me overthrown, to enter lists with God,
His Deity comparing and preferring
Before the God of *Abraham.* He, be sure,
Will not connive, or linger, thus provok'd,
But will arise and his great name assert:
Dagon must stoop, and shall e're long receive
Such a discomfit, as shall quite despoil him
Of all these boasted Trophies won on me,   470
And with confusion blank his Worshippers.
    Man. With cause this hope relieves thee, and these words
I as a Prophecy receive: for God,

Nothing more certain, will not long defer
To vindicate the glory of his name
Against all competition, nor will long
Endure it, doubtful whether God be Lord,
Or *Dagon*. But for thee what shall be done?
Thou must not in the mean while here forgot
Lie in this miserable loathsom plight   480
Neglected. I already have made way
To some *Philistian* Lords, with whom to treat
About thy ransom: well they may by this
Have satisfi'd thir utmost of revenge
By pains and slaveries, worse then death inflicted
On thee, who now no more canst do them harm.
   Sam. Spare that proposal, Father, spare the trouble
Of that sollicitation; let me here,
As I deserve, pay on my punishment;
And expiate, if possible, my crime,   490
Shameful garrulity. To have reveal'd
Secrets of men, the secrets of a friend,
How hainous had the fact been, how deserving
Contempt, and scorn of all, to be excluded
All friendship, and avoided as a blab,
The mark of fool set on his front?
But I Gods counsel have not kept, his holy secret
Presumptuously have publish'd, impiously,
Weakly at least, and shamefully: A sin
That Gentiles in thir Parables condemn   500
To thir abyss and horrid pains confin'd.
   Man. Be penitent and for thy fault contrite,
But act not in thy own affliction, Son,
Repent the sin, but if the punishment
Thou canst avoid, self-preservation bids;
Or th' execution leave to high disposal,
And let another hand, not thine, exact
Thy penal forfeit from thy self; perhaps
God will relent, and quit thee all his debt;
Who evermore approves and more accepts   510
(Best pleas'd with humble and filial submission)
Him who imploring mercy sues for life,
Then who self-rigorous chooses death as due;
Which argues over-just, and self-displeas'd
For self-offence, more then for God offended.
Reject not then what offerd means, who knows
But God hath set before us, to return thee
Home to thy countrey and his sacred house,
Where thou mayst bring thy off'rings, to avert
His further ire, with praiers and vows renew'd.   520
   Sam. His pardon I implore; but as for life,
To what end should I seek it? when in strength
All mortals I excell'd, and great in hopes
With youthful courage and magnanimous thoughts
Of birth from Heav'n foretold and high exploits,
Full of divine instinct, after some proof

Of acts indeed heroic, far beyond
The Sons of *Anac,* famous now and blaz'd,
Fearless of danger, like a petty God
I walk'd about admir'd of all and dreaded   530
On hostile ground, none daring my affront.
Then swoll'n with pride into the snare I fell
Of fair fallacious looks, venereal trains,
Softn'd with pleasure and voluptuous life;
At length to lay my head and hallow'd pledge
Of all my strength in the lascivious lap
Of a deceitful Concubine who shore me
Like a tame Weather, all my precious fleece,
Then turn'd me out ridiculous, despoil'd,
Shav'n, and disarm'd among my enemies.   540
    Chor. Desire of wine and all delicious drinks,
Which many a famous Warriour overturns,
Thou couldst repress, nor did the dancing Rubie
Sparkling, out-pow'rd, the flavor, or the smell,
Or taste that cheers the heart of Gods and men,
Allure thee from the cool Crystalline stream.
    Sam. Where ever fountain or fresh current flow'd
Against the Eastern ray, translucent, pure.
With touch ætherial of Heav'ns fiery rod
I drank, from the clear milkie juice allaying   550
Thirst, and refresht; nor envy'd them the grape
Whose heads that turbulent liquor fills with fumes.
    Chor. O madness, to think use of strongest wines
And strongest drinks our chief support of health,
When God with these forbid'n made choice to rear
His mighty Champion, strong above compare,
Whose drink was only from the liquid brook.
    Sam. But what avail'd this temperance, not compleat
Against another object more enticing?
What boots it at one gate to make defence,   560
And at another to let in the foe
Effeminatly vanquish't? by which means,
Now blind, disheartn'd, sham'd, dishonour'd, quell'd,
To what can I be useful, wherein serve
My Nation, and the work from Heav'n impos'd,
But to sit idle on the houshold hearth,
A burdenous drone; to visitants a gaze,
Or pitied object, these redundant locks
Robustious to no purpose clustring down,
Vain monument of strength; till length of years   570
And sedentary numness craze my limbs
To a contemptible old age obscure.
Here rather let me drudge and earn my bread,
Till vermin or the draff of servil food
Consume me, and oft-invocated death
Hast'n the welcom end of all my pains.
    Man. Wilt thou then serve the *Philistines* with that gift
Which was expresly giv'n thee to annoy them?
Better at home lie bed-rid, not only idle,

Inglorious, unimploy'd, with age out-worn. 580
But God who caus'd a fountain at thy prayer
From the dry ground to spring, thy thirst to allay
After the brunt of battel, can as easie
Cause light again within thy eies to spring,
Wherewith to serve him better then thou hast;
And I perswade me so; why else this strength
Miraculous yet remaining in those locks?
His might continues in thee not for naught,
Nor shall his wondrous gifts be frustrate thus.
 Sam. All otherwise to me my thoughts portend, 590
That these dark orbs no more shall treat with light,
Nor th' other light of life continue long,
But yield to double darkness nigh at hand:
So much I feel my genial spirits droop,
My hopes all flat, nature within me seems
In all her functions weary of herself;
My race of glory run, and race of shame,
And I shall shortly be with them that rest.
 Man. Believe not these suggestions which proceed
From anguish of the mind and humours black, 600
That mingle with thy fancy. I however
Must not omit a Fathers timely care
To prosecute the means of thy deliverance
By ransom or how else: mean while be calm,
And healing words from these thy friends admit.
 Sam. O that torment should not be confin'd
To the bodies wounds and sores
With maladies innumerable
In heart, head, brest, and reins;
But must secret passage find 610
To th' inmost mind,
There exercise all his fierce accidents,
And on her purest spirits prey,
As on entrails, joints, and limbs,
With answerable pains, but more intense,
Though void of corporal sense.
 My griefs not only pain me
As a lingring disease,
But finding no redress, ferment and rage,
Nor less then wounds immedicable 620
Ranckle, and fester, and gangrene,
To black mortification.
Thoughts my Tormenters arm'd with deadly stings
Mangle my apprehensive tenderest parts,
Exasperate, exulcerate, and raise
Dire inflammation which no cooling herb
Or medcinal liquor can asswage,
Nor breath of Vernal Air from snowy *Alp.*
Sleep hath forsook and giv'n me o're
To deaths benumming Opium as my only cure. 630
Thence faintings, swounings of despair,
And sense of Heav'ns desertion.

I was his nursling once and choice delight,
His destin'd from the womb,
Promisd by Heavenly message twice descending.
Under his special eie
Abstemious I grew up and thriv'd amain;
He led me on to mightiest deeds
Above the nerve of mortal arm
Against the uncircumcis'd, our enemies.   640
But now hath cast me off as never known,
And to those cruel enemies,
Whom I by his appointment had provok't,
Left me all helpless with th' irreparable loss
Of sight, reserv'd alive to be repeated
The subject of thir cruelty, or scorn.
Nor am I in the list of them that hope;
Hopeless are all my evils, all remediless;
This one prayer yet remains, might I be heard,
No long petition, speedy death,   650
The close of all my miseries, and the balm.
    Chor. Many are the sayings of the wise
In antient and in modern books enroll'd;
Extolling Patience as the truest fortitude;
And to the bearing well of all calamities,
All chances incident to mans frail life
Consolatories writ
With studied argument, and much perswasion sought
Lenient of grief and anxious thought,
But with th' afflicted in his pangs thir sound   660
Little prevails, or rather seems a tune,
Harsh, and of dissonant mood from his complaint,
Unless he feel within
Some sourse of consolation from above;
Secret refreshings, that repair his strength,
And fainting spirits uphold.
   God of our Fathers, what is man!
That thou towards him with hand so various,
Or might I say contrarious,
Temperst thy providence through his short course,   670
Not evenly, as thou rul'st
The Angelic orders and inferiour creatures mute,
Irrational and brute.
Nor do I name of men the common rout,
That wandring loose about
Grow up and perish, as the summer flie,
Heads without name no more rememberd,
But such as thou hast solemnly elected,
With gifts and graces eminently adorn'd
To some great work, thy glory,   680
And peoples safety, which in part they effect:
Yet toward these thus dignifi'd, thou oft
Amidst thir highth of noon,
Changest thy countenance, and thy hand with no regard
Of highest favours past

From thee on them, or them to thee of service.
    Nor only dost degrade them, or remit
To life obscur'd, which were a fair dismission,
But throw'st them lower then thou didst exalt them high,
Unseemly falls in human eie,   690
Too grievous for the trespass or omission,
Oft leav'st them to the hostile sword
Of Heathen and prophane, thir carkasses
To dogs and fowls a prey, or else captiv'd:
Or to the unjust tribunals, under change of times,
And condemnation of the ingrateful multitude.
If these they scape, perhaps in poverty
With sickness and disease thou bow'st them down,
Painful diseases and deform'd,
In crude old age;   700
Though not disordinate, yet causless suffring
The punishment of dissolute days, in fine,
Just or unjust, alike seem miserable,
For oft alike, both come to evil end.
    So deal not with this once thy glorious Champion,
The Image of thy strength, and mighty minister.
What do I beg? how hast thou dealt already?
Behold him in this state calamitous, and turn
His labours, for thou canst, to peaceful end.
    But who is this, what thing of Sea or Land?   710
Femal of sex it seems,
That so bedeckt, ornate, and gay,
Comes this way sailing
Like a stately Ship
Of *Tarsus,* bound for th' Isles
Of *Javan* or *Gadier*
With all her bravery on, and tackle trim,
Sails fill'd, and streamers waving,
Courted by all the winds that hold them play,
An Amber sent of odorous perfume   720
Her harbinger, a damsel train behind;
Some rich *Philistian* Matron she may seem,
And now at nearer view, no other certain
Then *Dalila* thy wife.
    Sam. My Wife, my Traytress, let her not come near me.
    Cho. Yet on she moves, now stands & eies thee fixt,
About t' have spoke, but now, with head declin'd
Like a fair flower surcharg'd with dew, she weeps
And words addrest seem into tears dissolv'd,
Wetting the borders of her silk'n veil: 730
But now again she makes address to speak.
    Dal. With doubtful feet and wavering resolution
I came, still dreading thy displeasure, *Samson,*
Which to have merited, without excuse,
I cannot but acknowledge; yet if tears
May expiate (though the fact more evil drew
In the perverse event then I foresaw)
My penance hath not slack'n'd, though my pardon

No way assur'd. But conjugal affection
Prevailing over fear, and timerous doubt   740
Hath led me on desirous to behold
Once more thy face, and know of thy estate.
If aught in my ability may serve
To light'n what thou suffer'st, and appease
Thy mind with what amends is in my power,
Though late, yet in some part to recompense
My rash but more unfortunate misdeed.
  Sam. Out, out *Hyæna;* these are thy wonted arts,
And arts of every woman false like thee,
To break all faith, all vows, deceive, betray,   750
Then as repentant to submit, beseech,
And reconcilement move with feign'd remorse,
Confess, and promise wonders in her change,
Not truly penitent, but chief to try
Her husband, how far urg'd his patience bears,
His vertue or weakness which way to assail:
Then with more cautious and instructed skill
Again transgresses, and again submits;
That wisest and best men full oft beguil'd
With goodness principl'd not to reject   760
The penitent, but ever to forgive,
Are drawn to wear out miserable days,
Entangl'd with a poysnous bosom snake,
If not by quick destruction soon cut off
As I by thee, to Ages an example.
  Dal. Yet hear me *Samson;* not that I endeavour
To lessen or extenuate my offence,
But that on th' other side if it be weigh'd
By it self, with aggravations not surcharg'd,
Or else with just allowance counterpois'd,   770
I may, if possible, thy pardon find
The easier towards me, or thy hatred less.
First granting, as I do, it was a weakness
In me, but incident to all our sex,
Curiosity, inquisitive, importune
Of secrets, then with like infirmity
To publish them, both common female faults:
Was it not weakness also to make known
For importunity, that is for naught,
Wherein consisted all thy strength and safety?   780
To what I did thou shewdst me first the way.
But I to enemies reveal'd, and should not.
Nor shouldst thou have trusted that to womans frailty
E're I to thee, thou to thy self wast cruel.
Let weakness then with weakness come to parl
So near related, or the same of kind,
Thine forgive mine; that men may censure thine
The gentler, if severely thou exact not
More strength from me, then in thy self was found.
And what if Love, which thou interpret'st hate,   790
The jealousie of Love, powerful of sway

In human hearts, nor less in mine towards thee,
Caus'd what I did? I saw thee mutable
Of fancy, feard lest one day thou wouldst leave me
As her at *Timna,* sought by all means therefore
How to endear, and hold thee to me firmest:
No better way I saw then by importuning
To learn thy secrets, get into my power
Thy key of strength and safety: thou wilt say,
Why then reveal'd? I was assur'd by those   800
Who tempted me, that nothing was design'd
Against thee but safe custody, and hold:
That made for me, I knew that liberty
Would draw thee forth to perilous enterprises,
While I at home sate full of cares and fears
Wailing thy absence in my widow'd bed;
Here I should still enjoy thee day and night
Mine and Loves prisoner, not the *Philistines,*
Whole to my self, unhazarded abroad,
Fearless at home of partners in my love.   810
These reasons in Loves law have past for good,
Though fond and reasonless to some perhaps;
And Love hath oft, well meaning, wrought much wo,
Yet always pity or pardon hath obtain'd.
Be not unlike all others, not austere
As thou art strong, inflexible as steel.
If thou in strength all mortals dost exceed,
In uncompassionate anger do not so.
      Sam. How cunningly the sorceress displays
Her own transgressions, to upbraid me mine?   820
That malice not repentance brought thee hither,
By this appears: I gave, thou say'st, th' example,
I led the way; bitter reproach, but true,
I to my self was false e're thou to me,
Such pardon therefore as I give my folly,
Take to thy wicked deed: which when thou seest
Impartial, self-severe, inexorable,
Thou wilt renounce thy seeking, and much rather
Confess it feign'd, weakness is thy excuse,
And I believe it, weakness to resist   830
Philistian gold: if weakness may excuse,
What Murtherer, what Traytor, Parricide,
Incestuous, Sacrilegious, but may plead it?
All wickedness is weakness: that plea therefore
With God or Man will gain thee no remission.
But Love constrain'd thee; call it furious rage
To satisfie thy lust: Love seeks to have Love;
My love how couldst thou hope, who tookst the way
To raise in me inexpiable hate,
Knowing, as needs I must, by thee betray'd?   840
In vain thou striv'st to cover shame with shame,
Or by evasions thy crime uncoverst more.
      Dal. Since thou determinst weakness for no plea
In man or woman, though to thy own condemning,

Hear what assaults I had, what snares besides,
What sieges girt me round, e're I consented;
Which might have aw'd the best resolv'd of men,
The constantest to have yielded without blame.
It was not gold, as to my charge thou lay'st,
That wrought with me: thou know'st the Magistrates   850
And Princes of my countrey came in person,
Sollicited, commanded, threatn'd, urg'd,
Adjur'd by all the bonds of civil Duty
And of Religion, press'd how just it was,
How honourable, how glorious to entrap
A common enemy, who had destroy'd
Such numbers of our Nation: and the Priest
Was not behind, but ever at my ear,
Preaching how meritorious with the gods
It would be to ensnare an irreligious   860
Dishonourer of *Dagon*: what had I
To oppose against such powerful arguments?
Only my love of thee held long debate;
And combated in silence all these reasons
With hard contest: at length that grounded maxim
So rife and celebrated in the mouths
Of wisest men; that to the public good
Private respects must yield; with grave authority
Took full possession of me and prevail'd;
Vertue, as I thought, truth, duty so enjoyning.   870
    Sam. I thought where all thy circling wiles would end;
In feign'd Religion, smooth hypocrisie.
But had thy love, still odiously pretended,
Bin, as it ought, sincere, it would have taught thee
Far other reasonings, brought forth other deeds.
I before all the daughters of my Tribe
And of my Nation chose thee from among
My enemies, lov'd thee, as too well thou knew'st,
Too well, unbosom'd all my secrets to thee,
Not out of levity, but over-powr'd   880
By thy request, who could deny thee nothing;
Yet now am judg'd an enemy. Why then
Didst thou at first receive me for thy husband?
Then, as since then, thy countries foe profest:
Being once a wife, for me thou wast to leave
Parents and countrey; nor was I their subject,
Nor under their protection but my own,
Thou mine, not theirs: if aught against my life
Thy countrey sought of thee, it sought unjustly,
Against the law of nature, law of nations,   890
No more thy countrey, but an impious crew
Of men conspiring to uphold thir state
By worse then hostile deeds, violating the ends
For which our countrey is a name so dear;
Not therefore to be obey'd. But zeal mov'd thee;
To please thy gods thou didst it; gods unable
To acquit themselves and prosecute their foes

But by ungodly deeds, the contradiction
Of their own deity, Gods cannot be:
Less therefore to be pleas'd, obey'd, or fear'd,
These false pretexts and varnish'd colours failing,
Bare in thy guilt how foul must thou appear?
   Dal. In argument with men a woman ever
Goes by the worse, whatever be her cause.
   Sam. For want of words no doubt, or lack of breath,
Witness when I was worried with thy peals.
   Dal. I was a fool, too rash, and quite mistaken
In what I thought would have succeeded best.
Let me obtain forgiveness of thee, *Samson,*
Afford me place to shew what recompence
Towards thee I intend for what I have misdone,
Misguided; only what remains past cure
Bear not too sensibly, nor still insist
To afflict thy self in vain: though sight be lost,
Life yet hath many solaces, enjoy'd
Where other senses want not their delights
At home in leisure and domestic ease,
Exempt from many a care and chance to which
Eye-sight exposes daily men abroad.
I to the Lords will intercede, not doubting
Thir favourable ear, that I may fetch thee
From forth this loathsom prison-house, to abide
With me, where my redoubl'd love and care
With nursing diligence, to me glad office,
May ever tend about thee to old age
With all things gratful chear'd, and so suppli'd,
That what by me thou hast lost thou least shalt miss.
   Sam. No, no, of my condition take no care;
It fits not; thou and I long since are twain;
Nor think me so unwary or accurst
To bring my feet again into the snare
Where once I have been caught; I know thy trains
Though dearly to my cost, thy ginns, and toyls;
Thy fair enchanted cup, and warbling charms
No more on me have power, their force is null'd,
So much of Adders wisdom I have learn't
To fence my ear against thy sorceries.
If in my flower of youth and strength, when all men
Lov'd, honour'd, fear'd me, thou alone could hate me
Thy Husband, slight me, sell me, and forgo me;
How wouldst thou use me now, blind, and thereby
Deceiveable, in most things as a child
Helpless, thence easily contemn'd, and scorn'd,
And last neglected? How wouldst thou insult
When I must live uxorious to thy will
In perfect thraldom, how again betray me,
Bearing my words and doings to the Lords
To gloss upon, and censuring, frown or smile?
This Gaol I count the house of Liberty
To thine whose doors my feet shall never enter.

900

910

920

930

940

950

Dal. Let me approach at least, and touch thy hand.
Sam. Not for thy life, lest fierce remembrance wake
My sudden rage to tear thee joint by joint.
At distance I forgive thee, go with that;
Bewail thy falshood, and the pious works
It hath brought forth to make thee memorable
Among illustrious women, faithful wives:
Cherish thy hast'n'd widowhood with the gold
Of Matrimonial treason: so farewel.
   Dal. I see thou art implacable, more deaf   960
To prayers, then winds and seas, yet winds to seas
Are reconcil'd at length, and Sea to Shore:
Thy anger, unappeasable, still rages,
Eternal tempest never to be calm'd.
Why do I humble thus my self, and suing
For peace, reap nothing but repulse and hate?
Bid go with evil omen and the brand
Of infamy upon my name denounc't?
To mix with thy concernments I desist
Henceforth, nor too much disapprove my own.   970
Fame if not double-fac't is double-mouth'd,
And with contrary blast proclaims most deeds,
On both his wings, one black, th' other white,
Bears greatest names in his wild aerie flight.
My name perhaps among the Circumcis'd
In *Dan,* in *Judah,* and the bordering Tribes,
To all posterity may stand defam'd,
With malediction mention'd, and the blot
Of falshood most unconjugal traduc't.
But in my countrey where I most desire,   980
In *Ecron, Gaza, Asdod,* and in *Gath*
I shall be nam'd among the famousest
Of Women, sung at solemn festivals,
Living and dead recorded, who to save
Her countrey from a fierce destroyer, chose
Above the faith of wedlock-bands, my tomb
With odours visited and annual flowers.
Not less renown'd then in Mount *Ephraim,*
Jael, who with inhospitable guile
Smote *Sisera* sleeping through the Temples nail'd.   990
Nor shall I count it hainous to enjoy
The public marks of honour and reward
Conferr'd upon me, for the piety
Which to my countrey I was judg'd to have shewn.
At this who ever envies or repines
I leave him to his lot, and like my own.
   Chor. She's gone, a manifest Serpent by her sting
Discover'd in the end, till now conceal'd.
   Sam. So let her go, God sent her to debase me,
And aggravate my folly who committed   1000
To such a viper his most sacred trust
Of secresie, my safety, and my life.
   Chor. Yet beauty, though injurious, hath strange power,

After offence returning, to regain
Love once possest, nor can be easily
Repuls't, without much inward passion felt
And secret sting of amorous remorse.
    Sam. Love-quarrels oft in pleasing concord end,
Not wedlock-trechery endangering life.
    Chor. It is not vertue, wisdom, valour, wit,   1010
Strength, comliness of shape, or amplest merit
That womans love can win or long inherit;
But what it is, hard is to say,
Harder to hit,
(Which way soever men refer it)
Much like thy riddle, *Samson,* in one day
Or seven, though one should musing sit;
    If any of these or all, the *Timnian* bride
Had not so soon preferr'd
Thy Paranymph, worthless to thee compar'd,   1020
Successour in thy bed,
Nor both so loosly disally'd
Thir nuptials, nor this last so trecherously
Had shorn the fatal harvest of thy head.
Is it for that such outward ornament
Was lavish't on thir Sex, that inward gifts
Were left for hast unfinish't, judgment scant,
Capacity not rais'd to apprehend
Or value what is best
In choice, but oftest to affect the wrong?   1030
Or was too much of self-love mixt,
Of constancy no root infixt,
That either they love nothing, or not long?
    What e're it be, to wisest men and best
Seeming at first all heavenly under virgin veil,
Soft, modest, meek, demure,
Once join'd, the contrary she proves, a thorn
Intestin, far within defensive arms
A cleaving mischief, in his way to vertue
Adverse and turbulent, or by her charms   1040
Draws him awry enslav'd
With dotage, and his sense deprav'd
To folly and shameful deeds which ruin ends.
What Pilot so expert but needs must wreck
Embarqu'd with such a Stears-mate at the Helm?
    Favour'd of Heav'n who finds
One vertuous rarely found,
That in domestic good combines:
Happy that house! his way to peace is smooth:
But vertue which breaks through all opposition,   1050
And all temptation can remove,
Most shines and most is acceptable above.
    Therefore Gods universal Law
Gave to the man despotic power
Over his female in due awe,
Nor from that right to part an hour,

Smile she or lowre:
So shall he least confusion draw
On his whole life, not sway'd
By female usurpation, nor dismay'd.   1060
  But had we best retire, I see a storm?
  Sam. Fair days have oft contracted wind and rain.
  Chor. But this another kind of tempest brings.
  Sam. Be less abstruse, my riddling days are past.
  Chor. Look now for no inchanting voice, nor fear
The bait of honied words; a rougher tongue
Draws hitherward, I know him by his stride,
The Giant *Harapha* of *Gath,* his look
Haughty as is his pile high-built and proud.
Comes he in peace? what wind hath blown him hither   1070
I less conjecture then when first I saw
The sumptuous *Dalila* floating this way:
His habit carries peace, his brow defiance.
  Sam. Or peace or not, alike to me he comes.
  Chor. His fraught we soon shall know, he now arrives.
  Har. I come not *Samson,* to condole thy chance,
As these perhaps, yet wish it had not been,
Though for no friendly intent. I am of *Gath*
Men call me *Harapha,* of stock renown'd
As *Og* or *Anak* and the *Emims* old   1080
That *Kiriathaim* held, thou knowst me now
If thou at all art known. Much I have heard
Of thy prodigious might and feats perform'd
Incredible to me, in this displeas'd,
That I was never present on the place
Of those encounters where we might have tri'd
Each others force in camp or listed field:
And now am come to see of whom such noise
Hath walk'd about, and each limb to survey,
If thy appearance answer loud report.   1090
  Sam. The way to know were not to see but taste.
  Har. Dost thou already single me; I thought
Gives and the Mill had tam'd thee; O that fortune
Had brought me to the field where thou art fam'd
To have wrought such wonders with an Asses Jaw;
I should have forc'd thee soon with other arms,
Or left thy carkass where the Ass lay thrown:
So had the glory of Prowess been recover'd
To *Palestine,* won by a *Philistine*
From the unforeskinn'd race, of whom thou bear'st   1100
The highest name for valiant Acts, that honour
Certain to have won by mortal duel from thee,
I lose, prevented by thy eyes put out.
  Sam. Boast not of what thou wouldst have done, but do
What then thou would'st, thou seest it in thy hand.
  Har. To combat with a blind man I disdain,
And thou hast need much washing to be toucht.
  Sam. Such usage as your honourable Lords
Afford me assassinated and betrav'd,

Who durst not with thir whole united powers   1110
In fight withstand me single and unarm'd,
Nor in the house with chamber Ambushes
Close-banded durst attaque me, no not sleeping,
Till they had hir'd a woman with their gold
Breaking her Marriage Faith to circumvent me.
Therefore without feign'd shifts let be assign'd
Some narrow place enclos'd, where sight may give thee,
Or rather flight, no great advantage on me;
Then put on all thy gorgeous arms, thy Helmet
And Brigandine of brass, thy broad Habergeon,   1120
Vant-brass and Greves, and Gauntlet, add thy Spear
A Weavers beam, and seven-times-folded shield,
I only with an Oak'n staff will meet thee,
And raise such out-cries on thy clatter'd Iron,
Which long shall not with-hold mee from thy head,
That in a little time while breath remains thee,
Thou oft shalt wish thy self at *Gath* to boast
Again in safety what thou wouldst have done
To *Samson,* but shalt never see *Gath* more.
    Har. Thou durst not thus disparage glorious arms   1130
Which greatest Heroes have in battel worn,
Thir ornament and safety, had not spells
And black enchantments, some Magicians Art
Arm'd thee or charm'd thee strong, which thou from Heaven
Feigndst at thy birth was giv'n thee in thy hair,
Where strength can least abide, though all thy hairs
Were bristles rang'd like those that ridge the back
Of chaf't wild Boars, or ruffl'd Porcupines.
    Sam. I know no Spells, use no forbidden Arts;
My trust is in the living God who gave me   1140
At my Nativity this strength, diffus'd
No less through all my sinews, joints and bones,
Then thine, while I preserv'd these locks unshorn,
The pledge of my unviolated vow.
For proof hereof, if *Dagon* be thy god,
Go to his Temple, invocate his aid
With solemnest devotion, spread before him
How highly it concerns his glory now
To frustrate and dissolve these Magic spells,
Which I to be the power of *Israel's* God   1150
Avow, and challenge *Dagon* to the test,
Offering to combat thee his Champion bold,
With th' utmost of his Godhead seconded:
Then thou shalt see, or rather to thy sorrow
Soon feel, whose God is strongest, thine or mine.
    Har. Presume not on thy God, what e're he be,
Thee he regards not, owns not, hath cut off
Quite from his people, and delivered up
Into thy Enemies hand, permitted them
To put out both thine eyes, and fetter'd send thee   1160
Into the common Prison, there to grind
Among the Slaves and Asses thy comrades,

As good for nothing else, no better service
With those thy boyst'rous locks, no worthy match
For valour to assail, nor by the sword
Of noble Warriour, so to stain his honour,
But by the Barbers razor best subdu'd.
   Sam. All these indignities, for such they are
From thine, these evils I deserve and more,
Acknowledge them from God inflicted on me   1170
Justly, yet despair not of his final pardon
Whose ear is ever open; and his eye
Gracious to re-admit the suppliant;
In confidence whereof I once again
Defie thee to the trial of mortal fight,
By combat to decide whose god is god,
Thine or whom I with *Israel's* Sons adore.
   Har. Fair honour that thou dost thy God, in trusting
He will accept thee to defend his cause,
A Murtherer, a Revolter, and a Robber.   1180
   Sam. Tongue-doubtie Giant, how dost thou prove me these?
   Har. Is not thy Nation subject to our Lords?
Their Magistrates confest it, when they took thee
As a League-breaker and deliver'd bound
Into our hands: for hadst thou not committed
Notorious murder on those thirty men
At *Askalon,* who never did thee harm,
Then like a Robber stripdst them of thir robes?
The *Philistines,* when thou hadst broke the league,
Went up with armed powers thee only seeking,   1190
To others did no violence nor spoil.
   Sam. Among the Daughters of the *Philistines*
I chose a Wife, which argu'd me no foe;
And in your City held my Nuptial Feast:
But your ill-meaning Politician Lords,
Under pretence of Bridal friends and guests,
Appointed to await me thirty spies,
Who threatning cruel death constrain'd the bride
To wring from me and tell to them my secret,
That solv'd the riddle which I had propos'd.   1200
When I perceiv'd all set on enmity,
As on my enemies, where ever chanc'd,
I us'd hostility, and took thir spoil
To pay my underminers in thir coin.
My Nation was subjected to your Lords.
It was the force of Conquest; force with force
Is well ejected when the Conquer'd can.
But I a private person, whom my Countrey
As a league-breaker gave up bound, presum'd
Single Rebellion and did Hostile Acts.   1210
I was no private but a person rais'd
With strength sufficient and command from Heav'n
To free my Countrey; if their servile minds
Me their Deliverer sent would not receive,
But to thir Masters gave me up for nought,

Th' unworthier they; whence to this day they serve.
I was to do my part from Heav'n assign'd,
And had perform'd it if my known offence
Had not disabl'd me, not all your force:
These shifts refuted, answer thy appellant   1220
Though by his blindness maim'd for high attempts,
Who now defies thee thrice to single fight,
As a petty enterprise of small enforce.
    Har. With thee a Man condemn'd, a Slave enrol'd,
Due by the Law to capital punishment?
To fight with thee no man of arms will deign.
    Sam. Cam'st thou for this, vain boaster, to survey me,
To descant on my strength, and give thy verdit?
Come nearer, part not hence so slight inform'd;
But take good heed my hand survey not thee.   1230
    Har. O *Baal-zebub!* can my ears unus'd
Hear these dishonours, and not render death?
    Sam. No man with-holds thee, nothing from thy hand
Fear I incurable; bring up thy van,
My heels are fetter'd, but my fist is free.
    Har. This insolence other kind of answer fits.
    Sam. Go baffl'd coward, lest I run upon thee,
Though in these chains, bulk without spirit vast,
And with one buffet lay thy structure low,
Or swing thee in the Air, then dash thee down   1240
To the hazard of thy brains and shatter'd sides.
    Har. By *Astaroth* e're long thou shalt lament
These braveries in Irons loaden on thee.
    Chor. His Giantship is gone somewhat crest-fall'n,
Stalking with less unconsci'nable strides,
And lower looks, but in a sultrie chafe.
    Sam. I dread him not, nor all his Giant-brood,
Though Fame divulge him Father of five Sons
All of Gigantic size, *Goliah* chief.
    Chor. He will directly to the Lords, I fear,   1250
And with malitious counsel stir them up
Some way or other yet further to afflict thee.
    Sam. He must allege some cause, and offer'd fight
Will not dare mention, lest a question rise
Whether he durst accept the offer or not,
And that he durst not plain enough appear'd.
Much more affliction then already felt
They cannot well impose, nor I sustain;
If they intend advantage of my labours
The work of many hands, which earns my keeping   1260
With no small profit daily to my owners.
But come what will, my deadliest foe will prove
My speediest friend, by death to rid me hence,
The worst that he can give, to me the best.
Yet so it may fall out, because thir end
Is hate, not help to me, it may with mine
Draw thir own ruin who attempt the deed.
    Chor. Oh how comely it is and how reviving

To the Spirits of just men long opprest!
When God into the hands of thir deliverer   1270
Puts invincible might
To quell the mighty of the Earth, th' oppressour,
The brute and boist'rous force of violent men
Hardy and industrous to support
Tyrannic power, but raging to pursue
The righteous and all such as honour Truth;
He all thir Ammunition
And feats of War defeats
With plain Heroic magnitude of mind
And celestial vigour arm'd,   1280
Thir Armories and Magazins contemns,
Renders them useless, while
With winged expedition
Swift as the lightning glance he executes
His errand on the wicked, who surpris'd
Lose thir defence distracted and amaz'd.
　　But patience is more oft the exercise
Of Saints, the trial of thir fortitude,
Making them each his own Deliverer,
And Victor over all   1290
That tyrannie or fortune can inflict,
Either of these is in thy lot,
Samson, with might endu'd
Above the Sons of men; but sight bereav'd
May chance to number thee with those
Whom Patience finally must crown.
This Idols day hath bin to thee no day of rest,
　　Labouring thy mind
More then the working day thy hands,
And yet perhaps more trouble is behind.   1300
For I descry this way
Some other tending, in his hand
A Scepter or quaint staff he bears,
Comes on amain, speed in his look.
By his habit I discern him now
A Public Officer, and now at hand.
His message will be short and voluble.
　　Off. *Ebrews,* the Pris'ner *Samson* here I seek.
　　Chor. His manacles remark him, there he sits.
　　Off. *Samson,* to thee our Lords thus bid me say;   1310
This day to *Dagon* is a solemn Feast,
With Sacrifices, Triumph, Pomp, and Games;
Thy strength they know surpassing human rate,
And now some public proof thereof require
To honour this great Feast, and great Assembly;
Rise therefore with all speed and come along,
Where I will see thee heartn'd and fresh clad
To appear as fits before th' illustrious Lords.
　　Sam. Thou knowst I am an *Ebrew,* therefore tell them,
Our Law forbids at thir Religious Rites   1320
My presence; for that cause I cannot come.

Off. This answer, be assur'd, will not content them.
Sam. Have they not Sword-players, and ev'ry sort
Of Gymnic Artists, Wrestlers, Riders, Runners,
Juglers and Dancers, Antics, Mummers, Mimics,
But they must pick me out with shackles tir'd,
And over-labour'd at thir publick Mill,
To make them sport with blind activity?
Do they not seek occasion of new quarrels
On my refusal to distress me more,   1330
Or make a game of my calamities?
Return the way thou cam'st, I will not come.
    Off. Regard thy self, this will offend them highly.
    Sam. My self? my conscience and internal peace.
Can they think me so broken, so debas'd
With corporal servitude, that my mind ever
Will condescend to such absurd commands?
Although thir drudge, to be thir fool or jester,
And in my midst of sorrow and heart-grief
To shew them teats and play before thir god,   1340
The worst of all indignities, yet on me
Joyn'd with extream contempt? I will not come.
    Off. My message was impos'd on me with speed,
Brooks no delay: is this thy resolution?
    Sam. So take it with what speed thy message needs.
    Off. I am sorry what this stoutness will produce.
    Sam. Perhaps thou shalt have cause to sorrow indeed.
    Chor. Consider, *Samson;* matters now are strain'd
Up to the highth, whether to hold or break;
He's gone, and who knows how he may report   1350
Thy words by adding fuel to the flame?
Expect another message more imperious,
More Lordly thund'ring then thou well wilt bear.
    Sam. Shall I abuse this Consecrated gift
Of strength, again returning with my hair
After my great transgression, so requite
Favour renew'd, and add a greater sin
By prostituting holy things to Idols;
A *Nazarite* in place abominable
Vaunting my strength in honour to thir *Dagon?*   1360
Besides, how vile, contemptible, ridiculous,
What act more execrably unclean, prophane?
    Chor. Yet with this strength thou serv'st the *Philistines,*
Idolatrous, uncircumcis'd, unclean.
    Sam. Not in thir Idol-worship, but by labour
Honest and lawful to deserve my food
Of those who have me in thir civil power.
    Chor. Where the heart joins not, outward acts defile not.
    Sam. Where outward force constrains, the sentence holds
But who constrains me to the Temple of *Dagon,*   1370
Not dragging? the *Philistian* Lords command.
Commands are no constraints. If I obey them,
I do it freely; venturing to displease
God for the fear of Man, and Man prefer,

Set God behind: which in his jealousie
Shall never, unrepented, find forgiveness.
Yet that he may dispense with me or thee
Present in Temples at Idolatrous Rites
For some important cause, thou needst not doubt.
   Chor. How thou wilt here come off surmounts my reach.   1380
   Sam. Be of good courage, I begin to feel
Some rouzing motions in me which dispose
To something extraordinary my thoughts.
I with this Messenger will go along,
Nothing to do, be sure, that may dishonour
Our Law, or stain my vow of *Nazarite*.
If there be aught of presage in the mind,
This day will be remarkable in my life
By some great act, or of my days the last.
   Chor. In time thou hast resolv'd, the man returns.   1390
   Off. Samson, this second message from our Lords
To thee I am bid say. Art thou our Slave,
Our Captive, at the public Mill our drudge,
And dar'st thou at our sending and command
Dispute thy coming? come without delay;
Or we shall find such Engines to assail
And hamper thee, as thou shalt come of force,
Though thou wert firmlier fastn'd then a rock.
   Sam. I could be well content to try thir Art,
Which to no few of them would prove pernicious.   1400
Yet knowing thir advantages too many,
Because they shall not trail me through thir streets
Like a wild Beast, I am content to go.
Masters commands come with a power resistless
To such as owe them absolute subjection;
And for a life who will not change his purpose?
(So mutable are all the ways of men)
Yet this be sure, in nothing to comply
Scandalous or forbidden in our Law.
   Off. I praise thy resolution, doff these links: 1410
By this compliance thou wilt win the Lords
To favour, and perhaps to set thee free.
   Sam. Brethren farewel, your company along
I will not wish, lest it perhaps offend them
To see me girt with Friends; and how the sight
Of me as of a common Enemy,
So dreaded once, may now exasperate them
I know not. Lords are Lordliest in thir wine;
And the well-feasted Priest then soonest fir'd
With zeal, if aught Religion seem concern'd: 1420
No less the people on thir Holy-days
Impetuous, insolent, unquenchable;
Happ'n what may, of me expect to hear
Nothing dishonourable, impure, unworthy
Our God, our Law, my Nation, or my self,
The last of me or no I cannot warrant.
   Chor. Go, and the Holy One

Of *Israel* be thy guide
To what may serve his glory best, & spread his name
Great among the Heathen round: 1430
Send thee the Angel of thy Birth, to stand
Fast by thy side, who from thy Fathers field
Rode up in flames after his message told
Of thy conception, and be now a shield
Of fire; that Spirit that first rusht on thee
In the camp of *Dan*
Be efficacious in thee now at need.
For never was from Heaven imparted
Measure of strength so great to mortal seed,
As in thy wond'rous actions hath been seen.   1440
But wherefore comes old *Manoa* in such hast
With youthful steps? much livelier then e're while
He seems: supposing here to find his Son,
Or of him bringing to us some glad news?
    Man. Peace with you brethren; my inducement hither
Was not at present here to find my Son,
By order of the Lords new parted hence
To come and play before them at thir Feast.
I heard all as I came, the City rings
And numbers thither flock, I had no will,   1450
Lest I should see him forc't to things unseemly.
But that which mov'd my coming now, was chiefly
To give ye part with me what hope I have
With good success to work his liberty.
    Chor. That hope would much rejoyce us to partake
With thee; say reverend Sire, we thirst to hear.
    Man. I have attempted one by one the Lords
Either at home, or through the high street passing,
With supplication prone and Fathers tears
To accept of ransom for my Son thir pris'ner,   1460
Some much averse I found and wondrous harsh,
Contemptuous, proud, set on revenge and spite;
That part most reverenc'd *Dagon* and his Priests,
Others more moderate seeming, but thir aim
Private reward, for which both God and State
They easily would set to sale, a third
More generous far and civil, who confess'd
They had anough reveng'd, having reduc't
Thir foe to misery beneath thir fears,
The rest was magnanimity to remit,   1470
If some convenient ransom were propos'd.
What noise or shout was that? it tore the Skie.
    Chor. Doubtless the people shouting to behold
Thir once great dread, captive, & blind before them,
Or at some proof of strength before them shown.
    Man. His ransom, if my whole inheritance
May compass it, shall willingly be paid
And numberd down: much rather I shall chuse
To live the poorest in my Tribe, then richest,
And he in that calamitous prison left.   1480

No, I am fixt not to part hence without him.
For his redemption all my Patrimony,
If need be I am ready to forgo
And quit: not wanting him, I shall want nothing.
   Chor. Fathers are wont to lay up for thir Sons,
Thou for thy Son art bent to lay out all;
Sons wont to nurse thir Parents in old age,
Thou in old age car'st how to nurse thy Son
Made older then thy age through eye-sight lost.
   Man. It shall be my delight to tend his eyes,   1490
And view him sitting in the house, enobl'd
With all those high exploits by him atchiev'd,
And on his shoulders waving down those locks,
That of a Nation arm'd the strength contain'd:
And I perswade me God had not permitted
His strength again to grow up with his hair
Garrison'd round about him like a Camp
Of faithful Souldiery, were not his purpose
To use him further yet in some great service,
Not to sit idle with so great a gift   1500
Useless, and thence ridiculous about him.
And since his strength with eye-sight was not lost,
God will restore him eye-sight to his strength.
   Chor. Thy hopes are not ill founded nor seem vain
Of his delivery, and thy joy thereon
Conceiv'd, agreeable to a Fathers love,
In both which we, as next participate.
   Man. I know your friendly minds and—O what noise!
Mercy of Heav'n what hideous noise was that!
Horribly loud unlike the former shout.   1510
   Chor. Noise call you it or universal groan
As if the whole inhabitation perish'd,
Blood, death, and deathful deeds are in that noise,
Ruin, destruction at the utmost point.
   Man. Of ruin indeed methought I heard the noise,
Oh it continues, they have slain my Son.
   Chor. Thy Son is rather slaying them, that outcry
From slaughter of one foe could not ascend.
   Man. Some dismal accident it needs must be;
What shall we do, stay here or run and see?   1520
   Chor. Best keep together here, lest running thither
We unawares run into dangers mouth.
This evil on the *Philistines* is fall'n,
From whom could else a general cry be heard?
The sufferers then will scarce molest us here,
From other hands we need not much to fear.
What if his eye-sight (for to *Israels* God
Nothing is hard) by miracle restor'd,
He now be dealing dole among his foes,
And over heaps of slaughter'd walk his way?   1530
   Man. That were a joy presumptuous to be thought.
   Chor. Yet God hath wrought things as incredible
For his people of old; what hinders now?

Man. He can I know, but doubt to think he will;
Yet Hope would fain subscribe, and tempts Belief.
A little stay will bring some notice hither.
   Chor. Of good or bad so great, of bad the sooner;
For evil news rides post, while good news baits.
And to our wish I see one hither speeding,
An *Ebrew,* as I guess, and of our Tribe.   1540
   Mess. O whither shall I run, or which way flie
The sight of this so horrid spectacle
Which earst my eyes beheld and yet behold;
For dire imagination still persues me.
But providence or instinct of nature seems,
Or reason though disturb'd, and scarse consulted
To have guided me aright, I know not how,
To thee first reverend *Manoa,* and to these
My Countreymen, whom here I knew remaining,
As at some distance from the place of horrour,   1550
So in the sad event too much concern'd.
   Man. The accident was loud, & here before thee
With rueful cry, yet what it was we hear not,
No Preface needs, thou seest we long to know.
   Mess. It would burst forth, but I recover breath
And sense distract, to know well what I utter.
   Man. Tell us the sum, the circumstance defer.
   Mess. Gaza yet stands, but all her Sons are fall'n,
All in a moment overwhelm'd and fall'n.
   Man. Sad, but thou knowst to *Israelites* not saddest   1560
The desolation of a Hostile City.
   Mess. Feed on that first, there may in grief be surfet.
   Man. Relate by whom. *Mess.* By *Samson.*
     Man. That still lessens
The sorrow, and converts it nigh to joy.
   Mess. Ah *Manoa* I refrain, too suddenly
To utter what will come at last too soon;
Lest evil tidings with too rude irruption
Hitting thy aged ear should pierce too deep.
   Man. Suspense in news is torture, speak them out.
   Mess. Then take the worst in brief, *Samson* is dead.   1570
   Man. The worst indeed, O all my hope's defeated
To free him hence! but death who sets all free
Hath paid his ransom now and full discharge.
What windy joy this day had I conceiv'd
Hopeful of his Delivery, which now proves
Abortive as the first-born bloom of spring
Nipt with the lagging rear of winters frost.
Yet e're I give the rains to grief, say first,
How dy'd he? death to life is crown or shame.
All by him fell thou say'st, by whom fell he,   1580
What glorious hand gave *Samson* his deaths wound?
   Mess. Unwounded of his enemies he fell.
   Man. Wearied with slaughter then or how? explain.
   Mess. By his own hands. *Man.* Self-violence? what cause
Brought him so soon at variance with himself

Among his foes? *Mess.* Inevitable cause
At once both to destroy and be destroy'd;
The Edifice where all were met to see him
Upon thir heads and on his own he pull'd.
   Man. O lastly over-strong against thy self!   1590
A dreadful way thou took'st to thy revenge.
More then anough we know; but while things yet
Are in confusion, give us if thou canst,
Eye-witness of what first or last was done,
Relation more particular and distinct.
   Mess. Occasions drew me early to this City,
And as the gates I enter'd with Sun-rise,
The morning Trumpets Festival proclaim'd
Through each high street: little I had dispatch't
When all abroad was rumour'd that this day   1600
Samson should be brought forth to shew the people
Proof of his mighty strength in feats and games;
I sorrow'd at his captive state, but minded
Not to be absent at that spectacle.
The building was a spacious Theatre
Half round on two main Pillars vaulted high,
With seats where all the Lords and each degree
Of sort, might sit in order to behold,
The other side was op'n, where the throng
On banks and scaffolds under Skie might stand;   1610
I among these aloof obscurely stood.
The Feast and noon grew high, and Sacrifice
Had fill'd thir hearts with mirth, high chear, & wine,
When to thir sports they turn'd. Immediately
Was *Samson* as a public servant brought,
In thir state Livery clad; before him Pipes
And Timbrels, on each side went armed guards,
Both horse and foot before him and behind
Archers, and Slingers, Cataphracts and Spears.
At sight of him the people with a shout   1620
Rifted the Air clamouring thir god with praise,
Who had made thir dreadful enemy thir thrall.
He patient but undaunted where they led him,
Came to the place, and what was set before him
Which without help of eye, might be assay'd,
To heave, pull, draw, or break, he still perform'd
All with incredible, stupendious force,
None daring to appear Antagonist.
At length for intermission sake they led him
Between the pillars; he his guide requested   1630
(For so from such as nearer stood we heard)
As over-tir'd to let him lean a while
With both his arms on those two massie Pillars
That to the arched roof gave main support.
He unsuspitious led him; which when *Samson*
Felt in his arms, with head a while enclin'd,
And eyes fast fixt he stood, as one who pray'd,
Or some great matter in his mind revolv'd.

At last with head erect thus cryed aloud,
Hitherto, Lords, what your commands impos'd 1640
I have perform'd, as reason was obeying,
Not without wonder or delight beheld.
Now of my own accord such other tryal
I mean to shew you of my strength, yet greater,
As with amaze shall strike all who behold.
This utter'd, straining all his nerves he bow'd,
As with the force of winds and waters pent,
When Mountains tremble, those two massie Pillars
With horrible convulsion to and fro,
He tugg'd, he shook, till down they came and drew 1650
The whole roof after them, with burst of thunder
Upon the heads of all who sate beneath,
Lords, Ladies, Captains, Councellors, or Priests,
Thir choice nobility and flower, not only
Of this but each *Philistian* City round
Met from all parts to solemnize this Feast.
Samson with these immixt, inevitably
Pulld down the same destruction on himself;
The vulgar only scap'd who stood without.
  Chor. O dearly-bought revenge, yet glorious! 1660
Living or dying thou hast fulfill'd
The work for which thou wast foretold
To *Israel,* and now ly'st victorious
Among thy slain self-kill'd
Not willingly, but tangl'd in the fold
Of dire necessity, whose law in death conjoin'd
Thee with thy slaughter'd foes in number more
Then all thy life had slain before.
  Semichor. While thir hearts were jocund and sublime,
Drunk with Idolatry, drunk with Wine, 1670
And fat regorg'd of Bulls and Goats,
Chaunting thir Idol, and preferring
Before our living Dread who dwells
In *Silo* his bright Sanctuary:
Among them he a spirit of phrenzie sent,
Who hurt thir minds,
And urg'd them on with mad desire
To call in hast for thir destroyer;
They only set on sport and play
Unweetingly importun'd 1680
Thir own destruction to come speedy upon them.
So fond are mortal men
Fall'n into wrath divine,
As thir own ruin on themselves to invite,
Insensate left, or to sense reprobate,
And with blindness internal struck.
  Semichor. But he though blind of sight,
Despis'd and thought extinguish't quite,
With inward eyes illuminated
His fierie vertue rouz'd 1690
From under ashes into sudden flame,

And as an ev'ning Dragon came,
Assailant on the perched roosts,
And nests in order rang'd
Of tame villatic Fowl; but as an Eagle
His cloudless thunder bolted on thir heads.
So vertue giv'n for lost,
Deprest, and overthrown, as seem'd,
Like that self-begott'n bird
In the *Arabian* woods embost,   170c
That no second knows nor third,
And lay e're while a Holocaust,
From out her ashie womb now teem'd,
Revives, reflourishes, then vigorous most
When most unactive deem'd,
And though her body die, her fame survives,
A secular bird ages of lives.
   Man. Come, come, no time for lamentation now,
Nor much more cause, *Samson* hath quit himself
Like *Samson,* and heroicly hath finish'd   1710
A life Heroic, on his Enemies
Fully reveng'd, hath left them years of mourning,
And lamentation to the Sons of *Caphtor*
Through all *Philistian* bounds. To *Israel*
Honour hath left, and freedom, let but them
Find courage to lay hold on this occasion,
To himself and Fathers house eternal fame;
And which is best and happiest yet, all this
With God not parted from him, as was feard,
But favouring and assisting to the end.   1720
Nothing is here for tears, nothing to wail
Or knock the breast, no weakness, no contempt,
Dispraise, or blame, nothing but well and fair,
And what may quiet us in a death so noble.
Let us go find the body where it lies
Sok't in his enemies blood, and from the stream
With lavers pure and cleansing herbs wash off
The clotted gore. I with what speed the while
(*Gaza* is not in plight to say us nay)
Will send for all my kindred, all my friends   1730
To fetch him hence and solemnly attend
With silent obsequie and funeral train
Home to his Fathers house: there will I build him
A Monument, and plant it round with shade
Of Laurel ever green, and branching Palm,
With all his Trophies hung, and Acts enroll'd
In copious Legend, or sweet Lyric Song.
Thither shall all the valiant youth resort,
And from his memory inflame thir breasts
To matchless valour, and adventures high: 1740
The Virgins also shall on feastful days
Visit his Tomb with flowers, only bewailing
His lot unfortunate in nuptial choice,
From whence captivity and loss of eyes.

Chor. All is best, though we oft doubt,
What th' unsearchable dispose
Of highest wisdom brings about,
And ever best found in the close.
Oft he seems to hide his face,
But unexpectedly returns   1750
And to his faithful Champion hath in place
Bore witness gloriously; whence *Gaza* mourns
And all that band them to resist
His uncontroulable intent,
His servants he with new acquist
Of true experience from this great event
With peace and consolation hath dismist,
And calm of mind all passion spent.

The End.

OF REFORMATION IN ENGLAND,

AND THE

CAUSES THAT HITHERTO HAVE HINDERED IT.

IN TWO BOOKS.

WRITTEN TO A FRIEND.

[The text is that of the first edition, 1641.]

THE FIRST BOOK.

Sir,—Amidst those deep and retired thoughts, which, with every man Christianly instructed, ought to be most frequent, of God, and of his miraculous ways and works amongst men, and of our religion and worship, to be performed to him; after the story of our Saviour Christ, suffering to the lowest bent of weakness in the flesh, and presently triumphing to the highest pitch of glory in the spirit, which drew up his body also; till we in both be united to him in the revelation of his kingdom, I do not know of anything more worthy to take up the whole passion of pity on the one side, and joy on the other, than to consider first the foul and sudden corruption, and then, after many a tedious age, the long deferred, but much more wonderful and happy reformation of the church in these latter days. Sad it is to think how that doctrine of the gospel, planted by teachers divinely inspired, and by them winnowed and sifted from the chaff of overdated ceremonies, and refined to such a spiritual height and temper of purity, and knowledge of the Creator, that the body, with all the circumstances of time and place, were purified by the affections of the regenerate soul, and nothing left impure but sin; faith needing not the weak and fallible office of the senses, to be either the ushers or interpreters of heavenly mysteries, save where our Lord himself in his sacraments ordained; that such a doctrine should, through the grossness and blindness of her professors, and the fraud of deceivable traditions, drag so downwards, as to backslide one way into the Jewish beggary of old cast rudiments, and stumble forward another way into the new-vomited paganism of sensual idolatry, attributing purity or impurity to things indifferent, that they might bring the inward acts of the spirit to the outward and customary eye-service of the body, as if they could make God earthly and fleshly, because they could not make themselves heavenly and spiritual; they began to draw down all the divine intercourse betwixt God and the soul, yea, the very shape of God himself, into an exterior and bodily form, urgently pretending a necessity and obligement of joining the body in a formal reverence and worship circumscribed; they hallowed it, they fumed it, they sprinkled it, they bedecked it, not in robes of pure innocency, but of pure linen, with other deformed and fantastic dresses, in palls and mitres, gold, and gewgaws fetched from Aaron's old wardrobe, or the flamins vestry; then was the priest set to con his motions and his postures, his liturgies and his lurries,

441

till the soul by this means of overbodying herself, given up justly to fleshly delights, bated her wing apace downward: and finding the ease she had from her visible and sensuous colleague, the body, in performance of religious duties, her pinions now broken, and flagging, shifted off from herself the labor of high soaring any more, forgot her heavenly flight, and left the dull and droiling carcase to plod on in the old road, and drudging trade of outward conformity. And here out of question from her perverse conceiting of God and holy things, she had fallen to believe no God at all, had not custom and the worm of conscience nipped her incredulity: hence to all the duties of evangelical grace, instead of the adoptive and cheerful boldness which our new alliance with God requires, came servile and thrallike fear: for in very deed, the superstitious man by his good will is an atheist; but being scared from thence by the pangs and gripes of a boiling conscience, all in a pudder shuffles up to himself such a God and such a worship as is most agreeable to remedy his fear; which fear of his, as also is his hope, fixed only upon the flesh, renders likewise the whole faculty of his apprehension carnal; and all the inward acts of worship, issuing from the native strength of the soul, run out lavishly to the upper skin, and there harden into a crust of formality. Hence men came to scan the scriptures by the letter, and in the covenant of our redemption, magnified the external signs more than the quickening power of the Spirit; and yet, looking on them through their own guiltiness with a servile fear, and finding as little comfort, or rather terror from them again, they knew not how to hide their slavish approach to God's behests, by them not understood, nor worthily received, but by cloaking their servile crouching to all religious presentments, sometimes lawful, sometimes idolatrous, under the name of humility, and terming the piebald frippery and ostentation of ceremonies, decency.

Then was baptism changed into a kind of exorcism, and water, sanctified by Christ's institute, thought little enough to wash off the original spot, without the scratch or cross impression of a priest's forefinger: and that feast of free grace and adoption to which Christ invited his disciples to sit as brethren, and coheirs of the happy covenant, which at that table was to be sealed to them, even that feast of love and heavenly-admitted fellowship, the seal of filial grace, became the subject of horror, and glouting adoration, pageanted about like a dreadful idol; which sometimes deceives well-meaning men, and beguiles them of their reward, by their voluntary humility; which indeed is fleshly pride, preferring a foolish sacrifice, and the rudiments of the world, as St. Paul to the Colossians explaineth, before a savory obedience to Christ's example. Such was Peter's unseasonable humility, as then his knowledge was small, when Christ came to wash his feet; who at an impertinent time would needs strain courtesy with his master, and falling troublesomely upon the lowly, all-wise, and unexaminable intention of Christ, in what he went with resolution to do, so provoked by his interruption the meek Lord, that he threatened to exclude him from his heavenly portion, unless he could be content to be less arrogant and stiffnecked in his humility.

But to dwell no longer in characterizing the depravities of the church, and how they sprung, and how they took increase; when I recall to mind at last, after so many dark ages, wherein the huge overshadowing train of error had almost swept all the stars out of the firmament of the church; how the bright and blissful Reformation (by divine power) struck through the black and settled night of ignorance and antichristian tyranny, methinks a sovereign and reviving joy must needs rush into the bosom of him that reads or hears; and the sweet odor of the returning gospel imbathe his soul with the fragrancy of heaven. Then was the sacred Bible sought out of the dusty corners where profane falsehood and neglect had thrown it, the schools opened, divine and human learning raked out of the embers of forgotten tongues, the princes and cities trooping apace to the new erected banner of salvation; the martyrs, with the unresistible might of weakness, shaking the powers of darkness, and scorning the fiery rage of the old red dragon.

The pleasing pursuit of these thoughts hath ofttimes led me into a serious question and debatement with myself, how it should come to pass that England (having had this grace and honor from God, to be the first that should set up a standard for the recovery of lost truth, and blow the first evangelic trumpet to the nations, holding up, as from a hill, the new lamp of saving light to all Christendom) should now be last and most unsettled in the enjoyment of that peace, whereof she taught the way to others; although indeed our Wickliffe's preaching, at which all the succeeding reformers more effectually lighted their tapers, was to his countrymen but a short [10] blaze, soon damped and stifled by the pope and prelates for six or seven kings' reigns; yet methinks the precedency which God gave this island, to be first restorer of buried truth, should have been followed with more happy success, and sooner attained perfection; in which as yet we are amongst the last: for, albeit in purity of doctrine we agree with our brethren; yet in discipline, which is the execution and applying of doctrine home, and [20] laying the salve to the very orifice of the wound, yea, tenting and searching to the core, without which pulpit preaching is but shooting at rovers; in this we are no better than a schism from all the Reformation, and a sore scandal to them: for while we hold ordination to belong only to bishops, as our prelates do, we must of necessity hold also their ministers to be no ministers, and shortly after their church to be no church: not to speak [30] of those senseless ceremonies which we only retain, as a dangerous earnest of sliding back to Rome, and serving merely, either as a mist to cover nakedness where true grace is extinguished, or as an interlude to set out the pomp of prelatism. Certainly it would be worth the while therefore, and the pains, to inquire more particularly, what, and how many the chief causes have been, that have still hindered our uniform consent to the [40] rest of the churches abroad, at this time especially when the kingdom is in a good propensity thereto, and all men in prayers, in hopes, or in disputes, either for or against it.

Yet I will not insist on that which may seem to be the cause on God's part; as his judgment on our sins, the trial of his own, the unmasking of hypocrites: nor shall I stay to speak of the continual eagerness and extreme diligence of the pope and papists to [50] stop the furtherance of reformation, which know they have no hold or hope of England, their lost darling, longer than the government

of bishops bolsters them out; and therefore plot all they can to uphold them, as may be seen by the book of Santa Clara, the popish priest, in defence of bishops, which came out piping hot much about the time that one of our own prelates, out of ominous fear, had writ on the same argument; as if they had joined their forces, like good confederates, to support one falling Babel.

But I shall chiefly endeavor to declare those causes that hinder the forwarding of true discipline, which are among ourselves. Orderly proceeding will divide our inquiry into our forefathers' days, and into our times. Henry VIII. was the first that rent this kingdom from the pope's subjection totally; but his quarrel being more about supremacy, than other faultiness in religion that he regarded, it is no marvel if he stuck where he did. The next default was in the bishops, who though they had renounced the pope, they still hugged the popedom, and shared the authority among themselves, by their six bloody articles, persecuting the protestants no slacker than the pope would have done. And doubtless, whenever the pope shall fall, if his ruin be not like the sudden downcome of a tower, the bishops, when they see him tottering, will leave him, and fall to scrambling, catch who may, he a patriarchdom, and another what comes next hand; as the French cardinal of late and the see of Canterbury hath plainly affected.

In Edward the Sixth's days, why a complete reformation was not effected, to any considerate man may appear. First, he no sooner entered into his kingdom, but into a war with Scotland; from whence the protector returning with victory, had but newly put his hand to repeal the six articles, and throw the images out of churches, but rebellions on all sides, stirred up by obdurate papists, and other tumults, with a plain war in Norfolk, holding tack against two of the king's generals, made them of force content themselves with what they had already done. Hereupon followed ambitious contentions among the peers, which ceased not but with the protector's death, who was the most zealous in this point: and then Northumberland was he that could do most in England, who little minding religion, (as his apostasy well showed at his death,) bent all his wit how to bring the right of the crown into his own line. And for the bishops, they were so far from any such worthy attempts, as that they suffered themselves to be the common stales, to countenance with their prostituted gravities every politic fetch that was then on foot, as oft as the potent statists pleased to employ them. Never do we read that they made use of their authority and high place of access, to bring the jarring nobility to Christian peace, or to withstand their disloyal projects: but if a toleration for mass were to be begged of the king for his sister Mary, lest Charles the Fifth should be angry, who but the grave prelates, Cranmer and Ridley, must be sent to extort it from the young king? But out of the mouth of that godly and royal child, Christ himself returned such an awful repulse to those halting and time-serving prelates, that after much bold importunity, they went their way not without shame and tears.

Nor was this the first time that they discovered to be followers of this world; for when the protector's brother, Lord Sudley, the admiral, through private malice and malengine, was to lose his life, no man could be found fitter than bishop Latimer (like another Dr. Shaw) to divulge in his sermon the forged accusations laid to his charge, thereby to defame him with the people, who else was thought would take ill the innocent man's death, unless the reverend bishop could warrant them there was no foul play. What could be more impious than to debar the children of the king from their right to the crown? to comply with the ambitious usurpation of a traitor, and to make void the last will of Henry VIII., to which the breakers had sworn observance? Yet bishop Cranmer, one of the executors, and the other bishops, none refusing, (lest they should resist the duke of Northumberland,) could find in their consciences to set their hands to the disenabling and defeating not only of the princess Mary the papist, but of Elizabeth the protestant, and (by the bishops' judgment) the lawful issue of king Henry.

Who then can think (though these prelates had sought a further reformation) that the least wry face of a politician would not have hushed them? But it will be said, these men were martyrs: what then? though every true

Christian will be a martyr when he is called to it, not presently does it follow, that every one suffering for religion is, without exception. St. Paul writes, that "a man may give his body to be burnt, (meaning for religion,) and yet not have charity:" he is not therefore above all possibility of erring, because he burns for some points of truth.

Witness the Arians and Pelagians, which were slain by the heathen for Christ's sake, yet we take both these for no true friends of Christ. If the martyrs (saith Cyprian in his 30th epistle) decree one thing, and the gospel another, either the martyrs must lose their crown by not observing the gospel for which they are martyrs, or the majesty of the gospel must be broken and lie flat, if it can be overtopped by the novelty of any other decree.

And here withal I invoke the Immortal Deity, revealer and judge of secrets, that wherever I have in this book plainly and roundly (though worthily and truly) laid open the faults and blemishes of fathers, martyrs, or Christian emperors, or have otherwise inveighed against error and superstition with vehement expressions; I have done it neither out of malice, nor list to speak evil, nor any vain glory, but of mere necessity to vindicate the spotless truth from an ignominious bondage, whose native worth is now become of such a low esteem, that she is like to find small credit with us for what she can say, unless she can bring a ticket from Cranmer, Latimer, and Ridley; or prove herself a retainer to Constantine, and wear his badge. More tolerable it were for the church of God, that all these names were utterly abolished, like the brazen serpent, than that men's fond opinion should thus idolize them, and the heavenly truth be thus captivated.

Now to proceed, whatsoever the bishops were, it seems they themselves were unsatisfied in matters of religion as they then stood, by that commission granted to eight bishops, eight other divines, eight civilians, eight common lawyers, to frame ecclesiastical constitutions; which no wonder if it came to nothing, for (as Hayward relates) both their professions and their ends were different. Lastly, we all know by examples, that exact reformation is not perfected at the first push, and those unwieldy times of Edward VI. may hold some plea by this excuse. Now let any reasonable man judge whether that king's reign be a fit time from whence to pattern out the constitution of a church discipline, much less that it should yield occasion from whence to foster and establish the continuance of imperfection, with the commendatory subscriptions of confessors and martyrs, to entitle and engage a glorious name to a gross corruption. It was not episcopacy that wrought in them the heavenly fortitude of martyrdom, as little is it that martyrdom can make good episcopacy; but it was episcopacy that led the good and holy men, through the temptation of the enemy, and the snare of this present world, to many blameworthy and opprobrious actions. And it is still episcopacy that before all our eyes worsens and slugs the most learned and seeming religious of our ministers, who no sooner advanced to it, but, like a seething pot set to cool, sensibly exhale and reak out the greatest part of that zeal and those gifts which were formerly in them, settling in a skinny congealment of ease and sloth at the top; and if they keep their learning by some potent sway of nature, it is a rare chance; but their devotion most commonly comes to that queazy temper of lukewarmness, that gives a vomit to God himself.

But what do we suffer misshapen and enormous prelatism, as we do, thus to blanch and varnish her deformities with the fair colors, as before of martyrdom, so now of episcopacy? They are not bishops, God and all good men know they are not, that have filled this land with late confusion and violence; but a tyrannical crew and corporation of imposters, that have blinded and abused the world so long under that name. He that, enabled with gifts from God, and the lawful and primitive choice of the church assembled in convenient number, faithfully from that time forward feeds his parochial flock, has his coequal and compresbyterial power to ordain ministers and deacons by public prayer, and vote of Christ's congregation in like sort as he himself was ordained, and is a true apostolic bishop. But when he steps up into the chair of pontifical pride, and changes a moderate and exemplary house for a misgoverned and haughty palace, spiritual dignity for carnal precedence, and secular high office and employment for the high negotiations of his heavenly embassage, then he degrades, then he unbishops himself; he that makes him bishop, makes him no bishop. No marvel therefore if St. Martin complained to Sulpitius Severus, that since he was bishop he felt inwardly a sensible decay of those virtues and graces that God had given him in great measure before; although the same Sulpitius write that he was nothing tainted or altered in his habit, diet, or personal demeanor from that simple plainness to which he first betook himself. It was not therefore that thing alone which God took displeasure at in the bishops of those times, but rather an universal rottenness and gangrene in the whole function.

From hence then I pass to queen Elizabeth, the next protestant prince, in whose days why religion attained not a perfect reducement in the beginning of her reign, I suppose the hindering causes will be found to be common with some formerly alleged for king Edward VI.; the greenness of the times, the weak estate which queen Mary left the realm in, the great places and offices executed by papists, the judges, the lawyers, the justices of peace for the most part popish, the bishops firm to Rome; from whence was to be expected the furious flashing of excommunications, and absolving the people from their obedience. Next, her private counsellors, whoever they were, persuaded her (as Camden writes) that the altering of ecclesiastical policy would move sedition. Then was the liturgy given to a number of moderate divines, and Sir Thomas Smith, a statesman, to be purged and physicked: and surely they were moderate divines indeed, neither hot nor cold; and Grindal, the best of them, afterwards archbishop of Canterbury, lost favor in the court, and I think was discharged the government of his see, for favoring the ministers, though Camden seem willing to find another cause: therefore about her second year, in a parliament of men and minds some scarce well grounded, others belching the sour crudities of yesterday's popery, those constitutions of Edward VI., which, as you heard before, no way satisfied the men that made them, are now established for best, and not to be mended. From that time followed nothing but imprisonments, troubles, disgraces on all those that found fault with the decrees of the convocation, and straight were they branded with the name of puritans. As for the queen herself, she was made believe that by putting down bishops her prerogative would be infringed, of which shall be spoken anon as the course of method brings it in: and why the prelates labored it should be so thought, ask not them, but ask their bellies. They had found a good tabernacle, they sat under a spreading vine, their lot was fallen in a fair inheritance. And these perhaps were the chief impeachments of a more sound rectifying the church in the queen's time.

From this period I count to begin our times, which because they concern us more nearly, and our own eyes and ears can give us the ampler scope to judge, will require a more exact search; and to effect this the speedier, I shall distinguish such as I esteem to be the hinderers of reformation into three sorts, Antiquitarians (for so I had rather call them than antiquaries, whose labors are useful and laudable). 2. Libertines. 3. Politicians.

To the votarists of antiquity I shall think to have fully answered, if I shall be able to prove out of antiquity, First, that if they will conform our bishops to the purer times, they must mew their feathers, and their pounces, and make but curtailed bishops of them; and we know they hate to be docked and clipped, as much as to be put down outright. Secondly, that those purer times were corrupt, and their books corrupted soon after. Thirdly, that the best of those that then wrote disclaim that any man should repose on them, and send all to the scriptures.

First therefore, if those that overaffect antiquity will follow the square thereof, their bishops must be elected by the hands of the whole church. The ancientest of the extant fathers, Ignatius, writing to the Philadelphians, saith "that it belongs to them as to the church of God to choose a bishop." Let no man cavil, but take the church of God as meaning the whole consistence of orders and members, as St. Paul's epistles express, and this likewise being read over: besides this, it is there to be marked, that those Philadelphians are exhorted to choose a bishop of Antioch. Whence it seems by the way that there was not that wary limitation of diocese in those times, which is confirmed even by a fast friend of episcopacy, Camden, who cannot but love bishops as well as old coins, and his much lamented monasteries, for antiquity's sake. He writes in his description of Scotland, that "over all the world bishops had no certain diocese till pope Dionysius about the year 268 did cut them out; and that the bishops of Scotland executed their function in what place soever they came indifferently, and without distinction, till king Malcolm the Third, about the year 1070." Whence may be guessed what their function was: was it to go about circled with a band of rooking officials, with cloakbags full of citations, and processes to be served by a corporality of griffonlike promoters and apparitors? Did he go about to pitch down his court, as an empiric does his bank, to inveigle in all the money of the country? No, certainly, it would not have been permitted him to exercise any such function indifferently wherever he came. And verily some such matter it was as want of a fat diocese that kept our Britain bishops so poor in the primitive times, that being called to the council of Ariminum in the year 359, they had not wherewithal to defray the charges of their journey, but were fed and lodged upon the emperor's cost; which must needs be no accidental but usual poverty in them: for the author, Sulpitius Severus, in his 2nd book of Church History, praises them, and avouches it praiseworthy in a bishop to be so poor as to have nothing of his own. But to return to the ancient election of bishops, that it could not lawfully be without the consent of the people is so express in Cyprian, and so often to be met with, that to cite each place at large were to translate a good part of the volume; therefore touching the chief passages, I refer the rest to whom so list peruse the author himself. In the 24th epistle, "If a bishop," saith he, "be once made and allowed by the testimony and judgment of his colleagues and the people, no other can be made." In the 55th, "When a bishop is made by the suffrage of all the people in peace." In the 68th mark but what he says: "The people chiefly hath power either of choosing worthy ones, or refusing unworthy;" this he there proves by authorities out of the Old and

New Testament, and with solid reasons: these were his antiquities.

This voice of the people, to be had ever in episcopal elections, was so well known before Cyprian's time, even to those that were without the church, that the emperor Alexander Severus desired to have his governors of provinces chosen in the same manner, as Lampridius can tell; so little thought it he offensive to monarchy. And if single authorities persuade not, hearken what the whole general council of Nicæa, the first and famousest of all the rest, determines, writing a synodical epistle to the African churches, to warn them of Arianism: it exhorts them to choose orthodox bishops in the place of the dead, so they be worthy, and the people choose them; whereby they seem to make the people's assent so necessary, that merit without their free choice were not sufficient to make a bishop. What would ye say now, grave fathers, if you should wake and see unworthy bishops, or rather no bishops, but Egyptian taskmasters of ceremonies thrust purposely upon the groaning church, to the affliction and vexation of God's people? It was not of old that a conspiracy of bishops could frustrate and fob off the right of the people; for we may read how St. Martin, soon after Constantine, was made bishop of Turon in France, by the people's consent from all places thereabout, maugre all the opposition that the bishops could make. Thus went matters of the church almost 400 years after Christ, and very probably far lower: for Nicephorus Phocas, the Greek emperor, whose reign fell near the 1000th year of our Lord, having done many things tyrannically, is said by Cedrenus to have done nothing more grievous and displeasing to the people, than to have enacted that no bishop should be chosen without his will; so long did this right remain to the people in the midst of other palpable corruptions. Now for episcopal dignity, what it was, see out of Ignatius, who, in his epistle to those of Trallis, confesseth, that "the presbyters are his fellow-counsellors and fellow-benchers." And Cyprian in many places, as in the 6th, 41st, 52nd epistles, speaking of presbyters, calls them his compresbyters, as if he deemed himself no other, whenas by the same place it appears he was a bishop; he calls them brethren, but that will be thought his meekness; yea, but the presbyters and deacons writing to him think they do him honor enough, when they phrase him no higher than brother Cyprian, and dear Cyprian, in the 26th epistle. For their authority it is evident not to have been single, but depending on the counsel of the presbyters, as from Ignatius was erewhile alleged; and the same Cyprian acknowledges as much in the 6th epistle, and adds thereto, that he had determined, from his entrance into the office of bishop, to do nothing without the consent of his people; and so in the 31st epistle, for it were tedious to course through all his writings, which are so full of the like assertions, insomuch that even in the womb and centre of apostasy, Rome itself, there yet remains a glimpse of this truth; for the pope himself, as a learned English writer notes well, performeth all ecclesiastical jurisdiction as in consistory among his cardinals, which were originally but the parish priests of Rome. Thus then did the spirit of unity and meekness inspire and animate every joint and sinew of the mystical body: but now the gravest and worthiest minister, a true bishop of his fold, shall be reviled and ruffled by an insulting and only canon-wise prelate, as if he were some slight paltry companion: and the people of God, redeemed and washed with Christ's blood, and dignified with so many glorious titles of saints and sons in the gospel, are now no better reputed than impure ethnics and lay dogs; stones, and pillars, and crucifixes, have now the honor and the alms due to Christ's living members; the table of communion, now become a table of separation, stands like an exalted platform upon the brow of the choir, fortified with bulwark and barricado, to keep off the profane touch of the laics, whilst the obscene and surfeited priest scruples not to paw and mammoc the sacramental bread, as familiarly as his tavern biscuit. And thus the people, vilified and rejected by them, give over the earnest study of virtue and godliness, as a thing of greater purity than they need, and the search of divine knowledge as a mystery too high for their capacities, and only for churchmen to meddle with; which is that the prelates desire, that when they have brought us back to popish blindness, we might commit to their dispose the whole managing of our salvation; for they think it was never fair world with them since that time. But he that will mold a modern bishop into a primitive, must yield him to be elected by the popular voice, undiocesed, unrevenued, unlorded, and leave him nothing but brotherly equality, matchless temperance, frequent fasting, incessant prayer and preaching, continual watchings and labors in his ministry; which what a rich booty it would be, what a plump endowment to the many-benefice-gaping-mouth of a prelate, what a relish it would give to his canary-sucking and swan-eating palate, let old bishop Mountain judge for me.

How little therefore those ancient times make for modern bishops hath been plainly discoursed; but let them make for them as much as they will, yet why we ought not to stand to their arbitrement, shall now appear by a threefold corruption which will be found upon them. 1. The best times were spreadingly infected. 2. The best men of those times foully tainted. 3. The best writings of those men dangerously adulterated. These positions are to be made good out of those times witnessing of themselves. First, Ignatius in his early days testifies to the churches of Asia, that even then heresies were sprung up, and rife every where, as Eusebius relates in his 3rd book, 35th chap. after the Greek number. And Hegesippus, a grave church writer of prime antiquity, affirms in the same book of Eusebius, c. 32, "that while the apostles were on earth, the depravers of doctrine did but lurk; but they once gone, with open forehead they durst preach down the truth with falsities." Yea, those that are reckoned for orthodox, began to make sad and shameful rents in the church about the trivial celebration of feasts, not agreeing when to keep Easter-day; which controversy grew so hot, that Victor, the bishop of Rome, excommunicated all the churches of Asia for no other cause, and was worthily thereof reproved by Irenæus. For can any sound theologer think, that these great fathers understood what was gospel, or what was excommunication? Doubtless that which led the good men into fraud and error was, that they attended more to the near tradition of what they heard the apostles sometimes did, than to what they had left written, not considering that many things which they did were by the apostles themselves professed to be done only for the present, and of mere indulgence to some scrupulous converts of the circumcision, but what they writ was of firm decree to all future ages. Look but a century lower in the 1st. cap. of Eusebius's 8th book. What a universal tetter of impurity had envenomed every part, order, and degree of the church! to omit the lay herd, which will be little regarded, "Those that seem to be our pastors," saith he, "overturning the law of God's worship, burnt in contentions one towards another, and increasing in hatred and bitterness, outrageously sought to uphold lordship, and command as it were a tyranny." Stay but a little, magnanimous bishops, suppress your aspiring thoughts, for there is nothing wanting but Constantine to reign, and then tyranny herself shall give up all her citadels into your hands, and count ye thenceforward her trustiest agents. Such were these that must be called the ancientest and most virgin times between Christ and Constantine. Nor was this general contagion in their actions, and not in their writings. Who is ignorant of the foul errors, the ridiculous wresting of Scripture, the heresies, the vanities thick sown through the volumes of Justin Martyr, Clemens, Origen, Tertullian, and others of eldest time? Who would think him fit to write an apology for Christian faith to the Roman senate, that would tell them "how of the angels," which he must needs mean those in Genesis, called the sons of God, "mixing with women were begotten the devils," as good Justin Martyr in his Apology told them? But more indignation would it move to any Christian that shall read Tertullian, terming St. Paul a novice, and raw in grace, for reproving St. Peter at Antioch, worthy to be blamed, if we believe the epistle to the Galatians. Perhaps from this hint the blasphemous Jesuits presumed in Italy to give their judgment of St. Paul, as of a hotheaded person, as Sandys in his relations tells us.

Now besides all this, who knows not how many surreptitious works are ingraffed into the legitimate writings of the fathers? And of those books that pass for authentic, who knows what hath been tampered withal, what hath been razed out, what hath been inserted? Besides the late legerdemain of the papists, that which Sulpitius writes concerning Origen's books gives us cause vehemently to suspect there hath been packing of old. In the third chapter of his 1st Dialogue we may read what wrangling the bishops and monks had about the reading or not reading of Origen; some objecting that he was corrupted by heretics; others answering that all such books had been so dealt with. How then shall I trust these times to lead me, that testify so ill of leading themselves? Certainly of their defects their own witness may be best received, but of the rectitude and sincerity of their life and doctrine, to judge rightly, we must judge by that which was to be their rule.

But it will be objected, that this was an unsettled state of the church, wanting the temporal magistrate to suppress the licence of false brethren, and the extravagancy of still new opinions; a time not imitable for church government, where the temporal and spiritual power did not close in one belief, as under Constantine. I am not of opinion to think the church a vine in this respect, because, as they take it, she cannot subsist without clasping about the elm of worldly strength and felicity, as if the heavenly city could not support itself without the props and buttresses of secular authority. They extol Constantine because he extolled them; as our homebred monks in their histories blanch the kings their benefactors, and brand those that went about to be their correctors. If he had curbed the growing pride, avarice, and luxury of the clergy, then every page of his story should have swelled with his faults, and that which Zozimus the heathen writes of him should have come in to boot; we should have heard then in every declamation how he slew his nephew Commodus, a worthy man, his noble and eldest son Crispus, his wife Fausta, besides numbers of his friends: then his cruel exactions, his unsoundness in religion, favoring the Arians that had been condemned in a council, of which himself sat as it were president; his hard measure and banishment of the faithful and invincible Athanasius; his living unbaptized almost to his dying day: these blurs are too apparent in his life. But since he must needs be the loadstar of reformation, as some men clatter, it will be good to see further his knowledge of religion what it was, and by that we may likewise guess at the sincerity of his times in those that were not heretical, it being likely that he would converse with the famousest prelates (for so he had made them) that were to be found for learning.

Of his Arianism we heard, and for the rest a pretty scantling of his knowledge may be taken by his deferring to be baptized so many years, a thing not usual, and repugnant to the tenor of scripture; Philip knowing nothing that should hinder the eunuch to be baptized after profession of his belief. Next, by the excessive devotion, that I may not say superstition, both of him and his mother Helena, to find out the cross on which Christ suffered, that had long lain under the rubbish of old ruins; (a thing which the disciples and kindred of our Saviour might with more ease have done, if they had thought it a pious duty;) some of the nails whereof he put into his helmet, to bear off blows in battle; others he fastened among the studs of his bridle, to fulfil (as he thought or his court bishops persuaded him) the prophecy of Zachariah: "And it shall be that that which is in the bridle shall be holy to the Lord." Part of the cross, in which he thought such virtue to reside, as would prove a kind of palladium to save the city wherever it remained, he caused to be laid up in a pillar of porphyry by his statue. How he or his teachers could trifle thus with half an eye open upon St. Paul's principles, I know not how to imagine.

How should then the dim taper of this emperor's age that had such need of snuffing, extend any beam to our times, wherewith we might hope to be better lighted, than by those luminaries that God hath set up to shine to us far nearer hand? And what reformation he wrought for his own time, it will not be amiss to consider. He appointed certain times for fasts and feasts, built stately churches, gave large immunities to the clergy, great riches and promotions to bishops, gave and ministered occasion to bring in a deluge of ceremonies, thereby either to draw in the heathen by a resemblance of their rites, or to set a gloss upon the simplicity and plainness of Christianity; which, to the gorgeous solemnities of paganism, and the sense of the world's children, seemed but a homely and yeomanly religion; for the beauty of inward sanctity was not within their prospect.

So that in this manner the prelates, both then and ever since, coming from a mean and plebeian life on a sudden to be lords of stately palaces, rich furniture, delicious fare, and princely attendance, thought the plain and homespun verity of Christ's gospel unfit any longer to hold their lordships acquaintance, unless the poor threadbare matron were put into better clothes: her chaste and modest veil, surrounded with celestial beams, they overlaid with wanton tresses, and in a flaring tire bespeckled her with all the gaudy allurements of a whore.

Thus flourished the church with Constantine's wealth, and thereafter were the effects that followed: his son Constantius proved a flat Arian, and his nephew Julian an apostate, and there his race ended; the church that before by insensible degrees welked and impaired, now with large steps went down hill decaying; at this time antichrist began first to put forth his horn, and that saying was common, that former times had wooden chalices and golden priests, but they, golden chalices and wooden priests. "Formerly," saith Sulpitius, "martyrdom by glorious death was sought more greedily than now bishoprics by vile ambition are hunted after," speaking of these times. And in another place, "They gape after possessions, they tend lands and livings, they cower over their gold, they buy and sell: and if there be any that neither possess nor traffic, that which is worse, they sit still, and expect gifts, and prostitute every endowment of grace, every holy thing, to sale." And in the end of his history thus he concludes: "All things went to wrack by the faction, wilfulness, and avarice of the bishops; and by this means God's people, and every good man, was had in scorn and derision;" which St. Martin found truly to be said by his friend Sulpitius; for, being held in admiration of all men, he had only the bishops his enemies, found God less favorable to him after he was bishop than before, and for his last sixteen years would come at no bishop's meeting.

Thus you see, sir, what Constantine's doings in the church brought forth, either in his own or in his son's reign.

Now, lest it should be thought that something else might ail this author thus to hamper the bishops of those days, I will bring you the opinion of three the famousest men for wit and learning that Italy at this day glories of, whereby it may be concluded for a received opinion, even among men professing the Romish faith, that Constantine marred all in the church. Dante, in his 19th Canto of Inferno, hath thus, as I will render it you in English blank verse:

"Ah Constantine! of how much ill was cause,
 Not thy conversion, but those rich domains
 That the first wealthy pope receiv'd of thee!"

So, in his 20th Canto of Paradise, he makes the like complaint; and Petrarch seconds him in the same mind in his 108th sonnet, which is wiped out by the inquisitor in some editions; speaking of the Roman antichrist as merely bred up by Constantine:—

"Founded in chaste and humble poverty,
 'Gainst them that rais'd thee dost thou lift thy
   horn,
 Impudent whore, where hast thou plac'd thy
   hope?
 In thy adulterers, or thy ill-got wealth?
 Another Constantine comes not in haste."

Ariosto of Ferrara, after both these in time, but equal in fame, following the scope of his poem in a difficult knot how to restore Orlando, his chief hero, to his lost senses, brings Astolfo, the English knight, up into the moon, where St. John, as he feigns, met him. Cant. 34:

"And, to be short, at last his guide him brings
 Into a goodly valley, where he sees
 A mighty mass of things strangely confus'd,
 Things that on earth were lost, or were abus'd."

And amongst these so abused things listen what he met withal, under the conduct of the Evangelist:

"Then pass'd he to a flowery mountain green,
 Which once smelt sweet, now stinks as odiously:
 This was that gift (if you the truth will have)
 That Constantine to good Sylvestro gave."

And this was a truth well known in England before this poet was born, as our Chaucer's Ploughman shall tell you by and by upon another occasion. By all these circumstances laid together, I do not see how it can be disputed what good this emperor Constantine wrought to the church; but rather whether ever any, though perhaps not wittingly, set open a door to more mischief in Christendom. There is just cause therefore, that when the prelates cry out, Let the church be reformed according to Constantine, it should sound to a judicious ear no otherwise than if they should say, Make us rich, make us lofty, make us lawless; for if any under him were not so, thanks to those ancient remains of integrity which were not yet quite worn out, and not to his government.

Thus finally it appears, that those purer times were no such as they are cried up, and not to be followed without suspicion, doubt, and danger. The last point wherein the antiquary is to be dealt with at his own weapon, is to make it manifest that the ancientest and best of the fathers have disclaimed all sufficiency in themselves that men should rely on, and sent all comers to the scriptures, as all-sufficient: that this is true, will not be unduly gathered, by showing what esteem they had of antiquity themselves, and what validity they thought in it to prove doctrine or discipline. I must of necessity begin from the second rank of fathers, because till then antiquity could have no plea. Cyprian in his 63d epistle: "If any," saith he, "of our ancestors, either ignorantly or out of simplicity, hath not observed that which the Lord taught us by his example," speaking of the Lord's supper, "his simplicity God may pardon of his mercy; but we cannot be excused for following him, being instructed by the Lord." And have not we the same instructions? and will not this holy man, with all the whole consistory of saints and martyrs that lived of old, rise up and stop our mouths in judgment, when we shall go about to father our errors and opinions upon their authority? In the 73d epistle he adds, "In vain do they oppose custom to us, if they be overcome by reason: as if custom were greater than truth, or that in spiritual things that were not to be followed which is revealed for the better by the Holy Ghost."

In the 74th: "Neither ought custom to hinder that truth should not prevail; for custom without truth is but agedness of error."

Next Lactantius, he that was preferred to have the bringing up of Constantine's children, in his second book of Institutions, chap. 7 and 8, disputes against the vain trust in antiquity, as being the chiefest argument of the heathen against the Christians: "They do not consider," saith he, "what religion is, but they are confident it is true, because the ancients delivered it; they count it a trespass to examine it." And in the eighth: "Not because they went before us in time, therefore in wisdom; which being given alike to all ages, cannot be prepossessed by the ancients: wherefore, seeing that to seek the truth is inbred to all, they bereave themselves of wisdom, the gift of God, who without judgment follow the ancients, and are led by others like brute beasts." St. Austin writes to Fortunatian, that "he counts it lawful, in the books of whomsoever, to reject that which he finds otherwise than true; and so he would have others deal by him." He neither accounted, as it seems, those fathers that went before, nor himself, nor others of his rank, for men of more than ordinary spirit, that might equally deceive, and be deceived: and ofttimes setting our servile humors aside, yea, God so ordering, we may find truth with one man, as soon as in a council, as Cyprian agrees, 71st epistle: "Many things," saith he, "are better revealed to single persons." At Nicæa, in the first and best-reputed council of all the world, there had gone out a canon to divorce married priests, had not one old man, Paphnutius, stood up and reasoned against it.

Now remains it to show clearly that the fathers refer all decision of controversy to the scriptures, as all-sufficient to direct, to resolve, and to determine. Ignatius, taking his last leave of the Asian churches, as he went to martyrdom, exhorted them to adhere close to the written doctrine of the apostles, necessarily written for posterity: so far was he from unwritten traditions, as may be read in the 36th chap. of Eusebius, 3rd book. In the 74th epistle of Cyprian against Stefan, bishop of Rome, imposing upon him a tradition: "Whence," quoth he, "is this tradition? Is it fetched from the authority of Christ in the gospel, or of the apostles in their epistles? for God testifies that those things are to be done which are written." And then thus, "What obstinacy, what presumption is this, to prefer human tradition before divine ordinance?" And in the same epistle: "If we shall return to the head and beginning of divine tradition, (which we all know he means the Bible,) human error ceases; and the reason of heavenly mysteries unfolded, whatsoever was obscure becomes clear." And in the 14th distinct. of the same epistle, directly against our modern fantasies of a still visible church, he teaches, "that succession of truth may fail; to renew which, we must have recourse to the fountains;" using this excellent similitude, "If a channel, or conduit-pipe which brought in water plentifully before, suddenly fail, do we not go to the fountain to know the cause, whether the spring affords no more, or whether the vein be stopped, or turned aside in the midcourse? Thus ought we to do, keeping God's precepts, that if in aught the truth shall be changed, we may repair to the gospel and to the apostles, that thence may arise the reason of our doings, from whence our order and beginning arose." In the 75th he inveighs bitterly against pope Stephanus, "for that he could boast his succession from Peter, and yet foist in traditions that were not apostolical." And in his book of the unity of the church, he compares those that, neglecting God's word, follow the doctrines of men, to Corah, Dathan, and Abiram. The very first page of Athanasius against the Gentiles avers the scriptures to be sufficient of themselves for the declaration of truth; and that if his friend Macarius read other religious writers, it was but φιλοκάλος, come un vertuoso, (as the Italians say,) as a lover of elegance: and in his second tome, the 39th page, after he hath reckoned up the canonical books, "In these only," saith he, "is the doctrine of godliness taught; let no man add to these, or take from these." And in his Synopsis, having again set down all the writers of the Old and New Testament, "These," saith he, "be the anchors and props of our faith." Besides these, millions of other books have been written by great and wise men according to rule, and agreement with these, of which I will not now speak, as being of infinite number and mere dependence on the canonical books. Basil, in his 2nd tome, writing of true faith, tells his auditors, he is bound to teach them that which he hath learned out of the Bible: and in the same treatise he saith, "that seeing the commandments of the Lord are faithful, and sure for ever, it is a plain falling from the faith, and a high pride, either to make void anything therein, or to introduce anything not there to be found:" and he gives the reason: "For Christ saith, My sheep hear my voice: they will not follow another, but fly from him, because they know not his voice." But not to be endless in quotations, it may chance to be objected, that there be many opinions in the fathers which have no ground in scripture; so much the less, may I say, should we follow them, for their own words shall condemn them, and acquit us, that lean not on them; otherwise these their words shall acquit them, and condemn us. But it will be replied, The scriptures are difficult to be understood, and therefore require the explanation of the fathers. It is true, there be some books, and especially some places in those books, that remain clouded; yet ever that which is most necessary to be known is most easy; and that which is most difficult, so far expounds itself ever, as to tell us how little it imports our saving knowledge. Hence, to infer a general obscurity over all the text, is a mere suggestion of the devil to dissuade men from reading it, and casts an aspersion of dishonor both upon the mercy, truth, and wisdom of God. We count it no gentleness or fair dealing in a man of power amongst us, to require strict and punctual obedience, and yet give out all his commands ambiguous and obscure: we should think he had a plot upon us; certainly such commands were no commands, but snares. The very essence of truth is plainness and brightness; the darkness and crookedness is our own. The wisdom of God created understanding, fit and proportionable to truth, the object and end of it, as the eye to the thing visible. If our understanding have a film of ignorance over it, or be blear with gazing on other false glisterings, what is that to truth? If we will but purge with sovereign eyesalve that intellectual ray which God hath planted in us, then we would believe the scriptures protesting their own plainness and perspicuity, calling to them to be instructed, not only the wise and learned, but the simple, the poor, the babes, foretelling an extraordinary effusion of God's Spirit upon every age and sex, attributing to all men, and requiring from them the ability of searching, trying, examining all things, and by the Spirit discerning that which is good; and as the scriptures themselves pronounce their own plainness, so do the fathers testify of them.

I will not run into a paroxysm of citations again in this point, only instance Athanasius in his forementioned first page: "The knowledge of truth," saith he, "wants no human lore, as being evident in itself, and by the preaching of Christ now opens brighter than the sun." If these doctors, who had scarce half the light that we enjoy, who all, except two or three, were ignorant of the Hebrew tongue, and many of the Greek, blundering upon the dangerous and suspectful translations of the apostate Aquila, the heretical Theodotion, the judaized Symmachus, the erroneous Origen; if these could yet find the Bible so easy, why should we doubt, that have all the helps of learning and faithful industry that man in this life can look for, and the assistance of God as near now to us as ever? But let the scriptures be hard; are they more hard, more crabbed, more abstruse than the fathers? He that cannot understand the sober, plain, and unaffected style of the scriptures, will be ten times more puzzled with the knotty Africanisms, the pampered metaphors, the intricate and involved sentences of the fathers, besides the fantastic and declamatory flashes, the crossjingling periods which cannot but disturb, and come thwart a settled devotion, worse than the din of bells and rattles.

Now, sir, for the love of holy reformation, what can be said more against these importunate clients of antiquity than she herself their patroness hath said? Whether, think ye, would she approve still to dote upon immeasurable, innumerable, and therefore unnecessary and unmerciful volumes, choosing rather to err with the specious name of the fathers, or to take a sound truth at the hand of a plain upright man, that all his days hath been diligently reading the holy scriptures, and thereto imploring God's grace, while the admirers of antiquity have been beating their brains about their ambones, their dyptichs, and meniaias? Now, he that cannot tell of stations and indictions, nor has wasted his precious hours in the endless conferring of councils and conclaves that demolish one another, (although I know many of those that pretend to be great rabbies in these studies, have scarce saluted them from the strings, and the titlepage; or, to give them more, have been but the ferrets and mousehunts of an index:) yet what pastor or minister, how learned, religious, or discreet soever, does not now bring both his cheeks full blown with œcumenical and synodical, shall be counted a lank, shallow, insufficient man, yea, a dunce, and not worthy to speak about reformation of church discipline. But I trust they for whom God hath reserved the honor of reforming this church, will easily perceive their adversaries' drift in thus calling for antiquity: they fear the plain field of the scriptures; the chase is too hot; they seek the dark, the bushy, the tangled forest, they would imbosk: they feel themselves struck in the transparent streams of divine truth; they would plunge, and tumble, and think to lie hid in the foul weeds and muddy waters, where no plummet can reach the bottom. But let them beat themselves like whales, and spend their oil till they be dragged ashore: though wherefore should the ministers give them so much line for shifts and delays? wherefore should they not urge only the gospel, and hold it ever in their faces like a mirror of diamond, till it dazzle and pierce their misty eyeballs? maintaining it the honor of its absolute sufficiency and supremacy inviolable: for if the scripture be for reformation, and antiquity to boot, it is but an advantage to the dozen, it is no winning cast: and though antiquity be against it, while the scriptures be for it, the cause is as good as ought to be wished, antiquity itself sitting judge.

But to draw to an end: the second sort of those that may be justly numbered among the hinderers of reformation, are libertines; these suggest that the discipline sought would be intolerable: for one bishop now in a diocese, we should then have a pope in every parish. It will not be requisite to answer these men, but only to discover them; for reason they have none, but lust and licentiousness, and therefore answer can have none. It is not any discipline that they could live under, it is the corruption and remissness of discipline that they seek. Episcopacy duly executed, yea, the Turkish and Jewish rigor against whoring and drinking, the dear and tender discipline of a father, the sociable and loving reproof of a brother, the bosom admonition of a friend, is a presbytery, and a consistory to them. It is only the merry friar in Chaucer can disple them.

"Full sweetly heard he confession,
And pleasant was his absolution,
He was an easy man to give penance."

And so I leave them; and refer the political discourse of episcopacy to a second book.

THE SECOND BOOK.

Sir,—It is a work good and prudent to be able to guide one man; of larger extended virtue to order well one house: but to govern a nation piously and justly, which only is to say happily, is for a spirit of the greatest size, and divinest mettle. And certainly of no less a mind, nor of less excellence in another way, were they who by writing laid the solid and true foundations of this science, which being of greatest importance to the life of man, yet there is no art that hath been more cankered in her principles, more soiled and slubbered with aphorising pedantry, than the art of policy; and that most, where a man would think should least be, in Christian commonwealths. They teach not, that to govern well, is to train up a nation in true wisdom and virtue, and that which springs from thence, magnanimity, (take heed of that,) and that which is our beginning, regeneration, and happiest end, likeness to God, which in one word we call godliness; and that this is the true flourishing of a land, other things follow as the shadow does the substance: to teach thus were mere pulpitry to them. This is the masterpiece of a modern politician, how to qualify and mold the sufferance and subjection of the people to the length of that foot that is to tread on their necks; how rapine may serve itself with the fair and honorable pretences of public good; how the puny law may be brought under the wardship and control of lust and will: in which attempt if they fall short, then must a superficial color of reputation by all means, direct or indirect, be gotten to wash over the unsightly bruise of honor. To make men governable in this manner, their precepts mainly tend to break a national spirit and courage, by countenancing open riot, luxury, and ignorance, till having thus disfigured and made men beneath men, as Juno in the fable of Io, they deliver up the poor transformed heifer of the commonwealth to be stung and vexed with the breese and goad of oppression, under the custody of some Argus with a hundred eyes of jealousy. To be plainer, sir, how to solder, how to stop a leak, how to keep up the floating carcase of a crazy and diseased monarchy or state, betwixt wind and water swimming still upon her own dead lees, that now is the deep design of a politician. Alas, sir! a commonwealth ought to be but as one huge Christian personage, one mighty growth and stature of an honest man, as big and compact in virtue as in body; for look what the grounds and causes are of single happiness to one man, the same ye shall find them to a whole state, as Aristotle, both in his Ethics and Politics, from the principles of reason, lays down: by consequence, therefore, that which is good and agreeable to monarchy, will appear soonest to be so, by being good and agreeable to the true welfare of every Christian; and that which can be justly proved hurtful and offensive to every true Christian, will be evinced to be alike hurtful to monarchy: for God forbid that we should separate and distinguish the end and good of a monarch, from the end and good of the monarchy, or of that, from Christianity. How then this third and last sort that hinder reformation will justify that it stands not with reason of state, I much muse, for certain I am, the Bible is shut against them, as certain that neither Plato nor Aristotle is for their turns. What they can bring us now from the schools of Loyola with his

Jesuits, or their Malvezzi, that can cut Tacitus into slivers and steaks, we shall presently hear. They allege, 1. That the church-government must be conformable to the civil polity; next, That no form of church-government is agreeable to monarchy, but that of bishops. Must church-government that is appointed in the gospel, and has chief respect to the soul, be conformable and pliant to civil, that is arbitrary, and chiefly conversant about the visible and external part of man? This is the very maxim that molded the calves of Bethel and of Dan; this was the quintessence of Jeroboam's policy, he made religion conform to his politic interests; and this was the sin that watched over the Israelites till their final captivity. If this state principle come from the prelates, as they affect to be counted statists, let them look back to Eleutherius bishop of Rome, and see what he thought of the policy of England; being required by Lucius, the first Christian king of this island, to give his counsel for the founding of religious laws, little thought he of this sage caution, but bids him betake himself to the Old and New Testament, and receive direction from them how to administer both church and commonwealth; that he was God's vicar, and therefore to rule by God's laws; that the edicts of Cæsar we may at all times disallow, but the statutes of God for no reason we may reject. Now certain, if church-government be taught in the gospel, as the bishops dare not deny, we may well conclude of what late standing this position is, newly calculated for the altitude of bishop-elevation, and lettuce for their lips. But by what example can they show, that the form of church-discipline must be minted and modelled out to secular pretences? The ancient republic of the Jews is evident to have run through all the changes of civil estate, if we survey the story from the giving of the law to the Herods; yet did one manner of priestly government serve without inconvenience to all these temporal mutations; it served the mild aristocracy of elective dukes, and heads of tribes joined with them; the dictatorship of the judges, the easy or hardhanded monarchies, the domestic or foreign tyrannies: lastly, the Roman senate from without, the Jewish senate at home, with the Galilean

tetrarch; yet the Levites had some right to deal in civil affairs: but seeing the evangelical precept forbids churchmen to intermeddle with worldly employments, what interweavings or interworkings can knit the minister and the magistrate in their several functions, to the regard of any precise correspondency! Seeing that the churchman's office is only to teach men the Christian faith, to exhort all, to encourage the good, to admonish the bad, privately the less offender, publicly the scandalous and stubborn; to censure and separate, from the communion of Christ's flock, the contagious and incorrigible, to receive with joy and fatherly compassion the penitent: all this must be done, and more than this is beyond any church-authority. What is all this either here or there, to the temporal regiment of weal public, whether it be popular, princely, or monarchical? Where doth it entrench upon the temporal governor? where does it come in his walk? where does it make inroad upon his jurisdiction? Indeed if the minister's part be rightly discharged, it renders him the people more conscionable, quiet, and easy to be governed; if otherwise, his life and doctrine will declare him. If, therefore, the constitution of the church be already set down by divine prescript, as all sides confess, then can she not be a handmaid to wait on civil commodities and respects; and if the nature and limits of church-discipline be such, as are either helpful to all political estates indifferently, or have no particular relation to any, then is there no necessity, nor indeed possibility, of linking the one with the other in a special conformation.

Now for their second conclusion, "That no form of church-government is agreeable to monarchy, but that of bishops," although it fall to pieces of itself by that which hath been said; yet to give them play, front and rear, it shall be my task to prove that episcopacy, with that authority which it challenges in England, is not only not agreeable, but tending to the destruction of monarchy. While the primitive pastors of the church of God labored faithfully in their ministry, tending only their sheep, and not seeking, but avoiding all worldly matters as clogs, and indeed derogations and debasements to their high calling, little needed the princes and potentates of the earth, which way soever the gospel was spread, to study ways how to make a coherence between the church's polity and theirs: therefore, when Pilate heard once our Saviour Christ professing that "his kingdom was not of this world," he thought the man could not stand much in Cæsar's light nor much endamage the Roman empire; for if the life of Christ be hid to this world, much more is his sceptre inoperative, but in spiritual things. And thus lived, for two or three ages, the successors of the apostles. But when, through Constantine's lavish superstition, they forsook their first love, and set themselves up two gods instead, Mammon and their belly; then taking advantage of the spiritual power which they had on men's consciences, they began to cast a longing eye to get the body also, and bodily things into their command: upon which their carnal desires, the spirit daily quenching and dying in them, they knew no way to keep themselves up from falling to nothing, but by bolstering and supporting their inward rottenness by a carnal and outward strength. For a while they rather privily sought opportunity, than hastily disclosed their project; but when Constantine was dead, and three or four emperors more, their drift became notorious and offensive to the whole world; for while Theodosius the younger reigned, thus writes Socrates the historian, in his 7th book, chap. 11. "Now began an ill name to stick upon the bishops of Rome and Alexandria, who beyond their priestly bounds now long ago had stepped into principality:" and this was scarce eighty years since their raising from the meanest worldly condition. Of courtesy now let any man tell me, if they draw to themselves a temporal strength and power out of Cæsar's dominion, is not Cæsar's empire thereby diminished? But this was a stolen bit, hitherto he was but a caterpillar secretly gnawing at monarchy; the next time you shall see him a wolf, a lion, lifting his paw against his raiser, as Petrarch expressed it, and finally an open enemy and subverter of the Greek empire. Philippicus and Leo, with divers other emperors after them, not without the advice of their patriarchs, and at length of a whole eastern council of three hundred and thirty-eight bishops, threw the images out of churches as being decreed idolatrous.

Upon this goodly occasion the bishop of Rome not only seizes the city, and all the territory about, into his own hands, and makes himself lord thereof, which till then was governed by a Greek magistrate, but absolves all Italy of their tribute and obedience due to the emperor, because he obeyed God's commandment in abolishing idolatry.

Mark, sir, here, how the pope came by St. Peter's patrimony, as he feigns it; not the donation of Constantine, but idolatry and rebellion got it him. Ye need but read Sigonius, one of his own sect, to know the story at large. And now to shroud himself against a storm from the Greek continent, and provide a champion to bear him out in these practices, he takes upon him by papal sentence to unthrone Chilpericus, the rightful king of France, and gives the kingdom to Pepin, for no other cause, but that he seemed to him the more active man. If he were a friend herein to monarchy, I know not; but to the monarch I need not ask what he was.

Having thus made Pepin his fast friend, he calls him into Italy against Aistulphus the Lombard, that warred upon him for his late usurpation of Rome, as belonging to Ravenna, which he had newly won. Pepin, not unobedient to the pope's call, passing into Italy, frees him out of danger, and wins for him the whole exarchate of Ravenna; which though it had been almost immediately before the hereditary possession of that monarchy, which was his chief patron and benefactor, yet he takes and keeps it to himself as lawful prize, and given to St. Peter. What a dangerous fallacy is this, when a spiritual man may snatch to himself any temporal dignity or dominion, under pretence of receiving it for the church's use? Thus he claims Naples, Sicily, England, and what not? To be short, under show of his zeal against the errors of the Greek church, he never ceased baiting and goring the successors of his best lord Constantine, what by his barking curses and excommunications, what by his hindering the western princes from aiding them against the Saracens and Turks, unless when they humored him; so that it may be truly affirmed, he was the subversion and fall of that monarchy which was the hoisting of him. This, besides Petrarch, whom I have cited, our Chaucer also hath observed, and gives from hence a caution to England, to beware of her bishops in time, for that their ends and aims are no more friendly to monarchy than the pope's.

Thus he brings in the Ploughman speaking, part ii, stanza 28:

"The emperor yafe the pope sometime
    So high lordship him about,
That at last the silly kime,
    The proud pope put him out;
So of this realm is no doubt,
    But lords beware and them defend;
For now these folks be wonders stout,
    The king and lords now this amend."

And in the next stanza, which begins the third part of the tale, he argues that they ought not to be lords:

"Moses law forbode it tho
    That priests should no lordships welde,
Christ's gospel biddeth also
    That they should no lordships held:
Ne Christ's apostles were never so bold
    No such lordships to hem embrace,
But smeren her sheep and keep her fold."

And so forward. Whether the bishops of England have deserved thus to be feared by men so wise as our Chaucer is esteemed; and how agreeable to our monarchy and monarchs their demeanor has been, he that is but meanly read in our chronicles needs not be instructed. Have they not been as the Canaanites and Philistines to this kingdom? What treasons, what revolts to the pope, what rebellions, and those the basest and most pretenceless, have they not been chief in? What could monarchy think, when Becket durst challenge the custody of Rochester Castle, and the Tower of London, as appertaining to his signory? to omit his other insolencies and affronts to regal majesty, until the lashes inflicted on the anointed body of the king, washed off the holy unction with his blood drawn by the polluted hands of bishops, abbots, and monks. What good upholders of royalty were the bishops, when, by their rebellious opposition against king John, Normandy was lost, he himself deposed, and this kingdom made over to the pope? When the bishop of Winchester durst tell the nobles, the pillars of the realm, that there were no peers in England, as in France, but that the king might do what he pleased, what could tyranny say more? It would be petty now if I should insist upon the rendering up of Tournay by Wolsey's treason, the excommunications, cursings, and interdicts upon the whole land; for haply I shall be cut off short by a reply, that these were the faults of the men and their popish errors, not of episcopacy, that hath now renounced the pope, and is a protestant. Yes, sure; as wise and famous men have suspected and feared the protestant episcopacy in England, as those that have feared the papal.

You know, sir, what was the judgment of Padre Paolo, the great Venetian antagonist of the pope, for it is extant in the hands of many men, whereby he declares his fear, that when the hierarchy of England shall light into the hands of busy and audacious men, or shall meet with princes tractable to the prelacy, then much mischief is like to ensue. And can it be nearer at hand than when bishops shall openly affirm that, "No bishop no king?" A trim paradox, and that ye may know where they have been a begging for it, I will fetch you the twin brother to it out of the Jesuits' cell: they feeling the axe of God's reformation, hewing at the old and hollow trunk of papacy, and finding the Spaniard their surest friend, and safest refuge, to soothe him up in his dream of a fifth monarchy, and withal to uphold the decrepit papalty, have invented this superpolitic aphorism, as one terms it, "One pope and one king."

Surely there is not any prince in Christendom, who, hearing this rare sophistry, can choose but smile; and if we be not blind at home, we may as well perceive that this worthy motto, "No bishop no king," is of the same batch, and infanted out of the same fears, a mere ague-cake, coagulated of a certain fever they have, presaging their time to be but short: and now, like those that are sinking, they catch round at that which is likeliest to hold them up; and would persuade regal power that if they dive, he must after. But what greater debasement can there be to royal dignity, whose towering and steadfast height rests upon the unmovable foundations of justice, and heroic virtue, than to chain it in a dependence of subsisting, or ruining, to the painted battlements and gaudy rottenness of prelatry, which want but one puff of the king's to blow them down like a pasteboard house built of courtcards? Sir, the little ado which methinks I find in untacking these pleasant sophisms, puts me into the mood to tell you a tale ere I proceed further; and Menenius Agrippa speed us.

Upon a time the body summoned all the members to meet in the guild, for the common good: (as Æsop's chronicles aver many stranger accidents:) the head by right takes the first seat, and next to it a huge and monstrous wen, little less than the head itself, growing to it by a narrower excrescency. The members, amazed, began to ask one another what he was that took place next their chief? None could resolve. Whereat the wen, though unwieldy, with much ado gets up, and bespeaks the assembly to this purpose: "That as in place he was second to the head, so by due of merit; that he was to it an ornament, and strength, and of special near relation; and that if the head should fail, none were fitter than himself to step into his place: therefore he thought it for the honor of the body, that such dignities and rich endowments should be decreed him, as did adorn and set out the noblest members." To this was answered, that it should be consulted. Then was a wise and learned philosopher sent for, that knew all the charters, laws, and tenures of the body. On him it is imposed by all, as chief committee, to examine, and discuss the claim and petition of right put in by the wen; who soon perceiving the matter, and wondering at the boldness of such a swoln tumor, "Wilt thou," quoth he, "that art but a bottle of vicious and hardened excrements, contend with the lawful and freeborn members, whose certain number is set by ancient and unrepealable statute? Head thou art none, though thou receive this huge substance from it. What office bearest thou? what good canst thou show by thee done to the commonweal?" The wen, not easily dashed, replies that his office was his glory; for so oft as the soul would retire out of the head from over the steaming vapors of the lower parts to divine contemplation, with him she found the purest and quietest retreat, as being most remote from soil and disturbance. "Lourdan," quoth the philosopher, "thy folly is as great as thy filth: know that all the faculties of the soul are confined of old to their several vessels and ventricles, from which they cannot part without dissolution of the whole body; and that thou containest no good thing in thee, but a heap of hard and loathsome uncleanness, and art to the head a foul disfigurement and burden, when I have cut thee off, and opened thee, as by the help of these implements I will do, all men shall see."

But to return whence was digressed: seeing that the throne of a king, as the wise king Solomon often remembers us, "is established in justice," which is the universal justice that Aristotle so much praises, containing in it all other virtues, it may assure us that the fall of prelacy, whose actions are so far distant from justice, cannot shake the least fringe that borders the royal canopy; but that their standing doth continually oppose and lay battery to regal safety, shall by that which follows easily appear. Amongst many secondary and accessory causes that support monarchy, these are not of least reckoning, though common to all other states; the love of the subjects, the multitude and valor of the people, and store of treasure. In all these things hath the kingdom been of late sore weakened, and chiefly by the prelates. First, let any man consider, that if any prince shall suffer under him a commission of authority to be exercised, till all the land groan and cry out, as against a whip of scorpions, whether this be not likely to lessen and keel the affections of the subject. Next, what numbers of faithful and freeborn Englishmen, and good Christians, have been constrained to forsake their dearest home, their friends and kindred, whom nothing but the wide ocean, and the savage deserts of America, could hide and shelter from the fury of the bishops? O, sir, if we could but see the shape of our dear mother England, as poets are wont to give a personal form to what they please, how would she appear, think ye, but in a mourning weed, with ashes upon her head, and tears abundantly flowing from her eyes, to behold so many of her children exposed at once, and thrust from things of dearest necessity, because their conscience could not assent to things which the bishops thought indifferent? What more binding than conscience? What more free than indifferency? Cruel then must that indifferency needs be, that shall violate the strict necessity of conscience; merciless and inhuman that free choice and liberty that shall break asunder the bonds of religion! Let the astrologer be dismayed at the portentous blaze of comets, and impressions in the air, as foretelling troubles and changes to states: I shall believe there cannot be a more ill-boding sign to a nation (God turn the omen from us!) than when the inhabitants, to avoid insufferable grievances at home, are enforced by heaps to forsake their native country. Now, whereas the only remedy and amends against the depopulation and thinness of a land within, is the borrowed strength of firm alliance from without, these priestly policies of theirs having thus exhausted our domestic forces, have gone the way also to leave us as naked of our firmest and faithfullest neighbors abroad, by disparaging and alienating from us all protestant princes and commonwealths; who are not ignorant that our prelates, and as many as they can infect, account them no better than a sort of sacrilegious and puritanical rebels, preferring the Spaniard, our deadly enemy, before them, and set all orthodox writers at nought in comparison of the Jesuits, who are indeed the only corrupters of youth and good learning: and I have heard many wise and learned men in Italy say as much. It cannot be that the strongest knot of confederacy should not daily slacken, when religion, which is the chief engagement of our league, shall be turned to their reproach. Hence it is that the prosperous and prudent states of the United Provinces, (whom we ought to love, if not for themselves, yet for our own good work in them, they having been in a manner planted and erected by us, and having been since to us the faithful watchmen and discoverers of many a popish and Austrian complotted treason, and with us the partners of many a bloody and victorious battle,) whom the similitude of manners and language, the commodity of traffic, which founded the old Burgundian league betwixt us, but chiefly religion, should bind to us immortally; even such friends as these, out of some principles instilled into us by the prelates, have been often dismissed with distasteful answers, and sometimes unfriendly actions: nor is it to be considered but the breach of confederate nations, whose mutual interest is of such high consequence, though their merchants bicker in the East Indies; neither is it safe, or wary, or indeed Christianly, that the French king, of a different faith, should afford our nearest allies as good protection as we. Sir, I persuade myself, if our zeal to true religion, and the brotherly usage of our truest friends, were as notorious to the world as our prelatical schism, and captivity to rochet apophthegms, we had ere this seen our old conquerors, and afterwards liegemen, the Normans, together with the Britains, our proper colony, and all the Gascoins that are the rightful dowry of our ancient kings, come with cap and knee, desiring the shadow of the English sceptre to defend them from the hot persecutions and taxes of the French. But when they come hither, and see a tympany of Spaniolized bishops swaggering in the foretop of the state, and meddling to turn and dandle the royal ball with unskilful and pedantic palms, no marvel though they think it as unsafe to commit religion and liberty to their arbitrating as to a synagogue of Jesuits.

But what do I stand reckoning upon advantages and gains lost by the misrule and turbulency of the prelates? What do I pick up so thriftily their scatterings and diminishings of the meaner subject, whilst they by their seditious practices have endangered to lose the king one third of his main stock? What have they not done to banish him from his own native country? But to speak of this as it ought, would ask a volume by itself.

Thus as they have unpeopled the kingdom by expulsion of so many thousands, as they have endeavored to lay the skirts of it bare by disheartening and dishonoring our loyalest confederates abroad, so have they hamstrung the valor of the subject by seeking to effeminate us all at home. Well knows every wise nation, that their liberty consists in manly and honest labors, in sobriety and rigorous honor to the marriage-bed, which in both sexes should be bred up from chaste hopes to loyal enjoyments; and when the people slacken, and fall to looseness and riot, then do they as much as if they laid down their necks for some wily tyrant to get up and ride. Thus learnt Cyrus to tame the Lydians, whom by arms he could not whilst they kept themselves from luxury; with one easy proclamation to set up stews, dancing, feasting, and dicing, he made them soon his slaves. I know not what drift the prelates had, whose brokers they were to prepare, and supple us either for a foreign invasion or domestic oppression: but this I am sure, they took the ready way to despoil us both of manhood and grace at once, and that in the shamefullest and ungodliest manner, upon that day which God's law, and even our own reason hath consecrated, that we might have one day at least of seven set apart wherein to examine and increase our knowledge of God, to meditate and commune of our faith, our hope, our eternal city in heaven, and to quicken withal the study and exercise of charity; at such a time that men should be plucked from their soberest and saddest thoughts, and by bishops, the pretended fathers of the church, instigated, by public edict, and with earnest endeavor pushed forward to gaming, jigging, wassailing, and mixed dancing, is a horror to think! Thus did the reprobate hireling priest Balaam seek to subdue the Israelites to Moab, if not by force, then by this devilish policy, to draw them from the sanctuary of God to the luxurious and ribald feasts of Baal-peor. Thus have they trespassed not only against the monarchy of England, but of Heaven also, as others, I doubt not, can prosecute against them.

I proceed within my own bounds to show you next what good agents they are about the revenues and riches of the kingdom, which declares of what moment they are to monarchy, or what avail. Two leeches they have that still suck and suck the kingdom— their ceremonies and their courts. If any man will contend that ceremonies be lawful under the gospel, he may be answered otherwhere. This doubtless, that they ought to be many and overcostly, no true protestant will affirm. Now I appeal to all wise men, what an excessive waste of treasury hath been within these few years in this land, not in the expedient, but in the idolatrous erection of temples beautified exquisitely to outvie the papists, the costly and dear-bought scandals and snares of images, pictures, rich copes, gorgeous altar-cloths: and by the courses they took, and the opinions they held, it was not likely any stay would be, or any end of their madness, where a pious pretext is so ready at hand to cover their insatiate desires. What can we suppose this will come to? What other materials than these have built up the spiritual Babel to the height of her abominations? Believe it, sir, right truly it may be said, that Antichrist is Mammon's son. The sour leaven of human traditions, mixed in one putrefied mass with the poisonous dregs of hyprocrisy in the hearts of prelates, that lie basking in the sunny warmth of wealth and promotion, is the serpent's egg that will hatch an Antichrist wheresoever, and engender the same monster as big, or little, as the lump is which breeds him. If the splendor of gold and silver begin to lord it once again in the church of England, we shall see Antichrist shortly wallow here, though his chief kennel be at Rome. If they had one thought upon God's glory, and the advancement of Christian faith, they would be a means that with these expenses, thus profusely thrown away in trash, rather churches and schools might be built, where they cry out for want, and more added where too few are; a moderate maintenance distributed to every painful minister, that now scarce sustains his family with bread, while the prelates revel like Belshazzar with their full carouses in goblets, and vessels of gold snatched from God's temple; which (I hope) the worthy men of our land will consider. Now then for their courts. What a mass of money is drawn from the veins into the ulcers of the kingdom this way; their extortions, their open corruptions, the multitude of hungry and ravenous harpies that swarm about their offices, declare sufficiently. And what though all this go not over sea? It were better it did: better a penurious kingdom, than where excessive wealth flows into the graceless and injurious hands of common sponges, to the impoverishing of good and loyal men, and that by such execrable, such irreligious courses.

If the sacred and dreadful works of holy discipline, censure, penance, excommunication, and absolution, where no profane thing ought to have access, nothing to be assistant but sage and Christianly admonition, brotherly love, flaming charity and zeal; and then according to the effects, paternal sorrow, or paternal joy, mild severity, melting compassion: if such divine ministeries as these, wherein the angel of the church represents the person of Christ Jesus, must lie prostitute to sordid fees, and not pass to and fro between our Saviour that of free grace redeemed us, and the submissive penitent, without the truckage of perishing coin, and the butcherly execution of tormentors, rooks, and rakeshames sold to lucre; then have the Babylonish merchants of souls just excuse. Hitherto, sir, you have heard how the prelates have weakened and withdrawn the external accomplishments of kingly prosperity, the love of the people, their multitude, their valor, their wealth; mining and sapping the outworks and redoubts of monarchy. Now hear how they strike at the very heart and vitals.

We know that monarchy is made up of two parts, the liberty of the subject, and the supremacy of the king. I begin at the root. See what gentle and benign fathers they have been to our liberty! Their trade being, by the same alchemy that the pope uses, to extract heaps of gold and silver out of the drossy bullion of the people's sins; and justly fearing that the quick-sighted protestant's eye, cleared in great part from the mist of superstition, may at one time or other look with a good judgment into these their deceitful pedleries; to gain as many associates of guiltiness as they can, and to infect the temporal magistrate with the like lawless, though not sacrilegious extortion, see awhile what they do! they engage themselves to preach, and persuade an assertion for truth the most false, and to this monarchy the most pernicious and destructive that could be chosen. What more baneful to monarchy than a popular commotion? for the dissolution of monarchy slides aptest into a democracy; and what stirs the Englishmen, as our wisest writers have observed, sooner to rebellion, than violent and heavy hands upon their goods and purses? Yet these devout prelates, spite of our Great Charter, and the souls of our progenitors that wrested their liberties out of the Norman gripe with their dearest blood and highest prowess, for these many years have not ceased in their pulpits wrenching and spraining the text, to set at nought and trample under foot all the most sacred and lifeblood laws, statutes, and acts of parliament, that are the holy covenant of union and marriage between the king and his realm, by proscribing and confiscating from us all the right we have to our own bodies, goods, and liberties. What is this but to blow a trumpet, and proclaim a firecross to a hereditary and perpetual civil war? Thus much against the subjects' liberty hath been assaulted by them. Now how they have spared supremacy, or likely are hereafter to submit to it, remains lastly to be considered.

The emulation that under the old law was in the king towards the priest, is now so come about in the gospel, that all the danger is to be feared from the priest to the king. Whilst the priest's office in the law was set out with an exterior lustre of pomp and glory, kings were ambitious to be priests; now priests, not perceiving the heavenly brightness and inward splendor of their more glorious evangelic ministry, with as great ambition affect to be kings, as in all their courses is easy to be observed. Their eyes ever imminent upon worldly matters, their desires ever thirsting after worldly employments, instead of diligent and fervent study in the Bible, they covet to be expert in canons and decretals, which may enable them to judge and interpose in temporal causes, however pretended ecclesiastical. Do they not hoard up pelf, seek to be potent in secular strength, in state affairs, in lands, lordships, and domains, to sway and carry all before them in high courts and privy-councils, to bring into their grasp the high and principal offices of the kingdom? Have they not been bold of late to check the common law, to slight and brave the indiminishable majesty of our highest court, the lawgiving and sacred parliament? Do they not plainly labor to exempt churchmen from the magistrate? Yea, so presumptuously as to question and menace officers that represent the king's person for using their authority against drunken priests? The cause of protecting murderous clergymen was the first heart-burning that swelled up the audacious Becket to the pestilent and odious vexation of Henry the Second. Nay, more: have not some of their devoted scholars begun, I need not say to nibble, but openly to argue against the king's supremacy? Is not the chief of them accused out of his own book, and his late canons, to effect a certain unquestionable patriarchate, independent, and unsubordinate to the crown? From whence having first brought us to a servile state of religion and manhood, and having predisposed his conditions with the pope, that lays claim to this land, or some Pepin of his own creating, it were all as likely for him to aspire to the monarchy among us, as that the pope could find means so on the sudden both to bereave the emperor of the Roman territory with the favor of Italy, and by an unexpected friend out of France, while he was in danger to lose his new-got purchase, beyond hope to leap into the fair exarchate of Ravenna.

A good while the pope subtly acted the lamb, writing to the emperor, "my lord Tiberius, my lord Mauritius;" but no sooner did this his lord pluck at the images and idols, but he threw off his sheep's clothing, and started up a wolf, laying his paws upon the emperor's right, as forfeited to Peter. Why may not we as well, having been fore-warned at home by our renowned Chaucer, and from abroad by the great and learned Padre Paolo, from the like beginnings, as we see they are, fear the like events? Certainly a wise and provident king ought to suspect a hierarchy in his realm, being ever attended, as it is, with two such greedy purveyors, ambition and usurpation; I say, he ought to suspect a hierarchy to be as dangerous and derogatory from his crown as a tetrarchy or a heptarchy. Yet now that the prelates had almost attained to what their insolent and unbridled minds had hurried them; to thrust the laity under the despotical rule of the monarch, that they themselves might confine the monarch to a kind of pupilage under their hierarchy, observe but how their own principles combat one another, and supplant each one his fellow.

Having fitted us only for peace, and that a servile peace, by lessening our numbers, draining our estates, enfeebling our bodies, cowing our free spirits by those ways as you have heard, their impotent actions cannot sustain themselves the least moment, unless they rouse us up to a war fit for Cain to be the leader of, an abhorred, a cursed, a fraternal war. England and Scotland, dearest brothers both in nature and in Christ, must be set to wade in one another's blood; and Ireland, our free denizen, upon the back of us both, as occasion should serve: a piece of service that the pope and all his factors have been compassing to do ever since the Reformation.

But ever blessed be He, and ever glorified, that from his high watchtower in the heavens, discerning the crooked ways of perverse and cruel men, hath hitherto maimed and infatuated all their damnable inventions, and deluded their great wizards with a delusion fit for fools and children: had God been so minded, he could have sent a spirit of mutiny amongst us, as he did between Abimelech and the Sechemites, to have made our funerals, and slain heaps more in number than the miserable surviving remnant; but he, when we least deserved, sent out a gentle gale and message of peace from the wings of those his cherubims that fan his mercy-seat. Nor shall the wisdom, the moderation, the Christian piety, the constancy of our nobility and commons of England, be ever forgotten, whose calm and temperate connivance could sit still and smile out the stormy bluster of men more audacious and precipitant than of solid and deep reach, till their own fury had run itself out of breath, assailing by rash and heady approaches the impregnable situation of our liberty and safety, that laughed such weak enginery to scorn, such poor drifts to make a national war of a surplice brabble, a tippet scuffle, and engage the unattainted honor of English knighthood to unfurl the streaming red cross, or to rear the horrid standard of those fatal guly dragons, for so unworthy a purpose, as to force upon their fellow-subjects that which themselves are weary of, the skeleton of a mass-book. Nor must the patience, the fortitude, the firm obedience of the nobles and people of Scotland, striving against manifold provocations; nor must their sincere and moderate proceedings hitherto be unremembered, to the shameful conviction of all their detractors.

Go on both hand in hand, O nations, never to be disunited; be the praise and the heroic song of all posterity; merit this, but seek only virtue, not to extend your limits; (for what needs to win a fading triumphant laurel out of the tears of wretched men?) but to settle the pure worship of God in his church, and justice in the state: then shall the hard- est difficulties smooth out themselves before ye; envy shall sink to hell, craft and malice be confounded, whether it be homebred mischief or outlandish cunning: yea, other nations will then covet to serve ye, for lordship and victory are but the pages of justice and virtue. Commit securely to true wisdom the vanquishing and uncasing of craft and subtlety, which are but her two runagates: join your invincible might to do worthy and godlike deeds; and then he that seeks to break your union, a cleaving curse be his inheritance to all generations.

Sir, you have now at length this question for the time, and as my memory would best serve me in such a copious and vast theme, fully handled, and you yourself may judge whether prelacy be the only church-govern- ment agreeable to monarchy. Seeing there- fore the perilous and confused estate into which we are fallen, and that, to the certain knowledge of all men, through the irreligious pride and hateful tyranny of prelates, (as the innumerable and grievous complaints of every shire cry out,) if we will now resolve to settle affairs either according to pure religion or sound policy, we must first of all begin roundly to cashier and cut away from the public body the noisome and diseased tumor of prelacy, and come from schism to unity with our neighbor reformed sister-churches, which with the blessing of peace and pure doctrine have now long time flourished; and doubtless with all hearty joy and gratulation will meet and welcome our Christian union with them, as they have been all this while grieved at our strange- ness, and little better than separation from them. And for the discipline propounded, seeing that it hath been inevitably proved, that the natural and fundamental causes of political happiness in all governments are the same and that this church-discipline is taught in the word of God, and, as we see, agrees according to wish with all such states as have received it; we may infallibly assure ourselves that it will as well agree with mon- archy, though all the tribe of Aphorismers and Politicasters would persuade us there be secret and mysterious reasons against it. For upon the settling hereof mark what nourishing and cordial restorements to the state will follow, the ministers of the gospel attending only to the work of salvation, every one within his limited charge; besides the diffusive blessings of God upon all our actions, the king shall sit without an old disturber, a daily encroacher and intruder; shall rid his kingdom of a strong sequestered and collateral power; a confronting mitre, whose potent wealth and wakeful ambition he had just cause to hold in jealousy: not to repeat the other present evils which only their removal will remove, and because things simply pure are inconsistent in the mass of nature, nor are the elements or humors in a man's body exactly homogeneal; and hence the best-founded commonwealths and least barbarous have aimed at a certain mixture and temperament, partaking the several vir- tues of each other state, that each part drawing to itself may keep up a steady and even uprightness in common.

There is no civil government that hath been known, no not the Spartan, not the Roman, though both for this respect so much praised by the wise Polybius, more divinely and harmoniously tuned, more equally balanced as it were by the hand and scale of justice, than is the commonwealth of England; where, under a free and untutored monarch, the noblest, worthiest, and most prudent men, with full approbation and suffrage of the people, have in their power the supreme and final determination of highest affairs. Now if conformity of church-discipline to the civil be so desired, there can be nothing more parallel, more uniform, than when under the sovereign prince, Christ's viceger- ent, using the sceptre of David, according to God's law, the godliest, the wisest, the learnedest ministers in their several charges have the instructing and disciplining of God's people, by whose full and free election they are consecrated to that holy and equal aristoc- racy. And why should not the piety and conscience of Englishmen, as members of the church, be trusted in the election of pastors to functions that nothing concern a monarch, as well as their worldly wisdoms are privileged as members of the state in suffraging their knights and burgesses to matters that concern him nearly? And if in weighing these several offices, their difference in time and quality be cast in, I know they will not turn the beam of equal judgment the moiety of a scruple. We therefore having already a kind of apostolical and ancient church election in our state, what a perverseness would it be in us of all others to retain forcibly a kind of imperious and stately election in our church! And what a blindness to think that what is already evangelical, as it were by a happy chance in our polity, should be repugnant to that which is the same by divine command in the ministry! Thus then we see that our ecclesial and political choices may consent and sort as well together without any rupture in the state, as Christians and freeholders. But as for honor, that ought indeed to be different and distinct, as either office looks a several way; the minister whose calling and end is spiritual, ought to be honored as a father and physician to the soul, (if he be found to be so,) with a sonlike and disciplelike reverence, which is indeed the dearest and most affectionate honor, most to be desired by a wise man, and such as will easily command a free and plentiful provision of outward necessaries, without his further care of this world.

The magistrate, whose charge is to see to our persons and estates, is to be honored with a more elaborate and personal courtship, with large salaries and stipends, that he himself may abound in those things whereof his legal justice and watchful care give us the quiet enjoyment. And this distinction of honor will bring forth a seemly and graceful uniformity over all the kingdom.

Then shall the nobles possess all the dignities and offices of temporal honor to themselves, sole lords without the improper mixture of scholastic and pusillanimous upstarts; the parliament shall void her upper house of the same annoyances; the common and civil laws shall be both set free, the former from the control, the other from the mere vassalage and copyhold of the clergy.

And whereas temporal laws rather punish men when they have transgressed, than form them to be such as should transgress seldomest, we may conceive great hopes, through the showers of divine benediction watering the unmolested and watchful pains of the ministry, that the whole inheritance of God will grow up so straight and blameless, that the civil magistrate may with far less toil and difficulty, and far more ease and delight, steer the tall and goodly vessel of the commonwealth through all the gusts and tides of the world's mutability.

Here I might have ended, but that some objections, which I have heard commonly flying about, press me to the endeavor of an answer. We must not run, they say, into sudden extremes. This is a fallacious rule, unless understood only of the actions of virtue about things indifferent: for if it be found that those two extremes be vice and virtue, falsehood and truth, the greater extremity of virtue and superlative truth we run into, the more virtuous and the more wise we become; and he that, flying from degenerate and traditional corruption, fears to shoot himself too far into the meeting embraces of a divinely warranted reformation, had better not have run at all. And for the suddenness, it cannot be feared. Who should oppose it? The papists? They dare not. The protestants otherwise affected? They were mad. There is nothing will be removed but what to them is professedly indifferent. The long affection which the people have borne to it, what for itself, what for the odiousness of prelates, is evident: from the first year of queen Elizabeth it hath still been more and more propounded, desired, and beseeched, yea, sometimes favorably forwarded by the parliaments themselves. Yet if it were sudden and swift, provided still it be from worse to better, certainly we ought to hie us from evil like a torrent, and rid ourselves of corrupt discipline, as we would shake fire out of our bosoms.

Speedy and vehement were the reformations of all the good kings of Judah, though the people had been nuzzled in idolatry never so long before; they feared not the bugbear danger, nor the lion in the way that the sluggish and timorous politician thinks he sees; no more did our brethren of the reformed churches abroad, they ventured (God being their guide) out of rigid popery, into that which we in mockery call precise puritanism, and yet we see no inconvenience befell them.

Let us not dally with God when he offers us a full blessing, to take as much of it as we think will serve our ends, and turn him back the rest upon his hands, lest in his anger he snatch all from us again. Next, they allege the antiquity of episcopacy through all ages. What it was in the apostles' time, that questionless it must be still; and therein I trust the ministers will be able to satisfy the parliament. But if episcopacy be taken for prelacy, all the ages they can deduce it through, will make it no more venerable than papacy.

Most certain it is, (as all our stories bear witness,) that ever since their coming to the see of Canterbury, for near twelve hundred years, to speak of them in general, they have been in England to our souls a sad and doleful succession of illiterate and blind guides; to our purses and goods a wasteful band of robbers, a perpetual havoc and rapine; to our state a continual hydra of mischief and molestation, the forge of discord and rebellion; this is the trophy of their antiquity, and boasted succession through so many ages. And for those prelate-martyrs they glory of, they are to be judged what they were by the gospel, and not the gospel to be tried by them.

And it is to be noted, that if they were for bishoprics and ceremonies, it was in their prosperity and fulness of bread; but in their persecution, which purified them, and near their death, which was their garland, they plainly disliked and condemned the ceremonies, and threw away those episcopal ornaments wherein they were installed as foolish and detestable; for so the words of Ridley at his degradement, and his letter to Hooper, expressly show. Neither doth the author of our church-history spare to record sadly the fall (for so he terms it) and infirmities of these martyrs, though we would deify them. And why should their martyrdom more countenance corrupt doctrine or discipline, than their subscriptions justify

their treason to the royal blood of this realm, by diverting and entailing the right of the crown from the true heirs, to the houses of Northumberland and Suffolk? which had it took effect, this present king had, in all likelihood, never sat on this throne, and the happy union of this island had been frustrated.

Lastly, whereas they add that some the learnedest of the reformed abroad admire our episcopacy; it had been more for the strength of the argument to tell us that some of the wisest statesmen admire it, for thereby we might guess them weary of the present discipline, as offensive to their state, which is the bug we fear, but being they are churchmen, we may rather suspect them for some prelatizing spirits that admire our bishoprics, not episcopacy.

The next objection vanishes of itself, propounding a doubt, whether a greater inconvenience would not grow from the corruption of any other discipline than from that of episcopacy. This seems an unseasonable foresight, and out of order, to defer and put off the most needful constitution of one right discipline, while we stand balancing the discommodities of two corrupt ones. First constitute that which is right, and of itself it will discover and rectify that which swerves, and easily remedy the pretended fear of having a pope in every parish, unless we call the zealous and meek censure of the church a popedom, which whoso does, let him advise how he can reject the pastorly rod and sheephook of Christ, and those cords of love, and not fear to fall under the iron sceptre of his anger, that will dash him to pieces like a potsherd.

At another doubt of theirs I wonder, whether this discipline which we desire be such as can be put in practice within this kingdom; they say it cannot stand with the common law nor with the king's safety, the government of episcopacy is now so weaved into the common law. In God's name let it weave out again; let not human quillets keep back divine authority. It is not the common law, nor the civil, but piety and justice that are our foundresses; they stoop not, neither change color for aristocracy, democracy, or monarchy, nor yet at all interrupt their just courses; but far above the taking notice of these inferior niceties, with perfect sympathy, wherever they meet, kiss each other. Lastly, they are fearful that the discipline which will succeed cannot stand with the king's safety. Wherefore? it is but episcopacy reduced to what it should be: were it not that the tyranny of prelates under the name of bishops hath made our ears tender and startling, we might call every good minister a bishop, as every bishop, yea, the apostles themselves, are called ministers, and the angels ministering spirits, and the ministers again angels. But wherein is this propounded government so shrewd? Because the government of assemblies will succeed. Did not the apostles govern the church by assemblies? How should it else be catholic? How should it have communion? We count it sacrilege to take from the rich prelates their lands and revenues, which is sacrilege in them to keep, using them as they do; and can we think it safe to defraud the living church of God of that right which God has given her in assemblies? O but the consequence! assemblies draw to them the supremacy of ecclesiastical jurisdiction. No, surely, they draw no supremacy, but that authority which Christ, and St. Paul in his name, confers upon them. The king may still retain the same supremacy in the assemblies, as in the parliament; here he can do nothing alone against the common law, and there neither alone, nor with consent, against the scriptures. But is this all? No: this ecclesiastical supremacy draws to it the power to excommunicate kings; and then follows the worst that can be imagined. Do they hope to avoid this, by keeping prelates that have so often done it? Not to exemplify the malapert insolence of our own bishops in this kind towards our kings, I shall turn back to the primitive and pure times, which the objectors would have the rule of reformation to us.

Not an assembly, but one bishop alone, St. Ambrose of Milan, held Theodosius, the most Christian emperor, under excommunication above eight months together, drove him from the church in the presence of his nobles; which the good emperor bore with heroic humility, and never ceased by prayers and tears, till he was absolved; for which coming to the bishop with supplication into the salutatory, some out-porch of the church, he was charged by him with tyrannical madness against God, for coming into holy ground. At last, upon conditions absolved, and after great humiliation approaching to the altar to offer, (as those thrice pure times then thought meet,) he had scarce withdrawn his hand, and stood awhile, when a bold archdeacon comes in the bishop's name, and chases him from within the rails, telling him peremptorily, that the place wherein he stood was for none but the priests to enter, or to touch: and this is another piece of pure primitive divinity! Think ye, then, our bishops will forego the power of excommunication on whomsoever? No, certainly, unless to compass sinister ends, and then revoke when they see their time. And yet this most mild, though withal dreadful and inviolable prerogative of Christ's diadem, excommunication, serves for nothing with them, but to prog and pander for fees, or to display their pride, and sharpen their revenge, debarring men the protection of the law; and I remember not whether in some cases it bereave not men all right to their worldly goods and inheritances, besides the denial of Christian burial. But in the evangelical and reformed use of this sacred censure, no such prostitution, no such Iscariotical drifts are to be doubted, as that spiritual doom and sentence should invade worldly possession, which is the rightful lot and portion even of the wickedest men, as frankly bestowed upon them by the all-dispensing bounty as rain and sunshine. No, no, it seeks not to bereave or destroy the body; it seeks to save the soul by humbling the body, not by imprisonment, or pecuniary mulct, much less by stripes, or bonds, or disinheritance, but by fatherly admonishment and Christian rebuke, to cast it into godly sorrow, whose end is joy, and ingenuous bashfulness to sin: if that cannot be wrought, then as a tender mother takes her child and holds it over the pit with scaring words, that it may learn to fear where danger is; so doth excommunication as dearly and as freely, without money, use her wholesome and saving terrors, she is instant, she beseeches, by all the dear and sweet promises of salvation, she entices and woos; by all the threatenings and thunders of the law, and rejected gospel, she charges and adjures: this is all her armory, her munition, her artillery; then she awaits with longsufferance, and yet ardent zeal. In brief, there is no act in all the errand of God's ministers to mankind wherein passes more loverlike contestation between Christ and the soul of a regenerate man lapsing, than before, and in, and after the sentence of excommunication. As for the fogging proctorage of money, with such an eye as struck Gehazi with leprosy and Simon Magus with a curse, so does she look, and so threaten her fiery whip against that banking den of thieves that dare thus baffle, and buy and sell the awful and majestic wrinkles of her brow. He that is rightly and apostolically sped with her invisible arrow, if he can be at peace in his soul, and not smell within him the brimstone of hell, may have fair leave to tell all his bags over undiminished of the least farthing, may eat his dainties, drink his wine, use his delights, enjoy his lands and liberties, not the least skin raised, not the least hair misplaced, for all that excommunication has done: much more may a king enjoy his rights and prerogatives undeflowered, untouched, and be as absolute and complete a king, as all his royalties and revenues can make him. And therefore little did Theodosius fear a plot upon his empire, when he stood excommunicate by Saint Ambrose, though it were done either with much haughty pride, or ignorant zeal. But let us rather look upon the reformed churches beyond the seas, the Grizons, the Swisses, the Hollanders, the French, that have a supremacy to live under, as well as we: where do the churches in all these places strive for supremacy? Where do they clash and justle supremacies with the civil magistrate? In France, a more severe monarchy than ours, the protestants under this church government carry the name of the best subjects the king has; and yet presbytery, if it must be so called, does there all that it desires to do: how easy were it, if there be such great suspicion, to give no more scope to it in England! But let us not for fear of a scarecrow, or else through hatred to be reformed, stand hankering and politizing, when God with spread hands testifies to us, and points us out the way to our peace.

Let us not be so over-credulous, unless God hath blinded us, as to trust our dear souls into the hands of men that beg so devoutly for the pride and gluttony of their own backs and bellies, that sue and solicit so eagerly, not for the saving of souls, the consideration of which can have here no place at all, but for their bishoprics, deaneries, prebends, and canonries: how can these men not be corrupt, whose very cause is the bribe of their own pleading, whose mouths cannot open without the strong breath and loud stench of avarice, simony, and sacrilege, embezzling the treasury of the church on painted and gilded walls of temples, wherein God hath testified to have no delight, warming their palace kitchens, and from thence their unctuous and epicurean paunches, with the alms of the blind, the lame, the impotent, the aged, the orphan, the widow? for with these the treasury of Christ ought to be, here must be his jewels bestowed, his rich cabinet must be emptied here; as the constant martyr St. Lawrence taught the Roman prætor. Sir, would you know what the remonstrance of these men would have, what their petition implies? They entreat us that we would not be weary of those insupportable grievances that our shoulders have hitherto cracked under; they beseech us that we would think them fit to be our justices of peace, our lords, our highest officers of state, though they come furnished with no more experience than they learnt between the cook and the maniple, or more profoundly at the college audit, or the regent house, or to come to their deepest insight, at their patron's table; they would request us to endure still the rustling of their silken cassocks, and that we would burst our midriffs, rather than laugh to see them under sail in all their lawn and sarcenet, their shrouds and tackle, with a geometrical rhomboides upon their heads: they would bear us in hand that we must of duty still appear before them once a year in Jerusalem, like good circumcised males and females, to be taxed by the poll, to be sconced our head-money, our twopences, in their chandlerly shopbook of Easter. They pray us that it would please us to let them still hale us, and worry us with their bandogs and pursuivants; and that it would please the parliament that they may yet have the whipping, fleecing, and flaying of us in their diabolical courts, to tear the flesh from our bones, and into our wide wounds instead of balm, to pour in the oil of tartar, vitriol, and mercury: surely, a right reasonable, innocent, and soft-hearted petition. O the relenting bowels of the fathers! Can this be granted them, unless God have smitten us with frenzy from above, and with a dazzling giddiness at noonday? Should not those men rather be heard that come to plead against their own preferments, their worldly advantages, their own abundance; for honor and obedience to God's word, the conversion of souls, the Christian peace of the land, and union of the reformed catholic church, the unappropriating and unmonopolizing the rewards of learning and industry, from the greasy clutch of ignorance and high feeding? We have tried already, and miserably felt what ambition, worldly glory, and immoderate wealth, can do; what the boisterous and contradictional hand of a temporal, earthly, and corporeal spirituality can avail to the edifying of Christ's holy church; were it such a desperate hazard to put to the venture the universal votes of Christ's congregation, the fellowly and friendly yoke of a teaching and laborious ministry, the pastor-like and apostolic imitation of meek and unlordly discipline, the gentle and benevolent mediocrity of church-maintenance, without the ignoble hucksterage of piddling tithes? Were it such an incurable mischief to make a little trial, what all this would do to the flourishing and growing up of Christ's mystical body? as rather to use every poor shift, and if that serve not, to threaten uproar and combustion, and shake the brand of civil discord?

O, sir, I do now feel myself inwrapped on the sudden into those mazes and labyrinths of dreadful and hideous thoughts, that which way to get out, or which way to end, I know not, unless I turn mine eyes, and with your help lift up my hands to that eternal and propitious throne, where nothing is readier than grace and refuge to the distresses of mortal suppliants: and it were a shame to leave these serious thoughts less piously than the heathen were wont to conclude their graver discourses.

Thou, therefore, that sittest in light and glory unapproachable, parent of angels and men! next, thee I implore, omnipotent King, Redeemer of that lost remnant whose nature thou didst assume, ineffable and everlasting Love! and thou, the third subsistence of divine infinitude, illumining Spirit, the joy and solace of created things! one Tripersonal godhead! look upon this thy poor and almost spent and expiring church, leave her not thus a prey to these importunate wolves, that wait and think long till they devour thy tender flock; these wild boars that have broke into thy vineyard, and left the print of their polluting hoofs on the souls of thy servants. O let them not bring about their damned designs, that stand now at the entrance of the bottomless pit, expecting the watchword to open and let out those dreadful locusts and scorpions, to reinvolve us in that pitchy cloud of infernal darkness, where we shall never more see the sun of thy truth again, never hope for the cheerful dawn, never more hear the bird of morning sing. Be moved with pity at the afflicted state of this our shaken monarchy, that now lies laboring under her throes, and struggling against the grudges of more dreaded calamities.

O thou, that, after the impetuous rage of five bloody inundations, and the succeeding sword of intestine war, soaking the land in her own gore, didst pity the sad and ceaseless revolution of our swift and thick-coming sorrows; when we were quite breathless, of thy free grace didst motion peace, and terms of covenant with us; and having first well nigh freed us from antichristian thraldom, didst build up this Britannic empire to a glorious and enviable height, with all her daughter-islands about her; stay us in this felicity, let not the obstinacy of our half-obedience and will-worship bring forth that viper of sedition, that for these fourscore years hath been breeding to eat through the entrails of our peace; but let her cast her abortive spawn without the danger of this travailing and throbbing kingdom: that we may still remember in our solemn thanksgivings, how for us, the northern ocean even to the frozen Thule was scattered with the proud shipwrecks of the Spanish armada, and the very maw of hell ransacked, and made to give up her concealed destruction, ere she could vent it in that horrible and damned blast.

O how much more glorious will those former deliverances appear, when we shall know them not only to have saved us from greatest miseries past, but to have reserved us for greatest happiness to come! Hitherto thou hast but freed us, and that not fully, from the unjust and tyrannous claim of thy foes; now unite us entirely, and appropriate us to thyself, tie us everlastingly in willing homage to the prerogative of thy eternal throne.

And now we know, O thou our most certain hope and defence, that thine enemies have been consulting all the sorceries of the great whore, and have joined their plots with that sad intelligencing tyrant that mischiefs the world with his mines of Ophir, and lies thirsting to revenge his naval ruins that have larded our seas: but let them all take counsel together, and let it come to nought; let them decree, and do thou cancel it; let them gather themselves, and be scattered; let them embattle themselves, and be broken; let them embattle, and be broken, for thou art with us.

Then, amidst the hymns and hallelujahs of saints, some one may perhaps be heard offering at high strains in new and lofty measures to sing and celebrate thy divine mercies and marvellous judgments in this land throughout all ages; whereby this great and warlike nation, instructed and inured to the fervent and continual practice of truth and righteousness, and casting far from her the rags of her old vices, may press on hard to that high and happy emulation to be found the soberest, wisest, and most Christian people at that day, when thou, the eternal and shortly expected King, shalt open the clouds to judge the several kingdoms of the world, and distributing national honors and rewards to religious and just commonwealths, shalt put an end to all earthly tyrannies, proclaiming thy universal and mild monarchy through heaven and earth; where they undoubtedly, that by their labors, counsels, and prayers, have been earnest for the common good of religion and their country, shall receive above the inferior orders of the blessed, the regal addition of principalities, legions, and thrones into their glorious titles, and in

supereminence of beatific vision, progressing the dateless and irrevoluble circle of eternity, shall clasp inseparable hands with joy and bliss, in overmeasure for ever.

But they contrary, that by the impairing and diminution of the true faith, the distresses and servitude of their country, aspire to high dignity, rule, and promotion here, after a shameful end in this life, (which God grant them,) shall be thrown down eternally into the darkest and deepest gulf of hell, where, under the despiteful control, the trample and spurn of all the other damned, that in the anguish of their torture, shall have no other ease than to exercise a raving and bestial tyranny over them as their slaves and negroes, they shall remain in that plight for ever, the basest, the lowermost, the most dejected, most underfoot, and downtrodden vassals of perdition.

OF PRELATICAL EPISCOPACY,

AND WHETHER IT MAY BE DEDUCED FROM THE APOSTOLICAL TIMES, BY VIRTUE OF THOSE TESTIMONIES WHICH ARE ALLEGED TO THAT PURPOSE IN SOME LATE TREATISES; ONE WHEREOF GOES UNDER THE NAME OF JAMES, ARCHBISHOP OF ARMAGH.

[The text is that of the first edition, 1641.]

EPISCOPACY, as it is taken for an order in the church above a presbyter, or, as we commonly name him, the minister of a congregation, is either of divine constitution or of human. If only of human, we have the same human privilege that all men have ever had since Adam, being born free, and in the mistress island of all the British, to retain this episcopacy, or to remove it, consulting with our own occasions and conveniences, and for the prevention of our own dangers and disquiets, in what best manner we can devise, without running at a loss, as we must needs in those stale and useless records of either uncertain or unsound antiquity; which, if we hold fast to the grounds of the reformed church, can neither skill of us, nor we of it, so oft as it would lead us to the broken reed of tradition. If it be of divine constitution, to satisfy us fully in that, the scripture only is able, it being the only book left us of divine authority, not in anything more divine than in the all-sufficiency it hath to furnish us, as with all other spiritual knowledge, so with this in particular, setting out to us a perfect man of God, accomplished to all the good works of his charge: through all which book can be nowhere, either by plain text or solid reasoning, found any difference between a bishop and a presbyter, save that they be two names to signify the same order. Notwithstanding this clearness, and that by all evidence of argument, Timothy and Titus (whom our prelates claim to imitate only in the controlling part of their office) had rather the vicegerency of an apostleship committed to them, than the ordinary charge of a bishopric, as being men of an extraordinary calling; yet to verify that which St. Paul foretold of succeeding times, when men began to have itching ears, then not contented with the plentiful and wholesome fountains of the gospel, they began after their own lusts to heap to themselves teachers, and as if the divine scripture wanted a supplement, and were to be eked out, they cannot think any doubt resolved, and any doctrine confirmed, unless they run to that indigested heap and fry of authors which they call antiquity. Whatsoever time, or the heedless hand of blind chance, hath drawn down from of old to this present, in her huge drag-net, whether fish or seaweed, shells or shrubs, unpicked, unchosen, those are the fathers. Seeing, therefore, some men, deeply conversant in books, have had so little care of late to give the world a better account of their reading, than by divulging needless tractates stuffed with specious names of Ignatius and Polycarpus; with fragments of old martyrologies and legends, to distract and stagger the multitude of credulous readers, and mislead them from their strong guards and places of safety, under the tuition of holy writ; it came into my thoughts to persuade myself, setting all distances and nice respects aside, that I could do religion and my country no better service for the time, than doing my utmost endeavor to recall the people of God from this vain foraging after straw, and to reduce them to their firm stations under the standard of the gospel; by making appear to them. first the insufficiency, next the incon-

venience, and lastly the impiety of these gay testimonies, that their great doctors would bring them to dote on. And in performing this, I shall not strive to be more exact in method, than as their citations lead me.

First, therefore, concerning Ignatius shall be treated fully, when the author shall come to insist upon some places in his epistles. Next, to prove a succession of twenty-seven bishops from Timothy, he cites one Leontius, bishop of Magnesia, out of the 11th act of the Chalcedonian council: this is but an obscure and single witness, and for his faithful dealing who shall commend him to us, with this his catalogue of bishops? What know we further of him, but that he might be as factious and false a bishop as Leontius of Antioch, that was a hundred years his predecessor? For neither the praise of his wisdom or his virtue hath left him memorable to posterity, but only this doubtful relation, which we must take at his word: and how shall this testimony receive credit from his word, whose very name had scarce been thought on but for this bare testimony? But they will say, he was a member of the council, and that may deserve to gain him credit with us. I will not stand to argue, as yet with fair allowance I might, that we may as justly suspect there were some bad and slippery men in that council, as we know there are wont to be in our convocations: nor shall I need to plead at this time, that nothing hath been more attempted, nor with more subtlety brought about, both anciently by other heretics, and modernly by papists, than to falsify the editions of the councils, of which we have none but from our adversaries' hands, whence canons, acts, and whole spurious councils are thrust upon us; and hard it would be to prove in all, which are legitimate, against the lawful rejection of an urgent and free disputer. But this I purpose not to take advantage of; for what avails it to wrangle about the corrupt editions of councils, whenas we know that many years ere this time, which was almost five hundred years after Christ, the councils themselves were foully corrupted with ungodly prelatism, and so far plunged into worldly ambition, as that it stood them upon long ere this to uphold their now well tasted hierarchy by what fair pretext soever they could, in like manner as they had now learned to defend many other gross corruptions by as ancient and supposed authentic tradition as episcopacy? And what hope can we have of this whole council to warrant us a matter, four hundred years at least above their time, concerning the distinction of bishop and presbyter, whenas we find them such blind judges of things before their eyes, in their decrees of precedency between bishop and bishop, acknowledging Rome for the apostolic throne, and Peter, in that see, for the rock, the basis, and the foundation of the catholic church and faith, contrary to the interpretation of more ancient fathers? And therefore from a mistaken text did they give to Leo, as Peter's successor, a kind of pre-eminence above the whole council, as Evagrius expresses; (for now the pope was come to that height, as to arrogate to himself by his vicars incompetible honors;) and yet having thus yielded to Rome the universal primacy for spiritual reasons, as they thought, they conclude their sitting with a carnal and ambitious decree, to give the second place of dignity to Constantinople from reason of state, because it was New Rome; and by like consequence doubtless of earthly privileges annexed to each other city, was the bishop thereof to take his place.

I may say again therefore, what hope can we have of such a council, as, beginning in the spirit, ended thus in the flesh? Much rather should we attend to what Eusebius the ancientest writer extant of church-history, nowithstanding all the helps he had above these, confesses in the 4th chapter of his third book, that it was no easy matter to tell who were those that were left bishops of the churches by the apostles, more than by what a man might gather from the Acts of the Apostles, and the Epistles of St. Paul, in which number he reckons Timothy for bishop of Ephesus. So as may plainly appear, that this tradition of bishoping Timothy over Ephesus was but taken for granted out of that place in St. Paul, which was only an entreating him to tarry at Ephesus, to do something left him in charge. Now, if Eusebius, a famous writer, thought it so difficult to tell who were appointed bishops by the apostles, much more may we think it difficult to Leontius, an obscure bishop, speaking beyond his own diocese: and certainly much more hard was it for either of them to determine what kind of bishops those were, if they had so little means to know who they were; and much less reason have we to stand to their definitive sentence, seeing they have been so rash to raise up such lofty bishops and bishoprics out of places in scripture merely misunderstood. Thus while we leave the Bible to gad after these traditions of the ancients, we hear the ancients themselves confessing, that what knowledge they had in this point was such as they had gathered from the Bible.

Since therefore antiquity itself hath turned over the controversy to that sovereign book which we had fondly straggled from, we shall do better not to detain this venerable apparition of Leontius any longer, but dismiss him with his list of seven and twenty, to sleep unmolested in his former obscurity.

Now for the word προεστώς, it is more likely that Timothy never knew the word in that sense: it was the vanity of those next succeeding times not to content themselves with the simplicity of scripture phrase, but must make a new lexicon, to name themselves by; one will be called προεστώς, or antistes, a word of precedence; another would be termed a gnostic, as Clemens; a third, sacerdos, or priest, and talks of altars; which was a plain sign that their doctrine began to change, for which they must change their expressions. But that place of Justin Martyr serves rather to convince the author, than to make for him, where the name προεστώς τῶν ἀδελφῶν, the president or pastor of the brethren, (for to what end is he their president, but to teach them?) cannot be limited to signify a prelatical bishop, but rather communicates that Greek appellation to every ordinary presbyter: for there he tells what the Christians had wont to do in their several congregations, to read and expound, to pray and administer, all which he says the προεστώς, or antistes, did. Are these the offices only of a bishop, or shall we think that every congregation where these things were done, which he attributes to this antistes, had a bishop present among them? Unless they had as many antistites as presbyters, which this place rather seems to imply; and so we may infer even from their own alleged authority, that "antistes was nothing else but presbyter."

As for that nameless treatise of Timothy's martyrdom, only cited by Photius that lived almost nine hundred years after Christ, it handsomely follows in that author the martyrdom of the seven sleepers, that slept (I tell you but what mine author says) three hundred seventy and two years; for so long they had been shut up in a cave without meat, and were found living. This story of Timothy's Ephesian bishopric, as it follows in order, so may it for truth, if it only subsist upon its own authority, as it doth; for Photius only saith he read it, he does not aver it. That other legendary piece found among the lives of the saints, and sent us from the shop of the Jesuits at Louvain, does but bear the name of Polycrates; how truly, who can tell? and shall have some more weight with us when Polycrates can persuade us of that which he affirms in the same place of Eusebius's fifth book, that St. John was a priest, and wore the golden breastplate: and why should he convince us more with his traditions of Timothy's episcopacy, than he could convince Victor, bishop of Rome, with his traditions concerning the feast of Easter, who, not regarding his irrefragable instances of examples taken from Philip and his daughters that were prophetesses, or from Polycarpus, no, nor from St. John himself, excommunicated both him and all the Asian churches, for celebrating their Easter judaically? He may therefore go back to the seven bishops his kinsmen, and make his moan to them, that we esteem his traditional ware as lightly as Victor did.

Those of Theodoret, Felix, and John of Antioch, are authorities of later times, and therefore not to be received for their antiquity's sake to give in evidence concerning an allegation, wherein writers, so much their elders, we see so easily miscarry. What if they had told us that Peter, who, as they say, left Ignatius bishop of Antioch, went afterwards to Rome, and was bishop there, as this Ignatius, and Irenæus, and all antiquity with one mouth deliver? there be nevertheless a number of learned and wise protestants, who have written, and will maintain, that Peter's being at Rome as bishop

cannot stand with concordance of scripture.

Now come the epistles of Ignatius to show us, first, that Onesimus was bishop of Ephesus; next, to assert the difference of bishop and presbyter: wherein I wonder that men, teachers of the protestant religion, make no more difficulty of imposing upon our belief a supposititious offspring of some dozen epistles, whereof five are rejected as spurious, containing in them heresies and trifles; which cannot agree in chronology with Ignatius, entitling him archbishop of Antioch Theopolis, which name of Theopolis that city had not till Justinian's time, long after, as Cedrenus mentions; which argues both the barbarous time, and the unskilful fraud of him that foisted this epistle upon Ignatius. In the epistle to those of Tarsus, he condemns them for ministers of Satan, that say, "Christ is God above all." To the Philippians, them that kept their Easter as the Asian churches, and Polycarpus did, and them that fasted upon any Saturday or Sunday, except one, he counts as those that had slain the Lord. To those of Antioch, he salutes the subdeacons, chanters, porters, and exorcists, as if these had been orders of the church in his time: those other epistles less questioned, are yet so interlarded with corruptions, as may justly endue us with a wholesome suspicion of the rest. As to the Trallians, he writes, that "a bishop hath power over all beyond all government and authority whatsoever." Surely then no pope can desire more than Ignatius attributes to every bishop; but what will become then of the archbishops and primates, if every bishop in Ignatius's judgment be as supreme as a pope? To the Ephesians, near the very place from whence they fetch their proof for episcopacy, there stands a line that casts an ill hue upon all the epistle; "Let no man err," saith he: "unless a man be within the rails or enclosure of the altar, he is deprived of the bread of life." I say not but this may be stretched to a figurative construction; but yet it has an ill look, especially being followed beneath with the mention of I know not what sacrifices. In the other epistle to Smyrna, wherein is written that "they should follow their bishop as Christ did his Father, and the presbytery as the apostles;" not to speak of the insulse, and ill laid comparison, this cited place lies upon the very brim of a noted corruption, which, had they that quote this passage ventured to let us read, all men would have readily seen what grain the testimony had been of, where it is said, "that it is not lawful without a bishop to baptize, nor to offer, nor to do sacrifice." What can our church make of these phrases but scandalous? And but a little further he plainly falls to contradict the Spirit of God in Solomon, judged by the words themselves; "My son," saith he, "honor God and the king; but I say, honor God and the bishop as high-priest, bearing the image of God according to his ruling, and of Christ according to his priesting; and after him honor the king." Excellent Ignatius! Can ye blame the prelates for making much of this epistle? Certainly, if this epistle can serve you to set a bishop above a presbyter, it may serve you next to set him above a king. These, and other like places in abundance through all those short epistles, must either be adulterate, or else Ignatius was not Ignatius, nor a martyr, but most adulterate, and corrupt himself. In the midst, therefore, of so many forgeries, where shall we fix to dare say this is Ignatius? As for his style, who knows it, so disfigured and interrupted as it is? except they think that where they meet with anything sound, and orthodoxal, there they find Ignatius. And then they believe him, not for his own authority, but for a truth's sake, which they derive from elsewhere: to what end then should they cite him as authentic for episcopacy, when they cannot know what is authentic in him, but by the judgment which they brought with them, and not by any judgment which they might safely learn from him? How can they bring satisfaction from such an author, to whose very essence the reader must be fain to contribute his own understanding? Had God ever intended that we should have sought any part of useful instruction from Ignatius, doubtless he would not have so ill provided for our knowledge, as to send him to our hands in this broken and disjointed plight; and if he intended no such thing, we do injuriously in thinking to taste better the pure evangelic manna, by seasoning our mouths with the tainted scraps and fragments of an unknown table; and

searching among the verminous and polluted rags dropped overworn from the toiling shoulders of time, with these deformedly to quilt and interlace the entire, the spotless, and undecaying robe of truth, the daughter not of time, but of Heaven, only bred up here below in Christian hearts, between two grave and holy nurses, the doctrine and discipline of the gospel.

Next follows Irenæus, bishop of Lyons, who is cited to affirm, that Polycarpus "was made bishop of Smyrna by the apostles;" and this, it may seem, none could better tell than he who had both seen and heard Polycarpus: but when did he hear him? Himself confesses to Florinus, when he was a boy. Whether that age in Irenæus may not be liable to many mistakings; and whether a boy may be trusted to take an exact account of the manner of a church constitution, and upon what terms, and within what limits, and with what kind of commission Polycarpus received his charge, let a man consider, ere he be credulous. It will not be denied that he might have seen Polycarpus in his youth, a man of great eminence in the church, to whom the other presbyters might give way for his virtue, wisdom, and the reverence of his age; and so did Anicetus, bishop of Rome, even in his own city, give him a kind of priority in administering the sacrament, as may be read in Eusebius: but that we should hence conclude a distinct and superior order from the young observation of Irenæus, nothing yet alleged can warrant us; unless we shall believe such as would face us down, that Calvin and, after him, Beza were bishops of Geneva, because that in the unsettled state of the church, while things were not fully composed, their worth and learning cast a greater share of business upon them, and directed men's eyes principally towards them: and yet these men were the dissolvers of episcopacy. We see the same necessity in state affairs; Brutus, that expelled the kings out of Rome, was for the time forced to be as it were a king himself, till matters were set in order, as in a free commonwealth. He that had seen Pericles lead the Athenians which way he listed, haply would have said he had been their prince; and yet he was but a powerful and eloquent man in a democracy, and had no more at any time than a temporary and elective sway, which was in the will of the people when to abrogate. And it is most likely that in the church, they which came after these apostolic men, being less in merit, but bigger in ambition, strove to invade those privileges by intrusion and plea of right, which Polycarpus, and others like him possessed, from the voluntary surrender of men subdued by the excellency of their heavenly gifts; which because their successors had not, and so could neither have that authority, it was their policy to divulge that the eminence which Polycarpus and his equals enjoyed, was by right of constitution, not by free will of condescending. And yet thus far Irenæus makes against them, as in that very place to call Polycarpus an apostolical presbyter. But what fidelity his relations had in general, we cannot sooner learn than by Eusebius, who, near the end of his third book, speaking of Papias, a very ancient writer, one that had heard St. John, and was known to many that had seen and been acquainted with others of the apostles, but being of a shallow wit, and not understanding those traditions which he received, filled his writings with many new doctrines, and fabulous conceits: he tells us there, that "divers ecclesiastical men, and Irenæus among the rest, while they looked at his antiquity, became infected with his errors." Now, if Irenæus were so rash as to take unexamined opinions from an author of so small capacity, when he was a man, we should be more rash ourselves to rely upon those observations which he made when he was a boy. And this may be a sufficient reason to us why we need no longer muse at the spreading of many idle traditions so soon after the apostles, while such as this Papias had the throwing them about, and the inconsiderate zeal of the next age, that heeded more the person than the doctrine, had the gathering them up. Wherever a man, who had been any way conversant with the apostles, was to be found, thither flew all the inquisitive ears, the exercise of right instructing was changed into the curiosity of impertinent fabling: where the mind was to be edified with solid doctrine, there the fancy was soothed with solemn stories: with less fervency was studied what St. Paul or St.

John had written, than was listened to one that could say, Here he taught, here he stood, this was his stature; and thus he went habited; and, O happy this house that harbored him, and that cold stone whereon he rested, this village wherein he wrought such a miracle, and that pavement bedewed with the warm effusion of his last blood, that sprouted up into eternal roses to crown his martyrdom. Thus, while all their thoughts were poured out upon circumstances, and the gazing after such men as had sat at table with the apostles, (many of which Christ hath professed, yea, though they had cast out devils in his name, he will not know at the last day,) by this means they lost their time, and truanted in the fundamental grounds of saving knowledge, as was seen shortly by their writings. Lastly, for Irenæus, we have cause to think him less judicious in his reports from hand to hand of what the apostles did, when we find him so negligent in keeping the faith which they writ, as to say in his third book against heresies, that "the obedience of Mary was the cause of salvation to herself and all mankind;" and in his fifth book, that "as Eve was seduced to fly God, so the virgin Mary was persuaded to obey God, that the virgin Mary might be made the advocate of the virgin Eve." Thus if Irenæus, for his nearness to the apostles, must be the patron of episcopacy to us, it is no marvel though he be the patron of idolatry to the papist, for the same cause. To the epistle of those brethren of Smyrna, that write the martyrdom of Polycarpus, and style him an apostolical and prophetical doctor, and bishop of the church of Smyrna, I could be content to give some credit for the great honor and affection which I see those brethren bear him; and not undeservedly, if it be true, which they there say, that he was a prophet, and had a voice from heaven to comfort him at his death, which they could hear, but the rest could not for the noise and tumult that was in the place; and besides, if his body were so precious to the Christians, that he was never wont to pull off his shoes for one or other that still strove to have the office, that they might come to touch his feet, yet a light scruple or two I would gladly be resolved in; if Polycarpus (who, as they say, was a prophet that never failed in what he fore-told) had declared to his friends, that he knew, by vision, he should die no other death than burning, how it came to pass that the fire, when it came to proof, would not do his work, but starting off like a full sail from the mast, did but reflect a golden light upon his unviolated limbs, exhaling such a sweet odor, as if all the incense of Arabia had been burning; insomuch that when the [10] billmen saw that the fire was overawed, and could not do the deed, one of them steps to him and stabs him with a sword, at which wound such abundance of blood gushed forth as quenched the fire. By all this relation it appears not how the fire was guilty of his death: and then how can his prophecy be fulfilled? Next, how the standers-by could be so soon weary of such a glorious sight, and such a fragrant smell, as to hasten the [20] executioner to put out the fire with the mar-tyr's blood; unless perhaps they thought, as in all perfumes, that the smoke would be more odorous than the flame: yet these good brethren say he was bishop of Smyrna. No man questions it, if bishop and presbyter were anciently all one: and how does it ap-pear by anything in this testimony that they were not? If among his other high titles of prophetical, apostolical, and most admired of [30] those times, he be also styled bishop of the church of Smyrna in a kind of speech, which the rhetoricans call κατ' ἐξοχὴν, for his ex-cellence sake, as being the most famous of all the Smyrnian presbyters; it cannot be proved neither from this nor that other place of Irenæus, that he was therefore in distinct and monarchical order above the other presbyters; it is more probable, that if the whole presbytery had been as renowned [40] as he, they would have termed every one of them severally bishop of Smyrna. Hence it is, that we read sometimes of two bishops in one place; and had all the presbyters there been of like worth, we might perhaps have read of twenty.

Tertullian accosts us next, (for Polycrates hath had his answer,) whose testimony, state but the question right, is of no more force to deduce episcopacy, than the two former. [50] He says that the church of Smyrna had Polycarpus placed there by John, and the church of Rome, Clement ordained by Peter;

and so the rest of the churches did show what bishops they had received by the ap-pointment of the apostles. None of this will be contradicted, for we have it out of the scripture that bishops, or presbyters, which were the same, were left by the apostles in every church, and they might perhaps give some special charge to Clement, or Poly-carpus, or Linus, and put some special trust in them for the experience they had of their faith and constancy; it remains yet to be evinced out of this and the like places, which will never be, that the word bishop is other-wise taken than in the language of St. Paul and the Acts for an order above presbyters. We grant them bishops, we grant them worthy men, we grant them placed in sev-eral churches by the apostles, we grant that Irenæus and Tertullian affirm this; but that they were placed in a superior order above the presbytery, show from all these words why we should grant. It is not enough to say the apostle left this man bishop in Rome, and that other in Ephesus; but to show when they altered their own decree set down by St. Paul, and made all the presbyters under-lings to one bishop. But suppose Tertullian had made an imparity where none was originally, should he move us, that goes about to prove an imparity between God the Father and God the Son, as these words im-port in his book against Praxeas?—"The Father is the whole substance, but the Son a derivation, and portion of the whole, as he himself professes, 'Because the Father is greater than me.'" Believe him now for a faithful relater of tradition, whom you see such an unfaithful expounder of the scrip-ture. Besides, in his time, all allowable tra-dition was now lost. For this same author whom you bring to testify the ordination of Clement to the bishopric of Rome by Peter, testifies also, in the beginning of his treatise concerning chastity, that the bishop of Rome did then use to send forth his edicts by the name of Pontifex Maximus, and Episcopus Episcoporum, Chief Priest, and Bishop of Bishops: for shame then do not urge that authority to keep up a bishop, that will neces-sarily engage you to set up a pope. As little can your advantage be from Hegesippus, an historian of the same time, not extant, but cited by Eusebius: his words are, that "in every city all things so stood in his time as the law, and the prophets, and our Lord did preach." If they stood so, then stood not bishops above presbyters; for what our Lord and his disciples taught, God be thanked, we have no need to go learn of him: and you may as well hope to persuade us out of the same author, that James, the brother of our Lord, was a Nazarite, and that to him only it was lawful to enter into the holy of holies; that his food was not upon anything that had life, fish or flesh; that he used no woollen garments, but only linen, and so as he trifles on.

If therefore the tradition of the church were now grown so ridiculous, and disconsenting from the doctrine of the apostles, even in those points which were of least moment to men's particular ends, how well may we be assured it was much more degenerated in point of episcopacy and precedency, things which could afford such plausible pretences, such commodious traverses for ambition and avarice to lurk behind!

As for those Britain bishops which you cite, take heed what you do; for our Britain bishops, less ancient than these, were remarkable for nothing more than their poverty, as Sulpitius Severus and Beda can remember you of examples good store.

Lastly, (for the fabulous Metaphrastes is not worth an answer,) that authority of Clemens Alexandrinus is not to be found in all his works; and wherever it be extant, it is in controversy, whether it be Clement's or no; or if it were, it says only that St. John in some places constituted bishops: questionless he did; but where does Clement say he set them above presbyters? No man will gainsay the constitution of bishops: but the raising them to a superior and distinct order above presbyters, seeing the gospel makes them one and the same thing, a thousand such allegations as these will not give prelatical episcopacy one chapel of ease above a parish church. And thus much for this cloud I cannot say rather than petty fog of witnesses, with which episcopal men would cast a mist before us, to deduce their exalted episcopacy from apostolic times. Now, although, as all men well know, it be the wonted shift of error, and fond opinion, when they find themselves outlawed by the

Bible, and forsaken of sound reason, to betake them with all speed to their old starting-hole of tradition, and that wild and overgrown covert of antiquity, thinking to farm there at large room, and find good stabling, yet thus much their own deified antiquity betrays them to inform us, that tradition hath had very seldom or never the gift of persuasion; as that which church histories report of those east and western pascalists, formerly spoken of, will declare. Who would have thought that Polycarpus, on the one side, could have erred in what he saw St. John do? or Anicetus, bishop of Rome, on the other side, in what he or some of his friends might pretend to have seen St. Peter or St. Paul do? and yet neither of these could persuade either when to keep Easter. The like frivolous contention troubled the primitive English churches, while Colmanus and Wilfride on either side deducing their opinions, the one from the undeniable example of St. John, and the learned bishop Anatolius, and lastly the miraculous Columba, the other from St. Peter and the Nicene council, could gain no ground each of other, till king Oswy, perceiving no likelihood of ending the controversy that way, was fain to decide it himself, good king, with that small knowledge wherewith those times had furnished him. So when those pious Greek emperors began, as Cedrenus relates, to put down monks, and abolish images, the old idolaters, finding themselves blasted, and driven back by the prevailing light of the scripture, sent out their sturdy monks, called the Abramites, to allege for images the ancient fathers Dionysius, and this our objected Irenæus; nay, they were so highflown in their antiquity, that they undertook to bring the apostles, and Luke the evangelist, yea, Christ himself, from certain records that were then current, to patronize their idolatry: yet for all this the worthy emperor Theophilus, even in those dark times, chose rather to nourish himself and his people with the sincere milk of the gospel, than to drink from the mixed confluence of so many corrupt and poisonous waters, as tradition would have persuaded him to, by most ancient seeming authorities. In like manner all the reformed churches abroad, unthroning episcopacy, doubtless were not ignorant of these testimonies alleged to draw it in a line from the apostles' days: for surely the author will not think he hath brought us now any new authorities or considerations into the world, which the reformers in other places were not advised of: and yet we see, the intercession of all these apostolic fathers could not prevail with them to alter their resolved decree of reducing into order their usurping and over-provendered episcopants; and God hath blessed their work this hundred years with a prosperous and steadfast, and still happy success. And this may serve to prove the insufficiency of these present episcopal testimonies, not only in themselves but in the account of those ever that have been the followers of truth. It will next behoove us to consider the inconvenience we fall into, by using ourselves to be guided by these kind of testimonies. He that thinks it the part of a well-learned man to have read diligently the ancient stories of the church, and to be no stranger in the volumes of the fathers, shall have all judicious men consenting with him; not hereby to control and new fangle the scripture, God forbid! but to mark how corruption and apostasy crept in by degrees, and to gather up wherever we find the remaining sparks of original truth, wherewith to stop the mouths of our adversaries, and to bridle them with their own curb, who willingly pass by that which is orthodoxal in them, and studiously cull out that which is commentitious, and best for their turns, not weighing the fathers in the balance of scripture, but scripture in the balance of the fathers. If we, therefore, making first the gospel our rule and oracle, shall take the good which we light on in the fathers, and set it to oppose the evil which other men seek from them, in this way of skirmish we shall easily master all superstition and false doctrine; but if we turn this our discreet and wary usage of them into a blind devotion towards them, and whatsoever we find written by them; we both forsake our own grounds and reasons which led us at first to part from Rome, that is, to hold to the scriptures against all antiquity; we remove our cause into our adversaries' own court, and take up there those cast principles, which will soon cause us to solder up with them again; inasmuch as believing antiquity for itself in any one point, we bring an engagement upon ourselves of assenting to all that it charges upon us. For suppose we should now, neglecting that which is clear in Scripture, that a bishop and presbyter is all one both in name and office, and that what was done by Timothy and Titus, executing an extraordinary place, as fellow-laborers with the apostles, and of a universal charge in planting Christianity through divers regions, cannot be drawn into particular and daily example; suppose that neglecting this clearness of the text, we should, by the uncertain and corrupted writings of succeeding times determine that bishop and presbyter are different, because we dare not deny what Ignatius, or rather the Perkin Warbeck of Ignatius, says; then must we be constrained to take upon ourselves a thousand superstitions and falsities, which the papists will prove us down in, from as good authorities, and as ancient as these that set a bishop above a presbyter. And the plain truth is, that when any of our men, of those that are wedded to antiquity, come to dispute with a papist, and leaving the scriptures put themselves without appeal to the sentence of synods and councils, using in the cause of Sion the hired soldiery of revolted Israel; where they give the Romanists one buff, they receive two counterbuffs. Were it therefore but in this regard, every true bishop should be afraid to conquer in his cause by such authorities as these, which if we admit for the authority's sake, we open a broad passage for a multitude of doctrines, that have no ground in scripture, to break in upon us.

Lastly, I do not know, it being undeniable that there are but two ecclesiastical orders, bishops and deacons, mentioned in the gospel, how it can be less than impiety to make a demur at that, which is there so perspicuous, confronting and paralleling the sacred verity of St. Paul with the offals and sweepings of antiquity, that met as accidentally and absurdly, as Epicurus's atoms, to patch up a Leucippean Ignatius, inclining rather to make this phantasm an expounder, or indeed a depraver of St. Paul, than St. Paul an examiner, and discoverer of this impostership; nor caring how slightly they put off the verdict of holy text unsalved, that says plainly there be but two orders, so they maintain the reputation of their imaginary doctor that proclaims three. Certainly if Christ's apostle have set down but two, then according to his own words, though he himself should unsay it, and not only the angel of Smyrna, but an angel from heaven, should bear us down that there be three, St. Paul has doomed him twice: "Let him be accursed;" for Christ has pronounced that no tittle of his word shall fall to the ground: and if one jot be alterable, it is as possible that all should perish; and this shall be our righteousness, our ample warrant, and strong assurance, both now and at the last day, never to be ashamed of, against all the heaped names of angels and martyrs, councils and fathers, urged upon us, if we have given ourselves up to be taught by the pure and living precept of God's word only; which, without more additions, nay, with a forbidding of them hath, within itself the promise of eternal life, the end of all our wearisome labors, and all our sustaining hopes. But if any shall strive to set up his ephod and teraphim of antiquity against the brightness and perfection of the gospel; let him fear lest he and his Baal be turned into Bosheth. And thus much may suffice to show, that the pretended episcopacy cannot be deduced from the apostolical times.

ANIMADVERSIONS

UPON THE

REMONSTRANT'S DEFENCE AGAINST SMECTYMNUUS.

[The text is that of the first edition, 1641.]

PREFACE.

ALTHOUGH it be a certain truth, that they who undertake a religious cause need not care to be men-pleasers; yet because the satisfaction of tender and mild consciences is far different from that which is called menpleasing, to satisfy such, I shall address myself in few words to give notice beforehand of something in this book, which to some men perhaps may seem offensive, that when I have rendered a lawful reason of what is done, I may trust to have saved the labor of defending or excusing hereafter. We all know that in private and personal injuries,

yea, in public sufferings for the cause of Christ, his rule and example teaches us to be so far from a readiness to speak evil, as not to answer the reviler in his language, though never so much provoked: yet in the detecting and convincing of any notorious enemy to truth and his country's peace, especially that is conceited to have a voluble and smart fluence of tongue, and in the vain confidence of that, and out of a more tenacious cling to worldly respects, stands up for all the rest to justify a long usurpation and convicted pseudepiscopy of prelates, with all their ceremonies, liturgies, and tyrannies, which God and man are now ready to explode and hiss out of the land; I suppose, and more than suppose, it will be nothing disagreeing from Christian meekness to handle such a one in a rougher accent, and to send home his haughtiness well bespurted with his own holy water. Nor to do thus are we unautoritied either from the moral precept of Solomon, to answer him thereafter that prides him in his folly; nor from the example of Christ, and all his followers in all ages, who, in the refuting of those that resisted sound doctrine, and by subtile dissimulations corrupted the minds of men, have wrought up their zealous souls into such vehemencies, as nothing could be more killingly spoken: for who can be a greater enemy to mankind, who a more dangerous deceiver, than he who, defending a traditional corruption, uses no common arts, but with a wily stratagem of yielding to the time a greater part of his cause, seeming to forego all that man's invention hath done therein, and driven from much of his hold in scripture; yet leaving it hanging by a twined thread, not from divine command, but from apostolical prudence or assent; as if he had the surety of some rolling trench, creeps up by this means to his relinquished fortress of divine authority again, and still hovering between the confines of that which he dares not be openly, and that which he will not be sincerely, trains on the easy Christian insensibly within the close ambushment of worst errors, and with a sly shuffle of counterfeit principles, chopping and changing till he have gleaned all the good ones out of their minds, leaves them at last, after a slight resemblance of sweeping and garnishing, under the sevenfold possession of a desperate stupidity? And, therefore, they that love the souls of men, which is the dearest love, and stirs up the noblest jealousy, when they meet with such collusion, cannot be blamed though they be transported with the zeal of truth to a well-heated fervency; especially, seeing they which thus offend against the souls of their brethren, do it with delight to their great gain, ease, and advancement in this world; but they that seek to discover and oppose 10 their false trade of deceiving, do it not without a sad and unwilling anger, not without many hazards; but without all private and personal spleen, and without any thought of earthly reward, whenas this very course they take stops their hopes of ascending above a lowly and unenviable pitch in this life. And although in the serious uncasing of a grand imposture, (for, to deal plainly with you, readers, prelaty is no better,) there be 20 mixed here and there such a grim laughter, as may appear at the same time in an austere visage, it cannot be taxed of levity or insolence: for even this vein of laughing (as I could produce out of grave authors) hath ofttimes a strong and sinewy force in teaching and confuting; nor can there be a more proper object of indignation and scorn together, than a false prophet taken in the greatest, dearest, and most dangerous cheat, 30 the cheat of souls: in the disclosing whereof, if it be harmful to be angry, and withal to cast a lowering smile, when the properest object calls for both, it will be long enough ere any be able to say, why those two most rational faculties of human intellect, anger and laughter, were first seated in the breast of man. Thus much, readers, in favor of the softer spirited Christian; for other exceptioners there was no thought taken. Only if 40 it be asked, why this close and succinct manner of coping with the adversary was rather chosen, this was the reason chiefly, that the ingenuous reader, without further amusing himself in the labyrinth of controversial antiquity, may come the speediest way to see the truth vindicated, and sophistry taken short at the first false bound. Next, that the Remonstrant himself, as oft as he pleases to be frolic, and brave it with others, may find 50 no gain of money, and may learn not to insult in so bad a cause. But now he begins.

SECTION I.

REMONSTRANT. My single Remonstrance is encountered with a plural adversary.

Answer. Did not your single Remonstrance bring along with it a hot scent of your more than singular affection to spiritual pluralities, your singleness would be less suspected with all good Christians than it is.

Remonst. Their names, persons, qualities, numbers, I care not to know.

Answ. Their names are known to the all-knowing Power above; and in the meanwhile, doubtless, they reck not whether you or your nomenclator know them or not.

Remonst. But could they say my name is Legion, for we are many?

Answ. Wherefore should you begin with the devil's name, descanting upon the number of your opponents? Wherefore that conceit of Legion with a by-wipe? Was it because you would have men take notice how you esteem them, whom through all your book so bountifully you call your brethren? We had not thought that Legion could have furnished the Remonstrant with so many brethren.

Remonst. My cause, ye gods, would bid me meet them undismayed, &c.

Answ. Ere a foot further we must be content to hear a preambling boast of your valor, what a St. Dunstan you are to encounter Legions, either infernal or human.

Remonst. My cause, ye gods.

Answ. What gods? Unless your belly, or the god of this world be he? Show us any one point of your Remonstrance that does not more concern superiority, pride, ease, and the belly, than the truth and glory of 40 God, or the salvation of souls?

Remonst. My cause, ye gods, would bid me meet them undismayed, and to say with holy David, "Though a host, &c."

Answ. Do not think to persuade us of your undaunted courage, by misapplying to yourself the words of holy David; we know you fear, and are in an agony at this present, lest you should lose that superfluity of riches and honor, which your party usurp. And 50 whosoever covets, and so earnestly labors to keep such an encumbering surcharge of earthly things, cannot but have an earthquake still in his bones. You are not armed,

Remonstrant, nor any of your band, you are not dieted, nor your loins girt, for spiritual valor, and Christian warfare, the luggage is too great that follows your camp; your hearts are there, you march heavily; how shall we think you have not carnal fear, while we see you so subject to carnal desires?

Remonst. I do gladly fly to the bar.

Answ. To the bar with him then. Gladly, you say. We believe you as gladly as your whole faction wished and longed for the assembling of this parliament; as gladly as your beneficiaries the priests came up to answer the complaints and outcries of all the shires.

Remonst. The Areopagi! who were those? Truly, my masters, I had thought this had been the name of the place, not of the men.

Answ. A soar-eagle would not stoop at a fly; but sure some pedagogue stood at your elbow, and made it itch with this parlous criticism; they urged you with a decree of the sage and severe judges of Athens, and you cite them to appear for certain paragogical contempts, before a capricious pedantry of hot-livered grammarians. Mistake not the matter, courteous Remonstrant, they were not making Latin: if in dealing with an outlandish name, they thought it best not to screw the English mouth to a harsh foreign termination, so they kept the radical word, they did no more than the elegantest authors among the Greeks, Romans, and at this day the Italians, in scorn of such a servility use to do. Remember how they mangle our British names abroad: what trespass were it, if we in requital should as much neglect theirs? And our learned Chaucer did not stick to do so, writing Semyramus for Semiramis, Amphiorax for Amphiaraus, K. Sejes for K. Ceyx, the husband of Alcyone, with many other names strangely metamorphosed from the true orthography, if he had made any account of that in these kind of words.

Remonst. Lest the world should think the press had of late forgot to speak any language other than libellous, this honest paper hath broken through the throng.

Answ. Mince the matter while you will, it showed but green practice in the laws of discreet rhetoric to blurt upon the ears of a judicious parliament with such a presumptuous and overweening proem: but you do well to be the sewer of your own mess.

Remonst. That which you miscall the preface, was a too just complaint of the shameful number of libels.

Answ. How long is it that you and the prelatical troop have been in such distaste with libels? Ask your Lysimachus Nicanor what defaming invectives have lately flown abroad against the subjects of Scotland, and our poor expulsed brethren of New England, the prelates rather applauding than showing any dislike: and this hath been ever so, insomuch that Sir Francs Bacon in one of his discourses complains of the bishops' uneven hand over these pamphlets, confining those against bishops to darkness, but licensing those against puritans to be uttered openly, though with the greater mischief of leading into contempt the exercise of religion in the persons of sundry preachers, and disgracing the higher matter in the meaner person.

Remonst. A point no less essential to that proposed remonstrance.

Answ. We know where the shoe wrings you, you fret and are galled at the quick; and O what a death it is to the prelates to be thus unvisarded, thus uncased, to have the periwigs plucked off that cover your baldness, your inside nakedness thrown open to public view! The Romans had a time once every year, when their slaves might freely speak their minds; it were hard if the freeborn people of England, with whom the voice of truth for these many years, even against the proverb, hath not been heard but in corners, after all your monkish prohibitions, and expurgatorius indexes, your gags and snaffles, your proud Imprimaturs not to be obtained without the shallow surview, but not shallow hand of some mercenary, narrow-souled, and illiterate chaplain; when liberty of speaking, than which nothing is more sweet to man, was girded and straitlaced almost to a broken-winded phthisic, if now at a good time, our time of parliament, the very jubilee and resurrection of the state, if now the concealed, the aggrieved, and long-persecuted truth, could not be suffered speak; and though she burst out with some efficacy of words, could not be excused after such an injurious strangle of silence, nor avoid the censure of libelling, it were hard, it were something pinching in a kingdom of free spirits. Some princes, and great statists, have thought it a prime piece of necessary policy to thrust themselves under disguise into a popular throng, to stand the night long under eaves of houses, and low windows, that they might hear everywhere the free utterances of private breasts, and amongst them find out the precious gem of truth, as amongst the numberless pebbles of the shore, whereby they might be the abler to discover, and avoid, that deceitful and close-couched evil of flattery that ever attends them, and misleads them, and might skilfully know how to apply the several redresses to each malady of state, without trusting the disloyal information of parasites and sycophants; whereas now this permission of free writing, were there no good else in it, yet at some times thus licensed, is such an unripping, such an anatomy of the shyest and tenderest particular truths, as makes not only the whole nation in many points the wiser, but also presents and carries home to princes, and men most remote from vulgar concourse, such a full insight of every lurking evil, or restrained good among the commons, as that they shall not need hereafter, in old cloaks and false beards, to stand to the courtesy of a nightwalking cudgeller for eaves-dropping, nor to accept quietly as a perfume, the overhead emptying of some salt lotion. Who could be angry, therefore, but those that are guilty, with these free-spoken and plain-hearted men, that are the eyes of their country, and the prospective glasses of their prince? But these are the nettlers, these are the blabbing-books that tell, though not half, your fellows' feats. You love toothless satires; let me inform you, a toothless satire is as improper as a toothed sleek-stone, and as bullish.

Remonst. I beseech you, brethren, spend your logic upon your own works.

Answ. The peremptory analysis that you call it, I believe will be so hardy as once more to unpin your spruce fastidious oratory, to rumple her laces, her frizzles, and her bobbins, though she wince and fling never so peevishly.

Remonst. Those verbal exceptions are but light froth, and will sink alone.

Answ. O rare subtlety, beyond all that Cardan ever dreamed of! when, I beseech you, will light things sink? when will light froth sink alone? Here in your phrase, the same day that heavy plummets will swim alone. Trust this man, readers, if you please, whose divinity would reconcile England with Rome, and his philosophy make friends nature with the chaos, sine pondere habentia pondus.

Remonst. That scum may be worth taking off which follows.

Answ. Spare your ladle, sir, it will be as bad as the bishop's foot in the broth; the scum will be found upon your own Remonstrance.

Remonst. I shall desire all indifferent eyes to judge, whether these men do not endeavor to cast unjust envy upon me.

Answ. Agreed.

Remonst. I had said that the civil polity, as in general notion, hath sometimes varied, and that the civil came from arbitrary imposers; these gracious interpreters would needs draw my words to the present and particular government of our monarchy.

Answ. And deservedly have they done so; take up your logic else and see: civil polity, say you, hath sometimes varied, and came from arbitrary imposers; what proposition is this? Bishop Downam, in his Dialectics, will tell you it is a general axiom, though the universal particle be not expressed, and you yourself in your Defence so explain in these words as in general notion. Hence is justly inferred, he that says civil polity is arbitrary, says that the civil polity of England is arbitrary. The inference is undeniable, a thesi ad hypothesin, or from the general to the particular, an evincing argument in logic.

Remonst. Brethren, whiles ye desire to seem godly, learn to be less malicious.

Answ. Remonstrant, till you have better learnt your principles of logic, take not upon you to be a doctor to others.

Remonst. God bless all good men from such charity.

Answ. I never found that logical maxims were uncharitable before; yet, should a jury of logicians pass upon you, you would never be saved by the book.

Remonst. And our sacred monarchy from such friends.

Answ. Add, as the prelates.

Remonst. If episcopacy have yoked monarchy, it is the insolence of the persons, not the fault of the calling.

Answ. It was the fault of the persons, and of no calling: we do not count prelaty a calling.

Remonst. The testimony of a pope (whom these men honor highly).

Answ. That slanderous insertion was doubtless a pang of your incredible charity, the want whereof you lay so often to their charge; a kind token of your favor lapped up in a parenthesis, a piece of the clergy benevolence laid by to maintain the episcopal broil, whether the 1000 horse or no, time will discover: for certainly had those cavaliers come on to play their parts, such a ticket as this of highly honoring the pope, from the hand of a prelate, might have been of special use and safety to them that had cared for such a ransom.

Remonst. And what says Antichrist?

Answ. Ask your brethren the prelates, that hold intelligence with him, ask not us. But is the pope Antichrist now? Good news! take heed you be not shent for this; for it is verily thought that, had this bill been put in against him in your last convocation, he would have been cleared by most voices.

Remonst. Anything serves against episcopacy.

Answ. See the frowardness of this man! he would persuade us that the succession and divine right of bishopdom hath been unquestionable through all ages; yet, when they bring against him kings, they were irreligious; popes, they are antichrist. By what era of computation, through what fairyland, would the man deduce this perpetual beadroll of uncontradicted episcopacy? The pope may as well boast his ungainsaid authority to them that will believe that all his contradictors were either irreligious or heretical.

Remonst. If the bishops, saith the pope, be declared to be of divine right, they would be exempted from regal power; and if there might be this danger in those kingdoms, why is this enviously upbraided to those of ours? who do gladly profess, &c.

Answ. Because your dissevered principles were but like the mangled pieces of a gashed serpent, that now begun to close, and grow together popish again. Whatsoever you now gladly profess out of fear, we know what your drifts were when you thought yourselves secure.

Remonst. It is a foul slander to charge the name of episcopacy with a faction, for the fact imputed to some few.

Answ. The more foul your faction that hath brought a harmless name into obloquy; and the fact may justly be imputed to all of ye that ought to have withstood it, and did not.

Remonst. Fie, brethren! are ye the presbyters of the church of England, and dare challenge episcopacy of faction?

Answ. Yes, as oft as episcopacy dares be factious.

Remonst. Had you spoken such a word in the time of holy Cyprian, what had become of you?

Answ. They had neither been haled into your Gehenna at Lambeth, nor strapadoed with an oath ex officio by your bowmen of the arches: and as for Cyprian's time, the cause was far unlike, he indeed succeeded into an episcopacy that began then to prelatize; but his personal excellence, like an antidote, overcame the malignity of that breeding corruption, which was then a disease that lay hid for a while under show of a full and healthy constitution, as those hydropic humors not discernible at first from a fair and juicy fleshiness of body; or that unwonted ruddy color, which seems graceful to a cheek otherwise pale, and yet arises from evil causes, either of some inward obstruction or inflammation, and might deceive the first physicians till they had learned the sequel, which Cyprian's days did not bring forth; and the prelatism of episcopacy, which began then to burgeon and spread, had as yet, especially in famous men, a fair, though a false imitation of flourishing.

Remonst. Neither is the wrong less to make application of that which was most justly charged upon the practices, and combinations of libelling separatists, whom I deservedly censured, &c.

Answ. To conclude this section, our Remonstrant we see is resolved to make good that which was formerly said of his book, that it was neither humble nor a remonstrance, and this his Defence is of the same complexion. When he is constrained to mention the notorious violence of his clergy, attempted on the church of Scotland, he slightly terms it a fact imputed to some few;

but when he speaks of that which the parliament vouchsafes to name the city petition, "which I," saith he, (as if the state had made him public censor,) "deservedly censured." And how? As before for a tumultuary and underhand way of procured subscriptions, so now in his Defence more bitterly, as the practices and combinations of libelling separatists, and the miszealous advocates thereof, justly to be branded for incendiaries. Whether this be for the honor of our chief city to be noted with such an infamy for a petition, which not without some of the magistrates, and great numbers of sober and considerable men, was orderly and meekly presented, although our great clerks think that these men, because they have a trade, (as Christ himself and St. Paul had,) cannot therefore attain to some good measure of knowledge, and to a reason of their actions, as well as they that spend their youth in loitering, bezzling, and harlotting, their studies in unprofitable questions and barbarous sophistry, their middle age in ambition and idleness, their old age in avarice, dotage, and diseases. And whether this reflect not with a contumely upon the parliament itself, which thought this petition worthy, not only of receiving, but of voting to a commitment, after it had been advocated, and moved for by some honorable and learned gentlemen of the house, to be called a combination of libelling separatists, and the advocates thereof to be branded for incendiaries; whether this appeach not the judgment and approbation of the parliament, I leave to equal arbiters.

SECTION II.

Remonst. After the overflowing of your gall, you descend to liturgy and episcopacy.

Answ. The overflow being past, you cannot now in your own judgment impute any bitterness to their following discourses.

Remonst. Dr. Hall, whom you name I dare say for honor's sake.

Answ. You are a merry man, sir, and dare say much.

Remonst. And why should I not speak of martyrs, as the authors and users of this holy liturgy?

Answ. As the authors! the translators, you

might perhaps have said: for Edward the Sixth, as Hayward hath written in his story, will tell you, upon the word of a king, that the order of the service, and the use thereof in the English tongue, is no other than the old service was, and the same words in English which were in Latin, except a few things omitted, so fond, that it had been a shame to have heard them in English; these are his words: whereby we are left uncertain who the author was, but certain that part of the work was esteemed so absurd by the translators thereof, as was to be ashamed of in English. O but the martyrs were the refiners of it, for that only is left you to say. Admit they were, they could not define a scorpion into a fish, though they had drawn it, and rinsed it with never so cleanly cookery, which made them fall at variance among themselves about the use either of it, or the ceremonies belonging to it.

Remonst. Slight you them as you please, we bless God for such patrons of our good cause.

Answ. O Benedicite! Qui color ater erat, nunc est contrarius atro. Are not these they which one of your bishops in print scornfully terms the Foxian confessors? Are not these they whose acts and monuments are not only so contemptible, but so hateful to the prelates, that their story was almost come to be a prohibited book, which for these two or three editions hath crept into the world by stealth, and at times of advantage, not without the open regret and vexation of the bishops, as many honest men that had to do in setting forth the book will justify? And now at a dead lift for your liturgies you bless God for them: out upon such hypocrisy!

Remonst. As if we were bound to make good every word that falls from the mouth of every bishop.

Answ. Your faction then belike is a subtile Janus, and hath two faces: your bolder face to set forward any innovations or scandals in the church, your cautious and wary face to disavow them if they succeed not, that so the fault may not light upon the function, lest it should spoil the whole plot by giving it an irrecoverable wound. Wherefore else did you not long ago, as a good bishop should have done, disclaim and protest against them? Wherefore have you sat still, and complied and hood-winked, till the general complaints of the land have squeezed you to a wretched, cold, and hollow-hearted confession of some prelatical riots both in this and other places of your book? Nay, what if you still defend them as follows?

Remonst. If a bishop have said that our liturgy hath been so wisely and charitably framed, as that the devotion of it yieldeth no cause of offence to a very pope's ear.

Answ. O new and never heard of supererogative height of wisdom and charity in our liturgy! Is the wisdom of God or the charitable framing of God's word otherwise inoffensive to the pope's ear, than as he may turn it to the working of his mysterious iniquity? A little pulley would have stretched your wise and charitable frame it may be three inches further, that the devotion of it might have yielded no cause of offence to the very devil's ear, and that had been the same wisdom and charity surmounting to the highest degree. For antichrist we know is but the devil's vicar; and therefore please him with your liturgy, and you please his master.

Remonst. Would you think it requisite, that we should chide and quarrel when we speak to the God of peace?

Answ. Fie, no sir, but forecast our prayers so, that Satan and his instruments may take as little exception against them as may be, lest they should chide and quarrel with us.

Remonst. It is no little advantage to our cause and piety, that our liturgy is taught to speak several languages for use and example.

Answ. The language of Ashdod is one of them, and that makes so many Englishmen have such a smattering of their Philistian mother. And indeed our liturgy hath run up and down the world like an English galloping nun proffering herself; but we hear of none yet that bids money for her.

Remonst. As for that sharp censure of learned Mr. Calvin, it might well have been forborne by him in aliena republica.

Answ. Thus this untheological remonstrant would divide the individual catholic church into several republics: know, therefore, that every worthy pastor of the church of Christ hath universal right to admonish over all the world within the church; nor can that care be aliened from him by any distance or distinction of nation, so long as in Christ all nations and languages are as one household.

Remonst. Neither would you think it could become any of our greatest divines, to meddle with his charge.

Answ. It hath ill become them indeed to meddle so maliciously, as many of them have done, though that patient and Christian city hath borne hitherto all their profane scoffs with silence.

Remonst. Our liturgy passed the judgment of no less reverend heads than his own.

Answ. It bribed their judgment with worldly engagements, and so passed it.

Remonst. As for that unparalleled discourse concerning the antiquity of liturgies, I cannot help your wonder, but shall justify mine own assertion.

Answ. Your justification is but a miserable shifting off those testimonies of the ancientest fathers alleged against you, and the authority of some synodal canons, which are no warrant to us. We profess to decide our controversies only by the scriptures; but yet to repress your vain-glory, there will be voluntarily bestowed upon you a sufficient conviction of your novelties out of succeeding antiquity.

Remonst. I cannot see how you will avoid your own contradiction, for I demand, is this order of praying and administration set or no? If it be not set, how is it an order? And if it be a set order both for matter and form——

Answ. Remove that form, lest you tumble over it, while you make such haste to clap a contradiction upon others.

Remonst. If the forms were merely arbitrary, to what use was the prescription of an order?

Answ. Nothing will cure this man's understanding but some familiar and kitchen physic, which, with pardon, must for plainness sake be administered to him. Call hither your cook. The order of breakfast, dinner, and supper, answer me, is it set or no? Set. Is a man therefore bound in the morning to poached eggs and vinegar, or at noon to brawn or beef, or at night to fresh salmon, and French kickshose? May he not make his meals in order, though he be not bound to this or that viand? Doubtless the neat-fingered artist will answer, Yes, and help us out of this great controversy without more trouble. Can we not understand an order in church-assemblies of praying, reading, expounding, and administering, unless our prayers be still the same crambe of words?

Remonst. What a poor exception is this, that liturgies were composed by some particular men?

Answ. It is a greater presumption in any particular men, to arrogate to themselves that which God universally gives to all his ministers. A minister that cannot be trusted to pray in his own words without being chewed to, and fescued to a formal injunction of his rote lesson, should as little be trusted to preach, besides the vain babble of praying over the same things immediately again; for there is a large difference in the repetition of some pathetical ejaculation raised out of the sudden earnestness and vigor of the inflamed soul, (such as was that of Christ in the garden,) from the continual rehearsal of our daily orisons; which if a man shall kneel down in a morning, and say over, and presently in another part of the room kneel down again, and in other words ask but still for the same things as it were out of one inventory, I cannot see how he will escape that heathenish battology of multiplying words, which Christ himself, that has the putting up of our prayers, told us would not be acceptable in heaven. Well may men of eminent gifts set forth as many forms and helps to prayer as they please; but to impose them upon ministers lawfully called, and sufficiently tried, as all ought to be ere they be admitted, is a supercilious tyranny, impropriating the Spirit of God to themselves.

Remonst. Do we abridge this liberty by ordaining a public form?

Answ. Your bishops have set as fair to do it as they durst for that old pharisaical fear that still dogs them, the fear of the people; though you will say you are none of those, still you would seem not to have joined with the worst, and yet keep aloof off from that which is best. I would you would either mingle, or part: most true it is what Savonarola complains, that while he endeavored to reform the church, his greatest enemies were still these lukewarm ones.

Remonst. And if the Lord's Prayer be an ordinary and stinted form, why not others?

Answ. Because there be no other lords that can stint with like authority.

Remonst. If Justin Martyr said, that the instructor of the people prayed (as they falsely term it) "according to his ability."

Answ. Ὅση δύναμις αὐτῷ will be so rendered to the world's end by those that are not to learn Greek of the Remonstrant, and so Langus renders it to his face, if he could see; and this ancient father mentions no antiphonies or responsories of the people here, but the only plain acclamation of Amen.

Remonst. The instructor of the people prayed according to his ability, it is true, so do ours: and yet we have a liturgy, and so had they.

Answ. A quick come-off. The ancients used pikes and targets, and therefore guns and great ordnance, because we use both.

Remonst. Neither is this liberty of pouring out ourselves in our prayers ever the more impeached by a public form.

Answ. Yes: the time is taken up with a tedious number of liturgical tautologies and impertinencies.

Remonst. The words of the council are full and affirmative.

Answ. Set the grave councils up upon their shelves again, and string them hard, lest their various and jangling opinions put their leaves into a flutter. I shall not intend this hot season to bid you the base through the wide and dusty champaign of the councils, but shall take counsel of that which counselled them—reason: and although I know there is an obsolete reprehension now at your tongue's end, yet I shall be bold to say, that reason is the gift of God in one man as well as in a thousand: by that which we have tasted already of their cisterns, we may find that reason was the only thing, and not any divine command that moved them to enjoin set forms of liturgy. First, lest anything in general might be missaid in their public prayers through ignorance, or want of care, contrary to the faith; and next, lest the Arians, and Pelagians in particular, should infect the people by their hymns, and forms of prayer. By the leave of these ancient fathers, this was no solid prevention of spreading heresy, to debar the ministers of God the use of their noblest talent, prayer in the congregation; unless they had forbid the use of sermons, and lectures too, but such as were ready made to their hands, as our homilies: or else he that was heretically disposed, had as fair an opportunity of infecting in his discourse as in his prayer or hymn. As insufficiently, and to say truth, as imprudently, did they provide by their contrived liturgies, lest anything should be erroneously prayed through ignorance, or want of care in the ministers. For if they were careless and ignorant in their prayers, certainly they would be more careless in their preaching, and yet more careless in watching over their flock; and what prescription could reach to bound them in both these? What if reason, now illustrated by the word of God, shall be able to produce a better prevention than these councils have left us against heresy, ignorance, or want of care in the ministry, that such wisdom and diligence be used in the education of those that would be ministers, and such strict and serious examination to be undergone, ere their admission, as St. Paul to Timothy sets down at large, and then they need not carry such an unworthy suspicion over the preachers of God's word, as to tutor their unsoundness with the Abcie of a liturgy, or to diet their ignorance, and want of care, with the limited draught of a matin, and even-song drench. And this may suffice after all your laborsome scrutiny of the councils.

Remonst. Our Saviour was pleased to make use in the celebration of his last and heavenly banquet both of the fashions and words which were usual in the Jewish feasts.

Answ. What he pleased to make use of, does not justify what you please to force.

Remonst. The set forms of prayer at the Mincha.

Answ. We will not buy your rabbinical fumes; we have one that calls us to buy of him pure gold tried in the fire.

Remonst. In the Samaritan chronicle.

Answ. As little do we esteem your Samaritan trumpery, of which people Christ himself testifies, Ye worship ye know not what.

Remonst. They had their several songs.

Answ. And so have we our several psalms for several occasions, without gramercy to your liturgy.

Remonst. Those forms which we have under the names of St. James, &c., though they have some insertions which are plainly spurious, yet the substance of them cannot be taxed for other than holy and ancient.

Answ. Setting aside the odd coinage of your phrase, which no mint-master of language would allow for sterling, that a thing should be taxed for no other than holy and ancient, let it be supposed the substance of them may savor of something holy or ancient, this is but the matter; the form, and the end of the thing, may yet render it either superstitious, fruitless, or impious, and so worthy to be rejected. The garments of a strumpet are often the same, materially, that clothe a chaste matron, and yet ignominious for her to wear: the substance of the tempter's words to our Saviour were holy, but his drift nothing less.

Remonst. In what sense we hold the Roman a true church, is so cleared that this iron is too hot for their fingers.

Answ. Have a care it be not the iron to sear your own conscience.

Remonst. You need not doubt but that the alteration of the liturgy will be considered by wiser heads than your own.

Answ. We doubt it not, because we know your head looks to be one.

Remonst. Our liturgy symbolizeth not with popish mass, neither as mass nor as popish.

Answ. A pretty slipskin conveyance to sift mass into no mass, and popish into not popish; yet saving this passing fine sophistical boulting hutch, so long as she symbolizes in form, and pranks herself in the weeds of popish mass, it may be justly feared she provokes the jealousy of God, no otherwise than a wife affecting whorish attire kindles a disturbance in the eye of her discerning husband.

Remonst. If I find gold in the channel, shall I throw it away because it was ill laid?

Answ. You have forgot that gold hath been anathematized for the idolatrous use; and to eat the good creatures of God once offered to idols, is, in St. Paul's account, to have fellowship with devils, and to partake of the devil's table. And thus you throttle yourself with your own similes.

Remonst. If the devils confessed the Son of God, shall I disclaim that truth?

Answ. You sifted not so clean before, but you shuffle as foully now; as if there were the like necessity of confessing Christ, and using the liturgy: we do not disclaim that truth, because we never believed it for his testimony; but we may well reject a liturgy which had no being that we can know of, but from the corruptest times: if therefore the devil should be given never so much to prayer, I should not therefore cease from that duty, because I learned it not from him; but if he would commend to me a new Paternoster, though never so seeming holy, he should excuse me the form which was his; but the matter, which was none of his, he could not give me, nor I be said to take it from him. It is not the goodness of matter therefore which is not, nor can be owed to the liturgy, that will bear it out, if the form, which is the essence of it, be fantastic and superstitious, the end sinister, and the imposition violent.

Remonst. Had it been composed into this frame on purpose to bring papists to our churches.

Answ. To bring them to our churches? alas! what was that? unless they had been first fitted by repentance and right instruction. You will say, the word was there preached which is the means of conversion; you should have given so much honor then to the word preached, as to have left it to God's working without the interloping of a liturgy baited for them to bite at.

Remonst. The project had been charitable and gracious.

Answ. It was pharisaical, and vain-glorious, a greedy desire to win proselytes by conforming to them unlawfully; like the desire of Tamar, who, to raise up seed to her husband, sate in the common road drest like a courtezan, and he that came to her committed incest with her. This was that which made the old Christians paganize, while by their scandalous and base conforming to heathenism they did no more, when they had done their utmost, but bring some pagans to Christianize; for true Christians they neither were themselves, nor could make others such in this fashion.

Remonst. If there be found aught in liturgy that may endanger a scandal, it is under careful hands to remove it.

Answ. Such careful hands as have shown themselves sooner bent to remove and expel the men from the scandals, than the scandals from the men; and to lose a soul rather than a syllable or a surplice.

Remonst. It is idolized, they say, in England, they mean at Amsterdam.

Answ. Be it idolized therefore where it will, it is only idolatrized in England.

Remonst. Multitudes of people they say distaste it; more shame for those that have so mistaught them.

Answ. More shame for those that regard not the troubling of God's church with things by themselves confessed to be indifferent, since true charity is afflicted, and burns at the offence of every little one. As for the Christian multitude, which you affirm to be so mistaught, it is evident enough, though you would declaim never so long to the contrary, that God hath now taught them to detest your liturgy and prelacy; God who hath promised to teach all his children, and to deliver them out of your hands that hunt and worry their souls: hence is it that a man shall commonly find more savory knowledge in one layman, than in a dozen of cathedral prelates; as we read in our Saviour's time that the common people had a reverend esteem of him, and held him a great prophet, whilst the gowned rabbies, the incomparable and invincible doctors, were of opinion that he was a friend of Beelzebub.

Remonst. If the multitude distaste wholesome doctrine, shall we, to humor them, abandon it?

Answ. Yet again! as if there were the like necessity of saving doctrine, and arbitrary, if not unlawful, or inconvenient liturgy: who would have thought a man could have thwacked together so many incongruous similitudes, had it not been to defend the motley incoherence of a patched missal?

Remonst. Why did not other churches conform to us? I may boldly say ours was, and is, the more noble church.

Answ. O Laodicean, how vainly and how carnally dost thou boast of nobleness and precedency! more lordly you have made our church indeed, but not more noble.

Remonst. The second quære is so weak, that I wonder it could fall from the pens of wise men.

Answ. You are but a bad fencer, for you never make a proffer against another man's weakness, but you leave your own side always open: mark what follows.

Remonst. Brethren, can ye think that our reformers had any other intentions than all other the founders of liturgies, the least part of whose care was the help of the minister's weakness?

Answ. Do you not perceive the noose you have brought yourself into, whilst you were so brief to taunt other men with weakness? It is clean out of your mind what you cited from among the councils; that the principal scope of those liturgy-founders was to prevent either the malice or the weakness of the ministers; their malice, of infusing heresy in their forms of prayer; their weakness, lest something might be composed by them through ignorance or want of care contrary to the faith? Is it not now rather to be wondered, that such a weakness could fall from the pen of such a wise remonstrant man?

Remonst. Their main drift was the help of the people's devotion, that they knowing before the matter that should be sued for,—

Answ. A solicitous care, as if the people could be ignorant of the matter to be prayed for, seeing the heads of public prayer are either ever constant, or very frequently the same.

Remonst. And the words wherewith it should be clothed, might be the more prepared, and be so much the more intent and less distracted.

Answ. As for the words, it is more to be feared lest the same continually should make them careless or sleepy, than that variety on the same known subject should distract; variety (as both music and rhetoric teacheth us) erects and rouses an auditory, like the masterful running over many chords and divisions; whereas if men should ever be thumbing the drone of one plain song, it would be a dull opiate to the most wakeful attention.

Remonst. Tell me, is this liturgy good or evil?

Answ. It is evil. Repair the acheloian horn of your dilemma how you can against the next push.

Remonst. If it be evil, it is unlawful to be used.

Answ. We grant you; and we find you have not your salve about you.

Remonst. Were the imposition amiss, what is that to the people?

Answ. Not a little; because they bear an equal part with the priest in many places, and have their cues and versets as well as he.

Remonst. The ears and hearts of our people look for a settled liturgy.

Answ. You deceive yourself in their ears and hearts; they look for no such matter.

Remonst. The like answer serves for homilies; surely, were they enjoined to all, &c.

Answ. Let it serve for them that will be ignorant; we know that Hayward their own creature writes, that for defect of preachers, homilies were appointed to be read in churches while Edward VI. reigned.

Remonst. Away then with the book, whilst it may be supplied with a more profitable nonsense.

Answ. Away with it rather, because it will be hardly supplied with a more unprofitable nonsense, than is in some passages of it to be seen.

SECTION III.

Remonst. Thus their cavils concerning liturgy are vanished.

Answ. You wanted but hey pass, to have made your transition like a mystical man of Sturbridge. But for all your sleight of hand, our just exceptions against liturgy are not vanished, they stare you still in the face.

Remonst. Certainly had I done so, I had been no less worthy to be spit upon for my saucy uncharitableness, than they are now for their uncharitable falsehood.

Answ. We see you are in choler, therefore till you cool awhile we turn us to the ingenuous reader. See how this Remonstrant would invest himself conditionally with all the rheum of the town, that he might have sufficient to bespaul his brethren. They are accused by him of uncharitable falsehood, whereas their only crime hath been, that they have too credulously thought him, if not an over-logical, yet a well-meaning man; but now we find him either grossly deficient in his principles of logic, or else purposely bent to delude the parliament with equivocal sophistry, scattering among his periods ambiguous words, whose interpretation he will afterwards dispense according to his pleasure, laying before us universal propositions, and then thinks when he will to pinion them with a limitation: for say, Remonstrant.

Remonst. Episcopal government is cried down abroad by either weak or factious persons.

Answ. Choose you whether you will have this proposition proved to you to be ridiculous or sophistical; for one of the two it must be. Step again to bishop Downam, your patron, and let him gently catechise you in the grounds of logic; he will show you that this axiom, "episcopal government is cried down abroad by either weak or factious persons," is as much as to say, they that cry down episcopacy abroad, are either weak or factious persons. He will tell you that this axiom contains a distribution, and that all such axioms are general; and lastly, that a distribution in which any part is wanting, or abundant, is faulty, and fallacious. If therefore distributing by the adjuncts of faction and weakness, the persons that decry episcopacy, you made your distribution imperfect for the nonce, you cannot but be guilty of fraud intended toward the honorable court to whom you wrote. If you had rather vindicate your honesty, and suffer in your want of art, you cannot condemn them of uncharitable falsehood, that attributed to you more skill than you had, thinking you had been able to have made a distribution, as it ought to be, general and full; and so any man would take it, the rather as being accompanied with that large word, (abroad,) and so take again either your manifest leasing, or manifest ignorance.

Remonst. Now come these brotherly slanderers.

Answ. Go on, dissembling Joab, as still your use is, call brother and smite; call brother and smite, till it be said of you, as the like was of Herod, a man had better be your hog than your brother.

Remonst. Which never came within the verge of my thoughts.

Answ. Take a metaphor or two more as good—the precinct, or the diocese of your thoughts.

Remonst. Brethren, if you have any remainders of modesty or truth, cry God mercy.

Answ. Remonstrant, if you have no groundwork of logic, or plain dealing in you, learn both as fast as you can.

Remonst. Of the same strain is their witty descant of my confoundedness.

Answ. Speak no more of it: it was a fatal word that God put into your mouth when you began to speak for episcopacy, as boding confusion to it.

Remonst. I am still, and shall ever be thus self-confounded, as confidently to say, that he is no peaceable and right-affected son of the church of England, that doth not wish well to liturgy and episcopacy.

Answ. If this be not that saucy uncharitableness, with which, in the foregoing page, you voluntarily invested yourself, with thought to have shifted it off, let the parliament judge, who now themselves are deliberating whether liturgy and episcopacy be to be well wished to or no.

Remonst. This they say they cannot but rank amongst my notorious—speak out, masters; I would not have that word stick in your teeth or in your throat.

Answ. Take your spectacles, sir, it sticks in the paper, and was a pectoral roll we prepared for you to swallow down to your heart.

Remonst. Wanton wits must have leave to play with their own stern.

Answ. A meditation of yours doubtless observed at Lambeth from one of the archiepiscopal kittens.

Remonst. As for that form of episcopal government, surely could those look with my eyes, they would see cause to be ashamed of this their injurious misconceit.

Answ. We must call the barber for this wise sentence; one Mr. Ley the other day writ a treatise of the sabbath, and the preface puts the wisdom of Balaam's ass upon one of our bishops, bold man for his labor; but we shall have more respect to our Remonstrant, and liken him to the ass's master though the story say he was not so quicksighted as his beast. Is not this Balaam the son of Beor, the man whose eyes are open, that said to the parliament, Surely, could those look with my eyes? Boast not of your eyes, 'tis feared you have Balaam's disease, a pearl in your eye, Mammon's prestriction.

Remonst. Alas, we could tell you of China, Japan, Peru, Brazil, New England, Virginia, and a thousand others, that never had any bishops to this day.

Answ. O do not foil your cause thus, and trouble Ortelius; we can help you, and tell you where they have been ever since Constantine's time at least, in a place called Mundus alter et idem, in the spacious and rich countries of Crapulia, Pamphagonia, Yvronia, and in the dukedom of Orgilia, and Variana, and their metropolis of Ucalegonium. It was an oversight that none of your prime antiquaries could think of these venerable monuments to deduce episcopacy by; knowing that Mercurius Britannicus had them forthcoming.

———

SECTION IV.

Remonst. Hitherto they have flourished, now I hope they will strike.

Answ. His former transition was in the fair about the jugglers, now he is at the pageants among the whifflers.

Remonst. As if arguments were almanacks.

Answ. You will find some such as will prognosticate your date, and tell you that, after your long summer solstice, the Equator calls for you, to reduce you to the ancient and equal house of Libra.

Remonst. Truly, brethren, you have not well taken the height of the pole.

Answ. No marvel, there be many more that do not take well the height of your pole; but will take better the declination of your altitude.

Remonst. He that said, "I am the way," said that the old way was the good way.

Answ. He bids ask of the old paths, or for the old ways, where or which is the good way; which implies that all old ways are not good, but that the good way is to be searched with diligence among the old ways; which is a thing that we do in the oldest records we have—the gospel. And if others may chance to spend more time with you in canvassing later antiquity, I suppose it is not for that they ground themselves thereon; but that they endeavor by showing the corruptions,

uncertainties, and disagreements of those volumes, and the easiness of erring, or overslipping in such a boundless and vast search, if they may not convince those that are so strongly persuaded thereof; yet to free ingenuous minds from that overawful esteem of those more ancient than trusty fathers, whom custom and fond opinion, weak principles, and the neglect of sounder and superior knowledge hath exalted so high as to have gained them a blind reverence; whose books in bigness and number so endless and immeasurable, I cannot think that either God or nature, either divine or human wisdom, did ever mean should be a rule or reliance to us in the decision of any weighty and positive doctrine; for certainly every rule and instrument of necessary knowledge that God hath given us, ought to be so in proportion, as may be wielded and managed by the life of man, without penning him up from the duties of human society; and such a rule and instrument of knowledge perfectly is the holy Bible. But he that shall bind himself to make antiquity his rule, if he read but part, besides the difficulty of choice, his rule is deficient, and utterly unsatisfying; for there may be other writers of another mind which he hath not seen; and if he undertake all, the length of man's life cannot extend to give him a full and requisite knowledge of what was done in antiquity. Why do we therefore stand worshipping and admiring this unactive and lifeless Colossus, that, like a carved giant terribly menacing to children and weaklings, lifts up his club, but strikes not, and is subject to the muting of every sparrow? If you let him rest upon his basis, he may perhaps delight the eyes of some with his huge and mountainous bulk, and the quaint workmanship of his massy limbs; but if ye go about to take him in pieces, ye mar him; and if you think, like pigmies, to turn and wind him whole as he is, besides your vain toil and sweat, he may chance to fall upon your own heads. Go, therefore, and use all your art, apply your sledges, your levers, and your iron crows, to heave and hale your mighty Polypheme of antiquity to the delusion of novices and inexperienced Christians. We shall adhere close to the scriptures of God, which he hath left us as the just and adequate measure of truth, fitted and proportioned to the diligent study, memory, and use of every faithful man, whose every part consenting, and making up the harmonious symmetry of complete instruction, is able to set out to us a perfect man of God, or bishop thoroughly furnished to all the good works of his charge: and with this weapon, without stepping a foot further, we shall not doubt to batter and throw down your Nebuchadnezzar's image, and crumble it like the chaff of the summer threshing-floors, as well the gold of those apostolic successors that you boast of, as your Constantinian silver, together with the iron, the brass, and the clay of those muddy and strawy ages that follow.

Remonst. Let the boldest forehead of them all deny that episcopacy hath continued thus long in our island, or that any till this age contradicted it.

Answ. That bold forehead you have cleanly put upon yourself, it is you who deny that any till this age contradicted it; no forehead of ours dares do so much: you have rowed yourself fairly between the Scylla and Charybdis, either of impudence or nonsense, and now betake you to whither you please.

Remonst. As for that supply of accessory strength, which I not beg.

Answ. Your whole Remonstrance does nothing else but beg it, and your fellow-prelates do as good as whine to the parliament for their fleshpots of Egypt, making sad orations at the funeral of your dear prelacy, like that doughty centurion Afranius in Lucian; who, to imitate the noble Pericles in his epitaphian speech, stepping up after the battle to bewail the slain Severianus, falls into a pitiful condolement, to think of those costly suppers and drinking banquets, which he must now taste of no more: and by then he had done, lacked but little to lament the dear-loved memory and calamitous loss of his capon and white broth.

Remonst. But raise and evince from the light of nature, and the rules of just policy, for the continuance of those things which long use and many laws have firmly established as necessary and beneficial.

Answ. Open your eyes to the light of grace, a better guide than nature. Look upon the mean condition of Christ and his apostles, without that accessory strength you take such pains to raise from the light of nature and policy: take divine counsel, "Labor not for the things that perish:" you would be the salt of the earth; if that savor be not found in you, do not think much that the time is now come to throw you out, and tread you under-foot. Hark how St. Paul, writing to Timothy, informs a true bishop: "Bishops (saith he) must not be greedy of filthy lucre; and having food and raiment, let us be therewith content; but they (saith he, meaning, more especially in that place, bishops) that will be rich, fall into temptation and a snare, and into many foolish and hurtful lusts, which drown men in destruction and perdition: for the love of money is the root of all evil, which while some coveted after, they have erred from the faith." How can we therefore expect sound doctrine, and the solution of this our controversy, from any covetous and honor-hunting bishop, that shall plead so stiffly for these things, while St. Paul thus exhorts every bishop: "But thou, O man of God, fly these things?" As for the just policy, that long use and custom, and those many laws which you say have conferred these benefits upon you; it hath been nothing else but the superstitious devotion of princes and great men that knew no better, or the base importunity of begging friars, haunting and harassing the deathbeds of men departing this life, in a blind and wretched condition of hope to merit heaven for the building of churches, cloisters, and convents. The most of your vaunted possessions, and those proud endowments that ye as sinfully waste, what are they but the black revenues of purgatory, the price of abused and murdered souls, the damned simony of Trentals, and indulgences to mortal sin? How can ye choose but inherit the curse that goes along with such a patrimony? Alas! if there be any releasement, any mitigation, or more tolerable being for the souls of our misguided ancestors; could we imagine there might be any recovery to some degree of ease left for as many of them as are lost, there cannot be a better way than to take the misbestowed wealth which they were cheated of from these our prelates, who are the true successors of those that popped them into the other world with this conceit of meriting by their goods, which was their final undoing; and to bestow their beneficent gifts upon places and means of Christian education, and the faithful laborers in God's harvest, that may incessantly warn the posterity of Dives, lest they come where their miserable forefather was sent by the cozenage and misleading of avaricious and worldly prelates.

Remonst. It will stand long enough against the battery of their paper pellets.

Answ. That must be tried without a square cap in the council; and if pellets will not do, your own canons shall be turned against you.

Remonst. They cannot name any man in this nation, that ever contradicted episcopacy, till this present age.

Answ. What an overworn and bedridden argument is this! the last refuge ever of old falsehood, and therefore a good sign, I trust, that your castle cannot hold out long. This was the plea of judaism and idolatry against Christ and his apostles, of papacy against reformation; and perhaps to the frailty of flesh and blood in a man destitute of better enlightening may for some while be pardonable: for what has fleshly apprehension other to subsist by than succession, custom, and visibility; which only hold, if in his weakness and blindness he be loath to lose, who can blame? But in a protestant nation, that should have thrown off these tattered rudiments long ago, after the many strivings of God's Spirit, and our fourscore years' vexation of him in this our wilderness since reformation began, to urge these rotten principles, and twit us with the present age, which is to us an age of ages wherein God is manifestly come down among us, to do some remarkable good to our church or state, is, as if a man should tax the renovating and reingendering Spirit of God with innovation, and that new creature for an upstart novelty; yea, the new Jerusalem, which, without your admired link of succession, descends from heaven, could not escape some such like censure. If you require a further answer, it will not misbecome a Christian to be either more magnanimous or more devout than Scipio was; who, instead of other answer to the frivolous accusations of Petilius the tribune, "This day, Romans, (saith he,) I fought with Hannibal prosperously; let us all go and thank the gods that gave us so great a victory:" in like manner will we now say, not caring otherwise to answer this unprotestant-like objection: In this age, Britons, God hath reformed his church after many hundred years of popish corruption; in this age he hath freed us from the intolerable yoke of prelates and papal discipline; in this age he hath renewed our protestation against all those yet remaining dregs of superstition. Let us all go, every true protested Briton, throughout the three kingdoms, and render thanks to God the Father of light, and Fountain of heavenly grace, and to his Son Christ our Lord, leaving this Remonstrant and his adherents to their own designs; and let us recount even here without delay, the patience and long-suffering that God hath used towards our blindness and hardness time after time. For he being equally near to his whole creation of mankind, and of free power to turn his beneficent and fatherly regard to what region or kingdom he pleases, hath yet ever had this island under the special indulgent eye of his providence; and pitying us the first of all other nations, after he had decreed to purify and renew his church that lay wallowing in idolatrous pollutions, sent first to us a healing messenger to touch softly our sores, and carry a gentle hand over our wounds: he knocked once and twice, and came again opening our drowsy eyelids leisurely by that glimmering light which Wickliff and his followers dispersed; and still taking off by degrees the inveterate scales from our nigh perished sight, purged also our deaf ears, and prepared them to attend his second warning trumpet in our grandsire's days. How else could they have been able to have received the sudden assault of his reforming Spirit, warring against human principles, and carnal sense, the pride of flesh, that still cried up antiquity, custom, canons, councils, and laws; and cried down the truth for novelty, schism, profaneness, and sacrilege? whenas we that have lived so long in abundant light, besides the sunny reflection of all the neighboring churches, have yet our hearts rivetted with those old opinions, and so obstructed and benumbed with the same fleshly reasonings, which in our forefathers soon melted and gave way, against the morning beam of reformation. If God hath left undone this whole work, so contrary to flesh and blood, till these times, how should we have yielded to his heavenly call had we been taken, as they were, in the starkness of our ignorance; that yet, after all these spiritual preparatives and purgations, have our earthly apprehensions so clammed and furred with the old leaven? O if we freeze at noon after their early thaw, let us fear lest the sun for ever hide himself, and turn his orient steps from our ingrateful horizon, justly condemned to be eternally benighted. Which dreadful judgment, O thou the ever-begotten Light and perfect Image of the Father! intercede, may never come upon us, as we trust thou hast; for thou hast opened our difficult and sad times, and given us an unexpected breathing after our long oppressions: thou hast done justice upon those that tyrannized over us, while some men wavered and admired a vain shadow of wisdom in a tongue nothing slow to utter guile, though thou hast taught us to admire only that which is good, and to count that only praiseworthy, which is grounded upon thy divine precepts. Thou hast discovered the plots, and frustrated the hopes, of all the wicked in the land, and put to shame the persecutors of thy church: thou hast made our false prophets to be found a lie in the sight of all the people, and chased them with sudden confusion and amazement before the redoubled brightness of thy descending cloud, that now covers thy tabernacle. Who is there that cannot trace thee now in thy beamy walk through the midst of thy sanctuary, amidst those golden candlesticks, which have long suffered a dimness amongst us through the violence of those that had seized them, and were more taken with the mention of their gold than of their starry light; teaching the doctrine of Balaam, to cast a stumbling-block before thy servants, commanding them to eat things sacrificed to idols, and forcing them to fornication? Come therefore, O thou that hast the seven stars in thy right hand, appoint thy chosen priests according to their orders and courses of old, to minister before thee, and duly to dress and pour out the consecrated oil into thy holy and ever-burning lamps. Thou hast sent out the spirit of prayer upon thy servants over all the land to this effect, and stirred up their vows as the sound of many waters about thy throne. Every one can say, that now certainly thou hast visited this land, and hast not forgotten the utmost corners of the earth, in a time when men had thought that thou wast gone up from us to the furthest end of the heavens, and hadst left to do marvellously among the sons of these last ages. O perfect and accomplish thy glorious acts! for men may leave their works unfinished, but thou art a God, thy nature is perfection: shouldst thou bring us thus far onward from Egypt to destroy us in this wilderness, though we deserve, yet thy great name would suffer in the rejoicing of thine enemies, and the deluded hope of all thy servants. When thou hast settled peace in the church, and righteous judgment in the kingdom, then shall all thy saints address their voices of joy and triumph to thee, standing on the shore of that Red Sea into which our enemies had almost driven us. And he that now for haste snatches up a plain ungarnished present as a thank-offering to thee, which could not be deferred in regard of thy so many late deliverances wrought for us one upon another, may then perhaps take up a harp, and sing thee an elaborate song to generations. In that day it shall no more be said as in scorn, this or that was never held so till this present age, when men have better learnt that the times and seasons pass along under thy feet to go and come at thy bidding: and as thou didst dignify our fathers' days with many revelations above all the foregoing ages, since thou tookest the flesh; so thou canst vouchsafe to us (though unworthy) as large a portion of thy Spirit as thou pleasest: for who shall prejudice thy all-governing will? seeing the power of thy grace is not passed away with the primitive times, as fond and faithless men imagine, but thy kingdom is now at hand, and thou standing at the door. Come forth out of thy royal chambers, O Prince of all the kings of the earth! put on the visible robes of thy imperial majesty, take up that unlimited sceptre which thy Almighty Father hath bequeathed thee; for now the voice of thy bride calls thee, and all creatures sigh to be renewed.

———

SECTION V.

REMONST. Neglect not the gift which was given thee by prophecy, and by laying on the hands of presbytery.

Answ. The English translation expresses the article, (the,) and renders it the presbytery, which you do injury to omit.

Remonst. Which I wonder ye can so press, when Calvin himself takes it of the office, and not of the men.

Answ. You think then you are fairly quit of this proof, because Calvin interprets it for you, as if we could be put off with Calvin's name, unless we be convinced with Calvin's reason! The word πρεσβυτέριον is a collective noun, signifying a certain number of men in one order, as the word privy-council with us; and so Beza interprets, that knew Calvin's mind doubtless, with whom he lived. If any amongst us should say the privy-council ordained it, and thereby constrain us to understand one man's authority, should we not laugh at him? And therefore when you have used all your cramping-irons to the text, and done your utmost to cram a presbytery into the skin of one person, it will be but a piece of frugal nonsense. But if your meaning be with a violent and bold hyperbaton to transpose the text, as if the words lay thus in order, "neglect not the gift of presbytery," this were a construction like a harquebuss shot over a file of words twelve deep, without authority to bid them stoop; or to make the word gift, like the river Mole in Surrey, to run under the bottom of a long line, and so start up to govern the word presbytery, as in immediate syntaxis: a device ridiculous enough to make good that old wife's tale of a certain queen of England that sunk at Charing-cross, and rose up at Queenhithe. No marvel though the prelates be a troublesome generation, and, which way soever they turn them, put all things into a foul discomposure, when, to maintain their domineering, they seek thus to rout and disarray the wise and well-couched order of St. Paul's own words, using either a certain textual riot to chop off the hands of the word presbytery, or else a like kind of simony to clap the word gift between them. Besides, if the verse must be read according to this transposition, μὴ ἀμέλει τοῦ ἐν σοὶ χαρίσματος τοῦ πρεσβυτερίου, it would be improper to call ordination χάρισμα, whenas it is rather only χείρισμα, an outward testimony of approbation; unless they will make it a sacrament, as the papists do: but surely the prelates would have St. Paul's

words ramp one over another, as they use to climb into their livings and bishoprics.

Remonst. Neither need we give any other satisfaction to the point than from St. Paul himself, 2 Timothy i. 6: "Stir up the gift of God which is in thee by the imposition of my hands;" mine, and not others.

Answ. Ye are too quick: this last place is to be understood by the former; as the law of method, which bears chief sway in the art of teaching, requires that clearest and plainest expressions be set foremost, to the end they may enlighten any following obscurity; and wherefore we should not attribute a right method to the teachableness of scripture, there can be no reason given: to which method, if we shall now go contrary, besides the breaking of a logical rule, which the Remonstrant hitherto we see hath made little account of, we shall also put a manifest violence and impropriety upon a known word against his common signification, in binding a collective to a singular person. But if we shall, as logic (or indeed reason) instructs us, expound the latter place by the former cited, and understand "by the imposition of my hands," that is, of mine chiefly as an apostle, with the joint authority and assistance of the presbytery, there is nothing more ordinary or kindly in speech than such a phrase as expresses only the chief in any action, and understands the rest. So that the imposition of St. Paul's hands, without more expression in this place, cannot exclude the joint act of the presbytery affirmed by the former text.

Remonst. In the mean while see, brethren, how you have with Simon fished all night, and caught nothing.

Answ. If we fishing with Simon the apostle can catch nothing, see what you can catch with Simon Magus; for all his hooks and fishing implements he bequeathed among you.

SECTION XIII.

Remonst. We do again profess, that if our bishops challenge any other power than was delegated to and required of Timothy and Titus, we shall yield them usurpers.

Answ. Ye cannot compare an ordinary bishop with Timothy, who was an extraordinary man, foretold and promised to the church by many prophecies, and his name joined as collateral with St. Paul, in most of his apostolic epistles, even where he writes to the bishops of other churches, as those in Philippi. Nor can you prove out of the scripture that Timothy was bishop of any particular place; for that wherein it is said in the third verse of the first epistle, "As I besought thee to abide still at Ephesus," will be such a gloss to prove the constitution of a bishop by, as would not only be not so good as a Bourdeaux gloss, but scarce be received to varnish a vizard of Modona. All that can be gathered out of holy writ concerning Timothy is, that he was either an apostle, or an apostle's extraordinary vicegerent, not confined to the charge of any place. The like may be said of Titus, (as those words import in the 5th verse,) that he was for that cause left in Crete, that he might supply or proceed to set in order that which St. Paul in apostolic manner had begun, for which he had his particular commission, as those words sound, "As I had appointed thee." So that what he did in Crete, cannot so much be thought the exercise of an ordinary function, as the direction of an inspired mouth. No less also may be gathered from 2 Cor. viii. 23.

Remonst. You descend to the angels of the seven Asian churches; your shift is, that the angel is here taken collectively, not individually.

Answ. That the word is collective, appears plainly, Rev. ii.

First, Because the text itself expounds it so; for having spoken all the while as to the angel, the seventh verse concludes, that this was spoken to the churches. Now if the spirit conclude collectively, and kept the same tenor all the way, for we see not where he particularizes, then, certainly, he must begin collectively, else the construction can be neither grammatical nor logical.

Secondly, If the word angel be individual, then are the faults attributed to him individual: but they are such as for which God threatens to remove the candlestick out of his place, which is as much as to take away from that church the light of his truth; and we cannot think he will do so for one bishop's fault. Therefore, those faults must be understood collective, and by consequence the subject of them collective.

Thirdly, An individual cannot branch itself into sub-individuals; but this word angel doth in the tenth verse. "Fear none of those things which thou shalt suffer; behold the devil shall cast some of you into prison." And the like from other places of this and the following chapter may be observed. Therefore it is no individual word, but a collective.

Fourthly, In the 24th verse this word Angel is made capable of a pronoun plural, which could not be, unless it were a collective. As for the supposed manuscript of Tecla, and two or three other copies that have expunged the copulative, we cannot prefer them before the more received reading, and we hope you will not, against the translation of your mother the church of England, that passed the revise of your chiefest prelates: besides this, you will lay an unjust censure upon the much-praised bishop of Thyatira, and reckon him among those that had the doctrine of Jezebel, when the text says, he only suffered her. Whereas, if you will but let in a charitable conjunction, as we know your so much called for charity will not deny, then you plainly acquit the bishop, if you comprehend him in the name of angel; otherwise you leave his case very doubtful.

Remonst. "Thou sufferest thy wife Jezebel:" was she wife to the whole company, or to one bishop alone?

Answ. Not to the whole company doubtless, for that had been worse than to have been the Levite's wife in Gibeah: but here among all those that constantly read it otherwise, whom you trample upon, your good mother of England is down again in the throng, who with the rest reads it, "that woman Jezebel:" but suppose it were wife, a man might as well interpret that word figuratively, as her name Jezebel no man doubts to be a borrowed name.

Remonst. Yet what makes this for a diocesan bishop? Much every way.

Answ. No more than a special endorsement could make to puff up the foreman of a jury. If we deny you more precedence than as the senior of any society, or deny you this priority to be longer than annual, prove you the contrary from hence, if you can. That you think to do from the title of eminence, Angel: alas! your wings are too short. It is not ordination nor jurisdiction that is angelical, but the heavenly message of the gospel, which is the office of all ministers alike; in which sense John the Baptist is called an Angel, which in Greek signifies a messenger, as oft as it is meant by a man, and might be so rendered here without treason to the hierarchy; but that the whole book soars to a prophetic pitch in types and allegories. Seeing then the reason of this borrowed name is merely to signify the preaching of the gospel, and that this preaching equally appertains to the whole ministry, hence maybe drawn a fifth argument, that if the reason of this borrowed name Angel be equally collective and communicative to the whole preaching ministry of the place, then must the name be collectively and communicatively taken; but the reason, that is to say, the office, of preaching and watching over the flock, is equally collective and communicative: therefore the borrowed name itself is to be understood as equally collective and communicative to the whole preaching ministry of the place. And if you will contend still for a superiority in one person, you must ground it better than from this metaphor, which you may now deplore as the axehead that fell into the water, and say, "Alas, master! for it was borrowed;" unless you have as good a faculty to make iron swim, as you had to make light froth sink.

Remonst. What is, if this be not, ordination and jurisdiction?

Answ. Indeed, in the constitution and founding of a church, that some men inspired from God should have an extraordinary calling to appoint, to order, and dispose, must needs be. So Moses, though himself no priest, sanctified and ordained Aaron and his sons; but when all needful things be set, and regulated by the writings of the apostles, whether it be not a mere folly to keep up a superior degree in the church only for ordination and jurisdiction, it will be no hurt to debate awhile. The apostles were the builders, and, as it were, the architects of the Christian church: wherein consisted their excellence above ordinary ministers? A prelate would say, In commanding, in controlling, in appointing, in calling to them, and sending from about them, to all countries, their bishops and archbishops as their deputies, with a kind of legantine power.

No, no, vain prelates; this was but as the scaffolding of a new edifice, which for the time must board and overlook the highest battlements; but if the structure once finished, any passenger should fall in love with them, and pray that they might still stand, as being a singular grace and strengthening to the house, who would otherwise think, but that the man were presently to be laid hold on, and sent to his friends and kindred? The eminence of the apostles consisted in their powerful preaching, their unwearied laboring in the word, their unquenchable charity, which, above all earthly respects, like a working flame, had spun up to such a height of pure desire, as might be thought next to that love which dwells in God to save souls; which, while they did, they were contented to be the offscouring of the world, and to expose themselves willingly to all afflictions, perfecting thereby their hope through patience to a joy unspeakable. As for ordination, what is it, but the laying on of hands, an outward sign or symbol of admission? It creates nothing, it confers nothing; it is the inward calling of God that makes a minister, and his own painful study and diligence that manures and improves his ministerial gifts. In the primitive times, many, before ever they had received ordination from the apostles, had done the church noble service, as Apollos and others. It is but an orderly form of receiving a man already fitted, and committing to him a particular charge; the employment of preaching is as holy, and far more excellent; the care also and judgment to be used in the winning of souls, which is thought to be sufficient in every worthy minister, is an ability above that which is required in ordination: for many may be able to judge who is fit to be made a minister, that would not be found fit to be made ministers themselves; as it will not be denied that he may be the competent judge of a neat picture, or elegant poem, that cannot limn the like. Why, therefore, we should constitute a superior order in the church to perform an office which is not only every minister's function, but inferior also to that which he has a confessed right to, and why this superiority should remain thus usurped, some wise Epimenides tell us. Now for jurisdiction, this dear saint of the prelates, it will be best to consider, first, what it is: that sovereign Lord, who in the discharge of his holy anointment from God the Father, which made him supreme bishop of our souls, was so humble as to say, "Who made me a judge, or a divider over ye?" hath taught us that a churchman's jurisdiction is no more but to watch over his flock in season, and out of season, to deal by sweet and efficacious instructions, gentle admonitions, and sometimes rounder reproofs: against negligence or obstinacy, will be required a rousing volley of pastoral threatenings; against a persisting stubbornness, or the fear of a reprobate sense, a timely separation from the flock by that interdictive sentence, lest his conversation unprohibited, or unbranded, might breathe a pestilential murrain into the other sheep. In sum, his jurisdiction is to see to the thriving and prospering of that which he hath planted: what other work the prelates have found for chancellors and suffragans, delegates and officials, with all the hell-pestering rabble of sumners and apparitors, is but an invasion upon the temporal magistrate, and affected by them as men that are not ashamed of the ensign and banner of antichrist. But true evangelical jurisdiction or discipline is no more, as was said, than for a minister ·to see to the thriving and prospering of that which he hath planted. And which is the worthiest work of these two, to plant as every minister's office is equally with the bishops, or to tend that which is planted, which the blind and undiscerning prelates call jurisdiction, and would appropriate to themselves as a business of higher dignity? Have patience, therefore, a little, and hear a law case. A certain man of large possessions had a fair garden, and kept therein an honest and laborious servant, whose skill and profession was to set or sow all wholesome herbs, and delightful flowers, according to every season, and whatever else was to be done in a well-husbanded nursery of plants and fruits. Now, when the time was come that he should cut his hedges, prune his trees, look to his tender slips, and pluck up the weeds that hindered their growth, he gets him up by break of day, and makes account to do what was needful in his garden: and who would think that any other should know better than he how the day's work was to be spent? Yet, for all this, there comes another strange gardener, that never knew the soil, never handled a dibble or spade to set the least potherb that grew there, much less had endured an hour's sweat or chillness, and yet challenges as his right the binding or unbinding of every flower, the clipping of every bush, the weeding and worming of every bed, both in that and all other gardens thereabout. The honest gardener, that ever since the daypeep, till now the sun was grown somewhat rank, had wrought painfully about his banks and seed-plots, at this commanding voice turns suddenly about with some wonder; and although he could have well beteemed to have thanked him of the ease he proffered, yet loving his own handiwork, modestly refused him, telling him withal, that, for his part, if he had thought much of his own pains, he could for once have committed the work to one of his fellow-laborers, for as much as it is well known to be a matter of less skill and less labor to keep a garden handsome, than it is to plant it, or contrive it; and that he had already performed himself. No, said the stranger, this is neither for you nor your fellows to meddle with, but for me only that am for this purpose in dignity far above you; and the provision which the lord of the soil allows me in this office is, and that with good reason, tenfold your wages. The gardener smiled and shook his head; but what was determined, I cannot tell you till the end of this parliament.

Remonst. If in time you shall see wooden chalices, and wooden priests, thank yourselves.

Answ. It had been happy for this land, if your priests had been but only wooden; all England knows they have been to this island not wood, but wormwood, that have infected the third part of our waters, like that apostate star in the Revelation, that many souls have died of their bitterness; and if you mean by wooden, illiterate or contemptible, there was no want of that sort among you; and their number increasing daily, as their laziness, their tavern-hunting, their neglect of all sound literature, and their liking of doltish and monastical schoolmen daily increased. What, should I tell you how the universities, that men look should be fountains of learning and knowledge, have been poisoned and choked under your governance? And if to be wooden be to be base, where could there be found among all the reformed churches, nay, in the church of Rome itself, a baser brood of flattering and time-serving priests? according as God pronounces by Isaiah, the prophet that teacheth lies, he is the tail. As for your young scholars, that petition for bishoprics and deaneries to encourage them in their studies, and that many gentlemen else will not put their sons to learning, away with such young mercenary striplings, and their simoniacal fathers; God has no need of such, they have no plot or lot in his vineyard: they may as well sue for nunneries, that they may have some convenient stowage for their withered daughters, because they cannot give them portions answerable to the pride and vanity they have bred them in. This is the root of all our mischief, that which they allege for the encouragement of their studies should be cut away forewith as the very bait of pride and ambition, the very garbage that draws together all the fowls of prey and ravine in the land to come and gorge upon the church. How can it be but ever unhappy to the church of England, while she shall think to entice men to the pure service of God by the same means that were used to tempt our Saviour to the service of the devil, by laying before him honor and preferment? Fit professors indeed are they like to be, to teach others that godliness with content is great gain, whenas their godliness of teaching had not been but for worldly gain. The heathen philosophers thought that virtue was for its own sake inestimable, and the greatest gain of a teacher to make a soul virtuous; so Xenophon writes of Socrates, who never bargained with any for teaching them; he feared not lest those who had received so high a benefit from him would not of their own free will return him all possible thanks. Was moral virtue so lovely, and so alluring, and heathen men so enamored of her, as to teach and study her with greatest neglect and contempt of worldly profit and advancement? And is Christian piety so homely and so unpleasant, and Christian men so cloyed with her, as that none will study and teach her but for lucre and preferment? O stale grown piety! O gospel rated as cheap as thy Master, at thirty pence, and not

worth the study, unless thou canst buy those that will sell thee! O race of Capernaïtans senseless of divine doctrine, and capable only of loaves and belly-cheer! But they will grant, perhaps, piety may thrive, but learning will decay: I would fain ask these men at whose hands they seek inferior things, as wealth, honor, their dainty fare, their lofty houses? No doubt but they will soon answer, that all these things they seek at God's hands. Do they think then that all these meaner and superfluous things come from God, and the divine gift of learning from the den of Plutus, or the cave of Mammon? Certainly never any clear spirit nursed up from brighter influences, with a soul enlarged to the dimensions of spacious art and high knowledge, ever entered there but with scorn, and thought it ever foul disdain to make pelf or ambition the reward of his studies; it being the greatest honor, the greatest fruit and proficiency of learned studies to despise these things. Not liberal science, but illiberal must that needs be, that mounts in contemplation merely for money. And what would it avail us to have a hireling clergy, though never so learned? For such can have neither true wisdom nor grace; and then in vain do men trust in learning where these be wanting. If in less noble and almost mechanic arts, according to the definitions of those authors, he is not esteemed to deserve the name of a complete architect, an excellent painter, or the like, that bears not a generous mind above the peasantly regard of wages and hire; much more must we think him a most imperfect and incomplete divine, who is so far from being a contemner of filthy lucre, that his whole divinity is molded and bred up in the beggarly and brutish hopes of a fat prebendary, deanery, or bishopric; which poor and low-pitched desires, if they do but mix with those other heavenly intentions that draw a man to this study, it is justly expected that they should bring forth a baseborn issue of divinity, like that of those imperfect and putrid creatures that receive a crawling life from two most unlike procreants, the sun and mud. And in matters of religion, there is not anything more intolerable than a learned fool, or a learned hypocrite: the one is ever cooped up at his empty speculations, a sot, an idiot for any use that mankind can make of him, or else sowing the world with nice and idle questions, and with much toil and difficulty wading to his auditors up to the eyebrows in deep shallows that wet not the instep: a plain unlearned man that lives well by that light which he has, is better and wiser, and edifies others more towards a godly and happy life than he. The other is still using his sophisticated arts, and bending all his studies how to make his insatiate avarice and ambition seem pious and orthodoxal, by painting his lewd and deceitful principles with a smooth and glossy varnish in a doctrinal way, to bring about his wickedest purposes. Instead of the great harm therefore that these men fear upon the dissolving of prelates, what an ease and happiness will it be to us, when tempting rewards are taken away, that the cunningest and most dangerous mercenaries will cease of themselves to frequent the fold, whom otherwise scarce all the prayers of the faithful could have kept back from devouring the flock! But a true pastor of Christ's sending hath this especial mark, that for greatest labors and greatest merits in the church, he requires either nothing, if he could so subsist, or a very common and reasonable supply of human necessaries. We cannot therefore do better than to leave this care of ours to God: he can easily send laborers into his harvest, that shall not cry, Give, give, but be contented with a moderate and beseeming allowance; nor will he suffer true learning to be wanting, where true grace and our obedience to him abounds: for if he give us to know him aright, and to practise this our knowledge in right-established discipline, how much more will he replenish us with all abilities in tongues and arts, that may conduce to his glory and our good! He can stir up rich fathers to bestow exquisite education upon their children, and so dedicate them to the service of the gospel; he can make the sons of nobles his ministers, and princes to be his Nazarites; for certainly there is no employment more honorable, more worthy to take up a great spirit, more requiring a generous and free nurture, than to be the messenger and herald of heavenly truth from God to man, and, by the faithful work of holy doctrine, to procreate a number of faithful men, making a kind of creation like to God's, by in-

fusing his spirit and likeness into them, to their salvation, as God did into him; arising to what climate soever he turn him, like that Sun of Righteousness that sent him, with healing in his wings, and new light to break in upon the chill and gloomy hearts of his hearers, raising out of darksome barrenness a delicious and fragrant spring of saving knowledge, and good works. Can a man, thus employed, find himself discontented, or dishonored for want of admittance to have a pragmatical voice at sessions and jail deliveries? or because he may not as a judge sit out the wrangling noise of litigious courts to shrive the purses of unconfessing and unmortified sinners, and not their souls, or be discouraged though men call him not lord, whenas the due performance of his office would gain him, even from lords and princes, the voluntary title of father? Would he tug for a barony to sit and vote in parliament, knowing that no man can take from him the gift of wisdom and sound doctrine, which leaves him free, though not to be a member, yet a teacher and persuader of the parliament? And in all wise apprehensions the persuasive power in man to win others to goodness by instruction is greater, and more divine, than the compulsive power to restrain men from being evil by terror of the law; and therefore Christ left Moses to be the lawgiver, but himself came down amongst us to be a teacher, with which office his heavenly wisdom was so well pleased, as that he was angry with those that would have put a piece of temporal judicature into his hands, disclaiming that he had any commission from above for such matters.

Such a high calling therefore as this sends not for those drossy spirits that need the lure and whistle of earthly preferment, like those animals that fetch and carry for a morsel; no. She can find such as therefore study her precepts, because she teaches to despise preferment. And let not those wretched fathers think they shall impoverish the church of willing and able supply, though they keep back their sordid sperm, begotten in the lustiness of their avarice, and turn them to their malting kilns; rather let them take heed what lessons they instil into that lump of flesh which they are the cause of; lest, thinking to offer him as a present to

God, they dish him out for the devil. Let the novice learn first to renounce the world and so give himself to God, and not therefore give himself to God, that he may close the better with the world, like that false shepherd Palinode in the eclogue of May, under whom the poet lively personates our prelates, whose whole life is a recantation of their pastoral vow, and whose profession to forsake the world, as they use the matter, bogs them deeper into the world. Those our admired Spenser inveighs against, not without some presage of these reforming times:

"The time was once and may again return,
(For oft may happen that hath been beforn,)
When shepherds had none inheritance,
Ne of land nor fee in sufferance,
But what might arise of the bare sheep,
(Were it more or less,) which they did keep.
Well ywis was it with shepherds tho,
Nought having, nought feared they to forego:
For Pan himself was their inheritance,
And little them served for their maintenance:
The shepherds God so well them guided,
That of nought they were unprovided.
Butter enough, honey, milk and whey,
And their flock fleeces them to array.
But tract of time, and long prosperity
(That nurse of vice, this of insolency)
Lulled the shepherds in such security,
That not content with loyal obeysance,
Some gan to gape for greedy governance,
And match themselves with mighty potentates,
Lovers of lordships, and troublers of states.
Tho gan shepherds swains to looke aloft,
And leave to live hard, and learne to lig soft.
Tho under color of shepherds some while
There crept in wolves full of fraud and guile,
That often devoured their own sheep,
And often the shepherd that did them keep.
This was the first source of shepherds sorrow,
That now nill be quit with bale, nor borrow."

By all this we may conjecture how little we need fear that the ungilding of our prelates will prove the woodening of our priests. In the meanwhile let no man carry in his head either such narrow or such evil eyes, as not to look upon the churches of Belgia and Helvetia, and that envied city Geneva: where in the Christian world doth learning more flourish than in these places? Not among your beloved Jesuits, nor their favorers, though you take all the prelates into the number, and instance in what kind of

learning you please. And how in England all noble sciences attending upon the train of Christian doctrine may flourish more than ever; and how the able professors of every art may with ample stipends be honestly provided; and finally, how there may be better care had that their hearers may benefit by them, and all this without the prelates; the courses are so many and so easy, that I shall pass them over.

Remonst. It is God that makes the bishop, the king that gives the bishopric: what can you say to this?

Answ. What you shall not long stay for: we say it is God that makes a bishop, and the devil that makes him take a prelatical bishopric; as for the king's gift, regal bounty may be excusable in giving, where the bishop's covetousness is damnable in taking.

Remonst. Many eminent divines of the churches abroad have earnestly wished themselves in our condition.

Answ. I cannot blame them, they were not only eminent but supereminent divines, and for stomach much like to Pompey the Great, that could endure no equal.

Remonst. The Babylonian note sounds well in your ears, "Down with it, down with it, even to the ground!"

Answ. You mistake the matter, it was the Edomitish note. But change it, and if you be an angel, cry with the angel, "It is fallen, it is fallen!"

Remonst. But the God of heaven will, we hope, vindicate his own ordinance so long perpetuated to his church.

Answ. Go rather to your god of this world, and see if he can vindicate your lordships, your temporal and spiritual tyrannies, and all your pelf; for the God of heaven is already come down to vindicate his own ordinance from your so long perpetuated usurpation.

Remonst. If yet you can blush.

Answ. This is a more Edomitish conceit than the former, and must be silenced with a counter quip of the same country. So often and so unsavorily has it been repeated, that the reader may well cry, Down with it, down with it, for shame. A man would think you had eaten over-liberally of Esau's red porridge, and from thence dream continually of blushing; or perhaps, to heighten your fancy in writing, are wont to sit in your doctor's scarlet, which through your eyes infecting your pregnant imaginative with a red suffusion, begets a continual thought of blushing; that you thus persecute ingenuous men over all your book, with this one over-tired rubrical conceit still of blushing: but if you have no mercy upon them, yet spare yourself, lest you bejade the good galloway, your own opiniatre wit, and make the very conceit itself blush with spurgalling.

Remonst. The scandals of our inferior ministers I desired to have had less public.

Answ. And what your superior archbishop or bishops! O forbid to have it told in Gath! say you. O dauber! and therefore remove not impieties from Israel. Constantine might have done more justly to have punished those clergical faults which he could not conceal, than to leave them unpunished, that they might remain concealed: better had it been for him, that the heathen had heard the fame of his justice, than of his wilful connivance and partiality; and so the name of God and his truth had been less blasphemed among his enemies, and the clergy amended, which daily, by this impunity, grew worse and worse. But, O, to publish it in the streets of Ascalon; sure some colony of puritans have taken Ascalon from the Turk lately, that the Remonstrant is so afraid of Ascalon. The papists we know condole you, and neither Constantinople nor your neighbors of Morocco trouble you. What other Ascalon can you allude to?

Remonst. What a death it is to think of the sport and advantage these watchful enemies, these opposite spectators, will be sure to make of our sin and shame!

Answ. This is but to fling and struggle under the inevitable net of God, that now begins to environ you round.

Remonst. No one clergy in the whole Christian world yields so many eminent scholars, learned preachers, grave, holy, and accomplished divines, as this church of England doth at this day.

Answ. Ha, ha, ha!

Remonst. And long, and ever may it thus flourish.

Answ. O pestilent imprecation! flourish as it does at this day in the prelates.

Remonst. But O forbid to have it told in Gath!

Answ. Forbid him rather, sacred parliament, to violate the sense of scripture, and turn that which is spoken of the afflictions of the church under her pagan enemies, to a pargetted concealment of those prelatical crying sins: for from these is profaneness gone forth into all the land; they have hid their eyes from the sabbaths of the Lord; they have fed themselves, and not their flocks; with force and cruelty have they ruled over God's people: they have fed his sheep (contrary to that which St. Peter writes) not of a ready mind, but for filthy lucre; not as examples to the flock, but as being lords over God's heritage: and yet this dauber would daub still with his untempered mortar. But hearken what God says by the prophet Ezekiel, "Say unto them that daub this wall with untempered mortar, that it shall fall; there shall be an overflowing shower, and ye, O great hailstones, shall fall, and a stormy wind shall rend it, and I will say unto you, the wall is no more, neither they that daubed it."

Remonst. Whether of us shall give a better account of our charity to the God of peace, I appeal.

Answ. Your charity is much to your fellow-offenders, but nothing to the numberless souls that have been lost by their false feeding: use not therefore so sillily the name of charity, as most commonly you do, and the peaceful attribute of God to a preposterous end.

Remonst. In the next section, like illbred sons, you spit in the face of your mother, the church of England.

Answ. What should we do or say to this Remonstrant, that by his idle and shallow reasonings seems to have been conversant in no divinity but that which is colorable to uphold bishoprics? We acknowledge, and believe, the catholic reformed church; and if any man be disposed to use a trope or figure, as St. Paul once did in calling her the common mother of us all, let him do as his own rhetoric shall persuade him. If therefore we must needs have a mother, and if the catholic church only be, and must be she, let all genealogy tell us, if it can, what we must call the church of England, unless we shall make every English protestant a kind of poetical Bacchus, to have two mothers. But mark, readers, the crafty scope of these prelates; they endeavor to impress deeply into weak and superstitious fancies the awful notion of a mother, that hereby they might cheat them into a blind and implicit obedience to whatsoever they shall decree or think fit. And if we come to ask a reason of aught from our dear mother, she is invisible, under the lock and key of the prelates, her spiritual adulterers; they only are the internuncios, or the go-betweens, of this trim devised mummery: whatsoever they say, she says must be a deadly sin of disobedience not to believe. So that we, who by God's special grace have shaken off the servitude of a great male tyrant, our pretended father the pope, should now, if we be not betimes aware of these wily teachers, sink under the slavery of a female notion, the cloudy conception of a demy-island mother; and, while we think to be obedient sons, should make ourselves rather the bastards, or the centaurs of their spiritual fornications.

Remonst. Take heed of the ravens of the valley.

Answ. The ravens we are to take heed on are yourselves, that would peck out the eyes of all knowing Christians.

Remonst. Sit you merry, brethren.

Answ. So we shall when the furies of prelatical consciences will not give them leave to do so.

Queries. Whether they would not jeopard their ears rather &c.

Answ. A punishment that awaits the merits of your bold accomplices, for the lopping and stigmatizing of so many freeborn Christians.

Remonst. Whether the professed slovenliness in God's service, &c.

Answ. We have heard of Aaron and his linen amice, but those days are past; and for your priest under the gospel, that thinks himself the purer or the cleanlier in his office for his new-washed surplice, we esteem him for sanctity little better than Apollonius Thyanæus in his white frock, or the priest of Isis in his lawn sleeves; and they may all for holiness lie together in the suds.

Remonst. Whether it were not most lawful and just to punish your presumption and disobedience.

Answ. The punishing of that which you call our presumption and disobedience lies not now within the execution of your fangs; the merciful God above, and our just parliament, will deliver us from your Ephesian beasts, your cruel Nimrods, with whom we shall be ever fearless to encounter.

Remonst. God give you wisdom to see the truth, and grace to follow it.

Answ. I wish the like to all those that resist not the Holy Ghost; for of such God commands Jeremiah, saying, "Pray not thou for them, neither lift up cry or prayer for them, neither make intercession to me, for I will not hear thee;" and of such St. John saith, "He that bids them God speed, is partaker of their evil deeds."

———

TO THE POSTCRIPT.

Remonst. A goodly pasquin borrowed for a great part out of Sion's plea, or the breviate consisting of a rhapsody of histories.

Answ. How wittily you tell us what your wonted course is upon the like occasion: the collection was taken, be it known to you, from as authentic authors in this kind, as any in a bishop's library; and the collector of it says moreover, that if the like occasion come again, he shall less need the help of breviates, or historical rhapsodies, than your reverence to eke out your sermonings shall need repair to postils or poliantheas.

Remonst. They were bishops, you say; true, but they were popish bishops.

Answ. Since you would bind us to your jurisdiction by their canon law, since you would enforce upon us the old riffraff of Sarum, and other monastical relics; since you live upon their unjust purchases, allege their authorities, boast of their succession, walk in their steps, their pride, their titles, their covetousness, their persecuting of God's people; since you disclaim their actions, and build their sepulchres, it is most just that all their faults should be imputed to you, and their iniquities visited upon you.

Remonst. Could you see no colleges, no hospitals built?

Answ. At that primero of piety, the pope and cardinals are the better gamesters, and will cog a die into heaven before you.

Remonst. No churches re-edified?

Answ. Yes, more churches than souls.

Remonst. No learned volumes writ?

Answ. So did the miscreant bishop of Spalato write learned volumes against the pope, and run to Rome when he had done: ye write them in your closets, and unwrite them in your courts; hot volumnists and cold bishops; a swashbuckler against the pope, and a dormouse against the devil, while the whole diocese be sown with tares, and none to resist the enemy, but such as let him in at the postern; a rare superintendent at Rome, and a cipher at home. Hypocrites! the gospel faithfully preached to the poor, the desolate parishes visited and duly fed, loiterers thrown out, wolves driven from the fold, had been a better confutation of the pope and mass, than whole hecatontomes of controversies; and all this careering with spear in rest, and thundering upon the steel cap of Baronius or Bellarmine.

Remonst. No seduced persons reclaimed?

Answ. More reclaimed persons seduced.

Remonst. No hospitality kept?

Answ. Bacchanalian good store in every bishop's family, and good gleeking.

Remonst. No great offenders punished?

Answ. The trophies of your high commission are renowned.

Remonst. No good offices done for the public?

Answ. Yes: the good office of reducing monarchy to tyranny, of breaking pacifications, and calumniating the people to the king.

Remonst. No care of the peace of the church?

Answ. No, nor of the land; witness the two armies in the north, that now lie plundered and overrun by a liturgy.

Remonst. No diligence in preaching?

Answ. Scarce any preaching at all.

Remonst. No holiness in living?

Answ. No.

Remonst. Truly, brethren, I can say no more, but that the fault is in your eyes.

Answ. If you can say no more than this, you were a proper Remonstrant to stand up for the whole tribe!

Remonst. Wipe them and look better.

Answ. Wipe your fat corpulencies out of our light.

Remonst. Yea, I beseech God to open them rather that they may see good.

Answ. If you mean good prelates, let be your prayer. Ask not impossibilities.

Remonst. As for that proverb, "the bishop's foot hath been in it," it were more fit for a Scurra in Trivio, or some ribald upon an alebench.

Answ. The fitter for them then of whom it was meant.

Remonst. I doubt not but they will say, the bishop's foot hath been in your book, for I am sure it is quite spoiled by this just confutation; for your proverb, Sapit ollam.

Answ. Spoiled, quoth ye? Indeed it is so spoiled, as a good song is spoiled by a lewd singer; or, as the saying is, "God sends meat, but the cooks work their wills:" in that sense we grant your bishop's foot may have spoiled it, and made it "Sapere ollam," if not "Sapere aulam;" which is the same in old Latin, and perhaps in plain English. For certain your confutation hath achieved nothing against it, and left nothing upon it but a foul taste of your skillet foot, and a more perfect and distinguishable odor of your socks, than of your nightcap. And how the bishop should confute a book with his foot, unless his brains were dropped into his great toe, I cannot meet with any man that can resolve me; only they tell me that certainly such a confutation must needs be gouty. So much for the bishop's foot.

Remonst. You tell us of Bonner's broth; it is the fashion in some countries to send in their keal in the last service, and this it seems is the manner among our Smectymnuans.

Answ. Your latter service at the high altar you mean. But soft, sir, the feast was but begun, the broth was your own, you have been inviting the land to it this fourscore years; and so long we have been your slaves to serve it up for you, much against our wills: we know you have the beef to it, ready in your kitchens, we are sure it was almost sod before this parliament begun; what direction you have given since to your cooks, to set it by in the pantry till some fitter time, we know not, and therefore your dear jest is lost; this broth was but your first service: alas, sir! why do you delude your guests? Why do not those goodly flanks and briskets march up in your stately chargers? Doubtless, if need be, the pope that owes you for mollifying the matter so well with him, and making him a true church, will furnish you with all the fat oxen of Italy.

Remonst. Learned and worthy Dr. Moulin shall tell them.

Answ. Moulin says, in his book of the calling of pastors, that because bishops were the reformers of the English church, therefore they were left remaining: this argument is but of small force to keep you in your cathedrals. For first it may be denied that bishops were our first reformers, for Wickliff was before them, and his egregious labors are not to be neglected: besides, our bishops were in this work but the disciples of priests, and began the reformation before they were bishops. But what though Luther and other monks were the reformers of other places? Does it follow, therefore, that monks ought to continue? No, though Luther had taught so. And lastly, Moulin's argument directly makes against you; for if there be nothing in it but this, bishops were left remaining because they were the reformers of the church, by as good a consequence, therefore, they are now to be removed, because they have been the most certain deformers and ruiners of the church. Thus you see how little it avails you to take sanctuary among those churches which in the general scope of your actions formerly you have disregarded and despised; however, your fair words would now smooth it over otherwise.

Remonst. Our bishops, some whereof being crowned with martyrdom, subscribed the gospel with their blood.

Answ. You boast much of martyrs to uphold your episcopacy; but if you would call to mind what Eusebius in his fifth book recites from Apollinarius of Hierapolis, you should then hear it esteemed no other than an old heretical argument, to prove a position true, because some that held it were martyrs; this was that which gave boldness to the Marcionists and Cataphryges to avouch their impious heresies for pious doctrine, because they could reckon many martyrs of their sect; and when they were confuted in other points, this was ever their last and stoutest plea.

Remonst. In the mean time I beseech the God of heaven to humble you.

Answ. We shall beseech the same God to give you a more profitable and pertinent humiliation than yet you know, and a less mistaken charitableness, with that peace which you have hitherto so perversely misaffected.

THE

REASON OF CHURCH GOVERNMENT URGED AGAINST PRELATY.

IN TWO BOOKS.

[The text is that of the first edition, 1641–42.]

THE FIRST BOOK.

THE PREFACE.

In the publishing of human laws, which for the most part aim not beyond the good of civil society, to set them barely forth to the people without reason or preface, like a physical prescript, or only with threatenings, as it were a lordly command, in the judgment of Plato was thought to be done neither generously nor wisely. His advice was, seeing that persuasion certainly is a more winning and more manlike way to keep men in obedience than fear, that to such laws as were of principal moment, there should be used as an induction some well-tempered discourse, showing how good, how gainful, how happy it must needs be to live according to honesty and justice; which being uttered with those native colors and graces of speech, as true eloquence, the daughter of virtue, can best bestow upon her mother's praises, would so incite, and in a manner charm, the multitude into the love of that which is really good, as to embrace it ever after, not of custom and awe, which most men do, but of choice and purpose, with true and constant delight. But this practice we may learn from a better and more ancient authority than any heathen writer hath to give us; and indeed being a point of so high wisdom and worth, how could it be but we should find it in that book, within whose sacred context all wisdom is unfolded? Moses, therefore, the only lawgiver that we can believe to have been visibly taught of God, knowing how vain it was to write laws to men whose hearts were not first seasoned with the knowledge of God and of his works, began from the book of Genesis, as a prologue to his laws; which Josephus right well hath noted: that the nation of the Jews, reading therein the universal goodness of God to all creatures in the creation, and his peculiar favor to them in his election of Abraham, their ancestor, from whom they could derive so many blessings upon themselves, might be moved to obey sincerely, by knowing so good a reason of their obedience. If then, in the administration of civil justice, and under the obscurity of ceremonial rites, such care was had by the wisest of the heathen, and by Moses among the Jews, to instruct them at least in a general reason of that government to which their subjection was required; how much more ought the members of the church, under the gospel, seek to inform their understanding in the reason of that government which the church claims to have over them! Especially for that the church hath in her immediate care those inner parts and affections of the mind, where the seat of reason is, having power to examine our spiritual knowledge, and to demand from us, in God's behalf, a service entirely reasonable. But because about the manner and order of this government, whether it ought to be presbyterial or prelatical, such endless question, or rather uproar, is arisen in this land, as may be justly termed what the fever is to the physicians, the eternal reproach of our divines, whilst other profound clerks of late, greatly, as they conceive, to the advancement of prelaty, are so earnestly meting out the Lydian proconsular Asia, to make good the prime metropolis of Ephesus, as if some of our prelates in all haste meant to change their soil, and become neighbors to the English bishop of Chalcedon; and whilst good Breerwood as busily bestirs himself in our vulgar tongue, to divide precisely the three patriarchates of Rome, Alexandria, and Antioch; and whether to any of these England doth belong: I shall in the meanwhile not cease to hope through the mercy and grace of Christ, the head and husband of his church, that England shortly is to belong, neither to see patriarchal nor see prelatical, but to the faithful feeding and disciplining of that ministerial order, which the blessed apostles constituted throughout the churches: and this, I shall essay to prove, can be no other than that of presbyters and deacons. And if any man incline to think I undertake a task too difficult for my years, I trust through the supreme enlightening assistance far otherwise; for my years, be they few or many, what imports it? So they bring reason, let that be looked on: and for the task, from hence that the question in hand is so needful to be known at this time, chiefly by every meaner capacity, and contains in it the explication of many admirable and heavenly privileges reached out to us by the gospel, I conclude the task must be easy: God having to this end ordained his gospel to be the revelation of his power and wisdom in Christ Jesus. And this is one depth of his wisdom, that he could so plainly reveal so great a measure of it to the gross distorted apprehension of decayed mankind. Let others, therefore, dread and shun the scriptures for their darkness; I shall wish I may deserve to be reckoned among those who admire and dwell upon them for their clearness. And this seems to be the cause why in those places of holy writ, wherein is treated of church government, the reasons thereof are not formally and professedly set down, because to him that heeds attentively the drift and scope of Christian profession, they easily imply themselves; which thing further to explain, having now prefaced enough, I shall no longer defer.

_____

CHAPTER I.

That Church Government is prescribed in the Gospel; and that to say otherwise is unsound.

THE first and greatest reason of church government we may securely, with the assent of many on the adverse part, affirm to be, because we find it so ordained and set out to us by the appointment of God in the scriptures; but whether this be presbyterial, or prelatical, it cannot be brought to the scanning, until I have said what is meet to some who do not think it for the ease of their inconsequent opinions, to grant that the church discipline is platformed in the Bible, but that it is left to the discretion of men. To this conceit of theirs I answer, that it is both unsound and untrue; for there is not that thing in the world of more grave and urgent importance throughout the whole life of man, than is discipline. What need I instance! He that hath read with judgment of nations and commonwealths, of cities and camps, of peace and war, sea and land, will readily agree that the flourishing and decaying of all civil societies, all the moments and turnings of human occasions are moved to and fro as upon the axle of discipline. So that whatsoever power or sway in mortal things weaker men have attributed to fortune, I durst with more confidence (the honor of Divine Providence ever saved) ascribe either to the vigor or the slackness of discipline. Nor is there any sociable perfection in this life, civil or sacred, that can be above discipline; but she is that which with her musical chords preserves and holds all the parts thereof together. Hence in those perfect armies of Cyrus in Xenophon, and Scipio in the Roman stories, the excellence of military skill was esteemed, not by the not needing, but by the readiest submitting to the edicts of their commander. And certainly discipline is not only the removal of disorder; but if any visible shape can be given to divine things, the very visible shape and image of virtue, whereby she is not only seen in the regular gestures and motions of her heavenly paces as she walks, but also makes the harmony of her voice audible to mortal ears. Yea, the angels themselves, in whom no disorder is feared, as the apostle that saw them in his rapture describes, are distinguished and quaternioned into their celestial princedoms and satrapies, according as God himself has writ his imperial decrees through the great provinces of heaven. The state also of the blessed in paradise, though never so perfect, is not therefore left without discipline, whose golden surveying reed marks out and measures every quarter and circuit of New Jerusalem. Yet is it not to be conceived, that those eternal effluences of sanctity and love in the glorified saints should by this means be confined and cloyed with repetition of that which is prescribed, but that our happiness may orb itself into a thousand vagancies of glory and delight, and with a kind of

eccentrical equation be, as it were, an invariable planet of joy and felicity; how much less can we believe that God would leave his frail and feeble, though not less beloved church here below, to the perpetual stumble of conjecture and disturbance in this our dark voyage, without the card and compass of discipline? Which is so hard to be of man's making, that we may see even in the guidance of a civil state to worldly happiness, it is not for every learned, or every wise man, though many of them consult in common, to invent or frame a discipline: but if it be at all the work of man, it must be of such a one as is a true knower of himself, and himself in whom contemplation and practice, wit, prudence, fortitude, and eloquence, must be rarely met, both to comprehend the hidden causes of things, and span in his thoughts all the various effects that passion or complexion can work in man's nature; and hereto must his hand be at defiance with gain, and his heart in all virtues heroic; so far is it from the ken of these wretched projectors of ours, that bescrawl their pamphlets every day with new forms of government for our church. And therefore all the ancient lawgivers were either truly inspired, as Moses, or were such men as with authority enough might give it out to be so, as Minos, Lycurgus, Numa, because they wisely forethought that men would never quietly submit to such a discipline as had not more of God's hand in it than man's. To come within the narrowness of household government, observation will show us many deep counsellors of state and judges to demean themselves incorruptly in the settled course of affairs, and many worthy preachers upright in their lives, powerful in their audience: but look upon either of these men where they are left to their own disciplining at home, and you shall soon perceive, for all their single knowledge and uprightness, how deficient they are in the regulating of their own family; not only in what may concern the virtuous and decent composure of their minds in their several places, but, that which is of a lower and easier performance, the right possessing of the outward vessel, their body, in health or sickness, rest or labor, diet or abstinence, whereby to render it more pliant to the soul, and useful to the commonwealth: which if men were but as good to discipline themselves, as some are to tutor their horses and hawks, it could not be so gross in most households. If then it appear so hard, and so little known how to govern a house well, which is thought of so easy discharge, and for every man's undertaking, what skill of man, what wisdom, what parts can be sufficient to give laws and ordinances to the elect household of God? If we could imagine that he had left it at random without his provident and gracious ordering, who is he so arrogant, so presumptuous, that durst dispose and guide the living ark of the Holy Ghost, though he should find it wandering in the field of Bethshemesh, without the conscious warrant of some high calling? But no profane insolence can parallel that which our prelates dare avouch, to drive outrageously, and shatter the holy ark of the church, not borne upon their shoulders with pains and labor in the word, but drawn with rude oxen, their officials, and their own brute inventions. Let them make shows of reforming while they will, so long as the church is mounted upon the prelatical cart, and not, as it ought, between the hands of the ministers, it will but shake and totter; and he that sets to his hand, though with a good intent to hinder the shogging of it, in this unlawful waggonry wherein it rides, let him beware it be not fatal to him, as it was to Uzza. Certainly if God be the father of his family the church, wherein could he express that name more, than in training it up under his own allwise and dear economy, not turning it loose to the havoc of strangers and wolves, that would ask no better plea than this, to do in the church of Christ whatever humor, faction, policy, or licentious will would prompt them to? Again, if Christ be the church's husband, expecting her to be presented before him a pure unspotted virgin; in what could he show his tender love to her more than in prescribing his own ways, which he best knew would be to the improvement of her health and beauty, with much greater care doubtless than the Persian king could appoint for his queen Esther those maiden dietings and set prescriptions of baths and odors, which may render her at last the more amiable to his eye? For of any age or sex, most unfitly may a virgin be left to an uncertain and arbitrary education. Yea, though she be well instructed, yet is she still under a more strait tuition, especially if betrothed. In like manner the church bearing the same resemblance, it were not reason to think she should be left destitute of that care which is as necessary and proper to her as instruction. For public preaching indeed is the gift of the Spirit, working as best seems to his secret will; but discipline is the practic work of preaching directed and applied, as is most requisite, to particular duty; without which it were all one to the benefit of souls, as it would be to the cure of bodies, if all the physicians in London should get into the several pulpits of the city, and assembling all the diseased in every parish, should begin a learned lecture of pleurisies, palsies, lethargies, to which perhaps none there present were inclined; and so, without so much as feeling one pulse, or giving the least order to any skilful apothecary, should dismiss them from time to time, some groaning, some languishing, some expiring, with this only charge, to look well to themselves, and do as they hear. Of what excellence and necessity then church-discipline is, how beyond the faculty of man to frame, and how dangerous to be left to man's invention, who would be every foot turning it to sinister ends; how properly also it is the work of God as father, and of Christ as husband, of the church, we have by thus much heard.

CHAPTER II.

That Church Government is set down in Holy Scripture; and that to say otherwise is untrue.

As therefore it is unsound to say, that God hath not appointed any set government in his church, so is it untrue. Of the time of the law there can be no doubt; for to let pass the first institution of priests and Levites, which is too clear to be insisted upon, when the temple came to be built, which in plain judgment could breed no essential change, either in religion, or in the priestly government; yet God, to show how little he could endure that men should be tampering and contriving in his worship, though in things of less regard, gave to David for

Solomon not only a pattern and model of the temple, but a direction for the courses of the priests and Levites, and for all the work of their service. At the return from the captivity things were only restored after the ordinance of Moses and David; or if the least alteration be to be found, they had with them inspired men, prophets; and it were not sober to say they did aught of moment without divine intimation. In the prophecy of Ezekiel, from the 40th chapter onward, after the destruction of the temple, God, by his prophet, seeking to wean the hearts of the Jews from their old law, to expect a new and more perfect reformation under Christ, sets out before their eyes the stately fabric and constitution of his church, with all the ecclesiastical functions appertaining: indeed the description is, as sorted best to the apprehension of those times, typical and shadowy, but in such manner as never yet came to pass, nor never must literally, unless we mean to annihilate the gospel. But so exquisite and lively the description is in portraying the new state of the church, and especially in those points where government seems to be most active, that both Jews and Gentiles might have good cause to be assured, that God, whenever he meant to reform his church, never intended to leave the government thereof, delineated here in such curious architecture, to be patched afterwards, and varnished over with the devices and embellishings of man's imagination. Did God take such delight in measuring out the pillars, arches, and doors of a material temple? Was he so punctual and circumspect in lavers, altars, and sacrifices soon after to be abrogated, lest any of these should have been made contrary to his mind? Is not a far more perfect work, more agreeable to his perfection in the most perfect state of the church militant, the new alliance of God to man? Should not he rather now by his own prescribed discipline have cast his line and level upon the soul of man, which is his rational temple, and, by the divine square and compass thereof, form and regenerate in us the lovely shapes of virtues and graces, the sooner to edify and accomplish that immortal stature of Christ's body, which is his church, in all her glorious lineaments and proportions? And that this indeed God hath done for us in the gospel we shall see with open eyes, not under a veil. We may pass over the history of the Acts and other places, turning only to those epistles of St. Paul to Timothy and Titus; where the spiritual eye may discern more goodly and gracefully erected, than all the magnificence of temple or tabernacle, such a heavenly structure of evangelical discipline, so diffusive of knowledge and charity to the prosperous increase and growth of the church, that it cannot be wondered if that elegant and artful symmetry of the promised new temple in Ezekiel, and all those sumptuous things under the law, were made to signify the inward beauty and splendor of the Christian church thus governed. And whether this be commanded, let it now be judged. St. Paul, after his preface to the first of Timothy, which he concludes in the 17th verse with Amen, enters upon the subject of his epistle, which is to establish the church government, with a command: "This charge I commit to thee, son Timothy; according to the prophecies which went before on thee, that thou by them mightest war a good warfare." Which is plain enough thus expounded: This charge I commit to thee, wherein I now go about to instruct thee how thou shalt set up church discipline, that thou mightest war a good warfare, bearing thyself constantly and faithfully in the ministry, which, in the first to the Corinthians, is also called a warfare; and so after a kind of parenthesis concerning Hymenæus, he returns to his command, though under the mild word of exhorting, chap. ii. ver. 1, "I exhort therefore;" as if he had interrupted his former command by the occasional mention of Hymenæus. More beneath in the 14th verse of the third chapter, when he hath delivered the duties of bishops or presbyters, and deacons, not once naming any other order in the church, he thus adds; "These things write I unto thee, hoping to come unto thee shortly; (such necessity it seems there was;) but if I tarry long, that thou mayest know how thou oughtest to behave thyself in the house of God." From this place it may be justly asked, whether Timothy by this here written, might know what was to be known concerning the orders of church governors or no? If he might, then, in such a clear text as this, may we know too without further jangle; if he might not, then did St. Paul write insufficiently, and moreover said not true, for he saith here he might know; and I persuade myself he did know ere this was written, but that the apostle had more regard to the instruction of us, than to the informing of him. In the fifth chapter, after some other church-precepts concerning discipline, mark what a dreadful command follows, ver. 21: "I 10 charge thee before God and the Lord Jesus Christ, and the elect angels, that thou observe these things." And as if all were not yet sure enough, he closes up the epistle with an adjuring charge thus: "I give thee charge in the sight of God, who quickeneth all things, and before Christ Jesus, that thou keep this commandment:" that is, the whole commandment concerning discipline, being the main purpose of the epistle: although 20 Hooker would fain have this denouncement referred to the particular precept going before, because the word commandment is in the singular number, not remembering that even in the first chapter of this epistle, the word commandment is used in a plural sense, ver. 5: "Now the end of the commandment is charity;" and what more frequent than in like manner to say the law of Moses? So that either to restrain the significance too 30 much, or too much to enlarge it, would make the adjuration either not so weighty or not so pertinent. And thus we find here that the rules of church discipline are not only commanded, but hedged about with such a terrible impalement of commands, as he that will break through wilfully to violate the least of them, must hazard the wounding of his conscience even to death. Yet all this notwithstanding, we shall find them broken 40 well nigh all by the fair pretenders even of the next ages. No less to the contempt of him whom they feign to be the archfounder of prelaty, St. Peter, who, by what he writes in the fifth chap. of his first epistle, should seem to be far another man than tradition reports him: there he commits to the presbyters only full authority both of feeding the flock and episcopating; and commands that obedience be given to them as to the 50 mighty hand of God, which is his mighty ordinance. Yet all this was as nothing to repel the venturous boldness of innovation that ensued, changing the decrees of God that are immutable, as if they had been breathed by man. Nevertheless when Christ by those visions of St. John, foreshows the reformation of his church, he bids him take his reed, and mete it out again after the first pattern, for he prescribes him no other. "Arise," said the angel, "and measure the temple of God, and the altar, and them that worship therein." What is there in the world can measure men but discipline? Our word ruling imports no less. Doctrine indeed is the measure, or at least the reason of the measure, it is true; but unless the measure be applied to that which it is to measure, how can it actually do its proper work? Whether therefore discipline be all one with doctrine, or the particular application thereof to this or that person, we all agree that doctrine must be such only as is commanded; or whether it be something really differing from doctrine, yet was it only of God's appointment, as being the most adequate measure of the church and her children, which is here the office of a great evangelist, and the reed given him from heaven. But that part of the temple which is not thus measured, so far is it from being in God's tuition or delight, that in the following verse he rejects it; however in show and visibility it may seem a part of his church, yet inasmuch as it lies thus unmeasured, he leaves it to be trampled by the Gentiles, that is to be polluted with idolatrous and gentilish rites and ceremonies. And that the principal reformation here foretold is already come to pass, as well in discipline as in doctrine, the state of our neighbor churches afford us to behold. Thus, through all the periods and changes of the church, it hath been proved, that God hath still reserved to himself the right of enacting church government.

CHAPTER III.

That it is dangerous and unworthy the Gospel, to hold that Church Government is to be patterned by the Law, as Bishop Andrews and the Primate of Armagh maintain.

WE may return now from this interposing difficulty thus removed, to affirm, that since church government is so strictly commanded in God's word, the first and greatest reason why we should submit thereto is, because God hath so commanded. But whether of these two, prelaty or presbytery, can prove itself to be supported by this first and greatest reason, must be the next dispute; wherein this position is to be first laid down, as granted, that I may not follow a chase rather than an argument, that one of these two, and none other, is of God's ordaining; and if it be, that ordinance must be evident in the gospel. For the imperfect and obscure institution of the law, which the apostles themselves doubt not ofttimes to vilify, cannot give rules to the complete and glorious ministration of the gospel, which looks on the law as on a child, not as on a tutor. And that the prelates have no sure foundation in the gospel, their own guiltiness doth manifest; they would not else run questing up as high as Adam to fetch their original, as it is said one of them lately did in public. To which assertion, had I heard it, because I see they are so insatiable of antiquity, I should have gladly assented, and confessed them yet more ancient: for Lucifer, before Adam, was the first prelate angel; and both he, as is commonly thought, and our forefather Adam, as we all know, for aspiring above their orders, were miserably degraded. But others, better advised, are content to receive their beginning from Aaron and his sons, among whom bishop Andrews of late years, and in these times the primate of Armagh, for their learning are reputed the best able to say what may be said in this opinion. The primate, in his discourse about the original of episcopacy newly revised, begins thus: "The ground of episcopacy is fetched partly from the pattern prescribed by God in the Old Testament, and partly from the imitation thereof brought in by the apostles." Herein I must entreat to be excused of the desire I have to be satisfied, how for example the ground of episcopacy is fetched partly from the example of the Old Testament, by whom next, and by whose authority. Secondly, how the church government under the gospel can be rightly called an imitation of that in the Old Testament; for that the gospel is the end and fulfilling of the law, our liberty also from the bondage of the law, I plainly read. How then

the ripe age of the gospel should be put to school again, and learn to govern herself from the infancy of the law, the stronger to imitate the weaker, the freeman to follow the captive, the learned to be lessoned by the rude, will be a hard undertaking to evince from any of those principles which either art or inspiration hath written. If anything done by the apostles may be drawn howsoever to a likeness of something Mosaical, if it cannot be proved that it was done of purpose in imitation, as having the right thereof grounded in nature, and not in ceremony or type, it will little avail the matter. The whole Judaic law is either political (and to take pattern by that, no Christian nation ever thought itself obliged in conscience) or moral, which contains in it the observation of whatsoever is substantially and perpetually true and good, either in religion or course of life. That which is thus moral, besides what we fetch from those unwritten laws and ideas which nature hath engraven in us, the gospel, as stands with her dignity most, lectures to us from her own authentic handwriting and command, not copies out from the borrowed manuscript of a subservient scroll, by way of imitating: as well might she be said in her sacrament of water, to imitate the baptism of John. What though she retain excommunication used in the synagogue, retain the morality of the Sabbath? She does not therefore imitate the law, her underling, but perfect her. All that was morally delivered from the law to the gospel, in the office of the priests and Levites, was, that there should be a ministry set apart to teach and discipline the church; both which duties the apostles thought good to commit to the presbyters. And if any distinction of honor were to be made among them, they directed it should be to those not that only rule well, but especially to those that labor in the word and doctrine. By which we are taught that laborious teaching is the most honorable prelaty that one minister can have above another in the gospel; if, therefore, the superiority of bishopship be grounded on the priesthood as a part of the moral law, it cannot be said to be an imitation; for it were ridiculous that morality should imitate morality, which ever was the same thing. This very word of patterning or imitating excludes episcopacy from the solid and grave ethical law, and betrays it to be a mere child of ceremony, or likelier some misbegotten thing, that having plucked the gay feathers of her obsolete bravery, to hide her own deformed bareness, now vaunts and glories in her stolen plumes. In the mean while, what danger there is against the very life of the gospel, to make in anything the typical law her pattern, and how impossible in that which touches the priestly government, I shall use such light as I have received to lay open. It cannot be unknown by what expressions the holy apostle St. Paul spares not to explain to us the nature and condition of the law, calling those ordinances which were the chief and essential offices of the priests, the elements and rudiments of the world, both weak and beggarly. Now to breed, and bring up the children of the promise, the heirs of liberty and grace, under such a kind of government as is professed to be but an imitation of that ministry which engendered to bondage the sons of Agar; how can this be but a foul injury and derogation, if not a cancelling of that birthright and immunity, which Christ hath purchased for us with his blood? For the ministration of the law, consisting of carnal things, drew to it such a ministry as consisted of carnal respects, dignity, precedence, and the like. And such a ministry established in the gospel, as is founded upon the points and terms of superiority, and nests itself in worldly honors, will draw to it, and we see it doth, such a religion as runs back again to the old pomp and glory of the flesh: for doubtless there is a certain attraction and magnetic force betwixt the religion and the ministerial form thereof. If the religion be pure, spiritual, simple, and lowly as the gospel most truly is, such must the face of the ministry be. And in like manner, if the form of the ministry be grounded in the worldly degrees of authority, honor, temporal jurisdiction, we see it with our eyes it will turn the inward power and purity of the gospel into the outward carnality of the law; evaporating and exhaling the internal worship into empty conformities, and gay shows. And what remains then, but that we should run into as dangerous and deadly apostasy as our lamented neighbors the papists, who, by this very snare and pitfall of imitating the ceremonial law, fell into that irrecoverable superstition, as must needs make void the covenant of salvation to them that persist in this blindness?

CHAPTER IV.

That it is impossible to make the Priesthood of Aaron a Pattern whereon to ground Episcopacy.

THAT which was promised next is, to declare the impossibility of grounding evangelic government in the imitation of the Jewish priesthood; which will be done by considering both the quality of the persons, and the office itself. Aaron and his sons were the princes of their tribe, before they were sanctified to the priesthood: that personal eminence, which they held above the other Levites, they received not only from their office, but partly brought it into their office; and so from that time forward the priests were not chosen out of the whole number of the Levites, as our bishops, but were born inheritors of the dignity. Therefore, unless we shall choose our prelates only out of the nobility, and let them run in a blood, there can be no possible imitation of lording over their brethren in regard of their persons altogether unlike. As for the office, which was a representation of Christ's own person more immediately in the high-priest, and of his whole priestly office in all the other, to the performance of which the Levites were but as servitors and deacons, it was necessary there should be a distinction of dignity between two functions of so great odds. But there being no such difference among our ministers, unless it be in reference to the deacons, it is impossible to found a prelaty upon the imitation of this priesthood: for wherein, or in what work, is the office of a prelate excellent above that of a pastor? In ordination, you will say; but flatly against Scripture: for there we know Timothy received ordination by the hands of the presbytery, notwithstanding all the vain delusions that are used to evade that testimony, and maintain an unwarrantable usurpation. But wherefore should ordination be a cause of setting up a superior degree in the church? Is not that whereby Christ became our Saviour a higher and greater work than that whereby he did ordain messengers to preach and publish him our Saviour? Every minister sustains the person of Christ in his highest work of communicating to us the mysteries of our salvation, and hath the power of binding and absolving; how should he need a higher dignity, to represent or execute that which is an inferior work in Christ? Why should the performance of ordination, which is a lower office, exalt a prelate, and not the seldom discharge of a higher and more noble office, which is preaching and administering, much rather depress him? Verily, neither the nature nor the example of ordination doth any way require an imparity between the ordainer and the ordained; for what more natural than every like to produce his like, man to beget man, fire to propagate fire? And in examples of highest opinion the ordainer is inferior to the ordained: for the pope is not made by the precedent pope, but by cardinals, who ordain and consecrate to a higher and greater office than their own.

CHAPTER V.

To the Arguments of Bishop Andrews and the Primate.

IT follows here to attend to certain objections in a little treatise lately printed among others of like sort at Oxford, and in the title said to be out of the rude drafts of bishop Andrews: and surely they be rude drafts indeed, insomuch that it is marvel to think what his friends meant, to let come abroad such shallow reasonings with the name of a man so much bruited for learning. In the twelfth and twenty-third pages he seems most notoriously inconstant to himself; for in the former place he tells us he forbears to take any argument of prelaty from Aaron, as being the type of Christ. In the latter he can forbear no longer, but repents him of his rash gratuity, affirming, that to say, Christ being come in the flesh, his figure in the high priest ceaseth, is the shift of an anabaptist; and stiffly argues that Christ being as well king as priest, was as well foreresembled by the kings then, as by the high priest: so that if his coming take away the one type, it must also the other. Marvellous piece of divinity! and well worth that the land should pay six thousand pounds a year

for in a bishopric; although I read of no sophister among the Greeks that was so dear, neither Hippias nor Protagoras, nor any whom the Socratic school famously refuted without hire. Here we have the type of the king sewed to the tippet of the bishop, subtly to cast a jealousy upon the crown, as if the right of kings, like Meleager in the Metamorphosis, were no longer lived than the firebrand of prelaty. But more likely the prelates fearing (for their own guilty carriage protests they do fear) that their fair days cannot long hold, practise by possessing the king with this most false doctrine, to engage his power for them, as in his own quarrel, that when they fall they may fall in a general ruin; just as cruel Tiberius would wish:

"When I die let the earth be rolled in flames."

But where, O bishop, doth the purpose of the law set forth Christ to us as a king? That which never was intended in the law can never be abolished as part thereof. When the law was made, there was no king: if before the law, or under the law, God by a special type in any king would foresignify the future kingdom of Christ, which is not yet visibly come; what was that to the law? The whole ceremonial law (and types can be in no law else) comprehends nothing but the propitiatory office of Christ's priesthood, which being in substance accomplished, both law and priesthood fades away of itself, and passes into air like a transitory vision, and the right of kings neither stands by any type nor falls. We acknowledge that the civil magistrate wears an authority of God's giving, and ought to be obeyed as his vicegerent. But to make a king a type, we say is an abusive and unskilful speech, and of a moral solidity makes it seem a ceremonial shadow: therefore your typical chain of king and priest must unlink. But is not the type of priest taken away by Christ's coming? No, saith this famous protestant bishop of Winchester, it is not; and he that saith it is, is an anabaptist. What think ye, readers? Do ye not understand him? What can be gathered hence, but that the prelate would still sacrifice? Conceive him, readers: he would missificate. Their altars, indeed, were in a fair forwardness: and by such arguments as these they were setting up the molten calf of their mass again, and of their great hierarch the pope. For if the type of priest be not taken away, then neither of the high priest; it were a strange beheading; and high priest more than one there cannot be, and that one can be no less than a pope. And this doubtless was the bent of his career, though never so covertly. Yea, but there was something else in the high priest, besides the figure, as is plain by St. Paul's acknowledging him. It is true that in the 17th of Deuteronomy, whence this authority arises to the priest in matters too hard for the secular judges, as must needs be many in the occasions of those times, involved so with ceremonial niceties, no wonder though it be commanded to inquire at the mouth of the priests, who besides the magistrates their colleagues, had the oracle of Urim to consult with. And whether the high priest Ananias had not encroached beyond the limits of his priestly authority, or whether used it rightly, was no time then for St. Paul to contest about. But if this instance be able to assert any right of jurisdiction to the clergy, it must impart it in common to all ministers, since it were a great folly to seek for counsel in a hard intricate scruple from a dunce prelate, when there might be found a speedier solution from a grave and learned minister, whom God hath gifted with the judgment of Urim, more amply ofttimes than all the prelates together; and now in the gospel hath granted the privilege of this oraculous ephod alike to all his ministers. The reason, therefore, of imparity in the priests, being now, as is aforesaid, really annulled both in their person and in their representative office, what right of jurisdiction soever can be from this place Levitically bequeathed, must descend upon the ministers of the gospel equally, as it finds them in all other points equal. Well, then, he is finally content to let Aaron go; Eleazar will serve his turn, as being a superior of superiors, and yet no type of Christ in Aaron's lifetime. O thou that wouldest wind into any figment or phantasm, to save thy mitre! yet all this will not fadge, though it be cunningly interpolished by some second hand with crooks and emendations: hear then the type of Christ in some one particular, as of entering yearly into the holy of holies,

and such-like, rested upon the high priest only as more immediately personating our Saviour: but to resemble his whole satisfactory office, all the lineage of Aaron was no more than sufficient. And all or any of the priests, considered separately without relation to the highest, are but as a lifeless trunk, and signify nothing. And this shows the excellence of Christ's sacrifice, who at once and in one person fulfilled that which many hundreds of priests many times repeating had enough to foreshow. What other imparity there was among themselves, we may safely suppose it depended on the dignity of their birth and family, together with the circumstances of a carnal service, which might afford many priorities. And this I take to be the sum of what the bishop hath laid together to make plea for prelaty by imitation of the law: though, indeed, if it may stand, it will infer popedom all as well. Many other courses he tries, enforcing himself with much ostentation of endless genealogies, as if he were the man that St. Paul forewarns us of in Timothy, but so unvigorously, that I do not fear his winning of many to his cause, but such as doting upon great names are either over-weak, or over-sudden of faith. I shall not refuse, therefore, to learn so much prudence as I find in the Roman soldier that attended the cross, not to stand breaking of legs, when the breath is quite out of the body, but pass to that which follows. The primate of Armagh, at the beginning of his tractate, seeks to avail himself of that place in the sixty-sixth of Isaiah, "I will take of them for priests and Levites, saith the Lord," to uphold hereby such a form of superiority among the minsters of the gospel, succeeding those in the law, as the Lord's-day did the sabbath. But certain if this method may be admitted of interpreting those prophetical passages concerning Christian times in a punctual correspondence, it may with equal probability be urged upon us, that we are bound to observe some monthly solemnity answerable to the new moons, as well as the Lord's-day, which we keep in lieu of the sabbath: for in the 23rd verse the prophet joins them in the same manner together, as before he did the priests and Levites, thus: "And it shall come to pass that from one new moon to another, and from one sabbath to another, shall all flesh come to worship before me, saith the Lord." Undoubtedly with as good consequence may it be alleged from hence, that we are to solemnize some religious monthly meeting different from the sabbath, as from the other any distinct formality of ecclesiastical orders may be inferred. This rather will appear to be the lawful and unconstrained sense of the text, that God, in taking of them for priests and Levites, will not esteem them unworthy, though Gentiles, to undergo any function in the church, but will make of them a full and perfect ministry, as was that of the priests and Levites in their kind. And bishop Andrews himself, to end the controversy, sends us a candid exposition of this quoted verse from the 24th page of his said book, plainly deciding that God, by those legal names there of priests and Levites, means our presbyters and deacons; for which either ingenuous confession, or slip of his pen, we give him thanks, and withal to him that brought these treatises into one volume, who, setting the contradictions of two learned men so near together, did not foresee. What other deducements or analogies are cited out of St. Paul, to prove a likeness between the ministers of the Old and New Testament, having tried their sinews, I judge they may pass without harm-doing to our cause. We may remember, then, that prelaty neither hath nor can have foundation in the law, nor yet in the gospel; which assertion, as being for the plainness thereof a matter of eyesight rather than of disquisition, I voluntarily omit; not forgetting, to specify this note again, that the earnest desire which the prelates have to build their hierarchy upon the sandy bottom of the law, gives us to see abundantly the little assurance which they find to rear up their high roofs by the authority of the gospel, repulsed as it were from the writings of the apostles, and driven to take sanctuary among the Jews. Hence that open confession of the primate before mentioned: "Episcopacy is fetched partly from the pattern of the Old Testament, and partly from the New, as an imitation of the Old;" though nothing can be more rotten in divinity than such a position as this, and is all one as to say, Episcopacy is partly of divine institution, and partly of man's own carving. For who gave the authority to

fetch more from the pattern of the law, than what the apostles had already fetched, if they fetched anything at all, as hath been proved they did not? So was Jeroboam's episcopacy partly from the pattern of the law, and partly from the pattern of his own carnality; a party-colored and a party-membered episcopacy: and what can this be less than a monstrous? Others therefore among the prelates, perhaps not so well able to brook or rather to justify, this foul relapsing to the old law, have condescended at last to a plain confessing, that both the names and offices of bishops and presbyters at first were the same, and in the scriptures nowhere distinguished. This grants the Remonstrant in the fifth section of his Defence, and in the preface to his last short Answer. But what need respect be had whether he grant or grant it not, whenas through all antiquity, and even in the loftiest times of prelaty, we find it granted? Jerome, the learnedst of the fathers, hides not his opinion, that custom only, which the proverb calls a tyrant, was the maker of prelaty; before his audacious workmanship the churches were ruled in common by the presbyters; and such a certain truth this was esteemed, that it became a decree among the papal canons compiled by Gratian. Anselm also, of Canterbury, who, to uphold the points of his prelatism, made himself a traitor to his country, yet commenting the epistles to Titus and the Philippians, acknowledges, from the clearness of the text, what Jerome and the church rubric hath before acknowledged. He little dreamed then that the weeding-hook of reformation would after two ages pluck up his glorious poppy from insulting over the good corn. Though since, some of our British prelates, seeing themselves pressed to produce scripture, try all their cunning, if the New Testament will not help them, to frame of their own heads, as it were with wax, a kind of mimic bishop limned out to the life of a dead priesthood: or else they would strain us out a certain figurative prelate, by wringing the collective allegory of those seven angels into seven single rochets. Howsoever, since it thus appears that custom was the creator of prelaty, being less ancient than the government of presbyters, it is an extreme folly to give them the hearing that tells us of bishops through so many ages: and if against their tedious muster of citations, sees, and successions, it be replied that wagers and church antiquities, such as are repugnant to the plain dictate of scripture, are both alike the arguments of fools, they have their answer. We rather are to cite all those ages to an arraignment before the word of God, wherefore, and what pretending, how presuming they durst alter that divine institution of presbyters, which the apostles, who were no various and inconstant men, surely had set up in the churches; and why they choose to live by custom and catalogue, or, as St. Paul saith, by sight and visibility, rather than by faith? But, first, I conclude from their own mouths, that God's command in scripture, which doubtless ought to be the first and greatest reason of church government, is wanting to prelaty. And certainly we have plenteous warrant in the doctrine of Christ, to determine that the want of this reason is of itself sufficient to confute all other pretences, that may be brought in favor of it.

CHAPTER VI.

That Prelaty was not set up for Prevention of Schism, as is pretended; or if it were, that it performs not what it was first set up for, but quite the contrary.

YET because it hath the outside of a specious reason, and specious things we know are aptest to work with human lightness and frailty, even against the solidest truth that sounds not plausibly, let us think it worth the examining, for the love of infirmer Christians, of what importance this their second reason may be. Tradition they say hath taught them, that, for the prevention of growing schism, the bishop was heaved above the presbyter. And must tradition then ever thus to the world's end be the perpetual cankerworm to eat out God's commandments? Are his decrees so inconsiderate and so fickle, that when the statutes of Solon or Lycurgus shall prove durably good to many ages, his, in forty years, shall be found defective, illcontrived, and for needful causes to be altered? Our Saviour and his apostles did not only foresee, but foretell and forewarn us to look for schism. Is it a thing to be imagined of God's wisdom, or at least of apostolic prudence, to set up such a government in the tenderness of the church, as should incline, or not be more able than any other to oppose itself to schism? It was well known what a bold lurker schism was, even in the household of Christ, between his own disciples and those of John the Baptist, about fasting; and early in the Acts of the Apostles the noise of schism had almost drowned the proclaiming of the gospel; yet we read not in scripture that any thought was had of making prelates, no, not in those places where dissension was most rife. If prelaty had been then esteemed a remedy against schism, where was it more needful than in that great variance among the Corinthians, which St. Paul so labored to reconcile? And whose eye could have found the fittest remedy sooner than his? And what could have made the remedy more available, than to have used it speedily? And, lastly, what could have been more necessary, than to have written it for our instruction? Yet we see he neither commended it to us, nor used it himself. For the same division remaining there, or else bursting forth again more than twenty years after St. Paul's death, we find in Clement's epistle, of venerable authority, written to the yet factious Corinthians, that they were still governed by presbyters. And the same of other churches out of Hermas, and divers other the scholars of the apostles, by the late industry of the learned Salmasius appears. Neither yet did this worthy Clement, St. Paul's disciple, though writing to them to lay aside schism, in the least word advise them to change the presbyterian government into prelaty. And therefore if God afterward gave or permitted this insurrection of episcopacy, it is to be feared he did it in his wrath, as he gave the Israelites a king. With so good a will doth he use to alter his own chosen government once established. For mark whether this rare device of man's brain, thus preferred before the ordinance of God, had better success than fleshly wisdom, not counselling with God, is wont to have. So far was it from removing schism, that if schism parted the congregations before, now it rent and mangled, now it raged. Heresy begat heresy with a certain monstrous haste of pregnancy in her birth, at once born and bringing forth. Contentions, before brotherly, were now hostile. Men went to choose their bishop as they went to a pitched field, and the day of his election was like the sacking of a city, sometimes ended with the blood of thousands. Nor this among heretics only, but men of the same belief, yea, confessors; and that with such odious ambition, that Eusebius, in his eighth book, testifies he abhorred to write. And the reason is not obscure, for the poor dignity, or rather burden, of a parochial presbyter could not engage any great party, nor that to any deadly feud: but prelaty was a power of that extent and sway, that if her election were popular, it was seldom not the cause of some faction or broil in the church. But if her dignity came by favor of some prince, she was from that time his creature, and obnoxious to comply with his ends in state, were they right or wrong. So that, instead of finding prelaty an impeacher of schism or faction, the more I search, the more I grow into all persuasion to think rather that faction and she, as with a spousal ring, are wedded together, never to be divorced. But here let every one behold the just and dreadful judgment of God meeting with the audacious pride of man, that durst offer to mend the ordinances of heaven. God, out of the strife of men, brought forth by his apostles to the church that beneficent and ever-distributing office of deacons, the stewards and ministers of holy alms: man, out of the pretended care of peace and unity, being caught in the snare of his impious boldness to correct the will of Christ, brought forth to himself upon the church that irreconcilable schism of perdition and apostasy, the Roman antichrist; for that the exaltation of the pope arose out of the reason of prelaty, it cannot be denied. And as I noted before, that the pattern of the high priest pleaded for in the gospel, (for take away the head priest, the rest are but a carcase,) sets up with better reason a pope than an archbishop; for if prelaty must still rise and rise till it come to a primate, why should it stay there? whenas the catholic government is not to follow the division of kingdoms, the temple best representing the universal church, and the high priest the universal head: so I ob-

serve here, that if to quiet schism there must be one head of prelaty in a land, or monarchy, rising from a provincial to a national primacy, there may, upon better grounds of repressing schism, be set up one catholic head over the catholic church. For the peace and good of the church is not terminated in the schismless estate of one or two kingdoms, but should be provided for by the joint consultation of all reformed christendom: that all controversy may end in the final pronounce or canon of one archprimate or protestant pope: although by this means, for aught I see, all the diameters of schism may as well meet and be knit up in the centre of one grand falsehood. Now let all impartial men arbitrate what goodly inference these two main reasons of the prelates have, that by a natural league of consequence make more for the pope than for themselves; yea, to say more home, are the very womb for a new subantichrist to breed in, if it be not rather the old force and power of the same man of sin counterfeiting protestant. It was not the prevention of schism, but it was schism itself, and the hateful thirst of lording in the church, that first bestowed a being upon prelaty; this was the true cause, but the pretence is still the same. The prelates, as they would have it thought, are the only mauls of schism. Forsooth if they be put down, a deluge of innumerable sects will follow; we shall be all Brownists, Familists, Anabaptists. For the word Puritan seems to be quashed, and all that heretofore were counted such, are now Brownists. And thus do they raise an evil report upon the expected reforming grace that God hath bid us hope for; like those faithless spies, whose carcases shall perish in the wilderness of their own confused ignorance, and never taste the good of reformation. Do they keep away schism? If to bring a numb and chill stupidity of soul, an unactive blindness of mind, upon the people by their leaden doctrine, or no doctrine at all; if to persecute all knowing and zealous Christians by the violence of their courts, be to keep away schism, they keep away schism indeed: and by this kind of discipline all Italy and Spain is as purely and politicly kept from schism as England hath been by them. With as good a plea might the dead palsy boast to a man, It is

I that free you from stitches and pains, and the troublesome feeling of cold and heat, of wounds and strokes: if I were gone, all these would molest you. The winter might as well vaunt itself against the spring, I destroy all noisome and rank weeds, I keep down all pestilent vapors; yes, and all wholesome herbs, and all fresh dews, by your violent and hide-bound frost: but when the gentle west winds shall open the fruitful bosom of the earth, thus overgirded by your imprisonment, then the flowers put forth and spring, and then the sun shall scatter the mists, and the manuring hand of the tiller shall root up all that burdens the soil without thank to your bondage. But far worse than any frozen captivity is the bondage of prelates; for that other, if it keep down anything which is good within the earth, so doth it likewise that which is ill; but these let out freely the ill, and keep down the good, or else keep down the lesser ill, and let out the greatest. Be ashamed at last to tell the parliament ye curb schismatics, whenas they know ye cherish and side with papists, and are now as it were one party with them, and it is said they help to petition for ye. Can we believe that your government strains in good earnest at the petty gnats of schism, whenas we see it makes nothing to swallow the camel heresy of Rome, but that indeed your throats are of the right pharisaical strain? where are those schismatics, with whom the prelates hold such hot skirmish? show us your acts, those glorious annals which your courts of loathed memory lately deceased have left us? Those schismatics I doubt me will be found the most of them such as whose only schism was to have spoken the truth against your high abominations and cruelties in the church; this is the schism ye hate most, the removal of your criminous hierarchy. A politic government of yours, and of a pleasant conceit, set up to remove those as a pretended schism, that would remove you as a palpable heresy in government. If the schism would pardon ye that, she might go jagged in as many cuts and slashes as she pleased for you. As for the rending of the church, we have many reasons to think it is not that which ye labor to prevent, so much as the rending of your pontifical sleeves: that schism would be the sorest schism to you;

that would be Brownism and Anabaptism indeed. If we go down, say you, (as if Adrian's wall were broken,) a flood of sects will rush in. What sects? What are their opinions? Give us the inventory. It will appear both by your former prosecutions and your present instances, that they are only such to speak of, as are offended with your lawless government, your ceremonies, your liturgy, an extract of the mass-book translated. But that they should be contemners of public prayer, and churches used without superstition, I trust God will manifest it ere long to be as false a slander as your former slanders against the Scots. Noise it till ye be hoarse, that a rabble of sects will come in; it will be answered ye, No rabble, sir priest; but an unanimous multitude of good protestants will then join to the church, which now, because of you, stand separated. This will be the dreadful consequence of your removal. As for those terrible names of sectaries and schismatics which ye have got together, we know your manner of fight, when the quiver of your arguments, which is ever thin, and weakly stored, after the first brunt is quite empty, your course is to betake ye to your other quiver of slander, wherein lies your best archery. And whom you could not move by sophistical arguing, them you think to confute by scandalous misnaming; thereby inciting the blinder sort of people to mislike and deride sound doctrine and good Christianity, under two or three vile and hateful terms. But if we could easily endure and dissolve your doughtiest reasons in argument, we shall more easily bear the worst of your unreasonableness in calumny and false report: especially being foretold by Christ, that if he our master were by your predecessors called Samaritan and Beelzebub, we must not think it strange if his best disciples in the reformation, as at first by those of your tribe they were called Lollards and Hussites, so now by you be termed Puritans and Brownists. But my hope is, that the people of England will not suffer themselves to be juggled thus out of their faith and religion by a mist of names cast before their eyes, but will search wisely by the scriptures, and look quite through this fraudulent aspersion of a disgraceful name into the things themselves: knowing that the primitive Christians in their times were accounted such as are now called Familists and Adamites, or worse. And many on the prelatic side, like the church of Sardis, have a name to live, and yet are dead; to be protestants, and are indeed papists in most of their principles. Thus persuaded, this your old fallacy we shall soon unmask, and quickly apprehend how you prevent schism, and who are your schismatics. But what if ye prevent and hinder all good means of preventing schism? That way which the apostles used, was to call a council: from which, by anything that can be learned from the fifteenth of the Acts, no faithful Christian was debarred, to whom knowledge and piety might give entrance. Of such a council as this every parochial consistory is a right homogeneous and constituting part, being in itself, as it were, a little synod, and towards a general assembly moving upon her own basis in an even and firm progression, as those smaller squares in battle unite in one great cube, the main phalanx, an emblem of truth and steadfastness. Whereas, on the other side, prelaty ascending by a gradual monarchy from bishop to archbishop, from thence to primate, and from thence, for there can be no reason yielded neither in nature nor in religion, wherefore, if it have lawfully mounted thus high, it should not be a lordly ascendant in the horoscope of the church, from primate to patriarch, and so to pope: I say, prelaty thus ascending in a continual pyramid upon pretence to perfect the church's unity, if notwithstanding it be found most needful, yea, the utmost help to darn up the rents of schism by calling a council, what does it but teach us that prelaty is of no force to effect this work, which she boasts to be her masterpiece; and that her pyramid aspires and sharpens to ambition, not to prefection or unity? This we know, that as often as any great schism disparts the church, and synods be proclaimed, the presbyters have as great right there, and as free vote of old, as the bishops, which the canon law conceals not. So that prelaty, if she will seek to close up divisions in the church, must be forced to dissolve and unmake her own pyramidal figure, which she affirms to be of such uniting power, whenas indeed it is the most dividing and schismatical form that geometricians know of, and must be fain to inglobe or incube herself among the presbyters;

which she hating to do, sends her haughty prelates from all parts with their forked mitres, the badge of schism, or the stamp of his cloven foot whom they serve, I think, who, according to their hierarchies acuminating still higher and higher in a cone of prelaty, instead of healing up the gashes of the church, as it happens in such pointed bodies meeting, fall to gore one another with their sharp spires for upper place and precedence, till the council itself proves the greatest schism of all. And thus they are so far from hindering dissension, that they have made unprofitable, and even noisome, the chiefest remedy we have to keep Christendom at one, which is by councils: and these, if we rightly consider apostolic example, are nothing else but general presbyteries. This seemed so far from the apostles to think much of, as if hereby their dignity were impaired, that, as we may gather by those epistles of Peter and John, which are likely to be latest written, when the church grew to a settling, like those heroic patricians of Rome (if we may use such comparison) hastening to lay down their dictatorship, they rejoiced to call themselves, and to be as fellow-elders among their brethren; knowing that their high office was but as the scaffolding of the church yet unbuilt, and would be but a troublesome disfigurement, so soon as the building was finished. But the lofty minds of an age or two after, such was their small discerning, thought it a poor indignity, that the high-reared government of the church should so on a sudden, as it seemed to them, squat into a presbytery. Next, or rather, before councils, the timeliest prevention of schism is to preach the gospel abundantly and powerfully throughout all the land, to instruct the youth religiously, to endeavor how the scriptures may be easiest understood by all men; to which the proceedings of these men have been on set purpose contrary. But how, O prelates, should you remove schism? and how should you not remove and oppose all the means of removing schism? when prelaty is a schism itself from the most reformed and most flourishing of our neighbor churches abroad, and a sad subject of discord and offence to the whole nation at home. The remedy which you allege, is the very disease we groan under; and never can be to us a remedy but by removing itself. Your predecessors were believed to assume this pre-eminence above their brethren, only that they might appease dissension. Now God and the church calls upon you, for the same reason, to lay it down, as being to thousands of good men offensive, burdensome, intolerable. Surrender that pledge, which, unless you foully usurped it, the church gave you, and now claims it again, for the reason she first lent it. Discharge the trust committed to you, prevent schism; and that ye can never do, but by discharging yourselves. That government which ye hold, we confess, prevents much, hinders much, removes much: but what? the schisms and grievances of the church? no, but all the peace and unity, all the welfare not of the church alone, but of the whole kingdom. And if it be still permitted ye to hold, will cause the most sad, I know not whether separation be enough to say, but such a wide gulf of distraction in this land, as will never close her dismal gap until ye be forced, (for of yourselves you will never do as that Roman, Curtius, nobly did,) for the church's peace and your country's, to leap into the midst, and be no more seen. By this we shall know whether yours be that ancient prelaty, which you say was first constituted for the reducement of quiet and unanimity into the church, for then you will not delay to prefer that above your own preferment. If otherwise, we must be confident that your prelaty is nothing else but your ambition, an insolent preferring of yourselves above your brethren; and all your learned scraping in antiquity, even to disturb the bones of old Aaron and his sons in their graves, is but to maintain and set upon our necks a stately and severe dignity, which you call sacred, and is nothing in very deed but a grave and reverend gluttony, a sanctimonious avarice; in comparison of which, all the duties and dearnesses which ye owe to God or to his church, to law, custom, or nature, ye have resolved to set at naught. I could put you in mind what counsel Clement, a fellow-laborer with the apostles, gave to the presbyters of Corinth, whom the people, though unjustly, sought to remove. "Who among you," saith he, "is noble-minded, who is pitiful, who is charitable? let him say thus, If for me this sedition, this enmity, these differences be, I

willingly depart, I go my ways; only let the flock of Christ be at peace with the presbyters that are set over it. He that shall do this," saith he, "shall get him great honor in the Lord, and all places will receive him." This was Clement's counsel to good and holy men, that they should depart rather from their just office, than by their stay to ravel out the seamless garment of concord in the church. But I have better counsel to give the prelates, and far more acceptable to their ears; this advice in my opinion is fitter for them: Cling fast to your pontifical sees, bate not, quit yourselves like barons, stand to the utmost for your haughty courts and votes in parliament. Still tell us, that you prevent schism, though schism and combustion be the very issue of your bodies, your first-born; and set your country a bleeding in a prelatical mutiny, to fight for your pomp, and that ill-favored weed of temporal honor, that sits dishonorably upon your laic shoulders, that ye may be fat and fleshy, swollen with high thoughts and big with mischievous designs, when God comes to visit upon you all this fourscore years' vexation of his church under your Egyptian tyranny. For certainly of all those blessed souls which you have persecuted, and those miserable ones which you have lost, the just vengeance does not sleep.

CHAPTER VII.

That those many Sects and Schisms by some supposed to be among us, and that Rebellion in Ireland, ought not to be a Hindrance, but a Hastening of Reformation.

As for those many sects and divisions rumored abroad to be amongst us, it is not hard to perceive, that they are partly the mere fictions and false alarms of the prelates, thereby to cast amazements and panic terrors into the hearts of weaker Christians, that they should not venture to change the present deformity of the church, for fear of I know not what worse inconveniences. With the same objected fears and suspicions, we know that subtle prelate Gardner sought to divert the first reformation. It may suffice us to be taught by St. Paul, that there must be sects for the manifesting of those that are sound-hearted. These are but winds and flaws to try the floating vessel of our faith, whether it be stanch and sail well, whether our ballast be just, our anchorage and cable strong. By this is seen who lives by faith and certain knowledge, and who by credulity and the prevailing opinion of the age; whose virtue is of an unchangeable grain, and whose of a slight wash. If God come to try our constancy, we ought not to shrink or stand the less firmly for that, but pass on with more steadfast resolution to establish the truth, though it were through a lane of sects and heresies on each side. Other things men do to the glory of God: but sects and errors, it seems, God suffers to be for the glory of good men, that the world may know and reverence their true fortitude and undaunted constancy in the truth. Let us not therefore make these things an incumbrance, or an excuse of our delay in reforming, which God sends us as an incitement to proceed with more honor and alacrity: for if there were no opposition, where were the trial of an unfeigned goodness and magnanimity? Virtue that wavers is not virtue, but vice revolted from itself, and after a while returning. The actions of just and pious men do not darken in their middle course; but Solomon tells us, they are as the shining light, that shineth more and more unto the perfect day. But if we shall suffer the trifling doubts and jealousies of future sects to overcloud the fair beginnings of purposed reformation, let us rather fear that another proverb of the same wise man be not upbraided to us, that "the way of the wicked is as darkness; they stumble at they know not what." If sects and schisms be turbulent in the unsettled estate of a church, while it lies under the amending hand, it best beseems our Christian courage to think they are but as the throes and pangs that go before the birth of reformation, and that the work itself is now in doing. For if we look but on the nature of elemental and mixed things, we know they cannot suffer any change of one kind or quality into another, without the struggle of contrarieties. And in things artificial, seldom any elegance is wrought without a superfluous waste and refuse in the transaction. No marble statue can be politely carved, no fair edifice built, without almost as much rubbish and sweeping. Insomuch that even in the spiritual conflict of St. Paul's conversion, there fell scales from his eyes, that were not perceived before. No wonder then in the reforming of a church, which is never brought to effect without the fierce encounter of truth and falsehood together, if, as it were, the splinters and shares of so violent a jousting, there fall from between the shock many fond errors and fanatic opinions, which, when truth has the upper hand, and the reformation shall be perfected, will easily be rid out of the way, or kept so low, as that they shall be only the exercise of our knowledge, not the disturbance or interruption of our faith. As for that which Barclay, in his "Image of Minds," writes concerning the horrible and barbarous conceits of Englishmen in their religion, I deem it spoken like what he was, a fugitive papist traducing the island whence he sprung. It may be more judiciously gathered from hence, that the Englishman of many other nations is least atheistical, and bears a natural disposition of much reverence and awe towards the Deity, but in his weakness and want of better instruction, which among us too frequently is neglected, especially by the meaner sort, turning the bent of his own wits, with a scrupulous and ceaseless care, what he might do to inform himself aright of God and his worship, he may fall not unlikely sometimes, as any other landman, into an uncouth opinion. And verily if we look at his native towardliness in the roughcast without breeding, some nation or other may haply be better composed to a natural civility and right judgment than he. But if he get the benefit once of a wise and well-rectified nurture, which must first come in general from the godly vigilance of the church, I suppose that wherever mention is made of countries, manners, or men, the English people, among the first that shall be praised, may deserve to be accounted a right pious, right honest, and right hardy nation. But thus while some stand dallying and deferring to reform for fear of that which should mainly hasten them forward, lest schism and error should increase, we may now thank ourselves and our delays, if instead of schism a bloody and inhuman rebellion be strook in between our slow movings. Indeed against violent and powerful opposition there can be no just blame of a lingering dispatch. But this I urge against those that discourse it for a maxim, as if the swift opportunities of establishing or reforming religion were to attend upon the phlegm of state-business. In state many things at first are crude and hard to digest, which only time and deliberation can supple and concoct. But in religion, wherein is no immaturity, nothing out of season, it goes far otherwise. The door of grace turns upon smooth hinges, wide opening to send out, but soon shutting to recall the precious offers of mercy to a nation: which, unless watchfulness and zeal, two quicksighted and ready-handed virgins, be there in our behalf to receive, we lose: and still the ofter we lose, the straiter the door opens, and the less is offered. This is all we get by demurring in God's service. It is not rebellion that ought to be the hindrance of reformation, but it is the want of this which is the cause of that. The prelates which boast themselves the only bridlers of schism, God knows, have been so cold and backward both there and with us to repress heresy and idolatry, that either, through their carelessness, or their craft, all this mischief is befallen. What can the Irish subject do less in God's just displeasure against us, than revenge upon English bodies the little care that our prelates have had of their souls? Nor hath their negligence been new in that island, but ever notorious in Queen Elizabeth's days, as Camden, their known friend, forbears not to complain. Yet so little are they touched with remorse of these their cruelties, (for these cruelties are theirs, the bloody revenge of those souls which they have famished,) that whenas against our brethren the Scots, who, by their upright and loyal deeds, have now bought themselves an honorable name to posterity, whatsoever malice by slander could invent, rage in hostility attempt, they greedily attempted; toward these murderous Irish, the enemies of God and mankind, a cursed offspring of their own connivance, no man takes notice but that they seem to be very calmly and indifferently affected. Where then should we begin to extinguish a rebellion that hath his cause from the misgovernment of the church? where, but at the church's reformation, and the removal of that government which pursues and wars with all good Christians under the name of schismatics, but maintains and fosters all papists and idolaters as tolerable Christians? And if the sacred Bible may be our light, we are neither without example, nor the witness of God himself, that the corrupted estate of the church is both the cause of tumult and civil wars, and that to stint them, the peace of the church must first be settled. "Now, for a long season," saith Azariah to King Asa, "Israel hath been without the true God, and without a teaching priest and without law: and in those times there was no peace to him that went out, nor to him that came in, but great vexations were upon all the inhabitants of the countries. And nation was destroyed of nation, and city of city, for God did vex them with all adversity. Be ye strong therefore," saith he to the reformers of that age, "and let not your hands be weak, for your work shall be rewarded." And in those prophets that lived in the times of reformation after the captivity, often doth God stir up the people to consider, that while establishment of church-matters was neglected, and put off, there "was no peace to him that went out or came in; for I," saith God, "had set all men every one against his neighbor." But from the very day forward that they went seriously and effectually about the welfare of the church, he tells them, that they themselves might perceive the sudden change of things into a prosperous and peaceful condition. But it will here be said, that the reformation is a long work, and the miseries of Ireland are urgent of a speedy redress. They be indeed; and how speedy we are, the poor afflicted remnant of our martyred countrymen that sit there on the seashore, counting the hours of our delay with their sighs, and the minutes with their falling tears, perhaps with the distilling of their bloody wounds, if they have not quite by this time cast off, and almost cursed the vain hope of our foundered ships and aids, can best judge how speedy we are to their relief. But let their succors be hasted, as all need and reason is; and let not therefore the reformation, which is the chiefest cause of success and victory, be still procrastinated. They of the captivity in their greatest extremities could find both counsel and hands enough at once to build, and to expect the enemy's assault.

And we, for our parts, a populous and mighty nation, must needs be fallen into a strange plight either of effeminacy or confusion, if Ireland, that was once the conquest of one single earl with his private forces, and the small assistance of a petty Kernish prince, should now take up all the wisdom and prowess of this potent monarchy, to quell a barbarous crew of rebels, whom, if we take but the right course to subdue, that is, beginning at the reformation of our church, their own horrid murders and rapes will so fight against them, that the very sutlers and horseboys of the camp will be able to rout and chase them, without the staining of any noble sword. To proceed by other method in this enterprise, be our captains and commanders never so expert, will be as great an error in the art of war, as any novice in soldiership ever committed. And thus I leave it as a declared truth, that neither the fear of sects, no, nor rebellion, can be a fit plea to stay reformation, but rather to push it forward with all possible diligence and speed.

THE SECOND BOOK.

How happy were it for this frail, and as it may be truly called mortal life of man, since all earthly things which have the name of good and convenient in our daily use, are withal so cumbersome and full of trouble, if knowledge, yet which is the best and lightsomest possession of the mind, were, as the common saying is, no burden; and that what it wanted of being a load to any part of the body, it did not with a heavy advantage overlay upon the spirit! For not to speak of that knowledge that rests in the contemplation of natural causes and dimensions, which must needs be a lower wisdom, as the object is low, certain it is, that he who hath obtained in more than the scantiest measure to know anything distinctly of God, and of his true worship, and what is infallibly good and happy in the state of man's life, what in itself evil and miserable, though vulgarly not so esteemed; he that hath obtained to know this, the only high valuable wisdom indeed, remembering also that God, even to a strictness, requires the improvement of these his intrusted gifts, cannot but sustain a sorer burden of mind, and more pressing, than any supportable toil or weight which the body can labor under, how and in what manner he shall dispose and employ those sums of knowledge and illumination, which God hath sent him into this world to trade with. And that which aggravates the burden more, is, that, having received amongst his allotted parcels certain precious truths, of such an orient lustre as no diamond can equal, which nevertheless he has in charge to put off at any cheap rate, yea, for nothing to them that will; the great merchants of this world, fearing that this course would soon discover and disgrace the false glitter of their deceitful wares, wherewith they abuse the people, like poor Indians with beads and glasses, practise by all means how they may suppress the vending of such rarities, and such a cheapness as would undo them, and turn their trash upon their hands. Therefore by gratifying the corrupt desires of men in fleshly doctrines, they stir them up to persecute with hatred and contempt all those that seek to bear themselves uprightly in this their spiritual factory: which they foreseeing, though they cannot but testify of truth, and the excellence of that heavenly traffic which they bring, against what opposition or danger soever, yet needs must it sit heavily upon their spirits, that being, in God's prime intention and their own, selected heralds of peace, and dispensers of treasure inestimable, without price, to them that have no pence, they find in the discharge of their commission, that they are made the greatest variance and offence, a very sword and fire both in house and city over the whole earth. This is that which the sad prophet Jeremiah laments: "Wo is me, my mother, that thou hast borne me, a man of strife and contention!" And although divine inspiration must certainly have been sweet to those ancient prophets, yet the irksomeness of that truth which they brought was so unpleasant to them, that everywhere they call it a burden. Yea, that mysterious book of revelation, which the great evangelist was bid to eat, as it had been some eye-brightening electuary of knowledge and foresight, though it were sweet in his mouth, and in the learning, it was bitter in his belly, bitter in the denouncing. Nor was this hid from the wise poet Sophocles, who in that place of his tragedy where Tiresias is called to resolve king Œdipus in a matter which he knew would be grievous, brings him in bemoaning his lot, that he knew more than other men. For surely to every good and peaceable man, it must in nature needs be a hateful thing to be the displeaser and molester of thousands; much better would it like him doubtless to be the messenger of gladness and contentment, which is his chief intended business to all 10 mankind, but that they resist and oppose their own true happiness. But when God commands to take the trumpet, and blow a dolorous or a jarring blast, it lies not in man's will what he shall say, or what he shall conceal. If he shall think to be silent as Jeremiah did, because of the reproach and derision he met with daily, "And all his familiar friends watched for his halting," to to be revenged on him for speaking the truth, 20 he would be forced to confess as he confessed: "His word was in my heart as a burning fire shut up in my bones; I was weary with forbearing, and could not stay." Which might teach these times not suddenly to condemn all things that are sharply spoken or vehemently written as proceeding out of stomach, virulence, and ill-nature; but to consider rather, that if the prelates have leave to say the worst that can be said, and 30 do the worst that can be done, while they strive to keep to themselves, to their great pleasure and commodity, those things which they ought to render up, no man can be justly offended with him that shall endeavor to impart and bestow, without any gain to himself, those sharp but saving words which would be a terror and a torment in him to keep back. For me, I have determined to lay up as the best treasure and solace of a good 40 old age, if God vouchsafe it me, the honest liberty of free speech from my youth where I shall think it available in so dear a concernment as the church's good. For if I be, either by disposition or what other cause, too inquisitive, or suspicious of myself and mine own doings, who can help it? But this I foresee, that should the church be brought under heavy oppression, and God have given me ability the while to reason against that 50 man that should be the author of so foul a deed; or should she, by blessing from above on the industry and courage of faithful men,

change this her distracted estate into better days, without the least furtherance or contribution of those few talents, which God at that present had lent me; I foresee what stories I should hear within myself, all my life after, of discourage and reproach. Timorous and ingrateful, the church of God is now again at the foot of her insulting enemies, and thou bewailest. What matters it for thee, or thy bewailing? When time was, thou couldst not find a syllable of all that thou hadst read, or studied, to utter in her behalf. Yet ease and leisure was given thee for thy retired thoughts, out of the sweat of other men. Thou hadst the diligence, the parts, the language of a man, if a vain subject were to be adorned or beautified; but when the cause of God and his church was to be pleaded, for which purpose that tongue was given thee which thou hast, God listened if he could hear thy voice among his zealous servants, but thou wert dumb as a beast; from henceforward be that which thine own brutish silence hath made thee. Or else I should have heard on the other ear: Slothful, and ever to be set light by, the church hath now overcome her late distresses after the unwearied labors of many her true servants that stood up in her defence; thou also wouldst take upon thee to share amongst them of their joy: but wherefore thou? Where canst thou show any word or deed of thine which might have hastened her peace? Whatever thou dost now talk, or write, or look, is the alms of other men's active prudence and zeal. Dare not now to say or do anything better than thy former sloth and infancy; or if thou darest, thou dost impudently to make a thrifty purchase of boldness to thyself, out of the painful merits of other men; what before was thy sin is now thy duty, to be abject and worthless. These, and suchlike lessons as these, I know would have been my matins duly, and my even-song. But now by this little diligence, mark what a privilege I have gained with good men and saints, to claim my right of lamenting the tribulations of the church, if she should suffer, when others, that have ventured nothing for her sake, have not the honor to be admitted mourners. But if she lift up her drooping head and prosper, among those that have something more than wished her welfare, I have my charter and freehold of rejoicing to me and my heirs. Concerning therefore this wayward subject against prelaty, the touching whereof is so distasteful and disquietous to a number of men, as by what hath been said I may deserve of charitable readers to be credited, that neither envy nor gall hath entered me upon this controversy, but the enforcement of conscience only, and a preventive fear lest the omitting of this duty should be against me, when I would store up to myself the good provision of peaceful hours: so, lest it should be still imputed to me, as I have found it hath been, that some self-pleasing humor of vain-glory hath incited me to contest with men of high estimation, now while green years are upon my head; from this needless surmisal I shall hope to dissuade the intelligent and equal auditor, if I can but say successfully that which in this exigent behooves me; although I would be heard only, if it might be, by the elegant and learned reader, to whom principally for a while I shall beg leave I may address myself. To him it will be no new thing, though I tell him that if I hunted after praise, by the ostentation of wit and learning, I should not write thus out of mine own season when I have neither yet completed to my mind the full circle of my private studies, although I complain not of any insufficiency to the matter in hand; or were I ready to my wishes, it were a folly to commit anything elaborately composed to the careless and interrupted listening of these tumultuous times. Next, if I were wise only to my own ends, I would certainly take such a subject as of itself might catch applause, whereas this hath all the disadvantages on the contrary, and such a subject as the publishing whereof might be delayed at pleasure, and time enough to pencil it over with all the curious touches of art, even to the perfection of a faultless picture; whenas in this argument the not deferring is of great moment to the good speeding, that if solidity have leisure to do her office, art cannot have much. Lastly, I should not choose this manner of writing, wherein knowing myself inferior to myself, led by the genial power of nature to another task, I have the use, as I may account it, but of my left hand. And though I shall be foolish in saying more to this purpose. yet, since it will

be such a folly, as wisest men go about to commit, having only confessed and so committed, I may trust with more reason, because with more folly, to have courteous pardon. For although a poet, soaring in the high region of his fancies, with his garland and singing robes about him, might, without apology, speak more of himself than I mean to do; yet for me sitting here below in the cool element of prose, a mortal thing among many readers of no empyreal conceit, to venture and divulge unusual things of myself, I shall petition to the gentler sort, it may not be envy to me. I must say, therefore, that after I had for my first years, by the ceaseless diligence and care of my father, (whom God recompense!) been exercised to the tongues, and some sciences, as my age would suffer, by sundry masters and teachers, both at home and at the schools, it was found that whether aught was imposed me by them that had the overlooking, or betaken to of mine own choice in English, or other tongue, prosing or versing, but chiefly this latter, the style, by certain vital signs it had, was likely to live. But much latelier in the private academies of Italy, whither I was favored to resort, perceiving that some trifles which I had in memory, composed at under twenty or thereabout, (for the manner is, that every one must give some proof of his wit and reading there,) met with acceptance above what was looked for; and other things, which I had shifted in scarcity of books and conveniences to patch up amongst them, were received with written encomiums, which the Italian is not forward to bestow on men of this side the Alps; I began thus far to assent both to them and divers of my friends here at home, and not less to an inward prompting which now grew daily upon me, that by labor and intense study, (which I take to be my portion in this life,) joined with the strong propensity of nature, I might perhaps leave something so written to aftertimes, as they should not willingly let it die. These thoughts at once possessed me, and these other; that if I were certain to write as men buy leases, for three lives and downward, there ought no regard be sooner had than to God's glory, by the honor and instruction of my country. For which cause, and not only for that I knew it would be hard to arrive at the second rank among the Latins, I applied myself to that resolution, which Ariosto followed against the persuasions of Bembo, to fix all the industry and art I could unite to the adorning of my native tongue; not to make verbal curiosities the end, (that were a toilsome vanity,) but to be an interpreter and relater of the best and sagest things among mine own citizens throughout this island in the mother dialect. That what the greatest and choicest wits of Athens, Rome, or modern Italy, and those Hebrews of old did for their country, I, in my proportion, with this over and above, of being a Christian, might do for mine; not caring to be once named abroad, though perhaps I could attain to that, but content with these British islands as my world; whose fortune hath hitherto been, that if the Athenians, as some say, made their small deeds great and renowned by their eloquent writers, England hath had her noble achievements made small by the unskilful handling of monks and mechanics.

Time serves not now, and perhaps I might seem too profuse to give any certain account of what the mind at home, in the spacious circuits of her musing, hath liberty to propose to herself, though of highest hope and hardest attempting; whether that epic form whereof the two poems of Homer, and those other two of Virgil and Tasso, are a diffuse, and the book of Job a brief model: or whether the rules of Aristotle herein are strictly to be kept, or nature to be followed, which in them that know art, and use judgment, is no transgression, but an enriching of art: and lastly, what king or knight, before the conquest, might be chosen in whom to lay the pattern of a Christian hero. And as Tasso gave to a prince of Italy his choice whether he would command him to write of Godfrey's expedition against the Infidels, or Belisarius against the Goths, or Charlemain against the Lombards; if to the instinct of nature and the emboldening of art aught may be trusted, and that there be nothing adverse in our climate, or the fate of this age, it haply would be no rashness, from an equal diligence and inclination, to present the like offer in our own ancient stories; or whether those dramatic constitutions, wherein Sophocles and Euripides reign, shall be found more doctrinal and exemplary to a nation. The scrip-

ture also affords us a divine pastoral drama in the Song of Solomon, consisting of two persons, and a double chorus, as Origen rightly judges. And the Apocalypse of St. John is the majestic image of a high and stately tragedy, shutting up and intermingling her solemn scenes and acts with a sevenfold chorus of hallelujahs and harping symphonies: and this my opinion the grave authority of Pareus, commenting that book, is sufficient to confirm. Or if occasion shall lead, to imitate those magnific odes and hymns, wherein Pindarus and Callimachus are in most things worthy, some others in their frame judicious, in their matter most an end faulty. But those frequent songs throughout the law and prophets beyond all these, not in their divine argument alone, but in the very critical art of composition, may be easily made appear over all the kinds of lyric poesy to be incomparable. These abilities, wheresoever they be found, are the inspired gift of God, rarely bestowed, but yet to some (though most abuse) in every nation; and are of power, beside the office of a pulpit, to imbreed and cherish in a great people the seeds of virtue and public civility, to allay the perturbations of the mind, and set the affections in right tune; to celebrate in glorious and lofty hymns the throne and equipage of God's almightiness, and what he works, and what he suffers to be wrought with high providence in his church; to sing the victorious agonies of martyrs and saints, the deeds and triumphs of just and pious nations, doing valiantly through faith against the enemies of Christ; to deplore the general relapses of kingdoms and states from justice and God's true worship. Lastly, whatsoever in religion is holy and sublime, in virtue amiable or grave, whatsoever hath passion or admiration in all the changes of that which is called fortune from without, or the wily subtleties and refluxes of man's thoughts from within; all these things with a solid and treatable smoothness to paint out and describe. Teaching over the whole book of sanctity and virtue, through all the instances of example, with such delight to those especially of soft and delicious temper, who will not so much as look upon truth herself, unless they see her elegantly dressed; that whereas the paths of honesty and good life appear now rugged and difficult, though they be indeed easy and pleasant, they will then appear to all men both easy and pleasant, though they were rugged and difficult indeed. And what a benefit this would be to our youth and gentry, may be soon guessed by what we know of the corruption and bane which they suck in daily from the writings and interludes of libidinous and ignorant poetasters, who having scarce ever heard of that which is the main consistence of a true poem, the choice of such persons as they ought to introduce, and what is moral and decent to each one; do for the most part lap up vicious principles in sweet pills to be swallowed down, and make the taste of virtuous documents harsh and sour. But because the spirit of man cannot demean itself lively in this body, without some recreating intermission of labor and serious things, it were happy for the commonwealth, if our magistrates, as in those famous governments of old, would take into their care, not only the deciding of our contentious lawcases and brawls, but the managing of our public sports and festival pastimes; that they might be, not such as were authorized a while since, the provocations of drunkenness and lust, but such as may inure and harden our bodies by martial exercises to all warlike skill and performance; and may civilize, adorn, and make discreet our minds by the learned and affable meeting of frequent academies, and the procurement of wise and artful recitations, sweetened with eloquent and graceful enticements to the love and practice of justice, temperance, and fortitude, instructing and bettering the nation at all opportunities, that the call of wisdom and virtue may be heard everywhere, as Solomon saith: "She crieth without, she uttereth her voice in the streets, in the top of high places, in the chief concourse, and in the openings of the gates." Whether this may not be, not only in pulpits, but after another persuasive method, at set and solemn paneguries, in theatres, porches, or what other place or way may win most upon the people to receive at once both recreation and instruction, let them in authority consult. The thing which I had to say and those intentions which have lived within me ever since I could conceive myself anything worth to my country, I return to crave excuse that urgent reason

hath plucked from me, by an abortive and foredated discovery. And the accomplishment of them lies not but in a power above man's to promise; but that none hath by more studious ways endeavored, and with more unwearied spirit that none shall, that I dare almost aver of myself, as far as life and free leisure will extend; and that the land had once enfranchised herself from this impertinent yoke of prelaty, under whose inquisitorious and tyrannical duncery, no free and splendid wit can flourish. Neither do I think it shame to covenant with any knowing reader, that for some few years yet I may go on trust with him toward the payment of what I am now indebted, as being a work not to be raised from the heat of youth, or the vapors of wine; like that which flows at waste from the pen of some vulgar amorist, or the trencher fury of a rhyming parasite; nor to be obtained by the invocation of dame memory and her siren daughters, but by devout prayer to that eternal Spirit, who can enrich with all utterance and knowledge, and sends out his seraphim, with the hallowed fire of his altar, to touch and purify the lips of whom he pleases: to this must be added industrious and select reading, steady observation, insight into all seemly and generous arts and affairs; till which in some measure be compassed, at mine own peril and cost, I refuse not to sustain this expectation from as many as are not loth to hazard so much credulity upon the best pledges that I can give them. Although it nothing content me to have disclosed thus much beforehand, but that I trust hereby to make it manifest with what small willingness I endure to interrupt the pursuit of no less hopes than these, and leave a calm and pleasing solitariness, fed with cheerful and confident thoughts, to embark in a troubled sea of noises and hoarse disputes, put from beholding the bright countenance of truth in the quiet and still air of delightful studies, to come into the dim reflection of hollow antiquities sold by the seeming bulk, and there be fain to club quotations with men whose learning and belief lies in marginal stuffings, who, when they have, like good sumpters, laid ye down their horse-loads of citations and fathers at your door with a rhapsody of who and who were bishops here or there, ye may take off their packsaddles, their day's work is done, and episcopacy, as they think, stoutly vindicated. Let any gentle apprehension, that can distinguish learned pains from unlearned drudgery imagine what pleasure or profoundness can be in this, or what honor to deal against such adversaries. But were it the meanest under-service, if God by his secretary conscience enjoin it, it were sad for me if I should draw back; for me especially, now when all men offer their aid to help, ease, and lighten the difficult labors of the church, to whose service, by the intentions of my parents and friends, I was destined of a child, and in mine own resolutions: till coming to some maturity of years, and perceiving what tyranny had invaded the church, that he who would take orders must subscribe slave, and take an oath withal, which, unless he took with a conscience that would retch, he must either straight perjure, or split his faith; I thought it better to prefer a blameless silence before the sacred office of speaking, bought and begun with servitude and forswearing. Howsoever, thus church-outed by the prelates, hence may appear the right I have to meddle in these matters, as before the necessity and constraint appeared.

CHAPTER I.

That Prelaty opposeth the Reason and End of the Gospel three Ways: and first, in her outward Form.

AFTER this digression, it would remain that I should single out some other reason, which might undertake for prelaty to be a fit and lawful church-government; but finding none of like validity with these that have already sped according to their fortune, I shall add one reason why it is not to be thought a church government at all, but a church tyranny, and is at hostile terms with the end and reason of Christ's evangelic ministry. Albeit I must confess to be half in doubt whether I should bring it forth or no, it being so contrary to the eye of the world, and the world so potent in most men's hearts, that I shall endanger either not to be regarded, or not to be understood; for who is there almost that

measures wisdom by simplicity, strength by suffering, dignity by lowliness? Who is there that counts it first to be last, something to be nothing, and reckons himself of great command in that he is a servant? Yet God, when he meant to subdue the world and hell at once, part of that to salvation, and this wholly to perdition, made choice of no other weapons or auxiliaries than these, whether to save or to destroy. It had been a small mastery for him to have drawn out his legions into array, and flanked them with his thunder; therefore he sent foolishness to confute wisdom, weakness to bind strength, despisedness to vanquish pride: and this is the great mystery of the gospel made good in Christ himself, who, as he testifies, came not to be ministered to, but to minister; and must be fulfilled in all his ministers till his second coming. To go against these principles St. Paul so feared, that if he should but affect the wisdom of words in his preaching, he thought it would be laid to his charge, that he had made the cross of Christ to be of none effect. Whether, then, prelaty do not make of none effect the cross of Christ, by the principles it hath so contrary to these, nullifying the power and end of the gospel, it shall not want due proof, if it want not due belief. Neither shall I stand to trifle with one that would tell me of quiddities and formalities, whether prelaty or prelateity, in abstract notion, be this or that; it suffices me that I find it in his skin, so I find it inseparable, or not oftener otherwise than a phœnix hath been seen; although I persuade me, that whatever faultiness was but superficial to prelaty at the beginning, is now, by the just judgment of God, long since branded and inworn into the very essence thereof. First, therefore, if to do the work of the gospel, Christ our Lord took upon him the form of a servant, how can his servant in this ministry take upon him the form of a lord? I know Bilson hath deciphered us all the gallantries of signore and monsignore, and monsieur, as circumstantially as any punctualist of Castile, Naples, or Fountain-Bleau could have done: but this must not so compliment us out of our right minds, as to be to learn that the form of a servant was a mean, laborious, and vulgar life, aptest to teach; which form Christ thought fittest, that he might bring about his will according to his own principles, choosing the meaner things of this world, that he might put under the high. Now, whether the pompous garb, the lordly life, the wealth, the haughty distance of prelaty, be those meaner things of the world, whereby God in them would manage the mystery of his gospel, be it the verdict of common sense. For Christ saith, in St. John, "The servant is not greater than his lord, nor he that is sent greater than he that sent him;" and adds, "If ye know these things, happy are ye if ye do them." Then let the prelates well advise, if they neither know, nor do these things, or if they know, and yet do them not, wherein their happiness consists. And thus is the gospel frustrated by the lordly form of prelaty.

CHAPTER II.

That the ceremonious Doctrine of Prelaty opposeth the Reason and End of the Gospel.

THAT which next declares the heavenly power and reveals the deep mystery of the gospel, is the pure simplicity of doctrine, accounted the foolishness of this world, yet crossing and confounding the pride and wisdom of the flesh. And wherein consists this fleshly wisdom and pride? In being altogether ignorant of God and his worship? No, surely; for men are naturally ashamed of that. Where then? It consists in a bold presumption of ordering the worship and service of God after man's own will in traditions and ceremonies. Now if the pride and wisdom of the flesh were to be defeated and confounded, no doubt but in that very point wherein it was proudest, and thought itself wisest, that so the victory of the gospel might be the more illustrious. But our prelates, instead of expressing the spiritual power of their ministry, by warring against this chief bulwark and stronghold of the flesh, have entered into fast league with the principal enemy against whom they were sent, and turned the strength of fleshly pride and wisdom against the pure simplicity of saving truth. First, mistrusting to find the authority of their order in the immediate institution of Christ,

or his apostles, by the clear evidence of scripture, they fly to the carnal supportment of tradition; when we appeal to the Bible, they to the unwieldy volumes of tradition: and do not shame to reject the ordinance of him that is eternal, for the perverse iniquity of sixteen hundred years; choosing rather to think truth itself a liar, than that sixteen ages should be taxed with an error; not considering the general apostacy that was foretold, and the church's flight into the wilderness. Nor is this enough; instead of showing the reason of their lowly condition from divine example and command, they seek to prove their high pre-eminence from human consent and authority. But let them chant while they will of prerogatives, we shall tell them of scripture; of custom, we of scripture; of acts and statutes, still of scripture; till the quick and piercing word enter to the dividing of their souls, and the mighty weakness of the gospel throw down the weak mightiness of man's reasoning. Now for their demeanor within the church, how have they disfigured and defaced that more than angelic brightness, the unclouded serenity of Christian religion, with the dark overcasting of superstitious copes and flaminical vestures, wearing on their backs, and, I abhor to think, perhaps in some worse place, the inexpressible image of God the Father? Tell me, ye priests, wherefore this gold, wherefore these robes and surplices over the gospel? Is our religion guilty of the first trespass, and hath need of clothing to cover her nakedness? What does this else but cast an ignominy upon the perfection of Christ's ministry, by seeking to adorn it with that which was the poor remedy of our shame? Believe it, wondrous doctors, all corporeal resemblances of inward holiness and beauty are now past; he that will clothe the gospel now, intimates plainly that the gospel is naked, uncomely, that I may not say reproachful. Do not, ye church maskers, while Christ is clothing upon our barrenness with his righteous garment to make us acceptable in his Father's sight; do not, as ye do, cover and hide his righteous verity with the polluted clothing of your ceremonies, to make it seem more decent in your own eyes. "How beautiful," saith Isaiah, "are the feet of him that bringeth good tidings, that publisheth salvation!" Are the feet so beautiful, and is the very bringing of these tidings so decent of itself? What new decency then can be added to this by your spinstry? Ye think by these gaudy glisterings to stir up the devotion of the rude multitude; ye think so, because ye forsake the heavenly teaching of St. Paul for the hellish sophistry of papism. If the multitude be rude, the lips of the preacher must give knowledge, and not cere- monies. And although some Christians be new-born babes comparatively to some that are stronger, yet in respect of ceremony, which is but a rudiment of the law, the weakest Christian hath thrown off the robes of his minority, and is a perfect man, as to legal rites. What children's food there is in the gospel we know to be no other than the "sincerity of the word, that they may grow thereby." But is here the utmost of your out- braving the service of God? No. Ye have been bold, not to set your threshold by his threshold, or your posts by his posts; but your sacrament, your sign, call it what you will, by his sacrament, baptizing the Christian infant with a solemn sprinkle, and unbaptizing for your own part with a profane and impious forefinger; as if when ye had laid the purifying element upon his forehead, ye meant to cancel and cross it out again with a character not of God's bidding. O but the innocence of these ceremonies! O rather the sottish absurdity of this excuse. What could be more innocent than the washing of a cup, a glass, or hands, before meat, and that under the law, when so many washings were commanded, and by long tradition? yet our Saviour detested their customs, though never so seeming harmless, and charges them severely, that they had transgressed the commandments of God by their traditions, and worshipped him in vain. How much more then must these, and much grosser ceremonies now in force, delude the end of Christ's coming in the flesh against the flesh, and stifle the sincerity of our new covenant, which hath bound us to forsake all carnal pride and wisdom, especially in matters of religion? Thus we see again how prelaty, sailing in opposition to the main end and power of the gospel, doth not join in that mysterious work of Christ, by lowliness to confound height; by simplicity of doctrine,

the wisdom of the world; but contrariwise hath made itself high in the world and the flesh, to vanquish things by the world accounted low, and made itself wise in tradition and fleshly ceremony, to confound the purity of doctrine which is the wisdom of God.

CHAPTER III.

That prelatical Jurisdiction opposeth the Reason and End of the Gospel and of State.

THE third and last consideration remains, whether the prelates in their function do work according to the gospel, practising to subdue the mighty things of this world by things weak, which St. Paul hath set forth to be the power and excellence of the gospel; or whether in more likelihood they band themselves with the prevalent things of this world, to overrun the weak things which Christ hath made choice to work by: and this will soonest be discerned by the course of their jurisdiction. But here again I find my thoughts almost in suspense betwixt yea and no, and am nigh turning mine eye which way I may best retire, and not proceed in this subject, blaming the ardency of my mind that fixed me too attentively to come thus far. For truth, I know not how, hath this unhappiness fatal to her, ere she can come to the trial and inspection of the understanding; being to pass through many little wards and limits of the several affections and desires, she cannot shift it, but must put on such colors and attire as those pathetic handmaids of the soul please to lead her in to their queen: and if she find so much favor with them, they let her pass in her own likeness; if not, they bring her into the presence habited and colored like a notorious falsehood. And contrary, when any falsehood comes that way, if they like the errand she brings, they are so artful to counterfeit the very shape and visage of truth, that the understanding not being able to discern the fucus which these enchantresses with such cunning have laid upon the feature sometimes of truth, sometimes of falsehood interchangeably, sentences for the most part one for the other at the first blush, according to the subtle imposture of these sensual mistresses, that keep the ports and passages between her and the object. So that were it not for leaving imperfect that which is already said, I should go near to relinquish that which is to follow. And because I see that most men, as it happens in this world, either weakly or falsely principled, what through ignorance, and what through custom of licence, both in discourse and writing, by what hath been of late written in vulgar, have not seemed to attain the decision of this point: I shall likewise assay those wily arbitresses who in most men have, as was heard, the sole ushering of truth and falsehood between the sense and the soul, with what loyalty they will use me in convoying this truth to my understanding; the rather for that, by as much acquaintance as I can obtain with them, I do not find them engaged either one way or other. Concerning therefore ecclesial jurisdiction, I find still more controversy, who should administer it, than diligent inquiry made to learn what it is: for had the pains been taken to search out that, it had been long ago enrolled to be nothing else but a pure tyrannical forgery of the prelates; and that jurisdictive power in the church there ought to be none at all. It cannot be conceived that what men now call jurisdiction in the church, should be other thing than a Christian censorship; and therefore is it most commonly and truly named ecclesiastical censure. Now if the Roman censor, a civil function, to that severe assize of surveying and controlling the privatest and slyest manners of all men and all degrees, had no jurisdiction, no courts of plea or indictment, no punitive force annexed; whether it were that to this manner of correction the entanglement of suits was improper, or that the notice of those upright inquisitors extended to such the most covert and spirituous vices as would slip easily between the wider and more material grasp of law or that it stood more with the majesty of that office to have no other sergeants or maces about them but those invisible ones of terror and shame; or, lastly, were it their fear, lest the greatness of this authority and honor, armed with jurisdiction, might step with ease into a tyranny: in all these respects, with much more reason undoubtedly ought the censure of the church be quite divested and disentailed of all jurisdiction whatsoever. For if the course of judicature to a political

censorship seem either too tedious, or too contentious, much more may it to the discipline of church, whose definitive decrees are to be speedy, but the execution of rigor slow, contrary to what in legal proceedings is most usual; and by how much the less contentious it is, by so much will it be the more Christian. And if the Censor, in his moral episcopy being to judge most in matters not answerable by writ or action, could not use an instrument so gross and bodily as jurisdiction is, how can the minister of gospel manage the corpulent and secular trial of bill and process in things merely spiritual? Or could that Roman office, without this juridical sword or saw, strike such a reverence of itself into the most undaunted hearts, as with one single dash of ignominy to put all the senate and knighthood of Rome into a tremble? Surely much rather might the heavenly ministry of the evangel bind herself about with far more piercing beams of majesty and awe, by wanting the beggarly help of halings and amercements in the use of her powerful keys. For when the church without temporal support is able to do her great works upon the unforced obedience of men, it argues a divinity about her. But when she thinks to credit and better her spiritual efficacy, and to win herself respect and dread by strutting in the false vizard of worldly authority, it is evident that God is not there, but that her apostolic virtue is departed from her, and hath left her keycold; which she perceiving as in a decayed nature, seeks to the outward fomentations and chafings of worldly help, and external flourishes, to fetch, if it be possible, some motion into her extreme parts, or to hatch a counterfeit life with the crafty and artificial heat of jurisdiction. But it is observable, that so long as the church, in true imitation of Christ, can be content to ride upon an ass, carrying herself and her government along in a mean and simple guise, she may be, as he is, a lion of the tribe of Judah; and in her humility all men with loud hosannas will confess her greatness. But when, despising the mighty operation of the Spirit by the weak things of this world, she thinks to make herself bigger and more considerable, by using the way of civil force and jurisdiction, as she sits upon this lion she changes into an ass, and instead of hosannas every man pelts her with stones and dirt. Lastly, if the wisdom of the Romans feared to commit jurisdiction to an office of so high esteem and dread as was the censor's, we may see what a solecism in the art of policy it hath been, all this while through Christendom to give jurisdiction to ecclesiastical censure. For that strength, joined with religion, abused and pretended to ambitious ends, must of necessity breed the heaviest and most quelling tyranny not only upon the necks, but even to the souls of men: which if Christian Rome had been so cautelous to prevent in her church, as pagan Rome was in her state, we had not had such a lamentable experience thereof as now we have from thence upon all Christendom. For although I said before, that the church coveting to ride upon the lionly form of jurisdiction, makes a transformation of herself into an ass, and becomes despicable, that is, to those whom God hath enlightened with true knowledge; but where they remain yet in the reliques of superstition, this is the extremity of their bondage and blindness, that while they think they do obeisance to the lordly visage of a lion, they do it to an ass, that through the just judgment of God is permitted to play the dragon among them because of their wilful stupidity. And let England here well rub her eyes, lest by leaving jurisdiction and church censure to the same persons, now that God hath been so long medicining her eyesight, she do not with her over-politic fetches mar all, and bring herself back again to worship this ass bestriding a lion. Having hitherto explained, that to ecclesiastical censure no jurisdictive power can be added, without a childish and dangerous oversight in polity, and a pernicious contradiction in evangelic discipline, as anon more fully, it will be next to declare wherein the true reason and force of church censure consists, which by then it shall be laid open to the root; so little is it that I fear lest any crookedness, any wrinkle or spot should be found in presbyterial government, that if Bodin, the famous French writer, though a papist, yet affirms that the commonwealth which maintains this discipline will certainly flourish in virtue and piety I dare assure myself, that every true protestant will admire the integrity, the uprightness, the divine and gracious purposes

thereof, and even for the reason of it so coherent with the doctrine of the gospel, besides the evidence of command in Scripture, will confess it to be the only true church government; and that, contrary to the whole end and mystery of Christ's coming in the flesh, a false appearance of the same is exercised by prelaty. But because some count it rigorous, and that hereby men shall be liable to a double punishment, I will begin somewhat higher, and speak of punishment; which, as it is an evil, I esteem to be of two sorts, or rather two degrees only, a reprobate conscience in this life, and hell in the other world. Whatever else men call punishment or censure, is not properly an evil, so it be not an illegal violence, but a saving medicine ordained of God both for the public and private good of man; who consisting of two parts, the inward and the outward, was by the eternal Providence left under two sorts of cure, the church and the magistrate. The magistrate hath only to deal with the outward part, I mean not of the body alone, but of the mind in all her outward acts, which in scripture is called the outward man. So that it would be helpful to us if we might borrow such authority as the rhetoricians by patent may give us, with a kind of Promethean skill to shape and fashion this outward man into the similitude of a body, and set him visible before us; imagining the inner man only as the soul. Thus then the civil magistrate looking only upon the outward man, (I say as a magistrate, for what he doth further, he doth it as a member of the church,) if he find in his complexion, skin, or outward temperature the signs and marks, or in his doings the effects of injustice, rapine, lust, cruelty, or the like, sometimes he shuts up as in frenetick or infectious diseases; or confines within doors, as in every sickly estate. Sometimes he shaves by penalty or mulct, or else to cool and take down those luxuriant humors which wealth and excess have caused to abound. Otherwhiles he sears, he cauterizes, he scarifies, lets blood; and finally, for utmost remedy cuts off. The patients, which most an-end are brought into his hospital, are such as are far gone, and beside themselves, (unless they be falsely accused,) so that force is necessary to tame and quiet them in their unruly fits, before they can be made capable of a more human cure. His general end is the outward peace and welfare of the commonwealth, and civil happiness in this life. His particular end in every man is, by the infliction of pain, damage, and disgrace, that the senses and common perceivance might carry this message to the soul within, that it is neither easeful, profitable, nor praiseworthy in this life to do evil. Which must needs tend to the good of man, whether he be to live or die; and be undoubtedly the first means to a natural man, especially an offender, which might open his eyes to a higher consideration of good and evil, as it is taught in religion. This is seen in the often penitence of those that suffer, who, had they escaped, had gone on sinning to an immeasurable heap, which is one of the extremest punishments. And this is all that the civil magistrate, as so being, confers to the healing of man's mind, working only by terrifying plasters upon the rind and orifice of the sore; and by all outward appliances, as the logicians say, a posteriori, at the effect, and not from the cause; not once touching the inward bed of corruption, and that hectic disposition to evil, the source of all vice and obliquity against the rule of law. Which how insufficient it is to cure the soul of man, we cannot better guess than by the art of bodily physic. Therefore God, to the intent of further healing man's depraved mind, to this power of the magistrate, which contents itself with the restraint of evil-doing in the external man, added that which we call censure, to purge it and remove it clean out of the inmost soul. In the beginning this authority seems to have been placed, as all both civil and religious rites once were, only in each father of family; afterwards, among the heathen, in the wise men and philosophers of the age; but so as it was a thing voluntary, and no set government. More distinctly among the Jews, as being God's peculiar people, where the priests, Levites, prophets, and at last the scribes and pharisees, took charge of instructing and overseeing the lives of the people. But in the gospel, which is the straightest and the dearest covenant can be made between God and man, we being now his adopted sons, and nothing fitter for us to think on than to be like him, united to him, and, as he pleases to express it, to

have fellowship with him; it is all necessity that we should expect this blest efficacy of healing our inward man to be ministered to us in a more familiar and effectual method than ever before. God being now no more a judge after the sentence of the law, nor, as it were, a schoolmaster of perishable rites, but a most indulgent father, governing his church as a family of sons in their discreet age; and therefore, in the sweetest and mildest manner of paternal discipline, he hath committed this other office of preserving in healthful constitution the inner man, which may be termed the spirit of the soul, to his spiritual deputy the minister of each congregation; who being best acquainted with his own flock, hath best reason to know all the secretest diseases likely to be there. And look by how much the internal man is more excellent and noble than the external, by so much is his cure more exactly, more thoroughly, and more particularly to be performed. For which cause the Holy Ghost by the apostles, joined to the minister, as assistant in this great office, sometimes a certain number of grave and faithful brethren, (for neither doth the physician do all in restoring his patient; he prescribes, another prepares the medicine; some tend, some watch, some visit,) much more may a minister partly not see all, partly err as a man: besides, that nothing can be more for the mutual honor and love of the people to their pastor and his to them, than when in select numbers and courses they are seen partaking and doing reverence to the holy duties of discipline by their serviceable and solemn presence, and receiving honor again from their employment, not now any more to be separated in the church by veils and partitions, as laics and unclean, but admitted to wait upon the tabernacle as the rightful clergy of Christ, a chosen generation, a royal priesthood, to offer up spiritual sacrifice in that meet place, to which God and the congregation shall call and assign them. And this all Christians ought to know, that the title of clergy St. Peter gave to all God's people, till pope Higinus and the succeeding prelates took it from them, appropriating that name to themselves and their priests only; and condemning the rest of God's inheritance to an injurious and alienate condition of laity, they separated from them by local partitions in churches, through their gross ignorance and pride imitating the old temple, and excluded the members of Christ from the property of being members, the bearing of orderly and fit offices in the ecclesiastical body; as if they had meant to sew up that Jewish veil, which Christ by his death on the cross rent in sunder. Although these usurpers could not so presently overmaster the liberties and lawful titles of God's freeborn church; but that Origen, being yet a layman, expounded the scriptures publicly, and was therein defended by Alexander of Jerusalem, and Theoctistus of Cæsarea, producing in his behalf divers examples, that the privilege of teaching was anciently permitted to many worthy laymen: and Cyprian in his epistles professes he will do nothing without the advice and assent of his assistant laics. Neither did the first Nicene council, as great and learned as it was, think it any robbery to receive in, and require the help and presence of many learned lay-brethren, as they were then called. Many other authorities to confirm this assertion, both out of scripture and the writings of next antiquity, Golartius hath collected in his notes upon Cyprian; whereby it will be evident that the laity, not only by apostolic permission, but by consent of many the ancientest prelates, did participate in church offices as much as is desired any lay-elder should now do. Sometimes also not the elders alone, but the whole body of the church is interested in the work of discipline, as oft as public satisfaction is given by those that have given public scandal. Not to speak now of her right in elections. But another reason there is in it, which though religion did not commend to us, yet moral and civil prudence could not but extol. It was thought of old in philosophy, that shame, or to call it better, the reverence of our elders, our brethren, and friends, was the greatest incitement to virtuous deeds, and the greatest dissuasion from unworthy attempts that might be. Hence we may read in the Iliad, where Hector being wished to retire from the battle, many of his forces being routed, makes answer, that he durst not for shame, lest the Trojan knights and dames should think he did ignobly. And certain it is, that whereas terror is thought such a great stickler in a common-

wealth, honorable shame is a far greater, and has more reason: for where shame is, there is fear; but where fear is, there is not presently shame. And if anything may be done to inbreed in us this generous and Christianly reverence one of another, the very nurse and guardian of piety and virtue, it cannot sooner be than by such a discipline in the church, as may use us to have in awe the assemblies of the faithful, and to count it a thing most grievous, next to the grieving of God's Spirit, to offend those whom he hath put in authority, as a healing superintendence over our lives and behaviors, both to our own happiness, and that we may not give offence to good men, who, without amends by us made, dare not, against God's command, hold communion with us in holy things. And this will be accompanied with a religious dread of being outcast from the company of saints, and from the fatherly protection of God in his church, to consort with the devil and his angels. But there is yet a more ingenuous and noble degree of honest shame, or, call it, if you will, an esteem, whereby men bear an inward reverence toward their own persons. And if the love of God, as a fire sent from heaven to be ever kept alive upon the altar of our hearts, be the first principle of all godly and virtuous actions in men, this pious and just honoring of ourselves is the second, and may be thought as the radical moisture and fountain-head, whence every laudable and worthy enterprise issues forth. And although I have given it the name of a liquid thing, yet it is not incontinent to bound itself, as humid things are, but hath in it a most restraining and powerful abstinence to start back, and glob itself upward from the mixture of any ungenerous and unbeseeming motion, or any soil wherewith it may peril to stain itself. Something I confess it is to be ashamed of evil-doing in the presence of any; and to reverence the opinion and the countenance of a good man rather than a bad, fearing most in his sight to offend, goes so far as almost to be virtuous; yet this is but still the fear of infamy, and many such, when they find themselves alone, saving their reputation, will compound with other scruples, and come to a close treaty with their dearer vices in secret. But he that holds himself in reverence and due esteem, both for the dignity of God's image upon him, and for the price of his redemption, which he thinks is visibly marked upon his forehead, accounts himself both a fit person to do the noblest and godliest deeds, and much better worth than to deject and defile, with such a debasement, and such a pollution as sin is, himself so highly ransomed and ennobled to a new friendship and filial relation with God. Nor can he fear so much the offence and reproach of others, as he dreads and would blush at the reflection of his own severe and modest eye upon himself, if it should see him doing or imagining that which is sinful, though in the deepest secrecy. How shall a man know to do himself this right, how to perform this honorable duty of estimation and respect towards his own soul and body? which way will lead him best to this hill-top of sanctity and goodness, above which there is no higher ascent but to the love of God, which from this self-pious regard cannot be asunder? No better way doubtless, than to let him duly understand, that as he is called by the high calling of God, to be holy and pure, so is he by the same appointment ordained, and by the church's call admitted, to such offices of discipline in the church, to which his own spiritual gifts, by the example of apostolic institution, have authorized him. For we have learned that the scornful term of laic, the consecrating of temples, carpets, and table-cloths, the railing in of a repugnant and contradictive mount Sinai in the gospel, as if the touch of a lay-christian, who is nevertheless God's living temple, could profane dead judaisms, the exclusion of Christ's people from the offices of holy discipline through the pride of a usurping clergy, causes the rest to have an unworthy and abject opinion of themselves, to approach to holy duties with a slavish fear, and to unholy doings with a familiar boldness. For seeing such a wide and terrible distance between religious things and themselves, and that in respect of a wooden table, and the perimeter of holy ground about it, a flagon pot, and a linen corporal, the priest esteems their layships unhallowed and unclean, they fear religion with such a fear as loves not, and think the purity of the gospel too pure for them, and that any uncleanness is more suitable to their unconsecrated estate. But when every good Christian,

thoroughly acquainted with all those glorious privileges of sanctification and adoption, which render him more sacred than any dedicated altar or element, shall be restored to his right in the church, and not excluded from such place of spiritual government, as his Christian abilities, and his approved good life in the eye and testimony of the church shall prefer him to, this and nothing sooner will open his eyes to a wise and true valuation of himself, (which is so requisite and high a point of Christianity,) and will stir him up to walk worthy the honorable and grave employment wherewith God and the church hath dignified him; not fearing lest he should meet with some outward holy thing in religion, which his lay-touch or presence might profane; but lest something unholy from within his own heart should dishonor and profane in himself that priestly unction and clergy-right whereto Christ hath entitled him. Then would the congregation of the Lord soon recover the true likeness and visage of what she is indeed, a holy generation, a royal priesthood, a saintly communion, the household and city of God. And this I hold to be another considerable reason why the functions of church government ought to be free and open to any Christian man, though never so laic, if his capacity, his faith, and prudent demeanor, commend him. And this the apostles warrant us to do. But the prelates object, that this will bring profaneness into the church: to whom may be replied, that none have brought that in more than their own irreligious courses, nor more driven holiness out of living into lifeless things. For whereas God, who hath cleansed every beast and creeping worm, would not suffer St. Peter to call them common or unclean, the prelate bishops, in their printed orders hung up in churches, have proclaimed the best of creatures, mankind, so unpurified and contagious, that for him to lay his hat or his garment upon the chancel table, they have defined it no less heinous, in express words, than to profane the table of the Lord. And thus have they by their Canaanitish doctrine, (for that which was to the Jew but Jewish, is to the Christian no better than Canaanitish,) thus have they made common and unclean, thus have they made profane that nature which God hath not only cleansed, but Christ also hath assumed.

And now that the equity and just reason is so perspicuous, why in ecclesiastic censure the assistance should be added of such as whom not the vile odor of gain and fees, (forbid it, God, and blow it with a whirlwind out of our land!) but charity, neighborhood, and duty to church government hath called together, where could a wise man wish a more equal, gratuitous, and meek examination of any offence, that he might happen to commit against Christianity, than here? Would he prefer those proud simoniacal courts? Thus therefore the minister assisted attends his heavenly and spiritual cure: where we shall see him both in the course of his proceeding, and first in the excellence of his end, from the magistrate far different, and not more different than excelling. His end is to recover all that is of man, both soul and body, to an everlasting health; and yet as for worldly happiness, which is the proper sphere wherein the magistrate cannot but confine his motion without a hideous exorbitancy from law, so little aims the minister, as his intended scope, to procure the much prosperity of this life, that ofttimes he may have cause to wish much of it away, as a diet puffing up the soul with a slimy fleshiness, and weakening her principal organic parts. Two heads of evil he has to cope with, ignorance and malice. Against the former he provides the daily manna of incorruptible doctrine, not at those set meals only in public, but as oft as he shall know that each infirmity or constitution requires. Against the latter with all the branches thereof, not meddling with that restraining and styptic surgery, which the law uses, not indeed against the malady, but against the eruptions, and outermost effects thereof; he on the contrary, beginning at the prime causes and roots of the disease, sends in those two divine ingredients of most cleansing power to the soul, admonition and reproof; besides which two there is no drug or antidote that can reach to purge the mind, and without which all other experiments are but vain, unless by accident. And he that will not let these pass into him, though he be the greatest king, as Plato affirms, must be thought to remain impure within, and unknowing of those things wherein his pureness and his knowledge should most appear. As soon therefore as it

may be discerned that the Christian patient, by feeding otherwhere on meats not allowable, but of evil juice, hath disordered his diet, and spread an ill-humor through his veins, immediately disposing to a sickness, the minister, as being much nearer both in eye and duty than the magistrate, speeds him betimes to overtake that diffused malignance with some gentle potion of admonishment; or if aught be obstructed, puts in his opening and discussive confections. This not succeeding after once or twice, or oftener, in the presence of two or three his faithful brethren appointed thereto, he advises him to be more careful of his dearest health, and what it is that he so rashly hath let down into the divine vessel of his soul, God's temple. If this obtain not, he then, with the counsel of more assistants, who are informed of what diligence hath been already used, with more speedy remedies lays nearer siege to the entrenched causes of his distemper, not sparing such fervent and well-aimed reproofs as may best give him to see the dangerous estate wherein he is. To this also his brethren and friends entreat, exhort, adjure; and all these endeavors, as there is hope left, are more or less repeated. But if neither the regard of himself, nor the reverence of his elders and friends prevail with him to leave his vicious appetite, then as the time urges, such engines of terror God hath given into the hand of his minister, as to search the tenderest angles of the heart: one while he shakes his stubbornness with racking convulsions nigh despair; otherwhiles with deadly corrosives he gripes the very roots of his faulty liver to bring him to life through the entry of death. Hereto the whole church beseech him, beg of him, deplore him, pray for him. After all this performed with what patience and attendance is possible, and no relenting on his part, having done the utmost of their cure, in the name of God and of the church they dissolve their fellowship with him, and holding forth the dreadful sponge of excommunion, pronounce him wiped out of the list of God's inheritance, and in the custody of Satan till he repent. Which horrid sentence, though it touch neither life nor limb, nor any worldly possession, yet has it such a penetrating force, that swifter than any chemical sulphur, or that lightning which harms not the skin, and rifles the entrails, it scorches the inmost soul. Yet even this terrible denouncement is left to the church for no other cause but to be as a rough and vehement cleansing medicine, where the malady is obdurate, a mortifying to life, a kind of saving by undoing. And it may be truly said, that as the mercies of wicked men are cruelties, so the cruelties of the church are mercies. For if repentance sent from Heaven meet this lost wanderer, and draw him out of that steep journey wherein he was hasting towards destruction, to come and reconcile to the church, if he bring with him his bill of health, and that he is now clear of infection, and of no danger to the other sheep; then with incredible expressions of joy all his brethren receive him, and set before him those perfumed banquets of Christian consolation; with precious ointments bathing and fomenting the old, and now to be forgotten stripes, which terror and shame had inflicted; and thus with heavenly solaces they cheer up his humble remorse, till he regain his first health and felicity. This is the approved way, which the gospel prescribes, these are the "spiritual weapons of holy censure, and ministerial warfare, not carnal, but mighty through God to the pulling down of strong holds, casting down imaginations, and every high thing that exalteth itself against the knowledge of God, and bringing into captivity every thought to the obedience of Christ." What could be done more for the healing and reclaiming that divine particle of God's breathing, the soul? and what could be done less? he that would hide his faults from such a wholesome curing as this, and count it a twofold punishment, as some do, is like a man that having foul diseases about him, perishes for shame, and the fear he has of a rigorous incision to come upon his flesh. We shall be able by this time to discern whether prelatical jurisdiction be contrary to the gospel or no. First, therefore, the government of the gospel being economical and paternal, that is, of such a family where there be no servants, but all sons in obedience, not in servility, as cannot be denied by him that lives but within the sound of scripture; how can the prelates justify to have turned the fatherly orders of Christ's household, the blessed meekness of his lowly roof, those ever-open and inviting doors of his dwellinghouse, which delight to be frequented with only filial accesses; how can they justify to have turned these domestic privileges into the bar of a proud judicial court, where fees and clamors keep shop and drive a trade, where bribery and corruption solicits, paltering the free and moneyless power of discipline with a carnal satisfaction by the purse? Contrition, humiliation, confession, the very sighs of a repentant spirit, are there sold by the penny. That undeflowered and unblemishable simplicity of the gospel, not she herself, for that could never be, but a false-whited, a lawny resemblance of her, like that airborn Helena in the fables, made by the sorcery of prelates, instead of calling her disciples from the receipt of custom, is now turned publican herself; and gives up her body to a mercenary whoredom under those fornicated arches, which she calls God's house, and in the sight of those her altars, which she hath set up to be adored, makes merchandise of the bodies and souls of men. Rejecting purgatory for no other reason, as it seems, than because her greediness cannot defer, but had rather use the utmost extortion of redeemed penances in this life. But because these matters could not be thus carried without a begged and borrowed force from worldly authority, therefore prelaty, slighting the deliberate and chosen council of Christ in his spiritual government, whose glory is in the weakness of fleshly things, to tread upon the crest of the world's pride and violence by the power of spiritual ordinances, hath on the contrary made these her friends and champions, which are Christ's enemies in this his high design, smothering and extinguishing the spiritual force of his bodily weakness in the discipline of his church with the boisterous and carnal tyranny of an undue, unlawful, and ungospel-like jurisdiction. And thus prelaty, both in her fleshly supportments, in her carnal doctrine of ceremony and tradition, in her violent and secular power, going quite counter to the prime end of Christ's coming in the flesh, that is, to reveal his truth, his glory, and his might, in a clean contrary manner than prelaty seeks to do, thwarting and defeating the great mystery of God; I do not conclude that prelaty is antichristian, for what need I? the things themselves conclude it. Yet if such like practices, and not many worse than these of our prelates, in that great darkness of the Roman church, have not exempted both her and her present members from being judged to be antichristian in all orthodoxal esteem; I cannot think but that it is the absolute voice of truth and all her children to pronounce this prelaty, and these her dark deeds in the midst of this great light wherein we live, to be more antichristian than antichrist himself.

THE CONCLUSION.

The Mischief that Prelaty does in the State.

I ADD one thing more to those great ones that are so fond of prelaty: this is certain, that the gospel being the hidden might of Christ, as hath been heard, hath ever a victorious power joined with it, like him in the Revelation that went forth on the white horse with his bow and his crown, conquering and to conquer. If we let the angel of the gospel ride on his own way, he does his proper business, conquering the high thoughts, and the proud reasonings of the flesh, and brings them under to give obedience to Christ with the salvation of many souls. But if ye turn him out of his road, and in a manner force him to express his irresistible power by a doctrine of carnal might, as prelaty is, he will use that fleshly strength, which ye put into his hands, to subdue your spirits by a servile and blind superstition; and that again shall hold such dominion over your captive minds, as returning with an insatiate greediness and force upon your worldly wealth and power, wherewith to deck and magnify herself, and her false worships, she shall spoil and havoc your estates, disturb your ease, diminish your honor, enthral your liberty under the swelling mood of a proud clergy, who will not serve or feed your souls with spiritual food; look not for it, they have not wherewithal, or if they had, it is not in their purpose. But when they have glutted their ingrateful bodies, at least, if it be possible that those open sepulchres should ever be glutted, and when they have stuffed their idolish temples with the wasteful pillage of your estates, will they yet have any

compassion upon you, and that poor pittance which they have left you; will they be but so good to you as that ravisher was to his sister, when he had used her at his pleasure; will they but only hate ye, and so turn ye loose? No, they will not, lords and commons, they will not favor ye so much. What will they do then, in the name of God and saints, what will these manhaters yet with more despite and mischief do? I will tell ye, or at least remember ye: (for most of ye know it already:) that they may want nothing to make them true merchants of Babylon, as they have done to your souls, they will sell your bodies, your wives, your children, your liberties, your parliaments, all these things; and if there be ought else dearer than these, they will sell at an outcry in their pulpits to the arbitrary and illegal dispose of any one that may hereafter be called a king, whose mind shall serve him to listen to their bargain. And by their corrupt and servile doctrines boring our ears to an everlasting slavery, as they have done hitherto, so will they yet do their best to repeal and erase every line and clause of both our great charters. Nor is this only what they will do, but what they hold as the main reason and mystery of their advancement that they must do; be the prince never so just and equal to his subjects, yet such are their malicious and depraved eyes, that they so look on him, and so understand him, as if he required no other gratitude or piece of service from them than this. And indeed they stand so opportunely for the disturbing or the destroying of a state, being a knot of creatures, whose dignities, means, and preferments have no foundation in the gospel, as they themselves acknowledge, but only in the prince's favor, and to continue so long to them, as by pleasing him they shall deserve: whence it must needs be they should bend all their intentions and services to no other ends but to his, that if it should happen that a tyrant (God turn such a scourge from us to our enemies) should come to grasp the sceptre, here were his spearmen and his lances, here were his firelocks ready, he should need no other pretorian band nor pensionary than these, if they could once with their perfidious preachments awe the people. For although the prelates in time of popery were sometimes

friendly enough to Magna Charta, it was because they stood upon their own bottom,
without their main dependence on the royal
nod: but now being well acquainted that the
protestant religion, if she will reform herself
rightly by the scriptures, must undress them
of all their gilded vanities, and reduce them
as they were at first to the lowly and equal
order of presbyters, they know it concerns
them nearly to study the times more than the
text, and to lift up their eyes to the hills of
the court, from whence only comes their
help; but if their pride grow weary of this
crouching and observance, as ere long it
would, and that yet their minds climb still
to a higher ascent of worldly honor, this only
refuge can remain to them, that they must
of necessity contrive to bring themselves and
us back again to the pope's supremacy; and
this we see they had by fair degrees of late
been doing. These be the two fair supporters
between which the strength of prelaty is
borne up, either of inducing tyranny, or of
reducing popery. Hence also we may judge
that prelaty is mere falsehood. For the property of truth is, where she is publicly taught
to unyoke and set free the minds and spirits
of a nation first from the thraldom of sin and
superstition, after which all honest and legal
freedom of civil life cannot be long absent;
but prelaty, whom the tyrant custom begot,
a natural tyrant in religion, and in state the
agent and minister of tyranny, seems to have
had this fatal gift in her nativity, like another Midas, that whatsoever she should
touch or come near either in ecclesial or political government, it should turn, not to gold,
though she for her part could wish it, but to
the dross and scum of slavery, breeding and
settling both in the bodies and the souls of
all such as do not in time, with the sovereign
treacle of sound doctrine, provide to fortify
their hearts against her hierarchy. The service of God, who is truth, her liturgy confesses
to be perfect freedom; but her works and her
opinions declare, that the service of prelaty
is perfect slavery, and by consequence perfect falsehood. Which makes me wonder much
that many of the gentry, studious men as I
hear, should engage themselves to write and
speak publicly in her defence; but that I believe their honest and ingenuous natures coming to the universities to store themselves
with good and solid learning, and there unfortunately fed with nothing else but the
scragged and thorny lectures of monkish and
miserable sophistry, were sent home again
with such a scholastical bur in their throats,
as hath stopped and hindered all true and generous philosophy from entering, cracked their
voices for ever with metaphysical gargar-
isms, and hath made them admire a sort of
formal outside men prelatically addicted,
whose unchastened and unwrought minds
never yet initiated or subdued under the
true lore of religion or moral virtue, which
two are the best and greatest points of
learning; but either slightly trained up in
a kind of hypocritical and hackney course
of literature to get their living by, and dazzle the ignorant, or else fondly over-studied
in useless controversies, except those which
they use with all the specious and delusive
subtlety they are able, to defend their prelatical Sparta; having a gospel and church
government set before their eyes, as a fair
field wherein they might exercise the greatest
virtues and the greatest deeds of Christian
authority, in mean fortunes and little furniture of this world; (which even the sage
heathen writers, and those old Fabritii and
Curii well knew to be a manner of working,
than which nothing could liken a mortal
man more to God, who delights most to
work from within himself, and not by the
heavy luggage of corporeal instruments;) they
understand it not, and think no such matter, but admire and dote upon worldly riches
and honors, with an easy and intemperate
life, to the bane of Christianity: yea, they
and their seminaries shame not to profess,
to petition, and never lin pealing our ears,
that unless we fat them like boars, and
cram them as they list with wealth, with
deaneries and pluralities, with baronies and
stately preferments, all learning and religion
will go underfoot. Which is such a shameless, such a bestial plea, and of that odious
impudence in churchmen, who should be to
us a pattern of temperance and frugal
mediocrity, who should teach us to contemn
this world and the gaudy things thereof, according to the promise which they themselves require from us in baptism, that should
the scripture stand by and be mute, there is
not that sect of philosophers among the

heathen so dissolute, no not Epicurus, nor Aristippus with all his Cyrenaic rout, but would shut his school-doors against such greasy sophisters; not any college of mountebanks, but would think scorn to discover in themselves with such a brazen forehead the outrageous desire of filthy lucre. Which the prelates make so little conscience of, that they are ready to fight, and if it lay in their power, to massacre all good Christians under the names of horrible schismatics, for only finding fault with their temporal dignities, their unconscionable wealth and revenues, their cruel authority over their brethren, that labor in the word, while they snore in their luxurious excess: openly proclaiming themselves now in the sight of all men, to be those which for a while they sought to cover under sheep's clothing, ravenous and savage wolves, threatening inroads and bloody incursions upon the flock of Christ, which they took upon them to feed, but now claim to devour as their prey. More like that huge dragon of Egypt, breathing out waste and desolation to the land, unless he were daily fattened with virgin's blood. Him our old patron St. George by his matchless valor slew, as the prelate of the garter that reads his collect can tell. And if our princes and knights will imitate the fame of that old champion, as by their order of knighthood solemnly taken they vow, far be it that they should uphold and side with this English dragon; but rather to do as indeed their oath binds them, they should make it their knightly adventure to pursue and vanquish this mighty sail-winged monster, that menaces to swallow up the land, unless her bottomless gorge may be satisfied with the blood of the king's daughter, the church; and may, as she was wont, fill her dark and infamous den with the bones of the saints. Nor will any one have reason to think this as too incredible or too tragical to be spoken of prelaty, if he consider well from what a mass of slime and mud the slothful, the covetous, and ambitious hopes of church-promotions and fat bishoprics, she is bred up and nuzzled in, like a great Python, from her youth, to prove the general poison both of doctrine and good discipline in the land. For certainly such hopes and such principles of earth as these wherein she welters from a young one, are the immediate generation both of a slavish and tyrannous life to follow, and a pestiferous contagion to the whole kingdom, till like that fen-born serpent she be shot to death with the darts of the sun, the pure and powerful beams of God's word. And this may serve to describe to us in part what prelaty hath been, and what, if she stand, she is like to be toward the whole body of people in England. Now that it may appear how she is not such a kind of evil as hath any good or use in it, which many evils have, but a distilled quintessence, a pure elixir of mischief, pestilent alike to all, I shall show briefly, ere I conclude, that the prelates, as they are to the subjects a calamity, so are they the greatest underminers and betrayers of the monarch, to whom they seem to be most favorable. I cannot better liken the state and person of a king than to that mighty Nazarite Samson; who being disciplined from his birth in the precepts and the practice of temperance and sobriety, without the strong drink of injurious and excessive desires, grows up to a noble strength and perfection with those his illustrious and sunny locks, the laws, waving and curling about his godlike shoulders. And while he keeps them about him undiminished and unshorn, he may with the jawbone of an ass, that is, with the word of his meanest officer, suppress and put to confusion thousands of those that rise against his just power. But laying down his head among the strumpet flatteries of prelates, while he sleeps and thinks no harm, they wickedly shaving off all those bright and weighty tresses of his laws, and just prerogatives, which were his ornament and strength, deliver him over to indirect and violent counsels, which, as those Philistines, put out the fair and far-sighted eyes of his natural discerning, and make him grind in the prison-house of their sinister ends and practices upon him: till he, knowing this prelatical razor to have bereft him of his wonted might, nourish again his puissant hair, the golden beams of law and right; and they sternly shook, thunder with ruin upon the heads of those his evil counsellors, but not without great affliction to himself. This is the sum of their loyal service to kings; yet these are the men that still cry, The king, the king, the Lord's anointed! We grant it; and wonder how they came to light upon anything so true; and wonder more, if kings be the Lord's anointed, how they dare thus oil over and besmear so holy an unction with the corrupt and putrid ointment of their base flatteries, which while they smooth the skin, strike inward and envenom the lifeblood. What fidelity kings can expect from prelates, both examples past, and our present experience of their doings at this day, whereon is grounded all that hath been said, may suffice to inform us. And if they be such clippers of regal power, and shavers of the laws, how they stand affected to the lawgiving parliament, yourselves, worthy peers and commons, can best testify; the current of whose glorious and immortal actions hath been only opposed by the obscure and pernicious designs of the prelates, until their insolence broke out to such a bold affront, as hath justly immured their haughty looks within strong walls. Nor have they done anything of late with more diligence, than to hinder or break the happy assembling of parliaments, however needful to repair the shattered and disjointed frame of the commonwealth; or if they cannot do this, to cross, to disenable, and traduce all parliamentary proceedings. And this, if nothing else, plainly accuses them to be no lawful members of the house, if they thus perpetually mutiny against their own body. And though they pretend, like Solomon's harlot, that they have right thereto, by the same judgment that Solomon gave, it cannot belong to them, whenas it is not only their assent, but their endeavor continually to divide parliaments in twain; and not only by dividing, but by all other means to abolish and destroy the free use of them to all posterity. For the which, and for all their former misdeeds, whereof this book and many volumes more cannot contain the moiety, I shall move ye, lords, in the behalf I dare say of many thousand good Christians, to let your justice and speedy sentence pass against this great malefactor, prelaty. And yet in the midst of rigor I would beseech ye to think of mercy; and such a mercy, (I fear I shall overshoot with a desire to save this falling prelaty,) such a mercy (if I may venture to say it) as may exceed that which for only ten righteous persons would have saved Sodom. Not that I dare advise ye to contend with God, whether he or you shall be more merciful, but in your wise esteems to balance the offences of those peccant cities with these enormous riots of ungodly misrule, that prelaty hath wrought both in the church of Christ, and in the state of this kingdom. And if ye think ye may with a pious presumption strive to go beyond God in mercy, I shall not be one now that would dissuade ye. Though God for less than ten just persons would not spare Sodom, yet if you can find, after due search, but only one good thing in prelaty, either to religion or civil government, to king or parliament, to prince or people, to law, liberty, wealth, or learning, spare her, let her live, let her spread among ye, till with her shadow all your dignities and honors, and all the glory of the land be darkened and obscured. But on the contrary, if she be found to be malignant, hostile, destructive to all these, as nothing can be surer, then let your severe and impartial doom imitate the divine vengeance; rain down your punishing force upon this godless and oppressing government, and bring such a dead sea of subversion upon her, that she may never in this land rise more to afflict the holy reformed church, and the elect people of God.

AN

APOLOGY FOR SMECTYMNUUS

[The text is that of the first edition, 1642.]

IF, readers, to that same great difficulty of well-doing what we certainly know, were not added in most men as great a carelessness of knowing what they and others ought to do, we had been long ere this, no doubt but all of us, much farther on our way to some degree of peace and happiness in this kingdom. But since our sinful neglect of practising that which we know to be undoubtedly true and good, hath brought forth among us, through God's just anger, so great a difficulty now to know that which otherwise might be soon learnt, and hath divided us by a controversy of great importance indeed, but of no hard solution, which is the more our punishment; I resolved (of what small moment soever I might be thought) to stand on that side where I saw both the plain authority of scripture leading, and the reason of justice and equity persuading; with this opinion, which esteems it more unlike a Christian to be a cold neuter in the cause of the church, than the law of Solon made it punishable after a sedition in the state.

And because I observe that fear and dull disposition, lukewarmness and sloth, are not seldomer wont to cloak themselves under the affected name of moderation, than true and lively zeal is customably disparaged with the term of indiscretion, bitterness, and choler; I could not to my thinking honor a good cause more from the heart, than by defending it earnestly, as oft as I could judge it to behoove me, notwithstanding any false name that could be invented to wrong or undervalue an honest meaning. Wherein although I have not doubted to single forth more than once such of them as were thought the chief and most nominated opposers on the other side, whom no man else undertook; if I have done well either to be confident of the truth, whose force is best seen against the ablest resistance, or to be jealous and tender of the hurt that might be done among the weaker by the entrapping authority of great names titled to false opinions; or that it be lawful to attribute somewhat to gifts of God's imparting, which I boast not, but thankfully acknowledge, and fear also lest at my certain account they be reckoned to me many rather than few; or if lastly it be but justice not to defraud of due esteem the wearisome labors and studious watchings, wherein I have spent and tired out almost a whole youth, I shall not distrust to be acquitted of presumption: knowing, that if heretofore all ages have received with favor and good acceptance the earliest industry of him that hath been hopeful, it were but hard measure now if the freedom of any timely spirit should be oppressed merely by the big and blunted fame of his elder adversary; and that his sufficiency must be now sentenced, not by pondering the reason he shows, but by calculating the years he brings.

However, as my purpose is not, nor hath been formerly, to look on my adversary abroad, through the deceiving glass of other men's great opinion of him, but at home, where I may find him in the proper light of his own worth, so now against the rancor of an evil tongue, from which I never thought so absurdly, as that I of all men should be exempt, I must be forced to proceed from the unfeigned and diligent inquiry of my own conscience at home, (for better way I know not, readers,) to give a more true account of myself abroad than this modest confuter, as he calls himself, hath given of me. Albeit, that in doing this I shall be sensible of two things which to me will be nothing pleasant; the one is, that not unlikely I shall be thought too much a party in mine own cause, and therein to see least: the other, that I shall be put unwillingly to molest the public view with the vindication of a private name; as if it were worth the while that the people should care whether such a one were thus, or thus. Yet those I entreat who have found the leisure to read that name, however of small repute, unworthily defamed, would be so good and so patient as to hear the same person not unneedfully defended.

I will not deny but that the best apology against false accusers is silence and sufferance, and honest deeds set against dishonest words. And that I could at this time most easily and securely, with the least loss of reputation, use no other defence, I need not despair to win belief; whether I consider both the foolish contriving and ridiculous aiming of these his slanderous bolts, shot so wide of any suspicion to be fastened on me, that I have oft with inward contentment perceived my friends congratulating themselves in my innocence, and my enemies ashamed of their partner's folly: or whether I look at these present times, wherein most men, now scarce permitted the liberty to think over their own concernments, have removed the seat of their thoughts more outward to the expectation of public events: or whether the examples of men, either noble or religious, who have sat down lately with a meek silence and sufferance under many libellous endorsements, may be a rule to others, I might well appease myself to put up any reproaches in such an honorable society of fellow-sufferers, using no other defence.

And were it that slander would be content to make an end where it first fixes, and not seek to cast out the like infamy upon each thing that hath but any relation to the person traduced, I should have pleaded against this confuter by no other advocates than those which I first commended, silence and sufferance, and speaking deeds against faltering words. But when I discerned his intent was not so much to smite at me, as through me to render odious the truth which I had written, and to stain with ignominy that evangelic doctrine which opposes the tradition of prelaty, I conceived myself to be now not as mine own person, but as a member incorporate into that truth whereof I was persuaded, and whereof I had declared openly to be a partaker. Whereupon I thought it my duty, if not to myself, yet to the religious cause I had in hand, not to leave on my garment the least spot or blemish in good name, so long as God should give me to say that which might wipe it off; lest those disgraces which I ought to suffer, if it so befall me, for my religion, through my default religion be made liable to suffer for me. And, whether it might not something reflect upon those reverent men, whose friend I may be thought in writing the Animadversions, was not my last care to consider: if I should rest under these reproaches, having the same common adversary with them, it might be counted small credit for their cause to have found such an assistant, as this babbler hath devised me. What other thing in his book there is of dispute or question, in answering thereto I doubt not to be justified; except there be who will condemn me to have wasted time in throwing down that which could not keep itself up. As for others, who notwithstanding what I can allege have yet decreed to misinterpret the intents of my reply, I suppose they would have found as many causes to have misconceived the reasons of my silence.

To begin, therefore, an Apology for those Animadversions, which I writ against the Remonstrant in defence of Smectymnuus; since the preface, which was purposely set before them, is not thought apologetical enough, it will be best to acquaint ye, readers, before other things, what the meaning was to write them in that manner which I did. For I do not look to be asked wherefore I writ the book, it being no difficulty to answer, that I did it to those ends which the best men propose to themselves when they write; but wherefore in that manner, neglecting the main bulk of all that specious antiquity, which might ˙ stun children, but not men, I chose rather to observe some kind of military advantages, to await him at his foragings, at his waterings, and whenever he felt himself secure, to solace his vein in derision of his more serious opponents.

And here let me have pardon, readers, if the remembrance of that which he hath licensed himself to utter contemptuously of those reverend men, provoke me to do that over again, which some expect I should excuse as too freely done, since I have two provocations—his latest insulting in his short answer, and their final patience. I had no fear, but that the authors of Smectymnuus, to all the show of solidity, which the Remonstrant could bring, were prepared both with skill and purpose to return a sufficing answer, and were able enough to lay the dust and pudder in antiquity, which he and his, out of stratagem, are wont to raise. But when I saw his weak arguments headed with sharp taunts, and that his design was if he could not refute them, yet at least with quips and snapping adages to vapor them out, which they, bent only upon the business, were minded to let pass; by how much I saw them taking little thought for their own injuries, I must confess I took it as my part the less to endure that my respected friends, through their own unnecessary patience, should thus lie at the mercy of a coy flirting style; to be girded with frumps and curtal gibes, by one who makes sentences by the statute, as if all above three inches long were confiscate. To me it seemed an indignity, that whom his whole wisdom could not move from their place, them his impetuous folly should presume to ride over. And if I were more warm than was meet in any passage of that book, which yet I do not yield, I might use therein the patronage of no worse an author than Gregory Nyssen, who mentioning his sharpness against Eunomius in the defence of his brother Basil, holds himself irreprovable in that "it was not for himself, but in the cause of his brother; and in such cases," saith he, "perhaps it is worthier pardon to be angry than to be cooler."

And whereas this confuter taxes the whole discourse of levity, I shall show ye, readers, wheresoever it shall be objected in particular, that I have answered with as little lightness as the Remonstrant hath given example. I have not been so light as the palm of a bishop, which is the lightest thing in the world when he ·brings out his book of ordination: for then, contrary to that which is wont in releasing out of prison, any one that will pay his fees is laid hands on. Another reason, it would not be amiss though the Remonstrant were told, wherefore he was in that unusual manner beleaguered; and this was it, to pluck out of the heads of his admirers the conceit that all who are not prelatical, are gross-headed, thick-witted, illiterate, shallow. Can nothing then but episcopacy teach men to speak good English, to pick and order a set of words judiciously? Must we learn from canons and quaint sermonings, interlined with barbarous Latin, to illumine a period, to wreathe an enthymema with masterous dexterity? I rather incline, as I have heard it observed, that a Jesuit's Italian, when he writes, is ever naught, though he be born and bred a Florentine, so to think, that from like causes we may go near to observe the same in the style of a prelate.

For doubtless that indeed according to art is most eloquent, which returns and approaches nearest to nature, from whence it came; and they express nature best, who in their lives least wander from her safe leading, which may be called regenerate reason. So that how he should be truly eloquent who is not withal a good man, I see not. Nevertheless, as oft as is to be dealt with men who pride themselves in their supposed art, to leave them unexcusable wherein they will not be bettered; there be of those that esteem prelaty a figment, who yet can pipe if they can dance, nor will be unfurnished to show, that what the prelates admire and have not, others have and admire not. The knowledge whereof, and not of that only, but of what the scripture teacheth us how we ought to withstand the perverters of the gospel, were those other motives which gave the Animadversions no leave to remit a continual vehemence throughout the book. For as in teaching doubtless the spirit of meekness is most powerful, so are the meek only fit persons to be taught: as for the proud, the obstinate, and false doctors of men's devices, be taught they will not, but discovered and laid open they must be.

For how can they admit of teaching, who have the condemnation of God already upon them for refusing divine instruction? That is, to be filled with their own devices, as in the Proverbs we may read: therefore we may safely imitate the method that God uses, "with the froward to be froward, and to throw scorn upon the scorner," whom if anything, nothing else will heal. And if the "righteous shall laugh at the destruction of the ungodly," they may also laugh at their pertinacious and incurable obstinacy, and at the same time be moved with detestation of their seducing malice, who employ all their wits to defend a prelaty usurped, and to deprave that just government which pride and ambition, partly by fine fetches and pretences, partly by force, hath shouldered out of the church. And against such kind of deceivers openly and earnestly to protest, lest any one should be inquisitive wherefore this or that man is forwarder than others, let him know that this office goes not by age or youth, but to whomsoever God shall give apparently the will, the spirit, and the utterance. Ye have heard the reasons for which I thought not myself exempted from associating with good men in their labors towards the church's welfare; to which if any one brought opposition, I brought my best resistance. If in requital of this, and for that I have not been negligent toward the reputation of my friends, I have gained a name bestuck, or as I may say, bedecked with the reproaches and reviles of this modest confuter; it shall be to me neither strange nor unwelcome, as that which could not come in a better time.

Having rendered an account what induced me to write those Animadversions in that manner as I writ them, I come now to see what the Confutation hath to say against them; but so as the confuter shall hear first what I have to say against his Confutation. And because he pretends to be a great conjector at other men by their writings, I will not fail to give ye, readers, a present taste of him from his own title, hung out like a tolling sign-post to call passengers, not simply a confutation, but "a Modest Confutation," with a laudatory of itself obtruded in the very first word. Whereas a modest title should only inform the buyer what the book contains without further insinuation; this officious epithet so hastily assuming the modesty which others are to judge of by reading, not the author to anticipate to himself by forestalling, is a strong presumption that his modesty, set there to sale in the frontispiece, is not much addicted to blush. A surer sign of his lost shame he could not have given, than seeking thus unseasonably to prepossess men of his modesty. And seeing he hath neither kept his word in the sequel, nor omitted any kind of boldness in slandering, it is manifest his purpose was only to rub the forehead of his title with this word Modest, that he might not want color to be the more impudent throughout his whole Confutation.

Next, what can equally savor of injustice and plain arrogance, as to prejudice and forecondemn his adversary in the title for "slanderous and scurrilous," and as the Remonstrant's fashion is, for frivolous, tedious, and false, not staying till the reader can hear him proved so in the following discourse? Which is one cause of a suspicion that in setting forth this pamphlet the Remonstrant was not unconsulted with. Thus his first address was, "An humble Remonstrance by a dutiful Son of the Church," almost as if he had said, her whiteboy. His next was "a Defence" (a wonder how it escaped some praising adjunct) "against the frivolous and false Exceptions of Smectymnuus," sitting in the chair of his title-page upon his poor cast adversaries both as a judge and party, and that before the jury of readers can be impannelled. His last was "A short answer to a tedious Vindication;" so little can he suffer a man to measure, either with his eye or judgment, what is short or what tedious, without his preoccupying direction: and from hence is begotten this "Modest Confutation against a slanderous and scurrilous Libel."

I conceive, readers, much may be guessed at the man and his book, what depth there is, by the framing of his title; which being in this Remonstrant so rash and unadvised as ye see, I conceit him to be near akin to him who set forth a passion sermon with a formal dedicatory in great letters to our Saviour. Although I know that all we do ought to begin and end to his praise and glory, yet to inscribe him in a void place with flourishes, as a man in compliment uses to trick up the name of some esquire, gentleman, or lord paramount at common law, to be his book-patron, with the appendant form of a ceremonious presentment, will ever appear among the judicious to be but an insulse and frigid affectation. As no less was that before his book against the Brownists, to write a letter to a Prosopopœia, a certain rhetorized woman whom he calls mother, and complains of some that laid whoredom to her charge; and certainly had he folded his epistle with a superscription to be delivered to that female figure by any post or carrier, who were not an ubiquitary, it had been a most miraculous greeting. We find the primitive doctors, as oft as they writ to churches, speaking to them as to a number of faithful brethren and sons; and not to make a cloudy transmigration of sexes in such a familiar way of writing as an epistle ought to be, leaving the tract of common address, to run up, and tread the air in metaphorical compellations, and many fond utterances better let alone.

But I step again to this emblazoner of his title-page, (whether it be the same man or no, I leave it in the midst,) and here I find him pronouncing without reprieve those Animadversions to be a slanderous and scurrilous libel. To which I, readers, that they are neither slanderous, nor scurrilous, will answer in what place of his book he shall be found with reason, and not ink only, in his mouth. Nor can it be a libel more than his own, which is both nameless and full of slanders; and if in this that it freely speaks of things amiss in religion, but established by act of state, I see not how Wickliff and

Luther, with all the first martyrs and reformers, could avoid the imputation of libelling. I never thought the human frailty of erring in cases of religion, infamy to a state, no more than to a council. It had therefore been neither civil nor Christianly, to derogate the honor of the state for that cause, especially when I saw the parliament itself piously and magnanimously bent to supply and reform the defects and oversights of their forefathers; which to the godly and repentant ages of the Jews were often matter of humble confessing and bewailing, not of confident asserting and maintaining. Of the state therefore I found good reason to speak all honorable things, and to join in petition with good men that petitioned: but against the prelates, who were the only seducers and misleaders of the state to constitute the government of the church not rightly, methought I had not vehemence enough. And thus, readers, by the example which he hath set me, I have given ye two or three notes of him out of his title-page; by which his firstlings fear not to guess boldly at his whole lump, for that guess will not fail ye; and although I tell him keen truth, yet he may bear with me, since I am like to chase him into some good knowledge, and others, I trust, shall not misspend their leisure. For this my aim is, if I am forced to be unpleasing to him whose fault it is, I shall not forget at the same time to be useful in something to the stander-by.

As therefore he began in the title, so in the next leaf he makes it his first business to tamper with his reader by sycophanting, and misnaming the work of his adversary. He calls it "a mime thrust forth upon the stage, to make up the breaches of those solemn scenes between the prelates and the Smectymnuans." Wherein while he is so over-greedy to fix a name of ill sound upon another, note how stupid he is to expose himself or his own friends to the same ignominy, likening those grave controversies to a piece of stagery, or scenework, where his own Remonstrant, whether in buskin or sock, must of all right be counted the chief player, be it boasting Thraso, or Davus that troubles all things, or one who can shift into any shape, I meddle not; let him explicate who hath resembled the whole argument

to a comedy, for "tragical," he says, "were too ominous." Nor yet doth he tell us what a mime is, whereof we have no pattern from ancient writers, except some fragments, which contain many acute and wise sentences. And this we know in Laertius, that the mimes of Sophron were of such reckoning with Plato, as to take them nightly to read on, and after make them his pillow. Scaliger describes a mime to be a poem imitating any action to stir up laughter. But this being neither poem, nor yet ridiculous, how is it but abusively taxed to be a mime? For if every book, which may by chance excite to laugh here and there, must be termed thus, then may the dialogues of Plato, who for those his writings hath obtained the surname of divine, be esteemed as they are by that detractor in Athenæus, no better than mimes: because there is scarce one of them, especially wherein some notable sophister lies sweating and turmoiling under the inevitable and merciless dilemmas of Socrates, but that he who reads, were it Saturn himself, would be often robbed of more than a smile. And whereas he tells us, that "scurrilous Mime was a personated grim lowering fool," his foolish language unwittingly writes fool upon his own friend, for he who was there personated was only the Remonstrant; the author is ever distinguished from the person he introduces.

But in an ill hour hath this unfortunate rashness stumbled upon the mention of miming, that he might at length cease, which he hath not yet since he stepped in, to gall and hurt him whom he would aid. Could he not beware, could he not bethink him, was he so uncircumspect as not to foresee, that no sooner would that word mime be set eye on in the paper, but it would bring to mind that wretched pilgrimage over Minsheu's dictionary called "Mundus alter et idem," the idlest and the paltriest mime that ever mounted upon bank? Let him ask "the author of those toothless satires," who was the maker, or other the anticreator of that universal foolery, who he was, who like that other principal of the Manichees, the arch evil one, when he had looked upon all that he had made and mapped out, could say no other but contrary to the divine mouth, that it was all very foolish. That grave and

noble invention, which the greatest and sublimest wits in sundry ages, Plato in Critias,
and our two famous countrymen, the one
in his "Utopia," the other in his "New
Atlantis," chose, I may not say as a field, but
as a mighty continent, wherein to display the
largeness of their spirits, by teaching this
our world better and exacter things than
were yet known or used; this petty prevari-
cator of America, the zany of Columbus,
(for so he must be till his world's end,)
having rambled over the huge topography of
his own vain thoughts, no marvel if he
brought us home nothing but a mere tankard
drollery, a venereous parjetory for stews.
Certainly, he that could endure with a sober
pen to sit and devise laws for drunkards to
carouse by, I doubt me whether the very
soberness of such a one, like an unliquored
Silenus, were not stark drunk. Let him go
now and brand another man injuriously with
the name of mime, being himself the loosest
and most extravagant mime that hath been
heard of, whom no less than almost half the
world could serve for stage-room to play
the mime in. And let him advise again with
Sir Francis Bacon, whom he cites to confute
others, what it is "to turn the sins of Christendom into a mimical mockery, to rip up
the saddest vices with a laughing countenance," especially where neither reproof nor
better teaching is adjoined. Nor is my meaning, readers, to shift off a blame from myself, by charging the like upon my accuser,
but shall only desire that sentence may be
respited till I can come to some instance
whereto I may give answer.

Thus having spent his first onset, not in confuting, but in a reasonless defaming of the
book, the method of his malice hurries him
to attempt the like against the author; not
by proofs and testimonies, but "having no
certain notice of me," as he professes,
"further than what he gathers from the
Animadversions," blunders at me for the
rest, and flings out stray crimes at a venture, which he could never, though he be a
serpent, suck from anything that I have
written, but from his own stuffed magazine
and hoard of slanderous inventions, over and
above that which he converted to venom in
the drawing. To me, readers, it happens as
a singular contentment, and let it be to

good men no slight satisfaction, that the
slanderer here confesses he has "no further
notice of me than his own conjecture."
Although it had been honest to have inquired, before he uttered such infamous
words, and I am credibly informed he did
inquire; but finding small comfort from the
intelligence which he received, whereon to
ground the falsities which he had provided,
thought it his likeliest course, under a pretended ignorance, to let drive at random,
lest he should lose his odd ends, which
from some penurious book of characters he
had been culling out and would fain apply.
Not caring to burden me with those vices,
whereof, among whom my conversation hath
been, I have been ever least suspected; perhaps not without some subtlety to cast me
into envy, by bringing on me a necessity to
enter into mine own praises. In which argument I know every wise man is more unwillingly drawn to speak, than the most
repining ear can be averse to hear.

Nevertheless, since I dare not wish to pass
this life unpersecuted of slanderous tongues,
for God hath told us that to be generally
praised is woeful, I shall rely on his promise
to free the innocent from causeless aspersions: whereof nothing sooner can assure
me, than if I shall feel him now assisting
me in the just vindication of myself, which
yet I could defer, it being more meet, that
to those other matters of public debatement
in this book I should give attendance first,
but that I fear it would but harm the truth
for me to reason in her behalf, so long as
I should suffer my honest estimation to lie
unpurged from these insolent suspicions. And
if I shall be large, or unwonted in justifying myself to those who know me not, for
else it would be needless, let them consider
that a short slander will ofttimes reach
further than a long apology; and that he
who will do justly to all men, must begin
from knowing how, if it so happen, to be
not unjust to himself. I must be thought,
if this libeller (for now he shows himself
to be so) can find belief, after an inordinate
and riotous youth spent at the university,
to have been at length "vomited out thence."
For which commodious lie, that he may be
encouraged in the trade another time, I
thank him; for it hath given me an apt

occasion to acknowledge publicly with all grateful mind, that more than ordinary favor and respect, which I found above any of my equals at the hands of those courteous and learned men, the fellows of that college wherein I spent some years: who at my parting, after I had taken two degrees, as the manner is, signified many ways how much better it would content them that I would stay; as by many letters full of kindness and loving respect, both before that time, and long after, I was assured of their singular good affection towards me. Which being likewise propense to all such as were for their studious and civil life worthy of esteem, I could not wrong their judgments and upright intentions, so much as to think I had that regard from them for other cause, than that I might be still encouraged to proceed in the honest and laudable courses, of which they apprehended I had given good proof. And to those ingenuous and friendly men, who were ever the countenancers of virtuous and hopeful wits, I wish the best and happiest things, that friends in absence wish one to another.

As for the common approbation or dislike of that place, as now it is, that I should esteem or disesteem myself, or any other the more for that, too simple and too credulous is the confuter, if he think to obtain with me, or any right discerner. Of small practice were that physician, who could not judge by what both she or her sister hath of long time vomited, that the worser stuff she strongly keeps in her stomach, but the better she is ever kecking at, and is queasy. She vomits now out of sickness; but ere it be well with her, she must vomit by strong physic. In the meanwhile that suburb sink, as this rude scavenger calls it, and more than scurrilously taunts it with the plague, having a worse plague in his middle entrail, that suburb wherein I dwell shall be in my account a more honorable place than his university. Which as in the time of her better health, and mine own younger judgment, I never greatly admired, so now much less. But he follows me to the city, still usurping and forging beyond his book notice, which only he affirms to have had; "and where my morning haunts are, he wisses not." It is wonder that, being so

rare an alchymist of slander, he could not extract that, as well as the university vomit, and the suburb sink which his art could distil so cunningly; but because his limbec fails him to give him and envy the more vexation, I will tell him.

Those morning haunts are where they should be, at home; not sleeping, or concocting the surfeits of an irregular feast, but up and stirring, in winter often ere the sound of any bell awake men to labor, or to devotion; in summer as oft with the bird that first rouses, or not much tardier, to read good authors, or cause them to be read, till the attention be weary, or memory have his full fraught: then, with useful and generous labors preserving the body's health and hardiness to render lightsome, clear, and not lumpish obedience to the mind, to the cause of religion, and our country's liberty, when it shall require firm hearts in sound bodies to stand and cover their stations, rather than to see the ruin of our protestation, and the inforcement of a slavish life.

These are the morning practices: proceed now to the afternoon; "in playhouses," he says, "and the bordelloes." Your intelligence, unfaithful spy of Canaan? He gives in his evidence, that "there he hath traced me." Take him at his word, readers; but let him bring good sureties ere ye dismiss him, that while he pretended to dog others, he did not turn in for his own pleasure: for so much in effect he concludes against himself, not contented to be caught in every other gin, but he must be such a novice as to be still hampered in his own hemp. In the Animadversions, saith he, I find the mention of old cloaks, false beards, night-walkers, and salt lotion; therefore, the animadverter haunts playhouses and bordelloes; for if he did not, how could he speak of such gear? Now that he may know what it is to be a child, and yet to meddle with edged tools, I turn his antistrophon upon his own head; the confuter knows that these things are the furniture of playhouses and bordelloes, therefore, by the same reason, "the confuter himself hath been traced in those places." Was it such a dissolute speech, telling of some politicians who were wont to eavesdrop in disguise, to say they were often liable to a nightwalking cudgeller, or the emptying of a urinal? What if I had written as your friend the author of the aforesaid mime, "Mundus alter et idem," to have been ravished like some young Cephalus or Hylas, by a troop of camping housewives in Viraginea, and that he was there forced to swear himself an uxorious varlet; then after a long servitude to have come into Aphrodisia that pleasant country, that gave such a sweet smell to his nostrils among the shameless courtezans of Desvergonia? Surely he would have then concluded me as constant at the bordello, as the galley-slave at his oar.

But since there is such necessity to the hearsay of a tire, a periwig, or a vizard, that plays must have been seen, what difficulty was there in that? when in the colleges so many of the young divines, and those in next aptitude to divinity, have been seen so often upon the stage, writhing and unboning their clergy limbs to all the antic and dishonest gestures of Trinculoes, buffoons, and bawds; prostituting the shame of that ministry, which either they had, or were nigh having, to the eyes of courtiers and court ladies, with their grooms and mademoiselles. There, while they acted and overacted, among other young scholars, I was a spectator; they thought themselves gallant men, and I thought them fools; they made sport, and I laughed; they mispronounced, and I misliked; and, to make up the atticism, they were out, and I hissed. Judge now whether so many good textmen were not sufficient to instruct me of false beards and vizards, without more expositors; and how can this confuter take the face to object to me the seeing of that which his reverend prelates allow, and incite their young disciples to act? For if it be unlawful to sit and behold a mercenary comedian personating that which is least unseemly for a hireling to do, how much more blameful is it to endure the sight of as vile things acted by persons either entered, or presently to enter into the ministry; and how much more foul and ignominious for them to be the actors!

But because as well by this upbraiding to me the bordelloes, as by other suspicious glancings in his book, he would seem privily to point me out to his readers, as one whose custom of life were not honest, but licentious, I shall entreat to be borne with, though I digress; and in a way not often trod, acquaint ye with the sum of my thoughts in this matter, through the course of my years and studies: although I am not ignorant how hazardous it will be to do this under the nose of the envious, as it were in skirmish to change the compact order, and instead of outward actions, to bring inmost thoughts into front. And I must tell ye, readers, that by this sort of men I have been already bitten at; yet shall they not for me know how slightly they are esteemed, unless they have so much learning as to read what in Greek ἀπειροκαλία is, which, together with envy, is the common disease of those who censure books that are not for their reading. With me it fares now, as with him whose outward garment hath been injured and ill-bedighted; for having no other shift, what help but to turn the inside outwards, especially if the lining be of the same, or, as it is sometimes, much better? So if my name and outward demeanor be not evident enough to defend me, I must make trial if the discovery of my inmost thoughts can: wherein of two purposes, both honest and both sincere, the one perhaps I shall not miss; although I fail to gain belief with others, of being such as my perpetual thoughts shall here disclose me, I may yet not fail of success in persuading some to be such really themselves, as they cannot believe me to be more than what I feign.

I had my time, readers, as others have, who have good learning bestowed upon them, to be sent to those places where, the opinion was, it might be soonest attained; and as the manner is, was not unstudied in those authors which are most commended. Whereof some were grave orators and historians, whose matter methought I loved indeed, but as my age then was, so I understood them, others were the smooth elegiac poets, whereof the schools are not scarce, whom both for the pleasing sound of their numerous writing, which in imitation I found most easy, and most agreeable to nature's part in me, and for their matter, which what it is, there be few who know not, I was so allured to read, that no recreation came to me better welcome. For that it was then those years with me which are excused, though they be least severe, I may be saved the labor to remember ye. Whence having observed them to account it the chief glory of their wit, in that they were ablest to judge, to praise, and by that could esteem themselves worthiest to love those high perfections, which under one or other name they took to celebrate; I thought with myself by every instinct and presage of nature, which is not wont to be false, that what emboldened them to this task, might with such diligence as they used emboldened me; and that what judgment, wit, or elegance was my share, would herein best appear, and best value itself, by how much more wisely, and with more love of virtue I should choose (let rude ears be absent) the object of not unlike praises. For albeit these thoughts to some will seem virtuous and commendable, to others only pardonable, to a third sort perhaps idle; yet the mentioning of them now will end in serious.

Nor blame it, readers, in those years to propose to themselves such a reward, as the noblest dispositions above other things in this life have sometimes preferred: whereof not to be sensible when good and fair in one person meet, argues both a gross and shallow judgment, and withal an ungentle and swainish breast. For by the firm settling of these persuasions, I became, to my best memory, so much a proficient, that if I found those authors anywhere speaking unworthy things of themselves, or unchaste of those names which before they had extolled; this effect it wrought with me, from that time forward their art I still applauded, but the men I deplored; and above them all, preferred the two famous renowners of Beatrice and Laura, who never write but honor of them to whom they devote their verse, displaying sublime and pure thoughts, without transgression. And long it was not after, when I was confirmed in this opinion, that he who would not be frustrate of his hope to write well hereafter in laudable things, ought himself to be a true poem; that is, a composition and pattern of the best and honorablest things; not presuming to sing high praises of heroic men, or famous cities, unless he have in himself the experience and the practice of all that which is praiseworthy. These reasonings, together

with a certain niceness of nature, an honest haughtiness, and self-esteem either of what I was, or what I might be, (which let envy call pride,) and lastly that modesty, whereof, though not in the title-page, yet here I may be excused to make some beseeming profession; all these uniting the supply of their natural aid together, kept me still above those low descents of mind, beneath which he must deject and plunge himself, that can agree to saleable and unlawful prostitutions.

Next, (for hear me out now, readers,) that I may tell ye whither my younger feet wandered; I betook me among those lofty fables and romances, which recount in solemn cantos the deeds of knighthood founded by our victorious kings, and from hence had in renown over all Christendom. There I read it in the oath of every knight, that he should defend to the expense of his best blood, or of his life, if it so befell him, the honor and chastity of virgin or matron; from whence even then I learnt what a noble virtue chastity sure must be, to the defence of which so many worthies, by such a dear adventure of themselves, had sworn. And if I found in the story afterward, any of them, by word or deed, breaking that oath, I judged it the same fault of the poet, as that which is attributed to Homer, to have written undecent things of the gods. Only this my mind gave me, that every free and gentle spirit, without that oath, ought to be born a knight, nor needed to expect the gilt spur, or the laying of a sword upon his shoulder to stir him up both by his counsel and his arm, to secure and protect the weakness of any attempted chastity. So that even these books, which to many others have been the fuel of wantonness and loose living, I cannot think how, unless by divine indulgence, proved to me so many incitements, as you have heard, to the love and steadfast observation of that virtue which abhors the society of bordelloes.

Thus, from the laureat fraternity of poets, riper years and the ceaseless round of study and reading led me to the shady spaces of philosophy; but chiefly to the divine volumes of Plato, and his equal Xenophon: where, if I should tell ye what I learnt of chastity and love, I mean that which is truly so, whose charming cup is only virtue, which she bears in her hand to those who are worthy; (the rest are cheated with a thick intoxicating potion, which a certain sorceress, the abuser of love's name, carries about;) and how the first and chiefest office of love begins and ends in the soul, producing those happy twins of her divine generation, knowledge and virtue. With such abstracted sublimities as these, it might be worth your listening, readers, as I may one day hope to have ye in a still time, when there shall be no chiding; not in these noises, the adversary, as ye know, barking at the door, or searching for me at the bordelloes, where it may be has lost himself, and raps up without pity the sage and rheumatic old prelatess, with all her young Corinthian laity, to inquire for such a one.

Last of all, not in time, but as perfection is last, that care was ever had of me, with my earliest capacity, not to be negligently trained in the precepts of Christian religion: this that I have hitherto related, hath been to show, that though Christianity had been but slightly taught me, yet a certain reservedness of natural disposition, and moral discipline, learnt out of the noblest philosophy, was enough to keep me in disdain of far less incontinences than this of the bordello. But having had the doctrine of holy scripture unfolding those chaste and high mysteries, with timeliest care infused, that "the body is for the Lord, and the Lord for the body;" thus also I argued to myself, that if unchastity in a woman, whom St. Paul terms the glory of man, be such a scandal and dishonor, then certainly in a man, who is both the image and glory of God, it must, though commonly not so thought, be much more deflouring and dishonorable; in that he sins both against his own body, which is the perfecter sex, and his own glory, which is in the woman; and, that which is worst, against the image and glory of God, which is in himself. Nor did I slumber over that place expressing such high rewards of ever accompanying the Lamb with those celestial songs to others inapprehensible, but not to those who were not defiled with women, which doubtless means fornication; for marriage must not be called a defilement.

Thus large I have purposely been, that if I have been justly taxed with this crime, it may come upon me, after all this my confession, with a tenfold shame: but if I have hitherto deserved no such opprobious word, or suspicion, I may hereby engage myself now openly to the faithful observation of what I have professed. I go on to show you the unbridled impudence of this loose railer, who, having once begun his race, regards not how far he flies out beyond all truth and shame; who from the single notice of the Animadversions, as he protests, will undertake to tell ye the very clothes I wear, though he be much mistaken in my wardrobe; and like a son of Belial, without the hire of Jezebel, charges me "of blaspheming God and the king," as ordinarily as he imagines "me to drink sack and swear," merely because this was a shred in his common-place book, and seemed to come off roundly, as if he were some empiric of false accusations, to try his poisons upon me, whether they would work or no. Whom what should I endeavor to refute more, whenas that book, which is his only testimony, returns the lie upon him; not giving him the least hint of the author to be either a swearer or a sack-drinker. And for the readers, if they can believe me, principally for those reasons which I have alleged, to be of life and purpose neither dishonest nor unchaste, they will be easily induced to think me sober both of wine and of word; but if I have been already successless in persuading them, all that I can further say will be but vain; and it will be better thrift to save two tedious labors, mine of excusing, and theirs of needless hearing.

Proceeding further, I am met with a whole ging of words and phrases not mine, for he hath maimed them, and, like a sly depraver, mangled them in this his wicked limbo, worse than the ghost of Deiphobus appeared to his friend Æneas. Here I scarce know them; and he that would, let him repair to the place in that book where I set them: for certainly this tormentor of semicolons is as good at dismembering and slitting sentences, as his grave fathers the prelates have been at stigmatizing and slitting noses. By such handicraft as this what might he not traduce? Only that odor, which being his own must needs offend his sense of smelling, since he will needs bestow his foot among us, and not allow us to think he wears a sock, I shall endeavor it may be offenceless to other men's ears. The Remonstrant having to do with grave and reverend men his adversaries, thought it became him to tell them in scorn, that "the bishop's foot had been in their book and confuted it;" which when I saw him arrogate to have done that with his heels that surpassed the best consideration of his head, to spurn a confutation among respected men, I questioned not the lawfulness of moving his jollity to bethink him, what odor a sock would have in such a painful business. And this may have chanced to touch him more nearly than I was aware, for indeed a bishop's foot that hath all his toes maugre the gout, and a linen sock over it, is the aptest emblem of the prelate himself; who being a pluralist, may under one surplice, which is also linen, hide four benefices, besides the metropolitan toe, and sends a fouler stench to heaven than that which this young queasiness retches at. And this is the immediate reason here why our enraged confuter, that he may be as perfect a hypocrite as Caiaphas, ere he be a high priest, cries out, "Horrid blasphemy!" and, like a recreant Jew, calls for stones. I beseech ye, friends, ere the brickbats fly, resolve me and yourselves, is it blasphemy, or any whit disagreeing from Christian meekness, whenas Christ himself, speaking of unsavory traditions, scruples not to name the dunghill and the jakes, for me to answer a slovenly wincer of a confutation, that if he would needs put his foot to such a sweaty service, the odor of his sock was like to be neither musk nor benjamin? Thus did that foolish monk in a barbarous declamation accuse Petrarch of blasphemy for dispraising the French wines.

But this which follows is plain bedlam stuff; this is the demoniac legion indeed, which the Remonstrant feared had been against him, and now he may see, is for him. "You that love Christ," saith he, "and know this miscreant wretch, stone him to death, lest you smart for his impunity." What thinks the Remonstrant? does he like that such words as these should come out of his shop, out of his *Trojan horse?* to give the watchword like a Guisian of Paris to a mutiny or massacre; to proclaim a crusade against his fellow-christian now in this troublous and divided time of the kingdom? If he do, I shall

say that to be the Remonstrant, is no better than to be a Jesuit; and that if he and his accomplices could do as the rebels have done in Ireland to the protestants, they would do in England the same to them that would no prelates. For a more seditious and butcherly speech no cell of Loyola could have belched against one who in all his writing spake not, that any man's skin should be rased.

And yet this cursing Shimei, a hurler of stones, as well as a railer, wants not the face instantly to make as though he "despaired of victory, unless a modest defence would get it him." Did I err at all, readers, to foretell ye, when first I met with his title, that the epithet of modest there was a certain red portending sign, that he meant ere long to be most tempestuously bold and shameless? Nevertheless, he dares not say but there may be hid in his nature as much venomous atheism and profanation, as he thinks hath broke out at his adversary's lips; but he hath not "the sore running upon him," as he would intimate I have. Now trust me not, readers, if I be not already weary of pluming and footing this sea-gull, so open he lies to strokes, and never offers at another but brings home the dorre upon himself. For if the sore be running upon me, in all judgment I have escaped the disease; but he who hath as much infection hid in him, as he hath voluntarily confessed, and cannot expel it, because he is dull, (for venomous atheism were no treasure to be kept within him else,) let him take the part he hath chosen, which must needs follow, to swell and burst with his own inward venom.

But mark, readers, there is a kind of justice observed among them that do evil; but this man loves injustice in the very order of his malice. For having all this while abused the good name of his adversary with all manner of licence in revenge of his Remonstrant, if they be not both one person, or as I am told, father and son, yet after all this he calls for satisfaction, whenas he himself hath already taken the utmost farthing. "Violence hath been done," says he, "to the person of a holy and religious prelate." To which, something in effect to what St. Paul answered of Ananias, I answer, "I wist not, brethren, that he was a holy and religious prelate;" for evil is written of those who would be prelates. And finding him thus in disguise without his superscription or phylactery either of holy or prelate, it were no sin to serve him as Longchamp bishop of Ely was served in his disguise at Dover: he hath begun the measure nameless, and when he pleases we may all appear as we are. And let him be then what he will, he shall be to me so as I find him principled. For neither must prelate or archprelate hope to exempt himself from being reckoned as one of the vulgar, which is for him only to hope whom true wisdom and the contempt of vulgar opinions exempts, it being taught us in the Psalms, that he who is in honor and understandeth not, is as the beasts that perish.

And now first "the manner of handling that cause," which I undertook, he thinks is suspicious, as if the wisest and the best words were not ever to some or other suspicious. But where is the offence, the disagreement from Christian meekness, or the precept of Solomon in answering folly? When the Remonstrant talks of froth and scum, I tell him there is none, and bid him spare his ladle: when he brings in the mess with keal, beef, and brewess, what stomach in England could forbear to call for flanks and briskets? Capon and white broth having been likely sometimes in the same room with Christ and his apostles, why does it trouble him, that it should be now in the same leaf, especially where the discourse is not continued, but interrupt? And let him tell me, is he wont to say grace, doth he not then name holiest names over the steam of costliest superfluities? Does he judge it foolish or dishonest, to write that among religious things, which, when he talks of religious things, he can devoutly chew? Is he afraid to name Christ where those things are written in the same leaf, whom he fears not to name while the same things are in his mouth? Doth not Christ himself teach the highest things by the similitude of old bottles and patched clothes? Doth he not illustrate best things by things most evil? his own coming to be as a thief in the night, and the righteous man's wisdom to that of an unjust steward? He might therefore have done better to have kept in his canting beggars, and heathen altar, to sacrifice his threadbare criticism of Bomolochus to an unseasonable goddess fit for him called Importunity, and have

reserved his Greek derivation till he lecture to his freshmen, for here his itching pedantry is but flouted.

But to the end that nothing may be omitted, which may farther satisfy any conscionable man, who, notwithstanding what I could explain before the Animadversions, remains yet unsatisfied concerning that way of writing which I there defended, but this confuter, whom it pinches, utterly disapproves; I shall assay once again, and perhaps with more success. If therefore the question were in oratory, whether a vehement vein throwing out indignation or scorn upon an object that merits it, were among the aptest *ideas* of speech to be allowed, it were my work, and that an easy one, to make it clear both by the rules of best rhetoricians, and the famousest examples of the Greek and Roman orations. But since the religion of it is disputed, and not the art, I shall make use only of such reasons and authorities as religion cannot except against. It will be harder to gainsay, than for me to evince, that in the teaching of men diversely tempered, different ways are to be tried. The Baptist, we know, was a strict man, remarkable for austerity and set order of life. Our Saviour, who had all gifts in him, was Lord to express his indoctrinating power in what sort him best seemed; sometimes by a mild and familiar converse; sometimes with plain and impartial homespeaking, regardless of those whom the auditors might think he should have had in more respect; otherwhiles, with bitter and ireful rebukes, if not teaching, yet leaving excuseless those his wilful impugners.

What was all in him, was divided among many others the teachers of his church; some to be severe and ever of a sad gravity, that they may win such, and check sometimes those who be of nature over-confident and jocund; others were sent more cheerful, free, and still as it were at large, in the midst of an untrespassing honesty; that they who are so tempered, may have by whom they might be drawn to salvation, and they who are too scrupulous, and dejected of spirit, might be often strengthened with wise consolations and revivings: no man being forced wholly to dissolve that groundwork of nature which God created in him, the sanguine to empty out all his sociable liveliness, the choleric to expel quite the unsinning predominance of his anger; but that each radical humor and passion, wrought upon and corrected as it ought, might be made the proper mold and foundation of every man's peculiar gifts and virtues. Some also were indued with a staid moderation and soundness of argument, to teach and convince the rational and soberminded; yet not therefore that to be thought the only expedient course of teaching, for in times of opposition, when either against new heresies arising, or old corruptions to be reformed, this cool unpassionate mildness of positive wisdom is not enough to damp and astonish the proud resistance of carnal and false doctors, then (that I may have leave to soar awhile as the poets use) Zeal, whose substance is ethereal, arming in complete diamond, ascends his fiery chariot, drawn with two blazing meteors, figured like beasts, but of a higher breed than any the zodiac yields, resembling two of those four which Ezekiel and St. John saw; the one visaged like a lion, to express power, high authority, and indignation; the other of countenance like a man, to cast derision and scorn upon perverse and fraudulent seducers: with these the invincible warrior, Zeal, shaking loosely the slack reins, drives over the heads of scarlet prelates, and such as are insolent to maintain traditions, bruising their stiff necks under his flaming wheels.

Thus did the true prophets of old combat with the false; thus Christ himself, the fountain of meekness, found acrimony enough to be still galling and vexing the prelatical pharisees. But ye will say, these had immediate warrant from God to be thus bitter; and I say, so much the plainlier is it proved, that there may be a sanctified bitterness against the enemies of truth. Yet that ye may not think inspiration only the warrant thereof, but that it is as any other virtue, of moral and general observation, the example of Luther may stand for all, whom God made choice of before others to be of highest eminence and power in reforming the church; who, not of revelation, but of judgment, writ so vehemently against the chief defenders of old untruths in the Romish church, that his own friends and favorers were many times offended with the fierceness of his spirit; yet he being cited before Charles the

Fifth to answer for his books, and having divided them into three sorts, whereof one was of those which he had sharply written, refused, though upon deliberation given him, to retract or unsay any word therein, as we may read in Sleidan. Yea, he defends his eagerness, as being "of an ardent spirit, and one who could not write a dull style:" and affirmed, "he thought it God's will, to have the inventions of men thus laid open, seeing that matters quietly handled were quickly forgot."

And herewithal how useful and available God hath made this tart rhetoric in the church's cause, he often found by his own experience. For when he betook himself to lenity and moderation, as they call it, he reaped nothing but contempt both from Cajetan and Erasmus, from Cocleus, from Ecchius, and others; insomuch that blaming his friends, who had so counselled him, he resolved never to run into the like error. If at other times he seem to excuse his vehemence, as more than what was meet, I have not examined through his works, to know how far he gave way to his own fervent mind; it shall suffice me to look to mine own. And this I shall easily aver, though it may seem a hard saying, that the Spirit of God, who is purity itself, when he would reprove any fault severely, or but relate things done or said with indignation by others, abstains not from some words not civil at other times to be spoken. Omitting that place in Numbers at the killing of Zimri and Cosbi, done by Phineas in the height of zeal, related, as the rabbins expound, not without an obscene word; we may find in Deuteronomy and three of the prophets, where God, denouncing bitterly the punishments of idolaters, tells them in a term immodest to be uttered in cool blood, that their wives shall be defiled openly.

But these, they will say, were honest words in that age when they were spoken. Which is more than any rabbin can prove; and certainly had God been so minded, he could have picked such words as should never have come into abuse. What will they say to this? David going against Nabal, in the very same breath when he had just before named the name of God, he vows not "to leave any alive of Nabal's house that pisseth against the wall." But this was unadvisedly spoke, you will answer, and set down to aggravate his infirmity. Turn then to the First of Kings, where God himself uses the phrase, "I will cut off from Jeroboam him that pisseth against the wall;" which had it been an unseemly speech in the heat of an earnest expression, then we must conclude that Jonathan or Onkelos the targumists were of cleaner language than he that made the tongue; for they render it as briefly, "I will cut off all who are at years of discretion," that is to say, so much discretion as to hide nakedness. Whereas God, who is the author both of purity and eloquence, chose this phrase as fittest in that vehement character wherein he spake. Otherwise that plain word might have easily been forborne: which the mazoreths and rabbinical scholiasts, not well attending, have often used to blur the margin with Keri instead of Ketiv, and gave us this insulse rule out of their Talmud, "That all words which in the law are written obscenely, must be changed to more civil words:" fools, who would teach men to read more decently than God thought good to write. And thus I take it to be manifest, that indignation against men and their actions notoriously bad hath leave and authority ofttimes to utter such words and phrases, as in common talk were not so mannerly to use. That ye may know, not only as the historian speaks, "that all those things for which men plough, build, or sail, obey virtue," but that all words, and whatsoever may be spoken, shall at some time in an unwonted manner wait upon her purposes.

Now that the confutant may also know as he desires, what force of teaching there is sometimes in laughter, I shall return him in short, that laughter, being one way of answering "a fool according to his folly," teaches two sorts of persons: first, the fool himself, "not to be wise in his own conceit," as Solomon affirms; which is certainly a great document to make an unwise man know himself. Next, it teacheth the hearers, inasmuch as scorn is one of those punishments which belong to men carnally wise, which is oft in scripture declared; for when such are punished, "the simple are thereby made wise," if Solomon's rule be true. And I would ask, to what end Eliah mocked the false prophets? was it to show his wit, or to fulfil

his humor? Doubtless we cannot imagine that great servant of God had any other end, in all which he there did but to teach and instruct the poor misled people. And we may frequently read, that many of the martyrs in the midst of their troubles were not sparing to deride and scoff their superstitious persecutors. Now may the confutant advise again with Sir Francis Bacon, whether Eliah and the martyrs did well to turn religion into a comedy or satire; "to rip up the wounds of idolatry and superstition with a laughing countenance:" so that for pious gravity his author here is matched and overmatched, and for wit and morality in one that follows:

"——laughing to teach the truth
What hinders? as some teachers give to boys
  Junkets and knacks, that they may learn apace."

Thus Flaccus in his first satire, and his tenth:

"——Jesting decides great things
  Stronglier and better oft than earnest can."

I could urge the same out of Cicero and Seneca, but he may content him with this. And henceforward, if he can learn, may know as well what are the bounds and objects of laughter and vehement reproof, as he hath known hitherto how to deserve them both. But lest some may haply think, or thus expostulate with me after all this debatement, who made you the busy almoner to deal about this dole of laughter and reprehension, which no man thanks your bounty for? To the urbanity of that man I should answer much after this sort: that I, friend objector, having read of heathen philosophers, some to have taught, that whosoever would but use his ear to listen, might hear the voice of his guiding genius ever before him, calling, and as it were pointing to that way which is his part to follow; others, as the stoics, to account reason, which they call the Hegemonicon, to be the common Mercury conducting without error those that give themselves obediently to be led accordingly. Having read this, I could not esteem so poorly of the faith which I profess, that God had left nothing to those who had forsaken all other doctrines for his, to be an inward witness and warrant of what they have to do, as that they should need to measure themselves by other men's measures, how to give scope or limit to their proper actions; for that were to make us the most at a stand, the most uncertain and accidental wanderers in our doings, of all religions in the world. So that the question ere while moved, who is he that spends thus the benevolence of laughter and reproof so liberally upon such men as the prelates, may return with a more just demand, who he is not of place and knowledge never so mean, under whose contempt and jerk these men are not deservedly fallen? Neither can religion receive any wound by disgrace thrown upon the prelates, since religion and they surely were never in such amity. They rather are the men who have wounded religion, and their stripes must heal her. I might also tell them what Electra in Sophocles, a wise virgin, answered her wicked mother, who thought herself too violently reproved by her the daughter:

" 'Tis you that say it, not I; you do the deeds,
And your ungodly deeds find me the words."

If therefore the Remonstrant complain of libels, it is because he feels them to be right aimed. For I ask again, as before in the Animadversions, how long is it since he hath disrelished libels? We never heard the least mutter of his voice against them while they flew abroad without control or check, defaming the Scots and Puritans. And yet he can remember of none but Lysimachus Nicanor, and "that he misliked and censured." No more but of one can the Remonstrant remember? What if I put him in mind of one more? What if of one more whereof the Remonstrant in many likelihoods may be thought the author? Did he never see a pamphlet intitled after his own fashion, "A Survey of that foolish, sedious, scandalous, prophane Libel, the Protestation protested?" The child doth not more expressly refigure the visage of his father, than that book resembles the style of the Remonstrant, in those idioms of speech, wherein he seems most to delight: and in the seventeenth page three lines together are taken out of the Remonstrance word for word, not as a citation, but as an author borrows from himself. Whoever it be, he may as justly be said to have libelled, as he against whom he writes: there ye shall find another man than is here made show of, there he bites as fast as this whines. "Vinegar in the ink," is there "the antidote of vipers." Laughing in a religious controversy is there "a thrifty physic to expel his melancholy."

In the meantime the testimony of Sir Francis Bacon was not misalleged, complaining that libels on the bishops' part were uttered openly; and if he hoped the prelates had no intelligence with the libellers, he delivers it but as his favorable opinion. But had he contradicted himself, how could I assoil him here, more than a little before, where I know not how, by entangling himself, he leaves an aspersion upon Job, which by any else I never heard laid to his charge? For having affirmed that "there is no greater confusion than the confounding of jest and earnest," presently he brings the example of Job, "glancing at conceits of mirth, when he sat among the people with the gravity of a judge upon him." If jest and earnest be such a confusion, then were the people much wiser than Job, for "he smiled, and they believed him not." To defend libels, which is that whereof I am next accused, was far from my purpose. I had not so little share in good name, as to give another that advantage against myself. The sum of what I said was, that a more free permission of writing at some times might be profitable, in such a question especially wherein the magistrates are not fully resolved; and both sides have equal liberty to write, as now they have. Not as when the prelates bore sway, in whose time the books of some men were confuted, when they who should have answered were in close prison, denied the use of pen or paper. And the divine right of episcopacy was then valiantly asserted, when he who would have been respondent must have bethought himself withal how he could refute the Clink or the Gatehouse. If now therefore they be pursued with bad words, who persecuted others with bad deeds, it is a way to lessen tumult rather than to increase it; whenas anger thus freely vented spends itself ere it break out into action, though Machiavel, whom he cites, or any Machiavelian priest, think the contrary.

Now, readers, I bring ye to his third section; wherein very cautiously and no more than needs, lest I should take him for some chaplain at hand, some squire of the body to his prelate, one that serves not at the altar only, but at the court cupboard, he will bestow on us a pretty model of himself; and sobs me out half-a-dozen phthisical mottoes, wherever he had them, hopping short in the measure of convulsion-fits; in which labor the agony of his wit having escaped narrowly, instead of well-sized periods, he greets us with a quantity of thumb-ring posies. "He has a fortune therefore good, because he is content with it." This is a piece of sapience not worth the brain of a fruit trencher; as if content were the measure of what is good or bad in the gift of fortune: for by this rule a bad man may have a good fortune, because he may be ofttimes content with it for many reasons which have no affinity with virtue, as love of ease, want of spirit to use more, and the like. "And therefore content," he says, "because it neither goes before, nor comes behind his merit." Belike then if his fortune should go before his merit, he would not be content, but resign, if we believe him; which I do the less, because he implies, that if it came behind his merit, he would be content as little. Whereas if a wise man's content should depend upon such a therefore, because his fortune came not behind his merit, how many wise men could have content in this world?

In his next pithy symbol I dare not board him, for he passes all the seven wise masters of Greece, attributing to himself that which, on my life, Solomon durst not: "to have affections so equally tempered, that they neither too hastily adhere to the truth before it be fully examined, nor too lazily afterward:" which unless he only were exempted out of the corrupt mass of Adam, born without sin original, and living without actual, is impossible. Had Solomon, (for it behooves me to instance in the wisest, dealing with such a transcendent sage as this,) had Solomon affections so equally tempered, as "not adhering too lazily to the truth," when God warned him of his halting in idolatry? do we read that he repented hastily? did not his affections lead him hastily from an examined truth, how much more would they lead him slowly to it? Yet this man, beyond a stoic apathy, sees truth as in a rapture, and cleaves to it; not as through the dim glass of his affections, which, in this frail mansion of flesh, are ever unequally tempered, pushing forward to error, and keeping back from truth ofttimes the best of men. But how far this boaster is from knowing himself, let his preface speak. Something I thought it was that made him so quick-sighted to gather such strange things out of the Animadversions, whereof the least conception could not be drawn from thence, of "suburb-sinks," sometimes "out of wit and clothes," sometimes "in new serge, drinking sack, and swearing;" now I know it was this equal temper of his affections, that gave him to see clearer than any fennel-rubbed serpent. Lastly, he has resolved "that neither person nor cause shall improper him." I may mistake his meaning, for the word ye hear is "improper." But whether if not a person, yet a good personage or impropriation bought out for him, would not "improper" him, because there may be a quirk in the word, I leave it for a canonist to resolve.

And thus ends this section or rather dissection, of himself, short ye will say both in breath and extent, as in our own praises it ought to be, unless wherein a good name hath been wrongfully attainted. Right; but if ye look at what he ascribes to himself, "that temper of his affections," which cannot anywhere be but in Paradise, all the judicious panegyrics in any language extant are not half so prolix. And that well appears in his next removal. For what with putting his fancy to the tiptoe in this description of himself, and what with adventuring presently to stand upon his own legs without the crutches of his margin, which is the sluice most commonly that feeds the drought of his text, he comes so lazily on in a simile, with his "armful of weeds," and demeans himself in the dull expression so like a dough-kneaded thing, that he has not spirit enough left him so far to look to his syntax, as to avoid nonsense. For it must be understood there that the stranger, and not he who brings the bundle, would be deceived in censuring the field, which this hip-shot grammarian cannot set into right frame of construction, neither here in the similitude, nor in the following reddition thereof; which being to this purpose, that "the faults of the best picked out, and presented in gross, seem monstrous; this," saith he, "you have done, in pinning on his sleeve the faults of others;" as if to pick out his own faults, and to pin the faults of others upon him, were to do the same thing.

To answer therefore how I have culled out the evil actions of the Remonstrant from his virtues, I am acquitted by the dexterity and conveyance of his nonsense, losing that for which he brought his parable. But what of other men's faults I have pinned upon his sleeve, let him show. For whether he were the man who termed the martyrs "Foxian confessors," it matters not; he that shall step up before others to defend a church government, which wants almost no circumstance, but only a name, to be a plain popedom, a government which changes the fatherly and ever-teaching discipline of Christ into that lordly and uninstructing jurisdiction, which properly makes the pope Antichrist, makes himself an accessory to all the evil committed by those who are armed to do mischief by that undue government; which they, by their wicked deeds, do, with a kind of passive and unwitting obedience to God, destroy; but he, by plausible words and traditions against the scripture, obstinately seeks to maintain. They, by their own wickedness ruining their own unjust authority, make room for good to succeed; but he, by a show of good upholding the evil which in them undoes itself, hinders the good which they by accident let in. Their manifest crimes serve to bring forth an ensuing good, and hasten a remedy against themselves; and his seeming good tends to reinforce their self-punishing crimes and his own, by doing his best to delay all redress. Shall not all the mischief which other men do be laid to his charge, if they do it by that unchurch-like power which he defends? Christ saith, "He that is not with me is against me; and he that gathers not with me, scatters." In what degree of enmity to Christ shall we place that man, then, who so is with him, as that it makes more against him; and so gathers with him, that it scatters more from him? Shall it avail

that man to say he honors the martyrs' memory, and treads in their steps? No; the pharisees confessed as much of the holy prophets. Let him, and such as he, when they are in their best actions, even at their prayers, look to hear that which the pharisees heard from John the Baptist when they least expected, when they rather looked for praise from him: "Generation of vipers, who hath warned ye to flee from the wrath to come?"

Now that ye have started back from the purity of scripture, which is the only rule of reformation, to the old vomit of your traditions; now that ye have either troubled or leavened the people of God, and the doctrine of the gospel, with scandalous ceremonies and mass-borrowed liturgies, do ye turn the use of that truth which ye profess, to countenance that falsehood which ye gain by? We also reverence the martyrs, but rely only upon the scriptures. And why we ought not to rely upon the martyrs, I shall be content with such reasons as my confuter himself affords me; who is, I must needs say for him, in that point as officious an adversary as I would wish to any man. For, "first," saith he, "there may be a martyr in a wrong cause, and as courageous in suffering as the best; sometimes in a good cause with a forward ambition displeasing to God. Otherwhiles they that story of them out of blind zeal or malice, may write many things of them untruly. If this be so, as ye hear his own confession, with what safety can the Remonstrant rely upon the martyrs as "patrons of his cause," whenas any of those who are alleged for the approvers of our liturgy or prelaty, might have been, though not in a wrong cause, martyrs? Yet whether not vainly ambitious of that honor, or whether not misreported or misunderstood in those their opinions, God only knows. The testimony of what we believe in religion must be such as the conscience may rest on to be infallible and incorruptible, which is only the word of God.

His fifth section finds itself aggrieved that the Remonstrant should be taxed with the illegal proceedings of the high commission, and oath *ex officio;* and first, "whether they were illegal or no, 'tis more than he knows." See this malevolent fox! that tyranny which the whole kingdom cried out against as stung with adders and scorpions, that tyranny which the parliament, in compassion of the church and commonwealth, hath dissolved and fetched up by the roots, for which it hath received the public thanks and blessings of thousands, this obscure thorn-eater of malice and detraction as well as of quodlibets and sophisms, knows not whether it were illegal or not. Evil, evil would be your reward, ye worthies of the parliament, if this sophister and his accomplices had the censuring or the sounding forth of your labors. And that the Remonstrant cannot wash his hands of all the cruelties exercised by the prelates, is past doubting. They scourged the confessors of the gospel; and he held the scourgers' garments. They executed their rage; and he, if he did nothing else, defended the government with the oath that did it, and the ceremonies which were the cause of it: does he think to be counted guiltless?

In the following section I must foretell ye, readers, the doings will be rough and dangerous, the baiting of a satire. And if the work seem more trivial or boisterous than for this discourse, let the Remonstrant thank the folly of this confuter, who could not let a private word pass, but he must make all this blaze of it. I had said, that because the Remonstrant was so much offended with those who were tart against the prelates, sure he loved toothless satires, which I took were as improper as a toothed sleekstone. This champion from behind the arras cries out, that those toothless satires were of the Remonstrant's making; and arms himself here tooth and nail, and horn to boot, to supply the want of teeth, or rather of gums in the satires; and for an onset tells me, that the simile of a sleekstone "shows I can be as bold with a prelate as familiar with a laundress." But does it not argue rather the lascivious promptness of his own fancy, who, from the harmless mention of a sleekstone, could neigh out the remembrance of his old conversation among the viragian trollops? For me, if he move me, I shall claim his own oath, the oath *ex officio*, against any priest or prelate in the kingdom, to have ever as much hated such pranks as the best and chastest of them all. That exception which I made against toothless satires, the confuter hopes I had from the satirist, but is far deceived: neither had I ever read the hobbling distich which he means.

For this good hap I had from a careful education, to be inured and seasoned betimes with the best and elegantest authors of the learned tongues, and thereto brought an ear that could measure a just cadence, and scan without articulating: rather nice and humorous in what was tolerable, than patient to read every drawling versifier. Whence lighting upon this title of "toothless satires," I will not conceal ye what I thought, readers, that sure this must be some sucking satyr, who might have done better to have used his coral, and made an end of breeding, ere he took upon him to wield a satire's whip. But when I heard him talk of "scouring the rusted swords of elvish knights," do not blame me if I changed my thought, and concluded him some desperate cutler. But why "his scornful muse could never abide with tragic shoes her ankles for to hide," the pace of the verse told me that her mawkin knuckles were never shapen to that royal buskin. And turning by chance to the sixth satire of his second book, I was confirmed; where having begun loftily "in heaven's universal alphabet," he falls down to that wretched poorness and frigidity, as to talk of "Bridge Street in heaven, and the ostler of heaven," and there wanting other matter to catch him a heat, (for certain he was in the frozen zone miserably benumbed,) with thoughts lower than any beadle betakes him to whip the signposts of Cambridge alehouses, the ordinary subject of freshmen's tales, and in a strain as pitiful. Which for him who would be counted the first English satire, to abase himself to, who might have learned better among the Latin and Italian satirists, and in our own tongue from the "Vision and Creed of Piers Plowman," besides others before him, manifested a presumptuous undertaking with weak and unexamined shoulders. For a satire as it was born out of a tragedy, so ought to resemble his parentage, to strike high, and adventure dangerously at the most eminent vices among the greatest persons, and not to creep into every blind tap-house, that fears a constable more than a satire. But that such a poem should be toothless, I still affirm it to be a bull, taking away the essence of that which it calls itself. For if it bite neither the persons nor the vices, how is it a satire? And if it bite either, how is it toothless? So that toothless satires are as much as if he had said toothless teeth. What we should do, therefore, with this learned comment upon teeth and horns, which hath brought this confutant into his pedantic kingdom of cornucopia, to reward him for glossing upon horns even to the Hebrew root, I know not; unless we should commend him to be lecturer in Eastcheap upon St. Luke's day, when they send their tribute to that famous haven by Deptford. But we are not like to escape him so; for now the worm of criticism works in him, he will tell us the derivation of "German rutters, of meat, and of ink," which doubtless, rightly applied with some gall in it, may prove good to heal this tetter of pedagogism that bespreads him, with such a tenesmus of originating, that if he be an Arminian, and deny original sin, all the etymologies of his book shall witness, that his brain is not meanly tainted with that infection.

His seventh section labors to cavil out the flaws which were found in the Remonstrant's logic; who having laid down for a general proposition, that "civil polity is variable and arbitrary," from whence was inferred logically upon him, that he had concluded the polity of England to be arbitrary, for general includes particular; here his defendant is not ashamed to confess, that the Remonstrant's proposition was sophistical by a fallacy called *ad plures interrogationes,* which sounds to me somewhat strange, that a Remonstrant of that pretended sincerity should bring deceitful and doubledealing propositions to the parliament. The truth is, he had let slip a shrewd passage ere he was aware, not thinking the conclusion would turn upon him with such a terrible edge, and not knowing how to wind out of the briers, he, or his substitute, seems more willing to lay the integrity of his logic to pawn, and grant a fallacy in his own major, where none is, than be forced to uphold the inference. For that distinction of possible and lawful, is ridiculous to be sought for in that proposition; no man doubting that it is possible to change the form of civil polity; and that it is held lawful by that major, the word "arbitrary" implies. Nor will this help him to deny that it is arbitrary, "at any time, or by any undertakers," (which are two limitations invented by him since,) for when it stands as he will have it now by his second edition, "civil polity is variable, but not at any time or by any undertakers," it will result upon him, belike then at some time, and by some undertakers it may. And so he goes on mincing the matter, till he meets with something in Sir Francis Bacon; then he takes heart again, and holds his major at large. But by and by, as soon as the shadow of Sir Francis hath left him, he falls off again, warping and warping, till he come to contradict himself in diameter; and denies flatly that it is "either variable or arbitrary, being once settled." Which third shift is no less a piece of laughter: for, before the polity was settled, how could it be variable, whenas it was no polity at all, but either an anarchy or a tyranny? That limitation, therefore, of after-settling, is a mere tautology. So that, in fine, his former assertion is now recanted, and "civil polity is neither variable nor arbitrary."

Whatever else may persuade me, that this Confutation was not made without some assistance or advice of the Remonstrant, yet in this eighth section that his hand was not greatly intermixed, I can easily believe. For it begins with this surmise, that "not having to accuse the Remonstrant to the king, I do it to the parliament:" which conceit of the man cleanly shoves the king out of the parliament, and makes two bodies of one. Whereas the Remonstrant, in the epistle to his last "Short Answer," gives his supposal, "that they cannot be severed in the rights of their several concernments." Mark, readers, if they cannot be severed in what is several, (which casts a bull's eye to go yoke with the toothless satires,) how should they be severed in their common concernments, the welfare of the land, by due accusation of such as are the common grievances, among which I took the Remonstrant to be one? And therefore if I accused him to the parliament, it was the same as to accuse him to the king.

Next he casts it into the dish of I know not whom, "that they flatter some of the house, and libel others whose consciences made them vote contrary to some proceedings." Those some proceedings can be understood of nothing else but the deputy's execution. And can this private concoctor of malcontent, at the very instant when he pretends to extol the parliament, afford thus to blur over, rather than to mention that public triumph of their justice and constancy, so high, so glorious, so reviving to the fainted commonwealth, with such a suspicious and murmuring expression as to call it some proceedings? And yet immediately he falls to glossing, as if he were the only man that rejoiced at these times. But I shall discover to ye, readers, that this his praising of them is as full of nonsense and scholastic foppery, as his meaning he himself discovers to be full of close malignity. His first encomium is, "that the sun looks not upon a braver, nobler convocation than is that of king, peers, and commons."

One thing I beg of ye, readers, as ye bear any zeal to learning, to elegance, and that which is called decorum in the writing of praise, especially on such a noble argument, ye would not be offended, though I rate this cloistered lubber according to his deserts. Where didst thou learn to be so aguish, so pusillanimous, thou losel bachelor of art, as against all custom and use of speech to term the high and sovereign court of parliament, a convocation? Was this the flower of all thy synonimas and voluminous papers, whose best folios are predestined to no better end than to make winding-sheets in Lent for pilchers? Couldst thou presume thus, with one word's speaking, to clap, as it were under hatches, the king with all his peers and gentry into square caps and monkish hoods? How well dost thou now appear to be a chip of the old block, that could find, "Bridge Street and alehouses in heaven?" Why didst thou not, to be his perfect imitator, liken the king to the vice-chancellor, and the lords to the doctors? Neither is this an indignity only, but a reproach, to call that inviolable residence of justice and liberty by such an odious name as now a "convocation" is become, which would be nothing injured, though it were

styled the house of bondage, whereout so many cruel tasks, so many unjust burdens have been laden upon the bruised consciences of so many Christians throughout the land.

But which of those worthy deeds, whereof we and our posterity must confess this parliament to have done so many and so noble, which of those memorable acts comes first into his praises? None of all, not one. What will he then praise them for? Not for anything doing, but for deferring to do, for deferring to chastise his lewd and insolent compriests: not that they have deferred all, but that he hopes they will remit what is yet behind. For the rest of his oratory that follows, so just is it in the language of stall epistle nonsense, that if he who made it can understand it, I deny not but that he may deserve for his pains a cast doublet. When a man would look he should vent something of his own, as ever in a set speech the manner is with him that knows anything; he, lest we should not take notice enough of his barren stupidity, declares it by alphabet, and refers us to odd remnants in his topics. Nor yet content with the wonted room of his margin, but he must cut out large docks and creeks into his text, to unlade the foolish frigate of his unseasonable authorities, not wherewith to praise the parliament, but to tell them what he would have them do. What else there is, he jumbles together in such a lost construction, as no man, either lettered or unlettered, will be able to piece up. I shall spare to transcribe him, but if I do him wrong let me be so dealt with.

Now although it be a digression from the ensuing matter, yet because it shall not be said I am apter to blame others than to make trial myself, and that I may, after this harsh discord, touch upon a smoother string, awhile to entertain myself and him that list, with some more pleasing fit, and not the least to testify the gratitude which I owe to those public benefactors of their country, for the share I enjoy in the common peace and good by their incessant labors; I shall be so troublesome to this disclaimer for once, as to show him what he might have better said in their praise; wherein I must mention only some few things of many, for more than that to a digression may not be granted. Although certainly their actions are worthy not thus to be spoken of by the way, yet if hereafter it befall me to attempt something more answerable to their great merits, I perceive how hopeless it will be to reach the height of their praises at the accomplishment of that expectation that waits upon their noble deeds, the unfinishing whereof already surpasses what others before them have left enacted with their utmost performance through many ages. And to the end we may be confident that what they do proceeds neither from uncertain opinion nor sudden counsels, but from mature wisdom, deliberate virtue, and dear affection to the public good, I shall begin at that which made them likeliest in the eyes of good men to effect those things for the recovery of decayed religion and the commonwealth, which they who were best minded had long wished for, but few, as the times then were desperate, had the courage to hope for.

First, therefore, the most of them being either of ancient and high nobility, or at least of known and well-reputed ancestry, which is a great advantage towards virtue one way, but in respect of wealth, ease, and flattery, which accompanies a nice and tender education, is as much a hindrance another way: the good which lay before them they took, in imitating the worthiest of their progenitors: and the evil which assaulted their younger years by the temptation of riches, high birth, and that usual bringing up, perhaps too favorable and too remiss, through the strength of an inbred goodness, and with the help of divine grace, that had marked them out for no mean purposes, they nobly overcame. Yet had they a greater danger to cope with; for being trained up in the knowledge of learning, and sent to those places which were intended to be the seed-plots of piety and the liberal arts, but were become the nurseries of superstition and empty speculation, as they were prosperous against those vices which grow upon youth out of idleness and superfluity, so were they happy in working off the harms of their abused studies and labors; correcting, by the clearness of their own judgment, the errors of their misinstruction, and were, as David was, wiser than their teachers. And

although their lot fell into such times, and to be bred in such places, where if they chanced to be taught anything good, or of their own accord had learnt it, they might see that presently untaught them by the custom and ill example of their elders; so far in all probability was their youth from being misled by the single power of example, as their riper years were known to be unmoved with the baits of preferment, and undaunted for any discouragement and terror, which appeared often to those that loved religion and their native liberty; which two things God hath inseparably knit together, and hath disclosed to us, that they who seek to corrupt our religion, are the same that would enthral our civil liberty.

Thus in the midst of all disadvantages and disrespects, (some also at last not without imprisonment and open disgraces in the cause of their country,) having given proof of themselves to be better made and framed by nature to the love and practice of virtue, than others under the holiest precepts and best examples have been headstrong and prone to vice; and having, in all the trials of a firm ingrafted honesty, not oftener buckled in the conflict than given every opposition the foil; this moreover was added by favor from Heaven, as an ornament and happiness to their virtue, that it should be neither obscure in the opinion of men, nor eclipsed for want of matter equal to illustrate itself; God and man consenting in joint approbation to choose them out as worthiest above others to be both the great reformers of the church, and the restorers of the commonwealth. Nor did they deceive that expectation which with the eyes and desires of their country was fixed upon them: for no sooner did the force of so much united excellence meet in one globe of brightness and efficacy, but encountering the dazzled resistance of tyranny, they gave not over, though their enemies were strong and subtle, till they had laid her grovelling upon the fatal block; with one stroke winning again our lost liberties and charters, which our forefathers after so many battles could scarce maintain.

And meeting next, as I may so resemble, with the second life of tyranny, (for she was grown an ambiguous monster, and to be slain in two shapes,) guarded with superstition, which hath no small power to captivate the minds of men otherwise most wise, they neither were taken with her mitred hypocrisy, nor terrified with the push of her bestial horns, but breaking them, immediately forced her to unbend the pontifical brow, and recoil; which repulse only given to the prelates (that we may imagine how happy their removal would be) was the producement of such glorious effects and consequences in the church, that if I should compare them with those exploits of highest fame in poems and panegyrics of old, I am certain it would but diminish and impair their worth, who are now my argument; for those ancient worthies delivered men from such tyrants as were content to enforce only an outward obedience, letting the mind be as free as it could; but these have freed us from a doctrine of tyranny, that offered violence and corruption even to the inward persuasion. They set at liberty nations and cities of men good and bad mixed together; but these, opening the prisons and dungeons, called out of darkness and bonds the elect martyrs and witnesses of their Redeemer. They restored the body to ease and wealth; but these, the oppressed conscience to that freedom which is the chief prerogative of the gospel; taking off those cruel burdens imposed not by necessity, as other tyrants are wont or the safeguard of their lives, but laid upon our necks by the strange wilfulness and wantonness of a needless and jolly persecutor, called Indifference. Lastly, some of those ancient deliverers have had immortal praises for preserving their citizens from a famine of corn. But these, by this only repulse of an unholy hierarchy, almost in a moment replenished with saving knowledge their country, nigh famished for want of that which should feed their souls. All this being done while two armies in the field stood gazing on: the one in reverence of such nobleness quietly gave back and dislodged; the other, spite of the unruliness, and doubted fidelity in some regiments, was either persuaded or compelled to disband and retire home.

With such a majesty had their wisdom begirt itself, that whereas others had levied war to subdue a nation that sought for peace, they sitting here in peace could so many miles extend the force of their single words, as to overawe the dissolute stoutness of an armed power, secretly stirred up and almost hired against them. And having by a solemn protestation vowed themselves and the kingdom anew to God and his service, and by a prudent foresight above what their fathers thought on, prevented the dissolution and frustrating of their designs by an untimely breaking up; notwithstanding all the treasonous plots against them, all the rumors either of rebellion or invasion, they have not been yet brought to change their constant resolution, ever to think fearlessly of their own safeties, and hopefully of the commonwealth: which hath gained them such an admiration from all good men, that now they hear it as their ordinary surname, to be saluted the fathers of their country, and sit as gods among daily petitions and public thanks flowing in upon them. Which doth so little yet exalt them in their own thoughts, that, with all gentle affability and courteous acceptance, they both receive and return that tribute of thanks which is tendered them; testifying their zeal and desire to spend themselves as it were piece-meal upon the grievances and wrongs of their distressed nation; insomuch that the meanest artisans and laborers, at other times also women, and often the younger sort of servants assembling with their complaints, and that sometimes in a less humble guise than for petitioners, have gone with confidence, that neither their meanness would be rejected, nor their simplicity contemned; nor yet their urgency distasted either by the dignity, wisdom, or moderation of that supreme senate; nor did they depart unsatisfied.

And, indeed, if we consider the general concourse of suppliants, the free and ready admittance, the willing and speedy redress in what is possible, it will not seem much otherwise, than as if some divine commission from heaven were descended to take into hearing and commiseration the long remediless afflictions of this kingdom; were it not that none more than themselves labor to remove and divert such thoughts, lest men should place too much confidence in their persons, still referring us and our prayers to him that can grant all, and appointing the monthly return of public fasts and supplications. Therefore the more they seek to humble themselves, the more does God, by manifest signs and testimonies, visibly honor their proceedings; and sets them as the mediators of this his covenant, which he offers us to renew. Wicked men daily conspire their hurt, and it comes to nothing; rebellion rages in our Irish province, but, with miraculous and lossless victories of few against many, is daily discomfited and broken; if we neglect not this early pledge of God's inclining towards us, by the slackness of our needful aids. And whereas at other times we count it ample honor when God vouchsafes to make man the instrument and subordinate worker of his gracious will, such acceptation have their prayers found with him, that to them he hath been pleased to make himself the agent, and immediate performer of their desires; dissolving their difficulties when they are thought inexplicable, cutting out ways for them where no passage could be seen; as who is there so regardless of divine Providence, that from late occurrences will not confess? If, therefore, it be so high a grace when men are preferred to be but the inferior officers of good things from God, what is it when God himself condescends, and works with his own hands to fulfil the requests of men? Which I leave with them as the greatest praise that can belong to human nature: not that we should think they are at the end of their glorious progress, but that they will go on to follow his Almighty leading, who seems to have thus covenanted with them; that if the will and the endeavor shall be theirs, the performance and the perfecting shall be his. Whence only it is that I have not feared, though many wise men have miscarried in praising great designs before the utmost event, because I see who is their assistant, who their confederate, who hath engaged his omnipotent arm to support and crown with success their faith, their fortitude, their just and magnanimous actions, till he have brought to pass all that expected good which, his servants trust, is in his thoughts to bring upon this land in the full and perfect reformation of his church.

Thus far I have digressed, readers, from my former subject: but into such a path, as I doubt not ye will agree with me, to be much fairer and more delightful than the roadway I was in. And how to break off suddenly into those jarring notes which this confuter hath set me, I must be wary, unless I can provide against offending the ear, as some musicians are wont skilfully to fall out of one key into another, without breach of harmony. By good luck, therefore, his ninth section is spent in mournful elegy, certain passionate soliloquies, and two whole pages of interrogatories that praise the Remonstrant even to the sonneting of "his fresh cheeks, quick eyes, round tongue, agile hand, and nimble invention."

In his tenth section he will needs erect figures, and tell fortunes: "I am no bishop," he says; "I was never born to it." Let me tell, therefore, this wizard, since he calculates so right, that he may know there be in the world, and I among those, who nothing admire his idol—a bishopric; and hold that it wants so much to be a blessing, as that I rather deem it the merest, the falsest, the most unfortunate gift of fortune. And were the punishment and misery of being a prelate bishop terminated only in the person, and did not extend to the affliction of the whole diocese, if I would wish anything in the bitterness of soul to mine enemy, I would wish him the biggest and fattest bishopric. But he proceeds, and the familiar belike informs him, that "a rich widow, or a lecture, or both, would content me:" whereby I perceive him to be more ignorant in his art of divining than any gipsy. For this I cannot omit without ingratitude to that Providence above, who hath ever bred me up in plenty, although my life hath not been unexpensive in learning, and voyaging about; so long as it shall please him to lend me what he hath hitherto thought good, which is enough to serve me in all honest and liberal occasions, and something over besides, I were unthankful to that highest bounty, if I should make myself so poor, as to solicit needily any such kind of rich hopes as this fortune-teller dreams of. And that he may further learn how his astrology is wide all the houses of heaven in spelling marriages, I care not if I tell him thus much professedly, though it be to the losing of my rich hopes, as he calls them, that I think with them who, both in prudence and elegance of spirit, would choose a virgin of mean fortunes, honestly bred, before the wealthiest widow. The fiend, therefore, that told our Chaldean the contrary, was a lying fiend.

His next venom he utters against a prayer, which he found in the Animadversions, angry it seems to find any prayers but in the service-book; he dislikes it, and I therefore like it the better. "It was theatrical," he says; and yet it consisted most of scripture language; it had no rubric to be sung in an antic cope upon the stage of a high altar. "It was big-mouthed," he says; no marvel, if it were framed as the voice of three kingdoms; neither was it a prayer, so much as a hymn in prose, frequent both in the prophets, and in human authors; therefore, the style was greater than for an ordinary prayer. "It was an astounding prayer." I thank him for that confession, so it was intended to astound and to astonish the guilty prelates; and this confuter confesses, that with him it wrought that effect. But in that which follows, he does not play the soothsayer, but the diabolic slanderer of prayers. "It was made," he says, "not so much to please God, or to benefit the weal public," (how dares the viper judge that?) "but to intimate," saith he, "your good abilities to her that is your rich hopes, your Maronilla."

How hard it is when a man meets with a fool to keep his tongue from folly! That were miserable indeed to be a courtier of Maronilla, and withal of such a hapless invention, as that no way should be left me to present my meaning but to make myself a canting probationer of orisons. The Remonstrant, when he was as young as I, could

"Teach each hollow grove to sound his love,
Wearying echo with one changeless word."
　　　　　　　　　Toothless Satires.

And so he well might and all his auditory besides, with his "teach each."

'Whether so me list my lovely thoughts to sing,
Come dance ye nimble dryads by my side,
Whiles I report my fortunes or my loves."
　　　　　　　　　Toothless Satires.

Delicious! he had that whole bevy at command whether in morrice or at maypole; whilst I by this figure-caster must be imagined in such distress as to sue to Maronilla, and yet left so impoverished of what to say, as to turn my liturgy into my lady's psalter. Believe it, graduate, I am not altogether so rustic, and nothing so irreligious, but as far distant from a lecturer as the merest laic, for any consecrating hand of a prelate that shall ever touch me. Yet I shall not decline the more for that, to speak my opinion in the controversy next moved, "whether the people may be allowed for competent judges of a minister's ability." For how else can be fulfilled that which God hath promised, to pour out such abundance of knowledge upon all sorts of men in the times of the gospel? How should the people examine the doctrine which is taught them, as Christ and his apostles continually bid them do? How should they "discern and beware of false prophets, and try every spirit," if they must be thought unfit to judge of the minister's abilities? The apostles ever labored to persuade the Christian flock, that they "were called in Christ to all perfectness of spiritual knowledge, and full assurance of understanding in the mystery of God." But the non-resident and plurality-gaping prelates, the gulfs and whirlpools of benefices, but the dry pits of all sound doctrine, that they may the better preach what they list to their sheep, are still possessing them that they are sheep indeed, without judgment, without understanding, "the very beasts of Mount Sinai," as this confuter calls them; which words of theirs may serve to condemn them out of their own mouths, and to show the gross contrarieties that are in their opinions. For while none think the people so void of knowledge as the prelates think them, none are so backward and malignant as they to bestow knowledge upon them; both by suppressing the frequency of sermons, and the printed explanations of the English Bible.

No marvel if the people turn beasts, when their teachers themselves, as Isaiah calls them, "are dumb and greedy dogs that can never have enough; ignorant, blind, and cannot understand; who, while they all look their own way, every one for his gain from his quarter," how many parts of the land are fed with windy ceremonies instead of sincere milk; and while one prelate enjoys the nourishment and right of twenty ministers, how many waste places are left as dark as "Galilee of the Gentiles, sitting in the region and shadow of death," without preaching minister, without light. So little care they of beasts to make them men, that by their sorcerous doctrine of formalities, they take the way to transform them out of Christian men into judaizing beasts. Had they but taught the land, or suffered it to be taught, as Christ would it should have been in all plenteous dispensation of the word; then the poor mechanic might have so accustomed his ear to good teaching, as to have discerned between faithful teachers and false. But now, with a most inhuman cruelty, they who have put out the people's eyes, reproach them of their blindness; just as the pharisees their true fathers were wont, who could not endure that the people should be thought competent judges of Christ's doctrine, although we know they judged far better than those great rabbis; yet "this people," said they, "that knows not the law is accursed."

We need not the authority of Pliny brought to tell us the people cannot judge of a minister: yet that hurts not. For as none can judge of a painter, or statuary, but he who is an artist, that is either in the practice or theory, which is often separated from the practice, and judges learnedly without it; so none can judge of a Christian teacher, but he who hath either the practice, or the knowledge of Christian religion, though not so artfully digested in him. And who almost of the meanest Christians hath not heard the scriptures often read from his childhood, besides so many sermons and lectures, more in number than any student hath heard in philosophy, whereby he may easily attain to know when he is wisely taught, and when weakly? whereof, three ways I remember are set down in scripture; the one is to read often that best of books written to this purpose, that not the wise only, but the simple and ignorant, may learn by them; the other way to know of a minister is, by the life he leads, whereof the meanest understanding

may be apprehensive. The last way to judge aright in this point is, when he who judges, lives a Christian life himself. Which of these three will the confuter affirm to exceed the capacity of a plain artisan? And what reason then is there left, wherefore he should be denied his voice in the election of his minister, as not thought a competent discerner?

It is but arrogance therefore, and the pride of a metaphysical fume, to think that "the mutinous rabble" (for so he calls the Christian congregation) "would be so mistaken in a clerk of the university," that were to be their minister. I doubt me those clerks, that think so, are more mistaken in themselves; and what with truanting and debauchery, what with false grounds and the weakness of natural faculties in many of them, (it being a maxim in some men to send the simplest of their sons thither,) perhaps there would be found among them as many unsolid and corrupted judgments, both in doctrine and life, as in any other two corporations of like bigness. This is undoubted, that if any carpenter, smith, or weaver were such a bungler in his trade, as the greater number of them are in their profession, he would starve for any custom. And should he exercise his manufacture as little as they do their talents, he would forget his art; and should he mistake his tools as they do theirs, he would mar all the work he took in hand. How few among them that know to write or speak in a pure style; much less to distinguish the ideas and various kinds of style in Latin barbarous, and oft not without solecisms, declaiming in rugged and miscellanous gear blown together by the four winds, and in their choice preferring the gay rankness of Apuleius, Arnobius, or any modern fustianist, before the native Latinisms of Cicero. In the Greek tongue most of them unlettered, or "unentered to any sound proficiency in those Attic masters of moral wisdom and eloquence." In the Hebrew text, which is so necessary to be understood, except it be some few of them, their lips are utterly uncircumcised.

No less are they out of the way in philosophy, pestering their heads with the sapless dotages of old Paris and Salamanca. And that which is the main point, in their sermons affecting the comments and postils of friars and jesuits, but scorning and slighting the reformed writers; insomuch that the better sort among them will confess it a rare matter to hear a true edifying sermon, in either of their great churches: and that such as are most hummed and applauded there, would scarce be suffered the second hearing in a grave congregation of pious Christians. Is there cause why these men should overwean, and be so queasy of the rude multitude, lest their deep worth should be undervalued for want of fit umpires? No, my matriculated confutant, there will not want in any congregation of this island, that hath not been altogether famished or wholly perverted with prelatish leaven; there will not want divers plain and solid men, that have learned by the experience of a good conscience, what it is to be well taught, who will soon look through and through both the lofty nakedness of your Latinizing barbarian, and the finical goosery of your neat sermon actor. And so I leave you and your fellow "stars," as you term them, "of either horizon," meaning I suppose either hemisphere, unless you will be ridiculous in your astronomy; for the rational horizon in heaven is but one, and the sensible horizons in earth are innumerable; so that your allusion was as erroneous as your stars. But that you did well to prognosticate them all at lowest in the horizon; that is, either seeming bigger than they are through the mist and vapor which they raise, or else sinking and wasted to the snuff in their western socket.

His eleventh section intends I know not what, unless to clog us with the residue of his phlegmatic sloth, discussing with a heavy pulse the "expedience of set forms;" which no question but to some, and for some time, may be permitted, and perhaps there may be usefully set forth by the church a common directory of public prayer, especially in the administration of the sacraments. But that it should therefore be enforced where both minister and people profess to have no need, but to be scandalized by it, that, I hope, every sensible Christian will deny; and the reasons of such denial the confuter himself, as his bounty still is to his adversary, will give

us out of his affirmation. First, saith he, "God in his providence hath chosen some to teach others, and pray for others, as ministers and pastors." Whence I gather, that however the faculty of others may be, yet that they whom God hath set apart to his ministry, are by him endued with an ability of prayer; because their office is to pray for others, and not to be the lip-working deacons of other men's appointed words. Nor is it easily credible, that he who can preach well, should be unable to pray well; whenas it is indeed the same ability to speak affirmatively, or doctrinally, and only by changing the mood, to speak prayingly.

In vain, therefore, do they pretend to want utterance in prayer, who can find utterance to preach. And if prayer be the gift of the Spirit, why do they admit those to the ministry who want a main gift of their function, and prescribe gifted men to use that which is the remedy of another man's want; setting them their tasks to read, whom the Spirit of God stands ready to assist in his ordinance with the gift of free conceptions? What if it be granted to the infirmity of some ministers (though such seem rather to be half-ministers) to help themselves with a set form, shall it therefore be urged upon the plenteous graces of others? And let it be granted to some people while they are babes in Christian gifts, were it not better to take it away soon after, as we do loitering books and interlineary translations from children: to stir up and exercise that portion of the Spirit which is in them, and not impose it upon congregations who not only deny to need it, but as a thing troublesome and offensive, refuse it?

Another reason which he brings for liturgy, is "the preserving of order, unity, and piety;" and the same shall be my reason against liturgy. For I, readers, shall always be of this opinion, that obedience to the Spirit of God, rather than to the fair seeming pretences of men, is the best and most dutiful order that a Christian can observe. If the Spirit of God manifest the gift of prayer in his minister, what more seemly order in the congregation than to go along with that man in our devoutest affections? For him to abridge himself by reading, and to forestall himself in those petitions, which he must either omit, or vainly repeat, when he comes into the pulpit under a show of order, is the greatest disorder. Nor is unity less broken, especially by our liturgy, though this author would almost bring the communion of saints to a communion of liturgical words. For what other reformed church holds communion with us by our liturgy, and does not rather dislike it? And among ourselves, who knows it not to have been a perpetual cause of disunion?

Lastly, it hinders piety rather than sets it forward, being more apt to weaken the spiritual faculties, if the people be not weaned from it in due time; as the daily pouring in of hot waters quenches the natural heat. For not only the body and the mind, but also the improvement of God's Spirit, is quickened by using. Whereas they who will ever adhere to liturgy, bring themselves in the end to such a pass, by overmuch leaning, as to lose even the legs of their devotion. These inconveniences and dangers follow the compelling of set forms: but that the toleration of the English liturgy now in use is more dangerous than the compelling of any other which the reformed churches use, these reasons following may evince. To contend that it is fantastical, if not senseless in some places, were a copious argument, especially in the Responsories. For such alternations as are there used must be by several persons; but the minister and the people cannot so sever their interests, as to sustain several persons; he being the only mouth of the whole body which he presents. And if the people pray, he being silent, or they ask one thing, and he another, it either changes the property, making the priest the people, and the people the priest, by turns, or else makes two persons and two bodies representative where there should be but one. Which, if it be nought else, must needs be a strange quaintness in ordinary prayer.

The like, or worse, may be said of the litany, wherein neither priest nor people speak any entire sense of themselves throughout the whole, I know not what to name it; only by the timely contribution of their parted stakes, closing up as it were, the schism of a sliced prayer, they pray not in vain, for by this means they keep life between them in a piece of gasping sense, and keep down the sauciness of a continual rebounding nonsense. And hence it is, that as it hath been far from the imitation of any warranted prayer, so we all know it hath been obvious to be the pattern of many a jig. And he who hath but read in good books of devotion, and no more, cannot be so either of ear or judgment unpractised to distinguish what is grave, pathetical, devout, and what not, but will presently perceive this liturgy all over in conception lean and dry, of affections empty and unmoving; of passion, or any height whereto the soul might soar upon the wings of zeal, destitute and barren; besides errors, tautologies, impertinencies, as those thanks in the woman's churching for her delivery from sunburning and moonblasting, as if she had been travailing not in her bed, but in the deserts of Arabia.

So that while some men cease not to admire the incomparable frame of our liturgy, I cannot but admire as fast what they think is become of judgment and taste in other men, that they can hope to be heard without laughter. And if this were all, perhaps it were a compliable matter. But when we remember this our liturgy, where we found it, whence we had it, and yet where we left it, still serving to all the abominations of the antichristian temple, it may be wondered how we can demur whether it should be done away or no, and not rather fear we have highly offended in using it so long. It hath indeed been pretended to be more ancient than the mass; but so little proved, that whereas other corrupt liturgies have had withal such a seeming antiquity, as that their publishers have ventured to ascribe them, with their worst corruptions, either to St. Peter, St. James, St. Mark, or at least to Chrysostom or Basil, ours hath been never able to find either age or author allowable, on whom to father those things therein which are least offensive, except the two creeds, for Te Deum has a smatch in it of Limbus Patrum: as if Christ had not "opened the kingdom of heaven" before he had "overcome the sharpness of death." So that having received it from the papal church as an original creature, for aught can be shown to the contrary, formed and fashioned by workmasters ill to be trusted, we may be assured that if God loathe the best of an idolater's prayer, much more the conceited fangle of his prayer.

This confuter himself confesses that a community of the same set form in prayers, is that which "makes church and church truly one;" we then using a liturgy far more like to the mass-book than to any Protestant set form, by his own words must have more communion with the Romish church, than with any of the reformed. How can we then not partake with them the curse and vengeance of their superstition, to whom we come so near in the same set form and dress of our devotion? Do we think to sift the matter finer than we are sure God in his jealousy will, who detested both the gold and the spoil of idolatrous cities, and forbid the eating of things offered to idols? Are we stronger than he, to brook that which his heart cannot brook? It is not surely because we think that prayers are nowhere to be had but at Rome! That were a foul scorn and indignity cast upon all the reformed churches, and our own: if we imagine that all the godly ministers of England are not able to now mold a better and more pious liturgy than this which was conceived and infanted by an idolatrous mother, how basely were that to esteem of God's Spirit, and all the holy blessings and privileges of a true church above a false!

Hark ye, prelates, is this your glorious mother of England, who, whenas Christ hath taught her to pray, thinks it not enough unless she add thereto the teaching of Antichrist? How can we believe ye would refuse to take the stipend of Rome, when ye shame not to live upon the almsbasket of her prayers? Will ye persuade us that ye can curse Rome from your hearts, when none but Rome must teach ye to pray? Abraham disdained to take so much as a thread or a shoe-lachet from the king of Sodom, though no foe of his, but a wicked king; and shall we receive our prayers at the bounty of our more wicked enemies, whose gifts are no gifts, but the instruments of our bane? Alas! that the Spirit of God should blow as an uncertain wind, should so mistake his inspiring, to misbestow his gifts, promised only to the elect, that the idolatrous should find words acceptable to present God with, and abound to their neighbors, while the true professors of the gospel can find nothing of their own worth the constituting, wherewith to worship God in public! Consider if this be to magnify the church of England, and not rather to display her nakedness to all the world.

Like, therefore, as the retaining of this Romish liturgy is a provocation to God, and a dishonor to our church, so is it by those ceremonies, those purifyings and offerings at the altar, a pollution and disturbance to the gospel itself; and a kind of driving us with the foolish Galatians to another gospel. For that which the apostles taught hath freed us in religion from the ordinances of men, and commands that "burdens be not laid" upon the redeemed of Christ; though the formalist will say, "What! no decency in God's worship?" Certainly, readers, the worship of God singly in itself, the very act of prayer and thanksgiving, with those free and unimposed expressions which from a sincere heart unbidden come into the outward gesture, is the greatest decency that can be imagined. Which to dress up and garnish with a devised bravery abolished in the law, and disclaimed by the gospel, adds nothing but a deformed ugliness; and hath ever afforded a colorable pretence to bring in all those traditions and carnalities that are so killing to the power and virtue of the gospel. What was that which made the Jews, figured under the names of Aholah and Aholibah, go a whoring after all the heathen's inventions, but that they saw a religion gorgeously attired and desirable to the eye? What was all that the false doctors of the primitive church and ever since have done, but "to make a fair show in the flesh," as St. Paul's words are?

If we have indeed given a bill of divorce to popery and superstition, why do we not say as to a divorced wife, "Those things which are yours take them all with you, and they shall sweep after you?" Why were not we thus wise at our parting from Rome? Ah! like a crafty adulteress, she forgot not all her smooth looks and enticing words at her parting: "Yet keep these letters, these tokens, and these few ornaments; I am not all so greedy of what is mine, let them preserve with you the memory"—of what I am? No, but—"of what I was; once fair and lovely in your eyes." Thus did those tenderhearted reformers dotingly suffer themselves to be overcome with harlot's language. And she, like a witch, but with a contrary policy, did not take something of theirs, that she might still have power to bewitch them, but for the same intent left something of her own behind her. And that her whorish cunning should prevail to work upon us her deceitful ends, though it be sad to speak, yet, such is our blindness, that we deserve. For we are deep in dotage. We cry out sacrilege and misdevotion against those who in zeal have demolished the dens and cages of her unclean wallowings. We stand for a popish liturgy as for the ark of our covenant. And so little does it appear our prayers are from the heart, that multitudes of us declare, they know not how to pray but by rote. Yet they can learnedly invent a prayer of their own to the parliament, that they may still ignorantly read the prayers of other men to God. They object, that if we must forsake all that is Rome's, we must bid adieu to our creed; and I had thought our creed had been of the apostles, for so it bears title. But if it be hers, let her take it. We can want no creed, so long as we want not the scriptures. We magnify those who, in reforming our church, have inconsiderately and blamefully permitted the old leaven to remain and sour our whole lump. But they were martyrs: true; and he that looks well into the book of God's providence, if he read there that God, for this their negligence and halting, brought all that following persecution upon this church, and on themselves, perhaps will be found at the last day not to have read amiss.

But now, readers, we have the port within sight; his last section, which is no deep one, remains only to be forded, and then the wished shore. And here first it pleases him much, that he hath descried me, as he conceives, to be unread in the councils. Concerning which matter it will not be unnecessary to shape him this answer; that some years I had spent in the stories of those Greek and Roman exploits, wherein I found many things both nobly done, and worthily spoken: when, coming in the method of time to that age wherein the church had obtained a Christian emperor, I so prepared myself, as being now to read examples of wisdom and goodness among those who were foremost in the church, not elsewhere to be paralleled; but to the amazement of what I expected, readers, I found it all quite contrary: excepting in some very few, nothing but ambition, corruption, contention, combustion; insomuch that I could not but love the historian, Socrates, who, in the proem to his fifth book professes, "he was fain to intermix affairs of state; for that it would be else an extreme annoyance to hear, in a continued discourse, the endless brabbles and counterplottings of the bishops."

Finding, therefore, the most of their actions in single to be weak, and yet turbulent, full of strife and yet flat of spirit; and the sum of their best councils there collected, to be most commonly in questions either trivial or vain, or else of short and easy decision, without that great bustle which they made; I concluded that if their single ambition and ignorance was such, then certainly united in a council it would be much more; and if the compendious recital of what they there did was so tedious and unprofitable, then surely to sit out the whole extent of their tattle in a dozen volumes would be a loss of time irrecoverable. Besides that which I had read of St. Martin, who for his last sixteen years could never be persuaded to be at any council of the bishops. And Gregory Nazianzen betook him to the same resolution, affirming to Procopius, "that of any council or meeting of bishops he never saw good end; nor any remedy thereby of evil in the church, but rather an increase. For," saith he, "their contentions and desire of lording no tongue is able to express."

I have not therefore, I confess, read more of the councils, save here and there; I should be sorry to have been such a prodigal of my time; but, that which is better, I can assure this confuter, I have read into them all. And if I want anything yet I shall reply something toward that which in the defence of Murena was answered by Cicero to Sulpitius the lawyer. If ye provoke me (for at no hand else will I undertake such a frivolous labor) I will in three months be an expert councilist. For, be not deceived, readers, by men that would overawe your ears with big names and huge tomes that contradict and repeal one another, because they can cram a margin with citations. Do but winnow their chaff from their wheat, ye shall see their great heap shrink and wax thin, past belief.

From hence he passes to inquire wherefore I should blame the vices of the prelates only, seeing the inferior clergy is known to be as faulty. To which let him hear in brief; that those priests whose vices have been notorious, are all prelatical, which argues both the impiety of that opinion, and the wicked remissness of that government. We hear not of any which are called nonconformists, that have been accused for scandalous living; but are known to be pious or at least sober men: which is a great good argument that they are in the truth and prelates in the error. He would be resolved next, "What the corruptions of the universities concern the prelates?" And to that let him take this, that the Remonstrant having spoken as if learning would decay with the removal of prelates, I showed him that while books were extant and in print, learning could not readily be at a worse pass in the universities than it was now under their government. Then he seeks to justify the pernicious sermons of the clergy, as if they upheld sovereignty; whenas all Christian sovereignty is by law, and to no other end but to the maintenance of the common good. But their doctrine was plainly the dissolution of law, which only sets up sovereignty, and the erecting of an arbitrary sway, according to private will, to which they would enjoin a slavish obedience without law; which is the known definition of a tyrant, and a tyrannized people.

A little beneath he denies that great riches in the church are the baits of pride and ambition; of which error to undeceive him I shall allege a reputed divine authority, as ancient as Constantine, which his love to antiquity must not except against; and to add the more weight, he shall learn it rather in the words of our old poet, Gower, than in mine, that he may see it is no new opinion, but a truth delivered of old by a voice from heaven, and ratified by long experience.

"This Constantine which heal hath found,
Within Rome anon let found
Two churches which he did make
For Peter and for Paul's sake:
Of whom he had a vision,
And yafe thereto possession
Of lordship and of world's good;
But how so that his will was good
Toward the pope and his franchise,
Yet hath it proved otherwise
To see the working of the deed;
For in cronick thus I read,
Anon as he hath made the yeft,
A voice was heard on high the left,
Of which all Rome was adrad,
And said, this day venim is shad
In holy Church, of temporall
That meddleth with the spiritual;
And how it stant in that degree,
Yet may a man the sooth see,
God amend it when he will,
I can thereto none other skill."

But there were beasts of prey, saith he, before wealth was bestowed on the church. What, though, because the vultures had then but small picking, shall we therefore go and fling them a full gorge? If they, for lucre, use to creep into the church undiscernibly, the more wisdom will it be so to provide that no revenue there may exceed the golden mean; for so good pastors will be content, as having need of no more, and knowing withal the precept and example of Christ and his apostles, and also will be less tempted to ambition. The bad will have but small matter whereon to set their mischief awork; and the worst and subtlest heads will not come at all, when they shall see the crop nothing answerable to their capacious greediness; for small temptations allure but dribbling offenders; but a great purchase will call such as both are most able of themselves, and will be most enabled hereby to compass dangerous projects.

"But," saith he, "a widow's house will tempt as well as a bishop's palace." Acutely spoken! because neither we nor the prelates can abolish widows' houses, which are but an occasion taken of evil without the church, therefore we shall set up within the church a lottery of such prizes as are the direct inviting causes of avarice and ambition, both unnecessary and harmful to be proposed, and most easy, most convenient, and needful to be removed. "Yea, but they are in a wise dispenser's hand." Let them be in whose hand they will, they are most apt to blind, to puff up, and pervert the most seeming good. And how they have been kept from vultures, whatever the dispenser's care hath been, we have learned by our miseries.

But this which comes next in view, I know not what good vein or humor took him when he let drop into his paper; I that was erewhile the ignorant, the loiterer, on the sudden by his permission am now granted "to know something." And that "such a volley of expressions" he hath met withal, "as he would never desire to have them better clothed." For me, readers, although I cannot say that I am utterly untrained in those rules which best rhetoricians have given, or unacquainted with those examples which the prime authors of eloquence have written in any learned tongue; yet true eloquence I find to be none, but the serious and hearty love of truth: and that whose mind soever is fully possessed with a fervent desire to know good things, and with the dearest charity to infuse the knowledge of them into others, when such a man would speak, his words, (by what I can express,) like so many nimble and airy servitors, trip about him at command, and in well-ordered files, as he would wish, fall aptly into their own places.

But now to the remainder of our discourse. Christ refused great riches and large honors at the devil's hand. But why? saith he, "as they were tendered by him from whom it was a sin to receive them." Timely remembered: why is it not therefore as much a sin to receive a liturgy of the masses' giving, were it for nothing else but for the giver? "But he could make no use of such a high estate," quoth the confuter, opportunely. For why then should the servant take upon him to use those things which his master had unfitted himself to use, that he might teach his ministers to follow his steps in the same ministry? But "they were offered him to a bad end." So they prove to the prelates, who, after their preferment, most usually change the teaching labor of the word, into the unteaching ease of lordship over consciences and purses. But he proceeds: "God enticed the Israelites with the promise of Canaan;" did not the prelates bring as slavish minds with them, as the Jews brought out of Egypt, they had left out that instance. Besides that it was then the time, whenas the best of them, as St. Paul saith, "was shut unto the faith under the law, their schoolmaster," who was forced to entice them as children with childish enticements. But the gospel is our manhood, and the ministry should be the manhood of the gospel, not to look after, much less so basely to plead for earthly rewards.

"But God incited the wisest man, Solomon, with these means." Ah, confuter of thyself, this example hath undone thee; Solomon asked an understanding heart, which the prelates have little care to ask. He asked no riches, which is their chief care; therefore was the prayer of Solomon pleasing to God: he gave him wisdom at his request, and riches without asking, as now he gives the prelates riches at their seeking, and no wisdom, because of their perverse asking. But he gives not over yet. "Moses had an eye to the reward." To what reward, thou man that lookest with Balaam's eyes? To what reward had the faith of Moses an eye to? He that had forsaken all the greatness of Egypt, and chose a troublesome journey in his old age through the wilderness, and yet arrived not at his journey's end. His faithful eyes were fixed upon that incorruptible reward, promised to Abraham and his seed in the Messiah; he sought a heavenly reward, which could make him happy, and never hurt him; and to such a reward every good man may have a respect; but the prelates are eager of such rewards as cannot make them happy, but can only make them worse. Jacob, a prince born, vowed that if God would "but give him bread to eat, and raiment to put on, then the Lord should be his God." But the prelates of mean birth, and ofttimes of lowest, making show as if they were called to the spiritual and humble ministry of the gospel, yet murmur, and think it a hard service, unless, contrary to the tenor of their profession, they may eat the bread and wear the honors of princes: so much more covetous and base they are than Simon Magus, for he proffered a reward to be admitted to that work, which they will not be meanly hired to.

But, saith he, "Are not the clergy members of Christ: why should not each member thrive alike?" Carnal text man! as if worldly thriving were one of the privileges we have by being in Christ, and were not a providence ofttimes extended more liberally to the infidel than to the Christian. Therefore must the ministers of Christ not be over rich or great in the world, because their calling is spiritual, not secular; because they have a special warfare, which is not to be entangled with many impediments; because their master, Christ, gave them this precept, and set them this example, told them this was the mystery of his coming, by mean things and persons to subdue mighty ones; and lastly, because a middle estate is most proper to the office of teaching, whereas higher dignity teaches far less, and blinds the teacher. Nay, saith the confuter, fetching his last endeavor, "the prelates will be very loath to let go their baronies, and votes in parliament," and calls it "God's cause," with an insufferable impudence. "Not that they love the honors and the means," good men and generous! "but that they would not have their country made guilty of such a sacrilege and injustice!"

A worthy patriot for his own corrupt ends. That which he imputes as sacrilege to his country, is the only way left them to purge that abominable sacrilege out of the land, which none but the prelates are guilty of; who for the discharge of one single duty, receive and keep that which might be enough to satisfy the labors of many painful ministers better deserving than themselves; who possess huge benefices for lazy performances, great promotions only for the execution of a cruel disgospelling jurisdiction; who engross many pluralities under a non-resident and slubbering dispatch of souls; who let hundreds of parishes famish in one diocese, while they, the prelates, are mute, and yet enjoy that wealth that would furnish all those dark places with able supply: and yet they eat, and yet they live at the rate of earls, and yet hoard up; they

who chase away all the faithful shepherds of the flock, and bring in a dearth of spiritual food, robbing thereby the church of her dearest treasure, and sending herds of souls starveling to hell, while they feast and riot upon the labors of hireling curates, consuming and purloining even that which by their foundation is allowed, and left to the poor, and to reparations of the church. These are they who have bound the land with the sin of sacrilege, from which mortal engagement we shall never be free, till we have totally removed, with one labor, as one individual thing, prelaty and sacrilege. And herein will the king be a true defender of the faith, not by paring or lessening, but by distributing in due proportion the maintenance of the church, that all parts of the land may equally partake the plentiful and diligent preaching of the faith; the scandal of ceremonies thrown out that delude and circumvent the faith; and the usurpation of prelates laid level, who are in words the fathers, but in their deeds the oppugners of the faith. This is that which will best confirm him in that glorious title.

Thus ye have heard, readers, how many shifts and wiles the prelates have invented to save their ill-got booty. And if it be true, as in scripture it is foretold, that pride and covetousness are the sure marks of those false prophets which are to come; then boldly conclude these to be as great seducers as any of the latter times. For between this and the judgment-day do not look for any arch deceivers, who in spite of reformation will use more craft, or less shame to defend their love of the world and their ambition, than these prelates have done. And if ye think that soundness of reason, or what force of argument soever, will bring them to an ingenuous silence, ye think that which will never be. But if ye take that course which Erasmus was wont to say Luther took against the pope and monks; if ye denounce war against their mitres and their bellies, ye shall soon discern that turban of pride, which they wear upon their heads, to be no helmet of salvation, but the mere metal and hornwork of papal jurisdiction; and that they have also this gift, like a certain kind of some that are possessed, to have their voice in their bellies, which being well-drained and taken down, their great oracle, which is only there, will soon be dumb; and the divine right of episcopacy, forthwith expiring, will put us no more to trouble with tedious antiquities and disputes.

THE DOCTRINE AND DISCIPLINE

OF

DIVORCE;

RESTORED TO THE GOOD OF BOTH SEXES, FROM THE BONDAGE OF CANON LAW, AND OTHER MISTAKES, TO THE TRUE MEANING OF SCRIPTURE IN THE LAW AND GOSPEL COMPARED.

WHEREIN ALSO ARE SET DOWN THE BAD CONSEQUENCES OF ABOLISHING, OR CONDEMNING AS SIN, THAT WHICH THE LAW OF GOD ALLOWS, AND CHRIST ABOLISHED NOT.

NOW THE SECOND TIME REVISED AND MUCH AUGMENTED, IN TWO BOOKS:

TO THE PARLIAMENT OF ENGLAND WITH THE ASSEMBLY.

The Author J. M.

MATTH. xiii. 52. "Every scribe instructed to the kingdom of heaven is like the master of a house, which bringeth out of his treasury things new and old."

PROV. xviii. 13. "He that answereth a matter before he heareth it, it is folly and shame unto him."

London, Imprinted in the year 1644.

[The text is that of the second edition, 1644.]

TO THE PARLIAMENT OF ENGLAND, WITH THE ASSEMBLY.

IF it were seriously asked, (and it would be no untimely question,) renowned parliament, select assembly! who of all teachers and masters, that have ever taught, hath drawn the most disciples after him, both in religion and in manners, it might be not untruly answered, custom. Though virtue be commended for the most persuasive in her theory, and conscience in the plain demonstration of the spirit finds most evincing; yet whether it be the secret of divine will, or the original blindness we are born in, so it happens for the most part that custom still is silently received for the best instructor. Except it be, because her method is so glib and easy, in some manner like to that vision of Ezekiel rolling up her sudden book of implicit knowledge, for him that will to take and swallow down at pleasure; which proving but of bad nourishment in the concoction, as it was heedless in the devouring, puffs up unhealthily a certain big face of pretended learning, mistaken among credulous men for the wholesome habit of soundness and good constitution, but is indeed no other than that swollen visage of counterfeit knowledge and literature, which not only in private mars our education, but also in public is the common climber into every chair, where either religion is preached, or law reported; filling each estate of life and profession with abject and servile principles, depressing the high and heaven-born spirit of man, far beneath the condition wherein either God created him, or sin hath sunk him. To pursue the allegory, custom being but a mere face, as echo is a mere voice, rests not in her unaccomplishment, until by secret inclination she accorporate herself with error, who being a blind and serpentine body without a head, willingly accepts what he wants, and supplies what her incompleteness went seeking. Hence it is, that error supports custom, custom countenances error; and these two between them would persecute and chase away all truth and solid wisdom out of human life, were it not that God, rather than man, once in many ages calls together the prudent and religious counsels of men, deputed to repress the incroachments, and to work off the inveterate blots and obscurities wrought upon our minds by the subtle insinuating of error and custom; who, with the numerous and vulgar train of their followers, make it their chief design to envy and cry down the industry of free reasoning, under the terms of humor and innovation; as if the womb of teeming truth were to be closed up, if she presume to bring forth aught that sorts not with their unchewed notions and suppositions. Against which notorious injury and abuse of man's free soul, to testify and oppose the utmost that study and true labor can attain, heretofore the incitement of men reputed grave hath led me among others; and now the duty and the right of an instructed Christian calls me through the chance of good or evil report, to be the sole advocate of a discountenanced truth: a high enterprise, lords and commons! a high enterprise and a hard, and such as every seventh son of a seventh son does not venture on. Nor have I amidst the clamor of so much envy and impertinence whither to appeal, but to the concourse of so much piety and wisdom here assembled. Bringing in my hands an ancient and most necessary, most charitable, and yet most injured statute of Moses: not repealed ever by him who only had the authority, but thrown aside with much inconsiderate neglect, under the rubbish of canonical ignorance; as once the whole law was by some such like conveyance in Josiah's time. And he who shall endeavor the amendment of any old neglected grievance in church or state, or in the daily course of life, if he be gifted with abilities of mind, that may raise him to so high an undertaking, I grant he hath already much whereof not to repent him; yet let me aread him, not to be the foreman of any misjudged opinion, unless his resolutions be firmly seated in a square and constant mind, not conscious to itself of any deserved blame, and regardless of ungrounded suspicions. For this let him be sure, he shall be boarded presently by the ruder sort, but not by discreet and well-nurtured men, with a thousand idle descants and surmises. Who when they cannot confute the least joint or sinew of any passage in the book; yet God forbid that truth should be truth, because they have a boisterous conceit of some pretences in the writer. But were they not more busy and inquisitive than the apostle commends, they would hear him at least, "rejoicing so the truth be preached, whether of envy or other pretence whatsoever:" for truth is as impossible to be soiled by any outward touch, as the sunbeam; though this ill hap wait on her nativity, that she never comes into the world, but like a bastard, to the ignominy of him that brought her forth; till time, the midwife rather than the mother of truth, have washed and salted the infant, declared

her legitimate, and churched the father of his young Minerva, from the needless causes of his purgation. Yourselves can best witness this, worthy patriots! and better will, no doubt hereafter: for who among ye of the foremost that have travailed in her behalf to the good of church or state, hath not been often traduced to be the agent of his own by-ends, under pretext of reformation? So much the more I shall not be unjust to hope, that however infamy or envy may work in other men to do her fretful will against this discourse, yet that the experience of your own uprightness misinterpreted will put ye in mind, to give it free audience and generous construction. What though the brood of Belial, the draff of men, to whom no liberty is pleasing, but unbridled and vagabond lust without pale or partition, will laugh broad perhaps, to see so great a strength of scripture mustering up in favor, as they suppose, of their debaucheries; they will know better when they shall hence learn, that honest liberty is the greatest foe to dishonest licence. And what though others, out of a waterish and queasy conscience, because ever crazy and never yet sound, will rail and fancy to themselves that injury and licence is the best of this book? Did not the distemper of their own stomachs affect them with a dizzy megrim, they would soon tie up their tongues and discern themselves like that Assyrian blasphemer, all this while reproaching not man, but the Almighty, the Holy One of Israel, whom they do not deny to have belawgiven his own sacred people with this very allowance, which they now call injury and licence, and dare cry shame on, and will do yet a while, till they get a little cordial sobriety to settle their qualming zeal. But this question concerns not us perhaps: indeed man's disposition, though prone to search after vain curiosities, yet when points of difficulty are to be discussed, appertaining to the removal of unreasonable wrong and burden from the perplexed life of our brother, it is incredible how cold, how dull, and far from all fellow-feeling we are, without the spur of self-concernment. Yet if the wisdom, the justice, the purity of God be to be cleared from foulest imputations, which are not yet avoided; if charity be not to be degraded and trodden down under a civil ordinance; if matrimony be not to be advanced like that exalted perdition written of to the Thessalonians, "above all that is called God," or goodness, nay, against them both; then I dare affirm, there will be found in the contents of this book that which may concern us all. You it concerns chiefly, worthies in parliament! on whom, as on our deliverers, all our grievances and cares, by the merit of your eminence and fortitude, are devolved. Me it concerns next, having with much labor and faithful diligence first found out, or at least with a fearless and communicative candor first published, to the manifest good of Christendom, that which, calling to witness everything mortal and immortal, I believe unfeignedly to be true. Let not other men think their conscience bound to search continually after truth, to pray for enlightening from above, to publish what they think they have so obtained, and debar me from conceiving myself tied by the same duties. Ye have now, doubtless, by the favor and appointment of God, ye have now in your hands a great and populous nation to reform; from what corruption, what blindness in religion, ye know well; in what a degenerate and fallen spirit from the apprehension of native liberty, and true manliness, I am sure ye find; with what unbounded licence rushing to whoredoms and adulteries, needs not long inquiry: insomuch that the fears, which men have of too strict a discipline, perhaps exceed the hopes that can be in others of ever introducing it with any great success. What if I should tell ye now of dispensations and indulgences, to give a little the reins, to let them play and nibble with the bait awhile; a people as hard of heart as that Egyptian colony that went to Canaan. This is the common doctrine that adulterous and injurious divorces were not connived only, but with eye open allowed of old for hardness of heart. But that opinion, I trust, by then this following argument hath been well read, will be left for one of the mysteries of an indulgent Antichrist to farm out incest by, and those his other tributary pollutions. What middle way can be taken then, may some interrupt, if we must neither turn to the right,

nor to the left, and that the people hate to be reformed? Mark then, judges and lawgivers and ye whose office is to be our teachers, for I will utter now a doctrine, if ever any other, though neglected or not understood, yet of great and powerful importance to the governing of mankind. He who wisely would restrain the reasonable soul of man within due bounds, must first himself know perfectly, how far the territory and dominion extends of just and honest liberty. As little must he offer to bind that which God hath loosened, as to loosen that which he hath bound. The ignorance and mistake of this high point hath heaped up one huge half of all the misery that hath been since Adam. In the gospel we shall read a supercilious crew of masters, whose holiness, or rather whose evil eye, grieving that God should be so facile to man, was to set straiter limits to obedience than God had set, to enslave the dignity of man, to put a garrison upon his neck of empty and over-dignified precepts: and we shall read our Saviour never more grieved and troubled than to meet with such a peevish madness among men against their own freedom. How can we expect him to be less offended with us, when much of the same folly shall be found yet remaining where it least ought, to the perishing of thousands? The greatest burden in the world is superstition, not only of ceremonies in the church, but of imaginary and scarecrow sins at home. What greater weakening, what more subtle stratagem against our Christian warfare, when besides the gross body of real transgressions to encounter, we shall be terrified by a vain and shadowy menacing of faults that are not? When things indifferent shall be set to overfront us under the banners of sin, what wonder if we be routed, and by this art of our adversary, fall into the subjection of worst and deadliest offences? The superstition of the papist is, "Touch not, taste not," when God bids both; and ours is, "Part not, separate not," when God and charity both permits and commands. "Let all your things be done with charity," saith St. Paul; and his master saith, "She is the fulfilling of the law." Yet now a civil, an indifferent, a sometime dissuaded law of marriage, must be forced upon us to fulfil, not only without charity but against her. No place in heaven or earth, except hell, where charity may not enter: yet marriage, the ordinance of our solace and contentment, the remedy of our loneliness, will not admit now either of charity or mercy, to come in and mediate, or pacify the fierceness of this gentle ordinance, the unremedied loneliness of this remedy. Advise ye well, supreme senate, if charity be thus excluded and expulsed, how ye will defend the untainted honor of your own actions and proceedings. He who marries, intends as little to conspire his own ruin, as he that swears allegiance: and as a whole people is in proportion to an ill government, so is one man to an ill marriage. If they, against any authority, covenant, or statute, may, by the sovereign edict of charity, save not only their lives but honest liberties from unworthy bondage, as well may he against any private covenant, which he never entered to his mischief, redeem himself from unsupportable disturbances to honest peace and just contentment. And much the rather, for that to resist the highest magistrate though tyrannizing, God never gave us express allowance, only he gave us reason, charity, nature, and good example to bear us out; but in this economical misfortune thus to demean ourselves, besides the warrant of those four **great** directors, which doth as justly belong hither, we have an express law of God, and such a law, as whereof our Saviour with a solemn threat forbade the abrogating. For no effect of tyranny can sit more heavy on the commonwealth, than this household unhappiness on the family. And farewell all hope of true reformation in the state, while such an evil as this lies undiscerned or unregarded in the house: on the redress whereof depends not only the spiritful and orderly life of our grown men, but the willing and careful education of our children. Let this therefore be new examined, this tenure and freehold of mankind, this native and domestic charter given us by a greater lord than that Saxon king the Confessor. Let the statutes of God be turned over, be scanned anew, and considered not altogether by the narrow intellectuals of quotationists and common placers, but (as was the ancient right of councils) by men of what liberal profession soever, of eminent spirit and breeding, joined with a diffuse and various knowledge of divine and human things; able to balance and define good and evil, right and wrong, throughout every state of life; able to show us the ways of the Lord straight and faithful as they are, not full of cranks and contradictions, and pitfalling dispenses, but with divine insight and benignity measured out to the proportion of each mind and spirit, each temper and disposition created so different each from other, and yet by the skill of wise conducting, all to become uniform in virtue. To expedite these knots, were worthy a learned and memorable synod; while our enemies expect to see the expectation of the church tired out with dependencies and independencies, how they will compound and in what calends. Doubt not, worthy senators! to vindicate the sacred honor and judgment of Moses your predecessor, from the shallow commenting of scholastics and canonists. Doubt not after him to reach out your steady hands to the misinformed and wearied life of man; to restore this his lost heritage, into the household state: wherewith be sure that peace and love, the best subsistence of a Christian family, will return home from whence they are now banished; places of prostitution will be less haunted, the neighbor's bed less attempted, the yoke of prudent and manly discipline will be generally submitted to; sober and well-ordered living will soon spring up in the commonwealth. Ye have an author great beyond exception, Moses; and one yet greater, he who hedged in from abolishing every smallest jot and tittle of precious equity contained in that law, with a more accurate and lasting Masoreth, than either the synagogue of Ezra or the Galilæan school at Tiberias hath left us. Whatever else ye can enact, will scarce concern a third part of the British name: but the benefit and good of this your magnanimous example, will easily spread far beyond the banks of Tweed and the Norman isles. It would not be the first or second time, since our ancient druids, by whom this island was the cathedral of philosophy to France, left off their pagan rights, that England hath had this honor vouchsafed from heaven, to give out reformation to the world. Who was it but our English Constantine that baptized the Roman empire? Who but the Northumbrian Willibrode and Winifride of Devon, with their followers, were the first apostles of Germany? Who but Alcuin and Wickliff our countrymen, opened the eyes of Europe, the one in arts, the other in religion? Let not England forget her precedence of teaching nations how to live.

Know, worthies; know and exercise the privilege of your honored country. A greater title I here bring ye than is either in the power or in the policy of Rome to give her monarchs; this glorious act will style ye the defenders of charity. Nor is this yet the highest inscription that will adorn so religious and so holy a defence as this; behold here the pure and sacred law of God, and his yet purer and more sacred name, offering themselves to you first, of all Christian reformers, to be acquitted from the long-suffered ungodly attribute of patronizing adultery. Defer not to wipe off instantly these imputative blurs and stains cast by rude fancies upon the throne and beauty itself of inviolable holiness: lest some other people more devout and wise than we bereave us this offered immortal glory, our wonted prerogative, of being the first asserters in every great vindication. For me, as far as my part leads me, I have already my greatest gain, assurance and inward satisfaction to have done in this nothing unworthy of an honest life, and studies well employed. With what event, among the wise and right understanding handful of men, I am secure. But how among the drove of custom and prejudice this will be relished by such whose capacity, since their youth run ahead into the easy creek of a system or a medulla, sails there at will under the blown physiognomy of their unlabored rudiments; for them, what their taste will be, I have also surety sufficient, from the entire league that hath been ever between formal ignorance and grave obstinacy. Yet when I remember the little that our Saviour could prevail about this doctrine of charity against the crabbed textuists of his time, I make no wonder, but rest confident, that whoso prefers either matrimony or other ordinance before the good of man and the plain ex-

igence of charity, let him profess papist, or protestant, or what he will, he is no better than a pharisee, and understands not the gospel: whom as a misinterpreter of Christ I openly protest against; and provoke him to the trial of this truth before all the world: and let him bethink him withal how **he will solder** up the shifting flaws of his ungirt permissions, his venial and unvenial dispenses, wherewith the law of God pardoning and unpardoning hath been shamefully branded for want of heed in glossing, to have eluded and baffled out all faith and chastity from the marriage-bed of that holy seed, with politic and judicial adulteries. I seek not to seduce the simple and illiterate; my errand is to find out the choicest and the learnedest, who have this high gift of wisdom to answer solidly, or to be convinced. I crave it from the piety, the learning, and the prudence which is housed in this place. It might perhaps more fitly have been written in another tongue: and I had done so, but that the esteem I have of my country's judgment, and the love I bear to my native language to serve it first with what I endeavor, make me speak it thus, ere I assay the verdict of outlandish readers. And perhaps also here I might have ended nameless, but that the address of these lines chiefly to the parliament of England might have seemed ingrateful not to acknowledge by whose religious care, unwearied watchfulness, courageous and heroic resolutions, I enjoy the peace and studious leisure to remain,

The Honorer and Attendant of their noble Worth and Virtues,

JOHN MILTON.

THE DOCTRINE AND DISCIPLINE OF DIVORCE;

RESTORED TO THE GOOD OF BOTH SEXES.

BOOK I.

THE PREFACE.

That Man is the Occasion of his own Miseries in most of those evils which he imputes to God's inflicting. The Absurdity

of our Canonists in their Decrees about Divorce. The Christian inperial Laws framed with more Equity. The opinion of Hugo Grotius and Paulus Fagius: And the Purpose in General of this Discourse.

MANY men, whether it be their fate or fond opinion, easily persuade themselves, if God would but be pleased a while to withdraw his just punishments from us, and to restrain what power either the devil or any earthly enemy hath to work us woe, that then man's nature would find immediate rest and re- leasement from all evils. But verily they who think so, if they be such as have a mind large enough to take into their thoughts a general survey of human things, would soon prove themselves in that opinion far deceived. For though it were granted us by divine indulgence to be exempt from all that can be harmful to us from without, yet the perverseness of our folly is so bent, that we should never lin hammering out of our own hearts, as it were out of a flint, the seeds and sparkles of new misery to ourselves, till all were in a blaze again. And no marvel if out of our own hearts, for they are evil; but even out of those things which God meant us, either for a principal good, or a pure contentment, we are still hatching and contriving upon ourselves matter of continual sorrow and perplexity. What greater good to man than that revealed rule, whereby God vouchsafes to show us how he would be worshipped? And yet that not rightly understood became the cause, that once a famous man in Israel could not but oblige his conscience to be the sacrificer; or if not, the jailor of his innocent and only daughter; and was the cause ofttimes that armies of valiant men have given up their throats to a heathenish enemy on the sab- bath day; fondly thinking their defensive resistance to be as then a work unlawful. What thing more instituted to the solace and delight of man than marriage? And yet the misinterpreting of some scripture, directed mainly against the abusers of the law for divorce given by Moses, hath changed the blessing of matrimony not seldom into a familiar and coinhabiting mischief; at least into a drooping and disconsolate household captivity, without refuge or redemption. So ungoverned and so wild a race doth supersti- tion run us, from one extreme of abused liberty into the other of unmerciful restraint. For although God in the first ordaining of marriage taught us to what end he did it, in words expressly implying the apt and cheerful conversation of man with woman, to comfort and refresh him against the evil of solitary life, not mentioning the purpose of generation till afterwards, as being but a secondary end in dignity, though not in necessity: yet now, if any two be but once handed in the church, and have tasted in any sort the nuptial bed, let them find them- selves never so mistaken in their disposi- tions through any error, concealment, or misadventure, that through their different tempers, thoughts, and constitutions, they can neither be to one another a remedy against loneliness, nor live in any union or contentment all their days; yet they shall, so they be but found suitably weaponed to the least possibility of sensual enjoyment, be made, spite of antipathy, to fadge to- gether, and combine as they may to their unspeakable wearisomeness, and despair of all sociable delight in the ordinance which God established to that very end. What a calamity is this, and, as the wise man, if he were alive, would sigh out in his own phrase, what a "sore evil is this under the sun!" All which we can refer justly to no other author than the canon law and her adherents, not consulting with charity, the interpreter and guide of our faith, but rest- ing in the mere element of the text; doubt- less by the policy of the devil to make that gracious ordinance become unsupportable, that what with men not daring to venture upon wedlock, and what with men wearied out of it, all inordinate licence might abound. It was for many ages that mar- riage lay in disgrace with most of the ancient doctors, as a work of the flesh, al- most a defilement, wholly denied to priests, and the second time dissuaded to all, as he that reads Tertullian or Jerome may see at large. Afterwards it was thought so sacramental, that no adultery or desertion could dissolve it; and this is the sense of our canon courts in England to this day, but in no other reformed church else: yet there remains in them also a burden on it as heavy as the other two were disgraceful or superstitious, and of as much iniquity, crossing a law not only written by Moses, but charactered in us by nature, of more antiquity and deeper ground than marriage itself; which law is to force nothing against the faultless proprieties of nature, yet that this may be colorably done, our Saviour's words touching divorce are as it were congealed into a stony rigor, inconsistent both with his doctrine and his office; and that which he preached only to the conscience is by canonical tyranny snatched into the compulsive censure of a judicial court; where laws are imposed even against the venerable and secret power of nature's impression, to love, whatever cause be found to loathe: which is a heinous barbarism both against the honor of marriage, the dignity of man and his soul, the goodness of Christianity, and all the human respects of civility. Notwithstanding that some the wisest and gravest among the Christian emperors, who had about them, to consult with, those of the fathers then living, who for their learning and holiness of life are still with us in great renown, have made their statutes and edicts concerning this debate far more easy and relenting in many necessary cases, wherein the canon is inflexible. And Hugo Grotius, a man of these times, one of the best learned, seems not obscurely to adhere in his persuasion to the equity of those imperial decrees, in his notes upon the Evangelists; much allaying the outward roughness of the text, which hath for the most part been too immoderately expounded; and excites the diligence of others to inquire further into this question, as containing many points that have not yet been explained. Which ever likely to remain intricate and hopeless upon the suppositions commonly stuck to, the authority of Paulus Fagius, one so learned and so eminent in England once, if it might persuade, would straight acquaint us with a solution of these differences no less prudent than compendious. He, in his comment on the Pentateuch, doubted not to maintain that divorces might be as lawfully permitted by the magistrate to Christians, as they were to the Jews. But because he is but brief, and these things of great consequence not to be kept obscure,

I shall conceive it nothing above my duty, either for the difficulty or the censure that may pass thereon, to communicate such thoughts as I also have had, and do offer them now in this general labor of reformation to the candid view both of church and magistrate: especially because I see it the hope of good men, that those irregular and unspiritual courts have spun their utmost date in this land, and some better course must now be constituted. This therefore shall be the task and period of this discourse to prove, first, that other reasons of divorce, besides adultery, were by the law of Moses, and are yet to be allowed by the Christian magistrate as a piece of justice, and that the words of Christ are not hereby contraried. Next, that to prohibit absolutely any divorce whatsoever, except those which Moses excepted, is against the reason of law, as in due place I shall show out of Fagius, with many additions. He therefore who by adventuring, shall be so happy as with success to light the way of such an expedient liberty and truth as this, shall restore the much-wronged and oversorrowed state of matrimony, not only to those merciful and life-giving remedies of Moses, but, as much as may be, to that serene and blissful condition it was in at the beginning, and shall deserve of all apprehensive men, (considering the troubles and distempers, which, for want of this insight, have been so oft in kingdoms, in states, and families,) shall deserve to be reckoned among the public benefactors of civil and human life, above the inventors of wine and oil; for this is a far dearer, far nobler, and more desirable cherishing to man's life, unworthily exposed to sadness and mistake, which he shall vindicate. Not that licence, and levity, and unconsented breach of faith should herein be countenanced, but that some conscionable and tender pity might be had of those who have unwarily, in a thing they never practised before, made themselves the bondmen of a luckless and helpless matrimony. In which argument, he whose courage can serve him to give the first onset, must look for two several oppositions: the one from those who having sworn themselves to long custom, and the letter of the text, will not out of the road; the other from those whose gross and vulgar apprehensions conceit but low of matrimonial purposes, and in the work of male and female think they have all. Nevertheless, it shall be here sought by due ways to be made appear, that those words of God in the institution, promising a meet help against loneliness, and those words of Christ, that "his yoke is easy, and his burden light," were not spoken in vain: for if the knot of marriage may in no case be dissolved but for adultery, all the burdens and services [10] of the law are not so intolerable. This only is desired of them who are minded to judge hardly of thus maintaining, that they would be still, and hear all out, nor think it equal to answer deliberate reason with sudden heat and noise; remembering this, that many truths now of reverend esteem and credit, had their birth and beginning once from singular and private thoughts, while the most of men were otherwise possessed; and [20] had the fate at first to be generally exploded and exclaimed on by many violent opposers; yet I may err perhaps in soothing myself, that this present truth revived will deserve on all hands to be not sinisterly received, in that it undertakes the cure of an inveterate disease crept into the best part of human society; and to do this with no smarting corrosive, but with a smooth and pleasing lesson, which received hath the vir- [30] tue to soften and dispel rooted and knotty sorrows, and without enchantment, if that be feared, or spell used, hath regard at once both to serious pity and upright honesty; that tends to the redeeming and restoring of none but such as are the object of compassion, having in an ill hour hampered themselves, to the utter dispatch of all their most beloved comforts and repose for this life's term. But if we shall obstinately dis- [40] like this new overture of unexpected ease and recovery, what remains but to deplore the frowardness of our hopeless condition, which neither can endure the estate we are in, nor admit of remedy either sharp or sweet? Sharp we ourselves distaste; and sweet, under whose hands we are, is scrupled and suspected as too luscious. In such a posture Christ found the Jews, who were neither won with the austerity of John the [50] Baptist, and thought it too much licence to follow freely the charming pipe of him who sounded and proclaimed liberty and relief

to all distresses: yet truth in some age or other will find her witness, and shall be justified at last by her own children.

CHAPTER I.

The Position. Proved by the Law of Moses. That Law expounded and asserted to a moral and charitable Use, first by Paulus Fagius, next with other Additions.

To remove therefore, if it be possible, this great and sad oppression, which through the strictness of a literal interpreting hath invaded and disturbed the dearest and most peaceable estate of household society, to the overburdening, if not the overwhelming of many Christians better worth than to be so deserted of the church's considerate care, this position shall be laid down, first proving, then answering what may be objected either from scripture or light of reason.

"That indisposition, unfitness, or contrariety of mind, arising from a cause in nature unchangeable, hindering, and ever likely to hinder the main benefits of conjugal society, which are solace and peace; is a greater reason of divorce than natural [30] frigidity, especially if there be no children, and that there be mutual consent."

This I gather from the law in Deut. xxiv. 1: "When a man hath taken a wife and married her, and it come to pass that she find no favor in his eyes, because he hath found some uncleanness in her, let him write her a bill of divorcement, and give it in her hand, and send her out of his house," &c. This law, if the words of Christ may be [40] admitted into our belief, shall never, while the world stands, for him be abrogated. First therefore I here set down what learned Fagius hath observed on this law: "The law of God," saith he, "permitted divorce for the help of human weakness. For every one that of necessity separates, cannot live single. That Christ denied divorce to his own, hinders not; for what is that to the unregenerate, who hath not attained such [50] perfection? Let not the remedy be despised, which was given to weakness. And when Christ saith, who marries the divorced commits adultery, it is to be understood if he had any plot in the divorce." The rest I reserve until it be disputed, how the magistrate is to do herein. From hence we may plainly discern a twofold consideration in this law: first, the end of the lawgiver, and the proper act of the law, to command or to allow something just and honest, or indifferent. Secondly, his sufferance from some accidental result of evil by this allowance, which the law cannot remedy. For if this law have no other end or act but only the allowance of a sin, though never to so good intention, that law is no law, but sin muffled in the robe of law, or law disguised in the loose garment of sin. Both which are too foul hypotheses, to save the phenomenon of our Saviour's answer to the pharisees about this matter. And I trust anon, by the help of an infallible guide, to perfect such Prutenic tables, as shall mend the astronomy of our wide expositors.

The cause of divorce mentioned in the law is translated "some uncleanness," but in the Hebrew it sounds "nakedness of aught, or any real nakedness:" which by all the learned interpreters is referred to the mind as well as to the body. And what greater nakedness or unfitness of mind than that which hinders ever the solace and peaceful society of the married couple? And what hinders that more than the unfitness and defectiveness of an unconjugal mind? The cause therefore of divorce expressed in the position cannot but agree with that described in the best and equallest sense of Moses's law. Which, being a matter of pure charity, is plainly moral, and more now in force than ever; therefore surely lawful. For if under the law such was God's gracious indulgence, as not to suffer the ordinance of his goodness and favor through any error to be seared and stigmatized upon his servants to their misery and thraldom; much less will he suffer it now under the covenant of grace, by abrogating his former grant of remedy and relief. But the first institution will be objected to have ordained marriage inseparable. To that a little patience until this first part have amply discoursed the grave and pious reasons of this divorcive law; and then I doubt not but with one gentle stroking to wipe away ten thousands tears out of the life of man. Yet thus much I shall now insist on, that whatever the institution were, it could not be so enormous, nor so rebellious against both nature and reason as to exalt itself above the end and person for whom it was instituted.

CHAPTER II.

The first Reason of this Law grounded on the prime Reason of Matrimony. That no Covenant whatsoever obliges against the main End both of itself, and of the parties covenanting.

For all sense and equity reclaims, that any law or covenant, how solemn or strait soever, either between God and man, or man and man, though of God's joining, should bind against a prime and principal scope of its own institution, and of both or either party covenanting; neither can it be of force to engage a blameless creature to his own perpetual sorrow, mistaken for his expected solace, without suffering charity to step in and do a confessed good work of parting those whom nothing holds together but this of God's joining, falsely supposed against the express end of his own ordinance. And what his chief end was of creating woman to be joined with man, his own instituting words declare, and are infallible to inform us what is marriage, and what is no marriage; unless we can think them set there to no purpose: "It is not good," saith he, "that man should be alone. I will make him a help meet for him." From which words, so plain, less cannot be concluded, nor is by any learned interpreter, than that in God's intention a meet and happy conversation is the chiefest and the noblest end of marriage: for we find here no expression so necessarily implying carnal knowledge, as this prevention of loneliness to the mind and spirit of man. To this, Fagius, Calvin, Pareus, Rivetus, as willingly and largely assent as can be wished. And indeed it is a greater blessing from God, more worthy so excellent a creature as man is, and a higher end to honor and sanctify the league of marriage, whenas the solace and satisfaction of the mind is regarded and provided for before the sensitive pleasing of the body. And with all generous persons married thus it is, that where the mind and person pleases aptly, there some unaccomplishment of the body's delight may be better borne with, than when the mind hangs off in an unclosing disproportion, though the body be as it ought; for there all corporal delight will soon become unsavory and contemptible. And the solitariness of man, which God had namely and principally ordered to prevent by marriage, hath no remedy, but lies under a worse condition than the loneliest single life: for in single life the absence and remoteness of a helper might inure him to expect his own comforts out of himself, or to seek with hope; but here the continual sight of his deluded thoughts, without cure, must needs be to him, if especially his complexion incline him to melancholy, a daily trouble and pain of loss, in some degree like that which reprobates feel. Lest therefore so noble a creature as man should be shut up incurably under a worse evil by an easy mistake in that ordinance which God gave him to remedy a less evil, reaping to himself sorrow while he went to rid away solitariness, it cannot avoid to be concluded, that if the woman be naturally so of disposition, as will not help to remove, but help to increase that same Godforbidden loneliness, which will in time draw on with it a general discomfort and dejection of mind, not beseeming either Christian profession or moral conversation, unprofitable and dangerous to the commonwealth, when the household estate, out of which must flourish forth the vigor and spirit of all public enterprises, is so ill-contented and procured at home, and cannot be supported; such a marriage can be no marriage, whereto the most honest end is wanting; and the aggrieved person shall do more manly, to be extraordinary and singular in claiming the due right whereof he is frustrated, than to piece up his lost contentment by visiting the stews, or stepping to his neighbor's bed, which is the common shift in this misfortune; or else by suffering his useful life to waste away, and be lost under a secret affliction of an unconscionable size to human strength. Against all which evils the mercy of this Mosaic law was graciously exhibited.

CHAPTER III.

The Ignorance and Iniquity of Canon-law, providing for the Right of the Body in Marriage, but nothing for the Wrongs and Grievances of the Mind. An Objection, that the Mind should be better looked to before contract, answered.

How vain, therefore, is it, and how preposterous in the canon law, to have made such careful provision against the impediment of carnal performance, and to have had no care about the unconversing inability of mind so defective to the purest and most sacred end of matrimony; and that the vessel of voluptuous enjoyment must be made good to him that has taken it upon trust, without any caution; whenas the mind, from whence must flow the acts of peace and love, a far more precious mixture than the quintessence of an excrement, though it be found never so deficient and unable to perform the best duty of marriage in a cheerful and agreeable conversation, shall be thought good enough, however flat and melancholious it be, and must serve, though to the eternal disturbance and languishing of him that complains him. Yet wisdom and charity, weighing God's own institution, would think that the pining of a sad spirit wedded to loneliness should deserve to be freed, as well as the impatience of a sensual desire so providently relieved. It is read to us in the liturgy, that "we must not marry to satisfy the fleshly appetite, like brute beasts, that have no understanding;" but the canon so runs, as if it dreamt of no other matter than such an appetite to be satisfied; for if it happen that nature hath stopped or extinguished the veins of sensuality, that marriage is annulled. But though all the faculties of the understanding and conversing part after trial appear to be so ill and so aversely met through nature's unalterable working, as that neither peace, nor any sociable contentment can follow, 'tis as nothing; the contract shall stand as firm as ever, betide what will. What is this but secretly to instruct us, that however many grave reasons are pretended to the married life, yet that nothing indeed is thought worth regard therein, but the prescribed satisfaction of an irrational heat? Which cannot be but ignominious to the state of marriage, dishonorable to the undervalued soul of man, and even to Christian doctrine itself: while it seems more moved at the disappointing of an impetuous nerve, than at the ingenuous grievance of a mind unreasonably yoked; and to place more of marriage in the channel of concupiscence, than in the pure influence of peace and love, whereof the soul's lawful contentment is the only fountain.

But some are ready to object, that the disposition ought seriously to be considered before. But let them know again, that for all the wariness can be used, it may yet befall a discreet man to be mistaken in his choice: and we have plenty of examples. The soberest and best governed men are least practised in these affairs; and who knows not that the bashful muteness of a virgin may ofttimes hide all the unliveliness and natural sloth which is really unfit for conversation? Nor is there that freedom of access granted or presumed, as may suffice to a perfect discerning till too late; and where any indisposition is suspected, what more usual than the persuasion of friends, that acquaintance, as it increases, will amend all? And lastly, it is not strange though many, who have spent their youth chastely, are in some things not so quick-sighted, while they haste too eagerly to light the nuptial torch; nor is it, therefore, that for a modest error a man should forfeit so great a happiness, and no charitable means to release him, since they who have lived most loosely, by reason of their bold accustoming, prove most successful in their matches, because their wild affections unsettling at will, have been as so many divorces to teach them experience. Whenas the sober man honoring the appearance of modesty, and hoping well of every social virtue under that veil, may easily chance to meet, if not with a body impenetrable, yet often with a mind to all other due conversation inaccessible, and to all the more estimable and superior purposes of matrimony useless and almost lifeless; and what a solace, what a fit help such a consort would be through the whole life of a man, is less pain to conjecture than to have experience.

CHAPTER IV.

The second Reason of this Law, because without it Marriage, as it happens oft, is not a Remedy of that which it promises, as any rational Creature would expect. That Marriage, if we pattern from the Beginning, as our Saviour bids, was not properly the Remedy of Lust, but the fulfilling of conjugal Love and Helpfulness.

AND that we may further see what a violent cruel thing it is to force the continuing of those together whom God and nature in the gentlest end of marriage never joined; divers evils and extremities, that follow upon such a compulsion, shall here be set in view. Of evils, the first and greatest is, that hereby a most absurd and rash imputation is fixed upon God and his holy laws, of conniving and dispensing with open and common adultery among his chosen people; a thing which the rankest politician would think it shame and disworship that his laws should countenance: how and in what manner this comes to pass I shall reserve till the course of method brings on the unfolding of many scriptures. Next, the law and gospel are hereby made liable to more than one contradiction, which I refer also thither. Lastly, the supreme dictate of charity is hereby many ways neglected and violated; which I shall forthwith address to prove. First, we know St. Paul saith, "It is better to marry than to burn." Marriage, therefore, was given as a remedy of that trouble: but what might this burning mean? Certainly not the mere motion of carnal lust, not the mere goad of a sensitive desire: God does not principally take care for such cattle. What is it then but that desire which God put into Adam in Paradise, before he knew the sin of incontinence; that desire which God saw it was not good that man should be left alone to burn in; the desire and longing to put off an unkindly solitariness by uniting another body, but not without a fit soul to his, in the cheerful society of wedlock? Which if it were so needful before the fall, when man was much more perfect in himself, how much more is it needful now against all the sorrows and casualties of this life, to have an intimate and speaking help, a ready and reviving associate in marriage? Whereof who misses, by chancing on a mute and spiritless mate, remains more alone than before, and in a burning less to be contained than that which is fleshly, and more to be considered; as being more deeply rooted even in the fault-less innocence of nature. As for that other burning, which is but as it were the venom of a lusty and over-abounding concoction, strict life and labor, with the abatement of a full diet, may keep that low and obedient enough; but this pure and more inbred desire of joyning to itself in conjugal fellow-ship a fit conversing soul (which desire is properly called love) "is stronger than death," as the spouse of Christ thought: "many waters cannot quench it, neither can the floods drown it." This is that rational burning that marriage is to remedy, not to be allayed with fasting, nor with any pen-ance to be subdued: which how can he assuage who by mishap hath met the most unmeetest and unsuitable mind? Who hath the power to struggle with an intelligible flame, not in Paradise to be resisted, become now more ardent by being failed of what in reason it looked for; and even then most unquenched, when the importunity of a provender burning is well enough appeased; and yet the soul hath obtained nothing of what it justly desires. Certainly such a one forbidden to divorce, is in effect forbidden to marry, and compelled to greater diffi-culties than in a single life; for if there be not a more human burning which marriage must satisfy, or else may be dissolved, than that of copulation, marriage cannot be honorable for the meet reducing and ter-minating of lust between two; seeing many beasts in voluntary and chosen couples live together as unadulterously, and are as truly married in that respect. But all ingenuous men will see that the dignity and blessing of marriage is placed rather in the mutual enjoyment of that which the wanting soul needfully seeks, than of that which the plenteous body would joyfully give away. Hence it is that Plato in his festival dis-course brings in Socrates relating what he feigned to have learned from the prophetess Diotima, how Love was the son of Penury, begot of Plenty in the garden of Jupiter. Which divinely sorts with that which in effect Moses tells us, that Love was the son of Loneliness, begot in Paradise by that sociable and helpful aptitude which God im-planted between man and woman toward each other. The same, also, is that burning mentioned by St. Paul, whereof marriage ought to be the remedy: the flesh hath other mutual and easy curbs which are in the power of any temperate man. When, therefore, this original and sinless penury, or loneliness of the soul, cannot lay itself down by the side of such a meet and accept-able union as God ordained in marriage, at least in some proportion, it cannot conceive and bring forth love, but remains utterly unmarried under a former wedlock, and still burns in the proper meaning of St. Paul. Then enters Hate; not that hate that sins, but that which only is natural dis-satisfaction, and the turning aside from a mistaken object: if that mistake have done injury, it fails not to dismiss with recom-pense; for to retain still, and not be able to love, is to heap up more injury. Thence this wise and pious law of dismission now de-fended took beginning: he, therefore, who lacking of his due in the most native and human end of marriage, thinks it better to part than to live sadly and injuriously to that cheerful covenant, (for not to be be-loved, and yet retained, is the greatest in-jury to a gentle spirit,) he, I say, who therefore seeks to part, is one who highly honors the married life and would not stain it: and the reasons which now move him to divorce are equal to the best of those that could first warrant him to marry; for, as was plainly shown, both the hate which now diverts him, and the loneli-ness which leads him still powerfully to seek a fit help, hath not the least grain of a sin in it, if he be worthy to understand him-self.

CHAPTER V.

The third Reason of this Law, because with-out it, he who has happened where he finds nothing but remediless offences and discontents, is in more and greater temptations than ever before.

THIRDLY, Yet it is next to be feared, if he must be still bound without reason by a deaf rigor, that when he perceives the just expectance of his mind defeated, he will begin even against law to cast about where he may find his satisfaction more complete, unless he be a thing heroically virtuous; and that are not the common lump of men, for whom chiefly the laws ought to be made; though not to their sins, yet to their unsinning weaknesses, it being above their strength to endure the lonely estate, which while they shunned they are fallen into. And yet there follows upon this a worse temptation: for if he be such as hath spent his youth unblamably, and laid up his chiefest earthly comforts in the enjoyment of a contented marriage, nor did neglect that furtherance which was to be obtained therein by constant prayers; when he shall find himself bound fast to an uncomplying discord of nature, or, as it oft happens, to an image of earth and phlegm, with whom he looked to be the copartner of a sweet and gladsome society, and sees withal that his bondage is now inevitable; though he be almost the strongest Christian, he will ·be ready to despair in virtue, and mutiny against Divine Providence: and this doubtless is the reason of those lapses, and that melancholy despair, which we see in many wedded persons, though they understand it not, or pretend other causes, because they know no remedy; and is of extreme danger: therefore when human frailty surcharged is at such a loss, charity ought to venture much, and use bold physic, lest an overtossed faith endanger to shipwreck.

CHAPTER VI.

The fourth Reason of this Law, that God regards Love and Peace in the Family, more than a compulsive Performance of Marriage, which is more broke by a grievous Continuance, than by a needful Divorce.

FOURTHLY, Marriage is a covenant, the very being whereof consists not in a forced cohabitation, and counterfeit performance of duties, but in unfeigned love and peace: and of matrimonial love, no doubt but that was chiefly meant, which by the ancient sages was thus parabled; that Love, if he be not twin born, yet hath a brother wondrous like him, called Anteros; whom while he seeks all about, his chance is to meet with many false and feigning desires, that wander singly up and down in his likeness: by them in their borrowed garb, Love, though not wholly blind, as poets wrong him, yet having but one eye, as being born an archer aiming, and that eye not the quickest in this dark region here below, which is not Love's proper sphere, partly out of the simplicity and credulity which is native to him, often deceived, embraces and consorts him with these obvious and suborned striplings, as if they were his mother's own sons; for so he thinks them, while they subtly keep themselves most on his blind side. But after a while, as his manner is, when soaring up into the high tower of his Apogæum, above the shadow of the earth, he darts out the direct rays of his then most piercing eyesight upon the impostures and trim disguises that were used with him, and discerns that this is not his genuine brother, as he imagined; he has no longer the power to hold fellowship with such a personated mate: for straight his arrows lose their golden heads, and shed their purple feathers, his silken braids untwine, and slip their knots, and that original and fiery virtue given him by fate all on a sudden goes out, and leaves him undeified and despoiled of all his force; till finding Anteros at last, he kindles and repairs the almost-faded ammunition of his deity by the reflection of a coequal and homogeneal fire. Thus mine author sung it to me: and by the leave of those who would be counted the only grave ones, this is no mere amatorious novel; (though to be wise and skilful in these matters, men heretofore of greatest name in virtue have esteemed it one of the highest arcs, that human contemplation circling upwards can make from the glassy sea whereon she stands;) but this is a deep and serious verity, showing us that love in marriage cannot live nor subsist unless it be mutual; and where love cannot be, there can be left of wedlock nothing but the empty husk of an outside matrimony, as undelightful and unpleasing to God as any other kind of hypocrisy. So far is his command from tying men to the observance of duties which there is no help for, but they must be dissembled. If Solomon's advice be not over-frolic, "Live joyfully," saith he, "with the wife whom thou lovest, all thy days, for that is thy portion:" how then, where we find it impossible to rejoice or to love, can we obey this precept? How miser-[10] ably do we defraud ourselves of that comfortable portion, which God gives us, by striving vainly to glue an error together, which God and nature will not join, adding but more vexation and violence to that blissful society by our importunate superstition, that will not hearken to St. Paul, I Cor. vii., who, speaking of marriage and divorce, determines plain enough in general, that God therein "hath called us to peace, and [20] not to bondage!" Yea, God himself commands in his law more than once, and by his prophet Malachi, as Calvin and the best translations read, that "he who hates, let him divorce," that is, he who cannot love. Hence it is that the rabbins, and Maimonides, famous among the rest, in a book of his set forth by Buxtorfius, tells us, that "divorce was permitted by Moses to preserve peace in marriage, and quiet in the family." [30] Surely the Jews had their saving peace about them as well as we; yet care was taken that this wholesome provision for household peace should also be allowed them: and must this be denied to Christians? O perverseness! that the law should be made more provident of peace-making than the gospel! that the gospel should be put to beg a most necessary help of mercy from the law, but must not have it! and that to grind in the [40] mill of an undelighted and servile copulation, must be the only forced work of a Christian marriage, ofttimes with such a yokefellow, from whom both love and peace, both nature and religion mourns to be separated. I cannot therefore be so diffident, as not securely to conclude, that he who can receive nothing of the most important helps in marriage, being thereby disenabled to return that duty which is his, with a clear and [50] hearty countenance, and thus continues to grieve whom he would not, and is no less

grieved; that man ought even for love's sake and peace to move divorce upon good and liberal conditions to the divorced. And it is a less breach of wedlock to part with wise and quiet consent betimes, than still to soil and profane that mystery of joy and union with a polluting sadness and perpetual distemper: for it is not the outward continuing of marriage that keeps whole that covenant, but whosoever does most according to peace and love, whether in marriage or in divorce, he it is that breaks marriage least; it being so often written, that "Love only is the fulfilling of every commandment."

CHAPTER VII.

The fifth Reason, that nothing more hinders and disturbs the whole Life of a Christian, than a Matrimony found to be incurably unfit, and doth the same in effect that an idolatrous Match.

FIFTHLY, As those priests of old were not to be long in sorrow, or if they were, they could not rightly execute their function; so every true Christian in a higher order of priesthood, is a person dedicate to joy and peace, offering himself a lively sacrifice of praise and thanksgiving, and there is no Christian duty that is not to be seasoned and set off with cheerfulness; which in a thousand outward and intermitting crosses may yet be done well, as in this vale of tears: but in such a bosom affliction as this, crushing the very foundation of his inmost nature, when he shall be forced to love against a possibility, and to use dissimulation against his soul in the perpetual and [40] ceaseless duties of a husband; doubtless his whole duty of serving God must needs be blurred and tainted with a sad unpreparedness and dejection of spirit, wherein God has no delight. Who sees not therefore how much more Christianity it would be to break by divorce that which is more broken by undue and forcible keeping, rather than "to cover the altar of the Lord with continual tears, so that he regardeth not the offering [50] any more," rather than that the whole worship of a Christian man's life should languish and fade away beneath the weight of an immeasurable grief and discouragement? And because some think the children of a second matrimony succeeding a divorce would not be a holy seed, it hindered not the Jews from being so; and why should we not think them more holy than the offspring of a former ill-twisted wedlock, begotten only out of a bestial necessity, without any true love or contentment, or joy to their parents? So that in some sense we may call them the "children of wrath" and anguish, which will as little conduce to their sanctifying, as if they had been bastards: for nothing more than disturbance of mind suspends us from approaching to God; such a disturbance especially, as both assaults our faith and trust in God's providence, and ends, if there be not a miracle of virtue on either side, not only in bitterness and wrath, the canker of devotion, but in a desperate and vicious carelessness, when he sees himself, without fault of his, trained by a deceitful bait into a snare of misery, betrayed by an alluring ordinance, and then made the thrall of heaviness and discomfort by an undivorcing law of God, as he erroneously thinks, but of man's iniquity, as the truth is; for that God prefers the free and cheerful worship of a Christian, before the grievous and exacted observance of an unhappy marriage, besides that the general maxims of religion assure us, will be more manifest by drawing a parallel argument from the ground of divorcing an idolatress, which was, lest she should alienate his heart from the true worship of God: and, what difference is there whether she pervert him to superstition by her enticing sorcery, or disenable him in the whole service of God through the disturbance of her unhelpful and unfit society; and so drive him at last, through murmuring and despair, to thoughts of atheism? Neither doth it lessen the cause of separating, in that the one willingly allures him from the faith, the other perhaps unwillingly drives him; for in the account of God it comes all to one, that the wife loses him a servant: and therefore by all the united force of the Decalogue she ought to be disbanded, unless we must set marriage above God and charity, which is a doctrine **of devils**, no less than forbidding to marry.

CHAPTER VIII.

That an idolatrous Heretic ought to be divorced, after a convenient Space given to hope of Conversion. That Place of I Cor. vii. restored from a twofold erroneous Exposition; and that the common Expositors flatly contradict the moral Law.

AND here by the way, to illustrate the whole question of divorce, ere this treatise end, I shall not be loath to spend a few lines, in hope to give a full resolve of that which is yet so much controverted: whether an idolatrous heretic ought to be divorced. To the resolving whereof we must first know, that the Jews were commanded to divorce an unbelieving Gentile for two causes: First, because all other nations, especially the Canaanites, were to them unclean. Secondly, to avoid seducement. That other nations were to the Jews impure, even to the separating of marriage, will appear out of Exod. xxxiv. 16, Deut. vii. 3, 6, compared with Ezra ix. 2, also chap. x. 10, 11, Neh. xiii. 30. This was the ground of that doubt raised among the Corinthians by some of the circumcision, whether an unbeliever were not still to be counted an unclean thing, so as that they ought to divorce from such a person. This doubt of theirs St. Paul removes by an evangelical reason, having respect to that vision of St. Peter, wherein the distinction of clean and unclean being abolished, all living creatures were sanctified to a pure and Christian use, and mankind especially, now invited by a general call to the covenant of grace. Therefore, saith St. Paul, "The unbelieving wife is sanctified by the husband;" that is, made pure and lawful to his use, so that he need not put her away for fear lest her unbelief should defile him; but that if he found her love still towards him, he might rather hope to win her. The second reason of that divorce was to avoid seducement, as is proved by comparing those places of the law to that which Ezra and Nehemiah did by divine warrant in compelling the Jews to forego their wives. And this reason is moral and perpetual in the rule of Christian faith without evasion; therefore, saith the apostle, 2 Cor. vi. "Misyoke not together with infidels," which is interpreted of marriage in the first place. And although the former legal pollution be now done off, yet there is a spiritual contagion in idolatry as much to be shunned; and though seducement were not to be feared, yet where there is no hope of converting, there always ought to be a certain religious aversation and abhorring, which can no way sort with marriage: therefore saith St. Paul, "What fellowship hath righteousness with unrighteousness? What communion hath light with darkness? What concord hath Christ with Belial? What part hath he that believeth with an infidel?" And in the next verse but one he moralizes, and makes us liable to that command of Isaiah, "Wherefore come out from among them, and be ye separate, saith the Lord; touch not the unclean thing, and I will receive ye." And this command thus gospelized to us, hath the same force with that whereon Ezra grounded the pious necessity of divorcing. Neither had he other commission for what he did, than such a general command in Deuteronomy as this, nay, not so direct as this; for he is bid there not to marry, but not bid to divorce; and yet we see with what a zeal and confidence he was the author of a general divorce between the faithful and the unfaithful seed. The gospel is more plainly on his side, according to three of the evangelists, than the words of the law; for where the case of divorce is handled with such a severity, as was fittest to aggravate the fault of unbounded licence; yet still in the same chapter, when it comes into question afterwards, whether any civil respect, or natural relation which is dearest, may be our plea to divide, or hinder or but delay our duty to religion we hear it determined th.t father, and mother, and wife also, is not only to be hated, but forsaken, if we mean to inherit the great reward there promised. Nor will it suffice to be put off by saying we must forsake them only by not consenting or not complying with them, for that were to be done, and roundly too, though being of the same faith, they should but seek out of a fleshly tenderness to weaken our Christian fortitude with worldly persuasions, or but to unsettle our constancy with timorous and softening suggestions; as we may read with what a vehemence Job,

the patientest of men, rejected the desperate counsels of his wife; and Moses, the meekest, being thoroughly offended with the profane speeches of Zippora, sent her back to her father. But if they shall perpetually, at our elbow, seduce us from the true worship of God, or defile and daily scandalize our conscience by their hopeless continuance in misbelief; then even in the due progress of reason, and that ever equal proportion which justice proceeds by, it cannot be imagined that this cited place commands less than a total and final separation from such an adherent; at least that no force should be used to keep them together; while we remember that God commanded Abraham to send away his irreligious wife and her son for the offences which they gave in a pious family. And it may be guessed that David for the like cause disposed of Michal in such a sort, as little differed from a dismission. Therefore, against reiterated scandals and seducements, which never cease, much more can no other remedy or retirement be found but absolute departure. For what kind of matrimony can that remain to be, what one duty between such can be performed as it should be from the heart, when their thoughts and spirits fly asunder as far as heaven from hell; especially if the time that hope should send forth her expected blossoms, be past in vain? It will easily be true, that a father or brother may be hated zealously, and loved civilly or naturally; for those duties may be performed at distance, and do admit of any long absence: but how the peace and perpetual cohabitation of marriage can be kept, how that benevolent and intimate communion of body can be held, with one that must be hated with a most operative hatred, must be forsaken and yet continually dwelt with and accompanied; he who can distinguish, hath the gift of an affection very oddly divided and contrived: while others both just and wise, and Solomon, among the rest, if they may not hate and forsake as Moses enjoins, and the gospel imports, will find it impossible not to love otherwise than will sort with the love of God, whose jealousy brooks no corrival. And whether is more likely, that Christ bidding to forsake wife for religion, meant it by divorce as Moses meant it, whose law, grounded on moral reason, was both his office and his essence to maintain; or that he should bring a new morality into religion, not only new, but contrary to an unchangeable command, and dangerously derogating from our love and worship of God? As if when Moses had bid divorce absolutely, and Christ had said, hate and forsake, and his apostle had said, no communion with Christ and Belial; yet that Christ after all this could be understood to say, Divorce not; no, not for religion, seduce, or seduce not. What mighty and invisible remora is this in matrimony, able to demur and to contemn all the divorcive engines in heaven or earth! both which may now pass away, if this be true; for more than many jots or tittles, a whole moral law is abolished. But if we dare believe it is not, then in the method of religion, and to save the honor and dignity of our faith, we are to retreat and gather up ourselves from the observance of an inferior and civil ordinance, to the strict maintaining of a general and religious command, which is written, "Thou shalt make no covenant with them," Deut. vii. 2, 3: and that covenant which cannot be lawfully made, we have directions and examples lawfully to dissolve. Also 2 Chron. ii. 19, "Shouldest thou love them that hate the Lord?" No, doubtless; for there is a certain scale of duties, there is a certain hierarchy of upper and lower commands, which for want of studying in right order, all the world is in confusion.

Upon these principles I answer, that a right believer ought to divorce an idolatrous heretic, unless upon better hopes: however, that it is in the believer's choice to divorce or not.

The former part will be manifest thus first, that an apostate idolater, whether husband or wife seducing, was to die by the decree of God, Deut. xiii. 6, 9; that marriage, therefore, God himself disjoins: for others born idolaters, the moral reason of their dangerous keeping, and the incommunicable antagony that is between Christ and Belial, will be sufficient to enforce the commandment of those two inspired reformers, Ezra and Nehemiah, to put an idolater away as well under the gospel.

The latter part, that although there be no seducement feared, yet if there be no hope given, the divorce is lawful, will appear by this; that idolatrous marriage is still hateful to God, therefore still it may be divorced by the pattern or that warrant that Ezra had, and by the same everlasting reason: neither can any man give an account wherefore, if those whom God joins no man may separate, it should not follow, that whom he joins not, but hates to join, those men ought to separate. But saith the lawyer, "That which ought not have been done, once done, avails." I answer, "This is but a crotchet of the law, but that brought against it is plain scripture." As for what Christ spake concerning divorce, 'tis confessed by all knowing men, he meant it between them of the same faith. But what shall we say then to St. Paul, who seems to bid us not divorce an infidel willing to stay? We may safely say thus, that wrong collections have been hitherto made out of those words by modern divines. His drift, as was heard before, is plain; not to command our stay in marriage with an infidel, that had been a flat renouncing of the religious and moral law; but to inform the Corinthians that the body of an unbeliever was not defiling, if his desire to live in Christian wedlock showed any likelihood that his heart was opening to the faith; and therefore advises to forbear departure so long till nothing have been neglected to set forward a conversion: this, I say, he advises, and that with certain cautions, not commands, if we can take up so much credit for him, as to get him believed upon his own word: for what is this else but his counsel in a thing indifferent, "To the rest speak I, not the Lord?" for though it be true that the Lord never spake it, yet from St. Paul's mouth we should have took it as a command, had not himself forewarned us, and disclaimed; which notwithstanding if we shall still avouch to be a command, he palpably denying it, this is not to expound St. Paul, but to outface him. Neither doth it follow but that the apostle may interpose his judgment in a case of Christian liberty, without the guilt of adding to God's word. How do we know marriage or single life to be of choice, but by such like words as these, "I speak this by permission, not of commandment; I have no command of the Lord, yet I give my judgment"? Why shall not the like words have leave to signify a freedom in this our present question, though Beza deny? Neither is the scripture hereby less inspired, because St. Paul confesses to have written therein what he had not of command: for we grant that the Spirit of God led him thus to express himself to Christian prudence, in a matter which God thought best to leave uncommanded. Beza, therefore, must be warily read, when he taxes St. Austin of blasphemy, for holding that St. Paul spake here as of a thing indifferent. But if it must be a command, I shall yet the more evince it to be a command that we should herein be left free; and that out of the Greek word used in the 12th verse, which instructs us plainly, there must be a joint assent and good liking on both sides: he that will not deprave the text must thus render it: "If a brother have an unbelieving wife, and she join in consent to dwell with him," (which cannot utter less to us than a mutual agreement,) let him not put her away for the mere surmise of Judaical uncleanness: and the reason follows, for the body of an infidel is not polluted, neither to benevolence, nor to procreation. Moreover, this note of mutual complacency forbids all offer of seducement, which to a person of zeal cannot be attempted without great offence: if, therefore, seducement be feared, this place hinders not divorce. Another caution was put in this supposed command, of not bringing the believer into "bondage" hereby, which doubtless might prove extreme, if Christian liberty and conscience were left to the humor of a pagan staying at pleasure to play with, or to vex and wound with a thousand scandals and burdens, above strength to bear. If, therefore, the conceived hope of gaining a soul come to nothing, then charity commands that the believer be not wearied out with endless waiting under many grievances sore to his spirit; but that respect be had rather to the present suffering of a true Christian, than the uncertain winning of an obdured heretic. The counsel we have from St. Paul to hope, cannot countermand the moral and evangelic charge we have

from God to fear seducement, to separate from the misbeliever, the unclean, the obdurate. The apostle wisheth us to hope; but does not send us a wool-gathering after vain hope; he saith, "How knowest thou, O man, whether thou shalt save thy wife?" that is, till he try all due means, and set some reasonable time to himself, after which he may give over washing an Ethiop, if he will hear the advice of the gospel; "Cast not pearls before swine," saith Christ himself. "Let him be to thee as a heathen." "Shake the dust off thy feet." If this be not enough, "hate and forsake" what relation soever. And this also that follows must appertain to the precept, "Let every man wherein he is called, therein abide with God," v. 24, that is, so walking in his inferior calling of marriage, as not, by dangerous subjection to that ordinance, to hinder and disturb the higher calling of his Christianity. Last, and never too oft remembered, whether this be a command or an advice, we must look that it be so understood as not to contradict the least point of moral religion that God hath formerly commanded; otherwise what do we but set the moral law and the gospel at civil war together? and who then shall be able to serve those two masters?

CHAPTER IX.

That Adultery is not the greatest breach of Matrimony: that there may be other violations as great.

Now whether idolatry or adultery be the greatest violation of marriage, if any demand let him thus consider; that among Christian writers touching matrimony, there be three chief ends thereof agreed on: godly society; next, civil; and thirdly, that of the marriage bed. Of these the first in name to be the highest and most excellent, no baptized man can deny, nor that idolatry smites directly against this prime end; nor that such as the violated end is, such is the violation: but he who affirms adultery to be the highest breach, affirms the bed to be the highest of marriage, which is in truth a gross and boorish opinion, how common soever; as far from the countenance of scripture, as from the light of all clean philosophy or civil nature. And out of question the cheerful help that may be in marriage toward sanctity of life, is the purest, and so the noblest end of that contract: but if the particular of each person be considered, then of those three ends which God appointed, that to him is greatest which is most necessary; and marriage is then most broken to him when he utterly wants the fruition of that which he most sought therein, whether it were religious, civil, or corporal society. Of which wants to do him right by divorce only for the last and meanest is a perverse injury, and the pretended reason of it as frigid as frigidity itself, which the code and canon are only sensible of. Thus much of this controversy. I now return to the former argument. And having shown that disproportion, contrariety, or numbness of mind may justly be divorced, by proving already that the prohibition thereof opposes the express end of God's institution, suffers not marriage to satisfy that intellectual and innocent desire which God himself kindled in man to be the bond of wedlock, but only to remedy a sublunary and bestial burning, which frugal diet, without marriage, would easily chasten. Next, that it drives many to transgress the conjugal bed, while the soul wanders after that satisfaction which it had hope to find at home, but hath missed; or else it sits repining, even to atheism, finding itself hardly dealt with, but misdeeming the cause to be in God's law, which is in man's unrighteous ignorance. I have shown also how it unties the inward knot of marriage, which is peace and love, (if that can be untied which was never knit,) while it aims to keep fast the outward formality: how it lets perish the Christian man, to compel impossibly the married man.

CHAPTER X.

The sixth Reason of this Law; that to prohibit Divorce sought for natural Causes, is against Nature.

THE sixth place declares this prohibition to be as respectless of human nature as it is of religion, and therefore is not of God.

He teaches, that an unlawful marriage may be lawfully divorced; and that those who having thoroughly discerned each other's disposition, which ofttimes cannot be till after matrimony, shall then find a powerful reluctance and recoil of nature on either side, blasting all the content of their mutual society, that such persons are not lawfully married, (to use the apostle's words,) "Say I these things as a man; or saith not the law also the same? For it is written, Deut. xxii. 'Thou shalt not sow thy vineyard with divers seeds, lest thou defile both. Thou shalt not plough with an ox and an ass together;'" and the like. I follow the pattern of St. Paul's reasoning: "Doth God care for asses and oxen," how ill they yoke together? "or is it not said altogether for our sakes? For our sakes no doubt this is written." Yea, the apostle himself, in the forecited 2 Cor. vi. 14, alludes from that place of Deut. to forbid misyoking marriage, as by the Greek word is evident; though he instance but in one example of mismatching with an infidel, yet next to that, what can be a fouler incongruity, a greater violence to the reverend secret of nature, than to force a mixture of minds that cannot unite, and to sow the furrow of man's nativity, with seed of two incoherent and uncombining dispositions? which act being kindly and voluntary, as it ought, the apostle in the language he wrote called "eunoia," and the Latins "benevolence," intimating the original thereof to be in the understanding and the will; if not, surely there is nothing which might more properly be called a malevolence rather; and is the most injurious and unnatural tribute that can be extorted from a person endued with reason, to be made pay out the best substance of his body, and of his soul too, as some think, when either for just and powerful causes he cannot like, or from unequal causes finds not recompense. And that there is a hidden efficacy of love and hatred in man as well as in other kinds, not moral but natural, which though not always in the choice, yet in the success of marriage will ever be most predominant: besides daily experience, the author of Ecclesiasticus, whose wisdom hath set him next the Bible, acknowledges, xiii. 16, "A man," saith he, "will cleave to his like."

But what might be the cause, whether each one's allotted genius or proper star, or whether the supernal influence of schemes and angular aspects, or this elemental crasis here below; whether all these jointly or singly meeting friendly, or unfriendly in either party, I dare not, with the men I am likest to clash, appear so much a philosopher as to conjecture. The ancient proverb in Homer, less abstruse, entitles this work of leading each like person to his like, peculiarly to God himself: which is plain enough also by his naming of a meet or like help in the first espousal instituted; and that every woman is meet for every man, none so absurd as to affirm. Seeing then there is indeed a twofold seminary, or stock in nature, from whence are derived the issues of love and hatred, distinctly flowing through the whole mass of created things, and that God's doing ever is to bring the due likenesses and harmonies of his works together, except when out of two contraries met to their own destruction, he molds a third existence; and that it is error, or some evil angel which either blindly or maliciously hath drawn together, in two persons ill embarked in wedlock, the sleeping discords and enmities of nature, lulled on purpose with some false bait, that they may wake to agony and strife, later than prevention could have wished, if from the bent of just and honest intentions beginning what was begun and so continuing, all that is equal, all that is fair and possible hath been tried, and no accommodation likely to succeed; what folly is it still to stand combating and battering against invincible causes and effects, with evil upon evil, till either the best of our days be lingered out, or ended with some speeding sorrow! The wise Ecclesiasticus advises rather, xxxvii. 27, "My son, prove thy soul in thy life; see what is evil for it, and give not that unto it." Reason he had to say so; for if the noisomeness or disfigurement of body can soon destroy the sympathy of mind to wedlock duties, much more will the annoyance and trouble of mind infuse itself into all the faculties and acts of the body, to render them invalid, unkindly, and even unholy against the fundamental lawbook of nature, which Moses never thwarts but reverences; therefore he commands us

to force nothing against sympathy or natural order, no, not upon the most abject creatures; to show that such an indignity cannot be offered to man without an impious crime. And certainly those divine meditating words of finding out a meet and like help to man, have in them a consideration of more than the indefinite likeness of womanhood; nor are they to be made waste paper on, for the dulness of canon divinity: no, nor those other allegoric precepts of beneficence fetched out of the closet of nature, to teach us goodness and compassion in not compelling together unmatchable societies; or if they meet through mischance, by all consequence to disjoin them, as God and nature signifies, and lectures to us not only by those recited decrees, but even by the first and last of all his visible works; when by his divorcing command the world first rose out of chaos, nor can be renewed again out of confusion, but by the separating of unmeet consorts.

CHAPTER XI.

The seventh Reason, that sometimes Continuance in Marriage may be evidently the Shortening or Endangering of Life to either Party; both Law and Divinity concluding, that Life is to be preferred before Marriage, the intended Solace of Life.

SEVENTHLY, The canon law and divines consent, that if either party be found contriving against another's life, they may be severed by divorce: for a sin against the life of marriage is greater than a sin against the bed; the one destroys, the other but defiles. The same may be said touching those persons who being of a pensive nature and course of life, have summed up all their solace in that free and lightsome conversation which God and man intends in marriage; whereof when they see themselves deprived by meeting an unsociable consort, they ofttimes resent one another's mistake so deeply, that long it is not ere grief end one of them. When therefore this danger is foreseen, that the life is in peril by living together, what matter is it whether helpless grief or wilful practice be the cause? This is certain, that the preservation of life is more worth than the compulsory keeping of marriage; and it is no less than cruelty to force a man to remain in that state as the solace of his life, which he and his friends know will be either the undoing or the disheartening of his life. And what is life without the vigor and spiritful exercise of life? How can it be useful either to private or public employment? Shall it therefore be quite dejected, though never so valuable, and left to molder away in heaviness, for the superstitious and impossible performance of an ill-driven bargain? Nothing more inviolable than vows made to God; yet we read in Numbers, that if a wife had made such a vow, the mere will and authority of her husband might break it: how much more may he break the error of his own bonds with an unfit and mistaken wife, to the saving of his welfare, his life, yea, his faith and virtue, from the hazard of overstrong temptations! For if man be lord of the sabbath, to the curing of a fever, can he be less than lord of marriage in such important causes as these?

CHAPTER XII.

The eighth Reason, It is probable, or rather certain, that every one who happens to marry hath not the Calling; and therefore upon Unfitness found and considered, Force ought not to be used.

EIGHTHLY, It is most sure that some even of those who are not plainly defective in body, yet are destitute of all other marriageable gifts, and consequently have not the calling to marry unless nothing be requisite thereto but a mere instrumental body; which to affirm, is to that unanimous covenant a reproach: yet it is as sure that many such, not of their own desire, but by the persuasion of friends, or not knowing themselves, do often enter into wedlock; where finding the difference at length between the duties of a married life, and the gifts of a single life, what unfitness of mind, what wearisomeness, what scruples, and doubts, to an incredible offence and displeasure, are like to follow between, may be soon imagined; whom thus to shut up, and immure, and shut up together, the one with a mischosen mate, the other in a mistaken calling, is not a course that

Christian wisdom and tenderness ought to use. As for the custom that some parents and guardians have of forcing marriages, it will be better to say nothing of such a savage inhumanity, but only thus: that the law which gives not all freedom of divorce to any creature endued with reason so assassinated, is next in cruelty.

CHAPTER XIII.

The ninth Reason; because Marriage is not a mere carnal Coition, but a human Society: where that cannot reasonably be had, there can be no true Matrimony. Marriage compared with all other Covenants and Vows warrantably broken for the good of Man. Marriage the Papists' Sacrament, and unfit Marriage the Protestants' Idol.

NINTHLY, I suppose it will be allowed us that marriage is a human society, and that all human society must proceed from the mind rather than the body, else it would be but a kind of animal or beastish meeting: if the mind therefore cannot have that due company by marriage that it may reasonably and humanly desire, that marriage can be no human society, but a certain formality; or gilding over of little better than a brutish congress, and so in very wisdom and pureness to be dissolved.

But marriage is more than human, "the covenant of God," Prov. ii. 17; therefore man cannot dissolve it. I answer, if it be more than human, so much the more it argues the chief society thereof to be in the soul rather than in the body, and the greatest breach thereof to be unfitness of mind rather than defect of body: for the body can have least affinity in a covenant more than human, so that the reason of dissolving holds good the rather. Again, I answer, that the sabbath is a higher institution, a command of the first table, for the breach whereof God hath far more and oftener testified his anger than for divorces, which from Moses to Malachi he never took displeasure at, nor then neither if we mark the text; and yet as oft as the good of man is concerned, he not only permits, but commands to break the sabbath. What covenant more contracted with God and less in man's power, than the vow which hath once passed his lips? yet if it be found rash, if offensive, if unfruitful either to God's glory or the good of man, our doctrine forces not error and unwillingness irksomely to keep it, but counsels wisdom and better thoughts boldly to break it; therefore to enjoin the indissoluble keeping of a marriage found unfit against the good of man both soul and body, as hath been evidenced, is to make an idol of marriage, to advance it above the worship of God and the good of man, to make it a transcendent command, above both the second and first table; which is a most prodigious doctrine.

Next, whereas they cite out of the Proverbs, that it is the covenant of God, and therefore more than human, that consequence is manifestly false: for so the covenant which Zedekiah made with the infidel king of Babel is called the covenant of God, Ezk. xvii. 19, which would be strange to hear counted more than a human covenant. So every covenant between man and man, bound by oath, may be called the covenant of God, because God therein is attested. So of marriage he is the author and the witness; yet hence will not follow any divine astriction more than what is subordinate to the glory of God, and the main good of either party: for as the glory of God and their esteemed fitness one for the other, was the motive which led them both at first to think without other revelation that God had joined them together; so when it shall be found by their apparent unfitness, that their continuing to be man and wife is against the glory of God and their mutual happiness, it may assure them that God never joined them, who hath revealed his gracious will not to set the ordinance above the man for whom it was ordained; not to canonize marriage either as a tyranness or a goddess over the enfranchised life and soul of man; for wherein can God delight, wherein be worshipped, wherein be glorified by the forcible continuing of an improper and ill-yoking couple? He that loved not to see the disparity of several cattle at the plough, cannot be pleased with any vast unmeetness in marriage. Where can be the peace and love which must invite God to such a house? May it not be feared that the not divorcing of such a helpless disagreement will be the divorcing of God finally from such a place? But it is a trial of our patience, they say: I grant it; but which of Job's afflictions were sent him with that law, that he might not use means to remove any of them if he could? And what if it subvert our patience and our faith too? Who shall answer for the perishing of all those souls, perishing by stubborn expositions of particular and inferior precepts against the general and supreme rule of charity? They dare not affirm that marriage is either a sacrament or a mystery, though all those sacred things give place to man; and yet they invest it with such an awful sanctity, and give it such adamantine chains to bind with, as if it were to be worshipped like some Indian deity, when it can confer no blessing upon us, but works more and more to our misery. To such teachers the saying of St. Peter at the council of Jerusalem will do well to be applied: "Why tempt ye God to put a yoke upon the necks of" Christian men, which neither the Jews, God's ancient people, "nor we are able to bear;" and nothing but unwary expounding hath brought upon us?

CHAPTER XIV.

Considerations concerning Familism, Antinomianism; and why it may be thought that such Opinions may proceed from the undue Restraint of some just Liberty, than which no greater Cause to contemn Discipline.

To these considerations this also may be added as no improbable conjecture, seeing that sort of men who follow Anabaptism, Familism, Antinomianism, and other fanatic dreams, (if we understand them not amiss,) be such most commonly as are by nature addicted to religion, of life also not debauched, and that their opinions having full swing, do end in satisfaction of the flesh; it may be come with reason into the thoughts of a wise man, whether all this proceed not partly, if not chiefly, from the restraint of some lawful liberty, which ought to be given men, and is denied them? As by physic we learn in menstruous bodies, where nature's current hath been stopped, that the suffocation and upward forcing of some lower part affects the head and inward sense with dotage and idle fancies. And on the other hand, whether the rest of vulgar men not so religiously professing, do not give themselves much the more to whoredom and adulteries, loving the corrupt and venial discipline of clergy-courts, but hating to hear of perfect reformation; whenas they foresee that then fornication shall be austerely censured, adultery punished, and marriage, the appointed refuge of nature, though it hap to be never so incongruous and displeasing, must yet of force be worn out, when it can be to no other purpose but of strife and hatred, a thing odious to God? This may be worth the study of skilful men in theology, and the reason of things. And lastly, to examine whether some undue and ill-grounded strictness upon the blameless nature of man, be not the cause in those places where already reformation is, that the discipline of the church, so often, and so unavoidably broken, is brought into contempt and derision? And if it be thus, let those who are still bent to hold this obstinate literality, so prepare themselves, as to share in the account for all these transgressions, when it shall be demanded at the last day, by one who will scan and sift things with more than a literal wisdom of equity: for if these reasons be duly pondered, and that the gospel is more jealous of laying on excessive burdens than ever the law was, lest the soul of a Christian, which is inestimable, should be overtempted and cast away; considering also that many properties of nature, which the power of regeneration itself never alters, may cause dislike of conversing, even between the most sanctified; which continually grating in harsh tune together, may breed some jar and discord, and that end in rancor and strife, a thing so opposite both to marriage and to Christianity, it would perhaps be less scandal to divorce a natural disparity, than to link violently together an unchristian dissension, committing two insnared souls inevitably to kindle one another, not with the fire of love, but with a hatred inconcileable; who, were they dissevered, would be straight friends in any other relation. But if an alphabetical servility must be still urged, it may so fall out, that the true church may unwittingly use as much cruelty in forbidding to divorce, as the church of antichrist doth wilfully in forbidding to marry.

BOOK II.

CHAPTER I.

The Ordinance of Sabbath and Marriage compared. Hyperbole no unfrequent Figure in the Gospel. Excess cured by contrary Excess. Christ neither did nor could abrogate the Law of Divorce, but only reprove the Abuse thereof.

HITHERTO the position undertaken has been declared, and proved by a law of God, that law proved to be moral, and unabolishable, for many reasons equal, honest, charitable, just, annexed thereto. It follows now, that those places of scripture, which have a seeming to revoke the prudence of Moses, or rather that merciful decree of God, be forthwith explained and reconciled. For what are all these reasonings worth, will some reply, whenas the words of Christ are plainly against all divorce, "except in case of fornication?" to whom he whose mind were to answer no more but this, "except also in case of charity," might safely appeal to the more plain words of Christ in defence of so excepting. "Thou shalt do no manner of work," saith the commandment of the sabbath. Yes, saith Christ, works of charity. And shall we be more severe in paraphrasing the considerate and tender gospel, than he was in expounding the rigid and peremptory law? What was ever in all appearance less made for man, and more for God alone, than the sabbath? Yet when the good of man comes into the scales, we hear that voice of infinite goodness and benignity, that "sabbath was made for man, not man for sabbath." What thing ever was more made for man alone, and less for God, than marriage? And shall we load it with a cruel and senseless bondage utterly against both the good of man, and the glory of God? Let whoso will now listen, I want neither pall nor mitre, I stay neither for ordination nor induction; but in the firm faith of a knowing Christian, which is the best and truest endowment of the keys, I pronounce, the man, who shall bind so cruelly a good and gracious ordinance of God, hath not in that the spirit of Christ. Yet that every text of scripture seeming opposite may be attended with a due exposition, this other part ensues, and makes account to find no slender arguments for this assertion, out of those very scriptures, which are commonly urged against it.

First therefore let us remember, as a thing not to be denied, that all places of scripture, wherein just reason of doubt arises from the letter, are to be expounded by considering upon what occasion everything is set down, and by comparing other texts. The occasion, which induced our Saviour to speak of divorce, was either to convince the extravagance of the pharisees in that point, or to give a sharp and vehement answer to a tempting question. And in such cases, that we are not to repose all upon the literal terms of so many words, many instances will teach us: wherein we may plainly discover how Christ meant not to be taken word for word, but like a wise physician, administering one excess against another to reduce us to a perfect mean: where the pharisees were strict, there Christ seems remiss; where they were too remiss, he saw it needful to seem most severe: in one place he censures an unchaste look to be adultery already committed; another time he passes over actual adultery with less reproof than for an unchaste look; not so heavily condemning secret weakness, as open malice: so here he may be justly thought to have given this rigid sentence against divorce, not to cut off all remedy from a good man, who finds himself consuming away in a disconsolate and unenjoyed matrimony, but to lay a bridle upon the bold abuses of those overweening rabbies; which he could not more effectually do, than by a countersway of restraint curbing their wild exorbitance almost in to the other extreme; as when we bow things the contrary way, to make them come to their natural straightness. And that this was the only intention of Christ is most evident, if we attend but to his own words and protestation made in the same sermon, not many verses before he treats of divorcing, that he came not to abrogate from the law "one jot or tittle," and denounces against them that shall so teach.

But St. Luke, the verse immediately foregoing that of divorce, inserts the same caveat, as if the latter could not be understood without the former; and as a witness to produce against this our wilful mistake of abrogating, which must needs confirm us, that whatever else in the political law of more special relation to the Jews might cease to us; yet that of those precepts concerning divorce, not one of them was repealed by the doctrine of Christ, unless we have vowed not to believe his own cautious and immediate profession; for if these our Saviour's words inveigh against all divorce, and condemn it as adultery, except it be for adultery, and be not rather understood against the abuse of those divorces permitted in the law, then is that law of Moses, Deut. xxiv. 1, not only repealed and wholly annulled against the promise of Christ, and his known profession not to meddle in matters judicial; but that which is more strange, the very substance and purpose of that law is contradicted, and convinced both of injustice and impurity, as having authorized and maintained legal adultery by statute. Moses also cannot scape to be guilty of unequal and unwise decrees, punishing one act of secret adultery by death, and permitting a whole life of open adultery by law. And albeit lawyers write, that some political edicts, though not approved, are yet allowed to the scum of the people, and the necessity of the times; these excuses have but a weak pulse: for first, we read, not that the scoundrel people, but the choicest, the wisest, the holiest of that nation have frequently used these laws, or such as these, in the best and holiest times. Secondly, be it yielded, that in matters not very bad or impure, a human lawgiver may slacken something of that which is exactly good, to the disposition of the people and the times: but if the perfect, the pure, the righteous law of God, (for so are all his statutes and his judgments,) be found to have allowed smoothly, without any certain reprehension, that which Christ afterward declares to be adultery, how can we free this law from the horrible indictment of being both impure, unjust, and fallacious?

CHAPTER II.

How Divorce was permitted for Hardness of Heart, cannot be understood by the common Exposition. That the Law cannot permit, much less enact a Permission of Sin.

NEITHER will it serve to say this was permitted for the hardness of their hearts, in that sense as it is usually explained; for the law were then but a corrupt and erróneous schoolmaster, teaching us to dash against a vital maxim of religion, by doing foul evil in hope of some uncertain good.

This only text not to be matched again throughout the whole scripture, whereby God in his perfect law should seem to have granted to the hard hearts of his holy people, under his own hand, a civil immunity and free charter to live and die in a long successive adultery, under a covenant of works, till the Messiah, and then that indulgent permission to be strictly denied by a covenant of grace; besides, the incoherence of such a doctrine cannot, must not be thus interpreted, to the raising of a paradox never known till then, only hanging by the twined thread of one doubtful scripture, against so many other rules and leading principles of religion, of justice, and purity of life. For what could be granted more either to the fear, or to the lust of any tyrant or politician, than this authority of Moses thus expounded; which opens him a way at will to dam up justice, and not only to admit of any Romish or Austrian dispenses, but to enact a statute of that which he dares not seem to approve, even to legitimate vice, to make sin itself, the ever alien and vassal sin, a free citizen of the commonwealth, pretending only these or these plausible reasons? And well he might, all the while that Moses shall be alleged to have done as much without showing any reason at all. Yet this could not enter into the heart of David, Psalm xciv. 20, how any such authority, as endeavors to "fashion wickedness by a law," should derive itself from God. And Isaiah lays "Wo upon them that decree unrighteous decrees," chap. x. 1. Now which of these two is the better lawgiver, and which deserves most a wo, he that gives out an edict singly unjust, or he that confirms to generations a fixed and unmolested impunity of that which is not only held to be unjust, but also unclean, and both in a high degree; not only, as they themselves affirm, an injurious expulsion of one wife, but also an unclean freedom by more than a patent to wed another adulterously? How can we therefore with safety thus dangerously confine the free simplicity of our Saviour's meaning to that which merely amounts from so many letters, whenas it can consist neither with his former and cautionary words, nor with other more pure and holy principles, nor finally with a scope of charity, commanding by his express commission in a higher strain? But all rather of necessity must be understood as only against the abuse of that wise and ingenuous liberty, which Moses gave, and to terrify a roving conscience from sinning under that pretext.

CHAPTER III.

That to allow Sin by Law, is against the Nature of Law, the End of the Lawgiver, and the Good of the People. Impossible therefore in the Law of God. That it makes God the Author of Sin more than anything objected by the Jesuits or Arminians against Predestination.

BUT let us yet further examine upon what consideration a law of licence could be thus given to a holy people for the hardness of heart. I suppose all will answer, that for some good end or other. But here the contrary shall be proved. First, that many ill effects, but no good end of such a sufferance can be shown; next, that a thing unlawful can, for no good end whatever, be either done or allowed by a positive law. If there were any good end aimed at, that end was then good either as to the law or to the lawgiver licensing; or as to the person licensed. That it could not be the end of the law, whether moral or judicial, to license a sin, I prove easily out of Rom. v. 20: "The law entered, that the offence might abound;" that is, that sin might be made abundantly manifest to be heinous and displeasing to God, that so his offered grace might be the more esteemed. Now if the law, instead of aggravating and terrifying sin, shall give out licence, it foils itself and turns recreant from its own end: it forestalls the pure grace of Christ, which is through righteousness, with impure indulgences, which are through sin. And instead of discovering sin, for "by the law is the knowledge thereof," saith St. Paul, and that by certain and true light for men to walk in safely, it holds out false and dazzling fires to stumble men; or, like those miserable flies, to run into with delight and be burnt: for how many souls might easily think that to be lawful which the law and magistrate allowed them? Again, we read, I Tim. i. 5, "The end of the commandment is charity out of a pure heart, and of a good conscience, and of faith unfeigned." But never could that be charity, to allow a people what they could not use with a pure heart, but with conscience and faith both deceived, or else despised. The more particular end of the judicial law is set forth to us clearly, Rom. xiii. That God hath given to that law "a sword not in vain, but to be a terror to evil works, a revenge to execute wrath upon him that doth evil." If this terrible commission should but forbear to punish wickedness, were it other to be accounted than partial and unjust? But if it begin to write indulgence to vulgar uncleanness, can it do more to corrupt and shame the end of its own being? Lastly, if the law allow sin, it enters into a kind of covenant with sin; and if it do, there is not a greater sinner in the world than the law itself. The law, to use an allegory something different from that in Philo-Judæus concerning Amalek, though haply more significant, the law is the Israelite, and hath this absolute charge given it, Deut. xxv. "To blot out the memory of sin, the Amalekite, from under heaven, not to forget it." Again, the law is the Israelite, and hath this express repeated command, "to make no covenant with sin, the Canaanite," but to expel him, lest he prove a snare. And to say truth, it were too rigid and reasonless to proclaim such an enmity between man and man, were it not the type of a greater enmity between law and sin. I spake even now, as if sin were condemned in a perpetual villanage never to be free by law, never to be manumitted: but sure sin can have no tenure by law, at all, but is rather an eternal outlaw, and in hostility with law past all atonement: both diagonal contraries, as much allowing one another, as day and night together in one hemisphere. Or if it be possible, that sin with his darkness may come to composition, it cannot be without a foul eclipse and twilight to the law, whose brightness ought to surpass the noon. Thus we see how this unclean permittance defeats the sacred and glorious end both of the moral and judicial law.

As little good can the lawgiver propose to equity by such a lavish remissness as this: if to remedy hardness of heart, Paræus and other divines confess, it more increases by this liberty, than is lessened: and how is it probable that their hearts were more hard in this, that it should be yielded to, than in any other crime? Their hearts were set upon usury, and are to this day, no nation more; yet that which was the endamaging only of their estates was narrowly forbid: this, which is thought the extreme injury and dishonor of their wives and daughters, with the defilement also of themselves, is bounteously allowed. Their hearts were as hard under their best kings to offer in high places, though to the true God: yet that, but a small thing, it strictly forewarned; this, accounted a high offence against one of the greatest moral duties, is calmly permitted and established. How can it be evaded, but that the heavy censure of Christ should fall worse upon this lawgiver of theirs, than upon all the scribes and pharisees? For they did but omit judgment and mercy to trifle in mint and cummin, yet all according to law; but this their lawgiver, altogether as punctual in such niceties, goes marching on to adulteries, through the violence of divorce by law against law. If it were such a cursed act of Pilate, a subordinate judge to Cæsar, overswayed by those hard hearts, with much ado to suffer one transgression of law but once, what is it then with less ado to publish a law of transgression for many ages? Did God for this come down and cover the mount of Sinai with his glory, uttering in thunder those his sacred ordinances out of the bottomless treasures of his wisdom and infinite pureness, to patch up an ulcerous and rotten commonwealth with strict and stern injunctions, to wash the skin and garments for every unclean touch; and such easy permission given to pollute the soul with adulteries by public authority, without disgrace or question? No; it had been better that man had never known law or matrimony, than that such foul iniquity should be fastened upon the Holy One of Israel, the Judge of all the earth; and such a piece of folly as Beelzebub would not commit, to divide against himself, and pervert his own ends: or if he, to compass more certain mischief, might yield perhaps to feign some good deed, yet that God should enact a licence of certain evil for uncertain good against his own glory and pureness, is abominable to conceive. And as it is destructive to the end of law, and blasphemous to the honor of the lawgiver licensing, so is it as pernicious to the person licensed. If a private friend admonish not, the scripture saith, "He hates his brother, and lets him perish;" but if he soothe him and allow him in his faults, the Proverbs teach us, "He spreads a net for his neighbor's feet, and worketh ruin." If the magistrate or prince forget to administer due justice, and restrain not sin, Eli himself could say, "It made the Lord's people to transgress." But if he countenance them against law by his own example, what havoc it makes both in religion and virtue among the people may be guessed, by the anger it brought upon Hophni and Phineas not to be appeased "with sacrifice nor offering for ever." If the law be silent to declare sin, the people must needs generally go astray, for the apostle himself saith, "he had not known lust but by the law:" and surely such a nation seems not to be under the illuminating guidance of God's law, but under the horrible doom rather of such as despise the gospel: "He that is filthy, let him be filthy still." But where the law itself gives a warrant for sin, I know not what condition of misery to imagine miserable enough for such a people, unless that portion of the wicked, or rather of the damned, on whom God threatens, in Psalm xi. "to rain snares;" but that questionless cannot be by any law, which the apostle saith is "a ministry ordained of God unto our good," and not so many ways and in so high a degree to our

destruction, as we have now been graduating. And this is all the good can come to the person licensed in his hardness of heart.

I am next to mention that, which because it is a ground in divinity, Rom. iii., will save the labor of demonstrating, unless her given axioms be more doubted than in other arts, that a thing unlawful can for no good whatsoever be done, much less allowed by a positive law (although it be no less firm in the precepts of philosophy). And this is the matter why interpreters upon that passage in Hosea will not consent it to be a true story, that the prophet took a harlot to wife: because God, being a pure spirit, could not command a thing repugnant to his own nature, no, not for so good an end as to exhibit more to the life a wholesome and perhaps a converting parable to many an Israelite. Yet that he commanded the allowance of adulterous and injurious divorces for hardness of heart, a reason obscure and in a wrong sense, they can very savorily persuade themselves; so tenacious is the leaven of an old conceit. But they shift it: he permitted only. Yet silence in the law is consent, and consent is accessory: why then is not the law, being silent, or not active against a crime, accessory to its own conviction, itself judging? For though we should grant, that it approves not, yet it wills: and the lawyers' maxim is, that "the will compelled is yet the will." And though Aristotle in his ethics call this "a mixed action," yet he concludes it to be voluntary and inexcusable, if it be evil. How justly, then, might human law and philosophy rise up against the righteousness of Moses, if this be true which our vulgar divinity fathers upon him, yea, upon God himself, not silently, and only negatively to permit, but in his law to divulge a written and general privilege to commit and persist in unlawful divorces with a high hand, with security and no ill fame? For this is more than permitting or contriving, this is maintaining: this is warranting, this is protecting, yea, this is doing evil, and such an evil as that reprobate lawgiver did, whose lasting infamy is engraven upon him like a surname, "he who made Israel to sin." This is the lowest pitch contrary to God that public fraud and injustice can descend.

If it be affirmed, that God, as being Lord, may do what he will, yet we must know, that God hath not two wills, but one will, much less two contrary. If he once willed adultery should be sinful, and to be punished by death, all his omnipotence will not allow him to will the allowance that his holiest people might, as it were, by his own antinomy, or counterstatute, live unreproved in the same fact as he himself esteemed it, according to our common explainers. The hidden ways of his providence we adore and search not, but the law is his revealed will, his complete, his evident and certain will: herein he appears to us, as it were, in human shape, enters into covenant with us, swears to keep it, binds himself like a just lawgiver to his own prescriptions, gives himself to be understood by men, judges and is judged, measures and is commensurate to right reason; cannot require less of us in one cantle of his law than in another, his legal justice cannot be so fickle and so variable, sometimes like a devouring fire, and by and by connivant in the embers, or, if I may so say, oscitant and supine. The vigor of his law could no more remit, than the hallowed fire on his altar could be let go out. The lamps that burnt before him might need snuffing, but the light of his law never. Of this also more beneath, in discussing a solution of Rivetus.

The Jesuits, and that sect among us which is named of Arminius, are wont to charge us of making God the author of sin, in two degrees especially, not to speak of his permission: 1. Because we hold, that he hath decreed some to damnation, and consequently to sin, say they; next, Because those means, which are of saving knowledge to others, he makes to them an occasion of greater sin. Yet considering the perfection wherein man was created, and might have stood, no decree necessitating his freewill, but subsequent, though not in time, yet in order to causes, which were in his own power; they might methinks be persuaded to absolve both God and us. Whenas the doctrine of Plato and Chrysippus, with their followers, the academics and the stoics, who knew not what a consummate and most adorned Pandora was bestowed upon Adam, to be the nurse and guide of his arbitrary happiness and perseverance, I mean, his native innocence and perfection, which might have kept him from being our true Epimetheus; and though they taught of virtue and vice to be both the gift of divine destiny, they could yet find reasons not invalid, to justify the councils of God and fate from the insulsity of mortal tongues: that man's own freewill self-corrupted, is the adequate and sufficient cause of his disobedience besides fate; as Homer also wanted not to express, both in his Iliad and Odyssey. And Manilius the poet, although in his fourth book he tells of some "created both to sin and punishment;" yet without murmuring, and with an industrious cheerfulness, he acquits the Deity. They were not ignorant in their heathen lore, that it is most godlike to punish those who of his creatures became his enemies with the greatest punishment; and they could attain also to think, that the greatest, when God himself throws a man furthest from him; which then they held he did, when he blinded, hardened, and stirred up his offenders, to finish and pile up their desperate work since they had undertaken it. To banish for ever into a local hell, whether in the air or in the centre, or in that uttermost and bottomless gulf of chaos, deeper from holy bliss than the world's diameter multiplied; they thought had not a punishing so proper and proportionate for God to inflict as to punish sin with sin. Thus were the common sort of Gentiles wont to think, without any wry thoughts cast upon divine governance. And therefore Cicero, not in his Tusculan or Campanian retirements among the learned wits of that age, but even in the senate to a mixed auditory, (though he were sparing otherwise to broach his philosophy among statists and lawyers,) yet as to this point, both in his Oration against Piso, and in that which is about the answers of the soothsayers against Clodius, he declares it publicly as no paradox to common ears, that God cannot punish man more, nor make him more miserable, than still by making him more sinful. Thus we see how in this controversy the justice of God stood upright even among heathen disputers. But if any one be truly, and not pretendedly zealous for God's honor, here I call him forth, before men and angels, to use his best and most advised skill, lest God more unavoidably than ever yet, and in the guiltiest manner, be made the author of sin: if he shall not only deliver over and incite his enemies by rebukes to sin as a punishment, but shall by patent under his own broad seal allow his friends whom he would sanctify and save, whom he would unite to himself and not disjoin, whom he would correct by wholesome chastening, and not punish as he doth the damned by lewd sinning; if he shall allow these in his law, the perfect rule of his own purest will, and our most edified conscience, the perpetrating of an odious and manifold sin without the least contesting. It is wondered how there can be in God a secret and revealed will; and yet what wonder, if there be in man two answerable causes. But here there must be two revealed wills grappling in a fraternal war with one another without any reasonable cause apprehended. This cannot be less than to engraft sin into the substance of the law, which law is to provoke sin by crossing and forbidding, not by complying with it. Nay, this is, which I tremble in uttering, to incarnate sin into the unpunishing and well-pleased will of God. To avoid these dreadful consequences, that tread upon the heels of those allowances to sin, will be a task of far more difficulty than to appease those minds, which perhaps out of a vigilant and wary conscience except against predestination. Thus finally we may conclude, that a law wholly giving licence cannot upon any good consideration be given to a holy people, for hardness of heart in the vulgar sense.

CHAPTER IV.

That if Divorce be no Command, no more is Marriage. That Divorce could be no Dispensation, if it were sinful. The Solution of Rivetus, that God dispensed by some unknown Way, ought not to satisfy a Christian Mind.

OTHERS think to evade the matter by not granting any law of divorce, but only a dispensation which is contrary to the words of Christ, who himself calls it a "law," Mark x. 5: or if we speak of a command in the strictest definition, then marriage itself is no more a command than divorce, but only a free permission to him who cannot contain. But as to dispensation, I affirm the same as before of the law, that it can never be given to the allowance of sin: God cannot give it neither in respect of himself, nor in respect of man; not in respect of himself, being a most pure essence, the just avenger of sin; neither can he make that cease to be a sin, which is in itself unjust and impure, as all divorces, they say, were, which were not for adultery. Not in respect of man, for then it must be either to his good, or to his evil. Not to his good; for how can that be imagined any good to a sinner, whom nothing but rebuke and due correction can save, to hear the determinate oracle of divine law louder than any reproof dispensing and providing for the impunity and convenience of sin; to make that doubtful, or rather lawful, which the end of the law was to make most evidently hateful? Nor to the evil of man can a dispense be given; for if "the law were ordained unto life," Rom. vii. 10, how can the same God publish dispenses against that law, which must needs be unto death? Absurd and monstrous would that dispense be, if any judge or law should give it a man to cut his own throat, or to damn himself. Dispense, therefore, presupposes full pardon, or else it is not a dispense, but a most baneful and bloody snare. And why should God enter covenant with a people to be holy, as "the command is holy, and just, and good," Rom. vii. 12, and yet suffer an impure and treacherous dispense, to mislead and betray them under the vizard of law to a legitimate practice of uncleanness? God is no covenant-breaker; he cannot do this.

Rivetus, a diligent and learned writer, having well weighed what hath been written by those founders of dispense, and finding the small agreement among them, would fain work himself aloof these rocks and quicksands, and thinks it best to conclude that God certainly did dispense, but by some way to us unknown, and so to leave it. But to this I oppose that a Christian by no means ought rest himself in such an ignorance; whereby so many absurdities will straight reflect both against the purity, justice, and wisdom of God, the end also both of law and gospel, and the comparison of them both together. God indeed in some ways of his providence is high and secret, past finding out: but in the delivery and execution of his law, especially in the managing of a duty so daily and so familiar as this is whereof we reason, hath plain enough revealed himself, and requires the observance thereof not otherwise, than to the law of nature and of equity imprinted in us seems correspondent. And he hath taught us to love and to extol his laws, not only as they are his, but as they are just and good to every wise and sober understanding. Therefore Abraham, even to the face of God himself, seemed to doubt of divine justice, if it should swerve from that irradiation wherewith it had enlightened the mind of man, and bound itself to observe its own rule: "Wilt thou destroy the righteous with the wicked? that be far from thee; shall not the judge of the earth do right?" Thereby declaring that God hath created a righteousness in right itself, against which he cannot do. So David, Psalm cxix. "The testimonies which thou hast commanded are righteous and very faithful; thy word is very pure, therefore thy servant loveth it." Not only then for the author's sake, but for its own purity. "He is faithful," saith St. Paul, "he cannot deny himself;" that is, cannot deny his own promises, cannot but be true to his own rules. He often pleads with men the uprightness of his ways by their own principles. How should we imitate him else, to "be perfect as he is perfect"? If at pleasure he can dispense with golden poetic ages of such pleasing licence, as in the fabled reign of old Saturn, and this perhaps before the law might have some covert; but under such an undispensing covenant as Moses made with them, and not to tell us why and wherefore, indulgence cannot give quiet to the breast of any intelligent man. We must be resolved how the law can be pure and perspicuous, and yet throw a polluted skirt over these Eleusinian mysteries, that no man can utter what they mean: worse in this than the worst obscenities of heathen superstition; for their filthiness was hid, but the mystic reason thereof known to their sages. But this Jewish imputed filthiness was daily and open, but the reason of it is not known to our divines. We know of no design the gospel can have to impose new righteousness upon works, but to remit the old by faith without works, if we mean justifying works: we know no mystery our Saviour could have to lay new bonds upon marriage in the covenant of grace which himself had loosened to the severity of law. So that Rivetus may pardon us, if we cannot be contented with his nonsolution, to remain in such a peck of uncertainties and doubts, so dangerous and ghastly to the fundamentals of our faith.

CHAPTER V.

What a Dispensation is.

THEREFORE to get some better satisfaction, we must proceed to inquire as diligently as we can what a dispensation is, which I find to be either properly so called, or improperly. Improperly so called, is rather a particular and exceptive law, absolving and disobliging from a more general command for some just and reasonable cause. As Numb. ix. they who were unclean, or in a journey, had leave to keep the passover in the second month, but otherwise ever in the first. As for that in Leviticus of marrying the brother's wife, it was a penal statute rather than a dispense: and commands nothing injurious or in itself unclean, only prefers a special reason of charity before an institutive decency, and perhaps is meant for lifetime only, as is expressed beneath in the prohibition of taking two sisters. What other edict of Moses, carrying but the semblance of a law in any other kind, may bear the name of a dispense, I have not readily to instance. But a dispensation most properly is some particular accident rarely happening, and therefore not specified in the law, but left to the decision of charity, even under the bondage of Jewish rites, much more under the liberty of the gospel. Thus did "David enter into the house of God, and did eat the shewbread, he and his followers, which was" ceremonially "unlawful." Of such dispenses as these it was that Verdune the French divine so gravely disputed in the council of Trent against friar Adrian, who held that the pope might dispense with anything. "It is a fond persuasion," saith Verdune, "that dispensing is a favor; nay, it is as good distributive justice as what is most, and the priest sins if he give it not, for it is nothing else but a right interpretation of law." Thus far that I can learn touching this matter wholesomely decreed. But that God, who is the giver of every good and perfect gift, Jam. i. should give out a rule and directory to sin by, should enact a dispensation as longlived as a law, whereby to live in privileged adultery for hardness of heart, (and yet this obdurate disease cannot be conceived how it was the more amended by this unclean remedy,) is the most deadly and scorpionlike gift, that the enemy of mankind could have given to any miserable sinner, and is rather such a dispense as that was, which the serpent gave to our first parents. God gave quails in his wrath, and kings in his wrath, yet neither of these things evil in themselves: but that he whose eyes cannot behold impurity, should in the book of his holy covenant, his most unpassionate law, give licence and statute for uncontrolled adultery, although it go for the received opinion, I shall ever dissuade my soul from such a creed, such an indulgence as the shop of Antichrist never forged a baser.

CHAPTER VI.

That the Jew had no more Right to this supposed Dispense than the Christian hath; and rather not so much.

But if we must needs dispense, let us for a while so far dispense with truth, as to grant that sin may be dispensed; yet there will be copious reason found to prove, that the Jew had no more right to such a supposed indulgence than the Christian; whether we look at the clear knowledge wherein he lived, or the strict performance of works whereto he was bound. Besides visions and prophecies, they had the law of God, which in the Psalms and Proverbs is chiefly praised for sureness and certainty, both easy and perfect to the enlightening of the simple. How could it be so obscure then, or they so sottishly blind in this plain, moral, and household duty? They had the same precepts about marriage; Christ added nothing to

their clearness, for that had argued them imperfect; he opens not the law, but removes the pharisaic mists raised between the law and the people's eyes: the only sentence which he adds, "What God hath joined let no man put asunder," is as obscure as any clause fetched out of Genesis, and hath increased a yet undecided controversy of clandestine marriages. If we examine over all his sayings, we shall find him not so much interpreting the law with his words, as referring his own words to be interpreted by the law, and oftener obscures his mind in short, and vehement, and compact sentences, to blind and puzzle them the more, who would not understand the law. The Jews therefore were as little to be dispensed with for lack of moral knowledge as we.

Next, none I think will deny, but that they were as much bound to perform the law as any Christian. That severe and rigorous knife not sparing the tender foreskin of any male infant, to carve upon his flesh the mark of that strict and pure covenant whereinto he entered, might give us to understand enough against the fancy of dispensing. St. Paul testifies, that every "circumcised man is a debtor to the whole law," Gal. v., or else "circumcision is in vain," Rom. ii. 25. How vain then, and how preposterous must it needs be to exact a circumcision of the flesh from an infant unto an outward sign of purity, and to dispense an uncircumcision in the soul of a grown man to an inward and real impurity! How vain again was that law, to impose tedious expiations for every slight sin of ignorance and error, and to privilege without penance or disturbance an odious crime whether of ignorance or obstinacy! How unjust also inflicting death and extirpation for the mark of circumstantial pureness omitted, and proclaiming all honest and liberal indemnity to the act of a substantial impureness committed, making void the covenant that was made against it! Thus if we consider the tenor of the law, to be circumcised and to perform all, not pardoning so much as the scapes of error and ignorance, and compare this with the condition of the gospel, "believe and be baptized," I suppose it cannot be long ere we grant, that the Jew was bound as strictly to the performance of every duty as was possible; and therefore could not be dispensed with more than the Christian, perhaps not so much.

CHAPTER VII.

That the Gospel is apter to dispense than the Law. Paræus answered.

IF then the law will afford no reason why the Jew should be more gently dealt with than the Christian, then surely the gospel can afford as little why the Christian should be less gently dealt with than the Jew. The gospel indeed exhorts to highest perfection, but bears with weakest infirmity more than the law. Hence those indulgences, "All cannot receive this saying," "Every man hath his proper gift," with express charges not to "lay on yokes, which our fathers could not bear." The nature of man still is as weak, and yet as hard; and that weakness and hardness as unfit and as unteachable to be harshly used as ever. Ay, but, saith Paræus, there is a greater portion of spirit poured upon the gospel, which requires from us perfecter obedience. I answer, this does not prove that the law therefore might give allowance to sin more than the gospel; and if it were no sin, we know it the work of the spirit to "mortify our corrupt desires and evil concupiscence;" but not to root up our natural affections and disaffections, moving to and fro even in wisest men upon just and necessary reasons, which were the true ground of that Mosaic dispense, and is the utmost extent of our pleading. What is more or less perfect we dispute not, but what is sin or no sin. And in that I still affirm the law required as perfect obedience as the gospel: besides that the prime end of the gospel is not so much to exact our obedience, as to reveal grace, and the satisfaction of our disobedience. What is now exacted from us, it is the accusing law that does it, even yet under the gospel; but cannot be more extreme to us now than to the Jews of old; for the law ever was of works, and the gospel ever was of grace.

Either then the law by harmless and needful dispenses, which the gospel is now made to deny, must have anticipated and exceeded the grace of the gospel, or else must be found to have given politic and superficial graces without real pardon, saying in general, "Do this and live," and yet deceiving and damning underhand with unsound and hollow permissions; which is utterly abhorring from the end of all law, as hath been showed. But if those indulgences were safe and sinless, out of tenderness and compassion, as indeed they were, and yet shall be abrogated by the gospel, then the law, whose end is by rigor to magnify grace, shall itself give grace, and pluck a fair plume from the gospel; instead of hastening us thither, alluring us from it. And whereas the terror of the law was as a servant to amplify and illustrate the mildness of grace; now the unmildness of evangelic grace shall turn servant to declare the grace and mildness of the rigorous law. The law was harsh to extol the grace of the gospel, and now the gospel by a new affected strictness of her own shall extenuate the grace which herself offers. For by exacting a duty which the law dispensed, if we perform it, then is grace diminished, by how much performance advances, unless the apostle argue wrong: if we perform it not, and perish for not performing, then are the conditions of grace harder than those of rigor. If through faith and repentance we perish not, yet grace still remains the less, by requiring that which rigor did not require, or at least not so strictly. Thus much therefore to Paræus; that if the gospel require perfecter obedience than the law as a duty, it exalts the law and debases itself, which is dishonorable to the work of our redemption. Seeing therefore that all the causes of any allowance that the Jews might have remain as well to the Christians; this is a certain rule, that so long as the causes remain, the allowance ought. And having thus at length inquired the truth concerning law and dispense, their ends, their uses, their limits, and in what manner both Jew and Christian stand liable to the one or capable of the other; we may safely conclude, that to affirm the giving of any law or lawlike dispense to sin for hardness of heart, is a doctrine of that extravagance from the sage principles of piety, that whoso considers thoroughly cannot but admire how this hath been digested all this while.

CHAPTER VIII.

The true Sense how Moses suffered Divorce for Hardness of Heart.

WHAT may we do then to salve this seeming inconsistence? I must not dissemble, that I am confident it can be done no other way than this:

Moses, Deut. xxiv. 1, established a grave and prudent law, full of moral equity, full of due consideration towards nature, that cannot be resisted, a law consenting with the laws of wisest men and civilest nations; that when a man hath married a wife, if it come to pass, that he cannot love her by reason of some displeasing natural quality or unfitness in her, let him write her a bill of divorce. The intent of which law undoubtedly was this, that if any good and peaceable man should discover some helpless disagreement or dislike either of mind or body, whereby he could not cheerfully perform the duty of a husband without the perpetual dissembling of offence and disturbance to his spirit; rather than to live uncomfortably and unhappily both to himself and to his wife; rather than to continue undertaking a duty, which he could not possibly discharge, he might dismiss her whom he could not tolerably and so not conscionably retain. And this law the Spirit of God by the mouth of Solomon, Prov. xxx. 21, 23, testifies to be a good and a necessary law, by granting it that "a hated woman," (for so the Hebrew word signifies, rather than "odious," though it come all to one,) that "a hated woman, when she is married, is a thing that the earth cannot bear." What follows then, but that the charitable law must remedy what nature cannot undergo? Now that many licentious and hardhearted men took hold of this law to cloak their bad purposes, is nothing strange to believe. And these were they, not for whom Moses made the law, (God forbid!) but whose hardness of heart taking ill-advantage by this law he held it better to suffer as by accident, where it could not be detected, rather than good men should lose their just and lawful privilege of remedy; Christ therefore having to answer these

tempting pharisees, according as his custom was, not meaning to inform their proud ignorance what Moses did in the true intent of the law, which they had ill cited, suppressing the true cause for which Moses gave it, and extending it to every slight matter, tells them their own, what Moses was forced to suffer by their abuse of his law. Which is yet more plain, if we mark that our Saviour, in Matt. v., cites not the law of Moses, but the pharisaical tradition falsely grounded upon that law. And in those other places, chap. xix. and Mark x., the pharisees cite the law, but conceal the wise and humane reason there expressed; which our Saviour corrects not in them, whose pride deserved not his instruction, only returns them what is proper to them: "Moses for the hardness of your heart suffered you," that is, such as you, "to put away your wives; and to you he wrote this precept for that cause," which ("to you") must be read with an impression, and understood limitedly of such as covered ill purposes under that law; for it was seasonable, that they should hear their own unbounded licence rebuked, but not seasonable for them to hear a good man's requisite liberty explained. But us he hath taught better, if we have ears to hear. He himself acknowledged it to be a law, Mark x., and being a law of God, it must have an undoubted "end of charity, which may be used with a pure heart, a good conscience, and faith unfeigned," as was heard: it cannot allow sin, but is purposely to resist sin, as by the same chapter to Timothy appears. There we learn also, "that the law is good, if a man use it lawfully." Out of doubt then there must be a certain good in this law, which Moses willingly allowed, and there might be an unlawful use made thereof by hypocrites; and that was it which Moses unwillingly suffered, foreseeing it in general, but not able to discern it in particulars. Christ therefore mentions not here what Moses and the law intended; for good men might know that by many other rules; and the scornful pharisees were not fit to be told, until they could employ that knowledge they had less abusively. Only he acquaints them with what Moses by them was put to suffer.

CHAPTER IX.

The Words of the Institution how to be understood; and of our Saviour's Answer to his Disciples.

AND to entertain a little their overweening arrogance as best befitted, and to amaze them yet further, because they thought it no hard matter to fulfil the law, he draws them up to that unseparable institution, which God ordained in the beginning before the fall, when man and woman were both perfect, and could have no cause to separate: just as in the same chapter he stands not to contend with the arrogant young man, who boasted his observance of the whole law, whether he had indeed kept it or not, but screws him up higher to a task of that perfection, which no man is bound to imitate. And in like manner, that pattern of the first institution he set before the opinionative pharisees, to dazzle them, and not to bind us. For this is a solid rule, that every command, given with a reason, binds our obedience no otherwise than that reason holds. Of this sort was that command in Eden, "Therefore shall a man cleave to his wife, and they shall be one flesh;" which we see is no absolute command, but with an inference "therefore:" the reason then must be first considered, that our obedience be not misobedience. The first is, for it is not single, because the wife is to the husband "flesh of his flesh," as in the verse going before. But this reason cannot be sufficient of itself: for why then should he for his wife leave his father and mother, with whom he is far more "flesh of flesh, and bone of bone," as being made of their substance? And besides, it can be but a sorry and ignoble society of life, whose unseparable injunction depends merely upon flesh and bones. Therefore we must look higher, since Christ himself recalls us to the beginning, and we shall find, that the primitive reason of never divorcing was that sacred and not vain promise of God to remedy man's loneliness by "making him a meet help for him," though not now in perfection, as at first; yet still in proportion as things now are. And this is repeated, verse 20, when all other creatures were fitly associated and brought to Adam, as if the Divine Power had been in some care and deep thought, because "there was not yet found a help meet for man." And can we so slightly depress the all-wise purpose of a deliberating God, as if his consultation had produced no other good for man, but to join him with an accidental companion of propagation, which his sudden word had already made for every beast? Nay, a far less good to man it will be found, if she must at all adventures be fastened upon him individually. And therefore even plain sense and equity, and, which is above them both, the all-interpreting voice of charity herself cries loud, that this primitive reason, this consulted promise of God, "to make a meet help," is the only cause that gives authority to this command of not divorcing, to be a command. And it might be further added, that if the true definition of a wife were asked in good earnest, this clause of being "a meet help" would show itself so necessary and so essential, in that demonstrative argument, that it might be logically concluded: Therefore she who naturally and perpetually is no "meet help," can be no wife; which clearly takes away the difficulty of dismissing such a one. If this be not thought enough, I answer yet further, that marriage, unless it mean a fit and tolerable marriage, is not inseparable neither by nature nor institution. Not by nature, for then those Mosaic divorces had been against nature, if separable and inseparable be contraries, as who doubts they be? And what is against nature is against law, if soundest philosophy abuse us not; by this reckoning Moses should be most unmosaic, that is, most illegal, not to say most unnatural. Nor is it inseparable by the first institution; for then no second institution in the same law for so many causes could dissolve it; it being most unworthy a human, (as Plato's judgment is in the fourth book of his laws,) much more a divine lawgiver, to write two several decrees upon the same thing. But what would Plato have deemed, if one of these were good, and the other evil to be done? Lastly, suppose it be inseparable by institution, yet in competition with higher things, as religion and charity in mainest matters, and when the chief end is frustrate for which it was ordained, as hath been shown; if still it must remain inseparable, it holds a strange and lawless propriety from all other works of God (or under heaven). From these many considerations, we may safely gather, that so much of the first institution as our Saviour mentions, for he mentions not all, was but to quell and put to nonplus the tempting pharisees, and to lay open their ignorance and shallow understanding of the scriptures. For, saith he, "Have ye not read that he which made them at the beginning, made them male and female, and said, For this cause shall a man cleave to his wife?" which these blind usurpers of Moses's chair could not gainsay: as if this single respect of male and female were sufficient, against a thousand inconveniences and mischiefs, to clog a rational creature to his endless sorrow unrelinquishably, under the guileful superscription of his intended solace and comfort. What if they had thus answered? "Master, if thou mean to make wedlock as inseparable as it was from the beginning, let it be made also a fit society, as God meant it, which we shall soon understand it ought to be, if thou recite the whole reason of the law." Doubtless our Saviour had applauded their just answer. For then they had expounded this command of Paradise, even as Moses himself expounds it by his laws of divorce, that is, with due and wise regard had to the premises and reasons of the first command; according to which, without unclean and temporizing permissions, he instructs us in this imperfect state what we may lawfully do about divorce.

But if it be thought that the disciples, offended at the rigor of Christ's answer, could yet obtain no mitigation of the former sentence pronounced to the pharisees, it may be fully answered, that our Saviour continues the same reply to his disciples, as men leavened with the same customary licence which the pharisees maintained, and displeased at the removing of a traditional abuse, whereto they had so long not unwillingly been used: it was no time then to contend with their slow and prejudicial belief, in a thing wherein an ordinary measure of light in scripture, with some attention, might afterwards inform them well enough. And yet ere Christ had finished this argument, they might have picked out of his own concluding words an answer more to their minds, and in effect the same with that which hath been all this while entreating audience: "All men," saith he, "cannot receive this saying, save they to whom it is given; he that is able to receive it, let him receive it." What saying is this which is left to a man's choice to receive, or not receive? what but the married life? Was our Saviour then so mild and favorable to the weakness of a single man, and is he turned on the sudden so rigorous and inexorable, to the distresses and extremities of an ill-wedded man? Did he so graciously give leave to change the better single life for the worse married life? Did he open so to us this hazardous and accidental door of marriage, to shut upon us like the gate of death, without retracting or returning, without permitting to change the worst, most insupportable, most unchristian mischance of marriage, for all the mischiefs and sorrows that can ensue, being an ordinance which was especially given as a cordial and exhilarating cup of solace, the better to bear our other crosses and afflictions? Questionless this were a hardheartedness of undivorcing, worse than that in the Jews, which, they say, extorted the allowance from Moses, and is utterly dissonant from all the doctrine of our Saviour. After these considerations, therefore, to take a law out of Paradise given in time of original perfection, and to take it barely without those just and equal inferences and reasons which mainly establish it, nor so much as admitting those needful and safe allowances, wherewith Moses himself interprets it to the fallen condition of man; argues nothing in us but rashness and contempt of those means that God left us in his pure and chaste law, without which it will not be possible for us to perform the strict imposition of this command: or if we strive beyond our strength, we shall strive to obey it otherwise than God commands it. And lamented experience daily teaches the bitter and vain fruits of this our presumption, forcing men in a thing wherein we are not able to judge either of their strength or of their sufferance. Whom neither one vice nor other by natural addiction, but only marriage ruins, which doubtless is not the fault of that ordinance, for God gave it as a blessing, nor always of man's mischoosing, it being an error above wisdom to prevent, as examples of wisest men so mistaken manifest: it is the fault therefore of a perverse opinion, that will have it continued in despite of nature and reason, when indeed it was never truly joined. All those expositors upon the fifth Matthew confess the law of Moses to be the law of the Lord, wherein no addition or diminution hath place; yet coming to the point of divorce, as if they feared not to be called least in the kingdom of heaven, any slight evasion will content them, to reconcile those contradictions, which they make between Christ and Moses, between Christ and Christ.

CHAPTER X.

The vain Shift of those who make the Law of Divorce to be only the Premises of a succeeding Law.

SOME will have it no law, but the granted premises of another law following, contrary to the words of Christ, Mark x. 5, and all other translations of gravest authority, who render it in form of a law, agreeable to Mal. ii. 16, as it is most anciently and modernly expounded. Besides, the bill of divorce, and the particular occasion therein mentioned, declares it to be orderly and legal. And what avails this to make the matter more righteous, if such an adulterous condition shall be mentioned to build a law upon without either punishment or so much as forbidding? They pretend it is implicitly reproved in these words, Deut. xxiv. 4, "after she is defiled;" but who sees not that this defilement is only in respect of returning to her former husband after an intermixed marriage? else why was not the defiling condition first forbidden, which would have saved the labor of this after-law? Nor is it seemly or piously attributed to the justice of God and his known hatred of sin, that such a heinous fault as this through all the law should be only wiped with an implicit and oblique touch, (which yet is falsely supposed,) and that his peculiar people should be let wallow in adulterous marriages almost two thousand years, for want of a direct law to prohibit them: it is rather to be confidently assumed, that this was granted to apparent necessities,

as being of unquestionable right and reason in the law of nature, in that it still passes without inhibition, even when greatest cause is given us to expect it should be directly forbidden.

CHAPTER XI.

The other Shift of saying Divorce was permitted by Law, but not approved. More of the Institution.

BUT it was not approved. So much the worse that it was allowed; as if sin had over-mastered the law of God, to conform her steady and straight rule to sin's crookedness, which is impossible. Besides, what needed a positive grant of that which was not approved? It restrained no liberty to him that could but use a little fraud; it had been better silenced, unless it were approved in some case or other. But still it was not approved. Miserable excusers! he who doth evil, that good may come thereby, approves not what he doth; and yet the grand rule forbids him, and counts his damnation just if he do it. The sorceress Medea did not approve her own evil doings, yet looked not to be excused for that: and it is the constant opinion of Plato in Protagoras, and other of his dialogues, agreeing with that proverbial sentence among the Greeks, that "no man is wicked willingly." Which also the Peripatetics do rather distinguish than deny. What great thank then if any man, reputed wise and constant, will neither do, nor permit others under his charge to do, that which he approves not, especially in matter of sin? but for a judge, but for a magistrate, the shepherd of his people, to surrender up his approbation against law, and his own judgment, to the obstinacy of his herd, what more unjudgelike, unmagistratelike, and in war more uncommanderlike? Twice in a short time it was the undoing of the Roman state, first when Pompey, next when Marcus Brutus, had not magnanimity enough but to make so poor a resignation of what they approved, to what the boisterous tribunes and soldiers bawled for. Twice it was the saving of two the greatest commonwealths in the world, of Athens by Themistocles at the seafight of Salamis, of Rome by Fabius Maximus in the Punic war; for that these two matchless generals had the fortitude at home, against the rashness and the clamors of their own captains and confederates, to withstand the doing or permitting of what they could not approve in the duty of their great command. Thus far of civil prudence. But when we speak of sin, let us look again upon the old reverend Eli, who in his heavy punishment found no difference between the doing and permitting of what he did not approve. If hardness of heart in the people may be any excuse, why then is Pilate branded through all memory? He approved not what he did, he openly protested, he washed his hands, and labored not a little ere he would yield to the hard hearts of a whole people, both princes and plebeians, importuning and tumulting unto the fear of a revolt. Yet is there any will undertake his cause? If therefore Pilate for suffering but one act of cruelty against law, though with much unwillingness testified, at the violent demand of a whole nation, shall stand so black upon record to all posterity; alas for Moses! what shall we say for him, while we are taught to believe he suffered not one act only both of cruelty and uncleanness in one divorce, but made it a plain and lasting law against law, whereby ten thousand acts accounted both cruel and unclean might be daily committed, and this without the least suit or petition of the people, that we can read of?

And can we conceive without vile thoughts, that the majesty and holiness of God could endure so many ages to gratify a stubborn people in the practice of a foul polluting sin? and could he expect they should abstain, he not signifying his mind in a plain command, at such time especially when he was framing their laws and them to all possible perfection? But they were to look back to the first institution; nay, rather why was not that individual institution brought out of Paradise, as was that of the sabbath, and repeated in the body of the law, that men might have understood it to be a command? For that any sentence that bears the resemblance of a precept, set there so out of place in another world, at such a distance from the whole law, and not once mentioned there, should be an obliging command to us, is very disputable; and perhaps it might be denied to be a command without further dispute: however, it commands not absolutely, as hath been cleared, but only with reference to that precedent promise of God, which is the very ground of his institution: if that appear not in some tolerable sort, how can we affirm such a matrimony to be the same which God instituted? in such an accident it will best behoove our soberness to follow rather what moral Sinai prescribes equal to our strength, than fondly to think within our strength all that lost Paradise relates.

CHAPTER XII.

The third Shift of them who esteem it a mere Judicial Law Proved again to be a Law of moral Equity.

ANOTHER while it shall suffice them, that it was not a moral but a judicial law, and so was abrogated: nay, rather not abrogated because judicial: which law the ministry of Christ came not to deal with. And who put it in man's power to exempt, where Christ speaks in general of not abrogating "the least jot or tittle," and in special not that of divorce, because it follows among those laws which he promised expressly not to abrogate, but to vindicate from abusive traditions? which is most evidently to be seen in the 16th of Luke, where this caution of not abrogating is inserted immediately, and not otherwise than purposely, when no other point of the law is touched but that of divorce. And if we mark the 31st verse of Matt. v. he there cites not the law of Moses, but the licentious gloss which traduced the law; that therefore which he cited, that he abrogated, and not only abrogated, but disallowed and flatly condemned; which could not be the law of Moses, for that had been foully to the rebuke of his great servant. To abrogate a law made with God's allowance, had been to tell us only that such a law was now to cease: but to refute it with an ignominious note of civilizing adultery, casts the reproof, which was meant only to the pharisees, even upon him who made the law. But yet if that be judicial, which belongs to a civil court, this law is less judicial than nine of the ten commandments: for antiquaries affirm, that divorces proceeded among the Jews without knowledge of the magistrate, only with hands and seals under the testimony of some rabbies to be then present. Perkins, in a "Treatise of Conscience," grants, that what in the judicial law is of common equity binds also the Christian: and how to judge of this, prescribes two ways: if wise nations have enacted the like decree; or if it maintain the good of family, church, or commonwealth. This therefore is a pure moral economical law, too hastily imputed of tolerating sin; being rather so clear in nature and reason, that it was left to a man's own arbitrement to be determined between God and his own conscience; not only among the Jews, but in every wise nation: the restraint whereof, who is not too thick-sighted, may see how hurtful and distractive it is to the house, the church, and commonwealth. And that power which Christ never took from the master of family, but rectified only to a right and wary use at home; that power the undiscerning canonist hath improperly usurped into his court-leet, and bescribbled with a thousand trifling impertinences, which yet have filled the life of man with serious trouble and calamity. Yet grant it were of old a judicial law, it need not be the less moral for that, being conversant as it is about virtue or vice. And our Saviour disputes not here the judicature, for that was not his office, but the morality of divorce, whether it be adultery or no; if therefore he touch the law of Moses at all, he touches the moral part thereof, which is absurd to imagine, that the covenant of grace should reform the exact and perfect law of works, eternal and immutable; or if he touch not the law at all, then is not the allowance thereof disallowed to us.

CHAPTER XIII.

The ridiculous Opinion that Divorce was permitted from the Custom in Egypt. That Moses gave not this Law unwillingly. Perkins confesses this Law was not abrogated.

OTHERS are so ridiculous as to allege, that this licence of divorcing was given them because they were so accustomed in Egypt. As if an ill custom were to be kept to all posterity; for the dispensation is both universal and of time unlimited, and so indeed no dispensation at all; for the overdated dispensation of a thing unlawful, serves for nothing but to increase hardness of heart, and makes men but wax more incorrigible; which were a great reproach to be said of any law or allowance that God should give us. In these opinions it would be more religion to advise well, lest we make ourselves juster than God, by censuring rashly that for sin, which his unspotted law without rebuke allows, and his people without being conscious of displeasing him have used: and if we can think so of Moses, as that the Jewish obstinacy could compel him to write such impure permissions against the rule of God and his own judgment; doubtless it was his part to have protested publicly what straits he was driven to, and to have declared his conscience, when he gave any law against his mind: for the law is the touchstone of sin and of conscience, must not be intermixed with corrupt indulgences; for then it loses the greatest praise it has of being certain, and infallible, not leading into error as all the Jews were led by this connivance of Moses, if it were a connivance. But still they fly back to the primitive institution, and would have us re-enter paradise against the sword that guards it. Whom I again thus reply to, that the place in Genesis contains the description of a fit and perfect marriage, with an interdict of ever divorcing such a union: but where nature is discovered to have never joined indeed, but vehemently seeks to part, it cannot be there conceived that God forbids it; nay, he commands it both in the law and in the prophet Malachi, which is to be our rule. And Perkins upon this chapter of Matthew deals plainly, that our Saviour here confutes not Moses's law, but the false glosses that depraved the law; which being true, Perkins must needs grant, that something then is left to that law which Christ found no fault with; and what can that be but the conscionable use of such liberty, as the plain words import? so that by his own inference, Christ did not absolutely intend to restrain all divorces to the only cause of adultery. This therefore is the true scope of our Saviour's will, that he who looks upon the law concerning divorce, should look also back upon the first institution, that he may endeavor what is perfectest: and he that looks upon the institution should not refuse as sinful and unlawful those allowances which God affords him in his following law, lest he make himself purer than his Maker, and presuming above strength, slip into temptations irrecoverably. For this is wonderful, that in all those decrees concerning marriage, God should never once mention the prime institution to dissuade them from divorcing, and that he should forbid smaller sins as opposite to the hardness of their hearts, and let this adulterous matter of divorce pass ever unreproved.

This is also to be marvelled, that seeing Christ did not condemn whatever it was that Moses suffered, and that thereupon the Christian magistrate permits usury and open stews, and here with us adultery to be so slightly punished, which was punished by death to these hard-hearted Jews; why we should strain thus at the matter of divorce, which may stand so much with charity to permit, and make no scruple to allow usury esteemed to be so much against charity? But this it is to embroil ourselves against the righteous and all-wise judgments and statutes of God; which are not variable and contrarious, as we would make them, one while permitting, and another while forbidding, but are most constant and most harmonious each to other. For how can the uncorrupt and majestic law of God, bearing in her hand the wages of life and death, harbor such a repugnance within herself, as to require an unexempted and impartial obedience to all her decrees, either from us or from our Mediator, and yet debase herself to falter so many ages with circumcised adulteries by unclean and slubbering permissions?

CHAPTER XIV.

That Beza's Opinion of regulating Sin by apostolic Law cannot be sound.

YET Beza's opinion is, that a politic law (but what politic law I know not, unless one of Machiavel's) may regulate sin; may bear indeed, I grant, with imperfection for a time, as those canons of the apostles did in ceremonial things; but as for sin, the essence of it cannot consist with rule; and if the law fall to regulate sin, and not to take it utterly away, it necessarily confirms and establishes sin. To make a regularity of sin by law, either the law must straighten sin into no sin, or sin must crook the law into no law. The judicial law can serve to no other end than to be the protector and champion of religion and honest civility, as is set down plainly, Rom. xiii., and is but the arm of moral law, which can no more be separate from justice, than justice from virtue. Their office also, in a different manner, steers the same course; the one teaches what is good by precept, the other unteaches what is bad by punishment. But if we give way to politic dispensations of lewd uncleanness, the first good consequence of such a relax will be the justifying of papal stews, joined with a toleration of epidemic whoredom. Justice must revolt from the end of her authority, and become the patron of that whereof she was created the punisher. The example of usury, which is commonly alleged, makes against the allegation which it brings, as I touched before. Besides that usury, so much as is permitted by the magistrate, and demanded with common equity, is neither against the word of God, nor the rule of charity; as hath been often discussed by men of eminent learning and judgment. There must be therefore some other example found out to show us wherein civil policy may with warrant from God settle wickedness by law, and make that lawful which is lawless. Although I doubt not but, upon deeper consideration, that which is true in physic will be found as true in policy, that as of bad pulses those that beat most in order, are much worse than those that keep the most inordinate circuit; so of popular vices, those that may be committed legally will be more pernicious than those that are left to their own course at peril, not under a stinted privilege to sin orderly and regularly, which is an implicit contradiction, but under due and fearless execution of punishment.

The political law, since it cannot regulate vice, is to restrain it by using all means to root it out. But if it suffer the weed to grow up to any pleasurable or contented height upon what pretext soever, it fastens the root, it prunes and dresses vice, as if it were a good plant. Let no man doubt therefore to affirm, that it is not so hurtful or dishonorable to a commonwealth, nor so much to the hardening of hearts, when those worse faults pretended to be feared are committed, by who so dares under strict and executed penalty, as when those less faults tolerated for fear of greater, harden their faces, not their hearts only, under the protection of public authority. For what less indignity were this, than as if justice herself, the queen of virtues, descending from her sceptered royalty, instead of conquering, should compound and treat with sin, her eternal adversary and rebel, upon ignoble terms? or as if the judicial law were like that untrusty steward in the gospel, and instead of calling in the debts of his moral master, should give out subtile and sly acquittances to keep himself from begging? or let us person him like some wretched itinerary judge, who, to gratify his delinquents before him, would let them basely break his head, lest they should pull him from the bench, and throw him over the bar. Unless we had rather think both moral and judicial, full of malice and deadly purpose, conspired to let the debtor Israelite, the seed of Abraham, run on upon a bankrupt score, flattered with insufficient and ensnaring discharges, that so he might be haled to a more cruel forfeit for all the indulgent arrears which those judicial acquitments had engaged him in. No, no, this cannot be, that the law whose integrity and faithfulness is next to God, should be either the shameless broker of our impunities, or the intended instrument of our destruction. The method of holy correction, such as became the commonwealth of Israel, is not to bribe sin with sin, to capitulate and hire out one crime with another; but with more noble and graceful severity than Popilius the Roman legate used with Antiochus, to limit and level out the direct way from vice to virtue, with straightest and exactest lines on either side, not winding or indenting so much as to the right hand of fair pretences. Violence indeed and insurrection may force the law to suffer what it cannot mend; but to write a decree in allowance of sin, as soon can the hand of justice rot off. Let this be ever concluded as a truth that will outlive the faith of those that seek to bear it down.

CHAPTER XV.

That Divorce was not given for Wives only, as Beza and Parœus write. More of the Institution.

LASTLY, if divorce were granted, as Beza and others say, not for men, but to release afflicted wives; certainly, it is not only a dispensation, but a most merciful law: and why it should not yet be in force, being wholly as needful, I know not what can be in cause but senseless cruelty. But yet to say, divorce was granted for relief of wives rather than of husbands, is but weakly conjectured, and is manifest the extreme shift of a huddled exposition. Whenas it could not be found how hardness of heart should be lessened by liberty of divorce, a fancy was devised to hide the flaw, by commenting that divorce was permitted only for the help of wives. Palpably uxorious! who can be ignorant, that woman was created for man, and not man for woman, and that a husband may be injured as insufferably in marriage as a wife? What an injury is it after wedlock not to be beloved! what to be slighted! what to be contended with in point of house-rule who shall be the head; not for any parity of wisdom, for that were something reasonable, but out of a female pride! "I suffer not," saith St. Paul, "the woman to usurp authority over the man." If the apostle could not suffer it, into what mold is he mortified that can? Solomon saith, "that a bad wife is to her husband as rottenness to his bones, a continual dropping. Better dwell in the corner of the house-top, or in the wilderness," than with such a one. "Whoso hideth her, hideth the wind, and one of the four mischiefs that the earth cannot bear." If the Spirit of God wrote such aggravations as these, and (as may be guessed by these similitudes) counsels the man rather to divorce than to live with such a colleague; and yet on the other side expresses nothing of the wife's suffering with a bad husband; is it not most likely that God in his law had more pity towards man thus wedlocked, than towards the woman that was created for another? The same Spirit relates to us the course which the Medes and Persians took by occasion of Vashti, whose mere denial to come at her husband's sending lost her the being queen any longer, and set up a wholesome law, "that every man should bear rule in his own house." And the divine relater shows us not the least sign of disliking what was done; how should he, if Moses long before was nothing less mindful of the honor and pre-eminence due to man? So that to say divorce was granted for woman rather than man, was but fondly invented. Esteeming therefore to have asserted thus an injured law of Moses, from the unwarranted and guilty name of a dispensation, to be again a most equal and requisite law, we have the word of Christ himself, that he came not to alter the least tittle of it; and signifies no small displeasure against him that shall teach to do so. On which relying, I shall not much waver to affirm, that those words which are made to intimate as if they forbade all divorce but for adultery, (though Moses have constituted otherwise,) those words taken circumscriptly, without regard to any precedent law of Moses, or attestation of Christ himself, or without care to preserve those his fundamental and superior laws of nature and charity, to which all other ordinances give up their seals, are as much against plain equity and the mercy of religion, as those words of "Take, eat; this is my body," elementally understood, are against nature and sense.

And surely the restoring of this degraded law hath well recompensed the diligence was used by enlightening us further to find out wherefore Christ took off the pharisees from alleging the law, and referred them to the first institution; not condemning, altering, or abolishing this precept of divorce, which is plainly moral, for that were against his truth, his promise, and his prophetic office; but knowing how fallaciously they had cited and concealed the particular and natural reason of the law, that they might justify any froward reason of their own, he lets go that sophistry unconvinced; for that had been to teach them else, which his purpose was not. And since they had taken a liberty which the law gave not, he amuses and repels their tempting pride with a perfection of Paradise, which the law required not; not thereby to oblige our performance to that whereto the law never enjoined the fallen estate of man: for if the first institution must make wedlock, whatever happened, inseparable to us, it must make it also as perfect, as meetly helpful, and as comfortable as God promised it should be, at least in some degree; otherwise it is not equal or proportionable to the strength of man, that he should be reduced into such indissoluble bonds to his assured misery, if all the other conditions of that covenant be manifestly altered.

CHAPTER XVI.

How to be understood, that they must be one Flesh; and how that those whom God hath joined, Man should not sunder.

NEXT he saith, "They must be one flesh;" which when all conjecturing is done, will be found to import no more but to make legitimate and good the carnal act, which else might seem to have something of pollution in it; and infers thus much over, that the fit union of their souls be such as may even incorporate them to love and amity: but that can never be where no correspondence is of the mind; nay, instead of being one flesh, they will be rather two carcasses chained unnaturally together; or, as it may happen, a living soul bound to a dead corpse; a punishment too like that inflicted by the tyrant Mezentius, so little worthy to be received as that remedy of loneliness which God meant us: Since we know it is not the joining of another body will remove loneliness, but the uniting of another compliable mind; and that it is no blessing but a torment, nay, a base and brutish condition to be one flesh, unless where nature can in some measure fix a unity of disposition. The meaning therefore of these words, "For this cause shall a man leave his father and his mother, and shall cleave to his wife," was first to show us the dear affection which naturally grows in every not unnatural marriage, even to the leaving of parents, or other familiarity whatsoever. Next, it justifies a man in so doing, that nothing is done undutifully to father or mother. But he that should be here sternly commanded to cleave to his error, a disposition which to his he finds will never cement, a quotidian of sorrow and discontent in his house; let us be excused to pause a little, and bethink us every way round ere we lay such a flat solecism upon the gracious, and certainly not inexorable, not rushless and flinty ordinance of marriage. For if the meaning of these words must be thus blocked up within their own letters from all equity and fair deduction, they will serve then well indeed their turn, who affirm divorce to have been granted only for wives; whenas we see no word of this text binds women, but men only, what it binds. No marvel then if Salomith (sister to Herod) sent a writ of ease to Costobarus her husband, which (as Josephus there attests) was lawful only to men. No marvel though Placidia, the sister of Honorius, threatened the like to earl Constantius for a trivial cause, as Photius relates from Olympiodorus. No marvel anything, if letters must be turned into palisadoes, to stake out all requisite sense from entering to their due enlargement.

Lastly, Christ himself tells who should not be put asunder, namely, those whom God hath joined. A plain solution of this great controversy, if men would but use their eyes. For when is it that God may be said to join? when the parties and their friends consent? No, surely; for that may concur to lewdest ends. Or is it when church rites are finished? Neither; for the efficacy of those depends upon the presupposed fitness of either party. Perhaps after carnal knowledge. Least of all; for that may join persons whom neither law nor nature dares join. It is left, that only then when the minds are fitly disposed and enabled to maintain a cheerful conversation, to the solace and love of each other, according as God intended and promised in the very first foundation of matrimony, "I will make him a help-meet for him;" for surely what God intended and promised, that only can be thought to be his joining, and not the contrary. So likewise the apostle witnesseth, 1 Cor. vii. 15, that in marriage "God hath called us to peace." And doubtless in what respect he hath called us to marriage, in that also he hath joined

us. The rest, whom either disproportion, or deadness of spirit, or something distasteful and averse in the immutable bent of nature renders unconjugal, error may have joined, but God never joined against the meaning of his own ordinance. And if he joined them not, then is there no power above their own consent to hinder them from unjoining, when they cannot reap the soberest ends of being together in any tolerable sort. Neither can it be said properly that such twain were ever divorced, but only parted from each other, as two persons unconjunctive and unmarriable together. But if, whom God hath made a fit help, frowardness or private injuries hath made unfit, that being the secret of marriage, God can better judge than man, neither is man indeed fit or able to decide this matter: however it be, undoubtedly a peaceful divorce is a less evil, and less in scandal than a hateful, hardhearted, and destructive continuance of marriage in the judgment of Moses and of Christ, that justifies him in choosing the less evil; which if it were an honest and civil prudence in the law, what is there in the gospel forbidding such a kind of legal wisdom, though we should admit the common expositors?

CHAPTER XVII.

The Sentence of Christ concerning Divorce how to be expounded. What Grotius hath observed. Other Additions.

HAVING thus unfolded those ambiguous reasons, wherewith Christ (as his wont was) gave to the pharisees that came to sound him, such an answer as they deserved, it will not be uneasy to explain the sentence itself that now follows; "Whosoever shall put away his wife, except it be for fornication, and shall marry another, committeth adultery." First therefore I will set down what is observed by Grotius upon this point, a man of general learning. Next, I produce what mine own thoughts gave me before I had seen his annotations. Origen, saith he, notes that Christ named adultery rather as one example of other like cases, than as one only exception; and that it is frequent not only in human but in divine laws, to express one kind of fact, whereby other causes of like nature may have the like plea, as Exod. xxi. 18, 19, 20, 26; Deut. xix. 5. And from the maxims of civil law he shows, that even in sharpest penal laws the same reason hath the same right; and in gentler laws, that from like causes to like the law interprets rightly. But it may be objected, saith he, that nothing destroys the end of wedlock so much as adultery. To which he answers, that marriage was not ordained only for copulation, but for mutual help and comfort of life: and if we mark diligently the nature of our Saviour's commands, we shall find that both their beginning and their end consists in charity: whose will is that we should so be good to others, as that we be not cruel to ourselves: and hence it appears why Mark, and Luke, and St. Paul to the Corinthians, mentioning this precept of Christ, add no exception, because exceptions that arise from natural equity are included silently under general terms: it would be considered therefore, whether the same equity may not have place in other cases less frequent. Thus far he. From hence is what I add: First, that this saying of Christ, as it is usually expounded, can be no law at all, that a man for no cause should separate but for adultery, except it be a supernatural law, not binding us as we now are. Had it been the law of nature, either the Jews, or some other wise and civil nation, would have pressed it: or let it be so, yet that law, Deut. xxiv. 1, whereby a man hath leave to part, whenas for just and natural cause discovered he cannot love, is a law ancienter and deeper engraven in blameless nature than the other: therefore the inspired lawgiver Moses took care, that this should be specified and allowed; the other he let vanish in silence, not once repeated in the volume of his law, even as the reason of it vanished with Paradise. Secondly, this can be no new command, for the gospel enjoins no new morality, save only the infinite enlargement of charity, which in this respect is called the new commandment by St. John, as being the accomplishment of every command. Thirdly, it is no command of perfection further than it partakes of charity, which is "the bond of perfection." Those commands therefore, which compel us to self-cruelty above our strength, so hardly will help forward to perfection, that they hinder and set backward in all the common rudiments of Christianity, as was proved. It being thus clear, that the words of Christ can be no kind of command as they are vulgarly taken, we shall now see in what sense they may be a command, and that an excellent one, the same with that of Moses, and no other. Moses had granted, that only for a natural annoyance, defect, or dislike, whether in body or mind, (for so the Hebrew words plainly note,) which a man could not force himself to live with, he might give a bill of divorce, thereby forbidding any other cause, wherein amendment or reconciliation might have place. This law the pharisees depraving extended to any slight contentious cause whatsoever. Christ therefore seeing where they halted, urges the negative part of that law, which is necessarily understood, (for the determinate permission of Moses binds them from further licence,) and checking their supercilious drift, declares that no accidental, temporary, or reconcilable offence (except fornication) can justify a divorce. He touches not here those natural and perpetual hinderances of society, whether in body or mind, which are not to be removed; for such as they are aptest to cause an unchangeable offence, so are they not capable of reconcilement, because not of amendment: they do not break indeed, but they annihilate the bands of marriage more than adultery. For that fault committed argues not always a hatred either natural or incidental against whom it is committed; neither does it infer a disability of all future helpfulness, or loyalty, or loving agreement, being once past and pardoned, where it can be pardoned: but that which naturally distastes, and "finds no favor in the eyes" of matrimony, can never be concealed, never appeased, never intermitted, but proves a perpetual nullity of love and contentment, a solitude and dead vacation of all acceptable conversing. Moses therefore permits divorce, but in cases only that have no hands to join, and more need separating than adultery. Christ forbids it, but in matters only that may accord, and those less than fornication. Thus is Moses's law here plainly confirmed, and those causes which he permitted not a jot gainsaid. And that this is the true meaning of this place,

I prove also by no less an author than St. Paul himself, 1 Cor. vii. 10, 11; upon which text interpreters agree, that the apostle only repeats the precept of Christ: where while he speaks of the "wife's reconcilement to her husband," he puts it out of controversy, that our Saviour meant chiefly matters of strife and reconcilement; of which sort he would not that any difference should be the occasion of divorce, except fornication. And that we may learn better how to value a grave and prudent law of Moses, and how unadvisedly we smatter with our lips, when we talk of Christ's abolishing any judicial law of his great Father, except in some circumstances which are judaical rather than judicial, and need no abolishing, but cease of themselves; I say again, that this recited law of Moses contains a cause of divorce greater beyond compare than that for adultery: and whoso cannot so conceive it, errs and wrongs exceedingly a law of deep wisdom for want of well fathoming. For let him mark, no man urges the just divorcing of adultery as it is a sin, but as it is an injury to marriage; and though it be but once committed, and that without malice, whether through importunity or opportunity, the gospel does not therefore dissuade him who would therefore divorce; but that natural hatred whenever it arises, is a greater evil in marriage than the accident of adultery, a greater defrauding, a greater injustice, and yet not blameable, he who understands not after all this representing, I doubt his will, like a hard spleen, draws faster than his understanding can well sanguify: nor did that man ever know or feel what it·is to love truly, nor ever yet comprehend in his thoughts what the true intent of marriage is. And this also will be somewhat above his reach, but yet no less a truth for lack of his perspective, that as no man apprehends what vice is. so well as he who is truly virtuous, no man knows hell like him who converses most in heaven; so there is none that can estimate the evil and the affliction of a natural hatred in matrimony, unless he have a soul gentle enough and spacious enough to contemplate what is true love.

And the reason why men so disesteem this wise judging law of God, and count hate, or "the not finding of favor," as it is there termed, a humorous, a dishonest, and slight cause of divorce, is because themselves apprehend so little of what true concord means: for if they did, they would be juster in their balancing between natural hatred and casual adultery; this being but a transient injury, and soon amended, I mean as to the party against whom the trespass is: but that other being an unspeakable and unremitting sorrow and offence, whereof no amends can be made, no cure, no ceasing but by divorce, which like a divine touch in one moment heals all, and like the word of God in one instant hushes outrageous tempests into a sudden stillness and peaceful calm. Yet all this so great a good of God's own enlarging to us is, by the hard reins of them that fit us, wholly diverted and embezzled from us. Maligners of mankind! But who hath taught you to mangle thus, and make more gashes in the miseries of a blameless creature, with the leaden daggers of your literal decrees, to whose ease you cannot add the tithe of one small atom, but by letting alone your unhelpful surgery? As for such as think wandering concupiscence to be here newly and more precisely forbidden than it was before; if the apostle can convince them, we know that we are to "know lust by the law," and not by any new discovery of the gospel. The law of Moses knew what it permitted, and the gospel knew what it forbid; he that under a peevish conceit of debarring concupiscence, shall go about to make a novice of Moses, (not to say a worse thing, for reverence sake,) and such a one of God himself, as is a horror to think, to bind our Saviour in the default of a downright promise-breaking; and to bind the disunions of complaining nature in chains together, and curb them with a canon bit; 'tis he that commits all the whoredom and adultery which himself adjudges, besides the former guilt so manifold that lies upon him. And if none of these considerations, with all their weight and gravity, can avail to the dispossessing him of his precious literalism, let some one or other entreat him but to read on in the same 19th of Matt. till he come to that place that says, "Some make themselves eunuchs for the kingdom of heaven's sake." And if then he please to make use of Origen's knife, he may do well to be his own carver.

CHAPTER XVIII.

Whether the Words of our Saviour be rightly expounded only of actual Fornication to be the Cause of Divorce. The Opinion of Grotius, with other Reasons.

BUT because we know that Christ never gave a judicial law, and that the word fornication is variously significant in scripture, it will be much right done to our Saviour's words, to consider diligently whether it be meant here, that nothing but actual fornication, proved by witness, can warrant a divorce; for so our canon law judges. Nevertheless, as I find that Grotius on this place hath observed the Christian emperors, Theodosius the Second and Justinian, men of high wisdom and reputed piety, decreed it to be a divorcive fornication, if the wife attempted either against the knowledge, or obstinately against the will of her husband, such things as gave open suspicion of adulterizing, as the wilful haunting of feasts, and invitations with men not of her near kindred, the lying forth of her house, without probable cause, the frequenting of theatres against her husband's mind, her endeavor to prevent or destroy conception. Hence that of Jerome, "Where fornication is suspected, the wife may lawfully be divorced:" not that every motion of a jealous mind should be regarded, but that it should not be exacted to prove all things by the visibility of law witnessing, or else to hoodwink the mind: for the law is not able to judge of these things but by the rule of equity, and by permitting a wise man to walk the middle way of prudent circumspection, neither wretchedly jealous, nor stupidly and tamely patient. To this purpose hath Grotius in his notes. He shows also, that fornication is taken in scripture for such a continual headstrong behavior, as tends to plain contempt of the husband, and proves it out of Judges xix. 2, where the Levite's wife is said to have played the whore against him; which Josephus and the Septuagint, with the Chaldean, interpret only of stubbornness and rebellion against her husband: and to this I add, that Kimchi, and the two other rabbies who gloss the text, are in the same opinion. Ben Gersom reasons, that had it been whoredom, a Jew and a Levite would have disdained to fetch her again. And this I shall contribute, that had it been whoredom, she would have chosen any other place to run to than to her father's house, it being so infamous for a Hebrew woman to play the harlot, and so opprobrious to the parents. Fornication then in this place of the Judges is understood for stubborn disobedience against the husband, and not for adultery. A sin of that sudden activity, as to be already committed when no more is done, but only looked unchastely, which yet I should be loath to judge worthy a divorce, though in our Saviour's language it be called adultery. Nevertheless when palpable and frequent signs are given, the law of God, Numb. v., so far gave way to the jealousy of a man, as that the woman, set before the sanctuary with her head uncovered, was adjured by the priest to swear whether she were false or no, and constrained to drink that "bitter water," with an undoubted "curse of rottenness and tympany" to follow, unless she were innocent. And the jealous man had not been guiltless before God, as seems by the last verse, if having such a suspicion in his head, he should neglect this trial; which if to this day it be not to be used, or be thought as uncertain of effect as our antiquated law of Ordalium, yet all equity will judge, that many adulterous demeanors, which are of lewd suspicion and example, may be held sufficient to incur a divorce, though the act itself hath not been proved. And seeing the generosity of our nation is so, as to account no reproach more abominable than to be nicknamed the husband of an adulteress; that our law should not be as ample as the law of God, to vindicate a man from that ignoble sufferance, is our barbarous unskilfulness, not considering that the law should be exasperated according to our estimation of the injury. And if it must be suffered till the act be visibly proved, Solomon himself, whose judgment will be granted to surpass the acuteness of any canonist, confesses, Prov. xxx. 19, 20, that for the act of adultery it is as difficult to be found as the "track of an eagle in the air, or the way of a ship in the sea;" so that a man may be put to unmanly indignities ere it be found out. This therefore may be enough to inform us that divorcive adultery is not limited by our Saviour to the utmost act, and that to be attested always by eyewitness, but may be extended also to divers obvious actions, which either plainly lead to adultery, or give such presumption whereby sensible men may suspect the deed to be already done. And this the rather may be thought, in that our Saviour chose to use the word fornication, which word is found to signify other matrimonial transgressions of main breach to that covenant besides actual adultery. For that sin needed not the riddance of divorce, but of death by the law, which was active even till then by the example of the woman taken in adultery; or if the law had been dormant, our Saviour was more likely to have told them of their neglect, than to have let a capital crime silently scape into a divorce: or if it be said, his business was not to tell them what was criminal in the civil courts, but what was sinful at the bar of conscience, how dare they then, having no other ground than these our Saviour's words, draw that into trial of law, which both by Moses and our Saviour was left to the jurisdiction of conscience? But we take from our Saviour, say they, only that it was adultery, and our law of itself applies the punishment. But by their leave that so argue, the great Lawgiver of all the world, who knew best what was adultery, both to the Jew and to the Gentile, appointed no such applying, and never likes when mortal men will be vainly presuming to outstrip his justice.

CHAPTER XIX.

Christ's manner of teaching. St. Paul adds to this matter of Divorce without command, to show the matter to be of Equity, not of Rigor. That the Bondage of a Christian may be as much, and his Peace as little, in some other Marriages besides idolatrous. If those Arguments, therefore, be good in that one Case, why not in those other? Therefore the Apostle himself adds, ἐν τοῖς τοιούτοις.

THUS at length we see, both by this and by other places, that there is scarce any one saying in the gospel but must be read with limitations and distinctions to be rightly understood; for Christ gives no full comments or continued discourses, but (as Demetrius the rhetorician phrases it) speaks oft in monosyllables, like a master scattering the heavenly grain of his doctrine like pearl here and there, which requires a skilful and laborious gatherer, who must compare the words he finds with other precepts, with the end of every ordinance, and with the general analogy of evangelic doctrine: otherwise many particular sayings would be but strange repugnant riddles, and the church would offend in granting divorce for frigidity, which is not here excepted with adultery, but by them added. And this was it undoubtedly which gave reason to St. Paul of his own authority, as he professes, and without command from the Lord, to enlarge the seeming construction of those places in the gospel, by adding a case wherein a person deserted (which is something less than divorced) may lawfully marry again. And having declared his opinion in one case, he leaves a further liberty for Christian prudence to determine in cases of like importance, using words so plain as not to be shifted off, "that a brother or a sister is not under bondage in such cases;" adding also, that "God hath called us to peace" in marriage.

Now if it be plain that a Christian may be brought into unworthy bondage, and his religious peace not only interrupted now and then, but perpetually and finally hindered in wedlock, by misyoking with a diversity of nature as well as of religion, the reasons of St. Paul cannot be made special to that one case of infidelity, but are of equal moment to a divorce, wherever Christian liberty and peace are without fault equally obstructed: that the ordinance which God gave to our comfort may not be pinned upon us to our undeserved thraldom, to be cooped up, as it were, in mockery of wedlock, to a perpetual betrothed loneliness and discontent, if nothing worse ensue. There being nought else of marriage left between such but a displeasing and forced remedy against the sting of a brute desire; which fleshly accustoming without the soul's union and commixture of intellectual delight, as it is rather a soiling than a fulfilling of marriage rites, so is it enough to imbase the mettle of a generous spirit, and sinks him to a low and vulgar pitch of endeavor in all his actions; or, which is worse, leaves him in a despairing plight of abject and hardened thoughts: which condition rather than a good man should fall into, a man, useful in the service of God and mankind, Christ himself hath taught us to dispense with the most sacred ordinance of his worship, even for a bodily healing to dispense with that holy and speculative rest of sabbath, much more than with the erroneous observance of an ill-knotted marriage, for the sustaining of an overcharged faith and perseverance.

CHAPTER XX.

The Meaning of St. Paul, that "Charity believeth all Things." What is to be said to the Licence which is vainly feared will grow hereby. What to those who never have done prescribing Patience in this Case. The Papist most severe against Divorce, yet most easy to all Licence. Of all the Miseries in Marriage God is to be cleared, and the Fault to be laid on Man's unjust Laws.

AND though bad causes would take licence by this pretext, if that cannot be remedied, upon their conscience be it who shall so do. This was that hardness of heart, and abuse of a good law, which Moses was content to suffer, rather than good men should not have it at all to use needfully. And he who, to run after one lost sheep, left ninety-nine of his own flock at random in the wilderness, would little perplex his thoughts for the obduring of nine hundred and ninety such as will daily take worse liberties, whether they have permission or not. To conclude, as without charity God hath given no commandment to men, so without it neither can men rightly believe any commandment given. For every act of true faith, as well that whereby we believe the law as that whereby we endeavor the law, is wrought in us by charity, according to that in the divine hymn of St. Paul, 1 Cor. xiii., "Charity believeth all things;" not as if she were so credulous, which is the exposition hitherto current, for that were a trivial praise, but to teach us that charity is the high governess of our belief, and that we cannot safely assent to any precept written in the Bible, but as charity commends it to us. Which agrees with that of the same apostle to the Eph. iv. 14, 15; where he tells us, that the way to get a sure undoubted knowledge of things, is to hold that for truth which accords most with charity. Whose unerring guidance and conduct having followed as a loadstar, with all diligence and fidelity, in this question, I trust, through the help of that illuminating Spirit which hath favored me, to have done no every day's work, in asserting, after many ages, the words of Christ, with other scriptures of great concernment, from burdensome and remorseless obscurity, tangled with manifold repugnances, to their native lustre and consent between each other; hereby also dissolving tedious and Gordian difficulties; which have hitherto molested the church of God, and are now decided, not with the sword of Alexander, but with the immaculate hands of charity, to the unspeakable good of Christendom. And let the extreme literalist sit down now, and revolve whether this in all necessity be not the due result of our Saviour's words; or if he persist to be otherwise opinioned, let him well advise, lest thinking to gripe fast the gospel, he be found instead with the canon law in his fist; whose boisterous edicts tyrannizing the blessed ordinance of marriage into the quality of a most unnatural and unchristianly yoke, hath given the flesh this advantage to hate it, and turn aside, ofttimes unwillingly, to all dissolute uncleanness, even till punishment itself is weary and overcome by the incredible frequency of trading lust and uncontrolled adulteries. Yet men whose creed is custom, I doubt not will be still endeavoring to hide the sloth of their own timorous capacities with this pretext, that for all this it is better to endure with patience and silence this affliction which God hath sent. And I agree 'tis true, if this be exhorted and not enjoined; but withal it will be wisely done to be as sure as may be, that what man's iniquity hath laid on be not imputed to God's sending, lest under the color of an affected patience we detain ourselves at the gulf's mouth of many hideous temptations, not to be withstood without proper gifts, which, as Perkins well notes, God gives not ordinarily, no, not to most earnest prayers. Therefore we pray, "Lead us not into temptation;" a vain prayer, if, having led ourselves thither, we love to stay in that perilous condition. God sends remedies as well as evils, under which he who lies and groans, that may lawfully acquit himself, is accessory to his own ruin; nor will it excuse him though he suffer through a sluggish fearfulness to search thoroughly what is lawful, for fear of disquieting the secure falsity of an old opinion. Who doubts not but that it may be piously said to him who would dismiss frigidity, Bear your trial; take it as if God would have you live this life of continence? If he exhort this, I hear him as an angel, though he speak without warrant; but if he would compel me, I know him for Satan. To him who divorces an adulteress, piety might say, Pardon her; you may show much mercy, you may win a soul: yet the law both of God and man leaves it freely to him; for God loves not to plough out the heart of our endeavors with overhard and sad tasks. God delights not to make a drudge of virtue, whose actions must be all elective and unconstrained. Forced virtue is as a bolt overshot: it goes neither forward nor backward, and does no good as it stands. Seeing, therefore, that neither scripture nor reason hath laid this unjust austerity upon divorce, we may resolve that nothing else hath wrought it but that letter-bound servility of the canon doctors, supposing marriage to be a sacrament, and out of the art they have to lay unnecessary burdens upon all men, to make a fair show in the fleshly observance of matrimony, though peace and love, with all other conjugal respects fare never so ill. And, indeed, the papists, who are the strictest forbidders of divorce, are the easiest libertines to admit of grossest uncleanness; as if they had a design by making wedlock a supportless yoke, to violate it most, under color of preserving it most inviolable; and

withal delighting (as their mystery is) to make men the day laborers of their own afflictions, as if there were such a scarcity of miseries from abroad, that we should be made to melt our choicest home blessings, and coin them into crosses, for want whereby to hold commerce with patience. If any, therefore, who shall hap to read this discourse, hath been through misadventure ill engaged in this contracted evil here complained of, and finds the fits and workings of a high impatience frequently upon him; of all those wild words which men in misery think to ease themselves by uttering, let him not open his lips against the providence of Heaven, or tax the ways of God and his divine truth; for they are equal, easy, and not burdensome; nor do they ever cross the just and reasonable desires of men, nor involve this our portion of mortal life into a necessity of sadness and malcontent, by laws commanding over the unreducible antipathies of nature, sooner or later found, but allow us to remedy and shake off those evils into which human error hath led us through the midst of our best intentions, and to support our incident extremities by that authentic precept of sovereign charity, whose grand commission is to do and to dispose over all the ordinances of God to man, that love and truth may advance each other to everlasting. While we, literally superstitious, through customary faintness of heart, not venturing to pierce with our free thoughts into the full latitude of nature and religion, abandon ourselves to serve under the tyranny of usurped opinions; suffering those ordinances which were allotted to our solace and reviving, to trample over us, and hale us into a multitude of sorrows, which God never meant us. And where he set us in a fair allowance of way, with honest liberty and prudence to our guard, we never leave subtilizing and casuisting till we have straightened and pared that liberal path into a razor's edge to walk on; between a precipice of unnecessary mischief on either side, and starting at every false alarm, we do not know which way to set a foot forward with manly confidence and Christian resolution, through the confused ringing in our ears of panic scruples and amazements.

CHAPTER XXI.

That the Matter of Divorce is not to be tried by Law, but by Conscience, as many other Sins are. The Magistrate can only see that the Condition of the Divorce be just and equal. The Opinion of Fagius, and the Reasons of this Assertion.

ANOTHER act of papal encroachment it was to pluck the power and arbitrement of divorce from the master of family, into whose hands God and the law of all nations had put it, and Christ so left it, preaching only to the conscience, and not authorizing a judicial court to toss about and divulge the unaccountable and secret reasons of disaffection between man and wife, as a thing most improperly answerable to any such kind of trial. But the popes of Rome, perceiving the great revenue and high authority it would give them even over princes, to have the judging and deciding of such a main consequence in the life of man as was divorce, wrought so upon the superstition of those ages, as to divest them of that right, which God from the beginning had entrusted to the husband: by which means they subjected that ancient and natural domestic prerogative to an external and unbefitting judicature. For although differences in divorce about dowries, jointures, and the like, besides the punishing of adultery, ought not to pass without referring, if need be, to the magistrate; yet that the absolute and final hindering of divorce cannot belong to any civil or earthly power, against the will and consent of both parties, or of the husband alone, some reasons will be here urged as shall not need to decline the touch. But first I shall recite what hath been already yielded by others in favor of this opinion. Grotius and many more agree, that notwithstanding what Christ spake therein to the conscience, the magistrate is not thereby enjoined aught against the preservation of civil peace, of equity, and of convenience. Among these Fagius is most remarkable, and gives the same liberty of pronouncing divorce to the Christian magistrate as the Mosaic had. "For whatever," saith he, "Christ spake to the regenerate, the judge hath to deal with the vulgar: if therefore any through hardness of heart will not be a tolerable wife or husband, it will be lawful as well now as of old to pass the bill of divorce, not by private but by public authority. Nor doth man separate them then, but God by his law of divorce given by Moses. What can hinder the magistrate from so doing, to whose government all outward things are subject, to separate and remove from perpetual vexation, and no small danger, those bodies whose minds are already separate; it being his office to procure peaceable and convenient living in the commonwealth; and being as certain also, that they so necessarily separated cannot all receive a single life?" And this I observe, that our divines do generally condemn separation of bed and board, without the liberty of second choice: if that therefore in some cases be most purely necessary, (as who so blockish to deny?) then is this also as needful. Thus far by others is already well stepped, to inform us that divorce is not a matter of law, but of charity; if there remain a furlong yet to end the question, these following reasons may serve to gain it with any apprehension not too unlearned or too wayward. First, because ofttimes the causes of seeking divorce reside so deeply in the radical and innocent affections of nature, as is not within the diocese of law to tamper with. Other relations may aptly enough be held together by a civil and virtuous love: but the duties of man and wife are such as are chiefly conversant in that love which is most ancient and merely natural, whose two prime statutes are to join itself to that which is good, and acceptable, and friendly; and to turn aside and depart from what is disagreeable, displeasing, and unlike: of the two this latter is the strongest, and most equal to be regarded; for although a man may often be unjust in seeking that which he loves, yet he can never be unjust or blameable in retiring from his endless trouble and distaste, whenas his tarrying can redound to no true content on either side. Hate is of all things the mightest divider; nay, is division itself. To couple hatred therefore, though wedlock try all her golden links, and borrow to her aid all the iron manacles and fetters of law, it does but seek to twist a rope of sand, which was a task they say that posed the devil: and that sluggish fiend in hell, Ocnus, whom the poems tell of, brought his idle cordage to as good effect, which never served to bind with, but to feed the ass that stood at his elbow. And that the restrictive law against divorce attains as little to bind anything truly in a disjointed marriage, or to keep it bound, but serves only to feed the ignorance and definitive impertinence of a doltish canon, were no absurd allusion. To hinder therefore those deep and serious regresses of nature in a reasonable soul, parting from that mistaken help, which he justly seeks in a person created for him, recollecting himself from an unmeet help which was never meant, and to detain him by compulsion in such an unpredestined misery as this, is in diameter against both nature and institution: but to interpose a jurisdictive power upon the inward and irremediable disposition of man, to command love and sympathy, to forbid dislike against the guiltless instinct of nature, is not within the province of any law to reach; and were indeed an uncommodious rudeness, not a just power: for that law may bandy with nature, and traverse her sage motions, was an error in Callicles the rhetorician, whom Socrates from high principles confutes in Plato's Gorgias. If therefore divorce may be so natural, and that law and nature are not to go contrary; then to forbid divorce compulsively, is not only against nature but against law.

Next, it must be remembered, that all law is for some good, that may be frequently attained without the admixture of a worse inconvenience; and therefore many gross faults, as ingratitude and the like, which are too far within the soul to be cured by constraint of law, are left only to be wrought on by conscience and persuasion. Which made Aristotle, in the 10th of his Ethics to Nicomachus, aim at a kind of division of law into private or persuasive, and public or compulsive. Hence it is, that the law forbidding divorce never attains to any good end of such prohibition, but rather multiplies evil. For if nature's resistless sway in love or hate be once compelled, it grows careless of itself, vicious, useless to friend, unserviceable and spiritless to the commonwealth. Which Moses rightly foresaw, and all wise lawgivers that ever knew man, what kind of creature he was. The parliament also and clergy of England were not ignorant of this, when they consented that Harry VIII. might put away his queen Anne of Cleve, whom he could not like after he had been wedded half a year; unless it were that, contrary to the proverb, they made a necessity of that which might have been a virtue in them to do; for even the freedom and eminence of man's creation gives him to be a law in this matter to himself, being the head of the other sex which was made for him: whom therefore though he ought not to injure, yet neither should he be forced to retain in society to his own overthrow, nor to hear any judge therein above himself: it being also an unseemly affront to the sequestered and veiled modesty of that sex, to have her unpleasingness and other concealments bandied up and down, and aggravated in open court by those hired masters of tongue-fence. Such uncomely exigencies it befel no less a majesty than Henry VIII. to be reduced to, who, finding just reason in his conscience to forego his brother's wife, after many indignities of being deluded, and made a boy of by those his two cardinal judges, was constrained at last, for want of other proof that she had been carnally known by prince Arthur, even to uncover the nakedness of that virtuous lady, and to recite openly the obscene evidence of his brother's chamberlain. Yet it pleased God to make him see all the tyranny of Rome, by discovering this which they exercised over divorce, and to make him the beginner of a reformation to this whole kingdom, by first asserting into his familiary power the right of just divorce. It is true, an adulteress cannot be shamed enough by any public proceeding; but that woman whose honor is not appeached is less injured by a silent dismission, being otherwise not illiberally dealt with, than to endure a clamoring debate of utterless things, in a business of that civil secrecy and difficult discerning as not to be overmuch questioned by nearest friends. Which drew that answer from the greatest and worthiest Roman of his time,

Paulus Emilius, being demanded why he would put away his wife for no visible reason? "This shoe," said he, and held it out on his foot, "is a neat shoe, a new shoe, and yet none of you know where it wrings me:" much less by the unfamiliar cognizance of a feed gamester can such a private difference be examined, neither ought it.

Again, if law aim at the firm establishment and preservation of matrimonial faith, we know that cannot thrive under violent means, but is the more violated. It is not when two unfortunately met are by the canon forced to draw in that yoke an unmerciful day's work of sorrow till death unharness them, that then the law keeps marriage most unviolated and unbroken; but when the law takes order that marriage be accountant and responsible to perform that society, whether it be religious, civil, or corporal, which may be conscionably required and claimed therein, or else to be dissolved if it cannot be undergone. This is to make marriage most indissoluble, by making it a just and equal dealer, a performer of those due helps, which instituted the covenant; being otherwise a most unjust contract, and no more to be maintained under tuition of law, than the vilest fraud, or cheat, or theft, that may be committed. But because this is such a secret kind of fraud or theft, as cannot be discerned by law but only by the plaintiff himself; therefore to divorce was never counted a political or civil offence, neither to Jew nor Gentile, nor by any judicial intendment of Christ, further than could be discerned to transgress the allowance of Moses, which was of necessity so large, that it doth all one as if it sent back the matter undeterminable at law, and intractable by rough dealing, to have instructions and admonitions bestowed about it by them whose spiritual office is to adjure and to denounce, and so left to the conscience. The law can only appoint the just and equal conditions of divorce; and is to look how it is an injury to the divorced, which in truth it can be none, as a mere separation; for if she consent, wherein has the law to right her? or consent not, then is it either just, and so deserved; or if unjust, such in all likelihood was the divorcer: and to part from an unjust man is a happiness, and no injury to be lamented. But suppose it be an injury, the law is not able to amend it, unless she think it other than a miserable redress, to return back from whence she was expelled, or but entreated to be gone, or else to live apart still married without marriage, a married widow. Last, if it be to chasten the divorcer, what law punishes a deed which is not moral but natural, a deed which cannot certainly be found to be an injury; or how can it be punished by prohibiting the divorce, but that the innocent must equally partake both in the shame and in the smart? So that which way soever we look, the law can to no rational purpose forbid divorce; it can only take care that the conditions of divorce be not injurious. Thus then we see the trial of law, how impertinent it is to this question of divorce, how helpless next, and then how hurtful.

CHAPTER XXII.

The last Reason why Divorce is not to be restrained by Law, it being against the Law of Nature and of Nations. The larger Proof whereof referred to Mr. Selden's Book, "De Jure Naturali et Gentium." An Objection of Paræus answered. How it ought to be ordered by the Church. That this will not breed any worse Inconvenience, nor so bad as is now suffered.

THEREFORE the last reason, why it should not be, is the example we have, not only from the noblest and wisest commonwealths, guided by the clearest light of human knowledge, but also from the divine testimonies of God himself, lawgiving in person to a sanctified people. That all this is true, whoso desires to know at large with least pains, and expects not here overlong rehearsals of that which is by others already so judiciously gathered, let him hasten to be acquainted with that noble volume written by our learned Selden, "Of the Law of Nature and of Nations," a work more useful and more worthy to be perused by whosoever studies to be a great man in wisdom, equity, and justice, than all those "decretals and sumless sums," which the pontifical clerks have doted on, ever since that unfortunate mother famously sinned thrice, and died impenitent of her bringing into the world those two misbegotten infants, and for ever infants, Lombard and Gratian, him the compiler of canon iniquity, the other the Tubalcain of scholastic sophistry, whose overspreading barbarism hath not only infused their own bastardy upon the fruitfullest part of human learning, not only dissipated and dejected the clear light of nature in us, and of nations, but hath tainted also the fountains of divine doctrine, and rendered the pure and solid law of God unbeneficial to us by their calumnious dunceries. Yet this law, which their unskilfulness hath made liable to all ignominy, the purity and wisdom of this law shall be the buckler of our dispute. Liberty of divorce we claim not, we think not but from this law; the dignity, the faith, the authority thereof is now grown among Christians, O astonishment! a labor of no mean difficulty and envy to defend. That it should not be counted a faltering dispense, a flattering permission of sin, the bill of adultery, a snare, is the expense of all this apology. And all that we solicit is, that it may be suffered to stand in the place where God set it, amidst the firmament of his holy laws, to shine, as it was wont, upon the weaknesses and errors of men, perishing else in the sincerity of their honest purposes: for certain there is no memory of whoredoms and adulteries left among us now, when this warranted freedom of God's own giving is made dangerous and discarded for a scroll of licence. It must be your suffrages and votes, O Englishmen, that this exploded decree of God and Moses may scape and come off fair, without the censure of a shameful abrogating: which, if yonder sun ride sure, and mean not to break word with us to-morrow, was never yet abrogated by our Saviour. Give sentence if you please, that the frivolous canon may reverse the infallible judgment of Moses and his great director. Or if it be the reformed writers, whose doctrine persuades this rather, their reasons I dare affirm are all silenced, unless it be only this. Paræus, on the Corinthians, would prove, that hardness

of heart in divorce is no more now to be permitted, but to be amerced with fine and imprisonment. I am not willing to discover the forgettings of reverend men, yet here I must: what article or clause of the whole new covenant can Paræus bring, to exasperate the judicial law upon any infirmity under the gospel? I say infirmity, for if it were the high hand of sin, the law as little would have endured it as the gospel; it would not stretch to the dividing of an inheritance; it refused to condemn adultery, not that these things should not be done at law, but to show that the gospel hath not the least influence upon judicial courts, much less to make them sharper and more heavy, least of all to arraign before a temporal judge that which the law without summons acquitted. "But," saith he, "the law was the time of youth, under violent affections; the gospel in us is mature age, and ought to subdue affections." True, and so ought the law too, if they be found inordinate, and not merely natural and blameless. Next I distinguish, that the time of the law is compared to youth and pupilage in respect of the ceremonial part, which led the Jews as children through corporal and garish rudiments, until the fulness of time should reveal to them the higher lessons of faith and redemption. This is not meant of the moral part; therein it soberly concerned them not to be babies, but to be men in good earnest: the sad and awful majesty of that law was not to be jested with: to bring a bearded nonage with lascivious dispensations before that throne, had been a lewd affront, as it is now a gross mistake. But what discipline is this, Paræus, to nourish violent affections in youth, by cockering and wanton indulgencies, and to chastise them in mature age with a boyish rod of correction? How much more coherent is it to scripture, that the law, as a strict schoolmaster, should have punished every trespass without indulgence so baneful to youth, and that the gospel should now correct that by admonition and reproof only, in free and mature age, which was punished with stripes in the childhood and bondage of the law? What, therefore, it allowed them so fairly, much less is to be whipped now, especially in penal courts: and if it ought now to trouble the conscience, why did that angry accuser and condemner law reprieve it? So then, neither from Moses nor from Christ hath the magistrate any authority to proceed against it. But what, shall then the disposal of that power return again to the master of family? Wherefore not, since God there put it, and the presumptuous canon thence bereft it? This only must be provided, that the ancient manner be observed in the presence of the minister and other grave selected elders, who after they shall have admonished and pressed upon him the words of our Saviour, and he shall have protested in the faith of the eternal gospel, and the hope he has of happy resurrection, that otherwise than thus he cannot do, and thinks himself and this his case not contained in that prohibition of divorce which Christ pronounced, the matter not being of malice, but of nature, and so not capable of reconciling; to constrain him further were to unchristian him, to unman him, to throw the mountain of Sinai upon him, with the weight of the whole law to boot, flat against the liberty and essence of the gospel; and yet nothing available either to the sanctity of marriage, the good of husband, wife, or children, nothing profitable either to church or commonwealth, but hurtful and pernicious to all these respects. But this will bring in confusion: yet these cautious mistrusters might consider, that what they thus object lights not upon this book, but upon that which I engage against them, the book of God and of Moses, with all the wisdom and providence which had forecast the worst of confusion that could succeed, and yet thought fit of such a permission. But let them be of good cheer, it wrought so little disorder among the Jews, that from Moses till after the captivity, not one of the prophets thought it worth rebuking; for that of Malachi well looked into will appear to be not against divorcing, but rather against keeping strange concubines, to the vexation of their Hebrew wives. If, therefore, we Christians may be thought as good and tractable as the Jews were, (and certainly the prohibitors of divorce presume us to be better,) then less confusion is to be feared for this among us than was

among them. If we be worse, or but as bad, which lamentable examples confirm we are, then have we more, or at least as much, need of this permitted law, as they to whom God therefore gave it (as they say) under a harsher covenant. Let not, therefore, the frailty of man go on thus inventing needless troubles to itself, to groan under the false imagination of a strictness never imposed from above; enjoining that for duty which is an impossible and vain supererogating. "Be not righteous overmuch," is the counsel of Ecclesiastes; "why shouldest thou destroy thyself?" Let us not be thus overcurious to strain at atoms, and yet to stop every vent and cranny of permissive liberty, lest nature, wanting those needful pores and breathing-places, which God hath not debarred our weakness, either suddenly break out into some wide rupture of open vice and frantic heresy, or else inwardly fester with repining and blasphemous thoughts, under an unreasonable and fruitless rigor of unwarranted law. Against which evils nothing can more beseem the religion of the church, or the wisdom of the state, than to consider timely and provide. And in so doing let them not doubt but they shall vindicate the misreputed honor of God and his great lawgiver, by suffering him to give his own laws according to the condition of man's nature best known to him, without the unsufferable imputation of dispensing legally with many ages of ratified adultery. They shall recover the misattended words of Christ to the sincerity of their true sense from manifold contradictions, and shall open them with the key of charity. Many helpless Christians they shall raise from the depth of sadness and distress, utterly unfitted as they are to serve God or man: many they shall reclaim from obscure and giddy sects, many regain from dissolute and brutish licence, many from desperate hardness, if ever that were justly pleaded. They shall set free many daughters of Israel not wanting much of her sad plight whom "Satan had bound eighteen years." Man they shall restore to his just dignity and prerogative in nature, preferring the soul's free peace before the promiscuous draining of a carnal rage. Marriage, from a perilous hazard and snare, they shall reduce to be a more certain haven and retirement of happy society; when they shall judge according to God and Moses, (and how not then according to Christ,) when they shall judge it more wisdom and goodness to break that covenant seemingly, and keep it really, than by compulsion of law to keep it seemingly, and by compulsion of blameless nature to break it really, at least if it were ever truly joined. The vigor of discipline they may 10 then turn with better success upon the prostitute looseness of the times, when men, finding in themselves the infirmities of former ages, shall not be constrained above the gift of God in them to unprofitable and impossible observances, never required from the civilest, the wisest, the holiest nations, whose other excellencies in moral virtue they never yet could equal. Last of all, to those whose mind still is to maintain 20 textual restrictions, whereof the bare sound cannot consist sometimes with humanity, much less with charity; I would ever answer, by putting them in remembrance of a command above all commands, which they seem to have forgot, and who spake it: in comparison whereof, this which they so exalt is but a petty and subordinate precept. "Let them go," therefore, with whom I am loath to couple them, yet they will needs 30 run into the same blindness with the pharisees; "let them go therefore," and consider well what this lesson means, "I will have mercy and not sacrifice:" for on that "saying all the law and prophets depend;" much more the gospel, whose end and excellence is mercy and peace. Or if they cannot learn that, how will they hear this? which yet I shall not doubt to leave with them as a conclusion, that God the Son hath put all 40 other things under his own feet, but his commandments he hath left all under the feet of charity.

THE JUDGMENT OF MARTIN BUCER,

CONCERNING DIVORCE:

WRITTEN TO EDWARD THE SIXTH, IN HIS 50 SECOND BOOK OF THE KINGDOM OF CHRIST: AND NOW ENGLISHED. WHEREIN A LATE BOOK, RESTORING THE "DOCTRINE AND DISCIPLINE OF DIVORCE," IS HERE CONFIRMED AND JUSTIFIED BY THE AUTHORITY OF MARTIN BUCER.

TO THE PARLIAMENT OF ENGLAND.

John iii. 10, "Art thou a teacher of Israel, and knowest not these things?"

PUBLISHED BY AUTHORITY.

———————

[The text is that of the first edition, 1644.]

TESTIMONIES OF THE HIGH APPROBATION WHICH LEARNED MEN HAVE GIVEN OF MARTIN BUCER.

Simon Grinæus, 1533.

AMONG all the Germans, I give the palm to Bucer, for excellence in the scriptures. Melancthon in human learning is wonderous fluent; but greater knowledge in the scripture I attribute to Bucer, and speak it unfeignedly.

John Calvin, 1539.

Martin Bucer, a most faithful doctor of the church of Christ, besides his rare learning, and copious knowledge of many things, besides his clearness of wit, much reading, and other many and various virtues, wherein he is almost by none now living excelled, hath few equals, and excels most; hath this praise peculiar to himself, that none in this age hath used exacter diligence in the exposition of scripture.

And a little beneath.

Bucer is more large than to be read by overbusied men; and too high to be easily understood by unattentive men, and of a low capacity.

Sir John Cheek, Tutor to King Edward VI. 1551.

We have lost our master, than whom the world scarce held a greater, whether we consider his knowledge of true religion, or his integrity and innocence of life, or his incessant study of holy things, or his matchless labor of promoting piety, or his authority and amplitude of teaching, or whatever else was praiseworthy and glorious in him.—Script. Anglicana, pag. 864.

John Sturmius of Strasburgh.

No man can be ignorant what a great and constant opinion and estimation of Bucer there is in Italy, France, and England. Whence the saying of Quintilian hath oft come to my mind, that he hath well profited in eloquence whom Cicero pleases. The same say I of Bucer, that he hath made no small progress in divinity whom Bucer pleases; for in his volumes, which he wrote very many, there is the plain impression to be discerned of many great virtues, of diligence, of charity, of truth, of acuteness, of judgment, of learning. Wherein he hath a certain proper kind of writing, whereby he doth not only teach the reader, but affects him with the sweetness of his sentences, and with the manner of his arguing, which is so teaching, and so logical, that it may be perceived how learnedly he separates probable reasons from necessary, how forcibly he confirms what he has to prove, how subtly he refutes, not with sharpness, but with truth.

Theodore Beza, on the Portraiture of M. Bucer.

This is that countenance of Bucer, the mirror of mildness tempered with gravity, to whom the city of Strasburgh owes the reformation of her church; whose singular learning, and eminent zeal, joined with excellent wisdom, both his learned books, and public disputations in the general diets of the empire, shall witness to all ages. Him the German persecution drove into England; where, honorably entertained by Edward the Sixth, he was for two years chief professor of divinity in Cambridge, with greatest frequency and applause of all learned and pious men until his death, 1551.
—Bezæ Icones.

Mr. Fox's Book of Martyrs, vol. iii. p. 763.

Bucer, what by writing, but chiefly by reading and preaching openly, wherein, being painful in the word of God, he never spared himself, nor regarded his health, brought all men into such an admiration of him, that neither his friends could sufficiently praise him, nor his enemies in any point find fault with his singular life and sincere doctrine. A most certain token whereof may be his sumptuous burial at Cambridge, solemnized with so great an assistance of all the university, that it was not possible to devise more to the setting out and amplifying of the same.

Dr. Pern, the Popish Vice-Chancellor of Cambridge, his adversary.

Cardinal Pool, about the fourth year of Queen Mary, intending to reduce the university of Cambridge to popery again, thought no way so effectual, as to cause the bones of Martin Bucer and Paulus Fagius, which had been four years in the grave, to be taken up and burnt openly with their books, as knowing that those two worthy men had been of greatest moment to the reformation of that place from popery, and had left such powerful seeds of their doctrine behind them, as would never die, unless the men themselves were digged up, and openly condemned for heretics by the university itself. This was put in execution, and Doctor Pern, vice-chancellor, appointed to preach against Bucer: who, among other things, laid to his charge the opinions which he held of the marriage of priests, of divorcement, and of usury. But immediately after his sermon, or somewhat before, as the Book of Martyrs for a truth relates, vol. iii. p. 770, the said Doctor Pern, smiting himself on the breast, and in manner weeping, wished with all his heart, that God would grant his soul might then presently depart and remain with Bucer's; for he knew his life was such, that if any man's soul were worthy of heaven, he thought Bucer's in special to be most worthy.
—Histor. de Combust. Buceri et Fagii.

Acworth, the University-orator.

Soon after that Queen Elizabeth came to the crown, this condemnation of Bucer and Fagius by the cardinal and his doctors was solemnly repealed by the university; and the memory of those two famous men celebrated in an oration by Acworth, the University-orator, which is yet extant in the book of Martyrs, vol. iii. p. 773, and in Latin, Scripta Anglic. p. 936.

Nicholas Carre, a learned man; Walter Hadden, master of the requests to Queen Elizabeth; Matthew Parker, afterwards primate of England; with other eminent men, in their funeral orations and sermons, express abundantly how great a man Martin Bucer was; what an incredible loss England sustained in his death; and that with him died the hope of a perfect reformation for that age—Ibid.

Jacobus Verheiden of Grave, in his elegies of famous divines.

Though the name of Martin Luther be famous, yet thou, Martin Bucer, for piety, learning, labor, care, vigilance, and writing, art not to be held inferior to Luther. Bucer was a singular instrument of God, so was Luther. By the death of this most learned and most faithful man, the church of Christ sustained a heavy loss, as Calvin witnesseth; and they who are studious of Calvin are not ignorant how much he ascribes to Bucer; for thus he writes in a letter to Viretus: "What a manifold loss befell the church of God in the death of Bucer! as oft as I call to mind, I feel my heart almost rent asunder."

Peter Martyr Epist. to Conradus Hubertus.

He is dead, who hath overcome in many battles of the Lord. God lent us for a time this our father, and our teacher, never enough praised. Death hath divided me from a most unanimous friend, one truly according to mine own heart. My mind is overpressed with grief, insomuch that I have not power to write more. I bid thee in Christ farewell, and wish thou mayst be able to bear the loss of Bucer better than I can bear it.

Testimonies given by learned men to Paulus Fagius, who held the same opinion with Martin Bucer concerning divorce.

Paulus Fagius, born in the Palatinate, became most skilful in the Hebrew tongue. Being called to the ministry at Isna, he published many ancient and profitable Hebrew books, being aided in the expenses

by a senator of that city, as Origen sometimes was by a certain rich man called Ambrosius. At length invited to Strasburgh, he there famously discharged the office of a teacher; until the same persecution drove him and Bucer into England, where he was preferred to a professor's place in Cambridge, and soon after died.—Bezæ Icones.

Melchior Adamus writes his life among the famous German divines.

Sleidan and Thuanus mention him with honor in their history; and Verheiden in his elegies.

TO THE PARLIAMENT.

THE book which, among other great and high points of reformation, contains, as a principal part thereof, this treatise here presented, supreme court of parliament! was, by the famous author Martin Bucer, dedicated to Edward the Sixth; whose incomparable youth doubtless had brought forth to the church of England such a glorious manhood, had his life reached it, as would have left in the affairs of religion nothing without an excellent pattern for us now to follow. But since the secret purpose of divine appointment hath reserved no less perhaps than the just half of such a sacred work to be accomplished in this age, and principally, as we trust, by your successful wisdom and authority, religious lords and commons! what wonder if I seek no other, to whose exactest judgment and review I may commend these last and worthiest labors of this renowned teacher; whom living all the pious nobility of those reforming times, your truest and best-imitated ancestors, reverenced and admired. Nor was he wanting to a recompense as great as was himself; when both at many times before, and especially among his last sighs and prayers, testifying his dear and fatherly affection to the church and realm of England, he sincerely wished in the hearing of many devout men, "that what he had in this his last book written to king Edward concerning discipline might have place in this kingdom. His hope was then, that no calamity, no confusion, or deformity would happen to the commonwealth; but otherwise he feared, lest in the midst of all this ardency to know God, yet by the neglect of discipline, our good endeavors would not succeed." These remarkable words of so godly and so eminent a man at his death, as they are related by a sufficient and well-known witness, who heard them, and inserted by Thuanus into his grave and serious history; so ought they to be chiefly considered by that nation for whose sake they were uttered, and more especially by that general 10 council, which represents the body of that nation. If therefore the book, or this part thereof, for necessary causes, be now revived and recommended to the use of this indisciplined age; it hence appears, that these reasons have not erred in the choice of a fit patronage for a discourse of such importance. But why the whole tractate is is not here brought entire, but this matter of divorcement selected in particular, to 20 prevent the full speed of some misinterpreter, I hasten to disclose. First, it will be soon manifest to them who know what wise men should know, that the constitution and reformation of a commonwealth, if Ezra and Nehemiah did not misreform, is, like a building, to begin orderly from the foundation thereof, which is marriage and the family, to set right first whatever is amiss therein. How can there else grow up a race 30 of warrantable men, while the house and home that breeds them is troubled and disquieted under a bondage not of God's constraining, with a natureless constraint, (if his most righteous judgments may be our rule,) but laid upon us imperiously in the worst and weakest ages of knowledge, by a canonical tyranny of stupid and malicious monks? who having rashly vowed themselves to a single life, which they could not 40 undergo, invented new fetters to throw on matrimony, that the world thereby waxing more dissolute, they also in a general looseness might sin with more favor. Next, there being yet among many such a strange iniquity and perverseness against all necessary divorce, while they will needs expound the words of our Saviour, not duly by comparing other places, as they must do in the resolving of a hundred other scriptures, but 50 by persisting deafly in the abrupt and papistical way of a literal apprehension against the direct analogy of sense, reason,

law, and gospel; it therefore may well seem more than time, to apply the sound and holy persuasions of this apostolic man to that part in us, which is not yet fully dispossessed of an error as absurd, as most that we deplore in our blindest adversaries; and to let his authority and unanswerable reasons be vulgarly known, that either his name, or the force of his doctrine, may work a wholesome effect. Lastly, I find it clear to be the author's intention, that this point of divorcement should be held and received as a most necessary and prime part of discipline in every Christian government. And therefore having reduced his model of reformation to fourteen heads, he bestows almost as much time about this one point of divorce, as about all the rest; which also was the judgment of his heirs and learned friends in Germany, best acquainted with his meaning; who first publishing this his book by Oporinus at Basil, (a city for learning and constancy in the true faith honorable among the first,) added a special note in the title, "that there the reader should find the doctrine of divorce handled so solidly, and so fully, as scarce the like in any writer of that age:" and with this particular commendation they doubted not to dedicate the book, as a most profitable and exquisite discourse, to Christian the Third, a worthy and pious king of Denmark, as the author himself had done before to our Edward the Sixth. Yet did not Bucer in that volume only declare what his constant opinion was herein, but also in his comment upon Matthew, written at Strasburgh divers years before, he treats distinctly and copiously the same argument in three several places; touches it also upon the seventh to the Romans, and promises the same solution more largely upon the First to the Corinthians, omitting no occasion to weed out this last and deepest mischief of the canon law, sown into the opinions of modern men, against the laws and practice both of God's chosen people, and the best primitive times. Wherein his faithfulness and powerful evidence prevailed so far with all the church of Strasburgh, that they published this doctrine of divorce as an article of their confession, after they had taught so eight and twenty years, through all those times, when that city flourished, and excelled most, both in religion, learning, and good government, under those first restorers of the gospel there, Zellius, Hedio, Capito, Fagius, and those who incomparably then governed the commonwealth, Farrerus and Sturmius. If therefore God in the former age found out a servant, and by whom he had converted and reformed many a city, by him thought good to restore the most needful doctrine of divorce from rigorous and harmful mistakes on the right hand; it can be no strange thing, if in this age he stir up by whatsoever means whom it pleases him, to take in hand and maintain the same assertion. Certainly if it be in man's discerning to sever providence from chance, I could allege many instances, wherein there would appear cause to esteem of me no other than a passive instrument under some power and counsel higher and better than can be human, working to a general good in the whole course of this matter. For that I owe no light or leading received from any man in the discovery of this truth, what time I first undertook it in "the Doctrine and Discipline of Divorce," and had only the infallible grounds of scripture to be my guide. He who tries the inmost heart, and saw with what severe industry and examination of myself I set down every period, will be my witness. When I had almost finished the first edition, I chanced to read in the notes of Hugo Grotius upon the fifth of Matthew, whom I straight understood inclining to reasonable terms in this controversy: and something he whispered rather than disputed about the law of charity, and the true end of wedlock. Glad therefore of such an able assistant, however at much distance, I resolved at length to put off into this wild and calumnious world. For God, it seems, intended to prove me, whether I durst alone take up a rightful cause against a world of disesteem, and found I durst. My name I did not publish, as not willing it should sway the reader either for me or against me. But when I was told that the style, which what it ails to be so soon distinguishable I cannot tell, was known by most men, and that some of the clergy began to inveigh and exclaim on what I was credibly informed they had not read; I took it then for my proper season, both to show them a name that could easily contemn such an indiscreet kind of censure, and to reinforce the question with a more accurate diligence: that if any of them would be so good as to leave railing, and to let us hear so much of his learning and Christian wisdom, as will be strictly demanded of him in his answering to this problem, care was had he should not spend his preparations against a nameless pamphlet. By this time I had learned that Paulus Fagius, one of the chief divines in Germany, sent for by Frederic the Palatine, to reform his dominion, and after that invited hither in king Edward's days, to be professor of divinity in Cambridge, was of the same opinion touching divorce, which these men so lavishly traduced in me. What I found, I inserted where fittest place was, thinking sure they would respect so grave an author, at least to the moderating of their odious inferences. And having now prefected a second edition, I referred the judging thereof to your high and impartial sentence, honored lords and commons! For I was confident, if anything generous, anything noble, and above the multitude, were left yet in the spirit of England; it could be nowhere sooner found, and nowhere sooner understood, than in that house of justice and true liberty where ye sit in council. Nor doth the event hitherto, for some reasons which I shall not here deliver, fail me of what I conceived so highly. Nevertheless, being far otherwise dealt with by some, of whose profession and supposed knowledge I had better hope, and esteemed the deviser of a new and pernicious paradox, I felt no difference within me from that peace and firmness of mind, which is of nearest kin to patience and contentment: both for that I knew I had divulged a truth linked inseparably with the most fundamental rules of Christianity, to stand or fall together, and was not uninformed, that divers learned and judicious men testified their daily approbation of the book. Yet at length it hath pleased God, who had already given me satisfaction in myself, to afford me now a means whereby I may be fully justified also in the eyes of men. When the book had been now the second time set forth well-nigh three months, as I best remember, I then first came to hear that Martin Bucer had written much concerning divorce: whom, earnestly turning over, I soon perceived, but not without amazement, in the same opinion, confirmed with the same reasons which in that published book, without the help or imitation of any precedent writer, I had labored out, and laid together. Not but that there is some difference in the handling, in the order, and the number of arguments, but still agreeing in the same conclusion. So as I may justly gratulate mine own mind with due acknowledgment of assistance from above, which led me, not as a learner, but as a collateral teacher, to a sympathy of judgment with no less a man than Martin Bucer. And he, if our things here below arrive him where he is, does not repent him to see that point of knowledge, which he first and with an unchecked freedom preached to those more knowing times of England, now found so necessary, though what he admonished were lost out of our memory; yet that God doth now again create the same doctrine in another unwritten table, and raises it up immediately out of his pure oracle to the convincement of a perverse age, eager in the reformation of names and ceremonies, but in realities as traditional and as ignorant as their forefathers. I would ask now the foremost of my profound accusers, whether they dare affirm that to be licentious, new, and dangerous, which Martin Bucer so often and so urgently avouched to be most lawful, most necessary, and most Christian, without the least blemish to his good name, among all the worthy men of that age, and since, who testify so highly of him? If they dare, they must then set up an arrogance of their own against all those churches and saints who honored him without this exception: if they dare not, how can they now make that licentious doctrine in another, which was never blamed or confuted in Bucer, or in Fagius? The truth is, there will be due to them for this their unadvised rashness the best donative that can be given them; I mean, a round reproof; now that where they thought to be most magisterial, they have displayed their own want, both of reading, and of judgment. First, to be so unacquainted in the writings of Bucer, which are so obvious and so useful in their own faculty; next, to be so caught in a prejudicating weakness, as to condemn that for lewd, which (whether they knew or not) these elect servants of Christ commended for lawful; and for new, that which was taught by these almost the first and greatest authors of reformation, who were never taxed for so teaching; and dedicated without scruple to a royal pair of the first reforming kings in Christendom, and confessed in the public confession of a most orthodoxal church and state in Germany. This is also another fault which I must tell them, that they have stood now almost this whole year clamoring afar off, while the book hath been twice printed, twice brought up, and never once vouchsafed a friendly conference with the author, who would be glad and thankful to be shown an error, either by private dispute, or public answer, and could retract, as well as wise men before him; might also be worth the gaining, as one who heretofore hath done good service to the church by their own confession. Or if he be obstinate, their confutation would have rendered him without excuse, and reclaimed others of no mean parts, who incline to his opinion. But now their work is more than doubled; and how they will hold up their heads against the sudden aspect of these two great and reverend saints, whom they have defamed, how they will make good the censuring of that, for a novelty of licence, which Bucer constantly taught to be a pure and holy law of Christ's kingdom, let them advise. For against these my adversaries, who, before the examining of a propounded truth in a fit time of reformation, have had the conscience to oppose nought else but their blind reproaches and surmises, that a single innocence might not be oppressed and overborne by a crew of mouths, for the restoring of a law and doctrine falsely and unlearnedly reputed new and scandalous; God, that I may ever magnify and record this his goodness, hath unexpectedly raised up as it were from the dead more than one famous light of the first reformation, to bear witness with me, and to do me honor in that very thing, wherein these men thought to have blotted me; and hath given them the proof of a capacity, which they despised, running equal, and authentic with some of their chiefest masters unthought of, and in a point of sagest moment. However, if we know at all when to ascribe the occurrences of this life to the work of a special Providence, as nothing is more usual in the talk of good men, what can be more like to a special Providence of God, than in the first reformation of England, that this question of divorce, as a main thing to be restored to just freedom, was written, and seriously commended to Edward the Sixth, by a man called from another country to be the instructor of our nation; and now in this present renewing of the church and commonwealth, which we pray may be more lasting, that the same question should be again treated and presented to this parliament, by one enabled to use the same reasons without the least sight or knowledge of what was done before? It were no trespass, lords and commons! though something of less note were attributed to the ordering of a heavenly power; this question therefore of such prime concernment both to Christian and civil welfare, in such an extraordinary manner, not recovered, but plainly twice born to these latter ages, as from a divine hand I tender to your acceptance, and most considerate thoughts. Think not that God raised up in vain a man of greatest authority in the church, to tell a trivial and licentious tale in the ears of that good prince, and to bequeath it as his last will and testament, nay, rather as the testament and royal law of Christ, to this nation; or that it should of itself, after so many years, as it were in a new field where it was never sown, grow up again as a vicious plant in the mind of another, who had spoke honestest things to the nation; though he knew not that what his youth then reasoned without a pattern had been heard already, and well allowed from the gravity and worth of Martin Bucer: till meeting with the envy of men ignorant in their own undertaken calling, God directed him to the forgotten writings of this faithful evangelist, to be his defence and warrant against the gross imputation of broaching licence. Ye are now in the glorious way to high virtue, and matchless deeds, trusted with a most inestimable trust, the asserting of our just liberties. Ye have a nation that expects now, and from mighty sufferings aspires to be the example of all Christendom to a perfectest reforming. Dare to be as great, as ample, and as eminent in the fair progress of your noble designs, as the full and goodly stature of truth and excellence itself; as unlimited by petty precedents and copies, as your unquestionable calling from Heaven gives ye power to be. What are all our public immunities and privileges worth, and how shall it be judged, that we fight for them with minds worthy to enjoy them, if we suffer ourselves in the meanwhile not to understand the most important freedom, that God and nature hath given us in the family; which no wise nation ever wanted, till the popery and superstition of some former ages attempted to remove and alter divine and most prudent laws for human and most imprudent canons: whereby good men in the best portion of their lives, and in that ordinance of God which entitles them from the beginning to most just and requisite contentments, are compelled to civil indignities, which by the law of Moses bad men were not compelled to? Be not bound about, and straitened in the spacious wisdom of your free spirits, by the scanty and unadequate and inconsistent principles of such as condemn others for adhering to traditions, and are themselves the prostrate worshippers of custom; and of such a tradition as they can deduce from no antiquity, but from the rudest and thickest barbarism of antichristian times. But why do I anticipate the more acceptable and prevailing voice of learned Bucer himself, the pastor of nations? And O that I could set him living before ye in that doctoral chair, where once the learnedest of England thought it no disparagement to sit at his feet! He would be such a pilot, and such a father to ye, as ye would soon find the difference of his hand and skill upon the helm of reformation. Nor do I forget that faithful associate of his labors, Paulus Fagius; for these their great names and merits, how precious soever, God hath now joined with me necessarily, in the good or evil report of this doctrine, which I leave with you. It was written to a religious king of this land; written earnestly as a main matter wherein this kingdom needed a reform, if it purposed to be the kingdom of Christ: written by him, who if any, since the days of Luther, merits to be counted the apostle of our church: whose unwearied pains and watching for our sakes, as they spent him quickly here among us, so did they, during the shortness of his life, incredibly promote the gospel throughout this realm. The authority, the learning, the godliness of this man consulted with, is able to outbalance all that the lightness of a vulgar opposition can bring to counterpoise. I leave him also as my complete surety and testimonial, if truth be not the best witness to itself, that what I formerly presented to your reading on this subject was good, and just, and honest, not licentious. Not that I have now more confidence by the addition of these great authors to my party: for what I wrote was not my opinion, but my knowledge; even then when I could trace no footstep in the way I went: nor that I think to win upon your apprehensions with numbers and with names, rather than with reasons; yet certainly the worst of my detractors will not except against so good a bail of my integrity and judgment, as now appears for me. They must else put in the fame of Bucer and of Fagius, as my accomplices and confederates, into the same indictment; they must dig up the good name of these prime worthies, (if their names could be ever buried,) they must dig them up and brand them as the papists did their bodies; and those their pure unblameable spirits, which live not only in heaven, but in their writings, they must attaint with new attaintures, which no protestant ever before aspersed them with. Or if perhaps we may obtain to get our appeachment new drawn a writ of error, not of libertinism, that those two principal leaders of reformation may not come now to be sued in a bill of licence, to the scandal of our church, the brief result will be, that for the error, if their own works be not thought sufficient to defend them, there lives yet, who will be ready, in a fair and Christianly discussive way, to debate and sift this matter to the utmost

ounce of learning and religion, in him that shall lay it as an error, either upon Martin Bucer, or any other of his opinion. If this be not enough to qualify my traducers, and that they think it more for the wisdom of their virulence not to recant the injuries they have bespoke me, I shall not, for much more disturbance than they can bring me, intermit the prosecution of those thoughts, which may render me best serviceable, either to this age, or, if it so happen, to posterity; following the fair path, which your illustrious exploits, honored lords and commons! against the breast of tyranny have opened; and depending so on your happy successes in the hopes that I have conceived either of myself, or of the nation, as must needs conclude me one who most affectionately wishes and awaits the prosperous issue of your noble and valorous counsels.

JOHN MILTON.

THE JUDGMENT OF MARTIN BUCER,

TOUCHING DIVORCE:

TAKEN OUT OF THE SECOND BOOK, ENTITLED, "OF THE KINGDOM OF CHRIST;" WRITTEN BY MARTIN BUCER TO EDWARD THE SIXTH, KING OF ENGLAND.

CHAPTER XV.

The seventh Law of the Sanctifying and Ordering of Marriage. That the Ordering of Marriage belongs to the civil Power. That the Popes have evaded by Fraud and Force the Ordering of Marriage.

BESIDES these things, Christ our king, and his churches, require from your sacred majesty, that you would take upon you the just care of marriages. For it is unspeakable how many good consciences are hereby entangled, afflicted, and in danger, because there are no just laws, no speedy way constituted according to God's word, touching this holy society and fountain of mankind. For seeing matrimony is a civil thing, men, that they may rightly contract, inviolably keep, and not without extreme necessity dissolve marriage, are not only to be taught by the doctrine and discipline of the church, but also are to be acquitted, aided, and compelled by laws and judicature of the commonwealth. Which thing pious emperors acknowledging, and therein framing themselves to the law of nations, gave laws both of contracting and preserving, and also, where an unhappy need required, of divorcing marriages. As may be seen in the Code of Justinian, the 5th book, from the beginning through twenty-four titles. And in the authentic of Justinian the 22nd, and some others.

But the antichrists of Rome, to get the imperial power into their own hands, first by fraudulent persuasion, afterwards by force, drew to themselves the whole authority of determining and judging as well in matrimonial causes, as in most other matters. Therefore it hath been long believed, that the care and government thereof doth not belong to the civil magistrate. Yet where the gospel of Christ is received, the laws of antichrist should be rejected. If therefore kings and governors take not this care, by the power of law and justice, to provide that marriages be piously contracted, religiously kept, and lawfully dissolved, if need require, who sees not what confusion and trouble is brought upon this holy society; and what a rack is prepared, even for many of the best consciences, while they have no certain laws to follow, no justice to implore, if any intolerable thing happen? And how much it concerns the honor and safety of the commonwealth, that marriages, according to the will of Christ, be made, maintained, and not without just cause dissolved, who understands not? For unless that first and holiest society of man and woman be purely constituted, that household discipline may be upheld by them according to God's law, how can we expect a race of good men? Let your majesty therefore know, that this is your duty, and in the first place, to reassume to yourself the just ordering of matrimony, and by firm laws to establish and defend the religion of this first and divine society among men, as all wise lawgivers of old, and Christian emperors, have carefully done.

The two next chapters, because they chiefly treat about the degrees of consanguinity and affinity, I omit: only setting down a passage or two concerning the judicial laws of Moses, how fit they be for Christians to imitate rather than any other.

CHAPTER XVII., towards the end.

I CONFESS that we, being free in Christ, are not bound to the civil laws of Moses in every circumstance; yet seeing no laws can be more honest, just, and wholesome, than those which God himself gave, who is eternal wisdom and goodness, I see not why Christians, in things which no less appertain to them, ought not to follow the laws of God, rather than of any men. We are not to use circumcision, sacrifice, and those bodily washings prescribed to the Jews; yet by these things we may rightly learn, with what purity and devotion both baptism and the Lord's supper should be administered and received. How much more is it our duty to observe diligently what the Lord hath commanded, and taught by the examples of his people concerning marriage, whereof we have the use no less than they!

And because this same worthy author hath another passage to this purpose, in his comment upon Matthew, chap. v. 19, I here insert it from p. 46.

Since we have need of civil laws, and the power of punishing, it will be wisest not to contemn those given by Moses; but seriously rather to consider what the meaning of God was in them, what he chiefly required, and how much it might be to the good of every nation, if they would borrow thence their manner of governing the commonwealth; yet freely all things and with the Spirit of Christ. For what Solon, or Plato, or Aristotle, what lawyers or Cæsars could make better laws than God? And it is no light argument, that many magistrates at this day do not enough acknowledge the kingdom of Christ, though they would seem most Christian, in that they govern their states by laws so diverse from those of Moses.

The 18th chapter I only mention as determining a thing not here in question, that marriage without consent of parents ought not to be held good; yet with this qualification fit to be known.

That if parents admit not the honest desires of their children, but shall persist to abuse the power they have over them; they are to be mollified by admonitions, entreaties, and persuasions, first of their friends and kindred, next of the church-elders, whom, if still the hard parents refuse to hear, then ought the magistrate to interpose his power, lest any, by the evil mind of their parents, be detained from marriage longer than is meet, or forced to an unworthy match: in which case the Roman laws also provided.—C. de Nupt. l. 11, 13, 26.

CHAPTER XIX.

Whether it may be permitted to revoke the Promise of Marriage.

HERE ariseth another question concerning contracts, when they ought to be unchangeable; for religious emperors decreed, that the contract was not indissoluble, until the spouse were brought home, and the solemnities performed. They thought it a thing unworthy of divine and human equity, and the due consideration of man's infirmity in deliberating and determining, when space is given to renounce other contracts of much less moment, which are not yet confirmed before the magistrate, to deny that to the most weighty contract of marriage which requires the greatest care and consultation. Yet, lest such a covenant should be broken for no just cause, and to the injury of that person to whom marriage was promised, they decreed a fine, that he who denied marriage to whom he had promised, and for some cause not approved by the judges, should pay the double of that pledge which was given at making sure, or as much as the judge should pronounce might satisfy the damage, or the hindrance of either party. It being most certain, that ofttimes after contract just and honest causes of departing from promise come to be known and found out, it cannot be other than the duty of pious princes, to give men the same liberty of unpromising in these cases, as pious emperors granted; especially where there is only a promise, and not carnal knowledge. And as there is no true marriage between them, who agree not in true consent of mind; so it will be the part of godly magistrates to procure that no matrimony be

among their subjects, but what is knit with love and consent. And though your majesty be not bound to the imperial laws, yet it is the duty of a Christian king to embrace and follow whatever he knows to be anywhere piously and justly constituted, and to be honest, just, and well-pleasing to his people. But why in God's law and the examples of his saints nothing hereof is read, no marvel; seeing his ancient people had power, yea, a precept, that whoso could not bend his mind to the true love of his wife, should give her a bill of divorce, and send her from him, though after carnal knowledge and long dwelling together. This is enough to authorize a godly prince in that indulgence which he gives to the changing of a contract, both because it is certainly the invention of Antichrist, that the promise of marriage "de præsenti," as they call it, should be indissoluble, and because it should be a prince's care, that matrimony be so joined, as God ordained; which is, that every one should love his wife with such a love as Adam expressed to Eve: so as we may hope, that they who marry may become one flesh, and one also in the Lord.

CHAPTER XX.

CONCERNS only the celebration of marriage.

CHAPTER XXI.

The Means of preserving Marriage holy and pure.

Now since there ought not to be less care, that marriage be religiously kept, than that it be piously and deliberately contracted, it will be meet, that to every church be ordained certain grave and godly men, who may have this care upon them, to observe whether the husband bear himself wisely toward the wife, loving and inciting her to all piety, and the other duties of this life; and whether the wife be subject to her husband, and study to be truly a meet help to him, as first to all godliness, so to every other use of life: And if they shall find each to other failing of their duty, or the one long absent from the other without just and urgent cause, or giving suspicion of irreligious and impure life, or of living in manifest wickedness, let it be admonished them in time. And if their authority be contemned, let the names of such contemners be brought to the magistrate, who may use punishment to compel such violators of marriage to their duty, that they may abstain from all probable suspicion of transgressing; and if they admit of suspected company, the magistrate is to forbid them; whom they not therein obeying, are to be punished as adulterers, according to the law of Justinian, Authent. 117. For if holy wedlock, the fountain and seminary of good subjects, be not vigilantly preserved from all blots and disturbances, what can be hoped, as I said before, of the springing up of good men, and a right reformation of the commonwealth? We know it is not enough for Christians to abstain from foul deeds, but from the appearance and suspicion thereof.

CHAPTER XXII.

Of lawful Divorce, what the ancient Churches have thought.

Now we shall speak about that dissolving of matrimony which may be approved in the sight of God, if any grievous necessity require. In which thing Roman antichrists have knit many a pernicious entanglement to distressed consciences: for that they might here also exalt themselves above God, as if they would be wiser and chaster than God himself is; for no cause, honest or necessary, will they permit a final divorce: in the meanwhile, whoredoms and adulteries, and worse things than these, not only tolerating in themselves and others, but cherishing and throwing men headlong into these evils. For although they also disjoin married persons from board and bed, that is, from all conjugal society and communion, and this not only for adultery, but for ill usage, and matrimonial duties denied; yet they forbid those thus parted to join in wedlock with others: but, as I said before, any dishonest associating they permit. And they pronounce the bond of marriage to remain between those whom they have thus separated: as if the bond of marriage, God so teaching and pronouncing, were not such a league as binds the married couple to all society of life, and

communion in divine and human things; and so associated keeps them. Something, indeed, out of the later fathers they may pretend for this their tyranny, especially out of Austin and some others, who were much taken with a preposterous admiration of single life; yet though these fathers, from the words of Christ not rightly understood, taught that it was unlawful to marry again while the former wife lived, whatever cause there had been either of desertion or divorce; yet if we mark the custom of the church, and the common judgment which both in their times and afterwards prevailed, we shall perceive, that neither these fathers did ever cast out of the church any one for marrying after a divorce, approved by the imperial laws.

Nor only the first Christian emperors, but the latter also, even to Justinian, and after him, did grant, for certain causes approved by judges, to make a true divorce; which made and confirmed by law, it might be lawful to marry again; which, if it could not have been done without displeasing Christ and his church, surely it would not have been granted by Christian emperors, nor had the fathers then winked at those doings in the emperors. Hence ye may see that Jerome also, though zealous of single life more than enough, and such a condemner of second marriage, though after the death of either party, yet, forced by plain equity, defended Fabiola, a noble matron of Rome, who, having refused her husband for just causes, was married to another. For that the sending of a divorce to her husband was not blameworthy, he affirms because the man was heinously vicious; and that if an adulterer's wife may be discarded, an adulterous husband is not to be kept. But that she married again, while yet her husband was alive; he defends in that the apostle hath said, "It is better to marry than to burn;" and that young widows should marry, for such was Fabiola, and could not remain in widowhood.

But some one will object, that Jerome adds, "Neither did she know the vigor of the gospel, wherein all cause of marrying is debarred from women, while their husbands live; and again, while she avoided many wounds of Satan, she received one ere she was aware." But let the equal reader mind also what went before: "Because," saith he, soon after the beginning, "there is a rock and storm of slanderers opposed against her, I will not praise her converted, unless I first absolve her guilty." For why does he call them slanderers, who accused Fabiola of marrying again, if he did not judge it a matter of Christian equity and charity, to pass by and pardon that fact, though in his own opinion he held it a fault? And what can this mean, "I will not praise her, unless I first absolve her?" For how could he absolve her, but by proving that Fabiola, neither in rejecting her vicious husband, nor in marrying another, had committed such a sin as could be justly condemned? Nay, he proves both by evident reason, and clear testimonies of scripture, that she avoided sin.

This also is hence understood, that Jerome by "the vigor of the gospel," meant that height and perfection of our Saviour's precept, which might be remitted to those that burn; for he adds, "But if she be accused in that she remained not unmarried, I shall confess the fault, so I may relate the necessity." If then he acknowledged a necessity, as he did, because she was young, and could not live in widowhood, certainly he could not impute her second marriage to her much blame: but when he excuses her out of the word of God, does he not openly declare his thoughts, that the second marriage of Fabiola was permitted her by the Holy Ghost himself, for the necessity which he suffered, and to shun the danger of fornication, though she went somewhat aside from the vigor of the gospel? But if any urge, that Fabiola did public penance for her second marriage, which was not imposed but for great faults; 'tis answered, she was not enjoined to this penance, but did it of her own accord "and not till after her second husband's death." As in the time of Cyprian, we read that many were wont to do voluntary penance for small faults, which were not liable to excommunication.

CHAPTER XXIII.

That Marriage was granted by the ancient Fathers, even after the Vow of single life.

I omit his testimonies out of Cyprian, Gelasius, Epiphanius, contented only to relate what he thence collects to the present purpose.

SOME will say perhaps, Wherefore all this concerning marriage after vow of single life, whenas the question was of marriage after divorce? For this reason, that they whom it so much moves, because some of the fathers thought marriage after any kind of divorce to be condemned of our Saviour, may see that this conclusion follows not. The fathers thought all marriage after divorce to be forbidden of our Saviour, therefore they thought such marriage was not to be tolerated in a Christian. For the same fathers judged it forbidden to marry after vow; yet such marriages they neither dissolved nor excommunicated; for these words of our Saviour, and of the Holy Ghost, stood in their way: "All cannot receive this saying, but they to whom it is given." "Every one hath his proper gift from God, one after this manner, another after that." "It is better to marry than to burn." "I will that younger widows marry;" and the like.

So there are many canons and laws extant, whereby priests, if they married, were removed from their office; yet is it not read that their marriage was dissolved, as the papists now-a-days do, or that they were excommunicated; nay, expressly they might communicate as laymen. If the consideration of human infirmity, and those testimonies of divine scripture which grant marriage to every one that wants it, persuaded those fathers to bear themselves so humanely toward them who had married with breach of vow to God, as they believed, and with divorce of that marriage wherein they were in a manner joined to God; who doubts but that the same fathers held the like humanity was to be afforded to those, who after divorce and faith broken with men, as they thought, entered into second marriage? For among such are also found no less weak, and no less burning.

CHAPTER XXIV.

Who of the ancient Fathers have granted Marriage after Divorce.

THIS is clear both by what hath been said, and by that which Origen relates of certain bishops in his time, Homil. 7, in Matt. "I know some," saith he, "which are over churches, who without scripture have permitted the wife to marry while her former husband lived. And did this against scripture, which saith, the wife is bound to her husband so long as he lives; and she shall be called an adulteress, if, her husband living, she take another man; yet did they not permit this without cause, perhaps for the infirmity of such as had not continence, they permitted evil to avoid worse." Ye see Origen and the doctors of his age, not without all cause, permitted women after divorce to marry, though their former husbands were living; yet writes that they permitted against scripture. But what cause could they have to do so, unless they thought our Saviour in his precepts of divorce had so forbidden, as willing to remit such perfection to his weaker ones, cast into danger of worse faults?

The same thought Leo, bishop of Rome, Ep. 85, to the African bishops of Mauritania Cæsariensis, wherein complaining of a certain priest, who divorcing his wife, or being divorced by her, as other copies have it, had married another, neither dissolves the matrimony, nor excommunicates him, only unpriests him. The fathers therefore, as we see, did not simply and wholly condemn marriage after divorce.

But as for me, this remitting of our Saviour's precepts, which these ancients allow to the infirm in marrying after vow and divorce, I can in no ways admit; for whatsoever plainly consents not with the commandment, cannot, I am certain, be permitted, or suffered in any Christian: for heaven and earth shall pass away, but not a tittle from the commands of God among them who expect life eternal. Let us therefore consider, and weigh the words of our Lord concerning marriage and divorce, which he pronounced both by himself, and by his apostle, and let us compare them with other oracles of God; for whatsoever is contrary to these, I shall not persuade the least tolerating thereof. But if it can be taught to agree with the word of God, yea, to be commanded, that most men may have permission given them to divorce and marry again, I must prefer the authority of God's word before the opinion of fathers and doctors, as they themselves teach.

CHAPTER XXV.

The Words of our Lord, and of the Holy Ghost by the Apostle Paul, concerning Divorce, are explained. The 1st Axiom, that Christ could not condemn of Adultery that which he once commanded.

BUT the words of our Lord, and of the Holy Ghost, out of which Austin and some others of the fathers think it concluded, that our Saviour forbids marriage after any divorce, are these: Matt. v. 31, 32, "It hath been said," &c.; and Matt. xix. 7, "They say unto him, why did Moses then command," &c.: and Mark x., and Luke xvi., Rom. vii. 1, 2, 3, 1 Cor. vii. 10, 11. Hence therefore they conclude, that all marriage after divorce is called adultery; which to commit, being no ways to be tolerated in any Christian, they think it follows, that second marriage is in no case to be permitted either to the divorcer, or to the divorced.

But that it may be more fully and plainly perceived what force is in this kind of reasoning, it will be the best course, to lay down certain grounds whereof no Christian can doubt the truth. First, it is a wickedness to suspect that our Saviour branded that for adultery, which himself, in his own law which he came to fulfil, and not to dissolve, did not only permit, but also command; for by him, the only Mediator, was the whole law of God given. But that by this law of God marriage was permitted after any divorce, is certain by Deut. xxiv. 1.

CHAPTER XXVI.

That God in his Law did not only grant, but also command Divorce to certain Men.

DEUT. xxiv. 1, "When a man hath taken a wife," &c. But in Mal. ii. 15, 16, is read the Lord's command to put her away whom a man hates, in these words: "Take heed to your spirit, and let none deal injuriously against the wife of his youth. If he hate, let him put away, saith the Lord God of Israel. And he shall hide thy violence with his garment," that marries her divorced by thee, "saith the Lord of hosts; but take heed to your spirit, and do no injury." By these testimonies of the divine law, we see, that the Lord did not only permit, but also expressly and earnestly commanded his people, by whom he would that all holiness and faith of marriage covenant should be observed, that he who could not induce his mind to love his wife with a true conjugal love, might dismiss her, that she might marry to another.

CHAPTER XXVII.

That what the Lord permitted and commanded to his ancient People concerning Divorce belongs also to Christians.

Now what the Lord permitted to his first-born people, that certainly he could not forbid to his own among the Gentiles, whom he made coheirs, and into one body with his people; nor could he ever permit, much less command, aught that was not good for them, at least so used as he commanded. For being God, he is not changed as man. Which thing who seriously considers, how can he imagine, that God would make that wicked to them that believe, and serve him under grace, which he granted and commanded to them that served him under the law? Whenas the same causes require the same permission. And who that knows but human matters, and loves the truth, will deny that many marriages hang as ill together now, as ever they did among the Jews? So that such marriages are liker to torments than true marriages. As therefore the Lord doth always succor and help the oppressed, so he would ever have it provided for injured husbands and wives, that under pretence of the marriage bond, they be not sold to perpetual vexations, instead of the loving and comfortable marriage duties. And lastly, as God doth always detest hypocrisy and fraud, so neither doth he approve that among his people, that should be counted marriage, wherein none of those duties remain, whereby the league of wedlock is chiefly preserved. What inconsiderate neglect than of God's law is this, that I may not call it worse, to hold that Christ our Lord would not grant the same remedies both of divorce and second marriage to the weak, or to the evil, if they will needs have it so, but especially to the innocent and wronged; whenas the same urgent causes remain as before, when the discipline of the church and magistrate hath tried what may be tried?

CHAPTER XXVIII.

That our Lord Christ intended not to make new Laws of Marriage and Divorce, or of any civil Matters. Axiom 2.

It is agreed by all who determine of the kingdom and offices of Christ, by the holy scriptures, as all godly men ought to do, that our Saviour upon earth took not on him either to give new laws in civil affairs, or to change the old. But it is certain, that matrimony and divorce are civil things. Which the Christian emperors knowing, gave conjugal laws, and reserved the administration of them to their own courts; which no true ancient bishop ever condemned.

Our Saviour came to preach repentance and remission: seeing therefore those who put away their wives without any just cause, were not touched with conscience of the sin, through misunderstanding of the law, he recalled them to a right interpretation, and taught, that the woman in the beginning was so joined to the man, that there should be a perpetual union both in body and spirit: where this is not, the matrimony is already broke, before there be yet any divorce made, or second marriage.

CHAPTER XXIX.

That it is wicked to strain the Words of Christ beyond their Purpose.

This is his third axiom whereof there needs no explication here.

CHAPTER XXX.

That all Places of Scripture about the same Thing are to be joined, and compared, to avoid Contradictions. Axiom 4.

This he demonstrates at large out of sundry places in the gospel, and principally by that precept against swearing, which compared with many places of the law and prophets, is a flat contradiction of them all, if we follow superstitiously the letter. Then having repeated briefly his four axioms, he thus proceeds:

THESE things thus preadmonished, let us inquire what the undoubted meaning is of our Saviour's words, and inquire according to the rule which is observed by all learned and good men in their expositions; that praying first to God, who is the only opener of our hearts, we may first with fear and reverence consider well the words of our Saviour touching this question. Next, that we may compare them with all other places of scripture treating of this matter, to see how they consent with our Saviour's words, and those of his apostle.

CHAPTER XXXI.

THIS chapter disputes against Austin and the papists, who deny second marriage even to them who divorce in case of adultery; which because it is not controverted among true protestants, but that the innocent person is easily allowed to marry, I spare the translating.

CHAPTER XXXII.

That a manifest Adulteress ought to be divorced, and cannot lawfully be retained in marriage by any true Christian.

THIS though he prove sufficiently, yet I let pass, because this question was not handled in "the Doctrine and Discipline of Divorce;" to which book I bring so much of this treatise as runs parallel.

CHAPTER XXXIII.

That Adultery is to be punished with Death.

THIS chapter also I omit for the reason last alleged.

CHAPTER XXXIV.

That it is lawful for a Wife to leave an Adulterer, and to marry another Husband.

THIS is generally granted, and therefore excuses me the writing out.

CHAPTER XXXV.

Places in the Writings of the Apostle Paul, touching Divorce, explained.

LET us consider the answers of the Lord given by the apostle severally. Concerning the first, which is Rom. vii. 1, "Know ye not, brethren, for I speak to them that know the law," &c. Ver. 2, "The woman is bound by the law to her husband so long as he liveth." Here it is certain that the Holy Ghost had no purpose to determine aught of marriage or divorce, but only to bring an example from the common and ordinary law of wedlock, to show, that as no covenant holds either party being dead, so now that we are not bound to the law, but to Christ our Lord, seeing that through him we are dead to sin, and to the law; and so joined to Christ, that we may bring forth fruit in him from a willing godliness, and not by the compulsion of law, whereby our sins are more excited, and become more violent. What therefore the Holy Spirit here speaks of matrimony cannot be extended beyond the general rule.

Besides it is manifest, that the apostle did allege the law of wedlock, as it was delivered to the Jews; for, saith he, "I speak to them that know the law." They knew no law of God, but that by Moses, which plainly grants divorce for several reasons. It cannot therefore be said, that the apostle cited this general example out of the law, to abolish the several exceptions of that law, which God himself granted by giving authority to divorce.

Next, when the apostle brings an example out of God's law concerning man and wife, it must be necessary, that we understand such for man and wife, as are so indeed according to the same law of God; that is, who are so disposed, as that they are both willing and able to perform the necessary duties of marriage; not those who, under a false title of marriage, keep themselves mutually bound to injuries and disgraces; for such twain are nothing less than lawful man and wife.

The like answer is to be given to all the other places both of the gospel and the apostle, that whatever exception may be proved out of God's law, be not excluded from those places. For the Spirit of God doth not condemn things formerly granted and allowed, where there is like cause and reason. Hence Ambrose, upon that place, 1 Cor. vii. 15, "A brother or a sister is not under bondage in such cases," thus expounds: "The reverence of marriage is not due to him who abhors the author of marriage; nor is that marriage ratified which is without devotion to God: he sins not therefore, who is put away for God's cause, though he join himself to another. For the dishonor of the Creator dissolves the right of matrimony to him who is deserted, that he be not accused, though marrying to another. The faith of wedlock is not to be kept with him who departs, that he might not hear the God of Christians to be the author of wedlock. For if Ezra caused the misbelieving wives and husbands to be divorced, that God might be appeased, and not offended, though they took others of their own faith, how much more shall it be free, if the misbeliever depart, to marry one of our own religion. For this is not to be counted matrimony, which is against the law of God."

Two things are here to be observed toward the following discourse, which truth itself and the force of God's word hath drawn from this holy man. For those words are very large, "Matrimony is not ratified, without devotion to God." And, "The dishonor of the Creator dissolves the right of matrimony." For devotion is far off, and dishonor is done to God by all who persist in any wickedness and heinous crime.

CHAPTER XXXVI.

That although it seem in the Gospel, as if our Saviour granted Divorce only for Adultery, yet in very deed he granted it for other Causes also.

Now is to be dealt with this question, whether it be lawful to divorce and marry again for other causes besides adultery, since our Saviour expressed that only? To this question, if we retain our principles already laid, and must acknowledge it to be a cursed blasphemy, if we say that the words of God do contradict one another, of necessity we must confess, that our Lord did grant divorce, and marriage after that, for other causes besides adultery, notwithstanding what he said in Matthew. For, first, they who consider but only that place, 1 Cor. vii., which treats of believers and misbelievers matched together, must of force, confess, that our Lord granted just divorce and second marriage in the cause of desertion, which is other than the cause of fornication. And if there be one other cause found lawful, then is it most true, that divorce was granted not only for fornication.

Next, it cannot be doubted, as I showed before, by them to whom it is given to know God and his judgments out of his own word, but that, what means of peace and safety God ever granted and ordained to his elected people, the same he grants and ordains to men of all ages, who have equally need of the same remedies. And who, that is but a knowing man, dares say there be not husbands and wives now to be found in such a hardness of heart, that they will not perform either conjugal affection, or any requisite duty thereof, though it be most deserved at their hands?

Neither can any one defer to confess, but that God, whose property it is to judge the cause of them that suffer injury, hath provided for innocent and honest persons wedded, how they might free themselves by lawful means of divorce, from the bondage and iniquity of those who are falsely termed their husbands or their wives. This is clear out of Deut. xxiv. 1; Mal. ii.; Matt. xix; 1 Cor. vii.; and out of those principles which the scripture everywhere teaches, that God changes not his mind, dissents not from himself, is no accepter of persons; but allows the same remedies to all men, oppressed with the same necessities and infirmities; yea, requires that we should use them. This he will easily perceive, who considers these things in the Spirit of the Lord.

Lastly, it is most certain, that the Lord hath commanded us to obey the civil laws, every one of his own commonwealth, if they be not against the laws of God.

CHAPTER XXXVII.

For what Causes Divorce is permitted by the civil Law ex l. Consensu Codic. de Repudiis.

IT is also manifest, that the law of Theodosius and Valentinian, which begins, "Consensu," &c., touching divorce, and many other decrees of pious emperors agreeing herewith, are not contrary to the word of God; and therefore may be recalled into use by any Christian prince or commonwealth; nay, ought to be with due respect had to every nation; for whatsoever is equal and just, that in everything is to be sought and used by Christians. Hence it is plain, that divorce is granted by divine approbation, both to husbands and to wives, if either party can convict the other of these following offences before the magistrate.

If the husband can prove the wife to be an adulteress, a witch, a murderess; to have bought or sold to slavery, any one free born, to have violated sepulchres, committed sacrilege, favored thieves and robbers, desirous of feasting with strangers, the husband not knowing, or not willing; if she lodge forth without a just and probable cause, or frequent theatres and sights, he forbidding; if she be privy with those that plot against the state, or if she deal falsely, or offer blows. And if the wife can prove her husband guilty of any those forenamed crimes, and frequent the company of lewd women in her sight, or if he beat her, she had the like liberty to quit herself; with this difference, that the man after divorce might forthwith marry again; the woman not till a year after, lest she might chance to have conceived.

CHAPTER XXXVIII.

An Exposition of those Places wherein God declares the Nature of holy Wedlock.

Now to the end it may be seen, that this agrees with the divine law, the first institution of marriage is to be considered, and those texts in which God established the joining of male and female, and described the duties of them both. When God had determined to make woman, and give her as a wife to man, he spake thus, Gen. ii. 18: "It is not good for man to be alone: I will make him a help meet for him. And Adam said," but in the Spirit of God, ver. 23, 24, "This is now bone of my bone, and flesh of my flesh: therefore shall a man leave his father and mother, and shall cleave to his wife, and they shall be one flesh."

To this first institution did Christ recall his own, when answering the pharisees, he condemned the licence of unlawful divorce. He taught therefore by his example, that we, according to this first institution, and what God hath spoken thereof, ought to determine what kind of covenant marriage is, how to be kept, and how far, and lastly, for what causes to be dissolved. To which decrees of God these also are to be joined, which the Holy Ghost hath taught by his apostle, that neither the husband nor the wife "hath power of their own body, but mutually each of either's." That "the husband shall love the wife as his own body, yea, as Christ loves his church; and that the wife ought to be subject to her husband, as the church is to Christ."

By these things the nature of holy wedlock is certainly known; whereof if only one be wanting in both or either party, and that either by obstinate malevolence, or too deep inbred weakness of mind, or lastly, through incurable impotence of body, it cannot then be said, that the covenant of matrimony holds good between such, if we mean that covenant which God instituted and called marriage, and that whereof only it must be understood that our Saviour said, "Those whom God hath joined, let no man separate."

And hence is concluded, that matrimony requires continual cohabitation and living together, unless the calling of God be otherwise evident; which union if the parties themselves disjoin either by mutual consent, or one against the other's will depart, the marriage is then broken. Wherein the papists, as in other things, oppose themselves against God; while they separate for many causes from bed and board, and yet will have the bond of matrimony remain, as if this covenant could be other than the conjunction and communion not only of bed and board, but of all other loving and helpful duties. This we may see in these words: "I will make him a help meet for him; bone of his bone, and flesh of his flesh: for this cause shall he leave father and mother, and cleave to his wife, and they twain shall be one flesh." By which words who discerns not, that God requires of them both so to live together, and to be united not only in body but in mind also, with such an affection as none may be dearer and more ardent among all the relations of mankind, nor of more efficacy to the mutual offices of love and loyalty? They must communicate and consent in all things both divine and human, which have any moment to well and happy living. The wife must honor and obey her husband, as the church honors and obeys Christ, her head. The husband must love and cherish his wife, as Christ his church. Thus they must be to each other, if they will be true man and wife in the sight of God, whom certainly the churches ought to follow in their judgment. Now the proper and ultimate end of marriage is not copulation, or children, for then there was not true matrimony between Joseph and Mary the mother of Christ, nor between many holy persons more; but the full and proper and main end of marriage is the communicating of all duties both divine and human, each to other with utmost benevolence and affection.

CHAPTER XXXIX.

The Properties of a true and Christian Marriage more distinctly repeated.

By which definition we may know that God esteems and reckons upon these four necessary properties to be in every true marriage. 1. That they should live together, unless the calling of God require otherwise for a time. 2. That they should love one another to the height of dearness, and that in the Lord, and in the communion of true religion. 3. That the husband bear himself as the head and preserver of his wife, instructing her to all godliness and integrity of life; that the wife also be to her husband a help, according to her place, especially furthering him in the true worship of God, and next in all the occasions of civil life. And 4. That they defraud not each other of conjugal benevolence, as the apostles commands, 1 Cor. vii. Hence it follows, according to the sentence of God, which all Christians ought to be

ruled by, that between those who either through obstinacy, or helpless inability, cannot or will not perform these repeated duties, between those there can be no true matrimony, nor ought they to be counted man and wife.

CHAPTER XL.

Whether those crimes recited chap. xxxvii. out of the civil Law, dissolve Matrimony in God's account.

Now if a husband or wife be found guilty of any those crimes which by the law "consensu" are made causes of divorce, 'tis manifest, that such a man cannot be the head and preserver of his wife, nor such a woman be a meet help to her husband, as the divine law in true wedlock requires; for these faults are punished either by death, or deportation, or extreme infamy, which are directly opposite to the covenant of marriage. If they deserve death, as adultery and the like, doubtless God would not that any should live in wedlock with them whom he would not have to live at all. Or if it be not death, but the incurring of notorious infamy, certain it is neither just, nor expedient, nor meet, that an honest man should be coupled with an infamous woman, nor an honest matron with an infamous man. The wise Roman princes had so great regard to the equal honor of either wedded person, that they counted those marriages of no force which were made between the one of good repute, and the other of evil note. How much more will all honest regard of Christian expedience and comeliness beseem and concern those who are set free and dignified in Christ, than it could the Roman senate, or their sons, for whom that law was provided?

And this all godly men will soon apprehend, that he who ought to be the head and preserver not only of his wife, but also of his children and family, as Christ is of his church, had need be one of honest name: so likewise the wife, which is to be the meet help of an honest and good man, the mother of an honest offspring and family, the glory of the man, even as the man is the glory of Christ, should not be tainted with ignominy; as neither of them can avoid to be, having been justly appeached of those forenamed crimes; and therefore cannot be worthy to hold their place in a Christian family: yea, they themselves turn out themselves and dissolve that holy covenant. And they who are true brethren and sisters in the Lord are no more in bondage to such violators of marriage.

But here the patrons of wickedness and dissolvers of Christian discipline will object, that it is the part of man and wife to bear one another's cross, whether in calamity or infamy, that they might gain each other, if not to a good name, yet to repentance and amendment. But they who thus object, seek the impunity of wickedness, and the favor of wicked men, not the duties of true charity; which prefers public honesty before private interest, and had rather the remedies of wholesome punishment appointed by God should be in use, than that by remissness the licence of evil doing should increase. For if they who, by committing such offences, have made void the holy knot of marriage, be capable of repentance, they will be sooner moved when due punishment is executed on them, than when it is remitted.

We must ever beware, lest, in contriving what will be best for the soul's health of delinquents, we make ourselves wiser and discreeter than God. He that religiously weighs his oracles concerning marriage, cannot doubt that they, who have committed the foresaid transgressions, have lost the right of matrimony, and are unworthy to hold their dignity in an honest and Christian family.

But if any husband or wife see such signs of repentance in their transgressor, as that they doubt not to regain them by continuing with them, and partaking of their miseries and attaintures, they may be left to their own hopes, and their own mind; saving ever the right of church and commonwealth, that it receive no scandal by the neglect of due severity, and their children no harm by this invitation to licence, and want of good education.

From all these considerations, if they be thought on, as in the presence of God, and out of his word, any one may perceive, who desires to determine of these things by the scripture, that those causes of lawful divorce, which the most religious emperors Theodosius and Valentinian set forth in the forecited place, are according to the law of God, and the prime institution of marriage; and were still more and more straitened, as the church and state of the empire still more and more corrupted and degenerated. Therefore pious princes and commonwealths both may and ought establish them again, if they have a mind to restore the honor, sanctity, and religion of holy wedlock to their people, and disentangle many consciences from a miserable and perilous condition, to a chaste and honest life.

To those recited causes wherefore a wife might send a divorce to her husband, Justinian added four more, Constit. 117; and four more for which a man might put away his wife. Three other causes were added in the Code, de Repudiis, 1. Jubemus. All which causes are so clearly contrary to the first intent of marriage, that they plainly dissolve it. I set them not down, being easy to be found in the body of the civil law.

It was permitted also by Christian emperors, that they who would divorce by mutual consent, might without impediment. Or if there were any difficulty at all in it, the law expresses the reason, that it was only in favor of the children; so that if there were none, the law of those godly emperors made no other difficulty of a divorce by consent. Or if any were minded without consent of the other to divorce, and without those causes which have been named, the Christian emperors laid no other punishment upon them, than that the husband wrongfully divorcing his wife should give back her dowry, and the use of that which was called "Donatio propter nuptias;" or if there were no dowry nor no donation, that he should then give her the fourth part of his goods. The like penalty was inflicted on the wife departing without just cause. But that they who were once married should be compelled to remain so ever against their wills, was not exacted. Wherein those pious princes followed the law of God in Deut. xxiv. 1, and his express charge by the prophet Malachi, to dismiss from him the wife whom he hates. For God never meant in marriage to give to man a perpetual torment instead of a meet help. Neither can God approve, that to the violation of this holy league (which is violated as soon as true affection ceases and is lost) should be added murder, which is already committed by either of them who resolvedly hates the other, as I showed out of 1 John iii. 15, "Whoso hateth his brother, is a murderer."

CHAPTER XLI.

Whether the Husband or Wife deserted may marry to another.

THE wife's desertion of her husband the Christian emperors plainly decreed to be a just cause of divorce, whenas they granted him the right thereof, if she had but lain out one night against his will without probable cause. But of the man deserting his wife they did not so determine: yet if we look into the word of God, we shall find, that he who though but for a year without just cause forsakes his wife, and neither provides for her maintenance, nor signifies his purpose of returning, and good will towards her, whenas he may, hath forfeited his right in her so forsaken. For the Spirit of God speaks plainly, that both man and wife have such power over one another's person, as that they cannot deprive each other of living together, but by consent, and for a time.

Hither may be added, that the Holy Spirit grants desertion to be a cause of divorce, in those answers given to the Corinthians concerning a brother or sister deserted by a misbeliever. "If he depart, let him depart; a brother or a sister is not under bondage in such cases." In which words, who sees not that the Holy Ghost openly pronounced, that the party without cause deserted is not bound for another's wilful desertion, to abstain from marriage, if he have need thereof?

But some will say, that this is spoken of a misbeliever departing. But I beseech ye, doth not he reject the faith of Christ in his deeds, who rashly breaks the holy covenant of wedlock instituted by God? And besides this, the Holy Spirit does not make the misbelieving of him who departs, but the departing of him who misbelieves, to be the just cause of freedom to the brother or sister.

Since therefore it will be agreed among Christians, that they who depart from wedlock without just cause, do not only deny the faith of matrimony, but of Christ also, whatever they profess with their mouths; it is but reason to conclude, that the party deserted is not bound in case of causeless desertion, but that he may lawfully seek another consort, if it be needful to him, toward a pure and blameless conversation.

CHAPTER XLII.

That Impotence of Body, Leprosy, Madness, &c., are just Causes of Divorce.

OF this, because it was not disputed in "the Doctrine and Discipline of Divorce," him that would know further, I commend to the Latin original.

CHAPTER XLIII.

That to grant Divorce for all the Causes which have been hitherto brought, disagrees not from the Words of Christ, naming only the Cause of Adultery.

Now we must see how these things can stand with the words of our Saviour, who seems directly to forbid all divorce except it be for adultery. To the understanding whereof, we must ever remember this: That in the words of our Saviour there can be no contrariety: That his words and answers are not to be stretched beyond the question proposed: That our Saviour did not there purpose to treat of all the causes for which it might be lawful to divorce and marry again; for then that in the Corinthians of marrying again without guilt of adultery could not be added: That it is not good for that man to be alone, who hath not the special gift from above: That it is good for every such one to be married, that he may shun fornication.

With regard to these principles, let us see what our Lord answered to the tempting pharisees about divorce and second marriage, and how far his answer doth extend.

First, no man who is not very contentious will deny, that the pharisees asked our Lord whether it were lawful to put away such a wife, as was truly, and according to God's law, to be counted a wife; that is, such a one as would dwell with her husband, and both would and could perform the necessary duties of wedlock tolerably. But she who will not dwell with her husband is not put away by him, but goes of herself: and she who denies to be a meet help, or to be so hath made herself unfit by open misdemeanors, or through incurable impotencies cannot be able, is not by the law of God to be esteemed a wife; as hath been shown both from the first institution, and other places of scripture. Neither certainly would the pharisees propound a question concerning such an unconjugal wife; for their depravation of the law had brought them to that pass, as to think a man had right to put away his wife for any cause, though never so slight. Since therefore it is manifest, that Christ answered the pharisees concerning a fit and meet wife according to the law of God, whom he forbade to divorce for any cause but fornication; who sees not that it is a wickedness so to wrest and extend that answer of his, as if it forbade to divorce her who hath already forsaken, or hath lost the place and dignity of a wife, by deserved infamy, or hath undertaken to be that which she hath not natural ability to be?

This truth is so powerful, that it hath moved the papists to grant their kind of divorce for other causes besides adultery—as for ill usage, and the not performing of conjugal duty; and to separate from bed and board for these causes, which is as much divorce as they grant for adultery.

But some perhaps will object, that though it be yielded that our Lord granted divorce not only for adultery, yet it is not certain, that he permitted marriage after divorce, unless for that only cause. I answer, first, that the sentence of divorce and second marriage is one and the same. So that when the right of divorce is evinced to belong not only to the cause of fornication, the power of second marriage is also proved to be not limited to that cause only; and that most evidently whenas the Holy Ghost, 1 Cor. vii., so frees the deserted party from bondage, as that he may not only send a just divorce in case of desertion, but may seek another marriage.

Lastly, seeing God will not that any should live in danger of fornication and utter ruin for the default of another, and hath commanded the husband to send away with a bill of divorce her whom he could not love; it is impossible that the charge of adultery should belong to him who for lawful causes divorces and marries, or to her who marries after she hath been unjustly rejected, or to him who

receives her without all fraud to the former wedlock. For this were a horrid blasphemy against God, so to interpret his words, as to make him dissent from himself; for who sees not a flat contradiction in this, to enthral blameless men and women to miseries and injuries, under a false and soothing title of marriage, and yet to declare by his apostle, that a brother or sister is not under bondage in such cases? No less do these two things conflict with themselves, to enforce the innocent and faultless to endure the pain and misery of another's perverseness, or else to live in unavoidable temptation; and to affirm elsewhere that he lays on no man the burden of another man's sin, nor doth constrain any man to the endangering of his soul.

CHAPTER XLIV.

That to those also who are justly divorced, second Marriage ought to be permitted.

THIS although it be well proved, yet because it concerns only the offender, I leave him to search out his own charter himself in the author.

CHAPTER XLV.

That some Persons are so ordained to Marriage, as that they cannot obtain the Gift of Continence, no, not by earnest Prayer; and that therein every one is to be left to his own Judgment and Conscience, and not to have a Burden laid upon him by any other.

CHAPTER XLVI.

The Words of the Apostle concerning the Praise of single Life unfolded.

THESE two chapters not so immediately debating the right of divorce, I choose rather not to insert.

CHAPTER XLVII.

The Conclusion of this Treatise.

THESE things, most renowned king, I have brought together, both to explain for what causes the unhappy but sometimes most necessary help of divorce ought to be granted, according to God's word, by princes and rulers; as also to explain how the words of Christ do consent with such a grant. I have been large indeed both in handling those oracles of God, and in laying down those certain principles, which he who will know what the mind of God is in this matter, must ever think on and remember. But if we consider what mist and obscurity hath been poured out by antichrist upon this question, and how deep this pernicious contempt of wedlock, and admiration of single life, even in those who are not called thereto, hath sunk into many men's persuasions; I fear lest all that hath been said be hardly enough to persuade such, that they would cease at length to make themselves wiser and holier than God himself, in being so severe to grant lawful marriage, and so easy to connive at all, not only whoredoms but deflowerings and adulteries: whenas, among the people of God, no whoredom was to be tolerated.

Our Lord Jesus Christ, who came to destroy the works of Satan, send down his Spirit upon all Christians, and principally upon Christian governors, both in church and commonwealth, (for of the clear judgment of your royal majesty I nothing doubt, revolving the scripture so often as ye do,) that they may acknowledge how much they provoke the anger of God against us, whenas all kind of unchastity is tolerated, fornications and adulteries winked at; but holy and honorable wedlock is oft withheld by the mere persuasion of antichrist, from such as without this remedy cannot preserve themselves from damnation. For none who hath but a spark of honesty will deny, that princes and states ought to use diligence toward the maintaining of pure and honest life among all men, without which all justice, all fear of God, and true religion decays.

And who knows not, that chastity and pureness of life can never be restored, or continued in the commonwealth, unless it be first established in private houses, from whence the whole breed of men is to come forth? To effect this, no wise man can doubt, that it is necessary for princes and magistrates, first, with severity to punish whoredom and adultery; next, to see that marriages be lawfully contracted, and in the Lord; then, that they be faithfully kept; and lastly, when that unhappiness urges, that they be lawfully dissolved, and other marriage granted, according as the law of God, and of nature, and the constitutions of pious princes have decreed; as I have shown both by evident authorities of scripture, together with the writings of the ancient fathers, and other testimonies. Only the Lord grant that we may learn to prefer his ever just and saving word, before the comments of antichrist, too deeply rooted in many, and the false and blasphemous exposition of our Saviour's words. Amen.

A POSTSCRIPT

THUS far Martin Bucer: whom, where I might without injury to either part of the cause, I deny not to have epitomized; in the rest observing a well-warranted rule, not to give an inventory of so many words, but to weigh their force. I could have added that eloquent and right Christian discourse, written by Erasmus on this argument, not disagreeing in effect from Bucer. But this, I hope, will be enough to excuse me with the mere Englishman, to be no forger of new and loose opinions. Others may read him in his own phrase on the First to the Corinthians, and ease me who never could delight in long citations, much less in whole traductions; whether it be natural disposition or education in me, or that my mother bore me a speaker of what God made mine own, and not a translator. There be others also whom I could reckon up, of no mean account in the church, (and Peter Martyr among the first,) who are more than half our own in this controversy. But this is a providence not to be slighted, that as Bucer wrote this tractate of divorce in England and for England, so Erasmus professes he begun here among us the same subject, especially out of compassion, for the need he saw this nation had of some charitable redress herein; and seriously exhorts others to use their best industry in the clearing of this point, wherein custom hath a greater sway than verity. That therefore which came into the mind of these two admired strangers to do for England, and in a touch of highest prudence, which they took to be not yet recovered from monastic superstition, if I a native am found to have done for mine own country, altogether suitably and conformably to their so large and clear understanding, yet without the least help of theirs; I suppose that henceforward among conscionable and judicious persons it will no more be thought to my discredit, or at all to this nation's dishonor. And if these their books the one shall be printed often with best allowance in most religious cities, the other with express authority of Leo the Tenth, a pope, shall, for the propagating of truth, be published and republished, though against the received opinion of that church, and mine containing but the same thing, shall in a time of reformation, a time of free speaking, free writing, not find a permission to the press; I refer me to wisest men, whether truth be suffered to be truth, or liberty to be liberty, now among us, and be not again in danger of new fetters and captivity after all our hopes and labors lost: and whether learning be not (which our enemies too prophetically feared) in the way to be trodden down again by ignorance. Whereof while time is, out of the faith owing to God and my country, I bid this kingdom beware; and doubt not but God who hath dignified this parliament already to so many glorious degrees, will also give them (which is a singular blessing) to inform themselves rightly in the midst of an unprincipled age, and to prevent this working mystery of ignorance and ecclesiastical thraldom, which under new shapes and disguises begins afresh to grow upon us.

TETRACHORDON:

EXPOSITIONS

UPON THE FOUR CHIEF PLACES IN SCRIPTURE WHICH TREAT OF MARRIAGE, OR NULLITIES IN MARRIAGE.

ON

GEN. i. 27, 28, COMPARED AND EXPLAINED BY GEN. ii. 18, 23, 24. DEUT. xxiv. 1, 2. MATT. v. 31, 32, WITH MATT. xix. FROM VER. 3 TO 11. I COR. vii. FROM VER. 10 TO 16.

WHEREIN THE DOCTRINE AND DISCIPLINE OF DIVORCE, AS WAS LATELY PUBLISHED, IS CONFIRMED BY EXPLANATION OF SCRIPTURE: BY TESTIMONY OF ANCIENT FATHERS; OF CIVIL LAWS IN THE PRIMITIVE CHURCH; OF FAMOUSEST REFORMED DIVINES; AND LASTLY,

BY AN INTENDED ACT OF THE PARLIAMENT AND CHURCH OF ENGLAND IN THE LAST YEAR OF EDWARD THE SIXTH.

—— Σκαιοῖσι καινὰ προσφέρων σοφὰ
Δόξεις ἀχρεῖος, κοὐ σοφὸς πεφυκέναι·
Τῶν δ' αὖ δοκούντων εἰδέναι τι ποικίλον,
Κρείσσων νομισθεὶς ἐν πόλει, λυπρὸς φανῇ.
—*Euripid. Medea.*

[The text is that of the first edition, 1645.]

TO THE PARLIAMENT.

THAT which I knew to be the part of a good magistrate, aiming at true liberty through the right information of religious and civil life, and that which I saw, and was partaker of, your vows and solemn covenants, parliament of England! your actions also manifestly tending to exalt the truth, and to depress the tyranny of error and ill custom, with more constancy and prowess than ever yet any, since that parliament which put the first sceptre of this kingdom into his hand whom God and extraordinary virtue made their monarch; were the causes that moved me, one else not placing much in the eminence of a dedication, to present your high notice with a discourse, conscious to itself of nothing more than of diligence, and firm affection to the public good. And that ye took it so as wise and impartial men, obtaining so great power and dignity, are wont to accept, in matters both doubtful and important, what they think offered them well meant, and from a rational ability, I had no less than to persuade me. And on that persuasion am returned, as to a famous and free port, myself also bound by more than a maritime law, to expose as freely what fraughtage I conceive to bring of no trifles. For although it be generally known, how and by whom ye have been instigated to a hard censure of that former book, entitled, "The Doctrine and Discipline of Divorce," an opinion held by some of the best among reformed writers without scandal or confutement, though now thought new and dangerous by some of our severe Gnostics, whose little reading, and less meditating, holds ever with hardest obstinacy that which it took up with easiest credulity; I do not find yet that aught, for the furious incitements which have been used, hath issued by your appointment, that might give the least interruption or disrepute either to the author, or to the book. Which he who will be better advised than to call your neglect or connivance at a thing imagined so perilous, can attribute it to nothing more justly, than to the deep and quiet stream of your direct and calm deliberations, that gave not way either to the fervent rashness or the imma- terial gravity of those who ceased not to exasperate without cause. For which uprightness and incorrupt refusal of what ye were incensed to, lords and commons! (though it were done to justice, not to me, and was a peculiar demonstration how far your ways are different from the rash vulgar,) besides those allegiances of oath and duty, which are my public debt to your public labors, I have yet a store of gratitude laid up, which cannot be exhausted; and such thanks perhaps they may live to be, as shall more than whisper to the next ages. Yet that the author may be known to ground himself upon his own innocence, and the merit of his cause, not upon the favor of a diversion, or a delay to any just censure, but wishes rather he might see those his detractors at any fair meeting, as learned debatements are privileged with a due freedom under equal moderators; I shall here briefly single one of them, (because he hath obliged me to it,) who I persuade me having scarce read the book, nor knowing him who writ it, or at least feigning the latter, hath not forborne to scandalize him, unconferred with, unadmonished, undealt with by any pastorly or brotherly convincement, in the most open and invective manner, and at the most bitter opportunity that drift or set design could have invented. And this, whenas the canon law, though commonly most favoring the boldness of their priests, punishes the naming or traducing of any person in the pulpit, was by him made no scruple. If I shall, therefore, take licence by the right of nature, and that liberty wherein I was born, to defend myself publicly against a printed calumny, and do willingly appeal to those judges to whom I am accused, it can be no immoderate or unallowable course of seeking so just and needful reparations. Which I had done long since, had not these employments, which are now visible, deferred me. It was

preached before ye, lords and commons! in August last upon a special day of humiliation, that "there was a wicked book abroad," and ye were taxed of sin that it was yet "uncensured, the book deserving to be burnt;" and "impudence" also was charged upon the author, who durst "set his name to it, and dedicate it to yourselves!" First, lords and commons! I pray to that God, before whom ye then were prostrate, so to forgive ye those omissions and trespasses, which ye desire most should find forgiveness, as I shall soon show to the world how easily ye absolve yourselves of that which this man calls your sin, and is indeed your wisdom, and your nobleness, whereof to this day ye have done well not to repent. He terms it "a wicked book," and why but "for allowing other causes of divorce, than Christ and his apostles mention?" and with the same censure condemns of wickedness not only Martin Bucer, that elect instrument of reformation, highly honored, and had in reverence by Edward the Sixth, and his whole parliament, whom also I had published in English by a good providence, about a week before this calumnious digression was preached; so that if he knew not Bucer then, as he ought to have known, he might at least have known him some months after, ere the sermon came in print; wherein notwithstanding he persists in his former sentence, and condemns again of wickedness, either ignorantly or wilfully, not only Martin Bucer, and all the choicest and holiest of our reformers, but the whole parliament and church of England in those best and purest times of Edward the Sixth. All which I shall prove with good evidence, at the end of these explanations. And then let it be judged and seriously considered with what hope the affairs of our religion are committed to one among others, who hath now only left him which of the twain he will choose, whether this shall be his palpable ignorance, or the same wickedness of his own book, which he so lavishly imputes to the writings of other men: and whether this of his, that thus peremptorily defames and attaints of wickedness unspotted churches, unblemished parliaments, and the most eminent restorers of Christian doctrine, deserve not to be burnt first. And if his heat had burst out only against the opinion, his wonted passion had no doubt been silently borne with wonted patience. But since, against the charity of that solemn place and meeting, it served him further to inveigh opprobriously against the person, branding him with no less than impudence, only for setting his name to what he had written; I must be excused not to be so wanting to the defence of an honest name, or to the reputation of those good men who afford me their society, but to be sensible of such a foul endeavored disgrace: not knowing aught either in mine own deserts, or the laws of this land, why I should be subject, in such a notorious and illegal manner, to the intemperances of this man's preaching choler. And indeed to be so prompt and ready in the midst of his humbleness, to toss reproaches of this bulk and size, argues as if they were the weapons of his exercise, I am sure not of his ministry, or of that day's work. Certainly to subscribe my name at what I was to own, was what the state had ordered and requires. And he who lists not to be malicious, would call it ingenuity, clear conscience, willingness to avouch what might be questioned, or to be better instructed. And if God were so displeased with those, Isa. lviii., who "on the solemn fast were wont to smite with the fist of wickedness," it could be no sign of his own humiliation accepted, which disposed him to smite so keenly with a reviling tongue. But if only to have writ my name must be counted "impudence," how doth this but justify another, who might affirm with as good warrant, that the late discourse of "Scripture and Reason," which is certain to be chiefly his own draught, was published without a name, out of base fear, and the sly avoidance of what might follow to his detriment, if the party at court should hap to reach him? And I, to have set my name, where he accuses me to have set it, am so far from recanting, that I offer my hand also if need be, to make good the same opinion which I there maintain, by inevitable consequences drawn parallel from his own principal arguments in that of "Scripture and Reason:" which I shall pardon him if he can deny, without shaking his own composition to pieces. The "impudence," therefore, since he weighed so little what a gross revile that was to give his equal, I send him back again for a phylactery to stitch upon his arrogance, that censures not only before conviction, so bitterly without so much as one reason given, but censures the congregation of his governors to their faces, for not being so hasty as himself to censure.

And whereas my other crime is, that I addressed the dedication of what I had studied to the parliament; how could I better declare the loyalty which I owe to that supreme and majestic tribunal, and the opinion which I have of the high entrusted judgment, and personal worth assembled in that place? With the same affections therefore, and the same addicted fidelity, parliament of England! I here again have brought to your perusal on the same argument these following expositions of scripture. The former book, as pleased some to think, who were thought judicious, had of reason in it to a sufficiency; what they required was, that the scriptures there alleged might be discussed more fully. To their desires thus much further hath been labored in the scriptures. Another sort also, who wanted more authorities and citations, have not been here unthought of. If all this attain not to satisfy them, as I am confident that none of those our great controversies, at this day hath had a more demonstrative explaining, I must confess to admire what it is; for doubtless it is not reason now-a-days that satisfies or suborns the common credence of men, to yield so easily, and grow so vehement in matters much more disputable, and far less conducing to the daily good and peace of life. Some whose necessary shifts have long inured them to cloak the defects of their unstudied years, and hatred now to learn, under the appearance of a grave solidity, (which estimation they have gained among weak perceivers,) find the ease of slighting what they cannot refute, and are determined, as I hear, to hold it not worth the answering. In which number I must be forced to reckon that doctor, who in a late equivocating treatise plausibly set afloat against the Dippers, diving the while himself with a more deep prelatical malignance against the present state and church government, mentions with ignominy "the Tractate of Divorce;" yet answers nothing, but instead thereof (for which I do not commend his marshalling) sets Moses also among the crew of his Anabaptists, as one who to a holy nation, the commonwealth of Israel, gave laws "breaking the bonds of marriage to inordinate lust." These are no mean surges of blasphemy, not only dipping Moses the divine lawgiver, but dashing with a high hand against the justice and purity of God himself; as these ensuing scriptures plainly and freely handled shall verify, to the launching of that old apostemated error. Him therefore I leave now to his repentance.

Others, which is their courtesy, confess that wit and parts may do much to make that seem true which is not; as was objected to Socrates by them who could not resist his efficacy, that he ever made the worst cause seem the better; and thus thinking themselves discharged of the difficulty, love not to wade further into the fear of a convincement. These will be their excuses to decline the full examining of this serious point. So much the more I press it and repeat it, lords and commons! that ye beware while time is, ere this grand secret and only art of ignorance affecting tyranny, grow powerful, and rule among us. For if sound argument and reason shall be thus put off, either by an undervaluing silence, or the masterly censure of a railing word or two in the pulpit, or by rejecting the force of truth, as the mere cunning of eloquence and sophistry; what can be the end of this, but that all good learning and knowledge will suddenly decay? Ignorance, and illiterate presumption, which is yet but our disease, will turn at length into our very constitution, and prove the hectic evil of this age: worse to be feared, if it get once to reign over us, than any fifth monarchy. If this shall be the course, that what was wont to be a chief commendation, and the ground of other men's confidence in an author, his diligence, his learning, his elocution, whether by right or by ill meaning granted him, shall be turned now to a disadvantage and suspicion against him, that what he writes, though unconfuted, must therefore be mistrusted, therefore not received for the industry, the exactness, the labor in it, confessed to be more than ordinary; as if wisdom had now forsaken the thirsty and laborious inquirer, to dwell against her nature with the arro-

gant and shallow babbler; to what purpose all those pains and that continual searching required of us by Solomon to the attainment of understanding? Why are men bred up with such care and expense to a life of perpetual studies? Why do yourselves with such endeavor seek to wipe off the imputation of intending to discourage the progress and advance of learning? He therefore, whose heart can bear him to the high pitch of your noble enterprises, may easily assure himself, that the prudence and far-judging circumspectness of so grave a magistracy sitting in parliament, who have before them the prepared and purposed act of their most religious predecessors to imitate in this question, cannot reject the clearness of these reasons, and these allegations both here and formerly offered them; nor can overlook the necessity of ordaining more wholesomely and more humanely in the casualties of divorce, than our laws have yet established, if the most urgent and excessive grievances happening in domestic life be worth the laying to heart; which, unless charity be far from us, cannot be neglected. And that these things, both in the right constitution, and in the right reformation of a commonwealth, call for speediest redress, and ought to be the first considered, enough was urged in what was prefaced to that monument of Bucer, which I brought to your remembrance, and the other time before. Henceforth, except new cause be given, I shall say less and less. For if the law make not timely provision, let the law, as reason is, bear the censure of those consequences, which her own default now more evidently produces. And if men want manliness to expostulate the right of their due ransom, and to second their own occasions, they may sit hereafter and bemoan themselves to have neglected through faintness the only remedy of their sufferings, which a seasonable and well-grounded speaking might have purchased them. And perhaps in time to come, others will know how to esteem what is not every day put into their hands, when they have marked events, and better weighed how hurtful and unwise it is, to hide a secret and pernicious rupture under the ill counsel of a bashful silence. But who would distrust aught, or not be ample in his hopes of your wise and Christian determination? who have the prudence to consider, and should have the goodness, like gods as ye are called, to find out readily, and by just law to administer those redresses, which have of old, not without God ordaining, been granted to the adversities of mankind, ere they who needed were put to ask. Certainly, if any other have enlarged his thoughts to expect from this government, so justly undertaken, and by frequent assistances from Heaven so apparently upheld, glorious changes and renovations both in church and state, he among the foremost might be named, who prays that the fate of England may tarry for no other deliverers.

JOHN MILTON.

TETRACHORDON:

EXPOSITIONS

UPON THE FOUR CHIEF PLACES IN SCRIPTURE WHICH TREAT OF MARRIAGE OR NULLITIES IN MARRIAGE.

Genesis i. 27.

"So God created man in his own image, in the image of God created he him; male and female created he them.

28. "And God blessed them, and God said unto them, Be fruitful," &c.

Genesis ii. 18.

"And the Lord God said, It is not good that man should be alone; I will make him a help meet for him.

23. "And Adam said, This is now bone of my bones, and flesh of my flesh; she shall be called Woman, because she was taken out of man.

24. "Therefore shall a man leave his father and his mother, and shall cleave unto his wife, and they shall be one flesh."

Genesis i. 27.

"So God created man in his own image."] To be informed aright in the whole history of marriage, that we may know for certain, not by a forced yoke, but by an impartial definition, what marriage is, and what is not marriage, it will undoubtedly be safest, fairest, and most with our obedience, to inquire, as our Saviour's direction is, how it was in the beginning. And that we begin so high as man created after God's own image, there want not earnest causes. For nothing now-a-days is more degenerately forgotten, than the true dignity of man, almost in every respect, but especially in this prime institution of matrimony, wherein his native preeminence ought most to shine. Although if we consider that just and natural privileges men neither can rightly seek, nor dare fully claim, unless they be allied to inward goodness and steadfast knowledge, and that the want of this quells them to a servile sense of their own conscious unworthiness; it may save the wondering why in this age many are so opposite both to human and to Christian liberty, either while they understand not, or envy others that do; contenting, or rather priding themselves in a specious humility and strictness, bred out of low ignorance, that never yet conceived the freedom of the gospel; and is therefore by the apostle to the Colossians ranked with no better company than "will-worship and the mere show of wisdom." And how injurious herein they are, if not to themselves, yet to their neighbors, and not to them only, but to the all-wise and bounteous grace offered us in our redemption, will orderly appear.

"In the image of God created he him."] It is enough determined, that this image of God, wherein man was created, is meant wisdom, purity, justice, and rule over all creatures. All which, being lost in Adam, was recovered with gain by the merits of Christ. For albeit our first parent had lordship over sea, and land, and air, yet there was a law without him, as a guard set over him. But Christ having "cancelled the handwriting of ordinances which was against us," Col. ii. 14, and interpreted the fulfilling of all through charity, hath in that respect set us over law, in the free custody of his love, and left us victorious under the guidance of his living Spirit, not under the dead letter; to follow that which most edifies, most aids and furthers a religious life, makes us holiest and likest to his immortal image, not that which makes us most conformable and captive to civil and subordinate precepts: whereof the strictest observance may ofttimes prove the destruction not only of many innocent persons and families, but of whole nations: although indeed no ordinance, human or from heaven, can bind against the good of man; so that to keep them strictly against that end, is all one with to break them. Men of most renowned virtue have sometimes by transgressing most truly kept the law; and wisest magistrates have permitted and dispensed it; while they looked not peevishly at the letter, but with a greater spirit at the good of mankind, if always not written in the characters of law, yet engraven in the heart of man by a divine impression. This heathens could see, as the well-read in story can recount of Solon and Epaminondas, whom Cicero, in his first book of "Invention," nobly defends. "All law," saith he, "we ought refer to the common good, and interpret by that, not by the scroll of letters. No man observes law for law's sake, but for the good of them for whom it was made." The rest might serve well to lecture these times, deluded through belly doctrines into a devout slavery. The scripture also affords us David in the shewbread, Hezekiah in the passover, sound and safe transgressors of the literal command, which also dispensed not seldom with itself; and taught us on what just occasions to do so: until our Saviour, for whom that great and godlike work was reserved, redeemed us to a state above prescriptions, by dissolving the whole law into charity. And have we not the soul to understand this, and must we against this glory of God's transcendent love towards us be still the servants of a literal indictment?

"Created he him."] It might be doubted why he saith, "In the image of God created he him," not them, as well as "male and female" them; especially since that image might be common to them both, but male and female could not, however the Jews fable and please themselves with the accidental concurrence of Plato's wit, as if man at first had been created hermaphrodite: but then it must have been male and female created he him. So had the image of God been equally common to them both, it had no doubt been said, "In the image of God created he them." But St. Paul ends the controversy, by explaining, that the woman is not primarily and immediately the image of God, but in reference to the man: "The head of the woman," saith he, 1 Cor. xi., "is the man;" "he the image and glory of God, she the glory of the man;" he not for her, but she for him. Therefore his precept is, "Wives, be subject to your husbands, as is fit in the Lord," Col. iii. 18; "in everything," Eph. v. 24. Nevertheless man is not to hold her as a servant, but receives her into a part of that empire which God proclaims him to, though not equally, yet largely, as his own image and glory: for it is no small glory to him, that a creature so like him should be made subject to him. Not but that particular exceptions may have place, if she exceed her husband in prudence and dexterity, and he contentedly yield: for then a superior and more natural law comes in, that the wiser should govern the less wise, whether male or female. But that which far more easily and obediently follows from this verse is, that, seeing woman was purposely made for man, and he her head, it cannot stand before the breath of this divine utterance, that man, the portraiture of God, joining to himself for his intended good and solace an inferior sex, should so become her thrall, whose wilfulness or inability to be a wife frustrates the occasional end of her creation; but that he may acquit himself to freedom by his natural birthright, and that indelible character of priority, which God crowned him with. If it be urged, that sin hath lost him this, the answer is not far to seek, that from her the sin first proceeded, which keeps her justly in the same proportion still beneath. She is not to gain by being first in the transgression, that man should further lose to her, because already he hath lost by her means. Oft it happens, that in this matter he is without fault; so that his punishment herein is causeless: and God hath the praise in our speeches of him, to sort his punishment in the same kind with the offence. Suppose he erred; it is not the intent of God or man to hunt an error so to the death with a revenge beyond all measure and proportion. But if we argue thus, This affliction is befallen him for his sin, therefore he must bear it, without seeking the only remedy: first, it will be false, that all

affliction comes for sin, as in the case of
Job, and of the man born blind, John ix. 3, was
evident: next, by that reason, all miseries
coming for sin, we must let them all lie
upon us like the vermin of an Indian
Catharist, which his fond religion forbids
him to molest. Were it a particular punishment inflicted through the anger of God
upon a person, or upon a land, no law hinders
us in that regard, no law but bids us remove it if we can; much more if it be a
dangerous temptation withal; much more
yet, if it be certainly a temptation, and not
certainly a punishment, though a pain. As
for what they say we must bear with patience: to bear with patience, and to seek
effectual remedies, implies no contradiction.
It may no less be for our disobedience, our
unfaithfulness, and other sins against God,
that wives become adulterous to the bed;
and questionless we ought to take the affliction as patiently as Christian prudence
would wish: yet hereby is not lost the right of
divorcing for adultery. No, you say; because our Saviour excepted that only. But
why, if he were so bent to punish our sins,
and try our patience in binding on us a
disastrous marriage, why did he except
adultery? Certainly to have been bound from
divorce in that case also had been as plentiful a punishment to our sins, and not too
little work for the patientest. Nay, perhaps
they will say it was too great a sufferance;
and with as slight a reason, for no wise man
but would sooner pardon the act of adultery
once and again committed by a person worth
pity and forgiveness, than to lead a wearisome life of unloving and unquiet conversation with one who neither affects nor is
affected, much less with one who exercises
all bitterness, and would commit adultery
too, but for envy lest the persecuted condition should thereby get the benefit of his
freedom. It is plain therefore, that God enjoins not this supposed strictness of not
divorcing either to punish us, or to try our
patience.

Moreover, if man be the image of God,
which consists in holiness, and woman ought
in the same respect to be the image and
companion of man, in such wise to be loved
as the church is beloved of Christ; and if,
as God is the head of Christ, and Christ

the head of man, so man is the head of
woman; I cannot see by this golden dependence of headship and subjection, but
that piety and religion is the main tie of
Christian matrimony: so as if there be
found between the pair a notorious disparity
either of wickedness or heresy, the husband
by all manner of rights is disengaged from
a creature, not made and inflicted on him to
the vexation of his righteousness: the wife
also, as her subjection is terminated in the
Lord, being herself the redeemed of Christ,
is not still bound to be the vassal of him,
who is the bondslave of Satan: she being
now neither the image nor the glory of such
a person, nor made for him, nor left in
bondage to him; but hath recourse to the
wing of charity, and protection of the church,
unless there be a hope on either side; yet
such a hope must be meant, as may be a
rational hope, and not an endless servitude.
Of which hereafter.

But usually it is objected, that if it be
thus, then there can be no true marriage
between misbelievers and irreligious persons.
I might answer, Let them see to that who
are such; the church hath no commission to
judge those without, 1 Cor. v. But this they
will say, perhaps, is but penuriously to resolve a doubt. I answer therefore, that
where they are both irreligious, the marriage may be yet true enough to them in a
civil relation. For there are left some remains
of God's image in man, as he is merely man;
which reason God gives against the shedding
of man's blood, Gen. ix., as being made in
God's image, without expression whether he
were a good man or bad, to exempt the slayer
from punishment. So that in those marriages where the parties are alike void of
religion, the wife owes a civil homage and
subjection, the husband owes a civil loyalty.
But where the yoke is misyoked, heretic
with faithful, godly with ungodly, to the
grievance and manifest endangering of a
brother or sister, reasons of a higher strain
than matrimonial bear sway; unless the
gospel, instead of freeing us, debase itself
to make us bondmen, and suffer evil to
control good.

"Male and female created he them."] This
contains another end of matching man and
woman, being the right and lawfulness of

the marriage-bed; though much inferior to the former end of her being his image and help in religious society. And who of weakest insight may not see, that this creating of them male and female cannot in any order of reason, or Christianity, be of such moment against the better and higher purposes of their creation, as to enthral husband or wife to duties or to sufferings, unworthy and unbeseeming the image of God in them? Now whenas not only men, but good men, do stand upon their right, their estimation, their dignity, in all other actions and deportments, with warrant enough and good conscience, as having the image of God in them, it will not be difficult to determine what is unworthy and unseemly for a man to do or suffer in wedlock: and the like proportionally may be found for woman, if we love not to stand disputing below the principles of humanity. He that said, "Male and female created he them," immediately before that said also in the same verse, "In the image of God created he him," and redoubled it, that our thoughts might not be so full of dregs as to urge this poor consideration of male and female, without remembering the nobleness of that former repetition; lest when God sends a wise eye to examine our trivial glosses, they be found extremely to creep upon the ground: especially since they confess, that what here concerns marriage is but a brief touch, only preparative to the institution which follows more expressly in the next chapter; and that Christ so took it, as desiring to be briefest with them who came to tempt him, account shall be given in due place.

Ver. 28. "And God blessed them, and God said unto them, Be fruitful and multiply, and replenish the earth," &c.

This declares another end of matrimony, the propagation of mankind; and is again repeated to Noah and his sons. Many things might be noted on this place not ordinary, nor unworthy the noting; but I undertook not a general comment. Hence therefore we see the desire of children is honest and pious; if we be not less zealous in our Christianity than Plato was in his heathenism; who, in the sixth of his Laws, counts offspring therefore desirable, that we may leave in our stead sons of our sons, continual servants of God: a religious and prudent desire, if people knew as well what were required to breeding as to begetting; which desire perhaps was a cause why the Jews hardly could endure a barren wedlock; and Philo, in his book of special laws, esteem him only worth pardon, that sends not barrenness away. Carvilius, the first recorded in Rome to have sought divorce, had it granted him for the barrenness of his wife, upon his oath that he married to the end he might have children; as Dionysius and Gellius are authors. But to dismiss a wife only for barrenness, is hard: and yet in some the desire of children is so great, and so just, yea, sometimes so necessary, that to condemn such a one to a childless age, the fault apparently not being in him, might seem perhaps more strict than needed. Sometimes inheritances, crowns, and dignities are so interested and annexed in their common peace and good to such or such lineal descent, that it may prove of great moment both in the affairs of men and of religion, to consider thoroughly what might be done herein, notwithstanding the waywardness of our school doctors.

Genesis ii. 18.

"And the Lord said, It is not good that man should be alone; I will make him a help meet for him."
Ver. 23. "And Adam said," &c. Ver. 24. "Therefore shall a man leave," &c.

This second chapter is granted to be a commentary on the first, and these verses granted to be an exposition of that former verse, "Male and female created he them:" and yet when this male and female is by the explicit words of God himself here declared to be not meant other than a fit help, and meet society, some, who would engross to themselves the whole trade of interpreting, will not suffer the clear text of God to do the office of explaining itself.

"And the Lord God said. It is not good."] A man would think, that the consideration of who spake should raise up the attention of our minds to inquire better, and obey the purpose of so great a speaker: for as we order the business of marriage, that which he here speaks is all made vain; and in the decision of matrimony, or not matrimony, nothing at all regarded. Our presumption hath utterly changed the state and condition of this ordinance: God ordained it in love and helpfulness to be indissoluble, and we in outward act and formality to be a forced bondage; so that being subject to a thousand errors in the best men, if it prove a blessing to any, it is of mere accident, as man's law hath handled it, and not of institution.

"It is not good for man to be alone."] Hitherto all things that have been named, were approved of God to be very good: loneliness is the first thing which God's eye named not good: whether it be a thing, or the want of something, I labor not; let it be their tendance, who have the art to be industriously idle. And here "alone" is meant alone without woman; otherwise Adam had the company of God himself, and angels to converse with; all creatures to delight him seriously, or to make him sport. God could have created him out of the same mold a thousand friends and brother Adams to have been his consorts; yet for all this, till Eve was given him, God reckoned him to be alone.

"It is not good."] God here presents himself like to a man deliberating; both to show us that the matter is of high consequence, and that he intended to found it according to natural reason, not impulsive command; but that the duty should arise from the reason of it, not the reason be swallowed up in a reasonless duty. "Not good," was as much to Adam before his fall, as not pleasing, not expedient; but since the coming of sin into the world, to him who hath not received the continence, it is not only not expedient to be alone, but plainly sinful. And therefore he who wilfully abstains from marriage, not being supernaturally gifted, and he who by making the yoke of marriage unjust and intolerable, causes men to abhor it, are both in a diabolical sin, equal to that of antichrist, who forbids to marry. For what difference at all whether he abstain men from marrying, or restrain them in a marriage happening totally discommodious, distasteful, dishonest, and pernicious to him,

without the appearance of his fault? For God does not here precisely say, I make a female to this male, as he did briefly before; but expounding himself here on purpose, he saith, because it is not good for man to be alone, I make him therefore a meet help. God supplies the privation of not good, with the perfect gift of a real and positive good; it is man's perverse cooking, who hath turned this bounty of God into a scorpion, either by weak and shallow constructions, or by proud arrogance and cruelty to them who neither in their purposes nor in their actions have offended against the due honor of wedlock.

Now whereas the apostle's speaking in the spirit, 1 Cor. vii., pronounces quite contrary to this word of God, "It is good for a man not to touch a woman," and God cannot contradict himself; it instructs us, that his commands and words, especially such as bear the manifest title of some good to man, are not to be so strictly wrung, as to command without regard to the most natural and miserable necessities of mankind. Therefore the apostle adds a limitation in the 26th verse of that chapter, for the present necessity it is good; which he gives us doubtless as a pattern how to reconcile other places by the general rule of charity.

"For man to be alone."] Some would have the sense hereof to be in respect of procreation only; and Austin contests that manly friendship in all other regard had been a more becoming solace for Adam, than to spend so many secret years in an empty world with one woman. But our writers deservedly reject this crabbed opinion; and defend that there is a peculiar comfort in the married state besides the genial bed, which no other society affords. No mortal nature can endure, either in the actions of religion, or study of wisdom, without sometimes slackening the cords of intense thought and labor, which, lest we should think faulty, God himself conceals us not his own recreations before the world was built: "I was," saith the Eternal Wisdom, "daily his delight, playing always before him." And to him, indeed, wisdom is as a high tower of pleasure, but to us a steep hill, and we toiling ever about the bottom. He executes with ease the exploits of his omnipotence, as easy as with us it is to will; but no worthy enterprise can be done by us without continual plodding and wearisomeness to our faint and sensitive abilities. We cannot, therefore, always be contemplative, or pragmatical abroad, but have need of some delightful intermissions, wherein the enlarged soul may leave off a while her severe schooling, and, like a glad youth in wandering vacancy, may keep her holidays to joy and harmless pastime; which as she cannot well do without company, so in no company so well as where the different sex in most resembling unlikeness, and most unlike resemblance, cannot but please best, and be pleased in the aptitude of that variety. Whereof lest we should be too timorous, in the awe that our flat sages would form us and dress us, wisest Solomon among his gravest proverbs countenances a kind of ravishment and erring fondness in the entertainment of wedded leisures; and in the Song of Songs, which is generally believed, even in the jolliest expressions, to figure the spousals of the church with Christ, sings of a thousand raptures between those two lovely ones far on the hither side of carnal enjoyment. By these instances, and more which might be brought, we may imagine how indulgently God provided against man's loneliness; that he approved it not, as by himself declared not good; that he approved the remedy thereof, as of his own ordaining, consequently good; and as he ordained it, so doubtless proportionably to our fallen estate he gives it; else were his ordinance at least in vain, and we for all his gifts still empty handed. Nay, such an unbounteous giver we should make him, as in the fables Jupiter was to Ixion, giving him a cloud instead of Juno; giving him a monstrous issue by her, the breed of Centaurs, a neglected and unloved race, the fruits of a delusive marriage; and lastly, giving him her with a damnation to that wheel in hell, from a life thrown into the midst of temptations and disorders. But God is no deceitful giver, to bestow that on us for a remedy of loneliness, which if it bring not a sociable mind as well as a conjunctive body, leaves us no less alone than before; and if it bring a mind perpetually averse and disagreeable, betrays us to a worse condition than the most deserted loneliness. God cannot in the justice of his own promise and institution so unexpectedly mock us, by forcing that upon us as the remedy of solitude, which wraps us in a misery worse than any wilderness, as the Spirit of God himself judges, Prov. xix.; especially knowing that the best and wisest men amidst the sincere and most cordial designs of their heart, do daily err in choosing. We may conclude, therefore, seeing orthodoxal expositors confess to our hands, that by loneliness is not only meant the want of copulation, and that man is not less alone by turning in a body to him, unless there be within it a mind answerable; that it is a work more worthy the care and consultation of God to provide for the worthiest part of man, which is his mind, and not unnaturally to set it beneath the formalities and respects of the body, to make it a servant of its own vassal: I say, we may conclude that such a marriage, wherein the mind is so disgraced and vilified below the body's interest, and can have no just or tolerable contentment, is not of God's institution, and therefore no marriage. Nay, in concluding this, I say we conclude no more than what the common expositors themselves give us, both in that which I have recited, and much more hereafter. But the truth is, they give us in such a manner, as they who leave their own mature positions like the eggs of an ostrich in the dust; I do but lay them in the sun; their own pregnancies hatch the truth; and I am taxed of novelties and strange producements, while they, like that inconsiderate bird, know not that these are their own natural breed.

"I will make him a help meet for him."] Here the heavenly institutor, as if he labored not to be mistaken by the supercilious hypocrisy of those that love to master their brethren, and to make us sure that he gave us not now a servile yoke, but an amiable knot, contents not himself to say, I will make him a wife; but resolving to give us first the meaning before the name of a wife, saith graciously, "I will make him a help meet for him." And here again, as before, I do not require more full and fair deductions than the whole consent of our divines usually raise from this text, that in matrimony there must be first a mutual help to piety; next, to civil fellowship of love and amity; then, to generation; so to household affairs; lastly, the remedy of incontinence. And commonly they reckon them in such order, as leaves generation and incontinence to be last considered. This I amaze me at, that though all the superior and nobler ends both of marriage and of the married persons be absolutely frustrate, the matrimony stirs not, loses no hold, remains as rooted as the 10 centre: but if the body bring but in a complaint of frigidity, by that cold application only this adamantine Alp of wedlock has leave to dissolve; which else all the machinations of religious or civil reason at the suit of a distressed mind, either for divine worship or human conversation violated, cannot unfasten. What courts of concupiscence are these, wherein fleshly appetite is heard before right reason, lust before love or devo- 20 tion? They may be pious Christians together, they may be loving and friendly, they may be helpful to each other in the family, but they cannot couple; that shall divorce them, though either party would not. They can neither serve God together, nor one be at peace with the other, nor be good in the family one to other; but live as they were dead, or live as they were deadly enemies in a cage together: it is all one, they can 30 couple, they shall not divorce till death, no, though this sentence be their death. What is this besides tyranny, but to turn nature upside down, to make both religion and the mind of man wait upon the slavish errands of the body, and not the body to follow either the sanctity or the sovereignty of the mind, unspeakably wronged, and with all equity complaining? what is this but to abuse the sacred and mysterious bed of 40 marriage to be the compulsive sty of an ingrateful and malignant lust, stirred up only from a carnal acrimony, without either love or peace, or regard to any other thing holy or human? This I admire, how possibly it should inhabit thus long in the sense of so many disputing theologians, unless it be the lowest lees of a canonical infection liver-grown to their sides, which, perhaps, will never uncling, without the strong abstersive 50 of some heroic magistrate, whose mind, equal to his high office, dares lead him both to know and to do without their frivolous

case-putting. For certain he shall have God and this institution plainly on his side. And if it be true both in divinity and law, that consent alone, though copulation never follow, makes a marriage, how can they dissolve it for the want of that which made it not, and not dissolve it for that not continuing which made it and should not preserve it in love and reason, and difference it from a brute conjugality?

"Meet for him."] The original here is more expressive than other languages word for word can render it; but all agree effectual conformity of disposition and affection to be hereby signified; which God, as it were, not satisfied with the naming of a help, goes on describing another self, a second self, a very self itself. Yet now there is nothing in the life of man, through our misconstruction, made more uncertain, more hazardous and full of chance, than this divine blessing with such favorable significance here conferred upon us; which if we do but err in our choice, the most unblameable error that can be, err but one minute, one moment after those mighty syllables pronounced, which take upon them to join heaven and hell together unpardonably till death pardon; this divine blessing that looked but now with such a humane smile upon us, and spoke such gentle reason, straight vanishes like a fair sky, and brings on such a scene of cloud and tempest, as turns all to shipwreck without haven or shore, but to a ransomless captivity; and then they tell us it is our sin; but let them be told again, that sin, through the mercy of God, hath not made such waste upon us, as to make utterly void to our use any temporal benefit, much less any so much availing to a peaceful and sanctified life, merely for a most incident error, which no wariness can certainly shun. And wherefore serves our happy redemption, and the liberty we have in Christ, but to deliver us from calamitous yokes, not to be lived under without the endangerment of our souls, and to restore us in some competent measure to a right in every good thing both of this life and the other? Thus we see how treatably and distinctly God hath here taught us what the prime ends of marriage are—mutual solace and help. That we are now, upon the most irreprehensible mistake in choosing, defeated and defrauded of all this original benignity, was begun first through the snare of antichristian canons long since obtruded upon the church of Rome, and not yet scoured off by reformation, out of a lingering vainglory that abides among us to make fair shows in formal ordinances, and to enjoin continence and bearing of crosses in such a garb as no scripture binds us, under the thickest arrows of temptation, where we need not stand. Now we shall see with what acknowledgment and assent Adam received this new associate which God brought him.

> Ver. 23. "And Adam said, This is now bone of my bones and flesh of my flesh; she shall be called Woman, because she was taken out of man."

That there was a nearer alliance between Adam and Eve, than could be ever after between man and wife, is visible to any. For no other woman was ever molded out of her husband's rib, but of mere strangers for the most part they come to have that consanguinity, which they have by wedlock. And if we look nearly upon the matter, though marriage be most agreeable to holiness, to purity, and justice, yet is it not a natural, but a civil and ordained relation. For if it were in nature, no law or crime could disannul it, to make a wife or husband otherwise than still a wife or husband, but only death; as nothing but that can make a father no father, or a son no son. But divorce for adultery or desertion, as all our churches agree but England, not only separates, but nullifies, and extinguishes the relation itself of matrimony, so that they are no more man and wife; otherwise the innocent party could not marry elsewhere, without the guilt of adultery. Next, were it merely natural, why was it here ordained more than the rest of moral law to man in his original rectitude, in whose breast all that was natural or moral was engraven without external constitutions and edicts? Adam, therefore, in these words does not establish an indissoluble bond of marriage in the carnal ligaments of flesh and bones; for if he did, it would belong only to himself in the literal sense, every one of us being nearer in flesh of flesh and bone of bones to

our parents than to a wife; they therefore were not to be left for her in that respect. But Adam, who had the wisdom given him to know all creatures, and to name them according to their properties, no doubt but had the gift to discern perfectly that which concerned him much more; and to apprehend at first sight the true fitness of that consort which God provided him. And therefore spake in reference to those words which God pronounced before; as if he had said, "This is she by whose meet help and society I shall no more be alone; this is she who was made my image, even as I the image of God, not so much in body, as in unity of mind and heart." And he might as easily know what were the words of God, as he knew so readily what had been done with his rib while he slept so soundly. He might well know if God took a rib out of his inside to form of it a double good to him, he would far sooner disjoin it from his outside, to prevent a treble mischief to him; and far sooner cut it quite off from all relation for his undoubted ease, than nail it into his body again, to stick for ever there a thorn in his heart. Whenas nature teaches us to divide any limb from the body to the saving of its fellows, though it be the maiming and deformity of the whole; how much more is it her doctrine to sever by incision, not a true limb so much, though that be lawful, but an adherent, a sore, the gangrene of a limb, to the recovery of a whole man? But if in these words we shall make Adam to erect a new establishment of marriage in the mere flesh, which God so lately had instituted, and founded in the sweet and mild familiarity of love and solace and mutual fitness; what do we but use the mouth of our general parent, the first time it opens, to an arrogant opposition and correcting of God's wiser ordinance? These words, therefore, cannot import anything new in marriage, but either that which belongs to Adam only, or to us in reference only to the instituting words of God, which made a meet help against loneliness. Adam spake like Adam the words of flesh and bones, the shell and rind of matrimony; but God spake like God, of love, and solace, and meet help, the soul both of Adam's words and of matrimony.

Ver. 24. "Therefore shall a man leave his father and his mother, and shall cleave unto his wife; and they shall be one flesh."

This verse, as our common heed expounds it, is the great knot-tier, which hath undone by tying, and by tangling, millions of guiltless consciences: this is that grisly porter, who having drawn men, and wisest men, by subtle allurement within the train of an unhappy matrimony, claps the dungeon-gate upon them, as irrecoverable as the grave. But if we view him well, and hear him with not too hasty and prejudicant ears, we shall find no such terror in him. For first it is not here said absolutely without all reasons he shall cleave to his wife, be it to his weal or to his destruction as it happens, but he shall do this upon the premises and considerations of that meet help and society before mentioned. "Therefore he shall cleave to his wife," no otherwise a wife than a fit help. He is not bid to leave the dear cohabitation of his father, mother, brothers, and sisters, to link himself inseparably with the mere carcass of a marriage, perhaps an enemy. This joining particle "Therefore" is in all equity, nay, in all necessity of construction, to comprehend first and most principally what God spake concerning the inward essence of marriage in his institution, that we may learn how far to attend what Adam spake of the outward materials thereof in his approbation. For if we shall bind these words of Adam only to a corporal meaning, and that the force of this injunction upon all us his sons, to live individually with any woman which hath befallen us in the most mistaken wedlock, shall consist not in those moral and relative causes of Eve's creation, but in the mere anatomy of a rib, and that Adam's insight concerning wedlock reached no further, we shall make him as very an idiot as the Socinians make him; which would not be reverently done of us. Let us be content to allow our great forefather so much wisdom, as to take the instituting words of God along with him into this sentence, which if they be well minded, will assure us that flesh and ribs are but of a weak and dead efficacy to keep marriage united where there is no other fitness. The

rib of marriage, to all since Adam, is a relation much rather than a bone; the nerves and sinews thereof are love and meet help, they knit not every couple that marries, and where they knit they seldom break; but where they break, which for the most part is where they never truly joined, to such at the same instant both flesh and rib cease to be in common: so that here they argue nothing to the continuance of a false or violated marriage, but must be led back to receive their meaning from those institutive words of God, which give them all the life and vigor they have.

"Therefore shall a man leave his father," &c.] What to a man's thinking more plain by this appointment, that the fatherly power should give place to conjugal prerogative? Yet it is generally held by reformed writers against the papist, that though in persons at discretion the marriage in itself be never so fit, though it be fully accomplished with benediction, board, and bed, yet the father not consenting, his main will without dispute shall dissolve all. And this they affirm only from collective reason, not any direct law; for that in Exod. xxii. 17, which is most particular, speaks that a father may refuse to marry his daughter to one who hath deflowered her, not that he may take her away from one who hath soberly married her. Yet because the general honor due to parents is great, they hold he may, and perhaps hold not amiss. But again, when the question is of harsh and rugged parents, who defer to bestow their children seasonably, they agree jointly, that the church or magistrate may bestow them, though without the father's consent: and for this they have no express authority in scripture. So that they may see by their own handling of this very place, that it is not the stubborn letter must govern us, but the divine and softening breath of charity, which turns and winds the dictate of every positive command, and shapes it to the good of mankind. Shall the outward accessory of a father's will wanting rend the fittest and most affectionate marriage in twain, after all nuptial consummations; and shall not the want of love, and the privation of all civil and religious concord, which is the inward essence of wedlock, do as much to part those who were never truly wedded? Shall a father have this power to vindicate his own wilful honor and authority to the utter breach of a most dearly united marriage; and shall not a man in his own power have the permission to free his soul, his life, and all his comfort of life from the disaster of a no-marriage? Shall fatherhood, which is but man, for his own pleasure dissolve matrimony; and shall not matrimony, which is God's ordinance, for its own honor and better conservation dissolve itself when it is wrong, and not fitted to any of the chief ends which it owes us?

"And they shall be one flesh."] These words also infer that there ought to be an individuality in marriage; but without all question presuppose the joining causes. Not a rule yet that we have met with, so universal in this whole institution, but hath admitted limitations and conditions, according to human necessity. The very foundation of matrimony, though God laid it so deliberately, "that is not good for man to be alone," holds not always, if the apostle can secure us. Soon after we are bid leave father and mother, and cleave to a wife, but must understand the father's consent withal, else not. "Cleave to a wife," but let her be a wife, let her be a meet help, a solace, not a nothing, not an adversary, not a desertrice: can any law or command be so unreasonable as to make men cleave to calamity, to ruin, to perdition? In like manner here, "They shall be one flesh;" but let the causes hold, and be made really good which only have the possibility to make them one flesh. We know that flesh can neither join nor keep together two bodies of itself; what is it then must make them one flesh, but likeness, but fitness of mind and disposition, which may breed the spirit of concord and union between them? If that be not in the nature of either, and that there has been a remediless mistake, as vain we go about to compel them into one flesh, as if we undertook to weave a garment of dry sand. It were more easy to compel the vegetable and nutritive power of nature to assimilations and mixtures, which are not alterable each by other; or force the concoctive stomach to turn that into flesh, which is so totally unlike that substance, as not to be wrought on. For as the unity of mind is nearer and greater than the union of bodies, so doubtless is the dissimilitude greater and more dividual, as that which makes between bodies all difference and distinction. Especially whenas besides the singular and substantial differences of every soul, there is an intimate quality of good or evil, through the whole progeny of Adam, which, like a radical heat or mortal chillness, joins them, or disjoins them irresistibly. In whom therefore either the will or the faculty is found to have never joined, or now not to continue so, it is not to say, they shall be one flesh, for they cannot be one flesh. God commands not impossibilities; and all the ecclesiastical glue that liturgy or laymen can compound, is not able to solder up two such incongruous natures into the one flesh of a true beseeming marriage. Why did Moses then set down their uniting into one flesh? And I again ask, why the gospel so oft repeats the eating of our Saviour's flesh, the drinking of his blood? "That we are one body with him, the members of his body, flesh of his flesh, and bone of his bone," Ephes. v. Yet lest we should be Capernaitans, as we are told there, that the flesh profiteth nothing; so we are told here, if we be not as deaf as adders, that this union of the flesh proceeds from the union of a fit help and solace. We know that there was never a more spiritual mystery than this gospel taught us under the terms of body and flesh; yet nothing less intended than that we should stick there. What a stupidness then is it, that in marriage, which is the nearest resemblance of our union with Christ, we should deject ourselves to such a sluggish and underfoot philosophy, as to esteem the validity of marriage merely by the flesh, though never so broken and disjointed from love and peace, which only can give a human qualification to that act of the flesh, and distinguish it from bestial! The text therefore uses this phrase, that "they shall be one flesh," to justify and make legitimate the rites of marriage-bed; which was not unneedful, if for all this warrant they were suspected of pollution by some sects of philosophy, and religions of old, and latelier among the papists, and other heretics elder than they. Some think there is a high mystery in those words, from that which Paul saith of them, Ephes. v. "This is a great mystery, but I speak of Christ and the church:" and thence they would conclude marriage to ·be inseparable. For me, I dispute not now whether matrimony be a mystery or no: if it be of Christ and his church, certainly it is not meant of every ungodly and miswedded marriage; but then only mysterious, when it is a holy, happy, and peaceful match. But when a saint is joined with a reprobate, or both alike wicked with wicked, fool with fool, a he-drunkard with a she; when the bed hath been nothing else for twenty years or more, but an old haunt of lust and malice mixed together, no love, no goodness, no loyalty, but counterplotting, and secret wishing one another's dissolution; this is to me the greatest mystery in the world, if such a marriage as this can be the mystery of aught, unless it be the mystery of iniquity: according to that which Paræus cities out of Chrysostom, that a bad wife is a help for the devil, and the like may be said of a bad husband. Since therefore none but a fit and pious matrimony can signify the union of Christ and his church, there cannot hence be any hindrance of divorce to that wedlock wherein there can be no good mystery. Rather it might to a Christian conscience be matter of finding itself so much less satisfied than before, in the continuance of an unhappy yoke, wherein there can be no representation either of Christ or of his church.

Thus having inquired the institution how it was in the beginning, both from the first chap. of Gen., where it was only mentioned in part, and from the second, where it was plainly and evidently instituted, and having attended each clause and word necessary with a diligence not drowsy, we shall now fix with some advantage, and by a short view backward gather up the ground we have gone, and sum up the strength we have into one argumentative head, with that organic force that logic proffers us. All arts acknowledge, that then only we know certainly, when we can define; for definition is that which refines the pure essence of things from the circumstance. If therefore we can attain in this our controversy to define exactly what marriage is, we shall soon learn when there is a nullity thereof, and when a divorce.

The part therefore of this chapter, which hath been here treated, doth orderly and readily resolve itself into a definition of marriage, and a consectary from thence. To the definition these words chiefly contribute, "It is not good," &c. "I will make," &c. Where the consectary begins this connexion, "Therefore," informs us, "Therefore shall a man," &c. Definition is decreed by logicians to consist only of causes constituting the essence of a thing. What is not therefore among the causes constituting marriage, must not stay in the definition. Those causes are concluded to be matter, and, as the artist calls it, Form. But inasmuch as the same thing may be a cause more ways than one, and that in relations and institutions which have no corporal subsistence, but only a respective being, the Form, by which the thing is what it is, is oft so slender and undistinguishable, that it would soon confuse, were it not sustained by the efficient and final causes, which concur to make up the form, invalid otherwise of itself, it will be needful to take in all the four causes into the definition. First therefore the material cause of matrimony is man and woman; the author and efficient, God and their consent; the internal Form and soul of this relation is conjugal love arising from a mutual fitness to the final causes of wedlock, help and society in religious, civil, and domestic conversation, which includes as an inferior end the fulfilling of natural desire, and specifical increase: these are the final causes both moving the Efficient, and perfecting the Form. And although copulation be considered among the ends of marriage, yet the act thereof in a right esteem can no longer be matrimonial, than it is an effect of conjugal love. When love finds itself utterly unmatched, and justly vanishes, nay, rather, cannot but vanish, the fleshly act indeed may continue, but not holy, not pure, not beseeming the sacred bond of marriage; being at best but an animal excretion, but more truly worse and more ignoble than that mute kindliness among the herds and flocks: in that proceeding as it ought from intellective principles, it participates of nothing rational, but that which the field and the fold equals. For in human actions the soul is the agent, the body in a manner passive. If then the body do out of sensitive force what the soul complies not with, how can man, and not rather something beneath man, be thought the doer?

But to proceed in the pursuit of an accurate definition, it will avail us something, and whet our thoughts, to examine what fabric hereof others have already reared. Paræus on Gen. defines marriage to be "an indissoluble conjunction of one man and one woman to an individual and intimate conversation and mutual benevolence," &c. Wherein is to be marked his placing of intimate conversation before bodily benevolence; for bodily is meant, though indeed "benevolence" rather sounds will than body. Why then shall divorce be granted for want of bodily performance, and not for want of fitness to intimate conversation, whenas corporal benevolence cannot in any human fashion be without this? Thus his definition places the ends of marriage in one order, and esteems them in another. His tautology also of indissoluble and individual is not to be imitated; especially since neither indissoluble nor individual hath aught to do in the exact definition, being but a consectary flowing from thence, as appears by plain scripture, "Therefore shall a man leave," &c. For marriage is not true marriage by being individual, but therefore individual, if it be true marriage. No argument but causes enter the definition: a consectary is but the effect of those causes. Besides, that marriage is indissoluble, is not catholicly true; we know it dissoluble for adultery and for desertion by the verdict of all reformed churches. Dr. Ames defines it "an individual conjunction of one man and one woman, to communion of body and mutual society of life;" but this perverts the order of God, who in the institution places meet help and society of life before communion of body. And vulgar estimation undervalues beyond comparison all society of life and communion of mind beneath the communion of body; granting no divorce, but to the want, or miscommunicating of that. Hemingius, an approved author, Melancthon's scholar, and who, next to Bucer and Erasmus, writes of divorce most like a divine, thus comprises, "Marriage is a conjunction of one man and one woman, lawfully consenting, into one flesh, for mutual help's sake, ordained of God." And in his explanation stands punctually upon the conditions of consent, that it be not in any main matter deluded, as being the life of wedlock, and no true marriage without a true consent. "Into one flesh" he expounds into one mind, as well as one body, and makes it the formal cause: herein only missing, while he puts the effect into his definition instead of the cause which the text affords him. For "one flesh" is not the formal essence of wedlock, but one end, or one effect of "a meet help:" the end ofttimes being the effect and fruit of the form, as logic teaches; else many aged and holy matrimonies, and more eminently that of Joseph and Mary, would be no true marriage. And that maxim, generally received, would be false, that "consent alone, though copulation never follow, makes the marriage." Therefore to consent lawfully into one flesh, is not the formal cause of matrimony, but only one of the effects. The civil lawyers, and first Justinian or Tribonian, defines matrimony a "conjunction of man and woman containing individual accustom of life." Wherein, first, individual is not so bad as indissoluble put in by others: and although much cavil might be made in the distinguishing between indivisible and individual, yet the one taken for possible, the other for actual, neither the one nor the other can belong to the essence of marriage; especially when a civilian defines, by which law marriage is actually divorced for many causes, and with good leave, by mutual consent. Therefore where "conjunction" is said, they who comment the Institutes agree, that conjunction of mind is by the law meant, not necessarily conjunction of body. That law then had good reason attending to its own definition, that divorce should be granted for the breaking of that conjunction which it holds necessary, sooner than for the want of that conjunction which it holds not necessary. And whereas Tuningus, a famous lawyer, excuses individual as the purpose of marriage, not always the success, it suffices not. Purpose is not able to constitute the essence of a thing. Nature herself, the universal mother, intends nothing but her own perfection and preservation; yet is not the more indissoluble for that. The Pandects out of Modestinus, though not define, yet well describe marriage "the conjunction of male and female, the society of all life, the communion of divine and human right:" which Bucer also imitates on the [10] fifth to the Ephesians. But it seems rather to comprehend the several ends of marriage than to contain the more constituting cause that makes it what it is.

That I therefore among others (for who sings not Hylas?) may give as well as take matter to be judged on, it will be looked I should produce another definition than these which have not stood the trial. Thus then I suppose that marriage by the natural and [20] plain order of God's institution in the text may be more demonstratively and essentially defined: "Marriage is a divine institution, joining man and woman in a love fitly disposed to the helps and comforts of domestic life." "A divine institution." This contains the prime efficient cause of marriage: as for consent of parents and guardians, it seems rather a concurrence than a cause; for as many that marry are in their own power as [30] not; and where they are not their own, yet are they not subjected beyond reason. Now though efficient causes are not requisite in a definition, yet divine institution hath such influence upon the Form, and is so a conserving cause of it, that without it the Form is not sufficient to distinguish matrimony from other conjunctions of male and female, which are not to be counted marriage. "Joining man and woman in a love," &c. This [40] brings in the parties' consent; until which be, the marriage hath no true being. When I say "consent," I mean not error, for error is not properly consent: and why should not consent be here understood with equity and good to either part, as in all other friendly covenants, and not be strained and cruelly urged to the mischief and destruction of both? Neither do I mean that singular act of consent which made the contract, for [50] that may remain, and yet the marriage not true nor lawful; and that may cease, and yet the marriage both true and lawful, to their

sin that break it. So that either as no efficient at all, or but a transitory, it comes not into the definition. That consent I mean, which is a love fitly disposed to mutual help and comfort of life: this is that happy form of marriage naturally arising from the very heart of divine institution in the text, in all the former definitions either obscurely, and under mistaken terms expressed, or not at [10] all. This gives marriage all her due, all her benefits, all her being, all her distinct and proper being. This makes a marriage not a bondage, a blessing not a curse, a gift of God not a snare. Unless there be a love, and that love born of fitness, how can it last? Unless it last, how can the best and sweetest purpose of marriage be attained? And they not attained, which are the chief ends, and with a lawful love constitute the formal [20] cause itself of marriage, how can the essence thereof subsist? How can it be indeed what it goes for? Conclude therefore by all the power of reason, that where this essence of marriage is not, there can be no true marriage; and the parties, either one of them or both, are free, and without fault, rather by a nullity than by a divorce, may betake them to a second choice, if their present condition be not tolerable to them. If any shall [30] ask, why, "domestic" in the definition? I answer, that because both in the scriptures, and in the gravest poets and philosophers, I find the properties and excellencies of a wife set out only from domestic virtues; if they extend further, it diffuses them into the notion of some more common duty than matrimonial.

Thus far of the definition. The consectary which flows from thence, and altogether depends thereon, is manifestly brought in by [40] this connexive particle "therefore;" and branches itself into a double consequence: First, individual society: "Therefore shall a man leave father and mother." Secondly, conjugal benevolence: "And they shall be one flesh." Which, as was shown, is not without cause here mentioned, to prevent and to abolish the suspect of pollution in that natural and undefiled act. These consequences therefore cannot either in religion, [50] law, or reason, be bound, and posted upon mankind to his sorrow and misery, but receive what force they have from the meet-ness of help and solace, which is the formal cause and end of that definition that sustains them. And although it be not for the majesty of scripture, to humble herself in artificial theorems, and definitions, and corollaries, like a professor in the schools, but looks to be analysed, and interpreted by the logical industry of her disciples and followers, and to be reduced by them, as oft as need is, into those sciential rules which are the implements of instruction; yet Moses, as if foreseeing the miserable work that man's ignorance and pusillanimity would make in this matrimonious business, and endeavoring his utmost to prevent it, condescends in this place to such a methodical and school-like way of defining and consequencing, as in no place of the whole law more.

Thus we have seen, and, if we be not contentious, may know what was marriage in the beginning, to which in the gospel we are referred; and what from hence to judge of nullity, or divorce. Here I esteem the work done; in this field the controversy decided; but because other places of scripture seem to look aversely upon this our decision, (although indeed they keep all harmony with it,) and because it is a better work to reconcile the seeming diversities of scripture, than the real dissensions of nearest friends; I shall assay in three following discourses to perform that office.

Deut. xxiv. 1, 2.

1. "When a man hath taken a wife, and married her, and it come to pass that she find no favor in his eyes, because he hath found some uncleanness in her, then let him write her a bill of divorcement, and give it in her hand, and send her out of his house.
2. "And when she is departed out of his house, she may go and be another man's wife."

That which is the only discommodity of speaking in a clear matter, the abundance of argument that presses to be uttered, and the suspense of judgment what to choose, and how in the multitude of reason to be not tedious, is the greatest difficulty which I expect here to meet with. Yet much hath been said formerly concerning this law in "the Doctrine of Divorce." Whereof I shall repeat no more than what is necessary. Two things are here doubted: First, and that but of late, whether this be a law or no; next, what this reason of "uncleanness" might mean, for which the law is granted. That it is a plain law no man ever questioned, till Vatablus within these hundred years professed Hebrew at Paris, a man of no religion, as Beza deciphers him. Yet some there be who follow him, not only against the current of all antiquity, both Jewish and Christian, but the evidence of scripture also, Malachi ii. 16, "Let him who hateth put away, saith the Lord God of Israel." Although this place also hath been tampered with, as if it were to be thus rendered, "The Lord God saith, that he hateth putting away." But this new interpretation rests only in the authority of Junius: for neither Calvin, nor Vatablus himself, nor any other known divine so interpreted before. And they of best note who have translated the scripture since, and Diodati for one, follow not his reading. And perhaps they might reject it, if for nothing else, for these two reasons: first, it introduces in a new manner the person of God speaking less majestic than he is ever wont: when God speaks by his prophet, he ever speaks in the first person, thereby signifying his majesty and omnipresence. He would have said, "I hate putting away, saith the Lord;" and not sent word by Malachi in a sudden fallen style," "The Lord God saith, that he hateth putting away:" that were a phrase to shrink the glorious omnipresence of God speaking, into a kind of circumscriptive absence. And were as if a herald, in the achievement of a king, should commit the indecorum to set his helmet sideways and close, not full-faced and open in the posture of direction and command. We cannot think therefore that this last prophet would thus in a new fashion absent the person of God from his own words, as if he came not along with them. For it would also be wide from the proper scope of this place; he that reads attentively will soon perceive, that God blames not here the Jews for putting away their wives, but for keeping strange concubines, to the "profaning of Juda's holiness," and the vexation of their Hebrew wives, ver. 11 and 14, "Judah hath married the daughter of a strange god:" and exhorts them rather to put their wives away whom they hate, as the law permitted, than to keep them under such affronts. And it is received, that this prophet lived in those times of Ezra and Nehemiah, (nay, by some is thought to be Ezra himself,) when the people were forced by these two worthies to put their strange wives away. So that what the story of those times, and the plain context of the eleventh verse, from whence this rebuke begins, can give us to conjecture of the obscure and curt Ebraisms that follow; this prophet does not forbid putting away, but forbids keeping, and commands putting away according to God's law, which is the plainest interpreter both of what God will and what he can best suffer. Thus much evinces, that God there commanded divorce by Malachi; and this confirms, that he commands it also here by Moses.

I may the less doubt to mention by the way an author, though counted apocryphal, yet of no small account for piety and wisdom, the author of Ecclesiasticus. Which book begun by the grandfather of that Jesus, who is called the son of Sirach, might have been written in part, not much after the time when Malachi lived; if we compute by the reign of Ptolemæus Euergetes. It professes to explain the law and the prophets; and yet exhorts us to divorce for incurable causes, and to cut off from the flesh those whom it there describes, Ecclesiastic. xxv. 26. Which doubtless that wise and ancient writer would never have advised, had either Malachi so lately forbidden it, or the law by a full precept not left it lawful. But I urge not this for want of better proof; our Saviour himself allows divorce to be a command, Mark x. 3, 5. Neither do they weaken this assertion, who say it was only a sufferance, as shall be proved at large in that place of Matthew. But suppose it were not a written law, they never can deny it was a custom, and so effect nothing. For the same reasons that induce them why it should not be a law will straiten them as hard why it should be allowed a custom. All custom is either evil or not evil; if it be evil, this is the very end of lawgiving, to abolish evil customs by

wholesome laws; unless we imagine Moses weaker than every negligent and startling politician. If it be, as they make this of divorce to be, a custom against nature, against justice, against chastity, how, upon this most impure custom tolerated, could the God of pureness erect a nice and precise law, that the wife married after divorce could not return to her former husband, as being defiled? What was all this following niceness worth, built upon the lewd foundation of a wicked thing allowed? In few words then, this custom of divorce either was allowable, or not allowable: if not allowable, how could it be allowed? if it were allowable, all who understand law will consent that a tolerated custom hath the force of a law, and is indeed no other but an unwritten law, as Justinian calls it, and is as prevalent as any written statute. So that their shift of turning this law into a custom wheels about, and gives the onset upon their own flanks; not disproving, but concluding it to be the more firm law, because it was without controversy a granted custom; as clear in the reason of common life, as those given rules whereon Euclid builds his propositions.

Thus being every way a law of God, who can without blasphemy doubt it to be a just and pure law? Moses continually disavows the giving them any statute, or judgment, but what he learnt of God; of whom also in his song he saith, Deut. xxxii., "He is the rock, his work is perfect, all his ways are judgment, a God of truth and without iniquity, just and right is he." And David testifies, the judgments of the Lord "are true and righteous altogether." Not partly right and partly wrong, much less wrong altogether, as divines of now-a-days dare censure them. Moses again, of that people to whom he gave this law, saith, Deut. xiv., "Ye are the children of the Lord your God, the Lord hath chosen thee to be a peculiar people to himself above all the nations upon the earth, that thou shouldst keep all his commandments, and be high in praise, in name, and in honor, holy to the Lord!" chap. xxvi. And in the fourth, "Behold, I have taught you statutes and judgments, even as the Lord my God commanded me: keep therefore and do them. For this is your wisdom and your understanding in the sight of nations that shall hear all these statutes, and say, Surely this great nation is a wise and understanding people. For what nation is there so great, who hath God so nigh to them? and what nation that hath statutes and judgments so righteous as all this law which I set before you this day?" Thus whether we look at the purity and justice of God himself, the jealousy of his honor among other nations, the holiness and moral perfection which he intended by his law to teach this people, we cannot possibly think how he could endure to let them slug and grow inveterately wicked, under base allowances, and whole adulterous lives by dispensation. They might not eat, they might not touch an unclean thing; to what hypocrisy then were they trained up, if by prescription of the same law, they might be unjust, they might be adulterous for term of life? forbid to soil their garments with a coy imaginary pollution, but not forbid, but countenanced and animated by law, to soil their souls with deepest defilements. What more unlike to God, what more like that God should hate, than that his law should be so curious to wash vessels and vestures, and so careless to leave unwashed, unregarded, so foul a scab of Egypt in their souls? What would we more? The statutes of the Lord are all pure and just: and if all, then this of divorce.

"Because he hath found some uncleanness in her."] That we may not esteem this law to be a mere authorizing of licence, as the pharisees took it, Moses adds the reason: for "some uncleanness found." Some heretofore have been so ignorant, as to have thought that this uncleanness means adultery. But Erasmus, who, for having writ an excellent treatise of divorce, was wrote against by some burly standard divine, perhaps of Cullen, or of Lovain, who calls himself Phimostomus, shows learnedly out of the fathers, with other testimonies and reasons, that uncleanness is not here so understood; defends his former work, though new to that age, and perhaps counted licentious, and fears not to engage all his fame on the argument. Afterward, when expositors began to understand the Hebrew text, which they had not done of many ages before, they translated word for word not "uncleanness," but "the nakedness of anything;" and considering that nakedness is usually referred in scripture to the mind as well as to the body, they constantly expound it any defect, annoyance, or ill quality in nature, which to be joined with, makes life tedious, and such company worse than solitude. So that here will be no cause to vary from the general consent of exposition, which gives us freely that God permitted divorce, for whatever was unalterably distasteful, whether in body or mind. But with this admonishment, that if the Roman law, especially in contracts and doweries, left many things to equity with these cautions, "ex fide bona, quod æquius melius erit, ut inter bonos bene agier;" we will not grudge to think, that God intended not licence here to every humor, but to such remediless grievances as might move a good and honest and faithful man then to divorce, when it can no more be peace or comfort to either of them continuing thus joined. And although it could not be avoided, but that men of hard hearts would abuse this liberty, yet doubtless it was intended, as all other privileges in law are, to good men principally, to bad only by accident. So that the sin was not in the permission, nor simply in the action of divorce, (for then the permitting also had been sin,) but only in the abuse. But that this law should, as it were, be wrung from God and Moses, only to serve the hardheartedness and the lust of injurious men, how remote it is from all sense, and law, and honesty, and therefore surely from the meaning of Christ, shall abundantly be manifest in due order.

Now although Moses needed not to add other reason of this law than that one there expressed, yet to these ages wherein canons, and Scotisms, and Lombard laws, have dulled, and almost obliterated the lively sculpture of ancient reason and humanity; it will be requisite to heap reason upon reason, and all little enough to vindicate the whiteness and the innocence of this divine law, from the calumny it finds at this day, of being a door to licence and confusion. Whenas indeed there is not a judicial point in all Moses, consisting of more true equity, high wisdom, and godlike pity than this law; not derogating, but preserving the honor and peace of marriage, and exactly agreeing with the sense and mind of that institution in Genesis.

For, first, if marriage be but an ordained relation, as it seems not more, it cannot take place above the prime dictates of nature: and if it be of natural right, yet it must yield to that which is more natural, and before it by eldership and precedence in nature. Now it is not natural, that Hugh marries Beatrice, or Thomas, Rebecca, being only a civil contract, and full of many chances; but that these men seek them meet helps, that only is natural; and that they espouse them such, that only is marriage. But if they find them neither fit helps nor tolerable society, what thing more natural, more original, and first in nature, than to depart from that which is irksome, grievous, actively hateful, and injurious even to hostility, especially in a conjugal respect, wherein antipathies are invincible, and where the forced abiding of the one can be no true good, no real comfort to the other? For if he find no contentment from the other, how can he return it from himself? or no acceptance, how can he mutually accept? What more equal, more pious, than to untie a civil knot for a natural enmity held by violence from parting, to dissolve an accidental conjunction of this or that man and woman, for the most natural and most necessary disagreement of meet from unmeet, guilty from guiltless, contrary from contrary? It being certain, that the mystical and blessed unity of marriage can be no way more unhallowed and profaned, than by the forcible uniting of such disunions and separations. Which if we see ofttimes they cannot join or piece up to a common friendship, or to a willing conversation in the same house, how should they possibly agree to the most familiar and united amity of wedlock? Abraham and Lot, though dear friends and brethren in a strange country, chose rather to part asunder, than to infect their friendship with the strife of their servants: Paul and Barnabas, joined together by the Holy Ghost to a spiritual work, thought it better to separate, when once they grew at variance. If these great saints, joined by nature, friendship, religion, high providence, and revelation, could not so govern a casual difference, a sudden passion,

but must in wisdom divide from the outward duties of a friendship, or a colleagueship in the same family, or in the same journey, lest it should grow to a worse division; can anything be more absurd and barbarous, than that they whom only error, casualty, art, or plot, hath joined, should be compelled, not against a sudden passion, but against the permanent and radical discords of nature, to the most intimate and incorporating duties of love and embracement, therein only rational and human, as they are free and voluntary; being else an abject and servile yoke, scarce not brutish? and that there is in man such a peculiar sway of liking or disliking in the affairs of matrimony, is evidently seen before marriage among those who can be friendly, can respect each other, yet to marry each other would not for any persuasion. If then this unfitness and disparity be not till after marriage discovered, through many causes, and colors, and concealments, that may overshadow; undoubtedly it will produce the same effects, and perhaps with more vehemence, that such a mistaken pair would give the world to be unmarried again. And their condition Solomon to the plain justification of divorce expresses, Prov. xxx. 21, 23, where he tells us of his own accord, that a "hated, or a hateful woman, when she is married, is a thing for which the earth is disquieted, and cannot bear it;" thus giving divine testimony to this divine law, which bids us nothing more than is the first and most innocent lesson of nature, to turn away peaceably from what afflicts and hazards our destruction; especially when our staying can do no good, and is exposed to all evil.

Secondly, It is unjust that any ordinance, ordained to the good and comfort of man, where that end is missing, without his fault, should be forced upon him to an unsufferable misery and discomfort, if not commonly ruin. All ordinances are established in their end; the end of law is the virtue, is the righteousness of law: and therefore him we count an ill expounder, who urges law against the intention thereof. The general end of every ordinance, of every severest, every divinest, even of sabbath, is the good of man; yea, his temporal good not excluded. But marriage is one of the benignest ordinances of God to man, whereof both the general and particular end is the peace and contentment of man's mind, as the institution declares. Contentment of body they grant, which if it be defrauded, the plea of frigidity shall divorce: but here lies the fathomless absurdity, that granting this for bodily defect, they will not grant it for any defect of the mind, any violation of religious or civil society. Whenas, if the argument of Christ be firm against the ruler of the synagogue, Luke xiii., "Thou hypocrite, doth not each of you on the sabbath-day loosen his ox or his ass from the stall, and lead him to watering? and should not I unbind a daughter of Abraham from this bond of Satan?" it stands as good here; ye have regard in marriage to the grievance of body, should you not regard more the grievances of the mind, seeing the soul as much excels the body, as the outward man excels the ass, and more? for that animal is yet a living creature, perfect in itself; but the body without the soul is a mere senseless trunk. No ordinance therefore, given particularly to the good both spiritual and temporal of man, can be urged upon him to his mischief; and if they yield this to the unworthier part, the body, whereabout are they in their principles, that they yield it not to the more worthy, the mind of a good man?

Thirdly, As no ordinance, so no covenant, no, not between God and man, much less between man and man, being, as all are, intended to the good of both parties, can hold to the deluding or making miserable of them both. For equity is understood in every covenant, even between enemies, though the terms be not expressed. If equity therefore made it, extremity may dissolve it. But marriage, they used to say, is the covenant of God. Undoubted: and so is any covenant frequently called in scripture, wherein God is called to witness: the covenant of friendship between David and Jonathan is called "the covenant of the Lord," 1 Sam. xx. The covenant of Zedekiah with the king of Babel, a covenant to be doubted whether lawful or no, yet, in respect of God invoked thereto, is called "the oath, and the covenant of God," Ezek. xvii. Marriage also is called "the covenant of God," Prov. ii. 17. Why, but, as before, because God is the witness thereof? Mal. ii. 14. So that this denomination adds nothing to the covenant of marriage above any other civil and solemn contract: nor is it more indissoluble for this reason than any other against the end of its own ordination; nor is any vow or oath to God exacted with such a rigor, where superstition reigns not. For look how much divine the covenant is, so much the more equal, so much the more to be expected that every article thereof should be fairly made good; no false dealing or unperforming should be thrust upon men without redress, if the covenant be so divine. But faith, they say, must be kept in covenant, though to our damage. I answer, that only holds true, where the other side performs; which failing, he is no longer bound. Again, this is true, when the keeping of faith can be of any use or benefit to the other. But in marriage, a league of love and willingness, if faith be not willingly kept, it scarce is worth the keeping; nor can be any delight to a generous mind, with whom it is forcibly kept: and the question still supposes the one brought to an impossibility of keeping it as he ought, by the other's default; and to keep it formally, not only with a thousand shifts and dissimulations, but with open anguish, perpetual sadness and disturbance, no willingness, no cheerfulness, no contentment, cannot be any good to a mind not basely poor and shallow, with whom the contract of love is so kept. A covenant therefore brought to that pass, is on the unfaulty side without injury dissolved.

Fourthly, The law is not to neglect men under greatest sufferances, but to see covenants of greatest moment faithfullest performed. And what injury comparable to that sustained in a frustrate and false-dealing marriage, to lose, for another's fault against him, the best portion of his temporal comforts, and of his spiritual too, as it may fall out? It was the law that for man's good and quiet reduced things to propriety, which were at first in common: how much more lawlike were it to assist nature in disappropriating that evil, which by continuing proper becomes destructive? But he might have bewared. So he might in any other covenant, wherein the law does not constrain error to so dear a forfeit. And yet in these matters wherein the wisest are apt to err, all the wariness that can be ofttimes nothing avails. But the law can compel the offending party to be more duteous. Yes, if all these kind of offences were fit in public to be complained on, or being compelled were any satisfaction to a mate not sottish, or malicious. And these injuries work so vehemently, that if the law remedy them not, by separating the cause when no way else will pacify, the person not relieved betakes him either to such disorderly courses, or to such a dull dejection, as renders him either infamous, or useless to the service of God and his country. Which the law ought to prevent as a thing pernicious to the commonwealth: and what better prevention than this which Moses used?

Fifthly, The law is to tender the liberty and the human dignity of them that live under the law, whether it be the man's right above the woman or the woman's just appeal against wrong and servitude. But the duties of marriage contain in them a duty of benevolence, which to do by compulsion against the soul, where there can be neither peace, nor joy, nor love, but an enthralment to one who either cannot or will not be mutual in the godliest and the civilest ends of that society, is the ignoblest and the lowest slavery that a human shape can be put to. This law therefore justly and piously provides against such an unmanly task of bondage as this. The civil law, though it favored the setting free of a slave, yet if he proved ungrateful to his patron, reduced him to a servile condition. If that law did well to reduce from liberty to bondage for an ingratitude not the greatest, much more became it the law of God, to enact the restorement of a freeborn man from an unpurposed and unworthy bondage to a rightful liberty, for the most unnatural fraud and ingratitude that can be committed against him. And if that civilian emperor, in his title of "Donations," permit the giver to recall his gift from him who proves unthankful towards him; yea, though he had subscribed and signed in the deed of his gift not to recall it, though for this very cause of ingratitude; with much more equity doth Moses permit here the giver to recall no petty gift, but the gift of himself, from one who most injuriously and deceitfully uses him against the main ends and conditions of his giving himself, expressed in God's institution.

Sixthly, Although there be nothing in the plain words of this law, that seems to regard the afflictions of a wife, how great soever; yet expositors determine, and doubtless determine rightly, that God was not uncompassionate of them also in the framing of this law. For should the rescript of Antoninus in the civil law give release to servants flying for refuge to the emperor's statute, by giving leave to change their cruel masters; and should God, who in his law also is good to injured servants, by granting them their freedom in divers cases, not consider the wrongs and miseries of a wife, which is no servant? Though herein the countersense of our divines to me, I must confess, seems admirable; who teach that God gave this as a merciful law, not for man whom he here names, and to whom by name he gives this power; but for the wife, whom he names not, and to whom by name he gives no power at all. For certainly if man be liable to injuries in marriage, as well as woman, and man be the worthier person, it were a preposterous law to respect only the less worthy; her whom God made for marriage, and not him at all for whom marriage was made.

Seventhly, The law of marriage gives place to the power of parents; for we hold, that consent of parents not had may break the wedlock, though else accomplished. It gives place to masterly power, for the master might take away from a Hebrew servant the wife which he gave him, Exod. xxi. If it be answered, that the marriage of servants is no matrimony; it is replied, that this in the ancient Roman law is true, not in the Mosaic. If it be added, she was a stranger, not a Hebrew, therefore easily divorced; it will be answered, that strangers not being Canaanites, and they also being converts, might be lawfully married, as Rahab was. And her conversion is here supposed; for a Hebrew master could not lawfully give a heathen wife to a Hebrew servant. However, the divorcing of an Israelitish woman was as easy by the law, as the divorcing of a stranger, and almost in the same words permitted, Deut. xxiv. and Deut. xxi. Lastly, it gives place to the right of war; for a captive woman lawfully married, and afterwards not beloved, might be dismissed, only without ransom, Deut. xxi. If marriage may be dissolved by so many exterior powers, not superior, as we think, why may not the power of marriage itself, for its own peace and honor, dissolve itself, where the persons wedded be free persons? Why may not a greater and more natural power complaining dissolve marriage? For the ends, why matrimony was ordained, are certainly and by all logic above the ordinance itself; why may not that dissolve marriage, without which that institution hath no force at all? For the prime ends of marriage are the whole strength 10 and validity thereof, without which matrimony is like an idol, nothing in the world. But those former allowances were all for hardness of heart. Be that granted, until we come where to understand it better: if the law suffer thus far the obstinacy of a bad man, is it not more righteous here, to do willingly what is but equal, to remove in season the extremities of a good man?

Eighthly, If a man had deflowered a virgin, 20 or brought an ill name on his wife, that she came not a virgin to him, he was amerced in certain shekels of silver, and bound never to divorce her all his days, Deut. xxii.; which shows that the law gave no liberty to divorce, where the injury was palpable; and that the absolute forbidding to divorce was in part the punishment of a deflowerer, and a defamer. Yet not so but that the wife questionless might depart when she pleased. Other- 30 wise this course had not so much righted her, as delivered her up to more spite and cruel usage. This law, therefore, doth justly distinguish the privilege of an honest and blameless man in the matter of divorce, from the punishment of a notorious offender.

Ninthly, suppose it might be imputed to a man, that he was too rash in his choice, and why took he not better heed, let him now smart, and bear his folly as he may; al- 40 though the law of God, that terrible law, do not thus upbraid the infirmities and unwilling mistakes of man in his integrity: but suppose these and the like proud aggravations of some stern hypocrite, more merciless in his mercies, than any literal law in the vigor of severity, must be patiently heard; yet all law, and God's law especially, grants everywhere to error easy remitments, even where the utmost penalty exacted were no undoing. 50 With great reason therefore and mercy doth it here not torment an error, if it be so, with the endurance of a whole life lost to all

household comfort and society, a punishment of too vast and huge dimension for an error, and the more unreasonable for that the like objection may be opposed against the plea of divorcing for adultery: he might have looked better before to her breeding under religious parents: why did he not then more diligently inquire into her manners, into what company she kept? every glance of her eye, every step of her gait, would have prophesied adultery, if the quick scent of these discerners had been took along; they had the divination to have foretold you all this, as they have now the divinity to punish an error inhumanly. As good reason to be content, and forced to be content with your adulteress, if these objectors might be the judges of human frailty. But God, more mild and good to man, than man to his brother, in all this liberty given to divorcement, mentions not a word of our past errors and mistakes, if any were; which these men objecting from their own inventions prosecute with all violence and iniquity. For if the one be to look so narrowly what he takes, at the peril of ever keeping, why should not the other be made as wary what is promised, by the peril of losing? for without those promises the treaty of marriage had not proceeded. Why should his own error bind him, rather than the other's fraud acquit him? Let the buyer beware, saith the old law-beaten termer. Belike then there is no more honesty, nor ingenuity in the bargain of a wedlock, than in the buying of a colt: we must, it seems, drive it on as craftily with those whose affinity we seek, as if they were a pack of sale men and complotters. But the deceiver deceives himself in the unprosperous marriage, and therein is sufficiently punished. I answer, that the most of those who deceive are such as either understand not, or value not the true purposes of marriage; they have the prey they seek, not the punishment: yet say it prove to them some cross, it is not equal that error and fraud should be linked in the same degree of forfeiture, but rather that error should be acquitted, and fraud bereaved his morsel, if the mistake were not on both sides; for then on both sides the acquitment will be reasonable, if the bondage be intolerable; which this law graciously determines, not unmindful of the wife, as was granted willingly to the common expositors, though beyond the letter of this law, yet not beyond the spirit of charity.

Tenthly, Marriage is a solemn thing, some say a holy, the resemblance of Christ and his church; and so, indeed, it is where the persons are truly religious; and we know all sacred things, not performed sincerely as they ought, are no way acceptable to God in their outward formality. And that wherein it differs from personal duties, if they be not truly done, the fault is in ourselves; but marriage to be a true and pious marriage is not in the single power of any person; the essence whereof, as of all other covenants, is in relation to another, the making and maintaining causes thereof are all mutual, and must be a communion of spiritual and temporal comforts. If, then, either of them cannot, or obstinately will not, be answerable in these duties, so as that the other can have no peaceful living, or enduring the want of what he justly seeks, and sees no hope, then straight from that dwelling, love, which is the soul of wedlock, takes his flight, leaving only some cold performances of civil and common respects; but the true bond of marriage, if there were ever any there, is already burst like a rotten thread. Then follows dissimulation, suspicion, false colors, false pretences, and, worse than these, disturbance, annoyance, vexation, sorrow, temptation even in the faultless person, weary of himself, and of all action, public or domestic; then comes disorder, neglect, hatred, and perpetual strife; all these the enemies of holiness and Christianity, and, every one of these persisted in, a remediless violation to matrimony. Therefore God, who hates all feigning and formality, where there should be all faith and sincereness, and abhors to see the inevitable discord, where there should be greatest concord, when through another's default faith and concord cannot be, counts it neither just to punish the innocent with the transgressor, nor holy, nor honorable for the sanctity of marriage, that should be the union of peace and love, to be made the commitment and close fight of enmity and hate. And therefore doth in this law what best agrees with his goodness, loosening a sacred thing to peace and charity, rather than binding it to hatred and contention; loosening only the outward and formal tie of that which is already inwardly and really broken, or else was really never joined.

Eleventhly, One of the chief matrimonial ends is said to seek a holy seed; but where an unfit marriage administers continual cause of hatred and distemper, there, as was heard before, cannot choose but much unholiness abide. Nothing more unhallows a man, more unprepares him to the service of God in any duty, than a habit of wrath and perturbation, arising from the importunity of troublous causes never absent. And where the household stands in this plight, what love can there be to the unfortunate issue, what care of their breeding, which is of main conducement to their being holy? God, therefore, knowing how unhappy it would be for children to be born in such a family, gives this law either as a prevention, that, being an unhappy pair, they should not add to be unhappy parents, or else as a remedy that if there be children, while they are fewest, they may follow either parent, as shall be agreed or judged, from the house of hatred and discord to a place of more holy and peaceable education.

Twelfthly, All law is available to some good end; but the final prohibition of divorce avails to no good end, causing only the endless aggravation of evil; and therefore this permission of divorce was given to the Jews by the wisdom and fatherly providence of God; who knew that law cannot command love, without which matrimony hath no true being, no good, no solace, nothing of God's instituting, nothing but so sordid and so low, as to be disdained of any generous person. Law cannot enable natural inability either of body or mind, which gives the grievance; it cannot make equal those inequalities, it cannot make fit those unfitnesses; and where there is malice more than defect of nature, it cannot hinder ten thousand injuries, and bitter actions of despite, too subtle and too unapparent for law to deal with. And while it seeks to remedy more outward wrongs, it exposes the injured person to other more inward and more cutting. All these evils unavoidably will redound upon the children, if any be, and the whole family. It degenerates and disorders the best spirits, leaves them to unsettled imaginations, and degraded hopes, careless of themselves, their households, and their friends, unactive to all public service, dead to the commonwealth; wherein they are by one mishap, and no willing trespass of theirs, outlawed from all the benefits and comforts of married life and posterity. It confers as little to the honor and inviolable keeping of matrimony, but sooner stirs up temptations and occasions to secret adulteries and unchaste roving. But it maintains public honesty. Public folly rather: who shall judge of public honesty? The law of God and of ancientest Christians, and all civil nations; or the illegitimate law of monks and canonists, the most malevolent, most unexperienced, and incompetent judges of matrimony?

These reasons, and many more that might be alleged, afford us plainly to perceive both what good cause this law had to do for good men in mischances, and what necessity it had to suffer accidentally the hardheartedness of bad men, which it could not certainly discover, or discovering could not subdue, no, nor endeavor to restrain without multiplying sorrow to them for whom all was endeavored. The guiltless, therefore, were not deprived their needful redresses, and the hard hearts of others, unchastisable in those judicial courts, were so remitted there, as bound over to the higher session of conscience.

Notwithstanding all this, there is a loud exception against this law of God, nor can the holy Author save his law from this exception, that it opens a door to all licence and confusion. But this is the rudest, I was almost saying the most graceless objection, and with the least reverence to God and Moses, that could be devised: this is to cite God before man's tribunal, to arrogate a wisdom and holiness above him. Did not God then foresee what event of licence or confusion could follow? Did not he know how to ponder these abuses with more prevailing respects, in the most even balance of his justice and pureness, till these correctors came up to show him better? The law is, if it stir up sin any way, to stir it up by forbidding, as one contrary excites another, Rom. vii.; but if it once come to provoke sin, by granting licence to sin, according to laws that have no other honest end, but only to permit the fulfilling of obstinate lust, how is God not made the contradicter of himself? No man denies that best things may be abused; but it is a rule resulting from many pregnant experiences, that what doth most harm in the abusing, used rightly doth most good. And such a good to take away from honest men, for being abused by such as abuse all things, is the greatest abuse of all. That the whole law is no further useful, than as a man uses it lawfully, St. Paul teaches, 1 Tim. i. And that Christian liberty may be used for an occasion to the flesh, the same apostle confesses, Gal. v.; yet thinks not of removing it for that, but bids us rather "stand fast in the liberty wherewith Christ hath freed us, and not be held again in the yoke of bondage." The very permission, which Christ gave to divorce for adultery, may be foully abused, by any whose hardness of heart can either feign adultery, or dares commit, that he may divorce. And for this cause the pope, and hitherto the church of England, forbid all divorce from the bond of marriage, though for openest adultery. If then it be righteous to hinder, for the fear of abuse, that which God's law, notwithstanding that caution, hath warranted to be done, doth not our righteousness come short of Antichrist? or do we not rather herein conform ourselves to his unrighteousness in this undue and unwise fear? For God regards more to relieve by this law the just complaints of good men, than to curb the licence of wicked men, to the crushing withal, and the overwhelming of his afflicted servants. He loves more that his law should look with pity upon the difficulties of his own, than with rigor upon the boundless riots of them who serve another master, and, hindered here by strictness, will break another way to worse enormities. If this law, therefore, have many good reasons for which God gave it, and no intention of giving scope to lewdness, but as abuse by accident comes in with every good law, and every good thing; it cannot be wisdom in us, while we can content us with God's wisdom, nor can be purity, if his purity will suffice us, to except against this law, as if it fostered licence. But if they affirm this law had no other end, but to permit obdurate lust, because it would be obdurate, making the law of God intentionally to proclaim and enact sin lawful, as if the will of God were become sinful, or sin stronger than his direct and lawgiving will; the men would be admonished to look well to it, that while they are so eager to shut the door against licence, they do not open a worse door to blasphemy. And yet they shall be here further shown their iniquity: what more foul and common sin among us than drunkenness? And who can be ignorant, that if the importation of wine, and the use of all strong drink, were forbid, it would both clean rid the possibility of committing that odious vice, and men might afterwards live happily and healthfully without the use of those intoxicating liquors? Yet who is there, the severest of them all, that ever propounded to lose his sack, his ale, toward the certain abolishing of so great a sin? who is there of them, the holiest, that less loves his rich canary at meals, though it be fetched from places that hazard the religion of them who fetch it, and though it make his neighbor drunk out of the same tun? While they forbid not, therefore, the use of that liquid merchandise, which forbidden would utterly remove a most loathsome sin, and not impair either the health or the refreshment of mankind, supplied many other ways, why do they forbid a law of God, the forbidding whereof brings into an excessive bondage ofttimes the best of men, and betters not the worse? He, to remove a national vice, will not pardon his cups, nor think it concerns him to forbear the quaffing of that outlandish grape, in his unnecessary fulness, though other men abuse it never so much; nor is he so abstemious as to intercede with the magistrate, that all matter of drunkenness be banished the commonwealth; and yet for the fear of a less inconvenience unpardonably requires of his brethren, in their extreme necessity, to debar themselves the use of God's permissive law, though it might be their saving, and no man's endangering the more. Thus this peremptory strictness we may discern of what sort it is, how unequal, and how unjust.

But it will breed confusion. What confusion it would breed, God himself took the care to prevent in the fourth verse of this chapter, that the divorced, being married to another, might not return to her former husband. And Justinian's law counsels the same in his title of "Nuptials." And what confusion else can there be in separation, to separate upon extreme urgency the religious from the irreligious, the fit from the unfit, the willing from the wilful, the abused from the abuser? Such a separation is quite contrary to confusion. But to bind and mix together holy with atheist, heavenly with hellish, fitness with unfitness, light with darkness, antipathy with antipathy, the injured with the injurer, and force them into the most inward nearness of a detested union; this doubtless is the most horrid, the most unnatural mixture, the greatest confusion that can be confused.

Thus by this plain and Christian Talmud, vindicating the law of God from irreverent and unwary expositions, I trust, where it shall meet with intelligible perusers, some stay at least of men's thoughts will be obtained, to consider these many prudent and righteous ends of this divorcing permission: that it may have, for the great Author's sake, hereafter some competent allowance to be counted a little purer than the prerogative of a legal and public ribaldry, granted to that holy seed. So that from hence we shall hope to find the way still more open to the reconciling of those places which treat this matter in the gospel. And thither now without interruption the course of method brings us.

<hr />

MATTHEW v. 31, 32.

31. "It hath been said, Whosoever shall put away his wife, let him give her a writing of divorcement.

32. "But I say unto you, That whosoever shall put away his wife," &c.

Matt. xix, 3, 4, &c.

3. "And the Pharisees also came unto him, tempting him," &c.

"IT hath been said."] What hitherto hath been spoke upon the law of God touching matrimony or divorce, he who will deny to have been argued according to reason and all equity of scripture, I cannot edify how, or by what rule of proportion, that man's virtue calculates, what his elements are, nor what his analytics. Confidently to those who have read good books, and to those whose reason is not an illiterate book to themselves, I appeal, whether they would not confess all this to be the commentary of truth and justice, were it not for these recited words of our Saviour. And if they take not back that which they thus grant, nothing sooner might persuade them that Christ here teaches no new precept, and nothing sooner might direct them to find his meaning than to compare and measure it by the rules of nature and eternal righteousness, which no written law extinguishes, and the gospel least of all. For what can be more opposite and disparaging to the covenant of love, of freedom, and of our manhood in grace, than to be made the yoking pedagogue of new severities, the scribe of syllables and rigid letters, not only grievous to the best of men, but different and strange from the light of reason in them, save only as they are fain to stretch and distort their apprehensions, for fear of displeasing the verbal straitness of a text, which our own servile fear gives us not the leisure to understand aright? If the law of Christ shall be written in our hearts, as was promised to the gospel, Jer. xxxi., how can this in the vulgar and superficial sense be a law of Christ, so far from being written in our hearts, that it injures and disallows not only the free dictates of nature and moral law, but of charity also and religion in our hearts? Our Saviour's doctrine is that the end and the fulfilling of every command is charity; no faith without it, no truth without it, no worship, no works pleasing to God but as they partake of charity. He himself sets us an example, breaking the solemnest and strictest ordinance of religious rest, and justified the breaking, not to cure a dying man, but such whose cure might without danger have been deferred. And wherefore needs must the sick man's bed be carried home on that day by his appointment? And why were the disciples, who could not forbear on that day to pluck the corn, so industriously defended, but to show us that, if he preferred the slightest occasions of man's good before the observing of highest and severest ordinances, he gave us much more easy leave to break the intolerable yoke of a never well-joined wedlock for the removing of our heaviest afflictions? Therefore it is, that the most of evangelic precepts are given us in proverbial forms, to drive us from the letter, though we love ever to be sticking there. For no other cause did Christ assure us that whatsoever things we bind or slacken on earth, are so in heaven, but to signify that the Christian arbitrement of charity is supreme decider of all contro-

versy, and supreme resolver of all scripture, not as the pope determines for his own tyranny, but as the church ought to determine for its own true liberty. Hence Eusebius, not far from beginning his history, compares the state of Christians to that of Noah and the patriarchs before the law. And this indeed was the reason why apostolic tradition in the ancient church was counted nigh equal to the written word, though it carried them at length awry, for want of considering that tradition was not left to be imposed as law, but to be a pattern of that Christian prudence and liberty, which holy men by right assumed of old; which truth was so evident, that it found entrance even into the council of Trent, when the point of tradition came to be discussed. And Marinaro, a learned Carmelite, for approaching too near the true cause that gave esteem to tradition, that is to say, the difference between the Old and New Testament, the one punctually prescribing written law, the other guiding by the inward spirit, was reprehended by Cardinal Pool as one that had spoken more worthy a German Colloquy, than a general council. I omit many instances, many proofs and arguments of this kind, which alone would compile a just volume, and shall content me here to have shown briefly, that the great and almost only commandment of the gospel is, to command nothing against the good of man, and much more no civil command against his civil good. If we understand not this, we are but cracked cymbals, we do but tinkle, we know nothing, we do nothing, all the sweat of our toilsomest obedience will but mock us. And what we suffer superstitiously returns us no thanks. Thus medicining our eyes, we need not doubt to see more into the meaning of these our Saviour's words, than many who have gone before us.

"It hath been said, Whosoever shall put away his wife."] Our Saviour was by the doctors of his time suspected of intending to dissolve the law. In this chapter he wipes off this aspersion upon his accusers, and shows, how they were the lawbreakers. In every commonwealth, when it decays, corruption makes two main steps: first, when men cease to do according to the inward and uncompelled actions of virtue, caring only to live by the outward constraint of law, and turn the simplicity of real good into the craft of seeming so by law. To this hypocritical honesty was Rome declined in that age wherein Horace lived, and discovered it to Quintius.

"Whom do we count a good man, whom but he
Who keeps the laws and statutes of the Senate?
Who judges in great suits and controversies?
Whose witness and opinion wins the cause?
But his own house, and the whole neighbourhood
Sees his foul inside through his whited skin."

The next declining is, when law becomes now too strait for the secular manners, and those too loose for the cincture of law. This brings in false and crooked interpretations to eke out law, and invents the subtle encroachment of obscure traditions hard to be disproved. To both these descents the pharisees themselves were fallen. Our Saviour therefore shows them both where they broke the law, in not marking the divine intent thereof, but only the letter; and where they depraved the letter also with sophistical expositions. This law of divorce they had depraved both ways: first, by teaching that to give a bill of divorce was all the duty which that law required, whatever the cause were; next, by running to divorce for any trivial, accidental cause; whenas the law evidently stays in the grave causes of natural and immutable dislike. "It hath been said," saith he. Christ doth not put any contempt or disesteem upon the law of Moses, by citing it so briefly; for in the same manner God himself cites a law of greatest caution, Jer. iii.; "They say, If a man put away his wife, shall he return to her again?" &c. Nor doth he more abolish it than the law of swearing, cited next with the same brevity, and more appearance of contradicting: for divorce hath an exception left it; but we are charged there, as absolutely as words can charge us, "not to swear at all;" yet who denies the lawfulness of an oath, though here it be in no case permitted? And what shall become of his solemn protestation not to abolish one law, or one tittle of any law, especially of those which he mentions in this chapter? And that he meant more particularly the not abolishing of Mosaic divorce, is beyond all cavil manifest in Luke xvi. 17, 18, where this clause against abrogating is inserted immediately before the sentence against divorce, as if it were called thither on purpose to defend the equity of this particular law against the foreseen rashness of common textuaries, who abolish laws, as the rabble demolish images, in the zeal of their hammers oft violating the sepulchres of good men: like Pentheus in the tragedies, they see that for Thebes which is not, and take that for superstition, as these men in the heat of their annulling perceive not how they abolish right, and equal, and justice, under the appearance of judicial. And yet are confessing all the while, that these sayings of Christ stand not in contradiction to the law of Moses, but to the false doctrine of the pharisees raised from thence; that the law of God is perfect, not liable to additions or diminutions: and Paræus accuses the Jesuit Maldonatus of greatest falsity for limiting the perfection of that law only to the rudeness of the Jews. He adds, "That the law promiseth life to the performers thereof, therefore needs not perfecter precepts than such as bring to life; that if the corrections of Christ stand opposite, not to the corruptions of the pharisees, but to the law itself of God, the heresy of Manes would follow—one God of the Old Testament, and another of the New. That Christ saith not here, Except your righteousness exceed the righteousness of Moses' law, but of the scribes and pharisees." That all this may be true: whither is common sense flown asquint, if we can maintain that Christ forbade the Mosaic divorce utterly, and yet abolished not the law that permits it? For if the conscience only were checked, and law not repealed, what means the fanatic boldness of this age, that dares tutor Christ to be more strict than he thought fit? Ye shall have the evasion: it was a judicial law. What could infancy and slumber have invented more childish? Judicial or not judicial, it was one of those laws expressly which he forewarned us with protestation, that his mind was not to abrogate: and if we mark the steerage of his words, what course they hold, we may perceive that what he protested not to dissolve (that he might faithfully and not deceitfully remove a suspicion from himself) was principally concerning the judicial law; for of that sort are all these here which he vindicates, except the last. Of the ceremonial law he told them true, that nothing of it should pass "until all were fulfilled." Of the moral law he knew the pharisees did not suspect he meant to nullify that; for so doing would soon have undone his authority, and advanced theirs. Of the judicial law therefore chiefly this apology was meant: for how is that fulfilled longer than the common equity thereof remains in force? And how is this our Saviour's defence of himself not made fallacious, if the pharisees' chief fear be lest he should abolish the judicial law, and he, to satisfy them, protests his good intention to the moral law? It is the general grant of divines, that what in the judicial law is not merely judaical, but reaches to human equity in common, was never in the thought of being abrogated. If our Saviour took away aught of law, it was the burdensome of it, not the ease of burden; it was the bondage, not the liberty of any divine law, that he removed; this he often professed to be the end of his coming. But what if the law of divorce be a moral law, as most certainly it is fundamentally, and hath been so proved in the reasons thereof? For though the giving of a bill may be judicial, yet the act of divorce is altogether conversant in good or evil, and so absolutely moral. So far as it is good, it never can be abolished, being moral; so far as it is simply evil, it never could be judicial, as hath been shown at large in "the Doctrine of Divorce," and will be reassumed anon. Whence one of these two necessities follow, that either it was never established, or never abolished. Thus much may be enough to have said on this place. The following verse will be better unfolded in the 19th chapter, where it meets us again, after a large debatement on the question between our Saviour and his adversaries.

Matt. xix. 3, 4, &c.

Ver. 3. "And the pharisees came unto him, tempting him, and saying unto him."

"Tempting him."] The manner of these men coming to our Saviour, not to learn, but to tempt him, may give us to expect, that their answer will be such as is fittest for them; not so much a teaching, as an entangling. No man, though never so willing or so well enabled to instruct, but if he discern his willingness and candor made use of to entrap him, will suddenly draw in himself, and laying aside the facile vein of perspicuity, will know his time to utter clouds and riddles; if he be not less wise than that noted fish, whenas he should be not unwiser than the serpent. Our Saviour at no time expressed any great desire to teach the obstinate and unteachable pharisees; but when they came to tempt him, then least of all. As now about the liberty of divorce, so another time about the punishment of adultery, they came to sound him; and what satisfaction got they from his answer, either to themselves, or to us, that might direct a law under the gospel, new from that of Moses, unless we draw his absolution of adultery into an edict? So about the tribute, who is there can pick out a full solution, what and when we must give to Cæsar, by the answer which he gave the pharisees? If we must give to Cæsar that which is Cæsar's and all be Cæsar's which hath his image, we must either new stamp our coin, or we may go new stamp our foreheads with the superscription of slaves instead of freemen. Besides, it is a general precept not only of Christ, but of all other sages, not to instruct the unworthy and the conceited, who love tradition more than truth, but to perplex and stumble them purposely with contrived obscurities. No wonder then if they who would determine of divorce by this place, have ever found it difficult and unsatisfying through all the ages of the church, as Austin himself and other great writers confess. Lastly, it is manifest to be the principal scope of our Saviour, both here and in the fifth of Matthew, to convince the pharisees of what they being evil did licentiously, not to explain what others being good and blameless men might be permitted to do in case of extremity. Neither was it seasonable to talk of honest and conscientious liberty among them, who had abused legal and civil liberty to uncivil licence. We do not say to a servant what we say to a son; nor was it expedient to preach freedom to those who had transgressed in wantonness. When we rebuke a prodigal, we admonish him of thrift, not of magnificence, or bounty. And to school a proud man, we labor to make him humble, not magnanimous.

So Christ, to retort these arrogant inquisitors their own, took the course to lay their haughtiness under a severity which they deserved; not to acquaint them, or to make them judges either of the just man's right and privilege, or of the afflicted man's necessity. And if we may have leave to conjecture, there is a likelihood offered us by Tertullian in his fourth against Marcion, whereby it may seem very probable, that the pharisees had a private drift of malice against our Saviour's life in proposing this question; and our Saviour had a peculiar aim in the rigor of his answer, both to let them know the freedom of his spirit, and the sharpness of his discerning. "This I must now show," saith Tertullian, "whence our Lord deduced this sentence, and which way he directed it, whereby it will more fully appear, that he intended not to dissolve Moses." And thereupon tells us, that the vehemence of this our Saviour's speech was chiefly darted against Herod and Herodias. The story is out of Josephus. Herod had been a long time married to the daughter of Aretas, king of Petra, till happening on his journey towards Rome to be entertained at his brother Philip's house, he cast his eye unlawfully and unguestlike upon Herodias there, the wife of Philip, but daughter to Aristobulus, their common brother, and durst make words of marrying her his niece from his brother's bed. She assented, upon agreement he should expel his former wife. All was accomplished, and by the Baptist rebuked with the loss of his head. Though doubtless that stayed not the various discourses of men upon the fact, which while the Herodian flatterers, and not a few perhaps among the pharisees, endeavored to defend by wresting the law, it might be a means to bring the question of divorce into a hot agitation among the people, how far Moses gave allowance. The pharisees therefore knowing our Saviour to be a friend of John the Baptist, and no doubt but having heard much of his sermon in the mount, wherein he spake rigidly against the licence of divorce, they put him this question, both in hope to find him a contradictor of Moses, and a condemner of Herod; so to insnare him within compass of the same accusation which had ended his friend; and our Saviour so orders his answer, as that they might perceive Herod and his adulteress, only not named; so lively it concerned them both what he spake. No wonder then if the sentence of our Saviour sounded stricter than his custom was; which his conscious attempters doubtless apprehended sooner than his other auditors. Thus much we gain from hence to inform us, that what Christ intends to speak here of divorce, will be rather the forbidding of what we may not do herein passionately and abusively, as Herod and Herodias did, than the discussing of what herein we may do reasonably and necessarily.

"Is it lawful for a man to put away his wife?"] It might be rendered more exactly from the Greek, "to loosen, or to set free;" which though it seem to have a milder signification than the two Hebrew words commonly used for divorce, yet interpreters have noted that the Greek also is read in the Septuagint for an act which is not without constraint.

As when Achish drove from his presence David, counterfeiting madness, Psalm xxxiv., the Greek word is the same with this here, "to put away." And Erasmus quotes Hilary, rendering it by an expression not so soft. Whence may be doubted whether the pharisees did not state this question in the strict right of the man, not tarrying for the wife's consent. And if our Saviour answered directly according to what was asked in the term of putting away, it may be questionable whether the rigor of his sentence did not forbid only such putting away as is without mutual consent, in a violent and harsh manner, or without any reason but will, as the tetrarch did. Which might be the cause that those Christian emperors feared not in their constitutions to dissolve marriage by mutual consent; in that our Saviour seems here, as the case is most likely, not to condemn all divorce, but all injury and violence in divorce. But no injury can be done to them, who seek it, as the ethics of Aristotle sufficiently prove. True it is, that an unjust thing may be done to one though willing, and so may justly be forbidden: but divorce being in itself no unjust or evil thing, but only as it is joined with injury or lust; injury it cannot be at law, if consent be, and Aristotle err not. And lust it may as frequently not be, while charity hath the judging of so many private grievances in a misfortuned wedlock, which may pardonably seek a redemption. But whether it be or not, the law cannot discern or examine lust, so long as it walks from one lawful term to another, from divorce to marriage, both in themselves indifferent. For if the law cannot take hold to punish many actions apparently covetous, ambitious, ingrateful, proud, how can it forbid and punish that for lust, which is but only surmised so, and can no more be certainly proved in the divorcing now, than before in the marrying? Whence if divorce be no unjust thing, but through lust, a cause not discernible by law as law is wont to discern in other cases, and can be no injury, where consent is; there can be nothing in the equity of law, why divorce by consent may not be lawful: leaving secrecies to conscience, the thing which our Saviour here aims to rectify, not to revoke the statutes of Moses. In the meanwhile the word "to put away," being in the Greek to loosen or dissolve, utterly takes away that vain papistical distinction of divorce from bed, and divorce from bond, evincing plainly, that both Christ and the pharisees mean here that divorce which finally dissolves the bond, and frees both parties to a second marriage.

"For every cause."] This the pharisees held, that for every cause they might divorce, for every accidental cause, any quarrel or difference that might happen. So both Josephus and Philo, men who lived in the same age, explain; and the Syriac translator, whose antiquity is thought parallel to the Evangelists themselves, reads it conformably, "upon any occasion or pretence." Divines also generally agree, that thus the pharisees meant. Cameron, a late writer, much applauded, commenting this place not undiligently, affirms that the Greek preposition κατὰ, translated unusually "for," hath a force in it implying the suddenness of those pharisaic divorces; and that their question was to this effect, "whether for any cause, whatever it chanced to be, straight as it rose, the divorce might be lawful." This he freely gives, whatever

moved him, and I as freely take, nor can deny his observation to be acute and learned. If therefore we insist upon the word of "putting away," that it imports a constraint without consent, as might be insisted, and may enjoy what Cameron bestows on us, that "for every cause" is to be understood, "according as any cause may happen," with a relation to the speediness of those divorces, and that Herodian act especially, as is already brought us, the sentence of our Saviour will appear nothing so strict a prohibition as hath been long conceived, forbidding only to divorce for casual and temporary causes, that may be soon ended, or soon remedied: and likewise forbidding to divorce rashly, and on the sudden heat, except it be for adultery. If these qualifications may be admitted, as partly we offer them, partly are offered them by some of their own opinion, and that where nothing is repugnant why they should not be admitted, nothing can wrest them from us; the severe sentence of our Saviour will straight unbend the seeming frown into that gentleness and compassion which was so abundant in all his actions, his office, and his doctrine, from all which otherwise it stands off at no mean distance.

Ver. 4. "And he answered and said unto them, Have ye not read, that he which made them at the beginning, made them male and female?

Ver. 5. "And said, For this cause shall a man leave father and mother, and shall cleave to his wife, and they twain shall be one flesh.

Ver. 6. "Wherefore they are no more twain, but one flesh. What therefore God hath joined together, let no man put asunder."

4 and 5. "Made them male and female; and said, For this cause," &c.] We see it here undeniably, that the law which our Saviour cites to prove that divorce was forbidden, is not an absolute and tyrannical command without reason, as now-a-days we make it little better, but is grounded upon some rational cause not difficult to be apprehended, being in a matter which equally concerns the meanest and the plain-

est sort of persons in a household life. Our next way then will be to inquire if there be not more reasons than one; and if there be, whether this be the best and chiefest. That we shall find by turning to the first institution, to which Christ refers our own reading: he himself, having to deal with treacherous assailants, useth brevity, and lighting on the first place in Genesis that mentions anything tending to marriage in the first chapter, joins it immediately to the twenty-fourth verse of the second chapter, omitting all the prime words between which create the institution, and contain the noblest and purest ends of matrimony; without which attained, that conjunction hath nothing in it above what is common to us with beasts. So likewise beneath in this very chapter, to the young man, who came not tempting him, but to learn of him, asking him which commandments he should keep, he neither repeats the first table, nor all the second, nor that in order which he repeats. If here then being tempted, he desire to be the shorter, and the darker in his conference, and omit to cite that from the second of Genesis, which all divines confess is a commentary to what he cites out of the first, the "making them male and female," what are we to do, but to search the institution ourselves? And we shall find there his own authority, giving other manner of reasons why such firm union is to be in matrimony; without which reasons, their being male and female can be no cause of joining them unseparably: for if it be, then no adultery can sever. Therefore the prohibition of divorce depends not upon this reason here expressed to the pharisees, but upon the plainer and more eminent causes omitted here, and referred to the institution; which causes not being found in a particular and casual matrimony, this sensitive and materious cause alone can no more hinder a divorce against those higher and more human reasons urging it, than it can alone without them to warrant a copulation, but leaves it arbitrary to those who in their chance of marriage find not why divorce is forbid them, but why it is permitted them; and find both here and in Genesis, that the forbidding is not absolute, but according to the reasons there taught us, not here. And that our Saviour taught them no better, but uses the most vulgar, most animal and corporal argument to convince them, is first to show us, that as through their licentious divorces they made no more of marriage, than as if to marry were no more than to be male and female, so he goes no higher in his confutation; deeming them unworthy to be talked with in a higher strain, but to be tied in marriage by the mere material cause thereof, since their own licence testified that nothing matrimonial was in their thought, but to be male and female. Next, it might be done to discover the brute ignorance of these carnal doctors, who taking on them to dispute of marriage and divorce, were put to silence with such a slender opposition as this, and outed from their hold with scarce one quarter of an argument. That we may believe this, his entertainment of the young man soon after may persuade us. Whom, though he came to preach eternal life by faith only, he dismisses with a salvation taught him by works only. On which place Paræus notes, "that this man was to be convinced by a false persuasion; and that Christ is wont otherwise to answer hypocrites, otherwise those that are docible." Much rather then may we think, that, in handling these tempters, he forgot not so to frame his prudent ambiguities and concealments, as was to the troubling of those peremptory disputants most wholesome. When therefore we would know what right there may be, in ill accidents, to divorce, we must repair thither where God professes to teach his servants by the prime institution, and not where we see him intending to dazzle sophisters: we must not read, "He made them male and female," and not understand he made them more intendedly "a meet help" to remove the evil of being "alone." We must take both these together, and then we may infer completely, as from the whole cause, why a man shall cleave to his wife, and they twain shall be one flesh: but if the full and chief cause why we may not divorce be wanting here, this place may skirmish with the rabbies while it will, but to the true

Christian it prohibits nothing beyond the full reason of its own prohibiting, which is best known by the institution.

Ver. 6. "Wherefore they are no more twain, but one flesh." This is true in the general right of marriage, but not in the chance-medley of every particular match. For if they who were once undoubtedly one flesh, yet become twain by adultery, then sure they who were never one flesh rightly, never helps meet for each other according to the plain prescript of God, may with less ado than a volume be concluded still twain. And so long as we account a magistrate no magistrate, if there be but a flaw in his election, why should we not much rather count a matrimony no matrimony, if it cannot be in any reasonable manner according to the words of God's institution.

"What therefore God hath joined, let no man put asunder."] But here the Christian prudence lies to consider what God hath joined. Shall we say that God hath joined error, fraud, unfitness, wrath, contention, perpetual loneliness, perpetual discord; whatever lust, or wine, or witchery, threat or enticement, avarice or ambition hath joined together, faithful with unfaithful, Christian with antichristian, hate with hate, or hate with love; shall we say this is God's joining?

"Let not man put asunder."] That is to say, what God hath joined; for if it be, as how oft we see it may be, not of God's joining, and his law tells us he joins not unmatchable things, but hates to join them, as an abominable confusion, then the divine law of Moses puts them asunder, his own divine will in the institution puts them asunder, as oft as the reasons be not extant, for which only God ordained their joining. Man only puts asunder when his inordinate desires, his passion, his violence, his injury makes the breach: not when the utter want of that which lawfully was the end of his joining, when wrongs and extremities and unsupportable grievances compel him to disjoin: when such as Herod and the pharisees divorce beside law, or against law, then only man separates, and to such only this prohibition belongs. In a word, if it be unlawful for man to put asunder that which

God hath joined, let man take heed it be not detestable to join that by compulsion which God hath put asunder.

Ver. 7. "They say unto him, Why did Moses then command to give a writing of divorcement, and to put her away?
Ver. 8. "He saith unto them, Moses because of the hardness of your hearts suffered you to put away your wives; but from the beginning it was not so."

"Moses because of the hardness of your hearts suffered you."] Hence the divinity now current argues, that this judicial Moses is abolished. But suppose it were so, though it hath been proved otherwise, the firmness of such right to divorce, as here pleads is fetched from the prime institution, does not stand or fall with the judicial Jew, but is as moral as what is moralest. Yet as I have shown positively, that this law cannot be abrogated, both by the words of our Saviour pronouncing the contrary, and by that unabolishable equity which it conveys to us; so I shall now bring to view those appearances of strength which are levied from this text to maintain the most gross and massy paradox that ever did violence to reason and religion, bred only under the shadow of these words, to all other piety or philosophy strange and insolent, that God by act of law drew out a line of adultery almost two thousand years long: although to detect the prodigy of this surmise, the former book set forth on this argument hath already been copious. I shall not repeat much, though I might borrow of mine own; but shall endeavor to add something either yet untouched, or not largely enough explained. First, it shall be manifest, that the common exposition cannot possibly consist with Christian doctrine; next, a truer meaning of this our Saviour's reply shall be left in the room. The received exposition is, that God, though not approving, did enact a law to permit adultery by divorcement simply unlawful. And this conceit they feed with fond supposals, that have not the least footing in scripture; as that the Jews learnt this custom of divorce in Egypt, and therefore God would not un-teach it them till Christ came, but let it stick as a notorious botch of deformity in the midst of his most perfect and severe law. And yet he saith, Lev. xviii., "After the doings of Egypt ye shall not do." Another while they invent a slander, (as what thing more bold than teaching ignorance when he shifts to hide his nakedness?) that the Jews were naturally to their wives the cruellest men in the world; would poison, brain, and do I know not what, if they might not divorce. Certain, if it were a fault heavily punished, to bring an evil report upon the land which God gave, what is it to raise a groundless calumny against the people which God made choice of? But that this bold interpretament, how commonly soever sided with, cannot stand a minute with any competent reverence to God, or his law, or his people, nor with any other maxim of religion, or good manners, might be proved through all the heads and topics of argumentation; but I shall willingly be as concise as possible. First, the law, not only the moral, but the judicial, given by Moses, is just and pure; for such is God who gave it. "Hearken, O Israel," saith Moses, Deut. iv., "unto the statutes and the judgments which I teach you, to do them, that ye may live, &c. Ye shall not add unto the word which I command you, neither shall ye diminish aught from it, that ye may keep the commandments of the Lord your God, which I command you." And onward in the chapter, "Behold, I have taught you statutes and judgments, even as the Lord my God commanded me. Keep therefore and do them; for this is your wisdom and your understanding. For what nation hath God so nigh unto them, and what nation hath statutes and judgments so righteous as all this law, which I set before ye this day?" Is it imaginable there should be among these a law which God allowed not, a law giving permissions laxative to unmarry a wife, and marry a lust, a law to suffer a kind of tribunal adultery? Many other scriptures might be brought to assert the purity of this judicial law, and many I have alleged before; this law therefore is pure and just. But if it permit, if it teach, if it defend that which is both unjust and impure, as by the common doctrine it doth,

what think we? The three general doctrines of Justinian's laws are, "To live in honesty, To hurt no man, To give every one his due." Shall the Roman civil law observe these three things, as the only end of law, and shall a statute be found in the civil law of God, enacted simply and totally against all these three precepts of nature and morality?

Secondly, the gifts of God are all perfect; and certainly the law is of all his other gifts one of the perfectest. But if it give that outwardly which it takes away really, and give that seemingly, which if a man take it, wraps him into sin and damns him, what gift of an enemy can be more dangerous and destroying than this?

Thirdly, Moses everywhere commends his laws, prefers them before all of other nations, and warrants them to be the way of life and safety to all that walk therein, Lev. xviii. But if they contain statutes which God approves not, and train men unweeting to commit injustice and adultery under the shelter of law; if those things be sin, and death sin's wages, what is this law but the snare of death?

Fourthly, The statutes and judgments of the Lord, which, without exception, are often told us to be such as doing we may live by them, are doubtless to be counted the rule of knowledge and of conscience. "For I had not known lust," saith the apostle, "but by the law." But if the law come down from the state of her incorruptible majesty to grant lust his boon, palpably it darkens and confounds both knowledge and conscience; it goes against the common office of all goodness and friendliness, which is at least to counsel and admonish; it subverts the rules of all sober education, and is itself a most negligent and debauching tutor.

Fifthly, If the law permit a thing unlawful, it permits that which elsewhere it hath forbid; so that hereby it contradicts itself, and transgresses itself. But if the law become a transgressor, it stands guilty to itself: and how then shall it save another? It makes a confederacy with sin: how then can it justly condemn a sinner? And thus reducing itself to the state of neither saving nor condemning, it will not fail to expire solemnly ridiculous.

Sixthly, The prophets in scripture declare severely against the decreeing of that which is unjust, Psalm xciv. 20; Isaiah x. But it was done, they say, for hardness of heart: to which objection the apostle's rule, "not to do evil that good may come thereby," gives an invincible repulse; and here especially, where it cannot be shown how any good came by doing this evil; how rather more evil did not hereon abound: for the giving way to hardness of heart hardens the more, and adds more to the number. God to an evil and adulterous generation would not "grant a sign;" much less would he for their hardness of heart pollute his law with an adulterous permission. Yea, but to permit evil, is not to do evil. Yes, it is in a most eminent manner to do evil: where else are all our grave and faithful sayings, that he whose office is to forbid and forbids not, bids, exhorts, encourages? Why hath God denounced his anger against parents, masters, friends, magistrates, neglectful of forbidding what they ought, if law, the common father, master, friend, and perpetual magistrate, shall not only not forbid, but enact, exhibit, and uphold with countenance and protection, a deed every way dishonest, whatever the pretence be? If it were of those inward vices, which the law cannot by outward constraint remedy, but leaves to conscience and persuasion, it had been guiltless in being silent: but to write a decree of that which can be no way lawful, and might with ease be hindered, makes law by the doom of law itself accessory in the highest degree.

Seventhly, It makes God the direct author of sin: for although he be not made the author of what he silently permits in his providence, yet in his law, the image of his will, when in plain expression he constitutes and ordains a fact utterly unlawful: what wants he to authorize it? and what wants that to be the author?

Eighthly, To establish by law a thing wholly unlawful and dishonest, is an affirmation was never heard of before in any law, reason, philosophy, or religion, till it was raised by inconsiderate glossists from the mistake of this text. And though the civilians have been contented to chew this opinion, after the canon had subdued them, yet they never could bring example or authority, either from divine writ, or human learning, or human practice in any nation, or well-formed republic, but only from the customary abuse of this text. Usually they allege the epistle of Cicero to Atticus; wherein Cato is blamed for giving sentence to the scum of Romulus, as if he were in Plato's commonwealth. Cato would have called some great one into judgment for bribery; Cicero, as the time stood, advised against it. Cato, not to endamage the public treasury, would not grant to the Roman knights that the Asian taxes might be farmed them at a less rate. Cicero wished it granted. Nothing in all this will be like the establishing of a law to sin; here are no laws made, here only the execution of law is craved might be suspended: between which and our question is a broad difference. And what if human lawgivers have confessed they could not frame their laws to that perfection which they desired? We hear of no such confession from Moses concerning the laws of God, but rather all praise and high testimony of perfection given them. And although man's nature cannot bear exactest laws, yet still within the confines of good it may and must, so long as less good is far enough from altogether evil. As for what they instance of usury, let them first prove usury to be wholly unlawful, as the law allows it; which learned men as numerous on the other side will deny them. Or if it be altogether unlawful, why is it tolerated more than divorce? He who said, "Divorce not," said also, "Lend, hoping for nothing again," Luke vi. 35. But then they put in, that trade could not stand; and so to serve the commodity of insatiable trading, usury shall be permitted: but divorce, the only means ofttimes to right the innocent and outrageously wronged, shall be utterly forbid. This is egregious doctrine, and for which one day charity will much thank them. Beza, not finding how to salve this perplexity, and Cameron since him, would secure us; although the latter confesses, that to "permit a wicked thing by law, is a wickedness from which God abhors; yet to limit sin, and prescribe it a certain measure, is good." First, this evasion will not help here; for this law bounded no man: he might put away whatever found not favor in his eyes. And how could it forbid to divorce, whom it could not forbid to dislike, or command to love? If these be the limits of law to restrain sin, who so lame a sinner, but may hop over them more easily than over those Romulean circumscriptions, not as Remus did with hard success, but with all indemnity? Such a limiting as this were not worth the mischief that accompanies it. This law therefore, not bounding the supposed sin, by permitting enlarges it, gives it enfranchisement. And never greater confusion than when law and sin move their landmarks, mix their territories, and correspond, have intercourse, and traffic together. When law contracts a kindred and hospitality with transgression, becomes the godfather of sin, and names it lawful; when sin revels and gossips within the arsenal of law, plays and dandles the artillery of justice that should be bent against her, this is a fair limitation indeed. Besides, it is an absurdity to say that law can measure sin, or moderate sin: sin is not in a predicament to be measured and modified, but is always an excess. The least sin that is exceeds the measure of the largest law that can be good; and is as boundless as that vacuity beyond the world. If once it square to the measure of law, it ceases to be an excess, and consequently ceases to be a sin; or else law conforming itself to the obliquity of sin, betrays itself to be not straight, but crooked, and so immediately no law. And the improper conceit of moderating sin by law will appear, if we can imagine any lawgiver so senseless as to decree, that so far a man may steal, and thus far be drunk, that moderately he may couzen, and moderately commit adultery. To the same extent it would be as pithily absurd to publish, that a man may moderately divorce, if to do that be entirely naught. But to end this moot: the law of Moses is manifest to fix no limit therein at all, or such at least as impeaches the fraudulent abuser no more than if it were not set; only requires the dismissive writing without other caution, leaves that to the inner man, and the bar of conscience. But it stopped other sins. This is as vain as the rest, and dangerously uncertain: the contrary to be feared rather, that one sin, admitted courteously by law, opened the gate to another. However, evil must not be done for good. And it were a fall to be lamented, and indignity unspeakable, if law should become tributary to sin, her slave, and forced to yield up into his hands her awful minister, punishment, should buy out her peace with sin for sin, paying, as it were, her so many Philistian foreskins to the proud demand of transgression. But suppose it any way possible to limit sin, to put a girdle about that chaos, suppose it also good; yet if to permit sin by law be an abomination in the eyes of God, as Cameron acknowledges, the evil of permitting will eat out the good of limiting. For though sin be not limited, there can but evil come out of evil; but if it be permitted and decreed lawful by divine law, of force then sin must proceed from the Infinite Good, which is a dreadful thought. But if the restraining of sin by this permission being good, as this author testifies, be more good than the permission of more sin by the restraint of divorce, and that God weighing both these like two ingots, in the perfect scales of his justice and providence, found them so, and others, coming without authority from God, shall change this counterpoise, and judge it better to let sin multiply by setting a judicial restraint upon divorce which Christ never set; then to limit sin by this permission, as God himself thought best to permit it, it will behoove them to consult betimes whether these their balances be not false and abominable, and this their limiting that which God loosened, and their loosening the sins that he limited, which they confess was good to do: and were it possible to do by law, doubtless it would be most morally good; and they so believing, as we hear they do, and yet abolishing a law so good and moral, the limiter of sin, what are they else but contrary to themselves? For they can never bring us to that time wherein it will not be good to limit sin, and they can never limit it better than so as God prescribed in his law.

Others conceive it a more defensible retirement to say, This permission to divorce sinfully for hardness of heart was a dispensation; but surely they either know not, or attend not what a dispensation means. A dispensation is for no long time; is particular to some persons, rather than general to a whole people; always hath charity the end; is granted to necessities and infirmities, not to obstinate lust. This permission is another creature, hath all those evils and absurdities following the name of a dispensation, as when it was named a law; and is the very antarctic pole against charity, nothing more adverse, ensnaring and ruining those that trust in it or use it: so lewd and criminous as never durst enter into the head of any politician, Jew, or proselyte, till they became the apt scholars of this canonistic exposition. Aught in it that can allude in the least manner to charity, or goodness, belongs with more full right to the Christian under grace and liberty, than to the Jew under law and bondage. To Jewish ignorance it could not be dispensed, without a horrid imputation laid upon the law, to dispense foully, instead of teaching fairly; like that dispensation that first polluted Christendom with idolatry, permitting to laymen images instead of books and preaching. Sloth or malice in the law would they have this called? But what ignorance can be pretended for the Jews, who had all the same precepts about marriage, that we now? for Christ refers all to the institution. It was as reasonable for them to know then as for us now, and concerned them alike; for wherein hath the gospel altered the nature of matrimony? All these considerations, or many of them, have been further amplified in "the Doctrine of Divorce." And what Rivetus and Paræus have objected or given over as past cure, hath been there discussed. Whereby it may be plain enough to men of eyes, that the vulgar exposition of a permittance by law to an entire sin, whatever the color may be, is an opinion both ungodly, unpolitic, unvirtuous, and void of all honesty and civil sense. It appertains, therefore, to every zealous Christian, both for the honor of God's law, and the vindication of our Saviour's words, that such an irreligious depravement no longer may be soothed and flattered through custom, but with all diligence and speed solidly refuted, and in the room a better explanation given; which is now our next endeavor.

"Moses suffered you to put away," &c.] Not commanded you, says the common observer, and therefore cared not how soon it were abolished, being but suffered; herein declaring his annotation to be slight, and nothing law-prudent. For in this place "commanded" and "suffered" are interchangeably used in the same sense both by our Saviour and the pharisees. Our Saviour, who here saith, "Moses suffered you," in the 10th of Mark saith, "Moses wrote you this command." And the pharisees, who here say, "Moses commanded," and would mainly have it a command, in that place of Mark say, "Moses suffered," which had made against them in their own mouths, if the word of "suffering" had weakened the command. So that suffered and commanded is here taken for the same thing on both sides of the controversy, as Cameron also and others on this place acknowledge. And lawyers know that all the precepts of law are divided into obligatory and permissive, containing either what we must do, or what we may do; and of this latter sort are as many precepts as of the former, and all as lawful. Tutelage, an ordainment than which nothing more just, being for the defence of orphans, the Institutes of Justinian say, "is given and permitted by the civil law:" and "to parents it is permitted to choose and appoint by will the guardians of their children." What more equal? And yet the civil law calls this "permission." So likewise to "manumise," to adopt, to make a will, and to be made an heir, is called "permission" by law. Marriage itself, and this which is already granted, to divorce for adultery, obliges no man, is but a permission by law, is but suffered. By this we may see how weakly it hath been thought, that all divorce is utterly unlawful, because the law is said to suffer it: whenas to "suffer" is but the legal phrase denoting what by law a man may do or not do.

"Because of the hardness of your hearts."] Hence they argue that therefore he allowed it not, and therefore it must be abolished. But the contrary to this will sooner follow, that because he suffered it for a cause, therefore in relation to that cause he allowed it. Next, if he in his wisdom, and in the midst of his severity, allowed it for hardness of heart, it can be nothing better than arrogance and presumption to take stricter courses against hardness of heart, than God ever set an example; and that under the gospel, which warrants them to no judicial act of compulsion in this matter, much less to be more severe against hardness of extremity, than God thought good to be against hardness of heart. He suffered it rather than worse inconveniences; these men wiser, as they make themselves, will suffer the worst and heinousest inconveniences to follow, rather than they will suffer what God suffered. Although they can know when they please, that Christ spake only to the conscience, did not judge on the civil bench, but always disavowed it. What can be more contrary to the ways of God than these their doings? If they be such enemies to hardness of heart, although this groundless rigor proclaims it to be in themselves, they may yet learn, or consider, that hardness of heart hath a twofold acception in the gospel. One, when it is in a good man taken for infirmity, and imperfection, which was in all the apostles, whose weakness only, not utter want of belief, is called hardness of heart, Mark xvi. Partly for this hardness of heart, the imperfection and decay of man from original righteousness, it was that God suffered not divorce only, but all that which by civilians is termed the "secondary law of nature and of nations." He suffered his own people to waste and spoil and slay by war, to lead captives, to be some masters, some servants; some to be princes, others to be subjects; he suffered propriety to divide all things by several possession, trade, and commerce, not without usury; in his commonwealth some to be undeservedly rich, others to be undeservingly poor. All which, till hardness of heart came in, was most unjust; whenas prime nature made us all equal, made us equal coheirs by common right and dominion over all creatures. In the same manner, and for the same cause, he suffered divorce as well as marriage, our imperfect and degenerate condition of necessity requiring this law among the rest, as a remedy against intolerable wrong and servitude above the patience of man to bear. Nor was it given only because our infirmity,

or if it must be so called, hardness of heart, could not endure all things; but because the hardness of another's heart might not inflict all things upon an innocent person, whom far other ends brought into a league of love, and not of bondage and indignity. If, therefore, we abolish divorce as only suffered for hardness of heart, we may as well abolish the whole law of nations, as only suffered for the same cause; it being shown us by St. Paul, 1 Cor. vi., that the very seeking of a man's right by law, and at the hands of a worldly magistrate, is not without the hardness of our hearts. "For why do ye not rather take wrong," saith he, "why suffer ye not rather yourselves to be defrauded?" If nothing now must be suffered for hardness of heart, I say the very prosecution of our right by way of civil justice can no more be suffered among Christians, for the hardness of heart wherewith most men pursue it. And that would next remove all our judicial laws, and this restraint of divorce also in the number; which would more than half end the controversy. But if it be plain, that the whole juridical law and civil power is only suffered under the gospel, for the hardness of our hearts, then wherefore should not that which Moses suffered be suffered still by the same reason?

In a second signification, hardness of heart is taken for a stubborn resolution to do evil. And that God ever makes any law purposely to such, I deny; for he vouchsafes not to enter covenant with them, but as they fortune to be mixed with good men, and pass undiscovered, much less that he should decree an unlawful thing only to serve their licentiousness. But that God "suffers" this reprobate hardness of heart I affirm, not only in this law of divorce, but throughout all his best and purest commandments. He commands all to worship in singleness of heart according to all his ordinances; and yet suffers the wicked man to perform all the rites of religion hypocritically, and in the hardness of his heart. He gives us general statutes and privileges in all civil matters, just and good of themselves, yet suffers unworthiest men to use them, and by them to prosecute their own right, or any color of right, though for the most part maliciously, covetously, rigorously, revengefully. He allowed by law the discreet father and husband to forbid, if he thought fit, the religious vows of his wife or daughter, Numb. xxx.; and in the same law suffered the hardheartedness of impious and covetous fathers or husbands abusing this law, to forbid their wives or daughters in their offerings and devotions of greatest zeal. If, then, God suffer hardness of heart equally in the best laws, as in this of divorce, there can be no reason that for this cause this law should be abolished. But other laws, they object, may be well used, this never. How often shall I answer, both from the institution of marriage, and from other general rules in scripture, that this law of divorce hath many wise and charitable ends besides the being suffered for hardness of heart, which is indeed no end, but an accident happening through the whole law; which gives to good men right, and to bad men, who abuse right under false pretences, gives only sufferance? Now although Christ express no other reasons here, but only what was suffered, it nothing follows that this law had no other reason to be permitted but for hardness of heart. The scripture seldom nor never in one place sets down all the reasons of what it grants or commands, especially when it talks to enemies and tempters. St. Paul permitting marriage, 1 Cor. vii., seems to permit even that also for hardness of heart only, lest we should run into fornication; yet no intelligent man thence concludes marriage allowed in the gospel only to avoid an evil, because no other end is there expressed. Thus Moses of necessity suffered many to put away their wives for hardness of heart; but enacted the law of divorce doubtless for other good causes, not for this only sufferance. He permitted not divorce by law as an evil, for that was impossible to divine law, but permitted by accident the evil of them who divorced against the law's intention undiscoverably. This also may be thought not improbably, that Christ, stirred up in his spirit against these tempting pharisees, answered them in a certain form of indignation usual among good authors; whereby the question or the truth is not directly answered, but something which is fitter for them who ask to hear. So in the ecclesiastical stories, one demanding how God employed himself before the world was made, had answer, that he was making hell for curious questioners. Another (and Libanius, the sophist, as I remember) asking in derision some Christian what the carpenter, meaning our Saviour, was doing, now that Julian so prevailed, had it returned him, that the carpenter was making a coffin for the apostate. So Christ being demanded maliciously why Moses made the law of divorce, answers them in a vehement scheme, not telling them the cause why he made it, but what was fittest to be told them, that "for the hardness of their hearts" he suffered them to abuse it. And albeit Mark say not, "He suffered" you, but, "To you he wrote this precept," Mark may be warrantably expounded by Matthew the larger. And whether he suffered, or gave precept, being all one, as was heard, it changes not the trope of indignation, fittest account for such askers. Next, for the hardness of "your hearts, to you he wrote this precept," infers not therefore for this cause only he wrote it, as was paralleled by other scriptures. Lastly, it may be worth the observing, that Christ, speaking to the pharisees, does not say in general that for hardness of heart he gave this precept, but, "You he suffered, and to you he gave this precept, for your hardness of heart." It cannot be easily thought, that Christ here included all the children of Israel under the person of these tempting pharisees, but that he conceals wherefore he gave the better sort of them this law, and expresses by saying emphatically, "To you," how he gave it to the worser, such as the pharisees best represented, that is to say, for the hardness of your hearts: as indeed to wicked men and hardened hearts he gives the whole law and the gospel also, to harden them the more. Thus many ways it may orthodoxally be understood how God or Moses suffered such as the demanders were, to divorce for hardness of heart. Whereas the vulgar expositor, beset with contradictions and absurdities round, and resolving at any peril to make an exposition of it, (as there is nothing more violent and boisterous than a reverend ignorance in fear to be convicted,) rushes brutely and impetuously against all the principles both of nature, piety, and moral goodness; and in the fury of his literal expounding overturns them all.

"But from the beginning it was not so."] Not how from the beginning? Do they suppose that men might not divorce at all, not necessarily, not deliberately, except for adultery, but that some law, like canon law, presently attached them, both before and after the flood, till stricter Moses came, and with law brought licence into the world? That were a fancy indeed to smile at. Undoubtedly as to point of judicial law, divorce was more permissive from the beginning before Moses than under Moses. But from the beginning, that is to say, by the institution in Paradise, it was not intended that matrimony should dissolve for every trivial cause, as you pharisees accustom. But that it was not thus suffered from the beginning ever since the race of men corrupted, and laws were made, he who will affirm must have found out other antiquities than are yet known. Besides, we must consider now, what can be so as from the beginning, not only what should be so. In the beginning, had men continued perfect, it had been just that all things should have remained as they began to Adam and Eve. But after that the sons of men grew violent and injurious, it altered the lore of justice, and put the government of things into a new frame. While man and woman were both perfect each to other, there needed no divorce; but when they both degenerated to imperfection, and ofttimes grew to be an intolerable evil each to other, then law more justly did permit the alienating of that evil which mistake made proper, than it did the appropriating of that good which nature at first made common. For if the absence of outward good be not so bad as the presence of a close evil, and that propriety, whether by covenant or possession, be but the attainment of some outward good, it is more natural and righteous that the law should sever us from an intimate evil, than appropriate any outward good to us from the community of nature. The gospel indeed, tending ever to that which is perfectest, aimed at the restorement of all things as they were in the beginning; and therefore all things were in common to those primitive Christians in the Acts, which Ananias and Sapphira dearly felt. That custom also continued more or less till the time of Justin Martyr, as may be read in his second Apology, which might be writ after that act of communion perhaps some forty years above a hundred. But who will be the man shall introduce this kind of commonwealth, as Christianity now goes? If then marriage must be as in the beginning, the persons that marry must be such as then were; the institution must make good, in some tolerable sort, what it promises to either party. If not, it is but madness to drag this one ordinance back to the beginning, and draw down all other to the present necessity and condition, far from the beginning, even to the tolerating of extortions and oppressions. Christ only told us, that from the beginning it was not so; that is to say, not so as the pharisees manured the business; did not command us that it should be forcibly so again in all points, as at the beginning; or so at least in our intentions and desires, but so in execution, as reason and present nature can bear. Although we are not to seek, that the institution itself from the first beginning was never but conditional, as all covenants are: because thus and thus, therefore so and so; if not thus, then not so. Then moreover was perfectest to fulfill each law in itself; now as perfectest in this estate of things, to ask of charity how much law may be fulfilled: else the fulfilling ofttimes is the greatest breaking. If any therefore demand, which is now most perfection, to ease an extremity by divorce, or to enrage and fester it by the grievous observance of a miserable wedlock, I am not destitute to say, which is most perfection (although some, who believe they think favorably of divorce, esteem it only venial to infirmity). Him I hold more in the way to perfection, who foregoes an unfit, ungodly, and discordant wedlock, to live according to peace and love, and God's institution in a fitter choice, than he who debars himself the happy experience of all godly, which is peaceful conversation in his family, to live a contentious and unchristian life not to be avoided, in temptations not to be lived in, only for the false keeping of a most unreal nullity, a marriage that hath no affinity with God's intention, a daring phantasm, a mere toy of terror awing weak senses, to the lamentable superstition of ruining themselves; the remedy whereof God in his law vouchsafes us. Which not to dare use, he warranting, is not our perfection, is our infirmity, our little faith, our timorous and low conceit of charity: and in them who force us, it is their masking pride and vanity, to seem holier and more circumspect than God. So far is it that we need impute to him infirmity, who thus divorces: since the rule of perfection is not so much that which was done in the beginning, as that which now is nearest to the rule of charity. This is the greatest, the perfectest, the highest commandment.

Ver. 9. "And I say unto you, whoso shall put away his wife, except it be for fornication, and shall marry another, committeth adultery: and whoso marrieth her which is put away, doth commit adultery."

"And I say unto you."] That this restrictive denouncement of Christ contradicts and refutes that permissive precept of Moses common expositors themselves disclaim: and that it does not traverse from the closet of conscience to the courts of civil or canon law, with any Christian rightly commenced, requires not long evincing. If Christ then did not here check permissive Moses, nor did reduce matrimony to the beginning more than all other things, as the reason of man's condition could bear, we would know precisely what it was which he did, and what the end was of his declaring thus austerely against divorce. For this is a confessed oracle in law, that he who looks not at the intention of a precept, the more superstitious he is of the letter, the more he misinterprets. Was it to shame Moses? that had been monstrous. Or all those purest ages of Israel, to whom the permission was granted? that were as incredible. Or was it that he who came to abrogate the burden of law, not the equity, should put this yoke upon a blameless person, to league himself in chains with a begirting mischief, not to separate till death? He who taught us, that

no man puts a piece of new cloth upon an old garment, nor new wine into old bottles, that he should sew this patch of strictness upon the old apparel of our frailty, to make a rent more incurable, whenas in all other amendments his doctrine still charges, that regard be had to the garment, and to the vessel, what it can endure; this were an irregular and single piece of rigor, not only sounding disproportion to the whole gospel, but outstretching the most rigorous nerves of law and rigor itself. No other end therefore can be left imaginable of this excessive restraint, but to bridle those erroneous and licentious postillers the pharisees; not by telling them what may be done in necessity, but outstretching the most rigorous nerves abusively, which their tetrarch had done. And as the offence was in one extreme, so the rebuke, to bring more efficaciously to a rectitude and mediocrity, stands not in the middle way of duty, but in the other extreme. Which art of powerful reclaiming, wisest men have also taught in their ethical precepts and gnomologies, resembling it, as when we bend a crooked wand the contrary way; not that it should stand so bent, but that the overbending might reduce it to a straightness by its own reluctance. And as the physician cures him who hath taken down poison, not by the middling temper of nourishment, but by the other extreme of antidote; so Christ administers here a sharp and corrosive sentence against a foul and putrid licence; not to eat into the flesh, but into the sore. And knowing that our divines through all their comments make no scruple, where they please, to soften the high and vehement speeches of our Saviour, which they call hyperboles: why in this one text should they be such crabbed Masorites of the letter, as not to mollify a transcendence of literal rigidity, which they confess to find often elsewhere in his manner of delivery, but must make their exposition here such an obdurate Cyclops, to have but one eye for this text, and that only open to cruelty and enthralment, such as no divine or human law before ever heard of? No, let the foppish canonist, with his fardel of matrimonial cases, go and be vendible where men be so unhappy as to cheapen him: the words of Christ shall be asserted from such elemental notaries, and resolved by the now only lawgiving mouth of charity; which may be done undoubtedly by understanding them as follows.

"Whosoever shall put away his wife."] That is to say, shall so put away as the propounders of this question, the pharisees, were wont to do, and covertly defended Herod for so doing; whom to rebuke, our Saviour here mainly intends, and not to determine all the cases of divorce, as appears by St. Paul. Whosoever shall put away, either violently without mutual consent for urgent reasons, or conspiringly by plot of lust, or cunning malice, shall put away for any sudden mood, or contingency of disagreement, which is not daily practice, but may blow soon over, and be reconciled, except it be fornication; whosoever shall put away rashly, as his choler prompts him, without due time of deliberating, and think his conscience discharged only by the bill of divorce given, and the outward law satisfied; whosoever, lastly, shall put away his wife, that is, a wife indeed, and not in name only, such a one who both can and is willing to be a meet help toward the chief ends of marriage both civil and sanctified, except fornication be the cause, that man, or that pair, commit adultery. Not he who puts away by mutual consent, with all the considerations and respects of humanity and gentleness, without malicious or lustful drift. Not he who after sober and cool experience, and long debate within himself, puts away, whom though he cannot love or suffer as a wife with that sincere affection that marriage requires, yet loves at least with that civility and goodness, as not to keep her under a neglected and unwelcome residence, where nothing can be hearty, and not being, it must needs be both unjoyous and injurious to any perceiving person so detained, and more injurious than to be freely and upon good terms dismissed. Nor doth he put away adulterously who complains of causes rooted in immutable nature, utter unfitness, utter disconformity, not conciliable, because not to be amended without a miracle. Nor he who puts away an unquenchable vexation from his bosom, and flies an evil, than which a greater cannot befall human society. Nor he who puts away with

the full suffrage and applause of his conscience, not relying on the written bill of law, but claiming by faith and fulness of persuasion the rights and promises of God's institution, of which he finds himself in a mistaken wedlock defrauded. Doubtless this man hath bail enough to be no adulterer, giving divorce for these causes.

"His wife."] This word is not to be idle here, a mere word without a sense, much less a fallacious word signifying contrary to what it pretends; but faithfully signifies a wife, that is, a comfortable help and society, as God instituted; does not signify deceitfully under this name an intolerable adversary, not a helpless, unaffectionate, and sullen mass, whose very company represents the visible and exactest figure of loneliness itself. Such an associate he who puts away, divorces not a wife, but disjoins a nullity which God never joined, if she be neither willing, nor to her proper and requisite duties sufficient, as the words of God institute her. And this also is Bucer's explication of this place.

"Except it be for fornication," or "saving for the cause of fornication," as Matt. v.] This declares what kind of causes our Saviour meant; fornication being no natural and perpetual cause, but only accidental and temporary; therefore shows that head of causes from whence it is excepted, to be meant of the same sort. For exceptions are not logically deduced from a diverse kind, as to say whoso puts away for any natural cause except fornication, the exception would want salt. And if they understand it, whoso for any cause whatever, they cast themselves; granting divorce for frigidity a natural cause of their own allowing, though not here expressed, and for desertion without infidelity, whenas he who marries, as they allow him for desertion, deserts as well as is deserted, and finally puts away for another cause besides adultery. It will with all due reason therefore be thus better understood, whoso puts away for any accidental and temporary causes, except one of them, which is fornication. Thus this exception finds out the causes from whence it is excepted to be of the same kind, that is, casual, not continual.

"Saving for the cause of fornication."]

The New Testament, though it be said originally writ in Greek, yet hath nothing near so many Atticisms as Hebraisms, and Syriacisms, which was the majesty of God, not filing the tongue of scripture to a Gentilish idiom, but in a princely manner offering to them as to Gentiles and foreigners grace and mercy, though not in foreign words, yet in a foreign style that might induce them to the fountains; and though their calling were high and happy, yet still to acknowledge God's ancient people their betters, and that language the metropolitan language. He therefore who thinks to scholiaze upon the gospel, though Greek, according to his Greek analogies, and hath not been auditor to the oriental dialects, shall want in the heat of his analysis no accommodation to stumble. In this place, as the 5th of Matth. reads it, "Saving for the cause of fornication," the Greek, such as it is, sounds it, except for the "word, report, speech, or proportion" of fornication. In which regard, with other inducements, many ancient and learned writers have understood this exception, as comprehending any fault equivalent and proportional to fornication. But truth is, the evangelist here Hebraizes, taking "word or speech" for "cause or matter," in the common Eastern phrase, meaning perhaps no more than if he had said "for fornication," as in this 19th chapter. And yet the word is found in the 5th of Exodus also signifying proportion, where the Israelites are commanded to do their tasks, "the matter of each day in his day." A task, we know, is a proportion of work, not doing the same thing absolutely every day, but so much. Whereby it may be doubtful yet, whether here be not excepted not only fornication itself, but other causes equipollent, and proportional to fornication. Which very word also to understand rightly, we must of necessity have recourse again to the Hebrew. For in the Greek and Latin sense, by fornication is meant the common prostitution of body for sale. So that they who are so exact for the letter shall be dealt with by the Lexicon, and the Etymologicon too if they please, and must be bound to forbid divorce for adultery also, until it come to open whoredom and trade, like that for which Claudius divorced Mes-

salina. Since therefore they take not here the word fornication in the common significance, for an open exercise in the stews, but grant divorce for one single act of privatest adultery, notwithstanding that the word speaks a public and notorious frequency of fact, not without price; we may reason with as good leave, and as little straining to the text, that our Saviour on set purpose chose this word fornication, improperly applied to the lapse of adultery, that we might not think ourselves bound from all divorce, except when that fault hath been actually committed. For the language of scripture signifies by fornication (and others besides St. Austin so expounded it) not only the trespass of body, nor perhaps that between married persons, unless in a degree or quality as shameless as the bordello; but signifies also any notable disobedience, or intractable carriage of the wife to the husband, as Judg. xix. 2, whereof at large in "the Doctrine of Divorce," l. 2, c. 18. Secondly, signifies the apparent alienation of mind not to idolatry, (which may seem to answer the act of adultery,) but far on this side, to any point of will-worship, though to the true God; sometimes it notes the love of earthly things, or worldly pleasures, though in a right believer, sometimes the least suspicion of unwitting idolatry. As Numb. xv. 39, wilful disobedience to any of the least of God's commandments is called fornication: Psalm. lxxiii. 26, 27; a distrust only in God, and withdrawing from that nearness of zeal and confidence which ought to be, is called fornication. We may be sure it could not import thus much less than idolatry in the borrowed metaphor between God and man, unless it signified as much less than adultery in the ordinary acception between man and wife. Add also, that there was no need our Saviour should grant divorce for adultery, it being death by law, and law then in force. Which was the cause why Joseph sought to put away his betrothed wife privately, lest he should make her an example of capital punishment, as learnedest expounders affirm, Herod being a great zealot of the Mosaic law, and the pharisees great masters of the text, as the woman taken in adultery doubtless had cause to fear. Or if they can prove it was neglected, which they cannot do, why did our Saviour shape his answer to the corruption of that age, and not rather tell them of their neglect? If they say he came not to meddle with their judicatures, much less then was it in his thought to make them new ones, or that divorce should be judicially restrained in a stricter manner by these his words, more than adultery judicially acquitted by those his words to the adulteress. His sentence doth no more by law forbid divorce here, than by law it doth absolve adultery there. To them therefore, who have drawn this yoke upon Christians from his words thus wrested, nothing remains but the guilt of a presumption and perverseness, which will be hard for them to answer. Thus much that the word fornication is to be understood as the language of Christ understands it for a constant alienation and disaffection of mind, or for the continual practice of disobedience and crossness from the duties of love and peace; that is, in sum, when to be a tolerable wife is either naturally not in their power, or obstinately not in their will: and this opinion also is St. Austin's, lest it should hap to be suspected of novelty. Yet grant the thing here meant were only adultery, the reason of things will afford more to our assertion, than did the reason of words. For why is divorce unlawful but only for adultery? because, say they, that crime only breaks the matrimony. But this, I reply, The institution itself gainsays: for that which is most contrary to the words and meaning of the institution, that most breaks the matrimony; but a perpetual unmeetness and unwillingness to all the duties of help, of love, and tranquillity, is most contrary to the words and meaning of the institution; that therefore much more breaks matrimony than the act of adultery, though repeated. For this, as it is not felt, nor troubles him who perceives it not, so being perceived, may be soon repented, soon amended: soon, if it can be pardoned, may be redeemed with the more ardent love and duty in her who hath the pardon. But this natural unmeetness both cannot be unknown long, and ever after cannot be amended, if it be natural; and will not, if it be far gone obstinate. So that wanting aught in the instant to be as great a breach as adultery, it gains it in the perpetuity to be greater. Next, adultery does not exclude her other fitness, her other pleasingness: she may be otherwise both loving and prevalent, as many adulteresses be; but in this general unfitness or alienation she can be nothing to him that can please. In adultery nothing is given from the husband, which he misses, or enjoys the less, as it may be subtly given; but this unfitness defrauds him of the whole contentment which is sought in wedlock. And what benefit be given by the stealth of adultery to another, if that which there is to give, whether it be solace, or society, be not such as may justly content him? and so not only deprives him of what it should give him, but gives him sorrow and affliction, which it did not owe him. Besides, is adultery the greatest breach of matrimony in respect of the offence to God, or of the injury to man? If in the former, then other sins may offend God more, and sooner cause him to disunite his servants from being one flesh with such an offender. If in respect of the latter, other injuries are demonstrated therein more heavy to man's nature than the iterated act of adultery. God therefore, in his wisdom, would not so dispose his remedies, as to provide them for the less injuries, and not allow them for the greater. Thus is won both from the word fornication, and the reason of adultery, that the exception of divorce is not limited to that act, but enlarged to the causes above specified.

"And whoso marrieth her which is put away doth commit adultery."] By this clause alone, if by nothing else, we may assure us that Christ intended not to deliver here the whole doctrine of divorce, but only to condemn abuses. Otherwise to marry after desertion, which the apostle, and the reformed churches at this day permit, is here forbid, as adultery. Be she never so wrongfully deserted, or put away, as the law then suffered, if thus forsaken and expulsed, she accept the refuge and protection of any honester man who would love her better, and give herself in marriage to him; by what the letter guides us, it shall be present adultery to them both. This is either harsh and cruel, or all the churches, teaching as they do to the contrary, are loose and remiss; besides that the apostle himself stands deeply fined in a contradiction against our Saviour. What shall we make of this? what rather the common interpreter can make of it, for they be his own markets, let him now try; let him try which way he can wind in his Vertumnian distinctions and evasions, if his canonical gabardine of text and letter do not now sit too close about him, and pinch his activity: which if I err not, hath here hampered itself in a spring fit for those who put their confidence in alphabets. Spanheim, a writer of "Evangelic Doubts," comes now and confesses, that our Saviour's words are "to be limited beyond the limitation there expressed, and excepted beyond their own exception," as not speaking of what happened rarely, but what most commonly. Is it so rare, Spanheim, to be deserted? or was it then so rare to put away injuriously, that a person so hatefully expelled, should to the heaping of more injury be turned like an infectious thing out of all marriage fruition upon pain of adultery, as not considerable to the brevity of this half sentence? Of what then speaks our Saviour? "Of that collusion," saith he, "which was then most frequent among the Jews, of changing wives and husbands through inconstancy and unchaste desires." Colluders yourself, as violent to this law of God by your unmerciful binding, as the pharisees by their unbounded loosening? Have thousands of Christian souls perished as to this life, and God knows what hath betided their consciences, for want of this healing explanation; and is it now at last obscurely drawn forth, only to cure a scratch, and leave the main wound spouting? "Whosoever putteth away his wife, except for fornication, committeth adultery." That shall be spoke of all ages, and all men, though never so justly otherwise moved to divorce: in the very next breath, "And whoso marrieth her which is put away committeth adultery:" the men are new and miraculous, they tell you now, "you are to limit it to that age, when it was in fashion to chop matrimonies, and must be meant of him who puts away with his wife's consent through the lightness and lewdness of them both." But what rule of logic, or indeed of reason, is our commission to understand the antecedent one way and the consequent another? for in that habitude this whole verse may be considered: or at least to take the parts of a copulate axiom, both absolutely affirmative, and to say, the first is absolutely true, the other not, but must be limited to a certain time and custom; which is no less than to say they are both false? For in this compound axiom, be the parts never so many, if one of them do but falter, and be not equally absolute and general, the rest are all false. If, therefore, that "he who marries her which is put away commits adultery," be not generally true, neither is it generally true that "he commits adultery who puts away for other cause than fornication." And if the marrying her which is put away must be understood limited, which they cannot but yield it must, with the same limitation must be understood the putting away. Thus doth the common exposition confound itself and justify this which is here brought, that our Saviour, as well in the first part of this sentence as in the second, prohibited only such divorces as the Jews then made through malice or through plotted licence, not those which are for necessary and just causes; where charity and wisdom disjoins that which not God, but error and disaster, joined.

And there is yet to this our exposition, a stronger siding friend, than any can be an adversary, unless St. Paul be doubted, who repeating a command concerning divorce, 1 Cor. vii., which is agreed by writers to be the same with this of our Saviour, and appointing that the "wife remain unmarried, or be reconciled to her husband," leaves it infallible, that our Saviour spake chiefly against putting away for casual and choleric disagreements, or any other cause which may with human patience and wisdom be reconciled; not hereby meaning to hale and dash together the irreconcileable aversations of nature, nor to tie up a faultless person like a parricide, as it were into one sack with an enemy, to be his causeless tormentor and executioner the length of a long life. Lastly, let this sentence of Christ be understood how it will, yet that it was never intended for a judicial law, to be enforced by the magistrate, besides that the office of our Saviour had no such purpose in the gospel, this latter part of the sentence may assure us, "And whoso marrieth her which is put away, commits adultery." Shall the exception for adultery belong to this clause or not? If not, it would be strange, that he who marries a woman really divorced for adultery, as Christ permitted, should become an adulterer by marrying one who is now no other man's wife, himself being also free, who might by this means reclaim her from common whoredom. And if the exception must belong hither, then it follows that he who marries an adulteress divorced commits no adultery; which would soon discover to us what an absurd and senseless piece of injustice this would be, to make a civil statute of in penal courts: whereby the adulteress put away may marry another safely, and without a crime to him that marries her; but the innocent and wrongfully divorced shall not marry again without the guilt of adultery both to herself and to her second husband. This saying of Christ, therefore, cannot be made a temporal law, were it but for this reason. Nor is it easy to say what coherence there is at all in it from the letter, to any perfect sense not obnoxious to some absurdity, and seems much less agreeable to whatever else of the gospel is left us written: doubtless by our Saviour spoken in that fierceness and abstruse intricacy, first, to amuse his tempters, and admonish in general the abusers of that Mosaic law; next, to let Herod know a second knower of his unlawful act, though the Baptist were beheaded; last, that his disciples and all good men might learn to expound him in this place, as in all other his precepts, not by the written letter, but by that unerring paraphrase of Christian love and charity, which is the sum of all commands, and the perfection.

Ver. 10. "His disciples say unto him, If the case of the man be so with his wife, it is not good to marry."

This verse I add, to leave no objection behind unanswered: for some may think, if this our Saviour's sentence be so fair, as not commanding aught that patience or nature cannot brook, why then did the disciples murmur and say, "It is not good to marry?" I answer, that the disciples had been longer bred up under the pharisæan doctrine, than under that of Christ, and so no marvel though they yet retained the infection of loving old licentious customs; no marvel though they thought it hard they might not for any offence, that thoroughly angered them, divorce a wife, as well as put away a servant, since it was but giving her a bill, as they were taught. Secondly, it was no unwonted thing with them not to understand our Saviour in matters far easier. So that be it granted their conceit of this text was the same which is now commonly conceived, according to the usual rate of their capacity then, it will not hurt a better interpretation. But why did not Christ, seeing their error, inform them? for good cause: it was his professed method not to teach them all things at all times, but each thing in due place and season. Christ said, Luke xxii., that "he who had no sword, should sell his garment and buy one:" the disciples took it in a manifest wrong sense, yet our Saviour did not there inform them better. He told them, "it was easier for a camel to go through a needle's eye," than a rich man in at heaven-gate. They were "amazed exceedingly:" he explained himself to mean of those "who trust in riches," Mark x. "They were amazed then out of measure," for so Mark relates it; as if his explaining had increased their amazement in such a plain case, and which concerned so nearly their calling to be informed in. Good reason, therefore, if Christ at that time did not stand amplifying, to the thick prejudice and tradition wherein they were, this question of more difficulty, and less concernment to any perhaps of them in particular. Yet did he not omit to sow within them the seeds of a sufficient determining, against the time that his promised Spirit should bring all things to their memory. He had declared in their hearing not long before, how distant he was from abolishing the law itself of divorce; he had referred them to the institution; and after all this, gives them a set answer, from which they might collect what was clear enough, that "all men cannot receive all sayings," ver. 11. If such regard be had to each man's receiving of marriage or single life, what can arise, that the same Christian regard should not be had in most necessary divorce? All which instructed both them and us, that it beseemed his disciples to learn the deciding of this question, which hath nothing new in it, first by the institution, then by the general grounds of religion, not by a particular saying here or there, tempered and levelled only to an incident occasion, the riddance of a tempting assault. For what can this be but weak and shallow apprehension, to forsake the standard principles of institution, faith and charity; then to be blank and various at every occurrence in scripture, and in a cold spasm of scruple, to rear peculiar doctrines upon the place, that shall bid the gray authority of most unchangeable and sovereign rules to stand by and be contradicted? Thus to this evangelic precept of famous difficulty, which for these many ages weakly understood, and violently put in practice, hath made a shambles rather than an ordinance of matrimony, I am firm a truer exposition cannot be given. If this or that argument here used please not every one, there is no scarcity of arguments, any half of them will suffice. Or should they all fail, as truth itself can fail as soon, I should content me with the institution alone to wage this controversy, and not distrust to evince. If any need it not, the happier; yet Christians ought to study earnestly what may be another's need. But if, as mortal mischances are, some hap to need it, let them be sure they abuse not, and give God his thanks, who hath revived this remedy, not too late for them, and scoured off an inveterate misexposition from the gospel: a work not to perish by the vain breath or doom of this age. Our next industry shall be, under the same guidance, to try with what fidelity that remaining passage in the Epistles touching this matter hath been commented.

1 Cor. vii. 10, &c.

10. "And unto the married I command," &c.

11. "And let not the husband put away his wife."

This intimates but what our Saviour taught before, that divorce is not rashly to be made, but reconcilement to be persuaded and endeavored, as oft as the cause can have to do with reconcilement, and is not under the dominion of blameless nature; which may have reason to depart, though seldomest and last from charitable love, yet sometimes from friendly, and familiar, and something oftener from conjugal love, which requires not only moral, but natural causes to the making and maintaining; and may be warrantably excused to retire from the deception of what it justly seeks, and the ill requitals which unjustly it finds. For nature hath her zodiac also, keeps her great annual circuit over human things, as truly as the sun and planets in the firmament; hath her anomalies, hath her obliquities in ascensions and declinations, accesses and recesses, as blamelessly as they in heaven. And sitting in her planetary orb with two reins in each hand, one strait, the other loose, tempers the course of minds as well as bodies to several conjunctions and oppositions, friendly or unfriendly aspects, consenting oftest with reason, but never contrary. This in the effect no man of meanest reach but daily sees; and though to every one it appear not in the cause, yet to a clear capacity, well nurtured with good reading and observation, it cannot but be plain and visible. Other exposition, therefore, than hath been given to former places, that give light to these two summary verses, will not be needful: save only that these precepts are meant to those married who differ not in religion.

"But to the rest speak I, not the Lord: if any brother hath a wife that believeth not, and she be pleased to dwell with him, let him not put her away."

Now follows what is to be done, if the persons wedded be of a different faith. The common belief is, that a Christian is here commanded not to divorce, if the infidel please to stay, though it be but to vex, or to deride, or to seduce the Christian. This doctrine will be the easy work of a refutation. The other opinion is, that a Christian is here conditionally permitted to hold wedlock with a misbeliever only, upon hopes limited by Christian prudence, which without much difficulty shall be defended. That this here spoken by Paul, not by the Lord, cannot be a command, these reasons avouch. First, the law of Moses, Exod. xxxiv. 16; Deut. vii. 3, 6, interpreted by Ezra and Nehemiah, two infallible authors, commands to divorce an infidel not for the fear only of a ceremonious defilement, but of an irreligious seducement, feared both in respect of the believer himself, and of his children in danger to be perverted by the misbelieving parent, Nehem. xiii. 24, 26. And Peter Martyr thought this a convincing reason. If therefore the legal pollution vanishing have abrogated the ceremony of this law, so that a Christian may be permitted to retain an infidel without uncleanness, yet the moral reason of divorcing stands to eternity, which neither apostle nor angel from heaven can countermand. All that they reply to this is their human warrant, that God will preserve us in our obedience to this command against the danger of seducement. And so undoubtedly he will, if we understand his commands aright; if we turn not this evangelic permission into a legal, and yet illegal, command; if we turn not hope into bondage, the charitable and free hope of gaining another into the forced and servile temptation of losing ourselves: but more of this beneath. Thus these words of Paul by common doctrine made a command, are made a contradiction to the moral law.

Secondly, Not the law only, but the gospel from the law, and from itself, requires even in the same chapter, where divorce between them of one religion is so narrowly forbid, rather than our Christian love should come into danger of backsliding, to forsake all relations, how near soever, and the wife expressly, with promise of a high reward, Matt. xix. And he who hates not father or mother, wife or children, hindering his Christian course, much more if they despise or assault it, cannot be a disciple, Luke xiv. How can the apostle then command us to love and continue in that matrimony, which our Saviour bids us hate and forsake? They can as soon teach our faculty of respiration to contract and to dilate itself at once, to breathe and to fetch breath in the same instant, as teach our minds how to do such contrary acts as these towards the same object, and as they must be done in the same moment. For either the hatred of her religion, and her hatred to our religion, will work powerfully against the love of her society, or the love of that will by degrees flatter out all our zealous hatred and forsaking, and soon ensnare us to unchristianly compliances.

Thirdly, In marriage there ought not only to be a civil love, but such a love as Christ loves his church; but where the religion is contrary without hope of conversion, there can be no love, no faith, no peaceful society; (they of the other opinion confess it;) nay, there ought not to be, further than in expectation of gaining a soul: when that ceases, we know God hath put enmity between the seed of the woman, and the seed of the serpent. Neither should we "love them that hate the Lord," as the prophet told Jehoshaphat, 2 Chron. xix. And this apostle himself in another place warns us, that we "be not unequally yoked with infidels," 2 Cor. vi.; for that there can be no fellowship, no communion, no concord between such. Outward commerce and civil intercourse cannot perhaps be avoided; but true friendship and familiarity there can be none. How vainly therefore, not to say how impiously, would the most inward and dear alliance of marriage or continuance in marriage be commanded, where true friendship is confessed impossible! For, say they, we are forbid here to marry with an infidel, not bid to divorce. But to rob the words thus of their full sense, will not be allowed them: it is not said, Enter not into yoke, but, "Be not unequally yoked;" which plainly forbids the thing in present act, as well as in purpose: and his manifest conclusion is, not only that "we should not touch," but that having touched, "we should come out from among them, and be separate;" with the promise of a blessing thereupon, that "God will receive us, will be our Father, and we his sons and daughters," ver. 17, 18. Why we should stay with an infidel after the expense of all our hopes can be but for a civil relation; but why we should depart from a seducer, setting aside the misconstruction of this place, is from a religious necessity of departing. The worse cause therefore of staying (if it be any cause at all, for civil government forces it not) must not overtop the religious cause of separating, executed with such an urgent zeal, and such a prostrate humiliation, by Ezra and Nehemiah. What God hates to join, certainly he cannot love should continue joined; it being all one in matter of ill consequence, to marry, or to continue married with an infidel, save only so long as we wait willingly, and with a safe hope. St. Paul therefore, citing here a command of the Lord Almighty, for so he terms it, that we should separate, cannot have bound us with that which he calls his own, whether command or counsel, that we should not separate.

Which is the fourth reason, for he himself takes care lest we should mistake him: "but to the rest speak I, not the Lord." If the Lord spake not, then man spake it, and man hath no lordship to command the conscience: yet modern interpreters will have it a command, maugre St. Paul himself; they will make him a prophet like Caiaphas, to speak the word of the Lord, not thinking, nay, denying to think; though he disavow to have received it from the Lord, his word shall not be taken; though an apostle, he shall be borne down in his own epistle, by a race of expositors who presume to know from whom he spake, better than he himself. Paul deposes, that the Lord speaks not this; they, that the Lord speaks it: can this be less than to brave him with a full-faced contradiction? Certainly to such a violence as this, for I cannot call it an expounding, what a man should answer I know not, unless that if it be their pleasure next to put a gag into the apostle's mouth, they are already furnished with a commodious audacity toward the attempt. Beza would seem to shun the contradictory, by telling us that the Lord spake it not in person, as he did the former precept. But how many other doctrines doth St. Paul deliver, which the Lord spake not in person, and yet never uses this preamble but in things indifferent? So long as we receive him for a messenger of God, for him to stand sorting sentences, what the Lord spake in person, and what he, not the Lord in person, would be but a chill trifling, and his readers might catch an ague the while. But if we shall supply the grammatical ellipsis regularly, and as we must in the same tense, all will be then clear; for we cannot supply it thus, To the rest I speak, the Lord spake not; but, I speak, the Lord speaks not. If then the Lord neither spake in person, nor speaks it now, the apostle testifying both, it follows duly, that this can be no command. Forsooth the fear is, lest this, not being a command, would prove an evangelic counsel, and so make way for supererogations. As if the apostle could not speak his mind in things indifferent, as he doth in four or five several places of this chapter with the like preface of not commanding, but that the doubted inconvenience of supererogating must needs rush in. And how adds it to the word of the Lord, (for this also they object,) whenas the apostle by his Christian prudence guides us in the liberty which God hath left us to, without command? Could not the Spirit of God instruct us by him what was free, as well as what was not? But what need I more, when Cameron, an ingenuous writer, and in high esteem, solidly confutes the surmise of a command here, and among other words hath these, that "when Paul speaks as an apostle, he uses this form," The Lord saith, not I, ver. 10; "but as a private man he saith, I speak, not the Lord." And thus also all the prime fathers, Austin, Jerome, and the rest, understood this place.

Fifthly, The very stating of the question declares this to be no command: "If any brother hath an unbelieving wife, and she be pleased to dwell with him, let him not put her away." For the Greek word συνευδοκεῖ does not imply only her being pleased to stay, but his being pleased to let her stay: it must be a consent of them both. Nor can the force of this word be rendered less, without either much negligence or iniquity of him that otherwise translates it. And thus the Greek church also and their synods understood it, who best knew what their own language meant, as appears by Matthæus Monachus, an author set forth by Leunclavius, and of antiquity perhaps not inferior to Balsamon, who writes upon the canons of the apostles: this author in his chap. "That marriage is not to be made with heretics," thus recites the second canon of the 6th synod: "As to the Corinthians, Paul determines, If the believing wife choose to live with the unbelieving husband, or the believing husband with the unbelieving wife. Mark," saith he, "how the apostle here condescends: if the believer please to dwell with the unbeliever; so that if he please not, out of doubt the marriage is dissolved. And I am persuaded it was so in the beginning, and thus preached." And thereupon gives an example of one, who though not deserted, yet by the decree of Theodotus the patriarch divorced an unbelieving wife. What therefore depends in the plain state of this question on the consent and well liking of them both must not be a command. Lay next the latter end of the 11th verse to the 12th, (for wherefore else is logic taught us?) in a discreet axiom, as it can be no other by the phrase; "The Lord saith, Let not the husband put away his wife: but I say, Let him not put away a misbelieving wife." This sounds as if by the judgment of Paul a man might put away any wife but the misbelieving; or else the parts are not discrete, or dissentary, for both conclude not putting away, and consequently in such a form the proposition is ridiculous. Of necessity therefore the former part of this sentence must be conceived, as understood, and silently granted, that although the Lord command to divorce an infidel, yet I, not the Lord, command you. No; but give my judgment, that for some evangelic reasons a Christian may be permitted not to divorce her. Thus while we reduce the brevity of St. Paul to a plainer sense, by the needful supply of that which was granted between him and the Corinthians, the very logic of his speech extracts him confessing, that the Lord's command lay in a seeming contrariety to this his counsel: and that he meant not to thrust out a command of the Lord by a new one of his own, as one nail drives another, but to release us from the rigor of it, by the right of the gospel, so far forth as a charitable cause leads us on in the hope of winning another soul without the peril of losing our own. For this is the glory of the gospel, to teach us that "the end of the commandment is charity," 1 Tim. i., not the drudging out a poor and worthless duty forced from us by the tax and tale of so many letters. This doctrine therefore can be no command, but it must contradict the moral law, the gospel, and the apostle himself, both elsewhere and here also even in the act of speaking.

If then it be no command, it must remain to be a permission; and that not absolute, for so it would be still contrary to the law, but with such a caution as breaks not the law, but, as the manner of the gospel is, fulfils it through charity. The law had two reasons: the one was ceremonial, the pollution that all Gentiles were to the Jews; this the vision of Peter had abolished, Acts x., and cleansed all creatures to the use of a Christian. The Corinthians understood not this, but feared lest dwelling in matrimony with an unbeliever, they were defiled. The apostle discusses that scruple with an evangelic reason, showing them that although God

heretofore under the law, not intending the conversion of the Gentiles, except some special ones, held them as polluted things to the Jew, yet now purposing to call them in, he hath purified them from that legal uncleanness wherein they stood, to use and to be used in a pure manner.

For saith he, "The unbelieving husband is sanctified by the wife, and the unbelieving wife is sanctified by the husband, else were your children unclean; but now they are holy." That is, they are sanctified to you, from that legal impurity which you so fear; and are brought into a near capacity to be holy, if they believe, and to have free access to holy things. In the mean time, as being God's creatures, a Christian hath power to use them according to their proper use; in as much as now, "all things to the pure are become pure." In this legal respect therefore ye need not doubt to continue in marriage with an unbeliever. Thus others also expound this place, and Cameron especially. This reason warrants us only what we may do without fear of pollution, does not bind us that we must. But the other reason of the law to divorce an infidel was moral, the avoiding of enticement from the true faith. This cannot shrink; but remains in as full force as ever, to save the actual Christian from the snare of a misbeliever. Yet if a Christian full of grace and spiritual gifts, finding the misbeliever not frowardly affected, fears not a seducing, but hopes rather a gaining, who sees not that this moral reason is not violated by not divorcing, which the law commanded to do, but better fulfilled by the excellence of the gospel working through charity? For neither the faithful is seduced, and the unfaithful is either saved, or with all discharge of love and evangelic duty sought to be saved. But contrariwise, if the infirm Christian shall be commanded here against his mind, against his hope, and against his strength, to dwell with all the scandals, the household persecutions, or alluring temptations of an infidel, how is not the gospel by this made harsher than the law, and more yoking? Therefore the apostle, ere he deliver this other reason why we need not in all haste put away an infidel, his mind misgiving him, lest he should seem to be the imposer of a new command, stays not for method, but with an abrupt speed inserts the declaration of their liberty in this matter.

"But if the unbelieving depart, let him depart; a brother or a sister is not under bondage in such cases: but God hath called us to peace."

"But if the unbelieving depart."] This cannot be restrained to local departure only; for who knows not that an offensive society is worse than a forsaking? If his purpose of cohabitation be to endanger the life, or the conscience, Beza himself is half persuaded, that this may purchase to the faithful person the same freedom that a desertion may; and so Gerard, and others whom he cites. If, therefore, he depart in affection; if he depart from giving hope of his conversion, if he disturb, or scoff at religion, seduce or tempt; if he rage, doubtless not the weak only, but the strong may leave him; if not for fear, yet for the dignity's sake of religion, which cannot be liable to all base affronts, merely for the worshipping of a civil marriage. I take therefore "departing" to be as large as the negative of being well pleased; that is, if he be not pleased for the present to live lovingly, quietly, inoffensively, so as may give good hope; which appears well by that which follows.

"A brother or a sister is not under bondage in such cases."] If St. Paul provide seriously against the bondage of a Christian, it is not the only bondage to live unmarried for a deserting infidel, but to endure his presence intolerably, to bear indignities against his religion in words or deeds, to be wearied with seducements, to have idolatries and superstitions ever before his eyes, to be tormented with impure and profane conversation; this must needs be bondage to a Christian: is this left all unprovided for, without remedy, or freedom granted? Undoubtedly, no; for the apostle leaves it further to be considered with prudence, what bondage a brother or sister is not under, not only in this case, but as he speaks himself plurally, "in such cases."

"But God hath called us to peace."] To peace, not to bondage, not to brabbles and contentions with him who is not pleased to live peaceably, as marriage and Christianity require. And where strife arises from a cause hopeless to be allayed, what better way to peace than by separating that which is ill

joined? It is not divorce that first breaks the peace of family, as some fondly comment on this place; but it is peace already broken, which, when other cures fail, can only be restored to the faultless person by a necessary divorce. And St. Paul here warrants us to seek peace, rather than to remain in bondage. If God hath called us to peace, why should we not follow him? why should we miserably stay in perpetual discord under a servitude not required?

"For what knowest thou, O wife, whether thou shalt save thy husband," &c.] St. Paul having thus cleared himself, not to go about the mining of our Christian liberty, not to cast a snare upon us, which to do he so much hated, returns now to the second reason of that law, to put away an infidel for fear of seducement, which he does not here contradict with a command now to venture that; but if neither the infirmity of the Christian, nor the strength of the unbeliever, be feared, but hopes appearing that he may be won, he judges it no breaking of that law, though the believer be permitted to forbear divorce, and can abide, without the peril of seducement, to offer the charity of a salvation to wife or husband, which is the fulfilling, not the transgressing, of that law; and well worth the undertaking with much hazard and patience. For what knowest thou whether thou shalt save thy wife that is, till all means convenient and possible with discretion and probability, as human things are, have been used? For Christ himself sends not our hope on pilgrimage to the world's end; but sets it bounds, beyond which we need not wait on a brother, much less on an infidel. If after such a time we may count a professing Christian no better than a heathen, after less time perhaps we may cease to hope of a heathen, that he will turn Christian. Otherwise, to bind us harder than the law, and tell us we are not under bondage, is mere mockery. If, till the unbeliever please to part, we may not stir from the house of our bondage, then certain this our liberty is not grounded in the purchase of Christ, but in the pleasure of a miscreant. What knows the loyal husband, whether he may not save the adulteress? he is not therefore bound to receive her. What knows the wife, but she may reclaim her husband who hath deserted her? Yet the reformed churches do not enjoin her to wait longer than after the contempt of an ecclesiastical summons. Beza himself here befriends us with a remarkable speech:—"What could be firmly constituted in human matters, if under pretence of expecting grace from above, it should be never lawful for us to seek our right?" And yet in other cases not less reasonable to obtain a most just and needful remedy by divorce, he turns the innocent party to a task of prayers beyond the multitude of beads and rosaries, to beg the gift of chastity in recompense of an injurious marriage. But the apostle is evident enough: "We are not under bondage;" trusting that he writes to those who are not ignorant what bondage is, to let supercilious determiners cheat them of their freedom. God hath called us to peace, and so doubtless hath left in our hands how to obtain it seasonably, if it be not our own choice to sit ever like novices wretchedly servile.

Thus much the apostle on this question between Christian and pagan, to us now of little use; yet supposing it written for our instruction, as it may be rightly applied, I doubt not but that the difference between a true believer and a heretic, or any one truly religious, either deserted or seeking divorce from any one grossly erroneous or profane, may be referred hither. For St. Paul leaves us here the solution not of this case only, which little concerns us, but of such like cases, which may occur to us. For where the reasons directly square, who can forbid why the verdict should not be the same? But this the common writers allow us not. And yet from this text, which in plain words gives liberty to none, unless deserted by an infidel, they collect the same freedom, though the desertion be not for religion, which, as I conceive, they need not do; but may, without straining, reduce it to the cause of fornication. For first, they confess that desertion is seldom without a just suspicion of adultery: next, it is a breach of marriage in the same kind, and in some sort worse: for adultery, though it give to another, yet it bereaves not all; but the deserter wholly denies all right, and makes one flesh twain, which is counted the absolutest breach of matrimony, and causes the other, as much as in him lies, to commit sin, by being so left. Nevertheless, those reasons, which they bring

of establishing by this place the like liberty from any desertion, are fair and solid: and if the thing be lawful, and can be proved so, more ways than one, so much the safer. Their arguments I shall here recite, and that they may not come idle, shall use them to make good the like freedom to divorce for other causes; and that we are no more under bondage to any heinous default against the main ends of matrimony, than to a desertion: first, they allege that, 1 Tim. v. 8, "If any provide not for those of his own house, he hath denied the faith, and is worse than an infidel." But a deserter, say they, can have no care of them who are most his own; therefore the deserted party is not less to be righted against such a one than against an infidel. With the same evidence I argue, that man or wife, who hates in wedlock, is perpetually unsociable, unpeaceful, or unduteous, either not being able, or not willing to perform what the main ends of marriage demand in help and solace, cannot be said to care for who should be dearest in the house; therefore is worse than an infidel in both regards, either in undertaking a duty which he cannot perform, to the undeserved and unspeakable injury of the other party so defrauded and betrayed, or not performing what he hath undertaken, whenas he may or might have, to the perjury of himself, more irreligious than heathenism. The blameless person, therefore, hath as good a plea to sue out his delivery from this bondage, as from the desertion of an infidel. Since most writers cannot but grant that desertion is not only a local absence but an intolerable society; or if they grant it not, the reasons of St. Paul grant it, with all as much leave as they grant to enlarge a particular freedom from paganism into a general freedom from any desertion. Secondly, they reason from the likeness of either fact, "the same loss redounds to the deserted by a Christian, as by an infidel, the same peril of temptation." And I in like manner affirm, that if honest and free persons may be allowed to know what is most to their own loss, the same loss and discontent, but worse disquiet, with continual misery and temptation, resides in the company, or better called the persecution of an unfit, or an unpeaceable consort, than by his desertion. For then the deserted may enjoy himself at least. And he who deserts is more favorable to the party whom his presence afflicts, than that importunate thing, which is and will be ever conversant before the eyes, a loyal and individual vexation. As for those who still rudely urge it no loss to marriage, no desertion, so long as the flesh is present, and offers a benevolence that hates, or is justly hated, I am not of that vulgar and low persuasion to think such forced embracements as these worth the honor or the humanity of marriage, but far beneath the soul of a rational and freeborn man. Thirdly, they say, "It is not the infidelity of the deserter, but the desertion of the infidel, from which the apostle gives this freedom:" and I join, that the apostle could as little require our subjection to an unfit and injurious bondage present, as to an infidel absent. To free us from that which is an evil by being distant, and not from that which is an inmate, and in the bosom evil, argues an improvident and careless deliverer. And thus all occasions, which way soever they turn, are not unofficious to administer something which may conduce to explain or to defend the assertion of this book touching divorce. I complain of nothing, but that it is indeed too copious to be the matter of a dispute, or a defence, rather to be yielded, as in the best ages, a thing of common reason, not of controversy. What have I left to say? I fear to be more elaborate in such a perspicuity as this, lest I should seem not to teach, but to upbraid the dulness of an age; not to commune with reason in men, but to deplore the loss of reason from among men: this only, and not the want of more to say, is the limit of my discourse.

Who among the fathers have interpreted the words of Christ concerning divorce, as is here interpreted; and what the civil law of Christian emperors in the primitive church determined.

Although testimony be in logic an argument rightly called "inartificial," and doth not solidly fetch the truth by multiplicity of authors, nor argue a thing false by the few that hold so; yet seeing most men from their youth so accustom, as not to scan reason, nor clearly to apprehend it, but to trust for that the names and numbers of such, as have got, and many times undeservedly, the reputation among them to know much; and because there is a vulgar also of teachers, who are as blindly by whom they fancy led, as they lead the people, it will not be amiss for them who had rather list themselves under this weaker sort, and follow authorities, to take notice that this opinion which I bring, hath been favored, and by some of those affirmed, who in their time were able to carry what they taught, had they urged it, through all Christendom; or to have left it such a credit with all good men, as they who could not boldly use the opinion, would have feared to censure it. But since by his appointment on whom the times and seasons wait, every point of doctrine is not fatal to be thoroughly sifted out in every age, it will be enough for me to find, that the thoughts of wisest heads heretofore, and hearts no less reverenced for devotion, have tended this way, and contributed their lot in some good measure towards this which hath been here attained. Others of them, and modern especially, have been as full in the assertion, though not so full in the reason; so that either in this regard, or in the former, I shall be manifest in a middle fortune to meet the praise or dispraise of being something first.

But I defer not what I undertook to show, that in the church both primitive and reformed, the words of Christ have been understood to grant divorce for other causes than adultery; and that the word fornication in marriage hath a larger sense than that commonly supposed.

Justin Martyr in his first Apology, written within fifty years after St. John died, relates a story which Eusebius transcribes, that a certain matron of Rome, the wife of a vicious husband, herself also formerly vicious, but converted to the faith, and persuading the same to her husband, at least the amendment of his wicked life; upon his not yielding to her daily entreaties and persuasions in this behalf, procured by law to be divorced from him. This was neither for adultery, nor desertion, but as the relation says, "esteeming it an ungodly thing to be the consort of bed with him, who against the law of nature and of right sought out voluptuous ways." Suppose he endeavored some unnatural abuse, as the Greek admits that meaning, it cannot yet be called adultery; it therefore could be thought worthy of divorce no otherwise than as equivalent, or worse; and other vices will appear in other respects as much divorcive. Next, 'tis said her friends advised her to stay a while; and what reason gave they; not because they held unlawful what she purposed, but because they thought she might longer yet hope his repentance. She obeyed, till the man going to Alexandria, and from thence reported to grow still more impenitent, not for any adultery or desertion, whereof neither can be gathered, but saith the Martyr, and speaks it like one approving, "lest she should be partaker of his unrighteous and ungodly deeds, remaining in wedlock, the communion of bed and board with such a person, she left him by a lawful divorce." This cannot but give us the judgment of the church in those pure and next to apostolic times. For how else could the woman have been permitted, or here not reprehended? and if a wife might then do this without reproof, a husband certainly might no less, if not more.

Tertullian, in the same age, writing his fourth Book against Marcion, witnesses "that Christ, by his answer to the pharisees, protected the constitution of Moses as his own, and directed the institution of the Creator," for I alter not his Carthaginian phrase: "He excused rather than destroyed the constitution of Moses; I say, he forbade conditionally, 'If any one therefore put away, that he may marry another;' so that if he prohibited conditionally, then not wholly: and what he forbade not wholly, he permitted otherwise, where the cause ceases for which he prohibited:" that is, when a man makes it not the cause of his putting away, merely that he may marry again. "Christ teaches not contrary to Moses, the justice of divorce hath Christ the asserter; he would not have marriage separate, nor kept with ignomy, permitting then a divorce;" and guesses that this vehemence of our Saviour's sentence was chiefly bent against Herod, as was cited before. Which leaves it evident how Tertullian interpreted this prohibition of our Saviour: for whereas the text is, "Whosoever putteth away, and marrieth another;" wherefore should Tertullian explain it, "Whosoever putteth away that he may marry another," but to signify his opinion, that our Saviour did not forbid divorce from an unworthy yoke, but forbid the malice or the lust of a needless change, and chiefly those plotted divorces then in use?

Origen in the next century testifies to have known certain who had the government of churches in his time, who permitted some to marry, while yet their former husbands lived, and excuses the deed, as done "not without cause, though without scripture," which confirms that cause not to be adultery; for how then was it against scripture that they married again? And a little beneath, for I cite his seventh homily on Matthew, saith he, "to endure faults worse than adultery and fornication, seems a thing unreasonable;" and disputes therefore that Christ did not speak by "way of precept, but as it were expounding." By which and the like speeches, Origen declares his mind, far from thinking that our Saviour confined all the causes of divorce to actual adultery.

Lactantius, of the age that succeeded, speaking of this matter in the 6th of his "Institutions," hath these words: "But lest any think he may circumscribe divine precepts, let this be added, that all misinterpreting, and occasion of fraud or death may be removed, he commits adultery who marries the divorced wife; and besides the crime of adultery, divorces a wife that he may marry another." To divorce and marry another, and to divorce that he may marry another, are two different things; and imply that Lactantius thought not this place the forbidding of all necessary divorce, but such only as proceeded from the wanton desire of a future choice, not from the burden of a present affliction.

About this time the council of Eliberis in Spain decreed the husband excommunicate, "if he kept his wife being an adulteress; but if he left her, he might after ten years be received into communion, if he retained her any while in his house after the adultery known." The council of Neocaesarea, in the year 314, decreed, That if the wife of any laic were convicted of adultery, that man could not be admitted into the ministry: if after ordination it were committed, he was to divorce her; if not, he could not hold his ministry. The council of Nantes condemned in seven years' penance the husband that would reconcile with an adulteress. But how proves this that other causes may divorce?

It proves thus: There can be but two causes why these councils enjoined so strictly the divorcing of an adulteress, either as an offender against God, or against the husband; in the latter respect they could not impose on him to divorce; for every man is the master of his own forgiveness: who shall hinder him to pardon the injuries done against himself? It follows therefore, that the divorce of an adulteress was commanded by these three councils, as it was a sin against God; and by all consequence they could not but believe that other sins as heinous might with equal justice be the ground of a divorce.

Basil in his 73rd rule, as Chamier numbers it, thus determines: "That divorce ought not to be, unless for adultery, or the hindrance to a godly life." What doth this but proclaim aloud more causes of divorce than adultery, if by other sins besides this, in wife or husband, the godliness of the better person may be certainly hindered and endangered?

Epiphanius, no less ancient, writing against heretics, and therefore should himself be orthodoxal above others, acquaints us in his second book, tom. i., not that his private persuasion was, but that the whole church in his time generally thought other causes of divorce lawful besides adultery, as comprehended under that name: "If," saith he, "a divorce happen for any cause, either fornication or adultery, or any heinous fault, the word of God blames not either the man or wife marrying again, nor cuts them off from the congregation, or from life, but bears with the infirmity; not that he may keep both wives, but that leaving the former he may be lawfully joined to the latter: the holy word and the holy church of God, commiserates this man, especially if he be otherwise of good conversation, and live according to God's law." This place is clearer than exposition, and needs no comment.

Ambrose, on the 16th of Luke, teaches "that all wedlock is not God's joining:" and to the 19th of Prov., "That a wife is prepared of the Lord," as the old Latin translates it, he answers, that the Septuagint renders it, "a wife is fitted by the Lord, and tempered to a kind of harmony; and where that harmony is, there God joins; where it is not, there dissension reigns, which is not from God, for God is love." This he brings to prove the marrying of Christian with Gentile to be no marriage, and consequently divorced without sin; but he who sees not this argument how plainly it serves to divorce any untunable, or unatonable matrimony, sees little. On the First to the Cor. vii. he grants a woman may leave her husband not for only fornication, "but for apostacy, and inverting nature, though not marry again; but the man may:" here are causes of divorce assigned other than adultery. And going on he affirms, "that the cause of God is greater than the cause of matrimony; that the reverence of wedlock is not due to him who hates the author thereof; that no matrimony is firm without devotion to God; that dishonor done to God acquits the other being deserted from the bond of matrimony; that the faith of marriage is not to be kept with such." If these contorted sentences be aught worth, it is not the desertion that breaks what is broken, but the impiety; and who then may not for that cause better divorce, than tarry to be deserted? or these grave sayings of St. Ambrose are but knacks.

Jerome on the 19th of Matthew explains, that for the cause of fornication, or the "suspicion thereof, a man may freely divorce." What can breed that suspicion, but sundry faults leading that way? By Jerome's consent therefore divorce is free not only for actual adultery, but for any cause that may incline a wise man to the just suspicion thereof.

Austin also must be remembered among those who hold, that this instance of fornication gives equal inference to other faults equally hateful, for which to divorce: and therefore in his books to Pollentius he disputes, "that infidelity, as being a greater sin than adultery, ought so much the rather cause a divorce." And on the sermon in the mount, under the name of fornication, will have "idolatry, or any harmful superstition," contained, which are not thought to disturb matrimony so directly as some other obstinacies and disaffections, more against the daily duties of that covenant, and in the Eastern tongues not unfrequently called fornication, as hath been shown. "Hence is understood," saith he, "that not only for bodily fornication, but for that which draws the mind from God's law, and foully corrupts it, a man may without fault put away his wife, and a wife her husband, because the Lord excepts the cause of fornication, which fornication we are constrained to interpret in a general sense." And in the first book of his "Retractions," chap. 16, he retracts not this his opinion, but commends it to serious consideration; and explains that he counted not there all sin to be fornication, but the more detestable sort of sins. The cause of fornication therefore is not in this discourse newly interpreted to signify other faults infringing the duties of wedlock, besides adultery.

Lastly, the council of Agatha in the year 506, can. 25, decreed, that "if laymen who divorced without some great fault, or giving no probable cause, therefore divorced, that they might marry some unlawful person, or some other man's, if before the provincial bishops were made acquainted, or judgment passed, they presumed this, excommunication was the penalty." Whence it follows, that if the cause of divorce were some great offence, or that they gave probable causes for what they did, and did not therefore divorce, that they might presume with some unlawful person, or what was another man's, the censure of church in those days did not touch them.

Thus having alleged enough to show, after what manner the primitive church for above five hundred years understood our Saviour's words touching divorce, I shall now, with a labor less dispersed, and sooner dispatched, bring under view what the civil law of those times constituted about this matter: I say the civil law, which is the honor of every true civilian to stand for, rather than to count that for law, which the pontifical canon had enthralled them to, and instead of interpreting a generous and elegant law, made them the drudges of a blockish rubric.

Theodosius and Valentinian, pious emperors both, ordained that, "as by consent lawful marriages were made, so by consent, but not without the bill of divorce, they might be dissolved; and to dissolve was the more difficult, only in favor of the children." We see the wisdom and piety of that age, one of the purest and learnedest since Christ, conceived no hinderance in the words of our Saviour, but that a divorce, mutually consented, might be suffered by the law, especially if there were no children; or if there were, careful provision was made. And fur-

ther saith that law, (supposing there wanted the consent of either,) "We design the causes of divorce by this most wholesome law; for as we forbid the dissolving of marriage without just cause, so we desire that a husband or a wife distressed by some adverse necessity, should be freed though by an unhappy, yet a necessary relief." What dram of wisdom or religion (for charity is truest religion) could there be in that knowing age, which is not virtually summed up in this most just law? As for those other Christian emperors, from Constantine, the first of them, finding the Roman law in this point so answerable to the Mosaic, it might be the likeliest cause why they altered nothing to restraint; but if aught, rather to liberty, for the help and consideration of the weaker sex, according as the gospel seems to make the wife more equal to her husband in these conjugal respects, than the law of Moses doth. Therefore "if a man were absent from his wife four years, and in that space not heard of, though gone to war in the service of the empire," she might divorce, and marry another, by the edict of Constantine to Dalmatius, Cod. 1, 5, tit. 17. And this was an age of the church, both ancient and cried up still for the most flourishing in knowledge and pious government since the apostles. But to return to this law of Theodosius, with this observation by the way, that still as the church corrupted, as the clergy grew more ignorant and yet more usurping on the magistrate, who also now declined, so still divorce grew more restrained; though certainly if better times permitted the thing that worse times restrained, it would not weakly argue that the permission was better, and the restraint worse. This law therefore of Theodosius, wiser in this than the most of his successors, though not wiser than God and Moses, reduced the causes of divorce to a certain number, which by the judicial law of God, and all recorded humanity, were left before to the breast of each husband, provided that the dismiss was not without reasonable conditions to the wife. But this was a restraint not yet come to extremes. For besides adultery, and that not only actual, but suspected by many signs there set down, any fault equally punishable with adultery, or equally infamous, might be the cause of a divorce. Which informs how the wisest of those ages understood that place in the gospel, whereby not the pilfering of a benevolence was considered as the main and only breach of wedlock, as is now thought, but the breach of love and peace, a more holy union than that of the flesh; and the dignity of an honest person was regarded not to be held in bondage with one whose ignominy was infectious. To this purpose was constituted Cod. l. 5, tit. 17, and Authent. collat. 4, tit. i. Novell. 22, where Justinian added three causes more. In the 117 Novell., most of the same causes are allowed, but the liberty of divorcing by consent is repealed: but by whom? by Justinian, not a wiser, not a more religious emperor than either of the former, but noted by judicious writers for his fickle head in making and unmaking laws; and how Procopius, a good historian, and a counsellor of state, then living, deciphers him in his other actions, I willingly omit. Nor was the church then in better case, but had the corruption of a hundred declining years swept on it, when the statute of "Consent" was called in; which, as I said, gives us every way more reason to suspect this restraint, more than that liberty: which therefore in the reign of Justin, the succeeding emperor, was recalled, Novell. 140, and established with a preface more wise and Christianly than for those times, declaring the necessity to restore that Theodosian law, if no other means of reconcilement could be found. And by whom this law was abrogated, or how long after, I do not find; but that those other causes remained in force as long as the Greek empire subsisted, and were assented by that church, is to be read in the canons and edicts compared by Photius the patriarch, with the avertiments of Balsamon and Matthæus Monachus thereon.

But long before those days, Leo, the son of Basilius Macedo, reigning about the year 886, and for his excellent wisdom surnamed the "Philosopher," constituted, "that in case of madness, the husband might divorce after three years, the wife after five." Constit. Leon. 111, 112. This declares how he expounded our Saviour, and derived his reasons from the institution, which in his preface with great eloquence are set down; whereof a passage or two may give some proof, though

better not divided from the rest. "There is not," saith he, "a thing more necessary to preserve mankind, than the help given him from his own rib; both God and nature so teaching us: which being so, it was requisite that the providence of law, or if any other care be to the good of man, should teach and ordain those things which are to the help and comfort of married persons, and confirm the end of marriage purposed in the beginning, not those things which afflict and bring perpetual misery to them." Then answers the objection, that they are one flesh: "If matrimony had held so as God ordained it, he were wicked that would dissolve it. But if we respect this in matrimony, that it be contracted to the good of both, how shall he, who for some great evil feared, persuades not to marry, though contracted, not persuade to unmarry, if after marriage a calamity befall? Should we bid beware lest any fall into an evil, and leave him helpless who by human error is fallen therein? This were as if we should use remedies to prevent a disease, but let the sick die without remedy." The rest will be worth reading in the author.

And thus we have the judgment first of primitive fathers; next, of the imperial law not disallowed by the universal church in ages of her best authority; and lastly, of the whole Greek church and civil state, incorporating their canons and edicts together, that divorce was lawful for other causes equivalent to adultery, contained under the word fornication. So that the exposition of our Saviour's sentence here alleged hath all these ancient and great asserters; is therefore neither new nor licentious, as some now would persuade the commonalty; although it be nearer truth that nothing is more new than those teachers themselves, and nothing more licentious than some known to be, whose hypocrisy yet shames not to take offence at this doctrine for licence; whenas indeed they fear it would remove licence, and leave them but few companions.

That the pope's canon law, encroaching upon civil magistracy, abolished all divorce even for adultery. What the reformed divines have recovered; and that the famousest of them have taught according to the assertion of this book.

But in these western parts of the empire, it will appear almost unquestionable, that the cited law of Theodosius and Valentinian stood in force until the blindest and corruptest times of popedom displaced it. For, that the volumes of Justinian never came into Italy, or beyond Illyricum, is the opinion of good antiquaries. And that only manuscript thereof found in Apulia, by Lotharius, the Saxon, and given to the state of Pisa, for their aid at sea against the Normans of Sicily, was received as a rarity not to be matched. And although the Goths, and after them the Lombards and Franks, who overrun the most of Europe, except this island, (unless we make our Saxons and Normans a limb of them,) brought in their own customs, yet that they followed the Roman laws in their contracts in marriages, Agathias the historian is alleged. And other testimonies relate, that Alaricus and Theodoric, their kings, writ their statutes out of this Theodosian code, which hath the recited law of divorce. Nevertheless, while the monarchs of Christendom were yet barbarous, and but half-christian, the popes took this advantage of their weak superstition, to raise a corpulent law out of the canons and decretals of audacious priests; and presumed also to set this in the front: "That the constitutions of princes are not above the constitutions of clergy, but beneath them:" using this very instance of divorce, as the first prop of their tyranny; by a false consequence drawn from a passage of Ambrose upon Luke, where he saith, though "man's law grant it, yet God's law prohibits it:" whence Gregory the pope, writing to Theoctista, infers that ecclesiastical courts cannot be dissolved by the magistrate. A fair conclusion from a double error: first, in saying that the divine law prohibited divorce; (for what will he make of Moses?) next, supposing that it did, how will it follow, that whatever Christ forbids in his evangelic precepts, should be haled into a judicial constraint against the pattern of a divine law? Certainly the gospel came not to enact such compulsions. In the mean while we may note here, that the restraint of divorce was one of the first fair seeming pleas which the pope had, to step into secular authority, and with his antichristian rigor to abolish the permissive law of Christian princes conforming to a sacred lawgiver.

Which if we consider, this papal and unjust restriction of divorce need not be so dear to us, since the plausible restraining of that was in a manner the first loosening of antichrist, and, as it were, the substance of his eldest horn. Nor do we less remarkably owe the first means of his fall here in England, to the contemning of that restraint by Henry the Eighth, whose divorce he opposed. Yet was not that rigor executed anciently in spiritual courts, until Alexander the Third, who trod upon the neck of Frederic Barbarossa the emperor, and summoned our Henry the Second into Normandy, about the death of Becket. He it was, that the worthy author may be known, who first actually repealed the imperial law of divorce, and decreed this tyrannous decree, that matrimony for no cause should be dissolved, though for many causes it might separate; as may be seen Decret. Gregor. 1. 4, tit. 19, and in other places of the canonical tomes. The main good of which invention, wherein it consists, who can tell? but that it hath one virtue incomparable, to fill all Christendom with whoredoms and adulteries, beyond the art of Balaams, or of devils. Yet neither can these, though so perverse, but acknowledge that the words of Christ, under the name of fornication, allow putting away for other causes than adultery, both from "bed and board," but not from the "bond;" their only reason is, because marriage they believe to be a "sacrament." But our divines, who would seem long since to have renounced that reason, have so forgot themselves, as yet to hold the absurdity, which but for that reason, unless there be some mystery of Satan in it, perhaps the papist would not hold. It is true, we grant divorce for actual and proved adultery, and not for less than many tedious and unrepairable years of desertion, wherein a man shall lose all his hope of posterity, which great and holy men have bewailed, ere he can be righted; and then perhaps on the confines of his old age, when all is not worth the while. But grant this were seasonably done; what are these two cases to many other, which afflict the state of marriage as bad, and yet find no redress? What hath the soul of man deserved, if it be in the way of salvation, that it should be mortgaged thus, and may not redeem itself according to conscience out of the hands of such ignorant and slothful teachers as these, who are neither able nor mindful to give due tendance to that precious cure which they rashly undertake; nor have in them the noble goodness, to consider these distresses and accidents of man's life, but are bent rather to fill their mouths with tithe and oblation? Yet if they can learn to follow, as well as they can seek to be followed, I shall direct them to a fair number of renowned men, worthy to be their leaders, who will commend to them a doctrine in this point wiser than their own; and if they be not impatient, it will be the same doctrine which this treatise hath defended.

Wickliff, that Englishman honored of God to be the first preacher of a general reformation to all Europe, was not in this thing better taught of God, than to teach among his chiefest recoveries of truth, "that divorce is lawful to the Christian for many other causes equal to adultery." This book, indeed, through the poverty of our libraries, I am forced to cite from "Arnisæus of Halberstad on the Rite of Marriage," who cites it from Corasius of Toulouse, c. 4, Cent. Sect., and he from Wickliff, l. 4, Dial. c. 21. So much the sorrier, for that I never looked into an author cited by his adversary upon this occasion, but found him more conducible to the question than his quotation rendered him.

Next, Luther, how great a servant of God! in his book of "Conjugal Life," quoted by Gerard out of the Dutch, allows divorce for the obstinate denial of conjugal duty; and "that a man may send away a proud Vashti, and marry an Esther in her stead." It seems, if this example shall not be impertinent, that Luther meant not only the refusal of benevolence, but a stubborn denial of any main conjugal duty; or, if he did not, it will be evinced from what he allows. For, out of question, with men that are not barbarous, love, and peace, and fitness, will be yielded as essential to marriage, as corporal benevolence. "Though I give my body to be burnt," saith St. Paul, "and have not charity, it profits me nothing." So, though the body prostitute itself to whom the mind affords no other love or peace, but constant malice and vexation, can this bodily benevolence deserve to be called a marriage between Christians and rational creatures?

Melancthon, the third great luminary of reformation, in his book, "Concerning Marriage," grants divorce for cruel usage, and danger of life, urging the authority of that Theodosian law, which he esteems written with the grave deliberation of godly men; "and that they who reject this law, and think it disagreeing from the gospel, understand not the difference of law and gospel; that the magistrate ought not only to defend life, but to succour the weak conscience; lest, broke with grief and indignation, it relinquish prayer, and turn to some unlawful thing." What if this heavy plight of despair arise from other discontents in wedlock, which may go to the soul of a good man more than the danger of his life, or cruel using, which a man cannot be liable to? suppose it be ingrateful usage, suppose it be perpetual spite and disobedience, suppose a hatred; shall not the magistrate free him from this disquiet which interrupts his prayers, and disturbs the course of his service to God and his country all as much, and brings him such a misery, as that he more desires to leave his life than fears to lose it? Shall not this equally concern the office of civil protection, and much more the charity of a true church, to remedy?

Erasmus, who for learning was the wonder of his age, both in his Notes on Matthew, and on the first to the Corinthians, in a large and eloquent discourse, and in his answer to Phimostomus, a papist, maintains (and no protestant then living contradicted him) that the words of Christ comprehend many other causes of divorce under the name of fornication.

Bucer, (whom our famous Dr. Rainolds was wont to prefer before Calvin,) in his comment on Matthew, and in his second book "of the Kingdom of Christ," treats of divorce at large, to the same effect as is written in "the Doctrine and Discipline of Divorce," lately published, and the translation is extant: whom, lest I should be thought to have wrested to mine own purpose, take something more out of his 49th chapter, which I then for brevity omitted. "It will be the duty of pious princes, and all who govern church or commonwealth, if any, whether husband or wife, shall affirm their want of such, who either will or can tolerably perform the necessary duties of married life, to grant that they may seek them such, and marry them, if they make it appear that such they have not." This book he wrote here in England, where he lived the greatest admired man; and this he dedicated to Edward VI.

Fagius, ranked among the famous divines of Germany, whom Frederic, at that time the Palatine, sent for to be the reformer of his dominion, and whom afterwards England sought to, and obtained of him to come and teach her, differs not in this opinion from Bucer, as his notes on the Chaldee Paraphast well testify.

The whole church of Strasburgh in her most flourishing time, when Zellius, Hedio, Capito, and other great divines, taught there, and those two renowned magistrates, Farrerus and Sturmius, governed that commonwealth and academy to the admiration of all Germany, hath thus in the 21st article: "We teach, that if, according to the word of God, yea, or against it, divorces happen, to do according to God's word, Deut. xxiv. 1, Matt. xix., 1 Cor. vii., and the observation of the primitive church, and the Christian constitution of pious Cæsars."

Peter Martyr seems in word our easy adversary, but is, indeed, for us; toward which, though it be something when he saith of this opinion, "that it is not wicked, and can hardly be refuted," this which follows is much more. "I speak not here," saith he, "of natural impediments, which may so happen, that the matrimony can no longer hold:" but adding, that he often wondered "how the ancient and most Christian emperors established those laws of divorce, and neither Ambrose, who had such influence upon the laws of Theodosius, nor any of those holy fathers found fault, nor any of the churches, why the magistrates of this day should be so loath to constitute the same. Perhaps they fear an inundation of divorces, which is not likely; whenas we read not either among the Hebrews, Greeks, or Romans, that they were much frequent where they were most permitted. If they judge Christian men worse than Jews or pagans, they both injure that name, and by this reason will be constrained to grant divorces the rather, because it was permitted as a remedy of evil: for who would remove the medicine, while the disease is yet so rife?" This being read both in "his Commonplaces," and on the first to the Corinthians, with what we shall relate more of him yet ere the end, sets him absolutely on this side: not to insist that in both these, and other places of his commentaries, he grants divorce not only for desertion, but for the seducement and scandalous demeanor of an heretical consort.

Musculus, a divine of no obscure fame, distinguishes between the religious and the civil determination of divorce; and, leaving the civil wholly to the lawyers, pronounces a conscionable divorce for impotence not only natural, but accidental, if it be durable. His equity, it seems, can enlarge the words of Christ to one cause more than adultery: why may not the reason of another man as wise enlarge them to another cause?

Gualter, of Zuric, a well-known judicious commentator, in his homilies on Matthew, allows divorce for "leprosy, or any other cause which renders unfit for wedlock," and calls this rather "a nullity of marriage than a divorce." And who, that is not himself a mere body, can restrain all the unfitness of marriage only to a corporeal defect?

Hemingius, an author highly esteemed, and his works printed at Geneva, writing of divorce, confesses that learned men "vary in this question, some granting three causes thereof, some five, others many more;" he himself gives us six, "adultery, desertion, inability, error, evil usage, and impiety," using argument "that Christ under one special contains the whole kind, and under the name and example of fornication, he includes other causes equipollent." This discourse he wrote at the request of many who had the judging of these causes in Denmark and Norway, who by all likelihood followed his advice.

Hunnius, a doctor of Wittenberg, well known both in divinity and other arts, on the 19th of Matt. affirms, "That the exception of fornication expressed by our Saviour excludes not other causes equalling adultery, or destructive to the substantials of matrimony; but was opposed to the custom of the Jews, who made divorce for every light cause."

Felix Bidenbachius, an eminent divine in the duchy of Wirtemberg, affirms, "That the obstinate refusal of conjugal due is a lawful cause of divorce;" and gives an instance, "that the consistory of that state so judged."

Gerard cites Harbardus, an author not un-known, and Arnisæus cites Wigandus, both yielding divorce in case of cruel usage; and another author, who testifies to "have seen, in a dukedom of Germany, marriages dis-joined for some implacable enmities arising."

Beza, one of the strictest against divorce, denies it not "for danger of life from a her-etic, or importunate solicitation to do aught against religion;" and counts it "all one whether the heretic desert, or would stay upon intolerable conditions." But this de-cision, well examined, will be found of no solidity. For Beza would be asked why, if God so strictly exact our stay in any kind of wedlock, we had not better stay and hazard a murdering for religion at the hand of a wife or husband, as he and others enjoin us to stay and venture it for all other causes but that? and why a man's life is not as well and warrantably saved by divorcing from an orthodox murderer as an heretical? Again, if desertion be confessed by him to consist not only in the forsaking, but in the unsufferable conditions of staying, a man may as well deduce the lawfulness of divorcing from any intolerable conditions, (if his grant be good, that we may divorce thereupon from a heretic,) as he can deduce it lawful to divorce from any deserter, by finding it lawful to divorce from a deserting infidel. For this is plain, if St. Paul's permission to divorce an infidel deserter infer it lawful for any mali-cious desertion, then doth Beza's definition of a deserter transfer itself with like facility from the cause of religion to the cause of malice, and proves it as good to divorce from him who intolerably stays as from him who purposely departs; and leaves it as lawful to depart from him who urgently requires a wicked thing, though professing the same religion, as from him who urges a heathenish or superstitious compliance in a different faith. For, if there be such necessity of our abiding, we ought rather to abide the utmost for religion than for any other cause; seeing both the cause of our stay is pretended our religion to marriage, and the cause of our suffering is supposed our constant marriage to religion. Beza, therefore, by his own defi-nition of a deserter, justifies a divorce from any wicked or intolerable conditions rather in the same religion than in a different.

Aretius, a famous divine of Bern, approves many causes of divorce in his "Problems," and adds, "that the laws and consistories of Switzerland approve them also." As first "adultery, and that not actual only, but in-tentional;" alleging Matthew v., "Whosoever looketh to lust, hath committed adultery al-ready in his heart. Whereby," saith he, "our Saviour shows, that the breach of matrimony may be not only by outward act, but by the heart and desire; when that hath once pos-sessed, it renders the conversation intolerable, and commonly the fact follows." Other causes, to the number of nine or ten, con-senting in most with the imperial laws, may be read in the author himself, who avers them to be "grave and weighty." All these are men of name in divinity; and to these, if need were, might be added more. Nor have the civilians been all so blinded by the canon as not to avouch the justice of those old per-missions touching divorce.

Alciat of Milan, a man of extraordinary wisdom and learning, in the sixth book of his "Parerga," defends those imperial laws, "not repugnant to the gospel," as the church then interpreted. "For," saith he, "the ancients understood him separate by man, whom pas-sions and corrupt affections divorced, not if the provincial bishops first heard the mat-ter, and judged, as the council of Agatha declares:" and on some part of the Code he names Isidorus Hispalensis, the first com-puter of canons, "to be in the same mind." And in the former place gives his opinion, "that divorce might be more lawfully per-mitted than usury."

Corasius, recorded by Helvicus among the famous lawyers, hath been already cited of the same judgment.

Wesembechius, a much-named civilian, in his comment on this law, defends it, and affirms, "That our Saviour excluded not other faults equal to adultery; and that the word fornication signifies larger among the Hebrews than with us, comprehending every fault which alienates from him to whom obedience is due; and that the primitive church interpreted so."

Grotius, yet living, and of prime note among learned men, retires plainly from the canon to the ancient civility, yea, to the Mo-saic law, "as being most just and undeceivable." On the 5th of Matth. he saith, "That Christ made no civil laws, but taught us how to use law: that the law sent not a husband to the judge about this matter of divorce, but left him to his own conscience; that Christ, therefore, cannot be thought to send him; that adultery may be judged by a vehement suspicion; that the exception of adultery seems an example of other like offences;" proves it "from the manner of speech, the maxims of law, the reason of charity, and common equity."

These authorities, without long search, I had to produce, all excellent men, some of them such as many ages had brought forth none greater: almost the meanest of them might deserve to obtain credit in a singularity: what might not then all of them joined in an opinion so consonant to reason? For although some speak of this cause, others of that, why divorce may be, yet all agreeing in the necessary enlargement of that textual straitness, leave the matter to equity, not to literal bondage; and so the opinion closes. Nor could I have wanted more testimonies, had the cause needed a more solicitous inquiry. But herein the satisfaction of others hath been studied, not the gaining of more assurance to mine own persuasion: although authorities contributing reason withal be a good confirmation and a welcome. But God (I solemnly attest him!) withheld from my knowledge the consenting judgment of these men so late, until they could not be my instructors, but only my unexpected witnesses to partial men, that in this work I had not given the worst experiment of an industry joined with integrity, and the free utterance, though of an unpopular truth. Which yet to the people of England may, if God so please, prove a memorable informing; certainly a benefit which was intended them long since by men of highest repute for wisdom and piety, Bucer and Erasmus. Only this one authority more, whether in place or out of place, I am not to omit, which if any can think a small one, I must be patient; it is no smaller than the whole assembled authority of England both church and state, and in those times which are on record for the purest and sincerest that ever shone yet on the reformation of this island—the time of Edward the Sixth. That worthy prince, having utterly abolished the canon law out of his dominions, as his father did before him, appointed by full vote of parliament a committee of two-and-thirty chosen men, divines and lawyers, of whom Cranmer the archbishop, Peter Martyr, and Walter Haddon, (not without the assistance of Sir John Cheeke, the king's tutor, a man at that time counted the learnedest of Englishmen, and for piety not inferior,) were the chief, to frame anew some ecclesiastical laws, that might be instead of what was abrogated. The work with great diligence was finished, and with as great approbation of that reforming age was received; and had been doubtless, as the learned preface thereof testifies, established by act of parliament, had not the good king's death, so soon ensuing, arrested the further growth of religion also, from that season to this. Those laws, thus founded on the memorable wisdom and piety of that religious parliament and synod, allow divorce and second marriage, "not only for adultery or desertion, but for any capital enmity or plot laid against the other's life, and likewise for evil and fierce usage:" nay, the twelfth chapter of that title by plain consequence declares, "that lesser contentions, if they be perpetual, may obtain divorce:" which is all one really with the position by me held in the former treatise published on this argument, herein only differing, that there the cause of perpetual strife was put for example in the unchangeable discord of some natures, but in these laws intended us by the best of our ancestors, the effect of continual strife is determined no unjust plea of divorce, whether the cause be natural or wilful. Whereby the wariness and deliberation, from which that discourse proceeded, will appear, and that God hath aided us to make no bad conclusion of this point; seeing the opinion, which of late hath undergone ill censures among the vulgar, hath now proved to have done no violence to scripture, unless all these famous authors alleged have done the like; nor hath affirmed aught more than what indeed the most nominated fathers of the church, both ancient and modern, are unexpectedly found affirming; the laws of God's peculiar people, and of primitive Christendom found to have practised, reformed churches and states to have imitated, and especially the most pious church-times of this kingdom to have framed and published, and, but for sad hindrances in the sudden change of religion, had enacted by parliament. Henceforth let them, who condemn the assertion of this book for new and licentious, be sorry; lest, while they think to be of the graver sort, and take on them to be teachers, they expose themselves rather to be pledged up and down by men who intimately know them, to the discovery and contempt of their ignorance and presumption.

COLASTERION:

A REPLY TO A NAMELESS ANSWER AGAINST THE DOCTRINE AND DISCIPLINE OF DIVORCE.

WHEREIN THE TRIVIAL AUTHOR OF THAT ANSWER IS DISCOVERED, THE LICENSER CONFERRED WITH, AND THE OPINION, WHICH THEY TRADUCE, DEFENDED.

PROV. XXVI. 5. "Answer a fool according to his folly, lest he be wise in his own conceit."

[The text is that of the first edition, 1645.]

AFTER many rumors of confutations and convictions, forthcoming against the "Doctrine and Discipline of Divorce," and now and then a by-blow from the pulpit, feathered with a censure strict indeed, but how true, more beholden to the authority of that devout place, which it borrowed to be uttered in, than to any sound reason which it could oracle; while I still hoped as for a blessing to see some piece of diligence, or learned discretion, come from them, it was my hap at length, lighting on a certain parcel of queries, that seek and find not, to find not seeking, at the tail of anabaptistical, antinomian, heretical, atheistical epithets, a jolly slander, called "Divorce at Pleasure." I stood awhile and wondered, what we might do to a man's heart, or what anatomy use, to find in it sincerity; for all our wonted marks every day fail us, and where we thought it was, we see it is not, for alter and change residence it cannot sure. And yet I see no good of body or of mind secure to a man for all his past labors, without perpetual watchfulness and perseverance: whenas one above others, who hath suffered much and long in the defence of truth, shall after all this give her cause to leave him so destitute and so vacant of her defence, as to yield his mouth to be the common road of truth and falsehood, and such falsehood as is joined with a rash and heedless calumny of his neighbor. For what book hath he ever met with, as his complaint is, "printed in the city," maintaining either in the title, or in the whole pursuance, "Divorce at Pleasure"? It is true, that to divorce upon extreme necessity, when through the perverseness, or the apparent unfitness of either, the continuance can be to both no good at all, but an intolerable injury and temptation to the wronged and the defrauded; to divorce then, there is a book that writes it lawful. And that this law is a pure and wholesome national law, not to be withheld from good men because others likely enough may abuse it to their pleasure, cannot be charged upon that book, but must be entered a bold and impious accusation against God himself; who did not for this abuse withhold it from his own people. It will be just, therefore, and best for the reputation of him who in his Subitanes hath thus censured, to recall his sentence. And if, out of the abundance of his volumes, and the readiness of his quill, and the vastness of his other employments, especially in the great audit for accounts, he can spare us aught to the better understanding of this point, he shall be thanked in public; and what hath offended in the book shall willingly submit to his correction. Provided he be sure not to come with those old and stale suppositions, unless he can take away clearly what that discourse hath urged against them, by one who will expect other arguments to be persuaded the good health of a sound answer, than the gout and dropsy of a big margin, littered and overlaid with crude and huddled quotations. But as I still was waiting, when these light-armed refuters would have done pelting at their three lines uttered with a sage delivery of no reason, but an impotent and worse than Bonnerlike censure, to burn that which provokes them to a fair dispute; at length a book was brought to my hands, intitled "An Answer to the Doctrine and Discipline of Divorce." Gladly I received it, and very attentively composed myself to read; hoping that now some good man had vouchsafed the pains to instruct me better than I could yet learn out of all the volumes which for this purpose I had visited. Only this I marvelled, and other men have since, whenas I, in a subject so new to this age, and so hazardous to please, concealed not my name, why this author, defending that part which is so creeded by the people, would conceal his. But ere I could enter three leaves into the pamphlet, (for I defer the peasantly rudeness, which by the licenser's leave I met with afterwards,) my satisfaction came in abundantly, that it could be nothing why he durst not name himself, but the guilt of his own wretchedness. For first, not to speak of his abrupt and bald beginning, his very first page notoriously bewrays him an illiterate and arrogant presumer in that which he understands not, bearing us in hand as if he knew both Greek and Hebrew, and is not able to spell it which had he been, it had been either written as it ought, or scored upon the printer. If it be excused as the carelessness of his deputy, be it known, the learned author himself is inventoried, and summed up to the utmost value of his livery-cloak. Whoever he be, though this to some may seem a slight contest, I shall yet continue to think that man full of other secret injustice, and deceitful pride, who shall offer in public to assume the skill though it be but of a tongue which he hath not, and would catch his readers to believe of his ability, that which is not in him. The licenser indeed, as his authority now stands, may license much; but if these Greek orthographies were of his licensing, the boys at school might reckon with him at his grammar. Nor did I find this his want of the pretended languages alone, but accompanied with such a low and homespun expression of his mother English all along, without joint or frame, as made me, ere I knew further of him, often stop and conclude, that this author could for certain be no other than some mechanic. Nor was the style flat and rude, and the matter grave and solid, for then there had been pardon; but so shallow and so unwary was that also, as gave sufficiently the character of a gross and sluggish, yet a contentious and overweening, pretender. For first, it behooving him to show,

as he promises, what divorce is, and what the true doctrine and discipline thereof, and this being to do by such principles and proofs as are received on both sides, he performs neither of these; but shows it first from the judaical practice, which he himself disallows; and next from the practice of canon law, which the book he would confute utterly rejects, and all laws depending thereon: which this puny clerk calls "the Laws of England," and yet pronounceth them by an ecclesiastical judge: as if that were to be accounted the law of England which depended on the popery of England; or if it were, this parliament he might know hath now damned that judicature. So that whether his meaning were to inform his own party, or to confute his adversary, instead of showing us the true doctrine and discipline of divorce, he shows us nothing but his own contemptible ignorance. For what is the Mosaic law to his opinion? And what is the canon, utterly now antiquated, either to that, or to mine? Ye see already what a faithful definer we have him. From such a wind-egg of definition as this, they who expect any of his other arguments to be well hatched, let them enjoy the virtue of their worthy champion. But one thing more I observed, a singular note of his stupidity, and that his trade is not to meddle with books, much less with confutations: whenas the "Doctrine of Divorce" had now a whole year been published the second time, with many arguments added, and the former ones bettered and confirmed, this idle pamphlet comes reeling forth against the first edition only; as may appear to any by the pages quoted: which put me in mind of what by chance I had notice of to this purpose the last summer, as nothing so serious but happens ofttimes to be attended with a ridiculous accident: it was then told me, that the "Doctrine of Divorce" was answered, and the answer half printed against the first edition, not by one, but by a pack of heads; of whom the chief, by circumstance, was intimated to me, and since ratified to be no other, if any can hold laughter, and I am sure none will guess him lower, than an actual serving-man. This creature, for the story must on, (and what though he be the lowest person of an interlude, he may deserve a canvassing,) transplanted himself, and to the improvement of his wages, and your better notice of his capacity, turned solicitor. And having conversed much with a stripling divine or two of those newly-fledge probationers, that usually come scouting from the university, and lie here no lame legers to pop into the Bethesda of some knight's chaplainship, where they bring grace to his good cheer, but no peace or benediction else to his house; these made the cham-party, he contributed the law, and both joined in the divinity. Which made me intend following the advice also of friends, to lay aside the thought of misspending a reply to the buz of such a drone's nest. But finding that it lay, whatever was the matter, half-a-year after unfinished in the press, and hearing for certain that a divine of note, out of his goodwill to the opinion, had taken it into his revise, and something had put out, something put in, and stuck it here and there with a clove of his own calligraphy, to keep it from tainting; and further, when I saw the stuff, though very coarse and threadbare, garnished and trimly faced with the commendations of a licenser, I resolved, so soon as leisure granted me the recreation, that my man of law should not altogether lose his soliciting. Although I impute a share of the making to him whose name I find in the approbation, who may take, as his mind serves him, this reply. In the meanwhile it shall be seen, I refuse no occasion, and avoid no adversary, either to maintain what I have begun, or to give it up for better reason.

To begin then with the licenser and his censure. For a licenser is not contented now to give his single Imprimatur, but brings his chair into the title-leaf; there sits and judges up, or judges down, what book he pleases: if this be suffered, what worthless author, or what cunning printer, will not be ambitious of such a stale to put off the heaviest gear; which may in time bring in round fees to the licenser, and wretched misleading to the people? But to the matter: he "approves the publishing of this book, to preserve the strength and honor of marriage against those sad breaches and dangerous abuses of it." Belike then the wrongful suffering of all those sad breaches and abuses in marriage to a remediless thraldom is the strength and honor of marriage; a boisterous and bestial strength, a dishonorable honor, an infatuated doctrine,

worse than the "salvo jure" of tyrannizing, which we all fight against. Next he saith, that "common discontents make these breeches in unstaid minds, and men given to change." His words may be apprehended, as if they disallowed only to divorce for common discontents, in unstaid minds, having no cause, but a desire of change, and then we agree. But if he take all discontents on this side adultery, to be common, that is to say, not difficult to endure, and to affect only unstaid minds, it might administer just cause to think him the unfittest man that could be, to offer at a comment upon Job; as seeming by this to have no more true sense of a good man in his afflictions, than those Edomitish friends had, of whom Job complains, and against whom God testifies his anger. Shall a man of your own coat, who hath espoused his flock, and represents Christ more in being the true husband of his congregation, than an ordinary man doth in being the husband of his wife, (and yet this representment is thought a chief cause why marriage must be inseparable,) shall this spiritual man ordinarily for the increase of his maintenance or any slight cause, forsake that wedded cure of souls, that should be dearest to him, and marry another and another? And shall not a person wrongfully afflicted, and persecuted even to extremity, forsake an unfit, injurious, and pestilent mate, tied only by a civil and fleshly covenant? If you be a man so much hating change, hate that other change; if yourself be not guilty, counsel your brethren to hate it; and leave to be the supercilious judge of other men's miseries and changes, that your own be not judged. "The reasons of your licensed pamphlet," you say, "are good;" they must be better than your own then; I shall wonder else how such a trivial fellow was accepted and commended, to be the confuter of so dangerous an opinion as ye give out mine.

Now therefore to your attorney, since no worthier an adversary makes his appearance; nor this neither his appearance, but lurking under the safety of his nameless obscurity: such as ye turn him forth at the postern, I must accept him; and in a better temper than Ajax do mean to scourge this ram for ye, till I meet with his Ulysses.

He begins with law, and we have it of him as good cheap as any huckster at law, newly

set up, can possibly afford, and as impertinent; but for that he hath received his handsel.
He presumes also to cite the civil law, which
I perceive, by his citing, never came within
his dormitory: yet what he cites makes but
against himself.

His second thing therefore is to refute
the adverse position, and very methodically,
three pages before he sets it down; and sets
his own in the place, "that disagreement of
mind or disposition, though showing itself in
much sharpness, is not by the law of God
or man a just cause of divorce."

To this position I answer, That it lays no
battery against mine, no, nor so much as
faces it, but tacks about, long ere it come
near, like a harmless and respectful confutement. For I confess that disagreement of
mind or disposition, though in much sharpness, is not always a just cause of divorce:
for much may be endured. But what if the
sharpness be much more than his much? To
that point it is our mishap we have not here
his grave decision. He that will contradict
the positive which I alleged, must hold that
no disagreement of mind or disposition can
divorce, though shown in most sharpness;
otherwise he leaves a place for equity to appoint limits, and so his following arguments
will either not prove his own position, or not
disprove mine.

His first argument, all but what hobbles to
no purpose, is this: "Where the scripture
commands a thing to be done, it appoints
when, how, and for what, as in the case of
death, or excommunication. But the scripture
directs not what measure of disagreement or
contrariety may divorce: therefore the scripture allows not any divorce for disagreement."—Answer. First, I deny your major;
the scripture appoints many things, and yet
leaves the circumstance to man's discretion,
particularly in your own examples: excommunication is not taught when and for what
to be, but left to the church. How could the
licenser let pass this childish ignorance, and
call it "good"? Next, in matters of death, the
laws of England, whereof you have intruded
to be an opiniastrous subadvocate, and are
bound to defend them, conceive it not enjoined in scripture, when or for what cause
they shall put to death, as in adultery, theft,
and the like. Your minor also is false. for

the scripture plainly sets down for what
measure of disagreement a man may divorce,
Deut. xxiv. 1. Learn better what that phrase
means, "if she find no favor in his eyes."

Your second argument, without more tedious fumbling, is briefly thus: "If diversity
in religion, which breeds a greater dislike
than any natural disagreement, may not cause
a divorce, then may not the lesser disagreement. But diversity of religion may not.
Ergo."

Answ. First, I deny in the major, that
diversity of religion breeds a greater dislike
to marriage-duties than natural disagreement.
For between Israelite, or Christian, and infidel, more often hath been seen too much
love: but between them who perpetually
clash in natural contrarieties, it is repugnant
that there should be ever any married love
or concord. Next, I deny your minor, that
it is commanded not to divorce in diversity
of religion, if the infidel will stay: for that
place in St. Paul commands nothing, as that
book at large affirmed, though you over-
skipped it.

Secondly, If it do command, it is but with
condition that the infidel be content, and
well-pleased to stay; which cuts off the supposal of any great hatred or disquiet between
them, seeing the infidel had liberty to depart
at pleasure; and so this comparison avails
nothing.

Your third argument is from Deut. xxii.:
"If a man hate his wife, and raise an ill report, that he found her no virgin;" if this
were false, "he might not put her away,"
though hated never so much.

Answ. This was a malicious hatred, bent
against her life, or to send her out of doors
without her portion. Such a hater loses by
due punishment that privilege, Deut. xxiv. 1,
to divorce for a natural dislike; which,
though it could not love conjugally, yet sent
away civilly, and with just conditions. But
doubtless the wife in that former case had liberty to depart from her false accuser, lest his
hatred should prove mortal; else that law peculiarly made to right the woman, had turned
to her greatest mischief.

Your fourth argument: "One Christian
ought to bear the infirmities of another, but
chiefly of his wife."

Answ. I grant infirmities; but not outrages,

not perpetual defraudments of truest conjugal society, not injuries and vexations as important as fire. Yet to endure very much might do well an exhortation, but not a compulsive law. For the Spirit of God himself, by Solomon, declares that such a consort "the earth cannot bear," and "better dwell in a corner on the house-top, or in the wilderness." Burdens may be borne, but still with consideration to the strength of an honest man complaining. Charity indeed bids us forgive our enemies, yet doth not force us to continue friendship and familiarity with those friends who have been false or unworthy towards us; but is contented in our peace with them, at a fair distance. Charity commands not the husband to receive again into his bosom the adulterous wife; but thinks it enough, if he dismiss her with a beneficent and peaceful dismission. No more doth charity command, nor can her rule compel, to retain in nearest union of wedlock one whose other grossest faults, or disabilities to perform what was covenanted, are the just causes of as much grievance and dissension in a family, as the private act of adultery. Let not therefore, under the name of fulfilling charity, such an unmerciful and more than legal yoke be padlocked upon the neck of any Christian.

Your fifth argument: "If the husband ought love his wife, as Christ his church, then ought she not to be put away for contrariety of mind."

Answ. This similitude turns against him: for if the husband must be as Christ to the wife, then must the wife be as the church to her husband. If there be a perpetual contrariety of mind in the church toward Christ, Christ himself threatens to divorce such a spouse, and hath often done it. If they urge This was no true church, I urge again, That was no true wife.

His sixth argument is from Matth. v. 32, which he expounds after the old fashion, and never takes notice of what I brought against that exposition; let him therefore seek his answer there. Yet can he not leave this argument, but he must needs first show us a curvet of his madness, holding out an objection, and running himself upon the point. "For," saith he, "if Christ except no cause but adultery, then all other causes, as frigidity, incestuous

marriage, &c. are no causes of divorce;" and answers, "that the speech of Christ holds universally, as he intended it; namely, to condemn such divorce as was groundlessly practised among the Jews, for every cause which they thought sufficient; not checking the law of consanguinities or affinities, or forbidding other cause which makes marriage void, ipso facto."

Answ. Look to it now, you be not found taking fees on both sides; for if you once bring limitations to the universal words of Christ, another will do as much with as good authority, and affirm, that neither did he check the law, Deut. xxiv. 1, nor forbid the causes that make marriage void actually; which if anything in the world doth, unfitness doth, and contrariety of mind: yea, more than adultery; for that makes not the marriage void, nor much more unfit, but for the time, if the offended party forgive: but unfitness and contrariety frustrates and nullifies for ever, unless it be a rare chance, all the good and peace of wedded conversation; and leaves nothing between them enjoyable, but a prone and savage necessity, not worth the name of marriage, unaccompanied with love. Thus much his own objection hath done against himself.

Argument seventh. He insists, "that man and wife are one flesh, therefore must not separate." But must be sent to look again upon the 35th page of that book, where he might have read an answer, which he stirs not. Yet can he not abstain, but he must do us another pleasure ere he goes; although I call the common pleas to witness, I have not hired his tongue, whatever men may think by his arguing. For besides adultery, he excepts other causes which dissolve the union of being one flesh, either directly, or by consequence. If only adultery be excepted by our Saviour, and he voluntarily can add other exceptions that dissolve that union, both directly and by consequence; these words of Christ, the main obstacle of divorce, are open to us by his own invitation, to include whatever causes dissolve that union of flesh, either directly or by consequence. Which, till he name other causes more likely, I affirm to be done soonest by unfitness and contrariety of mind; for that induces hatred, which is the greatest dissolver both of spiritual and corporal union, turning the mind, and consequently the body, to other objects. Thus our doughty adversary, either directly or by consequence, yields us the question with his own mouth: and the next thing he does, recants it again.

His eighth argument shivers in the uttering, and he confesseth to be "not overconfident of it:" but of the rest it may be sworn he is. St. Paul, 1 Cor. vii, saith, that the "married have trouble in the flesh:" therefore we must bear it, though never so intolerable.

I answer, if this be a true consequence, why are not all troubles to be borne alike? Why are we suffered to divorce adulteries, desertions, or frigidities? Who knows not that trouble and affliction is the decree of God upon every state of life? Follows it therefore, that, though they grow excessive and insupportable, we must not avoid them? If we may in all other conditions, and not in marriage, the doom of our suffering ties us not by the trouble, but by the bond of marriage: and that must be proved inseparable from other reasons, not from this place. And his own confession declares the weakness of this argument, yet his ungoverned arrogance could not be dissuaded from venting it.

His ninth argument is, "that a husband must love his wife as himself; therefore he may not divorce for any disagreement no more than he may separate his soul from his body."

I answer: if he love his wife as himself, he must love her so far as he may preserve himself to her in a cheerful and comfortable manner, and not so as to ruin himself by anguish and sorrow, without any benefit to her. Next, if the husband must love his wife as himself, she must be understood a wife in some reasonable measure, willing and sufficient to perform the chief duties of her covenant; else by the hold of this argument it would be his great sin to divorce either for adultery or desertion. The rest of this will run circuit with the union of one flesh, which was answered before. And that to divorce a relative and metaphorical union of two bodies into one flesh cannot be likened in all things to the dividing of that natural union of soul and body into one person, is apparent of itself.

His last argument he fetches "from the inconveniences that would follow upon his freedom of divorce, to the corrupting of men's minds, and the overturning of all human society."

But for me let God and Moses answer this blasphemer, who dares bring in such a foul indictment against the divine law. Why did God permit this to his people the Jews, but that the right and good, which came directly thereby, was more in his esteem than the wrong and evil, which came by accident? And for those weak supposes of infants that would be left in their mothers' belly, (which must needs be good news for chamber-maids, to hear a serving-man grown so provident for great bellies,) and portions and jointures likely to incur embezzlement hereby, the ancient civil law instructs us plentifully how to award, which our profound opposite knew not, for it was not in his tenures.

His arguments are spun; now follows the chaplain with his antiquities, wiser if he had refrained, for his very touching aught that is learned soils it, and lays him still more and more open, a conspicuous gull. There being both fathers and councils more ancient, wherewith to have served his purpose better than with what he cites, how may we do to know the subtle drift that moved him to begin first with the "twelfth council of Toledo"? I would not undervalue the depth of his notion; but perhaps he had heard that the men of Toledo had store of good blademettle, and were excellent at cuttling; who can tell but it might be the reach of his policy, that these able men of decision would do best to have the prime stroke among his testimonies in deciding this cause? But all this craft avails him not; for seeing they allow no cause of divorce but fornication, what do these keen doctors here, but cut him over the sinews with their toledoes, for holding in the precedent page other causes of divorce besides, both directly and by consequence? As evil doth that Saxon council, next quoted, bestead him. For if it allow divorce precisely for no cause but fornication, it thwarts his own exposition: and if it understand fornication largely, it sides with whom he would confute. However, the authority of that synod can be but small, being under Theodorus, the Canterbury bishop, a Grecian monk of Tarsus, revolted from his own church to the pope. What have we next? the civil law stuffed in between two councils, as if the Code had been some synod; for that he understood himself in this quotation, is incredible; where the law, Cod. l. 3, tit. 38, leg. 11, speaks not of divorce, but against the dividing of possessions to divers heirs. whereby the married servants of a great family were divided, perhaps into distant countries and colonies, father from son, wife from husband, sore against their will. Somewhat lower he confesseth, that the civil law allows many reasons of divorce, but the canon law decrees otherwise; a fair credit to his cause! And I amaze me, though the fancy of this dolt be as obtuse and sad as any mallet, how the licenser could sleep out all this, and suffer him to uphold his opinion by canons and Gregorian decretals; a law which not only his adversary, but the whole reformation of this church and state hath branded and rejected. As ignorantly, and too ignorantly to deceive any reader but an unlearned, he talks of Justin Martyr's Apology, not telling us which of the twain; for that passage in the beginning of his first, which I have cited elsewhere, plainly makes against him: so doth Tertullian, cited next, and next Erasmus; the one against Marcion, the other in his annotations on Matthew, and to the Corinthians. And thus ye have the list of his choice antiquities, as pleasantly chosen as ye would wish from a man of his handy vocation, puffed up with no luck at all above the stint of his capacity.

Now he comes to the position, which I set down whole; and, like an able textman, slits it into four, that he may the better come at it with his barber-surgery, and his sleeves turned up. Wherein first, he denies "that any disposition, unfitness, or contrariety of mind, is unchangeable in nature; but that by the help of diet and physic it may be altered."

I mean not to dispute philosophy with this pork, who never read any. But I appeal to all experience, though there be many drugs to purge those redundant humors and circulations, that commonly impair health, and are not natural, whether any man can with the safety of his life bring a healthy constitution into physic with this design, to alter his natural temperament and disposition of mind. How much more vain and ridiculous would it be, by altering and rooting up the grounds of nature, which is most likely to produce death or madness, to hope the reducing of a mind to this or that fitness, or two disagreeing minds to a mutual sympathy! Suppose they might, and that with great danger of their lives and right senses, alter one temperature, how can they know that the succeeding disposition will not be as far from fitness and agreement? They would perhaps change melancholy into sanguine; but what if phlegm and choler in as great a measure come instead, the unfitness will be still as difficult and troublesome? But lastly, whether these things be changeable or not, experience teaches us, and our position supposes that they seldom do change in any time commensurable to the necessities of man, or convenient to the ends of marriage: and if the fault be in the one, shall the other live all his days in bondage and misery for another's perverseness, or immedicable disaffection? To my friends, of which may fewest be so unhappy, I have a remedy, as they know, more wise and manly to prescribe: but for his friends and followers, (of which many may deserve justly to feel themselves the unhappiness which they consider not in others,) I send them by his advice to sit upon the stool and strain, till their cross dispositions and contrarieties of mind shall change to a better correspondence, and to a quicker apprehension of common sense, and their own good.

His second reason is as heedless: "Because that grace may change the disposition, therefore no indisposition may cause divorce."

Answ. First, It will not be deniable that many persons, gracious both, may yet happen to be very unfitly married, to the great disturbance of either. Secondly, What if one have grace, the other not, and will not alter, as the scripture testifies there be of those, in whom we may expect a change, when "the blackamoor changes his color, or the leopard his spots," Jer. xiii, 23. shall the gracious therefore dwell in torment all his life for the ungracious? We see that holiest precepts, than which there can no better physic be administered to the mind of man, and set on with powerful preaching, cannot work this cure, no, not in the family, not in the wife of him that preaches day and night to her. What an unreasonable thing it is, that men, and clergymen especially, should exact such wonderous changes in another man's house, and are seen to work so little in their own!

To the second point of the position, that this unfitness hinders the main ends and benefits of marriage, he answers, "if I mean the unfitness of choler, or sullen disposition, that soft words, according to Solomon, pacify wrath."

But I reply, that the saying of Solomon is a proverb, frequently true, not universally, as both the event shows, and many other sentences written by the same author, particularly of an evil woman, Prov. xxi. 9, 19, and in other chapters, that she is better shunned than dwelt with, and a desert is preferred before her society. What need the Spirit of God put this choice into our heads, if soft words could always take effect with her? How frivolous is not only this disputer, but he that taught him thus, and let him come abroad!

To his second answer I return this, that although there be not easily found such an antipathy, as to hate one another like a toad or poison; yet that there is oft such a dislike in both, or either, to conjugal love, as hinders all the comfort of matrimony, scarce any can be so simple as not to apprehend. And what can be that favor, found or not found, in the eyes of the husband, but a natural liking or disliking; whereof the law of God, Deut. xxiv., bears witness, as of an ordinary accident, and determines wisely and divinely thereafter? And this disaffection happening to be in the one, not without the unspeakable discomfort of the other, must he be left like a thing consecrated to calamity and despair, without redemption?

Against the third branch of the position, he denies that "solace and peace, which is contrary to discord and variance, is the main end of marriage." What then? He will have it "the solace of male and female." Came this doctrine out of some school, or some sty? Who but one forsaken of all sense and civil nature, and chiefly of Christianity, will deny that peace, contrary to discord, is the calling and the general end of every Christian, and of all his actions, and more especially of marriage, which is the dearest league of love, and the dearest resemblance of that love which in Christ is dearest to his church?

How then can peace and comfort, as it is contrary to discord, which God hates to dwell with, not be the main end of marriage? Discord then we ought to fly, and to pursue peace, far above the observance of a civil covenant already broken, and the breaking daily iterated on the other side. And what better testimony than the words of the institution itself, to prove that a conversing solace and peaceful society, is the prime end of marriage, without which no other help or office can be mutual, beseeming the dignity of reasonable creatures, that such as they should be coupled in the rites of nature by the mere compulsion of lust, without love or peace, worse than wild beasts? Nor was it half so wisely spoken as some deem, though Austin spake it, that if God had intended other than copulation in marriage, he would for Adam have created a friend, rather than a wife, to converse with; and our own writers blame him for this opinion; for which and the like passages, concerning marriage, he might be justly taxed of rusticity in these affairs. For this cannot but be with ease conceived, that there is one society of grave friendship, and another amiable and attractive society of conjugal love, besides the deed of procreation, which of itself soon cloys, and is despised, unless it be cherished and reincited with a pleasing conversation. Which if ignoble and swainish minds cannot apprehend, shall such merit therefore to be the censurers of more generous and virtuous spirits?

Against the last point of the position, to prove that contrariety of mind is not a greater cause of divorce than corporal frigidity, he enters into such a tedious and drawling tale "of burning, and burning, and lust and burning," that the dull argument itself burns too for want of stirring; and yet all this burning is not able to expel the frigidity of his brain. So long therefore as that cause in the position shall be proved a sufficient cause of divorce, rather than spend words with this phlegmy clod of an antagonist, more than of necessity and a little merriment, I will not now contend whether it be a greater cause than frigidity or no.

His next attempt is upon the arguments which I brought to prove the position. And for the first, not finding it of that structure as to be scaled with his short ladder, he retreats with a bravado, that it deserves no answer. And I as much wonder what the whole book deserved, to be thus troubled and solicited by such a paltry solicitor. I would he had not cast the gracious eye of his duncery upon the small deserts of a pamphlet, whose every line meddled with uncases him to scorn and laughter.

That which he takes for the second argument, if he look better, is no argument, but an induction to those that follow. Then he stumbles that I should say, "the gentlest ends of marriage," confessing that he understands it not. And I believe him heartily: for how should he, a serving-man both by nature and by function, an idiot by breeding, and a solicitor by presumption, ever come to know or feel within himself what the meaning is of "gentle"? He blames it for "a neat phrase," for nothing angers him more than his own proper contrary. Yet altogether without art sure he is not; for who could have devised to give us more briefly a better description of his own servility?

But what will become now of the business I know not; for the man is suddenly taken with a lunacy of law, and speaks revelations out of the attorney's academy only from a lying spirit: for he says, "that where a thing is void ipso facto, there needs no legal proceeding to make it void:" which is false; for marriage is void by adultery or frigidity, yet not made void without legal proceeding. Then asks my opinion of John-a-Noaks and John-a-Stiles: and I answer him, that I, for my part, think John Dory was a better man than both of them; for certainly they were the greatest wranglers that ever lived, and have filled all our law-books with the obtunding story of their suits and trials.

After this he tells us a miraculous piece of antiquity, how "two Romans, Titus and Sempronius, made feoffments," at Rome, sure, and levied fines by the common law. But now his fit of law past, yet hardly come to himself, he maintains, that if marriage be void, as being neither of God nor nature, "there needs no legal proceeding to part it," and I tell him that offends not me; then quoth he, "this is nothing to your book, being the Doctrine and Discipline of Divorce." But that I deny him; for all discipline is not legal that is to say, juridical, but some is personal, some economical, and some ecclesiastical.

Lastly, If I prove that contrary dispositions are joined neither of God nor nature, and so the marriage void, "he will give me the controversy." I have proved it in that book to any wise man, and without more ado the institution proves it.

Where I answer an objection usually made, that "the disposition ought to be known before marriage," and show how difficult it is to choose a fit consort, and how easy to mistake, the servitor would know "what I mean by conversation," declaring his capacity nothing refined since his law-puddering, but still the same it was in the pantry, and at the dresser. Shall I argue of conversation with this hoyden, to go and practise at his opportunities in the larder? To men of quality I have said enough; and experience confirms by daily example, that wisest, soberest, justest men are sometimes miserably mistaken in their choice. Whom to leave thus without remedy, tossed and tempested in a most unquiet sea of afflictions and temptations, I say is most unchristianly.

But he goes on to untruss my arguments, imagining them his master's points. Only in the passage following I cannot but admire the ripeness and the pregnance of his native treachery, endeavoring to be more a fox than his wit will suffer him. Whereas I briefly mentioned certain heads of discourse, which I referred to a place more proper according to my method, to be treated there at full with all their reasons about them, this brainworm, against all the laws of dispute, will needs deal with them here. And as a country hind, sometimes ambitious to show his betters that he is not so simple as you take him, and that he knows his advantages, will teach us a new trick to confute by. And would you think to what a pride he swells in the contemplation of his rare stratagem, offering to carp at the language of a book, which yet he confesses to be generally commended; while himself will be acknowledged, by all that read him, the basest and the hungriest enditer, that could take the boldness to look abroad. Observe now the arrogance of a groom, how it will mount. I had written, that common adultery is a thing which the rankest politician would think it shame and diswor-

ship, that his law should countenance. First,
It offends him, that "rankest" should signify
aught but his own smell: who that knows
English would not understand me, when I
say a rank serving-man, a rank pettifogger, to
mean a mere serving-man, a mere and arrant pettifogger who lately was so hardy, as
to lay aside his buckram-wallet, and make
himself a fool in print, with confuting books
which are above him? Next, the word "politician" is not used to his maw; and thereupon he plays the most notorious hobby-
horse, jesting and frisking in the luxury of
his nonsense with such poor fetches to cog
a laughter from us, that no antic hobnail at
a morris, but is more handsomely facetious.

Concerning that place Deut. xxiv. 1, which
he saith to be "the main pillar of my opinion,"
though I rely more on the institution than on
that: these two pillars I do indeed confess
are to me as those two in the porch of the
temple, Jachin and Boaz, which names import establishment and strength; nor do I
fear who can shake them. The exposition of
Deut. which I brought is the received exposition, both ancient and modern, by all
learned men, unless it be a monkish papist
here and there; and the gloss, which he and
his obscure assistant would persuade us to,
is merely new and absurd, presuming out
of his utter ignorance in the Hebrew to interpret those words of the text, first, in a
mistaken sense of uncleanness, against all approved writers; secondly, in a limited sense,
whenas the original speaks without limitation, "some uncleanness, or any." And it had
been a wise law indeed to mean itself particular, and not to express the case which
this acute rabbi hath all this while been hook-
ing for; whereby they who are most partial
to him may guess that something is in this
doctrine which I allege, that forces the adversary to such a new and strained exposition; wherein he does nothing for above four
pages, but founder himself to and fro in his
own objections; one while denying that divorce was permitted, another while affirming
that it was permitted for the wife's sake,
and after all, distrusts himself. And for his
surest retirement, betakes him to those old
suppositions, "that Christ abolished the Mosaic law of Divorce; that the Jews had not
sufficient knowledge in this point, through

the darkness of the dispensation of heavenly
things; that under the plenteous grace of the
gospel we are tied by cruellest compulsion
to live in marriage till death with the wickedest, the worst, the most persecuting mate."
These ignorant and doting surmises he might
have read confuted at large, even in the first
edition; but found it safer to pass that part
over in silence. So that they who see not the
sottishness of this his new and tedious exposition, are worthy to love it dearly.

His explanation done, he charges me with
a wicked gloss, and almost blasphemy, for
saying that Christ in teaching meant not always to be taken word for word; but like a
wise physician, administering one excess
against another, to reduce us to a perfect
mean. Certainly to teach thus were no dishonest method: Christ himself hath often
used hyperboles in his teaching; and gravest
authors, both Aristotle in the second of his
"Ethics to Nichomachus," and Seneca in his
seventh "de Beneficiis," advise us to stretch
out the line of precept ofttimes beyond measure, that while we tend further, the mean
might be the easier attained. And whoever
comments that 5th of Matthew, when he
comes to the turning of cheek after cheek
to blows, and the parting both with cloak
and coat, if any please to be the rifler, will be
forced to recommend himself to the same exposition, though this catering lawmonger be
bold to call it wicked. Now note another
precious piece of him: Christ, saith he, "doth
not say that an unchaste look is adultery,
but the lusting after her;" as if the looking
unchastely could be without lusting. This gear
is licensed for good reason: "Imprimatur."

Next he would prove, that the speech of
Christ is not uttered in excess against the
pharisees, first, "because he speaks it to his
disciples," Matt. v.; which is false, for he
spake it to the multitude, as by the first verse
is evident, among which in all likelihood were
many pharisees; but out of doubt all of them
pharisean disciples, and bred up in their doctrine; from which extremes of error and falsity Christ throughout his whole sermon labors to reclaim the people. Secondly, saith
he, "because Christ forbids not only putting
away, but marrying her who is put away."
Acutely! as if the pharisees might not have
offended as much in marrying the divorced,

as in divorcing the married. The precept may bind all, rightly understood; and yet the vehement manner of giving it may be occasioned only by the pharisees.

Finally, he winds up his text with much doubt and trepidation; for it may be his trenchers were not scraped, and that which never yet afforded corn of savor to his noddle, the saltcellar was not rubbed; and therefore in this haste easily granting that his answers fall foul upon each other, and praying you would not think he writes as a prophet, but as a man, he runs to the black jack, fills his flagon, spreads the table, and serves up dinner.

After waiting and voiding, he thinks to void my second argument, and the contradictions that will follow both in the law and gospel, if the Mosaic law were abrogated by our Saviour, and a compulsive prohibition fixed instead; and sings his old song, "that the gospel counts unlawful that which the law allowed," instancing in circumcision, sacrifices, washings. But what are these ceremonial things to the changing of a moral point in household duty, equally belonging to Jew and Gentile? Divorce was then right, now wrong; then permitted in the rigorous time of law, now forbidden by law, even to the most extremely afflicted, in the favorable time of grace and freedom. But this is not for an unbuttoned fellow to discuss in the garret at his trestle, and dimension of candle by the snuff, which brought forth his cullionly paraphrase on St. Paul, whom he brings in discoursing such idle stuff to the maids and widows, as his own servile inurbanity forbears not to put into the apostle's mouth, "of the soul's conversing;" and this he presumes to do, being a bayard, who never had the soul to know what conversing means, but as his provender and the familiarity of the kitchen schooled his conceptions.

He passes to the third argument, like a boar in a vineyard, doing nought else, but still as he goes champing and chewing over what I could mean by this chimæra of a "fit conversing soul," notions and words never made for those chops; but like a generous wine, only by overworking the settled mud of his fancy, to make him drunk, and disgorge his vileness the more openly. All persons of gentle breeding (I say "gentle," though this barrow grunt at the word) I know will apprehend, and be satisfied in what I spake, how unpleasing and discontenting the society of body must needs be between those whose minds cannot be sociable. But what should a man say more to a snout in this pickle? What language can be low and degenerate enough?

The fourth argument which I had was, that marriage being a covenant, the very being whereof consists in the performance of unfeigned love and peace: if that were not tolerably performed, the covenant became broke and revokable. Which how can any, in whose mind the principles of right reason and justice are not cancelled, deny? For how can a thing subsist, when the true essence thereof is dissolved? Yet this he denies, and yet in such a manner as alters my assertion; for he puts in, "though the main end be not attained in full measure:" but my position is, if it be not tolerably attained, as throughout the whole discourse is apparent.

Now for his reasons:—"Heman found not that peace and solace which is the main end of communion with God: should he therefore break off that communion?"

I answer, that if Heman found it not, the fault was certainly his own. But in marriage it happens far otherwise: sometimes the fault is plainly not his who seeks divorce; sometimes it cannot be discerned whose fault it is, and therefore cannot in reason or equity be the matter of an absolute prohibition.

His other instance declares what a right handicraftsman he is of petty cases, and how unfit to be aught else at highest but a hackney of the law. "I change houses with a man; it is supposed I do it for my own ends; I attain them not in this house; I shall not therefore go from my bargain." How without fear might the young Charinus in Andria now cry out, "What likeness can be here to a marriage?" In this bargain was no capitulation, but the yielding of possession to one another, wherein each of them had his several end apart. In marriage there is a solmen vow of love and fidelity each to other: this bargain is fully accomplished in the change: in marriage the covenant still is in performing. If one of them perform nothing tolerably, but instead of love, abound in disaffection, disobedience, fraud, and hatred, what thing in the nature of a covenant shall bind the other to such a perdurable mischief? Keep to your problems of ten groats; these matters are not for pragmatics and folkmooters to babble in.

Concerning the place of Paul, "that God hath called us to peace," 1 Cor. vii., and therefore, certainly, if anywhere in this world, we have a right to claim it reasonably in marriage; it is plain enough in the sense which I gave, and confessed by Paræus, and other orthodox divines, to be a good sense; and this answerer does not weaken it. The other place, that "he who hateth, may put away," which if I show him, he promises to yield the whole controversy, is, besides Deut. xxiv. 1, Deut. xxi. 14. and before this, Exod. xxi. 8. Of Malachi I have spoken more in another place; and say again, that the best interpreters, all the ancient, and most of the modern, translate it as I cite it, and very few otherwise, whereof, perhaps, Junius is the chief.

Another thing troubles him, that marriage is called "the mystery of joy." Let it still trouble him; for what hath he to do either with joy or with mystery? He thinks it frantic divinity to say, it is not the outward continuance of marriage that keeps the covenant of marriage whole; but whosoever doth most according to peace and love, whether in marriage or divorce, he breaks marriage least. If I shall spell it to him, he breaks marriage least, is to say, he dishonors not marriage; for least is taken in the Bible, and other good authors, for not at all. And a particular marriage a man may break, if for a lawful cause, and yet not break, that is, not violate, or dishonor the ordinance of marriage. Hence those two questions that follow are left ridiculous; and the maids at Aldgate, whom he flouts, are likely to have more wit than the serving-man at Addle-gate.

Whereas he taxes me of adding to the scripture in that I said, Love only is the fulfilling of every commandment, I cited no particular scripture, but spake a general sense, which might be collected from many places. For seeing love includes faith, what is there that can fulfil every commandment but only love? and I meant, as any intelligent reader might apprehend, every positive and civil commandment, whereof Christ hath taught us that man is the lord. It is not the formal duty of worship, or the sitting still, that keeps

the holy rest of sabbath; but whosoever doth most according to charity, whether he works or works not, he breaks the holy rest of sabbath least. So marriage being a civil ordinance, made for man, not man for it; he who doth that which most accords with charity, first to himself, next to whom he next owes it, whether in marriage or divorce, he breaks the ordinance of marriage least. And what in religious prudence can be charity to himself, and what to his wife, either in continuing or in dissolving the marriage-knot, hath been already oft enough discoursed. So that what St. Paul saith of circumcision, the same I stick not to say of a civil ordinance, made to the good and comfort of man, not to his ruin: marriage is nothing, and divorce is nothing, "but faith which worketh by love." And this I trust none can mistake.

Against the fifth argument, that a Christian, in a higher order of priesthood than that Levitical, is a person dedicate to joy and peace, and therefore needs not in subjection to a civil ordinance, made to no other end but for his good, (when without his fault he finds it impossible to be decently or tolerably observed,) to plunge himself into immeasurable distractions and temptations above his strength: against this he proves nothing; but gads into silly conjectures of what abuses would follow, and with as good reason might declaim against the best things that are.

Against the sixth argument, that to force the continuance of marriage between minds found utterly unfit and disproportional, is against nature, and seems forbid under that allegorical precept of Moses, "not to sow a field with divers seed, lest both be defiled; not to plough with an ox and an ass together," which I deduced by the pattern of St. Paul's reasoning what was meant by not muzzling the ox: he rambles over a long narration, to tell us that "by the oxen are meant the preachers;" which is not doubted. Then he demands, "if this my reasoning be like St. Paul's." And I answer him, Yes. He replies, that sure St. Paul would be ashamed to reason thus. And I tell him, No. He grants that place which I alleged, 2 Cor. vi., of unequal yoking, may allude to that of Moses, but says, "I cannot prove it makes to my purpose," and shows not first how he can disprove it. Weigh, gentlemen, and consider, whether my affirmations, backed with reason, may hold balance against the bare denials of this ponderous confuter, elected by his ghostly patrons to be my copesmate.

Proceeding on to speak of mysterious things in nature, I had occasion to fit the language thereafter; matters not, for the reading of this odious fool, who thus ever, when he meets with aught above the cogitation of his breeding, leaves the noisome stench of his rude slot behind him, maligning that anything should be spoke or understood above his own genuine baseness; and gives sentence that his confuting hath been employed about a frothy, immeritous, and undeserving discourse. Who could have believed so much insolence durst vent itself from out the hide of a varlet, as thus to censure that which men of mature judgment have applauded to be writ with good reason? But this contents him not; he falls now to rave in his barbarous abusiveness. And why? A reason befitting such an artificer, because, he saith, the book is contrary to all human learning; whenas the world knows that all, both human and divine learning, till the canon law, allowed divorce by consent, and for many causes without consent. Next he dooms it as contrary to truth; whenas it hath been disputable among learned men, ever since it was prohibited: and is by Peter Martyr thought an opinion not impious, but hard to be refuted; and by Erasmus deemed a doctrine so charitable and pious, as if it cannot be used, were to be wished it could; but is by Martin Bucer, a man of dearest and most religious memory in the church, taught and maintained to be either most lawfully used, or most lawfully permitted. And for this, for I affirm no more than Bucer, what censure do you think, readers, he hath condemned the book to? To a death no less infamous than to be burnt by the hangman. Mr. Licenser, (for I deal not now with this caitiff, never worth my earnest, and now not seasonable for my jest,) you are reputed a man discreet enough, religious enough, honest enough, that is to an ordinary competence, in all these. But now your turn is, to hear what your own hand hath earned ye; that when you suffered this nameless hangman to cast into public such a despiteful contumely upon a name and person deserving of the church and state equally to yourself; and one who hath done more to the present advancement of your own tribe, than you or many of them have done for themselves; you forgot to be either honest, religious, or discreet. Whatever the state might do concerning it, supposed a matter to expect evil from, I should not doubt to meet among them with wise, and honorable, and knowing men: but as to this brute libel, so much the more impudent and lawless for the abused authority which it bears, I say again, that I abominate the censure of rascals and their licensers.

With difficulty I return to what remains of this ignoble task, for the disdain I have to change a period more with the filth and venom of this gourmand, swelled into a confuter; yet for the satisfaction of others I endure all this.

Against the seventh argument, that if the canon law and divines allow divorce for conspiracy of death, they may as well allow it to avoid the same consequence from the likelihood of natural causes.

First, he denies that the canon so decrees.

I answer, that it decrees for danger of life, as much as for adultery, Decret. Gregor. l. 4, tit. 19, and in other places: and the best civilians, who cite the canon law, so collect, as Schneidewin in Instit. tit. 10, p. 4, de divort. And indeed, who would have denied it, but one of a reprobate ignorance in all he meddles with?

Secondly, he saith the case alters; for there the offender, "who seeks the life, doth implicitly at least act a divorce."

And I answer, that here nature, though no offender, doth the same. But if an offender, by acting a divorce, shall release the offended, this is an ample grant against himself. He saith, Nature teaches to save life from one who seeks it. And I say, she teaches no less to save it from any other cause that endangers it. He saith, that here they are both actors. Admit they were, it would not be uncharitable to part them; yet sometimes they are not both actors, but the one of them most lamentedly passive. So he concludes, we must not take advantage of our own faults and corruptions, to release us from our duties. But shall we take no advantage to save ourselves from the faults of another, who hath annulled his right to our duty? "No," saith he; "let them die of the sullens, and try who will pity them." Barbarian, the shame of all honest attorneys! why do they not hoist him over the bar and blanket him?

Against the eighth argument, that they who are destitute of all marriageable gifts, except a body not plainly unfit, have not the calling to marry, and consequently married and so found, may be divorced: this, he saith, is nothing to the purpose, and not fit to be answered. I leave it therefore to the judgment of his masters.

Against the ninth argument, that marriage is a human society, and so chiefly seated in agreement and unity of mind: if therefore the mind cannot have that due society by marriage, that it may reasonably and humanly desire, it can be no human society, and so not without reason divorcible: here he falsifies, and turns what the position required of a reasonable agreement in the main matters of society, into an agreement in all things, which makes the opinion not mine, and so he leaves it.

At last, and in good hour, we are come to his farewell, which is to be a concluding taste of his jabberment at in law, the flashiest and the fustiest that ever corrupted in such an unswilled hogshead.

Against my tenth argument, as he calls it, but as I intended it, my other position, "That divorce is not a thing determinable by a compulsive law, for that all law is for some good that may be frequently attained without the admixture of a worse inconvenience; but the law forbidding divorce never attains to any good end of such prohibition, but rather multiplies evil; therefore the prohibition of divorce is no good law." Now for his attorney's prize: but first, like a right cunning and sturdy logician, he denies my argument, not mattering whether in the major or minor: and saith, "there are many laws made for good, and yet that good is not attained, through the defaults of the party, but a greater inconvenience follows."

But I reply, that this answer builds upon a shallow foundation, and most unjustly supposes every one in default, who seeks divorce from the most injurious wedlock. The default therefore will be found in the law itself; which is neither able to punish the offender, but the innocent must withal suffer: nor can right the innocent in what is chiefly sought, the obtainment of love or quietness. His instances out of the common law are all so quite beside the matter which he would prove, as may be a warning to all clients how they venture their business with such a cockbrained solicitor. For being to show some law of England, attaining to no good end, and yet through no default of the party, who is thereby debarred all remedy, he shows us only how some do lose the benefit of good laws through their own default. His first example saith, "It is a just law that every one shall peaceably enjoy his estate in lands or otherwise." Does this law attain to no good end? The bar will blush at this most incogitant woodcock. But see if a draught of Littleton will recover him to his senses. "If this man, having fee-simple in his lands, yet will take a lease of his own lands from another, this shall be an estopple to him in an assize from the recovering of his own land."

Mark now and register him! How many are there of ten thousand who have such a fee-simple in their sconce, as to take a lease of their own lands from another? So that this inconvenience lights upon scarce one in an age, and by his own default; and the law of enjoying each man his own is good to all others. But on the contrary, this prohibition of divorce is good to none, and brings inconvenience to numbers, who lie under intolerable grievances without their own default, through the wickedness or folly of another; and in all this iniquity the law remedies not, but in a manner maintains. His other cases are directly to the same purpose, and might have been spared, but that he is a tradesman of the law, and must be borne with at his first setting up, to lay forth his best ware, which is only gibberish.

I have now done that, which for many causes I might have thought could not likely have been my fortune, to be put to this underwork of scouring and unrubbishing the low and sordid ignorance of such a presumptuous lozel. Yet Hercules had the labor once imposed upon him to carry dung out of the Augean stable. At any hand I would be rid of him: for I had rather, since the life of man is likened to a scene, that all my entrances and exits might mix with such persons only, whose worth erects them and their actions to a grave and tragic deportment, and not to have to do with clowns and vices. But if a man cannot

peaceably walk into the world, but must be
infested, sometimes at his face with dorrs
and horseflies, sometimes beneath with bawl-
ing whippets and shin-barkers, and these to
be set on by plot and consultation with a junto
of clergymen and licensers, commended also
and rejoiced in by those whose partiality
cannot yet forego old papistical principles;
have I not cause to be in such a manner defensive, as may procure me freedom to pass
more unmolested hereafter by these incumbrances, not so much regarded for themselves,
as for those who incite them? And what defence can properly be used in such a despicable
encounter as this, but either the flap or the
spurn? If they can afford me none but a
ridiculous adversary, the blame belongs not
to me, though the whole dispute be strewed
and scattered with ridiculous. And if he have
such an ambition to know no better who are
his mates, but among those needy thoughts,
which though his two faculties of serving-
man and solicitor should compound into one
mongrel, would be but thin and meagre, if in
this penury of soul he can be possible to have
the lustiness to think of fame, let him but
send me how he calls himself, and I may
chance not fail to endorse him on the backside of posterity, not a golden, but a brazen
ass. Since my fate extorts from me a talent of
sport, which I had thought to hide in a nap-
kin, he shall be my Batrachomuomachia, my
Bavius, my Calandrino, the common adagy
of ignorance and overweening: nay, perhaps,
as the provocation may be, I may be driven to
curl up this gilding prose into a rough sotadic,
that shall rhyme him into such a condition,
as instead of judging good books to be burnt
by the executioner, he shall be readier to be
his own hangman. Thus much to this nui-
sance.

But as for the subject itself, which I have
writ and now defend, according as the opposition bears; if any man equal to the matter
shall think it appertains him to take in hand
this controversy, either excepting against
aught written, or persuaded he can show better
how this question, of such moment to be
thoroughly known, may receive a true determination, not leaning on the old and rotten
suggestions whereon it yet leans; if his intents be sincere to the public, and shall carry
him on without bitterness to the opinion, or

to the person dissenting; let him not, I entreat him, guess by the handling, which meri-
toriously hath been bestowed on this object
of contempt and laughter, that I account it
any displeasure done me to be contradicted
in print, but as it leads to the attainment of
anything more true, shall esteem it a benefit;
and shall know how to return his civility and
fair argument in such a sort, as he shall confess that to do so is my choice, and to have
done thus was my chance.

OF EDUCATION.

[The text is that of the first edition, 1644.]

TO MASTER SAMUEL HARTLIB.

Mr. Hartlib,

I am long since persuaded that to say or do
aught worth memory and imitation, no purpose or respect should sooner move us than
simply the love of God, and of mankind.
Nevertheless to write now the reforming of
education, though it be one of the greatest
and noblest designs that can be thought on,
and for the want whereof this nation perishes; I had not yet at this time been induced, but by your earnest entreaties and
serious conjurements; as having my mind
for the present half diverted in the pursuance of some other assertions, the knowledge
and the use of which cannot but be a great
furtherance both to the enlargement of truth,
and honest living with much more peace. Nor
should the laws of any private friendship
have prevailed with me to divide thus, or
transpose my former thoughts, but that I
see those aims, those actions, which have won
you with me the esteem of a person sent
hither by some good providence from a far
country to be the occasion and the incitement
of great good to this island.

And, as I hear, you have obtained the same
repute with men of most approved wisdom,
and some of highest authority among us; not
to mention the learned correspondence which
you hold in foreign parts, and the extraordinary pains and diligence which you have used
in this matter, both here and beyond the
seas; either by the definite will of God so
ruling, or the peculiar sway of nature, which
also is God's working. Neither can I think that

so reputed and so valued as you are, you would, to the forfeit of your own discerning ability, impose upon me an unfit and overponderous argument; but that the satisfaction which you profess to have received, from those incidental discourses which we have wandered into, hath pressed and almost constrained you into a persuasion, that what you require from me in this point, I neither ought nor can in conscience defer beyond this time both of so much need at once, and so much opportunity to try what God hath determined.

I will not resist, therefore, whatever it is, either of divine or human obligement, that you lay upon me; but will forthwith set down in writing, as you request me, that voluntary idea, which hath long, in silence, presented itself to me, of a better education, in extent and comprehension far more large, and yet of time far shorter, and of attainment far more certain, than hath been yet in practice. Brief I shall endeavor to be; for that which I have to say, assuredly this nation hath extreme need should be done sooner than spoken. To tell you, therefore, what I have benefited herein among old renowned authors, I shall spare; and to search what many modern Januas and Didactics, more than ever I shall read, have projected, my inclination leads me not. But if you can accept of these few observations which have flowered off, and are as it were the burnishing of many studious and contemplative years, altogether spent in the search of religious and civil knowledge, and such as pleased you so well in the relating, I here give you them to dispose of.

The end then of learning is to repair the ruins of our first parents by regaining to know God aright, and out of that knowledge to love him, to imitate him, to be like him, as we may the nearest by possessing our souls of true virtue, which being united to the heavenly grace of faith, makes up the highest perfection. But because our understanding cannot in this body found itself but on sensible things, nor arrive so clearly to the knowledge of God and things invisible, as by orderly conning over the visible and inferior creature, the same method is necessarily to be followed in all discreet teaching. And seeing every nation affords not experience and tradition enough for all kind of learning, therefore we are chiefly taught the languages of those people who have at any time been most industrious after wisdom; so that language is but the instrument conveying to us things useful to be known. And though a linguist should pride himself to have all the tongues that Babel cleft the world into, yet if he have not studied the solid things in them, as well as the words and lexicons, he were nothing so much to be esteemed a learned man, as any yeoman or tradesman competently wise in his mother dialect only.

Hence appear the many mistakes which have made learning generally so unpleasing and so unsuccessful; first, we do amiss to spend seven or eight years merely in scraping together so much miserable Latin and Greek, as might be learned otherwise easily and delightfully in one year. And that which casts our proficiency therein so much behind, is our time lost partly in too oft idle vacancies given both to schools and universities; partly in a preposterous exaction, forcing the empty wits of children to compose themes, verses, and orations, which are the acts of ripest judgment, and the final work of a head filled by long reading and observing, with elegant maxims and copious invention. These are not matters to be wrung from poor striplings, like blood out of the nose, or the plucking of untimely fruit. Besides the ill habit which they get of wretched barbarizing against the Latin and Greek idiom, with their untutored Anglicisms, odious to be read, yet not to be avoided without a wellcontinued and judicious conversing among pure authors digested, which they scarce taste. Whereas, if after some preparatory grounds of speech by their certain forms got into memory, they were led to the praxis thereof in some chosen short book lessoned thoroughly to them, they might then forthwith proceed to learn the substance of good things, and arts in due order, which would bring the whole language quickly into their power. This I take to be the most rational and most profitable way of learning languages, and whereby we may best hope to give account to God of our youth spent herein.

And for the usual method of teaching arts, I deem it to be an old error of universities, not yet well recovered from the scholastic grossness of barbarous ages, that instead of beginning with arts most easy, (and those be such as are most obvious to the sense,) they present their young unmatriculated novices, at first coming, with the most intellective abstractions of logic and metaphysics; so that they having but newly left those grammatic flats and shallows, where they stuck unreasonably to learn a few words with lamentable construction, and now on the sudden transported under another climate, to be tossed and turmoiled with their unballasted wits in fathomless and unquiet deeps of controversy, do for the most part grow into hatred and contempt of learning, mocked and deluded all this while with ragged notions and babblements, while they expected worthy and delightful knowledge; till poverty or youthful years call them importunately their several ways, and hasten them, with the sway of friends, either to an ambitious and mercenary, or ignorantly zealous divinity: some allured to the trade of law, grounding their purposes not on the prudent and heavenly contemplation of justice and equity, which was never taught them, but on the promising and pleasing thoughts of litigious terms, fat contentions, and flowing fees; others betake them to state affairs, with souls so unprincipled in virtue and true generous breeding, that flattery and court-shifts and tyrannous aphorisms appear to them the highest points of wisdom; instilling their barren hearts with a conscientious slavery; if, as I rather think, it be not feigned. Others, lastly, of a more delicious and airy spirit, retire themselves (knowing no better) to the enjoyments of ease and luxury, living out their days in feast and jollity; which indeed is the wisest and the safest course of all these, unless they were with more integrity undertaken. And these are the fruits of misspending our prime youth at the schools and universities as we do, either in learning mere words, or such things chiefly as were better unlearned.

I shall detain you no longer in the demonstration of what we should not do, but straight conduct you to a hillside, where I will point you out the right path of a virtuous and noble education; laborious indeed at the first ascent, but else so smooth, so green, so full of goodly prospect, and melodious sounds on every side, that the harp of Orpheus was not more charming. I doubt not but ye shall have more ado to drive our dullest and laziest youth, our stocks and stubs, from the infinite desire of such a happy nurture, than we have now to hale and drag our choicest and hopefullest wits to that asinine feast of sowthistles and brambles, which is commonly set before them as all the food and entertainment of their tenderest and most docible age. I call therefore a complete and generous education, that which fits a man to perform justly, skilfully, and magnanimously all the offices, both private and public, of peace and war. And how all this may be done between twelve and one and twenty, less time than is now bestowed in pure trifling at grammar and sophistry, is to be thus ordered.

First, to find out a spacious house and ground about it fit for an academy, and big enough to lodge a hundred and fifty persons, whereof twenty or thereabout may be attendants, all under the government of one, who shall be thought of desert sufficient, and ability either to do all, or wisely to direct and oversee it done. This place should be at once both school and university, not needing a remove to any other house of scholarship, except it be some peculiar college of law, or physic, where they mean to be practitioners; but as for those general studies which take up all our time from Lily to the commencing, as they term it, master of art, it should be absolute. After this pattern, as many edifices may be converted to this use as shall be needful in every city throughout this land, which would tend much to the increase of learning and civility everywhere. This number, less or more thus collected, to the convenience of a foot company, or interchangeably two troops of cavalry, should divide their day's work into three parts as it lies orderly: their studies, their exercise, and their diet.

For their studies: first, they should begin with the chief and necessary rules of some good grammar, either that now used, or any better; and while this is doing, their speech is to be fashioned to a distinct and clear pronunciation, as near as may be to the Italian, especially in the vowels. For we Englishmen being far northerly, do not open our mouths in the cold air wide enough to grace a southern tongue; but are observed by all other nations to speak exceeding close and inward, so that to smatter Latin with an English mouth, is as ill a hearing as law French. Next, to make them expert in the usefullest points of grammar, and withal to season them and win them early to the love of virtue and true labor, ere any flattering seducement or vain principle seize them wandering, some easy and delightful book of education would be read to them, whereof the Greeks have store, as Cebes, Plutarch, and other Socratic discourses. But in Latin we have none of classic authority extant, except the two or three first books of Quintilian, and some select pieces elsewhere.

But here the main skill and groundwork will be, to temper them such lectures and explanations, upon every opportunity, as may lead and draw them in willing obedience, inflamed with the study of learning and the admiration of virtue; stirred up with high hopes of living to be brave men, and worthy patriots, dear to God, and famous to all ages. That they may despise and scorn all their childish and ill-taught qualities, to delight in manly and liberal exercises, which he who hath the art and proper eloquence to catch them with, what with mild and effectual persuasions, and what with the intimation of some fear, if need be, but chiefly by his own example, might in a short space gain them to an incredible diligence and courage, infusing into their young breasts such an ingenuous and noble ardor, as would not fail to make many of them renowned and matchless men. At the same time, some other hour of the day, might be taught them the rules of arithmetic; and soon after the elements of geometry, even playing, as the old manner was. After evening repast, till bedtime, their thoughts would be best taken up in the easy grounds of religion, and the story of scripture.

The next step would be to the authors of agriculture, Cato, Varro, and Columella, for the matter is most easy; and, if the language be difficult, so much the better, it is not a difficulty above their years. And here will be an occasion of inciting, and enabling them hereafter to improve the tillage of their country, to recover the bad soil, and to remedy the waste that is made of good; for this was one of Hercules' praises. Ere half these authors be read (which will soon be with plying hard and daily) they cannot choose but be masters of any ordinary prose. So that it will be then seasonable for them to learn in any modern author the use of the globes, and all the maps, first, with the old names, and then with the new; or they might be then capable to read any compendious method of natural philosophy.

And at the same time might be entering into the Greek tongue, after the same manner as was before prescribed in the Latin; whereby the difficulties of grammar being soon overcome, all the historical physiology of Aristotle and Theophrastus are open before them, and, as I may say, under contribution. The like access will be to Vitruvius, to Seneca's natural questions, to Mela, Celsus, Pliny, or Solinus. And having thus passed the principles of arithmetic, geometry, astronomy, and geography, with a general compact of physics, they may descend in mathematics to the instrumental science of trigonometry, and from thence to fortification, architecture, enginery, or navigation. And in natural philosophy they may proceed leisurely from the history of meteors, minerals, plants, and living creatures, as far as anatomy.

Then also in course might be read to them, out of some not tedious writer, the institution of physic, that they may know the tempers, the humours, the seasons, and how to manage a crudity; which he who can wisely and timely do, is not only a great physician to himself and to his friends, but also may, at some time or other, save an army by this frugal and expenseless means only; and not let the healthy and stout bodies of young men rot away under him for want of this discipline; which is a great pity, and no less a shame to the commander. To set forward all these proceedings in nature and mathematics, what hinders but that they may procure, as oft as shall be needful, the helpful experiences of hunters, fowlers, fishermen, shepherds, gardeners, apothecaries; and in the other sciences, architects, engineers, mariners, anatomists; who doubtless would be ready, some for reward, and some to favor such a hopeful seminary. And this will give them such a real tincture of natural knowledge, as they shall never forget, but daily augment with delight. Then also those poets which are now counted most hard, will be both facile and pleasant, Orpheus, Hesiod, Theocritus, Aratus, Nicander, Oppian, Dionysius; and in Latin, Lucretius, Manilius, and the rural part of Virgil.

By this time, years and good general precepts, will have furnished them more distinctly with that act of reason which in ethics is called Proairesis; that they may with some judgment contemplate upon moral good and evil. Then will be required a special reinforcement of constant and sound indoctrinating, to set them right and firm, instructing them more amply in the knowledge of virtue and the hatred of vice; while their young and pliant affections are led through all the moral 10 works of Plato, Xenophon, Cicero, Plutarch, Laertius, and those Locrian remnants; but still to be reduced in their nightward studies wherewith they close the day's work, under the determinate sentence of David or Solomon, or the evangelists and apostolic scriptures. Being perfect in the knowledge of personal duty, they may then begin the study of economics. And either now or before this, they may have easily learnt, at any odd hour, 20 the Italian tongue. And soon after, but with wariness and good antidote, it would be wholesome enough to let them taste some choice comedies, Greek, Latin, or Italian; those tragedies also, that treat of household matters, as Trachiniæ, Alcestis, and the like.

The next remove must be to the study of politics; to know the beginning, end, and reasons of political societies; that they may not, in a dangerous fit of the commonwealth, 30 be such poor, shaken, uncertain reeds, of such a tottering conscience, as many of our great counsellors have lately shown themselves, but steadfast pillars of the state. After this, they are to dive into the grounds of law, and legal justice; delivered first and with best warrant by Moses; and as far as human prudence can be trusted, in those extolled remains of Grecian lawgivers, Lycurgus, Solon, Zaleucus, Charondas, and thence to all the Roman edicts 40 and tables with their Justinian and so down to the Saxon and common laws of England, and the statutes.

Sundays also and every evening may be now understandingly spent in the highest matters of theology, and church history, ancient and modern; and ere this time the Hebrew tongue at a set hour might have been gained, that the scriptures may be now read in their own original; whereto it would be no impos- 50 sibility to add the Chaldee and the Syrian dialect. When all these employments are well conquered, then will the choice histories, heroic poems, and Attic tragedies of stateliest and most regal argument, with all the famous political orations, offer themselves; which if they were not only read, but some of them got by memory, and solemnly pronounced with right accent and grace, as might be taught, would endue them even with the spirit and vigor of Demosthenes or Cicero, Euripedes or Sophocles.

And now, lastly, will be the time to read with them those organic arts, which enable men to discourse and write perspicuously, elegantly, and according to the fittest style, of lofty, mean, or lowly. Logic, therefore, so much as is useful, is to be referred to this due place with all her well-couched heads and topics, until it be time to open her contracted palm into a graceful and ornate rhetoric, taught out of the rule of Plato, Aristotle, Phalereus, Cicero, Hermogenes, Longinus. To which poetry would be made subsequent, or indeed rather precedent, as being less subtile and fine, but more simple, sensuous, and passionate. I mean not here the prosody of a verse, which they could not but have hit on before among the rudiments of grammar; but that sublime art which in Aristotle's poetics, in Horace, and the Italian commentaries of Castelvetro, Tasso, Mazzoni, and others, teaches what the laws are of a true epic poem, what of a dramatic, what of a lyric, what decorum is, which is the grand masterpiece to observe. This would make them soon perceive what despicable creatures our common rhymers and play-writers be; and show them what religious, what glorious and magnificent use might be made of poetry, both in divine and human things.

From hence, and not till now, will be the right season of forming them to be able writers and composers in every excellent matter, when they shall be thus fraught with an universal insight into things. Or whether they be to speak in parliament or council, honor and attention would be waiting on their lips. There would then also appear in pulpits other visages, other gestures, and stuff otherwise wrought than what we now sit under, ofttimes to as great a trial of our patience as any other that they preach to us. These are the studies wherein our noble and our gentle youth ought to bestow their time, in a disciplinary way, from twelve to one and twenty: unless they rely more upon their ancestors dead, than upon themselves living. In which methodical course it is so supposed they must proceed by the steady pace of learning onward, as at convenient times, for memory's sake, to retire back into the middle ward, and sometimes into the rear of what they have been taught, until they have confirmed and solidly united the whole body of their perfected knowledge, like the last embattling of a Roman legion. Now will be worth the seeing, what exercises and recreations may best agree, and become these studies.

The course of study hitherto briefly described is, what I can guess by reading, likest to those ancient and famous schools of Pythagoras, Plato, Isocrates, Aristotle, and such others, out of which were bred up such a number of renowned philosophers, orators, historians, poets, and princes all over Greece, Italy, and Asia, besides the flourishing studies of Cyrene and Alexandria. But herein it shall exceed them, and supply a defect as great as that which Plato noted in the commonwealth of Sparta; whereas that city trained up their youth most for war, and these in their academies and Lycæum all for the gown, this institution of breeding which I here delineate shall be equally good both for peace and war. Therefore about an hour and a half ere they eat at noon should be allowed them for exercise, and due rest afterwards; but the time for this may be enlarged at pleasure, according as their rising in the morning shall be early.

The exercise which I commend first, is the exact use of their weapon, to guard, and to strike safely with edge or point; this will keep them healthy, nimble, strong, and well in breath; is also the likeliest means to make grow large and tall, and to inspire them with a gallant and fearless courage, which being tempered with seasonable lectures and precepts to them of true fortitude and patience, will turn into a native and heroic valor, and make them hate the cowardice of doing wrong. They must be also practised in all the locks and gripes of wrestling, wherein Englishmen were wont to excel, as need may often be in fight to tug, or grapple, and to close. And this perhaps will be enough, wherein to prove and heat their single strength.

The interim of unsweating themselves regularly, and convenient rest before meat, may,

both with profit and delight, be taken up in recreating and composing their travailed spirits with the solemn and divine harmonies of music, heard or learned; either whilst the skilful organist plies his grave and fancied descant in lofty fugues, or the whole symphony with artful and unimaginable touches adorn and grace the well-studied chords of some choice composer; sometimes the lute or soft organ-stop waiting on elegant voices, either to religious, martial, or civil ditties; which, if wise men and prophets be not extremely out, have a great power over dispositions and manners, to smooth and make them gentle from rustic harshness and distempered passions. The like also would not be inexpedient after meat, to assist and cherish nature in her first concoction, and send their minds back to study in good tune and satisfaction. Where having followed it close under vigilant eyes, till about two hours before supper, they are, by a sudden alarum or watchword, to be called out to their military motions, under sky or covert, according to the season, as was the Roman wont; first on foot, then, as their age permits, on horseback, to all the art of cavalry; that having in sport, but with much exactness and daily muster, served out the rudiments of their soldiership, in all the skill of embattling, marching, encamping, fortifying, besieging, and battering, with all the helps of ancient and modern stratagems, tactics, and warlike maxims, they may as it were out of a long war come forth renowned and perfect commanders in the service of their country. They would not then, if they were trusted with fair and hopeful armies, suffer them, for want of just and wise discipline, to shed away from about them like sick feathers, though they be never so oft supplied; they would not suffer their empty and unrecruitable colonels of twenty men in a company, to quaff out or convey into secret hoards, the wages of a delusive list, and a miserable remnant; yet in the meanwhile to be overmastered with a score or two of drunkards, the only soldiery left about them, or else to comply with all rapines and violences. No, certainly, if they knew aught of that knowledge that belongs to good men or good governors, they would not suffer these things.

But to return to our own institute: besides these constant exercises at home, there is another opportunity of gaining experience to be won from pleasure itself abroad; in those vernal seasons of the year when the air is calm and pleasant, it were an injury and sullenness against nature, not to go out and see her riches, and partake in her rejoicing with heaven and earth. I should not therefore be a persuader to them of studying much then, after two or three years that they have well laid their grounds, but to ride out in companies, with prudent and staid guides, to all the quarters of the land: learning and observing all places of strength, all commodities of building and of soil, for towns and tillage, harbors and ports for trade. Sometimes taking sea as far as to our navy, to learn there also what they can in the practical knowledge of sailing and of sea-fight.

These ways would try all their peculiar gifts of nature; and if there were any secret excellence among them would fetch it out, and give it fair opportunities to advance itself by, which could not but mightily redound to the good of this nation, and bring into fashion again those old admired virtues and excellencies, with far more advantage now in this purity of Christian knowledge. Nor shall we then need the monsieurs of Paris to take our hopeful youth into their slight and prodigal custodies, and send them over, back again, transformed into mimics, apes, and kickshaws. But if they desire to see other countries at three or four and twenty years of age, not to learn principles, but to enlarge experience, and make wise observation, they will by that time be such as shall deserve the regard and honor of all men where they pass, and the society and friendship of those in all places who are best and most eminent. And, perhaps, then other nations will be glad to visit us for their breeding, or else to imitate us in their own country.

Now, lastly, for their diet there cannot be much to say, save only that it would be best in the same house; for much time else would be lost abroad, and many ill habits got; and that it should be plain, healthful, and moderate, I suppose is out of controversy. Thus, Mr. Hartlib, you have a general view in writing, as your desire was, of that which at several times I had discoursed with you concerning the best and noblest way of education; not beginning, as some have done, from the

cradle, which yet might be worth many considerations, if brevity had not been my scope; many other circumstances also I could have mentioned, but this, to such as have the worth in them to make trial, for light and direction may be enough. Only I believe that this is not a bow for every man to shoot in, that counts himself a teacher; but will require sinews almost equal to those which Homer gave Ulysses; yet I am withal persuaded that it may prove much more easy in the assay, than it now seems at distance, and much more illustrious; howbeit, not more difficult than I imagine, and that imagination presents me with nothing but very happy, and very possible according to best wishes; if God have so decreed, and this age have spirit and capacity enough to apprehend.

AREOPAGITICA:

A SPEECH FOR

THE LIBERTY OF UNLICENSED PRINTING.

TO THE PARLIAMENT OF ENGLAND.

———

Τουλεύθερον δ' ἐκεῖνο. Τίς θέλει πόλει
χρηστόν τι βούλευμ' ἐς μέσον φέρειν ἔχων;
καὶ ταῦθ' ὁ χρῄζων λαμπρός ἐσθ', ὁ μὴ θέλων
σιγᾷ. τί τούτων ἔστ' ἰσαίτερον πόλει;
— *Euripid. Hicetid.*

"This is true liberty, when free-born men,
Having to advise the public, may speak free,
Which he who can, and will, deserves high praise;
Who neither can, nor will, may hold his peace:
What can be juster in a state than this?"
— *Euripid. Hicetid.*

[The text is that of the first edition, 1644.]

THEY, who to states and governors of the commonwealth direct their speech, high court of parliament! or wanting such access in a private condition, write that which they foresee may advance the public good; I suppose them, as at the beginning of no mean endeavor, not a little altered and moved inwardly in their minds; some with doubt of what will be the success, others with fear of what will be the censure; some with hope, others with confidence of what they have to speak. And me perhaps each of these dispositions, as the subject was whereon I entered, may have at other times variously affected; and likely might in these foremost expressions now also disclose which of them swayed most, but that the very attempt of this address thus made, and the thought of whom it hath recourse to, hath got the power within me to a passion, far more welcome than incidental to a preface.

Which though I stay not to confess ere any ask, I shall be blameless, if it be no other than the joy and gratulation which it brings to all who wish and promote their country's liberty; whereof this whole discourse proposed will be a certain testimony, if not a trophy. For this is not the liberty which we can hope, that no grievance ever should arise in the commonwealth: that let no man in this world expect; but when complaints are freely heard, deeply considered, and speedily reformed, then is the utmost bound of civil liberty attained that wise men look for. To which if I now manifest, by the very sound of this which I shall utter, that we are already in good part arrived, and yet from such a steep disadvantage of tyranny and superstition grounded into our principles, as was beyond the manhood of a Roman recovery, it will be attributed first, as is most due, to the strong assistance of God, our deliverer; next, to your faithful guidance and undaunted wisdom, lords and commons of England! Neither is it in God's esteem, the diminution of his glory, when honorable things are spoken of good men, and worthy magistrates; which if I now first should begin to do, after so fair a progress of your laudable deeds, and such a long obligement upon the whole realm to your indefatigable virtues, I might be justly reckoned among the tardiest and the unwillingest of them that praise ye.

Nevertheless there being three principal things, without which all praising is but courtship and flattery: first, when that only is praised which is solidly worth praise; next, when greatest likelihoods are brought, that such things are truly and really in those persons to whom they are ascribed; the other, when he who praises, by showing that such his actual persuasion is of whom he writes, can demonstrate that he flatters not; the former two of these I have heretofore endeavored, rescuing the employment from him who went about to impair your merits with a

trivial and malignant encomium; the latter as belonging chiefly to mine own acquital, that whom I so extolled I did not flatter, hath been reserved opportunely to this occasion. For he who freely magnifies what hath been nobly done, and fears not to declare as freely what might be done better, gives ye the best covenant of his fidelity; and that his loyalest affection and his hope waits on your proceedings. His highest praising is not flattery, and his plainest advice is a kind of praising; for though I should affirm and hold by argument, that it would fare better with truth, with learning, and the commonwealth, if one of your published orders, which I should name, were called in; yet at the same time it could not but much redound to the lustre of your mild and equal government, whenas private persons are hereby animated to think ye better pleased with public advice than other statists have been delighted heretofore with public flattery. And men will then see what difference there is between the magnanimity of a triennial parliament, and that jealous haughtiness of prelates and cabin counsellors that usurped of late, whenas they shall observe ye in the midst of your victories and successes more gently brooking written exceptions against a voted order, than other courts, which had produced nothing worth memory but the weak ostentation of wealth, would have endured the least signified dislike at any sudden proclamation.

If I should thus far presume upon the meek demeanor of your civil and gentle greatness, lords and commons! as what your published order hath directly said, that to gainsay, I might defend myself with ease, if any should accuse me of being new or insolent, did they but know how much better I find ye esteem it to imitate the old and elegant humanity of Greece, than the barbaric pride of a Hunnish and Norwegian stateliness. And out of those ages, to whose polite wisdom and letters we owe that we are not yet Goths and Jutlanders, I could name him who from his private house wrote that discourse to the parliament of Athens, that persuades them to change the form of democracy which was then established. Such honor was done in those days to men who professed the study of wisdom and eloquence, not only in their own country, but in other lands, that cities and signiories heard them gladly, and with great respect, if they had aught in public to admonish the state. Thus did Dion Prusæus, a stranger and a private orator, counsel the Rhodians against a former edict; and I abound with other like examples, which to set here would be superfluous. But if from the industry of a life wholly dedicated to studious labors, and those natural endowments haply not the worst for two and fifty degrees of northern latitude, so much must be derogated, as to count me not equal to any of those who had this privilege, I would obtain to be thought not so inferior, as yourselves are superior to the most of them who received their counsel; and how far you excel them, be assured, lords and commons! there can no greater testimony appear, than when your prudent spirit acknowledges and obeys the voice of reason, from what quarter soever it be heard speaking; and renders ye as willing to repeal any act of your own setting forth, as any set forth by your predecessors.

If ye be thus resolved, as it were injury to think ye were not, I know not what should withhold me from presenting ye with a fit instance wherein to show both that love of truth which ye eminently profess, and that uprightness of your judgment which is not wont to be partial to yourselves; by judging over again that order which ye have ordained "to regulate printing: that no book, pamphlet, or paper shall be henceforth printed, unless the same be first approved and licensed by such, or at least one of such, as shall be thereto appointed." For that part which preserves justly every man's copy to himself, or provides for the poor, I touch not; only wish they be not made pretences to abuse and persecute honest and painful men, who offend not in either of these particulars. But that other cause of licensing books, which we thought had died with his brother quadragesimal and matrimonial when the prelates expired, I shall now attend with such a homily, as shall lay before ye, first, the inventors of it to be those whom ye will be loath to own; next, what is to be thought in general of reading, whatever sort the books be; and that this order avails nothing to the suppressing of scandalous, seditious, and libellous books, which were mainly intended to be suppressed. Last, that it will be primely to the discourage-

ment of all learning, and the stop of truth, not only by disexercising and blunting our abilities, in what we know already, but by hindering and cropping the discovery that might be yet further made, both in religious and civil wisdom.

I deny not, but that it is of greatest concernment in the church and commonwealth, to have a vigilant eye how books demean themselves, as well as men; and thereafter to confine, imprison, and do sharpest justice on them as malefactors; for books are not absolutely dead things, but do contain a potency of life in them to be as active as that soul was whose progeny they are; nay, they do preserve as in a vial the purest efficacy and extraction of that living intellect that bred them. I know they are as lively, and as vigorously productive, as those fabulous dragon's teeth: and being sown up and down, may chance to spring up armed men. And yet, on the other hand, unless wariness be used, as good almost kill a man as kill a good book: who kills a man kills a reasonable creature, God's image; but he who destroys a good book, kills reason itself, kills the image of God, as it were, in the eye. Many a man lives a burden to the earth; but a good book is the precious life-blood of a master-spirit, embalmed and treasured up on purpose to a life beyond life. 'Tis true, no age can restore a life, whereof, perhaps, there is no great loss; and revolutions of ages do not oft recover the loss of a rejected truth, for the want of which whole nations fare the worse. We should be wary, therefore, what persecution we raise against the living labors of public men, how we spill that seasoned life of man, preserved and stored up in books; since we see a kind of homicide may be thus committed, sometimes a martyrdom; and if it extend to the whole impression, a kind of massacre, whereof the execution ends not in the slaying of an elemental life, but strikes at that ethereal and fifth essence, the breath of reason itself; slays an immortality rather than a life. But lest I should be condemned of introducing licence, while I oppose licensing, I refuse not the pains to be so much historical, as will serve to show what hath been done by ancient and famous commonwealths, against this disorder, till the very time that this project of licensing crept out of the inquisition, was catched up by our prelates, and hath caught some of our presbyters.

In Athens, where books and wits were ever busier than in any other part of Greece, I find but only two sorts of writings which the magistrate cared to take notice of; those either blasphemous and atheistical, or libellous. Thus the books of Protagoras were by the judges of Areopagus, commanded to be burnt, and himself banished the territory for a discourse, begun with his confessing not to know "whether there were gods, or whether not." And against defaming, it was decreed that none should be traduced by name, as was the manner of Vetus Comœdia, whereby we may guess how they censured libelling; and this course was quick enough, as Cicero writes, to quell both the desperate wits of other atheists, and the open way of defaming, as the event showed. Of other sects and opinions, though tending to voluptuousness, and the denying of divine Providence, they took no heed. Therefore we do not read that either Epicurus, or that libertine school of Cyrene, or what the Cynic impudence uttered, was ever questioned by the laws. Neither is it recorded that the writings of those old comedians were suppressed, though the acting of them were forbid; and that Plato commended the reading of Aristophanes, the loosest of them all, to his royal scholar, Dionysius, is commonly known, and may be excused, if holy Chrysostom, as is reported, nightly studied so much the same author, and had the art to cleanse a scurrilous vehemence into the style of a rousing sermon.

That other leading city of Greece, Lacedæmon, considering that Lycurgus their lawgiver was so addicted to elegant learning, as to have been the first that brought out of Ionia the scattered works of Homer, and sent the poet Thales from Crete, to prepare and mollify the Spartan surliness with his smooth songs and odes, the better to plant among them law and civility; it is to be wondered how museless and unbookish they were, minding nought but the feats of war. There needed no licensing of books among them, for they disliked all but their own laconic apophthegms, and took a slight occasion to chase Archilochus out of their city, perhaps for composing in a higher strain than their own soldiery ballads and roundels could reach to; or if it were for

his broad verses, they were not therein so cautious, but they were as dissolute in their promiscuous conversing; whence Euripedes affirms, in Andromache, that their women were all unchaste.

Thus much may give us light after what sort of books were prohibited among the Greeks. The Romans also for many ages trained up only to a military roughness, resembling most the Lacedæmonian guise, knew of learning little but what their twelve tables and the pontific college with their augurs and flamens taught them in religion and law; so unacquainted with other learning, that when Carneades and Critolaus, with the stoic Diogenes, coming ambassadors to Rome, took thereby occasion to give the city a taste of their philosophy, they were suspected for seducers by no less a man than Cato the Censor, who moved it in the senate to dismiss them speedily, and to banish all such Attic babblers out of Italy. But Scipio and others of the noblest senators withstood him and his old Sabine austerity; honored and admired the men; and the censor himself at last, in his old age, fell to the study of that whereof before he was so scrupulous. And yet, at the same time, Nævius and Plautus, the first Latin comedians, had filled the city with all the borrowed scenes of Menander and Philemon. Then, began to be considered there also what was to be done to libellous books and authors; for Nævius was quickly cast into prison for his unbridled pen, and released by the tribunes upon his recantation: we read also that libels were burnt, and the makers punished, by Augustus.

The like severity, no doubt, was used, if aught were impiously written against their esteemed gods. Except in these two points, how the world went in books, the magistrate kept no reckoning. And therefore Lucretius, without impeachment, versifies his Epicurism to Memmius, and had the honor to be set forth the second time by Cicero, so great a father of the commonwealth; although himself disputes against that opinion in his own writings. Nor was the satirical sharpness or naked plainness of Lucilius, or Catullus, or Flaccus, by any order prohibited. And for matters of state, the story of Titus Livius, though it extolled that part which Pompey held, was not therefore suppressed by Octavius Cæsar, of the other faction. But that Naso was by him banished in his old age, for the wanton poems of his youth, was but a mere covert of state over some secret cause; and besides, the books were neither banished nor called in. From hence we shall meet with little else but tyranny in the Roman empire, that we may not marvel, if not so often bad as good books were silenced. I shall therefore deem to have been large enough, in producing what among the ancients was punishable to write, save only which, all other arguments were free to treat on.

By this time the emperors were become Christians, whose discipline in this point I do not find to have been more severe than what was formerly in practice. The books of those whom they took to be grand heretics were examined, refuted, and condemned in the general councils; and not till then were prohibited, or burnt, by authority of the emperor. As for the writings of heathen authors, unless they were plain invectives against Christianity, as those of Porphyrius and Proclus, they met with no interdict that can be cited, till about the year 400, in a Carthaginian council, wherein bishops themselves were forbid to read the books of Gentiles, but heresies they might read; while others long before them, on the contrary, scrupled more the books of heretics, than of Gentiles. And that the primitive councils and bishops were wont only to declare what books were not commendable, passing no further, but leaving it to each one's conscience to read or to lay by, till after the year 800, is observed already by Padre Paolo, the great unmasker of the Trentine council. After which time the popes of Rome, engrossing what they pleased of political rule into their own hands, extended their dominion over men's eyes, as they had before over their judgments, burning and prohibiting to be read what they fancied not; yet sparing in their censures, and the books not many which they so dealt with; till Martin the Fifth, by his bull, not only prohibited, but was the first that excommunicated the reading of heretical books; for about that time Wickliff and Husse growing terrible, were they who first drove the papal court to a stricter policy of prohibiting. Which course Leo the Tenth and his successors followed, until the council of Trent and the Spanish inquisition, engendering together, brought forth or perfected those catalogues and expurging indexes, that rake through the entrails of many an old good author, with a violation worse than any could be offered to his tomb.

Nor did they stay in matters heretical, but any subject that was not to their palate, they either condemned in a prohibition, or had it straight into the new purgatory of an index. To fill up the measure of encroachment, their last invention was to ordain that no book, pamphlet, or paper should be printed (as if St. Peter had bequeathed them the keys of the press also out of Paradise) unless it were approved and licensed under the hands of two or three glutton friars. For example:—

"Let the chancellor Cini be pleased to see if in this present work be contained aught that may withstand the printing.
    "Vincent Rabbata, Vicar of Florence."
"I have seen this present work, and find nothing athwart the catholic faith and good manners: in witness whereof I have given, &c.
    "Nicolo Cini, Chancellor of Florence."
"Attending the precedent relation, it is allowed that this present work of Davanzati may be printed.   "Vincent Rabbata," &c.
"It may be printed, July 15.
    "Friar Simon Mompei d'Amelia, Chancellor of the Holy Office in Florence."

Sure they have a conceit, if he of the bottomless pit had not long since broke prison, that this quadruple exorcism would bar him down. I fear their next design will be to get into their custody the licensing of that which they say Claudius intended, * but went not through with. Vouchsafe to see another of their forms, the Roman stamp:—

"Imprimatur, if it seems good to the reverend master of the Holy Palace,
    "Belcastro, Vicegerent."
"Imprimatur,
    "Friar Nicholo Rodolphi, Master of the Holy Palace."

Sometimes five imprimaturs are seen together, dialogue wise, in the piazza of one titlepage, complimenting and ducking each to other with their shaven reverences, whether the author, who stands by in perplexity at the

---

* "Quo veniam daret flatum crepitumque ventris in convivio emittendi."—(*Sueton. in Claudio.*)

foot of his epistle, shall to the press or to the spunge. These are the pretty responsories, these are the dear antiphonies, that so bewitched of late our prelates and their chaplains, with the goodly echo they made; and besotted us to the gay imitation of a lordly imprimatur, one from Lambeth-house, another from the west end of Paul's; so apishly romanizing, that the word of command still was set down in Latin; as if the learned grammatical pen that wrote it would cast no ink without Latin; or perhaps, as they thought, because no vulgar tongue was worthy to express the pure conceit of an imprimatur; but rather, as I hope, for that our English, the language of men ever famous and foremost in the achievements of liberty, will not easily find servile letters enow to spell such a dictatory presumption English.

And thus ye have the inventors and the original of book licensing ripped up and drawn as lineally as any pedigree. We have it not, that can be heard of, from any ancient state, or polity, or church, nor by any statute left us by our ancestors elder or later; nor from the modern custom of any reformed city or church abroad; but from the most antichristian council, and the most tyrannous inquisition that ever inquired. Till then books were ever as freely admitted into the world as any other birth; the issue of the brain was no more stifled than the issue of the womb: no envious Juno sat cross-legged over the nativity of any man's intellectual offspring; but if it proved a monster, who denies but that it was justly burnt, or sunk into the sea? But that a book, in worse condition than a peccant soul, should be to stand before a jury ere it be born to the world, and undergo yet in darkness the judgment of Radamanth and his colleagues, ere it can pass the ferry backward into light, was never heard before, till that mysterious iniquity, provoked and troubled at the first entrance of reformation, sought out new limbos and new hells wherein they might include our books also within the number of their damned. And this was the rare morsel so officiously snatched up, and so illfavoredly imitated by our inquisiturient bishops, and the attendant minorites, their chaplains. That ye like not now these most certain authors of this licensing order, and that all sinister intention was far distant from your thoughts, when ye were importuned the passing it, all men who knew the integrity of your actions, and how ye honor truth, will clear ye readily.

But some will say, what though the inventors were bad, the thing for all that may be good. It may so; yet if that thing be no such deep invention, but obvious and easy for any man to light on, and yet best and wisest commonwealths through all ages and occasions have forborne to use it, and falsest seducers and oppressors of men were the first who took it up, and to no other purpose but to obstruct and hinder the first approach of reformation; I am of those who believe, it will be a harder alchymy than Lullius ever knew, to sublimate any good use out of such an invention. Yet this only is what I request to gain from this reason, that it may be held a dangerous and suspicious fruit, as certainly it deserves, for the tree that bore it, until I can dissect one by one the properties it has. But I have first to finish, as was propounded, what is to be thought in general of reading books, whatever sort they be, and whether be more the benefit or the harm that thence proceeds.

Not to insist upon the examples of Moses, Daniel, and Paul, who were skilful in all the learning of the Egyptians, Chaldeans, and Greeks, which could not probably be without reading their books of all sorts, in Paul especially, who thought it no defilement to insert into holy scripture the sentences of three Greek poets, and one of them a tragedian; the question was notwithstanding sometimes controverted among the primitive doctors, but with great odds on that side which affirmed it both lawful and profitable, as was then evidently perceived, when Julian the Apostate, and subtlest enemy to our faith, made a decree forbidding Christians the study of heathen learning; for, said he, they wound us with our own weapons, and with our own arts and sciences they overcome us. And indeed the Christians were put so to their shifts by this crafty means, and so much in danger to decline into all ignorance, that the two Apollinarii were fain, as a man may say, to coin all the seven liberal sciences out of the Bible, reducing it into divers forms of orations, poems, dialogues, even to the calculating of a new Christian grammar.

But, saith the historian, Socrates, the providence of God provided better than the industry of Appollinarius and his son, by taking away that illiterate law with the life of him who devised it. So great an injury they then held it to be deprived of Hellenic learning; and thought it a persecution more undermining, and secretly decaying the church, than the open cruelty of Decius or Diocletian. And perhaps it was the same politic drift that the devil whipped St. Jerome in a lenten dream, for reading Cicero; or else it was a phantasm, bred by the fever which had then seized him. For had an angel been his discipliner, unless it were for dwelling too much upon Ciceronianisms, and had chastised the reading, not the vanity, it had been plainly partial, first, to correct him for grave Cicero, and not for scurril Plautus, whom he confesses to have been reading not long before; next to correct him only, and let so many more ancient fathers wax old in those pleasant and florid studies, without the lash of such a tutoring apparition; insomuch that Basil teaches how some good use may be made of Margites, a sportful poem, not now extant, writ by Homer; and why not then of Morgante, an Italian romance much to the same purpose?

But if it be agreed we shall be tried by visions, there is a vision recorded by Eusebius, far ancienter than this tale of Jerome, to the nun Eustochium, and besides, has nothing of a fever in it. Dionysius Alexandrinus was, about the year 240, a person of great name in the church, for piety and learning, who had wont to avail himself much against heretics, by being conversant in their books; until a certain presbyter laid it scrupulously to his conscience, how he durst venture himself among those defiling volumes. The worthy man, loath to give offence, fell into a new debate with himself, what was to be thought; when suddenly a vision sent from God (it is his own epistle that so avers it) confirmed him in these words: "Read any books whatever come to thy hands, for thou art sufficient both to judge aright, and to examine each matter." To this revelation he assented the sooner, as he confesses, because it was answerable to that of the apostle to the Thessalonians: "Prove all things, hold fast that which is good."

And he might have added another remarkable saying of the same author: "To the pure, all things are pure;" not only meats and drinks, but all kind of knowledge, whether of good or evil: the knowledge cannot defile, nor consequently the books, if the will and conscience be not defiled. For books are as meats and viands are; some of good, some of evil substance; and yet God in that unapocryphal vision said without exception, "Rise, Peter, kill and eat;" leaving the choice to each man's discretion. Wholesome meats to a vitiated stomach differ little or nothing from unwholesome; and best books to a naughty mind are not unapplicable to occasions of evil. Bad meats will scarce breed good nourishment in the healthiest concoction; but herein the difference is of bad books, that they to a discreet and judicious reader serve in many respects to discover, to confute, to forewarn, and to illustrate. Whereof what better witness can ye expect I should produce, than one of your own now sitting in parliament, the chief of learned men reputed in this land, Mr. Selden; whose volume of natural and national laws proves, not only by great authorities brought together, but by exquisite reasons and theorems almost mathematically demonstrative, that all opinions, yea, errors, known, read, and collated, are of main service and assistance toward the speedy attainment of what is truest.

I conceive, therefore, that when God did enlarge the universal diet of man's body, (saving ever the rules of temperance,) he then also, as before, left arbitrary the dieting and repasting of our minds; as wherein every mature man might have to exercise his own leading capacity. How great a virtue is temperance, how much of moment through the whole life of man! Yet God commits the managing so great a trust, without particular law or prescription, wholly to the demeanor of every grown man. And therefore when he himself tabled the Jews from heaven, that omer, which was every man's daily portion of manna, is computed to have been more than might have well sufficed the heartiest feeder thrice as many meals. For those actions which enter into a man, rather than issue out of him, and therefore defile not, God uses not to captivate under a perpetual childhood of prescription, but trusts him with the gift of reason to be his own chooser; there were but little work left for preaching, if law and compulsion should grow so fast upon those things which heretofore were governed only by exhortation. Solomon informs us, that much reading is a weariness to the flesh; but neither he, nor other inspired author, tells us that such or such reading is unlawful; yet certainly had God thought good to limit us herein, it had been much more expedient to have told us what was unlawful, than what was wearisome.

As for the burning of those Ephesian books by St. Paul's converts; it is replied, the books were magic, the Syriac so renders them. It was a private act, a voluntary act, and leaves us to a voluntary imitation: the men in remorse burnt those books which were their own; the magistrate by this example is not appointed; these men practised the books, another might perhaps have read them in some sort usefully. Good and evil we know in the field of this world grow up together almost inseparably; and the knowledge of good is so involved and interwoven with the knowledge of evil, and in so many cunning resemblances hardly to be discerned, that those confused seeds which were imposed upon Psyche as an incessant labor to cull out, and sort asunder, were not more intermixed. It was from out the rind of one apple tasted, that the knowledge of good and evil, as two twins cleaving together, leaped forth into the world. And perhaps this is that doom which Adam fell into of knowing good and evil; that is to say, of knowing good by evil.

As therefore the state of man now is; what wisdom can there be to choose, what continence to forbear, without the knowledge of evil? He that can apprehend and consider vice with all her baits and seeming pleasures, and yet abstain, and yet distinguish, and yet prefer that which is truly better, he is the true warfaring Christian. I cannot praise a fugitive and cloistered virtue unexercised and unbreathed, that never sallies out and sees her adversary, but slinks out of the race, where that immortal garland is to be run for, not without dust and heat. Assuredly we bring not innocence into the world, we bring impurity much rather; that which purifies us is trial, and trial is by what is contrary. That virtue therefore which is but a youngling in the contemplation of evil, and knows not the utmost that vice promises to her followers, and rejects it, is but a blank virtue, not a pure; her whiteness is but an excremental whiteness; which was the reason why our sage and serious poet Spenser, (whom I dare be known to think a better teacher than Scotus or Aquinas,) describing true temperance under the person of Guion, brings him in with his palmer through the cave of Mammon, and the bower of earthly bliss, that he might see and know, and yet abstain.

Since therefore the knowledge and survey of vice is in this world so necessary to the constituting of human virtue, and the scanning of error to the confirmation of truth, how can we more safely, and with less danger, scout into the regions of sin and falsity, than by reading all manner of tractates, and hearing all manner of reason? And this is the benefit which may be had of books promiscuously read. But of the harm that may result hence, three kinds are usually reckoned. First, is feared the infection that may spread; but then, all human learning and controversy in religious points must remove out of the world, yea, the Bible itself; for that ofttimes relates blasphemy not nicely, it describes the carnal sense of wicked men not unelegantly, it brings in the holiest men passionately murmuring against Providence through all the arguments of Epicurus: in other great disputes it answers dubiously and darkly to the common reader; and ask a Talmudist what ails the modesty of his marginal Keri, that Moses and all the prophets cannot persuade him to pronounce the textual Chetiv. For these causes we all know the Bible itself put by the papist into the first rank of prohibited books. The ancientest fathers must be next removed, as Clement of Alexandria, and that Eusebian book of evangelic preparation, transmitting our ears through a hoard of heathenish obscenities to receive the gospel. Who finds not that Irenæus, Epiphanius, Jerome, and others discover more heresies than they well confute, and that oft for heresy which is the truer opinion?

Nor boots it to say for these, and all the heathen writers of greatest infection, if it must be thought so, with whom is bound up the life of human learning, that they writ in an unknown tongue, so long as we are sure those languages are known as well to the worst of men, who are both most able and most diligent to instil the poison they suck, first into the courts of princes, acquainting them with the choicest delights, and criticisms of sin. As perhaps did that Petronius, whom Nero called his arbiter, the master of his revels; and that notorious ribald of Arezzo, dreaded and yet dear to the Italian courtiers. I name not him, for posterity's sake, whom Henry the Eighth named in merriment his vicar of hell. By which compendius way all the contagion that foreign books can infuse will find a passage to the people far easier and shorter than an Indian voyage, though it could be sailed either by the north of Cataio eastward, or of Canada westward, while our Spanish licensing gags the English press never so severely.

But, on the other side, that infection which is from books of controversy in religion, is more doubtful and dangerous to the learned than to the ignorant; and yet those books must be permitted untouched by the licenser. It will be hard to instance where any ignorant man hath been ever seduced by papistical book in English, unless it were commended and expounded to him by some of that clergy; and indeed all such tractates, whether false or true, are as the prophecy of Isaiah was to the eunuch, not to be "understood without a guide." But of our priests and doctors how many have been corrupted by studying the comments of Jesuits and Sorbonists, and how fast they could transfuse that corruption into the people, our experience is both late and sad. It is not forgot, since the acute and distinct Arminius was perverted merely by the perusing of a nameless discourse written at Delft, which at first he took in hand to confute.

Seeing therefore that those books, and those in great abundance, which are likeliest to taint both life and doctrine, cannot be suppressed without the fall of learning, and of all ability in disputation, and that these books of either sort are most and soonest catching to the learned, (from whom to the common people whatever is heretical or dissolute may quickly be conveyed,) and that evil manners are as perfectly learnt without books a thousand other ways which cannot be stopped, and evil doctrine not with books can propagate, except a teacher guide, which he might also do without writing, and so beyond prohibiting;

I am not unable to unfold, how this cautelous enterprise of licensing can be exempted from the number of vain and impossible attempts. And he who were pleasantly disposed, could not well avoid to liken it to the exploit of that gallant man, who thought to pound up the crows by shutting his park gate.

Besides another inconvenience, if learned men be the first receivers out of books, and dispreaders both of vice and error, how shall the licensers themselves be confided in, unless we can confer upon them, or they assume to themselves, above all others in the land, the grace of infallibility, and uncorruptedness? And again, if it be true, that a wise man, like a good refiner, can gather gold out of the drossiest volume, and that a fool will be a fool with the best book, yea, or without book; there is no reason that we should deprive a wise man of any advantage to his wisdom, while we seek to restrain from a fool that which being restrained will be no hindrance to his folly. For if there should be so much exactness always used to keep that from him which is unfit for his reading, we should in the judgment of Aristotle not only, but of Solomon, and of our Saviour, not vouchsafe him good precepts, and by consequence not willingly admit him to good books; as being certain that a wise man will make better use of an idle pamphlet, than a fool will do of sacred scripture.

'Tis next alleged, we must not expose ourselves to temptations without necessity, and next to that, not employ our time in vain things. To both these objections one answer will serve, out of the grounds already laid, that to all men such books are not temptations, nor vanities; but useful drugs and materials wherewith to temper and compose effective and strong medicines, which man's life cannot want. The rest, as children and childish men, who have not the art to qualify and prepare these working minerals, well may be exhorted to forbear; but hindered forcibly they cannot be, by all the licensing that sainted inquisition could ever yet contrive; which is what I promised to deliver next: that this order of licensing conduces nothing to the end for which it was framed; and hath almost prevented me by being clear already while thus much hath been explaining. See the ingenuity of truth, who, when she gets a free and willing hand, opens herself faster than the pace of method and discourse can overtake her. It was the task which I began with, to show that no nation, or well instituted state, if they valued books at all, did ever use this way of licensing; and it might be answered, that this is a piece of prudence lately discovered.

To which I return, that as it was a thing slight and obvious to think on, so if it had been difficult to find out, there wanted not among them long since, who suggested such a course; which they not following, leave us a pattern of their judgment that it was not the not knowing, but the not approving, which was the cause of their not using it. Plato, a man of high authority indeed, but least of all for his Commonwealth, in the book of his laws, which no city ever yet received, fed his fancy with making many edicts to his airy burgomasters, which they who otherwise admire him, wish had been rather buried and excused in the genial cups of an academic night sitting. By which laws he seems to tolerate no kind of learning, but by unalterable decree, consisting most of practical traditions, to the attainment whereof a library of smaller bulk than his own dialogues would be abundant. And there also enacts, that no poet should so much as read to any private man what he had written, until the judges and law keepers had seen it, and allowed it; but that Plato meant this law peculiarly to that commonwealth which he had imagined, and to no other, is evident. Why was he not else a lawgiver to himself, but a transgressor, and to be expelled by his own magistrates, both for the wanton epigrams and dialogues which he made, and his perpetual reading of Sophron Mimus and Aristophanes, books of grossest infamy; and also for commending the latter of them, though he were the malicious libeller of his chief friends, to be read by the tyrant Dionysius, who had little need of such trash to spend his time on? But that he knew this licensing of poems had reference and dependence to many other provisoes there set down in his fancied republic, which in this world could have no place; and so neither he himself, nor any magistrate or city, ever imitated that course, which, taken apart from those other collateral injunctions, must needs be vain and fruitless.

For if they fell upon one kind of strictness, unless their care were equal to regulate all other things of like aptness to corrupt the mind, that single endeavor they knew would be but a fond labor; to shut and fortify one gate against corruption, and be necessitated to leave others round about wide open. If we think to regulate printing, thereby to rectify manners, we must regulate all recreations and pastimes, all that is delightful to man. No music must be heard, no song be set or sung, but what is grave and doric. There must be licensing dancers, that no gesture, motion, or deportment be taught our youth, but what by their allowance shall be thought honest; for such Plato was provided of. It will ask more than the work of twenty licensers to examine all the lutes, the violins, and the guitars in every house; they must not be suffered to prattle as they do, but must be licensed what they may say. And who shall silence all the airs and madrigals that whisper softness in chambers? The windows also, and the balconies, must be thought on; there are shrewd books, with dangerous frontispieces, set to sale: who shall prohibit them, shall twenty licensers? The villages also must have their visitors to inquire what lectures the bagpipe and the rebec reads, even to the balatry and the gamut of every municipal fiddler; for these are the countryman's Arcadias, and his Montemayors.

Next, what more national corruption, for which England hears ill abroad, than household gluttony? Who shall be the rectors of our daily rioting? And what shall be done to inhibit the multitudes that frequent those houses where drunkenness is sold and harbored? Our garments also should be referred to the licensing of some more sober workmasters, to see them cut into a less wanton garb. Who shall regulate all the mixed conversation of our youth, male and female together, as is the fashion of this country? Who shall still appoint what shall be discoursed, what presumed, and no further? Lastly, who shall forbid and separate all idle resort, all evil company? These things will be, and must be; but how they shall be least hurtful, how least enticing, herein consists the grave and governing wisdom of a state.

To sequester out of the world into Atlantic and Utopian polities, which never can be drawn into use, will not mend our condition; but to ordain wisely as in this world of evil, in the midst whereof God hath placed us unavoidably. Nor is it Plato's licensing of books will do this, which necessarily pulls along with it so many other kinds of licensing, as will make us all both ridiculous and weary, and yet frustrate; but those unwritten, or at least unconstraining laws of virtuous education, religious and civil nurture, which Plato there mentions, as the bonds and ligaments of the commonwealth, the pillars and the sustainers of every written statute; these they be, which will bear chief sway in such matters as these, when all licensing will be easily eluded. Impunity and remissness for certain are the bane of a commonwealth; but here the great art lies, to discern in what the law is to bid restraint and punishment, and in what things persuasion only is to work. If every action which is good or evil in man at ripe years were to be under pittance, and prescription, and compulsion, what were virtue but a name, what praise could be then due to well-doing, what gramercy to be sober, just, or continent?

Many there be that complain of divine Providence for suffering Adam to transgress. Foolish tongues! when God gave him reason, he gave him freedom to choose, for reason is but choosing; he had been else a mere artificial Adam, such an Adam as he is in the motions. We ourselves esteem not of that obedience, or love, or gift, which is of force; God therefore left him free, set before him a provoking object ever almost in his eyes; herein consisted his merit, herein the right of his reward, the praise of his abstinence. Wherefore did he create passions within us, pleasures round about us, but that these rightly tempered are the very ingredients of virtue? They are not skilful considerers of human things, who imagine to remove sin, by removing the matter of sin; for, besides that it is a huge heap increasing under the very act of diminishing, though some part of it may for a time be withdrawn from some persons, it cannot from all, in such a universal thing as books are; and when this is done, yet the sin remains entire. Though ye take from a covetous man all his treasures, he has yet one jewel left, ye cannot bereave him of his covetousness. Banish all objects of lust, shut up all youth into the severest discipline that

can be exercised in any hermitage, ye cannot make them chaste, that came not thither so: such great care and wisdom is required to the right managing of this point.

Suppose we could expell sin by this means; look how much we thus expell of sin, so much we expel of virtue: for the matter of them both is the same: remove that, and ye remove them both alike. This justifies the high providence of God, who, though he command us temperance, justice, continence, yet pours out before us even to a profuseness all desirable things, and gives us minds that can wander beyond all limit and satiety. Why should we then affect a rigor contrary to the manner of God and of nature, by abridging or scanting those means, which books freely permitted, are both to the trial of virtue, and the exercise of truth?

It would be better done, to learn that the law must needs be frivolous, which goes to restrain things, uncertainly and yet equally working to good and to evil. And were I the chooser, a dram of well-doing should be preferred before many times as much the forcible hindrance of evil-doing. For God sure esteems the growth and completing of one virtuous person, more than the restraint of ten vicious. And albeit, whatever thing we hear or see, sitting, walking, travelling, or conversing, may be fitly called our book, and is of the same effect that writings are; yet grant the thing to be prohibited were only books, it appears that this order hitherto is far insufficient to the end which it intends. Do we not see, not once or oftener, but weekly, that continued court-libel against the parliament and city, printed, as the wet sheets can witness, and dispersed among us for all that licensing can do? Yet this is the prime service a man would think wherein this order should give proof of itself. If it were executed, you will say. But certain, if execution be remiss or blindfold now, and in this particular, what will it be hereafter, and in other books?

If then the order shall not be vain and frustrate, behold a new labor, lords and commons, ye must repeal and proscribe all scandalous and unlicensed books already printed and divulged; after ye have drawn them up into a list, that all may know which are condemned, and which not; and ordain that no foreign books be delivered out of custody, till they have been read over. This office will require the whole time of not a few overseers, and those no vulgar men. There be also books which are partly useful and excellent, partly culpable and pernicious; this work will ask as many more officials, to make expurgations and expunctions, that the commonwealth of learning be not damnified. In fine, when the multitude of books increase upon their hands, ye must be fain to catalogue all those print- ers who are found frequently offending, and forbid the importation of their whole suspected typography. In a word, that this your order may be exact, and not deficient, ye must reform it perfectly, according to the model of Trent and Sevil, which I know ye abhor to do.

Yet though ye should condescend to this, which God forbid, the order still would be but fruitless and defective to that end whereto ye meant it. If to prevent sects and schisms, who is so unread or uncatechised in story, that hath not heard of many sects refusing books as a hindrance, and preserving their doctrine unmixed for many ages, only by unwritten traditions? The Christian faith (for that was once a schism!) is not unknown to have spread all over Asia, ere any gospel or epistle was seen in writing. If the amendment of manners be aimed at, look into Italy and Spain, whether those places be one scruple the better, the honester, the wiser, the chaster, since all the inquisitional rigor that hath been executed upon books.

Another reason, whereby to make it plain that this order will miss the end it seeks, consider by the quality which ought to be in every licenser. It cannot be denied, but that he who is made judge to sit upon the birth or death of books whether they may be wafted into this world or not, had need to be a man above the common measure, both studious, learned, and judicious; there may be else no mean mistakes in the censure of what is passable or not; which is also no mean injury. If he be of such worth as behooves him, there cannot be a more tedious and unpleasing journeywork, a greater loss of time levied upon his head, than to be made the perpetual reader of unchosen books and pamphlets, oft-times huge volumes. There is no book that is acceptable, unless at certain seasons; but to be enjoined the reading of that at all times,

and in a hand scarce legible, whereof three pages would not down at any time in the fairest print, is an imposition which I cannot believe how he that values time, and his own studies, or is but of a sensible nostril, should be able to endure. In this one thing I crave leave of the present licensers to be pardoned for so thinking: who doubtless took this office up, looking on it through their obedience to the parliament, whose command perhaps made all things seem easy and unlaborious to them; but that this short trial hath wearied them out already, their own expressions and excuses to them who make so many journeys to solicit their license, are testimony enough. Seeing therefore those, who now possess the employment, by all evident signs wish themselves well rid of it, and that no man of worth, none that is not a plain unthrift of his own hours, is ever likely to succeed them, except he mean to put himself to the salary of a press corrector, we may easily foresee what kind of licensers we are to expect hereafter, either ignorant, imperious, and remiss, or basely pecuniary. This is what I had to show, wherein this order cannot conduce to that end whereof it bears the intention.

I lastly proceed from the no good it can do, to the manifest hurt it causes, in being first the greatest discouragement and affront that can be offered to learning and to learned men. It was the complaint and lamentation of prelates, upon every least breath of a motion to remove pluralities, and distribute more equally church revenues, that then all learning would be for ever dashed and discouraged. But as for that opinion, I never found cause to think that the tenth part of learning stood or fell with the clergy: nor could I ever but hold it for a sordid and unworthy speech of any churchman, who had a competency left him. If therefore ye be loath to dishearten utterly and discontent, not the mercenary crew of false pretenders to learning, but the free and ingenuous sort of such as evidently were born to study and love learning for itself, not for lucre, or any other end, but the service of God and of truth, and perhaps that lasting fame and perpetuity of praise, which God and good men have consented shall be the reward of those whose published labors advance the good of mankind: then know, that so far to distrust the judgment and the honesty of one who hath but a common repute in learning, and never yet offended, as not to count him fit to print his mind without a tutor and examiner, lest he should drop a schism, or something of corruption, is the greatest displeasure and indignity to a free and knowing spirit that can be put upon him.

What advantage is it to be a man, over it is to be a boy at school, if we have only escaped the ferula, to come under the fescue of an imprimatur? if serious and elaborate writings, as if they were no more than the theme of a grammar-lad under his pedagogue, must not be uttered without the cursory eyes of a temporizing and extemporizing licenser? He who is not trusted with his own actions, his drift not being known to be evil, and standing to the hazard of law and penalty, has no great argument to think himself reputed in the commonwealth wherein he was born for other than a fool or a foreigner. When a man writes to the world, he summons up all his reason and deliberation to assist him; he searches, meditates, is industrious, and likely consults and confers with his judicious friends; after all which done, he takes himself to be informed in what he writes, as well as any that writ before him; if in this, the most consummate act of his fidelity and ripeness, no years, no industry, no former proof of his abilities, can bring him to that state of maturity, as not to be still mistrusted and suspected, unless he carry all his considerate diligence, all his midnight watchings, and expense of Palladian oil, to the hasty view of an unleisured licenser, perhaps much his younger, perhaps far his inferior in judgment, perhaps one who never knew the labor of bookwriting; and if he be not repulsed, or slighted, must appear in print like a puny with his guardian, and his censor's hand on the back of his title to be his bail and surety, that he is no idiot or seducer; it cannot be but a dishonor and derogation to the author, to the book, to the privilege and dignity of learning.

And what if the author shall be one so copious of fancy, as to have many things well worth the adding, come into his mind after licensing, while the book is yet under the press, which not seldom happens to the best and diligentest writers; and that perhaps a dozen times in one book. The printer dares not go beyond his licensed copy; so often then must the author trudge to his leave-giver, that those his new insertions may be viewed; and many a jaunt will be made, ere that licenser, for it must be the same man, can either be found, or found at leisure; meanwhile either the press must stand still, which is no small damage, or the author lose his accuratest thoughts, and send the book forth worse than he had made it, which to a diligent writer is the greatest melancholy and vexation that can befall.

And how can a man teach with authority, which is the life of teaching; how can he be a doctor in his book, as he ought to be, or else had better be silent, whenas all he teaches, all he delivers, is but under the tuition, under the correction of his patriarchial licenser, to blot or alter what precisely accords not with the hide-bound humor which he calls his judgment? When every acute reader, upon the first sight of a pedantic license, will be ready with these like words to ding the book a quoit's distance from him:—"I hate a pupil teacher; I endure not an instructor that comes to me under the wardship of an overseeing fist. I know nothing of the licenser, but that I have his own hand here for his arrogance; who shall warrant me his judgment?" "The state, sir," replies the stationer: but has a quick return:—"The state shall be my governors, but not my critics; they may be mistaken in the choice of a licenser, as easily as this licenser may be mistaken in an author. This is some common stuff:" and he might add from Sir Francis Bacon, that "such authorized books are but the language of the times." For though a licenser should happen to be judicious more than ordinary, which will be a great jeopardy of the next succession, yet his very office and his commission enjoins him to let pass nothing but what is vulgarly received already.

Nay, which is more lamentable, if the work of any deceased author, though never so famous in his lifetime, and even to this day, come to their hands for license to be printed, or reprinted, if there be found in his book one sentence of a venturous edge, uttered in the height of zeal, (and who knows whether it might not be the dictate of a divine spirit?) yet, not suiting with every low decrepit humor of their own, though it were Knox himself, the reformer of a kingdom, that spake it, they will not pardon him their dash; the sense of that great man shall to all posterity be lost, for the fearfulness, or the presumptuous rashness of a perfunctory licenser. And to what an author this violence hath been lately done, and in what book, of greatest consequence to be faithfully published, I could now instance, but shall forbear till a more convenient season. Yet if these things be not resented seriously and timely by them who have the remedy in their power, but that such ironmolds as these shall have authority to gnaw out the choicest periods of exquisitest books, and to commit such a treacherous fraud against the orphan remainders of worthiest men after death, the more sorrow will belong to that hapless race of men, whose misfortune it is to have understanding. Henceforth let no man care to learn, or care to be more than worldly wise; for certainly in higher matters to be ignorant and slothful, to be a common steadfast dunce, will be the only pleasant life, and only in request.

And as it is a particular disesteem of every knowing person alive, and most injurious to the written labors and monuments of the dead, so to me it seems an undervaluing and vilifying of the whole nation. I cannot set so light by all the invention, the art, the wit, the grave and solid judgment which is in England, as that it can be comprehended in any twenty capacities, how good soever; much less that it should not pass except their superintendence be over it, except it be sifted and strained with their strainers, that it should be uncurrent without their manual stamp. Truth and understanding are not such wares as to be monopolized and traded in by tickets, and statutes, and standards. We must not think to make a staple commodity of all the knowledge in the land, to mark and license it like our broad-cloth and our woolpacks. What is it but a servitude like that imposed by the Philistines, not to be allowed the sharpening of our own axes and coulters, but we must repair from all quarters to twenty licensing forges?

Had any one written and divulged erroneous things and scandalous to honest life, misusing and forfeiting the esteem had of his reason among men, if after conviction this only censure were adjudged him, that he should never henceforth write, but what were first examined by an appointed officer, whose hand should be annexed to pass his credit for him, that now he might be safely read; it could not be apprehended less than a disgraceful punishment. Whence to include the whole nation, and those that never yet thus offended, under such a diffident and suspectful prohibition, may plainly be understood what a disparagement it is. So much the more whenas debtors and delinquents may walk abroad without a keeper, but unoffensive books must not stir forth without a visible jailor in their title. Nor is it to the common people less than a reproach; for if we be so jealous over them, as that we dare not trust them with an English pamphlet, what do we but censure them for a giddy, vicious, and ungrounded people; in such a sick and weak estate of faith and discretion, as to be able to take nothing down but through the pipe of a licenser? That this is care or love of them, we cannot pretend, whenas in those popish places, where the laity are most hated and despised, the same strictness is used over them. Wisdom we cannot call it, because it stops but one breach of licence, nor that neither: whenas those corruptions, which it seeks to prevent, break in faster at other doors, which cannot be shut.

And in conclusion it reflects to the disrepute of our ministers also, of whose labors we should hope better, and of the proficiency which their flock reaps by them, than that after all this light of the gospel which is, and is to be, and all this continual preaching, they should be still frequented with such an unprincipled, unedified, and laic rabble, as that the whiff of every new pamphlet should stagger them out of their catechism and Christian walking. This may have much reason to discourage the ministers, when such a low conceit is had of all their exhortations, and the benefiting of their hearers, as that they are not thought fit to be turned loose to three sheets of paper without a licenser; that all the sermons, all the lectures preached, printed, vended in such numbers, and such volumes, as have now well-nigh made all other books unsaleable, should not be armor enough against one single Enchiridion, without the castle of St. Angelo of an imprimatur.

And lest some should persuade ye, lords and commons, that these arguments of learned men's discouragement at this your order are mere flourishes, and not real, I could recount what I have seen and heard in other countries, where this kind of inquisition tyrannizes; when I have sat among their learned men, (for that honor I had,) and been counted happy to be born in such a place of philosophic freedom, as they supposed England was, while themselves did nothing but bemoan the servile condition into which learning amongst them was brought; that this was it which had damped the glory of Italian wits; that nothing had been there written now these many years but flattery and fustian. There it was that I found and visited the famous Galileo, grown old, a prisoner to the inquisition, for thinking in astronomy otherwise then the Franciscan and Dominican licensers thought. And though I knew that England then was groaning loudest under the prelatical yoke, neverthlesss I took it as a pledge of future happiness, that other nations were so persuaded of her liberty.

Yet was it beyond my hope, that those worthies were then breathing in her air, who should be her leaders to such a deliverance, as shall never be forgotten by any revolution of time that this world hath to finish. When that was once begun, it was as little in my fear, that what words of complaint I heard among learned men of other parts uttered against the inquisition, the same I should hear, by as learned men at home, uttered in time of parliament against an order of licensing; and that so generally, that when I had disclosed myself a companion of their discontent, I might say, if without envy, that he whom an honest quæstorship had endeared to the Sicilians, was not more by them importuned against Verres, than the favorable opinion which I had among many who honor ye, and are known and respected by ye, loaded me with entreaties and persuasions, that I would not despair to lay together that which just reason should bring into my mind, towards the removal of an undeserved thraldom upon learning.

That this is not therefore the disburdening of a particular fancy, but the common grievance of all those who had prepared their minds and studies above the vulgar pitch, to advance truth in others, and from others to entertain it, thus much may satisfy. And in their name I shall for neither friend nor foe conceal what the general murmur is; that if it come to in-

quisitioning again, and licensing, and that we are so timorous of ourselves, and so suspicious of all men, as to fear each book, and the shaking of every leaf, before we know what the contents are; if some who but of late were little better than silenced from preaching, shall come now to silence us from reading, except what they please, it cannot be guessed what is intended by some but a second tyranny over learning: and will soon put it out of controversy, that bishops and presbyters are the same to us, both name and thing.

That those evils of prelaty which before from five or six and twenty sees were distributively charged upon the whole people will now light wholly upon learning, is not obscure to us: whenas now the pastor of a small unlearned parish, on the sudden shall be exalted archbishop over a large diocess of books, and yet not remove, but keep his other cure too, a mystical pluralist. He who but of late cried down the sole ordination of every novice bachelor of art, and denied sole jurisdiction over the simplest parishioner, shall now at home in his private chair, assume both these over worthiest and excellentest books, and ablest authors that write them. This is not the covenants and protestations that we have made! This is not to put down prelacy; this is but to chop an episcopacy; this is but to translate the palace metropolitan from one kind of dominion into another; this is but an old canonical sleight of commuting our penance. To startle thus betimes at a mere unlicensed pamphlet, will, after a while, be afraid of every conventicle, and a while after will make a conventicle of every Christian meeting.

But I am certain, that a state governed by the rules of justice and fortitude, or a church built and founded upon the rock of faith and true knowledge, cannot be so pusillanimous. While things are yet not constituted in religion, that freedom of writing should be restrained by a discipline imitated from the prelates, and learned by them from the inquisition to shut us up all again into the breast of a licenser, must needs give cause of doubt and discouragement to all learned and religious men; who cannot but discern the fineness of this politic drift, and who are the contrivers; that while bishops were to be baited down, then all presses might be open; it was the people's birthright and privilege in time of parliament, it was the breaking forth of light.

But now the bishops abrogated and voided out of the church, as if our reformation sought no more, but to make room for others into their seats under another name; the episcopal arts begin to bud again; the cruise of truth must run no more oil; liberty of printing must be enthralled again, under a prelatical commission of twenty; the privilege of the people nullified; and, which is worse, the freedom of learning must groan again, and to her old fetters: all this the parliament yet sitting. Although their own late arguments and defences against the prelates might remember them, that this obstructing violence meets for the most part with an event utterly opposite to the end which it drives at: instead of suppressing sects and schisms, it raises them and invests them with a reputation: "The punishing of wits enhances their authority," saith the Viscount St. Albans; "and a forbidden writing is thought to be a certain spark of truth, that flies up in the faces of them who seek to tread it out." This order, therefore, may prove a nursing mother to sects, but I shall easily show how it will be a stepdame to truth: and first, by disenabling us to the maintenance of what is known already.

Well knows he who uses to consider, that our faith and knowledge thrives by exercise, as well as our limbs and complexion. Truth is compared in scripture to a streaming fountain; if her waters flow not in a perpetual progression, they sicken into a muddy pool of conformity and tradition. A man may be a heretic in the truth; and if he believe things only because his pastor says so, or the assembly so determines, without knowing other reason, though his belief be true, yet the very truth he holds becomes his heresy. There is not any burden that some would gladlier post off to another, than the charge and care of their religion. There be, who knows not that there be? of protestants and professors, who live and die in as errant and implicit faith, as any lay papist of Loretto.

A wealthy man, addicted to his pleasure and to his profits, finds religion to be a traffic so entangled, and of so many piddling accounts, that of all mysteries he cannot skill to keep a stock going upon that trade. What should he do? Fain he would have the name to be religious, fain he would bear up with his neighbors in that. What does he therefore, but resolves to give over toiling, and to find himself out some factor, to whose care and credit he may commit the whole managing of his religious affairs; some divine of note and estimation that must be. To him he adheres, resigns the whole warehouse of his religion, with all the locks and keys, into his custody; and indeed makes the very person of that man his religion; esteems his associating with him a sufficient evidence and commendatory of his own piety. So that a man may say his religion is now no more within himself, but is become a dividual moveable, and goes and comes near him, according as that good man frequents the house. He entertains him, gives him gifts, feasts him, lodges him; his religion comes home at night, prays, is liberally supped, and sumptuously laid to sleep; rises, is saluted, and after the malmsey, or some well-spiced bruage, and better breakfasted, than He whose morning appetite would have gladly fed on green figs between Bethany and Jerusalem, his religion walks abroad at eight, and leaves his kind entertainer in the shop trading all day without his religion.

Another sort there be, who when they hear that all things shall be ordered, all things regulated and settled; nothing written but what passes through the custom-house of certain publicans that have the tonnaging and poundaging of all free-spoken truth, will straight give themselves up into your hands, make them and cut them out what religion ye please: there be delights, there be recreations and jolly pastimes, that will fetch the day about from sun to sun, and rock the tedious year as in a delightful dream. What need they torture their heads with that which others have taken so strictly, and so unalterably into their own purveying? These are the fruits which a dull ease and cessation of our knowledge will bring forth among the people. How goodly, and how to be wished were such an obedient unanimity as this! What a fine conformity would it starch us all into! Doubtless a staunch and solid piece of framework, as any January could freeze together.

Nor much better will be the consequence even among the clergy themselves: it is no new thing never heard of before, for a parochial minister, who has his reward and is at his Hercules' pillars in a warm benefice, to be easily inclinable, if he have nothing else that may rouse up his studies, to finish his circuit in an English Concordance and a topic folio, the gatherings and savings of a sober graduateship, a Harmony and a Catena, treading the constant round of certain common doctrinal heads, attended with their uses, motives, marks, and means; out of which, as out of an alphabet or sol-fa, by forming and transforming, joining and disjoining variously, a little bookcraft, and two hours' meditation, might furnish him unspeakably to the performance of more than a weekly charge of sermoning: not to reckon up the infinite helps of interlinearies, breviaries, synopses, and other loitering gear. But as for the multitude of sermons ready printed and piled up, on every text that is not difficult, our London trading St. Thomas in his vestry, and add to boot St. Martin and St. Hugh, have not within their hallowed limits more vendible ware of all sorts ready made: so that penury he never need fear of pulpit provision, having where so plenteously to refresh his magazine. But if his rear and flanks be not impaled, if his back door be not secured by the rigid licenser, but that a bold book may now and then issue forth, and give the assault to some of his old collections in their trenches, it will concern him then to keep waking, to stand in watch, to set good guards and sentinels about his received opinions, to walk the round and counter-round with his fellow-inspectors, fearing lest any of his flock be seduced who also then would be better instructed, better exercised, and disciplined. And God send that the fear of this diligence, which must then be used, do not make us affect the laziness of a licensing church.

For if we be sure we are in the right, and do not hold the truth guiltily, which becomes not, if we ourselves condemn not our own weak and frivolous teaching, and the people for an untaught and irreligious gadding rout; what can be more fair, than when a man judicious, learned, and of a conscience, for aught we know, as good as theirs that taught us what we know, shall not privily from house to house, which is more dangerous, but openly by writing, publish to the world what his opinion is, what his reasons, and wherefore that which is now thought cannot be sound?

Christ urged it as wherewith to justify himself, that he preached in public; yet writing is more public than preaching; and more easy to refutation if need be, there being so many whose business and profession merely it is to be the champions of truth; which if they neglect, what can be imputed but their sloth or inability?

Thus much we are hindered and disinured by this course of licensing towards the true knowledge of what we seem to know. For how much it hurts and hinders the licensers themselves in the calling of their ministry, more than any secular employment, if they will discharge that office as they ought, so that of necessity they must neglect either the one duty or the other, I insist not, because it is a particular, but leave it to their own conscience, how they will decide it there.

There is yet behind of what I purposed to lay open, the incredible loss and detriment that this plot of licensing puts us to, more than if some enemy at sea should stop up all our havens, and ports, and creeks; it hinders and retards the importation of our richest merchandise,—truth: nay, it was first established and put in practice by anti-christian malice and mystery, on set purpose to extinguish, if it were possible, the light of reformation, and to settle falsehood; little differing from that policy wherewith the Turk upholds his Alcoran, by the prohibition of printing. 'Tis not denied, but gladly confessed, we are to send our thanks and vows to heaven, louder than most of nations, for that great measure of truth which we enjoy, especially in those main points between us and the pope, with his appurtenances the prelates: but he who thinks we are to pitch our tent here, and have attained the utmost prospect of reformation that the mortal glass wherein we contemplate can show us, till we come to beatific vision, that man by this very opinion declares that he is yet far short of truth.

Truth indeed came once into the world with her divine master, and was a perfect shape most glorious to look on: but when he ascended, and his apostles after him were laid asleep, then straight arose a wicked race of deceivers, who, as that story goes of the Egyptian Typhon with his conspirators, how they dealt with the good Osiris, took the virgin Truth, hewed her lovely form into a thousand

pieces, and scattered them to the four winds. From that time ever since, the sad friends of Truth, such as durst appear, imitating the careful search that Isis made for the mangled body of Osiris, went up and down gathering up limb by limb still as they could find them. We have not yet found them all, lords and commons, nor ever shall do, till her Master's second coming; he shall bring together every joint and member, and shall mold them into an immortal feature of loveliness and perfection. Suffer not these licensing prohibitions to stand at every place of opportunity forbidding and disturbing them that continue seeking, that continue to do our obsequies to the torn body of our martyred saint.

We boast our light; but if we look not wisely on the sun itself, it smites us into darkness. Who can discern those planets that are oft combust, and those stars of brightest magnitude that rise and set with the sun, until the opposite motion of their orbs bring them to such a place in the firmament, where they may be seen evening or morning? The light which we have gained was given us, not to be ever staring on, but by it to discover onward things more remote from our knowledge. It is not the unfrocking of a priest, the unmitring of a bishop, and the removing him from off the presbyterian shoulders, that will make us a happy nation: no; if other things as great in the church, and in the rule of life both economical and political, be not looked into and reformed, we have looked so long upon the blaze that Zuinglius and Calvin have beaconed up to us, that we are stark blind.

There be who perpetually complain of schisms and sects, and make it such a calamity that any man dissents from their maxims. It is their own pride and ignorance which causes the disturbing, who neither will hear with meekness, nor can convince, yet all must be suppressed which is not found in their Syntagma. They are the troublers, they are the dividers of unity, who neglect and permit not others to unite those dissevered pieces, which are yet wanting to the body of truth. To be still searching what we know not, by what we know, still closing up truth to truth as we find it, (for all her body is homogeneal, and proportional,) this is the golden rule in theology as well as in arithmetic, and makes up the best harmony in a church; not the forced and outward union of cold, and neutral, and inwardly divided minds.

Lords and commons of England! consider what nation it is whereof ye are, and whereof ye are the governors: a nation not slow and dull, but of a quick, ingenious, and piercing spirit; acute to invent, subtile and sinewy to discourse, not beneath the reach of any point the highest that human capacity can soar to. Therefore the studies of learning in her deepest sciences have been so ancient, and so eminent among us, that writers of good antiquity and ablest judgment have been persuaded, that even the school of Pythagoras, and the Persian wisdom, took beginning from the old philosophy of this island. And that wise and civil Roman, Julius Agricola, who governed once here for Cæsar, preferred the natural wits of Britain before the labored studies of the French.

Nor is it for nothing that the grave and frugal Transylvanian sends out yearly from as far as the mountainous borders of Russia, and beyond the Hercynian wilderness, not their youth, but their staid men, to learn our language and our theological arts. Yet that which is above all this, the favor and the love of Heaven, we have great argument to think in a peculiar manner propitious and propending towards us. Why else was this nation chosen before any other, that out of her, as out of Sion, should be proclaimed and sounded forth the first tidings and trumpet of reformation to all Europe? And had it not been the obstinate perverseness of our prelates against the divine and admirable spirit of Wickliff, to suppress him as a schismatic and innovator, perhaps neither the Bohemian Husse and Jerome, no, nor the name of Luther or of Calvin, had been ever known: the glory of reforming all our neighbors had been completely ours. But now, as our obdurate clergy have with violence demeaned the matter, we are become hitherto the latest and the backwardest scholars, of whom God offered to have made us the teachers.

Now once again by all concurrence of signs, and by the general instinct of holy and devout men, as they daily and solemnly express their thoughts, God is decreeing to begin some new and great period in his church, even to the reforming of reformation itself; what does he then but reveal himself to his servants, and as his manner is, first to his Englishmen? I say, as his manner is, first to us, though we mark not the method of his counsels, and are unworthy. Behold now this vast city, a city of refuge, the mansion-house of liberty, encompassed and surrounded with his protection; the shop of war hath not there more anvils and hammers waking, to fashion out the plates and instruments of armed justice in defence of beleaguered truth, than there be pens and heads there, sitting by their studious lamps, musing, searching, revolving new notions and ideas wherewith to present, as with their homage and their fealty, the approaching reformation: others as fast reading, trying all things, assenting to the force of reason and convincement.

What could a man require more from a nation so pliant and so prone to seek after knowledge? What wants there to such a towardly and pregnant soil, but wise and faithful laborers, to make a knowing people, a nation of prophets, of sages, and of worthies? We reckon more than five months yet to harvest; there need not be five weeks, had we but eyes to lift up, the fields are white already. Where there is much desire to learn, there of necessity will be much arguing, much writing, many opinions; for opinion in good men is but knowledge in the making. Under these fantastic terrors of sect and schism, we wrong the earnest and zealous thirst after knowledge and understanding, which God hath stirred up in this city. What some lament of, we rather should rejoice at, should rather praise this pious forwardness among men, to reassume the ill-deputed care of their religion into their own hands again. A little generous prudence, a little forbearance of one another, and some grain of charity might win all these diligencies to join and unite into one general and brotherly search after truth; could we but forego this prelatical tradition of crowding free consciences and Christian liberties into canons and precepts of men. I doubt not, if some great and worthy stranger should come among us, wise to discern the mold and temper of a people, and how to govern it, observing the high hopes and aims, the diligent alacrity of our extended thoughts and reasonings in the pursuance of truth and freedom, but that he would cry out as Pyrrhus did, admiring the Roman docility and

courage, "If such were my Epirots, I would not despair the greatest design that could be attempted to make a church or kingdom happy."

Yet these are the men cried out against for schismatics and sectaries, as if, while the temple of the Lord was building, some cutting, some squaring the marble, others hewing the cedars, there should be a sort of irrational men, who could not consider there must be many schisms and many dissections made in the quarry and in the timber ere the house of God can be built. And when every stone is laid artfully together, it cannot be united into a continuity, it can but be contiguous in this world: neither can every piece of the building be of one form; nay, rather the perfection consists in this, that out of many moderate varieties and brotherly dissimilitudes that are not vastly disproportional, arises the goodly and the graceful symmetry that commends the whole pile and structure.

Let us therefore be more considerate builders, more wise in spiritual architecture, when great reformation is expected. For now the time seems come, wherein Moses, the great prophet, may sit in heaven rejoicing to see that memorable and glorious wish of his fulfilled, when not only our seventy elders, but all the Lord's people, are become prophets. No marvel then though some men, and some good men too perhaps, but young in goodness, as Joshua then was, envy them. They fret, and out of their own weakness are in agony, lest these divisions and subdivisions will undo us. The adversary again applauds, and waits the hour: when they have branched themselves out, saith he, small enough into parties and partitions, then will be our time. Fool! he sees not the firm root, out of which we all grow, though into branches; nor will beware, until he see our small divided maniples cutting through at every angle of his ill-united and unwieldy brigade. And that we are to hope better of all these supposed sects and schisms, and that we shall not need that solicitude, honest perhaps, though overtimorous, of them that vex in this behalf, but shall laugh in the end at those malicious applauders of our differences, I have these reasons to persuade me.

First, when a city shall be as it were besieged and blocked about, her navigable river infested, inroads and incursions round, defiance and battle oft rumored to be marching up, even to her walls and suburb trenches; that then the people, or the greater part, more than at other times, wholly taken up with the study of highest and most important matters to be reformed, should be disputing, reasoning, reading, inventing, discoursing, even to a rarity and admiration, things not before discoursed or written of, argues first a singular good will, contentedness, and confidence in your prudent foresight, and safe government, lords and commons; and from thence derives itself to a gallant bravery and well-grounded contempt of their enemies, as if there were no small number of as great spirits among us, as his was who, when Rome was nigh besieged by Hannibal, being in the city, bought that piece of ground at no cheap rate whereon Hannibal himself encamped his own regiment.

Next, it is a lively and cheerful presage of our happy success and victory. For as in a body when the blood is fresh, the spirits pure and vigorous, not only to vital, but to rational faculties, and those in the acutest and the pertest operations of wit and subtlety, it argues in what good plight and constitution the body is; so when the cheerfulness of the people is so sprightly up, as that it has not only wherewith to guard well its own freedom and safety, but to spare, and to bestow upon the solidest and sublimest points of controversy and new invention, it betokens us not degenerated, nor drooping to a fatal decay, but casting off the old and wrinkled skin of corruption to outlive these pangs, and wax young again, entering the glorious ways of truth and prosperous virtue, destined to become great and honorable in these latter ages. Methinks I see in my mind a noble and puissant nation rousing herself like a strong man after sleep, and shaking her invincible locks: methinks I see her as an eagle mewing her mighty youth, and kindling her undazzled eyes at the full midday beam; purging and unscaling her long-abused sight at the fountain itself of heavenly radiance; while the whole noise of timorous and flocking birds, with those also that love the twilight, flutter about, amazed at what she means, and in their envious gabble would prognosticate a year of sects and schisms.

What should ye do then, should ye suppress all this flowery crop of knowledge and new light sprung up and yet springing daily in this city? Should ye set an oligarchy of twenty engrossers over it, to bring a famine upon our minds again, when we shall know nothing but what is measured to us by their bushel? Believe it, lords and commons! they who counsel ye to such a suppressing, do as good as bid ye suppress yourselves; and I will soon show how. If it be desired to know the immediate cause of all this free writing and free speaking, there cannot be assigned a truer than your own mild, and free, and humane government; it is the liberty, lords and commons, which your own valorous and happy counsels have purchased us; liberty which is the nurse of all great wits: this is that which hath rarefied and enlightened our spirits like the influence of heaven: this is that which hath enfranchised, enlarged, and lifted up our apprehensions, degrees above themselves. Ye cannot make us now less capable, less knowing, less eagerly pursuing of the truth, unless ye first make yourselves, that made us so, less the lovers, less the founders of our true liberty. We can grow ignorant again, brutish, formal, and slavish, as ye found us; but you then must first become that which ye cannot be, oppressive, arbitrary, and tyrannous, as they were from whom ye have freed us. That our hearts are now more capacious, our thoughts more erected to the search and expectation of greatest and exactest things, is the issue of your own virtue propagated in us; ye cannot suppress that unless ye reinforce an abrogated and merciless law, that fathers may dispatch at will their own children. And who shall then stick closest to ye and excite others? Not he who takes up arms for coat and conduct, and his four nobles of Danegelt. Although I dispraise not the defence of just immunities, yet love my peace better, if that were all. Give me the liberty to know, to utter, and to argue freely according to conscience, above all liberties.

What would be best advised then, if it be found so hurtful and so unequal to suppress opinions for the newness or the unsuitableness to a customary acceptance, will not be my task to say; I only shall repeat what I have learnt from one of your own honorable number, a right noble and pious lord, who had he not sacrificed his life and fortunes to the church and commonwealth, we had not now missed and bewailed a worthy and undoubted patron of this argument. Ye know him, I am sure; yet I for honor's sake, and may it be eternal to him, shall name him, the Lord Brooke. He writing of episcopacy, and by the way treating of sects and schisms, left ye his vote, or rather now the last words of his dying charge, which I know will ever be of dear and honored regard with ye, so full of meekness and breathing charity, that next to His last testament, who bequeathed love and peace to his disciples, I cannot call to mind where I have read or heard words more mild and peaceful. He there exhorts us to hear with patience and humility those, however they be miscalled, that desire to live purely, in such a use of God's ordinances, as the best guidance of their conscience gives them, and to tolerate them, though in some disconformity to ourselves. The book itself will tell us more at large, being published to the world, and dedicated to the parliament by him, who both for his life and for his death deserves, that what advice he left be not laid by without perusal.

And now the time in special is, by privilege to write and speak what may help to the further discussing of matters in agitation. The temple of Janus, with his two controversial faces, might now not unsignificantly be set open. And though all the winds of doctrine were let loose to play upon the earth, so truth be in the field, we do injuriously by licensing and prohibiting to misdoubt her strength. Let her and falsehood grapple; who ever knew truth put to the worse, in a free and open encounter? Her confuting is the best and surest suppressing. He who hears what praying there is for light and clearer knowledge to be sent down among us, would think of other matters to be constituted beyond the discipline of Geneva, framed and fabricked already to our hands.

Yet when the new light which we beg for shines in upon us, there be who envy and oppose, if it come not first in at their casements. What a collusion is this, whenas we are exhorted by the wise man to use diligence, "to seek for wisdom as for hidden treasures," early and late, that another order shall enjoin us, to know nothing but by statute? When a man hath been laboring the hardest labor in the deep mines of knowledge, hath furnished out his findings in all their equipage, drawn forth his reasons as it were a battle ranged, scattered and defeated all objections in his way, calls out his adversary into the plain, offers him the advantage of wind and sun, if he please, only that he may try the matter by dint of argument; for his opponents then to skulk, to lay ambushments, to keep a narrow bridge of licensing where the challenger should pass, though it be valor enough in soldiership, is but weakness and cowardice in the wars of truth. For who knows not that truth is strong, next to the Almighty; she needs no policies, nor stratagems, nor licensings to make her victorious; those are the shifts and the defences that error uses against her power: give her but room, and do not bind her when she sleeps, for then she speaks not true, as the old Proteus did, who spake oracles only when he was caught and bound, but then rather she turns herself into all shapes except her own, and perhaps tunes her voice according to the time, as Micaiah did before Ahab, until she be adjured into her own likeness.

Yet is it not impossible that she may have more shapes than one? What else is all that rank of things indifferent, wherein truth may be on this side, or on the other, without being unlike herself? What but a vain shadow else is the abolition of "those ordinances, that hand-writing nailed to the cross?" What great purchase is this Christian liberty which Paul so often boasts of? His doctrine is, that he who eats or eats not, regards a day or regards it not, may do either to the Lord. How many other things might be tolerated in peace, and left to conscience, had we but charity, and were it not the chief stronghold of our hypocrisy to be ever judging one another? I fear yet this iron yoke of outward conformity hath left a slavish print upon our necks; the ghost of a linen decency yet haunts us. We stumble, and are impatient at the least dividing of one visible congregation from another, though it be not in fundamentals; and through our forwardness to suppress, and our backwardness to recover, any enthralled piece of truth out of the gripe of custom, we care not to keep truth separated from truth, which is the fiercest rent and disunion of all. We do not see that while we still affect by all means a rigid external formality, we may as soon fall again into a gross conforming stupidity, a stark and dead congealment of "wood and hay and stubble" forced and frozen together, which is more to the sudden degenerating of a church than many subdichotomies of petty schisms.

Not that I can think well of every light separation; or that all in a church is to be expected "gold and silver, and precious stones:" it is not possible for man to sever the wheat from the tares, the good fish from the other fry; that must be the angels' ministry at the end of mortal things. Yet if all cannot be of one mind, as who looks they should be? this doubtless is more wholesome, more prudent, and more Christian, that many be tolerated rather than all compelled. I mean not tolerated popery, and open superstition, which as it extirpates all religions and civil supremacies, so itself should be extirpate, provided first that all charitable and compassionate means be used to win and regain the weak and the misled: that also which is impious or evil absolutely either against faith or manners, no law can possibly permit, that intends not to unlaw itself: but those neighboring differences, or rather indifferences, are what I speak of, whether in some point of doctrine or of discipline, which though they may be many, yet need not interrupt the unity of spirit, if we could but find among us the bond of peace.

In the meanwhile, if any one would write, and bring his helpful hand to the slow-moving reformation which we labor under, if truth have spoken to him before others, or but seemed at least to speak, who hath so bejesuited us, that we should trouble that man with asking licence to do so worthy a deed; and not consider this, that if it come to prohibiting, there is not aught more likely to be prohibited than truth itself: whose first appearance to our eyes, bleared and dimmed with prejudice and custom, is more unsightly and unplausible than many errors; even as the person is of many a great man slight and contemptible to see to. And what do they tell us vainly of new opinions, when this very opinion of theirs, that none must be heard but whom they like, is the worst and newest opinion of all others; and is the chief cause why sects and schisms do so much abound, and true knowledge is kept at distance from us; besides yet a greater danger which is in it. For when God shakes a kingdom, with strong and healthful commotions, to a general reforming, 'tis not untrue that many sectaries and false teachers are then busiest in seducing.

But yet more true it is, that God then raises to his own work men of rare abilities, and more than common industry, not only to look back and revise what hath been taught heretofore, but to gain further, and go on some new enlightened steps in the discovery of truth. For such is the order of God's enlightening his church, to dispense and deal out by degrees his beam, so as our earthly eyes may best sustain it. Neither is God appointed and confined, where and out of what place these his chosen shall be first heard to speak; for he sees not as man sees, chooses not as man chooses, lest we should devote ourselves again to set places and assemblies, and outward callings of men; planting our faith one while in the old convocation house; and another while in the chapel at Westminster; when all the faith and religion that shall be there canonized, is not sufficient without plain convincement, and the charity of patient instruction, to supple the least bruise of conscience, to edify the meanest Christian, who desires to walk in the spirit, and not in the letter of human trust, for all the number of voices that can be there made; no, though Harry the Seventh himself there, with all his liege tombs about him, should lend them voices from the dead to swell their number.

And if the men be erroneous who appear to be the leading schismatics, what withholds us but our sloth, our self-will, and distrust in the right cause, that we do not give them gentle meetings and gentle dismissions, that we debate not and examine the matter thoroughly with liberal and frequent audience; if not for their sakes yet for our own? Seeing no man who hath tasted learning, but will confess the many ways of profiting by those who, not contented with stale receipts, are able to manage and set forth new positions to the world. And were they but as the dust and cinders of our feet, so long as in that notion they may yet serve to polish and brighten the armory of truth, even for that respect they were not utterly to be cast away. But if they be of those whom God hath fitted for the special use of these times with eminent and ample gifts, and those perhaps neither among the priests, nor among the Pharisees, and we, in the haste of a precipitant zeal, shall make no distinction, but resolve to stop their mouths, because we fear they come with new and dangerous opinions, as we commonly forejudge them ere we understand them; no less than woe to us, while, thinking thus to defend the gospel, we are found the persecutors!

There have been not a few since the beginning of this parliament, both of the presbytery and others, who by their unlicensed books to the contempt of an imprimatur first broke that triple ice clung about our hearts, and taught the people to see day; I hope that none of those were the persuaders to renew upon us this bondage, which they themselves have wrought so much good by contemning. But if neither the check that Moses gave to young Joshua, nor the countermand which our Saviour gave to young John, who was so ready to prohibit those whom he thought unlicensed, be not enough to admonish our elders how unacceptable to God their testy mood of prohibiting is; if neither their own remembrance what evil hath abounded in the church by this let of licensing, and what good they themselves have begun by transgressing it, be not enough, but that they will persuade and execute the most Dominican part of the inquisition over us, and are already with one foot in the stirrup so active at suppressing, it would be no unequal distribution in the first place to suppress the suppressors themselves; whom the change of their condition hath puffed up, more than their late experience of harder times hath made wise.

And as for regulating the press, let no man think to have the honor of advising ye better than yourselves have done in that order published next before this, "That no book be printed, unless the printer's and the author's name, or at least the printer's be registered."

Those which otherwise come forth, if they be found mischievous and libellous, the fire and the executioner will be the timeliest and the most effectual remedy that man's prevention can use. For this authentic Spanish policy of licensing books, if I have said aught, will prove the most unlicensed book itself within a short while; and was the immediate image of a star-chamber decree to that purpose made in those very times when that court did the rest of those her pious works, for which she is now fallen from the stars with Lucifer. Whereby ye may guess what kind of state prudence, what love of the people, what care of religion or good manners there was at the contriving, although with singular hypocrisy it pretended to bind books to their good behavior. And how it got the upper hand of your precedent orders so well constituted before, if we may believe those men whose profession gives them cause to inquire most, it may be doubted there was in it the fraud of some old patentees and monopolizers, in the trade of bookselling; who, under pretence of the poor in their company not to be defrauded, and the just retaining of each man his several copy, (which God forbid should be gainsaid,) brought divers glossing colors to the house, which were indeed but colors, and serving to no end except it be to exercise a superiority over their neighbors; men who do not therefore labor in an honest profession, to which learning is indebted, that they should be made other men's vassals. Another end is thought was aimed at by some of them in procuring by petition this order, that having power in their hands, malignant books might the easier escape abroad, as the event shows. But of these sophisms and elenches of merchandise I skill not: this I know, that errors in a good government and in a bad are equally almost incident; for what magistrate may not be misinformed, and much the sooner, if liberty of printing be reduced into the power of a few? But to redress willingly and speedily what hath been erred, and in highest authority to esteem a plain advertisement more than others have done a sumptuous bride, is a virtue (honored lords and commons!) answerable to your highest actions, and whereof none can participate but greatest and wisest men.

THE

TENURE OF KINGS AND MAGISTRATES:

[The text is that of the first edition, 1649.]

PROVING

THAT IT IS LAWFUL, AND HATH BEEN HELD SO THROUGH ALL AGES, FOR ANY, WHO HAVE THE POWER, TO CALL TO ACCOUNT A TYRANT, OR WICKED KING, AND AFTER DUE CONVICTION, TO DEPOSE, AND PUT HIM TO DEATH, IF THE ORDINARY MAGISTRATE HAVE NEGLECTED, OR DENIED TO DO IT. AND THAT THEY WHO OF LATE SO · MUCH BLAME DEPOSING, ARE THE MEN THAT DID IT THEMSELVES.

IF men within themselves would be governed by reason, and not generally give up their understanding to a double tyranny of custom from without, and blind affections within, they would discern better what it is to favor and uphold the tyrant of a nation. But, being slaves within doors, no wonder that they strive so much to have the public state conformably governed to the inward vicious rule by which they govern themselves. For, indeed, none can love freedom heartily but good men; the rest love not freedom but licence, which never hath more scope or more indulgence than under tyrants. Hence is it that tyrants are not oft offended, nor stand much in doubt of bad men, as being all naturally servile; but in whom virtue and true worth most is eminent, them they fear in earnest, as by right their masters; against them lies all their hatred and suspicion. Consequently, neither do bad men hate tyrants, but have been always readiest, with the falsified names of loyalty and obedience, to color over their base compliances.

And although sometimes for shame, and when it comes to their own grievances, of purse especially, they would seem good patriots and side with the better cause, yet when others for the deliverence of their country endued with fortitude and heroic virtue to fear nothing but the curse written against those "that do the work of the Lord negligently," would go on to remove, not only the calamities and thraldoms of a people, but the roots and causes whence they spring;

straight these men, and sure helpers at need, as if they hated only the miseries, but not the mischiefs, after they have juggled and paltered with the world, bandied and borne arms against their king, divested him, disanointed him, nay, cursed him all over in their pulpits, and their pamphlets, to the engaging of sincere and real men beyond what is possible or honest to retreat from, not only turn revolters from those principles which only could at first move them, but lay the stain of disloyalty, and worse, on those proceedings which are the necessary consequences of their own former actions; nor disliked by themselves, were they managed to the entire advantages of their own faction; not considering the while that he toward whom they boasted their new fidelity, counted them accessory; and by those statutes and laws, which they so impotently brandish against others, would have doomed them to a traitor's death for what they have done already.

'Tis true, that most men are apt enough to civil wars and commotions as a novelty, and for a flash hot and active; but through sloth or inconstancy, and weakness of spirit, either fainting ere their own pretences, though never so just, be half attained, or through an inbred falsehood and wickedness, betray, ofttimes to destruction with themselves, men of noblest temper joined with them for causes whereof they in their rash undertakings were not capable. If God and a good cause give them victory, the prosecution whereof for the most part inevitably draws after it the alteration of laws, change of government, downfall of princes with their families; then comes the task to those worthies which are the soul of that enterprise, to be sweat and labored out amidst the throng and noises of vulgar and irrational men. Some contesting for privileges, customs, forms, and that old entanglement of iniquity, their gibberish laws, though the badge of their ancient slavery. Others, who have been fiercest against their prince, under the notion of a tyrant, and no mean incendiaries of the war against him, when God, out of his providence and high disposal, hath delivered him into the hand of their brethren, on a sudden and in a new garb of allegiance, which their doings have long since cancelled, they plead for him, pity him, extol him, protest against those that talk of bringing him to the trial of justice, which is the sword of God, superior to all mortal things, in whose hand soever by apparent signs his testified will is to put it.

But certainly, if we consider who and what they are, on a sudden grown so pitiful, we may conclude their pity can be no true and Christian commiseration, but either levity and shallowness of mind or else a carnal admiring of that worldly pomp and greatness from whence they see him fallen; or rather, lastly, a dissembled and seditious pity, feigned of industry to beget new discord. As for mercy, if it be to a tyrant, under which name they themselves have cited him so oft in the hearing of God, of angels, and the holy church assembled, and there charged him with the spilling of more innocent blood by far then ever Nero did, undoubtedly the mercy which they pretend is the mercy of wicked men; and "their mercies," we read, "are cruelties;" hazarding the welfare of a whole nation, to have saved one whom so oft they have termed Agag, and vilifying the blood of many Jonathans that have saved Israel; insisting with much niceness on the unnecessariest clause of their covenant wrested, wherein the fear of change and the absurd contradiction of a flattering hostility had hampered them, but not scrupling to give away for compliments, to an implacable revenge, the heads of many thousand Christians more.

Another sort there is, who coming in the course of these affairs to have their share in great actions above the form of law or custom, at least to give their voice and approbation, begin to swerve and almost shiver at the majesty and grandeur of some noble deed, as if they were newly entered into a great sin; disputing precedents, forms, and circumstances, when the commonwealth nigh perishes for want of deeds in substance, done with just and faithful expedition. To these I wish better instruction, and virtue equal to their calling; the former of which, that is to say, instruction, I shall endeavor, as my duty is, to bestow on them; and exhort them not to startle from the just and pious resolution of adhering, with all their strength and assistance, to the present parliament and army,

in the glorious way wherein justice and victory hath set them—the only warrants through all ages, next under immediate revelation, to exercise supreme power—in those proceedings, which hitherto appear equal to what hath been done in any age or nation heretofore justly or magnanimously.

Nor let them be discouraged or deterred by any new apostate scarecrows, who, under show of giving counsel, send out their barking monitories and mementoes, empty of aught else but the spleen of a frustrated faction. For how can that pretended counsel be either sound or faithful, when they that give it see not, for madness and vexation of their ends lost, that those statutes and scriptures which both falsely and scandalously they wrest against their friends and associates, would, by sentence of the common adversary, fall first and heaviest upon their own heads? Neither let mild and tender dispositions be foolishly softened from their duty and perseverance with the unmasculine rhetoric of any puling priest or chaplain, sent as a friendly letter of advice, for fashion sake in private, and forthwith published by the sender himself, that we may know how much of friend there was in it, to cast an odious envy upon them to whom it was pretended to be sent in charity. Nor let any man be deluded by either the ignorance or the notorious hypocrisy and self-repugnance of our dancing divines, who have the conscience and the boldness to come with scripture in their mouths, glossed and fitted for their turns with a double contradictory sense, transforming the sacred verity of God to an idol with two faces, looking at once two several ways; and with the same quotations to charge others, which in the same case they made serve to justify themselves. For while the hope to be made classic and provincial lords led them on, while pluralities greased them thick and deep, to the shame and scandal of religion, more than all the sects and heresies they exclaim against; then to fight against the king's person, and no less a party of his lords and commons, or to put force upon both the houses, was good, was lawful, was no resisting of superior powers; they only were powers not to be resisted, who countenanced the good and punished the evil.

But now that their censorious domineering

is not suffered to be universal, truth and conscience to be freed, tithes and pluralities to be no more, though competent allowance provided, and the warm experience of large gifts, and they so good at taking them; yet now to exclude and seize upon impeached members, to bring delinquents without exemption to a fair tribunal by the common national law against murder, is now to be no less than Korah, Dathan, and Abiram. He who but erewhile in the pulpits was a cursed tyrant, an enemy to God and saints, laden with all the innocent blood spilt in three kingdoms, and so to be fought against, is now, though nothing penitent or altered from his first principles, a lawful magistrate, a sovereign lord, the Lord's anointed, not to be touched, though by themselves imprisoned. As if this only were obedience, to preserve the mere useless bulk of his person, and that only in prison, not in the field, and to disobey his commands, deny him his dignity and office, everywhere to resist his power, but where they think it only surviving in their own faction.

But who in particular is a tyrant, cannot be determined in a general discourse, otherwise than by supposition; his particular charge, and the sufficient proof of it, must determine that: which I leave to magistrates, at least to the uprighter sort of them, and of the people, though in number less by many, in whom faction least hath prevailed above the law of nature and right reason, to judge as they find cause. But this I dare own as part of my faith, that if such a one there be, by whose commission whole massacres have been committed on his faithful subjects, his provinces offered to pawn or alienation, as the hire of those whom he had solicited to come in and destroy whole cities and countries; be he king, or tyrant, or emperor, the sword of justice is above him; in whose hand soever is found sufficient power to avenge the effusion, and so great a deluge of innocent blood. For if all human power to execute, not accidentally but intendedly, the wrath of God upon evil-doers without exception, be of God; then that power, whether ordinary, or if that fail, extraordinary, so executing that intent of God, is lawful, and not to be resisted. But to unfold more at large this whole question, though with all expedient brevity, I shall here set down, from first beginning, the original, of kings; how and wherefore exalted to that dignity above their brethren; and from thence shall prove, that turning to tyranny they may be as lawfully deposed and punished, as they were at first elected: this I shall do by authorities and reasons, not learnt in corners among schisms and heresies, as our doubling divines are ready to calumniate, but fetched out of the midst of choicest and most authentic learning, and no prohibited authors; nor many heathen, but Mosaical, Christian, orthodoxal, and, which must needs be more convincing to our adversaries, presbyterial.

No man, who knows aught, can be so stupid to deny, that all men naturally were born free, being the image and resemblance of God himself, and were, by privilege above all the creatures, born to command, and not to obey: and that they lived so, till from the root of Adam's transgression falling among themselves to do wrong and violence, and foreseeing that such courses must needs tend to the destruction of them all, they agreed by common league to bind each other from mutual injury, and jointly to defend themselves against any that gave disturbance or opposition to such agreement. Hence came cities, towns, and commonwealths. And because no faith in all was found sufficiently binding, they saw it needful to ordain some authority that might restrain by force and punishment what was violated against peace and common right.

This authority and power of self-defence and preservation being originally and naturally in every one of them, and unitedly in them all; for ease, for order, and lest each man should be his own partial judge, they communicated and derived either to one, whom for the eminence of his wisdom and integrity they chose above the rest, or to more than one, whom they thought of equal deserving: the first was called a king; the other, magistrates: not to be their lords and masters, (though afterward those names in some places were given voluntarily to such as have been authors of inestimable good to the people,) but to be their deputies and commissioners, to execute, by virtue of their intrusted power, that justice, which else every man by the bond of nature and of covenant must have executed for himself, and for one another. And to him that shall consider well, why among free persons one man by civil right should bear authority and jurisdiction over another, no other end or reason can be imaginable.

These for a while governed well, and with much equity decided all things at their own arbitrement; till the temptation of such a power, left absolute in their hands, perverted them at length to injustice and partiality. Then did they, who now by trial had found the danger and inconveniencies of committing arbitrary power to any, invent laws, either framed or consented to by all, that should confine and limit the authority of whom they chose to govern them: that so man, of whose failing they had proof, might no more rule over them, but law and reason, abstracted as much as might be from personal errors and frailities. While, as the magistrate was set above the people, so the law was set above the magistrate. When this would not serve, but that the law was either not executed, or misapplied, they were constrained from that time, the only remedy left them, to put conditions and take oaths from all kings and magistrates at their first instalment, to do impartial justice by law: who, upon those terms and no other, received allegiance from the people, that is to say, bond or covenant to obey them in execution of those laws, which they, the people, had themselves made or assented to. And this ofttimes with express warning, that if the king or magistrate proved unfaithful to his trust, the people would be disengaged. They added also counsellors and parliaments, not to be only at his beck, but, with him or without him, at set times, or at all times, when any danger threatened, to have care of the public safety. Therefore saith Claudius Sesell, a French statesman, "The parliament was set as a bridle to the king;" which I instance rather, not because our English lawyers have not said the same long before, but because that French monarchy is granted by all to be a far more absolute than ours. That this and the rest of what hath hitherto been spoken is most true, might be copiously made appear throughout all stories, heathen and Christian; even of those nations where kings and emperors have sought means to abolish all an-

cient memory of the people's right by their encroachments and usurpations. But I spare long insertions, appealing to the known constitutions of both the latest Christian Empires in Europe, the Greek and German, besides the French, Italian, Arragonian, English, and not least the Scottish histories: not forgetting this only by the way, that William the Norman, though a conqueror, and not unsworn at his coronation, was compelled a second time to take oath at St. Alban's ere the people would be brought to yield obedience.

It being thus manifest, that the power of kings and magistrates is nothing else but what is only derivative, transferred, and committed to them in trust from the people to the common good of them all, in whom the power yet remains fundamentally, and cannot be taken from them, without a violation of their natural birthright; and seeing that from hence Aristotle, and the best of political writers, have defined a king, "him who governs to the good and profit of his people, and not for his own ends;" it follows from necessary causes, that the titles of sovereign lord, natural lord, and the like, are either arrogancies or flatteries, not admitted by emperors and kings of best note, and disliked by the church both of Jews, Isa. xxvi. 13 and ancient Christians, as appears by Tertullian and others. Although generally the people of Asia, and with them the Jews also, especially since the time they chose a king against the advice and counsel of God, are noted by wise authors much inclinable to slavery.

Secondly, that to say, as is usual, the king hath as good right to his crown and dignity as any man to his inheritance, is to make the subject no better than the king's slave, his chattel, or his possession that may be bought and sold: and doubtless, if hereditary title were sufficiently inquired, the best foundation of it would be found either but in courtesy or convenience. But suppose it to be of right hereditary, what can be more just and legal, if a subject for certain crimes be to forfeit by law from himself and posterity all his inheritance to the king, than that a king, for crimes proportional, should forfeit all his title and inheritance to the people? Unless the people must be thought created all for him, he not for them, and they all in one body inferior to him single; which were a kind of treason against the dignity of mankind to affirm.

Thirdly, it follows, that to say kings are accountable to none but God, is the overturning of all law and government. For if they may refuse to give account, then all covenants made with them at coronation, all oaths are in vain, and mere mockeries; all laws which they swear to keep, made to no purpose: for if the king fear not God, (as how many of them do not,) we hold then our lives and estates by the tenure of his mere grace and mercy, as from a god, not a mortal magistrate; a position that none but courtparasites or men besotted would maintain! Aristotle, therefore, whom we commonly allow for one of the best interpreters of nature and morality, writes in the fourth of his Politics, chap. x. that "monarchy unaccountable is the worst sort of tyranny, and least of all to be endured by free-born men."

And surely no Christian prince, not drunk with high mind, and prouder than those pagan Cæsars that deified themselves, would arrogate so unreasonably above human condition, or derogate so basely from a whole nation of men, his brethren, as if for him only subsisting, and to serve his glory, valuing them in comparison of his own brute will and pleasure no more than so many beasts, or vermin under his feet, not to be reasoned with, but to be trod on; among whom there might be found so many thousand men for wisdom, virtue, nobleness of mind, and all other respects but the fortune of his dignity, far above him. Yet some would persuade us that this absurd opinion was King David's, because in the 51st Psalm he cries out to God, "Against thee only have I sinned;" as if David had imagined, that to murder Uriah and adulterate his wife had been no sin against his neighbor, whenas that law of Moses was to the king expressly, Deut. xvii., not to think so highly of himself above his brethren. David, therefore, by those words, could mean no other, than either that the depth of his guiltiness was known to God only, or to so few as had not the will or power to question him, or that the sin against God was greater beyond compare than against Uriah. Whatever his meaning were, any wise man will see, that the pathetical words of a psalm can be no certain decision to a point that hath abundantly more certain rules to go by.

How much more rationally spake the heathen king Demophoön, in a tragedy of Euripides, than these interpreters would put upon king David! "I rule not my people by tyranny, as if they were barbarians; but am myself liable, if I do unjustly, to suffer justly." Not unlike was the speech of Trajan, the worthy emperor, to one whom he made general of his prætorian forces: "Take this drawn sword," saith he, "to use for me if I reign well; if not, to use against me." Thus Dion relates. And not Trajan only, but Theodosius, the younger, a Christian emperor, and one of the best, caused it to be enacted as a rule undeniable and fit to be acknowledged by all kings and emperors, that a prince is bound to the laws; that on the authority of law the authority of a prince depends, and to the laws ought submit. Which edict of his remains yet in the Code of Justinian, l. i. tit. 24, as a sacred constitution to all the succeeding emperors. How then can any king in Europe maintain and write himself accountable to none but God, when emperors in their own imperial statutes have written and decreed themselves accountable to law? And indeed where such account is not feared, he that bids a man reign over him above law, may bid as well a savage beast.

It follows, lastly, that since the king or magistrate holds his authority of the people, both originally and naturally for their good, in the first place, and not his own, then may the people, as oft as they shall judge it for the best, either choose him or reject him, retain him or depose him, though no tyrant, merely by the liberty and right of free-born men to be governed as seems to them best. This, though it cannot but stand with plain reason, shall be made good also by Scripture: Deut. xvii. 14: "When thou art come into the land which the Lord thy God giveth thee, and shalt say, I will set a king over me, like as all the nations about me." These words confirm us that the right of choosing, yea of changing their own government, is by the grant of God himself in the people. And therefore when they desired a king, though then under another form of government, and though their changing displeased him, yet he that was himself their king, and rejected by them, would not be a hindrance to what they intended, further than by persuasion, but that they might do therein as they saw good, 1 Sam. viii., only he reserved to himself the nomination of who should reign over them. Neither did that exempt the king, as if he were to God only accountable, though by his especial command anointed. Therefore "David first made a covenant with the elders of Israel, and so was by them anointed king," 2 Sam. v. 3; 1 Chron. xi. And Jehoiada the priest, making Jehoash king, made a covenant between him and the people, 2 Kings, xi. 17. Therefore when Rehoboam, at his coming to the crown, rejected those conditions which the Israelites brought him, hear what they answer him: "What portion have we in David, or inheritance in the son of Jesse? See to thine own house, David." And for the like conditions not performed, all Israel before that time deposed Samuel; not for his own default, but for the misgovernment of his sons.

But some will say to both these examples, it was evilly done. I answer, that not the latter, because it was expressly allowed them in the law, to set up a king if they pleased; and God himself joined with them in the work; though in some sort it was at that time displeasing to him, in respect of old Samuel, who had governed them uprightly. As Livy praises the Romans, who took occasion from Tarquinius, a wicked prince, to gain their liberty, which to have extorted, saith he, from Numa, or any of the good kings before, had not been seasonable. Nor was it in the former example done unlawfully; for when Rehoboam had prepared a huge army to reduce the Israelites, he was forbidden by the prophet: 1 Kings, xii. 24: "Thus saith the Lord, ye shall not go up, nor fight against your brethren, for this thing is from me." He calls them their brethren, not rebels, and forbids to be proceeded against them, owning the thing himself, not by single providence, but by approbation, and that not only of the act, as in the former example, but of the fit season also; he had not otherwise forbid to molest them. And those grave and wise counsellors, whom Rehoboam first advised with, spake no such thing as our old gray-headed flatterers now are wont—stand upon your birthright, scorn to capitulate; you

hold of God, not of them;—for they knew no such matter, unless conditionally, but gave him politic counsel, as in a civil transaction.

Therefore kingdom and magistracy, whether supreme or subordinate, is without difference called "a human ordinance," 1 Pet. ii. 13, &c., which we are there taught is the will of God we should alike submit to, so far as for the punishment of evil-doers, and the encouragement of them that do well. "Submit," saith he, "as free men." But to any civil power, unaccountable, unquestionable, and not to be resisted, no, not in wickedness, and violent actions, how can we submit as free men? "There is no power but of God," saith Paul; Rom. xiii.; as much as to say, God put it into man's heart to find out that way at first for common peace and preservation, approving the exercise thereof; else it contradicts Peter, who calls the same authority an ordinance of man. It must be also understood of lawful and just power, else we read of great power in the affairs and kingdoms of the world permitted to the devil: for saith he to Christ, Luke iv. 6, "All this power will I give thee, and the glory of them, for it is delivered to me, &c. to whomsoever I will, I give it:" neither did he lie, or Christ gainsay what he affirmed; for in the thirteenth of the Revelation, we read how the dragon gave to the beast his power, his seat, and great authority: which beast so authorized most expound to be the tyrannical powers and kingdoms of the earth. Therefore Saint Paul in the fore-cited chapter tells us, that such magistrates he means, as are not a terror to the good, but to the evil; such as bear not the sword in vain, but to punish offenders, and to encourage the good.

If such only be mentioned here as powers to be obeyed, and our submission to them only required, then doubtless those powers that do the contrary are no powers ordained of God; and by consequence no obligation laid upon us to obey or not to resist them. And it may be well observed, that both these apostles, whenever they give this precept, express it in terms not concrete, but abstract, as logicians are wont to speak; that is, they mention the ordinance, the power, the authority, before the persons that execute it; and what that power is, lest we should be deceived, they describe exactly. So that if the power be not such, or the person execute not such power, neither the one nor the other is of God, but of the devil, and by consequence to be resisted. From this exposition Chrysostom also, on the same place, dissents not; explaining that these words were not written in behalf of a tyrant. And this is verified by David, himself a king, and likeliest to be author of the Psalm xciv. 20 which saith, "Shall the throne of iniquity have fellowship with thee?" And it were worth the knowing, since kings in these days, and that by Scripture, boast the justness of their title, by holding it immediately of God, yet cannot show the time when God ever set on the throne them or their forefathers, but only when the people chose them; why ·by the same reason, since God ascribes as oft to himself the casting down of princes from the throne, it should not be thought as lawful, and as much from God, when none are seen to do it but the people, and that for just causes. For if it needs must be a sin in them to depose, it may as likely be a sin to have elected. And contrary, if the people's act in election be pleaded by a king, as the act of God, and the most just title to enthrone him, why may not the people's act of rejection be as well pleaded by the people as the act of God, and the most just reason to depose him? So that we see the title and just right of reigning or deposing, in reference to God, is found in Scripture to be all one; visible only in the people, and depending merely upon justice and demerit. Thus far hath been considered briefly the power of kings and magistrates; how it was and is originally the people's, and by them conferred in trust only to be employed to the common peace and benefit; with liberty therefore and right remaining in them, to reassume it to themselves, if by kings or magistrates it be abused; or to dispose of it by any alteration, as they shall judge most conducing to the public good.

We may from hence with more ease and force of argument determine what a tyrant is, and what the people may do against him. A tyrant, whether by wrong or by right coming to the crown, is he who, regarding neither law nor the common good, reigns only for himself and his faction: thus St. Basil, among others, defines him. And because his power is great, his will boundless and exorbitant,

the fulfilling whereof is for the most part accompanied with innumerable wrongs and oppressions of the people, murders, massacres, rapes, adulteries, desolation, and subversion of cities and whole provinces; look how great a good and happiness a just king is, so great a mischief is a tyrant; as he the public father of his country, so this the common enemy. Against whom what the people lawfully may do, as against a common pest and destroyer of mankind, I suppose no man of clear judgment need go further to be guided than by the very principles of nature in him.

But because it is the vulgar folly of men to desert their own reason, and shutting their eyes, to think they see best with other men's, I shall show, by such examples as ought to have most weight with us, what hath been done in this case heretofore. The Greeks and Romans, as their prime authors witness, held it not only lawful, but a glorious and heroic deed, rewarded publicly with statues and garlands, to kill an infamous tyrant at any time without trial; and but reason, that he, who trod down all law, should not be vouchsafed the benefit of law. Insomuch that Seneca, the tragedian, brings in Hercules, the grand suppressor of tyrants, thus speaking:—

"——— Victima haud ulla amplior
Potest, magisque opima mactari Jovi
Quam rex iniquus ——— "

"——— There can be slain
No sacrifice to God more acceptable
Than an unjust and wicked king ———."

But of these I name no more, lest it be objected they were heathen; and come to produce another sort of men, that had the knowledge of true religion. Among the Jews this custom of tyrant-killing was not unusual. First, Ehud, a man whom God had raised to deliver Israel from Eglon king of Moab, who had conquered and ruled over them eighteen years, being sent to him as an ambassador with a present, slew him in his own house. But he was a foreign prince, an enemy, and Ehud besides had special warrant from God. To the first I answer, it imports not whether foreign or native: for no prince so native but professes to hold by law; which when he himself overturns, breaking all the covenants and oaths that gave him title to his dignity, and were the bond and alliance between him and his people, what differs he from an outlandish king, or from an enemy?

For look how much right the king of Spain hath to govern us at all, so much right hath the king of England to govern us tyrannically. If he, though not bound to us by any league, coming from Spain in person to subdue us, or to destroy us, might lawfully by the people of England either be slain in fight, or put to death in captivity, what hath a native king to plead, bound by so many covenants, benefits, and honors, to the welfare of his people; why he through the contempt of all laws and parliaments, the only tie of our obedience to him, for his own will's sake, and a boasted prerogative unaccountable, after seven years' warring and destroying of his best subjects, overcome, and yielded prisoner, should think to scape unquestionable, as a thing divine, in respect of whom so many thousand Christians destroyed should lie unaccounted for, polluting with their slaughtered carcasses all the land over, and crying for vengeance against the living that should have righted them? Who knows not that there is a mutual bond of amity and brotherhood between man and man over all the world, neither is it the English sea that can sever us from that duty and relation: a straiter bond yet there is between fellow-subjects, neighbors, and friends. But when any of these do one to another so as hostility could do no worse, what doth the law decree less against them, than open enemies and invaders? or if the law be not present or too weak, what doth it warrant us to less than single defence or civil war? and from that time forward the law of civil defensive war differs nothing from the law of foreign hostility. Nor is it distance of place that makes enmity, but enmity that makes distance. He, therefore, that keeps peace with me, near or remote, of whatsoever nation, is to me, as far as all civil and human offices, an Englishman and a neighbor: but if an Englishman, forgetting all laws, human, civil, and religious, offend against life and liberty, to him offended, and to the law in his behalf, though born in the same womb, he is no better than a Turk, a Saracen, a heathen.

This is gospel, and this was ever law among equals; how much rather then in force against any king whatever, who in respect of the people is confessed inferior and not equal: to distinguish, therefore, of a tyrant by outlandish, or domestic, is a weak evasion. To the second, that he was an enemy, I answer, what tyrant is not? yet Eglon by the Jews had been acknowledged as their sovereign, they had served him eighteen years, as long almost as we our William the Conqueror, in all which time he could not be so unwise a statesman, but to have taken of them oaths of fealty and allegiance; by which they made themselves his proper subjects, as their homage and present sent by Ehud testified. To the third, that he had special warrant to kill Eglon in that manner, it cannot be granted, because not expressed; 'tis plain that he was raised by God to be a deliverer, and went on just principles, such as were then and ever held allowable to deal so by a tyrant, that could no otherwise be dealt with.

Neither did Samuel, though a prophet, with his own hand abstain from Agag; a foreign enemy no doubt; but mark the reason: "As thy sword hath made women childless;" a cause that by the sentence of law itself nullifies all relations. And as the law is between brother and brother, father and son, master and servant, wherefore not between king, or rather tyrant, and people? And whereas Jehu had special command to slay Jehoram, a successive and hereditary tyrant, it seems not the less imitable for that; for where a thing grounded so much on natural reason hath the addition of a command from God, what does it but establish the lawfulness of such an act? Nor is it likely that God, who had so many ways of punishing the house of Ahab, would have sent a subject against his prince, if the fact in itself, as done to a tyrant, had been of bad example. And if David refused to lift his hand against the Lord's anointed, the matter between them was not tyranny, but private enmity; and David, as a private person, had been his own revenger, not so much the people's: but when any tyrant at this day can show to be the Lord's anointed, the only mentioned reason why David withheld his hand, he may then, but not till then, presume on the same privilege.

We may pass, therefore, hence to Christian times. And first, our Saviour himself, how much he favored tyrants, and how much intended they should be found or honored among Christians, declares his mind not obscurely; accounting their absolute authority no better than Gentilism, yea, though they flourished it over with the splendid name of benefactors; charging those that would be his disciples to usurp no such dominion; but that they, who were to be of most authority among them, should esteem themselves ministers and servants to the public: Matt. xx. 25: "The princes of the Gentiles exercise lordship over them;" and Mark x. 42: "They that seem to rule," saith he, either slighting or accounting them no lawful rulers; "but ye shall not be so, but the greatest among you shall be your servant." And although he himself were the meekest, and came on earth to be so, yet to a tyrant we hear him not vouchsafe an humble word: but, "Tell that fox," Luke xiii. So far we ought to be from thinking that Christ and his gospel should be made a sanctuary for tyrants from justice, to whom his law before never gave such protection. And wherefore did his mother, the Virgin Mary, give such praise to God in her prophetic song, that he had now, by the coming of Christ, cut down dynastas, or proud monarchs, from the throne, if the church, when God manifests his power in them to do so, should rather choose all misery and vassalage to serve them, and let them still sit on their potent seats to be adored for doing mischief?

Surely it is not for nothing that tyrants, by a kind of natural instinct, both hate and fear none more than the true church and saints of God, as the most dangerous enemies and subverters of monarchy, though indeed of tyranny; hath not this been the perpetual cry of courtiers and court-prelates? whereof no likelier cause can be alleged, but that they well discerned the mind and principles of most devout and zealous men, and indeed the very discipline of church, tending to the dissolution of all tyranny. No marvel then if since the faith of Christ received, in purer or impurer times, to depose a king and put him to death for tyranny, hath been accounted so just and requisite, that neighbor kings have both upheld and taken part with subjects in the action. And Ludovicus Pius, himself an emperor, and son of Charles the Great, being made judge (du Haillan is my author) between Milegast, king of the

Vultzes, and his subjects, who had deposed him, gave his verdict for the subjects, and for him whom they had chosen in his room. Note here, that the right of electing whom they please is, by the impartial testimony of an emperor, in the people: for, said he, "A just prince ought to be preferred before an unjust, and the end of government before the prerogative."

And Constantinus Leo, another emperor, in the Byzantine laws, saith, "That the end of a king is for the general good, which he not performing, is but the counterfeit of a king." And to prove, that some of our own monarchs have acknowledged that their high office exempted them not from punishment, they had the sword of St. Edward borne before them by an officer, who was called earl of the palace, even at the times of their highest pomp and solemnities; to mind them, saith Matthew Paris, the best of our historians, "that if they erred, the sword had power to restrain them." And what restraint the sword comes to at length, having both edge and point, if any sceptic will doubt, let him feel. It is also affirmed from diligent search made in our ancient books of law, that the peers and barons of England had a legal right to judge the king: which was the cause most likely, (for it could be no slight cause,) that they were called his peers, or equals. This, however, may stand immovable, so long as man hath to deal with no better than man; that if our law judge all men to the lowest by their peers, it should, in all equity, ascend also, and judge the highest.

And so much I find both in our own and foreign story, that dukes, earls, and marquisses were at first not hereditary, not empty and vain titles, but names of trust and office, and with the office ceasing; as induces me to be of opinion, that every worthy man in parliament, (for the word baron imports no more,) might for the public good be thought a fit peer and judge of the king, without regard had to petty caveats and circumstances, the chief impediment in high affairs, and ever stood upon most by circumstantial men. Whence doubtless our ancestors who were not ignorant with what rights either nature or ancient constitution had endowed them, when oaths both at coronation and renewed in parliament would not serve, thought it no way illegal, to depose and put to death their tyrannous kings. Insomuch that the parliament drew up a charge against Richard the Second, and the commons requested to have judgment decreed against him, that the realm might not be endangered. And Peter Martyr, a divine of foremost rank, on the third of Judges approves their doings. Sir Thomas Smith also, a protestant, and a statesman, in his Commonwealth of England, putting the question, "whether it be lawful to rise against a tyrant;" answers, "that the vulgar judge of it according to the event, and the learned according to the purpose of them that do it."

But far before these days, Gildas, the most ancient of all our historians, speaking of those times wherein the Roman empire decaying, quitted and relinquished what right they had by conquest to this island, and resigned it all into the people's hands, testifies that the people thus reinvested with their own original right, about the year 446, both elected them kings, whom they thought best, (the first Christian British kings that ever reigned here since the Romans,) and by the same right, when they apprehended cause, usually deposed and put them to death. This is the most fundamental and ancient tenure that any king of England can produce or pretend to; in comparison of which, all other titles and pleas are but of yesterday. If any object, that Gildas condemns the Britons for so doing, the answer is as ready; that he condemns them no more for so doing than he did before for choosing such; for, saith he, "They anointed them kings not of God, but such as were more bloody than the rest." Next, he condemns them not at all for deposing or putting them to death, but for doing it over hastily, without trial or well examining the cause, and for electing others worse in their room.

Thus we have here both domestic and most ancient examples, that the people of Britain have deposed and put to death their kings in those primitive Christian times. And to couple reason with example, if the church in all ages, primitive, Romish, or protestant, held it ever no less their duty than the power of their keys, though without express warrant of Scripture, to bring indifferently both king and peasant under the utmost rigor of their canons and censures ecclesiastical, even to the smiting him with a final excommunion, if he persist impenitent; what hinders but that the temporal law both may and ought, though without a special text or precedent, extend with like indifference the civil sword, to the cutting off, without exemption, him that capitally offends, seeing that justice and religion are from the same God, and works of justice ofttimes more acceptable? Yet because that some lately, with the tongues and arguments of malignant backsliders, have written that the proceedings now in parliament against the king are without precedent from any protestant state or kingdom, the examples which follow shall be all protestant, and chiefly presbyterian.

In the year 1546, the Duke of Saxony, Landgrave of Hesse, and the whole protestant league, raised open war against Charles the Fifth, their emperor, sent him a defiance, renounced all faith and allegiance toward him, and debated long in council whether they should give him so much as the title of Cæsar. Sleidan l. 17. Let all men judge what this wanted of deposing or of killing, but the power to do it.

In the year 1559, the Scots protestants claiming promise of their queen-regent for liberty of conscience, she answering that promises were not to be claimed of princes beyond what was commodious for them to grant, told her to her face in the parliament then at Stirling, that if it were so, they renounced their obedience; and soon after betook them to arms. Buch. Hist. l. 16. Certainly, when allegiance is renounced, that very hour the king or queen is in effect deposed.

In the year 1564, John Knox, a most famous divine, and the reformer of Scotland to the presbyterian discipline, at a general assembly maintained openly, in a dispute against Lethington the secretary of state, that subjects might and ought to execute God's judgments upon their king; that the fact of Jehu and others against their king, having the ground of God's ordinary command to put such and such offenders to death, was not extraordinary, but to be imitated of all that preferred the honor of God to the affection of flesh and wicked princes; that kings, if they offend, have no privilege to be exempted from the punishments of law more than any other subject: so that if the king be a murderer, adulterer, or idolater, he should suffer, not as a king, but as an offender; and this position he repeats again and again before them. Answerable was the opinion of John Craig, another learned divine, and that laws made by the tyranny of princes, or the negligence of people, their posterity might abrogate, and reform all things according to the original institution of commonwealths. And Knox being commanded by the nobility to write to Calvin and other learned men for their judgments in that question, refused, alleging, that both himself was fully resolved in conscience, and had heard their judgments, and had the same opinion under handwriting of many the most godly and most learned that he knew in Europe; that if he should move the question to them again, what should he do but show his own forgetfulness or inconstancy? All this is far more largely in the ecclesiastical history of Scotland, l. iv. with many other passages to this effect all the book over, set out with diligence by Scotsmen of best repute among them at the beginning of these troubles; as if they labored to inform us what we were to do, and what they intended upon the like occasion.

And to let the world know, that the whole church and protestant state of Scotland in those purest times of reformation were of the same belief, three years after, they met in the field Mary their lawful and hereditary queen, took her prisoner, yielding before fight, kept her in prison, and the same year deposed her. (Buchan. Hist. l. xviii.)

And four years after that, the Scots, in justification of their deposing Queen Mary, sent ambassadors to Queen Elizabeth, and in a written declaration alleged, that they had used towards her more lenity than she deserved; that their ancestors had heretofore punished their kings by death or banishment; that the Scots were a free nation, made king whom they freely chose, and with the same freedom unkinged him if they saw cause, by right of ancient laws and ceremonies yet remaining, and old customs yet among the highlanders in choosing the head of their clans or families; all which, with many other arguments, bore witness, that regal power was nothing else but a mutual covenant or stipulation between king and people. (Buch. Hist.

l. xx.) These were Scotchmen and presbyterians: but what measure then have they lately offered, to think such liberty less beseeming us than themselves, presuming to put him upon us for a master, whom their law scarce allows to be their own equal? If now then we hear them in another strain than heretofore in the purest times of their church, we may be confident it is the voice of faction speaking in them, not of truth and reformation. Which no less in England than in Scotland, by the mouths of those faithful witnesses commonly called puritans and nonconformists, spake as clearly for the putting down, yea, the utmost punishing of kings, as in their several treatises may be read; even from the first reign of Elizabeth to these times. Insomuch that one of them, whose name was Gibson, foretold King James he should be rooted out, and conclude his race, if he persisted to uphold bishops. And that very inscription, stamped upon the first coins at his coronation, a naked sword in a hand with these words, "*Si mereor, in me,*" "Against me, if I deserve," not only manifested the judgment of that state, but seemed also to presage the sentence of divine justice in this event upon his son.

In the year 1581, the states of Holland, in a general assembly at the Hague, abjured all obedience and subjection to Philip king of Spain; and in a declaration justify their so doing; for that by his tyrannous government, against faith so many times given and broken, he had lost his right to all the Belgic provinces; that therefore they deposed him, and declared it lawful to choose another in his stead. Thuan. l. 74. From that time to this, no state or kingdom in the world hath equally prospered: but let them remember not to look with an evil and prejudicial eye upon their neighbors, walking by the same rule.

But what need these examples to presbyterians, I mean to those who now of late would seem so much to abhor deposing, when as they to all Christendom have given the latest and the liveliest example of doing it themselves? I question not the lawfulness of raising war against a tyrant in defence of religion, or civil liberty; for no protestant church, from the first Waldenses of Lyons and Languedoc to this day, but have done it round, and maintained it lawful. But this I doubt not to affirm, that the presbyterians, who now so much condemn deposing, were the men themselves that deposed the king, and cannot, with all their shifting and relapsing, wash off the guiltiness from their own hands. For they themselves, by these their late doings, have made it guiltiness, and turned their own warrantable actions into rebellion.

There is nothing that so actually makes a king of England, as rightful possession and supremacy in all causes both civil and ecclesiastical: and nothing that so actually makes a subject of England as those two oaths of allegiance and supremacy observed without equivocating, or any mental reservation. Out of doubt then, when the king shall command things already constituted in church or state, obedience is the true essence of a subject, either to do, if it be lawful, or if he hold the thing unlawful, to submit to that penalty which the law imposes, so long as he intends to remain a subject. Therefore when the people, or any part of them, shall rise against the king and his authority, executing the law in anything established, civil or ecclesiastical, I do not say it is rebellion, if the thing commanded though established be unlawful, and that they sought first all due means of redress; (and no man is further bound to law;) but I say it is an absolute renouncing both of supremacy and allegiance, which, in one word, is an actual and total deposing of the king, and the setting up of another supreme authority over them.

And whether the presbyterians have not done all this and much more, they will not put me, I suppose, to reckon up a seven years' story, fresh in the memory of all men. Have they not utterly broke the oath of allegiance, rejecting the king's command and authority sent them from any part of the kingdom, whether in things lawful or unlawful? Have they not abjured the oath of supremacy, by setting up the parliament without the king, supreme to all their obedience; and though their vow and covenant bound them in general to the parliament, yet sometimes adhering to the lesser part of lords and commons that remained faithful, as they term it, and even of them, one while to the commons without the lords, another while to the lords without the commons? Have they not still declared their meaning, whatever their oath

were, to hold them only for supreme, whom they found at any time most yielding to what they petitioned? Both these oaths, which were the straitest bond of an English subject in reference to the king, being thus broke and made void; it follows undeniably, that the king from that time was by them in fact absolutely deposed, and they no longer in reality to be thought his subjects, notwithstanding their fine clause in the covenant to preserve his person, crown, and dignity, set there by some dodging casuist with more craft than sincerity, to mitigate the matter, in case of ill success and not taken, I suppose, by any honest man, but as a condition subordinate to every the least particle, that might more concern religion, liberty, or the public peace.

To prove it yet more plainly, that they are the men who have deposed the king, I thus argue. We know, that king and subject are relatives, and relatives have no longer being than in the relation; the relation between king and subject can be no other than regal authority and subjection. Hence I infer, past their defending, that if the subject, who is one relative, take away the relation, of force he takes away also the other relative; but the presbyterians, who were one relative, that is to say, subjects, have for this seven years taken away the relation, that is to say, the king's authority, and their subjection to it; therefore the presbyterians for these seven years have removed and extinguished the other relative, that is to say, the king; or, to speak more in brief, have deposed him; not only by depriving him the execution of his authority, but by conferring it upon others.

If then their oaths of subjection broken, new supremacy obeyed, new oaths and covenants taken, notwithstanding frivolous evasions, have in plain terms unkinged the king, much more than hath their seven years' war, not deposed him only, but outlawed him, and defied him as an alien, a rebel to law, and enemy to the state, it must needs be clear to any man not averse from reason, that hostility and subjection are two direct and positive contraries, and can no more in one subject stand together in respect of the same king, than one person at the same time can be in two remote places. Against whom therefore the subject is in act of hostility, we may be confident, that to him he is in no subjection: and in whom hostility takes place of subjection, for they can by no means consist together, to him the king can be not only no king, but an enemy.

So that from hence we shall not need dispute, whether they have deposed him, or what they have defaulted towards him as no king, but show manifestly how much they have done towards the killing him. Have they not levied all these wars against him, whether offensive or defensive, (for defence in war equally offends, and most prudently beforehand,) and given commission to slay, where they knew his person could not be exempt from danger? And if chance or flight had not saved him, how often had they killed him, directing their artillery, without blame or prohibition, to the very place where they saw him stand? Have they not sequestered him, judged or unjudged, and converted his revenue to other uses, detaining from him, as a grand delinquent, all means of livelihood, so that for them long since he might have perished, or have starved? Have they not hunted and pursued him round about the kingdom with sword and fire? Have they not formerly denied to treat with him, and their now recanting ministers preached against him, as a reprobate incurable, an enemy to God and his church, marked for destruction, and therefore not to be treated with? Have they not besieged him, and to their power forbid him water and fire, save what they shot against him to the hazard of his life? Yet while they thus assaulted and endangered it with hostile deeds, they swore in words to defend it, with his crown and dignity; not in order, as it seems now, to a firm and lasting peace, or to his repentance after all this blood; but simply, without regard, without remorse, or any comparable value of all the miseries and calamities suffered by the poor people, or to suffer hereafter, through his obstinancy or impenitence.

No understanding man can be ignorant, that covenants are ever made according to the present state of persons and of things; and have ever the more general laws of nature and of reason included in them, though not expressed. If I make a voluntary covenant, as with a man to do him good, and he prove afterward a monster to me, I should conceive a disobligement. If I covenant, not to hurt an enemy, in favor of him and forbearance, and hope of his amendment, and he, after that, shall do me tenfold injury and mischief to what he had done when I so covenanted, and still be plotting what may tend to my destruction, I question not but that his after-actions release me; nor know I covenant so sacred, that withholds me from demanding justice on him.

Howbeit, had not their distrust in a good cause, and the fast and loose of our prevaricating divines, overswayed, it had been doubtless better not to have inserted in a covenant unnecessary obligations, and words, not works of supererogating allegiance to their enemy; no way advantageous to themselves, had the king prevailed, as to their cost many would have felt; but full of snare and distraction to our friends, useful only, as we now find, to our adversaries, who under such a latitude and shelter of ambiguous interpretation have ever since been plotting and contriving new opportunities to trouble all again. How much better had it been, and more becoming an undaunted virtue, to have declared openly and boldly whom and what power the people were to hold supreme, as on the like occasion protestants have done before, and many conscientious men now in these times have more than once besought the parliament to do, that they might go on upon a sure foundation, and not with a riddling covenant in their mouths, seeming to swear counter, almost in the same breath, allegiance and no allegiance; which doubtless had drawn off all the minds of sincere men from siding with them, had they not discerned their actions far more deposing him than their words upholding him; which words, made now the subject of cavillous interpretations, stood ever in the covenant, by judgment of the more discerning sort, an evidence of their fear, not of their fidelity.

What should I return to speak on, of those attempts for which the king himself hath often charged the presbyterians of seeking his life, whenas, in the due estimation of things, they might without a fallacy be said to have done the deed outright? Who knows not, that the king is a name of dignity and office, not of person? Who therefore kills a king, must kill him while he is a king. Then they certainly, who by deposing him have long since taken from him the life of a king, his office and his dignity, they in the truest sense may be said to have killed the king: nor only by their deposing and waging war against him, which besides the danger to his personal life, set him in the furthest opposite point from any vital function of a king, but by their holding him in prison, vanquished and yielded into their absolute and despotic power, which brought him to the lowest degradement and incapacity of the regal name. I say not by whose matchless valor, next under God, lest the story of their ingratitude thereupon carry me from the purpose in hand, which is to convince them that they, which I repeat again, were the men who in the truest sense killed the king, not only as is proved before, but by depressing him, their king, far below the rank of a subject to the condition of a captive, without intention to restore him, as the chancellor of Scotland in a speech told him plainly at Newcastle, unless he granted fully all their demands, which they knew he never meant.

Nor did they treat, or think of treating, with him, till their hatred to the army that delivered them, not their love or duty to the king, joined them secretly with men sentenced so oft for reprobates in their own mouths, by whose subtle inspiring they grew mad upon a most tardy and improper treaty. Whereas if the whole bent of their actions had not been against the king himself, but only against his evil counsellors, as they feigned, and published, wherefore did they not restore him all that while to the true life of a king, his office, crown, and dignity, when he was in their power, and they themselves his nearest counsellors? The truth, therefore, is, both that they would not, and that indeed they could not without their own certain destruction, having reduced him to such a final pass, as was the very death and burial of all in him that was regal, and from whence never king of England yet revived, but by the new reinforcement of his own party, which was a kind of resurrection to him.

Thus having quite extinguished all that could be in him of a king, and from a total privation clad him over, like another specifical thing, with forms and habitudes destructive to the former, they left in his person, dead as to law and all the civil right either of king or subject, the life only of a prisoner, a captive, and a malefactor: whom the equal and impartial hand of justice finding, was no more to spare than another ordinary man: not only made obnoxious to the doom of law, by a charge more than once drawn up against him, and his own confession to the first article at Newport, but summoned and arraigned in the sight of God and his people, cursed and devoted to perdition worse than any Ahab, or Antiochus, with exhortation to curse all those in the name of God, that made not war against him, as bitterly as Meroz was to be cursed, that went not out against a Canaanitish king, almost in all the sermons, prayers, and fulminations, that have been uttered this seven years, by those cloven tongues of falsehood and dissension, who now, to the stirring up of new discord, acquit him; and against their own discipline, which they boast to be the throne and sceptre of Christ, absolve him, unconfound him, though unconverted, unrepentant, unsensible of all their precious saints and martyrs, whose blood they have so often laid upon his head. And now again, with a new sovereign anointment, can wash it all off, as if it were as vile, and no more to be reckoned for than the blood of so many dogs in a time of pestilence: giving the most opprobious lie to all the acted zeal that for these many years hath filled their bellies, and fed them fat upon the foolish people. Ministers of sedition, not of the gospel, who, while they saw it manifestly tend to civil war and bloodshed, never ceased exasperating the people against him; and now that they see it likely to breed new commotion, cease not to incite others against the people, that have saved them from him, as if sedition were their only aim, whether against him or for him.

But God, as we have cause to trust, will put other thoughts into the people, and turn them from giving ear or heed to these mercenary noisemakers, of whose fury and false prophecies we have enough experience; and from the murmurs of new discord will incline them to hearken rather with erected minds to the voice of our supreme magistracy, calling us to liberty, and the flourishing deeds of a reformed commonwealth; with this hope, that as God was heretofore angry with the Jews who rejected him and his form of government to choose a king, so that he will bless us, and be propitious to us, who reject a king to make him only our leader, and supreme governor, in the conformity, as near as may be, of his own ancient government; if we have at least but so much worth in us to entertain the sense of our future happiness, and the courage to receive what God vouchsafes us; wherein we have the honor to precede other nations, who are now laboring to be our followers.

For as to this question in hand, what the people by their just right may do in change of government, or of governor, we see it cleared sufficiently besides other ample authority, even from the mouths of princes themselves. And surely they that shall boast, as we do, to be a free nation, and not have in themselves the power to remove or to abolish any governor supreme, or subordinate, with the government itself upon urgent causes, may please their fancy with a ridiculous and painted freedom, fit to cozen babies; but are indeed under tyranny and servitude, as wanting that power, which is the root and source of all liberty, to dispose and economize in the land which God hath given them, as masters of family in their own house and free inheritance. Without which natural and essential power of a free nation, though bearing high their heads, they can in due esteem be thought no better than slaves and vassals born, in the tenure and occupation of another inheriting lord; whose government, though not illegal, or intolerable, hangs over them as a lordly scourge, not as a free government; and therefore to be abrogated.

How much more justly then may they fling off tyranny, or tyrants; who being once deposed can be no more than private men, as subject to the reach of justice and arraignment as any other transgressors? And certainly if men, not to speak of heathen, both wise and religious, have done justice upon tyrants what way they could soonest, how much more mild and human then is it, to give them fair and open trial; to teach lawless kings, and all who so much adore them, that not mortal man, or his imperious will, but justice, is the only true sovereign and supreme majesty upon earth? Let men cease therefore, out of faction and hypocrisy, to make outcries and horrid things of things so just and honorable. Though perhaps till now, no protestant state or kingdom can be alleged to have openly put to death their king, which lately some have written, and imputed to their great glory; much mistaking the matter. It is not, neither ought to be, the glory of a protestant state never to have put their king to death; it is the glory of a protestant king never to have deserved death. And if the parliament and military council do what they do without precedent, if it appear their duty, it argues the more wisdom, virtue, and magnanimity, that they know themselves able to be a precedent to others; who perhaps in future ages, if they prove not too degenerate, will look up with honor, and aspire towards these exemplary and matchless deeds of their ancestors, as to the highest top of their civil glory and emulation; which heretofore, in the pursuance of fame and foreign dominion, spent itself vaingloriously abroad; but henceforth may learn a better fortitude, to dare execute highest justice on them that shall by force of arms endeavor the oppressing and bereaving of religion and their liberty at home. That no unbridled potentate or tyrant, but to his sorrow, for the future may presume such high and irresponsible licence over mankind, to havoc and turn upside down whole kingdoms of men, as though they were no more in respect of his perverse will than a nation of pismires.

As for the party called presbyterian, of whom I believe very many to be good and faithful Christians, though misled by some of turbulent spirit, I wish them, earnestly and calmly, not to fall off from their first principles, nor to affect rigor and superiority over men not under them; not to compel unforcible things, in religion especially, which, if not voluntary, becomes a sin; nor to assist the clamor and malicious drifts of men whom they themselves have judged to be the worst of men, the obdurate enemies of God and his church: nor to dart against the actions of their brethren, for want of other argument, those wrested laws and scriptures thrown by prelates and malignants against their own sides, which though they hurt not otherwise, yet taken up by them to the condemnation of their own doings, give scandal to all men, and discover in themselves either extreme passion or apostasy. Let them not oppose their best friends and associates, who molest them not at all, infringe not the least of their liberties, unless they call it their liberty to bind other men's consciences, but are still seeking to live at peace with them and brotherly accord. Let them beware an old and perfect enemy, who, though he hope by sowing discord to make them his instruments, yet cannot forbear a minute the open threatening of his destined revenge upon them, when they have served his purposes. Let them fear therefore, if they be wise, rather what they have done already, than what remains to do, and be warned in time they put no confidence in princes whom they have provoked, lest they be added to the examples of those that miserably have tasted the event.

Stories can inform them how Christiern the Second, king of Denmark, not much above a hundred years past, driven out by his subjects, and received again upon new oaths and conditions, broke through them all to his most bloody revenge; slaying his chief opposers, when he saw his time, both them and their children, invited to a feast for that purpose. How Maximilian dealt with those of Bruges, though by meditation of the German princes reconciled to them by solemn and public writings drawn and sealed. How the massacre at Paris was the effect of that credulous peace, which the French protestants made with Charles IX. their king: and that the main visible cause, which to this day hath saved the Netherlands from utter ruin, was their final not believing the perfidious cruelty, which, as a constant maxim of state, hath been used by the Spanish kings on their subjects that have taken arms, and after trusted them; as no later age but can testify, heretofore in Belgia itself, and this very year in Naples. And to conclude with one past exception, though far more ancient, David, whose sanctified prudence might be alone sufficient, not to warrant us only, but to instruct us, when once he had taken arms, never after that trusted Saul, though with tears and much relenting he twice promised not to hurt him. These instances, few of many, might admonish them, both English and Scotch, not to let their own ends, and the driving on of a faction, betray them blindly into the snare of those enemies whose revenge looks on them as the men who first begun, fomented, and carried on, beyond the cure of any sound or safe accommodation, all the evil which hath since unavoidably befallen them and their king.

I have something also to the divines, though brief to what were needful; not to be disturbers of the civil affairs, being in hands better able and more belonging to manage them; but to study harder, and to attend the office of good pastors, knowing that he, whose flock is least among them, hath a dreadful charge, not performed by mounting twice into the chair with a formal preachment huddled up at the odd hours of a whole lazy week, but by incessant pains and watching, in season and out of season, from house to house, over the souls of whom they have to feed. Which if they ever well considered, how little leisure would they find, to be the most pragmatical sidesmen of every popular tumult and sedition! and all this while are to learn what the true end and reason is of the gospel which they teach; and what a world it differs from the censorious and supercilious lording over conscience. It would be good also they lived so as might persuade the people they hated covetousness, which, worse than heresy, is idolatry; hated pluralities, and all kind of simony; left rambling from benefice to benefice, like ravenous wolves seeking where they may devour the biggest. Of which if some, well and warmly seated from the beginning, be not guilty, 'twere good they held not conversation with such as are. Let them be sorry, that, being called to assemble about reforming the church, they fell to progging and soliciting the parliament, though they had renounced the name of priests, for a new settling of their tithes and oblations; and double-lined themselves with spiritual places of commodity beyond the possible discharge of their duty. Let them assemble in consistory with their elders and deacons, according to ancient ecclesiastical rule, to the preserving of church discipline, each in his several charge, and not a pack of clergymen by themselves to bellycheer in their presump-

tuous Sion, or to promote designs, abuse and
gull the simple laity, and stir up tumult, as
the prelates did, for the maintenance of their
pride and avarice.

These things if they observe, and wait with
patience, no doubt but all things will go well
without their importunities or exclamations;
and the printed letters, which they send subscribed with the ostentation of great characters and little moment, would be more considerable than now they are. But if they be
the ministers of mammon instead of Christ,
and scandalize his church with the filthy love
of gain, aspiring also to sit the closest and
the heaviest of all tyrants upon the conscience, and fall notoriously into the same
sins, whereof so lately and so loud they accused the prelates; as God rooted out those
wicked ones immediately before, so will he
root out them, their imitators; and, to vindicate his own glory and religion, will uncover
their hypocrisy to the open world; and visit
upon their own heads that "Curse ye Meroz,"
the very motto of their pulpits, wherewith so
frequently, not as Meroz, but more like atheists, they have blasphemed the vengeance of
God, and traduced the zeal of his people.

And that they be not what they go for,
true ministers of the protestant doctrine,
taught by those abroad, famous and religious
men, who first reformed the church, or by
those no less zealous, who withstood corruption and the bishops here at home, branded
with the name of puritans and nonconformists, we shall abound with testimonies to make
appear that men may yet more fully know
the difference between protestant divines and
these pulpit-firebrands. "Such is the state
of things at this day, that men neither can,
nor will, nor indeed, ought to endure longer
the domination of you princes," * "Neither is
Cæsar to make war as head of Christendom,
protector of the church, defender of the
faith; these titles being false and windy, and
most kings being the greatest enemies to religion." * What hinders then, but that we may
depose or punish them? These also are recited by Cochlæus in his Miscellanies to be
the words of Luther, or some other eminent

divine, then in Germany, when the protestants
there entered into solemn covenant at Smal-
caldia: "Ut ora iis obturem," &c. "That I
may stop their mouths, the pope and emperor
are not born, but elected; and may also be
deposed, as hath been often done." If Luther,
or whoever else, thought so, he could not stay
there; for the right of birth or succession can
be no privilege in nature, to let a tyrant sit
irremovable over a nation freeborn, without
transforming that nation from the nature and
condition of men born free, into natural,
hereditary, and successive slaves. Therefore
he saith further; "To displace and throw
down this exactor, this Phalaris, this Nero,
is a work well pleasing to God;" namely, for
being such a one: which is a moral reason.
Shall then so slight a consideration as his hap
to be not elective simply, but by birth, which
was a mere accident, overthrow that which
is moral, and make unpleasing to God that
which otherwise had so well pleased him?
Certainly not: for if the matter be rightly
argued, election, much rather than chance,
binds a man to content himself with what he
suffers by his own bad election. Though indeed neither the one nor other binds any man,
much less any people, to a necessary sufferance of those wrongs and evils, which they
have ability and strength enough given them
to remove.

"When kings reign perfidiously, and against
the rule of Christ, they may, according to
the word of God be deposed." † "I know not
how it comes to pass that kings reign by succession, unless it be with consent of the whole
people." ‡ "But when by suffrage and consent
of the whole people, or the better part of
them, a tyrant is deposed or put to death, God
is the chief leader in that action." § "Now
that we are so lukewarm in upholding public
justice, we endure the vices of tyrants to
reign now-a-days with impunity; justly therefore by them we are trod underfoot, and shall
at length with them be punished. Yet ways
are not wanting by which tyrants may be removed, but there wants public justice." *
"Beware, ye tyrants! for now the gospel of
Jesus Christ, spreading far and wide, will

* "Is est hodie rerum status, &c.—Luther. Lib. contra rusticos apud Sleidan. l. 5.
* "Neque vero Cæsarem," &c.—Lib. de Bello contra Turcas, apud Sleid. l. xiv.
† "Quando vero perfidè," &c.—Zwinglius, tom. i. articul. 42.
‡ "Mihi ergo compertum non est," &c.—Ibid.
§ "Quum vero consensu," &c.—Ibid.
* "Nunc cum tam tepidi sumus," &c.—Zwinglius.

renew the lives of many to love innocence and justice; which if ye also shall do, ye shall be honored. But if ye shall go on to rage and do violence, ye shall be trampled on by all men." † "When the Roman empire, or any other, shall begin to oppress religion, and we negligently suffer it, we are as much guilty of religion so violated, as the oppressors themselves." ‡

"Now-a-days monarchs pretend always in their titles to be kings by the grace of God; but how many of them to this end only pretend it, that they may reign without control! For to what purpose is the grace of God mentioned in the title of kings, but that they may acknowledge no superior? In the meanwhile God, whose name they use to support themselves, they willingly would tread under their feet. It is therefore a mere cheat, when they boast to reign by the grace of God." § "Earthly princes depose themselves, while they rise against God; yea, they are unworthy to be numbered among men: rather it behooves us to spit upon their heads, than to obey them." ‖

"If a sovereign prince endeavor by arms to defend transgressors, to subvert those things which are taught in the word of God, they, who are in authority under him, ought first to dissuade him; if they prevail not, and that he now bears himself not as a prince but as an enemy, and seeks to violate privileges and rights granted to inferior magistrates or commonalties, it is the part of pious magistrates, imploring first the assistance of God, rather to try all ways and means, than to betray the flock of Christ to such an enemy of God: for they also are to this end ordained, that they may defend the people of God, and maintain those things which are good and just. For to have supreme power lessens not the evil committed by that power, but makes it the less tolerable, by how much the more generally hurtful.* Then certainly the less tolerable, the more unpardonably to be punished." Of Peter Martyr we have spoken before. "They whose part it is to set up magistrates, may restrain them also from outrageous deeds, or pull them down; but all magistrates are set up either by parliament or by electors, or by other magistrates; they, therefore, who exalted them may lawfully degrade and punish them." †

Of the Scots divines I need not mention others than the famousest among them, Knox, and his fellow-laborers in the reformation of Scotland; whose large treatises on this subject defend the same opinion. To cite them sufficiently, were to insert their whole books, written purposely on this argument. "Knox's Appeal;" and "to the reader;" where he promises in a postscript, that the book which he intended to set forth, called, "The Second Blast of the Trumpet," should maintain more at large, that the same men most justly may depose and punish him whom unadvisedly they have elected, notwithstanding birth, succession, or any oath of allegiance. Among our own divines, Cartwright and Fenner, two of the learnedest, may in reason satisfy us what was held by the rest. Fenner, in his book of Theology, maintaining, that they who have power, that is to say, a parliament, may either by fair means or by force depose a tyrant, whom he defines to be him that wilfully breaks all or the principal conditions made between him and the commonwealth.* And Cartwright, in a prefixed epistle, testifies his approbation of the whole book.

"Kings have their authority of the people, who may upon occasion reassume it to themselves." † "The people may kill wicked princes, as monsters and cruel beasts." ‡ "When kings or rulers become blasphemers of God, oppressors and murderers of their subjects, they ought no more to be accounted kings, or lawful magistrates, but as private men to be examined, accused, condemned and punished by the law of God; and being convicted and punished by that law, it is not man's but God's doing." § "By the civil laws, a fool or idiot born, and so proved, shall lose the lands and inheritance whereto he is born, because he is not able to use them aright:

† "Cavete vobis ô tyranni."—Ibid.
‡ "Romanum imperium imô quodque," &c.—Idem. Epist. ad Conrad Somium.
§ "Hodie monarchæ semper in suis titulis," &c.—Calvin on Daniel c. iv. v. 25.
‖ "Abdicant se terreni principes," &c.—On Dan. c. vi. v. 22.
* "Si princeps superior," &c.—Bucer on Matth. c. v.
† "Quorum est constituere magistratus," &c.—Paræus in Rom. xiii.
* Fen. Sac. Theolog. c. 13.
† Gilby de Obedientiâ, p. 25 and 105.
‡ England's Complaint against the Canons.
§ Christopher Goodman of Obedience, c. x. p. 139.

and especially ought in no case be suffered to have the government of a whole nation; but there is no such evil can come to the commonwealth by fools and idiots, as doth by the rage and fury of ungodly rulers; such, therefore, being without God, ought to have no authority over God's people, who by his word requireth the contrary." ‖ "No person is exempt by any law of God from this punishment: be he king, queen, or emperor, he must die the death; for God hath not placed them above others, to transgress his laws as they list, but to be subject to them as well as others; and if they be subject to his laws, then to the punishment also, so much the more as their example is more dangerous." ¶ "When magistrates cease to do their duty, the people are, as it were, without magistrates, yea, worse, and then God giveth the sword into the people's hand, and he himself is become immediately their head." * "If princes do right, and keep promise with you, then do you owe to them all humble obedience; if not, ye are discharged, and your study ought to be in this case how ye may depose and punish according to the law such rebels against God, and oppressors of their country." †

This Goodman was a minister of the English church at Geneva, as Dudley Fenner was at Middleburgh, or some other place in that country. These were the pastors of those saints and confessors, who, flying from the bloody persecution of Queen Mary, gathered up at length their scattered members into many congregations; whereof some in Upper, some in Lower Germany, part of them settled at Geneva; where this author having preached on this subject, to the great liking of certain learned and godly men who heard him, was by them sundry times and with much instance required to write more fully on that point. Who thereupon took it in hand, and conferring with the best learned in those parts, (among whom Calvin was then living in the same city,) with their special approbation he published this treatise, aiming principally, as is testified by Whittingham in the Preface, that his brethren of England, the protestants, might be persuaded in the truth of that doctrine concerning obedience to magistrates.‡

These were the true protestant divines of England, our fathers in the faith we hold; this was their sense, who for so many years laboring under prelacy, through all storms and persecutions, kept religion from extinguishing; and delivered it pure to us, till there arose a covetous and ambitious generation of divines, (for divines they call themselves!) who, feigning on a sudden to be new converts and proselytes from episcopacy, under which they had long temporised, opened their mouths at length, in show against pluralities and prelacy, but with intent to swallow them down both; gorging themselves like harpies on those simonious places and preferments of their outed predecessors as the quarry for which they hunted, not to plurality only but to multiplicity; for possessing which they had accused them, their brethren, and aspiring under another title to the same authority and usurpation over the consciences of all men.

Of this faction, divers reverend and learned divines (as they are styled in the philactery of their own title-page) pleading the lawfulness of defensive arms against this king, in a treatise called "Scripture and Reason," seem in words to disclaim utterly the deposing of a king; but both the scripture, and the reasons which they use, draw consequences after them, which, without their bidding, conclude it lawful. For if by scripture, and by that especially to the Romans, which they most insist upon, kings, doing that which is contrary to St. Paul's definition of a magistrate, may be resisted, they may altogether with as much force of consequence be deposed or punished. And if by reason the unjust authority of kings "may be forfeited in part, and his power be reassumed in part, either by the parliament or people, for the case in hazard and the present necessity," as they affirm, p. 34, there can no scripture be alleged, no imaginable reason given, that necessity continuing, as it may always, and they in all prudence and their duty may take upon them to foresee it, why in such a case they may not finally amerce him with the loss of his kingdom, of whose amendment they have no hope. And if one wicked action persisted in against religion, laws, and liberties, may warrant us to thus much in part, why may not forty

‖ C. xi. 143, 144
* P. 185.
¶ C. xiii. p. 184.
† P. 190.
‡ Whittingham in Prefat.

times as many tyrannies, by him committed, warrant us to proceed on restraining him, till the restraint become total? For the ways of justice are exactest proportion; if for one trespass of a king it require so much remedy or satisfaction, then for twenty more as heinous crimes, it requires of him twenty-fold; and so proportionably, till it come to what is utmost among men. If in these proceedings against their king they may not finish, by the usual course of justice, what they have begun, they could not lawfully begin at all. For this golden rule of justice and morality, as well as of arithmetic, out of three terms which they admit, will as certainly and unavoidably bring out the fourth as any problem that ever Euclid or Appollonius made good by demonstration.

And if the parliament, being undeposable but by themselves, as is affirmed, p. 37, 38, might for his whole life, if they saw cause, take all power, authority, and the sword out of his hand, which in effect is to unmagistrate him, why might they not, being then themselves the sole magistrates in force, proceed to punish him, who, being lawfully deprived of all things that define a magistrate, can be now no magistrate to be degraded lower, but an offender to be punished. Lastly, whom they may defy, and meet in battle, why may they not as well prosecute by justice? For lawful war is but the execution of justice against them who refuse law. Among whom if it be lawful (as they deny not, p. 19, 20,) to slay the king himself coming in front at his own peril, wherefore may not justice do that intendedly, which the chance of a defensive war might without blame have done casually, nay, purposely, if there it find him among the rest? They ask, p. 19, "By what rule of conscience or God a state is bound to sacrifice religion, laws, and liberties, rather than a prince defending such as subvert them, should come in hazard of his life." And I ask by what conscience, or divinity, or law, or reason, a state is bound to leave all these sacred concernments under a perpetual hazard and extremity of danger, rather than cut off a wicked prince, who sits plotting day and night to subvert them.

They tell us, that the law of nature justifies any man to defend himself, even against the king in person: let them show us then, why the same law may not justify much more a state or whole people, to do justice upon him, against whom each private man may lawfully defend himself; seeing all kind of justice done is a defence to good men, as well as a punishment to bad; and justice done upon a tyrant is no more but the necessary self-defence of a whole commonwealth. To war upon a king, that his instruments may be brought to condign punishment, and thereafter to punish them the instruments, and not to spare only, but to defend and honor him the author, is the strangest piece of justice to be called Christian, and the strangest piece of reason to be called human, that by men of reverence and learning, as their style imports them, ever yet was vented. They maintain in the third and fourth section, that a judge or inferior magistrate is anointed of God, is his minister, hath the sword in his hand, is to be obeyed by St. Peter's rule, as well as the supreme, and without difference anywhere expressed: and yet will have us fight against the supreme till he remove and punish the inferior magistrate; (for such were greatest delinquents;) whenas by scripture, and by reason, there can no more authority be shown to resist the one than the other; and altogether as much, to punish or depose the supreme himself, as to make war upon him, till he punish or deliver up his inferior magistrates, whom in the same terms we are commanded to obey, and not to resist.

Thus while they, in a cautious line or two here and there stuffed in, are only verbal against the pulling down or punishing of tyrants, all the scripture and the reason which they bring, is in every leaf direct and rational, to infer it altogether as lawful, as to resist them. And yet in all their sermons, as hath by others been well noted, they went much further. For divines if ye observe them have their postures, and their motions no less expertly, and with no less variety, than they that practise feats in the Artillery-ground. Sometimes they seem furiously to march on, and presently march counter: by and by they stand, and then retreat; or if need be, can face about, or wheel in a whole body, with that cunning and dexterity as is almost unperceivable, to wind themselves by shifting ground into places of more advantage. And providence only must be the drum, providence the word of command, that calls them from above, but always to some larger benefice, or acts them into such or such figures and promotions. At their turns and doublings no men readier, to the right, or to the left; for it is their turns which they serve chiefly; herein only singular, that with them there is no certain hand right or left, but as their own commodity thinks best to call it. But if there come a truth to be defended, which to them and their interest of this world seems not so profitable, straight these nimble motionists can find no even legs to stand upon; and are no more of use to reformation thoroughly performed, and not superficially, or to the advancement of truth, (which among mortal men is always in her progress,) than if on a sudden they were struck maim and crippled.

Which the better to conceal, or the more to countenance by a general conformity to their own limping, they would have scripture, they would have reason also made to halt with them for company; and would put us off with impotent conclusions, lame and shorter than the premises.

In this posture they seem to stand with great zeal and confidence on the wall of Sion; but like Jebusites, not like Israelites, or Levites: blind also as well as lame, they discern not David from Adonibezec: but cry him up for the Lord's anointed, whose thumbs and great toes not long before they had cut off upon their pulpit cushions. Therefore he who is our only King, the Root of David, and whose kingdom is eternal righteousness, with all those that war under him, whose happiness and final hopes are laid up in that only just and rightful kingdom, (which we pray incessantly may come soon, and in so praying wish hasty ruin and destruction to all tyrants,) even he our immortal King, and all that love him, must of necessity have in abomination these blind and lame defenders of Jerusalem; as the soul of David hated them, and forbid them entrance into God's house, and his own. But as to those before them, which I cited first (and with an easy search, for many more might be added) as they there stand, without more in number, being the best and chief of protestant divines, we may follow them for faithful guides, and without doubt-

ing may receive them, as witnesses abundant of what we here affirm concerning tyrants. And indeed I find it generally the clear and positive determination of them all, (not prelatical, or of this late faction subprelatical,) who have written on this argument; that to do justice on a lawless king is to a private man unlawful; to an inferior magistrate lawful: or if they were divided in opinion, yet greater than these here alleged, or of more authority in the church, there can be none produced.

If any one shall go about, by bringing other testimonies to disable these, or by bringing these against themselves in other cited passages of their books, he will not only fail to make good that false and impudent assertion of those mutinous ministers, that the deposing and punishing of a king or tyrant "is against the constant judgment of all protestant divines," it being quite the contrary; but will prove rather what perhaps he intended not, that the judgment of divines, if it be so various and inconstant to itself, is not considerable, or to be esteemed at all. Ere which be yielded, as I hope it never will, these ignorant assertors in their own art will have proved themselves more and more, not to be protestant divines, whose constant judgment in this point they have so audaciously belied, but rather to be a pack of hungry churchwolves, who in the steps of Simon Magus their father, following the hot scent of double livings and pluralities, advowsons, donatives, inductions, and augmentations, though uncalled to the flock of Christ, but by the mere suggestion of their bellies, like those priests of Bel, whose pranks Daniel found out; have got possession, or rather seized upon the pulpit, as the stronghold and fortress of their sedition and rebellion against the civil magistrate. Whose friendly and victorious hand having rescued them from the bishops, their insulting lords, fed them plentously, both in public and in private, raised them to be high and rich of poor and base; only suffered not their covetousness and fierce ambition (which as the pit that sent out their fellow-locusts hath been ever bottomless and boundless) to interpose in all things, and over all persons, their impetuous ignorance and importunity?

EIKONOKLASTES:

IN ANSWER TO A BOOK ENTITLED

"EIKON BASILIKE,

THE PORTRAITURE OF HIS SACRED MAJESTY IN HIS SOLITUDES AND SUFFERINGS."

"As a roaring lion and raging bear, so is a wicked ruler over the poor people.

"The prince that wanteth understanding, is also a great oppressor; but he that hateth covetousness, shall prolong his days.

"A man that doth violence to the blood of any person, shall fly to the pit, let no man stay him."—PROV. xxviii. 15, 16, 17.

SALLUST. CONJURAT. CATLIN.

"Regium imperium, quod initio, conservandæ libertatis, atque augendæ reipublicæ causâ fuerat, in superbiam, dominationemque, se convertit.

"Regibus boni, quam mali suspectiores sunt, semperque his aliena virtus formidolosa est.

"Impunè quælibet facere, id est regem esse."

IDEM, BELL. JUGURTH.

PUBLISHED BY AUTHORITY.

[The text is that of the second edition, 1650.]

THE PREFACE.

To descant on the misfortunes of a person fallen from so high a dignity, who hath also paid his final debt both to nature and his faults, is neither of itself a thing commendable, nor the intention of this discourse. Neither was it fond ambition, or the vanity to get a name, present or with posterity, by writing against a king: I never was so thirsty after fame, nor so destitute of other hopes and means, better and more certain to attain it; for kings have gained glorious titles from their favorers by writing against private men, as Henry VIII. did against Luther; but no man ever gained much honor by writing against a king, as not usually meeting with that force of argument in such courtly antagonists, which to convince might add to his reputation. Kings most commonly, though strong in legions, are but weak at arguments; as they who ever have accustomed from the cradle to use their will only as their right hand, their reason always as their left. Whence unexpectedly constrained to that kind of combat, they prove but weak and puny adversaries: nevertheless, for their sakes, who through custom, simplicity, or want of better teaching, have not more seriously considered kings, than in the gaudy name of majesty, and admire them and their doings, as if they breathed not the same breath with other mortal men, I shall make no scruple to take up (for it seems to be the challenge both of him and all his party) to take up this gauntlet, though a king's, in the behalf of liberty and the commonwealth.

And further, since it appears manifestly the cunning drift of a factious and defeated party, to make the same advantage of his book which they did before of his regal name and authority, and intend it not so much the defence of his former actions, as the promoting of their own future designs; (making thereby the book their own rather than the king's, as the benefit now must be their own more than his;) now the third time to corrupt and disorder the minds of weaker men, by new suggestions and narrations, either falsely or fallaciously representing the state of things to the dishonor of this present government, and the retarding of a general peace, so needful to this afflicted nation, and so nigh obtained; I suppose it no injury to the dead, but a good deed rather to the living, if by better information given them, or, which is enough, by only remembering them the truth of what they themselves know to be here misaffirmed, they may be kept from entering the third time unadvisedly into war and bloodshed. For as to any moment of solidity in the book itself, (save only that a king is said to be the author, a name than which there needs no more among the blockish vulgar, to make it wise, and excellent, and admired, nay to set it next the Bible, though otherwise containing little else but the common grounds of tyranny and popery, dressed up the better to deceive, in a new protestant guise, and trimly garnished over,) or as to any need of answering, in respect of staid and well-principled men, I take it on me as a work assigned rather, than by me chosen or affected: which was the cause both of beginning it so late, and finishing it so leisurely in the midst of other employments and diversions.

And though well it might have seemed in vain to write at all, considering the envy and almost infinite prejudice likely to be stirred up among the common sort, against whatever can be written or gainsaid to the king's book, so advantageous to a book it is only to be a king's; and though it be an irksome labor, to write with industry and judicious pains, that which, neither weighed nor well read, shall be judged without industry or the pains of well-judging, by faction and the easy literature of custom and opinion; it shall be ventured yet, and the truth not smothered, but sent abroad, in the native confidence of her single self, to earn, how she can, her entertainment in the world, and to find out her own readers: few perhaps, but those few, such of value and substantial worth, as truth and wisdom, not respecting numbers and big names, have been ever wont in all ages to be contented with.

And if the late king had thought sufficient those answers and defences made for him in his lifetime, they who on the other side accused his evil government, judging that on their behalf enough also hath been replied, the heat of this controversy was in likelihood drawing to an end; and the further mention of his deeds, not so much unfortunate as faulty, had in tenderness to his late sufferings been willingly forborne; and perhaps for the present age might have slept with him unrepeated, while his adversaries, calmed and assuaged with the success of their cause, had been the less unfavorable to his memory. But since he himself, making new appeal to truth and the world, hath left behind him this book, as the best advocate and interpreter of his own actions, and that his friends, by publishing, dispersing, commending, and almost adoring it, seem to place therein the chief strength and nerves of their cause; it would argue doubtless in the other party great deficience and distrust of themselves, not to meet the force of his reason in any field whatsoever, the force and equipage of whose arms they have so often met victoriously. And he who at the bar stood excepting against the form and manner of his judicature, and complained that he was not heard; neither he nor his friends shall have that cause now to find fault, being met and debated with in this open and monumental court of his own erecting; and not only heard uttering his whole mind at large, but answered: which to do effectually, if it be necessary, that to his book nothing the more respect be had for being his, they of his own party can have no just reason to exclaim.

For it were too unreasonable that he, because dead, should have the liberty in his book to speak all evil of the parliament; and they, because living, should be expected to have less freedom, or any for them, to speak home the plain truth of a full and pertinent reply. As he, to acquit himself, hath not spared his adversaries to load them with all sorts of blame and accusation, so to him, as in his book alive, there will be used no more courtship than he uses; but what is properly his own guilt, not imputed any more to his evil counsellors, (a ceremony used longer by the parliament than he himself desired,) shall be laid here without circumlocutions at his own door. That they who from the first beginning, or but now of late, by what unhappiness I know not, are so much affatuated, not with his person only, but with his palpable faults, and dote upon his deformities, may have none to blame but their own folly, if they live and die in such a stricken blindness, as next to that of Sodom hath not happened to any sort of men more gross, or more misleading. Yet neither let his enemies expect to find recorded here all that hath been whispered in the court, or alleged openly, of the king's bad actions; it being the proper scope of this work in hand, not to rip up and relate the misdoings of his whole life, but to answer only and refute the missayings of his book.

First, then, that some men (whether this were by him intended, or by his friends) have by policy accomplished after death that revenge upon their enemies, which in life they were not able, hath been oft related. And among other examples we find, that the last will of Cæsar being read to the people, and what bounteous legacies he had bequeathed them, wrought more in that vulgar audience to the avenging of his death, than all the art he could ever use to win their favor in his lifetime. And how much their intent, who published these over-late apologies and meditations of the dead king, drives to the same end of stirring up the people to bring him that honor, that affection and by consequence that revenge to his dead corpse, which he himself living could never gain to his person, it appears both by the conceited portraiture before his book, drawn out to the full measure of a masking scene, and set there to catch fools and silly gazers; and by those Latin words after the end, *Vota dabunt quæ bella negarunt;* intimating, that what he could not compass by war, he should achieve by his meditations: for in words which admit of various sense, the liberty is ours, to choose that interpretation, which may best mind us of what our restless enemies endeavor, and what we are timely to prevent.

And here may be well observed the loose and negligent curiosity of those, who took upon them to adorn the setting out of this book; for though the picture set in front would martyr him and saint him to befool the people, yet the Latin motto in the end, which they understand not, leaves him, as it were, a politic contriver to bring about that interest, by fair and plausible words, which the force of arms denied him. But quaint emblems and devices, begged from the old pageantry of some twelfthnight's entertainment at Whitehall, will do but ill to make a saint or martyr: and if the people resolve to take him sainted at the rate of such a canonizing, I shall suspect their calendar more than the Gregorian. In one thing I must commend his openness, who gave the title to this book, Εικών Βασιλική, that is to say, The King's Image; and by the shrine he dresses out for him, certainly would have the people come and worship him. For which reason this answer also is entitled, Eikonoklastes, the famous surname of many Greek emperors, who, in their zeal to the command of God, after long tradition of idolatry in the church, took courage and broke all superstitious images to pieces.

But the people, exorbitant and excessive in all their motions, are prone ofttimes not to a religious only, but to a civil kind of idolatry, in idolizing their kings: though never more mistaken in the object of their worship; heretofore being wont to repute for saints those faithful and courageous barons, who

lost their lives in the field, making glorious war against tyrants for the common liberty; as Simon de Montfort, Earl of Leicester, against Henry III.; Thomas Plantagenet, Earl of Lancaster, against Edward II. But now, with a besotted and degenerate baseness of spirit, except some few who yet retain in them the old English fortitude and love of freedom, and have testified it by their matchless deeds, the rest, imbastardized from the ancient nobleness of their ancestors, are ready to fall flat, and give adoration to the image and memory of this man, who hath offered at more cunning fetches to undermine our liberties, and put tyranny into an art, than any British king before him. Which low dejection and debasement of mind in the people, I must confess, I cannot willingly ascribe to the natural disposition of an Englishman, but rather to two other causes; first, to the prelates and their fellow-teachers, though of another name and sect, whose pulpit-stuff, both first and last, hath been the doctrine and perpetual infusion of servility and wretchedness to all their hearers; whose lives the type of worldliness and hypocrisy, without the least true pattern of virtue, righteousness, or self-denial in their whole practice. I attribute it, next to the factious inclination of most men divided from the public by several ends and humors of their own.

At first no man less beloved, no man more generally condemned, than was the king; from the time that it became his custom to break parliaments at home, and either wilfully or weakly to betray protestants abroad, to the beginning of these combustions. All men inveighed against him; all men, except court-vassals, opposed him and his tyrannical proceedings; the cry was universal; and this full parliament was at first unanimous in their dislike and protestation against his evil government. But when they, who sought themselves and not the public, began to doubt, that all of them could not by one and the same way attain to their ambitious purposes, then was the king, or his name at least, as a fit property, first made use of, his doings made the best of, and by degrees justified; which begot him such a party, as, after many wiles and strugglings with his inward fears, emboldened him at length to set up his standard against the parliament: when-as before that time, all his adherents, consisting most of dissolute swordmen and suburb-roysterers, hardly amounted to the making up of one ragged regiment strong enough to assault the unarmed house of commons. After which attempt seconded by a tedious and bloody war on his subjects, wherein he hath so far exceeded those his arbitrary violences in time of peace, they who before hated him for his high misgovernment, nay, fought against him with displayed banners in the field, now applaud him and extol him for the wisest and most religious prince that lived. By so strange a method amongst the mad multitude is a sudden reputation won, of wisdom by wilfulness and subtle shifts, of goodness by multiplying evil, of piety by endeavoring to root out true religion.

But it is evident that the chief of his adherents never loved him, never honored either him or his cause, but as they took him to set a face upon their own malignant designs, nor bemoan his loss at all, but the loss of their own aspiring hopes: like those captive women, whom the poet notes in his Illiad, to have bewailed the death of Patroclus in outward show, but indeed their own condition.

Πάτροκλον πρόφασιν, σφῶν δ' αὐτῶν κήδε' ἑκάστη.
        Hom. Iliad. τ. 302.

And it needs must be ridiculous to any judgment unenthralled, that they, who in other matters express so little fear either of God or man, should in this one particular outstrip all precisianism with their scruples and cases, and fill men's ears continually with the noise of their conscientious loyalty and allegiance to the king, rebels in the meanwhile to God in all their actions besides: much less that they, whose professed loyalty and allegiance led them to direct arms against the king's person, and thought him nothing violated by the sword of hostility drawn by them against him, should now in earnest think him violated by the unsparing sword of justice, which undoubtedly so much the less in vain she bears among men, by how much greater and in highest place the offender. Else justice, whether moral or political, were not justice, but a false counterfeit of that impartial and godlike virtue. The only grief is, that the head was not struck off to the best advantage and commodity of them that held it by the hair: an ingrateful and perverse generation, who having first cried to God to be delivered from their king, now murmur against God that heard their prayers, and cry as loud for their king against those that delivered them.

But as to the author of these soliloquies, whether it were undoubtedly the late king, as is vulgarly believed, or any secret coadjutor, and some stick not to name him; it can add nothing, nor shall take from the weight, if any be, of reason which he brings. But allegations, not reasons, are the main contents of this book, and need no more than other contrary allegations to lay the question before all men in an even balance; though it were supposed, that the testimony of one man, in his own cause affirming, could be of any moment to bring in doubt the authority of a parliament denying. But if these his fair-spoken words shall be here fairly confronted, and laid parallel to his own far differing deeds, manifest and visible to the whole nation, then surely we may look on them who, notwithstanding, shall persist to give to bare words more credit than to open deeds, as men whose judgment was not rationally evinced and persuaded, but fatally stupefied and bewitched into such a blind and obstinate belief: for whose cure it may be doubted, not whether any charm, though never so wisely murmured, but whether any prayer can be available.

This however would be remembered and well noted, that while the king, instead of that repentance which was in reason and in conscience to be expected from him, without which we could not lawfully readmit him, persists here to maintain and justify the most apparent of his evil-doings, and washes over with a court-fucus the worst and foulest of his actions, disables and uncreates the parliament itself, with all our laws and native liberties that ask not his leave, dishonors and attaints all protestant churches not prelatical and what they piously reformed, with the slander of rebellion, sacrilege, and hypocrisy; they, who seemed of late to stand up hottest for the covenant, can now sit mute and much pleased to hear all these opprobrious things uttered against their faith, their freedom, and themselves in their own doings made traitors to boot. The divines, also, their wizards, can be so brazen as to cry Hosanna to this his book, which cries louder against them for no disciples of Christ, but of Iscariot; and to seem now convinced with these withered arguments and reasons here, the same which in some other writings of that party, and in his own former declarations and expresses, they have so often heretofore endeavored to confute and to explode; none appearing all this while to vindicate church or state from these calumnies and reproaches but a small handful of men, whom they defame and spit at with all the odious names of schism and sectarism. I never knew that time in England, when men of truest religion were not counted sectaries: but wisdom now, valor, justice, constancy, prudence united and embodied to defend religion and our liberties, both by word and deed, against tyranny, is counted schism and faction.

Thus in a graceless age things of highest praise and imitation under a right name, to make them infamous and hateful to the people, are miscalled. Certainly, if ignorance and perverseness will needs be national and universal, then they who adhere to wisdom and to truth, are not therefore to be blamed, for being so few as to seem a sect or faction. But in my opinion it goes not ill with that people where these virtues grow so numerous and well joined together, as to resist and make head against the rage and torrent of that boisterous folly and superstition, that possesses and hurries on the vulgar sort. This therefore we may conclude to be a high honor done us from God, and a special mark of his favor, whom he hath selected as the sole remainder, after all these changes and commotions, to stand upright and steadfast in his cause; dignified with the defence of truth and public liberty; while others, who aspired to be the top of zealots, and had almost brought religion to a kind of trading monopoly, have not only by their late silence and neutrality belied their profession, but foundered themselves and their consciences, to comply with enemies in that wicked cause and interest, which they have too often cursed in others, to prosper now in the same themselves.

CHAPTER I.

Upon the King's calling this last Parliament.

THAT which the king lays down as his first foundation, and as it were the head-stone of his whole structure, that "he called this last parliament, not more by others' advice, and the necessity of his affairs, than by his own choice and inclination," is to all knowing men so apparently not true, that a more unlucky and inauspicious sentence, and more betokening the downfall of his whole fabric, hardly could have come into his mind. For who knows not, that the inclination of a prince is best known either by those next about him, and most in favor with him, or by the current of his own actions? Those nearest to this king, and most his favorites, were courtiers and prelates; men whose chief study was to find out which way the king inclined, and to imitate him exactly: how these men stood affected to parliaments cannot be forgotten. No man but may remember, it was their continual exercise to dispute and preach against them; and in their common discourse nothing was more frequent, than that "they hoped the king should now have no need of parliaments any more." And this was but the copy which his parasites had industriously taken from his own words and actions, who never called a parliament but to supply his necessities; and having supplied those, as suddenly and ignominiously dissolved it, without redressing any one grievance of the people; sometimes choosing rather to miss of his subsidies, or to raise them by illegal courses, than that the people should not still miss of their hopes to be relieved by parliaments.

The first he broke off at his coming to the crown, for no other cause than to protect the Duke of Buckingham against them who had accused him, besides other heinous crimes, of no less than poisoning the deceased king, his father; concerning which matter the declaration of "No more addresses" hath sufficiently informed us. And still the latter breaking was with more affront and indignity put upon the house and her worthiest members, than the former. Insomuch that in the fifth year of his reign, in a proclamation, he seems offended at the very rumor of a parliament divulged among the people; as if he had taken it for a kind of slander, that men should think him that way exorable, much less inclined: and forbids it as a presumption, to prescribe him any time for parliaments; that is to say, either by persuasion or petition, or so much as the reporting of such a rumor: for other manner of prescribing was at that time not suspected. By which fierce edict, the people, forbidden to complain, as well as forced to suffer, began from thenceforth to despair of parliaments. Whereupon such illegal actions, and especially to get vast sums of money, were put in practice by the king and his new officers, as monopolies, compulsive knighthoods, coat, conduct, and ship-money, the seizing not of one Naboth's vineyard, but of whole inheritances, under the pretence of forest or crown-lands; corruption and bribery compounded for, with impunities granted for the future, as gave evident proof, that the king never meant, nor could it stand with the reason of his affairs, ever to recall parliaments: having brought by these irregular courses the people's interest and his own to so direct an opposition, that he might foresee plainly, if nothing but a parliament could save the people, it must necessarily be his undoing.

Till eight or nine years after, proceeding with a high hand in these enormities, and having the second time levied an injurious war against his native country, Scotland; and finding all those other shifts of raising money, which bore out his first expedition, now to fail him, not "of his own choice and inclination," as any child may see, but urged by strong necessities, and the very pangs of state, which his own violent proceedings had brought him to, he calls a parliament; first in Ireland, which only was to give him four subsidies, and so to expire; then in England, where his first demand was but twelve subsidies, to maintain a Scots war, condemned and abominated by the whole kingdom: promising their grievances should be considered afterwards. Which when the parliament, who judged that war itself one of their main grievances, made no haste to grant, not enduring the delay of his impatient will, or else fearing the conditions of their grant, he breaks off the whole session, and dismisses them and their grievances with scorn and frustration.

Much less therefore did he call this last parliament by his own choice and inclination; but having first tried in vain all undue ways to procure money, his army of their own accord being beaten in the north, the lords petitioning, and the general voice of the people almost hissing him and his ill-acted regality off the stage, compelled at length both by his wants and by his fears, upon mere extremity he summoned this last parliament. And how is it possible, that he should willingly incline to parliaments, who never was perceived to call them but for the greedy hope of a whole national bribe, his subsidies; and never loved, never fulfilled, never promoted the true end of parliaments, the redress of grievances; but still put them off, and prolonged them, whether gratified or not gratified; and was indeed the author of all those grievances? To say, therefore, that he called this parliament of his own choice and inclination, argues how little truth we can expect from the sequel of this book, which ventures in the very first period to affront more than one nation with an untruth so remarkable; and presumes a more implicit faith in the people of England, than the pope ever commanded from the Romish laity; or else a natural sottishness fit to be abused and ridden: while in the judgment of wise men, by laying the foundation of his defence on the avouchment of that which is so manifestly untrue, he hath given a worse foil to his own cause, than when his whole forces were at any time overthrown. They, therefore, who think such great service done to the king's affairs in publishing this book, will find themselves in the end mistaken; if sense and right mind, or but any mediocrity of knowledge and remembrance, hath not quite forsaken men.

But to prove his inclination to parliaments, he affirms here, "to have always thought the right way of them most safe for his crown, and best pleasing to his people." What he thought, we know not, but that he ever took the contrary way we saw; and from his own actions we felt long ago what he thought of parliaments or of pleasing his people: a surer evidence than what we hear now too late in words.

He alleges, that "the cause of forbearing to convene parliaments was the sparks which some men's distempers there studied to kindle." They were indeed not tempered to his temper; for it neither was the law, nor the rule, by which all other tempers were to be tried; but they were esteemed and chosen for the fittest men, in their several counties, to allay and quench those distempers, which his own inordinate doings had inflamed. And if that were his refusing to convene, till those men had been qualified to his temper, that is to say, his will, we may easily conjecture what hope there was of parliaments, had not fear and his insatiate poverty, in the midst of his excessive wealth, constrained him.

"He hoped by his freedom and their moderation to prevent misunderstandings." And wherefore not by their freedom and his moderation? But freedom he thought too high a word for them, and moderation too mean a word for himself: this was not the way to prevent misunderstandings. He still "feared passion and prejudice in other men;" not in himself: "and doubted not by the weight of his" own "reason, to counterpoise any faction; it being so easy for him, and so frequent, to call his obstinacy reason, and other men's reason, faction. We in the meanwhile must believe that wisdom and all reason came to him by title with his crown; passion, prejudice, and faction came to others by being subjects.

"He was sorry to hear, with what popular heat elections were carried in many places." Sorry rather, that court-letters and intimations prevailed no more, to divert or to deter the people from their free election of those men whom they thought best affected to religion and their country's liberty, both at that time in danger to be lost. And such men they were, as by the kingdom were sent to advise him, not sent to be cavilled at, because elected, or to be entertained by him with an undervalue and misprison of their temper, judgment, or affection. In vain was a parliament thought fittest by the known laws of our nation, to advise and regulate unruly kings, if they, instead of hearkening to advice, should be permitted to turn it off, and refuse it by vilifying and traducing their advisers, or by accusing of a popular heat those that lawfully elected them.

"His own and his children's interest obliged him to seek, and to preserve the love and welfare of his subjects." Who doubts it? But the same interest, common to all kings, was never yet available to make them all seek that which was indeed best for themselves and their posterity. All men by their own and their children's interest are obliged to honesty and justice: but how little that consideration works in private men, how much less in kings, their deeds declare best.

"He intended to oblige both friends and enemies, and to exceed their desires, did they but pretend to any modest and sober sense;" mistaking the whole business of a parliament; which met not to receive from him obligations, but justice; nor he to expect from them their modesty, but their grave advice, uttered with freedom in the public cause. His talk of modesty in their desires of the common welfare, argues him not much to have understood what he had to grant, who misconceived so much the nature of what they had to desire. And for "sober sense," the expression was too mean, and recoils with as much dishonor upon himself, to be a king where sober sense could possibly be so wanting in a parliament.

"The odium and offences, which some men's rigor, or remissness in church and state, had contracted upon his government, he resolved to have expiated with better laws and regulations." And yet the worst of misdemeanors committed by the worst of all his favorites in the height of their dominion, whether acts of rigor or remissness, he hath from time to time continued, owned, and taken upon himself by public declarations, as often as the clergy, or any other of his instruments, felt themselves overburdened with the people's hatred. And who knows not the superstitious rigor of his Sunday's chapel, and the licentious remissness of his Sunday's theatre; accompanied with that reverend statute for dominical jigs and maypoles, published in his own name, and derived from the example of his father, James? Which testifies all that rigor in superstition, all that remissness in religion, to have issued out originally from his own house, and from his own authority.

Much rather then may those general miscarriages in state, his proper sphere, be imputed to no other person chiefly than to himself. And which of all those oppressive acts or impositions did he ever disclaim or disavow, till the fatal awe of this parliament hung ominiously over him? Yet here he smoothly seeks to wipe off all the envy of his evil government upon his substitutes and under officers; and promises, though much too late, what wonders he purposed to have done in the reforming of religion: a work wherein all his undertakings heretofore declare him to have had little or no judgment: neither could his breeding, or his course of life, acquaint him with a thing so spiritual. Which may well assure us what kind of reformation we could expect from him; either some politic form of an imposed religion, or else perpetual vexation and persecution to all those that complied not with such a form.

The like amendment he promises in state; not a step further "than his reason and conscience told him was fit to be desired;" wishing "he had kept within those bounds, and not suffered his own judgment to have been overborne in some things," of which things one was the Earl of Strafford's execution. And what signifies all this, but that still his resolution was the same, to set up an arbitrary government of his own, and that all Britain was to be tied and chained to the conscience, judgment, and reason of one man; as if those gifts had been only his peculiar and prerogative, entailed upon him with his fortune to be a king? Whenas doubtless no man so obstinate, or so much a tyrant, but professes to be guided by that which he calls his reason and his judgment, though never so corrupted; and pretends also his conscience. In the meanwhile, for any parliament or the whole nation to have either reason, judgment, or conscience, by this rule was altogether in vain, if it thwarted the king's will; which was easy for him to call by any other more plausible name. He himself hath many times acknowledged to have no right over us but by law; and by the same law to govern us: but law in a free nation hath been ever public reason, the enacted reason of a parliament; which he denying to enact, denies to govern us by that which ought to be our law; interposing his own private reason, which to us is no law. And thus we find these fair and specious promises, made upon the experience of many hard sufferings, and his most mortified retirements, being thoroughly sifted, to contain nothing in them much different from his former practices, so cross, and so averse to all his parliaments, and both the nations of this island. What

fruits they could in likelihood have produced in his restorement, is obvious to any prudent foresight.

And this is the substance of his first section, till we come to the devout of it, modelled into the form of a private psalter. Which they who so much admire, either for the matter or the manner, may as well admire the archbishop's late breviary, and many other as good manuals and handmaids of devotion, the lip-work of every prelatical liturgist, clapped together and quilted out of Scripture phrase, with as much ease and as little need of Christian diligence or judgment, as belongs to the compiling of any ordinary and saleable piece of English divinity, that the shops value. But he who from such a kind of psalmistry, or any other verbal devotion, without the pledge and earnest of suitable deeds, can be persuaded of a zeal and true righteousness in the person, hath much yet to learn; and knows not that the deepest policy of a tyrant hath been ever to counterfeit religious. And Aristotle, in his Politics, hath mentioned that special craft among twelve other tyrannical sophisms. Neither want we examples: Andronicus Comnenus, the Byzantine emperor, though a most cruel tyrant, is reported by Nicetas to have been a constant reader of Saint Paul's Epistles; and by continual study had so incorporated the phrase and style of that transcendent apostle into all his familiar letters, that the imitation seemed to vie with the original. Yet this availed not to deceive the people of that empire, who, notwithstanding his saint's vizard, tore him to pieces for his tyranny.

From stories of this nature both ancient and modern which abound, the poets also, and some English, have been in this point so mindful of decorum, as to put never more pious words in the mouth of any person, than of a tyrant. I shall not instance an abtruse author, wherein the king might be less conversant, but one whom we well know was the closest companion of these his solitudes, William Shakespeare; who introduces the person of Richard the Third, speaking in as high a strain of piety and mortification as is uttered in any passage of this book, and sometimes to the same sense and purpose with some words in this place: "I intended," saith he, "not only to oblige my friends, but my enemies." The like saith Richard, act ii. scene 1.

"I do not know that Englishman alive,
With whom my soul is any jot at odds,
More than the infant that is born to-night;
I thank my God for my humility."

Other stuff of this sort may be read throughout the whole tragedy, wherein the poet used not much licence in departing from the truth of history, which delivers him a deep dissembler, not of his affections only, but of religion.

In praying, therefore, and in the outward work of devotion, this king we see hath not at all exceeded the worst of kings before him. But herein the worst of kings, professing Christianism, have by far exceeded him. They, for aught we know, have still prayed their own, or at least borrowed from fit authors. But this king, not content with that which, although in a thing holy, is no holy theft, to attribute to his own making other men's whole prayers, hath as it were unhallowed and unchristened the very duty of prayer itself, by borrowing to a Christian use prayers offered to a heathen god. Who would have imagined so little fear in him of the true all-seeing Deity, so little reverence of the Holy Ghost, whose office is to dictate and present our Christian prayers, so little care of truth in his last words, or honor to himself, or to his friends, or sense of his afflictions, or of that sad hour which was upon him, as immediately before his death to pop into the hand of that grave bishop who attended him, for a special relique of his saintly exercises, a prayer stolen word for word from the mouth of a heathen fiction praying to a heathen god; and that in no serious book, but the vain amatorious poem of Sir Philip Sidney's Arcadia; a book in that kind full of worth and wit, but among religious thoughts and duties not worthy to be named; nor to be read at any time without good caution, much less in time of trouble and affliction to be a Christian's prayer-book?

They who are yet incredulous of what I tell them for a truth, that this philippic prayer is no part of the king's goods, may satisfy their own eyes at leisure in the third book of Sir Philip's Arcadia, p. 248, comparing Pamela's prayer with the first prayer of his majesty, delivered to Dr. Juxon immediately before his death, and entitled a Prayer in Time of Captivity, printed in all the best editions of his book. And since there be a crew of lurking railers, who in their libels, and their fits of railing up and down, as I hear from others, take it so currishly, that I should dare to tell abroad the secrets of their Ægyptian Apis; to gratify their gall in some measure yet more, which to them will be a kind of alms, (for it is the weekly vomit of their gall, which to most of them is the sole means of their feeding,) that they may not starve for me, I shall gorge them once more with this digression somewhat larger than before: nothing troubled or offended at the working upward of their sale-venom thereupon, though it happen to asperse me; being, it seems, their best livelihood, and the only use or good digestion that their sick and perishing minds can make of truth charitably told them.

However, to the benefit of others much more worth the gaining, I shall proceed in my assertion; that if only but to taste wittingly of meat or drink offered to an idol be in the doctrine of St. Paul judged a pollution, much more must be his sin who takes a prayer so dedicated into his mouth, and offers it to God. Yet hardly it can be thought upon (though how sad a thing!) without some kind of laughter at the manner and solemn transaction of so gross a cozenage, that he, who had trampled over us so stately and so tragically, should leave the world at last so ridiculously in his exit, as to bequeath among his deifying friends that stood about him such a precious piece of mockery to be published by them, as must needs cover both his and their heads with shame, if they have any left. Certainly, they that will may now see at length how much they were deceived in him, and were ever like to be hereafter, who cared not, so near the minute of his death, to deceive his best and dearest friends with the trumpery of such a prayer, not more secretly than shamefully purloined; yet given them as the royal issue of his own proper zeal. And sure it was the hand of God to let them fall, and be taken in such a foolish trap, as hath exposed them to all derision; if for nothing else, to throw contempt and disgrace in the sight of all men upon this his idolized book, and the whole rosary of his prayers; thereby testifying how little he accepted them from those who thought no better of the living God than of a buzzard idol, fit to be so served and worshipped in reversion, with the polluted orts and refuse of Arcadias and romances, without being able to discern the affront rather than the worship of such an ethnic prayer.

But leaving what might justly be offensive to God, it was a trespass also more than usual against human right, which commands, that every author should have the property of his own work reserved to him after death, as well as living. Many princes have been rigorous in laying taxes on their subjects by the head; but of any king heretofore that made a levy upon their wit, and seized it as his own legitimate, I have not whom besides to instance. True it is, I looked rather to have found him gleaning out of books written purposely to help devotion. And if in likelihood he have borrowed much more out of prayer-books than out of pastorals, then are these painted feathers, that set him off so gay among the people, to be thought few or none of them his own. But if from his divines he have borrowed nothing, nothing out of all the magazine, and the rheum of their mellifluous prayers and meditations, let them who now mourn for him as for Thammuz, them who howl in their pulpits, and by their howling declare themselves right wolves, remember and consider in the midst of their hideous faces, when they do only not cut their flesh for him like those rueful priests whom Elijah mocked; that he who was once their Ahab, now their Josiah, though feigning outwardly to reverence churchmen, yet here hath so extremely set at nought both them and their praying faculty, that being at a loss himself what to pray in captivity, he consulted neither with the liturgy, nor with the directory, but, neglecting the huge fardell of all their honey-comb devotions, went directly where he doubted not to find better praying to his mind with Pamela, in the Countess's Arcadia.

What greater argument of disgrace and ignominy could have been thrown with cunning upon the whole clergy, than that the king, among all his priestery, and all those numberless volumes of their theological distillations, not meeting with one man or book of that coat that could befriend him with a prayer in captivity, was forced to rob Sir Philip and his captive shepherdess of their heathen orisons, to supply in any fashion his miserable indigence, not of bread, but of a single prayer to God? I say therefore not of bread, for that want may befall a good man, and yet not make him totally miserable: but he who wants a prayer to beseech God in his necessity, it is inexpressible how poor he is; far poorer within himself than all his enemies can make him. And the unfitness, the indecency of that pitiful supply which he sought, expresses yet further the deepness of his poverty.

Thus much be said in general to his prayers, and in special to that Arcadian prayer used in his captivity; enough to undeceive us what esteem we are to set upon the rest. For he certainly, whose mind could serve him to seek a Christian prayer out of a pagan legend, and assume it for his own, might gather up the rest God knows from whence; one perhaps out of the French Astræa, another out of the Spanish Diana; Amadis and Palmerin could hardly scape him. Such a person we may be sure had it not in him to make a prayer of his own, or at least would excuse himself the pains and cost of his invention, so long as such sweet rhapsodies of heathenism and knight-errantry could yield him prayers. How dishonorable then, and how unworthy of a Christian king, were these ignoble shifts to seem holy and to get a saintship among the ignorant and wretched people; to draw them by this deception, worse than all his former injuries, to go a whoring after him! And how unhappy, how forsook of grace, and unbeloved of God that people who resolve to know no more of piety or of goodness, than to account him their chief saint and martyr, whose bankrupt devotion came not honestly by his very prayers; but having sharked them from the mouth of a heathen worshipper, (detestable to teach him prayers!) sold them to those that stood and honored him next to the Messiah, as his own heavenly compositions in adversity; for hopes no less vain and presumptuous (and death at that time so imminent upon him) than by these goodly relics to be held a saint and martyr in opinion with the people!

And thus far in the whole chapter we have seen and considered, and it cannot but be clear to all men, how, and for what ends, what concernments and necessities, the late king was no way induced, but every way constrained to call this last parliament; yet here in his first prayer he trembles not to avouch, as in the ears of God, "That he did it with an upright intention to his glory, and his people's good:" of which dreadful attestation, how sincerely meant, God, to whom it was avowed, can only judge; and he hath judged already, and hath written his impartial sentence in characters legible to all Christendom; and besides hath taught us, that there be some, whom he hath given over to delusion, whose very mind and conscience is defiled; of whom St. Paul to Titus makes mention.

CHAPTER II.

Upon the Earl of Strafford's Death.

THIS next chapter is a penitent confession of the king, and the strangest, if it be well weighed, that ever was auricular. For he repents here of giving his consent, though most unwillingly, to the most seasonable and solemn piece of justice, that had been done of many years in the land: but his sole conscience thought the contrary. And thus was the welfare, the safety, and, within a little, the unanimous demand of three populous nations, to have attended still on the singularity of one man's opinionated conscience; if men had always been so tame and spiritless, and had not unexpectedly found the grace to understand, that, if his conscience were so narrow and peculiar to itself, it was not fit his authority should be so ample and universal over others: for certainly a private conscience sorts not with a public calling, but declares that person rather meant by nature for a private fortune. And this also we may take for truth, that he, whose conscience thinks it sin to put to death a capital offender, will as oft think it meritorious to kill a righteous person.

But let us hear what the sin was, that lay so sore upon him, and, as one of his prayers given to Dr. Juxon testifies, to the very day of his death; it was his signing the bill of Strafford's execution; a man whom all men looked upon as one of the boldest and most impetuous instruments that the king had, to advance any violent or illegal design. He had ruled Ireland, and some parts of England, in an arbitrary manner; had endeavored to subvert fundamental laws, to subvert parliaments, and to incense the king against them; he had also endeavored to make hostility between England and Scotland: he had counselled the king to call over that Irish army of papists, which he had cunningly raised, to reduce England, as appeared by good testimony then present at the consultation: for which and many other crimes alleged and proved against him in twenty-eight articles, he was condemned of high-treason by the parliament.

The commons by far the greater number cast him: the lords, after they had been satisfied in a full discourse by the king's solicitor, and the opinions of many judges delivered in their house, agreed likewise to the sentence of treason. The people universally cried out for justice. None were his friends but courtiers and clergymen, the worst, at that time, and most corrupted sort of men; and court ladies, not the best of women; who when they grow to that insolence as to appear active in state affairs, are the certain sign of a dissolute, degenerate, and pusillanimous commonwealth. Last of all, the king, or rather first, for these were but his apes, was not satisfied in conscience to condemn him of high-treason; and declared to both houses, "that no fears or respects whatsoever should make him alter that resolution founded upon his conscience." Either then his resolution was indeed not founded upon his conscience, or his conscience received better information, or else both his conscience and this his strong resolution struck sail, notwithstanding these glorious words, to his stronger fear; for within a few days after, when the judges, at a privy-council, and four of his elected bishops had picked the thorn out of his conscience, he was at length persuaded to sign the bill for Strafford's execution. And yet perhaps that it wrung his conscience to condemn the earl of high-treason is not unlikely; not because he thought him guiltless of highest treason, had half those crimes been committed against his own private interest or person, as appeared plainly by his charge against the six members; but because he knew himself a principal in what the earl was but his accessory, and thought nothing treason against the commonwealth, but against himself only.

Had he really scrupled to sentence that for treason, which he thought not treasonable, why did he seem resolved by the judges and the bishops? and if by them resolved, how comes this scruple here again? It was not then, as he now pretends, "the importunities of some, and the fear of many," which made him sign, but the satisfaction given him by those judges and ghostly fathers of his own choosing. Which of him shall we believe? for he seems not one, but double; either here we must not believe him professing that his satisfaction was but seemingly received and out of fear, or else we may as well believe that the scruple was no real scruple, as we can believe him here against himself before, that the satisfaction then received was no real satisfaction. Of such a variable and fleeting conscience what hold can be taken?

But that indeed it was a facile conscience, and could dissemble satisfaction when it pleased, his own ensuing actions declared; being soon after found to have the chief hand in a most detested conspiracy against the parliament and kingdom, as by letters and examinations of Percy, Goring, and other conspirators came to light; that his intention was to rescue the Earl of Strafford, by seizing on the Tower of London; to bring up the English army out of the North, joined with eight thousand Irish papists raised by Strafford, and a French army to be landed at Portsmouth, against the parliament and their friends. For which purpose the king, though requested by both houses to disband those Irish papists, refused to do it, and kept them still in arms to his own purposes. No marvel then, if being as deeply criminous as the earl himself, it stung his conscience to adjudge to death those misdeeds, whereof himself had been the chief author: no marvel though instead of blaming and detesting his ambition, his evil counsel, his violence, and oppression of the people, he fall to praise his great abilities; and with scholastic flourishes, beneath the decency of a king, compares him to the sun, which in all figurative use and significance bears allusion to a king, not to a subject: no marvel though he knit contradictions as close as words can lie together, "not approving in his judgment," and yet approving in his subsequent reason all that Strafford did, as "driven by the necessity of times, and the temper of that people;" for this excuses all his misdemeanors. Lastly, no marvel that he goes on building many fair and pious conclusions upon false and wicked premises, which deceive the common reader, not well discerning the antipathy of such connections: but this is the marvel, and may be the astonishment, of all that have a conscience, how he durst in the sight of God (and with the same words of contrition wherewith David repents the murdering of Uriah) repent his lawful compliance to that just act of not saving him, whom he ought to have delivered up to speedy punishment; though himself the guiltier of the two.

If the deed were so sinful, to have put to death so great a malefactor, it would have taken much doubtless from the heaviness of his sin, to have told God in his confession how he labored, what dark plots he had contrived, into what a league entered, and with what conspirators, against his parliament and kingdoms, to have rescued from the claim of justice so notable and so dear an instrument of tyranny; which would have been a story, no doubt, as pleasing in the ears of heaven, as all these equivocal repentances. For it was fear, and nothing else, which made him feign before both the scruple and the satisfaction of his conscience, that is to say, of his mind: his first fear pretended conscience, that he might be borne with to refuse signing; his latter fear, being more urgent, made him find a conscience both to sign and to be satisfied. As for repentance, it came not on him till a long time after; when he saw "he could have suffered nothing more, though he had denied that bill." For how could he understandingly repent of letting that be treason, which the parliament and whole nation so judged? This was that which repented him, to have given up to just punishment so stout a champion of his designs, who might have been so useful to him in his following civil broils. It was a worldly repentance, not a conscientious; or else it was a strange tyranny, which his conscience had got over him, to vex him like an evil spirit for doing one act of justice, and by that means to "fortify his resolution" from ever doing so any more. That mind must needs be irrecoverably depraved, which either by chance or importunity, tasting but once of one just deed, spatters at it, and abhors the relish ever after.

To the Scribes and Pharisees wo was denounced by our Saviour, for straining at a gnat and swallowing a camel, though a gnat were to be strained at: but to a conscience with whom one good deed is so hard to pass down as to endanger almost a choking, and bad deeds without number, though as big and bulky as the ruin of three kingdoms, go down currently without straining, certainly a far greater wo appertains. If his conscience were come to that unnatural dyscrasy, as to digest poison and to keck at wholesome food, it was not for the parliament or any of his kingdoms, to feed with him any longer. Which to conceal he would persuade us, that the parliament also in their conscience escaped not "some touches of remorse," for putting Strafford to death, in forbidding it by an after-act to be a precedent for the future. But, in a fairer construction, that act implied rather a desire in them to pacify the king's mind, whom they perceived by this means quite alienated: in the meanwhile not imagining that this after-act should be retorted on them to tie up justice for the time to come upon like occasion, whether this were made a precedent or not, no more than the want of such a precedent, if it had been wanting, had been available to hinder this.

But how likely is it, that this after-act argued in the parliament their least repenting for the death of Strafford, when it argued so little in the king himself; who, notwithstanding this after-act, which had his own hand and concurrence, if not his own instigation, within the same year accused of high-treason no less than six members at once for the same pretended crimes, which his conscience would not yield to think treasonable in the earl? So that this his subtle argument to fasten a repenting, and, by that means a guiltiness of Strafford's death upon the parliament, concludes upon his own head; and shows us plainly, that either nothing in his judgment was treason against the commonwealth, but only against the king's person; (a tyrannical principle!) or that his conscience was a perverse and prevaricating conscience, to scruple that the commonwealth should punish for treasonous in one eminent offender that which

he himself sought so vehemently to have punished in six guiltless persons. If this were "that touch of conscience which he bore with greater regret" than for any sin committed in his life, whether it were that proditory aid sent to Rochelle and religion abroad, or that prodigality of shedding blood at home to a million of his subjects' lives not valued in comparison of one Strafford; we may consider yet at last, what true sense and feeling could be in that conscience, and what fitness to be the master-conscience of three kingdoms.

But the reason why he labors, that we should take notice of so much "tenderness and regret in his soul for having any hand in Strafford's death," is worth the marking ere we conclude: "he hoped it would be some evidence before God and man to all posterity, that he was far from bearing that vast load and guilt of blood" laid upon him by others: which hath the likeness of a subtle dissimulation; bewailing the blood of one man, his commodious instrument, put to death, most justly, though by him unwillingly, that we might think him too tender to shed willingly the blood of those thousands whom he counted rebels. And thus by dipping voluntarily his finger's end, yet with show of great remorse, in the blood of Strafford, whereof all men clear him, he thinks to scape that sea of innocent blood, wherein his own guilt inevitably hath plunged him all over. And we may well perceive to what easy satisfactions and purgations he had inured his secret conscience, who thought by such weak policies and ostentations as these to gain belief and absolution from understanding men.

CHAPTER III.

Upon his going to the House of Commons.

CONCERNING his inexcusable and hostile march from the court to the house of commons, there needs not much be said; for he confesses it to be an act, which most men, whom he calls "his enemies," cried shame upon, "indifferent men grew jealous of and fearful, and many of his friends resented, as a motion rising rather from passion than reason." He himself, in one of his answers to both houses, made profession to be convinced, that it was a plain breach of their privilege; yet here, like a rotten building newly trimmed over, he represents it speciously and fraudulently, to impose upon the simple reader; and seeks by smooth and supple words, not here only, but through his whole book, to make some beneficial use or other even of his worst miscarriages.

"These men," saith he, meaning his friends, "knew not the just motives and pregnant grounds with which I thought myself furnished;" to wit, against the five members, whom he came to drag out of the house. His best friends indeed knew not, nor could ever know, his motives to such a riotous act; and had he himself known any just grounds, he was not ignorant how much it might have tended to his justifying, had he named them in this place, and not concealed them. But suppose them real, suppose them known, what was this to that violation and dishonor put upon the whole house, whose very door, forcibly kept open, and all the passages near it, he beset with swords and pistols cocked and menaced in the hands of about three hundred swaggerers and ruffians, who but expected, nay, audibly called for, the word of onset to begin a slaughter.

"He had discovered, as he thought, unlawful correspondences, which they had used, and engagements to embroil his kingdoms;" and remembers not his own unlawful correspondences and conspiracies with the Irish army of papists, with the French to land at Portsmouth, and his tampering both with the English and Scots army to come up against the parliament: the least of which attempts, by whomsoever, was no less than manifest treason against the commonwealth.

If to demand justice of the five members were his plea, for that which they with more reason might have demanded justice upon him, (I use his own argument,) there needed not so rough assistance. If he had "resolved to bear that repulse with patience," which his queen by her words to him at his return little thought he would have done, wherefore, did he provide against it, with such an armed and unusual force? but his heart served him not to undergo the hazard that such a desperate scuffle would have brought him to. But wherefore did he go at all, it behooving

him to know there were two statutes, that declared he ought first to have acquainted the parliament, who were the accusers, which he refused to do, though still professing to govern by law, and still justifying his attempts against law? And when he saw it was not permitted him to attaint them but by a fair trial, as was offered him from time to time, for want of just matter which yet never came to light, he let the business fall of his own accord; and all those pregnancies and just motives came to just nothing.

"He had no temptation of displeasure or revenge against those men:" none but what he thirsted to execute upon them, for the constant opposition which they made against his tyrannous proceedings, and the love and reputation which they therefore had among the people; but most immediately, for that they were supposed the chief, by whose activity those twelve protesting bishops were but a week before committed to the Tower.

"He missed but little to have produced writings under some men's own hands." But yet he missed, though their chambers, trunks, and studies were sealed up and searched; yet not found guilty. "Providence would not have it so." Good Providence! that curbs the raging of proud monarchs, as well as of mad multitudes. "Yet he wanted not such probabilities" (for his pregnant is come now to probable) "as were sufficient to raise jealousies in any king's heart." And thus his pregnant motives are at last proved nothing but a tympany, or a Queen Mary's cushion; for in any king's heart, as kings go now, what shadowy conceit or groundless toy will not create a jealousy?

"That he had designed to assault the house of commons," taking God to witness, he utterly denies; yet in his answer to the city, maintains that "any course of violence had been very justifiable." And we may then guess how far it was from his design: however, it discovered in him an excessive eagerness to be avenged on them that crossed him; and that to have his will, he stood not to do things never so much below him. What a becoming sight it was, to see the king of England one while in the house of commons, and by and by in the Guildhall among the liveries and manufacturers, prosecuting so greedily the track of five or six fled subjects;

himself not the solicitor only, but the pursuivant and the apparitor of his own partial cause! And although in his answers to the parliament, he hath confessed, first that his manner of prosecution was illegal, next "that as he once conceived he had ground enough to accuse them, so at length that he found as good cause to desert any prosecution of them;" yet here he seems to reverse all, and against promise takes up his old deserted accusation, that he might have something to excuse himself, instead of giving due reparation, which he always refused to give them whom he had so dishonored.

"That I went," saith he of his going to the house of commons, "attended with some gentlemen;" gentlemen indeed; the ragged infantry of stews and brothels; the spawn and shipwreck of taverns and dicing-houses: and then he pleads, "it was no unwonted thing for the majesty and safety of a king to be so attended, especially in discontented times." An illustrious majesty no doubt, so attended! a becoming safety for the king of England, placed in the fidelity of such guards and champions! happy times, when braves and hacksters, the only contented members of his government, were thought the fittest and the faithfullest to defend his person against the discontents of a parliament and all good men! Were those the chosen ones to "preserve reverence to him," while he entered "unassured," and full of suspicions, into his great and faithful council! Let God then and the world judge, whether the cause were not in his own guilty and unwarrantable doings: the house of commons, upon several examinations of this business, declared it sufficiently proved, that the coming of those soldiers, papists and others, with the king, was to take away some of their members; and in case of opposition or denial, to have fallen upon the house in a hostile manner.

This the king here denies; adding a fearful imprecation against his own life, "if he purposed any violence or oppression against the innocent, then," saith he, "let the enemy persecute my soul, and tread my life to the ground, and lay my honor in the dust." What need then more disputing? He appealed to God's tribunal, and behold! God hath judged and done to him in the sight of all men according to the verdict of his own mouth:

to be a warning to all kings hereafter how they use presumptuously the words and protestations of David, without the spirit and conscience of David. And the king's admirers may here see their madness, to mistake this book for a monument of his worth and wisdom, whenas indeed it is his doomsday book; not like that of William the Norman, his predecessor, but the record and memorial of his condemnation; and discovers whatever hath befallen him to have been hastened on from divine justice by the rash and inconsiderate appeal of his own lips. But what evasions, what pretences, though never so unjust and empty, will he refuse in matters more unknown, and more involved in the mists and intricacies of state, who, rather than not justify himself in a thing so generally odious, can flatter his integrity with such frivolous excuses against the manifest dissent of all men, whether enemies, neuters, or friends? But God and his judgments have not been mocked; and good men may well perceive what a distance there was ever like to be between him and his parliament, and perhaps between him and all amendment, who for one good deed, though but consented to, asks God forgiveness; and from his worst deeds done, takes occasion to insist upon his righteousness!

CHAPTER IV.

Upon the Insolency of the Tumults.

WE have here, I must confess, a neat and well-couched invective against tumults, expressing a true fear of them in the author; but yet so handsomely composed, and withal so feelingly, that, to make a royal comparison, I believe Rehoboam the son of Solomon could not have composed it better. Yet Rehoboam had more cause to inveigh against them; for they had stoned his tribute-gatherer, and perhaps had as little spared his own person, had he not with all speed betaken him to his chariot. But this king hath stood the worst of them in his own house without danger, when his coach and horses, in a panic fear, have been to seek: which argues, that the tumults at Whitehall were nothing so dangerous as those at Sechem.

But the matter here considerable, is not

whether the king or his household rhetorician have made a pithy declamation against tumults; but first, whether these were tumults or not; next, if they were, whether the king himself did not cause them. Let us examine therefore how things at that time stood. The king, as before hath been proved, having both called this parliament unwillingly, and as unwillingly from time to time condescended to their several acts, carrying on a disjoint and private interest of his own; and not enduring to be so crossed and overswayed, especially in the executing of his chief and boldest instrument, the deputy of Ireland, first tempts the English army, with no less reward than the spoil of London, to come up and destroy the parliament. That being discovered by some of the officers, who, though bad enough, yet abhorred so foul a deed; the king, hardened in his purpose, tempts them the second time at Burrowbridge, promises to pawn his jewels for them, and that they should be met and assisted (would they but march on) with a gross body of horse under the Earl of Newcastle. He tempts them yet the third time, though after discovery, and his own abjuration to have ever tempted them, as is affirmed in the declaration of "No more addresses." Neither this succeeding, he turns him next to the Scotch army, and by his own credential letters given to O'Neal and Sir John Henderson, baits his temptation with a richer reward; not only to have the sacking of London, but four northern counties to be made Scottish, with jewels of great value to be given in pawn the while.

But neither would the Scots, for any promise of reward, be bought to such an execrable and odious treachery: but with much honesty gave notice of the king's design both to the parliament and city of London. The parliament moreover had intelligence, and the people could not but discern, that there was a bitter and malignant party grown up now to such a boldness, as to give out insolent and threatening speeches against the parliament itself. Besides this, the rebellion in Ireland was now broke out; and a conspiracy in Scotland had been made, while the king was there, against some chief members of that parliament; great numbers here of unknown and suspicious persons resorted to the city.

The king, being returned from Scotland,

presently dismisses that guard, which the parliament thought necessary in the midst of so many dangers to have about them, and puts another guard in their place, contrary to the privilege of that high court, and by such a one commanded as made them no less doubtful of the guard itself. Which they therefore, upon some ill effects thereof first found, discharged; deeming it more safe to sit free, though without a guard, in open danger, than enclosed with a suspected safety. The people, therefore, lest their worthiest and most faithful patriots, who had exposed themselves for the public, and whom they saw now left naked, should want aid, or be deserted in the midst of these dangers, came in multitudes, though unarmed, to witness their fidelity and readiness in case of any violence offered to the parliament. The king, both envying to see the people's love thus devolved on another object, and doubting lest it might utterly disable him to do with parliaments as he was wont, sent a message into the city forbidding such resorts.

The parliament also, both by what was discovered to them, and what they saw in a malignant party, (some of which had already drawn blood in a fray or two at the court-gate, and even at their own gate in Westminsterhall,) conceiving themselves to be still in danger where they sate, sent a most reasonable and just petition to the king, that a guard might be allowed them out of the city, whereof the king's own chamberlain, the Earl of Essex, might have command; it being the right of inferior courts to make choice of their own guard. This the king refused to do; and why he refused the very next day made manifest: for on that day it was that he sallied out from Whitehall, with those trusty myrmidons, to block up or give assault to the house of commons. He had, besides all this, begun to fortify his court, and entertained armed men not a few; who, standing at his palace gate, reviled, and with drawn swords wounded many of the people, as they went by unarmed, and in a peaceable manner, whereof some died. The passing by of a multitude, though neither to St. George's feast, nor to a tilting, certainly of itself was no tumult; the expression of their loyalty and steadfastness to the parliament, whose lives and safeties by more than slight rumours they doubted to be in danger, was no tumult. If it grew to be so, the cause was in the king himself and his injurious retinue, who, both by hostile preparations in the court, and by actual assailing of the people, gave them just cause to defend themselves.

Surely those unarmed and petitioning people needed not have been so formidable to any, but to such whose consciences misgave them how ill they had deserved of the people; and first began to injure them, because they justly feared it from them; and then ascribe that to popular tumult, which was occasioned by their own provoking. And that the king was so emphatical and elaborate on this theme against tumults, and expressed with such a vehemence his hatred of them, will redound less perhaps than he was aware to the commendation of his government. For, besides that in good governments they happen seldomest, and rise not without cause, if they prove extreme and pernicious, they were never counted so to monarchy, but to monarchial tyranny; and extremes one with another are at most antipathy. If then the king so extremely stood in fear of tumults, the inference will endanger him to be the other extreme. Thus far the occasion of this discourse against tumults: now to the discourse itself, voluble enough, and full of sentence, but that, for the most part, either specious rather than solid, or to his cause nothing pertinent.

"He never thought anything more to presage the mischiefs that ensued, than those tumults." Then was his foresight but short, and much mistaken. Those tumults were but the mild effects of an evil and injurious reign; not signs of mischiefs to come, but seeking relief for mischiefs past: those signs were to be read more apparent in his rage and purposed revenge of those free expostulations and clamors of the people against his lawless government. "Not anything," saith he, "portends more God's displeasure against a nation, than when he suffers the clamors of the vulgar to pass all bounds of law and reverence to authority." It portends rather his displeasure against a tyrannous king, whose proud throne he intends to overturn by that contemptible vulgar; the sad cries and oppressions of whom his royalty regarded not. As for that supplicating people, they did no hurt either to law or authority, but stood for it rather in the parliament against whom they feared would violate it.

"That they invaded the honor and freedom of the two houses," is his own officious accusation, not seconded by the parliament, who, had they seen cause, were themselves best able to complain. And if they "shook and menaced" any, they were such as had more relation to the court than to the commonwealth; enemies, not patrons of the people. But if their petitioning unarmed were an invasion of both houses, what was his entrance into the house of commons, besetting it with armed men? In what condition then was the honor and freedom of that house? "They forebore not rude deportments, contemptuous words and actions, to himself and his court." It was more wonder, having heard what treacherous hostility he had designed against the city and his whole kingdom, that they forbore to handle him as people in their rage have handled tyrants heretofore for less offences.

"They were not a short ague, but a fierce quotidian fever." He indeed may best say it, who most felt it; for the shaking was within him, and it shook him, by his own description, "worse than a storm, worse than an earthquake;" Belshazzar's palsy. Had not worse fears, terrors, and envies made within him that commotion, how could a multitude of his subjects, armed with no other weapon than petitions, have shaken all his joints with such a terrible ague? Yet that the parliament should entertain the least fear of bad intentions from him or his party he endures not; but would persuade us, that "men scare themselves and others without cause:" for he thought fear would be to them a kind of armor, and his design was, if it were possible, to disarm all, especially of a wise fear and suspicion; for that he knew would find weapons.

He goes on therefore with vehemence, to repeat the mischiefs done by these tumults. "They first petitioned, then protested; dictate next, and lastly overawe the parliament. They removed obstructions, they purged the houses, cast out rotten members." If there were a man of iron, such as Talus, by our poet Spenser is feigned to be, the page of Justice, who with his iron flail could do all this, and expeditiously, without those deceitful forms and circumstances of law; worse than ceremonies in religion; I say, God send it done, whether by one Talus, or by a thousand.

"But they subdued the men of conscience in parliament, backed and abetted all seditious and schismatical proposals against government, ecclesiastical and civil." Now we may perceive the root of his hatred, whence it springs. It was not the king's grace, or 10 princely goodness, but this iron flail, the people, that drove the bishops out of their baronies, out of their cathedrals, out of the lords' house, out of their copes and surplices, and all those papistical innovations, threw down the high-commission and star-chamber, gave us a triennial parliament, and what we most desired; in revenge whereof he now so bitterly inveighs against them; these are those seditious and schismatical proposals then by 20 him condescended to as acts of grace, now of another name; which declares him, touching matters of church and state, to have been no other man in the deepest of his solitude, than he was before at the highest of his sovereignty.

But this was not the worst of these tumults: they played the hasty "midwives, and would not stay the ripening, but went straight to ripping up, and forcibly cut out abortive votes." They would not stay perhaps the 30 Spanish demurring, and putting off such wholesome acts and counsels, as the politic cabinet at Whitehall had no mind to. But all this is complained here as done to the parliament, and yet we heard not the parliament at that time complain of any violence from the people, but from him. Wherefore intrudes he to plead the cause of parliament against the people, while the parliament was pleading their own cause against him; and against him 40 were forced to seek refuge of the people? It is plain then, that those confluxes and resorts interrupted not the parliament, nor by them were thought tumultuous, but by him only and his court faction.

"But what good man had not rather want anything he most desired for the public good, than attain it by such unlawful and irreligious means?" As much as to say, had not rather sit still, and let his country be tyrannized, 50 than that the people, finding no other remedy, should stand up like men, and demand their rights and liberties. This is the artificialest

piece of fineness to persuade men into slavery that the wit of court could have invented. But hear how much better the moral of this lesson would befit the teacher. What good man had not rather want a boundless and arbitrary power, and those fine flowers of the crown, called prerogatives, than for them to use force and perpetual vexation to his faithful subjects, nay, to wade for them through 10 blood and civil war? So that this and the whole bundle of those following sentences may be applied better to the convincement of his own violent courses, than of those pretended tumults.

"Who were the chief demagogues to send for those tumults, some alive are not ignorant." Setting aside the affrightment of this goblin word; for the king, by his leave, cannot coin English, as he could money, to be 20 current, (and 'tis believed this wording was above his known style and orthography, and accuses the whole composure to be conscious of some other author,) yet if the people were sent for, emboldened and directed by those demagogues, who, saving his Greek, were good patriots, and by his own confession "men of some repute for parts and piety," it helps well to assure us there was both urgent cause, and the less danger of their coming.

"Complaints were made, yet no redress 30 could be obtained." The parliament also complained of what danger they sat in from another party, and demanded of him a guard; but it was not granted. What marvel then if it cheered them to see some store of their friends, and in the Roman, not the pettifogging sense, their clients so near about them! a defence due by nature both from whom it was offered, and to whom, as due 40 as to their parents; though the court stormed and fretted to see such honor given to them, who were then best fathers of the commonwealth. And both the parliament and people complained, and demanded justice for those assaults, if not murders, done at his own doors by that crew of rufflers; but he, instead of doing justice on them, justified and abetted them in what they did, as in his public answer to a petition from the city 50 may be read. Neither is it slightly to be passed over, that in the very place where blood was first drawn in this cause, as the beginning of all that followed, there was his own blood shed by the executioner: according to that sentence of divine justice, "In the place where dogs licked the blood of Naboth, shall dogs lick thy blood, even thine."

From hence he takes occasion to excuse that improvident and fatal error of his absenting from the parliament. "When he found that no declaration of the bishops could take place against those tumults." Was that worth his considering that foolish and self-undoing declaration of twelve cipher bishops, who were immediately appeached of treason for that audacious declaring? The bishops peradventure were now and then pulled by the rochets, and deserved another kind of pulling; but what amounted this to "the fear of his own person in the streets?" Did he not the very next day after his irruption into the house of commons, than which nothing had more exasperated the people, go in his coach unguarded into the city? Did he receive the least affront, much less violence, in any of the streets, but rather humble demeanors and supplications? Hence may be gathered, that however in his own guiltiness he might have justly feared, yet that he knew the people so full of awe and reverence to his person, as to dare commit himself single among the thickest of them, at a time when he had most provoked them.

Besides, in Scotland they had handled the bishops in a more robustious manner: Edinburgh had been full of tumults; two armies from thence had entered England against him: yet after all this he was not fearful, but very forward to take so long a journey to Edinburgh; which argues first, as did also his rendition afterward to the Scots army, that to England he continued still, as he was indeed, a stranger, and full of diffidence; to the Scots only a native king, in his confidence, though not in his dealing towards them. It shows us next beyond doubting, that all this his fear of tumults was but a mere color and occasion taken of his resolved absence from the parliament, for some other end not difficult to be guessed. And those instances, wherein valor is not to be questioned for not "scuffling with the sea, or an undisciplined rabble," are but subservient to carry on the solemn jest of his fearing tumults; if they discover not withal the true reason why he departed, only to turn his slashing at the court-gate to

slaughtering in the field; his disorderly bickering to an orderly invading; which was nothing else but a more orderly disorder.

"Some suspected and affirmed that he meditated a war when he went first from Whitehall." And they were not the worst heads that did so, nor did any of his former acts weaken him to that, as he alleges for himself; or if they had, they clear him only for the time of passing them, not for whatever thoughts might come after into his mind. Former actions of improvidence or fear, not with him unusual, cannot absolve him of all after meditations. He goes on protesting his "no intention to have left Whitehall," had these horrid tumults given him but fair quarter; as if he himself, his wife, and children had been in peril. But to this enough hath been answered. "Had this parliament, as it was in its first election," namely, with the lord and baron bishops, "sat full and free," he doubts not but all had gone well. What warrant this of his to us, whose not doubting was all good men's greatest doubt? "He was resolved to hear reason, and to consent so far as he could comprehend." A hopeful resolution! what if his reason were found by oft experience to comprehend nothing beyond his own advantages; was this a reason fit to be intrusted with the common good of three nations? "But," saith he, "as swine are to gardens, so are tumults to parliaments." This the parliament, had they found it so, could best have told us. In the meanwhile, who knows not that one great hog may do as much mischief in a garden as many little swine?

"He was sometimes prone to think, that had he called this last parliament to any other place in England, the sad consequences might have been prevented." But change of air changes not the mind. Was not his first parliament at Oxford dissolved after two subsidies given him, and no justice received? Was not his last in the same place, where they sat with as much freedom, as much quiet from tumults, as they could desire; a parliament, both in his account and their own, consisting of all his friends, that fled after him, and suffered for him, and yet by him nicknamed and cashiered for a "mongrel parliament, that vexed his queen with their base and mutinous motions," as his cabinet-letter tells us? Whereby the world may see plainly, that no shifting of place, no sifting of members to his own mind, no number, no paucity, no freedom from tumults, could ever bring his arbitrary wilfulness, and tyrannical designs, to brook the least shape or similitude, the least counterfeit of a parliament. Finally, instead of praying for his people as a good king should do, he prays to be delivered from them, as "from wild beasts, inundations, and raging seas, that had overborne all loyalty, modesty, laws, justice, and religion." God save the people from such intercessors!

CHAPTER V.

Upon the Bill for Triennial Parliaments, and for settling this, &c.

THE bill for a triennial parliament was but the third part of one good step toward that which in times past was our annual right. The other bill for settling this parliament was new indeed, but at that time very necessary; and, in the king's own words, no more than what the world "was fully confirmed he might in justice, reason, honor, and conscience grant them;" for to that end he affirms to have done it.

But whereas he attributes the passing of them to his own act of grace and willingness, (as his manner is to make virtues of his necessities,) and giving to himself all the praise, heaps ingratitude upon the parliament, a little memory will set the clean contrary before us; that for those beneficial acts we owe what we owe to the parliament, but to his granting them neither praise nor thanks. The first bill granted much less than two former statutes yet in force by Edward the Third; that a parliament should be called every year, or oftener, if need were; nay, from a far ancienter law-book, called the "Mirror," it is affirmed in a late treatise called "Rights of the Kingdom;" that parliaments by our old laws ought twice a year to be at London. From twice in one year to once in three years, it may be soon cast up how great a loss we fell into of our ancient liberty by that act, which in the ignorant and slavish minds we then were, was thought a great purchase.

Wisest men perhaps were contented (for the present, at least) by this act to have recovered parliaments, which were then upon the brink of danger to be for ever lost. And this is that which the king preaches here for a special token of his princely favor, to have abridged and overreached the people five parts in six of what their due was, both by ancient statute and originally. And thus the taking from us all but a triennial remnant of that English freedom which our fathers left us double, in a fair annuity enrolled, is set out, and sold to us here for the gracious and over-liberal giving of a new enfranchisement. How little, may we think, did he ever give us, who in the bill of his pretended givings writes down imprimis that benefit or privilege once in three years given us, which by so giving he more than twice every year illegally took from us: such givers as give single to take away sixfold, be to our enemies! for certainly this commonwealth, if the statutes of our ancestors be worth aught, would have found it hard and hazardous to thrive under the damage of such a guileful liberality.

The other act was so necessary, that nothing in the power of man more seemed to be the stay and support of all things from that steep ruin to which he had nigh brought them, than that act obtained. He had by his illstewardship, and, to say no worse, the needless raising of two armies, intended for a civil war, beggared both himself and the public; and besides had left us upon the score of his needy enemies for what it cost them in their own defence against him. To disengage him and the kingdom great sums were to be borrowed, which would never have been lent, nor could ever be repaid, had the king chanced to dissolve this parliament as heretofore. The errors also of his government had brought the kingdom to such extremes, as were incapable of all recovery without the absolute continuance of a parliament. It had been else in vain to go about the settling of so great distempers, if he, who first caused the malady, might, when he pleased, reject the remedy. Notwithstanding all which, that he granted both these acts unwillingly, and as a mere passive instrument, was then visible even to most of those men who now will see nothing.

At passing of the former act he himself concealed not his unwillingness; and testifying a general dislike of their actions, which they then proceeded in with great approbation of the whole kingdom, he told them with a masterly brow, that "by this act he had obliged them above what they had deserved," and gave a piece of justice to the commonwealth six times short of his predecessors, as if he had been giving some boon or begged office to a sort of his desertless grooms.

That he passed the latter act against his will, no man in reason can hold it questionable. For if the February before he made so dainty, and were so loath to bestow a parliament once in three years upon the nation, because this had so opposed his courses, was it likely that the May following he should bestow willingly on this parliament an indissoluble sitting, when they had offended him much more by cutting short and impeaching of high-treason his chief favorites? It was his fear then, not his favor, which drew from him that act, lest the parliament, incensed by his conspiracies against them, about the same time discovered, should with the people have resented too heinously those his doings, if to the suspicion of their danger from him he had also added the denial of this only means to secure themselves.

From these acts therefore in which he glories, and wherewith so oft he upbraids the parliament, he cannot justly expect to reap aught but dishonor and dispraise; as being both unwillingly granted, and the one granting much less than was before allowed by statute, the other being a testimony of his violent and lawless custom, not only to break privileges, but whole parliaments; from which enormity they were constrained to bind him first of all his predecessors; never any before him having given like causes of distrust and jealousy to his people. As for this parliament, how far he was from being advised by them as he ought, let his own words express.

He taxes them with "undoing what they found well done," and yet knows they undid nothing in the church, but lord bishops, liturgies, ceremonies, high-commission, judged worthy by all true protestants to be thrown out of the church. They undid nothing in the state but irregular and grinding courts, the main grievances to be removed; and if these were the things which in his opinion they found well done, we may again from hence

be informed with what unwillingness he removed them; and that those gracious acts, whereof so frequently he makes mention, may be Englished more properly acts of fear and dissimulation against his mind and conscience.

The bill preventing dissolution of this parliament he calls "an unparalleled act, out of the extreme confidence that his subjects would not make ill use of it." But was it not a greater confidence of the people, to put into one man's hand so great a power, till he abused it, as to summon and dissolve parliaments? He would be thanked for trusting them, and ought to thank them rather for trusting him: the trust issuing first from them, not from him.

And that it was a mere trust, and not his prerogative, to call and dissolve parliaments at his pleasure; and that parliaments were not to be dissolved, till all petitions were heard, all grievances redressed, is not only the assertion of this parliament, but of our ancient law-books, which aver it to be an unwritten law of common right, so engraven in the hearts of our ancestors, and by them so constantly enjoyed and claimed, as that it needed not enrolling. And if the Scots in their declaration could charge the king with breach of their laws for breaking up that parliament without their consent, while matters of greatest moment were depending; it were unreasonable to imagine, that the wisdom of England should be so wanting to itself through all ages, as not to provide by some known law, written or unwritten, against the not calling, or the arbitrary dissolving, of parliaments; or that they who ordained their summoning twice a year, or as oft as need required, did not tacitly enact also, that as necessity of affairs called them, so the same necessity should keep them undissolved, till that were fully satisfied.

Were it not for that, parliaments, and all the fruit and benefit we receive by having them, would turn soon to mere abusion. It appears then, that if this bill of not dissolving were an unparalleled act, it was a known and common right, which our ancestors under other kings enjoyed as firmly as if it had been graven in marble; and that the infringement of this king first brought it into a written act: who now boasts that as a great favor done us, which his own less fidelity than was in former kings constrained us only of an old undoubted right to make a new written act. But what needed written acts, whenas anciently it was esteemed part of his crown oath, not to dissolve parliaments till all grievances were considered? whereupon the old "Modi of Parliament" calls it flat perjury, if he dissolve them before: as I find cited in a book mentioned at the beginning of this chapter, to which and other law tractates I refer the more lawyerly mooting of this point, which is neither my element, nor my proper work here; since the book which I have to answer, pretends reason, not authorities and quotations: and I hold reason to be the best arbitrator, and the law of law itself.

It is true, that "good subjects think it not just, that the king's condition should be worse by bettering theirs." But then the king must not be at such a distance from the people in judging what is better and what worse; which might have been agreed, had he known (for his own words condemn him) "as well with moderation to use, as with earnestness to desire his own advantages." "A continual parliament, he thought, would keep the commonwealth in tune." Judge, commonwealth! what proofs he gave, that this boasted profession was ever in his thought. "Some," saith he, "gave out, that I repented me of that settling act." His own actions gave it out beyond all supposition; for doubtless it repented him to have established that by law, which he went about so soon after to abrogate by the sword.

He calls those acts, which he confesses "tended to their good, not more princely than friendly contributions." As if to do his duty were of courtesy, and the discharge of his trust a parcel of his liberality; so nigh lost in his esteem was the birthright of our liberties, that to give them back again upon demand, stood at the mercy of his contribution. "He doubts not but the affections of his people will compensate his sufferings for those acts of confidence:" and imputes his sufferings to a contrary cause. Not his confidence, but his distrust, was that which brought him to those sufferings, from the time that he forsook his parliament; and trusted them never the sooner for what he tells "of their piety and religious strictness," but rather hated them as puritans, whom he always sought to extirpate.

He would have it believed, that "to bind his hands by these acts, argued very short foresight of things, and extreme fatuity of mind in him," if he had meant a war. If we should conclude so, that were not the only argument: neither did it argue that he meant peace; knowing that what he granted for the present out of fear, he might as soon repeal by force, watching his time; and deprive them the fruit of those acts, if his own designs, wherein he put his trust, took effect.

Yet he complains, "that the tumults threatened to abuse all acts of grace, and turn them into wantonness." I would they had turned his wantonness into the grace of not abusing scripture. Was this becoming such a saint as they would make him to adulterate those sacred words from the grace of God to the acts of his own grace? Herod was eaten up of worms for suffering others to compare his voice to the voice of God; but the borrower of this phrase gives much more cause of jealousy, that he likened his own acts of grace to the acts of God's grace.

From profaneness he scarce comes off with perfect sense. "I was not then in a capacity to make war," therefore, "I intended not." "I was not in a capacity," therefore "I could not have given my enemies greater advantage, than by so unprincely inconstancy to have scattered them by arms, whom but lately I had settled by parliament." What place could there be for his inconstancy in that thing whereto he was in no capacity? Otherwise his inconstancy was not so unwonted, or so nice, but that it would have easily found pretences to scatter those in revenge, whom he settled in fear.

"It had been a course full of sin, as well as of hazard and dishonor." True; but if those considerations withheld him not from other actions of like nature, how can we believe they were of strength sufficient to withhold him from this? And that they withheld him not, the event soon taught us. "His letting some men go up to the pinnacle of the temple, was a temptation to them to cast him down headlong." In this simile we have himself compared to Christ, the parliament to the devil, and his giving them that act of settling, to his letting them go up to the "pinnacle of the temple." A tottering and giddy act rather than a settling. This was goodly use made of scripture in his solitudes: but it was no pinnacle of the temple, it was a pinnacle of Nebuchadnezzar's palace, from whence he and monarchy fell headlong together.

He would have others see that "all the kingdoms of the world are not worth gaining by ways of sin which hazard the soul;" and hath himself left nothing unhazarded to keep three. He concludes with sentences, that, rightly scanned, make not so much for him as against him, and confesses, that "the act of settling was no sin of his will;" and we easily believe him, for it hath been clearly proved a sin of his unwillingness. With his orisons I meddle not, for he appeals to a high audit. This yet may be noted, that at his prayers he had before him. the sad presage of his ill success, "as of a dark and dangerous storm, which never admitted his return to the port from whence he set out." Yet his prayer-book no sooner shut, but other hopes flattered him; and their flattering was his destruction.

CHAPTER VI.

Upon his Retirement from Westminster.

THE simile wherewith he begins I was about to have found fault with, as in a garb somewhat more poetical than for a statist: but meeting with many strains of like dress in other of his essays, and hearing him reported a more diligent reader of poets than of politicians, I began to think that the whole book might perhaps be intended a piece of poetry. The words are good, the fiction smooth and cleanly; there wanted only rhyme, and that, they say, is bestowed upon it lately. But to the argument.

"I stayed at Whitehall, till I was driven away by shame more than fear." I retract not what I thought of the fiction, yet here, I must confess it lies too open. In his messages and declarations, nay, in the whole chapter next but one before this, he affirms, that "the danger wherein his wife, his children, and his own person" were by those tumults, was the main cause that drove him from Whitehall, and appeals to God as witness: he affirms here that it was "shame more than fear."

And Digby, who knew his mind as well as any, tells his new-listed guard, "that the principal cause of his majesty's going thence was to save them from being trod in the dirt." From whence we may discern what false and frivolous excuses are avowed for truth, either in those declarations, or in this penitential book.

Our forefathers were of that courage and severity of zeal to justice and their native liberty, against the proud contempt and misrule of their kings, that when Richard the Second departed but from a committee of lords, who sat preparing matter for the parliament not yet assembled, to the removal of his evil counsellors, they first vanquished and put to flight Robert de Vere, his chief favorite; and then, coming up to London with a huge army, required the king, then withdrawn for fear, but no further off than the Tower, to come to Westminster. Which he refusing, they told him flatly, that unless he came they would choose another. So high a crime it was accounted then for kings to absent themselves, not from a parliament, which none ever durst, but from any meeting of his peers and counsellors, which did but tend towards a parliament. Much less would they have suffered, that a king, for such trivial and various pretences, one while for fear of tumults, another while "for shame to see them," should leave his regal station, and the whole kingdom bleeding to death of those wounds, which his own unskilful and perverse government had inflicted.

Shame then it was that drove him from the parliament, but the shame of what? Was it not the shame of his manifold errors and misdeeds, and to see how weakly he had played the king? No; "but to see the barbarous rudeness of those tumults to demand anything." We have started here another, and I believe the truest cause of his deserting the parliament. The worst and strangest of that "Anything" which the people then demanded, was but the unlording of bishops, and expelling them the house, and the reducing of church-discipline to a conformity with other protestant churches; this was the barbarism of those tumults: and that he might avoid the granting of those honest and pious demands, as well demanded by the parliament as the people, for this very cause more than for fear, by his own confession here, he left the city; and in a most tempestuous season forsook the helm and steerage of the commonwealth. This was that terrible "Anything," from which his conscience and his reason chose to run, rather than not deny. To be importuned the removing of evil counsellors, and other grievances in church and state, was to him "an intolerable oppression." If the people's demanding were so burdensome to him, what was his denial and delay of justice to them?

But as the demands of his people were to him a burden and oppression, so was the advice of his parliament esteemed a bondage; "Whose agreeing votes," as he affirms, "were not by any law or reason conclusive to his judgment." For the law, it ordains a parliament to advise him in his great affairs; but if it ordain also, that the single judgment of a king shall out-balance all the wisdom of his parliament, it ordains that which frustrates the end of its own ordaining. For where the king's judgment may dissent, to the destruction, as it may happen, both of himself and the kingdom, their advice, and no further, is a most insufficient and frustraneous means to be provided by law in case of so high concernment. And where the main and principal law of common preservation against tyranny is left so fruitless and infirm, there it must needs follow, that all lesser laws are to their several ends and purposes much more weak and ineffectual. For that nation would deserve to be renowned and chronicled for folly and stupidity, that should by law provide force against private and petty wrongs, advice only against tyranny and public ruin.

It being therefore most unlike a law, to ordain a remedy so slender and unlawlike, to be the utmost means of all our safety or prevention, as advice is, which may at any time be rejected by the sole judgment of one man, the king, and so unlike the law of England, which lawyers say is the quintessence of reason and mature wisdom; we may conclude, that the king's negative voice was never any law, but an absurd and reasonless custom, begotten and grown up either from the flattery of basest times, or the usurpation of immoderate princes. Thus much to the law of it, by a better evidence than rolls and records—reason. But is it possible he should pretend also to reason, that the judgment of one man, not

as a wise or good man, but as a king, and ofttimes a wilful, proud, and wicked king, should outweigh the prudence and all the virtue of an elected parliament? What an abusive thing were it then to summon parliaments, that by the major part of voices greatest matters may be there debated and resolved, whenas one single voice after that shall dash all their resolutions?

He attempts to give a reason why it should: "Because the whole parliament represents not him in any kind." But mark how little he advances; for if the parliament represent the whole kingdom, as is sure enough they do, then doth the king represent only himself; and if a king without his kingdom be in a civil sense nothing, then without or against the representative of his whole kingdom, he himself represents nothing; and by consequence his judgment and his negative is as good as nothing. And though we should allow him to be something, yet not equivalent or comparable to the whole kingdom, and so neither to them who represent it; much less that one syllable of his breath put into the scales should be more ponderous than the joint voice and efficacy of a whole parliament, assembled by election, and endued with the plenipotence of a free nation, to make laws, not to be denied laws; and with no more but "no!" a sleeveless reason, in the most pressing times of danger and disturbance to be sent home frustrate and remediless.

Yet here he maintains, "to be no further bound to agree with the votes of both houses, than he sees them to agree with the will of God, with his just rights as a king, and the general good of his people." As to the freedom of his agreeing or not agreeing, limited with due bounds, no man reprehends it; this is the question here, or the miracle rather, why his only not agreeing should lay a negative bar and inhibition upon that which is agreed to by a whole parliament, though never so conducing to the public good or safety? To know the will of God better than his whole kingdom, whence should he have it? Certainly court-breeding and his perpetual conversation with flatterers was but a bad school. To judge of his own rights could not belong to him, who had no right by law in any court to judge of so much as felony or treason, being held a party in both these cases, much more in this; and his rights however should give place to the general good, for which end all his rights were given him.

Lastly, to suppose a clearer insight and discerning of the general good, allotted to his own singular judgment, than to the parliament and all the people, and from that self-opinion of discerning, to deny them that good which they, being all freemen, seek earnestly and call for, is an arrogance, and iniquity beyond imagination rude and unreasonable; they undoubtedly having most authority to judge of the public good, who for that purpose are chosen out and sent by the people to advise him. And if it may be in him to see oft "the major part of them not in the right," had it not been more his modesty, to have doubted their seeing him more often in the wrong?

He passes to another reason of his denials: "Because of some men's hydropic unsatiableness, and thirst of asking, the more they drank, whom no fountain of regal bounty was able to overcome." A comparison more properly bestowed on those that came to guzzle in his wine-cellar, than on a free-born people that came to claim in parliament their rights and liberties, which a king ought therefore to grant, because of right demanded; not to deny them for fear his bounty should be exhaust, which in these demands (to continue the same metaphor) was not so much as broached; it being his duty, not his bounty, to grant these things. He who thus refuses to give us law, in that refusal gives us another law, which is his will, another name also, and another condition; of freemen to become his vassals.

Putting off the courtier, he now puts on the philosopher, and sententiously disputes to this effect, "that reason ought to be used to men, force and terror to beasts; that he deserves to be a slave, who captivates the rational sovereignty of his soul and liberty of his will to compulsion; that he would not forfeit that freedom, which cannot be denied him as a king, because it belongs to him as a man and a Christian, though to preserve his kingdom; but rather die enjoying the empire of his soul, than live in such a vassalage as not to use his reason and conscience, to like or dislike as a king." Which words, of themselves, as far as they are sense, good and

philosophical, yet in the mouth of him, who, to engross this common liberty to himself would tread down all other men into the condition of slaves and beasts, they quite lose their commendation. He confesses a rational sovereignty of soul and freedom of will in every man, and yet with an implicit repugnancy would have his reason the sovereign of that sovereignty, and would captivate and make useless that natural freedom of will in all other men but himself.

But them that yield him this obedience he so well rewards, as to pronounce them worthy to be slaves. They who have lost all to be his subjects, may stoop and take up the reward. What that freedom is, which "cannot be denied him as a king, because it belongs to him as a man and a Christian," I understand not. If it be his negative voice, it concludes all men, who have not such a negative as his against a whole parliament, to be neither men nor Christians: and what was he himself then, all this while that we denied it him as a king? Will he say, that he enjoyed within himself the less freedom for that? Might not he, both as a man and as a Christian, have reigned within himself in full sovereignty of soul, no man repining, but that his outward and imperious will must invade the civil liberties of a nation? Did we therefore not permit him to use his reason or his conscience, not permitting him to bereave us the use of ours? And might not he have enjoyed both as a king, governing us as freemen by what laws we ourselves would be governed? It was not the inward use of his reason and of his conscience, that would content him, but to use them both as a law over all his subjects, "in whatever he declared as a king to like or dislike." Which use of reason, most reasonless and unconscionable, is the utmost that any tyrant ever pretended over his vassals.

In all wise nations the legislative power, and the judicial execution of that power, have been most commonly distinct, and in several hands; but yet the former supreme, the other subordinate. If then the king be only set up to execute the law, which is indeed the highest of his office, he ought no more to make or forbid the making of any law, agreed upon in parliament, than other inferior judges, who are his deputies. Neither can he more reject a law offered him by the commons, than he can new make a law, which they reject. And yet the more to credit and uphold his cause, he would seem to have philosophy on his side; straining her wise dictates to unphilosophical purposes. But when kings come so low, as to fawn upon philosophy, which before they neither valued nor understood, it is a sign that fails not, they are then put to their last trump. And philosophy as well requites them, by not suffering her golden sayings either to become their lips, or to be used as masks and colors of injurious and violent deeds. So that what they presume to borrow from her sage and virtuous rules, like the riddle of Sphinx not understood, breaks the neck of their own cause.

But now again to politics: "He cannot think the majesty of the crown of England to be bound by any coronation oath in a blind and brutish formality, to consent to whatever its subjects in parliament shall require." What tyrant could presume to say more, when he meant to kick down all law, government, and bond of oath? But why he so desires to absolve himself the oath of his coronation would be worth the knowing. It cannot but be yielded, that the oath, which binds him to performance of his trust, ought in reason to contain the sum of what his chief trust and office is. But if it neither do enjoin, nor mention to him, as a part of his duty, the making or the marring of any law, or scrap of law, but requires only his assent to those laws which the people have already chosen, or shall choose; (for so both the Latin of that oath, and the old English; and all reason admits, that the people should not lose under a new king what freedom they had before;) then that negative voice so contended for, to deny the passing of any law which the commons choose, is both against the oath of his coronation, and his kingly office.

And if the king may deny to pass what the parliament hath chosen to be a law, then doth the king make himself superior to his whole kingdom; which not only the general maxims of policy gainsay, but even our own standing laws, as hath been cited to him in remonstrances heretofore, that "the king hath two superiors, the law, and his court of parliament." But this he counts to be a blind and brutish formality, whether it be law, or oath, or his duty, and thinks to turn it off with wholesome words and phrases, which he then first learnt of the honest people, when they were so often compelled to use them against those more truly blind and brutish formalities thrust upon us by his own command, not in civil matters only, but in spiritual. And if his oath to perform what the people require, when they crown him, be in his esteem a brutish formality, then doubtless those other oaths of allegiance and supremacy, taken absolute on our part, may most justly appear to us in all respects as brutish and as formal; and so by his own sentence no more binding to us, than his oath to him.

As for his instance, in case "he and the house of peers attempted to enjoin the house of commons," it bears no equality; for he and the peers represent but themselves, the commons are the whole kingdom. Thus he concludes "his oath to be fully discharged in governing by laws already made," as being not bound to pass any new, "if his reason bids him deny." And so may infinite mischiefs grow, and he with a pernicious negative may deny us all things good, or just, or safe, whereof our ancestors, in times much differing from ours, had either no foresight, or no occasion to foresee; while our general good and safety shall depend upon the private and overweening reason of one obstinate man, who against all the kingdom, if he list, will interpret both the law and his oath of coronation by the tenor of his own will. Which he himself confesses to be an arbitrary power, yet doubts not in his argument to imply, as if he thought it more fit the parliament should be subject to his will, than he to their advice; a man neither by nature nor by nurture wise. How is it possible, that he, in whom such principles as these were so deep rooted, could ever, though restored again, have reigned otherwise than tyrannically?

He objects. "That force was but a slavish method to dispel his error." But how often shall it be answered him, that no force was used to dispel the error out of his head, but to drive it from off our necks? for his error was imperious, and would command all other men to renounce their own reason and understanding, till they perished under the injunction of his all-ruling error. He alleges the uprightness of his intentions to excuse his possible failings, a position false both in law and divinity: yea, contrary to his own better principles, who affirms in the twelfth chapter, that "the goodness of a man's intention will not excuse the scandal and contagion of his example." His not knowing, through the corruption of flattery and court-principles, what he ought to have known, will not excuse his not doing what he ought to have done; no more than the small skill of him, who undertakes to be a pilot, will excuse him to be misled by any wandering star mistaken for the pole. But let his intentions be never so upright, what is that to us? What answer for the reason and the national rights, which God hath given us, if, having parliaments, and laws, and the power of making more, to avoid mischief, we suffer one man's blind intentions to lead us all with our eyes open to manifest destruction?

And if arguments prevail not with such a one, force is well used; not "to carry on the weakness of our counsels, or to convince his error," as he surmises, but to acquit and rescue our own reason, our own consciences, from the force and prohibition laid by his usurping error upon our liberties and understandings. "Never thing pleased him more, than when his judgment concurred with theirs." That was to the applause of his own judgment, and would as well have pleased any self-conceited man.

"Yea, in many things he chose rather to deny himself than them." That is to say, in trifles. For "of his own interests" and personal rights he conceives himself "master." To part with, if he please; not to contest for, against the kingdom, which is greater than he, whose rights are all subordinate to the kingdom's good. And "in what concerns truth, justice, the right of church, or his crown, no man shall gain his consent against his mind." What can be left then for a parliament, but to sit like images, while he still thus, either with incomparable arrogance assumes to himself the best ability of judging for other men what is truth, justice, goodness, what his own or the church's right, or with unsufferable tyranny restrains all men from the enjoyment

of any good which his judgment, though erroneous, thinks not fit to grant them; notwithstanding that the law and his coronal oath require his undeniable assent to what laws the parliament agree upon?

"He had rather wear a crown of thorns with our Saviour." Many would be all one with our Saviour, whom our Saviour will not know. They who govern ill those kingdoms which they had a right to, have to our Saviour's crown of thorns no right at all. Thorns they may find enow of their own gathering, and their own twisting; for thorns and snares, saith Solomon, are in the way of the froward: but to wear them as our Saviour wore them, is not given to them that suffer by their own demerits. Nor is a crown of gold his due, who cannot first wear a crown of lead; not only for the weight of that great office, but for the compliance which it ought to have with them who are to counsel him, which here he terms in scorn, "an imbased flexibleness to the various and oft contrary dictates of any factions," meaning his parliament: for the question hath been all this while between them two. And to his parliament, though a numerous and choice assembly of whom the land thought wisest, he imputes, rather than to himself, "want of reason, neglect of the public, interest of parties, and particularity of private will and passion;" but with what modesty or likelihood of truth, it will be wearisome to repeat so often.

He concludes with a sentence fair in seeming, but fallacious. For if the conscience be ill edified, the resolution may more befit a foolish than a Christian king, to prefer a self-willed conscience before a kingdom's good; especially in the denial of that, which law and his regal office by oath bids him grant to his parliament and whole kingdom rightfully demanding. For we may observe him throughout the discourse to assert his negative power against the whole kingdom; now under the specious plea of his conscience and his reason, but heretofore in a louder note: "Without us, or against our consent, the votes of either or of both houses together, must not, cannot, shall not." (Declar. May 4, 1642.) With these and the like deceivable doctrines he leavens also his prayer.

CHAPTER VII.

Upon the Queen's Departure.

To this argument we shall soon have said; for what concerns it us to hear a husband divulge his household privacies, extolling to others the virtues of his wife? an infirmity not seldom incident to those who have least cause. But how good she was a wife, was to himself, and be it left to his own fancy; how bad a subject, is not much disputed. And being such, it need be made no wonder, though she left a protestant kingdom with as little honor as her mother left a popish.

That this "is the first example of any protestant subjects, that have taken up arms against their king, a protestant," can be to protestants no dishonor, when it shall be heard, that he first levied war on them, and to the interest of papists more than of protestants. He might have given yet the precedence of making war upon him to the subjects of his own nation, who had twice opposed him in the open field long ere the English found it necessary to do the like. And how groundless, how dissembled is that fear, lest she, who for so many years had been averse from the religion of her husband, and every year more and more, before these disturbances broke out, should for them be now the more alienated from that, to which we never heard she was inclined? But if the fear of her delinquency, and that justice which the protestants demanded on her, was any cause of her alienating the more, to have gained her by indirect means had been no advantage to religion, much less then was the detriment to lose her further off. It had been happy if his own actions had not given cause of more scandal to the protestants, than what they did against her could justly scandalize any papist.

Them who accused her, well enough known to be the parliament, he censures for "men yet to seek their religion, whether doctrine, discipline, or good manners;" the rest he soothes with the name of true English protestants, a mere schismatical name, yet he so great an enemy of schism. He ascribes "rudeness and barbarity, worse than Indian," to the English parliament; and "all virtue" to his wife, in strains that come almost to sonnetting:

how fit to govern men, undervaluing and aspersing the great council of his kingdom, in comparison of one woman! Examples are not far to seek, how great mischief and dishonor hath befallen to nations under the government of effeminate and uxorious magistrates; who being themselves governed and overswayed at home under a feminine usurpation, cannot but be far short of spirit and authority without doors, to govern a whole nation.

"Her tarrying here he could not think safe among them, who were shaking hands with allegiance, to lay faster hold on religion;" and taxes them of a duty rather than a crime, it being just to obey God rather than man, and impossible to serve two masters: I would they had quite shaken off what they stood shaking hands with; the fault was in their courage, not in their cause. In his prayer he prays that the disloyalty of his protestant subjects may not be a hindrance to her love of the true religion; and never prays, that the dissoluteness of his court, the scandals of his clergy, the unsoundness of his own judgment, the lukewarmness of his life, his letter of compliance to the pope, his permitting agents at Rome, the pope's nuncio, and her jesuited mother here, may not be found in the sight of God far greater hindrances to her conversion.

But this had been a subtle prayer indeed, and well prayed, though as duly as a Paternoster, if it could have charmed us to sit still, and have religion and our liberties one by one snatched from us, for fear lest rising to defend ourselves we should fright the queen, a stiff papist, from turning protestant! As if the way to make his queen a protestant, had been to make his subjects more than halfway papists. He prays next, "that his constancy may be an antidote against the poison of other men's example." His constancy in what? Not in religion, for it is openly known, that her religion wrought more upon him, than his religion upon her; and his open favoring of papists, and his hatred of them called puritans, (the ministers also that prayed in churches for her conversion, being checked from court,) made most men suspect she had quite perverted him. But what is it, that the blindness of hypocrisy dares not do? It dares pray, and thinks to hide that from the eyes of God, which it cannot hide from the open view of man.

CHAPTER VIII.

Upon his Repulse at Hull, and the Fate of the Hothams.

HULL, a town of great strength and opportunity both to sea and land affairs, was at that time the magazine of all those arms which the king had bought with money most illegally extorted from his subjects of England, to use in a causeless and most unjust civil war against his subjects of Scotland. The king in high discontent and anger had left the parliament, and was gone towards the north, the queen into Holland, where she pawned and set to sale the crown jewels; (a crime heretofore counted treasonable in kings;) and to what intent these sums were raised, the parliament was not ignorant. His going northward in so high a chafe they doubted was to possess himself of that strength which the storehouse and situation of Hull might add suddenly to his malignant party. Having first therefore in many petitions earnestly prayed him to dispose and settle, with consent of both houses, the military power in trusty hands, and he as oft refusing, they were necessitated by the turbulence and danger of those times, to put the kingdom by their own authority into a posture of defence; and very timely sent Sir John Hotham, a member of the house, and knight of that county, to take Hull into his custody, and some of the trained bands to his assistance.

For besides the general danger, they had, before the king's going to York, notice given them of his private commissions to the Earl of Newcastle, and to Colonel Legg, one of those employed to bring the army up against the parliament; who had already made some attempts, and the latter of them under a disguise, to surprise that place for the king's party. And letters of the Lord Digby were intercepted, wherein was wished, that the king would declare himself, and retire to some safe place; other information came from abroad, that Hull was the place designed for some new enterprise. And accordingly Digby himself not long after, with many other commanders, and much foreign ammunition, landed in those parts. But these attempts not succeeding, and that town being now in custody of the parliament, he sends a message to them, that he had firmly resolved to go in person into Ireland, to chastise those wicked rebels, (for these and worse words he then gave them,) and that towards this work he intended forthwith to raise by his commissions, in the counties near Westchester, a guard for his own person, consisting of two thousand foot, and two hundred horse, that should be armed from his magazine at Hull.

On the other side, the parliament, foreseeing the king's drift, about the same time send him a petition, that they might have leave for necessary causes to remove the magazine of Hull to the Tower of London, to which the king returns his denial; and soon after going to Hull attended with about four hundred horse, requires the governor to deliver him up the town: whereof the governor besought humbly to be excused, till he could send notice to the parliament, who had intrusted him. Whereat the king much incensed proclaims him traitor before the town walls, and gives immediate order to stop all passages between him and the parliament. Yet he himself dispatches post after post to demand justice, as upon a traitor; using a strange iniquity to require justice upon him, whom he then waylaid, and debarred from his appearance. The parliament no sooner understood what had passed, but they declare, that Sir John Hotham had done no more than was his duty, and was therefore no traitor.

This relation, being most true, proves that which is affirmed here to be most false; seeing the parliament, whom he accounts his "greatest enemies," had "more confidence to abet and own," what Sir John Hotham had done, than the king had confidence to let him answer in his own behalf. To speak of his patience, and in that solemn manner, he might better have forborne; "God knows," saith he, "it affected me more with sorrow for others, than with anger for myself; nor did the affront trouble me so much as their sin." This is read, I doubt not, and believed: and as there is some use of everything, so is there of this book, were it but to show us, what a miserable, credulous, deluded thing that creature is, which is called the vulgar; who, notwithstanding what they might know, will believe such vain glories as these. Did not that choleric and vengeful act of proclaiming him traitor before due process of law, having been convinced so late before of his illegality with the five members, declare his anger to be incensed? Doth not his own relation confess as much? And his second message left him fuming three days after, and in plain words testifies "his impatience of delay" till Hotham be severely punished, for that which he there terms an insupportable affront.

Surely if his sorrow for Sir John Hotham's sin were greater than his anger for the affront, it was an exceeding great sorrow indeed, and wondrous charitable. But if it stirred him so vehemently to have Sir John Hotham punished, and not at all, that we hear, to have him repent, it had a strange operation to be called a sorrow for his sin. He who would persuade us of his sorrow for the sins of other men, as they are sins, not as they are sinned against himself, must give us first some testimony of a sorrow for his own sins, and next for such sins of other men as cannot be supposed a direct injury to himself. But such compunction in the king no man hath yet observed; and till then his sorrow for John Hotham's sin will be called no other than the resentment of his repulse; and his labor to have the sinner only punished will be called by a right name, his revenge.

And "the hand of that cloud, which cast all soon after into darkness and disorder," was his own hand. For, assembling the inhabitants of Yorkshire and other counties, horse and foot, first under color of a new guard to his person, soon after, being supplied with ammunition from Holland, bought with the crown jewels, he begins an open war by laying siege to Hull: which town was not his own, but the kingdom's; and the arms there, public arms, bought with the public money, or not his own. Yet had they been his own by as good right as the private house and arms of any man are his own; to use either of them in a way not private, but suspicious to the commonwealth, no law permits. But the king had no propriety at all either in Hull or in the magazine: so that the following maxims, which he cites, "of bold and disloyal under-

takers," may belong more justly to whom he least meant them. After this, he again relapses into the praise of his patience at Hull, and by his overtalking of it seems to doubt either his own conscience or the hardness of other men's belief. To me the more he praises it in himself, the more he seems to suspect that in very deed it was not in him; and that the lookers on so likewise thought.

Thus much of what he suffered by Hotham, and with what patience; now of what Hotham suffered, as he judges, for opposing him: "he could not but observe how God, not long after, pleaded and avenged his cause." Most men are too apt, and commonly the worst of men, so to interpret, and expound the judgments of God, and all other events of Providence or chance, as makes most to the justifying of their own cause, though never so evil; and attribute all to the particular favor of God towards them. Thus when Saul heard that David was in Keilah, "God," saith he, "hath delivered him into my hands, for he is shut in." But how far that king was deceived in his thought that God was favoring to his cause, that story unfolds; and how little reason this king had to impute the death of Hotham to God's avengement of his repulse at Hull, may easily be seen.

For while Hotham continued faithful to his trust, no man more safe, more successful, more in reputation than he: but from the time he first sought to make his peace with the king, and to betray into his hands that town, into which before he had denied him entrance, nothing prospered with him. Certainly had God purposed him such an end for his opposition to the king, he would not have deferred to punish him till then, when of an enemy he was changed to be the king's friend, nor have made his repentance and amendment the occasion of his ruin. How much more likely is it, since he fell into the act of disloyalty to his charge, that the judgment of God concurred with the punishment of man, and justly cut him off for revolting to the king; to give the world an example, that glorious deeds done to ambitious ends find reward answerable, not to their outward seeming, but to their inward ambition! In the meanwhile, what thanks he had from the king for revolting to his cause, and what good opinion for dying in his service, they who have ventured like him, or intend, may here take notice.

He proceeds to declare, not only in general wherefore God's judgment was upon Hotham, but undertakes by fancies and allusions to give a criticism upon every particular, "that his head was divided from his body, because his heart was divided from the king; two heads cut off in one family for affronting the head of the commonwealth; the eldest son being infected with the sin of his father, against the father of his country." These petty glosses and conceits on the high and secret judgments of God, besides the boldness of unwarrantable commenting, are so weak and shallow, and so like the quibbles of a court sermon, that we may safely reckon them either fetched from such a pattern, or that the hand of some household priest foisted them in; lest the world should forget how much he was a disciple of those cymbal doctors. But that argument, by which the author would commend them to us, discredits them the more; for if they be so "obvious to every fancy," the more likely to be erroneous, and to misconceive the mind of those high secrecies, whereof they presume to determine. For God judges not by human fancy.

But however God judged Hotham, yet he had the king's pity. But mark the reason, how preposterous; so far he had his pity, "as he thought he at first acted more against the light of his conscience, than many other men in the same cause." Questionless they who act against conscience, whether at the bar of human or divine justice, are pitied least of all. These are the common grounds and verdicts of nature, whereof when he who hath the judging of a whole nation is found destitute under such a governor that nation must needs be miserable. By the way he jerks at "some men's reforming to models of religion, and that they think all is gold of piety, that doth but glister with a show of zeal." We know his meaning, and apprehend how little hope there could be of him from such language as this; but are sure that the piety of his prelatic model glistered more upon the posts and pillars which their zeal and fervency gilded over, than in the true works of spiritual edification.

"He is sorry that Hotham felt the justice of others, and fell not rather into the hands of his mercy." But to clear that, he should have shown us what mercy he had ever used to such as fell into his hands before, rather than what mercy he intended to such as never could come to ask it. Whatever mercy one man might have expected, 'tis too well known the whole nation found none; though they besought it often, and so humbly; but had been swallowed up in blood and ruin, to set his private will above the parliament, had not his strength failed him. "Yet clemency he counts a debt, which he ought to pay to those that crave it; since we pay not anything to God for his mercy but prayers and praises." By this reason we ought as freely to pay all things to all men; for of all that we receive from God, what do we pay for, more than prayers and praises? We looked for the discharge of his office, the payment of his duty to the kingdom, and are paid court-payment, with empty sentences that have the sound of gravity, but the significance of nothing pertinent.

Yet again after his mercy past and granted, he returns back to give sentence upon Hotham; and whom he tells us he would so fain have saved alive, him he never leaves killing with a repeated condemnation, though dead long since. It was ill that somebody stood not near to whisper him, that a reiterating judge is worse than a tormentor. "He pities him, he rejoices not, he pities him" again; but still is sure to brand him at the tail of his pity with some ignominious mark, either of ambition or disloyalty. And with a kind of censorious pity aggravates rather than lessens or conceals the fault: to pity thus, is to triumph. He assumes to foreknow, that "after times will dispute whether Hotham were more infamous at Hull, or at Tower-hill." What knew he of after times, who, while he sits judging and censuring without end the fate of that unhappy father and his son at Tower-hill, knew not the like fate attended him before his own palace-gate; and as little knew whether after times reserve not a greater infamy to the story of his own life and reign?

He says but over again in his prayer what his sermon hath preached: how acceptably to those in heaven we leave to be decided by that precept, which forbids "vain repetitions." Sure enough it lies as heavy as he can lay it upon the head of poor Hotham. Needs he will fasten upon God a piece of revenge as done for his sake; and takes it for a favor, before he know it was intended him: which in his closet had been excusable, but in a written and published prayer too presumptuous. Ecclesiastes hath a right name for such kind of sacrifices.

Going on he prays thus: "Let not thy justice prevent the objects and opportunities of my mercy." To folly, or to blasphemy, or to both, shall we impute this? Shall the justice of God give place, and serve to glorify the mercies of a man? All other men, who know what they ask, desire of God that their doings may tend to his glory; but in this prayer God is required, that his justice would forbear to prevent, and as good have said to intrench upon the glory of a man's mercy. If God forbear his justice, it must be, sure, to the magnifying of his own mercy: how then can any mortal man, without presumption little less than impious, take the boldness to ask that glory out of his hand? It may be doubted now by them who understand religion, whether the king were more unfortunate in this his prayer, or Hotham in those his sufferings.

———

CHAPTER IX.

Upon the listing and raising Armies, &c.

It were an endless work to walk side by side with the verbosity of this chapter; only to what already hath not been spoken, convenient answer shall be given. He begins again with tumults: all demonstration of the people's love and loyalty to the parliament was tumult; their petitioning tumult; their defensive armies were but listed tumults; and will take no notice that those about him, those in a time of peace listed into his own house, were the beginners of all these tumults, abusing and assaulting not only such as came peaceably to the parliament at London, but those that came petitioning to the king himself at York. Neither did they abstain from doing violence and outrage to the messengers sent from parliament; he himself either countenancing or conniving at them.

He supposes that "his recess gave us confidence, that he might be conquered." Other men suppose both that and all things else, who knew him neither by nature warlike, nor experienced, nor fortunate; so far was any man, that discerned aught, from esteeming him unconquerable; yet such are readiest to embroil others. "But he had a soul invincible." What praise is that? The stomach of a child is ofttimes invincible to all correction. The unteachable man hath a soul to all reason and good advice invincible; and he who is intractable, he whom nothing can persuade, may boast himself invincible; whenas in some things to be overcome, is more honest and laudable than to conquer.

He labors to have it thought, "that his fearing God more than man" was the ground of his sufferings; but he should have known that a good principle not rightly understood may prove as hurtful as a bad; and his fear of God may be as faulty as a blind zeal. He pretended to fear God more than the parliament, who never urged him to do otherwise; he should also have feared God more than he did his courtiers, and the bishops, who drew him as they pleased to things inconsistent with the fear of God. Thus boasted Saul to have "performed the commandment of God," and stood in it against Samuel; but it was found at length, that he had feared the people more than God, in saving those fat oxen for the worship of God, which were appointed to destruction. Not much unlike, if not much worse, was that fact of his, who, for fear to displease his court and mongrel clergy, with the dissolutest of the people, upheld in the church of God, while his power lasted, those beasts of Amalec, the prelates, against the advice of his parliament and the example of all reformation; in this more unexcusable than Saul, that Saul was at length convinced, he to the hour of death fixed in his false persuasion; and soothes himself in the flattering peace of an erroneous and obdurate conscience; singing to his soul vain psalms of exultation, as if the parliament had assailed his reason with the force of arms, and not he on the contrary their reason with his arms; which hath been proved already, and shall be more hereafter.

He twits them with "his acts of grace;" proud, and unselfknowing words in the mouth of any king, who affects not to be a god, and such as ought to be as odious in the ears of a free nation. For if they were unjust acts, why did he grant them as of grace? If just, it was not of his grace, but of his duty and his oath to grant them. "A glorious king he would be, though by his sufferings:" but that can never be to him whose sufferings are his own doings. He feigns "a hard choice" put upon him, "either to kill his own subjects, or be killed." Yet never was king less in danger of any violence from his subjects, till he unsheathed his sword against them; nay, long after that time, when he had spilt the blood of thousands, they had still his person in a foolish veneration.

He complains "that civil war must be the fruits of his seventeen years reigning with such a measure of justice, peace, plenty, and religion, as all nations either admired or envied." For the justice we had, let the counciltable, star-chamber, high-commission speak the praise of it; not forgetting the unprincely usage, and as far as might be, the abolishing of parliaments, the displacing of honest judges, the sale of offices, bribery, and exaction, not found out to be punished, but to be shared in with impunity for the time to come. Who can number the extortions, the oppressions, the public robberies and rapines committed on the subject both by sea and land, under various pretences? their possessions also taken from them, one while as forest-land, another while as crown-land; nor were their goods exempted, no, not the bullion in the mint; piracy was become a project owned and authorized against the subject.

For the peace we had, what peace was that which drew out the English to a needless and dishonorable voyage against the Spaniard at Cales? Or that which lent our shipping to a treacherous and antichristian war against the poor protestants of Rochelle our suppliants? What peace was that which fell to rob the French by sea, to the embarring of all our merchants in that kingdom? which brought forth that unblest expedition to the Isle of Rhé, doubtful whether more calamitous in the success, or in the design, betraying all the flower of our military youth and best commanders to a shameful surprisal and execution. This was the peace we had, and the peace we gave, whether to friends or to foes abroad. And if at home any peace were intended us, what meant those Irish billetted soldiers in all parts of the kingdom, and the design of German horse to subdue us in our peaceful houses?

For our religion, where was there a more ignorant, profane, and vicious clergy, learned in nothing but the antiquity of their pride, their covetousness, and superstition? whose unsincere and leavenous doctrine, corrupting the people, first taught them looseness, then bondage; loosening them from all sound knowledge and strictness of life, the more to fit them for the bondage of tyranny and superstition. So that what was left us for other nations not to pity, rather than admire or envy, all those seventeen years, no wise man could see. For wealth and plenty in a land where justice reigns not is no argument of a flourishing state, but of a nearness rather to ruin or commotion.

These were not "some miscarriages" only of government, "which might escape," but a universal distemper, and reducement of law to arbitrary power; not through the evil counsels of "some men," but through the constant course and practice of all that were in highest favor: whose worst actions frequently avowing he took upon himself; and what faults did not yet seem in public to be originally his, such care he took by professing and proclaiming openly, as made them all at length his own adopted sins. The persons also, when he could no longer protect, he esteemed and favored to the end; but never otherwise than by constraint yielded any of them to due punishment; thereby manifesting that what they did was by his own authority and approbation.

Yet here he asks, "whose innocent blood he hath shed, what widows' or orphans' tears can witness against him?" After the suspected poisoning of his father, not inquired into but smothered up, and him protected and advanced to the very half of his kingdom, who was accused in parliament to be author of the fact; (with much more evidence than duke Dudley, that false protector, is accused upon record to have poisoned Edward the Sixth;) after all his rage and persecution, after so many years of cruel war on his people in three kingdoms! Whence the author of "Truths Manifest," a Scotsman, not unacquainted with affairs, positively affirms, "that there hath been more Christian blood shed by the commission, approbation, and connivance of king Charles, and his father, James, in the latter end of their reign, than in the ten Roman persecutions." Not to speak of those many whippings, pillories, and other corporal inflictions, wherewith his reign also, before this war, was not unbloody; some have died in prison under cruel restraint, others in banishment, whose lives were shortened through the rigor of that persecution wherewith so many years he infested the true church.

And those six members all men judged to have escaped no less than capital danger, whom he so greedily pursuing into the house of commons, had not there the forbearance to conceal how much it troubled him, "that the birds were flown." If some vulture in the mountains could have opened his beak intelligibly and spoke, what fitter words could he have uttered at the loss of his prey? The tyrant Nero, though not yet deserving that name, set his hand so unwillingly to the execution of a condemned person, as to wish "he had not known letters." Certainly for a king himself to charge his subjects with high-treason, and so vehemently to prosecute them in his own cause, as to do the office of a searcher, argued in him no great aversation from shedding blood, were it but to "satisfy his anger," and that revenge was no unpleasing morsel to him, whereof he himself thought not much to be so diligently his own caterer. But we insist rather upon what was actual, than what was probable.

He now falls to examine the causes of this war, as a difficulty which he had long "studied" to find out. "It was not," saith he, "my withdrawing from Whitehall; for no account in reason could be given of those tumults, where an orderly guard was granted." But if it be a most certain truth, that the parliament could never yet obtain of him any guard fit to be confided in, then by his own confession some account of those pretended tumults "may in reason be given;" and both concerning them and the guards enough hath been said already.

"Whom did he protect against the justice of parliament?" Whom did he not to his utmost power? Endeavoring to have rescued Strafford from their justice, though with the destruction of them and the city; to that end expressly commanding the admittance of new soldiers into the Tower, raised by Suckling and other conspirators under pretence for the Portugal: though that ambassador being sent to, utterly denied to know of any such commission from his master. And yet, that listing continued: not to repeat his other plot of bringing up the two armies. But what can be disputed with such a king, in whose mouth and opinion the parliament itself was never but a faction, and their justice no justice, but "the dictates and overswaying insolence of tumults and rabbles?" and under that excuse avouches himself openly the general patron of most notorious delinquents, and approves their flight out of the land, whose crimes were such, as that the justest and the fairest trial would have soonest condemned them to death.

But did not Catiline plead in like manner against the Roman senate, and the injustice of their trial, and the justice of his flight from Rome? Cæsar also, then hatching tyranny, injected the same scrupulous demurs, to stop the sentence of death in full and free senate decreed on Lentulus and Cethegus, two of Catiline's accomplices, which were renewed and urged for Strafford. He vouchsafes to the reformation, by both kingdoms intended, no better name than "innovation and ruin both in church and state." And what we would have learned so gladly of him in other passages before, to know wherein, he tells us now of his own accord. The expelling of bishops out of the house of peers, this was "ruin to the state;" the "removing" them "root and branch," this was "ruin to the church." How happy could this nation be in such a governor, who counted that their ruin, which they thought their deliverance; the ruin both of church and state, which was the recovery and the saving of them both?

To the passing of those bills against bishops how is it likely that the house of peers gave so hardly their consent, which they gave so easily before to the attaching them of high-treason, twelve at once, only for protesting that the parliament could not act without them? Surely if their rights and privileges were thought so undoubted in that house, as is here maintained; then was that protestation, being meant and intended in the name of their whole spiritual order, no treason; and so that house itself will become liable to a just construction either of injustice to appeach them for so consenting, or of usurpation, representing none but themselves, to expect that their voting or not voting should obstruct the commons: who not for "five repulses of the lords," no, not for fifty, were to desist from what in name of the whole kingdom they demanded, so long as those lords were none of our lords. And for the bill against root and branch, though it passed not in both houses till many of the lords and some few of the commons, either enticed away by the king, or overawed by the sense of their own malignancy not prevailing, deserted the parliament, and made a fair riddance of themselves; that was no warrant for them who remained faithful, being far the greater number, to lay aside that bill of root and branch, till the return of their fugitives; a bill so necessary and so much desired by themselves as well as by the people.

This was the partiality, this degrading of the bishops, a thing so wholesome in the state, and so orthodoxal in the church, both ancient and reformed; which the king rather than assent to "will either hazard both his own and the kingdom's ruin," by our just defence against his force of arms; or prostrate our consciences in a blind obedience to himself, and those men, whose superstition, zealous or unzealous, would enforce upon us an antichristian tyranny in the church, neither primitive, apostolical, nor more anciently universal than some other manifest corruptions.

But "he was bound, besides his judgment, by a most strict and undispensable oath, to preserve that order and the rights of the church." If he mean the oath of his coronation, and that the letter of that oath admit not to be interpreted either by equity, reformation, or better knowledge, then was the king bound by that oath, to grant the clergy all those customs, franchises, and canonical privileges granted to them by Edward the Confessor; and so might one day, under pretence of that oath and his conscience, have brought us all again to popery. But had he so well remembered as he ought the words to which he swore, he might have found himself no otherwise obliged there, than "according to the laws of God, and true profession of the gospel." For if those following words, "established in this kingdom," be set there to limit and lay prescription on the laws of God and truth of the gospel by man's establishment, nothing can be more absurd or more injurious to religion. So that however, the German emperors or other kings have levied all those wars on their protestant subjects under the color of a blind and literal observance to an oath, yet this king had least pretence of all; both sworn to the laws of God and evangelic truth, and disclaiming, as we heard him before, "to be bound by any coronation oath, in a blind and brutish formality." Nor is it to be imagined, if what shall be established come in question, but that the parliament should oversway the king and not he the parliament. And by all law and reason that which the parliament will not is no more established in this kingdom, neither is the king bound by oath to uphold it as a thing established. And that the king (who of princely grace, as he professes, hath so oft abolished things that stood firm by law, as the star-chamber and high commission) ever thought himself bound by oath to keep them up, because established; he who will believe, must at the same time condemn him of as many perjuries, as he is well known to have abolished both laws and jurisdictions that wanted no establishment.

"Had he gratified," he thinks, "their anti-episcopal faction with his consent, and sacrificed the church-government and revenues to the fury of their covetousness," &c. an army had not been raised. Whereas it was the fury of his own hatred to the professors of true religion, which first incited him to persecute them with the sword of war, when whips, pillories, exiles, and imprisonments were not thought sufficient. To color which he cannot find wherewithal, but that stale pretence of Charles V., and other popish kings, that the protestants had only an intent to lay hands upon church revenues, a thing never in the thoughts of this parliament, till, exhausted by his endless war upon them, their necessity seized on that for the commonwealth, which the luxury of prelates had abused before to a common mischief.

His consent to the unlording of bishops, (for to that he himself consented, and at Canterbury the chief seat of their pride, so God would have it!) "was from his firm persuasion of their contentedness to suffer a present diminution of their rights." Can any man reading this, not discern the pure mockery of a royal consent, to delude us only for "the present," meaning, it seems, when time should serve, to revoke all? By this reckoning, his consents and his denials come all to one pass: and we may hence perceive the small wisdom and integrity of those votes, which voted his concessions of the Isle of Wight for grounds of a lasting peace. This he alleges, this controversy about bishops, "to be the true state" of that difference between him and the parliament. For he held episcopacy "both very sacred and divine; with this judgment, and for this cause, he withdrew from the parliament, and confesses that some men knew "he was like to bring again the same judgment which he carried with him:" A fair and unexpected justification from his own mouth afforded to the parliament, who, notwithstanding what they knew of his obstinate mind, omitted not to use all those means and that patience to have gained him.

As for delinquents, "he allows them to be but the necessary consequences of his and their withdrawing and defending:" a pretty shift! to mince the name of a delinquent into a necessary consequent. What is a traitor, but the necessary consequence of his treason? What a rebel, but of his rebellion? From this conceit he would infer a pretext only in the parliament "to fetch in delinquents," as if there had indeed been no such cause, but all the delinquency in London tumults. Which is the overworn theme and stuffing of all his discourses.

This he thrice repeats to be the true state and reason of all that war and devastation in the land; and that "of all the treaties and propositions" offered him, he was resolved "never to grant the abolishing of episcopal, or the establishment of presbyterian, government." I would demand now of the Scots and covenanters, (for so I call them, as misobservers of the covenant,) how they will reconcile "the preservation of religion and their liberties, and the bringing of delinquents to condign punishment," with the freedom, honor, and safety of this vowed resolution here, that esteems all the zeal of their prostituted covenant no better than "a noise and show of piety, a heat for reformation, filling them with prejudice, and obstructing all equality and clearness of judgment in them?" With these principles who knows but that at length he might have come to take the covenant, as others, whom they brotherly admit, have done before him? And then all, no doubt, had gone well, and ended in a happy peace.

His prayer is most of it borrowed out of David; but what if it be answered him as the Jews, who trusted in Moses, were answered by our Saviour: "There is one that accuseth you, even David, whom you misapply." He tells God, "that his enemies are many;" but tells the people, when it serves his turn, they are but "a faction of some few, prevailing over the major part of both houses." God knows he had no passion, design, or preparation to embroil his kingdom in a civil war." True; for he thought his kingdom to be Issachar, a "strong ass that would have couched down between two burdens," the one of prelatical superstition, the other of civil tyranny: but what passion and design, what close and open preparation he had made, to subdue us to both these by terror and preventive force, all the nation knows.

"The confidence of some men had almost persuaded him to suspect his own innocence." As the words of Saint Paul had almost persuaded Agrippa to be a Christian. But almost, in the work of repentance, is as good as not at all. "God," saith he, "will find out bloody and deceitful men, many of whom have not lived out half their days." It behooved him to have been more cautious how he tempted God's finding out of blood and deceit, till his own years had been further spent, or that he had enjoyed longer the fruits of his own violent counsels.

But instead of wariness he adds another temptation, charging God "to know, that the chief design of this war was either to destroy his person, or to force his judgment." And thus his prayer, from the evil practice of unjust accusing men to God, arises to the hideous rashness of accusing God before men, to know that for truth which all men know to be most false. He prays "that God would forgive the people, for they know not what they do." It is an easy matter to say over what our Saviour said; but how he loved the people other arguments than affected sayings must demonstrate. He who so oft hath presumed rashly to appeal the knowledge and testimony of God in things so evidently untrue, may be doubted what belief or esteem he had of his forgiveness, either to himself, or those for whom he would so feign that men should hear he prayed.

———

CHAPTER X.

Upon their seizing the Magazines, Forts, &c.

To put the matter soonest out of controversy who was the first beginner of this civil war, since the beginning of all war may be discerned not only by the first act of hostility, but by the counsels and preparations foregoing, it shall evidently appear that the king was still foremost in all these. No king had ever at his first coming to the crown more love and acclamation from a people; never any people found worse requital of their loyalty and good affection: first, by his extraordinary fear and mistrust, that their liberties and rights were the impairing and diminishing of his regal power, the true original of tyranny; next, by his hatred to all those who were esteemed religious; doubting that their principles too much asserted liberty. This was quickly seen by the vehemence, and the causes alleged of his persecuting, the other by his frequent and opprobrious dissolution of parliaments; after he had demanded more money of them, and they to obtain their rights had granted him, than would have bought the Turk out of Morea, and set free all the Greeks.

But when he sought to extort from us, by way of tribute, that which had been offered him conditionally in parliament, as by a free people, and that those extortions were now consumed and wasted by the luxury of his court, he began then, (for still the more he did wrong, the more he feared,) before any tumult or insurrection of the people, to take counsel how he might totally subdue them to his own will. Then was the design of German horse, while the duke reigned; and, which was worst of all, some thousands of the Irish papists were in several parts billetted upon us, while a parliament was then sitting. The pulpits resounded with no other doctrine than that which gave all property to the king, and passive obedience to the subject. After which, innumerable forms and shapes of new exactions and exactors overspread the land: nor was it enough to be impoverished, unless we were disarmed. Our trained bands, which are the trustiest and most proper strength of a free nation not at war within itself, had their arms in divers counties taken from them;

other ammunition by design was ingrossed and kept in the Tower, not to be bought without a licence, and at a high rate.

Thus far and many other ways were his counsels and preparations beforehand with us, either to a civil war, if it should happen, or to subdue us without a war, which is all one, until the raising of his two armies against the Scots, and the latter of them raised to the most perfidious breaking of a solemn pacification: the articles whereof though subscribed with his own hand, he commanded soon after to be burned openly by the hangman. What enemy durst have done him that dishonor and affront, which he did therein to himself?

After the beginning of this parliament, whom he saw so resolute and unanimous to relieve the commonwealth, and that the Earl of Strafford was condemned to die, other of his evil counsellors impeached and imprisoned; to show there wanted not evil counsel within himself sufficient to begin a war upon his subjects, though no way by them provoked, he sends an agent with letters to the King of Denmark, requiring aid against the parliament: and that aid was coming, when Divine Providence, to divert them, sent a sudden torrent of Swedes into the bowels of Denmark. He then endeavors to bring up both armies, first the English, with whom eight thousand Irish papists, raised by Strafford, and a French army were to join; then the Scots at Newcastle, whom he thought to have encouraged by telling them what money and horse he was to have from Denmark.

I mention not the Irish conspiracy till due place. These and many other were his counsels toward a civil war. His preparations, after those two armies were dismissed, could not suddenly be too open: nevertheless there were eight thousand Irish papists, which he refused to disband, though entreated by both houses, first for reasons best known to himself, next under pretence of lending them to the Spaniard; and so kept them undisbanded till very near the month wherein that rebellion broke forth. He was also raising forces in London, pretendedly to serve the Portugal, but with intent to seize the Tower; into which divers cannoniers were by him sent with many fireworks and grenadoes; and many great battering pieces were mounted against the city. The court was fortified with ammunition, and soldiers new listed, who followed the king from London, and appeared at Kingston, some hundreds of horse, in a warlike manner, with waggons of ammunition after them; the queen in Holland was buying more; of which the parliament had certain knowledge, and had not yet so much as once demanded the militia to be settled, till they knew both of her going over sea, and to what intent. For she had packed up the crown jewels to have been going long before, had not the parliament, suspecting by the discoveries at Burrowbridge what was intended with the jewels, used means to stay her journey till the winter. Hull and the magazine there had been secretly attempted under the king's hand; from whom (though in his declarations renouncing all thought of war) notes were sent oversea for supply of arms; which were no sooner come, but the inhabitants of Yorkshire and other counties were called to arms, and actual forces raised, while the parliament were yet petitioning in peace, and had not one man listed.

As to the act of hostility, though not much material in whom first it began, or by whose commissions dated first, after such counsels and preparations discovered, and so far advanced by the king, yet in that act also he will be found to have had precedency, if not at London by the assault of his armed court upon the naked people, and his attempt upon the house of commons, yet certainly at Hull: first, by his close practices on that town; next, by his siege. Thus whether counsels, preparations, or acts of hostility be considered, it appears with evidence enough, though much more might be said, that the king is truly charged to be the first beginner of these civil wars. To which may be added as a close, that in the Isle of Wight he charged it upon himself at the public treaty, and acquitted the parliament.

But as for the securing of Hull and the public stores therein, and in other places, it was no "surprisal of his strength;" the custody whereof by authority of parliament was committed into hands most fit and most responsible for such a trust. It were a folly beyond ridiculous, to count ourselves a free nation, if the king, not in parliament, but in his own person, and against them, might appropriate to himself the strength of a whole nation as his proper goods. What the laws of the land are, a parliament should know best, having both the life and death of laws in their law-giving power: and the law of England is, at best, but the reason of parliament. The parliament, therefore, taking into their hands that whereof most properly they ought to have the keeping, committed no surprisal. If they prevented him, that argued not at all either his "innocency or unpreparedness," but their timely foresight to use prevention.

But what needed that? "They knew his chiefest arms left him were those only which the ancient Christians were wont to use against their persecutors, prayers and tears." O sacred reverence of God! respect and shame of men! whither were ye fled when these hypocrisies were uttered? Was the kingdom then at all that cost of blood to remove from him none but prayers and tears? What were those thousands of blaspheming cavaliers about him, whose mouths let fly oaths and curses by the volley: were those the prayers; and those carouses drunk to the confusion of all things good or holy, did those minister the tears? Were they prayers and tears that were listed at York, mustered on Heworth Moor, and laid siege to Hull for the guard of his person? Were prayers and tears at so high a rate in Holland, that nothing could purchase them but the crown jewels? Yet they in Holland (such word was sent us) sold them for guns, carabines, mortarpieces, cannons, and other deadly instruments of war; which, when they came to York, were all, no doubt but by the merit of some great saint, suddenly transformed into prayers and tears: and, being divided into regiments and brigades, were the only arms that mischieved us in all those battles and encounters.

These were his chief arms, whatever we must call them, and yet such arms as they who fought for the commonwealth have, by the help of better prayers, vanquished and brought to nothing. He bewails his want of the militia, "not so much in reference to his own protection, as the people's, whose many and sore oppressions grieve him." Never considering how ill for seventeen years together he had protected them, and that these miseries of the people are still his own handiwork, having smitten them, like a forked arrow, so sore into the kingdom's sides, as not to be drawn out and cured without the incision of more flesh.

He tells us, that "what he wants in the hand of power," he has in "the wings of faith and prayer." But they who made no reckoning of those wings while they had that power in their hands, may easily mistake the wings of faith for the wings of presumption, and so fall headlong. We meet next with a comparison, how apt let them judge who have travelled to Mecca, "that the parliament have hung the majesty of kingship in an airy imagination of regality, between the privileges of both houses, like the tomb of Mahomet." He knew not that he was prophesying the death and burial of a Turkish tyranny, that spurned down those laws which gave it life and being, so long as it endured to be a regulated monarchy.

He counts it an injury "not to have the sole power in himself to help or hurt any;" and that the "militia, which he holds to be his undoubted right, should be disposed as the parliament thinks fit:" and yet confesses that, if he had it in his actual disposing, he would defend those whom he calls "his good subjects from those men's violence and fraud, who would persuade the world that none but wolves are fit to be trusted with the custody of the shepherd and his flock." Surely, if we may guess whom he means here, by knowing whom he hath ever most opposed in this controversy, we may then assure ourselves that by violence and fraud he means that which the parliament hath done in settling the militia, and those the wolves into whose hands it was by them intrusted: which draws a clear confession from his own mouth, that if the parliament had left him sole power of the militia, he would have used it to the destruction of them and their friends.

As for sole power of the militia, which he claims as a right no less undoubted than the crown, it hath been oft enough told him that he hath no more authority over the sword than over the law: over the law he hath none, either to establish or to abrogate, to interpret or to execute, but only by his courts and in his courts, whereof the parliament is highest; no more, therefore, hath he power of the militia, which is the sword, either to use or to dispose, but with consent of parliament; give him but that, and as good give him in a lump all our laws and liberties. For if the power of the sword were anywhere separate and undepending from the power of law, which is originally seated in the highest court, then would that power of the sword be soon master of the law: and being at one man's disposal might, when he pleased, control the law; and in derision of our Magna Charta, which were but weak resistance against an armed tyrant, might absolutely enslave us. And not to have in ourselves, though vaunting to be free-born, the power of our own freedom, and the public safety, is a degree lower than not to have the property of our own goods. For liberty of persons, and the right of self-preservation, is much nearer, much more natural, and more worth to all men, than the propriety of their goods and wealth. Yet such power as all this did the king in open terms challenge to have over us, and brought thousands to help him win it; so much more good at fighting than at understanding, as to persuade themselves, that they fought then for the subject's liberty.

He is contented, because he knows no other remedy, to resign this power "for his own time, but not for his successors:" so diligent and careful he is, that we should be slaves, if not to him, yet to his posterity, and fain would leave us the legacy of another war about it. But the parliament have done well to remove that question: whom as his manner is to dignify with some good name or other, he calls now a "many-headed hydra of government, full of factious distractions, and not more eyes than mouths." Yet surely not more mouths, or not so wide, as the dissolute rabble of all his courtiers had, both hees and shees, if there were any males among them.

He would prove, that to govern by parliament hath "a monstrosity rather than perfection;" and grounds his argument upon two or three eminent absurdities: first, by placing counsel in the senses; next, by turning the senses out of the head, and in lieu thereof placing power supreme above sense and reason: which be now the greater monstrosities? Further to dispute what kind of government is best would be a long debate; it sufficeth that his reasons here for monarchy are found weak and inconsiderable.

He bodes much "horror and bad influence

after his eclipse." He speaks his wishes; but they who by weighing prudently things past foresee things to come, the best divination, may hope rather all good success and happiness, by removing that darkness, which the misty cloud of his prerogative made between us and a peaceful reformation, which is our true sunlight, and not he, though he would be taken for our sun itself. And wherefore should we not hope to be governed more happily without a king, whenas all our misery and trouble hath been either by a king, or by our necessary vindication and defence against him?

He would be thought "inforced to perjury," by having granted the militia, by which his oath bound him to protect the people. If he can be perjured in granting that, why doth he refuse for no other cause the abolishing of episcopacy? But never was any oath so blind as to swear him to protect delinquents against justice, but to protect all the people in that order, and by those hands, which the parliament should advise him to, and the protected confide in; not under the show of protection to hold a violent and incommunicable sword over us, as ready to be let fall upon our own necks, as upon our enemies; nor to make our own hands and weapons fight against our own liberties.

By his parting with the militia he takes to himself much praise of his "assurance in God's protection;" and to the parliament imputes the fear "of not daring to adventure the injustice of their actions upon any other way of safety." But wherefore came not this assurance of God's protection to him till the militia was wrung out of his hands? It should seem by his holding it so fast, that his own actions and intentions had no less of injustice in them, than what he charges upon others, whom he terms Chaldeans, Sabeans, and the devil himself. But Job used no such militia against those enemies, nor such a magazine as was at Hull, which this king so contended for, and made war upon us, that he might have wherewithal to make war against us. He concludes, that, "although they take all from him, yet can they not obstruct his way to heaven." It was no handsome occasion, by feigning obstructions where they are not, to tell us whither he was going:

he should have shut the door, and prayed in secret, not here in the high street. Private prayers in public ask something of whom they ask not, and that shall be their reward.

CHAPTER XI.

Upon the Nineteen Propositions, &c.

Of the nineteen propositions he names none in particular, neither shall the answer: but he insists upon the old plea of "his conscience, honor, and reason;" using the plausibility of large and indefinite words, to defend himself at such a distance as may hinder the eye of common judgment from all distinct view and examination of his reasoning. "He would buy the peace of his people at any rate, save only the parting with his conscience and honor." Yet shows not how it can happen that the peace of a people, if otherwise to be bought at any rate, should be inconsistent or at variance with the conscience and honor of a king. Till then, we may receive it for a better sentence, that nothing should be more agreeable to the conscience and honor of a king, than to preserve his subjects in peace; especially from civil war.

And which of the propositions were "obtruded on him with the point of the sword," till he first with the point of the sword, thrust from him both the propositions and the propounders? He never reckons those violent and merciless obtrusions, which for almost twenty years he had been forcing upon tender consciences, by all sorts of persecution, till through the multitude of them that were to suffer, it could no more be called a persecution, but a plain war. From which when first the Scots, then the English, were constrained to defend themselves, this their just defence is that which he calls here, "their making war upon his soul."

He grudges that "so many things are required of him, and nothing offered him in requital of those favors which he had granted." What could satiate the desires of this man, who being king of England, and master of almost two millions yearly, what by hook or crook, was still in want; and those acts of justice which he was to do in duty, counts done as favors; and such favors as were not done without the avaricious hope of other rewards besides supreme honor, and the constant revenue of his place?

"This honor," he saith, "they did him, to put him on the giving part." And spake truer than he intended, it being merely for honor's sake that they did so; not that it belonged to him of right: for what can he give to a parliament, who receives all he hath from the people, and for the people's good? Yet now he brings his own conditional rights to contest and be preferred before the people's good; and yet, unless it be in order to their good, he hath no rights at all; reigning by the laws of the land, not by his own; which laws are in the hands of parliament to change or abrogate as they shall see best for the commonwealth, even to the taking away of kingship itself, when it grows too masterful and burdensome.

For every commonwealth is in general defined, a society sufficient of itself, in all things conducible to well-being and commodious life. Any of which requisite things, if it cannot have without the gift and favor of a single person, or without leave of his private reason or his conscience, it cannot be thought sufficient of itself, and by consequence no commonwealth, nor free; but a multitude of vassals in the possession and domain of one absolute lord, and wholly obnoxious to his will. If the king have power to give or deny anything to his parliament, he must do it either as a person several from them, or as one greater: neither of which will be allowed him: not to be considered severally from them; for as the king of England can do no wrong, so neither can he do right but in his courts and by his courts; and what is legally done in them, shall be deemed the king's assent, though he as a several person shall judge or endeavor the contrary; so that indeed without his courts, or against them, he is no king. If therefore he obtrude upon us any public mischief, or withhold from us any general good, which is wrong in the highest degree, he must do it as a tyrant, not as a king of England, by the known maxims of our law. Neither can he, as one greater, give aught to the parliament which is not in their own power, but he must be greater also than the kingdom which they represent: so that to honor him with the

giving part was a mere civility, and may be well termed the courtesy of England, not the king's due.

"But the "incommunicable jewel of his conscience" he will not give, "but reserve to himself." It seems that his conscience was none of the crown jewels; for those we know were in Holland, not incommunicable, to buy arms against his subjects. Being therefore but a private jewel, he could not have done a greater pleasure to the kingdom, than by reserving it to himself. But he, contrary to what is here professed, would have his conscience not an incommunicable, but a universal conscience, the whole kingdom's conscience. Thus what he seems to fear lest we should ravish from him, is our chief complaint that he obtruded upon us; we never forced him to part with his conscience, but it was he that would have forced us to part with ours.

Some things he taxes them to have offered him, "which, while he had the mastery of his reason, he would never consent to." Very likely; but had his reason mastered him as it ought, and not been mastered long ago by his sense and humor, (as the breeding of most kings hath been ever sensual and most humored,) perhaps he would have made no difficulty. Meanwhile at what a fine pass is the kingdom, that must depend in greatest exigencies upon the phantasy of a king's reason, be he wise or fool, who arrogantly shall answer all the wisdom of the land, that what they offer seems to him unreasonable!

He prefers his "love of truth" before his love of the people. His love of truth would have led him to the search of truth, and have taught him not to lean so much upon his own understanding. He met at first with doctrines of unaccountable prerogative; in them he rested, because they pleased him; they therefore pleased him because they gave him all; and this he calls his love of truth, and prefers it before the love of his people's peace.

Some things they proposed, "which would have wounded the inward peace of his conscience." The more our evil hap, that three kingdoms should be thus pestered with one conscience; who chiefly scrupled to grant us that, which the parliament advised him to, as the chief means of our public welfare and reformation. These scruples to many perhaps will seem pretended; to others, upon as good grounds, may seem real; and that it was the just judgment of God, that he who was so cruel and so remorseless to other men's consciences, should have a conscience within him as cruel to himself; constraining him, as he constrained others, and ensnaring him in such ways and counsels as were certain to be his destruction.

"Other things though he could approve, yet in honor and policy he thought fit to deny, lest he should seem to dare deny nothing." By this means he will be sure, what with reason, conscience, honor, policy, or punctilios, to be found never unfurnished of a denial; whether it were his envy not to be overbounteous, or that the submissness of our asking stirred up in him a certain pleasure of denying. Good princes have thought it their chief happiness to be always granting; if good things, for the things' sake; if things indifferent, for the people's sake; while this man sits calculating variety of excuses how he may grant least; as if his whole strength and royalty were placed in a mere negative.

Of one proposition especially he laments him much, that they would bind him "to a general and implicit consent for whatever they desired." Which though I find not among the nineteen, yet undoubtedly the oath of his coronation binds him to no less; neither is he at all by his office to interpose against a parliament in the making or not making of any law; but to take that for just and good legally, which is there decreed, and to see it executed accordingly. Nor was he set over us to vie wisdom with his parliament, but to be guided by them; any of whom possibly may as far excel him in the gift of wisdom, as he them in place and dignity. But much nearer is it to impossibility, that any king alone should be wiser than all his council; sure enough it was not he, though no king ever before him so much contended to have it thought so. And if the parliament so thought not, but desired him to follow their advice and deliberation in things of public concernment, he accounts it the same proposition as if Samson had been moved "to the putting out his eyes, that the Philistines might abuse him." And

thus out of an unwise or pretended fear, lest others should make a scorn of him for yielding to his parliament, he regards not to give cause of worse suspicion, that he made a scorn of his regal oath.

But "to exclude him from all power of denial seems an arrogance;" in the parliament he means: what in him then to deny against the parliament? None at all, by what he argues: for "by petitioning, they confess their inferiority, and that obliges them to rest, if not satisfied, yet quieted with such an answer as the will and reason of their superior thinks fit to give." First, petitioning, in better English, is no more than requesting or requiring; and men require not favors only, but their due; and that not only from superiors, but from equals, and inferiors also. The noblest Romans, when they stood for that which was a kind of regal honor, the consulship, were wont in a submissive manner to go about, and beg that highest dignity of the meanest plebeians, naming them man by man; which in their tongue was called *petitio consulatus*. And the parliament of England petitioned the king, not because all of them were inferior to him, but because he was superior to any one of them, which they did of civil custom, and for fashion's sake, more than of duty; for by plain law cited before, the parliament is his superior.

But what law in any trial or dispute enjoins a freeman to rest quieted, though not satisfied with the will and reason of his superior? It were a mad law that would subject reason to superiority of place. And if our highest consultations and purposed laws must be terminated by the king's will, then is the will of one man our law, and no subtlety of dispute can redeem the parliament and nation from being slaves: neither can any tyrant require more than that his will or reason, though not satisfying, should yet be rested in, and determine all things. We may conclude, therefore, that when the parliament petitioned the king, it was but merely form, let it be as "foolish and absurd" as he pleases. It cannot certainly be so absurd as what he requires, that the parliament should confine their own and all the kingdom's reason to the will of one man, because it was his hap to succeed his father. For neither God nor the laws have subjected us to his will, nor set his reason to be our sovereign above law, (which must needs be, if he can strangle it in the birth,) but set his person over us in the sovereign execution of such laws as the parliament establish. The parliament, therefore, without any usurpation, hath had it always in their power to limit and confine the exorbitancy of kings, whether they call it their will, their reason, or their conscience.

But this above all was never expected, nor is to be endured, that a king, who is bound by law and oath to follow the advice of his parliament, should be permitted to except against them as "young statesmen," and proudly to suspend his following their advice, "until his seven years' experience had shown him how well they could govern themselves." Doubtless the law never supposed so great an arrogance could be in one man; that he whose seventeen years' unexperience had almost ruined all, should sit another seven years schoolmaster to tutor those who were sent by the whole realm to be his counsellors and teachers. And with what modesty can he pretend to be a statesman himself, who with his father's kingcraft and his own, did never that of his own accord, which was not directly opposite to his professed interest both at home and abroad; discontenting and alienating his subjects at home, weakening and deserting his confederates abroad, and with them the common cause of religion; so that the whole course of his reign, by an example of his own furnishing, hath resembled Phaeton more than Phœbus, and forced the parliament to drive like Jehu; which omen taken from his own mouth, God hath not diverted?

And he on the other side might have remembered, that the parliament sit in that body, not as his subjects, but as his superiors, called, not by him, but by the law; not only twice every year, but as oft as great affairs require, to be his counsellors and dictators, though he stomach it; nor to be dissolved at his pleasure, but when all grievances be first removed, all petitions heard and answered. This is not only reason, but the known law of the land.

"When he heard that propositions would be sent him," he sat conjecturing what they would propound; and because they propounded what he expected not, he takes that to be a warrant for his denying them. But what did he expect? He expected that the parliament would reinforce "some old laws." But if those laws were not a sufficient remedy to all grievances, nay, were found to be grievances themselves, when did we lose that other part of our freedom to establish new? "He thought some injuries done by himself and others to the commonwealth were to be repaired." But how could that be, while he, the chief offender, took upon him to be sole judge both of the injury and the reparation?

"He stayed till the advantages of his crown considered, might induce him to condescend to the people's good." Whenas the crown itself with all those advantages were therefore given him, that the people's good should be first considered; not bargained for, and bought by inches with the bribe of more offertures and advantages to his crown. He looked "for moderate desires of due reformation;" as if any such desires could be immoderate. He looked for such a reformation, "both in church and state, as might preserve" the roots of every grievance and abuse in both still growing, (which he calls "the foundation and essentials,") and would have only the excrescences of evil pruned away for the present, as was plotted before, that they might grow fast enough between triennial parliaments, to hinder them, by work enough besides, from ever striking at the root.

He alleges, "They should have had regard to the laws in force, to the wisdom and piety of former parliaments, to the ancient and universal practice of Christian churches." As if they who come with full authority to redress public grievances, which ofttimes are laws themselves, were to have their hands bound by laws in force, or the supposition of more piety and wisdom in their ancestors, or the practice of churches heretofore; whose fathers, notwithstanding all these pretences, made as vast alterations to free themselves from ancient popery. For all antiquity that adds or varies from the scripture, is no more warranted to our safe imitation, than what was done the age before at Trent. Nor was there need to have despaired of what could be established in lieu of what was to be annulled, having before his eyes the government of so many churches beyond the seas; whose pregnant and solid reasons wrought so with the parliament, as to desire a uniformity rather with all other Protestants, than to be a schism divided from them under a conclave of thirty bishops, and a crew of irreligious priests that gaped for the same preferment.

And whereas he blames those propositions for not containing what they ought, what did they mention, but to vindicate and restore the rights of parliament invaded by cabin councils, the courts of justice obstructed, and the government of church innovated and corrupted? All these things he might easily have observed in them, which he affirms he could not find; but found "those demanding" in parliament, who were "looked upon before as factious in the state, and schismatical in the church; and demanding not only tolerations for themselves in their vanity, novelty, and confusion, but also an extirpation of that government, whose rights they had a mind to invade." Was this man ever likely to be advised, who with such a prejudice and disesteem sets himself against his chosen and appointed counsellors? likely ever to admit of reformation, who censures all the government of other Protestant churches, as bad as any papist could have censured them? And what king had ever his whole kingdom in such contempt, so to wrong and dishonor the free elections of his people, as to judge them, whom the nation thought worthiest to sit with him in parliament, few else but such as were "punishable by laws"? yet knowing that time was, when to be a protestant, to be a Christian, was by law as punishable as to be a traitor; and that our Saviour himself, coming to reform his church, was accused of an intent to invade Cæsar's right, as good a right as the prelate bishops ever had: the one being got by force, the other by spiritual usurpation; and both by force upheld.

He admires and falls into an ecstasy, that the parliament should send him such a "horrid proposition," as the removal of episcopacy. But expect from him in an ecstasy no other reasons of his admiration than the dream and tautology of what he hath so oft repeated, law, antiquity, ancestors, prosperity, and the like, which will be therefore not worth a second answer, but may pass with his own comparison into the common sewer of other popish arguments.

"Had the two houses sued out their livery from the wardship of tumults," he could sooner have believed them. It concerned them first to sue out their livery from the unjust wardship of his encroaching prerogative. And had he also redeemed his overdated minority from a pupilage under bishops, he would much less have mistrusted his parliament; and never would have set so base a character upon them, as to count them no better than the vassals of certain nameless men, whom he charges to be such as "hunt after faction with their hounds, the tumults." And yet the bishops could have told them that Nimrod, the first that hunted after faction, is reputed by ancient tradition the first that founded monarchy; whence it appears, that to hunt after faction is more properly the king's game; and those hounds, which he calls the vulgar, have been often hallooed to from court, of whom the mongrel sort have been enticed; the rest have not lost their scent, but understood aright that the parliament had that part to act, which he had failed in; that trust to discharge, which he had broken; that estate and honor to preserve, which was far beyond his, the estate and honor of the commonwealth, which he had embezzled.

Yet so far doth self-opinion or false principles delude and transport him, as to think "the concurrence of his reason" to the votes of parliament, not only political, but natural, "and as necessary to the begetting," or bringing forth of any one "complete act of public wisdom as the sun's influence is necessary to all nature's productions." So that the parliament, it seems, is but a female, and without his procreative reason, the laws which they can produce are but wind-eggs; wisdom, it seems, to a king is natural, to a parliament not natural, but by conjunction with the king; yet he professes to hold his kingly right by law; and if no law could be made but by the great council of a nation, which we now term a parliament, then certainly it was a parliament that first created kings; and not only made laws before a king was in being, but those laws especially whereby he holds his crown.

He ought then to have so thought of a parliament, if he count it not male, as of his mother, which to civil being created both him and the royalty he wore. And if it hath been anciently interpreted the presaging sign of a future tyrant, but to dream of copulation with his mother, what can it be less than actual tyranny to affirm waking, that the parliament, which is his mother, can neither conceive or bring forth "any authoritative act" without his masculine coition? Nay, that his reason is as celestial and lifegiving to the parliament, as the sun's influence is to the earth: what other notions but these, or such like, could swell up Caligula to think himself a god?

But to be rid of these mortifying propositions, he leaves no tyrannical evasion unessayed; first, "that they are not the joint and free desires of both houses, or the major part;" next, "that the choice of many members was carried on by faction." The former of these is already discovered to be an old device put first in practice by Charles V., since the Reformation: who, when the Protestants of Germany for their own defence joined themselves in league, in his declarations and remonstrances laid the fault only upon some few, (for it was dangerous to take notice of too many enemies,) and accused them, that under color of religion they had a purpose to invade his and the church's right; by which policy he deceived many of the German cities, and kept them divided from that league, until they saw themselves brought into a snare. That other cavil against the people's choice puts us in mind rather what the court was wont to do, and how to tamper with elections: neither was there at that time any faction more potent or more likely to do such a business, than they themselves who complain most.

But "he must chew such morsels as propositions, ere he let them down." So let him; but if the kingdom shall taste nothing but after his chewing, what does he make of the kingdom but a great baby? "The straitness of his conscience will not give him leave to swallow down such camels of sacrilege and injustice as others do." This is the pharisee up and down: "I am not as other men are." But what camels of injustice he could devour all his three realms were witness, which

was the cause that they almost perished for want of parliaments. And he that will be unjust to man, will be sacrilegious to God; and to bereave a Christian conscience of liberty, for no other reason than the narrowness of his own conscience, is the most unjust measure to man, and the worst sacrilege to God.

That other, which he calls sacrilege, of taking from the clergy that superfluous wealth, which antiquity as old as Constantine, from the credit of a divine vision, counted "poison in the church," hath been ever most opposed by men, whose righteousness in other matters hath been least observed. He concludes, as his manner is, with high commendation of his own "unbiassed rectitude," and believes nothing to be in them that dissent from him but faction, innovation, and particular designs. Of these repetitions I find no end, no, not in his prayer; which being founded upon deceitful principles, and a fond hope that God will bless him in those his errors, which he calls "honest," finds a fit answer of St. James: "Ye ask and receive not, because ye ask amiss." As for the truth and sincerity, which he prays may be always found in those his declarations to the people, the contrariety of his own actions will bear eternal witness, how little careful or solicitous he was what he promised or what he uttered there.

CHAPTER XII.

Upon the Rebellion in Ireland.

THE rebellion and horrid massacre of English protestants in Ireland, to the number of 154,000 in the province of Ulster only, by their own computation; which, added to the other three, makes up the total sum of that slaughter in all likelihood four times as great; although so sudden and so violent, as at first to amaze all men that were not accessary; yet from whom and from what counsels it first sprung, neither was nor could be possibly so secret as the contrivers thereof, blinded with vain hope, or the despair that other plots would succeed, supposed. For it cannot be imaginable, that the Irish, guided by so many subtle and Italian heads of the Romish party should so far have lost the use of reason, and indeed of common sense, as, not supported with other strength than their own, to begin a war so desperate and irreconcilable against both England and Scotland at once. All other nations, from whom they could expect aid, were busied to the utmost in their own most necessary concernments.

It remains then that either some authority, or some great assistance promised them from England, was that whereon they chiefly trusted. And as it is not difficult to discern from what inducing cause this insurrection first arose, so neither was it hard at first to have applied some effectual remedy, though not prevention. And yet prevention was not hopeless, when Strafford either believed not, or did not care to believe, the several warnings and discoveries thereof, which more than once by papists and by friars themselves were brought him; besides what was brought by deposition, divers months before that rebellion, to the Archbishop of Canterbury and others of the king's council; as the declaration of "No addresses" declares. But the assurance which they had in private, that no remedy should be applied, was, it seems, one of the chief reasons that drew on their undertaking. And long it was ere that assurance failed them; until the bishops and popish lords, who, while they sat and voted, still opposed the sending aid to Ireland, were expelled the house.

Seeing then the main incitement and authority for this rebellion must be needs derived from England, it will be next inquired, who was the prime author. The king here denounces a malediction temporal and eternal, not simply to the author, but to the "malicious author" of this bloodshed: and by that limitation may exempt, not himself only, but perhaps the Irish rebels themselves, who never will confess to God or man that any blood was shed by them maliciously; but either in the catholic cause, or common liberty, or some other specious plea, which the conscience, from grounds both good and evil, usually suggests to itself: thereby thinking to elude the direct force of that imputation which lies upon them.

Yet he acknowledges, "it fell out as a most unhappy advantage of some men's malice against him:" but indeed of most men's just suspicion, by finding in it no such wide departure or disagreement from the scope of his former counsels and proceedings. And that he himself was the author of that rebellion, he denies both here and elsewhere, with many imprecations, but no solid evidence. What on the other side against his denial hath been affirmed in three kingdoms, being here briefly set in view, the reader may so judge as he finds cause.

This is most certain, that the king was ever friendly to the Irish papists; and in his third year, against the plain advice of parliament, like a kind of pope, sold them many indulgences for money; and upon all occasions advancing the popish party, and negotiating underhand by priests, who were made his agents, engaged the Irish papists in a war against the Scotch protestants. To that end he furnished them, and had them trained in arms, and kept them up, either openly or underhand, the only army in his three kingdoms, till the very burst of that rebellion. The summer before that dismal October, a committee of most active papists, all since in the head of that rebellion, were in great favor at Whitehall; and admitted to many private consultations with the king and queen. And to make it evident that no mean matters were the subject of those conferences, at their request he gave away his peculiar right to more than five Irish counties, for the payment of an inconsiderable rent. They departed not home till within two months before the rebellion; and were either from the first breaking out, or soon after, found to be the chief rebels themselves.

But what should move the king besides his own inclination to popery, and the prevalence of his queen over him, to hold such frequent and close meetings with a committee of Irish papists in his own house, while the parliament of England sat unadvised with, is declared by a Scotch author, and of itself is clear enough. The parliament at the beginning of that summer, having put Strafford to death, imprisoned others his chief favorites, and driven the rest to fly, the king, who had in vain tempted both the Scotch and the English army to come up against the parliament and city, finding no compliance answerable to his hope from the protestant armies, betakes himself last to the Irish; who had in readiness an army of eight thousand papists, which he had refused so often to disband, and a committee here of the same religion. With them, who thought the time now come, (which to bring about they had been many years before not wishing only, but with much industry complotting, to do some eminent service for the church of Rome and their own perfidious natures, against a puritan parliament and the hated English their masters,) he agrees and concludes, that so soon as both armies in England were disbanded, the Irish should appear in arms, master all the protestants, and help the king against his parliament. And we need not doubt, that those five counties were given to the Irish for other reason than the four northern counties had been a little before offered to the Scots. The king, in August, takes a journey into Scotland; and overtaking the Scotch army then on their way home, attempts the second time to pervert them, but without success.

No sooner come into Scotland, but he lays a plot, so saith the Scotch author, to remove out of the way such of the nobility there as were most likely to withstand, or not to further his designs. This being discovered, he sends from his side one Dillon, a papist lord, soon after a chief rebel, with letters into Ireland; and dispatches a commission under the great seal of Scotland, at that time in his own custody, commanding that they should forthwith, as had been formerly agreed, cause all the Irish to rise in arms. Who no sooner had received such command but obeyed, and began in massacre; for they knew no other way to make sure the protestants, which was commanded them expressly; and the way, it seems, left to their discretion. He who hath a mind to read the commission itself, and sound reason added why it was not likely to be forged, besides the attestation of so many Irish themselves, may have recourse to a book, entitled, "The Mystery of Iniquity." Besides what the parliament itself in the declaration of "No more addresses" hath affirmed, that they have one copy of that commission in their own hands, attested by the oaths of some that were eyewitnesses, and had seen it under the seal: others of the principal rebels have confessed, that this commission was the summer before promised at London to the Irish commissioners; to whom the king then discovered in plain words his great desire to be revenged on the parliament of England.

After the rebellion broken out, which in words only he detested, but underhand favored and promoted by all the offices of friendship, correspondence, and what possible aid he could afford them, the particulars whereof are too many to be inserted here; I suppose no understanding man could longer doubt who was "author or instigator" of that rebellion. If there be who yet doubt, I refer them especially to that declaration of July 1643, with that of "No addresses," 1647, and another full volume of examinations to be set out speedily concerning this matter. Against all which testimonies, likelihoods, evidences, and apparent actions of his own, being so abundant, his bare denial, though with imprecation, can no way countervail; and least of all in his own cause.

As for the commission granted them, he thinks to evade that by retorting, that "some in England fight against him, and yet pretend his authority." But though a parliament, by the known laws, may affirm justly to have the king's authority inseparable from that court, though divided from his person, it is not credible that the Irish rebels, who so much tendered his person above his authority, and were by him so well received at Oxford, would be so far from all humanity, as to slander him with a particular commission, signed and sent them by his own hand.

And of his good affection to the rebels this chapter itself is not without witness. He holds them less in fault than the Scots, as from whom they might allege to have fetched "their imitation;" making no difference between men that rose necessarily to defend themselves, which no protestant doctrine ever disallowed, against them who threatened war, and those who began a voluntary and causeless rebellion, with the massacre of so many thousands, who never meant them harm.

He falls next to flashes, and a multitude of words, in all which is contained no more than what might be the plea of any guiltiest offender:—he was not the author, because "he hath the greatest share of loss and dishonor by what is committed." Who is there that offends God, or his neighbor, on whom the greatest share of loss and dishonor lights not in the end? But in the act of doing evil, men use not to consider the event of their evil doing; or if they do, have then no power to curb the sway of their own wickedness; so that the greatest share of loss and dishonor to happen upon themselves, is no argument that they were not guilty. This other is as weak, that "a king's interest, above that of any other man, lies chiefly in the common welfare of his subjects;" therefore no king will do aught against the common welfare. For by this evasion any tyrant might as well purge himself from the guilt of raising troubles or commotions among the people, because undoubtedly his chief interest lies in their sitting still.

I said but now, that even this chapter, if nothing else, might suffice to discover his good affection to the rebels, which in this that follows too notoriously appears; imputing this insurrection to "the preposterous rigor, and unreasonable severity, the covetous zeal and uncharitable fury, of some men;" (these "some men," by his continual paraphrase, are meant the parliament;) and, lastly, "to the fear of utter extirpation." If the whole Irishry of rebels had fee'd some advocate to speak partially and sophistically in their defence, he could have hardly dazzled better; yet nevertheless would have proved himself no other than a plausible deceiver. And, perhaps (nay, more than perhaps, for it is affirmed and extant under good evidence that) those feigned terrors and jealousies were either by the king himself, or the popish priests which were sent by him, put into the head of that inquisitive people, on set purpose to engage them. For who had power "to oppress" them, or to relieve them being oppressed, but the king, or his immediate deputy? This rather should have made them rise against the king, than against the parliament.

Who threatened or ever thought of their extirpation, till they themselves had begun it to the English? As for "preposterous rigor, covetous zeal, and uncharitable fury," they had more reason to suspect those evils first from his own commands, whom they saw using daily no greater argument to prove the truth of his religion, than by enduring no

other but his own prelatical; and, to force it upon others, made episcopal, ceremonial, and common-prayer-book wars. But the papists understood him better than by the outside; and knew that those wars were their wars. Although if the commonwealth should be afraid to suppress open idolatry; lest the papists thereupon should grow desperate, this were to let them grow and become our persecutors, while we neglected what we might have done evangelically to be their reformers: or to do as his father James did, who instead of taking heart and putting confidence in God by such a deliverance as from the powder-plot, though it went not off, yet with the mere conceit of it, as some observe, was hit into such a hectic shivering between protestant and papist all his life after, that he never durst from that time do otherwise than equivocate or collogue with the pope and his adherents.

He would be thought to commiserate the sad effects of that rebellion, and to lament that "the tears and blood spilt there did not quench the sparks of our civil" discord here. But who began these dissensions? And what can be more openly known than those retardings and delays, which by himself were continually devised, to hinder and put back the relief of those distressed protestants? which undoubtedly, had it not been then put back, might have saved many streams of those tears and that blood, whereof he seems here so sadly to bewail the spilling. His manifold excuses, diversions, and delays, are too well known to be recited here in particular, and too many.

But "he offered to go himself in person upon that expedition," and reckons up many surmises why he thinks they would not suffer him. But mentions not that by his underdealing to debauch armies here at home, and by his secret intercourse with the chief rebels, long ere that time everywhere known, he had brought the parliament into so just a diffidence of him, as that they durst not leave the public arms to his disposal, much less an army to his conduct. He concludes, "That next the sin of those who began that rebellion, theirs must needs be who hindered the suppressing, or diverted the aids." But judgment rashly given ofttimes involves the judge himself. He finds fault with those "who threatened all extremity to the rebels," and pleads much that mercy should be shown them. It seems he found himself not so much concerned as those who had lost fathers, brothers, wives, and children by their cruelty; whom in justice to retaliate is not, as he supposes, "unevangelical," so long as magistracy and war is not laid down under the gospel. If this his sermon of affected mercy were not too pharisaical, how could he permit himself to cause the slaughter of so many thousands here in England for mere prerogatives, the toys, and gewgaws of his crown, for copes and surplices, the trinkets of his priests; and not perceive his zeal, while he taxes others, to be most preposterous and unevangelical?

Neither is there the same cause to destroy a whole city for the ravishing of a sister, not done out of villany, and recompence offered by marriage: nor the same case for those disciples to summon fire from heaven upon the whole city where they were denied lodging; and for a nation by just war and execution to slay whole families of them, who so barbarously had slain whole families before. Did not all Israel do as much against the Benjamites for one rape committed by a few, and defended by the whole tribe? And did they not the same to Jabesh-Gilead for not assisting them in that revenge? I speak not this that such measure should be meted rigorously to all the Irish, or as remembering that the parliament ever so decreed; but to show that this his homily hath more craft and affectation in it, than of sound doctrine.

But it was happy that his going into Ireland was not consented to; for either he had certainly turned his raised forces against the parliament itself, or not gone at all; or had he gone, what work he would have made there, his own following words declare. "He would have punished some;" no question; for some, perhaps, who were of least use, must of necessity have been sacrificed to his reputation, and the convenience of his affairs. Others he "would have disarmed;" that is to say, in his own time: but "all of them he would have protected from the fury of those that would have drowned them, if they had refused to swim down the popular stream." These expressions are too often met, and too well understood, for any man to doubt his meaning. By the "fury of those," he means no other than the justice of parliament, to whom yet he had committed the whole business. Those who would have refused to swim down the popular stream, our constant key tells us to be papists, prelates, and their faction; these, by his own confession here, he would have protected against his puritan parliament: and by this who sees not that he and the Irish rebels had but one aim, one and the same drift, and would have forthwith joined in one body against us?

He goes on still in his tenderness of the Irish rebels, fearing lest "our zeal should be more greedy to kill the bear for his skin, than for any harm he hath done." This either justifies the rebels to have done no harm at all, or infers his opinion that the parliament is more bloody and rapacious in the prosecution of their justice, than those rebels were in the execution of their barbarous cruelty. Let men doubt now, and dispute to whom the king was a friend most—to his English parliament, or to his Irish rebels.

With whom, that we may yet see further how much he was their friend, after that the parliament had brought them everywhere either to famine or a low condition, he, to give them all the respite and advantages they could desire, without advice of parliament, to whom he himself had committed the managing of that war, makes a cessation; in pretence to relieve the protestants, "overborne there with numbers;" but, as the event proved, to support the papists, by diverting and drawing over the English army there, to his own service here against the parliament. For that the protestants were then on the winning hand, it must needs be plain; who, notwithstanding the miss of those forces, which at their landing here mastered without difficulty great part of Wales and Cheshire, yet made a shift to keep their own in Ireland. But the plot of this Irish truce is in good part discovered in that declaration of September 30, 1643. And if the protestants were but handfuls there, as he calls them, why did he stop and waylay, both by land and sea, to his utmost power, those provisions and supplies which were sent by the parliament? How were so many handfuls called over, as for a while stood him in no small stead, and against our main forces here in England?

Since therefore all the reasons that can be given of this cessation appear so false and frivolous, it may be justly feared, that the design itself was most wicked and pernicious. What remains then? He "appeals to God," and is cast; likening his punishments to Job's trials, before he saw them to have Job's ending. But how could charity herself believe there was at all in him any religion, so much as but to fear there is a God; whenas, by what it noted in the declaration of "No more addresses," he vowed solemnly to the parliament, with imprecations upon himself and his posterity, if ever he consented to the abolishing of those laws which were in force against papists; and, at the same time, as appeared plainly by the very date of his own letters to the queen and Ormond, consented to the abolishing of all penal laws against them both in Ireland and England? If these were acts of a religious prince, what memory of man, written or unwritten, can tell us news of any prince that ever was irreligious? He cannot stand "to make prolix apologies." Then surely those long pamphlets set out for declarations and protestations in his name were none of his; and how they should be his, indeed, being so repugnant to the whole course of his actions, augments the difficulty.

But he usurps a common saying, "That it is kingly to do well, and hear ill." That may be sometimes true; but far more frequently to do ill and hear well; so great is the multitude of flatterers, and them that deify the name of king! Yet not content with these neighbors, we have him still a perpetual preacher of his own virtues, and of that especially which who knows not to be patience perforce? He "believes it will at last appear, that they who first began to embroil his other kingdoms, are also guilty of the blood of Ireland." And we believe so too; for now the cessation is become a peace by published articles, and commission to bring them over against England, first only ten thousand by the Earl of Glamorgan, next all of them, if possible, under Ormond, which was the last of all his transactions done as a public person. And no wonder; for he looked upon the blood spilt, whether of subjects or of rebels,

with an indifferent eye, "as exhausted out of his own veins;" without distinguishing, as he ought, which was good blood and which corrupt; the not letting out whereof endangers the whole body.

And what the doctrine is, ye may perceive also by the prayer, which, after a short ejaculation for the "poor protestants," prays at large for the Irish rebels, that God would not give them over, or "their children, to the covetousness, cruelty, fierce and cursed anger" of the parliament. He finishes with a deliberate and solemn curse "upon himself and his father's house." Which how far God hath already brought to pass, is to the end, that men, by so eminent an example, should learn to tremble at his judgments, and not play with imprecations.

CHAPTER XIII.

Upon the calling in of the Scots, and their coming.

IT must needs seem strange, where men accustom themselves to ponder and contemplate things in their first original and institution, that kings, who as all other officers of the public, were at first chosen and installed only by consent and suffrage of the people, to govern them as freemen by laws of their own framing, and to be, in consideration of that dignity and riches bestowed upon them, the entrusted servants of the commonwealth, should, notwithstanding, grow up to that dishonest encroachment, as to esteem themselves masters, both of that great trust which they serve, and of the people that betrusted them; counting what they ought to do, both in discharge of their public duty, and for the great reward of honor and revenue which they receive, as done all of mere grace and favor; as if their power over us were by nature, and from themselves, or that God had sold us into their hands.

Indeed, if the race of kings were eminently the best of men, as the breed at Tutbury is of horses, it would in some reason then be their part only to command, ours always to obey. But kings by generation no way excelling others, and most commonly not being the wisest or the worthiest by far of whom they claim to have the governing; that we should yield them subjection to our own ruin, or hold of them the right of our common safety, and our natural freedom by mere gift, (as when the conduit pisses wine at coronations,) from the superfluity of their royal grace and beneficence, we may be sure was never the intent of God, whose ways are just and equal; never the intent of nature, whose works are also regular; never of any people not wholly barbarous, whom prudence, or no more but human sense, would have better guided when they first created kings, than so to nullify and tread to dirt the rest of mankind, by exalting one person and his lineage without other merit looked after, but the mere contingency of a begetting, into an absolute and unaccountable dominion over them and their posterity.

Yet this ignorant or wilful mistake of the whole matter had taken so deep root in the imagination of this king, that whether to the English or to the Scot, mentioning what acts of his regal office (though God knows how unwillingly) he had passed, he calls them, as in other places, acts of grace and bounty; so here "special obligations, favors to gratify active spirits, and the desires of that party." Words not only sounding pride and lordly usurpation, but injustice, partiality, and corruption. For to the Irish he so far condescended, as first to tolerate in private, then to covenant openly the tolerating of popery: so far to the Scot, as to remove bishops, establish presbytery, and the militia in their own hands; "preferring, as some thought, the desires of Scotland before his own interest and honor." But being once on this side Tweed, his reason, his conscience, and his honor became so straitened with a kind of false virginity, that to the English neither one nor other of the same demands could be granted, wherewith the Scots were gratified; as if our air and climate on a sudden had changed the property and the nature both of conscience, honor, and reason, or that he found none so fit as English to be the subjects of his arbitrary power. Ireland was as Ephraim, the strength of his head; Scotland as Judah was his lawgiver; but over England, as over Edom, he meant to cast his shoe: and yet so many sober Englishmen, not sufficiently awake to consider this, like men enchanted with the Circæan cup of servitude, will not be held back from running their own heads into the yoke of bondage.

The sum of his discourse is against "settling of religion by violent means;" which, whether it were the Scots' design upon England, they are best able to clear themselves. But this of all may seem strangest, that the king, who, while it was permitted him, never did thing more eagerly than to molest and persecute the consciences of most religious men; he who had made a war, and lost all, rather than not uphold a hierarchy of persecuting bishops, should have the confidence here to profess himself so much an enemy of those that force the conscience. For was it not he, who upon the English obtruded new ceremonies, upon the Scots a new Liturgy, and with his sword went about to score a bloody rubric on their backs? Did he not forbid and hinder all effectual search of truth; nay, like a besieging enemy, stopped all her passages both by word and writing? Yet here can talk of "fair and equal disputations:" where, notwithstanding, if all submit not to his judgment, as not being "rationally convicted," they must submit (and he conceals it not) to his penalty, as counted obstinate. But what if he himself, and those his learned churchmen, were the convicted or the obstinate part long ago; should reformation suffer them to sit lording over the church in their fat bishoprics and pluralities, like the great whore that sitteth upon many waters, till they would vouchsafe to be disputed out? Or should we sit disputing, while they sat plotting and persecuting? Those clergymen were not "to be driven into the fold like sheep," as his simile runs, but to be driven out of the fold like wolves or thieves, where they sat fleecing those flocks which they never fed.

He believes "that presbytery, though proved to be the only institution of Jesus Christ, were not by the sword to be set up without his consent;" which is contrary both to the doctrine and the known practice of all protestant churches, if his sword threaten those who of their own accord embrace it. And although Christ and his apostles, being to civil affairs but private men, contended not with magistrates; yet when magistrates themselves, and especially parliaments, who have greatest right to dispose of the civil sword, come to know religion, they ought in conscience to defend all those who receive it willingly, against the violence of any king or tyrant whatsoever. Neither is it therefore true, "that Christianity is planted or watered with Christian blood;" for there is a large difference between forcing men by the sword to turn presbyterians, and defending those who willingly are so from a furious inroad of bloody bishops, armed with the militia of a king, their pupil. And if "covetousness and ambition be an argument that presbytery hath not much of Christ," it argues more strongly against episcopacy; which, from the time of her first mounting to an order above the presbyters, had no other parents than "covetousness and ambition." And those sects, schisms, and heresies, which he speaks of, "if they get but strength and numbers," need no other pattern than episcopacy and himself, to "set up their ways by the like method of violence."

Nor is there anything that hath more marks of schism and sectarism than English episcopacy; whether we look at apostolic times, or at reformed churches; for "the universal way of church-government before," may as soon lead us into gross error, as their universally corrupted doctrine. And government, by reason of ambition, was likeliest to be corrupted much the sooner of the two. However, nothing can be to us catholic or universal in religion, but what the scripture teaches; whatsoever without scripture pleads to be universal in the church, in being universal is but the more schismatical. Much less can particular laws and constitutions impart to the church of England any power of consistory or tribunal above other churches, to be the sole judge of what is sect or schism, as with much rigor, and without scripture, they took upon them. Yet these the king resolves here to defend and maintain to his last, pretending, after all those conferences offered, or had with him, "not to see more rational and religious motives than soldiers carry in their knapsacks." With one thus resolved, it was but folly to stand disputing.

He imagines his "own judicious zeal to be most concerned in his tuition of the church." So thought Saul when he presumed to offer sacrifice, for which he lost his king-dom; so thought Uzziah when he went into the temple, but was thrust out with a leprosy for his opinioned zeal, which he thought judicious. It is not the part of a king, because he ought to defend the church, therefore to set himself supreme head over the church, or to meddle with ecclesial government, or to defend the church otherwise than the church would be defended; for such defence is bondage; nor to defend abuses, and stop all reformation, under the name of "new molds fancied and fashioned to private designs."

The holy things of church are in the power of other keys than were delivered to his keeping. Christian liberty, purchased with the death of our Redeemer, and established by the sending of his free Spirit to inhabit in us, is not now to depend upon the doubtful consent of any earthly monarch; nor to be again fettered with a presumptuous negative voice, tyrannical to the parliament, but much more tyrannical to the church of God; which was compelled to implore the aid of parliament, to remove his force and heavy hands from off our consciences, who therefore complains now of that most just defensive force, because only it removed his violence and persecution. If this be a violation to his conscience, that it was hindered by the parliament from violating the more tender consciences of so many thousand good Christians, let the usurping conscience of all tyrants be ever so violated!

He wonders (fox wonder!) how we could so much "distrust God's assistance," as to call in the protestant aid of our brethren in Scotland. Why then did he, if his trust were in God and the justice of his cause, not scruple to solicit and invite earnestly the assistance both of papists and of Irish rebels? If the Scots were by us at length sent home, they were not called to stay here always; neither was it for the people's ease to feed so many legions longer than their help was needful.

"The government of their kirk we despised" not, but their imposing of that government upon us, not presbytery, but archpresbytery, classical, provincial, and diocesan presbytery, claiming to itself a lordly power and superintendency both over flocks and pastors, over persons and congregations no way their own. But these debates, in his judgment, would have been ended better "by the best divines in Christendom in a full and free synod." A most improbable way, and such as never yet was used, at least with good success, by any protestant kingdom or state since the Reformation: every true church having wherewithal from heaven, and the assisting Spirit of Christ implored, to be complete and perfect within itself. And the whole nation is not easily to be thought so raw, and so perpetually a novice, after all this light, as to need the help and direction of other nations, more than what they write in public of their opinion, in a matter so familiar as church-government.

In fine, he accuses piety with the want of loyalty, and religion with the breach of allegiance, as if God and he were one master, whose commands were so often contrary to the commands of God. He would persuade the Scots that their "chief interest consists in their fidelity to the crown." But true policy will teach them to find a safer interest in the common friendship of England, than in the ruins of one ejected family.

CHAPTER XIV.

Upon the Covenant.

UPON this theme his discourse is long, his matter little but repetition, and therefore soon answered. First, after an abusive and strange apprehension of covenants, as if men "pawned their souls" to them with whom they covenant, he digresses to plead for bishops; first, from the antiquity of their "possession here, since the first plantation of Christianity in this island;" next from "a universal prescription since the apostles, till this last century." But what avails the most primitive antiquity against the plain sense of scripture? which, if the last century have best followed, it ought in our esteem to be the first. And yet it hath been often proved by learned men, from the writings and epistles of most ancient Christians, that episcopacy crept not up into an order above the presbyters, till many years after that the apostles were deceased.

He next is "unsatisfied with the covenant,"

not only for "some passages in it referring to himself," as he supposes, "with very dubious and dangerous limitations," but for binding men "by oath and covenant" to the reformation of church discipline. First, those limitations were not more dangerous to him, than he to our liberty and religion; next, that which was there vowed, to cast out of the church an antichristian hierarchy which God had not planted, but ambition and corruption had brought in, and fostered to the church's great damage and oppression, was no point of controversy to be argued without end, but a thing of clear moral necessity to be forthwith done. Neither was the "covenant superfluous, though former engagements, both religious and legal, bound us before;" but was the practice of all churches heretofore intending reformation. All Israel, though bound enough before by the law of Moses "to all necessary duties;" yet with Asa their king entered into a new covenant at the beginning of a reformation: and the Jews, after captivity, without consent demanded of that king who was their master, took solemn oath to walk in the commandments of God.

All protestant churches have done the like, notwithstanding former engagements to their several duties. And although his aim were to sow variance between the protestation and the covenant, to reconcile them is not difficult. The protestation was but one step, extending only to the doctrine of the church of England, as it was distinct from church discipline; the covenant went further, as it pleased God to dispense his light and our encouragement by degrees, and comprehended church-government;—former with latter steps, in the progress of well-doing need not reconcilement. Nevertheless he breaks through to his conclusion, "that all honest and wise men ever thought themselves sufficiently bound by former ties of religion;" leaving Asa, Ezra, and the whole church of God, in sundry ages, to shift for honesty and wisdom from some other than his testimony. And although after-contracts absolve not till the former be made void, yet he first having done that, our duty returns back, which to him was neither moral nor eternal, but conditional.

Willing to persuade himself that many "good men" took the covenant, either un-

warily or out of fear, he seems to have bestowed some thoughts how these "good men,"
following his advice, may keep the covenant
and not keep it. The first evasion is presuming "that the chief end of covenanting in
such men's intentions was to preserve religion in purity, and the kingdom's peace."
But the covenant will more truly inform them
that purity of religion and the kingdom's
peace was not then in state to be preserved, [10]
but to be restored; and therefore binds them
not to a preservation of what was, but to a
reformation of what was evil, what was traditional, and dangerous, whether novelty or
antiquity, in church or state. To do this
clashes with "no former oath" lawfully sworn
either to God or the king, rightly understood.

In general, he brands all "such confedera-
tions by league and covenant, as the common [20]
road used in all factious perturbations of
state and church." This kind of language reflects, with the same ignominy, upon all the
protestant reformations that have been since
Luther; and so indeed doth his whole book,
replenished throughout with hardly other
words or arguments than papists, and especially popish kings, have used heretofore
against their protestant subjects, whom he
would persuade to be "every man his own [30]
pope, and to absolve himself of those ties,"
by the suggestion of false or equivocal interpretations too oft repeated to be now answered.

The parliament, he saith, "made their
covenant, like manna, agreeable to every
man's palate." This is another of his glosses
upon the covenant; he is content to let it be
manna, but his drift is that men should loathe
it, or at least expound it by their own "rel- [40]
ish" and "latitude of sense;" wherein, lest
any one of the simpler sort should fail to
be his craftsmaster, he furnishes him with
two or three laxative, he terms them "general clauses, which may serve somewhat to
relieve them" against the covenant taken:
intimating, as if "what were lawful and
according to the word of God," were no otherwise so, than as every man fancied to
himself. For such learned explications and [50]
resolutions as these upon the covenant, what
marvel if no royalist or malignant refuse to
take it, as having learnt from these princely

instructions his many "salvoes, cautions, and
reservations," how to be a covenanter and an-
ticovenanter, how at once to be a Scot, and
an Irish rebel. He returns again to disallow
of "that reformation which the covenant"
vows, "as being the partial advice of a few
divines." But matters of this moment, as
they were not to be decided there by those divines, so neither are they to be determined
here by essays and curtal aphorisms, but by
solid proofs of scripture.

The rest of his discourse he spends, highly
accusing the parliament, "that the main
reformation by" them "intended was to rob
the church," and much applauding himself
both for "his forwardness" to all due reformation, and his averseness from all such kind
of sacrilege. All which, with his glorious title
of the "Church's Defender," we leave him
to make good by "Pharaoh's divinity," if he
please, for to Joseph's piety it will be a task
unsuitable. As for "the parity and poverty
of ministers," which he takes to be so sad of
"consequence," the scripture reckons them
for two special legacies left by our Saviour
to his disciples; under which two primitive
nurses, for such they were indeed, the church
of God more truly flourished than ever after,
since the time that imparity and church-
revenue rushing in, corrupted and belepered
all the clergy with a worse infection than
Gehazi's; some one of whose tribe, rather
than a king, I should take to be compiler
of that unsalted and Simonical prayer annexed: although the prayer itself strongly
prays against them. For never such holy
things as he means were given to more swine,
nor the church's bread more to dogs, than
when it fed ambitious, irreligious, and dumb
[40] prelates.

CHAPTER XV

Upon the many Jealousies, &c.

To wipe off jealousies and scandals, the
best way had been by clear actions, or till
actions could be cleared, by evident reasons:
but mere words we are too well acquainted
[50] with. Had "his honor and reputation been
dearer to him" than the lust of reigning, how
could the parliament of either nation have
laid so often at his door the breach of words,

promises, acts, oaths, and execrations, as they do avowedly in many of their petitions and addresses to him? Thither I remit the reader. And who can believe that whole parliaments, elected by the people from all parts of the land, should meet in one mind and resolution not to advise him, but to conspire against him, in a worse powder-plot than Catesbie's "to blow up," as he terms it, "the people's affection towards him, and batter down their loyalty by the engines of foul aspersions." Water-works rather than engines to batter with, yet those aspersions were raised from the foulness of his own actions; whereof to purge himself, he uses no other argument than a general and so often iterated commendation of himself; and thinks that court holy-water hath the virtue of expiation, at least with the silly people; to whom he familiarly imputes sin where none is, to seem liberal of his forgiveness where none is asked or needed.

What ways he hath taken towards the prosperity of his people, which he would seem "so earnestly to desire," if we do but once call to mind, it will be enough to teach us, looking on the smooth insinuations here, that tyrants are not more flattered by their slaves, than forced to flatter others whom they fear. For the people's "tranquillity he would willingly be the Jonah;" but lest he should be taken at his word, pretends to foresee within ken two imaginary "winds" never heard of in the compass, which threaten, if he be cast overboard, "to increase the storm;" but that controversy divine lot hath ended.

"He had rather not rule, than that his people should be ruined;" and yet, above these twenty years, hath been ruining the people about the niceties of his ruling. He is accurate "to put a difference between the plague of malice and the ague of mistakes; the itch of novelty, and the leprosy of disloyalty." But had he as well known how to distinguish between the venerable gray hairs of ancient religion and the old scurf of superstition, between the wholesome heat of well governing and the feverous rage of tyrannizing, his judgment in state physic had been of more authority.

Much he prophesies, "that the credit of those men, who have cast black scandals on him, shall ere long be quite blasted by the same furnace of popular obloquy, wherein they sought to cast his name and honor." I believe not that a Romish gilded portraiture gives better oracle than a Babylonish golden image could do, to tell us truly who heated that furnace of obloquy, or who deserves to be thrown in, Nebuchadnezzar or the three kingdoms. It "gave him great cause to suspect his own innocence," that he was opposed by "so many who professed singular piety." But this qualm was soon over, and he concluded rather to suspect their religion than his own innocence, affirming that "many with him were both learned and religious above the ordinary size." But if his great seal, without the parliament, were not sufficient to create lords, his parole must needs be far more unable to create learned and religious men; and who shall authorize his unlearned judgment to point them out?

He guesses that "many well-minded men were by popular preachers urged to oppose him." But the opposition undoubtedly proceeded and continues from heads far wiser, and spirits of a nobler strain; those priest-led Herodians, with their blind guides, are in the ditch already; travelling as they thought, to Sion, but moored in the Isle of Wight. He thanks God "for his constancy to the protestant religion both abroad and at home." Abroad, his letter to the pope; at home, his innovations in the church, will speak his constancy in religion what it was, without further credit to this vain boast. His "using the assistance of some papists," as the cause might be, could not hurt his religion; but, in the settling of protestantism, their aid was both unseemly and suspicious, and inferred that the greatest part of protestants were against him and his obtruded settlement.

But this is strange indeed, that he should appear now teaching the parliament, what no man, till this was read, thought ever he had learnt, "that difference of persuasion in religious matters may fall out where there is the sameness of allegiance and subjection." If he thought so from the beginning, wherefore was there such compulsion used to the puritans of England, and the whole realm of Scotland, about conforming to a Liturgy? Wherefore no bishop, no king? Wherefore episcopacy more agreeable to monarchy, if different persuasions in religion, may agree in one duty and allegiance? Thus do court maxims, like court minions, rise or fall as the king pleases.

Not to tax him for want of elegance as a courtier, in writing Oglio for Olla, the Spanish word, it might be well affirmed, that there was a greater medley and disproportioning of religions, to mix papists with protestants in a religious cause, than to entertain all those diversified sects, who yet were all protestants, one religion, though many opinions. Neither was it any "shame to protestants," that he, a declared papist, if his own letter to the pope, not yet renounced, belie him not, found so few protestants of his religion, as enforced him to call in both the counsel and the aid of papists to help establish protestancy, who were led on, not "by the sense of their allegiance," but by the hope of his apostacy to Rome, from disputing to warring; his own voluntary and first appeal.

His hearkening to evil counsellors, charged upon him so often by the parliament, he puts off as "a device of those men who were so eager to give him better counsel." That "those men" were the parliament, and that he ought to have used the counsel of none but those, as a king, is already known. What their civility laid upon evil counsellors, he himself most commonly owned; but the event of those evil counsels, "the enormities, the confusions, the miseries," he transfers from the guilt of his own civil broils to the just resistance made by parliament; and imputes what miscarriages of his they could not yet remove for his opposing, as if they were some new misdemeanors of their bringing in, and not the inveterate diseases of his own bad government; which, with a disease as bad, he falls again to magnify and commend. And may all those who would be governed by his "retractions and concessions," rather than by laws of parliament, admire his self-encomiums, and be flattered with that "crown of patience," to which he cunningly exhorted them, that his monarchical foot might have the setting it upon their heads!

That trust which the parliament faithfully discharged in the asserting of our liberties, he calls "another artifice to withdraw the people from him to their designs." What piece of justice could they have demanded for the people, which the jealousy of a king

might not have miscalled a design to disparage his government, and to ingratiate themselves? To be more just, religious, wise, or magnanimous than the common sort, stirs up in a tyrant both fear and envy; and straight he cries out popularity, which, in his account, is little less than treason. The sum is, they thought to limit or take away the remora of his negative voice, which, like to that little pest at sea, took upon it to arrest and stop the commonwealth steering under full sail to a reformation. They thought to share with him in the militia, both or either of which he could not possibly hold without consent of the people, and not be absolutely a tyrant. He professes "to desire no other liberty than what he envies not his subjects according to law;" yet fought with might and main against his subjects, to have a sole power over them in his hand, both against and beyond law. As for the philosophical liberty which in vain he talks of, we may conclude him very ill trained up in those free notions, who to civil liberty was so injurious.

He calls the conscience "God's sovereignty:" why, then, doth he contest with God about that supreme title? why did he lay restraints, and force enlargements, upon our consciences in things for which we were to answer God only and the church? God bids us "be subject for conscience sake;" that is, as to a magistrate and in the laws; not usurping over spiritual things, as Lucifer beyond his sphere. And the same precept bids him likewise, for conscience sake, be subject to the parliament, both his natural and his legal superior.

Finally, having laid the fault of these commotions not upon his own misgovernment, but upon the "ambition of others, the necessity of some men's fortune, and thirst after novelty," he bodes himself "much honor and reputation, that, like the sun, shall rise and recover itself to such a splendor, as owls, bats, and such fatal birds shall be unable to bear." Poets, indeed, use to vapor much after this manner. But to bad kings, who, without cause, expect future glory from their actions, it happens as to bad poets, who sit and starve themselves with a delusive hope to win immortality by their bad lines. For though men ought not to "speak evil of dignities" which are just, yet nothing hinders us to speak evil, as oft as it is the truth, of those who in their dignities do evil. Thus did our Saviour himself, John the Baptist, and Stephen the Martyr. And those black veils of his own misdeeds he might be sure would ever keep "his face from shining," till he could "refute evil speaking with well doing," which grace he seems here to pray for; and his prayer doubtless as it was prayed, so it was heard. But even his prayer is so ambitious of prerogative, that it dares ask away the prerogative of Christ himself, "To become the headstone of the corner."

CHAPTER XVI.

Upon the Ordinance against the Common-Prayer Book.

WHAT to think of liturgies, both the sense of scripture and apostolical practice would have taught him better than his human reasonings and conjectures. Nevertheless, what weight they have, let us consider: if it "be no news to have all innovations ushered in with the name of reformation," sure it is less news to have all reformation censured and opposed under the name of innovation, by those who, being exalted in high place above their merit, fear all change, though of things never so ill, or so unwisely settled. So hardly can the dotage of those that dwell upon antiquity allow present times any share of godliness or wisdom.

The removing of liturgy he traduces to be done only as a "thing plausible to the people;" whose rejection of it he likens, with small reverence, to the crucifying of our Saviour; next, that it was done "to please these men who gloried in their extemporary vein," meaning the ministers. For whom it will be best to answer, as was answered for the man born blind, "They are of age, let them speak for themselves;" not how they came blind, but whether it were liturgy that held them tongue-tied.

"For the matter contained in that book," we need no better witness than king Edward the Sixth, who to the Cornish rebels confesses it was no other than the old mass-book done into English, all but some few words that were expunged. And by this argument, which king Edward so promptly had to use against that irreligious rabble, we may be assured it was the carnal fear of those divines and politicians that modelled the liturgy no further off from the old mass, lest by too great an alteration they should incense the people, and be destitute of the same shifts to fly to, which they had taught the young king.

"For the manner of using set forms, there is no doubt but that, wholesome" matter and good desires rightly conceived in the heart, wholesome words will follow of themselves. Neither can any true Christian find a reason why liturgy should be at all admitted, a prescription not imposed or practised by those first founders of the church, who alone had that authority: without whose precept or example, how constantly the priest puts on his gown and surplice, so constantly doth his prayer put on a servile yoke of liturgy. This is evident, that they "who use no set forms of prayer," have words from their affections; while others are to seek affections fit and proportionable to a certain dose of prepared words; which as they are not rigorously forbid to any man's private infirmity, so to imprison and confine by force, into a pinfold of set words, those two most unimprisonable things, our prayers, and that divine spirit of utterance that moves them, is a tyranny that would have longer hands than those giants who threatened bondage to heaven. What we may do in the same form of words is not so much the question, as whether liturgy may be forced as he forced it. It is true that we "pray to the same God;" must we, therefore, always use the same words? Let us then use but one word, because we pray to one God. "We profess the same truths:" but the liturgy comprehends not all truths: "we read the same scriptures," but never read that all those sacred expressions, all benefit and use of scripture, as to public prayer, should be denied us, except what was barrelled up in a common-prayer book with many mixtures of their own, and, which is worse, without salt.

But suppose them savory words and unmixed, suppose them manna itself, yet, if they shall be hoarded up and enjoined us, while God every morning rains down new expressions into our hearts; instead of being fit to use, they will be found, like reserved manna, rather to breed worms and stink. "We have the same duties upon us, and feel the same wants;" yet not always the same, nor at all times alike; but with variety of circumstances, which ask variety of words, whereof God hath given us plenty; not to use so copiously upon all other occasions, and so niggardly to him alone in our devotions. As if Christians were now in a worse famine of words fit for prayer, than was of food at the siege of Jerusalem, when perhaps the priests being to remove the shewbread, as was accustomed, were compelled every sabbath-day, for want of other loaves, to bring again still the same. If the "Lord's Prayer" had been the "warrant, or the pattern of set liturgies," as is here affirmed, why was neither that prayer, nor any other set form, ever after used, or so much as mentioned by the apostles, much less commended to our use? Why was their care wanting in a thing so useful to the church? so full of danger and contention to be left undone by them to other men's penning, of whose authority we could not be so certain? Why was this forgotten by them, who declare that they have revealed to us the whole counsel of God? who, as he left our affections to be guided by his sanctifying Spirit, so did he likewise our words to be put into us without our premeditations; not only those cautious words to be used before Gentiles and tyrants, but much more those filial words, of which we have so frequent use in our access with freedom of speech to the throne of grace. Which to lay aside for other outward dictates of men, were to injure him and his perfect gift, who is the spirit, and the giver of our ability to pray: as if his ministration were incomplete, and that to whom he gave affections, he did not also afford utterance to make his gift of prayer a perfect gift; to them especially, whose office in the church is to pray publicly.

And although the gift were only natural, yet voluntary prayers are less subject to formal and superficial tempers than set forms. For in those, at least for words and matter, he who prays must consult first with his heart, which in likelihood may stir up his affections; in these, having both words and matter ready made to his lips, which is enough to make up the outward act of prayer, his affections grow lazy, and come not up easily at the call of words not their own. The prayer also having less intercourse and sympathy with a heart wherein it was not conceived, saves itself the labor of so long a journey downward, and flying up in haste on the specious wings of formality, if it fall not back again headlong, instead of a prayer which was expected, presents God with a set of stale and empty words.

No doubt but "ostentation and formality" may taint the best duties; we are not therefore to leave duties for no duties, and to turn prayer into a kind of lurry. Cannot unpremeditated babblings be rebuked and restrained in whom we find they are, but the Spirit of God must be forbidden in all men? But it is the custom of bad men and hypocrites, to take advantage at the least abuse of good things, that under that covert they may remove the goodness of those things, rather than the abuse. And how unknowingly, how weakly is the using of set forms attributed here to "constancy," as if it were constancy in the cuckoo to be always in the same liturgy.

Much less can it be lawful that an Englished mass-book, composed, for aught we know, by men neither learned nor godly, should justle out, or at any time deprive us the exercise of that heavenly gift, which God by special promise pours out daily upon his church, that is to say, the spirit of prayer. Whereof to help those many infirmities, which he reckons up, "rudeness, impertinency, flatness," and the like, we have a remedy of God's finding out, which is not liturgy, but his own free Spirit. Though we know not what to pray as we ought, yet he with sighs unutterable by any words much less by a stinted liturgy, dwelling in us makes intercession for us, according to the mind and will of God, both in private and in the performance of all ecclesiastical duties. For it is his promise also, that where two or three gathered together in his name shall agree to ask him anything, it shall be granted; for he is there in the midst of them. If then ancient churches, to remedy the infirmities of prayer, or rather the infections of Arian and Pelagian heresies, neglecting that ordained and promised help of the Spirit, betook them almost four hundred years after Christ to liturgy, (their own invention,) we are not to imitate them; nor to distrust God in the removal of that truant help to our devotion, which by him never was appointed. And what is said of liturgy is said also of directory, if it be imposed: although to forbid the service-book there be much more reason, as being of itself superstitious, offensive, and indeed, though Englished, yet still the mass-book; and public places ought to be provided of such as need not the help of liturgies or directories continually, but are supported with ministerial gifts answerable to their calling.

Lastly, that the common-prayer book was rejected because it "prayed so oft for him," he had no reason to object: for what large and laborious prayers were made for him in the pulpits, if he never heard, 'tis doubtful they were never heard in heaven. We might now have expected, that his own following prayer should add much credit to set forms; but on the contrary we find the same imperfections in it, as in most before, which he lays here upon extemporal. Nor doth he ask of God to be directed whether liturgies be lawful, but presumes, and in a manner would persuade him, that they be so; praying, "that the church and he may never want them." What could be prayed worse extempore? unless he mean by wanting, that they may never need them.

CHAPTER XVII.

Of the Differences in point of Church-Government.

THE government of church by bishops hath been so fully proved from the scriptures to be vicious and usurped, that whether out of piety or policy maintained, it is not much material; for piety grounded upon error can no more justify king Charles, than it did queen Mary, in the sight of God or man. This, however, must not be let pass without a serious observation; God having so disposed the author in this chapter as to confess and discover more of mystery and combination between tyranny and false religion, than from any other hand would have been credible. Here we may see the very dark roots of them both turned up, and how they twine and interweave one another in the earth, though above ground shooting up in two severed branches.

We may have learnt, both from sacred history and times of reformation, that the kings of this world have both ever hated and instinctively feared the church of God. Whether it be for that their doctrine seems much to favor two things to them so dreadful, liberty and equality; or because they are the children of that kingdom, which, as ancient prophecies have foretold, shall in the end break to pieces and dissolve all their great power and dominion. And those kings and potentates who have strove most to rid themselves of this fear, by cutting off or suppressing the true church, have drawn upon themselves the occasion of their own ruin, while they thought with most policy to prevent it. Thus Pharaoh, when once he began to fear and wax jealous of the Israelites, lest they should multiply and fight against him, and that his fear stirred him up to afflict and keep them under, as the only remedy of what he feared, soon found that the evil which before slept, came suddenly upon him, by the preposterous way he took to shun it.

Passing by examples between, and not shutting wilfully our eyes, we may see the like story brought to pass in our own land. This king, more than any before him, except perhaps his father, from his first entrance to the crown, harboring in his mind a strange fear and suspicion of men most religious, and their doctrine, which in his own language he here acknowledges, terming it "the seditious exorbitancy" of ministers' tongues, and doubting "lest they," as he not Christianly expresses it, "should with the keys of heaven let out peace and loyalty from the people's hearts." Though they never preached or attempted aught that might justly raise in him such apprehensions, he could not rest, or think himself secure, so long as they remained in any of his three kingdoms unrooted out.

But outwardly professing the same religion with them, he could not presently use violence as Pharaoh did; and that course had with others before but ill succeeded. He chooses therefore a more mystical way, a newer method of antichristian fraud, to the church more dangerous; and, like to Balak the son of Zippor, against a nation of prophets thinks it best to hire other esteemed prophets, and to undermine and wear out the true church by a false ecclesiastical policy. To this drift he found the government of bishops most serviceable; an order in the church, as by men first corrupted, so mutually corrupting them who receive it, both in judgment and manners. He, by conferring bishoprics and great livings on whom he thought most pliant to his will, against the known canons and universal practice of the ancient church, whereby those elections were the people's right, sought, as he confesses to have "greatest influence upon churchmen." They on the other side finding themselves in a high dignity, neither founded by scripture, nor allowed by reformation, nor supported by any spiritual gift or grace of their own, knew it their best course to have dependence only upon him; and wrought his fancy by degrees to that degenerate and unkingly persuasion of "No bishop, no king." Whenas on the contrary all prelates in their own subtle sense are of another mind; according to that of Pius IV., remembered in the Trentine story, that bishops then grow to be most vigorous and potent, when princes happen to be most weak and impotent.

Thus when both interests of tyranny and episcopacy were incorporate into each other, the king, whose principal safety and establishment consisted in the righteous execution of his civil power, and not in bishops and their wicked counsels, fatally driven on, set himself to the extirpating of those men whose doctrine and desire of church-discipline he so feared would be the undoing of his monarchy. And because no temporal law could touch the innocence of their lives, he begins with the persecution of their consciences, laying scandals before them; and makes that the argument to inflict his unjust penalties both on their bodies and estates. In this war against the church, if he hath sped so, as other haughty monarchs whom God heretofore hath hardened to the like enterprise, we ought to look up with praises and thanksgiving to the Author of our deliverance, to whom victory and power, majesty, honor, and dominion belongs for ever.

In the meanwhile, from his own words we may perceive easily that the special motives which he had to endear and deprave his judgment to the favoring and utmost defending of episcopacy, are such as here we represent them; and how unwillingly, and with what mental reservation, he condescended against his interest to remove it out of the peer's house, hath been shown already. The reasons, which, he affirms, wrought so much upon his judgment, shall be so far answered as they be urged.

Scripture he reports, but distinctly produces none; and next the "constant practice of all Christian churches, till of late years tumult, faction, pride, and covetousness invented new models under the title of Christ's government." Could any papist have spoke more scandalously against all reformation? Well may the parliament and best affected people not now be troubled at his calumnies and reproaches, since he binds them in the same bundle with all other the reformed churches; who also may now further see, besides their own bitter experience, what a cordial and well-meaning helper they had of him abroad, and how true to the protestant cause.

As for histories to prove bishops, the Bible, —if we mean not to run into errors, vanities, and uncertainties,—must be our only history. Which informs us that the apostles were not properly bishops; next, that bishops were not successors of apostles, in the function of apostleship. And that if they were apostles, they could not be precisely bishops; if bishops, they could not be apostles; this being universal, extraordinary, and immediate from God; that being an ordinary, fixed, and particular charge, the continual inspection over a certain flock. And although an ignorance and deviation of the ancient churches afterward may with as much reason and charity be supposed as sudden in point of prelaty, as in other manifest corruptions, yet that "no example since the first age for fifteen hundred years can be produced of any settled church, wherein were many ministers and congregations, which had not some bishops above them;" the ecclesiastical story, to which he appeals for want of scripture, proves clearly to be a false and over-confident assertion.

Sozomenus, who wrote above twelve hundred years ago, in his seventh book, relates from his own knowledge, that in the churches of Cyprus and Arabia (places near to Jerusalem, and with the first frequented by apostles) they had bishops in every village; and what could those be more than presbyters? The like he tells of other nations; and that episcopal churches in those days did not condemn them. I add, that many Western churches, eminent for their faith and good works, and settled above four hundred years ago in France, in Piedmont and Bohemia, have both taught and practised the same doctrine, and not admitted of episcopacy among them. And if we may believe what the papists themselves have written of these churches, which they call Waldenses, I find it in a book written almost four hundred years since, and set forth in the Bohemian history, that those churches in Piedmont have held the same doctrine and government since the time that Constantine with his mischievous donations poisoned Sylvester and the whole church.

Others affirm they have so continued there since the apostles; and Theodorus Belvederensis in his relation of them confesseth, that those heresies, as he names them, were from the first times of Christianity in that place. For the rest I refer me to that famous testimony of Jerome, who upon this very place which he only roves at here, the Epistle to Titus, declares openly that bishop and presbyter were one and the same thing, till by the instigation of Satan, partialities grew up in the church, and that bishops, rather by custom than any ordainment of Christ, were exalted above presbyters; whose interpretation we trust shall be received before this intricate stuff tattled here of Timothy and Titus, and I know not whom their successors, far beyond court-element, and as far beneath true edification. These are his "fair grounds both from scripture canons and ecclesiastical examples;" how undivinelike written, and how like a worldly gospeller that understands nothing of these matters, posterity no doubt will be able to judge; and will but little regard what he calls apostolical, who in his letter to the pope calls apostolical the Roman religion.

Nor let him think to plead, that therefore "it was not policy of state," or obstinacy in him which upheld episcopacy, because the injuries and losses which he sustained by so doing were to him "more considerable than episcopacy itself;" for all this might Pharaoh have had to say in his excuse of detaining the Israelites, that his own and his kingdom's safety, so much endangered by his denial, was to him more dear than all their building labors could be worth to Egypt. But whom God hardens, them also he blinds.

He endeavors to make good episcopacy not only in "religion, but from the nature of all civil government, where parity breeds confusion and faction." But of faction and confusion, to take no other than his own testimony, where hath more been ever bred than under the imparity of his own monarchical government? of which to make at this time longer dispute, and from civil constitutions and human conceits to debate and question the convenience of divine ordinations, is neither wisdom nor sobriety. And to confound Mosaic priesthood with evangelic presbytery against express institution, is as far from warrantable. As little to the purpose is it, that we should stand polling the reformed churches, whether they equalize in number "those of his three kingdoms;" of whom so lately the far greater part,—what they have long desired to do,—have now quite thrown off episcopacy.

Neither may we count it the language or religion of a protestant, so to vilify the best reformed churches (for none of them but Lutherans retain bishops) as to fear more the scandalizing of papists, because more numerous, than of our protestant brethren, because a handful. It will not be worth the while to say what "schismatics or heretics" have had no bishops: yet, lest he should be taken for a great reader, he who prompted him, if he were a doctor, might have remembered the forementioned place in Sozomenus; which affirms that besides the Cyprians and Arabians, who were counted Orthodoxal, the Novatians also, and Montanists in Phrygia, had no other bishops than such as were in every village. And what presbyter hath a narrower diocese? As for the Aërians, we know of no heretical opinion justly fathered upon them, but that they held bishops and presbyters to be the same. Which he in this place not obscurely seems to hold a heresy in all the reformed churches; with whom why the church of England desired conformity, he can find no reason, with all his "charity, but the coming in of the Scots' army;" such a high esteem he had of the English!

He tempts the clergy to return back again to bishops, from the fear of "tenuity and contempt," and the assurance of better "thriving under the favor of princes;" against which temptations if the clergy cannot arm themselves with their own spiritual armor, they are indeed as "poor a carcass" as he terms them. Of secular honors and great revenues added to the dignity of prelates, since the subject of that question is now removed, we need not spend time: but this perhaps will never be unseasonable to bear in mind out of Chrysostom, that when ministers came to have lands, houses, farms, coaches, horses, and the like lumber, then religion brought forth riches in the church, and the daughter devoured the mother.

But if his judgment in episcopacy may be judged by the goodly choice he made of bishops, we need not much amuse ourselves with the consideration of those evils, which by his foretelling, will "necessarily follow" their pulling down, until he prove that the apostles, having no certain diocese or appointed place of residence, were properly "bishops over those presbyters whom they ordained, or churches they planted;" wherein ofttimes their labors were both joint and promiscuous; or that the apostolic power must "necessarily descend to bishops, the use and end" of either function being so different. And how the church hath flourished under episcopacy, let the multitude of their ancient and gross errors testify, and the words of some learnedest and most zealous bishops among them; Nazianzen in a devout passion, wishing prelacy had never been: Basil terming them the slaves of slaves: Saint Martin, the enemies of saints; and confessing that after he was made a bishop, he found much of that grace decay in him which he had before.

Concerning his "coronation oath," what it was, and how far it bound him, already hath been spoken. This we may take for certain, that he was never sworn to his own particular conscience and reason, but to our conditions as a free people, which required him to give us such laws as ourselves shall choose. This the Scots could bring him to, and would not be baffled with the pretence of a coronation oath, after that episcopacy had for many years been settled there. Which concession of his to them, and not to us, he seeks here to put off with evasions that are ridiculous. And, to omit no shifts, he alleges that the presbyterian manners gave him no encouragement to like their modes of government. If that were so, yet certainly those men are in most likelihood nearer to amendment, who seek a stricter church-discipline than that of episcopacy, under which the most of them learned their manners. If estimation were to be made of God's law by their manners, who, leaving Egypt, received it in the wilderness, it could reap from such an inference as this nothing but rejection and disesteem. For the prayer wherewith he closes, it had been good some safe liturgy, which he so commends, had rather been in his way; it would perhaps in some measure have performed the end for which they say liturgy was first invented; and have hindered him both here, and at other times, from turning his notorious errors into his prayers.

CHAPTER XVIII.

Upon the Uxbridge Treaty, &c.

"IF the way of treaties be looked upon" in general, "as a retiring" from bestial force to human reason, his first aphorism here is in part deceived. For men may treat like beasts as well as fight. If some fighting were not manlike, then either fortitude were no virtue, or no fortitude in fighting. And as politicians ofttimes through dilatory purposes and emulations handle the matter, there hath been nowhere found more bestiality than in treating; which hath no more commendation in it, than from fighting to come to undermining, from violence to craft; and when they can no longer do as lions, to do as foxes.

The sincerest end of treating after war once proclaimed is either to part with more, or to demand less, than was at first fought for, rather than to hazard more lives, or worse mischiefs. What the parliament in that point were willing to have done, when first after the war begun, they petitioned him at Colnbrook to vouchsafe a treaty, is unknown.

For after he had taken God to witness of his continual readiness to treat, or to offer treaties to the avoiding of bloodshed, had named Windsor the place of treaty, and passed his royal word not to advance further, till commissioners by such a time were speeded towards him; taking the advantage of a thick mist, which fell that evening—weather that soon invited him to a design no less treacherous and obscure—he follows at the heels those messengers of peace with a train of covert war; and with a bloody surprise falls on our secure forces, which lay quartering at Brentford, in the thoughts and expectation of a treaty. And although in them who make a trade of war, and against a natural enemy, such an onset might in the rigor of military law have been excused, while arms were not yet by agreement suspended; yet by a king who seemed so heartily to accept of treating with his subjects, and professes here, "he never wanted either desire or disposition to it," professes to have "greater confidence in his reason than in his sword, and as a Christian to seek peace and ensue it," such bloody and deceitful advantages would have been forborne one day at least, if not much longer; in whom there had not been a thirst rather than a detestation of civil war and blood, and a desire to subdue rather than to treat.

In the midst of a second treaty, not long after sought by the parliament, and after much ado obtained with him at Oxford, what subtle and unpeaceable designs he then had in chase, his own letters discovered; what attempts of treacherous hostility, successful and unsuccessful, he made against Bristol, Scarborough, and other places, the proceedings of that treaty will soon put us in mind; and how he was so far from granting more of reason after so much of blood, that he denied then to grant what before he had offered; making no other use of treaties pretending peace, than to gain advantages that might enable him to continue war. What marvel then if "he thought it no diminution of himself," as oft as he saw his time, to be "importunate for treaties," when he sought them only, as by the upshot appeared, "to get opportunities"? And once to a most cruel purpose, if we remember, May 1643: and that messenger of peace from Oxford, whose secret message and commission, had it been effected, would have drowned the innocence of our treating, in the blood of a designed massacre. Nay, when treaties from the parliament sought out him no less than seven times, (oft enough to testify the willingness of their obedience, and too oft for the majesty of a parliament to court their subjection,) he, in the confidence of his own strength, or of our divisions, returned us nothing back but denials, or delays, to their most necessary demands; and being at lowest, kept up still and sustained his almost famished hopes with the hourly expectation of raising up himself the higher, by the greater heap which he sat promising himself of our sudden ruin through dissension.

But he infers, as if the parliament would have compelled him to part with something of "his honor as a king." What honor could he have or call his, joined not only with the offence or disturbance, but with the bondage and destruction of three nations? whereof, though he be careless and improvident, yet the parliament, by our laws and freedom, ought to judge, and use prevention; our laws else were but cobweb laws. And what were all his most rightful honors, but the people's gift, and the investment of that lustre, majesty, and honor, which for the public good, and no otherwise, redounds from a whole nation into one person? So far is any honor from being his to a common mischief and calamity. Yet still he talks on equal terms with the grand representative of that people, for whose sake he was a king; as if the general welfare and his subservient rights were of equal moment or consideration. His aim indeed hath ever been to magnify and exalt his borrowed rights and prerogatives above the parliament and kingdom, of whom he holds them. But when a king sets himself to bandy against the highest court and residence of all his regal power, he then, in the single person of a man, fights against his own majesty and kingship, and then indeed sets the first hand to his own deposing.

"The treaty at Uxbridge," he saith, "gave the fairest hopes of a happy composure;" fairest indeed, if his instructions to bribe our commissioners with the promise of security, rewards, and places, were fair. What other hopes it gave, no man can tell. There being but three main heads whereon to be treated—Ireland, episcopacy, and the militia; the first was anticipated and forestalled by a peace at any rate to be hastened with the Irish rebels, ere the treaty could begin, that he might pretend his word and honor passed against "the specious and popular arguments" (he calls them no better) which the parliament would urge upon him for the continuance of that just war. Episcopacy he bids the queen be confident he will never quit; which informs us by what patronage it stood; and the sword he resolves to clutch as fast, as if God with his own hand had put it into his. This was the "moderation which he brought;" this was, "as far as reason, honor, conscience," and the queen, who was his regent in all these, "would give him leave."

Lastly, "for composure," instead of happy, how miserable it was more likely to have been, wise men could then judge; when the English, during treaty, were called rebels; the Irish, good and catholic subjects; and the parliament beforehand, though for fashion's sake called a parliament, yet, by a jesuitical sleight, not acknowledged, though called so; but privately in the council books enrolled no parliament: that if accommodation had succeeded, upon what terms soever, such a devilish fraud was prepared, that the king in his own esteem had been absolved from all performance, as having treated with rebels and no parliament; and they, on the other side, instead of an expected happiness, had been brought under the hatchet. Then no doubt "war had ended," that massacre and tyranny might begin. These jealousies, however raised, let all men see whether they be diminished or allayed by the letters of his own cabinet opened. And yet the breach of this treaty is laid all upon the parliament and their commissioners, with odious names of "pertinacy, hatred of peace, faction, and covetousness," nay, his own brat, "superstition," is laid to their charge; notwithstanding his here professed resolution to continue both the order, maintenance, and authority of prelates, as a truth of God.

And who "were most to blame in the unsuccessfulness of that treaty," his appeal is to God's decision; believing to be very excusable at that tribunal. But if ever man gloried in an unflexible stiffness, he came not behind any; and that grand maxim, always to put something into his treaties which might give color to refuse all that was in other things granted, and to make them signify nothing, was his own principal maxim and particular instructions to his commissioners. Yet all, by his own verdict, must be construed reason in the king, and depraved temper in the parliament.

That the "highest tide of success," with these principles and designs, "set him not above a treaty," no great wonder. And yet if that be spoken to his praise, the parliament therein surpassed him; who, when he was their vanquished and their captive, his forces utterly broken and disbanded, yet offered him three several times no worse proposals or demands, than when he stood fair to be their conqueror. But that imprudent surmise that his lowest ebb could not set him "below a fight," was a presumption that ruined him.

He presaged the future "unsuccessfulness of treaties by the unwillingness of some men to treat;" and could not see what was present, that their unwillingness had good cause to proceed from the continual experience of his own obstinacy and breach of word. His prayer, therefore, of forgiveness to the guilty of that treaty's breaking, he had good reason to say heartily over, as including no man in that guilt sooner than himself. As for that protestation following in his prayer, "How oft have I entreated for peace, but when I speak thereof they make them ready to war;" unless he thought himself still in that perfidious mist between Colnbrook and Hounslow, and thought that mist could hide him from the eye of Heaven as well as of man, after such a bloody recompence given to our first offers of peace, how could this in the sight of heaven without horrors of conscience be uttered?

CHAPTER XIX.

Upon the various Events of the War.

It is no new or unwonted thing, for bad men to claim as much part in God as his best servants; to usurp and imitate their words, and appropriate to themselves those properties which belong only to the good and righteous. This not only in scripture is familiarly to be found, but here also in this chapter of Apocrypha. He tells us much why "it pleased God" to send him victory or loss, (although what in so doing was the intent of God, he might be much mistaken as to his own particular,) but we are yet to learn what real good use he made thereof in his practice.

Those numbers, which he grew to "from small beginnings," were not such as out of love came to protect him, for none approved his actions as a king, except courtiers and prelates, but were such as fled to be protected by him from the fear of that reformation which the pravity of their lives would not bear. Such a snowball he might easily gather by rolling through those cold and dark provinces of ignorance and lewdness, where on a sudden he became so numerous. He imputes that to God's "protection" which, to them who persist in a bad cause, is either his long-suffering or his hardening, and that to wholesome "chastisement" which were the gradual beginnings of a severe punishment. For if neither God nor nature put civil power in the hands of any whomsoever, but to a lawful end, and commands our obedience to the authority of law only, not to the tyrannical force of any person; and if the laws of our land have placed the sword in no man's single hand, so much as to unsheath against a foreign enemy, much less upon the native people; but have placed it in that elective body of the parliament, to whom the making, repealing, judging, and interpreting of law itself was also committed, as was fittest, so long as we intended to be a free nation, and not the slaves of one man's will; then was the king himself disobedient and rebellious to that law by which he reigned: and by authority of parliament to raise arms against him in defence of law and liberty, we do not only think, but believe and know, was justifiable both "by the word of God, the laws of the land, and all lawful oaths;" and they who sided with him, fought against all these.

The same allegations which he uses for himself and his party, may as well fit any tyrant in the world; for let the parliament be called a faction when the king pleases, and that no law must be made or changed, either civil or religious, because no law will content all sides, then must be made or changed no law at all, but what a tyrant, be he protestant or papist, thinks fit. Which tyrannous assertion forced upon us by the sword, he who fights against, and dies fighting, if his other sins overweigh not, dies a martyr undoubtedly both of the faith and of the commonwealth; and I hold it not as the opinion, but as the full belief and persuasion, of far holier and wiser men than parasitic preachers; who, without their dinner-doctrine, know that neither king, law, civil oaths, or religion, was ever established without the parliament. And their power is the same to abrogate as to establish; neither is anything to be thought established, which that house declares to be abolished. Where the parliament sits, there inseparably sits the king, there the laws, there our oaths, and whatsoever can be civil in religion. They who fought for the parliament, in the truest sense, fought for all these; who fought for the king divided from his parliament, fought for the shadow of a king against all these; and for things that were not, as if they were established. It were a thing monstrously absurd and contradictory, to give the parliament a legislative power, and then to upbraid them for transgressing old establishments.

But the king and his party having lost in this quarrel their heaven upon earth, begin to make great reckoning of eternal life, and at an easy rate *in forma pauperis* canonize one another into heaven; he them in his book, they him in the portraiture before his book. But, as was said before, stage-work will not do it, much less the "justness of their cause," wherein most frequently they died in a brutish fierceness, with oaths and other damning words in their mouths; as if such had been all "the oaths" they fought for; which undoubtedly sent them full sail on another voyage than to heaven. In the meanwhile they to whom God gave victory never brought to the king at Oxford the state of their consciences, that he should presume without confession, more than a pope presumes, to tell abroad what "conflicts and accusations" men whom he never spoke with have "in their own thoughts." We never read of any English king but one that was a confessor, and his name was Edward; yet sure it passed his skill to know thoughts, as this king takes upon him. But they who will not stick to slander men's inward consciences, which they can neither see nor know, much less will care to slander outward actions, which they pretend to see, though with senses never so vitiated.

To judge of "his conditions conquered," and the manner of "dying" on that side, by the sober men that chose it, would be his small advantage: it being most notorious, that they who were hottest in his cause, the most of them were men oftener drunk, than by their good-will sober, and very many of them so fought and so died. And that the conscience of any man should grow suspicious, or be now convicted by any pretensions in the parliament, which are now proved false and unintended, there can be no just cause. For neither did they ever pretend to establish his throne without our liberty and religion, nor religion without the word of God, nor to judge of laws by their being established, but to establish them by their being good and necessary.

He tells the world "he often prayed, that all on his side might be as faithful to God and their own souls, as to him." But kings, above all other men, have in their hands not to pray only, but to do. To make that prayer effectual, he should have governed as well as prayed. To pray and not to govern, is for a monk, and not a king. Till then he might be well assured, they were more faithful to their lust and rapine than to him. In the wonted predication of his own virtues he goes on to tell us, that to "conquer he never desired, but only to restore the laws and liberties of his people." It had been happy then he had known at last, that by force to restore laws abrogated by the legislative parliament, is to conquer absolutely both them and law itself. And for our liberties none ever oppressed them more, both in peace and war: first, like a master by his arbitrary power; next, as an enemy by hostile invasion.

And if his best friends feared him, and "he himself, in the temptation of an absolute conquest," it was not only pious but friendly in the parliament, both to fear him and resist him; since their not yielding was the only means to keep him out of that temptation wherein he doubted his own strength. He

takes himself to be "guilty in this war of nothing else, but of confirming the power of some men." Thus all along he signifies the parliament, whom to have settled by an act he counts to be his only guiltiness. So well he knew that to continue a parliament, was to raise a war against himself; what were his actions then, and his government the while? For never was it heard in all our story, that parliaments made war on their kings, but on their tyrants; whose modesty and gratitude was more wanting to the parliament than theirs to any of such kings.

What he yielded was his fear; what he denied was his obstinacy. Had he yielded more, fear might perchance have saved him; had he granted less, his obstinacy had perhaps the sooner delivered us. "To review the occasions of this war," will be to them never too late, who would be warned by his example from the like evils: but to wish only a happy conclusion, will never expiate the fault of his unhappy beginnings. 'Tis true, on our side the sins of our lives not seldom fought against us: but on their side, besides those, the grand sin of their cause. How can it be otherwise, when he desires here most unreasonably, and indeed sacrilegiously, that we should be subject to him, though not further, yet as far as all of us may be subject to God; to whom this expression leaves no precedency? He who desires from men as much obedience and subjection as we may all pay to God, desires not less than to be a God: a sacrilege far worse than meddling with the bishops' lands, as he esteems it.

His prayer is a good prayer and a glorious; but glorying is not good, if it know not that a little leaven leavens the whole lump. It should have purged out the leaven of untruth, in telling God that the blood of his subjects by him shed was in his just and necessary defence. Yet this is remarkable; God hath here so ordered his prayer, that as his own lips acquitted the parliament, not long before his death, of all the blood spilt in this war, so now his prayer unwittingly draws it upon himself. For God imputes not to any man the blood he spills in a just cause; and no man ever begged his not imputing of that, which he in his justice could not impute; so that now, whether purposely or unaware, he hath confessed both to God and man the blood-guiltiness of all this war to lie upon his own head.

CHAPTER XX.

Upon the Reformation of the Times.

THIS chapter cannot punctually be answered without more repetitions than now can be excusable; which perhaps have already been more humored than was needful. As it presents us with nothing new, so with his exceptions against reformation pitifully old, and tattered with continual using; not only in his book, but in the words and writings of every papist and popish king. On the scene he thrusts out first an antimask of two bugbears, novelty and perturbation; that the ill looks and noise of those two may as long as possible drive off all endeavors of a reformation. Thus sought pope Adrian, by representing the like vain terrors, to divert and dissipate the zeal of those reforming princes of the age before in Germany. And if we credit Latimer's sermons, our papists here in England pleaded the same dangers and inconveniences against that which was reformed by Edward VI. Whereas if those fears had been available, Christianity itself had never been received: which Christ foretold us would not be admitted, without the censure of novelty, and many great commotions. These therefore are not to deter us.

He grants reformation to be "a good work," and confesses "what the indulgence of times and corruption of manners might have depraved." So did the forementioned pope, and our grandsire papists in this realm. Yet all of them agree in one song with this here, that "they are sorry to see so little regard had to laws established, and the religion settled." "Popular compliance, dissolution of all order and government in the church, schisms, opinions, undecencies, confusions, sacrilegious invasions, contempt of the clergy and their liturgy, diminution of princes;" all these complaints are to be read in the messages and speeches almost of every legate from the pope to those states and cities which began reformation. From whence he either learned the same pretences, or had them naturally in

him from the same spirit. Neither was there ever so sincere a reformation that hath escaped these clamors.

He offered a "synod or convocation rightly chosen." So offered all those popish kings heretofore; a course the most unsatisfactory, as matters have been long carried, and found by experience in the church liable to the greatest fraud and packing; no solution or redress of evil, but an increase rather; detested therefore by Nazianzen, and some other of the fathers. And let it be produced, what good hath been done by synods from the first times of reformation. Not to justify what enormities the vulgar may commit in the rudeness of their zeal, we need but only instance how he bemoans "the pulling down of crosses" and other superstitious monuments, as the effect "of a popular and deceitful reformation." How little this savors of a protestant is too easily perceived.

What he charges in defect of "piety, charity, and morality," hath been also charged by papists upon the best reformed churches; not as if they the accusers were not tenfold more to be accused, but out of their malignity to all endeavor of amendment; as we know who accused to God the sincerity of Job; an accusation of all others the most easy, whenas there lives not any mortal man so excellent, who in these things is not always deficient. But the infirmities of best men, and the scandals of mixed hypocrites in all times of reforming, whose bold intrusion covets to be ever seen in things most sacred, as they are most specious, can lay no just blemish upon the integrity of others, much less upon the purpose of reformation itself. Neither can the evil doings of some be the excuse of our delaying or deserting that duty to the church, which for no respect of times or carnal policies can be at any time unseasonable.

He tells with great show of piety what kind of persons public reformers ought to be, and what they ought to do. 'Tis strange that in above twenty years, the church growing still worse and worse under him, he could neither be as he bids others be, nor do as he pretends here so well to know; nay, which is worst of all, after the greatest part of his reign spent in neither knowing nor doing aught toward a reformation either in church or state, should spend the residue in hindering those by a seven years' war, whom it concerned, with his consent or without it, to do their parts in that great performance.

'Tis true that the "method of reforming" may well subsist without "perturbation of the state;" but that it falls out otherwise for the most part, is the plain text of scripture. And if by his own rule he had allowed us to "fear God first," and the king in due order, our allegiance might have still followed our religion in a fit subordination. But if Christ's kingdom be taken for the true discipline of the church, and by "his kingdom" be meant the violence he used against it, and to uphold an antichristian hierarchy, then sure enough it is, that Christ's kingdom could not be set up without pulling down his: and they were best Christians who were least subject to him. "Christ's government," out of question meaning it prelatical, he thought would confirm his: and this was that which overthrew it.

He professes "to own his kingdom from Christ, and to desire to rule for his glory, and the church's good." The pope and the king of Spain profess everywhere as much; and both his practice and all his reasonings, all his enmity against the true church we see hath been the same with theirs, since the time that in his letter to the pope he assured them both of his full compliance. "But evil beginnings never bring forth good conclusions:" they are his own words, and he ratified them by his own ending. To the pope he engaged himself to hazard life and estate for the Roman religion, whether in compliment he did it, or in earnest; and God, who stood nearer than he for complimenting minded, writ down those words; that according to his resolution, so it should come to pass. He prays against "his hypocrisy and pharisaical washings," a prayer to him most pertinent; but chokes it straight with other words, which pray him deeper into his old errors and delusions.

CHAPTER XXI.

Upon his Letters taken and divulged.

THE king's letters taken at the battle of Naseby, being of greatest importance to let the people see what faith there was in all his promises and solemn protestations, were transmitted to public view by special order of the parliament. They discovered his good affection to papists and Irish rebels, the straight intelligence he held, the pernicious and dishonorable peace he made with them, not solicited, but rather soliciting, which by all invocations that were holy he had in public abjured. They revealed his endeavors to bring in foreign forces, Irish, French, Dutch, Lorrainers, and our old invaders the Danes, upon us. besides his subtleties and mysterious arts in treating; to sum up all, they showed him governed by a woman. All which, though suspected vehemently before, and from good grounds believed, yet by him and his adherents peremptorily denied, were by the opening of that cabinet visible to all men under his own hand.

The parliament, therefore, to clear themselves of aspersing him without cause, and that the people might no longer be abused and cajoled, as they call it, by falsities and court impudence, in matters of so high concernment; to let them know on what terms their duty stood, and the kingdom's peace, conceived it most expedient and necessary that those letters should be made public. This the king affirms was by them done without "honor and civility;" words, which if they contain not in them, as in the language of a courtier most commonly they do not, more of substance and reality, than compliment, ceremony, court-fawning, and dissembling, enter not I suppose further than the ear into any wise man's consideration. Matters were not then between the parliament, and a king their enemy, in that state of trifling, as to observe those superficial vanities. But if honor and civility mean, as they did of old, discretion, honesty, prudence, and plain truth, it will be then maintained against any sect of those Cabalists, that the parliament, in doing what they did with those letters, could suffer in their honor and civility no diminution. The reasons are already heard.

And that it is with none more familiar than with kings, to transgress the bounds of all honor and civility, there should not want examples good store, if brevity would permit: in point of letters, this one shall suffice. The duchess of Burgundy, and heir of duke Charles, had promised to her subjects, that she intended no otherwise to govern than by advice of the three estates; but to Louis, the French king, had written letters, that she had resolved to commit wholly the managing of her affairs to four persons, whom she named. The three estates, not doubting the sincerity of her princely word, send ambassadors to Louis, who then besieged Arras belonging to the duke of Burgundy. The king, taking hold of this occasion to set them at division among themselves, questioned their credence: which when they offered to produce with their instructions, he not only shows them the private letter of their duchess, but gives it them to carry home, wherewith to affront her; which they did, she denying it stoutly; till they, spreading it before her face in a full assembly, convicted her of an open lie. Which although Comines the historian much blames, as a deed too harsh and dishonorable in them who were subjects, and not at war with their princess, yet to his master Louis, who first divulged those letters, to the open shaming of that young governess, he imputes no incivility or dishonor at all, although betraying a certain confidence reposed by that letter in his royal secrecy.

With much more reason then may letters not intercepted only, but won in battle from an enemy, be made public to the best advantages of them that win them, to the discovery of such important truth or falsehood. Was it not more dishonorable in himself to feign suspicions and jealousies, which we first found among those letters, touching the chastity of his mother, thereby to gain assistance from the king of Denmark, as in vindication of his sister? The damsel of Burgundy at sight of her own letter was soon blank, and more ingenuous than to stand outfacing; but this man, whom nothing will convince, thinks by talking world without end, to make good his integrity and fair dealing, contradicted by his own hand and seal. They who can pick nothing out of them but phrases, shall be counted bees: they that discern further both there and here, that constancy to his wife is set in place before laws and religion, are in his naturalities no better than spiders.

He would work the people to a persuasion, that "if he be miserable, they cannot be happy." What should hinder them? Were they all born twins of Hippocrates with him and his fortune, one birth, one burial? It were a nation miserable indeed, not worth the name of a nation, but a race of idiots, whose happiness and welfare depended upon one man. The happiness of a nation consists in true religion, piety, justice, prudence, temperance, fortitude, and the contempt of avarice and ambition. They in whomsoever these virtues dwell eminently, need not kings to make them happy, but are the architects of their own happiness; and, whether to themselves or others, are not less than kings. But in him which of these virtues were to be found, that might extend to the making happy, or the well-governing of so much as his own household, which was the most licentious and ill-governed in the whole land?

But the opening of his letters was designed by the parliament "to make all reconciliation desperate." Are the lives of so many good and faithful men, that died for the freedom of their country, to be so slighted, as to be forgotten in a stupid reconcilement without justice done them? What he fears not by war and slaughter, should we fear to make desperate by opening his letters? Which fact he would parallel with Cham's revealing of his father's nakedness: when he at that time could be no way esteemed the father of his country, but the destroyer; nor had he ever before merited that former title.

"He thanks God he can not only bear this with patience, but with charity forgive the doers." Is not this mere mockery to thank God for what he can do, but will not? For is it patience to impute barbarism and inhumanity to the opening of an enemy's letter, or is it charity to clothe them with curses in his prayer, whom he hath forgiven in his discourse? In which prayer, to show how readily he can return good for evil to the parliament, and that if they take away his coat he can let them have his cloak also; for the dismantling of his letters he wishes "they may be covered with the cloak of confusion." Which I suppose they do resign with much willingness, both livery, badge, and cognizance, to them who chose rather to be the slaves and vassals of his will, than to stand against him, as men by nature free; born and created with a better title to their freedom than any king hath to his crown.

CHAPTER XXII.

Upon his going to the Scots.

THE king's coming in, whether to the Scots or English, deserved no thanks: for necessity was his counsellor; and that he hated them both alike, his expressions everywhere manifest. Some say his purpose was to have come to London, till hearing how strictly it was proclaimed, that no man should conceal him, he diverted his course. But that had been a frivolous excuse: and besides, he himself rehearsing the consultations had, before he took his journey, shows us clearly that he was determined to adventure "upon their loyalty who first began his troubles." And that the Scots had notice of it before, hath been long since brought to light. What prudence there could be in it, no man can imagine; malice there might be, by raising new jealousies to divide friends. For besides his diffidence of the English, it was no small dishonor that he put upon them, when, rather than yield himself to the parliament of England, he yielded to a hireling army of Scots in England, paid for their service here, not in Scotch coin, but in English silver; nay, who from the first beginning of these troubles, what with brotherly assistance, and what with monthly pay, have defended their own liberty and consciences at our charge. However, it was a hazardous and rash journey taken, "to resolve riddles in men's loyalty," who had more reason to mistrust the riddle of such a disguised yielding; and to put himself in their hands whose loyalty was a riddle to him, was not the course to be resolved of it, but to tempt it. What Providence denied to force, he thought it might grant to fraud, which he styles prudence; but Providence was not cozened with disguises, neither outward nor inward.

To have known "his greatest danger in his supposed safety, and his greatest safety in his supposed danger," was to him a fatal riddle never yet resolved; wherein rather to have employed his main skill, had been much more to his preservation. Had he "known when the game was lost," it might have saved much contest; but the way to give over fairly, was not to slip out of open war into a new disguise. He lays down his arms, but not his wiles; nor all his arms; for in obstinacy he comes no less armed than ever capà-pé. And what were they but wiles, continually to move for treaties, and yet to persist the same man, and to fortify his mind beforehand, still purposing to grant no more than what seemed good to that violent and lawless triumvirate within him, under the falsified names of his reason, honor, and conscience, the old circulating dance of his shifts and evasions?

The words of a king, as they are full of power, in the authority and strength of law, so, like Samson, without the strength of that Nazarite's lock, they have no more power in them than the words of another man. He adores reason as Domitian did Minerva, and calls her the "divinest power," thereby to intimate as if at reasoning, as at his own weapon, no man were so able as himself. Might we be so happy as to know where these monuments of his reason may be seen; for in his actions and his writing they appear as thinly as could be expected from the meanest parts, bred up in the midst of so many ways extraordinary to know something. He who reads his talk, would think he had left Oxford not without mature deliberation: yet his prayer confesses, that "he knew not what to do." Thus is verified that Psalm: "He poureth contempt upon princes, and causeth them to wander in the wilderness where there is no way." Psal. cvii.

———

CHAPTER XXIII.

Upon the Scots delivering the King to the English.

THAT the Scots in England should "sell their king," as he himself here affirms, and for a "price so much above that" which the covetousness of Judas was contented with to sell our Saviour, is so foul an infamy and dishonor cast upon them, as befits none to vindicate but themselves. And it were but friendly counsel to wish them beware the son, who comes among them with a firm belief, that they sold his father. The rest of this chapter he sacrifices to the echo of his conscience, out-babbling creeds and aves: glorying in his resolute obstinacy, and, as it were, triumphing how "evident it is now, that not evil counsellors," but he himself, hath been the author of all our troubles. Herein only we shall disagree to the world's end; while he, who sought so manifestly to have annihilated all our laws and liberties, hath the confidence to persuade us, that he hath fought and suffered all this while in their defence.

But he who neither by his own letters and commissions under hand and seal, nor by his own actions held as in a mirror before his face, will be convinced to see his faults, can much less be won upon by any force of words, neither he, nor any that take after him; who in that respect are no more to be disputed with, than they who deny principles. No question then but the parliament did wisely in their decree at last, to make no more addresses. For how unalterable his will was, that would have been our lord, how utterly averse from the parliament and reformation during his confinement, we may behold in this chapter. But to be ever answering fruitless repetitions, I should become liable to answer for the same myself. He borrows David's Psalms, as he charges the assembly of divines in his twentieth discourse, "to have set forth old catechisms and confessions of faith new dressed:" had he borrowed David's heart, it had been much the holier theft. For such kind of borrowing as this, if it be not bettered by the borrower, among good authors is accounted plagiary. However, this was more tolerable than Pamela's prayer stolen out of Sir Philip.

CHAPTER XXIV.

Upon the Denying him the Attendance of his Chaplains.

A CHAPLAIN is a thing so diminutive and inconsiderable, that how he should come here among matters of so great concernment, to take such room up in the discourses of a prince, if it be not wondered, is to be smiled at. Certainly by me, so mean an argument shall not be written; but I shall huddle him, as he does prayers. The scripture owns no such order, no such function in the church; and the church not owning them, they are left, for aught I know, to such a further examining as the sons of Sceva, the Jew, met with.

Bishops or presbyters we know, and deacons we know: but what are chaplains? In state perhaps they may be listed among the upper serving-men of some great household, and be admitted to some such place as may style them the sewers, or the yeomen-ushers of devotion, where the master is too resty or too rich to say his own prayers, or to bless his own table.

Wherefore should the parliament then take such implements of the court cupboard into their consideration? They knew them to have been the main corrupters at the king's elbow; they knew the king to have been always their most attentive scholar and imitator, and of a child to have sucked from them and their closet-work all his impotent principles of tyranny and superstition. While therefore they had any hope left of his reclaiming, these sowers of malignant tares they kept asunder from him, and sent to him such of the ministers and other zealous persons as they thought were best able to instruct him, and to convert him. What could religion herself have done more, to the saving of a soul? But when they found him past cure, and that he to himself was grown the most evil counsellor of all, they denied him not his chaplains, as many as were fitting, and some of them attended him, or else were at his call, to the very last. Yet here he makes more lamentation for the want of his chaplains, than superstitious Micah did to the Danites, who had taken away his household priest: "Ye have taken away my gods which I made, and the priest: and what have I more?" And perhaps the whole story of Micah might square not unfitly to this argument: "Now know I," saith he, "that the Lord will do me good, seeing I have a Levite to my priest." Micah had as great a care that his priest should be Mosaical, as the king had, that his should be apostolical; yet both in an error touching their priests.

Household and private orisons were not to be officiated by priests; for neither did public prayer appertain only to their office. Kings heretofore, David, Solomon, and Jehoshaphat, who might not touch the priesthood, yet might pray in public, yea, in the temple, while the priests themselves stood and heard. What ailed this king then, that he could not chew his own matins without the priest's

Ore tenus? Yet is it like he could not pray at home, who can here publish a whole prayer-book of his own, and signifies in some part of this chapter, almost as good a mind to be a priest himself, as Micah had to let his son be? There was doubtless therefore some other matter in it, which made him so desirous to have his chaplains about him, who were not only the contrivers, but very oft the instruments also of his designs.

The ministers which were sent him, no marvel he endured not; for they preached repentance to him: the others gave him easy confession, easy absolution, nay, strengthened his hands, and hardened his heart, by applauding him in his wilful ways. To them he was an Ahab, to these a Constantine: it must follow then, that they to him were as unwelcome as Elijah was to Ahab; these, as dear and pleasing as Amaziah, the priest of Bethel, was to Jeroboam. These had learned well the lesson that would please: "Prophesy not against Bethel, for it is the king's chapel, the king's court;" and had taught the king to say of those ministers, which the parliament had sent, "Amos hath conspired against me, the land is not able to bear all his words."

Returning to our first parallel, this king looked upon his prelates "as orphans under the sacrilegious eyes of many rapacious reformers;" and there was as great fear of sacrilege between Micah and his mother, till with their holy treasure, about the loss whereof there was such cursing, they made a graven and a molten image, and got a priest of their own. To let go his criticising about the "sound of prayers, imperious, rude, or passionate," modes of his own devising, we are in danger to fall again upon the flats and shallows of liturgy. Which, if I should repeat again would turn my answers into responsaries, and beget another liturgy, having too much of one already.

This only I shall add, that if the heart, as he alleges, cannot safely "join with another man's extemporal sufficiency," because we know not so exactly what they mean to say; then those public prayers made in the temple by those forenamed kings, and by the apostles in the congregation, and by the ancient Christians for above three hundred years before liturgies came in, were with the people made in vain.

After he hath acknowledged that kings heretofore prayed without chaplains, even publicly in the temple itself, and that every "private believer is invested with a royal priesthood;" yet like one that relished not what he "tasted of the heavenly gift, and the good word of God," whose name he so confidently takes into his mouth, he frames to himself impertinent and vain reasons, why he should rather pray by the officiating mouth of a closet chaplain. "Their prayers," saith he, "are more prevalent, they flow from minds more enlightened, from affections less distracted." Admit this true, which is not, this might be something said as to their prayers for him, but what avails it to their praying with him? If his own mind "be encumbered with secular affairs," what helps it his particular prayer, though the mind of his chaplain be not wandering, either after new preferment, or his dinner? The fervency of one man in prayer cannot supererogate for the coldness of another; neither can his spiritual defects in that duty be made out, in the acceptance of God, by another man's abilities. Let him endeavor to have more light in himself, and not to walk by another man's lamp, but to get oil into his own. Let him cast from him, as in a Christian warfare, that secular encumbrance, which either distracts or overloads him; his load else will never be the less heavy, because another man's is light. Thus these pious flourishes and colors, examined thoroughly, are like the apples of Asphaltis, appearing goodly to the sudden eye; but look well upon them, or at least but touch them, and they turn into cinders.

In his prayer he remembers what "voices of joy and gladness" there were in his chapel, "God's house," in his opinion, between the singing men and the organs; and this was "unity of spirit in the bond of peace;" the vanity, superstition, and misdevotion of which place was a scandal far and near: wherein so many things were sung and prayed in those songs, which were not understood; and yet he who makes a difficulty how the people can join their hearts to extemporal prayers, though distinctly heard and understood, makes no question how they should join their hearts in unity to songs not understood.

I believe that God is no more moved with a prayer elaborately penned, than men truly charitable are moved with the penned speech of a beggar. Finally, O ye ministers, ye pluralists, whose lips preserve not knowledge, but the way ever open to your bellies, read here what work he makes among your wares, your gallipots, your balms and cordials, in print; and not only your sweet sippets in widows' houses, but the huge gobbets wherewith he charges you to have devoured houses. and all; the "houses of your brethren, your king, and your God." Cry him up for a saint in your pulpits, while he cries you down for atheists into hell.

CHAPTER XXV.

Upon his Penitential Meditations and Vows at Holmby.

It is not hard for any man who hath a Bible in his hands, to borrow good words and holy sayings in abundance; but to make them his own, is a work of grace, only from above. He borrows here many penitential verses out of David's psalms. So did many among those Israelites, who had revolted from the true worship of God, "invent to themselves instruments of music, like David," and probably psalms also like his: and yet the prophet Amos complains heavily against them. But to prove how short this is of true repentance, I will recite the penitence of others, who have repented in words not borrowed, but their own, and yet, by the doom of scripture itself, are judged reprobates.

"Cain said unto the Lord: My iniquity is greater than I can bear: behold thou hast driven me this day from the face of the earth, and from thy face shall I be hid."

"And when Esau heard the words of his father, he cried with an exceeding bitter cry and said, Bless me, even me also, O my father; yet found no place of repentance, though he sought it carefully with tears." (Heb. xii.)

"And Pharaoh said to Moses, The Lord is righteous, I and my people are wicked; I have sinned against the Lord your God, and against you."

"And Balaam said, Let me die the death of the righteous, and let my last end be like his."

"And Saul said to Samuel, I have sinned, for I have transgressed the commandment of the Lord; yet honor me now, I pray thee, before the elders of my people."

"And when Ahab heard the words of Elijah he rent his clothes, and put sackcloth upon his flesh, and fasted, and lay in sackcloth, and went softly."

"Jehoram also rent his clothes, and the people looked, and behold he had sackcloth upon his flesh;" yet in the very act of his humiliation he could say, "God do so, and more also to me, if the head of Elisha shall stand on him this day."

"Therefore, saith the Lord, They have not cried unto me with their heart, when they howled upon their beds. They return, but not to the Most High." (Hosea vii.)

"And Judas said, I have sinned, in that I have betrayed innocent blood."

"And Simon Magus said, Pray ye to the Lord for me, that none of these things come upon me."

All these took the pains both to confess and to repent in their own words, and many of them in their own tears, not in David's. But transported with the vain ostentation of imitating David's language, not his life, observe how he brings a curse upon himself and his father's house (God so disposing it) by his usurped and ill-imitated prayer: "Let thy anger, I beseech thee, be against me and my father's house; as for these sheep, what have they done?" For if David indeed sinned in numbering the people, of which fault he in earnest made that confession, and acquitted the whole people from the guilt of that sin; then doth this king, using the same words, bear witness against himself to be the guilty person; and either in his soul and conscience here acquits the parliament and the people, or else abuses the words of David, and dissembles grossly to the very face of God; which is apparent in the next line; wherein he accuses even the church itself to God, as if she were the church's enemy, for having overcome his tyranny by the powerful and miraculous might of God's manifest arm: for to other strength, in the midst of our divisions and disorders, who can attribute our victories? Thus had this miserable man no worse enemies to solicit and mature his own destruction, from the hastened sentence of divine justice, than the obdurate curses which proceeded against himself out of his own mouth.

Hitherto his meditations, now his vows; which, as the vows of hypocrites used to be, are most commonly absurd, and some wicked. Jacob vowed that God should be his God, if he granted him but what was necessary to perform that vow, life and subsistence: but the obedience proffered here is nothing so cheap. He, who took so heinously to be offered nineteen propositions from the parliament, capitulates here with God almost in as many articles.

"If he will continue that light," or rather that darkness of the gospel, which is among his prelates, settle their luxuries, and make them gorgeous bishops;

If he will "restore" the grievances and mischiefs of those obsolete and popish laws, which the parliament without his consent had abrogated, and will suffer justice to be executed according to his sense;

"If he will suppress the many schisms in church," to contradict himself in that which he hath foretold must and shall come to pass, and will remove reformation as the greatest schism of all, and factions in state, by which he means in every leaf, the parliament;

If he will "restore him" to his negative voice and the militia, as much to say, as arbitrary power, which he wrongfully avers to be the "right of his predecessors;"

"If he will turn the hearts of his people" to their old cathedral and parochial service in the liturgy, and their passive obedience to the king;

"If he will quench" the army, and withdraw our forces from withstanding the piracy of Rupert, and the plotted Irish invasion;

"If he will bless him with the freedom" of bishops again in the house of peers, and of fugitive delinquents in the house of commons, and deliver the honor of parliament into his hands, from the most natural and due protection of the people that entrusted them with the dangerous enterprise of being faithful to their country against the rage and malice of his tyrannous opposition;

"If he will keep him from that great offence," of following the counsel of his parliament, and enacting what they advise him to: which in all reason, and by the known law, and oath of his coronation, he ought to do, and not to call that sacrilege, which necessity, through the continuance of his own civil war, hath compelled them to; necessity, which made David eat the shewbread, made Hezekiah take all the silver which was found in God's house, and cut off the gold which overlaid those doors and pillars, and gave it to Sennacherib; necessity, which ofttimes made the primitive church to sell her sacred utensils, even to the communion-chalice;

"If he will restore him to a capacity of glorifying him by doing" that both in church and state, which must needs dishonor and pollute his name;

"If he will bring him again with peace, honor, and safety to his chief city," without repenting, without satisfying for the blood spilt, only for a few politic concessions, which are as good as nothing;

"If he will put again the sword into his hand, to punish" those that have delivered us, and to protect delinquents against the justice of parliament;

Then, if it be possible to reconcile contradictions, he will praise him by displeasing him, and serve him by disserving him.

"His glory," in the gaudy copes and painted windows, mitres, rochets, altars, and the chanted service-book, "shall be dearer to him," than the establishing his crown in righteousness, and the spiritual power of religion. "He will pardon those that have offended him in particular;" but there shall want no subtle ways to be even with them upon another score of their supposed offences against the commonwealth; whereby he may at once affect the glory of a seeming justice, and destroy them pleasantly, while he feigns to forgive them as to his own particular, and outwardly bewails them.

These are the conditions of his treating with God, to whom he bates nothing of what he stood upon with the parliament: as if commissions of array could deal with him also. But of all these conditions, as it is now evident in our eyes, God accepted none, but that final petition, which he so oft, no doubt but by the secret judgment of God, importunes against his own head; praying God, "That his mercies might be so toward him, as his resolutions of truth and peace were toward his people." It follows then, God having cut him off without granting any of these mercies, that his resolution were as feigned as his vows were frustrate.

CHAPTER XXVI.

Upon the Army's Surprisal of the King at Holmby.

To give account to royalists what was done with their vanquished king, yielded up into our hands, is not to be expected from them whom God hath made his conquerors. And for brethren to debate and rip up their falling out in the ear of a common enemy, thereby making him the judge, or at least the well-pleased auditor of their disagreement, is neither wise nor comely. To the king therefore, were he living, or to his party yet remaining, as to this action, there belongs no answer. Emulations, all men know, are incident among military men; and are, if they exceed not, pardonable. But some of the former army, eminent enough for their own martial deeds, and prevalent in the house of commons, touched with envy to be so far outdone by a new model, which they contemned, took advantage of presbyterian and independent names, and the virulence of some ministers, to raise disturbance. And the war being then ended, thought slightly to have discarded them who had faithfully done the work, without their due pay, and the reward of their invincible valor.

But they who had the sword yet in their hands, disdaining to be made the first objects of ingratitude and oppression, after all that expense of their blood for justice, and the common liberty, seized upon the king, their prisoner, whom nothing but their matchless deeds had brought so low as to surrender up his person: though he, to stir up new discord, chose rather to give up himself a captive to his own countrymen, who less had won him. This in likelihood might have grown to some height of mischief, partly through the strife which was kindling between our elder and our younger warriors, but chiefly through the seditious tongues of some false ministers, more zealous against schisms than against their own simony and pluralities or watchful of the common enemy, whose subtle insinuations had got so far in among them, as with all diligence to blow the coals. But it pleased God not to embroil and put to confusion his whole people for the perverseness of a few. The growth of our dissension was either prevented, or soon quieted: the enemy soon deceived of his rejoicing, and the king especially disappointed of - not the meanest morsel that his hope presented him, to ruin us by our division. And being now so nigh the end, we may the better be at leisure to stay a while, and hear him commenting upon his own captivity.

He saith of his surprisal, that it was a "motion eccentric and irregular." When then? his own allusion from the celestial bodies puts us in mind, that irregular motions may be necessary on earth sometimes, as well as constantly in heaven. That is not always best, which is most regular to written law. Great worthies heretofore, by disobeying law, ofttimes have saved the commonwealth; and the law afterward by firm decree hath approved that planetary motion, that unblamable exorbitancy in them.

He means no good to either independent or presbyterian, and yet his parable, like that of Balaam, is overruled to portend them good, far beside his intention. Those twins, that strove enclosed in the womb of Rebecca, were the seed of Abraham: the younger undoubtedly gained the heavenly birthright; the elder, though supplanted in his simile, shall yet no question find a better portion than Esau found, and far above his uncircumcised prelates.

He censures, and in censuring seems to hope it will be an ill omen, that they who build Jerusalem divide their tongues and hands. But his hope failed him with his example; for that there were divisions both of tongues and hands at the building of Jerusalem, the story would have certified him; and yet the work prospered; and, if God will, so may this, notwithstanding all the craft and malignant wiles of Sanballat and Tobiah, adding what fuel they can to our dissensions; or the indignity of his comparison, that likens us to those seditious zealots, whose intestine fury brought destruction to the last Jerusalem.

It being now no more in his hand to be revenged on his opposers, he seeks to satiate his fancy with the imagination of some revenge upon them from above; and, like one who in a drouth observes the sky, he sits and watches when anything will drop, that might solace him with the likeness of a punishment from heaven upon us; which he straight expounds how he pleases. No evil can befall the parliament or city but he positively interprets it a judgment upon them for his sake; as if the very manuscript of God's judgments had been delivered to his custody and exposition. But his reading declares it well to be a false copy which he uses; dispensing often to his own bad deeds and successes the testimony of divine favor, and to the good deeds and successes of other men divine wrath and vengeance.

But to counterfeit the hand of God is the boldest of all forgery. And he who without warrant but his own fantastic surmise, takes upon him perpetually to unfold the secret and unsearchable mysteries of high providence, is likely for the most part to mistake and slander them; and approaches to the madness of those reprobate thoughts that would wrest the sword of justice out of God's hand, and employ it more justly in their own conceit. It was a small thing to contend with the parliament about sole power of the militia, when we see him doing little less than laying hands on the weapons of God himself, which are his judgments, to wield and manage them by the sway and bent of his own frail cogitations. Therefore "they that by tumults first occasioned the raising of armies" in his doom must needs "be chastened by their own army for new tumults."

First, note here his confession, that those tumults were the first occasion of raising armies, and by consequence that he himself raised them first, against those supposed tumults. But who occasioned those tumults, or who made them so, being at first nothing more than the unarmed and peaceable concourse of people, hath been discussed already. And that those pretended tumults were chastised by their own army for new tumults, is not proved by a game at tic-tac with words; "tumults and armies, armies and tumults," but seems more like the method of a justice irrational than divine.

If the city were chastened by the army for new tumults, the reason is by himself set down evident and immediate, "their new tumults." With what sense can it be referred then to another far-fetched and imaginary cause, that happened so many years before, and in his supposition only as a cause? Manlius defended the capitol and the Romans from their enemies the Gauls; Manlius for sedition afterward was by the Romans thrown headlong from the capitol; therefore Manlius was punished by divine justice for defending the capitol, because in that place punished for sedition, and by those whom he defended. This is his logic upon divine justice; and was the same before upon the death of Sir John Hotham. And here again, "such as were content to see him driven away by unsuppressed tumults, are now forced to fly to an army." Was this a judgment? Was it not a mercy rather, that they had a noble and victorious army so near at hand to fly to?

From God's justice he comes down to man's justice. Those few of both houses who at first withdrew with him for the vain pretence of tumults, were counted deserters; therefore those many must be also deserters, who withdrew afterwards from real tumults: as if it were the place that made a parliament, and not the end and cause. Because it is denied that those were tumults, from which the king made show of being driven, is it therefore of necessity implied, that there could be never any tumults for the future? If some men fly in craft, may not other men have cause to fly in earnest? But mark the difference between their flight and his: they soon return in safety to their places, he not till after many years, and then a captive to receive his punishment. So that their flying, whether the cause be considered, or the event, or both, neither justified him, nor condemned themselves.

But he will needs have vengeance to pursue and overtake them; though to bring it in, it cost him an inconvenient and obnoxious comparison, "As the mice and rats overtook a German bishop." I would our mice and rats had been as orthodoxal here, and had so pursued all his bishops out of England; then vermin had rid away vermin, which now hath lost the lives of too many thousand honest men to do.

"He cannot but observe this divine justice, yet with sorrow and pity." But sorrow and pity in a weak and overmastered enemy is looked upon no otherwise than as the ashes of his revenge burnt out upon itself, or as the damp of a cooled fury, when we say, it gives. But in this manner to sit spelling and observing divine justice upon every accident and slight disturbance that may happen humanly to the affairs of men, is but another fragment of his broken revenge; and yet the shrewdest and the cunningest obloquy that can be thrown upon their actions. For if he can persuade men that the parliament and their cause is pursued with divine vengeance, he hath attained his end, to make all men forsake them, and think the worst that can be thought of them.

Nor is he only content to suborn divine justice in his censure of what is past, but he assumes the person of Christ himself, to prognosticate over us what he wishes would come. So little is any thing or person sacred from him, no not in heaven, which he will not use, and put on, if it may serve him plausibly to wreak his spleen, or ease his mind upon the parliament. Although, if ever fatal blindness did both attend and punish wilfulness, if ever any enjoyed not comforts for neglecting counsel belonging to their peace, it was in none more conspicuously brought to pass than in himself; and his predictions against the parliament and their adherents have for the most part been verified upon his own head, and upon his chief counsellors.

He concludes with high praises of the army. But praises in an enemy are superfluous, or smell of craft; and the army shall not need his praises, nor the parliament fare worse for his accusing prayers that follow. Wherein, as his charity can be no way comparable to that of Christ, so neither can his assurance, that they whom he seems to pray for, in doing what they did against him, "knew not what they did." It was but arrogance therefore, and not charity, to lay such ignorance to others in the sight of God, till he himself had been infallible, like him whose peculiar words he overweeningly assumes.

CHAPTER XXVII.

Entitled, To the Prince of Wales.

WHAT the king wrote to his son, as a father concerns not us; what he wrote to him as a king of England, concerns not him; God and the parliament having now otherwise disposed of England. But because I see it done with some artifice and labor, to possess the people that they might amend their present condition by his or by his son's restorement, I shall show point by point, that although the king had been reinstalled to his desire, or that his son admitted should observe exactly all his father's precepts, yet that this would be so far from conducing to our happiness, either as a remedy to the present distempers, or a prevention of the like to come, that it would inevitably throw us back again into all our past and fulfilled miseries; would force us to fight over again all our tedious wars, and put us to another fatal struggling for liberty and life, more dubious than the former. In which as our success hath been no other than our cause; so it will be evident to all posterity, that his misfortunes were the mere consequence of his perverse judgment.

First, he argues from the experience of those troubles, which both he and his son have had, to the improvement of their piety and patience; and by the way bears witness in his own words, that the corrupt education of his youth, which was but glanced at only in some former passages of this answer, was a thing neither of mean consideration, nor untruly charged upon him or his son: himself confessing here, that "court-delights are prone either to root up all true virtue and honor, or to be contented only with some leaves and withering formalities of them, without any real fruits tending to the public good." Which presents him still in his own words another Rehoboam, softened by a far worse court than Solomons's, and so corrupted by flatteries, which he affirms to be unseparable, to the overturning of all peace, and the loss of his own honor and kingdoms.

That he came therefore thus bred up and nurtured to the throne far worse than Rehoboam, unless he be of those who equalized his father to king Solomon, we have here his own confession. And how voluptuously, how idly reigning in the hands of other men, he either tyrannized or trifled away those seventeen years of peace, without care or thought, as if to be a king had been nothing else in his apprehension, but to eat and drink, and have his will, and take his pleasure; though there be who can relate his domestic life to the exactness of a diary, there shall be here no mention made. This yet we might have then foreseen, that he who spent his leisure so remissly and so corruptly to his own pleasing, would one day or other be worse busied and employed to our sorrow. And that he acted in good earnest what Rehoboam did but threaten, to make his little finger heavier than his father's loins, and to whip us with two twisted scorpions, both temporal, and spiritual tyranny, all his kingdoms have felt. What good use he made afterward of his adversity, both his impenitence and obstinacy to the end, (for he was no Manasseh,) and the sequel of these his meditated resolutions, abundantly express: retaining, commending, teaching to his son all those putrid and pernicious documents, both of state and of religion, instilled by wicked doctors and received by him as in a vessel nothing better seasoned, which were the first occasion both of his own and all our miseries.

And if he, in the best maturity of his years and understanding made no better use to himself or others of his so long and manifold afflictions, either looking up to God, or looking down upon the reason of his own affairs; there can be no probability, that his son, bred up, not in the soft effeminacies of a court only, but in the rugged and more boisterous licence of undisciplined camps and garrisons, for years unable to reflect with judgment upon his own condition, and thus ill-instructed by his father, should give his mind to walk by any other rules than these, bequeathed him as on his father's death-bed, and as the choicest of all that experience, which his most serious observation and retirement in good or evil days had taught him. David indeed, by suffering without just cause, learned that meekness and that wisdom by adversity, which made him much the fitter man to reign. But they who suffer as oppressors, tyrants, violators of law, and persecutors of reformation, without appearance of repenting, if they once get hold again of that dignity and power, which they had lost, are but whetted and enraged by what they suffered, against those whom they look upon as them that caused their sufferings.

How he hath been "subject to the sceptre of God's word and Spirit," though acknowledged to be the best government; and what his dispensation of civil power hath been, with what justice, and what honor to the public peace, it is but looking back upon the whole catalogue of his deeds, and that will be sufficient to remember us. "The cup of God's physic," as he calls it, what alteration it wrought in him to a firm healthfulness from any surfeit, or excess whereof the people generally thought him sick, if any man would go about to prove, we have his own testimony following here, that it wrought none at all.

First, he hath the same fixed opinion and esteem of his old Ephesian goddess, called the church of England, as he had ever; and charges strictly his son after him to persevere in that antipapal schism, (for it is not much better,) as that which will be necessary both for his soul's and the kingdom's peace. But if this can be any foundation of the kingdom's peace, which was the first cause of our distractions, let common sense be judge. It is a rule and principle worthy to be known by Christians, that no scripture, no, nor so much as any ancient creed, binds our faith, or our obedience to any church whatsoever, denominated by a particular name; far less, if it be distinguished by a several government from that which is indeed catholic. No man was ever bid be subject to the church of Corinth, Rome, or Asia, but to the church without addition, as it held faithful to the rules of scripture, and the government established in all places by the apostles; which at first was universally the same in all churches and congregations; not differing or distinguished by the diversity of countries, territories, or civil bounds. That church, that from the name of a distinct place takes authority to set up a distinct faith of government, is a schism and faction, not a church. It were an injury to condemn the papist of absurdity and contradiction, for adhering to his catholic Romish religion, if we, for the pleasure of a king and his politic considerations, shall adhere to a catholic English.

But suppose the church of England were as it ought to be, how is it to us the safer by being so named and established, whenas that very name and establishment, by his contriving or approbation, served for nothing else but to delude us and amuse us, while the church of England insensibly was almost changed and translated into the church of Rome? Which as every man knows in general to be true, so the particular treaties and transactions tending to that conclusion are at large discovered in a book entitled the "English Pope." But when the people, discerning these abuses, began to call for reformation, in order to which the parliament demanded of the king to unestablish that prelatical government, which without scripture had usurped over us; straight, as Pharaoh accused of idleness the Israelites that sought leave to go and sacrifice to God, he lays faction to their charge.

And that we may not hope to have ever anything reformed in the church either by him or his son, he forewarns him, "that the devil of rebellion doth most commonly turn himself into an angel of reformation:" and says enough to make him hate it, as the worst of evils, and the bane of his crown: nay, he counsels him to "let nothing seem little or despicable to him, so as not speedily and effectually to suppress errors and schisms." Whereby we may perceive plainly, that our consciences were destined to the same servitude and persecution, if not worse than before, whether under him, or if it should so happen, under his son; who count all protestant churches erroneous and schismatical, which are not episcopal.

His next precept is concerning our civil liberties; which by his sole voice and predominant will must be circumscribed, and not permitted to extend a hand's breadth further than his interpretation of the laws already settled. And although all human laws are but the offspring of that frailty, that fallibility and imperfection, which was in their authors, whereby many laws in the change of ignorant and obscure ages, may be found both scandalous, and full of grievance to their posterity that made them, and no law is further good than mutable upon just occasion; yet if the removing of an old law, or the making of a new, would save the kingdom, we shall not have it, unless his arbitrary voice will so far slacken the stiff

curb of his prerogative, as to grant it us; who are as free-born to make our own laws, as our fathers were who made these we have.

Where are then the English liberties, which we boast to have been left us by our progenitors? To that he answers, that "our liberties consist in the enjoyment of the fruits of our industry, and the benefit of those laws to which we ourselves have consented." First, for the enjoyment of those fruits, which our industry and labors have made our own upon our own, what privilege is that above what the Turks, Jews, and Moors enjoy under the Turkish monarchy? For without that kind of justice, which is also in Algiers, among thieves and pirates between themselves, no kind of government, no society, just or unjust, could stand; no combination or conspiracy could stick together. Which he also acknowledges in these words: "That if the crown upon his head be so heavy as to oppress the whole body, the weakness of inferior members cannot return anything of strength, honor, or safety to the head; but that a necessary debilitation must follow." So that this liberty of the subject concerns himself and the subsistence of his own regal power in the first place, and before the consideration of any right belonging to the subject. We expect therefore something more, that must distinguish free government from slavish. But instead of that this king, though ever talking and protesting as smooth as now, suffered it in his own hearing to be preached and pleaded without control or check, by them whom he most favored and upheld, that the subject had no property of his own goods, but that all was the king's right.

Next, for the "benefit of those laws, to which we ourselves have consented," we never had it under him; for, not to speak of laws ill executed, when the parliament, and in them the people, have consented to divers laws, and, according to our ancient rights, demanded them, he took upon him to have a negative will, as the transcendent and ultimate law above all our laws; and to rule us forcibly by laws, to which we ourselves did not consent, but complained of. Thus these two heads, wherein the utmost of his allowance here will give our liberties leave to

consist, the one of them shall be so far only
made good to us, as may support his own
interest and crown from ruin or debilitation;
and so far Turkish vassals enjoy as much
liberty under Mahomet and the Grand
Signior: the other we neither yet have enjoyed under him, nor were ever like to do
under the tyranny of a negative voice, which
he claims above the unanimous consent and
power of a whole nation, virtually in the
parliament.

In which negative voice to have been cast
by the doom of war, and put to death by
those who vanquished him in their own defence, he reckons to himself more than a
negative martyrdom. But martyrs bear witness to the truth, not to themselves. "If I
bear witness of myself," saith Christ, "my
witness is not true." He who writes himself
martyr by his own inscription, is like an ill
painter, who, by writing on the shapeless picture which he hath drawn, is fain to tell
passengers what shape it is: which else no
man could imagine; no more than how a
martyrdom can belong to him, who therefore
dies for his religion because it is established.
Certainly if Agrippa had turned Christian,
as he was once turning, and had put to death
scribes and pharisees for observing the law
of Moses, and refusing Christianity, they had
died a truer martyrdom. For those laws were
established by God and Moses, these by no
warrantable authors of religion, whose laws
in all other best reformed churches are rejected. And if to die for an establishment of
religion be martyrdom, then Romish priests
executed for that, which had so many hundred years been established in this land, are
no worse martyrs than he. Lastly, if to die
for the testimony of his own conscience be
enough to make him martyr, what heretic
dying for direct blasphemy, as some have
done constantly, may not boast a martyrdom?

As for the constitution or repeal of civil
laws, that power lying only in the parliament,
which he by the very law of his coronation
was to grant them, not to debar them, nor
to preserve a lesser law with the contempt
and violation of a greater; it will conclude
him not so much as in a civil and metaphorical sense to have died a martyr of our
laws, but a plain transgressor of them. And

should the parliament, endued with legislative
power, make our laws, and be after to dispute them piecemeal with the reason,
conscience, humor, passion, fancy, folly,
obstinacy, or other ends of one man, whose
sole word and will shall baffle and unmake
what all the wisdom of a parliament hath
been deliberately framing; what a ridiculous
and contemptible thing a parliament would
soon be, and what a base unworthy nation
we, who boast our freedom, and send them
with the manifest peril of their lives to
preserve it, they who are not marked by
destiny for slaves may apprehend! In this
servile condition to have kept us still under
hatches, he both resolves here to the last,
and so instructs his son.

As to those offered condescensions of "charitable connivance, or toleration," if we consider what went before, and what follows,
they molder into nothing. For, what with
not suffering ever so little to seem a despicable schism, without effectual suppression, as
he warned him before, and what with no opposition of law, government, or established
religion to be permitted, which is his following proviso, and wholly within his own construction, what a miserable and suspected
toleration, under spies and haunting promoters, we should enjoy, is apparent. Besides that it is so far beneath the honor of
a parliament and free nation, to beg and
supplicate the godship of one frail man, for
the bare and simple toleration of what they
all consent to be both just, pious, and best
pleasing to God, while that which is erroneous,
unjust, and mischievous in the church or
state shall by him alone against them all
be kept up and established, and they censured the while for a covetous, ambitious,
and sacrilegious faction.

Another bait to allure the people is the
charge he lays upon his son to be tender
of them. Which if we should believe in part,
because they are his herd, his cattle, the
stock upon his ground, as he accounts them,
whom to waste and destroy would undo himself, yet the inducement, which he brings to
move him, renders the motion itself something suspicious. For if princes need no palliations, as he tells his son, wherefore is it
that he himself hath so often used them?
Princes, of all other men, have not more

change of raiment in their wardrobes, than variety of shifts and palliations in their solemn actings and pretences to the people.

To try next if he can ensnare the prime men of those who have opposed him, whom, more truly than his meaning was, he calls the "patrons and vindicators of the people," he gives out indemnity, and offers acts of oblivion. But they who with a good conscience and upright heart did their civil duties in the sight of God, and in their several places, to resist tyranny and the violence of superstitution banded both against them, he may be sure will never seek to be forgiven that, which may be justly attributed to their immortal praise; nor will assent ever to the guilty blotting out of those actions before men, by which their faith assures them they chiefly stand approved, and are had in remembrance before the throne of God.

He exhorts his son "not to study revenge." But how far he, or at least they about him, intend to follow that exhortation, was seen lately at the Hague, and now lateliest at Madrid; where to execute in the basest manner, though but the smallest part of that savage and barbarous revenge, which they do nothing else but study and contemplate, they cared not to let the world know them for professed traitors and assassinators of all law, both divine and human even of that last and most extensive law kept inviolable to public persons among all fair enemies in the midst of uttermost defiance and hostility. How implacable therefore they would be, after any terms of closure or admittance for the future, or any like opportunity given them hereafter, it will be wisdom and our safety to believe rather, and prevent, than to make trial. And it will concern the multitude, though courted here, to take heed how they seek to hide or color their own fickleness and instability with a bad repentance of their well-doing, and their fidelity to the better cause; to which at first so cheerfully and conscientiously they joined themselves.

He returns again to extol the church of England, and again requires his son, by the joint authority of "a father and a king, not to let his heart receive the least check or disaffection against it." And not without cause; for by that means, "having sole influence upon the clergy, and they upon the people, after long search and many disputes," he could not possibly find a more compendious and politic way to uphold and settle tyranny, than by subduing first the consciences of vulgar men, with the insensible poison of their slavish doctrine: for then the body and besotted mind without much reluctancy was likeliest to admit the yoke.

He commends also "parliaments held with freedom and with honor." But I would ask how that can be, while he only must be the sole free person in that number; and would have the power with his unaccountable denial, to dishonor them by rejecting all their counsels, to confine their lawgiving power, which is the foundation of our freedom, and to change at his pleasure the very name of a parliament into the name of a faction.

The conclusion therefore must needs be quite contrary to what he concludes; that nothing can be more unhappy, more dishonorable, more unsafe for all, than when a wise, grave, and honorable parliament shall have labored, debated, argued, consulted, and, as he himself speaks, "contributed" for the public good all their counsels in common, to be then frustrated, disappointed, denied, and repulsed by the single whiff of a negative, from the mouth of one wilful man; nay, to be blasted, to be struck as mute and motionless as a parliament of tapestry in the hangings; or else, after all their pains and travel, to be dissolved, and cast away like so many noughts in arithmetic, unless it be to turn the O of their insignificance into a lamentation with the people, who had so vainly sent them. For this is not to "enact all things by public consent," as he would have us be persuaded; this is to enact nothing but by the private consent and leave of one not negative tyrant; this is mischief without remedy, a stifling and obstructing evil that hath no vent, no outlet, no passage through. Grant him this, and the parliament hath no more freedom than if it sate in his noose, which when he pleases to draw together with one twitch of his negative, shall throttle a whole nation, to the wish of Caligula, in one neck.

This with the power of the militia in his own hands over our bodies and estates, and the prelates to enthral our consciences either by fraud or force, is the sum of that happiness and liberty we were to look for, whether in his own restitution, or in these precepts given to his son. Which unavoidably would have set us in the same state of misery wherein we were before; and have either compelled us to submit like bondslaves, or put us back to a second wandering over that horrid wilderness of distraction and civil slaughter, which, not without the strong and miraculous hand of God assisting us, we have measured out, and survived. And who knows, if we make so slight of this incomparable deliverance, which God hath bestowed upon us, but that we shall, like those foolish Israelites, who deposed God and Samuel to set up a king, "cry out" one day, "because of our king," which we have been mad upon; and then God, as he foretold them, will no more deliver us.

There remains now but little more of his discourse, whereof yet to take a short view will not be amiss. His words make semblance as if he were magnanimously exercising himself, and so teaching his son, "to want as well as to wear a crown;" and would seem to account it "not worth taking up or enjoying, upon sordid, dishonorable, and irreligious terms;" and yet to his very last did nothing more industriously, than strive to take up and enjoy again his sequestered crown, upon the most sordid, disloyal, dishonorable, and irreligious terms, not of making peace only, but of joining and incorporating with the murderous Irish, formerly by himself declared against, for "wicked and detestable rebels, odious to God and all good men." And who but those rebels now are the chief strength and confidence of his son? While the presbyter Scot that woos and solicits him is neglected and put off, as if no terms were to him sordid, irreligious, and dishonorable, but the Scottish and presbyterian, never to be complied with, till the fear of instant perishing starve him out at length to some unsound and hypocritical agreement.

He bids his son "keep to the true principles of piety, virtue, and honor, and he shall never want a kingdom." And I say, people of England! keep ye to those principles, and ye shall never want a king. Nay, after such a fair deliverance as this, with so much fortitude and valor shown against a tyrant, that people that should seek a king claiming what this man claims, would show themselves to be by nature slaves and arrant beasts; not fit for that liberty which they cried out and bellowed for, but fitter to be led back again into their old servitude, like a sort of clamoring and fighting brutes, broke loose from their copyholds, that know not how to use or possess the liberty which they fought for, but with the fair words and promises of an old exasperated foe, are ready to be stroked and tamed again, into the wonted and well-pleasing state of their true Norman villanage, to them best agreeable.

The last sentence, whereon he seems to venture the whole weight, of all his former reasons and argumentations, "that religion to their God, and loyalty to their king, cannot be parted, without the sin and infelicity of a people," is contrary to the plain teaching of Christ, that "No man can serve two masters; but, if he hold to the one, he must reject and forsake the other." If God, then, and earthly kings be for the most part not several only, but opposite masters, it will as oft happen, that they who will serve their king must forsake their God; and they who will serve God must forsake their king: which then will neither be their sin, nor their infelicity; but their wisdom, their piety, and their true happiness; as to be deluded by these unsound and subtle ostentations here, would be their misery; and in all likelihood much greater than what they hitherto have undergone: if now again intoxicated and moped with these royal, and therefore so delicious because royal, rudiments of bondage, the cup of deception, spiced, and tempered to their bane, they should deliver up themselves to these glozing words and illusions of him, whose rage and utmost violence they have sustained, and overcome so nobly.

CHAPTER XXVIII.

Entitled, Meditations upon Death.

It might be well thought by him who reads no further than the title of this last essay, that it required no answer. For all other human things are disputed, and will be variously thought of to the world's end. But this business of death is a plain case, and admits no controversy: in that centre all opinions meet. Nevertheless, since out of those few mortifying hours that should have been entirest to themselves, and most at peace from all passion and disquiet, he can afford spare time to inveigh bitterly against that justice which was done upon him; it will be needful to say something in defence of those proceedings, though briefly, in regard so much on this subject hath been written lately.

It happened once, as we find in Esdras and Josephus, authors not less believed than any under sacred, to be a great and solemn debate in the court of Darius, what thing was to be counted strongest of all other. He that could resolve this, in reward of his excelling wisdom, should be clad in purple, drink in gold, sleep on a bed of gold, and sit next Darius. None but they, doubtless, who were reputed wise, had the question propounded to them; who after some respite given them by the king to consider, in full assembly of all his lords and gravest counsellors, returned severally what they thought. The first held that wine was strongest; another, that the king was strongest; but Zorobabel, prince of the captive Jews, and heir to the crown of Judah, being one of them, proved women to be stronger than the king, for that he himself had seen a concubine take his crown from off his head to set it upon her own; and others beside him have lately seen the like feat done, and not in jest. Yet he proved on, and it was so yielded by the king himself, and all his sages, that neither wine, nor women, nor the king, but truth of all other things was the strongest.

For me, though neither asked, nor in a nation that gives such rewards to wisdom, I shall pronounce my sentence somewhat different from Zorobabel; and shall defend that either truth and justice are all one, (for truth is but justice in our knowledge, and justice is but truth in our practice;) and he indeed so explains himself, in saying that with truth is no accepting of persons, which is the property of justice, or else if there be any odds, that justice, though not stronger than truth, yet by her office, is to put forth and exhibit more strength in the affairs of mankind. For truth is properly no more than contemplation; and her utmost efficiency is but teaching: but justice in her very essence is all strength and activity; and hath a sword put into her hand, to use against all violence and oppression on the earth. She it is most truly, who accepts no person, and exempts none from the severity of her stroke. She never suffers injury to prevail, but when falsehood first prevails over truth; and that also is a kind of justice done on them who are so deluded. Though wicked kings and tyrants counterfeit her sword, as some did that buckler fabled to fall from heaven into the capitol, yet she communicates her power to none but such as, like herself, are just, or at least will do justice. For it were extreme partiality and injustice, the flat denial and overthrow of herself, to put her own authentic sword into the hand of an unjust and wicked man, or so far to accept and exalt one mortal person above his equals, that he alone shall have the punishing of all other men transgressing, and not receive like punishment from men, when he himself shall be found the highest transgressor.

We may conclude, therefore, that justice, above all other things, is and ought to be the strongest; she is the strength, the kingdom, the power, and majesty of all ages. Truth herself would subscribe to this, though Darius and all the monarchs of the world should deny. And if by sentence thus written it were my happiness to set free the minds of Englishmen from longing to return poorly under that captivity of kings from which the strength and supreme sword of justice hath delivered them, I shall have done a work not much inferior to that of Zorobabel; who, by well-praising and extolling the force of truth, in that contemplative strength conquered Darius, and freed his country and the people of God from the captivity of Babylon. Which I shall yet not despair to do, if they in this land, whose minds are yet captive, be but as ingenuous to acknowledge the strength and supremacy of justice, as that heathen king was to confess the strength of truth: or let them but, as he did, grant that, and they will soon perceive that truth resigns all her outward strength to justice: justice therefore must needs be strongest, both in her own, and in the strength of truth. But if a king may do among men whatsoever is his will and pleasure, and notwithstanding be unaccountable to men, then, contrary to this magnified wisdom of Zorobabel, neither truth nor justice, but the king, is strongest of all other things, which that Persian monarch himself, in the midst of all his pride and glory, durst not assume.

Let us see, therefore, what this king hath to affirm, why the sentence of justice, and the weight of that sword, which she delivers into the hands of men, should be more partial to him offending, than to all others of human race. First, he pleads, that "no law of God or man gives to subjects any power of judicature without or against him." Which assertion shall be proved in every part to be most untrue. The first express law of God given to mankind was that to Noah, as a law, in general, to all the sons of men. And by that most ancient and universal law, "Whosoever sheddeth man's blood, by man shall his blood be shed," we find here no exception. If a king therefore do this, to a king, and that by men also, the same shall be done. This in the law of Moses, which came next, several times is repeated, and in one place remarkably, Numb. xxxv. "Ye shall take no satisfaction for the life of a murderer, but he shall surely be put to death: the land cannot be cleansed of the blood that is shed therein, but by the blood of him that shed it." This is so spoken as that which concerned all Israel, not one man alone, to see performed; and if no satisfaction were to be taken, then certainly no exception. Nay, the king, when they should set up any, was to observe the whole law, and not only to see it done, but to "do it; that his heart might not be lifted up above his brethren;" to dream of vain and reasonless prerogatives or exemptions, whereby the law itself must needs be founded in unrighteousness.

And were that true, which is most false, that all kings are the Lord's anointed, it were yet absurd to think that the anointment of God should be, as it were, a charm against law, and give them privilege, who punish others, to sin themselves unpunishably. The high priest was the Lord's anointed as well as any king, and with the same consecrated oil; yet Solomon had put to death Abiathar, had it not been for other respects than that anointment. If God himself say to kings, "Touch not mine anointed," meaning his chosen people, as is evident in that Psalm, yet no man will argue thence, that he protects them from civil laws if they offend; then certainly, though David, as a private man, and in his own cause, feared to lift his hand against the Lord's anointed, much less can this forbid the law, or disarm justice from having legal power against any king. No other supreme magistrate, in what kind of government soever, lays claim to any such enormous privilege; wherefore then should any king, who is but one kind of magistrate, and set over the people for no other end than they?

Next in order of time to the laws of Moses are those of Christ, who declares professedly his judicature to be spiritual, abstract from civil managements, and therefore leaves all nations to their own particular laws, and way of government. Yet because the church hath a kind of jurisdiction within her own bounds, and that also, though in process of time much corrupted and plainly turned into a corporal judicature, yet much approved by this king; it will be firm enough and valid against him, if subjects, by the laws of church also, be "invested with a power of judicature" both without and against their king, though pretending, and by them acknowledged, "next and immediately under Christ supreme head and governor." Theodosius, one of the best Christian emperors, having made a slaughter of the Thessalonians for sedition, but too cruelly, was excommunicated to his face by St. Ambrose, who was his subject; and excommunion is the utmost of ecclesiastical judicature, a spiritual putting to death.

But this, ye will say, was only an example. Read then the story; and it will appear, both that Ambrose avouched it for the law of God, and Theodosius confessed it of his own accord to be so; "and that the law of God was not to be made void in him, for any reverence to his imperial power." From hence, not to be tedious, I shall pass into our own land of Britain; and show that subjects here have exercised the utmost of spiritual judicature, and more than spiritual, against their kings, his predecessors. Vortiger, for committing incest with his daughter, was by St. German, at that time his subject, cursed and condemned in a British council, about the year 448; and thereupon soon after was deposed. Mauricus, a king in Wales, for breach of oath and murder of Cynetus, was excommunicated and cursed, with all his offspring, by Oudoceus, bishop of Llandaff, in full synod, about the year 560, and not restored till he had repented. Morcant, another king in Wales, having slain Frioc his uncle, was fain to come in person, and receive judgment from the same bishop and his clergy; who upon his penitence acquitted him, for no other cause than lest the kingdom should be destitute of a successor in the royal line.

These examples are of the primitive, British, and episcopal church; long ere they had any commerce or communion with the church of Rome. What power afterward of deposing kings, and so consequently of putting them to death, was assumed and practised by the canon law, I omit, as a thing generally known. Certainly, if whole councils of the Romish church have in the midst of their dimness discerned so much of truth, as to decree at Constance, and at Basil, and many of them to avouch at Trent also, that a council is above the pope, and may judge him, though by them not denied to be the vicar of Christ; we in our clearer light may be ashamed not to discern further, that a parliament is by all equity and right above a king, and may judge him, whose reasons and pretensions to hold of God only, as his immediate vicegerent, we know how far-fetched they are, and insufficient.

As for the laws of man, it would ask a volume to repeat all that might be cited in this point against him from all antiquity. In Greece, Orestes, the son of Agamemnon, and by succession king of Argos, was in that country judged and condemned to death for killing his mother: whence escaping, he was judged again, though a stranger, before the great council of Areopagus in Athens. And this memorable act of judicature was the first that brought the justice of that grave senate into fame and high estimation over all Greece for many ages after. And in the same city tyrants were to undergo legal sentence by the laws of Solon.

The kings of Sparta, though descended lineally from Hercules, esteemed a god among them, were often judged, and sometimes put to death, by the most just and renowned laws of Lycurgus; who, though a king, thought it most unequal to bind his subjects by any law, to which he bound not himself. In Rome, the laws made by Valerius Publicola, soon after the expelling of Tarquin and his race, expelled without a written law, the law being afterward written; and what the senate decreed against Nero, that he should be judged and punished according to the laws of their ancestors, and what in like manner was decreed against other emperors, is vulgarly known; as it was known to those heathen, and found just by nature ere any law mentioned it. And that the Christian Civil law warrants like power of judicature to subjects against tyrants, is written clearly by the best and famousest civilians. For if it was decreed by Theodosius, and stands yet firm in the code of Justinian, that the law is above the emperor, then certainly the emperor being under law, the law may judge him; and if judge him, may punish him, proving tyrannous: how else is the law above him, or to what purpose? These are necessary deductions; and thereafter hath been done in all ages and kingdoms, oftener than to be here recited.

But what need we any further search after the law of other lands, for that which is so fully and so plainly set down lawful in our own? Where ancient books tell us, Bracton, Fleta, and others, that the king is under law, and inferior to his court of parliament; that although his place "to do justice" be highest, yet that he stands as liable "to receive justice" as the meanest of his kingdom. Nay, Alfred, the most worthy king, and by some accounted first absolute monarch of the Saxons here, so ordained; as is cited out of an ancient law-book called "the Mirror;" in "Rights of the Kingdom," p. 31, where it is complained on, "as the sovereign abuse of all," that the king should be deemed above the law, whereas he ought to be subject to it by his oath. Of which oath anciently it was the last clause, that the king "should be as liable, and obedient to suffer right, as others of his people." And indeed it were but fond and senseless, that the king should be accountable to every petty suit in lesser courts as we all know he was, and not be subject to the judicature of parliament in the main matters of our common safety or destruction; that he should be answerable in the ordinary course of law for any wrong done to a private person, and not answerable in court of parliament for destroying the whole kingdom.

By all this, and much more that might be added, as in an argument over-copious rather than barren, we see it manifest that all laws, both of God and man, are made without exemption of any person whomsoever; and that if kings presume to overtop the law by which they reign for the public good, they are by law to be reduced into order; and that can no way be more justly, than by those who exalted them to that high place. For who should better understand their own laws, and when they are transgressed, than they who are governed by them, and whose consent first made them? And who can have more right to take knowledge of things done within a free nation than they within themselves?

Those objected oaths of allegiance and supremacy we swore, not to his person, but as it was invested with his authority; and his authority was by the people first given him conditionally, in law, and under law, and under oath also for the kingdom's good, and not otherwise; the oaths then were interchanged, and mutual; stood and fell together; he swore fidelity to his trust; (not as a deluding ceremony, but as a real condition of their admitting him for king; and the Conqueror himself swore it oftener than at his crowning;) they swore homage and fealty to his person in that trust. There was no reason why the kingdom should be further bound by oaths to him, than he by his coronation oath to us, which he hath every way broken: and having broken, the ancient crown oath of Alfred above mentioned conceals not his penalty.

As for the covenant, if that be meant, certainly no discreet person can imagine it should bind us to him in any stricter sense than those oaths formerly. The acts of hostility, which we received from him, were no such dear obligements, that we should owe him more fealty and defence for being our enemy, than we could before when we took him only for a king. They were accused by him and his party, to pretend liberty and reformation, but to have no other end than to make themselves great, and to destroy the king's person and authority. For which reason they added that third article, testifying to the world, that as they were resolved to endeavor first a reformation in the church, to extirpate prelacy, to preserve the rights of parliament, and the liberties of the kingdom, so they intended, so far as it might consist with the preservation and defence of these, to preserve the king's person and authority; but not otherwise. As far as this comes to, they covenant and swear in the sixth article to preserve and defend the persons and authority of one another, and all those that enter into that league; so that this covenant gives no unlimitable exemption to the king's person, but gives to all as much defence and preservation as to him, and to him as much as to their own persons, and no more; that is to say, in order and subordination to those main ends, for which we live and are a nation of men joined in society either Christian, or, at least, human.

But if the covenant were made absolute, to preserve and defend any one whomsoever, without respect had, either to the true religion, or those other superior things to be defended and preserved however, it cannot then be doubted, but that the covenant was rather a most foolish, hasty, and unlawful vow, than a deliberate and well-weighed covenant; swearing us into labyrinths and repugnances, no way to be solved or reconciled, and therefore no way to be kept; as first offending against the law of God, to vow the absolute preservation, defence, and maintaining of one man, though in his sins and offences never so great and heinous against God or his neighbor; and to except a person from justice, whereas his law excepts none. Secondly, it offends against the law of this nation, wherein, as hath been proved, kings in receiving justice, and undergoing due trial, are not differenced from the meanest subject.

Lastly, it contradicts and offends against the covenant itself, which vows in the fourth article to bring to open trial and condign punishment all those that shall be found guilty of such crimes and delinquences, whereof the king, by his own letters, and other undeniable testimonies not brought to light till afterward, was found and convicted to be chief actor in what they thought him, at the time of taking that covenant, to be overruled only by evil counsellors; and those, or whomsoever they should discover to be principal, they vowed to try, either by their own "supreme judicatories," (for so even then they called them,) "or by others having power from them to that effect." So that to have brought the king to condign punishment hath not broke the covenant, but it would have broke the covenant to have saved him from those judicatories, which both nations declared in that covenant to be supreme against any person whatsoever.

And besides all this, to swear in covenant the bringing of his evil counsellors and accomplices to condign punishment, and not only to leave unpunished and untouched the grand offender, but to receive him back again from the accomplishment of so many violences and mischiefs, dipped from head to foot, and stained over with the blood of thousands that were his faithful subjects, forced to their own defence against a civil war by him first raised upon them; and to receive him thus, in this gory pickle, to all his dignities and honors, covering the ignominious and horrid purple robe of innocent blood, that sat so close about him, with the glorious purple of royalty and supreme rule, the reward of highest excellence and virtue here on earth, were not only to swear and covenant the performance of an unjust vow, the strangest and most impious to the face of God, but were the most unwise and unprudential act as to civil government.

For so long as a king shall find by experience that, do the worst he can, his subjects, overawed by the religion of their own covenant, will only prosecute his evil instruments, not dare to touch his person; and that whatever hath been on his part offended or transgressed, he shall come off at last with the same reverence to his person, and the same honor as for well-doing, he will not fail to find them work; seeking far and near, and inviting to his court all the concourse of evil counsellors, or agents, that may be found: who, tempted with preferments and his promise to uphold them, will hazard easily their own heads, and the chance of ten to one but they shall prevail at last over men so quelled and fitted to be slaves by the false

conceit of a religious covenant. And they in that superstition neither wholly yielding, nor to the utmost resisting, at the upshot of all their foolish war and expense, will find to have done no more but fetched a compass only of their miseries, ending at the same point of slavery, and in the same distractions wherein they first began.

But when kings themselves are made as liable to punishment as their evil counsellors, it will be both as dangerous from the king himself as from his parliament, to those that evil-counsel him: and they, who else would be his readiest agents in evil, will then not fear to dissuade or to disobey him, not only in respect of themselves and their own lives, which for his sake they would not seem to value, but in respect of that danger which the king himself may incur, whom they would seem to love and serve with greatest fidelity. On all these grounds therefore of the covenant itself, whether religious or political, it appears likeliest, that both the English parliament and the Scotch commissioners, thus interpreting the covenant, (as indeed at that time they were the best and most authentical interpreters joined together,) answered the king unanimously, in their letters dated January the 13th, 1645, that till security and satisfaction first given to both kingdoms for the blood spilled, for the Irish rebels brought over, and for the war in Ireland by him fomented, they could in nowise yield their consent to his return.

Here was satisfaction, full two years and upward after the covenant taken, demanded of the king by both nations in parliament for crimes at least capital, wherewith they charged him. And what satisfaction could be given for so much blood, but justice upon him that spilled it? till which done, they neither took themselves bound to grant him the exercise of his regal office by any meaning of the covenant which they then declared, (though other meanings have been since contrived,) not so much regarded the safety of his person, as to admit of his return among them from the midst of those whom they declared to be his greatest enemies; nay, from himself as from an actual enemy, not as from a king, they demanded security. But if the covenant, all this notwithstanding, swore otherwise to preserve him than in the preservation of true religion and our liberties, against which he fought, if not in arms, yet in resolution, to his dying day, and now after death still fights against in this his book, the covenant was better broken, than he saved. And God hath testified by all propitious and the most evident signs, whereby in these latter times he is wont to testify what pleases him, that such a solemn and for many ages unexampled act of due punishment was no mockery of justice, but a most grateful and well-pleasing sacrifice. Neither was it to cover their perjury, as he accuses, but to uncover his perjury to the oath of his coronation.

The rest of his discourse quite forgets the title; and turns his meditations upon death into obloquy and bitter vehemence against his "judges and accusers;" imitating therein, not our Saviour, but his grandmother, Mary queen of Scots, as also in the most of his other scruples, exceptions, and evasions; and from whom he seems to have learnt, as it were by heart, or else by kind, that which is thought by his admirers to be the most virtuous, most manly, most Christian, and most martyr-like, both of his words and speeches here, and of his answers and behavior at his trial.

"It is a sad fate," he saith, "to have his enemies both accusers, parties, and judges." Sad indeed, but no sufficient plea to acquit him from being so judged. For what malefactor might not sometimes plead the like? If his own crimes have made all men his enemies, who else can judge him? They of the powder-plot against his father might as well have pleaded the same. Nay, at the resurrection it may as well be pleaded, that the saints, who then shall judge the world, are "both enemies, judges, parties, and accusers."

So much he thinks to abound in his own defence, that he undertakes an unmeasurable task, to bespeak "the singular care and protection of God over all kings," as being the greatest patrons of law, justice, order and religion on earth. But what patrons they be, God in the Scripture oft enough hath expressed; and the earth itself hath too long groaned under the burden of their injustice, disorder, and irreligion. Therefore "to bind their kings in chains, and their nobles with links of iron," is an honor belonging to his saints; not to build Babel, (which was Nimrod's work, the first king, and the beginning of his kingdom was Babel,) but to destroy it, especially that spiritual Babel: and first to overcome those European kings, which receive their power, not from God, but from the beast; and are counted no better than his ten horns. "These shall hate the great whore," and yet "shall give their kingdoms to the beast that carries her; they shall commit fornication with her," and yet "shall burn her with fire," and yet "shall lament the fall of Babylon," where they fornicated with her. Rev. xvii. xviii.

Thus shall they be to and fro, doubtful and ambiguous in all their doings, until at last, "joining their armies with the beast," whose power first raised them, they shall perish with him by the "King of kings," against whom they have rebelled; and "the fowls shall eat their flesh." This is their doom written, Rev. xix., and the utmost that we find concerning them in these latter days; which we have much more cause to believe, than his unwarranted revelation here, prophesying what shall follow after his death, with the spirit of enmity, not of St. John.

He would fain bring us out of conceit with the good success, which God hath vouchsafed us. We measure not our cause by our success, but our success by our cause. Yet certainly in a good cause success is a good confirmation; for God hath promised it to good men almost in every leaf of scripture. If it argue not for us, we are sure it argues not against us; but as much or more for us, than ill success argues for them; for to the wicked God hath denounced ill success in all they take in hand.

He hopes much of those "softer tempers," as he calls them, and "less advantaged by his ruin, that their consciences do already" gripe them. 'Tis true, there be a sort of moody, hotbrained, and always unedified consciences; apt to engage their leaders into great and dangerous affairs past retirement, and then upon a sudden qualm and swimming of their conscience, to betray them basely in the midst of what was chiefly undertaken for their sakes. Let such men never meet with any faithful parliament to hazard for them; never with any noble spirit to conduct and lead them out: but let them live and die in servile condition and their scrupulous queasiness, if no instruction will confirm them! Others there be, in whose consciences the loss of gain, and those advantages they hoped for, hath sprung a sudden leak. These are they that cry out, "The covenant broken!" and, to keep it better, slide back into neutrality, or join actually with incendiaries and malignants. But God hath eminently begun to punish those, first in Scotland, then in Ulster, who have provoked him with the most hateful kind of mockery, to break his covenant under pretence of strictest keeping it; and hath subjected them to those malignants, with whom they scrupled not to be associates. In God therefore we shall not fear what their false fraternity can do against us.

He seeks again with cunning words to turn our success into our sin: but might call to mind, that the scripture speaks of those also, who "when God slew them, then sought him;" yet did but "flatter him with their mouth, and lied to him with their tongues: for their heart was not right with him." And there was one, who in the time of his affliction trespassed more against God. This was that king Ahaz.

He glories much in the forgiveness of his enemies; so did his grandmother at her death. Wise men would sooner have believed him, had he not so often told us so. But he hopes to erect "the trophies of his charity over us." And trophies of charity no doubt will be as glorious as trumpets before the alms of hypocrites; and more especially the trophies of such an aspiring charity, as offers in his prayer to share victory with God's compassion, which is over all his works. Such prayers as these may haply catch the people, as was intended: but how they please God is to be much doubted, though prayed in secret, much less written to be divulged. Which perhaps may gain him after death, a short, contemptible, and soon fading reward; not what he aims at, to stir the constancy and solid firmness of any wise man, or to unsettle the conscience of any knowing Christian, (if he could ever aim at a thing so hopeless, and above the genius of his cleric elocution,) but to catch the worthless approbation of an inconstant, irrational, and

image-doting rabble; that like a credulous and hapless herd, begotten to servility, and enchanted with these popular institutes of tyranny, subscribed with a new device of the king's picture at his prayers, hold out both their ears with such delight and ravishment to be stigmatized and bored through, in witness of their own voluntary and beloved baseness. The rest, whom perhaps ignorance without malice, or some error, less than fatal, hath for the time misled, on this side sorcery or obduration, may find the grace and good guidance, to bethink themselves and recover.

A TREATISE

OF

CIVIL POWER IN ECCLESIASTICAL CAUSES;

SHOWING THAT IT IS NOT LAWFUL FOR ANY POWER ON EARTH TO COMPEL IN MATTERS OF RELIGION.

[The text is that of the first edition, 1659.]

TO THE PARLIAMENT OF THE COMMONWEALTH OF ENGLAND, WITH THE DOMINIONS THEREOF.

I HAVE prepared, supreme council! against the much-expected time of your sitting, this treatise; which, though to all Christian magistrates equally belonging, and therefore to have been written in the common language of Christendom, natural duty and affection hath confined, and dedicated first to my own nation; and in a season wherein the timely reading thereof, to the easier accomplishment of your great work, may save you much labor and interruption: of two parts usually proposed, civil and ecclesiastical, recommending civil only to your proper care; ecclesiastical, to them only from whom it takes both that name and nature. Yet not for this cause only do I require or trust to find acceptance, but in a twofold respect besides: first, as bringing clear evidence of scripture and protestant maxims to the parliament of England, who in all their late acts, upon occasion, have professed to assert only the true protestant Christian religion, as it is contained in the holy scriptures: next, in regard that your power being but for a time, and having in yourselves a Christian liberty of your own, which at one time or other may be oppressed, thereof truly sensible, it will concern you while you are in power, so to regard other men's consciences, as you would your own should be regarded in the power of others; and to consider that any law against conscience is alike in force against any conscience, and so may one way or other justly redound upon yourselves. One advantage I make no doubt of, that I shall write to many eminent persons of your number, already perfect and resolved in this important article of Christianity. Some of whom I remember to have heard often for several years, at a council next in authority to your own, so well joining religion with civil prudence, and yet so well distinguishing the different power of either; and this not only voting, but frequently reasoning why it should be so, that if any there present had been before of an opinion contrary, he might doubtless have departed thence a convert in that point, and have confessed, that then both commonwealth and religion will at length, if ever, flourish in Christendom, when either they who govern discern between civil and religious, or they only who so discern shall be admitted to govern. Till then, nothing but troubles, persecutions, commotions can be expected; the inward decay of true religion among ourselves, and the utter overthrow at last by a common enemy. Of civil liberty I have written heretofore by the appointment, and not without the approbation of civil power: of Christian liberty I write now, which others long since having done with all freedom under heathen emperors, I shall do wrong to suspect, that I now shall with less under Christian governors, and such especially as profess openly their defence of Christian liberty; although I write this, not otherwise appointed or induced, than by an inward persuasion of the Christian duty, which I may usefully discharge herein to the common Lord and Master of us all, and the certain hope of his approbation, first and chiefest to be sought: in the hand of whose providence I remain, praying all success and good event on your public councils, to the defence of true religion and our civil rights. JOHN MILTON.

A TREATISE OF CIVIL POWER IN ECCLESIASTICAL CAUSES.

Two things there be, which have been ever found working much mischief to the church of God and the advancement of truth: force on one side restraining, and hire on the other side corrupting, the teachers thereof. Few ages have been since the ascension of our Saviour, wherein the one of these two, or both together, have not prevailed. It can be at no time, therefore, unseasonable to speak of these things; since by them the church is either in continual detriment and oppression, or in continual danger. The former shall be at this time my argument; the latter as I shall find God disposing me, and opportunity inviting. What I argue shall be drawn from the scripture only; and therein from true fundamental principles of the gospel, to all knowing Christians undeniable. And if the governors of this commonwealth, since the rooting out of prelates, have made least use of force in religion, and most have favored Christian liberty of any in this island before them since the first preaching of the gospel, for which we are not to forget our thanks to God, and their due praise; they may, I doubt not, in this treatise, find that which not only will confirm them to defend still the Christian liberty which we enjoy, but will incite them also to enlarge it, if in aught they yet straiten it. To them who perhaps hereafter, less experienced in religion, may come to govern or give us laws, this or other such, if they please, may be a timely instruction: however, to the truth it will be at all times no unneedful testimony, at least some discharge of that general duty, which no Christian, but according to what he hath received, knows is required of him, if he have aught more conducing to the advancement of religion, than what is usually endeavored, freely to impart it.

It will require no great labor of exposition to unfold what is here meant by matters of religion; being as soon apprehended as defined, such things as belong chiefly to the knowledge and service of God; and are either above the reach and light of nature without revelation from above, and therefore liable to be variously understood by human reason, or such things as are enjoined or forbidden by divine precept, which else by the light of reason would seem indifferent to be done or not done; and so likewise must needs appear to every man as the precept is understood. Whence I here mean by conscience or religion that full persuasion, whereby we are assured, that our belief and practice, as far as we are able to apprehend and probably make appear, is according to the will of God and his Holy Spirit within us, which we ought to follow much rather than any law of man, as not only his word everywhere bids us, but the very dictate of reason tells us: Acts iv. 19, "Whether it be right in the sight of God, to hearken to you more than to God, judge ye." That for belief or practice in religion, according to this conscientious persuasion, no man ought be punished or molested by any outward force on earth whatsoever, I distrust not, through God's implored assistance, to make plain by these following arguments.

First, it cannot be denied, being the main foundation of our protestant religion, that we of these ages, having no other divine rule or authority from without us, warrantable to one another as a common ground, but the holy scripture, and no other within us but the illumination of the Holy Spirit, so interpreting that scripture as warrantable only to ourselves, and to such whose consciences we can so persuade, can have no other ground in matters of religion but only from the scriptures. And these being not possible to be understood without this divine illumination, which no man can know at all times to be in himself, much less to be at any time for certain in any other, it follows clearly, that no man or body of men in these times can be the infallible judges or determiners in matters of religion to any other men's consciences but their own. And therefore those Bereans are commended, Acts xvii. 11, who after the preaching even of St. Paul, "searched the scriptures daily, whether those things were so." Nor did they more than what God himself in many places commands us by the same apostle, to search, to try, to judge of these things ourselves: and gives us reason also, Gal. vi. 4, 5: "Let every man prove his own work, and then shall he have rejoicing in himself alone, and not in another: for every man shall bear his own

burden." If then we count it so ignorant and irreligious in the papist, to think himself discharged in God's account, believing only as the church believes, how much greater condemnation will it be to the protestant his condemner, to think himself justified, believing only as the state believes? With good cause, therefore, it is the general consent of all sound protestant writers, that neither traditions, councils, nor canons of any visible church, much less edicts of any magistrate or civil session, but the scripture only, can be the final judge or rule in matters of religion, and that only in the conscience of every Christian to himself. Which protestation made by the first public reformers of our religion against the imperial edicts of Charles the Fifth, imposing church traditions without scripture, gave first beginning to the name of Protestant; and with that name hath ever been received this doctrine, which prefers the scripture before the church, and acknowledges none but the scripture sole interpreter of itself to the conscience. For if the church be not sufficient to be implicitly believed, as we hold it is not, what can there else be named of more authority than the church but the conscience, than which God only is greater? 1 John iii. 20. But if any man shall pretend that the scripture judges to his conscience for other men, he makes himself greater not only than the church, but also than the scripture, than the consciences of other men: a presumption too high for any mortal, since every true Christian, able to give a reason of his faith, hath the word of God before him, the promised Holy Spirit, and the mind of Christ within him, 1 Cor. ii. 16; a much better and safer guide of conscience, which as far as concerns himself he may far more certainly know, than any outward rule imposed upon him by others, whom he inwardly neither knows nor can know; at least knows nothing of them more sure than this one thing, that they cannot be his judges in religion: 1 Cor. ii. 15: "The spiritual man judgeth all things, but he himself is judged of no man." Chiefly for this cause do all true protestants account the pope antichrist, for that he assumes to himself this infallibility over both the conscience and the scripture; "sitting in the temple of God," as it were opposite to God, "and exalting himself above all that is called God, or is worshipped," 2 Thes. ii. 4. That is to say, not only above all judges and magistrates, who though they be called gods, are far beneath infallible; but also above God himself, by giving law both to the scripture, to the conscience, and to the Spirit itself of God within us. Whenas we find, James iv. 12, "There is one lawgiver, who is able to save and to destroy: Who art thou that judgest another?" That Christ is the only lawgiver of his church, and that it is here meant in religious matters, no well-grounded Christian will deny. Thus also St. Paul, Rom. xiv. 4, "Who art thou that judgest the servant of another? to his own lord he standeth or falleth: but he shall stand; for God is able to make him stand." As therefore of one beyond expression bold and presumptuous, both these apostles demand, "Who art thou," that presumest to impose other law or judgment in religion than the only lawgiver and judge Christ, who only can save and can destroy, gives to the conscience? And the forecited place to the Thessalonians, by compared effects, resolves us, that be he or they who or wherever they be or can be, they are of far less authority than the church, whom in these things as protestants they receive not, and yet no less antichrist in this main point of antichristianism, no less a pope or popedom than he at Rome, if not much more, by setting up supreme interpreters of scripture either those doctors whom they follow, or, which is far worse, themselves as a civil papacy assuming unaccountable supremacy to themselves, not in civil only, but ecclesiastical causes. Seeing then that in matters of religion, as hath been proved, none can judge or determine here on earth, no, not church governors themselves, against the consciences of other believers, my inference is, or rather not mine but our Saviour's own, that in those matters they neither can command nor use constraint, lest they run rashly on a pernicious consequence, forewarned in that parable, Matt. xiii. from ver. 26 to 31: "Lest while ye gather up the tares, ye root up also the wheat with them. Let both grow together until the harvest: and in the time of harvest I will say to the reapers, Gather ye together first the tares," &c. Whereby he declares, that this work neither his own

ministers nor any else can discerningly enough or judgingly perform without his own immediate direction, in his own fit season; and that they ought till then not to attempt it. Which is further confirmed, 2 Cor. i. 24, "Not that we have dominion over your faith, but are helpers of your joy." If apostles had no dominion or constraining power over faith or conscience, much less have ordinary ministers: 1 Pet. v. 2, 3, "Feed the flock of God, not by constraint &c., neither as being lords over God's heritage." But some will object, that this overthrows all church discipline, all censure of errors, if no man can determine. My answer is, that what they hear is plain scripture, which forbids not church sentence or determining, but as it ends in violence upon the conscience unconvinced. Let whoso will interpret or determine, so it be according to true church discipline, which is exercised on them only who have willingly joined themselves in that covenant of union, and proceeds only to a separation from the rest, proceeds never to any corporal enforcement or forfeiture of money, which in spiritual things are the two arms of Antichrist, not of the true church; the one being an inquisition, the other no better than a temporal indulgence of sin for money, whether by the church exacted or by the magistrate; both the one and the other a temporal satisfaction for what Christ hath satisfied eternally; a popish commuting of penalty, corporal for spiritual; a satisfaction to man, especially to the magistrate, for what and to whom we owe none: these and more are the injustices of force and fining in religion, besides what I most insist on, the violation of God's express commandment in the gospel, as hath been shown. Thus then, if church governors cannot use force in religion, though but for this reason, because they cannot infallibly determine to the conscience without convincement, much less have civil magistrates authority to use force where they can much less judge; unless they mean only to be the civil executioners of them who have no civil power to give them such commission, no, nor yet ecclesiastical, to any force or violence in religion. To sum up all in brief, if we must believe as the magistrate appoints, why not rather as the church? If not as either without convincement, how can force be lawful? But some are ready to cry out, what shall then be done to blasphemy? Them I would first exhort, not thus to terrify and pose the people with a Greek word; but to teach them better what it is, being a most usual and common word in that language to signify any slander, any malicious or evil speaking, whether against God or man, or anything to good belonging: blasphemy or evil speaking against God maliciously, is far from conscience in religion, according to that of Mark ix. 39, "There is none who doth a powerful work in my name, and can lightly speak evil of me." If this suffice not, I refer them to that prudent and well deliberated act, August 9, 1650, where the parliament defines blasphemy against God, as far as it is a crime belonging to civil judicature, "plenius ac melius Chrysippo et Crantore;" in plain English, more warily, more judiciously, more orthodoxally than twice their number of divines have done in many a prolix volume: although in all likelihood they whose whole study and profession these things are, should be most intelligent and authentic therein, as they are for the most part; yet neither they nor these unerring always, or infallible. But we shall not carry it thus; another Greek apparition stands in our way, Heresy and Heretic; in like manner also railed at to the people as in a tongue unknown. They should first interpret to them that heresy, by what it signifies in that language, is no word of evil note, meaning only the choice or following of any opinion, good or bad, in religion, or any other learning; and thus not only in heathen authors, but in the New Testament itself, without censure or blame; Acts xv. 5, "Certain of the heresy of the pharisees which believed;" and xxvi. 5, "After the exactest heresy of our religion I lived a Pharisee." In which sense presbyterian or independent may without reproach be called a heresy. Where it is mentioned with blame, it seems to differ little from schism: 1 Cor. xi. 18, 19, "I hear that there be schisms among you," &c. "for there must also heresies be among you," &c. Though some, who write of heresy after their own heads, would make it far worse than schism; whenas on the contrary, schism signifies division, and in the worst sense; heresy, choice only of one opinion before

another, which may be without discord. In apostolic times, therefore, ere the scripture was written, heresy was a doctrine maintained against the doctrine by them delivered; which in these times can be no otherwise defined than a doctrine maintained against the light which we now only have of the scripture. Seeing, therefore, that no man, no synod, no session of men, though called the church, can judge definitively the sense of scripture to another man's conscience, which is well known to be a general maxim of the protestant religion; it follows plainly, that he who holds in religion that belief, or those opinions, which to his conscience and utmost understanding appear with most evidence or probability in the scripture, though to others he seem erroneous, can no more be justly censured for a heretic than his censurers; who do but the same thing themselves, while they censure him for so doing. For ask them, or any protestant, which hath most authority, the church or the scripture? They will answer, doubtless, that the scripture: and what hath most authority, that no doubt but they will confess is to be followed. He then, who to his best apprehension follows the scripture, though against any point of doctrine by the whole church received, is not the heretic; but he who follows the church against his conscience and persuasion grounded on the scripture. To make this yet more undeniable, I shall only borrow a plain simile, the same which our own writers, when they would demonstrate plainest, that we rightly prefer the scripture before the church, use frequently against the papist in this manner. As the Samaritans believed Christ, first for the woman's word, but next and much rather for his own, so we the scripture: first on the church's word, but afterwards and much more for its own, as the word of God; yea, the church itself we believe then for the scripture. The inference of itself follows: If by the protestant doctrine we believe the scripture, not for the church's saying, but for its own, as the word of God, then ought we to believe what in our conscience we apprehend the scripture to say, though the visible church, with all her doctors, gainsay: and being taught to believe them only for the scripture, they who so do are not heretics, but the best protestants: and by their opinions, whatever they be, can hurt no protestant, whose rule is not to receive them but from the scripture: which to interpret convincingly to his own conscience, none is able but himself guided by the Holy Spirit; and not so guided, none than he to himself can be a worse deceiver. To protestants, therefore, whose common rule and touchstone is the scripture, nothing can with more conscience, more equity, nothing more protestantly can be permitted, than a free and lawful debate at all times by writing, conference, or disputation of what opinion soever, disputable by scripture: concluding that no man in religion is properly a heretic at this day, but he who maintains traditions or opinions not probable by scripture, who, for aught I know, is the papist only; he the only heretic, who counts all heretics but himself. Such as these, indeed, were capitally punished by the law of Moses, as the only true heretics, idolaters, plain and open deserters of God and his known law: but in the gospel such are punished by excommunion only: Tit. iii. 10, "An heretic, after the first and second admonition, reject." But they who think not this heavy enough, and understand not that dreadful awe and spiritual efficacy which the apostle hath expressed so highly to be in church discipline, 2 Cor. x., of which anon, and think weakly that the church of God cannot long subsist but in a bodily fear, for want of other proof will needs wrest that place of St. Paul, Rom. xiii., to set up civil inquisition, and give power to the magistrate both of civil judgment and punishment in causes ecclesiastical. But let us see with what strength of argument: "Let every soul be subject to the higher powers." First, how prove they that the apostle means other powers than such as they to whom he writes were then under; who meddled not at all in ecclesiastical causes, unless as tyrants and persecutors? And from them, I hope, they will not derive either the right of magistrates to judge in spiritual things, or the duty of such our obedience. How prove they next, that he entitles them here to spiritual causes, from whom he withheld, as much as in him lay, the judging of civil? 1 Cor. vi. 1, &c. If he himself appealed to Cæsar, it was to judge his innocence, not his religion. "For rulers are not a terror to good works, but to the evil:" then are they not a terror to conscience, which is the rule or judge of good works grounded on the scripture. But heresy, they say, is reckoned among evil works, Gal. v. 20, as if all evil works were to be punished by the magistrate; whereof this place, their own citation, reckons up besides heresy a sufficient number to confute them; "uncleanness, wantonness, enmity, strife, emulations, animosities, contentions, envyings;" all which are far more manifest to be judged by him than heresy, as they define it; and yet I suppose they will not subject these evil works, nor many more suchlike, to his cognizance and punishment. "Wilt thou then not be afraid of the power? Do that which is good, and thou shalt have praise of the same." This shows that religious matters are not here meant; wherein from the power here spoken of, they could have no praise. "For he is the minister of God to thee for good:" true; but in that office, and to that end, and by those means, which in this place must be clearly found, if from this place they intend to argue. And how, for thy good by forcing, oppressing, and ensnaring thy conscience? Many are the ministers of God, and their offices no less different than many; none more different than state and church government. Who seeks to govern both, must needs be worse than any lord prelate, or church pluralist: for he in his own faculty and profession, the other not in his own, and for the most part not thoroughly understood, makes himself supreme lord or pope of the church, as far as his civil jurisdiction stretches; and all the ministers of God therein, his ministers, or his curates rather in the function only, not in the government; while he himself assumes to rule by civil power things to be ruled only by spiritual: whenas this very chapter, verse 6, appointing him his peculiar office, which requires utmost attendance, forbids him this worse than church plurality from that full and weighty charge, wherein alone he is "the minister of God, attending continually on this very thing." To little purpose will they here instance Moses, who did all by immediate divine direction; no, nor yet Asa, Jehoshaphat, or Josiah, who both might, when they pleased, receive answer from God, and had a commonwealth by him delivered them, incorporated with a national church, exercised more in bodily than in spiritual worship: so as that the church might be called a commonwealth, and the whole commonwealth a church: nothing of which can be said of Christianity, delivered without the help of magistrates, yea, in the midst of their opposition; how little then with any reference to them, or mention of them, save only of our obedience to their civil laws, as they countenance good, and deter evil? which is the proper work of the magistrate, following in the same verse, and shows distinctly wherein he is the minister of God, "a revenger to execute wrath on him that doth evil." But we must first know who it is that doth evil: the heretic they say among the first. Let it be known then certainly who is a heretic; and that he who holds opinions in religion professedly from tradition, or his own inventions, and not from scripture, but rather against it, is the only heretic: and yet though such, not always punishable by the magistrate, unless he do evil against a civil law, properly so called, hath been already proved, without need of repetition: "But if thou do that which is evil, be afraid." To do by scripture and the gospel, according to conscience, is not to do evil; if we thereof ought not to be afraid, he ought not by his judging to give cause: causes therefore of religion are not here meant: "For he beareth not the sword in vain." Yes, altogether in vain, if it smite he knows not what; if that for heresy, which not the church itself, much less he, can determine absolutely to be so; if truth for error, being himself so often fallible, he bears the sword not in vain only, but unjustly and to evil. "Be subject not only for wrath, but for conscience sake:" How for conscience sake, against conscience? By all these reasons it appears plainly, that the apostle in this place gives no judgment or coercive power to magistrates, neither to those then, nor these now, in matters of religion; and exhorts us no otherwise than he exhorted those Romans. It hath now twice befallen me to assert, through God's assistance, this most wrested and vexed place of scripture: heretofore against Salmasius, and regal tyranny over the state; now against Erastus, and state

tyranny over the church. If from such uncertain, or rather such improbable grounds as these, they endue magistracy with spiritual judgment, they may as well invest him in the same spiritual kind with power of utmost punishment, excommunication; and then turn spiritual into corporal, as no worse authors did than Chrysostom, Jerome, and Austin, whom Erasmus and others in their notes on the New Testament have cited, to interpret that cutting off which St. Paul wished to them who had brought back the Galatians to circumcision, no less than the amercement of their whole virility: and Grotius adds, that this concising punishment of circumcisers became a penal law thereupon among the Visigoths: a dangerous example of beginning in the spirit to end so in the flesh; whereas that cutting off much likelier seems meant a cutting off from the church, not unusually so termed in scripture, and a zealous imprecation, not a command. But I have mentioned this passage to show how absurd they often prove who have not learned to distinguish rightly between civil power and ecclesiastical. How many persecutions, then imprisonments, banishments, penalties, and stripes; how much bloodshed have the forcers of conscience to answer for, and protestants rather than papists! For the papist, judging by his principles, punishes them who believe not as the church believes, though against the scripture; but the protestant, teaching every one to believe the scripture, though against the church, counts heretical, and persecutes against his own principles, them who in any particular so believe as he in general teaches them; them who most honor and believe divine scripture, but not against it any human interpretation though universal; them who interpret scripture only to themselves, which by his own position, none but they to themselves can interpret: them who use the scripture no otherwise by his own doctrine to their edification, than he himself uses it to their punishing; and so whom his doctrine acknowledges a true believer, his discipline persecutes as a heretic. The papist exacts our belief as to the church due above scripture; and by the church, which is the whole people of God, understands the pope, the general councils, prelatical only, and the surnamed fathers: but the forcing protestant, though he deny such belief to any church whatsoever, yet takes it to himself and his teachers, of far less authority than to be called the church, and above scripture believed: which renders his practice both contrary to his belief, and far worse than that belief, which he condemns in the papist. By all which, well considered, the more he professes to be a true protestant, the more he hath to answer for his persecuting than a papist. No protestant therefore, of what sect soever, following scripture only, which is the common sect wherein they all agree, and the granted rule of every man's conscience to himself, ought by the common doctrine of protestants to be forced or molested for religion. But as for popery and idolatry, why they also may not hence plead to be tolerated, I have much less to say. Their religion the more considered, the less can be acknowledged a religion; but a Roman principality rather, endeavoring to keep up her old universal dominion under a new name, and mere shadow of a catholic religion; being indeed more rightly named a catholic heresy against the scripture, supported mainly by a civil, and, except in Rome, by a foreign, power: justly therefore to be suspected, not tolerated, by the magistrate of another country. Besides, of an implicit faith which they profess, the conscience also becomes implicit, and so by voluntary servitude to man's law, forfeits her Christian liberty. Who then can plead for such a conscience, as being implicitly enthralled to man instead of God, almost becomes no conscience, as the will not free, becomes no will? Nevertheless, if they ought not to be tolerated, it is for just reason of state, more than of religion; which they who force, though professing to be protestants, deserve as little to be tolerated themselves, being no less guilty of popery in the most popish point. Lastly, for idolatry, who knows it not to be evidently against all scripture, both of the Old and New Testament, and therefore a true heresy, or rather an impiety, wherein a right conscience can have nought to do; and the works thereof so manifest, that a magistrate can hardly err in prohibiting and quite removing at least the public and scandalous use thereof?

From the riddance of these objections, I proceed yet to another reason why it is unlawful for the civil magistrate to use force in matters of religion; which is, because to judge in those things, though we should grant him able, which is proved he is not, yet as a civil magistrate he hath no right. Christ hath a government of his own, sufficient of itself to all his ends and purposes in governing his church, but much different from that of the civil magistrate; and the difference in this very thing principally consists, that it governs not by outward force; and that for two reasons: First, Because it deals only with the inward man and his actions, which are all spiritual, and to outward force not liable. Secondly, To show us the divine excellence of his spiritual kingdom, able, without worldly force, to subdue all the powers and kingdoms of this world, which are upheld by outward force only. That the inward man is nothing else but the inward part of man, his understanding and his will; and that his actions thence proceeding, yet not simply thence, but from the work of divine grace upon them, are the whole matter of religion under the gospel, will appear plainly by considering what that religion is; whence we shall perceive yet more plainly that it cannot be forced. What evangelic religion is, is told in two words,—faith and charity, or belief and practice. That both these flow, either, the one from the understanding, the other from the will, or both jointly from both, once indeed naturally free, but now only as they are regenerate and wrought on by divine grace, is in part evident to common sense and principles unquestioned, the rest by scripture: concerning our belief, Matt. xvi. 17, "Flesh and blood hath not revealed it unto thee, but my Father which is in heaven;" concerning our practice, as it is religious, and not merely civil, Gal. v. 22, 23, and other places, declare it to be the fruit of the spirit only. Nay, our whole practical duty in religion is contained in charity, or the love of God and our neighbor, no way to be forced, yet the fulfilling of the whole law; that is to say, our whole practice in religion. If then both our belief and practice, which comprehend our whole religion, flow from faculties of the inward man, free and unconstrainable of themselves by nature, and our practice not only from faculties endued with freedom, but from love and charity besides, incapable of force, and all these things by transgression lost, but renewed and regenerated in us by the power and gift of God alone; how can such religion as this admit of force from man, or force be any way applied to such religion, especially under the free offer of grace in the gospel, but it must forthwith frustrate and make of no effect both the religion and the gospel? And that to compel outward profession, which they will say perhaps ought to be compelled, though inward religion cannot, is to compel hypocrisy, not to advance religion, shall yet, though of itself clear enough, be ere the conclusion, further manifest. The other reason why Christ rejects outward force in the government of his church, is, as I said before, to show us the divine excellence of his spiritual kingdom, able without worldly force to subdue all the powers and kingdoms of this world, which are upheld by outward force only: by which to uphold religion otherwise than to defend the religious from outward violence, is no service to Christ or his kingdom, but rather a disparagement, and degrades it from a divine and spiritual kingdom, to a kingdom of this world: which he denies it to be, because it needs not force to confirm it: John xviii. 36: "If my kingdom were of this world, then would my servants fight, that I should not be delivered to the Jews." This proves the kingdom of Christ not governed by outward force, as being none of this world, whose kingdoms are maintained all by force only; and yet disproves not that a Christian commonwealth may defend itself against outward force, in the cause of religion as well as in any other: though Christ himself coming purposely to die for us, would not be so defended. 1 Cor. i. 27: "God hath chosen the weak things of the world, to confound the things which are mighty." Then surely he hath not chosen the force of this world to subdue conscience, and conscientious men, who in this world are counted weakest; but rather conscience, as being weakest, to subdue and regulate force, his adversary, not his aid or instrument in governing the church: 2 Cor. x. 3, 4, 5, 6: "For though we walk in the flesh, we do not war after the flesh: for the weapons of our warfare are not carnal, but mighty through God to the pulling down of strongholds, casting down imaginations, and every high thing that exalts itself against the knowledge of God, and bringing into captivity every thought to the obedience of Christ: and having in a readiness to avenge all disobedience." It is evident by the first and second verses of this chapter, that the apostle here speaks of that spiritual power by which Christ governs his church, how all-sufficient it is, how powerful to reach the conscience, and the inward man with whom it chiefly deals, and whom no power else can deal with. In comparison of which, as it is here thus magnificently described, how uneffectual and weak is outward force with all her boisterous tools, to the shame of those Christians, and especially those churchmen, who to the exercising of church-discipline, never cease calling on the civil magistrate to interpose his fleshly force? An argument that all true ministerial and spiritual power is dead within them; who think the gospel, which both began and spread over the whole world for above three hundred years, under heathen and persecuting emperors, cannot stand or continue, supported by the same divine presence and protection, to the world's end, much easier under the defensive favor only of a Christian magistrate, unless it be enacted and settled, as they call it, by the state, a statute or a state religion; and understand not that the church itself cannot, much less the state, settle or impose one tittle of religion upon our obedience implicit, but can only recommend or propound it to our free and conscientious examination: unless they mean to set the state higher than the church in religion, and with a gross contradiction give to the state in their settling petition that command of our implicit belief which they deny in their settled confession both to the state and to the church. Let them cease then to importune and interrupt the magistrate from attending to his own charge in civil and moral things, the settling of things just, things honest, the defence of things religious, settled by the churches within themselves; and the repressing of their contraries, determinable by the common light of nature; which is not to constrain or to repress religion probable by scripture, but the violaters and persecuters thereof: of all which things he hath enough and more than enough to do, left yet undone; for which the land groans, and justice goes to wrack the while. Let him also forbear force where he hath no right to judge, for the conscience is not his province, lest a worst woe arrive him, for worse offending, than was denounced by our Saviour, Matt. xxiii. 23, against the pharisees: Ye have forced the conscience, which was not to be forced; but judgment and mercy ye have not executed; this ye should have done, and the other let alone. And since it is the counsel and set purpose of God in the gospel, by spiritual means which are counted weak, to overcome all power which resists him; let them not go about to do that by worldly strength, which he hath decreed to do by those means which the world counts weakness, lest they be again obnoxious to that saying, which in another place is also written of the pharisees, Luke vii. 30, that "they frustrated the counsel of God." The main plea is, and urged with much vehemence to their imitation, that the kings of Judah, as I touched before, and especially Josiah, both judged and used force in religion: 2 Chron. xxxiv. 33, "He made all that were present in Israel to serve the Lord their God:" an argument, if it be well weighed, worse than that used by the false prophet Shemaia to the high-priest, that in imitation of Jehoiada, he ought to put Jeremiah in the stocks, Jer. xxix. 24, 26, &c.; for which he received his due denouncement from God. But to this besides I return a threefold answer: First, That the state of religion under the gospel is far differing from what it was under the law. Then was the state of rigor, childhood, bondage, and works, to all which force was not unbefitting; now is the state of grace, manhood, freedom, and faith, to all which belongs willingness and reason, not force: the law was then written on tables of stone, and to be performed according to the letter, willingly or unwillingly; the gospel, our new covenant, upon the heart of every believer, to be interpreted only by the sense of charity and inward persuasion: the law had no distinct government or governors of church and commonwealth, but the priests and Levites judged in all causes, not ecclesiastical only, but civil, Deut. xvii. 8, &c.; which under the gospel is forbidden to all church ministers,

as a thing which Christ their Master in his ministry disclaimed, Luke xii. 14, as a thing beneath them, 1 Cor. vi. 4, and by many other statutes, as to them who have a peculiar and far-differing government of their own. If not, why different the governors? Why not church ministers in state affairs, as well as state ministers in church affairs? If church and state shall be made one flesh again, as under the law, let it be withal considered, that God, who then joined them, hath now severed them; that which, he so ordaining, was then a lawful conjunction, to such on either side as join again what he hath severed would be nothing now but their own presumptuous fornication. Secondly, the kings of Judah, and those magistrates under the law, might have recourse, as I said before, to divine inspiration; which our magistrates under the gospel have not, more than to the same spirit, which those whom they force have ofttimes in greater measure than themselves: and so, instead of forcing the Christian, they force the Holy Ghost; and, against that wise forewarning of Gamaliel, fight against God. Thirdly, those kings and magistrates used force in such things only as were undoubtedly known and forbidden in the law of Moses, idolatry and direct apostacy from that national and strict enjoined worship of God; whereof the corporal punishment was by himself expressly set down; but magistrates under the gospel, our free, elective, and rational worship, are most commonly busiest to force those things which in the gospel are either left free, nay, sometimes abolished when by them compelled, or else controverted equally by writers on both sides, and sometimes with odds on that side which is against them. By which means they either punish that which they ought to favor and protect, or that with corporal punishment, and of their own inventing, which not they, but the church, hath received command to chastise with a spiritual rod only. Yet some are so eager in their zeal of forcing, that they refuse not to descend at length to the utmost shift of that parabolical proof, Luke xiv. 16, &c., "Compel them to come in:" therefore magistrates may compel in religion. As if a parable were to be strained through every word or phrase, and not expounded by the general scope thereof; which is no other here than the earnest expression of God's displeasure on those recusant Jews, and his purpose to prefer the Gentiles on any terms before them: expressed here by the word compel. But how compels he? Doubtless no other wise than he draws, without which no man can come to him, John vi. 44; and that is by the inward persuasive motions of his Spirit, and by his ministers; not by the outward compulsions of a magistrate or his officers. The true people of Christ, as is foretold, Psalm cx. 3, "are a willing people in the day of his power;" then much more now when he rules all things by outward weakness, that both his inward power and their sincerity may the more appear. "God loveth a cheerful giver:" then certainly is not pleased with an uncheerful worshipper: as the very words declare of his evangelical invitations, Isa. lv. 1, "Ho, every one that thirsteth, come." John vii. 37, "If any man thirsteth." Rev. iii. 18, "I counsel thee." And xxii. 17, "Whosoever will, let him take of the water of life freely." And in that grand commission of preaching, to invite all nations, Mark xvi. 16, as the reward of them who come, so the penalty of them who come not, is only spiritual. But they bring now some reason with their force, which must not pass unanswered, that the church of Thyatira was blamed, Rev. ii. 20, for suffering the false "prophetess to teach and to seduce." I answer, That seducement is to be hindered by fit and proper means ordained in church discipline, by instant and powerful demonstration to the contrary; by opposing truth to error, no unequal match; truth the strong, to error the weak, though sly and shifting. Force is no honest confutation, but uneffectual, and for the most part unsuccessful, ofttimes fatal to them who use it: sound doctrine, diligently and duly taught, is of herself both sufficient, and of herself (if some secret judgment of God hinder not) always prevalent against seducers. This the Thyatirians had neglected, suffering against church discipline, that woman to teach and seduce among them: civil force they had not then in their power, being the Christian part only of that city, and then especially under one of those ten great persecutions, whereof this the second was raised by Domitian: force therefore in these matters could not be required of them who were then under force themselves.

I have shown, that the civil power hath neither right, nor can do right, by forcing religious things; I will now show the wrong it doth, by violating the fundamental privilege of the gospel, the new birthright of every true believer, Christian liberty: 2 Cor. iii. 17, "Where the Spirit of the Lord is, there is liberty." Gal. iv. 26, "Jerusalem which is above is free; which is the mother of us all." And ver. 31, "We are not children of the bondwoman, but of the free." It will be sufficient in this place to say no more of Christian liberty, than that it sets us free not only from the bondage of those ceremonies, but also from the forcible imposition of those circumstances, place and time, in the worship of God: which though by him commanded in the old law, yet in respect of that verity and freedom which is evangelical, St. Paul comprehends both kinds alike, that is to say, both ceremony and circumstance, under one and the same contemptuous name of "weak and beggarly rudiments," Gal. iv. 3, 9, 10; Col. ii. 8 with 16; conformable to what our Saviour himself taught, John iv. 21, 23, "Neither in this mountain, nor yet at Jerusalem. In spirit and in truth; for the Father seeketh such to worship him:" that is to say, not only sincere of heart, for such he sought ever; but also, as the words here chiefly import, not compelled to place, and by the same reason, not to any set time; as his apostle by the same spirit hath taught us, Rom. xiv. 6, &c. "One man esteemeth one day above another," &c.; Gal. iv. 10, "Ye observe days and months," &c.; Col. ii. 16. These and other such places of scripture the best and learnedest reformed writers have thought evident enough to instruct us in our freedom, not only from ceremonies, but from those circumstances also, though imposed with a confident persuasion of morality in them, which they hold impossible to be in place or time. By what warrant then our opinions and practices herein are of late turned quite against all other protestants, and that which is to them orthodoxal, to us becomes scandalous and punishable by statute, I wish were once again better considered; if we mean not to proclaim a schism in this point from the best and most reformed churches abroad. They who would seem more knowing, confess that these things are indifferent, but for that very cause by the magistrate may be commanded. As if God of his special grace in the gospel had to this end freed us from his own commandments in these things, that our freedom should subject us to a more grievous yoke, the commandments of men. As well may the magistrate call that common or unclean which God hath cleansed, forbidden to St. Peter, Acts x. 15; as well may he loosen that which God hath straitened or straiten that which God hath loosened, as he may enjoin those things in religion which God hath left free, and lay on that yoke which God hath taken off. For he hath not only given us this gift as a special privilege and excellence of the free gospel above the servile law, but strictly also hath commanded us to keep it and enjoy it: Gal. v. 13, "You are called to liberty." 1 Cor. vii. 23, "Be not made the servants of men." Gal. v. 14, "Stand fast therefore in the liberty wherewith Christ hath made us free; and be not entangled again with the yoke of bondage." Neither is this a mere command, but for the most part in these forecited places, accompanied with the very weightiest and inmost reasons of Christian religion: Rom. xiv. 9, 10, "For to this end Christ both died, and rose, and revived, that he might be Lord both of the dead and living. But why dost thou judge thy brother?" &c. How presumest thou to be his lord, to be whose only Lord, at least in these things, Christ both died, and rose, and lived again? "We shall all stand before the judgment-seat of Christ." Why then dost thou not only judge, but persecute in these things for which we are to be accountable to the tribunal of Christ only, our Lord and lawgiver? 1 Cor. vii. 23. "Ye are bought with a price: be not made the servants of men." Some trivial price belike, and for some frivolous pretences paid in their opinion, if bought and by him redeemed, who is God, from what was once the service of God, we shall be enthralled again, and forced by men to what now is but the service of men: Gal. iv. 31, with v. 1, "We are not children of the bondwoman, &c.; stand fast therefore," &c. Col. ii. 8, "Beware lest any man spoil you, &c., after the rudiments of the world, and not after Christ." Solid reasons whereof are continued through the whole chapter. Ver. 10, "Ye are complete in him, which is the head of all principality and power:" not completed therefore or made the more religious by those ordinances of civil power from which Christ their head hath discharged us; "blotting out the handwriting of ordinances that was against us, which was contrary to us; and took it out of the way, nailing it to his cross," ver. 14. Blotting out ordinances written by God himself, much more those so boldly written over again by men; ordinances which were against us, that is, against our frailty, much more those which are against our conscience. "Let no man therefore judge you in respect of," &c., ver. 16; Gal. iv. 3, &c. "Even so we, when we were children, were in bondage under the rudiments of the world: but when the fulness of time was come, God sent forth his Son, &c., to redeem them that were under the law, that we might receive the adoption of sons, &c. Wherefore thou art no more a servant, but a son, &c. But now, &c. how turn ye again to the weak and beggarly rudiments, whereunto ye desire again to be in bondage? Ye observe days," &c. Hence it plainly appears, that if we be not free, we are not sons, but still servants unadopted; and if we turn again to those weak and beggarly rudiments, we are not free; yea, though willingly, and with a misguided conscience, we desire to be in bondage to them; how much more then if unwillingly and against our conscience? Ill· was our condition changed from legal to evangelical, and small advantage gotten by the gospel, if for the spirit of adoption to freedom promised us, we receive again the spirit of bondage to fear; if our fear, which was then servile towards God only, must be now servile in religion towards men: strange also and preposterous fear, if when and wherein it hath attained by the redemption of our Saviour to be filial only towards God, it must be now servile towards the magistrate: who, by subjecting us to his punishment in these things, brings back into religion that law of terror and satisfaction belonging only to civil crimes; and thereby in effect abolishes the gospel, by establishing again the law to a far worse yoke of servitude upon us than before. It will therefore not misbecome the meanest Christian to put in mind

Christian magistrates, and so much the more freely by how much the more they desire to be thought Christian, (for they will be thereby, as they ought to be in these things, the more our brethren and the less our lords,) that they meddle not rashly with Christian liberty, the birthright and outward testimony of our adoption; lest while they little think it, nay, think they do God service, they themselves, like the sons of that bondwoman, be found persecuting them who are free-born of the Spirit, and by a sacrilege of not the least aggravation, bereaving them of that sacred liberty, which our Saviour with his own blood purchased for them.

A fourth reason why the magistrate ought not to use force in religion, I bring from the consideration of all those ends which he can likely pretend to the interposing of his force therein; and those hardly can be other than first the glory of God; next, either the spiritual good of them whom he forces, or the temporal · punishment of their scandal to others. As for the promoting of God's glory, none, I think, will say that his glory ought to be promoted in religious things by unwarrantable means, much less by means contrary to what he hath commanded. That outward force is such, and that God's glory in the whole administration of the gospel according to his own will and counsel ought to be fulfilled by weakness, at least so refuted, not by force; or if by force, inward and spiritual, not outward and corporeal, is already proved at large. That outward force cannot tend to the good of him, who is forced in religion, is unquestionable. For in religion whatever we do under the gospel, we ought to be thereof persuaded without scruple; and are justified by the faith we have, not by the work we do: Rom. xiv. 5, "Let every man be fully persuaded in his own mind." The other reason which follows necessarily is obvious, Gal. ii. 16, and in many other places of St. Paul, as the groundwork and foundaton of the whole gospel, that we are "justified by the faith of Christ, and not by the works of the law." If not by the works of God's law, how then by the injunctions of man's law? Surely force cannot work persuasion, which is faith; cannot therefore justify nor pacify the conscience, and that which justifies not in the gospel, condemns; is not only not

good, but sinful to do; Rom. xiv. 23, "Whatsoever is not of faith, is sin." It concerns the magistrate, then, to take heed how he forces in religion conscientious men, lest by compelling them to do that whereof they cannot be persuaded, that wherein they cannot find themselves justified, but by their own consciences condemned, instead of aiming at their spiritual good, he force them to do evil; and while he thinks himself Asa, Josiah, Nehemiah, he be found Jeroboam, who caused Israel to sin; and thereby draw upon his own head all those sins and shipwrecks of implicit faith and conformity, which he hath forced, and all the wounds given to those little ones, whom to offend he will find worse one day than that violent drowning mentioned Matt. xviii. 6. Lastly, as a preface to force, it is the usual pretence, that although tender consciences shall be tolerated, yet scandals thereby given shall not be unpunished, profane and licentious men shall not be encouraged to neglect the performance of religious and holy duties by color of any law giving liberty to tender consciences. By which contrivance the way lies ready open to them hereafter, who may be so minded, to take away by little and little that liberty which Christ and his gospel, not any magistrate, hath right to give: though this kind of his giving be but to give with one hand, and take away with the other, which is a deluding, not a giving. As for scandals, if any man be offended at the conscientious liberty of another, it is a taken scandal, not a given. To heal one conscience, we must not wound another: and men must be exhorted to beware of scandals in Christian liberty not forced by the magistrate; lest while he goes about to take away the scandal, which is uncertain whether given or taken, he take away our liberty, which is the certain and the sacred gift of God, neither to be touched by him, nor to be parted with by us. None more cautious of giving scandal than St. Paul. Yet while he made himself "servant to all," that he "might gain the more," he made himself so of his own accord, was not made so by outward force, testifying at the same time that he "was free from all men," 1 Cor. ix. 19; and thereafter exhorts us also, Gal. v. 13, "Ye were called to liberty, &c., but by love serve one another:" then not by force. As for that fear, lest profane and licentious men should be encouraged to omit the performance of religious and holy duties, how can that care belong to the civil magistrate, especially to his force? For if profane and licentious persons must not neglect the performance of religious and holy duties, it implies, that such duties they can perform, which no protestant will affirm. They who mean the outward performance, may so explain it; and it will then appear yet more plainly, that such performance of religious and holy duties, especially by profane and licentious persons, is a dishonoring rather than a worshipping of God; and not only by him not required, but detested: Prov. xxi. 27, "The sacrifice of the wicked is an abomination; how much more when he bringeth it with a wicked mind?" To compel, therefore, the profane to things holy in his profaneness, is all one under the gospel, as to have compelled the unclean to sacrifice in his uncleanness under the law. And I add withal, that to compel the licentious in his licentiousness, and the conscientious against his conscience, comes all to one: tends not to the honor of God, but to the multiplying and the aggravating of sin to them both. We read not that Christ ever exercised force but once, and that was to drive profane ones out of his temple, not to force them in; and if their being there was an offence, we find by many other scriptures that their praying there was an abomination: and yet to the Jewish law, that nation, as a servant, was obliged; but to the gospel each person is left voluntary, called only, as a son, by the preaching of the word; not to be driven in by edicts and force of arms. For if by the apostle, Rom. xii. 1, we are "beseeched as brethren by the mercies of God to present our bodies a living sacrifice, holy, acceptable to God, which is our reasonable service," or worship, then is no man to be forced by the compulsive laws of men to present his body a dead sacrifice; and so under the gospel most unholy and unacceptable, because it is his unreasonable service, that is to say, not only unwilling but unconscionable. But if profane and licentious persons may not omit the performance of holy duties, why may they not partake of holy things? Why are they prohibited the Lord's supper, since both the one and the other action may be outward; and outward performance of duty may attain at least an outward participation of benefit? The church denying them that communion of grace and thanksgiving, as it justly doth, why doth the magistrate compel them to the union of performing that which they neither truly can, being themselves unholy, and to do seemingly is both hateful to God and perhaps no less dangerous to perform holy duties irreligiously, than to receive holy signs or sacraments unworthily? All profane and licentious men, so known, can be considered but either so without the church as never yet within it, or departed thence of their own accord, or excommunicate: if never yet within the church, whom the apostle, and so, consequently, the church have nought to do to judge, as he professes, 1 Cor. v. 12, then by what authority doth the magistrate judge; or, which is worse, compel in relation to the church? If departed of his own accord, like that lost sheep, Luke xv. 4, &c., the true church, either with her own or any borrowed force, worries him not in again, but rather in all charitable manner sends after him; and if she find him, lays him gently on her shoulders, bears him, yea, bears his burdens, his errors, his infirmities any way tolerable, "so fulfilling the law of Christ," Gal. vi. 2. If excommunicate, whom the church hath bid go out, in whose name doth the magistrate compel to go in? The church, indeed, hinders none from hearing in her public congregation, for the doors are open to all: nor excommunicates to destruction; but, as much as in her lies, to a final saving. Her meaning, therefore, must needs be, that as her driving out brings on no outward penalty, so no outward force or penalty of an improper and only a destructive power should drive in again her infectious sheep; therefore sent out because infectious, and not driven in but with the danger not only of the whole and sound, but also of his own utter perishing. Since force neither instructs in religion, nor begets repentance or amendment of life, but, on the contrary, hardness of heart, formality, hypocrisy, and, as I said before, every way increase of sin; more and more alienates the mind from a violent religion, expelling out and compelling in, and reduces it to a condition like that which the

Britons complain of in our story, driven to and fro between the Picts and the sea. If, after excommunion, he be found intractable, incurable, and will not hear the church, he becomes as one never yet within her pale, "a heathen or a publican," Matt. xviii. 17, not further to be judged, no, not by the magistrate, unless for civil causes; but left to the final sentence of that Judge, whose coming shall be in flames of fire; that Maranathà, 1 Cor. xvi. 22, than which to him so left nothing can be more dreadful, and ofttimes to him particularly nothing more speedy, that is to say, The Lord cometh: in the mean while delivered up to Satan, 1 Cor. v. 5. 1 Tim. i. 20, that is, from the fold of Christ and kingdom of grace to the world again, which is the kingdom of Satan; and as he was received "from darkness to light, and from the power of Satan to God," Acts xxvi. 18, so now delivered up again from light to darkness, and from God to the power of Satan; yet so as is in both places manifested, to the intent of saving him, brought sooner to contrition by spiritual than by any corporal severity. But grant it belonging any way to the magistrate, that profane and licentious persons omit not the performance of holy duties, which in them were odious to God even under the law, much more now under the gospel; yet ought his care both as a magistrate and a Christian, to be much more that conscience be not inwardly violated, than that licence in these things be made outwardly conformable: since his part is undoubtedly as a Christian, which puts him upon this office much more than as a magistrate, in all respects to have more care of the conscientious than of the profane; and not for their sakes to take away (while they pretend to give) or to diminish the rightful liberty of religious consciences.

On these four scriptural reasons, as on a firm square, this truth, the right of Christian and evangelic liberty, will stand immovable against all those pretended consequences of licence and confusion, which for the most part men most licentious and confused themselves, or such as whose severity would be wiser than divine wisdom, are ever aptest to object against the ways of God: as if God without them, when he gave us this liberty, knew not of the worst which these men in their arrogance pretend will follow: yet knowing all their worst, he gave us this liberty as by him judged best. As to those magistrates who think it their work to settle religion, and those ministers or others, who so oft call upon them to do so, I trust, that having well considered what hath been here argued, neither they will continue in that intention, nor these in that expectation from them; when they shall find that the settlement of religion belongs only to each particular church by persuasive and spiritual means within itself, and that the defence only of the church belongs to the magistrate. Had he once learned not further to concern himself with church affairs, half his labor might be spared, and the commonwealth better tended. To which end, that which I premised in the beginning, and in due place treated of more at large, I desire now concluding, that they would consider seriously what religion is; and they will find it to be, in sum, both our belief and our practice depending upon God only. That there can be no place then left for the magistrate or his force in the settlement of religion, by appointing either what we shall believe in divine things, or practice in religious, (neither of which things are in the power of man either to perform himself, or to enable others,) I persuade me in the Christian ingenuity of all religious men, the more they examine seriously, the more they will find clearly to be true; and find how false and deceivable that common saying is, which is so much relied upon, that the Christian magistrate is "Custos utriusque Tabulæ," Keeper of both Tables, unless is meant by keeper the defender only: neither can that maxim be maintained by any proof or argument, which hath not in this discourse first or last been refuted. For the two tables, or ten commandments, teach our duty to God and our neighbor from the love of both; give magistrates no authority to force either: they seek that from the judicial law, though on false grounds, especially in the first table, as I have shown; and both in first and second execute that authority for the most part, not according to God's judicial laws, but their own. As for civil crimes, and of the outward man, which all are not, no, not of those against the second table, as that of coveting; in them what power they have, they had from the beginning, long before Moses or the two tables were in being. And whether they be not now as little in being to be kept by any Christian as they are two legal tables, remains yet as undecided, as it is sure they never were yet delivered to the keeping of any Christian magistrate. But of these things, perhaps, more some other time; what may serve the present hath been above discoursed sufficiently out of the scriptures: and to those produced, might be added testimonies, examples, experiences, of all succeeding ages to these times, asserting this doctrine: but having herein the scripture so copious and so plain, we have all that can be properly called true strength and nerve; the rest would be but pomp and encumbrance. Pomp and ostentation of reading is admired among the vulgar; but doubtless, in matters of religion, he is learnedest who is plainest. The brevity I use, not exceeding a small manual, will not therefore, I suppose, be thought the less considerable, unless with them, perhaps, who think that great books only can determine great matters. I rather choose the common rule, not to make much ado, where less may serve; which in controversies, and those especially of religion, would make them less tedious, and by the consequence read ofter by many more, and with more benefit.

CONSIDERATIONS

TOUCHING THE LIKELIEST MEANS TO

REMOVE HIRELINGS OUT OF THE CHURCH

WHEREIN IS ALSO DISCOURSED

OF TITHES, CHURCH FEES, AND CHURCH-REVENUES;

AND

WHETHER ANY MAINTENANCE OF MINISTERS CAN BE SETTLED BY LAW.

[The text is that of the first edition, 1659.]

TO THE PARLIAMENT OF THE COMMONWEALTH OF ENGLAND, WITH THE DOMINIONS THEREOF.

OWING to your protection, supreme senate! this liberty of writing, which I have used these eighteen years on all occasions to assert the just rights and freedoms both of church and state, and so far approved, as to have been trusted with the representment and defence of your actions to all Christendom against an adversary of no mean repute; to whom should I address what I still publish on the same argument, but to you, whose magnanimous councils first opened and unbound the age from a double bondage under prelatical and regal tyranny; above our own hopes heartening us to look up at last, like men and Christians, from the slavish dejection, wherein from father to son we were bred up and taught; and thereby deserving of these nations, if they be not barbarously ingrateful, to be acknowledged, next under God, the authors and best patrons of religious and civil liberty, that ever these islands brought forth? The care and tuition of whose peace and safety, after a short but scandalous night of interruption, is now again, by a new dawning of God's miraculous providence among us, revolved upon your shoulders. And to whom more appertain these considerations, which I propound, than to yourselves, and the debate before you, though I trust of no difficulty, yet at present of great expectation, not whether ye will gratify, were it no more than so, but whether ye will hearken to the just petition of many thousands best affected both to religion and to this your return, or whether ye will satisfy, which you never can, the covetous pretences and demands of insatiable hirelings, whose disaffection ye well know both to yourselves and your resolutions? That I, though among many others in this common concernment, interpose to your deliberations what my thoughts also are; your own judgment and the success thereof hath given me the confidence: which requests but this, that if I have prosperously, God so favoring me, defended the public cause of this commonwealth to foreigners, ye would not think the reason and ability, whereon ye trusted once (and repent not) your whole reputation to the world, either grown less by more maturity and longer study, or less available in English than in another tongue: but that if it sufficed some years past to convince and satisfy the unengaged of other nations in the justice of your doings, though then held paradoxal, it may as well suffice now against weaker opposition in matters, except here in England with a spirituality of men devoted to their temporal gain, of no controversy else among protestants. Neither do I doubt, seeing daily the acceptance which they find who in their petitions venture to bring advice also, and new models of a commonwealth, but that you will interpret it much more the duty of a Christian to offer what his conscience persuades him may be of moment to the freedom and better constituting of the church: since it is a deed of highest charity to help undeceive the people, and a work worthiest your authority, in all things else authors, assertors, and now recoverers of our liberty, to deliver us, the only people of all protestants left still undelivered, from the oppressions of a simonious decimating clergy, who shame not, against the judgment and practice of all other churches reformed, to maintain, though very weakly, their popish and oft refuted positions; not in a point of conscience wherein they might be blameless, but in a point of covetousness and unjust claim to other men's goods; a contention foul and odious in any man, but most of all in ministers of the gospel, in whom contention, though for their own right, scarce is allowable. Till which grievances be removed, and religion set free from the monopoly of hirelings, I dare affirm that no model whatsoever of a commonwealth will prove successful or undisturbed; and so persuaded, implore divine assistance on your pious counsels and proceedings to unanimity in this and all other truth.

JOHN MILTON.

THE former treatise, which leads in this, began with two things ever found working much mischief to the church of God and the advancement of truth, force on the one side restraining, and hire on the other side corrupting, the teachers thereof. The latter of these is by much the more dangerous: for under force, though no thank to the forcers, true religion ofttimes best thrives and flourishes; but the corruption of teachers, most commonly the effect of hire, is the very bane of truth in them who are so corrupted. Of force not to be used in matters of religion, I have already spoken; and so stated matters of conscience and religion in faith and divine worship, and so severed them from blasphemy and heresy, the one being such properly as is despiteful, the other such as stands not to the rule of scripture, and so both of them not matters of religion, but rather against it, that to them who will yet use force, this only choice can be left, whether they will force them to believe, to whom it is not given from above, being not forced thereto by any principle of the gospel, which is now the only dispensation of God to all men; or whether being protestants, they will punish in those things wherein the protestant religion denies them to be judges, either in themselves infallible, or to the consciences of other men; or whether, lastly, they think fit to punish error, supposing they can be infallible that it is so, being not wilful but conscientious, and, according to the best light of him who errs, grounded on scripture: which kind of error all men religious, or but only reasonable, have thought worthier of pardon, and the growth thereof to be prevented by spiritual means and church discipline, not by civil laws and outward force, since it is God only who gives as well to believe aright, as to believe at all; and by those means, which he ordained sufficiently in his church to the full execution of his divine purpose in the gospel. It remains now to speak of hire, the other evil so mischievous in religion: whereof I promised then to speak further, when I should find God disposing me, and opportunity inviting. Opportunity I find now inviting; and apprehend therein the concurrence of God disposing; since the maintenance of church ministers, a thing not properly belonging to the magistrate, and yet with such importunity called for, and expected from him, is at present under public debate. Wherein lest anything may happen to be determined and established prejudicial to the right and freedom of church, or advantageous to such as may be found hirelings therein, it will be now most seasonable, and in these matters, wherein every Christian hath his free suffrage, no way misbecoming Christian meekness to offer freely, without disparagement to the wisest, such advice as God shall incline him and enable him to propound: since heretofore in commonwealths of most fame for government, civil laws were not established till they had been first for certain days published to the view of all men, that whoso pleased might speak freely his opinion thereof, and give in his exceptions, ere the law could pass to a full establishment. And where ought this equity to have more place, than in the liberty which is unseparable from Christian religion? This, I am not ignorant, will be a work unpleasing to some: but what truth is not hateful to some or other, as this, in likelihood, will be to none but hirelings. And if there be among them who hold it their duty to speak impartial truth, as the work of their ministry, though not performed without money, let them not envy others who think the same no less their duty by the general office of Christianity, to speak truth, as in all reason may be thought, more impartially and unsuspectedly without money.

Hire of itself is neither a thing unlawful, nor a word of any evil note, signifying no more than a due recompence or reward; as when our Saviour saith, "The laborer is worthy of his hire." That which makes it so dangerous in the church, and properly makes the hireling, a word always of evil signification, is either the excess thereof, or the undue manner of giving and taking it. What harm the excess thereof brought to the church, perhaps was not found by experience till the days of Constantine; who out of his zeal thinking he could be never too liberally a nursing father of the church, might be not unfitly said to have either overlaid it or choked it in the nursing. Which was foretold, as is recorded in ecclesiastical traditions, by a voice heard from heaven, on the very day that those great donations and church revenues were given, crying aloud, "This day is poison poured into the church." Which the event soon after verified, as appears by another no less ancient observation, "That religion brought forth wealth, and the daughter devoured the mother." But long ere wealth came into the church, so soon as any gain appeared in religion, hirelings were apparent; drawn in long before by the very scent thereof. Judas therefore, the first hireling, for want of present hire answerable to his coveting, from the small number or the meanness of such as then were the religious, sold the religion itself with the founder thereof, his master. Simon Magus the next, in hope only that preaching and the gifts of the Holy Ghost would prove gainful, offered beforehand a sum of money to obtain them. Not long after, as the apostle foretold, hirelings like wolves came in by herds: Acts xx. 29, "For I know this, that after my departing shall grievous wolves enter in among you, not sparing the flock." Tit. i. 11, "Teaching things which they ought not, for filthy lucre's sake." 2 Pet. ii. 3, "And through covetousness shall they with feigned words make merchandise of you." Yet they taught not false doctrine only, but seeming piety: 1 Tim. vi. 5, "Supposing that gain is godliness." Neither came they in of themselves only, but invited ofttimes by a corrupt audience: 2 Tim. iv. 3, "For the time will come, when they will not endure sound doctrine, but after their own lusts they will heap to themselves teachers, having itching ears;" and they on the other side, as fast heaping to themselves disciples, Acts xx. 30, doubtless had as itching palms: 2 Pet. ii. 15, "Following the way of Balaam, the son of Bosor, who loved the wages of unrighteousness." Jude 11, "They ran greedily after the error of Balaam for reward." Thus we see, that not only the excess of hire in wealthiest times, but also the undue and vicious taking or giving it, though but small or mean, as in the primitive times, gave to hirelings occasion, though not intended, yet sufficient to creep at first into the church. Which argues also the difficulty, or rather the impossibility, to remove them quite, unless every minister were, as St. Paul, contented to teach gratis; but few such are to be found. As therefore we cannot justly take away all hire in the church, because we cannot otherwise quite remove all hirelings, so are we not, for the impossibility of removing them all, to use therefore no endeavor that fewest may come in; but rather, in regard the evil, do what we can, will always be incumbent and unavoidable, to use our utmost diligence how it may be least dangerous: which will be likeliest effected, if we consider, first, what recompence God hath ordained should be given to ministers of the church; (for that a recompence ought to be given them, and may by them justly be re-received, our Saviour himself from the very light of reason and of equity hath declared, Luke x. 7, "The laborer is worthy of his hire;") next, by whom; and lastly, in what manner.

What recompence ought to be given to church ministers, God hath answerably ordained according to that difference which he hath manifestly put between those his two great dispensations, the law and the gospel. Under the law he gave them tithes; under the gospel, having left all things in his church to charity and Christian freedom, he hath given them only what is justly given them. That, as well under the gospel as under the law, say our English divines, and they only of all protestants, is tithes; and they say true, if any man be so minded to give them of his own the tenth or twentieth; but that the law therefore of tithes is in force under the gospel, all other protestant divines, though equally concerned, yet constantly deny. For although hire to the laborer be of moral and perpetual right, yet that special kind of hire, the tenth, can be of no right or necessity, but to that special labor for which God ordained it. That special labor was the Levitical and ceremonial service of the tabernacle, Numb. xviii. 21, 31, which is now abolished: the right therefore of that special hire must needs be withal abolished, as being also ceremonial. That tithes were ceremonial, is plain, not being given to the Levites till they had been first offered a heave-offering to the Lord, ver. 24, 28. He then who by that law brings tithes into the gospel, of necessity brings in withal a sacrifice, and an altar; without which tithes by that law were unsanctified and polluted, ver. 32, and therefore never thought on in the first Christian times, till ceremonies, altars, and oblations, by an ancienter corruption, were brought back long before. And yet the Jews, ever since their temple was destroyed, though they have rabbies and teachers of their law, yet pay no tithes, as having no Levites to whom, no temple where, to pay them, no altar whereon to hallow them; which argues that the Jews

themselves never thought tithes moral, but ceremonial only. That Christians therefore should take them up, when Jews have laid them down, must needs be very absurd and preposterous. Next, it is as clear in the same chapter, that the priests and Levites had not tithes for their labor only in the tabernacle, but in regard they were to have no other part nor inheritance in the land, ver. 20, 24, and by that means for a tenth, lost a twelfth. But our Levites undergoing no such law of deprivement, can have no right to any such compensation: nay, if by this law they will have tithes, can have no inheritance of land, but forfeit what they have. Besides this, tithes were of two sorts, those of every year, and those of every third year: of the former, every one that brought his tithes was to eat his share: Deut. xiv. 23, "Thou shalt eat before the Lord thy God, in the place which he shall choose to place his name there, the tithe of thy corn, of thy wine, and of thine oil," &c. Nay, though he could not bring his tithe in kind, by reason of his distant dwelling from the tabernacle or temple, but was thereby forced to turn it into money, he was to bestow that money on whatsoever pleased him, oxen, sheep, wine, or strong drink; and to eat and drink thereof there before the Lord, both he and his household, ver. 24, 25, 26. As for the tithes of every third year, they were not given only to the Levite, but to the stranger, the fatherless, and the widow, ver. 28, 29, and chap. xxvi. 12, 13. So that ours, if they will have tithes, must admit of these shares with them. Nay, these tithes were not paid in at all to the Levite, but the Levite himself was to come with those his fellow-guests, and eat his share of them only at his house who provided them; and this not in regard of his ministerial office, but because he had no part nor inheritance in the land. Lastly, the priests and Levites, a tribe, were of a far different constitution from this of our ministers under the gospel: in them were orders and degrees both by family, dignity, and office, mainly distinguished; the high priest, his brethren and his sons, to whom the Levites themselves paid tithes, and of the best, were eminently superior, Numb. xviii. 28, 29. No protestant, I suppose, will liken one of our ministers to a high priest, but rather to a common Levite. Unless then, to keep their tithes, they mean to bring back again bishops, archbishops, and the whole gang of prelaty, to whom will they themselves pay tithes, as by that law it was a sin to them if they did not? ver. 32. Certainly this must needs put them to a deep demur, while the desire of holding fast their tithes without sin may tempt them to bring back again bishops, as the likeness of that hierarchy that should receive tithes from them; and the desire to pay none may advise them to keep out of the church all orders above them. But if we have to do at present, as I suppose we have, with true reformed protestants, not with papists or prelates, it will not be denied that in the gospel there be but two ministerial degrees, presbyters and deacons; which if they contend to have any succession, reference, or conformity with those two degrees under the law, priests and Levites, it must needs be such whereby our presbyters or ministers may be answerable to priests, and our deacons to Levites; by which rule of proportion it will follow that we must pay our tithes to the deacons only, and they only to the ministers. But if it be truer yet, that the priesthood of Aaron typified a better reality, 1 Pet. ii. 5, signifying the Christian true and "holy priesthood to offer up spiritual sacrifice;" it follows hence, that we are now justly exempt from paying tithes to any who claim from Aaron, since that priesthood is in us now real, which in him was but a shadow. Seeing then by all this which has been shown, that the law of tithes is partly ceremonial, as the work was for which they were given, partly judicial, not of common, but of particular right to the tribe of Levi, nor to them alone, but to the owner also and his household, at the time of their offering, and every three year to the stranger, the fatherless, and the widow, their appointed sharers, and that they were a tribe of priests and deacons improperly compared to the constitution of our ministry; and the tithes given by that people to those deacons only; it follows that our ministers at this day, being neither priests nor Levites, nor fitly answering to either of them, can have no just title or pretence to tithes, by any consequence drawn from the law of Moses. But they think they have yet a better plea in the example of Melchisedec, who took tithes of Abram ere the law was given; whence they would infer tithes to be of moral right. But they ought to know, or to remember, that not examples, but express commands, oblige our obedience to God or man: next, that whatsoever was done in religion before the law written, is not presently to be counted moral, whenas so many things were then done both ceremonial and judaically judicial, that we need not doubt to conclude all times before Christ more or less under the ceremonial law. To what end served else those altars and sacrifices, that distinction of clean and unclean entering into the ark, circumcision, and the raising up of seed to the elder brother? Gen. xxxviii. 8. If these things be not moral, though before the law, how are tithes, though in the example of Abram and Melchisedec? But this instance is so far from being the just ground of a law, that after all circumstances duly weighed both from Gen. xiv. and Heb. vii., it will not be allowed them so much as an example. Melchisedec, besides his priestly benediction, brought with him bread and wine sufficient to refresh Abram and his whole army; incited to do so, first, by the secret providence of God, intending him for a type of Christ and his priesthood; next, by his due thankfulness and honor to Abram, who had freed his borders of Salem from a potent enemy: Abram on the other side honors him with the tenth of all, that is to say, (for he took not sure his whole estate with him to that war) of the spoils, Heb. vii. 4. Incited he also by the same secret providence, to signify as grandfather of Levi, that the Levitical priesthood was excelled by the priesthood of Christ. For the giving of a tenth declared, it seems, in those countries and times, him the greater who received it. That which next incited him was partly his gratitude to requite the present, partly his reverence to the person and his benediction: to his person, as a king and priest, greater therefore than Abram, who was a priest also, but not a king. And who unhired will be so hardy as to say, that Abram at any other time ever paid him tithes, either before or after; or had then, but for this accidental meeting and obligement; or that else Melchisedec had demanded or exacted them, or took them otherwise than as the voluntary gift of Abram? But our ministers, though neither priests nor kings more than any other Christian, greater in their own esteem than Abraham and all his seed, for the verbal labor of a seventh day's preachment, not bringing, like Melchisedec, bread or wine at their own cost, would not take only at the willing hand of liberality or gratitude, but require and exact as due, the tenth, not of spoils, but of our whole estates and labors; nor once, but yearly. We then it seems, by the example of Abram, must pay tithes to these Melchisedecs: but what if the person of Abram can either no way represent us, or will oblige the ministers to pay tithes no less than other men? Abram had not only a priest in his loins, but was himself a priest, and gave tithes to Melchisedec either as grandfather of Levi, or as father of the faithful. If as grandfather (though he understood it not) of Levi, he obliged not us, but Levi only, the inferior priest, by that homage (as the apostle to the Hebrews clearly enough explains) to acknowledge the greater. And they who by Melchisedec claim from Abram as Levi's grandfather, have none to seek their tithes of but the Levites, where they can find them. If Abram, as father of the faithful, paid tithes to Melchisedec, then certainly the ministers also, if they be of that number, paid in him equally with the rest. Which may induce us to believe, that as both Abram and Melchisedec, so tithes also in that action typical and ceremonial, signified nothing else but that subjection which all the faithful, both ministers and people, owe to Christ, our high priest and king.

In any literal sense, from this example, they never will be able to extort that the people in those days paid tithes to priests, but this only, that one priest once in his life, of spoils only, and in requital partly of a liberal present, partly of a benediction, gave voluntary tithes, not to a greater priest than himself, as far as Abram could then understand, but rather to a priest and king joined in one person. They will reply, perhaps, that if one priest paid tithes to another, it must needs be understood that the people did no less to the priest. But I shall easily remove that necessity, by remembering them that in those days was no priest, but the father, or the first-born of each family; and by

consequence no people to pay him tithes, but his own children and servants, who had not wherewithal to pay him, but of his own. Yet grant that the people then paid tithes, there will not yet be the like reason to enjoin us; they being then under ceremonies, a mere laity, we now under Christ, a royal priesthood, 1 Pet. ii. 9, as we are coheirs, kings and priests with him, a priest for ever after the order, or manner, of Melchisedec. As therefore Abram paid tithes to Melchisedec because Levi was in him, so we ought to pay none because the true Melchisedec is in us, and we in him, who can pay to none greater, and hath freed us, by our union with himself, from all compulsive tributes and taxes in his church. Neither doth the collateral place, Heb. vii., make other use of this story than to prove Christ, personated by Melchisedec, a greater priest than Aaron: ver. 4, "Now consider how great this man was," &c.; and proves not in the least manner that tithes be of any right to ministers, but the contrary: first, the Levites had "a commandment to take tithes of the people according to the law," that is, of their brethren, though they come out of the loins of Abraham, ver. 5. The commandment then was, it seems, to take tithes of the Jews only, and according to the law. That law changing of necessity with the priesthood, no other sort of ministers, as they must needs be another sort under another priesthood, can receive that tribute of tithes which fell with that law, unless renewed by another express command, and according to another law: no such law is extant. Next, Melchisedec not as a minister, but as Christ himself in person, blessed Abraham, who "had the promises," ver. 6, and in him blessed all, both ministers and people, both of the law and gospel: that blessing declared him greater and better than whom he blessed, ver. 7, receiving tithes from them all, not as a maintenance, which Melchisedec needed not, but as a sign of homage and subjection to their king and priest; whereas ministers bear not the person of Christ in his priesthood or kingship, bless not as he blesses, are not by their blessing greater than Abraham, and all the faithful with themselves included in him; cannot both give and take tithes in Abram, cannot claim to themselves that sign of our allegiance due only to our eternal King and Priest; cannot therefore derive tithes from Melchisedec. Lastly, the eighth verse hath thus; "Here men that die receive tithes: there he received them, of whom it is witnessed that he liveth." Which words intimate, that as he offered himself once for us, so he received once of us in Abraham, and in that place the typical acknowledgment of our redemption: which had it been a perpetual annuity to Christ, by him claimed as his due, Levi must have paid it yearly as well as then, ver. 9; and our ministers ought still, to some Melchisedec or other, as well now as they did in Abraham. But that Christ never claimed any such tenth as his annual due, much less resigned it to the ministers, his so officious receivers, without express commission or assignment, will be yet clearer as we proceed. Thus much may at length assure us, that this example of Abram and Melchisedec, though I see of late they build most upon it, can so little be the ground of any law to us, that it will not so much avail them as to the authority of an example. Of like impertinence is that example of Jacob, Gen. xxviii. 22, who of his free choice, not enjoined by any law, vowed the tenth of all that God should give him; which for aught appears to the contrary, he vowed as a thing no less indifferent before his vow, than the foregoing part thereof: that the stone, which he had set there for a pillar, should be God's house. And to whom vowed he this tenth but to God? Not to any priest, for we read of none to him greater than himself: and to God, no doubt but he paid what he vowed, both in the building of that Bethel, with other altars elsewhere, and the expense of his continual sacrifices, which none but he had right to offer. However, therefore, he paid his tenth, it could in no likelihood, unless by such an occasion as befell his grandfather, be to any priest. But, say they, "All the tithe of the land, whether of the seed of the land, or of the fruit of the tree, is the Lord's, holy unto the Lord," Lev. xxvii. 30. And this before it was given to the Levites; therefore since they ceased. No question; for "the whole earth is the Lord's, and the fulness thereof," Psal. xxiv. 1; and the light of nature shows us no less: but that the tenth is his more than the rest, how know I, but as he so declares it? He declares it so here of the land of Canaan only, as by all circumstance appears, and passes, by deed of gift, this tenth to the Levite; yet so as offered to him first a heave-offering, and consecrated on his altar, Numb. xviii., all which I had as little known, but by that evidence. The Levites are ceased, the gift returns to the giver. How then can we know that he hath given it to any other? Or how can these men presume to take it unoffered first to God, unconsecrated, without another clear and express donation, whereof they show no evidence or writing? Besides, he hath now alienated that holy land: who can warrantably affirm, that he hath since hallowed the tenth of this land, which none but God hath power to do or can warrant? Their last proof they cite out of the gospel, which makes as little for them, Matt. xxiii. 23, where our Saviour, denouncing woe to the scribes and pharisees, who paid tithes so exactly, and omitted weightier matters, tells them, that these they ought to have done, that is, to have paid tithes. For our Saviour spake then to those who observed the law of Moses, which was yet not fully abrogated, till the destruction of the temple. And by the way here we may observe, out of their own proof, that the scribes and pharisees, though then chief teachers of the people, such at least as were not Levites, did not take tithes, but paid them: so much less covetous were the scribes and pharisees in those worse times than ours at this day. This is so apparent to the reformed divines of other countries, that when any one of ours hath attempted in Latin to maintain this argument of tithes, though a man would think they might suffer him without opposition, in a point equally tending to the advantage of all ministers, yet they forbear not to oppose him, as in a doctrine not fit to pass unopposed under the gospel. Which shows the modesty, the contentedness of those foreign pastors, with the maintenance given them, their sincerity also in the truth, though less gainful, and the avarice of ours; who through the love of their old papistical ties, consider not the weak arguments or rather conjectures and surmises, which they bring to defend them. On the other side, although it be sufficient to have proved in general the abolishing of tithes, as part of the judaical or ceremonial law, which is abolished all, as well that before as that after Moses; yet I shall further prove them abrogated by an express ordinance of the gospel, founded not on any type, or that municipal law of Moses, but on moral and general equity, given us instead: 1 Cor. ix. 13, 14, "Know ye not, that they who minister about holy things, live of the things of the temple; and they which wait at the altar, are partakers with the altar? So also the Lord hath ordained, that they who preach the gospel, should live of the gospel." He saith not, should live on things which were of the temple, or of the altar, of which were tithes, for that had given them a clear title; but, abrogating that former law of Moses, which determined what and how much, by a later ordinance of Christ, which leaves the what and how much indefinite and free, so it be sufficient to live on, he saith, "The Lord hath so ordained, that they who preach the gospel, should live of the gospel;" which hath neither temple, altar, nor sacrifice: Heb. vii. 13, "For he of whom these things are spoken, pertaineth to another tribe, of which no man gave attendance at the altar:" his ministers therefore cannot thence have tithes. And where the Lord hath so ordained, we may find easily in more than one evangelist: Luke x. 7, 8, "In the same house remain, eating and drinking such things as they give: for the laborer is worthy of his hire, &c. And into whatsoever city you enter, and they receive you, eat such things as are set before you." To which ordinance of Christ it may seem likeliest, that the apostle refers us both here, and 1 Tim. v. 18, where he cites this as the saying of our Saviour, that "the laborer is worthy of his hire." And both by this place of Luke, and that of Matt. x. 9, 10, 11, it evidently appears, that our Saviour ordained no certain maintenance for his apostles or ministers, publicly or privately, in house or city received, but that, whatever it were, which might suffice to live on: and this not commanded or proportioned by Abram or by Moses, whom he might easily have here cited, as his manner was, but declared only by a rule of common equity, which proportions the hire as well to the ability of him who gives, as to the labor of him who receives, and recommends him only as worthy, not invests him with a legal right. And mark whereon he grounds this his ordinance; not on a perpetual right

of tithes from Melchisedec, as hirelings pretend, which he never claimed, either for himself, or for his ministers, but on the plain and common equity of rewarding the laborer; worthy sometimes of single, sometimes of double honor, not proportionable by tithes. And the apostle in this forecited chapter to the Corinthians, ver. 11, affirms it to be no great recompence, if carnal things be reaped for spiritual sown; but to mention tithes, neglects here the fittest occasion that could be offered him, and leaves the rest free and undetermined. Certainly if Christ or his apostles had approved of tithes, they would have, either by writing or tradition, recommended them to the church; and that soon would have appeared in the practice of those primitive and the next ages. But for the first three hundred years and more, in all the ecclesiastical story, I find no such doctrine or example: though error by that time had brought back again priests, altars, and oblations; and in many other points of religion had miserably judaized the church. So that the defenders of tithes, after a long pomp, and tedious preparation out of heathen authors, telling us that tithes were paid to Hercules and Apollo, which perhaps was imtated from the Jews, and as it were bespeaking our expectation, that they will abound much more with authorities out of Christian story, have nothing of general approbation to begin with from the first three or four ages, but that which abundantly serves to the confutation of their tithes; while they confess that churchmen in those ages lived merely upon freewill-offering. Neither can they say, that tithes were not then paid for want of a civil magistrate to ordain them, for Christians had then also lands, and might give out of them what they pleased; and yet of tithes then given we find no mention. And the first Christian emperors, who did all things as bishops advised them, supplied what was wanting to the clergy not out of tithes, which were never motioned, but out of their own imperial revenues; as is manifest in Eusebius, Theodore, and Sozomen, from Constantine to Arcadius. Hence those ancientest reformed churches of the Waldenses, if they rather continued not pure since the apostles, denied that tithes were to be given, or that they were ever given in the primitive church, as appears by an ancient tractate inserted in the Bohemian history. Thus far hath the church been always, whether in her prime or in her ancientest reformation, from the approving of tithes: nor without reason; for they might easily perceive that tithes were fitted to the Jews only, a national church of many incomplete synagogues, uniting the accomplishment of divine worship in one temple; and the Levites there had their tithes paid where they did their bodily work; to which a particular tribe was set apart by divine appointment, not by the people's election: but the Christian church is universal; not tied to nation, diocese, or parish, but consisting of many particular churches complete in themselves, gathered not by compulsion, or the accident of dwelling nigh together, but by free consent, choosing both their particular church and their church officers. Whereas if tithes be set up, all these Christian privileges will be disturbed and soon lost, and with them Christian liberty.

The first authority which our adversaries bring, after those fabulous apostolic canons, which they dare not insist upon, is a provincial council held at Cullen, where they voted tithes to be God's rent, in the year 356; at the same time perhaps when the three kings reigned there, and of like authority. For to what purpose do they bring these trivial testimonies, by which they might as well prove altars, candles at noon, and the greatest part of those superstitions fetched from paganism or Jewism, which the papist, inveigled by this fond argument of antiquity, retains to this day? To what purpose those decrees of I know not what bishops, to a parliament and people who have thrown out both bishops and altars, and promised all reformation by the word of God? And that altars brought tithes hither, as one corruption begot another, is evident by one of those questions which the monk Austin propounded to the pope, "concerning those things, which by offerings of the faithful came to the altar;" as Beda writes, 1. i. c. 27. If then by these testimonies we must have tithes continued, we must again have altars. Of fathers, by custom so called, they quote Ambrose, Augustine, and some other ceremonial doctors of the same leaven: whose assertion, without pertinent scripture, no reformed church can

admit; and what they vouch is founded on the law of Moses, with which, everywhere pitifully mistaken, they again incorporate the gospel; as did the rest also of those titular fathers, perhaps an age or two before them, by many rites and ceremonies, both Jewish and heathenish, introduced; whereby thinking to gain all, they lost all: and instead of winning Jews and pagans to be Christians, by too much condescending they turned Christians into Jews and pagans. To heap such unconvincing citations as these in religion, whereof the scripture only is our rule, argues not much learning nor judgment, but the lost labor of much unprofitable reading. And yet a late hot querist for tithes, whom ye may know, by his wits lying ever beside him in the margin, to be ever beside his wits in the text, a fierce reformer once, now rankled with a contrary heat, would send us back, very reformedly indeed, to learn reformation from Tyndarus and Rebuffus, two canonical promoters. They produce next the ancient constitutions of this land, Saxon laws, edicts of kings and their councils, from Athelstan, in the year 928, that tithes by statute were paid: and might produce from Ina, above 200 years before, that Romescot or Peter's penny was by as good statute-law paid to the pope, from 725, and almost as long continued. And who knows not that this law of tithes was enacted by those kings and barons upon the opinion they had of their divine right? as the very words import of Edward the Confessor, in the close of that law: "For so blessed Austin preached and taught;" meaning the monk, who first brought the Romish religion into England from Gregory the pope. And by the way I add, that by these laws, imitating the law of Moses, the third part of tithes only was the priest's due; the other two were appointed for the poor, and to adorn or repair churches; as the canons of Ecbert and Elfric witness. Concil. Brit. If then these laws were founded upon the opinion of divine authority, and that authority be found mistaken and erroneous, as hath been fully manifested, it follows, that these laws fall of themselves with their false foundation. But with what face or conscience can they allege Moses or these laws for tithes, as they now enjoy or exact them; whereof Moses ordains the owner, as we heard before, the stranger, the fatherless, and the widow, partakers of the Levite; and these fathers which they cite, and these though Romish rather than English laws, allotted both to priest and bishop the third part only? But these our protestant, these our new reformed English presbyterian divines, against their own cited authors, and to the shame of their pretended reformation, would engross to themselves all tithes by statute; and, supported more by their wilful obstinacy and desire of filthy lucre, than by these both insufficient and impertinent authorities, would persuade a Christian magistracy and parliament, whom we trust God hath restored for a happier reformation, to impose upon us a judaical ceremonial law, and yet from that law to be more irregular and unwarrantable, more complying with a covetous clergy, than any of those popish kings and parliaments alleged. Another shift they have to plead, that tithes may be moral as well as the sabbath, a tenth of fruits as well as a seventh of days: I answer, that the prelates who urge this argument have least reason to use it, denying morality in the sabbath, and therein better agreeing with reformed churches abroad than the rest of our divines. As therefore the seventh day is not moral, but a convenient recourse of worship in fit season, whether seventh or other number; so neither is the tenth of our goods, but only a convenient subsistence morally due to ministers. The last and lowest sort of their arguments, that men purchased not their tithe with their land, and such like pettifoggery, I omit; as refuted sufficiently by others: I omit also their violent and irreligious exactions, related no less credibly; their seizing of pots and pans from the poor, who have as good right to tithes as they; from some, the very beds; their suing and imprisoning, worse than when the canon-law was in force; worse than when those wicked sons of Eli were priests, whose manner was thus to seize their pretended priestly due by force: 1 Sam. ii. 12, &c., "Whereby men abhorred the offering of the Lord." And it may be feared, that many will as much abhor the gospel, if such violence as this be suffered in her ministers, and in that which they also pretend to be the offering of the Lord. For those sons of Belial within some limits made seizure of what they knew was their own by an undoubted law; but these, from whom there is no sanctuary, seize out of men's grounds, out of men's houses, their other goods of double, sometimes of treble value, for that which, did not covetousness and rapine blind them, they know to be not their own by the gospel which they preach. Of some more tolerable than these, thus severely God hath spoken: Isa. xlvi. 10, "They are greedy dogs; they all look to their own way, every one for his gain, from his quarter." With what anger then will he judge them who stand not looking, but, under color of a divine right, fetch by force that which is not their own, taking his name not in vain, but in violence? Not content, as Gehazi was, to make a cunning, but a constrained advantage of what their master bids them give freely, how can they but return smitten, worse than that sharking minister, with a spiritual leprosy? And yet they cry out sacrilege that men will not be gulled and baffled the tenth of their estates, by giving credit to frivolous pretences of divine right. Where did God ever clearly declare to all nations, or in all lands, (and none but fools part with their estates without clearest evidence, on bare supposals and presumptions of them who are the gainers thereby,) that he required the tenths as due to him or his Son perpetually and in all places? Where did he demand it, that we might certainly know, as in all claims of temporal right is just and reasonable? or if demanded, where did he assign it, or by what evident conveyance to ministers? Unless they can demonstrate this by more than conjectures, their title can be no better to tithes than the title of Gehazi was to those things which by abusing his master's name he rooked from Naaman. Much less where did he command that tithes should be fetched by force, where left not under the gospel, whatever his right was, to the freewill-offerings of men? Which is the greater sacrilege, to belie divine authority, to make the name of Christ accessory to violence, and robbing him of the very honor which he aimed at in bestowing freely the gospel, to commit simony and rapine, both secular and ecclesiastical; or, on the other side, not to give up the tenth of civil right and propriety to the tricks and impostures of clergymen, contrived with all the art and argument that their bellies can invent or suggest; yet so ridiculous and presuming on the people's dulness or superstition, as to think they prove the divine right of their maintenance by Abram paying tithes to Melchisedec, whenas Melchisedec in that passage rather gave maintenance to Abram; in whom all, both priests and ministers as well as laymen, paid tithes, not received them? And because I affirmed above, beginning this first part of my discourse, that God hath given to ministers of the gospel that maintenance only which is justly given them, let us see a little what hath been thought of that other maintenance besides tithes, which of all protestants our English divines either only or most apparently both require and take. Those are fees for christenings, marriages, and burials: which, though whoso will may give freely, yet being not of right, but of free gift, if they be exacted or established, they become unjust to them who are otherwise maintained; and of such evil note, that even the council of Trent, l. ii. p. 240, makes them liable to the laws against simony, who take or demand fees for the administering of any sacrament: "Che la sinodo volendo levare gli abusi introdotti," &c. And in the next page, with like severity, condemns the giving or taking for a benefice, and the celebrating of marriages, christenings, and burials, for fees exacted or demanded: nor counts it less simony to sell the ground or place of burial. And in a state-assembly at Orleans, 1561, it was decreed, "Che non si potesse essiger cosa alcuna, &c., p. 429, That nothing should be exacted for the administering of sacraments, burials, or any other spiritual function." Thus much that council, of all others the most popish, and this assembly of papists, though, by their own principles, in bondage to the clergy, were induced, either by their own reason and shame, or by the light of reformation then shining in upon them, or rather by the known canons of many councils and synods long before, to condemn of simony spiritual fees demanded. For if the minister be maintained for his whole ministry, why should he be twice paid for any part thereof? Why should he, like a servant, seek vails over and above his wages? As for christenings, either they themselves call men to baptism, or men of themselves come: if ministers invite, how ill had it become John the Baptist to demand fees for his baptizing, or Christ for his christenings? Far less becomes it these now, with a greediness lower than that of tradesmen calling passengers to their shop, and yet paid beforehand, to ask again for doing that which those their founders did freely. If men of themselves come to be baptized, they are either brought by such as already pay the minister, or come to be one of his disciples and maintainers: of whom to ask a fee as it were for entrance is a piece of paltry craft or caution, befitting none but beggarly artists. Burials and marriages are so little to be any part of their gain, that they who consider well may find them to be no part of their function. At burials their attendance they alleged on the corpse; all the guests do as much unhired. But their prayers at the grave; superstitiously required: yet if required, their last performance to the deceased of their own flock. But the funeral sermon: at their choice; or if not, an occasion offered them to preach out of season, which is one part of their office. But something must be spoken in praise: if due, their duty; if undue, their corruption: a peculiar simony of our divines in England only. But the ground is broken, and especially their unrighteous possession, the chancel. To sell that, will not only raise up in judgment the council of Trent against them, but will lose them the best champion of tithes, their zealous antiquary, Sir Henry Spelman; who, in a book written to that purpose, by many cited canons, and some even of times corruptest in the church, proves that fees exacted or demanded for sacraments, marriages, burials, and especially for interring, are wicked, accursed, simoniacal, and abominable: yet thus is the church, for all this noise of reformation, left still unreformed, by the censure of their own synods, their own favorers, a den of thieves and robbers. As for marriages, that ministers should meddle with them, as not sanctified or legitimate without their celebration, I find no ground in scripture either of precept or example. Likeliest it is (which our Selden hath well observed, l. ii, c. 28, Ux. Eb.) that in imitation of heathen priests, who were wont at nuptials to use many rites and ceremonies, and especially, judging it would be profitable, and the increase of their authority, not to be spectators only in business of such concernment to the life of man, they insinuated that marriage was not holy without their benediction, and for the better color, made it a sacrament; being of itself a civil ordinance, a household contract, a thing indifferent and free to the whole race of mankind, not as religious, but as men: best, indeed, undertaken to religious ends, and, as the apostle saith, 1 Cor. vii., "in the Lord." Yet not therefore invalid or unholy without a minister and his pretended necessary hallowing, more than any other act, enterprise, or contract of civil life, which ought all to be done also in the Lord and to his glory: all which, no less than marriage, were by the cunning of priests heretofore, as material to their profit, transacted at the altar. Our divines deny it to be a sacrament; yet retained the celebration, till prudently a late parliament recovered the civil liberty of marriage from their encroachment, and transferred the ratifying and registering thereof from the canonical shop to the proper cognizance of civil magistrates. Seeing then, that God hath given to ministers under the gospel that only which is justly given them, that is to say, a due and moderate livelihood, the hire of their labor, and that the heave-offering of tithes is abolished with the altar; yea, though not abolished, yet lawless, as they enjoy them; their Melchisedechian right also trivial and groundless, and both tithes and fees, if exacted or established, unjust and scandalous; we may hope, with them removed, to remove hirelings in some good measure, whom these tempting baits, by law especially to be recovered, allure into the church.

The next thing to be considered in the maintenance of ministers, is by whom it should be given. Wherein though the light of reason might sufficiently inform us, it will be best to consult the scripture. Gal. vi. 6, "Let him that is taught in the word, communicate to him that teacheth, in all good things:" that is to say, in all manner of gratitude, to his ability. 1 Cor. ix. 11, "If we have sown unto you spiritual things, is it a great matter if we reap your carnal things?" To whom therefore hath not been sown, from him wherefore should be reaped? 1 Tim. v. 17, "Let the elders that rule well, be counted worthy of double honor; espe-

cially they who labor in word and doctrine." By these places we see, that recompense was given either by every one in particular who had been instructed, or by them all in common, brought into the church-treasury, and distributed to the ministers according to their several labors: and that was judged either by some extraordinary person, as Timothy, who by the apostle was then left evangelist at Ephesus, 2 Tim. iv. 5, or by some to whom the church deputed that care. This is so agreeable to reason, and so clear, that any one may perceive what iniquity and violence hath prevailed since in the church, whereby it hath been so ordered, that they also shall be compelled to recompense the parochial minister, who neither chose him for their teacher, nor have received instruction from him, as being either insufficient, or not resident, or inferior to whom they follow; wherein to bar them their choice, is to violate Christian liberty. Our law books testify, that before the council of Lateran, in the year 1179, and the fifth of our Henry II., or rather before a decretal Epistle of pope Innocent the Third, about 1200, and the first of king John, "any man might have given his tithes to what spiritual person he would:" and as the Lord Coke notes on that place, Instit. part ii., that "this decretal bound not the subjects of this realm, but as it seemed just and reasonable." The pope took his reason rightly from the above-cited place, 1 Cor. ix. 11, but falsely supposed every one to be instructed by his parish priest. Whether this were then first so decreed, or rather long before, as may seem by the laws of Edgar and Canute, that tithes were to be paid, not to whom he would that paid them, but to the cathedral church or the parish priest, it imports not; since the reason which they themselves bring, built on false supposition, becomes alike infirm and absurd, that he should reap from me, who sows not to me; be the cause either his defect, or my free choice. But here it will be readily objected, What if they who are to be instructed be not able to maintain a minister, as in many villages? I answer, that the scripture shows in many places what ought to be done herein. First, I offer it to the reason of any man, whether he think the knowledge of Christian religion harder than any other art or science to attain. I suppose he will grant that it is far easier, both of itself, and in regard of God's assisting Spirit, not particularly promised us to the attainment of any other knowledge, but of this only: since it was preached as well to the shepherds of Bethlehem by angels, as to the Eastern wise men by that star: and our Saviour declares himself anointed to preach the gospel to the poor, Luke iv. 18; then surely to their capacity. They who after him first taught it, were otherwise unlearned men: they who before Husse and Luther first reformed it, were for the meanness of their condition called, "the poor men of Lyons:" and in Flanders at this day, "les Gueus," which is to say, beggars. Therefore are the scriptures translated into every vulgar tongue, as being held in main matters of belief and salvation, plain and easy to the poorest: and such no less than their teachers have the spirit to guide them in all truth, John xiv. 26, and xvi. 13. Hence we may conclude, if men be not all their lifetime under a teacher to learn logic, natural philosophy, ethics, or mathematics, which are more difficult, that certainly it is not necessary to the attainment of Christian knowledge, that men should sit all their life long at the feet of a pulpited divine; while he, a lollard indeed over his elbow cushion, in almost the seventh part of forty or fifty years teaches them scarce half the principles of religion; and his sheep ofttimes sit the while to as little purpose of benefiting, as the sheep in their pews at Smithfield; and for the most part by some simony or other bought and sold like them: or if this comparison be too low, like those women, 1 Tim. iii. 7, "Ever learning and never attaining;" yet not so much through their own fault, as through the unskilful and immethodical teaching of their pastor, teaching here and there at random out of this or that text, as his ease or fancy, and ofttimes as his stealth, guides him. Seeing then that Christian religion may be so easily attained, and by meanest capacities, it cannot be much difficult to find ways, both how the poor, yea, all men, may be soon taught what is to be known of Christianity, and they who teach them, recompensed. First, if ministers of their own accord, who pretend that they are called and sent to preach the gospel, those especially

who have no particular flock, would imitate our Saviour and his disciples, who went preaching through the villages, not only through the cities, Matt. ix. 35, Mark vi. 6, Luke xiii. 22, Acts viii. 25, and there preached to the poor as well as to the rich, looking for no recompense but in heaven: John iv. 35, 36, "Look on the fields, for they are white already to harvest: and he that reapeth, receiveth wages, and gathereth fruit unto life eternal." This was their wages. But they will soon reply, We ourselves have not wherewithal; who shall bear the charges of our journey? To whom it may as soon be answered, that in likelihood they are not poorer than they who did thus; and if they have not the same faith which those disciples had to trust in God and the promise of Christ for their maintenance as they did, and yet intrude into the ministry without any livelihood of their own, they cast themselves into a miserable hazard or temptation, and ofttimes into a more miserable necessity, either to starve, or to please their paymasters rather than God; and give men just cause to suspect, that they came neither called nor sent from above to preach the word, but from below, by the instinct of their own hunger, to feed upon the church. Yet grant it needful to allow them both the charges of their journey and the hire of their labor, it will belong next to the charity of richer congregations, where most commonly they abound with teachers, to send some of their number to the villages round, as the apostles from Jerusalem sent Peter and John to the city and villages of Samaria, Acts viii. 14, 25; or as the church at Jerusalem sent Barnabas to Antioch, chap. xi. 22, and other churches joining sent Luke to travel with Paul, 2 Cor. viii. 19; though whether they had their charges borne by the church or no, it be not recorded. If it be objected, that this itinerary preaching will not serve to plant the gospel in those places, unless they who are sent abide there some competent time; I answer, that if they stay there a year or two, which was the longest time usually stayed by the apostles in one place, it may suffice to teach them who will attend and learn all the points of religion necessary to salvation; then sorting them into several congregations of a moderate number, out of the ablest and zealous-est among them to create elders, who, exercising and requiring from themselves what they have learned, (for no learning is retained without constant exercise and methodical repetition,) may teach and govern the rest: and so exhorted to continue faithful and steadfast, they may securely be committed to the providence of God and the guidance of his Holy Spirit, till God may offer some opportunity to visit them again, and to confirm them: which when they have done, they have done as much as the apostles were wont to do in propagating the gospel. Acts xiv. 23, "And when they had ordained them elders in every church, and had prayed with fasting, they commended them to the Lord, on whom they believed." And in the same chapter, ver. 21, 22, "When they had preached the gospel to that city, and had taught many, they returned again to Lystra, and to Iconium and Antioch, confirming the souls of the disciples, and exhorting them to continue in the faith." And chap. xv. 36, "Let us go again, and visit our brethren." And ver. 41, "He went through Syria and Cilicia, confirming the churches." To these I might add other helps, which we enjoy now, to make more easy the attainment of Christian religion by the meanest: the entire scripture translated into English with plenty of notes; and somewhere or other, I trust, may be found some wholesome body of divinity, as they call it, without school-terms and metaphysical notions, which have obscured rather than explained our religion, and made it seem difficult without cause. Thus taught once for all, and thus now and then visited and confirmed, in the most destitute and poorest places of the land, under the government of their own elders performing all ministerial offices among them, they may be trusted to meet and edify one another, whether in church or chapel, or, to save them the trudging of many miles thither, nearer home, though in a house or barn. For notwithstanding the gaudy superstition of some devoted still ignorantly to temples, we may be well assured, that he who disdained not to be laid in a manger, disdains not to be preached in a barn; and that by such meetings as these, being indeed most apostolical and primitive, they will in a short time advance more in Christian knowledge and reformation of life, than by the many

years' preaching of such incumbent, I may say, such an incubus ofttimes, as will be meanly hired to abide long in those places. They have this left perhaps to object further; that to send thus, and to maintain, though but for a year or two, ministers and teachers in several places, would prove chargeable to the churches, though in towns and cities round about. To whom again I answer, that it was not thought so by them who first thus propagated the gospel, though but few in number to us, and much less able to sustain the expense. Yet this expense would be much less than to hire incumbents, rather incumbrances, for lifetime; and a great means (which is the subject of this discourse) to diminish hirelings. But be the expense less or more, if it be found burdensome to the churches, they have in this land an easy remedy in their recourse to the civil magistrate; who hath in his hands the disposal of no small revenues, left perhaps anciently to superstitious, but meant undoubtedly to good and best uses; and therefore, once made public, appliable by the present magistrate to such uses as the church, or solid reason from whomsoever, shall convince him to think best. And those uses may be, no doubt, much rather than as glebes and argumentations are now bestowed, to grant such requests as these of the churches; or to erect in greater number, all over the land, schools, and competent libraries to those schools, where languages and arts may be taught free together, without the needless, unprofitable, and inconvenient removing to another place. So all the land would be soon better civilized, and they who are taught freely at the public cost might have their education given them on this condition, that therewith content, they should not gad for preferment out of their own country, but continue there thankful for what they received freely, bestowing it as freely on their country, without soaring above the meanness wherein they were born. But how they shall live when they are thus bred and dismissed, will be still the sluggish objection. To which is answered, that those public foundations may be so instituted, as the youth therein may be at once brought up to a competence of learning and to an honest trade; and the hours of teaching so ordered, as their study may be no hindrance to their labor or other calling. This was the breeding of St. Paul, though born of no mean parents, a free citizen of the Roman empire: so little did his trade debase him, that it rather enabled him to use that magnanimity of preaching the gospel through Asia and Europe at his own charges. Thus those preachers among the poor Waldenses, the ancient stock of our reformation, without these helps which I 10 speak of, bred up themselves in trades, and especially in physic and surgery, as well as in the study of scripture, (which is the only true theology,) that they might be no burden to the church; and by the example of Christ, might cure both soul and body; through industry joining that to their ministry, which he joined to his by gift of the Spirit. Thus relates Peter Gilles in his History of the Waldenses in Piemont. But our ministers 20 think scorn to use a trade, and count it the reproach of this age, that tradesmen preach the gospel. It were to be wished they were all tradesmen; they would not then so many of them, for want of another trade, make a trade of their preaching: and yet they clamor that tradesmen preach; and yet they preach, while they themselves are the worst tradesmen of all. As for church endowments and possessions, I meet with none considerable 30 before Constantine, but the houses and gardens where they met, and their places of burial; and I persuade me, that from them the ancient Waldenses, whom deservedly I cite so often, held, "That to endow churches is an evil thing; and that the church then fell off and turned whore, sitting on that beast in the Revelation, when under pope Sylvester she received those temporal donations." So the fore-cited tractate of their 40 doctrine testifies. This also their own traditions of that heavenly voice witnessed, and some of the ancient fathers then living foresaw and deplored. And, indeed, how could these endowments thrive better with the church, being unjustly taken by those emperors, without suffrage of the people, out of the tributes and public lands of each city, whereby the people became liable to be oppressed with other taxes. Being therefore 50 given for the most part by kings and other public persons, and so likeliest out of the public, and if without the people's consent,

unjustly, however to public ends of much concernment, to the good or evil of a commonwealth, and in that regard made public though given by private persons, or, which is worse, given, as the clergy then persuaded men, for their souls' health, a pious gift; but as the truth was, ofttimes a bribe to God or to Christ for absolution, as they were then taught, from murders, adulteries, and other heinous crimes; what shall be found heretofore given by kings or princes out of the public, may justly by the magistrate be recalled and reappropriated to the civil revenue: what by private or public persons out of their own, the price of blood or lust, or to some such purgatorious and superstitious uses, not only may, but ought to be taken off from Christ, as a foul dishonor laid upon him, or not impiously given, nor in particular to any one, but in general to the church's good, may be converted to that use, which shall be judged tending more directly to that general end. Thus did the princes and cities of Germany in the first reformation; and defended their so doing by many reasons, which are set down at large in Sleidan, lib. vi. anno 1526, and lib. xi. anno 1537, and lib. xiii. anno 1540. But that the magistrate either out of that church revenue which remains yet in his hand, or establishing any other maintenance instead of tithe, should take into his own power the stipendiary maintenance of church-ministers, or compel it by law, can stand neither with the people's right, nor with Christian liberty, but would suspend the church wholly upon the state, and turn her ministers into state pensioners. And for the magistrate in person of a nursing father to make the church his mere ward, as always in minority, the church to whom he ought as a magistrate, Isa. xlix. 23, "to bow down with his face toward the earth, and lick up the dust of her feet;" her to subject to his political drifts or conceived opinions, by mastering her revenue; and so by his examinant committees to circumscribe her free election of ministers, is neither just nor pious; no honor done to the church, but a plain dishonor: and upon her whose only head is in heaven, yea, upon him, who is her only head, sets another in effect, and which is most monstrous, a human on a heavenly, a carnal on a spiritual, a political head on an ecclesiastical body; which at length, by such heterogeneal, such incestuous conjunction, transforms her ofttimes into a beast of many heads and many horns. For if the church be of all societies the holiest on earth, and so to be reverenced by the magistrate; not to trust her with her own belief and integrity, and therefore not with the keeping, at least with the disposing, of what revenue should be found justly and lawfully her own, is to count the church not a holy congregation, but a pack of giddy or dishonest persons, to be ruled by civil power in sacred affairs. But to proceed further in the truth yet more freely, seeing the Christian church is not national, but consisting of many particular congregations, subject to many changes, as well through civil accidents, as through schism and various opinions, not to be decided by any outward judge, being matters of conscience, whereby these pretended church revenues, as they have been ever, so are like to continue endless matter of dissension, both between the church and magistrate, and the churches among themselves, there will be found no better remedy to these evils, otherwise incurable, than by the incorruptest council of those Waldenses, our first reformers, to remove them as a pest, an apple of discord in the church, (for what else can be the effect of riches, and the snare of money in religion?) and to convert them to those more profitable uses above expressed, or other such as shall be judged most necessary; considering that the church of Christ was founded in poverty rather than in revenues, stood purest and prospered best without them, received them unlawfully from them who both erroneously and unjustly, sometimes impiously, gave them, and so justly was ensnared and corrupted by them. And lest it be thought that, these revenues withdrawn and better employed, the magistrate ought instead to settle by statute some maintenance of ministers, let this be considered first, that it concerns every man's conscience to what religion he contributes; and that the civil magistrate is entrusted with civil rights only, not with conscience, which can have no deputy or representer of itself, but one of the same mind: next, that what each man gives to the minister, he gives either as to God, or as to his teacher: if as to God, no civil power can

justly consecrate to religious uses any part either of civil revenue, which is the people's, and must save them from other taxes, or of any man's propriety, but God by special command, as he did by Moses, or the owner himself by voluntary intention and the persuasion of his giving it to God. Forced consecrations out of another man's estate are no better than forced vows, hateful to God, "who loves a cheerful giver;" but much more hateful, wrung out of men's purses to maintain a disapproved ministry against their conscience; however unholy, infamous, and dishonorable to his ministers and the free gospel, maintained in such unworthy manner as by violence and extortion. If he give it as to his teacher, what justice or equity compels him to pay for learning that religion which leaves freely to his choice whether he will learn it or no, whether of this teacher or another, and especially to pay for what he never learned, or approves not; whereby, besides the wound of his conscience, he becomes the less able to recompense his true teacher? Thus far hath been inquired by whom church-ministers ought to be maintained, and hath been proved most natural, most equal and agreeable with scripture, to be by them who receive their teaching; and by whom, if they be unable. Which ways well observed can discourage none but hirelings, and will much lessen their number in the church.

It remains lastly to consider, in what manner God hath ordained that recompense be given to ministers of the gospel; and by all scripture it will appear, that he hath given it them not by civil law and freehold, as they claim, but by the benevolence and free gratitude of such as receive them: Luke x. 7, 8, "Eating and drinking such things as they give you. If they receive you, eat such things as are set before you." Matt. x. 7, 8, "As ye go, preach, saying, The kingdom of God is at hand, &c. Freely ye have received, freely give." If God have ordained ministers to preach freely, whether they receive recompense or not, then certainly he hath forbid both them to compel it, and others to compel it for them. But freely given, he accounts it as given to himself: Phil. iv. 16, 17, 18, "Ye sent once and again to my necessity: not because I desire a gift; but I desire fruit, that may abound to your account. Having received of Epaphroditus the things which were sent from you, an odor of sweet smell, a sacrifice acceptable, well-pleasing to God;" which cannot be from force or unwillingness. The same is said of alms: Heb. xiii. 16, "To do good and to communicate, forget not; for with such sacrifices God is well pleased." Whence the primitive church thought it no shame to receive all their maintenance as the alms of their auditors. Which they who defend tithes, as if it made for their cause, whenas it utterly confutes them, omit not to set down at large; proving to our hands out of Origen, Tertullian, Cyprian, and others, that the clergy lived at first upon the mere benevolence of their hearers; who gave what they gave, not to the clergy, but to the church; out of which the clergy had their portions given them in baskets, and were thence called sportularii, basket-clerks: that their portion was a very mean allowance, only for a bare livelihood; according to those precepts of our Saviour, Matt. x. 7, &c., the rest was distributed to the poor. They cite also out of Prosper, the disciple of St. Austin, that such of the clergy as had means of their own might not without sin partake of church maintenance; not receiving thereby food which they abound with, but feeding on the sins of other men: that the Holy Ghost saith of such clergymen, they eat the sins of my people; and that a council at Antioch, in the year 340, suffered not either priest or bishop to live on church maintenance without necessity. Thus far tithers themselves have contributed to their own confutation, by confessing that the church lived primitively on alms. And I add, that about the year 359, Constantius the emperor having summoned a general council of bishops to Ariminium in Italy, and provided for their subsistence there, the British and French bishops judging it not decent to live on the public, chose rather to be at their own charges. Three only out of Britain, constrained through want, yet refusing offered assistance from the rest, accepted the emperor's provision; judging it more convenient to subsist by public than by private sustenance. Whence we may conclude, that bishops then in this island had their livelihood only from benevolence; in which regard this relater, Sulpitius

Severus, a good author of the same time, highly praises them. And the Waldenses, our first reformers, both from the scripture and these primitive examples, maintained those among them who bore the office of ministers by alms only. Take their very words from the history written of them in French, part iii. lib. ii. chap. 2: "La nouriture et ce de quoy nous sommes couverts, &c. Our food and clothing is sufficiently administered and given to us by way of gratuity and alms, by the good people whom we teach." If then by alms and benevolence, not by legal force, not by tenure of freehold or copyhold: for alms, though just, cannot be compelled: and benevolence forced is malevolence rather, violent and inconsistent with the gospel; and declares him no true minister thereof, but a rapacious hireling rather, who by force receiving it, eats the bread of violence and exaction, no holy or just livelihood, no, not civilly counted honest; much less beseeming such a spiritual ministry. But, say they, our maintenance is our due, tithes the right of Christ, unseparable from the priest, no where repealed; if then, not otherwise to be had, by law to be recovered: for though Paul were pleased to forego his due, and not to use his power, 1 Cor. ix. 12, yet he had a power, ver. 4, and bound not others. I answer first, because I see them still so loath to unlearn their decimal arithmetic, and still grasp their tithes as inseparable from a priest, that ministers of the gospel are not priests; and therefore separated from tithes by their own exclusion, being neither called priests in the New Testament, nor of any order known in scripture: not of Melchisedec, proper to Christ only, not of Aaron, as they themselves will confess; and the third priesthood only remaining, is common to all the faithful. But they are ministers of our high priest. True, but not of his priesthood, as the Levites were to Aaron; for he performs that whole office himself incommunicably. Yet tithes remain, say they, still unreleased, the due of Christ; and to whom payable, but to his ministers? I say again, that no man can so understand them, unless Christ in some place or other so claim them. That example of Abram argues nothing but his voluntary act; honor once only done, but on what consideration, whether to a priest or to a king, whether due the honor, arbitrary that kind of honor or not, will after all contending be left still in mere conjecture: which must not be permitted in the claim of such a needy and subtle spiritual corporation, pretending by divine right to the tenth of all other men's estates; nor can it be allowed by wise men or the verdict of common law. And the tenth part, though once declared holy, is declared now to be no holier than the other nine, by that command to Peter, Acts x. 15, 28, whereby all distinction of holy and unholy is removed from all things. Tithes therefore, though claimed, and holy under the law, yet are now released and quitted both by that command to Peter, and by this to all ministers, above-cited, Luke x.: "Eating and drinking such things as they give you:" made holy now by their free gift only. And therefore St. Paul, 1 Cor. ix. 4, asserts his power indeed; but of what? not of tithes, but "to eat and drink such things as are given" in reference to this command; which he calls not holy things, or things of the gospel, as if the gospel had any consecrated things in answer to things of the temple, ver. 13; but he calls them "your carnal things," ver. 11, without changing their property. And what power had he? Not the power of force, but of conscience only, whereby he might lawfully and without scruple live on the gospel; receiving what was given him, as the recompense of his labor. For if Christ the Master hath professed his kingdom to be not of this world, it suits not with that profession, either in him or his ministers, to claim temporal right from spiritual respects. He who refused to be the divider of an inheritance between two brethren, cannot approve his ministers, by pretended right from him, to be dividers of tenths and freeholds out of other men's possessions, making thereby the gospel but a cloak of carnal interest, and, to the contradiction of their master, turning his heavenly kingdom into a kingdom of this world, a kingdom of force and rapine; to whom it will be one day thundered more terribly than to Gehazi, for thus dishonoring a far greater master and his gospel; "Is this a time to receive money, and to receive garments, and oliveyards, and vineyards, and sheep, and oxen?" The leprosy of Naaman linked with that apostolic curse of perishing imprecated on Simon Magus, may be feared, will "cleave to such and to their seed for ever." So that when all is done, and belly hath used in vain all her cunning shifts, I doubt not but all true ministers, considering the demonstration of what hath been here proved, will be wise, and think it much more tolerable to hear, that no maintenance of ministers, whether tithes or any other, can be settled by statute, but must be given by them who receive instruction; and freely given, as God hath ordained. And indeed what can be a more honorable maintenance to them than such, whether alms or willing oblations, as these; which being accounted both alike as given to God, the only acceptable sacrifices now remaining, must needs represent him who receives them much in the care of God, and nearly related to him, when not by worldly force and constraint, but with religious awe and reverence, what is given to God, is given to him; and what to him, accounted as given to God. This would be well enough, say they; but how many will so give? I answer, As many, doubtless, as shall be well taught, as many as God shall so move. Why are ye so distrustful, both of your own doctrine and of God's promises, fulfilled in the experience of those disciples first sent? Luke xxii. 35, "When I sent you without purse, and scrip, and shoes, lacked ye anything? And they said, Nothing." How then came ours, or who sent them thus destitute, thus poor and empty both of purse and faith? who style themselves ambassadors of Jesus Christ, and seem to be his tithe-gatherers, though an office of their own setting up to his dishonor, his exactors, his publicans rather, not trusting that he will maintain them in their embassy, unless they bind him to his promise by a statute-law, that we shall maintain them. Lay down for shame that magnific title, while ye seek maintenance from the people: it is not the manner of ambassadors to ask maintenance of them to whom they are sent. But he who is Lord of all things, hath so ordained. Trust him then; he doubtless will command the people to make good his promises of maintenance more honorably unasked, unraked for. This they know, this they preach, yet believe not: but think it as impossible, without a statute-law, to live of the gospel, as if by those words they were bid go eat their Bibles, as Ezekiel and John did their books; and such doctrines as these are as bitter to their bellies; but will serve so much the better to discover hirelings, who can have nothing, though but in appearance, just and solid to answer for themselves against what hath been here spoken, unless perhaps this one remaining pretence, which we shall quickly see to be either false or uningenuous.

They pretend that their education, either at school or university, hath been very chargeable, and therefore ought to be repaired in future by a plentiful maintenance: whenas it is well known, that the better half of them, (and ofttimes poor and pitiful boys, of no merit or promising hopes that might entitle them to the public provision, but their poverty and the unjust favor of friends,) have had the most of their breeding, both at school and university, by scholarships, exhibitions, and fellowships, at the public cost, which might engage them the rather to give freely, as they have freely received. Or if they have missed of these helps at the latter place, they have after two or three years left the course of their studies there, if they ever well began them, and undertaken, though furnished with little else but ignorance, boldness, and ambition, if with no worse vices, a chaplainship in some gentleman's house, to the frequent embasing of his sons with illiterate and narrow principles. Or if they have lived there upon their own, who knows not that seven years' charge of living there, to them who fly not from the government of their parents to the licence of a university, but come seriously to study, is no more than may be well defrayed and reimbursed by one year's revenue of an ordinary good benefice? If they had then means of breeding from their parents, it is likely they have more now; and if they have, it needs must be mechanic and uningenuous in them to bring a bill of charges for the learning of those liberal arts and sciences, which they have learned (if they have indeed learned them, as they seldom have) to their own benefit and accomplishment. But they will say, we had betaken us to some other trade or profession, had we not expected to find a better livelihood by the ministry. This is that which I looked for, to discover them openly neither true lovers of learning, and so very seldom guilty of it,

nor true ministers of the gospel. So long ago out of date is that old true saying, 1 Tim. iii. 1, "If a man desire a bishopric, he desires a good work:" for now commonly he who desires to be a minister, looks not at the work, but at the wages; and by that lure or lowbell, may be tolled from parish to parish all the town over. But what can be plainer simony, than thus to be at charges beforehand, to no other end than to make their ministry doubly or trebly beneficial? To whom it might be said, as justly as to that Simon, "Thy money perish with thee, because thou hast thought that the gift of God may be purchased with money: thou hast neither part nor lot in this matter." Next it is a fond error, though too much believed among us to think that the university makes a minister of the gospel; what it may conduce to other arts and sciences, I dispute not now: but that which makes fit a minister, the scripture can best inform us to be only from above, whence also we are bid to seek them: Matt. ix. 38, "Pray ye therefore to the Lord of the harvest, that he will send forth laborers into his harvest." Acts xx. 28, "The flock, over which the Holy Ghost hath made you overseers." Rom. x. 15, "How shall they preach, unless they be sent?" By whom sent? by the university, or the magistrate, or their belly? No, surely; but sent from God only, and that God who is not their belly. And whether he be sent from God, or from Simon Magus, the inward sense of his calling and spiritual ability will sufficiently tell him; and that strong obligation felt within him, which was felt by the apostle, will often express from him the same words: 1 Cor. ix. 16, "Necessity is laid upon me, yea, woe is me if I preach not the gospel." Not a beggarly necessity, and the woe feared otherwise of perpetual want, but such a necessity as made him willing to preach the gospel gratis, and to embrace poverty, rather than as a woe to fear it. 1 Cor. xii. 28, "God hath set some in the church, first apostles," &c. Ephes. iv. 11, &c. "He gave some apostles, &c. For the perfecting of the saints, for the work of the ministry, for the edifying of the body of Christ, till we all come to the unity of the faith." Whereby we may know, that as he made them at the first, so he makes them still, and to the world's end. 2 Cor. iii. 6, "Who hath also made us fit or able ministers of the New Testament." 1 Tim. iv. 14, "The gift that is in thee, which was given thee by prophecy, and the laying on of the hands of the presbytery." These are all the means, which we read of, required in scripture to the making of a minister. All this is granted, you will say; but yet that it is also requisite he should be trained in other learning: which can be nowhere better had than at universities. I answer, that what learning, either human or divine, can be necessary to a minister, may as easily and less chargeably be had in any private house. How deficient else, and to how little purpose, are all those piles of sermons, notes and comments on all parts of the Bible, bodies and marrows of divinity, besides all other sciences, in our English tongue; many of the same books which in Latin they read at the university? And the small necessity of going thither to learn divinity I prove first from the most part of themselves, who seldom continue there till they have well got through logic, their first rudiments; though, to say truth, logic also may much better be wanting in disputes of divinity, than in the subtle debates of lawyers, and statesmen, who yet seldom or never deal with syllogisms. And those theological disputations there held by professors and graduates are such, as tend least of all to the edification or capacity of the people, but rather perplex and leaven pure doctrine with scholastical trash, than enable any minister to the better preaching of the gospel. Whence we may also compute, since they come to reckonings, the charges of his needful library; which, though some shame not to value at £600, may be competently furnished for £60. If any man for his own curiosity or delight be in books further expensive, that is not to be reckoned as necessary to his ministerial, either breeding or function. But papists and other adversaries cannot be confuted without fathers and councils, immense volumes, and of vast charges. I will show them therefore a shorter and a better way of confutation: Tit. i. 9, "Holding fast the faithful word, as he hath been taught, that he may be able by sound doctrine, both to exhort and to convince gainsayers:" who are confuted as soon as heard, bringing that which is either not in scripture, or against it. To pursue them further through the obscure and entangled wood of antiquity, fathers and councils fighting one against another, is needless, endless, not requisite in a minister, and refused by the first reformers of our religion. And yet we may be confident, if these things be thought needful, let the state but erect in public good store of libraries, and there will not want men in the church, who of their own inclinations will become able in this kind against papist or any other adversary. I have thus at large examined the usual pretences of hirelings, colored over most commonly with the cause of learning and universities; as if with divines learning stood and fell, wherein for the most part their pittance is so small; and, to speak freely, it were much better there were not one divine in the university, no school-divinity known, the idle sophistry of monks, the canker of religion; and that they who intended to be ministers, were trained up in the church only by the scripture, and in the original languages thereof at school; without fetching the compass of other arts and sciences, more than what they can well learn at secondary leisure, and at home. Neither speak I this in contempt of learning, or the ministry, but hating the common cheats of both; hating that they, who have preached out bishops, prelates, and canonists, should, in what serves their own ends, retain their false opinions, their pharisaical leaven, their avarice, and closely their ambition, their pluralities, their nonresidences, their odious fees, and use their legal and popish arguments for tithes: that independents should take that name, as they may justly from the true freedom of Christian doctrine and church discipline, subject to no superior judge but God only, and seek to be dependents on the magistrate for their maintenance; which two things, independence and state-hire in religion, can never consist long or certainly together. For magistrates at one time or other, not like these at present our patrons of Christian liberty, will pay none but such whom by their committees of examination they find conformable to their interests and opinions: and hirelings will soon frame themselves to that interest, and those opinions which they see best pleasing to their paymasters; and to seem right themselves, will force others as to the truth. But most of all they are to be reviled and shamed, who cry out with the distinct voice of notorious hirelings, that if ye settle not our maintenance by law, farewell the gospel; than which nothing can be uttered more false, more ignominious, and I may say, more blasphemous against our Saviour; who hath promised without this condition, both his Holy Spirit, and his own presence with his church to the world's end: nothing more false, (unless with their own mouths they condemn themselves for the unworthiest and most mercenary of all other ministers,) by the experience of 300 years after Christ, and the churches at this day in France, Austria, Polonia, and other places, witnessing the contrary under an adverse magistrate, not a favorable: nothing more ignominious, levelling, or rather undervaluing Christ beneath Mahomet. For if it must be thus, how can any Christian object it to a Turk, that his religion stands by force only, and not justly fear from him this reply, Yours both by force and money, in the judgment of your own preachers? This is that which makes atheists in the land, whom they so much complain of: not the want of maintenance, or preachers, as they allege, but the many hirelings and cheaters that have the gospel in their hands; hands that still crave, and are never satisfied. Likely ministers indeed, to proclaim the faith, or to exhort our trust in God, when they themselves will not trust him to provide for them in the message whereon, they say, he sent them; but threaten, for want of temporal means, to desert it; calling that want of means, which is nothing else but the want of their own faith; and would force us to pay the hire of building our faith to their covetous incredulity! Doubtless, if God only be he who gives ministers to his church till the world's end; and through the whole gospel never sent us for ministers to the schools of philosophy, but rather bids us beware of such "vain deceit," Col. ii. 8, (which the primitive church, after two or three ages not remembering, brought herself quickly to confusion,) if all the faithful be now "a holy and a royal priesthood," 1 Pet. ii. 5, 9, not excluded from the dispensation of things holiest, after free election of the church, and imposition of hands, there will not want ministers elected out of all sorts and orders of men, for the gospel makes no difference from the magistrate himself to the meanest artificer, if God evidently favor him with spiritual gifts, as he can easily, and oft hath done, while those bachelor divines and doctors of the tippet have been passed by. Heretofore in the first evangelic times, (and it were happy for Christendom if it were so again,) ministers of the gospel were by nothing else distinguished from other Christians, but by their spiritual knowledge and sanctity of life, for which the church elected them to be her teachers and overseers, though not thereby to separate them from whatever calling she then found them following besides; as the example of St. Paul declares, and the first times of Christianity. When once they affected to be called a clergy, and became, as it were, a peculiar tribe of Levites, a party, a distinct order in the commonwealth, bred up for divines in babbling schools, and fed at the public cost, good for nothing else but what was good for nothing, they soon grew idle: that idleness, with fulness of bread, begat pride and perpetual contention with their feeders, the despised laity, through all ages ever since; to the perverting of religion, and the disturbance of all Christendom. And we may confidently conclude, it never will be otherwise while they are thus upheld undepending on the church, on which alone they anciently depended, and are by the magistrate publicly maintained, a numerous faction of indigent persons, crept for the most part out of extreme want and bad nurture, claiming by divine right and freehold the tenth of our estates, to monopolize the ministry as their peculiar, which is free and open to all able Christians, elected by any church. Under this pretence, exempt from all other employment, and enriching themselves on the public, they last of all prove common incendiaries, and exalt their horns against the magistrate himself that maintains them, as the priest of Rome did soon after against his benefactor the emperor, and the presbyters of late in Scotland. Of which hireling crew, together with all the mischiefs, dissensions, troubles, wars merely of their kindling, Christendom might soon rid herself and be happy, if Christians would but know their own dignity, their liberty, their adoption, and let it not be wondered if I say their spiritual priesthood, whereby they have all equally access to any ministerial function, whenever called by their own abilities, and the church, though they never came near commencement or university. But while protestants, to avoid the due labor of understanding their own religion, are content to lodge it in the breast, or rather in the books, of a clergyman, and to take it thence by scraps and mammocks, as he dispenses it in his Sunday's dole, they will be always learning and never knowing; always infants; always either his vassals, as lay papists are to their priests; or at odds with him, as reformed principles give them some light to be not wholly conformable; whence infinite disturbances in the state, as they do, must needs follow. Thus much I had to say; and, I suppose, what may be enough to them who are not avariciously bent otherwise, touching the likeliest means to remove hirelings out of the church; than which nothing can more conduce to truth, to peace and all happiness, both in church and state. If I be not heard nor believed, the event will bear me witness to have spoken truth: and I in the meanwhile have borne my witness, not out of season, to the church and to my country.

THE PRESENT MEANS AND BRIEF DELINEATION

OF

A FREE COMMONWEALTH,

EASY TO BE PUT IN PRACTICE, AND WITHOUT DELAY.

IN A LETTER TO GENERAL MONK.

[The text is that of Toland, 1698.]

FIRST, All endeavors speedily to be used, that the ensuing election be of such as are already firm, or inclinable to constitute a free commonwealth, (according to the former qualifications decreed in parliament, and not yet repealed, as I hear,) without single person, or house of lords. If these be not such, but the contrary, who foresees not, that our liberties will be utterly lost in this next parliament, without some powerful course taken, of speediest prevention? The speediest way will be to call up forthwith the chief gentlemen out of every county: to lay before them (as your excellency hath already, both in your published letters to the army, and your declaration recited to the members of parliament) the danger and confusion of readmitting kingship in this land; especially against the rules of all prudence and example, in a family once ejected, and thereby not to be trusted with the power of revenge. That you will not longer delay them with vain expectation, but will put into their hands forthwith the possession of a free commonwealth; if they will first return immediately and elect them, by such at least of the people as are rightly qualified, a standing council in every city and great town, which may then be dignified with the name of city, continually to consult the good and flourishing state of that place, with a competent territory adjoined; to assume the judicial laws, either these that are, or such as they themselves shall new make severally, in each commonalty, and all judicatures, all magistracies, to the administration of all justice between man and man, and all the ornaments of public civility, academies, and such like, in their own hands. Matters appertaining to men of several counties or territories, may be determined as they are here at London, or in some more convenient place, under equal judges.

Next, That in every such capital place, they will choose them the usual number of ablest knights and burgesses, engaged for a commonwealth, to make up the parliament, or (as it will from henceforth be better called) the Grand or General Council of the Nation: whose office must be, with due caution, to dispose of forces both by sea and land, under the conduct of your excellency, for the preservation of peace, both at home and abroad; must raise and manage the public revenue, but with provided inspection of their accompts; must administer all foreign affairs, make all general laws, peace or war, but not without assent of the standing council in each city, or such other general assemby as may be called on such occasion, from the whole territory, where they may, without much trouble, deliberate on all things fully, and send up their suffrages within a set time, by deputies appointed.

Though this grand council be perpetual,

(as in that book I proved would be best and most conformable to best examples,) yet they will then, thus limited, have so little matter in their hands, or power to endanger our liberty; and the people so much in theirs, to prevent them, having all judicial laws in their own choice, and free votes in all those which concern generally the whole commonwealth, that we shall have little cause to fear the perpetuity of our general senate; which will be then nothing else but a firm foundation and custody of our public liberty, peace and union, through the whole commonwealth, and the transactors of our affairs with foreign nations. If this yet be not thought enough, the known expedient may at length be used, of a partial rotation.

Lastly, if these gentlemen convocated refuse these fair and noble offers of immediate liberty, and happy condition, no doubt there be enough in every county who will thankfully accept them; your excellency once more declaring publicly this to be your mind, and having a faithful veteran army, so ready and glad to assist you in the prosecution thereof. For the full and absolute administration of law in every county, which is the difficultest of these proposals, hath been of most long desired: and the not granting it held a general grievance. The rest, when they shall see the beginnings and proceedings of these constitutions proposed, and the orderly, the decent, the civil, the safe, the noble effects thereof, will be soon convinced, and by degrees come in of their own accord, to be partakers of so happy a government.

THE READY AND EASY WAY

TO ESTABLISH

A FREE COMMONWEALTH,

AND THE EXCELLENCE THEREOF COMPARED WITH THE INCONVENIENCES AND DANGERS OF READMITTING KINGSHIP IN THIS NATION.

——————————————— "Et nos
Consilium dedimus Syllæ, demus populo nunc."

[The text is that of the second edition, 1660.]

ALTHOUGH, since the writing of this treatise, the face of things hath had some change, writs for new elections have been recalled, and the members at first chosen re-admitted from exclusion; yet not a little rejoicing to hear declared the resolution of those who are in power, tending to the establishment of a free commonwealth, and to remove, if it be possible, this noxious humor of returning to bondage, instilled of late by some deceivers, and nourished from bad principles and false apprehensions among too many of the people; I thought best not to suppress what I had written, hoping that it may now be of much more use and concernment to be freely published, in the midst of our elections to a free parliament, or their sitting to consider freely of the government; whom it behooves to have all things represented to them that may direct their judgment therein; and I never read of any state, scarce of any tyrant, grown so incurable, as to refuse counsel from any in a time of public deliberation, much less to be offended. If their absolute determination be to enthrall us, before so long a Lent of servitude, they may permit us a little shroving-time first, wherein to speak freely, and take our leaves of liberty. And because in the former edition, through haste, many faults escaped, and many books were suddenly dispersed, ere the note to mend them could be sent, I took the opportunity from this occasion to revise and somewhat to enlarge the whole discourse, especially that part which argues for a perpetual senate. The treatise thus revised and enlarged, is as follows:

The Parliament of England, assisted by a great number of the people who appeared and stuck to them faithfulest in defence of religion and their civil liberties, judging kingship by long experience a government unnecessary, burdensome, and dangerous, justly and magnanimously abolished it, turning regal bondage into a free commonwealth, to the admiration and terror of our emulous neighbors. They took themselves not bound by the light of nature or religion to any former covenant, from which the king himself, by many forefeitures of a latter date or discovery, and our own longer consideration thereon, had more and more unbound us, both to himself and his posterity; as hath been ever the justice and the prudence of all wise nations that have ejected tyranny. They covenanted "To preserve the king's person and authority, in the preservation of the true religion, and our liberties;" not in his endeavoring to bring in upon our consciences a popish religion; upon our liberties, thraldom; upon our lives, destruction, by his occasioning, if not complotting, as was after discovered, the Irish massacre; his fomenting and arming the rebellion; his covert leaguing with the rebels against us; his refusing, more than seven times, propositions most just and necessary to the true religion and our liberties, tendered him by the parliament both of England and Scotland. They made not their covenant concerning him with no difference between a king and a God; or promised him, as Job did to the Almighty, "to trust in him though he slay us:" they understood that the solemn engagement, wherein we all forswore kingship, was no more a breach of the covenant, than the covenant was of the protestation before, but a faithful and prudent going on both in the words well weighed, and in the true sense of the covenant "without respect of persons," when we could not serve two contrary masters, God and the king, or the king and that more supreme law, sworn in the first place to maintain our safety and our liberty. They knew the people of England to be a free people, themselves the representers of that freedom; and although many were excluded, and as many fled (so they pretended) from tumults to Oxford, yet they were left a sufficient number to act in parliament, therefore not bound by any statute of preceding parliaments, but by the law of nature only, which is the only law of laws truly and properly to all mankind fundamental; the beginning and the end of all government; to which no parliament or people that will throughly reform, but may and must have recourse, as they had, and must yet have, in church reformation (if they throughly intend it) to evangelic rules; not to ecclesiastical canons, though never so ancient, so ratified and established in the land by statutes which for the most part are mere positive laws, neither natural nor moral: and so by any parliament, for just and serious considerations, without scruple to be at any time repealed.

If others of their number in these things were under force, they were not, but under free conscience; if others were excluded by a power which they could not resist, they were not therefore to leave the helm of government in no hands, to discontinue their care of the public peace and safety, to desert the people in anarchy and confusion, no more than when so many of their members left them, as made up in outward formality a more legal parliament of three estates against them. The best affected also, and best principled of the people, stood not numbering or computing, on which side were most voices in parliament, but on which side appeared to them most reason, most safety, when the house divided upon main matters. What was well motioned and advised, they examined not whether fear or persuasion carried it in the vote, neither did they measure votes and counsels by the intentions of them that voted; knowing that intentions either are but guessed at, or not soon enough known; and although good, can neither make the deed such, nor prevent the consequence from being bad. Suppose bad intentions in things otherwise well done; what was well done, was by them who so thought, not the less obeyed or followed in the state; since in the church, who had not rather follow Iscariot or Simon, the magician, though to covetous ends, preaching, than Saul, though in the uprightness of his heart persecuting the gospel?

Safer they, therefore, judged what they thought the better counsels, though carried on by some perhaps to bad ends, than the worse by others, though endeavored with best intentions. And yet they were not to learn that a greater number might be corrupt within the walls of a parliament, as well as of a city; whereof in matters of nearest concernment all men will be judges; nor easily permit that the odds of voices in their greatest council shall more endanger them by corrupt or credulous votes, than the odds of enemies by open assaults; judging that most voices ought not always to prevail, where main matters are in question. If others hence will pretend to disturb all counsels; what is that to them who pretend not, but are in real danger; not they only so judging, but a great, though not the greatest number of their chosen patriots, who might be more in weight than the others in number: there being in number little virtue, but by weight and measure wisdom working all things, and the dangers on either side they seriously thus weighed?

From the treaty, short fruits of long labors, and seven years' war; security for twenty years, if we can hold it; reformation in the church for three years: then put to shift again with our vanquished master. His justice, his honor, his conscience declared quite contrary to ours; which would have furnished him with many such evasions, as in a book entitled "An Inquisition for Blood," soon after were not concealed: bishops not totally removed, but left, as it were, in ambush, a reserve, with ordination in their sole power; their lands already sold, not to be alienated, but rented, and the sale of them called "sacrilege;" delinquents, few of many brought to condign punishment; accessories punished, the chief author, above pardon, though, after utmost resistance, vanquished; not to give, but to receive, laws; yet besought, treated with, and to be thanked for his gracious concessions, to be honored, worshipped, glorified.

If this we swore to do, with what righteousness in the sight of God, with what assurance that we bring not by such an oath, the whole sea of blood-guiltiness upon our own heads? If on the other side we prefer a free government, though for the present not obtained, yet all those suggested fears and difficulties, as the event will prove, easily overcome, we remain finally secure from the exasperated regal power, and out of snares; shall retain the best part of our liberty, which is our religion, and the civil part will be from these who defer us, much more easily recovered, being neither so subtle nor so awful as a king reinthroned. Nor were their actions less both at home and abroad, that might become the hopes of a glorious rising commonwealth: nor were the expressions both of army and people, whether in their public declarations, or several writings, other than such as testified a spirit in this nation, no less noble and well-fitted to the liberty of a commonwealth, than in the ancient Greeks or Romans. Nor was the heroic cause unsuccessfully defended to all Christendom, against the tongue of a famous and thought invincible adversary; nor the constancy and fortitude, that so nobly vindicated our liberty, our victory at once against two the most prevailing usurpers over mankind, superstition and tyranny, unpraised or uncelebrated in a written monument, likely to outlive detraction, as it hath hitherto convinced or silenced not a few of our detractors, especially in parts abroad.

After our liberty and religion thus prosperously fought for, gained, and many years possessed, except in those unhappy interruptions, which God hath removed; now that nothing remains, but in all reason the certain hopes of a speedy and immediate settlement forever in a firm and free commonwealth, for this extolled and magnified nation, regardless both of honor won, or deliverances vouchsafed from heaven, to fall back, or rather to creep back so poorly, as it seems the multitude would, to their once abjured and detested thraldom of kingship, to be ourselves the slanderers of our own just and religious deeds, though done by some to covetous and ambitious ends, yet not therefore to be stained with their infamy, or they to asperse the integrity of others; and yet these now by revolting from the conscience of deeds well done, both in church and state, to throw away and forsake, or rather to betray a just and noble cause for the mixture of bad men who have ill-managed and abused it, (which had our fathers done heretofore, and on the same pretence deserted true religion, what had long ere this become of our gospel, and all protestant reformation so much intermixed with the avarice and ambition of some reformers?) and by thus relapsing, to verify all the bitter predictions of our triumphing enemies, who will now think they wisely discerned and justly censured both us and all our actions as rash, rebellious, hypocritical, and impious; not only argues a strange, degenerate contagion suddenly spread among us, fitted and prepared for new slavery, but will render us a scorn and derision to all our neighbors.

And what will they at best say of us, and of the whole English name, but scoffingly, as of that foolish builder mentioned by our Saviour, who began to build a tower, and was not able to finish it? Where is this goodly tower of a commonwealth, which the English boasted they would build to overshadow kings, and be another Rome in the west? The foundation indeed they laid gallantly, but fell into a worse confusion, not of tongues, but of factions, than those at the tower of Babel; and have left no memorial of their work behind them remaining but in the common laughter of Europe! Which must needs redound the more to our shame, if we but look on our neighbors the United Provinces, to us inferior in all outward advantages; who notwithstanding, in the midst of greater difficulties, courageously, wisely, constantly went through with the same work, and are settled in all the happy enjoyments of a potent and flourishing republic to this day.

Besides this, if we return to kingship, and soon repent, (as undoubtedly we shall, when we begin to find the old encroachments coming on by little and little upon our consciences, which must necessarily proceed from king and bishop united inseparably in one interest,) we may be forced perhaps to fight over again all that we have fought, and spend over again all that we have spent, but are never like to attain thus far as we are now advanced to the recovery of our freedom, never to have it in possession as we now have it, never to be vouchsafed hereafter the like mercies and signal assistances from Heaven in our cause, if by our ingrateful backsliding we make these fruitless; flying now to regal concessions from his divine condescensions and gracious answers to our once importuning prayers against the tyranny which we then groaned under; making vain and viler than dirt the blood of so many thousand faithful and valiant Englishmen, who left us in this liberty, bought with their lives; losing by a strange aftergame of folly all the battles we have won, together with all Scotland as to our conquest, hereby lost, which never any of our kings could conquer, all the treasure we have spent, not that corruptible treasure only, but that far more precious of all our late miraculous deliverances; treading back again with lost labor all our happy steps in the progress of reformation, and most pitifully depriving ourselves the instant fruition of that free government, which we have so dearly purchased, a free commonwealth, not only held by wisest men in all ages the noblest, the manliest, the equallest, the justest government, the most agreeable to all due liberty and proportioned equality, both human, civil, and Christian, most cherishing to virtue and true religion, but also (I may say it with greatest probability) plainly commended, or rather enjoined by our Saviour himself, to all Christians, not without remarkable disallowance, and the brand of Gentilism upon kingship.

God in much displeasure gave a king to the Israelites, and imputed it a sin to them that they sought one; but Christ apparently forbids his disciples to admit of any such heathenish government: "The kings of the Gentiles," saith he, "exercise lordship over them," and they that "exercise authority upon them are called benefactors: but ye shall not be so; but he that is greatest among you, let him be as the younger; and he that is chief, as he that serveth." The occasion of these his words was the ambitious desire of Zebedee's two sons to be exalted above their brethren in his kingdom, which they thought was to be ere long upon earth. That he speaks of civil government, is manifest by the former part of the comparison, which infers the other part to be always in the same kind. And what government comes nearer to this precept of Christ, than a free commonwealth; wherein they who are greatest, are perpetual servants and drudges to the public at their own cost and charges, neglect their own affairs, yet are not elevated above their brethren; live soberly in their families, walk the streets as other men, may be spoken to freely, familiarly, friendly, without adoration? Whereas a king must be adored like a demigod, with a dissolute and haughty court about him, of vast expense and luxury, masks and revels, to the debauching of our prime gentry, both male and female; not in their pastimes only, but in earnest, by the loose employments of court-service, which will be then thought honorable. There will be a queen also of no less charge; in most likelihood outlandish and a papist; besides a queen-mother such already; together with both their courts and numerous train: then a royal issue, and ere long severally their sumptuous courts; to the multiplying of a servile crew, not of servants only, but of nobility and gentry, bred up then to the hopes not of public, but of court-offices, to be stewards, chamberlains, ushers, grooms even of the close-stool; and the lower their minds debased with court-opinions, contrary to all virtue and reformation, the haughtier will be their pride and profuseness. We may well remember this not long since at home; nor need but look at present into the French court, where enticements and preferments daily draw away and pervert the protestant nobility.

As to the burden of expense, to our cost we shall soon know it; for any good to us deserving to be termed no better than the vast and lavish price of our subjection, and their debauchery, which we are now so greedily cheapening, and would so fain be paying most inconsiderately to a single person: who, for anything wherein the public really needs him, will have little else to do, but to bestow the eating and drinking of excessive dainties, to set a pompous face upon the superficial actings of state, to pageant himself up and down in progress among the perpetual bowings and cringings of an abject people, on either side deifying and adoring him for nothing done that can deserve it. For what can he more than another man? who, even in the expression of a late court-poet, sits only like a great cipher set to no purpose before a long row of other significant figures. Nay, it is well and happy for the people, if their king be but a cipher, being ofttimes a mischief, a pest, a scourge of the nation, and, which is worse, not to be removed, not to be controlled, much less accused or brought to punishment, without the danger of a common ruin, without the shaking and almost subversion of the whole land; whereas in a free commonwealth, any governor or chief counsellor offending may be removed and punished, without the least commotion.

Certainly then that people must needs be mad or strangely infatuated, that build the chief hope of their common happiness or safety on a single person; who, if he happen to be good, can do no more than another man; if to be bad, hath in his hands to do more evil without check, than millions of other men. The happiness of a nation must needs be firmest and certainest in a full and free council of their own electing, where no single person, but reason only, sways. And what madness is it for them who might manage nobly their own affairs themselves, sluggishly and weakly to devolve all on a single person; and, more like boys under age than men, to commit all to his patronage and disposal, who neither can perform what he undertakes; and yet for undertaking it, though royally paid, will not be their servant, but their lord? How unmanly must it needs be, to count such a one the breath of our nostrils, to hang all our felicity on him, all our safety, our well-being, for which if we were aught else but sluggards or babies, we need depend on none but God and our own counsels, our own active virtue and industry! "Go to the ant, thou sluggard," saith Solomon; "consider her ways, and be wise; which having no prince, ruler, or lord, provides her meat in the summer, and gathers her food in the harvest:" which evidently shows us, that they who think the nation undone without a king, though they look grave or haughty, have not so much true spirit and understanding in them as a pismire: neither are these diligent creatures hence concluded to live in lawless anarchy, or that commended; but are set the examples to imprudent and ungoverned men, of a frugal and self-governing democracy or commonwealth: safer and more thriving in the joint providence and counsel of many industrious equals than under the single domination of one imperious lord.

It may be well wondered that any nation, styling themselves free, can suffer any man to pretend hereditary right over them as their lord; whenas, by acknowledging that right, they conclude themselves his servants and his vassals, and so renounce their own freedom. Which how a people and their leaders especially can do, who have fought so gloriously for liberty; how they can change their noble words and actions, heretofore so becoming the majesty of a free people, into the base necessity of court flatteries and prostrations, is not only strange and admirable, but lamentable to think on. That a nation should be so valorous and courageous to win their liberty in the field, and when they have won it, should be so heartless and unwise in their counsels, as not to know how to use it, value it, what to do with it, or with themselves; but after ten or twelve years' prosperous war and contestation with tyranny, basely and besottedly to run their necks again into the yoke which they have broken, and prostrate all the fruits of their victory for nought at the feet of the vanquished, besides our loss of glory, and such an example as kings or tyrants never yet had the like to boast of, will be an ignominy if it befall us, that never yet befell any nation possessed of their liberty; worthy indeed themselves, whatsoever they be, to be for ever slaves, but that part of the nation which consents not with them, as I persuade me of a great number, far worthier than by their means to be brought into the same bondage.

Considering these things so plain, so rational, I cannot but yet further admire on the other side, how any man, who hath the true principles of justice and religion in him, can presume or take upon him to be a king and lord over his brethren, whom he cannot but know, whether as men or Christians, to be for the most part every way equal or superior to himself: how he can display with such vanity and ostentation his regal splendor, so supereminently above other mortal men; or, being a Christian, can assume such extraordinary honor and worship to himself, while the kingdom of Christ, our common king and lord, is hid to this world, and such gentilish imitation forbid in express words by himself to all his disciples. All protestants hold that Christ in his church hath left no vicegerent of his power; but himself, without deputy, is the only head thereof governing it from heaven: how then can any Christian man derive his kingship from Christ, but with worse usurpation than the pope his headship over the church, since Christ not only hath not left the least shadow of a command for any such vicegerence from him in the state, as the pope pretends for his in the church, but hath expressly declared that such regal dominion is from the gentiles, not from him, and hath strictly charged us not to imitate them therein?

I doubt not but all ingenuous and knowing men will easily agree with me, that a free commonwealth without single person or house of lords is by far the best government, if it can be had; but we have all this while, say they, been expecting it, and cannot yet attain it. It is true, indeed, when monarchy was dissolved, the form of a commonwealth should have forthwith been framed, and the practice thereof immediately begun; that the people might have soon been satisfied and delighted with the decent order, ease, and benefit thereof; we had been then by this time firmly rooted, past fear of commotions or mutations, and now flourishing; this care of timely settling a new government instead of the old, too much neglected, hath been our mischief. Yet the cause thereof may be ascribed with most reason to the frequent disturbances, interruptions, and dissolutions, which the parliament hath had partly from the impatient or disaffected people, partly from some ambitious leaders in the army; much contrary, I believe, to the mind and approbation of the army itself, and their other commanders, once undeceived, or in their own power.

Now is the opportunity, now the very season, wherein we may obtain a free commonwealth, and establish it for ever in the land, without difficulty or much delay. Writs are sent out for elections, and, which is worth observing, in the name, not of any king, but of the keepers of our liberty, to summon a free parliament; which then only will indeed be free, and deserve the true honor of that supreme title, if they preserve us a free people. Which never parliament was more free to do, being now called not as heretofore, by the summons of a king, but by the voice of liberty. And if the people, laying aside prejudice and impatience, will seriously and calmly now consider their own good, both religious and civil, their own liberty and the only means thereof, as shall be here laid before them, and will elect their knights and burgesses able men, and according to the just and necessary qualifications, (which, for aught I hear, remain yet in force unrepealed, as they were formerly decreed in parliament,) men not addicted to a single person or house of lords, the work is done; at least the foundation firmly laid of a free commonwealth, and good part also erected of the main structure. For the ground and basis of every just and free government, (since men have smarted so oft for committing all to one person,) is a general council of ablest men, chosen by the people to consult of public affairs from time to time for the common good. In this grand council must the sovereignty, not transferred, but delegated only, and as it were deposited, reside; with this caution, they must have the forces by sea and land committed to them for preservation of the common peace and liberty; must raise and manage the public revenue, at least with some inspectors deputed for satisfaction of the people, how it is employed; must make or propose, as more expressly shall be said anon, civil laws, treat of commerce, peace or war with foreign nations; and, for the carrying on some particular affairs with more secrecy and expedition, must elect, as they have already out of their own number and others, a council of state.

And, although it may seem strange at first hearing, by reason that men's minds are prepossessed with the notion of successive parliaments, I affirm, that the grand or general council, being well chosen, should be perpetual: for so their business is or may be, and ofttimes urgent; the opportunity of affairs gained or lost in a moment. The day of council cannot be set as the day of a festival; but must be ready always to prevent or answer all occasions. By this continuance they will become every way skilfullest, best provided of intelligence from abroad, best acquainted with the people at home, and the people with them. The ship of the commonwealth is always under sail; they sit at the stern, and if they steer well, what need is there to change them, it being rather dangerous? Add to this, that the grand council is both foundation and main pillar of the whole state; and to move pillars and foundations, not faulty, cannot be safe for the building.

I see not, therefore, how we can be advantaged by successive and transitory parliaments; but that they are much likelier continually to unsettle rather than to settle a free government, to breed commotions, changes, novelties, and uncertainties, to bring neglect upon present affairs and opportunities, while all minds are suspense with expectation of a new assembly, and the assembly, for a good space, taken up with the new settling of itself. After which, if they find no great work to do, they will make it, by altering or repealing former acts, or making and multiplying new; that they may seem to see what their predecessors saw not, and not to have assembled for nothing; till all law be lost in the multitude of clashing statutes. But if the ambition of such as think themselves injured, that they also partake not of the government, and are impatient till they be chosen, cannot brook the perpetuity of others chosen before them; or if it be feared, that long continuance of power may corrupt sincerest men, the known expedient is, and by some lately propounded, that annually (or if the space be longer, so much perhaps the better) the third part of senators may go out according to the precedence of their election, and the like number be chosen in their places, to prevent the settling of too absolute a power, if it should be perpetual: and this they call "partial rotation."

But I could wish, that this wheel, or partial wheel in state, if it be possible, might be avoided, as having too much affinity with the wheel of Fortune. For it appears not how this can be done, without danger and mischance of putting out a great number of the best and ablest: in whose stead new elections may bring in as many raw, unexperienced, and otherwise affected, to the weakening and much altering for the worse of public transactions. Neither do I think a perpetual senate, especially chosen and entrusted by the people, much in this land to be feared, where the well-affected either in a standing army, or in a settled militia, have their arms in their own hands. Safest therefore to me it seems, and of least hazard or interruption to affairs, that none of the grand council be moved, unless by death, or just conviction of some crime: for what can be expected firm or steadfast from a floating foundation? However, I forejudge not any probable expedient, any temperament that can be found in things of this nature, so disputable on either side.

Yet lest this which I affirm be thought my single opinion, I shall add sufficient testimony. Kingship itself is therefore counted the more safe and durable because the king, and for the most part his council, is not changed during life. But a commonwealth is held immortal, and therein firmest, safest, and most above fortune; for the death of a king causeth ofttimes many dangerous alterations; but the death now and then of a senator is not felt, the main body of them still continuing permanent in greatest and noblest commonwealths and as it were eternal. Therefore among the Jews, the supreme council of seventy, called the Sanhedrim, founded by Moses, in Athens that of Areopagus, in Sparta that of the ancients, in Rome the senate, consisted of members chosen for term of life; and by that means remained as it were still the same to generations. In Venice they change indeed oftener than every year some particular councils of state, as that of six, or such other: but the true senate, which upholds and sustains the government, is the whole aristocracy immovable. So in the United Provinces, the states-general, which are indeed but a council of state deputed by the whole union, are not usually the same persons for above three or six years; but the states of every city, in whom the sovereignty hath been placed time out of mind, are a standing senate, without succession, and accounted chiefly in that regard the main prop of their liberty. And why they should be so in every well-ordered commonwealth, they who write of policy give these reasons: That to make the senate successive, not only impairs the dignity and lustre of the senate, but weakens the whole commonwealth, and brings it into manifest danger; while by this means the secrets of state are frequently divulged, and matters of greatest consequence committed to inexpert and novice counsellors, utterly to seek in the full and intimate knowledge of affairs past.

I know not therefore what should be peculiar in England, to make successive parliaments thought safest, or convenient here more than in other nations, unless it be the fickleness which is attributed to us as we are islanders. But good education and acquisite wisdom ought to correct the fluxible fault, if any such be, of our watery situation. It will be objected, that in those places where they had perpetual senates, they had also popular remedies against their growing too imperious: as in Athens, besides Areopagus, another senate of four or five hundred; in Sparta, the Ephori; in Rome, the tribunes of the people.

But the event tells us, that these remedies either little availed the people, or brought them to such a licentious and unbridled democracy, as in fine ruined themselves with their own excessive power. So that the main reason urged why popular assemblies are to be trusted with the people's liberty, rather than a senate of principal men, because great men will be still endeavoring to enlarge their power, but the common sort will be contented to maintain their own liberty, is by experience found false; none being more immoderate and ambitious to amplify their power, than such popularities, which were seen in the people of Rome; who, at first contented to have their tribunes, at length contended with the senate that one consul, then both; soon after, that the censors and prætors also should be created plebeian, and the whole empire put into their hands; adoring lastly those, who most

were adverse to the senate, till Marius, by fulfilling their inordinate desires, quite lost them all the power for which they had so long been striving, and left them under the tyranny of Sylla. The balance therefore must be exactly so set, as to preserve and keep up due authority on either side, as well in the senate as in the people. And this annual rotation of a senate to consist of three hundred, as is lately propounded, requires also another popular assembly upward of a thousand, with an answerable rotation. Which, besides that it will be liable to all those inconveniences found in the aforesaid remedies, cannot but be troublesome and chargeable, both in their motion and their session, to the whole land, unwieldy with their own bulk, unable in so great a number to mature their consultations as they ought, if any be allotted them, and that they meet not from so many parts remote to sit a whole year lieger in one place, only now and then to hold up a forest of fingers, or to convey each man his bean or ballot into the box, without reason shown or common deliberation; incontinent of secrets, if any be imparted to them; emulous and always jarring with the other senate. The much better way doubtless will be, in this wavering condition of our affairs, to defer the changing or circumscribing of our senate, more than may be done with ease, till the commonwealth be thoroughly settled in peace and safety, and they themselves give us the occasion.

Military men hold it dangerous to change the form of battle in view of an enemy: neither did the people of Rome bandy with their senate, while any of the Tarquins lived, the enemies of their liberty; nor sought, by creating tribunes, to defend themselves against the fear of their patricians, till, sixteen years after the expulsion of their kings, and in full security of their state, they had or thought they had just cause given them by the senate. Another way will be, to well qualify and refine elections: not committing all to the noise and shouting of a rude multitude, but permitting only those of them who are rightly qualified, to nominate as many as they will; and out of that number others of a better breeding, to choose a less number more judiciously, till after a third or fourth sifting and refining of exactest choice, they only be left chosen who are the due number, and seem by most voices the worthiest.

To make the people fittest to choose, and the chosen fittest to govern, will be to mend our corrupt and faulty education, to teach the people faith, not without virtue, temperance, modesty, sobriety, parsimony, justice; not to admire wealth or honor; to hate turbulence and ambition; to place every one his private welfare and happiness in the public peace, liberty, and safety. They shall not then need to be much mistrustful of their chosen patriots in the grand council; who will be then rightly called the true keepers of our liberty, though the most of their business will be in foreign affairs. But to prevent all mistrust, the people then will have their several ordinary assemblies (which will henceforth quite annihilate the odious power and name of committees) in the chief towns of every county, without the trouble, charge, or time lost of summoning and assembling from far in so great a number, and so long residing from their own houses, or removing of their families, to do as much at home in their several shires, entire or subdivided, toward the securing of their liberty, as a numerous assembly of them all formed and convened on purpose with the wariest rotation. Whereof I shall speak more ere the end of this discourse; for it may be referred to time, so we be still going on by degrees to perfection. The people well weighing and performing these things, I suppose would have no cause to fear, though the parliament abolishing that name, as originally signifying but the parley of our lords and commons with their Norman king when he pleased to call them, should, with certain limitations of their power, sit perpetual, if their ends be faithful and for a free commonwealth, under the name of a grand or general council.

Till this be done, I am in doubt whether our state will be ever certainly and throughly settled; never likely till then to see an end of our troubles and continual changes, or at least never the true settlement and assurance of our liberty. The grand council being thus firmly constituted to perpetuity, and still, upon the death or default of any member, supplied and kept in full number, there can be no cause alleged, why peace, justice, plentiful trade, and all prosperity should not there-

upon ensue throughout the whole land; with as much assurance as can be of human things that they shall so continue (if God favor us, and our wilful sins provoke him not) even to the coming of our true and rightful, and only to be expected King, only worthy as he is our only Saviour, the Messiah, the Christ, the only heir of his eternal Father, the only by him anointed and ordained since the work of our redemption finished, universal Lord of all mankind.

The way propounded is plain, easy, and open before us; without intricacies, without the introducement of new or obsolete forms or terms, or exotic models; ideas that would effect nothing; but with a number of new injunctions to manacle the native liberty of mankind; turning all virtue into prescription, servitude, and necessity, to the great impairing and frustrating of Christian liberty. I say again, this way lies free and smooth before us; is not tangled with inconveniencies; invents no new incumbrances; requires no perilous, no injurious alteration or circumscription of men's lands and properties; secure, that in this commonwealth, temporal and spiritual lords removed, no man or number of men can attain to such wealth or vast possession, as will need the hedge of an agrarian law (never successful, but the cause rather of sedition, save only where it began seasonably with first possession) to confine them from endangering our public liberty. To conclude, it can have no considerable objection made against it, that it is not practicable; lest it be said hereafter, that we gave up our liberty for want of a ready way or distinct form proposed of a free commonwealth. And this facility we shall have above our next neighboring commonwealth, (if we can keep us from the fond conceit of something like a duke of Venice, put lately into many men's heads, by some one or other subtly driving on under that notion his own ambitious ends to lurch a crown,) that our liberty shall not be hampered or hovered over by any engagement to such a potent family as the house of Nassau, of whom to stand in perpetual doubt and suspicion, but we shall live the clearest and absolutest free nation in the world.

On the contrary, if there be a king, which the inconsiderate multitude are now so mad upon, mark how far short we are like to come of all those happinesses which in a free state we shall immediately be possessed of. First, the grand council, which, as I showed before, should sit perpetually, (unless their leisure give them now and then some intermissions or vacations, easily manageable by the council of state left sitting,) shall be called, by the king's good will and utmost endeavor, as seldom as may be. For it is only the king's right, he will say, to call a parliament; and this he will do most commonly about his own affairs rather than the kingdom's, as will appear plainly so soon as they are called. For what will their business then be, and the chief expense of their time, but an endless tugging between petition of right and royal prerogative, especially about the negative voice, militia, or subsidies, demanded and ofttimes extorted without reasonable cause appearing to the commons, who are the only true representatives of the people and their liberty, but will be then mingled with a court-faction; besides which, within their own walls, the sincere part of them who stand faithful to the people will again have to deal with two troublesome counter-working adversaries from without, mere creatures of the king, spiritual, and the greater part, as is likeliest of temporal lords, nothing concerned with the people's liberty.

If these prevail not in what they please, though never so much against the people's interest, the parliament shall be soon dissolved, or sit and do nothing; not suffered to remedy the least grievance, or enact aught advantageous to the people. Next, the council of state shall not be chosen by the parliament, but by the king, still his own creatures, courtiers, and favorites; who will be sure in all their counsels to set their master's grandeur and absolute power, in what they are able, far above the people's liberty. I deny not but that there may be such a king, who may regard the common good before his own, may have no vicious favorite, may hearken only to the wisest and incorruptest of his parliament: but this rarely happens in a monarchy not elective; and it behooves not a wise nation to commit the sum of their well-being, the whole state of their safety to fortune. What need they? and how absurd would it be, whenas they themselves, to whom his chief virtue will be but to hearken, may with much better management and dispatch, with much more commendation of their own worth and magnanimity, govern without a master? Can the folly be paralleled, to adore and be the slaves of a single person, for doing that which it is ten thousand to one whether he can or will do, and we without him might do more easily, more effectually, more laudably ourselves? Shall we never grow old enough to be wise, to make seasonable use of gravest authorities, experiences, examples? Is it such an unspeakable joy to serve, such felicity to wear a yoke? to clink our shackles, locked on by pretended law of subjection, more intolerable and hopeless to be ever shaken off, than those which are knocked on by illegal injury and violence?

Aristotle, our chief instructor in the universities, lest this doctrine be thought sectarian, as the royalist would have it thought, tells us in the third of his Politics, that certain men at first, for the matchless excellence of their virtue above others, or some great public benefit, were created kings by the people, in small cities and territories, and in the scarcity of others to be found like them; but when they abused their power, and governments grew larger, and the number of prudent men increased, that then the people, soon deposing their tyrants, betook them, in all civilest places, to the form of a free commonwealth. And why should we thus disparage and prejudicate our own nation, as to fear a scarcity of able and worthy men united in counsel to govern us, if we will but use diligence and impartiality, to find them out and choose them, rather yoking ourselves to a single person, the natural adversary and oppressor of liberty; though good, yet far easier corruptible by the excess of his singular power and exaltation, or at best, not comparably sufficient to bear the weight of government, nor equally disposed to make us happy in the enjoyment of our liberty under him?

But admit that monarchy of itself may be convenient to some nations; yet to us who have thrown it out, received back again, it cannot but prove pernicious. For kings to come, never forgetting their former ejection, will be sure to fortify and arm themselves sufficiently for the future against all such attempts hereafter from the people; who shall be then so narrowly watched and kept so low, that though they would never so fain, and at the same rate of their blood and treasure, they never shall be able to regain what they now have purchased and may enjoy, or to free themselves from any yoke imposed upon them. Nor will they dare to go about it; utterly disheartened for the future, if these their highest attempts prove unsuccessful; which will be the triumph of all tyrants hereafter over any people that shall resist oppression; and their song will then be, to others, How sped the rebellious English? to our posterity, How sped the rebels, your fathers?

This is not my conjecture, but drawn from God's known denouncement against the gentilizing Israelites, who, though they were governed in a commonwealth of God's own ordaining, he only their king, they his peculiar people, yet affecting rather to resemble heathen, but pretending the misgovernment of Samuel's sons, no more a reason to dislike their commonwealth, than the violence of Eli's sons was imputable to that priesthood or religion, clamored for a king. They had their longing, but with this testimony of God's wrath: "Ye shall cry out in that day, because of your king whom ye shall have chosen, and the Lord will not hear you in that day." Us if he shall hear now, how much less will he hear when we cry hereafter, who once delivered by him from a king, and not without wondrous acts of his providence, insensible and unworthy of those high mercies, are returning precipitantly, if he withhold us not, back to the captivity from whence he freed us!

Yet neither shall we obtain or buy at an easy rate this new gilded yoke, which thus transports us: a new royal revenue must be found, a new episcopal; for those are individual: both which being wholly dissipated, or bought by private persons, or assigned for service done, and especially to the army, cannot be recovered without a general detriment and confusion to men's estates, or a heavy imposition on all men's purses; benefit to none but to the worst and ignoblest sort of men, whose hope is to be either the ministers of court riot and excess, or the gainers by it. But not to speak more of losses and extraordinary levies on our estates, what will then be the revenges and offences remembered and returned, not only by the chief person, but by all his adherents; accounts and reparations that will be required, suits, indictments, inquiries, discoveries, complaints, informations, who knows against whom or how many, though perhaps neuters, if not to utmost infliction, yet to imprisonment, fines, banishment, or molestation? if not these, yet disfavor, discountenance, disregard, and contempt on all but the known royalist, or whom he favors, will be plenteous.

Nor let the new royalized presbyterians persuade themselves, that their old doings, though now recanted, will be forgotten; whatever conditions be contrived or trusted on. Will they not believe this; nor remember the pacification, how it was kept to the Scots; how other solemn promises many a time to us? Let them but now read the diabolical forerunning libels, the faces, the gestures, that now appear foremost and briskest in all public places, as the harbingers of those, that are in expectation to reign over us; let them but hear the insolencies, the menaces, the insultings, of our newly animated common enemies, crept lately out of their holes, their hell I might say, by the language of their infernal pamphlets, the spew of every drunkard, every ribald; nameless, yet not for want of license, but for very shame of their own vile persons, not daring to name themselves, while they traduce others by name; and give us to foresee, that they intend to second their wicked words, if ever they have power, with more wicked deeds.

Let our zealous backsliders forethink now with themselves how their necks yoked with these tigers of Bacchus, these new fanatics of not the preaching, but the sweating-tub, inspired with nothing holier than the venereal pox, can draw one way under monarchy to the establishing of church discipline with these new disgorged atheisms. Yet shall they not have the honor to yoke with these, but shall be yoked under them; these shall plough on their backs. And do they among them, who are so forward to bring in the single person, think to be by him trusted or long regarded? So trusted they shall be, and so regarded, as by kings are wont reconciled enemies; neglected, and soon after discarded, if not prosecuted for old traitors; the first inciters, beginners, and more than to the third part actors, of all that followed.

It will be found also, that there must be then, as necessarily as now, (for the contrary part will be still feared,) a standing army; which for certain shall not be this, but of the fiercest cavaliers, of no less expense, and perhaps again under Rupert. But let this army be sure they shall be soon disbanded, and likeliest without arrear or pay; and being disbanded, not be sure but they may as soon be questioned for being in arms against their king. The same let them fear who have contributed money; which will amount to no small number; that must then take their turn to be made delinquents and compounders. They who past reason and recovery are devoted to kingship perhaps will answer, that a greater part by far of the nation will have it so, the rest therefore must yield.

Not so much to convince these, which I little hope, as to confirm them who yield not, I reply, that this greatest part have both in reason, and the trial of just battle, lost the right of their election what the government shall be. Of them who have not lost that right, whether they for kingship be the greater number, who can certainly determine? Suppose they be, yet of freedom they partake all alike, one main end of government; which if the greater part value not, but will degenerately forego, is it just or reasonable, that most voices against the main end of government should enslave the less number that would be free? More just it is, doubtless, if it come to force, that a less number compel a greater to retain, which can be no wrong to them, their liberty, than that a greater number, for the pleasure of their baseness, compel a less most injuriously to be their fellow-slaves. They who seek nothing but their own just liberty, have always right to win it and to keep it, whenever they have power, be the voices never so numerous that oppose it. And how much we above others are concerned to defend it from kingship, and from them who in pursuance thereof so perniciously would betray us and themselves to most certain misery and thraldom, will be needless to repeat.

Having thus far shown with what ease we may now obtain a free commonwealth, and by it, with as much ease, all the freedom, peace, justice, plenty, that we can desire; on the other side, the difficulties, troubles, un-

certainties, nay, rather impossibilities, to enjoy these things constantly under a monarch; I will now proceed to show more particularly wherein our freedom and flourishing condition will be more ample and secure to us under a free commonwealth, than under kingship.

The whole freedom of man consists either in spiritual or civil liberty. As for spiritual, who can be at rest, who can enjoy anything in this world with contentment, who hath not liberty to serve God, and save his own soul, according to the best light which God hath planted in him to that purpose, by the reading of his revealed will, and the guidance of his Holy Spirit? That this is best pleasing to God, and that the whole protestant church allows no supreme judge or rule in matters of religion, but the Scriptures; and these to be interpreted by the Scriptures themselves, which necessarily infers liberty of conscience, I have heretofore proved at large in another treatise; and might yet further, by the public declarations, confessions, and admonitions of whole churches and states, obvious in all histories since the reformation.

This liberty of conscience, which above all other things ought to be to all men dearest and most precious, no government more inclinable not to favor only, but to protect, than a free commonwealth; as being most magnanimous, most fearless, and confident of its own fair proceedings. Whereas kingship, though looking big, yet indeed most pusillanimous, full of fears, full of jealousies, startled at every umbrage, as it hath been observed of old to have ever suspected most and mistrusted them who were in most esteem for virtue and generosity of mind, so it is now known to have most in doubt and suspicion them who are most reputed to be religious. Queen Elizabeth, though herself accounted so good a protestant, so moderate, so confident of her subjects' love, would never give way so much as to presbyterian reformation in this land, though once and again besought, as Camden relates; but imprisoned and persecuted the very proposers thereof, alleging it as her mind and maxim unalterable, that such reformation would diminish regal authority.

What liberty of conscience can we then expect of others, far worse principled from the cradle, trained up and governed by popish and Spanish counsels, and on such depending hitherto for subsistence? Especially what can this last parliament expect, who having revived lately and published the covenant, have re-engaged themselves, never to readmit episcopacy? Which no son of Charles returning but will most certainly bring back with him, if he regard the last and strictest charge of his father, "to persevere in, not the doctrine only, but government of the church of England, not to neglect the speedy and effectual suppressing of errors and schisms;" among which he accounted presbytery one of the chief.

Or if, notwithstanding that charge of his father, he submit to the covenant, how will he keep faith to us, with disobedience to him; or regard that faith given, which must be founded on the breach of that last and solemnest paternal charge, and the reluctance, I may say the antipathy, which is in all kings, against presbyterian and independent discipline? For they hear the gospel speaking much of liberty; a word which monarchy and her bishops both fear and hate, but a free commonwealth both favors and promotes; and not the word only, but the thing itself. But let our governors beware in time, lest their hard measure to liberty of conscience be found the rock whereon they shipwreck themselves, as others have now done before them in the course wherein God was directing their steerage to a free commonwealth; and the abandoning of all those whom they call sectaries, for the detected falsehood and ambition of some, be a wilful rejection of their own chief strength and interest in the freedom of all protestant religion, under what abusive name soever calumniated.

The other part of our freedom consists in the civil rights and advancements of every person according to his merit: the enjoyment of those never more certain, and the access to these never more open, than in a free commonwealth. Both which, in my opinion, may be best and soonest obtained, if every county in the land were made a kind of subordinate commonalty or commonwealth, and one chief town or more, according as the shire is in circuit, made cities, if they be not so called already; where the nobility and chief gentry, from a proportionable compass of territory annexed to each city, may build houses or palaces befitting their quality; may bear part in the government, make their own judicial laws, or use these that are, and execute them by their own elected judicatures and judges without appeal, in all things of civil government between man and man. So they shall have justice in their own hands, law executed fully and finally in their own counties and precincts, long wished and spoken of, but never yet obtained. They shall have none then to blame but themselves, if it be not well administered; and fewer laws to expect or fear from the supreme authority; or to those that shall be made, of any great concernment to public liberty, they may, without much trouble in these commonalties, or in more general assemblies called to their cities from the whole territory on such occasion, declare and publish their assent or dissent by deputies, within a time limited, sent to the grand council; yet so as this their judgment declared shall submit to the greater number of other counties or commonalties, and not avail them to any exemption of themselves, or refusal of agreement with the rest, as it may in any of the United Provinces, being sovereign within itself, ofttimes to the great disadvantage of that union.

In these employments they may, much better than they do now, exercise, and fit themselves till their lot fall to be chosen into the grand council, according as their worth and merit shall be taken notice of by the people. As for controversies that shall happen between men of several counties, they may repair, as they do now, to the capital city, or any other more commodious, indifferent place, and equal judges. And this I find to have been practised in the old Athenian commonwealth, reputed the first and ancientest place of civility in all Greece; that they had in their several cities a peculiar, in Athens a common government; and their right, as it befell them, to the administration of both.

They should have here also schools and academies at their own choice, wherein their children may be bred up in their own sight to all learning and noble education; not in grammar only, but in all liberal arts and exercises. This would soon spread much more knowledge and civility, yea, religion, through all parts of the land, by communicating the natural heat of government and culture more distributively to all extreme parts, which now lie numb and neglected; would soon make the whole nation more industrious, more ingenuous at home, more potent, more honorable abroad. To this a free commonwealth will easily assent; (nay, the parliament hath had already some such thing in design;) for of all governments a commonwealth aims most to make the people flourishing, virtuous, noble, and high-spirited. Monarchs will never permit; whose aim is to make the people wealthy indeed perhaps, and well fleeced, for their own shearing, and the supply of regal prodigality; but otherwise softest, basest, viciousest, servilest, easiest to be kept under. And not only in fleece, but in mind also sheepishest; and will have all the benches of judicature annexed to the throne, as a gift of royal grace, that we have justice done us, whenas nothing can be more essential to the freedom of a people, than to have the administration of justice, and all public ornaments, in their own election, and within their own bounds, without long travelling or depending on remote places to obtain their right, or any civil accomplishment; so it be not supreme, but subordinate to the general power and union of the whole republic.

In which happy firmness, as in the particular above mentioned, we shall also far exceed the United Provinces, by having not as they, (to the retarding and distracting ofttimes of their counsels or urgentest occasions,) many sovereignties united in one commonwealth, but many commonwealths under one united and intrusted sovereignty. And when we have our forces by sea and land either of a faithful army, or a settled militia, in our own hands, to the firm establishing of a free commonwealth, public accounts under our own inspection, general laws and taxes, with their causes in our own domestic suffrages, judicial laws, offices, and ornaments at home in our own ordering and administration, all distinction of lords and commoners, that may any way divide or sever the public interest, removed; what can a perpetual senate have then, wherein to grow corrupt, wherein to encroach upon us, or usurp? Or if they do, wherein to be formidable? Yet if all this avail not to remove the fear or envy of a perpetual sitting, it may be easily provided, to change a third part of them yearly, or every two or three years, as was above mentioned; or that it be at those

times in the people's choice, whether they will change them, or renew their power, as they shall find cause.

I have no more to say at present: few words will save us, well considered; few and easy things, now seasonably done. But if the people be so affected as to prostitute religion and liberty to the vain and groundless apprehension, that nothing but kingship can restore trade, not remembering the frequent plagues and pestilences that then wasted this city, such as through God's mercy we never have felt since; and that trade flourishes nowhere more than in the free commonwealths of Italy, Germany, and the Low Countries, before their eyes at this day; yet if trade be grown so craving and importunate through the profuse living of tradesmen, that nothing can support it but the luxurious expenses of a nation upon trifles or superfluities; so as if the people generally should betake themselves to frugality, it might prove a dangerous matter, lest tradesmen should mutiny for want of trading; and that therefore we must forego and set to sale religion, liberty, honor, safety, all concernments divine or human, to keep up trading: if, lastly, after all this light among us, the same reason shall pass for current, to put our necks again under kingship, as was made use of by the Jews to return back to Egypt, and to the worship of their idol queen, because they falsely imagined that they then lived in more plenty and prosperity; our condition is not sound, but rotten, both in religion and all civil prudence; and will bring us soon, the way we are marching, to those calamities, which attend always and unavoidably on luxury, all national judgments under foreign or domestic slavery: so far we shall be from mending our condition by monarchizing our government, whatever new conceit now possesses us.

However, with all hazard I have ventured what I thought my duty to speak in season, and to forewarn my country in time; wherein I doubt not but there be many wise men in all places and degrees, but am sorry the effects of wisdom are so little seen among us. Many circumstances and particulars I could have added in those things whereof I have spoken: but a few main matters now put speedily in execution, will suffice to recover us, and set all right: and there will want at no time who are good at circumstances; but men who set their minds on main matters, and sufficiently urge them, in these most difficult times I find not many.

What I have spoken, is the language of that which is not called amiss "The good old Cause:" if it seem strange to any, it will not seem more strange, I hope, than convincing to backsliders. Thus much I should perhaps have said, though I was sure I should have spoken only to trees and stones; and had none to cry to, but with the prophet, "O earth, earth, earth!" to tell the very soil itself, what her perverse inhabitants are deaf to. Nay, though what I have spoke should happen (which thou suffer not, who didst create mankind free! nor thou next, who didst redeem us from being servants of men!) to be the last words of our expiring liberty. But I trust I shall have spoken persuasion to abundance of sensible and ingenuous men; to some, perhaps, whom God may raise of these stones to become children of reviving liberty; and may reclaim, though they seem now choosing them a captain back for Egypt, to bethink themselves a little, and consider whither they are rushing; to exhort this torrent also of the people, not to be so impetuous, but to keep their due channel; and at length recovering and uniting their better resolutions, now that they see already how open and unbounded the insolence and rage is of our common enemies, to stay these ruinous proceedings, justly and timely fearing to what a precipice of destruction the deluge of this epidemic madness would hurry us, through the general defection of a misguided and abused multitude.

OF TRUE RELIGION, HERESY, SCHISM, TOLERATION;

AND WHAT BEST MEANS MAY BE USED AGAINST THE GROWTH OF POPERY.

[The text is that of the first edition, 1673.]

IT is unknown to no man, who knows aught of concernment among us, that the increase of popery is at this day no small trouble and offence to greatest part of the nation; and the rejoicing of all good men that it is so: the more their rejoicing, that God hath given a heart to the people, to remember still their great and happy deliverance from popish thraldom, and to esteem so highly the precious benefit of his gospel, so freely and so peaceably enjoyed among them. Since, therefore, some have already in public, with many considerable arguments, exhorted the people to beware the growth of this Romish weed, I thought it no less than a common duty to lend my hand, how unable soever, to so good a purpose. I will not now enter into the labyrinth of councils and fathers, an entangled wood, which the papist loves to fight in, not with hope of victory, but to obscure the shame of an open overthrow, which yet in that kind of combat many heretofore, and one of late, hath eminently given them. And such manner of dispute with them to learned men is useful and very commendable. But I shall insist on what is plainer to common apprehension, and what I have to say without longer introduction.

True religion is the true worship and service of God, learned and believed from the word of God only. No man or angel can know how God would be worshipped and served unless God reveal it: he hath revealed and taught it us in the holy scriptures by inspired ministers, and in the gospel by his own Son and his apostles, with strictest command, to reject all other traditions or additions whatsoever: according to that of St. Paul, "Though we or an angel from heaven preach any other gospel unto you than that which we have preached unto you, let him be anathema, or accursed." And Deut. iv. 2. "Ye shall not add to the word which I command you, neither shall you diminish aught from it." Rev. xxii. 18, 19: "If any man shall add, &c. If any man shall take away from the words," &c. With good and religious reason, therefore, all protestant churches with one consent, and particularly the church of England in her thirty-nine articles, article 6th, 19th, 20th, 21st, and elsewere, maintain these two points, as the main principles of true religion—that the rule of true religion is the word of God only; and that their faith ought not to be an implicit faith, that is, to believe, though as the church believes, against or without express authority of scripture. And if all protestants, as universally as they hold these two principles, so attentively and religiously would observe them, they would avoid and cut off many debates and contentions, schisms and persecutions, which too oft have been among them, and more firmly unite against the common adversary. For hence it directly follows, that no true protestant can persecute, or not tolerate, his fellow-protestant, though dissenting from him in some opinions, but he must flatly deny and renounce these two his own main principles, whereon true religion is founded; while he compels his brother from that which he believes as the manifest word of God, to an implicit faith (which he himself condemns) to the endangering of his brother's soul, whether by rash belief, or outward conformity: for "whatsoever is not of faith is sin."

I will now as briefly show what is false religion, or heresy, which will be done as easily; for of contraries the definitions must needs be contrary. Heresy, therefore, is a religion taken up and believed from the traditions of men, and additions to the word of God. Whence also it follows clearly, that of all known sects, or pretended religions, at this day in Christendom, popery is the only or the greatest heresy; and he, who is so forward to brand all others for heretics, the obstinate papist, the only heretic. Hence one of their own famous writers found just cause to style the Romish church "Mother of error, school of heresy." And whereas the papist boasts himself to be a Roman Catholic, it is a mere contradiction, one of the pope's bulls, as if he should say, universal particular, a catholic schismatic. For catholic in Greek signifies universal; and the Christian church was so called, as consisting of all nations to whom the gospel was to be preached, in contradistinction to the Jewish church which consisted for the most part of Jews only.

Sects may be in a true church as well as in a false, when men follow the doctrine too much for the teacher's sake, whom they think almost infallible; and this becomes, through infirmity, implicit faith; and the name sectary pertains to such a disciple.

Schism is a rent or division in the church, when it comes to the separating of congregations; and may also happen to a true church, as well as to a false; yet in the true needs not tend to the breaking of communion, if they can agree in the right administration of that wherein they communicate, keeping their other opinions to themselves, not being destructive to faith. The pharisees and saddu-

cees were two sects, yet both met together in their common worship of God at Jerusalem. But here the papist will angrily demand, What! are Lutherans, Calvinists, Anabaptists, Socinians, Arminians, no heretics? I answer, All these may have some errors, but are no heretics. Heresy is in the will and choice professedly against scripture; error is against the will, in misunderstanding the scripture after all sincere endeavors to understand it rightly: hence it was said well by one of the ancients, "Err I may, but a heretic I will not be." It is a human frailty to err, and no man is infallible here on earth. But so long as all these profess to set the word of God only before them as the rule of faith and obedience; and use all diligence and sincerity of heart, by reading, by learning, by study, by prayer for illumination of the Holy Spirit, to understand the rule and obey it, they have done what man can do: God will assuredly pardon them, as he did the friends of Job; good and pious men, though much mistaken, as there it appears, in some points of doctrine. But some will say, with Christians it is otherwise, whom God hath promised by his Spirit to teach all things. True, all things absolutely necessary to salvation: but the hottest disputes among protestants, calmly and charitably inquired into, will be found less than such. The Lutheran holds consubstantiation; an error indeed, but not mortal. The Calvinist is taxed with predestination, and to make God the author of sin; not with any dishonorable thought of God, but it may be over-zealously asserting his absolute power, not without plea of scripture. The anabaptist is accused of denying infants their right to baptism; again they say, they deny nothing but what the scripture denies them. The Arian and Socinian are charged to dispute against the Trinity, they affirm to believe the Father, Son, and Holy Ghost, according to scripture and the apostolic creed; as for terms of trinity, triniunity, coessentiality, tripersonality, and the like, they reject them as scholastic notions, not to be found in scripture, which by a general protestant maxim is plain and perspicuous abundantly to explain its own meaning in the properest words, belonging to so high a matter, and so necessary to be known; a mystery indeed in their sophistic subtleties, but in scripture a plain doctrine. Their other opinions are of less moment. They dispute the satisfaction of Christ or rather the word "satisfaction," as not scriptural: but they acknowledge him both God and their Saviour. The Arminian, lastly, is condemned for setting up free will against free grace; but that imputation he disclaims in all his writings, and grounds himself largely upon scripture only. It cannot be denied, that the authors or late revivers of all these sects or opinions were learned, worthy, zealous, and religious men, as appears by their lives written, and the same of their many eminent and learned followers, perfect and powerful in the scriptures, holy and unblamable in their lives: and it cannot be imagined that God would desert such painful and zealous laborers in his church, and ofttimes great sufferers for their conscience, to damnable errors and a reprobate sense, who had so often implored the assistance of his Spirit; but rather, having made no man infallible, that he hath pardoned their errors, and accepts their pious endeavors, sincerely searching all things according to the rule of scripture, with such guidance and direction as they can obtain of God by prayer. What protestant then, who himself maintains the same principles, and disavows all implicit faith, would persecute, and not rather charitably tolerate, such men as these, unless he mean to abjure the principles of his own religion? If it be asked, how far they should be tolerated; I answer, doubtless equally, as being all protestants; that is, on all occasions to give account of their faith, either by arguing, preaching in their several assemblies, public writing, and the freedom of printing. For if the French and Polonian protestants enjoy all this liberty among papists, much more may a protestant justly expect it among protestants; and yet sometimes here among us, the one persecutes the other upon every slight pretence.

But he is wont to say, he enjoins only things indifferent. Let them be so still; who gave him authority to change their nature by enjoining them? If by his own principles, as is proved, he ought to tolerate controverted points of doctrine not slightly grounded on scripture, much more ought he not impose things indifferent without scripture. In religion nothing is indifferent; but if it come once to be imposed, is either a command or a prohibition, and so consequently an addition to the word of God, which he professes to disallow. Besides, how unequal, how uncharitable must it needs be, to impose that which his conscience cannot urge him to impose, upon him whose conscience forbids him to obey! What can it be but love of contention for things not necessary to be done, to molest the conscience of his brother, who holds them necessary to be not done? To conclude, let such a one but call to mind his own principles above mentioned, and he must necessarily grant, that neither he can impose, nor the other believe or obey, aught in religion, but from the word of God only. More amply to understand this, may be read the 14th and 15th chapters to the Romans, and the contents of the 14th, set forth no doubt but with full authority of the church of England: the gloss is this: "Men may not contemn or condemn one the other for things indifferent." And in the 6th article above mentioned, "Whatsoever is not read in holy scripture, nor may be proved thereby, is not to be required of any man as an article of faith, or necessary to salvation." And certainly what is not so, is not to be required at all, as being an addition to the word of God expressly forbidden.

Thus this long and hot contest, whether protestants ought to tolerate one another, if men will be but rational and not partial, may be ended without need of more words to compose it.

Let us now inquire whether popery be tolerable or no. Popery is a double thing to deal with, and claims a twofold power, ecclesiastical and political, both usurped, and the one supporting the other.

But ecclesiastical is ever pretended to political. The pope by this mixed faculty pretends right to kingdoms and states, and especially to this of England, thrones and unthrones kings, and absolves the people from their obedience to them; sometimes interdicts to whole nations the public worship of God, shutting up their churches: and was wont to drain away greatest part of the wealth of this then miserable land, as part of his patrimony, to maintain the pride and luxury of his court and prelates; and now, since, through the infinite mercy and favor of God, we have shaken off his Babylonish yoke, hath not ceased by his spies and agents, bulls and emissaries, once to destroy both king and parliament; perpetually to seduce, corrupt, and pervert as many as they can of the people. Whether therefore it be fit or reasonable to tolerate men thus principled in religion towards the state, I submit it to the consideration of all magistrates, who are best able to provide for their own and the public safety. As for tolerating the exercise of their religion, supposing their state-activities not to be dangerous, I answer, that toleration is either public or private; and the exercise of their religion, as far as it is idolatrous, can be tolerated neither way: not publicly, without grievous and unsufferable scandal given to all conscientious beholders; not privately, without great offence to God, declared against all kind of idolatry, though secret. Ezek. viii. 7, 8: "And he brought me to the door of the court; and when I looked, behold, a hole in the wall. Then said he unto me, Son of man, dig now in the wall: and when I had digged, behold a door; and he said unto me, Go in, and behold the wicked abominations that they do here." And ver. 12: "Then said he unto me, Son of man, hast thou seen what the ancients of the house of Israel do in the dark?" &c. And it appears by the whole chapter, that God was no less offended with these secret idolatries than with those in public; and no less provoked, than to bring on and hasten his judgments on the whole land for these also.

Having shown thus, that popery, as being idolatrous, is not to be tolerated either in public or in private; it must be now thought how to remove it, and hinder the growth thereof, I mean in our natives, and not foreigners, privileged by the law of nations. Are we to punish them by corporal punishment, or fines in their estates, upon account of their religion? I suppose it stands not with the clemency of the gospel, more than what appertains to the security of the state: but first we must remove their idolatry, and all the furniture thereof, whether idols or the mass wherein they adore their God under bread and wine: for the commandment forbids to adore, not only "any graven image, but the likeness of anything in heaven above, or in the earth beneath, or in the water under the earth; thou shalt not bow down to them nor worship them, for I the Lord thy God am a jealous God." If they say, that by removing their idols we violate their consciences, we have no warrant to regard conscience which is not grounded on scripture: and they themselves confess in their late defences, that they hold not their images necessary to salvation, but only as they are enjoined them by tradition.

Shall we condescend to dispute with them? The scripture is our only principle in religion; and by that only they will not be judged, but will add other principles of their own, which, forbidden by the word of God, we cannot assent to. And the common maxim also in logic is, "against them who deny principles, we are not to dispute." Let them bound their disputations on the scripture only, and an ordinary protestant, well read in the Bible, may turn and wind their doctors. They will not go about to prove their idolatries by the word of God, but run to shifts and evasions, and frivolous distinctions; idols they say are laymen's books, and a great means to stir up pious thoughts and devotion in the learnedest. I say, they are no means of God's appointing, but plainly the contrary: let them hear the prophets. Jer. x. 8: "The stock is a doctrine of vanities." Hab. ii. 18: "What profiteth the graven image, that the maker thereof hath graven it; the molten image and a teacher of lies?" But they allege in their late answers, that the laws of Moses, given only to the Jews, concern not us under the gospel; and remember not that idolatry is forbidden as expressly [in several places of the gospel] but with these wiles and fallacies "compassing sea and land, like the pharisees of old, to make one proselyte," they lead away privily many simple and ignorant souls, men or women, "and make them twofold more the children of hell than themselves," Matt. xxiii. 15. But the apostle hath well warned us, I may say, from such deceivers as these, for their mystery was then working. "I beseech you, brethren," saith he, "mark them which cause divisions and offences, contrary to the doctrine which ye have learned, and avoid them; for they that are such, serve not our Lord Jesus Christ, but their own belly, and by good words and fair speeches deceive the heart of the simple." Rom. xvi. 17, 18.

The next means to hinder the growth of popery will be, to read duly and diligently the holy scriptures, which, as St. Paul saith to Timothy, who had known them from a child, "are able to make wise unto salvation." And to the whole church of Colossi: "Let the word of Christ dwell in you plentifully, with all wisdom," Col. iii. 16. The papal antichristian church permits not her laity to read the Bible in their own tongue: our church, on the contrary, hath proposed it to all men, and to this end translated it into English, with profitable notes on what is met with obscure, though what is most necessary to be known be still plainest; that all sorts and degrees of men, not understanding the original, may read it in their mother tongue. Neither let the countryman, the tradesman, the lawyer, the physician, the statesman, excuse himself by his much business from the studious reading thereof. Our Saviour saith, Luke x. 41, 42, "Thou art careful and troubled about many things; but one thing is needful." If they were asked, they would be loath to set earthly things, wealth or honor, before the wisdom of salvation. Yet most men in the course and practice of their lives are found to do so; and through unwillingness to take the pains of understanding their religion by their own diligent study, would fain be saved by a deputy. Hence comes implicit faith, ever learning and never taught, much hearing and small proficience, till want of fundamental knowledge easily turns to superstition or popery: therefore the apostle admonishes, Eph. iv. 14, "That we henceforth be no more children, tossed to and fro and carried about with every wind of doctrine, by the sleight of men, and cunning craftiness whereby they lie in wait to deceive." Every member of the church, at least of any breeding or capacity, so well ought to be grounded in spiritual knowledge, as, if need be, to examine their teachers themselves. Acts xvii. 11: "They searched the scriptures daily, whether those things were so." Rev. ii. 2: "Thou hast tried them which say they are apostles, and are not." How should any private Christian try his teachers, unless he be well grounded himself in the rule of scripture, by which he is taught? As therefore among papists their ignorance in scripture chiefly upholds popery; so among protestant people, the frequent and serious reading thereof will soonest pull popery down.

Another means to abate popery arises from the constant reading of scripture, wherein believers, who agree in the main, are everywhere exhorted to mutual forbearance and charity one towards the other, though dissenting in some opinions. It is written, that the coat of our Saviour was without seam; whence some would infer that there should be no division in the church of Christ. It should be so indeed; yet seams in the same cloth neither hurt the garment nor misbecome it; and not only seams, but schisms will be while men are fallible: but if they who dissent in matters not essential to belief, while the common adversary is in the field, shall stand jarring and pelting at one another, they will be soon routed and subdued. The papist with open mouth makes much advantage of our several opinions; not that he is able to confute the worst of them, but that we by our continual jangle among ourselves make them worse than they are indeed. To save ourselves, therefore, and resist the common enemy, it concerns us mainly to agree within ourselves, that with joint forces we may not only hold our own, but get ground: and why should we not? The gospel commands us to tolerate one another, though of various opinions, and hath promised a good and happy event thereof. Phil. iii. 15: "Let us therefore, as many as be perfect, be thus minded; and if in anything ye be otherwise minded God shall reveal even this unto you." And we are bid, 1 Thess. v. 21, "Prove all things, hold fast that which is good." St. Paul judged, that not only to tolerate, but to examine and prove all things, was no danger to our holding fast of that which is good. How shall we prove all things, which includes all opinions at least founded on scripture, unless we not only tolerate them, but patiently hear them, and seriously read them? If he who thinks himself in the truth professes to have learnt it, not by implicit faith, but by attentive study of the scriptures, and full persuasion of heart, with what equity can he refuse to hear or read him who demonstrates to have gained his knowledge by the same way? Is it a fair course to assert truth, by arrogating to himself the only freedom of speech, and stopping the mouths of others equally gifted? This is the direct way to bring in that papistical implicit faith, which we all disclaim. They pretend it would unsettle the weaker sort; the same groundless fear is pretended by the Romish clergy in prohibiting the scripture. At least, then, let them have leave to write in Latin, which the common people understand not; that what they hold may be discussed among the learned only. We suffer the idolatrous books of papists, without this fear, to be sold and read as common as our own: why not much rather of Anabaptists, Arians, Arminians, and Socinians? There is no learned man but will confess he hath much profited by reading controversies, his senses awakened, his judgment sharpened, and the truth which he holds more firmly established. If then it be profitable for him to read, why should it not at least be tolerable and free for his adversary to write? In logic they teach, that contraries laid together more evidently appear: it follows, then, that all controversies being permitted, falsehood will appear more false, and truth the more true; which must needs conduce much, not only to the confounding of popery, but to the general confirmation of unimplicit truth.

The last means to avoid popery is, to amend our lives. It is a general complaint, that this nation of late years is grown more numerously and excessively vicious than heretofore; pride, luxury, drunkenness, whoredom, cursing, swearing, bold and open atheism everywhere abounding: where these grow, no wonder if popery also grow apace. There is no man so wicked but sometimes his conscience will wring him with thoughts of another world, and the peril of his soul; the trouble and melancholy, which he conceives of true repentance and amendment, he endures not, but inclines rather to some carnal superstition, which may pacify and lull his conscience with some more pleasing doctrine. None more ready and officious to offer herself than the Romish, and opens wide her office, with all her faculties, to receive him; easy confession, easy absolution, pardons, indulgences, masses for him both quick and dead, Agnus Deis, relics, and the like: and he, instead of "working out his salvation with fear and trembling," straight thinks in his heart, (like another kind of fool than he in the Psalms,) to bribe God as a corrupt judge; and by his proctor, some priest, or friar, to buy out his peace with money, which he cannot with his repentance. For God, when men sin outrageously, and will not be admonished, gives over chastising them, perhaps by pestilence, fire, sword, or famine, which may all turn to their good, and takes up his severest

punishments, hardness, besottedness of heart, and idolatry, to their final perdition. Idolatry brought the heathen to heinous transgressions, Rom. ii. And heinous transgressions ofttimes bring the slight professors of true religion to gross idolatry: 1 Thes. ii. 11, 12, "For this cause God shall send them strong delusion, that they should believe a lie, that they all might be damned who believe not the truth, but had pleasure in unrighteousness." And Isaiah xliv. 18, speaking of idolaters, "They have not known nor understood, for he hath shut their eyes that they cannot see, and their hearts that they cannot understand." Let us therefore, using this last means, last here spoken of, but first to be done, amend our lives with all speed; lest through impenitency we run into that stupidly which we now seek all means so warily to avoid, the worst of superstitions, and the heaviest of all God's judgments—popery.

JOHN MILTON,
THE CHRISTIAN DOCTRINE

[The translation is that of Bishop Sumner, 1825, as revised in the Bohn Library.]

TO ALL THE CHURCHES OF CHRIST

AND TO ALL

WHO PROFESS THE CHRISTIAN FAITH THROUGHOUT THE WORLD, PEACE, AND THE RECOGNITION OF THE TRUTH, AND ETERNAL SALVATION IN GOD THE FATHER, AND IN OUR LORD JESUS CHRIST.

SINCE the commencement of the last century, when religion began to be restored from the corruptions of more than thirteen hundred years to something of its original purity, many treatises of theology have been published, conducted according to sounder principles, wherein the chief heads of Christian doctrine are set forth sometimes briefly, sometimes in a more enlarged and methodical order. I think myself obliged, therefore, to declare in the first instance why, if any works have already appeared as perfect as the nature of the subject will admit, I have not remained contented with them—or, if all my predecessors have treated it unsuccessfully, why their failure has not deterred me from attempting an undertaking of a similar kind.

If I were to say that I had devoted myself to the study of the Christian religion because nothing else can so effectually rescue the lives and minds of men from those two detestable curses, slavery and superstition, I should seem to have acted rather from a regard to my highest earthly comforts, than from a religious motive.

But since it is only to the individual faith of each that the Deity has opened the way of eternal salvation, and as he requires that he who would be saved should have a personal belief of his own, I resolved not to repose on the faith or judgment of others in matters relating to God; but on the one hand, having taken the grounds of my faith from divine revelation alone, and on the other, having neglected nothing which depended on my own industry, I thought fit to scrutinize and ascertain for myself the several points of my religious belief, by the most careful perusal and meditation of the Holy Scriptures themselves.

If therefore I mention what has proved beneficial in my own practice, it is in the hope that others, who have a similar wish of improving themselves, may be thereby invited to pursue the same method. I entered upon an assiduous course of study in my youth, beginning with the books of the Old and New Testament in their original languages, and going diligently through a few of the shorter systems of divines, in imitation of whom I was in the habit of classing under certain heads whatever passages of Scripture occurred for extraction, to be made use of hereafter as occasion might require. At length I resorted with increased confidence to some of the more copious theological treatises, and to the examination of the arguments advanced by the conflicting parties respecting certain disputed points of faith. But, to speak the truth with freedom as well as candor, I was concerned to discover in many instances adverse reasonings either evaded by wretched shifts, or attempted to be refuted, rather speciously than with solidity, by an affected display of formal sophisms, or by a constant recourse to the quibbles of the grammarians; while what was most pertinaciously espoused as the true doctrine, seemed often defended, with more vehemence than strength of argument, by misconstructions of Scripture, or by the hasty deduction of erroneous inferences. Owing to these causes, the truth was sometimes as strenuously opposed as if it had been an error or a heresy—while errors and heresies were substituted for the truth, and valued rather from deference to custom and the spirit of party than from the authority of Scripture.

According to my judgment, therefore, neither my creed nor my hope of salvation could be safely trusted to such guides; and yet it appeared highly requisite to possess some methodical tractate of Christian doctrine, or at least to attempt such a disquisition as might be useful in establishing my faith or assisting my memory. I deemed it therefore safest and most advisable to compile for myself, by my own labor and study, some original treatise which should be always at hand, derived solely from the word of God itself, and executed with all possible fidelity, seeing that I could have no wish to practise any imposition on myself in such a matter.

After a diligent perseverance in this plan for several years, I perceived that the strong holds of the reformed religion were sufficiently fortified, as far as it was in danger from the Papists,—but neglected in many other quarters; neither competently strengthened with works of defence, nor adequately provided with champions. It was also evident to me, that, in religion as in other things, the offers of God were all directed, not to an indolent credulity, but to constant diligence, and to an unwearied search after truth; and that more than I was aware of still remained, which required to be more rigidly examined by the rule of Scripture, and reformed after a more accurate model. I so far satisfied myself in the prosecution of this plan as at length to trust that I had discovered, with regard to religion, what was matter of belief, and what only matter of opinion. It was also a great solace to me to have compiled, by God's assistance, a precious aid for my faith,—or rather to have laid up for myself a treasure which would be a provision for my future life, and would remove from my mind all grounds for hesitation, as often as it behooved me to render an account of the principles of my belief.

If I communicate the result of my inquiries to the world at large; if, as God is my witness, it be with a friendly and benignant feeling towards mankind, that I readily give as wide a circulation as possible to what I esteem my best and richest possession, I hope to meet with a candid reception from all parties, and that none at least will take unjust offence, even though many things should be brought to light which will at once be seen to differ from certain received opinions. I earnestly beseech all lovers of truth, not to cry out that the Church is thrown into confusion by that freedom of discussion and inquiry which is granted to the schools, and ought certainly to be refused to no believer, since we are ordered "to prove all things," and since the daily progress of the light of truth is productive far less of disturbance to the Church, than of illumination and edification. Nor do I see how the Church can be more disturbed by the investigation of truth, than were the Gentiles by the first promulgation of the gospel; since so far from recommending or imposing anything on my own authority, it is my particular advice that every one should suspend his opinion on whatever points he may not feel himself fully satisfied, till the evidence of Scripture prevail, and persuade his reason into assent and faith. Concealment is not my object; it is to the learned that I address myself, or if it be thought that the learned are not the best umpires and judges of such things, I should at least wish to submit my opinions to men of a mature and manly understanding, possessing a thorough knowledge of the doctrines of the gospel; on whose judgments I should rely with far more confidence, than on those of novices in these matters. And whereas the greater part of those who have written most largely on these subjects have been wont to fill whole pages with explanations of their own opinions, thrusting into the margin the texts in support of their doctrine with a summary reference to the chapter and verse, I have chosen, on the contrary, to fill my pages even to redundance with quotations from Scripture, that so as little space as possible might be left for my own words, even when they arise from the context of revelation itself.

It has also been my object to make it appear from the opinions I shall be found to have advanced, whether new or old, of how much consequence to the Christian religion is the liberty not only of winnowing and sifting every doctrine, but also of thinking and even writing respecting it, according to our individual faith and persuasion; an inference which will be stronger in proportion to the weight and importance of those opinions, or rather in proportion to the authority of Scripture, on the abundant testimony of which they rest. Without this liberty there is neither religion nor gospel—force alone prevails,—by which it is disgraceful for the Christian religion to be supported. Without this liberty we are still enslaved, not indeed, as formerly, under the divine law, but, what is worst of all, under the law of man, or to speak more truly, under a barbarous tyranny. But I do not expect from candid and judicious readers a conduct so unworthy of them,—that like certain unjust and foolish men, they should stamp with the invidious name of heretic or heresy whatever appears to them to differ from the received opinions, without trying the doctrine by a comparison with Scripture testimonies. According to their notions, to have branded any one at random with this opprobrious mark, is to have refuted him without any trouble, by a single word. By the simple imputation of the name of heretic, they think that they have despatched their man at one blow. To men of this kind I answer, that in the time of the apostles, ere the New Testament was written, whenever the charge of heresy was applied as a term of reproach, that alone was considered as heresy which was at variance with their doctrine orally delivered,—and that those only were looked upon as heretics, who according to Rom. xvi. 17, 18. "caused divisions and offences contrary to the doctrine" of the apostles. . . . "serving not our Lord Jesus Christ, but their own belly." By parity of reasoning therefore, since the compilation of the New Testament, I maintain that nothing but what is in contradiction to it can properly be called heresy.

For my own part, I adhere to the Holy Scriptures alone—I follow no other heresy or sect. I had not even read any of the works of heretics, so called, when the mistakes of those who are reckoned for orthodox, and their incautious handling of Scripture first taught me to agree with their opponents whenever those opponents agreed with Scripture. If this be heresy, I confess with St. Paul, Acts xxiv. 14. "that after the way which they call heresy, so worship I the God of my fathers, believing all things which are written in the law and the prophets"—to which I add, whatever is written in the New Testament. Any other judges or paramount interpreters of the Christian belief, together with all implicit faith, as it is called, I, in common with the whole Protestant Church, refuse to recognise.

For the rest, brethren, cultivate truth with brotherly love. Judge of my present undertaking according to the admonishing of the Spirit of God—and neither adopt my sentiments nor reject them, unless every doubt has been removed from your belief by the clear testimony of revelation. Finally, live in the faith of our Lord and Saviour Jesus Christ. Farewell.

———

BOOK I.

CHAP. I.—Of the Definition of Christian Doctrine, and the several parts thereof.

The Christian Doctrine is that *divine revelation* disclosed in various ages by Christ (though he was not known under that name in the beginning) concerning the nature and worship of the Deity, for the promotion of the glory of God, and the salvation of mankind.

It is not unreasonable to assume that Christians believe in the Scriptures whence this doctrine is derived—but the authority of those Scriptures will be examined in the proper place. Under the name *Christ* are also comprehended Moses and the Prophets, who were his forerunners, and the Apostles whom he sent.

Divine Revelation. This doctrine, therefore, is to be obtained, not from the schools of the philosophers, nor from the laws of man, but from the Holy Scriptures alone, under the guidance of the Holy Spirit.

In this treatise, then, no novelties of doctrine are taught; but, for the sake of assisting the memory, what is dispersed throughout the different parts of the Holy Scriptures is conveniently reduced into one compact body as it were, and digested under certain heads. This method might be easily defended on the ground of Christian prudence, but it seems better to rest its authority on the divine command. This usage of the Christians was admirably suited for Catechumens when first professing their faith in the Church. Allusion is made to the same system in Rom. vi. 17. "ye have obeyed from the heart that form of doctrine which was delivered you." In this passage the Greek word $\tau\upsilon\pi\grave{o}s$, as well as $\upsilon\pi o\tau\acute{\upsilon}\pi\omega\sigma\iota s$, 2 Tim. i. 13. seems to signify either that part of the evangelical Scriptures which were then written (as in Rom. ii. 20. $\mu\acute{o}\rho\phi\omega\sigma\iota s$, "the form of knowledge and of the truth in the law" signified the law itself) or some systematic course of instruction derived from them or from the whole doctrine of the gospel. Acts xx. 27. "I have not shunned to declare unto you all the counsel of God"—which must mean some entire body of doctrine, formed according to a certain plan, though probably not of great extent, since the whole was gone through, and perhaps even repeated several times during St. Paul's stay at Ephesus, which was about the space of three years.

Christian doctrine is comprehended under two divisions,—*Faith, or the knowledge of God,*—and *Love, or the worship of God.* These two divisions, though they are distinct in their own nature, and put asunder for the convenience of teaching, cannot be separated in practice. Besides, obedience and love are always the best guides to knowledge, and often lead the way from small beginnings to a greater and more flourishing degree of proficiency. It must be observed, that Faith in this division does not mean the habit of believing, but the things to be habitually believed.

———

CHAP. II.—Of God.

Though there be not a few who deny the existence of *God,* for "the fool hath said in his heart, There is no God," Psal. xiv. 1. yet the Deity has imprinted upon the human mind so many unquestionable tokens of himself, and so many traces of him are apparent throughout the whole of nature, that no one in his senses can remain ignorant of the truth. There can be no doubt but that every thing in the world, by the beauty of its order, and the evidence of a determinate and beneficial purpose which pervades it, testifies that some supreme efficient Power must have pre-existed, by which the whole was ordained for a specific end.

There are some who pretend that nature or fate is this supreme Power: but the very name of nature implies that it must owe its birth to some prior agent, or, to speak properly, signifies in itself nothing; but means either the essence of a thing, or that general law which is the origin of every thing, and under which every thing acts. On the other hand, fate can be nothing but a divine decree emanating from some almighty power.

Further, those who attribute the creation of every thing to nature, must necessarily associate chance with nature as a joint divinity; so that they gain nothing by this theory, except that in the place of that one God, whom they cannot tolerate, they are obliged, however reluctantly, to substitute two sovereign rulers of affairs, who must almost always be in opposition to each other. In short, many visible proofs, the verification of numberless predictions, a multitude of wonderful works have compelled all nations to believe, either that God, or that some evil power whose name was unknown, presided over the affairs of the world. Now that evil should prevail over good, and be the true supreme power, is as unmeet as it is incredible. Hence it follows as a necessary consequence, that God exists.

Again: the existence of God is further proved by that feeling, whether we term it conscience, or right reason, which even in the worst of characters, is not altogether extinguished. If there were no God, there would be no distinction between right and wrong; the estimate of virtue and vice would entirely depend on the blind opinion of men; none would follow virtue, none would be restrained from vice and by any sense of shame, or fear of the laws, unless conscience or right reason did from time to time convince every one, however unwilling, of the existence of God, the Lord and ruler of all things, to whom, sooner or later, each must give an account of his own actions, whether good or bad.

The whole tenor of Scripture proves the same thing; and the disciples of the doctrine of Christ may fairly be required to give assent to this truth before all others, according to Heb. xi. 6. "he that cometh to God must believe that he is." It is proved also by the dispersion of the ancient nation of the Jews throughout the whole world, conformably to what God often forewarned them would happen on account of their sins. Nor is it only to pay the penalty of their own guilt that they have been reserved in their scattered state, among the rest of the nations, through the revolution of successive ages, and even to the present day; but also to be a perpetual and living testimony to all people under heaven, of the existence of God, and of the truth of the Holy Scripture. No one, however, can have right thoughts of God, with nature or reason alone as his guide, independent of the word, or message of God.

God is known, so far as he is pleased to make us acquainted with himself, either from his own nature, or from his efficient power. When we speak of knowing God, it must be understood with reference to the imperfect comprehension of man; for to know God as he really is, far transcends the powers of man's thoughts, much more of his perception. God therefore has made as full a revelation of himself as our minds can conceive, or the weakness of our nature can bear.

Our safest way is to form in our minds such a conception of God, as shall correspond with his own delineation and representation of himself in the sacred writings. For granting that both in the literal and figurative descriptions of God, he is exhibited not as he really is, but in such a manner as may be within the scope of our comprehension, yet we ought to entertain such a conception of him, as he, in condescending to accommodate himself to our capacities, has shown that he desires we should conceive. For it is on this very account that he has lowered himself to our level, lest in our flights above the reach of human understanding, and beyond the written word of Scripture, we should be tempted to indulge in vague cogitations and subtleties.

There is no need then that theologians

should have recourse here to what they call anthropopathy—a figure invented by the grammarians to excuse the absurdities of the poets on the subject of the heathen divinities. We may be sure that sufficient care has been taken that the Holy Scriptures should contain nothing unsuitable to the character or dignity of God, and that God should say nothing of himself which could derogate from his own majesty. It is better therefore to contemplate the Deity, and to conceive of him, not with reference to human passions, that is, after the manner of men, who are never weary of forming subtle imaginations respecting him, but after the manner of Scripture, that is, in the way wherein God has offered himself to our contemplation; nor should we think that he would say or direct anything to be written of himself, which is inconsistent with the opinion he wishes us to entertain of his character. Let us require no better authority than God himself for determining what is worthy or unworthy of him. If "it repented Jehovah that he had made man," Gen. vi. 6. and "because of their groanings," Judges ii. 18, let us believe that it did repent him, only taking care to remember that what is called repentance when applied to God, does not arise from inadvertency, as in men; for so he has himself cautioned us, Num. xxiii. 19. Again, if "it grieved the Lord at his heart," Gen. vi. 6. and if "his soul were grieved for the misery of Israel," Judges x. 16, let us believe that it did grieve him. For the affections which in a good man are good, and rank with virtues, in God are holy. If after the work of six days it be said of God that "he rested and was refreshed," Exod. xxxi. 17. if it be said that "he feared the wrath of the enemy," Deut. xxxii. 27, let us believe that it is not beneath the dignity of God to grieve in that for which he is grieved, or to be refreshed in that which refresheth him, or to fear in that he feareth. For however we may attempt to soften down such expressions by a latitude of interpretation, when applied to the Deity, it comes in the end to precisely the same. If God be said "to have made man in his own image, after his likeness," Gen. i. 26. and that too not only as to his soul, but also as to his outward form (unless the same words have different significations here and in chap. v. 3. "Adam begat a son in his own likeness, after his image") and if God habitually assign to himself the members and form of man, why should we be afraid of attributing to him what he attributes to himself, so long as what is imperfection and weakness when viewed in reference to ourselves be considered as most complete and excellent when imputed to God? Questionless the glory and majesty of the Deity must have been so dear to him, that he would never say anything of himself which could be humiliating or degrading, and would ascribe to himself no personal attribute which he would not willingly have ascribed to him by his creatures. Let us be convinced that those have acquired the truest apprehension of the nature of God who submit their understandings to his word; considering that he has accommodated his word to their understandings, and has shown what he wishes their notion of the Deity should be.

In a word, God either is, or is not, such as he represents himself to be. If he be really such, why should we think otherwise of him? If he be not such, on what authority do we say what God has not said? If it be his will that we should thus think of him, why does our imagination wander into some other conception? Why should we hesitate to conceive God according to what he has not hesitated to declare explicitly respecting himself? For such knowledge of the Deity as was necessary for the salvation of man, he has himself of his goodness been pleased to reveal abundantly.

In arguing thus, we do not say that God is in fashion like unto man in all his parts and members, but that as far as we are concerned to know, he is of that form which he attributes to himself in the sacred writings. If therefore we persist in entertaining a different conception of the Deity than that which it is to be presumed he desires should be cherished, inasmuch as he has himself disclosed it to us, we frustrate the purposes of God instead of rendering him submissive obedience. As if, forsooth, we wished to show that it was not we who had thought too meanly of God, but God who had thought too meanly of us.

It is impossible to comprehend accurately under any form of definition the *divine nature*, for so it is called, 2 Pet. i. 4. "that ye might be partakers of the divine nature"—though nature does not here signify essence, but the divine image, as in Gal. iv. 8. and θεοτὴς Col. ii. 9. θειοτὴς Rom. i. 20. τὸ θεῖον Acts xvii. 29. which words are all translated *Godhead*. But though the nature of God cannot be defined, since he who has no efficient cause is essentially greatest of all, some description of it at least may be collected from his names and attributes.

The names and attributes of God either show his nature, or his divine power and excellence. There are three names which seem principally to intimate the nature of God,— יהוה *Jehovah*—יָּה *Jah*— אהיה *Ehie*. Even the name of Jehovah was not forbidden to be pronounced, provided it was with due reverence. It seems to be introduced in the same way, 1 Kings xvii. 12. "as Jehovah thy God liveth," and also in many óther places. This name both in the New Testament and in the Greek version of the Old is always translated Κύριος—*the Lord*,—probably for no other reason than because the word Jehovah could not be expressed in Greek letters. Its signification is, *"he who is,"* or, *"which is, and which was, and which is to come,"* Rev. i. 4. *Jah*, which is a sort of contraction of the former name, has the same signification. *Ehie*, "I am that I am," or "will be;" and if the first person be changed into the third of the kindred verb, *Jave*, who is, or will be,—meaning the same as Jehovah, as some think, and more properly expressed thus than by the other words; but the name Jave appears to signify not only the existence of his nature, but also of his promises, or rather the completion of his promises; whence it is said, Exod. vi. 3. "by my name *Jehovah* was I not known to them." And with what vowel points this name Jehovah ought to be pronounced, is shown by those proper names into the composition of which two of them enter, as Jehosaphat, Jehoram, Jehoiada, and the like. The third, or final vowel point may be supplied by analogy from the two other divine names, אהי and יָּה.

I. The first of those attributes which show the inherent nature of God, is *Truth*.

II. God considered in his most simple nature is a *Spirit*. What a spirit is, or rather what it is not, is shown, Isai. xxxi. 3. "flesh, and not spirit." Whence it is evident that the essence of God, being in itself most simple, can admit no compound quality; so that the term hypostasis, Heb. i. 3. which is differently translated *substance,* or *subsistence,* or *person,* can be nothing else but that most perfect essence by which God subsists by himself, in himself, and through himself. For neither *substance* nor *subsistence* make any addition to what is already a most perfect essence; and the word *person* in its later acceptation signifies any individual thing gifted with intelligence, whereas *hypostasis* denotes not the ens itself, but the essence of the ens in the abstract. Hypostasis, therefore, is clearly the same as essence, and thus many of the Latin commentators render it in the passage already quoted. Therefore, as God is a most simple essence, so is he also a most simple subsistence.

III. *Immensity and infinity*.

IV. *Eternity*. It is universally acknowledged that nothing is eternal, strictly speaking, but what has neither beginning nor end, both which properties are attributed to God, not indeed in each of the following passages separately, but as a plain deduction from the several texts when compared together. The evidence of the New Testament is still clearer, because the Greek word signifies *always existent*.

But all the words used in Scripture to denote eternity, often signify only of old time, or antiquity. Gen. vi. 4. "mighty men which were of old." David also seems to have understood that the term *for ever* only intimated *a great while to come. 2* Sam. vii. 13. "I will establish the throne of his kingdom for ever," compared with v. 19. "thou hast spoken also of thy servant's house for a great while to come." In Heb. xi. 3. the word is also used to signify this world, where the Syriac version translates it,—*before the worlds were framed.* From these and many similar texts it appears that the idea of eternity, properly so called. is conveyed in the Hebrew language rather by comparison and deduction than in express words.

V. The *immutability* of God has ·an immediate connection with the last attribute.

VI. His *incorruptibility* is also derived from the fourth attribute.

VII. The *omnipresence* of God, which is his next attribute, is the consequence of his infinity. Our thoughts of the omnipresence of God, whatever may be the nature of the attributes, should be such as appear most suitable to the reverence due to the Deity.

VIII. *Omnipotence.* There seems, therefore, an impropriety in the term of *actus purus,* or the active principle, which Aristotle applies to God, for thus the Deity would have no choice of act, but what he did he would do of necessity, and could do in no other way, which would be inconsistent with his omnipotence and free agency. It must be remembered, however, that the power of God is not exerted in things which imply a contradiction.

IX. The ninth attribute, or the *Unity* of God, may be considered as proceeding necessarily from all the foregoing attributes. Separate proof for it, however, is not wanting. Is. xliv. 21. "there is no God else beside me. . . . there is none beside me." v. 22. "I am God, and there is none else"—that is, no spirit, no person, no being beside him is God; for *none* is an universal negative, xlvi. 9. "I am God, and there is none else; I am God, and there is none like me." What can be plainer, what more distinct, what more suitable to general comprehension and the ordinary forms of speech for the purpose of impressing on the people of God that there was numerically one God and one Spirit, in the common acceptation of numerical unity. It was in truth fitting and highly agreeable to reason, that the first and consequently the greatest commandment, to which even the lowest of the people were required to pay scrupulous obedience, should be delivered in so plain a manner, that no ambiguous or obscure expressions might lead his worshippers into error, or keep them in suspense or doubt. Accordingly, the Israelites under the law and the prophets always understood it to mean, that God was numerically one God, beside whom there was none other, much less any equal. For the schoolmen had not as yet appeared, who, through their confidence in their own sagacity, or, more properly speaking, on arguments purely contradictory, impugned the doctrine itself of the unity of God which they pretended to assert. But as with regard to the omnipotence of the Deity, it is universally allowed, as has been stated before, that he can do nothing which involves a contradiction; so must it also be remembered in this place, that nothing can

be said of the one God, which is inconsistent with his unity, and which assigns to him at the same time the attributes of unity and plurality.

Proceeding to the evidence of the New Testament, we find it equally clear, so far as it goes over the former ground, and in one respect even clearer, inasmuch as it testifies that the Father of our Lord Jesus Christ is that one God. Christ having been asked, Mark xii. 28. which was the first commandment of all, answers, from Deut. vi. 4.—a passage quoted before, and evidently understood by our Lord in the same sense which had been always applied to it—"hear, O Israel, the Lord our God is one Lord." To which answer the scribe assented, "well, Master, thou hast said the truth; for there is one God, and there is none other but he."

Hitherto those attributes only have been mentioned which describe the nature of God, partly in an affirmative, partly in a negative sense, inasmuch as they deny the existence of those imperfections in the Deity, which belong to created things,—as, for instance, when we speak of his immensity, his infinity, his incorruptibility. I now proceed to notice those which show his divine power and excellence under the ideas of *vitality, intelligence,* and *will.*

I. *Vitality.* Deut. xxxii. 40. "I live for ever," whence he is called "the living God." Psal. xlii. 2. and in many other passages.

II. Under the head of the *intelligence* of God must be classed his attribute of *omniscience.* So extensive is the prescience of God, that he knows beforehand the thoughts and actions of free agents as yet unborn, and many ages before those thoughts or actions have their origin.

III. As regards the *will* of God, he is, 1st, infinitely pure and holy.

2. He is most gracious. Another proof of the immutability of God may be also derived from the consideration of his infinite wisdom and goodness; since a being infinitely wise and good would neither wish to change an infinitely good state for another, nor would be able to change it without contradicting his own attributes.

3. As God is true in respect of his nature, so is he also true and faithful in respect of his will.

4. He is also just. There is no need for discussing at large in this place what is consistent or inconsistent with the justice of God, since it is either plain in itself, or where any remarks are necessary, they will be introduced as the occasion requires in other parts of this work. Severity also is attributed to God, Rom. xi. 22.

From all these attributes springs that infinite excellence which constitutes the true perfection of God, and causes him to abound in glory, and to be most deservedly and justly the supreme Lord of all things, as he is so often called. Some description of this divine glory has been revealed, as far as it falls within the scope of human comprehension.

It follows, finally that God must be styled by us wonderful, and incomprehensible.

CHAP. III.—OF THE DIVINE DECREES.

HITHERTO I have considered that knowledge of God which his nature affords. That which is derived from his efficiency is the next subject of inquiry.

The *efficiency of God* is either *internal* or *external*.

The *internal efficiency* of God is that which is independent of all extraneous agency. Such are his decrees.

The *decrees of God* are *general* or *special*.

God's general decree is that *whereby he has decreed from all eternity of his own most free and wise and holy purpose, whatever he himself willed, or was about to do.*

Whatever. Eph. i. 11. "who worketh all things after the counsel of his own will;" that is, whatever he himself works or wills singly, not what is done by others, or by himself in co-operation with those to whom he has conceded the natural power of free agency. The creation of the world, and the removal of the curse from the ground, Gen. viii. 21, are among his sole decrees.

Of his own most free—; that is, without control, impelled by no necessity, but according to his own will.

Most wise—; that is, according to his perfect foreknowledge of all things that were to be created. Hence it is absurd to separate the decrees or will of the Deity from his eternal counsel and foreknowledge, or to give

them priority of order. For the foreknowledge of God is nothing but the wisdom of God, under another name, or that idea of every thing, which he had in his mind, to use the language of men before he decreed anything.

We must conclude, therefore, that God decreed nothing absolutely, which he left in the power of free agents,—a doctrine which is shown by the whole canon of Scripture. God had said, 2 Kings xx. 1, that Hezekiah should die immediately, which event, however did not happen, and therefore could not have been decreed without reservation. The death of Josiah was not decreed peremptorily, but he would not hearken to the voice of Necho when he warned him according to the word of the Lord, not to come out against him; 2 Chron. xxxv. 22. Again, Jer. xviii. 9, 10. "at what instant I shall speak concerning a nation, and concerning a kingdom, to build and to plant it; if it do evil in my sight, that it obey not my voice, then I will repent of the good wherewith I said I would benefit them,"—that is, I will rescind the decree, because that people hath not kept the condition on which the decree depended. Here then is a rule laid down by God himself, according to which he would always have his decrees understood,—namely, that regard should be paid to the conditionate terms attached to them. So also God had not even decreed absolutely the burning of Jerusalem. Jer. xxxviii. 17. Jonah iii. iv. "yet forty days, and Nineveh shall be overthrown"—whereas it appears from the tenth verse, that when God saw that they turned from their evil way, he repented of his purpose, notwithstanding the anger of Jonah, who thought the change unworthy of God. Acts xxvii. 24, 31. "God hath given thee all them that sail with thee" —and again—"except these abide in the ship, ye cannot be saved," where Paul revokes the declaration he had previously made on the authority of God; or rather, God revokes the gift he had made to Paul, except on condition that they should consult for their own safety by their own personal exertions.

It appears, therefore, from these passages of Scripture, as well as from many others of the same kind, to which we must bow, as to a paramount authority, that the most high God has not decreed all things absolutely.

If, however, it be allowable to examine the divine decrees by the laws of human reason, since so many arguments have been maintained on this subject by controvertists on both sides, with more of subtlety than of solid argument, this theory of contingent decrees may be defended even on the principles of men, as most wise, and in no respect unworthy of the Deity. For if those decrees of God which have been referred to above, and such others of the same class as occur perpetually, were to be understood in an absolute sense, without any implied conditions, God would contradict himself, and appear inconsistent.

It is argued, however, that in such instances not only was the ultimate purpose predestinated, but even the means themselves were predestinated with a view to it. So, indeed, it is asserted, but not on the authority of Scripture; and the silence of Scripture would alone be a sufficient reason for rejecting the doctrine. But it is also attended by this additional inconvenience, that it would entirely take away from human affairs all liberty of action, all endeavor and desire to do right. For we might argue thus—if God have at all events decreed my salvation, however I may act, I shall not perish. But God has also decreed as the means of salvation that you should act rightly. I cannot, therefore, but act rightly at some time or other, since God has so decreed—in the mean time I will do as I please; if I never act rightly, it will be seen that I was never predestinated to salvation, and that whatever good I might have done would have been to no purpose. See more on this subject in the following Chapter.

Nor is it sufficient to affirm in reply, that it is not compulsory necessity which is here intended, but a necessity arising from the immutability of God, whereby all things are decreed, or a necessity arising from his infallibility or prescience, whereby all things are foreknown. I shall dispose hereafter of this twofold necessity of the schools; in the meantime no other law of necessity can be admitted than what logic, or, in other words, what sound reason teaches; that is to say, when the efficient either causes some determinate and uniform effect by its own inherent propensity, as for example, when fire burns, which kind is denominated physical necessity; or when the efficient is compelled by some extraneous force to operate the effect, which is called compulsory necessity, and in the latter case, whatever effect the efficient produces, it produces *per accidens*. Now any necessity arising from external causes influences the agent either determinately or compulsorily; and it is apparent that on either alternative his liberty must be wholly annihilated. But though a certain immutable and internal necessity of acting rightly, independent of all extraneous influence whatever, may exist in God conjointly with the most perfect liberty, both which principles in the same divine nature tend to the same point, it does not therefore follow that the same thing can be conceded with regard to two different natures, as the nature of God and the nature of man, in which case the external immutability of one party may be in opposition to the internal liberty of the other, and may prevent unity of will. Nor is it admitted that the actions of God are in themselves necessary, but only that he has a necessary existence; for Scripture itself testifies that his decrees, and therefore his actions, of what kind soever they be, are perfectly free.

But it is objected that divine necessity, or a first cause, imposes no constraint upon the liberty of free agents. I answer,—if it do not constrain, it either determines, or co-operates, or is wholly inefficient. If it determine or co-operate, it is either the sole or the joint and principal cause of every action, whether good or bad, of free agents. If it be wholly inefficient, it cannot be called a cause in any sense, much less can it be termed necessity.

Nor do we imagine anything unworthy of God, when we assert that those conditional events depend on the human will, which God himself has chosen to place at the free disposal of man; since the Deity purposely framed his own decrees with reference to particular circumstances, in order that he might permit free causes to act conformably to that liberty with which he had endued them. On the contrary, it would be much more unworthy of God, that man should nominally enjoy a liberty of which he was virtually deprived, which would be the case were that liberty to be oppressed or even obscured under the pretext of some sophistical necessity of immutability or infallibility, though not of compulsion,—a notion which has led, and still continues to lead, many individuals into error.

However, properly speaking, the divine counsels can be said to depend on nothing, but on the wisdom of God himself, whereby he perfectly foreknew in his own mind from the beginning what would be the nature and event of every future occurrence when its appointed season should arrive.

But it is asked how events, which are uncertain, inasmuch as they depend on the human will, can harmonize with the decrees of God, which are immutably fixed? for it is written, Psal. xxxiii. 11. "the counsel of Jehovah standeth for ever." To this objection it may be answered, first, that to God the issue of events is not uncertain, but foreknown with the utmost certainty, though they be not decreed necessarily, as will appear hereafter.—Secondly, in all the passages referred to, the divine counsel is said to stand against all human power and counsel, but not against liberty of will in things which God himself has placed at man's disposal, and had determined so to place from all eternity. For otherwise one of God's decrees would be in direct opposition to another, which would lead to the very consequence imputed by the objector to the doctrines of his opponents, inasmuch as by considering those things as necessary which the Deity has left to the uncontrolled decision of man, God would be rendered mutable. But God is not mutable, so long as he decrees nothing absolutely which could happen otherwise through the liberty assigned to man. He would indeed be mutable, neither would his *counsel stand*, if he were to obstruct by another decree that liberty which he had already decreed, or were to darken it with the least shadow of necessity.

It follows, therefore, that the liberty of man must be considered entirely independent of necessity, nor can any admission be made in favor of that modification of the principle which is founded on the doctrine of God's immutability and prescience. If there be any necessity at all, as has been stated before, it either determines free agents to a particular line of conduct, or it constrains them against their will, or it co-operates with them in conjunction with their will, or it is altogether inoperative. If it determine free agents to a particular line of conduct, man will be rendered the natural cause of all his actions, and consequently of his sins, and formed as it were with an inclination for sinning. If it constrain them against their will, man being subject to this compulsory decree, becomes the cause of sins only *per accidens,* God being the cause of sins *per se.* If it co-operate with them in conjunction with their will, then God becomes either the principal or the joint cause of sins with man. If finally it be altogether inoperative, there is no such thing as necessity, it virtually destroys itself by being without operation. For it is wholly impossible, that God should have fixed by a necessary decree what we know at the same time to be in the power of man; or that that should be immutable which it remains for subsequent contingent circumstances either to fulfil or frustrate.

Whatever, therefore, was left to the free will of our first parents, could not have been decreed immutably or absolutely from all eternity; and questionless, the Deity must either have never left any thing in the power of man, or he cannot be said to have determined finally respecting whatever was so left without reference to possible contingencies.

If it be objected, that this doctrine leads to absurd consequences, we reply, either the consequences are not absurd, or they are not the consequences of the doctrine. For it is neither impious nor absurd to say, that the idea of certain things or events might be suggested to God from some extraneous source; since inasmuch as God had determined from all eternity, that man should so far be a free agent, that it remained with himself to decide whether he would stand or fall, the idea of that evil event, or of the fall of man, was suggested to God from an extraneous source, —a truth which all confess.

Nor does it follow from hence, that what is temporal becomes the cause of, or a restriction upon what is eternal, for it was not any thing temporal, but the wisdom of the eternal mind that gave occasion for framing the divine counsel.

Seeing, therefore that, in assigning the gift of free will, God suffered both men and angels to stand or fall at their own uncontrolled choice, there can be no doubt that the decree itself bore a strict analogy to the object which the divine counsel regarded, not necessitating the evil consequences which ensued, but leaving them contingent; hence the covenant was of this kind—if thou stand, thou shalt abide in Paradise; if thou fall, thou shalt be cast out: if thou eat not the forbidden fruit, thou shalt live; if thou eat, thou shalt die.

Hence, those who contend that the liberty of actions is subject to an absolute decree, erroneously conclude that the decree of God is the cause of his foreknowledge, and antecedent in order of time. If we must apply to God a phraseology borrowed from our own habits and understanding, to consider his decrees as consequent upon his foreknowledge seems more agreeable to reason, as well as to Scripture, and to the nature of the Deity himself, who, as has just been proved, decreed everything according to his infinite wisdom by virtue of his foreknowledge.

That the will of God is the first cause of all things, is not intended to be denied, but his prescience and wisdom must not be separated from his will, much less considered as subsequent to the latter in point of time. The will of God, in fine, is not less the universal first cause, because he has himself decreed that some things should be left to our own free will, than if each particular event had been decreed necessarily.

To comprehend the whole matter in a few words, the sum of the argument may be thus stated in strict conformity with reason. God of his wisdom determined to create men and angels reasonable beings, and therefore free agents; foreseeing at the same time which way the bias of their will would incline, in the exercise of their own uncontrolled liberty. What then? shall we say that this foresight or foreknowledge on the part of God imposed on them the necessity of acting in any definite way? No more than if the future event had been foreseen by any human being. For what any human being has foreseen as certain to happen, will not less certainly happen than what God himself has predicted. Thus Elisha foresaw how much evil Hazael would bring upon the children of Israel in the course of a few years, 2 Kings viii. 12. Yet no one would affirm that the evil took place necessarily on account of the foreknowledge of Elisha; for had he never foreknown it, the event

would have occurred with equal certainty, through the free will of the agent. In like manner nothing happens of necessity, because God has foreseen it; but he foresees the event of every action, because he is acquainted with their natural causes, which, in pursuance of his own decree, are left at liberty to exert their legitimate influence. Consequently the issue does not depend on God who foresees it, but on him alone who is the object of his foresight. Since, therefore, as has before been shown, there can be no absolute decree of God regarding free agents, undoubtedly the prescience of the Deity (which can no more bias free agents than the prescience of man, that is, not at all, since the action in both cases is intransitive, and has no external influence,) can neither impose any necessity of itself, nor can it be considered at all as the cause of free actions. If it be so considered, the very name of liberty must be altogether abolished as an unmeaning sound; and that not only in matters of religion, but even in questions of morality and indifferent things. There can be nothing but what will happen necessarily, since there is nothing but what is foreknown by God.

That this long discussion may be at length concluded by a brief summary of the whole matter, we must hold that God foreknows all future events, but that he has not decreed them all absolutely: lest the consequence should be that sin in general would be imputed to the Deity, and evil spirits and wicked men exempted from blame. Does my opponent avail himself of this, and think the concession enough to prove either that God does not foreknow every thing, or that all future events must therefore happen necessarily, because God has foreknown them? I allow that future events which God has foreseen, will happen certainly, but not of necessity. They will happen certainly, because the divine prescience cannot be deceived, but they will not happen necessarily, because prescience can have no influence on the object foreknown, inasmuch as it is only an intransitive action. What therefore is to happen according to contingency and the free will of man, is not the effect of God's prescience, but is produced by the free agency of its own natural causes, the future spontaneous inclination of which is perfectly known to God. Thus God foreknew that Adam would fall of his own free will; his fall was therefore certain, but not necessary, since it proceeded from his own free will, which is incompatible with necessity. Thus also God foreknew that the Israelites would turn from the true worship to strange gods, Deut. xxxi. 16. If they were to be led to revolt necessarily on account of this prescience on the part of God, it was unjust to threaten them with the many evils which he was about to send upon them, ver. 17. it would have been to no purpose that a song was ordered to be written, which should be a witness for him against the children of Israel, because their sin would have been of necessity. The truth is, that the prescience of God, like that of Moses, v. 27. had no extraneous influence, and God testifies, v. 16. that he foreknew they would sin from their own voluntary impulse, and of their own accord,—"this people will rise up," and v. 18. "I will surely hide my face in that day. . . . in that they are turned unto other gods." Hence the subsequent revolt of the Israelites was not the consequence of God's foreknowledge, but his foreknowledge led him to know that, although they were free agents, they would certainly revolt, owing to causes with which he was well acquainted.

From what has been said it is sufficiently evident, that free causes are not impeded by any law of necessity arising from the decrees or prescience of God. There are some who in their zeal to oppose this doctrine, do not hesitate even to assert that God is himself the cause and origin of sin. Such men, if they are not to be looked upon as misguided rather than mischievous, should be ranked among the most abandoned of all blasphemers. An attempt to refute them, would be nothing more than an argument to prove that God was not the evil spirit.

Thus far of the *general decree* of God. Of his *special decrees* the first and most important is that which regards his *Son,* and from which he primarily derives his name of *Father.* From all these passages it appears that the Son of God was begotten by the decree of the Father. There is no express mention made of any *special decree* respecting *the angels,* but its existence seems to be implied.

CHAP. IV.—Of Predestination.

The principal *special decree* of God *relating to man* is termed *predestination,* whereby *God in pity to mankind, though foreseeing that they would fall of their own accord, predestinated to eternal salvation before the foundation of the world those who should believe and continue in the faith; for a manifestation of the glory of his mercy, grace, and wisdom, according to his purpose in Christ.*

It has been the practice of the schools to use the word predestination, not only in the sense of election, but also of reprobation. This is not consistent with the caution necessary on so momentous a subject, since wherever it is mentioned in Scripture, election alone is uniformly intended. In other modes of expression, where predestination is alluded to, it is always in the same sense of election alone. For when it is said negatively, 1 Thess. v. 9. "God hath not appointed us to wrath, but to obtain salvation by our Lord Jesus Christ," we are not obliged to imply that there are others who are appointed to wrath. Nor does the expression in 1 Pet. ii. 8. "whereunto also they were appointed," signify that they were appointed from all eternity, but from some time subsequent to their defection, as the Apostles are said to be *chosen* in time, *and ordained* by Christ to their office, John xv. 16.

Again, if an argument of any weight in the discussion of so controverted a subject can be derived from allegorical and metaphorical expressions, mention is frequently made of those who are written among the living, and of the book of life, but never of the book of death. Enrolment in the book of life, however, does not appear to signify eternal predestination, which is general, but some temporary and particular decision of God applied to certain men, on acount of their works. Psal. lxix. 28. "let them be blotted out of the book of the living, and not be written with the righteous;" whence it appears that they had not been written from everlasting. Rev. xx. 12. "the dead were judged out of those things which were written in the books, according to their works;" whereby it is evident that it was not the book of eternal predestination, but of their works. Nor were those ordained from everlasting who are said, Jude 4, to have been "before of old ordained to this condemnation." For why should we give so extensive a signification to the term *of old,* instead of defining it to mean, from the time when they had become inveterate and hardened sinners? Why must we understand it to imply so remote a period, either in this text, or in the passage whence it seems to be taken? 2 Pet. ii. 3. "whose judgment now of a long time lingereth not, and their damnation slumbereth not,"—that is, from the time of their apostacy, however long they had dissembled it.

The text, Prov. xvi. 4. is also objected,—"Jehovah hath made all things for himself; yea, even the wicked for the day of evil." But God did not make man wicked, much less did he make him so *for himself.* All that he did was to sentence the wicked to deserved punishment, as was most fitting, but he did not predestinate him who was innocent to the same fate. It is more clearly expressed, Eccles. vii. 29. "God hath made man upright; but they have sought out many inventions;" whence the day of evil ensues as certainly, as if the wicked had been made for it.

Predestination, therefore, must always be understood with reference to election, and seems often to be used instead of the latter term. What St. Paul says, Rom. viii. 29. "whom he did foreknow, he also did predestinate," is thus expressed, 1 Pet. i. 2. "elect according to the foreknowledge." Rom. ix. 11. "the purpose of God according to election." xi. 5. "according to the election of grace." "Eph. i. 4. "he hath chosen us in him." Col. iii. 12. "as the elect of God, holy and beloved." 2 Thess. ii. 13. "because God hath from the beginning chosen you to salvation." Reprobation, therefore, could not be included under predestination. 1 Tim. ii. 4. "who will have all men to be saved, and to come unto the knowledge of the truth." 2 Pet. iii. 9. "the Lord . . . is long-suffering to us-ward, not willing that any should perish, but that all should come to repentance,"—*to us-ward,* that is, towards all men, not towards the elect only, as some interpret it, but particularly towards the wicked, as it is said, Rom. ix. 22. "God endured . . . the vessels of wrath." For if, as some object, Peter would scarcely have included himself among the unbelievers, much less would he have numbered himself among such of the elect as had not yet come to repentance. Nor does God delay, but rather hastens the times on account of the elect.

I do not understand by the term election, that general or national election, by which God chose the whole nation of Israel for his own people. Nor do I mean that sense of the word election in which God, after rejecting the Jews, is said to have chose that the Gospel should be announced to the Gentiles, to which the apostle particularily alludes, Rom. ix. and xi.; nor that in which an individual is said to be selected for the performance of some office, as 1 Sam. x. 24. "see ye him whom the Lord hath chosen?" John vi. 70. "have not I chosen you twelve, and one of you is a devil?" whence those are sometimes called elect who are eminent for any particular excellence, as 2 John 1. "the elect lady," that is, most precious. But that special election is here intended, which is nearly synonymous with eternal predestination. Election, therefore, is not a part of predestination; much less then is reprobation. For, speaking accurately, the ultimate purpose of predestination is salvation of believers,—a thing in itself desirable,—whereas the object which reprobation has in view is the destruction of unbelievers, a thing in itself ungrateful and odious; whence it is clear that God could never have predestinated reprobation, or proposed it to himself as an end. If therefore the Deity have no pleasure either in sin or in the death of the sinner, that is, either in the cause or the effect of reprobation, certainly he cannot delight in reprobation itself. It follows, that reprobation forms no part of what is meant by the divine predestination.

In pity to mankind, though foreseeing that they would fall of their own accord. It was not simply man as a being who was to be created, but man as a being who was to fall of his own accord, that was the matter or object of predestination; for that manifestation of divine grace and mercy which God designed as the ultimate purpose of predestination, presupposes the existence of sin and misery in man, originating from himself alone. That the fall of man was not necessary, is admitted on all sides; but if such, nevertheless, was the nature of the divine decree, that his fall became really inevitable (both which opinions, however contradictory, are sometimes held by the same persons), then the restoration of man, after he had lapsed of necessity, became no longer a matter of grace on the part of God, but of simple justice. For if it be granted that he lapsed, though not against his own will, yet of necessity, it will be impossible not to think that the admitted necessity must have overruled or influenced his will by some secret force or guidance. But if God foresaw that man would fall of his own free will, there was no occasion for any decree relative to the fall itself, but only relative to the provision to be made for man, whose future fall was foreseen. Since then the apostasy of the first man was not decreed, but only foreknown by the infinite wisdom of God, it follows that predestination was not an absolute decree before the fall of man; and even after his fall, it ought always to be considered and defined as arising, not so much from a decree itself, as from the immutable condition of a decree.

Predestinated; that is, designated, elected: proposed to himself the salvation of man as the scope and end of his counsel. Hence may be refuted the notion of a preterition and desertion from all eternity, in direct opposition to which God explicitly and frequently declares, as has been quoted above, that he desires not the death of any one, but the salvation of all; that he hates nothing that he has made; and that he has omitted nothing which might suffice for universal salvation.

For *a manifestation of the glory of his mercy, grace, and wisdom.* This is the chief end of predestination.

According to his purpose in Christ. Eph. iii. 10, 11. "the manifold wisdom of God, according to the eternal purpose which he purposed in Christ Jesus our Lord." This is the source of that love of God, declared to us in Christ. Hence there was no grace decreed for man who was to fall, no mode of reconciliation with God, independently of the foreknown sacrifice of Christ; and since God has so plainly declared that predestination is the effect of his mercy, and love, and grace,

and wisdom in Christ, it is to these qualities that we ought to attribute it, and not, as is generally done, to his absolute and secret will, even in those passages where mention is made of his will only. Exod. xxxiii. 19. "I will be gracious to whom I will be gracious," that is, not to enter more largely into the causes of this graciousness at present, Rom. ix. 18. "he hath mercy on whom he will have mercy," by that method, namely, which he had appointed in Christ. It will appear, moreover, on examination of the particular texts, that in passages of this kind God is generally speaking of some extraordinary manifestation of his grace and mercy. James i. 18. "of his own will,"—that is, in Christ, who is the word and truth of God,—"begat he us with the word of truth."

Those who should believe, and continue in the faith. This condition is immutably attached to the decree, nor does it attribute mutability either to God or to his decrees; 2 Tim. ii. 19. "the foundation of God standeth sure, having this seal, The Lord knoweth them that are his:" or according to the explanation in the same verse, all who "name the name of Christ, and depart from iniquity;" that is, whoever believes: the mutability is entirely on the side of them who renounce their faith, as it is said, 2 Tim. ii. 13. "if we believe not, yet he abideth faithful; he cannot deny himself." It seems, then, that there is no particular predestination or election, but only general,—or in other words, that the privilege belongs to all who heartily believe and continue in their belief,—that none are predestinated or elected irrespectively, e. g. that Peter is not elected as Peter, or John as John, but inasmuch as they are believers, and continue in their belief,—and that thus the general decree of election becomes personally applicable to each particular believer, and is ratified to all who remain stedfast in the faith.

This is most explicitly declared by the whole of Scripture, which offers salvation and eternal life equally to all, under the condition of obedience in the Old Testament, and of faith in the New. There can be no doubt that the tenor of the decree as promulged was in conformity with the decree itself,—otherwise the integrity of God would be impugned, as expressing one intention, and concealing another within his breast. Such a charge is in effect made by the scholastic distinction which ascribes a twofold will to God; his revealed will, whereby he prescribes the way in which he desires us to act, and his hidden will, whereby he decrees that we shall never so act; which is much the same as to attribute to the Deity two distinct wills, whereof one is in direct contradiction to the other. It is, however, asserted that the Scriptures contain two opposite statements respecting the same thing;—it was the will of God that Pharaoh should let the people go, for such was the divine command,—but it was also not his will, for he hardened Pharaoh's heart. The truth however is, that it was God alone who willed their departure, and Pharaoh alone who was unwilling; and that he might be the more unwilling, God hardened his heart, and himself deferred the execution of his own pleasure, which was in opposition to that of Pharaoh, that he might afflict him with heavier punishment on account of the reluctance of his will. Neither in his mode of dealing with our common father Adam, nor with those whom he calls and invites to accept of grace, can God be charged with commanding righteousness, while he decrees our disobedience to the command. What can be imagined more absurd than a necessity which does not necessitate, and a will without volition?

The tenor of the decree as promulged (which was the other point to be proved) is uniformly conditional. Gen. ii. 17. "thou shalt not eat of it; for in the day that thou eatest thereof thou shalt surely die,"—which is the same as if God had said, I will that thou shalt not eat of it; I have not therefore decreed that thou shalt eat of it; for if thou eatest thou shalt die; if thou eatest not, thou shalt live. Thus the decree itself was conditional before the fall; which from numberless other passages appears to have been also conditional after the fall. Exod. xxxii. 32, 33. "blot me, I pray thee, out of thy book which thou hast written . . . whosoever hath sinned against me, him will I blot out of my book." Such was the love of Moses for his nation, that either he did not remember that believers, so long as they continued such, could not be blotted out, or the prayer must be understood in a modified sense, as in Rom. ix. 1. "I could wish, if it were possible." The reply of God,

however, although metaphorical, explains with sufficient clearness that the principle of predestination depends upon a condition,—"whosoever hath sinned, him will I blot out." This is announced more fully in the enforcement of the legal covenant, Deut. vii. 6—8. where God pointedly declares his choice and love of his people to have been gratuitous; and in v. 9. where he desires to be known as "a faithful God which keepeth his covenant and mercy," yet he adds as a condition, "with them that love him and keep his commandments." Again, it is said still more clearly, v. 12. "it shall come to pass, if ye hearken to these judgments, and keep and do them, that Jehovah thy God shall keep unto thee the covenant and the mercy which he sware unto thy fathers." Though these and similar passages seem chiefly to refer either to the universal election of a nation to the service of God, or of a particular individual or family to some office (for in the Old Testament scarcely a single expression can be discovered referring to election properly so called, that is, election to eternal life), yet the principle of the divine decree is in all cases the same. Thus it is said of Solomon, as of another Christ, 1 Chron. xxviii. 6, 7, 9. "I have chosen him to be my son, and I will be his father." But what are the terms of the covenant?— "if he be constant to do my commandments and my judgments, as at this day . . . if thou seek him, he will be found of thee; but if thou forsake him, we will cast thee off for ever." The election of his posterity also depended on the same stipulation.

The same must be remembered with respect to the covenant of grace, as often as the condition itself is not expressly added. It is, however, rarely omitted. Mark xvi. 16, "he that believeth and is baptised shall be saved; but he that believeth not shall be damned." If we figure to ourselves that God originally predestinated mankind on such conditional terms as these, endless controversies might be decided by this single sentence, or by John iii. 16. "God so loved the world, that he gave his only begotten Son, that whosoever believeth in him should not perish, but have everlasting life." No man was more evidently one of the elect than Peter, and yet a condition is expressly reserved, John xiii. 8. "if I wash thee not, thou hast no part with me." What then ensued? Peter readily complied, and consequently had part with his Lord; had he not complied, he would have had no part with him. For though Judas is not only said to have been chosen, which may refer to his apostleship, but even to have been given to Christ by the Father, he yet attained not salvation. John xvii. 12. "those that thou gavest me I have kept, and none of them is lost, but the son of perdition; that the Scripture might be fulfilled." i. 11, 12. "he came unto his own, and his own received him not. But as many as received him, to them gave he power," that is, to those who believed in his name; to whom he did not give power before they had received and believed in him, not even to those who were specially called his own. So St. Paul, Eph. i. 13. Undoubtedly those whom in the beginning of his epistle he calls holy, were not sealed till after that they had believed, were not individually predestinated before that period.

Again, if God have predestinated us *in Christ,* as has been proved already, it certainly must be on condition of faith in Christ. 2 Thes. ii. 13. whence it appears that it is only those who will believe that are chosen. Heb. xi. 6. "without faith it is impossible to please God,"—and thus become one of the elect; whence I infer that believers are the same as the elect, and that the terms are used indiscriminately. So Matt. xx. 16. "many be called, but few chosen," only signifies that they which believe are few. Rom. viii. 33. "who shall lay anything to the charge of God's elect?" that is, of believers: otherwise by separating election from faith, and therefore from Christ, we should be entangled in hard, not to say detestable and absurd doctrines. So also Rom. xi. 7. "the election have obtained it;" that is, believers, as is clear from the twentieth verse, "thou," that is, thou that art elect, "standest by faith." Such is St. Paul's interpretation of the doctrine in his own case; 1 Cor. ix. 27.

Two difficult texts remain to be explained from analogy by the aid of so many plainer passages; for what is obscure must be illustrated by what is clear, not what is clear by what is obscure. The first passage occurs Acts xiii. 48. the other Rom. viii. 28—30, which, as being in my judgment the least difficult of the two, I shall discuss first. It is as follows: "we know that all things work together for good to them that love God, to them who are the called according to his purpose: for whom he did foreknow, he also did predestinate to be conformed to the image of his Son, &c. moreover whom he did predestinate, them he also called; and whom he called, them he also justified; and whom he justified, them he also glorified."

In the first place it must be remarked, that it appears from v. 28. that those "who love God" are the same as those "who are the called according to his purpose," and consequently as those "whom he did foreknow," and "whom he did predestinate," for "them he also called," as is said in v. 30. Hence it is apparent that the apostle is here propounding the scheme and order of predestination in general, not of the predestination of certain individuals in preference to others. As if he had said, We know that all things work together for good to those who love God, that is, to those who believe, for those who love God believe in him. Further, as regards the order, God originally foreknew those who should believe, that is, he decreed or announced it as his pleasure that it should be those alone who should find grace in his sight through Christ, that is, all men, if they would believe. These he predestinated to salvation, and to this end he in various ways called all mankind to believe, or in other words, to acknowledge God in truth; those who actually thus believed he justified; and those who continued in the faith unto the end he finally glorified. But that it may be more clear who those are whom God has foreknown, it must be observed that there are three ways in which any person or thing is said to be known to God. First, by his universal knowledge, as Acts xv. 18. "known unto God are all his works from the beginning of the world." Secondly, by his approving or gracious knowledge, which is an Hebraism, and therefore requires more explanation. Exod. xxxiii. 12. "I know thee by name, and thou hast also found grace in my sight." Thirdly, by knowledge attended with displeasure. In the passage under discussion it is evident that the approving knowledge of God can be alone intended; but he foreknew or approved no one, except in Christ, and no one in Christ except a believer. Those therefore who were about to love, that is, to believe in God, God foreknew or approved;—or in general all men, if they should believe; those whom he thus foreknew, he predestinated, and called them that they might believe; those who believed, he justified. But if God justified believers, and believers only, inasmuch as it is faith alone that justifieth, he foreknew those only who would believe, for those whom he foreknew he justified; those therefore whom he justified he also foreknew, namely, those alone who were about to believe. So Rom. xi. 2. "God hath not cast away his people which he foreknew," that is, believers, as appears from v. 20. 2 Tim. ii. 19. "the Lord knoweth them that are his," that is, all who name the name of Christ, and depart from iniquity; or in other words, all believers. 1 Pet. i. 2. "elect according to the foreknowledge of God the Father, through sanctification of the Spirit, unto obedience and sprinkling of the blood of Jesus Christ." This can be applicable to none but believers, whom the Father has chosen, according to his foreknowledge and approbation of them, through the sanctification of the Spirit and faith, without which the sprinkling of the blood of Christ would avail them nothing. Hence it seems that the generality of commentators are wrong in interpreting the foreknowledge of God in these passages in the sense of prescience; since the prescience of God seems to have no connection with the principle or essence of predestination; for God has predestinated and elected whoever believes and continues in the faith. Of what consequence is it to us to know whether the prescience of God foresees who will, or will not, subsequently believe? for no one believes because God has foreseen his belief, but God foresees his belief because he was about to believe. Nor is it easy to understand how the prescience or foreknowledge of God with regard to particular persons can be brought to bear at all upon the doctrine of predestination, except for the purpose of raising a number of useless and utterly inapplicable questions. For why should God foreknow particular individuals, or what could he foreknow in them which should induce him to predestinate them in particular, rather than all in general, when the condition of faith, which was common to all mankind, had been once laid down. Without searching deeper into this subject, let us be contented to know nothing more than that God, out of his infinite mercy and grace in Christ, has predestinated to salvation all who should believe.

The other passage is Acts xiii. 48. "when the Gentiles heard this, they were glad, and glorified the word of the Lord; and as many as were ordained to eternal life, believed." The difficulty is caused by the abrupt manner in which the sacred historian introduces an assertion, which appears at first sight to contradict himself as well as the rest of Scripture, for he had before attributed to Peter this saying, chap. x. 34, 35. "of a truth I perceive that God is no respecter of persons; but in every nation he that feareth him, and worketh righteousness, is accepted with him." *Accepted* certainly means chosen; and lest it should be urged that Cornelius was a proselyte previously, St. Paul says the same even of those who had never known the law, Rom. ii. 10, 14. Now those who hold the doctrine that a man believes because he is ordained to eternal life, not that he is ordained to eternal life because he will believe, cannot avoid attributing to God the character of a respecter of persons, which he so constantly disclaims. Besides, if the Gentiles believed because they were ordained to eternal life, the same must have been the primary cause of the unbelief of the Jews, which will plead greatly in their excuse, since it would seem that eternal life had only been placed in their view, not offered to their acceptance. Nor would such a dispensation be calculated to encourage the other nations, who would immediately conclude from it that there was no occasion for any will or works of their own in order to obtain eternal life, but that the whole depended on some appointed decree, whereas, on the contrary, Scripture uniformly shows in the clearest manner, that as many as have been ordained to eternal life believe, not simply because they have been so ordained, but because they have been ordained on condition of believing.

For these reasons other interpreters of more sagacity, according to my judgment, have thought that there is some ambiguity in the Greek word τεταγμένοι, which is translated *ordained*, and that it has the same force as εὖ ἤτοι μετρίως διατεθειμένοι, *well or moder-*

ately disposed or affected, of a composed, attentive, upright, and not disorderly mind; of a different spirit from those Jews, as touching eternal life, who had *put from them the word of God,* and had shown themselves *unworthy of everlasting life.* The Greeks use the word in a similar sense, as in Plutarch, and 2 Thess. iii. 6, 11. "there are some which walk disorderly," certainly with reference to eternal life. This sense of the word, and even the particular application which is here intended, frequently occurs in Scripture in other terms. Luke ix. 62. "εὔθετος, well disposed *or* fit for the kingdom of God." Mark xii. 34. "not far from the kingdom of God." 2 Tim. ii. 21. "a vessel . . . meet for the master's use, and prepared for every good work." For, as will be shown hereafter, there are some remnants of the divine image left in man, the union of which in one individual renders him more fit and disposed for the kingdom of God than another. Since therefore we are not merely senseless stocks, some cause at least must be discovered in the nature of man himself, why divine grace is rejected by some and embraced by others. One thing appears certain, that though all men be dead in sin and children of wrath, yet some are worse than others; and this difference may not only be perceived daily in the nature, disposition, and habits of those who are most alienated from the grace of God, but may also be inferred from the expressions used in the parable, Matt. xiii. where the nature of the soil is variously described in three or four ways, part as stony ground, part overrun with thorns, part good ground, at least in comparison of the rest, before it had as yet received any seed. How could any one be worthy before the Gospel had been preached, unless on account of his being *ordained,* that is, well inclined or disposed, to eternal life? a truth which Christ teaches will be made evident to others by the measure of their own punishment after death. And, lastly, the gift of reason has been implanted in all, by which they may of themselves resist bad desires, so that no one can complain of, or allege in excuse, the depravity of his own nature compared with that of others.

But, it is objected, God has no regard to the less depraved among the wicked in his choice, but often selects the worse rather than the better. Deut. ix. 5. "not for thy righteousness, or for the uprightness of thine heart, dost thou go to possess their land." Luke x. 13. "if the mighty works had been done in Tyre and Sidon, which have been done in you, they had a great while ago repented, sitting in sackcloth and ashes." I answer, that it cannot be determined from these passages, what God regards in those whom he chooses; for in the first place, I have not argued that he has regarded righteousness even in the least degree. Secondly, in the former passage the question is not respecting election to life eternal, but concerning the gift of the land of Canaan to the Israelites, a gift assigned them for other reasons than those for which eternal life would have been given,—partly on account of the wickedness of the original inhabitants, and partly that the promise might be fulfilled which had been ratified by an oath to their forefathers; wherein there is nothing that contradicts my doctrine. In the latter passage, it is not the elect who are compared with the reprobate, but the reprobate who are compared with each other, the Tyrians with the unbelieving Jews, neither of which nations had repented. Nor would the Tyrians ever have truly repented, even if those mighty works had been wrought among them, for, if God had foreseen that they would have repented, he would never have forsaken them; but the expression is to be understood in the same sense as Matt. xxi. 31. "the publicans and the harlots go into the kingdom of God before you."

Lastly, it will be objected that "it is not of him that willeth, nor of him that runneth, but of God that showeth mercy," Rom. ix. 16. I answer, that my argument does not presuppose one that willeth or that runneth, but one that is less reluctant, less backward, less resisting than another—though it is God, nevertheless, that showeth mercy, and is at once infinitely wise and just. On the other hand, whoever affirms that "it is not of him that willeth nor of him that runneth," admits that there is one who wills, and one who runs, but only guards against assigning him any portion of merit or praise. When, however, God determined to restore mankind, he also without doubt decreed that the liberty of will which they had lost should be at least partially regained, which was but reasonable. Whomsoever therefore in the exercise of that degree of freedom which their will had acquired either previously to their call, or by reason of the call itself, God had seen in any respect willing or running, (who it is probable are here meant by the ordained) to them he gave a greater power of willing and running, that is, of believing. Thus it is said, 1 Sam. xvi. 7, "Jehovah looketh on the heart," namely, on the disposition of men either as it is by nature, or after grace has been received from him that calleth them. To the same purport is that well-known saying, "to him that hath shall be given." This may be illustrated by example, as in the case of the centurion, Matt. viii. 10. "I have not found so great faith, no, not in Israel,"—in that of the woman of Canaan, Matt. xv. 28. "O woman, great is thy faith,"—in that of the father of the demoniac, Mark ix. 24. "Lord, I believe; help thou mine unbelief,"—and in that of Zaccheus, Luke xix. 3. "he sought to see Jesus who he was," whence, v. 9. "Jesus said unto him, This day is salvation come to this house." Zacheus therefore had not been ordained from all eternity, but from the time when he had shown himself eagerly desirous of knowing Christ.

Nor is it less on this account "of God that showeth mercy," since the principal is often not improperly put for the sole cause by logicians themselves as well as in common discourse; and it is certain that unless God had first shown mercy, it would have been in the power of no one either to will or to run. 2 Cor. iii. 5. "not that we are sufficient of ourselves to think any thing as of ourselves; but our sufficiency is of God," without whose mercy he that willeth or he that runneth would gain nothing.

Reasoning, therefore, from the analogy of all the other passages of Scripture, I think there can be no difficulty in determining who those are that are said in the verse quoted from the Acts to have been ordained to eternal life. On a review of the whole subject, I should conclude that Luke did not intend to advance in so abrupt a manner any new doctrine, but simply to confirm by a fresh example the saying of Peter respecting Cornelius, Acts x. 34, 35. Cornelius and the Gentiles with him believed, as many at least as feared God and worked righteousness, for such were accepted of God in every nation. So in the other passage, those of the Gentiles whose thoughts were already devoted to serious subjects, worthy the attention of men, believed, and gave themselves up to instruction with docility and gladness of heart, glorifying the word of the Lord. Such Peter declared were accepted of God in every nation, and such Luke, in conformity with Peter's opinion, asserts to be ordained to, that is, qualified for eternal life, even though they were Gentiles.

But an objection of another kind may perhaps be made. If God be said to have predestinated men only on condition that they believe and continue in the faith, predestination will not be altogether of grace, but must depend on the will and belief of mankind; which is derogatory to the exclusive efficacy of divine grace. I maintain on the contrary that, so far from the doctrine of grace being impugned, it is thus placed in a much clearer light than by the theory of those who make the objection. For the grace of God is seen to be infinite, in the first place, by his showing any pity at all for man whose fall was to happen through his own fault. Secondly, by his "so loving the world, that he gave his only begotten Son" for its salvation. Thirdly, by his granting us again the power of volition, that is, of acting freely, in consequence of recovering the liberty of the will by the renewing of the Spirit. It was thus that he opened the heart of Lydia, Acts xvi. 14. Admitting, however, that the condition whereon the decree depends, (that is to say, the will enfranchised by God himself, and that faith which is required of mankind), is left in the power of free agents, there is nothing in the doctrine either derogatory to grace, or inconsistent with justice; since the power of willing and believing is either the gift of God, or, so far as it is inherent in man, partakes not of the nature of merit or of good works, but only of a natural faculty. Nor does this reasoning represent God as depending upon the human will, but as fulfilling his own pleasure, whereby he has chosen that man should always use his own will with a regard to the love and worship of the Deity, and consequently with a regard to his own salvation. If this use of the will be not admitted, whatever worship or love we render to God is entirely vain and of no value; the acceptableness of duties done under a law of necessity is diminished, or rather is annihilated altogether, inasmuch as freedom can no longer be attributed to that will over which some fixed decree is inevitably suspended.

The objections, therefore, which some urge so vehemently against this doctrine, are of no force whatever;—namely, that the repentance and faith of the predestinated having been foreseen, predestination becomes posterior in point of time to works,—that it is rendered dependent on the will of man,—that God is defrauded of part of the glory of our salvation,—that man is puffed up with pride, —that the foundations of all Christian consolation in life and in death are shaken,— that gratuitous justification is denied. On the contrary, the scheme, and consequently the glory, not only of the divine grace, but also of the divine wisdom and justice, is thus displayed in a clearer manner than on the opposite hypothesis; and consequently the principal end is effected which God proposed to himself in predestination.

Seeing, then, that God has predestinated from eternity all those who should believe and continue in the faith, it follows that none can be reprobated, except they do not believe or continue in the faith, and even this rather as a consequence than a decree; there can therefore be no reprobation of individuals from all eternity. For God has predestinated to salvation, on the proviso of a general condition, all who enjoy freedom of will; while none are predestinated to destruction, except through their own fault, and as it were *per accidens*, in the same manner as the gospel itself is said to be a stumbling-block and a savor of death to some. This shall be proved on the testimony of Scripture no less explicitly than the doctrine asserted in the former part of the chapter. Rev. xiii. 8. "all that dwell upon the earth shall worship him, whose names are not written in the book of life of the lamb slain from the foundation of the world;" those, namely, who have not believed, whom God has expressly deserted because they "wandered after the beast," v. 3. Nor should I call the decree in Zephaniah ii. 1—3. a decree of eternal reprobation, but rather of temporal punishment, and at any rate not an absolute decree, as the passage itself is sufficient to show: "gather yourselves together, . . . before the decree bring forth . . . it may be ye shall be hid in the day of the anger of Jehovah."

If God had decreed any to absolute reprobation, which we nowhere read in Scripture, the system of those who affirm that reprobation is an absolute decree, requires that he should have also decreed the means whereby his own decree might be fulfilled. Now these means are neither more nor less than sin. Nor will it avail to reply that God did not decree sin, but only permitted it; for there is a fatal objection to this common subterfuge, namely, that it implies more than simple permission. Further, he who permits a thing does not decree it, but leaves it free.

But even if there be any decree of reprobation, Scripture everywhere declares, that as election is established and confirmed by faith, so reprobation is rescinded by repentance.

If then God reject none but the disobedient and unbelieving, he undoubtedly gives grace to all, if not in equal measure, at least sufficient for attaining knowledge of the truth and final salvation. I have said, not in equal measure, because not even to the reprobate, as they are called, has he imparted uniformly the same degree of grace. For God, as any other proprietor might do with regard to his private possessions, claims to himself the right of determining concerning his own creatures according to his pleasure, nor can he be called to account for his decision, though, if he chose, he could give the best reasons for it. That an equal portion of grace should not be extended to all, is attributable to the supreme will of God alone; that there are none to whom he does not vouchsafe grace sufficient for their salvation, is attributable to his justice. Undoubtedly if he desire that the wicked should turn from their way and live, Ezek. xxxiii. 11.—if he would have all men to be saved, 1 Tim. ii. 4.—if he be unwilling that any should perish, 2 Pet. iii. 9. he must also will that an adequate proportion of saving grace shall be withholden from no man; for if otherwise, it does not appear how his truth towards mankind can be justified. Nor is it enough that only so much grace shall be bestowed, as will suffice to take away all excuse; for our condemnation would have been reasonable, even had no grace at all been bestowed. But the offer of grace having been once proclaimed, those who perish will always have some excuse, and will perish unjustly, unless it be evident that the grace imparted is actually sufficient for salvation. So that what Moses said in his address to the Israelites, Deut. xxix. 4. "Jehovah hath not given you an heart to perceive, and eyes to see, and ears to hear, unto this day," must be understood as having been dictated by the kindness and tenderness of his feelings, which led him to avoid the appearance of harshness and asperity in selecting that particular time for openly reproving the hardness of the hearts of so large an assembly of the people, who were then on the point of entering into covenant with God. Since, therefore, there were two causes to which their impenitence might be ascribed,—either that a heart had not yet been given by God, who was at liberty to give it when he pleased, or, that they had not yielded obedience to God,—he made mention only of God's free will, leaving their hardness of heart to be suggested silently by their own consciences: for no one could be at a loss to perceive either that their own stubbornness must have been the principal cause, if to that day God had not given them an understanding heart, or, on the contrary, that God, who had wrought so many miracles for their sakes, had abundantly given them a heart to perceive, and eyes to see, and ears to hear, but that they had refused to make use of these gifts.

Thus much, therefore, may be considered as a certain and irrefragable truth—that God excludes no one from the pale of repentance and eternal salvation, till he has despised and rejected the propositions of sufficient grace, offered even to a late hour, for the sake of manifesting the glory of his long-suffering and justice. So far from God having anywhere declared in direct and precise terms that reprobation is the effect of his arbitrary will, the reasons which influence him in cases of this kind, are frequently stated,—namely, the grievous sins of the reprobate previously committed, or foreseen before actual commission, —want of repentance,—contempt of grace, —deafness to the repeated calls of God. For reprobation must not be attributed, like the election of grace, to the divine will alone. For the exercise of mercy requires no vindication;

it is unnecessary to assign any cause for it, except God's own merciful will; whereas before reprobation, which is followed by punishment, can be looked upon as just, the sin of the individual, not the arbitrary will of God, must be its primary cause—sin, that is to say, either committed or foreseen, grace having been repeatedly rejected, or sought at length too late, and only through fear of punishment, when the prescribed time was already past. For God does not reprobate for one cause, and condemn or assign to death for another, according to the distinction commonly made; but those whom he has condemned on account of sin, he has also reprobated on account of sin, as in time, so from all eternity. And this reprobation lies not so much in the divine will, as in the obstinacy of their own minds; nor is it the decree of God, but rather of the reprobate themselves, by their refusal to repent while it is in their power. Nor would it be less unjust to decree reprobation, than to condemn for any other cause than sin. Inasmuch, therefore, as there is no condemnation except on account of unbelief or of sin, the texts themselves which are produced in confirmation of the decree of reprobation will prove that no one is excluded by any decree of God from the pale of repentance and eternal salvation, unless it be after the contempt and rejection of grace and that at a very late hour.

I will begin with the case of Jacob and Esau, Rom. ix., because many are of opinion that it is decisive respecting the question at issue. It will be seen that predestination is not so much the subject of discussion in this passage as the unmerited calling of the Gentiles after the Jews had been deservedly rejected.

St. Paul shows in the sixth verse that the word which God spake to Abraham had not been frustrated, though so far from the whole of his posterity having received Christ, more had believed among the Gentiles than among the Jews. For the promise was not made in all the children of Abraham, but in Isaac, v. 7; that is to say, "they which are the children of the flesh, these are not the children of God but the children of the promise are counted for the seed." v. 8. The promise therefore was not made to the children of Abraham according to the flesh, but to the children of God, who are therefore called the children of the promise. But since Paul does not say in this passage who are the children of God, an explanation must be sought from John i. 11, 12. where this very promise is briefly referred to; "he came unto his own, and his own received him not: but as many as received him, to them gave he power to become the sons of God, even to them that believe on his name." The promise, therefore, is not to the children of Abraham in the flesh, but to as many of the children of his faith as received Christ, namely, to the children of God and of the promise, that is, to believers; for where there is a promise, there must be also a faith in that promise.

St. Paul then shows by another example, that God did not grant mercy in the same degree to all the posterity even of Isaac, but much more abundantly to the children of the promise, that is, to believers; and that this difference originates in his own will: lest any one should arrogate anything to himself on the score of his own merits. v. 11, 12. "for the children being not yet born, neither having done any good or evil, that the purpose of God according to election might stand, not of works, but of him that calleth, it was said unto her, The elder shall serve the younger." The purpose of God, according to what election? Doubtless according to the election to some benefit, to some privilege, and in this instance specially to the right of primogeniture transferred from the elder to the younger of the sons or of the nations; whence it arises that God now prefers the Gentiles to the Jews. Here then I acknowledge that his *purpose of election* is expressly mentioned, but not of reprobation. St. Paul contents himself with establishing the general principle of election to any mercy or benefit whatever from this single example. Why should we endeavor to extort from the words a harsh and severe meaning, which does not belong to them? If the elder shall serve the younger, whether the individual or the people be intended, (and in this case it certainly applies best to the people) it does not therefore follow that the elder shall be reprobated by a perpetual decree; nor, if the younger be favored with a larger amount of grace, that the elder shall be favored with none. For this cannot be said of Esau, who was taught the

true worship of God in the house of his father, nor of his posterity, whom we know to have been called to the faith with the rest of the Gentiles. Hence this clause is added in Esau's blessing, Gen. xxvii. 40. "it shall come to pass when thou shalt have the dominion, that thou shalt break his yoke from off thy neck;" which, if the servitude of Esau implies his reprobation, must certainly imply that it was not to last for ever. There is, however, an expression in the same chapter which is alleged as decisive; "Jacob have I loved, but Esau have I hated," v. 13. But how did God evince his love or hatred? He gives his own answer, Mal. i. 2, 3. "I hated Esau, and laid his mountains and his heritage waste." He evinced his love therefore to Jacob, by bringing him back again into his country from the land of Babylon; according to the purpose of that same election by which he now calls the Gentiles, and abandons the Jews. At the same time even this text does not prove the existence of any decree of reprobation, though St. Paul subjoins it incidentally, as it were, to illustrate the former phrase,—"the elder shall serve the younger;" for the text in Mal. i. 2, 3. differs from the present passage, inasmuch as it does not speak of the children yet unborn, but of the children when they had been long dead, after the one had eagerly accepted, and the other had despised the grace of God. Nor does this derogate in the least from the freedom of grace, because Jacob himself openly confesses that he was undeserving of the favor which he had obtained; Gen. xxxiii. 10. St. Paul therefore asserts the right of God to impart whatever grace he chooses even to the undeserving, v. 14, 15. and concludes —"so then it is not of him that willeth, or of him that runneth, (not even of Jacob, who had openly confessed himself undeserving, nor of the Jews who followed after the law of righteousness) but of God that showeth mercy," v. 16. Thus St. Paul establishes the right of God with respect to any election whatever, even of the undeserving, such as the Gentiles then seemed to be.

The apostle then proceeds to prove the same with regard to the rejection of the Jews, by considering God's right to exercise justice upon sinners in general: which justice, however, he does not display by reprobation, and hatred towards the children yet unborn, but by judicially hardening the heart, and punishing flagrant offenders. v. 17, 18. "the Scripture saith unto Pharaoh, Even for this same purpose have I raised thee up," &c. He does not say, "I have decreed," but, "I have raised up;" that is, in raising up Pharaoh, he only called into action, by means of a most reasonable command, that hardness of heart, with which he was already acquainted. So too 1 Pet. ii. (in which chapter much has been borrowed from the ninth of Romans,) v. 7, 8. "unto them which be disobedient, the stone which the builders disallowed . . . even to them that stumble at the word, being disobedient; whereunto also they were appointed." They therefore first disallowed Christ, before they were disallowed by him; they were then finally appointed for punishment, when they persisted in disobedience.

To return, however, to the chapter in Romans. We read in the next verses, 19–21. "thou wilt say then unto me, Why doth he yet find fault? why hast thou made me thus" —that is, hard-hearted, and a vessel unto dishonor, while thou showest mercy to others? In answer to which the apostle proves the reasonableness, not indeed of a decree of reprobation, but of that penal hardness of heart, which, after much long-suffering on the part of God, is generally the final punishment reserved for the more atrocious sins. v. 21. "hath not the potter power over the clay?" that is, the material fitted for his own purposes, to put honor upon whom he chooses, provided it be not on the disobedient; as it is said, 2 Tim. ii. 21. "if a man purge himself from these, he shall be a vessel unto honor," while he hardens still more the hearts of the contumacious, that is, he punishes them, according to the next verse of this chapter— "he endured with much long-suffering the vessels of wrath fitted to destruction." Whence then were they fitted, except from their own hardness of heart, whereby the measure of their iniquity was completed! Nor does the use of the passive voice always imply the sufferance of some external force; for we speak of one being given up to vice, or inclined to this or that propensity, meaning only that such is the bias of his own disposition. Finally, the three last verses of the chapter, which contain the conclusion of the whole question, are a convincing proof that St.

Paul only intended to show on the one hand, the free and gratuitous mercy of God in calling the Gentiles to salvation, who would be obedient to the faith, and, on the other, the justice of his judgments in hardening the hearts of the Jews and others, who obstinately adhered to the law of works. v. 30— 32. "what shall we say then? that the Gentiles . . . have attained to righteousness which is of faith"—not therefore of election independent of faith: "but Israel . . . hath not attained; wherefore? because they sought it not by faith"—not therefore of a decree of reprobation independent of unbelief.

After having passed this difficulty, those which remain will scarcely interrupt our course. Psal. xcv. 10, 11. "forty years long was I grieved with this generation," "unto whom I sware in my wrath that they should not enter into my rest." Here we must observe how long it was before God passed his decree, and that (if we may reason by analogy respecting spiritual things, from types of this kind, as was done before in the case of Esau) he excluded from his eternal rest only those who tempted him, and whose hearts were hardened. Isai. xxix. 10. "for Jehovah hath poured out upon you the spirit of deep sleep, and hath closed your eyes." The reason is given, v. 13, 14. where it appears that it was not on account of God's decree, but of their own grievous wickedness; "forasmuch as this people draw near me with their mouth, but have removed their heart far from me . . . therefore the wisdom of their wise men shall perish." Matt. xi. 25, 26. "I thank thee, O Father, because thou hast hid these things from the wise and prudent, and hast revealed them unto babes: even so, Father, for so it seemed good in thy sight." Lest we should attribute this solely to the arbitrary will of God, the verses preceding will explain why *it seemed good,* and why Christ ascribes glory to the Father on this account, v. 21— 23: where it is disclosed what those wise men had first shown themselves to be, namely, despisers of the divine grace. See also xiii. 11. "it is given unto you to know the mysteries of the kingdom of heaven, but to them it is not given." Do we ask why? the next verse subjoins the reason: "whosoever hath, to him shall be given, and he shall have more abundance; but whosoever hath not, from him shall be taken away even that he hath." This can only be applied to those who have first voluntarily rejected divine grace, in the sense in which nearly the same words are addressed to the slothful servant, xxv. 29. In the same manner must be explained xiii. 13. "therefore speak I to them in parables, because they seeing see not." Hence an easy solution is afforded for other texts. John viii. 43. "ye cannot hear my word;"—because when ye were able, ye would not, ye are now unable, not on account of any decree of God, but through unbelief in which you are hardened, or through pride, on account of which you cannot endure to hear the word; or lastly, as it is expressed in the following verse, because "ye are of your father the devil, and the lusts of your father ye will do." Again, v. 46. "if I say the truth, why do ye not believe me?" Christ himself answers the question, v. 47. "ye therefore hear not, because ye are not of God." Not to be of God cannot signify not elect, but means, as it is said in v. 44. "to be of the devil," that is, to follow the devil rather than God. So too, x. 26. "ye believe not, because ye are not of my sheep." Why "not of my sheep?" Because it was so decreed? By no means,—but because ye do not hear the word; because ye do not follow me; "my sheep hear my voice, and they follow me," v. 27. Ye, as I repeatedly tell you, do not believe. v. 25, 26. "I told you, and ye believed not; the works that I do in my Father's name, they bear witness of me: but ye believe not, because ye are not of my sheep, as I said unto you." The argument runs thus—ye do not believe, because ye are not of my sheep; ye are not of my sheep, because ye neither hear my word, nor follow me. Christ certainly intended to give such a reason for their unbelief as would throw the fault of it upon themselves, not as would exempt them from blame; whereas if not to be of his sheep, be interpreted to mean not to be of the elect, a privilege which had never been within their option, his words would contain an excuse for their conduct, rather than a reproof, which would be contrary to his obvious purpose. Again, xii. 39, 40, compared with Isai. vi. 10. "therefore they could not believe, because that Esaias saith again, He hath blinded their eyes." Not because the words of Isaiah, or the decree of God delivered by his mouth,

had previously taken away from them the grace or power of believing irrespectively; but, as the prophet declares, alleging the reason why they could not believe, because God had blinded their eyes. Why he had blinded their eyes the preceding chapter explains, v. 4, because nothing more remained to be done to his unfruitful vineyard, but to cut it down. 1 Pet. ii. 7, 8. "the stone which the builders disallowed, and a stone of stumbling and rock of offence, even to them which stumble at the word, being disobedient; whereunto also they were appointed,"—that is, to be disobedient. And why? Because they had disallowed that stone, and had stumbled upon it, disallowing Christ themselves before they were disallowed by him. Attention to these points will show that mistakes arise on the doctrine in question as often as the proper distinction between the punishment of hardening the heart and the decree of reprobation is omitted to be made; according to Prov. xix. 3. "the foolishness of man perverteth his way, and his heart fretteth against Jehovah." For such do in effect impugn the justice of God, however vehemently they may disclaim the intention; and might justly be reproved in the words of the heathen Homer:

> . . . they perish'd, self-destroyed
> By their own fault.
> *Odyss.* Book I. 1. 9. Cowper's Translation.

And again, in the person of Jupiter:

> Perverse mankind! whose wills, created free,
> Charge all their woes on absolute decree:
> All to the dooming gods their guilt translate,
> And follies are miscall'd the crimes of fate.
> *Odyss.* Book I. l. 40. Pope's Translation.

CHAP. V.—PREFATORY REMARKS.

I CANNOT enter upon subjects of so much difficulty as the *Son of God* and the *Holy Spirit*, without again premising a few introductory remarks. If indeed I were a member of the Church of Rome, which requires implicit obedience to its creed on all points of faith, I should have acquiesced from education or habit in its simple decree and authority, even though it denies that the doctrine of the Trinity, as now received, is capable of being proved from any passage of Scripture. But since I enrol myself among the number of those who acknowledge the word of God alone as the rule of faith, and freely advance what appears to me much more clearly deducible from the Holy Scriptures than the commonly received opinion, I see no reason why any one who belongs to the same Protestant or Reformed Church, and professes to acknowledge the same rule of faith as myself, should take offence at my freedom, particularly as I impose my authority on no one, but merely propose what I think more worthy of belief than the creed in general acceptation. I only entreat that my readers will ponder and examine my statements in a spirit which desires to discover nothing but the truth, and with a mind free from prejudice. For without intending to oppose the authority of Scripture, which I consider inviolably sacred, I only take upon myself to refute human interpretations as often as the occasion requires, conformably to my right, or rather to my duty as a man. If indeed those with whom I have to contend were able to produce direct attestation from heaven to the truth of the doctrine which they espouse, it would be nothing less than impiety to venture to raise, I do not say a clamor, but so much as a murmur against it. But inasmuch as they can lay claim to nothing more than human powers, assisted by that spiritual illumination which is common to all, it is not unreasonable that they should on their part allow the privileges of diligent research and free discussion to another inquirer, who is seeking truth through the same means and in the same way as themselves, and whose desire of benefiting mankind is equal to their own.

In reliance, therefore, upon the divine assistance, let us now enter upon the subject itself.

OF THE SON OF GOD.

Hitherto I have considered the *internal efficiency* of God, as manifested in his decrees.

His *external efficiency,* or the execution of his decrees, whereby he carries into effect by external agency whatever decrees he has purposed within himself, may be comprised under the heads of *Generation, Creation,* and the *Government of the Universe.*

First, *Generation,* whereby God, in pursuance of his decree, has begotten his only Son; whence he chiefly derives his appellation of Father.

Generation must be an external efficiency, since the Father and Son are different persons; and the divines themselves acknowledge this, who argue that there is a certain emanation of the Son from the Father (which will be explained when the doctrine concerning the Holy Spirit is under examination); for though they teach that the Spirit is co-essential with the Father, they do not deny its emanation, procession, spiration, and issuing from the Father,—which are all expressions denoting external efficiency. In conjunction with this doctrine they hold that the Son is also co-essential with the Father, and generated from all eternity. Hence this question, which is naturally very obscure, becomes involved in still greater difficulties if the received opinion respecting it be followed; for though the Father be said in Scripture to have begotten the Son in a double sense, the one literal, with reference to the production of the Son, the other metaphorical, with reference to his exaltation, many commentators have applied the passages which allude to the exaltation and mediatorial functions of Christ as proof of his generation from all eternity. They have indeed this excuse, if any excuse can be received in such a case, that it is impossible to find a single text in all Scripture to prove the eternal generation of the Son. Certain, however, it is, whatever some of the moderns may allege to the contrary, that the Son existed in the beginning, under the name of the logos or word, and was the first of the whole creation, by whom afterwards all other things were made both in heaven and earth.

All these passages prove the existence of the Son before the world was made, but they conclude nothing respecting his generation from all eternity. The other texts which are produced relate only to his metaphorical generation, that is, to his resuscitation from the dead, or to his unction to the mediatorial office, according to St. Paul's own interpretation of the second Psalm: "I will declare the decree; Jehovah hath said unto me, Thou art my Son; this day have I begotten thee"— which the apostle thus explains, Acts xiii. 32, 33. "God hath fulfilled the promise unto us their children, in that he hath raised up

Jesus again; as it is also written in the second Psalm, Thou art my Son; this day have I begotten thee." Further, it will be apparent from the second Psalm, that God has begotten the Son, that is, has made him a king: v. 6. "yet have I set my King upon my holy hill of Sion;" and then in the next verse, after having anointed his King, whence the name of *Christ* is derived, he says, "this day have I begotten thee." Heb. i. 4, 5. "being made so much better than the angels, as he hath by inheritance obtained a more excellent name than they." No other name can be intended but that of Son, as the following verse proves: "for unto which of the angels said he at any time, Thou art my Son; this day have I begotten thee?" The Son also declares the same of himself. John x. 35, 36. "say ye of Him whom the Father hath sanctified, and sent into the world, Thou blasphemest, because I said, I am the Son of God?" By a similar figure of speech, though in a much lower sense, the saints are also said to be begotten of God.

It is evident however upon a careful comparison and examination of all these passages, and particularly from the whole of the second Psalm, that however the generation of the Son may have taken place, it arose from no natural necessity, as is generally contended, but was no less owing to the decree and will of the Father than his priesthood or kingly power, or his resuscitation from the dead. Nor is it any objection to this that he bears the title of begotten, in whatever sense that expression is to be understood, or of God's *own Son*, Rom. viii. 32. For he is called the own Son of God merely because he had no other Father besides God, whence he himself said, that *God was his Father,* John v. 18. For to Adam God stood less in the relation of Father, than of Creator, having only formed him from the dust of the earth; whereas he was properly the Father of the Son made of his own substance. Yet it does not follow from hence that the Son is co-essential with the Father, for then the title of Son would be least of all applicable to him, since he who is properly the Son is not coeval with the Father, much less of the same numerical essence, otherwise the Father and the Son would be one person; nor did the Father beget him from any natural necessity, but of his own free will,—a mode more perfect and more agreeable to the paternal dignity; particularly since the Father is God, all whose works, and consequently the works of generation, are executed freely according to his own good pleasure, as has been already proved from Scripture.

For questionless, it was in God's power consistently with the perfection of his own essence not to have begotten the Son, inasmuch as generation does not pertain to the nature of the Deity, who stands in no need of propagation; but whatever does not pertain to his own essence or nature, he does not effect like a natural agent from any physical necessity. If the generation of the Son proceeded from a physical necessity, the Father impaired himself by physically begetting a co-equal; which God could no more do than he could deny himself; therefore the generation of the Son cannot have proceeded otherwise than from a decree, and of the Father's own free will.

Thus the Son was begotten of the Father in consequence of his decree, and therefore within the limits of time, for the decree itself must have been anterior to the execution of the decree, as is sufficiently clear from the insertion of the word *to-day.* Nor can I discover on what passage of Scripture the assertors of the eternal generation of the Son ground their opinion, for the text in Micah v. 2. does not speak of his generation, but of his works, which are only said to have been wrought *from of old.* But this will be discussed more at large hereafter.

The Son is also called *only begotten.* Yet he is not called one with the Father in essence, inasmuch as he was visible to sight, and given by the Father, by whom also he was sent, and from whom he proceeded; but he enjoys the title of only begotten by way of superiority, as distinguished from many others who are also said to have been born of God. But since throughout the Scriptures the Son is never said to be begotten, except, as above, in a metaphorical sense, it seems probable that he is called *only begotten* principally because he is the one mediator between God and man.

So also the Son is called the *first born;* all which passages preclude the idea of his co-essentiality with the Father, and of his generation from all eternity. Thus it is said of Israel, Exod. iv. 22. and of Ephraim, Jer. xxxi. 9. and of all the saints, Heb. xii. 23.

Hitherto only the metaphorical generation of Christ has been considered; but since to generate another who had no previous existence, is to give him being, and that if God generate by a physical necessity, he can generate nothing but a co-equal Deity, which would be inconsistent with self-existence, an essential attribute of Divinity; (so that according to the one hypothesis there would be two infinite Gods, or according to the other the *first* or *efficient cause* would become the *effect,* which no man in his senses will admit) it becomes necessary to inquire how or in what sense God the Father can have begotten the Son. This point also will be easily explained by reference to Scripture. For when the Son is said to be *the first born of every creature,* and *the beginning of the creation of God,* nothing can be more evident than that God of his own will created, or generated, or produced the Son before all things, endued with the divine nature, as in the fulness of time he miraculously begat him in his human nature of the Virgin Mary. The generation of the divine nature is described by no one with more sublimity and copiousness than by the apostle to the Hebrews, i. 2, 3. "whom he hath appointed heir of all things, by whom also he made the worlds; who being the brightness of his glory, and the express image of his person. . . ." It must be understood from this, that God imparted to the Son as much as he pleased of the divine nature, nay of the divine substance itself, care being taken not to confound the substance with the whole essence, which would imply, that the Father had given to the Son what he retained numerically the same himself; which would be a contradiction of terms instead of a mode of generation. This is the whole that is revealed concerning the generation of the Son of God. Whoever wishes to be wiser than this, becomes foiled in his pursuit after wisdom, entangled in the deceitfulness of vain philosophy, or rather of sophistry, and involved in darkness.

Since, however, Christ not only bears the name of the only begotten Son of God, but is also several times called in Scripture God, notwithstanding the universal doctrine that there is but one God, it appeared to many, who had no mean opinion of their own acuteness, that there was an inconsistency in this; which gave rise to an hypothesis no less strange than repugnant to reason, namely, that the Son, although personally and numerically another, was yet essentially one with the Father, and that thus the unity of God was preserved.

But unless the terms unity and duality mean the same with God as with man, it would have been to no purpose that God had so repeatedly inculcated that first commandment, that he was the one and only God, if another could be said to exist besides, who also himself ought to be believed in as the one God. Unity and duality cannot consist of one and the same essence. God is one ens, not two; one essence and one subsistence, which is nothing but a substantial essence, appertain to one ens; if two subsistences or two persons be assigned to one essence, it involves a contradiction of terms, by representing the essence as at once simple and compound. If one divine essence be common to two persons, that essence or divinity will either be in the relation of a whole to its several parts, or of a genus to its several species, or lastly of a common subject to its accidents. If none of these alternatives be conceded, there is no mode of escaping from the absurd consequences that follow, such as that one essence may be the third part of two or more.

There would have been no occasion for the supporters of these opinions to have offered such violence to reason, nay even to so much plain scriptural evidence, if they had duly considered God's own words addressed to kings and princes, Psal. lxxxii. 6. "I have said, Ye are gods, and all of you are children of the Most High;" or those of Christ himself, John x. 35. "if he called them Gods, unto whom the word of God came, and the Scripture cannot be broken—;" or those of St. Paul, 1 Cor. viii. 5, 6. "for though there be that are called gods, whether in heaven or earth, (for there be gods many and lords many,) but to us there is but one God, the Father, of whom are all things;" or lastly of St. Peter, ii. 1, 4. "that by these ye might be partakers of the divine nature," which implies much more than the title of gods in the sense in which that title is applied to kings; though no one would conclude from this expression that the saints were co-essential with God.

Let us then discard reason in sacred matters, and follow the doctrine of Holy Scripture exclusively. Accordingly, no one need expect that I should here premise a long metaphysical discussion, and advocate in all its parts the drama of the personalities in the Godhead: since it is most evident, in the first place, from numberless passages of Scripture, that there is in reality but one true independent and supreme God; and as he is called one, (inasmuch as human reason and the common language of mankind, and the Jews, the people of God, have always considered him as one person only, that is, one in a numerical sense) let us have recourse to the sacred writings in order to know who this one true and supreme God is. This knowledge ought to be derived in the first instance from the Gospel, since the clearest doctrine respecting the one God must necessarily be that copious and explanatory revelation concerning him which was delivered by Christ himself to his apostles, and by the apostles to their followers. Nor is it to be supposed that the gospel would be ambiguous or obscure on this subject; for it was not given for the purpose of promulgating new and incredible doctrines respecting the nature of God, hitherto utterly unheard of by his own people, but to announce salvation to the Gentiles through Messiah the Son of God, according to the promise of the God of Abraham. "No man hath seen God at any time; the only begotten Son, which is in the bosom of the Father, he hath declared him," John i. 18. Let us therefore consult the Son in the first place respecting God.

According to the testimony of the Son, delivered in the clearest terms, the Father is that one true God, by whom are all things. Being asked by one of the scribes, Mark xii. 28, 29, 32, which was the first commandment of all, he answered from Deut. vi. 4, "the first of all the commandments is, 'Hear, O Israel, the Lord our God is one Lord;'" or as it is in the Hebrew, "Jehovah our God is one Jehovah." The scribe assented; "there is one God, and there is none other one but he;" and in the following verse Christ approves this answer. Nothing can be more clear than that it was the opinion of the scribe, as well as of the other Jews, that by the unity of God is intended his oneness of person. That this God was no other than God the Father, is proved from John viii. 41, 54, "we have one Father, even God. . . . it is my Father that honoreth me; of whom ye say that he is your God." Christ therefore agrees with the whole people of God, that the Father is that one and only God. For who can believe it possible for the very first of the commandments to have been so obscure, and so ill understood by the Church through such a succession of ages, that two other persons, equally entitled to worship, should have remained wholly unknown to the people of God, and debarred of divine honors even to that very day? especially as God, where he is teaching his own people respecting the nature of their worship under the gospel, forewarns them that they would have for their God the one Jehovah whom they had always served, and David, that is, Christ, for their King and Lord. Jer. xxx. 9. "they shall serve Jehovah their God, and David their King, whom I will raise up unto them." In this passage Christ, such as God willed that he should be known or worshipped by his people under the gospel, is expressly distinguished from the one God Jehovah, both by nature and title. Christ himself therefore, the Son of God, teaches us nothing in the gospel respecting the one God but what the law had before taught, and every where clearly asserts him to be his Father. John xx. 17. "I ascend unto my Father and your Father; and to my God and your God:" if therefore the Father be the God of Christ, and the same be our God, and if there be none other God but one, there can be no God beside the Father.

Paul, the apostle and interpreter of Christ, teaches the same in so clear and perspicuous a manner, that one might almost imagine the inculcation of this truth to have been his sole object. No teacher of catechumens in the church could have spoken more plainly and expressly of the one God, according to the sense in which the universal consent of mankind has agreed to understand unity of number. 1 Cor. viii. 4—6. "we know that an idol is nothing in the world, and that there is none other God but one: for though there be that are called gods, whether in heaven or in earth, (as there be gods many and lords many), but to us there is but one God, the Father, of whom are all things, and we in him; and one Lord Jesus Christ, by whom are all things, and we by him." Here the expression *there is none other God but one,* excludes not only all other essences, but all other persons whatever; for it is expressly said in the sixth verse, "that the Father is that one God;" wherefore there is no other person but one; at least in that sense which is intended by divines, when they argue from John xiv. 16. that there is *another,* for the sake of asserting the personality of the Holy Spirit. Again, to those *who are called gods, whether in heaven or in earth, God the Father of whom are all things* is opposed singly; he who is numerically *one God,* to *many gods.* Though the Son be another God, yet in this passage he is called merely *Lord;* he *of whom are all things* is clearly distinguished from him *by whom are all things,* and if a difference of causation prove a difference of essence, he is distinguished also in essence. Besides, since a numerical difference originates in difference of essence, those who are two numerically, must be also two essentially. There is *one Lord,* namely, he whom "God the Father hath made," Acts ii. 36. much more therefore is the Father Lord, who made him, though he be not here called Lord. For he who calls the Father *one God,* also calls him one Lord above all, as Psal. cx. 1. "the Lord saith unto my Lord," —a passage which will be more fully discussed hereafter. He who calls Jesus Christ *one Lord,* does not call him one God, for this reason among others, that "God the Father hath made him both Lord and Christ," Acts ii. 36. Elsewhere therefore he calls the Father both God and Lord of him whom he here calls "one Lord Jesus Christ." Eph. i. 17. "the God of our Lord Jesus Christ." 1 Cor. xi. 3. "the head of Christ is God." xv. 28. "the Son also himself shall be subject unto him." If in truth the Father be called the *Father of Christ,* if he be called *the God of Christ,* if he be called *the head of Christ,* if he be called the God to whom Christ described as *the Lord,* nay, even as *the Son himself, is subject, and shall be subjected,* why should not the Father be also the Lord of the same Lord Christ, and the God of the same God Christ; since Christ must also be God in the same relative manner that he is Lord and Son? Lastly, the Father is he *of whom,* and *from whom,* and *by whom,* and *for whom are all things;* Rom. xi. 36. The Son is not he *of whom,* but only *by whom;* and that not without an exception, viz. *"all things* which were made," John i. 3. "All things, except him which did put all things under him," 1 Cor. xv. 27. It is evident therefore that when it is said "all things were by him," it must be understood of a secondary and delegated power; and that when the particle *by* is used in reference to the Father, it denotes the primary cause, as John vi. 57. "I live by the Father;" when in reference to the Son, the secondary and instrumental cause: which will be explained more clearly on a future occasion.

Again, Eph. iv. 4–6. "there is one body and one Spirit, even as ye are called in one hope of your calling; one Lord, one faith, one baptism; one God and Father of all, who is above all, and through all, and in you all." Here there is one Spirit, and one Lord; but the Father is one, and therefore God is one in the same sense as the remaining objects of which unity is predicated, that is, numerically one, and therefore one also in person. 1 Tim. ii. 5. "there is one God, and one mediator between God and men, the man Christ Jesus." Here the mediator, though not purely human, is purposely named man, by the title derived from his inferior nature, lest he should be thought equal to the Father, or the same God, the argument distinctly and expressly referring to one God. Besides, it cannot be explained how any one can be a mediator to himself on his own behalf; according to Gal. iii. 20. "a mediator is not a mediator of one, but God is one." How then can God be a mediator of God? Not to mention that he himself uniformly testifies of himself, John viii. 28. "I do nothing of myself," and v. 42. "neither came I of myself." Undoubtedly therefore he does not act as a mediator to himself; nor return as a mediator to himself. Rom. v. 10. "we were reconciled to God by the death of his Son." To whatever God we were reconciled, if he be one God, he cannot be the God by whom we are reconciled, inasmuch as that God is another person; for if he be one and the same, he must be a mediator between himself and us, and reconcile us to himself by himself; which is an insurmountable difficulty.

Though all this be so self-evident as to require no explanation,—namely, that the Father alone is a self-existent God, and that a being which is not self-existent cannot be God,—it is wonderful with what futile subtleties, or rather with what juggling artifices, certain individuals have endeavored to elude or obscure the plain meaning of these passages; leaving no stone unturned, recurring to every shift, attempting every means, as if their object were not to preach the pure and unadulterated truth of the gospel to the poor and simple, but rather by dint of vehemence and obstinacy to sustain some absurd paradox from falling, by the treacherous aid of sophisms and verbal distinctions, borrowed from the barbarous ignorance of the schools.

They defend their conduct, however, on the ground, that though these opinions may seem inconsistent with reason, they are to be received for the sake of other passages of Scripture, and that otherwise Scripture will not be consistent with itself. Setting aside reason therefore, let us have recourse again to the language of Scripture.

The passages in question are two only. The first is John x. 30. "I and my Father are one,"—that is, one in essence, as it is commonly interpreted. But God forbid that we should decide rashly on any point relative to the Deity. Two things may be called one in more than one way. Scripture saith, and the Son saith, *I and my Father are one,*—I bow to their authority. Certain commentators conjecture that they are one in essence,—I reject what is merely man's invention. For the Son has not left us to conjecture in what manner he is one with the Father, (whatever member of the Church may have first arrogated to himself the merit of the discovery,) but explains the doctrine himself most fully, so far as we are concerned to know it. The Father and the Son are one, not indeed in essence, for he had himself said the contrary in the preceding verse, "my Father, which gave them me, is greater than all," (see also xiv. 28. "my Father is greater than I,") and in the following verses he distinctly denies that he made himself God in saying, "I and my Father are one;" he insists that he had only said as follows, which implies far less, v. 36, "say ye of him whom the Father hath sanctified, and sent into the world, Thou blasphemest; because I said, I am the Son of God?" This must be spoken of two persons not only not co-essential, but not co-equal. Now if the Son be laying down a doctrine respecting the unity of the divine essence in two persons of the Trinity, how is it that he does not rather attribute the same unity of essence to the three persons? Why does he divide the indivisible Trinity? For there cannot be unity without totality. Therefore, on the authority of the opinions holden by my opponents themselves, the Son and the Father without the Spirit are not one in essence. How then are they one? It is the province of Christ alone to acquaint us with this, and accordingly he does acquaint us with it. In the first place, they are one, inasmuch as they speak and act with unanimity; and so he explains himself in the same chapter, after the Jews had misunderstood his saying: x. 38. "believe the works; that ye may know and believe that the Father is in me, and I in him." xiv. 10. "believest thou not that I am in the Father, and the Father in me? the words that I speak unto you, I speak not of myself, but the Father that dwelleth in me, he doeth the works." Here he evidently distinguishes the Father from himself in his whole capacity, but asserts at the same time that the Father remains in him; which does not denote unity of essence, but only intimacy of communion. Secondly, he declares himself to be one with the Father in the same manner as we are one with him,—that is, not in essence, but in love, in communion, in agreement, in charity, in spirit, in glory. When the Son has shown in so many modes how he and the Father are one, why should I set them all aside? why should I, on the strength of my own reasoning, though in opposition to reason itself, devise another mode, which makes them one in essence; or why, if already devised by some other person, adopt it, in preference to Christ's own mode? If it be proposed on the single authority of the Church, the true doctrine of the orthodox Church herself teaches me otherwise; inasmuch as it instructs me to listen to the words of Christ before all other.

The other passage, and which according to the general opinion affords the clearest foundation for the received doctrine of the essential unity of the three persons, is 1 John v. 7. "there are three that bear record in heaven, the Father, the Word, and the Holy Ghost, and these three are one." But not to mention that this verse is wanting in the Syriac and the other two Oriental versions, the Arabic and the Ethiopic, as well as in the greater part of the ancient Greek manuscripts, and that in those manuscripts which actually contain it many various readings occur, it no more necessarily proves those to be essentially one, who are said to be one in heaven, than it proves those to be essentially one, who are said in the following verse to be one on earth. And not only Erasmus, but even Beza, however unwillingly, acknowledged (as may be seen in their own writings) that if John be really the author of the verse, he is only speaking here, as in the last quoted passage, of an unity of agreement and testimony. Besides, who are the three who are said to bear witness? That they are three Gods, will not be admitted; therefore neither is it the one God, but one record or one testimony of three witnesses, which is implied. But he who is not co-essential with God the Father, cannot be co-equal with the Father. This text, however, will be discussed more at large in the following chapter.

But, it is objected, although Scripture does not say in express words that the Father and Son are one in essence, yet reason proves the truth of the doctrine from the texts quoted above, as well as from other passages of Scripture.

In the first place, granting, (which I am far from doing,) that this is the case, yet on a subject so sublime, and so far above our reason, where the very elements and first postulates, as it were, of our faith are concerned, belief must be founded, not on mere reason, but on the word of God exclusively, where the language of the revelation is most clear and particular. Reason itself, however, protests strongly against the doctrine in question; for how can reason establish (as it must in the present case) a position contrary to reason? Undoubtedly the product of reason must be something consistent with reason, not a notion as absurd as it is removed from all human comprehension. Hence we conclude, that this opinion is agreeable neither to Scrip-

ture nor reason. The other alternative therefore must be adopted, namely, that if God be one God, and that one God be the Father, and if notwithstanding the Son be also called God, the Son must have received the name and nature of Deity from God the Father, in conformity with his decree and will, after the manner stated before. This doctrine is not disproved by reason, and Scripture teaches it in innumerable passages.

But those who insist that the Son is one God with the Father, consider their point as susceptible of ample proof, even without the two texts already examined, (on which indeed some admit that no reliance is to be placed) if it can be demonstrated from a sufficient number of Scripture testimonies that the name, attributes, and works of God, as well as divine honors, are habitually ascribed to the Son. To proceed therefore in the same line of argument, I do not ask them to believe that the Father alone and none else is God, unless I shall have proved, first, that in every passage each of the particulars abovementioned is attributed in express terms only to one God the Father, as well by the Son himself as by his apostles. Secondly, that wherever they are attributed to the Son, it is in such a manner that they are easily understood to be attributable in their original and proper sense to the Father alone; and that the Son acknowledges himself to possess whatever share of Deity is assigned to him by virtue of the peculiar gift and kindness of the Father; as the apostles also testify. And lastly, that the Son himself and his apostles acknowledge throughout the whole of their discourses and writings, that the Father is greater than the Son in all things.

I am aware of the answer which will be here made by those who, while they believe in the unity of God, yet maintain that the Father alone is not God. I shall therefore meet their objection in the outset, lest they should raise a difficulty and outcry at each individual passage. They twice beg the question, or rather require us to make two gratuitous concessions. In the first place, they insist, that wherever the name of God is attributed to the Father alone, it should be understood οὐσιωδῶς, not ὑποστατικᾶς, that is to say, that the name of the Father, who is unity, should be understood to signify the three persons, or the whole essence of the Trinity, not the single person of the Father. This is on many accounts a ridiculous distinction, and invented solely for the purpose of supporting their peculiar opinion; although in reality, instead of supporting it, it will be found to be dependent on it, and therefore if the opinion itself be invalidated, for which purpose a simple denial is sufficient, the futile distinction falls to the ground at the same time. For the fact is, not merely that the distinction is a futile one, but that it is no distinction at all; it is a mere verbal quibble, founded on the use of synonymous words, and cunningly dressed up in terms borrowed from the Greek to dazzle the eyes of novices. For since essence and hypostasis mean the same thing, as has been shown in the second chapter, it follows that there can be no real difference of meaning between the adverbs *essentially* and *substantially*, which are derived from them. If then the name of God be attributed to the Father alone *essentially,* it must also be attributed to the Father alone *substantially;* since one substantial essence means nothing else than one hypostasis, and vice versa. I would therefore ask my adversaries, whether they hold the Father to be an abstract ens or not? Questionless they will reply, the primary ens of all. I answer, therefore, that as he has one hypostasis, so must he have one essence proper to himself, incommunicable in the highest degree, and participated by no one, that is, by no person besides, for he cannot have his own proper hypostasis, without having his own proper essence. For it is impossible for any ens to retain its own essence in common with any other thing whatever, since by this essence it is what it is, and is numerically distinguished from all others. If therefore the Son, who has his own proper hypostasis, have not also his own proper essence, but the essence of the Father, he becomes on the hypothesis either no ens at all, or the same ens with the Father; which strikes at the very foundation of the Christian religion. The answer which is commonly made, is ridiculous—namely, that although one finite essence can pertain to one person only, one infinite essence may pertain to a plurality of persons; whereas in reality the infinitude of the essence affords an additional reason why it can pertain to only one

person. All acknowledge that both the essence and the person of the Father are infinite; therefore the essence of the Father cannot be communicated to another person, for otherwise there might be two, or any imaginable number of infinite persons.

The second postulate is, that wherever the Son attributes Deity to the Father alone, and as to one greater than himself, he must be understood to speak in his human character, or as mediator. Wherever the context and the fact itself require this interpretation, I shall readily concede it, without losing anything by the concession; for however strongly it may be contended, that when the Son attributes every thing to the Father alone, he speaks in his human or mediatorial capacity, it can never be inferred from hence that he is one God with the Father. On the other hand, I shall not scruple to deny the proposition, whenever it is to be conceded not to the sense of the passage, but merely to serve their own theory; and shall prove that what the Son attributes to the Father, he attributes in his filial or even in his divine character to the Father as God of God, and not to himself under any title or pretence whatever.

With regard to the name of God, wherever simultaneous mention is made of the Father and the Son, that name is uniformly ascribed to the Father alone, except in such passages as shall be hereafter separately considered. I shall quote in the first place the texts of the former class, which are by far the more considerable in point of number, and form a large and compact body of proofs. John iii. 16. "so God loved the world, that he gave his own Son." vi. 27. "him hath God the Father sealed." v. 29. "this is the work of God, that ye believe on him whom he hath sent." xiv. 1. "ye believe in God, believe also in me." What is meant by believing in any one, will be explained hereafter; in the mean time it is clear that two distinct things are here intended—*in God* and *in me*. Thus all the apostles in conjunction, Acts iv. 24. The same thing may be observed in the very outset of all the Epistles of St. Paul and of the other apostles, where, as is natural, it is their custom to declare in express and distinct terms who he is by whose divine authority they have been sent.

The Son likewise teaches that the attributes of divinity belong to the Father alone, to the exclusion even of himself. With regard to omniscience. Matt. xxiv. 36. "of that day and hour knoweth no man, no not the angels of heaven, but my Father only;" and still more explicitly, Mark xiii. 32.

With regard to supreme dominion both in heaven and earth, the unlimited authority and full power of decreeing according to his own independent will. Matt. xx. 23. "to sit on my right hand and on my left, is not mine to give, but it shall be given to them for whom it is prepared of my Father. It is not mine—," in my mediatorial capacity, as it is commonly interpreted. But questionless when the ambition of the mother and her two sons incited them to prefer this important demand, they addressed their petition to the entire nature of Christ, how exalted soever it might be, praying him to grant their request to the utmost extent of his power whether as God or man. Christ also answers with reference to his whole nature—*it is not mine to give;* and lest for some reason they might still believe the gift belonged to him, he declares that it was altogether out of his province, and the exclusive privilege of the Father. If his reply was meant solely to refer to his mediatorial capacity, it would have bordered on sophistry, which God forbid that we should attribute to him; as if he were capable of evading the request of Salome and her sons by the quibble which the logicians call *expositio prava* or *æquivoca,* when the respondent answers in a sense or with a mental intention different from the meaning of the questioner. The same must be said of other passages of the same kind, where Christ speaks of himself; for after the hypostatical union of two natures in one person, it follows that whatever Christ says of himself, he says not as the possessor of either nature separately, but with reference to the whole of his character, and in his entire person, except where he himself makes a distinction. Those who divide this hypostatical union at their own discretion, strip the discourses and answers of Christ of all their sincerity; they represent every thing as ambiguous and uncertain, as true and false at the same time; it is not Christ that speaks, but some unknown substitute, sometimes one, and sometimes another; so that the words of Horace may be justly applied to such disputants:

Quo teneam vultus mutantem Protea nodo?

Christ himself says, Matt. xxvi. 39. "O my Father, if it be possible, let this cup pass from me; nevertheless not as I will, but as thou wilt." Now it is manifest that those who have not the same will, cannot have the same essence. It appears, however, from many passages, that the Father and Son have not, in a numerical sense, the same intelligence or will. Those therefore whose understanding and will are not numerically the same, cannot have the same essence. Nor is there any mode of evading this conclusion, inasmuch as this is the language of the Son himself respecting his own divine nature. If these prayers be uttered only in his human capacity, which is the common explanation, why does he petition these things from the Father alone instead of from himself, if he were God? Or rather, supposing him to be at once man and the supreme God, why does he ask at all for what was in his own power? What need was there for the union of the divine and human nature in one person, if he himself, being equal to the Father, gave back again into his hands everything that he had received from him?

With regard to his supreme goodness. Matt. xix. 17 "why callest thou me good? there is none good but one, that is, God." We need not be surprised that Christ should refuse to accept the adulatory titles which were wont to be given to the Pharisees, and on this account should receive the young man with less kindness than usual; but when he says, *there is none good but one, that is, God,* it is evident that he did not choose to be considered essentially the same with that one God; for otherwise this would only have been disclaiming the credit of goodness in one character, for the purpose of assuming it in another. John vi. 65. "no man can come unto me"—that is, to me, both God and man—"except it were given unto him of my Father."

With regard to his supreme glory. John xvii. 4. "I have glorified thee on the earth." Nay, it is to those who obey the Father that the promise of true wisdom is made even with regard to the knowing Christ himself, which is the very point now in question.

Thus Christ assigns every attribute of the Deity, to the Father alone. The apostles uniformly speak in a similar manner.

With regard to his works. So many are the texts wherein the Son is said to be raised up by the Father alone, which ought to have greater weight than the single passage in St. John, ii. 19. "destroy the temple, and in three days I will raise it up"—where he spake briefly and enigmatically, without explaining his meaning to enemies who were unworthy of a fuller answer, on which account he thought it necessary to mention the power of the Father.

With regard to divine honors. For as the Son uniformly pays worship and reverence to the Father alone, so he teaches us to follow the same practice. Here however my opponents quote the passage from Malachi iii. 1. "the Lord whom ye seek shall suddenly come to his temple, even the messenger of the covenant." I answer, that in prophetical language these words signify the coming of the Lord into the flesh, or into the temple of the body, as it is expressed John ii. 21. For the Jews sought no one in the temple as an object of worship, except the Father; and Christ himself in the same chapter has called the temple his Father's house, and not his own. Nor were they seeking God, but *that Lord and messenger of the covenant;* that is, him who was sent from God as the mediator of the covenant;—he it was who should come to his Church, which the prophets generally express figuratively under the image of the temple. So also where the terms God and man are put in opposition to each other, the Father stands exclusively for the one God.

But it is strenuously urged on the other hand, that the Son is sometimes called God, and even Jehovah; and that all the attributes of the Deity are assigned to him likewise in many passages both of the Old and New Testament. We arrive therefore at the other point which I originally undertook to prove; and since it has been already shown from the analogy of Scripture, that where the Father and the Son are mentioned together, the name, attributes, and works of the Deity, as well as divine honors, are always assigned to the one and only God the Father, I will now demonstrate, that whenever the same properties are assigned to the Son, it is in such

a manner as to make it easily intelligible that they ought all primarily and properly to be attributed to the Father alone.

It must be observed in the first place, that the name of God is not unfrequently ascribed, by the will and concession of God the Father, even to angels and men,—how much more then to the only begotten Son, the image of the Father. To angels. Psal. xcvii. 7, 9. compared with Heb. i. 6. See also Psal. viii. 5. To judges. Exod. xxii. 28. See also, in the Hebrew, Exod. xxi. 6. xxii. 8, 9. Psal. lxxxii. 1, 6. To the whole house of David, or to all the Saints. Zech. xii. 8. The word אלהים, though it be of the plural number, is also employed to signify a single angel, in case it should be thought that the use of the plural implies a plurality of persons in the Godhead: Judges xiii. 21. The same word is also applied to a single false god. Exod. xx. 3. To Dagon. Judges xvi. 23. To single idols. 1 Kings xi. 33. To Moses. Exod. iv. 16. and vii. 1. To God the Father alone. Psal. ii. 7. xlv. 7. and in many other places. Similar to this is the use of the word אדנים, *the Lord,* in the plural number with a singular meaning; and with a plural affix according to the Hebrew mode. The word אדני also with the vowel *Patha* is frequently employed to signify one man, and with the vowel *Kamets* to signify one God, or one angel bearing the character of God. This peculiarity in the above words has been carefully noticed by the grammarians and lexicographers themselves, as well as in בעל used appellatively. The same thing may perhaps be remarked of the proper names בעלים and עשתרות. For even among the Greeks, the word δεσπότης, that is, Lord, is also used in the plural number in the sense of the singular, when extraordinary respect and honor are intended to be paid. Thus in the Iphigenia in Aulis of Euripides. It is also used in Rhesus and Bacchæ in the same manner.

Attention must be paid to these circumstances, lest any one through ignorance of the language should erroneously suppose, that whenever the word Elohim is joined with a singular, it is intended to intimate a plurality of persons in unity of essence. But if there be any significance at all in this peculiarity, the word must imply as many gods as it does persons. Besides, a plural adjective or a plural verb is sometimes joined to the word Elohim, which, if a construction of this kind could mean anything, would signify not a plurality of persons only, but also of natures. Further, the singular אֱלוֹהַּ also sometimes occurs, Deut. xxxii. 18. and elsewhere. It is also attributed to Christ with the singular affix. Psal. cx. 1. לַאדֹנִי "Jehovah said unto my Lord," in which passage the Psalmist speaks of Christ (to whom the name of *Lord* is assigned, as a title of the highest honor) both as distinct from Jehovah, and, if any reliance can be placed on the affix, as inferior to Jehovah. But when he addresses the Father, the affix is changed, and he says, v. 5. אֲדֹנָי, "the Lord at thy right hand shall strike through kings in the day of his wrath."

The name of God seems to be attributed to angels because as heavenly messengers they bear the appearance of the divine glory and person, and even speak in the very words of the Deity. For the expression so frequently in the mouth of the prophets, and which is elsewhere often omitted, is here inserted, for the purpose of showing that angels and messengers do not declare their own words, but the commands of God who sends them, even though the speaker seem to bear the name and character of the Deity himself. Isai. vi. 1, 2. "I saw the Lord sitting upon a throne. . . . above it stood the seraphim." I repeat, it was not God himself that he saw, but perhaps one of the angels clothed in some modification of the divine glory, or the son of God himself, the image of the glory of his Father, as John understands the vision, xii. 41. "these things said Esaias, when he saw his glory." For if he had been of the same essence, he could no more have been seen or heard than the Father himself, as will be more fully shown hereafter. Hence even the holiest of men were troubled in mind when they had seen an angel, as if they had seen God himself.

The name of God is ascribed to judges, because they occupy the place of God to a certain degree in the administration of judgment. The Son, who was entitled to the name of God both in the capacity of a messenger and of a judge, and indeed in virtue of a much better right, did not think it foreign to his character, when the Jews accused him of blasphemy because he made himself God, to allege in his own defence the very reason which has been advanced. John x. 34–36.

Even the principal texts themselves which are brought forward to prove the divinity of the Son, if carefully weighed and considered, are sufficient to show that the Son is God in the manner which has been explained. John i. 1. "in the beginning was the Word, and the Word was with God, and the Word was God." It is not said, from everlasting, but *in the beginning. The Word,*—therefore the Word was audible. But God, as he cannot be seen, so neither can he be heard; John v. 37. The Word therefore is not of the same essence with God. *The Word was with God, and was God,*—namely, because he was with God, that is, in the bosom of the Father, as it is expressed v. 18. Does it follow therefore that he is one in essence with him with whom he was? It no more follows, than that the disciple *who was lying on Jesus' breast,* John xiii. 23. was one in essence with Christ. Reason rejects the Doctrine; Scripture nowhere asserts it; let us therefore abandon human devices, and follow the evangelist himself, who is his own interpreter. Rev. xix. 13. "his name is called the Word of God"—that is, of the one God: he himself is a distinct person. If therefore he be a distinct person, he is distinct from God, who is unity. How then is he himself also God? By the same right as he enjoys the title of the Word, or of the only begotten Son, namely, by the will of the one God. This seems to be the reason why it is repeated in the second verse—"the same was in the beginning with God;" which enforces what the apostle wished we should principally observe, not that he was in the beginning God, but in the beginning with God; that he might show him to be God only by proximity and love, not in essence; which doctrine is consistent with the subsequent explanations of the evangelist in numberless passages of his gospel.

Another passage is the speech of Thomas, John xx. 28. "my Lord and my God." He must have an immoderate share of credulity who attempts to elicit a new confession of faith, unknown to the rest of the disciples, from this abrupt exclamation of the apostle, who invokes in his surprise not only Christ his own Lord, but the God of his ancestors, namely, God the Father;—as if he had said, Lord! what do I see—what do I hear—what do I handle with my hands? He whom Thomas is supposed to call God in this passage, had acknowledged respecting himself not long before, v. 17. "I ascend unto my God and your God." Now the God of God cannot be essentially one with him whose God he is. On whose word therefore can we ground our faith with most security; on that of Christ, whose doctrine is clear, or of Thomas, a new disciple, first incredulous, then suddenly breaking out into an abrupt exclamation in an ecstasy of wonder, if indeed he really called Christ his God? For having reached out his fingers, he called the man whom he touched, as if unconscious of what he was saying, by the name of God. Neither is it credible that he should have so quickly understood the hypostatic union of that person whose resurrection he had just before disbelieved. Accordingly the faith of Peter is commended—*blessed art thou, Simon*—for having only said—"thou art the Son of the living God," Matt. xvi. 16. The faith of Thomas, although as it is commonly explained, it asserts the divinity of Christ in a much more remarkable manner, is so far from being praised, that it is undervalued, and almost reproved in the next verse— "Thomas, because thou hast seen me, thou hast believed; blessed are they that have not seen, and yet have believed." And yet, though the slowness of his belief may have deserved blame, the testimony borne by him to Christ as God, which, if the common interpretation be received as true, is clearer than occurs in any other passage, would undoubtedly have met with some commendation; whereas it obtains none whatever. Hence there is nothing to invalidate that interpretation of the passage which has been already suggested, referring the words—*my Lord*—to Christ,— *my God*—to God the Father, who had just testified that Christ was his Son, by raising him up from the dead in so wonderful a manner.

So to Heb. i. 8. But in the next verse it follows, "thou hast loved righteousness, therefore God, even thy God, hath anointed thee with the oil of gladness above thy fellows," where almost every word indicates the sense in which Christ is here termed God; and the words of Jehovah put into the mouth of the

bridal virgins, Psal. xlv. might have been more properly quoted by this writer for any other purpose than to prove that the Son is co-equal with the Father, since they are originally applied to Solomon, to whom, as appropriately as to Christ, the title of God might have been given on account of his kingly power, conformably to the language of Scripture.

These three passages are the most distinct of all that are brought forward; for the text in Matt. i. 23. "they shall call (for so the great majority of the Greek manuscripts read it) his name Immanuel, which being interpreted is, God with us," does not prove that he whom they were so to call should necessarily be God, but only a messenger from God, according to the song of Zacharias, Luke i. 68, 69. Nor can anything certain be inferred from Acts xvi. 31, 34. "believe on the Lord Jesus Christ,—and he rejoiced, believing in God with all his house." For it does not follow from hence that Christ is God, since the apostles have never distinctly pointed out Christ as the ultimate object of faith; but these are merely the words of the historian, expressing briefly what the apostles doubtless inculcated in a more detailed manner,—faith in God the Father through Christ. Nor is the passage in Acts xx. 28. more decisive,—"the church of God, which he hath purchased with his own blood;" that is, with his own Son, as it is elsewhere expressed, for God properly speaking has no blood; and no usage is more common than the substitution of the figurative term blood for offspring. But the Syriac version reads, not *the Church of God,* but *the Church of Christ;* and in our own recent translation it is, *the Church of the Lord.* Nor can any certain dependence be placed on the authority of the Greek manuscripts, five of which read τοῦ Κυρίου καὶ Θεοῦ, according to Beza, who suspects that the words τοῦ Κυρίου have crept in from the margin, though it is more natural to suppose the words καὶ Θεοῦ to have crept in, on account of their being an addition to the former. The same must be said respecting Rom. ix. 5. "who is over all, God blessed for ever. Amen." For in the first place, Hilary and Cyprian do not read the word *God* in this passage, nor do some of the other Fathers, if we may believe the authority of Erasmus; who has also shown that the difference of punctuation may raise a doubt with regard to the true meaning of the passage, namely, whether the clause in question should not rather be understood of the Father than of the Son. But waiving these objections, and supposing that the words are spoken of the Son; they have nothing to do with his essence, but only intimate that divine honor is communicated to the Son by the Father, and particularly that he is called God; which is nothing more than what has been already fully shown by other arguments. But, it is said, the same words which were spoken of the Father, Rom. i. 25. "the Creator, who is blessed for ever. Amen," are here repeated of the Son; therefore the Son is equal to the Father. If there be any force in this reasoning, it will rather prove that the Son is greater than the Father; for according to the ninth chapter, he is *over all*, which, however, they remind us, ought to be understood in the same sense as John iii. 31, 32. "he that cometh from above, is above all; he that cometh from heaven is above all." In these words even the divine nature is clearly implied, and yet, *what he hath seen and heard, that he testifieth*, which language affirms that he came not of himself, but was sent from the Father, and was obedient to him. It will be answered, that it is only his mediatorial character which is intended. But he never could have become a mediator, nor could he have been sent from God, or have been obedient to him, unless he had been inferior to God and the Father as to his nature. Therefore also after he shall have laid aside his functions as mediator, whatever may be his greatness, or whatever it may previously have been, he must be subject to God and the Father. Hence he is to be accounted above all, with this reservation, that He is always to be excepted "who did put all things under him," 1 Cor. xv. 27. and who consequently is above him under whom He has put all things. If lastly he be termed *blessed*, it must be observed that he received blessing as well as divine honor, not only as God, but even as man.

There is a still greater doubt respecting the reading in 1 Tim. iii. 19. "God was manifest in the flesh." Here again Erasmus asserts that neither Ambrose nor the Vetus Interpres read the word God in this verse, and that it does not appear in a considerable number of the early copies. However this may be it will be clear, when the context is duly examined, that the whole passage must be understood of God the Father in conjunction with the Son. For it is not Christ who is *the great mystery of godliness*, but God the Father in Christ, as appears from 2 Cor. v. 18, 19. "all things are of God, who hath reconciled us to himself by Jesus Christ . . . to wit, that God was in Christ, reconciling the world unto himself, not imputing their trespasses unto them." Why therefore should God the Father not be in Christ through the medium of all those offices of reconciliation which the apostle enumerates in this passage of Timothy? *God was manifest in the flesh*—namely, in the Son, his own image; in any other way he is invisible: nor did Christ come to manifest himself, but his Father, John xiv. 8, 9. "justified in the Spirit"—and who should be thereby justified, if not the Father? "Seen of angels"—inasmuch as they desired to look into this mystery. 1 Pet. i. 12. "Preached unto the Gentiles"—that is, the Father in Christ. "Believed on in the world"—and to whom is faith so applicable, as to the Father through Christ? "Received up into glory"—namely, he who was in the Son from the beginning, after reconciliation had been made, returned with the Son into glory, or was received into that supreme glory which he had obtained in the Son. But there is no need of discussing this text at greater length: those who are determined to defend at all events the received opinion, according to which these several propositions are predicated not of the Father but of the Son alone, when they are in fact applicable both to the one and the other, though on different grounds, may easily establish that the Son is God, a truth which I am far from denying—but they will in vain attempt to prove from this passage that he is the supreme God, and one with the Father.

The next passage is Tit. ii. 13. "the glorious appearing of the great God and our Saviour Jesus Christ.". Here also the glory of God the Father may be intended, with which Christ is to be invested on his second advent, Matt. xvi. 27. as Ambrose understands the passage from the analogy of Scripture. For the whole force of the proof depends upon the definitive article, which may be inserted or omitted before the two nouns in the Greek without affecting the sense; or the article prefixed to one may be common to both. Besides, in other languages, where the article is not used, the words may be understood to apply indifferently either to one or two persons; and nearly the same words are employed without the article in reference to two persons, Philipp. i. 2. and Philem. 3. except that in the latter passages the word *Father* is substituted for great. So also 2 Pet. i. 1. "through the righteousness of [our] God and our Saviour Jesus Christ." Here the repetition of the pronoun ἡμῶν without the article, as it is read by some of the Greek manuscripts, shows that two distinct persons are spoken of. And surely what is proposed to us as an object of belief, especially in a matter involving a primary article of faith, ought not be an inference forced and extorted from passages relating to an entirely different subject, in which the readings are sometimes various, and the sense doubtful,—nor hunted out by careful research from among articles and particles,—nor elicited by dint of ingenuity, like the answers of an oracle, from sentences of dark or equivocal meaning—but should be susceptible of abundant proof from the clearest sources. For it is in this that the superiority of the gospel to the law consists; this, and this alone, is consistent with its open simplicity; this is that true light and perspicuity which we had been taught to expect would be its characteristic. Lastly, he who calls God, *great,* does not necessarily call him supreme, or essentially one with the Father; nor on the other hand does he thereby deny that Christ is *the great God,* in the sense in which he has been above proved to be such.

Another passage which is also produced is 1 John iii. 16. "hereby perceive we the love of God, because he laid down his life for us." Here, however, the Syriac version reads *illius* instead of *Dei,* and it remains to be seen whether other manuscripts do the same. The pronoun *he,* ἐκεῖνος, seems not to be referred to God, but to the Son of God, as may be concluded from a comparison of the former chapters of this epistle, and the first, second, fifth and eighth verses of the chapter before us, as well as from Rom. v. 8. *The love of God,* therefore, is the love of the Father, whereby he so loved the world, that "he purchased it

with his own blood," Acts xx. 28. and for it *laid down his life,* that is, the life of his only begotten Son, as it may be explained from John iii. 16. and by analogy from many other passages. Nor is it extraordinary that by the phrase, *his life,* should be understood the life of his beloved Son, since we are ourselves in the habit of calling any much-loved friend by the title of life, or part of our life, as a term of endearment in familiar discourse.

But the passage which is considered most important of all, is 1 John v. part of the twentieth verse—for if the whole be taken, it will not prove what it is adduced to support. "We know that the Son of God is come, and hath given us an understanding, that we may know him that is true, and we are in him that is true, (even) in his Son Jesus Christ: this is the true God, and eternal life." For *we are in him that is true in his Son,*—that is, so far as we are in the Son of him that is true:—*this is the true God;* namely, he who was just before called *him that was true,* the word *God* being omitted in the one clause, and subjoined in the other. For he it is that is *he that is true* (whom that we might know, *we know that the Son of God is come, and hath given us an understanding*) not he who is called *the Son of him that is true,* though that be the nearest antecedent,—for common sense itself requires that the article *this* should be referred to *him that is true,* (to whom the subject of the context principally relates,) not to *the Son of him that is true.* Examples of a similar construction are not wanting. Compare also John xvii. 3. with which passage the verse in question seems to correspond exactly in sense, the position of the words alone being changed. But it will be objected, that according to some of the texts quoted before, Christ is God; now if the Father be the only true God, Christ is not the true God; but if he be not the true God, he must be a false God. I answer, that the conclusion is too hastily drawn; for it may be that he is not *he that is true,* either because he is the only image of him that is true, or because he uniformly declares himself to be inferior to him that is true. We are not obliged to say of Christ what the Scriptures do not say. The Scriptures call him *God,* but not *him that is the true God;* why are we not at liberty to acquiesce in the same distinction? At all events *he* is not to be called a false God, to whom, as to his beloved Son, he that is the true God has communicated his divine power and glory.

They also adduce Philipp. ii. 6. "who being in the form of God"—But this no more proves him to be God than the phrase which follows —"took upon him the form of a servant"— proves that he was really a servant, as the sacred writers nowhere use the word *form* for actual being. But if it be contended that *the form of God* is here taken in a philosophical sense for the essential form, this consequence cannot be avoided; that when Christ laid aside the form, he laid aside also the substance and the efficiency of God; a doctrine against which they protest, and with justice. *To be in the form of God,* therefore, seems to be synonymous with being in the image of God; which is often predicated of Christ, even as man is also said, though in a much lower sense, to be the image of God, and to be in the image of God, that is, by creation. More will be added respecting this passage hereafter.

The last passage that is quoted is from the the epistle of Jude, v. 4. "denying the only Lord God, and our Lord Jesus Christ." Who will not agree that this is too verbose a mode of description, if all these words are intended to apply to one person? or who would not rather conclude, on a comparison of many other passages which tend to confirm the same opinion, that they were spoken of two persons, namely, the Father the only God, and our Lord Jesus Christ? Those, however, who are accustomed to discover some extraordinary force in the use of the article, contend that both names must refer to the same person, because the article is prefixed in the Greek to the first of them only, which is done to avoid weakening the structure of the sentence. If the force of the articles is so great, I do not see how other languages can dispense with them.

The passages quoted in the New Testament from the Old will have still less weight than the above, if produced to prove anything more than what the writer who quoted them intended. Of this class are, Psal. lxviii. 17–19. Here (to say nothing of several ellipses, which the interpreters are bold enough to fill up in various ways, as they think proper)

mention is made of two persons, *God* and *the Lord,* which is in contradiction to the opinions of those who attempt to elicit a testimony to the supreme divinity of Christ, by comparing this passage with Eph. iv. 5–8. Such a doctrine was never intended by the apostle, who argues very differently in the ninth verse—"now that he ascended, what is it but that he also descended first into the lower parts of the earth?"—from which he only meant to show that the Lord Christ, who had lately died, and was now received into heaven, *gave gifts unto men* which he had received from the Father.

It is singular, however, that those who maintain the Father and the Son to be one in essence, should revert from the gospel to the times of the law, as if they would make a fruitless attempt to illustrate light by darkness. They say that the Son is not only called God, but also Jehovah, as appears from a comparison of several pasages in both testaments. Now Jehovah is the one supreme God; therefore the Son and the Father are one in essence. It will be easy, however, to expose the weakness of an argument derived from the ascription of the name of Jehovah to the Son. For the name of Jehovah is conceded even to the angels, in the same sense as it has been already shown that the name of God is applied to them, namely, when they represent the divine presence and person, and utter the very words of Jehovah. So Exod. iii. 2, 4. "the angel of Jehovah . . . when Jehovah saw that he turned aside to see, God called unto him"—compared with Acts vii. 30. "there appeared to him an angel of the Lord in a flame of fire in a bush." If that angel had been Christ or the supreme God, it is natural to suppose that Stephen would have declared it openly, especially on such an occasion, where it might have tended to strengthen the faith of the other believers, and strike his judges with alarm. In Exod. xx. on the delivery of the law to Moses, no mention is made of any one, except Jehovah, and yet Acts vii. 38. the same Stephen says, "this is he that was in the church in the wilderness with the angel which spake to him in the Mount Sinai;" and v. 53. he declares that "the law was received by the disposition of angels." Therefore what is said in Exodus to have been spoken by Jehovah, was not spoken by himself personally, but by angels in the name of Jehovah. Nor is this extraordinary, for it would seem unsuitable that Christ the minister of the gospel should also have been the minister of the law: "by how much more also he is the mediator of a better covenant," Heb. viii. 6. On the other hand it would indeed have been wonderful if Christ had actually appeared as the mediator of the law, and none of the apostles had ever intimated it. Nay, the contrary seems to be asserted Heb. i. 1.

But it may be urged, that the name of Jehovah is sometimes assigned to two persons in the same sentence. Gen. xix. 24. 1 Sam. iii. 21. I answer, that in these passages either one of the two persons is an angel, according to that usage of the word which has been already explained; or it is to be considered as a peculiar form of speaking, in which, for the sake of emphasis, the name of Jehovah is repeated, though with reference to the same person; "for Jehovah the God of Israel is one Jehovah." If in such texts as these both persons are to be understood properly and in their own nature as Jehovah, there is no longer one Jehovah, but two; whence it follows that the repetition of the name can only have been employed for the purpose of giving additional force to the sentence. 1 Thess. iii. 12, 13. Here whether it be *God, even our Father,* or *our Lord Jesus,* who is in the former verse called *Lord,* in either case there is the same redundance. If the Jews had understood the passages quoted above, and others of the same kind, as implying that there were two persons, both of whom were Jehovah, and both of whom had an equal right to the appellation, there can be no doubt that, seeing the doctrine so frequently enforced by the prophets, they would have adopted the same belief which now prevails among us, or would at least have labored under considerable scruples on the subject: whereas I suppose no one in his senses will venture to affirm that the Jewish Church ever so understood the passages in question, or believed that there were two persons, each of whom was Jehovah, and had an equal right to assume the title. It would seem, therefore, that they interpreted them in the manner above mentioned. Thus in allusion to a human being, 1 Kings viii. 1. No one is so absurd as to suppose that the name of Solomon is here applied to two

persons in the same sentence. It is evident, therefore, both from the declaration of the sacred writer himself, and from the belief of those very persons to whom the angels appeared, that the name of Jehovah was attributed to an angel: and not to an angel only, but also to the whole church, Jer. xxxiii. 16.

But as Placæus of Saumur thinks it incredible that an angel should bear the name of Jehovah, and that the dignity of the supreme Deity should be degraded by being personated, as it were on a stage, I will produce a passage in which God himself declares that his name is in an angel. Exod. xxiii. 20. "behold, I send an angel before thee, to keep thee in the way." The angel who from that time forward addressed the Israelites, and whose voice they were commanded to hear, was always called Jehovah, though the appellation did not properly belong to him. To this they reply, that he was really Jehovah, for that angel was Christ. I answer, that it is of no importance to the present question, whether it were Christ or not; the subject of inquiry now is, whether the children of Israel understood that angel to be really Jehovah? If they did so understand, it follows that they must have conceived either that there were two Jehovahs, or that Jehovah and the angel were one in essence; which no rational person will affirm to have been their belief. But even if such an assertion were advanced, it would be refuted by chap. xxxiii. 2, 3, 5. If the people had believed that Jehovah and that angel were one in essence, equal in divinity and glory, why did they mourn, and desire that Jehovah should go up before them, notwithstanding his anger, rather than the angel? who, if he had indeed been Christ, would have acted as a mediator and peacemaker. If, on the contrary, they did not consider the angel as Jehovah, they must necessarily have understood that he bore the name of Jehovah in the sense in which I suppose him to have borne it, wherein there is nothing either absurd or histrionic. Being at length prevailed upon to go up with them in person, he grants thus much only, v. 14. "my presence shall go with thee,"—which can imply nothing else than a representation of his name and glory in the person of some angel. But whoever this was, whether Christ, or some angel different from the preceding, the very words of Jehovah himself show that he was neither one with Jehovah, nor co-equal, for the Israelites are commanded to hear his voice, not on the authority of his own name, but because the name of Jehovah was in him. If on the other hand it is contended that the angel was Christ, this proves no more than that Christ was an angel, according to their interpretation of Gen. xlviii. 16. and Isai. lxiii. 9. "the angel of his presence saved them"— that is, he who represented his presence or glory, and bore his character; an angel, or messenger, as they say, by office, but Jehovah by nature. But to whose satisfaction will they be able to prove this? He is called indeed, Mal. iii. 1. "the messenger of the covenant." But it does not therefore follow, that whenever an angel is sent from heaven, that angel is to be considered as Christ; nor where Christ is sent, that he is to be considered as one God with the Father. Nor ought the obscurity of the law and the prophets to be brought forward to refute the light of the gospel, but on the contrary the light of the gospel ought to be employed to illustrate the obscurity necessarily arising from the figurative language of the prophets. However this may be, Moses says, prophesying of Christ, Deut. xviii. 15. "Jehovah thy God will raise up unto thee a prophet from the midst of thee, of thy brethren, like unto me; unto him ye shall hearken." It will be answered, that he here predicts the human nature of Christ. I reply that in the following verse he plainly takes away from Christ that divine nature which it is wished to make co-essential with the Father, "according to all that thou desiredst of Jehovah thy God in Horeb . . . saying, Let me not hear again the voice of Jehovah my God." In hearing Christ, therefore, as Moses himself predicts and testifies, they were not to hear the God Jehovah, nor were they to consider Christ as Jehovah.

The style of the Prophetical book of Revelations, as respects this subject, must be regarded in the same light. Chap. i. 1, 8, 11. "he sent and signified it by his angel." Afterwards this angel (who is described nearly in the same words as the angel, Dan. x. 5.) "I am Alpha and Omega, the beginning and the ending, saith the Lord, which is, and which was, and which is to come." v. 13 ff. These passages so perplexed Beza, that he was compelled to reconcile the imaginary difficulty by supposing that the order of a few verses in the last chapter had been confused and transposed by some Arian, (which he attributed to the circumstance of the book having been acknowledged as canonical by the Church at a comparatively late period, and therefore less carefully preserved,) whence he thought it necessary to restore them to what he considered their proper order. This supposition would have been unnecessary, had he remarked, what may be uniformly observed throughout the Old Testament, that angels are accustomed to assume the name and person, and the very words of God and Jehovah, as their own; and that occasionally an angel represents the person and the very words of God, without taking the name either of Jehovah or God, but only in the character of an angel, or even of a man, as Junius himself acknowledges, Judges ii. 1. But according to divines the name of Jehovah signifies two things, either the nature of God, or the completion of his word and promises. If it signify the nature, and therefore the person of God, why should not he who is invested with his person and presence, be also invested with the name which represents them? If it signify the completion of his word and promises, why should not he, to whom words suitable to God alone are so frequently attributed, be permitted also to assume the name of Jehovah, whereby the completion of these words and promises is represented? Or if that name be so acceptable to God, that he has always chosen to consider it as sacred and peculiar to himself alone, why has he uniformly disused it in the New Testament, which contains the most important fulfilment of his prophecies; retaining only the name of the Lord, which had always been common to him with angels and men? If, lastly, any name whatever can be so pleasing to God, why has he exhibited himself to us in the gospel without any proper name at all?

They urge, however, that Christ himself is sometimes called Jehovah in his own name and person; as in Isai. viii. 13, 14. compared with 1 Pet. ii. 7. I answer, that it appears on a comparison of the thirteenth with the eleventh verse, that these are not the words of Christ exhorting the Israelites to sanctify and fear himself, whom they had not yet known, but of the Father threatening, as in other places, that he would be "for a stone of stumbling, to both the houses of Israel," that is, to the Israelites and especially to the Israelites of that age. But supposing the words to refer to Christ, it is not unusual among the prophets for God the Father to declare that he would work himself, what afterwards under the gospel he wrought by means of his Son. Hence Peter says—"the same is made the head of the corner, and a stone of stumbling." By whom made, except by the Father? And in the third chapter, a quotation of part of the same passage of Isaiah clearly proves that the Father was speaking of himself; v. 15. "but sanctify the Lord God"—under which name no one will assert that Christ is intended. Again, they quote Zech. xi. 13. "Jehovah said unto me, Cast it unto the potter; a goodly price that I was prized at of them." That this relates to Christ I do not deny; only it must be remembered, that this is not his own name, but that the name of Jehovah was in him, as will presently appear more plainly. At the same time there is no reason why the words should not be understood of the Father speaking in his own name, who would consider the offences which the Jews should commit against his Son, as offences against himself; in the same sense as the Son declares that whatever is done to those who believed in him, is done to himself. An instance of the same kind occurs Acts ix. 4, 5. "Saul, Saul, why persecutest thou me?" The same answer must be given respecting Zech. xii. 10. especially on a comparison with Rev. i. 7. "every eye shall see him;" for none have seen Jehovah at any time, much less have they seen him as a man; least of all have they pierced him. Secondly, they pierced him who "poured upon them the spirit of grace," v. 10. Now it was the Father who poured the spirit of grace through the Son; Acts ii. 33. Therefore it was the Father whom they pierced in the Son. Accordingly, John does not say, "they shall look upon me," but, "they shall look upon him whom they pierced," chap. xix. 37. So also in the verse of Zechariah alluded to, a change of persons takes place—"they shall look upon me whom they have pierced, and they shall mourn for him as one mourneth for his only Son;" as if Jehovah were not properly alluding to himself, but spoke of another, that is,

of the Son. The passage in Malachi iii. 1. admits of a similar interpretation: "behold I will send my messenger, and he shall prepare the way before me, and Jehovah, whom ye seek, shall suddenly come to his temple, even the messenger of the covenant, whom ye delight in: behold he shall come, saith Jehovah of hosts." From which passage Placæus argues thus: He before whose face the Baptist is to be sent as a messenger, is the God of Israel; but the Baptist was not sent before the face of the Father; therefore Christ is that God of Israel. But if the name of Elias could be ascribed to John the Baptist, inasmuch as he "went before him in the spirit and power of Elias," why may not the Father be said to send him before his own face, inasmuch as he sends him before the face of him who was to come in the name of the Father? for that it was the Father who sent the messenger, is proved by the subsequent words of the same verse, since the phrases "I who sent," and "the messenger of the covenant who shall come," and "Jehovah of hosts who saith these things," can scarcely be understood to apply all to the same person. Nay, even according to Christ's own interpretation, the verse implies that it was the Father who sent the Messenger; Matt. xi. 10. "behold, I send my messenger before thy face." Who was it that sent?—the Son, according to Placæus. Before the face of whom?—of the Son: therefore the Son addresses himself in this passage, and sends himself before his own face, which is a new and unheard of figure of speech; not to mention that the Baptist himself testifies that he was sent by the Father, John i. 33. God the Father therefore sent the messenger before the face of his Son, inasmuch as that messenger preceded the advent of the Son; he sent him before his own face, inasmuch as he was himself in Christ, or, which is the same thing, in the Son, "reconciling the world unto himself," 2 Cor. v. 19. That the name and presence of God is used to imply his vicarious power and might resident in the Son, is proved by another prophecy concerning John the Baptist, Isai. xl. 3.

Recurring, however, to the Gospel itself, on which, as on a foundation, our dependence should chiefly be placed, and adducing my proofs more especially from the evangelist John, the leading purpose of whose work was to declare explicitly the nature of the Son's divinity, I proceed to demonstrate the other proposition announced in my original division of the subject—namely, that the Son himself professes to have received from the Father, not only the name of God and of Jehovah, but all that pertains to his own being,—that is to say, his individuality, his existence itself, his attributes, his works, his divine honors; to which doctrine the apostles also, subsequent to Christ, bear their testimony.

But here perhaps the advocates of the contrary opinion will interpose with the same argument which was advanced before; for they are constantly shifting the form of their reasoning, Vertumnus-like, and using the twofold nature of Christ developed in his office of mediator, as a ready subterfuge by which to evade any arguments that may be brought against them. What Scripture says of the Son generally, they apply, as suits their purpose, in a partial and restricted sense; at one time to the Son of God, at another to the Son of Man,—now to the Mediator in his divine, now in his human capacity, and now again in his union of both natures. But the Son himself says expressly, "the Father loveth the Son, and hath given all things into his hand," John iii. 35.—namely, because *he loveth him,* not because he hath begotten him—and he hath given all things to him as *the Son,* not as Mediator only. If the words had been meant to convey the sense attributed to them by my opponents, it would have been more satisfactory and intelligible to have said, *the Father loveth Christ,* or *the Mediator,* or *the Son of Man.* None of these modes of expression are adopted, but it is simply said, *the Father loveth the Son;* that is, whatever is comprehended under the name of the Son. The same question may also be repeated which was asked before, whether from the time that he became the Mediator, his Deity, in their opinion, remained what it had previously been, or not? If it remained the same, why does he ask and receive every thing from the Father, and not from himself? If all things come from the Father, why is it necessary (as they maintain it to be) for the mediatorial office, that he should be the true and supreme God; since he has received from the Father whatever belongs to him, not only in his me-

diatorial, but in his filial character? If his Deity be not the same as before, he was never the Supreme God. From hence may be understood John xvi. 15. "all things that the Father hath are mine,"—that is, by the Father's gift.

In the first place, then, it is most evident that he receives his name from the Father. Isai. ix. 6. "his name shall be called Wonderful, . . . the everlasting Father;" if indeed this elliptical passage be rightly understood: for, strictly speaking, the Son is not the Father, and cannot properly bear the name, nor is it elsewhere ascribed to him, even if we should allow that in some sense or other it is applied to him in the passage before us. The last clause, however, is generally translated not *the everlasting Father,* but *the Father of the age to come,*—that is, its teacher, the name of father being often attributed to a teacher. Philipp. ii. 9. "wherefore God also hath highly exalted him, and hath given him (καὶ ἐχαρίσατο) a name which is above every name." There is no reason why that name should not be Jehovah, or any other name pertaining to the Deity, if there be any still higher: but the imposition of a name is allowed to be uniformly the privilege of the greater personage, whether father or lord.

We need be under no concern, however, respecting the name, seeing that the Son receives his very being in like manner from the Father. John vii. 29. The same thing is implied John i. 1. For the notion of his eternity it here excluded not only by the decree, as has been stated before, but by the name of Son, and by the phrases—*this day have I begotten thee,* and *I will be to him a father.* Besides, the word *beginning* can only here mean *before the foundation of the world,* according to John xvii. 5. as is evident from Col. i. 15–17. "the first born of every creature: for by him were all things created that are in heaven, and that are in earth, and he is before all things, and by him all things consist." Here the Son, not in his human or mediatorial character, but in his capacity of creator, is himself called the first born of every creature. Him who was begotten from all eternity the Father cannot have begotten for what was made from all eternity was never in the act of being made; him whom the

Father begat from all eternity he still begets; he whom he still begets is not yet begotten, and therefore is not yet a son; for an action which has no beginning can have no completion. Besides, it seems to be altogether impossible that the Son should be either begotten or born from all eternity. If he is the Son, either he must have been originally in the Father, and have proceeded from him, or he must always have been as he is now, separate from the Father, self-existent and independent. If he was originally in the Father, but now exists separately, he has undergone a certain change at some time or other, and is therefore mutable. If he always existed separately from, and independently of, the Father, how is he from the Father, how begotten, how the Son, how separate in subsistence, unless he be also separate in essence? since (laying aside metaphysical trifling) a substantial essence and a subsistence are the same thing. However this may be, it will be universally acknowledged that the Son now at least differs numerically from the Father; but that those who differ numerically must differ also in their proper essences, as the logicians express it, is too clear to be denied by any one possessed of common reason. Hence it follows that the Father and the Son differ in essence.

That this is the true doctrine, reason shows on every view of the subject; that it is contrary to Scripture, which my opponents persist in maintaining, remains to be proved by those who make the assertion. Nor does the type of Melchisedec, on which so much reliance is placed, involve any difficulty. Heb. vii. 3. "without father, without mother, without descent; having neither beginning of days, nor end of life; but made like unto the Son of God." For inasmuch as the Son was without any earthly father, he is in one sense said to have had no beginning of days; but it no more appears that he had no beginning of days from all eternity, than that he had no Father, or was not a Son. If, however, he derived his essence from the Father, let it be shown how that essence can have been supremely divine, that is, identically the same with the essence of the Father; since the divine essence, whose property it is to be always one, cannot possibly generate the same essence by which it is generated, nor can

a subsistence or person become an agent or patient under either of the circumstances supposed, unless the entire essence be simultaneously agent or patient in the same manner also. Now as the effect of generation is to produce something which shall exist independently of the generator, it follows that God cannot beget a co-equal Deity, because unity and infinity are two of his essential attributes. Since therefore the Son derives his essence from the Father, he is posterior to the Father not merely in rank (a distinction unauthorized by Scripture, and by which many are deceived) but also in essence; and the filial character itself, on the strength of which they are chiefly wont to build his claim to supreme divinity, affords the best refutation of their opinion. For the supreme God is self-existent; but he who is not self-existent, who did not beget, but was begotten, is not the first cause, but the effect, and therefore is not the supreme God. He who was begotten from all eternity, must have been from all eternity; but if he can have been begotten who was from all eternity, there is no reason why the Father himself should not have been begotten, and have derived his origin also from some paternal essence. Besides, since father and son are relative terms, distinguished from each other both in theory and in fact, and since according to the laws of contraries the father cannot be the son, nor the son the father, if (which is impossible from the nature of relation) they were of one essence, it would follow that the father stood in a filial relation to the son, and the son in a paternal relation to the father,—a position, of the extravagance of which any rational being may judge. For the doctrine which holds that a plurality of hypostasis is consistent with a unity of essence, has already been sufficiently confuted. Lastly, if the Son be of the same essence with the Father, and the same Son after his hypostatical union coalesce in one person with man, I do not see how to evade the inference, that man also is the same person with the Father, an hypothesis which would give birth to not a few paradoxes. But more may perhaps be said on this point, when the incarnation of Christ comes under consideration.

With regard to his existence. John vi. 57. "as the living Father hath sent me, and I live by the Father, so he that eateth me." This gift of life is for ever.

With regard to the divine attributes. And first, that of Omnipresence; for if the Father has given all things to the Son, even his very being and life, he has also given him to be wherever he is. In this sense is to be understood John i. 48. "before that Philip called thee. . . . I saw thee." For Nathanael inferred nothing more from this than what he professes in the next verse,—"thou art the Son of God," and iii. 13. "the Son of man which is in heaven." These words can never prove that the Son, whether of man or of God, is of the same essence with the Father; but only that the Son of man came down from heaven at the period of his conception in the womb of the Virgin, that though he was ministering on earth in the body, his whole spirit and mind, as befitted a great prophet, were in the Father,—or that he, who when made man was endowed with the highest degree of virtue, by reason of that virtue, or of a superior nature given to him in the beginning, is even now *in heaven;* or rather *which was in heaven,* the Greek ὤν having both significations. Again, Matt. xviii. 20. "there am I in the midst of them." xxviii. 20. "I am with you alway, even unto the end of the world." Even these texts, however, do not amount to an assertion of absolute omnipresence, as will be demonstrated in the following chapter.

Omniscience. Matt. xi. 27. "all things are delivered unto me of my Father, and no man knoweth the Son, but the Father, neither knoweth any man the Father, save the Son, and he to whomsoever the Son will reveal him." Even the Son, however, knows not all things absolutely; there being some secret purposes, the knowledge of which the Father has reserved to himself alone.

Authority. Matt. xxviii. 18. "all power is given unto me in heaven and in earth."

Omnipotence. John v. 19. "the Son can do nothing of himself, but what he seeth the Father do; for what thing soever he doeth, these also doeth the Son likewise." Rev. i. 8. "I am . . . the Almighty:" though it may be questioned whether this is not said of God the Father by the Son or the angel representing his authority, as has been explained before.

Works. John v. 20, 21. "for the Father . . .

will show him greater works than these . . . for as the Father raiseth up the dead, and quickeneth them; even so the Son quickeneth whom he will." v. 36. "the works that my Father hath given me to finish, the same works that I do, bear witness of me that the Father hath sent me:"—it is not therefore his divinity of which they bear witness, but his mission from God; and so in other places. So likewise in working miracles, even where he does not expressly implore the divine assistance, he nevertheless acknowledges it. Yet the nature of these works, although divine, was such, that angels were not precluded from performing similar miracles at the same time and in the same place where Christ himself abode daily. The disciples also performed the same works.

The following gifts also, great as they are, were received by him from the Father. First, the power of conversion. Wherever Christ is said to have chosen any one, he must be understood to speak only of the election to the apostolic office.

Secondly, creation—but with this peculiarity, that it is always said to have taken place *per eum,* through him, not by him, but by the Father. Isai. li. 16. "I have put my words in thy mouth, and I have covered thee in the shadow of mine hand, that I may plant the heavens, and lay the foundations of the earth, and say unto Zion, Thou art my people." Whether this be understood of the old or the new creation, the inference is the same. Rom. xi. 36. "for of him," (*ex eo*)—that is, of the Father—"and through him, (*per eum*), and to him, are all things; to whom be glory for ever." 1 Cor. viii. 6. "to us there is but one God, the Father, of whom (*a quo*) are all things, and we in him; and one Lord Jesus Christ, by whom (*per quem*) are all things." The remaining passages on the same subject will be cited in the seventh chapter, on the Creation. But the preposition *per* must signify the secondary efficient cause, whenever the *efficiens a quo,* that is, the principal efficient cause, is either expressed or understood. Now it appears from all the texts which have been already quoted, as well as from those which will be produced hereafter, that the Father is the first or chief cause of all things. This is evident even from the single passage, Heb. iii. 1–6. "consider the Apostle . . .

who was faithful to him that appointed him . . . who hath builded the house," that is, the Church. But he "that appointed him," v. 2. and "builded all things, is God," that is, the Father, v. 4.

Thirdly, the remission of sins, even in his human nature.

Fourthly, preservation. John xvii. 11, 12. Heb. i. 3. "upholding all things by the word of his power," where it is read in the Greek, not *of his own power,* but *of his,* namely, of the Father's power. But this subject will come under consideration again in the eighth chapter, on Providence, where the chief government of all things will be shown to belong primarily to the Father alone; whence the Father, Jehovah, is often called by the prophets not only the Preserver, but also the Saviour. Those who refer these passages to the Son, on account of the appellation of Saviour, seem to conceive that they hereby gain an important argument for his divinity; as if the same title were not frequently applied to the Father in the New Testament, as will be shown in the thirteenth chapter.

Fifthly, renovation. Acts v. 31. "him hath God exalted with his right hand, to be a Prince and a Saviour, for to give repentance to Israel." Sixthly, the power of conferring gifts—namely, that vicarious power which he has received from the Father. John xvii. 18. Seventhly, his mediatorial work itself, or rather his passion. Matt. xxvi. 39. For if the Son was able to accomplish by his own independent power the work of his passion, why did he forsake himself; why did he implore the assistance of his Father; why was an angel sent to strengthen him? How then can the Son be considered co-essential and co-equal with the Father? So too he exclaimed upon the cross—*My God, my God, why hast thou forsaken me?* He whom the Son, himself God, addresses as God, must be the Father,—why then did the Son call upon the Father? Because he felt even his divine nature insufficient to support him under the pains of death. Thus also he said, when at the point of death, Luke xxiii. 46. "Father, into thy hands I commend my spirit." To whom rather than to himself as God would he have commended himself in his human nature, if by his own divine nature alone he had possessed sufficient power to deliver him-

self from death? It was therefore the Father only who raised him again to life; which is the next particular to be noticed. Eighthly, his resuscitation from death. Ninthly, his future judicial advent. Tenthly, divine honors. It appears therefore that when we call upon the Son of God, it is only in his capacity of advocate with the Father. Eleventhly, baptism in his name. Twelfthly, belief in him; if indeed this ought to be considered as an honor peculiar to divinity; for the Israelites are said, Exod. xiv. 31. "to believe Jehovah and his servant Moses." Whence it would seem, that *to believe in any one* is nothing more than an Hebraism, which the Greeks or Latins express by the phrase *to believe any one;* so that whatever trifling distinction may be made between the two, originates in the schools, and not in Scripture. For in some cases *to believe in any one* implies no faith at all. On the other hand, *to believe any one* often signifies the highest degree of faith. This honor, however, like the others, is derived from the Father. It may therefore be laid down as certain, that *believing in Christ* implies nothing more than that we believe Christ to be the Son of God, sent from the Father for our salvation. Thirteenthly, divine glory. No one doubts that the Father restored the Son, on his ascent into heaven, to that original place of glory of which he here speaks. That place will be universally acknowledged to be the right hand of God; the same therefore was his place of glory in the beginning, and from which he had descended. But the right hand of God primarily signifies a glory, not in the highest sense divine, but only next in dignity to God. In these, as in other passages, we are taught that the nature of the Son is indeed divine, but distinct from and clearly inferior to the nature of the Father,—for to be with God, πρὸς Θεὸν, and to be from God, παρὰ Θεῷ,—to be God, and to be in the bosom of God the Father,—to be God, and to be from God,—to be the one invisible God, and to be the only-begotten and visible, are things so different that they cannot be predicated of one and the same essence. Besides, considering that his glory even in his divine nature before the foundation of the world, was not self-derived, but given by the love of the Father, it is plainly demonstrated to be inferior to the Father. These passages most clearly evince that Christ has received his fulness from God, in the sense in which we shall receive our fulness from Christ. For the term *bodily,* which is subjoined, either means *substantially,* in opposition to the *vain deceit* mentioned in the preceding verse, or is of no weight in proving that Christ is of the same essence with God. For though the Son be *another* than the Father, God only means that he will not give his glory to graven images and strange gods,—not that he will not give it to the Son, who is the brightness of his glory, and the express image of his person, and upon whom he had promised that he would put his Spirit. For the Father does not alienate his glory from himself in imparting it to the Son, inasmuch as the Son uniformly glorifies the Father. Hence it becomes evident on what principle the attributes of the Father are said to pertain to the Son. Lastly, his coming to judgment.

Christ therefore, having received all these things from the Father, and "being in the form of God, thought it not robbery to be equal with God," Philipp. ii. 5. namely, because he had obtained them by gift, not by robbery. For if this passage imply his co-equality with the Father, it rather refutes than proves his unity of essence; since equality cannot exist but between two or more essences. Further, the phrases *he did not think it,—he made himself of no reputation,* (literally, *he emptied himself,*) appear inapplicable to the supreme God. For *to think* is nothing else than to entertain an opinion, which cannot be properly said of God. Nor can the infinite God be said to empty himself, any more than to contradict himself; for infinity and emptiness are opposite terms. But since he emptied himself of that form of God in which he had previously existed, if the form of God is to be taken for the essence of the Deity itself, it would prove to have emptied himself to that essence, which is impossible.

Again, the Son himself acknowledges and declares openly, that the Father is greater than the Son; which was the last proposition I undertook to prove. John xiv. 28. "my Father is greater than I." It will be answered, that Christ is speaking of his human nature. But did his disciples understand him as speaking merely of his human nature? Was this the belief in himself which Christ required? Such an opinion will scarcely be maintained. If therefore he saith this, not of his human nature only, (for that the Father was greater than he in his human nature could not admit of a doubt), but in the sense in which he himself wished his followers to conceive of him both as God and man, it ought undoubtedly to be understood as if he had said, My Father is greater than I, whatsoever I am, both in my human and divine nature; otherwise the speaker would not have been he in whom they believed, and instead of teaching them, he would only have been imposing upon them with an equivocation. He must therefore have intended to compare the nature with the person, not the nature of God the Father with the nature of the Son in his human form. So v. 31. "as the Father gave me commandment, even so I do." John v. 18, 19. Being accused by the Jews of having made himself equal with God, he expressly denies it: "the Son can do nothing of himself." vi. 38. "I came down from heaven, not to do mine own will, but the will of him that sent me." Now he that was sent was the only begotten Son; therefore the will of the Father is other and greater than the will of the only begotten Son. viii. 29. "he that sent me is with me: the Father hath not left me alone; for I do always those things that please him." If he says this as God, how could he be left by the Father, with whom he was essentially one? if as man, what is meant by his being *left alone,* who was sustained by a Godhead of equal power? And why *did not the Father leave him alone?*—not because he was essentially one with him, but because he *did always those things that pleased him,* that is, as the less conforms himself to the will of the greater. v. 42. "neither came I of myself," —not therefore of his own Godhead,—*but he sent me:* he that sent him was therefore another and greater than himself.

Thus far we have considered the testimony of the Son respecting the Father; let us now inquire what is the testimony of the Father respecting the Son: for it is written, Matt. xi. 27. "no man knoweth the Son, but the Father; neither knoweth any man the Father, save the Son, and he to whomsoever the Son will reveal him." The apostles every where teach the same doctrine; as the Baptist had done before them. The terms here used, being all relative, and applied numerically to two persons, prove, first, that there is no unity of essence, and secondly, that the one is inferior to the other. Here, if any where, it might have been expected that Christ would have been designated by the title of God; yet it is only said that he is *of God*.

Such was the faith of the saints respecting the Son of God; such is the tenor of the celebrated confession of that faith; such is the doctrine which alone is taught in Scripture, which is acceptable to God, and has the promise of eternal salvation. Finally, this is the faith proposed to us in the Apostles' Creed, the most ancient and universally received compendium of belief in the possession of the Church.

CHAP. VI.—OF THE HOLY SPIRIT.

HAVING concluded what relates to the Father and the Son, the next subject to be discussed is that of the Holy Spirit, inasmuch as this latter is called the Spirit of the Father and the Son. With regard to the nature of the Spirit, in what manner it exists, or whence it arose, Scripture is silent; which is a caution to us not to be too hasty in our conclusions on the subject. For though it be a Spirit, in the same sense in which the Father and Son are properly called Spirits; though we read that Christ by breathing on his disciples gave to them the Holy Ghost, or rather perhaps some symbol or pledge of the Holy Ghost, yet in treating of the nature of the Holy Spirit, we are not authorized to infer from such expressions, that the Spirit was breathed from the Father and the Son. The terms *emanation* and *procession,* employed by theologians on the authority of John xv. 26. do not relate to the nature of the Holy Spirit; *the Spirit of truth,* ὁ παρὰ τοῦ Πατρὸς ἐκπορεύεται, *who proceedeth or goeth forth from the Father;* which single expression is too slender a foundation for the full establishment of so great a mystery, especially as these words relate rather to the mission than to the nature of the Spirit; in which sense the Son also is often said ἐξελθεῖν, which in my opinion may be translated either *to go forth* or to *proceed* from the Father, without making any difference in the meaning. Nay, we are even said "to live by every word (ἐκπορευομένῳ) that proceedeth, *or* goeth forth from the mouth of God," Matt. iv. 4. Since therefore the Spirit is neither said to be generated nor created, nor is any other mode of existence specifically attributed to it in Scripture, we must be content to leave undetermined a point on which the sacred writers have preserved so uniform a silence.

The name of Spirit is also frequently applied to God and angels, and to the human mind. When the phrase, the Spirit of God, or the Holy Spirit, occurs in the Old Testament, it is to be variously interpreted; sometimes it signifies God the Father himself,—as Gen. vi. 3. "my Spirit shall not always strive with man;" sometimes the power and virtue of the Father, and particularly that divine breath or influence by which every thing is created and nourished. In this sense many both of the ancient and modern interpreters understand the passage in Gen. i. 2. "the Spirit of God moved upon the face of the waters." Here, however, it appears to be used with reference to the Son, through whom the Father is so often said to have created all things. Sometimes it means an angel. Sometimes it means Christ, who according to the common opinion was sent by the Father to lead the Israelites into the land of Canaan. Sometimes it means that impulse or voice of God by which the prophets were inspired. Sometimes it means that light of truth, whether ordinary or extraordinary, wherewith God enlightens and leads his people. Undoubtedly neither David, nor any other Hebrew, under the old covenant, believed in the personality of that *good* and *Holy Spirit,* unless perhaps as an angel. More particularly, it implies that light which was shed on Christ himself. It is also used to signify the spiritual gifts conferred by God on individuals, and the act of gift itself.

Nothing can be more certain, than that all these passages, and many others of a similar kind in the Old Testament, were understood of the virtue and power of God the Father, inasmuch as the Holy Spirit was not yet given, nor believed in, even by those who prophesied that it should be poured forth in the latter times. So likewise under the Gospel, what is called the Holy Spirit, or the Spirit of God, sometimes means the Father himself.

Again, it sometimes means the virtue and power of the Father. For thus the Scripture teaches throughout, that Christ was raised by the power of the Father, and thereby declared to be the Son of God. See particularly Acts xiii. 32, 33. quoted in the beginning of the last chapter. But the phrase, "according to the Spirit" (*secundum Spiritum*) seems to have the same signification as Eph. iv. 24. "which after God (*secundum Deum*) is created in righteousness and true holiness." Acts x. 38. "God anointed Jesus of Nazareth with the Holy Ghost and with power." i. 2. "after that he through the Holy Ghost had given commandments unto the apostles whom he had chosen." It is more probable that these phrases are to be understood of the power of the Father, than of the Holy Spirit himself; for how could it be necessary that Christ should be filled with the Holy Spirit, of whom he had himself said, John xvi. 15. "he shall take of mine?" For the same reason I am inclined to believe that the Spirit descended upon Christ at his baptism, not so much in his own name, as in virtue of a mission from the Father, and as a symbol and minister of the divine power. For what could the Spirit confer on Christ, from whom he was himself to be sent, and to receive all things? Was his purpose to bear witness to Christ? But as yet he was himself not so much as known. Was it meant that the Spirit should be then manifested for the first time to the Church? But at the time of his appearance nothing was said to him or of his office; nor did that voice from heaven bear any testimony to the Spirit, but only to the Son. The descent therefore and appearance of the Holy Spirit in the likeness of a dove, seems to have been nothing more than a representation of the ineffable affection of the Father for the Son, communicated by the Holy Spirit under the appropriate image of a dove, and accompanied by a voice from heaven declaratory of that affection.

Thirdly, the Spirit signifies a divine impulse, or light, or voice, or word, transmitted from above either through Christ, who is the Word of God, or by some other channel. It appears to me, that these and similar passages cannot be considered as referring to the express person of the Spirit, both because the Spirit was not yet given, and because Christ alone, as has been said before, is, properly speaking, and in a primary sense, the Word of God, and the prophet of the Church; though "God at sundry times and in divers manners spake in time past unto the Fathers by the prophets," Heb. i. 1. whence it appears that he did not speak by the Holy Spirit alone, unless the term be understood in the signification which I have proposed, and in a much wider sense than was subsequently attributed to it. Hence, 1 Pet. i. 11. "searching what or what manner of time the Spirit of Christ which was in them"—that is, in the prophets—*did signify,* must either be understood of Christ himself,—as iii. 18, 19. "quickened by the Spirit, by which also he went and preached unto the spirits in prison," —or it must be understood of the Spirit which supplied the place of Christ the Word and the Chief Prophet.

Further, the Spirit signifies the person itself of the Holy Spirit, or its symbol. John i. 32, 33. "like a dove." Nor let it be objected, that a dove is not a person; for an intelligent substance, under any form whatever, is a person; as for instance, the four living creatures seen in Ezekiel's vision, ch. i. John xx. 22. "he breathed on them, and saith unto them, Receive ye the Holy Ghost,"—which was a kind of symbol, and sure pledge of that promise, the fulfilment of which is recorded Acts ii. 2–4, 33. "having received of the Father the promise of the Holy Ghost, he hath shed forth this." Lastly, it signifies the donation of the Spirit itself, and of its attendant gifts. Who this Holy Spirit is, and whence he comes, and what are his offices, no one has taught us more explicitly than the Son of God himself, Matt. x. 20. "it is not ye that speak, but the Spirit of your Father than speaketh in you."

If it be the divine will that a doctrine which is to be understood and believed as one of the primary articles of our faith, should be delivered without obscurity or confusion, and explained, as is fitting, in clear and precise terms,—if it be certain that particular care ought to be taken in every thing connected with religion, lest the objection urged by Christ against the Samaritans should be applicable to us—"ye worship ye know not what," if our Lord's saying should be held sacred wherever points of faith are in question—"we know what we worship"—the particulars which have been stated seem to contain all that we are capable of knowing, or are required to know respecting the Holy Spirit, inasmuch as revelation has declared nothing else expressly on the subject. The nature of these particulars is such, that although the Holy Spirit be nowhere said to have taken upon himself any mediatorial 10 functions, as is said of Christ, nor to be engaged by the obligations of a filial relation to pay obedience to the Father, yet he must evidently be considered as inferior to both Father and Son, inasmuch as he is represented and declared to be subservient and obedient in all things; to have been promised, and sent, and given; to speak nothing of himself; and even to have been given as an earnest. There is no room here for any sophistical distinction 20 founded on a twofold nature; all these expressions refer to the Holy Spirit, who is maintained to be the supreme God; whence it follows, that wherever similar phrases are applied to the Son of God, in which he is distinctly declared to be inferior to the Father, they ought to be understood in reference to his divine as well to his human character. For what those, who believe in the Holy Spirit's co-equality with the Father, deem to 30 be not unworthy of him, cannot be considered unworthy of the Son, however exalted may be the dignity of his Godhead. Wherefore it remains now to be seen on what grounds, and by what arguments, we are constrained to believe that the Holy Spirit is God, if Scripture nowhere expressly teach the doctrine of his divinity, not even in the passages where his office is explained at large, nor in those where the unity of God 40 is explicitly asserted, nor where God is either described, or introduced as sitting upon his throne,—if, further, the Spirit be frequently named the Spirit of God, and the Holy Spirit of God, so that the Spirit of God being actually and numerically distinct from God himself, cannot possibly be essentially one God with him whose Spirit he is, (except on certain strange and absurd hypotheses, which have no foundation in Holy Scripture, but were de- 50 vised by human ingenuity, for the sole purpose of supporting this particular doctrine) —if, wherever the Father and the Holy Spirit are mentioned together, the Father alone be called God, and the Father alone, omitting all notice of the Spirit, be acknowledged by Christ himself to be the one true God, as has been proved in the former chapter by abundant testimony;—if he be God who "stablisheth us in Christ," who "hath anointed us," who "hath sealed us," and "given us the earnest of the Spirit," if that God be one God, and that one God the Father;—if, finally, "God hath sent forth the Spirit of his Son into our hearts, crying, Abba, Father," whence it follows that he who sent both the Spirit of his Son and the Son himself, he on whom we are taught to call, and on whom the Spirit himself calls, is the one God and the only Father. It seems exceedingly unreasonable, not to say dangerous, that in a matter of so much difficulty, believers should be required to receive a doctrine, represented by its advocates as of primary importance and of undoubted certainty, on anything less than the clearest testimony of Scripture; and that a point which is confessedly contrary to human reason, should nevertheless, be considered as susceptible of proof from human reason only, or rather from doubtful and obscure disputations.

First, then, it is usual to defend the divinity of the Holy Spirit on the ground, that the name of God seems to be attributed to the Spirit: Acts v. 3, 4. "why hath Satan filled thine heart to lie to the Holy Ghost? . . . thou hast not lied unto men, but unto God." But if attention be paid to what has been stated before respecting the Holy Ghost on the authority of the Son, this passage will appear too weak for the support of so great a doctrinal mystery. For since the Spirit is expressly said to be sent by the Father, and in the name of the Son, he who lies to the Spirit must lie to God, in the same sense as he who receives an apostle, receives God who sent him. St. Paul himself removes all ground of controversy from this passage, and explains it most appositely by implication, 1 Thess. iv. 8. where his intention is evidently to express the same truth more at large: "he therefore that despiseth, despiseth not man, but God, who hath also given unto us his Holy Spirit." Besides, it may be doubted whether the Holy Spirit in this passage does not signify God the Father; for Peter afterwards says, v. 9. "how is it that ye have agreed together to tempt the Spirit of the Lord?" that is, God the Father himself, and his divine intelligence, which no one can elude or deceive. And in v. 32. the Holy Spirit is not called God, but a witness of Christ with the apostles, "whom God hath given to them that obey him."

The second passage is Acts xxviii. 25. compared with Isai. vi. 8, 9. "I heard the voice of the Lord, saying . . . well spake the Holy Ghost by Esaias the prophet." But it has been shown above, that the names Lord and Jehovah are throughout the Old Testament attributed to whatever angel God may entrust with the execution of his commands; and in the New Testament the Son himself openly testifies of the Holy Spirit, John xvi. 13. that "he shall not speak of himself, but whatsoever he shall hear, that shall he speak." It cannot therefore be inferred from this passage, any more than from the preceding, that the Holy Ghost is God.

The third place is 1 Cor. iii. 16. compared with vi. 19. and 2 Cor. vi. 16. "the temple of God . . . the temple of the Holy Ghost." But neither is it here said, nor does it in any way follow from hence, that the Holy Spirit is God; for it is not because the Spirit alone, but because the Father also and the Son *make their abode with us,* that we are called *the temple of God.* Therefore in 1 Cor. vi. 19, where we are called "the temple of the Holy Ghost," St. Paul has added, "which ye have of God," as if with the purpose of guarding against any error which might arise respecting the Holy Spirit in consequence of his expression. How then can it be deduced from this passage, that he whom we have of God, is God himself? In what sense we are called *the temple of the Holy Ghost,* the same apostle has explained more fully Eph. ii. 22. "in whom ye also are builded together for an habitation of God through the Spirit."

The next evidence which is produced for this purpose, is the ascription of the divine attributes to the Spirit. And first, Omniscience; as if the Spirit were altogether of the same essence with God. 1 Cor. ii. 10, 11. "the Spirit searcheth all things, yea the deep things of God: for what man knoweth the things of a man, save the spirit of man which is in him? even so the things of God knoweth

no man, but the Spirit of God." With regard to the tenth verse, I reply, that in the opinion of divines, the question here is not respecting the divine omniscience, but only respecting those deep things "which God hath revealed unto us by his Spirit"—the words immediately preceding. Besides, the phrase *all things* must be restricted to mean whatever it is expedient for us to know: not to mention that it would be absurd to speak of God searching God, with whom he was one in essence. Next, as to the eleventh verse, the essence of the Spirit is not the subject in question; for the consequences would be full of absurdity, if it were to be understood that the Spirit of God was with regard to God, as the spirit of a man is with regard to man. Allusion therefore is made only to the intimate relationship and communion of the Spirit with God, from whom he originally proceeded. That no doubt may remain as to the truth of this interpretation, the following verse is of the same import: "we have received . . . the Spirit which is of God." That which is *of* God, cannot be actually God, who is unity. The Son himself disallows the omniscience of the Spirit still more plainly. Matt. xi. 27. "no man knoweth the Son, but the Father, neither knoweth any man the Father, save the Son, and he to whomsoever the Son will reveal him." What then becomes of the Holy Spirit? for according to this passage, no third person whatever knoweth either the Father or the Son, except through their medium. Mark xiii. 32. "of that day and that hour knoweth no man, no, not the angels which are in heaven, neither the Son, but the Father." If not even the Son himself, who is also in heaven, then certainly not the Spirit of the Son, who receiveth all things from the Son himself.

Secondly, Omnipresence, on the ground that *the Spirit of God dwelleth in us.* But even if it filled with its presence the whole circle of the earth, with all the heavens, that is, the entire fabric of this world, it would not follow that the Spirit is omnipresent. For why should not the Spirit easily fill with the influence of its power, what the Sun fills with its light; though it does not necessarily follow that we are to believe it infinite? If that lying spirit, 1 Kings xxii. 22. were able to fill four hundred prophets at once, how many thousands ought we not to think the Holy Spirit capable of pervading, even without the attributes of infinity or immensity?

Thirdly, divine works. Acts. ii. 4. "the Spirit gave them utterance." A single remark will suffice for the solution of all these passages, if it be only remembered what was the language of Christ respecting the Holy Spirit, the Comforter; namely, that he was sent by the Son from the Father, that he spake not of himself, nor in his own name, and consequently that he did not act in his own name; therefore that he did not even move others to speak of his own power, but that what he gave he had himself received. Again, 1 Cor. xii. 11. the Spirit is said "to divide to every man severally as he will." In answer to this it may be observed, that the Spirit himself is also said to be divided to each according to the will of God the Father, Heb. ii. 4. and that even "the wind bloweth where it listeth," John iii. 8. With regard to the annunciation made to Joseph and Mary, that the Holy Spirit was the author of the miraculous conception, Matt. i. 18, 20. Luke i. 35. it is not to be understood with reference to his own person alone. For it is certain that, in the Old Testament, under the name of the Spirit of God, or of the Holy Spirit, either God the Father himself, or his divine power was signified; nor had Joseph and Mary at that time heard anything of any other Holy Spirit, inasmuch as the personality and divinity of the Holy Spirit are not acknowledged by the Jews even to the present day. Accordingly, in both the passages quoted, πνεῦμα ἅγιον is without the customary article; or if this be not considered as sufficiently decisive, the angel speaks in a more circumstantial manner in St. Luke: "the Holy Ghost shall come upon thee, and the power of the Highest shall overshadow thee; therefore that holy thing which shall be born of these shall be called the Son of God,"—that is, of the Father: unless we suppose that there are two Fathers,—one Father of the Son of God, another Father of the Son of man.

Fourthly, divine honors. Matt. xxviii. 19. "baptizing them in the name of the Father, and of the Son, and of the Holy Ghost." Here mention is undoubtedly made of three persons; but there is not a word that determines the divinity, or unity, or equality of these three. To be baptized therefore *in their name*,

is to be admitted to those benefits and gifts which we have received through the Son and the Holy Spirit. Hence St. Paul rejoiced that no one could say he had been baptized in his name. It was not the imputation of making himself God that he feared, but that of affecting greater authority than was suitable to his character. From all which it is clear that when we are baptized in the name of the Father, Son, and Holy Ghost, this is not done to impress upon our minds the inherent or relative natures of these three persons, but the benefits conferred by them in baptism on those who believe,—namely, that our eternal salvation is owing to the Father, our redemption to the Son, and our sanctification to the Spirit. The power of the Father is inherent in himself, that of the Son and the Spirit is received from the Father; for it has been already proved on the authority of the Son, that the Son does everything in the name of the Father, and the Spirit every thing in the name of the Father and the Son; and a confirmation of the same truth may be derived from the words immediately preceding the verse under discussion; 1 Cor. vi. 11. "but ye are washed, but ye are sanctified, but ye are justified in the name of the Lord Jesus, and by the Spirit of our God." Here the same three are mentioned as in baptism, *the Son, the Spirit*, and *our God;* it follows therefore that the Father alone is our God, of whom are both the Son and the Spirit.

But invocation is made to the Spirit, 2 Cor. xiii. 14. "the grace of the Lord Jesus Christ, and the love of God, and the communion of the Holy Ghost, be with you all." This, however, is not so much an invocation as a benediction, in which the Spirit is not addressed as a person, but sought as a gift, from him who alone is there called God, namely, the Father, from whom Christ himself directs us to seek the communication of the Spirit. If the Spirit were ever to be invoked personally, it would be then especially, when we pray for him; yet we are commanded not to ask him of himself, but only of the Father. Why do we not call upon the Spirit himself, if he be God, to give himself to us? He who is sought from the Father, and given by him, not by himself, can neither be God, nor an object of invocation. The same form of benediction occurs. Rev. i. 4. "grace be unto you and peace from him which is . . . and from the seven spirits." It is clear that in this passage the seven spirits, of whom more will be said hereafter, are not meant to be invoked. Besides that in this benediction the order or dignity of the things signified should be considered, rather than that of the persons; for it is by the Son that we come to the Father, from whom finally the Holy Spirit is sent. So 1 Cor. xii. 4–6. "there are diversities of gifts, but the same Spirit: and there are differences of administrations, but the same Lord: and there are diversities of operations, but it is the same God which worketh all in all." Here the three are again mentioned in an inverse order; but it is one God which worketh all in all, even in the Son and the Spirit, as we are taught throughout the whole of Scripture.

Hence it appears that what is said Matt. xii. 31, 32. has no reference to the personality of the Holy Spirit. For if to sin against the Holy Spirit were worse than to sin against the Father and Son, and if that alone were an unpardonable sin, the Spirit truly would be greater than the Father and the Son. The words must therefore apply to that illumination, which, as it is highest in degree, so it is last in order of time, whereby the Father enlightens us through the Spirit, and which if any one resist, no method of salvation remains open to him. I am inclined to believe, however, that it is the Father himself who is here called the Holy Spirit, by whose *Spirit*, v. 28. or *finger*, Luke xi. 20. Christ professed to cast out devils; when therefore the Pharisees accused him falsely of acting in concern with Beelzebub, they are declared to sin unpardonably, because they said of him who had the Spirit of his Father, "he hath an unclean spirit," Mark iii. 30. Besides, it was to the Pharisees that he spoke thus, who acknowledged no other Spirit than the Father himself. If this be the true interpretation of the passage, which will not be doubted by any one who examines the whole context from v. 24 to v. 32. that dreaded sin against the Holy Spirit will be in reality a sin against the Father, who is the Spirit of holiness; of which he would be guilty, who should affirm that the Spirit of the Father which was working in Christ was the prince of the devils, or an unclean spirit;—as Mark clearly shows in the passage quoted above.

But the spirit bestows grace and blessing upon the churches in conjunction with the Father and the Son; Rev. i. 4, 5. "grace be unto you and peace from him which is . . . and from the seven spirits which are before his throne, and from Jesus Christ." It is clear, however, that the Holy Spirit is not here meant to be implied; the number of the spirits is inconsistent with such a supposition, as well as the place which they are said to occupy, standing like angels before the throne. See also iv. 5. and v. 6. where the same spirits are called "seven lamps of fire burning before the throne," and the "seven horns" and "seven eyes" of the Lamb. Those who reduce these spirits to one Holy Spirit, and consider them as synonymous with his sevenfold grace, (an opinion which is deservedly refuted by Beza) ought to beware, lest, by attributing to mere virtues the properties of persons, they furnish arguments to those commentators who interpret the Holy Spirit as nothing more than the virtue and power of the Father. This may suffice to convince us, that in this kind of threefold enumerations the sacred writers have no view whatever to the doctrine of three divine persons, or to the equality or order of those persons;—not even in that verse which has been mentioned above, and on which commentators in general lay so much stress, 1 John v. 7. "there are three that bear record in heaven, the Father, the Word, and the Holy Ghost, and these three are one," where there is in reality nothing which implies either divinity or unity of essence. As to divinity, God is not the only one who is said to bear record in heaven; 1 Tim. v. 21. "I charge thee before God, and the Lord Jesus Christ, and the elect angels," where it might have been expected that the Holy Spirit would have been named in the third place, if such ternary forms of expression really contained the meaning which is commonly ascribed to them. What kind of unity is intended, is sufficiently plain from the next verse, in which *the spirit, the water, and the blood* are mentioned, which *are to bear record to one,* or *to that one thing.* Beza himself, who is generally a staunch defender of the Trinity, understands the phrase *unum sunt* to mean, *agree in one*. What it is that they testify, appears in the fifth and sixth verses—namely, that *he that overcometh the world is he that believeth that Jesus is the Son of God, even Jesus Christ,* that is, *the anointed;* therefore he is not one with, nor equal to, him that anointed him. Thus the very record that they bear is inconsistent with the essential unity of the witnesses, which is attempted to be deduced from the passage. For the Word is both Son and Christ, that is, as I say, *anointed;* and as he is the image, as it were, by which we see God, so is he the word by which we hear him. But if such be his nature, he cannot be essentially one with God, whom no one can see or hear. The same has been already proved, by other arguments, with regard to the Spirit; it follows, therefore, that these three are not one in essence. I say nothing of the suspicion of spuriousness attached to the passage, which is a matter of criticism rather than of doctrine. Further, I would ask whether there is one Spirit that bears record in heaven, and another which bears record in earth, or whether both are the same Spirit. If the same, it is extraordinary that we nowhere else read of his bearing witness in heaven, although his witness has always been most conspicuously manifested in earth, that is, in our hearts. Christ certainly brings forward himself and his Father as the only witnesses of himself, John viii. 16, 19. Why then, in addition to two other perfectly competent witnesses, should the Spirit twice bear witness to the same thing. On the other hand, if it be another Spirit, we have here a new and unheard-of doctrine. There are besides other circumstances, which in the opinion of many render the passage suspicious; and yet it is on the authority of this text, almost exclusively, that the whole doctrine of the Trinity has been hastily adopted.

Lest, however, we should be altogether ignorant who or what the Holy Spirit is, although Scripture nowhere teaches us in express terms, it may be collected from the passages quoted above, that the Holy Spirit, inasmuch as he is a minister of God, and therefore a creature, was created or produced of the substance of God, not by a natural necessity, but by the free will of the agent, probably before the foundations of the world

were laid, but later than the Son, and far inferior to him. It will be objected, that thus the Holy Spirit is not sufficiently distinguished from the Son. I reply, that the Scriptural expressions themselves, "to come forth, to go out from the Father, to proceed from the Father," which mean the same in the Greek, do not distinguish the Son from the Holy Spirit, inasmuch as these terms are used indiscriminately with reference to both persons, and signify their mission, not their nature. There is, however, sufficient reason for placing the name as well as the nature of the Son above that of the Holy Spirit in the discussion of topics relative to the Deity; inasmuch as the brightness of the glory of God, and the express image of his person, are said to have been impressed on the one, and not on the other.

––––––––

CHAP. VII.—OF THE CREATION.

THE second species of external efficiency is commonly called *Creation*. As to the actions of God before the foundation of the world, it would be the height of folly to inquire into them, and almost equally so to attempt a solution of the question. With regard to the account which is generally given from 1 Cor. ii. 7. "he ordained his wisdom in a mystery, even the hidden mystery which God ordained before the world,"—or, as it is explained, that he was occupied with election and reprobation, and with decreeing other things relative to these subjects,—it is not imaginable that God should have been wholly occupied from eternity in decreeing that which was to be created in a period of six days, and which, after having been governed in divers manners for a few thousand years, was finally to be received into an immutable state with himself, or to be rejected from his presence for all eternity. That the world was created, is an article of faith: Heb. xi. 3.

Creation is that act whereby *God the Father produced every thing that exists by his Word and Spirit,* that is, *by his will, for the manifestation of the Glory of his power and goodness.*

Whereby God the Father. Isai. xlv. 6, 7. "that they may know from the rising of the sun, and from the west, that there is none beside me: I am Jehovah, and there is none else: I form the light, and create darkness." If there be any thing like a common meaning, or universally received usage of words, this language not only precludes the possibility of there being any other God, but also of there being any co-equal person, of any kind whatever.

By his word. Gen. i. throughout the whole chapter.—"God said." 2 Pet. iii. 5. "by the word of God the heavens were of old," that is, as is evident from other passages, by the Son, who appears hence to derive his title of Word. The preposition *per* sometimes signifies the primary cause, as Matt. xii. 28. "I cast out devils (*per Spiritum*) by the Spirit of God." 1 Cor. i. 9. "God is faithful, (*per quem*) by whom ye are called," sometimes the instrumental, or less principal cause, as in the passages quoted above, where it cannot be taken as the primary cause, for if so, the Father himself, of whom are all things, would not be the primary cause; nor is it the joint cause, for in such case it would have been said that the Father created all things, not by, but with the Word and Spirit; or collectively, the Father, the Word, and the Spirit created; which phrases are nowhere to be found in Scripture. Besides, the expressions *to be of the Father,* and *to be by the Son,* do not denote the same kind of efficient cause. If it be not the same cause, neither is it a joint cause; and if not a joint cause, certainly the Father, of whom are all things, must be the principal cause, rather than the Son by whom are all things; for the Father is not only he *of* whom, but also from whom, and for whom, and through whom, and on account of whom are all things, as has been proved above, inasmuch as he comprehends within himself all lesser causes; whereas the Son is only he by whom are all things; wherefore he is the less principal cause. Hence it is often said that the Father created the world by the Son,—but never, in the same sense, that the Son created the world by the Father. It is, however, sometimes attempted to be proved from Rev. iii. 14. that the Son was the joint, or even the principal cause of the creation with the Father; *the beginning of the creation of God;* where the word *beginning* in interpreted

in an active sense, on the authority of Aristotle. But in the first place, the Hebrew language, whence the expression is taken, no where admits of this sense, but rather requires a contrary usage, as Gen. xlix. 3. "Reuben, thou art . . . the beginning of my strength." Secondly, there are two passages in St. Paul referring to Christ himself, which clearly prove that the word *beginning* is here used in a passive signification. Col. i. 15, 18. "the first born of every creature . . . the beginning, the first born from the dead,"— where the position of the Greek accent, and the passive verbal πρωτότοκος, show that the Son of God was the first born of every creature precisely in the same sense as the Son of man was the first born of Mary, πρωτότοκος, Matt. i. 25. The other passage is Rom. viii. 29. "first born among many brethren;" that is, in a passive signification. Lastly, it should be remarked, that he is not called simply *the beginning of the creation,* but *of the creation of God;* which can mean nothing else than the first of those things which God created; how therefore can he be himself God? Nor can we admit the reason devised by some of the Fathers for his being called, Col. i. 15. "the first born of every creature," —namely, because it is said v. 16. "by him all things were created." For had St. Paul intended to convey the meaning supposed, he would have said, *who was before every creature,* (which is what these Fathers contend the words signify, though not without violence to the language) not, *who was the first born of every creature,* an expression which clearly has a superlative, and at the same time to a certain extent a partitive sense, in so far as production may be considered as a kind of generation and creation; but by no means in so far as the title of first born among men may be here applied to Christ, seeing that he is termed first born, not only in respect of dignity, but also of time.

Nor is the passage in Prov. viii. 22, 23. of more weight, even if it be admitted that the chapter in general is to be understood with reference to Christ: "Jehovah possessed me in the beginning of his way before his works of old; I was set up from everlasting." For that which was *possessed* and *set up,* could not be the primary cause. Even a creature, however, is called the beginning of the ways of God, Job xl. 19. "he (behemoth) is the chief (*principium*) of the ways of God." As to the eighth chapter of Proverbs, it appears to me that it is not the Son of God who is there introduced as the speaker, but a poetical personification of wisdom, as in Job xxviii. 20–27. "whence then cometh wisdom?—then did he see it."

Another argument is brought from Isai. xlv. 12, 23. "I have made the earth . . . unto me every knee shall bow." It is contended that this is spoken of Christ, on the authority of St. Paul, Rom. xiv. 10, 11. "we shall all stand before the judgment seat of Christ: for it is written, As I live, saith the Lord, every knee shall bow to me." But it is evident from the parallel passage Philipp. ii. 9—11. that this is said of God the Father, by whose gift the Son has received that judgment seat, and all judgment, "that at the name of Jesus every knee shall bow . . . to the glory of God the Father;" or, which means the same thing, "every tongue shall confess to God."

And Spirit. Gen. i. 2. "the Spirit of God moved upon the face of the waters;" that is, his divine power, rather than any person, as has been already shown in the sixth chapter, on the Holy Spirit. For if it were a person, why is the Spirit named, to the exclusion of the Son, by whom we so often read that the world was created? unless, indeed, that Spirit were Christ, to whom, as has been before proved, the name of Spirit is sometimes given in the Old Testament. However this may be, and even if it should be admitted to have been a person, it seems at all events to have been only a subordinate minister: God is first described as creating the heaven and the earth; the Spirit is only represented as moving upon the face of the waters already created. Psal. xxxiii. 6. "by the word of Jehovah were the heavens made, and all the host of them by the breath (*spiritu*) of his mouth." Now the person of the Spirit does not seem to have proceeded more from the mouth of God than from that of Christ, who "shall consume that wicked one with the spirit of his mouth," 2 Thess. ii. 8. compared with Isai. xi. 4. "the rod of his mouth."

Thus far it has appeared that God the Father is the primary and efficient cause of all things. With regard to the original matter of the universe, however, there has been much difference of opinion. Most of the moderns contend that it was formed from nothing, a basis as unsubstantial as that of their own theory. In the first place, it is certain that neither the Hebrew verb בָּרָא, nor the Greek κτίζειν, nor the Latin *creare*, can signify to create of nothing. On the contrary, these words uniformly signify to create out of matter. To allege, therefore, that creation signifies production out of nothing, is, as logicians say, to lay down premises without a proof; for the passages of Scripture commonly quoted for this purpose, are so far from confirming the received opinion, that they rather imply the contrary, namely, that all things were not made out of nothing. 2 Cor. iv. 6. "God, who commanded the light to shine out of darkness." That this darkness was far from being a mere negation, is clear from Isai. xlv. 7. "I am Jehovah; I form the light, and create darkness." If the darkness be nothing, God in creating darkness, created nothing, or in other words, he created and did not create, which is a contradiction. Again, what we are required *to understand through faith* respecting *the worlds,* is merely this, that "the things which were seen were not made of things which do appear," Heb. xi. 3. Now *the things which do not appear* are not to be considered as synonymous with nothing, (for nothing does not admit of a plural, nor can a thing be made and compacted together out of nothing, as out of a number of things,) but the meaning is, that they do not appear as they now are. The apocryphal writers, whose authority may be considered as next to that of the Scriptures, speak to the same effect. The expression in Matt. ii. 18. may be quoted, "the children of Rachel are not." This, however, does not mean properly that they are nothing, but that (according to a common Hebraism) they are no longer among the living.

It is clear then that the world was framed out of matter of some kind or other. For since action and passion are relative terms, and since, consequently, no agent can act externally, unless there be some patient, such as matter, it appears impossible that God could have created this world out of nothing; not from any defect of power on his part, but because it was necessary that something should have previously existed capable of receiving passively the exertion of the divine efficacy. Since, therefore, both Scripture and reason concur in pronouncing that all these things were made, not out of nothing, but out of matter, it necessarily follows, that matter must either have always existed independently of God, or have originated from God at some particular point of time. That matter should have been always independent of God, (seeing that it is only a passive principle, dependent on the Deity, and subservient to him; and seeing, moreover, that, as in number, considered abstractedly, so also in time or eternity there is no inherent force or efficacy) that matter, I say, should have existed of itself from all eternity, is inconceivable. If on the contrary it did not exist from all eternity, it is difficult to understand from whence it derives its origin. There remains, therefore, but one solution of the difficulty, for which moreover we have the authority of Scripture, namely, that all things are of God.

In the first place, there are, as is well known to all, four kinds of causes,—*efficient, material, formal,* and *final.* Inasmuch then as God is the primary, and absolute, and sole cause of all things, there can be no doubt but that he comprehends and embraces within himself all the causes above mentioned. Therefore the material cause must be either God, or nothing. Now nothing is no cause at all; and yet it is contended that forms, and above all, that human forms, were created out of nothing. But matter and form, considered as internal causes, constitute the thing itself; so that either all things must have had two causes only, and those external, or God will not have been the perfect and absolute cause of every thing. Secondly, it is an argument of supreme power and goodness, that such diversified, multiform, and inexhaustible virtue should exist and be *substantially* inherent in God (for that virtue cannot be *accidental* which admits of degrees, and of augmentation or remission, according to his pleasure) and that this diversified and substantial virtue should not remain dormant within the Deity, but should be diffused and propagated and extended as far and in such manner as he himself may will. For the original matter of which we speak, is not to be looked upon as an evil or trivial thing, but as intrinsically

good, and the chief productive stock of every subsequent good. It was a substance, and derivable from no other source than from the fountain of every substance, though at first confused and formless, being afterwards adorned and digested into order by the hand of God.

Those who are dissatisfied because, according to this view, substance was imperfect, must also be dissatisfied with God for having originally produced it out of nothing in an imperfect state, and without form. For what difference does it make, whether God produced it in this imperfect state out of nothing, or out of himself? By this reasoning, they only transfer that imperfection to the divine efficiency, which they are unwilling to admit can properly be attributed to substance considered as an efflux of the Deity. For why did not God create all things out of nothing in an absolutely perfect state at first? It is not true, however, that matter was in its own nature originally imperfect; it merely received embellishment from the accession of forms, which are themselves material. And if it be asked how what is corruptible can proceed from incorruption, it may be asked in return how the virtue and efficacy of God can proceed out of nothing. Matter, like the form and nature of the angels itself, proceeded incorruptible from God; and even since the fall it remains incorruptible as far as concerns its essence.

But the same, or even a greater difficulty still remains—how that which is in its nature peccable can have proceeded (if I may so speak) from God? I ask in reply, how anything peccable can have originated from the virtue and efficacy which proceeded from God? Strictly speaking, indeed it is neither matter nor form that sins; and yet having proceeded from God, and become in the power of another party, what is there to prevent them, inasmuch as they have now become mutable, from contracting taint and contamination through the enticements of the devil, or those which originate in man himself? It is objected, however, that body cannot emanate from spirit. I reply, much less then can body emanate from nothing. For spirit being the more excellent substance, virtually and essentially contains within itself the inferior one; as the spiritual and rational faculty contains the corporeal, that is, the sentient and vegetative faculty. For not even divine virtue and efficiency could produce bodies out of nothing, according to the commonly received opinion, unless there had been some bodily power in the substance of God; since no one can give to another what he does not himself possess. Nor did St. Paul hesitate to attribute to God something corporeal; Col. ii. 9. "in him dwelleth all the fulness of the Godhead bodily." Neither is it more incredible that a bodily power should issue from a spiritual substance, than that what is spiritual should arise from body; which nevertheless we believe will be the case with our own bodies at the resurrection. Nor, lastly, can it be understood in what sense God can properly be called infinite, if he be capable of receiving any accession whatever; which would be the case if anything could exist in the nature of things, which had not first been of God and in God.

Since therefore it has (as I conceive) been satisfactorily proved, under the guidance of Scripture, that God did not produce everything out of nothing, but of himself, I proceed to consider the necessary consequence of this doctrine, namely, that if all things are not only from God, but of God, no created thing can be finally annihilated. And, not to mention that not a word is said of this annihilation in the sacred writings, there are other reasons, besides that which has been just alleged, and which is the strongest of all, why this doctrine should be altogether exploded. First, because God is neither willing, nor, properly speaking, able to annihilate anything altogether. He is not willing, because he does everything with a view to some end,—but nothing can be the end neither of God, nor of anything whatever. Not of God, because he is himself the end of himself; not of anything whatever, because good of some kind is the end of everything. Now nothing is neither good, nor in fact anything. Entity is good, non-entity consequently is not good; wherefore it is neither consistent with the goodness or wisdom of God to make out of entity, which is good, that which is not good, or nothing. Again, God is not able to annihilate anything altogether, because by creating nothing he would create and not create at the same time, which involves a contradiction. If it be said that the creative power of God continues to operate, inasmuch as he makes that not to exist which did exist; I answer, that there are two things necessary to constitute a perfect action, motion and the effect of motion: in the present instance the motion is the act of annihilation; the effect of motion is none, that is, nothing, no effect. Where then there is no effect there is no efficient.

Creation is either of things invisible or visible. The things invisible, or which are at least such to us, are, the highest heaven, which is the throne and habitation of God, and the heavenly powers, or angels. Such is the division of the apostle, Col. i. 16. The first place is due to things invisible, if not in respect of origin, at least of dignity. For the highest heaven is as it were the supreme citadel and habitation of God.

It is improbable that God should have formed to himself such an abode for his majesty only at so recent a period as at the beginning of the world. For if there be any one habitation of God, where he diffuses in an eminent manner the glory and brightness of his majesty, why should it be thought that its foundations are only coeval with the fabric of this world, and not of much more ancient origin? At the same time it does not follow that heaven should be eternal, nor, if eternal, that it should be God; for it was always in the power of God to produce any effect he pleased at whatever time and in whatever manner seemed good to him. We cannot form any conception of light independent of a luminary; but we do not therefore infer that a luminary is the same as light, or equal in dignity. In the same manner we do not think that what are called *the back parts* of God, Exod. xxxiii. are, properly speaking, God; though we nevertheless consider them to be eternal. It seems more reasonable to conceive in the same manner of the heaven of heavens, the throne and habitation of God, than to imagine that God should have been without a heaven till the first of the six days of creation. At the same time I give this opinion, not as venturing to determine anything certain on such a subject, but rather with a view of showing that others have been too bold in affirming that the invisible and highest heaven was made on the first day, contemporaneously with that **heaven** which is within our sight. For since it was of the latter heaven alone, and of the visible world, that Moses undertook to write, it would have been foreign to his purpose to have said anything of what was above the world.

In this highest heaven seems to be situated the heaven of the blessed; which is sometimes called Paradise, Luke xxiii. 43. and Abraham's bosom, Luke xvi. 22. compared with Matt. viii. 11. where also God permits himself to be seen by the angels and saints (as far as they are capable of enduring his glory), and will unfold himself still more fully to their view at the end of the world, 1 Cor. xiii. 12.

It is generally supposed that the angels were created at the same time with the visible universe, and that they are considered as comprehended under the general name of heavens. That the angels were created at some particular period, we have the testimony of Numb. xvi. 22. and xxvii. 16. "God of the spirits." But that they were created on the first, or on any one of the six days, seems to be asserted (like most received opinions) with more confidence than reason, chiefly on the authority of the repetition in Gen. ii. 1. "thus the heavens and the earth were finished, and all the host of them,"—unless we are to suppose that more was meant to be implied in the concluding summary than in the previous narration itself, and that the angels are to be considered as the host who inhabit the visible heavens. For when it is said Job xxxviii. 7. that they shouted for joy before God at the creation, it proves rather that they were then already in existence, than that they were then first created. Many at least of the Greek, and some of the Latin Fathers, are of opinion that angels, as being spirits, must have existed long before the material world; and it seems even probable, that the apostasy which caused the expulsion of so many thousands from heaven, took place before the foundations of this world were laid. Certainly there is no sufficient foundation for the common opinion, that motion and time (which is the measure of motion) could not, according to the ratio of priority and subsequence, have existed before this world was made; since Aristotle, who teaches that no ideas of motion and time can be formed except in reference to this world, nevertheless pronounces the world itself to be eternal.

Angels are spirits, inasmuch as a legion of devils is represented as having taken possession of one man, Luke viii. 30. They are of ethereal nature, 1 Kings xxii. 21. Heb. i. 7. "as lightning," Luke x. 18. whence also they are called Seraphim. Immortal, Luke xx. 36. "neither can they die any more." Excellent in wisdom; 2 Sam. xiv. 20. Most powerful in strength; Psal. ciii. 20. Endued with the greatest swiftness, which is figuratively denoted by the attribute of wings; Ezek. i. 6. In number almost infinite; Deut. xxxiii. 2. Created in perfect holiness and righteousness; Luke ix. 26. Hence they are also called sons of God, Job. i. 6. and even Gods, Psal. viii. 5. But they are not to be compared with God; Job. iv. 18. They are distinguished one from another by offices and degrees; Matt. xxv. 41. Cherubim, Gen. iii. 24. Seraphim, Isai. vi. 2. and by proper names; Dan. viii. 16. See more on this subject in the ninth chapter. To push our speculations further on this subject, is to incur the apostle's reprehension, Col. ii. 18.

The visible creation comprises the material universe, and all that is contained therein; and more especially the human race.

The creation of the world in general, and of its individual parts, is related Gen. i. It is also described Job xxvi. and xxxviii. and in various passages of the Psalms and Prophets. Previously, however, to the creation of man, as if to intimate the superior importance of the work, the Deity speaks like to a man deliberating: Gen. i. 26. "God said, Let us make man in our own image, after our own likeness." So that it was not the body alone that was then made, but the soul of man also (in which our likeness to God principally consists); which precludes us from attributing pre-existence to the soul which was then formed,—a groundless notion sometimes entertained, but refuted by Gen. ii. 7. "God formed man of the dust of the ground, and breathed into his nostrils the breath of life; thus man became a living soul." Nor did God merely breathe that spirit into man, but molded it in each individual, and infused it throughout, enduing and embellishing it with its proper faculties.

We may understand from other passages

of Scripture, that when God infused the breath of life into man, what man thereby received was not a portion of God's essence, or a participation of the divine nature, but that measure of the divine virtue or influence, which was commensurate to the capabilities of the recipient. For it appears from Psal. civ. 29, 30. that he infused the breath of life into other living beings also;—"thou takest away their breath, they die . . . thou sendest forth thy spirit, they are created;" whence we learn that every living thing receives animation from one and the same source of life and breath; inasmuch as when God takes back to himself that spirit or breath of life, they cease to exist. Eccles. iii. 19. "they have all one breath." Nor has the word *spirit* any other meaning in the sacred writings, but that breath of life which we inspire, or the vital, or sensitive, or rational faculty, or some action or affection belonging to those faculties.

Man having been created after this manner, it is said, as a consequence, that *man became a living soul;* whence it may be inferred (unless we had rather take the heathen writers for our teachers respecting the nature of the soul) that man is a living being, intrinsically and properly one and individual, not compound or separable, not, according to the common opinion, made up and framed of two distinct and different natures, as of soul and body,—but that the whole man is soul, and the soul man, that is to say, a body, or substance individual, animated, sensitive, and rational; and that the breath of life was neither a part of the divine essence, nor the soul itself, but as it were an inspiration of some divine virtue fitted for the exercise of life and reason, and infused into the organic body; for man himself, the whole man, when finally created, is called in express terms *a living soul.* Hence the word used in Genesis to signify *soul,* is interpreted by the apostle, 1 Cor. xv. 45. "animal." Again, all the attributes of the body are assigned in common to the soul: the touch, Lev. v. 2.—the act of eating, vii. 18. "the soul that eateth of it shall bear his iniquity;" and in other places:—hunger, Prov. xiii. 25.—thirst, xxv. 25.—capture, 1 Sam. xxiv. 11.

Where, however, we speak of the body as of a mere senseless stock, there the soul must be understood as signifying either the spirit, or its secondary faculties, the vital or sensitive faculty for instance.—Thus it is as often distinguished from the spirit, as from the body itself. But that the spirit of man should be separate from the body, so as to have a perfect and intelligent existence independently of it, is nowhere said in Scripture, and the doctrine is evidently at variance both with nature and reason, as will be shown more fully hereafter. For the word *soul* is also applied to every kind of living being; Gen. i. 30. yet it is never inferred from these expressions that the soul exists separate from the body in any of the brute creation.

On the seventh day, God ceased from his work, and ended the whole business of creation: Gen. ii. 2, 3.

It would seem, therefore, that the human soul is not created daily by the immediate act of God, but propagated from father to son in a natural order; which was considered as the more probable opinion by Tertullian and Apollinarius, as well as by Augustine, and the whole western church in the time of Jerome, as he himself testifies, Tom. II. Epist. 82. and Gregory of Nyssa in his treatise on the soul. God would in fact have left his creation imperfect, and a vast, not to say, a servile task would yet remain to be performed, without even allowing time for rest on each successive Sabbath, if he still continued to create as many souls daily as there are bodies multiplied throughout the whole world, at the bidding of what is not seldom the flagitious wantonness of man. Nor is there any reason to suppose that the influence of the divine blessing is less efficacious in imparting to man the power of producing after his kind, than to the other parts of animated nature. Thus it was from one of the ribs of the man that God made the mother of all mankind, without the necessity of infusing the breath of life a second time, Gen. ii. 22. and Adam himself begat a son in his own likeness after his image, v. 3. Thus 1 Cor. xv. 49. "as we have borne the image of the earthy;" and this not only in the body, but in the soul, as it was chiefly with respect to the soul that Adam was made in the divine image. Heb. vii. 10. "Levi was in the loins of Abraham:" whence in Scripture an offspring is called *seed,* and Christ is denominated *the seed of the woman.*

But besides the testimony of revelation, some arguments from reason may be alleged in confirmation of this doctrine. Whoever is born, or shapen and conceived in sin, (as we all are, not David only, Psal. li. 5.) if he receive his soul immediately from God, cannot but receive it from him shapen in sin; for to be generated and conceived, means nothing else than to receive a soul in conjunction with the body. If we receive the soul immediately from God, it must be pure, for who in such case will venture to call it impure? But if it be pure, how are we conceived in sin in consequence of receiving a pure soul, which would rather have the effect of cleansing the impurities of the body; or with what justice is the pure soul charged with the sin of the body? But, it is contended, God does not create souls impure, but only impaired in their nature, and destitute of original righteousness; I answer that to create pure souls, destitute of original righteousness,—to send them into contaminated and corrupt bodies,—to deliver them up in their innocence and helplessness to the prison house of the body, as to an enemy, with understanding blinded and with will enslaved,—in other words, wholly deprived of sufficient strength for resisting the vicious propensities of the body—to create souls thus circumstanced, would argue as much injustice, as to have created them impure would have argued impurity; it would have argued as much injustice, as to have created the first man Adam himself impaired in his nature, and destitute of original righteousness.

Again, if sin be communicated by generation, and transmitted from father to son, it follows that what is the πρῶτον δεκτικὸν, or original subject of sin, namely, the rational soul, must be propagated in the same manner; for that it is from the soul that all sin in the first instance proceeds, will not be denied. Lastly, on what principle of justice can sin be imputed through Adam to that soul, which was never either in Adam, or derived from Adam? In confirmation of which Aristotle's argument may be added, the truth of which in my opinion is indisputable. If the soul be equally diffused throughout any given whole, and throughout every part of that whole, how can the human seed, the noblest and most intimate part of all the body, be imagined destitute and devoid of the soul of the par-

ents, or at least of the father, when communicated to the son by the laws of generation? It is acknowledged by the common consent of almost all philosophers, that every *form,* to which class the human soul must be considered as belonging, is produced by the power of matter.

It was probably by some such considerations as these that Augustine was led to confess that he could neither discover by study, nor prayer, nor any process of reasoning, how the doctrine of original sin could be defended on the supposition of the creation of souls. The texts which are usually advanced, Eccles. xii. 7. 1 Isai. vii. 16. Zech. xii. 1. certainly indicate that nobler origin of the soul implied in its being breathed from the mouth of God; but they no more prove that each soul is severally and immediately created by the Deity, than certain other texts, which might be quoted, prove that each individual body is formed in the womb by the immediate hand of God. We are not to infer from these passages, that natural causes do not contribute their ordinary efficacy for the propagation of the body; nor on the other hand that the soul is not received by traduction from the father, because at the time of death it again betakes itself to different elements than the body, in conformity with its own origin.

With regard to the passage, Heb. xii. 9. where *the fathers of the flesh* are opposed to *the Father of spirits,* I answer, that it is to be understood in a theological, not in a physical sense, as if the father of the body were opposed to the father of the soul; for *flesh* is taken neither in this passage, nor probably any where else, for the body without the soul; nor *the father of spirits* for the father of the soul, in respect of the work of generation; but *the father of the flesh* here means nothing else than the earthly or natural father, whose offspring are begotten in sin; *the father of spirits* is either the heavenly father, who in the beginning created all spirits, angels as well as the human race, or the spiritual father, who bestows a second birth on the faithful; according to John iii. 6. "that which is born of the flesh is flesh, and that which is born of the Spirit is spirit." The argument, too, will proceed better, if the whole be understood as referring to edification and correction, not to generation; for the point in question is not, from what source each individual originated, or what part of him thence originated, but who had proved most successful in employing chastisement and instruction. By parity of reasoning, the apostle might exhort the converts to bear with his rebuke, on the ground that he was their spiritual father. God indeed is as truly the father of the flesh as of *the spirits of flesh,* Numb. xvi. 22. but this is not the sense intended here, and all arguments are weak which are deduced from passages of Scripture originally relating to a different subject.

With regard to the soul of Christ, it will be sufficient to answer that its generation was supernatural, and therefore cannot be cited as an argument in the discussion of this controversy. Nevertheless, even he is called *the seed of the woman, the seed of David according to the flesh;* that is, undoubtedly, according to his human nature.

There seems therefore no reason, why the soul of man should be made an exception to the general law of creation. For, as has been shown before, God breathed the breath of life into other living beings, and blended it so intimately with matter, that the propagation and production of the human form were analogous to those of other forms, and were the proper effect of that power which had been communicated to matter by the Deity.

Man being formed after the image of God, it followed as a necessary consequence that he should be endued with natural wisdom, holiness, and righteousness. Certainly without extraordinary wisdom he could not have given names to the whole animal creation with such sudden intelligence, Gen. ii. 20.

CHAP. VIII.—OF THE PROVIDENCE OF GOD, OR OF HIS GENERAL GOVERNMENT OF THE UNIVERSE.

THE remaining species of God's external efficiency, is his *government of the whole creation.*

This government is either *general* or *special.*

His *general government* is that whereby *God the Father regards, preserves, and governs the whole of creation with infinite wisdom and holiness according to the conditions of his decree.*

God the Father. To this truth Christ himself bears witness everywhere, even as regards the Son himself. The preservation of the universe is attributed to the Son also, but in what sense, and on what grounds, may be seen in the fifth chapter, on the Son of God.

According to the conditions of his decree. It is necessary to add this qualification, inasmuch as God preserves neither angels, nor men, nor any other part of creation absolutely, but always with reference to the conditions of his decree. For he preserves mankind, since their spontaneous fall, and all other things with them, only so far as regards their existence, and not as regards their primitive perfection. Generally speaking, however, no distinction is made between the righteous and the wicked, with regard to the final issue of events, at least in this life.

The whole of creation, Gen. viii. 1. "God remembered Noah, and every living thing, and all the cattle." Even the smallest objects. At the same time, God does not extend an equal share of his providential care to all things indiscriminately. 1 Cor. ix. 9. "doth God take care for oxen?" that is, as much care as he takes for man? Natural things. Exod. iii. 21. "I will give this people favor in the sight of the Egyptians;" that is, by operating a change in their natural affections. Even such as are supernatural. Events contingent or fortuitous. Nor does Scripture intimate anything derogatory to divine providence, even where (as sometimes happens) the names of fortune or chance are not scrupled to be employed; all that is meant is to exclude the idea of human causation. Voluntary actions. In this, however, there is no infringement on the liberty of the human will; otherwise man would be deprived of the power of free agency, not only with regard to what is right, but with regard to what is indifferent, or even positively wrong. Lastly, temporal evils no less than blessings. Isai. xlv. 7. "I make peace and create evil,"—that is, what afterwards became evil, and now remains so; for whatever God created was originally good, as he himself testifies, Gen. i.

God, however, is concerned in the production of evil only in one of these two ways; either, first, he permits its existence by throwing no impediment in the way of natural causes and free agents, or, secondly, he causes evil by the infliction of judgments, which is called the evil of punishment.

If (inasmuch as I do not address myself to such as are wholly ignorant, but to those who are already competently acquainted with the outlines of Christian doctrine) I may be permitted, in discoursing on the general providence of God, so far to anticipate the natural order of arrangement, as to make an allusion to a subject which belongs properly to another part of my treatise, that of sin, I might remark, that even in the matter of sin God's providence finds its exercise, not only in permitting its existence, or in withdrawing his grace, but also in impelling sinners to the commission of sin, in hardening their hearts, and in blinding their understandings.

But though in these, as well as in many other passages of the Old and New Testament, God distinctly declares that it is himself who impels the sinner to sin, who hardens his heart, who blinds his understanding, and leads him into error; yet on account of the infinite holiness of the Deity, it is not allowable to consider him as in the smallest instance the author of sin. 1 John ii. 16. "for all that is in the world, the lust of the flesh, and the lust of the eyes, and the pride of life, is not of the Father, but is of the world." For it is not the human heart in a state of innocence and purity, and repugnance to evil, that is induced by him to act wickedly and deceitfully; but after it has conceived sin, and when it is about to bring forth, he, in his character of sovereign disposer of all things, inclines and biasses it in this or that direction, or towards this or that object. Psal. xciv. 23. "he shall bring upon them their own iniquity, and shall cut them off in their own wickedness, yea, Jehovah our God shall cut them off;"—that is to say, by the infliction of punishment. Nor does God make that will evil which was before good, but the will being already in a state of perversion, he influences it in such a manner, that out of its own wickedness it either operates good for others, or punishment for itself, though unknowingly, and with the intent of producing a very different result. Thus Ezek. xxi. 21, 22. when the king of Babylon stood at the parting of the way, in doubt whether he should go to war against the Ammonites or against the Jews, God so ordered the divination, as to determine him on going against Jerusalem. Or, to use the common simile, as a rider who urges on a stumbling horse in a particular direction is the cause of its increasing its speed, but not of its stumbling,—so God, who is the supreme governor of the universe, may instigate an evil agent, without being in the least degree the cause of the evil. I shall recur again to this simile hereafter. For example, —God saw that the mind of David was so elated and puffed up by the increase of his power, that even without any external impulse he was on the point of giving some remarkable token of his pride; he therefore excited in him the desire of numbering the people; he did not inspire him with the passion of vain glory, but impelled him to display in this manner, rather than in any other, that latent arrogance of his heart, which was ready to break forth. God therefore was the author of the act itself, but David alone was responsible for its pride and wickedness. Further, the end which a sinner has in view is generally something evil and unjust, from which God uniformly educes a good and just result, thus as it were creating light out of darkness. By this means he proves the inmost intentions of men, that is, he makes man to have a thorough insight into the latent wickedness of his own heart, that he may either be induced thereby to forsake his sins, or if not, that he may become notorious and inexcusable in the sight of all; or lastly, to the end that both the author and the sufferer of the evil may be punished for some former transgression. At the same time, the common maxim, that God makes sin subservient to the punishment of sin, must be received with caution; for the Deity does not effect his purpose by compelling any one to commit crime, or by abetting him in it, but by withdrawing the ordinary grace of his enlightening spirit, and ceasing to strengthen him against sin. There is indeed a proverb which says, that he who is able to forbid an action, and forbids it not, virtually commands it. This maxim is indeed binding on man, as a moral precept; but it is otherwise with regard to God. When, in conformity with the language of mankind, he is spoken of as instigating, where he only does not prohibit evil, it does not follow that he therefore bids it, inasmuch as there is no obligation by which he is bound to forbid it. Hence it is said, Rom. i. 24. "wherefore God also gave them up to uncleanness,"—that is, he left them to be actuated by their own lusts, to walk in them; for properly speaking God does not instigate, or give up, him whom he leaves entirely to himself, that is, to his own desires and counsels, and to the suggestions of his ever active spiritual enemy. In the same sense the Church is said to give up to Satan the contumacious member, whom it interdicts from its communion. With regard to the case of David's numbering the people, a single word will be sufficient. For it is not God, but Satan who is said to have instigated him, 2 Sam. xxiv. 1. As to the popular simile of the stumbling horse, the argument drawn from it is itself a lame one; for the sinner, if he really instigated, is not instigated simply to act, as in the case of the horse, but to act amiss,—or in other words, he is instigated to stumble, because he stumbles. In both the instances above adduced, God had determined to punish openly the secret adultery of David: he saw Absolom's propensity to every act of wickedness; he saw the mischievous counsels of Ahithophel, and did nothing more than influence their minds, which were already in a state of preparation for any atrocity, to perpetrate one crime in preference to another, when opportunity should offer. For to offer an occasion of sinning, is only to manifest the wickedness of the sinner, not to create it. The other position, that God eventually converts every evil deed into an instrument of good, contrary to the expectation of sinners, and overcomes evil with good, is sufficiently illustrated in the example of Joseph's sale by his brethren, Gen. xlv. 8. Thus also in the crucifixion of Christ the sole aim of Pilate was to preserve the favor of Cæsar; that of the Jews to satisfy their own hatred and vengeance; but God, whose "hand and counsel had determined before every thing that was to be done," Acts iv. 28. made use of their cruelty and violence as instruments for effecting the general redemption of mankind.

Again, as God's instigating the sinner does not render him the author of sin, so neither does his hardening the heart or blinding the understanding involve that consequence; inasmuch as he does not produce these effects by infusing an evil disposition, but on the contrary by employing such just and kind methods, as ought rather to soften the hearts of sinners than harden them. First, by his long-suffering. Secondly, by urging his own good and reasonable commands in opposition to the obstinacy of the wicked; as an anvil, or adamant, is said to be hardened under the hammer. Thus Pharaoh became more furious and obdurate in proportion as he resisted the commands of God. Thirdly, by correction or punishment. The hardening of the heart, therefore, is usually the last punishment inflicted on inveterate wickedness and unbelief in this life. God often hardens in a remarkable manner the powerful and rebellious princes of this world, in order that through their insolence and haughtiness his glory may be magnified among the nations. Yet the act of hardening is not so exclusively the work of God, but that the wicked themselves fully co-operate in it, though with any view rather than that of fulfilling the divine will.

Thus also with regard to the blinding of the understanding. Lastly, God is said to deceive men, not in the sense of seducing them to sin, but of beguiling them to their own punishment, or even to the production of some good end. God first deceived the already corrupt and covetous prophet, by disposing his mind to prophesy things acceptable to the people, and then deservedly cut off both the people who inquired of him, and the prophet of whom they inquired, to deter others from sinning in a similar manner; because on the one hand a bad intention had been displayed on the part of the inquirers, and on the other a false answer had been returned, which God had not commanded.

To this view of providence must be referred what is called temptation, whereby God either tempts men, or permits them to be tempted by the devil or his agents.

Temptation is either for evil or for good.

An evil temptation is when God, as above described, either withdraws his grace, or presents occasions of sin, or hardens the heart, or blinds the understanding. This is generally an evil temptation in respect of him who is tempted, but most equitable on the part of the Deity, for the reason above-mentioned. It also serves the purpose of unmasking hypocrisy; for God tempts no one in the sense of enticing or persuading to sin, though there be some towards whom he deservedly permits the devil to employ such temptations. We are taught in the Lord's prayer to deprecate temptations of this kind.

A good temptation is that whereby God tempts even the righteous for the purpose of proving them, not as though he were ignorant of the disposition of their hearts, but for the purpose of exercising or manifesting their faith or patience, as in the case of Abraham and Job; or of lessening their self-confidence, and reproving their weakness, that both they themselves may become wiser by experience, and others may profit by their example: as in the case of Hezekiah, 2 Chron. xxxii. 31. whom "God left"—partially, or for a time—"to try him, that he might know all that was in his heart." He tempted the Israelites in the wilderness with the same view. This kind of temptation is therefore rather to be desired. God also promises a happy issue.

Yet even believers are not always sufficiently observant of these various operations of divine providence, until they are led to investigate the subject more deeply, and become more intimately conversant with the word of God.

Having said in the prefatory definition, that the providence of God extends to all things, and that certain immutable laws have been enacted, by which every part of the creation is administered, it may not be an useless digression to inquire in this place, whether, among other fixed regulations, a limit has been set to the duration of human life, which is not to be passed. That such is the case, Scripture clearly intimates. From these and similar passages, and especially from the early history of the world, it is evident that God, at least after the fall of man, limited human life to a certain term, which in the progress of ages, from Adam to David, gradually became more and more contracted; so that whether this term be one and the same to all, or appointed differently to each individual, it is in the power of no one to prolong or exceed its limits. This is the province of God alone, as is proved beyond all doubt by the promise of long life made by him to his people, and by his addition of fifteen years to the life of Hezekiah when at the point of death. The power of shortening or anticipating the term in question, on the other hand, is not the exclusive privilege of God, though this also is exercised by him, both for purposes of reward and punishment; the same effect may be, and in fact frequently is, produced by the crimes or vices of mortals themselves. Psal. lv. 23. "bloody and deceitful men shall not live out half their days," that is, they shall not live to the end of that term, to which by the constitution of their bodies they might otherwise have arrived; in which class are to be placed all those who lay violent hands on themselves, or who accelerate death by intemperate living. The providence of God is either ordinary or extraordinary. His ordinary providence is that whereby he upholds and preserves the immutable order of causes appointed by him in the beginning. This is commonly, and indeed too frequently, described by the name of nature; for nature cannot possibly mean anything but the mysterious power and efficacy of that divine voice which went forth in the beginning, and to which, as to a perpetual command, all things have since paid obedience. The extraordinary providence of God is that whereby God produces some effect out of the usual order of nature, or gives the power of producing the same effect to whomsoever he may appoint. This is what we call a miracle. Hence God alone is the primary author of miracles, as he only is able to invert that order of things which he has himself appointed. The use of miracles is to manifest the divine power, and confirm our faith. Miracles are also designed to increase the condemnation of unbelievers, by taking away all excuse for unbelief.

CHAP. IX.—OF THE SPECIAL GOVERNMENT OF ANGELS.

The general government of Providence has been hitherto the subject of consideration. *The special government* is that which embraces with peculiar regard angels and men, as beings far superior to the rest of the creation.

Angels are either good or evil, Luke ix. 26. viii. 2. for it appears that many of them revolted from God of their own accord before the fall of man. Some are of opinion that the good angels are now upheld, not so much by their own strength, as by the grace of God. 1 Tim. v. 21. "the elect angels," that is, who have not revolted. Hence arises, in their opinion, the delighted interest which the angels take in the mystery of man's salvation; Pet. i. 12. "which things the angels desire to look into." They assign the same reason for their worshipping Christ. Heb. i. 6. It seems, however, more agreeable to reason, to suppose that the good angels are upheld by their own strength no less than man himself was before his fall;—that they are called *elect*, in the sense of beloved, or excellent;—that it is not from any interest of their own, but from their love to mankind, that they desire to look into the mystery of our salvation;—that they are not comprehended in the covenant of reconciliation;— that, finally, they are included under Christ as their head, not as their Redeemer.

For the rest, they are represented as standing dispersed around the throne of God in the capacity of ministering agents, praising God. They are obedient to God in all respects. Their ministry relates especially to believers. 1 Cor. xi. 10. "for this cause ought the woman to have power on her head because of the angels," namely, as some think, (and numerous examples in confirmation of their opinion are not wanting) those angels whose office it was to be present at the religious assemblies of believers.

Seven of these, in particular, are described as traversing the earth in the execution of their ministry.

It appears also probable that there are certain angels appointed to preside over nations, kingdoms, and particular districts.

They are sometimes sent from heaven as messengers of the divine vengeance, to punish the sins of men. They destroy cities and nations.

There appears to be one who presides over the rest of the good angels, to whom the name of Michael is often given. It is generally thought that Michael is Christ. But Christ vanquished the devil, and trampled him under foot singly; Michael, the leader of the angels, is introduced in the capacity of a hostile commander waging war with the prince of the devils, the armies on both sides being drawn out in battle array, and separating after a doubtful conflict. Rev. xii. 7; 8. Jude also says of the same angel, "when contending with the devil he disputed about the body of Moses, he durst not bring against him a railing accusation,"—which would be an improper expression to use with reference to Christ, especially if he be God. Besides it seems strange that an apostle of Christ, in revealing things till then so new and unheard-of concerning his master, should express himself thus obscurely, and should even shadow the person of Christ under a difference of name.

The good angels do not look into all the secret things of God, as the Papists pretend; some things indeed they know by revelation, and others by means of the excellent intelligence with which they are gifted; there is much, however, of which they are ignorant. An angel is introduced inquiring Dan. viii. 13. "how long shall be the vision?" The evil angels are reserved for punishment. They are sometimes, however, permitted to wander throughout the whole earth, the air, and heaven itself, to execute the judgments of God. They are even admitted into the presence of God. Their proper place, however, is the bottomless pit, from which they cannot escape without permission. Nor can they do anything without the command of God.

Their knowledge is great, but such as tends rather to aggravate than diminish their misery; so that they utterly despair of their salvation. James ii. 19. "the devils believe and tremble," knowing that they are reserved for punishment, as has been shown.

The devils also have their prince. Matt. xii. 24. "Beelzebub, the prince of the devils." They retain likewise their respective ranks. Their leader is the author of all wickedness, and the opponent of all good. Hence he has obtained many names corresponding to his actions. He is frequently called "Satan," that is, an enemy or adversary, Job i. 6.

CHAP. X. —OF THE SPECIAL GOVERN-
MENT OF MAN BEFORE THE FALL,
INCLUDING THE INSTITUTIONS OF
THE SABBATH AND OF MARRIAGE.

THE Providence of God as regards mankind, relates to man either in his state of rectitude, or since his fall.

With regard to that which relates to man in his state of rectitude, God, having placed him in the garden of Eden, and furnished him with whatever was calculated to make life happy, commanded him, as a test of his obedience, to refrain from eating of the single tree of knowledge of good and evil, under penalty of death if he should disregard the injunction. This is sometimes called "the covenant of works," though it does not appear from any passage of Scripture to have been either a covenant, or of works. No works whatever were required of Adam; a particular act only was forbidden. It was necessary that something should be forbidden or commanded as as a test of fidelity, and that an act in its own nature indifferent, in order that man's obedience might be thereby manifested. For since it was the disposition of man to do what was right, as a being naturally good and holy, it was not necessary that he should be bound by the obligation of a covenant to perform that to which he was of himself inclined; nor would he have given any proof of obedience by the performance of works to which he was led by a natural impulse, independently of the divine command. Not to mention, that no command, whether proceeding from God or from a magistrate, can properly be called a covenant, even where rewards and punishments are attached to it; but rather an exercise of jurisdiction.

The tree of knowledge of good and evil was not a sacrament, as it is generally called; for a sacrament is a thing to be used, not abstained from: but a pledge, as it were, and memorial of obedience. It was called the tree of knowledge of good and evil from the event; for since Adam tasted it, we not only know evil, but we know good only by means of evil. For it is by evil that virtue is chiefly exercised, and shines with greater brightness. The tree of life, in my opinion, ought not to be considered so much a sacrament, as a symbol of eternal life, or rather perhaps the nutriment by which that life is sustained.

Seeing, however, that man was made in the image of God, and had the whole law of nature so implanted and innate in him, that he needed no precept to enforce its observance, it follows, that if he received any additional commands, whether respecting the tree of knowledge, or the institution of marriage, these commands formed no part of the law of nature, which is sufficient of itself to teach whatever is agreeable to right reason, that is to say, whatever is intrinsically good. Such commands therefore must have been founded on what is called positive right, whereby God, or any one invested with lawful power, commands or forbids what is in itself neither good nor bad, and what therefore would not have been obligatory on any one, had there been no law to enjoin or prohibit it. With regard to the Sabbath, it is clear that God hallowed it to himself, and dedicated it to rest, in remembrance of the consummation of his work. Whether its institution was ever made known to Adam, or whether any commandment relative to its observance was given previous to the delivery of the law on Mount Sinai, much less whether any such was given before the fall of man, cannot be ascertained, Scripture being silent on the subject. The most probable supposition is, that Moses, who seems to have written the book of Genesis much later than the promulgation of the law, inserted this sentence from the fourth commandment, into what appeared a suitable place for it; where an opportunity was afforded for reminding the Israelites, by a natural and easy transition, of the reason assigned by God, many ages after the event itself, for his command with regard to the observance of the Sabbath by the covenanted people. The injunction respecting the celebration of the Sabbath in the wilderness, a short time previous to the delivery of the law, namely, that no one should go out to gather manna on the seventh morning, because God had said that he would not rain it from heaven on that day, seems rather to have been intended as a preparatory notice, the groundwork, as it were, of a law for the Israelites, to be delivered shortly afterwards in a clearer manner; they having been previously ignorant of the mode of observing the Sabbath. For the rulers of the congregation, who ought to have been better acquainted than the rest with the commandment of the Sabbath, if any such institution then existed, wondered why the people gathered twice as much on the sixth day, and appealed to Moses; who then, as if announcing something new, proclaimed to them that the morrow would be the Sabbath. After which, as if he had already related in what manner the Sabbath was for the first time observed, he proceeds, "so the people rested on the seventh day." That the Israelites had not so much as heard of the Sabbath before this time, seems to be confirmed by several passages of the prophets.

With regard to marriage, that it was instituted, if not commanded, at the creation, is clear, and that it consisted in the mutual love, society, help, and comfort of the husband and wife, though with a reservation of superior rights to the husband. The power of the husband was even increased after the fall. Therefore the word בַּעַל in the Hebrew signifies both husband and lord. Thus Sarah is represented as calling her husband Abraham *lord*, 1 Pet. iii. 6.

Marriage, therefore, is a most intimate connection of man with woman, ordained by God, for the purpose either of the procreation of children, or of the relief and solace of life. Hence it is said, Gen. ii. 24. "therefore shall a man leave his father and his mother, and shall cleave unto his wife, and they shall be one flesh." This is neither a law nor a commandment, but an effect or natural consequence of that most intimate union which would have existed between them in the perfect state of man; nor is the passage intended to serve any other purpose, than to account for the origin of families.

In the definition which I have given, I have not said, in compliance with the common opinion, *of one man with one woman*, lest I should by implication charge the holy patriarchs and pillars of our faith, Abraham, and the others who had more than one wife at the same time, with habitual fornication and adultery; and lest I should be forced to exclude from the sanctuary of God as spurious, the holy offspring which sprang from them, yea, the whole of the sons of Israel,

for whom the sanctuary itself was made. For it is said, Deut. xxiii. 2. "a bastard shall not enter into the congregation of Jehovah, even to his tenth generation." Either therefore polygamy is a true marriage, or all children born in that state are spurious; which would include the whole race of Jacob, the twelve holy tribes chosen by God. But as such an assertion would be absurd in the extreme, not to say impious, and as it is the height of injustice, as well as an example of most dangerous tendency in religion, to account as sin what is not such in reality; it appears to me, that, so far from the question respecting the lawfulness of polygamy being trivial, it is of the highest importance that it should be decided.

Those who deny its lawfulness, attempt to prove their position from Gen. ii. 24. "a man shall cleave unto his wife, and they shall be one flesh," compared with Matt. xxix. 5. "they twain shall be one flesh." A man shall cleave, they say, to his wife, not to his wives, and they twain, and no more, shall be one flesh. This is certainly ingenious; and I therefore subjoin the passage in Exod. xx. 17. "thou shalt not covet thy neighbor's house, nor his man-servant, nor his maid-servant, nor his ox nor his ass;" whence it would follow that no one had more than a single house, a single man-servant, a single maid-servant, a single ox or ass. It would be ridiculous to argue, that it is not said houses, but house, not man-servants, but man-servant, not even neighbors, but neighbor; as if it were not the general custom, in laying down commandments of this kind, to use the singular number, not in a numerical sense, but as designating the species of the thing intended. With regard to the phrase, *they twain*, and not more, *shall be one flesh*, it is to be observed, first, that the context refers to the husband and that wife only whom he was seeking to divorce, without intending any allusion to the number of his wives, whether one or more. Secondly, marriage is in the nature of a relation; and to one relation there can be no more than two parties. In the same sense therefore as if a man has many sons, his paternal relation towards them all is manifold, but towards each individually is single and complete in itself; by parity of reasoning, if a man has many wives, the relation which he bears to each will not be less perfect in itself, nor will the husband be *less one flesh* with each of them, than if he had only one wife. Thus it might be properly said of Abraham, with regard to Sarah and Hagar respectively, *these twain were one flesh*. And with good reason; for whoever consorts with harlots, however many in number, is still said to be *one flesh* with each. The expression may therefore be applied as properly to the husband who has many wives, as to him who has only one. Hence it follows that the commandment in question (though in fact it is no commandment at all, as has been shown) contains nothing against polygamy, either in the way of direct prohibition or implied censure; unless we are to suppose that the law of God, as delivered by Moses, was at variance with his prior declarations; or that, though the passage in question had been frequently looked into by a multitude of priests, and Levites, and prophets, men of all ranks, of holiest lives and most acceptable to God, the fury of their passions was such as to hurry them by a blind impulse into habitual fornication; for to this supposition are we reduced, if there be anything in the present precept which renders polygamy incompatible with lawful marriage.

Another text from which the unlawfulness of polygamy is maintained, is Lev. xvii. 18. "neither shalt thou take a wife to her sister, to vex her, to uncover her nakedness, beside the other in her life time." Here Junius translates the passage *mulierem unam ad alteram,* instead of *mulierem ad sororem suam,* in order that from this forced and inadmissible interpretation he may elicit an argument against polygamy. In drawing up a law, as in composing a definition, it is necessary that the most exact and appropriate words should be used, and that they should be interpreted not in their metaphorical, but in their proper signification. He says, indeed, that the same words are found in the same sense in other passages. This is true; but it is only where the context precludes the possibility of any ambiguity, as in Gen. xxvi. 31. *juraverunt vir fratri suo,* that is *alteri, they sware one to another.* No one would infer from this passage that Isaac was the brother of Abimelech; nor would any one, on the other hand, entertain a doubt that the passage in Leviticus was intended as a prohibition against taking a wife to her sister; particularly as the preceding verses of this chapter treat of the degrees of affinity to which intermarriage is forbidden. Moreover, this would be *to uncover her nakedness,* the evil against which the law in question was intended to guard; whereas the caution would be unnecessary in the case of taking another wife not related or allied to the former; for no nakedness would be thereby uncovered. Lastly, why is the clause *in her life time* added? For there could be no doubt of its being lawful after her death to marry another who was neither related nor allied to her, though it might be questionable whether it were lawful to marry a wife's sister. It is objected, that marriage with a wife's sister is forbidden by analogy in the sixteenth verse, and that therefore a second prohibition was unnecessary. I answer, first, that there is in reality no analogy between the two passages; for that by marrying a brother's wife, the brother's nakedness is uncovered; whereas by marrying a wife's sister, it is not a sister's nakedness, but only that of a kinswoman by marriage, which is uncovered. Besides, if nothing were to be prohibited which had been before prohibited by analogy, why is marriage with a mother forbidden, when marriage with a father had been already declared unlawful? or why marriage with a mother's sister, when marriage with a father's sister had been prohibited? If this reasoning be allowed, it follows that more than half the laws relating to incest are unnecessary. Lastly, considering that the prevention of enmity is alleged as the principal motive for the law before us, it is obvious, that if the intention had been to condemn polygamy, reasons of a much stronger kind might have been urged from the nature of the original institution, as was done in the ordinance of the Sabbath.

A third passage which is advanced, Deut. xvii. 17. is so far from condemning polygamy, either in a king, or in any one else, that it expressly allows it; and only imposes the same restraints upon this condition which are laid upon the multiplication of horses, or the accumulation of treasure; as will appear from the seventeenth and eighteenth verses.

Except the three passages which are thus irrelevantly adduced, not a trace appears of the interdiction of polygamy throughout the whole law; nor even in any of the prophets, who were at once the rigid interpreters of the law, and the habitual reprovers of the vices of the people. The only shadow of an exception occurs in a passage of Malachi, the last of the prophets, which some consider as decisive against polygamy. It would be indeed a late and postliminous enactment, if that were for the first time prohibited after the Babylonish captivity which ought to have been prohibited many ages before. For if it had been really a sin, how could it have escaped the reprehension of so many prophets who preceded him? We may safely conclude that if polygamy be not forbidden in the law, neither is it forbidden here; for Malachi was not the author of a new law. Let us however see the words themselves as translated by Junius, ii. 15. *Nonne unum effecit? quamvis reliqui spiritus ipsi essent: quid autem unum?* It would be rash and unreasonable indeed, if, on the authority of so obscure a passage, which has been tortured and twisted by different interpreters into such a variety of meanings, we were to form a conclusion on so momentous a subject, and to impose it upon others as an article of faith. But whatever be the signification of the words *nonne unum effecit,* what do they prove? are we, for the sake of drawing an inference against polygamy, to understand the phrase thus—*did not he make one woman?* But the gender, and even the case, are at variance with this interpretation; for nearly all the other commentators render the words as follows: *annon unus fecit? et residuum spiritus ipsi? et quid ille unus?* We ought not therefore to draw any conclusion from a passage like the present in behalf of a doctrine which is either not mentioned elsewhere, or only in doubtful terms; but rather conclude that the prophet's design was to reprove a practice which the whole of Scripture concurs in reproving, and which forms the principal subject of the very chapter in question, v. 11–16. namely, marriage with *the daughter of a strange god;* a corruption very prevalent among the Jews of that time, as we learn from Ezra and Nehemiah.

With regard to the words of Christ, Matt. v. 32. and xix. 5. the passage from Gen. ii. 24. is repeated not for the purpose of condemning polygamy, but of reproving the unrestrained liberty of divorce, which is a very different thing; nor can the words be made to apply to any other subject without evident violence to their meaning. For the argument which is deduced from Matt. v. 32. that if a man who marries another after putting away his first wife, committeth adultery, much more must he commit adultery who retains the first and marries another, ought itself to be repudiated as an illegitimate conclusion. For in the first place, it is the divine precepts themselves that are obligatory, not the consequences deduced from them by human reasoning; for what appears a reasonable inference to one individual, may not be equally obvious to another of not inferior discernment. Secondly, he who puts away his wife and marries another, is not said to commit adultery because he marries another, but because in consequence of his marriage with another he does not retain his former wife, to whom also he owed the performance of conjugal duties; whence it is expressly said, Mark x. 11. "he committeth adultery against her." That he is in a condition to perform his conjugal duties to the one, after having taken another to her, is shown by God himself, Exod. xxi. 10. "if he take him another wife, her food, her raiment, and her duty of marriage shall he not diminish." It cannot be supposed that the divine forethought intended to provide for adultery.

Nor is it allowable to argue, from 1 Cor. vii. 2. "let every man have his own wife," that therefore none should have more than one; for the meaning of the precept is, that every man should have his own wife to himself, not that he should have but one wife. That bishops and elders should have no more than one wife is explicitly enjoined 1 Tim. iii. 2. and Tit. i. 6. "he must be the husband of one wife," in order probably that they may discharge with greater diligence the ecclesiastical duties which they have undertaken. The command itself, however, is a sufficient proof that polygamy was not forbidden to the rest, and that it was common in the church at that time.

Lastly, in answer to what is urged from 1 Cor. vii. 4. "likewise also the husband hath not power of his own body, but the wife," it is easy to reply, as was done above, that the word *wife* in this passage is used with reference to the species, and not to the number. Nor can the power of the wife over the body of her husband be different now from what it was under the law, where it is called עֹנָה, Exod. xxi 10. which signifies "her stated times," expressed by St. Paul in the present chapter by the phrase, "her due benevolence." With regard to what is *due,* the Hebrew word is sufficiently explicit.

On the other hand, the following passages clearly admit the lawfulness of polygamy. Exod. xxi. 10. "if he take him another wife, her food, her raiment, and her duty of marriage shall he not diminish." Deut. xvii. 17. "neither shall he multiply wives to himself, that his heart turn not away." Would the law have been so loosely worded, if it had not been allowable to take more wives than one at the same time? Who would venture to subjoin as an inference from this language, therefore let him have one only? In such case, since it is said in the preceding verse, "he shall not multiply horses to himself," it would be necessary to subjoin there also, therefore he shall have one horse only. Nor do we want any proof to assure us, that the first institution of marriage was intended to bind the prince equally with the people; if therefore it permits only one wife, it permits no more even to the prince. But the reason given for the law is this, *that his heart turn not away;* a danger which would arise if he were to marry many, and especially strange women, as Solomon afterwards did. Now if the present law had been intended merely as a confirmation and vindication of the primary institution of marriage, nothing could have been more appropriate than to have recited the institution itself in this place, and not to have advanced that reason alone which has been mentioned.

Let us hear the words of God himself, the author of the law, and the best interpreter of his own will. 2 Sam. xii. 8. "I gave thee thy master's wives into thy bosom . . . and if that had been too little, I would moreover have given unto thee such and such things." Here there can be no subterfuge; God gave him wives, he gave them to the man whom he loved, as one among a number of great benefits; he would have given him more, if these had not been enough. Besides, the very argument which God uses towards David, is of more force when applied to the gift of wives, than to any other,—thou oughtest at least to have abstained from the wife of an-

other person, not so much because I had given thee thy master's house, or thy master's kingdom, as because I had given thee the wives of the king. Beza indeed objects, that David herein committed incest, namely, with the wives of his father-in-law. But he had forgotten what is indicated by Esther ii. 12, 13. that the kings of Israel had two houses for the women, one appointed for the virgins, the other for the concubines, and that it was the former and not the latter which were given to David. This appears also from 1 Kings i. 4. "the king knew her not." Cantic. vi. 8. "there are fourscore concubines, and virgins without number." At the same time, it might be said with perfect propriety that God had given him his master's wives, even supposing that he had only given him as many in number and of the same description, though not the very same; even as he gave him, not indeed the identical house and retinue of his master, but one equally magnificent and royal.

It is not wonderful, therefore, that what the authority of the law, and the voice of God himself has sanctioned, should be alluded to by the holy prophets in their inspired hymns as a thing lawful and honorable. Psal. xlv. 9. (which is entitled *A song of loves*) "kings' daughters were among thy honorable women," v. 14. "the virgins her companions that follow her shall be brought unto thee." Nay, the words of this very song are quoted by the apostle to the Hebrews, i. 8. "unto the Son he saith, Thy throne, O God," as the words wherein God the father himself addresses the Son, and in which his divinity is asserted more clearly than in any other passage. Would it have been proper for God the Father to speak by the mouth of harlots, and to manifest his holy Son to mankind as God in the amatory songs of adulteresses? Thus also in Cantic. vi. 8–10. the queens and concubines are evidently mentioned with honor, and are all without distinction considered worthy of celebrating the praises of the bride: "there are threescore queens, and fourscore concubines, and virgins without number . . . the daughters saw her and blessed her; yea, the queens and the concubines, and they praised her." Nor must we omit 2 Chron. xxiv. 2, 3. "Joash did that which was right in the sight of the Lord all the days of Jehoiada the priest: and Jehoiada took for him two wives." For the two clauses are not placed in contrast, or disjoined from each other, but it is said in one and the same connection that under the guidance of Jehoiada he did that which was right, and that by the authority of the same individual he married two wives. This is contrary to the usual practice in the eulogies of the kings, where, if anything blameable be subjoined, it is expressly excepted from the present character. Since therefore the right conduct of Joash is mentioned in unqualified terms, in conjunction with his double marriage, it is evident that the latter was not considered matter of censure; for the sacred historian would not have neglected so suitable an opportunity of making the customary exception, if there had really been anything which deserved disapprobation.

Moreover, God himself, in an allegorical fiction, Ezek. xxiii. 4. represents himself as having espoused two wives, Aholah and Aholibah; a mode of speaking which he would by no means have employed, especially at such length, even in a parable, nor indeed have taken on himself such a character at all, if the practice which it implied had been intrinsically dishonorable or shameful.

On what grounds, however, can a practice be considered dishonorable or shameful, which is prohibited to no one even under the gospel? for that dispensation annuls none of the merely civil regulations which existed previous to its introduction. It is only enjoined that elders and deacons should be chosen from such as were husbands of one wife. This implies, not that to be the husband of more than one wife would be a sin, for then the restriction would have been equally imposed on all; but that, in proportion as they were less entangled in domestic affairs, they would be more at leisure for the business of the church. Since therefore polygamy is interdicted in this passage to the ministers of the church alone, and that not on account of any sinfulness in the practice, and since none of the other members are precluded from it either here or elsewhere, it follows that it was permitted, as abovesaid, to all the remaining members of the church, and that it was adopted by many without offence.

Lastly, I argue as follows from Heb. xiii. 4. Polygamy is either marriage, or fornication, or adultery; the apostle recognizes no fourth state. Reverence for so many patriarchs who were polygamists will, I trust, deter any one from considering it as fornication or adultery; for "whoremongers and adulterers God will judge;" whereas the patriarchs were the objects of his especial favor, as he himself testifies. If then polygamy be marriage properly so called, it is also lawful and honorable, according to the same apostle: "marriage is honorable in all, and the bed undefiled."

It appears to me sufficiently established by the above arguments that polygamy is allowed by the law of God: lest however any doubt should remain, I will subjoin abundant examples of men whose holiness renders them fit patterns for imitation, and who are among the lights of our faith. Foremost I place Abraham, the father of all the faithful, and of the holy seed, and, if I mistake not, Moses, Numb. xii. 1. It is not likely that the wife of Moses, who had been so often spoken of before by her proper name of Zipporah, should now be called by the new title of a Cushite; or that the anger of Aaron and Miriam should at this time be suddenly kindled, because Moses forty years before had married Zipporah; nor would they have acted thus scornfully towards one whom the whole house of Israel had gone out to meet on her arrival with her father Jethro. If then he married the Cushite during the lifetime of Zipporah, his conduct in this particular received the express approbation of God himself, who moreover punished with severity the unnatural opposition of Aaron and his sister. Next I place Gideon, that signal example of faith and piety, and Elkanah, a rigid Levite, the father of Samuel; who was so far from believing himself less acceptable to God on account of his double marriage, that he took with him his two wives every year to the sacrifices and annual worship, into the immediate presence of God; nor was he therefore reproved, but went home blessed with Samuel, a child of excellent promise. Passing over several other examples, though illustrious, such as Caleb, the sons of Issachar, in number "six and thirty thousand men, for they had many wives and sons," contrary to the modern European practice, where in many places the land is suffered to remain uncultivated for want of population; and also Manasseh, the son of Joseph, I come to the prophet David, whom God loved beyond all men, and who took two wives, besides Michal; and this not in a time of pride and prosperity, but when he was almost bowed down by adversity, and when, as we learn from many of the psalms, he was entirely occupied in the study of the word of God and in the right regulation of his conduct. Such were the motives, such the honorable and holy thoughts whereby he was influenced, namely, by the consideration of God's kindness toward him for his people's sake. His heavenly and prophetic understanding saw not in that primitive institution what we in our blindness fancy we discern so clearly; nor did he hesitate to proclaim in the supreme council of the nation the pure and honorable motives to which, as he trusted, his children born in polygamy owed their existence. I say nothing of Solomon, notwithstanding his wisdom, because he seems to have exceeded due bounds; although it is not objected to him that he had taken many wives, but that he had married strange women. His son Rehoboam *desired many wives,* not in the time of his iniquity, but during the three years in which he is said to have walked in the way of David. Of Joash mention has already been made; who was induced to take two wives, not by licentious passion, or the wanton desires incident to uncontrolled power, but by the sanction and advice of a most wise and holy man, Jehoiada the priest. Who can believe, either that so many men of the highest character should have sinned through ignorance for so many ages; or that their hearts should have been so hardened; or that God should have tolerated such conduct in his people? Let therefore the rule received among theologians have the same weight here as in other cases: "The practice of the saints is the best interpretation of the commandments."

It is the peculiar province of God to make marriage prosperous and happy. The consent of the parents, if living, should not be wanting. But the mutual consent of the parties themselves is naturally the first and most important requisite; for there can be no love or good will, and consequently no marriage, without mutual consent. In order that marriage may be valid, the consent must be free from every kind of fraud, especially in respect of chastity. It will be obvious to every sensible person that maturity of age is requisite.

The degrees of affinity which constitute incest are to be determined by the law of God, and not by ecclesiastical canons or legal decrees. We are moreover to interpret the text in its plain and obvious meaning, without attempting to elicit more from it than is really contains. To be wise beyond this point, savors of superstitious folly, and a spurious preciseness.

It is also necessary that the parties should be of one mind in matters of religion. Under the law this precept was understood as applying to marriages already contracted, as well as those in contemplation. A similar provision was made under the gospel for preventing the contraction of any marriage where a difference of religious opinion might exist. But if the marriage be already contracted, it is not to be dissolved, while any hope remains of doing good to the unbeliever. For the rest, what kind of issue generally follows such marriages may be seen in the case of the antediluvian world, of Ahab, of Jehoshaphat, who gave his son Jehoram a wife of the daughters of Ahab.

The *form* of marriage consists in the mutual exercise of benevolence, love, help, and solace between the espoused parties, as the institution itself, or its definition, indicates.

The end of marriage is nearly the same with the form. Its proper fruit is the procreation of children; but since Adam's fall, the provision of a remedy against incontinency has become in some degree a secondary end. 1 Cor. vii. 2. Hence marriage is not a command binding on all, but only on those who are unable to live with chastity out of this state.

Marriage is honorable in itself, and prohibited to no order of men; wherefore the Papists act contrary to religion in excluding the ministers of the church from this rite.

Marriage, by its definition, is an union of the most intimate nature; but not indissoluble or indivisible, as some contend on the ground of its being subjoined, Matt. xix. 5. "they two shall be one flesh." These words, properly considered, do not imply that marriage is absolutely indissoluble, but only that it ought not to be lightly dissolved. For it is upon the institution itself, and the due observance of all its parts, that what follows respecting the indissolubility of marriage depends, whether the words be considered in the light of a command, or of a natural consequence. Hence it is said, "for this cause shall a man leave father and mother . . . and they two shall be one flesh;" that is to say, if, according to the nature of the institution as laid down in the preceding verses, Gen. ii. 18, 20. the wife will be an help meet for the husband; or in other words, if good will, love, help, comfort, fidelity, remain unshaken on both sides, which, according to universal acknowledgment, is the *essential form* of marriage. But if the essential form be dissolved, it follows that the marriage itself is virtually dissolved.

Great stress, however, is laid upon an expression in the next verse; "what God hath joined together, let not man put asunder." What it is that God hath joined together, the institution of marriage itself declares. God has joined only what admits of union, what is suitable, what is good, what is honorable; he has not made provision for unnatural and monstrous associations, pregnant only with dishonor, with misery, with hatred, and with calamity. It is not God who forms such unions, but violence, or rashness, or error, or the influence of some evil genius. Why then should it be unlawful to deliver ourselves from so pressing an intestine evil? Further, our doctrine does not separate those whom God has joined together in the spirit of his sacred institution, but only those whom God has himself separated by the authority of his equally sacred law; an authority which ought to have the same force with us now, as with his people of old. As to Christian perfection, the promotion of which is urged by some as an argument for the indissolubility of marriage, that perfection is not to be forced upon us by compulsion and penal laws, but must be produced, if at all, by exhortation and Christian admonition. Then only can man be properly said to dissolve a marriage lawfully contracted, when, adding to the divine ordinance what the ordinance itself does not contain, he separates, under pretence of religion, whomsoever it suits his purpose. For it ought to be remembered that God in his just and pure and holy law, has not only permitted divorce on a variety of grounds, but has even ratified it in some cases, and enjoined it in others, under the severest penalties.

But this, it is objected, was "because of the hardness of their hearts." I reply, that these words of Christ, though a very appropriate answer to the Pharisees who tempted him, were never meant as a general explanation of the question of divorce. His intention was, as usual, to repress the arrogance of the Pharisees, and elude their snares; for his answer was only addressed to those who taught from Deut. xxiv. 1. that it was lawful to put away a wife for any cause whatever, provided a bill of divorcement were given. This is evident from the former part of the same chapter, v. 3. "is it lawful for a man to put away his wife for every cause?" not for the sole reason allowed by Moses, namely, if "some uncleanness were found in her," which might convert love into hatred; but because it had become a common practice to give bills of divorce, under the pretence of uncleanness, without just cause; an abuse which, since the law was unable to restrain it, he thought it advisable to tolerate, notwithstanding the hardness of heart which it implied, rather than to prevent the dissolution of unfortunate marriages, considering that the balance of earthly happiness or misery rested principally on this institution.

For, if we examine the several causes of divorce enumerated in the law, we shall find that wherever divorce was permitted, it was not in compliance with the hardness of the human heart, but on grounds of the highest equity and justice. The first passage is Exod. xxi. 1–4. Nothing could be more just than this law, which, so far from conceding anything to the hardness of their hearts, rather restrained it; inasmuch as, while it provided against the possibility of any Hebrew, at whatever price he might have been purchased, remaining more than seven years in bondage, it at the same time established the claim of the master as prior to that of the husband. This law is remarkable for its consummate humanity and equity; for while it does not permit the husband to put away his wife through the mere hardness of his heart, it allows the wife to leave her husband on the most reasonable of all grounds, that of inhumanity and unkindness. Again, Deut. xxi. 13, 14. it was permitted by the right of war, both to take a female captive to wife, and to divorce her afterwards; but it was not conceded to the hardness of their hearts, that she should be subsequently sold, or that the master should derive any profit from the possession of her person as a slave.

The third passage is Deut. xxiv. 1. There is no room here for the charge of hardness of heart, supposing the cause alleged to be true, and not a fictitious one. For since, as is evident from the institution itself, God gave a wife to man at the beginning to the intent that she should be his help and solace and delight, if, as often happens, she should eventually prove to be rather a source of sorrow, of disgrace, of ruin, of torment, of calamity, why should we think that we are displeasing God by divorcing such a one? I should attribute hardness of heart rather to him who retained her, than to him who sent her away under such circumstances; and not I alone, but Solomon himself, or rather the Spirit of God himself speaking by the mouth of Solomon. God therefore appears to have enacted this law by the mouth of Moses, and reiterated it by that of the prophet, with the view, not of giving scope to the hardheartedness of the husband, but of rescuing the unhappy wife from its influence wherever the case required it. For there is no hardheartedness in dismissing honorably and freely her whose own fault it is that she is not loved. That one who is not beloved, who is, on the contrary, deservedly neglected, and an object of dislike and hatred; that a wife thus situated should be retained, in pursuance of a most vexatious law, under a yoke of the heaviest slavery (for such is marriage without love) to one who entertains for her neither attachment nor friendship, would indeed be a hardship more cruel than any divorce whatever. God therefore gave laws of divorce, in their proper use most equitable and humane; he even extended the benefit of them to those whom he knew would abuse them through the hardness of their hearts, thinking it better to bear with the obduracy of the wicked, than to refrain from alleviating the misery of the righteous, or suffer the institution itself to be subverted, which, from a divine blessing, was in danger of becoming the bitterest of all calamities.

The two next passages, Ezra x. 3. and Nehem. xiii. 23, 30. do not merely tolerate divorce on account of the people's hardness of heart, but positively command it for the most sacred religious reasons. On what authority did these prophets found their precept? They were not the promulgators of a new law; the law of Moses alone could be their warrant. But the law of Moses nowhere commands the dissolution of marriages of this kind; it only forbids the contracting of such: Deut. vii. 3, 4. whence they argued, that the marriage which ought never to have been contracted, ought, if contracted, to be dissolved. So groundless is the vulgar maxim, that what ought not to have been done, is valid when done.

Marriage therefore gives place to religion; it gives place, as has been seen, to the right of the master; and the right of a husband, as appears from the passages of Scripture above quoted, as well as from the whole tenor of the civil law, and the custom of nations in general, is nearly the same as that of the master. It gives way, finally, to irresistible antipathies, and to that natural aversion with which we turn from whatever is unclean; but it is nowhere represented as giving way to hardness of heart, if this latter motive be really alleged as the sole or principal reason for enacting the law. This appears still more evidently from Deut. xxii. 19. Now if the law of Moses did not give way to his hardness of heart who was desirous of putting away the virgin whom he had humbled, or to his who was willing to put away the wife against whom he had brought up an evil report, why should we imagine that it would give way to his alone who was averse from uncleanness, supposing that such aversion could properly be included under the definition of hardness of heart? Christ therefore reproves the hardness of heart of those who abused this law, that is, of the Pharisees and others, when he says, "on account of the hardness of your hearts he permitted you to put away your wives;" but he does not abrogate the law itself, or the legitimate use of it; for he says that Moses permitted it on account of the hardness of their hearts, not that he permitted it wrongfully or improperly. In this sense almost the whole of the civil law might be said to have been given on account of the hardness of their hearts: whence St. Paul reproves the brethren, because they had recourse to it, though no one argues from hence that the civil law is, or ought to be abrogated. How much less then can any one who understands the spirit of the Gospel believe, that this latter denies what the law did not scruple to concede, either as a matter of right or of indulgence, to the infirmity of human nature?

The clause of the eighth verse, "from the beginning it was not so," means nothing more than what is more clearly intimated above in the fourth verse, "he which made them at the beginning, made them male and female;" namely, that marriage in its original institution was not capable of being dissolved even by death, for sin and death were not then in existence. If however the purpose of the institution should be violated by the offence of either, it was obvious that death, the consequence of that offence, must in the course of things dissolve the bond; and reason taught them that separation must frequently take place even before that period. No age or record, since the fall of man, gives a tradition of any other beginning in which it was not so. In the earliest ages of our faith, Abraham himself, the father of the faithful, put away his contentious and turbulent wife Hagar by the command of God.

Christ himself permitted divorce for the cause of fornication; which could not have been, if those whom God had once joined in the bands of matrimony were never afterwards to be disunited. According to the idiom of the eastern languages, however, the word fornication signifies, not adultery only, but either what is called *any unclean thing,* or a defect in some particular which might justly be required in a wife, Deut. xxiv. 1. (as Selden was the first to prove by numerous testimonies in his *Uxor Hebræa*) or it signifies whatever is found to be irreconcileably at variance with love, or fidelity, or help, or society, that is, with the objects of the original institution; as Selden proves, and as I have myself shown in another treatise from several texts of Scripture. For it would have been absurd, when the Pharisees asked, whether it was allowable to put away a wife for every cause, to answer, that it was not lawful except in case of adultery, when it was well known already to be not only lawful but necessary to put away an adulteress,

and that not by divorce, but by death. Fornication, therefore, must be here understood in a much wider sense than that of simple adultery, as is clear from many passages of Scripture, and particularly from Judg. xix. 2. "his concubine played the whore against him;" not by committing adultery, for in that case she would not have dared to flee to her father's house, but by refractory behavior towards her husband. Nor could St. Paul have allowed divorce in consequence of the departure of an unbeliever, unless this also were a species of fornication. It does not affect the question, that the case alluded to is that of a heathen; since whoever deserts her family "is worse than an infidel," 1 Tim. v. 8. Nor could anything be more natural, or more agreeable to the original institution, than that the bond which had been formed by love, and the hope of mutual assistance through life, and honorable motives, should be dissolved by hatred and implacable enmity, and disgraceful conduct on either side. For man, therefore, in his state of innocence in Paradise, previously to the entrance of sin into the world, God ordained that marriage should be indissoluble; after the fall, in compliance with the alteration of circumstances, and to prevent the innocent from being exposed to perpetual injury from the wicked, he permitted its dissolution: and this permission forms part of the law of nature and of Moses, and is not disallowed by Christ. Thus every covenant, when originally concluded, is intended to be perpetual and indissoluble, however soon it may be broken by the bad faith of one of the parties; nor has any good reason yet been given why marriage should differ in this respect from all other compacts; especially since the apostle has pronounced that "a brother or a sister is not under bondage," not merely in case of desertion, but *in such cases,* that is, in all cases that produce an unworthy bondage. 1 Cor. vii. 15. "a brother or a sister is not under bondage in such cases, but God hath called us in peace, or to peace;" he has not therefore called us to the end that we should be harassed with constant discord and vexations; for the object of our call is peace and liberty, not marriage, much less perpetual discord and the slavish bondage of an unhappy union, which the apostle declares to be above all things unworthy of a free man and a Christian. It is not to be supposed that Christ would expunge from the Mosaic law any enactment which could afford scope for the exercise of mercy towards the wretched and afflicted, or that his declaration on the present occasion was intended to have the force of a judicial decree, ordaining new and severer regulations on the subject; but that having exposed the abuses of the law, he proceeded after his usual manner to lay down a more perfect rule of conduct, disclaiming on this, as on all other occasions, the office of a judge, and inculcating truth by simple admonition, not by compulsory decrees. It is therefore a most flagrant error to convert a gospel precept into a civil statute, and enforce it by legal penalties.

It may perhaps be asked, if the disciples understood Christ as promulgating nothing new or more severe than the existing law on the subject of divorce, how it happened that they were so little satisfied with his explanation, as to say, v. 10. "if the case of the man be so with his wife, it is not good to marry"? I answer, that it is no wonder if the disciples, who had imbibed the doctrines of their time, thought and felt like the Pharisees with regard to divorce; so that the declaration of our Lord, that it was not lawful to put away a wife for every cause, only having given her a writing of divorcement, must have appeared to them a new and hard saying.

The whole argument may be summed up in brief as follows. It is universally admitted that marriage may lawfully be dissolved, if the prime end and form of the institution be violated; which is generally alleged as the reason why Christ allowed divorce in cases of adultery only. But the prime end and form of marriage, as almost all acknowledge, is not the nuptial bed, but conjugal love, and mutual assistance through life; for that must be regarded as the prime end and form of a rite, which is alone specified in the original institution. Mention is there made of the pleasures of society, which are incompatible with the isolation consequent upon aversion, and of conjugal assistance, which is afforded by love alone; not of the nuptial bed, or of the production of offspring, which may take place even without love: for whence it is evident that conjugal affection is of more importance and higher excellence than the nuptial bed

itself, and more worthy to be considered as the prime end and form of the institution. No one can surely be so base and sensual as to deny this. The very cause which renders the pollution of the marriage bed so heavy a calamity, is, that in its consequences it interrupts peace and affection; much more therefore must the perpetual interruption of peace and affection by mutual differences and unkindness be a sufficient reason for granting the liberty of divorce. And that it is such, Christ himself declares in the above passage; for it is certain, and has been proved already, that fornication signifies, not so much adultery, as the constant enmity, faithlessness, and disobedience of the wife, arising from the manifest and palpable alienation of the mind, rather than of the body. Not to mention, that the common, though false interpretation, by which adultery is made the sole ground of divorce, so far from vindicating the law, does in effect abrogate it; for it was ordained by the law of Moses, not that an adulteress should be put away, but that she should be brought to judgment, and punished with death.

CHAP. XI.—OF THE FALL OF OUR FIRST PARENTS, AND OF SIN.

THE Providence of God as regards the fall of man, is observable in the sin of man, and the misery consequent upon it, as well as in his restoration.

Sin, as defined by the apostle, is ἀνομία, or the *transgression of the law,* 1 John iii. 4.

By the law is here meant, in the first place, that rule of conscience which is innate, and engraven upon the mind of man; secondly, the special command which proceeded out of the mouth of God, (for the law written by Moses was long subsequent).

Sin is distinguished into *that which is common to all men,* and *the personal sin of each individual.*

The sin which is common to all men is that which our first parents, and in them all their posterity committed, when, casting off their obedience to God, they tasted the fruit of the forbidden tree.

Our first parents. This sin originated, first, in the instigation of the devil, as is clear from the narrative in Gen. iii. and from 1 John iii. 8. "he that committeth sin is of the devil, for the devil sinneth from the beginning." Secondly, in the liability to fall with which man was created, whereby he, as the devil had done before him, "abode not in the truth." If the circumstances of this crime are duly considered, it will be acknowledged to have been a most heinous offence, and a transgression of the whole law. For what sin can be named, which was not included in this one act? It comprehended at once distrust in the divine veracity, and a proportionate credulity in the assurances of Satan; unbelief; ingratitude; disobedience; gluttony; in the man excessive uxoriousness, in the woman a want of proper regard for her husband, in both an insensibility to the welfare of their offspring, and that offspring the whole human race; parricide, theft, invasion of the rights of others, sacrilege, deceit, presumption in aspiring to divine attributes, fraud in the means employed to attain the object, pride, and arrogance.

And in them all their posterity for even such as were not then born are judged and condemned in them, so that without doubt they also sinned in them, and at the same time with them. Undoubtedly therefore all sinned in Adam. For Adam being the common parent and head of all, it follows that, as in the covenant, that is, in receiving the commandment of God, so also in the defection from God, he either stood or fell for the whole human race; in the same manner as "Levi also payed tithes in Abraham, whilst he was yet in the loins of his father," Heb. vii. 9, 10. For if all did not sin in Adam, why has the condition of all become worse since his fall? Some of the modern commentators reply, that the deterioration was not moral, but physical. To which I answer, that it was as unjust to deprive the innocent of their physical, as of their moral perfection; especially since the former has so much influence on the latter, that is on the practical conduct of mankind.

It is, however, a principle uniformly acted upon in the divine proceedings, and recognized by all nations and under all religions from the earliest period, that the penalty incurred by the violation of things sacred (and such was the tree of knowledge of good and evil) attaches not only to the criminal himself, but to the whole of his posterity, who thus become accursed and obnoxious to punishment. It was thus in the deluge, and in the destruction of Sodom; in the swallowing up of Korah, and in the punishment of Achan. In the burning of Jericho the children suffered for the sins of their fathers, and even the cattle were devoted to the same slaughter with their masters. A like fate befel the posterity of Eli the priest, and the house of Saul, because their father had slain the Gibeonites.

God declares this to be the method of his justice. He himself explains the principle by which this justice is regulated, Lev. xxvi. 39. The difficulty is solved with respect to infants, by the consideration that all souls belong to God; that these, though guiltless of actual sin, were the offspring of sinful parents, and that God foresaw that, if suffered to live, they would grow up similar to their parents. With respect to others, it is obviated by the consideration, that no one perishes, except he himself sin. Thus Agag and his people were smitten for the crime of their fathers, four hundred years after their ancestors had lain wait for Israel in the way, when he came up out of Egypt, but at the same time they were themselves justly obnoxious to punishment for sins of their own. So too Hoshea king of Israel was better than the kings that were before him, but having fallen into the idolatry of the Gentiles, he was punished at once for his own sins and for those of his fathers, by the loss of his kingdom.

Hence the penitent are enjoined to confess not only their own sins, but those of their fathers. Thus also entire families become obnoxious to punishment for the guilt of their head. Subjects also are afflicted for the sins of their rulers; thus the whole of Egypt was smitten for the offence of Pharaoh. It is remarkable that David, even while remonstrating against the hardship of punishing the people for the sins of their king, yet thought it not unjust that the sons should suffer for and with their father. Sometimes a whole nation is punished for the iniquity of one of the people, and the trespass of one is imputed to all. We may add, that even just men have not thought it inconsistent with equity to visit offences against themselves, not only on the offender, but on his posterity. Thus Noah scrupled not to pronounce the condemnation of Canaan for the wickedness of his father Ham.

This principle of divine justice in the infliction of piacular punishments was not unknown to other nations, nor was it ever by them accounted unjust. So Thucydides, Book I. Sect. 126. ἀπὸ τούτου ἐναγεῖς καὶ ἀλιτήριοι τῆς Θεοῦ εκεῖνοί τε ἐκαλοῦντο, καὶ τὸ γενὸς τὸ ἀπ' ἐκείνῶν. And Virgil, Æn. I. 39.

. . . Pallasne exurere classem
Argivûm, atque ipsos potuit submergere ponto
Unius ob noxam?

The same might be easily shown by a multitude of other Pagan testimonies and examples.

Again, the possessions and right of citizenship of one convicted of high treason, a crime between man and man, are forfeited, not only as respects himself, but all his posterity; and legal authorities decide similarly in other analogous cases. We all know what are the recognized rights of war, not only with regard to the immediate parties themselves, but all who fall into the power of the enemy, such as women and children, and those who have contributed nothing to the progress of the war either in will or deed.

The personal sin of each individual is that which each in his own person has committed, independently of the sin which is common to all. Here likewise all men are guilty. Both kinds of sin, as well that which is common to all, as that which is personal to each individual, consist of the two following parts, whether we term them gradations, or divisions, or modes of sin, or whether we consider them in the light of cause and effect; namely, evil concupiscence, or the desire of sinning, and the act of sin itself. This is not ill expressed by the poet:

Mars videt hanc, visamque cupit, potiturque
  cupita.   Ovid. *Fast*. III, 21.

Evil concupiscence is that of which our original parents were first guilty, and which they transmitted to their posterity, as shares in the primary transgression, in the shape of an innate propensity to sin. This is called in Scripture "the old man, and the body of sin."

The first who employed the phrase *original sin* is said to have been Augustine in his writings against Pelagius; probably because in the *origin,* that is, in the generation of man, it was handed down from our first parents to their posterity. If however this were his meaning, the term is too limited; for that evil concupiscence, that law of sin, was not only naturally bred in us, but dwelt also in Adam after the fall, in whom it could not properly be called original. This general depravity of the human mind and its propensity to sin is described Gen. vi. 5. This depravity was engendered in us by our first parents. For faith, though it takes away the personal imputation of guilt, does not altogether remove indwelling sin. It is not therefore man as a regenerate being, but man in his animal capacity, that propagates his kind; as seed, though cleared from the chaff and stubble, produces not only the ear or grain, but also the stalk and husk. Christ alone was exempt from this contagion, being born by supernatural generation, although descended from Adam.

Some contend that this original sin is specially guiltiness; but guiltiness is not so properly sin, as the imputation of sin, which is also called *the judgement of God,* whereby sinners are accounted *worthy of death,* and become ὑπόδικοι, that is, "guilty before God," and "are under sin." Thus our first parents, in whom, as above observed, there could have been no original sin, were involved in guiltiness immediately upon their fall; and their posterity, before original sin was yet engendered, were involved in the same guiltiness in Adam; besides, guiltiness is taken away in those who are regenerate, while original sin remains.

Others define original sin to be the loss of original righteousness, and the corruption of the whole mind. But before this loss can be attributed to us, it must be attributed to our first parents, to whom, as was argued before, original sin could not attach; in them therefore it was what is called actual sin, which these divines themselves distinguish from original sin. At any rate it was the consequence of sin, rather than sin itself; or if it were sin, it was a sin of ignorance; for they expected nothing less than that they should lose any good by eating the fruit, or suffer harm in any way whatever. I shall therefore consider this loss of original righteousness in the following chapter, under the head of punishment, rather than in the present, which relates to sin.

The second thing in sin, after evil concupiscence, is the crime itself, or the act of sinning, which is commonly called Actual Sin. This may be incurred, not only by actions commonly so called, but also by words and thoughts, and even by the omission of good actions. It is called Actual Sin, not that sin in properly an action, for in reality it implies defect; but because it commonly consists in some act. For every act is in itself good; it is only its irregularity, or deviation from the line of right, which properly speaking is evil. Wherefore the act itself is not the matter of which sin consists, but only the ὑποκείμενον or *subject* in which it is committed, by words, by thoughts, and by omission. See also Luke xi. 23. and vi. 9. where to omit saving the life of a man is accounted the same as to destroy it.

All sins however are not, as the Stoics maintained, of equal magnitude. This inequality arises from the various circumstances of person, place, time, and the like. The distinction between mortal and venial sin will come more properly under consideration in another place. In the mean time it is certain, that even the least sin renders the sinner obnoxious to condemnation.

CHAP. XII.—Of the Punishment of Sin.

Thus far of Sin. After sin came death, as the calamity or punishment consequent upon it. Under the head of death, in Scripture, all evils whatever, together with every thing which in its consequence tends to death, must be understood as comprehended; for mere bodily death, as it is called, did not follow the sin of Adam on the self-same day, as God had threatened.

Hence divines, not inappropriately, reckon up four several degrees of death. The first, as before said, comprehends *all those evils which lead to death, and which it is agreed came into the world immediately upon the fall of man,* the most important of which I proceed to enumerate. In the first place, guiltiness; which though in its primary sense it is

an imputation made by God to us, yet is it also, as it were, a commencement or prelude of death dwelling in us, by which we are held as by a bond, and rendered subject to condemnation and punishment. Guiltiness, accordingly, is accompanied or followed by terrors of conscience. It is attended likewise with the sensible forfeiture of the divine protection and favor; whence results a diminution of the majesty of the human countenance, and a conscious degradation of mind. Hence the whole man becomes polluted; whence arises shame.

The second degree of death is called *spiritual death;* by which is meant the loss of divine grace, and that of innate righteousness, wherein man in the beginning lived unto God. And this death took place not only on the very day, but at the very moment of the fall. They who are delivered from it are said to be *regenerated,* to be *born again,* and to be *created afresh;* which is the work of God alone, as will be shown in the chapter on Regeneration.

This death consists, first, in the loss, or at least in the obscuration to a great extent of that right reason which enabled man to discern the chief good, and in which consisted as it were the life of the understanding. It consists, secondly, in that deprivation of righteousness and liberty to do good, and in that slavish subjection to sin and the devil, which constitutes, as it were, the death of the will. All have committed sin in Adam; therefore all are born servants of sin. Lastly, sin is its own punishment, and produces, in its natural consequences, the death of the spiritual life: more especially gross and habitual sin. Rom. i. 26. "for this cause God gave them up unto vile affections." The reason of this is evident; for in proportion to the increasing amount of his sins, the sinner becomes more liable to death, more miserable, more vile, more destitute of the divine assistance and grace, and farther removed from his primitive glory. It ought not to be doubted that sin in itself alone is the heaviest of all evils, as being contrary to the chief good, that is, to God; whereas punishment seems to be at variance only with the good of the creature, and not always with that.

It cannot be denied, however, that some remnants of the divine image still exist in us, not wholly extinguished by this spiritual death.

This is evident, not only from the wisdom and holiness of many of the heathen, manifested both in words and deeds, but also from what is said Gen. ix. 2. These vestiges of original excellence are visible, first, in the understanding. Psal. xix. 1. "the heavens declare the glory of God;" which could not be if man were incapable of hearing their voice. Nor, again, is the liberty of the will entirely destroyed. First, with regard to things indifferent, whether natural or civil. Secondly, the will is clearly not altogether inefficient in respect of good works, or at any rate of good endeavors; at least after the grace of God has called us: but its power is so small and insignificant, as merely to deprive us of all excuse for inaction, without affording any subject of boasting. Hence almost all mankind profess some desire of virtue, and turn with abhorrence from some of the more atrocious crimes.

There can be no doubt that for the purpose of vindicating the justice of God, especially in his calling of mankind, it is much better to allow to man, (whether as a remnant of his primitive state, or as restored through the operation of the grace whereby he is called) some portion of free will in respect of good works, or at least of good endeavors, rather than in respect of things which are indifferent. For if God be conceived to rule with absolute disposal all the actions of men, natural as well as civil, he appears to do nothing which is not his right, neither will any one murmur against such a procedure. But if he inclines the will of man to moral good or evil according to his own pleasure, and then rewards the good, and punishes the wicked, the course of equity seems to be disturbed; and it is entirely on this supposition that the outcry against divine justice is founded. It would appear, therefore, that God's general government of the universe, to which such frequent allusion is made, should be understood as relating to natural and civil concerns, to things indifferent and fortuitous, in a word, to anything rather than to matters of morality and religion. And this is confirmed by many passages of Scripture. For if our personal religion were not in some degree dependent on ourselves, and in our own power, God could not properly enter into a covenant with us; neither

could we perform, much less swear to perform, the conditions of that covenant.

CHAP. XIII.—OF THE DEATH OF THE BODY.

THE third degree of death is what is called *the death of the Body*. To this all the labors, sorrows, and diseases which afflict the body, are nothing but the prelude. All nature is likewise subject to mortality and a curse on account of man. Even the beasts are not exempt, Gen. iii. 14. vi. 7. So the *first-born of beasts* in the land of Egypt perished for the sins of their masters.

The death of the body is to be considered in the light of a punishment for sin, no less than the other degrees of death, notwithstanding the contrary opinion entertained by some. 1 Cor. xv. 21. "since by man came death;" that is to say, temporal as well as eternal death; as is clear from the corresponding member of the sentence, "by man came also the resurrection from the dead;" therefore that bodily death from which we are to rise again originated in sin, and not in nature; contrary to the opinion of those who maintain that temporal death is the result of natural causes, and that eternal death alone is due to sin.

The death of the body is the loss or extinction of life. The common definition, which supposes it to consist in the separation of soul and body, is inadmissible. For what part of man is it that dies when this separation takes place? Is it the soul? This will not be admitted by the supporters of the above definition. Is it then the body? But how can that be said to die, which never had any life of itself? Therefore the separation of soul and body cannot be called the death of man.

Here then arises an important question, which, owing to the prejudice of divines in behalf of their preconceived opinions, has usually been dismissed without examination, instead of being treated with the attention it deserves. Is it the whole man, or the body alone, that is deprived of vitality? And as this is a subject which may be discussed without endangering our faith or devotion, whichever side of the controversy we espouse, I shall declare freely what seems to me the true doctrine, as collected from numberless passages of Scripture; without regarding the opinion of those, who think that truth is to be sought in the schools of philosophy, rather than in the sacred writings.

Inasmuch then as the whole man is uniformly said to consist of body, spirit, and soul, (whatever may be the distinct provinces severally assigned to these divisions,) I shall first show that the whole man dies, and, secondly, that each component part suffers privation of life. It is to be observed, first of all, that God denounced the punishment of death against the whole man that sinned, without excepting any part. For what could be more just, than that he who had sinned in his whole person, should die in his whole person? Or, on the other hand, what could be more absurd than that the mind, which is the part principally offending, should escape the threatened death; and that the body alone, to which immortality was equally allotted, before death came into the world by sin, should pay the penalty of sin by undergoing death, though not implicated in the transgression?

It is evident that the saints and believers of old, the patriarchs, prophets and apostles, without exception, held this doctrine. The belief of David was the same, as is evident from the reason so often given by him for deprecating the approach of death. Certainly if he had believed that his soul would survive, and be received immediately into heaven, he would have abstained from all such remonstrances, as one who was shortly to take his flight where he might praise God unceasingly. It appears that the belief of Peter respecting David was the same as David's belief respecting himself; Acts ii. 29. 34. Again, it is evident that Hezekiah fully believed that he should die entirely, where he laments that it is impossible to praise God in the grave. God himself bears testimony to the same truth. Isai. lvii. 1, 2. It is on the same principle that Christ himself proves God to be a God of the living, arguing from their future resurrection; for if they were then living, it would not necessarily follow from his argument that there would be a resurrection of the body: hence, he says, John xi. 25. "I am the resur-

rection and the life." Accordingly he declares expressly, that there is not even a place appointed for the abode of the saints in heaven, till the resurrection: John xiv. 2, 3. There is no sufficient reason for interpreting this of the body; it is clear therefore that it was spoken, and should be understood, of the reception of the soul and spirit conjointly with the body into heaven, and that not till the coming of the Lord. 1 Cor. xv. 17–19. whence it appears that there were only two alternatives, one of which must ensue; either they must rise again or perish: for "if in this life only we have hope in Christ, we are of all men most miserable;" which again indicates that we must either believe in the resurrection, or have our hope in this life only. v. 32. "let us eat and drink, for to-morrow we die;" that is, die altogether, for otherwise the argument would have no force. In the verses which follow, from v. 42. to v. 50. the reasoning proceeds on the supposition that there are only two states, the mortal and the immortal, death and resurrection; not a word is said of any intermediate condition. Nay, Paul himself affirms that the crown of righteousness which was laid up for him was not to be received before that last day. If a crown were *laid up* for the apostle, it follows that it was not to be received immediately after death. At what time then was it to be received? At the same time when it was to be conferred on the rest of the saints, that is, not till the appearance of Christ in glory. Our conversation therefore is in heaven, not where we are now dwelling, but in that place from whence we look for the coming of the Saviour, who shall conduct us thither. Luke xx. 35, 36.—that is, when they finally become such; whence it follows, that previous to the resurrection they are not admitted to that heavenly world.

Thus far proof has been given of the death of the whole man. But lest recourse should be had to the sophistical distinction, that although the whole man dies, it does not therefore follow that the whole *of* man should die, I proceed to give similar proof with regard to each of the parts, the body, the spirit, and the soul, according to the division above stated.

First, then, as to the body, no one doubts that it suffers privation of life. Nor will the same be less evident as regards the spirit, if it be allowed that the spirit, according to the doctrine laid down in the seventh chapter, has no participation in the divine nature, but is purely human; and that no reason can be assigned, why, if God has sentenced to death the whole of man that sinned, the spirit, which is the part principally offending, should be alone exempt from the appointed punishment; especially since previous to the entrance of sin into the world, all parts of man were alike immortal; and that since that time, in pursuance of God's denunciation, all have become equally subject to death. But to come to the proofs. The Preacher himself, the wisest of men, expressly denies that the spirit is exempt from death: iii. 18–20. "as the beast dieth, so dieth the man; yea, they have all one breath . . . all go unto one place." And in the twenty-first verse, he condemns the ignorance of those who venture to affirm that the way of the spirits of men and of beasts after death is different: "who knoweth the spirit of man (*an sursum ascendat*), whether it goeth upward?" Now the thoughts are in the mind and the spirit, not in the body; and if they perish, we must conclude that the mind and spirit undergo the same fate as the body.

Lastly, there is abundant testimony to prove that the soul (whether we understand by this term the whole human composition, or whether it is to be considered as synonymous with the spirit) is subject to death, natural as well as violent. Numb. xxiii. 10. "let me (*anima mea*, Lat. Vulg.) die the death of the righteous." Such are the words of Balaam, who, though not the most upright of prophets, yet in this instance uttered the words which the Lord put into his mouth. The just and sufficient reason assigned above for the death of the soul, is the same which is given by God himself; Ezek. xviii. 20. "the soul that sinneth, it shall die:" and therefore, on the testimony of the prophet and the apostle, as well as of Christ himself, the soul even of Christ was for a short time subject unto death on account of our sins. Nor do we anywhere read that the souls assemble, or are summoned to judgment, from heaven or from hell, but that they are all called out of the tomb, or at least that they were previously in the state of the dead. John v. 28, 29. In this passage those who rise again, those who hear, those who come forth, are all

described as being in the graves, the righteous as well as the wicked. They *were asleep;* whereas the lifeless body does not sleep, unless inanimate matter can be said to sleep. *That ye sorrow not, even as others which have no hope,*—but why should they sorrow and have no hope, if they believed that their souls would be in a state of salvation and happiness even before the resurrection, whatever might become of the body? The rest of the world, indeed, who had no hope, might with reason despair concerning the soul as well as the body, because they did not believe in the resurrection: and therefore it is to the resurrection that St. Paul directs the hope of all believers. *Them which sleep in Jesus will God bring with him;* that is, to heaven from the grave. *We which are alive and remain unto the coming of the Lord shall not prevent them which are asleep.* But there would have been no reason to fear lest the survivors should prevent them, if they who were asleep had long since been received into heaven; in which case the latter would not come *to meet the Lord,* but would return with him. *We* however *which are alive shall be caught up together with them,* not after them, *and so shall we ever be with the Lord,* namely, after, not before the resurrection. And then at length "the wicked shall be severed from among the just." In such a sleep I should suppose Lazarus to have been lying, if it were asked whither his soul betook itself during those four days of death. For I cannot believe that it would have been called back from heaven to suffer again the inconveniences of the body, but rather that it was summoned from the grave, and roused from the sleep of death. The words of Christ themselves lead to this conclusion: John xi. 11, 13. which death, if the miracle were true, must have been real. This is confirmed by the circumstances of Christ's raising him; v. 43. If the soul of Lazarus, that is, if Lazarus himself was not within the grave, why did Christ call on the lifeless body which could not hear? If it were the soul which he addressed, why did he call it from a place where it was not? Had he intended to intimate that the soul was separated from the body, he would have directed his eyes to the quarter whence the soul of Lazarus might be expected to return, namely, from heaven: for to call from the grave what is not there, is like seeking the living among the dead, which the angel reprehended as ignorance in the disciples, Luke xxiv. 5. The same is apparent in the raising of the widow's son: Luke vii. 14.

On the other hand, those who assert that the soul is exempt from death, and that when divested of the body, it wings its way, or is conducted by angels, directly to its appointed place of reward or punishment, where it remains in a separate state of existence to the end of the world, found their belief principally on the following passages of Scripture. Psal. xlix. 15. "God will redeem my soul from the power of the grave." But this proves rather that the soul enters the grave with the body, as was shown above, from whence it needs to be redeemed, namely, at the resurrection, when *God shall receive it,* as follows in the same verse.

The second text is Eccles. xii. 7. "the spirit shall return unto God that gave it." But neither does this prove what is required; for the phrase, *the spirit returning to God,* must be understood with considerable latitude; since the wicked do not return to God at death, but depart far from him. The preacher had moreover said before, iii. 20. "all go unto one place;" and God is said both to have given, and to gather unto himself the spirit of every living thing, whilst the body returns to dust, Job. xxxiv. 14, 15. Euripides in the *Suppliants* has, without being aware of it, given a far better interpretation of this passage than the commentators in question.

Each various part
That constitutes the frame of man, returns
Whence it was taken; to th' ethereal sky
The soul, the body to its earth.
Line 519. *Potter's Transl.*

That is, every constituent part returns at dissolution to its elementary principle. This is confirmed by Ezek. xxxvii. 9. "come from the four winds, O breath;" it is certain therefore that the spirit of man must have previously departed thither from whence it is now summoned to return. Hence perhaps originates the expression in Matt. xxiv. 31. "they shall gather together the elect from the four winds." For why should not the spirits of the elect be as easily gathered together as the smallest particles of their bodies, sometimes

most widely dispersed throughout different countries? In the same manner is to be understood 1 Kings xvii. 21. "let this child's soul come into him again." This, however, is a form of speech applied to fainting in general. For there are many passages of Scripture, some of which have been already quoted, which undoubtedly represent the dead as devoid of all vital existence; but what was advanced above respecting the death of the spirit affords a sufficient answer to the objection.

The third passage is Matt. x. 28. "fear not them which kill the body, but are not able to kill the soul." It may be answered that, properly speaking, the body cannot be killed, as being in itself a thing inanimate; the body therefore, as is common in Scripture, must be taken for the whole human compound, or for the animal and temporal life; the soul for that spiritual life with which we shall be clothed after the end of the world, as appears from the remainder of the verse, and from 1 Cor. xv. 44.

The fourth text is Philipp. i. 23. "having a desire to depart" (*cupiens dissolvi,* having a desire for dissolution) "and to be with Christ." But, to say nothing of the uncertain and disputed sense of the word ἀναλῦσαι, which signifies anything rather than *dissolution,* it may be answered, that although Paul desired to obtain immediate possession of heavenly perfection and glory, in like manner as every one is desirous of attaining as soon as possible to that, whatever it may be, which he regards as the ultimate object of his being, it by no means follows that, when the soul of each individual leaves the body, it is received immediately either into heaven or hell. For he *had a desire to be with Christ;* that is, at his appearing, which all the believers hoped and expected was then at hand. In the same manner one who is going on a voyage desires to set sail and to arrive at the destined port, (such is the order in which his wishes arrange themselves) omitting all notice of the intermediate passage. If, however, it be true that there is no time without motion, which Aristotle illustrates by the examples of those who were fabled to have slept in the temple of the heroes, and who, on awaking, imagined that the moment in which they awoke had succeeded without an interval to that in which they fell asleep; how much more must intervening time be annihilated to the departed, so that to them to die and to be with Christ will seem to take place at the same moment? Christ himself, however, expressly indicates the time at which we shall be with him; John xiv. 3.

The fifth text evidently favors my view of the subject: 1 Pet. iii. 19. "by which also he went and preached to the spirits that are in prison," literally, *in guard*, or, as the Syriac version renders it, *in sepulchro*, "in the grave," which means the same; for the grave is the common guardian of all till the day of judgment. What therefore the apostle says more fully, iv. 5, 6. "who shall give account to him that is ready to judge the quick and the dead; for, for this cause was the gospel preached also to them that are dead," he expresses in this place by a metaphor, "the spirits that are in guard;" it follows, therefore, that the spirits are dead.

The sixth text is Rev. vi. 9. "I saw under the altar the souls of them that were slain." I answer, that in the Scripture idiom the soul is generally often put for the whole animate body, and that in this passage it is used for the souls of those who were not yet born; unless indeed the fifth seal was already opened in the time of John: in the same manner as in the parable of Dives and Lazarus, though Christ, for the sake of the lesson to be conveyed, speaks of that as present which was not to take place till after the day of judgment, and describes the dead as placed in two distinct states, he by no means intimates any separation of the soul from the body.

The seventh text is Luke xxiii. 43. "Jesus said unto him, Verily I say unto thee, To-day shalt thou be with me in paradise." This passage has on various accounts occasioned so much trouble, that some have not hesitated to alter the punctuation, as if it had been written, *I say unto thee to-day;* that is, although I seem to-day the most despised and miserable of all men, yet I declare to thee and assure thee, that thou shalt hereafter be with me in paradise, that is, in some pleasant place, (for, properly speaking, paradise is not heaven) or in the spiritual state allotted to the soul and body. The same expedient has been resorted to Matt. xxvii. 52, 53. At the time of the earthquake, on the same day

(not three days after, as is generally supposed) the graves were opened, the dead arose and came out, v. 52. καὶ ἐξελθόντες, and having come out, at length after the resurrection of Christ they went into the holy city; for so, according to Erasmus, the ancient Greeks pointed the passage; and with this the Syriac agrees. That spiritual state in which the souls as well as bodies of the arising saints previously abode, might not improperly be called paradise; and it was in this state, as appears to me, that the penitent thief was united to the other saints without polluting them by his company. Nor is it necessary to take the word *to-day* in its strict acceptation, but rather for a short time. However this may be, so much clear evidence should not be rejected on account of a single passage, of which it is not easy to give a satisfactory interpretation.

The eighth text is the forty-sixth verse of the same chapter; "into thy hands I commend my spirit." But the spirit is not therefore separated from the body, or incapable of death; for David uses the same language Psal. xxxi. 5. although he was not then about to die: "into thine hand I commit my spirit," while it was yet abiding in, and with the body. So Stephen, Acts vii. 59. "Lord Jesus, receive my spirit . . . and when he had said this, he fell asleep." It was not the bare spirit divested of the body that he commended to Christ, but *the whole spirit and soul and body,* as it is expressed 1 Thess. v. 23. Thus the spirit of Christ was to be raised again with the body on the third day, while that of Stephen was to be reserved till the appearing of the Lord.

The ninth passage is 2 Cor. v. 1–20. It is sufficiently apparent, however, that the object of this passage is not to inculcate the separation of the soul from the body, but to contrast the animal and terrestrial life of the whole man with the spiritual and heavenly. Hence in the first verse "the house of this tabernacle" is opposed, not to the soul, but to "a building of God, an house not made with hands," that is, to the final renewal of the whole man, as Beza also explains it, whereby "we are clothed upon" in the heavens, "being clothed . . . not naked," v. 3. This distinctly appears from the fourth verse: "not for that we would be unclothed, but clothed upon, that mortality might be swallowed up of life," not for the separation of the soul from the body, but for the perfecting of both. Wherefore the clause in the eighth verse, "to be absent from the body, and to be present with the Lord," must be understood of the consummation of our happiness; and *the body* must be taken for this frail life, as is common in the sacred writers, and the *absence* spoken of, v. 9. for our eternal departure to a heavenly world; or perhaps to be "at home in the body, and to be absent from the Lord," v. 6. may mean nothing more than to be entangled in worldly affairs, and to have little leisure for heavenly things; the reason of which is given v. 7. "for we walk by faith, not by sight:" whence it follows, v. 8. "we are confident and willing rather to be absent from the body, and to be present with the Lord;" that is, to renounce the worldly things as much as possible, and to be occupied with things heavenly. The ninth verse proves still more clearly that the expressions *to be present* and *to be absent* both refer to this life: "wherefore we labor that whether present or absent, we may be accepted of God:" for no one supposes that the souls of men are occupied from the time of death to that of the resurrection in endeavors to render themselves acceptable to God in heaven; that is the employment of the present life, and its reward is not to be looked for till the second coming of Christ. For the apostle says, v. 10. "we must all appear before the judgment-seat of Christ, that every one may receive the things done in his body, according to that he hath done, whether it be good or bad." There is consequently no recompense of good or bad after death, previous to the day of judgment. Compare 1 Cor. xv. the whole of which chapter throws no small light on this passage. The same sense is to be ascribed to 2 Pet. i. 13–15; "as long as I am in this tabernacle," that is, in this life. It is however unnecessary to prolong this discussion, as there is scarcely one of the remaining passages of Scripture which has not been already explained by anticipation.

The fourth and last degree of death, is *death eternal, the punishment of the damned;* which will be considered in the twenty-seventh chapter.

CHAP. XIV.—Of Man's Restoration and of Christ as Redeemer.

We have hitherto considered the Providence of God in relation to the fall of man; we are now to consider it as operating in his restoration.

The restoration of Man is the act whereby man, being delivered from sin and death by God the Father through Jesus Christ, is raised to a far more excellent state of grace and glory than that from which he had fallen. In this restoration are comprised the *redemption* and *renovation of man.*

Redemption is that act whereby *Christ, being sent in the fulness of time, redeemed all believers at the price of his own blood, by his own voluntary act, conformably to the eternal counsel and grace of God the Father.*

Grace. Even before man had, properly speaking, confessed his guilt, that is, before he had avowed it ingenuously and in the spirit of repentance, God nevertheless, in pronouncing the punishment of the serpent, previously to passing sentence on man, promised that he would raise up from the seed of the woman one who should bruise the serpent's head, Gen. iii. 15. and thus anticipated the condemnation of mankind by a gratuitous redemption. Hence the Father is often called *our Saviour,* inasmuch as it is by his eternal counsel and grace alone that we are saved. There is no other Redeemer or Mediator besides Christ. There was a promise made to all mankind, and an expectation of the Redeemer, more or less distinct, even from the time of the fall. At the appointed time he was sent into the world.

Two points are to be considered in relation to Christ's character as Redeemer; his *nature* and *office.* His *nature* is twofold; divine and human. Col. ii. 9. "in him dwelleth all the fulness of the Godhead bodily;" which passage I understand, not in the divine nature of Christ, but of the entire virtue of the Father, and the full completion of his promises, (for so I would interpret the word, rather than *fulness,*) dwelling in, not hypostatically united with, Christ's human nature; and this *bodily,* that is, not in ceremonies and the rudiments of the world, but really and substantially. 1 Tim. iii. 16. "God was manifest in the flesh," that is, in the incarnate Son.

his own image. With regard to Christ's divine nature, the reader is referred to what was proved in a former chapter concerning the Son of God; from whence it follows, that he by whom all things were made both in heaven and earth, even the angels themselves, he who in the beginning was the Word, and God with God, and although not supreme, yet the first born of every creature, must necessarily have existed previous to his incarnation, whatever subtleties may have been invented to evade this conclusion by those who contend for the merely human nature of Christ.

This incarnation of Christ, whereby he, being God, took upon him the human nature, and was made flesh, without thereby ceasing to be numerically the same as before, is generally considered by theologians as, next to the Trinity in Unity, the greatest mystery of our religion. Of the mystery of the Trinity, however, no mention is made in Scripture; whereas the incarnation is frequently spoken of as a mystery.

Since then this mystery is so great, we are admonished by that very consideration not to assert anything respecting it rashly or presumptuously, on mere grounds of philosophical reasoning; not to add to it anything of our own; not even to adduce in its behalf any passage of Scripture of which the purport may be doubtful, but to be contented with the clearest texts, however few in number. If we listen to such passages, and are willing to acquiesce in the simple truth of Scripture, unencumbered by metaphysical comments, to how many prolix and preposterous arguments shall we put an end! how much occasion of heresy shall we remove! how many ponderous volumes of dabblers in theology shall we cast out, purging the temple of God from the contamination of their rubbish! Nothing would be more plain, and agreeable to reason, nothing more suitable to the understanding even of the meanest individual, than such parts of the Christian faith as are declared in Scripture to be necessary for salvation, if teachers, even of the reformed church, were as yet sufficiently impressed with the propriety of insisting on nothing but divine authority in matters relating to God, and of limiting themselves to the contents of the sacred volume. What is essential would easily appear, when freed from the perplexities of controversy; what is mysterious would be suffered to remain inviolate, and we should be fearful of overstepping the bounds of propriety in its investigation.

The opinion, however, which now prevails, or rather which has prevailed for many ages, is this; that whereas it was contended in a former stage of the controversy respecting Christ, that the three persons of the Trinity were united in one nature, it is now asserted, on the other hand, that two natures are so combined in the one person of Christ, that he has a real and perfect subsistence in the one nature independently of that which properly belongs to the other; insomuch that two natures are comprehended in one person. That is what is called in the schools the hypostatic union. Such is the explanation of Zanchius, Vol. I. Part II. Book II. Chap. 7. 'He took upon him not man, properly speaking, but the human nature. For the Logos being in the womb of the virgin assumed the human nature by forming a body of the substance of Mary, and creating at the same time a soul to animate it. Moreover, such was his intimate and exclusive assumption of this nature, that it never had any separate subsistence, independent of the Logos; but did then first subsist, and has ever since subsisted, in the Logos alone.' I say nothing of the silence of Scripture respecting the above arcana, though they are promulgated with as much confidence, as if he who thus ventures to deliver them on his own authority, had been a witness in the womb of Mary to the mysteries which he describes. He argues as if it were possible to assume human nature, without at the same time assuming man; for human nature, that is, the form of man in a material mold, wherever it exists, constitutes at once the proper and entire man, deficient in no part of his essence, not even (if the words have any meaning) in subsistence and personality. In reality, however, subsistence is the same as substantial existence; and personality is nothing but a word perverted from its proper use to patch up the threadbare theories of theologians. It is certain that the Logos was made that which he assumed; if then he assumed the human nature, not man, he was made not man, but the human nature; these two things being inseparable.

But before I proceed to demonstrate the

weakness of the received opinion, it is necessary to explain the meaning of the three terms so frequently recurring, *nature, person,* and *hypostasis,* which word is translated in Latin, *substantia* or *subsistentia, substance* or *subsistence. Nature* in the present instance can signify nothing, but either the actual essence or the properties of that essence. Since however these properties are inseparable from the essence, and the union of the natures is *hypostatical* not *accidental,* we must conclude that the term *nature* can here mean only the essence itself. *Person* is a metaphorical word, transferred from the stage to the schools of theology, signifying any one individual being, as the logicians express it; any intelligent ens, numerically one, whether God, or angel, or man. The Greek word *hypostasis* can signify nothing in the present case but what is expressed in Latin by *substantia* or *subsistentia, substance* or *subsistence;* that is to say, a perfect essence existing *per se;* whence it is generally put in opposition to merely *accidents.*

Hence the union of two natures in Christ must be considered as the mutual hypostatic union of two essences; for where there is a perfect substantial essence, there must also be an hypostasis or subsistence, inasmuch as they are the same thing; so that one Christ, one ens, one person, is formed of this mutual hypostatic union of two natures or essences. For it is no more to be feared that the union of two hypostases should constitute two persons, than that the same consequence should result from the union of two natures, that is to say, of two essences. If however the human nature of Christ never had any proper and independent subsistence, or if the Son did not take upon himself that subsistence, it would have been no more possible for him to have been made very man, or even to have assumed the real and perfect substance or essence of man, than for the body of Christ to be present in the sacrament without quantity or local extinction, as the Papists assert. This indeed they explain by his divine power, their usual resort in such cases. It is however of no use to allege a divine power, the existence of which cannot be proved on divine authority. There is then in Christ a mutual hypostatic union of two natures, that is to say, of two essences, of two substances, and conse-

quently of two persons; nor does this union prevent the respective properties of each from remaining individually distinct. That the fact is so, is sufficiently certain; the mode of union is unknown to us; and it is best to be ignorant of what God wills should remain unknown. If indeed it were allowable to define and determine with precision in mysteries of this kind, why should not our philosophical inquisitiveness lead us to inquire respecting the external form common to the two natures? For if the divine and human nature have coalesced in one person, that is to say, as my opponents themselves admit, in a reasonable being, numerically one, it follows that these two natures must have also coalesced in one external form. The consequence would be, either that the divine form must have been annihilated or blended with the human, which would be absurd, unless they were previously the same; or, vice versa, that the human must have been annihilated or blended with the divine, unless it exactly resembled the latter; or, which is the only remaining alternative, Christ must be considered as having two forms. How much better is it for us to know merely that the Son of God, our Mediator, was made flesh, that he is called both God and Man, and is such in reality, which is expressed in Greek by the single and appropriate term Θεάνθρωπος. Since however God has not revealed the mode in which this union is effected, it behooves us to cease from devising subtle explanations, and to be contented with remaining wisely ignorant.

It may however be observed, that the opinion here given respecting the hypostatic union agrees with what was advanced relative to the Son of God in the fifth chapter, namely, that his essence is not the same with that of the Father; for if it were the same, it could not have coalesced in one person with man, unless the Father were also included in the same union, nay, unless man became one person with the Father as well as with the Son; which is impossible.

The reasons, therefore, which are given to prove that he who was made flesh must necessarily be the supreme God, may safely be dismissed. It is urged, first, from Heb. vii. 26, 27. that "such an high priest became us, who is holy, harmless, undefiled, separate from sinners, and made higher than the heavens."

These words, however, do not even prove that he is God, much less that it was necessary that he should be so; not to mention, that he is *holy,* not only as God but as man conceived of the Holy Spirit by the power of the Most High; nor is he said to be higher than the heavens, but to be "made higher than the heavens." Again, what is said of him, v. 24. "he continueth ever," is a property which he has in common with both men and angels; nor does it follow that he is God, because "he is able to save them to the uttermost that come unto God by him," v. 25. Lastly, "the word of the oath, which was since the law, maketh the Son, who is consecrated for evermore." v. 28. so that he is not on this account necessarily God. Besides, Scripture nowhere teaches that none but God is able to approach God, to take away sin, to fulfil the law, to endure and vanquish the anger of God, the power of Satan, temporal as well as eternal death, in a word, to restore to us the blessings which we had lost; but it teaches that *he* has power to effect this "to whom the Father has given it;" that is to say, the beloved Son of God, in whom he has himself testified that he is well pleased.

That Christ therefore, since his assumption of human flesh, remains one Christ, is a matter of faith; whether he retains his two-fold will and understanding, is a point respecting which, as Scripture is silent, we are not concerned to inquire. For after having *emptied himself,* he might "increase in wisdom," Luke ii. 52. by means of the understanding which he previously possessed, and might "know all things," John xxi. 17. namely, through the teaching of the Father, as he himself acknowledged. Nor is this two-fold will implied in the single passage Matt. xxvi. 39. "not as I will, but as thou wilt," unless he be the same with the Father, which, as has been already shown, cannot be admitted.

That Christ was very man, is evident from his having a body, a soul and a spirit. It is true that God attributes to himself also a soul and spirit; but there are reasons most distinctly assigned in Scripture, why Christ should be very man. Inasmuch, however, as the two natures constitute one Christ, certain particulars appear to be predicated of him absolutely, which properly apply to one of his natures.

This is what is called *communicatio idiomatum* or *proprietatum,* where by the customary forms of language what is peculiar to one of two natures is attributed to both jointly. Accordingly, these and similar passages, wherever they occur, are to be understood κατ' ἄλλο καὶ ἄλλο, as theologians express it; (for in speaking of Christ the proper expression is not ἄλλος καὶ ἄλλος, but ἄλλο καὶ ἄλλο, inasmuch as it refers, not to himself, but to his person, or in other words, his office of mediator: for as to the subject of his two natures, it is too profound a mystery, in my judgment at least, to warrant any positive assertion respecting it).

It sometimes happens, on the other hand, that what properly belongs to the compound nature of Christ, is attributed to one of his natures only, 1 Tim. ii. 5. Now he is not mediator inasmuch as he is man, but inasmuch as he is Θεάνθρωπς. Scripture, however, more frequently distinguishes what is peculiar to his human nature. 1 Pet. iii. 18. "being put to death in the flesh," that is to say, being affected chiefly and most visibly in his human nature.

The incarnation of Christ consists of two parts; his conception and his nativity. Of his conception the efficient cause was the Holy Spirit. Luke i. 35. "the Holy Ghost shall come upon thee, and the power of the Highest shall overshadow thee;" by which words I am inclined to understand the power and spirit of the Father himself, as has been shown before. The object of this miraculous conception was to obviate the contamination consequent upon the sin of Adam.

The nativity of Christ is predicted by all the prophets. That the Messiah is already come is proved, in contradiction to the belief of the Jews, by the following arguments. First, the cities of Bethlehem and Nazareth, (where according to prophecy Christ was to be born and educated,) are no longer in existence. Secondly, it was predicted that his advent should take place while the second temple and the Jewish government were yet in being. Lastly, because the Gentiles have long since put away the worship of other gods and embraced the faith of Christ, which event, according to the prophecies, was not to take place till after his coming.

———

CHAP. XV.—OF THE OFFICE OF THE MEDIATOR AND OF HIS THREEFOLD FUNCTIONS.

The mediatorial office of Christ is that whereby, *at the special appointment of God the Father, he voluntarily performed, and continues to perform, on behalf of man, whatever is requisite for obtaining reconciliation with God, and eternal salvation.*

The name and office of mediator is in a certain sense ascribed to Moses, as a type of Christ. In treating of the office of the Mediator, we are to consider his three-fold functions as *prophet, priest* and *king,* and his manner of administering the same.

His function as a prophet is to instruct his church in heavenly truth, and to declare the whole will of his father. His prophetical function consists of two parts; one external, namely, the promulgation of divine truth; the other internal, to wit, the illumination of the understanding. Christ's prophetical functions began with the creation of the world, and will continue till the end of all things.

Christ's sacerdotal function is that whereby *he once offered himself to God the Father as a sacrifice for sinners, and has always made, and still continues to make intercession for us.*

Once offered; virtually, and as regarded the efficacy of his sacrifice, from the foundation of the world, as above stated.

Himself as a sacrifice. He offered himself, however, more particularly in his human nature, as many passages of Scripture expressly indicate.

He makes intercession, first, by "appearing in the presence of God for us." Secondly, by rendering our prayers agreeable to God. Gal. iv. 6. "God hath sent forth the Spirit of his Son into your hearts, crying, Abba, Father;" that is, encouraging and persuading us to address God as our Father through faith. This is easily distinguished from the intercession which Christ makes for us in his sacerdotal capacity.

The Kingly function of Christ is that whereby *being made King by God the Father, he governs and preserves, chiefly by an inward law and spiritual power. The Church* which he has purchased for himself, and conquers and subdues its enemies.

Hence the law of the kingdom, the gift of the Spirit, was given at Jerusalem on the fiftieth day from the crucifixion, as the Mosaic law was given on the fiftieth day from the passover in Mount Sinai, Acts ii. 1. in sign that the old law was superseded by the new, the law of bondage and of the flesh by the law of the Spirit and of freedom. Herein it is that the pre-eminent excellency of Christ's kingdom over all others, as well as the divine principles on which it is founded, are manifested; inasmuch as he governs not the bodies of men alone, as the civil magistrate, but their minds and consciences, and that not by force and fleshly weapons, but by what the world esteems the weakest of all instruments. Hence external force ought never to be employed in the administration of the kingdom of Christ, which is the church.

The kingdom of Christ is also styled the kingdom of grace, and the kingdom of glory. The kingdom of grace is the same as the kingdom of heaven, which *is at hand.* The kingdom of glory is that which is destined to be made more manifest at his second advent.

The kingdom of Christ, as appears from the authorities just quoted, is, like his priesthood, eternal; that is, it will endure as long as the world shall last, and as long as there shall be occasion for his mediatorial office. This is clearly taught by the apostle, 1 Cor. xv. 24, 28. In like manner as a period is assigned to his priestly office (although that also is called eternal) as well as to his prophetical office, *that God may be all in all.*

CHAP. XVI.—OF THE MINISTRY OF REDEMPTION.

The humiliation of Christ is that state in which under his character of God-man he voluntarily submitted himself to the divine justice, as well in life as in death, for the purpose of undergoing all things requisite to accomplish our redemption.

Under his character of God-man. Luke xxii. 43. "there appeared an angel unto him from heaven, strengthening him." Now the presence of an angel would have been superfluous, unless the divine nature of Christ, as well as his human, had needed support. Matt. xxvii. 46. "My God, why hast thou forsaken me?" If his divine nature had not partaken of the trial, why was it not at hand to sustain him when he demanded succour? or, if it had the ability, but not the will to help him, of what avail was it to call upon his Father, whose will was identically one with his own?

In Life. This is conspicuous even from his birth, Luke ii. 7. in his circumcision, Rom. xv. 8. by which he became "a debtor to do the whole law," Gal. v. 3. whence an offering was made for him, Luke ii. 24; in his flight into Egypt, Matt. iii.; in his subjection to his parents, Luke ii. 51; in his submitting to manual labor, Mark vi. 3.; in his baptism, Matt. iii.; in his temptation, Matt. iv.; in his poverty, Matt. viii. 20.; in the persecutions, insults and dangers which he underwent; for an account of which, together with the whole of his passion, it is better to refer to the gospels, than to cite the passages at length. To the same purport is the prediction of Isaiah, 1. 6.

This death was ignominious in the highest degree. The curse also to which we were obnoxious, was transferred to him, accompanied with a dreadful consciousness of the pouring out of the divine wrath upon his head, which extorted from him the dying exclamation, Matt. xxvii. 46. Lastly, he was detained in the grave three days after death. And here may be found the solution of the difficulty respecting the descent into hell, which has occasioned so much acrimonious controversy among divines; for if Christ's death was real, his soul must have died on the same day with his body, as was above shown. There is another question which seems less easy of solution; namely, whether he yielded to death in his divine nature likewise. For not a few passages of Scripture intimate that his divine nature was subjected to death conjointly with his human; passages too clear to be explained away by the supposition of idiomatic language. Him whom we ought to confess with the mouth, God raised from the dead. But he whom we ought to confess with the mouth is *the Lord Jesus,* that is, the whole person of Jesus; therefore God raised from the dead the

whole person of the Lord Jesus. Christ therefore was not raised in his human nature alone, but in the whole of his person; and Paul received his mission from him not as man, but as God-man. The only uncertainty, therefore, arises from the words of Christ to the thief, *this day thou shalt be with me in Paradise;* a passage which has on other accounts given much trouble to the learned. As to the conciseness of expression in 1 Pet. iii. 18. I consider it as of comparatively little importance; "being put to death in the flesh, but quickened by (or *in*) the Spirit;" since, if the antithesis be correct, the apostle's intention is to specify, on the one hand, the part in which he died, and on the other, that in which he was quickened. Now that which was quickened must have been previously dead. But if *the Spirit* be here put for that which causes life, it must be understood, on comparing it with less obscure texts of Scripture, to signify the Spirit of God the Father. The fact, that Christ became a sacrifice both in his divine and human nature, is denied by none; and as it was requisite that the whole of the sacrifice should be slain, Christ, who was the sacrificial lamb, must be considered as slain in the whole of his nature.

The humiliation of Christ was succeeded by his exaltation. *The exaltation of Christ* is that by which, *having triumphed over death, and laid aside the form of a servant, he was exalted by God the Father to a state of immortality and of the highest glory, partly by his own merits, partly by the gift of the Father, for the benefit of mankind; wherefore he rose again from the dead, ascended into heaven, and sitteth on the right hand of God.* This exaltation consists of three degrees; his resurrection, his ascension into heaven, and his sitting on the right hand of God; all of which are specified with sufficient clearness in the gospels and apostolical writings. The human nature of Christ, although exalted to a state of the highest glory, exists nevertheless in one definite place, and has not, as some contend, the attribute of ubiquity. As Christ emptied himself in both his natures, so both participate in his exaltation; his Godhead, by its restoration and manifestation; his manhood, by an accession of glory. The effect and design of the whole ministry of mediation is, the satisfaction of divine justice on behalf of all men, and the conformation of the faithful to the image of Christ.

The satisfaction of Christ is the complete reparation made by him in his two-fold capacity of God and man, by the fulfilment of the law, and payment of the required price for all mankind.

Christ fulfilled the law by perfect love to God and his neighbor, until the time when he laid down his life for his brethren, being made obedient unto his Father in all things.

By *payment of the required price for,* that is to say, *instead of all mankind.* Matt. xx. 28. λύτρον ἀντὶ πολλων, "a ransom for many." 1 Tim. ii. 6. ἀντίλυτρον ὑπερ πάντων, "a ransom for all." The expressions in the Greek clearly denote the substitution of one person in the place of another. It is in vain that the evidence of these texts is endeavored to be evaded by those who maintain that Christ died, not in our stead, and for our redemption, but merely for our advantage in the abstract, and as an example to mankind. At the same time I confess myself unable to perceive how those who consider the Son as of the same essence with the Father, can explain either his incarnation, or his satisfaction.

For all mankind. 2 Cor. v. 14. "if one died for all, then were all dead." If this deduction be true, then the converse is also true, namely, that if all were dead, because Christ died for all, Christ died for all who were dead; that is, for all mankind. Eph. i. 10. "that he might gather together in one all things in Christ, both which are in heaven, and which are on earth;" all things therefore on earth, without a single exception, as well as in heaven. Further, Christ is said in many places to have been given for the whole world. They however who maintain that Christ made satisfaction for the elect alone, reply, that these passages are to be understood only of the elect who are in the world; and that this is confirmed by its being said elsewhere that Christ made satisfaction *for us,* that is, as they interpret it, for the elect. That the elect, however, cannot be alone intended, will be obvious to any one who examines these texts with attention, if in the first passage from St. John (for instance) the term *elect* be subjoined by way of explanation to that of *the world. So God loved the world* (that is, the elect) *that whosoever* (of the elect) *believeth in him should not*

perish. This would be absurd; for which of the elect does not believe? It is obvious therefore that God here divides the world into believers and unbelievers; and that in declaring, on the one hand, that *whosoever believeth in him shall not perish,* he implies on the other, as a necessary consequence, that whosoever believeth not, shall perish. Besides, where *the world* is not used to signify all mankind, it is most commonly put for the worst characters in it. Again, where Christ is said to be given *for us,* it is expressly declared that the rest of the world is not excluded. 1 John ii. 2. "not for ours only, but also for the sins of the whole world;" words the most comprehensive that could possibly have been used. The same explanation applies to the texts in which Christ is said to lay down his life *for his sheep,* John x. 16. or *for the church,* Acts xx. 28. Besides, if, as has been proved above, a sufficiency of grace be imparted to all, it necessarily follows that a full and efficacious satisfaction must have been made for all by Christ, so far at least as depended on the counsel and will of God; inasmuch as without such satisfaction not the least portion of grace could possibly have been vouchsafed. The passages in which Christ is said to have *given a ransom for many,* as Matt. xx. 28. afford no argument against the belief that he has given a ransom *for all;* for *all* are emphatically *many.* If however it should be argued, that because Christ gave his life *for many,* therefore he did not give it *for all,* many other texts expressly negative this interpretation, and especially Rom. v. 19. Or even if the expression *for all* should be explained to mean *for some,* or, in their own words, for classes of individuals, not for individuals in every class, nothing is gained by this interpretation; not to mention the departure from the usual signification of the word for the sake of a peculiar hypothesis. For the testimony of the sacred writings is not less strong to Christ's having made satisfaction for each individual in every class (as appears from the frequent assertions that he died *for all,* and *for the whole world,* and that he is *not willing that any should perish,*) than the single text Rev. v. 9. is to his having died for classes of individuals: "thou hast redeemed us to God by thy blood out of every kindred, and tongue, and people, and nation." It will be proved, however, that Christ has made satisfaction not for the elect alone, but also for the reprobate, as they are called. Now all were lost; he therefore came to save all, the reprobate as well as those who are called elect. John iii. 17. "God sent not his Son into the world to condemn the world" (which doctrine, nevertheless, must be maintained by those who assert that Christ was sent for the elect only, to the heavier con- 10 demnation of the reprobate) "but that the world through him might be saved;" that is, the reprobate; for it would be superfluous to make such a declaration with regard to the elect. Those whom he will judge, he undoubtedly calls to repentance: but he will judge all the world individually; therefore he calls all the world individually to repentance. But this gracious call could have been vouchsafed to none, had not Christ interfered to make 20 such a satisfaction as should be not merely sufficient in itself, but effectual, so far as the divine will was concerned, for the salvation of all mankind; unless we are to suppose that the call is not made in earnest. Now the call to repentance and the gift of grace are from the Deity; their acceptance is the result of faith: if therefore the efficacy of Christ's satisfaction be lost through want of faith, this does not prove that an effectual satisfaction 30 has not been made, but that the offer has not been accepted. Forasmuch then as all mankind are divided into elect and reprobate, in behalf of both of whom Christ has made satisfaction, he has made satisfaction for all. So far indeed is this satisfaction from regarding the elect alone, as is commonly believed, to the exclusion of sinners in general, that the very contrary is the case; it regards all sinners whatever, and it regards them ex- 40 pressly as sinners; whereas it only regards the elect in so far as they were previously sinners. But it is objected, Christ *does not pray for the world,* John xvii. 9. This is true of that particular prayer, which was dedicated chiefly to the benefit of his disciples; but on the cross he prayed even for his murderers. He exhorts us likewise by the mouth of the apostle, 1 Tim. ii. 1. They also object Tit. ii. 14. "who gave himself for us, that he might 50 redeem us from all iniquity, and purify unto himself a peculiar people, zealous of good works:" a peculiar people, not therefore the

whole of mankind. I reply, that redemption is not purification; Christ has redeemed all transgressors, but he purifies only such as are zealous of good works, that is, believers; for no works are good, unless done in faith. All are redeemed, even those who know not of it, or who are yet *enemies* and *sinners,* but none are purified, except their wills be consenting, and they have faith; as Scripture everywhere testifies.

That the satisfaction made by Christ was the effect and end proposed by the whole of his ministry, appears from the following passages. First, of his humiliation. Isai. lii. 4–11. Secondly, of his exaltation. Rom. v. 10. The effect of Christ's satisfaction is sufficient to produce the reconciliation of God the Father with man.

The second object of the ministry of the Mediator is, *that we may be conformed to the image of Christ, as well in his state of humiliation as of exaltation.*

So far, therefore, as regards the satisfaction of Christ, and our conformity to his humiliation, the restoration of man is of merit; in which sense those texts are to be understood which convey a notion of recompense and reward. Nor need we fear, lest in maintaining this belief we should lend any support to the doctrine of human merits. For our conformity to the image of Christ is as far from adding anything to the full and perfect satisfaction made by him, as our works are from adding to faith; it is faith that justifies, but a faith not destitute of works: and in like manner, if we deserve anything, if there be any worthiness in us on any ground whatever, it is God that hath made us worthy in Christ.

On the other hand, so far as regards the election of Christ to the office of Mediator by God the Father, and our own election to life by the same Father, the restoration of man is purely of grace; whence the Father is so often said in the gospel to have given those that are the Son's to the Son, and the Son to those that are the Son's.

The fable of a purgatory, in which, as the Papists feign, the sins of men are cleansed and purged away by fire, is refuted by many considerations, but above all by that of the full satisfaction of Christ. For (besides that there is no mention of any such place in Scripture) if it be true that the blood of Christ has made complete expiation for us, and purified us thoroughly from all stains, it follows that there is nothing left for the fire to purge. To those who understand the *fire* mentioned in 1 Cor. iii. 13, 15. of a real fire, I reply, that the apostle is not here speaking of the flames of purgatory, but of a metaphorical fire, appointed to try, not mankind in general, but the false teachers, whose doctrine *the day,* that is, the light of truth, *shall declare,* whether it was on the one hand disguised and impaired by false ornaments, or whether, on the other hand, it remained neglected and without cultivation. Like the *fiery trial* mentioned 1 Pet. iv. 12. it proves us in this world, not purges us in the next. Besides, all retribution, all endurance of good or evil subsequent to this life, is deferred till the day when Christ shall sit in judgment. And if it be true, as shown in a preceding chapter, that the soul as well as the body sleeps till the day of resurrection, no stronger argument can be urged against the existence of a purgatory. Lastly, it is certain that to those who are to be saved there is nothing intervening, except death, between *the earthly house* of this life, and *the house eternal in the heavens.*

CHAP. XVII.—OF MAN'S RENOVATION, INCLUDING HIS CALLING.

HAVING concluded the subject of man's *redemption,* his *renovation* is next to be considered.

The renovation of man is that change whereby *he who was before under the curse, and obnoxious to the divine wrath, is brought into a state of grace.*

In renovation two things are to be considered; the mode by which man is renewed, and the manifestation of that mode.

The mode by which man is renewed, is either *natural* or *supernatural.*

By the natural mode, I mean that which influences the natural affections alone. This includes the calling of the natural man, and the consequent change in his character.

The calling of man is that natural mode of renovation whereby *God the Father, according to his purpose in Christ, invites fallen man to a knowledge of the way in which he is to be propitiated and worshipped; insomuch that believers, through his gratuitous kindness, are called to salvation, and such as refuse to believe are left without excuse.*

This calling is either general or special. The general calling is that whereby God invites the whole of mankind, in various ways, but all of them sufficient for the purpose, to the knowledge of the true Deity. It may be objected, that all have not known Christ. I answer, that this proves nothing against the doctrine, that all are called in Christ alone; inasmuch as, had he not been given to the world, God would have called no one: and as the ransom he has paid is in itself sufficient for the redemption of all mankind, all are called to partake of its benefits, though all may not be aware of the source from which the benefits flow. For if Job believed that his sacrifice could avail for his sons, who were not present at its offering, and were perhaps thinking of nothing less; if the returned Jews believed that their sacrifices could be available for the ten tribes, who were then far distant, and ignorant of what was passing at Jerusalem; how much more ought we to believe that the perfect sacrifice of Christ may be abundantly sufficient even for those who have never heard of the name of Christ, and who believe only in God? This will be treated more at large under the head of faith.

God's special calling is that whereby he, at the time which he thinks proper, invites particular individuals, elect as well as reprobate, more frequently, and with a more marked call than others.

Particular individuals in preference to others. Thus he called Abraham from his father's house, who probably expected no such call, and who was even an idolator at the time. So also he called the people of Israel, for his name's sake and for the sake of the promises made to their fathers.

The change which takes place in man by reason of his calling, is that whereby the natural mind and will of man being partially renewed by a divine impulse, are led to seek the knowledge of God, and for the time, at least, undergo an alteration for the better.

Inasmuch as this change is from God, those in whom it takes place are said to be enlightened, and to be endued with power to will what is good. This is ascribed sometimes to the Father; sometimes to the Son; sometimes to the Holy Spirit.

As this change is of the nature of an effect produced on man, and an answer, as it were, to the call of God, it is sometimes spoken of under the metaphor of hearing or hearkening, (this faculty itself, however, being usually described as a gift from God) sometimes under that of tasting. This can only imply that he works in us the power of acting freely, of which, since our fall, we were incapable, except by means of a calling and renewal. For the power of volition cannot be wrought in us, without the power of free agency being at the same time imparted; since it is in this power that the will itself consists.

The parts of this change, considered as an effect, are two: repentance, and a corresponding faith. Both the one and the other of these feelings may be either the genuine beginnings of conversion, or the mere effect of nature, or, lastly, they may be altogether fictitious; and repentance of this kind, or a transient sorrow for past sin, bears the same relation to solid and lasting repentance, which the faith corresponding to it bears to a saving faith. I distinguish between the two species of repentance for the sake of clearness, although I do not deny that the same word is indiscriminately employed to denote the temporary and the permanent affection; in like manner as the various kinds of faith are all expressed in Scripture by the same term. This secondary species of repentance (in Greek μεταμέλεια) is that whereby a man abstains from sin through fear of punishment, and obeys the call of God merely for the sake of his own salvation.

This kind of repentance is common to the regenerate and to the unregenerate. Examples among the unregenerate are Cain, Esau, Pharaoh, Saul, Ahab, Judas, and many others, in whom contrition, and confession of sins, and other marks of repentance, are perceptible. All exhortation, however, would be addressed in vain to such as were not in some measure renewed, at least in the natural mode here described; that is to say, who were not endued with some portion of mental judgment and liberty of will.

The faith corresponding to this species of repentance is an assent, likewise natural, yielded to the call of God, and accompanied by a trust which is in like manner natural, and often vain. I have described this assent as yielded to the call of God, inasmuch as faith, of whatever kind, can only be founded on divine testimony in matters relating to God. This faith is commonly distinguished into the several degrees of historical faith, temporary faith, and faith in miracles. Any faith, however, may be temporary; so may repentance itself: as will be hereafter shown. Historical faith consists in an assent to the truth of the scripture history, and to sound doctrine. This faith is necessary to salvation, but is not in itself a saving faith.

Temporary faith is that which assents to hearing, and exercises a certain degree of trust in God, but generally of that kind only which is termed natural. I say generally, because there is no reason why a regenerate faith should not itself sometimes prove merely temporary, owing to the remains of human frailty still inherent in us; this however seldom happens, as will be argued hereafter under the head of final perseverance. Faith in miracles is that whereby any one is endued with the power of working miracles in the name of God, or whereby he believes that another is endued with this power. Even without this species of faith, however, miracles have been sometimes wrought for unbelievers. The call of God, and the consequent change in the natural man, do not of themselves ensure his salvation, unless he be also regenerate; inasmuch as they are only parts of the natural mode of renovation.

——————

CHAP. XVIII.—Of Regeneration.

The intent of *supernatural renovation* is not only to restore man more completely than before to the use of his natural faculties as regards his power to form right judgment, and to exercise free will; but to create afresh, as it were, the inward man, and infuse from above new and supernatural faculties into the minds of the renovated. This is called *regeneration,* and the regenerate are said to be *planted in Christ.*

Regeneration is that change operated by the Word and the Spirit, whereby the old man being destroyed, the inward man is re-generated by God after his own image, in all the faculties of his mind, insomuch that he becomes as it were a new creature, and the whole man is sanctified both in body and soul, for the service of God, and the perform-ance of good works.

Is regenerated by God; namely, the Father; for no one generates, except the Father.

In all the faculties of his mind; that is to say, in understanding and will. This renewal of the will can mean nothing, but a restora-tion to its former liberty. If the choice were given us, we could ask nothing more of God, than that, being delivered from the slavery of sin, and restored to the divine image, we might have it in our power to obtain salva-tion if willing. Willing we shall undoubtedly be, if truly free, and he who is not willing, has no one to accuse but himself. But if the will of the regenerate be not made free, then we are not renewed, but compelled to em-brace salvation in an unregenerate state.

A new creature. 2 Cor. 5. 17. "if any man be in Christ, he is a new creature." Hence some, less properly, divide regeneration into two parts, *the mortification of the flesh,* and *the quickening of the Spirit;* whereas mortifi-cation cannot be a constituent part of re-generation, inasmuch as it partly precedes it, (that is to say, as corruption precedes genera-tion) and partly follows it; in which latter capacity it belongs rather to repentance. On the other hand, *the quickening of the spirit* is as often used to signify resurrection as re-generation. Sanctification is sometimes used in a more extended sense, for any kind of elec-tion or separation, either of a whole nation to some particular form of worship, or of an individual to some office. The external cause of regeneration or sanctification is the death and resurrection of Christ. Sanctifica-tion is attributed also to faith. Acts xv. 9. "purifying their hearts by faith;" not that faith is anterior to sanctification, but because faith is an instrumental and assisting cause in its gradual progress.

CHAP. XIX.—OF REPENTANCE.

THE effects of regeneration are *repentance* and *faith.*

Repentance, or rather that higher species of it called in Greek μετάνοια, is *the gift of God, whereby the regenerate man perceiving with sorrow that he has offended God by sin, detests and avoids it, humbly turning to God through a sense of the divine mercy, and heartily striving to follow right-eousness.*

The gift of God; namely, of the Father through the Son.

By a comparison of these and similar texts, we may distinguish certain progressive steps in repentance; namely, conviction of sin, con-trition, confession, departure from evil, con-version to good: all which, however, belong likewise in their respective degrees to the re-pentance of the unregenerate.

Confession of sin is made sometimes to God; sometimes to men: and that either pri-vately, or publicly; sometimes both to God and men. Confession of faith, which is another kind, does not belong to the present subject. Repentance is either general, which is also called conversion, when a man is converted from a state of sin to a state of grace; or par-ticular, when one who is already converted re-pents of some individual sin. General repent-ance is either primary or continued; from which latter even the regenerate are not ex-empt, through their sense of in-dwelling sin. Particular repentance is exemplified in the cases of David and Peter. Repentance, in re-generate man, is prior to faith. Therefore that sense of the divine mercy, which leads to re-pentance, ought not to be confounded with faith, as it is by the greater number of divines. Chastisement is often the instrumental cause of repentance. God however assigns a limit to chastisement, lest we should be overwhelmed, and supplies strength for our support even un-der those inflictions which (as is sometimes the case) appear to us too heavy to be borne. He even seems to repent of what he had done, and through his abounding mercy, as though he had in his wrath inflicted double punish-ment for our transgressions, compensates for our affliction with a double measure of con-solation. This compensation is more than an hundredfold, even an infinite weight of glory. We ought not therefore to form rash judg-ments respecting the afflictions of others. On the contrary, it is said of those who are not chastened, Psal. xvii. 14. "they have their portion in this life." Hence arises consolation to the afflicted.

CHAP. XX.—OF SAVING FAITH.

THE other effect of regeneration is *saving faith.*

Saving faith is a full persuasion operated in us through the gift of God, whereby we believe, on the sole authority of the promise itself, that whatsoever things he has promised in Christ are ours, and especially the grace of eternal life.

Hence implicit faith, which sees not the objects of hope, but yields belief with a blind assent, cannot possibly be genuine faith, except in the case of novices or first converts, whose faith must necessarily be for a time implicit, inasmuch as they believe even before they have entered upon a course of instruction. Such was that of the Samaritans, and of the disciples, who believed in Christ long before they were accurately acquainted with many of the articles of faith. Those also belong to this class, who are slow of understanding and inapt to learn, but who nevertheless believe according to the measure of their knowledge, and striving to live by faith, are acceptable to God. Faith is also called πεποίθεσις, or *trust*, with the same meaning.

As to the three divisions into which faith is commonly distinguished by divines, knowledge of the word, assent, and persuasion or trust, the two former equally belong to temporary, and even to historical faith, and both are comprehended in, or, more properly, precede a full persuasion.

Hence, as was shown in the fifth chapter, the ultimate object of faith is not Christ the Mediator, but God the Father; a truth which the weight of scripture evidence has compelled divines to acknowledge. For the same reason it ought not to appear wonderful if many, both Jews and others, who lived before Christ, and many also who have lived since his time, but to whom he has never been revealed, should be saved by faith in God alone: still however through the sole merits of Christ, inasmuch as he was given and slain from the beginning of the world, even for those to whom he was not known, provided they believed in God the Father. Hence honorable testimony is borne to the faith of the illustrious patriarchs who lived under the law, Abel, Enoch, Noah, &c. though it is expressly stated that they believed only in God.

Seeing, however, that faith necessarily includes a receiving of God, and coming to him, seeing also that we must have a right knowledge of God before we can receive him or come to him, for "he that cometh to God, must believe that he is, and that he is a rewarder of them that diligently seek him," it follows, that the source from which faith originally springs, and whence it proceeds onward in its progress to good, is a genuine, though possibly in the first instance imperfect, knowledge of God; so that, properly speaking, the seat of faith is not in the understanding, but in the will.

From faith arises hope, that is, a most assured expectation through faith of those future things which are already ours in Christ. Hope differs from faith, as the effect from the cause; it differs from it likewise in its object; for the object of faith is the promise; that of hope, the thing promised.

CHAP. XXI.—OF BEING INGRAFTED IN CHRIST, AND ITS EFFECTS.

Regeneration and its effects, repentance and faith, have been considered. Next follows *ingrafting in Christ.*

Believers are said *to be ingrafted in Christ,* when they are planted in Christ by God the Father, that is, are made partakers of Christ, and meet for becoming one with him.

Of this ingrafting, combined with regeneration, the effects are *newness of life* and *increase.* For the new spiritual life and its increase bear the same relation to the restoration of man, which spiritual death and its progress (as described above, on the punishment of sin) bear to his fall. *Newness of life* is that by which we are said to live unto God. This is also called self-denial.

The primary functions of the new life are comprehension of spiritual things, and love of holiness. And as the power of exercising these functions was weakened and in a manner destroyed by the spiritual death, so is the understanding restored in great part to its primitive clearness, and the will to its primitive liberty, by the new spiritual life in Christ.

The comprehension of spiritual things is a habit or condition of mind produced by God, whereby the natural ignorance of those who believe and are ingrafted in Christ is removed, and their understandings enlightened for the perception of heavenly things, so that, by the teaching of God, they know all that is necessary for eternal salvation and the true happiness of life. In the present life, however, we can only attain to an imperfect comprehension of spiritual things.

The other effect is *love or charity, arising from a sense of the divine love shed abroad in the hearts of the regenerate by the Spirit, whereby those who are ingrafted in Christ being influenced, become dead to sin, and alive again unto God, and bring forth good works spontaneously and freely.* This is also called *holiness.*

The love here intended is not brotherly love, which belongs to another place; nor even the ordinary affection which we bear to God, but one resulting from a consciousness and lively sense of the love wherewith he has loved us, and which in theology is reckoned the third after faith and hope. This is the offspring, as it were, of faith, and the parent of good works. It is described 1 Cor. xiii. and 1 John iv. 16.

Spontaneously and freely; for our own co-operation is uniformly required. In consequence of this love or sanctity all believers are called *saints.* Philipp. iv. 21, 22. "salute every saint in Christ Jesus;" and to the same effect in other passages. The holiness of the saints is nevertheless imperfect in this life.

Thus far of newness of life and its effects. It remains to speak of *the increase* operated in the regenerate. This increase is either absolute, which is internal, or relative, which is external. Absolute increase is an increase *derived from God the Father* of those gifts which we have received by regeneration and ingrafting in Christ. Spiritual increase, unlike physical growth, appears to be to a certain degree in the power of the regenerate themselves.

With regard to perfection, although not to be expected in the present life, it is our duty to strive after it with earnestness, as the ultimate object of our existence. Hence the struggle between the flesh and the Spirit in the regenerate. There is also a victory to be gained, over the world, over death and over Satan. Hence such as are strenuous in this conflict, and earnestly and unceasingly labor to attain perfection in Christ, though they be really imperfect, are yet, by imputation and through the divine mercy, frequently called in Scripture *perfect,* and *blameless,* and *without sin;* inasmuch as sin, though still dwelling in them, does not reign over them.

CHAP. XXII.—OF JUSTIFICATION.

HAVING considered the absolute or internal increase of the regenerate, I proceed to speak of that which is relative or external. This increase has reference either to the Father exclusively, or to the Father and Son conjointly. That which has reference to the Father exclusively is termed *justification* and *adoption.*

Justification is the gratuitous purpose of God, whereby those who are regenerate and ingrafted in Christ are absolved from sin and death through his most perfect satisfaction, and accounted just in the sight of God, not by the works of the law, but through faith.

As therefore our sins are imputed to Christ, so the merits or righteousness of Christ are imputed to us through faith. It is evident therefore that justification, in so far as we are concerned, is gratuitous: in so far as Christ is concerned, not gratuitous; inasmuch as Christ paid the ransom of our sins, which he took upon himself by imputation, and thus of his own accord, and at his own cost, effected their expiation; whereas man, paying nothing on his part, but merely believing, receives as a gift the imputed righteousness of Christ. Finally, the Father, appeased by this propitiation, pronounces the justification of all believers. A simpler mode of satisfaction could not have been devised, nor one more agreeable to equity. Hence we are said to be *clothed* with the righteousness of Christ. For the same reason we are also called the *friends* of God.

Accounted just in the sight of God. Eph. v. 27. On the same principle the faithful both before and under the law were accounted just. Nor is it in any other sense that we are said *not to sin,* except as our sins are not imputed unto us through Christ. In all these numerous passages we are said to be justified by faith, and through faith, and of faith; whether through faith as an instrument, according to the common doctrine, or in any other sense, is not said. Undoubtedly, if to believe be to act, faith is an action, or rather a frame of mind acquired and confirmed by a succession of actions, although in the first instance infused from above; and by this faith we are justified, as declared in the numerous texts above quoted. An action, however, is generally considered in the light of the effect, not of an instrument; or perhaps it may be more properly designated as the less principal cause. On the other hand, if faith be not in any degree acquired, but wholly infused from above, there will be the less hesitation in admitting it as the cause of our justification.

An important question here arises, which is discussed with much vehemence by the advocates on both sides; namely, whether faith alone justifies? Our divines answer in the affirmative; adding, that works are the effects of faith, not the cause of justification. Others contend that justification is not by faith alone, on the authority of James ii. 24. "by works a man is justified, and not by faith only." As however the two opinions appear at first sight inconsistent with each other, and incapable of being maintained together, the advocates of the former, to obviate the difficulty arising from the passage of St. James, allege that the apostle is speaking of justification in the sight of men, not in the sight of God. But whoever reads attentively from the fourteenth verse to the end of the chapter, will see that the apostle is expressly treating of justification in the sight of God. For the question there at issue relates to the faith which profits, and which is a living and a saving faith; consequently it cannot relate to that which justifies only in the sight of men, inasmuch as this latter may be hypocritical. When therefore the apostle says that we are justified by works, and not by faith only, he is speaking of the faith which profits, and which is a true, living, and saving faith. Considering then that the apostles, who treat this point of our religion with particular attention, nowhere, in summing up their doctrine, use words implying that a man is

justified by faith alone, but generally conclude as follows, that "a man is justified by faith without the deeds of the law," Rom. iii. 28. I am at a loss to conjecture why our divines should have narrowed the terms of the apostolical conclusion. Had they not so done, the declaration in the one text that "by faith a man is justified without the deeds of the law," would have appeared perfectly consistent with that in the other, "by works a man is justified, and not by faith only." For St. Paul does not say simply that a man is justified without works, but "without the works of the law:" nor yet by faith alone, but "by faith which worketh by love," Gal. v. 6. Faith has its own works, which may be different from the works of the law. We are justified therefore by faith, but by a living, not a dead faith; and that faith alone which acts is counted living. Hence we are justified by faith without the works of the law, but not without the works of faith; inasmuch as a living and true faith cannot consist without works, though these latter may differ from the works of the written law. Such were those of Abraham and Rahab, the two examples cited by St. James in illustration of the works of faith, when the former was prepared to offer up his son, and the latter sheltered the spies of the Israelites. To these may be added the instance of Phinehas, whose action "was counted unto him for righteousness," Psal. cvi. 31. the very same words being as in the case of Abraham, whose "faith was reckoned to him for righteousness," Gen. xv. 6. Nor will it be denied that Phinehas was justified in the sight of God rather than of men, and that his work recorded Numb. xxv. 11, 12. was a work of faith, not of law. Phinehas therefore was justified not by faith alone, but also by the works of faith. The principle of this doctrine will be developed more fully hereafter, when the subjects of the gospel and of Christian liberty are considered.

This interpretation, however, affords no countenance to the doctrine of human merit, inasmuch as both faith itself and its works are the works of the Spirit, not our own. Eph. ii. 8 —10. In this passage the works of which a man may boast are distinguished from those which do not admit of boasting, namely, the works of faith. Now what is the law of faith, but the works of faith? Hence, wherever after *works* the words *of the law* are omitted, as in Rom. iv. 2. we must supply either *the works of the law,* or, as in the present passage, *of the flesh,* with reference to xi. 1. (not *of the law,* since the apostle is speaking of Abraham, who lived before the law). Otherwise St. Paul would have contradicted himself as well as St. James; he would contradict himself, in saying that Abraham had whereof to glory through any works whatever, whereas he had declared in the preceding chapter, v. 27, 28. "that by the law of faith, that is, by the works of faith, boasting was excluded;" he would expressly contradict St. James, who affirms, as above, that "by works a man is justified, and not by faith stood only;" unless the expression be understood to mean the works of faith, not the works of the law. In the same sense is to be understood Matt. v. 20. "except your righteousness shall exceed the righteousness of the Scribes and Pharisees, ye shall in no case enter into the kingdom of heaven;" whereas their righteousness was of the exactest kind according to the law.

Nor does this doctrine derogate in any degree from Christ's satisfaction; inasmuch as, our faith being imperfect, the works which proceed from it cannot be pleasing to God, except in so far as they rest upon his mercy and the righteousness of Christ, and are sustained by that foundation alone.

The Papists argue, that it is no less absurd to say that a man is justified by the righteousness of another, than that a man is learned by the learning of another. But there is no analogy between the two cases, inasmuch as mankind are not one with each other in the same intimate manner as the believer is one with Christ his head. In the mean time they do not perceive the real and extreme absurdity of which they are themselves guilty, in supposing that the righteousness of the dead, or of monks, can be imputed to others. They likewise contend, on the authority of a few passages of Scripture, that man is justified by his own works. Rom. ii. 6. "who will render to every man according to his deeds." But to render to every man *according to his deeds* is one thing, to render to him *on account of his deeds* is another; nor does it follow from

hence that works have any inherent justifying power, or deserve anything as of their own merit; seeing that, if we do anything right, or if God assign any recompense to our right actions, it is altogether owing to his grace. Finally, the same Psalmist who attributes to himself righteousness, attributes to himself iniquity in the same sentence.

As to the expression in Matt. xxv. 34, 35. "inherit the kingdom . . . for I was an hungred, and ye gave me meat," our answer is, that the sentence which Christ shall pass on that day will not have respect to faith, which is the internal cause of justification, but to the effects and signs of that faith, namely, the works done in faith, that he may thereby make the equity of his judgment manifest to all mankind. When a man is said to be perfect and just in the sight of God, this is to be understood according to the measure of human righteousness, and as compared with the progress of others; or it may mean that they were endued with a sincere and upright heart, without dissimulation, which interpretation seems to be favored by the expression *in the sight of God.* Or, lastly, it may mean that they were declared righteous by God through grace and faith.

With regard to Luke vii. 47. "her sins, which are many, are forgiven, for she loved much," it is to be observed that this love was not the cause, but the token or effect of forgiveness, as is evident from the parable itself, v. 40. for the debtors were not forgiven because they had loved much, but they loved much because much had been forgiven. The same appears from what follows; *to whom little is forgiven, the same loveth little;* and still more plainly from v. 50. "thy faith hath saved thee." That which saved, the same also justified; namely, not love, but faith, which was itself the cause of the love in question. From a consciousness of justification proceed peace and real tranquillity of mind. This is that peace for which the apostles pray in their salutations addressed to the church.

———

CHAP. XXIII.—OF ADOPTION.

WE have considered *justification,* the first of those particulars connected with the increase of the regenerate which bear reference to the Father; that which remains to be treated of is *Adoption*.

Adoption is that act whereby *God adopts as his children those who are justified through faith.*

In one sense we are by nature sons of God, as well as the angels, inasmuch as he is the author of our being. But the sense here intended is that of adopted children, such as those probably were, though in profession only, who are mentioned Gen. vi. 2. "the sons of God saw the daughters of men that they were fair."

From adoption is derived, first, liberty; a privilege which was not unknown to the posterity of Abraham, in virtue of their title as children of God, even under the law of bondage. In the spirit of this liberty, they did not scruple even to infringe the ceremonies of religion, when their observance would have been inconsistent with the law of love. But the clearer and more perfect light in which liberty, like adoption itself, has been unfolded by the gospel, renders it necessary to reserve the fuller exposition of this privilege to that part of our work in which the subject of the Gospel is considered. By adoption we are also made heirs through Christ. This also confers the title of *first-born*, and of *brethren of Christ.* Hence we are said to be "of the household of God." Eph. ii. 19. Hence even the angels minister unto us. Heb. i. 14. Lastly, we become sons of God by a new generation; by the assumption, as it were, of a new nature, and by a conformity to his glory.

CHAP. XXIV.—OF UNION AND FELLOWSHIP WITH CHRIST AND HIS MEMBERS, WHEREIN IS CONSIDERED THE MYSTICAL OR INVISIBLE CHURCH.

HITHERTO the increase of the regenerate has been considered in its relation to the Father alone. We are now to consider that increase which has reference to the Father and Son conjointly. This consists in our *union* and *fellowship* with the father through Christ the Son, and our glorification after the image of Christ.

The fellowship arising from this union consists in a participation, through the Spirit, of the various gifts and merits of Christ. From this our fellowship with Christ arises the mutual fellowship of the members of Christ's body among themselves, called in the Apostles' Creed *The Communion of Saints.*

Lastly, from this union and fellowship of the regenerate with the Father and Christ, and of the members of Christ's body among themselves, results the mystical body called *The Invisible Church,* whereof Christ is the head. Seeing then that the body of Christ is mystically one, it follows that the fellowship of his members must also be mystical, and not confined to place or time, inasmuch as it is composed of individuals of widely separated countries, and of all ages from the foundation of the world.

The love of Christ towards his invisible and spotless Church is described by the appropriate figure of conjugal love. Christ is also called *the Shepherd,* by reason of his protecting and teaching the church.

———

CHAP. XXV.—OF IMPERFECT GLORIFICATION, WHEREIN ARE CONSIDERED THE DOCTRINES OF ASSURANCE AND FINAL PERSEVERANCE.

OF that increase which has reference to the Father and Son conjointly, the remaining part is *Glorification.*

Glorification is either *imperfect* or *perfect.*

Imperfect glorification is that state wherein, being *justified and adopted by God the Father, we are filled with a consciousness of present grace and excellency, as well as with an expectation of future glory, insomuch that our blessedness is in a manner already begun.*

St. Paul traces this glorification by progressive steps, from its original source in the foreknowledge of God himself. Both regeneration and increase are accompanied by confirmation, or preservation in the faith, which is also the work of God.

These three, *regeneration, increase* and *preservation in the faith,* considered as proximate causes on the part of God, and their effects, as *faith, love,* &c. considered as proximate causes on the part of man, or as acting in man, produce *assurance of salva-*

tion, and *the final perseverance of the saints.* On the part of God, however, the primary or more remote cause is his predestination or election of believers.

Hence *assurance of salvation is a certain degree or gradation of faith, whereby a man has a firm persuasion and conviction, founded on the testimony of the Spirit, that if he believe and continue in faith and love, having been justified and adopted, and partly glorified by union and fellowship with Christ and the Father, he will at length most certainly attain to everlasting life and the consummation of Glory.*

Has a firm persuasion; or, to speak more properly, ought, and is entitled to have a firm persuasion. 2 Pet. i. 10. "wherefore the rather, brethren, give diligence to make your calling and election sure," that is, the fruit of your calling and election, eternal life; for the calling itself cannot be made more sure, inasmuch as it is already past; but this is of no avail, unless we give diligence to make both sure. It follows, that, as far as this depends upon ourselves, it must be in our own power to make it sure. Hence we are enjoined to prove our faith, lest we should be reprobates; not our election, which cannot be sure without faith. This assurance of salvation produces a joy unspeakable.

The final perseverance of the saints is the gift of God's preserving power, whereby they who are foreknown, elect and born again, and sealed by the Holy Spirit, persevere to the end in the faith and grace of God, and never entirely fall away through any power or malice of the devil or the world, so long as nothing is wanting on their own parts, and they continue to the utmost in the maintenance of faith and love.

So long as nothing is wanting on their own parts. In adding this limitation, I was influenced by what I had observed to be the uniform tenor of Scripture. Psal. cxxv. 1, 2. "they that trust in Jehovah shall be as mount Sion, which cannot be removed, but abideth for ever." In promising to "put his fear in their hearts, that they shall not depart from him." God merely engages to perform what is requisite on his part, namely, to bestow such a supply of grace as should be sufficient, if properly employed, to retain them in his way. At the same time he enters into a convenant with them. Now a covenant implies certain conditions to be performed, not by one, but by both the parties. "They shall not depart from me; that is, from my external worship, as the whole of the context shows, from the thirty-seventh verse to the end of the chapter, compared with the twentieth and twenty-first verses of the following; "if ye can break my covenant of the day . . . then may also my covenant be broken with David my servant . . . and with the Levites." Lastly, it appears that these very persons, in whose hearts he promised to put his fear that they should not depart from him, did actually so depart; for the same promise is made to their children. The event therefore proved, that although God had according to compact put his fear into their hearts to the very end that they should not depart, they nevertheless departed through their own fault and depravity. Moreover, the words are addressed to, and include, the whole nation; but the whole nation was not elect; it follows therefore that the passage cannot refer to the elect exclusively, as is contended.

Thus the gifts of God are said to be "without repentence," inasmuch as he did not repent of his promise to Abraham and his seed, although the greater part of them had revolted; but it does not follow that he did not change his purpose towards those who had first changed theirs towards him. That a real believer, however, may fall irrecoverably, the same apostle shows, "they allure through the lusts of the flesh, through much wantonness, those that were clean escaped from them who live in error;" if indeed this be the right reading, and not, as others contend, *escaped a little:* not to mention, that it appears doubtful whether *the knowledge of the Lord* should be understood here of a saving faith, and not of an historical only; and whether their escape *from the pollutions of the world* implies a truly regenerate and Christian purity of life, and not a mere outward and philosophical morality: so that from this passage nothing certain can be inferred. The text in Ezekiel, xviii. 26. is clearer; "when a righteous man turneth away from his righteousness . . . he shall die." The righteousness here intended must necessarily be true righteousness, being that from which whosoever turns shall die. But, it is replied, the event is conditional, *if he turneth away;* which, on our hypothesis, will never happen. I answer, first, that the Hebrew does not express any condition, and secondly, that if it were so, an absurd and impracticable condition is inconsistent with the character of God.

Accordingly, not the elect, but those who continue to the end, are said to obtain salvation. John viii. 31. "if ye continue in my word, then are ye my disciples indeed." From this last passage, however, our opponents draw the inverse inference, *if ye be my disciples indeed, ye will continue;* in other words, your continuance will be a proof of your being really my disciples; in support of which they quote 1 John ii. 19. I reply, that these texts do not contradict each other, inasmuch as the apostle is not here laying down a rule applicable to believers in general, formally deduced from necessary causes; but merely giving his judgment concerning certain antichrists, which judgment, according to a common practice, he had formed from the event. He does not say, therefore, *if they had been of us, it was impossible but that they should have continued with us,* nor does he mention the causes of this impossibility; but he merely says, *they would have continued.* His argument is as follows; since it is very rare that a true disciple does not continue in the faith, it is natural to suppose that they would have continued in it, if they had been true disciples. But *they went out from us.* Why? Not to show that true believers could never depart from the faith, but that all who walked with the apostles were not true believers, inasmuch as true believers very rarely acted as they had done. In the same way it might be said of an individual, "if he had been a real friend, he would never have been unfaithful;" not because it is impossible that a real friend should ever ·be unfaithful, but because the case very seldom happens. That the apostle could not have intended to lay down a rule of universal application, may be shown by inverting the hypothesis; *If they had continued, they would no doubt have been of us;* whereas many hypocrites continue in outward communion with the church even till their death, and never go out from it. As therefore those who con-

tinue are not known to be real believers simply from their continuing, so neither are those who do not continue proved thereby never to have been real believers; this only is certain, that they were not real believers when they went out from the church, for neither does Christ, with whom John undoubtedly agreed, argue thus; *ye are my disciples indeed, if ye continue in my word,* but thus; *if ye continue indeed* (for this latter word must be taken with both members of the sentence) *then will ye be indeed my disciples;* therefore, *if ye do not continue, ye will not be my disciples.*

It is said, however, in the same epistle, chap. iii. 9. "whosoever is born of God doth not commit sin; for his seed remaineth in him, and he cannot sin, because he is born of God;" from which they argue as follows; if he cannot sin, much less can he depart from the faith. We are not at liberty, however, thus to separate a particular verse from its context, without carefully comparing its meaning with other verses of the same chapter and epistle, as well as with texts bearing on the same subject in other parts of Scripture; lest the apostle should be made to contradict either himself, or the other sacred writers. He is declaring, in the verse above quoted, the strength of that internal aid with which God has provided us against sin; having previously explained what is required on our own part, v. 3. "every man that hath this hope in him, purifieth himself, even as he is pure." He recurs again to the same point v. 18. "whosoever is born of God, sinneth not, but he that is begotten of God keepeth himself."—Whosoever, therefore, is born of God, cannot sin, and therefore cannot depart from the faith, provided that he at the same time purifieth himself to the utmost of his power, that he do righteousness, that he love his brother, that he remain himself in love, in order that God and his seed may also remain in him; that finally he keep himself. Further, in what sense is it said, *he cannot sin,* when the apostle has already declared, chap. i. 8. "if we say that we have no sin, we deceive ourselves, and the truth is not in us"? Doubtless we ought to understand by this phrase that he does not easily fall into sin, not voluntarily and intentionally, not wilfully and presumptuously, but with reluctance and remorse; and that he does not persist in the habit of sinning; for which reasons, and above all for Christ's sake, sin is not imputed to ·him. If then so much caution be necessary in explaining the word *sin,* we ought to proceed with no less care in the interpretation of the remaining part of the verse; and not to take advantage of the simplicity of style peculiar to this apostle, for the purpose of establishing a doctrine in itself absurd. For *not to be able,* as the Remonstrant divines have rightly observed, does not always signify absolute impossibility, either in common language or in Scripture. Thus we often say that a particular thing cannot be done, meaning that it cannot be done with convenience, honor, or facility, or with a safe conscience, or consistently with modesty, or credit, or dignity, or good faith. Matt. xii. 34. "how can ye, being evil, speak good things?" whereas it is easy even for hypocrites to *speak good things.* In like manner, when it is said in the present passage *he cannot sin,* the meaning is, that he cannot easily fall into sin, and therefore cannot easily depart from the faith. The same divines have displayed equal sagacity and research in their explanation of the reason assigned by the apostle, *for his seed remaineth in him;* where they show that *to remain in him* means the same as *to be in him.* So John xiv. 7. Thus also v. 14. *he that loveth not his brother, abideth in death;* that is, so long as he does not love his brother; for in any other sense it would be impossible for a man to escape death who had ever been guilty of not loving his brother. *Whosoever* therefore *is born of God cannot sin, because his seed remaineth,* or *is in him;* it is in him as long as he does not himself quench it, for even the Spirit can be quenched; it remains in him, moreover, as long as he himself remains in love.

Those, however, who do not persevere in the faith, are in ordinary cases to be accounted unregenerate and devoid of genuine belief: seeing that God who *keeps us* is faithful, and that he has given believers so many pledges of salvation, namely, election, regeneration, justification, adoption, union and fellowship with him conjointly with Christ and the Spirit, who is the earnest and seal of the covenant: seeing also that the work of glorification is in them already begun. Or perhaps they are to be considered as apostates from the faith, in that sense of faith in which it is the object, not the cause of belief. However this may be, it is our duty to entreat God with constant prayer, in the words of the apostle, 2 Thess. i. 11.

Thus far of the beginnings of glorification. As its perfection is not attainable in the present life, this part of the subject will be reserved for the concluding chapter of the present book.

CHAP. XXVI.—Of the Manifestation of the Covenant of Grace; including the Law of God.

The nature and process of renovation, so far as it is developed in this life, have been considered. We are now to trace its manifestation and exhibition in the covenant of Grace.

The covenant of grace itself, on the part of God, is first declared Gen. iii. 15. "I will put enmity between thee and the woman, and between thy seed and her seed; it shall bruise thy head and thou shalt bruise his heel;" compared with Rom. xvi. 20. "the God of peace shall bruise Satan under your feet shortly." On the part of man its existence may be considered as implied from the earliest period at which it is recorded that mankind worshipped God.

The manifestation of the covenant of grace consists in its exhibition and its ratification. Both existed under the law, and both continue under the gospel.

Even under the law the existence of a Redeemer and the necessity of redemption are perceptible, though obscurely and indistinctly. Heb. ix. 8. "the way into the holiest of all was not yet made manifest, while as the first tabernacle was yet standing;" which was a figure for the time then present, in which were offered both gifts and sacrifices, that could not make him that did the service perfect, as pertaining to the conscience; which stood only in meats and drinks, and divers washings, and carnal ordinances (or righteousness of the flesh), imposed on them until the time of reformation. Under the gospel both the Redeemer and the truth of his redemption are more explicitly understood.

The Law of God is either written or unwritten. The unwritten law is no other than that law of nature given originally to Adam, and of which a certain remnant, or imperfect illumination, still dwells in the hearts of all mankind; which, in the regenerate, under the influence of the Holy Spirit, is daily tending towards a renewal of its primitive brightness. Hence *the law* is often used for heavenly doctrine in the abstract, or the will of God, as declared under both covenants.

The manifestation of this gratuitous covenant under the law was partly anterior to, and partly coincident with, Moses. Even before Moses the law was already in part delivered, although not in a written form. A certain manifestation or shadowing forth of the covenant was exhibited under Moses, first, in the redemption from bondage by the liberation from Egypt under the guidance of Moses; secondly, in the brazen serpent. The symbols of expiation and redemption, both before and under Moses, were the sacrifices and the priests, Melchisedec and Aaron with his posterity.

The Mosaic law was a written code consisting of many precepts, intended for the Israelites alone, with a promise of life to such as should keep them, and a curse on such as should be disobedient; to the end that they, being led thereby to an acknowledgement of the depravity of mankind, and consequently of their own, might have recourse to the righteousness of the promised Saviour; and that they, and in process of time all other nations, might be led under the Gospel from the weak and servile rudiments of this elementary institution to the full strength of the new creature, and a manly liberty worthy the sons of God.

This wall of partition between the Gentiles and Israelites was at length broken down by the death of Christ, Eph. ii. 14. until which time the Gentiles were aliens from the whole of the covenant.

With a promise of life; namely, temporal life, as is obvious from the whole of the twenty-sixth chapter of Leviticus. Though the law, however, does not promise eternal life, this latter seems to be implied in the language of the prophets. To those who are not yet regenerate, the law of nature has the same obligatory force, and is intended to serve the same purposes, as the law of Moses to the Israelites.

The righteousness of the promised Saviour. Hence Christ's invitation, Matt. xi. 28. "come unto me, all ye that labor, and are heavy laden, and I will give you rest," that is, from the curse of the law. Hence also the conflict in the mind of Paul while under the curse of the law, and the thanks which he renders to God for the atonement of Christ; Rom. vii. 24, 25. Thus the imperfection of the law was manifested in the person of Moses himself; for Moses, who was a type of the law, could not bring the children of Israel into the land of Canaan, that is, into eternal rest; but an entrance was given to them under Joshua, or Jesus. Hence Peter testifies that eternal salvation was through Christ alone under the law, equally as under the gospel, although he was not then revealed.

CHAP. XXVII.—OF THE GOSPEL AND CHRISTIAN LIBERTY.

The Gospel is the new dispensation of the covenant of grace, far more excellent and perfect than the law, announced first obscurely by Moses and the prophets, afterwards in the clearest terms by Christ Himself, and his apostles and evangelists, written since by the Holy Spirit in the hearts of believers, and ordained to continue even to the end of the world, containing a promise of eternal life to all in every nation who shall believe in Christ when revealed to them, and a threat of eternal death to such as shall not believe.

The new dispensation. It is called the new testament," Matt. xxvi. 28. But the word διαθήκη, is generally used by the inspired writers for συνθήκη, *covenant,* and is rendered in Latin by the word *pactum,* 2 Cor. iii. 14. Gal. iv. 24. *veteris pacti.* The Gospel is only once called *testament* in a proper sense, and then for a particular reason which is subjoined.

On the introduction of the gospel, or new covenant through faith in Christ, the whole of the preceding covenant, in other words, the entire Mosaic law, was abolished. In Rom. iii. the apostle illustrates our emancipation from the law by the instance of a wife who is loosed from her husband who is dead. v. 7. It is in the decalogue that the injunction here specified is contained; we are therefore absolved from subjection to the decalogue as fully as to the rest of the law. Now not only the ceremonial code, but the whole positive law of Moses, was a law of commandments, and contained in ordinances; nor was it the ceremonial law which formed the sole ground of distinction between the Jews and Gentiles, as Zanchius on this passage contends, but the whole law; seeing that the Gentiles, v. 12, "were aliens from the commonwealth of Israel, and strangers from the covenant of promise," which promise was made to the works of the whole law, not to those of the ceremonial alone; nor was it to these latter only that the enmity between God and us was owing, v. 16.

It is generally replied, that all these passages are to be understood only of the abolition of the ceremonial law. This is refuted, first, by the definition of the law itself, as given in the preceding chapter, in which are specified all the various reasons for its enactment: if therefore, of the causes which led to the enactment of the law considered as a whole, every one is revoked or obsolete, it follows that the whole law itself must be annulled also. The principal reasons then which are given for the enactment of the law are as follows; that it might call forth and develop our natural depravity; that by this means it might work wrath; that it might impress us with a slavish fear through consciousness of divine enmity, and of the handwriting of accusation that was against us; that it might be a schoolmaster to bring us to the righteousness of Christ; and others of a similar description. Now the texts quoted above prove clearly, both that all these causes are now abrogated, and that they have not the least connection with the ceremonial law.

First then, the law is abolished principally on the ground of its being a law of works; that it might give place to the law of grace. Now the law of works was not solely the ceremonial law, but the whole law. Secondly, iv. 15. "the law worketh wrath; for where no law is, there is no transgression." It is not however a part, but the whole of the law that worketh wrath; inasmuch as the transgression is of the whole, and not of a part only. Seeing then that the law worketh wrath, but the gospel grace, and that wrath is incompatible with grace, it is obvious that the law cannot co-exist with the gospel. Thirdly, the law of which it was written, "the man that doeth them shall live in them," Gal. iii. 12. Now to fufil the ceremonial law could not have been a matter of difficulty; it must therefore have been the entire Mosaic law from which Christ delivered us. Again, as it was against those who did not fulfil the whole law that the curse was denounced, it follows that Christ could not have redeemed us from that curse, unless he had abrogated the whole law; if therefore he abrogated the whole, no part of it can be now binding upon us. Fourthly, we are taught, 2 Cor. iii. 7. that the law *written and engraven in stones* was *the ministration of death,* and therefore *was done away.* Now the law engraven in stones was not the ceremonial law, but the decalogue. Fifthly, that which was, as just stated, a law of sin and death, (of sin, because it is provocative to sin; of death, because it produces death, and is in opposition to the law of the spirit of life,) is certainly not the ceremonial law alone, but the whole law. But the law to which the above description applies, is abolished. Sixthly, it was undoubtedly not by the ceremonial law alone that "the motions of sin which were by the law, wrought in our members to bring forth fruit unto death," Rom. vii. 5. But of the law which thus operated it is said that we "are become dead thereto," v. 4. and "that being dead wherein we were held," v. 6. "we are delivered from it," as a wife is free "from the law of her husband who is dead," v. 3. We are therefore "delivered," v. 6. not from the ceremonial law alone, but from the whole law of Moses. Seventhly, all believers, inasmuch as they are justified by God through faith, are undoubtedly to be accounted righteous; but Paul expressly asserts that "the law is not made for a righteous man," 1 Tim. i. 9. If however any law were to be made for the righteous, it must needs be a law which should justify. Now the ceremonial law alone was so far from justifying, that even the entire Mosaic law had not power to effect this, as has been already shown in treating of justification. Therefore it must be the whole law, and not the ceremonial part alone, which is abrogated by reason of its inability in this respect.

To these considerations we may add, that that law which, not only cannot justify, but is the source of trouble and subversion to believers; which even tempts God if we endeavor to perform its requisitions; which has no promise attached to it, or, to speak more properly, which takes away and frustrates all promises, whether of inheritance, or adoption, or grace, or of the Spirit itself; nay, which even subjects us to a curse; must necessarily have been abolished. If then it can be shown that the above effects result, not from the ceremonial law alone, but from the whole law, that is to say, the law of works in a comprehensive sense, it will follow that the whole law is abolished; and that they do so result, I shall proceed to show from the clearest passages of Scripture. Therefore "all things which are written in the law," and not the things of the ceremonial law alone, render us obnoxious to the curse. Christ therefore, when "he redeemed us from the curse," redeemed us also from the causes of the curse, namely, the works of the law, which is the same, from the whole law of works; which, as has been shown above, is not the ceremonial part alone. Even supposing, however, that no such consequences followed, there could be but little inducement to observe the conditions of a law which has not the promise; it would be even ridiculous to attempt to observe that which is of no avail unless it be fulfilled in every part, and which nevertheless it is impossible for man so to fulfil; especially as it has been superseded by the more excellent law of faith, which God in Christ has given us both will and power to fulfil.

It appears therefore as well from the evidence of Scripture as from the arguments above adduced, that the whole of the Mosaic law is abolished by the gospel. It is to be observed, however, that the sum and essence of the law is not hereby abrogated; its purpose being attained in that love of God and our neighbor, which is born of the Spirit through faith. It was with justice therefore that Christ asserted the permanence of the law.

The common objection to this doctrine is anticipated by St. Paul himself, who expressly teaches that by this abrogation of the law, sin, if not taken away, is at least weakened rather than increased in power. Therefore, as was said above, the end for which the law was instituted, namely, the love of God and our neighbor, is by no means to be considered as abolished; it is the tablet of the law, so to speak, that is alone changed, its injunctions being now written by the Spirit in the hearts of believers; with this difference, that in certain precepts the Spirit appears to be at variance with the letter, namely, wherever by departing from the letter we can more effectually consult the love of God and our neighbor. Thus Christ departed from the letter of the law, Mark ii. 27. "the sabbath was made for man, and not man for the sabbath," if we compare his words with the fourth commandment. St. Paul did the same in declaring that a marriage with an unbeliever was not to be dissolved, contrary to the express injunction of the law; 1 Cor. vii. 12. "to the rest speak I, not the Lord." In the interpretation of these two commandments, of the sabbath and marriage, a regard to the law of love is declared to be better than a compliance with the whole written law; a rule which applies equally to every other instance. Matt. xxii. 37-40. "on these two commandments (namely, the love of God and our neighbor), hang all the law and the prophets." Now neither of these is propounded in express terms among the ten commandments, the former occurring for the first time Deut. vi. 5. the latter Lev. xix. 18. and yet these two precepts are represented as comprehending emphatically, not only the ten commandments, but the whole law and the prophets. Hence all rational interpreters have explained the precepts of Christ, in his sermon on the mount, not according to the letter, but in the spirit of the law of love. So also that of St. Paul, 1 Cor. xi. 4. "every man praying or prophesying, having his head covered, dishonoreth his head;" a text which will come under consideration in Book II. chap. iv. on the outward deportment befitting prayer. Hence it is said, Rom. iv. 15. "where no law is, there is no transgression;" that is, no transgression in disregarding the letter of the law, provided that under the direction of the Spirit the end of the institution be attained in the love of God and our neighbor.

On the united authority of so many passages of Scripture, I conceived that I had satisfactorily established the truth in question against the whole body of theologians, who, so far as my knowledge then extended, concurred in denying the abrogation of the entire Mosaic law. I have since, however, discovered, that Zanchius, in his commentary on the second chapter of Ephesians, declares himself of the same opinion, remarking, very justly, that 'no inconsiderable part of divinity depends on the right explanation of this question; and that it is impossible to comprehend the Scriptures properly, especially those parts which relate to justification and good works,' (he might have added, the whole of the New Testament) 'unless the subject of the abrogation of the law be thoroughly understood.' He proves his point with sufficient accuracy, but neglects to follow up his conclusions; losing himself in a multitude of minute exceptions, and apparently fluctuating between the two opinions, so as to leave the reader, if not extremely attentive, in a state of uncertainty. I have also observed that Cameron somewhere expresses the same opinion respecting the abolition of the whole law.

It is asserted, however, by divines in general, who still maintain the tenet of the converted Pharisees, that it is needful for those who are under the gospel to observe the law (a doctrine which in the infancy of the church was productive of much mischief) that the law may be highly useful, in various ways, even to us who are Christians; inasmuch as we are thereby led to a truer conviction of sin, and consequently to a more thankful acceptance of grace; as well as to a more perfect knowledge of the will of God. With regard to the first point, I reply, that I am not speaking of sinners, who stand in need of a preliminary impulse to come to Christ, but of such as are already believers, and consequently in the most intimate union with Christ; as to the second, the will of God is best learnt from the gospel itself under the promised guidance of the Spirit of truth, and from the divine law written in the hearts of believers. Besides, if the law

be the means of leading us to conviction of sin and an acceptance of the grace of Christ, this is effected by a knowledge of the law itself, not by the performance of its works; inasmuch as through the works of the law, instead of drawing nearer to Christ, we depart farther from him; as Scripture is perpetually inculcating.

In the next place, a distinction is made; and Polanus in particular observes, that 'when it is said that we are not under the law, it is not meant that we are not under an obligation to obey it, but that we are exempt from the curse and restraint of the law, as well as from the provocation to sin which results from it.' If this be the case, what advantage do believers reap from the gospel? since even under the law they at least were exempted from the curse and provocation to sin: and since to be free from the restraint of the law can mean nothing but that for which I contend, an entire exemption from the obligation of the law. For as long as the law exists, it constrains, because it is a law of bondage; constraint and bondage being as inseparable from the dispensation of the law, as liberty from the dispensation of the gospel; of which shortly.

Polanus contends, on Gal. iv. 4, 5. "to redeem them that were under the law," that 'when Christians are said to be redeemed from subjection to the law, and to be no longer under the law, this is not to be taken in an absolute sense, as if they owed no more obedience to it. What then do the words imply? They signify, that Christians are no longer under the necessity of perfectly fulfilling the law of God in this life, inasmuch as Christ has fulfilled it for them.' That this is contrary to the truth, is too obvious not to be acknowledged. So far from a less degree of perfection being exacted from Christians, it is expected of them that they should be more perfect than those who were under the law; as the whole tenor of Christ's precepts evinces. The only difference is, that Moses imposed the letter, or external law, even on those who were not willing to receive it; whereas Christ writes the inward law of God by his Spirit on the heart of believers, and leads them as willing followers. Under the law, those who trusted in God were justified by faith indeed, but not without the works of the law. The gospel, on the contrary, justifies by faith without the works of the law. Wherefore, we being freed from the works of the law, no longer follow the letter, but the spirit; doing the works of faith, not of the law. Neither is it said to us, *whatever is not of the law is sin*, but, *whatever is not of faith is sin;* faith consequently, and not the law, is our rule. It follows, therefore, that as faith cannot be made matter of compulsion, so neither can the works of faith.

From the abrogation, through the gospel, of the law of servitude, results Christian liberty; though liberty, strictly speaking, is the peculiar fruit of adoption, and consequently was not unknown during the time of the law, as observed in the twenty-third chapter. Inasmuch, however, as it was not possible for our liberty either to be perfected or made fully manifest till the coming of Christ our deliverer, liberty must be considered as belonging in an especial manner to the gospel, and as consorting therewith; first, because truth is principally known by the gospel. Secondly, because the peculiar gift of the gospel is the Spirit; but "where the Spirit of the Lord is, there is liberty." 2 Cor. iii. 17.

Christian liberty is that whereby *we are loosed as it were by enfranchisement, through Christ our deliverer, from the bondage of sin, and consequently from the rule of the law and of man; to the intent that being made sons instead of servants, and perfect men instead of children, we may serve God in love through the guidance of the Spirit of truth.* Hence we are freed from the yoke of human judgments, much more of civil decrees and penalties in religious matters. If we are forbidden to judge (or condemn) our brethren respecting matters of religion or conscience in common discourse, how much more in a court of law, which has confessedly no jurisdiction here; since St. Paul refers all such matters to the judgment-seat of Christ, not of man? James ii. 12. "so speak ye, and so do, as they that shall be judged by the law of liberty;" namely, by God, not by fallible men in things appertaining to religion; wherein if he will judge us according to the law of liberty, why should man prejudge us according to the law of bondage?

By the guidance of the Spirit of truth in love. Rom. xiv. throughout the whole of the chapter; and chap. xv. 1–15. In these chapters Paul lays down two especial cautions to be observed; first, that whatever we do in pursuance of this our liberty, we should do it in full assurance of faith, nothing doubting that it is permitted us. Secondly, that we should give no just cause of offence to a weak brother. 1 Cor. viii. 13. "if meat make my brother to offend, I will eat no flesh while the world standeth, lest I make my brother to offend;" which resolution, however, must be considered as an effect of the extraordinary love which the apostle bore his brethren, rather than a religious obligation binding on every believer to abstain from flesh for ever, in case a weak brother should think vegetable food alone lawful.

This appears to have been the sole motive for the command given to the churches, Acts xv. 28, 29. "to abstain from blood, and from things strangled;" namely, lest the Jews who were not yet sufficiently established in the faith should take offence. For that the abstinence from blood was purely ceremonial, is evident from the reason assigned Lev. xvii. 11. "the life of the flesh is in the blood, and I have given it to you upon the altar to make an atonement for your souls." Thus the eating of fat was forbidden by the law, yet no one infers from hence that the use of fat is unlawful, this prohibition applying only to the sacrificial times.

No regard, however, is to be paid to the scruples of the malicious or obstinate. Christ was not deterred by the fear of giving offence to the Pharisees from defending the practice of his disciples in eating bread with unwashen hands, and plucking the ears of corn, which it was considered unlawful to do on the sabbath-day. Nor would he have suffered a woman of condition to anoint his feet with precious ointment, and to wipe them with her hair, still less would he have vindicated and praised the action, neither would he have availed himself of the good offices and kindness of the women who ministered unto him whithersoever he went, if it were necessary on all occasions to satisfy the unreasonable scruples of malicious or envious persons. Nay, we must withstand the opinions of the brethren themselves, if they are influenced by motives unworthy of the gospel. Nor cught the weak believer to judge rashly of the liberty of a Christian brother whose faith is stronger than his own, but rather to give himself up to be instructed with the more willingness.

Neither this reason, therefore, nor a pretended consideration for the weaker brethren, afford a sufficient warrant for those edicts of the magistrate which constrain believers, or deprive them in any respect of their religious liberty. For so the apostle argues 1 Cor. ix. 19. "though I be free from all men, yet have I made myself servant unto all;" I was not made so by others, but became so of my own accord; free from all men, and consequently from the magistrate, in these matters at least. When the magistrate takes away this liberty, he takes away the gospel itself; he deprives the good and the bad indiscriminately of their privilege of free judgment, contrary to the spirit of the well known precept, Matt. xiii. 29, 30. "lest while ye gather up the tares ye root up also the wheat with them: let both grow together until the harvest."

CHAP. XXVIII.—OF THE EXTERNAL SEALING OF THE COVENANT OF GRACE.

The manifestation of the covenant of grace, under the law and the gospel respectively, has been considered; we are now to speak of the *sealing of that covenant,* or rather of its representation under certain outward signs.

This representation, like the covenant itself and its manifestation, is common both to the law and the gospel: under the former it consisted in *Circumcision* and the *Passover;* under the latter it consists in *Baptism* and the *Supper of the Lord.* These ceremonies, particularly the two latter, are generally known by the name of *Sacraments.*

A Sacrament is a visible sign ordained by God, whereby he sets his seal on believers in token of his saving grace, or of the satisfaction of Christ; and whereby we on our part testify our faith and obedience to God with a sincere heart and a grateful remembrance.

Respecting *circumcision,* compare Gen. xvii.

10. Sometimes, by a similar figure, it signifies sanctification even under the gospel. Subsequently, however, to the giving of the law circumcision seems to have typified the covenant of works. Rom. iv. 12. Respecting the *passover,* compare Exod. xii. 3. The passover typified the sacrifice of Christ, and the efficacy of the sprinkling of his blood for the salvation of such as celebrated the feast with purity of heart.

Under the gospel, the first of the sacraments commonly so called *is baptism, wherein the bodies of believers who engage themselves to pureness of life, are immersed in running water, to signify their regeneration by the Holy Spirit, and their union with Christ in his death, burial, and resurrection.*

Hence it follows that infants are not to be baptized, inasmuch as they are incompetent to receive instruction, or to believe, or to enter into a covenant, or to promise or answer for themselves, or even to hear the word. For how can infants, who understand not the word, be purified thereby; any more than adults can receive edification by hearing an unknown language? For it is not that outward baptism, which purifies only the filth of the flesh, that saves us, but "the answer of a good conscience," as Peter testifies, of which infants are incapable. Besides, baptism is not merely a covenant, containing a certain stipulation on one side, with a corresponding engagement on the other, which in the case of an infant is impossible; but it is also a vow, and as such can neither be pronounced by infants, nor required of them.

It is remarkable to what futile arguments those divines have recourse, who maintain the contrary opinion. They allege Matt. xix. 14. "suffer little children, and forbid them not to come unto me, for of such is the kingdom of heaven." It appears however that they were not brought to him for the purpose of being baptized. Seeing then that they were neither brought to Christ to be baptized, nor, when received, were actually baptized by him, it is impossible to admit the sophistical inference, that they were properly qualified for baptism; or, which is still more difficult to conceive, that not little children merely, but infants, are so qualified. For if competent to be baptized, they are competent on the same grounds to be partakers of the Lord's Supper.

Let the church therefore receive infants which come unto her, after the example of Christ, with imposition of hands and benediction, but not with baptism. Again, they remind us, that *of such is the kingdom of heaven.* Is this to be understood of all without distinction, or only of such as shall subsequently believe? How perfectly soever God may know them that are his, the church does not know them; what they are in the sight of God is one thing, and what they are by church privilege is another. It must mean, therefore, *of such* in respect of simplicity and innocence; whereas neither simplicity nor innocence, although they may be predicated of little children, can properly be attributed to infants, who have not as yet the faculty of reason; neither does it follow, that because any one is an inheritor of the kingdom of heaven, he is therefore admissible to every religious sacrament; or that, because he is included in the covenant, he has therefore the right of participating in such signs and seals of that covenant as demand the exercise of mature faith and reason. For the thing signified in the Supper of the Lord appertains no less to infants than the thing signified in baptism; and yet infants are not admitted to the former rite, although they were admitted to the passover, which held the same place in the former dispensation as the Lord's Supper in the present. Hence, by the way, we may perceive how weak it is to reason as follows: baptism has succeeded to circumcision; but infants were circumcised, therefore infants are to be baptized: seeing that it is equally certain that the Lord's Supper has succeeded to the passover, notwithstanding which, infants, who were admitted to the latter rite, are not admitted to the former.

They argue, again, that as it is said, "we were all baptized unto Moses in the cloud and in the sea," 1 Cor. x. 2. infants must be included in the general expression. I answer, that "all did eat the same spiritual meat, and did all drink the same spiritual drink," iii. 4. yet that infants are not on this ground admitted to partake of the Lord's Supper.

They lay much stress likewise on Gen. xvii. 7. "I will establish my covenant between me and thee and thy seed after thee . . . in their generations." No one, however, will seriously affirm that this is to be understood of infants,

and not of the adult posterity of Abraham *in their generations,* that is, successively. Otherwise, we must suppose that God intended to give the land also to infants, v. 8. and that infants are commanded to keep the covenant, v. 9. Again, Acts ii. 39. "the promise is unto you and to your children, and to all that are afar off, even as many as the Lord our God shall call." *Your children,* that is, as they understand it, your infants: in other words, God calls those who cannot understand, and addresses those who cannot hear; an interpretation which can only have proceeded from the infancy of reasoning. Had these commentators but read two verses farther, they would have found it expressly stated, *they that gladly received his word were baptized;* whence it appears that understanding and will were necessary qualifications for baptism, neither of which are possessed by infants. So also Acts viii. 37. "if thou believest with all thine heart thou mayest be baptized;" whereas infants, so far from believing with all their heart, are incapable of even the slightest degree of faith. With regard, however, to the text on which they insist so much, *the promise is unto you and to your children,* if they had attended sufficiently to Paul's interpretation of this passage, Rom. ix. 7, 8. they would have understood that the promise was not to all seed indiscriminately, seeing that it was not even to the *seed of Abraham* according to the *flesh,* but only to the *children of God,* that is, to believers, who alone under the gospel *are the children of the promise* and *are counted for the seed.* But none can be considered believers by the church, till they have professed their belief. To those therefore to whom it does not appear that the promise was ever made, the church cannot with propriety give the seal of the promise in baptism.

Again, they allege the analogy between baptism and circumcision, which latter was performed on infants. Coloss. ii. 11. In the first place, there is no other analogy between being *circumcised* and being *buried with him in baptism,* than that which exists among all sacraments by which the same thing is signified, the mode of signification being different. But, secondly, why is it necessary that things which are analogous should coincide in all points? Of circumcision, for instance, women were not partakers; in baptism they are equally included with men, whether as being a more perfect sign, or a symbol of more perfect things. For circumcision, although "a seal of the righteousness of faith," Rom. iv. 11, 12. was such only to Abraham, who being uncircumcised had already believed, and to others who should believe in like manner; not to his posterity, who in after-times were circumcised before they were of an age to exercise faith, and who, consequently, could not believe in the uncircumcision. To them it was a seal in the flesh, indistinctly and obscurely given, of that grace which was at some distant period to be revealed; whereas baptism is a seal of grace already revealed, of the remission of sins, of sanctification; finally, a sign of our death and resurrection with Christ. Circumcision was given under the law and the sacrifices, and bound the individual to the observance of the whole law, which was a service of bondage, and a schoolmaster to bring its followers to Christ; through baptism, on the other hand, we are initiated into the gospel, which is a reasonable, manly, and in the highest sense free service. For under the law men were not merely born, but grew up infants in a spiritual sense; under the gospel, in baptism, we are born men. Hence baptism requires, as from adults, the previous conditions of knowledge and faith; whereas in circumcision all conditions are omitted, as unnecessary in the case of servants, and impracticable in that of infants. Lastly, circumcision was performed not by the priests and Levites, but by the master of a family, Gen. xvii. by the mother, Exod. iv. 26. or by any other person, a surgical operator for instance; whereas baptism, according to our opponents themselves, can only be administered by a teacher of the gospel; and even those who hold a wider opinion on the subject, allow that it can only be performed by a believer, and by one who is neither a new convert, nor unlearned in the faith. To what purpose is this, unless that the person to be baptized may be previously instructed in the doctrines of the gospel? which in the case of an infant is impossible. There is therefore no necessary analogy between circumcision and baptism; and it is our duty not to build our belief on vague parallels, but to attend exclusively to the institution of the sacrament itself, and regard its au-

thority as paramount, according to the frequent admonition of our opponents themselves.

They contend, however, that circumcision was "the seal of the righteousness of faith," Rom. iv. 11, 12. notwithstanding which infants were circumcised, who were incapable of belief. I answered, as above, that it was indeed the seal of the righteousness of faith, but only to Abraham, and to such as after his example believed being yet uncircumcised; and in the case of infants it was a thing of entirely different import, namely, an outward and merely national consecration to the external service of God, and, by implication, to the Mosaic form of worship which was in due time to be ordained.

Lastly it is urged that the apostles baptized whole families, and consequently infants among the rest. The weakness of this argument is clearly shown by Acts viii. 12. "when they believed . . . they were baptized, both men and women," infants not being included. xvi. 31–34. Here the expression *all his house* obviously comprehends only those who believed in his house, not infants; therefore those alone unto whom *they spake the word of the Lord,* and who believed, were baptized. Even the baptism of John, which was but the prelude to that of Christ, is called "the baptism of repentance," and those who came to it "were baptized, confessing their sins," whereas infants are incapable either of repentance or confession. If then infants were not meet for the baptism of John, how can they be meet for the baptism of Christ, which requires knowledge, repentance, and faith, before it can be received?

Immersion. It is in vain alleged by those who, on the authority of Mark vii. 4. Luke xi. 38. have introduced the practice of affusion in baptism instead of immersion, that to dip and to sprinkle mean the same thing; since in washing we do not sprinkle the hands, but immerse them.

Hence it appears that baptism was intended to represent figuratively the painful life of Christ, his death and burial, in which he was immersed, as it were, for a season, Mark x 38.

The baptism of John was essentially the same as the baptism of Christ; but it differed in the form of words used in its administration, and in the comparative remoteness of its efficacy. If it had not been really the same, it would follow that we had not undergone the same baptism as Christ, that our baptism had not been sanctified by the person of Christ, "that Christ had not fulfilled all righteousness," finally, that the apostles would have needed to be rebaptized, which we do not read to have been the case. In some respects, however, there was a difference; for although both baptisms were from God, and both required repentance and faith, these requisites were less clearly propounded in the one case than in the other, and the faith required in the former instance was an imperfect faith, founded on a partial manifestation of Christ; in the latter, it was faith in a fully revealed Saviour. The baptism of Christ was also administered with a more solemn form of words, "in the name of the Father, and of the Son, and of the Holy Ghost," (although it is nowhere said that this form was ever expressly used by the apostles) and attended, as above observed, with a more immediate efficacy; inasmuch as the baptism of John was with water only, except in the single instance of Christ, the design of which exception was not to prove the virtue of John's baptism, but to bear testimony to the Son of God. Hence the apostles did not receive the Holy Ghost till a much later period, and the Ephesians, who had been baptized with the baptism of John, "had not so much as heard whether there was any Holy Ghost," whereas the baptism of Christ, which was with water and the Spirit, conferred the gifts of the Spirit from the very beginning.

It is usually replied, that in the places where the baptism of John is said to be with water only, it is not intended to oppose the baptism of John to baptism with water and the Spirit, but to distinguish between the part which Christ acts in baptism, and that of the mere minister of the rite. If however this were true, the same distinction would be made with respect to other ministers of baptism, the apostles for instance; which is not the case: on the contrary, it is abundantly evident that the apostles baptized both with water and the Holy Spirit.

Considering, therefore, that the baptism of John either did not confer the gifts of the Spirit at all, or not immediately, it would appear to have been rather a kind of initiatory measure, or purification preparatory to receiving the doctrine of the gospel, in conformity with the ancient Hebrew custom that all proselytes should be baptized, than an absolute sealing of the covenant; for this latter is the province of the Spirit alone.

Hence it appears that the baptism of Christ, although not indispensable, might without impropriety be superadded to the baptism of John. I have said, not indispensable, inasmuch as the apostles and many others appear to have rested in the baptism of John; according to which analogy, I should be inclined to conclude, that those persons who have been baptized while yet infants, and perhaps in other respects irregularly, have no need of second baptism when arrived at maturity: indeed, I should be disposed to consider baptism itself as necessary for proselytes alone, and not for those born in the church, had not the apostle taught that baptism is not merely an initiatory rite, but a figurative representation of our death, burial and resurrection with Christ. Previously to the promulgation of the Mosaic law, Noah's ark was the type of baptism: 1 Pet. iii. 20, 21. Under the law it was typified by the cloud.

The *Lord's Supper* is a solemnity in which the death of Christ is commemorated by the breaking of bread and pouring out of wine, both of which elements are tasted by each individual communicant, and the benefits of his death thereby sealed to believers. It is true that John vi. does not relate exclusively to the Lord's Supper, but to the participation in general, through faith, of any of the benefits of Christ's incarnation: for what is called so repeatedly, "eating the flesh of Christ" and "drinking his blood," is described as "coming to Christ" and "believing in him;" in the same manner as the phrase, "that living water, of which whosoever drinketh he shall never thirst," cannot be referred in a primary sense either to baptism, or to the Lord's Supper, but must be considered as an expression purely metaphorical. Nevertheless, the words of Christ to his disciples in this chapter throw a strong light, by anticipation, on the nature of the sacrament which was to be so shortly afterwards instituted (for "the passover was nigh"). They teach us, by an obvious inference, that *flesh,* or the mere bodily food received, has no more spiritual efficacy in the sacrament than it had in the miracle of the loaves there recorded; and that the flesh which he verily and indeed gives is not that which can be eaten with the teeth, and by any one indiscriminately, but the food of faith alone; a heavenly and spiritual bread, *which came down from heaven,* not earthly, (as it must be, if we suppose that what he gave on that occasion was his literal flesh born of the Virgin) but heavenly in a higher sense than manna itself, and of which "he that eateth shall live for ever." Were it, as the Papists hold, his literal flesh, and eaten by all in the Mass, the consequence would be that the very worst of the communicants (to say nothing of the mice and worms by which the eucharist is occasionally devoured) would through the virtue of this heavenly bread attain eternal life. That *living bread* therefore which Christ calls *his flesh,* and that *blood* which is *drink indeed,* can be nothing but the doctrine of Christ's having become man in order to shed his blood for us; a doctrine which whosoever receives by faith shall as surely attain eternal life, as the partaking of meats and drinks supports our brief term of bodily existence: nay, more surely; for thus, as above quoted, *Christ dwells in us, and we in him;* whereas the food which is received into the body does not dwell there, being carried off partly by natural transpiration, and partly in other ways, as soon as the process of digestion is completed.

This solemnity is called by St. Paul "the Lord's Supper," 1 Cor. xi. 20. and its original institution by Christ, together with an explanation of the rite, is given v. 23–30. Under the law, the Lord's Supper was typified by the manna, and the water flowing from the rock. 1 Cor. x. 3, 4. If they under a carnal covenant partook spiritually of the body of Christ, surely we do not partake of it carnally under a spiritual covenant.

I have quoted the above passages at length, inasmuch as in them is comprised the whole Scripture doctrine relative to the Lord's Supper. Whosoever interprets these with true Christian simplicity of heart according to their plain and obvious meaning, will be at a loss to account for the numberless absurd speculations on this subject, by which the peace of the church has been destroyed, and which have well nigh converted the Supper of the Lord into a banquet of cannibals.

Consubstantiation, and above all the papistical doctrine of transubstantiation (or rather anthropophagy, for it deserves no better name) are irreconcileable, not only with reason and common sense, and the habits of mankind, but with the testimony of Scripture, with the nature and end of a sacrament, with the analogy of baptism, with the ordinary forms of language, with the human nature of Christ, and finally with the state of glory in which he is to remain till the day of judgment.

In speaking of sacraments, as of most other subjects between whose parts an analogy exists, a figure is frequently employed, by which whatever illustrates or signifies any particular thing is used to denote, not what it is in itself, but what it illustrates or signifies. In sacraments, on account of the peculiarly close relation between the sign and the thing signified, this kind of identification is not uncommon; an inattention to which peculiarity has been, and continues to be, a source of error to numbers. Thus circumcision is called "a covenant," Gen. xvii. 10. and "a token of the covenant," v. 11. Again, a lamb is called "the passover," Exod. xii. 11. which text is defended against the exceptions of objectors by the similar passages, Luke xxii. 7. The object of the sacred writers, in thus expressing themselves, was probably to denote the close affinity between the sign and the thing signified, as well as, by a bold metaphor, to intimate the certainty with which the seal is thus set to spiritual blessings; the same form of speech being used in other instances, where the certainty of a thing is to be emphatically expressed.

Lastly, since every sacrament is, by its very definition, a seal of the covenant of grace, it is evident that the Papists err, when they attribute to the outward sign the power of bestowing salvation or grace by virtue of the mere *opus operatum;* seeing that sacraments can neither impart salvation nor grace of themselves; but are given as a pledge or symbol to believers of the actual blessings.

Hence it follows, that sacraments are not absolutely indispensable: first, because many have been saved without partaking of them; thus circumcision was dispensed with in the case of women, baptism in that of the thief on the cross, and doubtless of many infants and catechumens. Thus also many have obtained the gifts of the Spirit through the word and faith alone. Nor was John himself, the first who administered the rite, baptized, although he testified that he also had need of baptism. The same was not improbably the case with Apollos, inasmuch as he does not appear to have left his native city of Alexandria for Ephesus till long after the death of John; nor can it be inferred with certainty, from its being said of him that he *knew only the baptism of John,* that he had actually undergone the ceremony. Yet, as far as appears, Aquila and Priscilla considered a more thorough initiation in the gospel all that was wanting to him, without requiring that he should be baptized. Secondly, the seal does not constitute the covenant, but is only an evidence of it; whence Abraham, after that he had already believed and was justified, received circumcision as the seal of his righteousness. When therefore it is said John iii. 5. "except a man be born of water and of the Spirit, he cannot enter into the kingdom of God," this must be understood in a conditional sense, assuming that a fit opportunity has been offered, and that it has not been lost through neglect. When therefore the necessity of the sacraments is under discussion, it may in like manner be urged, that it is the Spirit which quickens, and that it is faith which feeds upon the body of Christ; that on the other hand the outward feeding of the body, as it cannot always take place conveniently, so neither is it absolutely necessary. Assuredly, if a sacrament be nothing more than what it is defined to be, a seal, or rather a visible representation of God's benefits to us, he cannot be wrong, who reposes the same faith in God's promises without this confirmation as with it, in cases where it is not possible for him to receive it duly and conveniently; especially as so many opportunities are open to him through life of evincing his gratitude to God, and commemorating the death of Christ, though not in the precise mode and form which God has instituted.

We nowhere read in Scripture of the Lord's Supper being distributed to the first Christians by an appointed minister; we are only told that they partook of it in common, and that frequently, and in private houses. I know no reason therefore why ministers refuse to permit the celebration of the Lord's Supper, except where they themselves are allowed to administer it; for if it be alleged that Christ gave the bread and wine to his disciples, it may be replied first, that we nowhere read of his giving them to each individually, and secondly, that he was then acting in the character, not of a minister, but of the founder of a new institution. With regard to the expression in 1 Cor. iv. 1. "let a man so account of us, as of the ministers of Christ, and stewards of the mysteries of God," it is evident that Paul is there speaking of himself and the other ministers of his own order, who were the exclusive stewards of the divine mysteries, that is, of the doctrine of the Gospel, before hidden, but then first revealed from God; not of bread and wine, for they did not "serve tables," Acts vi. 2. not even those at which we may suppose them to have met constantly for the celebration of the sacrament; in like manner as Paul himself was not sent "to baptize, but to preach the Gospel," 1 Cor. i. 17. That the *mysteries* in question are to be understood of doctrine, is evident from the verse following, "it is required in stewards that a man be found faithful;" for it would be derogating from the dignity of such a steward as Paul to consider faithfulness in administering bread and wine (which are mere elements, and not mysteries) as of sufficient importance to be specified in his case among the requisite qualifications for the office. So also chap. x. 16, 17. the cup of blessing and the breaking of bread is spoken of as common to all, who are qualified to participate in the communion itself. For Christ is the sole priest of the new covenant.

Even were it otherwise, however, it is not conceivable that there should be any such essential distinction between the passover and the Lord's Supper, that whereas under the law, when it was forbidden to all but the priests and Levites even to touch the sacred things, there was no ordinance restricting the celebration of the passover to the members of that body, under the gospel, by which these ceremonial sanctities have been abolished, and a wider scope given to the rights and liberties of believers, the dispensing of the elements, which in Scripture is committed to no one in particular, should be considered as an unfit office for any but the ministers of the church; so that the master of a family, or any one appointed by him, is not at liberty to celebrate the Lord's Supper from house to house, as was done in the dispensation of the passover; if indeed we are to suppose that any distribution of the elements by an individual officiator was then, or is now, requisite.

The sacraments are not to be approached without self-examination and renunciation of sin. The neglect, or the improper celebration of the sacraments, equally provokes the indignation of the Deity. Hence it is not only allowable, but necessary to defer partaking in them, till such time as a proper place and season, purity of heart and life, and a regular communion of believers, concur to warrant their celebration.

The Mass of the Papists differs from the Lord's Supper in several respects. In the first place, the one is an ordinance of our Lord, the other an institution of the Pope. Secondly, the Lord's Supper is celebrated in remembrance of Christ once offered, which offering he himself made by virtue of his own peculiar priesthood, whereas in the Mass the offering itself is supposed to be repeated daily, and that by innumerable petty priests at the same point of time. Thirdly, Christ offered himself, not at the holy Supper, but on the cross; whereas it is in the Mass that the pretended daily sacrifice takes place. Fourthly, in the Lord's Supper, the real body of the living Lord, made of the Virgin Mary, was personally present; in the Mass, by the mere muttering of the four mystical words, *this is my body*, it is supposed to be created out of the substance of the bread at some given moment, for the sole purpose of being broken in pieces as soon as created. Fifthly, in the Lord's Supper the bread and wine, after consecration, remain unchanged in substance as in name; in the Mass, if we believe the Papists, although the outward appearance remains the same, they are converted by a sudden metamorphosis into the body of our Lord. Sixthly, in the Lord's Supper, according to the original institution, all the communicants drink of the cup; in the Mass, the cup is refused to the laity. Lastly, in the Mass the sacred body of Christ, after having completed

its appointed course of hardship and suffering, is dragged back from its state of exaltation at the right hand of the Father to a condition even more wretched and degrading than before; it is again exposed to be broken, and crushed, and bruised by the teeth not only of men, but of brutes; till, having passed through the whole process of digestion, it is cast out at length into the draught; a profanation too horrible to be even alluded to without shuddering.

It is manifest from the very definition of the word, that the other sacraments so called by the Papists, namely, *confirmation, penance, extreme unction, orders,* and *marriage,* cannot be such in the proper sense of the term; inasmuch as they are not of divine institution, neither do they possess any sign appointed by God for the sealing of the covenant of grace.

Confirmation or *imposition of hands* was, it is true, administered by Christ, not however as a sacrament, but as a form of blessing, according to a common Jewish custom, derived probably from patriarchal times, when fathers were accustomed to lay their hands on their children in blessing them, and magistrates on those whom they appointed their successors, as Moses on Joshua, Numb. xxvii. 18. Hence the apostles usually laid hands on such as were baptized, or chosen to any ecclesiastical office; usually, I say, not always: for, although we read of imposition of hands on the seven deacons, Acts vi. 6. we do not find that this ceremony was practised towards Matthias, when he was numbered with the eleven apostles, Acts i. 26. In the case of the baptized, imposition of hands conferred, not indeed saving grace, but miraculous powers, and the extraordinary gifts of the Spirit. Hence, although the church rejects this ceremony as a sacrament, she retains it with great propriety and advantage as a symbol of blessing.

With respect to *orders,* and to the act of *penance* for sins committed subsequently to baptism (for to this penance alone the Papists apply the name of a sacrament) we have no objection to their being called sacraments, in the sense of religious emblems, or symbols of things sacred, analogous to the ancient custom of washing the feet of the poor, and the like. It is unnecessary to be very scrupulous

as to the sense of a word which nowhere occurs in Scripture. Penance however has no
peculiar sign attached to it, neither is it a
seal of the covenant, any more than faith.

With regard to *marriage,* inasmuch as it is
not an institution peculiar to Christian nations, but common to them all by the universal law of mankind, (unless it be meant to
restrict the word to the union of believers
properly so called,) it is not even a religious
ceremony, still less a sacrament, but a compact purely civil; nor does its celebration belong in any manner to the ministers of the
church.

As to the *unction of the sick,* it is true that
the apostles "anointed with oil many that
were sick, and healed them," Mark vi. 13.
and St. James enjoins the same custom, v.
14, 15. This rite, however, was not of the nature of a sacrament; and as it was employed
solely in conjunction with miraculous powers,
with the cessation of those powers its use
must have also ceased. There is therefore no
analogy between the anointing of the first
Christians, and the extreme unction of the
Papists in modern times; seeing that, in the
first place, the apostles anointed not only
those who were at the point of death, as is
now the custom, but all, as many as were
grievously sick; and that secondly, this unction was attended with the cure of their disorder.

To the above may be added, that sacraments, being instituted chiefly for purposes
in which all are concerned, namely, as tokens
of the sealing of the covenant of grace, and
for the confirmation of our faith, ought to be
imparted equally to all believers; whereas of
the five papistical sacraments above mentioned, four are exclusively appropriated to
particular classes of individuals; penance to
the lapsed, orders to the clergy, extreme unction to the sick, marriage to the lay members
of the church alone.

CHAP. XXIX.—OF THE VISIBLE CHURCH.

WE have hitherto treated of the vocation of
man, and of the effects thereby produced,
whether consisting in a mere outward change

of character, or in actual regeneration; of the
spiritual increase of the regenerate; of the
various manifestations of the offered covenant; and, finally, of the sealing of that
covenant by sacraments.

The assembly of those who are called is
termed the *visible Church.* By the *called,* I
mean those indiscriminately who have received the call, whether actually regenerate
or otherwise.

The tokens of the visible church are, pure
doctrine; the proper external worship of God;
genuine evangelical love, so far as it can be
distinguished from the fictitious by mere human perception; and a right administration
of the seals of the covenant.

As to what are called signs, Mark xvi. 17,
18. these are not to be considered as tokens
uniformly attending the visible church, but
as testimonies which, however necessary at
the time of its first establishment, when the
doctrines of Christianity were to Jews and
Gentiles alike, new, unheard of, and all but
incredible, are less requisite at the present
period, when men are educated in the apostolic faith, and begin their belief from their
earliest childhood. Under these circumstances,
the same end is answered by their hearing
and reading of the miracles performed at the
beginning by Christ and his apostles. The
working of miracles was sometimes permitted
even to impostors, and to a false church.

Neither is the re-establishment of the
church uniformly attended by miracles; in
like manner as this species of attestation was
not granted to several of the prophets, nor
to the Baptist, John x. 41. nor in all cases to
the apostles themselves, 2 Tim. iv. 20. "Tro-
phimus have I left at Miletum sick:" whence
it appears that Paul was unable to heal, not
only one who was a believer, but of note
among the believers. Miracles have no inherent efficacy in producing belief, any more
than simple preaching; it is God that gives
the right heart in the one case as in the other.
Those also are declared blessed who believe
without the testimony of miracles. So long
therefore as charity, the greatest of all gifts,
exists, and wheresoever it is found, we cannot doubt that the visible church there established is a true church. As Christ is the
head of the mystical church, so no one besides Christ has the right or power of presid-

ing over the visible church. They are therefore in error, who would set up an earthly head over the church in the person of the apostle Peter, and his successors commonly so called the Roman pontiffs; for which no authority can be found in Scripture. As to Peter, it does not appear that any preference was given to him over the other apostles, either with regard to his mission, or to any special command assigned to him, or to any authority reposed in him for the deciding of controversies, or to his knowledge of the faith, at least to his constancy in professing it, since he fell grievously in his denial of Christ, and was afterwards reprehensible, though in a less degree, in the matter for which he was reproved by Paul. He was *also an elder* like the others, neither is he promised any distinction of honors hereafter, nor is superiority of any kind attributed to him rather than to James, or John, or Paul and Barnabas. Nay, he was the apostle of the circumcision only, as was Paul of the Gentiles, who was "not a whit behind the very chiefest apostles." He was likewise sent as the colleague of John into Samaria, and gave an account of his apostleship to those who contended with him. Lastly, the church is not said to be *built upon the foundation* of Peter alone, but *of the apostles.* Even supposing, however, that it were otherwise, how can a *foundation* have any succession? Nor does the celebrated text, Matt. xvi. 18, 19, which is perverted by the Pope to form the charter of his authority, confer any distinction on Peter beyond what is enjoyed by other professors of the same faith. For inasmuch as many others confessed no less explicitly than Peter that Christ was the Son of God (as is clear from the narrative of the evangelists), the answer of Christ is not, *upon thee Peter,* but *upon this rock I will build my church,* that is, upon this faith which thou hast in common with other believers, not upon thee as an individual; seeing that, in the personal sense of the word, the true rock is Christ, nor is there any other foundation, whence also faith in Christ is called the foundation. And the same term is applied to the apostles as the original teachers of that faith, though not to the exclusion of others. Nor is it to Peter exclusively that the keys of the kingdom of heaven are committed, inasmuch as

the power of the keys, as it is called, or the right of binding and loosing, is not entrusted to him alone. Nor does the passage of St. John, xx. 15, imply that the office of feeding the flock of Christ was committed to Peter in any higher sense than to the others; the meaning of the repetition is, that he who had fallen by denying his master thrice, is here, by a confession as often repeated, restored to the place from whence he fell; and that he who in his overweening self-confidence had maintained that he loved Christ more than all the rest, is at once reminded of the event by which his weakness had been manifested, and admonished that if he really loved Christ more than the other disciples, he should show his love by a greater assiduity in feeding Christ's flock, and more particularly his lambs; being in effect a repetition of the charge he had shortly before received. For to feed the sheep of Christ, that is to teach all nations, was the common office of all the apostles. Granting, however, to Peter all that is claimed for him, what proof have we that the same privileges are continued to his successors? or that these successors are the Roman pontiffs?

The visible church is either universal or particular. The universal visible church is the whole multitude of those who are called in every part of the world, and who openly worship God the Father through Christ in any place whatever, either individually, or in conjunction with others.

Either individually, for although it is the duty of believers to join themselves, if possible, to a church duly constituted, yet such as cannot do this conveniently, or with full satisfaction of conscience, are not to be considered as excluded from the blessing bestowed by God on the churches.

The universal church consists of *ministers and people. Ministers are persons appointed by divine commission to perform various offices in the church of Christ.* Ministerial labors are of no efficacy in themselves, independently of divine grace. A reward, however, is laid up for such as are faithful in the ministry.

The ministers of the universal church are either *extraordinary or ordinary.* Eph. iv. 11—13. where it is observable that pastors and teachers are used synonymously; for the apostle does not say, *he gave some, pastors, some, teachers,* but merely adds the second or proper title as an explanation of the figurative term; whereby is evinced the futility of the modern academical title of doctor, as distinguishing its possessor from other ministers of the word. For the provinces of teaching and of exhortation are nowhere separated, but are both alike assigned to the pastor, no less than to the teacher so called; the functions are two- fold, but the office and the agent are one; although individuals may possess peculiar powers either of teaching or of exhortation, and may be distinguished as such.

Extraordinary ministers are persons inspired and sent on a special mission by God, for the purpose of planting the church where it did not before exist, or of reforming its corruptions, either through the medium of preaching or of writing. To this class belong the prophets, apostles, evangelists and the like.

Any believer is competent to act as an *ordinary minister,* according as convenience may require, supposing him to be endowed with the necessary gifts; these gifts constituting his mission. Such were, before the law, the fathers or eldest sons of families, as Abel, Noah, Abraham, &c. Such were, under the law, Aaron and his posterity, the whole tribe of Levi, and lastly the prophets. In like manner, any one appearing to be in other respects qualified, was allowed to teach openly in the synagogue, though he were neither priest nor Levite; a permission which was granted to Christ, and subsequently to Paul at Antioch. How much more then must every believer endowed with similar gifts enjoy the same liberty under the gospel? Accordingly, this liberty is expressly conceded. If our modern clergy, as they are called by way of distinction, who claim to themselves the exclusive right of preaching the gospel, had seen this grace imparted to those whom they are pleased to denominate the laity, it would have been to them a subject, not of rejoicing, but of censure and obloquy. Again 1 Pet. v. 3. "neither as being lords over God's heritage." If in this passage the word *heritage* (*clerus,* Lat. whence the term clergy, appropriated by the ecclesiastics to themselves) has any meaning at all, it must designate the whole body of the church. Nor is the name of prophet applied exclusively to such as foretell future events, but to any one endowed with extraordinary piety and wisdom for the purposes of teaching. Thus it was said of Abraham. So also Miriam is called a prophetess. Hence under the gospel likewise, the simple gift of teaching, especially of gospel teaching, is called *prophecy.* Pastors and teachers, therefore, are the gift of the same God who gave apostles and prophets, and not of any human institution whatever.

If therefore it be competent to any believer whatever to preach the gospel, provided he be furnished with the requisite gifts, it is also competent to him to administer the rite of baptism; inasmuch as the latter office is inferior to the former. Hence Ananias, who was only a disciple, baptized Paul. And if it be true that baptism has succeeded to the place of circumcision, and bears the analogy to it which is commonly supposed, why should not any Christian whatever (provided he be not a mere novice, and therefore otherwise incompetent) be qualified to administer baptism, in the same manner as any Jew was qualified to perform the rite of circumcision?

With regard to the Lord's Supper also, it has been shown in the preceding chapter that all are entitled to participate in that rite, but the privilege of dispensing the elements is confined to no particular man, or order of men. There can be still less shadow of reason for assigning to the ministers of the church the celebration of marriages or funerals, offices which hirelings were wont to assume to themselves exclusively, without even the feeble semblance of prescription derived from the Levitical law.

The people of the universal church comprise *all nations;* Matt. xxviii. 19, 20. "go ye and teach all nations;" whose conversion it is the duty of all men to promote to the utmost of their power.

CHAP. XXX.—OF THE HOLY SCRIPTURES.

THE writings of the prophets, apostles and evangelists, composed under divine inspiration, are called *The Holy Scriptures.*

With regard to the question, what books of the Old and New Testament are to be considered as *canonical,* that is to say, as the genuine writings of the prophets, apostles, and evangelists, there is little or no difference of opinion among the orthodox, as may be seen in the common editions of the Bible.

The books usually subjoined to these under the name of *apocryphal,* are by no means of equal authority with the canonical, neither can they be adduced as evidence in matters of faith.

The reasons for their rejection are, first, because, although written under the old dispensation, they are not in the Hebrew language, which they would undoubtedly be if genuine; for as the Gentiles were not then called, and the church consisted wholly of Hebrews, it would have been preposterous to write in the language of a people who had no concern in the things discoursed of. Secondly, their authority is deservedly called in question, inasmuch as they are never quoted in the New Testament. Lastly, they contain much that is at variance with the acknowledged parts of Scripture, besides some things fabulous, low, trifling, and contrary to true religion and wisdom.

The Holy Scriptures were not written for occasional purposes only, as is the doctrine of the Papists, but for the use of the church throughout all ages, as well under the gospel as under the law. Almost everything advanced in the New Testament is proved by citations from the Old. The use of the New Testament writings themselves is declared John xx. 31. "these are written that ye might believe—." It is true that the Scriptures which Timothy is said to have *known from a child,* and which were of themselves *able to make him wise unto salvation through faith in Christ,* were probably those of the Old Testament alone, since no part of the New Testament appears to have existed during the infancy of Timothy; the same is, however, predicated of the whole of Scripture in the succeeding verse, namely, that it is *profitable for doctrine;* even to such as are already wise and learned.

From all these passages it is evident, that the use of the Scriptures is prohibited to no one; but that, on the contrary, they are adapted for the daily hearing or reading of all classes and orders of men; of princes, of magistrates, of men of all descriptions, and for the whole people. To the same purpose may be adduced the testimony of a writer whom the opponents of this opinion regard as canonical. 1 Macc. i. 56, 57. The New Testament is still more explicit. Luke x. 26. "what is written in the law? how readest thou?" This was the question of Christ to one of the interpreters of the law, of whom there were many at that time, Pharisees and others, confessedly neither priests nor Levites; neither was expounding in the synagogue forbidden to Christ himself, whom we cannot suppose to have been considered as particularly learned in the law; much less therefore could it have been unlawful to read the Scriptures at home.

The Scriptures, therefore, partly by reason of their own simplicity, and partly through the divine illumination, are plain and perspicuous in all things necessary to salvation, and adapted to the instruction even of the most unlearned, through the medium of diligent and constant reading. Whence it follows that the liberty of investigating Scripture thoroughly is granted to all. Neither therefore is it to be interpreted by the judgment of man, that is, by our own unassisted judgment, but by means of that Holy Spirit promised to all believers. Hence the gift of prophecy, mentioned 1 Cor. i. 4.

If then the Scriptures be in themselves so perspicuous, and sufficient of themselves to *make men wise unto salvation through faith,* that *the man of God may be perfect, thoroughly furnished unto all good works,* through what infatuation is it, that even Protestant divines persist in darkening the most momentous truths of religion by intricate metaphysical comments, on the plea that such explanation is necessary; stringing together all the useless technicalities and empty distinctions of scholastic barbarism, for the purpose of elucidating those Scriptures, which they are continually extolling as models of plainness? As if Scripture, which possesses in itself the clearest light, and is sufficient for its own explanation, especially in matters of faith and holiness, required to have the simplicity of its divine truths more fully developed, and placed in a more distinct view, by illustrations drawn from the abstrusest of human sciences, falsely so called.

It is only to those who perish that the

Scriptures are obscure, especially in things necessary for salvation. No passage of Scripture is to be interpreted in more than one sense; in the Old Testament, however, this sense is sometimes a compound of the historical and typical. The custom of interpreting Scripture in the church is mentioned Nehem. viii. 8, 9.

The requisites for the public interpretation of Scripture have been laid down by divines with much attention to usefulness, although they have not been observed with equal fidelity. They consist in knowledge of languages; inspection of the originals; examination of the context; care in distinguishing between literal and figurative expressions; consideration of cause and circumstance, of antecedents and consequences; mutual comparison of texts; and regard to the analogy of faith. Attention must also be paid to the frequent anomalies of syntax; as for example, where the relative does not refer to the immediate antecedent, but to the principal word in the sentence, though more remote. Lastly, no inferences from the text are to be admitted, but such as follow necessarily and plainly from the words themselves; lest we should be constrained to receive what is not written for what is written, the shadow for the substance, the fallacies of human reasoning for the doctrines of God: for it is by the declarations of Scripture, and not by the conclusions of the schools, that our consciences are bound.

Every believer has a right to interpret the Scriptures for himself, inasmuch as he has the Spirit for his guide, and the mind of Christ is in him; nay, the expositions of the public interpreter can be of no use to him, except so far as they are confirmed by his own conscience. More will be added on this subject in the next chapter, which treats of the members of particular churches. The right of public interpretation for the benefit of others is possessed by all whom God has appointed apostles, or prophets, or evangelists, or pastors, or teachers, that is, by all who are endowed with the gift of teaching, "every scribe which is instructed unto the kingdom of heaven," Matt. xiii. 52. not by those whose sole commission is derived from human authority, or academical appointment; of whom it may too often be said in the words of Scripture, "woe unto you, lawyers, for ye have taken away the key of knowledge; ye enter not yourselves, and them that were entering in ye hindered," Luke xi. 52.

It is not therefore within the province of any visible church, much less of the civil magistrate, to impose their own interpretations on us as laws, or as binding on the conscience; in other words, as matter of implicit faith. If however there be any difference among professed believers as to the sense of Scripture, it is their duty to tolerate such difference in each other, until God shall have revealed the truth to all.

The rule and canon of faith, therefore, is Scripture alone. Scripture is the sole judge of controversies; or rather, every man is to decide for himself through its aid, under the guidance of the Spirit of God. For they who, on the authority of 1 Tim. iii. 15. "the church of the living God, the pillar and ground of the truth," claim for the visible church, however defined, the supreme right of interpreting Scripture and determining religious controversies, are confuted by the comparison of the words in question with the former part of the verse, and with the preceding verses. What St. Paul here writes to Timothy, and which is intended to have the force of Scripture with him, is a direction by which he may know *how he ought to behave himself in the house of God, which is the church;* that is, in any assembly of believers. It was not therefore *the house of God,* or *the Church,* which was to be a rule to him *that he might know,* but the Scripture which he had received from the hands of Paul. The church indeed is, or rather ought to be, (for it is not always such in fact) the *pillar and ground,* that is, the guardian, and repository, and support *of the truth;* even where it is all this, however, it is not on that account to be considered as the rule or arbiter of truth and the Scripture; inasmuch as the house of God is not a rule to itself, but receives its rule from the word of God, which it is bound, at least, to observe scrupulously. Besides, the writings of the prophets and the apostles, in other words the Scriptures themselves, are said to be the foundation of the church. Now the church cannot be the rule or arbiter of that on which it is itself founded.

That some of the instructions of the apostles to the churches were not committed to writing, or that, if written, they have not come down to us, seems probable from 2 John 12. "having many things to write unto you, I would not write with paper and ink." Seeing then that the lost particulars cannot be supposed to have contained anything necessary to salvation, but only matters profitable for doctrine, they are either to be collected from other passages of Scripture, or, if it be doubtful whether this is possible, they are to be supplied, not by the decrees of popes or councils, much less by the edicts of magistrates, but by the same Spirit which originally dictated them, enlightening us inwardly through the medium of faith and love.

Under the gospel we possess, as it were, a two-fold Scripture; one external, which is the written word, and the other internal, which is the Holy Spirit, written in the hearts of believers, according to the promise of God, and with the intent that it should by no means be neglected; as was shown above, chap. xxvii. on the gospel. Hence, although the external ground which we possess for our belief at the present day in the written word is highly important, and, in most instances at least, prior in point of reception, that which is internal, and the peculiar possession of each believer, is far superior to all, namely, the Spirit itself. For the external Scripture, or written word, particularly of the New Testament (to say nothing of the spurious books, with regard to which the apostle has long since cautioned us,) the written word, I say, of the New Testament, has been liable to frequent corruption, and in some instances has been corrupted, through the number, and occasionally the bad faith of those by whom it has been handed down, the variety and discrepancy of the original manuscripts, and the additional diversity produced by subsequent transcripts and printed editions. But the Spirit which leads to truth cannot be corrupted, neither is it easy to deceive a man who is really spiritual. An instance of a corrupted text pervading nearly all the manuscripts occurs in Matt. xxvii. 9. where a quotation is attributed to Jeremiah, which belongs only to Zechariah; and similar instances are to be found in almost every page of Erasmus, Beza, and other editors of the New Testament.

Previously to the Babylonish captivity,

the law of Moses was preserved in the sacred repository of the ark of the covenant; after that event, it was committed to the trust and guardianship of the priests and prophets, as Ezra, Zechariah, Malachi, and other men taught of God. There can be no doubt that these handed down the sacred volumes in an uncorrupted state to be preserved in the temple by the priests their successors, who were in all ages most scrupulous in preventing alterations, and who had themselves no grounds of suspicion to induce them to make any change. With regard to the remaining books, particularly the historical, although it be uncertain by whom and at what time they were written, and although they appear sometimes to contradict themselves on points of chronology, few or none have ever questioned the integrity of their doctrinal parts. The New Testament, on the contrary, has come down to us (as before observed) through the hands of a multitude of persons, subject to various temptations; nor have we in any instance the original copy in the author's handwriting, by which to correct the errors of the others. Hence Erasmus, Beza, and other learned men, have edited from the different manuscripts what in their judgment appeared most likely to be the authentic readings. It is difficult to conjecture the purpose of Providence in committing the writings of the New Testament to such uncertain and variable guardianship, unless it were to teach us by this very circumstance that the Spirit which is given to us is a more certain guide than Scripture, whom therefore it is our duty to follow.

For with regard to the visible church, which is also proposed as a criterion of faith, it is evident that, since the ascension of Christ, the *pillar and ground of the truth* has not uniformly been the church, but the hearts of believers, which are properly "the house and church of the living God." Certain it is, that the editors and interpreters of the New Testament (which is the chief authority for our faith) are accustomed to judge of the integrity of the text, not by its agreement with the visible church, but by the number and integrity of the manuscripts. Hence, where the manuscripts differ, the editors must necessarily be at a loss what to consider as the genuine word of God; as in the story of the woman taken in adultery, and some other passages.

The process of our belief in the Scriptures is, however, as follows: we set out with a general belief in their authenticity, founded on the testimony either of the visible church, or of the existing manuscripts; afterwards, by an inverse process, the authority of the church itself, and of the different books as contained in the manuscripts, is confirmed by the internal evidence implied in the uniform tenor of Scripture, considered as a whole; and, lastly, the truth of the entire volume is established by the inward persuasion of the Spirit working in the hearts of individual believers. So the belief of the Samaritans in Christ, though founded in the first instance on the word of the woman, derived its permanent establishment, less from her saying, than from the presence and discourses of Christ himself, John iv. 42. Thus, even on the authority of Scripture itself, everything is to be finally referred to the Spirit and the unwritten word.

Hence it follows, that when an acquiescence in human opinions or an obedience to human authority in matters of religion is exacted, in the name either of the church or of the Christian magistrate, from those who are themselves led individually by the Spirit of God, this is in effect to impose a yoke, not on man, but on the Holy Spirit itself. Certainly, if the apostles themselves, in a council governed by the inspiration of the Holy Spirit, determined that even the divinely instituted law was a yoke from which believers ought to be exempt, much less is any modern church, which cannot allege a similar claim to the presence of the Spirit, and least of all is the magistrate entitled to impose on believers a creed nowhere found in Scripture, or which is merely inferred from thence by human reasons, carrying with them no certain conviction.

We are expressly forbidden to pay any regard to human traditions, whether written or unwritten. Neither can we trust implicitly in matters of this nature to the opinions of our forefathers, or of antiquity. Jeremiah admonishes the people *to ask for the old paths,* in order to see *where is the good way,* and to choose that alone, for in any other sense the argument may be as justly employed to defend the idolatries of the heathen, and the errors of the Pharisees and Samaritans. Even to the venerable name of our mother church itself we are not to attach any undue authority.

CHAP. XXXI.—OF PARTICULAR CHURCHES.

THUS far of the *universal visible church. A particular church* is a society of persons professing the faith, united by a special bond of brotherhood, and so ordered as may best promote the ends of edification and mutual communion of the saints. The ordinary ministers of a particular church are *presbyters and deacons.*

Presbyters are otherwise called *bishops.* Acts xx. 17. compared with v. 28. The same office of bishop or presbyter is described 1 Tim. iii. 1, where no mention is made of any other minister except deacon. Lastly, in the first council of the church, held at Jerusalem, the apostles and elders alone are spoken of as present, no mention being made of bishops, Acts xv. 6. xvi. 4. bishops and presbyters must therefore have been the same. Of the presbyters, some were set apart for the office of teaching, others watched over the discipline of the church, while in particular instances both these functions were united.

The office of a *deacon* is properly to administer, in the character of a public servant, to the temporal wants of the church in general, and particularly of the poor, the sick, and strangers. The widows of the church are also associated with the deacons in the performance of their duty. The choice of ministers belongs to the people. It is proper that ministers should undergo a certain trial previous to their admission. The requisite qualifications of an elder, as well as of a deacon, are detailed at length in the epistles to Timothy and Titus. On such as were approved the presbyters laid their hands. The imposition of hands, however, was not confined to the election of presbyters, but was practised even towards veteran ministers, in the way of solemn benediction, on their engaging in any work of importance. The right of succession is consequently nugatory, and of no force.

With regard to the remuneration to be allotted to the ministers of the universal church, as well as to those of particular religious communities, it must be allowed that a certain recompense is both reasonable in itself, and sanctioned by the law of God and the declarations of Christ and his apostle. It is lawful and equitable, and the ordinance of God himself, 1 Cor. ix. 14. "that they which preach the gospel should live of the gospel." It is however more desirable for example's sake, and for the preventing of offence or suspicion, as well as more noble and honorable in itself, and conducive to our more complete glorying in God, to render an unpaid service to the church in this as well as in all other instances, and, after the example of our Lord, to minister and serve gratuitously. St. Paul proposed the same to the imitation of ministers in general, and recommended it by his example. And if at any time extreme necessity compelled him to accept the voluntary aid of the churches, such constraint was so grievous to him, that he accuses himself as if he were guilty of robbery.

If however such self-denial be thought too arduous for the ministers of the present day, they will most nearly approach to it, when, relying on the providence of God who called them, they shall look for the necessary support of life, not from the edicts of the civil power, but from the spontaneous good-will and liberality of the church in requital of their voluntary service.

For it does not necessarily follow that because a thing is in itself just, a matter of duty and conscience, and sanctioned by the word of God, the performance of it is therefore to be enjoined and compelled by the authority of the magistrate. The same argument, and nearly the same words, which are used by St. Paul to prove that provision should be made for the ministers of the church, are also used to prove that the Gentiles ought to contribute to the support of the poor saints at Jerusalem; it hath pleased them verily, and their debtors they are; for if the Gentiles have been made partakers of their spiritual things. their duty is also to minister unto

them in carnal things; yet no one contends that the giving of alms should be compelled by authority. If then in a case of merely moral and civil gratitude, force is not to be employed, how much more ought the gratitude which we owe for the benefits of the gospel to be exempt from the slightest shadow of force or constraint? On the same principle, pecuniary considerations ought by no means to enter into our motives for preaching the gospel. If it be a crime to purchase the gospel, what must it be to sell it? or what are we to think of the fate of those, whom I have so often heard exclaiming in the language of unbelief, If you take away church revenues, you destroy the gospel? If the Christian religion depends for its existence on no firmer supports than wealth and civil power, how is it more worthy of belief than the Mahometan superstition?

Hence to exact or bargain for tithes or other stipendiary payments under the gospel, to extort them from the flock under the alleged authority of civil edicts, or to have recourse to civil actions and legal processes for the recovery of allowances purely ecclesiastical, is the part of wolves rather than of ministers of the gospel. Acts xx. 33. "I have coveted no man's silver, or gold, or apparel;" whence it follows that the apostle neither exacted these things himself, nor approved of their exaction by ministers of the gospel in general. If it be scarcely allowable for a Christian to go to law with his adversary in defence even of his own property, what are we to think of an ecclesiastic, who for the sake of tithes, that is, of the property of others, which, either as an offering made out of the spoils of war, or in pursuance of the vow voluntarily contracted by an individual, or from an imitation of that agrarian law established among the Jews, but altogether foreign to our habits, and which is not only abolished itself, but of which all the causes have ceased to operate, were due indeed formerly, and to ministers of another sect, but are now due to no one; what are we to think of a pastor, who for the recovery of claims thus founded, (an abuse unknown to any reformed church but our own,) enters into litigation with his own flock, or, more properly speaking, with a flock which is not his own? If his own, how avaricious in him to be so eager in making a gain of his holy office! if not his own, how iniquitous! Moreover, what a piece of officiousness, to force his instructions on such as are unwilling to receive them; what extortion, to exact the price of teaching from one who disclaims the teacher, and whom the teacher himself would equally disclaim as a disciple, were it not for the profit! Many such there are in these days, who abandon their charge on the slightest pretences, and ramble from flock to flock, less through fear of the wolf than to gratify their own wolfish propensities, wherever a richer prey invites; who, unlike good shepherds, are for ever seeking out new and more abundant pastures, not for their flock, but for themselves.

"How then," ask they, "are we to live?" How ought they to live, but as the prophets and apostles lived of old? on their own private resources, by the exercise of some calling, by some industry, after the example of the prophets, who accounted it no disgrace to be able to hew their own wood, and build their own houses, of Christ, who wrought with his own hands as a carpenter, and of St. Paul, to whom the plea so importunately urged in modern times, of the expensiveness of a liberal education, and the necessity that it should be repaid out of the wages of the gospel, seems never to have occurred. Thus far of the ministers of particular churches.

With regard to the *people of the church* (especially in those particular churches where discipline is maintained in strictness) such only are to be accounted of that number, as are well taught in Scripture doctrine, and capable of trying by the rule of Scripture and the Spirit any teacher whatever, or even the whole collective body of teachers although arrogating to themselves the exclusive name of the church. Hence the people are warned not to take delight in vain teachers.

Every church consisting of the above parts, however small its numbers, is to be considered as in itself an integral and perfect church, so far as regards its religious rights; nor has it any superior on earth, whether individual, or assembly, or convention, to whom it can be lawfully required to render submission; inasmuch as no believer out of its pale, nor any order or council of men whatever, has a greater right than itself to expect a participation in the written word and the promises, in the presence of Christ, in the presiding influence of the Spirit, and in those gracious gifts which are the reward of united prayer. Hence all particular churches, whether in Judea, where there was originally one church comprehending the whole nation, or in any other country whatever, are properly called churches.

In this respect a particular church differs from the Jewish synagogue, which, although a particular assembly, and convened for religious purposes, was not a particular church, inasmuch as the entire worship of God could not be there duly celebrated, by reason that the sacrifices and ceremonies of the law were to be performed in the temple alone. Under the gospel, on the contrary, all that pertains to the worship of God and the salvation of believers, all, in short, that is necessary to constitute a church, may be duly and orderly transacted in a particular church, within the walls of a private house, and where the numbers assembled are inconsiderable. Nay, such a church, when in compliance with the interested views of its pastor it allows of an increase of numbers beyond what is convenient, deprives itself in a great measure of the advantages to be derived from meeting in common.

It was indeed necessary for Jews and proselytes to meet together at Jerusalem from all quarters of the world for religious purposes, because at that time there was only one national or universal Jewish church, and no particular churches; whereas at present there is no national church, but a number of particular churches, each complete and perfect in itself, and all co-equal in divine right and power; which like similar and homogeneous parts of the same body, connected by a bond of mutual equality, form in conjunction one catholic church: nor need any one church have recourse to another for a grace or privilege which it does not possess in its independent capacity. Particular churches, however, may communicate with each other in a spirit of brotherhood and agreement, and co-operate for purposes connected with the general welfare.

Of councils, properly so called, I find no

trace in Scripture; for the decision recorded Acts xv. 2, is rather to be considered as an oracular declaration obtained from the inspired apostles, to whom recourse was had in a doubtful matter, as to the supreme authority on controverted points, while there was yet no written word. This was very different from a modern council composed of bishops or elders, who have no gift of inspiration more than other men; whose authority is not, like that of the apostles, co-ordinate with the Scriptures; who are equally liable to error with their brethren, insomuch that they cannot pronounce with certainty, like the apostles, who nevertheless assume the right of imposing laws on the churches, and require the rest of mankind to obey their mandates; forgetting that at the assembly in Jerusalem the whole multitude of believers were present, and gave their voices. Where however they content themselves with the fraternal office of admonition, their counsel is not to be despised.

The enemies of the church are partly heretics, and partly profane opponents. The hostility of heretics originates either in their own evil dispositions, or in the imposition of some unnecessary yoke on the church. Yet even these are not without their use. The enemies of the church are various, but the destruction of all is portended. The great enemy of the church is called *Antichrist,* who according to prediction is to arise from the church itself.

The frauds and persecutions practised by the enemies of the church are of various kinds. Hence we are enjoined to flee from persecution, and the precept is confirmed by the example of Elijah, of Joseph, Christ, Matt. xii. 15. the disciples, Acts viii. 4. and of Paul and Barnabas, xiv. 6. except where flight would not be conducive to the glory of God. There are appropriate consolations for the persecuted. A compensation is also promised. Mark. x. 30. "he shall receive an hundred-fold."

CHAP. XXXII.—OF CHURCH
DISCIPLINE.

THE bond by which a particular church is held together. is its *discipline. Church dis-*cipline consists in a mutual agreement among the members of the church to fashion their lives according to Christian doctrine, and to regulate every thing in their public meetings decently and with order.

It is a prudent as well as a pious custom, to solemnize the formation or re-establishment of a particular church by a public renewal of the covenant; as was frequently done in the reformations of the Jewish church. So also, when an individual unites himself to a particular church, it is requisite that he should enter into a solemn covenant with God and the church, to conduct himself in all respects, both towards the one and the other, so as to promote his own edification and that of his brethren. This covenant ought properly to take place in baptism, as being the rite appointed for the admission of all persons (that is, of all adults) into the church. Seeing also that most men are liable to a frequent change of residence, it will be necessary that this promise should be repeated so often as they pass from one particular church to another, unless they are provided with the most satisfactory testimonials from some other orthodox church; this being apparently the only means by which discipline can be adequately maintained, or prevented from sinking into gradual decline and dissolution.

The custom of holding assemblies is to be maintained, not after the present mode, but according to the apostolical institution, which did not ordain that an individual, and he a stipendiary, should have the sole right of speaking from a higher place, but that each believer in turn should be authorized to speak, or prophesy, or teach, or exhort, according to his gifts; insomuch that even the weakest among the brethren had the privilege of asking questions, and consulting the elders and more experienced members of the congregation. This custom was derived by the apostles from the synagogue, and transferred by them to the churches. Luke ii. 46. Compare also other places where Christ is related to have taught in the synagogue, and even in the temple, a permission which was granted to him not as Christ, but simply as a gifted individual, in the same manner as it was afterwards granted to the apostles, Acts xiii. 5. These rulers of the synagogue were persons appointed to see that all things were done in order.

Women, however, are enjoined to keep silence in the church. 1 Cor. xiv. 34, 35. "let your women keep silence in the churches, for it is not permitted unto them to speak, but they are commanded to be under obedience, as saith the law (Gen. iii. 16); and if they will learn anything, let them ask their husbands at home; for it is a shame for women to speak in the church." 1 Tim. ii. 11, 12. "let the woman learn in silence in all subjection: but I suffer not a woman to teach, nor to usurp authority over the man, but to be in silence."

The administration of discipline is called *the power of the keys;* a power not committed to Peter and his successors exclusively, or to any individual pastor specifically, but to the whole particular church collectively, of whatever number of members composed.

The administration of discipline consists, first, in receiving and treating with gentleness the weak or lapsed members of the church. Secondly, in composing differences between the brethren. Thirdly, in admonishing or openly rebuking grievous offenders. Fourthly, in separating the disobedient from the communion of the church. Or even, lastly, in ejecting them from the church; not however for their destruction, but rather for their preservation, if so they may be induced to repent; as was done in the ancient synagogue. There are some, however, who may justly be considered irrecoverable.

The civil power differs from the ecclesiastical in the following respects. First, every man is subject to the civil power; that is to say, in matters properly civil. On the contrary, none but the members of the church are subject to ecclesiastical power, and that only in religious matters, with a liability to ecclesiastical punishment alone, that is, to punishment inflicted by their own body. Secondly, the civil power has dominion only over the body and external faculties of man; the ecclesiastical is exercised exclusively on the faculties of the mind, which acknowledge no other jurisdiction. Nay, we are expressly enjoined not to suffer ourselves to be governed by the commandments of men in matters of religion. Thirdly, the civil power punishes even such as confess their faults; the eccle-

siastical, on the contrary, pardons all who are penitent.

The power of the church against those who despise her discipline is exceedingly great and extensive. It is therefore highly derogatory to the power of the church as well as an utter want of faith, to suppose that her government cannot be properly administered without the intervention of the civil magistrate.

CHAP. XXXIII.—Of Perfect Glorification, including the Second Advent of Christ, the Resurrection of the Dead, and the General Conflagration.

IN the twenty-fifth chapter I treated of that *imperfect glorification* to which believers attain in this life. I now proceed to consider, lastly, that *perfect glorification* which is effected in eternity. Before the law this was typified by the translation of Enoch, as it was under the law by that of Elijah. Its fulfilment and consummation will commence from the period of Christ's second coming to judgment, and the resurrection of the dead.

The coming of the Lord to judgment, when he shall judge the world with his holy angels, was predicted, first, by Enoch and the prophets; afterwards by Christ himself and his apostles. The day and hour of Christ's coming are known to the Father only. The treatise of Zanchius *De fine sœculi,* tom. vii. may be likewise advantageously consulted on this subject. Hence it will be sudden. Certain signs however are pointed out by Christ and his apostles as indicative of its approach. These signs are either general or peculiar. The general signs are those which relate equally to the destruction of Jerusalem, the type of Christ's advent, and to the advent itself; such as false prophets, false Christs, wars, earthquakes, persecutions, pestilence, famine, and the gradual decay of faith and charity, down to the very day itself. The peculiar signs are, first, an extreme recklessness and impiety, and an almost universal apostasy. Secondly, the revealing of antichrist, and his destruction by the spirit of the mouth of Christ.

Some refer to the same event another sign, namely, the calling of the entire nation of the Jews, as well as of the ten dispersed tribes. Christ will delay his coming. His advent will be glorious. It will be terrible. The second advent of Christ will be followed by the resurrection of the dead and the last judgment.

A belief in the *resurrection of the dead* existed even before the time of the gospel. This expectation was confirmed under the gospel by the testimony of Christ. To these testimonies from Scripture, may be added several arguments from reason in support of the doctrine. First, the covenant with God is not dissolved by death. Secondly, "if there be no resurrection of the dead, then is Christ not risen." 1 Cor. xv. 13–20. Thirdly, were there no resurrection, the righteous would be of all men the most miserable, and the wicked, who have a better portion in this life, most happy; which would be altogether inconsistent with the providence and justice of God.

This resurrection will take place partly through the resuscitation of the dead, and partly through a sudden change operated upon the living. It appears indicated in Scripture that every man will rise numerically one and the same person. Otherwise we should not be conformed to Christ, who entered into glory with that identical body of flesh and blood, wherewith he had died and risen again. The change to be undergone by the living is predicted 1 Cor. xv. 51. "behold, I show you a mystery . . . we shall all be changed."

The last judgment is that wherein *Christ with the saints, arrayed in the glory and power of the Father, shall judge the evil angels, and the whole race of mankind.*

The rule of judgment will be the conscience of each individual, according to the measure of light which he has enjoyed.

Coincident, as appears, with the time of this last judgment (I use the indefinite expression time, as the word day is often employed to denote any given period, and as it is not easily imaginable that so many myriads of men and angels should be assembled and sentenced within a single day, beginning with its commencement, and extending a little beyond its conclusion, will take place that glorious reign of Christ on earth with his saints, so often promised in Scripture, even

until all his enemies shall be subdued. His kingdom of grace, indeed, which is also called *the kingdom of heaven,* began with his first advent, when its beginning was proclaimed by John the Baptist, as appears from testimony of Scripture; but his kingdom of glory will not commence till his second advent. Dan. vii. 13, 14. "behold, one like the Son of man came with the clouds of heaven . . . and there was given him dominion, and glory, and a kingdom;" given him, that is, from the time when he came with the clouds of heaven (in which manner his final advent is uniformly described) not to assume our nature, as Junius interprets it, (for then he would have been like the Son of man before he became man, which would be an incongruity) but to execute judgment; from the period so indicated, to the time when he should lay down the kingdom, 1 Cor. xv. 24. "then cometh the end," of which more shortly. That this reign will be on earth, is evident from many passages. It appears that the *judgment* here spoken of will not be confined to a single day, but will extend through a great space of time; and that the word is used to denote, not so much a judicial inquiry properly so called, as an exercise of dominion; in which sense Gideon, Jephthah, and the other judges are said to have judged Israel during many years.

After the expiration of the thousand years Satan will rage again, and assail the church at the head of an immense confederacy of its enemies; but will be overthrown by fire from heaven, and condemned to everlasting punishment. Rev. xx. 7–9.

After the evil angels and chief enemies of God have been sentenced, judgment will be passed upon the whole race of mankind. Rev. xx. 11–15.

Then, as appears, will be pronounced that sentence, Matt. xxv. 34. *Come, ye blessed of my Father, inherit the kingdom prepared for you from the foundation of the world.* v. 41. *depart from me, ye cursed, into everlasting fire, prepared for the devil and his angels.*

The passing of the sentence will be followed by its execution; that is to say, by the punishment of the wicked, and the perfect glorification of the righteous. Then will be the end, spoken of in 1 Cor. xv. 24–28. It may be asked, if Christ is to deliver up the kingdom to Go⸍ and the Father, what becomes of the declarations, Heb. i, 8. and Dan. vii. 14. I reply, there shall be no end of his kingdom, *for ages of ages,* that is, so long as the ages of the world endure, until *time* itself *shall be no longer,* Rev. x. 6. until every thing which his kingdom was intended to effect shall have been accomplished; insomuch that his kingdom will not *pass away* as insufficient for its purpose; it will not be *destroyed,* nor will its period be a period of dissolution, but rather of perfection and consummation, like the end of the law. In the same manner many other things are spoken of as never to pass away, but to remain eternally; as circumcision, the ceremonial law in general, the land of Canaan, the sabbath, the priesthood of Aaron, the memorial of stones at the river Jordan, the signs of heaven.

The second death is so termed with reference to the first, or death of the body. For the three other, or preparatory degrees of death, on the Punishment of Sin. The fourth and last gradation is that of which we are now speaking, namely, eternal death, or the punishment of the damned.

Under this death may be included the destruction of the present unclean and polluted world itself, namely, *its final conflagration.* Whether by this is meant the destruction of the substance of the world itself, or only a change in the nature of its constituent parts, is uncertain, and of no importance to determine; respecting the event itself, we are informed, so far as it concerns us to know, Job. xiv. 12.

The second death, or the punishment of the damned, seems to consist partly in the loss of the chief good, namely, the favor and protection of God, and the beatific vision of his presence, which is commonly called the punishment of loss; and partly in eternal torment, which is called the punishment of sense. The intensity and duration of these punishments are variously intimated. Punishment, however, varies according to the degree of guilt.

The place of punishment is called HELL; *Tophet,* Isai. xxx. 33. "hell fire," Matt. v. 22. and still more distinctly, x. 28. "outer darkness," viii. 12. xxii. 13. xxv. 30. "a furnace of fire," xiii. 42. *Hades,* Luke xvi. 23. and elsewhere: "a place of torment," v. 28. "the bottomless pit," Rev. ix. 1. "the lake of fire," xx. 15. "the lake which burneth with fire and brimstone," xxi. 8. Hell appears to be situated beyond the limits of this universe. Luke xvi. 26. "between us and you there is a great gulf fixed, so that they which would pass from hence to you cannot." Matt. viii. 12. "outer darkness." Rev. xxii. 14, 15. "they may enter in through the gates into the city; for without are dogs." Nor are reasons wanting for this locality; for as the place of the damned is the same as that prepared for the devil and his angels, Matt. xxv. 41. in punishment of their apostasy, which occurred before the fall of man, it does not seem probable that hell should have been prepared within the limits of this world, in the bowels of the earth, on which the curse had not as yet passed. This is said to have been the opinion of Chrysostom, as likewise of Luther and some later divines. Besides, if, as has been shown from various passages of the New Testament, the whole world is to be finally consumed by fire, it follows that hell, being situated in the centre of the earth, must share the fate of the surrounding universe, and perish likewise; a consummation more to be desired than expected by the souls in perdition. Thus far of the punishment of the wicked; it remains to speak of the perfect glorification of the righteous.

Perfect glorification consists in eternal life and perfect happiness, arising chiefly from the divine vision. It appears that all the saints will not attain to an equal state of glory.

Our glorification will be accomplished by the renovation of heaven and earth, and of all things therein adapted to our service or delight, to be possessed by us in perpetuity. Isai. lxv. 17.

BOOK II

OF THE WORSHIP OF GOD.

CHAP. I.—OF GOOD WORKS.

THE subject of the first Book was *Faith,* or *the Knowledge of God.* The second treats of *the Worship or Love of God.*

The true worship of God consists chiefly in the exercise of good works.

Good works are those which we perform by the Spirit of God working in us through true faith to the glory of God, the assured hope of our own salvation, and the edification of our neighbor.

Through faith. James ii. 22. "seest thou how faith wrought with his works, and by works was faith made perfect?" that is, how faith (to use a logical expression) constitutes the *form* of the works, and endows them with the quality of goodness; and how it is itself consummated by the works, as by its end and natural product.

As to the position of divines, that the essential form of good works is their accordance with the decalogue, so far as they are there prescribed, it is not easy to discover how this can be the case under the gospel. St. Paul certainly teaches a different doctrine, throughout the whole of Romans and elsewhere; declaring explicitly, Rom. xiv. 23. that "whatsoever is not of faith is sin." He does not say, "whatsoever is not of the decalogue, is sin," but "whatsoever is not of faith;" it is therefore an accordance with faith, not with the decalogue, that ought to be considered as the essential form of good works. Hence, if I observe the sabbath in compliance with the decalogue, but contrary to the dictates of my own faith, conformity with the decalogue, however exact, becomes in my case sin, and a violation of the law. For it is faith that justifies, not agreement with the decalogue; and that which justifies can alone render any work good; none therefore of our works can be good, but by faith; hence faith is the essential form of good works, the definition of form being, that by which a thing is what it is. With regard to the passages in which mention is made of keeping God's commandments, 1 John ii. 4. and elsewhere, it seems reasonable to understand this of the precepts of the gospel, in which faith is uniformly put before the works of the law. If then in the gospel faith be above the works of the law, it must be equally above its precepts; for works are the end and fulfilling of precepts. Since therefore under the gospel, although a man should observe the whole Mosaic law with the utmost punctuality, it would profit him nothing without faith, it is evident that good works must be defined to be of faith, not of the decalogue; whence it follows that conformity not with the written, but with the unwritten law, that is, with the law of the Spirit given by the Father to lead us into all truth, is to be accounted the true essential form of good works. For the works of believers are the works of the Spirit itself; and though such can never be in contradiction to the love of God and our neighbor, which is the sum of the law, they may occasionally deviate from the letter even of the gospel precepts, particularly of those which are merely special through a predominating regard to the law of love; as was shown by Christ himself in the abolition of Sabbatical observances, as well as on several other occasions.

The edification of our neighbor. Hence we are admonished so to act, that we may become examples to others. For a virtuous example excites, in the virtuous, an emulation of that virtue; a vicious example, on the contrary, is productive of vicious emulation; as well as of offences, by which the strong are scandalized, and the weaker brethren, if not absolutely led into sin, rendered more remiss in the performance of good works. In this sense a man is said to be a stumbling-block to himself, when he indulges himself in any vice to which his nature inclines him.

Where however the offence does not proceed from any fault of ours, but from the frowardness or malignity of the other party, the guilt rests not with him who gives, but with him who takes the offence. Matt. xv. 12, 13. Thus Christ did not break off his intercourse with the publicans through fear of scandalizing the Pharisees, but contented himself with giving reasons for his conduct.

As to what the Papists call works of supererogation, whereby more is done than the law prescribes, insomuch that some of the saints, through the superabundance of their works, have been enabled to purchase eternal life not only for themselves, but for others, such works are clearly impossible. For since we are commanded, under the gospel as well as under the law, to love and serve God with all our strength and with all our mind, and our neighbor as ourselves, and since, consequently, there can be no excess in piety and charity, it follows that no act which we are capable of performing can be of such excellence as to fulfil, still less to transcend the requisitions of duty. Those counsels of the gospel, therefore, which the Papists affirm to be of a higher nature than its precepts, insomuch that if a man follow them, not being compelled so to do, he performs a work of supererogation, are not in reality counsels, as distinguished from precepts, nor of a higher nature than the latter; but are to be considered as particular precepts, given, not to all mankind, but to certain individuals, for special reasons and under special circumstances. Thus we are told, Matt. xix. 11. that it is good for those who have the gift of continence and can receive the saying, not to marry, whenever by remaining single they can more effectually promote the glory of God and the good of the church. Again, v. 21. whether the words of Christ are to be considered as precept or as simple counsel, it is certain that, had the young man to whom they were addressed fulfilled them in their utmost extent, he would have done nothing beyond what duty required, any more than Abraham when he led forth his son to sacrifice: for the commands of God, whether addressed to mankind in general, or to a particular class, or to an individual, are equally obligatory on the kind, or class, or individual to whom they are addressed. In the example just cited, obedience to the general precept of loving God above all things was singled out as an instance of duty to be required from the self-sufficient young man, for the purpose of exposing his folly and unfounded confidence, and of showing him how far he was from the perfection to which he pretended. For it was not the selling all he had, which has been done without charity, but the leaving his possessions and following Christ, which was to be the test of his perfection. With regard to the other instance of celibacy, 1 Cor. vii. this is neither made expressly a matter of precept nor of counsel, but is left free to the discretion of individuals, according to seasons and circumstances. To the above may be added, that, if there be any such works as are here described, those precepts must needs be imperfect, which require to be amended by supplementary admonitions. If, moreover,

these latter are, as is alleged, of a higher order of excellence than the precepts themselves, who shall be sufficient to fulfil them? seeing that no one is able to perform entirely even the requisitions of the law. Not to mention, that the name of counsels is sometimes applied to precepts of universal application, and of the most imperative necessity. Lastly, that prayer for forgiveness, which by Christ's command we all daily offer, is utterly irreconcileable with the vain boasting of works implied in this doctrine.

It is true that in matters of choice and Christian liberty, one work may be more perfect than another; but it is not less the duty of every one to do whatever may most effectually promote the glory of God and the edification of his neighbor. St. Paul, had he so chosen, needed not have preached the gospel without charge, but believing, as he did, that a gratuitous service would be less open to suspicion, and tend more to the edification of the church, he did nothing more than his duty in preaching gratuitously. No work of supererogation was performed by Zaccheus, when he voluntarily gave half his goods to the poor, nor by the poor widow, when she cast into the treasury all that she had, nor by the disciples, when they sold their lands and divided the produce among the brethren; those who did such actions only proved that they loved their neighbors, and especially the believing part of them, as themselves. They were not however under any absolute obligation to give such extraordinary proofs of their love, for although perfection is proposed to all men as the end of their endeavors, it is not required of all.

Hence may be easily discerned the vanity of human merits; seeing that, in the first place, our good actions are not our own, but of God working in us; secondly, that, were they our own, they would still be equally due; and, thirdly, that, in any point of view, there can be no proportion between our duty and the proposed reward. Hence although Hezekiah asserts his uprightness in the sight of God, he is so far from considering this as constituting any claim to reward, that he acknowledges himself indebted to the free mercy of God for the pardon of his sins. So likewise Nehemiah. The declaration of God himself, Exod. xx. 6. is to the same purpose. Lastly, that of which God stands in no need, can deserve nothing of him.

Opposed to good works are evil works; the vanity and bitterness of which are forcibly described by Isaiah, lix. 4. A good man is known by his works. Sometimes, however, certain temporary virtues, or semblances of virtues, are discernible even in the wicked; as in Saul, 1 Sam. xix. and in the Jews, Jer. xxxiv. An outward show of liberality, gratitude, and equity, with a regard for the interest of his subjects, are visible in the king of Sodom, Gen. xiv. 21. The wicked man is described Psal. x. 3.

CHAP. II.—OF THE PROXIMATE CAUSES OF GOOD WORKS.

THE primary efficient cause of good works, as has been stated above, is God.

The *proximate causes of good works* are naturally, in ordinary cases at least, good habits, or, as they are called, *virtues;* in which is comprised the whole of our duty towards God and man. These are partly general, or such as pertain to the whole duty of man; and partly special, or such as apply to the particular branches of that duty. The general virtues belong partly to the understanding, and partly to the will.

Those which belong to the understanding are *wisdom* and *prudence.*

Wisdom is that whereby we earnestly search after the will of God, learn it with all diligence, and govern all our actions according to its rule.

The treasures of wisdom are not to be rashly lavished on such as are incapable of appreciating them. Prov. xxiii. 9. To wisdom is opposed folly; which consists, first and chiefly, in an ignorance of the will of God. Secondly, in a false conceit of wisdom. Yet folly cries aloud, and invites mankind to her instructions, as if she were the sole depositary of wisdom. Thirdly, in a prying into hidden things, after the example of our first parents, who sought after the knowledge of good and evil contrary to the command of God: and of Lot's wife. Fourthly, in human or carnal wisdom. We are frequently permitted to be deceived with false shows of human wisdom, in requital for our contempt of that which is true and divine.

Prudence is that virtue by which we discern what is proper to be done under the various circumstances of time and place. This quality is an indispensable seasoning to every virtue, as salt was to the ancient sacrifices. Hence the maxim, 'of the evils of sin choose none, of those of punishment the least.' If this be true with regard to the evils of sin, it is obvious how preposterously they interpret the law, who hold that usury, divorce, polygamy, and the like, were conceded to the hard-heartedness of the Jews as venial infirmities, or as evils which were to be abated or regulated by law; whereas the law can no more concede or tolerate the smallest degree of moral evil, than a good man can voluntarily choose it.

Thus much of the general virtues which belong to the understanding; those which belong to the will are *sincerity, promptitude,* and *constancy.*

Sincerity, which is also called integrity, and a good conscience, consists in acting rightly on all occasions, with a sincere desire and a hearty mental determination. Properly speaking, however, a good conscience is not in itself sincerity, but rather an approving judgment of the mind respecting its own actions, formed according to the light which we have received either from nature or from grace, whereby we are satisfied of our inward sincerity. The opposite to this is an evil conscience; that is to say (allowing some latitude of signification to the word) the judgment of each individual mind concerning its own bad action, and its consequent disapproval of them, according to the light enjoyed from nature or grace; which may be more properly called a consciousness of evil. Contrary to sincerity are, first, evil thoughts. Secondly, hypocrisy; the deeds of which, though plausible, are not good, or if good, are not done with a good design.

Promptitude or alacrity is that which excites us to act with a ready and willing spirit. Its opposites are, first, precipitancy. Secondly, a forced and not spontaneous discharge of duty.

Constancy is that virtue whereby we persevere in a determination to do right, from which nothing can divert us. The opposites of these are, first, inconstancy. Secondly, obstinacy in error, or in a wrong purpose.

CHAP. III.—OF THE VIRTUES BELONGING TO THE WORSHIP OF GOD.

Special virtues are those which pertain only to a particular branch of our duty; namely, to our duty towards God, or towards man.

Our duty towards God relates to *His immediate worship or service;* which is either internal or external.

Internal worship consists mainly in the acknowledgement of the one true God, and in the cultivation of devout affections towards him. Opposed to this is, first, atheism. Secondly, polytheism, or the acknowledgement of more gods than one, except in the sense authorized by Scripture itself.

Devout affections towards God are love, trust, hope, gratitude, fear, humility, patience, obedience. The love of God is that by which we prefer him above all other objects of affection, and desire his glory. Opposed to this is a hatred of God, and a love of the world or of created things. Of faith, in its primary sense, and as the instrumental cause of justification, I have spoken above; I now speak of *trust in God,* considered as an effect of love, and as a part of internal worship, whereby we wholly repose on him. Opposed to this is, first, distrust of God. Secondly, an overweening presumption. Thirdly, carnal reliance. Fourthly, a trust in idols.

Hope is that by which we expect with certainty the fulfilment of God's promises. Opposed to this virtue, as well as to faith, is doubt; to which even the pious are sometimes liable, at least for a time. Secondly, despair; which takes place only in the reprobate.

Gratitude towards God is that whereby we acknowledge his goodness in conferring benefits upon creatures so unworthy as ourselves. Opposed to this is, first, ingratitude towards God. Secondly, the bestowing on idols, or on created things, that gratitude which we owe to God.

The *fear of God* is that whereby we reverence God as the supreme Father and Judge of all men, and dread offending him above all things. Opposed to this is, first, carnal security. Secondly, a slavish fear. Thirdly, a fear of idols. And lastly, a fear of anything whatever except God.

Humility is that whereby we acknowledge our unworthiness in the sight of God. To this is opposed, first, pride towards God. Secondly, a false or superstitious humility.

Patience is that whereby we acquiesce in the promises of God, through a confident reliance on his divine providence, power, and goodness, and bear inevitable evils with equanimity, as the dispensation of the supreme Father, and sent for our good. Opposed to this is impatience under the divine decrees; a temptation to which the saints themselves are at times liable.

Obedience is that virtue whereby we propose to ourselves the will of God as the paramount rule of our conduct, and serve him alone. Opposed to this is disobedience.

CHAP. IV.—OF EXTERNAL WORSHIP.

THUS much of the internal worship of God. We are now to speak of his external worship, which is commonly denominated *religion;* not that internal worship is not also religion, but that it is not usually called so, except as it manifests itself in outward actions. Although external worship is, for the convenience of definition, distinguished from internal, it is our duty to unite them in practice, nor are they ever separated, except by the impiety of sinners.

True religion is that by which God is worshipped with sincerity after the form and manner which he has himself prescribed. Worship is expressed in Scripture by the verb λατρεύειν, Matt. iv. 10. and δουλεύειν, vi. 24. Gal. iv. 8. The Papists therefore err in explaining λατρεία, of the worship paid to God, δουλεία of that paid to holy men and angels.

Opposed to this is, first, superstition or will worship (ἐθελοθρησκεία), the offspring of man's invention. Thus Nadab and Abihu offered strange fire before Jehovah, for which they were forthwith punished with death. Levit. x. 1, 2. Some of the early teachers of the church are chargeable with this grievous error, in that they, to facilitate the conversion of the heathen to Christianity, retained the pagan rites with a slight alteration of names or things, to the infinite detriment of religion, and in direct violation of the precept, Deut. xii. 30, 31.

Secondly, an hypocritical worship, in which the external forms are duly observed, but without any accompanying affection of the mind; which is a high offence against God. The Shechemites (Gen. xxxiv.) were punished with slaughter and destruction for having adopted a new religion inconsiderately, and from secular motives. On the contrary, internal worship, or the worship of the heart, is accepted of God, even where external forms are not in all respects duly observed.

The parts and circumstances of true religion, or of the worship of God, are next to be considered. *The parts* into which *religion* is divided, are *the invocation or adoration of God,* and *the sanctification of his name in all the circumstances of life.* Under *invocation* are included, first, *supplication* and *thanksgiving;* secondly, *oaths* and the *casting of lots. Supplication* is that act whereby *under the guidance of the Holy Spirit we reverently ask of God things lawful, either for ourselves, or others, through faith in Christ.*

The Lord's Prayer was intended rather as a model of supplication, than as a form to be repeated verbatim by the apostles, or by Christian churches at the present day. Hence the superfluousness of set forms of worship; seeing that, with Christ for our master, and the Holy Spirit for our assistant in prayer, we can have no need of any human aid in either respect.

Reverence comprehends, first, the internal affection of the mind, and secondly, the voice and outward deportment of the body. Under the former is included, first, that we ask every thing aright, that is to say, to a right end. Secondly, that our supplications proceed from a pure and penitent heart. Thirdly, that we pray in a spirit of kindness and forgiveness towards our brethren. Fourthly, that we seek the Lord early. Fifthly, that we pray with all humility. Sixthly, that we pray earnestly; see the parable of the man who came to borrow bread of his friend, Luke xi. 5. and of the unjust judge, xviii. 2; Lastly, that we per-

severe in prayer. It is not necessary that our prayers should be always audible; the silent supplication of the mind, whispers, even groans and inarticulate exclamations in private prayer, are available. Thus, too, our devotions will be less conspicuous; according to the command, Matt. vi. 6.

Praying may be offered either alone, or in company. Christ appears seldom to have prayed in conjunction with his disciples, or even in their presence, but either wholly alone, or at some distance from them. It is moreover evident that the precepts, Matt. vi. have reference to private prayer alone. When however he inculcated on his disciples the duty of prayer in general, he gave no specific direction whether they should pray alone, or with others. It is certain that they were in the frequent practice of praying in assemblies; sometimes individually, each framing within himself his own particular petition relative to some subject on which they had agreed in common, Matt. xviii. 19. sometimes by the mouth of one chosen from their number, who spoke in the name of the rest; both which modes of prayer appear to have been used indiscriminately by the primitive Christians. Hence the impropriety of offering up public prayer in an unknown tongue, 1 Cor. xiv. 15, 16, as above; inasmuch as in public prayer consent is necessary. Both in private and in public prayer, vain repetitions and empty words are to be avoided. No particular posture of the body in prayer was injoined, even under the law.

Connected with the posture of the body, is the deportment to be observed in prayer. On this subject St. Paul says, 1 Cor. xi. 4. "every man praying or prophesying having his head covered, dishonoreth his head, but every woman that prayeth or prophesieth with her head uncovered, dishonoreth her head." Why was this? Because at that time covering the head was, with both sexes alike, a token of subjection; on which account it was usual for men to pray or prophesy with their heads uncovered. Now, on the contrary, since the covering the head has become a token of authority, and the uncovering it of submission, it is the custom with most churches, especially those of Europe, in compliance not so much with the letter as with the spirit of the law (which is always to be preferred), to worship God uncovered, as being the mark of reverence prescribed by modern custom; but to prophesy covered, in token of the authority with which the speaker is invested; and likewise to listen to his instructions covered, as the deportment most emblematic, according to modern ideas, of our freedom and maturity as sons of God. On the other hand, it will be easily inferred from hence, that in countries where the cold is intense, as Livonia or Russia, or where custom will not allow the head to be uncovered without great impropriety, as in Asia or Africa, it is allowable to pray covered; as has been shown by Cappellus in a learned note on this passage, and by other commentators.

With regard to the place of prayer, all are equally suitable. For private prayer, a retired place is most proper. To offer private prayer in public is hypocritical. It was lawful, however, to offer private prayer in the sanctuary, and afterwards in the temple of Jerusalem, as in the instances of Hannah, David, and others, quoted above. Neither is there any time at which prayer may not be properly offered. The seasons most appropriate for prayer, however, are evening, morning, and noon-day.

For ourselves or others; inasmuch as we are commanded not to pray for ourselves only, but for all mankind. Particularly for the universal church and its ministers. For all magistrates; especially with a view to the peace of the church. Even for our enemies. Much more for the brethren. If however there be any whom we know certainly to be past remedy, we are not to pray for them.

We are even commanded to call down curses publicly on the enemies of God and the church; as also on false brethren, and on such as are guilty of any grievous offence against God, or even against ourselves. The same may be lawfully done in private prayer, after the example of some of the holiest of men. It is expressly promised that supplications offered in a spirit of faith and obedience shall be heard. Hence our knowledge of God's will, or of his providence in the government of the world, ought not to render us less earnest in deprecating evil and desiring good, but the contrary. It frequently happens,

however, that believers are not heard in all that they ask for themselves or others; namely, when they seek what is contrary to their own good, or to the glory of God. The prayers even of unbelievers sometimes prevail with God, to the obtaining of bodily comforts or worldly advantages; for he is kind to all, and "maketh his sun to rise on the evil and on the good," Matt. v. 45. Hence he occasionally grants the requests even of devils. Sometimes he complies with our prayers in anger; as when the Israelites asked flesh, Num. xi. 18. So likewise when they asked a king, Hos. xiii. 11.

Among errors under the head of prayer may be classed rash imprecations, whereby we invoke God or the devil to destroy any particular person or thing: Rom. xii. 14. "bless and curse not;" an intemperance to which even the pious are occasionally liable. Undeserved curses, however, are of no force, and therefore not to be dreaded. Prayer is assisted by fasting and vows. A religious fast is that whereby a man abstains, not so much from eating and drinking, as from sin, that he may be enabled to devote himself more closely to prayer, for the obtaining some good, or deprecating some evil. Religious fasts are either private or public. A private fast is one imposed by an individual on himself or his family, for private reasons. A public fast is that which is proclaimed by the church or civil power for public reasons. To fasting were anciently added various inflictions for the mortification of the body, conformably to the customs of those nations. Even outward fasting sometimes averts the anger of God for a season. There is also a fasting which works miracles.

A vow is a promise respecting some lawful matter, solemnly made to God, sometimes with the sanction of an oath, and by which we testify our readiness and hearty resolution to serve God, or the gratitude with which we shall receive the fulfilment of our prayers. Vows are general or special. General vows relate to things which God has commanded, and are either public or private. A public vow is one which is vowed by the whole church; and is usually called in Scripture a covenant. A private vow is one which is vowed by an individual; as for instance the baptismal vow. Special vows relate to things lawful, but not expressly commanded; and are undertaken for special reasons.

We must be careful, however, not to interdict ourselves or others from those things which God intended for our use, as meat or drink; except in cases where the exercise of our liberty may be a stumbling-block to any of the brethren. The same rule applies to marriage: Matt. xix. 11. "all men cannot receive this saying, save them to whom it is given."

Vows of voluntary poverty are also to be accounted superstitious; inasmuch as poverty is enumerated among the greatest evils.

No one can make a special vow who is not his own master, and exempt from subjection to any other authority; as a son or a daughter to a parent, a wife to her husband, a male or female servant to their lord. Neither can a general or special vow be made by one who has not yet arrived at the full use of his judgment. Considering how generally this rule is received among divines, it is strange that they should so far forget their own doctrine, as to require the special vow of baptism from infants. Any one, who is in these respects qualified, may bind himself by a special vow; when once made, however, he is not at liberty to recall it, but must fulfil it at all hazards. An impious vow, however, is not binding, any more than an unjust oath. Here that which ought to have been applied to the support of the parents, had been vowed as a gift to God, so that either the vow could not be fulfilled, or the support of the parents must be withdrawn. Christ therefore decides that the parents are to be supported, and that the impious vow is of no force.

The opposite of a vow is sacrilege; which consists in the non-performance of a vow, or in the appropriation to private uses of things dedicated to God.

Thus far of prayer and its auxiliaries.

Thanksgiving consists in returning thanks with gladness for the divine benefits. Addresses to God, and particular thanksgivings, are frequently accompanied by singing, and hymns in honor of the divine name.

CHAP. V.—OF OATHS AND THE LOT.

Another species of Invocation consists in *Oaths*, and in *the Casting of the Lot. An Oath* is that whereby *we call God to witness the truth of what we say, with a curse upon ourselves, either implied or expressed, should it prove false.*

The lawfulness of oaths is evident from the express commandment, as well as example of God. Agreeable to this is the practice of angels and holy men. It is only in important matters, however, that recourse should be had to the solemnity of an oath. An oath involving a promise is to be observed, even contrary to our interest, provided the promise itself be not unlawful. In connexion with this subject, it has been made matter of discussion whether an oath sworn to a robber for the observance of secrecy, or for the payment of a stipulated ransom, is binding. Some answer, that the oath only which relates to ransom is to be observed, not that which relates to secrecy; inasmuch as every man is bound by a prior obligation to the civil magistrate to denounce any known robber, and that this obligation is of more force than the subsequent one of secrecy can possibly be. They conclude, therefore, that it is the duty of such person to give information to the magistrate, and to consider his compulsory oath as annulled by his prior engagement, the weaker obligation yielding to the stronger. If however this be just, why does it not apply equally to the oath respecting ransom? seeing that it is the positive duty of every good man not to support robbers with his substance, and that no one can be compelled to do a dishonorable action, even though bound by oath to its performance. This seems to be implied in the word *jusjurandum* itself, which is derived from *jus.* Considering the robber, therefore, as one with whom (at least while in the act of robbery) we can be under no engagement either of religious obligation, or civil right or private duty, it is clear that no agreement can be lawfully entered into with one thus circumstanced. If then under the influence of compulsion we have sworn to perform any such act as that above described, we have only committed a single offence; but if from religious scruples we observe on oath extorted under such circumstances, the sin is doubled, and instead of giving honor to God, and acquitting ourselves of an obligation which we ought never to have incurred, we are only entangling ourselves more deeply in the bonds of iniquity. Hence, if we fail to perform such agreement, it ought not to be imputed to us as a crime that we deceive one who is himself guilty of deceit or violence towards us, and refuse to ratify an unlawful compact. If therefore, a man has allowed himself to be involved in such an engagement, the point for consideration is, not whether a bond of faith extorted by a robber ought in conscience to be observed, but how he may best effect his escape.

To the fulfilment of oaths is opposed, first, a superstitious denial of their legality. For the precept of Christ, Matt. v. 33, &c. "swear not at all, neither by heaven," does not prohibit us from swearing by the name of God, any more than the passage James v. 12. inasmuch as it was foretold that even under the gospel "every tongue should swear by the God of truth," Isai. xlv. 22, 23. and lxv. 19. We are only commanded not to swear by heaven or by earth, or by Jerusalem, or by the head of any individual. Besides, the prohibition does not apply to serious subjects, but to our daily conversation, in which nothing can occur of such importance as to be worthy the attestation of God. Lastly, Christ's desire was that the conversation and manners of his disciples should bear such a stamp of truth and good faith, that their simple asseveration should be considered as equivalent to the oath of others.

Secondly, perjury; which consists in swearing to what we know to be false with the view of deceiving our neighbor, or in making a lawful promise under the sanction of an oath, without intending to perform it, or at least without actually performing it.

I have said *our neighbor*, with reference to the question discussed above. For as it would be a crime to make a sworn promise to a robber or assassin, who in committing the act has forfeited his title to the rights of social life, so to observe the oath would not be to repair the original offence, but to incur a second; at any rate, there can be nothing wrong in refusing to ratify the promise. Cases

however may occur in which a contrary decision will be necessary, owing to the degree of solemnity in the form of the oath, or to other accompanying circumstances. An instance of this occurs in the three kings, Hoshea, Hezekiah, and Zedekiah. 2 Kings xvii. 4. The fault of Hoshea seems to have been not so much his rebellion, as his reliance on So, king of Egypt. In Hezekiah it was considered meritorious and praiseworthy that he trusted in the Lord, rather than his enemy. To Zedekiah, on the contrary, it was objected, first, that his defection from the enemy was not accompanied by a return to the protection of God, and secondly, that he acted in opposition to God's special command. There is, however, this difference between a robber and a national enemy, that with the one the laws of war are to be observed, whereas the other is excluded from all rights, whether of war or social life.

Thirdly, common swearing. Fourthly, unlawful oaths; that is to say, oaths of which the purport is unlawful, or which are exacted from us by one to whom they cannot be lawfully taken. Of the former kind was the oath of David respecting the destructing of the house of Nabal, 1 Sam. xxv. 22. from which example we may also learn that the breach of such oaths is better than the performance, v. 33, 34. a rule disregarded by Herod, when he beheaded John for his oath's sake. Of the latter, David's oath to Shimei is an instance, 2 Sam. xix. 23. "the king sware unto him." Hence, although David himself did not violate his oath, he forbade his son to observe it, 1 Kings ii. 8, 9. Solomon therefore committed no breach of faith in punishing Shimei with death, of which the latter was doubly deserving, as being himself guilty of perjury. Fifthly, an idolatrous oath; which consists in swearing not by God but by some other object, contrary to the prohibition Matt. v. 33. and James v. 12.

Next in solemnity to an oath is a grave asseveration, as Gen. xlii. 15, 16. "by the life of Pharaoh;" or 1 Sam. i. 26. "as thy soul liveth, my lord;" that is, as surely as thou livest, or as I wish that thou mayest live. Such also is the expression of Christ, "verily, verily, I say unto you;" and that of Paul, 1 Cor. xv. 31. νὴ τὴν ἡμετέραν καύχησιν, "I protest by your rejoicing;" although, strictly speaking, the particle νή has the force of an oath.

To the same head belongs what is called adjuration; that is to say, the charging any one in the name of God, by oath or solemn asseveration, to speak the truth to be best of his knowledge respecting the subject of inquiry. There is no impropriety in adjuring even our dearest and most faithful friends. Gen. xlvii. 29. "put I pray thee, thy hand under my thigh." Adjurations are to be complied with, in matters not contrary to religion or equity. Thus Christ, Matt. xxvi. 63, 64. on the adjuration even of the impious high priest Caiaphas, no longer kept silence, but confessed openly that he was the Christ. Opposed to this are magical adjurations, and the superstitious or mercenary practice of exorcism.

Thus far of oaths. *In the Casting of the Lot we appeal to the Deity for the explanation of doubts, and the decision of controverted questions.*

Against the use of the lot it has been urged, that on successive repetitions the result is not invariably the same, and that therefore it must be considered as a matter of chance. This objection is of no force, inasmuch as the Deity, even in his direct verbal communications with the prophets of old, did not uniformly return the same answer, when tempted by importunate inquiries; as in the instance of Balaam, Num. xxii. 12, 20 "thou shalt not go with them . . . rise up and go with them." To this is opposed the casting of lots in jest, or with a superstitious or fraudulent purpose.

To the invocation or adoration of the Deity are opposed *idolatry,* and *invocation of angels or saints.*

Idolatry consists in *the making, worshipping, or trusting in idols, whether considered as representations of the true God, or of a false one.*

Whether of the true God—. It is indeed said, Exod. xxiv. 10. that Moses and the elders "saw the God of Israel, and there was under his feet as it were a paved work of a sapphire stone, and as it were the body of heaven in his clearness;" but it is clear, from the passage of Deuteronomy quoted above, that they saw the likeness of no living thing whatever. Hence to worship the true God

under the form of an idol was considered as criminal as to worship devils. 2 Chron. xi. 15. although Jeroboam doubtless imagined that he was appointing priests to Jehovah, while he was in reality officiating in the rites of those which were not gods.

Or of a false God. Num. xxxiii. 52. In pursuance of these injunctions, pious rulers in all ages have opposed idolatry. The cherubic images over the ark are not to be counted idols; first, as being representations not of false gods, but of the ministering spirits of Jehovah, and consequently not objects of worship; secondly, as being made by the special command of God himself. Even the brazen serpent, the type of Christ, was commanded to be demolished, as soon as it became an object of religious worship.

Hence the Papists err in calling idols laymen's books; their real nature whether considered as books or teachers, appears from Psal. cxv. 5. We are commanded to abstain, not only from idolatrous worship itself, but from all things and persons connected with it.

A question here arises, whether it be lawful for a professor of the true religion to be present at idol-worship, in cases where his attendance is necessary for the discharge of some civil duty. The affirmative seems to be established by the example of Naaman the Syrian, 2 Kings v. 17–19. who was permitted, as an additional mark of the divine approbation, to construct for himself a private altar of Israelitish earth, although, as a Gentile, he was uncircumcised. It is however safer and more consistent with the fear of God, to avoid, as far as possible, duties of this kind, even of a civil nature, or to relinquish them altogether.

The invocation of saints and angels is forbidden. Acts. x. 26. "stand up; I myself also am a man." The reason is, that God is kinder and more favorable to us than any saint or angel either is, or has power to be. Further, the charge of absurdity and folly which the prophets uniformly bring against the worshippers of idols, applies equally to those who worship images of saints or angels.

The subterfuges by which the Papists defend the worship of saints and angels, are truly frivolous. They allege Gen. xlviii. 15, 16. "the angel which redeemed me from evil, bless the lads." Jacob here was not praying, but conferring his benediction on the sons of Joseph; no one therefore will contend that the words are to be taken as an invocation, but simply as an expression of hope that God, and the redeeming angels as his minister, should bless the lads. Some indeed contend that the angel here spoken of was not a created being: but whether this be true, or whether it entered into the mind of Jacob or not, involves another and a far more difficult controversy. They urge also Job v. 1. "to which of the saints wilt thou turn?" which however may as properly be understood of living saints, as in James v. 14. "let him call for the elders of the church, and let them pray over him;" where it is not recommended that the dead should be invoked, but that those who are living and present should be entreated to pray for us.

Another opposite to invocation is the tempting of God.

A third consists in the invocation of devils, and the practice of magical arts. All study of the heavenly bodies, however, is not unlawful or unprofitable; as appears from the journey of the wise men, and still more from the star itself, divinely appointed to announce the birth of Christ, Matt. ii. 1, 2.

CHAP. VI.—Of Zeal.

We have treated of the first part of true religion, the invocation or adoration of the Deity; we proceed to the remaining part, *the sanctification of the divine name under all circumstances.*

An ardent desire of hallowing the name of God, together with an indignation against whatever tends to the violation or contempt of religion, is called *zeal.* Examples of this virtue are seen in Lot, 2 Pet. ii. 7, 8. in Moses, Exod. xxxii. 19. in Phinehas, Num. xxv. 7. in Elijah, 1 Kings xix. 10. in Jeremiah, Jer. xxiii. 9–11. In Christ, Matt. xii. 30. in Stephen, Acts vii. 51. in Paul and Barnabas, xiv. 14. Its opposites are, first, lukewarmness, as exemplified in Eli, 1 Sam. ii. 29. and iii. 13. in the chief rulers of the Jews, John xii. 43. in the Laodiceans, Rev. iii. 15, 16. Secondly, an ignorant and imprudent zeal. 2 Sam. xxi. 1, 3. Thirdly, a too fiery zeal. Jonah iv.

1–3. Fourthly, an hypocritical and boastful zeal, as that of Jehu, 2 Kings x. 16. The name of God is to be hallowed in word as well as in deed. To hallow it in word, is never to name it but with a religious purpose, and to make an open profession of the true faith, whenever it is necessary. The holy or reverential mention of God is inculcated Exod. xx. 7.

To this is opposed an impious or reproachful mention of God, or, as it is commonly called, blasphemy, from the Greek βλασφημία, as in the Hebrew בְּדִיבָח with the root בָּ, and הָלַּר with the root קָלַל. This was the crime of the Israelitish woman's son, Levit. xxiv. 11. "who blasphemed (*or* expressly named) the name of Jehovah, and cursed (*or* spake impiously)." Such also was that of Rabshakeh and other Assyrians, 2 Kings xix. 6. of the scribes, Mark iii. 22. compared with v. 29. for the scribes had said that the deeds of the Father working in Christ were the deeds of Beelzebub; of those whom Paul before his conversion compelled to blaspheme, Acts xxvi. 11. of the Jews at Corinth, xviii. 6. when they "opposed themselves and blasphemed—;" of Paul himself in his unconverted state, 1 Tim. i. 13. of Hymenæus and Alexander, v. 19, 20. of those profane persons mentioned in James ii. 7. of the beast, Rev. xiii. 5, 6. and of the followers of the beast, xvi. 11.

Considering, however, that all the Greek writers, sacred as well as profane, use the word *blasphemy* in a general sense, as implying any kind of reproach against any person whatever, which is also the received usage of the corresponding word in Hebrew, Isai. xliii. 28. Ezek. v. 15. that is, to the Jews, Zeph. ii. 8. in all which passages the same word is used, being that which we translate blasphemy: considering, I say, that such is the meaning invariably attached to the Greek word even by the sacred writers, I am of opinion that those who introduced this foreign term into the Latin language, did wrong in restricting it to the single sense of speaking evil of God; especially since, at the same time that they narrowed its meaning in one direction, they expanded it in another to an almost indefinite vagueness; insomuch that, presuming on the general ignorance as to the true signification of the word, they have not scrupled to brand as blasphemy every opinion differing from their own on the subject of God or religion. This is to resemble the scribes, Matt. ix. 3. who when Christ had simply said, v. 2. "thy sins be forgiven thee," immediately "said within themselves, This man blasphemeth;" whereas blasphemy, as is evident from the foregoing examples, consists solely in uttering reproaches against God openly, and with a high hand, Numb. xv. 30. and that whether against God or men. This sin therefore is not to be imputed to those, who in sincerity of heart, and with no contentious purpose, promulgate or defend their conscientious persuasions respecting God, founded, as appears to them, on the Scriptures. If on the other hand blasphemy is interpreted according to the Hebrew sense, it will comprehend too much; for in this sense every obstinate sinner will be a blasphemer, and as such, according to those who regard the law of Moses on this subject as still in force, punishable with death.

A second opposite is irreverent or jesting mention of the name of God, or of religious subjects. The most solemn mention of the name of God consists in dedicating to his glory whatever is intended for the use of man. Opposed to this are superstitious consecrations, such as are common among the Papists.

Thus far of the solemn and reverential mention of the name of God. We are next to consider the duty of making a consistent, and, when necessary, an open profession of his true worship. This is enjoined Matt. x. 32, 33. This profession, when it leads to death, or imprisonment, or torments, or disgrace, is called *martyrdom*. Matt. v. 11. It is generally through the means of martyrdom that the gospel is more extensively promulgated. Opposed to this is, first, the concealment of our religion. This was the fault of Nicodemus, John iii. 2. Secondly, apostasy. 2. Cron. xxviii. 6. Thirdly, an unseasonable profession. Matt. vii. 6.

Such are the means by which the name of God is hallowed in word. It is hallowed in deed, when our actions correspond with our religious profession. Matt. v. 16. Opposed to this, is a neglect to act conformably to our profession. Thus Moses and Aaron are said, contrary to their usual custom, not to have sanctified God in the eyes of the people, Numb. xx. 12. and David, a man otherwise holy, gave occasion to the Gentiles to think and speak ill of God, by reason of his adultery, 2 Sam. xii. 14. So also the Jews, of whom St. Paul writes, Rom. ii. 24.

CHAP. VII.—ON THE TIME FOR DIVINE WORSHIP; WHEREIN ARE CONSIDERED THE SABBATH, LORD'S DAY, AND FESTIVALS.

THUS far of the parts of divine worship. We are now to consider its circumstances. The circumstances of worship are the same as of all things natural, place and time.

Public worship, previously to the law of Moses, was not confined to any definite place; under the law it took place partly in the synagogues and partly in the temple; under the gospel any convenient place is proper. John iv. 21, 23.

With regard to the time of public worship, what this was before the law does not appear. Under the law it was the Sabbath, that is, the seventh day, which was consecrated to God from the beginning of the world, Gen. ii. 2, 3. but which (as stated in Book I. chap. x.) was not, so far as we can learn, observed, or commanded to be observed, till the second month of the departure of the Israelites from Egypt, Exod. xvi. 1, 23, 25, 29. when it was enforced with severe prohibitions.

The command to observe the Sabbath was given to the Israelites for a variety of reasons, mostly peculiar to themselves, and which are recorded in different parts of the Mosaic law. First, as a memorial of God's having completed the work of creation on the seventh day. Exod. xx. 11. 15–17. "wherefore the children of Israel shall keep the sabbath. Here, although the reason given for the celebration of the Sabbath applies equally to all other nations, the Israelites alone are enjoined to observe it; as is also the case with the command to abstain from creeping things, Levit. xi. 44. with the law against disfiguring the body, and other similar commands, Deut. xiv. 1. for the reasons on which these precepts are founded apply equally to believers in general and to all ages, although the precepts themselves are no longer obligatory. This has been remarked by our countryman Ames. 'Non est catholicæ veritatis illa regula interpretandi scripturas quæ tradi solet a quibusdam, officia illa omnia esse moralia et immutabilia quæ rationes morales et immutabiles habent sibi annexas; nisi sic intelligatur ut illa officia sequantur ex illis rationibus, nullo singulari Dei præcepto intercedente.' Ames *Medull. Theol.* lib. ii. c. 13. This, however, cannot be said either of the precepts above mentioned, or of the Sabbath. Secondly, because God was pleased by this distinguishing mark to separate the Israelites from other nations. Exod. xxxi. 13. Thirdly, that the slaves and cattle might enjoy a respite from labor. Exod. xxiii. 12. This reason applies only where servants are in a state of slavery, and subject to severe labor; the condition of hired servants, who are now generally employed, being much easier than that of purchased slaves in old time. Fourthly, in remembrance of their liberation from Egypt. Deut. v. 15. Fifthly, as a shadow or type of things to come. Col. ii. 16, 17. Of what things to come the sabbaths are a shadow, we are taught Heb. iv. 9, 10. namely, of that sabbatical rest or eternal peace in heaven, of which all believers are commanded to strive to be partakers through faith and obedience, following the example of Christ.

Works of charity and mercy were not forbidden on the Sabbath, upon the authority of Christ himself. Mark ii. 27. Even for a man to take up his bed, although consonant to the spirit of the law, was contrary to its letter.

Since then the Sabbath was originally an ordinance of the Mosaic law, imposed on the Israelites alone, and that for the express purpose of distinguishing them from other nations, it follows that, if (as was shown in the former book) those who live under the gospel are emancipated from the ordinances of the law in general, least of all can they be considered as bound by that of the Sabbath, the distinction being abolished which was the special cause of its institution. It was for asserting this in precept, and enforcing it by example, that Christ incurred the heavy censure of the Pharisees,

John ix. 16. If it be contended, that it is only the septennial, and not the seventh day sabbath which is said by St. Paul to be abrogated, I reply, first, that no exception is here made; and, secondly, that it may as well be contended that baptism is not meant, Heb. vi. 2. on account of the plural noun *baptisms*. Besides, it is certain that the words *sabbath* and *sabbaths* are used indiscriminately of the seventh day; Exod. xxxi. 13, 14. Isai. lvi. 2, 4, 6. Whoever therefore denies that under the words of the apostle, "in respect of an holy-day, or of the new moon, or of the sabbath-days," the Sabbath of the fourth commandment is comprehended, may as well deny that it is spoken of 2 Chron. ii. 4. or viii. 13. or xxxi. 3. from which passages the words of St. Paul seem to be taken.

The law of the Sabbath being thus repealed, that no particular day of worship has been appointed in its place, is evident from the same apostle, Rom. xiv. 5. For since, as was observed above, no particular place is designated under the gospel for the public worship of God, there seems no reason why time, the other circumstance of worship, should be more defined. If Paul had not intended to intimate the abolition of all sabbaths whatever, and of all sanctification of one day above another, he would not have added in the following verse, "he that regardeth not the day, to the Lord he doth not regard it." For how does he *not regard the day to the Lord,* if there be any commandment still in force by which a particular day, whether the Sabbath or any other, is to be observed?

It remains to be seen on what they ground their opinion, who maintain that the Lord's day is to be observed as set apart for public worship by divine institution, in the nature of a new sabbath. It is urged, first, that God rested on the seventh day. This is true; and with reason, inasmuch as he had finished a great work, the creation of heaven and earth; if then we are bound to imitate him in his rest, without any command to that effect, (and none has yet been produced,) we are equally bound to imitate his work, according to the fable of Prometheus of old; for rest implies previous labor. They rejoin, that God hallowed that day. Doubtless he hallowed it, as touching himself, for "on the seventh day he rested and was refreshed," Exod. xxxi. 17.

but not as touching us, unless he had added an express commandment to that effect; for it is by the precepts, not by the example, even of God himself that we are bound. They affirm again, that the Sabbath was observed previously to the Mosaic law. This is asserted with more confidence than probability; even if it were so, however, (a point as to which we are altogether ignorant) it is equally certain that sacrificial rites, and distinctions between things clean and unclean, and other similar observances, were in force during the same period, which nevertheless are not classed among moral duties.

They urge, however, that the celebration of the Sabbath was subsequently ordained by the fourth commandment. This is true, as regards the seventh day; but how does this apply to the first day? If, on the plea of a divine command, they impose upon us the observance of a particular day, how do they presume, without the authority of a divine command, to substitute another day in its place? or in other words to pronounce, that not merely the seventh day, which was appointed for the observation of the Israelites alone, but any one of the seven may, even on the authority of the fourth commandment itself, be kept holy; and that this is to be accounted an article of moral duty among all nations.

In the first place, I do not see how this assertion can be established, for it is impossible to extort such a sense from the words of the commandment; seeing that the reason for which the command itself was originally given, namely, as a memorial of God's having rested from the creation of the world, cannot be transferred from the seventh day to the first; nor can any new motive be substituted in its place, whether the resurrection of our Lord or any other, without the sanction of a divine commandment. Since then it is evident from more than one passage of Scripture, that the original Sabbath is abrogated, and since we are nowhere told that it has been transferred from one day to another, nor is any reason given why it should be so transferred, the church, when she sanctioned a change in this matter, evinced, not her obedience to God's command (inasmuch as the command existed no longer) but her own rightful liberty; for in any other view it can

only be termed folly. To make any change whatever in a commandment of God, whether we believe that commandment to be still in force or not, is equally dangerous, and equally reprehensible; inasmuch as in so doing we are either annulling what is not yet repealed, or re-enacting what is obsolete. It ought also to be shown what essential principle of morality is involved in the number seven; and why, when released from the obligation of the Sabbath, we should still be bound to respect a particular number possessing no inherent virtue or efficacy. The only moral sabbatical rest which remains for us under the gospel, is spiritual and eternal, pertaining to another life rather than the present. Heb. iv. 9–11. If then the commandment of the Sabbath was given to those alone whom God had *brought out of the land of Egypt, and out of the house of bondage,* it is evidently inapplicable to us as Christians; or if, as is contended, it is applicable to us inasmuch as we have been brought out of the slavery of a spiritual Egypt, the Sabbath ought to be such as the deliverance, spiritual and evangelical, not bodily and legal; above all, it ought to be a voluntary, not a constrained observance, lest we should be merely substituting one Egyptian bondage for another; for the Spirit cannot be forced. To contend therefore that what, under the new dispensation, ought to be our daily employment, has been enjoined as the business of the Sabbath exclusively, is to disparage the gospel worship, and to frustrate rather than enforce the commandments of God.

It is urged, however, that the church relies on the fourth commandment as its perpetual authority for the observance of public worship. That public worship is commended, and inculcated as a voluntary duty, even under the gospel, I allow; but that it is a matter of compulsory enactment, binding on believers from the authority of this commandment, or of any Sinaitical precept whatever, I deny. With regard to the doctrine of those who consider the decalogue as a code of universal morality, I am at a loss to understand how such an opinion should ever have prevailed; these commandments being evidently nothing more than a summary of the whole Mosaic law, as the fourth in particular is of the whole ceremonial law; which therefore can contain nothing applicable to the gospel worship.

Whether the festival of *the Lord's day* (an expression which occurs only once in Scripture, Rev. i. 10.) was weekly or annual, cannot be pronounced with certainty, inasmuch as there is not (as in the case of the Lord's Supper) any account of its institution, or command for its celebration, to be found in Scripture. If it was the day of his resurrection, why, we may ask, should this be considered as the Lord's day in any higher sense than that of his birth, or death, or ascension? why should it be held in higher consideration than the day of the descent of the Holy Spirit? and why should the celebration of the one recur weekly, whereas the commemoration of the others is not necessarily even annual, but remains at the discretion of each believer?

Neither can the circumstance of Christ's having appeared twice to his disciples on this day (if indeed the words *after eight days*, John xx. 26. are rightly interpreted the eighth day after) be safely adduced in proof of the divine institution of a new sabbath; inasmuch as there can be no doubt that he appeared on other days also, Luke xxiv. 36. and John xxi. 3, 4. "Peter saith unto them, I go a fishing," which was not lawful on the Sabbath; so that the day following, on the morning of which Christ appeared, could not have been the first day of the week. Even supposing, however, that it had been so, still the assigning this as a reason for the institution of a new sabbath is matter solely of human inference; since no commandment on this subject, nor any reason for such institution, is found in all Scripture.

From commandments, of which we have proved the non-existence, we pass to examples; although no example can weaken the force of a contrary precept. We shall proceed, however, to prove, that what are adduced as examples are not such in reality. First then, with regard to Acts xx. 7. where it is related that the disciples dwelling at Troas "came together to break bread upon the first day of the week," who shall determine with certainty whether this was a periodical meeting, or only held occasionally, and of their own accord; whether it was a religious festival, or a fraternal meal; whether a special assembly convoked on that particular day, or a daily meeting like those recorded in chap. ii. 42. compared with v. 46; lastly, whether this meeting was held by order of the apostles, or whether it was merely permitted by them in compliance with the popular custom, according to their frequent practice on other occasions?

The inference deduced from 1 Cor. xvi. 2. is equally unsatisfactory; for what the apostle is here enjoining, is not the celebration of the Lord's day, but that on the *first day of the week* (if this be the true interpretation of κατὰ μίαν σαββάτων, *per unam sabbathorum*) each should *lay by him* (that is, at home) for the relief of the poor; no mention being made of any public assembly, or of any collection at such assembly, on that day. He was perhaps led to select the first day of the week, from the idea that our alms ought to be set aside as a kind of first-fruits to God, previous to satisfying other demands; or because the first day of the week was most convenient for the arrangement of the family accounts. Granting, however, that the Corinthians were accustomed to assemble on that day for religious purposes, it no more follows that we are bound to keep it holy in conformity with their practice, without a divine command to that effect, than that we are bound to observe the Jewish sabbath in conformity with the practice of the Philippians, or of Paul himself, Acts xvi. 13.

Those therefore, who on the authority of an expression occurring only once in Scripture, keep holy a sabbath-day, for the consecration of which no divine command can be alleged, ought to consider the dangerous tendency of such an example, and the consequences with which it is likely to be followed in the interpretation of Scripture.

Hence we arrive at the following conclusions; first, that under the gospel no one day is appointed for divine worship in preference to another, except such as the church may set apart of its own authority for the voluntary assembling of its members, wherein, relinquishing all wordly affairs, we may dedicate ourselves wholly to religious services, so far as is consistent with the duties of charity; and, secondly, that this may conveniently take place once every seven days, and particularly on the first day of the week; provided always that it be observed in compliance with the authority of the church, and not in obedience to the edicts of the magistrate; and likewise that a snare be not laid for the conscience by the allegation of a divine commandment, borrowed from the decalogue; an error against which St. Paul diligently cautions us, Col. ii. 16. For if we under the gospel are to regulate the time of our public worship by the prescriptions of the decalogue, it will surely be far safer to observe the seventh day, according to the express commandment of God, than on the authority of mere human conjecture to adopt the first. I perceive also that several of the best divines, as *Bucer, Calvin, Peter Martyr, Musculus, Ursinus, Gomarus,* and others, concur in the opinions above expressed.

CHAP. VIII.—OF OUR DUTIES TO- WARDS MEN; AND THE GENERAL VIRTUES BELONGING THERETO.

HITHERTO we have treated of the virtues comprehended in our *duty towards God;* we are next to speak of those which belong to our *duty towards men;* although even in these we may be considered as serving God, so long as they are done in obedience to the divine command.

Inasmuch therefore as God is best served by internal worship, whereas man stands more in need of outward attention, the external service even of God is sometimes to be postponed to our duties towards men. The virtues connected with our duty towards man, are partly those which each individual owes to himself, and partly those which we owe to our neighbors. These virtues, like those relating to God, are either general or special.

The general virtues are *love* and *righteousness.* In the first book I treated of love generally, and in its wider sense as identified with holiness; I now proceed to define it more particularly, with reference to its object, as follows. *Love is a general virtue, infused into believers by God the Father in Christ through the Spirit, and comprehending the whole duty of love which each indi-*

vidual owes to himself and his neighbor. It is nowhere more fully described than in the whole thirteenth chapter of the first epistle to the Corinthians, to which we shall have frequently to refer. The opposite of this is uncharitableness; which renders all our other qualities and actions, however excellent in appearance, of no account.

The other general virtue belonging to the regenerate is *righteousness,* whereby we render to each his due, whether to ourselves, or to our neighbor.

Opposed to this is, first, unrighteousness, which excludes from the kingdom of heaven. Secondly, a pharisaical righteousness. Both these general virtues, as has been stated above, are exercised partly towards ourselves, and partly towards our neighbor.

The love of man towards himself consists in loving himself next to God, and in seeking his own temporal and eternal good. Prov. xi. 17. Opposed to this is, first, a perverse hatred of self. In this class are to be reckoned those who lay violent hands on themselves, (who nevertheless are not excluded from decent burial, 2 Sam. xvii. 23.) and all who are guilty of presumptuous sin. Secondly, an extravagant self-love, whereby a man loves himself more than God, or despises his neighbor in comparison of himself. In allusion to the former species of self-love Christ says, John xii. 25. "he that loveth his life shall lose it." Respecting the latter, see 2 Tim. iii. 2. On the contrary, those are commended, Rev. xii. 11. "who loved not their lives unto the death."

Righteousness towards ourselves consists in a proper method of self-government. 1 Cor. ix. 27. From this, as from a fountain, the special virtues in general derive their origin; inasmuch as under the head of righteousness towards ourselves are included, first, the entire regulation of the internal affections; secondly, the discriminating pursuit of external good, and the resistance to, or patient endurance of, external evil.

The affections are love, hatred; joy, sorrow; hope, fear; and anger.

Love is to be so regulated, that our highest affections may be placed on the objects most worthy of them; in like manner, hatred is to be proportioned to the intrinsic hatefulness of the object.

Our joy ought to be so regulated, that we may delight in things essentially good in proportion to their excellence, and in things indifferent so far only as is consistent with reason. The same rule is to be observed with regard to sorrow. In the proper regulation of hope and fear, the cause, the object, and the degree of excitation are chiefly to be considered. Concerning hope, see above; concerning fear, Matt. x. 28.

In anger, we are to consider the motive for the passion, its degree, and duration. Prov. xvi. 32.

The excess of anger is irascibility. From well-regulated affections proceeds the proper government of the tongue.

CHAP. IX.—OF THE FIRST CLASS OF SPECIAL VIRTUES CONNECTED WITH THE DUTY OF MAN TOWARDS HIMSELF.

THE *Special Virtues* which regulate our desire of external advantages, have reference either to bodily gratifications, or to the possessions which enrich and adorn life.

The virtue which prescribes bounds to the desire of bodily gratification is called *temperance*. Under temperance are comprehended sobriety and chastity, modesty and decency.

Sobriety consists in abstinence from immoderate eating and drinking. The opposites of this virtue are drunkenness and gluttony: instances of which may be seen in Noah, Gen. ix. Allied to sobriety is watchfulness. The opposite to this is an excessive love of sleep.

Chastity consists in temperance as regards the unlawful lusts of the flesh; which is also called sanctification. To chastity are opposed all kinds of impurity; effeminacy, sodomy, bestiality, &c. which are offences against ourselves in the first instance, and tending to our own especial injury.

Modesty consists in refraining from all obscenity of language or action, in short, from whatever is inconsistent with the strictest decency of behavior in reference to sex or person. The same ideas of womanly decorum existed even among the Gentiles. Thus Homer introduces Penelope:

> She . . . . beneath
> The portal of her stately mansion stood.
>> I. 414: *Cowper's Translation*

Opposed to this are obscene conversation, and filthy licentious gestures.

Decency consists in refraining from indecorum or lasciviousness in dress or personal appearance. Moderation in the enjoyment of temporal possessions manifests itself in the virtues of contentment, frugality, industry, and liberal spirit.

Contentment is that virtue whereby a man is inwardly satisfied with the lot assigned him by divine providence. Hence poverty is not to be accounted a disgrace. Prov. xvii. 5. We are forbidden to glory in riches, or to put our confidence in them. Prov. xi. 28. Opposed to this are, first, anxiety respecting the necessaries of life. Secondly, covetousness. Thirdly, a murmuring against the wisdom of God in making provision for the wants of this life.

Frugality consists in avoiding expense, so far as is seemly, and in wasting nothing which is capable of being applied to an useful purpose. The opposite of this is penuriousness.

Industry is that by which we honestly provide for ourselves the means of comfortable living. The opposite of this is remissness in making provision for the necessaries of life.

Liberality is a temperate use of our honest acquisitions in the provision of food and raiment, and of the elegancies of life. The opposite of this is luxury. Prov. xxi. 17. The virtues more peculiarly appropriate to a high station are lowliness of mind and magnanimity. Lowliness of mind consists in thinking humbly of ourselves, and in abstaining from self-commendation, except where occasion requires it. Opposed to this are, first, arrogance. Secondly, a desire of vain glory. Thirdly, boasting. Fourthly, a crafty or hypocritical extenuation of our own merits, for the purpose of extorting greater praises. Fifthly, a glorying in iniquity and misdeeds. Allied to lowliness is the love of an unspotted reputation, and of the praises of good men, with a proportionate contempt for those of the wicked. Opposed to this is a shameless disregard of reputation. Secondly, an excessive and indiscriminate passion for esteem and praise, from whatever quarter. Prov. xxvii. 2.

Magnanimity is shown, when in seeking or avoiding, the acceptance or refusal of riches, advantages, or honors, we are actuated by a regard to our own dignity, rightly understood. Thus Abraham did not refuse the gifts of the king of Egypt, though he rejected those of the king of Sodom, and though he declined to accept the field offered him by Ephron the Hittite, except on payment of its full value. Thus also Job, although restored to his former health and prosperity, did not disdain the congratulatory offerings of his friends. In this spirit Gideon refused the kingdom, Judges viii. 23. The same disposition accompanied Joseph in his exaltation from a prison to the first honors of the empire, Gen. xli. So also Daniel ii. 48, 49. He was actuated by the same temper in refusing and accepting dignities. Such was also the spirit of Nehemiah in asking honors, ii. 5. of Samuel in laying down his authority, 1 Sam. x. 1. of Elisha in refusing a reward for the cure he had wrought, 2 Kings v. 15, 16. of Christ in rejecting the empire of the world, Matt. iv. 9. in despising riches, 2 Cor. viii. 9. in accepting honors, Matt. xxi. 7. Such, finally, is the spirit by which every true Christian is guided in his estimate of himself.

Allied to this is indignation at the unfounded praises or undeserved prosperity of the wicked. When however this feeling exceeds due bounds, it ceases to be praiseworthy. The language of indignation is used, Job xxx. 1. The vehemence of its expression sometimes borders on indecency. See Ezek. xvi. 25, 36. Opposed to magnanimity are, first, an ambitious spirit. Secondly, pride, when a man values himself without merit, or more highly than his merits deserve, or is elated by some insignificant circumstance. 2 Sam. xxii. 28. Thirdly, pusillanimity; of which Saul when chosen king is an example, 1 Sam. x. 21, 22.

CHAP. X.—OF THE SECOND CLASS OF VIRTUES CONNECTED WITH THE DUTY OF MAN TOWARDS HIMSELF.

THE virtues which regulate our desire of external good have been spoken of; we are next to consider those which are exercised in the resistance to, or the endurance of evil. These virtues are fortitude and patience.

Fortitude is chiefly conspicuous in repelling evil or regarding its approach with equanimity. The great pattern of fortitude is our Saviour Jesus Christ, throughout the whole of his life, and in his death. Opposed to fortitude are, first, timidity. Secondly, rashness, which consists in exposing ourselves to danger unnecessarily.

Patience consists in the endurance of misfortunes and injuries. Compensation for injuries, nevertheless, is occasionally exacted even by pious men. The opposites to this are, first, impatience and an effeminate spirit. Secondly, an hypocritical patience, which voluntarily inflicts upon itself unnecessary evils. This is exemplified in the prophets of Baal, 1 Kings xviii. 28. and in the flagellations of the modern Papists. Lastly, a stoical apathy; for sensibility to pain, and even lamentations, are not inconsistent with true patience; as may be seen in Job and the other saints, when under the pressure of affliction.

CHAP. XI.—OF THE DUTIES OF MAN TOWARDS HIS NEIGHBOR, AND THE VIRTUES COMPREHENDED UNDER THOSE DUTIES.

HITHERTO we have treated of those duties of charity and justice which man owes *to himself;* we are next to consider the same virtues as exercised towards *our neighbor.*

Charity towards our neighbor consists in *loving him as ourselves.* Under the name of neighbor are comprehended all to whom we have the opportunity of rendering service or assistance. Luke x. 36, 37. Here the Samaritan showed mercy on the Jew, although estranged from him in so many respects. Chiefly however believers: inasmuch as, in addition to the ordinary tie of affinity, we are connected with them by a spiritual bond: Eph. iv. 3. Next in degree are those most closely allied to us by relationship or friendship Even our enemies are not to be excluded from the exercise of our charity, inasmuch as they are not excluded from our prayers. The opposite of this virtue is, first, uncharitableness towards our neighbor. Secondly, hypocritical charity. Thirdly, an excessive and preposterous love. Fourthly, hatred of our neighbor. Fifthly, a meddling disposition. Hatred, however, is in some cases a religious duty; as when we hate the enemies of God or the church. We are to hate even our dearest connections, if they endeavor to seduce or deter us from the love of God and true religion.

Love towards our neighbor is absolute or reciprocal. Under absolute love are comprised humanity, good will, and compassion. *Humanity* consists in the performance of those ordinary attentions which man owes to man, whether living or dead, as the partaker of one common nature. Towards the dead, humanity is shown by mourning for their loss, and by a decent sepulture. Mourning is the appropriate mark of respect paid to the memory of all who are not utterly worthless. Much more therefore to those of our own household. Even on such occasions, however, our grief ought not to be immoderate. Decent burial. To remain unburied is an indignity. Any place of sepulture which is consistent with decency, may be adopted without impropriety. Sarah, for instance, was buried in a cave, Gen. xxiii. 19. Rachel, not in Ephrath, but on the high road to that city, xxxv. 18. xlviii. 7. Samuel in his own house at Ramah, 1 Sam. xxv. 1. and Christ in a garden near the place of crucifixion. When Jacob and Joseph made it their especial request to be gathered unto the sepulchre of their fathers in the land of promise, this was in token of their reliance on the divine declarations, Gen. xlix. 29, 1. 25.

The opposite of humanity is, first, inhumanity; against which there are the severest prohibitions, Lev. xix. 14. Such was that of the Edomites towards the Israelites in their distress. Amos i. 6. Such too was that of the priest and Levite in the parable, who passed by on the other side, when the traveller who had fallen among thieves was lying half dead and plundered, Luke x. 31, 32. Secondly, an incautious and unadvised humanity; as for instance when we become responsible for another without due consideration. Thirdly, an officious humanity. Lastly, an excess of humanity, which makes provision for the idle and undeserving.

The second modification of love is *good will,* which consists in wishing well to all men. The opposite of this is, first, envy, or a grudging disposition; which is shown in various ways. First, when a man cannot bear that others should participate in his good fortune; as in the instance of the laborers who were hired first into the vineyard, Matt. xx. 11. and of the Jews who were unwilling that salvation should be extended to the Gentiles, as may be seen throughout the book of Acts. Secondly, when a man grudges another that which he cannot himself obtain; which is exemplified in the envy with which Satan regards the salvation of the human race; in Cain's anger against his brother, because God had more respect unto him, Gen. iv. in Esau, xxvii. 41. in Joseph's brethren, Acts vii. 9. in Saul, 1 Sam. xviii. 7, 8. and in the princes of Persia, Dan. vi. Thirdly, when a man is jealous that any should be endued with the same gifts as one of whom he is himself an admirer or follower; which is exemplified in Joshua, Num. xi. 28. in John's disciples, John iii. 26. and in those of Christ, Mark ix, 38. Envy is to be shunned, Matt. xx. 15. "is thine eye evil, because I am good?" partly as instigating to crimes, murder for instance, Gen. iv. and partly as being in its nature a self-tormentor. Secondly, pretended good will; which is exemplified in the Pharisees who invited Christ to eat bread, Luke xiv. 1.

The third modification of absolute love is *compassion.* The opposite of this is, first, unmercifulness. Secondly, a rejoicing in the misfortunes of others. Thirdly, pretended pity. Fourthly, a misplaced compassion. This is exemplified in the pity of Ahab for Benhadad.

Under reciprocal love are comprised brotherly love and friendship. *Brotherly* or *Christian love* is the strongest of all affections, whereby believers mutually love and assist each other as members of Christ, and are as far as possible of one mind; bearing at the same time to the utmost of their power with the weaker brethren, and with such as are of a different opinion. Bearing with the weaker brethren. Opposed to this are divisions, enmities, rivalries among brethren, &c.

Friendship is a most intimate union of two or more individuals, cemented by an interchange of all good offices, of a civil at least, if not of a religious kind. It takes precedence of all degrees of relationship. Deut. xiii. 6. Prov. xvii. 17. xviii. 24. xxvii. 10. Friendship, and even common companionship with good men, is safe and advantageous. The benefits of their friendship, however, extend not to the ensuring our salvation in a future life; not even in the instance of those who associated with Christ on earth. Opposed to this, are, first, pretended friendship. Of this crime the traitor Judas is an example. Secondly, friendship or social intercourse with the wicked. Thirdly, enmity.

CHAP. XII.—OF THE SPECIAL VIRTUES OR DUTIES WHICH REGARD OUR NEIGHBOR.

The special virtues, or *various modes of charity or justice as regards our neighbor,* relate to him either under the general acceptation of the word neighbor, as denoting simple proximity; or under some special acceptation, where our relationship arises from special circumstances. The discharge of our special duties towards our neighbor includes the regulation not only of our actions, but of our affections, as concerns him. Special duties towards our neighbor, using the word in its general sense, regard either his internal or external good. His internal good is consulted by a regard to his safety and honor; his external, by a concern for his good name and worldly interests. Our regard to his safety should extend not merely to the present life, but to the eternal state. The duty of preserving our neighbor's life is inculcated.

Under this class of virtues are comprehended innocence, meekness, and placability. *Innocence* consists in doing a voluntary injury to no one.

Meekness is that by which we are so far from offering or taking offence, that we conduct ourselves mildly and affectionately towards all men, as far as is practicable.

Placability consists in a readiness to forgive those by whom we have been injured.

Opposed to a regard for the life of our neighbor, is, first, the shedding his blood. Under this head is also included, first, every thing by which the life of our neighbor is endangered; as blows, wounds, mutilations, &c.

Secondly, hasty anger. Thirdly, revenge. To avenge the church, however, or to desire that she be avenged of her enemies, is not forbidden.

The *honor* of our neighbor is consulted by a respect to his personal modesty.

Opposed to this are unnatural vices, fornication, violation, adultery, incest, rape, whoredom, and similar offences. Hence the laws against fornication, Exod. xxii. 16, 17. and against incest. Hence also provision was expressly made for cases of jealousy. Even before the promulgation of the law, adultery was made capital by divine command. Some marriages, however, were prohibited by the Mosaic code, which appear to have been previously lawful. Respecting a menstruous woman, see Levit. xx. 18.

CHAP. XIII.—OF THE SECOND CLASS OF SPECIAL DUTIES TOWARDS OUR NEIGHBOR.

THE external good of our neighbor is consulted, as before said, by a regard to his good name and worldly interests.

We consult *our neighbor's good name,* when *in our deportment towards him, in our conversation with him, and in our manner of speaking of him, we preserve towards him a due respect, and avoid doing anything which may causelessly injure him in the opinion of others.* Nor are we anywhere told that obeisance was made even to kings otherwise than by a lowly inclination of the body, the same token of respect which was frequently paid to each other even by private individuals.

In our deportment towards him. To this head belongs that sense of delicacy, which precludes us from saying or doing everything indiscriminately, however proper in itself, in the presence of our neighbor. Opposed to this is impudence; as exemplified in the unjust judge. Luke xviii. 2.

In our manner of conversing with him. The virtues herein comprised are veracity and candor. *Veracity* consists in speaking the truth to all who are entitled to hear it, and in matters which concern the good of our neighbor. Opposed to this is, first, an improper concealment of the truth. I say improper, for it is not every concealment of the truth that is wrong, inasmuch as we are not on all occasions required to declare what we know; that concealment only is blameable, which proceeds from improper motives. Secondly, falsehood. Hence falsehood is not justifiable, even in the service of God. Falsehood is commonly defined to be a violation of truth either in word or deed, with the purpose of deceiving. Since however not only the dissimulation or concealment of truth, but even direct untruth with the intention of deceiving, may in many instances be beneficial to our neighbor, it will be necessary to define falsehood somewhat more precisely; for I see no reason why the same rule should not apply to this subject, which holds good with regard to homicide, and other cases hereafter to be mentioned, our judgment of which is formed not so much from the actions themselves, as from the intention in which they originated. No rational person will deny that there are certain individuals whom we are fully justified in deceiving. Who would scruple to dissemble with a child, with a madman, with a sick person, with one in a state of intoxication, with an enemy, with one who has himself a design of deceiving us, with a robber? unless indeed we dispute the trite maxim, *Cui nullum est jus, ei nulla fit injuria.* Yet, according to the above definition, it is not allowable to deceive either by word or deed in any of the cases stated. If I am under no obligation to restore to a madman a sword, or any other deposit, committed to me while in a sound mind, why should I be required to render the truth to one from whom I never received it, who is not entitled to demand it, and who will in all probability make a bad use of it? If every answer given to every interrogator with the intent of deceiving is to be accounted a falsehood, it must be allowed that nothing was more common even among the prophets and holiest of men.

Hence falsehood may perhaps be defined as follows: *Falsehood is incurred when any one, from a dishonest motive, either perverts the truth, or utters what is false to one to whom it is his duty to speak the truth.* Thus the devil, speaking in the serpent, was the first liar, Gen. iii. 4. So Cain subsequently, iv. 9. and Sarah xviii. 15. for when the angels were justly angry with her, she evaded a candid confession of her fault. So also Abraham xii. 13. and chap. xx. for his fiction concerning Sarah, as he might have learned from his previous experience in Egypt, though intended only for the preservation of his own life, was of a nature to lead others into a dangerous error, and a desire of what was not their own, through ignorance of the fact. Thus too David in his flight from Saul, 1 Sam. xxi. 3. inasmuch as he ought not to have concealed from the priest his situation with respect to the king, or to have exposed his host to danger. Ananias and Sapphira were guilty of the same crime, Acts v.

It follows from this definition, first, that parables, hyperboles, apologies and ironical modes of speech are not falsehoods, inasmuch as their object is not deception, but instruction. In this respect it agrees with the common definition. Secondly, that in the proper sense of the word deceit, no one can be deceived without being at the same time injured. When therefore, instead of injuring a person by a false statement, we either confer on him a positive benefit, or prevent him from inflicting or suffering injury, we are so far from being guilty of deceit towards him, however often the fiction may be repeated, that we ought rather to be considered as doing him a service against his will. Thirdly, it is universally admitted that feints and stratagems in war, when unaccompanied by perjury or breach of faith, do not fall under the description of falsehood. Now this admission is evidently fatal to the vulgar definition; inasmuch as it is scarcely possible to execute any of the artifices of war, without openly uttering the greatest untruths with the indisputable intention of deceiving; by which, according to the definition, the sin of falsehood is incurred. It is better therefore to say that stratagems, though coupled with falsehood, are lawful for the cause above assigned, namely, that where we are not under an obligation to speak the truth, there can be no reason why we should not, when occasion requires it, utter even what is false; nor do I perceive why this should be more allowable in war than in peace, especially in cases where, by an honest and beneficial kind of falsehood, we may be enabled to avert injury or danger from ourselves or our neighbor.

The denunciations against falsehood, therefore, which are cited from Scripture, are to be understood only of such violations of truth as are derogatory to the glory of God, or injurious to ourselves or our neighbor. Of this class, besides what were quoted above, are the following texts: Lev. xix. 11. Psal. ci.7. Prov. vi. 16, 17. Jer. ix. 5. In these and similar passages we are undoubtedly commanded to speak the truth; but to whom? not to an enemy, not to a madman, not to an oppressor, not to an assassin, but to *our neighbor,* to one with whom we are connected by the bonds of peace and social fellowship. If then it is to our neighbor only that we are commanded to speak the truth, it is evident that we are not forbidden to utter what is false, if requisite, to such as do not deserve that name. Should any one be of a contrary opinion, I would ask him, by which of the commandments falsehood is prohibited? He will answer, doubtless, by the ninth. Let him only repeat the words of that commandment, and he will be a convert to my opinion; for nothing is there prohibited but what is injurious to our neighbor; it follows, therefore, that a falsehood productive of no evil to him, if prohibited at all, is not prohibited by the commandment in question.

Hence we are justified in acquitting all those holy men who, according to the common judgment of divines, must be convicted of falsehood: Abraham for example, Gen. xxii. 5. when he told his young men, for the purpose of deceiving them and quieting their suspicions, that he would return with the lad: although he must at the same time have been persuaded in his own mind that his son would be offered up as a sacrifice and left on the mount; for had he expected otherwise, his faith would have been put to no severe trial. His wisdom therefore taught him, that as his servants were in no way interested in knowing what was to happen, so it was expedient for himself that it should be for a time concealed from them. So also Rebecca and Jacob, Gen. xxvii. when by subtlety and proper caution they opened a way to that birthright which Esau had held cheap, a birthright already belonging to Jacob by prophecy, as well as by right of purchase. It is objected, that in so doing he deceived his

father. Say rather that he interposed at the proper time to correct his father's error, who had been led by an unreasonable fondness to prefer Esau. So Joseph, Gen. xlii. 7. who according to the common definition must have been guilty of habitual falsehood, inasmuch as he deviated from the truth in numberless instances, with the express purpose of deceiving his brethren; not however to their injury, but to their exceeding advantage. The Hebrew midwives, Exod. i. 19. whose conduct received the approbation of God himself; for in deceiving Pharaoh, they were so far from doing him any injury, that they preserved him from the commission of a crime. Moses, Exod. iii. who by the express command of God asked permission for the Israelites to go three days' journey into the wilderness under the pretext of sacrificing to the Lord; his purpose being to impose on Pharaoh by alleging a false reason for their departure, or at least by substituting a secondary for the principal motive. The whole Israelitish people, who, by divine command likewise. borrowed from the Egyptians jewels of gold and silver and raiment, doubtless under a promise of restoring them, though with the secret purpose of deception; for by what obligation were they bound to keep faith with the enemies of God, the transgressors of the laws of hospitality, and the usurpers, for so long a period, of the property of those who now despoiled them? Rahab, whose magnanimous falsehood recorded Josh. ii. 4, 5. was no breach of duty, inasmuch as she only deceived those whom God willed to be deceived, though her own countrymen and magistrates, and preserved those whom God willed to be preserved; rightly preferring religious to civil obligations. Ehud, who deceived Eglon in two several instances, Judges iii. 19, 20. and that justifiably, considering that he was dealing with an enemy, and that he acted under the command of God himself. Jael, by whose enticements Sisera perished, Judges iv. 18, 19. although he was less her personal enemy than the enemy of God. Junius, indeed, considers this as a pious fraud, not as a falsehood; which is a distinction without a difference. Jonathan, who was prevailed upon to assign a fictitious reason for the absence of David, 1 Sam. xx. 6, 28. thinking it better to preserve the life of the innocent than to abet his father in an act of cruelty; and considering that the duties of charity were better fulfilled by favoring the escape of a friend under wrongful accusation, though at the expense of veracity, than by disclosing the truth unnecessarily, in obedience to the commands of a parent, for the purpose of aiding in the commission of a crime. All these, with numberless other saints, by a more careful inquiry into the nature of truth are rescued, as it were, from the new *limbus patrum* to which the vulgar definition had consigned them.

Under falsehood is included false witness; which is forbidden Exod. xx. ·16. It is again prohibited Deut. xix. 16. under a most severe penalty.

The other virtue included in a regard to the good name of our neighbor, whether present or absent, is *candor;* whereby we cheerfully acknowledge the gifts of God in our neighbor, and interpret all his words and actions in a favorable sense. Candor, however, is usually spoken of under the general name of charity or love. The same virtue appears also to be described under the name of equity or moderation. Opposed to this is, first, evil surmising. Secondly, a prying into the faults of others, and a precipitancy in passing judgment upon them, Matt. vii. 3. Thirdly, talebearing. Fourthly, calumny, which consists in a malicious construction of the motives of others. Fifthly, evil speaking and slandering. Sixthly, contumely and personal abuse. Seventhly, litigiousness. Opposed to candor, on the other side, are, first, flattery. Secondly, unmerited praise or blame.

Allied to candor are simplicity, faithfulness, gravity, taciturnity, courteousness, urbanity, freedom of speech, and the spirit of admonition.

Simplicity consists in an ingenuous and open dealing with our neighbor. Opposed to this are, first, duplicity. Secondly, credulity.

Faithfulness is shown in the performance of promises, and the safe custody of secrets. It has been made matter of inquiry, whether it be lawful to revoke a promise once made, or to recall a benefit once conferred. This would seem to be allowable, where the person on whom the promise or benefit was be-

stowed proves himself unworthy of our kindness. Thus the lord in the parable exacted the debt from his servant, in punishment for his cruelty towards his fellow-servant, although he had before forgiven it him; Matt. xviii. 27, 32, 34. Opposed to this are, first, precipitancy in making a promise, without due consideration of circumstances. Secondly, talkativeness. Thirdly, treachery; of which Judas Iscariot is a signal instance.

Gravity consists in an habitual self-government of speech and action, with a dignity of look and manner, befitting a man of holiness and probity. Opposed to this is levity.

Taciturnity preserves a due moderation in our speech. Opposed to this are, first, loquacity. Secondly, foolish talking. Thirdly, excess of taciturnity.

Courteousness consists in affability and readiness of access. Opposed to this are, first, churlishness. Secondly, frowardness. Thirdly, false or constrained courtesy; as that of Absalom, 2 Sam. xv. 3, 4.

Urbanity comprehends not only the innocent refinements and elegances of conversation, but acuteness and appropriateness of observation or reply. Opposed to this are obscenity and double meanings. Obscenity, properly speaking, consists neither in word nor in action, but in the filthiness of his mind, who out of derision or wantonness perverts them from their proper import. Hence those expressions in the Hebrew Scriptures, for which the Jewish commentators substitute others in the margin which they esteem more decent, are not to be considered as obscene, but are to be attributed to the vehemence or indignation of the speaker. Neither are the words of Deut. xxii. 17. to be regarded as indecent; "they shall spread the cloth before the elders of the city."

Freedom of speech consists in speaking the truth with boldness. This virtue is exemplified in Elijah and Elisha, 2 Kings vi. 32. and in many others. Opposed to this is timidity in speaking the truth. The spirit of admonition is that by which we freely warn sinners of their danger, without respect of persons. Admonition however is not to be thrown away on the scornful and obstinate.

CHAP. XIV.—The second Class of special Duties towards our Neighbor continued.

THE virtues by which we promote the *worldly interests of our neighbor,* are integrity and beneficence.

Integrity consists in refraining from the property of others, which is also called abstinence; and in honesty and uprightness as regards our dealings with our neighbor, which is called commutative justice.

Abstinence is exemplified in Moses, Numb. xvi. 15. "I have not taken one ass from them, neither have I hurt one of them;" and in Samuel, 1 Sam. xii. 3. "whose ox have I taken?" On this subject laws are given Deut. xxiii. 24, 25. "when thou comest into thy neighbor's vineyard," &c. The opposites to this are, first, theft. Secondly, fraud. Under the law, fraud could not be expiated unless restitution were previously made. Thirdly, oppression and robbery. Fourthly, injury. Fifthly, man-stealing.

Under *commutative justice* are included all transactions of purchase and sale, of letting and hire, of lending and borrowing, of keeping and restoring deposits. Transactions of sale and purchase. To justice in matters of sale and purchase, are opposed various frauds. So also when counterfeit or adulterated goods are sold for genuine. Or when false weights and measures are employed. Levit. xix. 35. Or when the buyer, on his part, uses dishonest artifices in the conclusion of a bargain. Transactions of letting or hire. Lending and borrowing.

In loans, justice is violated by the exaction of immoderate interest; under which denomination all interest is included, which is taken from the poor. This is the meaning of the command in Deut. xxiii. 19. As however much difference of opinion exists with regard to usury, and as the discussion belongs properly to this place, we will consider briefly what is to be determined on the subject. It is the opinion of most, that usury is not in all cases unlawful, but that its legality or illegality is determined by the purpose for which it is exacted, the rate of interest, and the party by whom it is paid; that with regard to the party, it may be lawfully received from any one possessed of sufficient property for payment; that the rate of interest should be such as is consistent with equity at least, if not with charity; and that in exacting it we should have a view not to our own interests exclusively, but also to those of our neighbor. Where these conditions are observed, they maintain that usury is perfectly allowable; nor is it without reason that these limitations are added, since without these there is scarcely any species of compact or commercial intercourse which can be considered as lawful. That usury is in itself equally justifiable with any other kind of civil contract, is evident from the following considerations; first, that if it were in itself reprehensible, God would not have permitted the Israelites to lend upon usury to strangers, Deut. xxiii. 20. especially as he elsewhere commands them to do no hurt to the stranger, but on the contrary to assist him with every kind of good office, especially in case of poverty. Secondly, if it be lawful to receive profit for the use of cattle, lands, houses, and the like, why not of money also? which, when borrowed, as it often is, not from necessity, but for purposes of gain, is apt to be more profitable to the borrower than to the lender. It is true that God prohibited the Israelites from lending upon usury on the produce of their land; but this was for a reason purely ceremonial, in like manner as he forbade them to sell their land in perpetuity. Levit. xxv. 23. Under the gospel, therefore, that usury only is to be condemned which is taken from the poor, or of which the sole object is gain, and which is exacted without a regard to charity and justice; even as any other species of lucrative commerce carried on in the same spirit would be equally reprehensible, and equally entitled to the Hebrew name נשך, signifying *a bite.* This therefore is the usury prohibited Exod. xxii. 25. These are the earliest passages in which the subject occurs; they ought therefore to be considered as illustrating by anticipation those which come after, and the exception contained in them as applying equally to all other occasions on which usury is mentioned: Deut. xxiii. 19. as above. Psal. xv. 5. Prov. xxviii. 8. Ezek. xviii. 8.

Justice as regards the safe custody of property, is concerned in the demand or restitution of pledges, and of deposits in trust; on which subject see Exod. xxii. 7. Under what limitations a pledge may be received from a poor man, is seen Exod. xxii. 26. The same chapter enjoins a regard to humanity in the taking of pledges, v. 10.

Thus far of commutative justice. Under the same head may be classed *moderation*, which consists in voluntarily conceding some portion of an acknowledged right, or in abandoning it altogether.

Beneficence consists in rendering willing assistance to our neighbor out of our own abundance; particularly to the poor within our reach.

Beneficence, as shown in public distributions of any kind, is called *liberality*. Opposed to liberality are, first, niggardliness, which gives nothing, or sparingly, or with a grudging mind. Secondly, prodigality.

Beneficence, whether private or public, when exercised on an extraordinary scale, is called *magnificence*. This is exemplified in David, 1 Chron. xxix. 2.

Corresponding with beneficence is *gratitude*, which is shown in the requital, or, where this is impossible, in the thankful sense of a kindness. Opposed to this is ingratitude.

CHAP. XV.—OF THE RECIPROCAL DUTIES OF MAN TOWARDS HIS NEIGHBOR AND SPECIALLY OF PRIVATE DUTIES.

THUS far we have treated of the virtues or special duties which man owes to his neighbor simply as such; we are next to consider those which originate in circumstances of particular relationship. These duties are either private or public.

The private duties are partly domestic, and partly such as are exercised towards those not of our own house. Under domestic duties are comprehended the reciprocal obligations of husband and wife, parent and child, brethren and kinsmen, master and servant.

The duties of husband and wife are mutual or personal. Mutual duties. 1 Cor. vii. 3. The personal duties appertaining to either party respectively are, first, those of the husband. Exod. xxi. 10, 11. The contrary is reproved Mal. ii. 13, 14.

Personal duties of the wife. Prov. xiv. 1. "every wise woman buildeth her house." xix. 14. "a prudent wife is from Jehovah." xxxi. 11. "the heart of her husband doth safely trust in her." 1 Cor. xi. 3. "the woman is the glory of the man; for the man is not of the woman, but the woman of the man." Eph. v. 22–24. "wives, submit yourselves unto your own husbands, as unto the Lord; for the husband is the head of the wife, even as Christ is the head of the church, and he is the Saviour of the body; therefore as the church is subject unto Christ, so let the wives be to their own husbands in every thing." Col. iii. 18. "wives, submit yourselves unto your own husbands, as it is fit in the Lord." Tit. ii. 4, 5. "that they may teach the young women to be sober, to love their husbands, to love their children, to be discreet, chaste, keepers at home, good, obedient to their own husbands, that the word of God be not blasphemed." 1 Pet. iii. 1. "likewise, ye wives, be in subjection to your own husbands," &c. The same is implied in the original formation of the woman: Gen. ii. 22. "the rib which Jehovah had taken from man, made he a woman;" it cannot therefore be fitting that a single member, and that not one of the most important, should be independent of the whole body, and even of the head. Finally, such is the express declaration of God: Gen. iii. 16. "he shall rule over thee."

Offences against these duties. Exod. iv. 25. "a bloody husband art thou to me." Job. ii. 9. "then said his wife unto him, Dost thou still retain thine integrity?" 2 Sam. vi. 20. "Michal the daughter of Saul came out to meet David, and said." Prov. ix. 13. "a foolish woman is clamorous." vii. 11. "her feet abide not in her house." xiv. 1. "the foolish plucketh it down with her hands." xix. 13. "the contentions of a wife are a continual dropping." See also xxvii. 15. xxi. 9. "it is better to dwell in a corner of the housetop, than with a brawling woman in a wide house." v. 19. "it is better to dwell in the wilderness, than with a contentious and an angry woman." See also xxv. 24. Eccles. vii.

26. "I find more bitter than death the woman whose heart is snares and nets, and her hands as bands: whoso pleaseth God shall escape from her, but the sinner shall be taken by her." Above all, adultery: Deut. xxii. 14, 20. "I took this woman, and when I came unto her, I found her not a maid . . . if this thing be true."

The duties of parents are inculcated Deut. iv. 9. The opposites are, first, unbounded indulgence; as that of Eli the priest, 1 Sam. ii. and of David towards his sons Absalom and Adonijah, 1 Kings i. 6. Secondly, excessive severity. 1 Sam. xiv. 44.

The duties of children are prescribed Gen. ix. 23. Contrary to the above is the conduct of Ham, Gen. ix. 22. Also an extravagant and preposterous regard. Matt. viii. 21, 22.

Analogous to the relation of parent and child are those of guardian and ward, teacher and pupil, elder and younger; in a word, of superior and inferior, whatever be the ground of distinction. For the duties of *Guardians*, see 2 Kings xi. 4, &c. The duties of *wards*. 2 Kings xii. 2.

The prophet Samuel did not consider it beneath his dignity in his old age, after having exercised the most important public functions, to discharge the office of *teacher* in the schools of the prophets. 1 Sam. xix. 20. The duties of *pupils*. 1 Kings xix. 21.

The duties of the *elder*. Prov. xvi. 31. Tit. ii. 2. The reverse. Job xx. 11. Isai. lxv. 20. The duties of the *younger*. Lev. xix. 32. Job xxxii. 4. Psal. xxv. 7. cxix. 9. Eccles. xi. 9, 10. xii 1–3. The reverse. 2 Kings ii. 23. Psal. lviii. 3. "the wicked are estranged from the womb."

The duties of *superiors*. Ruth ii. 4. The reverse. Prov. xxvi. 1.

We are forbidden to glory in nobility of birth, or in rank, however exalted. Deut. xxvi. 5. Job xii. 21. "he poureth contempt upon princes." Opposed to the proper duty of a superior, is an unauthorized assumption of censorial power. 1 Pet. iv. 15.

The duties of *inferiors*. Prov. xxvi. 8. Rom. xiii. 7. The reverse. James ii. 2.

The duties of *brethren* and *kinsmen*. Gen. iv. 7. The reverse. 2 Chron. xxi. 4.

The duties of *masters*. Exod. xxi. 26, 27. The reverse. Prov. iii. 33. xi. 29. xiv. 11. xv. v. 25.

Respecting the possession of slaves, and the extent of the master's authority, see Gen. xvii. 12. Levit. xix. 20. xxv. 44–46. 1 Cor. vii. 21, 22. See also the epistle to Philemon. Concerning the forfeiture, by insolvency, of the rights of freedom, see 2 Kings iv. 1. Respecting the punishment of slaves, see Gen. xvi. 6. Punishment, however, should not exceed due limits.

The duties of *servants*. Gen. xvi. 9.

CHAP. XVI.—OF THE REMAINING CLASS OF PRIVATE DUTIES.

THUS far of domestic duties. We are next to speak of those which are exercised towards strangers. The principal virtues in this class are almsgiving and hospitality.

Almsgiving consists in *affording relief to the poor, especially to such as are brethren, in proportion to our means, or even beyond them, without ostentation, and from the motive of true charity.* On this, as on similar occasions, we are to be guided by geometrical rather than by arithmetical proportion, regulating our bounty according to the rank and dignity, the education and previous condition of each individual; lest we fall into the absurdity of equalizing those whom nature never intended for an equality.

To the poor; that is, to such as are unable to support themselves by their own labor and exertions. Lev. xxv. 35. 2 Thess. iii. 10. "if any would not work, neither should he eat." Hence we are not bound to relieve those vagrants and beggars who are such of choice, and not of necessity. Among the poor are to be reckoned orphans and widows, on account of the desolate situation of the one, and the tender age of the other. Exod. xxii. 22–24. "ye shall not afflict any widow or fatherless child." To these may be added such as are weak or helpless from any cause whatever, and all who are in affliction, especially for religion's sake. Isai. lviii. 7.

Scripture everywhere declares that the reward of almsgiving is great. Job. xxix. 11–25. On the other hand, the neglect of this duty is condemned, Prov. xxi. 13. Matt. xxv. 45. "inasmuch as ye did it not to one of the least of these, ye did it not to me."

Hospitality consists in receiving under our own roof, or providing for the kind reception of the poor and strangers; especially such as are recommended to us by the churches, or by our brethren in the faith. The reward of a hospitable spirit is signally exemplified in the woman of Sarepta, and in the Shunammite, who received prophets under their roof.

Injury or oppression of guests or strangers was forbidden by various laws, recorded Exod. xxii. 21, &c. Levit. xix. 33, 34. Deut. x. 18, 19.

Opposed to this is inhospitality. Deut. xxvii. 19. "cursed be he that perverteth the judgment of the stranger." Ezek. xxii. 29. "they have vexed the poor and needy, yea. they have oppressed the stranger wrongfully." 3 John 10. "not content therewith, neither doth he himself receive the brethren, and forbiddeth them that would, and casteth them out of the church."

CHAP. XVII.—Of Public Duties
towards our Neighbor.

Hitherto we have treated of the private duties of man towards his neighbor. Public duties are of two kinds, political and ecclesiastical. Under political duties are comprehended the obligations of the magistrate and the people to each other, and to foreign nations.

The duties of the magistrate to the people are described Exod. xxiii. 8. Lev. xix. 15. "thou shalt not respect the person of the poor, nor honor the person of the mighty; but in righteousness shalt thou judge thy neighbor." Num. xi. 11, "wherefore have I not found favor in thy sight, that thou layest the burden of all this people upon me?"

In the matter of reward and punishment. Excessive punishment is forbidden. Deut. xxv. 3. 1 Kings ii. 26. The right of the magistrate as regards the sword. Gen. ix. 6. Psal. lxx. v. 6. Prov. viii. 15, 16.

Of the election of magistrates, see Exod. xviii. 21. Numb. xi. 16, 17, 25. Deut. i. 13. The following texts show what is contrary to the duties of the magistrate. Psal. xxvi. 10. xciv. 20. Prov. xvii. 23. xxi. 7. xxviii. 15, 16. xxix. 4. v. 12. Eccles. iv. 13. x. 5, 6. v. 16, 17.

Isai. i. 23. iii. 4. v. 12. v. 14. v. 23. x. 12. Ezek. xxix. 3. Amos v. 7. vii. 3. The licentiousness of courts is exposed, Gen. xii. 15.

It is especially the duty of the magistrate to encourage religion and the service of God (public worship in particular), and to reverence the church. Isai. xlix. 23. That the church, however, does not stand in need of the superintendence of the magistrate, but that, if left in peace, she is fully qualified, in the exercise of her own proper laws and discipline, to govern herself aright, and enlarge her boundaries, is evident from Acts ix. 31. Religion therefore is to be protected by the magistrate, not forced upon the people. Josh. xxiv. 15. If then kings are forbidden to exercise violence against religious persons in any matter whatever, much more are they forbidden to force the consciences of such persons in the matter of religion itself, especially on points where the magistrate is fully as liable to be mistaken as the pope, and is actually mistaken in many instances; unless indeed they are content, like him, to be accounted antichrist, a name given to the pope himself chiefly from his encroachments on the consciences of mankind. True it is, that the Jewish kings and magistrates interposed their judgment in matters of religion, and even employed force in the execution of their decrees: but this was only in cases where the law of God was clear and express, and where the magistrate might safely decide without danger of mistake or controversy. In our own times, on the contrary, Christians are on many occasions persecuted or subjected to punishment for matters either purely controversial, or left by Christian liberty to the judgment of each believer, or concerning which there is no express declaration of the gospel. Against such magistrates, Christians only in name, many heathen and Jewish rulers will rise in judgment, and among the rest Pontius Pilate himself, whose deference to Jewish opinions was such, that he did not think it derogatory to his proconsular dignity to go out to speak to the Jews, when they, from a religious scruple, declined entering the judgment-hall. John xviii. 28, 29. So also Gamaliel, Acts v. 39. and Gallio, xviii. 15.

For if even the ecclesiastical minister is not entitled to exercise absolute authority over the church, much less can the civil magistrate claim such authority. 2 Cor. i. 24. Coloss. ii. 18. 1 Pet. v. 3. Rom. xiv. 4. James iv. 12. For other arguments to the same effect, I refer to Book I. of this Treatise, under the heads of Christ's kingdom, Faith, the Gospel, Christian Liberty, Church Discipline and its objects. Undoubtedly, as the kingdom of Christ is not of this world, so neither is it sustained by force and compulsion, the supporters of earthly rule. Hence the outward profession of the gospel ought not to be made a matter of constraint; and as to the inner parts of religion, faith and liberty of conscience, these are beyond its power, being from their very nature matter of ecclesiastical discipline alone, and incapable of being affected by the determinations of human tribunals: not to mention the absurdity and impiety of compelling the conscientious to adopt a religion which they do not approve, or of constraining the profane to bear a part in that public worship from which God has interdicted them. Psal. l. 16, 17. Prov. xv. 8. and xxi. 27.

For the duties of the people towards the magistrate, see Exod. xxii. 28. 2 Sam. xxi. 17. Prov. xxiv. 21, 22. xxix. 26. Eccles. viii. 2. Matt. xxii. 21. Rom. xiii. 1. 1 Tim. ii. 1, 2. Tit. iii. 1. 1 Pet. ii. 13. Even towards unjust magistrates. Matt. xvii. 26, 27. Acts xxiii. 4. Those cases must be excepted, in which compliance with the commands of men would be incompatible with our duty towards God. Exod. i. 17. Opposed to this are, first, rebellion. Numb. xvi. 1. 2. Sam. xx. 1. Secondly, obedience in things unlawful. 1 Sam. xxii. 18. The opinion maintained by some, that obedience is due to the commands not only of an upright magistrate, but of an usurper, and that in matters contrary to justice, has no foundation in Scripture. For with regard to 1 Pet. ii. 13. "submit yourselves to every ordinance of man," it is evident from v. 14. that although this passage comprehends all human ordinances, all forms of government indiscriminately, it applies to them only so far as they are legitimately constituted. The eighteenth verse, which is alleged to the same purpose, relates to servants exclusively, and affords no rule for the conduct of free nations, whose rights are of a kind altogether distinct from those of purchased or hired

servants. As for the obedience of the Israelites to Pharaoh, we have no means of ascertaining whether it was voluntary or compulsory, or whether in obeying they acted rightly or otherwise, inasmuch as we are nowhere told, either that they were enjoined to obey him, or that their obedience was made matter of commendation. The conduct of Daniel in captivity is equally foreign to the purpose, as under his circumstances it was impossible for him to act otherwise. That it may be the part of prudence to obey the commands even of a tyrant in lawful things, or, more properly, to comply with the necessity of the times for the sake of public peace, as well as of personal safety, I am far from denying.

The duties of the magistrate and people *towards their neighbors* regard the transactions of peace and war. Under the head of *peace* are included international treaties. In order to ascertain whether, in particular cases, these may be lawfully contracted with the wicked, we ought to consider the purposes for which treaties are concluded, whether simply for the sake of peace, or of mutual defence and closer intimacy. Of the former class are the confederacy of Abraham with the men of Mamre, Gen. xiv. 13. and with Abimelech, xxi. 27. that of Isaac with Abimelech, xxvi. 29–31. that of Solomon with Hiram, 1 Kings v. 12. from which examples the lawfulness of such alliances appears evident. Of the latter class are the treaties of Asa with Benhadad, 1 Kings xv. 19. of Jehoshaphat with the house of Ahab, 2 Chron. xviii. 1. compared with xix. 2. of Amaziah with the Israelites, xxv. 6–8. of Ahaz with the Assyrians, 2 Kings xvi. 7. and that which the Jews sought to contract with the Egyptians, Isai. xxx. 2. These were unlawful, and led to calamitous results. Exod. xxiii. 32. Asa, 2 Chron. xvi. 3. and Zedekiah, xxxvi. 13. are examples of the violation of treaties. On the subject of asylums see Numb. xxxv. 6—15. Deut. xxiii. 15.

With regard to the duties of *war,* it is enjoined, first, that it be not undertaken without mature deliberation. Prov. xx. 18. xxiv. 6. Luke xiv. 31. Secondly, that it be carried on wisely and skilfully. 1 Sam. xiv. 28. Thirdly, that it be prosecuted with moderation. Deut. xx. 19. Fourthly, that it be waged in a spirit of godliness. Deut. xxiii. 9. Fifthly, that r mercy be shown to a merciless enemy. 1 Sam. xv. 33. Psal. xviii. 41, 42. lx. 8. Jer. xlviii. 10. Sixthly, that our confidence be not placed in human strength, but in God alone. Exod. xiv. 17, 18. Deut. xx. 1. 1 Sam. xiv. 6. xvii. 47. Seventhly, that the booty be distributed in equitable proportions. Numb. xxxi. 27.

There seems no reasons why war should be unlawful now, any more than in the time of the Jews: nor is it anywhere forbidden in the New Testament. Psal. cxlix. 6. Two centurions, namely, the man of Capernaum and Cornelius, are reckoned among believers, Matt. viii. Acts x. Neither does John exhort the soldiers to refrain from war, but only from wrong and robbery; Luke iii. 14. 1 Cor. ix. 7. Paul likewise availed himself of a guard of soldiers for his personal security; Acts xxiii. 17.

The observance of the divine commandments is the source of prosperity to nations. See Levit. xxvi. It renders them flourishing, wealthy, and victorious, Deut. xv. 4–6. lords over many nations, v. 6. xxvi. 17–19. exalted above all others, xxviii. a chapter which should be read again and again by those who have the direction of political affairs.

The consequences of impiety to nations are described, Isai. iii. 7.

Public ecclesiastical duties consist in the reciprocal obligations of ministers, and of the church considered collectively and individually. *The duties of ministers towards the church in general, and towards individual believers in particular,* are stated in the first book, in the chapter on ministers. Towards the church in general: Jer. i. 7, 8. Opposed to the above are the ignorant, the slothful, the timid, flatterers, the dumb, false teachers, the covetous, the ambitious. Isai. ix. 15. Ezek. xliv. 8. "ye have set keepers of my charge in my sanctuary for yourselves;" as was done by bishops formerly, and is not unfrequently practised by magistrates in the present day, thus depriving the people of their privilege of election. Isai. lvi. 10. For an example of flatterers, see 2 Chron. xviii. 5. Neh. vi. 12. Jer. ii. 8. In this class are to be placed Hananiah, chap. xxviii. with the two other prophets mentioned in chap. xxix. 21. and Shemaiah, v. 24.

The duties of the whole church and of individual believers towards their ministers

are stated Book I. in the chapter concerning the ministers and people; to which many of the following texts may also be referred. Matt. ix. 37, 38. See also John xiii. 29. Luke viii. 18. Philipp. iii. 17, 18. 1 Thess. v. 12, 13. Heb. xiii. 7. v. 17, 18. Jer. xxiii. 16. The contrary conduct is condemned, Isai. xxx. 9, 10. Jer. xliii. 2. Micah ii. 6. v. 11. Luke vii. 29. 30. 3 John 9.

FAMILIAR LETTERS.

[The following translation of the *Familiar Letters* is that made by Masson and printed in his *Life of Milton*. It is here used through the kindly courtesy of The Macmillan Company.]

THE PRINTER TO THE READER

(1674)

WITH respect to the public letters, having ascertained that those who alone had the power were for certain reasons averse to their publication, I, content with what I had got, was satisfied with giving to the world the Familiar Letters by themselves. When I found these Familiar Letters to be somewhat too scanty for a volume even of limited size, I resolved to treat with the author through a particular friend of both of us, in order that, if he chanced to have by him any little matter in the shape of a treatise, he might not grudge throwing it in, as a makeweight, to counter-balance the paucity of the Letters, or at least occupy the blank. He, influenced by the adviser, having turned over his papers, at last fell upon the accompanying juvenile compositions, scattered about, some here and others there, and, at my friend's earnest request, made them over to his discretion. These, therefore, when I perceived that, as they were sufficiently approved of by the common friend in whom I trusted, so the author did not seem to think he ought to be ashamed of them, I have not hesitated, juvenile as they are, to give to the light; hoping, as it is very much my interest to do, that they will be found not less vendible by me than originally, when they were recited, they were agreeable to their auditors.

1. *To* THOMAS YOUNG, *His Preceptor*

Although I had resolved with myself, most excellent Preceptor, to send you a certain small epistle composed in metrical numbers, yet I did not consider that I had done enough, unless I also wrote something in prose; for truly the boundless and singular gratitude of my mind, which your deserts justly claim from me, was not to be expressed in that cramped mode of speech, straitened by fixed feet and syllables, but in a free oration, nay rather, were it possible, in an Asiatic exuberance of words. Albeit, 'tis true, to express sufficiently how much I owe you were a work far greater than my strength, even if I should call into play all those commonplaces of argument which Aristotle or that Dialectician of Paris has collected, or even if I should exhaust all the fountains of oratory. You complain (as justly you may) that my letters have been to you very few and very short; but I, on the other hand, do not so much grieve that I have been remiss in a duty so pleasant and so enviable, as I rejoice, and all but exult, at having such a place in your friendship as that you should care to ask for frequent letters from me. That I should never have written to you for now more than three years, I pray you will not misconceive, but, in accordance with your wonderful indulgence and candor, put the more charitable construction upon it. For I call God to witness how much as a Father I regard you, with what singular devotion I have always followed you in thought, and how I feared to trouble you with my writings. In sooth I make it my first care that since there is nothing else to commend my letters, their rarity may commend them. Next, as out of that most vehement desire after you which I feel, I always fancy you with me, and speak to you and behold you as if you were present, and so (as almost happens in love) soothe my grief by a certain vain imagination of your presence, it is in truth my fear, as soon as I meditate sending you a letter, that it should suddenly come into my mind by what an interval of earth you are distant from me, and so the grief of your absence, already nearly lulled, should grow fresh, and break up my sweet dream. The Hebrew Bible, your truly most acceptable gift, I have already received. These lines I have written in London in the midst of town-distractions, not, as usual, surrounded by books: if, therefore, anything in this epistle should please you less than might be, and

disappoint your expectation, it will be made up for by another more elaborate one, as soon as I have returned to the haunts of the Muses.

London, March 26, 1625.

2. *To* ALEXANDER GILL

I received your letter, and, what wonderfully delighted me, your truly great verses, breathing everywhere a genuine poetical majesty, and a Vergilian genius. I knew, indeed, how impossible it would be for you and your genius to keep away from poetry, and to discharge out of the depths of your breast those heaven-inspired furies and the sacred and ethereal fire, seeing that (as Claudian says of himself) *Totum spirent præcordia Phœbum.* Therefore, if you have broken the promises made to yourself, I here praise your (as you call it) inconstancy; I praise the sin, if there be any; and that I should have been made by you the judge of so excellent a poem, I no less glory in and regard as an honor than if the contending musical gods themselves came to me for judgment, as they fable happened of old to Timolus, the popular god of the Lydian mountain. I know not truly whether I should more congratulate Henry of Nassau on the capture of the city or on your verses; for I think the victory he has obtained nothing more illustrious or more celebrated than this poetical tribute of yours. But, as we hear you sing the prosperous successes of the Allies in so sonorous and triumphal a strain, how great a poet we shall hope to have in you, if by chance our own affairs, turning at last more fortunate, should demand your congratulatory muses! Farewell, learned Sir, and believe that you have my best thanks for your verses.

London, May 20, 1628.

3. *To* ALEXANDER GILL

In my former letter I did not so much reply to you as stave off my turn of replying; and I silently promised with myself that another letter should soon follow, in which I should answer somewhat more at large to your most friendly challenge; but even if I had not promised this, it must be confessed on the highest grounds of right to be your due, seeing that I think that each single letter of yours could not be balanced except by two of mine, nay, if the account were more strict, not even by a hundred of mine. The matter respecting which I wrote to you rather obscurely, you will find contained in the accompanying sheets. When your letter reached me, I was (being hard put to by the shortness of the time) laboring upon it with all my might: for a certain Fellow of our house who had to act as Respondent in the philosophical disputation in this Commencement chanced to entrust to my puerility the composition of the verses according to annual custom required to be written on the questions in dispute, being himself already long past the age for trifles of that sort, and more intent on serious things. The result, committed to type, I have sent to you, as knowing you to be a very severe judge in poetical matters, and a very candid judge of my productions. But if you in turn shall deign to communicate to me yours, there will assuredly be no one who will more delight in them, though there may be, I admit, who will more rightly judge of them according to their worth. Indeed, as often as I recollect your almost constant conversations with me (which even in this Athens, the University itself, I long after and miss), I straightway think, and not without grief, of how much benefit my absence from you has deprived me—me who never left your company without a manifest increase and ἐπιδόσει of literary knowledge, just as if I had been to some emporium of learning. Truly, amongst us here, as far as I know, there are hardly one or two here and there, who do not fly off unfeathered to Theology, while all but rude and uneducated in Philology as well as Philosophy, content too lightly to pick up as much Theology as may suffice for anyhow sticking together a little sermon and stitching it over with worn rags from other quarters, insomuch that it is to be dreaded that by degrees there may spread among our clergy that priestly ignorance of a former age. And, finding as I do almost no companions in my studies here, I should certainly be looking to London, were I not thinking of retiring during this summer vacation into a deeply literary repose, and hiding myself, so to speak, in the bowers of the Muses. But, as this is what you do daily, I think it almost a crime longer to interrupt you with my din at present. Farewell.

Cambridge, July 2, 1628.

4. *To* THOMAS YOUNG

On looking at your letter, most excellent preceptor, this alone struck me as superfluous, that you excused your slowness in writing; for, though nothing could come to me more desirable than your letters, how could I or ought I to hope that you should have so much leisure from serious and more sacred affairs as to have time always to answer me—especially as that is a matter entirely of kindness, and not at all of duty? That, however, I should suspect that you had forgotten me, your so many recent kindnesses to me would by no means allow. I do not see how you could dismiss out of your memory one laden with so great benefits by you. Having been invited by you to your part of the country, as soon as Spring is a little advanced, I will gladly come to enjoy the delights of the year, and not less of your conversation; and will then withdraw myself from the din of town for a little to your Stoa of the Iceni as to that most celebrated porch of Zeno or the Tusculan Villa of Cicero—where you, with moderate means but regal spirit, like some Serranus or Curius, placidly reign in your little farm, and, contemning fortune, hold as it were a triumph over riches, ambition, pomp, luxury, and whatever the herd of men admire and are amazed by. But, as you have deprecated the blame of slowness, you will also, I hope, pardon me the fault of haste; for, having put off this letter to the last, I preferred writing little, and that in a rather slovenly manner, to not writing at all. Farewell, most to be respected Sir.

Cambridge, July 21, 1628.

5. *To* ALEXANDER GILL

If you had presented to me a gift of gold, or of preciously embossed vases, or whatever of that sort mortals admire, it were certainly to my shame not to have some time or other made you a remuneration in return, as far as my faculties might serve. Your gift of the day before yesterday, however, having been such a sprightly and elegant set of Hendecasyllabics, you have, just in proportion to the superiority of that gift to anything in the form of gold, made us the more anxious to find some dainty means by which to repay the kindness of so pleasant a favor. We had, indeed, at hand some things of our own of this same kind, but such as I could nowise deem fit to be sent in contest of equality of gift with yours. I send, therefore, what is not exactly mine, but belongs also to the truly divine poet, this ode of whom, only last week, with no deliberate intention certainly, but from I know not what sudden impulse before daybreak, I adapted, almost in bed, to the rule of Greek heroic verse: with the effect, it seems, that, relying on this coadjutor, who surpasses you no less in his subject than you surpass me in art, I should have something that might have a resemblance of approach to a balancing of accounts. Should anything meet you in it not coming up to your usual opinion of our productions, understand that, since I left your school, this is the first and only thing I have composed in Greek,—employing myself, as you know, more willingly in Latin and English matters; inasmuch as whoever spends study and pains in this age on Greek composition runs a risk of singing mostly to the deaf. Farewell, and expect me on Monday (if God will) in London among the booksellers. Meanwhile, if with such influence of friendship as you have with that Doctor, the annual President of the College, you can anything promote our business, take the trouble, I pray, to go to him as soon as possible in my behalf. Again, farewell.

From our suburban residence, Decemb. 4, 1634.

6. *To* CHARLES DIODATI

Now at length I see plainly that what you are driving at is to vanquish me sometimes in the art of obstinate silence; and, if it is so, bravo! have that little glory over us, for behold! we write first. All the same if ever the question should come into contention why neither has written to the other for so long, do not think but that I shall stand by many degrees the more excused of the two, —manifestly so indeed, as being one by nature slow and lazy to write, as you well know; while you, on the other hand, whether by nature or by habit, are wont without difficulty to be drawn into epistolary correspondence of this sort. It makes also for my favor that I know your method of studying to be so arranged that you frequently take breath in the middle, visit your friends, write much, sometimes make a journey, whereas my genius is such that no delay, no rest, no care or thought almost of anything, holds me aside until I reach the end I am making for, and round off, as it were, some great period of my studies. Wholly hence, and not from any other cause, believe me, has it happened that I am slower in approaching the voluntary discharge of good offices; but in replying to such, O our *Theodotus,* I am not so very dilatory; nor have I ever been guilty of not meeting any letter of yours by one of mine in due turn. How happens it that, as I hear, you have sent letters to the bookseller, to your brother too not infrequently, either of whom could, conveniently enough, on account of their nearness, have caused letters to have been delivered to me, if there had been any? What I complain of, however, is that, whereas you promised that you would take up your quarters with us for a passing visit on your departure from the city, you did not keep your promise, and that, if you had but once thought of this neglect of your promise, there would not have been wanting necessary occasion enough for writing. All this matter of deserved lecture, as I imagine, I have been keeping against you. What you will prepare in answer see for yourself. But, meanwhile, how is it with you, pray? Are you all right in health? Are there in those parts any smallish learned folks with whom you can willingly associate and chat, as we were wont together? When do you return? How long do you intend to remain among those *hyperboreans?* Please to answer me these questions one by one: not that you are to make the mistake of supposing that only now have I your affairs at heart,—for understand that, in the beginning of the autumn, I turned out of my way on a journey to see your brother for the purpose of knowing what you were doing. Lately also, when it had been fallaciously reported to me in London by some one that you were in town, straightway and as if by storm I dashed to your crib; but 'twas the vision of a shadow! for nowhere did you appear. Wherefore, if you can without inconvenience, fly hither all the sooner, and fix yourself in some place so situated that I may have a more pleasant hope that somehow or other we may be able at least sometimes to exchange visits,—though I would you were as much our neighbor in the country as you are when in town. But this as it pleases God! I would say more about myself and my studies, but would rather do so when we meet; and now tomorrow we are to return to that country-residence of ours, and the journey so presses that I have hardly had time to put all this on the paper. Farewell.

London: Septemb. 2, 1637.

7. *To* CHARLES DIODATI

While other friends generally in their letters think it enough to express a single wish for one's health, I see now how it is that you convey the same salutation so many times; for to those mere wishes on the subject which were all that you yourself could in former times offer, and which are all that others have to offer yet, you would now have me understand, I suppose, that there is the gigantic addition of your art and all the force of your medical practitionership. You bid me be well six hundred times, as well as I wish to be, well as I can be, and so forth even more superlatively. Verily you must have lately been made the very steward of the larder, the clerk of the kitchen, to Health, such havoc you make of the whole store of salubrity; or, doubtless, Health ought now to be your parasite, you so act the king over her and command her to be obedient. I therefore congratulate you, and find it consequently necessary to return you thanks on a double account,—your friendship, for one thing, and your excellence in your profession for another. I did indeed, since it had been so agreed, long expect letters from you; but, having never received any, I did not, believe me, on that account suffer my old good-will to you to cool in the least; nay, that very excuse for your delay which you have employed in the beginning of your letter I had anticipated in my own mind you would offer, and that rightly

and in accordance with our relations to each other. For I would not have true friendship turn on balances of letters and salutations, all which may be false, but that it should rest on both sides in the deep roots of the mind and sustain itself there, and that, once begun on sincere and sacred grounds, it should, though mutual good offices should cease, be free from suspicion and blame all life long. For fostering such a friendship as this what is wanted is not so much written correspondence as a loving recollection of virtues on both sides. Nor, even should you have persisted in not writing, would there be lack of means with me for supplying that good office. Your probity writes for me in your stead, and inscribes true letters on my inmost consciousness, your frank innocence of character writes to me, and your love of the good; your genius also, by no means an every-day one, writes to me and commends you to me more and more. Don't, therefore, now that you have possessed yourself of that tyrannic citadel of Medicine, wave those terrors before me, as if you meant to draw in bit by bit, and to demand lack from me your six hundred healths till only one was left, if by chance (which God forbid) I should become a traitor to friendship. Remove that terrible *battery* which you seem to have planted right at me in your resolution that it shall not be lawful for me to get ill without your good leave. For, lest you should threaten too much, know that it is impossible for me not to love men like you. What besides God has resolved concerning me I know not, but this at least: *He has instilled into me, if into anyone, a vehement love of the beautiful.* Not with so much labor, as the fables have it, is Ceres said to have sought her daughter Proserpina as it is my habit day and night to seek for this *idea of the beautiful,* as for a certain image of supreme beauty, through all the forms and faces of things (for many are the shapes of things divine) and to follow it as it leads me on by some sure traces which I seem to recognize. Hence it is that, when any one scorns what the vulgar opine in their depraved estimation of things, and dares to feel and speak and be that which the highest wisdom throughout all ages has taught to be best, to that man I attach myself forthwith by a kind of real necessity, wherever I find him. If, whether by nature or by my fate, I am so circumstanced that by no effort and labor of mine can I myself rise to such an honor and elevation, yet that I should always worship and look up to those who have attained that glory, or happily aspire to it, neither gods nor men, I reckon, have bidden nay.

But now I know you wish to have your curiosity satisfied. You make many anxious inquiries, even as to what I am at present thinking of. Hearken, Theodotus, but let it be in your private ear, lest I blush; and allow me for a little to use big language with you. You ask what I am thinking of? So may the good Deity help me, of immortality! And what am I doing? *Growing my wings* and meditating flight; but as yet our Pegasus raises himself on very tender pinions. Let us be lowly wise!

I will now tell you seriously what I am thinking of. I am thinking of migrating into some Inn of the Lawyers where I can find a pleasant and shady walking-ground, because there I shall have both a more convenient habitation among a number of companions if I wish to remain at home, and more *suitable* headquarters if I choose to make excursions in any direction. Where I am now, as you know, I live obscurely and in a cramped manner. You shall also have information respecting my studies. I have by continuous reading brought down the affairs of the Greeks as far as to the time when they ceased to be Greeks. I have been long engaged in the obscure business of the state of Italians under the Longobards, the Franks, and the Germans, down to the time when liberty was granted them by Rodolph, King of Germany: from that period it will be better to read separately what each City did by its own wars. But what are you doing? How long will you hang over domestic matters as a *filius familias*, forgetting your town companionships? Unless this step-motherly war be very bad indeed, worse than the Dacian or the Sarmatian, you will certainly have to make haste, so as to come to us at least for winter-quarters. Meanwhile, if it can be done without trouble to you, I beg you to send me Justiniani, the historian of the Venetians. I will, on my word, see that

he is well kept against your arrival, or, if you prefer it, that he is sent back to you not very long after receipt. Farewell.

London: Septemb. 23, 1637.

8. *To* BENEDETTO BONMATTEI *of Florence*

By this work of yours, Benedetto Bonmattei, the compilation of new institutes of your native tongue, now so far advanced that you are about to give it the finishing touch, you are entering on a path to renown shared with you by some intellects of the highest order, and have also, as I see, raised a hope and an opinion of yourself among your fellow-citizens, as of one that is to confer, by his own easy effort, either lucidity or richness, or, at least, polish and order, on what has been handed down by others. Under what extraordinary obligation you have laid your countrymen by this, they must be ungrateful if they do not perceive. For whoever in a state knows how to form wisely the manners of men and to rule them at home and in war with excellent institutes, him in the first place, above others, I should esteem worthy of all honor; but next to him the man who strives to establish in maxims and rules the method and habit of speaking and writing received from a good age of the nation, and, as it were, to fortify the same round with a kind of wall, any attempt to overleap which ought to be prevented by a law only short of that of Romulus. Should we compare the two in respect of utility, it is the former alone that can make the social existence of the citizens just and holy, but it is the latter alone that can make it splendid and beautiful,—which is the next thing to be wished. The one, as I believe, supplies a noble courage and intrepid counsels against an enemy invading the territory; the other takes to himself the task of extirpating and defeating, by means of a learned detective police of ears and a light cavalry of good authors, that barbarism which makes large inroads upon the minds of men, and is a destructive intestine enemy to genius. Nor is it to be considered of small consequence what language, pure or corrupt, a people has, or what is their customary degree of propriety in speaking it,—a matter which oftener than once involved the salva tion of Athens: nay, while it is Plato's opinion that by a change in the manner and habit of dressing serious commotions and mutations are portended in a commonwealth, I, for my part, would rather believe that the fall of that city and its low and obscure condition were consequent on the general vitiation of its usage in the matter of speech. For, let the words of a country be in part unhandsome and offensive in themselves, in part debased by wear and wrongly uttered, and what do they declare but, by no light indication, that the inhabitants of that country are an indolent, idly-yawning race, with minds already long prepared for any amount of servility? On the other hand, we have never heard that any empire, any state, did not flourish moderately at least as long as liking and care for its own language lasted. Therefore, Benedetto, if only you proceed to perform vigorously this labor of yours for your native state, behold clearly, even from this, what a fair and solid affection you will necessarily win from your countrymen. All this I say, not because I suppose you to be ignorant of any of it, but because I persuade myself that you are much more intent on the consideration of what you yourself can do for your country than of what your country will, by the best right, owe to you. I will now speak of foreigners. For obliging them, if that is at your heart, most certainly at present an ample opportunity is offered,—since what one is there among them that, happening to be more blooming than the rest in genius or in pleasing and elegant manners, and so counting the Tuscan tongue among his chief delights, does not also consider that it ought to have a place for him in the solid part of his literature, especially if he has imbibed Greek and Latin either not at all or but in slight tincture? I, certainly, who have not wet merely the tips of my lips with both those tongues, but have, as much as any, to the full allowance of my years, drained their deeper draughts, can yet sometimes willingly and eagerly go for a feast to that Dante of yours, and to Petrarch, and a good few more; nor has Attic Athens herself, with her pellucid Ilissus, nor that old Rome with her bank of the Tiber, been able so to hold me but that I love often to visit

your Arno and these hills of Fiesole. See now, I entreat, whether it has not been with enough of providential cause that I have been given to you for these few days, as your latest guest from the ocean, who am so great a lover of your nation that, as I think, there is no other more so. Wherefore you may, with more reason, remember what I am wont so earnestly to request of you,—to wit, that to your work already begun, and in greater part finished, you would, to the utmost extent that the case will permit, add yet, in behalf of us foreigners, some little appendix concerning the right pronunciation of the language. For with other authorities in your tongue hitherto the intention seems to have been to satisfy only their own countrymen, without care for us. Although, in my opinion, they would have consulted both their own fame and the glory of the Italian tongue much more certainly had they so delivered their precepts as if it concerned all mankind to acquire the knowledge of that language, yet, in so far as has depended on them, you might seem, you Italians, to regard nothing beyond the bounds of the Alps. This praise, therefore, untasted by any one before, will be wholly your own, and keeps itself till now untouched and entire for you; nor less another which I will venture to mention. Would you consider it too much trouble if you were to give information separately on such points as these:—who, in such a crowd of writers, can justly claim for himself the second place, next after the universally celebrated authors of the Florentine tongue; who is illustrious in Tragedy; who happy and sprightly in Comedy; who smart or weighty in Epistles or Dialogues; who noble in History? By this means the choice of the best in each kind would not be difficult for the willing student, while, whenever it might please him to range more widely, he would have ground on which to step intrepidly. In this matter you will have, among the ancients, Cicero and Fabius for examples; but whether any of your own men I know not. —Though I believe I have already (unless my memory deceive me) made these demands of you every time we have fallen on the matter in talk,—such is your politeness and kindly disposition,—I am unwilling to regard that as any reason for not entreating the same in set phrase, so to speak, and in an express manner. For while your own worth and candor would assign the lowest value and the lowest estimation to your own labors, my wish is that both their inherent dignity and my individual respect should set the just and exact value upon them; and certainly it is but fair everywhere that, the more easily one admits a request, the less defect should there be of due honor to his compliance.—For the rest, should you perchance wonder why, on such a subject, I use the Latin tongue rather than yours, please to understand that it is precisely because I wish to have this Italian tongue of yours cleared up for me in precepts by yourself that I employ Latin openly in my confession of poverty and want of skill. By this very method I have hoped to prevail more with you,—not without a belief at the same time that, by the very act of bringing with me that hoary and venerable mother from Latium as my helper in her daughter's cause, I should make sure that you would deny nothing to her venerable authority, her majesty august through so many ages. Farewell.

Florence, Septemb. 10, 1638.

9. *To* Lucas Holstenius *in the Vatican at Rome*

Although I both can and often do remember many courteous and most friendly acts done me by many in this my passage through Italy, yet, for so brief an acquaintance, I do not know whether I can justly say that from any one I have had greater proofs of goodwill than those which have come to me from you. For, when I went up to the Vatican for the purpose of meeting you, though a total stranger to you,—unless perchance anything had been previously said about me to you by Alexander Cherubini,—you received me with the utmost courtesy. Admitted at once with politeness into the Museum, I was allowed to behold the superb collection of books, and also very many manuscript Greek authors set forth with your explanations,—some of whom, not yet seen in our age, seemed now, in their array, like Vergil's

penitus convalle virenti
Inclusæ animæ superumque ad limen ituræ,

to demand the active hands of the printer, and a delivery into the world, while others, already edited by your care, are eagerly received everywhere by scholars:—dismissed, too, richer than I came, with two copies of one of these last presented to me by yourself. Then, I could not but believe that it was in consequence of the mention you made of me to the most excellent Cardinal Francesco Barberini that, when he, a few days after, gave that public musical entertainment with truly Roman magnificence, he himself, waiting at the doors, and seeking me out in so great a crowd, almost seizing me by the hand indeed, admitted me within in a truly most honorable manner. Further, when, on this account, I went to pay my respects to him next day, you again were the person that both made access for me and obtained me an opportunity of leisurely conversation with him—an opportunity such as, with so great a man,—than whom, on the topmost summit of dignity, nothing more kind, nothing more courteous,—was truly, place and time considered, too ample rather than too sparing. I am quite ignorant, most learned Holstenius, whether I am exceptional in having found you so friendly and hospitable, or whether, in respect of your having spent three years in study at Oxford, it is your express habit to confer such obligations on all Englishmen. If the latter, truly you are paying back finely to our England the expenses of your schooling there, and you eminently deserve equal thanks on private grounds from each of us and on public grounds for our country. If the former is the case, then that I should have been held distinguishable by you above the rest, and should have seemed worthy so far of a wish on your part to form a bond of friendship with me, while I congratulate myself on this opinion of yours, I would at the same time attribute it to your frankness rather than to my merit. The commission which you seemed to give me, relating to the inspection of a Medicean codex, I have already carefully reported to my friends; who, however, hold forth for the present very small hope of effecting that matter. In that library, I am told, nothing can be copied, unless by leave first obtained; it is not permitted even to bring a pen to the tables. But they tell me that Giovanni Battista Doni is now in Rome; having been called to Florence to undertake the public lectureship in Greek, he is daily expected; and through him, they say, it will be easy for you to compass what you want. Still it would have been truly a most gratifying accident for me if a matter of a kind so eminently desirable had advanced somewhat farther by my little endeavor, the disgrace being that, engaged as you are in work so honorable and illustrious, all men, methods, and circumstances, are not everywhere at your bidding.—For the rest, you will have bound me by a new obligation if you salute his Eminence the Cardinal with all possible respect in my name; whose great virtues, and regard for what is right, singularly evident in his readiness to forward all the liberal arts, are always present before my eyes, as well as that meek, and, if I may so say, submissive loftiness of mind, which alone has taught him to raise himself by self-depression; concerning which it may truly be said, as is said of Ceres in Callimachus, though with a turn of the sense: *Feet to the earth still cling, while the head is touching Olympus.* This may be a proof to most other princes how far asunder and alien from true magnanimity is the sour superciliousness and courtly haughtiness too common. Nor do I think that, while he is alive, men will miss any more the Este, the Farnesi, or the Medici, formerly the favored of learned men.—Farewell, most learned Holstenius; and, if there is any more than average lover of you and your studies, I should wish you to reckon me along with him, should you think that of such consequence, wheresoever in the world my future may be.

Florence, March 30, 1639.

10. *To* CHARLES DATI, *Nobleman of Florence*

With how great and what new pleasure I was filled, my Charles, on the unexpected arrival of your letter since it is impossible for me to describe it adequately, I wish you may in some degree understand from the very pain with which it was dashed, such pain as is almost the invariable accompaniment of any great delight yielded to me. For,

on running over that first portion of your letter, in which elegance contends so finely with friendship, I should have called my feeling one of unmixed joy, and the rather because I see your labor to make friendship the winner. Immediately, however, when I came upon that passage where you write that you had sent me three letters before, which I now know to have been lost, then, in the first place, that sincere gladness of mine at the receipt of this one began to be infected and troubled with a sad regret, and presently a something heavier creeps in upon me, to which I am accustomed in very frequent grievings over my own lot: the sense, namely, that those whom the mere necessity of neighborhood, or something else of a useless kind, has closely conjoined with me, whether by accident or by the tie of law, they are the persons, though in no other respect commendable, who sit daily in my company, weary me, nay, by heaven, all but plague me to death whenever they are jointly in the humor for it, whereas those whom habits, disposition, studies, had so handsomely made my friends, are now almost denied me, either by death or by most unjust separation of place, and are so far the most part snatched from my sight that I have to live well-nigh in a perpetual solitude. As to what you say, that from the time of my departure from Florence you have been anxious about my health and always mindful of me, I truly congratulate myself that a feeling has been equal and mutual in both of us, the existence **of** which on my side only I was perhaps claiming to my credit. Very sad to me also, I will not conceal from you, was that departure, and it planted stings in my heart which now rankle there deeper, as often as I think with myself of my reluctant parting, my separation as by a wrench, from so many companions at once, such good friends as they were, and living so pleasantly with each other in one city, far off indeed, but to me most dear. I call to witness that tomb of Damon, ever to be sacred and solemn to me, whose adornment with every tribute of grief was my weary task, till I betook myself at length to what comforts I could, and desired again to breathe a little—I call that sacred grave to witness that I have had no greater delight all this while than in recalling to my mind the most pleasant memory of all of you, and of yourself especially. This you must have read for yourself long ere now, if that poem reached you, as now first I hear from you it did. I had carefully caused it to be sent, in order that, however small a proof of talent, it might, even in those few lines introduced into it emblem-wise, be no obscure proof of my love towards you. My idea was that by this means I should lure either yourself or some of the others to write to me; for, if I wrote first, either I had to write to all, or I feared that, if I gave the preference to any one, I should incur the reproach of such others as came to know it, hoping as I do that very many are yet there alive who might certainly have a claim to this attention from me. Now, however, you first of all, both by this most friendly call of your letter, and by your thrice-repeated attention of writing before, have freed the reply for which I have been some while since in your debt from any expostulation from the others. There was, I confess, an additional cause for my silence in that most turbulent state of our Britain, subsequent to my return home, which obliged me to divert my mind shortly afterwards from the prosecution of my studies to the defence anyhow of life and fortune. What safe retirement for literary leisure could you suppose given one among so many battles of a civil war, slaughters, flights, seizures of goods? Yet, even in the midst of these evils, since you desire to be informed about my studies, know that we have published not a few things in our native tongue; which, were they not written in English, I would willingly send to you, my friends in Florence, to whose opinions I attach very much value. The part of the Poems which is in Latin I will send shortly, since you wish it; and I would have done so spontaneously long ago, but that, on account of the rather harsh sayings against the Pope of Rome in some of the pages, I had a suspicion they would not be quite agreeable to your ears. Now I beg of you that the indulgence you were wont to give, I say not to your own Dante and Petrarch in the same case, but with singular politeness to my own former freedom of speech, as you know, among you, the

same you, Dati, will obtain (for of yourself I am sure) from my other friends whenever I may be speaking of your religion in our peculiar way. I am reading with pleasure your description of the funeral ceremony to King Louis, in which I recognize your style —not that one of street bazaars and mercantile concerns which you say jestingly you have been lately practising, but the right eloquent one which the Muses like, and which befits the president of a club of wits. It remains that we agree on some method and plan by which henceforth our letters may go between us by a sure route. This does not seem very difficult, when so many of our merchants have frequent and large transactions with you, and their messengers run backwards and forwards every week, and their vessels sail from port to port not much seldomer. The charge of this I shall commit, rightly I hope, to Bookseller James, or to his master, my very familiar acquaintance. Meanwhile farewell, my Charles; and give best salutations in my name to Coltellini, Francini, Frescobaldi, Malatesta, Chimentelli the younger, anyone else you know that remembers me with some affection, and, in fine, to the whole Gaddian Academy. Again farewell!

London: April 21, 1647.

11. *To* HERMANN MYLIUS, *Agent for the Count of Oldenburg*

Before I reply, most noble Hermann, to your letter to me of the 17th of December, I must first of all, lest you should perchance consider me the person responsible for so long a silence, explain why I did not reply sooner. Understand then that a first cause of delay was, what is now almost a perpetual enemy of mine, bad health; next, on account of my health, there was a sudden and unavoidable removal to another house, and I had begun the same, as it chanced, on the very day on which your letter was brought me; finally, in truth, I was ashamed at then having nothing to report on your business that I thought would be agreeable to you. For, when, the day after, I met Mr. Frost accidentally, and carefully inquired of him whether any answer was yet under resolution for you (for, in my invalid state, I was often myself absent from the Council), he told me, and with some concern, that nothing was yet under resolution, and that he was having no success in his efforts to expedite the affair. I thought it better, therefore, to be silent for a time than to write at once what I knew would be annoying to you, and this in the expectation of afterwards being able to write, with full satisfaction, what I wanted to write and you so much desired. Today, as I hope, I have brought things to a conclusion; for, after I had in the council once and again reminded the President of your business, he reported it immediately, and with such effect that to-morrow is appointed for the consideration of an answer to be given to you as speedily as possible. I thought that, if I were the first, as was my purpose, to give you this information, you would be greatly pleased and it would also be a sign of my regard for you.

Westminster.

12. *To the most distinguished* LEONARD PHILARAS, *of Athens, Ambassador from the Duke of Parma to the King of France*

Your good will towards me, most honored LEONARD PHILARAS, as well as your high opinion of our *Defence for the English People,* I learnt from your letters, written partly on that subject, to MR. AUGIER, a man illustrious among us for his remarkable fidelity in diplomatic business for this Republic: after which I received, through the same, your kind greeting, with your portrait, and the accompanying eulogium, certainly most worthy of your virtues,—and then, finally, a most polite letter from yourself. Be assured that I, who am not in the habit of despising the genius of the Germans, or even of the Danes or Swedes, cannot but value much such an opinion of me from you, a native of Attic Athens, who have besides, after happily finishing a course of literary studies among the Italians, reached such ample honors by great handling of affairs. For, as the great Alexander himself, when carrying on war in the remotest parts of the earth, declared that he had undergone such great labors *for the sake of the good opinion of the Athenians,* why should not I congratulate myself, and think myself honored to the highest, in having received praises from one

in whom singly at this day the Arts of the old Athenians and all their celebrated excellencies appear, after so long an interval, to revive and rebloom? Remembering how many men of supreme eloquence were produced by that city, I have pleasure in confessing that whatever literary advance I have made I owe chiefly to steady intimacy with their writings from my youth upwards. But, were there in me, by direct gift from them, or a kind of transfusion, such a power of pleading that I could rouse our armies and fleets for the deliverance of Greece, the land of eloquence, from her Ottoman oppressor—to which mighty act you seem almost to implore our aid—truly there is nothing which it would be more or sooner in my desire to do. For what did even the bravest men of old, or the most eloquent, consider more glorious or more worthy of them than, whether by pleading or by bravely acting *to make the Greeks free and self-governing?* There is, however, something else besides to be tried, and in my judgment far the most important: namely that some one should, if possible, arouse and rekindle in the minds of the Greeks, by the relation of that old story, the old Greek valor itself, the old industry, the old patience of labor. Could some one do that—and from no one more than yourself ought we to expect it, looking to the strength of your feeling for your native land, and the combination of the same with the highest prudence, skill in military affairs, and a powerful passion for the recovery of the ancient political liberty— then, I am confident, neither would the Greeks be wanting to themselves, nor any other nation wanting to the Greeks. Farewell.

London, June 1652.

13. *To* RICHARD HEATH

If I have ever been able, my much respected Friend, to give aid, whether in promoting your studies or in procuring furtherance in them—and such aid has assuredly been either nothing or very slight—I am glad on more than one account that it should have been bestowed so well and fortunately on a nature of such promise, though known rather late, and that it has been so fruitful as to have produced an upright pastor of the church, a good citizen of his country, and at the same time an agreeable friend for myself. All this I am easily sure of, both from the rest of your life and your excellent state of sentiment about Religion and State, and also, and especially, from that singular affectionateness of your mind which can be extinguished or lessened by no amount of absence, no lapse of time. Nor is it possible, unless you had made more than ordinary progress in virtue and piety and in study of the best things, that you should be so grateful to those who have conferred even the least assistance towards those acquisitions. Wherefore, my Pupil (for I willingly call you by that name, if you allow it), I would have you believe that you have a high place in my regards, and that nothing would be more desirable for me than that, if your convenience and your plans permitted (and this I see to be also in your own wishes), you should be able to live somewhere near me, so that there might be more frequent and pleasant intercourse of life and studies between us. But of that as God pleases and you find expedient! Further, as to what you say about writing in English, do so if you please (though you have really made no small advance in Latin), lest at any time the trouble of writing should make either of us slow to write, and in order that our ideas, not being bound by any fetters of an alien speech, may the more freely express themselves. You will, I believe, with the greatest propriety entrust your letters to any one of the servants of the family I have mentioned to you. Farewell. Westminster, December 13, 1652.

14. *To* HENRY OLDENBURG, *Agent for Bremen*

Your former letter, Honored Sir, was given to me when your messenger, I was told, was on the point of return; whence it happened that there was no opportunity of reply at that time. While I was afterwards purposing an early reply, some unexpected business took me off; but for which I should certainly not have sent you my book, *Defence* though it is called, in such a naked condition, without accompanying excuse. And now I have your second letter, in which your thanks are quite disproportioned to the slenderness of the gift. It was in my mind too more than once to send you back English for your Latin, in order that, as you have learnt to speak our language more accurately and happily than any other foreigner of my acquaintance, you should not lose any opportunity of writing the same; which I believe you could do with equal accuracy. But in this, just as henceforward the impulse may be, let your choice regulate. As to the substance of your communication, you plainly think with me that a "Cry" of that kind "to Heaven" transcends all bounds of human sense; the more impudent, then, must be he who declares so boldly he has heard it. You throw in a scruple after all as to who he is: but, formerly, whenever we talked on this subject, just after you had come hither from Holland, you seemed to have no doubt whatever but MORUS was the author, inasmuch as that was the common report in those parts and no one else was named. If then, you have now at last any more certain information on the point, be so good as to inform me. As to the treatment of the argument, I should wish (why should I dissemble?) not to differ from you, if only because I would fain know what there is to which one would more readily yield than the sincere judgment of friendly men, like yourself, and praise free from all flattery. To prepare myself, as you suggest, for other labors,—whether nobler or more useful I know not, for what can be nobler or more useful in human affairs than the vindication of Liberty?—truly, if my health shall permit, and this blindness of mine, a sorer affliction than old age, and lastly the "cries" of such brawlers as there have been about me, I shall be induced to *that* easily enough. An idle ease has never had charms for me, and this unexpected contest with the Adversaries of Liberty took me off against my will when I was intent on far different and altogether pleasanter studies: not that in any way I repent of what I have done, since it was necessary; for I am far from thinking that I have spent my toil, as you seem to hint, on matters of inferior consequence. But of this at another time; meanwhile, learned Sir, not to detain you too long, farewell, and reckon me among your friends. Westminster, July 6, 1654.

15. *To* Leonard Philaras, *Athenian*

As I have been from boyhood an especial worshipper of all bearing the Greek name, and of your Athens in chief, so I have always had a firm private persuasion that that city would some time or other requite me splendidly for my affection towards her. Nor, in truth, has the ancient genius of your noble country failed my augury, since in you, an Athenian born, I have had bestowed upon me one of the most loving of friends. When I was known to you by writings only, and you were yourselves separated from me by place, you opened a communication with me most courteously by letter; and, coming afterwards unexpectedly to London, and visiting a man incapable any more of seeing his visitors, even in that calamity by which I am rendered an object of more regard to none, and perhaps of less regard to many, you continue now to show me the same kind attention. As you have, therefore, suggested to me that I should not give up all hope of recovering my sight, and told me that you have a friend and close companion in the Paris physician Thevenot, especially distinguished as an oculist, and that you will consult him about my eyes if I furnish you with means for his diagnosis of the causes and symptoms, I will do what you advise, that I may not haply seem to refuse any chance of help offered me providentially.

It is ten years, I think, more or less, since I felt my sight getting weak and dull, and at the same time my viscera generally out of sorts. In the morning, if I began, as usual, to read anything, I felt my eyes at once thoroughly pained, and shrinking from the act of reading, but refreshed after moderate bodily exercise. If I looked at a lit candle, a kind of iris seemed to snatch it from me. Not very long after, a darkness coming over the left part of my left eye (for that eye became clouded some years before the other) removed from my vision all objects situated on that side. Objects in front also, if I chanced to close the right eye, seemed smaller. The other eye also failing perceptibly and gradually through a period of three years, I observed, some months before my sight was wholly gone, that objects I looked at without myself moving seemed all to swim, now to the right, now to the left. Inveterate mists now seem to have settled in my forehead and temples, which weigh me down and depress me with a kind of sleepy heaviness, especially from meal-time to evening; so that not seldom there comes into my mind the description of the Salmydessian seer Phineus in the *Argonautics:*

All round him then there grew
A purple thickness; and he thought the Earth
Whirling beneath his feet, and so he sank,
Speechless at length, into a feeble sleep.

But I should not forget to mention that, while yet a little sight remained, when first I lay down in bed, and turned myself to either side, there used to shine out a copious glittering light from my shut eyes; then that, as my sight grew less from day to day, colors proportionally duller would burst from them, as with a kind of force and audible shot from within; but that now, as if the sense of lucency were extinct, it is a mere blackness, or a blackness dashed, and as it were inwoven, with an ashy grey, that is wont to pour itself forth. Yet the darkness which is perpetually before me, by night as well as by day, seems always nearer to a whitish than to a blackish, and such that, when the eye rolls itself, there is admitted, as through a small chink, a certain little trifle of light.

And so, whatever ray of hope also there may be for me from your famous physician, all the same, as in a case quite incurable, I prepare and compose myself accordingly, and my frequent thought is that, since many days of darkness, as the Wise Man warns us, are destined for every one, my darkness hitherto, by the singular kindness of God, amid rest and studies, and the voices and greetings of friends, has been much easier to bear than that deathly one. But if, as is written, "Man shall not live by bread alone, but by every word that proceedeth out of the mouth of God," what should prevent one from resting likewise in the belief that his eyesight lies not in his eyes alone, but enough for all purposes in God's leading and providence? Verily, while only He looks out for me and provides for me, as He doth, leading me and leading me forth as with

His hand through my whole life, I shall willingly, since it has seemed good to Him, have given my eyes their long holiday. And to you, dear Philaras, whatever may befall, I now bid farewell, with a mind not less brave and steadfast than if I were Lynceus himself for keenness of sight.

Westminster: September 28, 1654.

16. *To* Leo Van Aitzema

It is very gratifying to me that you retain the same amount of recollection of me as you very politely showed of good will by once and again visiting me while you resided among us. As regards the Book on Divorce which you tell me you have given to some one to be turned into Dutch, I would rather you had given it to be turned into Latin. For my experience in those books of mine has now been that the vulgar still receive according to their wont opinions not already common. I wrote a good while ago, I may mention, *three* treatises on the subject:— the first, in two books, in which *The Doctrine and Discipline of Divorce* is contained at large; a second, which is called *Tetrachordon,* and in which the four chief passages of Scripture concerning that doctrine are explicated; the third called *Colasterion,* in which answer is made to a certain sciolist. Which of these Treatises you have given to be translated, or what edition, I do not know: the first of them was twice issued, and was much enlarged in the second edition. Should you not have been made aware of this already, or should I understand that you desire anything else on my part, such as sending you the more correct edition or the rest of the Treatises, I shall attend to the matter carefully and with pleasure. For there is not anything at present that I should wish changed in them or added. Therefore, should you keep to your intention, I earnestly hope for myself a faithful translator, and for you all prosperity.

Westminster: Feb. 5, 1654–5.

17. *To* Ezekiel Spanheim *of Geneva.*

I know not by what accident it has happened that your letter has reached me little less than three months after date. There is clearly extreme need of a speedier conveyance of mine to you; for, though from day to day I was resolving to write it, I now perceive that, hindered by some constant occupations, I have put it off nearly another three months. I would not have you understand from this my tardiness in replying that my grateful sense of your kindness to me has cooled, but rather that the remembrance has sunk deeper from my longer and more frequent daily thinking of my duty to you in return. Late performance of duty has at least this excuse for itself, that there is a clearer confession of obligation to do a thing when it is done so long after than if it had been done immediately.

You are not wrong, in the first place, in the opinion of me expressed in the beginning of your letter—to wit, that I am not likely to be surprised at being addressed by a foreigner; nor could you, indeed, have a more correct impression of me than precisely by thinking that I regard no good man in the character of a foreigner or a stranger. That you are such I am readily persuaded by your being the son of a most learned and most saintly father, also by your being well esteemed by good men, and also finally by the fact that you hate the bad. With which kind of cattle as I too happen to have a warfare, Calandrini has but acted with his usual courtesy, and in accordance with my own sentiment, in signifying to you that it would be very gratifying to me if you lent me your help against a common adversary. This you have most obligingly done in this very letter, part of which, with the author's name not mentioned, I have not hesitated, trusting in your regard for me, to insert by way of evidence in my forthcoming *Defensio.* This book, as soon as it is published, I will direct to be sent to you, if there is anyone to whose care I may rightly entrust it. Any letters you may intend for me, meanwhile, you will not, I think, be unsafe if you send under cover to Turretin of Geneva, now staying in London, whose brother in Geneva you know; through whom as this of mine will reach you most conveniently, so will yours reach me. For the rest I would assure you that you have won a high place in my esteem, and that I particularly wish to be loved by you yet more.

Westminster: March 24, 1654–5.

18. *To* HENRY OLDENBURG, *Agent for Bremen with the English Government*

Your letter, brought by young Ranelagh, has found me rather busy; and so I am forced to be briefer than I should wish. You have indeed kept your departing promise of writing to me, and that with a punctuality surpassed, I believe, by no one hitherto in the payment of a debt. I congratulate you on your present retirement, to my loss though it be, since it gives pleasure to you; I congratulate you also on that happy state of mind which enables you so easily to set aside at once the ambition and the ease of city-life, and to lift your thoughts to higher matters of contemplation. What advantage that retirement affords, however, besides plenty of books, I know not; and those persons you have found there as fit associates in your studies I should suppose to be such rather from their own natural constitution than from the discipline of the place,—unless perchance, from missing you here, I do less justice to the place for keeping you away. Meanwhile you yourself rightly remark that there are too many there whose occupation it is to spoil divine and human things alike by their frivolous quibblings, that they may not seem to be doing absolutely nothing for those many endowments by which they are supported so much to the public detriment. All this you will understand better for yourself. Those ancient annals of the Chinese from the Flood downwards which you say are promised by the Jesuit Martini are doubtless very eagerly expected on account of the novelty of the thing; but I do not see what authority or confirmation they can add to the Mosaic books. Our Cyriack, whom you bade me salute, returns the salutation. Farewell.

Westminster: June 25, 1656.

19. *To the Noble Youth,* RICHARD JONES

Preparing again and again to reply to your last letter, I was first prevented, as you know, by some sudden pieces of business, of such a kind as are apt to be mine; then I heard you were off on an excursion to some places in your neighborhood; and now your most excellent mother, on her way to Ireland—whose departure ought to be a matter of no ordinary regret to both of us (for to me also she has stood in the place of all kith and kin)—carries you this letter herself. That you feel assured of my affection for you, right and well; and I would have you feel daily more and more assured of it, the more of good disposition and of good use of your advantages you give me to see in you. Which result, by God's grace, I see you not only engage for personally, but, as if I had provoked you by a wager on the subject, give solemn pledge and put in bail that you will accomplish,—not refusing, as it were, to abide judgment, and to pay the penalty of failure if judgment should be given against you. I am truly delighted with this so good hope you have of yourself; which you cannot now be wanting to, without appearing at the same time not only to have been faithless to your own promises but also to have run away from your bail. As to what you write to the effect that you do not dislike Oxford, you adduce nothing to make me believe that you have got any good there or been made any wiser: you will have to show me that by very different proofs. Victories of Princes, which you extol with praises, and matters of that sort in which force is of most avail, I would not have you admire too much, now that you are listening to Philosophers. For what should be the great wonder if in the native land of wethers there are born strong horns, able to ram down most powerfully cities and towns? Learn you, already from your early age, to weigh and discern great characters not by force and animal strength, but by justice and temperance. Farewell; and please to give best salutations in my name to the highly accomplished Henry Oldenburg, your chamber-fellow.

Westminster: Sept. 21, 1656.

20. *To the very accomplished youth,* PETER HEIMBACH

Most amply, my Heimbach, have you fulfilled your promises and all the other expectations one would have of your goodness, with the exception that I have still to long for your return. You promised that it would be within two months at farthest; and now, unless my desire to have you back makes me misreckon the time, you have been absent nearly three. In the matter of the Atlas you have abundantly performed all I requested of you; which was not that you should procure me one, but only that you should find out the lowest price of the book. You write that they ask 130 florins: it must be the Mauritanian mountain Atlas, I think, and not a book, that you tell me is to be bought at so huge a price. Such is now the luxury of Typographers in printing books that the furnishing of a library seems to have become as costly as the furnishing of a villa. Since to me at least, on account of my blindness, painted maps can hardly be of use, vainly surveying as I do with blind eyes the actual globe of the earth, I am afraid that the bigger the price at which I should buy that book the greater would seem to me my grief over my deprivation. Be good enough, pray, to take so much farther trouble for me as to be able to inform me, when you return, how many volumes there are in the complete work, and which of the two issues, that of Blæu or that of Jansen, is the larger and more correct. This I hope to hear from you personally, on your speedy return, rather than by another letter. Meanwhile, farewell, and come back to us as soon as you can.

Westminster: Nov. 8, 1656.

21. *To the most accomplished* EMERIC BIGOT.

That on your coming into England I had the honor of being thought by you more worth visiting and saluting than others was truly and naturally gratifying to me; and that now you renew your salutation by letter, even at such an interval, is somewhat more gratifying still. For in the first instance you might have come to me perhaps on the inducement of other people's opinion; but you could hardly return to me by letter save at the prompting of your own judgment, or, at least, good will. On this surely I have ground to congratulate myself. For many have made a figure by their published writings whose living voice and daily conversation have presented next to nothing that was not low and common: if, then, I can attain the distinction of seeming myself equal in mind and manners to any writings of mine that have been tolerably to the purpose,

there will be the double effect that I shall so have added weight personally to my writings, and shall receive back by way of reflection from them credit, how small soever it may be, yet greater in proportion. For, in that case, whatever is right and laudable in them, that same I shall seem not more to have derived from authors of high excellence than to have fetched forth pure and sincere from the inmost feelings of my own mind and soul. I am glad, therefore, to know that you are assured of my tranquillity of spirit in this great affliction of loss of sight, and also of the pleasure I have in being civil and attentive in the reception of visitors from abroad. Why, in truth, should I not bear gently the deprivation of sight, when I may hope that it is not so much lost as revoked and retracted inwards, for the sharpening rather than the blunting of my mental edge? Whence it is that I neither think of books with anger, nor quite intermit the study of them, grievously though they have mulcted me,—were it only that I am instructed against such moroseness by the example of King Telephus of the Mysians, who refused not to be cured in the end by the weapon that had wounded him. As to that book you possess, *On the Manner of Holding Parliaments,* I have caused the marked passages of it to be either amended, or, if they were doubtful, confirmed, by reference to the MS. in the possession of the illustrious Lord Bradshaw, and also to the Cotton MS., as you will see from your little paper returned herewith. In compliance with your desire to know whether also the autograph of this book is extant in the Tower of London, I sent one to inquire of the Herald who has the custody of the Deeds, and with whom I am on familiar terms. His answer is that no copy of that book is extant among those records. For the help you offer me in return in procuring literary material I am very much obliged. I want, of the Byzantine Historians, *Theophanis Chronographia* (folio: Greek and Latin), *Constantini Manassis Breviarium Historicum,* with *Codini Excerpta de Antiquitatibus Constantinopolitanis* (folio: Greek and Latin), *Anastasii Bibliothecarii Historia et Vitæ Romanorum Pontificum* (folio); to which be so good as to add, from the same press, *Michael Glycas,* and

Ioannes Cinnamus, the continuator of Anna Commena, if they are now out. I do not ask you to get them as cheap as you can, both because there is no need to put a very frugal man like yourself in mind of that, and because they tell me the price of these books is fixed and known to all. MR. STOUPE has undertaken the charge of the money for you in cash, and also to see about the most convenient mode of carriage. That you may have all you wish, and all you aspire after, is my sincere desire. Farewell.

Westminster: March 24, 1656–7.

22. *To the Noble Youth,* RICHARD JONES

I received your letter much after its date, —not till it had lain, I think, fifteen days, put away somewhere, at your mother's. Most gladly at last I recognized in it your continued affection for me and sense of gratitude. In truth my goodwill to you, and readiness to give you the most faithful admonitions, have never but justified, I hope, both your excellent mother's opinion of me and confidence in me, and your own disposition. There is, indeed, as you write, plenty of amenity and salubrity in the place where you now are; there are books enough for the needs of a University: if only the amenity of the spot contributed as much to the genius of the inhabitants as it does to pleasant living, nothing would seem wanting to the happiness of the place. The Library there, too, is splendidly rich; but, unless the minds of the students are made more instructed by means of it in the best kinds of study, you might more properly call it a book-warehouse than a Library. Most justly you acknowledge that to all these helps there must be added a spirit for learning and habits of industry. Take care, and steady care, that I may never have occasion to find you in a different state of mind; and this you will most easily avoid if you diligently obey the weighty and friendly precepts of the highly accomplished Henry Oldenburg beside you. Farewell, my well-beloved Richard; and allow me to exhort and incite you to virtue and piety, like another Timothy, by the example of that most exemplary woman, your mother.

Westminster.

23. *To the Very Distinguished* MR. HENRY DE BRASS

I see, Sir, that you, unlike most of our modern youth in their surveys of foreign lands, travel rightly and wisely, after the fashion of the old philosophers, not for ordinary youthful quests, but with a view to the acquisition of fuller erudition from every quarter. Yet, as often as I look at what you write, you appear to me to be one who has come among strangers not so much to receive knowledge as to impart it to others, to barter good merchandise rather than to buy it. I wish indeed it were as easy for me to assist and promote in every way those excellent studies of yours as it is pleasant and gratifying to have such help asked by a person of your uncommon talents.

As for the resolution you say you have taken to write to me and request my answers towards solving those difficulties about which for many ages writers of Histories seem to have been in the dark, I have never assumed anything of the kind as within my powers, nor should I dare now to do so. In the matter of Sallust, which you refer to me, I will say freely, since you wish me to tell plainly what I do think, that I prefer Sallust to any other Latin historian; which also was the almost uniform opinion of the Ancients. Your favourite Tacitus has his merits; but the greatest of them, in my judgment, is that he imitated Sallust with all his might. As far as I can gather from what you write, it appears that the result of my discourse with you personally on this subject has been that you are now nearly of the same mind with me respecting that most admirable writer; and hence it is that you ask me, with reference to what he has said, in the introduction to his *Catilinarian War*—as to the extreme difficulty of writing History, from the obligation that the expressions should be proportional to the deeds—by what method I think a writer of History might attain that perfection. This, then, is my view: that he who would write of worthy deeds worthily must write with mental endowments and experience of affairs not less than were in the doer of the same, so as to be able with equal mind to comprehend and measure even the greatest of them, and.

when he has comprehended them, to relate them distinctly and gravely in pure and chaste speech. That he should do so in ornate style, I do not much care about; for I want a Historian, not an Orator. Nor yet would I have frequent maxims, or criticisms on the transactions, prolixly thrown in, lest, by interrupting the thread of event, the Historian should invade the office of the Political Writer: for, if the Historian, in explicating counsels and narrating facts, follows truth most of all, and not his own fancy or conjecture, he fulfills his proper duty. I would add also that characteristic of Sallust, in respect of which he himself chiefly praised Cato,—to be able to throw off a great deal in few words: a thing which I think no one can do without the sharpest judgment and a certain temperance at the same time. There are many in whom you will not miss either elegance of style or abundance of information; but for conjunction of brevity with abundance, i.e., for the despatch of much in few words, the chief of the Latins, in my judgment, is Sallust. Such are the qualities that I think should be in the Historian that would hope to make his expressions proportional to the facts he records.

But why all this to you, who are sufficient, with the talent you have, to make it all out and who, if you persevere in the road you have entered, will soon be able to consult no one more learned than yourself. That you do persevere, though you require no one's advice for that, yet, that I may not seem to have altogether failed in replying correspondingly with the value you are pleased to put upon my authority with you, is my earnest exhortation and suggestion. Farewell; and all success to your real worth, and your zeal for acquiring wisdom.

Westminster: July 15, 1657.

24. *To* Henry Oldenburg

I am glad you have arrived safe at Saumur, the goal of your travel, as I believe. You are not mistaken in thinking the news would be very agreeable to me in particular, who both love you for your own merit, and know the cause of your undertaking the journey to be so honorable and praiseworthy.

As to the news you have heard, that so infamous a priest has been called to instruct so illustrious a church, I had rather anyone else had heard it in Charon's boat than you in that of Charenton; for it is mightily to be feared that whoever thinks to get to heaven under the auspices of so foul a guide will be a whole world awry in his calculations. Woe to that church (only God avert the omen!) where such ministers please, mainly by tickling the ears,—ministers whom the Church, if she would truly be called Reformed, would more fitly cast out than desire to bring in.

In not having given copies of my writings to anyone that does not ask for them, you have done well and discreetly, not in my opinion alone, but also in that of Horace:

Err not by zeal for us, nor on our books
Draw hatred by too vehement care.

A learned man, a friend of mine, spent last summer at Saumur. He wrote to me that the book was in demand in those parts; I sent only one copy; he wrote back that some of the learned to whom he had lent it had been pleased with it hugely. Had I not thought I should be doing a thing agreeable to them, I should have spared you trouble and myself expense. But,

If chance my load of paper galls your back,
Off with it now, rather than in the end
Dash down the panniers cursing.

To our Lawrence, as you bade me, I have given greetings in your name. For the rest, there is nothing I should wish you to do or care for more than see that yourself and your pupil get on in good health, and that you return to us as soon as possible with all your wishes fulfilled.

Westminster: Aug. 1, 1657.

25. *To the noble youth,* Richard Jones

That you made out so long a journey without inconvenience, and that, spurning the allurements of Paris, you have so quickly reached your present place of residence, where you can enjoy literary leisure and the society of learned persons, I am both heartily glad, and set down to the credit of your disposition. There, so far as you keep yourself in bounds, you will be in harbor; elsewhere you would have to beware the Syrtes, the Rocks, and the songs of the Sirens. All the same I would not have you thirst too much after the Saumur vintage, with which you think to delight yourself, unless it be also your intention to dilute that juice of Bacchus, more than a fifth part, with the freer cup of the Muses. But to such a course, even if I were silent, you have a first-rate adviser; by listening to whom you will indeed consult best for your own good, and cause great joy to your most excellent mother, and a daily growth of her love for you. Which that you may accomplish you ought every day to petition Almighty God. Farewell; and see that you return to us as good as possible, and as cultured as possible in good arts. That will be to me, beyond others, a most delightful result.

Westminster: Aug. 1, 1657.

26. *To the very distinguished* Mr. Henry de Brass

Having been hindered these days past by some occupation, illustrious Sir, I reply later than I meant. For I meant to do so all the more speedily because I saw that your present letter, full of learning as it is, did not so much leave me room for suggesting anything to you (a thing which you ask of me, I believe, out of compliment to me, not for your own need) as for simple congratulation. I congratulate myself especially on my good fortune in having, as it appears, so suitably explained Sallust's meaning, and you on your so careful perusal of that most wise author with so much benefit from the same. Respecting him I would venture to make the same assertion to you as Quintilian made respecting Cicero,—that a man may know himself no mean proficient in the business of History who enjoys his Sallust. As for that precept of Aristotle's in the Third Book of his Rhetoric which you would like explained—Use is to be made of maxims both in the narrative of a case and in the pleading, for it has a moral effect—I see not what it has in it that much needs explanation: only that the narration and the pleading (which last is usually also called the proof) are here understood to be such as the Orator uses, not the Historian; for the parts of the Orator and the Historian are different whether they narrate or prove, just as the Arts themselves are different. What is suitable for the historian you will have learnt more correctly from the ancient authors, Polybius, the Halicarnassian, Diodorus, Cicero, Lucian, and many others, who have handed down certain stray precepts concerning that subject. For me, I wish you heartily all happiness in your studies and travels, and success worthy of the spirit and diligence which I see you employ on everything of high excellence. Farewell.

Westminster: December 16, 1657.

27. *To the highly accomplished* Peter Heimbach

I have received your letter dated the Hague, Dec. 18, which, as I see it concerns your interests, I have thought I ought to answer on the very day it has reached me. After thanking me for I know not what favors of mine,—which, as one who desires everything good for you, I would were really of any consideration at all,—you ask me to recommend you, through Lord Lawrence, to our Minister appointed for Holland. I really regret that this is not in my power, both because of my very few intimacies with the men of influence, almost shut up at home as I am, and as I prefer to be, and also because I believe the gentleman is now embarking and on his way, and has with him in his company the person he wishes to be his Secretary—the very office about him you seek. But the post is this instant going. Farewell.

Westminster: December 18, 1657.

28. *To* Jean Labadie, *Minister of Orange*

If I answer you rather late, distinguished and reverend Sir, our common friend Durie, I believe, will not refuse to let me transfer the blame of the late answer from myself to him. For, now that he has communicated to me that paper which you wished read to me, on the subject of your doings and sufferings in behalf of the Gospel, I have not deferred preparing this letter for you, to be given to the first carrier, being really anxious as to the interpretation you may put upon my long silence. I owe very great thanks meanwhile to your Du Moulin of Mismes, who, by his speeches and most friendly talk concerning me, has procured me the good will of so many good men in those parts. And truly, though I am not ignorant that, from the fact that I did not, when publicly commissioned, decline the contest with an adversary of such name, or an account of the celebrity of the subject, or, finally, on account of my style of writing, I have become sufficiently known far and wide, yet my feeling is that I have real fame only in proportion to the good esteem I have among good men. That you also are of this way of thinking I see plainly—you who, kindled by the regard and love of Christian Truth, have borne so many labors, sustained the attacks of so many enemies, and who bravely do such actions every day as prove that, so far from seeking any fame from the bad, you do not fear rousing against you their most certain hatred and maledictions. O happy man thou! whom God, from among so many thousands, otherwise knowing and learned, has snatched singly from the very gates and jaws of Hell, and called to such an illustrious and intrepid profession of his Gospel! And at this moment I have cause for thinking that it has happened by the singular providence of God that I did not reply to you sooner. For, when I understood from your letter that, assailed and besieged as you are on all hands by bitter enemies, you were looking round, and no wonder, to see where you might, in the last extremity, should it come to that, find a suitable refuge, and that England was most to your mind, I rejoiced on more accounts than one that you had come to this conclusion,— one reason being the hope of having you here, and another the delight that you should have so high an opinion of my country; but the joy was counterbalanced by the regret that I did not then see any prospect of a becoming provision for you among us here, especially as you do not know English. Now, however, it has happened most opportunely that a certain French minister here, of great age, died a few days ago. The persons of most influence in the congregation, understanding that you are by no means safe where you are at present, are very desirous (I report this not from vague rumor, but on information from themselves) to have you chosen to the place of that minister: in fact,

they invite you; they have resolved to pay the expenses of your journey; they promise that you shall have an income equal to the best of any French minister here, and that nothing shall be wanting that can contribute to your pleasant discharge of the pastoral duty among them. Wherefore, take my advice, Reverend Sir, and fly hither as soon as possible, to people who are anxious to have you, and where you will reap a harvest, not perhaps so rich in the goods of this world, but, as men like you most desire, numerous, I hope, in souls; and be assured that you will be most welcome here to all good men, and the sooner the better. Farewell.

Westminster: April 21, 1659.

29. *To* Henry Oldenburg

That forgiveness which you ask for your silence you will give rather to mine; for, if I remember rightly, it was my turn to write to you. By no means has it been any diminution of my regard for you (of this I would have you fully persuaded) that has been the impediment, but only my employments or domestic cares; or perhaps it is mere sluggishness to the act of writing that makes me guilty of the intermitted duty. As you desire to be informed, I am, by God's mercy, as well as usual. Of any such work as compiling the history of our political troubles, which you seem to advise, I have no thought whatever: they are worthier of silence than of commemoration. What is needed is not one to compile a good history of our troubles, but one who can happily end the troubles themselves; for, with you, I fear lest, amid these our civil discords, or rather sheer madnesses, we shall seem to the lately confederated enemies of Liberty and Religion a too fit object of attack, though in truth they have not yet inflicted a severer wound on Religion than we ourselves have been long doing by our crimes. But God, as I hope, on His own account, and for his own glory, now in question, will not allow the counsels and onsets of the enemy to succeed as they themselves wish, whatever convulsions Kings and Cardinals meditate and design. Meanwhile, for the Protestant Synod of Loudom, which you tell me is soon to meet I pray —what has never happened to any Synod yet—a happy issue, not of the Nazianzenian sort, and am of opinion that the issue of this one will be happy enough if, should they decree nothing else, they should decree the expulsion of Morus. Of my posthumous adversary, as soon as he makes his appearance, be good enough to give me the earliest information. Farewell.

Westminster: December 20, 1659.

30. *To the Noble Youth*, RICHARD JONES

For the long break in your correspondence with me your excuses are truly modest, inasmuch as you might with more justice accuse me of the same fault; and, as the case stands, I am really at a loss to know whether I should have preferred your not having been in fault to your having apologized so finely. On no account let it ever come into your mind that I measure your gratitude, if anything of the kind is due to me from you, by your constancy in letter-writing. My feeling of your gratitude to me will be strongest when the fruits of those services of mine to you of which you speak shall appear not so much in frequent letters as in your perseverance and laudable proficiency in excellent pursuits. You have rightly marked out for yourself the path of virtue in that theatre of the world on which you have entered; but remember that the path is common so far to virtue and vice, and that you have yet to advance to where the path divides itself into two. And you ought now betimes to prepare yourself for leaving this common path, pleasant and flowery, and for being able the more readily, with your own will, though with labor and danger, to climb that arduous and difficult one which is the slope of virtue only. For this you have great advantages over others, believe me, in having secured so faithful and skillful a guide. Farewell.

Westminster: December 20, 1659.

31. *To the very distinguished* PETER HEIMBACH, *Councillor to the Elector of Brandenburg*

Small wonder if, in the midst of so many deaths of my countrymen, in a year of such heavy pestilence, you believed, as you write you did, on the faith of some special rumor, that I also had been cut off. Such a rumor

among your people is not displeasing, if it was the occasion of making known the fact that they were anxious for my safety, for then I can regard it as a sign of their goodwill to me. But, by the blessing of God, who had provided for my safety in a country retreat, I am still both alive and well, nor useless yet, I hope, for any duty that remains to be performed by me in this life.— That after so long an interval I should have come into your mind is very agreeable; although, from your exuberant expression of the matter, you seem to afford some ground for suspecting that you have rather forgotten me, professing as you do such an admiration of the marriage-union in me of so many different virtues. Truly, I should dread a too numerous progeny from so many forms of the marriage-union as you enumerate, were it not an established truth that virtues are nourished most and flourish most in straitened and hard circumstances; albeit I may say that one of the virtues on your list has not very handsomely requited to me the hospitable reception she had. For what you call policy, but I would rather have you call loyalty to one's country,—this particular lass, after inveigling me with her fair name, has almost expatriated me, so to speak. The chorus of the rest, however, makes a very fine harmony. One's country is wherever it is well with one.—And now I will conclude, after first begging you, if you find anything incorrectly written or without punctuation here, to impute that to the boy who has taken it down from my dictation, and who is utterly ignorant of Latin, so that I was forced, while dictating, not without misery, to spell out the letters of the words one by one. Meanwhile I am glad that the merits of one whom I knew as a young man of excellent hope have raised him to so honorable a place in his Prince's favor; and I desire and hope all prosperity for you otherwise. Farewell!

London, Aug. 15, 1666.

SOME ORATORICAL EXERCISES

OF

JOHN MILTON

I.

IN COLLEGE, &.

Whether Day is more excellent than Night

ALL of the most distinguished teachers of rhetoric far and wide have left behind the opinion—a fact which has not escaped your notice, my fellow students—that in every kind of speaking, whether demonstrative or deliberative or judicial, the exordium ought to be occupied with securing the goodwill of the listeners; otherwise the minds of the audience could not be persuaded nor could the cause be triumphant as one might wish. But if such is the fact, which—may I not depart from the truth—I know is surely fixed and established by the agreement of all scholars, have mercy on me! To what desperate straits am I reduced this day! I, who at the very beginning of my speech fear lest I may advance something not at all worthy of orators and lest I should have deviated unavoidably from the primary and principal duty of a speaker; indeed, how can I expect your goodwill, when, in this great assembly, I perceive almost as many persons hostile to me as I behold with my eyes? Hence it is that I seem to come as an orator to those who are inexorable. Great can be the rivalry even in schools for the production of hatreds, either among those pursuing different subjects, or among those following different methods in the same studies. I really am not disturbed.

Lest Polydamas and the Trojan women
Prefer Labeo to me; that is nonsense.

Truly, however, my soul cannot wholly despair, for I see here and there, unless I am deluded, those who signify, not at all secretly, by the very quietness of their countenances, that they wish me well. By these indeed, however few, for my part, I would prefer to be approved, than by innumerable companies of the ignorant, who have no brains, no power to reason correctly, no sound judgment, men who betray themselves by a cer-

tain boasting and quite laughable froth of words, from whom if you take away the medley begged from modern authors, immortal god! you will find them even more empty than a bean pod, and when they have exhausted their meagre supply of words and little maxims, they utter not even a grunt, being just as speechless as the little Seriphian frogs. But O with what difficulty would even Heraclitus himself, if he were alive, restrain his laughter, if by chance, the gods being willing, he could perceive these little speakers here, whom a short time ago he might have heard spouting in the buskined Orestes of Euripides, or more bombastically in the *Hercules* raging toward his death; at length their very slender supply of some little words being exhausted, parade in measured step with haughtiness laid aside, or crawl slowly off like certain little animals with their horns drawn in.

But I recover myself, having digressed a very little. If then there is anyone who, spurning the conditions of peace, would impose upon me "truceless war," him at the present moment I will not disdain to address and to ask that he put aside for a little while his animosity and that he be present as an impartial judge of this debate, nor that, on account of the fault of the orator, if there is any, he speak disparagingly of such a splendid and most noble subject. But if you should think these remarks a little too biting and steeped too much in vinegar, I acknowledge that I have done this very thing intentionally; for I wish that the beginning of my oration should resemble the very early dawn from whose gloomy clouds the clearest day is usually born.

Whether the day is more excellent than the night is surely no common question to dilate upon, one indeed which it is now my duty, fellow students, at this morning exercise, to examine carefully and completely, although this would seem more suitable for a poetical exercise than for an oratorical contest. However that may be, have I affirmed that night arranged a contest with day? What sort of question is this? What an undertaking is this? Do the Titans renew the ancient war, bringing to life the remains of the Phlegraean battle? Has the earth brought forth a new offspring of monstrous size against the gods above? Has Typhoeus forced himself out of the mass of Mount Aetna heaped upon him? Has Briareus at length by deceiving Cerberus released himself from the adamantine chains? What indeed at length is it that has aroused the divine shades now for the third time to a hope of heavenly dominion, even though the lightning of Jove must be defied? even though the unconquered valor of Pallas must [10] be thought worthless, by which at one time she produced so great a carnage among earth-born brothers? Has that remarkable victory of Father Liber over the shattered giants, throughout the circuit of heaven, escaped from her mind? Truly, by no means. She well remembers, not without tears, that many brothers were overwhelmed by Jove and that other survivors were also driven in flight to the lowermost depths of hell; and [20] certainly now, alarmed, she prepares for nothing less than war; rather she plans an accusation and a suit; and according to the fashion of women, after struggling bravely with nails and fists, she comes to a conference, or, more truly, a wrangle, about to test, I think, whether she is more effective with her tongue than with arms. But in truth how indiscreetly, how presumptuously, and with how slight a claim for a case does [30] she seek to gain supreme power in behalf of day, I hasten to relate; inasmuch as I behold even Day herself, aroused by the crowing of the cock, has advanced in her accustomed course more speedily in order to hear her own praises. And because each one thinks it contributes especially to honor and glory, if he ascertains himself to be born from a noble lineage and from the ancient stock of kings and gods, in the first place I [40] will consider which of the two in birth is more noble, next which is the more honored by antiquity, then whether the one or the other serves more suitably human needs.

Accordingly, I find it stated by the most ancient writers on Mythology that Demogorgon, ancestor of all the gods, whom I note was also called Chaos by antiquity, begot the Earth among many other children whom he had borne. She, by an undetermined father, [50] became the mother of Night; although somewhat differently Hesiod would wish her the offspring of Chaos, in this single line:

From Chaos, Erebus and black Night were born.

Whatsoever her origin, when she had grown to an age fit for marriage, Phanes, the shepherd, demanded her as his wife. Although her mother approved, she refused and said that she would not enter into marriage relations with an unknown man whom she had never seen and whose habits besides were so very different. Phanes, bearing with ill grace his repulse, his love turning to hatred, full of rage, followed this dark daughter of Earth through all the world seeking her death. Him whom she scorned as a lover, none the less she feared as an enemy. Wherefore, not deeming herself safe enough even among the farthest nations and in places separated as far as possible, indeed not in the very bosom of her mother, she furtively and secretly betook herself hastily into the incestuous embraces of her brother Erebus. At the same time she was released from her oppressive fear, and bore her husband a child very like himself in every respect. Accordingly, both Aether and Day are reported born to the beautiful pair of mates, on the authority of the same author, Hesiod, whom we have already mentioned:

From Night Aether and Day were born,
Whom she conceived and bore when inspired by love of Erebus.

However it may be, the gentler Muses, nay Philosophy itself, very close to the gods, forbids us to give credence in every way to the pictures of gods in the poets, especially to the Grecian. Nor should anyone think this statement libellous concerning them; since in a matter of great importance the authors seem not quite trustworthy. For if any of them deviated just a little from the truth, the swerving ought not be ascribed so much to their character, than which nothing is more divine, as to the perverse and blind ignorance of that age, an ignorance which pervaded everything in those days. As it is, they have won for themselves abundantly indeed of praise, enough of glory, because they have driven into one place men who were wandering in woods and mountains after the fashion of wild beasts, and they have established states, and, inspired by the divinity, they first have taught all learning whatsoever that has been handed down to this day, clad in the beautiful vestments of fiction. And this alone will be a not unworthy help to them for the attainment of an immortal name: that they have left a knowledge of the arts happily begun for posterity to finish.

Do not therefore, whoever you are, condemn me rashly on account of my assumption, as if I had already shattered and changed the principles of all the old poets, bound by no authority; for I do not affirm this of myself, but I attempt somehow or other to reduce these things to the norm of reason, being about to investigate in this fashion whether they can endure the test of strict truth.

Wherefore, in the first place, Antiquity has related learnedly and indeed in the best style that Night sprang from the Earth; for what else besides the Earth produces Night, except a dense and impenetrable earth interposed between the light of the sun and our horizon? Since the Mythologists are uncertain at one time about her paternity and at another time about her maternity, the story becomes a pleasant fiction; if indeed it is rightly considered to have been false or forged, or if the parents did not in the end acknowledge for shame off-spring so notorious and ignoble. But in truth, why they should believe that Phanes, a more than human being with an extraordinary countenance, had yearned for a union with Ethiopian and shadowy Night, would seem an exceedingly difficult matter to assert from the evidence, unless the remarkable scarcity of women up to that time furnished no abundant choice.

Let us, however, get at the matter closely and hand to hand. The ancients interpret Phanes as the Sun or Day. When, accordingly, they write that he sought at first a union with Night and then pursued her in revenge on account of the scorned connection, they wish to show nothing else than the alternate succession of day and night. In addition to this moreover, what was the necessity of representing Phanes seeking connection with Night, when that everlasting succession and as it were mutual impulse of these is better explained by an innate

and eternal animosity; since it happens that light and darkness have disagreed among themselves with bitterest hatred from the very beginning of things. And I truly believe that Night has received the cognomen *Euphrones* for this reason alone, that she cautiously and considerately refused to enter into marriage relationship with Phanes; for if she had admitted him to her chamber, beyond a doubt, devoured by his rays and by his unendurable brightness, she would either have been reduced to nothingness or she would have been burned to a crisp, just as once they say happened when Semele was consumed against his will by her lover Jupiter. On this account, not unmindful of her safety, she preferred Erebus; whence that witty and polished epigram of Martial:

Most wicked wife, most wicked husband;
I wonder that you don't get along well together.

Nor do I think I ought to pass over in silence how she enriched her husband with offspring, beautiful and worthy of herself: doubtless with Tribulation, Envy, Fear, Guile, Fraud, Obstinacy, Poverty, Wretchedness, Famine, Complaint, Sickness, Senility, Fright, Blindness, Sleep, Death, Charon, who was produced in a final birth, in order that she might on this occasion very fittingly complete what comes in the fashion of an adage: From a bad crow a bad egg.

Besides, there are not lacking those who relate that Night bore Aether and Day likewise to her Erebus. But how few there are in their right minds who do not disapprove and reject such a philosophic phantasy as smacking of Democritian fabrications or the stories of nurses? For does it bear any appearance of truth in its own behalf, that it is possible for cloudy and murky Night to produce offspring so beauteous, so lovable, so pleasing and agreeable to all? Furthermore, as soon as she had been conceived, she tortured her mother, rushing violently forth in premature birth; next drove away her father Erebus himself; and then compelled old Charon to hide his nocturnal eyes in the Stygian depths, and, if there are any dens under Hades, to betake him thither with oar and sails. Not only was Day not born in

Orcus; she never even appeared there: nor is it possible to enter there except against the will of the fates or through a very small crevice.

What shall be said to this: that I dare to say that Day is more ancient than Night; that this world, recently emerged from Chaos, was illuminated by diffused light before Night had begun her alternations; unless we wish erroneously to call Night that dense, foul obscurity, equivalent even to Demogorgon himself? Therefore, I think Day is the eldest daughter of Uranus, or rather, you will say, of his son, whom he is said to have begotten for the comfort of mankind and the terror of the Infernal Gods. Yea, forsooth, with Night occupying the position of a tyrant and situate with no interval between Earth and Tartarus, the Shades and Furies and all that infamous brood of monsters would continuously crawl up to the earth, leaving their home in the infernal regions; while wretched mankind, wrapped in dense fogs and pent up whithersoever they turn, would experience even in life the pangs of dead souls.

Up to this point, fellow students, we have shown the obscure origin of Night from black and most profound darkness; you shall straightway consider how she has proved herself worthy of her birthplace; but after I shall first have paid my ample tribute to the praises of Day, although she truly would surpass the eloquence of all encomiasts.

In the first place, what need is there to explain to you how pleasant and agreeable it is to the race of living creatures; since even the birds themselves cannot conceal their joy, but, coming from their nests at daybreak, or in the tops of trees, they describe all things with sweetest harmony; or, launching themselves on high, they fly as close to the sun as they are able, expressing thanks for his returning light. But first of all, the sleepless cock hails the approaching sun and like some herald seems to warn mankind, aroused from sleep, to come forth and rush out to greet the coming dawn. The she-goats caper in the fields. The whole race of quadrupeds is transported and leaps with joy. Yea, also, even mournful Clytie, awaiting almost the whole night her Phoebus, with her face turned toward the east, now smiles upon and invites her approaching lover. The marigold and also the rose, lest they add nothing to the common joy, opening their bosoms, breathe forth profusely their odors, reserved for the sun only, which they disdain to share with the night, concealing themselves in their leaflets as soon as evening approaches. And the other flowers, raising their heads which had been bowed a little and languishing with dew, almost surrender themselves to the sun and ask secretly that he wipe away with his kisses their tears, which his absences had produced. The Earth herself, at the coming of the sun, also clothes herself in more splendid attire. And the clouds in like manner with garments of varying hues, with festal show, and in long procession, seem to be maids in attendance on the rising god. Finally, that there may be nothing lacking to magnify his praises, to him the Persians, to him the Libyans, have decreed divine honors; the Rhodesians also have dedicated to him that very celebrated Colossus, of stupendous size, erected with wonderful skill by Chares of Lindos; to him even to this day we learn that the peoples of the Indian Occident sacrifice with incense and with other ceremonial. I call you to witness, fellow students, what a joyous, what a delightful daily expectation dawns upon you in the morning, seeing that it summons you again to the more gentle Muses, from whom the disagreeable night has separated you, insatiable and thirsty. I call to witness finally Saturn, driven from Heaven into Hell, how gladly he would wish to return from the hateful shades to the upper air, if only he might be permitted by Jove; for in very truth, it is indeed generally known that Light even to Pluto himself is more powerful by far than his own darkness, inasmuch as he has sought many times the dominion of heaven, concerning which Orpheus has beautifully and most truly sung in his Hymn to Aurora:

Thus rejoiceth she the race of clear-
    voiced mortals—
Nor doth a single one escape that watchful
    gaze, o'erhead.
When from their eyes, thou doth shake off
    sweet sleep,

Joy fills the soul of all,—of creeping beast, the host
Of quadrupeds, of birds, of the finny dwellers in the deep.

Nor is it to be wondered at, since Day brings no less of usefulness than of pleasure, and alone is adapted to the transaction of business; for who of mortals would undertake to cross the vast and boundless seas, if he should give up hope that day would come again? Indeed, they could no more sail the ocean than the shades could Lethe and Acheron, covered over everywhere doubtless with awful darkness. Also each one would confine himself in his hut, hardly ever daring to creep out of doors; so that it would be necessary immediately to dissolve human society. In vain would Apelles have attempted his Venus arising from the sea; in vain would Zeuxis have painted his Helen; if dark and cloudy night should so obscure the things which must be seen by our eyes. Then also in vain would the earth bring forth the vines, tangled in many folds and wandering flight; in vain the trees of most noble height; to no purpose in fine would she bedeck herself with gems and flowers like little stars, trying to imitate heaven. Then at length that most eminent faculty of seeing would be of no use to animals; so in a word, with the eye of the world put out, all things would fade and completely die away; nor indeed would men themselves long survive that disaster, men who should inhabit an earth shrouded in darkness, since nothing would produce the means of subsistence, nothing indeed would hinder all things from plunging to ancient Chaos. To these ideas it might be possible for someone with an unexhausted pen to add many things; but the modest day itself would not permit every item to be mentioned, and in its downward journey, hastening to the west, would by no means permit excessive adulation. Now, therefore, the day declines into eventide and quickly yields to night, unless you say wittily that, winter having come to maturity, the solstitial day has come.

May your patience permit only a few words which I cannot conveniently omit. Justly indeed the poets are wont to write that night arises from Hell; since it would be quite impossible from another source for so many and so great evils to assail mortals, except from that place. For on the appearance of night all things become murky and overspread with gloom; there is truly no difference between Helen and Canidia, none between the most precious and the common jewels, except that among the gems some conquer the obscurity of night. To this be it added that some most charming places do then inspire horror, which is increased by a certain deep and mournful silence, since indeed all who are anywhere in the fields, either of men or beasts, betake themselves speedily to home or to caves, where hidden in beds they close their eyes to the terrible visions of night. Nothing abroad do you see except thieves and light-shunning rogues, who, breathing out slaughter and rapine, lie in wait for the goods of citizens and wander along in the night, lest they be detected by day; since indeed day is not wont to track down any impious deed, not being able to endure that its light should be polluted by evils of this kind. You will have no assembly, except of ghosts and spectres and hobgoblins, which night brings with her as companions from subterranean places and which claim the lands of the earth to be during the whole night under their sway and shared by them with men. Accordingly, I believe night has rendered more acute our hearing, so that the groans of shades, the hoots of owls and the screeches of hags, and the roars of lions whom hunger calls forth, on that account more quickly stun the ears and spirits, and smite with a deeper fear. Hence, it is plainly evident how deceived is he who affirms that men are at night free from fear and that night lulls to sleep all cares; for all who have been conscious of any wickedness in themselves have learned by unhappy experience this opinion to be worthless and futile; whom at that time Sphinxes and Harpies, whom then Gorgons and Chimeras pursue with menacing aspect; they have learned, wretched creatures, who hurl bitter complaints at the senseless rocks, when no one is by to help or aid them, no one to soothe their sorrows with pleasant conversation, continually longing for the coming day. Therefore Ovid, most elegant of poets, with perfect justice, has called night the "greatest nurse of cares." That, however, at this time especially we refresh and renew with sleep our bodies, worn and fatigued by daily labors, this is a favor of the god, not a gift of night; but be it so, sleep is not of so much importance that we hold night in honor on account of it; because, when we set out to sleep, we tacitly confess ourselves in truth cowardly and wretched creatures, who are not able to take care of these weak little bodies for a short time without repose. And surely what else is sleep but the image and likeness of death? Hence, in Homer Death and Sleep are twins, begotten at one conception, born at one birth. Lastly, that the moon and other stars reveal their faces by night, this also is due to the sun; for these do not possess the light which they transmit, except that which they mutually receive from him.

Who, therefore, if not a swindler, if not a burglar, if not a gambler, if not one accustomed to spend whole nights among bands of strumpets and to pass entire days snoring; who, I say, except such a man would undertake to defend a cause so unseemly and so abominable in itself? And I am at a loss to know how he would dare to look at the sun here and how he could enjoy in safety the common light which he ungratefully disparages; surely worthy is he that the Sun slay him with the adverse strokes of its rays, like a new Python; worthy is he of spending a long and detested life shut up in Cimmerian darkness; worthy in short that his oration should put his audience asleep, so that what he might say would establish no greater credence than some dream or other; and who, asleep himself, is so deceived that he thinks his nodding and snoring auditors approve him and applaud his peroration.

But I see the black eyebrows of Night and I feel the dark shadows arising; I must retire lest Night overwhelm me unawares. You, therefore, my hearers, since Night is nothing else than the passing and as it were the death of Day, be unwilling to hold that Death should be preferred to Life; but deign to adorn my cause with your votes, so that the Muses may bless your studies. And may Aurora, the friend of the Muses, hearken; and may Phoebus give heed, who sees all

things and hears those promoters of his glory whom he has in this assembly. I have spoken.

II.

On the Music of the Spheres

IF THERE is any place for a man of my poor powers, fellow students, after so many speakers of consequence have been heard today. I shall attempt even at this moment to express, in accordance with my small ability, how well I wish the established exercise of the present occasion; and I shall follow, albeit far outdistanced, in the course of this day's demonstration of eloquence. Accordingly, while I avoid and shun entirely those common and ordinary topics of discourse, the purpose of this day and likewise of those who, I suspected, would speak appropriately concerning matters fitted to the time, kindles and straightway rouses my mind to attempt with ardor some new theme. These two reasons are able to furnish incentives or keenness to one somewhat sluggish and for the most part possessed of a dull wit. Wherefore, a few words at least suggest themselves to be pronounced, as they say, with open hand and with rhetorical embellishment, about that famous heavenly harmony, concerning which very shortly there is to be a disputation with the closed fist; consideration of the time being observed, which now presses me on and restrains me. I would prefer, however, that you, my hearers, should regard these things as said in jest.

Now what sane man would have thought that Pythagoras, that god of the philosophers, at whose name all mortals of his age stood up in very sacred veneration;—who, I say, would have thought that he would ever have expressed in public an opinion so uncertainly founded? Surely, if indeed he taught the harmony of the spheres and that the heavens revolved with melodious charm, he wished to signify by it, in his wise way, the very loving and affectionate relations of the orbs and their eternally uniform revolutions according to the fixed laws of necessity. Certainly, in this he imitated either the poets or, what is almost the same thing, the divine oracles, by whom no secret and hidden mystery is exhibited in public, unless clad in some covering or garment. That most skilful interpreter of Mother Nature, Plato, has followed him, since he affirms that certain sirens sit one upon each of the circles of the heavens and hold spell-bound gods and men by their most honey-sweet song. And finally, this agreement of things universal and this loving concord, which Pythagoras secretly introduced in poetic fashion by the term Harmony, Homer likewise suggested significantly and appropriately by means of that famous golden chain of Jove hanging down from heaven.

Aristotle, the envious and perpetual calumniator of Pythagoras and Plato, out of the shattered opinions of these great men, paved a way to renown by claiming that this symphony of the heavens was unheard, and he imputed to Pythagoras the tunes of the spheres. But if either fate or necessity had decreed that your soul, O Father Pythagoras, should have been translated into me, there would not have been lacking one who would easily have come to your rescue, however great the infamy under which you were laboring at the moment. Indeed, why should not the celestial bodies during their everlasting courses evolve musical sounds? Does it not seem fair to you, O Aristotle? Truly, I hardly believe your intelligence would be able to endure with patience that sedentary toil of the rolling heavens for so many ages, unless that ineffable song of the stars had prevented your departure and by the charm of its melody had persuaded a delay. It would be as if you were to take away from heaven those beautiful little goddesses and should deliver the ministering gods to mere drudgery and to condemn them to the treadmill. Nay indeed, Atlas himself long ago would have withdrawn his shoulders from a heaven that was about to fall, had not that sweet song soothed, with its most delightful charm, him, gasping and sweating under his great burden. In addition to these things the Dolphin, wearied of his constellation, would long ago have preferred his own seas to heaven, if he had not rightly been burning with the thought that the singing orbs of the sky excelled by far the sweetness of Arion's lyre. Why, credible it is that the lark itself should fly right up to the clouds at early dawn, and that the nightingale should spend the whole lonely night in song, in order that they may adjust their strains to the harmonic mode of the sky, to which they listen attentively. Thus also from the very beginning of things the story has prevailed about the Muses dancing day and night around the altar of Jove; hence from remote antiquity skill with the lyre has been attributed to Phoebus; for this reason the ancients believed Harmonia ought to be regarded as the daughter of Jove and Electra, whom the whole choir of heaven is said to have lauded in song when she had been given to Cadmus in marriage.

But supposing no one on earth had ever heard this symphony of the stars, does it therefore follow that all has been silent beyond the circle of the moon, and lulled to sleep by the benumbing silence? Nay rather, let us blame our feeble ears which are not able, or are not worthy to overhear the songs and such sweet tones. But this melody of the sky is not really unheard; for who, O Aristotle, would have conceived of your constellations as dancing in the mid-region of the air, except that, when they hear the singing heavens clearly on account of their nearness, they cannot restrain themselves from performing a choral dance?

But Pythagoras alone of mortals is said to have heard this song; unless that good man was both some deity and native of the sky, who perchance by direction of the gods had descended for the purpose of instructing the minds of men with holy knowledge and of calling upon them to improve. Certainly he was a man who combined in himself the whole gamut of virtues and who was worthy to converse with the very gods like unto himself and to enjoy the company of the celestials. Therefore, I do not wonder that the gods, loving him very much, permitted him to take part in the most secret mysteries of Nature.

Moreover, the boldness of the thieving Prometheus seems to be the reason why we hear so little this harmony, a deed which brought upon humanity so many ills and likewise took away this happiness from us, which we will never be permitted to enjoy so long as we remain brutish and overwhelmed by wicked animal desires; for how can those be susceptible of that heavenly sound whose souls, as Persius says, are bent toward the earth and absolutely devoid of celestial matters? But if we possessed hearts so pure, so spotless, so snowy, as once upon a time Pythagoras had, then indeed would our ears be made to resound and to be completely filled with that most delicious music of the revolving stars; and then all things would return immediately as it were to that golden age; then, at length, freed from miseries we would spend our time in peace, blessed and envied even by the gods.

At this moment, however, as it were in the midst of my speech, time has cut me off; and I suspect this has happened very opportunely indeed, lest I prove an obstacle to this whole occasion by a style, rude and quite lacking in rhythm compared with the harmony which I mentioned before; and lest I myself should be a hindrance, preventing you from hearing it. And so I am done.

III.

IN THE PUBLIC SCHOOLS

Against the Scholastic Philosophy

I was seeking lately with all my might, fellow collegians, very anxiously, how I might entertain you, my auditors, with the best possible exhibition of language; when suddenly there came into my mind an expression which Marcus Tullius, from whom by a fortunate omen my oration begins, frequently set down in his books; namely, that the function of the speaker has been established and determined as follows: that he instruct, please, and finally persuade. Accordingly, with that in view, I proposed to myself the task of departing as little as possible from this threefold requirement of the orator. But since to teach you, accomplished men from every quarter, is not what I should undertake, nor is it what you would endure, I may be permitted at least (and that is the next requirement) to suggest something perchance not altogether foreign to the occasion. Meanwhile, to please, which

I really fear very much is my weak point, will be nevertheless the height of my desire, which, if I shall attain it, certainly will be equal to persuasion. I will indeed persuade you fully at this time to my opinion, if I shall be able to induce you, my listeners, to open with sparer hand those huge and almost monstrous tomes of the, as they say, subtle doctors; and to indulge a little more mildly in the warty controversies of the sophists. But, although it is well known to everybody how that which I advocate is just and honored, I will show briefly during my little half hour that, by those studies mentioned, the mind is neither delighted nor instructed, nor indeed is any common good promoted.

And certainly at the beginning I challenge you, Academics, if by any means it can be done in accordance with my conception of your ability: what pleasure, I ask, can there be in these joyous wranglings of crabbed old men, which, born if not in the cave of Trophonius, then certainly in the cells of monks, are betrayed by their odor and exhale the savage sternness of their authors and exhibit the frowns of the fathers; and which, prolix beyond measure, in the midst of extreme brevity awaken disgust and loathing? Moreover, if ever more verbose authors are read, then indeed they breed in the readers an aversion almost natural and whatever is beyond inborn hatred. Frequently, my hearers, when by chance at different times the necessity of investigating a little while these quibbles was forced upon me, after the keenness of my eyes and mind had been dulled by long reading—frequently, I say, I halted to catch my breath, and, repeatedly measuring the weight with my mind's eye, I have sought a wretched relief from my disgust. But when I always saw more in sight than I had finished in my reading, often indeed I preferred, instead of these crammed-in fooleries, to clean out the Augean stables; and I declared Hercules a happy man, to whom the good-natured Juno had never set an exhausting hardship of this kind.

Nor does a more flowery style uplift from the earth or elevate this nerveless, languid, creeping stuff; but a diction dry and juiceless accompanies in such very close fashion the insignificance of the material that I could certainly believe without difficulty it had been written under gloomy Saturn; unless the harmless simplicity of that age was quite ignorant of those delusions and trifling inconsistencies with which these books everywhere abound. Believe me, most illustrious young men, while I survey unwillingly sometimes these empty little questions, I seem to myself to be undertaking a journey through rugged deserts and uneven roads and through vast solitudes and precipitous passes of mountains, because it is not likely that the charming and elegant Muses preside over these shrivelled and obscure subjects, or that the silly followers of these lay claim to their patronage. On the contrary, I think there never was a place for them on Parnassus, except perhaps some neglected corner at the bottom of the hill, dismal, rough and wild with brambles and thorns, covered over with thistles and dense nettles, far distant from the chorus and assembly of the goddesses —a place which neither yields laurels nor produces flowers, where in short the sound of Phoebus' lyre shall never reach.

Certainly divine Poetry, by that power which has been communicated from heaven, rousing to high flight the mind, buried in earthly dross, establishes quarters among the temples of the sky; and, as though inspiring with nectarean breath and besprinkling the whole with ambrosia, instils in a measure heavenly blessedness and suggests a kind of immortal joy.

Likewise Rhetoric captures the minds of men and so pleasantly draws after her in chains those who are enticed, that at one time it is able to move to pity, at another to transport into hatred, again to kindle to warlike ardor, and then to exalt to contempt of death.

History, nobly ordered, now soothes and composes the restless agitation of the mind, now causes anointment with joy, anon it produces tears, but these gentle and quiet, which even though moist bring with them something of pleasure.

But these useless and really dry controversies and verbal wranglings certainly have no power to stir up the passions of the soul;

they invite by their nature sluggishness only and torpidity. Likewise, they please nobody except one who is boorish and quite hairy of chest, and one who, inclined by some secret leanings to controversies and disagreements and moreover to excessive talkativeness, always shudders at and turns from a just and sound wisdom. Accordingly, let him be sent away with his quibbles, either into the Caucasian Mountain or wherever in the world dark Scythia holds sway, and there let him establish a workshop for his subtleties and illusions, and let him for his own pleasure twist and torment himself to no purpose about these matters until too much forethought shall have eaten up and consumed utterly his heart, like that Promethean vulture.

But these studies and those which add absolutely nothing to the knowledge of things are as fruitless as unpleasant. Truly, let us hold before our eyes all those bands of hooded old men, especially those moulders of sophistries:—what one is there who has adorned literature with anything worth while? Without doubt, indeed, he has rendered refined, cultured, and gentler philosophy quite odious by his rough harshness, and like an evil genius he has filled human breasts with thorns and briars, and has introduced perpetual discord into the schools, which indeed has hindered to an extraordinary degree the happy progress of those who are learning.

What then? Do the wily philosophasters toss arguments forward and backward? This fellow establishes ponderously his opinion in every way, that one on the other hand with great labor strives to overthrow; and what you believe fortified by an invincible argument, that the opponent at once refutes without much trouble. Meanwhile, the reader is perplexed, as though at a crossroad, uncertain where to stop, whither to turn, and hesitating in his decision; while so many weapons are hurled on both sides close together that they take away the light itself and produce a deep darkness in the subjects, so that, as a result, the labor of the reader now becomes such that, imitating the daily labors of Ceres, he seeks Truth over the whole surface of the earth with a burning torch and finds it nowhere, and at length is reduced to insanity, so that he wretchedly thinks he is blind, where there is nothing for him to see.

Furthermore, not seldom it happens that those who incline toward and devote themselves wholly to the soot of these disputations, if by chance they attempt some other subject foreign to their nonsense, betray in an astonishing manner their ignorance and ridiculous childishness.

Finally then, the whole fruit of the labor so earnestly performed will be that you emerge a more accurate simpleton, a manufacturer of trifles; and that there accrues to you, as it were a more expert ignorance. It is not astonishing, since all these things, about which toil has been spent so tormentingly and anxiously, exist nowhere in the nature of things; but certain airy visions flit before minds disordered by trifling ideas and destitute of more accurate wisdom.

As to the rest, that these fatuities conduce very little to uprightness of life and to refinement of manners, which is by far the most important, even if I do not mention it, is abundantly clear to you.

And indeed at this moment that which I proposed as the last point to be discussed by me is plainly evident: namely, that this distressing logomachy does not eventuate in public welfare, nor in any way does it bring to a country either honor or utility, in spite of the fact that among the sciences all consider it to be the most ancient. Since indeed I have observed that a country is especially honored and adorned by these two things chiefly: either by speaking excellently or by acting bravely; and since this quarrelsome contest of discordant views does not seem able to develop eloquence nor to teach wisdom, nor to incite to brave deeds; therefore, let cunning quibblers vanish with their formalities, upon whom after death there will be this appropriate punishment inflicted: that they shall twist ropes in hell with the famous Ocnus.

How much better it would be, fellow students, and how much more worthy of your name, to make at this time a tour as it were with your eyes about the whole earth as represented on the map and view the places trodden by ancient heroes, and to travel through the regions made famous by wars, by triumphs, and even by the tales of illustrious poets: now to cross the raging Adriatic, now to approach unharmed flame-capped Aetna; then to observe the customs of men and the governments of nations, so admirably arranged; thence to investigate and to observe the natures of all living creatures; from these to plunge the mind into the secret essences of stones and plants. Do not hesitate, my hearers, to fly even up to the skies, there to behold those multiform aspects of the clouds, the massy power of the snow, and the source of those tears of early morn; next to peer into the caskets of the hail and to survey the arsenals of the thunderbolts. Nor let what Jupiter or Nature veils from you be concealed when a baleful and enormous comet ofttimes threatens a conflagration from heaven; nor let the most minute little stars be hidden from you, however many there may be scattered and straying between the two poles. Yea, follow as companion the wandering sun, and subject time itself to a reckoning and demand the order of its everlasting journey. Nay, let not your mind suffer itself to be hemmed in and bounded by the same limits as the earth, but let it wander also outside the boundaries of the world. Finally, what is after all the most important matter, let it learn thoroughly to know itself and at the same time those holy beings and intelligences, with whom hereafter it will enter into everlasting companionship.

Why speak further? Let that famous man, Aristotle, be your teacher in all these subjects, who possess so much charm, who indeed has left to us almost all these things, which ought to be learned, written in a scientific manner and with much pains. I perceive you are suddenly moved by his name, fellow students, and are drawn gently to this opinion, and, as if by his allurement, are become more tractable. If this be so, clearly you owe to him praise on account of this matter, of whatever kind it is, and thanks. But in the meanwhile, as it concerns me, I am quite content if I shall have obtained indulgence by your courtesy for my prolixity. I have spoken.

IV.

IN COLLEGE, &.

Thesis

In the destruction of any substance a resolution to primary matter does not occur.

WHETHER Error broke forth from Pandora's box or from the lowest Stygian depth, or whether, in short, one of the sons of Earth conspired against the gods, is not to be investigated too closely at this time. Moreover it may easily be noted even by a careless observer that Error from the smallest beginnings, has grown to such enormous magnitude, as was once the case with Typhon or Ephialtes, son of Neptune, that I fear for Truth itself on account of him; for I behold Error contending not infrequently on equal terms with the goddess Aletheia herself; I behold him made richer after defeats, vigorous after wounds, and though conquered, rejoicing over the victors. A circumstance of this kind antiquity has related concerning the Lybian Anteus. Besides indeed, not for a light reason could anyone call into question that Ovidian story: whether, for instance, Astraea was the last of the goddesses to leave the earth; for I suspect that Peace and Truth would not have abandoned even hostile mortals many ages after her. Certainly, if she were sojourning up to this time on earth, who would be led to believe that Error, one-eyed and dim-sighted, could gaze at Truth, rivaling the sun, without surely losing the keenness of his eyes, without being himself driven to the lower regions again, whence he arose in the first place? But truly beyond a doubt she fled away to the skies, never to return to her home among wretched humanity; and foul Error is lord and master in all the schools and is the chief power in affairs, finding defenders who are certainly not sluggish and who are not few in numbers. By the addition of which powers, puffed up beyond what can be endured, what particle of matter, pray, is there, even quite minute, upon which he has not rushed, which he has not profaned with his dirty nails, even as we have heard that the Harpies polluted the tables of Phineus, king of the Arcadians?

Whence the matter has truly come to this point, that the choicest viands of philosophy, not less rich than those very delicacies upon which the supernals dine, now produce nausea in their feasts; for it happens again and again to one unrolling the huge tomes of the philosophers and to one wearing them out by daily and nightly handling, that he is dismissed in a more uncertain state than he was in the first place. For whatsoever one affirms and believes he supports by a sufficiently valid argument, another shows to be of no consequence, or at least he seems to refute it. And so the one has always almost without end the point that he affirms, and the other always what he replies; while the wretched reader in the meantime, long tossed and torn this way and that, as it were between two monsters, and almost killed with weariness, at length is left as though at a crossway, quite uncertain in mind whether to turn in one direction or the other. Upon which side Truth, however, may abide perhaps—I would not conceal the facts—it is not worth while to investigate with that industry which is profitable; for often a very great controversy is carried on by hundreds of philosophic investigators about a matter of exceedingly small importance.

But I seem to hear some persons murmuring, Whither is that fellow now racing? While he inveighs against error, he himself is errant over the universe. Indeed, I acknowledge the errancy; nor would I have done this had I not promised myself great things from your open minds. Now therefore at length let us gird our loins to begin the task. May the goddess Lua, as Lipsius says, happily deliver me from these great difficulties!

The question which is set before us today for elucidation is this: whether when anything whatever is destroyed a change to primary matter occurs. This men are accustomed to express in other words, as follows: whether any accidents which have existed in a disintegrated body still abide in the body that is produced. That is, whether when the form is destroyed, all the accidents perish which formerly existed in the compound. A great difference of opinion about this matter exists even among philosophers whose names are by no means obscure. Some contend very ardently that a change of this kind takes place; others maintain firmly that in no wise can it occur. As I understand the problem, my mind is inclined to follow the latter, being led both by reason and, as I think, by the authority of great men to differ very widely from the former. In what manner this can be proved remains for us to examine for a little while; and this as briefly as possible, and at first in this manner.

If a resolution to a primary substance occurs, then it is subjoined that that essential dictum, namely, that it is never to be found pure, is wrongly ascribed to primary matter. My opponents will reply: "This is said with respect to form." But let those numbskulls bear this in mind, that substantial forms are found nowhere in the world apart from accidental forms. But this is trivial; it does not grasp the case by the very throat; stronger arguments than these must be added.

Now in the first place, let us see whether we have any partisans among the old philosophers on our side. To us who are inquiring, behold of his own accord Aristotle presents himself and, with a very select band of his interpreters, attaches himself to our side; for indeed I would desire you to understand, my hearers, that this battle was started by Aristotle himself as leader and inciter, and, I hope, was begun under good auspices. He indeed seems to affirm the very thing that we hold as true, when he says in *Metaphysics 7, Text 8*, that quantity first of all is inherent in matter. Accordingly, whoever shall gainsay this opinion, I can boldly bring an indictment of heresy against him in conformity with the law of all wise men. Yea, indeed, in another place he clearly maintains that quantity is a property of primary matter, which the most of his adherents likewise affirm; but as to a property parting from its subject, who may assert upon the very best judgment even of an authority selected by the opposition?

But proceed, let us come to grips, and let us weigh carefully what reason recommends. The assertion, accordingly, is proved in the first place by this: that matter has its own real being by virtue of its own existence; therefore, it can support quantity, at least that kind which is called unbounded. Moreover, some confidently affirm that form does not take possession of matter unless with quantity as a mediant.

In the second place, if an accident is destroyed, it must necessarily follow that it is destroyed by these methods only: either by the introduction of a contrary, or by the cessation of a limit, or by the absence of another preservative cause, finally by the absence of the proper subject to which it belongs. By the first method, quantity cannot be destroyed, seeing that it may not have a contrary; and, although quality may be here present, it however is not supposed to be introduced. The second method does not tend in this direction, as being one that is the property of things related. Nor does the method "by the absence of a preservative cause," for that which the adversaries assign is form. Moreover, accidents are conceived to depend upon form in two ways: either in the class of the formal cause or of the efficient cause. In the first, the dependency is not immediate, for the substantial form does not give form to the accidents, nor can it be perceived what other function may be at work in respect to that cause in this class, and for that reason it is merely a go-between. Without doubt, to whatever extent matter depends upon form, that also in turn depends upon matter. The method of dependency next in order is in the class of the efficient cause. Nevertheless, there is doubt whether accidents in this class depend upon form or not. But although we may grant it is so, yet it does not follow that when form is destroyed the accidents in like manner also perish, for this reason: that to the cause which disappears another sufficiently like it in every respect instantly takes its place, to preserve exactly the same effect without interruption.

Lastly, the circumstance that quantity and, in respect to this class, other accidents do not vanish into nothingness on account of the disappearance of their own substance, is proved by the fact that the fundamental element of quantity is either a compound or form or matter. That it is not a compound will be clear from this, that the accident which is in the compound appertains at the same time, by its union, both to matter and form through the mode of unity. But in truth, quantity can by no means have any connection with a rational soul, so long as it is spiritual and is the effect of formal quantity; that is, capable to a very small extent of quantitative extension.

Next, that form is not its fundamental is easily perceived from what has been said before. There remains, therefore, that matter alone is the substratum of quantity, and thus the conclusion of total destruction in connection with quantity is smashed to pieces.

As to the pertinency of what is commonly adduced concerning a scar, I believe the argument is most powerful; for who can wrest my faith to the extent that I should believe it is quite different in a dead body from that which it was very recently in a living body, when no reason is at hand, no necessity for adjusting our impression which seldom indeed is deceived in respect to a proper object? Truly, I would more quickly and more easily hear one mentioning the wonders of ghosts and hobgoblins, than those harebrained philophasters growling stupidly and foolishly about their newly begotten accidents. For we have examined carefully in the very moment of death and likewise after death, heat and those other tensionable and relaxable animal qualities; for why should these be destroyed when others like them must be produced? So far it has happened that if they should be created afresh, they would last for a time not indeed short, nor would they arrive suddenly at the highest degree of tension, but gradually and as it were step by step. Add to this the most ancient axiom, that quantity follows matter and quality follows form. I could indeed, nay, I even ought to linger longer on this point, but I am not sure whether I am boring to you; certainly I am very much to myself.

There remains to say that we now descend to the arguments of the opponents, which might the Muses grant that I may reduce to prime matter, if it can be done, or rather into nothingness.

In regard to the first point, the asserted testimony of Aristotle, that the sensible subject does not abide during generation, we oppose that it ought to be understood concerning the complete and entire subject; i.e., concerning the substantial compound, which the ancient and scholarly writer, Philoponus, testifies. As to the second point, Aristotle says that matter is neither something, nor quantity, nor quality. This does not mean that it is not connected with quantity and quality, but that of itself and in its own entity it includes neither quantity nor quality. Thirdly, Aristotle says that when primary substances are destroyed all of the accidents are destroyed; because evidently we may not corrupt what is to be if another accident takes the place immediately of the very one destroyed. Lastly, he says form is admitted in pure matter; that is, in the pure state of the substantial form.

At this moment the battle becomes violent and victory sways to and fro, for they rush into the struggle anew in this fashion: Since indeed matter is pure potency, it has no existence except that which is obtained by begging from form; whence it has not enough power of itself to support accidents, unless at least it is united by nature to form, by which being may be recognized. For this error men are wont to provide a remedy in this way: that primary matter has its own proper being, which may be incomplete, although in the class of substance; nevertheless, if it is united with accident, it can be called conveniently being in a simple form. Nay, they even set up the argument that matter looks to the substantial form as a primary activity, but to accidents as secondary activities. I reply that matter looks to form first in the order of design, not of generation or of performance.

Now the argument blazes up and boils over; and as if about to struggle to extermination, they press us keenly after this fashion: Every property diffuses actively from the essence of that of which it is the property; but quantity cannot do this, because this power of emination is some efficiency; but matter of its own volition has no efficiency, since it is merely passive; therefore, etc. I reply, that the natural conjunction of matter with quantity can be understood in two ways: first, by reason alone of the passive power within demanding according to its own nature such a relation; for no necessity urges that every innate property be under obligation to a subject by reason of the active principle, for in the meantime the passive is sufficient, even as many think motion is natural in heaven;

second, it is possible also for motion to be understood through an inner emination, since it may have in itself a true and actual essence.

But all hope of victory has not yet been abandoned, for again making an attack, they approach with hostile intent, asserting indeed that form through the medium of quantity is admitted into matter, since it belongs first to matter. We, on the contrary, openly protest against this sequence, and the more so because we can reply in perfect safety that we employ this distinction: form in matter is admitted through the medium of quantity as by an arrangement or by an inevitable condition, but in no way, however, by a potency closely received from form.

Finally, they argue in this way: if quantity belongs to matter only, it follows that it is uncreated and indestructible. That seems to be contradictory, because motion by itself belongs to quantity. But we indeed grant the consequence, because quantity really is indestructible with respect to its own entity, although, with respect to the various limitations, it is possible to begin and to put an end to being by a union and a separation of quantity, for there is not in itself a movement for the production of quantity, but for the increment. And not for this reason does it come to pass that new quantity takes on being in the nature of things, but for this, that one quantity is added to another and what was foreign does become inherent.

I could indeed produce many arguments on both sides, which, however, I pass by for the sake of alleviating your fatigue. At this point, therefore, it will be enough to sound a retreat.

V.

IN THE PUBLIC SCHOOLS

Partial forms do not occur in an animal in addition to the whole.

THE Romans, once upon a time masters of the world, attained the highest reach of empire, such as neither Assyrian magnitude nor Macedonian valor were ever able to approach; to which no future power of kings will be able to raise itself again. Either Jupiter himself, now somewhat burdened with years and comfortable in his heaven, had wished to spend his days in peace by yielding to the Roman people as though to earthly gods the reins of human affairs; or he had granted to Father Saturn, cast down into Italy as a solace for his lost heaven, this: that the Roman citizens, his descendants, should be rulers over everything whatsoever on land and sea. However it may be, he did not grant this favor to them gratuitously, but he gave it reluctantly, accompanied by unceasing warfare and by tedious toil, seeking to find out, I believe, whether the Romans alone might appear worthy to perform the duties of great Jove among mortals. Accordingly, in a thrifty and rigorous way, they were compelled to spend their lives, since the sound of war and the clanking of armed men on every side always destroyed the incipient allurements of peace.

In addition, they were compelled to place, and frequently to renew, garrisons in every conquered city and province, and to send almost all the young men, sometimes into foreign service, sometimes into colonies. Furthermore, they did not always march home with bloodless victories; often indeed they were pursued by deadly swords. For instance, Brennus, leader of the Gauls, once almost destroyed the budding glory of the Romans; and little was lacking but that the most eminent city of Carthage had wrested from Rome the control of the world, though entrusted by the gods. And finally, the Goths and Vandals, under Alaric their king, and the Huns and the Panonians, under the leadership of Attila and Bleda, sweeping over the whole of Italy, tore in shreds the most flourishing resources of the empire, accumulated from the spoils of so many battles; drove the Romans, who a little while before were kings of men, in disgraceful flight; and took by the mere terror of their name the city itself, Rome, I say, itself; than which deed nothing more famous can be told or imagined: quite as if they had taken Victory herself either by love, or, terrified by force of arms, had dragged her off into their own country.

You have wondered sufficiently, my listeners, why I have mentioned all these things: now give heed. As often as I call up these matters and run them over in my mind, so often do I contemplate how great are the forces engaged in the struggle to uphold Truth, how great the zeal of all, how great the watchfulness demanded to defend from the assaults of enemies Truth, everywhere tottering and overcome. Nor is it possible to prevent the most loathsome mixture of error from entering every day all learning, which indeed is so potent or poisonous that it can either substitute its own image for snow-white Truth, or it can join to itself by some unknown artifice a brilliant appearance of Truth; by which art, so it seems, it frequently deceives even great philosophers and claims for itself honors and veneration due to Truth alone.

This fact you can perceive in today's question, which indeed has aroused contestants by no means sluggish and those of distinguished name; provided, by abandoning these opposing sides, they prefer to do honor to Truth. Accordingly, it will now be our task to return Error to its natal deformity, bare and stripped of its borrowed plumage; which, that it may be more speedily accomplished, I think can be done by setting forth the opinions of the most notable authors, for it must not be expected that I can add anything of myself to what perchance has escaped the notice of, and been neglected by, so many men preeminent in ability. Therefore, I will state briefly what is sufficient to make the matter clear, and I will fortify by argument on every side as by a mound; then, if anything is contradictory and presents an obstacle to our view, I will present such refutation as I am able. All of these things, however, I will touch briefly and graze them, as it were, with the tips of my wings.

Against the unity of form, which the more acute philosophers are wont always to posit in one and the same matter, we read that opinions at variance have arisen; for some maintain stoutly that many complete forms are present in the animal. And this they defend in a variety of ways, each according to his own notion. Others assert quite strongly that there is one only total (principal) form, but that numerous partial (subordinate) forms of the same matter are comfortably sustained. With the former for the moment, after the fashion of war, we agree to an armistice, while we turn the whole force and attack of battle against the latter.

Let there be placed in the front rank Aristotle, who plainly sides with us, and who, toward the end of his first book of the *De Anima,* in no obscure manner favors our assertion. It is not a work of long investigation to attach to this authority some other arguments. Especially on my side Chrysostomus Javellus presents himself, from whose dunghill, to be sure in shaggy and unkempt style, we may dig up gold and pearls, which, if any voluptuary lift up his nose, that famous fable of the Aesopian cock will fit in his case indeed somewhat neatly. He argues for the most part in this manner: That diversity and organization of dissimilar parts must precede the introduction of the soul, inasmuch as it is the moving impulse, not of any body whatsoever, but of the physical organism; wherefore, immediately before the production of a total form, it is necessary that those partial forms be destroyed, unless that generally accepted axiom is thoroughly overthrown, namely, "The generation of one is the destruction of another"; whose production the immediate production of like things does not follow, for that would be without cause and not accordant enough with the wisdom of Mother Nature.

Next, since every form whether perfect or imperfect, imparts specific being, it is necessary that that particular form abide as long as that same condition continues unchanged in accordance with its own substance, and in the same manner the total form dominates like an accident, not through generation but through *alteration.* It follows in turn that the total soul, whether divisible or indivisible, is not sufficient to give form fully and perfectly to all parts of a living creature, because, as we grant, no reason impels. It follows likewise that the one substantial form is as it were an arrangement closest to and persistent in an other, which is not accordant with truth, since indeed each form has established a complete essence in the class of substance.

Lastly, if in all parts, for example, of a man partial forms were to come into existence in numbers, surely from these one whole form distinct from the rational soul will arise, whence that will be the form either of an inanimate or of a corporeity, or of a mixture, which to be granted in addition to the soul in man is quite beyond belief, or it will be a soul either sensitive or vegetative. The more learned band of Philosophants will in no wise hear one affirming this. Of which matter I pass by more ample proof, since it is everywhere known and does not ad- 10 vance very much to the climax of the argument.

In truth, as to the chief point in the controversy, the adversaries present the objection that a part cut off from an animal continues actual after the separation, not in the complete form since it is away from the whole, nor through a form recently acquired, since there is present no producing force, no perceptible immanent activity, no 20 heralded change. Therefore, in its activity it exists through its own form which it had in the first place while it was one with the whole.

And especially do they think to butt over our side and upturn it completely by this argument: In other respects not less rightly than commonly the reply is made that form produced anew, since it happens very commonly in the case of a dead body and one 30 as it were on the way to resolution, does not demand much time, nor many arrangements, nor an orderly alteration. What if also some universal cause should agree with the nearest combination to produce any form whatever, would not matter be found void? Moreover, because numerous activities are seen in the animal, this ought not to be due to distinct partial forms, but to the preeminence of the total soul, which indeed is 40 equivalent to forms specifically distinct.

It is permissible, according to agreement, to pass over other objections of lesser importance, which the opponents bring up, for they are not convincing, and they can be banished more easily and be more satisfactorily refuted, if perchance they should be brought forward openly in the midst of the disputation.

In whatever way the matter may turn out, 50 although I may lose the cause, the cause is not lost: for Truth invincible is always more than sufficiently powerful in defend-

ing herself by her own exertions; nor to accomplish this does she need outside assistance. And even if she seem sometimes vanquished and trodden under foot, nevertheless she always preserves herself unharmed and unscarred by the claws of Error. In this she is not unlike the Sun, who often shows himself to the eyes of men, enshrouded as it were and befouled by clouds, when, for all that, having gathered his rays into himself and having summoned all his glory to himself, quite unstained by any blemish, he shines resplendent.

VI.

AT THE SUMMER HOLIDAYS OF THE COLLEGE, BUT, ACCORDING TO CUSTOM, WITH ALMOST ALL OF THE YOUNG MEN OF THE INSTITUTION ASSEMBLED.

ORATION

That sometimes sportive exercises are not prejudicial to philosophic studies.

WHEN I came back hither recently, Academicians, from that city which is the capital of cities, stuffed, I might almost say, to corpulence with all the pleasures in which that place overflows beyond measure, I hoped I might have again hereafter that literary leisure, a kind of life in which I believe the heavenly spirits rejoice; and there was deeply in my mind a desire now at last to bury myself in literature and to besiege by day and by night most gracious Philosophy: thus always the alteration of labor and pleasure is wont to banish the weariness of satiety and to bring it to pass that things neglected for a while are taken up again more eagerly. Me, on fire with these desires, the almost annual observance of a very old custom has suddenly summoned and dragged away; and that leisure which I had primarily designed for the acquisition of wisdom I have been ordered to transfer to foolish trifles and to the invention of novel absurdities, as if there were not already quite enough fools, as if that famous and likewise enchanted ship, Argo, laden with dolts, had met with shipwreck, and finally as if matter for jesting were wanting at this time to Democritus himself.

But grant me pardon, I beseech you, my hearers; for this exercise, which we are celebrating today, although I have been a little too free-spoken about it, is in truth really not senseless, but rather exceedingly praiseworthy; which fact indeed I have proposed to myself at this time to set forth at once more clearly. Wherefore if Junius Brutus, that second founder of the Roman state, that great punisher of royal lust, dared suppress, by feigning idiocy, a soul almost equal to the immortal gods, and a wondrous natural ability; surely there is no reason why I should be ashamed to play the fool for a while with silly wisdom, especially by order of him whose business it is, like an aedile, to preside over these presumably solemn diversions. Besides, to no small degree, your courteousness, very lately made known to me—you who are members of the same college with me—, has allured and enticed me to undertake these duties; for, when I was about to perform an oratorical function before you, some months gone by, and I thought that any lucubrations whatsoever of mine would certainly be quite disagreeable, and that Aeacus and Minos would be more lenient judges than almost any of you; truly, beyond my belief, beyond whatever slight hope I had, they were received, as I noted, nay rather, I myself felt, with unusual applause from all, yea even from those who at other times, on account of disagreements over our studies, possessed an absolutely hostile and unfriendly spirit: truly a magnanimous way of exercising rivalry and one not unworthy of a royal heart; since indeed, when friendship itself very frequently is wont to misrepresent many things done without bad intent, then truly bitter and hostile enmity did not unwillingly interpret in a kindly way and more indulgently than was my desert many things spoken perhaps erroneously and not a few doubtless unskilfully. Now, in a word, by this unparalleled example even foolish rage itself was seen to be sane of mind and by this circumstance had washed away the disgrace of madness.

But in truth, I am highly delighted and in wonderful fashion I am filled with pleasure when I behold myself surrounded and encompassed on every side by so great a concourse of most learned men. Yet on the other hand, however, when I descend into myself, and, as it were with my eyes turned inwardly, I secretly look upon my weakness, indeed too often conscious of myself alone. I blush, while a certain unexpected sadness, rushing in, presses down and chokes my leaping joy. But do not thus, fellow students, I beseech you, do not thus leave me in the lurch, me prostrate and dismayed, struck by the keenness of your eyes as though by lightning. May the breath of your goodwill stimulate me, half dead, as it can, and revive me. May it so happen, by your commands, that this torment be not too severe. Nevertheless, with you providing a remedy for the evil, I proceed more happily and more entertainingly; so much so that it will be exceedingly pleasant for me to be frequently scared out of my wits, provided that it be permitted me to be revived and refreshed as many times by you. But O, in the meanwhile, the remarkable power in you and the extraordinary virtue, which like that famous spear of Achilles, gift of Vulcan, wounds and heals!

Besides, let no one wonder if I, stationed as it were among the stars, rejoice exceedingly that so many men renowned for scholarship and that almost the whole flower of the academic world have flocked hither. Indeed, I can hardly believe that in olden times greater numbers came to Athens to hear the two most distinguished orators, Demosthenes and Aeschines, contending for oratorical supremacy; nor that ever this felicity happened to Hortensius when pleading; nor that so many men so remarkably versed in letters graced with their presence a Ciceronian display of oratory. Accordingly, although I may bring this task to a finish with little grace, nevertheless I shall regard it as an honor, not to be despised, to have even uttered words in so great a gathering and assemblage of most eminent men.

Moreover, by Hercules, I cannot but applaud myself at this moment with a little more unction because I am luckier by far in my body of judges than either Orpheus or Amphion; for they merely applied their fingers cunningly and skilfully to little strings, attuned with pleasing harmony; and an equal portion of the charm of both lay in the strings themselves and in the proper and correct movement of the hands; whereas, if I shall win any praise here today, it will certainly be wholly and truly mine by as much as a superior work of genius conquers and excels the craft of the hands. Further, they drew to themselves rocks, beasts, and trees, and, if there were any men, those who were rude and rustic: but I behold ears, most learned, loaned to me and hanging upon my lips. Lastly, those rustics and many wild beasts followed a harmony of strings already sufficiently known and clearly heard; but you, expectation alone has drawn hither and now detains.

But, however it be, Academicians, I wish you to bear in mind especially at this time, that I have not made these remarks boastingly, for would that just at this moment that honey-sweet, or, more truly, nectarian, flood of eloquence were granted to me, whatsoever once in former times saturated and bedewed as though from heaven the Attic and Roman genius. Would that it were permitted me to suck out from the innermost recesses all the marrow of Suada, and to filch from the chests of Mercury himself, and to empty to the bottom all the coffers of elegant sayings; so that I may be able to deliver something worthy of such great expectation, of such a renowned assembly, and finally of ears so pure and fastidious.

Behold, my auditors, whither a most violent desire and inclination for pleasing you carries me off and drives me; since unexpectedly I feel that I have been swept into a certain excessive desire to please, a sacrilege, but a pure and virtuous one, if such a thing can be. And undoubtedly, I am of the opinion that there is hardly any need for me to beseech and implore aid of the Muses, because I believe I am surrounded by those who are full of all the Muses and Graces; and I imagine that all Helicon, and whatsoever shrines of the Muses there are in addition, have poured forth all their foster children for the purpose of taking part in the exercises of this day; so that it is credible, on account of their absence at this very moment, that the laurels of Parnassus weep and drop their flowers; whence indeed it will be vain to seek anywhere on earth for the Muses and Graces and Goddesses of delight, except in this place. It this is so, it necessarily follows at once that Barbarism itself, Error, Ignorance, and all that sort, detested by the Muses, will flee as speedily as possible at the sight of you and hide themselves far away under a different sky; and then indeed what opposes the removal at once from my oration of any barbarous, inelegant, and obsolete expression; and, by your inspiration and secret instigation, my suddenly becoming fluent and polished?

At any rate, however, I conjure you, my hearers, not to repent that any of you have had just a little leisure for my foolish remarks; for all of the gods themselves, laying aside for a time the administration of heavenly affairs, are said to have been present frequently at the spectacle of little human beings violently contending; also at different times, not despising humble circumstances and housed in poor quarters, they are said to have partaken of beans and greens. Accordingly I hope and pray you, most excellent listeners, that this little so-so feast of mine may please your dainty and acute palates.

But even though I have known very many smatterers with whom it is quite the custom to contemn arrogantly and ignorantly in others that of which they know nothing, just as if it were a disgrace for any one to spend his energies upon it: for instance, one fellow rails foolishly at Dialectic, which he never will be able to comprehend; another regards Philosophy as of no value, because, forsooth, Nature, most beautifully formed of the goddesses, has never deemed him worthy of such an honor, that she would permit him to gaze upon her naked: nevertheless I shall not consider it a burden to praise, according to my ability, pleasantries and witty sallies, in which I acknowledge my capabilities are quite limited; if I shall have added first this one thing, which may seem rather difficult and not at all easy: that I am about to speak seriously today in praise of jocularity. And this is done not without cause indeed, for what is it that more quickly conciliates and retains friendships longer than a cheerful and agreeable disposition? And truly you will hardly find one is pleasing and welcome who lacks sportive remarks and pleasantries and elegant little witticisms.

Moreover, fellow students, if it were our daily custom to go to sleep and as it were to die of Philosophy and to grow grey among the brambles and thorns of Logic without any relaxation whatever, and never with any time granted for breathing; what difference would there be, I ask between philosophizing, and playing the soothsayer in the cave of Trophonius and following the doctrine of the too severely rigid Cato? Nay, even the very peasants would say that we dine on mustard.

Add this: that just as those who accustom themselves to wrestling and to field sports are rendered much more vigorous than others and better trained for every kind of work; so likewise it comes about by use that the sinews of the mind are much strengthened by this exercise of wit, and a better blood and spirit as it were is obtained; so that the native ability itself becomes finer and keener, both pliable and versatile for all things. But if anyone does not wish to be polished and elegant, let him not be irritated if he is called boorish and rustic. And well do we know a certain illiberal type of men, who, since they themselves are quite devoid of taste and elegance, valuing secretly in their own minds their contempt and ignorance, surmise at once that whatever by chance they hear spoken rather wittily is directed against them. Worthy indeed are they that that which they suspect without cause should really happen to them, that by all means they should be trounced by the witticisms of all, until they almost contemplate suicide. But these dregs of human society are not able to prevent a free use of neat little pleasantries.

Accordingly, my hearers, do you wish me to erect upon a foundation of reasons the confirmation of examples? Certainly these present themselves to me in great numbers. First of all Homer appears, that rising sun and morning star of more refined literature, with whom all learning like a twin was born; for he now and then, recalling his divine mind from the counsels of the gods and from things done in heaven and turning aside to drolleries, described most humorously a battle of the mice and frogs. Moreover Socrates, that most wise of mortals, by the testimony of Pytho, is said to have blunted often in witty fashion the nagging peevishness of his wife. Then we read the dialogs of the old philosophers, all sprinkled with wit, and everywhere crammed with charming humor. And certainly it was this alone that has given an eternity of name to all the ancient writers of comedies and epigrams, both Greek and Latin. Further, we hear that the "quips and wanton wiles" of Cicero filled three books, compiled by Tiro. And there is now in the hands of everyone that most clever "Praise of Folly," a work not by a writer of the lowest rank; and many other narratives of this kind on laughable topics by most distinguished orators are extant, exercises by no means lacking in humor.

Do you wish me to mention the greatest generals and kings and brave men? Be satisfied with Pericles, Epaminondas, Agesilaus, and Phillip of Macedon, who, if I may speak in the Gellian fashion, the historians say swarmed with whimsicalities and word-play. To these add Caius Laelius, Publius Cornelius Scipio, Cneius Pompeius, Caius Julius, and Octavius, Caesar, who, on the authority of Marcus Tullius, excelled all their contemporaries in this way.

Do you wish in addition greater names? The poets, who are the wisest delineators of truth, represent even Jove himself and the other heavenly beings lending themselves to jocularity in the midst of their banquets and potations.

Finally, Academicians, I may refer to your own guardianship and patronage, which will be to me worth them all. Indeed, that witticisms and jocosities are not displeasing to you, this great gathering of yours, taking place today, is a sure enough indication; and truly each and every head seems to nod its assent to me. Nor need it be a source of wonder, by Hercules, that this festive and elegant Humor thus diverts all worthy, and likewise distinguished men; since the very goddess herself may take a seat on high among the splendid ranks of Aristotelian perfections, and as though in some Pantheon may be resplendent among sister divinities.

But perhaps there are not wanting some bearded teachers of philosophy, exceedingly gloomy and dour, who, believing themselves great Catos, not to speak of little Catos, with their countenances set in Stoic severity, shaking their obstinate heads, complain querulously that everything nowadays is mixed up and perversely gone awry; and that, in place of an elucidation of Aristotle's Prior Analytics by the recently initiated bachelors, taunting expressions and silly trifles are shamelessly and unseasonably bandied about; also that the exercises of this day, rightly and truly established without doubt by our ancestors for the purpose of gathering some remarkable fruit, either in Rhetoric or Philosophy, have now of late been wrongly warped into tasteless witticisms.

But in truth I have ready and at hand what may prove a match for them: for let them know, if they are ignorant, that when the literary laws of our nation were first laid down, liberal studies had just been brought from foreign countries to these shores. Wherefore, since a mastery of the Greek and Latin tongues was quite rare and unusual, it was expedient on that account to struggle after, and to aspire to, these with keener desire and with more assiduous exertions. It will behoove us, since we are worse mannered, though better educated than our ancestors, having abandoned those studies which have not much difficulty, to take up those to which they would have applied themselves if they had been at leisure. Nor has it escaped your notice that some early lawmakers were accustomed always to issue decrees a little harsher and a trifle more severe than men were able to obey; so that by swerving from and lapsing a little they would fall into virtue itself. Finally, the conditions of things being now changed in every respect, it is necessary that laws and many customs, if they have not grown old or fallen into disuse, be at least limited and not observed at all points. But if such light bits of humor have been defended and approved openly and have merited public praise (for so they are wont with uplifted brows to assert), no one, with his mind not turned away from sober and solid learning, will attach himself forthwith to amusing trifles and almost histrionic frivolity, to such an extent that the very walks of the philosophers would be about to send forth jesters very much more shameless than clowns, instead of the learned and wise.

But in truth, I think that he who is wont to be so moved by stupid jokes as openly to neglect the serious and more useful things for them; he, I say would not be able to make much progress in the latter nor in the former line: not indeed in serious matters, because if he were adapted and framed by nature for managing serious affairs, I believe he would not so easily allow himself to be led away from them; nor in trifling matters, because hardly anyone can crack jokes delightfully and charmingly, unless he has also first learned to act seriously.

But I fear, Academicians, that I have spun out the thread of my discourse longer than is proper. I shall not present excuses, as I might, lest, by apologizing, the fault should be accentuated. Now, freed from oratorical laws, we will break forth into comic license; in which, if by chance I should swerve from my habit, if from the rigid laws of modesty, as they say, a finger's breadth, be it known, fellow students, that I have stripped off and laid aside for a short time my former custom out of good feeling for you; or, if anything shall be said loosely, if anything licentiously, you may consider that not my mind and disposition, but the procedure of the occasion and the genius of the place has indeed suggested it to me. Accordingly, like that which the comic actors used to beg at their exit, I at the very beginning entreat: "Clap your hands" and laugh.

EXERCISE

For the tottering, as it seems, and almost collapsing position, highest of fools, I know not indeed by what merit of mine I have been appointed Dictator. But why should I have been, when that distinguished leader and commander of all the Sophisters has gone around seeking eagerly for this office and would have been able to perform the duties in the very ablest manner? For that hardy soldier led valiantly through Barnwell's meadows not long ago about fifty Sophisters, armed with short little stakes; and, as if about to invest the town quite in soldierly fashion, overthrew the aqueduct, so that he might compel the town folk to surrender on account of thirst. But in truth, I grieve deeply because the gentleman has lately departed, since by his banishment he has left all of us Sophisters not only headless but also beheaded.

And now, my hearers, imagine that, although the first of April is not here, the feast of Hilaria, set apart for the mother of the gods, is at hand; or that a divine ceremony is due the God of Laughter. Accordingly, smile and raise loud laughter from your saucy spleen; smooth your brow; yield to wrinkled nostrils, but do not be hanged on your 10 hooked nose; let all places resound with most immoderate laughter; and let a more unfettered cachination evoke joyous tears, so that, when these are exhausted by laughter, grief may not have even a little drop with which to adorn her triumph. I, assuredly, if I shall behold anyone laughing with his jaw stretched too sparingly, will say that he is carefully concealing teeth that are scurfy and rotten and darkened with smut, or jut- 20 ting out in unsightly ranks; or that in the course of breakfast today he so stuffed his paunch that he dare not swell out his belly with laughter, lest not his Sphinx, but his sphincter anus, accompany his mouth in its incantations, and against his will babble some riddles, which I pass over to the doctors, not to Oedipus, for interpretation; for I am unwilling that the groan of a posterior by the sound of its cheery voice should make 30 a din in this assembly. Let the doctors who relax the bowels loosen up these questions. If anyone does not utter a loud and distinct roar, I shall assert that he breathes out such deep and deadly exhalations from his jaws that neither Aetna nor Avernus emits anything more noisome; or that he certainly has not long since eaten either garlic or leeks; so that as a result he dare not open his mouth lest he kill some of his neighbors with his 40 stinking breath.

But in truth, there is absent from this assembly that terrible and tartarian sound of hissing; for if it should be heard here today, I would believe the Furies and Eumenides had concealed themselves secretly among us and had let loose in your breasts their serpents and vipers; and in like manner that Athamantean frenzies had inflamed you.

But in very truth, Academicians, I wonder at and admire your goodwill toward me, you who have forced your way through fire and flames into this place in order to hear me. For on the one side of the very threshold that gleaming Cerberus of ours stands by. Horrible indeed with his smoky barking, and brilliant with his fiery staff, he emits glowing sparks from his ample mouth. On the other side, blazing and all devouring, our furnace belches forth lurid flames and rolls out tortuous balls of smoke. So that, as a result, the way to the infernal regions would not be more difficult, even with Pluto unwilling; and certainly not Jason himself attacked with less danger those fire-breathing oxen of Mars.

And now, my auditors, believe that you have been received into heaven, since you have left purgatory behind and have issued from the fiery furnace, saved by some new miracle. Nor indeed does there come to my mind any hero whose fortitude I can appropriately compare to yours, for that illustrious Bellerophon did not conquer with more spirit the flame-belching Chimaera; nor did those valiant knights of King Arthur overpower and rout more easily the enchantments of a burning and blazing stronghold And hence it comes to pass that I may promise myself spotless and most select auditors, for if any impurity has come hither after the testing of the furnace, I should say at once that our janitor's fires have been feeble.

But fortunate are we and safe will we be forever! For at Rome, during the long life of the empire, they fed perpetual fires carefully and conscientiously; we are protected by ever-burning and by living fires. Why have I called the fires, living and everburning? Truly this escaped by an unexpected slip, since just now I call to mind more correctly that these extinguish themselves at the approach of evening and do not come to life again until broad daylight There is hope, however, that our abode can be lighted brightly again after all, since nobody will be able to deny that the two greatest light tenders of the institution preside over our college, although they would never be held in higher honor than at Rome; for there, either virgins Vestal and sleepless, would keep those fires perpetually burning, even the whole night long; as flamen brothers, they would have been initiated into the seraphic order. Concerning these, in fine, that

Vergilian hemistich is especially applicable; "Fiery is the force in them." Yea, indeed, I have almost been led to believe that Horace has made mention of these our fire tenders; for the elder of these, when he tarries with his wife and children, shines among all like a moon among lesser lights. But I cannot pass by the shameful blunder of Ovid, who sang in this fashion: "Rising from the flame no bodies you see." For we see on all sides little fires wandering about, begot by this our fire. If Ovid should dispute this, it will be necessary to call the virtue of the wife into question.

I come back to you, my hearers. Do not be sorry on account of a journey so dangerous and fearful; behold for you a sumptuous banquet! Behold tables heaped even to Persian splendor, burdened with the choicest viands, which would even delight and sooth an Apician palate! Truly they report that eight whole wild boars were set before Antony and Cleopatra at a banquet; but before you, oho, in the first course fifty fatted boars, soaked for three years in pickled beer, and nevertheless still so tough that they can tire out even the teeth of a dog; then, besides, the same number of the choicest oxen extraordinarily tailed, just roasted before the doors by our servant fire; but I fear that they have tried out all the juice into the dripping pan. Besides these also, lo, as many calves heads, quite thick and meaty, but so lacking in brain that there is not enough for seasoning. Then, in addition, there are a hundred kids more or less; but I believe they are exceedingly lean from too frequent association with Venus. We looked for some rams, with splendid and spreading horns, but our cooks have not yet fetched those with them from the city. If any one prefers fowls, we have them in plenty, fattened a long while with balls of paste, with pellets, and with powdered cheese: first, I know not what kind of birds, as green in nature as in feather, whence I suspect they have been imported from the country of the parrots, which, because they always fly in flocks and make their nests generally in the same place, are also served from the same platter. But I am of the opinion that you should dine sparingly on

these, because, aside from the fact that they are rather indigestible and contain nothing in them of solid nourishment, they also push out the mange in the diners (provided the gourmand tells the truth).

Now, indeed, you may feast freely and jovially; for here present has been sent what I commend to you before all, namely, a huge snipe, of such oily fatness on account of three years of beech-mast, that for it one very full mess is hardly large enough; and its beak is so very long and very hard that it can without fear of punishment enter into a contest with an elephant or a rhinoceros. We have, however, rightly slaughtered it on this day, because it had begun, after the custom of the huge apes, to lie in ambush for the girls and to offer violence to the women.

Some Irish birds follow this—I do not know the name—, but they are very like cranes in gait and shape of body. As much as possible they are wont to be served in the last course. Here indeed is a new and rare, more than a healthy, food. Accordingly, I warn you to abstain from these, for they are very effective (provided the gourmand tells the truth) in the generation of inguinal lice. Therefore, I think they will be more suited to hostlers; for, since they are by nature lively, brisk, and dancing about, if they are injected into skinny horses through the fundament, they cause them instantly to become more vivacious and more speedy than if they had ten live eels in their inwards.

Also, behold very many geese, both of this year and of former years, exceedingly noisy and more sonorous than the frogs of Aristophanes; whom you will indeed easily recognize, for it is a wonder that they have not already made themselves known by hissing; straightway perhaps you will hear them.

Some eggs we have in addition; but these from a "bad crow."

The fruit to be sure is nothing except apples and medlars; and these from an unfortunate tree, not quite ripe; and so they will be the better to hang again in the sun.

You perceive our preparations. I beseech you, you who have an appetite, to fill up full. But I prophesy that you are about to say that these dishes, like those nocturnal feasts which are prepared by the devil for witches, are not seasoned with salt; and I fear that you may go away more hungry than you came.

But I pass on to those things which more nearly concern me. The Romans have their festival of flowers, the farmers their shepherds' feast, the bakers their oven fête; we also especially at this time, free from affairs and business, are accustomed to make sport in the Socratic manner. Likewise the Inns of the Pettifoggers have those whom they call Lords, even thereby indicating how ambitious of office they are. We, Academicians, however, wishing to approach as near as possible to paternity, desire to assume under a pseudonym that which we in truth do not even risk, except in secret; just as girls according to their custom imagine playful weddings and confinements, laying hold of and enjoying the shadows of those things which they pant for and eagerly desire.

For what reason, however, this annual festivity was dropped during the year which last ran its course, I really am unable to determine, unless it be that those who were about to become 'Fathers' conducted themselves so turbulently in town that he, to whom this duty was assigned, taking pity on their great exertions, of his own accord decreed that they should be relieved of this anxiety.

But indeed how comes it that I have so suddenly been made a 'Father'? Ye gods, grant me your protection! What prodigy is this, surpassing the strange tales of Pliny! Have I by killing a snake suffered the fate of Tiresias? Has some Thessalian witch smeared me with magic ointment? Or finally, violated by some god, like Caenus of old, have I bargained for manhood as a reward for dishonor, so that suddenly I might be changed from a woman into a man? From some I have lately heard the epithet 'Lady.' But why do I seem to those fellows insufficiently masculine? Was it any disgrace to Priscian? Really, the silly grammaticasters attribute to the feminine gender signs which belong to the masculine! Doubtless it was because I was never able to gulp down huge bumpers in pancratic fashion; or because my hand has not become calloused by holding the plow-handle; or because I never lay down on my back under the sun at mid-day, like a seven-year ox-driver; perhaps in fine, because I never proved myself a man in the same manner as those gluttons. But would that they could as easily lay aside their asshood as I whatever belongs to womanhood.

But notice how stupidly, **how** thoughtlessly they have taunted me about that which I, on the best authority, shall turn to my honor. For truly, even Demosthenes was called by his rivals and opponents a little man. Likewise Quintus Hortensius, most renowned of all the orators, after Marcus Tullius, was called by Lucius Torquatus "Dionysia the citharess." To him he replied: "I would prefer indeed to be Dionysia than what you are, Torquatus—unrefined, boorish, ill-bred." But I put far away and repel from me whatsoever pertains to Lord and Lady; I do not desire to be a 'Lord,' Academicians, except on your rostrum and in your tribunal. Who now will stop me from enjoying an omen so auspicious and happy, and from exulting with joy that I have been united in company with such great men under the same reproach! Meanwhile, as I think that all good and excellent men are placed above envy, so I believe these malicious fellows are so far the lowest down of all that they are not worth reviling.

And so I turn me as a 'Father' to my sons, of whom I perceive a brilliant band; and I behold also that the witty little rascals by secret nods do acknowledge me as 'Father.' Do you ask for names? Under the names of dishes I am unwilling to serve up my sons to you to be eaten, for that would be too closely bordering upon the savageness of Tantalus or Lycaon. I will not designate by the names of members, lest you think that I have begotten so many bits of men instead of complete men. Nor is it my pleasure to designate them by the kinds of wines, lest whatever I shall say be out of place, and no concern of Bacchus. I prefer that they be named after the band of Praedicaments, that in this way I may express both noble descent and free manner of life; and in the same manner, I shall take care that all have been advanced to some degree before my downfall.

But in respect to my salty sayings, I am unwilling that they should be toothless, for in so doing you may say that they are hackneyed and ancient, and that some little coughing old woman has spit them out. Accordingly, I believe no one will find fault with my dentate jokes, except some one who himself has no teeth, and therefore will find fault because they are not like his own. And certainly at the present moment I would prefer very much that the fortune of Horace should befall me; namely, that I might be the son of a salt-fish monger; for then my 'salties' would be perfect. Likewise, I would send you away so beautifully lashed by salty remarks that our soldiers who lately fled from the Isle of Re would not feel more sorry over the sought-for briny deep.

I do not wish to be excessively tiresome, my children, in giving advice to you, lest I should seem to have bestowed more labor in educating you than in begetting you; only let each one beware lest from a son he may become a scapegrace; and let not my sons worship (Father) Liber, if they wish me to be their 'Father.' If I should give any other pieces of advice, I feel these ought to be presented in the vernacular tongue, and I will try, according to my strength, to make you understand everything. Besides Neptune, Apollo, Vulcan, and all the tectonic gods must be entreated by me to be willing either to strengthen my flanks with slats or to bind me around with iron plates. Moreover, I must also supplicate the goddess Ceres, that, as she gave to Pelops an ivory shoulder, likewise she may deem it worth while to repair my almost ruined ribs; for there is no reason why anyone should wonder, if, after so great a racket and after begetting so many sons, they should be a trifle weaker. In these matters also I have tarried beyond what is enough, in a Neronian sense. Now, leaping over the academic laws, as over the walls of Romulus, I pass from Latin to English. You to whom such things are pleasing give now to me attentive ears and minds.

[At this point came the English verses, printed at p. 14.]

VII.

AN ORATION DELIVERED IN THE CHAPEL IN DEFENSE OF KNOWLEDGE

Knowledge renders man happier than ignorance.

ALTHOUGH, my hearers, nothing is more delightful and pleasing to me than your presence, than an attentive throng of gowned gentlemen, and also than this honor-bearing oratorical exhibition, in which at one time and another I have taken part among you, the task being not disagreeable; nevertheless, if it be allowable to mention what is a fact, it always so happens that, although neither my natural bent nor course of studies are very much at variance with this oratorical activity, I hardly ever undertake speaking of my own free will and accord. If it had been in my power, I would gladly indeed have avoided the exertion of this evening especially, because I have learned from books and from the opinions of the most learned men this, that in the orator as in the poet nothing commonplace or mediocre can be allowed, and that he who wishes deservedly to be and to be considered an orator ought to be equipped and perfected with a certain encompassing support of all the arts and of all science. Since my age does not permit this, I have preferred up to the present, while providing myself with these supports, to strive earnestly after that true reputation by long and severe toil, rather than to snatch a false reputation by a hurried and pre-mature mode of expression.

While I am wholly afire and ablaze every day with this plan and purpose of mind, I have never felt any hindrance and delay more pressing than this frequent annoyance of interruption; indeed nothing has more nourished my ability and conserved its good health, contrary to what takes place in the body, than learned and abundant leisure. This I have believed to be the prophetic sleep of Hesiod, those nocturnal trysts of Endymion with the moon, that retreat of Prometheus under the leadership of Mercury into the deepest solitudes of Mount Caucasus, where he became the wisest of gods and men, insomuch so that Jupiter himself is said to have asked his advice about the nuptials of Thetis.

I myself invoke the glades and streams and beloved elms of the villas, under which during the summer just gone by (if it be permitted to mention the secrets of the goddesses) I recall to mind with pleasant memories that I enjoyed the highest favor of the Muses, where amid fields and remote woodlands I have even seemed to myself to have been able to grow up as it were in a bygone age. In this place likewise I might have hoped for myself the same opportunity also of hiding, had not this inconvenient annoyance of speaking interposed itself quite unseasonably, which so hindered in a disagreeable way my sacred slumbers, so distracted a mind fixed on other things, and so impeded and burdened amid the rugged difficulties of the Arts, that having lost all hope of obtaining quiet, I began to think sorrowfully how far I was removed from that tranquillity which Letters at first promised me, that life would be painful among these surgings and tossings, that it would be better to forget the Arts completely. Accordingly, hardly master of myself, I undertook the rash design of praising Ignorance, which would certainly involve none of these commotions, and I advanced the proposition for debate: Which of the two, Knowledge or Ignorance, would render its devotees the happier?

I do not know what happened: either my Fate or my Genius did not wish me to depart from my early love of the Muses. Nay, even Blind Chance herself, become suddenly as it were prudent and foresighted, seemed likewise not to wish this. More speedily than I had supposed, Ignorance has found her champion; to me is left the defence of Knowledge. I truly rejoice that I was thus mocked, nor do I feel ashamed that Fortune, though blind, has restored my sight. For this boon I give thanks to her. Now at least I may praise the illustrious one from whose embrace I had been torn away, and by a speech I may almost console the grief of absence. Now this is clearly not an interruption; for who may call it an interruption when he praises and defends what he

loves, what he cherishes, what he wishes with all his heart to pursue.

In truth, my auditors, I think the power of eloquence is especially evinced in a matter which is praiseworthy to a moderate degree. Things which call for the highest laudation can scarcely be confined by any method, by any limits of language. In these the very abundance thwarts itself, and by the mass of material checks and restrains the ostentation of delivery from expanding itself. I am oppressed by this excessive abundance of evidence; the supplies themselves make me helpless; the means of defence render me defenceless. Accordingly, a selection must be made, or certainly it would be more truly an enumeration of the things which establish our case than a discussion, fixed and fortified by many strong proofs.

At this moment I perceive that one point ought especially to be emphasized by me: that I demonstrate what and how much weight on each side may contribute to that state of happiness toward which we all are hasting. Into this line of argument surely our speech will be turned with little trouble. Nor do I think there is very much need to fear what Stupidity may present against Knowledge, or Ignorance may present against Art, although this very thing which may present objections, which may cause discussion, which may even dare to open its mouth at this function of a most learned society, obtains everything from Knowledge by entreaty, or rather by begging.

I believe, my hearers, it is known and recognized by all, that the great framer of the universe, although he had founded all others things on change and decay, had intermingled in man, beyond what is mortal, a certain divine breath and as it were a part of himself, immortal, imperishable, immune from death and destruction: which, after it had sojourned spotlessly and chastely on earth for a while, a guest as it were from heaven, should wing itself upward to its native sky and should return to its destined mansion and native land. Whence it follows that nothing can be recounted justly among the causes of our happiness, unless in some way it takes into consideration both that eternal life and this temporal life. This is the sole contemplation, according to the judgment of almost everybody, by which our mind, without the aid of the body, remote and as it were wrapped up in itself, copies the eternal life of the immortal gods with an extraordinary delight.

This, however, without knowledge is altogether sterile and joyless, yea, indeed, worthless. For who can contemplate and examine seriously the ideal forms of things, human and divine, of which nothing can surely be known, unless he has a mind saturated and perfected by knowledge and training? So, in short, for one who lacks knowledge every approach to a happy life is seen to be cut off. This very soul, capable of deep wisdom and almost insatiable, God is seen to have given to us either in vain or in punishment, unless he had greatly wished us to climb the heights to a lofty knowledge of those things concerning which he had infused so great a desire in the nature of the human mind. In whatever way you are able, ponder over this entire scheme of things: the illustrious Artificer of the great work has built it for his own glory. The deeper we investigate its extraordinary plan, its remarkable structure, its wonderful variety, which, without knowledge, we cannot do, the more do we honor the author of this with our reverence and, as it were with a certain approbation, do we strive to follow what we believe is very pleasing, true, and altogether acceptable to him.

Will you believe, my auditors, that the great spaces of the enormous firmament, illuminated and adorned by the everlasting fires, sustain so many tremendously rapid motions, travel over such great paths of revolution, for this one reason: that they may furnish light for ignorant and stooping men? and present as it were a torch to us below, stupid and slothful? that nothing inheres in such a manifold increase of fruits and herbage, except a perishable adornment of verdure? Really, if we should be such unfair valuers of things that we follow nothing but the low inclination of the senses, we shall seem to be driven, not only slavishly and humbly, but also wickedly and maliciously, by the benign power; to whom, through our sluggishness and as it were through our ill will, a great part of the

honors and the reverence due so great a power will entirely perish. If therefore knowledge be for us the guide and introducer to happiness, if commanded and approved by a most powerful divinity and combined especially with his praise, certainly it is not possible for its devotees not to attain unto a high degree of happiness.

For I am not unaware, my hearers, that this contemplation, by which we strive toward that which ought to be highly desired, can have no flavor of true happiness without uprightness of life and blamelessness of character; moreover, that remarkably learned men have appeared impious, besides yielding to anger, hatred and low desires; that on the other hand many men unacquainted with Letters have proved themselves upright and most honest. What therefore? Is Ignorance more blessed? Truly, not in the least! So indeed it happens, my hearers, that the most corrupt customs and a rabble of illiterate men have lured into wickedness a few men preeminent perchance throughout their state; while the diligence of one scholarly and foresighted man has kept to their duty many human beings unrefined by knowledge. Undoubtedly, one family, one man endowed with knowledge and wisdom, like a great gift of God, may be sufficient to reform a whole state.

On the other hand, where no arts flourish, where all knowledge is banished, where indeed there is no trace of a good man, there savageness and frightful barbarism rage about. Of this fact I call to witness not one state or province or race, but a fourth part of the world, Europe, from the whole of which during several early centuries all good arts had perished; for a long time the presiding Muses had abandoned all the institutions of that age: blind Ignorance had pervaded and taken possession of everything; nothing was heard in the schools except the absurd dogmas of most stupid monks. Forsooth, having donned a gown, from empty platforms and pulpits, in filthy cathedrals, the profane and misshapen monster, Ignorance, vaunted itself. Then piety for the first time went into mourning, and religion expired and went to ruin; so that from its deep wound, late and with difficulty, it has hardly recovered even to this day.

But truly, my hearers, in Philosophy this appears to be sufficiently established and of long standing, that the perception of all art and of all science concerns only the intellect, but the home and the temple of the virtues and of uprightness is the will. Since, however, in the judgment of all, the human intellect, as head and ruler, surpasses in splendor the other faculties of the mind, it governs and illuminates with its splendor the will itself, otherwise blind and dark, that like the moon shines with another's light. Wherefore let us grant this truly and acknowledge of our own accord, that virtue without knowledge is more conducive to a happy life than knowledge without virtue; but where they have once been mutually associated in a happy union, as generally they ought and as very frequently happens, then indeed immediately, with bearing erect and lofty, Knowledge appears and shines forth far superior; it enthrones itself on high with the intellect as king and emperor, whence it views farther down, as it were lowly and underfoot, whatever is done by the will; and finally it easily takes to itself forever preeminence, renown, and majesty almost divine.

Come, let us proceed to the state. Let us observe both what takes place in private and what in public life. With respect to knowledge I pass over what is the most beautiful ornament of youth, the strong defence of the period of manhood, the adornment and comfort of old age. I also omit this, that many among their nobility, even the leaders of the Roman people, after extraordinary deeds and the glory of things accomplished, betook themselves out of the strife and din of ambition to literary study as though into a harbor and charming place of rest; that is to say, the most distinguished old men then perceived that the remaining best part of life ought to be invested in the best manner. Highest they were among men, yet in these arts they did not wish to be lowest among the gods. Honors they had sought, next immortality. In battling with the foes of the empire they employed a far different warfare; about to contend with death, the greatest plague of the human race, behold what weapons they select, what le-

gions they enroll, with what supplies they have been equipped.

But the greatest part of a social happiness has usually been lodged in human fellowship and in the friendships contracted. Many complain that the majority of the more learned class are hard to please, boorish, uncouth in manners, with no grace of speech for winning the minds of men. I acknowledge indeed that one who is commonly reclusive and withdrawn in studies is much more ready to address the gods than men; either because he is almost uninterruptedly at home among the higher powers, with little knowledge of, and quite inexperienced in, human affairs; or because, by the continuous contemplation of divine things, the mind, made as it were larger, tossing itself about with difficulty within the narrow confines of the body, becomes less adapted to the more exquisite gesticulations of greetings. But if worthy and suitable friendships have befallen, no one cultivates them more sacredly; for what can be imagined more delightful, what more happy than those conferences of learned and most eminent men, such as divine Plato is said to have held very frequently under that famous plane tree, which were certainly worthy of being heard with attentive silence by the whole of the confluent human race? Whereas to babble with one another stupidly, to gratify one another with splendor and licentiousness, this is indeed the friendship of ignorance, or really the ignorance of friendship.

Moreover, if this civic happiness consists in the noble and free pleasure of the mind; if this delight, which easily excels all others, has been reserved for learning and knowledge; what does it avail to have comprehended every law of the heavens and of the stars?—all the motions and shiftings of the air, whether it brings terror to sluggish minds by the august sound of thunders or by fiery locks, whether it becomes frozen in snow and hail, whether finally it falls soft and gentle in rain and dew; then to have learned perfectly the changing winds, all the vapors and gases which the earth and sea belch forth; next to become versed in the secret powers of plants and metals; and to have understood the nature and, if possible, the feelings of each living creature: thence the most exact structure and surgery of the human body; and finally the godlike power and force of mind; and whether any knowledge comes to us about those beings which are called Lares, Genii, and Demons? In addition to these there are infinite others, of which one might become acquainted with a goodly part before I could enumerate all.

So at length, my hearers, when once learning of all kinds shall have completed its cycles, that spirit of yours, not satisfied with this gloomy house of correction, will betake itself far and wide, until it shall have filled the world itself and far beyond with a certain divine extension of magnitude. Then at length many accidents and consequences of things will become clear so suddenly that nothing in life can happen quite unexpectedly, nothing by chance to one who has gained possession of this stronghold of wisdom. He will seem to be one whose power and authority the stars will obey, the land and the sea will follow implicitly, the winds and the storms will strive to please; one to whom Mother Nature even will hand over herself in surrender, quite as if some god, having abdicated power on earth, had delegated to him his court, his laws, his executive power, as though to some prefect. How great a pleasure is added hereto by flying through all the histories and problems of the races, by directing the attention, for the sake of practical judgment and morals, to the conditions and vicissitudes of kingdoms, nations, cities, peoples! This means, my hearers, to reside in every age as if alive, to be born as though a contemporary of time itself. Surely, when we have peered into the future for the glory of our name, this will be to extend and stretch life backward from the womb and wrest away from fate a certain preliminary immortality.

Do I pass by that to which what can be compared? To be the oracle of many races; to have a house like a temple; to be those whom kings and states summon to themselves; to be one, for the sake of seeing whom, neighbors and strangers flock together; one whom, even to have seen once, some shall brag about as though it possessed some honorable merit. These rewards of study, these fruits, Knowledge is able, and

frequently is wont, to confer upon her devotees in private life.

But what in public life? Truly to the height of majesty the reputation for learning has elevated few, nor for uprightness many more. Indisputably, these enjoy a kingdom in themselves far more glorious than all dominion over lands. And who lays hold of a double sovereignty without the disrepute of ambition? I will add this further, however, that there have been two men only up to this time who possessed the whole earth as by a gift of the gods, and have shared beyond all kings and princes a dominion equal to the gods themselves: namely, Alexander the Great and Octavius Caesar. And these both were disciples of Philosophy, just as if some pattern for emulation had been divinely produced for mankind, to which sort of man particularly the key and reins of affairs ought to be entrusted.

But many states have been renowned without learning, through deeds accomplished and through wealth. Of the Spartans indeed who betook themselves to the study of letters few are remembered. The Romans at a late date received Philosophy within the walls of the city. But the former profited by Lycurgus, the legislator, who was both a philosopher and fond of the poets, so much so that he first collected with the greatest care the writings of Homer which were scattered throughout Ionia. The latter, after various revolutions in the city and vigorous uprisings, maintained themselves with difficulty. Having sent ambassadors, they obtained by begging from Athens, at that time in highest repute for the study of the arts, the Decemviral Laws, which have also been called the Twelve Tables.

What can we say if our opponents put before us the argument that the modern Turks, ignorant of all literature, have obtained the mastery of affairs widely throughout the opulent kingdoms of Asia? Truly, in that state (if indeed that ought to be called a state in which the power has been continuously usurped by force and murder on the part of most cruel men whom a union of wickedness has brought together in one place) I have heard of nothing that may be within it noteworthy as a model. To provide the comforts of life, to guard possessions —that we owe to Nature, not to Art; to attack the property of others wantonly, to exist for themselves in mutual alliance for robbery, to conspire in villainy—this we owe to the depravity of Nature. A kind of justice is exercised among them; not to be wondered at. Other virtues easily take their flight; Justice, truly royal, compels reverence to herself; without her even the most unjust organizations would quickly be dissolved. Nor, to be sure, should I forget that the Saracens, in a sense the founders of the Turkish power, extended their dominion not more by devotion to arms than to good literature.

But if we go back to antiquity, we shall discover that the states were not only regulated by, but oftentimes were established on, knowledge. Some of the most ancient of the peoples, the indigenous, are said to have wandered in woods and mountains, seeking the advantage of food after the manner of wild beasts. With heads held high, in other respects bent over, you would have thought, aside from excellence of form, that they had nothing apart from brutes. The same caves, the same dens protected them from the weather and cold. Then no city, no temples of marble, no altars of the gods, or sanctuaries were resplendent. Not in those days was there a sacred law, not yet were the laws of men decreed in the forum. No nuptial torch, no chorus, no song at the joyous table, no burial rite, no lamentation, hardly a mound honored the dead. No banquets, no games, unheard the sound of the cithara; in those times all things were lacking which idleness now squanders in luxury. When suddenly the Arts and Sciences divinely inspired the rude hearts of men and allured within one wall those who were imbued with knowledge of them. Wherefore, indeed, according to some authors, the cities themselves were first founded, then established by laws. Afterward, protected by counsellors, they were able to stand firmly a very long time and very happily even under the same rulers.

What, on the other hand, has Ignorance to say? I feel, my hearers, she is veiled in darkness, is benumbed, is afar off, looks around for means of escape, complains that Life is short, Art is long. By all means in truth let us remove the two great stumbling blocks to our studies: the one of knowledge poorly taught, the other of our own slothfulness. With the permission of Galen, or whoever else it was, quite the contrary will it be: Life will be long, Art short. Nothing is more excellent than Art, and nothing also requiring more labor: nothing more sluggish than we, nothing more negligent. We permit ourselves to be outstripped by laborers and farmers in nightly and early morning toil. They are more unwearied in humble matters for common nourishment, than we in most noble matters for an abounding life. We, although we aspire to the highest and best in human affairs, are able to endure neither the exertion nor the disgrace of idleness; nay more, it causes shame to be that which we consider ourselves unworthy not to be.

We take care of our health with watchings and jealous care; shameful to say, we leave the mind uncultured. While we venerate the body, who would not reduce its powers, that greater powers may be won for the mind? Although indeed there are numerous most profligate creatures who dispute these things, having cast off all concern for time, character, or health by eating and drinking after the manner of sea beasts, by spending the nights in debauchery and gambling; they make no complaint that they have made themselves weaker. Since therefore they so weaken and accustom themselves that they are eager and keen for all kinds of turpitude, but sluggish and feeble for all actions of virtue and character; they falsely and wickedly transfer the blame to Nature or to the shortness of life. But if, by spending our life modestly and temperately, we prefer to subdue the primary impulses of the ungovernable age through reason and constant zeal in studies, preserving the heavenly vigor of the mind pure and unharmed from all contagion and defilement; it would be incredible to us, my hearers, on looking back after several years, how great a distance has been traversed, what a mighty sea of knowledge we shall seem to have sailed over with a quiet passage.

To this also a distinct gain would be added: if one could both know the useful arts and could properly choose the useful in the arts. In the first place, how many are the despicable trifles of the grammarians and the rhetoricians! You may hear the latter. in teaching their art, speaking ungrammatically; the former in a most childish manner. What shall we say of Logic? Queen she is indeed of the arts if she is handled in accordance with her worth. But alas, how great is the folly of the rational faculty! Here, not men, but just finches feed on thistles and thorns. "O hardy the bowels of the reapers!" Why should I mention that the subject which the Peripatetics call Metaphysics is not knowledge most abundant, as the authority of great men instructs me,—not knowledge, I say, for the most part, but "infamous rocks," but a kind of Lernian swamp of sophisms, contrived for shipwreck and destruction? Those things which I mentioned before are the wounds of gowned Ignorance. This same itch of the hoods has also spread widely into Natural Philosophy. The empty little glory of demonstrations infests Mathematics. With all of these things, which are of no value, despised and eliminated, it will be wonderful how many whole years we shall gain.

What of this, that a confused system makes especially obscure our legal science, and, what is worse, our speech is, I know not what, American, I suppose, or not even human! Wherefore, when I have sometimes heard our pettifoggers ranting, it has occurred to my mind to doubt whether a human mouth and speech belonged to them, or any human feelings dwelt in them. Certainly I am afraid that august Justice may not be able to respect us: I am afraid that she may not understand at any time our accusations and legal actions, the language of which she would not know how to speak. Accordingly, my hearers, if from childhood we permit no day to pass by without lessons and diligent study; if from knowledge we wisely omit the foreign, the superfluous, the useless; certainly within the age of Alexander the Great we shall have subdued something greater and more glorious than his circle of the earth; and we shall be so far from finding fault with the brevity of life or the irksomeness of knowledge that I believe we shall be more ready to weep and shed tears, as did that famous one long ago, because no

more worlds are left over which we may triumph.

Ignorance breathes its last! Now behold the final struggles and the dying effort!—We living mortals particularly are to be cheated out of glory, while a long chain and descent of years has made famous those illustrious ancients; we, in the decadent old age of the world, we, by the speedy destruction of all things, are to be overwhelmed, if we shall have left behind anything to be extolled with everlasting praise; our name is to abide but a short time, for hardly may any posterity succeed to its memory; vain is it now to produce so many books and eminent monuments of ability, which the approaching funeral pyre of the world will consume.

I do not deny that this can very likely take place. But, in truth, not to value fame when you have done well, that is beyond all glory. How little has the idle discourse of men enriched the departed and the dead, discourse of which no delight, no emotion could reach them? May we hope for an eternal life, which will never wipe out the memory at least of our good deeds on earth: in which, if we have nobly deserved anything here, we ourselves, being present, shall hear it; in which many have seriously reasoned that those would be exalted above all by a unique and supreme knowledge, who, first in this life, spent most temperately, have given all their time to good employments, and by them have aided mankind. Thenceforth let the lazy cease to cavil over whatever up to this time may have been to us uncertain and involved in the sciences; which, however, ought to be attributed not so much to science as to man. That it is, my hearers, which either disproves or mitigates or counterbalances both that Socratic ignorance and the cautious uncertainty of the Sceptics.

Now in faith what truly is the blessedness of Ignorance? To possess its own for itself, to be defamed by nobody, to avoid every care and trouble, to spend life as easily and calmly as possible. But this is the life of a beast or of some bird which has its nest for safety as close to the sky as possible, on the heights or in the deepest forests, which trains its young, which flies to the feeding ground without fear of the fowler, which at dawn and at evening sings sweet strains What does that ethereal vigor of the soul long for beyond these? Well, let it lay aside the human; it will surely become familiar with the Circean cup, stooping let it migrate to the beasts.

To the beasts, in truth? But they do not wish to receive such a vile guest, since they are either partakers of some low form of reasoning, as many argue, or they are wise with a certain powerful instinct; they employ among themselves either the arts or something like the arts. For, according to Plutarch, it is said that even the dogs are not ignorant of Logic, while tracking wild beasts; and if one should come by chance to a place where three ways meet, clearly he knows how to use a disjunctive syllogism. The nightingale, says Aristotle, is accustomed to teach its young certain rules, as it were, of music. Almost every animal is its own doctor; likewise many have given to mankind remarkable illustrations of the healing art. The Egyptian ibis shows the value of purging the bowels; the hippopotamus of letting blood. Who can say they are without knowledge of astronomy, from whom are obtained so many prognostications of winds, storms, floods, and pleasant weather? How, by a very wise and strict custom, do the geese, while flying over the Taurus mountain, lessen the danger of talkativeness by stopping their mouths with pebbles? Household affairs owe many things to the ants, the state to the bees. The beasts possess deeper wisdom than to deem Ignorance fit for their gatherings and associations; lower do they drive it.

What next? As to trees and rocks? But the trees themselves, the very bushes, and every grove once on a time, unfettered by roots, hastened after the most skilled songs of Orpheus. Often also, keepers of mysteries, like the Dodonian oak of old, they rendered divine oracles. Likewise the rocks reply with a certain docility to the sacred voice of the poets. Do not even these also drive Ignorance away from themselves? Will it then be permitted to find repose in that Not-Being of the Epicureans, below every kind of brute, below the trees and rocks, below every rank of Nature? Not even that, since it is necessary that what is more evil, what is more base, what is more wretched, that is lowest, be Ignorance.

I come to you, my most intelligent auditors; for, even though I myself had said nothing, I perceive that you are for me not so many arguments as weapons, which I will turn against Ignorance, even to its destruction. I have now sounded the trumpet; do you rush into battle; drive away this enemy from you; ward it off from your porticoes and walks. If you should permit it to become something, you yourselves will become that which you know is the most wretched of all. Yours therefore is this cause of all. Wherefore, if I have perchance been much more wordy than is permitted by the custom of this exercise, beyond that which the very dignity of the subject demanded, even you, my judges, will grant to me forbearance, I think, since you understand so much the better my opinion of you, how zealous I am for you, what labors, what vigils I have not refused in your behalf. I have spoken.

SECOND DRAFT OF A LETTER TO A FRIEND.

[The text is from the Cambridge MS. Probable date, early winter, 1631–32.]

SIR, besides that in sundry other respects I must acknowledge me to proffit by you when ever wee meet, you are often to me, & were yesterday especially, as a good watch man to admonish that the howres of the night passe on (for so I call my life as yet obscure, & unserviceable to mankind) & that the day with me is at hand wherin Christ commands all to labour while there is light. Which because I am persuaded you doe to no other purpose then out of a true desire that God should be honourd in every one, I therfore thinke my selfe bound though unask't, to give you account, as oft as occasion is, of this my tardie moving; according to the præcept of my conscience, which I firmely trust is not without God. Yet now I will not streine for any set apologie, but only referre my selfe to what my mynd shall have at any tyme to declare her selfe at her best ease.

But if you thinke, as you said, that too much love of Learning is in fault, & that I have given up my selfe to dreame away my yeares in the armes of studious retirement like Endymion with the Moone as the tale of Latmus goes, yet consider that if it were no more but the meere love of learning, whether it proceed from a principle bad, good, or naturall, it could not have held out thus long against so strong opposition on the other side of every kind. For if it be bad why should not all the fond hopes that forward Youth & Vanitie are fledge with together with Gaine, pride, & ambition call me forward more powerfully, then a poore regardlesse & unprofitable sin of curiosity should be able to withhold me; wherby a man cutts himselfe off from all action & becomes the most helplesse, pusilanimous & unweapon'd creature in the world, the most unfit & unable to doe that which all mortals most aspire to—either to defend & be usefull to his freinds, or to offend his enimies. Or, if it be to be thought an naturall pronenesse, there is against that a much more potent inclination & inbred, which about this tyme of a mans life sollicits most, the desire of house & family of his owne; to which nothing is esteemed more helpfull then the early entring into credible employment, & nothing more hindering then this affected solitarinesse. And though this were anough, yet there is to this another act, if not of pure, yet of refined nature no lesse available to dissuade prolonged obscurity,—a desire of honour & repute & immortall fame, seated in the brest of every true scholar; which all make hast to by the readiest ways of publishing & divulging conceived merits—as well those that shall, as those that never shall, obtaine it. Nature therfore would præsently worke the more prævalent way, if there were nothing but this inferiour bent of her selfe to restraine her. Lastly, the Love of Learning, as it is the pursuit of somthing good, it would sooner follow the more excellent & supreme good knowne & præsented, and so be quickly diverted from the emptie & fantastick chase of shadows & notions, to the solid good flowing from due & tymely obedience to that command in the gospell set out by the seasing of him that hid the talent.

It is more probable, therfore, that not the endlesse delight of speculation, but this very consideration of that great commandement, does not presse forward, as soone as

may be, to undergo, but keeps off, with a sacred reverence & religious advisement how best to undergoe—not taking thought of being late, so it give advantage to be more fit; for those that were latest lost nothing, when the maister of the vinyard came to give each one his hire. & heere I am come to a streame head, copious enough to disburden it selfe, like Nilus, at seven mouthes into an ocean. But then I should also run into a reciprocall contradiction of ebbing & flowing at once, & doe that which I excuse my selfe for not doing—preach & not preach. Yet, that you may see that I am something suspicious of selfe, & doe take notice of a certaine belatednesse in me I am the bolder to send you some of my nightward thoughts some while since, because they com in not altogether unfitly, made up in a Petrarchian stanza, which I told you of:—

[In the first draft, the sonnet, "How soon hath Time" is written at this place.]

After the stanza.

By this I beleeve you may well repent of having made mention at all of this matter; for, if I have not all this while won you to this, I have certainly wearied you to it. This, therefore, alone may be a sufficient reason for me to keepe me as I am, least having thus tired you singly, I should deale worse with a whole congregation, & spoyle all the patience of a Parish. For I my selfe doe not only see my owne tediousnesse, but now grow offended with it, that has hinderd m[e] thus long from comming to the last & best period of my letter, & that which must now cheifely worke my pardon that—I am

Your true & unfained freind.

SUBJECTS FOR POEMS AND PLAYS FROM THE CAMBRIDGE MANUSCRIPT

[I]

THE PERSONS

Michael
Heavenly Love
Chorus of Angels
Lucifer
Adam }
Eve } with the serpent
Conscience

Death

Labour ⎫
Sicknesse ⎪
Discontent ⎬ mutes
Ignorance ⎪
with others ⎭

Faith
Hope
Charity

[II]

THE PERSONS

Moses
Justice
Mercie
Wisdome
Heavenly Love
Hesperus the Evening Starre
Chorus of Angels
Lucifer
Adam
Eve
Conscience

Labour ⎫
Sicknesse ⎪
Discontent ⎪
Ignorance ⎬ mutes
Feare ⎪
Death ⎭

Faith
Hope
Charity

OTHER TRAGEDIES

Adam in Banishment
The flood
Abram in Ægypt.

—————————————

PARADISE LOST. THE PERSONS

Moses προλογίζει recounting how he as-
sum'd his true bodie, that it corrupts
not because of his [being] with God in
the mount declares the like of Enoch
and Eliah, besides the purity of the
pl[ace] that certaine pure winds, dues,
and clouds præserve it from corruption
whence [ex]horts to the sight of God,
tells they cannot se Adam in the state
of innocence by reason of thire sin

Justice ⎱ debating what should become of
Mercie ⎰   man if he fall

Wisdome
Chorus of Angels sing a hymne of the creation

Act 2

Heavenly Love
Evening starre
Chorus sing the marriage song and describe
Paradice

Act 3

Lucifer contriving Adams ruine
Chorus feares for Adam and relates Lucifers
rebellion and fall

Act 4

Adam ⎱ fallen
Eve ⎰
Conscience cites them to Gods examination
Chorus bewails and tells the good Adam
hath lost

Act 5

Adam and Eve, driven out of Paradice
præsented by an angel with
    Labour greife hatred Envie warre famine
        Pestilence
    sicknesse ⎫ mutes to whome he gives
    discontent ⎪ thire names likewise winter,
    Ignorance ⎬ heat Tempest &c enterd
    Feare ⎪ into the world
    Death ⎭
    Faith ⎫
    Hope ⎬ comfort him and instruct him
    Charity ⎭
Chorus breifly concludes

The Deluge.
Sodom.
Dinah vide Euseb. præ-
    parat.   Evang. 1. 9. c. 22
    The Persons
    Dina   Hamor
    Debora, Rebeccas
        nurse   Sichem
    Jacob   counselers 2.
    Simeon   nuncius
    Levi   Chorus.

Thamar Cüephorusa where Juda is found
to have bin the author of that crime which

he condemn'd in Tamar, Tamar excus'd in what she attempted.

The golden calfe or the massacre in Horeb.

The Quails. Num. 11.

The murmurers. Num. 14.

Corah, Dathan &c. Num. 16.17.

Moabitides. Num. 25.

Achan. Josue 7. et 8.

Josuah in Gibeon. Josu. 10.

Gideon Idoloclastes. Jud. 6.7.

Gideon pursuing. Jud. 8.

Abimelech the usurper. Jud. 9.

Samson pursophorus or Hybristes, or Samson marriing or in Ramath Lechi. Jud. 15.

Dagonalia. Jud. 16.

Comazontes or the Benjaminits. Jud. 19.20. &c. Or the Rioters.

Theristria. A Pastoral out cf Ruth.

Eliadæ, Hophni and Phinehas, Sam. 1.2.3.4. Beginning with the first over throw of Israel by the Philistims, interlac't with Samuels vision concerning Eli's familie.

Jonathan rescu'd. Sam. 1. 14.

Doeg slandering. Sam. 1. 22.

The sheepshearers in Carmel; a pastoral. 1 Sam. 25.

Saul in Gilboa. 1 Sam. 28. 31.

David revolted. 1 Sam. from the 27 c. to the 31.

David Adulterous. 2 Sam. c. 11. 12.

Tamar. 2 Sam. 13.

Achitophel. 2 Sam. 15.16.17.18.

Adoniah. 1 Reg. 2.

Salomon Gynæcocratumenus or Idolomargus aut Thysiazusæ. Reg. 1. 11.

Rehoboam. 1 Reg. 12. wher is disputed of a politick religion.

Abias Thersæus. 1 Reg. 14. The queen after much dispute as the last refuge sent to the profit Ahias of Shilo; receavs the message. The epitasis in that shee hearing the child shall die as she comes home refuses to return thinking therby to elude the oracle. The former part is spent in bringing the sick Prince forth as it were desirous to shift his chamber and couch as dying men use. His father telling him what sacrifize he had sent for his health to Bethel and Dan, his fearlesnesse of Death and puting his father in mind to set to Ahiah. The chorus of the Elders of Israel bemoning his vertues bereft them and at an other time wondring why

Jeroboam beeing bad himself should so greive for his son that was good. &c.

Imbres or the Showrs. 1 Reg. 18.

Naboth συκοφαντούμενος 1 Reg. 21.

Ahab. 1 Reg. 22. Beginning at th[e] synod of fals profets ending wi[th] relation cf Ahabs death; his bodie brought . . . [fr] einds for his seducing. Alleluiah, glory be &c. (See Lavater 2 Chron. 18.)

Elias in the mount. 2 Reg. 1. ὀρειβάτης or better Elias Polemistis.

Elisæus Hydrochóos. 2 Reg. 3. Hudrophantes Aquator.

Elisæus Adoradocétus.

Elisæus Menutes sive in Dothaimis. 2 Reg. 6.

Samaria liberata. 2 Reg. 7.

Achabæi Cunoboroomeni. 2 Reg. 9. The scene Jesrael. Beginning from the watchmans discovery of Jehu till he go out. In the mean while message of things passing brought to Jesebel, &c. Lastly the 70 heads of Ahabs [so]ns brought in .nd message brought of Ahaziah['s] brethren slain on the way. c. 10.

Jehu Belicola. 2 Reg 10.

Athaliah. 2 Reg 1.

Amaziah Doryalotus. 2 Reg. 14. 2 Chron. 25.

Hezechias πολιορκούμενος 2 Reg. 18. 19. infra.

Josiah Aiaζomenos. 2 Reg. 23.

Zedechiah νεοτερίζων. 2 Reg. but the story is larger in Jeremiah.

[Sa]lymωn Halosis which may [b]egin from a Message brought to [th]e citty of the judgment upon Zedechiah and his children in Ribla, and so seconded with the burning and destruction of citty & [t]emple by Nabuzaradan. Lamented by [J]eremiah.

Asa or Æthiopes. 2 Chron. 14. with the deposing his mother, and burning her Idol.

[D]ura. The three children. Dan. 3.

Hesechia beseig'd. The wicked hypocrysy of Shebna spoken of in the 11. or therabout of Isaiah & the commendation of Eliakim will afford αφορμας λογου together with a faction that sought help from Ægypt.

BRITISH TRAG.

Venutius, husband of Cartismandua.

The cloister king Constans set up by Vortiger.

2. Vortimer poison'd by Roena.
3. Vortiger immur'd. Vortiger marrying Roena. See Speed. Reproov'd by Vodin archbishop of London. Speed. The massacre of the Britains by Hengist in thire cups at Salisbyry plaine. Malmsbyry.
4. Sigher of the East Saxons revolted from the faith and reclaim'd by Jarumannus.
5. Ethelbert of the East Angles slaine by Offa the Mercian k. See Holinsh. l. 6. c. 5. Speed in the life of Offa & Ethelbert.
6. Sebert slaine by Penda after he had left his kingdom. See Holinshed. 116 p.
7. Wulfer slaying his tow sons for beeing Christians.
8. Osbert of Northumberland slain for ravishing the wife of Bernbocard and the Dans brought in. See Stow. Holinsh. l. 6. c. 12 and especially Speed l. 8. c. 2.
9. Edmond last k. of the East Angles martyr'd by Hinguar the Dane. See Speed l. 8. c. 2.
10. Sigebert tyrant of the West Saxons. Slain by a swinheard.
11. Edmund brother of Athelstan. Slain by a theefe at his owne table. Malmesb.
12. Edwin son to Edward the yonger for lust depriv'd of his kingdom. Or rather by faction of monks whome he hated together with the impostor Dunstan.
13. Edward son of Edgar murderd by his stepmother; to which may be inserted the tragedie stirrd up betwixt the monks and preists about mariage.
14. Etheldred son of Edgar a slothfull k.; the ruin of his land by the Danes.
15. Ceaulin k. of West Saxons for tyrannie depos'd, and banish't & dying.
16. The slaughter of the monks of Bangor by Edelfride, stirrd up as is said by Ethelbert, and he by Austine the monk, because the Britain would not receave the rites of the Roman Church. See Beda, Geffrey Monmouth, and Holinshed, p. 104. Which must begin with the convocat[ion] of British clergie by Austin to determin superfluous points which by them we[re] refused.
17. Edwin by vision promis'd the kingdom of Northumberland on promise of his conversion and therin establish't by Rodoald K. of East Angles.

18. Oswin k. of Deira slaine by Oswie his freind k. of Bernitia through instigation of flatterers. See Holinshed p. 115.
19. Sigibert of the East Angles keeping companie with a person excommunicated, slaine by the same man in his house according as the bishop Cedda had foretold.
20. Egfride k. of the Northumbers slaine in battel against the Picts having before wasted Ireland and made warre for no reason on men that ever lov'd the English; forewarnd also by Cutbert not to fight with the Picts.
21. Kinewulf k. of the West Saxons slaine by Kineard in the house of one of his concubins.
22. Gunthildis, the Danish ladie, with her husband Palingus and her son slaine by appointment of the traitor Edrick in k. Ethelreds days. Holinshed 7. l. c. 5. Together with the massacre of the Danes at Oxford. Speed.
23. Brightrick of West Saxons poyson'd by his wife Ethelburge, Offa's daughter, who dyes miserably also in beggery after adultery in an nunnery. Speed in Bithric.
24. Alfred in disguise of a ministrel discovers the Danes negligence; sets on with a mightie slaughter. About the same tyme the Devonshire men rout Hubba & slay him.

A Heroicall Poem may be founded somwhere in Alfreds reigne, especially at his issuing out of Edelingsey on the Danes; whose actions are wel like those of Ulysses.

25. Athelstan exposing his brother Edwin to the sea, and repenting.
26. Edgar slaying Ethelwold for false play in woing; wherin may be set out his pride, [and] lust, which he thought to close by favouring monks and building monasteries. Also the disposition of woman in Elfrida toward her husband.
27. Swane beseidging London and Etheldred repuls't by the Londoners.
28. Harold slaine in battel by William the Norman. The first scene may begin with the ghost of Alfred, the second son of Ethelred slaine in cruel manner by God-

win, Harolds father, his mother and
brother disuading him.

29. Edmund Ironside defeating the Danes at
Brentford with his combat with Canute.

30. Edmund Ironside murder'd by Edrick
the traitor and reveng'd by Canute.

31. Gunilda, daughter to k. Canute and
Emma wife to Henry, the third Emperour, accus'd of inchastitie, is defended by
her English page in combat against a
giantlike adversary, who by him at 2
blows is slaine, &c. Speed in the life of
Canute.

32. Hardiknute dying in his cups an example
to riot.

33. Edward Confessors divorsing and imprisoning his noble wife Editha, Godwins
daughter. Wherin is shewed his over
affection to strangers, the cause of
Godwins insurrection; wherein Godwins
forbearance of battel rais'd and the
[En]glish moderation [on] both sides
[m]agnifid; his slacknesse to redresse
the corrupt clergie and superstitious
prætence of chastitie.

Abram from Morea, or Isack redeemd.

The oiconomie may be thus: The fift or
sixt day after Abrahams departure, Eleazer,
Abrams steward, first alone, and then with
the chorus, discours of Abrahams strange
voiage, thire mistresse' sorrow and perplexity, accompanied with frigh[t]full dreams,
and tell the manner of his rising by night,
taking his servants and his son with him.
Next may come forth Sarah her self, after
the Chorus, or Ismael or Agar. Next, some
shepheard or companie of merchants, passing
through the mount in the time that Abram
was in the mid work, relate to Sarah what
they saw: hence lamentations, fears, wonders.
The matter in the mean while divulgd, Aner
or Eshcol or Mamre, Abrams confederats
come to the hous of Abram to be more certaine, or to bring news, in the mean while
discoursing, as the world would, of such an
action divers ways: bewayling the fate of so
noble a man faln from his reputation, either
through divin justice or superstition, or coveting to doe some notable act through zeal.
At length a servant sent from Abram relates
the truth, and last he himselfe comes in with

a great Train of Melchizedec, whose shep-
heards, beeing secret eye witnesses of all
passages, had related to thir master, and he
conducted his freind Abraham home with joy.

BAPTISTES.

The Scene. The Court.

Beginning from the morning of Herods
birth day. Herod by some counseler, or els
the Queen may plot under prætense of begging for his liberty to seek to draw him into
a snare by his freedom of speech, persuaded
on his birth day to release John Baptist,
purposes it. Causes him to be sent for to the
court from prison. The Queen hears of it;
takes occasion to passe wher he is on purpose, that under prætense of reconsiling to
him, or seeking to draw a kind retraction
from him of his censure on the marriage—
to which end she sends a courtier before to
sound whether he might be persuaded to mitigate his sentence; which not finding she her
selfe craftily assays, and on his constancie
founds an accusation to Herod of a contumacious affront on such a day before many
peers. Præpares the K. to some passion, and
at last by her daughters dancing effects it.
There may prologize the spirit of Philip,
Herods brother. It may also be thought that
Herod had well bedew'd himself with wine,
which made him grant the easier to his
wives daughter. Some of his disciples also,
as to congratulate his liberty, may be brought
in; with whom, after certain command
of his death, many compassioning words
of his disciples, bewayling his youth cut off
in his glorious cours—he telling them his
work is don and wishing them to follow
Christ his maister.

SODOM.

The Scene before Lots gate.

The Chorus consists of Lots Shepherds,
com [i]n to the citty about some affairs,
await in the evening thire maisters return
from his evening walk toward the citty
gates. He brings with him 2 yong men or
youth of noble form; after likely discourses,
præpares for thire entertainmen[t]. By then
supper is ended, the Gallantry of the town
passe by in Processio[n] with musick and

song to the temple of Venus Urania or Peor; and understanding of tow noble strangers arriv'd, they send 2 of thire choysest youth with the preist to invite them to thire citty solemnities, it beeing an honour that thire citty had decreed to all fair personages, as beeing sacred to thir goddesse. The angels beeing askt by the preist whence they are, say they are of Salem; the preist inveighs against the strict raigne of Melchizedeck. Lot, that knows thire drift, answers thwartly at last. Of which notice given to the whole assembly, they hasten thither, taxe him of præsumption, singularity, breach of citty customs; in fine, offer violence. The Chorus of Shepher[ds] præpare resistance in thire maisters defence, calling the rest of the serviture, but beeing forc't to give back, the Angels open the dore, rescue Lot, discover them selves, warne him to gather his freinds and sons in Law out of the citty. He goes, and returns as having met with some incredulous. Some other freind or son in law, out of the way when Lot came to his house, overtakes him to know his buisnes. Heer is disputed of incredulity of divine judgements & such like matter. At last is describ'd the parting from the citty. The Chorus depart with thir maister. The Angels doe the deed with all dreadfull execution. The K. and nobles of the citty may come forth and serve to set out the terror; a Chorus of Angels concluding and the Angels relating the event of Lots journy, & of his wife. The first Chorus beginning may relate the course of the citty, each eve[n]ing every one with mistresse, or Ganymed, gitterning along the streets, or solacing on the banks of Jordan, or down the stream. At the preists inviting the Angels to the Solemnity, the Angels, pittying thir beauty, may dispute of love & how it differs from lust, seeking to win them. In the last scene, to the king & nobles, when the firie thunders begin aloft, the Angel appeares all girt with flames, which he saith are the flames of true love, & tells the K., who falls down with terror, his just suffering, as also Athanes, id est, Gener, Lots son in law, for dispising the continuall admonitions of Lots. Then calling to the thunders, lightnings & fires, he bids them heare the call & command of God to come & destroy a godlesse nation. He brings them

down with some short warning to all other nations to take heed. The Title: Cupids funeral pile. Sodom Burning.

Herod massacring, or Rachel weeping. Math. 2.
Christ bound.
Christ crucifi'd.
Christ risen.
Lazarus. Joan. 11.

Adam unparadiz'd.

The angel Gabriel, either descending or entering, shewing since this globe was created, his frequency as much on earth as in heavn, describes Paradise. Next the Chorus, shewing the reason of his comming—to keep his watch in Paradise, after Lucifers rebellion, by command from God; & withall expressing his desire to see, & know more concerning this excellent new creature, man. The angel Gabriel, as by his name signifying a prince of power, tracing Paradise with a more free office, passes by the station of the chorus & desired by them, relates what he knew of man, as the creation of Eve, with thire love, & mariage. After this Lucifer appeares after his overthrow, bemoans himself, seeks revenge on man. The Chorus prepare resistance at his first approach. At last, after discourse of enmity on either side, he departs; wherat the chorus sings of the battell & victorie in heavn against him & his accomplices, as before after the first act was sung a hymn of the creation. Heer again may appear Lucifer relating & insulting in what he had don to the destruction of man. Man next & Eve, having by this time bin seduc't by the serpent, appeares confusedly cover'd with leaves. Conscience in a shape accuses him. Justice cites him to the place whither Jehova call'd for him. In the mean while the chorus entertains the stage, & is inform'd by some angel the manner of his fall. Heer the chorus bewailes Adams fall. Adam then & Eve returne, accuse one another; but especially Adam layes the blame to his wife, is stubborn in his offence. Justice appeares, reason[s] with him, convinces him. The Chorus admonisheth Adam, & bids him beware by Lucifers example of impenitence. The Angel is sent to banish them out of paradise; but before, causes to passe before his eyes in shapes a mask of all the evills of this life & world. He is humbl'd, relents, dispaires. At last appeares Mercy, comforts him, promises the Messiah; then calls in faith, hope, & charity; instructs him. He repents, gives God the glory, submitts to his penalty. The chorus breifly concludes. Compare this with the former draught.

Scotch stories, or rather Brittish of the north parts.

Athirco slain by Natholochus, whose daughters he had ravisht; and this Natholochus usurping theron the kingdom, seeks to slay the kindred of Athirco, who scape him & conspire against him. He sends to a witch to know the event. The witch tells the messenger that he is the man shall slay Natholochus. He detests it; but in his journie home changes his mind, & performs it, &c. Scotch Chron. English. p. 68, 69.

Duffe & Donwald. A strange story of witchcraft & murder discover'd & reveng'd. Scotch story, 149 &c.

Haie the plowman. Who with his towe sons that were at plow, running to the battell that was between the Scots & Danes in the next feild, staid the flight of his countrymen, renew'd the battell, & caus'd the victorie, &c. Scotch story p. 155.

Kenneth. Who having privily poison'd Malcolm Duffe, that his own son might succeed, is slain by Fenela. Scotch hist. p. 157, 158, &c.

Macbeth. Beginning at the arrivall of Malcolm at Mackduffe. The matter of Duncan may be express't by the appearing of his ghost.

Moabitides or Phineas.

The Epitasis wherof may lie in the contention first between the father of Zimri & Eleazer whether he [ought] to have slain his son without law. Next the Embassadors of the Moabite expostulating about Cosbi, a stranger & a noble woman, slain by Phineas. It may be argu'd about reformation & punishment illegal, & as it were, by tumult. After all arguments drivn home, then the

word of the Lord may be brought, acquitting & approving Phineas.

Christus patiens.

The Scene in the garden, beginning from the comming thither till Judas betraies, & the officers lead him away. The rest by message & chorus. His agony may receav noble expressions.

FROM THE FIRST DEFENCE.

[The translation is that of S. L. Wolff in the *Columbia Milton*.]

PREFACE.

IF I be as copious of words and empty of matter in my Defence of the People of England as most men think Salmasius has been in his Defence of the King, I fear that I shall apparently have deserved to be called a defender at once wordy and silly. Yet no man thinks he must make such haste, even in handling any ordinary subject, as not to employ an opening worthy of its importance. In handling well-nigh the greatest of all subjects, then, if I neither omit an introduction, nor overdo it, I am in hopes of attåining two things, both of which I earnestly desire: the one, that I be nowise wanting, as far as in me lies, to this cause, most renowned and most worth the remembrance of all the generations of men; the other, that I myself be yet deemed to have avoided the silliness and verbosity which I blame in my antagonist.

For I shall relate no common things, or mean; but how a most puissant king, when he had trampled upon the laws, and stricken down religion, and was ruling at his own lust and wantonness, was at last subdued in the field by his own people, who had served a long term of slavery; how he was thereupon put under guard, and when he gave no ground whatever, by either word or action, to hope better things of him, was finally by the highest council of the realm condemned to die, and beheaded before his very palace gate. I shall likewise relate (which will much conduce to the easing men's minds of a great superstition) under what system of laws, especially what laws of England, this judgment was rendered and executed; and shall easily defend my valiant and worthy countrymen, who have extremely well deserved of all subjects and nations in the world, from the most wicked calumnies of both domestic and foreign railers, and chiefly from the reproaches of this utterly empty sophister, who sets up to be captain and ringleader of all the rest. For what king's majesty high enthroned ever shone so bright as did the people's majesty of England, when, shaking off that age-old superstition which had long prevailed, they overwhelmed with judgment their very king (or rather him who from their king had become their enemy), ensnared in his own laws him who alone among men claimed by divine right to go unpunished, and feared not to inflict upon this very culprit the same capital punishment which he would have inflicted upon any other.

Yet why do I proclaim as done by the people these actions, which themselves almost utter a voice, and witness everywhere the presence of God? Who, as often as it hath seemed good to his infinite wisdom, useth to cast down proud unbridled kings, puffed up above the measure of mankind, and often uprooteth them with their whole house. As for us, it was by His clear command we were on a sudden resolved upon the safety and liberty that we had almost lost; it was He we followed as our Leader, and revered His divine footsteps imprinted everywhere; and thus we entered upon a path not dark but bright, and by His guidance shown and opened to us. I should be much in error if I hoped that by my diligence alone, such as it is, I might set forth all these matters as worthily as they deserve, and might make such records of them as, haply, all nations and all ages would read. For what eloquence can be august and magnificent enough, what man has parts sufficient, to undertake so great a task? Yea, since in so many ages as are gone over the world there has been but here and there a man found able to recount worthily the actions of great heroes and potent states, can any man have so good an opinion of himself as to think that by any style or language of his own he can compass these glorious and wonderful works—not of men, but, evidently, of almighty God?

Yet such is the office which the most eminent men of our commonwealth have by their influence prevailed upon me to undertake, and have wished this next best task assigned to me of defending their deeds from envy and calumny, against which steel and the furniture of war avail not—of defending, I say, with far other arms and other weapons, the works which under God's guidance they had gloriously wrought. Their decision, certainly, I count a great honor to myself—that they voted me, before all others, the one to render this never-to-be-regretted assistance to the valiant liberators of my country; and indeed from my youth upward I have been fired with a zeal which kept urging me, if not to do great deeds myself, at least to celebrate them. Yet, mistrusting these advantages, I have recourse to the divine assistance, and pray the great and holy God, dispenser of all gifts: Even as successfully and piously as those our glorious guides to freedom crushed in battle the royal insolence and tyranny uncontrolled, and then at last by a memorable punishment utterly ended them; even as easily as I, singlehanded, lately refuted and set aside the king himself when he, as it were, rose from the grave, and in that book published after his death tried to cry himself up before the people with new verbal sleights and harlotries; so, I pray, may I now as auspiciously and as truly refute and demolish this outlandish rhetorician's wanton lies.

Foreign born as he is, and (though he deny it a thousand times) a mere grammarian, yet, not satisfied with the grammarian's dole, he has chosen to mind everybody's business, and has presumed to mix in an affair of state, a foreign state at that, though he brings to the task neither moderation nor understanding nor anything else that so grand a judge would surely need, save his presumption and his grammar. Indeed if he had published here, and in English, the same things as he now has writ in Latin (such as it is) I think scarce any man would have thought it worth while to return an answer to them, but would partly despise them as common, and exploded over and over already and partly (even one who sided with the king) abhor them as foul despotic maxims, hardly to be endured by the most worthless of slaves. But as he unundertakes to puff his portentous sheet among outsiders, who are quite ignorant of our affairs, they, who thus get an utterly false no-

tion of them, certainly ought to be fully informed; and he, who is so very forward to
speak ill of others, should be treated in his
own kind.

If haply anyone wonder why, then, we all
have suffered him so long to strut unharmed,
swollen in triumph at our silence, I know not
what others may say, but for myself I can
boldly declare that I had neither words nor
arguments long to seek for the defence of so
good a cause, had I but found leisure, and
such health as could bear the toil of writing.
Yet as I still possess but slender strength, I
am forced to write by piece-meal, and break
off almost every hour, though the subject be
such as requires unremitted study and attention. If for this reason it be not given me
to clarion with right heraldry, befitting their
praises, those glorious fellow-citizens of mine,
their country's saviors, whose deathless deeds
already ring round the world, yet I hope it
will not be difficult for me to defend, at least,
and justify them, against the impertinence of
this bore of a pedant, and the squallings of
his professorial tongue. Nature and laws
would be in ill case if slavery were eloquent,
and liberty mute; if tyrants should find defenders, and they that are potent to master
and vanquish tyrants should find none. And
it were deplorable indeed, if the reason mankind is endued withal, which is God's gift,
should not furnish more arguments for men's
preservation, for their deliverance, and, as
much as the nature of the thing will bear, for
their equality, than for their oppression and
utter ruin under one man's dominion. Let me
therefore enter upon this noble cause with
cheerfulness grounded upon the assurance
that on the other side are cheating, and
trickery, and ignorance and outlandishness,
and on my side the light of truth and reason,
and the practice and theory of the best his-
toric ages.

[The Close of the 2nd edition of the *First
Defence, C. M.* p. 551.]

And now I think, through God's help, I
have finished the work I undertook at the beginning, namely to defend both at home and
abroad the noble actions of my countrymen
against the brainsick envious rage of this mad
sophist, and to assert the people's common
rights against the unrighteous despotism of
kings,—and this not out of any hatred of
kings, but of tyrants. Nor have I knowingly
left unanswered any argument or example or
document alleged by my adversary, that
seemed to possess any solid substance or
power to convince. Perhaps I have been
nearer the opposite fault, that by rather too
often answering also his sillinesses and
threadbare quibbles as if they were arguments, I may seem to have given them an importance that they nothing deserved.

One thing yet remains, haply the greatest,
and that is, that ye too, my countrymen,
yourselves refute this adversary of yours,
which to do I see no other way than by striving constantly to outdo all men's bad words
by your own good deeds. Your vows, your
burning prayers, when, crushed beneath more
than one kind of slavery, ye fled to God for
refuge, he hath graciously heard and granted.
Gloriously hath he delivered you before all
other nations from what surely are the two
greatest mischiefs of this life, and most pernicious to virtue—Tyranny and Superstition;
he hath inspired you with the greatness of
soul to be the first of mankind who, after having conquered their own king, and having him
delivered into their hands, have not hesitated
to judge him with a judgment that yet resounds in men's ears, and to condemn him,
and pursuant to that condemnation to put
him to death. After so glorious a deed, ye
ought to think, ye ought to do, nothing that
is mean and petty, nothing but what is great
and sublime. This praise that ye may attain,
there is but one path to tread: as ye have
subdued your enemies in the field, so ye shall
prove that unarmed and in the midst of peace
ye of all mankind have highest courage to
subdue what conquers the rest of the nations
of men—faction, avarice, the temptations of
riches, and the corruptions that wait upon
prosperity; and in maintaining your liberty
shall show as great justice, temperance, and
moderation as ye have shown courage in freeing yourselves from slavery. By these arguments and documents only can ye prove ye
are not such as this libeler reproaches you
with being—"Traitors, Robbers, Assassins,
Parricides, Madmen;" that what ye did was
not the slaughtering of a king because ye
were driven by factiousness, or desire to
usurp the rights of others, or mere quarrel-

someness, or perverse desires, or fury or madness, but was the punishing of a tyrant because ye were aflame with love of your liberty and your religion, of justice and honor, yea—and is not this the sum and end of all these?—with dear love of your country.

But if ye prove to be of other mind—which may the good God forbid forever!—if as ye have been valiant in war, ye should grow debauched in peace, if ye that have had such visible demonstrations of the goodness of God to yourselves, and of his wrath against your enemies, have not learned by so eminent and memorable an example before your eyes, to fear God and work righteousness, I for my part shall verily grant and confess, for I cannot deny, that the worst which slanderers and liars now speak or think of you is true. And in a little time ye will find God far more wrathful against you than either your adversaries have found him embittered, or ye have found him aforetime gracious and favorable beyond all other nations at this time on earth.

It is now several years since I published the foregoing, in haste, as reason of state then required, for I kept thinking that if ever I might take it in hand again at leisure, as occasionally happens, I might thereupon smooth out, or remove, maybe, or add somewhat. This I now judge that I have accomplished, though more briefly than I used to count upon doing it: a memorial which, such as it is, I see will not easily perish. Though someone may be found who may have defended civil freedom more freely than here it is defended, yet there shall hardly be found anyone who hath defended it in a greater and more glorious example. If, then, an action of example so high and illustrious is believed to have been as successfully accomplished as not without God's prompting undertaken, let this be reason good for thinking that in these my praises too it hath even by the same Might and Inspiration been glorified and defended. Indeed I had much rather all men thought so, than that any other success, whether of wit or judgment or industry, were allowed me. Yet as that famous Roman Consul, upon retiring from office, swore in the popular assembly that the state and the city owed their safety to his single efforts, even so, as I now put the

last touches to this work, so much only I dare assert, calling God and man to witness: that in this book I have indicated and brought to light, from the highest authors of wisdom both divine and human, matters whereby, I trust, not only the English people has been adequately defended in this cause, to the everlasting reputation of its posterity, but numerous other human beings as well, hitherto deluded by foul ignorance of their right and by false show of religion,—multitudes of men, I say, except such as themselves prefer and deserve to be slaves—have been quite set free. Now the oath of that Consul, great as were its claims, was in that same assembly ratified by oath of the whole Roman people with one mind and one voice; this conviction of mine, I have long understood, is fully ratified by the most excellent not only of my fellow-citizens, but of foreigners too, with the loud voice of nations everywhere.

This my zealous labor's fruit—the highest that I for my part have set before me in this life—I gratefully enjoy; yet therewith too consider chief how I may bear best witness—not only to my own country, to which I have paid the highest I possessed, but even to men of whatever nation, and to the cause of Christendom above all—that I am pursuing after yet greater things if my strength suffice (nay, it will if God grant), and for their sake meanwhile am taking thought, and studying to make ready.

From the Second Defence.

[The *Second Defence* was published in Latin in 1654. The selections are from the translation in the Bohn edition.]

RELYING on the divine assistance, they used every honorable exertion to break the yoke of slavery; of the praise of which, though I claim no share to myself, yet I can easily repel any charge which may be adduced against me, either of want of courage, or want of zeal. For though I did not participate in the toils or dangers of the war, yet I was at the same time engaged in a service not less hazardous to myself and more beneficial to my fellow-citizens; nor, in the adverse turns of our affairs, did I ever betray any symptoms of pusillanimity and dejection; or show myself more afraid than became me of malice or of death: For since from my youth I was devoted to the pursuits of literature, and my mind had always been stronger than my body, I did not court the labors of a camp, in which any common person would have been of more service than myself, but resorted to that employment in which my exertions were likely to be of most avail. Thus, with the better part of my frame I contributed as much as possible to the good of my country, and to the success of the glorious cause in which we were engaged; and I thought that if God willed the success of such glorious achievements, it was equally agreeable to his will that there should be others by whom those achievements should be recorded with dignity and elegance and that the truth, which had been defended by arms, should also be defended by reason; which is the best and only legitimate means of defending it. Hence, while I applaud those who were victorious in the field, I will not complain of the province which was assigned me; but rather congratulate myself upon it, and thank the Author of all good for having placed me in a station, which may be an object of envy to others rather than of regret to myself. I am far from wishing to make any vain or arrogant comparisons, or to speak ostentatiously of myself; but, in a cause so great and glorious, and particularly on an occasion when I am called by the the general suffrage to defend the very defenders of that cause, I can hardly refrain from assuming a more lofty and swelling tone than the simplicity of an exordium may seem to justify: and much as I may be surpassed in the powers of eloquence and copiousness of diction, by the illustrious orators of antiquity, yet the subject of which I treat was never surpassed in any age, in dignity, or in interest. It has excited such general and such ardent expectation, that I imagine myself not in the forum or on the rostra, surrounded only by the people of Athens or of Rome, but about to address in this, as I did in my former Defence, the whole collective body of people, cities, states, and councils of the wise and eminent, through the wide expanse of anxious and listening Europe. I seem to survey, as from a towering height, the far extended tracts of sea and land, and innumerable crowds of spectators, betraying in their looks the liveliest interest, and sensations the most congenial with my own. Here I behold the stout and manly prowess of the Germans disdaining servitude; there the generous and lively impetuosity of the French; on this side, the calm and stately valor of the Spaniard; on that, the composed and wary magnanimity of the Italian. Of all the lovers of liberty and virtue, the magnanimous and the wise, in whatever quarter they may be found, some secretly favor, others openly approve; some greet me with congratulations and applause; others, who had long been proof against conviction, at last yield themselves captive to the force of truth. Surrounded by congregated multitudes, I now imagine that, from the columns of Hercules to the Indian Ocean, I behold the nations of the earth recovering that liberty which they so long had lost; and that the people of this island are transporting to other countries a plant of more beneficial qualities, and more noble growth, than that which Triptolemus is reported to have carried from region to region; that they are disseminating the blessings of civilization and freedom among cities, kingdoms, and nations. Nor shall I approach unknown, nor perhaps unloved, if it be told that I am the same person who engaged in single-combat that fierce advocate of despotism; till then reputed invincible in the opinion of many, and in his own conceit; who insolently challenged us and our armies to the combat; but whom, while I repelled his virulence, I silenced with his own weapons; and over whom, if I may trust to the opinions of impartial judges, I gained a complete and glorious victory. That this is the plain unvarnished fact appears from this: that, after the most noble queen of Sweden, than whom there neither is nor ever was a personage more attached to literature and to learned men, had invited Salmasius or Salmasia (for to which sex he belonged is a matter of uncertainty) to her court, where he was received with great distinction, my Defence suddenly surprised him in the midst of his security. It was generally read, and by the queen among the rest, who, attentive to the dignity of her station, let the stranger experience no diminution of her former kindness and munificence. But, with respect to the rest, if I may assert what has been often told, and was matter of public notoriety, such a change was instantly effected in the public sentiment, that he, who but yesterday flourished in the highest degree of favor, seemed to-day to wither in neglect; and soon after receiving permission to depart, he left it doubtful among many whether he were more honored when he came, or more disgraced when he went away; and even in other places it is clear, that it occasioned no small loss to his reputation, and all this I have mentioned, not from any futile motives of vanity or ostentation, but that I might clearly show, as I proposed in the beginning, what momentous reasons I had for commencing this work with an effusion of gratitude to the Father of the universe. Such a preface was most honorable and appropriate, in which I might prove, by an enumeration of particulars, that I had not been without my share of human misery; but that I had, at the same time, experienced singular marks of the divine regard; that in topics of the highest concern, the most connected with the exigencies of my country, and the most beneficial to civil and religious liberty; the supreme wisdom and beneficence had invigorated and enlarged my faculties, to defend the dearest interests, not merely of one people, but of the whole human race, against the enemies of human liberty; as it were in a full concourse of all the nations on the earth: and I again invoke the same Almighty Being, that I may still be able with the same integrity, the same diligence, and the same success, to defend those actions which have been so gloriously achieved; while I vindicate the authors as well as myself, whose name has been associated with theirs, not so much for the sake of honor as disgrace, from unmerited ignominy and reproach. . . .

LET us now come to the charges that were brought against me. Is there anything reprehensible in my manners or my conduct? Surely nothing. What no one, not totally divested of all generous sensibility, would have done, he reproaches me with want of beauty and loss of sight.

"A monster huge and hideous, void of sight."

I certainly never supposed that I should have been obliged to enter into a competition for beauty with the Cyclops; but he immediately corrects himself, and says, "though not indeed huge, for there cannot be a more spare, shrivelled, and bloodless form." It is of no moment to say anything of personal appearance, yet lest (as the Spanish vulgar, implicitly confiding in the relations of their priests, believe of heretics) any one, from the representations of my enemies, should be led to imagine that I have either the head of a dog, or the horn of a rhinoceros, I will say something on the subject, that I may have an opportunity of paying my grateful acknowledgments to the Deity, and of refuting the most shameless lies. I do not believe that I was ever once noted for deformity, by any one who ever saw me; but the praise of beauty I am not anxious to obtain. My stature certainly is not tall; but it rather approaches the middle than the diminutive. Yet what if it were diminutive, when so many men, illustrious both in peace and war, have been the same? And how can that be called diminutive, which is great enough for every virtuous achievement? Nor, though very thin, was I ever deficient in courage or in strength; and I was wont constantly to exercise myself in the use of the broadsword, as long as it comported with my habit and my years. Armed with this weapon, as I usually was, I should have thought myself quite a match for any one, though much stronger than myself; and I felt perfectly secure against the assault of any open enemy. At this moment I have the same courage, the same strength, though not the same eyes; yet so little do they betray any external appearance of injury, that they are as unclouded and bright as the eyes of those who most distinctly see. In this instance alone I am a dissembler against my will. My face, which is said to indicate a total privation of blood, is of a complexion entirely opposite to the pale and the cadaverous; so that, though I am more than forty years old, there is scarcely any one to whom I do not appear ten years younger than I am; and the smoothness of my skin is not, in the least, affected by the wrinkles of age. If there be one particle of falsehood in this relation, I should deservedly incur the ridicule of many thousands of my country-men, and even many foreigners to whom I am personally known. But if he, in a matter so foreign to his purpose, shall be found to have asserted so many shameless and gratui-tous falsehoods, you may the more readily estimate the quantity of his veracity on other topics. Thus much necessity compelled me to assert concerning my personal appear-ance. Respecting yours, though I have been informed that it is most insignificant and contemptible, a perfect mirror of the worth-lessness of your character and the malevo-lence of your heart, I say nothing, and no one will be anxious that anything should be said. I wish that I could with equal facility refute what this barbarous opponent has said of my blindness; but I cannot do it; and I must submit to the affliction. It is not so wretched to be blind, as it is not to be capa-ble of enduring blindness. But why should I not endure a misfortune, which it behooves every one to be prepared to endure if it should happen; which may, in the common course of things, happen to any man; and which has been known to happen to the most distinguished and virtuous persons in history. Shall I mention those wise and an-cient bards, whose misfortunes the gods are said to have compensated by superior en-dowments, and whom men so much revered, that they chose rather to impute their want of sight to the injustice of heaven than to their own want of innocence or virtue? What is reported of the augur Tiresias is well known; of whom Apollonius sung thus in his Argonauts:

To men he dar'd the will divine disclose,
Nor fear'd what Jove might in his wrath impose.
The gods assigned him age, without decay,
But snatched the blessing of his sight away.

But God himself is truth; in propagating which, as men display a greater integrity and zeal, they approach nearer to the similitude of God, and possess a greater portion of his love. We cannot suppose the deity envious of truth, or unwilling that it should be freely communicated to mankind. The loss of sight, therefore, which this inspired sage, who was so eager in promoting knowledge among men, sustained, cannot be considered as a judicial punishment. Or shall I mention those wor-

thies who were as distinguished for wisdom in the cabinet, as for valor in the field? And first Timoleon of Corinth, who delivered his city and all Sicily from the yoke of slavery; than whom there never lived in any age, a more virtuous man, or a more incorrupt statesman: Next Appius Claudius, whose dis-creet counsels in the senate, though they could not restore sight to his own eyes, saved Italy from the formidable inroads of Pyr-rhus: then Cæcilius Metellus the high-priest, who lost his sight, while he saved, not only the city, but the palladium, the protection of the city, and the most sacred relics, from the destruction of the flames. On other occa-sions Providence has indeed given conspicu-ous proofs of its regard for such singular exertions of patriotism and virtue; what, therefore, happened to so great and so good a man, I can hardly place in the catalogue of misfortunes. Why should I mention others of later times, as Dandolo of Venice, the in-comparable Doge; or Boemar Zisca, the bravest of generals, and the champion of the cross; or Jerome Zanchius, and some other theologians of the highest reputation? For it is evident that the patriarch Isaac, than whom no man ever enjoyed more of the di-vine regard, lived blind for many years; and perhaps also his son Jacob, who was equally an object of the divine benevolence. And in short, did not our Saviour himself clearly declare that that poor man whom he restored to sight had not been born blind, either on account of his own sins or those of his progenitors? And with respect to my-self, though I have accurately examined my conduct, and scrutinized my soul, I call thee, O God, the searcher of hearts, to witness, that I am not conscious, either in the more early or in the later periods of my life, of having committed any enormity, which might deservedly have marked me out as a fit ob-ject for such a calamitous visitation. But since my enemies boast that this affliction is only a retribution for the transgressions of my pen, I again invoke the Almighty to wit-ness, that I never, at any time, wrote any-thing which I did not think agreeable to truth, to justice, and to piety. This was my persuasion then, and I feel the same per-suasion now. Nor was I ever prompted to such exertions by the influence of ambition, by the lust of lucre or of praise; it was only by the conviction of duty and the feeling of patriotism, a disinterested passion for the extension of civil and religious liberty. Thus, therefore, when I was publicly solicited to write a reply to the Defence of the royal cause, when I had to contend with the pressure of sickness, and with the apprehension of soon losing the sight of my remaining eye, and when my medical attendants clearly announced, that if I did engage in the work, it would be irreparably lost, their premonitions caused no hesitation and inspired no dismay. I would not have listened to the voice even of Esculapius himself from the shrine of Epidauris, in preference to the suggestions of the heavenly monitor within my breast; my resolution was unshaken, though the alternative was either the loss of my sight, or the desertion of my duty: and I called to mind those two destinies, which the oracle of Delphi announced to the son of Thetis:—

Two fates may lead me to the realms of night;
If staying here, around Troy's wall I fight,
To my dear home no more must I return;
But lasting glory will adorn my urn.
But, if I withdraw from the martial strife,
Short is my fame, but long will be my life. *Il.* ix.

I considered that many had purchased a less good by a greater evil, the meed of glory by the loss of life; but that I might procure great good by little suffering; that though I am blind, I might still discharge the most honorable duties, the performance of which, as it is something more durable than glory, ought to be an object of superior admiration and esteem; I resolved, therefore, to make the short interval of sight, which was left me to enjoy, as beneficial as possible to the public interest. Thus it is clear by what motives I was governed in the measures which I took, and the losses which I sustained. Let then the calumniators of the divine goodness cease to revile, or to make me the object of their superstitious imaginations. Let them consider, that my situation, such as it is, is neither an object of my shame or my regret, that my resolutions are too firm to be shaken, that I am not depressed by any sense of the divine displeasure; that, on the other hand,

in the most momentous periods, I have had full experience of the divine favor and protection; and that, in the solace and the strength which have been infused into me from above, I have been enabled to do the will of God; that I may oftener think on what he has bestowed, than on what he has withheld; that, in short, I am unwilling to exchange my consciousness of rectitude with that of any other person; and that I feel the recollection a treasured store of tranquillity and delight. But, if the choice were necessary, I would, sir, prefer my blindness to yours; yours is a cloud spread over the mind, which darkens both the light of reason and of conscience; mine keeps from my view only the colored surfaces of things, while it leaves me at liberty to contemplate the beauty and stability of virtue and of truth. How many things are there besides which I would not willingly see; how many which I must see against my will; and how few which I feel any anxiety to see! There is, as the apostle has remarked, a way to strength through weakness. Let me then be the most feeble creature alive, as long as that feebleness serves to invigorate the energies of my rational and immortal spirit; as long as in that obscurity, in which I am enveloped, the light of the divine presence more clearly shines, then, in proportion as I am weak, I shall be invincibly strong; and in proportion as I am blind, I shall more clearly see. O! that I may thus be perfected by feebleness, and irradiated by obscurity! And, indeed, in my blindness, I enjoy in no inconsiderable degree the favor of the Deity, who regards me with more tenderness and compassion in proportion as I am able to behold nothing but himself. Alas! for him who insults me, who maligns and merits public execration! For the divine law not only shields me from injury, but almost renders me too sacred to attack; not indeed so much from the privation of my sight, as from the overshadowing of those heavenly wings which seem to have occasioned this obscurity; and which, when occasioned, he is wont to illuminate with an interior light, more precious and more pure. To this I ascribe the more tender assiduities of my friends, their soothing attentions, their kind visits, their reverential observances; among whom there are some with whom I may interchange the Pyladean and Thesean dialogue of inseparable friends:—

OREST. Proceed, and be the rudder of my feet, by showing me the most endearing love.
Eurip. in Orest.

And in another place,

Lend your hand to your devoted friend, Throw your arm round my neck, and I will conduct you on the way.

This extraordinary kindness, which I experience, cannot be any fortuitous combination; and friends, such as mine, do not suppose that all the virtues of a man are contained in his eyes. Nor do the persons of principal distinction in the commonwealth suffer me to be bereaved of comfort, when they see me bereaved of sight, amid the exertions which I made, the zeal which I showed, and the dangers which I run for the liberty which I love. But, soberly reflecting on the casualties of human life, they show me favor and indulgence, as to a soldier who has served his time, and kindly concede to me an exemption from care and toil. They do not strip me of the badges of honor which I have once worn; they do not deprive me of the places of public trust to which I have been appointed; they do not abridge my salary or emoluments; which, though I may not do so much to deserve as I did formerly, they are too considerate and too kind to take away; and, in short, they honor me as much as the Athenians did those whom they determined to support at the public expense in the Prytaneum. Thus, while both God and man unite in solacing me under the weight of my affliction, let no one lament my loss of sight in so honorable a cause. And let me not indulge in unavailing grief, or want the courage either to despise the revilers of my blindness, or the forbearance easily to pardon the offence. . . .

But, good sir, I will by no means frustrate your endeavors: for, though I may wish to rival Ulysses in the merits of his patriotism, I am yet no competitor for the arms of Achilles. I am not solicitous for an Elysium painted on a shield, which others may see me brandish in the contest; but I desire to bear upon my shoulders a real not a painted weight, of which I may feel the pressure, but which may be imperceptible to others. For since I cherish no private rancor, nor hostility against any man, nor any man that I know of against me, I am well contented, for the sake of the public interest, to be so much aspersed and so much reviled. Nor, while I sustain the greatest weight of the disgrace, do I complain because I have the smallest share of the profit or the praise; for I am content to do what is virtuous, for the sake of the action itself, without any sinister expectations. Let others look to that; but do you, sir, know, that my hands were never soiled with the guilt of peculation; and that I never was even a shilling the richer by those exertions, which you most vehemently traduce. . . .

To grammarians and critics, who are principally occupied in editing the works of others, or in correcting the errors of copyists, we willingly concede the palm of industry and erudition; but we never bestow on them the name of great. He alone is worthy of the appellation, who either does great things, or teaches how they may be done, or describes them with a suitable majesty when they have been done; but those only are great things, which tend to render life more happy, which increase the innocent enjoyments and comforts of existence, or which pave the way to a state of future bliss more permanent and more pure. . . . But your penetrating mind, O serene queen of Sweden, soon detected his imposture; and, with a magnanimity almost above human, you taught sovereigns and the world to prefer truth to the interested clamors of faction. For though the splendor of his erudition, and the celebrity which he had acquired in the defence of the royal cause, had induced you to honor him with many marks of distinction, yet, when my answer appeared, which you perused with singular equanimity, you perceived that he had been convicted of the most palpable effrontery and misrepresentation; that he had betrayed the utmost indiscretion and intemperance, that he had uttered many falsehoods, many inconsistencies and contradictions. On this account, as it is said, you had him called into your presence; but when he was unable to vindicate himself, you were so visibly offended, that from that time you neither showed him the same attentions, nor held his talents nor his learning in the same esteem; and, what was entirely unexpected, you manifested a disposition to favor his adversary. You denied that what I had written against tyrants, could have any reference to you; whence, in your own breast you enjoyed the sweets, and among others the fame, of a good conscience. For, since the whole tenor of your conduct sufficiently proves, that you are no tyrant, this unreserved expression of your sentiments makes it still more clear, that you are not even conscious to yourself of being one. How happy am I beyond my utmost expectations! (for to the praise of eloquence, except as far as eloquence consists in the force of truth, I lay no claim,) that, when the critical exigencies of my country demanded that I should undertake the arduous and invidious task of impugning the rights of kings, I should meet with so illustrious, so truly a royal evidence to my integrity, and to this truth, that I had not written a word against kings, but only against tyrants, the spots and the pests of royalty? But you, O Augusta, possessed not only so much magnanimity, but were so irradiated by the glorious beams of wisdom and of virtue, that you not only read with patience, with incredible impartiality, with a serene complacency of countenance, what might seem to be levelled against your rights and dignity; but expressed such an opinion of the defender of those rights, as may well be considered an adjudication of the palm of victory to his opponent. You, O queen! will for ever be the object of my homage, my veneration, and my love; for it was your greatness of soul, so honorable to yourself and so auspicious to me, which served to efface the unfavorable impression against me at other courts, and to rescue me from the evil surmises of other sovereigns. What a high and favorable opinion must foreigners conceive, and your own subjects for ever entertain, of your impartiality and justice, when, in a matter which so nearly interested the fate of sovereigns and the rights of your crown, they saw you sit down to the discussion, with as much equanimity and composure, as you would to determine a dispute between two private individuals. It was not in vain that you made such large collections of books, and so many monuments of learning; not indeed, that they could contribute much to your instruction, but because they so well teach your subjects to appreciate the merits of your reign, and the rare excellence of your virtue and your wisdom. For the Divinity himself seems to have inspired you with a love of wisdom, and a thirst for improvement, beyond what any books ever could have produced. It excites our astonishment to see a force of intellect so truly divine, a particle of celestial flame so resplendently pure, in a region so remote; of which an atmosphere, so darkened with clouds, and so chilled with frosts, could not extinguish the light, nor repress the operations. The rocky and barren soil, which is often as unfavorable to the growth of genius as of plants, has not impeded the maturation of your faculties; and that country so rich in metallic ore, which appears like a cruel step-mother to others, seems to have been a fostering parent to you; and after the most strenuous attempts to have at last produced a progeny of pure gold. I would invoke you, Christina! as the only child of the renowned and victorious Adolphus, if your merit did not as much eclipse his, as wisdom excels strength, and the arts of peace the havoc of war. Henceforth, the queen of the south will not be alone renowned in history; for there is a queen of the north, who would not only be worthy to appear in the court of the wise king of the Jews, or any king of equal wisdom; but to whose court others may from all parts repair, to behold so fair a heroine, so bright a pattern of all the royal virtues; and to the crown of whose praise this may well be added, that neither in her conduct nor her appearance, is there any of the forbidding reserve, or the ostentatious parade, of royalty. She herself seems the least conscious of her own attributes of sovereignty; and her thoughts are always fixed on something greater and more sublime than the glitter of a crown. In this respect, her example may well make innumerable kings hide their diminished heads. She may, if such is the fatality of the Swedish nation, abdicate the sovereignty, but she can never lay aside the queen; for her reign has proved, that she is fit to govern, not only Sweden, but the world. . . .

"They fixed upon one John Milton, a

great hero truly, to oppose Salmasius." I did not know that I was a hero, though you perchance may be the progeny of some frail heroine, for you are nothing but a compound of iniquity. When I consider the good of the commonwealth, I may indeed lament, that I alone was selected to defend the people of England, though I could not readily have endured an associate in the fame. You say, that it is a matter of uncertainty who and whence I am. The same uncertainty attached to Homer and Demosthenes. Indeed, I had been early taught to hold my tongue and to say nothing; which Salmasius never could; and I accordingly buried those things within my breast, which if I had pleased to disclose, I could then have obtained as much celebrity as I now possess. But I was not eager to hasten the tardy steps of fame; nor willing to appear in public till a proper opportunity offered. For I did not regard the fame of anything so much as the proper time for the execution. Hence it happened, that I had not long been known to many, before Salmasius begun to know himself. "Whether he be a man or a worm!" Truly, I would rather be a worm in the way that David expresses it, ("I am a worm and no man,") than that my bosom, like yours, should be the seat of a never-dying worm. You say, that "the fellow having been expelled from the university of Cambridge, on account of his atrocities, had fled his country in disgrace and travelled into Italy." Hence we may discern what little reliance can be placed on the veracity of those from whom you derived your information; for all, who know me, know, that in this place, both you and they have uttered the most abominable falsehoods; as I shall soon make more fully appear. But, when I was expelled from Cambridge, why should I rather travel into Italy, than into France or Holland? where you, though a minister of the Gospel, and yet so vile a miscreant, not only enjoy impunity, but, to the great scandal of the church, pollute the pulpit and the altar by your presence. But why, sir, into Italy? Was it that, like another Saturn, I might find a hiding-place in Latium? No, it was because I well knew, and have since experienced, that Italy, instead of being, as you suppose, the general receptacle of vice, was the seat of civiliza-

tion and the hospitable domicile of every species of erudition. "When he returned, he wrote his book on divorce." I wrote nothing more than what Bucer on the Kingdom of Christ, Fagius on Deuteronomy, and Erasmus on the First Epistle to the Corinthians, which was more particularly designed for the instruction of the English, had written before me, for the most useful purposes and with the most disinterested views. Why what was not reprehensible in them, should constitute a charge of criminality against me, I cannot understand; though I regret that I published this work in English; for then it would not have been exposed to the view of those common readers, who are wont to be as ignorant of their own blessings, as they are insensible to others' sufferings. But shall you, base miscreant, set up a cry about divorce, who, having debauched Pontia, under the most solemn assurances of marriage, afterwards divorced her in a manner the most unprincipled and inhuman? And yet this servant of Salmasius is said to have been an Englishwoman, and a staunch royalist; so that you seem to have wooed her as a piece of royalty, and to have deserted her as the image of a republic, (res publica,) though you were the author of her degradation to that state of publicity, and, after having allured her from the service of Salmasius, reduced her to the condition of a public prostitute. In this manner, devotedly attached as you are to royalty, you are said to have founded many republics (res publicas) in one city, or to have undertaken the management of their concerns, after they have been founded by others. Such have been your divorces, or rather diversions, after which you proceed, as a ruffian, to attack my character. You now return to the invention of fresh lies. "When the conspirators were debating on the capital punishment of the king, he wrote to them, and, while they were wavering and irresolute, brought them over to determine on his death." But I neither wrote to them, nor could I have influenced the execution; for they had previously determined on the measure, without consulting me. But I will say more on this subject hereafter, as also on the publication of the Iconoclast. The fellow, (shall I call him a man, or only the excrement of a man?) next proceeding from his adulteries with servant maids and scullions, to the adulteration of the truth, endeavoured, by artfully fabricating a series of lies, to render me infamous abroad. I must, therefore, crave the indulgence of the reader if I have said already, or shall say hereafter, more of myself than I wish to say; that, if I cannot prevent the blindness of my eyes, the oblivion or the defamation of my name, I may at least rescue my life from that species of obscurity, which is the associate of unprincipled depravity. This it will be necessary for me to do on more accounts than one; first, that so many good and learned men among the neighbouring nations, who read my works, may not be induced by this fellow's calumnies to alter the favourable opinion which they have formed of me; but may be persuaded that I am not one who ever disgraced beauty of sentiment by deformity of conduct, or the maxims of a freeman by the actions of a slave; and that the whole tenor of my life has, by the grace of God, hitherto been unsullied by enormity or crime. Next, that those illustrious worthies, who are the objects of my praise, may know that nothing could afflict me with more shame than to have any vices of mine diminish the force or lessen the value of my panegyric upon them; and, lastly, that the people of England, whom fate, or duty, or their own virtues, have incited me to defend, may be convinced from the purity and integrity of my life, that my defence, if it do not redound to their honour, can never be considered as their disgrace. I will now mention who and whence I am. I was born at London, of an honest family; my father was distinguished by the undeviating integrity of his life; my mother, by the esteem in which she was held, and the alms which she bestowed. My father destined me from a child to the pursuits of literature; and my appetite for knowledge was so voracious, that, from twelve years of age, I hardly ever left my studies, or went to bed before midnight. This primarily led to my loss of sight. My eyes were naturally weak, and I was subject to frequent head-aches; which, however, could not chill the ardor of my curiosity, or retard the progress of my improvement. My father had me daily instructed in the grammar-school, and by other masters at home. He then, after I had acquired a proficiency in various languages, and had made a considerable progress in philosophy, sent me to the University of Cambridge. Here I passed seven years in the usual course of instruction and study, with the approbation of the good, and without any stain upon my character, till I took the degree of Master of Arts. After this I did not, as this miscreant feigns, run away into Italy, but of my own accord retired to my father's house, whither I was accompanied by the regrets of most of the fellows of the college, who showed me no common marks of friendship and esteem. On my father's estate, where he had determined to pass the remainder of his days, I enjoyed an interval of uninterrupted leisure, which I entirely devoted to the perusal of the Greek and Latin classics; though I occasionally visited the metropolis, either for the sake of purchasing books, or of learning something new in mathematics or in music, in which I, at that time, found a source of pleasure and amusement. In this manner I spent five years till my mother's death. I then became anxious to visit foreign parts, and particularly Italy. My father gave me his permission, and I left home with one servant. On my departure, the celebrated Henry Wotton, who had long been king James's ambassador at Venice, gave me a signal proof of his regard, in an elegant letter which he wrote, breathing not only the warmest friendship, but containing some maxims of conduct which I found very useful in my travels. The noble Thomas Scudamore, king Charles's ambassador, to whom I carried letters of recommendation, received me most courteously at Paris. His lordship gave me a card of introduction to the learned Hugo Grotius, at that time ambassador from the queen of Sweden to the French court; whose acquaintance I anxiously desired, and to whose house I was accompanied by some of his lordship's friends. A few days after, when I set out for Italy, he gave me letters to the English merchants on my route, that they might show me any civilities in their power. Taking ship at Nice, I arrived at Genoa, and afterwards visited Leghorn, Pisa, and Florence. In the latter city, which I have always more particularly esteemed for the elegance of its dialect, its genius, and its taste, I stopped about two months; when I contracted an intimacy with many persons of rank and learning; and was a constant attendant at their literary parties; a practice which prevails there, and tends so much to the diffusion of knowledge, and the preservation of friendship. No time will ever abolish the agreeable recollections which I cherish of Jacob Gaddi, Carolo Dati, Frescobaldo, Coltellino, Bonomatthei, Clementillo, Francini, and many others. From Florence I went to Siena, thence to Rome, where, after I had spent about two months in viewing the antiquities of that renowned city, where I experienced the most friendly attentions from Lucas Holstein, and other learned and ingenious men, I continued my route to Naples. There I was introduced by a certain recluse, with whom I had travelled from Rome, to John Baptista Manso, marquis of Villa, a nobleman of distinguished rank and authority, to whom Torquato Tasso, the illustrious poet, inscribed his book on friendship. During my stay, he gave me singular proofs of his regard: he himself conducted me round the city, and to the palace of the viceroy; and more than once paid me a visit at my lodgings. On my departure he gravely apologized for not having shown me more civility, which he said he had been restrained from doing, because I had spoken with so little reserve on matters of religion. When I was preparing to pass over into Sicily and Greece, the melancholy intelligence which I received of the civil commotions in England made me alter my purpose; for I thought it base to be travelling for amusement abroad, while my fellow-citizens were fighting for liberty at home. While I was on my way back to Rome, some merchants informed me that the English Jesuits had formed a plot against me if I returned to Rome, because I had spoken too freely on religion; for it was a rule which I laid down to myself in those places, never to be the first to begin any conversation on religion; but if any questions were put to me concerning my faith, to declare it without any reserve or fear. I, nevertheless, returned to Rome. I took no steps to conceal either my person or my character; and for about the space of two months I again openly defended, as I had done before, the reformed

religion in the very metropolis of popery. By the favor of God, I got safe back to Florence, where I was received with as much affection as if I had returned to my native country. There I stopped as many months as I had done before, except that I made an excursion for a few days to Lucca; and, crossing the Apennines, passed through Bologna and Ferrara to Venice. After I had spent a month in surveying the curiosities of this city, and had put on board a ship the books which I had collected in Italy, I proceeded through Verona and Milan, and along the Leman lake to Geneva. The mention of this city brings to my recollection the slandering More, and makes me again call the Deity to witness, that in all those places in which vice meets with so little discouragement, and is practised with so little shame, I never once deviated from the paths of integrity and virtue, and perpetually reflected that, though my conduct might escape the notice of men, it could not elude the inspection of God. At Geneva I held daily conferences with John Deodati, the learned professor of Theology. Then pursuing my former route through France, I returned to my native country, after an absence of one year and about three months; at the time when Charles, having broken the peace, was renewing what is called the episcopal war with the Scots, in which the royalists being routed in the first encounter, and the English being universally and justly disaffected, the necessity of his affairs at last obliged him to convene a parliament. As soon as I was able, I hired a spacious house in the city for myself and my books; where I again with rapture renewed my literary pursuits, and where I calmly awaited the issue of the contest, which I trusted to the wise conduct of Providence, and to the courage of the people. The vigor of the parliament had begun to humble the pride of the bishops. As long as the liberty of speech was no longer subject to control all mouths began to be opened against the bishops; some complained of the vices of the individuals, others of those of the order. They said that it was unjust that they alone should differ from the model of other reformed churches; that the government of the church should be according to the pattern of other churches, and particularly the word of God. This awakened all my attention and my zeal. I saw that a way was opening for the establishment of real liberty; that the foundation was laying for the deliverance of man from the yoke of slavery and superstition; that the principles of religion, which were the first objects of our care, would exert a salutary influence on the manners and constitution of the republic; and as I had from my youth studied the distinctions between religious and civil rights, I perceived that if I ever wished to be of use, I ought at least not to be wanting to my country, to the church, and to so many of my fellow-Christians, in a crisis of so much danger; I therefore determined to relinquish the other pursuits in which I was engaged, and to transfer the whole force of my talents and my industry to this one important object. I accordingly wrote two books to a friend concerning the reformation of the church of England. Afterwards, when two bishops of superior distinction vindicated their privileges against some principal ministers, I thought that on those topics, to the consideration of which I was led solely by my love of truth, and my reverence for Christianity, I should not probably write worse than those who were contending only for their own emoluments and usurpations. I therefore answered the one in two books, of which the first is inscribed, Concerning Prelatical Episcopacy, and the other Concerning the Mode of Ecclesiastical Government; and I replied to the other in some Animadversions, and soon after in an Apology. On this occasion it was supposed that I brought a timely succor to the ministers, who were hardly a match for the eloquence of their opponents; and from that time I was actively employed in refuting any answers that appeared. When the bishops could no longer resist the multitude of their assailants, I had leisure to turn my thoughts to other subjects; to the promotion of real and substantial liberty; which is rather to be sought from within than from without; and whose existence depends, not so much on the terror of the sword, as on sobriety of conduct and integrity of life. When, therefore, I perceived that there were three species of liberty which are essential to the happiness of social life—religious, domestic and civil; and as I had already writ-

ten concerning the first, and the magistrates were strenuously active in obtaining the third, I determined to turn my attention to the second, or the domestic species. As this seemed to involve three material questions, the conditions of the conjugal tie, the education of children, and the free publication of thought, I made them objects of distinct consideration. I explained my sentiments, not only concerning the solemnization of marriage, but the dissolution, if circumstances rendered it necessary; and I drew my arguments from the divine law, which Christ did not abolish, or publish another more grievous than that of Moses. I stated my own opinions, and those of others, concerning the exclusive exception of fornication, which our illustrious Selden has since, in his Hebrew Wife, more copiously discussed; for he in vain makes a vaunt of liberty in the senate or in the forum, who languishes under the vilest servitude, to an inferior at home. On this subject, therefore, I published some books which were more particularly necessary at that time, when man and wife were often the most inveterate foes, when the man often stayed to take care of his children at home, while the mother of the family was seen in the camp of the enemy, threatening death and destruction to her husband. I then discussed the principles of education in a summary manner, but sufficiently copious for those who attend seriously to the subject; than which nothing can be more necessary to principle the minds of men in virtue, the only genuine source of political and individual liberty, the only true safeguard of states. the bulwark of their prosperity and renown. Lastly, I wrote my Areopagitica, in order to deliver the press from the restraints with which it was encumbered; that the power of determining what was true and what was false, what ought to be published and what to be suppressed, might no longer be intrusted to a few illiterate and illiberal individuals, who refused their sanction to any work which contained views or sentiments at all above the level of the vulgar superstition. On the last species of civil liberty, I said nothing, because I saw that sufficient attention was paid to it by the magistrates; nor did I write anything on the prerogative of the crown, till the king voted an enemy by the parliament, and vanquished in the field, was summoned before the tribunal which condemned him to lose his head. But when, at length, some presbyterian ministers, who had formerly been the most bitter enemies to Charles, became jealous of the growth of the independents, and of their ascendancy in the parliament, most tumultuously clamored against the sentence, and did all in their power to prevent the execution, though they were not angry, so much on account of the act itself, as because it was not the act of their party; and when they dared to affirm, that the doctrine of the protestants, and of all the reformed churches, was abhorrent to such an atrocious proceeding against kings; I thought that it became me to oppose such a glaring falsehood; and accordingly, without any immediate or personal application to Charles, I showed, in an abstract consideration of the question, what might lawfully be done against tyrants; and in support of what I advanced, produced the opinions of the most celebrated divines; while I vehemently inveighed against the egregious ignorance or effrontery of men, who professed better things, and from whom better things might have been expected. That book did not make its appearance till after the death of Charles; and was written rather to reconcile the minds of the people to the event, than to discuss the legitimacy of that particular sentence which concerned the magistrates, and which was already executed. Such were the fruits of my private studies, which I gratuitously presented to the church and to the state; and for which I was recompensed by nothing but impunity; though the actions themselves procured me peace of conscience, and the approbation of the good; while I exercised that freedom of discussion which I loved. Others, without labor or desert, got possession of honors and emoluments; but no one ever knew me either soliciting anything myself or through the medium of my friends, ever beheld me in a supplicating posture at the doors of the senate, or the levees of the great. I usually kept myself secluded at home, where my own property, part of which had been withheld during the civil commotions, and part of which had been absorbed in the oppressive contributions which I had to sustain, afforded me a scanty subsistence. When I was released from these engagements, and thought that I was about to enjoy an interval of uninterrupted ease, I turned my thoughts to a continued history of my country, from the earliest times to the present period. I had already finished four books, when, after the subversion of the monarchy, and the establishment of a republic, I was surprised by an invitation from the council of state, who desired my services in the office for foreign affairs. A book appeared soon after, which was ascribed to the king, and contained the most invidious charges against the parliament. I was ordered to answer it; and opposed the Iconoclast to his Icon. I did not insult over fallen majesty, as is pretended; I only preferred queen Truth to king Charles. The charge of insult, which I saw that the malevolent would urge, I was at some pains to remove in the beginning of the work; and as often as possible in other places. Salmasius then appeared, to whom they were not, as More says, long in looking about for an opponent, but immediately appointed me, who happened at the time to be present in the council. I have thus, sir, given some account of myself, in order to stop your mouth, and to remove any prejudices which your falsehoods and misrepresentations might cause even good men to entertain against me. . . .

John Bradshaw (a name which will be repeated with applause wherever liberty is cherished or is known) was sprung from a noble family. All his early life he sedulously employed in making himself acquainted with the laws of his country; he then practised with singular success and reputation at the bar; he showed himself an intrepid and unwearied advocate for the liberties of the people: he took an active part in the most momentous affairs of the state, and occasionally discharged the function of a judge with the most inviolable integrity. At last, when he was entreated by the parliament to preside in the trial of the king, he did not refuse the dangerous office. To a profound knowledge of the law, he added the most comprehensive views, the most generous sentiments, manners the most obliging and the most pure. Hence he discharged that office with a propriety almost without a parallel; he inspired both respect and awe;

and, though menaced by the daggers of so many assassins, he conducted himself with so much consistency and gravity, with so much presence of mind and so much dignity of demeanor, that he seems to have been purposely destined by Providence for that part which he so nobly acted on the theatre of the world. And his glory is as much exalted above that of all other tyrannicides, as it is both more humane, more just, and more strikingly grand, judicially to condemn a tyrant, than to put him to death without a trial. In other respects there was no forbidding austerity, no moroseness in his manner; he was courteous and benign; but the great character which he then sustained, he with perfect consistency still sustains, so that you would suppose that not only then, but in every future period of his life, he was sitting in judgment upon the king. In the public business his activity is unwearied; and he alone is equal to a host. At home his hospitality is as splendid as his fortune will permit: in his friendships there is the most inflexible fidelity; and no one more readily discerns merit, or more liberally rewards it. Men of piety and learning, ingenious persons in all professions, those who have been distinguished by their courage or their misfortunes, are free to participate his bounty; and if they want not his bounty, they are sure to share his friendship and esteem. He never ceases to extol the merits of others, or to conceal his own; and no one was ever more ready to accept the excuses, or to pardon the hostility, of his political opponents. If he undertake to plead the cause of the oppressed, to solicit the favor or deprecate the resentment of the powerful, to reprove the public ingratitude towards any particular individual, his address and his perseverance are beyond all praise. On such occasions no one could desire a patron or a friend more able, more zealous, or more eloquent. No menace could divert him from his purpose; no intimidation on the one hand, and no promise of emolument or promotion on the other, could alter the serenity of his countenance, or shake the firmness of his soul. By these virtues, which endeared him to his friends and commanded the respect even of his enemies, he, sir, has acquired a name which, while you and such as you are moldering in oblivion, will flourish in every age, and in every country in the world. But I must proceed: the king was condemned to lose his head. "Against this atrocity almost all the pulpits in London thundered out their censures." We are not to be so easily scared by that thunder upon wood. We remember the fate of Salmoneus, and trust that these persons will one day see cause to repent of their fulminating temerity. These were the very persons who so lately, and with such vehemence, fulminated their censures against pluralists and non-residents. But some of these persons having grasped three, and others four of the livings, from which they had fulminated the episcopal clergy, they hence became non-residents themselves, guilty of the very sin against which they had inveighed, and the victims of their own fulminating rage. Nor have they any longer a spark of shame; they are now grown zealous abettors of the divine right of tithes; and truly as their thirst for tithes is so insatiable, they should be quite gorged with the commodity, and ordered to have, not only a tenth part of the fruits of the earth, but of the waves of the sea. They were the first to council a war of extermination against the king; but when the king was made prisoner, after having been convicted, according to their own repeated declarations, as the author of so much misery and bloodshed, they affected to compassionate his situation. Thus, in their pulpits, as in an auction-room, they retail what wares and trumpery they please to the people; and, what is worse, they reclaim what they have already sold. . . .

"The army is a Hydra-headed monster of accumulated heresies." Those who speak the truth, acknowledge that our army excels all others, not only in courage, but in virtue and in piety. Other camps are the scenes of gambling, swearing, riot, and debauchery; in ours, the troops employ what leisure they have in searching the Scriptures and hearing the word; nor is there one who thinks it more honorable to vanquish the enemy than to propagate the truth; and they not only carry on a military warfare against their enemies, but an evangelical one against themselves. And indeed if we consider the proper objects of war, what employment can be more becoming soldiers, who are raised to defend the laws, to be the support of our political and religious institutions? Ought they not then to be less conspicuous for ferocity than for the civil and the softer virtues, and to consider it as their true and proper destination, not merely to sow the seeds of strife, and reap the harvest of destruction, but to procure peace and security for the whole human race? If there be any who, either from the mistakes of others, or the infirmities of their own minds, deviate from these noble ends, we ought not to punish them with the sword, but rather labor to reform them by reason, by admonition, by pious supplications to God, to whom alone it belongs to dispel all the errors of the mind, and to impart to whom he will the celestial light of truth. We approve no heresies which are truly such; we do not even tolerate some; we wish them extirpated, but by those means which are best suited to the purpose—by reason and instruction, the only safe remedies for disorders of the mind; and not by the knife or the scourge, as if they were seated in the body. You say that "we have done another and equal injury to the temporal property of the church." . . . But that property did not belong to the church so much as the ecclesiastics, who, in this sense, might most justly be denominated churchmen; indeed they might have been more fully termed wolves than anything else; but could there be any impiety in applying to the necessary exigencies of a war which they themselves had occasioned, and which we had no other resource for carrying on, the property of these wolves, or rather the accumulated ravages of so many ages of ignorance and superstition? But it was expected that the wealth which was ravished from the bishops would be distributed among the parochial clergy. They expected, I know, and they desired, that the whole should be diffused among them; for there is no abyss so deep which it is not more easy to fill, than it is to satiate the rapacity of the clergy. In other places there may be an incompetent provision for the clergy; but ours have an abundant maintenance; they ought to be called sheep rather than shepherds; they themselves are fed more than they feed others. . . . They are stuffed with

tithes in a way disapproved by the rest of the reformed churches; and they have so little trust in God, that they choose to extort a maintenance, rather by judicial force, and magisterial authority, than to owe it to divine providence, or the gratitude and benevolence of their congregations. And, besides all this, they are so frequently entertained by their pious auditors of both sexes, that they hardly know what it is to dine or sup at home. Hence they luxuriate in superfluities, rather than languish in want; their wives and children vie with the wives and children of the rich in luxury and refinement. . . .

OLIVER CROMWELL was sprung from a line of illustrious ancestors, who were distinguished for the civil functions which they sustained under the monarchy, and still more for the part which they took in restoring and establishing true religion in this country. In the vigor and maturity of his life, which he passed in retirement, he was conspicuous for nothing more than for the strictness of his religious habits, and the innocence of his life; and he had tacitly cherished in his breast that flame of piety which was afterwards to stand him in so much stead on the greatest occasions, and in the most critical exigencies. In the last parliament which was called by the king, he was elected to represent his native town, when he soon became distinguished by the justness of his opinions, and the vigor and decision of his councils. When the sword was drawn, he offered his services, and was appointed to a troop of horse, whose numbers were soon increased by the pious and the good, who flocked from all quarters to his standard; and in a short time he almost surpassed the greatest generals in the magnitude and the rapidity of his achievements. Nor is this surprising; for he was a soldier disciplined to perfection in the knowledge of himself. He had either extinguished, or by habit had learned to subdue, the whole host of vain hopes, fears, and passions, which infest the soul. He first acquired the government of himself, and over himself acquired the most signal victories; so that on the first day he took the field against the external enemy, he was a veteran in arms, consummately practised in the toils and exigencies of war. It is not possible for me in the narrow limits in which I circumscribe myself on this occasion, to enumerate the many towns which he has taken, the many battles which he has won. The whole surface of the British empire has been the scene of his exploits, and the theatre of his triumphs; which alone would furnish ample materials for a history, and want a copiousness of narration not inferior to the magnitude and diversity of the transactions. This alone seems to be a sufficient proof of his extraordinary and almost supernatural virtue, that by the vigor of his genius, or the excellence of his discipline, adapted, not more to the necessities of war than to the precepts of Christianity, the good and the brave were from all quarters attracted to his camp, not only as to the best school of military talents, but of piety and virtue; and that during the whole war, and the occasional intervals of peace, amid so many vicissitudes of faction and of events, he retained and still retains the obedience of his troops, not by largesses or indulgence, but by his sole authority and the regularity of his pay. In this instance his fame may rival that of Cyrus, of Epaminondas, or any of the great generals of antiquity. Hence he collected an army as numerous and as well equipped as any one ever did in so short a time; which was uniformly obedient to his orders, and dear to the affections of the citizens; which was formidable to the enemy in the field, but never cruel to those who laid down their arms; which committed no lawless ravages on the persons or the property of the inhabitants; who, when they compared their conduct with the turbulence, the intemperance, the impiety, and the debauchery of the royalists, were wont to salute them as friends, and to consider them as guests. They were a stay to the good, a terror to the evil, and the warmest advocates for every exertion of piety and virtue. Nor would it be right to pass over the name of Fairfax, who united the utmost fortitude with the utmost courage; and the spotless innocence of whose life seemed to point him out as the peculiar favorite of Heaven. Justly, indeed, may you be excited to receive this wreath of praise; though you have retired as much as possible from the world, and seek those shades of privacy which were the delight of Scipio. Nor was it only the enemy whom you sub-

dued, but you have triumphed over that flame of ambition and that lust of glory which are wont to make the best and the greatest of men their slaves. The purity of your virtues and the splendor of your actions consecrate those sweets of ease which you enjoy, and which constitute the wished-for haven of the toils of man. Such was the ease which, when the heroes of antiquity possessed, after a life of exertion and glory not greater than yours, the poets, in despair of finding ideas or expressions better suited to the subject, feigned that they were received into heaven, and invited to recline at the tables of the gods. But whether it were your health, which I principally believe, or any other motive which caused you to retire, of this I am convinced, that nothing could have induced you to relinquish the service of your country, if you had not known that in your successor liberty would meet with a protector, and England with a stay to its safety, and a pillar to its glory. For, while you, O Cromwell, are left among us, he hardly shows a proper confidence in the Supreme, who distrusts the security of England; when he sees that you are in so special a manner the favored object of the divine regard. But there was another department of the war, which was destined for your exclusive exertions.

Without entering into any length of detail, I will, if possible, describe some of the most memorable actions, with as much brevity as you performed them with celerity. After the loss of all Ireland, with the exception of one city, you in one battle immediately discomfited the forces of the rebels: and were busily employed in settling the country, when you were suddenly recalled to the war in Scotland. Hence you proceeded with unwearied diligence against the Scots, who were on the point of making an irruption into England with the king in their train: and in about the space of one year you entirely subdued, and added to the English dominion, that kingdom which all our monarchs, during a period of 800 years, had in vain struggled to subject. In one battle you almost annihilated the remainder of their forces, who, in a fit of desperation had made a sudden incursion into England, then almost destitute of garrisons, and got as far as Worcester; where you came up with them by forced marches, and captured almost the whole of their nobility. A profound peace ensued; when we found, though indeed not then for the first time, that you was as wise in the cabinet as valiant in the field. It was your constant endeavor in the senate either to induce them to adhere to those treaties which they had entered into with the enemy, or speedily to adjust others which promised to be beneficial to the country. But when you saw that the business was artfully procrastinated, that every one was more intent on his own selfish interest than on the public good, that the people complained of the disappointments which they had experienced, and the fallacious promises by which they had been gulled, that they were the dupes of a few overbearing individuals, you put an end to their domination. A new parliament is summoned; and the right of election given to those to whom it was expedient. They meet; but do nothing; and, after having wearied themselves by their mutual dissensions, and fully exposed their incapacity to the observation of the country, they consent to a voluntary dissolution. In this state of desolation, to which we were reduced, you, O Cromwell! alone remained to conduct the government, and to save the country. We all willingly yield the palm of sovereignty to your unrivalled ability and virtue, except the few among us, who, either ambitious of honors which they have not the capacity to sustain, or who envy those which are conferred on one more worthy than themselves, or else who do not know that nothing in the world is more pleasing to God, more agreeable to reason, more politically just, or more generally useful, than that the supreme power should be vested in the best and the wisest of men. Such, O Cromwell, all acknowledge you to be; such are the services which you have rendered, as the leader of our councils, the general of our armies, and the father of your country. For this is the tender appellation by which all the good among us salute you from the very soul. Other names you neither have nor could endure; and you deservedly reject that pomp of title which attracts the gaze and admiration of the multitude. For what is a title but a certain definite mode of dignity; but actions such as yours surpass, not only the bounds of our admiration, but our titles; and, like the points of pyramids, which are lost in the clouds, they soar above the possibilities of titular commendation. But since, though it be not fit, it may be expedient, that the highest pitch of virtue should be circumscribed within the bounds of some human appellation, you endured to receive, for the public good, a title most like to that of the father of your country; not to exalt, but rather to bring you nearer to the level of ordinary men; the title of king was unworthy the transcendent majesty of your character. For if you had been captivated by a name over which, as a private man, you had so completely triumphed and crumbled into dust, you would have been doing the same thing as if, after having subdued some idolatrous nation by the help of the true God, you should afterwards fall down and worship the gods which you had vanquished. Do you then, sir, continue your course with the same unrivalled magnanimity; it sits well upon you;—to you our country owes its liberties; nor can you sustain a character at once more momentous and more august than that of the author, the guardian, and the preserver of our liberties; and hence you have not only eclipsed the achievements of all our kings, but even those which have been fabled of our heroes. Often reflect what a dear pledge the beloved land of your nativity has entrusted to your care; and that liberty which she once expected only from the chosen flower of her talents and her virtues, she now expects from you only, and by you only hopes to obtain. Revere the fond expectations which we cherish, the solicitudes of your anxious country; revere the looks and the wounds of your brave companions in arms, who, under your banners, have so strenuously fought for liberty; revere the shades of those who perished in the contest; revere also the opinions and the hopes which foreign states entertain concerning us, who promise to themselves so many advantages from that liberty which we have so bravely acquired, from the establishment of that new government which has begun to shed its splendor on the world, which, if it be suffered to vanish like a dream, would involve us in the deepest abyss of shame; and lastly, revere yourself; and, after having endured so many sufferings and encountered so many perils for the sake of liberty, do not suffer it, now it is obtained, either to be violated by yourself, or in any one instance impaired by others. You cannot be truly free unless we are free too; for such is the nature of things, that he who entrenches on the liberty of others, is the first to lose his own and become a slave. But if you, who have hitherto been the patron and tutelary genius of liberty, if you, who are exceeded by no one in justice, in piety, and goodness, should hereafter invade that liberty which you have defended, your conduct must be fatally operative, not only against the cause of liberty, but the general interests of piety and virtue. Your integrity and virtue will appear to have evaporated, your faith in religion to have been small; your character with posterity will dwindle into insignificance, by which a most destructive blow will be levelled against the happiness of mankind. The work which you have undertaken is of incalculable moment, which will thoroughly sift and expose every principle and sensation of your heart, which will fully display the vigor and genius of your character, which will evince whether you really possess those great qualities of piety, fidelity, justice, and self-denial, which made us believe that you were elevated by the special direction of the Deity to the highest pinnacle of power. At once wisely and discreetly to hold the sceptre over three powerful nations, to persuade people to relinquish inveterate and corrupt for new and more beneficial maxims and institutions, to penetrate into the remotest parts of the country, to have the mind present and operative in every quarter, to watch against surprise, to provide against danger, to reject the blandishments of pleasure and pomp of power;—these are exertions compared with which the labor of war is mere pastime; which will require every energy and employ every faculty that you possess; which demand a man supported from above, and almost instructed by immediate inspiration. These and more than these are, no doubt, the objects which occupy your attention and engross your soul; as well as the means by which you may accomplish these important ends, and render our liberty at once more ample and more secure. And this you can, in my opinion, in no other way so readily effect, as by associating in your councils the companions of your dangers and your toils; men of exemplary modesty, integrity, and courage; whose hearts have not been hardened in cruelty and rendered insensible to pity by the sight of so much ravage and so much death, but whom it has rather inspired with the love of justice, with a respect for religion, and with the feeling of compassion, and who are more zealously interested in the preservation of liberty, in proportion as they have encountered more perils in its defence. They are not strangers or foreigners, a hireling rout scraped together from the dregs of the people, but, for the most part, men of the better conditions in life, of families not disgraced if not ennobled, of fortunes either ample or moderate; and what if some among them are recommended by their poverty? for it was not the lust of ravage which brought them into the field; it was the calamitous aspect of the times, which, in the most critical circumstances, and often amid the most disastrous turn of fortune, roused them to attempt the deliverance of their country from the fangs of despotism. They were men prepared, not only to debate, but to fight; not only to argue in the senate, but to engage the enemy in the field. But unless we will continually cherish indefinite and illusory expectations, I see not in whom we can place any confidence, if not in these men and such as these. We have the surest and most indubitable pledge of their fidelity in this, that they have already exposed themselves to death in the service of their country; of their piety in this, that they have been always wont to ascribe the whole glory of their successes to the favor of the Deity, whose help they have so suppliantly implored, and so conspicuously obtained; of their justice in this, that they even brought the king to trial, and when his guilt was proved, refused to save his life; of their moderation in our own uniform experience of its effects, and because, if by any outrage, they should disturb the peace which they have procured, they themselves will be the first to feel the miseries which it will occasion, the first to meet the havoc of the sword, and the first again to risk their lives for all those comforts and distinctions which they have so happily acquired; and lastly, of their fortitude in this, that there is no instance of any people who ever recovered their liberty with so much courage and success; and therefore let us not suppose, that there can be any persons who will be more zealous in preserving it. I now feel myself irresistibly compelled to commemorate the names of some of those who have most conspicuously signalized themselves in these times: and first thine, O Fleetwood! whom I have known from a boy to the present blooming maturity of your military fame, to have been inferior to none in humanity, in gentleness, in benignity of disposition, whose intrepidity in the combat, and whose clemency in victory, have been acknowledged even by the enemy: next thine, O Lambert! who, with a mere handful of men, checked the progress, and sustained the attack, of the Duke of Hamilton, who was attended by the whole flower and vigor of the Scottish youth: next thine, O Desborough! and thine, O Hawley! who wast always conspicuous in the heat of the combat, and the thickest of the fight; thine, O Overton! who hast been most endeared to me now for so many years by the similitude of our studies, the suavity of your manners, and the more than fraternal sympathy of our hearts; you, who, in the memorable battle of Marston Moor, when our left wing was put to the rout, were beheld with admiration, making head against the enemy with your infantry and repelling his attack, amid the thickest of the carnage; and lastly you, who, in the Scotch war, when under the auspices of Cromwell, occupied the coast of Fife, opened a passage beyond Stirling, and made the Scotch of the west, and of the north, and even the remotest Orkneys, confess your humanity, and submit to your power. Besides these, I will mention some as celebrated for their political wisdom and their civil virtues, whom you, sir, have admitted into your councils, and who are known to me by friendship or by fame. Whitlocke, Pickering, Strickland, Sydenham, Sidney, (a name indissolubly attached to the interests of liberty,) Montacute, Lawrence, both of highly cultivated minds and polished taste; besides many other citizens of singular merit, some of whom were distinguished by their exertions in the senate, and others in the field. To these men, whose talents are so splendid, and whose worth has been so thoroughly tried, you would without doubt do right to trust the protection of our liberties; nor would it be easy to say to whom they might more safely be entrusted. Then, if you leave the church to its own government, and relieve yourself and the other public functionaries from a charge so onerous, and so incompatible with your functions; and will no longer suffer two powers, so different as the civil and ecclesiastical, to commit fornication together, and by their mutual and delusive aids in appearance to strengthen, but in reality to weaken and finally to subvert, each other; if you shall remove all power of persecution out of the church, (but persecution will never cease, so long as men are bribed to preach the gospel by a mercenary salary, which is forcibly extorted, rather than gratuitously bestowed, which serves only to poison religion and to strangle truth,) you will then effectually have cast those money-changers out of the temple, who do not merely truckle with doves but with the Dove itself, with the Spirit of the Most High. Then, since there are often in a republic men who have the same itch for making a multiplicity of laws, as some poetasters have for making many verses, and since laws are usually worse in proportion as they are more numerous, if you shall not enact so many new laws as you abolish old, which do not operate so much as warnings against evil, as impediments in the way of good; and if you shall retain only those which are necessary, which do not confound the distinctions of good and evil, which while they prevent the frauds of the wicked, do not prohibit the innocent freedoms of the good, which punish crimes, without interdicting those things which are lawful only on account of the abuses to which they may occasionally be exposed. For the intention of laws is to check the commission of vice; but liberty is the best school of virtue, and affords the strongest encouragements to the practice. Then, if you make a better provision for the education of our youth than has hitherto been made, if you prevent the promiscuous instruction of the docile and the indocile, of the idle and the diligent, at the public cost, but reserve the rewards of learning for the learned, and of merit for the meritorious. If you permit the free discussion of truth without any hazard to the author, or any subjection to the caprice of an individual, which is the best way to make truth flourish and knowledge abound, the censure of the half-learned, the envy, the pusillanimity, or the prejudice which measures the discoveries of others, and in short every degree of wisdom, by the measure of its own capacity, will be prevented from doling out information to us according to their own arbitrary choice. Lastly, if you shall not dread to hear any truth, or any falsehood, whatever it may be, but if you shall least of all listen to those who think that they can never be free till the liberties of others depend on their caprice, and who attempt nothing with so much zeal and vehemence as to fetter, not only the bodies but the minds of men, who labor to introduce into the state the worst of all tyrannies, the tyranny of their own depraved habits and pernicious opinions; you will always be dear to those who think not merely that their own sect or faction, but that all citizens of all descriptions, should enjoy equal rights and equal laws. If there be any one who thinks that this is not liberty enough, he appears to me to be rather inflamed with the lust of ambition or of anarchy, than with the love of a genuine and well-regulated liberty; and particularly since the circumstances of the country, which has been so convulsed by the storms of faction, which are yet hardly still, do not permit us to adopt a more perfect or desirable form of government.

For it is of no little consequence, O citizens, by what principles you are governed, either in acquiring liberty, or in retaining it when acquired. And unless that liberty which is of such a kind as arms can neither procure nor take away, which alone is the fruit of piety, of justice, of temperance, and unadulterated virtue, shall have taken deep root in your minds and hearts, there will not long be wanting one who will snatch from you by treachery what you have acquired by arms. War has made many great whom peace makes small. If after being released from the toils of war, you neglect the arts of peace, if your peace and your liberty be a state of warfare, if war be your only virtue, the summit of your praise, you will, believe me, soon find peace the most adverse to your in-

terests. Your peace will be only a more distressing war; and that which you imagined liberty will prove the worst of slavery. Unless by the means of piety, not frothy and loquacious, but operative, unadulterated, and sincere, you clear the horizon of the mind from those mists of superstition which arise from the ignorance of true religion, you will always have those who will bend your necks to the yoke as if you were brutes, who, notwithstanding all your triumphs, will put you up to the highest bidder, as if you were mere booty made in war; and will find an exuberant source of wealth in your ignorance and superstition. Unless you will subjugate the propensity to avarice, to ambition, and sensuality, and expel all luxury from yourselves and from your families, you will find that you have cherished a more stubborn and intractable despot at home, than you ever encountered in the field; and even your very bowels will be continually teeming with an intolerable progeny of tyrants. Let these be the first enemies whom you subdue; this constitutes the campaign of peace; these are triumphs, difficult indeed, but bloodless; and far more honorable than those trophies which are purchased only by slaughter and by rapine. Unless you are victors in this service, it is in vain that you have been victorious over the despotic enemy in the field. For if you think that it is a more grand, a more beneficial, or a more wise policy, to invent subtle expedients for increasing the revenue, to multiply our naval and military force, to rival in craft the ambassadors of foreign states, to form skilful treaties and alliances, than to administer unpolluted justice to the people, to redress the injured, and to succor the distressed, and speedily to restore to every one his own, you are involved in a cloud of error; and too late will you perceive, when the illusion of those mighty benefits has vanished, that in neglecting these, which you now think inferior considerations, you have only been precipitating your own ruin and despair. The fidelity of enemies and allies is frail and perishing, unless it be cemented by the principles of justice; that wealth and those honors, which most covet, readily change masters; they forsake the idle, and repair where virtue, where industry, where patience flourish most. Thus nation precipitates the downfall of nation; thus the more sound part of one people subverts the more corrupt; thus you obtained the ascendant over the royalists. If you plunge into the same depravity, if you imitate their excesses, and hanker after the same vanities, you will become royalists as well as they, and liable to be subdued by the same enemies, or by others in your turn; who, placing their reliance on the same religious principles, the same patience, the same integrity and discretion which made you strong, will deservedly triumph over you who are immersed in debauchery, in the luxury and the sloth of kings. Then, as if God was weary of protecting you, you will be seen to have passed through the fire, that you might perish in the smoke; the contempt which you will then experience will be great as the admiration which you now enjoy; and, what may in future profit others, but cannot benefit yourselves, you will leave a salutary proof what great things the solid reality of virtue and of piety might have effected, when the mere counterfeit and varnished resemblance could attempt such mighty achievements, and make such considerable advances towards the execution. For, if either through your want of knowledge, your want of constancy, or your want of virtue, attempts so noble, and actions so glorious, have had an issue so unfortunate, it does not therefore follow, that better men should be either less daring in their projects or less sanguine in their hopes. But from such an abyss of corruption into which you so readily fall, no one, not even Cromwell himself, nor a whole nation of Brutuses, if they were alive, could deliver you if they would, or would deliver you if they could. For who would vindicate your right of unrestrained suffrage, or of choosing what representatives you liked best, merely that you might elect the creatures of your own faction, whoever they might be, or him, however small might be his worth, who would give you the most lavish feasts, and enable you to drink to the greatest excess? Thus not wisdom and authority, but turbulence and gluttony, would soon exalt the vilest miscreants from our taverns and our brothels, from our towns and villages, to the rank and dignity of senators. For, should the management of the republic be entrusted to persons to whom no one would willingly entrust the management of his private concerns; and the treasury of the state be left to the care of those who had lavished their own fortunes in an infamous prodigality? Should they have the charge of the public purse, which they would soon convert into a private, by their unprincipled peculations? Are they fit to be the legislators of a whole people who themselves know not what law, what reason, what right and wrong, what crooked and straight, what licit and illicit means? who think that all power consists in outrage, all dignity in the parade of insolence? who neglect every other consideration for the corrupt gratification of their friendships, or the prosecution of their resentments? who disperse their own relations and creatures through the provinces, for the sake of levying taxes and confiscating goods; men, for the greater part, the most profligate and vile, who buy up for themselves what they pretend to expose to sale, who thence collect an exhorbitant mass of wealth, which they fraudulently divert from the public service; who thus spread their pillage through the country, and in a moment emerge from penury and rags to a state of splendor and of wealth? Who could endure such thievish servants, such vicegerents of their lords? Who could believe that the masters and the patrons of a banditti could be the proper guardians of liberty? or who would suppose that he should ever be made one hair more free by such a set of public functionaries, (though they might amount to five hundred elected in this manner from the counties and boroughs,) when among them who are the very guardians of liberty, and to whose custody it is committed, there must be so many, who know not either how to use or to enjoy liberty, who neither understand the principles nor merit the possession? But, what is worthy of remark, those who are the most unworthy of liberty are wont to behave most ungratefully towards their deliverers. Among such persons, who would be willing either to fight for liberty, or to encounter the least peril in its defence? It is not agreeable to the nature of things that such persons ever should be free. However much they may brawl about liberty, they are slaves, both at home and abroad, but without perceiving it; and when they do perceive it, like unruly horses that are impatient of the bit, they will endeavor to throw off the yoke, not from the love of genuine liberty, (which a good man only loves and knows how to obtain,) but from the impulses of pride and little passions. But though they often attempt it by arms, they will make no advances to the execution; they may change their masters, but will never be able to get rid of their servitude. This often happened to the ancient Romans, wasted by excess, and enervated by luxury: and it has still more so been the fate of the moderns; when, after a long interval of years, they aspired, under the auspices of Crescentius, Nomentanus, and afterwards of Nicolas Rentius, who had assumed the title of Tribune of the People, to restore the splendor and reestablish the government of ancient Rome. For, instead of fretting with vexation, or thinking that you can lay the blame on any one but yourselves, know that to be free is the same thing as to be pious, to be wise, to be temperate and just, to be frugal and abstinent, and lastly, to be magnanimous and brave; so to be the opposite of all these is is the same as to be a slave; and it usually happens, by the appointment, and as it were retributive justice, of the Deity, that that people which cannot govern themselves, and moderate their passions, but crouch under the slavery of their lusts, should be delivered up to the sway of those whom they abhor, and made to submit to an involuntary servitude. It is also sanctioned by the dictates of justice and by the constitution of nature, that he who from the imbecility or derangement of his intellect, is incapable of governing himself, should, like a minor, be committed to the government of another; and least of all should he be appointed to superintend the affairs of others or the interest of the state. You, therefore, who wish to remain free, either instantly be wise, or, as soon as possible, cease to be fools; if you think slavery an intolerable evil, learn obedience to reason and the government of yourselves; and finally bid adieu to your dissensions, your jealousies, your superstitions, your outrages, your rapine, and your lusts. Unless you will spare no pains to effect this, you must be judged unfit, both by God and mankind, to be entrusted with the possession of liberty and the administration of the government; but will rather, like a nation in a state of pupilage, want some active and courageous guardian to undertake the management of your affairs. With respect to myself, whatever turn things may take, I thought that my exertions on the present occasion would be serviceable to my country; and as they have been cheerfully bestowed, I hope that they have not been bestowed in vain. And I have not circumscribed my defence of liberty within any petty circle around me, but have made it so general and comprehensive, that the justice and the reasonableness of such uncommon occurrences, explained and defended, both among my countrymen and among foreigners, and which all good men cannot but approve, may serve to exalt the glory of my country, and to excite the imitation of posterity. If the conclusion do not answer to the beginning, that is their concern; I have delivered my testimony, I would almost say, have erected a monument, that will not readily be destroyed, to the reality of those singular and mighty achievements which were above all praise. As the epic poet, who adheres at all to the rules of that species of composition, does not profess to describe the whole life of the hero whom he celebrates, but only some particular action of his life, as the resentment of Achilles at Troy, the return of Ulysses, or the coming of Æneas into Italy; so it will be sufficient, either for my justification or apology, that I have heroically celebrated at least one exploit of my countrymen; I pass by the rest, for who could recite the achievements of a whole people? If after such a display of courage and of vigor, you basely relinquish the path of virtue, if you do anything unworthy of yourselves, posterity will sit in judgment on your conduct. They will see that the foundations were well laid; that the beginning (nay, it was more than a beginning) was glorious; but with deep emotions of concern will they regret, that those were wanting who might have completed the structure. They will lament that perseverance was not conjoined with such exertions and such virtues. They will see that there was a rich harvest of glory, and an opportunity afforded for the greatest achievements, but that men only were wanting for the execution; while they were not wanting who could rightly counsel, exhort, inspire, and bind an unfading wreath of praise round the brows of the illustrious actors in so glorious a scene.

From Pro Se Defensio.

[The selections are from the translation of George Burnett, London, 1809, as printed in the *Columbia Milton*, pp. 3, 13 and 107.]

At the time when I first undertook to vindicate the cause of liberty, I thought it would be no unheard of accident, nor, from the very beginning, was it at all foreign to my expectation, if I, who above the rest had publicly applauded my fellow-citizens as the deliverers of their country, and had confounded the unlimited and mischievous prerogative of tyrants, should have the hatred of all the unprincipled accumulated almost upon me alone. Englishmen! I foresaw, likewise, that your contest with the enemy would not be long; but that mine, with the fugitives and their hirelings, would be only not everlasting; because those, from whose hands you had wrested their arms, would therefore, with the greater bitterness, shower their curses and their reproaches upon me. Against you, then, the fury and violence of the enemy have abated. To me, it seems, alone it remains to terminate this war. These concluding attacks are indeed most contemptible; but like those from most low animals, they are full of venom. As all who are over-curious about other people's concerns, all who are the most mischievously busy and corrupt, whether among our own profligate citizens, or among foreigners, as all such fly upon me, against me will they point their venom and their stings. Whence it happens, that I am not at liberty, on the present occasion, to imitate the common practice of writers, with whom it is usual to premise something in commendation of their work, with a view to procure a favorable hearing, and thus to raise themselves by degrees from what may be low or ordinary in their subjects, to those topics which may be of the greatest weight and importance: On the contrary, I am now obliged to stoop from recounting achievements the most lofty and glorious, to things of no note or lustre,—to trace out the lurking holes of the nameless, and the haunts and the crimes of an adversary of the basest kind. Although this may appear little creditable to one who is making a beginning, and still less suited to gain the attention of the reader, yet, when we consider that the same thing has happened to the best and most illustrious of men, my situation, by presenting a parallel, is not without its circumstances of consolation. Even Scipio Africanus himself, after he had performed those exploits, than which nothing, in that line of glory, could be greater or more fortunate, after his affairs began to wane, which they continued to do without interruption, he seems always to have fed upon the substance of his own worth. At the outset of his career, he was the first of generals, superior even to Hannibal; afterwards he was sent to combat the Syrian, an unwarlike enemy; then he was harassed by the insolence of the tribunes, and last of all, he was constrained to fortify his own villa at Liternum, against thieves and robbers: yet, throughout this decline of his fortune, he is said to have been always the same, always equal to himself. Hence I am taught, as likewise from lessons derived from other sources, not to despise any condition or any office that may be allotted me by God however humble it may be, or however inferior to what I before enjoyed. But as a good general (for why should we not imitate the good in every kind of excellence?) will do the duty of a good general against an enemy of any description; or, if this comparison be too invidious, as a good shoe-maker (for thus philosophized a wise man of ancient times) will make the best shoe he is able of the leather he may happen to have in hand, so I will try, if, out of this shoe, (for when I had resolved on it, I was ashamed to call it an argument) though now worn and unsown, I cannot patch up something at least, which the ears of my readers may not disdain. Still, I should have spared myself altogether this trouble, if my enemy had not thrown out against me accusations and lies of such a nature, as I could not endure should adhere as a stain and a suspicion to my character. Forced then of necessity to undertake this task, I trust I shall be pardoned by all, if, as heretofore I was not found wanting to the people and to the commonwealth, I shall now show that I am not wanting to myself. . . .

It is now two years since was published, the opprobrious book entitled, *The Cry of the Royal Blood to Heaven against the English Parricides.* In this book, the commonwealth of England, and Cromwell in particular, (who was at that time the leader of our armies, but who is now the first man in the state) are loaded with the grossest calumnies of which language can be the interpreter. Next after Cromwell (for thus it seemed good to the anonymous scribbler) the largest share of the abuse falls upon me. The book was scarcely complete in sheets, before it was put into my hands in the council. Soon after that sitting, another copy is sent me by the person who was then president, accompanied with the intimation, that the commonwealth expected my services to stop the mouth of this importunate crier. But at that time, in an especial manner, I was oppressed with concerns of a far different nature My health was infirm, I was mourning the recent loss of two relatives, the light had now utterly vanished from my eyes. Besides, my old adversary abroad, a far more desirable one than the present, hovered for an attack, and now daily threatened to descend upon me with all his force. But considering myself relieved from a certain portion of my task, by his sudden death; and being somewhat reestablished in health, by its being in part restored and in part desperate; that I might not appear as disappointing altogether the expectation of persons of the first consequence, and amid so many calamities, to have abandoned all regard for reputation; as soon as an opportunity was given me of collecting any certain information concerning this anonymous crier, I commence my attack upon him. . . .

But I come now to that which has given offence to the sanctified More—that prodigy of the age for chastity. "I employ, (it seems) language of unwashed foulness, words naked and indelicate." O shameful, prostituted man! And do you censure words as foul, who without a blush can be guilty of deeds of unequalled foulness? Indeed, it would not repent me now, had I been a little more liberal of my words of this kind, had it been only to elicit this scoundrelly dissimulation, and hence openly to expose you (masked as you are to the eyes of the world) as the worst of hypocrites! But what expression, what word, will you point out to me, in any part of the book, more foul, than the word Morus itself? Yet, it is neither in the word nor in the thing, but in yourself exists all vice and all obscenity. Lewder than any fawn or naked satyr, your manners have converted words of chastest meaning into words of naked ribaldry. No shade could veil your filthiness, not even that notable fig-tree. Whoever speaks of you, and of your debaucheries, cannot choose but speak obscenely. And if I have uttered naked words in your reproach, I should be at no loss to defend myself by the practice of gravest authors; who have always been of opinion, that words naked and plain, indignantly uttered, have a meaning far different from obscenity—that they express the utmost vehemence of reproof. Whoever imputed it as a crime to Piso, the writer of the annals, who for his virtue and modest manners obtained the surname of *Frugi,* that, in those annals, he complained—"Adolescentes peni deditos esse?" Whoever censured Sallust, a very serious writer, for saying even in his history— "Ventre, manu, pene, alea, bona patria dilacerari": not to mention Herodotus, Seneca, Suetonius, Plutarch, the gravest of authors? and with whom you sufficiently proclaim your non-acquaintance, if you deny that they intermix, on divers occasions, words more than indelicate indeed, and subjects abundantly gross, with matters of greater seriousness. If this be indecorous at all times and places, how often will you have to charge with indecency, and obscenity, (shall I say?) Erasmus, that miracle of learning, whose brazen statue stands at Rotterdam; how often our own Thomas More, whose name you dishonour by pronouncing it at the same time with your own; lastly, how often the ancient fathers of the church, Clemens, Alexandrinus, Arnobius, Lactantius, Eusebius, when they uncover and cast derision upon the obscene mysteries of the old religions! But perhaps, as hypocrites are usually austere in words, though in things unclean, you will not suffer even Moses himself to escape unimpeached of this crime: for, as is usual with him in various other places, so if we are to believe the Hebrews, it is especially remarkable, in the passage where he speaks without any disguise, of the very part where the spear of Phinehas transfixed the woman. You will not spare even Job, most modest and patient of men, while, in naked and homely phrase, he imprecates on himself the curse of a harlot-wife, if he had ever lain in wait for the wife of another. Not the writings of Solomon the elegant, nor even of the prophets could escape your proscription of every petty indelicacy, though sometimes indeed of broad obscenity, whenever the Masorets and Rabins think proper to write their marginal *Keri*, to note the eloquent plainness of the text. As for me, I should choose rather to be plain-spoken with the sacred writers, than delicate with the futile Rabins. In vain will you call Marcus Tullius to your aid; for if he in that "golden book of offices," which you quote, deems of this kind of raillery as elegant, urbane, ingenious, witty, and of which not only Plautus and the ancient Attic comedy, but even the books of the Socratic philosophers, are full, as you might there have seen—it is not he who will be found to confine decorum within limits so narrow and strict, that it should be difficult for any one to restrain himself, and especially for me to restrain myself within those limits. Let us hear no more then, most polluted man, of your trifling about the honorable and the becoming; believe me, this becomes not you; nay, be assured, there is nothing less becoming, nothing more foreign to the very end of decorum, than for such a one as you to usurp the language of purity, or to censure that which is foul.

FROM THE HISTORY OF BRITAIN.

[The text is that of the original edition, 1670, as printed in the *Columbia Milton*, in the original spelling and punctuation.]

THE FIRST BOOK.

[*C. M.* pp. 1-3.]

THE beginning of Nations, those excepted of whom sacred Books have spok'n, is to this day unknown. Nor only the beginning, but the deeds also of many succeeding Ages, yea periods of Ages, either wholly unknown, or obscur'd and blemisht with Fables. Whether it were that the use of Letters came in long after, or were it the violence of barbarous inundations, or they themselves at certain revolutions of time, fatally decaying, and degenerating into Sloth and Ignorance; whereby the monuments of more ancient civility have bin som destroy'd, som lost. Perhaps dis-esteem and contempt of the public affairs then present, as not worth recording, might partly be in cause. Certainly oft-times we see that wise men, and of best abilitie have forborn to write the Acts of thir own daies, while they beheld with a just loathing and disdain, not only how unworthy, how pervers, how corrupt, but often how ignoble, how petty, how below all History the persons and thir actions were; who either by fortune, or som rude election had attain'd as a sore judgment, and ignominie upon the Land, to have cheif sway in managing the Commonwealth. But that any law, or superstition of our old Philosophers the *Druids* forbad the *Britans* to write thir memorable deeds, I know not why any out of *Cæsar* should allege: he indeed saith, that thir doctrine they thought not lawful to commit to Letters; but in most matters else, both privat, and public, among which well may History be reck'nd, they us'd the Greek Tongue: and that the *British Druids* who taught those in *Gaule* would be ignorant of any Language known and us'd by thir Disciples, or so frequently writing other things, and so inquisitive into highest, would for want of recording be ever Children in the Knowledge of Times and Ages, is not likely. What ever might be the reason, this we find, that of *British affairs,* from the first peopling of the Iland to the coming of *Julius Cæsar,* nothing certain, either by Tradition, History, or Ancient Fame hath hitherto bin left us. That which we have of oldest seeming, hath by the greater part of judicious Antiquaries bin long rejected for a modern Fable.

Nevertheless there being others besides the first suppos'd Author, men not unread, nor unlern'd in Antiquitie, who admit that for approved story, which the former explode for fiction, and seeing that oft-times relations heertofore accounted fabulous have bin after found to contain in them many footsteps, and reliques of somthing true, as what we read in Poets of the Flood, and Giants little beleev'd, till undoubted witnesses taught us, that all was not fain'd; I have therfore determin'd to bestow the telling over ev'n of these reputed Tales; be it for nothing else but

Cæs. l. 6.

in favour of our English Poets, and Rhetoricians, who by thir Art will know, how to use them judiciously.

I might also produce example, as *Diodorus* among the *Greeks, Livie* and others of the *Latines, Polydore* and *Virunnius* accounted among our own Writers. But I intend not with controversies and quotations to delay or interrupt the smooth course of History; much less to argue and debate long who were the first Inhabitants, with what probabilities, what authorities each opinion hath bin upheld, but shall endevor that which hitherto hath bin needed most, with plain, and lightsom brevity, to relate well and orderly things worth the noting, so as may best instruct and benefit them that read. Which, imploring divine assistance, that it may redound to his glory, and the good of the *British* Nation, *I now begin.*

FROM THE SECOND BOOK.

[*C. M.* pp. 32–34 and 86.]

I AM now to write of what befell the *Britans* from *fifty and three years before the Birth of our Saviour,* when first the *Romans* came in, till the decay and ceasing of that Empire; a story of much truth, and for the first hunderd years and somwhat more, collected without much labour. So many and so prudent were the Writers, which those two, the civilest, and the wisest of *European Nations,* both *Italy* and *Greece,* afforded to the actions of that Puissant Citty. For worthy deeds are not often destitute of worthy relaters: as by a certain Fate great Acts and great Eloquence have most commonly gon hand in hand, ːqualling and honouring each other in the same Ages. 'Tis true that in obscurest times, by shallow and unskilfull Writers, the indistinct noise of many Battels, and devastations, of many Kingdoms over-run and lost, hath come to our Eares. For what wonder, if in all Ages, Ambition and the love of rapine hath stirr'd up greedy and violent men to bold attempts in wasting and ruining Warrs, which to posterity have left the work of Wild Beasts and Destroyers, rather then the Deeds and Monuments of men and Conquerours. But he whose just and true valour uses the necessity of Warr and Dominion, not to destroy but to prevent destruction, to bring

in liberty against Tyrants, Law and Civility among barbarous Nations, knowing that when he Conquers all things else, he cannot Conquer *Time* or *Detraction,* wisely conscious of this his want as well as of his worth not to be forgott'n or conceal'd, honours and hath recourse to the aid of Eloquence, his freindliest and best supply; by whose immortal Record his noble deeds, which else were transitory, becoming fixt and durable against the force of Yeares and Generations, he fails not to continue through all Posterity, over *Envy, Death,* and *Time,* also victorious. Therfore when the esteem of Science, and liberal study waxes low in the Commonwealth, wee may presume that also there all civil Vertue, and worthy action is grown as low to a decline: and then Eloquence, as it were consorted in the same destiny, with the decrease and fall of vertue corrupts also and fades; at least resignes her office of relating to illiterat and frivolous Historians; such as the persons themselvs both deserv, and are best pleas'd with; whilst they want either the understanding to choose better, or the innocence to dare invite the examining, and searching stile of an intelligent, and faithfull Writer to the survay of thir unsound exploits, better befreinded by obscurity then *Fame.* As for these, the only Authors wee have of *Brittish* matters, while the power of *Rome* reach'd hither, (for *Gildas* affirms that of the *Roman* times noe *Brittish* Writer was in his daies extant, or if any ever were, either burnt by Enemies, or transported with such as fled the *Pictish* and *Saxon* invasions) these therfore only *Roman* Authors there bee who in the English Tongue have laid together, as much, and perhaps more then was requisite to a History of *Britain.* So that were it not for leaving an unsightly gap so neer to the beginning, I should have judg'd this labour, wherin so little seems to be requir'd above transcription, almost superfluous. Notwithstanding since I must through it, if ought by diligence may bee added, or omitted, or by other disposing may be more explain'd, or more express'd, I shall assay. . . .

While Peace held, the Empress *Julia* meeting on a time certain *British* Ladies, and discoursing with the Wife of *Argentocoxus* a *Caledonian,* cast out a scoff against the looseness of our Iland Women; whose manner then was to use promiscuously the company of divers men. Whom straight the *British* Woman boldly thus answer'd: *Much better do we* Britans *fulfill the work of Nature than you* Romans; *we with the best men accustom op'nly; you with the basest commit private adulteries.* Whether she thought this answer might serve to justifie the practice of her Countrie, as when vices are compar'd, the greater seems to justifie the less, or whether the law and custom wherein she was bred, had wip't out of her conscience the better dictate of Nature, and not convinc't her of the shame; certain it is that whereas other Nations us'd a liberty not unnatural for one man to have many Wives, the *Britans* altogether as licentious, but more absurd and preposterous in thir licence, had one or many Wives in common among ten or twelve Husbands; and those for the most part incestuously.

[*C. M.* pp. 101–104.]

Thus expir'd this great Empire of the *Romans;* first in *Britain,* soon after in *Italy* it self: having born chief sway in this Iland, though never throughly subdu'd, or all at once in subjection, if we reck'n from the coming in of *Julius* to the taking of *Rome* by *Alaric,* in which year *Honorius* wrote those Letters of discharge into *Britain,* the space of 462 years. And with the Empire fell also what before in this Western World was cheifly *Roman;* Learning, Valour, Eloquence, History, Civility, and eev'n Language it self, all these together, as it were, with equal pace diminishing, and decaying. Henceforth we are to stear by another sort of Authors; neer anough to the things they write, as in thir own Countrie, if that would serve; in time not much belated, some of equal age; in expression barbarous; and to say how judicious, I suspend a while: this we must expect; in civil matters to find them dubious Relaters, and still to the best advantage of what they term holy Church, meaning indeed themselves: in most other matters of Religion, blind, astonish'd, and strook with superstition as with a Planet; in one word, Monks. Yet these Guides, where can be had no better, must be follow'd; in gross, it may be true anough; in circumstance each man as his judgment gives him, may re-

serve his Faith, or bestow it. But so different a state of things requires a several relation.

THE THIRD BOOK.

THIS third Book having to tell of accidents as various and exemplary, as the intermission or change of Government hath any where brought forth, may deserve attention more than common, and repay it with like benefit to them who can judiciously read: considering especially that the late civil broils had cast us into a condition not much unlike to what the *Britans* then were in, when the imperial jurisdiction departing hence left them to the sway of thir own Councils; which times by comparing seriously with these later, and that confused Anarchy with this intereign, we may be able from two such remarkable turns of State, producing like events among us, to raise a knowledg of our selves both great and weighty, by judging hence what kind of men the *Britans* generally are in matters of so high enterprise, how by nature, industry, or custom fitted to attempt or undergoe matters of so main consequence: for if it be a high point of wisdom in every private man, much more is it in a Nation to know it self; rather than puft up with vulgar flatteries, and encomiums, for want of self knowledge, to enterprise rashly and come off miserably in great undertakings. The *Britans* thus as we heard being left without protection from the Empire, and the Land in a manner emptied of all her youth, consumed in Warrs abroad, or not caring to return home, themselves through long subjec-   *Gild. Bede. Malms.* tion, servile in mind, sloathful of body, and with the use of Arms unacquainted, sustain'd but ill for many years the violence of those barbarous Invaders, who now daily grew upon them. For although at first greedy of change, and to be   *Zozim. L. 6.* thought the leading Nation to freedom from the Empire, they seem'd a while to bestirr them with a shew of diligence in thir new affairs, som secretly aspiring to rule, others adoring the name of liberty, yet so soon as they felt by proof the weight of what it was to govern well themselves, and what was wanting within them, not stomach or the love of licence, but the wisdom, the virtu, the labour, to use and maintain true libertie, they soon remitted thir heat, and shrunk more wretchedly under the burden of thir own libertie, than before under a foren yoke. . . .

THE FOURTH BOOK

[C. M. pp. 142, 177, 185.]

THE *Northumbrians* had a custom at that time, and many hunder'd yeares after not abolish't, to sell thir Children for a small value into any Foren Land. Of which number, two comly youths were brought to *Rome*, whose fair and honest countnances invited *Gregory* Arch-Deacon of that Citty, among others that beheld them, pittying thir condition, to demand whence they were; it was answer'd by som who stood by, that they were *Angli* of the Province *Deira*, subjects to *Alla* King of *Northumberland*, and by Religion Pagans. Which last *Gregory* deploring, fram'd on a sudden this allusion to the three names he heard; that the *Angli* so like to Angels should be snatch't *de ira*, that is, from the wrath of God, to sing *Hallelujah*: and forthwith obtaining licence of *Benedict* the Pope, had come and preach't heer among them, had not the *Roman* people, whose love endur'd not the absence of so vigilant a Pastor over them, recall'd him then on his journey, though but deferr'd his pious intention. For a while after, succeeding in the Papal Seat, and now in his fourth year, admonisht, saith Beda, by divine instinct, he sent *Augustine* whom he had design'd for Bishop of the *English* Nation, and other zealous Monks with him, to preach to them the Gospel. Who being now on thir way, discourag'd by some reports, or thir own carnal fear, sent back *Austin,* in the name of all, to beseech *Gregory* they might return home, and not be sent a journey so full of hazard, to a fierce and infidel Nation, whose tongue they understood not. Gregory with pious and Apostolic perswasions exhorts them not to shrink back from so good a work, but cheerfully to go on in the strength of divine assistance. The Letter it self yet extant among our Writers of Ecclesiastic story, I omitt heer, as not professing to relate of those matters more then what mixes aptly with civil affairs. . . .

Three years after which, appear'd two Comets about the Sun, terrible to behold, the one before him in the Morning, the other after him in the Evening, for the space of two weeks in *January,* bending thir blaze toward the North, at which time the Saracens furiously invaded *France,* but were expell'd soon after with great overthrow. . . .

I am sensible how wearisom it may likely be to read of so many bare and reasonless Actions, so many names of Kings one after another, acting little more then Mute persons in a Scene: what would it be to have inserted the long Bead-roll of Archbishops, Bishops, Abbots, Abbesses, and thir doeings, neither to Religion profitable, nor to morality, swelling my Authors each to a voluminous body, by me studiously omitted; and left as their propriety, who have a mind to write the Ecclesiastical matters of those Ages; neither do I care to wrincle the smoothness of History with rugged names of places unknown, better harp'd at in *Camden,* and other Chorographers. . . .

THE FIFTH BOOK

[C. M. p. 197, 220.]

THE summe of things in this Iland, or the best part therof, reduc't now under the power of one man; and him one of the worthiest, which, as far as can be found in good Authors, was by none attain'd at any time heer before unless in Fables; men might with some reason have expected from such Union, peace and plenty, greatness, and the flourishing of all Estates and Degrees: but far the contrary fell out soon after, Invasion, Spoil, Desolation, slaughter of many, slavery of the rest, by the forcible landing of a fierce Nation; *Danes* commonly call'd, and somtimes *Dacians,* by others, the same with *Normans;* as barbarous as the *Saxons* themselves were at first reputed, and much more; for the *Saxons* first invited came hither to dwell; these unsent for, unprovok'd, came only to destroy. But if the *Saxons,* as is above related, came most of them from *Jutland* and *Anglen,* a part of *Denmarke,* as *Danish* Writers affirm, and that *Danes* and *Normans* are the same; then in this invasion, *Danes* drove out *Danes,* thir own posterity. And *Normans* afterwards, none but antienter *Normans.* Which invasion perhaps, had the Heptarchie stood divided as it was, had either not bin attempted, or not uneasily resisted; while each

Calvisius

hist. Dan Pontan.

Prince and people, excited by thir neerest concernments, had more industriously defended thir own bounds, then depending on the neglect of a deputed Governour, sent oft-times from the remote residence of a secure Monarch. Though as it fell out in those troubles, the lesser Kingdoms revolting from the *West-Saxon* yoke, and not aiding each other, too much concern'd with thir own safety, it came to no better pass; while severally they sought to repell the danger nigh at hand, rather then jointly to prevent it farre off. But when God hath decreed servitude on a sinful Nation, fitted by thir own vices for no condition but servile, all Estates of Government are alike unable to avoid it. God had purpos'd to punish our instrumental punishers, though now Christians, by other Heathen, according to his Divine retaliation; invasion for invasion, spoil for spoil, destruction for destruction. The *Saxons* were now full as wicked as the *Britans* were at their arrival, brok'n with luxurie and sloth, either secular or superstitious; for laying aside the exercise of Arms, and the study of all vertuous knowledge, some betook them to over-worldly or vitious practice, others to religious Idleness and Solitude, which brought forth nothing but vain and delusive visions; easily perceav'd such, by thir commanding of things, either not belonging to the Gospel, or utterly forbidden, Ceremonies, Reliques, Monasteries, Masses, Idols, add to these ostentation of Alms, got ofttimes by rapine and oppression, or intermixt with violent and lustfull deeds, sometimes prodigally bestow'd as the expiation of cruelty and bloodshed. What longer suffering could there be, when Religion it self grew so void of sincerity, and the greatest shews of purity were impur'd? . . . After which troublesome time, *Alfred* enjoying three years of peace, by him spent, as his manner was, not idely or voluptuously, but in all vertuous emploiments both of mind and body, becoming a Prince of his Renown, ended his daies in the year 900. the 51. of his Age, the 30*th* of his Reign, and was buried regally at *Winchester;* he was born at a place call'd *Wanading* in *Barkshire*, his Mother *Osburga* the Daughter of *Oslac* the Kings Cupbearer, a *Goth* by Nation, and of noble descent. He was of person comlier than all his Brethren, of pleasing Tongue and grace-

full behaviour, ready wit and memory; yet through the fondness of his Parents towards him, had not bin taught to read till the twelfth year of his Age; but the great desire of learning which was in him, soon appear'd. by his conning of *Saxon* Poems day and night, which with great attention he heard by others repeated. He was besides, excellent at Hunting, and the new Art then of Hawking, but more exemplary in devotion, having collected into a Book certain Prayers and Psalms, which he carried ever with him in his Bosome to use on all occasions. He thirsted after all liberal knowledge, and oft complain'd that in his youth he had no Teachers, in his middle Age so little vacancy from Wars and the cares of his Kingdome, yet leasure he found sometimes, not only to learn much himself, but to communicate therof what he could to his people, by translating Books out of Latin into English, *Orosius, Boethius, Beda's* History and others, permitted none unlern'd to bear Office, either in Court or Common-wealth; at twenty years of age not yet reigning, he took to Wife *Egelswitha* the Daughter of *Ethelred* a *Mercian* Earl. The extremities which befell him in the sixt of his Reign, *Neothan* Abbot told him, were justly come upon him for neglecting in his younger days the complaints of such as injur'd and oppress'd repair'd to him, as then second person in the Kingdome for redress; which neglect were it such indeed, were yet excusable in a youth, through jollity of mind unwilling perhaps to be detain'd long with sad and sorrowfull Narrations; but from the time of his undertaking regal charge, no man more patient in hearing causes, more inquisitive in examining, more exact in doing justice, and providing good Laws, which are yet extant; more severe in punishing unjust judges or obstinate offenders. Theeves especially and Robbers, to the terrour of whom in cross waies were hung upon a high Post certain Chains of Gold, as it were dareing any one to take them thence: so that justice seem'd in his daies not to flourish only, but to tryumph: no man then hee more frugal of two pretious things in mans life, his time and his revenue; no man wiser in the disposal of both. His time, the day, and night, he distributed by the burning of certain

Tapours into three equall portions: the one was for devotion, the other for publick or private affairs; the third for bodily refreshment: how each hour past, he was put in minde by one who had that Office. His whole annual revenue, which his first care was should be justly his own, he divided into two equall parts; the first he imploi'd to secular uses, and subdivided those into three, the first to pay his Souldiers, Household-Servants and Guard, of which divided into three Bands, one attended monthly by turn; the second was to pay his Architects and workmen, whom he had got together of several Nations; for he was also an Elegant Builder; above the Custome and conceit of Englishmen in those days: the third he had in readiness to releive or honour Strangers according to thir worth, who came from all parts to see him and to live under him. The other equall part of his yearly wealth he dedicated to religious uses, those of fowr sorts; the first to releive the poor, the second to the building and maintenance of two Monasteries, the third of a School, where he had perswaded the Sons of many Noblemen to study sacred knowledge and liberal Arts, some say at *Oxford;* the fourth was for the releif of Foreign Churches, as far as *India* to the shrine of St.

Malms. Thomas, sending thether *Sigelm* Bishop of *Sherburn,* who both return'd safe, and brought with him many rich Gems and Spices; guifts also and a letter he receav'd from the Patriarch of *Jerusalem,* sent many to *Rome,* and for them receav'd reliques. Thus far, and much more might be said of his noble mind, which rendered him the miror of Princes; his body was diseas'd in his youth with a great soreness in the Seige, and that ceasing of it self, with another inward pain of unknown cause, which held him by frequent fits to his dying day; yet not disinabl'd to sustain those many glorious labours of his life both in peace and war. . . .

THE SIXTH BOOK.

[*C. M.* pp. 299, 305 and 315.]

SIWARD but one year surviving his great Victory, dy'd at *Yorke;* reported by Huntingdon a man of Giant-like stature & by his own demeanour at point of Death manifested, of a rough and meer souldierly mind. For much disdaining to die in bed by a disease, not in the field fighting with his enemies, he caus'd himself compleatly arm'd, and weapon'd with battel-ax and shield to be set in a chair, whether to fight with death, if he could be so vain, or to meet him (when far other weapons and preparations were needful) in a Martial bravery; but true fortitude glories not in the feats of War, as they are such, but as they serve to end War soonest by a victorious Peace. . . .

After this King *Edward* [*the Confessor*] grew sickly, yet as he was able kept his *Christmas* at *London,* and was at the Dedication of St. *Peters* Church in *Westminster,* which he had rebuilt; but on the Eve of *Epiphanie,* or *Twelftide,* deceas'd much lamented, and in the Church was Entoomb'd. That he was harmless and simple, is conjecturd by his words in anger to a Peasant who had cross'd his Game (for with Hunting and Hawking he was much delighted) by God and Gods Mother, said hee, I shall do you as shrew'd a turn if I can; observing that Law-Maxim, the best of all his Successors, that the King of *England* can do no wrong. The softness of his Nature gave growth to factions of those about him, Normans especially and English; these complaining that *Robert* the Archbishop was a sower of dissention between the King and his people, a traducer of the English; the other side, that *Godwin* and his Sons bore themselves arrogantly and proudly towards the King, usurping to themselves equall share in the Government; ofttimes making sport with his simplicity, that through thir power in the land, they made no scruple to kill men of whose inheritance they took a likeing, and so to take possession. The truth is, that *Godwin* and his Sons did many things boistrously and violently, much against the Kings minde; which not able to resist, he had, as some say, his Wife *Edith Godwins* Daughter in such aversation, as in bed never to have touch'd her; whether for this cause or mistak'n Chastitie, not commendable; to enquire further is not material. His Laws held good and just, and long after desir'd by the English of thir Norman Kings, are yet extant. He is said to be at Table not excessive, at Festivals nothing puft up with the costly Robes he wore, which his Queen with curious Art had woven for him in Gold. He was full of Almsdeeds, and exhorted the Monks to like Charitie. He is said to be the first of English Kings that cur'd the Disease call'd thence the Kings Evil; yet *Malmsbury* blames them who attribute that Cure to his Royaltie, not to his Sanctitie; said also to have cur'd certain blinde men with the water wherin he had wash'd his hands. A little before his Death, lying speechless two days, the third day after a deep sleep, he was heard to pray, that if it were a true Vision, not an Illusion which he had seen, God would give him strength to utter it, otherwise not. Then he related how he had seen two devout Monks, whom he knew in *Normandy,* to have liv'd and dy'y well, who appearing told him they were sent Messengers from God to foretell, that because the great ones of *England,* Dukes, Lords, Bishops, and Abbots, were not Ministers of God but of the Devil, God had deliverd the Land to thir Enemies; and when he desir'd that he might reveal this Vision, to the end they might repent, it was answerd; they neither will repent, neither will God pardon them; at this relation others trembling, *Stigand* the Simonious Archbishop, whom *Edward* much to blame had suffered many years to sit Primate in the Church, is said to have laugh't, as at the feavourish Dream of a doteing old man; but the event prov'd it true. . . .

Coming to *London* with all his Army, he [William the Conqueror] was on *Christmass* day sollemly Crown'd in the great Church at *Westminster,* by *Aldred* Archbishop of *York,* having first giv'n his Oath at the Altar in presence of all the people, to defend the Church, well govern the people, maintain right Law; prohibit rapine and unjust judgment. Thus the English, while they agreed not about the choice of thir native King, were constrein'd to take the Yoke of an out-landish Conquerer. With what minds and by what course of life they had fitted themselves for this servitude, *William* of *Malmsbury* spares not to lay op'n. Not a few years before the Normans came, the Clergy, though in *Edward* the Confessors daies, had lost all good literature and

Religion, scarse able to read and understand thir Latin Service: he was a miracle to others who knew his Grammar. The Monks went clad in fine stuffs, and made no difference what they eat; which though in it self no fault, yet to their Consciences was irreligious. The great men giv'n to gluttony and dissolute life, made a prey of the common people, abuseing thir Daughters whom they had in service, then turning them off to the Stews, the meaner sort tipling together night and day, spent all they had in Drunk'ness, attended with other Vices which effeminate mens minds. Whence it came to pass, that carried on with fury and rashness more then any true fortitude or skill of War, they gave to *William* thir Conquerour so easie a Conquest. Not but that some few of all sorts were much better among them; but such was the generality. *And as the long suffering of God permits bad men to enjoy properous daies with the good, so his severity oft times exempts not good men from thir share in evil times with the bad.*

If these were the Causes of such misery and thraldom to those our Ancestors, with what better close can be concluded, then here in fit season to remember this Age in the midst of her security, to fear from like Vices without amendment the Revolution of like Calamities.

FINIS.

The Digression in Miltons History of England.

[*C. M.* p. 317.]

To come in Lib. 3. *C. M.* page 114. after these words.

[from one misery to another.]

BUT because the gaining or loosing of libertie is the greatest change to better or to worse that may befall a nation under civil government, and so discovers, as nothing more, what degree of understanding, or capacitie, what disposition to justice and civilitie there is among them, I suppose it will bee many wayes profitable to resume a while the whole discourse of what happn'd in this Iland soone after the Romans goeing out: and to consider what might bee the reason, why, seeing other nations both antient and modern with extreame hazard & danger have strove for libertie as a thing invaluable, & by the purchase thereof have soo enobl'd thir spirits, as from obscure and small to grow eminent and glorious commonwealths, why the Britans having such a smooth occasion giv'n them to free themselves as ages have not afforded, such a manumission as never subjects had a fairer, should let it pass through them as a cordial medcin through a dying man without the least effect of sence or natural vigor. And no less to purpose if not more usefully to us it may withal bee enquir'd, since god after 12 ages and more had drawne so neare a parallel betweene their state and ours in the late commotions, why they who had the chiefe mannagement ther-in having attain'd, though not so easilie, to a condition which had set before them civil goverment in all her formes, and giv'n them to bee masters of thir own choise, were not found able after so many years doeing and undoeing to hitt so much as into any good and laudable way that might show us hopes of a just and well amended common-wealth to come. For those our ancestors it is alledg'd, that thir youth and chiefe strength was carried over sea to serve the Empire, that the Scots and Picts and Saxons lay sore upon them without respit. And yet wee heare the Romans telling them that thir enimies were not stronger then they: when as one legion drove them twice out of the Ile at first encounter. Nor could the Brittans be so ignorant of warr whome the Romans had then newly instructed; or if they were to seeke, alike were thir enimies, rude and naked barbarians. But that they were so timorous and without heart, as Gildas reportes them, is no way credible; for the same hee reportes of those whom the Romans testifie to have found valiant. Wherof those alsoe gave not the least prooff, when a few of them, and these in thir greatest weakness takeing courage, not defended themselves onely against the Scots and Picts, but repuls'd them well beaten home. Of these who sway'd most in the late troubles, few words as to this point may suffice. They had armies, leaders and successes to thir wish;

but to make use of so great advantages was not thir skill. To other causes therefore and not to want of force, or warlike manhood in the Brittans, both those and these lately, wee must impute the ill husbanding of those faire opportunities, which might seeme to have put libertie, so long desir'd, like a bird into thir hands. Of which other causes equally belonging both to ruler, priest, and people above hath bin related: which as they brought those antient natives to miserie and ruin by libertie which rightly us'd might have made them happie, so brought they these of late after many labours, much blood-shed, & vast expence, to ridiculous frustration, in whom the like deffects, the like miscarriages notoriouslie appear'd, with vices not less hatefull or inexcusable; nor less inforcing, whosoever shall write thir storie, to revive those antient complaints of Gildas as deservedly on these lately as on those his times. For a parlament being call'd, and as was thought many things to redress, the people with great courage & expectation to be now eas'd of what discontented them chese to thir behoof in parlament such as they thought best affected to the public good, & some indeed men of wisdome and integritie. The rest, and to be sure the greatest part, whom wealth and ample possessions or bold and active ambition rather then merit had commended to the same place, when once the superficial zeale and popular fumes that acted thir new magistracie were cool'd and spent in them, straite every one betooke himself, setting the common-wealth behinde and his private ends before, to doe as his owne profit or ambition led him. Then was justice delai'd & soone after deny'd, spite and favour determin'd all: hence faction, then treacherie both at home & in the field, ev'ry where wrong & oppression, foule and dishonest things commited daylie, or maintain'd in secret or in op'n. Some who had bin call'd from shops & warehouses without other merit to sit in supreme councels & committies, as thir breeding was, fell to hucster the common-wealth; others did thereafter as men could sooth and humour them best: so that hee onely who could give most, or under covert of hypocritical zeal insinuate basest enjoy'd unworthylie the rewards of

learning & fidelitie, or escap'd the punishment of his crimes and misdeeds. Thir votes
and ordinances which men look'd should
have contain'd the repealing of bad laws &
the immediate constitution of better, resounded with nothing els but new impositions, taxes, excises, yearlie, monthlie,
weeklie, not to reck'n the offices, gifts, and
preferments bestow'd and shar'd among
themselves. They in the meane while who
were ever faithfullest to thir cause, and
freely aided them in person, or with thir
substance when they durst not compel either,
slighted soone after and quite bereav'd of
thir just debts by greedy sequestration, were
toss'd up and downe after miserable attendance from one committie to another with
petitions in thir hands, yet either miss'd the
obtaining of thir suit, or if it were at length
granted by thir orders, meere shame & reason oft times extorting from them at least a
show of justice, yet by thir sequestrators &
subcommitties abroad, men for the most
part of insatiable hands, & noted disloyaltie,
those orders were commonlie disobey'd;
which for certaine durst not have bin, without secret complyance if not compact with
some superiours able to beare them out.
Thus were thir friends confiscate in thir
enimies, while they forfeted thir debtors to
the state as they call'd it, but indeed to the
ravening seisure of innumerable theeves in
office, yet were withall no less burden'd in
all extraordinarie assessments and oppressions then whom they tooke to be disaffected.
Nor were wee happier creditours to the
state then to them who were sequester'd as
the states enimies; for that faith which
ought to bee kept as sacred and inviolable
as any thing holy, the public faith, after
infinite summs receiv'd & all the wealth of
the church, not better imploy'd, but swallow'd up into a private gulfe, was not ere
long asham'd to confess bankrupt. And now
besides the sweetness of briberie and other
gaine with the love of rule, thir owne guiltiness and the dreaded name of just account,
which the people had long call'd for, discover'd plainelie that there were of thir
owne number who secretly contriv'd and
fomented those troubles and combustions in
the land which openly they sate to remedy,
& would continually finde such worke, as

should keepe them from ever being brought
to the terrible stand of laying downe thir
authoritie for lack of new business, or not
drawing it out to any length of time though
upon the nesessarie ruin of a whole nation
And if the state were in this plight, religion
was not in much better: to reforme which a
certaine number of divines were call'd,
neither chosen by any rule or custome ecclesiastical, nor eminent for either piety or
knowledge above others left out; onelie as
each member of parlament in his private
fancie thought fit, so elected one by one.
The most of them were such as had preach'd
and cry'd downe with great show of zeal the
avarice & pluralities of bishops and prelates; that one cure of soules was a full im-
ployment for one spiritual pastor how able
so ever, if not a charge rather above humane
strength. Yet these conscientious men, ere
any part of the worke for which they came
together, and that on the public salarie,
wanted not impudence to the ignominie and
scandal of thir pastor-like profession & especially of thir boasted reformation, to seise
into thir hands or not unwillinglie to accept
(besides one sometimes two or more of the
best Livings) collegiat master-ships in the
universitie, rich lectures in the cittie, setting
saile to all windes that might blow gaine
into thir covetous bosomes. By which meanes
those great rebukers of nonresidence among
so many distant cures were not asham'd to
be seen so quicklie pluralists and nonresi-
dents themselves, to a feareful condemnation doubtless by thir owne mouthes. And
yet the main doctrin for which they tooke
such pay, and insisted upon with more vehemence then gospel, was but to tell us in
effect that thir doctrin was worth nothing
and the spiritual power of thir ministrie less
availeable then bodilie compulsion; perswading the magistrate to use it as a stronger
means to subdue & bring in conscience then
evangellic perswasion. But while they
taught compulsion without convincement
(which not long before they so much complain'd of as executed unchristianlie against
themselves) thir intents were cleere to be no
other then to have set up a spiritual tyrannie by a secular power to the advancing of
thir owne authoritie above the magistrate;
And well did thir disciples manifest them-

selves to be no better principl'd then thir teachers, trusted with committiships and other gainfull offices, upon their commendations for zealous &, as they stick'd not to term them, godlie men, but executing thir places more like children of the devil, unfaithfully, unjustly, unmercifully, and where not corruptly, stupidly. So that between them the teachers and these the disciples, there hath not bin a more ignominous and mortal wound to faith, to pietie, nor more cause of blaspheming giv'n to the enimies of god and of truth since the first preaching of reformation; which needed most to have begun in the forwardest reformers themselves. The people therefore looking one while on the statists, whom they beheld without constancie or firmness labouring doubtfully beneath the weight of thir own too high undertakings, busiest in pettie things, triffling in the maine, deluded & quite alienated, express'd divers wayes thir disaffection; some despising whom before they honour'd; some deserting, some inveighing, some conspireing against them. Then looking on the Church-men, most of whom they saw now to have preach't thir own bellies, rather then the gospel, many illiterate, persecutors more then lovers of the truth, covetous, worldlie, to whom not godliness with contentment seem'd great gaine, but godliness with gaine seem'd great contentment, like in many things whereof they had accus'd thir predecessors. Looking on all these the people, who had bin kept warme a while by the affected zele of thir pulpits, after a false heat became more cold & obdurate then before; som turning to leudness, som to flat atheisme, put beside thir old religion, & scandalis'd in what they expected should be new. Thus they who but of late were extoll'd as great deliverers, and had a people wholy at thir devotion, by so discharging thir trust as wee see, did not onely weak'n and unfitt themselves to be dispencers of what libertie they pretended, but unfitted also the people, now growne worse & more disordinate, to receave or to digest any libertie at all. For stories teach us that libertie sought out of season in a corrupt and degenerate age brought Rome it self into further slaverie. For libertie hath a sharp and double edge fitt onelie to be handl'd by just and vertuous men, to bad and dissolute it becomes a mischief unwieldie in thir own hands. Neither is it compleatlie giv'n, but by them who have the happie skill to know what is grievance and unjust to a people; and how to remove it wiselie; that good men may enjoy the freedom which they merit and the bad the curb which they need. But to doe this and to know these exquisit proportions, the heroic wisdom which is requir'd surmounted far the principles of narrow politicians: what wonder then if they sunke as those unfortunate Britans before them, entangl'd and oppress'd with things too hard and generous above thir straine and temper. For Britain (to speake a truth not oft spok'n) as it is a land fruitful enough of men stout and couragious in warr, so is it naturallie not over fertil of men able to govern justlie & prudently in peace; trusting onelie on thir Motherwitt, as most doo, & consider not that civilitie, prudence, love of the public more then of money or vaine honour are to this soile in a manner outlandish; grow not here but in minds well implanted with solid & elaborate breeding; too impolitic els and too crude, if not headstrong and intractable to the industrie and vertue either of executing or understanding true civil government. Valiant indeed and prosperous to winn a field but to know the end and reason of winning, unjudicious and unwise, in good or bad success alike unteachable. For the sunn, which wee want, ripens witts as well as fruits; and as wine and oyle are imported to us from abroad, so must ripe understanding and many civil vertues bee imported into our minds from forren writings & examples of best ages: wee shall else miscarry still and com short in the attempt of any great enterprise. Hence did thir victories prove as fruitless as thir losses dangerous, and left them still conquering under the same grievances that men suffer conquer'd, which was indeed unlikely to goe otherwise, unless men more then vulgar, bred up, as few of them were, in the knowledge of Antient and illustrious deeds, invincible against money, and vaine titles, impartial to friendships and relations had conducted thir affaires. But then from the chapman to the retaler many, whose ignorance was more audacious then the rest, were admitted with all thir sordid rudiments to beare no mean sway among them both in church and state. From the confluence of all these errors, mischiefs, & misdemeanors, what in the eyes of man could be expected but what befel those antient inhabitants whom they so much resembl'd, confusion in the end. But on these things and this parallel having anough insisted, I returne back to the storie which gave matter to this digression.

LETTERS OF STATE CONCERNING THE PIEDMONTESE.

[The translation of these selected Letters of State is that of Phillips, 1694.]

OLIVER, *the Protector, &c., to the most Serene Prince*, IMMANUEL *Duke of* SAVOY, *Prince of Piedmont, Greeting.*

Most Serene Prince,

LETTERS have been sent us from Geneva, as also from the Dauphinate, and many other places bordering upon your territories, wherein we are given to understand, that such of your royal highness's subjects as profess the reformed religion, are commanded by your edict, and by your authority, within three days after the promulgation of your edict, to depart their native seats and habitations, upon pain of capital punishment, and forfeiture of all their fortunes and estates, unless they will give security to relinquish their religion within twenty days, and embrace the Roman catholic faith. And that when they applied themselves to your royal highness in a most suppliant manner, imploring a revocation of the said edict, and that, being received into pristine favor, they might be restored to the liberty granted them by your predecessors, a part of your army fell upon them, most cruelly slew several, put others in chains, and compelled the rest to fly into desert places, and to the mountains covered with snow, where some hundreds of families are reduced to such distress, that it is greatly to be feared, they will in a short time all miserably perish through cold and hunger. These things, when they were related to us, we could not choose but be touched with extreme grief and compassion for the sufferings and calamities of this afflicted people. Now in regard we must acknowledge ourselves linked together not only by the same tie of humanity, but by joint communion of the same religion, we thought it impossible for us to satisfy our duty to God, to brotherly charity, or our profession of the same religion, if we should only be affected with a bare sorrow for the misery and calamity of our brethren, and not contribute all our endeavors to relieve and succor them in their unexpected adversity, as much as in us lies. Therefore in a greater measure we most earnestly beseech and conjure your royal highness, that you would call back to your thoughts the moderation of your most serene predecessors, and the liberty by them granted and confirmed from time to time to their subjects the Vaudois. In granting and confirming which, as they did that which without all question was most grateful to God, who has been pleased to reserve the jurisdiction and power over the conscience to himself alone, so there is no doubt, but that they had a due consideration of their subjects also, whom they found stout and most faithful in war, and always obedient in peace. And as your royal serenity in other things most laudably follows the footsteps of your immortal ancestors, so we again and again beseech your royal highness not to swerve from the path wherein they trod in this particular; but that you would vouchsafe to abrogate both this edict, and whatsoever else may be decreed to the disturbance of your subjects upon the account of the reformed religion; that you would ratify to them their conceded privileges and pristine liberty, and command their losses to be repaired, and that an end be put to their oppressions. Which if your royal highness shall be pleased to see performed, you will do a thing most acceptable to God, revive and comfort the miserable in dire calamity, and most highly oblige all your neighbors, that profess the reformed religion, but more especially ourselves, who shall be bound to look upon your clemency and benignity toward your subjects as the fruit of our earnest solicitation. Which will both engage us to a reciprocal return to all good offices, and lay the solid foundations not only of establishing, but increasing, alliance and friendship between this republic and your dominions. . . .

Whitehall, May—, 1655.

OLIVER, *Protector of the Republic of* ENGLAND, *to the most Serene Prince of* TRANSYLVANIA, *Greeting.*

Most Serene Prince,

By your letters of the 16th of November, sixteen hundred and fifty-four, you have made us sensible of your singular goodwill and affection towards us; and your envoy, who delivered those letters to us, more amply declared your desire of contracting alliance and friendship with us. Certainly for our parts we do not a little rejoice at this opportunity offered us, to declare and make manifest our affection to your highness, and how great a value we justly set upon your person. But after fame had reported to us your egregious merits and labors undertaken in behalf of the Christian republic, when you were pleased that all these things, and what you have further in your thoughts to do in the defence and for promoting the Christian interest, should be in friendly manner imparted to us by letters from yourself, this afforded us a more plentiful occasion of joy and satisfaction, to hear that God, in those remoter regions, had raised up to himself so potent and renowned a minister of his glory and providence: and that this great minister of heaven, so famed for his courage and success, should be desirous to associate with us in the common defence of the protestant religion, at this time wickedly assailed by words and deeds. Nor is it to be questioned but that God, who has infused into us both, though separated by such a spacious interval of many climates, the same desires and thoughts of defending the orthodox religion, will be our instructor and author of the ways and means whereby we may be assistant and useful to ourselves and the rest of the reformed cities; provided we watch all opportunities, that God shall put into our hands, and be not wanting to lay hold of them. In the mean time we cannot without an extreme and penetrating sorrow forbear putting your highness in mind how unmercifully the Duke of Savoy has persecuted his own subjects, professing the orthodox faith in certain valleys, at the feet of the Alps: whom he has not only constrained by a most severe edict, as many as refuse to embrace the catholic religion, to forsake their native habitations, goods, and estates, but has fallen upon them with his army, put several most cruelly to the sword, others more barbarously tormented to death, and driven the greatest number to the mountains, there to be consumed with cold and hunger, exposing their houses to the fury and their goods to the plunder of his executioners. These things, as they have already been related to your highness, so we readily assure ourselves that so much cruelty cannot but be grievously displeasing to your ears, and that you will not be wanting to afford your aid and succor to those miserable wretches, if there be any that survive so many slaughters and calamities. For our parts, we have written to the duke of Savoy, beseeching him to remove his incensed anger from his subjects; as also to the king of France, that he would vouchsafe to do the same; and, lastly, to the princes of the reformed religion, to the end they might understand our sentiments concerning so fell and savage a piece of cruelty. Which, though first begun upon those poor and helpless people, however, threatens all that profess the same religion, and therefore imposes upon all a greater necessity of providing for themselves in general, and consulting the common safety; which is the course that we shall always follow, as God shall be pleased to direct us. Of which your highness may be assured, as also of our sincerity and affection to your serenity, whereby we are engaged to wish all prosperous success to your affairs, and a happy issue of all your enterprises and endeavors, in asserting the liberty of the gospel, and the worshippers of it.

Whitehall, May—, 1655.

OLIVER, *Protector, to the most Serene Prince,* CHARLES GUSTAVUS ADOLPHUS, *King of* SWEDES, *Greeting.*

WE make no question but that the fame of that most rigid edict has reached your dominions, whereby the duke of Savoy has totally ruined his protestant subjects inhabiting the Alpine valleys, and commanded them to be exterminated from their native seats and habitations, unless they will give security to renounce their religion received from their forefathers, in exchange for the Roman catholic superstition, and that within twenty days at furthest: so that many being killed, the rest stripped to their skins, and exposed to most certain destruction, are now forced to wander over desert mountains, and through perpetual winter, together with their wives and children, half dead with cold and hunger: and that your majesty has laid it to heart, with a pious sorrow and compassionate consideration, we as little doubt. For that the protestant name and cause, although they differ among themselves in some things of little consequence, is nevertheless the same in general, and united in one common interest, the hatred of our adversaries, alike incensed against protestants, very easily demonstrates. Now there is nobody can be ignorant that the kings of the Swedes have always joined with the reformed, carrying their victorious arms into Germany in defence of the protestants without distinction. Therefore we make it our chief request, and that in a more especial manner to your majesty, that you would solicit the duke of Savoy by letters; and, by interposing your intermediating authority, endeavor to avert the horrid cruelty of this edict, if possible, from people no less innocent than religious. For we think it superfluous to admonish your majesty whither these rigorous beginnings tend, and what they threaten to all the protestants in general. But if he rather choose to listen to his anger, than to our joint entreaties and intercessions; if there be any tie, any charity or communion of religion to be believed and worshipped, upon consultations duly first communicated to your majesty, and the chief of the protestant princes, some other course is to be speedily taken, that such a numerous multitude of our innocent brethren may not miserably perish for want of succor and assistance. Which, in regard we make no question but that it is your majesty's opinion and determination, there can be nothing in our opinion more prudently resolved, than to join our reputation, authority, counsels, forces, and whatever else is needful, with all the speed that may be, in pursuance of so pious a design. In the mean time, we beseech Almighty God to bless your majesty.

OLIVER, *Protector, &c., to the High and Mighty Lords, the States of the* UNITED PROVINCES.

WE make no question but that you have already been informed of the duke of Savoy's edict, set forth against his subjects inhabiting the valley at the feet of the Alps, ancient professors of the orthodox faith; by which edict they are commanded to abandon their native habitations, stripped of all their fortunes, unless within twenty days they embrace the Roman faith; and with what cruelty the authority of this edict has raged against a needy and harmless people, many being slain by the soldiers, the rest plundered and driven from their houses, together with their wives and children, to combat cold and hunger among desert mountains, and perpetual snow. These things with what commotion of mind you heard related, what a fellow-feeling of the calamities of brethren pierced your breasts, we readily conjectured from the depth of our own sorrow, which certainly is most heavy and afflictive. For being engaged together by the same tie of religion, no wonder we should be so deeply moved with the same affections upon the dreadful and undeserved sufferings of our brethren. Besides, that your conspicuous piety and charity toward the orthodox, wherever overborne and oppressed, has been frequently experienced in the most urging straits and calamities of the churches. For my own part, unless my thoughts deceive me, there is nothing wherein I should desire more willingly to be overcome, than in goodwill and charity toward brethren of the same religion, afflicted and wronged in their quiet enjoyments; as being one that would be accounted always ready to prefer the peace and safety of the churches before my particular interests. So far, therefore, as hitherto lay in our power, we have written to the duke of Savoy, even almost to supplication, beseeching him that he would admit into his breast more placid thoughts and kinder effects of his favor towards his most innocent subjects and suppliants; that he would restore the miserable to their habitations and estates, and grant them their pristine freedom in the exercise of their religion. Moreover, we wrote to the chiefest princes and magistrates of the protestants, whom we thought most nearly concerned in these matters, that they would lend us their assistance to entreat and pacify the duke of Savoy in their behalf. And we make no doubt now but you have done the same, and perhaps much more. For this so dangerous a precedent, and lately renewed severity of utmost cruelty toward the reformed, if the authors of it meet with prosperous success, to what apparent dangers it reduces our religion, we need not admonish your prudence. On the other side, if the duke shall once but permit himself to be atoned and won by our united applications, not only our afflicted brethren, but we ourselves shall reap the noble and abounding harvest and reward of this laborious undertaking. But if he still persist in the same obstinate resolutions of reducing to utmost extremity those people, (among whom our religion was either disseminated by the first doctors of the gospel, and preserved from the defilement of superstition, or else restored to its pristine sincerity long before other nations obtained that felicity,) and determines their utter extirpation and destruction; we are ready to take such other course and counsels with yourselves, in common with the rest of our reformed friends and confederates, as may be most necessary for the preservation of just and good men, upon the brink of inevitable ruin; and to make the duke himself sensible that we can no longer neglect the heavy oppressions and calamities of our orthodox brethren. Farewell.

To the Evangelic Cities of SWITZERLAND.

WE make no question but the late calamity of the Piedmontese, professing our religion, reached your ears before the unwelcome news of it arrived with us: who being a people under the protection and jurisdiction of the duke of Savoy, and by a severe edict of their prince commanded to depart their native habitations, unless within three days they gave security to embrace the Roman religion, soon after were assailed by armed violence, that turned their dwellings into slaughterhouses, while others, without number, were terrified into banishment, where now naked and afflicted, without

house or home, or any covering from the weather, and ready to perish through hunger and cold, they miserably wander through desert mountains, and depths of snow, together with their wives and children. And far less reason have we to doubt but that so soon as they came to your knowledge, you laid these things to heart, with a compassion no less sensible of their multiplied miseries than ourselves; the more deeply imprinted perhaps in your minds, as being next neighbors to the sufferers. Besides that, we have abundant proof of your singular love and affection for the orthodox faith, of your constancy in retaining it, and your fortitude in defending it. Seeing then, by the most strict communion of religion, that you, together with ourselves, are all brethren alike, or rather one body with those unfortunate people, of which no member can be afflicted without the feeling, without pain, without the detriment and hazard of the rest; we thought it convenient to write to your lordships concerning this matter, and let you understand how much we believe it to be the general interest of us all, as much as in us lies, with our common aid and succor to relieve our exterminated and indigent brethren; and not only to take care for removing their miseries and afflictions, but also to provide that the mischief spread no further, nor encroach upon ourselves in general, encouraged by example and success. We have written letters to the duke of Savoy, wherein we have most earnestly besought him, out of his wonted clemency, to deal more gently and mildly with his most faithful subjects, and to restore them, almost ruined as they are, to their goods and habitations. And we are in hopes that, by these our entreaties, or rather by the united intercessions of us all, the most serene prince at length will be atoned, and grant what we have requested with so much importunity. But if his mind be obstinately bent to other determinations, we are ready to communicate our consultations with yours, by what most prevalent means to relieve and re-establish most innocent men, and our most dearly beloved brethren in Christ, tormented and overlaid with so many wrongs and oppressions, and preserve them from inevitable and undeserved ruin. Of whose welfare and safety, as I am assured that you, according to your wonted piety, are most cordially tender; so, for our own parts, we cannot but in our opinion prefer their preservation before our most important interests, even the safeguard of our own life. Farewell.

O. P.

Westminster, May 19th, 1655.

Superscribed, To the most Illustrious and [10] Potent Lords, the Consuls and Senators of the Protestant Cantons and Confederate Cities of Switzerland, Greeting.

To the most Serene and Potent Prince, Lewis, *King of* France.

Most Serene and Potent King,

By your majesty's letters, which you wrote in answer to ours of the twenty-fifth of May, [20] we readily understand that we failed not in our judgment, that the inhuman slaughter and barbarous massacres of those men, who profess the reformed religion in Savoy, perpetrated by some of your regiments, were the effects neither of your orders nor commands. And it afforded us a singular occasion of joy to hear that your majesty had so timely signified to your colonels and officers, whose violent precipitancy engaged them in those inhu- [30] man butcheries, without the encouragement of lawful allowance, how displeasing they were to your majesty; that you had admonished the duke himself to forbear such acts of cruelty; and that you had interposed with so much fidelity and humanity all the high veneration paid you in that court, your near alliance and authority, for restoring to their ancient abodes those unfortunate exiles. And it was our hopes that that prince would in some measure have [40] condescended to the good pleasure and intercessions of your majesty. But finding not anything obtained, either by your own, nor the entreaties and importunities of other princes in the cause of the distressed, we deemed it not foreign from our duty to send this noble person, under the character of our extraordinary envoy, to the duke of Savoy, more amply and fully to lay before him how deeply sensible we are of such exasperated cruelties, in- [50] flicted upon the professors of the same religion with ourselves, and all this too out of a hatred

of the same worship. And we have reason to hope a success of this negotiation so much the more prosperous, if your majesty would vouchsafe to employ your authority and assistance once again with so much the more urgent importunity; and as you have undertaken for those indigent people, that they will be faithful and obedient to their prince, so you would be graciously pleased to take care of their welfare and safety, that no further oppressions of this nature, no more such dismal calamities, may be the portion of the innocent and peaceful. This being truly royal and just in itself, and highly agreeable to your benignity and clemency, which everywhere protects in soft security so many of your subjects professing the same religion, we cannot but expect, as it behooves us, from your majesty. Which act of yours, as it will more closely [20] bind to your subjection all the protestants throughout your spacious dominions, whose affection and fidelity to your predecessors and yourself in most important distresses have been often conspicuously made known: so will it fully convince all foreign princes that the advice or intention of your majesty were no way contributory to this prodigious violence, whatever inflamed your ministers and officers to promote it. More especially if your majesty [30] shall inflict deserved punishment upon those captains and ministers who, of their own authority, and to gratify their own wills, adventured the perpetrating such dreadful acts of inhumanity. In the meanwhile, since your majesty has assured us of your justly-merited aversion to these most inhuman and cruel proceedings, we doubt not but you will afford a secure sanctuary and shelter within your kingdom to all those miserable exiles that shall [40] fly to your majesty for protection; and that you will not give permission to any of your subjects to assist the duke of Savoy to their prejudice. It remains that we make known to your majesty, how highly we esteem and value your friendship: in testimony of which, we further affirm, there shall never be wanting upon all occasions the real assurances and effects of our protestation.

Your majesty's most affectionate,

Oliver, Protector of the Commonwealth of England, &c.

Whitehall, July 29, 1655.

To the most Eminent Lord Cardinal
MAZARINE.

Most Eminent Lord Cardinal,

HAVING deemed it necessary to send this noble person to the king with letters, a copy of which is here enclosed, we gave him also further in charge to salute your excellency in our name, as having entrusted to his fidelity certain other matters to be communicated to your eminency. In reference to which affairs, I entreat your eminency to give him entire credit, as being a person in whom I have reposed a more than ordinary confidence.

Your eminency's most affectionate,
OLIVER, Protector of the Commonwealth of England.
Whitehall, July 29, 1655.

OLIVER, *Protector of the Commonwealth of* ENGLAND, *to the most Serene Prince,* FREDERIC III., *King of* DENMARK, NORWAY, &c.

WITH what a severe and unmerciful edict Immanuel, duke of Savoy, has expelled from their native seats his subjects inhabiting the valleys of Piedmont, men otherwise harmless, only for many years remarkably famous for embracing the purity of religion; and after a dreadful slaughter of some numbers, how he has exposed the rest to the hardships of those desert mountains, stripped to their skins, and barred from all relief, we believe your majesty has long since heard, and doubt not but your majesty is touched with a real commiseration of their sufferings, as becomes so puissant a defender and prince of the reformed faith: for indeed the institutions of Christian religion require, that whatever mischiefs and miseries any part of us undergo, it should behoove us all to be deeply sensible of the same: nor does any man better than your majesty foresee, if we may be thought able to give a right conjecture of your piety and prudence, what dangers the success and example of this fact portend to ourselves in particular, and to the whole protestant name in general. We have written the more willingly to yourself, to the end we might assure your majesty, that the same sorrow, which we hope you have conceived for the calamity of our most innocent brethren, the same opinion, the same judg-

ment you have of the whole matter, is plainly and sincerely our own. We have therefore sent our letters to the duke of Savoy, wherein we have most importunately besought him, to spare those miserable people, that implore his mercy, and that he would no longer suffer that dreadful edict to be in force: which if your majesty and the rest of the reformed princes would vouchsafe to do, as we are apt to believe they have already done, there is some hope that the anger of the most serene duke may be assuaged, and that his indignation will relent upon the intercession and importunities of his neighbor princes. Or if he persist in his determinations, we protest ourselves ready, together with your majesty, and the rest of our confederates of the reformed religion, to take such speedy methods, as may enable us, as far as in us lies, to relieve the distresses of so many miserable creatures, and provide for their liberty and safety. In the mean time we beseech Almighty God to bless your majesty with all prosperity.
Whithall, May —, 1655.

OLIVER, *Protector of the Commonwealth of* ENGLAND, &c. *to the most Noble the Consuls and Senators of the City of* GENEVA.

WE had before made known to your lordships our excessive sorrow for the heavy and unheard-of calamities of the protestants, inhabiting the valleys of Piedmont, whom the duke of Savoy persecutes with so much cruelty; but that we made it our business, that you should at the same time understand, that we are not only affected with the multitude of their sufferings, but are using the utmost of our endeavors to relieve them and comfort them in their distresses. To that purpose we have taken care for a gathering of alms to be made throughout this whole republic; which upon good grounds we expect will be such, as will demonstrate the affection of this nation toward their brethren, laboring under the burden of such horrid inhumanities; and that as the communion of religion is the same between both people, so the sense of their calamities is no less the same. In the mean time, while the collections of the money go forward, which in regard they will require some time to accomplish, and for that the wants and necessities of those deplorable people will admit of no delay, we thought it requisite to remit beforehand two thousand pounds of the value of England, with all possible speed, to be distributed among such as shall be judged to be most in present need of comfort and succor. Now in regard we are not ignorant how deeply the miseries and wrongs of those most innocent people have affected yourselves, and that you will not think amiss of any labor or pains where you can be assisting to their relief, we made no scruple to commit the paying and distributing this sum of money to your care; and to give ye this further trouble, that according to your wonted piety and prudence, you would take care, that the said money may be distributed equally to the most necessitous, to the end that though the sum be small, yet there may be something to refresh and revive the most poor and needy till we can afford them a more plentiful supply. And thus not making any doubt but you will take in good part the trouble imposed upon ye, we beseech Almighty God to stir up the hearts of all his people professing the orthodox religion, to resolve upon the common defence of themselves, and the mutual assistance of each other against their imbittered and most implacable enemies; in the prosecution of which, we should rejoice that our helping hand might be any way serviceable to the church. Farewell.

Fifteen hundred pounds of the foresaid two thousand will be remitted by Gerard Hench from Paris, and the other five hundred pounds will be taken care of by letters from the lord Stoup.

June 8, 1655.

TEXTUAL NOTES

The text in the present edition is that of the earliest editions, except when noted. Milton's shorter poems were first published in a volume in 1645; a second edition appeared in 1673. *Comus* was first published in 1637, with a preface, by Henry Lawes. *Paradise Lost* was published in 1667; but in the following years there were various issues of the first edition with varying title-pages, and with new front matter. The second edition was published in 1674. *Paradise Regained* and *Samson Agonistes* appeared in one volume in 1671. There are extant two manuscripts, referred to in the following notes. In the Library of Trinity College, Cambridge, is a manuscript, chiefly in Milton's hand, of many of the shorter poems. A few of the more significant readings from this manuscript have been given; where the word in the manuscript has been deleted, it may be assumed that the word in the present text has been written in by Milton. In the J. Pierpont Morgan Library is a manuscript of Book I of *Paradise Lost;* a few readings from this manuscript have also been given. References to additional texts will be readily understood. For a complete study of the variant readings of all manuscripts and editions, the student should consult the forthcoming Columbia University edition of the *Complete Works of John Milton,* Vols. I and II. The punctuation of the present text is that of the earlier editions. In the following notes the word before the bracket is from the text in the present volume.

The Stationer to the Reader] 1673 omits

On the Morning of Christ's Nativity 143–4 From 1673; 1645 has

Th' enameled Arras of the Rainbow wearing, And Mercy set between,

Psalm 136 10, 13, 17, 21, 25 who] from 1673; 1645 that

The Passion 22 latter] 1673 latest

On Time MS has a deleted sub-title: to be set on a clock case

At a Solemn Musick MS has two rough drafts and a fair copy, all in Milton's hand. 6 concent] 1673; MS in all three copies reads concent; 1645 content.

On Shakespear First printed in the *Second Folio Shakespeare* 1632; later *Shakespeare's Poems,* 1640 and in the *Third Folio Shakespeare,* 1663–64.
Title] 1632, 1640 and 1663 have An Epitaph on the admirable Dramaticke Poet, W. Shakespeare.
1 needs] 1632, 1640, 1663 neede
4 Star-ypointing] One issue of 1632 has starre-

ypointed, but the other issues, 1640, and 1663 have starre-ypointing
6 weak] 1632 dull 1640 weak 1663 dull
8 live-long] 1632, 1663 lasting
10 heart] 1632, 1663 part
13 her] 1632, 1663 her 1640 our

L'Allegro 104 And by the] From 1673; 1645 And he by

Sonnet VII The text occurs first in a letter to a friend in the MS.

Sonnet VIII MS gives a title in the hand of an amanuensis: On his dore when ye city expected an assault. Milton himself deleted this and wrote: When the assault was intended to ye city. In the margin is 1642, deleted. 3 from 1673; 1645 If ever deed of honour did thee please.

Sonnet X MS gives a deleted title: To the Lady Margaret Ley.

Sonnet XI In MS Sonnets XI and XII were written in reverse order.

Sonnet XII MS gives a deleted title: On the detraction which follow'd upon my writing certain treatises

Sonnet XIII First printed in 1648 in *Choice Psalms put into Musick for three voices: composed by Henry and William Lawes, Brothers and Servants to his Majestie.* MS has a rough draft and two fair copies. MS has the title: **To my freind Mr. Hen. Laws Feb 9. 1645 4 committing**] MS committing, deleted, then restored; in the margin, misjoyning. **9 lend**] 1648, and all three MSS. have lend, 1673 send. **11 story**] 1648 has story * with the note in the margin: **The story of Ariadne set by him in Music.**

Sonnet XIV MS gives a deleted title: **On the Religious Memorie of Mrs. Catharine Thomason my christian freind deceased Decem. 1646**

Sonnet XVII First printed in *The Life and Death of Sir Henry Vane, Kt.* by G. Sikes, where it is said that the sonnet was "composed by a learned Gentleman, and sent him, *July* 3, 1652." **10–11** MS had first:

**What powre the Church and what the civill meanes
Thou teachest best, which few have ever don**

Sonnet XXII The title is from the Phillips text, 1694. MS has no title.

On the New Forcers of Conscience **12 shallow**] MS **hare braind**, deleted **17** MS had first: **Cropp yee as close as Marginall P——s eares**

Lycidas The texts of Lycidas are (1) The Cambridge MS; (2) the King Memorial volume, 1638; (3) a presentation copy of 1638, corrected by Milton, in Cambridge University Library; (4) the edition of 1645; (5) the edition of 1673.
Title.] 1638 has no description under the title. MS has only: In this . . . 1637. Above is written, but deleted: Novem. 1637. **5** MS **and crop your young**, deleted
10 he knew] 1638, 1645, 1673. But Camb MS has **he well knew**; Milton also corrected the line to read **well** in the presentation copy of 1638, which is now in Camb. Univ. Lib. Milton undoubtedly meant the line to read **he well knew**, but perhaps the printer's consistent blunders finally reconciled him to the omission. The editor, though convinced himself that Milton wanted **well** inserted, has not cared, even on such good authority, to alter a line that is familiar to every reader of poetry. Cf. also the note on l. 64
26 opening] MS **glimmering**, deleted
30 MS and 1638 have **Oft till the e'vn-starre bright** MS then changed to **Oft till the starre that rose in Evning bright** Milton's final change of **in** to **at** is not in MS but in 1645 and 1673. **31 westering**] 1638 and MS. **burnisht;** deleted **47 wardrop**] MS **buttons**, deleted; 1638 wardrobe **58–63** Milton first wrote:

**What could the golden haryd Calliope
for her inchaunting son
when shee beheld (the gods farre sighted bee)
his goarie scalpe rowle downe the Thracian lee**

Not satisfied with this, he deleted ll. 1, 3, and 4; and revised:

**for her inchaunting son
whome universal nature might lament
and heaven and hel deplore
whenn his divine head downe the stream was sent
downe the swift Hebrus to the Lesbian shore.**

He then revised again, as in the present text. **64 uncessant**] MS incessant. This does not necessarily indicate that the printer blundered, but rather that Milton probably made the change himself in the proofs of 1645. Cf. the changes in 1.30
69 Or with] 1638 **Hid** in MS **Hid in** deleted
85 honour'd] MS **smooth** deleted
86 smooth] MS **soft** deleted
105 inwrought] MS **scrawl'd ore**
129 nothing] 1638 little. MS nothing, deleted. In the margin, little. Cf. ll. 30, 64
138 sparely] MS **faintly**, deleted
142–150 In MS written not in the body of the poem, but on a different page in two drafts. Draft 1 reads

**Bring the rathe primrose that unwedded dies
colouring the pale cheeke of uninjoyd love
and that sad floure that strove
to write his owne woes on the vermeil graine
next adde Narcissus that still weeps in vaine
the woodbine and ye pansie freak't with jet
the glowing violet
the cowslip wan that hangs his pensive head
and every bud that sorrows liverie weares
let Daffadillies fill thire cups with teares
bid Amaranthus all his beauty shed
to strew the laureat herse &c.**

Draft 2 is much the same as in the text.
157 whelming] 1638 **humming;** MS humming, deleted
160 Bellerus] MS **Corineus**, deleted

Comus The Letter to the Viscount Brackley and the letter by Sir Henry Wotton are omitted in 1673.

5 dim] MS dim, narrow. The last word is deleted

14 ope's] MS shews deleted

97 Atlantick] MS Tartessian deleted

155 blear] MS slight deleted; blind, deleted

164 snares] MS nets deleted

167–168 From 1673; 1645 has

Whom thrift keeps up about his Country gear,
But here she comes, I fairly step aside,
And hearken, if I may, her business here.

The change, involving the omission of one line and the transposition of the last two, must be Milton's. This is further proved by the insertion in the Errata of 1673 of directions to omit the comma after may (l. 168) and to read hear instead of here (l. 168)

207 that syllable mens names] MS that lure night wandering, deleted

213 hovering] MS flittering, deleted

214 unblemish't] MS unspotted, deleted

242 give resounding grace] MS hold a Counterpoint, deleted

254 potent] MS potent, deleted; powerful, deleted; mighty, deleted; potent, final reading.

316 Ere morrow wake] MS ere the larke rowse, deleted

355 MS adds three lines

so fares as did forsaken Proserpine
when the big rowling flakes of pitchie clowds
and darknesse wound her in. 1 Bro. Peace brother peace

447 unconquer'd] MS æternall, deleted; unvanquisht, deleted

492 father] MS fathers

546 meditate] 1673 meditate upon

552 frighted] MS flighted

556 steam] 1673 stream

580 furder] 1673 further

636 Hermes] MS Mercury, deleted

995 Elysian] MS manna, deleted; Sabæan, deleted

Psalm LXXXI 65 he] 1673 we

Paradise Lost In Paradisum Amissam] Not in 1667; from 1674
On Paradise Lost] Not in 1667; from 1674
The Printer to the Reader] Added in 1668, changed in 1669, omitted in 1674
I have procur'd it, and . . . not] From 1669; 1668 is procured
The Verse] Added in 1668
The Arguments were added in 1668, and printed as front matter. In 1674 they were distributed before the books. In 1667 the poem was printed

in ten books, in 1674 Book VII was divided to make the present Books VII and VIII, and Book X, to make the present Books XI and XII

Book I, 110 wrath] MS wrath, with u written above in a different hand, so treated throughout the MS

504–5 From 1674; 1667 has

In Gibeah, when hospitable Dores
Yielded thir Matrons to prevent worse rape.

703 found out] From 1674; 1667 founded

709 row of] MS hunderd deleted

530 fainted] 1674 fanting

Book II, 282 Where] 1674 were

375 Original] From 1674; 1667 Originals

414 wee] 1667 has we, but the Errata directs that the reading should be wee

483 thir] 1674 her

527 his] 1674 this

542 Œchalia] From 1674; 1667 Œalia

631 toward] 1674 towards

Book V, 627 now not in 1667; from 1674

636–640 From 1674; 1667 has

They eat, they drink, and with refection sweet
Are fill'd before th' all-bounteous King, who showrd

Book VIII, 1–4 Added in 1674, when Book VII was divided at line 640 to make the present Book VIII. Line 641 in 1667 reads To whom thus Adam gratefully repli'd.

827 then] Not in 1667; from 1674

Book IX, 186 Nor] From 1674; 1667 Not

Book X, Argument take] From 1674; 1667 taste

394 Likeliest] From 1674; 1667 Likest

827 then] From 1674; not in 1667

982 misery,] From 1674; 1667 misery.

Book XI, 485–487 From 1674; not in 1667

551–552 From 1674; 1667 has

Of rendring up. Michael to him repli'd.

651 tacks] 1674 makes

870 who] From 1674; 1667 that

Book XII, Argument The Angel . . . his Incarnation] From 1674; 1668 has thence from the Flood relates, and by degrees explains, who that Seed of the Woman shall be; his Incarnation

1–5 From 1674; added when the original Book X was divided to make Book XII

238 what they besaught] From 1674; 1667 them thir desire

ADDITIONAL TEXTUAL NOTES

Psalm 136 39 Smote] 1645 mote
On the Death of a Fair Infant 3 out-lasted]
    1673 out-lasted,
25 *Eurotas'*] 1673 *Eurota's*
34 no!] 1673 no?
54 c[r]own'd] 1673 cown'd
At A Vacation Exercise 3 tripps] 1673 tripp s
    The apostrophe failed to print; but space
    is left for it, or possibly for an **e**
On Shakespear. 1630 9 to th'] 1645 toth'
On the University Carrier 2 And] 1645 A
Il Penseroso. 57 In] 1645 Id
Sonnet IX 5 with *Ruth*] 1645 the *Ruth*
Sonnet XI 1 was] 1673 was was
Sonnet XVIII 10 sow] 1673 so corrected from
    Errata
On the new Forcers 17 bauk] 1673 bank
Lycidas 63 Lesbian] 1645 Letbian
113 swain] 1645 swain.
Comus 138 dues] 1645 due 1673 dues
168 aside.] 1673 aside
327 it.] 1645 it,
347 'Twould] 1645 T'would
605 *Africa*] 1645 *Africa,*
661 *Apollo.*] 1645 *Apollo,*
828 She] 1673 The
664 With all] 1645 Withall
Psalm I 13 judgment] 1673 jugdment
Psalm II 2 Muse] 1673 muse
5 dear.] 1673 dear
12 Anointed] 1673 anointed
Psalm V 23 if] 1673 If
Psalm VIII 8 oppose.] 1673 oppose
Psalm LXXX 8 dread.] 1673 dread
Psalm LXXXI 1 *clear,*] 1673 *clear*
8 *string.*] 1673 *string*
65 he] 1673 we
Psalm LXXXII 7 *might,*] 1673 *might.*
8 *strong?*] 1673 *strong*
18 on,] 1673 on
Psalm LXXXIII 34 *Coast.*] 1673 *Coast*
42 *speed.*] 1673 *speed*
59 due,] 1673 due;
Psalm LXXXV 48 Look] 1673 look
Psalm LXXXVI 4 With] 1673 with
18 Give] 1673 give
40 *slide.*] 1673 *slide*
PAGE 111. TEXT OF LATIN POEMS
[Præfatio]

2 præclaro] 1645 ˙preclaro 1673 præclaro
PAGE 114. JOANNI MILTONI
2 terrarum] 1645 *terra/rarum*
3 apprehenderet;] 1645 *apprehenderet.*
6 intelligat;] 1645, 1673 *intelligat.*
7 corporisque] 1645, 1673 *corporisque,*
8 venustate] From 1673; 1645 *vastitate*
9 adimunt;] 1645, 1673 *adimunt.*
10 Sapientia:] From 1673; 1645 *Sapientia.*
    gloriæ:] From 1673; 1645 *gloriæ.*
11 audienti;] 1645, 1673 *audienti,*
14 Lectione] 1645, 1673 *Lectione.*
15 percurrenti] 1645, 1673 *percurrenti.*
16 1645, 1673 have neither the parenthesis nor
    semicolon.
PAGE 114. ELEGIARUM
Élegia prima 2 nuntia] 1673 nuncia
13 *molles,*] 1645 *molles*
43 è] From 1673; 1645 e
Elegia secunda 12 à] From 1673; 1645 a
    tuo,] From 1673; 1645 tuo
Elegia Tertia 3 Imago] From 1673; 1645 imago
23 cœlo] From 1673; 1645 cælo
27 potestas,] 1645, 1673 potestas;
34 Phœbus,] From 1673; 1645 Phœbus
Elegia Quarta 47 multam] 1645, 1673 multam,
53 salutem;] From 1673; 1645 salutem
76 virûm] From 1673; 1645 virum
Elegia Quinta 33 opacæ,] 1645, 1673 opacæ
106 Litus] From 1673; 1645 Littus
110 Virgineos] From 1673; 1645 Virgineas
Elegia Sexta 24 merum,] 1645, 1673 merum.
27 Jaccho] 1673 Iaccho
48 sinus] From 1673; 1645 finus
79 si quid] From 1673; 1645 siquid
84 colit,] 1645, 1673 colit.
87 illa] From 1673; 1645 illa,
Elegia Septima 1 nôram] From 1673; 1645
    noram
2 fuit] 1645, 1673 suit
21 æterno] 1645 æreno
52 placent,] 1645, 1673 placent.
106 fuit,] 1645, 1673 fuit.
112 ipsa] 1645, 1673 ipse
PAGE 129. Ad Eandem (I) 6 lyræ;] 1645,
    1673 lyræ,
8 desipuisset] From the Errata of 1673; 1645
    desipuiiset; 1673 desipulisset
PAGE 130. SYLVARUM LIBER. In Quintum

74 hæres,] 1645, 1673 **hæres**
112 soleïs] 1673 **soleïs**; the reading of 1645 is not clear; in the N. Y. Public Library copy the mark above the i is apparently only a smudge
146 videntur,] 1645, 1673 **videntur**
149, 150 Manes/Exululat] See Professor **Trent's** note in the *Columbia Milton*
218 effætique] 1645, 1673 **effœtique**
219 omnem.] 1645, 1673 **omnem**
In Obitum 44 subterraneas.] 1645, 1673 **sub-terraneas**
Naturam non pati senium 38 Raptat] 1645 **Raptat,**
Ad Patrem 13 ista,] 1645, 1673 **ista**
49 Ætneo] From 1673; 1645 **Ætnæo**
90 Dimotáque] From 1673; 1645 **Dimotàque**
Ad Salsillum 5 lectum,] From 1673; 1645 **lec-tum.**
Mansus 83 adsit] From 1673; 1645 **ad sit**
Epitaphium Damonis 151 foliúmque] From 1673; 1645 **foliûmque**
172 sperâsse] From 1673; 1645 **sperasse**
211 nôrint] 1645 **norint**
Ad Joannem Rousium 7 umbras,] 1673 **umbras**
PAGE *157.* **PARADISE LOST**

The text of *Paradise Lost* is that of the first edition, 1667, revised by readings from the second edition, 1674, as made, evidently by Milton, in that edition. The editor is convinced that the revised second edition of 1674 should be the basis for all critical editions of the poem, but when this present text was originally prepared he felt that, perhaps in spelling and punctuation only, the first edition represented more nearly what Milton wished,—an opinion that he no longer holds. It is now too late to change the text,—and the difference between the two original editions in spelling and punctuation is not material to any but the specialist. All the changes in wording of the 1674 edition have, I believe, been incorporated into the present text, or at least explained in the notes.

Book I. 263 Heav'n.] 1667 **Heav'n**
409 *Horonaim*] From 1674. 1667 had *Heronaim* which in the Errata of the issue of 1668 was changed to *Horonaim*. But the printer of the 1669 issue was not as familiar with the Bible as was Milton, so that he printed *Honoraim* in the Errata. Thus the first edition in the 1669 issue remained in error. The printer of the second edition had no apparent trouble. This is one of many instances that shows how carefully the printer of the second edition worked and of the care that Milton himself took with that edition.
710 Anon] 1667 **A non**
756 Capital] MS. **Capitall**. The second **a** appears

to have been originally written **o** and then converted into **a**. Miss Darbishire has tried to prove that **o** is the correct reading as Milton wished it, but Professor Grierson was shown that **a** is probably the correct reading. See the discussions in the January and July issues, 1933, of the *Review of English Studies.*
PAGE 195. Book III 580 Starry] 1667 **Sarry**
592 Medal] 1667, 1674 both have this reading. Metal is probably the correct reading. Cf. l. 595.
PAGE 210. Book IV 841 be sure] 1667 **besure**
PAGE 264. Book VII 110] In 1667 and 1674 this line is indented, thus making a paragraph of a single line (109).
322 add] 1674 **and**
494 repeated] 1667 **repeaed**
588 for] 1667 **(for**
PAGE 312. Book X 423 inland] 1667 **in land**
982 misery,] 1667 **misery.**
PAGE 404. SAMSON AGONISTES 1665 fold] 1671 **fold,**

The Errata pages in Milton's original editions are important and interesting, for they reveal some of the characteristics of the poet as an editor. Especially interesting are the changes in spelling and punctuation. They prove how groundless was Bentley's principle that because Milton was blind he could not attend to the correction of his proof sheets. Few poets of the century were so careful if their proof reading. Modern editions almost uniformly omit these bits of evidence, though they should be printed; the changes, of course, have long since been incorporated into the text. The page numbers refer to the original editions.

Errata of 1673

The edition of 1645 had no errata; that of 1673 is as follows. Page 21. at the end of the Elegie should have come in the Verses *at a Vacation Exercise,* which follow afterwards, from pag. 64. to p. 68, p. 56. line 8. after *is* r. *it,* ib. l. 9. for *Colikto* r. *Colkitto,* p. 59, l. 4. for *so* r. *sow,* p. 69. l. 17. for *bank* r. *bauk,* p 90. l. 9. for *Heccat'* r. *Hecat',* p. 91. l. 19. leave out the Comma after *May,* and for *here* r. *hear,* p. 128. l. 3. leave out *that.* In the second part p. 43. l. 1. for *Canentam* r. *Canentem,* ibid. l. 4 for *desipulisset* r. *desipuisset,* p. 49. l. 2. for *Adamantius* r. *Adamantinus,* ibid. l. 9. for *Notat* r. *Natat,* p. 52. l. 2. for *Relliquas* r. *Relliquias,* P. 53. l. 17, 18 a Comma after *Manes,* none after *Exululat.* Some othre Errors and mispointings the Readers judgement may correct.

PARADISE LOST

The first edition of *Paradise Lost*, in the later issues, had an Errata page; the second edition had no Errata.

Lib. I. Vers. 25 for *th' Eternal*, Read *Eternal*.
Lib. I. V. 409. for *Heronaim*, r. *Horonaim*
[1668. 1669 Errata reads *Honoraim*.]
Lib. 1. V. 758 for *and Band* r. *Band and*.
Lib. 1. V. 760 for *hundreds* r. *hunderds*.
Lib. 2. V. 414 for *we* r. *wee*.
Lib. 2. V. 881 for *great* r. *grate*.
Lib. 3. V. 760 for *with* r. *in*.
Lib. 5. V. 193 for *breath* r. *breathe*.
Lib. 5. V. 598 for *whoseop* r. *whose top*.
Lib. 5. V. 656 for *more Heaven* r. *more in Heaven*.
Lib. 6. V. 184 for *blessed* r. *blest*.
Lib. 6. V. 215 for *sounder* r. *so under*.
Lib. 10. V. 575 for *lost* r. *last*.

Other literal faults the Reader of himself may Correct.

Errata in the former Poem. [Paradise Regain'd.]

Page 4. verse 62. after being no stop, p. 13 verse 226. for destroy, . *subdue*, p. 21. v. 373. for demuring, r. *demurring*, p. 22. v. 400. for never, r. *nearer*, p. 23. v. 407. for Imports, r. *Imparts*, p. 35. v. 127. after threat'ns, insert *then*, p. 44. v. 313. for Thebes, r. *Thebez*, p. 46. v. 341. for pill'd, r. *pil'd*, p. 47. v. 371. no comma after knowledge, but after works, p. 71. v. 323. for shower, r. *showers*, p. 83. v. 102. no stop after victor.

Errata in the latter Poem. [Samson Agonistes.]

Page 16. verse 127. for Irresistable, r. *Irresistible*, p. 17. v. 158. for complain'd, r. *complain*, p. 21. v. 222. for mention'd, r. *motion'd*, p. 28. v. 355. before, such r. *And*, p. 43. v. 657, no stop at the end, p. 44. v. 661. for to, r. *with*, p. 75. v. 259. for divulg'd, r. *divulge*, p. 78. v. 324. for race r. *rate*, p. 79. v. 336. for Mimirs, r. *Mimics*, p. 90. v. 553. for heard r. *here*.

1680 omits all errata.

GLOSSARY

For further information on the words in the glossary and others omitted necessarily, the student may consult the following:

The Dictionary of National Biography;
Allan H. Gilbert: *A Geographical Dictionary of Milton;*
Howe and Harper: *A Handbook of Classical Mythology*

and the following editions:

L'Allegro, Il Penseroso, Comus, and Lycidas, Ed. W. P. Trent;
Paradise Lost, Eds. Masson, Newton, Todd, Browne, Keightley, and Verity;
Paradise Regained, Ed. C. S. Jerram;
Samson Agonistes, Ed. H. M. Percival;
Areopagitica, Ed. J. W. Hales;
The Ready and Easy Way, Ed. E. M. Clarke;
Of Reformation, Ed. W. T. Hale

ABBREVIATIONS

A.	Arcades	L.	Lycidas
Ad P.	Ad Patrem	L'A.	L'Allegro
Anim.	Animadversions upon the Remonstrant's Defense against Smectymnuus	1–3 Leon.	Ad Leonoram Romæ Canentem (Three poems.)
Areop.	Areopagitica	Man.	Manso
C.	Comus	M.B.	The Judgment of Martin Bucer concerning Divorce
C.D.	The Christian Doctrine	Nat. Non.	Naturam non Pati Senium
C.P.	A Treatise of Civil Power in Ecclesiastical Causes	P.	The Passion
		P.E.	Of Prelatical Episcopacy
Ch.Gov.	The Reason of Church-government Urged against Prelaty	P.L.	Paradise Lost
		P.R.	Paradise Regained
Col.	Colasterion	Præs.	In Obitum Præsulis Eliensis
D.D.	The Doctrine and Discipline of Divorce	Procan.	In Obitum Procancellarii Medici
Da.	Epitaphium Damonis	1–4 Prod. B.	In Proditionem Bombardicam (Four poems.)
2 Def.	Defensio Secunda pro Populo Anglicano	Q.N.	In Quintum Novembris
Ed.	Of Education	Ref.	Of Reformation Touching Church Discipline in England
Eik.	Eikonoclastes		
Eleg.	Elegia		
F.C.	On the New Forcers of Conscience under the Long Parliament	Rous.	Ad Joannem Rousium
		S.	Sonnet
		S.A.	Samson Agonistes
Fr. Com.	The Ready and Easy Way to Establish a Free Commonwealth	S.M.	At a Solemn Music
		Sal.	Ad Salsillum Poetam Romanum
H.	On the Morning of Christ's Nativity	Sm.	Apology for Smectymnuus
Hir.	Considerations Touching the Likeliest Means to Remove Hirelings out of the Church	T.R.	Of True Religion, Heresie, Schism, Toleration
		Ten.	The Tenure of Kings and Magistrates
Idea	De Idea Platonica Quemadmodum Aristoteles Intellexit	Tet.	Tetrachordon
		V.E.	At a Vacation Exercise
Il P.	Il Penseroso	Win.	An Epitaph on the Marchioness of Winchester
Inf.	On the Death of a Fair Infant		

The last number in each item refers in the poetry to the line numbers; in the prose and the translation of the Latin, Greek, and Italian poems, to the page.

Aaron, the first high-priest of the Israelites, brother of Moses. See Exod. 28:17 ff. P.L. 3.598; 12.170; P.R. 3.15

Abaddon, the place of destruction, hell. Cf. Prov. 15.11. P.R. 4.624

Abarim, a wild, mountainous region east of the Dead Sea. P.L. 1.408

Abassin, Abyssinian. P.L. 4.280

Abbana, a small river flowing through Damascus, modern Barada. Abbana and Pharphar are mentioned together in 2 Kings 5.12. P.L. 1.469

Abdiel, "Servant of God." P.L. 5.805 ff.

Abiathar, a high-priest of Israel; 1 Kings 2.10 ff. Eik. 28.858

abide, ME. abyen, pay for. P.L. 4.87

Abimelech, son of Gideon, made king of Israel by the Shechemites; Judges 9. Ref. 2.462

Abiram, see Corah

abortive, L. ab, from, oriri, rise, grow. Producing nothing, chaotic. P.L. 2.441

Abram, Abraham, See Gen. 12 ff.

Abramites members of a Christian sect named from its founder, Abraham of Antioch, and charged with Gnostic errors. P.E. 476

ouse, deceive. P.R. 1.455

Academe, the Academy a public park and grove on the Cephissus about a mile n.w. of Athens, where Plato taught for nearly fifty years. P.R. 4.244

Academics, all the Platonic schools of philosophy down to the time of Cicero. P.R. 4.278

acanthus, acanthus spinosus and acanthus mollis, plants of southern Europe, having large, deeply cut, shiny leaves. The leaf of the first species was much used in Greek architecture, the second in Roman. P.L. 4.696

Accaron, Ekron (Vul. Accaron), one of the five chief cities of the Philistines, about 25 m. w. of Jerusalem, usually placed, in M's time, on the coast, 2 Kings 1.1–6. P. L. 1.466

accent, a stress on certain notes or parts of bars. S. 13.3

accident, one of the predicables. V.E. 74; an abnormal happening. S.A. 1552

accidents, unusual attributes. S.A. 612

Achæmenian maids, maids of Persia; Achæmenes, grandfather of Cyrus the Great, founded that famous line of Persian kings. Eleg. I. 86

acheloian, Achelous, a river-god, son of Oceanus and Tethys, who in fighting with Hercules assumed the form of a bull, and lost one of his horns. Anim. 2.488; 3 Leon 95

Acheron, the river of woe in Hades, over which Charon ferried the spirits of the dead. P.L. 2.578; C. 603

Achilles, the greatest of the Greek heroes in the Trojan war, aroused by the death of his comrade, Patroclus, sought revenge on the Trojans, esp. Hector, whom he dragged three times around the walls. P.L. 9.15

acquist, acquirement. S.A. 1755

acuminate, rise to a point. Ch.Gov. 1.6, 518

Acworth, George, LL.D., civilian and divine during the latter part of the 16th c.; University Orator at Cambridge. M.B. 627

Adamites, a sect that originated in n. Africa in the 2nd century; they claimed to have attained to the primitive innocence of Adam; accordingly they rejected marriage and refused to wear clothing. The sect soon died out, but reappeared during the Middle Ages and in the 17th c. Ch.Gov. 1.6.518

Adamus, Melchior, a German divine and biographer (d. 1622) who wrote the lives of German scholars and theologians of the 16th c. and about twenty other lives. M.B. 628

adamant, a very hard metal, a name first used by Homer, but adopted later by the poets for the name of the hardest substance, usually imaginary. P.L. 2.436; 6.110; 6.255; 10.318; P.R. 4.534

adamantean proof, either (1) proof as hard as adamant, or better, (2) proof against weapons of adamant. Cf. "rain-proof." S.A. 134

Addlegate, coined by M. after Aldgate, a gate in the e. wall of London. Col. 722

Ades, Aides, Hades, Pluto, king of the lower world. P.L. 2.964

Adiabene, a small Assyrian province on the Tigris. P.R. 3.320

admire, wonder, or wonder at. P.L. 2.677

Adonis, a beautiful youth, beloved by Aphrodite, killed by a boar; Zeus decreed that he should spend half the year in the lower world, half in the upper. The annual festival of Adonis in the spring was a favorite one with women. Also, a small river in Syria, rising in the Lebanon Mts. and flowing into the Mediterranean 13 m. n. of Beirut. In the spring freshets the river was discolored with a reddish sediment. P.L. 1.450

Adonis, Garden of, an imaginary garden, first mentioned by Pliny. Cf. Spenser, F.Q. 3.6.29. P.L. 9.440

Adramelec, a god of the Sepharvites, worshipped by burning children alive; see 2 Kings 17.17, 31. P.L. 6.365

Adria, that part of the Mediterranean lying between Crete and Sicily. P.L. 1.520

Adrian VI, pope from 1522 to 1523; dealt with the early stages of the Protestant revolt in Germany. Eik. 20.841

Adrian's Wall, an ancient wall between the Tyne and the Solway, believed to have been erected by Hadrian c. A.D. 122. Ch.Gov. 1.6.517

adust, burned with the heat. P.L. 12.635

advowson, the right of presentation to a vacant benefice. Ten. 774

Æacus, one of the judges of the lower world. Procan. 96

Ægialus, another name for Absyrtus, the brother of the Colchian princess Medea; as she fled with Jason, she is said to have dismembered her brother and scattered his limbs along their route in order to delay her father's pursuit. Procan. 96

Ælfric, c. 955–1020. Renowned English churchman and homilist.

Æmilian road, a Roman road built by M. Æmilius Lepidus, consul in B.C. 187; a continuation of the Via Flaminia, the Great North Road, traversing Cisalpine Gaul and terminating at Mediolanum (Milan). P.R. 4.69

Æneas, see Æneid vi. 494 ff. Sm. 550

Ænon, a place of unknown location near or on the Jordan; John 3.23. P.R. 2.21

Æolian, relating to Æolis, the n.w. coast region of Asia Minor. P.R. 4.257

Æolus, ruler of the winds, which at his will issued from and returned to their caverns in the Æolian Is. Eleg. IV. 88

Aerians, a reforming sect of the 4th c. that held that a presbyter does not differ from a bishop, repudiated prayers for the dead, and refused to keep the fasts; forerunners of the Presbyterians. Eik. 17.835

Æson, father of Jason, the leader of the Argonautic expedition in quest of the Golden Fleece; at Jason's request, his bride, the Colchian princess Medea, rejuvenated his aged father by her magic arts. Eleg. II. 86

Æthon, the sun god. Eleg. IV. 88

Afer, the s.w. wind. P.L. 10.702

afflict, L. afflictus, beaten down; usually employed by M. in this literal sense. P.L. 1.186; 4.939; 6.852; 10.863; 2.166; S.A. 114

Afric coast, the shore of n. Africa, noted for its delicate fish. P.R. 2.347

Africa, (1) famous from classical times as the home of fabulous monsters. C. 605; (2) see *African*

African, Publius Cornelius Scipio Africanus Maior; captured New Carthage in his twenty-fifth year, at that time he restored a noble captive Spanish lady to her lover; defeated Hannibal in 202 B.C. but later lost his popularity with the Romans; retired to his country estate, refusing to the end, it is said, even to allow himself to be buried in his ungrateful city. When he was accused, he proudly reminded the Romans that it was the anniversary of his defeat of Hannibal, and called upon them to follow him to the temple to return thanks. P.R. 2.199; 3.101

Agag, a king of the Amalekites. 1 Sam. 15. Ten. 755, 761

Agatha, Council of, held at Agde or Agatha in s. France in 506; its 47 genuine canons deal with ecclesiastical discipline and shed light on the social and moral conditions of the clergy and laity. Tet. 704

Agnus Deis (pl), waxen medallions, blessed by the pope, stamped with a figure of a lamb, and worn as a supplication against evil. T.R. 919

Agonistes, L. agonista, Gr. ἀγωνιστής, a combatant for a prize.

Agra, a city in n.w. India, in M's time the capital of the Mogul empire. P.L. 11.391

Agrican, in Boiardo's metrical romance, *Orlando Innamorato,* left unfinished in 1494, Agricane, king of Tartary, besieges the fortress of king Galafrone of Cathay to obtain Angelica, whose beauty won the hearts of all the Christian and Paynim heroes who beheld her. (Bk. 1. c. 10). P.R. 3.338

Agricola, C. Julius, Roman soldier and statesman, father-in-law of Tacitus; his just rule in Britain is related by Tacitus in his *Agric.* Bk. 21. Areop. 748

Agrippa II., Herod, king over n. Palestine; see Acts 26. Eik. 9.810

ague-cake, an enlarged spleen, caused by intermittent fevers. Ref. 2.457

Ahab, King, king of Israel and husband of the Tyrian Princess Jezabel; denounced by the Hebrew prophets for his disloyalty to Jehovah, and his vicious life; see 1 Kings 22.20 ff. P.R. 1.372; Eik. 24.846; Ten. 767; Eleg. 4.89

Ahaz, king of Judah "did that which was not right in the sight of the Lord his God." 2 Kings 16. P.L. 1.472; Eik. 28.863

Aialon, a valley 14 m. n.w. of Jerusalem where Joshua defeated the Canaanites. Joshua 1.12, 13. P.L. 12.266

Aistulphus, or Astolf, King of the Lombards, 749–756; lost his conquest of the exarchate of Ravenna to Pepin the Short in 754. Ref. 2.456

Ajax, one of the famous Gk. heroes in the Trojan war; when Agamemnon awarded the arms of Achilles to Odysseus, Ajax became mad, and furiously attacked the sheep of the Greeks, imagining that they were his enemies. Col. 713

alablaster, alabaster; the superfluous "l" usually appears in early mod. Eng.; a soft rock of various colors, as red, yellow, and gray, but most esteemed when of pure white. C. 659; P.L. 4.544; P.R. 4.548

Aladule, Armenia; its last king was Aladule. P.L. 10.435

alarm, It. all' arme, to arms! In P.L. 6.549 the word has much of this original meaning. Cf. also P.L. 2.103; P.L. 10.491; C. 364

Albracca, the castle of Galafrone in Cathay. See *Agrican.* P.R. 3.339

Alcairo, Cairo, built by the Moslems in the tenth c. near the ruins of ancient Memphis. M. means Memphis. P.L. 1.718

Alcestis, the wife of Admetus, brought to him from Hades by Hercules, and the subject of a drama by Euripides. S. 23.2; Ed. 729

alchymy, a composite metal, made by alchemists, used for trumpets. P.L. 2.517

Alciat, Andrea, 1492–1550; jurist of Milan; highly honored by Paul III. and Chas. V. for his writings on jurisprudence. Tet. 709

Alcides, Hercules, son of Jove, strove with Antæus, a giant who received fresh strength each time that he touched the earth; Hercules lifted him into the air and strangled him. P.R. 4.565. Eurytus, king of Œchalia, promised Hercules his daughter Iole if the hero defeated him in an archery contest; Hercules won. Deianira, his wife, becoming jealous, sent a poisoned robe to Hercules by his attendant Lichas; in his frenzy, Hercules threw Lichas into the sea. P.L. 2.542

Alcinous, king of a fabulous people in the *Odyssey.* The garden is described thus: "And without the courtyard hard by the door is a great garden, of four ploughgates, and a hedge runs round on either side. And there grow tall trees blossoming, pear-trees and pomegranates, and apple-trees with bright fruit, and sweet figs, and olives in their bloom. The fruit of these trees never perisheth, neither faileth, winter nor summer, enduring through the whole year. Evermore the West Wind blowing brings some fruits to birth, and ripens others. Pear upon pear waxes old, and apple on apple, yea and cluster ripens upon cluster of the grape, and fig upon fig. . . . There too, skirting the furthest line, are all manner of garden beds, planted trimly, that are perpetually fresh, and therein are two fountains. . . . These are the splendid gifts of the gods in the palace of Alcinous." Od. 7.112 ff. (Butcher and Lang). P.L. 5.341; P.L. 9.441; V.E. 49; Eleg. 3.87

Alcoran, the Koran, the sacred Book of Islam. Areop. 747

Alcuin, (c. 735–804) Eng. prelate, one of the most learned men of his age; called to court school of Charlemagne. Sm. 577

Aleian, see Bellerophon

Alexander, Bishop of Jerusalem, persecuted under Emperor Septimius Severus; d. in prison c. 250 Ch. Gov. 2.3.533

Alexander's tutor, Aristotle

Alexandria, a famous seaport of Egypt, founded by Alexander in 332 B.C., an important seat of Greek culture and learning. Ed. 730

Algarsife, see Chaucer's unfinished Squire's Tale. Il P. 111

allœostrophic, stanzas of different metrical patterns. S.A. Pref.

Almansor, the regent of Cordova under the sultan Hisbam II; died 1002: his realm extended to the w. coast of Africa and part of the n. coast. P.L. 11.403

aloof, prep., at a distance from. P.L. 3.577

Alpheus, the principal river of the Peloponnesus. As Alpheus, the river-god, madly in love with Arethusa, pursued her, she was changed into a fountain in Syracuse; he still pursued her, flowing under the sea to Sicily. A. 30; L. 132

Amadis, of Gaul, a medieval romance, especially popular in Spain. In 1540 Herberay translated the voluminous Spanish version into French; this translation was popular in England about 1649 and before. Eik. 1.784

Amalthea, (1) the nurse of Jove, sometimes represented as a nymph, sometimes a goat; possessed a miraculous horn, in which might be found anything that she wished for. P.R. 2.356 (2) the mistress of Lybian Jove; see *Ammon.* P.L. 4.278

Amara, a mountain of rock on the Abyssinian plateau where the Abyssinian kings hid their children for safety; see Gilbert. P.L. 4.281

amarant, an imaginary never-fading flower. P.L. 3.352

amaranthus, Gk. unfading, a name applied to a genus of plants, including many garden varieties, such as the cockscomb and love-lies-bleeding. L. 149

Amaziah, see Amos 7. 10–17. Eik. 24.846

ambones, in ancient churches, a pulpit, often richly ornamented, projecting from the wall. Ref. 1.453

Ambrose, St., one of the great church fathers, d. at Milan, 397; wrote *De officiis ministrorum.* Ref. 2.466; Hir. 886; Tet. 703; C.D. 5, 956

ambrosia, a celestial, mythical substance, bestowing immortality; the food of the gods, often spoken of as having a rich perfume. P.L. 5.57

Amalek, grandson of Esau, whose nomad descendants, the Amalekites, are described in the Old Testament as "the first of the nations," i. e., the most powerful, cf. Gen. 14, 7; Numb. 24, 20. Eik. 9.806

amerce, O.F. a merci, to be at the mercy (of a lord); to punish by an arbitrary fine or the loss of some right. P.L. 1.609; Ten. 772

Ames, Dr. William, (1576–1633) a highly revered Puritan divine who spent most of life in Europe, practically exiled by the high-church party. An English translation of his Latin treatise, *Medulla Theologiæ,* was ordered published by the Commons in 1642. Tet. 663; C.D. 2.7.1060

amice, a loose wrap, usually, as here, connected with the ritual. P.R. 4.427

ammiral, the ship that carries the admiral; hence the most important ship in a fleet. P.L. 1.294

Ammon, the chief deity of the Egyptians, identified with Jupiter by the Romans (Lybian Jove); according to Diodorus Siculus, bk. 3 (cf. Sir W. Raleigh, *Hist.* 1.6.5) Ammon hid his mistress, Amalthea and her son, Bacchus, from the jealous eyes of his wife, Rhea, on the island Nysa in the river Triton emptying into the Lybian coast of the Mediterranean. P.L. 4.277. In the form of a serpent he visited Olympias and became the father of Alexander the Great. P.L. 9.508

Amos, See Amos 7.10. Eik. 24.846

Amphiaraus, one of the seven chieftains who united to make war on Thebes; in one of the battles the earth opened and swallowed him and his chariot. Eleg. 7.93

Amphisbæna, a fabulous poisonous serpent, supposed to have a head at each end so as to be able to move in either direction. P.L. 10.524

Amphitrite, wife of Neptune and Queen of the Sea. C. 920

Amphitryoniades, Hercules, reputed son of Amphitryon, though really of Jupiter. Q.N. 96

Amram, the father of Moses. P.L. 1.339

amuse, causative verb, to cause to muse; to engage completely; hence to bewilder. P.L. 6. 581; 6.623

Amymone, a daughter of Danaus and beloved of Neptune. P.R. 2.188

Amyntor, father of Phœnix, a close friend of Achilles in the Trojan War. Eleg. 4.88

Anabaptists, Gk. rebaptize; a sect that held infant baptism invalid and required adults so baptized to be rebaptized upon joining their communion. T.R. 915

Anak, a giant, the father of the Anakim; Deut. 9.2. S.A. 528; 1080

Ananias, see Acts 5.1–11. Tet. 688. The name also of the high-priest whom Paul rebuked; Acts 23. 2 ff. Ch.Gov. 1.5.513

Anatolius, eminent philosopher of Alexandria during the latter part of the 3rd c; opened a school and was the first Christian to teach the philosophy of Aristotle. P.E. 476

Anchises, the father of Æneas. C. 922

Andrew, the brother of Peter. John 1. 40–42. P.R. 2.7

Andrews, Bishop Lancelot, (1555–1626) an English prelate and author, one of the translators of the Bible; wrote manuals of devotion. Ch. Gov. 1.3.509

Andromache, the wife of Hector and the heroine in the drama of that name by Euripides, in which the Spartan women are satirized; cf. *Androm.* 595 ff. Areop. 734

Andromeda, a northern constellation, supposed to represent the figure of a woman chained; beneath it is the sign of the Zodiac, Aries, the Ram (opposite Libra) which seems to bear Andromeda. P.L. 3.559

Angelica, the beautiful daughter of Galaphron, king of Cathay, and the beloved of Orlando in Boiardo's *Orlando Innamorato* and Ariosto's *Orlando Furioso.* P.R. 3.341

Angola, a district in Africa; Purchas' map places it "fardest south," though it is not. P.L. 11.401

Anicetus, Bishop of Rome from about 154 to 167; entertained St. Polycarpus. P.E. 473

Anna, see Luke 2. 36 ff. P.R. 1.255

Anselm, St., (1033–1109) archbishop of Canterbury; considered the reviver of metaphysics after the decline of the Roman empire Ch.Gov. 1.5. 514

Antæus, a giant, the son of Earth and Neptune, wrestling with Alcides (Hercules) in Irassa in North Africa, received fresh strength whenever he touched the earth; throttled by Hercules as he held him aloft. P.R. 4.563

Anteros, the god of the passion of love. D.D. 1.6.585

Antichrist, a powerful ruler to appear in time, whose essence will be enmity to God. See 1. John 2.18. Anim. 1.482

antics, clowns, buffoons with blackened faces and patched clothing. S.A. 1325

Antigonus, the last Maccabean king of Judea (c. 40–37 B.C.) supported on his throne by the Parthians. P.R. 3.367

antimask, a secondary mask, of a ludicrous character, introduced between parts of a serious mask. Eik. 20.841

Antioch, a flourishing and beautiful city from c. 300 B.C. until 65 B.C., the rich capital of the kings of Syria. P.R. 3.297 (2) a city in Asia Minor called also Cæsarea. C.D. 1.29.1038

Antiochus, IV. surnamed Epiphanes, king of Syria 175–164 B.C. Conquered Jerusalem and desecrated the temple. Said to have entered the Holy of Holies (2 Mac. 5. in the *Apocrypha.*) P.R. 3. 163; D.D. 2.14.612; Ten. 767

Antiopa, courted by Jupiter as a satyr; see Ovid. P.R. 2.187

Antinomianism, In M's time the doctrine that the sins of the elect are transferred to Christ and are no longer those of the actual sinner. D.D. 1.14.594

Antipater, the "Idumean," a man of great wealth, was made procurator of Judea by Pompey; the father of Herod the Great. P.R. 2.423

antistrophon, the turning of an argument against the one who made it. Sm. 547

Antonius, St., a learned archbishop of Florence 1387–1459); his *Summa Theologica* has often been reprinted. Tet. 670

Anubis, an Egyptian god, often represented with a dog's head. H. 212

Aonian mount, Mt. Helicon, the home of the Muses, in Bœotia, often in mythology and poetry called Aonia. P.L. 1.15

Aphrodisia, (from Aphrodite) the land of sexual pleasures. Sm. 548

Apis, the sacred bull of Memphis, in the religious worship of which were many mysteries. Eik. 1.783

Apocalypse, Gr. disclosure; The Revelation of St. John the Divine; P.L. 4.2; Ch. Gov. 2.525

Apogæum, apogee, that point in a planet's orbit when it is at the greatest distance from the earth; hence, figuratively, the greatest point, the climax. D.D. 1.4.585

Apollinarius, the Younger, Bishop of Laodicea in Syria (d. 390); collaborated with his father, the Elder, in reproducing the Old Testament in Homeric and Pindaric poetry and the New in Platonic dialogues. Areop. 737

Apollinarius of Hierapolis, a bishop of Phrygia in the 2nd C.; later canonized; wrote a defence of Christianity, not extant, which St. Jerome highly commends. Anim. P.S. 504; Areop. 737

Apollo, one of the chief and most honored gods of the Greeks and Romans, the son of Zeus and Leto; P.R. 2.190; as the god of poetry and music he is pictured as a youth with a lyre; C. 477; V.E. 37; Eleg. 6.92; Apollo loved Daphne, who, fleeing from him, was changed into a laurel tree; C. 662. He also loved a beautiful youth, Hyacinthus, whom he accidentally killed; from the blood sprang a purple flower, the hyacinth. Inf. 23. He had an important shrine at Delphi, called the Pythian oracle. H. 176

Apollonius of Perga, a Greek geometer of the Alexandrian school, about 262 B.C. Ten. 773

Apollonius Thyanæus, a Greek philosopher of the Neo-Pythagorean school, who travelled in the East, imbibing much of the teachings of the Magi and of oriental religions; on his return was said to have worked miracles, and received reverence from priests and the people. Anim. 13.502

apparitor, the lowest officer in an ecclesiastical court, whose duty was to serve the process; a sumner. Anim. 13.497

appellant, one who challenges another to single combat. S.A. 1220

Appian, the old Roman road leading south to Brundusium. P.R. 4.68

apply, to be busy about. P.L. 4.264

appoint, L. adpunctare, lit. to make a point at (with censure), hence arraign; or (2) arrange in order. Cf. "a well appointed house." S.A. 373

Apuleius, Lucius, b. c. 125 A.D., a Platonic philosopher and rhetorician; wrote the *Golden Ass;* his style is marked by meretricious ornament and affectation, but has also many excellent qualities. Sm. 565

Aquila, said to have been a kinsman of Hadrian; translated the O.T. into Greek; became a Christian but later apostatized; his translation was not generally approved by Christian scholars. Ref. 1.453

Aquilo, Boreas, the north wind. Inf. 8

Aquinas, Thomas, an Italian scholastic philosopher (c. 1227–1274) who has had great influence upon philosophy, theology, and religious poetry. Areop. 738

Arabia, a peninsula in s.w. Asia, noted for its deserts; P.R. 3.274; its fertile stretches, hence often called A. Felix, P.L. 4.163; and for its spices and frankincense, P.R. 2.364

Arachosia, a region w. of the Indus River. P.R. 3.316

Aracynthus, a mt. in Greece. Q.N. 97

Aratus, a Gr. poet of the Alexandrian school, b. c. 315 B.C.; though his poetry was highly considered, only two fragments remain. St. Paul quotes one verse, "For we are also his offspring," Acts 17.28. Ed. 728

Araxes, the Aras, flowing into the Caspian. P.R. 3.271

arbitress, the moon acts as a judge of their games. P.L. 1.785

Arcadia, a mountainous district of Greece, whose inhabitants were fond of music and dancing; hence, the ideal pastoral country. C. 340; A. 28, 95; P.L. 11.132; (2) a pastoral romance by Sir Philip Sidney, published in 1590; Eik. 1.783 (3) Any entertaining romance; Areop. 740

Arcadius, (c. 383–408) elder son of Theodosius; Byzantine emperor 395–408

Archetype of Man, the concept of man formed before any man was actually fashioned, but having nevertheless an objective and not merely intellectual existence. Idea. 101

Archilochus, celebrated Gk. lyric poet and satirist, fl. 680 or 700 B.C. Areop. 734

Areopagus, a hill in Athens, w. of the Acropolis, where the council of elders held sittings from unrecorded antiquity. Areop. 734; Fr. Com. 906

Arestor, father of Argus, the hundred-eyed. Q.N. 98

Aretas, king of Arabia, father-in-law of Herod Antipas; probably reigned in Damascus when Paul escaped from the city. Tet. 678

Aretius, Swiss Calvinist theologian and botanist, d. 1574. Tet. 709

Argus, the guardian appointed by Hera to protect Io, the beloved of Zeus; he had a hundred eyes and never slept; Hermes, sent by Zeus, put to sleep all the hundred eyes by music and story-telling, then killed him. P.L. 11.131

Arians, the followers of Arius (d. 336), who was excommunicated for heresy because he believed that the Son is similar to the Father, not the same as, and subordinate to him. Ref. 1, 444; Anim. 2, 485

Ariel, "Lion of God." P.L. 6.371

Aries, the Ram, a sign in the Zodiac. P.L. 10.329

Arimaspian, a mythical people dwelling in Scythia toward the n.; adorned their hair with gold stolen from the griphons. Herodotus 3.116; Pliny 7.2. P.L. 2.945

Arioch, "a fierce and terrible lion." P.L. 6.371

Arion, a famous poet and musician of Greece; thrown overboard by some avaricious sailors and rescued by a dolphin fascinated by his music. Ad P. 102

Ariosto, a celebrated Italian poet (1474–1533); wrote the *Orlando Furioso,* one of M's favorite romances. Ref. 1.450

Aristippus, the founder of the Cyrenaic school of philosophy; taught that happiness is the highest good, and indulged in all kinds of external luxury. Ch. Gov. Concl. 539

Aristobulus, brother of Mariamne, wife of Herod; made high priest at age of 17; put to death by Herod in 35 B.C. Tet. 678

Aristophanes, the great Greek comic dramatist. Areop. 734

ark, captive, see 1. Sam. 5.4. P.L. 1.458

Armagh, James Ussher (1580–1656), archbishop of Armagh and Primate of Ireland. P.E. 469; Ch. Gov. 1.3.509

Arminians, the followers of Jacobus Arminius (1560–1609), a Dutch theologian, who founded the anti-Calvinistic school of the Reformed religion known as the Remonstrant Church. Areop. 739; T.R. 915

Armoric, Breton. P.L. 1.581

Arnobius, rhetorician, eloquent apologist for Christianity; converted from paganism; fl. c. end of 3rd c. Sm. 565

Arnon, a river flowing westward into the Dead Sea. The Ammonites did not occupy this country, but the maps and references of M's time make the river flow southwest into the northeast corner of the Dead Sea; see Gilbert. P.L. 1.399

Aroer, a city of Palestine (Joshua 13.25) which M. identifies with a larger city of the same name on the north bank of the Arnon. P.L. 1.407

Arragon, a prominent kingdom in n.e. Spain united to Castile in 1479. Ten. 757

Arras, a city of n. France belonging to Burgundy; taken by Louis XI. in 1477. Eik. 21.843

arreed, counsel. P.L. 4.962

Arsaces, headed a revolt against Syria and established the Parthian kingdom about 250 B.C. P.R. 3.295

Artaxata, the chief city of Armenia. P.R. 3.292

Artaxerxes, king of Persia, defeated by Greeks at Salamis in Cyprus in 449 B.C. P.R. 4.271

artist, Tuscan, Galileo, who first employed the telescope in astronomy about 1609. P.L. 1.288

Asa, a good king of Judah. 2 Chron. 14; 15; 16. Ch. Gov. 1.7, 521; Eik. 14.827

Ascalon, one of the five cities of the Philistines, on the Mediterranean; see Judges 14.19. P.L. 1.465; S.A. 138; 1187; Anim. 13.501

Asdod, one of the five cities of the Philistines, near the Mediterranean, the center of the worship of Dagon. Vulgate, Azotus. S.A. 981; Anim. 2.484

Ashtaroth, the goddess of love among the Canaanites, identified with the moon. H. 200; P.L. 1.422; 1.438; P.R. 3. 417; S.A. 1242

Asmodeus, an evil spirit that loved Sara and destroyed her seven husbands in succession; the eighth husband, Tobias, instructed by the archangel, Raphael, drove him away by burning the liver of a fish. See the Book of Tobit in the *Apocrypha.* P.L. 4.168; 6.365; P.R. 2.151

Asphaltic pool, the Dead Sea. P.L. 1.411

asphodel, a kind of lily. C. 837; P.L. 9.1040

Aspramont, Aspromonte, a mountain in Provence where, according to the romances of Ariosto and Pulci, a battle was fought between the armies of Charlemagne and Agolant. P.L. 1.583

assassinated, maltreated. S.A. 1109

Assyria, an ancient Asiatic kingdom, bounded by Armenia on the north, the Lower Zab on the south, the Zagros Mts. on the east, and the Tigris on the west. P.L. 1.721; P.R. 3.270. *A. blasphemer,* Sennacherib; see 2 Kings 19. Pref. D.D. 574; *A. garden,* P.L. 4.285. *A. flood,* see Is. 11.15, 16. *A mount,* Niphates, in Armenia. P.L. 4.126. *A. Queen,* Astarte (Venus) grieving over Thammuz (Adonis). C. 1001

Astarte, see Ashtaroth. P.L. 1.439

Astoreth, see Ashtaroth

Astracan, a city on the Volga, near the Caspian Sea. P.L. 10.432

Astræa, (1) Virgo, one of the signs of the Zodiac. P.L. 4.998; (2) a popular French romance, written by Honoré d'Urfé, filled with discourses on love, developed with casuistry and long, elaborate delicacy. Eik. 1.784

Atabalipa, emperor of Peru, slain by Pizarro, 1533. P.L. 11.409

Athanasius, St., one of the fathers of the church, born in Alexandria c. 296. Ref. 1.453

atheist, means not only one who disbelieves in God, but also one who disregards his duty toward God. P.L. 1.495; 6.370; 11.625; S.A. 453

Athelstan (895–941), one of the wisest and ablest of A. S. Kings, grandson of Alfred. Hir. 886

Athenæus, a Gk. rhetorician of Naucratis in Egypt, fl. at the end of the 2nd c.; left a long work, *Deiphosophistæ*, relating an imaginary dinner conversation in dialogue form, filled with interesting information about dishes, dancing, music, literature. Sm. 545

Athenian damsel, Boreas carried off Orithyia, dau. of the king of Attica. Inf. 9

Athenian walls, Plutarch (Lys. 15) relates that a Phocian minstrel singing a chorus from the *Electra* of Euripides at a banquet in the camp of Lysander so affected the conquerors that they decided that the birthplace of such a famous man should be spared. S. 8.14

Atheous, ungodly, P.R. 1.487

Atlantean, As mighty as Atlas, who supported the heavens upon his shoulders. P.L. 2.306; Man. 105

Atlantic sisters, the Pleiades, the seven daughters of Atlas. P.L. 10.674

Atlantic stone, the citrus-wood which grew on Mt. Atlas; because of its beautiful veins and high polishing qualities, the Romans used it for tables. P.R. 4.115

Atlas, a mt. system in n. Africa. P.L. 4.987; 11.402

Atrides; refers sometimes to Agamemnon, sometimes to Menelaus, the two sons of Atreus. In this Elegy, Agamemnon is meant. Eleg. 2.86

Atropatia, the extreme n.w. of Media, s. of the Araxes. P.R. 3.319

Atropos, one of the three Fates that severed life. Win. 28

attent, attentive. P.R. 1.385

Attic bird, the nightingale. P.R. 4.245

Attic boy, Cephalus, beloved by Eos, the dawn. Il P. 124

attrite, worn by rubbing. P.L. 10.1073

Augustine, St., the most celebrated of the church fathers; see Austin

Augustus, the first Roman emperor, Areop. 734

Auran, Aurantis in Babylon. P.L. 4.211

Aurora, the dawn. P.L. 5.6; L'A. 19

Ausonian, Ausonia was an ancient name for Lower Italy. P.L. 1.739; Eleg. 1.86

Auster, the s. wind. Eleg. 4.88

Austin, St. Augustine. C.P. 869; Hir. 886; D.D.1. 8.590

authentic, belonging only to himself. P.L. 3.656; 4.719

Avernus, a lake in Campania, not far from Naples; anciently believed to be the entrance to the infernal regions. Eleg. 2.86

Avon, probably the Bristol Avon river, emptying into the Channel. V.E. 97

Azariah, a prophet. 2 Chron. 15.1–7. Ch. Gov. 1. 7.521

Azazel. Newton derives the name from two Heb. words meaning "brave in retreat," which seems to fit the context. Others claim it is the scape-goat, wrongly translated in Lev. 16.20. P.L. 1.534

Azores, due w. from Mesopotamia. P.L. 4.592

Azotus, see Asdod

Azza, see Gaza

Baal, the supreme god of the Canaanites. P.R. 3.417

Baalim, pl. of Baal, used by M. as a general name for the male gods of Syria from the Euphrates to Egypt. P.L. 1.422; H. 197

Baalzebub, Philistine god, worshipped chiefly at Ekron; 2 Kings 16. S.A. 1231

Babel, a tower and city which M. indentifies with Babylon; Gen. 11. P.L. 1.694; 3.466; 3.468; Eik. 28.862

Babylon, the capital of Babylonia, on the Euphrates, identified often by M. with Babel. P.L. 1.717; 12.343; 12.348; P.R. 3.280; 4.336

Babylonian woe, Babylon was the name often given by M. and his contemporaries to Rome. See Rev. 18 for the curse on B. and a description of the woe. S. 18.14

Babylonish golden image, see Daniel 3. Eik. 15.829

Bacchus, the son of Zeus, and god of wine; his rites were celebrated by many and various orgies. P.L. 7.33; his mother, Semele, was destroyed by lightning by her lover; the child, born after six months, was given to Ino, her sister. Anim. 13.501; or according to another story born to Amalthea. P.L. 4.279. In art his long, clustering hair is often confined by a fillet of ivy. L'A. 16. In his triumphal journey through all lands, when he taught the use of wine, he was drawn in a chariot by tigers. Fr. Com. 910; B. had many amours, of which M. imagines one was with Circe. C. 521

Bacon, Francis, Baron Verulam (1561–1626) a famous philosopher, jurist and statesman, whose writings had a great influence on 17th c. thought. He wrote the "New Atlantis," a philosophical romance, picturing an ideal state. Anim. 1.480; Sm. 554; Areop. 746

Balaam, a prophet, for whom Balak, the Moabite king, sent to curse the Israelites; see Numbers 22. Anim. 3.489; Eik. 26.849; Ref. 2.460

Balearis, relating to the Balearic Isles. Nat. Non. 100

Balsara, a city on the united Tigris and Euphrates, identified in M's time with Teredon. P.R. 3.321

bandog, a large, fierce dog, usually a mastiff; kept chained. Ref. 2.467

Barca, a district in n. Africa. P.L. 2.904

Barbarossa, Frederick I, noted emperor of the Holy Roman Empire, crowned in Rome by pope Hadrian IV in 1155; opposed the election of Alexander III. as pope, but was finally forced to recognize him, and in 1177 knelt before him and kissed his feet. Tet. 706

Barclay, John (1582–1621) a Scottish satirist and Latin poet; from 1605 to 1614 he published in four parts, *Satyricon,* a satire against the R.C. church; the fourth part (1614) is called *Icon Animorum.* In 1616 he went to Rome, where he seems to have made some kind of compromise with the church and became friendly with Cardinal Bellarmine; resided there until his death. Ch. Gov. 1.7.520

Baronius, Cæsar, (1538–1607) an Italian cardinal and ecclesiastical writer. Anim. P.S. 503

Basan, Bashan (Vulg. Basan) a tract of land on the e. side of the Jordan. P.L. 1.398

Basil, bishop of Cæsarea (370–379) a leading churchman and writer. Areop. 737; Ref. 1.452; Sm. 567; Tet. 703; Eik. 17.836

Basil, Basel, a city of Switzerland, where a great council of the church was held (1431–49). It early sided with the Reformation, and was noted as a literary center. Eik. 28.859

battening, making fat by good feeding. L. 29

Batrachomuomachia, an ancient Greek mock-heroic poem, a witty parody of the *Iliad.* Col. 725.

battology, the vain and idle repetition of words; see Mat. 6.7. Anim. 2.485

baulk, omit, to leave untouched F.C. 17

Bavius, an inferior Latin poet, envious of Vergil and Horace. Col. 725

bayard, one who is ignorant and self-confident. Col. 721

Bayona's hold, the castle of Bayona, a seaport in s.w. Galicia, Spain, due south over the ocean with no intervening land from the "guarded mount" in Land's End. L. 162

bays, the leaves of the laurel, signifying unusual merit; used here figuratively for poetry. Win. 57

bearth, produce, that which is born. P.L. 9.624

Beatrice, beloved of Dante, and celebrated in his poetry. Sm. 549

Becket, Thomas, (1118–1170) archbishop of Canterbury, stood firmly against Henry II. for what he considered the rights of the church; was so haughty that Henry prayed he might "be rid of this turbulent priest;" later murdered by four knights who overheard this hasty expression. Tet. 706; Ref. 2.457

Beda, The Venerable Bede, d. 735, a learned monk and ecclesiastical writer, author of the celebrated *Historia Ecclesiastica Gentis Anglorum.* P.E. 476

Beelzebub, an important god of the Philistines, worshipped at Ekron and described in Mat. 12.24 as the "Prince of devils." In P.L. next in power to Satan. P.L. 1.271; P.L. 2.299; 2.378

Beersaba, a town in s. Palestine. P.L. 3.536

Behemoth, Heb. "great beast," used in Job 40.15 of the hippopotamus, but by M. of the elephant. P.L. 7.471

Bel, a god of the Babylonians. Ten. 774

Belial, Heb, wickedness; the Heb. noun is translated in the Bible as the "son of Belial," not as the name of a god. P.L. 1.490; 1.502; 2.109; 2.226; 6.620; P.R. 2.150; 2.173; Sm. 550

Belisarius, (505–565) the greatest general of the Byzantine empire; fought against the Goths in Italy in 544. Ch. Gov. 2. Pref. 525

Bellerophon, had many successful adventures on his winged horse, Pegasus; at last through overweening pride attempted to ride to heaven, whereupon Zeus caused a gadfly so to sting Pegasus that he threw his rider, who wandered grief-stricken and aimless on the Aleian fields. P.L. 7.18

Bellerus, Land's End, called Bellerium by the Romans. L. 160

Bellona, L. bellum, war; the goddess of war. P.L. 2.922

Belus, Gk. Belos, same as Bel. P.L. 1.720

Bembo, Pietro, (1470–1547) Italian scholar and writer, celebrated for the classical elegance of his writings. Ch. Gov. 2 Pref. 525

Bengala, a country of India. P.L. 2.638

benjamin, a perfume made from benzoin. Sm. 551

Benjamites, see Judges 20, 21. Eik. 12.823

bespaul, to make foul with spittle. Anim. 3.488

Bethabara, the Ford of Jordan where John baptized Jesus. P.R. 1.184; 1.328; 2.20; 4.510

Bethel, Luz, a town 12 miles n. of Jerusalem. P.L. 1.485; 3.513; P.R. 3.431; Ref. 2.455; Eik. 24.846

Bethesda, a miraculous pool in Jerusalem; see John 5. Col. 713

Bethshemesh, a town of Palestine s.e. of Jerusalem, to which the ark was brought from the Philistines. Ch. Gov. 1.1.507

Beza, Theodore (1519–1605) a theologian, the biographer and successor of Calvin; wrote theological treatises; edited and translated the N.T. into Latin, thus influencing the Eng. versions of Geneva (1560) and London (1611). Anim. 5.494; D.D. 1.8.590; 2.14.611; M.B. 627; Tet. 709; C.D. 1.29.1041

bezzling, excessive drinking. Anim. 1.483

bickering, moving rapidly, quivering. P.L. 6.766

billman, a civic guardsman, armed with a bill (broadsword). P.E. 475

Bilson, Thos., (1536–1616) bishop of Worcester and Winchester; published several treatises on theological questions. Ch. Gov. 2.1.527

birds are flown, Chas. I. entered the House of Commons, against all precedent, with an armed force, attempting to capture five offending members, Pym, Hampden, Holles, Hesilrige, and Strode, Jan. 4, 1642; (Mandeville of the House of Lords was the sixth man wanted). The quotation is from his exclamation when he found them absent. Eik. 9.808

Biserta, a seaport of Tunis, formerly of great importance. P.L. 1.585

bituminous lake, the Dead Sea. P.L. 10.562

Bizance, Constantinople. P.L. 11.395

Blackmoor sea, that part of the Mediterranean bordering on Mauritania. P.R. 4.72

blain, a pustule, a blotch. P.L. 12.180

blank, white or pale. C. 452; P.L. 10.656; 3.48; 9.890; P.R. 2.120; S.A. 471

Boaz, the name of one of the pillars of the temple; 2. Chron. 3.17. Col. 720

Bocchus, king of Mauretania, about 110 B.C., father-in-law of Jugurtha. P.R. 4.72

Bodin, Jean, (1530–1596), an eminent French economic and political writer. Ch. Gov. 2.3.531

Bohemia, formerly a kingdom of Austria, revolted against the R.C. church under Huss (burned July 6, 1415) and his followers; ultimately established a protestant religion. Eik. 17.835

bolt, to sift the meal from the bran in the preparation of flour; hence, to consider arguments carefully. C. 760

Bomolochus, Gk. a beggar; literally, one who lingers about the altar to beg. Sm. 552

Bonner's broth, Edmund Bonner (1495–1569) an English bishop, who had a reputation for arbitrary persecution of the Protestants in Mary's reign. Anim. P.S. 503; Col. 711

Boötes, a star in the n. hemisphere close to the Great Bear. Eleg. 5.90

Bordeaux glass, A general name applied to dyestuffs which produce a vinous red color. Anim. 13.495

Boreas, the n. wind. P.L. 10.699

Bosheth, Heb. shameful thing, a word sometimes substituted for Baal by the Hebrew writers, because they would not write that unholy name. P.E. 478

Bosporus, the narrow strait between the Sea of Marmora and the Black Sea. P.L. 2.1018

Bracton, Henry de, English jurist and writer, d. 1268. Eik. 28.859

Breerwood, Sir Robert, (1588–1654), literary man and judge; retired to private life after the execution of Chas. I. Ch. Gov. 1. Pref. 505

breese, a gadfly. Ref. 2.454

Brentford, a village of Middlesex, sacked by Prince Rupert, 1642. Eik. 18.837

Briarios, a hundred-handed giant, not a Titan, who helped the gods. P.L. 1.199

bridegroom, see Matt. 25. 1 ff. S. 9.12

brigandine, a coat of armor made by fastening scales of steel to an undercoat of linen or leather. S.A. 1120

brewess, broth, and the bread soaked in broth. Sm. 552

brinded, of a gray or tawny color, marked with streaks of a darker tinge. C. 443; P.L. 7.466

Bristol, a town in Gloucestershire on the Avon. Eik. 18.837

Bromius, a name for Bacchus as the god of wild revelry. Q.N. 97

Brooke, Lord. Robert Greville (c. 1608–1643) was imprisoned at York in 1639 by Chas. I. for refusing to take the oath to support the king; wrote *The Nature of Truth,* 1640, an important book, and *A Discourse . . . of that Episcopacy . . . ,* 1641–42. Areop. 751

Brownists, followers of Robert Browne (1550–1633) who later developed into the Independents or Congregationists. Ch. Gov. 1.6. 517; Sm. 544

Brute, see Locrine. C. 828

Bucer, Martin, (1491–1551) a German reformer, invited by Cranmer to live in England; from his arrival, 1549, until his death was professor of divinity at Cambridge; highly regarded by all the English Protestants. M.B. 626 ff.; C.D. 2.7.1063

Buchanan, George, (1506–1582) celebrated Scot. historian, scholar, and Latin poet. Tet. 764

Buckingham, George Villiers, 1st Duke of, (1592–1628) an English statesman who exercised great influence over James I. and Chas. I. but who was unpopular with the people; killed by Fenton. Eik. 1.779

budge, austere, stiff, pedantic. There is also an entirely different word meaning lambskin dressed with the wool outward; much used in M.'s time, as an inexpensive fur. Probably the second definition is better here. The first is possible, but hardly as Miltonic. C. 707

Burgundy, once a kingdom, later a part of e. France. Eik. 21.842

Busiris, Pharaoh. Cf. Raleigh's *History of the World.* See Ex. 14, 15. P.L. 1.307

buskin, a half-boot or high shoe, worn anciently by actors in tragedy; hence pertaining to tragedy. Il P. 102; Sm. 545

Buxtorf, Johannes (1564–1629) a celebrated German Hebrew scholar. D.D. 1.6.586

cabalist, one versed in the mysteries of the Cabala, the body of Jewish mystic philosophy; hence, one skilled in mysterious niceties. Eik. 21.842

cabinet, a small private room. The King's letters were captured at Naseby, June 14, 1645, and afterwards published. Eik. 21.842

Cadmus, the mythical founder of Thebes in Bœotia; beset by many misfortunes, he left Thebes for the Enchelai, who made him their king; finally changed with his wife, Harmonia, into a serpent. P.L. 9.506

Cæsar, G. Julius, (100–44 B.C.) opposed the execution of the Catiline conspirators. Eik. Pref. 776; 9.808

Cæcias, the n.e. wind. P.L. 10.699

Caiaphas, a high priest of the Jews; see Jn. 11.49 ff. Sm. 551; Tet. 697

Cajetan, Cardinal, (1470–1534) Italian scholar and theologian; sent by the Pope as a papal legate into Germany; before him Luther was brought. Sm. 553

Calabria, s.w. part of Italy, the toe. P.L. 2.661

Calandrino, an unfortunate but amusing character in Boccaccio's *Decameron* (Eighth day, third tale). Col. 725

Calchas, soothsayer to the Greeks before Troy. Eleg. 6.92

Cales, (1) a city in Campania, noted for its wine. P.R. 4.117 (2) Cadiz, see Gades.

Caligula, the 3rd emperor of Rome (37–41) caused himself to be worshipped as a god; said to have once exclaimed: "Would that the Roman people had but one head!" Eik. 11.819; 27.856

Callicles, rhetorician and philosopher. D.D. 2.21.622

Callimachus, fl. 240 B.C. a famous Greek lyric poet, left 6 hymns to the gods. Ch. Gov. 2. Pref. 525

Callisto, beloved by Jupiter; Ovid, *Met.* 2.409. P.R. 2.186

Calvin, John, (1509–1564) a celebrated Protestant reformer. Areop. 748; Anim. 2.484; M.B. 626; C. D. 2.7.1063

Camball, see Chaucer's "Squire's Tale." Il P. 111

Cambalu, Pekin. P.L. 11.388

Cambuscan, see *Camball*

Camden, William, (1551–1623) a noted English antiquary. Ch. Gov. 1.7.521

Cameron, John, (1579–1623) Scottish theologian and Greek scholar. Tet. 684

Camus, the patron god of the River Cam and hence of Cambridge. L. 103

Canaan, spy of, see Num. 13.16 ff. Sm. 547

Canace, see *Camball*

Candaor, a city and province of Afghanistan. P.R. 3.316

canon-laws, rules or laws regarding faith, morals and discipline, enjoined on the members of a church, especially the Catholic. M. usually speaks with great scorn of canon-laws; note the implication here. C. 808

Canterbury, see *Laud*

Canute, (c. 995–1035) upheld and added to the laws of Edgar. Hir. 889

cany waggons, related in books of travels, as Heylin's *Cosmog.* P.L. 3.439

caparison, an ornamented covering thrown over the saddle. P.L. 9.35

Caphtor, sons of, the Philistines, because they came from Caphtor, i.e. Crete. S.A. 1713

capital, lit. "pertaining to the head." P.L. 12.383

Capito, Wolfgang Fabricius, (1478–1541) a German reformer; professor of Hebrew at Univ. of Heidelberg. M.B. 630; Tet. 708

Capreæ, an island, 10 m. s. of Naples, to which Tiberius retired. P.R. 4.92

carabine, carbine, a kind of firearm. Eik. 10.812

Cardan, Girolamo Cardano, (1501–1576) a celebrated Italian mathematician; student of medicine and science. Anim. 1.481

Carmel, a ridge extending to the s.e. of Palestine; cf. Jer. 46.18. P.L. 12.144

Carneades, (214–129 B.C.) a Gk. philosopher; on an embassy to Rome he delivered two speeches that so aroused the youth for philosophical speculation that Cato banished him. Areop. 734

Carpathian, Carpathus was an island in the Med. where Proteus had a cave. C. 871

Carre, Nicholas, M.D. (1524–1568), professor of Gk. at Trinity College, Cambridge. M.B. 628

Cartwright, Thos., (c. 1535–1603) a prominent Puritan scholar and divine. Ten. 771

Casbeen, Kasbin, a city of Persia, formerly a capital. P.L. 10.436

Casella. See Dante's *Purgatorio* 2.76 ff. S. 13.16

Casius, Mount, the summit of a range on the borders of Egypt and Arabia Petræa, close by the "Serbonian bog." P.L. 2.593

Caspian, according to travellers this sea was "always raging." P.L. 2.716; P.R. 3.271

Cassibelaunus, i. e. of St. Albans in Hertfordshire; but see Gilbert. Da. 108

Castalia, a spring at Delphi, the water of which was used for purification in connection with the worship of Apollo; supposed to impart poetical inspiration to those who drank of it. Eleg. 4.88; 5.89

Castalian Spring, a fountain at Daphne, named after the one at Delphi. P.L. 4.274

Castelvetro, Ludovico, (1505–1571) an Italian critic who first called the attention of modern poets to the unities, and emphasized the importance of the epic. Ed. 729

Cataio, Cathay, the n. half of China. P.L. 3. 438; 10.293; 11.388, 390; Areop. 739

cataphracts, mail armor for horses and men. S.A. 1619

Cataphryges, a sect of the 2nd c. that believed in the immediate 2nd coming of Christ, now called Montanists. Anim. P.S. 504

catena, a systematized selection of passages to prove or illustrate a doctrine. Areop. 747

cates, dainty and delicate foods. P.R. 2.348

Catesby, Robert, (1573–1605) an Eng. conspirator involved in the Gunpowder Plot. Eik. 15.829

Catiline, Lucius Sergius, (108–62 B.C.) a Roman politician and conspirator. Eik. 9.808

Cato, Marcus Porcius, (234–149 B.C.) the Censor, the earliest of the Latin prose writers, left a treatise on agriculture, his only extant work. Tet. 683; Ed. 728; Areop. 734

Catullus, G. Valerius (c. 84–54 B.C.) the greatest Latin lyric poet, some of whose poems are a stain on his reputation. Rous. 110; Areop. 734

causey, causeway, a raised road. P.L. 10.415

Cebes of Thebes, a disciple of Socrates; left the *Tabula* in which he shows that education is not erudition, but the formation of character. Ed. 728

Cecropian, Athenian, from Cecrops, first king of Attica. Da. 106

Cedrenus, Georgius (c. 1100) a Gk. writer; compiled the *Universal Chronicle.* Ref. 1.447

Celsus, A. Cornelius (fl. 50 A.D.) wrote an encyclopædia, of which only the eight bks. on medicine have survived. Ed. 728

Centaur, a sign of the Zodiac; Satan steering upward passed between Sagittarius and Scorpio, keeping far from the rising Sun. P.L. 10.328

centric, having the earth as a center. P.L. 8.83

Cephalus, beloved of Aurora; in love with Procris; had his fidelity tested by her in disguise. Eleg. 3.87; Sm. 548

Cerastes, a horned viper. P.L. 10.525

Ceraunian, the mts. in Epirus and part of the Caucasus. Nat. Non. 100

Cerberean, resembling Cerberus, the watch-dog of Hades. P.L. 2.655

Ceres, the Roman goddess of agriculture; see *Proserpine.* P.L. 4.271, 981; 9.395; Q.N. 96; Eleg. 5.91; Eleg. 6.92

Chæronea, a town in Bœotia, where Philip defeated the Athenians in 338 B.C.; Athens never regained complete liberty. S. 1.7

Chalcedon, a town on the Bosporus. P.E. 470; Ch. Gov. 1. Pref. 505

Chalcedonian Council, held in 451 to settle disputes between the Nestorians and Monophysites. P.E. 470

Chalcidian, pertaining to the region around Naples. 3 Leon. 95; Da. 108

Chaldæa, a part of ancient Babylonia. P.L. 12.130

Chaldeans, of Babylon had a wide culture, but also an unsavory reputation as soothsayers and magicians; see Daniel 2. Areop. 736; Eik. 10.814

Chaldee, a name formerly applied to the Aramaic portions of Ezra and Daniel and to the vernacular paraphrases of the O.T.; formerly supposed to have been written during the Babylonian captivity in the language of the Chaldeans. D.D. 2.18.617; Ed. 729

chalice, the cup containing the wine used in the celebration of the eucharist. Ref. 1.450

Chalybean, produced by the Chalybes, a race, s. of the Black Sea, famous as iron-workers. S.A. 133

Cham, Ham, the son of Noah, hence "old;" whose descendants were the inhabitants of Egypt and Lybia; hence their god. P.L. 4.276; Eik. 21.843

chandlery, belonging to a huckster. Ref. 2.467

Chaonia, a district of Epirus; Olympias, mother of Alexander the Great, was an Epirote princess. Eleg. 4.88

chaplain, an ecclesiastic officiating in a private chapel of a king, nobleman, or person of wealth. Eik. 24.845

Charing Cross, in London, near the present station of that name, where Edw. I erected the last of 13 crosses in memory of his queen, Eleanor; an extant ballad relates the tradition that the queen sank at Charing Cross and rose at Queene-Hithe, a haven in London. Anim. 5.494

Charlemain, (c. 742–814) the great king of the Franks; made war against the Lombards in 773; the C. medieval romances were concerned with him and his 12 peers. P.L. 1.586; P.R. 3.343; Ch. Gov. 2. Pref. 525

Charondas, a Sicilian lawgiver, born at Catana c. 500 B.C. Ed. 729

Charybdis, the name of a whirlpool in the narrows between Italy and Sicily, opposite Scylla, a sea-monster who lived in a rock of that name. C. 259; P.L. 2.1020; Anim. 4.491

Chebar, see Ezek. 8–10; esp. 10.15. P. 37

Cheek, Sir John, (1514–1557) a famous Eng. Gk. scholar, tutor to Edw. VI. and Professor of Gk. at Cambridge; a zealous Protestant. S. 12.14; M.B. 626; Tet. 710

Cherith, see 1 Kings 17. 3 ff. P.R. 2.266

Chersonese, a region e. of India, probably the peninsula of Malacca, fabled for its gold; hence called Aurea C. P.L. 11.392; P.R. 4.74

Chilpericus, I (d. 584) a Frankish king who tried to reduce the power of the church. Ref. 2.456

Chimæra, a fire-breathing monster of Lycia, part lion, part goat, part dragon; *Iliad* 6. 181. C. 516; P.L. 2.628

Chios, an island in the Ægean, famous for its wine. P.R. 4.118

Chloe, a maiden who is the subject of an ode by Horace. Eleg. 6.91

Chloris, goddess of growing things, esp. flowers, corresponding to the Roman goddess, Flora. Eleg. 3.87; Eleg. 4.88

Choaspes, a river of s. Persia; Herodotus may be M.'s authority; see Gilbert. P.R. 3.288

Christiern II, "the Cruel," king of Denmark and Norway, deposed and exiled in 1523. Ten. 769

Chrysippus, (280–207 B.C.) a Gk. Stoic philosopher, noted for his skill in logical reasoning. D.D. 2.3.600; C.P. 867

Chrysostom, (347–407) a father of the Gk. church; wrote many books on ecclesiastical matters. Sm. 567; Tet. 662; Areop. 734; Ten. 760; C.P. 867

Church's Defender, usually "Defender of the Faith," a title bestowed on Henry VIII. by Pope Leo X. for writing against Luther; adopted by later English sovereigns. Eik. 14.828

Cilicia, a district of n.w. Syria, in which was Tarsus, Paul's city. Eleg. 4.89

Cimbrian, pertaining to the Cimbri, a German tribe. Eleg. 4.88

Cimmerian, in Homer the C. dwelt in a land of perpetual darkness; *Od.* 11.12 ff. L'A. 10; Q.N. 97

Circe, an enchantress, daughter of the Sun, who by her magic arts changed the followers of Odysseus into swine; dwelt on the Island of Æaea, off the coast of Campania. C. 50, 153, 253, 521; Eleg. 1.86; P.L. 9.522; Eik. 13.825

Cirrha, a seaport in Greece, associated with Apollo. Procan. 96

Cithæron, a range of mts. in Greece. Q.N. 97

citron, an evergreen tree related to the lemon, bearing fragrant fruit, and having wood beautifully veined; highly prized by the Romans for tables. P.L. 5.22; P.R. 4.115

clammed, made cold and sticky. Anim. 4.493

classic, in the Presbyterian church each parish had its presbytery, several of which made a classis. F.C. 7; Ten. 755

Claudius, (1) Appius, censor of Rome in 312 B.C. Areop. 735; (2) Tiberius, emperor of Rome, 41–54. Tet. 691

Clemens Alexandrinus, (c. 130–220) a father of the primitive church and founder of the school of theology at Alexandria. P.E. 476; Ref. 1.448; Areop. 738

Clement, Romanus, (d. c. 106) reputed to have been the 3rd bishop of Rome after Peter; wrote 2 Epistles to the Corinthians, rediscovered by Patrick Young and published at Oxford in 1633. P.E. 476; Ch. Gov. 1.6.515

Cleombrotus, a Gk. youth who threw himself into the sea in order to enjoy at once the happiness of the future life as described by Plato in the *Phædon.* P.L. 3.473

Clinias, father of Alcibiades, favorite pupil of Socrates. Eleg. 4.88

Clink, a prison at the end of Bankside in London. Sm. 555

Clio, the muse of history; the name is often employed as representative of the muses in general. Eleg. 4.88

Clymene, a nymph loved by Apollo. P.R. 2.186

Cnidos, a city of Caria, having a famous temple of Venus. Eleg. 1.86

Cochlæus, Johannes, (1479–1552) a German R.C. theologian and controversialist; one of the leading German opponents of the Reformation; wrote among other works *Remarks on The Actions and Writings of Luther.* Ten. 770; Sm. 553

Cocleus, see Cochlæus

Cocytus, a branch of the Acheron in Epirus, transferred with Acheron to the lower world; Gk. lamentation. P.L. 2.579

Coke, Sir Edward, (1552–1634) chief justice of the King's Bench, 1613; tried Sir Walter Raleigh; later an advocate for English liberty. Hir. 889

Colchian, a region e. of the Black Sea, native land of Medea. Eleg. 4.88

Colkitto, one of the names of Alexander Macdonnel, a lieutenant under Montrose; another name was Galasp; the three names belong to one person; M. is making fun of the barbarity of Scottish names. S. 12.9

Colmanus, St. (d. 676) Irish monk, made Bishop of Lindisfarne by King Oswiu; was a notable figure at Synod of Whitby in 664, which decided in favor of the Roman church against Colmanus and his party. P.E. 476

Colne, a river near Horton, familiar to M. Da. 108

colonel, note the pronunciation, col-o-nel. S. 8.1

Columba, Irish saint and missionary to northern Britain, (563) where on the island of Iona he established a church and monastery; many miracles are credited to him. P.E. 476

Columella, born in Spain c. 40 A.D.; left 12 books on agriculture. Ed. 728

comedia vetus, the old comedy in Greece before Æschylus, up to 499 B.C. Areop. 734

Comines, Philippe de, (c. 1445–1519) French historian. Eik. 21.843

Commenus, Andronicus, (c. 1110–1185) Byzantine emperor. Eik. 1.782

committing, joining unsuitably, harshly. S. 13.4

Commodus, see Constantine

concoct, digest. P.L. 5.412; Ch. Gov. 1.521; (2) refine by removing extraneous matter. P.L. 6.514

confine, border upon. P.L. 2.977

conglobe, gather into a ball. P.L. 7.239, 292

conjure, swear together in a conspiracy against. P.L. 2.693

Constance, Council of, held 1414–18. Eik. 28. 859

Constantine the Great, (c. 288–337) the first Christian Roman emperor; made large grants to the church; while a young man in England he was an officer in the army. Ref. 1.444; Tet. 670, 704

Constantius II, (317–361) emperor of Rome, 3rd son of Constantine. Hir. 894

Constantius, Leo, (905–959) benevolent emperor of the East; wrote treatise on the government of the Empire. Ten. 762

convince, convict. P.R. 3.3

cope, (1) a covering. P.L. 1.345; (2) a large mantle usually of silk worn by priests at religious services. Eik. 25.848

copesmate, one who helps, a friend. Col. 723

copyhold, land occupied by tenure, as a manor. Eik. 27.856

Corah, Korah, Dathan and Abiram formed a rebellion against Moses; see Num. 16. Ref. 1.452

Corallæan fields, the country of the Coralli, on the w. shore of the Black Sea, to which Ovid was exiled. Eleg. 6.91

Corasius of Toulouse, eminent French jurist, killed in the Massacre of St. Bartholomew, 1572. Tet. 707

Corineus, a follower of Brut who killed Gogmagog, the legendary king of the Giants. Man. 105

Corinthian, Corinth was noted for its licentiousness. Sm. 550

Cornelius, a Roman centurion whom Peter received into the Church directly by baptism without circumcision. C.D. 1.4.936

Cornish rebels, rose against the imposition of the Book of Common Prayer in 1549. Eik. 16.831

Coronis, mother of Æsculapius, the God of Medicine and Healing Arts. Eleg. 2.86

Corus, also Caurus, the n.w. wind. Nat. Non. 100

Corydon, the typical shepherd in pastoral poetry. L'A. 83

Cosbi, see Numbers 25. Sm. 553

Cotytto, a Thracian goddess whose festivals, celebrated on hills, were riotous. C. 129

Crab, Cancer, a sign of the zodiac. P.L. 10.675

Craig, John, Scottish reformer, successor of Knox. Ten. 764

crambe, a game in which one side gives a line and the other side matches it with a rhyme. Anim. 2.485

Cranmer, Thomas, (1489–1556) archbishop of Canterbury. Ref. 1.444; Tet. 710

Crantor, (c. 325 B.C.) philosopher and first commentator on Plato. C.P. 867

Crapulia, the land of wine-drinking. Anim. 3.490

craze, break to pieces. P.L. 12.210; Ref. 2.454

creek, arm of the sea. P.L. 7.399

Cremona, the birth-place of Vida (1480–1566), an Italian poet who wrote the *Christiad.* P. 26

Creon, king of Thebes, brother of queen Jocaste, the ill-fated mother and wife of Œdipus. Eleg. 1.85

crescent, emblem of Turkey. P.L. 1.439; 10.434

cresset, a lamp. P.L. 1.728

Crete, an island s.e. of Greece, famous for its wines. P.L. 1.514; P.R. 4.118; Areop. 734

crew, a noisy, riotous band. P.L. 1.51

Crispus, eldest son of Constantine; by his military successes aroused the jealousy of his stepmother Fausta, who incited Constantine to sign an order for his death. Ref. 1.449

Critolaus, see Carneades. Areop. 734

Cromwell, Oliver, (1599–1658); see also M's eulogy in the 2nd Defence, p. 1076. S. 16.1

Cronian. Artic. P.L. 10.290

cry, pack. P.L. 2.654

Ctesiphon, an ancient city near Seleucia on the Tigris. P.R. 3.292; 3.300

cuckoo, the song of the c. heard before that of the nightingale portended bad fortune for the lover. S. 1.6

Cullen, Cologne. Tet. 667; Hir. 886

Curius, Dentatus, Roman general, a model of the older virtue of frugality; was said to have died so poor that the state provided dowries for his daughters. P.R. 2.446

Curtius, a Roman legendary hero who, when an earthquake opened a chasm in the city, jumped into it in obedience to the soothsayers' pronouncement that Rome could be saved only by sacrificing her dearest treasure. Ch. Gov. 1.6.519

Cusco, the capital of Peru. P.L. 11.408

Cybele, a Phrygian goddess, whose worship was brought to Rome at the close of the second Punic War; frequently called Magna Mater, the Earth Mother; often pictured with a crown of towers. Eleg. 5.91; A. 20

Cyclades, a group of 12 islands in the Ægean, so called because they were clustered around Delos. P.L. 5.264

Cyclops, a race of one-eyed, cruel, giant shepherds dwelling in Sicily. Tet. 689

Cydonian, Cretan. Eleg. 7.93

Cyllenius, or Cyllene, a mt. in Arcadia, sacred to Hermes (Cellenius). Eleg. 2.86; A. 98

cynic, referring to a sect of philosophers noted for their coarse mode of life. C. 707

cynosure, Gk. the dog's tail, the constellation of the Little Bear, containing the pole-star; hence an object which attracts. L'A. 80; C. 342

Cynthia, Diana, considered as the Moon Goddess. Eleg. 5.90; Il P. 59; H. 103

Cynthius, a name of Apollo, so called from Mt. Cynthus on the Island of Delos. Man. 105

Cyprian, (c. 200–258) bishop and martyr, left treatises and letters. Ref. 1.444; Hir. 894

Cypris, Venus, one of whose favorite dwelling places was the Island of Cyprus. Eleg. 3.87; 7.93

Cyprus, an island s. of Asia Minor; associated with the worship of Venus (Cypris). Eleg. 1.86; 3.87; 7.92; Eik. 17.835

Cyrene, a seat of Gk. learning in n. Africa. P.L. 2.904; Ch. Gov. 2 Concl. 339; Ed. 730

Cyriack Skinner, (1627–1700) a grandson of Sir Edw. Coke and a former pupil of M's. S. 21.1; 22.1

Cyrus the Great, (559–529 B.C.) founder of the Persian empire. P.R. 3.33; 3.284; Ref. 2.460

Cytherea, a name applied to Venus in connection with the belief that she rose from the sea off the island of Cythera. Eleg. 5.91. Her son was Æneas. P.L. 9.19

Dagon, the fish god of the Philistines. P.L. 1.462; S.A. 13

Dalila, Delilah; see Judges 16. P.L. 9.1061; S.A. 229

Dalmatius, a Roman prince, b. in Gaul, nephew of Emperor Constantine; was given

title of Cæsar in 335; killed by soldiers, 338. Tet. 704

Damasco, Damascus, an ancient city in Syria; Ariosto in *Orl. Fur.* can. 17, places a tournament there. Eleg. 4.89; P.L. 1.584; 1.468

Damiata, Damietta, a city near the mouth of the e. branch of the Nile. P.L. 2.593

Dan, (1) an ancient city of Palestine supposed in M's time to have been Paneas. P.L. 1.485; P.R. 3.431; Ref. 2.455; (2) one of the tribes of Israel. P.L. 9.1059; S.A. 332

Danaus, a king in Greece, father of the fifty daughters, the famous Danaides, who, with one exception, to gratify their father's desire for vengeance, slew their husbands on their wedding night. Eleg. 1.86

Danaw, the Danube. P.L. 1.353

Danegelt, an annual tax, first imposed in 991, to obtain funds to oppose the Danes. Areop. 750

Daniel, one of the prophets; see Dan. 1. ff. P.R. 2.278; 2.329; Ten. 774

Daphne, (1) a nymph loved by Apollo; prayed for help when pursued by him and was changed into a laurel-tree. C. 661; P.R. 2. 187; (2) a park near Antioch in Syria. P.L. 4.273

Daphnis, a shepherd, made famous by Theocritus. Da. 106

Dardanian, poetical for *Trojan.* Da. 108; Eleg. 1.86

Darien, the isthmus of Panama. P.L. 9.81

darkling, in the dark. P.L. 3.39

Darwen, a river in Lancashire, on which Cromwell routed the Scottish army, Aug. 17–19, 1648. S. 16.7

Dathan, see Corah. Areop. 756

Dati, an Italian poet. Da. 108

Daunian, poetical name for Apulia, meaning Italian. Rous. 109

Davus, a conventional name for a slave in Latin comedies. Sm. 545

debel, conquer by warring against; L. debellare. P.R. 4.605

Decan, the peninsula of Hindustan. P.L. 9.1103

Decius, C. M. Quintus Trajanus, emperor of Rome, 249–251. Areop. 737

Dee, a river flowing n. into the Irish Sea, the ancient boundary of Wales and England. Eleg. 1.85; L. 55; V.E. 99

defend, forbid. P.R. 2.370

Deiope, a nymph attendant upon Juno. Sca. 104

Deiphobus, son of Priam; see Æneid 6.494 ff. Sm. 550

Delft, a town in Holland. Areop. 739

Delia, the goddess of the woods, Diana. Nat. Non. 100; P.L. 9.387; 9.388

Delian god, Apollo, born on the island of Delos, in the Ægean Sea. Eleg. 5.89

Deliverer, a common title for rulers, as for Demetrius and Antigonus. P.R. 3.82

Delos, the central island of the Cyclades, believed to have been fixed by Zeus with chains of adamant to the bottom of the sea. P.L. 5.265; 10.296; Rous. 110; the birthplace of Apollo and Diana where later a famous temple of Apollo was built. Man. 105

Delphos, a town in Phocis, the seat of the oracle to Apollo. H. 178; P.L. 1.517; 10.530; P.R. 1.458

Denmark, in M's time more important than now; one of the great Protestant kingdoms. Eik. 10.811

Demetrius, Phalereus, (c. 345–283 B.C.) Gk. orator and critic; the rhetoric often ascribed to him is probably spurious. D.D. 2.19.618

Demodocus, singer for Alcinous, at whose song Odysseus wept; *Od.* 8.522. V.E. 48

Demogorgon, a late spirit of the infernal regions, first mentioned by Lactantius; then by Boccaccio and Ariosto. P.L. 2.965

Demophoon, a son of Theseus and Phædra, betrothed to Phyllis; after becoming king of Athens, aided the Heraclidæ in a war against Eurystheus. Ten. 758

derive, (1) divert. P.L. 10.77. (2) continue. P.L. 10.965

descant, a song with modulations. P.L. 4.603

Deucalion and Pyrrha, devoutly praying after the flood for the restoration of mankind, were directed to cast stones behind them; these turned into men and women. P.L. 11.12

Dian, Diana, goddess of the moon, skilled in hunting. C. 441; Eleg. 5.90; P.R. 2.355

Diana Enamorada, by Jorge de Montemayor, the most popular of the Spanish romances, first published in 1542. Eik. 1.784

Dictæan Jove, Mt. Dicte in e. Greece was associated with myths about Zeus. P.L. 10.584

Digby, George, 2nd Earl of Bristol (1612–1677) an ardent supporter of Chas. I. Eik. 6.797

Diocletian (245–313) Roman emperor, ordered a general persecution of the Christians throughout the empire in 303. Areop. 737

Diodati, Charles, an intimate friend of young M's, the son of Dr. Theodore Diodati, a London physician; died while M. was abroad; the subject of *Epitaphium Damonis*

Diogenes, (c. 412–383 B.C.) a Gk. Cynic philosopher. Areop. 734

Diomedean, relating to Diomedes, the bravest of the Greeks in the Trojan War. Eleg. 6.94

Dion, C. C. (c. 155–c. 230) a Roman historian. Ten. 758

Dion Prusæus, (b. c. 50 A.D.) surnamed Chrysostom; Gk. Sophist about eighty of whose orations are extant. Areop. 733

Dionysius (1) the Elder (c. 430–367 B.C.) a tyrant of Syracuse; student of Gk. literature and encourager of learning. Areop. 734, 740; (2) D. Halicarnassensis (d. c. 7 B.C.) a Gk. historian; wrote a history of Rome to 264 B.C. Tet. 655; (3) D. Periegetes wrote a description of the world in hexameter verse in an elegant style; popular in ancient times. Ed. 728; (4) D. Alexandrinus, St. (d. 265), patriarch of Alexandria; none of his various treatises extant. P.E. 476; Areop. 737

Dionysius, Pope, from 259 to 268, reorganized the church. Ref. 1.446

Dippers, Sects using immersion in Baptism, esp. Anabaptists or Baptists. Tet. 650

dipsas, a viper whose bite caused intense thirst. P.L. 10.526

Dircæa, a small river w. of Thebes, Idea 101; 2 Leon. 95

Dis, a name for Pluto, god of the Lower World. Nat. Non. 100; P.L. 4.270

discontinuous, physiologists defined a wound as "a solution of continuity." P.L. 6.329

discover, reveal. P.L. 3.547

dispence, dispensation, a privilege grant by the pope. P.L. 3.492

disple, contraction of discipline. Ref. 1.454

divine, prophetic. P.L. 9.845

dividual, (1) shared in common with others. P.L. 7.382. (2) divided, separate. P.L. 12.35

doctor, L. doctus, learned. S.A. 299

Dodona, a city in Epirus in which was a famous oracle of Zeus. P.L. 1.518

Dog-Star, Sirius, visible during the summer, when the heat is intense. Q.N. 98

Dominic, (1170–1221) the founder of the religious order of the black friars, Dominicans. P.L. 3.479; Areop. 753

Donations, see *Constantine*

doomsday book, a reference to the final judgment-day and also to the *Doomsday Book,* completed in 1086, containing a census with statistics. Eik. 2.789

Dorian lyric odes, those of Pindar, written in the D. dialect. P.R. 4.257

Dorian mood, severe, solemn music in the style of the Spartans, who were Doric in descent. P.L. 1.550

Doric, Greek; the Dorians were a Gk. tribe. P.L. 1.519

Doris, a goddess of the sea, wife of Nereus and mother of Nereids. Eleg. 4.88

dorr, (1) a beetle, probably the cockchafer. Col. 725; (2) trick, joke. Sm. 551

Downam, (d. 1634) Eng. theologian, one time chaplain to K. James I. Anim. 1.481

dragon's teeth—Cadmus, a legendary prince and supposed inventor of the alphabet, killed a dragon and planted its teeth, from which sprang armed men. Areop. 733

dryad, a tree nymph. C. 963; Eleg. 5.91; P.L. 9.387

Dryope, a shepherdess. Da. 107

Dudley, obtained chief control of govt. during reign of Edw. VI; persuaded Edw. to pronounce Lady Jane successor to the throne; at death of Edw. in 1553 vainly resisted accession of Mary and was executed for treason. Eik. 9.807

du Haillan, (1535–1610) French historian, commended by Chas. IX. Ten. 762

Dulichian hero, Dulichium, an island often mentioned in the *Odyssey*, probably near the island of Ithaca. Eleg. 6.92

Dun, the river Don, flowing into the Ouse, a tributary of the Humber. V.E. 92

Dunbar, a seaport near the mouth of the Forth; here the Scotch were defeated by Cromwell, Sept. 3, 1650. S. 16.8

dyscrasy, a general impairment of health. Eik. 2.787

Earl, James Ley (1550–1629) 1st Earl of Marlborough, appointed lord chief justice, 1622, and lord high treasurer, 1624. S. 10.1

Ecbatan, an ancient city of Media, now Hamadan, incorrectly identified by M. and his contemporaries with Tauris, the summer residence of the Persian kings. P.L. 11.393; P.R. 3.286

Ecbert, King of the West Saxons, 800–836. Hir. 886

eccentric, away from the center, i. e., have a circle away from the earth. P.L. 3.575; 5.623; 8.83

Ecchius, (1486–1543) German theologian, the able antagonist of Luther. Sm. 553

eccliptic, the sun's orbit. P.L. 3.740

Echionian, pertaining to Thebes, in Bœotia. Q.N. 97

Ecron, see Accaron

Eden, a large tract extending from the Euphrates e. to the Tigris, within which Paradise, a smaller tract, is situated. P.L. 4.210

Edgar, (944–975) king of England. Hir. 889

Edom, a district in Syria. P.R. 2.423; Eik. 13. 825; Col. 713

Edward the Confessor, (1004–1066) king of the West Saxons. Eik. 9.809

Edward VI., (1537–1553) religious boy king of Eng., a Protestant. Eik. 9.807

Edwards, Thomas, a Puritan preacher who dealt unsparingly with the Independent divines and opposed toleration; later wrote *Gangræna* (1646) in which he lists the heresies of the times. F.C. 12

Eikon Basilike, "the King's image," a book published in 1650, supposed to have been written by Chas. I as his Apologia; exceedingly popular with the Royalists, and widely read by all classes of Englishmen. Eik. Pref. 777

Eikonoklastes, "the image breaker," written by M. by order of Parl. to combat the influence on the popular mind of the E.B. Eik. Pref. 775

Egeria, an Italian nymph beloved by Numa, second King of Rome, whom she helped in the formulation of the religious system of the Romans. Sca. 104

eglantine, the wild rose, L'A. 48

eld, old age, Inf. 13

El Dorado, a fabulous city of gold supposed to be in n. of S. America. P.L. 11.411

Eleale, a town of Moab. P.L. 1.411

Eleazar, third son of Aaron; see Num. 3.2, 4, 32. Ch. Gov. 1.5.513

Electra, the subject of Euripides' drama of that name. S. 8.13

Elean, relating to Elis, a district of the western Peloponnesus, where the Olympic games were held every four years. Eleg. 6.91

Eleusis, a city of Attica. Eleg. 4.88

Eleusinian mysteries, the most famous of the Gk. mysteries. D.D. 2.4.602

Eleutherius, pope (c. 175–189) said to have had relations with the British king Lucius who desired to become a Christian. Ref. 2.455

Elfric, see *Alfric*

Eli's sons, see 1 Sam. 2.12 ff. P.L. 1.495

Eliah, Elijah, the greatest of the Hebrew prophets; see 1 Kings 17. P.R. 1.353; 2.19; 2.268; 2.277; Sm. 554

Eliberis, a ruined city of Spain, near Granada. Tet. 702

Elixir, the E. Vitæ, the water of life, an object of search by alchemists. P.L. 3.607

ellops, a sea serpent. P.L. 10.525

Elysium, the abode of the happy dead. Procan. 96; P.L. 3.472; C. 256

Emathian, Macedonian. Alex. the Gt. was said to have spared only the house of Pindar when he razed Thebes. S. 8.10; Procan. 96

Emathian city, Philippi, a city of Macedonia. Eleg. 4.89

embost, hidden in the woods. S.A. 1700

Emims, a race of giants dwelling e. of Canaan; Deut. 2.10. S.A. 1080

Empedocles, (490–430 B.C.) philosopher, poet and statesman of Agrigentum, Sicily. Tradition states that he threw himself into Ætna so that the people by his sudden disappearance might believe him a god. P.L. 3.471

empiric, experimental. P.L. 5.440

enchiridion, a manual. Areop. 744

Endymion, a beautiful young shepherd, beloved of Selene; lulled to sleep on Mt. Latmos in Asia Minor where, it was believed, the goddess stole down to caress him in his never-ending slumber. Eleg. 1.86

engine, any mechanical contrivance. L. 130

"English Pope, The," an anonymous book published in 1643. Eik. 27.853

Enna, a city of central Sicily. P.L. 4.269

enthymema, from Aristotle, meaning an inference from probabilities and signs. Sm. 543

Enyo, the goddess of war, the Roman Bellona. Eleg. 4.88

Epaminondas, (c. 412–c. 362 B.C.) illustrious Theban statesman and general. Tet. 653; 2 Def. 1077

Ephesian beasts, see 1 Cor. 15.32. Anim. 13.502

Ephesian goddess, Diana; see Acts. 19.26 ff. Eik. 27.852

Epicurus, Gk. philosopher (342–270 B.C.) founded the Epicurean school; taught that pleasure is the end of rational action. P.E. 477; Areop. 734; Ch. Gov. Concl. 539

Epicycle, a circle whose center moves on the circumference of another circle. P.L. 8.84

Epidaurus, a town on the east coast of the Peloponnesus, noted for its temple of Æsculapius, who was supposed to appear there as a serpent. P.L. 9.507

Epimenides, a Cretan poet and prophet of the 6th c. B.C. Anim. 13.496

Epimetheus, Gk. afterthought, brother of Prometheus; the "unwiser son of Japhet." P.L. 4.717; D.D. 2.3.600

Epiphanius, (c. 315–403), esp. active in combatting heresies. Areop. 738; M.B. 637; Tet. 703

Epirot, Pyrrhus, king of Epirus in Greece; defeated by the firm policy of the Roman Senate. S. 17.4; Areop. 749

episcopacy, government of the church by bishops, as practised in the Ch. of Eng.

Erasmus, a Dutch classical and theological scholar (1465–1536) who tried to reform, without disrupting, the R.C. church. C.D. 1.29.1041; Sm. 553

Erato, the muse of love poetry. Eleg. 6.92

Ercoco, on the w. coast of the Red Sea. P.L. 11.398

Erebus, son of Chaos; represents darkness; applied also to the infernal regions. C. 803; Q.N. 97; P.L. 2.883

Erechtheus, a mythical king of Athens. Rous. 110

erroneous, straying about. P.L. 7.20

Erymanth, a range in Arcadia. A. 100

Esau, see Gen. 28. 10 ff. P.L. 3.512

Eshtaol, a town belonging to the tribe of Dan. S.A. 181

essence, fifth, according to Aristotle there are five elementary ingredients, earth, water, air, fire, and the upper air. Areop. 733

Estotiland, a fabulous island near the e. coast of n. North America, often identified with Greenland. P.L. 10.686

Etham, a rock in the country of Judah. Judges 15.8 ff. S.A. 253

Ethiop line, Ethiopia included the country s. of the Desert and Egypt; hence E. line is the equator. Eleg. 5.90; P.L. 4.282

Ethiop queen, Andromeda, dau. of Cepheus, king of Ethiopia, was exposed to a sea-monster, sent by Poseidon into that country during a flood; she was later placed among the stars. Il P. 19

Ethiopian Sea, that part of the Atlantic south of the known world, between Africa and S. America. P.L. 2.641

ethnic, a pagan. Ref. 1.447

Etymologicon, a dictionary giving the derivations of words. Tet. 691

Etrurian, Tuscan. Q.N. 97; Man. 104; P.L. 1.303

Euan, a name for Bacchus, derived from a cry of the Bacchantes. Eleg. 6.91

Euboic Sea, at the foot of Mt. Œta, Thessaly. P.L. 2.546

Eumenides, the Furies when conceived of as gracious goddesses. Q.N. 96

Eunomius, of the extreme Arians (d. c. 393) Sm. 543

Euoe, the cry of the Bacchantes as they invoked Bacchus. Eleg. 6.91

euphrasy, an herb used to quicken failing eyesight. P.L. 11.414

Euphrosyne, one of the three graces; presided over festivals. L'A. 12

Euripides, (480–406 B.C.) M's favorite Gk. dramatist. Ed. 729; Areop. 731; Ten. 758; C.D. 1.12.1003

Eurotas, a river s.e. of Sparta. Inf. 25

Eurus, the e. wind. Da. 107; Eleg. 4.88; P.L. 10.705

Eurybates, herald to Agamemnon, commander of the Gk. forces before Troy. Eleg. 2.86

Eurydice, the wife of Orpheus. L'A. 150

Eurynome, see *Ophion*

Eurypylus, one of the Gk. warriors in the Trojan War. Procan. 96

Evander, a Gk. prince of Pallanteum, in Arcadia, whence he brought a colony to the Palatine Hill, long before the foundation of Rome itself. Sca. 104

expect, await; L. expecto. P.L. 6.186

explode, to hiss off the stage; L. explaudere, to drive out with disapproval by clapping. P.L. 10.546; 11.669; Anim. Pref. 478

Ezekiel, an Hebrew prophet, d. c. 572 B.C. For Hir. 895 and D.D. Pref. 573, see Ez. 3.1 ff.; for Sm. 553, see Ez. 1; for P.L. 1.455, see Ez. 8.12 ff.

Fabricius, a Roman consul sent as an ambassador to Pyrrhus, who tried unsuccessfully to bribe him. P.R. 2.446

fact, act. P.L. 2.124; 9.928; 9.980; 11.457; S.A. 493, 736

fadge, fit in with. Ch. Gov. 1.5.513

Fagius, Paulus, (1504–1550?), learned Protestant theologian and Hebraist, student and successor at Heidelberg of Wolfgang Capito. q.v. D.D. 1. Pref. 578; M.B. 627

Fairfax, Sir Thomas, (1612–1671) a Parliamentary leader and general in the Civil War; won the battles of Marston Moor and Naseby; organized the "New Model." S. 15.1

Falerne, a district in n. Campania, noted for its wines. P.R. 4.117

Familism, a sect founded by Hendrik Niclæs at Emden about 1540; spread into England about 1570; was repressed, but revived, 1640–1650; its leading principle, the "service of love," was highly idealistic, but subject to abuse. D.D. 1.14, 594; Ch. Gov. 1.6.516

Faunus, a Roman woodland deity, goat-footed. P.L. 4.708; Eleg. 5.91

Favonius, the w. wind. S. 20.6; Eleg. 3.87

Fawkes, a prime mover in the Gunpowder Plot, with which his name is practically synonymous. 1 Prod. b. 94

fee, in fee-simple, in full possession. S. 12.7; Col. 724

fennel-rubbed, serpents were supposed to be especially fond of fennel. P.L. 9.581; Sm. 556

Fenner, Dudley (c. 1558–1587) English Puritan divine. Ten. 771

fescue, a slender stick used to point out letters to pupils learning to read. Areop. 743; Anim. 2.485

Fesole, a town n.e. of Florence. P.L. 1.289

Fez, a part of n. Africa, now part of Morocco. P.L. 11.403

firecross, a burning cross used in Scotland in early times as a signal for war. Ref. 2.461

First Wheel of the Universe, the outermost of the concentric spheres whose centre is the earth. It is the sphere of the *primum mobile* and imparts motion to all the rest. Nat. Non. 100

Flaccus, Horace. Areop. 734; Sm. 554

flaw, a sudden gust of wind. P.L. 10.698; P.R. 4.454

Fleetwood. English general, commonly described as a fanatic and enthusiast of small capacity; married Bridget, daughter of Cromwell; d. 1692. 2 Def. 1080

Fleta, an anonymous Latin book on English law, c. 1290. Eikon. 28.859

Flora, goddess of spring and flowers. P.L. 5.16; P.R. 2.365

florid, flowery. P.L. 7.90

folkmooter, a frequenter of popular assemblies. Col. 722

Fontainebleau, a town 37 miles s.e. of Paris, the seat of the French court. Ch. Gov. 2.1.537

Fontarabbia, a town of n. Spain on the French border, near which at Roncesvalles occurred the defeat of Charlemagne and the death of Roland. P.L. 1.587

Fortunatian, St., a Latin poet, b. 530, became Bishop of Poitiers. Ref. 1.451

Fox, John (1516–1587) an active English Protestant, whose chief work is *Actes and Monuments,* usually known as the *Book of Martyrs,* M.B. 627; Anim. 2.483

Francini, an Italian poet, Da. 108

Francis, St. Francis of Assisi (1182–1226) Q.N. 97

Franciscans, the Gray Friars, founded by St. Francis of Assisi in 1210. P.L. 3.480

fucus, paint. Ch. Gov. 2.3.529

furred, coated with morbid matter. Anim. 4. 493

gaberdine, a long loose cloak. Tet. 693

Gabriel, "man of God," an archangel; Luke 1.26

Gades, Cadiz, an ancient city on an island, west of Gibraltar. P.R. 4.77; S.A. 716; Eik. 9.307

Gadire, Gades

Galasp, see *Colkitto*

Galatians see Gal. 3.1, Sm. 568

Galileo, (1564–1642) Italian astronomer, noticed the sun's spots in 1610. P.L. 1.288; 3.590; 5.262; Areop. 745

Gallaphrone, a city of Cathay, i.e. n. China. P.R. 3.340

Gallia, France. P.R. 4.77

galloway, a small-sized, spirited horse of a breed first raised in Galloway, Scotland. Anim. 13.501

Gallus, Cornelius, earliest of the four great writers of elegy in the Augustan age: Gallus, Tibullus, Propertius, and Ovid. Man. 104

Ganymede, a beautiful youth, the cup-bearer to Zeus. P.R. 2.353

Gardiner, Stephen. (c. 1490–1555) English prelate who did much to further the persecution of the Protestants under Mary. Ch. Gov. 1.6. 519

gargarism, a gargle. Ch. Gov. Concl. 538

Gate House, a London prison. Sm. 555

Gath, one of the five cities of the Philistines. S.A. 266

gauntlet, a glove. S.A. 1121

Gaza, the most southern of the five cities of the Philistines. S.A. 41

gear, affairs. C. 167 (note)

Gehazi, see 2 Kings 5.20 ff. Hir. 895; Ref. 2. 467

Gellius, A., a Latin grammarian and author of *Noctes Atticæ.* Tet. 655

Genezaret, the Sea of Galilee, formed by the expansion of the upper Jordan. P.R. 2.23

George, St., a Christian martyr under Diocletian; made the patron saint of England by Edw. III. Ch. Gov. Concl. 539

Gergessa, an ancient town on the Sea of Galilee. Eleg. 4.89

Gersom, Ben, (c. 1288–c. 1370) Jewish rationalistic writer; also wrote commentaries of Averroes. D.D. 2.13.617

Geryon's sons, the descendants of G., a fabulous king of Spain, whose oxen were carried away by Hercules. P.L. 11.410

Gibeah, a city of Palestine; see Judges 19. P.L. 1.504

Gibeon, see Josh. 10.12. P.L. 12.265

Gildas, British Latin historian; died c. 570. Ten. 763

Gilless, Peter, (b. c. 1570), Swiss Protestant, author of *History of the Church of Vandois.* Hir. 892

ging, a gang. Sm. 550

Glaucus, a Bœotian fisherman, who, eating an herb, was transformed into a sea-god with prophetic powers. C. 873

glebe, (1) ground, farming-land. P.R. 3.259. (2) the farming-land belonging to a parish church. Hir. 891

gleeking, frolicking. Anim. P.S. 503

glib, to make smooth. P.R. 1.375

globose, a globe. P.L. 5.753; 7.357

gloze, to flatter. C. 161; P.L. 9.549

Glycera, a maiden who is the subject of one Horace's Odes. Eleg. 6.91

gnomology, a collection of maxims. Tet. 689

Godfrey of Bouillon, (c. 1060–1100) a leader in the First Crusade. Ch. Gov. 2.525

Golgotha, Calvary, a place near Jerusalem where Jesus was crucified. P.L. 3.477

Gomarus, (1563–1641) celebrated Prot. theologian and controversialist.

gonfalon, a standard, usually with two or three streamers. P.L. 5.589

Goodman, Christopher (c. 1520–1603) puritan divine and author; friend of Knox. Exiled by Mary.

Gordian, complicated; the pole of Gordius' wagon was tied to the yoke with a knot of bark so intricate that no one could untie it. V.E. 90; P.L. 4.348

Gordon, a new name to Londoners, brought to their notice by the campaigns of Montrose and the Royalist army. S. 11.8

Gorgons, three frightful sisters with hideous features and snakes in their hair; see *Medusa.* P.L. 10.527; 2.611; 10.297; 2.628; C. 446; Nat. Non. 100

Goring, George, (1608–1657) officer in the Royalist army; connected with the "Army Plot" to which M. refers; the plan was to rescue Strafford by the army; when G's advice was not taken, he betrayed the plot to Pym. Eik. 2. 786

Goshen, a district on the borders of Egypt. P.L. 1.309

Gower, John, English poet, contemporary of Chaucer

Graces, three nymphs, Euphrosyne (Joy), Aglaia (Bright), and Thalia (Bloom). L'A. 15; C. 985; P.L. 4.267

Gratian, Italian canonist who compiled the *Decretals* c. 1150. Ch. Gov. 1.5.514; D.D. 2.22.624

greaves, armor for the legs. S.A. 1121

Greek poet, Archilochus, reputed inventor of satiric iambics. Præs. 99

gride, cut. P.L. 6.329

grisamber, gray amber, ambergris, a secretion of the sperm whale; when heated (steamed) it gives off a perfume; formerly used in cooking for state occasions. P.R. 2.344

Gregory I, pope from 590 to 604. Hir. 886

Gregory Nyssen, a father of the Eastern Church, brother of Basil. Sm. 543

gryfon, a fabulous creature said to guard the gold mines of Scythia from the Arimaspians. P.L. 2.943

Gualter of Zurich, (1518–1586) Swiss divine, son-in-law of Zwingli; first minister of Zurich; wrote several popular works. Tet. 708

Guendolen, see *Sabrina*

Grindal, Edmund, (1519–1583) Protestant divine, archbishop of Canterbury; vigorous opponent of the R.C. ch. Ref. 1.445

Grotius, Hugo, (1583–1645) Dutch jurist, theologian, statesman, and poet. D.D. 1. Pref. 578; Tet. 709; C.P. 869

Guildhall, the council hall of the city of London. Eik. 3. 788

Guisan of Paris, Cardinal de Lorraine (1525–1574), famous for his bitter hostility toward the Protestants; attempted to introduce Inquisition in France. Sm. 551

guly, of the red tincture (gules) used in heraldry. Ref. 2.462

habergeon, a shirt of mail. S.A. 1120

Habor, a tributary of the Euphrates. P.R. 3.376

Hadden, Walter, (1516–1572) Eng. scholar; contributed to revival of classical learning. M.B. 628; Tet. 710

Hæmonian, Thessalian, T. was n.e. Greece, called by poets Hæmonia; famous for magic, hence *hæmony.* Eleg. 2.86; cf. C. 637

Hæmus, mts. in Thrace. Nat. Non. 100

halings, draggings or hawlings. Ch. Gov. 2.3.530

Hall, Joseph, (1574–1656) English Bishop and author; in 1597 he published the first three books of *Toothless Satires;* published *Mundus alter et Idem* in 1605, Eng. translation in 1608; a rare book even in M's time, and one that the bishop must have blushed for. Sm. 558

Hamath, a city in n. Syria. P.L. 12.139

Hammon, Ammon, a deity who had an altar in the Libyan Desert. H. 203

handsel, a gift indicative of good will. Col. 714

Haran, a city in n.w. Mesopotamia. P.L. 12.131

Harefield House, in Middlesex, about 10 m. from Horton. A. (title)

Harapha, Heb. "giant," rendered in the margin of 2 Sam. 21.16 as *Rapha,* from which M. invents the name. S.A. 1068

harbinger, an officer who precedes royalty to prepare a lodging place; hence, a forerunner. P.L. 9.13

harpy, a filthy and ravenous winged monster. C. 604; P.R. 2.403

Hartlib, Samuel, (d. 1670) writer of many pamphlets on education and husbandry; highly thought of by M. Ed. 725

Hayward, Sir John, (c. 1564–1627) Eng. historian. Anim. 2.483; Ref. 1.444

heave-offering, in the Levitical law, an offering which was heaved or elevated by the priest; used also of other offerings. Hir. 881

Hebe, goddess of youth and spring; hence eternal and exuberant youth. C. 289; L'A. 29; V.E. 38; Sca. 104

Hebrides, islands w. of Scotland. L. 156

Hebron, a city 20 m. s.w. of Jerusalem. S.A. 148

Hebrus, a river of Thrace near Mt. Rhodope. L. 63

Hecate, the goddess of enchantment and magic arts. Procan. 96

hecatontome, a collection of 100 volumes, hence a large number. Anim. P.S. 503

Hecatompylos, a city of Parthia; the name means "of a hundred gates." P.R. 3.287

Hector, son of King Priam of Troy, and bravest of all the Trojan warriors. Procan. 96; Ch. Gov. 2.3.533

Hedio, Kaspar, (1494–1552) German Protestant divine; wrote a history of his times and other works. M.B. 630

Hegesippus, the first historian of the church, d. 180; only fragments of his works are extant. Ref. 1.448; P.E. 475

Helena, dau. of Zeus and wife of Menelaus; some stories relate that it was not Helen that was carried off to Troy by Paris, but a phantom. C. 675; Ch. Gov. 2.3.536

Helicon, a range of mts. in Bœotia, the haunt of the Muses. Win. 56; Procan. 96

Hellespont, the Dardanelles, a strait separating Asia and Europe. P.L. 10.309

Helvicus, (1581–1617) eminent German philologist and author of many tracts. Tet. 709

Hercules, son of Jupiter and Alcmena, the national hero of the Bœotians, famous for his twelve labors. Eleg. 7.93; Procan. 96

Heroides, maidens, one of whose parents was divine, the other human. Eleg. 1.86

Hermas, chief character in *The Shepherd of Hermas,* an early Christian allegorical and didactic book, written between 100 and 150 A.D., so highly esteemed by the church in some of the earlier periods as to be almost canonical. Ch. Gov. 1.6.515

Hermes, messenger of Zeus, who carried a *caduceus,* or rod; his Latin name was Mercury; hence in P.L. 3.603, "quick-silver." C. 636; P.L. 4.717; 11.133

Hermes, thrice-great, Hermes Trismegistus, an Egyptian king and sage, Thot, who was said to have written many occult bks. Il P. 88; Idea 101

Hermione, wife of Cadmus, q. v. P.L. 9.506

Hermogenes, Athenian philosopher, fl. c. 450 B.C.; is an interlocutor in the *Cratylus* of Plato. Ed. 729

Hermon, the highest mt. in Palestine. P.L. 12.141 ff.

Herod, the son of Antipater, made king of Judea by Mark Anthony under suspicion of bribery. P.R. 2.424

Hesebon, Heshebon (Vulgate, Hesebon) a city beyond Jordan. P.L. 1.408

Hesiod, a famous Gk. poet (fl. 750 B.C.). Ed. 728

Hesperian fields, western, i. e., Italy, because w. of Greece. Eleg. 3.87; Q.N. 97; P.L. 1.520

Hesperian gardens, mythical gardens in the w. where the golden apples grew. P.L. 3.568

Hesperian tree, a tree that bore golden apples. C. 392

Hesperides, nymphs who guarded the golden apples. P.R. 2.357

Hesperus, the king of the w. land, father of the Hesperides; changed into the evening star. C. 981; Eleg. 3.87; P.L. 4.605; 9.49

Heworth Moore, a village below Newcastle. Eik. 10.812

hey pass, an exclamation used by jugglers. Anim. 3.488

Hierapolis, a city in Phrygia. Anim. P.S. 504

Hilary, (c. 401–449) saint and Gaulish prelate. Tet. 678; C.D. 5.955

Himera, a river in Sicily. Da. 106

hinges, the cardinal points. P.R. 4.415

Hinnom, a ravine near Jerusalem P.L. 1.404

Hippias, (d. c. 490 B.C.) son of Pisistratus; succeeded him as tyrant of Athens; expelled in 510. Ch. Gov. 1.5.512

Hippocrates, (c. 460–c. 370) the "father of Gk. Medicine." Eik. 21.843

hippogrif, a monster in Ariosto's *Orlando,* who carries A's heroes about. P.R. 4.542

hip-shot, having a hip dislocated; hence, awkward. Sm. 556

Hippotades, a patronymic, meaning the "son of Hippotes"; i. e., Æolus. L. 96

Hispahan, a city of central Persia. P.L. 11.394

hobnail, a clown; used in contempt. Col. 720

Hobson, Thomas, drove the coach between Cambridge and London; died Jan. 1, 1631, at the age of 86; see Spectator 509 (Oct. 14, 1712) for an interesting reference

Holmby, a mansion near Northampton where Chas. was imprisoned in 1647. Eik. 26.849

holocaust, a sacrifice entirely consumed by fire; Gk. wholly burnt. S.A. 1702

Hooker, Richard, (c. 1553–1600) English divine; wrote *Of the Laws of Ecclesiastical Polity.* Ch. Gov. 1.2.509

Hooper, John. English bishop; burned at the stake, 1555. Ref. 2.465

Hophni, see 1 Sam. 4. D.D. 2.3.599

Horonaim, a city of Moab, site unknown. P.L. 1.409

horrent, bristling. P.L. 2.513

horrid, L. horridus, rough, bristling. P.L. 1.51

Hosea, see Hosea 1.2 ff. D.D. 2.3.599

hospital, an institution for dispensing hospitality to the needy. Anim. P.S. 502

hosting, a muster of armed men. P.L. 6.93

Hotham, Sir John, governor of Hull, played an important part in the defence of that city against Chas., but was finally executed for treason by the Parliament in 1645. Eik. 8.803; 26.850

Hounds-low, a village of Middlesex, w. of London, connected by a road with Colnbrook. Eik. 18.838

hull, toss about as if empty. P.L. 11.840

Humber, an estuary between Yorkshire and Lincolnshire; M. refers to the eagre made at flood tide about which he comments in the *Hist. of Brit.;* Spenser and Drayton also allude to it. V.E. 99; Da. 108

huddle, to run through hastily. C. 494; Eik. 24.845

Hugh, St., English prelate born in France, made bishop of Lincoln in 1186. Areop. 747

Hull, a town in Yorkshire important in the Civil War, because of munitions stored there. Eik. 8.803

Hunnius, (1550–1603) Lutheran theologian, noted for intolerance. Tet. 708

Huss, John, (1369–1415) Bohemian reformer. Hir. 890; Areop. 748

Hyacinth, a beautiful Spartan youth, beloved by Apollo, who slew him by accident; from his blood sprang the hyacinth. Inf. 25

hyacinthine, dark and curly, as the Gk. hyacinth. P.L. 4.301

Hydaspes, a river of India, modern Jehlam. P.L. 3.436

Hydra, a monster of the swamps with nine heads, slain by Hercules; when a head was cut off, three grew in its place. S. 15.7; C. 604; P.L. 2.628

Hyas, a shepherdess. Da. 107

Hydrus, a water snake. P.L. 10.525

Hylas, (1) a beautiful youth, beloved of Hercules, drawn down by the water nymphs as he stooped to drink from a pool. Eleg. 7.93; P.R. 2.353; Sm. 545; Tet. 664; Da. 106

Hymen, the god of marriage; also called Hymenæus L'A. 125; Eleg. 5.91; P.L. 11.591

Hymenæus, see Hymen. Eleg. 5.91; Ch. Gov. 1.2.508

Hymettus, a range near Athens, noted for its honey. Eleg. 5.90; P.R. 4.247

Hyperborean, pertaining to a mythical people of the far n. Q.N. 97

Hyperion, a Titan, in reality the father of the Sun God, but the name frequently indicates Helios himself, or Apollo. Ad. P. 102

Hyrcania, a land near the Caspian. P. R. 3.317

Hyrcanus, an aspirant for the throne of Syria, supported by the Romans, but captured by the Parthians and sent away at the age of 70. P.R. 3.367

Iapetus, father of Prometheus who, according to an ancient myth, fashioned human beings from the dust of the earth. Procan. 96

Iapetus's son, Prometheus who, to help man's progress in civilization, stole fire from heaven. Procan. 96

Iberian, Spanish. Q.N. 97; *I. dales,* modern Georgia, between the Black and Caspian Seas. P.R. 3.318; *I. fields,* Spain. C. 60; *I. maid,* see *Africanus*

Ibis, a poem in which Ovid launches a furious attack upon an unidentified person. Praes. 99

Icarus, son of the famous artificer Dædalus; the father and son attempted to escape from Crete with the help of wings fastened by wax to their shoulders. Icarus, however, flew too high, the wax melted, and he was drowned in the Ægean Sea. Eleg. 4.88

Iconium, a city in Asia Minor. Hir. 891

Ida, (1) a mt. in central Crete, one of the birthplaces of Zeus. Il P. 29; P.L. 1.515;

(2) a range around Troy. Eleg. 5.90; P.L. 5.382

idea, as used by Plato to denote a pure immaterial pattern. P.L. 7.557; Sm. 552

Idumanian, pertaining to the Blackwater River, Essex. Da. 107

Ignatius, bishop of Antioch, d.c. 117; wrote several epistles. Ref. 1.446; P.E. 477

Igraine, mother of Arthur. Da. 108

Ilissus, a small stream flowing by Athens. P.R. 4.249

illustrate, make glorious; L. illustris, lighted up. P.L. 5.739; 10.78; P.R. 1.370

Illyria, the country from Italy to Macedonia, and from the Danube to Epirus. P.L. 9.505

Ilus, a prince of Troy, builder of the city, which from his name was also known as Ilium. Eleg. 1.85

Imaus, the Himalaya mts. P.L. 3.431

imbosk, to conceal oneself. Ref. 2.453

imp, offspring. P.L. 9.89

impaled, surrounded. P.L. 2.647; 6.553

impediment, baggage; L. impedimenta. P.L. 6.548

implicit, L. implicitus, folded in; hence, involved. P.L. 7.323

incentive, kindling. P.L. 6.519

incubus, an imaginary being, supposed to cause nightmare. P.R. 2.152

indiction, a cycle of 15 yrs. Ref. 1.453

indorsed, placed on the back. P.R. 3.329

Indus, a river of India flowing into the Arabian Sea. P.L. 9.82; P.R. 3.272

infer, conclude. P.L. 7.116

infringed, broken to pieces. P.R. 1.62

inhabitation, the inhabited world; a Grecism. S.A. 1512

Inogenia, dau. of the British king, Pandrasus, wife of Brutus

instinct, infused with. P.L. 2.937; 6.752

insulse, dull, insipid, stupid. Sm. 544

interrupt, interposed. P.L. 3.84

inure, to establish by use. P.L. 8.239

Ion, son of Apollo by Creusa; the subject of an extant tragedy by Euripides. Rous. 30

Ionia, part of Asia Minor inhabited by Gks. Eleg. 1.85; P.L. 1.508

Ionian Homer, the birthplace of Homer, author of the two great epics, the *Iliad* and the *Odyssey,* was much disputed in ancient times, but was generally believed to be somewhere within the limits of Ionia, the central section of the w. coast of Asia Minor.

Irassa, a city mentioned by Pindar in connection with a different Antæus. P.R. 4.564

Iris, the rainbow. P.L. 11.244; C. 83.992

Isidorus Hispalensis, usually known as Isidore Mercator, fabricated in the 8th or 9th c. a famous code of canon law or collection of false decretals. Tet. 709

Isis, among the Egyptians, a goddess, sister and wife of Osiris, both deities representing the spiritual principle of good. Q.N. 98; P.L. 1.478; H. 212

Ismenian steep, a rock near Thebes from which the Sphinx hurled herself when Œdipus guessed her riddle. P.R. 4.575

Isocrates, (436–338 B.C.) one of the ten great Athenian orators; intimate friend of Plato; 21 of his orations are extant. Ed. 730

Ixion, a fabulous king of the Lapithæ, who, after committing a murder, was invited to the table of Jupiter; there he attempted to seduce Juno, a crime for which he was bound to a wheel that revolved eternally. Tet. 657

Jachin, see 1 Kings 7.21. Col. 720

Jacob, see Gen. 28.12; P.L. 3.510; see Gen. 32.1,2. P.L. 11.214

Jacobuses, Salmasius received 100 jacobuses from Chas. II. for writing his book. The j. was a gold coin struck in the reign of James I, value 22 s. Sal. 95

Jael, see Judges 418 ff. S.A. 989

Januas, L. gate; hence an introduction to some branch of learning. Ed. 726

Janus, a Roman deity of the beginnings of undertakings, usually represented wth two heads. P. L. 11. 129

Japan, visited by an Englishman in 1613; Gilbert. Anim. 3.490

Japhet, Iapetus, one of the Titans, father of Prometheus (forethought) and Epimetheus (afterthought), the "unwiser son." P.L. 4.717

jar, to make a tremulous and discordant sound. P.L. 5.793; S.M. 20

Javan, the son of Japheth (Gen. 10.2) identified with Ion, the mythical ancestor of the Ionians (Gks). P.L. 1.508; S.A. 716

Jehoram, Jehosophat, Jehu, for all these see 2 Kings 1 ff.

Jehu, a common name for a reckless coachman. Eik. 11.817

Jephthah, Judges 11. P.R. 2.439; S.A. 283

Jericho, a city, 5 m. from the Dead Sea. P.R. 2.20

Jeroboam, see 1 Kings 12 ff. Ref. 2.455; Ch. Gov. 1.5.514; Eik. 24.846

Jerome, (c. 340–420) a father of the Catholic church; made the Vulgate translation. M.B. 636; C.P. 869

Jerusalem, see 2 Chron. 36. P.R. 3.283

Jezebel, see 1 Kings 21. Sm. 550; see Rev. 2.18 ff. Anim. 13.495

Joab, see 2 Sam. 2 ff. Anim. 3.489

Joel, see Judges 4.21

John the Baptist, see Luke 3. P.R. 1.184; 2.84

John Dory, a favorite old ballad, often referred to in 17th c. lit. Col. 719

John a-Noakes, John (or **Tom**) **a-Stiles,** fictitious names used in cases of ejectment as we use "John Doe." Col. 719

Jonathan, see 1 Sam. 14. Ten. 755

Jonson, Ben, (c. 1573–1637) Eliz. dramatist and poet. L'A. 132

Josephus, (37-c. 95) a Jewish historian. Ch. Gov. 1 Pref. 503. D.D. 2.16.614; 2.17.614; Eik. 28.857

Josiah, see 2 Kings 22 ff. P.L. 1.418

jousted, took part in a tournament. P.L. 1.583

Julian the Apostate, (331–363) Roman emperor, at first a Christian, but later converted to paganism. Areop. 736; Ref. 1.450

Julius Cæsar, Roman dictator who became famous in middle life; said to have lamented while younger that he had done so little. P.R. 3.39

Juno, wife of Jupiter, angry at Æneas. C. 700; A. 22; P.L. 4.500; 9.18

Justin Martyr, a father of the Gk. church. d. c. 163. Ref. 1.488

Justinian, (483–563) Byzantine emperor. Tet. 682; Eik. 28.859

Justinian code, the body of Roman law compiled with notes by order of Justinian

justling rocks, the Symplegades at the entrance of the Bosporus. P.L. 2.1018

Jutland, the continental part of Denmark

Juxton, Wm., (1582–1663) English prelate, archbishop of Canterbury (1660), an adherent of Laud's. Eik. 1.783; 2.785

keal, a broth in which kale or cabbage is the chief ingredient. Sm. 552

kindly, natural. P.L. 4.228; 4.668

Keri, (d. 1685) Hungarian historian and Jesuit. Sm. 554; Areop. 738

key-cold, cold as a key. Ch. Gov. 2.3.530

kickshaws, performers of fantastic nothings. Ed. 731

kickshose, a light, unsubstantial food. Anim. 2.484

Kimchi, David, (1160–1232) influential Jewish grammarian and commentator. D.D. 2.18.617

Kiriathaim, a town e. of Jordan. S.A. 1081

Knox, John, (1505–1572) Scotch reformer. Ten. 763

Lactantius, (fl. 313) Christian writer and apologist. Ref. 1.451; Tet. 702

Ladon, a river in Arcadia, tributary to the Alpheus. A. 97

Laertes, father of Ulysses. P.L. 9.441

Laertius, Diogenes, (c. 211–235 A.D.) wrote important work on lives and doctrines of ancient philosophers. Sm. 545; Ed. 729

Lahor, the capital of the Punjab, India, formerly one of the capitals of the Moguls. P.L. 11.391

Lambeth, a palace in Lambeth, 1½ m. from St. Paul's Cathedral in London, the city residence of the Archbishop of Canterbury. Anim. 1.482; Areop. 736

Lampridius, (4th c.) one of the writers of the *Augustan History,* a collection of the lives of the Roman emperors. Ref. 1.447

Lancelot, one of the chief heroes of Arthur's Round Table. P.R. 2.361

lantskip, landscape. P.L. 2.491

Langland, author of *Piers the Plowman.* Sm. 558

Lapland, the traditional home of witches. P.L. 2.665

Laodicean, i.e., lukewarm; see Rev. 3.15, 16. Anim. 2.487

Lars, or Lares, household deities of the Romans. H. 191

Lateran, a palace in e. Rome, given by Constantine to the Bishop of Rome; a number of ecclesiastical councils were held here

Latimer, Hugh, (1485–1555) English prelate and reformer; burned at the stake. Ref. 1.444; Eik. 20.841

Latona, mother of Apollo and Artemis; sent forth by jealous Juno to wander about; at one time rustics mocked her and roiled the water she was about to drink, whereupon they were turned into frogs. A. 19; S. 12.6

Laud, Wm., (1573–1645) archbishop of Canterbury under Chas. I; the leader of the high church party; executed Jan. 10. Eik. 1.782

Laura, the heroine of Petrarch's poems. Sm. 549

Lavinia, dau. of the king of Latium, betrothed to Turnus, but later wedded Æneas. P.L. 9.17

Lawrence, Edward, son of Henry Lawrence, born in 1633; the father was President of Cromwell's Council. S. 20.1

Laws of Fate, decrees of destiny. Procan. 96

lawn, a cleared, open space in the woods. P.L. 4.252

Lebanon, a range in Syria, parallel with the Mediterranean. P.L. 1.447

Lee, a small river flowing into the Thames n. of London. V.E. 97

Lemnos, a large island in the Ægean Sea; see *Iliad.* 1.590 ff. P.L. 1.746; Eleg. 7.93; Nat. Nov. 100

Lemures, spirits of the dead, usually bent on doing mischief to the living. H. 191

lenient, assuasive, softening. S.A. 659

Leo, a sign of the Zodiac, Lion. P.L. 10.676

Leo, Bishop of Rome, pope, 440–461. M.B. 638

Leo X., pope, 1513–21. Areop. 735

Lesbian shore, Lesbos is an island in the Ægean near Mysia, to which the head of Orpheus was said to have been borne after leaving the mouth of the Hebrus. L. 63; Sal. 22; Sca. 104

Lethe, the river of forgetfulness in the lower world. Q.N. 98; Idea. 101; Dam. 108; Ad R. 109; P.L. 2.583, 604

Leucippus, Gk. philosopher (fl. 500 B.C.) founder of the atomic school. P.E. 477

Leucothea, a marine goddess of the Romans. C. 874; P.L. 11.135

Leunclavius, (1583–1593) German historian, author, and translator. Tet. 697

Leviathan, a Bible word, used for a large mythical creature. P.L. 1.201; 7.412

Levites, the descendants of Levi; the men formed a body of assistants to the priests in the temple service. Ch. Gov. 1.4.511; Hir. 886; C.D. 1.23.1021

Levite's wife, see Judges 19.16 ff. P.L. 1.505; Anim. 13.495

Levitical, pertaining to the old Jewish system of ritual of the Levites, the descendants of Levi, whose laws are recorded in Leviticus. Ch. Gov. 1.5.513

levy, raise. P.L. 2.501

Ley, John (1583–1662) minister at Great Bulworth, Cheshire, member of Westminster Assembly; author of several tracts; wrote *Sunday A Sabbath,* 1641. Anim. 3.489

Libanius, (314–390?) celebrated heathen sophist and rhetorician. Tet. 687

libbard, leopard. P.L. 7.467

Libecchio, the s.w. wind. P.L. 10.706

Libitina, a goddess of the dead and of funerals. Eleg. 3.87

Libra, the scales, a sign of the zodiac. P.L. 3.558

Libya, all Africa except Egypt. Q.N. 97

Libyan Jove, Jupiter Ammon, reputed father of Alexander the Great. Eleg. 4.88

Lichas, the servant of Hercules, who brought him the poisoned robe; thrown by H. into the sea. P.L. 2.545

Ligea, a siren. C. 879

Lily, Wm. (c. 1468–1522) wrote the Latin grammar used throughout England for many years. Ed. 727

limbec, an alembic, a still. P.L. 3.605

limbo, L. limbus, abl. limbo, a border; a region on the edge of hell; there were three: Of the fathers; of unbaptized infants; of fools. P.L. 3.495; Sm. 550; C.D. 2.13.1070

limitary, set to guard the limits. P.L. 4.971

lin, cease. Ch.Gov.Concl. 538

Linus, a mythical singer. Eleg. 6.92

Littleton, Sir Thomas, (1402–1481) a famous jurist, author of a noted bk. on law in French. Col. 724

Livius, Titus, (59 B.C.–17 A.D.) greatest Roman historian. Ten. 759; Areop. 734

Locrian, pertaining to e. Greece. Procan. 96

Locrian remnants, Timæus of Locris (fl. c. 390 B.C.), one of the masters of Plato, left a treatise: *On the Soul of the World, and Nature.* Ed. 729

Locrine, a mythical king of England, eldest son of Brutus, and father of Sabrina. C. 826; 921

Logres, Britain. P.R. 2.360

Lollards, the followers of Wyclif. Ch. Gov. 1.6.517

Lombard, Peter, (c. 1100–1160) Italian theologian; wrote 4 bks. of *Sentences.* D.D. 2.22.624

Longchamp, Wm of, (d. 1197) English prelate, Bishop of Ely, chancellor of Rich. I. See Holinshed for the story alluded to in Sm. 552

Longinus, (210–273) Gk. philosopher, supposed to have written the essay, *On Sublimity.* Ed. 729

lore, lesson. P.L. 2.815

Loreto, an episcopal see and pilgrimage resort of catholics in Ancona, Italy. Areop. 746

losel, worthless. Sm. 560

Lotharius (1075–1137) Emperor of Germany after death of Henry V. in 1125; crowned at Rome by Pope Innocent II. where he performed many acts of fealty to the papal see. Tet. 706

lotions, salt, referring to the common practice of emptying dishes from the windows into the street. Sm. 547

lourdan, a blockhead. Ref. 2.458

lowbell, a bell hung on the necks of animals. Hir. 896

Loyola, Ignatius, (1491–1556) Spanish prelate, founder of the Jesuits. Sm. 552; Ref. 2.455

Lucca, a city of Tuscany; in M's time an independent republic; home of the ancestors of Diodati. Da. 106

Lucifer, the morning star; used for Satan. P.L. 5.760; 7.131; 10.425; H. 74; Eleg. 3.87

Lucilius (148?–100? B.C.) Roman satiric poet of small poetical faculty but of great originality and force of character. Areop. 734

Lucina, Roman goddess of childbirth. Win. 26, 28

Lucretius, (c. 96 B.C.–55 B.C.) Roman philosophical poet. Ed. 728; Areop. 734

Lucrine Bay, a lagoon in Campania, famous for oysters. P.R. 2.347

Lucumo, see Lucca. Da. 107

Ludlow-Castle, in Shropshire on the Teme. C. 65

Ludovicus Pius, (Louis the Pious; 478–840) son and successor of Charlemagne, who was deposed by two of his sons. Ten. 762

Lyæus, a name for Bacchus, signifying his power to set men free from care. Eleg. 6.91

Lycæus, a mt. in Arcadia. A. 98

Lycambes, father of Neobule, who was betrothed to the poet Archilochus; Lycambes forced her to break her troth, whereupon A. lampooned them both so savagely that they committed suicide. Praes. 10

Lycaonian Boötes, Boötes is a star in the northern hemisphere close to the Great Bear; sometimes called Arctophylax, "the Bear Warden"; a myth declared that the Great Bear was Callisto, daughter of Lycaon, beloved of Jupiter, changed by jealous Juno into a bear. Eleg. 5.90

Lycurgus, (396 B.C.–323 B.C.) Spartan lawgiver. Ch. Gov. 1.1.506; Ed. 729; Eik. 28.859

Lydia, a country of w. Asia Minor. L'A. 136; C.D. 938; Ref. 2.460

Lyones, mythical country in Arthurian romances, probably Cornwall. P.R. 2.360

Macdonnel, see *Colkitto*

Macedonia, part of Greece n. of Thessaly. S. 8.10; P.R. 3.32, 290

Machaon, son of Æsculapius, god of medicine, and himself a famous physician in the Trojan War. Procan. 96

Machabeus, the family of Maccabees; Judas M. led a revolt vs. Antiochus Epiphanes; they were priests. P.R. 3.165

Machærus, a fortress e. of the Dead Sea. P.R. 2.22

Madian, a nomadic Arabian tribe. S.A. 281

Mæcenas, prime minister of Augustus; a famous patron of men of letters. Man. 104

Mænalus, a mt. in Arcadia, sacred to Pan. Eleg. 5.91; A. 102

Mæonides, Homer, according to one story born in Lydia (Mæonia) P.L. 3.35

Mæotis, the "Tauric Pool," the sea of Azof, on the n. side of the Black Sea. P.L. 9.78; P.R. 4.79

Magellan, the Straits of Magellan, s. of S. America. P.L. 10.687

magnetic, magnet. P.L. 3.583; P.R. 2.168

Mahanaim, a city of Palestine e. of Jordan; Gen. 32.1, 2. P.L. 11.214

Maia, mother of Hermes, messenger of Zeus. P.L. 5.285

Maid of Justice, Astræa, the goddess of just dealing, believed to have abandoned the earth in the Iron Age through her horror at its degeneracy. Eleg. 4.89

Malabar, the w. coast of Hindustan. P.L. 9.1103

Manlius, Roman consul, defended the Capitol from attacks of the Gauls, who captured Rome in 389 B.C.; according to tradition, an attempt of the Gauls to take the fortress by night was frustrated by Manlius, who was awakened by a flock of geese; later fell out of favor and was executed for treason. Eik. 26.850

Mauretania, now Morocco and w. Algeria. Ad P. 102

mammock, mangle, maul. Ref. 1.447

Manes, the spirits of the dead. Q.N. 98

manure, tend by hand. P.L. 4.628; 11.28

marasmus, consumption. P.L. 11.487

Marcion, a famous heretic of the 2nd c.; denied the incarnation and resurrection. Tet. 678; Col. 717; Anim. P.S. 504

Mareotis, a lake in Egypt. Q.N. 98

Margiana, a large district, s.e. of the Caspian. P.R. 3.317

marl, an earth, made of clay and carbonate of lime, but used vaguely for ground. P.L. 1.296

Margites, an ancient Gk. comic poem on a silly jack-of-all trades, considered by Aristotle to have been the germ of comedy. Areop. 737

Marini, (1569–1625) an Italian poet whose style was marked by whimsical comparison and overwrought descriptions. Man. 104

Marocco, Morocco. P.L. 1.584; 11.404

Massicus, a mt. in Campania, famous for wine. Eleg. 6.31

Marius, C. (155–86 B.C.) a Roman general, the rival of Sulla. Fr. Com. 907

Maro, Vergil, whose full name was Publius Vergilius Maro. Eleg. 1.85

Martin, St., a saint of the R.C. church, b. c. 316, bishop of Tours c. 371; his day is Nov. 11, Martinmas. Areop. 747; Ref. 1.445; Eik. 17.836

Martyr, Peter, (1455–1526) Italian scholar, statesman, and historian; left valuable historical work on progress of American discovery. M.B. 628; Tet. 710; C.D. 2.7.1063

Mavors, an old name for Mars, the god of War. Q.N. 97

masoreth, the text of the Jewish Bible with the traditional and critical marginalia of ancient scholars. D.D. Pref. 576; Tet. 689

Massic cups, from Massicus, a mt. in Campania, famous for its wine. Eleg. 6.91

materious, full of matter. Tet. 680

Matthew Paris, (c. 1200–1259) English chronicler, wrote the *Historia Major,* a history of the world from the creation to 1259. Ten. 762

Mazzoni, (1548–1598) Italian writer, intimate friend of Tasso; wrote several philosophical and critical works, the most important of which is his *Defence of Dante.* Ed. 729

mawkin, a kitchen servant. Sm. 558

Meander, a winding river in Asia Minor. C. 231

meath, a drink made by mixing wine and honey, but here used for unfermented wine. P.L. 5.345

Mecca, the capital of Arabia, birthplace of Mahomet, and the object of at least one pilgrimage for every pious Moslem. Eik. 10.813

Media, n.w. part of Persia. P.L. 4.171; P.R. 3.320, 376

medulla, a compendium or abridgment. D.D. Pref. 577

Medusa, a Gorgon who turned all beholders into stone; from each drop of her blood sprang a serpent; slain by Perseus who gave her head to Athene. P.L. 2.611

Medway, a river of s.e. England. V.E. 100

Megæra, a Fury, with snakes entwined in her hair. P.L. 10.560

megrim, a headache, often accompanied by dizziness. D.D. Pref. 574

Mela, a Roman geographer, fl. in 1st cent. Ed. 728

Melancthon, (1497–1560) German reformer, co-worker with Luther. M.B. 626; Tet. 707

Melanchætis, one of the four coursers of the chariot of Night. Q.N. 97

Melchisedec, see Gen. 14. Hir. 882; C.D. 1026

Melesigenes, Homer, so called because sometimes said to have been born at Meles. P.R. 4.259

Melibœan, a rich purple dye, named from Melibœa, a town in Thessaly. P.L. 11.242

Melind, a town on the coast of East Africa. P.L. 11.399

Memmius, Roman orator, poet, and politician; son-in-law of Sulla; often mentioned by Cicero; to him Lucretius dedicated his poem *De Rerum Natura.* Areop. 734

Memnon, an Ethiopian prince, famed for his beauty, who fought in the Trojan War. Il P. 18; P.L. 10.308

Memphian, Memphis was the ancient capital of Egypt. P.L. 1.307; 694; H. 214

Menalcas, a shepherd. Da. 108

Menander, Gk. dramatic poet, b. at Athens 341 B.C.; called the originator of the new comedy which attempted to portray actual life and manners. Areop. 734

Menenius Agrippa, the patrician ambassador to the plebeians, who related the fable of the belly and its members. Ref. 2.458

Mercury, in Roman mythology, M. was the father of Faunus. C. 962

Mercurius Britannicus, the assumed name of the author, probably Joseph Hall, of *Mundus Alter et Idem,* a satirical description of London. Anim. 3.490

Meroe, a district in the basin of the Nile, supposed by the ancients to be an island. P.R. 4.71

Michael, one of the archangels, was regarded as special protector of the Jewish nation; a festival was instituted in his honor by the Christians of the 9th c., which is still observed as Michaelmas Day (Sept. 29). C.D. 1.9.985

Midas, king of Phrygia, judging that Pan sang more sweetly than Apollo, had his ears changed into those of asses. S. 13.4; Ch. Gov. 2. Concl. 538

Middelburg, a prosperous commercial city in the Netherlands. Ten. 772

middle air, between earth and heaven. P.L. 1.516

middle shore, of the Mediterranean. P.L. 5.339

Mile-End Green, an open space, where troops exercised, about a mile e. of the center of London. S. 11.7

Mincius, tributary to the Po in Italy; Vergil lived on its shore. L. 86

Minerva, a Roman goddess, represented in art as holding a lance and a shield in one hand. C. 447

minims, minute things. P.L. 7.482

minute drops, drops that fall every minute. Il P. 130

Miriam, a prophetess, the sister of Moses; sang a song of triumph after the children of Israel had passed through the Red Sea. C.D. 1.29.1038

missive, hurled. P.L. 6.519

Moab, the country east of the Dead Sea. P.L. 1.406; Ten. 760

Modin, a city of Judea, location unknown, mentioned in Maccabees. P.R. 3.170

Mogul, a dynasty of Moslem emperors, reigning at Lahore. P.L. 11.391

Mole, a river in Surrey, which runs under ground for a short distance. V.E. 95

mole, mass. P.L. 10.300

Moloch, an Ammonite god, to whom human sacrifice was made. P.L. 1.392; 417; 2.43; 6.357; H. 205

moly, a fabulous herb, in Homer given by Hermes to Odysseus, powerful against charms C. 635

Mombaza, now the chief town of British East Africa. P.L. 11.399

Mona, an island n.w. of Wales. L. 54

monostrophic, of one stanza. S.A. Pref. 405

Montalban, Montauban, a castle of France, the scene of a battle between Charlemagne and the Saracens in the romances. P.L. 1.583

Montemayor, (c. 1520–1561) Spanish romancer. Areop. 740

Montezume, emperor of Mexico. P.L. 11.407

Mopsus, a shepherd. Da. 107

Moreh, see Gen. 12.6. P.L. 12.137; Eik. 10.811

Morgante, Maggiore, a serio-burlesque romantic poem by Pulci written 1485; the hero of the piece is the giant Morgante. Areop. 737

Morpheus, the god of sleep. Il P. 10

morrice, the morris dance. C. 116

Mosco, Moscow. P.L. 11.395

Moses' chair, see Matt. 23.2. P.R. 4.219

Moulin, (1568–1658?) eminent French Prot. theologian; author of *On the Recent Origin of Popery* and of other works. Anim. P.S. 504

Mountain, the Mount of the Temptation was probably Niphates, *q.v.*

Mount Ida, a mt. near Troy. Eleg. 5.90

Mozambic, in Portuguese East Africa. P.L. 4.161

Mulciber, Vulcan, the fire god. P.L. 1.740

mummer, a masked clown. S.A. 1325

murrain, a disease affecting cattle, esp. the foot-and-mouth disease. P.L. 12.179

Musæus, Mythical Greek poet supposed to have lived in the age of Homer. Il P. 104

Musculus, (1540–1581) German Lutheran theologian; author of *Compendium Theologicum.* Tet. 708; C.D. 2.7.1063

must, new wine. P.R. 4.16

Mycale, a mt. in Lydia. Man. 104

Myrmidons, the subjects and soldiers of Achilles in the Trojan War. Eleg. 4.88

Myrmidons, King of, Achilles. Eleg. 4.88

myrrhine, probably resembling porcelain. P.R. 4.119

Naaman, see Gehazi.

Naboth's vineyard, the property of Naboth, coveted by Ahab, who put him to death. Eik. 1.780

Nævius, Latin dramatic and epic poet, d. 204 B.C. Areop. 734

Naiades, water-nymphs. P.R. 2.355; C. 253

Narcissus, a beautiful youth who fell in love with his own image. C. 237

Naseby, a village 12 m. n. of Northampton, Eng., where on June 14, 1645, Fairfax and Cromwell defeated Charles I. Eik. 21.842

Naso, the poet Ovid, whose full name was Publius Ovidius Naso. Eleg. 6.91

Nathanæl, spoken of in John 1. 45–9, believed by many to be the same as Bartholomew, one of the apostles; stated by Eusebius to have preached the Gospel in India. C.D. 5.964

nathless, nevertheless. P.L. 1.299

Nazarites, religious devotees among the Hebrews, dedicated to God by a vow; see Num. 6. S.A. 318, 1359, 1386; Anim. 13.499

Neæra, the name of a maiden in Latin pastoral poetry. L. 69

Nebaioth, used for Ishmael, but the name of I's eldest son. Gen. 21.17. P.R. 2.309

Neocæsarea, a city in Asia Minor, where an important council was held in 315. Tet. 702

Nebo, a projecting headland in Moab, e. of the n. end of the Dead Sea; cf. 1 Chron. 5.8. P.L. 1.407

Negus, king of Abyssinia. P.L. 11.397

nepenthes, a drug given to Helen by Polydamna, wife of Thone. C. 674

Neptune, Roman god of the sea, enraged at Ulysses. P.L. 9.18

Nereus, the kindly old man of the sea, the father of 50 daughters, nymphs of the Mediterranean. C. 834; 870; Nat. Non. 100

Nessus, a centaur who, while attempting to carry off Deianira, Hercules' wife, was shot by him; in revenge he gave her some of his blood to be used if necessary as a charm to retain her husband's affection; she later smeared it on his sacrificial robe which then stuck fast to his flesh and fatally poisoned him; unable to bear his agony, Hercules ascended a funeral pyre on Mount Œta and was consumed in its flames. Procan. 96

Newcastle, Earl of, (1592–1676) Sir William Cavendish, British general and author; in the Civil War he commanded Chas.'s army in n. and gained important victories. Eik. 1.790

nice, fastidious. C. 139; P.L. 4.241; 5.433; 8.399; P.R. 4.157

Nicæa, Nice, in Asia Minor, the seat of two councils, one in 325 and one in 787. Ref. 1.447

Nicander, Gk. poet of the 2nd c. B.C. Ed. 728

Nicetas, a Byzantine historian, D.C. 1216. Eik. 1.782

Nichomachus, son of Aristotle, fl. c. 320 B.C.; little known of his life; some critics have ascribed to him works generally thought to have been written by his father. D.D. 2.21.622

night-foundered, lost in the night. C. 482; P.L. 1.204

Nineveh, a city on the Tigris, founded by Ninus. Eleg. 1.86; P.R. 3.275

Ninus, reputed founder of Nineveh. Idea 101

Niphates, a mt. range of w. Asia. P.L. 3.742

Nisibis, a city in n.w. Mesopotamia. P.R. 3.291

Nisroch, an Assyrian deity. P.L. 6.447

Norumbega, a district in N.A. corresponding roughly to the state of Maine. P.L. 10.696

Notus, the s. wind. P.L. 10.702

Novatians, a sect founded in the 3rd c., famous for its strict discipline. Eik. 17.835

numbering Israel, see 1 Chron. 21.1. P.R. 3.410

numerous, metrical. P.L. 5.150

Numa, the 2nd king in legendary Roman history, reputed to have founded many typical Roman institutions. Ten. 759; Ch.Gov. 1.1.506. Sca. 104

Nyseian Ile, Nysa was a city in n. Africa on an island in the river Triton. P.L. 4.275

Ob, a river of Siberia. P.L. 9.78

obdured, hardened. P.L. 2.568; 6.785

obnoxious, exposed. P.L. 9.170, 1094; S.A. 106

obsequious, obedient. P.L. 6.783; 8.509

obvious, L. in the way. P.L. 6.69; 11.374; S.A. 95

Ocean's trumpeter, Triton, who announced Jupiter's commands to the wind on his shell. Nat. Non. 100

Oceanus, orig. a swift stream encircling the known world; later, the Atlantic. C. 867

Odrysian, Thracian. Eleg. 4.89

Œchalia, a town in Eubœa, conquered by Hercules. P.L. 2.542

Œdipus, legendary king of Thebes, overcame the sphinx; involuntarily killed his father and married his mother; subject of Gk. drama. Ch. Gov. 2. Pref. 523; Nat. Non. 100

Œta, a mt. in s. Thessaly. P.L. 2.545; Procan. 96; Man. 105

Og, a giant of Bashan; Deut. 3.11. S.A. 1080

Ogygian, pertaining to Ogygius (Thebes). Eleg. 6.88

Olympian games, held in Elis, when all Greece participated. P.L. 2.530

Olympian hill, the mt. of the muses and gods on the border of Macedonia and Thessaly; sometimes M. means the high heaven. Nat. Non. 100

Olympiodorus, Gk. historian of the 5th c. of Thebes in Egypt. D.D. 2.16.614

Olympias, mother of Alex. the Gt. P.L. 9.509

Omnific, L. all-making. P.L. 7.217

Onesimus, St. disciple of Paul, martyred in 95. P.E. 472

Ophion, a Titan. P.L. 10.581

Ophir, a country, situation unknown, whence Solomon obtained gold. P.L. 11.400; Ref. 2.469

Ophiucus, a n. constellation, representing a man holding a serpent; "serpent-bearer." P.L. 2.709

Ophiusa, "abounding in snakes," applied to several islands near Minorca. P.L. 10.528

Oppian, Gk. poet of the 2nd c. A.D. Ed. 728

Opprobrious Hill, a peak of the Mt. of Olives, east of Jerusalem; 1. Kings 11.7. P.L. 1.403; 416; 443

Ops, wife of Saturn. P.L. 10.584; Eleg. 5.90

optic glass, telescope. P.L. 1.1.288; 3.590

orc, sea monster. P.L. 9.835

Orcus, name of the Roman king of the lower world. Eleg. 7.93; Ad P. 103; P.L. 2.964

Ordalium, a med. Latin adaptation of the word "ordeal." D.D. 2.18.617

oread, a mt. nymph. Eleg. 5.91; P.L. 9.387

Oreb, Mt. Sinai. P.L. 1.7; 484; 11.74

Orestes, pursued by the Furies for killing his mother; favorite subject for the Gk. tragic poets. Eik. 28.859

orient, bright, like the sunrise. P.L. 1.546

Origen, a Gk. father of the church; d. c. 253. Ref. 1.448; 2.453; D.D. 2.17.616; Hir. 894

Orion, a constellation represented as a man with a belt, supposed to bring storms. P.L. 1.305; Eleg. 7.93

Orkneys, a group of islands off n. Scotland, thought of by M. as the n. limit. Da. 108

Ormus, a city at the mouth of the Persian Gulf, a famous trading-place. P.L. 2.2

Orontes, the chief river of Syria. P.L. 4.273; 9.80

Orpheus, a legendary musician who visited Hades to bring back his wife, Eurydice, by the charm of his music; permission was given, on condition that he should not look back; he played so beautifully that trees and rocks were charmed and hastened to follow him; when he had almost reached the gates he looked around and his wife vanished. L. 58; L A. 145; Il P. 105; Ed. 728; Eleg. 6.92

Orus, an Egyptian deity. P.L. 1.478; H. 212

Osiris, an Egyptian deity who taught the people agriculture. H. 213; Idea 101; P.L. 1.478; Areop. 747

Oudoceus, Welsh bishop of the 6th c. Eik. 28.859

Ouse, a river rising in Oxfordshire. V.E. 92; Dam. 108

outlandish, simply foreign. P.R. 4.125

Oxus, a large river of central Asia, flowing into the Aral Sea. P.L. 11.389

Padan-Aram, apparently n.e. from Palestine; see Gen. 28. P.L. 3.513

Padre Paolo, Sarpi (1552–1623) Venetian historian, champion of free thought, interested in scientific thought; his great work, the *History of the Council of Trent,* was published in translation in London in 1619. Areop. 735; Ref. 2.457

Pæan, a name for Apollo, signifying "The Healer." Sca. 104

Palatine, one of the hills of Rome on wh. stood the palaces of the later emperors. P.R. 4.50

pall, a covering of silk or other material for the altar. Ref. 1.441

Palladian, referring to the goddess of wisdom, Pallas. Areop. 743

Pales, a Roman deity of flocks. Da. 107; P.L. 9.393

Palmerin, important Spanish romances of chivalry. Eik. 1.784

pampered, L. pampinus, overgrown; a vineyard in which the branches were full of leaves, and overgrown, was pampered. P.L. 5.214

Paphian, pertaining to Paphos, a city of Cyprus, famed for its temple. Eleg. 1.86; Eleg. 5.90; Eleg. 7.92; Man. 105

Pan, the Gk. god of nature, patron of shepherds; the word also means "all." P.L. 4.266; 4.707; P.R. 2.190; C. 175; 267; A. 106; H. 89; Da. 106

Pandemonium, the palace of "all the devils," after "Pantheon." P.L. 1.756; 10.424

Pandora, "all gifts," a woman created by the gods to betray men into ill fortune. P.L. 4.714; D.D. 2.3; 600

Paneas, in n. Palestine, where is a source of the Jordan. P.L. 3.535

panim, heathen. P.L. 1.765

Panope, "all-seeing," a sea nymph. L. 99

Papias, early Christian writer, fl. 130. P.E. 474

Paquin, Pekin. P.L. 11.390

paragon, to compare. P.L. 10.426

parallax, the effect of mirrors reflecting objects appearing in succession. P.R. 4.40

paramount, supreme lord. P.L. 2.508

paranymph, bridesman. S.A. 1020

Parcæ, the three goddesses of Fate. 1 Prod. b. 94; Procan. 96

Pareus, David (1548–1622), emiment German Divine of Reformed church; published "Neustadt Bible," commentaries on Scripture, and other works; his principles were Calvinistic. Ch. Gov. 2 Pref. 525; D.D. 2.22.624

parget, to gloss over. Anim. 13.501

Parker, Matthew, (1504–1575) learned and meritorious Eng. prelate, appointed archb. of Canterbury by Elizabeth in 1559. M.B. 628

Parthenope, one of the Sirens, who drowned herself when Ulysses sailed by without halting; she was buried at Naples where the sea cast her body. C. 878; 3 Leon. 95

Parthian, pertaining to an empire bounded by the Euphrates, the Caspian Sea, the Indus river and the Indian Ocean. Eleg. 7.93

peal, fill with noise. P.L. 2.920

Pegasus, the winged horse in mythology, associated with the Muses. P.L. 7.4; Rous. 109

Pelagius, an Eng. monk (fl. 400) who denied original sin, insisted on free will and rejected infant baptism. Anim. 2.485; Eik. 16.832; Ref. 1.444

Peleus, father of Achilles. Procan. 96

Pellean, Alex. the Gt., born at Pella; when 23,

he captured the wife and daughters of Darius, but dismissed them. P.R. 2.196

Pelion, a mt. in Thessaly, famous in mythology because the giants attempted to scale heaven by piling Mt. Ossa upon it. Q.N. 98

Pelleas, a knight of King Arthur. P.R. 2.361

Pellenore, a knight of King Arthur. P.R. 2.361

Pelops, a family whose misfortunes were the subject of many Gk. dramas. Il P. 99; Eleg. 1.86

Pelorus, n.e. promontory of Sicily. P.L. 1.232; Nat. Non. 100

Penelope, wife of Odysseus, famous for her constancy, and patient waiting for the long deferred return of her husband from the Trojan War. Eleg. 4.88

Peneus, a river of Thessaly flowing through the vale of Tempe. Eleg. 5.89; Eleg. 7.93; Man. 105

Pentheus, a king of Thebes in Gk. legend and drama. Tet. 676; 2 Leon. 95

Peor, Baal-peor, a licentious deity of the Philistines. P.L. 1.412; Ch. 197

Peræa, a district e. of the Jordan. P.R. 2.24

Pericles, (c. 495–429 B.C.) great Athenian statesman and orator. Anim. 4.491

Peripatetics, the followers of Aristotle, who walked about while teaching or disputing. D.D. 2.11.608

Perse's daughter, Circe, the famous enchantress. Eleg. 6.92

Persephone, the Gk. name for Proserpina, wife of Pluto and therefore Queen of the Lower World. Procan. 96

Persepolis, former capital of Persia. P.R. 3.284

person, personate, terms in the drama referring to the representation of characters on the stage. P.L. 10.156; P.R. 4.341

Peru, a country of w. S. America, but used by M. for all S.A. Ad P. 102

Peter's penny, an annual tax of one penny formerly paid to the R.C. ch. Hir. 886

Petsora, Petchora on the Artic. P.L. 10.292

Petronius, d. c. 66; Roman author; Arbiter of style. Areop. 739

Phaeton, a son of the sun-god Helios in Gk. myth. Eik. 11.817; Eleg. 5.90

Phalæcean, a trochaic verse composed of five feet, of which the first may be trochee, spondee, or even iambus. The second foot is regularly a dactyl; the next two trochees, and the last either trochee or spondee. Rous. post. 110

Phalaris, a Syracusan tyrant, d. c. 549 B.C. Ten. 770

Pharphar, a river of Damascus; see *Abbana*. P.L. 1.469

Pheretiades, Admetus, ruler of Pheræ, in Thessaly. Man. 105

Philemon, Gk. poet of the New Attic Comedy, d. 262 B.C. Areop. 734

Philip, father of Alex. the Gt.; Alex. reigned at 20, conquered Persia at 25, and d. at 33. P.R. 3.32

Philo, Hellenistic Jewish philosopher; d. c. 40 A.D. Tet. 679; D.D. 2.3.598

Philomel, daughter of Pandion, King of Attica, who was changed into a nightingale. Eleg. 5.90; (2) the nightingale. Il P. 56

Philyra, mother of the Centaur Thiron. Eleg. 4.88; Procan. 90

Phineus, (1) a blind soothsayer of Greece, whose cruelty as a Thracian prince Jupiter punished by sending the harpies, monstrous unclean birds, to torment him. P.L. 3.36; Rous. 109

Phlegeton, a river of fire in the infernal regions. P.L. 2.580; Q.N. 97

Phlegra, battle-field of the gods and giants. P.L. 1.577

Phœbus, Apollo, god of music and song. P.R. 4.260; Eik. 11.817

phœnix, a fabulous bird, supposed to live a thousand yrs. then to fly away to Thebes in Egypt where it burned itself, and a new bird arose from its ashes. P.L. 5.272; Ch. Gov. 2.1.527; Da. 108

Photius, famous Byzantine scholar and prelate; d. c. 891. P.E. 472; Tet. 705

Phrix, one of the coursers of the chariot of Night. Q.N. 97

Phyllis, a conventional name for a rustic maiden. L'A. 86; Eleg. 5.91

Piemont, see the State Letters on p. 1084. S. 18; Hir. 892; Eik. 17.835

Pierian, pertaining to Pierus, a mt. in Thessaly, sacred to the Muses. Ad P. 101; 2 Leon. 95; Eleg. 4.88

Pierides, the Muses, who inhabited Mt. Pierus. Man. 104

Pindarus, Gk. lyric poet; d. 443 B.C. S. 8.11; Ch. Gov. 2 Pref. 525

pinnacle, see Matt. 4.5 P.R. 4.549

Pirene, a fountain in Corinth, where Bellerophon caught Pegasus. Eleg. 5.89

Placæus of Saumur (c. 1605–1665) French Prot. theologian and author of many treatises. C.D. 1.5.959

platane, plane-tree. P.L. 4.478

Plautus, (c. 254–184 B.C.) most celebrated of Roman comic poets. Areop. 734

Pleione, mother of the Pleiades, one of whom, Maia, was the mother of Hermes (Mercury). Idea 101

Pliny, (23–79 A.D.) celebrated Roman naturalist, author of *Natural History;* perished in great eruption of Mt. Vesuvius. Ed. 728

Pluto, king of the lower world. L'A. 149; Il P. 107; P.L. 10.444

Plutarch, famous Gk. historian. Ed. 728

Polybius, Gk. historian of the 2nd c. B.C. Ref. 2.463

Polycarpus, eminent martyr and father of the Christian Church; suffered by fire at Smyrna c. 166 A.D. P.E. 473

Pomona, Roman goddess of fruits, wife of Vertumnus. P.L. 5.378; 9.393

Pompey, Roman general, distinguished at 23. P.R. 3.35; Eleg. 1.86

ponent, from the w. P.L. 10.704

Pontic King, Mithradates. P.R. 3.36

Pontus, the Black Sea. P.L. 5.340; 9.77; P.R. 2.347

Porphyrius, (233–c. 304 A.D.) celebrated neo-Platonic philosopher; friend of Plotinus, at whose request he wrote a famous work, in 5 books, against the Christians. Areop. 735

port, gate. P.L. 4.778

Portumnus, the god of harbors. Sal. 104

Posilipo, amt. near Naples. 3 Leon. 95

pretended, stretched like a screen. P.L. 10.872

prevenient, coming before. P.L. 11.3

prevent, anticipate

prick, ride rapidly. P.L. 2.536

primero, an old game of cards. Anim. P.S. 502

procinct, L. in procinctu, at hand. P.L. 6.19

Proclaimer, see Luke 3.4. P.R. 1.18

Procopius, a Byzantine historian, d. c. 565. Sm. 569

Proclus (412–485 A.D.) eminent Gk. philosopher and head of the neo-platonic school in Athens. Areop. 735

proem, prelude. P.L. 9.549

prog, to go a-begging for; prowl about and filch. Ref. 2.466

progeny, ancestry and birth. P.R. 4.554

Prometheus, stole fire from heaven to aid men; he was also the creator of man, endowing him with various qualities. Ch. Gov. 2.3.531

propense, inclined, either toward good or evil. Sm. 547

Proserpina, see *Persephone.* Procan. 96

Proserpine, dau. of Ceres, carried off to be the wife of Pluto. P.L. 4.269; 9.396

Protagoras, Gk. philosopher (c. 481–411 B.C.). Ch. Gov. 1.5.512; Areop. 734

Proteus, mythical "Old Man of the Sea"; he could transform himself into many shapes. P.L. 3.604; Areop. 751; Eleg. 3.87

prowest, most renowned, especially for bravery. P.R. 3.342

Prutenic tables, tables made by Reinhold in 1551; the first application of the Copernican theory. D.D. 1.1. 581

Prynne, see *querist*

Psyche, the soul, beloved by Eros (Cupid) who visited her only by night, forbidding her ever to look upon him; she disobeyed, he vanished, and she wandered disconsolately seeking him. She came finally to the temple of Ceres, where Venus imposed impossible tasks upon her, one of which was to sort the mixed grains in a large heap; Cupid sent ants to assist her. C. 1004; Areop. 738

pudder, bustle. Ref. 1.442

punctual, like a point. P.L. 8.23

Punic Coast, modern Tunisia. P.L. 5.340

purfled, fringed. C. 994

purlieus, neighborhood. P.L. 2.833

Pyrrha, wife of Deucalion, *q.v.* P.L. 11.12

Pyrrhus, Gk. general and king of Epirus; killed at Argos, 272 B.C. Areop. 749

Pythagoras, Gk. philosopher (c. 582-c. 500 B.C.). Areop. 748; Ed. 730

Pythian fields, below Delphi where the games were held. P.L. 2.530

Python, a monstrous serpent brained by Apollo. P.L. 10.531; Eleg. 7.21; Sal. 104

quaternion, fourfold; the four elements were air, water, earth and ether. P.L. 5.181

queasy, squeamish, inclining one to nausea. D.D. Pref. 574

Queenhithe, a haven in London; the reference is explained by an old ballad; see Gilbert. Anim. 5.494

Quiloa, a sea-port on the coast of German East Africa, near Zanzibar. P.L. 11.399

Quintilian, (c. 35-c. 95) Roman rhetorician. S. 11.11; Ed. 728

querist, one who asks questions; the reference is to Wm. Prynne (1600–1669); notice that M. never condescends to call him by name. Hir. 886; F.C. 17 note

Quintius, L. Cincinnatus, dictator of Rome, who was called from the plow and returned to it. P.R. 2.446

quodlibet, a scholastic argument, usually on theology. Sm. 558

quadragesimal, pertaining to the 40 days of Lent, referring to permissions not to observe the fast in all respects. Areop. 733

Quirini Arx, the citadel of Rome. Q.N. 53

Quirinus, the name under which the deified Romulus was worshipped. Q.N. 97

Rabba, a city of Palestine, later Philadelphia, e. of Jordan. P.L. 1.397

Rahab, mother of Boaz, an ancestor of David. See Josh. 2. C.D. 1.22. 1018

Ramath-lechi, a place in s. Palestine, means "the casting away of the jaw-bone"; location unknown. Jud. 15.17. S.A. 145

Ramiel, "exaltation of God." P.L. 6.372

Ramoth, a city of refuge in Gilead; 2 Chron. 18. P.R. 1.373

ramp, leap, S.A. 139

Raphael, an archangel; see *Asmodeus.* P.L. 5.221

rathe, coming too early. L. 142

realty, loyalty. P.L. 6.115

Saint Hugh, probably a church, but there was never a church of that name in London. Areop. 747

Saint Martin le Grand, a church in London, near which cheap articles such as beads were made. Areop. 747

Saint Thomas, the older name of the Mercers' Chapel in Cheapside, London. Areop. 747

Salamanca, city of Spain, famous for its great university. Sm. 565

Salamis, an island of Greece, opp. the harbor of Athens. D.D. 2.11.608

Salem, (1) W. of Jordan. P.R. 2.21; (2) unknown location, perhaps Jerusalem; see Gen. 14.18. Hir. 882

Salmanassar, king of Assyria; 2 Kings 17.1. P.R. 3.278

Salmasius, (1588–1653) a French classical scholar; defended Chas. I. in *Defensio regia pro Carolo I.* 1649; answered by M. Ch. Gov. 1.6.515; C.P. 869; Sal. 95

salve, save. P.R. 4.12

Samarchand, a city of central Asia, famous as the capital of Tamburlaine. P.L. 11.389

Samaria, part of Palestine n. of Judea; also its chief city. Anim. 486. Eleg. 4.115 (see 1 Kings 20); P.R. 3.359

Samian teacher, Pythagoras, b. at Samos. Eleg. 6.92

Samoed shore, part of n.e. Russia inhabited by the Samoeds. P.L. 10.696

Samos, an island off Asia Minor. P.L. 5.265; Eleg. 6.59

Sandys, George, (1577–1644) English traveller and writer. Ref. 1.448

Sanhedrin, the highest court of justice and supreme council of Jerusalem. Fr. Com. 906

sapient king, Solomon. P.L. 9.442

Sardis, a city in Lydia, Asia Minor; see Rev. 3.1. Ch. Gov. 1.6.518

Sarepta, a city in Sidonia; see 1 Kings 17.8 ff. C.D. 2.16.1074

Sarmatians, lived e. of Germany. P.R. 4.78

Sarra, Tyre. P.L. 11.243.

Sarum, Salisbury, Eng., seat of a strong bishopric in former times. Anim. P.S. 502

Satan, Heb. "adversary."

Saturn, a Titan who ruled until Zeus deposed him. P.L. 1.512

satyr, a sylvan deity, represented as having horns, a cloven hoof, and a goat's tail. L. 34; P.R. 2.191

scales, (1) a sign of the Zodiac. P.L. 10.676; (2) the ancients believed that the gods weigh in scales the fates of combatants. P.L. 4.997

Scaliger, Joseph Justus, (1540–1609) celebrated philologist, probably one of the great scholars of the 16 c. Sm. 545

Scazons, iambic lines in which the last foot is a spondee or trochee; the lines thus "limp." Sal. 103

Scipio, conqueror of Hannibal. P.R. 3.34

scull, a school. P.L. 7.402

Scylla, a rock in the Strait of Messina; see **Odyssey** 12.73 ff. C. 256; P.L. 2.660

Scythia, parts of Europe and Asia inhabited by nomads, extending from Russia to China. V. E. 99; Eleg. 4.11; Eleg. 4.88; Nat. Non. 100; P.R. 3.301; 4.78

Sechem, Vulgate form of Shechem, a city of Palestine; Gen. 12.6. P.L. 12.136

Scotus, Duns, (c. 1265-c. 1308) famous Scotch scholastic; his system contended with that of Aquinas for supremacy in medieval times. Areop. 738

secular, living for ages. S.A. 1707

secure, L. secura, without care

Selden, John, (1584–1654) English jurist and author, famed in his time for the breadth of his learning and the soundness of his opinions. D.D. 2.22.623; Hir. 888; Areop. 737; C.D. 1.10.995

Seleucia, a city on the Tigris. P.L. 4.212; P.R. 3.291

Semele, beloved of Zeus, the mother of Bacchus. P.R. 2.187; Eleg. 5.90

Seneca, (c. 5 B.C.–65 A.D.) eminent Roman stoic philosopher and moralist. Ed. 728; Ten. 760

seneschal, a steward of the household. P.L. 9.38

Sennaar. Shinar, prob. iden. with Babylonia; Gen. 11.2. P.L. 3.467

Seon's Realme, the land of Sihon, king of the Amorites, along the e. side of the Dead Sea. Ps. 136.67; P.L. 1.409

Serapis, an Egyptian deity. P.L. 1.720

Serbonian bog, a large swamp in the delta of the Nile. P.L. 2.592

serene, the *gutta serena,* a disease of the eyes. P.L. 3.25

Sericana, in China; wagons driven by wind are often mentioned in Eliz. books of travel in China. P.L. 3.438

Serraliona, a cape on the w. coast of Africa. P.L. 10.703

Setia, a city in Latium, famous for wine. P.R. 4.117

Seven Hills, the seven hills of Rome, 2 Prod. B. 94

Severn, a river of s.w. England, part of the ancient boundary between Wales and England, named from Sabrina who was drowned in it. C. 824, 841; V. E. 96

Severus, (c. 363–410) Christian historian, often styled "The Christian Sallust." Ref. 1.445

Sevil, a city in s. Spain, the center of the Inquisition. Areop. 742

sewer, a steward who arranged the dishes on the table. P.L. 9.38

Sibma, beyond Jordan, famous for its vineyards. P.L. 1.410

Sibyls, priestesses of Apollo, possessed of prophetic power; the Cumæan Sibyl is esp. famous. Ad Pat. 101

Sicanian, Sicilian. Eleg. 4.88; 5.90

Sidon, a seaport in Phœnicia. Eleg. 4.89; P.L. 1.441

Sigeum, a promontory and town in Troas, where was the tomb of Achilles. Eleg. 7.93

Silo, a town in Palestine where the ark was set up after the conquest of Canaan. S.A. 1674

Siloa, a pool, with a spring flowing from it, outside Jerusalem. P.L. 1.11

Simeon, see Luke 2.25. P.R. 1.255; 2.87

Simois, a small river in the Troad. Eleg. 1.86

Simon de Montfort, leader of the group of barons which defeated the army of Henry III. in 1264 and took the King prisoner; in the next year he called a parliament, which laid the groundwork for the House of Commons; Montfort was defeated and slain in the same year by royalist troops. Eik. Pref. 777

Simon Magus, a magician of Samaria who offered money to the disciples Peter and John if they would teach him the power of conferring the Holy Ghost. Ref. 2.467; Ten. 774

Sinæan, Chinese. P.L. 11.390

Sinai, Horeb or Oreb, a mt. in the Sinaitic peninsula, where the Law was given to Moses. P.L. 1.7; 12.227; H. 159; C.D. 15.1009

Sion, a hill in Jerusalem where the Temple stood. P.L. 1.10; C.D. 1.23.1021

Siope, one of the coursers of the chariot of Night. Q.N. 97

Sirens, lesser goddesses of the sea who lured mariners to destruction upon the rocks by their singing. C. 252, 877; A. 63; S.M. 1; 3 Leon. 95

sirocco, a hot s.e. wind. P.L. 10.706

Sittim, the last camping-place of the Israelites on the journey from Egypt; Num. 25.1 ff. P.L. 1.413

sleek-stone, a heavy smooth stone, used for polishing. Anim. 1.481

Sleidan, (1506–1556) German historian; wrote a valuable history of the Reformation. Sm. 553; M.B. 628; Hir. 892

sleight, trick. P.L. 9.92

slug, hinder. Ref. 1.445

Smectymnuus, the name affixed to a tract against episcopacy, made by using the initial letters of the five authors, Stephen Marshall, Edmund Calamy, Thomas Young, Matthew Newcomen, and William Spurstow. Anim. P.S. 503

Smith, Sir Thomas (c. 1512–1577) Eng. statesman and scholar; secretary of state under Edw. VI.; author of the work *The English Commonwealth.* Ten. 763

Smithfield, a famous cattle-market in London, n. of St. Paul's. Hir. 890

Socinians, a sect that followed L. Socinus (1525–1562) and F. Socinus (1539–1604); that believed that Christ was divinely endowed, but not to be worshipped, and other doctrines which place them midway between the Arians and the modern Unitarians. Tet. 660; T.R. 915

sock, a light shoe worn by ancient actors of comedy; hence, comedy. L'A. 132

Socrates, (470–399 B.C.) Athenian philosopher, put to death on a false charge of blasphemy and corrupting the youth by false doctrines. P.R. 3.96; 4.274; Tet. 651; Anim. 13.498

Socrates the historian, Gk. church historian, d. c. 440. Ref. 2.456

sod, boiled (obsolete pret. of seethe). Anim. P.S. 503

Solinus, Latin writer and naturalist of whom very little is known; fl. probably in 3rd c; left a work called *Polyhistor* published in an edition by Salmasius in 1629. Ed. 728

Solon, (c. 638–c. 558 B.C.) illustrious Athenian legislator; ranked among the Seven Sages of Greece. M.B. 634

Sozomenus, Gk. ecclesiastical historian, b. c. 400 A.D.; wrote a History of the Church from 323 to 439 A.D., which is extant. Eik. 17.835

Sodom, a city near the Dead Sea. P.L. 1.503; 10.562

Sofala, a seaport, formerly a district, in Portuguese E. Africa. P.L. 11.400

Sogdiana, a country of central Asia, the farthest conquest of Alexander. P.R. 3.302

Solomon, Garden of, See *Songs of Solomon.* P.L. 9.442

sooth, truth. Inf. 51

Sophocles, (c. 495–406 B.C.) Gk. tragic poet. Ed. 729

Sophi, the Shah. P.L. 10.433

Sophron, (fl. 440 B.C.) a Syracusan writer of comedy, famous for his mimes. Areop. 740; Sm. 545

sord, sward. P.L. 11.433

Sorec, a valley in Palestine; Judges 16.4. S.A. 229

sotadic, a palindrome, i. e., a verse which reads the same from right to left as from left to right. Col. 725

Spalato, a city on the Adriatic, Anim. P.S. 503

Spanheim, (1600–1649) German theologian and author of several treatises. Tet. 693

Specular Mount, see *Niphates*

Spelman, Sir Henry, (1562–1641) Eng. antiquary. Hir. 888

Spenser, Edmund, (c. 1552–1599) Eng. poet. Eik. 4.791; Areop. 738; Anim. 13.500

spet, spit, pierce. C. 132

spinstry, the work of spinning. Ch. Gov. 2.2.529

spring, young growth. P.L. 9.218

Stagirite, Aristotle, b. at Stagira, in Macedonia. Eleg. 4.88

stalls, fixed seats enclosed in the choir or chancel, richly canopied, occupied by the higher clergy. Sm. 560

Star Chamber, a court (so-called because the chamber ceiling was ornamented with stars) which sat at Westminster; it rendered its desions by arbitrary judgments, not by trial; abolished in 1630. Eik. 9.809

starve, perish with cold. P.L. 2.600; 4.769

statist, statesman. P.R. 4.354

Stoa, the Colonnade, or Painted Porch, in Athens where Zeno taught. P.R. 4.253

Stoics, followers of Zeno, who taught that men should be free from passion, unmoved by joy, grief, or fear; founded about 308 B.C. C.D. 1.11.999

Sturmius, Johann, (1507–1589) eminent scholar and teacher, surnamed the "German Cicero." M.B. 627

Stygian, belonging to Styx, a mighty river of the Lower World. P.L. 1.239

sublime, lifted high. P.L. 2.528

success, outcome. P.L. 2.9

succint, girt up. P.L. 3.643

Suckling, Sir John, (d. c. 1642) Eng. poet; implicated in a plot to free Strafford, May, 1641. Eik. 9.808

Summanus, an ancient deity who wielded the lightning. Q.N. 96

summed, a technical word, used in falconry, meaning when the wing feathers have reached their full growth. P.L. 7.421; P.R. 1.14

supplanted, thrown off his feet, P.L. 10.513

Sus, Tunis. P.L. 11.403

Susa, the chief city of s.w. Persia; summer residence of the Persian kings. P.L. 10.308; P.R. 3.288; Eleg. 1.86

Susiana, a province in s. w. Persia. P.R. 3.321

Syene, a town on the Nile near the first cataract. P.R. 4.70

Sylvan, a Roman deity of forests. C. 267; Il P. 134; P.L. 4.707; P.R. 2.191

Sylvanus, a deity of the woods. Eleg. 5.91

Sylvester, elected Pope 314 A.D.; under his pontificate the celebrated Council of Nice was held and the Arian controversy first promulgated; d. 335. Hir. 892

Symmachus, surnamed the Samaritan; fl. c. 200 A.D.; translated O.T. into Greek. Ref. 2.453

Syntagma, a systematically arranged treatise. Areop. 748

Syriacism, of or pertaining to the Syrian language. Tet. 691

Syrinx, a nymph beloved by Pan. A. 106; P.R. 2.188

Syrtis, two gulfs filled with quicksand on the n. coast of Africa; cf. Acts 27.17. P.L. 2.939

Talmud, the great work embodying the traditional interpretation of the Mosaic Law. Sm. 554; Tet. 674; Areop. 738

Tænarian abyss, 4 Prod. b. 94

Tænarum, a promontory in Laconia, where was a cave, the entrance to the Lower World. Eleg. 5.90; Procan. 96

Tagus, a river in Spain and Portugal, flowing into the Atlantic; Ovid (*Met.* 2.251) mentions its golden sand. Eleg. 3.87

Tamar, a river of s.w. Eng. Da. 108

Tantalus, was condemned to stand in water to his throat, but when he tried to drink, the water receded. P.L. 2.614

Taprobane, Ceylon. P.R. 4.75

Tarpeian, pertaining to the T. hill, or Capitoline, smallest of the seven hills of Rome. Eleg. 1.86

Tarpeian Rock, in front of the Capitoline Hill; from here malefactors were hurled down. P.R. 4.49

Tarsus, a city in Asia Minor. P.L. 1.200; S.A. 715

Tartarus, Hades, the infernal regions. Eleg. 5.89 P.L. 2.69; 2.858; 6.54; 7.238

Tartarean Jove, Pluto, the sovereign of the nether world, Tartarus, as Jupiter was of the upper world. Eleg. 3.87

Tartarean powder, gunpowder. Q.N. 98

Tasso, (1544–1595) Italian poet. Ch. Gov. 2 Pref. 525; Ed. 729

Tauric pool, sea of Azov. P.R. 4.79

Tauris, Tabriz, a city of Persia. P.L. 10.436

Taurus, a sign of the zodiac. P.L. 1.769; 10.673

teem, breed. P.L. 7.454; S.A. 1703; C. 174

Teian Muse, Anacreon, who was born at Teia, called by Ovid the Teian Muse. Eleg. 6.90

Telamon, father of Ajax and Teucer, two famous heroes of the Trojan War. Eleg. 4.88

Telassar, a place of unknown location in Mesopotamia. P.L. 4.214

Temesa, an ancient city on the w. coast of Calabria, Q.N. 99

Temir, Tamburlaine. P.L. 11.389

Teneriff, one of the Canary Islands, on which is the peak of the same name. P.L. 4.987

Teredon, an ancient city near the mouth of the united Tigris and Euphrates. P.R. 3.292

Ternate, an island of the Moluccas in the E. Indies. P.L. 2.639

Tertullian, (c. 150–c. 230) ecclesiastical writer, a father of the church. Ref. 1.448; P.E. 475; Hir. 894

Tethys, a sea deity, wife of Oceanus. C. 869; Eleg. 5.90

Tetrachordon, a musical instrument of four strings; also a diatonic series of four tones; M. had one of these in mind when he named his third divorce tract, treating four passages in Scripture that bear on divorce. S. 11.1

tetrarch, ruler of a fourth part; referring to the four elements. P.R. 4.201

Teucrigenæ, according to legend, Brutus the Trojan founded a colony in Britain.

Teumesian, pertaining to Teumessus, a range of mts. in Bœotia. Eleg. 6.91

Thalia, the goddess of comedy. Eleg. 6.92

Thammuz, Adonis, q.v. P.L. 1.446; 1.452; H. 204; Eik. 1.784

Thamyris, a blind Thracian poet. P.L. 3.35

Thaumas, father of Iris, goddess of the rainbow. Eleg. 3.87

Theban monster, the Sphinx. P.R. 4.572

Thebes, (1) a city in Bœotia, n. Greece, famous in Gk. lit. and hist. Il P. 99; P.L. 1.578; P.R. 4.572; (2) a city in upper Egypt on the Nile. P.L. 5.274

Thebez, a city in Palestine, belonging to the tribe of Ephraim. P.R. 2.16, 313

Themis, Gk. goddess of law, order, and justice. P.L. 11.14; S. 21.2

Theocritus, one of the most celebrated pastoral poets of antiquity; fl. c. 270 B.C. Ed. 728

Theodosius, "the Great" (c. 346–395) devout emperor of Roman Empire; active in the wars of Rome against the Goths. Ref. 2.466; Tet. 704

Theophilus, East Roman emperor (829–842) a pronounced iconoclast; his whole reign occupied in a war against the caliphs of Bagdad. P.E. 476

Thetis, a goddess of the sea. Q.N. 97

Thermodoön, a river of Pontus, on which the Amazons were fabled to dwell; the "puella" is Elizabeth. Q.N. 98

Thiodamas, father of Hylas., Eleg. 7.93

Thisbite, Elijah. P.R. 2.16

Thrascias, the n.n.w. wind. P.L. 10.700

Thuanus, (Fr. *de Thou*) (1553–1617) eminent Fr. historian and statesman. M.B. 628

Thucydides, (471–c. 401 B.C.) illustrious Gk. historian and general; author of the *History of the Peloponnesian War.* C.D. 1.11.998

Thule, an island which the ancients believed to be the n. limit of habitation, the "Utmost Isles." Ref. 2.468

Thyatira, a city of Asia Minor; see Rev. 2.18 ff. Anim. 13.495

Thyestean banquet, before Thyestes was set a banquet of the flesh of his sons. P.L. 10.688

Thyoneus, a name for Bacchus, indicative of wild revelry. Eleg. 6.91

Tidore, an island of the Moluccas. P.L. 2.639

Tigris, a river of Asia, supposed to have watered Paradise; see Gilbert. P.L. 9.71

timelessly, untimely. Inf. 2

tine, kindle. P.L. 10.1075

Tine, a river of n. Eng. V.E. 98

Tiresias, an ancient legendary Gk. poet. blind. P.L. 3.36; Eleg. 6.92

Tishbites, Elijah was a native of the town of Tishbe, in the Kingdom of Israel. Eleg. 4.89

Titans, ruled the universe before the advent of Zeus. P.L. 1.510

Titanian Rumor, Rumor, according to Gk. mythology, is descended from the Titans. Q.N. 97

Tithonia, in the extreme e. where Dawn, wife of Tithonus, dwells. Eleg. 5.90; Q.N. 98

Tityrus, a shepherd; Chaucer is here referred to. Man. 105

Tobias, see Asmodeus.

Tobit's son. Tobias. P.L. 4.170

Tomis, a town on the shores of the Black Sea, near the mouth of the Danube, the scene of Ovid's exile. Eleg. 1.85

Tomitanus Ager, Tomis, a town of Mœsia, to which Ovid was banished. Eleg. 1.22

Tophet, in the valley of Hinnom, *q.v.* P.L. 1.404

Torquato, Torquato Tasso, a famous Italian poet. 2 Leon. 95

Towerhill, an elevated spot near the Tower of London. Eik. 8.805

Trachinian, relating to Trachin, an old town in n.e. Thessaly. Man. 105

Trallis, an ancient town of Caria, Asia Minor, situated on the Enodon, a tributary of the Mæander. Ref. 1.447

Tremisen, a city in w. Algeria. P.L. 11.404

Trent, (1) a river of Eng. uniting with the Ouse. V.E. 93; Da. 108; (2) a city of Tyrol on the Adige, where a famous council of the R. C. Church was held from 1545 to 1563. F.C. 14; Areop. 735, 742; Eik. 29.859

Trinacrian, Sicilian. P.L. 2.661; Q.N. 99.

Trinculoes, clowns. Sm. 548

Triptolemus, founder of the art of agriculture, when a child was blessed and endowed with unusual powers by Ceres, goddess of agriculture. Eleg. 4.88

Triton, (1) an ancient river, now a salt lake, in n. Africa. P.L. 4.276; (2) a sea deity, son of Neptune. C. 872

turm, a troop of horse. P.R. 4.66

Turnus, rival of Æneas, betrothed to Lavinia. P.L. 9.17

Tuscan artist, Galileo. P.L. 1.288

Tweed, a river on the boundary between England and Scotland. V.E. 92; D.D. Pref. 576

Typhon, a monster who rebelled against Zeus. P.L. 1.199; H. 266

Tyrrhene, part of the Mediterranean w. of Italy. C. 49

Tyre, an ancient seaport of Phœnicia, famous for its dyes. H. 204; C. 342; P.L. 11.243

uncouth, unknown. P.L. 2.407

unexpressive, inexpressible. L. 176; H. 116

unfumed, not burned for scent. P.L. 5.349

Ur, on the w. bank of the Euphrates, below Babylon. P.L. 12.130

Urania, muse of the heavens, and of astronomy, but given a new meaning by M. P.L. 7.1

Uriel, "light of God." P.L. 3.648

Urim and Thummim, see Exod. 28.30. P.L. 6.761; P.R. 3.14

Ursinus, antipope 366–384. C.D. 2.7.1063

Uther's son, King Arthur. P.L. 1.580

Uz, a land e. of Palestine. P.R. 1.369; 3.94

Uzza, or Uzziah, fl. first of 8th c. B.C.; king of Judah; according to 2 Chron. was visited with leprosy as punishment for interfering with priestly prerogatives. Ch. Gov. 1.1.507

Valdarno, the valley in which Florence is situated, noted for its beauty and fertility. P.L. 1.290

Valentinian, able Roman Emperor of the West from 364–375. Tet. 704

Valerius Publicola, according to tradition, the colleague of Brutus in the first year of the Roman republic; introduced several liberal measures and was three times elected consul. Eik. 28.859

Vallombrosa, a beautiful valley near Florence; cf. Wordsworth's poem and Mrs. Browning's *Letters.* P.L. 1.303

van, wing. P.L. 2.535

Vane, Sir Henry (1612–1662) one of the greatest men of the Protectorate; argued for toleration in religious views; beheaded as a regicide. S. 17.1

vant-brace, mail for the arm. S.A. 1121

Vergivian Sea, the Irish Sea. Eleg. 1.85

Vertumnus, Roman deity who presided over gardens and orchards. P.L. 9.395; Tet. 693

Vesta, goddess of the hearth. Il P. 23; Eleg. 5.90

villatic, belonging to a villa, domestic. S.A. 1695

Vitruvius, Roman architect and engineer, author of a celebrated work on architecture; fl. during reign of Augustus. Ed. 728

volant, flying. P.L. 11.561

Vulcan, god of fire. C. 654

Waldenses, a body of reforming Christians, formed c. 1170, but inheritors of doctrines that long preceded that date. Hir. 885

wanton, sportive, sometimes with evil implied. P.L. 4.306

Wearer of the Triple Crown, the Pope. Q.N. 97

well-couched, well-hidden. P.R. 1.97

Whitehall, a palace in London built during the reign of Henry III. Eik. 777

Willibrode and Winifred, celebrated missionaries of the early 8th c. in Eng. D.D. Pref. 577

won, dwell. P.L. 7.457

worm, a serpent. P.R. 1.312

Xerxes, king of Persia, defeated at Salamis, 480 B.C. P.L. 10.307

Zaleucus, traditional lawgiver of the Locrians in Italy c. 7th c. B.C. Ed. 729

Zephyr, the w. wind. L'A. 19; Eleg. 3.87; P.L. 4.329; 10.705

Zodiac, the orbit studded with stars through which the earth revolves in its journey around the sun. Nat. Non. 100

zone, a magic girdle. P.R. 2.214

Zuinglius, (1484–1534) renowned Swiss reformer. Areop. 748

NOTES ON THE POETRY

The addresses of publishers to readers in the seventeenth century are usually worth careful study. As a piece of advertising, this preface by Moseley is skilful. It also expresses several ideas that were Milton's, such as "the love I have to our own language" and "trivial Airs may please thee better." Milton may have had a talk with the publisher.

PAGE 4. ON THE MORNING OF CHRISTS NATIVITY

When Milton first collected his poetry for publication in 1645, he exercised great care as to the position of the various pieces. Such care was a Renaissance characteristic; Ben Jonson had exercised a similar scrupulousness in the arrangement of his epigrams, as Herrick did later when he published his poetry in 1648. This care Milton never lost: in the Cambridge MS. are directions for changing the position of poems written shortly after 1645, and in the second edition of Milton's collected poetry in 1673—a year before his death —there is an errata page, which directs a change in position of the verses, *At a Vacation Exercise*. Milton here revealed his practical nature; he wished the poems to be arranged roughly in the order in which they were composed, but he was ready to abandon this order when a good practical reason presented itself. With Jonson, he knew the value of making a good first impression on his readers. He could not have chosen a better selection with which to open his first volume of poetry. The student will be interested in reading Milton to notice evidences of his practicality and of his ability as a critic of his own poetry. It may be worth while to read again *The Stationer to the Reader* with these points in mind. Notice that Moseley speaks highly of Spenser; watch for signs of Spenserian influence in Milton's writings and for any places where he definitely mentions him.

In this poem Milton shows himself a product of the Renaissance; the student should remember that throughout his life, both in his poetry and his prose, Milton was the ideal exponent of what Renaissance thought and art are; in seventeenth century England he was the embodiment of the Renaissance. No other influence, classical, Puritan, political, counted with him more; indeed, his ideas in every field were formed and shaped under the spirit of the Renaissance, which he had absorbed and with which he completely identified himself. Notice how thoroughly romantic this poem is. List several traits of romantic poetry shown here, such as a love for the far-away and for geographical names, and observe that the characteristics of romantic poetry as seen in the early nineteenth century do not vary greatly from those shown in Milton's poetry. Keep this suggestion in mind as you study other poems of Milton's.

Though Milton is thoroughly orthodox in this poem, it will be noticed that it is not the religious aspect of the theme, but the poetic and romantic aspects, that appeal to him. He is singing the coming of the King of Peace. Vergil, whom the Renaissance delighted to honor, had sung on the same general theme in his *Fourth Eclogue*.

Study the excellent art of the poem,—especially the skilful use of the prologue and the unity of thought and expression in the hymn itself. See if you can detect any so-called Miltonic traits of style. Is this poem "unpremeditated verse"? Are there evidences of careful planning and wording? Some one has said that this is a remarkable poem for a boy of twenty-one to have written; we may amend this opinion to read "for a person of any age to have written."

1 *the happy morn;* cf. *Elegy* vi, pp. 91, 92, especially the last paragraph, for Milton's comment upon this poem, and the time of its composition.

15 *Heav'nly Muse;* the Muse of sacred poetry, whom Milton invokes in the beginning of *P.L.* He discusses the characteristics of the Heavenly Muse, Urania, in *P.L.* VII. 1 ff.

23 *Wisards;* simply "wise men from the east" of *Matt.* ii. 1. The Vulgate has "Magi ab oriente."

24 *prevent;* anticipate, by writing first. *Ode;* observe the use of this word in the seventeenth century. It does not seem to have a very exact meaning.

27 *Quire,* choir. *Luke* ii, 13, 14.

39 *front;* literally, forehead; here, face.

48 *turning sphear;* the wheeling sphere of the whole Ptolemaic universe.

51 "Olive green", 47, "Turtle wing," 50, and "mirtle wand," are all emblems of peace.

55 *high up hung;* Probably, as Keightley suggests, an allusion to the custom of hanging up arms in the Roman temples in times of prolonged peace.

56 *hooked Chariot;* a chariot furnished with hooks, i. e. with scythes. Barbarian war chariots were often so equipped.

58 *the Trumpet;* the musical instrument of royal authority. Cf. *P.L.* ii. 515.

64 *whist;* hushed.

66 *Ocean;* o-ce-an.

71 *one way;* the stars were sending all their influence toward the Babe in Bethlehem; there was no malign influence.

74 *Lucifer;* the morning star.

85 *Lawn;* see glossary.

88 *than;* then.

89 *mighty Pan;* Christ is often referred to as a shepherd, and in Renaissance poetry he is often called Pan.

92 *silly;* innocent.

95 *strook;* notice how often Milton uses this form of the past tense and participle of the verb *strike.* Cf. the present tendency to use *proven* instead of the more correct *proved* in the perfect tense.

97 *noise;* concert. Cf. *At a Solemn Musick,* 18.

98 *took;* enchanted. Cf. *The Winter's Tale,* IV, iv, 118: Daffodils
That come before the swallow dares, and take
The winds of March with beauty.

100 *echo's;* the apostrophe in seventeenth century spelling is often hard to account for. In this case it stands for an omitted "e."

101 The effect of music upon nature is frequently alluded to in Milton's poetry. It will be interesting to collect examples as you read.

103 *Cynthia*'s; notice the care of the original printer; he italicizes the proper noun, but because the possessive "s" is no part of the name, he puts that in roman.

106 *its;* this neuter possessive form was just coming into use in Milton's time; he uses it only three times in his poetry.

108 *happier union;* i. e. than had prevailed since Adam's fall. For this idea of "keeping in tune with Heaven," study *At a Solemn Musick,* p. 19, where the theme is more fully developed.

116 *unexpressive;* inexpressible. Cf. *Ly.* 176.

117 ff See *Job* xxxviii. 4–11.

124 *weltring;* rolling to and fro. Cf. *Ly.* 13.

125 *Crystall sphears;* the Pythagorean notion of the music of the spheres. Milton alludes to the idea often, evidently attracted by its beauty.

126 *once;* the music of the spheres was not audible to mortal men. Milton asks that it may be audible this one time.

132 *consort;* chorus.

140 *peering;* appearing.

143, 144 Notice that the text of these two lines is from the edition of 1673. Study in the textual notes what Milton wrote first. What reasons do you see for the change? Is the figure better? Is the thought different? Finally, is the change an improvement? Your conclusion will probably be that in the years from 1629 to 1673 the poet improved greatly in his style and mellowed in his thought. Mercy no longer will be forced, but will come in her own right, as an equal with Truth and Justice. Cf. Shakspere's famous lines about mercy in the *Merchant of Venice.*

143 *Orb'd in;* surrounded by. Cf. *Rev.* x. 1.

146 *tissued;* referring to the cloth woven of silk and threads of gold or silver, much used on state occasions.

168 *Th' old Dragon;* Satan. *Rev.* xx. 2.

172 *Swindges;* lashes to and fro.

173 ff A tradition grew up among the early Christians that all oracles ceased with the birth of Christ. *P.R.* i. 455–464 give a good commentary on the text.

186 *Genius;* the god of a particular locality.

194 *service quaint;* Milton has none of the Puritan's shivering horror of all the wickedness that he is describing. He lingers over it because it has poetic beauty.

201 *Heav'ns Queen;* Selden, whom Milton admired, says in *De Diis Syriis,* that she was called *regina cœli* and *mater deum.*

240 *youngest teemed Star;* the one that appeared to the Wise Men.

Page 10. A PARAPHRASE ON PSALM 114

This and the following poem are interesting as the earliest of Milton's preserved poems. On reading, one is reminded of Aubrey's remark: "*Anno Domini* 1619 he was ten years old, as by his picture, and was then a poet." At least three characteristics of these poems are worth studying.
1. Carrying out Aubrey's suggestion, try to discover traits of the born poet. Is his style easy and natural? Notice that he turns naturally to poetic ideas and poetic words. Cf. this poem with the translation of the Psalm in the Authorized version and the translation from the Greek of Milton, p. 103. What has he added? Notice the firmness of the style, the lack of puerilities and the lack of flatness. *Psalm* 136 has simplicity and considerable strength; it is sung today in our

churches. 2. Literary influences seen in these two early poems are significant. The exuberance of style, especially in Psalm 114, and several phrases, have been traced to Sylvester's DuBartas, while traces of Buchanan's Latin version of the Psalms are not lacking. 3. The subject matter of these poems should also be studied. Hanford (*The Youth of Milton,* pp. 95–96) finds in the thought of the greatness and goodness of God, which runs through these poems, the beginning of a strain, from Sylvester, that culminates in *P.L.* It should also be observed that these two psalms are classed by Biblical scholars as Songs of Deliverance, and that they celebrate liberty won "after long toil."

1 *Terah;* the father of Abraham.

6 *was;* a compound subject usually takes a singular verb in seventeenth century English.

Page 12. ON THE DEATH OF A FAIR INFANT

The "fair infant" was the daughter of Milton's sister, Anne Phillips. Study how Milton uses the idea of contrasts to build up the poem. The stanza form is a Spenserian adaptation.

8 *Aquilo;* Boreas, the north wind, who dwelt in a cave in Thrace, carried off the daughter of Erechtheus, king of Athens.

39 *that high first-moving Spheare;* the Primum Mobile, or Tenth Sphere of the Ptolemaic system.

47 *earths Sonnes;* the Giants.

50 *just Maid;* Astræa, or Justice, who "forsook the hated earth" after the Golden Age. Cf. *Nat.* 135 and 141, 142.

53 *Youth;* probably Mercy as the older commentators suggest.

55 *heav'nly brood;* of virtues.

57 *golden-winged hoast;* the angels.

68 *pestilence;* a reference to the plague of the spring and summer of 1625.

Page 14. AT A VACATION EXERCISE

Milton's love for his native language, his belief that this language is a suitable vehicle for noble song, and his ability in handling the heroic couplet in the manner of Jonson, are among the chief points to observe in this poem. This enthusiasm for the vernacular was a trait of the Renaissance. Dante wrote a treatise on vulgar eloquence, Ariosto insisted on using it for his great romantic poem, Tasso praised those who had helped to establish its qualities; Du Bellay and Spenser both advocated its use. In Milton, this love for his native language probably began when he was a pupil in St. Paul's under Dr. Alexander Gill. Dr. Gill's son, under whom Mil-

ton also studied, published in 1621 a treatise on the use and spelling of English; Milton under him would naturally have had his attention called to the matter. This poem shows how thoroughly in touch with the tendencies of the time Milton was.

1 *Hail, native Language;* Milton's enthusiasm for English runs throughout his entire work. Cf. 577, 2.22; 863, 2.31; and 108, 2nd paragraph. The student will be able to add many other illustrations to these.

19 *new fangled toys;* probably a reference to some popular metaphysical poetasters of Cambridge now forgotten. Some critics see an allusion to Herbert's early poetry, but this is hardly probable. Anyway, the chief thing is that Milton declares his loyalty to the older school of Spenser.

37 *unshorn;* an epithet used in connection with Apollo by the Greek and Latin poets.
Then Ens; in the Aristotelian logic, Ens is Being, which is regarded as containing everything that is. Of each thing that is, one or more of what were called Prædicaments might be asserted. These Prædicaments, ten in number, were Substance, Quantity, Quality, Relation, Place, Time, Situation, Possession, Action, and Passion. These were all represented by different students, while Milton acted as Ens. The entire exercise was thus in the manner of a short, unpretentious mask.

74 *Accident;* in metaphysics, Substance, the eldest son of Ens, is dependent upon its accidents. These Accidents are the nine Prædicaments, after Substance, mentioned in the note above. Bearing these facts in mind, the student should be able to enjoy this bit of admirable academic fooling. If still doubtful and still curious, he may consult Masson's edition, i, 11 and iii, 238.

90 *Your learned hands;* addressed to the audience of students.

91 *Rivers;* the name of a student. Notice the continued pun on the name, and the aptness of the descriptive adjectives.

Page 16. THE PASSION

Composed probably in April, 1630. The first four lines refer to *On the Morning of Christs Nativity;* they also incidentally explain why the poem is not an inspired piece and why it is a fragment—perhaps almost the only thing that Milton ever attempted which he did not finish. The subject had little romantic appeal and the religious side did not interest the young poet. In fact, we may as well decide early in our study

that Milton was never primarily a religious poet.
Cf. what Milton says on 550, 1.19.

13 *Most perfect Heroe;* it is significant that
Milton before he was twenty-two should
mention Christ as the hero. It is interesting
to watch this idea develop as Milton grew
older.

25 *other where;* in Giles Fletcher's poem,
Christ's Victory, 1610.

26 *Cremona*'s; see glossary.

34, 35 An allusion to the mourning books of the
seventeenth century in some of which the
title-pages were black and the letters white.

36 An obvious effort to get some life into the
prosy poem, but without success.

37 *Prophet;* see *Ezekiel* viii.

Page 18. ON TIME

The student should study carefully the textual
notes. Why did Milton delete the sub-title of
the present poem?

3 *heavy Plummets pace;* the slow rate of
descent of the leaden weights of a clock.

12 *individual;* indivisible; i. e. everlasting.

18 *happy-making sight;* the Beatific Vision.

21 *Attir'd with Stars;* clothed with stars,
(Masson); crowned with stars, (Keightley);
or in the company of stars.

Page 18. UPON THE CIRCUMCISION

1 *flaming Powers;* the Seraphim. *winged Warriours;* probably the Cherubim.

Page 19. AT A SOLEMN MUSICK

This poem, celebrating a concert of sacred
music, shows Milton's enthusiasm for music, and
especially for sacred song. In the Cambridge MS.
are four drafts of this poem, showing Milton's
fastidious care in perfecting the lines. The advanced student should study the changes made
as recorded in the notes to the *Columbia Milton*
and should study also the MS. drafts as reproduced by the Facsimile Text Society, vol. 17. In
poetic value the poem is far superior to the two
preceding pieces; Milton has found a much more
congenial subject. The poetic form he has chosen,
practically one long continuous sentence, made
up of iambic lines of varying length, is suited to
the thought content and the organ music, the
effect of which he is trying to give. Milton's
success in choosing the best poetic form for the
thought that he is expressing is one of his most
marked poetic traits. Study in connection with
the ideas expressed in this poem, Milton's Latin
poem *To my Father,* p. 101.

2 *Sphear-born;* cf. *Comus* 240.

6 *concent;* harmony. See textual notes.

19 *once we did;* before the fall of man.

23 *Diapason;* all the eight notes of the scale.

Page 19. AN EPITAPH

The lady was Jane, daughter of Viscount
Savage, first wife of John, fifth Marquis of
Winchester. She died April 15, 1631, in her 23rd
year. For background read the biography of her
husband, John Paulet, in the D.N.B. Note that
he was a Catholic. On March 15, 1626, James
Howell addressed an interesting letter to the
Marchioness, praising both her beauty of body
and of mind. (*Fam. Letters,* Bk. I, Sect. 4, xiv.)
Jonson wrote an *Elegie* to her memory. Davenant
also wrote in her memory. Do you detect any
Jonsonian influences in the poem?

55 *tears of perfect moan;* poems probably written by Cambridge students, though no such
volume has been discovered (Warton and
Todd); poems by Jonson and others
(Keightley). For this use of *tears* cf. *Lycidas,*
14.

59 *Came;* i. e. Cambridge University.

Page 21. SONG ON MAY MORNING

This little poem is a typical Renaissance nature
song, examples of which may be found among
the poems of Drummond and his Continental
contemporaries. These songs in turn go back to
the *reverdie* of Provençal and Old French lyric
poetry. Though it is easy to find specimens of this
type of Renaissance poetry, it is not easy to find a
poem that equals Milton's in the free artistic expression of the spirit of spring and of May Day.
Study with this poem, *Sonnet* I and *Elegy* V,
p. 89.

Page 21. ON SHAKESPEAR

This tribute to Shakspere is the first of many
that Milton pays. Collect these references as you
advance and notice whether his attitude changes
from one of sincere admiration to one of qualified
approval. Try to formulate your own opinion as
to Milton's attitude toward Shakspere. It is possible to reconcile such a passage as that on 782,
2.43 with this present poem and *L'Allegro,*
131–134. To what class of poetry do these lines
belong? Be careful not to call the poem a
"sonnet." Is Milton's criticism of Shakspere
sound? Is Milton thinking of Shakspere's dramatic art or of his lyric art as seen in great passages in his plays? Milton praises Shakspere
chiefly for his "easy numbers." Notice his admiration for ease in writing, and cf. especially
P.L. iii. 37–38 and ix. 20–24.

Page 22. ON THE UNIVERSITY CARRIER

Thomas Hobson, born c. 1544, began his weekly trips from Cambridge to the Bull Inn, Bishopsgate, London, in 1564. Hobson was a beloved public character, and not unpopular with Cambridge students as can be understood from the affectionate manner in which Milton treats his memory. He died Jan. 1, 1630–1. In the *Spectator* for Oct. 14, 1712, (No. 509) Steele used his life as an example of thrift. See also D.N.B.

5 *'Twas;* an affectionate term for "he was".

Page 23. L'ALLEGRO

All critics unite in praising the charm, attractiveness and beauty of *L'Allegro* and its companion piece, *Il Penseroso*. They are not agreed, however, in interpreting the deeper significance of the poems. Masson sees in them the records of two ideal days of 12 hours each; Tillyard (Pamphlet No. 82 of The English Association, July, 1932) sees a study of the contrast between day and night, discovering in the *First Prolusion* the origin of the idea; and others have seen the two dominating moods of the century, Cavalier and Puritan, represented here. The present editor feels that there is some truth in all these views, but that they do not tell the whole story. Milton seems to be weighing and deciding one of the problems of his life—what kind of poet shall he become? In *Elegy* VI (p. 91) and in *Ad Patrem* (p. 101) he had written of certain phases of poetry and the life of a poet; he now asks if he is to be a poet, whether he shall devote his life to light, gay, careless, but innocent poetry, or to that which has all the high seriousness of the highest art. For already he believes that the true poet must be a true poem (549, 1.47). His decision is to do both, but to emphasize the high seriousness of *Il Penseroso*. The student will find many places where Milton is clearly concerned with the problem of his life work; he will also notice later that *Paradise Regain'd* deals with Christ's determination in regard to his future work and plans.

2 *Cerberus;* hell-dog, from two Greek words meaning heart-devouring, an appropriately invented sire for Melancholy.

4 *unholy;* because in the infernal regions.

5 *uncouth;* unknown.

6 *jealous;* suspiciously vigilant.

9 *ragged;* another form of *rugged*.

11 *free;* unrestrained in movement; hence, graceful and courteous.

14 The first parentage of the Graces is given by Servius in commenting on *Æn.* 1.720. (Keightley).

a; one.

17 *som Sager;* the second genealogy is found nowhere in the ancient poets. Professor Trent believes that Milton may have found the suggestion in Jonson's masks. He may be inventing it himself, as he often does. Anyway, Milton prefers the second possibility, which makes Mirth the daughter of Dawn and spring breezes, to the first, where she is the half-sister of Comus, the daughter of Wine and Love.

18 *frolick;* joyous, gay.

20 *a Maying;* the *a* is a weakened form of *on;* cf. our phrase, a-fishing. When one reads the many diatribes in seventeenth century writers against May-poles, one can readily see that the young Milton is far removed from the typical Puritan.

24 *bucksom;* pliant; here nearly the same as *free*. You will find the changes in the meaning of this interesting word in the N.E.D.

27 *Quips;* smart repartees. *Cranks;* sudden turns or twists of speech, with an element of humor; *wanton Wiles;* merry tricks.

30 *sleek;* soft, with a possible secondary meaning of sly.

34 *fantastick;* because dictated by fancy or whim.

36 Probably because mountain dwellers are traditionally strong lovers of freedom. In giving the *Mountain Nymph* the position of honor, Milton is beginning well his lifelong devotion to liberty.

40 *unreproved;* unreprovable. The past participle in -ed was frequently used by seventeenth century writers for the adjective ending in -able.

45 *to come;* in construction parallel with *to hear* (1.41). For a full discussion, see Trent.

43 *Sweet-Briar;* the wild rose.

44 *twisted Eglantine;* probably the honeysuckle.

50 *thin;* modifies the whole phrase, *rear of darknes*. Note the aptness of the military figure.

55 *Hoar Hill;* gray, as seen from a distance or through mist; or because of age; or because covered with frost. Which interpretation fits best with 1.53?

57 *not unseen;* part of the joy of living a life not too greatly troubled by deep thought.

60 *state;* stately march or progress.

67 *tells his tale;* counts his sheep.

83 *Corydon;* and the other names here are frequently used in pastoral poetry.

91 *secure;* see glossary.

94 *rebecks;* a kind of fiddle.

103–4 Study carefully the differences between 1645 and 1673. Were the changes due to Milton or the printer? Consider Hanford's suggestion that "she" and "he" are the Latin "illa" and "ille"; "one in the company, a woman," "another in the company, a man." (*Handbook*, p. 337.) Trent seems to think that Milton made the change. See his note.

110 *Fend;* fiend.

120 *weeds;* garments. Now used only of the black clothes of widows. *high triumphs;* tournaments and other gorgeous celebrations.

121 *store of;* abundance of.

122 *Rain influence;* as if the ladies were stars that poured out their influences according to the old astrology.

125 *Hymen;* the god of marriage.

127 *pomp;* as in Latin, a solemn procession.

132 *learned Sock;* the sock is a low, light shoe worn by actors in ancient comedy. Jonson was well versed in the ancient classics.

133 Compare the chief idea in *On Shakespear,* p. 21.

135 *eating Cares;* "Curas edaces," Horace, *Car.* ii. 11, 18. Cf. *Epitaphium Damonis,* l.46.

Moody says: "In spite of the epitaph, it is extremely doubtful whether Milton understood or rightly valued Shakespeare's genius." Do you agree?

136 *soft Lydian Aires;* one of the three recognized kinds of ancient music, soft and sweet. The following lines, describing the effect of Lydian airs, are as easy and free as such music itself—an effect probably intended by the poet.

138 *meeting;* the soul comes out to meet the music.

139 *bout;* a turn in the music.

149 *quite set free;* to have made no conditions as he did in the classical story.

151–2 Unconsciously reminiscent of the concluding lines of Marlowe's famous poem, *The Passionate Shepherd to His Love.* It is part of Milton's genius that he retained in memory lines of poetry that he admired and often adapted them, modified for his purpose, and usually bettered. Cf. his definition of plagiarism on 784, l.12, and cf. the note. The student should train himself to watch for these reminiscences of famous lines of poetry, and to enjoy them all the more because they call to mind places in other poems that have pleased readers and poets alike. He should also remember that this process seems to be largely unconscious on Milton's part.

Page 26. IL PENSEROSO

The student will find it enjoyable and profitable to work out the contrasts between this poem and the preceding one.

3 *bested;* satisfy.

4 *fixed;* firmly fixed upon thoughts of highest import.
toyes; trifles.

5 *idle;* empty, vacant.

6 *fond;* foolish.

7 Cf. "As thikke as motes in the sonne-beem." Chaucer's *Tale of the Wyf of Bathe,* l.12. Milton was a reader of Chaucer and other Middle English poets.

10 *pensioners;* paid members of a retinue, such as Queen Elizabeth's Gentlemen-pensioners; they were the tallest and handsomest young men in the kingdom and often accompanied her on her progresses.

13–14 The idea seems to come from the excessive brightness of Jehovah. *Ex.* xxxiii. 20. It is interesting to notice the presence, in this early poetry, of ideas which Milton used later in the most masterly fashion.

18 *Prince Memnons sister;* Prince Memnon was king of the "blameless Ethiopians," an ally of the Trojans, and a man of extraordinary beauty. (*Od.* xi. 522.) Milton assumes that his sister, Himera, must have been beautiful also.

21 *powers;* the sea-nymphs themselves.

23–24 *Vesta;* goddess of the chaste hearth, and *Saturn,* promoter of civilization, are fit parents for Milton's "divine Melancholy." Notice that she was born in the first great golden age.

31 *pensive;* note the thoughtful nature of melancholy.

32 *demure;* modest, with the idea also of being grave.

33 *All;* an adverb; dressed all over. *grain;* hue.

35 *stole;* veil or hood. *Cipres Lawn;* a thin crape-like tissue of fine quality.

36 *decent;* comely; Latin, *decens.*

38 *commercing;* communing.

41 *passion;* internal emotion.

42 Cf. *To Shakespear,* l.14.

43 *sad;* grave.

46 *Spare Fast;* an early statement of Milton's lifelong belief in the value of temperance.

51 See *Ezekiel* x.

55 Silence is to be allured by the only sound that she loves.

59 *Dragon yoke;* apparently only Demeter had a dragon yoke; Milton gives the moon a dragon team in *On the Death of the Bishop of Ely,* p. 100.

60 *accustom'd;* by the poet (Masson), by the nightingale (Trent), or by the moon?

65–66 The nightingale ceases to sing about July 1 when the meadows are first mown. Can you find other instances of close observation of nature in Milton's poetry?

71–72 Does the moon ever seem to be moving rather than the clouds? Cf. the preceding note.

79 Cf. *P.L.* I. 63.

87 As the constellation of the Bear never sets, this statement implies watching all night.

88 *or unsphear;* to call back the spirit of Plato from the unseen world by a careful study of his works.

95 *consent;* true relation with.

98 *Scepter'd;* an apparent, not a real, participle, meaning furnished with a scepter. *Pall;* a mantle. The two following lines tell why tragedy is described as royal.

101 *though rare;* what tragedies, of modern drama, besides Shakspere's four great ones, can compare favorably with the ancient Greek drama? Is Moody justified in saying that "rare" shows that Milton "was out of sympathy with the Elizabethan dramatic movement"? Is Milton's line essentially just?

102 *Buskind stage;* referring to a high shoe employed in ancient tragedy.

110–115 *story;* Chaucer's *Squire's Tale.* The names in the following lines are those of characters in the tale.

116 *great Bards;* such as Ariosto, Tasso, and Spenser.

120 I. e. the allegorical meaning inherent in such epic romances as the *Fairy Queen.*

122 *civil-suited;* in plain dress.

130 *minute drops;* see glossary.

147–150 The lines are condensed, but not difficult to interpret, if studied carefully. *wave at;* move to and fro. (Masson.) After forming his own opinions, the student may be interested in reading Professor Trent's note, where he will find undreamed-of possibilities of interpretation.

153 *spirit;* slur the second i in pronouncing. *good;* apparently modifies *spirit.*

155 *due;* because he would always resort to this walk.

156 *pale;* enclosure.

158 *massy proof;* being massive, they are proof against the weight of the heavy roof.

159 *storied;* the stained glass windows represented Biblical stories. Some commentators see a reference to the use of "story" for "history," but the context does not seem to warrant this meaning. Notice again the lack in the young Milton of typical Puritan feeling. If one insists on calling Milton a Puritan poet, one must use a very exact definition; he was far from being a Puritan in the ordinary sense of the word.

171 *shew;* notice the pronunciation.

Page 29. SONNETS

On the history of the sonnet, and especially on the form and content of the Miltonic sonnet, the student should consult J. S. Smart, *Milton's Sonnets.*

SONNET I

The theme of this sonnet is the medieval tradition that to hear the nightingale before the cuckoo in spring portended good luck to the lover. The Middle English poem, *The Cuckoo and the Nightingale,* formerly attributed to Chaucer, tells of this belief:

But as I lay this other night wakinge,
I thoght how lovers had a tokeninge,
And among hem it was a comune tale,
That it were good to here the nightingale
Rather than the lewde cukkow singe. . . .
And yet had I non herd of al this yere,
And hit was tho the thridde night of May.

Read in connection with this sonnet, *Elegy* VII, p. 92 where the tone is much the same.

4 *the jolly hours;* were Latin and Greek goddesses of the seasons. *jolly;* gay, festive. *lead on;* a metaphor taken from the dance (Verity).

6 *shallow;* in comparison with the "liquid notes" of the nightingale; with perhaps a secondary reference to the thoughtless repetition of its call, causing ill luck to the lover.

9 *rude Bird of Hate;* the cuckoo was unpropitious not only to lovers but to married people as well.

SONNET VII

This sonnet has no title in either of the printed editions of Milton's poems or in the MS. The date is, of course, December 1631. From the letter, in which the sonnet appears in the MS., we infer that a friend, perhaps imaginary, has been urging the young poet to settle down in some regular profession, and has especially advised the Church. Milton defends his present course, declaring that he has not forgotten "the terrible seasure of him that hid his talent." He then introduces the sonnet by writing: "Yet that you may see that I am somtyme suspicious of my selfe, & doe take notice of a certaine belatednesse in me, I am the bolder to send you some of my nightward thoughts some while since, since they come in fitly, in a Petrachian stanza." Read the entire letter on p. 1127.

5–6 Milton apparently long had a youthful appearance. Cf. the *Second Defence*, p. 1139, 2.44.

7 *inward ripenes;* cf. the opening lines of *Lycidas.*

8 Who were some of the "more timely-happy spirits"? Smart thinks Thomas Randolph was one, but, of course, this cannot be proved.

11–12 Cf. Pindar in the *Fourth Nemean Ode:* "But whatsoever merit King Fate has given to me, I well know that Time in its course will accomplish what is destined."

SONNET VIII

Study the textual notes; why did Milton change the title and finally delete it? After the battle of Edgehill, October 23, 1642, the Royalist army marched toward London, creating alarm in the city. Earthworks were thrown up, and on November 13 an army of 24,000 men was drawn up on Turnham Green to oppose the Royalists. But Charles gave orders for a retreat, and the danger passed. The sonnet may have been composed about this time. Edward Calamy, in a Thanksgiving Sermon preached before the House of Lords on June 15, 1643, mentions among other causes of thanksgiving, such as God's delivery of England from the Armada and from the Gunpowder Plot, that "when there was a designe to bring the Army up against London, God did then deliver us." *Sermon,* p. 58. The editor agrees with Masson that the sonnet is not to be taken too seriously; it is written "half in jest."

1 *Colonel;* pronounce in three syllables.

3 Why did Milton change the reading of this line? See textual notes.

12 *repeated air;* the repetition of the air. A Latinism.

12–14 The incident is told by Plutarch in his *Life of Lysander,* and quoted by Smart.

SONNET IX

This is not a love sonnet, but simply words of encouragement and sympathy addressed to a young girl of about twelve, some of whose friends had objected to her "growing virtues."

SONNET X

James Ley, the "good Earl" of this sonnet, born in 1550, became a lawyer, attained the office of Lord Chief Justice in 1622, and in that capacity presided over the trial of Lord Bacon and pronounced sentence. Later he became Lord High Treasurer and Lord President of the Council. He retired from office in 1628 at the advanced age

of seventy-eight. He died on March 14, 1629, four days after the dissolution of Charles's third Parliament. Milton implies that he had resigned because of disapproval of Charles's unconstitutional procedure, and that his death was hastened by the dissolution of Parliament. Lady Margaret was the elder of two daughters at home, and is described as "the staff of his age, the very prop." In December, 1641, Lady Margaret married Captain John Hobson. During the Civil War Hobson was on the side of Parliament, though the Marborough family were Royalists. Phillips in his life of Milton says: "This lady, being a woman of great wit and ingenuity, had a particuar honour for him, and took much delight in his company, as likewise Captain Hobson, her husband, a very accomplished gentleman; and what esteem he at same time had for her appears by a Sonnet he made in praise of her."

1 *that;* that well known. Latin *ille.* Note the repetition of the word in lines 5, 6, 8.

3 What historical event was probably in Milton's mind?

5 The dissolution of the Parliament in 1629 was tumultuous. The speaker was forcibly held down in his chair while a resolution was passed protesting against the king's policy. History does not record that the news of these violent times affected the aged earl's health, but, as Smart suggests, Milton would hardly have used the incident without a hint from Lady Margaret.

6 *dishonest;* disgraceful,—to those who won it. Latin *inhonestus.*

7 *Chæronéa;* the Athenians and Thebans united against their common enemy, Philip of Macedonia, and were defeated here. The Greek cities never recovered their independence.

8 Isocrates, then ninety-eight years old, was according to tradition so overwhelmed with grief that he voluntarily starved himself and died four days after the defeat.

9 What was Milton doing in the spring of 1629? Notice that he implies that most of his knowledge of the Earl's life has come from Lady Margaret. Observe the increasing strength and firmness of the sonnet as we approach the end.

SONNET XI

In the Cambridge MS. Sonnet XII is numbered XI and comes first. There is also a direction: "these sonnets follow ye 10 in ye printed booke," and a caution in the margin, "vide ante." Can you see any reason for Milton's departing from this order when he published them in 1673? Read the textual notes carefully and observe the effect of each change that Milton made.

1 *Tetrachordon;* printed at p. 648, was published on or about March 4, 1644. The word is a technical word in music, meaning the combination of four notes; naturally it was a queer and unknown word to the average reader.

2 All critics would agree that this line describes accurately certain characteristics of Milton's poetry, but not all would agree that the line applies equally well to his prose. Bear this line in mind as you read his prose works. Was Milton a good self-critic? It will be profitable to note, and even to gather together all the places you can where he speaks of his own style and to test his statements by modern standards.

4 Milton always prided himself on his good readers; on the poor intellects that read his divorce tracts, he poured out his scorn in *Colasterion,* p. 711. In the light of the reform that Milton hoped to bring about, the dying down of discussion among good intellects, in the excitements of the Civil War, must have been a disappointment to him.

5 *stall-reader;* the book stalls were located chiefly around St. Paul's, where persons curious, but not to the point of buying, could "stand spelling false" and gain a superficial knowledge of the books displayed. Milton is able to take a humorous view of their perplexities.

7–8 *Mile-End Green;* on the edge of town, a mile away.

8–9 Names of Scotch Civil War heroes, popular in London. Milton is not satirizing Scotchmen, but jestingly reproaching the typical Londoner for so easily forgetting his divorce tracts. Perhaps Milton also realizes that public events have pushed his program into the background.

10 *like;* our mouths (we) are as uncultured and harsh as the unfamiliar Scotch names once seemed. Notice how much is implied in the last lines of the sonnet, and how skilfully Milton is working up to the implication, nowhere stated, that, if the Londoners were really learned, they would understand and appreciate the arguments in *Tetrachordon.*

11 Quintilian discusses among other virtues of writing the desirability of choosing words that are pleasant in sound.

12 *Sir John Cheek;* see glossary. Cf. 710, 2.7: "Sir John Cheeke, the king's tutor, a man at that time counted the learnedest of Englishmen, and for piety not inferior."

13 *Hated not;* but they hated toad or asp as much as they possibly could. Get the full significance of the negative. *hated . . . wors then Toad;* cf. 718, 1.25: "as to hate one another like a toad."

14 Why is this line so often quoted? Is there a surprising turn in it? Notice how often Milton mentions King Edward in the prose works. He was something of a hero to the reforming Protestants. What is the implication in regard to Milton's works? Smart remarks that the sonnet shows the influence of the Latin epigram. Do you see any of the characteristics of Jonson's poetry in it?

SONNET XII

1 *cloggs;* literally, encumbrances fastened to animals to prevent straying.

2 *antient libertie;* Milton's ideals of liberty were formed and quickened largely by reading and re-reading the ancient classics. True liberty is often discussed by Cicero, Livy and other Latin writers.

3 *barbarous;* an especially well chosen word, when one considers the previous line.

4 Milton is thinking probably of the moral significance attached to these birds and animals by writers of natural history, such as Pliny. The owl, we are told, is an emblem of darkness; the cuckoo of ingratitude; the dog of quarrelsomeness and detraction.

10 *still;* always. Cf. *John* viii. 32: "The truth shall make you free."

11–12 Cf. other discussions by Milton of true liberty in the note on 459, 2.51. Cf. especially 754, 1.28: "For, indeed, none can love freedom heartily but good men; the rest love not freedom but licence."

SONNET XIII

Henry Lawes, who composed the music to the songs in *Comus,* was a musician of the court of Charles I. He set to music poems by Waller, Herrick, Lovelace, Carew and other contemporary poets. His distinction among composers is that he tried to adapt his music to the sense of the words of the song. It is said that in this he often succeeded admirably. Milton refers to this characteristic in this sonnet.

10 *Phœbus Quire;* the poets of his time.

12 *Dante;* watch for allusions to Dante. Do you think that the great Italian poet appealed greatly to Milton?

14 *milder;* than Hell, which Dante had described in the *Inferno.*

SONNET XIV

George Thomason was a bookseller and publisher, who had his shop in St. Paul's Churchyard. He is best known, however, for his collection of contemporary pamphlets, numbering about 22,000, now in the British Museum. He seems to have been a friend of Milton's, as several of Milton's treatises which he possessed are marked *Ex Dono Authoris*. Of his wife, who was Catharine Hutton, little is known. One of her daughters died in 1659. Dr. Edward Reynolds, who preached the funeral sermon, said: "She was, both in bodily resemblance and in moral imitation, the transcript of a gracious mother."

SONNET XV

Why were this sonnet and Sonnets XVI, XVII, and XXII omitted in 1673? With this sonnet compare a somewhat revised opinion in the *Second Defence*, p. 1151, 1.43. Fairfax began the siege of Colchester, June 13, 1648.

3 Because in this democratic uprising the kings of Europe read their own fate.

5 *vertue;* Latin, *virtus,* valor. Fairfax was noted for his unusual personal courage.

7 *Hydra;* see glossary.

7–8 The Scotch under Hamilton were invading England to support Charles, thus breaking the Solemn League and Covenant of 1643. *impe;* was a term in falconry, meaning to insert new feathers in the wing of a falcon, tying them with wire to the stumps of the old ones; thus, to strengthen.

12–14 The financial loss during the Civil War through dishonest and shameful acts of Parliament are familiar to readers of Scott's novels. Milton in many places takes occasion to notice it, and always with disapproval.

SONNET XVI

The Committee for the Propagation of the Gospel was appointed by Parliament to attempt to untangle the confusion in the church. One proposal received by them demanded that no one should be allowed to speak from a pulpit until he had secured a certificate from two or more godly and orthodox ministers. It was against this proposed restriction that Milton protested. Read with this sonnet Milton's eloquent tribute to Cromwell, written two years later, on pp. 1150 ff., and notice that even here, when he was writing for an European, as well as for an English, public, there is admonition as well as praise.

2 *detractions rude;* not only Royalists but even many adherents of Parliament misjudged Cromwell. Cf. the way in which Mrs. Hutchinson speaks of him in her *Memoirs.*

SONNET XVII

1 Sir Henry Vane was an able and energetic member of Parliament. He and Milton often agreed, especially upon religious toleration and the separation of church and state. He was nearly forty at this time.

5–6 War had already been declared with the Dutch, though the Dutch ambassadors still remained in London, declaring that hostilities had taken place against the wishes of their government.

SONNET XVIII

Most of the knowledge of historical events necessary to understand this sonnet will be obtained by reading the State letters at p. 1170. The massacre occurred on April 17–25, 1655. When Englishmen heard of it, they were horrified. Cromwell immediately dispatched vigorous letters through Milton to various states and princes. He then started a subscription for the refugees, which amounted by June 1 to £38,000; he himself contributed £2,000. Milton, having executed his public duties, gave further vent to his feelings in this sonnet, certainly the greatest that he ever wrote, and perhaps the greatest in English literature. Study especially the vowel sounds and their value and the sustained thought and sentence structure.

7 Jean Leger, the historian of the Vaudois, relates that the body of a mother was found dead, thrown from a rock, with her babe still living in her arms.

14 It had long been customary for Protestants, and even for Catholics, to refer to Rome as the Babylon, which would some day come to ruin.

SONNET XIX

This sonnet, the earliest reference by Milton in poetry to his blindness, was composed while the calamity was still fresh. Contrast the note of discouragement and then of resignation which dominates this poem with the staunch courage of Sonnet XXII.

2 *E're half my days;* Milton was 43 when he became blind.

3 Milton always felt keenly the responsibility of his genius. Cf. 522, 1.29 ff. Can you remember any other places where he shows this same solicitude? The parable of the talents, here alluded to, is given in *Matthew* xxv. 14–30. Milton naturally felt that his great poem that "the world would not willingly let die," must now remain unwritten; *that one Talent;* is his genius as a poet.

8 *fondly;* foolishly.

12 *Thousands;* of angelic beings. Cf. 984, 2.49.

SONNET XX

This sonnet and the following are in the lighter vein, suggested by Latin poems inviting friends to a dinner. Cf. especially Horace, II. *Carm.* xi. They show that Milton could write lighter poems successfully when he tried.

   1 *Lawrence;* probably Edward Lawrence, eldest son of Henry Lawrence, Lord President of the Council. See Smart. Edward Lawrence was born in 1633. *vertuous;* in the Latin sense, possessing eminence of character.

   4 *wast;* spend.

   8 Cf. *Matthew* vi. 28.

  9–10 The repasts of the Athenians were proverbially frugal.

  13 *And spare;* take care not to interpose them often.

SONNET XXI

Cyriack Skinner was the grandson of Sir Edward Coke, Chief Justice of the King's Bench. Coke is now unfortunately remembered for his cruel treatment of Sir Walter Raleigh; he was, however, a noble and upright judge. During his later career he was the consistent champion of Parliament against the usurpations of Charles I. Cyriack Skinner was one of Milton's pupils; his friendship with the poet lasted until Milton's death.

   8 *the Swede;* the Swedish nation under Charles X, who was then warring upon Poland and Denmark, and causing anxiety to Protestants in England. *the French;* under Cardinal Mazarin were also causing speculation.

SONNET XXII

Smart assigns this sonnet and the preceding one to the year 1655.

   1 *this three years day;* for three years.

  4–6 Cf. *P.L.* iii. 40 ff. Notice that in each passage the emphasis is placed upon the deprivation in regard to human relationships.

   9 *Right onward;* the MS. read at first "Uphillward." Why did Milton change the reading?

  12 *talks;* Phillips, who first published this sonnet in 1694, has "rings," suggested perhaps by l.1 of Sonnet XV. Modern editors often read "rings," though there is no authority in Milton for doing so. Phillips printed Sonnets XV, XVI, XVII and XXII, and in all of them his text is notoriously corrupt. In Sonnet XVI he even omitted a line. Ob-

viously his reading can be given little or no value in comparison with Milton's own manuscript.

SONNET XXIII

In 1656 Milton married Catherine Woodcock. In October, 1657, Mrs. Milton bore a child; she died in February, 1658, and the child a few weeks later. For more about her, see Smart.

   3 *Jove's great Son;* Hercules.

   6 See *Leviticus* xii.

  10 *Her face was veil'd;* as was Alcestis'. The allusion is to Milton's blindness.

Page 37. THE FIFTH ODE OF HORACE

Evidently Milton thought that translation of classical poetry into English verse kept him in good training. In the original edition he printed the Latin original, as if challenging comparison. The student may care to observe the closeness and felicity of the translation.

Page 38. ON THE NEW FORCERS OF CONSCIENCE

This poem belongs to the type known to Italian sonnet writers as the *Sonetto Caudato,* or the sonnet with a *coda* or tail. After the usual 14 lines the poem is continued by the addition of six short lines. In 1643 Parliament resolved to abolish the Prelatical government of the Church of England and to substitute a government by Presbyters, "nearer agreement with the Church of Scotland." The Westminster Assembly was called by Parliament for the purpose of revising the form of church government. A small group of Independents opposed this plan. Milton's growing anti-Presbyterianism, which may be profitably traced in his prose works, here found its culmination.

   1 *Prelate Lord;* church government by Bishops and Archbishops.

   2 The English Liturgy was the object of fierce attack by Milton and other anti-prelatical writers.

   5 Milton was always firm against any law compelling uniformity of religious worship. He believed strongly in the wholesomeness of schisms. Read his defence of sects and schisms on 748, 1.37 ff.

   7 *classic Hierarchy;* i.e. the Presbyterian church, which was divided into *classes.*

   8 *A. S.;* is Dr. Adam Stuart, an able Scotch divine and writer. Stuart was not a prominent figure in these discussions as he had been preaching abroad most of his mature life.

Probably *meer* means that Milton did not know what the initials signed to Stuart's tracts stood for. *Rotherford;* Samuel Rutherford, Professor of Divinity at St. Andrews. He always advocated strict censorship of religious opinions. In a book published about three years after the writing of this poem he argued for nothing less than a Protestant Inquisition.

9 Goodwin, Nye, Burroughs, and other Independent writers, with whom Milton agreed and sympathized.

10 *Paul;* the most learned of the Apostles.

12 *shallow Edwards;* Thomas Edwards was a divine and writer of extreme views against religious toleration. He replied to the men mentioned in the note to 9 in a book he called *Antapolgia.* Milton may, as Smart suggests, refer to this book, though it should be remembered that Edwards published a more famous book in 1645-6, *Gangræna*, in which he listed and discussed the heresies of his time. Milton was attacked for his opinions on divorce. The book is full of stories and gossip, without any thoughtful consideration of the problem. It well merits the epithet, *shallow.* Milton at first wrote *hare braind.* Considering the serious tone of Milton's poem, which epithet is better? *Scotch what d'ye call;* a contemptuous reference to some Scotch divine, probably Robert Baillie, Professor in Glasgow University and a member of the Westminster Assembly.

14 For Milton's opinion of councils, see 569, 1.44, and for his opinion of the Council of Trent, see 736, 1.20 ff.

15 Parliament had frequently rebuked the Westminster Assembly for its too zealous activity.

17 *bauk;* omit. Consider the original reading in the MS. *P----'s;* William Prynne, who had had his ears clipped on two occasions. *marginal;* because Prynne's works are filled with marginal notes, almost to the exclusion of the text in some instances. Why did Milton delete this line? Do you agree with Masson that Milton thought that Prynne had suffered enough? Masson's comment is probably much too generous. Milton seems rather to have thought that Prynne was too contemptible to merit naming, for in all his work he never calls him by name, though he refers to him frequently. Prynne was a lawyer of a narrow mind; his reliance upon historical precedents was especially irritating to Milton. When this poem was written, Prynne was engaged in a pamphlet war against Independents and Toleration.

20 *Presbyter* and *Priest* come from the same Greek root. Cf. with this line, *Areopagitica,* 745, 2.11: "bishops and presbyters are the same to us, both name and thing."

Page 38. ARCADES

The Countess Dowager of Derby was a daughter of Sir John Spencer. She and her two sisters had been celebrated by Spenser, who claimed kinship with the family. The first husband of the Countess, Lord Strange, died in 1594, leaving her with three daughters. In 1600 she married Sir Thomas Egerton, a widower, who became Viscount Brackley in 1616, and died in 1617. His son, Sir John Egerton, who married the second daughter of the Countess, became the Earl of Bridgewater, before whom *Comus* was presented. On the characteristics of the mask, the student may consult any good history of English literature. The date of composition is, according to Grierson, between 1630 and 1632.

1 A group of nymphs and shepherds, searching for their Arcadian Queen, the Countess, sing songs in her honor, when they find her.

Page 40. LYCIDAS

Whether or not one agrees with Pattison that in *Lycidas* we have the greatest short poem in the language, everyone will agree that no other poem affords so good a test by which to try one's true appreciation of poetry. No other poem more richly repays careful and minute study, while a full appreciation of it comes only after wide reading and years of mature study. English poets from Gray to Tennyson and after, have studied and appreciated the poem; echoes of words and phrases are found in many of their poems, especially in the *Prelude* and in *Adonais.* It is said that Tennyson used to measure the literary appreciation of his young poet visitors by questioning them upon *Lycidas;* if they showed enthusiastic appreciation, they were at once admitted to cordial relations, but if they were indifferent, they soon found their reception lacking in warmth. A poem that has commanded the study of the greatest minds of the nineteenth century demands justly of the present-day student careful preparation in wide reading, and thoughtful and repeated consideration extending to each word and phrase.

Undoubtedly the greatest difficulty in the first approach to *Lycidas,* as Hanford remarks, lies in its pastoral form, with which we today are completely out of touch, except through study. Before attempting this study, the student will do well to read some of the great pastorals, such as Nos. I, II, and VII of Theocritus, *The Lament for Adonis*, by Bion and *The Lament for Bion*, by Moschus, all beautifully translated into English prose by Andrew Lang (*Theocritus, Bion, and Moschus*); the last of Vergil's *Eclogues;* some of Spenser's pastoral poetry; and last, but obviously most important for many reasons, Milton's *Epitaphium Damonis*, translated at p. 106 of this volume.

It will help the reader to appreciate *Lycidas*, if he remembers that the poem is built upon a definite structural outline, for the first step always towards a real evaluation of a poem is an intelligent understanding of what the poet is trying to say and do. Milton imagines his tribute to his dead friend as a memorial service, held on a hillside, before the "sorrowing friends," also imagined to be present as "woful shepherds," mentioned on the title-page of the Memorial volume. In the first paragraph the occasion is stated, "For Lycidas is dead"; then follows the invocation, addressed to the muses of poetry, as is fitting in pastoral poetry. The address of Milton, the principal speaker, begins in the invocation, so closely and firmly knit are the thought and style. Milton then, in the manner of an effective speaker at such a service, tells of his associations with the deceased, their common studies at the University, their recreations, their love for nature, and their close associations with her, and lastly, the idealism and pursuit of fame by which they both had been animated. Then he imagines that other speakers are also present. Neptune has sent his representative, Triton, who, while lamenting the dead, is to clear the sea of blame. Cambridge University is properly represented, but grief is so deep that words are few. Lastly St. Peter, the spokesman for the profession for which the dead poet was actively preparing himself, speaks, emphasizing the loss, in an ill time, which the church has sustained. Then with the poet, we are invited to admire the floral tributes, only to be reminded that after all this is but a memorial service, for the body of Lycidas is not here but tossed in the whelming sea. Once more the chief speaker takes up the service; only the words of consolation remain to be spoken: Lycidas is not in the sea, but walks along other streams; and in the end of the paragraph we have the benediction. The concluding eight lines, the only stanza in the poem, is a part of the setting, corresponding to the opening lines, and describes the departure of the singer.

Less definite, but no less important, is the resemblance of *Lycidas* to a piece of music,—what we now call a symphony or a symphonic poem. In the poem there are, broadly speaking, two main movements, both beginning in the first paragraph, the second movement only occasionally and faintly heard, while the first is developing. The first movement is on fame,—worldly fame and true fame; it reaches its climax in the finality of the judgment of Jove in l.84 The second movement, the value of an able and good man in the world, which has been implied in the poem from the beginning, now becomes prominent and culminates in the famous St. Peter passage. Then follows the soft, gentle music of the flower passage, ending in a tremendous return of both movements. Finally the two are gently and skilfully blended into one in the closing words of consolation. Furthermore, the opening lines are processional music, while the closing ones are recessional. In the last line one feels a change in the tempo and spirit of the poem—a change that is almost startling. But this line is based upon a sound knowledge of human psychology. The one fact that usually most impresses bereaved friends, especially after a sudden and tragic death, is that the survivors must carry on, the living must face the duties of life. We see the exact parallel to this marvelous close in a military funeral, where, after the dead march, with the flag at half-mast, when taps has been sounded and all honors have been paid, the order is given to right about face, the flag is raised to full mast, and the troop marches away to a lively tune at double-quick time. It is but saying that the world is still before us.

Study the firm, compact form of the poem; there is not a phrase or word that has not its significance. Observe that the thought in one paragraph leads naturally to a development in the next; watch, for example, how subtly the thought in the first paragraph, *For Lycidas is dead*, is gradually changed in the development of the poem until in the end it has become, *For Lycidas, your sorrow, is not dead*. Notice the recurrence of certain phrases, with modifications, like the recurring strains in music, such as "once more," "no more." Some critics, who should know better, have followed Dr. Johnson in believing that the poem lacks real pathos; others have found the feeling of pathos in the author's fear that he too may, like King, die young. The last thought is undoubtedly in the poem, as it is in *Adonais*, but it is not there prominently. Masson took an unwarranted liberty in wresting the meaning of *my* in l.20 by italizing it; the word is not in an emphatic position, nor will it bear emphasis. A fair question to consider is whether the poem does not have all the real grief that the art form can properly sustain. Grief does not necessarily consist in wringing the hands, as some nineteenth century poets seem to think. In this connection, study the psychology in the poem, for in the final analysis no poet can be great who does not understand the working of the mind. Notice the reaction after l.153 and recall the law of psychology, now well known, that the bare mention of an object that we are trying to forget, brings that object forcibly into our minds. Some critics have thought that ll.152–164 are the most powerful in Milton. Title. *Lycidas;* in the Seventh Idyl of Theocritus *Lycidas* is the name of the "chiefest flute-player" among "herdsmen, yea and reapers." Whether King, judging from the Latin poems of his that remain, merits the name of poet, is not to the point; it is sufficient to know that Milton considers him a poet who could "build the lofty rhyme"; hence the name. *Monody;* the use of this word fits in with the structural outline given above. *And by occasion, etc.;* this sentence is not in the MS. nor in 1638. It was added by Milton in 1645, and is equivalent to saying: "Over seven years ago I foretold what now has gloriously taken place." Is there any implication here as to whether Milton considered the St. Peter passage a digression? Remember that it did not occur to him to mention it until 1645. *by occasion* means that in the course of this poem on a learned friend's death he had occasion, etc. Those who see a digression in this passage might well be asked to cite other passages in Milton that are digressions. To my knowledge this is the only passage that is seriously so considered.

1–2 *Laurels, Myrtles and Ivy;* are emblems of immortality, especially the immortality of poetry. Milton here refers to his immaturity, which he regretted in the seventh sonnet. He has been studying intensely for several years, yet he fears that inward ripeness has not yet arrived. Up to this time he had written no elegiac poem that he would be willing to consider more than a school exercise. Now he has attained years of manhood, he feels that he can no longer fall back on that excuse. The occasion demands that he write mature poetry, and he is forced reluctantly to try to reach the heights for which he has been preparing.

3 *Berries harsh and crude;* the immature fruits of poetic study. Observe the postpositive position of the adjectives. What effect does such a position have upon the meaning?

4 *forc'd fingers rude;* the last adjective, as usual in Milton's poetry, modifies, not exclusively the preceding noun, but rather the idea made by the union of the preceding adjective and noun combined.

5. *Shatter; scatter.* Milton wrote first: *and crop your young;* Watch the changes recorded in these notes and in the textual notes, and observe that uniformly the changes are an improvement. The student will benefit greatly by studying carefully the reproduction of Milton's own manuscript of *Lycidas* and other short poems, as printed in facsimile by the Facsimile Society, vol. 17 (July, 1933, Columbia University Press). *mellowing;* a proleptic use of the adjective, meaning, *the year that makes them mellow.*

7 *Compels;* in Elizabethan and seventeenth century English the verb belonging to a compound subject usually agrees with the subject nearest it. See *Abbott's Shakespearian Grammar* for rules governing the syntax of the time.

8 Study the skilful repetition. Cf. it with that in *On the Death of a Fair Infant,* 25–26, and in other early poems. Has Milton gained in the effective use of repetition? If so, just how?

11 *build the lofty rhyme;* Cf. Hor. *Ep.* I. iii. 24. "Seu condis amabile carmen." No attempt will be made to point out all the classical reminiscences in Milton's poetry, which from now on are numerous. To find in these poems words and phrases which one has formerly read, is a pleasure of which the classical student should not be deprived; to others the mere pointing out of such reminiscences will mean little. Those who wish to carry this subject further may consult Sir John Edwin Sandys, *The Literary Sources of Lycidas,* Transactions of the R.S.L. vol. xxxii.

13 *welter;* toss to and fro.

14 *melodious tear;* tears was a frequent Elizabethan name for elegiac poetry. Thus Drummond calls his elegy on Prince Henry, *Tears on the Death of Meliades.*

15 *Sisters of the sacred well;* the Muses, born at the Pierian fountain under Mt. Olympus.

18–22 Notice that these lines are naturally suggested by the first lines of the poem. *Muse;* poet. *lucky;* propitious.

23 Why do some modern editors err in beginning the next paragraph here? Observe the significance of the opening word. Milton here begins his account of his personal associations with King. Notice throughout the emphasis on their close relations: "self-same hill," "same flocks," "together both." These lines refer, of course, to their studies and recreations at Cambridge.

26 *opening;* notice the improvement over the original *glimmering.* Why is the later reading better? The line can be traced to a marginal reading on *Job* iii. 9: "Neither let it see the eye-lids of the morning."

28 *What time;* when; i. e. in the noon-tide heat. *Gray-fly;* the trumpet-fly.

29 *Batt'ning;* fattening.

30 Study carefully the various changes in this line.

34 *Rough Satyrs . . . Fauns;* the less brilliant and less polished Cambridge undergraduates; the "jolly, good fellows."

35 *Damœtas;* probably some well-beloved fellow of Christ's, such as Joseph Meade.

36 *gon;* notice Milton's consistent spelling of this word. How did he pronounce it?

38 *never must;* can never possibly return.

39 *desert;* why is this adjective used?

40 *gadding;* straying.

42–44 Here is Ruskin's "pathetic fallacy" used in a great poem. Does it add to or injure the poetry?

47 *wear;* Milton deleted this word and tried *beare;* but he finally restored *wear.*

49 *Such;* observe the appropriateness of each of the preceding similes.

60 *Universal nature;* contrasted with the named places in the preceding lines.

65 *homely slighted Shepherds trade;* the writing of serious poetry.

67–69 Either to engage in the writing of light amatory poetry, such as that of the Cavalier poets, or to occupy oneself with light love-making. Which interpretation fits in better with the text and with Milton's character?

70 This line and the following express despair at the outcome of their previous common efforts in securing fame. Cf. 549, 1.23: "Nor blame me, readers, in those years to propose to themselves such a reward, as the noblest dispositions above other things in this life have sometimes preferred." The reward is fame.

75 *blind Fury;* Atropos, one of the three Fates; she stood ready with her shears to cut the thread of life.

77 *trembling ears;* his ears were not trembling, as Masson suggests, because of the well-known superstition, that one's ears ring when one is being talked about, but because his being was in a highly nervous tension, brought about by the feeling of profound despair which had been accumulating since he first began to reflect upon his associations with the dead poet. Had Phœbus touched the poet's hand, he would have found it trembling.

75–84 Cf. *P.L.* VI. 29 ff.

83–84 Observe the finality of Jove's judgment. There is no appeal here nor hope of reconsideration. The thought and the rhyme scheme both unite to form a fitting close to the first movement, or "strain," as Milton called it.

85 *Arethuse;* a spring in the island of Ortygia at Syracuse; an allusion to Greek pastoral poetry, especially to that of Theocritus.

89 *Herald of the Sea;* Triton, who represents Neptune at this imaginary service. He gives the results of a court of investigation that Neptune had called to inquire into the cause of the shipwreck.

106 *sanguine flower;* the Greek hyacinth, a flower with dark purple patches.

117 *shearers feast;* the idea of Christ and his ministers as shepherds and the church as the flock, is thoroughly scriptural; but Milton carries the metaphor much further; evidently the shearers (herdmen) are entitled to a fair wage, but they should not greedily scramble to get more than their share. To what does Milton refer? What was "plurality"? Cf. *On the new Forcers,* p. 38.

119–127 Richard Baxter was born in 1615 at Eaton-Constantine, a village about five miles from Shrewsbury. In his Autobiography he thus describes the preachers to whom he listened in his youth: "We lived in a Country that had but little Preaching at all: In the Village where I was born there was four Readers successively in Six years time, ignorant Men, and two of them immoral in their lives. . . . In the Village, where my Father lived, there was a Reader about Eighty years of Age that never preached, and had two Churches about Twenty miles distant: His Eyesight failing him, he said Common-Prayer without Book; and for the Reading of the Psalms and Chapters, he got a Common Thresher and Day-Labourer one year, and a Taylor another year: (for the Clerk could not read well): And at last he had a kinsman of his own, (the excellentest Stage-player in all the Country, and a good Gamester and good Fellow) that got Orders and supplied one of his Places! After him another younger Kinsman, that could write and read, got Orders: And at the same time another Neighbour's Son that had been a while at School turn'd Minister, and who would needs go further than the rest, ventur'd to preach (and after got a Living in *Staffordshire,*) and when he had been a Preacher about Twelve or Sixteen years, he was fain to give over, it being discovered that his Orders were forged by the first ingenious Stage-Player. After him another Neighbour's Son took Orders, when he had been a while an Attorney's Clerk, and a common Drunkard, and tipled himself into so great Poverty that he had no other way to live: It was feared that he and more of them came by their Orders the same way with the forementioned Person. . . . Within a few miles about us, were near a dozen more Ministers that were near Eighty years old apiece, and never preached; poor ignorant Readers, and most of them of Scandalous Lives: only three or four constant competent Preachers lived near us, and those (though Conformable all save one) were the common Marks of the People's Obloquy and Reproach, and any that had but gone to hear them, when he had no Preaching at home, was made the Derision of the Vulgar Rabble, under the odious Name of a *Puritane.*" *Reliquiæ Baxterianæ*, 1696, p. 1. With this passage should also be compared 497, 2.44, where the clergy are described as "wooden, illiterate or contemptible," lazy, "tavern-hunting," and fond of "doltish and monastic schoolmen." Cf. also 565, 1.1: "How many parts of the land are fed with windy ceremonies instead of sincere milk; and while one prelate enjoys the nourishment and right of twenty ministers, how many waste places are left as dark as 'Galilee of the Gentiles, sitting in the region and shadow of death,' without preaching minister, without light. So little care they of beasts to make them men. . ."

128 *grim Woolf;* probably a reference to the activities of the Catholics, but notice that in *P.L.* IV, 183, Satan is compared to a wolf. Cf. also 825, 2.39: The selfish prelates ought "to be driven out of the fold like wolves or thieves, where they sat fleecing those flocks which they never fed."

130 *two-handed engine;* there have been many suggestions as to what Milton means by this "engine." Dorian, *PMLA* XLV (1930) 204 ff., makes a plausible case for the two houses of Parliament.

139 *Throw;* MS. read first, bring; deleted.

146 *the well attir'd Woodbine;* the second draft, given in the textual notes, had first, the garish columbine; deleted.

148 *sad embroidery wears;* the second draft has, sad escutcheon beares. In the margin is written, embroiderie. beares is deleted; above is weare; in the margin is beares; deleted. Above is the final reading, weares.

153 *frail;* MS. sad; deleted.

163 The Angel of the guarded Mount is bidden to look nearer home than off to Spain, and have pity on the hapless body of Lycidas tossed about in the sea.

164 The allusion is to the story of Arion, who, after being thrown overboard by angry sail-

ors, was carried to shore by dolphins that had been charmed by his song.

173 Cf. *Matthew* xiv. 25.

176 *And hears;* MS. listening: deleted.

183 *Genius;* Lord Herbert of Cherbury in *De Religione Gentilium* quotes Servius: "Genius is the natural God of every Place, Thing and Man." Translation by William Lewis, 1705.

Page 44. COMUS

Milton's friendship with Henry Lawes, the composer, undoubtedly led to his writing this mask, in which he develops the high value that he assigns to temperance and chastity,—a subject that was to be of the highest importance to him as long as he lived. His opinions on this subject, expressed in other works of prose and poetry, are too numerous to refer to here, but the student will be interested and profited by studying them as they occur from time to time. For Henry Lawes, see the note on Sonnet XIII. Notice that Lawes tells us that he acted the part of the Attendant Spirit, Thyrsis.

The Copy of a Letter; Sir Henry Wotton was the perfect type of the elegant, cultured man of the period. After serving as Ambassador to Venice and other European states for many years, he retired and became the Provost of Eton College. He should be known to every student of English literature for his exquisite lyric, "You meaner beauties of the night," addressed to Elizabeth, Queen of Bohemia, daughter of James I. Hebel and Hudson, *Poetry of the English Renaissance*, p. 551.

Mr. H.; undoubtedly the "ever memorable John Hales," who had retired to his fellowship at Eton and who was on intimate terms with Sir Henry. Read the interesting biographical sketch of Hales in the D.N.B.

Mr. R.; probably John Rouse, Librarian of Oxford. See Milton's poem addressed to him on p. 109 and the note.

the late R's Poems; a reference, probably, to an edition of Thomas Randolph's Poems. No edition with *Comus* bound with it has been discovered, but it may be that some stationer thus bound some of the copies. This letter alone from an old man to a young author sufficiently establishes Sir Henry's urbanity.

The texts of *Comus* are: (1) the Cambridge MS., where the mask, except for a few words, is in the hand of Milton; (2) the Bridgewater MS., in the hand of an amanuensis of Lawes's, used as the acting version; (3) the edition of 1637, in the dedication of which, printed at p. 44 of the present volume, Lawes states why he publishes the mask; (4) the edition of 1645, printed in this volume; and (5) the edition of 1673, containing a few alterations, probably by Milton. (6) The five songs, set to music, are also found in MS. Additional 11518 in the British Museum. The title, *Comus,* was first used in the stage version of 1737, and later by Dalton in his edition of 1747.

4 After this line, the Camb. MS. has a deleted passage of 14 lines which finally read as follows:

amidst th Hesperian gardens, on whose bancks
bedew'd with nectar, & celestiall songs
æternall roses grow, & hyacinth
& fruits of golden rind, on whose faire tree
the scalie-harnest dragon ever keeps
his uninchanted eye, & round the verge
& sacred limits of this blisfull Isle
the jealous ocean that old river winds
his farre-extended armes till with steepe fall
halfe his wast flood the wide Atlantique fills
& halfe the slow unfadom'd Stygian poole
but soft I was not sent to court your wonder
with distant worlds, & strange removed clim[es]
yet thence I come and oft from thence behold

7 *pester'd;* from a low Latin word meaning shackle, as when a horse is hobbled; hence, tied down. In the Cambridge MS., hereafter referred to as MS, line 7 is preceded by line 8, which in turn is followed by a deleted line: beyond the written date of mortall change. Milton interchanged the lines by marking them 2 and 1.

18 *task;* MS buisinesse now, deleted. *besides the;* MS whose, deleted.
21 *Imperial;* MS the, deleted. *of all the;* MS & title of each, deleted.
22 *rich, and;* MS rich gemms inlay, the last two words deleted.
25 *goverment;* notice the spelling. MS, Br, and 1645 have this spelling; 1637 and 1673 have the modern spelling.
27 *weild;* MS weild, deleted.
28 *the main;* MS his empire, deleted.
29 *blu-hair'd;* because the sea-gods were usually represented in the masks as having blue hair.
45 *From;* MS by, deleted.
48 Notice the absolute construction, a favorite form of expression with Milton, modeled on the Latin ablative absolute. Such constructions are not in good use today, though perhaps permissible in poetry. If you

are reading Milton's prose, observe whether he uses this construction in it.
49 *listed;* pleased.
54 *This;* The, deleted.
58 *Whom;* MS which, deleted. *Comus nam'd:* MS nam'd him, deleted.
60 *Celtick and Iberian fields;* France and Spain.
62 *shelter;* MS covert, deleted.
63 *mighty;* MS. potent, deleted.
65 *orient;* because of its rich, dark color. Cf. *P.L.* I.546. There may also be a reference here to the baleful and powerful Eastern drugs, not unknown in Europe in the seventeenth century.
67 *fond;* foolish. MS weake, deleted.
68 *potion;* MS potions, the s deleted.
69 *of;* MS of, deleted; followed by o', not deleted.
72 *were;* MS as before, deleted. Why did Milton delete and substitute? Why did he put in this prosaic line? Cf. the stage direction below.
83 *robes;* Br webs.
90 *Likeliest, and neerest;* this is the reading of 1637 as well as 1645 and Br. MS has, neerest & likliest, undeleted. When did Milton make the change? *the;* MS give, deleted, *ayd,* MS aide, deleted; chance, deleted; aide, restored.
93 The time is early evening; the star is not necessarily Vesper but any star that may first appear.
97 *Atlantick;* MS Tartessian, deleted.
99 *dusky;* MS northern, deleted.
108 *Advice;* MS nice . . . tom, deleted. MS is defective. *with;* MS with her, last word deleted.
114 *in;* MS with, deleted.
116 *Morrice;* a popular old country dance.
117 *Tawny;* MS yellow, deleted.
118 *pert;* brisk. *dapper;* spruce.
123 *hath;* MS, Br has.
125 *rights;* probably, rites.
131 *Dragon woom;* night is a being (a dragon) in whose womb fearful things are bred.
133 MS first had: and makes a blot of nature, deleted; then, and throws a blot, deleted.
134 *cloudy;* MS polisht, deleted.
136 MS first had: & favour our close revelrie; then jocondrie was tried in place of the last word; deleted.
137 *Of;* MS till, deleted. *dues;* 1645 misprints as due; all other texts have dues. *none;* MS nought, deleted.
144 *In;* MS with, deleted. *fantastick;* MS & frolic, deleted.
Stage Direction. MS has: the measure (in a wild rude & wanton antick).
145 *feel;* MS heare, deleted.

146 After this line MS has, deleted:
      some virgin sure benighted in these woods
      for so I can distinguish by myne art

147 MS and Br. have the stage direction in the
      margin: they all scatter

150 *charms;* MS trains, deleted.

151 *wily trains;* MS mothers charmes, deleted.

154 *dazling;* MS powder'd, deleted.

155 *blear;* MS sleight, deleted; blind, deleted.

156 *lest;* MS else, deleted.

164 *snares;* MS nets, deleted.

166–167 See textual notes. Study these lines
      carefully. Why should Milton have changed
      them? Or do you think it is all, including
      the Errata on this place in 1673, a patched-
      up printer's blunder?

173 *among;* MS amoungst, not deleted. Br.
      amonge. Who made the change and when?
      loose; MS rude, deleted.

174 *When;* Milton first wrote, when; then he
      tried, that; he finally restored, when.
      granges; MS garners, deleted. The line is
      written in the margin, but that fact does
      not necessarily mean that it was an after-
      thought, but that it may have been inad-
      vertently omitted when the present MS was
      copied from a preceding rough draft.

175 *they praise;* MS they praise, deleted, but
      restored; above, adore, deleted.

178 *O;* MS Oh, with the h deleted.

179 *inform;* Br acquainte, deleted. Can you sug-
      gest why the copyist made this error?

180 *mazes;* MS alleys, deleted. *this;* MS these,
      deleted. *tangl'd;* MS arched, deleted.

188 *weed;* MS and 1637, weeds. Why was the
      change made?

189 *wain;* MS chaire, deleted.

192 *wandring;* MS youthly, deleted.

193 *And envious;* MS to the soone parting light,
      deleted.

198 *due;* MS thire, deleted.

207 *that syllable mens names;* MS that lure
      night wandring, deleted. wandring had pre-
      viously to deletion been changed into wan-
      derers.

213 *hovering;* MS and 1637: flittering; in MS
      deleted and hov'ring written in the margin.

214 *unblemish't;* MS unspotted, deleted.

215 *and now beleeve;* MS
                & while I see yee
      this dusky hollow is a paradise
                & heaven gates ore my head
      These lines are deleted, followed by: & now
      I beleeve. The I is deleted.

218 *Guardian;* MS cherub, deleted.

228 *off;* MS and Br: hence, not deleted. When
      must the change have been made?

230 *shell;* MS shell, not deleted, but connected

by a sign with the margin, where cell is
written, undeleted.

242 *And give resounding grace;* MS, Br, and
      MS Add. all have: And hold a counterpoint.
      In MS the words are deleted, and the pres-
      ent line written in the margin. When was
      the change made and why? Watch for
      places in other poems where Milton may
      have changed his lines to avoid a technical
      phrase.

244 *inchanting;* MS enchaunting, with the u
      written in above the line. What significance
      has this?

251 *it;* MS, Br, 1637 she

253 *Amidst;* MS amidst, undeleted; but above,
      sitting, deleted.

254 *potent;* see textual notes.

256 *wept;* MS would weepe, deleted.

257 *chid;* MS chiding, changed into chide.

267 *Dwell'st;* MS liv'st, deleted.

269 *prosperous;* MS and Br: prospering; de-
      leted in MS.

275 *answer;* answere to give me; the last three
      words deleted. *Couch;* MS coutch; t above
      the line.

278 *neer-ushering;* MS thire ushering; the first
      word is deleted. *guides;* MS hands, deleted.

279 *weary;* MS wearied; d, deleted.

290 *Two such;* MS such tow, not deleted.

303 *them;* MS them out; the last word is de-
      leted.

309 *guess;* MS steerage of, deleted.

311 *wilde;* MS wide, with a line underneath,
      and an X, connected with a similar mark in
      the margin, where in a different hand, not
      Milton's, is written, wilde. Br. wide.

312 *bosky;* MS bosky, deleted; bosky, unde-
      leted.

315 *shroud;* MS shrouded; ed is deleted. *within;*
      MS within, deleted; written again above the
      line. *these;* MS these, in the right margin,
      shroudie, deleted. *I shall know;* MS I shall
      know, deleted; followed by I shall know,
      undeleted.

316 *Ere morrow wake;* MS ere the larke rowse,
      deleted.

320 *quest';* MS quest be made. The last two
      words deleted.

323 *with;* MS &, deleted.

325 *yet is most pretended;* MS is prætended yet,
      deleted.

326 *this;* MS this I cannot be. The last three
      words are deleted.

328 *eye;* MS eye, deleted; margin, eye. *my;*
      MS this, deleted.

339 *thy;* MS a, deleted.

348 *close;* MS lone, deleted; sad, deleted.

351 *amongst rude burrs and thistles;* MS in this

dead solitude, deleted; surrounding wilde, deleted; perhapps some cold hard banke, deleted.

354 *leans;* MS she leans; the first word is deleted. *unpillow'd;* MS thoughtfull, deleted. *fraught with sad fears;* MS musing at our unkindnesse, deleted.

355 *What if;* MS or else, deleted. Br. or els. MS and Br have three additional lines; see textual notes.

356 MS and Br omit 11. 356–364 at this place. They once existed on a loose, extra page in MS; Warton and Todd give readings from this lost sheet.

360 *For;* MS Which (Todd).

361 *his;* MS the (Warton and Todd).

364 *such;* MS this (Warton and Todd).

370 *constant;* MS steadie, deleted.

372 *see;* MS ad all her, deleted.

375 *Oft . . . Solitude;* MS oft seeks to solitarie sweet retire, deleted.

379 *were;* MS are, changed into, were.

383–384 MS and Br have:

walks in black vapours, though the noon-
    tyde brand
blaze in the summer solstice.

In MS, deleted; written in the margin.

387 *and;* MS and Br or; in MS, deleted.

389 *Weeds;* MS beads, deleted; gowne, deleted; beads, deleted.

390 *Beads;* MS hairie gowne, deleted.

399 *hope;* MS thinke, deleted.

402 *wilde surrounding wast;* MS vast & hideous wild; deleted, followed by: wide surrounding wast. Br has the last reading. 1637 has wild . . . wast.

408 *controversie;* MS and Br question, no. After this line MS and Br have five lines, omitted in all the printed editions:

I could be willing though now i'th darke
    to trie
a tough encounter with the shaggiest ruf-
    fian
that lurks by hedge or lane of this dead
    circuit
to have her by my side, though I were sure
she might be free from perill where she is

409 *Yet;* MS and Br but, undeleted.

421 MS has two additional lines, deleted:
& may (upon any needfull accident
be it not don in pride or wilfull tempting)
The word tempting was deleted and præsumption substituted, deleted.

422 *trace;* MS walke through, deleted.

426 *Will;* MS shall, deleted.

427 *there;* MS and Br even, not deleted.

428 Following this line MS, deleted, and Br have:

& yawning dens where glaring monsters
    house

431 *Som say;* MS some say, deleted; nay more, deleted; Some say, undeleted. Br. naye more. 1637 Some say.

432 *moorish;* MS moorie, not deleted.

433 *meager;* MS wrinckled, deleted; left margin, wrincl'd, deleted; above wrinckled is the final reading, meager.

447 *unconquer'd;* MS æternall, deleted, unvanquisht, deleted.

451 *and blank aw;* MS of her purenesse, deleted; of bright rays, deleted.

453 *a soul;* MS it finds, deleted.

464 *leud and lavish;* MS the lascivious, deleted. Br lewde lascivious.

470 *Sepulchers;* MS monume, deleted.

471 *Lingering;* MS hovering, not deleted; Br and 1637 Hovering.

473 *sensualty;* MS Sensualtie; Br, 1637 sensualitie; 1673 sensuality.

479 *List, list, I hear;* MS list, bro. list, me thought I heard, converted into the present reading.

484 *Som roaving Robber;* MS some curl'd man of the swoord, deleted; above man is, hedge, not deleted, probably accidentally left.

485 *agen agen;* MS yet agen, agen; first word deleted.

488 MS has: had best looke to his forehead. heere be brambles, deleted; left margin: he may chaunce scratch, with the u inserted above by a caret; right margin: a just Defence is a, all deleted. The re-written line as in the text follows.

490 *too neer;* MS too neere, deleted, but restored. *iron;* MS pointed, deleted.

492 *father;* MS and Br fathers; 1637, 1645, 1673, father.

495 *dale;* MS valley, deleted.

497 *Slipt from the fold;* MS leapt ore his penne, deleted.

522 *Deep skill'd;* MS enur'd, deleted; deepe learnt, deleted.

527 *the;* MS the; in the margin connected by a sign, makes, deleted.

530 *hilly crofts;* MS pastur'd lawns, deleted.

537 *sense;* MS spell, deleted.

544 *flaunting;* MS suckling, deleted; blowing, deleted; flaunting, deleted; blowing, deleted; flaunting, final reading.

545–546 MS has these lines in reversed order, but marked for transposition.

546 Only 1673 has, upon.

547 *a;* MS the, deleted.

552 See textual notes.

554 *soft;* MS soft, deleted; still, deleted; soft. deleted; sweet, deleted; soft, final reading

555 *a;* MS the softe, deleted. *steam;* MS, Br,
1637, 1645: steam; 1673, stream. *rich;* MS
slow, deleted; distill'd, deleted; slow, deleted, rich, final reading.
562 *did;* MS and Br might, not deleted.
573 *aidless;* MS helplesse, deleted.
579 *But;* MS and this, deleted.
587 *erring men call Chance;* cf 923, 1.12:
"There are some who pretend that nature or
fate is this supreme Power."
593 *And;* MS till all to place, deleted.
606 *restore;* MS release his new got prey, deleted.
607 *to a foul death;* MS, Br, and 1637: & cleave
his scalpe.
608 *Curs'd as his life;* MS, Br, and 1637: downe
to the hipps. In MS the last word is deleted, followed by lowest, deleted, followed
by hips.
610 *sword;* MS swo, deleted; steele, deleted;
above, swoord, deleted; left margin, 'swoord,
final reading. *little stead;* MS little stead,
deleted, but restored; small availe, deleted.
613 *unthred;* MS unquilt, deleted.
614 *all thy;* MS every, deleted.
626 *names;* MS hews, deleted.
631–636 Br omits these lines.
633 *and the dull swayn;* cf. 549, 1.27: "not to
be sensible when good and fair in one person meet, argues both a gross and shallow
judgment, and withal an ungentle and
swainish breast."
635 *more med'cinal;* cf. 549, 2.53: "whose
charming cup is only virtue," etc.; see also
Professor Hanford's letter to L. T. L. S.
August, 1932. *Moly;* MS ancient Moly;
first word deleted.
636 *That Hermes once;* MS that Mercury, deleted; above, which; below, Hermes once,
undeleted.
647 *when we go;* MS as wee goe), deleted;
when on the way, deleted.
648 *the;* MS his, deleted. *necromancers;* MS
necromantik, converted into necromancers.
64ʻ *dauntless hardihood;* MS suddaine violence,
deleted.
65ʻ *shed;* MS power, deleted. *liquor;* MS potion, deleted.
652 *But;* MS and, deleted.
657 MS has, deleted:
& good heaven cast his best regard upon
us Ex
659 *Alablaster;* all the texts have the superfluous
"l," a common spelling in the seventeenth
century.
660 *or;* MS fixt, deleted.
661–665 In MS these lines, Fool . . . frown, are
written in the margin. Lines 662–664 originally followed l 754 after traitor. In MS

Comus continued his speech with: why doe
ye frowne, deleted. Then: La: foole thou
art over proud; the last four words are deleted.
668 *fancy;* MS youth & fancie, deleted. *beget;*
MS beget, deleted; invent, deleted. *on;* MS
in converted into on.
669 *fresh;* MS brisk, deleted.
671 In MS we have the direction: that which
follows heere is in the pasted leafe begins
poore Ladie and first behold this &c. The
passage thus added consists of lines 671–
704. Lines 671–677 also appear in the passage following 1.754, where they are deleted. For a fuller statement of the changes
made, see the *Columbia Milton,* I, 543 ff.
677 After this line MS, deleted, and Br:
poore ladie thou hast need of some refreshing
678 MS has ll.678–686 in the right margin of
the pasted leaf, written as prose. Br. omits
these lines.
688 *have;* MS, deleted, and Br, hast. *but;* MS,
deleted, and Br, heere.
692 In MS lines 692–695 and 700–702 also appear, much altered, after while heaven sees
good (line 664) in the deleted passage after
1.754, referred to below as MS 2. These
changes are most easily followed line by
line, though the lines do not always exactly
correspond. Remember that MS 2 represents an earlier version of the lines in the
text, and is all deleted.
693 *Thou told'st me of;* MS 2 amongst these h
musl'd monsters. Above h musl'd is written
oughly. Right margin: these oughly headed
monsters. Left margin: thou toldst me of.
What grim aspects are these; MS 2 Mercie
guard me. Above what grim aspects are these
followed by (mercy guard me). Then as the
next line: O my simplicity what sights are
these? Above: how have I bin betrai'd.
Then as the last part of the regular line:
with darke disguises. In the next line MS 2
reads: and soothing lies; followed by: &
soothing flatteries. In the right margin is:
bruage; in the left margin, above; whether
deluded. The passage is so complicated by
variant readings that perhaps it will be of
help to reconstruct it as Milton finally left
it, before he shifted its position. As all the
words are deleted we cannot always be sure
of the order in which the deletion took
place, and in some cases when the words
are in the margin, we cannot be sure just
how the poet thought of using them. The
final reading of these lines in the deleted
passage was probably as follows:
Was this the cottage & the safe abode

amoung'st these oughly headed monsters
what grim aspects are these? mercie guard
  me
O my simplicitie how have I been betrai'd
whether deluded with darke disguises &
  soothing flatteries

695 For lines 695–700, MS 2 has:
hence with thy treacherous kindnesse
Below is: bru'd sorcerie. In the right margin, above:
  hence with thy hel bru'd liquor lest I
  throw it against the ground were it a
  draft &c
Below, in the main text:
  Thou man of lies & falshood, if thou give
  me it
  I throw it on the ground, were it a draft
  for Juno
brew'd inchantments; MS hel brewd opiate
foule.

696–699 MS 2 and Br omit these lines.

701 MS 2 has:
  I hate it from thy hands treasonous offer,
  none
Above the second word is, should reject.
None; cf. 568, 1.44.

703–704 MS 2 omits these lines.

706 *Furr;* MS gowne, deleted.

711 *fruits;* MS & with, deleted.

712 *Thronging;* MS cramming, deleted. MS has
for the next line
  the feilds with cattel & the aire with
  fowle.
Deleted; line 713 in the right margin.

716 *To deck;* MS to deck, deleted; to adorn.
The last word is deleted, followed by
deck.

720 *Pulse;* MS pulse, deleted; fetches, deleted.

726 *And live as;* MS living as; the first word is
converted into live, the last word is deleted;
left margin, &; above live as is written, for,
deleted.

731 *The Sea o'refraught;* MS the sea orefraught,
deleted; followed by: the ore, the last word
is deleted. *swell;* MS has:
  heave her waters up
  above the shoare,
deleted; above heave is swell.

732 MS has: would so be studde the center with
thire starrelight, deleted; right margin: and
so emblaze, etc. The first word is deleted;
above: would.

733 MS has: were they not taken thence, deleted; followed by: that they below. Above
the first part the present reading.

734 light; MS day, deleted.

736–754 Br omits these lines.

736 *and;* MS not, deleted, but restored; above:
and, deleted, preceded by nor, not deleted.

743 *with languish't head;* MS & fades away, deleted.

748 *thence;* MS from thence; the first word is
deleted. complexions; MS beetle, deleted;
bro, deleted, brows, deleted.

750 *sampler,* and; MS sample, or, not deleted.

754 *and be adviz'd, you are but young yet;* MS
has: and looke upon this cordial julep, deleted. Followed by lines 672–677. Then
comes:

  poore Ladie thou hast need of some refreshing
  that hast bin tir'd all day without repast
  & timely rest hast wanted heere sweet
  Ladie
  this will restore all soone La stand back
  false traitor

Then come lines 662–664. In the passage
given above, sweet Ladie, previously deleted, is followed by fairest virgin. The first
word is changed into faire. Then follows the
passage that stands for lines 692–702.

764 *Means;* MS intends, deleted.

777 *besotted;* MS a sottish, deleted.

778 Both MS and Br omit lines 778–805, shall
. . . strongly.

780 *contemptuous;* 1637 reproachfull. No other
text has reproachfull. When must Milton
have made the change?

805 *no more;* MS y'are too morall, deleted.

806 MS has:
  this is meere morall stuffe the very lees
  & setlings of a melancholy blood
Above the first line is: your morall stuffe;
above very is tilted. All the passage is deleted.

813 *scape;* MS spasse, deleted.

815 *rod;* MS art, deleted.

817 *sits here;* MS remaines, deleted; followed by
heere sits; Br. sitts heere.

820 *Som other means I have;* MS there is another way, deleted.

825 *Virgin pure;* MS virgin goddese chast; the
two last words are deleted.

830 *flood;* MS floud, deleted; streame, deleted.

833 *pearled;* MS white, deleted. *and;* MS to
converted to &. *took;* MS receave, deleted;
carie, deleted.

834 *Bearing;* MS and bore, deleted.

845 *make;* MS leave, deleted; followed by
makes; the last letter is deleted. After this
line MS has:
  and often takes our cattel with strange
  pinches.

846 Br omits this line.

848 *rustick;* MS lovely, deleted.

850 *pinks, and gaudy;* MS & of bonnie, deleted.

852 *The;* MS each, deleted. *thaw the numming spell;* MS secret holding spell, deleted; followed by, melt each numming spell; the first two words are deleted.

856 *In hard besetting need;* MS in honourd vertues cause, deleted.

857 *power;* MS power, deleted, but restored; call, deleted. *adjuring;* MS strong, deleted.

859 *Listen;* MS Listen virgin; the last word is deleted. *art sitting;* MS sit'st, deleted.

865 After this line MS in the right margin: to be said. Br: The verse to singe or not.

885 *coral-pav'n;* MS corall-paved. The last letter is changed into n.

894 *That in the channel strayes;* MS that my rich wheeles inlayes, deleted.

903 *charmed;* MS mag, deleted What probably did Milton start to write? Where did he perhaps get the word?

909 *Brightest;* MS vertuous, deleted.

920 *in;* MS on, changed to in.

923 *brimmed;* MS crystall, deleted.

926 *the;* MS from, deleted.

947 *met;* MS come, deleted.

955 *grow;* MS are, marked with X; in the margin, grow.

956 *sits;* MS raignes, deleted.

961 *Of lighter toes;* MS of speedier toeing; the second word and the ending of the third are deleted. The i in toeing is converted into s. Above, nimbler, deleted. *Court;* MS courtly, deleted; above, such neate, not deleted. In the margin, the line as in the text.

962 *As;* MS such, deleted. *Mercury;* MS Hermes, deleted.

970 *patience;* MS patience, deleted, but restored; temperance, deleted.

972 *With;* MS to, deleted. *Praise;* MS bays, deleted.

975 Br omits lines 975–1010 in this place; it transfers lines 975–982, lines 987–995 and lines 997–998 to the beginning of the mask, where, with a few slight alterations, they form a prologue. In MS there are two drafts of the remaining lines.

978 *broad;* MS plaine, deleted. After this line MS has:
farre beyond the earths end
where the welkin cleere doth bend.
The word, cleere, was first deleted and low written above. Then the two lines were cancelled.

981 *Hesperus;* MS Atlas, deleted. *daughters;* MS daughters, deleted, but restored; above, neeces, deleted.

982 MS 2 has: where grows the right-borne gold upon his native tree, deleted, followed by the line in the text.

983–986 MS 1 and Br omit these lines.

987 *That;* MS 1 and Br omit.

989 *cedar'n;* MS 1 myrtle, deleted.

990 *Nard;* MS 1 balme, deleted. *balmy;* MS 1 fragrant, deleted.

991 *humid;* MS 1 garnish't, deleted; garish, deleted.

994 *purfl'd;* MS 1 watchet, deleted. After this line MS 1 has:
yellow, watchet, greene, & blew
MS 2 has the same line deleted; Br has the same line.

995 *with;* MS 1 and Br oft with

996 MS 1 and Br omit this line; MS 2 has it in the margin.

998 *young Adonis oft;* MS 1, Br, and MS Add. many a cherub soft.

999 MS 1 and Br omit lines 999–1010.

1011 *But;* MS 1, Br, and MS Add. omit. *task;* MS 1 message, deleted; buisnesse, deleted. *is smoothly;* MS 1 well is; the first word is deleted and smoothly written above; underneath, the words are marked for transposition.

1013 *green earths;* MS 1 earths greene, marked for transposition.

1022 *stoop;* MS 1 bow, deleted.

Page 83. LATIN AND GREEK POEMS

The texts are printed on pp. 111 ff. and are from the edition of 1645, unless otherwise stated. Notice Milton's modest preface to the Encomiums. Not often did he allow himself the pleasure of prefatory poems, as was the usual custom of poets in the seventeenth century, though he himself wrote such poems for others. What other editions of Milton's had any prefatory matter of the laudatory kind?
Giovanni Battista Manso; now an aged man, remembered then and now as the generous patron of Tasso. See Milton's poem to him on p. 104. He was Milton's host in Naples. *Angle;* where have you read this pun before?
Selvaggi; observe that the substance of this epigram is repeated by Barrow in the last line of his poem on p. 157 and by Dryden in his famous, but rather mediocre lines on Milton.

Page 85. ELEGY I

In what sense does Milton use *elegy*? See the last line of the poem. Charles Diodati was the most intimate friend of Milton's youth. *Elegies* I and VI and two *Familiar Letters* are addressed to him. The *Epitaphium Damonis*, (translated at p. 106) was written in memory of this friend who had died while Milton was abroad.
near Chester; Diodati, who was a young phy-

sician, seems to have practiced near Chester for a time.

I am housed; this passage gives Milton's account of his rustication from Cambridge in the winter of 1625–26. One notices that he is not ashamed to write about it and that he does not seem to be in a very chastened mood. Do any of the four contemporary biographies say anything about this incident? Aubrey's parenthesis, "whipp't him," was added later, and is undoubtedly an interpolation, picked up from gossip.

Oh, that the poet; Ovid; notice the high esteem the young Milton has for this Latin poet. There is not much inherent Puritanism here.

When I am weary; his love for the theatre is keen. Try to identify some of the plays he seems to have in mind.

Here often; What new notion of Milton's character do we get in these Latin poems?

Page 86. ELEGY II

Anno ætatis 17 (Text, p. 116); not "in the seventeenth year of his age," but "at the age of seventeen." Milton was nearly eighteen when the beadle, Richard Ridding, died in October, 1626. *Beadle;* the beadle was an officer of the University with a host of multifarious duties, the chief of which was processional. When he attended the Chancellor or Vice-Chancellor, he carried a mace. Riddle had been beadle for thirty years.

Page 87. ELEGY III

The Bishop of Winchester was no other than the saintly and eloquent Lancelot Andrews, whom even his political enemies respected. Milton later did not agree with all the Bishop's views; see pp. 509–515.

deadly havoc; the plague raged in England in 1625 and 1626, claiming no fewer than 35,000 victims.

duke . . . brother; Christian, Duke of Brunswick, and Count Ernest of Mansfeld; they both fought on the Protestant side in the Thirty Years' War, and died in 1626.

The heavenly hosts; cf. *Lycidas* 178 ff.

Page 88. ELEGY IV

Thomas Young, a Scot, after graduating from St. Andrews, came to London, where he preached in the Puritan churches. He also acted as Milton's private tutor for some time,—how long and just when, we do not know. About 1622 Young went to Hamburg to act as minister for the Puritans who had fled to that city. Milton probably entered St. Paul's in 1620. Young returned to England in 1628. He soon became a well-known man, taking a part in the famous pamphlet by Smectymnuus. The first and fourth of the *Familiar Letters* are also addressed to him. *Fatherland, stern parent;* Milton early made up his mind about a policy that ultimately drove thousands of the best Englishmen away from their native land.

Page 89. ELEGY V

Many poets from Horace down through the Italian Renaissance had celebrated the coming of spring, so that the theme had become thoroughly conventionalized, but Milton succeeded in treating it with originality and freshness. Try to catch this spontaneity as you read it, either in the original or in the translation. Professor Rand says this poem "is Pagan from beginning to end, joyous in spirit, sensuous in flavor, perfect in form." (*Milton in Rustication.*)

Page 91. ELEGY VI

The date is fixed by the note which Milton prefixed and by the reference in the last lines to the poem, *On the Morning of Christs Nativity. Composed 1629.*

But the poet; up to now Milton has been bantering his friend upon his feeble excuses, but now he becomes serious as he writes of his ideals of great poetry and the life that a man who would write such poetry must live. This passage is of high importance in studying the development of Milton's poetic ideals. With these lines cf. *At a Vacation Exercise.*

live sparingly; Cf. 737, 2.39 ff.

a youth chaste; Cf. 548, 1.49 to 550, 1.51.

the poet is sacred to the gods; Cf. 525, 2.21 ff.; 738, 2.5; *P.L.* III. 51 ff.; *P.L.* IX. 20 ff. and other places where Milton expresses his belief in the divine character of poetry and its high value.

Page 92. ELEGY VII

This poem was written before Elegy VI, probably in May, 1627. Milton perhaps thought it a suitable poem to close the elegies, since they had opened with a love poem. This piece is not, however, similar to the first elegy, for it has much more of the personal note; one cannot help but feel that the poet is relating an actual experience.

Academy; not Cambridge, but the famous Academy where Plato taught.

Page 94. TO LEONORA

Leonora Baroni of Naples was one of the most famous singers of her day. Milton probably heard her on one of his two visits to Rome; Masson thinks it was on his first visit in October and November, 1638, for at that time Milton attended a magnificent concert in the palace of Cardinal Barberini.

Page 95. A FABLE

This is probably a later poem than the other Latin pieces as it was not included in 1645. Masson sees a "touch of political significance" in it; but surely there is not much, for Milton was not in the habit of hiding his political thoughts. Had he meant it as a political lesson, he would have added some pointed lines apprising the reader of the fact or else would have used it where the context would leave no doubt.

Page 95. AGAINST THE HUNDRED

This poem is part of the matter of the *First Defence* and the next, of the *Second Defence*. Since Milton never published them with his Latin poetry, they perhaps should not be separated from their context.

Page 96. POEMS IN VARIOUS METRES. SYLVARUM LIBER (Text, p. 130).

The classic Latin poets often grouped their poems, written in miscellaneous meters, under such titles as "Sylva." Cf. Jonson's "Underwoods."

Page 96. ON THE DEATH OF THE VICE-CHANCELLOR

The Vice-Chancellor was Dr. John Gostlin or Goslyn, who died in 1626. Before he was appointed as Vice-Chancellor in 1618, he had practiced medicine. In 1623 he was appointed Regius Professor of Medicine (MacKellar, *The Latin Poems of John Milton*, New Haven, 1930) and in 1625 he became Vice-Chancellor again.

Page 96. ON THE FIFTH OF NOVEMBER

The main facts concerning the Gunpowder Plot may be gleaned from any good history of England. It was customary to celebrate recurring anniversaries of the day. This poem and the four epigrams were probably written on different occasions as part of Milton's contribution.
good King James; as Milton grew older he revised his opinion of King James.
fierce tyrant; notice this early description of Satan; it is, as Warton suggested, and Masson agreed, "an early and promising prolusion" to *Paradise Lost.*
an adept in guile; cf. *P.L.* IV. 121. Many other

parallels to other phrases in this early poem can be found in *P.L.*
Francis; probably St. Francis of Assisi.
Sleepest thou; cf. *P.L.* V. 673.

Page 99. ON THE DEATH OF THE BISHOP

Nicholas Felton succeeded Lancelot Andrewes as Bishop of Ely and died in 1626. Fuller says he was known as a profound scholar and famous for his hospitality and charity.

Page 100. THAT NATURE

This was Milton's contribution on the side of modern thought in the controversy then raging as to whether nature were getting weaker as the world became more aged. This famous controversy early in the seventeenth century developed in the late seventeenth century into the "War between the Ancients and Moderns," in which Swift took a hand. See R. F. Jones, *The Background of the 'Battle of the Books.'* This piece and the next were probably written in Cambridge as academic exercises.

Page 101. TO MY FATHER

This autobiographical poem deserves careful study. It was probably written shortly after leaving Cambridge, when the question of choosing a profession was uppermost in the poet's mind. It would seem that his father had been using some mild persuasion to urge the youth to come to a decision. The final outcome is recorded in the poem.
trivial melodies; such as some of his earlier poetry. Suggest examples.
honored father; the influence upon the young poet of this remarkable father can hardly be over-estimated. The student should read sometime in connection with his studies the four contemporary biographies of Milton as reprinted in the present edition.
Do not look down; Milton's father, a prosperous man of business, may very naturally have been sceptical about his son's acknowledging the writing of poetry as a profession.
For song retains; cf. *Elegy* VI, p. 92. Notice that Milton does not allude to instrumental music, but to poetry set to music. Cf. his sonnet to Henry Lawes.
ill-guarded principles of national justice; though Milton had no desire to become a professional lawyer, the question of national justice had its interest for him, even at this time. Cf. 729, 1.27.
French language; it was Milton's father who

urged him to acquire a knowledge of the French and Italian languages; later he furnished the money, no inconsiderable sum, for an extensive foreign tour such as he doubtless had never himself been able to enjoy.

Go now, amass riches; remember this paragraph when you come to Milton's more mature poetry, and especially when he is discussing the choosing of one's life work in *Paradise Regain'd.*

Page 103. AGAINST A SCULPTOR

Look up in Vol. I of the *Columbia Milton* the reproduction of this portrait of Milton used as a frontispiece to the edition of 1645; you probably will agree that there is considerable point in Milton's little joke. The lines, written in Greek, were printed underneath the portrait, though probably the "sculptor" was none the wiser.

Page 104. TO MANSO

This delicate poetic tribute to a generous and noble old man should be carefully studied; there is no undue adulation, such as we find in many such poems of the day. Cf. the courteous social relations that are described delicately in *P.L.* between Adam and Eve, and between them and their angel guests. Milton had his faults, but lack of courtesy, kindliness of heart and urbanity were never among them. Legendary traditions, almost entirely unsupported, have had their share in obscuring this side of the great poet's character, and in leading even his admirers in past times into thinking him entirely a Puritan poet with all the Puritan characteristics; but the careful student finds little basis for such a judgment, but rather much evidence for the opposite view.

frozen north; Milton frequently mentions the cold and disagreeable climate of England. Cf. *P.L.* IX. 44.

call back into the realms of song; thoughts of his great poem are always with the young poet. He is now thinking of writing a poem, probably somewhat in the style of Spenser, upon King Arthur.

a life by no means silent; Milton worked up to the time of his death. In 1674, the year he died, *Paradise Lost* appeared in a revised and augmented edition; in the preceding year he had published his last prose pamphlet, *Of True Religion.*

that friend; cf. *Lycidas*, 19.

Page 106. DAMON'S EPITAPH

This poem, the greatest of Milton's Latin poems, should be carefully studied for its pas-toral form, its deep emotion and its auto-biographical significance. Milton wrote the poem immediately after his return from abroad. He first published it in 1640, as has recently been discovered from a copy of this hitherto unknown edition in the British Museum. (Leicester Bradner, *Milton's "Epitaphium Damonis,"* London Times Literary Supplement, Aug. 18, 1932.)

I shall sing; Milton has come home from his foreign tour, matured and confident, ready to start writing his great poem. He plans to sing of Arthur and his court, and he will write in English, content if Englishmen read his poetry. Mingled with his plans are the memories of his experiences abroad, his reception in Florence and his treatment by Manso. All this has begotten confidence, but he little dreams of the immediate years ahead, when he shall use only his left hand, as he later called it, in writing prose.

Page 109. TO JOHN ROUSE

John Rouse was the Librarian of the Bodleian in Oxford. The book of poems referred to was a copy of the 1645 edition of Milton's Poems. The original manuscript of this ode, sent to Rouse, is still in the Bodleian.

PARADISE LOST

Page 157. *S.B.* is Samuel Barrow, a London physician and friend of Milton's. You will be interested in reading the following translation of this poem by Professor McCrea.

On the Paradise Lost of John Milton, Consummate Poet

You who read *Paradise Lost,* sublime poem of mighty Milton, what do you read but the story of all things? All things and the first beginning of all things and their careers and ultimate destiny are contained within that book. The innermost recesses of the great universe are disclosed and whate'er lies hidden in all the world is there described: land and the expanse of the sea and the depths of the sky and the sulphurous flame-belching den of Erebus; all that dwell on earth and in the sea and in darksome Tartarus, and all that dwell in the bright realms of heaven above; whate'er is anywhere included within any boundaries, and illimitable Chaos and infinite Deity, and even more without limit, if there is aught that is more without limit, love towards mankind regained in Christ. Who that hoped for such a poem could have believed that it would come into existence? And yet this is the poem that the land of Britain reads today O, what warlike chieftains, what deeds of arms are here presented! What dire battles here sung and with how sonorous a trumpet! Celestial battle-lines and Heaven at war and fighting that befits the fields of Heaven! How magnificent is Lucifer, as he rises in his celestial armor, and as he strides scarce inferior to Michael himself! With what furious, with what deadly anger do they clash, while one fiercely protects the stars, the other makes them his prey! While they rend mountains and hurl them at each other as missiles and rain down fires that mortals do not know. Olympus stands doubtful to which side to yield and fears that it may not survive its own strife. But soon as the banners of Messiah gleam in the sky and His living chariot and His armor meet for God, soon as His wheels grind horribly, and the fierce lightnings of the wheels burst from those grim eyes, and the flames flash and veritable thunder with intermingled fires reverberates hoarsely in the skies, from His amazed foes departs all courage, all resistance, and from their empty hands their useless idle weapons fall. They flee to their punishment, and just as if Orcus were a refuge, they struggle to hide themselves in infernal darkness. Yield, ye writers of Rome, yield, ye writers of Greece, and all that Fame whether modern or ancient has celebrated. Whoso shall read this poem will think that Homer sang only of frogs, Vergil only of gnats.

Page 158. ON PARADISE LOST

A.M. is Andrew Marvell, for a time Milton's assistant in the office of Secretary for Foreign Tongues and a close personal friend. You will be interested in Marvell's estimate of the poem and in his sly hits at Dryden. Marvel enjoys taking a part in the popular controversy of the time in regard to the best and only manner of poetic expression.

Page 159. THE PRINTER TO THE READER

Masson thinks that Milton had a hand in changing this address in the second edition. See the textual notes. Why should Milton wish to change the wording?

Page 159. THE VERSE

This is Milton's defence for writing in blank verse He evidently has been drawn into the controversy, and probably censured by enthusiasts on the other side for not having written his poem in the heroic couplet.

Page 157. PARADISE LOST

In the early English and Latin poems we have been able with remarkable fulness to follow the development of the young Milton's mind and his attitude toward the writing of poetry. We saw him as a mere boy composing paraphrases of the Psalms, perhaps for his father to set to music. We found him at Cambridge celebrating local happenings in Latin verse, sending letters to his former friends in Latin poems, paying his respect to the memory of eminent University officials in fitting Latin memorials and writing in vacations and at other times English poems recording impressions and events that stirred his emotions. He had entered the University with the intention of studying for the church, the profession that promised most for a youth studiously inclined; when he left college, he had definitely abandoned any plans for such a profession, but had steadily been thinking more and more of devoting his life to writing. He had doubtless been encouraged to take this step by the success of his poetry, for he had, when only twenty-one, written a hymn for Christmas that promised more for the future than any poet then writing could pledge. This decision, arrived at during the course of more than seven years, brought other questions to be decided.

Does the life of the poet have any relation to his poetry? And if so, what kind of life should a serious poet live? The answer we have seen, for in the *Sixth Elegy,* written while he was composing his Nativity poem, he declares that he has resolved to live a frugal life, for such a life best befits a poet.

Involved in this question was another; what were the attractions for Milton in an innocent pleasure-seeking quest for beauty, with its consequent poetry, and a serious, studious, high-minded life of wide reading and deepest meditation? The answer was indicated in *Il Penseroso* and confirmed by five years of retirement at Horton, spent in wide reading in Latin and Greek classics and in the study of mathematics and music. But his life there was not unbalanced; it was simply full with intensive work, meditation, and suitable recreation.

There was another more basic question that had arisen while he was in college, and which he now considered carefully and thoughtfully. While an undergraduate he had been called "The Lady of Christ's," perhaps because of his handsome appearance, probably because of his refusal to join some of his classmates in their lives of undergraduate fast living. What should be the attitude toward love of a man who wished to lead a life of high ideals, yet full and well developed? His nature helped to an answer, for he was a full-blooded man of high spirits and deep emotions. One portion of his solution he expressed in *Comus,* where he celebrated the high protecting qualities of chastity and eloquently pictured the attractions of idealistic living. But *Comus* does not give the complete answer: Milton was never an ascetic; he was too normal a man for such a life. In the Italian poems and in the first and last of the *Elegies* we have seen the attractions that unusual beauty in women had for him. Part of his natural answer may easily be read in these poems. The complete answer waited for another ten years before being finally expressed in complete fulness in the *Doctrine and Discipline of Divorce,* the noblest and most impassioned expression in English prose of the old chivalric ideals of virtuous love.

Finally, in the Latin poem, *To His Father,* he had announced his purpose of devoting himself to a noble life and to the writing of serious poetry; others might amass riches, but he had other ambitions. The ideal of writing worthily had taken possession of him. But a great poem could not come from a little life; he would live life to the full—a noble, upright, ideal life to his fullest capacity.

But for all his serious study, maturity of thought and art seemed slow in arriving. In the fall of 1637, when, almost twenty-nine, he started to write his elegy for a dead friend, that thought came forcibly to him,—his fruit was still harsh and crude. That Milton was slow in developing, but of steady growth, even to the end, we have ample and convincing proof. In 1637 Milton's doubts concerning his poetic maturity came only from lack of confidence; the poem proved how false his fears were, for no other English poet has ever, in our twelve hundred years of English poetry, approached the perfect expression of thought, emotion and art found in this elegy.

It was undoubtedly part of his theory that such a full life required a prolonged residence abroad. His remarkable father, completely in sympathy with his son and now won over to the son's ambitions, readily and gladly furnished the means. In Florence Milton remained for some time, mingling freely and on terms of equality with the leading literary geniuses of the day; he then journeyed on to Rome and Naples. While in the last place he was entertained by the greatest literary patron of the age, the noble Marquis of Manso. That the generous but discriminating old man, the friend and patron of Tasso, the greatest Italian poet of the century, should treat the young Englishman as a literary and poetic genius was in itself a testimonial of the highest worth. Manso wrote a poem to him, and he wrote one to Manso. His reception in

Florence and in Naples, and the memory of his achievement at home in writing *Lycidas,* for we must never forget that Milton was always a competent judge of his own poetry, completed what years of study at college and in retirement had failed completely to achieve. Full confidence in his ability had come; inward ripeness, so earnestly desired, had at last arrived. With assurance he told his noble friend of the great poem that he should one day write; it might be about King Arthur, that noble idealistic knight, and his Round Table. At least, he would not be silent, but fill the years with study, meditation and work.

At home, so his letters informed him, his native countrymen were fighting for liberty; resolutely he turned back from his projected journey to Sicily and Athens. He must go home to take a hand in the fight for liberty. But underneath there was another motive that urged him on; he was now ready to start his great poem, and not only ready, but eager, to direct his study toward that end. He had seen a large portion of the worthwhile world; he must now get back to his work.

Milton's homecoming was not attended with omens of a happy life in England. Not only was the country torn with strife between an independent Parliament and an arbitrary king, with many signs that the strife might soon turn into civil war, but within his own private circle of friends Milton now learned how fraught with possibilities of tragedy human life is. While he was yet abroad he had been informed of the unexpected death of the dearest friend of his youth. His first duty upon his return was to the memory of that friendship: in 1640 he wrote and published his tender tribute to that friend. He had now an added motive for writing worthily,—it would please his departed friend, who once enjoyed his youthful poetry. He would write of England's early inhabitants, and maybe of King Arthur and his queen. And the poem should be in English, for it was by the English, first of all, that he wanted to be known.

But fate withstood. He had returned to fight for liberty, and he now wrote in quick succession five pamphlets attacking the government of the Church of England and the wide and powerful influences which the bishops, usually appointed arbitrarily by the king, or someone close to him, exerted over state government and the liberties of citizens. The whole structure of state religion needed a thorough reformation. Milton in powerful prose argument struck blow after blow for a wider toleration and a purer and better church. But he soon found, as others had before, and as others have since, that once one starts to war for liberty, the fighting is not all on one front. In his youth, as we have seen, he had been interested in the human relations brought about through love; in his Commonplace Book he had even entered quotations about divorce. When he had finished his open attack upon Prelacy, he turned to another phase of the extension of liberty,—a phase not at all unrelated to his previous fight. The Bishops, through their Ecclesiastical Courts, passed upon, among other things too numerous to mention, all cases of marriage and divorce. For centuries, marriage had not been a civil contract under the state, but a sacrament under the church. The Bishops, he claimed, in an arbitrary fashion controlled the happiness of every family in the realm. Here was an abuse that needed immediate correction, for was not marriage of concern to the state? Here was another case where the Bishops had altogether too much power.

Unfortunately or fortunately, while Milton was thinking about this problem, he had himself become involved, perhaps as early as 1642, in an unhappy marriage, from which he wished ardently to be released. He wrote his four divorce tracts which served to develop in his own mind his ideas about marriage,—one of the largest subjects in modern human life. That he thought clearly, deeply and nobly is proved by the fact that his main contention is now acknowledged by all liberal, progressive thinkers. Not all the details of a satisfactory solution have yet been worked out, but the high ideals of married love that dominate his tracts are still the goal of human endeavor.

While directly or indirectly he was attacking the clergy, and trying to extend the boundaries of liberty, he was always thinking of his great poem. Over and over again he reverted to the subject, as he took his reader into his confidence and enlarged upon many of the details related above. At home, when not engaged with his writing and teaching, he devoted himself to study and reading obscure writers as well as the great poets. He was thinking, meditating upon life and books, learning from the past and from the present. He even jotted down a long list of subjects that might lend themselves to a great poem or drama, and he drew up four synopses of a possible drama on Adam and Eve.

But liberty was not yet won; education was another field that needed reforming and modernizing. To that subject he had given considerable thought, and now, after being urged by a friend, he made his ideas known. He himself had discovered another aspect in which true liberty was being thwarted. He had found that in England even, a man might not publish freely what he had honestly thought out, but that he was bound by law to the narrow ideas of a state

censor. This was not liberty; it was tyranny inherited from an iniquitous institution. The killing of books, the precious life spirit of a great mind, was worse than killing a man. With consistent art and eloquence, coming only from the deepest sincerity and emotion, he pleaded for the removal of this blighting curse. And behind all this impassioned pleading was still the thought of his great life work, the unwritten poem, inspiring his paragraphs and directing unconsciously his eloquent appeals.

At home he was busy with odd tasks; he collected his scattered poems for publication; now and again he wrote a sonnet; and when the subject transcended the limit of fourteen lines, he extended the boundaries, though still true to form, as he poured out his righteous but vitriolic wrath upon those arch enemies of liberty, the Presbyterians. At first five years back, he had been rather favorably disposed towards a mild form of English Presbyterianism, but since the Scotch Presbyterians had arrived in London had grown from a luke-warm approval to open hostility. Arbitrary, dogmatic coercion he had always rebelled against. Conformity must never be forced upon unwilling people; in sects and schisms he found life and thought; liberty and chains were not consistent. Better have the Prelates back than endure these unthinking tyrants of thought.

While he had been thus engaged, occupied too with directing the studies of his increasing number of pupils, he had not forgotten the great issue, his poem. Meanwhile affairs in the state were becoming more serious each day. He must determine what he believed and why. What rights had the people and what rights had the king? Before the catastrophe of 1649 Milton had arrived at his conclusions and was writing them out. The king was only the chief magistrate of the people; from the people he derived whatever power he had. Government came from the people and existed for the people. Therefore the people might, whenever they chose, remove any king, good or bad. He had also reached his final conclusions in regard to the relation of church and state: he believed that the two should be entirely divorced, and that the state had no right whatever to force religious thought or practice upon those who disagreed with it. In religion neither state nor church had any rights beyond argument and persuasion; persecution could never, under any circumstances, be justified. For the next four years Milton was a public official, defending liberty wherever it was attacked, pouring scorn and wrath upon England's enemies, supporting Parliament, Cromwell and the great men around him, until his name was known throughout Europe as well as at home. There were no aspects of national liberty upon which Milton had not studied and upon which he had not done deep, original and creative thinking.

Sometime before this, probably, perhaps in the middle forties, he had studied another branch of human thinking, the subject of religion as expressed in theology. For his own benefit, he tells us, he had endeavored from a study of the Scriptures to arrive at his own beliefs in theology. His study led him away from many orthodox Protestant positions, but he stated them fearlessly and sincerely. Did he make this study for his soul's salvation? He says so; but back of this was another motive: a well rounded full life demanded religious expression and sincere belief and a great poem must not only be consistent with such a belief but must be founded upon it, for religion is too much a vital part of man's life to be passed over slightly. With characteristic thoroughness Milton thought out all his opinions on every vital point in religious theory and practice.

At last, but all too soon, blindness overtook him while writing in liberty's defence. His great poem had been delayed from year to year until now nearly twenty years had passed. But the thought and the ambition had been ever present; never had he ceased to write, to think, to study, and to grow. In the first affliction of his blindness it had seemed that all was lost; his one talent was lodged with him useless. But soon he found, as the blind usually find, that there are ways around the seemingly impossible obstacles. Anyway he could not rid himself of the thought of the poem that he had dreamed of writing all these years. Soon he set about his delayed work, and found that blindness had brought what the years of activity had denied, concentration and leisure such as he had never known since his return from abroad.

But the Milton of forty-four was a different Milton from the young radiant Englishman who had written to Manso. He had fought against Prelacy and had joined in the victory; he fought for divorce, and was preached against in Parliament, and scorned by the righteous as tainted and worse. He wrote on education, and had been unheeded. He asked for liberty of the press and he was a few years later made a censor. He wrote for political liberty and won a prominent place in the government, only to find himself disabled through blindness. He had known both affluence and adversity; he had experienced domestic unhappiness and bereavement; he had received into his home his aged father, his brother, who was on the wrong side politically, and relatives of his returned wife. He had known both triumphs and defeats. He had studied deeply into all the phases of liberty

that had come up in England for discussion, and he had brought up some of them himself; he had studied the relations between man and woman; he had studied and worked out his own religious beliefs. He had read and studied all the ancient Greek and Latin literature and history, and had read widely in the literature and history of modern and contemporary Europe. By experience, and by hard study and discipline, which he took to be his portion, his mind had become one of the most practical, reflective minds of his century.

The years of triumph and defeat, of domestic trouble and affliction, of reading and meditation, of work and struggle, had brought the understanding mind. At first he had wanted to write for England, but now that ambition had widened and the world was his audience. He then clearly perceived what we only now are beginning tardily to recognize that the whole world is one. "Who knows not," he had asked in 1649, "that there is a mutual bond of amity between man and man over all the world?" The Reformation now intended, the words that he had placed on the title-page to the first edition of his first divorce tract, had not fully taken place. The problem was still in the forefront; he saw its true nature more clearly now. He had advised Cromwell to preserve only the crags of liberty, and to abstain zealously from making new laws and prohibitions. Morality, he knew, could not be imposed from above; moral reformation comes from the people, and laws enacted against their wishes are worse than useless.

But the longed-for reformation was needed, sorely needed. How then proceed with it? He well knew, for his experience and deep study had brought him back to the words of that great teacher of mankind, "The kingdom of heaven is within you." Reform must begin with the individual, for he is the one and only unit in the nation.

No longer did the unreal, though highly idealistic, age of King Arthur appeal to him. His problem had changed. He now sought a subject that had a wide appeal to readers in every land. His audience need not be large; in fact he preferred an "audience fit but few." But he wanted an audience of thoughtful readers who should not willingly let his poem die. By writing for the thoughtful and studious he would help to bring about a better world. King Arthur and his knights had not a universal appeal in that day,— perhaps not so wide as now. But everyone read the Bible. Sympathy with his story was assured beforehand; allusions to detail would be readily understood. Again, he was about to study the causes of human error and the effects of that error. Milton was a sincere Christian, though a liberal one. What could be more natural than that he should turn to the Bible to find the first records of man's early perversity? His problem was a real living problem, his interest was in the living, pulsing present and in the future, not in imaginary pictures of a past that never existed. Mankind at present is in a sad way. How can we emerge triumphant and victorious? That now is the theme of the great poem. But Milton had partaken with Bacon of the insight into true progress. A study of present misery involves a study of past causes. Milton's great poem then is a study of how man became miserable and unhappy; from a study of first causes, a remedy will result.

Obviously Milton abandoned the drama form for the reason that no drama could include all the study that he wished to make, nor could it express all his life philosophy which the years had been accumulating. Only the epic, the form of poetry that the Renaissance considered the greatest, could hold all that he had to say,—and even that could not contain all, for the application of the remedy, the pattern of how the reformation should come about, was left for the sequel, *Paradise Regain'd*. That is why Milton could never bear to have the later poem, the climax of the entire study, disparaged. To him such disparagement was only new proof of the shallowness of the human mind.

It follows naturally from the account given above that Milton was no Puritan poet in any ordinary sense of the word. Milton was not a Puritan. Only in the sense that he lived in an age when English policies were dominated by Puritan leaders can he be called a Puritan. With many of their policies his own thought was at variance; against many of their ideas he fought with his whole strength all his life.

The Puritan distrusted all art, but Milton loved art and believed in its high ministrations to the human spirit. The Puritan regarded instrumental music as ungodly and removed the organs from many churches; Milton cultivated music, and loved especially the full melodious music of the pipe organ. This organ music that he loved and that he himself played formed a basic quality in his own poetic style. The Puritan abhorred sports and saw in them only the wiles of the devil; Milton found time even in his strenuous educational program for indulging in sports and recreation. The Puritan looked askance at learning; Milton, no less than Bacon, took all learning for his province. The Puritan read his Bible literally; Milton developed his own rules for Scriptural interpretation, rules that the leaders in liberal theological thought today still employ. The Puritan believed in a Mosaic God of justice and vengeance; Milton placed the em-

phasis on a God of love and mercy. The Puritan believed in a stationary world of dogmatic belief; Milton believed in a world of growth and change. The Puritan believed in imposing laws regarding moral acts from above; Milton believed in the utmost freedom of the human will. The Puritan excluded from his heaven all those who disagreed with him in such insignificant things as infant baptism, while he loved to argue that the poor heathen who had died before they had had a chance to hear the Gospel were damned beyond all hope; Milton tolerated sects and schisms; his charity was almost boundless; only when the adherents of a church tried to undermine the liberties of Englishmen did his wrath express itself against them; in Milton's heaven were Socrates and many another heathen who had lived life nobly. The Puritan hated ceremony and courted brusqueness of manners; Milton loved true courtesy and kindliness of spirit; he was not afraid to do reverence to superiors, so long as that reverence did not place him in any false position. The Puritan had many excellences, and in these Milton shared, but he was too large a man for any one group of men of his time. He was not a Puritan, unless Socrates and Plato, the writers of the Psalms and Jesus of Nazareth, Wordsworth and Shelley, Lincoln and Wilson, were Puritans.

Let us divest ourselves once for all of this wrong notion. We are approaching the greatest pleasure that a student of literature can have,— the thoughtful study of the life work of one of the greatest masters of English poetry—one of the greatest in art and in world-reaching thought. His ideas are not dead; his problems are still ours in this twentieth century of tumult and confusion. The great reformation has not yet been accomplished. We are not going to a prayer meeting or to a dreary pious church service. We are to listen to a man whose thoughts for three hundred years, consciously or unconsciously, have formed the basis of our American civilization. We have reached his ideas in many respects, but he yet has much to teach us; and that much he will offer us with an art always consistent and always pleasing and acceptable.

Page 159. BOOK I

1 *Of Mans First Disobedience, and the Fruit;* these words are the objects of the verb, *sing,* and state the theme of the poem. Remember always that the chief offence was disobedience; what particular form that disobedience took, we need not consider at present. Disobedience and the results of disobedience are to form our subject of study. But the disobedience is the *first* one that man in-

dulged in. Milton had learned from Bacon and the growing interest in science that a study of effects must proceed to the first causes. Notice throughout this poem how often he insists on *first*.

2 *Forbidden;* by whom? It is not a sufficient answer to reply, that God forbade. We should begin at once to formulate what we believe was Milton's conception of God. To this end it will be well to read through, if time allows, the entire *Christian Doctrine* before starting to study *Paradise Lost,* and then to refer to it continually throughout the reading of the poem. *mortal taste;* death-dealing taste. Why could not it mean deadly?

4 *one greater Man;* it is Christ as a man that most interests Milton. Notice how slightly the crucifixion is treated in this poem and in *Paradise Regain'd.*

5 What does Milton mean by this line? In what sense can one greater *Man* be said to have restored us? How did he regain the Garden of Eden for us? Milton's answer was not a theological one but, nevertheless, a deeply reflective and philosophical answer. The answer will be found briefly mentioned in the later parts of this poem and fully developed in *Paradise Regain'd.* It is obvious that no one can interpret this line literally. Accordingly, let us take heed of reading other parts of the poem too literally.

6 *Heav'nly Muse;* the heavenly power that inspired Moses, when he wrote the Creation poems in the Bible and David when he wrote some of the Psalms. On Milton's high regard for Hebrew poetry, see 525, 1.53.

9 *In the Beginning;* the first words of the Bible; three times so far we have had this idea of *first* mentioned.

10 *Rose out of Chaos;* Milton did not believe that the world was made out of nothing, the orthodox belief, but that God created it out of chaos. Who created Chaos? This seemingly slight variation in belief has deep possibilities; watch for them.

12 *Fast by;* right by.

13 *adventrous Song;* because it will treat of deepest Hell and highest Heaven.

14 *middle flight;* in no mediocre way. He intends to sing worthily of his divine subject.

15 *above th' Aonian Mount;* he will surpass the classic poets, Homer especially, because his subject is true.

16 *Things unattempted yet;* there had been epic poems before upon the story of the Creation, but Milton will tell the story on a vaster scheme, and with greater philo-

sophical import. Indeed, there had never been made such an attempt as he proposed.

17 *And chiefly Thou;* the second part of this double invocation is a personal prayer to the Holy Spirit for guidance and assistance Milton believed in a very real sense that he was inspired, and that all great poets are inspired. Cf. 525, 2.21 ff.

that dost prefer; cf. 1 *Cor.* iii. 16 and other passages.

26 *And justifie;* this is not the theme of the poem, but an incidental result of his theme. Many critics place a false emphasis on this thought by asserting that Milton's purpose is here stated. Milton well knows that God's ways demand no justification from him or any other mortal.

33 Cf. *Iliad* i. 8.

40 *to have equal'd;* is this an English or a Latin construction? What tense does the infinitive in English take after a verb in the past tense?

43 *impious;* why does Vergil usually speak of Æneas as *pius?* What is the meaning of *impious* here?

28–44 In these lines Milton restates his theme, dividing it into two parts: the war against God on earth and the war in Heaven. Then with remarkable smoothness of transition he continues without a break to develop that part of the epic plot that he has mentioned last.

54 *for now the thought;* cf. 985, 2.38: "Their knowledge is great, but such as tends rather to aggravate than diminish their misery; so that they utterly despair of their salvation."

58 Modifies *baleful eyes* in 56.

59 *kenn;* probably a verb.

63 *darkness visible;* cf. Job x. 22.

65–66 Why can not peace and rest dwell in Hell? The answer will be found in the text later, but we may as well be thinking about the problem now. *hope never comes;* reminiscent probably of what famous line in Dante?

68 *still urges;* always presses.

72 *utter;* another form of *outer.*

74 *Center;* of the earth. *Pole;* the extreme of the mundane universe.

81 *th' Arch-Enemy;* cf. 985, 2.47: "Their leader is the author of all wickedness, and the opponent of all good. Hence he has obtained many names corresponding to his actions. He is frequently called 'Satan,' that is, an enemy or adversary."

82 *Satan;* Hebrew, adversary.

84 The breaks and parentheses in this speech well indicate the mental state of the speaker.

89 *Glorious Enterprize;* observe the processes

91 *what Pit;* what awful kind of pit.

93 *who knew;* Satan is rationalizing and excusing his defeat.

97 *outward lustre;* the external appearance of
angels, like that of men, is determined by
their internal thoughts and purposes. Cf.
the familiar Platonic idea set forth in *Comus.*

105 *And shook his throne;* Satan, chiefly for his
own benefit, but also for Beëlzebub's, is
making the most of every favorable aspect
of the late war.

108 And what else does the phrase: "not to be
overcome" mean than, etc.? Are other interpretations possible? Which best fits the
context?

109 *wrath;* see textual notes, and observe that
beginning with Book II this longer spelling
is fairly uniform. How did Milton wish the
word pronounced?

115 *ignominy;* pronounce, ignomy; usually so
pronounced in Milton's poetry.

116 *by fate;* Satan implies that the angels were
not created by God, but he admits later that
he is a son of God. He is not always consistent even with himself. Here his self-
confidence and pride is rising to such a pitch
that he is almost back to his former position
of aspiring to equality with God.

117 *cannot fail;* Satan while in Heaven knew
that spirits are immortal, but he ignored the
conditions upon which that law acted. Belial
and Moloch, as is developed later, were not
so sure that evil spirits are immortal.

120 *successful hope;* hope of success.

121 *or guile;* the idea of such a war originated
with Satan; notice that he mentions it early.

128 Beëlzebub at first seems to have caught
some self-confidence from Satan's magnificent effort, but he soon lapses into a
more natural state of discouragement.

133 By which one of these is God upheld?

148 *do him mightier service;* cf. 985, 2.29:
"They are sometimes, however, permitted
to wander throughout the whole earth, the
air, and heaven itself, to execute the judgments of God."

156 *speedy words;* why speedy? What in the
preceding speech irritated Satan?

159 *We are decreed;* see the note on 1.53.

162 *If then his Providence;* cf. 983, 1.35: "The
other position, that God eventually converts
every evil deed into an instrument of good,
contrary to the expectation of sinners, and
overcomes evil with good, is sufficiently
illustrated. . ."

167 *if I fail not;* Lat. *ni fallor,* if I am not mistaken.

169 Note the dramatic quality of these words.

175 Milton often uses a concrete noun followed
by an abstract one. Watch for other examples.

186 *afflicted;* Lat. *afflictus,* struck down.

200 *that Sea-beast;* why should Milton develop
this simile at length when he passed over the
others with a bare mention?

201 *Leviathan; Job* xli. celebrates the prowess
of Leviathan; the commentators of Milton's
time believed that the word was used of
the whale, though it really means any huge
monster. The story of Leviathan was especially popular in medieval bestiaries. Cf.
the following translation from a Middle
English Bestiary, in the South Midland dialect of the early 13th century:

The Whale's Nature

The whale is the greatest fish that is in
the water. You would say—if you saw it
when it was floating—that it was an island
that sits on the sea-sand. . . . This fish
dwells on the bottom of the sea, and lives
there ever hale and sound, 'til there comes
a time when a storm stirs up all the sea,
when summer and winter contend with each
other. It may not remain there, so stirred
up is the sea's bottom—it may not remain
there a moment—but ascends to the top
and lies quiet. While the weather is so bad,
the ships that are driven about on the sea—
loath to them is death, and pleasant is
life—look about them and see this fish—
an island they think it is. Because of this,
they are very happy, and with their might
drag their ships to it, anchor them, and
disembark. . . They make a fire on this
wonder, warm themselves well, and eat and
drink. The whale feels the fire and sinks
them, for quickly he dives down to the
bottom; he destroys them all without
wound.

204 *night-founder'd;* lost in the night.

205 *as Sea-men tell;* it is interesting to watch
the characteristics of the scholar appearing
from time to time in Milton's poetry. Here
he protects himself: it is not his story.

206–208 Is this really a Homeric simile in which
while developing the beauty of the picture,
the poet loses all thought of the simile?

209 What makes this an especially good line?
Are there any words in it of more than one
syllable? What effect does this give?

210 *Chain'd on the burning lake:* cf. 985, 2.34:
"Their proper place however, is the bottomless pit, from which they cannot escape
without permission. Nor can they do anything without the command of God."

211–220 These lines should not be passed over
lightly. They raise several important ques-

tions that have large implications. The student may properly be cautioned about reading too much meaning into poetry, but, judging from the history of two hundred years of criticism of *Paradise Lost,* he may more appropriately be cautioned against reading too little into this poem. Read in all you can, and then you probably will not read in enough. But on the other hand, one may properly be cautious about reading into lines any autobiographical or historical significance where such significance is not plainly and easily implied. Here Milton tells us that evil is abroad in this world by permission of God. Why should God allow evil to go about freely? Did God create evil? What is its ultimate destiny? Was God entirely fair in allowing Satan to commit reiterated crimes? Did Milton believe in a millennium? Did he believe in man's growing to perfection? If so, under what conditions? Not all these questions are answered here; but be on the watch for every hint you can find. Read 741, 1.26 ff. and 738, 1.22 ff. Cf. *P.L.* III. 198 and the quotation given in the note on that passage.

221 *rears;* a dignified word in Milton's time, but in modern usage more restricted.

224 *horrid;* bristling, as almost always in Milton. In meaning, the word refers back to what word in 223?

234 *fewel'd;* furnished with fuel. This is an apparent participle, often used in Milton and Shakspere as well as in more modern writers. It is "apparent," because it is made from the noun, while the real participle is of verbal origin. Cf. Tennyson's line: "Weeded and worn the ancient thatch."
What does "weeded" mean here? What does "weeded" as a real participle mean? The apparent participle is always rendered by, "furnished with."

257 *all but less;* there are at least two possibilities of interpretation here. Work out which meaning fits best, but make your own decision and defend it.

260 *Here for his envy;* Satan is not without his humor, though it is a bitter satiric humor, as is fitting.

264 *But wherefore;* this line follows closely the thought expressed in the preceding line. It is an excellent example of the firmly knit character of Milton's style and thought. Satan says that if it is better to reign in Hell, he and Beëlzebub should get at it immediately.

274 *that voyce;* Milton is doing a bold thing in thus preparing us for the dreadful voice of Satan by frequently mentioning it and then

delaying while he is describing Satan and his fallen legions. By thus mentioning and delaying he emphasizes, and thereby raises our expectations. We expect a super-human voice, and we are not disappointed, but a poet of less ability than Milton might have made a fiasco of the speech. An interesting parallel, also successful, may be found in the curse in Act I of *Prometheus Unbound.*

282 *pernicious highth;* corresponding to the Latin construction of the accusative of extent of space.

284 *Was moving;* a classical use of the imperfect: began to move.

288 *Tuscan Artist;* Galileo. *Artist;* artisan, one who makes an instrument.

294 *Ammiral;* the first ship in a fleet.

302–304 Perhaps this is the most famous simile in English literature. Study it carefully to determine just where its beauty lies.

311 Milton carefully suggests the comparisons implied in each of the two similes. This union of two previous similes in the careful and appropriate working out of the application is a trait of Milton's style. You will easily find other examples as you read further.

318 *or have ye chos'n;* Satan, even in his most earnest speeches, cannot long refrain from satire. At least, we have learned the origin of this "dread evil."

335 *Nor . . . not;* a double negative, making an affirmative.

362 *blotted out and ras'd;* cf. 931, 2.38: "Again, if an argument of any weight in the discussion of so controverted a subject can be derived from allegorical and metaphorical expressions, mention is frequently made of those who are written among the living, and of the book of life, but never of the book of death." Bishop Sumner says: "This remark seems to justify Bentley's alteration of the plural to the singular number in *P.L.* I. 363."

363 *Books of Life;* what is the inference in regard to the immortality of these evil spirits?

366 Part of Milton's reasons for the existence of evil. What does Milton mean by *high?*

369 Milton is always careful that the reader shall be left with no false implications. Another one of Satan's wrong ideas is here corrected.

376 Here begins a list of the warriors, such as the catalogue of ships in Homer and the list of warriors in Vergil.

378 In this long poem we constantly come across ideas and words that often look forward to parts of the story that are soon to be developed and other lines that look backward at what has passed. This is part of Milton's

art. Thus not only is the plot made remarkably clear, but thought and style are knit in a firm compactness,—one of the characteristics of Milton's art and of his thinking.

380 Milton's attitude toward the common crowd is always an interesting subject for study, and one that throws much light on his own character and ability as well as upon tendencies of thought in his time. Milton was never more than mildly democratic. Cf. his attitude in the earlier tracts, especially the *Tenure,* and his latest utterances. And at each point decide how far you agree with him. But before arriving at any final conclusion, be sure that you understand his position thoroughly.

392 The older commentators blamed Milton for supposing that the fallen angels became heathen deities, and even Moody speaks of it as "a bold invention." As a matter of fact, there was no invention here, for medieval writers had often asserted this belief, and had written upon it. De Quincey was the first to justify Milton in an essay, printed in Vol. vi of his collected works.

396 ff. Why does Milton like to bring in all these geographical names? Do they add anything to the story? Do they help to make a convincing picture? Did the mere sound appeal to him? Does he work these hard names skilfully into his lines? Finally, do not forget Milton's description of two possible kinds of epics, 525, 1.24 ff.

423 Milton's serious explanation in this and the following lines seems to indicate that he has not mentioned these names for adornment only. In trying to arrive at the largest and truest interpretation of this poem, we must remember that we are naturally forced to read it in the terms of our own environment and training; the advantage is usually with us, for we have had nearly three hundred years more of high civilization than had his original readers; we should know more about the problems of reform than they. On the other hand, we must keep also in mind Milton's own immediate readers. It seems safe to assume that these allusions were much more familiar to them than they are to us.

433 *living strength;* let us not dismiss these words with the mere comment that they are a scriptural phrase. Milton has transmuted them into his own thought and feeling, where perhaps they have taken on an enlarged meaning.

444 *By that uxorious King;* cf. 992, 1.19: "I say nothing of Solomon, notwithstanding his wisdom, because he seems to have exceeded due bounds; although it is not objected to him that he had taken many wives, but that he had married strange women."

446 *Thammuz;* see glossary. It probably will be news to most of us to know that Adonis is mentioned in the Bible. Be sure to look up this scriptural reference anyway, even though you may not be so faithful in following up other Biblical allusions.

450 *Ran purple;* because of the sediment, caused by the spring freshets.

477 *crew;* always in Milton used in a slighting sense.

504–505 See textual notes. Why did Milton alter the reading of the lines?

506 *The Stygian Councel;* cf. 985, 2.46: "They retain likewise their respective ranks."

528 *recollecting;* re-collecting.

529 Observe how careful Milton is that none of these speeches shall be misunderstood. Brander Matthews, quoting a nineteenth century French critic of drama, used to instruct his students in dramatic writing: "Tell them you are going to do it, tell them you are doing it, tell them you have done it; and then maybe they will understand about it." Milton is especially careful to place literary sign-posts along the way. Were Shakspere and Molière equally careful?

530 *fainted;* can you find any justification for the reading of the 2nd edition, *fanting?* Their "looks" are still "down cast and damp." As for the spelling, the omission of the "i" is not an absolutely absurd typographical error. Watch for other cases of equally "absurd" spelling.

534 *Azazel;* see glossary. Saurat (*Milton, Man and Thinker,* p. 255) settles the matter by discovering that Azazel is mentioned in the apocryphal book of *Enoch* as the standard bearer of the fallen angels.

543 *Chaos and old Night;* not mentioned incidentally or accidentally, but subtly to prepare us for an experience later; another illustration of Milton's firmly knit style.

552 *Hero's old;* heroes of what race? Cf. 550. These lines, as do many others, reveal how thoroughly Milton by reading, studying, and thinking, had absorbed the best of the civilization and ideals of the ancient classic writers. His example should inspire us to read not once, but often, at least in translation, the greatest of these ancient poets, dramatists, historians and orators.

553 *in stead of rage;* why does Milton put this in? What suggested it?

557 Note the repetition of the conjunction. What is the effect?

578 ff. Milton mentions in these lines three of the sources of the most famous stories in European literature: Troy, King Arthur and Charlemagne.

591 *his form;* the effects of sin are gradual, not instantaneous. This gradual deterioration in Satan's external appearance should be observed as your study advances. Notice too that this faded appearance is mentioned or implied in other places in this paragraph.

603 *considerate;* thoughtful.

605 *remorse;* pity. *passion;* suffering, deep feeling.

609 *amerc't;* a legal term, deprived of.

611 *faithfull;* connected with what verb?

629 *the Adversary;* see the note on 81.

633 *emptied;* part of Satan's psychology in bolstering up his own courage and that of his followers is to exaggerate. The truth comes out later.

634 *self-rais'd;* Satan properly emphasizes their own ability. He continues the same strain in *native.*

635 *counsels different;* (1) different from what they should have been; (2) different from those held by others; or (3) differing among ourselves, divided counsels. Study the context carefully and decide which of these possible meanings you think is the best.

680–684 Cf. 493, 1.31: ". . . . . . amidst those golden candlesticks, which have long suffered a dimness amongst us through the violence of those that had seized them, and were more taken with the mention of their gold than of their starry light."

756 *Capital;* this word was originally written in MS as Capitoll. The "o" was then changed into "a," doubtless by Milton's direction. *high;* refers, not to the building, which is not mentioned, but to the place, and means "important." Cf. Milton's use of high constantly in connection with God.

759 *hunderds;* this word in 1667 was printed *hundreds;* Milton in the Errata corrected the spelling as he wished it to appear.

784 *Or dreams he sees;* the scholar again carefully limits his statement.

Page 175. BOOK II

5 *by merit rais'd;* even in Hell the law of merit holds.

11–42 What is Satan's chief purpose in this speech? Whom does he talk about most? Why does he talk about regaining Heaven? Does he mean it, or is he speaking somewhat figuratively? Is he misleading even them by covert guile, while he encourages them to recover their spirits? You will discover many excellences in this speech, traits of a great leader, and doubtless conclude, as Milton meant you to, that Satan held his place by merit.

16 Satan seems to think that even the defeat in Heaven may have been a good thing.

18 *Mee;* the vowel is often doubled for emphasis, according to Milton's scheme for spelling.

21 *yet this loss;* Hell has its advantages.

42 *who can advise, may speak;* the finality of these words indicate the confidence of a leader who is absolutely in command.

51 The next three speeches are character studies of types, much like the popular character writing of the seventeenth century. Moloch's speech is that of the professional military man, who is proud of his reckless courage and scornful of anything approaching watchful waiting.

61 *Hell flames and fury;* the concrete noun followed by an abstract one. Are there other examples in the following lines?

119 What type does Belial represent?

151 *the wide womb;* cf. 976, 2.2: "It was substance, and derivable from no other source than from the fountain of every substance, though at first confused and formless, being afterwards adorned and digested into order by the hand of God."

153 *Can give it;* has Belial any reason for thinking that God cannot have this power? Is God able to do anything?

185 Cf. *Hamlet* I.5: "Unhouseled, unanointed, unanealled." There are many unconscious echoes of Shakspere in *Paradise Lost.* Did you notice any in Moloch's speech?

226 Students invariably remark that at the end of each of these speeches they find themselves agreeing with the last speaker. This is, of course, the object of effective persuasion. These speeches owe much in their eloquence and oratory to the speeches of great heroes as given in the Greek and Latin historians. Is Milton just to Belial? Was not his policy the best for them? What was the fatal weakness in his argument?

229 Study this speech of the seeker of wealth for its arrangement and development as well as for its many other good points. It evidently was the strongest of the three; at least its reception inspired Beëlzebub to an immediate reply. When does Mammon first indicate that he has a plan of his own? When is the first hint given of that plan?

311 Satire is a powerful weapon with Beëlzebub. Why should he object so decidedly to Mammon's plan?

313 *doubtless;* note the culmination of satire in this single word.

329 *What;* why. Latin, *quid.*

330 *determin'd us* (1) our lot for us; or (2) marked our boundaries for us. Which is better?

344 *What if we find;* Beëlzebub up to this point has been shattering the arguments of the previous speakers; he now begins to present a constructive plan of his own.

379 *first devis'd;* cf. I.650 ff.

395 Beëlzebub, having won unanimous consent to his plan, can now afford to be generous. He first makes a concession to Moloch and then one to Mammon.

402 *whom;* this is the chief question to be settled. Whom has Beëlzebub in mind?

406 *palpable obscure;* darkness that can be felt.

430 Satan's masterly speech properly brings the great consult to a climactic close.

431 *demurr;* hesitation.

432 Satan gives a final interpretation to Vergil's famous line.

438 *void;* an adjective.

445 Satan with great skill shuts out all would-be competitors.

457 *intend;* attend to whatever concerns you.

476–77 Addison called this passage "very sublime and poetical."

492 *Scowls;* a transitive verb.

496 ff. Milton takes this occasion to remind us that the events which he has described as taking place outside our world still have their application here.

508 *In order;* another reminder that equality of merit does not exist anywhere.

526 Hell is above all else a mental state.

528 The games that figure in the classic epics.

534 The Northern Lights, the Aurora Borealis.

552 *partial;* partial to themselves; they did not consider all the truth.

561 *in wandring mazes lost;* an expression of Milton's own feeling in regard to the futility of metaphysical speculation when carried too far.

610 *fate withstands;* Vergil's *fata obstant.*

621 What is admirable about this line?

648 Milton drew upon many sources for this famous allegory of Sin and Death. It is a development of *James* i. 15: "Then when lust hath conceived, it bringeth forth sin: and sin, when it is finished, bringeth forth death." Be especially careful to work out the full significance of each part of this story.

678 *God and his Son except;* how should this be read? Was God created? Was the Son?

681 Accent thus: *Whénce and what árt thou, éxecráble shape.*

683 *miscreated;* Satan unwittingly describes the shape truly.

688 Observe how closely all of Satan's implications are answered.

696 *Hell-doomd;* this refers to what word in Satan's speech?

721 *once more;* when?

749 Cf. the description of the "crafty adulteress" on 568, 2.50.

761 What did Pope write about vice? Are these lines the original of his famous metaphor?

799 *return;* why? Cf. Sir Thomas Browne, *Religio Medici,* Part 2, section 10: "But it is the corruption that I fear within me, not the contagion of commerce without me. 'Tis that unruly regiment within me, that will destroy me; 'tis I that do infect myself."

807 When sin dies, death must also die.

990 The speech of the Anarch is purposely and admirably incoherent. He is a fit monarch for Chaos. Analyze his speech carefully and show just where he is confused.

1033 *God and good Angels;* cf. 985, 1.31: "They are obedient to God in all respects. Their ministry relates especially to believers."

1034 *sacred influence;* in direct preparation for the opening of Book III. When did Milton first begin to prepare us for this transition to light?

Page 195. BOOK III

1–2 Milton, in scholarly fashion, allows two interpretations: light is either the first created off-spring of God, or else it is uncreated and eternal. Is each possibility orthodox?

12 *Won from the void;* see the note on II.151.

32 *Nightly I visit;* we are told that Milton composed in his mind portions of his poem each night after he had retired; the next morning he dictated them.

44 *human face divine;* mentioned last as the most important. Observe the same order in Sonnet XXII.

49 *ras'd;* a figure from the Roman wax tablet.

62 *Beatitude past utterance;* what does Milton mean by this? Why should the angels receive such blessedness?

63 *The radiant image;* cf. 966, 1.8: "For though the Son be *another* than the Father, God only means that he will not give his glory to graven images and strange gods,—not that he will not give it to the Son, who is the brightness of his glory, and the express

image of his person, and upon whom he had promised that he would put his Spirit."

80 These speeches in Heaven are pregnant with meaning and must not be passed over lightly. They express and imply much of the philosophical meaning in the poem. *Onely begotten Son;* watch for any explanation as to what Milton means by this expression.

100 ff. With this entire passage cf. 741, 1.26 ff. Our ideas of Milton's conception of God should be enlarged by a careful understanding of these lines. What is free will? What does Milton think of Calvinistic predestination? How does he distinguish foreknowledge? How is reason also choice?

118 *Foreknowledge;* cf. 927, 2.1: "For the foreknowledge of God is nothing but the wisdom of God, under another name, or that idea of everything, which he had in his mind, to use the language of men, before he decreed anything. We must conclude, therefore, that God decreed nothing absolutely, which he left in the power of free agents,—a doctrine which is shown by the whole canon of Scripture"; cf. also 929, 1.32: "But God is not mutable, so long as he decrees nothing absolutely which could happen otherwise through the liberty assigned to man. He would indeed be mutable, neither would his counsel stand, if he were to obstruct by another decree that liberty which he had already decreed, or were to darken it with the least shadow of necessity."

120 Why is this line important?

135 The effect in Heaven of this high pronouncement was not more salutary than should be its effect upon us. Milton believed thoroughly in the infinite possibilities of human endeavor; he was no defeatist. What he would have thought of some modern psychologists that teach "scientific predestination," can easily be imagined.

138 *Beyond compare;* cf. 966, 1.3: "For the term *bodily,* which is subjoined, either means *substantially,* in opposition to the *vain deceit* mentioned in the preceding verse, or is of no weight in proving that Christ is of the same essence with God."

150 *should Man;* cf. 997, 1.4: This sin originated also "in the liability to fall with which man was created, whereby he, as the devil had done before him, 'abode not in the truth.'"

165-166 Milton uses the same argument in his prayer 493, 2.8: "Shouldst thou bring us thus far onward from Egypt to destroy us in this wilderness, though we deserve, yet thy great name would suffer in the rejoicing

of thine enemies, and the deluded hope of all thy servants."

173 Man, even though he fall, has possibilities beyond what the angels can perceive. Only the Son has read God's thought in its essence. On the whole passage cf. 938, 1.33: "and it is certain that unless God had first shown mercy, it would have been in the power of no one either to will or to run."

184 *Elect above the rest;* why are they elect? Cf. 939, 2.22: "If then God reject none but the disobedient and unbelieving, he undoubtedly gives grace to all, if not in equal measure, at least sufficient for attaining knowledge of the truth and final salvation."

191 *To prayer;* cf. 939, 2.17: "But even if there be any degree of reprobation, Scripture everywhere declares, that as election is established and confirmed by faith, so reprobation is rescinded by repentance."

198 *This my long sufferance;* cf. 934, 1.16: "The truth however is, that it was God alone who willed their departure, and Pharaoh alone who was unwilling. . . . God hardened his heart, and himself deferred the execution of his own pleasure, which was in opposition to that of Pharaoh that he might afflict him with heavier punishment on account of the reluctance of his will."

228 *man shall find grace;* cf. 938, 2.40: "since the power of willing and believing is either the gift of God, or, so far as it is inherent in man, partakes not of the nature of merit or of good works, but only of a natural faculty."

243 *thou hast givn me;* cf. 964, 1.1: "This gift of life [of the Son] is for ever."

287 *so in thee;* cf. 933, 1.48: "Hence there was no grace decreed for man who was to fall, no mode of reconciliation with God, independently of the foreknown sacrifice of Christ."

290 *His crime;* cf. 996, 2.47: "The sin which is common to all men is that which our first parents, and in them all their posterity committed. . . ."

309 Consider this line carefully; read what Milton says about the Son in the *Christian Doctrine,* 944; and begin to shape your opinions as to what Milton actually thought. Cf. also 964, 1.21: ". . . he, who when made man was endowed with the highest degree of virtue, by reason of that virtue, or of a superior nature given to him in the beginning, is even now in heaven. . . ."

313 *Therefore thy Humiliation;* cf. 1010, 2.47: "As Christ emptied himself in both his natures, so both participate in his exaltation;

his Godhead, by its restoration and manifestation; his manhood, by an accession of glory."

317 *all Power;* Milton gives "authority," as one of the attributes of the Son, 964, 1.43.

341 *God shall be All in All;* the ultimate goal of those who rise by merit.

372 This choral hymn, in which the angels celebrate the Father and the Son, comes appropriately after the revelation of God's plan for man. For the first time they comprehend somewhat completely the infinite possibilities of the human soul and they understand better the purpose of God in creating them and the greatness of his purpose as it shall work out in the eternal years of Heaven. The lyric beauty of the hymn serves to relieve the monotony of the epic, but this result is only incidental; its real purpose lies much deeper.

373 *Immortal, Infinite;* cf. the characteristics of God as given on 925, 2.19 ff.
The real issue between God and Satan is now apparent. It is not too much to say that God is the up-building, constructive power in the universe and that Satan is the destructive, negating power.

383 *of all creation first;* cf. 944, 2.33: "Certain it is . . . that the Son existed in the beginning, under the name of logos or word, and was the first of the whole creation, by whom afterwards all other things were made both in heaven and earth."

385 *In whose conspicuous;* see the note on *P.L.* VI.681.

390 *Hee Heav'n of Heavens;* cf. 974, 1.45: "Hence it is often said that the Father created the world by the Son,—but never, in the same sense, that the Son created the world by the Father."

443 *liveless;* lifeless.

484 Note the significance of *Wicket* (a small back gate) and *seems.*

520–521 Look up Dante's *Divine Comedy, Purgatory,* ii. 17 ff. This is one of the few places where Milton seems to have Dante's great poem in mind. Is there any direct reference to Dante's poem in Milton? See Sonnet XIII.

552 The effectiveness of much of Milton's philosophy depends upon the closeness of the parallel between Heaven and Earth and between God and the angels and man. Notice how often he mentions this parallel.

648 *Th' Arch-Angel;* cf. 985, 1.40: "Seven of these, in particular, are described as traversing the earth in the execution of their ministry."

654 Satan's versatility is remarkable; he has a

suitable manner for every occasion. His flattery here is as skilful as his boldness has been hitherto.

680 The arch-hypocrite is revealed by his words. Mr. Pecksniff in *Martin Chuzzlewit* is a hypocrite of Satan's own stamp. His words to Mrs. Todgers in Chapter ix are of a piece with Satan's expression. His daughters are introduced: " 'Mercy and Charity,' said Mr. Pecksniff, 'Charity and Mercy. Not unholy names, I hope?' "

705 Uriel has perhaps had his notions enlarged by the revelation of God's purposes in the speeches recorded in the early part of the book.

708 *I saw when;* see the note on II.151.

Page 210. BOOK IV

32 Phillips tells us that the ten lines beginning here were the earliest composed of any in the poem. They probably opened a projected drama on this theme. Notice how appropriately they fit in here. Satan is speaking in a soliloquy; we are therefore sure that he is speaking the truth as far as he knows it. At some points his speech reminds us of the King's speech in *Hamlet* III iii. 36.

66 *Hadst thou;* cf. 929, 2.49, quoted in the note on V.535.

73 *Me miserable;* see the note on I.54.

92 Satan in his sincerity finds it possible to indulge in satire against himself.

114–115 Satan is moved first by wrath, next by envy, and last by despair. Milton before the speech tells us of the first emotion; trace each emotion as it predominates in Satan's mind.

122 Milton never loses an opportunity to hit at religious hypocrisy. Observe what he says at different places about this sin.

151 *in;* Bentley suggested that we read, *on.* Which reading is better? Why? If you have not heard of Richard Bentley, look up his biography in the D.N.B.

180 What in Satan's nature led him to disdain due entrance?

181 The play on words is of course intentional.

192 The two similes are united in this one line of the application. The word "Thief" refers to which simile? And "Fould" to which?

193 The thought of present conditions is still in Milton's mind. Cf. *Lycidas* and the tract printed at p. 878.

209 In Professor Lowes' *The Road to Xanadu,* you will find significant comment upon this description of Eden, and see how profoundly it influenced another great poet; and more

important, you will discover a great modern work of criticism with which you ought to be familiar.

222 *bought dear by knowing ill;* cf. 986, 1.46: "It was called the tree of knowledge of good and evil from the event; for since Adam tasted it, we not only know evil, but we know good only by means of evil. For it is by evil that virtue is chiefly exercised, and shines with greater brightness." Cf. also 738, 1.33: "And perhaps this is that doom which Adam fell into of knowing good and evil; that is to say, of knowing good by evil."

241 Notice how much emphasis Milton places upon art. Was the taste of eighteenth century landscape gardening beginning to come in?

255 *irriguous;* full of springs.

347 The editor is content that you should defend this line, if you can.

358 *O Hell;* this is not simply an oath, but an integral part of the text; it reveals the deep anguish of Satan's envy, his wrath and despair—proper words to express his emotion as revealed by his soliloquy. Read the line as Milton meant it to be read. Notice the means that Satan uses later to recover his poise.

389 ff. G. Sikes, *Life of Sir H. Vane,* (1662) p. 122, says: "One main ground of the unjust proceeding of worldly powers against righteous and conscientious men, is Reason of State, which usually brings the most signal desolation upon them, by that very means whereby they thought to prevent it. With what a vengeance this thing called Reason of State has been repaid, we may observe in all times and places." He then cites examples from ancient history. Bishop Newton remarks that Milton probably had his own times in mind. Perhaps he may even have been thinking of the reason given for the execution of his friend, Vane.

426 *well thou knowst;* cf. 986, 1.11: "God, having placed him in the garden of Eden, and furnished him with whatever was calculated to make life happy, commanded him, as a test of his obedience, to refrain from eating of the single tree of knowledge of good and evil, under penalty of death if he should disregard the injunction."

438 There was work to be done in Eden before the Fall.

440 Notice the intellectual quality of Eve's speech, and read what Saurat has to say about Milton's treatment of woman.

451 *on;* 1674 has: *of.* Which is better?

618 Milton gives us part of his definition of man.

628 *manuring;* see glossary.

635 Milton shows his power as a poet as much in describing the content of domestic happiness as in the more sublime poetry that we often associate with his name. Why does he emphasize this part?

716 *unwiser son;* Epimetheus.

724 Their prayer is spontaneous and voluntary, not in set forms.

736 Milton's celebration of the purity of married love is the culmination of lifelong thought upon the relation of the sexes. With this passage cf. 583, 2.44: "What is it then but that desire which God put into Adam in Paradise, before he knew the sin of incontinence; that desire which God saw it was not good that man should be left alone to burn in; the desire and longing to put off an unkindly solitariness by uniting another body, but not without a fit soul to his, in the cheerful society of wedlock?" Also 584, 1.27: "Who hath the power to struggle with an intelligible flame, not in Paradise to be resisted . . . ?"

744 *Whatever Hypocrites;* cf. 992, 2.40: "Marriage is honorable in itself, and prohibited to no order of men."

830 Cf. *Samson Agonistes,* 1081.

970 *limitarie;* an angel set to guard the limits; from the Latin, *milites limitanei,* soldiers set to guard the frontiers.

Page 229. BOOK V

10 This dream experience of Eve's, really a part of the temptation that led to the Fall, is one of the most carefully worked out parts of the poem. It is so strikingly in accord with modern psychology that one is tempted to wonder if much of recent psychology is not simply the classification and naming of what the great poets have known and acted upon for many centuries. The knowledge that Milton shows of the causes and significance of dreams is not beneath the notice of scholars. Cf. 500, 2.48, and other places.

43 *sets off the face of things;* Landor thought this line was "worthier of Addison than Milton." What did he mean? Do you agree?

60 *Nor God, nor man;* cf. 954, 1.20: "The name of God seems to be attributed to angels because as heavenly messengers they bear the appearance of the divine glory and person, and even speak in the very words of the Deity."

99 *Yet evil whence;* cf. 980, 1.10: "If we receive the soul immediately from God, it

must be pure, for who in such case will venture to call it impure?"

100 *But know that;* cf. 976, 2.50: "For spirit being the more excellent substance, virtually and essentially contains within itself the inferior one; as the spiritual and rational faculty contains the corporeal, that is, the sentient and vegetative faculty."

117 A most important principle in Milton's philosophy. God is God because he puts evil out of his mind. Eve should do the same. This means that the holy angels, and perhaps God himself, are subject to discipline; God is God by merit; and the angels maintain their position and rise by merit. Cf. 506, 1.35: "Yea, the angels themselves, in whom no disorder is feared . . . are distinguished and quaternioned into their celestial princedoms and satrapies, according as God himself has writ his imperial degrees through the great provinces of heaven. The state also of the blessed in paradise, though never so perfect, is not therefore left without discipline. . . ."

144 *Lowly they bow'd;* cf. 1053, 1.30: "The Lord's Prayer was intended rather as a model of supplication, than as a form to be repeated verbatim by the apostles, or by Christian churches at the present day. Hence the superfluousness of set forms of worship; seeing that, with Christ for our master, and the Holy Spirit for our assistant in prayer, we can have no need of any human aid in either respect."

146 *In various style;* cf. 569, 1.20: "And so little does it appear our prayers are from the heart, that multitudes of us declare, they know not how to pray but by rote. Yet they [the prelates] can learnedly invent a prayer of their own to the parliament, that they may still ignorantly read the prayers of other men to God."

153 This choral hymn owes something to Psalm 148 and to the Canticle of the Three Children.

161 *yee behold him;* cf. 985, 1.28: "For the rest, they are represented as standing dispersed around the throne of God in the capacity of ministering angels, praising God."

202 *I;* the pronoun is singular, in the manner of the Greek chorus.

233 *such discourse;* cf. 929, 2.36: "since inasmuch as God had determined from all eternity that man should so far be a free agent, that it remained with himself to decide whether he would stand or fall."

236 *Left to his own free Will;* see the note on *P.L.* III.150.

345 *inoffensive moust;* unfermented, new wine. *meathes;* sweet drinks.

361 *Native of Heav'n;* Milton's epithets are far from the conventional ones used by the classical epic poets; they are a very real part of the content of the poem.

396 Do not miss the sly humor. There is considerable humor at various places in *Paradise Lost.* Have you found any other instances?

401–404 Another illustration of the principle that heaven and earth are closely united— that the same principles hold in both.

407 *And food alike;* see the note on V.100.

434 Why does Milton emphasize this idea?

469 This passage gives Milton's idea of evolution. How far is it consistent with modern evolutionary theory?

470 *All things;* inanimate as well as animate nature comes from God. Everything in the universe, if not depraved, is working toward God. Was this view orthodox? Think how much this implies, and what a large vision of the grandeur of creation Milton had. Why does Milton give these speeches to Raphael?

472 *one first matter;* cf. 976, 2.22: "It is not true, however, that matter was in its own nature originally imperfect; it merely received embellishment from the accession of forms, which are themselves material."

493 *time may come;* cf. 984, 1.40: "From these and similar passages, and especially from the early history of the world, it is evident that God, at least after the fall of man, limited human life to a certain term, which in the progress of ages, from Adam to David, gradually became more and more contracted." Sumner's note: "This seems to intimate a belief in the doctrine held by the Fathers and best divines, that if Adam had not sinned, he would not have died. The opinion is expressed in the same doubtful manner in a speech of Raphael." Cf. 1001, 1.20: "Or, on the other hand, what could be more absurd than that the mind, which is the part principally offending, should escape the threatened death; and that the body alone, to which immortality was equally alloted, before death came into the world by sin, should pay the penalty. . . ."

501 *If ye be found obedient;* Read all the meaning you can into this clause.

524 *God made thee perfect;* cf. 938, 2.51: "If this use of the will be not admitted, whatever worship or love we render to God is entirely vain and of no value; the acceptableness of duties done under a law of necessity is diminished, or rather is anni-

hilated altogether, inasmuch as freedom can no longer be attributed to that will over which some fixed decree is inevitably suspended." Cf. also 741, 1.26: "Many there be that complain of divine Providence for suffering Adam to transgress. Foolish tongues! when God gave him reason, he gave him freedom to choose, for reason is but choosing; he had been else a mere artificial Adam, such an Adam as he is in the motions. We ourselves esteem not of that obedience or love, or gift, which is of force; God therefore left him free, set before him a provoking object ever almost in his eyes; herein consisted his merit, herein the right of his reward, the praise of his abstinence."

535 *My self and all;* cf. 929, 2.49: "Seeing, therefore, that, in assigning the gift of free will, God suffered both men and angels to stand or fall at their own uncontrolled choice, there can be no doubt that the decree itself bore a strict analogy to the object which the divine counsel regarded, not necessitating the evil consequences which ensued, but leaving them contingent; hence the covenant was of this kind—if thou stand, thou shalt abide in Paradise; if thou fall, thou shalt be cast out: if thou eat not the forbidden fruit, thou shalt live; if thou eat, thou shalt die."

571 *what surmounts the reach;* cf. 924, 1.48: "If God be said 'to have made man in his own image, after his likeness,' Gen. i. 26. and that too not only as to his outward form (unless the same words have different significations here and in chap. v. 3. 'Adam begat a son in his own likeness, after his image') and if God habitually assign to himself the members and form of man, why should we be afraid of attributing to him what he attributes to himself, so long as what is imperfection and weakness when viewed in reference to ourselves be considered as most complete and excellent when imputed to God? Questionless the glory and majesty of the Deity must have been so dear to him, that he would never say anything of himself which could be humiliating or degrading, and would ascribe to himself no personal attribute which he would not willingly have ascribed to him by his creatures. Let us be convinced that those have acquired the truest apprehension of the nature of God who submit their understandings to his word; considering that he has accommodated his word to their understandings, and has shown what he wishes their notion of the Deity should be. In a word, God either is,

or is not, such as he represents himself to be. If he be really such, why should we think otherwise of him? If he be not such, on what authority do we say what God has not said? If it be his will that we should thus think of him, why does our imagination wander into some other conception? Why should we hesitate to conceive God according to what he has not hesitated to declare explicitly respecting himself? For such knowledge of the Deity as was necessary for the salvation of man, he has himself of his goodness been pleased to reveal abundantly."

580 *Time;* cf. 978, 1.46: "Certainly there is no sufficient foundation for the common opinion, that motion and time (which is the measure of motion) could not, according to the ratio of priority and subsequence, have existed before this world was made; since Aristotle, who teaches that no ideas of motion and time can be formed except in reference to this world, nevertheless pronounces the world itself to be eternal."

603 *This day I have begot;* evidently Milton does not use this expression in the ordinary sense. What does he mean?

611 *him who disobeyes;* cf. 961, 1.24: "At the same time there is no reason why the words should not be understood of the Father speaking in his own name, who would consider the offences which the Jews should commit against his Son, as offences against himself; in the same sense as the Son declares that whatever is done to those who believed in him, is done to himself."

719 *Son, thou in whom;* see the note on III.63.

833 *Thy self, though great;* cf. 974, 1.11: "'by the word of God the heavens were of old,' that is, as is evident from other passages, by the Son, who appears hence to derive his title of Word."

853 *That we were formd;* "The opinion that the angels were not created, but self-existent according to the Manichæan system, is with great propriety attributed to Satan." Sumner's note. Cf. 978, 1.21: "That the angels were created at some particular period, we have the testimony of Numb. xvi. 22 and xxvii. 16. 'God of the spirits.' But that they were created on the first, or on any one of the six days, seems to be asserted (like most received opinions) with more confidence than reason. . . ."

Page 247. BOOK VI

19 *in procinct;* in readiness.

29 It is hard not to think of Milton himself as we read this passage. What had he said

earlier in *Lycidas* about such a judgment?

34 What is peculiar about the meter of this line? What is the effect?

43 *by right of merit;* see the note on III.309.

44 *of Celestial Armies Prince;* cf. 985, 1.50: "There appears to be one who presides over the rest of the good angels, to whom the name of Michael is often given."

93 *hosting;* mustering.

171 ff. Here we have Milton's mature definition of liberty. Cf. with this passage the last pages of the *Second Defence,* especially the part beginning on p. 1155, 1.36.

137 *Who out of smallest things;* cf. 975, 1.52: "With regard to the original matter of the universe, however, there has been much difference of opinion. Most of the moderns contend that it was formed from nothing, a basis as unsubstantial as that of their own theory." Milton then gives the Hebrew, Greek and Latin words for *create.* These words, he concludes, cannot "signify to create out of nothing. On the contrary, these words uniformly signify to create out of matter."

203 *whereat Michael;* on this battle in heaven, cf. 985, 1.53: "It is generally thought that Michael is Christ. But Christ vanquished the devil, and trampled him under foot singly; Michael, the leader of the angels, is introduced in the capacity of a hostile commander waging war with the prince of devils, the armies on both sides being drawn out in battle array, and separating after a doubtful conflict. Rev. xii. 7, 8."

326 *shar'd;* cut.

329 *discontinuous wound;* an allusion to the old definition of a wound, a separation of the continuity of parts, *vulnus est solutio continui.*

344 *Spirits that live;* cf. 980, 1.43: "Lastly, on what principle of justice can sin be imputed through Adam to that soul, which was never either in Adam, or derived from Adam?"

374 *those elect / Angels;* cf. 985, 1.9: "1 Tim. v. 21: 'the elect angels,' that is, who have not revolted."

498 Ariosto in *Or. Fur.* ix. 91 ascribed the invention of firearms to the devil.

553 *impal'd;* fenced in.

680 *Effulgence of my Glorie;* see the note on III.63.

681 *Son in whose face;* cf. 965, 2.45: ". . . to be the one invisible God, and to be the only-begotten and visible, are things so different that they cannot be predicated of one and the same essence."

723 *O Father;* cf. 966, 1.15: "For the Father does not alienate his glory from himself in imparting it to the Son, inasmuch as the Son uniformly glorifies the Father."

730 *Scepter and Power;* see the note on III.317.

Page 264. BOOK VII

1 *Descend from Heav'n;* to treat of earthly affairs. *Urania;* the Heavenly Muse, called by the Greek name; but as Urania was never the muse of poetry of such high and divine content, he doubts if she is rightly called upon here.

8 Cf. *Proverbs* 8. 24, 25, 30. The Hebrew word is translated in King James' version as *rejoicing* and in the Vulgate as *ludens;* Milton follows, as often, the Vulgate. With this passage cf. 656, 2.46: ". . . God himself conceals us not his own recreations before the world was built: 'I was,' saith the Eternal Wisdom, 'daily his delight, playing always before him.' And to him, indeed, wisdom is as a high tower of pleasure, but to us a steep hill, and we toiling ever about the bottom. He executes with ease the exploits of his omnipotence, as easy as with us it is to will; but no worthy enterprise can be done by us without continual plodding and wearisomeness to our faint and sensitive abilities." Cf. also 973, 2.25: "As to the actions of God before the foundation of the world, it would be the height of folly to inquire into them, and almost equally so to attempt a solution of the question."

9 *didst converse;* what does this imply on the part of God?

14 *drawn;* breathed.

20 *Erroneous;* wandering. *forlorne;* utterly lost.

25 *though fall'n;* alluding to the political condition of England in the years immediately following the Restoration. This reference helps us in dating the writing of this part of the poem.

31 *fit audience find, though few;* a thoroughly Miltonic sentiment, though the thought can be traced to Horace, *Sat.* i. 10, 73: "Neque te ut miretur turba labores, Contentus paucis lectoribus."

41 *affable;* easy to talk with.

44 *least the like;* see the note on IV.426.

52 *Muse;* thoughtful, wondering meditation.

55 *Peace of God in bliss;* do not allow these frequent theological and scriptural expressions to pass by unchallenged. They all have meaning, else Milton would not have used them. What is the "bliss" of God? What is the "holy Rest" of 1.91?

70 Adam is decidedly curious about many

things that do not directly concern him, but he is also very tactful in approaching Raphael; he has the deep, kindly courtesy that comes from an understanding mind.

79–80 Gladstone used to maintain that Dante's line: "In la sua voluntade è nostra pace, In His will is our peace," is the greatest line of poetry ever written, because it contains the greatest thought that the human mind is capable of. Milton seems to have been impressed with Dante's thought, though he may not have been indebted to Dante for it.

92 *so late to build;* we have had many hints that the angels existed in Heaven long before the creation of the earth. Cf. V. 583.

116 *inferr;* prove.

120 *knowledge within bounds;* perhaps the chief principle in Milton's philosophy, moderation in all things. He develops this thought a few lines later.

170–173 Read what Saurat has to say about these lines in *Milton, Man and Thinker,* p. 124. The editor is rather inclined to doubt the validity of Saurat's interpretation. At any rate, a very simple explanation of these lines is possible, and more in accordance with Milton's thought elsewhere in the poem. *and put not forth;* cf. 973, 2.46: "Creation is that act whereby God the Father produced every thing that exists by his Word and Spirit, that is, by his will, for the manifestation of the Glory of his power and goodness."

216 Landor said of this line: "If we can imagine any thought or expression worthy of the Deity, we find it here." *Imaginary Conversations, Southey and Landor.*

450 *when God said;* cf. 979, 1.22: "Man having been created after this manner, it is said, as a consequence, that *man became a living soul;* whence it may be inferred . . . that man is a living being, intrinsicall: and properly one and individual, not compound or separable, not, according to the common opinion, made up and framed of two distinct and different natures, as of soul and body,— but that the whole man is soul, and the soul man, that is to say, a body, or substance individual, animated, sensitive, and rational; and that the breath of life was neither a part of the divine essence, nor the soul itself, but as it were an inspiration of some divine virtue fitted for the exercise of life and reason, and infused into the organic body; for man himself, the whole man, when finally created, is called in express terms *a living soul.*"

613 *Who seekes;* see the note on I.162.

. Page 277. BOOK VIII

1–3 P. W. Clayden in *The Early Life of Samuel Rogers,* p. 113, tells us that when Sir Joshua Reynolds delivered the last of his *Discourses on Art,* he finished with an eloquent tribute to "that divine man," Michael Angelo. After he had finished, Burke took him by the hand and repeated these lines from *Paradise Lost.* Rogers writes: "I was there and heard it." To us, perhaps the most significant comment on these lines is that they were added in the second edition, and that they must have been written when Milton was an old man, yet his pen has lost none of its cunning, nor his mind any of its ease or poetic imagination. In general, note that all the additions made to the second edition give no effect whatever of having been added years after the poem was finished.

70 In the first part of this passage, Raphael describes the Ptolemaic, in the last part, beginning at l.122, the Copernican, system of the universe. Does Milton seem to lean toward a preference for either of the systems?

172 ff. Is this any reflection upon advanced research? Is Milton's attitude still sensible today? Do not judge him entirely by what he says here, but gather other passages as you read, and consider them all. This is excess, as applied to study and research. Cf the note to IX. 1004.

167 Cf. 923, 2.47: "For it is on this very account that he has lowered himself to our level, lest in our flights above the reach of human understanding, and beyond the written word of Scripture, we should be tempted to indulge in vague cogitations and subtleties."

193 A good example of Milton's practical mind.

224 *Nor less think wee;* cf. 985, 1.10: "Hence arises, in their opinion, the delighted interest which the angels take in the mystery of man's salvation."

282 This line affords a good illustration of how ideas and expressions from one poet are used and subtly changed, usually bettered, by later poets,—a process that we have often seen illustrated by Milton himself. One of the best lines in Wordsworth occurs in *After-thought,* the last of the sonnets on the river Duddon: "We feel that we are greater than we know."

352 *I nam'd them;* cf. 981, 1.35: "Certainly without extraordinary wisdom he could not have given names to the whole animal creation with such sudden intelligence." Cf. also 659, 2.3: "But Adam, who had the wisdom

given him to know all creatures, and to name them according to their properties, no doubt but had the gift to discern perfectly that which concerned him much more; and to apprehend at first sight the true fitness of that consort which God provided him."

379 With this passage, cf. 656, 1.21: "And here 'alone' is meant alone without woman; otherwise Adam had the company of God himself, and angels to converse with; all creatures to delight him seriously, or to make him sport. God could have created him out of the same mold a thousand friends and brother Adams to have been his consorts; yet for all this, till Eve was given him, God reckoned him to be alone." Cf. also the note and the quotation given on IV. 736.

419 *No need that thou;* cf. 945, 2.8: "For questionless, it was in God's power consistently with the perfection of his own essence not to have begotten the Son, inasmuch as generation does not pertain to the nature of the Deity, who stands not in need of propagation; but whatever does not pertain to his own essence or nature, he does effect like a natural agent from any physical necessity."

560 What had Adam said that caused Raphael to frown?

571–573 The basis of Milton's own sense of self-esteem.

588 ff. The ultimate goal of human love—a Platonic and neo-Platonic conception, of course, and prominent in all of Milton's mature discussions of love.

595 *half abash't;* partly because of the angel's gentle reproof, partly because he was impressed by Raphael's explanation of the profound significance of love.

618 ff. This is not such a "curious" passage, neither is it thrown in as a pretty poetic diversion. We have noticed often before that life in Heaven has deep significance for us on earth. With Milton, this is no mere poetic parallel.

637 *thine and of all thy Sons;* cf. 929, 2.49, quoted in the note on V. 535.

Page 289. BOOK IX

2 *as with his Friend;* the seventeenth century poets, especially Herbert and Vaughan, often mention with longing regret that happy time when God talked to man as to a friend.

14 ff. The subjects of the Greek and Latin classical epics.

24 After long years of training this quality of ease that Milton had early admired in Shakspere, had now come to him. Is the

line a just description of the style in this poem? The following lines give us hints as to how Milton approached the writing of his great epic. Wars or courtly equipment, with their imaginary tournaments, did not now appeal to him.

44 *an age too late, or cold / Climat;* Macaulay in his *Essay on Milton* developed the first idea. Cf. 525, 1.47: "if . . . there be nothing adverse in our climate, or the fate of this age."

100 Satan frequently speaks of God as if he considered that God is capable of growing from past experience. Can you find any evidence that Milton ever expresses any possibility of such a conception? Did Milton ever conceive of God as some modern thinkers, such as Bergson, do?

145 *Whether such vertue;* see the note on V. 853.

155 *Subjected to his service;* see the note on II. 1033.

351 *But God left free the Will;* cf. 930, 1.34: "God of his wisdom determined to create men and angels reasonable beings, and therefore free agents; foreseeing at the same time which way the bias of their will would incline, in the exercise of their own uncontrolled liberty."

359 *Firm we subsist;* see the note on III. 150.

391–392 Again notice the choice that the poet gives us.

404 Observe the tenderness of the poet for the character that he has created.

446 A realistic picture of a typical city of Milton's time.

477 Satan as the negating, destroying spirit is well described here.

494 Satan has by now lost whatever heroic proportions he ever had. Who is the hero of *Paradise Lost?* Surely, in spite of some critical opinions, Satan never in his most heroic pose, could be seriously so considered by those who had studied the poem as a whole.

601 *to this shape retaind;* Latin, *retineo,* takes the dative.

613 *spirited;* possessed of a spirit.

647 Eve indulges in word play and shows other signs of her triviality of mind. Is this "triviality" Eve's essential sin, as Tillyard thinks, or is it only a characteristic of some tragic fault that lies deeper in her nature?

653 *Sole Daughter of his voice;* Another line of Milton's that Wordsworth used and improved. See the *Ode to Duty.*

671 Milton did not seem to have a high opinion of modern eloquence, even that of the Long Parliament

792 *And knew not eating Death;* this is a Greek

construction. In Greek, verbs of knowing and the like take the participle instead of a clause.

892–893 Why did the garland drop and the roses fade? Read what Saurat has to say. What hints have we had before to prepare us for this intimate association of man with all nature?

1004 What was the sin of which Adam and Eve were guilty? What does the apple represent? Saurat says it is sensuality. Tillyard says it is triviality. It seems to the editor that these critics take too narrow a view of the problem. Not only throughout this poem, but in all his works, and in his own life, Milton constantly objected to excess of any kind. Excess is always bad; in eating, in drinking, in study, in the literal interpretation of Scripture, in sex,—in almost every relation of life he urged moderation. Obedience to God and Nature demands moderation in all things. This principle of Greek civilization and art is the essence of right thinking and right living. "The rule of not too much" is Michael's advice to Adam later in the poem. It applies to every action of life. Adam, while in Eden, was naturally susceptible to only one excess,—that of sexual indulgence, for all the other possibilities have come with civilization. Before the Fall, Milton was particularly careful to tell us that sexual love between man and wife is holy; now he tells us that excess in this or other things is unholy. You will be able easily to find many other instances where Milton throughout his life urged and applied this principle of moderation in all things.

1173 beyond this had bin force; cf. 929, 1.41: "It follows, therefore, that the liberty of man must be considered entirely independent of necessity . . ."

Page 312. BOOK X

5 what can scape the Eye; cf. 930, 1.34, quoted in the note on IX. 351.

25 violated not thir bliss; Milton considers even little theoretical problems that sometimes trouble human thought. Why was it that the knowledge of earth's unhappiness did not violate their bliss? In what did their bliss consist?

43 no Decree of mine; cf. 931, 1.2: "Thus God foreknew that Adam would fall of his own free will; his fall was, therefore, certain, but not necessary, since it proceeded from his own free will, which is incompatible with necessity."

55 But whom send I; Christ's attributes include judicial power; 965, 2.4: "his future judicial advent."

63 unfoulding bright; see the note on III. 63.

146 was shee made thy guide; cf. 987, 1.18: "With regard to marriage, that it was instituted, if not commanded, at the creation, is clear, and that it consisted in the mutual love, society, help, and comfort of the husband and wife, though with a reservation of superior rights to the husband."

221 but inward nakedness; cf. 528, 2.45: "while Christ is clothing upon our barrenness with his righteous garment to make us acceptable in his Father's sight."

478 We know how outrageously Satan is lying.

678 Else had the Spring; cf. 1000, 2.12: "All nature is likewise subject to mortality and a curse on account of man."

764 yet him not thy election; cf. 945, 1.52: "nor did the Father beget him [the Son] from any natural necessity but of his own free will."

766 God made thee; cf. 939, 2.50: "Nor is it enough that only so much grace shall be bestowed, as will suffice to take away all excuse; for our condemnation would have been reasonable, even had no grace at all been bestowed."

784 Least that pure breath of Life; cf. 978, 2.48: "Nor did God merely breathe that spirit into man, but molded it in each individual, and infused it throughout, enduing and embellishing it with its proper faculties."

798 Can he make deathless Death; cf. 926, 1.11: "It must be remembered, however, that the power of God is not exerted in things which might imply a contradiction."

914 Eve is much superior to Adam at this unhappy time.

Page 333. BOOK XI

22–30 Even the Son says that the Fall was a good thing.

49 The law that God gave to nature forbids that man stay in Eden, because such a stay implies a contradiction, and God cannot break his own laws.

117 Even this early, Milton is preparing for the marvelous close of the poem From now on, watch how he is skilfully working to that close.

511 Why should not man; cf. 937, 1.18: "For, as will be shown hereafter, there are some remnants of the divine image left in man, the union of which in one individual renders him more fit and disposed for the kingdom of God than another.' Also 654, 2.33: "For

there are left some remains of God's image, as he is merely man, which reason God gives against the shedding of man's blood, Gen. ix., as being made in God's image without expression whether he were a good man or bad, to exempt the slayer from punishment."

531 *The rule of not too much;* this is the cardinal principle of Milton's philosophy. How does the rule fit in with the Fall? It applies in all aspects of life, as we have seen, and shall continue to see.

539 Is this pessimism, or rather a simple statement of the facts of life?

553–554 The rule of not too much receives a noble and dignified interpretation from Michael. Why in Book V and here are Milton's most serious ideas put into the mouths of visiting angels?

635 Michael will tolerate in Adam no self-justification, self-pity, or tendency to blame another for his own fault. How far were these traits characteristic of Milton? Have you caught any note of self-pity in any of his references to his blindness, his loss of property, or the loss of the cause for which he gave many of the best years of his life?

870 Adam is gradually becoming reconciled to the new order of things. Notice how subtly his thought changes from now on until in the next book he arrives at his final conclusion about the Fall.

Page 351. BOOK XII

6) *Man over men;* cf. 1036, 2.51: "As Christ is the head of the mystical church, so no one besides Christ has the right or power of presiding over the visible church."

79 Cf. with this passage on liberty the discussion at the end of the *Second Defence,* 1155, 1.36 and other passages that will readily occur to you, such as those given in the note on 459, 2.51.

84 *right Reason;* cf. 923, 1.41: "Again: the existence of God is further proved by that feeling, whether we term it conscience or right reason, which even in the worst of characters, is not altogether extinguished."

109 *resolving from thenceforth;* cf. 932, 2.10: "I do not understand by the term election that general or national election, by which God chose the whole nation of Israel for his own people."

115 *Bred up in Idol-worship;* cf. 1013, 2.39: "Thus he called Abraham from his father's house, who probably expected no such call and who was even an idolator at the time."

241 *Moses in figure beares;* cf. 1009, 1.12: "The name and office of mediator is in a certain sense ascribed to Moses, as a type of Christ."

308 *And therefore shall not Moses;* cf. 1024, 2.12: "Thus the imperfection of the law was manifested in the person of Moses himself; for Moses, who was a type of the law, could not bring the children of Israel into the land of Canaan, that is, into eternal rest; but an entrance was given to them under Joshua, or Jesus. Hence Peter testifies that eternal salvation was through Christ alone."

424 *Thy ransom paid;* cf. 936, 2.2: "Without searching deeper into this subject, let us be contented to know nothing more than that God, out of his infinite mercy and grace in Christ, has predestinated to salvation all who should believe."

513 *Left onely;* cf. 923, 2.21: "No one, however, can have right thoughts of God, with nature or reason alone as his guide, independent of the word, or message of God."

519 *The Spirit of God;* cf. 944, 1.29: "But inasmuch as they can lay claim to nothing more than human powers, assisted by that spiritual illumination which is common to all. . . ."

526 *what, but unbuild;* cf. 920, 1.12: "But since it is only to the individual faith of each that the Deity has opened the way of eternal salvation, and as he requires that he who would be saved should have a personal belief of his own. . . ."

561 As the end of the epic nears, we are brought back to the opening, where we first had the subject of the poem stated. Nor indeed at any time have we wandered from that theme, for disobedience is but an excess of will, or self-confidence, and of pride.

566 *by small;* see the note *P.R.* II. 473.

575 ff. This is Milton's mature and final conclusion. The great reformation can come only when each man rises to the greatest possibilities in himself.

583 *add Love;* the whole "knot of Christian graces," including all practical religion. Cf. 922, 2.32: "Christian doctrine is comprehended under two divisions,—Faith, or the knowledge of God,—and Love, or the worship of God."

587 The Paradise to be regained is within each man: "The Kingdom of Heaven is within you."

608 Tenderness, which we have noticed coming in, especially since the Fall, now becomes perhaps the dominating emotion.

624 *our Mother Eve;* this is the last time that

she is specially mentioned How do you feel about the epithet?

646–649 Even to the old poet life was still a great adventure. No painter or engraver has yet succeeded in picturing all that Milton in these last few lines describes. The ending is perfect as only Milton could make it. Succeeding poets studied Milton's endings, and in some cases profited greatly from that study. The manner in which Keats closed some of his great poems, such as the *Ode to a Nightingale* and *The Eve of St. Agnes*, shows a careful study of Milton.

PARADISE REGAIN'D

In *Paradise Lost* Milton has eloquently told us what the goal of human endeavor should be, but he has not given us any very definite ideas of how this goal can be attained. Having arrived at the same conclusion about human aspirations as did Jesus, he naturally turned to the life of that great Teacher for help in reaching that goal. But it was Jesus as a man that interested Milton most—Jesus the man showed the way to arrive at human grandeur. Accordingly he studied the most critical time in that man's life, that period in which he made his most far-reaching decisions. Jesus showed us how we can recover Paradise.

The student should read again Milton's description of the two kinds of epic, p. 525, 1.29, and remember that this poem is the short, unadorned epic.

Page 364. BOOK I

1–2 The reference is, of course, to *Paradise Lost*. Notice that the present poem is implied in the opening lines of the first epic. How do you reconcile Ellwood's statements? Obviously they cannot be literally true, as we have seen from our study of *Paradise Lost*. Perhaps it is best to decide that Milton was having a little fun with his naïve friend, and that what he said was spoken half-jokingly. Perhaps too Ellwood, writing many years after the conversation, unconsciously exaggerated the words and their importance.

17 *so long unsung;* Giles Fletcher had devoted a part of his poem to this subject and other poets also had written upon it; but no poet had made it the subject of deep philosophical study in a large plan such as Milton was developing. Before studying the poem, the student should read the passages of Scripture which are Milton's chief authorities: *Matthew* iii and iv. 1–11; *Mark* i. 1–15; *Luke* iii. 2–23, and iv. 1–14; and *John* i. These passages will explain many of the allusions that are here passed over.

83 *what e're it meant;* cf. 968, 1.39: "The descent therefore and appearance of the Holy Spirit in the likeness of a dove, seems to have been nothing more than a representation of the ineffable affection of the Father for the Son, communicated by the Holy Spirit under the appropriate image of a dove, and accompanied by a voice from heaven declaratory of that affection." Cf. the hesitant attitude expressed above with 282.

130 *by proof;* by experience.

166 *by merit call'd my Son;* see the note on *P.L.* III. 309.

132 *begin;* this idea of beginning is emphasized frequently throughout the poem.

157 Jesus went into the wilderness alone to determine how best he could develop the great power that he felt within him, and what the object of his life should be. The temptation took the form, for the most part, of attractively presenting different careers, all selfish, in which an ordinary man would like to develop and show his power. Thus the poem is at once made universal, for the choice of a life work is a problem that faces every young man and woman. Milton, as we have seen in various poems and in prose passages, was always interested in this problem as it affected himself. In what poems have we had more or less full discussions of this theme?

166 *by merit call'd my Son;* cf. 136. This is the second time that Milton has so spoken of Christ. He is emphasizing the human nature of Jesus.

200 ff. One cannot help but think that this is a fairly accurate picture of what Milton must have been when young. Cf. what Aubrey says of him.

217 This is to form the second temptation. What effect has its introduction here?

Page 374. BOOK II

63–65 This is a conceit in the seventeenth century fashion, probably the most thoroughgoing conceit to be found in Milton. *got head;* raised a force for a rebellion. Who were the soldiers? In what were they dressed?

169 *Women, when nothing else;* see the note on *P.L.* I. 444.

172 Why does Satan reject so quickly Belial's suggestion?

199–200 This story is worth reading in its original source; you will find it in *Livy* xxvi. 50 (Translation in Everyman's Library, *Livy*, iv, p. 64.)

240 *persons;* actors of parts in a drama.

337 It will be interesting to read Charles Lamb's criticism of this table, in his essay, "Grace before Meat," and then consider whether you agree. How does the "rule of not too much" apply here?

346 *exquisitest name;* alluding to the fanciful names that the Romans gave to some of their delicacies.

349 Milton many times in this poem refers back to events narrated in *Paradise Lost*.

369 Not a very tactful or subtle statement for Satan to make to Jesus.

378 *temperately;* the same great principle that applied in *Paradise Lost* is used here.

463 ff. Milton's picture of an ideal king.

473 *to guide nations;* cf. 1009, 2.10: "Herein it is that the preëminent excellency of Christ's kingdom over all others, as well as the divine principles on which it is founded, are manifested; inasmuch as he governs not the bodies of men alone, as the civil magistrate, but their minds and consciences, and that not by force and fleshly weapons, but by what the world esteems the weakest of all instruments."

481 ff. Milton probably had in mind the abdication of Queen Christina of Sweden. He praises her highly in the *Second Defence*.

Page 383. BOOK III

48–50 Milton's mature judgment. He once had had more faith in the common man; cf. his opinion throughout all the tracts of the Commonwealth period.

51 Things vulgar, and which when weighed, by judicious persons, are found to be scarce worth the praise.

60 *when God;* cf. 935, 2.44: Any person is said to be known to God, "by his approving or gracious knowledge."

101 Publius Scipio Africanus, after conquering Hannibal and putting an end to the long war with Carthage, finally died in self exile.

121 *fervently;* Jesus had answered temperately and patiently as long as Satan attacked only himself, but when he cast slights upon his Father, he justly resented them with warmth.

Page 392. BOOK IV

196 *Be not so sore offended;* cf. 954, 1.49: "The Son, who was entitled to the name of God

both in the capacity of a messenger and of a judge, and indeed in virtue of a much better right. . . ."

270 Some critics have found fault with this anachronism, and others have tried to justify it.

286 ff. Milton here expresses his mature conviction of the superiority of Christian religious philosophy over pagan Greek philosophy.

330 This line may be the source of Newton's famous simile.

333 *As in our native Language;* we have seen before Milton's high regard for the literature in the Bible.

334 *Story;* history, as often.

370–371 The contemplative life of retirement and study or religious devotion and meditation and the active life of the world were the two kinds of life, especially in the Middle Ages; there was a distinct leaning toward the contemplative life in many Englishmen of the seventeenth century.

372 *What dost thou in this World?* This is the counsel of despair: why not die?

388 Satan ruthlessly carries the suggestion of despair to its final conclusion. We feel in this passage perhaps best that Satan after all is a presentation of different thoughts that came to Jesus as he meditated on his future.

391 Satan as often indulges in some satiric humor.

420 That Jesus is the hero becomes apparent.

436 *Ruinous;* in its literal significance.

465 Satan still continues his temptations of despair. The suggestion is a natural one to come to Jesus at this time.

517–520 These statements are significant in any discussion of Milton's philosophy.

520 *All men are Sons of God;* cf. 945, 1.21: "By a similar figure of speech, though in a much lower sense, the saints are also said to be begotten of God."

551 Notice how carefully Milton has led up to this temptation. Satan has already suggested to Christ that this world is no place for him; let him now find it out more definitely.

562 The idea of Satan's falling is emphasized throughout this passage. Notice how many times the word "fall" occurs. In contrast, of course, Christ stands. This is the climax of the epic.

596 The hymn of triumph by the angels celebrates the victory by summing up the essence of the whole poem.

608 *lost Paradise;* thus we are brought back to the beginning of the poem and then to

NOTES ON THE PROSE

Page 441. OF REFORMATION

This, the first of Milton's prose works, and the first of five anti-Prelatical tracts, appeared about June, 1641. The Long Parliament had been summoned in 1640 and had taken measures to reform the political situation by impeaching Strafford. After that trial had been initiated, Parliament turned to the burning question of church reform. In June, 1641, a Root and Branch Bill had been introduced that provided for the complete abolishment of the system of Archbishops and Bishops and proposed to substitute a kind of Presbyterianism, somewhat resembling that of Scotland. This proposed measure met such heated opposition that a more moderate bill, curtailing the powers of the Bishops was then introduced. The pamphlet war was hot and heavy. Bishop Joseph Hall had published a tract in 1640, *Episcopacy by Divine Right,* and in January, 1641, another, *An Humble Remonstrance to the High Court of Parliament.* In March, 1641, a group of Puritan ministers, who signed themselves "Smectymnuus," issued *An Answer,* etc. Thomas Young, Milton's former tutor, seems to have been the leader of this group. Bishop Hall replied in the same month; in May James Ussher, Archbishop of Armagh, probably the most learned Englishman among the clergy, entered the field.

One needs to read some of the tracts mentioned above to realize the superiority of Milton's style and the care that he takes in the arrangement of his points, as well as the force with which he drives them home. The art in Milton's prose work has never been fully or properly studied, or, for that matter, appreciated.

1.6 *story;* history, as constantly in Milton's prose.

1.21 *winnowed and sifted;* cf. 921, 2.5: "is the liberty not only of winnowing and sifting every doctrine. . . ."

1.22 *overdated;* out of date, antiquated.

2.14 *God earthly and fleshly;* the passage beginning here gives part of Milton's objections against a formal ritual and against creating an anthropomorphic Deity. The subject is an important one,

not only for understanding all of Milton's work, but especially for a proper understanding of *Paradise Lost.*

2.27 *Aaron's old wardrobe, or the flaming vestry;* from the old Mosaic Hebrew ceremonies or from the pagan religion of Rome. Cf. 528, 2.28: "superstitious copes and flaminical vestures." 552, 1.51: "his . . . heathen altar."

2.29 *lurries;* confused patchwork.

Page 442, 1.9 *droiling;* slowly toiling.

1.13 *believe no God at all;* Milton's belief, often expressed, in regard to the tendency of ritual when carried too far.

1.32 *scan the scriptures by letter;* Milton is earnestly opposed to a too literal interpretation of the Bible. In no way does he show better his thoroughly modern characteristics than in his attitude toward Biblical interpretation, though in this he was by no means alone. Several liberal thinkers of the time used some or even all of his rules, and perhaps had others of their own. His principles may conveniently be gathered together here with references.

1. He is against a too literal interpretation. With the present passage cf. 577, 1.50: "crabbed textuists"; and many other places.

2. 494, 2.8: The "law of method" which requires that the clearest of a series of statements should come first.

3. 494, 2.20: The rules of grammar and of rhetoric must be observed in studying to get a correct interpretation: i. e. the Bible is well written.

4. 494, 2.23: The writers observed the rules of logic, and our interpretations must take these rules into consideration.

5. 494, 2.30: Often a "phrase expresses only the chief in any action, and understands the rest."

6. 505, 2.23: The scriptures are clear and simple in statement; but their drift must be studied as well as their explicit statements.

7. 577, 1.47: Not the words only but

the whole spirit must be understood.

8. 577, 1.53: The Gospel always keeps in mind the good of man.

9. 581, 2.17: No "law or covenant, how solemn or strait soever, either between God and man, or man and man, though of God's joining, should bind against a prime and principal scope of its own institution."

10. 687, 2.21: The Bible must be read as all other literature; i.e. its figures of speech must not be taken literally. "And whether he suffered, or gave precept, being all one, as was heard, it changes not the trope of indignation, fittest account for such askers." 689, 2.23: "Which art of powerful reclaiming, wisest men have also taught in their ethical precepts and gnomologies, resembling it, as when we bend a crooked wand the contrary way; not that it should stand so bent, but that the overbending might reduce it to a straightness by its own reluctance. And as the physician cures him who hath taken down poison, not by the middling temper of nourishment, but by the other extreme of antidote; so Christ administers here a sharp and corrosive sentence against a foul and putrid licence; not to eat into the flesh, but into the sore. And knowing that our divines through all their comments make no scruple, where they please, to soften the high and vehement speeches of our Saviour, which they call hyperboles: why in this one text should they be such crabbed Masorites of the letter . . , ?" 758, 1.53: "all men will see, that the pathetical words of a psalm can be no certain decision to a point that hath abundantly more certain rules to go by." 872, 2.50: "As if a parable were to be strained through every word or phrase, and not expounded by the general scope thereof."

11. 691, 2.1: An interpreter of the Bible must be a scholar who determines the exact meaning of a word as it occurs in its several places. 707, 2.29: "Erasmus . . . maintains . . . that the words of Christ comprehend many other causes of divorce under the name of fornication."

2.39 A good description of the early reformation and the revival of learning.

Page 443, 1.32 *earnest;* pledge.

1.42 *propensity;* inclination.

2.31 *French cardinal;* Cardinal Mazarin had been made a cardinal in 1641.

Page 444, 2.30 *spotless truth;* Milton's frequent descriptions of Truth in figurative and poetic language, showing, as they often do, profound insight, would make the basis for an unsurpassed essay on this subject. Toward such a collection, to which the student is encouraged to add, the editor offers the following passages:

1. 444, 2.30: "spotless truth."
2. 452, 2.43: "The very essence of truth is plainness and brightness."
3. 453, 2.28: "transparent streams of divine truth."
4. 468, 2.22: "sun of thy truth."
5. 473, 2.4: "the spotless, and undecaying robe of truth."
6. 477, 1.27: "to gather up wherever we find the remaining sparks of truth, wherewith to stop the mouths of our adversaries."
7. 481, 1.8: "the precious gem of truth, as amongst the numberless pebbles of the shore."
8. 522, 2.8: "certain precious truths, of such an orient lustre as no diamond can equal. . . ."
9. 525, 2.51: Some youths will not "look upon truth herself, unless they see her elegantly dressed."
10. 526, 2.44: "beholding the bright countenance of truth in the quiet and still air of delightful studies."
11. 529, 2.30: "For truth . . . hath this unhappiness fatal to her."
12. 541, 1.29: "truth, whose force is best seen against the ablest resistance."
13. 571, 1.24: "true eloquence I find to be none, but the serious and hearty love of truth."
14. 573, 2.47: "as if the womb of teeming truth were to be closed up."
15. 574, 1.46: "for truth is as impossible to be soiled by any outward touch, as the sunbeam."
16. 574, 1.49: "she never comes into the world, but like a bastard, to the ignominy of him that brought her forth."
17. 580, 2.1: "yet truth in some age or other will find her witness, and shall be justified at last by her own children."

18. 677, 2.29: "the unworthy and the conceited, who love tradition more than the truth."

19. 739, 2.52: "See the ingenuity of truth, who, when she gets a free and willing hand, opens herself faster than the pace of method and discourse can overtake her."

20. 746, 1.7: "the cruise of truth must run no more oil."

21. 746, 1.32: "Truth is compared in scripture to a streaming fountain; if her waters flow not in a perpetual progression, they sicken into a muddy pool of conformity and tradition."

22. 747, 2.22 "this plot of licensing . . . hinders and retards the importation of our richest merchandise,—truth."

23. 747, 2.45: "Truth indeed came once into the world with her divine master, and was a perfect shape most glorious to look on: but when he ascended, and his apostles after him were laid asleep, then straight arose a wicked race of deceivers, who . . . took the virgin Truth, hewed her lovely form into a thousand pieces, and scattered them to the four winds. From that time ever since, the sad friends of Truth, such as durst appear . . . went up and down gathering up limb by limb still as they could find them. We have not yet found them all, lords and commons, nor ever shall do. till her Master's second coming; he shall bring together every joint and member, and shall mold them into an immortal feature of loveliness and perfection."

24. 748, 1.47: "To be still searching what we know not, by what we know, still closing up truth to truth as we find it, (for all her body is homogeneal, and proportional,) this is the golden rule in theology as well as in arithmetic, and makes up the best harmony in a church."

25. 751, 2.15: "For who knows not that truth is strong, next to the Almighty; she needs no policies, nor stratagems, nor licensings to make her victorious; those are the shifts and the defences that error uses against her power; give her but room, and do not bind her when she sleeps, for then she speaks not true, . . . but then rather she turns herself into all shapes except her own, and

perhaps tunes her voice according to the time, . . . until she be adjured into her own likeness. . . . Yet is it not impossible that she may have more shapes than one?"

26. 774, 1.15: ". . . to the advancement of truth, (which among mortal men is always in her progress,) than if on a sudden they were struck maim and crippled."

27. 920, 2.37: "the offers of God were all directed, not to an indolent credulity, but to constant diligence and to an unwearied search after truth."

28. 1107, 1.9: Introduction to Prolusion IV, where he discusses the relations between truth and error. This discussion, though rather crude, is interesting, because it shows Milton's thought in its early stages of development.

29. 1111, 1.11: "snow-white Truth." Another early statement, with which we may compare later expressions, as given above.

30. 1112, 1.52: "Truth invincible is always more than sufficiently powerful in defending herself by her own exertions."

31. 1148, 2.17: "I only preferred queen Truth to king Charles."

Page 445, 1.19 *slugs;* hinders. On Milton's justification for using strong language, see the note on 478, 1.41.

1.29 *queazy;* nauseating.

1.36 *God and all good men;* an expression used so frequently by sixteenth and seventeenth century writers that it became almost a proverb.

1.51 *chair;* Milton probably had Archbishop Laud in mind as he wrote this passage.

2.6 *St. Martin;* Milton refers to the same incident at 450, 1.47

Page 446, 1.4 *puritans;* Milton's statement of the origin of this name should be noticed.

1.6 *her prerogative;* this was the first and constant argument of the bishops with the crown even in Elizabeth's reign; in Milton's time the Puritans turned the argument around and claimed that the bishops were in league against the king. Laud's attempts to strengthen the church in political power had given new validity to this argument.

1.30 *mew;* confine. This and *pounces* (l. 31), claws, are terms taken from falconry.

Page 447, 1.28 *fob off;* to put off slightingly or deceitfully.

2.35 *ethnics;* pagans.

2.38 *table of separation;* Laud ordered that the communion tables should be removed from the center of the church, placed near the altar and surrounded by a rail. This was, superficially at least, enacted in order to make a more dignified service, for the table had become the popular receptacle of hats, coats, and even babies. But the Puritans took the order hard; they insisted, whether rightly or not, the editor will leave to historians, that this was but another step toward Rome, that to remove the table meant a belief in the real presence in the sacrament, and was a further removal of religion from the people to the clergy.

Page 448, 1.5 *must yield him;* these conditions in which the primitive bishops lived, which Milton has established very skilfully and now drives home with equal skill, were not at all to the liking of the prelatical party.

1.6 *elected by the popular voice;* bishops in Milton's time were appointed by the king on the recommendation of the Archbishop of Canterbury. Thus the clergy had the matter really in their own hands.

1.12 *many-benefice-gaping-mouth;* plurality, the holding of two or more benefices by the same person at the same time, was much abused by the clergy, and roundly attacked by the Puritan writers.

1.43 *Easter-day;* Milton always has wrath and scorn for arguments upon trivial subjects of any kind.

Page 449, 1.6 *packing;* manipulating a statement so as to further one's own ends.

Page 450, 1.25 *welked;* faded, declined.

2.12 *Dante;* Milton shows a wide reading in the poets and likes to use them to strengthen his arguments. His references to Dante are more numerous in his prose than in his poetry. Cf. 549, 1.39: I . . . "preferred the two famous renowners of Beatrice and Laura," and other places.

2.20 *Petrarch;* Milton often quotes or refers to Petrarch in his prose. A few references are: 456, 1.47; 549, 1.40. See the note on 2.12 above.

2.34 *Ariosto;* Cf. 525, 1.2.

Page 451, 1.2 *Chaucer;* Among Milton's references to Chaucer in his prose works as they appear in this volume are: 454, 1.14; 462, 1.32; 480, 1.37.

2.20 *without judgment follow the ancients;* Milton cites this quotation with evident

approval; he was always firm against following anyone unless good judgment and sound thinking counseled such a course. In the famous argument of the century between those who praised the ancients and those who believed in the moderns he was emphatically on the side of the moderns.

Page 453, 1.34 *the sober, plain, and unaffected style of the scriptures;* the qualities that Milton admired in writing, those that he himself strove to attain, and the comments that he makes upon the art of writing, both in prose and in poetry, help us to appreciate his art and his quality as a thinker. With the present passage may be grouped the following:

2. 488, 1.36: Variety in writing.

3. 520, 1.49: The need for much revision and improving. See the MS copies of his poems for confirmation of his practice.

4. 524, 1.35: A suitable subject, leisurely worked at and elaborated with "all the curious touches of art."

5. 524, 1.43: A written piece compared to a painting.

6. 524, 2.25: The style must have vitality.

7. 524, 2.41: To write great poetry requires "labor and intense study." It therefore contains deep thought.

8. 542, 2.46: His long sentences justified.

9. 543, 1.39: "that indeed according to art is most eloquent, which returns and approaches nearest to nature."

10. 552, 2.12: A vehement vein justified.

11. 556, 2.25 and 558, 1.35: The selection of the proper words, used correctly.

12. 560, 1.25: Learning, elegance and "decorum in the writing of praise."

13. 560, 2.33: Close attention to the grammatical construction.

14. 563, 2.3: Variety without jarring notes.

15. 571, 1.19: Training in the rules given by the best rhetoricians and found in the best examples.

16. 571, 1.24: "true eloquence I find to be none, but the serious and hearty love of truth."

17. 583, 2.30: The "course of method": that is, the proper arrangement of arguments and exposition.

18. 712, 1.40: His care in writing English: "Nor did I find this his want of the pretended languages alone, but accompanied with such a low and homespun expression of his mother

English all along, without joint or frame, as made me, ere I knew further of him, often stop and conclude, that this author could for certain be no other than some mechanic."

19. 729, 2.30: He would have pupils read criticism that they know "what the laws are of a true epic poem, what of a dramatic, what of a lyric, what decorum is, which is the grand masterpiece to observe. This would . . . show them what religious, what glorious and magnificent use might be made of poetry, both in divine and human things."

20. 739, 2.53: "truth, who, when she gets a free and willing hand, opens herself faster than the pace of method and discourse can overtake her."

21. 1134, 2.24: The necessity of a good introduction. "Yet no man thinks he must make such haste, even in handling any ordinary subject, as not to employ an opening worthy of its importance."

2.13 *index;* superficial learning that is acquainted no further in a book than the index is often the object of Milton's scorn.

Page 454, 1.29 *to govern a nation;* it is interesting and useful to observe how early this scale of discipline occurs in Milton: first, to rule well oneself; next to guide well one's family; then, to guide a nation. No higher task or more responsible awaited any man than to influence well a nation, be it from a chair of state, a pulpit or the poet's study. Cf. 506, 2.34.

1.40 *the art of policy;* the art of politics or governing well.

1.43 *train up a nation in true wisdom and virtue;* many are the places, early and late, in which Milton insists upon this principle. Cf. 459, 2.50: "Well knows every wise nation, that their liberty consists in manly and honest labors"; 843, 2.5: "The happiness of a nation consists in true religion, piety, justice, prudence, temperance, fortitude, and the contempt of avarice and ambition."

1.48 *likeness to God;* Milton says that this is the end of all study, of all discipline, of all government, of life.

1.53 *modern politician;* no writer, not even today, has been more unsparing in describing the selfishness and crookedness of bad politicians and in damning their practices.

2.32 *single happiness to one man;* Milton is

an individualist in this: he insists that individuals are the units of which the state is composed. His deep classical studies, influenced by Renaissance enthusiasm and insight, gave him an immense advantage in all thinking. Observe here how solidly his opinion is stated and how firmly based it is.

2.34 *Aristotle;* Milton was well read in both Aristotle and Plato, upon whom he formed many of his political and philosophical principles. Some other references to Aristotle are: 525, 1.33; 909, 2.17.

2.51 *Plato;* Milton used Plato and Aristotle as well as the Bible in forming his principles of right living. The influence of Plato as revealed in Milton's poetry is very great from the time of his earliest English poems until his death. Some other direct references to this, the greatest of Greek philosophers, perhaps the greatest philosopher of all time, are: 504, 2.21: Laws should be set forth to the public with a pleasing preface. 545, 2.16: The divine dialogues of Plato have matter of laughter in them. 546, 1.2: Plato's ideal state. 622, 1.33: Socrates confutes Callicles who say that law can bandy with nature. 728, 1.7; 729, 1.11; 2.19; 730, 1.17.

Page 457, 2.26 *No bishop, no king;* the rally-cry of the prelatical party. They meant that if the bishops' power were destroyed, the king's would soon follow.

2.33. *the Spaniard;* the English people had been greatly agitated over the undue influence of Spain upon English policies— an uneasiness dating back to the time of Gondomar's influence over James and the unfortunate attempt at a Spanish match, and this feeling had not been much allayed by the king's marriage with a French catholic, Henrietta Maria. Milton's statement was sure to find sympathetic confirmation in Puritan minds. Cf. 459, 1.32; 459, 2.27.

Page 458, 1.12 Milton invents a fable after the manner of Æsop to point his moral; in structure and in application, this fable, however, is much nearer to the parables of Christ: it is applicable in all its details; so easy to understand that no one can mistake its meaning; and left entirely unexplained and unapplied. There is another parable thus used in 497, 1.38

2.3 *lourdan;* blockhead.

2.39 *scorpions;* cf. Rehoboam's answer to his people that justly complained, 2 *Chron* x. 14: "My father made your yoke heavy, but I will add thereto: my father chastised you with whips, but I will chastise you with scorpions."

2.40 *keel;* to make cool.

2.41. Milton's references to the American Pilgrims are of special interest to us. Remember that Thomas Young, one of his early tutors, greatly admired and loved by him, was for some time, after teaching Milton, a pastor of the emigrant Puritans in Holland. Other references are: 459, 2.36; 480, 2.9.

Page 459, 1.12 *blaze of comets;* Even in his prose works Milton often betrays an interest in such portents as comets and new stars. This is due in part to his natural curiosity about unexplained astronomical phenomena, but more to his wide reading in the Greek and Latin historians, who seldom miss an opportunity to relate such marvels and portents. The appearance of comets is frequently mentioned in the *History of Britain.*

2.18 *rochet;* a linen vestment worn by bishops.

2.26 *tympany;* a swelling.

2.51 *liberty;* among all our poets and reformers no one has ever surpassed, or perhaps equaled Milton, in his sound definitions of liberty, in his eloquent descriptions of its beauties, and in his stirring appeals for its extension to all phases of life. Some other passages are: 575, 2.7: "He who wisely would restrain the reasonable soul of man within due bounds, must first himself know perfectly, how far the territory and dominion extends of just and honest liberty." 574, 2.24: "honest liberty is the greatest foe to dishonest licence." 625, 2.14: "Let us not be thus overcurious to strain at atoms, and yet to stop every vent and cranny of permissive liberty, lest nature, wanting those needful pores and breathing-places, which God hath not debarred our weakness, either suddenly break out into some wide rupture of open vice and frantic heresy, or else inwardly fester with repining and blasphemous thoughts, under an unreasonable and fruitless rigor of unwarranted law." 754, 1.28: "For, indeed, none can love freedom heartily but good men; the rest love not freedom but licence, which never hath more scope or more indulgence than under tyrants." 843, 2.47: "them who chose rather to be the slaves and vassals of his will, than to stand against him, as men by nature free; born and created with a better title to their freedom than any king hath to his crown." 911, 2.27: "This liberty of

conscience, which above all other things ought to be to all men dearest and most precious, no government more inclinable not to favor only, but to protect, than a free commonwealth."

2.53 *rigorous honor to the marriage-bed;* this is the first mention in Milton's prose of the subject of marriage.

Page 460, 1.3 *people slacken . . . wily tyrant;* a theme that Milton never fails o drive home.

1.30 *gaming, jigging;* a reference to the encouragement by the court of the loosening of the moral restrictions which were urged by the Puritans; Milton probably had in mind chiefly the restoration of the famous "Declaration of Sports" which James had originally issued in 1617. In 1633 Charles had revived this order, which had, after 1618, been allowed to lie quiescent, owing to popular disapproval. Not only did Charles resurrect his father's unpopular order, but he insisted that it should be read in all the churches. The storm of protest that followed revealed and even increased the bitterness that preceded the actual outbreak of war.

1.47 *their courts;* before Milton wrote on divorce he was attacking the ecclesiastical courts; through these five anti-prelatical tracts one finds frequent and strong remarks about the undue powers that these courts possess. Cf. 464, 1.52; 468, 1.3: "diabolical courts." See the note on 573, 1.12.

2.2 *temples beautified exquisitely;* Laud constantly preached and put into execution his doctrine of "The Beauty of Holiness," by which he meant the dignity and beauty of the church service. This plan included the beautifying of churches by costly paintings, colored glass windows and other expensive decorations; it also involved costly and gorgeous clerical vestments, processions, the presence of many clergy at services in cathedrals, and all the display that naturally goes with a high church service. To Milton, who believed in the great value of a deep personal religion, this emphasis seemed misplaced.

2.34 *a moderate maintenance;* this is Milton's first expression of his opinion in regard to the compensation of ministers; this thought will grow and change until later it is to occupy one entire tract, "Means to remove Hirelings," 1659. Cf. 468, 1.34 where he speaks scornfully of "piddling tithes"; and 498, 1.32 where he says that ministers should never consider their monetary rewards.

Page 461, 1.48 *dissolution of a monarchy slides aptest into a democracy;* in 1641 when no one was dreaming of war, to say nothing of a democracy, Milton had seen the possibility and had foretold the outcome of the present troubles unless radical measures of reform were taken in time.

2.3 *Norman gripe;* this is one of the first references in the seventeenth century to the power that the Normans seized and exerted over the native English at the time of the Conquest. Norman tyranny over the English is constantly mentioned in the tracts of the Levelers and the Diggers, culminating apparently about 1649. Lilbourne seems to have meant by "Norman tyranny" oppression in general; Winstanley refers explicitly to oppression of the poor by the rich and the landlords.

2.43 *high and principal offices;* Laud had named the Lord High Treasurer and other important officials of the government under Charles.

Page 462, 2.7 *a fraternal war;* Charles, prompted by Laud, had attempted to force the liturgy of the church of England upon the Presbyterian Scotch. This had resulted in two wars, 1638–39 and 1640.

Page 463, 1.6 *not to extend your limits;* under Elizabeth there had grown up a definite policy of expansion and colonization; Milton, who had no faith in material success as such, could not look upon this growing empire with approval. See Green, *Short History.*

2.37 *than is the commonwealth of England;* eloquent praise of the English and ardent patriotism, when England seems to him to be right, are characteristic of Milton's prose and poetry. Cf. 468, 2.30; 492, 2.22.

Page 464, 2.5 *transgress seldomest;* acute criticism of the law-making of his age; even today in this enlightened time, our law-makers do not always bear this sound principle in mind.

2.6 *conceive great hopes;* the reforming party were all inspired with great hopes of the reform which they were trying to effect. Milton constantly refers to the great "reformation intended," (Title-page to the first edition of the *D and D*). Cf. 492, 1.35: "to us an age of ages wherein God is manifestly come down among us to do some remarkable good to our

church or state"; 577, 1.11; 726, 1.9: "I neither ought nor can in conscience defer beyond this time both of so much need at once, and so much opportunity to try what God hath determined."

2.51 *nuzzled;* nursed, reared.

Page 465, 2.47 *quillets;* quibbles, niceties.

Page 467, 1.37 *Swisses;* though Milton does not here explicitly mention the Waldenses, he evidently has them in mind. Other references are: 885, 2.50; 892, 1.9; 892, 1.34.

Page 468, 2.1 This eloquent prayer is thoroughly Miltonic; it has most of the characteristics in prose of such impassioned utterances in poetry as the sonnet, *On the late Massacher in Piemont,* and certain prayers in *P.L.* There is a similarly eloquent prayer at 493, 1.9; this prayer, however, did not escape the censure of Bishop Hall, who said that it was hypocritical and affected. For Milton's criticism of this last prayer, see 564, 1.7. 2.8 *one Tripersonal godhead;* Milton is still a good orthodox Trinitarian.

Page 469, 1.29 *some one may perhaps be heard;* Milton refers to his own intention of writing a great poem; perhaps he is thinking still of King Arthur as a possible subject.

Page 469. OF PRELATICAL EPISCOPACY

2.28 *James, Archbishop of Armagh;* James Ussher, often spelled, Usher, (1580–1656) took his M.A. degree from Trinity College, Dublin, in 1600; became Archbishop of Armagh and primate of Ireland in 1624; and at the outbreak of the civil war took sides with Charles; at this time he lost nearly all his property in Ireland, saving only his library. He established a chronology of the Old Testament which was used till disproved by modern research, in which he fixed the creation of the world at 4004 B.C.

2.46 *stale and useless records of either uncertain or unsound antiquity;* Milton here not only expresses his contempt for the over-valued church fathers, but he also hints early at one of the chief attacks that he is to make in this tract, that the text of the fathers is often corrupt. Cf. 490, 1.43.

2.51 *broken reed of tradition;* one of the evidences of Milton's radicalism is his distrust and outspoken hatred of tradition. He thought that every belief and every principle of action should be submitted to original and fresh inquiry; it should never be accepted simply because it had been accepted by our fathers. Cf. 677, 2.29: "the unworthy and conceited, who love tradition more than truth."

2.53 *scripture only is able;* this is the principle in which Milton and most of the Dissenters believed and upon which they founded all their religious beliefs: if any practice could be established from a study of the Bible, it was good and acceptable; if it were found to exist only in the Fathers or ecclesiastical literature, it would probably be damned, even though it might be good. To supplement this principle, some of the more liberal used also another which they called the "light of nature," about which more comment will be offered later. Cf. 478, 1.17; 528, 2.16.

Page 470, 1.28 *indigested heap and fry of . . . antiquity;* Milton's scorn of ecclesiastical antiquity is in marked contrast to his reverence for classical antiquity. Cf. 526, 2.47; 574, 1.18: "under the rubbish of canonical ignorance"; 576, 2.23: "shallow commenting of scholastics and canonists."

1.50 *foraging after straw;* Pharaoh refused to furnish the Israelites with straw with which to make bricks, so that they had to forage for it. *Ex.* v.

Page 472, 1.4 *nameless treatise;* this was perhaps one of the paragraphs that brought the scholar, Archbishop Ussher, to reexamine the whole Ignatius problem and to conclude that certain epistles hitherto assigned to that author were spurious.

1.19 *Louvain;* a city in Belgium that has always prided itself most on its theological teachings.

Page 473, 2.8 *doctrine and discipline;* theory and practice.

Page 477, 2.45 *Epicurus's atoms;* Milton's knowledge of Epicurus, which was in no way superficial, probably came largely through Lucretius. For Epicurus in England in the seventeenth century, see a forthcoming study by Thomas F. Mayo.

Page 478, 1.23 *ephod and teraphim of antiquity;* the ephod was a vestment worn by the Jewish high priest in ancient times; the teraphim (sing. teraph) were household images reverenced by ancient Hebrews. They seem to have been of human form and small size, and to have been worshiped as household gods or penates. Hence the phrase is equivalent to Milton's often repeated "ceremonies and superstitions."

Page 478. ANIMADVERSIONS

1.41 Milton is frequently criticized today for descending in his prose too often to personal abuse and the use of too sharp and strong language. His own defences of such language are therefore interesting to the student, and to some at least, convincing, though some idealists of the conservative type will doubtless continue sadly to shake their heads. Answering a tract, point by point, was a common method of reply at the time. Milton used this method also in *Eikonoclastes,* the three Defences and in other controversial tracts. In the present tract we find some of Milton's most interesting ideas as well as some of his noblest prose. Beside this opening paragraph, place the following: 552, 2.13, "a vehement vein" justified; 553, 2.22, obscene words justified on certain occasions.

Page 480, 1.27 *were not making Latin;* Milton never lost an opportunity of attacking an enemy for errors in language, whether in English or in a foreign or ancient tongue. Whether he is justified here or whether he is getting out of a bad situation as well as he can, the editor will leave to students of Latin and Greek. Cf. 712, 1.17: "For first, not to speak of his abrupt and baid beginning, his very first page notoriously bewrays him an illiterate and an arrogant presumer in that which he understands not, bearing us in hand as if he knew both Greek and Hebrew, and is not able to spell it, which had he been, it had been either written as it ought, or scored upon the printer."

2.36 *after all your monkish prohibitions;* this is one of Milton's first indications that he is revolting against the licencing of books; we now, with the aid of history, can easily see that he was bound to write *Areopagitica,* and that his own experiences, while undoubtedly they furnished the occasion for writing, must really have had, after all, little to do with the work.

Page 481, 1.8 *precious gem of truth, as amongst the numberless pebbles of the shore;* Cf. Isaac Newton's well-known simile.

Page 483, 1.17 *have a trade;* thus early Milton is defending those who work, and maintaining that even they have a right to be heard in government affairs; eighteen years later he was to insist that even ministers should have a trade. Cf. 892, 1.8. See also a forthcoming book on

Bunyan and his background by William Y. Tindall, where an account of the lay ministers is given.

1.21 *bezzling;* wasting money in riotous living.

2.25 *Qui color;* that which was black is now white; or more literally, is now the opposite of black.

Page 490, 1.8 *Ortelius;* a Flemish geographer (1527–1598) who published an atlas "Theatrum orbis terrarum" (1570).

1.10 *Mundus alter et idem;* an anonymous Latin tract in 4 books, published at Frankfort in 1605; translated by John Healey in 1608 as "The Discovery of a New World." Usually ascribed to Joseph Hall, though the uncertainty of authorship has never been cleared up. Nor is the purpose of the book clear; some scholars have called it a romance, others a kind of Utopia, and others a satirical description of London. At any rate, Milton makes the most of the opportunity offered him. Cf. 545, 2.43; 548, 1.3.

1.18 *Mercurius Britannicus;* pseudonym of Bishop Hall's.

Page 492, 1.46 *Scipio;* the story is beautifully related by Livy, Everyman's Lib. v. 300.

2.17 As this passage continues, Milton becomes more and more eloquent until towards the last he is a poet.

Page 493, 1.7 *orient;* attended with dazzling light.

2.18 *And he that now for haste;* a reference to the great poem that Milton was planning to write.

Page 496, 1.28 *Alas, master;* the quotation is taken from the story told in II *Kings* vi.

2.32 Milton's various descriptions of the ideal pastor are always interesting and valuable; they may well be compared with Chaucer's similar description. They should also be borne in mind when reading the scathing denunciation in *Lycidas* of the insufficient pastor.

2.40 Cf. Dr. Johnson's famous dictum to Boswell in regard to the critic, who is not a poet, criticizing poetry, and his illustration. Cf. 565, 1.31 and the note, for a supplementary distinction.

Page 497, 2.33 *I cannot tell you;* this is a telling and skilful application, if, indeed, such a slight hint can be called an application.

2.51 *universities:* the two universities were constant sources of irritation to Parliament and the reforming party, for they were stanchly conservative and royalist. The feeling that Milton expresses here was to culminate later in popular disap-

proval when the Puritans drove the royalists out of Cambridge, Cowley and Crashaw among them. This is the first of many places where Milton expresses his distrust and dislike of Cambridge. It is worth while to assemble all these places and study them together. To the present passage may be added: 547, 1.27; 565, 2.15; 726, 1.9: "I neither ought nor can in conscience defer beyond this time both of so much need at once, and so much opportunity to try what God hath determined"; 726, 2.49: "an error of universities, not yet well recovered from the scholastic grossness of barbarous ages. . ."

Page 498, 1.8 *young scholars;* a frequent argument with the prelatical writers was that the proposed reforms would harm education by discouraging aspiring young scholars from studying for the church. Milton expresses his opinion on this phase of the larger controversy in the following places: 538, 2.37; 897, 2.10: "I have thus at large examined the usual pretences of hirelings, colored over most commonly with the cause of learning and universities; as if with divines learning stood and fell."

2.32 *a complete architect;* Milton's high conceptions of the equipment, functions, and end of the profession of an artist, whether as here, an architect or painter, or, as elsewhere, a poet, reveal his deep and constant idealism. The following may be noted:
   1. He should have a generous mind above considerations of monetary rewards.
   2. 543, 1.39: That art is most eloquent which approaches closest to nature.
   3. 543, 1.42: Art is indissolubly knit with the life and character of the artist.
   4. 749, 2.5: Art requires variety.

Page 499, 2.20 *Would he tug for a barony;* a hard hit against the office-seeking higher clergy.

Page 503, 2.14 *Sapit ollam;* he knows his pot.

2.21 *aulam;* the archaic form of *ollam,* meaning a palace or the royal court.

2.46 *sod;* boiled.

Page 504. THE REASON OF CHURCH GOVERNMENT

2.21 *publishing of human laws;* Milton is always interested in the art of government. It is evident that many of his ideas came from Plato as in this passage: See the note on 454, 2.51.

Page 505, 2.4 *presbyters and deacons;* it should be noticed that Milton's idea of Presbyterianism was never that of Scotch Presbyterianism, and that, as we have seen, he was steadily developing in favor of a wide toleration that was soon to eliminate every form of a state church. His attitude of hostility to the Scotch Presbyterians developed actively only when he perceived their intolerance and narrowness.

2.6 *for my years;* he was 33 at this time.

Page 506, 1.4 *of more grave and urgent importance . . . than is discipline;* this is what may be called one foundation stone of all Milton's life. We easily observe how seriously it entered into his own private life, into all his study, and into his art. His remarks, therefore, on this subject are of great and peculiar interest to us, as students of Milton and as students of the art of living well.

1.32 *virtue;* in a large sense, somewhat as the Romans used the word. In a narrower sense it is used as the theme of *Comus.* This larger virtue is one of the prime elements in Milton's idealism, though he has never described it more beautifully than he has done here. Other passages are: 520, 1.8: "whose virtue is of an unchangeable grain, and whose of a slight wash." 520, 1.25: "Virtue that wavers is not virtue, but vice revolted from itself, and after a while returning." 549, 2.53: "whose charming cup is only virtue"; 573, 1.49: "Though virtue be commended for the most persuasive in her theory"; 612, 1.12: "justice herself, the queen of virtues"; 616, 1.42: "no man apprehends what vice is so well as he who is truly virtuous"; 726, 1.38: "to know God aright . . . by possessing our souls of true virtue, which being united to the heavenly grace of faith, makes up the highest perfection."

1.42 *blessed in Paradise . . . not . . . left without discipline;* upon a wide application of this principle rests a large part of the philosophical ideas in *Paradise Lost.* See the note on *P.L.* V. 117.

Page 512, 2.6 *tippet;* a silk cape, sometimes worn by dignitaries in place of the hood.

2.51 *missificate;* celebrate mass.

Page 515, 2.35 *Salmasius;* at this time Salmasius had an honored name with the Puritans, for he had written in defence of the reformed church against the custom of having bishops; it was a different story ten years later, when he turned around and supported the royalists.

Page 520, 1.50 *any elegance . . . without a superfluous waste;* a most enlightening remark upon Milton's own habits of composition, and the care and endless pains he took. Cf. 749, 2.5.

Page 522, 1.29 The first part of this preface is upon the responsibility for the gift of unusual talents or genius. One can easily see that Milton is writing after years of deep thought upon the subject. Interesting side-lights upon this and correlated themes are given in the following passages, selected from many that might be mentioned: Sonnet vii; *Lycidas,* opening lines; and Sonnet xix.

1.51 *God, even to a strictness requires;* a thought always constantly with Milton; this conviction and the equally important one, that his gifts were unusual, pushed him on always to accomplishment, even through the last year of his life. As a result no English writer has left a larger amount of significant work than has he. The fact that his own writing will fill eighteen volumes in the *Columbia Milton* speaks for itself. With this present passage, cf. Sonnet xix.

2.39 *Wo is me; Jer.* 15.10.

2.46 *book . . . was bid to eat; Rev.* 10.9.

2.53 *Sophocles:* Milton was as familiar with the Greek and Latin drama as we are with Shakspere's plays.

Page 523, 1.4 *For surely, to every good and peaceable man;* Milton was not naturally a contentious man; the early biographers give us a picture of a genial, urbane and cultured gentleman.

1.18 *And all his familiar friends;* cf. *Jer.* 20.10. "All my familiars watched for my halting."

1.22 *His word; Jer.* 20.9.

1.39 *I have determined to lay up;* Milton was constantly planning so to live that he might have a peaceful old age, in the consciousness of having God's approval—and he succeeded. Cf. 920, 1.31. 920, 2.50: "to have laid for myself a treasure which would be a provision for my future life. . ."

2.1 *distracted state;* other poets besides Milton found the times too troublesome for poetic endeavor. Herrick, and Cowley complained. Other passages in Milton are: 524, 1.35: "tumultuous times"; 526, 2.42: "to embark in a troubled sea of noises and hoarse disputes"; 550, 1.10: "as I may one day hope to have ye in a still time, when there shall be no chiding."

Page 524, 1.22 *elegant and learned reader;* Milton's natural aristocratic feeling resulted, not from birth or financial affluence, so much as from the knowledge of superior powers and superior ideals and achievements; he almost always deliberately appealed chiefly to the "elegant and learned reader." This attitude toward the common people is found frequently in Renaissance writers. Cf.: 577, 2.15: 'I seek not to seduce the simple and illiterate; my errand is to find out the choicest and the learnedest, who have this high gift of wisdom to answer solidly, or to be convinced"; 921, 1.33: "it is to the learned that I address myself."

1.28 *when I have neither yet completed . . . my private studies;* after finishing his university career of seven years with what must have been unusual brilliance, Milton had retired to Horton for private study; here his program seems to have included a reading, or re-reading, of all the Greek and Latin writers that he could obtain, a special study of European history through medieval times to the present, a further study of mathematics, some attention to music, and doubtless considerable study of modern Italian and French. After his return from Italy, he started to read the medieval Latin historians of England; then he was drawn into studying many of the ancient church fathers and church history—the full extent of his study is not known, but one can confidently assert that he was easily the most learned of any man who has attained an eminent place in English literature.

1.36 *Wise only to my own ends;* Milton seldom was "wise only to his own ends." It is hard to mention any poem that he wrote to catch "popular applause."

1.52 *left hand;* Milton himself has encouraged critics to regard his prose slightingly; but to one reader, at least, his left hand seems at all times no contemptible fellow for his right, and sometimes quite the equal.

2.5 *a poet, soaring;* this famous passage needs little comment, except to call attention to it.

2.16 *of my father;* Milton's father was alive at this time to read this public tribute; he died in 1647. Cf. the Latin poem, *Ad Patrem,* translated at p. 101.

2.24 *the style, by certain vital signs it had;* the essential *sine qua non* of all writing that lives.

2.28 *I had in memory;* evidently Milton did not take copies of his Latin poems with him, but depended on his tenacious memory.

2.37 *the Italian is not forward;* it would be interesting to know whether other English poets had experienced this reluctance to praise and, if so, had overcome it, as Milton did.

2.40 *inward prompting;* Milton evidently responded to the praises of his Italian friends; perhaps they should be given a larger share in his poetic career than we have been inclined to give them.

2.41 *labor and intense study;* an important statement for those who wish to understand Milton and his poetry.

2.49 *for three lives and downward;* Milton strove to write poetry that would last for at least 100 years.

2.51 *honor and instruction of my country;* one of the larger purposes of Milton's mature and serious poetry.

2.53 *second rank among the Latins;* this is one reason why we are not studying *Paradise Lost* in Latin today. Another is given or rather implied in the next line.

Page 525, 1.2 *Ariosto . . . Bembo;* cf. Giovan Battista Pigna in *I Romanzi,* pp. 73–75: "From this enterprise [of re-telling romantic stories in the vernacular] Bembo would fain have dissuaded him, telling him that he was more fitted for writing in Latin than in the vernacular, and that he would rise to greater eminence in the former than in the latter; but Ariosto answered that he would rather be one of the first among writers in Tuscan than barely the second among those in Latin; and he added that he felt certain to which his genius most inclined him." Quoted from Edmund G. Gardner, *The King of Court Poets,* London, 1906, p 264.

1.5 *not to make verbal curiosities the end;* probably he means that he would not follow the popular metaphysical school of poetry, and especially he would not imitate Marini in his verbal conceits.

1.10 *greatest and choicest wits of Athens, Rome, or modern Italy;* three of the sources of Milton's inspiration in writing; a fourth follows.

1.11 *those Hebrews;* Milton's admiration for Hebrew poetry often found expression.

1.14 *of being a Christian;* this is why he in

tended "to soar Above th' Aonian Mount,"
P.L. I. 14–15.

1.15 *not caring to be once named abroad;* Milton wrote his great poetry primarily for Englishmen, who, he hoped and believed, would read it for many years to come; there is not much indication that he often thought seriously of foreign nations reading it; there is, however, the well-known expression, "which the world would not willingly let die."

1.23 *monks and mechanics;* by monks he means the Latin historians of England in the Middle Ages, in whom he was now reading; by mechanics, he refers to their crude telling of unimportant events; they were mechanics compared with the great historians of Greece and Rome, in whom Milton especially delighted.

1.26 *the mind at home;* one of Milton's great secrets is that he was always meditating and studying for his great poetry; when he came to write it, he had already lived it for many years.

1.29 *epic form . . . Homer . . . Job . . . Aristotle;* a passage that explains fully and satisfactorily the kinds of epic represented by *P.L.* and *P.R. Samson Agonistes* represents Aristotle's concept of a Greek play as Milton interpreted him. These passages should always be borne in mind in every discussion of the form of these three poems.

1.37 *what knight or king;* see the head-note to *P.L.* for a suggested reason as to why Milton abandoned his idea of writing on King Arthur.

1.39 *Tasso;* the greatest of the more recent Renaissance poets; he had died only in 1595. Milton mentions him frequently and always favorably.

1.47 *fate of this age;* in 1825 when Macaulay wrote his essay on Milton, he advanced the idea that the age of writing great epic poetry was past. Milton may have had this idea in mind, or he may have referred only to the "tumultuous times."

1.51 *Sophocles;* one of Milton's favorite dramatists.

1.52 *Euripides;* critics have frequently claimed that Milton admired Euripides the most of all the Greek dramatists, and that the Euripidean influence is most felt in his work. The claim needs to be examined afresh.

2.2 *Song of Solomon;* this idea of considering parts of the Bible as answering the demands of classic literature was often entertained by Milton, and indeed by his contemporaries.

2.12 *magnific odes . . wherein Pindarus;* before Cowley published his *Pindaric Odes* in 1647, Milton was thinking of a strict imitation of Pindar in English.

2.22 *inspired gift of God;* Milton mentions so often his belief in the divine inspiration of poetry that we cannot doubt his absolute and sincere conviction on this point. Cf. 526, 2.23.

2.25 *beside . . the pulpit;* the function of the poet in the nation is placed beside that of the minister—the two most important teachers of "virtue and public civility." See 738, 2.6 and the note.

Page 526, 1.8 *writings and interludes of libidinous and ignorant poetasters;* here we get Milton's settled opinion of contemporary playwrights and poets. Shakspere and the Elizabethans are not included here. Milton's contemporaries were "ignorant" because they did not know or care for the high requirements of art that inspired the best ancient writers. Cf. Preface to *Samson Agonistes,* 405, 7.

1.14 *vicious principles;* a rather harsh but just criticism of some Caroline poetry.

1.17 *demean;* conduct.

1.18 *without some recreating;* Milton often insists on the necessity for recreation, holidays and change of work.

1.24 *managing of our public sports;* a modern idea, but, of course, as Milton hints, developed from ancient customs.

1.27 *drunkenness;* one of the forms of excess that troubled Milton as it has all serious thinkers and reformers. Cf. 539, 2.25; 674, 1.4.

1.29 *martial exercises;* one of the means of developing a sound mind in a sound body. *to all warlike skill;* Milton was no thorough-going believer in war; he seems to have believed only in a war for liberty, i. e. a war of defence against invasion from without or tyranny from within. On the other hand, he was no pacifist.

1.35 *to the love and practice of justice, temperance and fortitude;* these are the attainments of a life of moderation. In all this program for the attainment of national virtue, there are no prohibitions; all the ideas advanced are constructive and upbuilding. The scheme partakes of the nature of present-day preventive sociology In no way does Milton show better his modern tendencies than in this passage on the building of a nation in the ways of greatness.

1.46 *in theatres;* cf. our many civic opera houses, play houses and other institutions of similar nature.

2.10 *inquisitorius and tyrannical duncery;* England, for the most part, could not see the largeness and justice of this criticism, but it did so later.

2.13 *to covenant;* Milton's share in bringing about this ideal state is to write a great poem in which the principles may be laid down. It is interesting to observe that he is constantly thinking of his poem, and is perhaps doing more on it than we commonly think of his doing at this time.

2.20 *rhyming parasite;* evidently Milton did not have any great use for the court patronage that had grown up under James and Charles.

2.22 *dame memory;* a curious idea; Milton's tenacious memory must have made him especially susceptible to the danger of making his poems a mosaic of passages from other poets. He escaped that temptation well, though his poetry is still properly considered the most reminiscent of any poetry by our great poets; in fact, this quality of reminiscence is one of its charms.

2.28 *industrious and select reading;* work of the most highly disciplined kind went into the making of his poetry.

2.29 *steady observation;* we are glad to learn that Milton consciously cultivated the art of observation; his knowledge of psychology could hardly have been attained otherwise.

2.50 *marginal stuffings;* Milton had a genuine abhorrence of marginal notes. This was due to his hatred of what we may call "second-hand thinking." His own policy was to read widely and study deeply; then to arrive at his own conclusions. In this way he made use of other men's ideas, but was under no necessity of citing book and chapter; to have done so would have been pedantic. Cf.: 570, 1.7; 576, 1.51: "narrow intellectuals of quotationists and common placers"; 711, 2.42: "than the gout and dropsy of a big margin, littered and overlaid with crude and huddled quotations."

Page 527, 1.26 *church-outed;* Masson in his *Life* was considerably worried over this expression, as he found no law or regulation that would seem to justify Milton in such a strong statement. Obviously, the entire passage is not to be taken too literally; nevertheless, anyone who has followed the course of Milton's reactions to the Church of England as it was then governed, must be convinced that all his principles revolted against entering a profession with many of whose practices and even ideals he disagreed so thoroughly. The language is strong, but hardly too strong for the evolution through which he had been passing for the last ten years or more.

Page 531, 2.49 *most an end;* almost continuously.

Page 533, 2.30 *this pious and just honoring of ourselves;* another of Milton's cardinal principles. Cf. 549, 2.1: "an honest haughtiness, and self-esteem either of what I was, or what I might be, (which let envy call pride) . . . yet here I may be excused to make some beseeming profession."

Page 537, 2.23 *boring our ears to an everlasting slavery;* cf. *Ex.* 21.6: "and his master shall bore his ear through with an awl; and he shall serve him forever."

Page 539, 2.21 *liken . . . to that mighty Nazarite Samson;* this early reference to the subject of *Samson Agonistes* is interesting, for it shows us that even at this time Milton had selected some of the significant elements of the story as it appealed to him. It is especially important to note that it was Samson's practice of temperance and sobriety that impressed him. Cf. *S.A.* line 541.

Page 541. AN APOLOGY FOR SMECTYMNUUS

1.16 *lively zeal is customably disparaged;* a timely remark for enthusiastic Milton students to keep in mind.

1.40 *wearisome labors and studious watchings . . . tired out almost a whole youth;* another reference to Milton's disciplined life of studious and independent study.

2.22 *vindication of a private name;* Milton plainly foresaw that critics would say, whatever he argued, that he was thinking first of all of his own causes and needs; but he did not foresee that this sort of criticism would keep up and go to further lengths, even to this present time.

Page 542, 2.31 *pudder;* bustle, confusion.

2.45 *curtal;* cut short, brief.

2.46 *above three inches long . . . confiscate;* Milton's justification of his long sentences.

Page 543, 1.15 *lightest thing;* there is a double meaning here.

1.30 *barbarous Latin;* Milton's own Latin had

a classical elegance; in the opinion of those competent to judge, it is the best Latin written by any of our poets, with the possible exception of Landor.

2.42 *nature best;* a thought often expressed by Milton; he believed, contrary to some modern writers, that art is intimately associated with the private life and character of the artist. Cf. 549, 1.43: "And long it was not after, when I was confirmed in this opinion, that he would not be frustrate of his hope to write well hereafter in laudable things, ought himself to be a true poem."

Page 544, 1.43 *Whiteboy;* an old term of endearment; darling.

1.27 *Sir Francis Bacon;* by 1642 Bacon's influence upon thinking men was becoming perceptible; Milton mentions him several times, and always with respect. His quotations show that he had read Bacon's less known writings. Cf.: 554, 2.9; 555, 2.8; 743, 2.34; 746, 1.22.

1.47 *a serpent;* its reputed poisonous qualities are well known; the metaphor, as is always the case, is well chosen for the author's purposes.

2.13 *book of characters;* were popular at the time; Overbury and Earle were popular writers of characters; Bishop Hall had also tried his hand at the type, as had almost every other writer of English prose in the early part of the century.

2.51 *For which commodious lie . . . I thank him;* and so do we. This passage helps us to estimate such criticism as Dr. Johnson made of Milton's university career. Milton's friendly critics, from the time of the early biographers, have made good use of these few sentences.

Page 547, 1.3 *favor and respect;* Milton grew steadily in popularity with his fellow collegians as his university career advanced, —a testimony to his increasing urbanity as well as to his intellectual brilliance.

1.34 *she or her sister;* Cambridge and Oxford; see the note on 497, 2.51.

2.10 *ere the sound of any bell;* the first biographers mention his early rising.

2.17 *body's health and hardiness;* Milton's attention to physical health was much in advance of the average attention paid to such matters in his age. It shows how completely he had absorbed the best in ancient civilization.

2.21 *firm hearts in sound bodies;* the old Latin adage, *Mens sana in corpore sano.*

Page 548, 2.44 *smooth elegiac poets;* Milton here refers especially to his early admira-

tion of Ovid, whose influence is seen best in the Latin poems.

2.47 *numerous writing;* verse in meter and with accents or long and short syllables.

Page 549, 1.24 *such a reward, as the noblest dispositions;* the fame of a good poet. Cf. *Lycidas,* l. 70.

1.29 *ungentle and swainish breast;* cf. *Comus,* l. 633: "and the dull swayn / Treads on it daily with his clouted shoon," i. e., treads on the rare and precious moly.

2.5 *though not in the title-page;* a hit at Bishop Hall's title-page, "A Modest Confutation."

2.14 *those lofty fables and romances;* Milton was a voracious reader of romances, especially those by the Italian writers, Boiardo, Ariosto and others.

2.23 *what a noble virtue chastity sure must be;* the great single theme of Milton's youth, and in an enlarged sense, the theme of his whole life.

2.50 *Xenophon;* Milton seems to have given Xenophon a higher rank than most readers today; maybe he had in mind his historical works also, which go into the account to balance it.

2.53 *whose charming cup;* see *Comus,* l. 635, and the note.

Page 550, 1.5 *how the first . . . office of love;* the most enlightening passage on this broad and fundamental conception of love is the place in Plato's *Symposium* where Socrates tells how the wise woman instructed him in the philosophy of love.

1.21 *not to be negligently trained . . . though Christianity had been but slightly taught me;* this passage furnishes one of the clews to a proper approach to *Paradise Lost;* it is not primarily a theological or didactic poem, but, like most other great poems, one of religious-philosophical thought.

1.50 *for marriage;* thus early had Milton formed one of his lifelong principles in regard to marriage and chastity.

2.45 *tormentor of semicolons;* a good description of the pedantry that Milton hated.

Page 551, 1.1 Mr. H. W. Garrod in *Essays and Studies,* English Association, vol. xii, p. 9, note, suggests that for "ears" we should read "nares," and that at 549, 1.22 for "in serious" we should read, "insertions." These suggested changes are interesting and indeed plausible, but the editor has decided to retain the reading of the original texts. In Milton's works we find many evidences of his careful proof reading, frequently referred to in these notes.

Page 552, 1.13 *contempt of vulgar opinions;*

cf. *Paradise Regain'd* III, 51 and the note.

Page 554, 2.21 *Flaccus;* Horace; another classical poet who had his share of influence upon Milton. Cf. 676, 1.4.

2.26 *Cicero;* probably Milton's prose style at times is modeled more closely upon Cicero than we have realized.

2.27 *Seneca;* (c. 4 B.C.–65 A.D.) the celebrated Roman philosopher.

Page 555, 2.51 *Machiavel;* Milton's ideas about this great Italian were apparently not in advance of his time.

Page 558, 1.37 *toothless satires;* see glossary under *Hall.* Milton disliked these satires because of their inane quality and because of the improper word, "toothless," in the title. Cf. 564, 1.40.

2.41 *the first English satire;* Hall had boasted in the opening lines of his first satire: "Follow me who list / And be the second English satirist." In Milton's original text, *satire* is spelled *satyr,* which suggests a play upon the word.

2.43 *Italian satirists;* it is interesting to know that Milton had read not only the Italian romantic poets, but the satirists as well.

2.45 *Piers Plowman;* Milton seems to have been widely read in the less known Middle English poets; there appears also to have been a distinct revival of interest in Middle English poetry at this time. Milton quotes Gower on 570, 1.52.

2.48 *a satire . . . born out of a tragedy;* this is the correct historical account of the origin of satire.

Page 559, 1.23 *tetter;* a vague name for an itching skin disease.

1.24 *tenesmus;* a medical term for a straining to void, without accomplishment.

Page 560, 1.39 *pilchers;* one who wears a pilcher; i. e., a coarse garment.

2.42 *harsh discord;* Milton turns for his comparisons, in his remarks upon the art of writing, to music more naturally than to any other art. Cf. 563, 2.3.

2.46 *I owe to those public benefactors;* Milton often expresses his gratitude to Parliament, and his belief in their honesty and efficiency. Cf. 561, 1.24; 731, 2.42, where he addresses his *Areopagitica* to the Parliament; and numerous other places.

Page 561, 1.26 *well-reputed ancestry, which is a great advantage towards virtue;* Milton often traces good qualities to a noble stock.

Page 564, 1.7 *a prayer . . . Animadversions;* see the note on 468, 2.1.

2.45 *suppressing . . . the printed explanations of the English Bible;* Laud had suppressed the common pocket Geneva Bible, largely sold to people of little means, because it contained glosses of Calvinistic import that he did not like.

Page 565, 1.1 *how many parts of the land;* see *Lycidas,* l. 119 and the note.

1.29 *the authority of Pliny;* his book on Natural History had been an authoritative treatise throughout the Middle Ages, but was pretty well discredited by this time. The ironic satire in mentioning him is evident.

1.32 *none can judge;* this does not contradict what Milton has said previously on 496, 2.40. See the note on that passage.

2.2 *when he who judges, lives a Christian life himself;* life is the final test of all art, whether it be that of poetry or that of criticism.

2.15 *those clerks;* this unflinching criticism of the average university undergraduate of the time is typical of Milton's attitude. An interesting study could be made to see how far these criticisms were true, and whether they were fully justified. It would also be interesting to know how far they reflect Milton's own experience in Cambridge. See the note on 497, 2.51.

Page 568, 1.44 *Abraham disdained;* this is a principle that Milton mentions often in his poetry. Cf. *Comus* l. 701 "None / But such as are good men can give good things."

2.21 *What! no decency;* Laud's principle of the "beauty of Holiness." See the note on 460, 2.2.

Page 569, 2.22 *best councils;* Milton was too well read in the best the world has thought to have much interest in the records of church councils.

Page 570, 1.52 *Gower;* see the note on 558, 2.45.

Page 573. THE DOCTRINE AND DISCIPLINE OF DIVORCE

The first edition of the *Doctrine and Discipline* was published about August 1, 1643. On the title-page appeared the words: "Seasonable to be now thought on in the Reformation intended." The second edition, 1644, omitted this sentence from the title-page and substituted, "Now . . . J.M." It also added the appropriate second citation from the Bible. The first edition had no indication of authorship. The vexed question of the personal element in the Divorce tracts is still agitating scholars. Mr. B. A. Wright in the *Modern Language Review,* Dec., 1931 and Jan., 1932, has ably shown that the year usually assigned as that of Milton's marriage, 1643, rests on no authentic foundation, and that the year 1642 is the only likely, if indeed not the only possible, date. The acceptance of this date would do much to clear up our conceptions of the problem of Milton's personal relation to the subject discussed in these tracts. The editor's own feeling is that Milton, when he wrote the first edition of the *D. and D.* was not seriously involved in what later turned out to be an unhappy marriage, and that he would have written on the subject, even had he been happily married. When he wrote the second edition, however, his experience had been broadened.

1.7 *Doctrine and Discipline;* i. e., theory and practice. Cf. 443, 1.18.

1.12 *good of both sexes;* it has been objected that the divorce tracts are written chiefly from the stand-point of the man; it should be noticed, however, that the woman is often considered. Too much of Milton's own personal experiences can easily be read into this tract by unduly emphasizing his lack of consideration of the woman; it was not so much Milton as it was the attitude of his time.

1.12 *from the bondage of canon law;* this is an important function of the treatises that modern critics almost always forget. See the note on 577, 2.53.

1.28 *The author J.M.;* Milton did a bold thing when he put his initials on this title-page and printed his name in full at the end of the Preface. There is no printer's name, for the good reason that the tract had to be printed by the secret press; no licencer would permit such a book to be printed. But Milton did a bolder thing in thus defying the very tenets of popular morality. He had much to lose, and, if his own personal happiness were considered, little to gain, from the publication.

1.40 *To the Parliament of England;* with this sincere and eloquent tribute to the Parliament, cf. 560, 2.46; 561, 1.24; 574, 1.10; 577, 2.20.

1.45 *who of all teachers . . . that have ever taught, hath drawn the most disciples;* Milton has many important passages on the tyranny of custom. To accept principles, because they had always been accepted, was to him most repugnant: in theology, he insisted on going to the scriptures alone for his authority; in scholarship, he examined afresh each question in which he was interested; in history, he scorned the examples of his predecessors,

if they were unsound; in law, precedents had no weight with him,—any more than they had with former Justice Oliver Wendell Holmes; all things had to be studied anew. This present passage forms a good commentary on Wordsworth's lines:

And custom lie upon thee with a weight
Heavy as frost, and deep almost as life!

Cf. 754, 1.19: "If men within themselves would be governed by reason and not generally give up their understanding to a double tyranny of custom from without. . . ." Cf. also 760, 2.14: "But because it is the vulgar folly of men to desert their own reason, and shutting their eyes, to think they see best with other men's, I shall show . . ."

2.22 *depressing the high and heaven-born spirit of man;* Milton's Calvinistic belief in the doctrine of original sin seems to have progressively weakened. The idea was not congenial to him, and though he may sometimes state it, he never seems to take it too seriously. On the other hand, he emphasized always the utmost importance of the human spirit, and often as here revealed a Platonic reverence for the heavenly origin of the soul of man.

2.33 *error supports custom, custom countenances error;* a vicious circle that Milton spent his life in trying to break.

Page 574, 1.4 *through the chance of good or evil report;* most modern scholars have learned after patient research that in the statement of facts Milton can be trusted to tell the truth as he sees it; he has never yet been successfully proved to have misrepresented the truth. He is at times, of course, prejudiced and often one-sided, but never deliberately false. It is somewhat strange then to find many critics so over-emphasizing the personal element in these divorce tracts, some even going so far as to maintain that Milton would never have written on divorce at all, had he himself not been involved in an unhappy marriage. Professor Hanford has pointed out that several years before 1643, Milton had entered quotations concerning divorce in his *Commonplace Book.* The emphasis that Milton places on the undue powers of the ecclesiastical courts should also be borne in mind as one of his objects in writing these tracts. Nor should we ever forget the passage in the *Second Defence* where he reviews his purposes in writing the prose treatises, and says that he wrote for domestic liberty. Finally let us bear in mind his words here and elsewhere to the effect that he was entirely aware that people would say what they said then, and persist in saying now, that he wrote for his own personal ends.

1.5 *sole advocate of a discountenanced truth;* he frequently mentions that he alone and independently discovered the truths which he now advocated. Cf. 575, 1.12; 710, 1.31.

1.31 *not conscious to itself of any deserved blame;* cf. 577, 1.31: "For me . . . I have already my greatest gain, assurance and inward satisfaction to have done in this nothing unworthy of an honest life and studies well employed." Cf. also 710, 1.37.

Page 575, 1.27 *nation to reform;* cf. the words on the title-page to the first edition and the following: 577, 1.8: "Let not England forget her precedence of teaching nations how to live." 632, 2.4: "Ye have a nation that expects now, and from mighty sufferings aspires to be the example of all Christendom to a perfectest reforming."

2.32 *The greatest burden in the world is superstition;* a theme that Milton developed in almost every work of his mature life.

2.34 *imaginary and scarecrow sins;* Milton is startlingly modern in this thoroughly Freudian statement.

Page 577, 1.9 *teaching nations how to live;* England, when once she has set her own affairs in order, will be, as frequently in the past, the leader among nations. This ardent patriotism, in the best and most liberal sense, is met at almost every turn in Milton. Cf. 577, 2.24: "the esteem I have of my country's judgment"; and 748, 2.3 on the native characteristics of the English; cf. 750, 1.41: "Methinks I see in my mind a noble and puissant nation rousing herself like a strong man after sleep, and shaking her invincible locks: methinks I see her as an eagle mewing her mighty youth, and kindling her undazzled eyes at the full midday beam; purging and unscaling her long-abused sight at the fountain itself of heavenly radiance; while the whole noise of timorous and flocking birds, with those also that love the twilight, flutter about, amazed at what she means, and in their envious gabble would prognosticate a year of sects and schisms."

Page 577, 2.22 *more fitly written in another tongue;* Milton is thinking of readers outside of England as well as the learned Englishmen to whom he appeals. Many English scholars, such as Selden, wrote their treatises in Latin. Cf. 863, 2.35.

2.31 *might have seemed ingrateful.* Milton's courteous and urbane attitude toward Parliament is marked. This consistent manner, both before and after the publication of all the divorce tracts, makes absurd Masson's remark that Milton threatened Parliament to take action himself if it did not heed his advice. Cf. 863, 2.27; 878, 2.1.

2.53 *The Absurdity of our Canonists;* he places the ecclesiastical courts in the title to his Preface, and really makes them the chief object of attack in that introduction. Cf. especially 578, 2.32: "we can refer justly to no other author than the canon law and her adherents"; 579, 2.8: "those irregular and unspiritual courts have spun their utmost date in this land, and some better course must now be constituted."

Page 580, 1.14 *think it equal to answer deliberate reason with sudden heat and noise;* this is why he appeals to the learned and elegant reader; he well knew that the other kind could quickly answer and keep on answering, as they did.

2.22 *from scripture or light of reason;* the liberal movement in seventeenth century theology and in the Church of England began with the publication of Richard Hooker's *Of the Laws of Ecclesiastical Polity* about 1592. He was followed by William Chillingworth (1602–1644) and by Jeremy Taylor (1613–1667). These men and others of the same tendency believed in a liberal interpretation of the Bible (varying, of course, among themselves); this interpretation was supplemented by what they sometimes called "the law of reason," and sometimes "the light of nature."

2.24 *That indisposition;* this proposition of divorce for incompatibility, is carefully framed. In it Milton states exactly what he proposes to prove, defines his conception of marriage, and places careful restrictions.

Page 581, 2.40 *conversation;* manner of life.

Page 582, 1.34 *unprofitable and dangerous to the commonwealth;* this is one reason why these tracts form properly one phase of the fight for national liberty.

Page 583, 1.18 *a discreet man to be mistaken;* one cannot but feel that these lines fit Milton's own experience very closely.

2.44 Cf. *P.L.* IV, 736 and VIII, 379 and the notes on these lines.

Page 600, 1.1 *If it be affirmed;* cf. 934, 1.1: "Such a charge is in effect made by the scholastic distinction which ascribes a twofold will to God; his revealed will, whereby he prescribes the way in which he desires us to act, and his hidden will, whereby he decrees that we shall never so act; which is much the same as to attribute to the Deity two distinct wills, whereof one is in direct contradiction to the other."

Page 611, 2.49 *The political law;* Milton's ideas about the relation of law to morals, a subject that is especially engaging our attention in this age, are sensible and to the point. He here says that law can restrain vice, but not regulate it. Other statements are: 625, 2.14: "Let us not be overcurious to strain at atoms, and yet to stop every vent and cranny of permissive liberty, lest nature, wanting those needful pores and breathing-places, which God hath not debarred our weakness, either suddenly break out into some wide rupture of open vice and frantic heresy, or else inwardly fester with repining and blasphemous thoughts, under an unreasonable and fruitless rigor of unwarranted law."

2.25 *Palpably uxorious;* St. Paul is chiefly responsible for this typical seventeenth-century conception of the position of woman in relation to man.

Page 630, 1.49 *the style . . . was known by most men;* Milton's own age, at least, appreciated the virility of his style.

Page 631, 1.13 *So as I may justly gratulate . . . with . . . assistance from above;* another instance of Milton's belief in divine guidance.

Page 648. TETRACHORDON

2.28 *not placing much in the eminence of a dedication;* it is indicative of Milton's independence of character that he never dedicated one of his books or poems.

2.43 *by whom ye have been instigated to a hard censure;* i. e., by the clergy, especially by Herbert Palmer who preached against toleration and condemned the author of the *D. and D.* before the Houses of Parliament in August, 1644. Cf. 649, 1.53.

Page 649, 2.26 *about a week before;* this statement fixes pretty closely the time in 1644 when *Martin Bucer* was published.

Page 656, 2.46 *God himself conceals not;* see the note on *P.L.* VII. 8.

Page 660, 1.6 *heed;* interpretation.

Page 662, 1.46 *All arts acknowledge;* Milton's scholarship is nowhere better seen than in his careful and accurate definitions. This

whole passage may well be borne in mind as expressing a truth that we all need to heed.

Page 663, 1.26 *His tautology;* Milton's careful attention to the rules of good writing is evident at all turns. See the note on 453, 1.34.

Page 664, 1.6 *Pandects;* collections of Roman law; *Modestinus;* a Roman jurist who flourished about 250 B.C.

Page 665, 2.25 *Diodati;* Giovanni, (1576-1649) an Italian Protestant theologian, an uncle of Charles Diodati's; published in 1607 an Italian version of the Bible,— a name still known and honored.

2.30 *when God speaks;* this shows Milton's careful attention to every detail he could think of in his study of the Bible. Whether his statement would hold good today, the editor, for one, is not competent to judge.

Page 676, 2.28 *Manes;* the founder of Manicheism.

2.42 *judicial law;* one enacted by statute or promulgated by authority.

Page 686, 2.27 *juridical law;* the abstract conception of the law.

Page 706, 2.6 *horn;* so the original edition; one is tempted to amend to *born.*

Page 707, 1.23 *through the poverty of our libraries;* the handicaps of the scholar of that time might well appall us of this age of libraries. Even London could not afford Milton a copy of this book of Wycliff's.

Page 711. COLASTERION

2.28 *Subitanes;* sudden thoughts.

2.32 *in the great audit for accounts;* it was the irony of fate that the one kind of critic appeared that Milton had especially refrained from addressing; "the elegant and learned reader," with sound judgment, failed to answer. His use of satire is thus easily explained.

Page 713, 2.53 *as good cheap;* at as good a bargain.

Page 725. OF EDUCATION

2.18 *Master Samuel Hartlib;* see glossary. An interesting book in which Hartlib appears is *The Diary and Correspondence of John Worthington,* edited by James Crossley in the Chetham Society.

2.40 *of a person sent hither;* Comenius, who had probably been brought to London through the influence of Hartlib for the

purpose of advising Parliament in reforming education, a project in which
they were especially interested at this
time.

Page 726, 1.37 *The end;* this definition of a
real education has never been surpassed
except by that given on 727, 2.6; education does not stop with the schools, but
continues throughout life.

1.45 *sensible;* those things that can be apprehended by the senses.

2.4 *And though a linguist;* the important end
of studying foreign languages; it is the
thought in the languages, written or
spoken, that we study them for.

2.20 *idle vacancies;* the English school and university year is much shorter than ours,
even today.

2.22 *forcing the empty wits of children;* Milton rebelled at what we now consider an
absurd practice,—that of forcing mere
babes to compose themes in Latin on abstract moral subjects. Yet this custom was
followed in almost all the schools, and
continued in some form even through the
last century.

2.31 *barbarizing;* Milton's scholarly and fastidious taste was annoyed not only by offences against Latin and Greek, but by
those against English as well.

2.38 *praxis;* practice.

2.39 *some chosen short book;* one mistrusts
that Milton already had his plans for
writing a Latin grammar.

2.49 *an old error of universities;* see the note
on 497, 2.51.

Page 727, 2.3 *sowthistles;* a common weed
widely distributed over Europe and America.

2.6 *I call therefore a complete and generous
education;* it is important to comprehend
fully this liberal, but accurate, definition
of an education, for it throws light upon
all of Milton's life and upon all his writing. Some modern students may object
to his including a training for war, but
they may remember that, after all, life is
full of war, that the very struggle for
peace is a war; though of course, Milton
had the narrower idea of war in mind.
If we have found one place where we advanced moderns have caught up with
Milton, or perhaps have passed beyond
him, let us congratulate ourselves. Maybe
we are advancing.

2.42 *either that now used, or any better;* Lily,
or a better one, if available; another reference to the grammar which he was planning to write, and did write later, which

he called *Accidence commenc't Grammar;*
in the *Columbia Milton,* vi. Cf. the note
on 726, 2.39.

2.45 *as near as may be to the Italian;* Milton
mentions this method of pronunciation
often. Cf. Ellwood's experience in reading
Latin to him.

Page 728, 1.16 *stirred up with high hopes;* the
Tractate is marked by its constructive
criticism. We see this in these lines; the
end of education is learning how to live,
not in being learned. This high and large
purpose dominates everything that Milton
writes about education.

1.33 *the elements of geometry, even playing;*
Milton has something of an idea of the
modern project method, though he finds
that it was used in old times.

1.38 *The next step . . . agriculture;* this was
not such an absurd suggestion as it might,
on first thought, appear today. London,
though then the largest city in England,
was still a small city, and the other towns
would almost be called villages now. An
interest in farming and in large estates
was natural to youth. Furthermore at this
time, interest in improved methods of
agriculture was continually being stimu-
lated. Hartlib himself wrote several tracts
on the subject, and originated schemes for
draining the various marshes and other
improvements. He was the first, so far
as the editor knows, to suggest a college
where agriculture alone should be studied.
Doubtless he and his friend, Milton, had
talked often over these favorite plans of
his,—they may have furnished one of the
bonds between them.

1.41 *it is not a difficulty above their years;*
throughout the tract Milton is careful to
grade his studies to fit the age of the pupils. Cf. 548, 2.41.

2.5 *Greek tongue;* they are not to start Greek
until they have the elements of Latin well
mastered.

2.25 *physic;* the science of medicine. This study
amounts to what we call first aid. Milton
would not make physicians of his pupils.

2.27 *crudity;* an attack of indigestion.

Page 729, 1.15 *determinate;* concluding labor.
sentence; matter, thought-substance.

1.20 *may have easily learnt, at any odd hour,
the Italian tongue;* this feat may seem
quite impossible to the average college student, but it is accomplished by many
graduate students in English in exactly
this fashion.

1.47 *the Hebrew tongue;* Milton was a scholar
who would accept no translation blindly.

How far we have receded from this sound position may be judged by the fact that the ordinary graduate of a theological seminary today has no knowledge even of Greek, or at least, no adequate working knowledge of that language.

2.8 *Demosthenes or Cicero, Euripides or Sophocles;* it becomes increasingly evident, as we read on in this little tract, that Milton's idea of an education is not only wide reading, but intensive reading, in the best that has been thought and written in the world's history. His pupils are to get from the thought, the vigor and the style of the best writers, material and inspiration for right living. How far our teachers of the classics, ancient, and modern, fall short of this accomplishment is food for thought.

2.12 *discourse and write;* the ends and means of courses in public speaking and English composition are included in Milton's program.

2.48 *what we now sit under;* it takes no great effort to imagine how Milton must have been bored by the sermons that he listened to, nor is it hard to see why as his years advanced, he apparently found his little enthusiasm for listening to sermons much abated.

Page 730, 1.5 *retire back;* it is consoling to infer that even Milton, with his strong memory, found it necessary to review and to re-read more than once.

2.3 *solemn and divine harmonies of music;* music naturally found an important place in his program.

Page 731, 2.6 *this is not a bow for every man to shoot in;* for this saving remark, many a strong, successful and idealistic instructor is profoundly grateful.

Page 731. AREOPAGITICA

The note written by Professor William Haller in the *Columbia Milton,* IV, 366, is as follows: "*Areopagitica* . . . was published in London in 1644 without indication of printer or book-seller and without licence. On the title-page of the copy in the Thomason Collection appear in Thomason's autograph the words, 'Ex dono Authoris,' and the date, November 24. . . . The occasion of the work arose from the acrimonious discussion of toleration which followed the publication of *An Apologeticall Narration* on or before January 3, 1644, by the Independent members of the Westminster Assembly. This led to the attempt on the part of the Assembly to persuade Parliament to enforce against John Good-

win, Roger Williams, Milton and others the ordinance for licensing the press which had been adopted on June 14, 1643. On August 13, 1644, Herbert Palmer preached before Parliament a sermon against toleration in which Milton was condemned as the author of *The Doctrine and Discipline of Divorce.* On August 24, the Stationers' Company petitioned Parliament for stricter enforcement of the licensing ordinance and cited Milton as one of the transgressors of the law. (Masson, *Life,* III. 161, 265.) *Areopagitica* was Milton's reply to these attacks, specific reference being made in his concluding pages to the Stationers' Company. In his *Second Defence* Milton says: 'I wrote my Areopagitica, in order to deliver the press from the restraints with which it was encumbered.' "

Page 732, 2.41 *to imitate the old and elegant humanity of Greece;* Milton's subtlety in thus appealing to the learning and culture of his audience shows his skill and urbanity. The passage reveals also another trait of his style: he here incidentally introduces a thought which he is to employ for all it is worth later. The same trait was noticed in our study of *Paradise Lost.*

Page 733, 1.43 *had died with his brother quadragesimal and matrimonial;* civil war had now broken out; the church party was thoroughly discredited; Laud had been in prison for some time, and was awaiting his trial, and execution on January 10, of the next year. *quadragesimal;* pertaining to the observance of Lent; *matrimonial;* the ecclesiastical courts no longer existed; marriage had become a civil contract, and was no longer solely a sacrament of the church.

Page 736, 2.50 *all the seven liberal sciences out of the Bible;* other examples of finding in the Bible all culture and sometimes the original of such culture, will be found scattered throughout Milton's writings.

Page 737, 2.14 *best books to a naughty mind;* the principle of choice, based on reason (Reason also is choice, *P.L.* III. 108) is one of the foundation stones in Milton's philosophy of life. On it the doctrine of discipline rests.

2.39 *How great a virtue is temperance;* see the note on *P.L.* IX. 1004.

Page 738, 1.44 *warfaring;* the original edition has *wayfaring;* but in three copies which were apparently presentation copies from the author, the *y* has been corrected to *r,* apparently in Milton's hand. Cf. 480, 1.3: "and Christian warfare."

2.7 *a better teacher than;* the high value that Milton places on the poet as a teacher of how to live is observable throughout his work. He here states his belief that the poet is greater in this respect than the philosopher, though he does here limit the philosopher to the schoolmen. With this statement, cf. James Harvey Robinson, *The Mind in the Making*, New York, 1921, page 33. "The truest and most profound observations on Intelligence have in the past been made by the poets and, in recent times, by story-writers. They have been keen observers and recorders and reckoned freely with the emotions and sentiments. Most philosophers, on the other hand, have exhibited a grotesque ignorance of man's life and have built up systems that are elaborate and imposing, but quite unrelated to actual human affairs."

Page 739, 1.8 *notorious ribald of Arrezzo;* Pietro Aretino (1492–1557) wrote satirical and scandalous pieces against the high and powerful, unless bribed off. He was called "The Scourge of Princes."

1.33 *Sorbonists;* the Sorbonne was founded as a part of the University of Paris about 1250. Its predominant faculty was that of theology, which in the 17th century exercised a strong influence.

Page 741, 1.31 *motions;* puppet-shows.

2.37 *court-libel against the parliament;* books in large numbers were printed by the secret press in defiance of Parliament; even *Areopagitica* was so printed. Dr. Charles R. Gillett, in his two volumes, *Burned Books*, New York, 1932, gives an interesting and valuable account of the productions of the secret press during this period.

Page 743, 1.21 *When a man writes to the world;* Milton's own practice at least.

Page 749, 1.24 *We reckon more than five months yet to harvest;* this would seem to indicate that Milton was writing these words in March or thereabouts.

1.29 *for opinion in good men;* cf. 966, 1.34: "For *to think* is nothing else than to entertain an opinion, which cannot be properly said of God."

2.5 *cried out against for schismatics and sectaries;* Milton, although a Church of England man, had a tolerant attitude toward sects and schisms; rather, he approved of them. The reason will be found developed in the following pages. His chief reason is, that these differences indicate growing, thinking minds. Milton was never enthusiastic concerning one general large Christian church. Some critics have

thought that, under the influence of Hartlib and Durie, he may have had such a united protestant church in mind when he wrote the *Christian Doctrine;* but a study of his ideas about church union discountenances any such notion. His reason against church union is still valid: it shows why any such a scheme today is doomed to disappointment,—if indeed, it is not undesirable.

Page 754. THE TENURE OF KINGS AND MAGISTRATES

The Tenure of Kings and Magistrates was published in London in 1649. We learn from internal evidence that it was composed before or during the trial of Charles I, which began on January 20. The date on the copy in the Thomason Collection is February 13. Milton describes it in his *Second Defence* as a book to show "what might lawfully be done against tyrants." A second edition was published in about a year. See Professor Haller's note in the *Columbia Milton* V. 313.

2.3 *after they have juggled;* Milton is hitting at the Scotch Presbyterians who had now begun to argue for the king's cause.

Page 756, 2.17 *all men naturally were born free;* with this passage, cf. the note on 459, 2.51 and the passages on liberty there quoted.

2.20 *born to command;* not necessarily other men, but his own life and the affairs that concern him intimately.

Page 761, 1.3 *how much right the king of Spain;* this was a telling illustration at the time, when Spain was in especially bad repute in England.

1.25 *Who knows not that there is a mutual bond of amity;* even the germ of twentieth century internationalism may be here found.

Page 772, 1.29 *This Goodman;* see glossary. Goodman's important and famous book, from which Milton quotes, *How Superior Powers oght to be obeyd,* Geneva, 1558, was publicly burned. It was even in Milton's time one of the rarest books in the world. It was reproduced for the Facsimile Text Society in 1931.

Page 775. EIKONOCLASTES

The following note by Professor William Haller in the *Columbia Milton* (VI. 323) will form the best head-note here: "*Eikonoclastes* was published in London in 1649, . . . It was composed as a reply to *Eikon Basilike,* which was attributed at the time to Charles I and published immediately after his execution on January 30, 1649. On the title-page of the copy of the *Eikon Basilike* in the Thomason Collection there appears in Thomason's hand the date, February 9, and on the title-page of a copy of *Eikonoclastes* the date, October 6. Milton indicates in his preface that he wrote the book upon the instance of the Council of State. He says in the *Second Defence,* 'I was ordered to answer it; and opposed the Iconoclast to his Icon.' In composing the work he appears to have made use of *Eikon Alethine,* an anonymous reply to *Eikon Basilike,* which was published in the same year. . . . A second edition of *Eikonoclastes* appeared in 1650."

Page 778, 2.42 *court-fucus;* court-paint.

Page 779, 2.44 *no less than poisoning the deceased king;* a persistent rumor of the time, apparently without any foundation.

2.46 *No more addresses;* a resolution of the House of Commons, Jan. 3, 1647–48.

Page 781, 2.41 *published in his own name;* a reference to the Book of Sports.

Page 782, 2.47 *William Shakespeare;* this passage has been often quoted to prove that as Milton grew older, his early enthusiasm for the great dramatist decreased. The editor feels that the principle that Milton himself often insisted upon in interpreting passages of scripture should here apply: we must consider the circumstances. Milton says that Shakespeare is not suitable reading for a monarch in such deep trouble as was the king at that time. Such a statement is apparently sound. We may approve of angling on general principles, but to say that we disapprove of fishing for the president, when he should be making an important decision that will affect the welfare of the entire world, is not to cast any slur upon the honorable profession of angling. We should not forget that Milton pays the highest tribute to the dramatist when he imitates his phrases and lines countless times in *Paradise Lost* and his later work.

Page 783, 1.41 *Sir Philip Sidney;* the substance of the note given above on Shakespeare applies here also.

1.53 *the first prayer of his majesty;* some critics have claimed that Milton himself inserted this prayer in the king's book. It seems to be well established, however, that certain early copies actually contained this absurd plagiarism. Milton makes the best possible use of the error —he accepts it as the king's own action,

instead of using it to prove the spurious character of the book.

2.35 *his deifying friends;* the martyrdom of Charles and his beatification began almost before his execution, and has been continued to the present day by certain classes of conservatives who are horrified at the thought of royalty being judged as mere humanity. Some of the seventeenth-century royalists went so far as to say that his patience and nobility in suffering surpassed that of Jesus in his crucifixion.

Page 784, 1.8 *ethnic;* pagan.

1.12 *every author should have the property of his own work;* Milton's clear statement on plagiarism. Cf. 845, 1.30: "For such kind of borrowing as this, if it be not bettered by the borrower, among good authors is accounted plagiary."

Page 818, 2.43 *wind-egg;* an infertile egg.

Page 835, 1.18 *those churches in Piedmont;* Milton's first direct reference to the Waldenses.

1.30 *roves;* a term in archery: to aim at, especially in a casual manner.

Page 843, 1.53 *twins of Hippocrates;* we should say Siamese twins.

Page 845, 1.30 *For such kind of borrowing;* see the note on 784, 1.12.

Page 846, 1.1 *Ore tenus;* let us pray.

Page 847, 1.7 *sippets;* small pieces of bread in a drink.

Page 852, 1.11 *to whip us;* see the note on 458, 2.39.

Page 863, 2.7 *bored through;* see the note on 537, 2.23.

Page 864. A TREATISE OF CIVIL POWER

Milton in 1659 found time, while writing *Paradise Lost* and in the anxieties caused by the unsettled times that resulted from Cromwell's death in 1658, to write two treatises on the state of the church; in the first he advocated the complete separation of church and state, and protested against the use of force in matters of religious belief. In this wide toleration, he, Roger Williams and Henry Vane stood almost alone among the great men of the time. He had already given similar strong advice to Cromwell at the close of his *Second Defence.* See 1154, 2.5 ff. In the second tract, he returned to a theme that he had often mentioned incidentally,—that the clergy should not be supported by the state, but by each individual congregation.

Page 869, 1.53 *Erastus;* (1524–83) a Protestant

controversialist, who wrote on excommunication. To him is often ascribed erroneously the doctrine of state supremacy in church matters.

Page 878. CONSIDERATIONS TOUCHING THE LIKLIEST MEANS.

Page 886, 2.16 *a late hot querist for tithes;* William Prynne.

Page 891, 2.52 *to an honest trade;* Milton here anticipates the principle of University Extension for people who are working during the day.

Page 895, 2.53 *as Ezekiel and John; Ez.* 3.1 and *Rev.* 10.9

Page 896, 1.20 *exhibitions;* In English universities, benefactions settled for the maintenance of students.

Page 899. THE PRESENT MEANS

First published by Toland in 1698, who says that he printed it from the manuscript. The work is a summary of the argument of the next piece.

Page 900. THE READY AND EASY WAY

First published about March 3, 1660; a "second edition revised and augmented" appeared shortly before the Restoration, May 1, 1660. No work of Milton's shows better his utter fearlessness and his firm determination never to give up the fight while there remained the barest possibility of success.

1.50 *Et nos;* we have given advice to Sylla, let us now give it to the people. Milton probably refers to Monk and the letter he had sent him, as printed on 899. The motto was not in the first edition.

2.11 *false apprehensions;* as the army had the upper hand, many people feared a return to the times of confusion which they had experienced in the days following the success of the civil war.

2.28 *And because in the former edition;* what Milton says here, could, with suitable modifications, be applied to everything he wrote; he was always revising. Hence, it is the part of wisdom to follow generally the revised editions rather than the earlier ones. Cf. the title-page of the second edition of the *Doctrine and Discipline of Divorce,* 573; and the postscript to the second edition of the *First Defence,* 1137, 1.26.

2.45 *admiration and terror;* Masson (III, 715)

thinks that there was no terror among foreign nations; there was enough wonder, imagining what the mad English would do next. Cf. Sonnet XV. Rumors must have reached England, judging from our own experience of false newspaper reports in these days, that have not survived in the printed documents to which historians have to resort.

2.47 *light of nature or religion;* see the note on 469, 2.53.

Page 901, 2.52 *there being in number little virtue;* this is the theory of the superiority of the minority. Matthew Arnold once gave a notable address in New York on this subject, which later in his printed works he called, "Numbers." It is well worth reading in the light of present-day tendencies and experiences. See also the note on 904, 2.20.

Page 902, 2.1 *written monument;* his own *Defence of the English People.*

Page 904, 2.20 *in the joint providence and counsel of many industrious equals;* a hint at Milton's idea of government by the wisest leaders.

Page 919. THE CHRISTIAN DOCTRINE

In the early biographies we find frequent mention of Milton's treatise on the Christian religion. It was never published in his lifetime, and after his death the manuscript was lost sight of. It was discovered in the early nineteenth century; in 1825 Dr. (later Bishop) Charles R. Sumner edited it with a translation and notes in such a scholarly fashion that his edition has almost become a Milton classic. The reasons that prompted Milton to write this treatise are sufficiently stated by him in his preface, except that some interpretation should be added such as has been suggested in the head-note to *Paradise Lost,*—an explanation that Milton could hardly have made himself. We do not know exactly when Milton compiled this digest of his religious convictions; scholars have generally assigned it to some time between 1650 and 1658. It seems to the editor, however, that a much more probable date is between 1644 and 1648. During this period, Milton was curiously quiescent as far as publication was concerned. He was doing something,—of that we may be assured. His greatest work was his preparation for the great poem. We know that in these years some time he wrote four books of the *History of Britain;* that was part of his plan of preparation; it seems likely the determining of his final religious beliefs was also a part of that necessary preparation, and that this study may well have come in the same years. *The Christian Doctrine* throws light on many passages in Milton's work, and is especially helpful in a study of *Paradise Lost*. It should not, however, be taken as a final authority, for in some minor respects it seems to differ in thought from *Paradise Lost*. This fact in itself suggests that the treatise was written at an early date.

Page 1076. FAMILIAR LETTERS

2.17 The address of the printer may, in this case, be taken literally. Milton evidently made no effort to have his personal letters published, and probably with some reluctance consented to the printing of his juvenile exercises. His letters, scattered over a long period from his youth in 1628 to his old age in 1666, give valuable hints as to what he was doing, what his interests were, how his character developed, and how the years as they passed, mellowed his nature and ripened him into a "grand old man." His prolusions also furnish several bits of evidence concerning his interests and character as a young man that should not be overlooked. Masson in his *Life* used these letters and Prolusions, but it was not until recently, when Tillyard wrote on Milton (*Milton*, N. Y. 1930) that the evidence contained in these pieces was really employed to advantage. Even yet it is possible to secure fresh autobiographical hints and implications that have not been fully weighed. The enthusiasm of the youthful Milton, the business acumen and attention to practical matters of the mature man, always on the alert to attend to details concerned with the desired advancement of friends, and the culture and refinement of mature life and age are the chief characteristics that impress most of us in the letters, but none of us will overlook the genial and affectionate disposition that animates them from 1628 to 1666.

Page 1077, 2.6 *Alexander Gill;* was the son of the headmaster of St. Paul's, and was himself one of Milton's instructors. In 1621 he had published one of the first Anglo-Saxon grammars and had made interesting comments on the spelling and pronunciation of modern English words. His influence undoubtedly told in arousing, or at least in maintaining and increasing, Milton's interest in his native language.

Page 1078, 1.17 *The result, committed to type;*

this, so far as we know, was the first time that the young Milton appeared in print; one could hardly call this printed sheet, made only for the convenience of student auditors, a publication.

Page 1079, 2.8 *my genius is such;* in this passage we have valuable comment by Milton himself upon his own characteristics as seen in his habits of thinking and writing.

2.17 *Theodotus;* the word is put in italics, as some other expressions in the letters, because in the original it was written in Greek.

Page 1080, 2.43 *this idea of the beautiful;* the idealism and ideas of Platonic philosophy are evident especially in this letter, and will be found in other letters; the importance of Milton's deep admiration of this philosophy and its influence in shaping his thought in all his writings, and especially in *Comus* and *Paradise Lost* should be evident even to a casual student.

Page 1081, 1.18 *Growing my wings;* when we consider the date of this letter and what Milton must have been thinking of in late September, we cannot but conclude that he refers in this paragraph to *Lycidas* as the form and content of the poem is shaping itself in his mind and as, perhaps, he is writing the first drafts. There is present a new note of confidence.

Page 1084, 2.47 *tomb of Damon;* there is a hint in this sentence that Milton actually published an edition of the *Epitaphium Damonis* as soon as it was written, but scholars did not discover a copy of that edition until a year ago. Our experience in this case shows well how necessary for the scholar is careful examination of every statement that Milton makes,—seldom is he mistaken in his facts.

Page 1136, 1.47 *And now;* these paragraphs were in the first edition; the added postscript to the second edition begins at 1137, 1.26.

Page 1144, 2.13 *though I regret that I published this work in English;* cf. what he says at the end of the Preface to the second edition of the *D. and D.*, 577, 2.22 and what he says also in his letter to Leo Van Aitzema, 1089.

Page 1166, 2.35 *The Digression;* the Digression was omitted from the original edition of the *History of Britain* in 1670, perhaps at Milton's own discretion. It was first printed anonymously in 1681 as *Mr. John Miltons Character of the Long Parliament and Assembly of Divines in M DC XLI.* In the printed copy the place for the insertion of the *Digression* is given as well on in the third book, (in the *Columbia Milton* p. 114); there is, however, a manuscript copy of this Digression, now owned by Harvard University. This manuscript indicates a more appropriate place for it after the words "great undertakings," 1162, 2.6. In the letter to Henry Oldenburg, 1095. Milton refused to accept the suggestion that he give an account of the present state of political affairs in England. For us, this Digression briefly fills the place of such a history from Milton. It contains some of his maturest and most solid reflections on political subjects.